THE

HANDBOOK

OF

SCHOOL
PSYCHOLOGY

FOURTH EDITION

THE

HANDBOOK

OF

SCHOOL
PSYCHOLOGY

FOURTH EDITION

TERRY B. GUTKIN, PH.D.
Department of Counseling
San Francisco State University

CECIL R. REYNOLDS, PH.D.
Department of Educational Psychology
Texas A&M University

WILEY

JOHN WILEY & SONS, INC.

VICE PRESIDENT & PUBLISHER	Jay O'Callaghan
ACQUISITIONS EDITOR	Robert Johnston
SENIOR PRODUCTION EDITOR	Nicole Repasky
EXECUTIVE MARKETING MANAGER	Jeff Rucker
MARKETING MANAGER	Danielle Torio
SENIOR DESIGNER	Madelyn Lesure
PRODUCTION MANAGEMENT SERVICES	Pine Tree Composition, Inc.
SENIOR MEDIA EDITOR	Lynn Pearlman
EDITORIAL ASSISTANT	Katie Melega

This book was set in 9.5/11.5 Janson Text by Laserwords Private Limited, Chennai, India and printed and bound by Hamilton Printing. The cover was printed by Hamilton Printing.

The book is printed on acid-free paper. ∞

Library of Congress Cataloging-in-Publication Data:

The handbook of school psychology / [editors] Cecil R. Reynolds, Terry B. Gutkin. –4th ed.
   p. cm.
  Includes index.
  ISBN 978-0-471-70747-9 (cloth)
  1. Educational psychology–Handbooks, manuals, etc. 2. School psychology–Handbooks, manuals, etc.
I. Reynolds, Cecil R., 1952- II. Gutkin, Terry B., 1947-
  LB1051.H2356 2010
  370.15–dc22
                  2008021371

Printed in the United States of America

10 9 8 7 6 5 4 3 2 1

LIST
OF
CONTRIBUTORS

BRENDAN J. BARTLETT
School of Education and Professional Studies
Griffith University • Nathan, Australia

JOHN C. BEGENY
Department of Psychology
North Carolina State University • Raleigh, North
Carolina

MELISSA K. BERGSTROM
Department of Special Education and Communication
Disorders
Southern Illinois University–Edwardsville •
Edwardsville, Illinois

ANN E. BOEHM
Health and Behavior Studies, Teachers College
Columbia University • New York, New York

JESSICA BLOM-HOFFMAN
Department of Counseling and Applied Educational
Psychology
Northeastern University • Boston, Massachusetts

CAROLINE L. BOXMEYER
Department of Psychology
The University of Alabama • Tuscaloosa, Alabama

STEPHEN E. BROCK
Department of Special Education, Rehabilitation, School
Psychology, and Deaf Studies
California State University, Sacramento • Sacramento,
California

RONALD T. BROWN
Department of Public Health
Temple University • Philadelphia, Pennsylvania

KARLA BUERKLE
Department of Educational Psychology
University of Minnesota, Twin Cities • Minneapolis,
Minnesota

MATTHEW BURNS
Department of Educational Psychology
University of Minnesota, Twin Cities • Minneapolis,
Minnesota

THOMAS P. CAFFERTY
Department of Psychology
University of South Carolina • Columbia, South
Carolina

SANDRA L. CHRISTENSON
Department of Educational Psychology
University of Minnesota, Twin Cities • Minneapolis,
Minnesota

MARY M. CLARE
Department of Counseling Psychology
Lewis & Clark College • Portland, Oregon

STEPHANIE COLLINS
Department of Counseling, Educational Psychology,
and Special Education
Michigan State University • East Lansing,
Michigan

RICHARD J. COWAN
Department of Educational Foundations and Special
Services
Kent State University • Kent, Ohio

MICHAEL J. CURTIS
Department of Psychological and Social Foundations
University of South Florida • Tampa Florida

EDWARD J. DALY III
Department of Educational Psychology
University of Nebraska–Lincoln • Lincoln, Nebraska

SUE M. DAVIES
School of Education Studies and Social Inclusion
Trinity College • Carmarthen, United Kingdom

BETH DOLL
Department of Educational Psychology
University of Nebraska–Lincoln • Lincoln, Nebraska

ERIN DOWDY
Department of Counseling, Clinical, and School
Psychology
University of California–Santa Barbara • Santa Barbara,
California

NELL K. DUKE
Departments of Teacher Education and Counseling,
Educational Psychology, and Special Education
Michigan State University • East Lansing,
Michigan

JOSEPH A. DURLAK
Department of Psychology
Loyola University • Chicago, Illinois

STEPHEN N. ELLIOTT
Department of Special Education
Vanderbilt University • Nashville, Tennessee

PETER T. FARRELL
Department of Educational Support and Inclusion
University of Manchester • Manchester, United
Kingdom

LAUREN FINGERET
Department of Curriculum, Teaching, and Educational
Policy
Michigan State University • East Lansing, Michigan

MELISSA FISHER
Department of Educational Psychology
University of Texas at Austin • Austin, Texas

ELAINE FLETCHER-JANZEN
Private Practice • San Angelo, Texas

JENNIFER L. FRANK
Peabody College
Vanderbilt University • Nashville, Tennessee

PAUL J. FRICK
Department of Psychology
University of New Orleans • New Orleans,
Louisiana

CRAIG L. FRISBY
Department of Education, School, and Counseling
Psychology
University of Missouri • Columbia, Missouri

IRENE W. GASKINS
Benchmark School • Media, Pennsylvania

BRADLEY GERBER
Department of Educational Psychology
University of Texas at Austin • Austin, Texas

MARIBETH GETTINGER
Department of Educational Psychology
University of Wisconsin–Madison • Madison,
Wisconsin

DEBORAH GOLOS
Department of Communicative Disorders and Deaf
Education
Utah State University • Logan, Utah

TODD A. GRAVOIS
Department of Counseling and Personnel Services
University of Maryland, College Park • College Park,
Maryland

EMILY COOK GRAYBILL
College of Education
Georgia State University • Atlanta, Georgia

SARAH GROFF
Department of Counseling and Personnel Services
University of Maryland, College Park • College Park,
Maryland

TERRY B. GUTKIN
Department of Counseling
San Francisco State University • San Francisco,
California

JULIET L. HALLADAY
Department of Education
University of Vermont • Burlington, Vermont

AMY HAMILTON
Department of Educational Psychology
University of Texas at Austin • Austin, Texas

JENNIFER HARGRAVE
University of Texas Elementary School
University of Texas at Austin • Austin, Texas

PATTI L. HARRISON
Department of Educational Studies in Psychology,
Research Methodology, and Counseling
The University of Alabama • Tuscaloosa, Alabama

KATHERINE HILDEN
School of Teacher Education and Leadership
Radford University • Radford, Virginia

JOHN M. HINTZE
School Psychology Program
University of Massachusetts at Amherst • Amherst,
Massachusetts

KIMBERLY EATON HOAGWOOD
Department of Child and Adolescent Psychiatry
Columbia University • New York, New York

ANDY J. HOWES
Department of Educational Support and Inclusion
University of Manchester • Manchester, United
Kingdom

SHANE R. JIMERSON
Department of Counseling, Clinical, and School
Psychology
University of California, Santa Barbara • Santa Barbara,
California

JAMES W. KALAT
Department of Psychology
North Carolina State University • Raleigh, North
Carolina

RANDY W. KAMPHAUS
College of Education, Office of the Dean
Georgia State University • Atlanta, Georgia

TIMOTHY Z. KEITH
Department of Educational Psychology
University of Texas–Austin • Austin, Texas

THOMAS R. KRATOCHWILL
School Psychology Program
University of Wisconsin–Madison • Madison,
Wisconsin

SARAH KURIEN
Department of Educational Psychology
University of Nebraska–Lincoln • Lincoln, Nebraska

COURTNEY LECLAIR
Department of Educational Psychology
University of Nebraska–Lincoln • Lincoln, Nebraska

JESSICA MASS LEVITT
Department of Child and Adolescent Psychiatry
Columbia University • New York, New York

JOHN E. LOCHMAN
Department of Psychology
The University of Alabama • Tuscaloosa, Alabama

PATRICIA A. LOWE
Department of Psychology Research in Education
University of Kansas • Lawrence, Kansas

BRIAN K. MARTENS
Department of Psychology
Syracuse University • Syracuse, New York

ANN S. MASTEN
Institute of Child Development
University of Minnesota • Minneapolis, Minnesota

JENNIFER A. MAUTONE
Children's Hospital of Philadelphia • Philadelphia,
Pennsylvania

JOAN W. MAYFIELD
Our Children's House at Baylor • Dallas, Texas

KRISTEN L. MAYS
College of Education
Georgia State University • Atlanta, Georgia

FREDERIC J. MEDWAY
Department of Psychology
University of South Carolina • Columbia, South
Carolina

ADENA B. MEYERS
Department of Psychology
Illinois State University • Normal, Illinois

JOEL MEYERS
Department of Counseling and Psychological Services
Georgia State University • Atlanta, Georgia

LINDSEY MOHAN
Michigan State University • East Lansing, Michigan

FROSSO MOTTI-STEFANIDI
Department of Psychology
University of Athens • Athens, Greece

BONNIE KAUL NASTASI
Department of Psychology
Tulane University, New Orleans • New Orleans,
Louisiana

NANCY A. NEEF
College of Education and Human Ecology
Ohio State University • Columbus, Ohio

GEORGE H. NOELL
Department of Psychology
Louisiana State University • Baton Rouge, Louisiana

CEDAR W. O'DONNELL
Department of Psychology
University of New Orleans • New Orleans, Lousiana

SERENE OLIN
Department of Child and Adolescent Psychiatry
Columbia University • New York, New York

YONGHAN PARK
Department of Counseling, Educational Psychology,
and Special Education
Michigan State University • East Lansing, Michigan

ROBERT C. PIANTA
Center for Advanced Study of Teaching and Learning
University of Virginia • Charlottesville, Virginia

CLAIRE C. ST. PETER PIPKIN
Department of Psychology
West Virginia University • Morgantown, West Virginia

NICOLE R. POWELL
Department of Psychology
The University of Alabama • Tuscaloosa, Alabama

MICHAEL PRESSLEY
(deceased)
Departments of Teacher Education and Counseling,
Educational Psychology, and Special Education
Michigan State University • East Lansing, Michigan

SHERRIE LYNN PROCTOR
College of Education
Georgia State University • Atlanta, Georgia

LISA M. RAPHAEL
SEDL • Austin, Texas

FREDRICKA K. REISMAN
Goodwin College of Educational and Professional Studies
Drexel University • Philadelphia, Pennsylvania

KELLY REFFITT
Department of Curriculum, Teaching, and Educational Policy
Michigan State University • East Lansing, Michigan

DANIEL J. RESCHLY
Department of Education and Psychology
Vanderbilt University • Nashville, Tennessee

JORGE R. REYES
Department of Psychology
Westfield State College • Westfield, Massachusetts

CECIL R. REYNOLDS
Department of Educational Psychology
Texas A&M University • College Station, Texas

JULIA REYNOLDS
School of Education
Aquinas College • Grand Rapids, Missouri

MATTHEW R. REYNOLDS
Department of Psychology and Research in Education
University of Kansas • Lawrence, Kansas

PETER REYNOLDS
Clark County School District • Las Vegas, Nevada

LISA HUNTER ROMANELLI
Department of Child and Adolescent Psychiatry
Columbia University • New York, New York

SYLVIA ROSENFIELD
Department of Counseling and Personnel Services
University of Maryland, College Park • College Park, Maryland

NOA SAKA
Hebrew University of Jerusalem, Israel • Jerusalem, Israel

JONATHAN SANDOVAL
Department of Educational and School Psychology
University of the Pacific • Stockton, California

GREGORY SCHRAW
Department of Educational Psychology
University of Nevada–Las Vegas • Las Vegas, Nevada

EDWARD S. SHAPIRO
School Psychology Program
Lehigh University • Bethlehem, Pennsylvania

SUSAN M. SHERIDAN
Department of Educational Psychology
University of Nebraska–Lincoln • Lincoln, Nebraska

CHRISTOPHER H. SKINNER
Department of Educational Psychology and Counseling
University of Tennessee • Knoxville, Tennessee

KIMBERLY N. SLOMAN
The Graduate School of Applied and Professional Psychology
Rutgers University • New Brunswick, New Jersey

KATHRYN L. SOLIC
University of Tennessee • Knoxville, Tennessee

KEVIN D. STARK
Department of Educational Psychology
University of Texas at Austin • Austin, Texas

KAREN STOIBER
Department of Educational Psychology
University of Wisconsin–Milwaukee • Milwaukee, Wisconsin

KATHY STROUD
Carrollton-Farmers Branch Independent School District • Carrollton, Texas

TIMOTHY R. VOLLMER
Department of Psychology
University of Florida • Gainesville, Florida

MARLEY W. WATKINS
School Psychology Program
Arizona State University • Tempe, Arizona

ELIZABETH M. WHITEHOUSE
University of Minnesota, Twin Cities • Minneapolis, Minnesota

JIM YSSELDYKE
Department of Educational Psychology
University of Minnesota, Twin Cities • Minneapolis, Minnesota

SHENGLAN ZHANG
Department of Educational Foundations, Research, and Technology
Winona State University • Winona, Minnesota

DOLORES M. ZYGMONT
Temple University • Philadelphia, Pennsylvania

• DEDICATION •

To my wife, Barbara Gutkin; my children Laura Geduldig and Jeffrey Gutkin and their respective spouses Paul Geduldig and Helene Blatter; and my grandchildren Elijah Skye Geduldig, Hattie Rose Gutkin, Gabriel Sage Geduldig, and those that may be yet unborn. I wish for you and all peoples of this earth, a life of peace, justice, human dignity and love.

TBG

To Julia, as always, for always.
CRR

FOREWORD

The *Handbook* editors (Gutkin and Reynolds) continue to offer an invaluable service to psychology by their monumental efforts to synthesize trends, findings, and aspirations of our field. Such work has become even more valuable over the 26 year history of the Handbooks as information creation has exploded and school psychologists have disseminated their research and practice findings in an increasingly diverse array of scholarly vehicles. Both the amount and distribution of our knowledge make staying well informed increasingly difficult.

Handbooks in many fields play complementary roles of summarizing the biggest findings of an area, identifying the parameters of a field in terms of topics of inquiry, and making gaps in our knowledge more visible so as to facilitate next scholarly steps. A cursory review of the previous three editions of the *Handbook of School Psychology* illustrates how the field has developed. For example, gone is the early focus on roles of school psychologists in favor of the current emphasis on how school psychology as a field of research and practice is influenced and influences all of psychology. Further, topics of interest have changed over time as new developments in assessment and intervention have improved the technologies we have to offer each other as researchers and the public as consumers of services. Unlike many texts, the *Handbook is* not a history book.

The current edition of the *Handbook* offers us the latest information available about the scientific underpinnings of the field. The array is impressive covering research methods, and special contributions from educational, developmental, cognitive, social, and biological psychology. Such information is vital in all our school psychology roles as we attempt to meet the increasing expectations of evidence-based practice which now characterizes all areas of psychology.

Given the historic roots and current practice of school psychology, a whole section of the *Handbook is* devoted to psychological and educational assessment. Sophisticated and complementary approaches to assessment are necessary foundations for the development of scientifically based interventions. Assessment as a guide to intervention is provided through state of the art reviews of response to intervention, assessment of instructional environments, and curriculum based approaches in addition to more traditional approaches to assessment. Of special note are treatments of diagnostic decision making errors and problems of bias in psychological assessment.

At the heart of school psychology practice and research are attempts to intervene to prevent or alleviate childhood difficulties in learning, behavior, and emotional regulation. Section 3 of the *Handbook* provides a mixture of intervention and prevention strategies appropriate for use across a wide array of challenges faced by children and their families.

Prevention through universal capacity building in schools, families, and communities is certainly the preferred role for school psychology.

Calls for school psychologists to be the public health specialists in psychology have a long history. It is clear that a good education is a powerful driver of personal resilience (health, economic welfare, mental health) and so a focus on educational attainment is a decisive mental health intervention. Section 4 of the *Handbook* is more squarely focused on this important area.

Helping a child learn to read is a powerful psychological intervention. Teaching social skills enhances children's opportunities to construct supportive peer groups which in turn can be buffers against victimization and models for educational attainment. We have compartmentalized our psychological thought in ways that do not match human development. A thorough reading of the *Handbook* is an antidote for this recalcitrant problem in psychological science and practice.

Perhaps every scholarly field of the 21st Century has the simultaneous experiences of despair and hope. After more than a century of psychology why do so many problems in classrooms, families, and communities remain? We know a lot about how to be helpful to children, teachers, and parents, but childhood disorders are pervasive. Our delivery systems are broken. Our access to children is highly dependent on their families' wealth not on their need.

On the other hand, in just a tiny fraction of recent human history, the secrets of mind/body are being unlocked and translated into strategies unthinkable just a decade ago. There is reason to be hopeful that technological advances and guidelines for behavior will suggest exciting new ways to avoid childhood difficulties and to treat many more.

There are, however, also reasons to be wary about our future influence as a profession. Children, though not absolutely determined by context, are vulnerable to disruptions in families, communities, schools, and their own development. The *Handbook* is appearing at a time of significant economic dislocation among millions of families and at a time when public confidence in political systems and public institutions may be at an all time low. Many school psychologists have little training and lack the platforms to influence these powerful forces.

Are we up to the notion that instead of identifying deficits we must build on strengths? Can we grapple with roles that span all the adults in children's lives? Can we master the knowledge bases that inform working with developing humans in complex organizations? My questions are probably answered with a, "no," at an individual level, but with a resounding, "yes," at a profession level. The *Handbook's* contents speak to the range of expertise that is available and needed for school psychology to be a force for good and a driver of psychological science.

The promise of the public practice of psychology has intrigued and inspired me for 30 years. I have never wavered in my belief that schools can be the best platforms for positive psychological intervention. This belief is the basis for my choice to lead a school of education. My hopes for school psychology have sometimes wavered. These hopes are revitalized, however, by the newest edition of the *Handbook*. Many of the authors are distinguished and long time contributors to the psychology literature and many more are rising stars armed with sophisticated research skills.

In 2008 images of war and warfare are common place in our society and perhaps explain why I am reminded of the words of Sir Winston Churchill (1874–1965) in 1941 in a speech at Harrow School,

> *Never give in–never, never, never, never, in nothing great or small, large or petty, never give in except to convictions of honour and good sense. Never yield to force; never yield to the apparently overwhelming might of the enemy.*

I think the connection between our work as school psychologists and those who do battle is regrettably apt. The threats to human welfare are strong, continuous, and evolving. Cyber bullying and sexual exploitation are on the rise. Child poverty with its accompanying effects on health and nutrition is a relentless reality in the U.S. despite our position as a world super power. Racism and intolerance of differences of all types seem unabated. Public schools are awash in systemic difficulties that threaten their effectiveness with children. Families are struggling to manage the pressures of work, family, and an increasingly materialistic culture. In the face of these real enemies, psychologists must be armed not only with techniques but with a world view that makes sense of how nested levels of influence affect children's behavior.

The *Handbook is* a valiant attempt to arm us for this battle of our lifetimes. We are confronted by forces that demand action beyond individual assessment and therapy. We are challenged to expand our competence to work with people who present as very different from our individual histories and comfort zones. As a beginning psychologist, I often said that my goal was to work myself out of a job. Now I realize that my goal is to never give up, never surrender, and never give in. We can't be done, but we can be relentless. Thank you, Terry and Cecil, for giving us more tools for success in the service of keeping children first.

JANE CLOSE CONOLEY
Dean and Professor,
University of California Santa Barbara
April, 2008

PREFACE

With the publication of the fourth edition of *The Handbook of School Psychology*, we strive to continue the tradition of providing a unique and comprehensive outlet for disseminating the collective wisdom and insight of outstanding scholars working in the field of school psychology. Like its predecessors, the fourth edition of *The Handbook* brings to a single publication the field's latest developments in research and practice, highlighting domains in which there has emerged both growing consensus and vibrant crosscurrents of thought and analysis. Featuring chapters with new foci, new authors, and new content, this edition showcases the trajectory of our field and is intended to lead researchers, academicians, field-based practitioners, and students alike forward into an increasingly challenging and rewarding future.

Along with the accelerating pace of change that has characterized society's emergence into the twenty-first century, school psychology has also continued to evolve with increasing rapidity. Since the prior edition, scientific progress has been evident in all aspects of professional practice and research. These are addressed in the pages of this latest volume by many of the very scholars who have pioneered and contributed directly to these advancements in our field.

In 2008 as we write this preface, the need for more effective school psychological services has never been more apparent. As detailed by Gutkin (this volume), our country faces pandemics in both mental health and education. Exemplifying this are distressing reports by: (a) the Center for Disease Control and Prevention revealing that anti-depressant medication has become the most frequently prescribed category of pharmaceuticals in the United States of America (Burt, McCaig, & Rechtsteiner, 2007), and (b) the Surgeon General concluding that "the nation is facing a public crisis in mental healthcare for infants, children and adolescents" (U.S. Public Health Service, 2000) and that the "foremost finding is that most children in need of mental health services do not get them." (U.S. Department of Health and Human Services, 1999, p. 180). Against this backdrop, school psychology finds itself at the nexus of ameliorative treatment, early intervention, prevention, public health services and health promotion for America's children, youth and their families. The potential impact of our professional contributions has never been greater.

The dominant theme pervading all prior editions of *The Handbook* is very evident yet again in this latest volume. Progress in the field of school psychology depends on a growing and increasingly sophisticated body of scientific knowledge. The fourth edition of *The Handbook* undergirds that perspective yet again. As quoted by Reynolds (1982) beginning in our first edition, "In God we trust, all others must have data" (p. 178). For us, as editors of *The Handbook* series, this remains a truism.

With each passing edition of *The Handbook* other truisms have also begun to emerge. Perhaps the most compelling and demanding of these is the reality that we, as school psychologists, do not function in a vacuum. Everything we do takes place in a larger context, one that includes teachers, parents, administrators, communities, and society itself. The traditional view of isolated "patients" being "cured" in our isolated offices is utterly inconsistent with the reality of interconnected and reciprocally influential social systems that pervade, buttress, and often challenge every action we take or wish to take in behalf of the clients we strive to serve. Our best science and wisest professional insights must be directed effectively toward the systems and ecologies surrounding our clients just as surely as they must be responsive to the needs of our clients themselves. It is our belief that coming to grips with "the ecology of school psychology" (Sheridan & Gutkin, 2000, p. 485) will be essential if our field is to play a central rather than a peripheral role in reversing and recovering from our nation's mental health and educational pandemics noted earlier. The fourth edition of *The Handbook* is intended to underscore this truism and advance those bases of knowledge necessary to nourish this perspective.

Naturally, we could never have completed the fourth edition of *The Handbook* successfully without the assistance of more people than we have space to acknowledge. First and foremost there are our respective wives, Barbara Gutkin and Julia Hickman, who somehow found it in their hearts to give us the time and space necessary to bring this work to fruition—many times over the years. Their love, support, perseverance, and patience made this, and virtually everything else in our careers, possible. We would never have been able to achieve this without them. We are completely indebted to our authors, who produced works that we, as editors, felt were up to the high standards of scholarship we strove to establish for *The Handbook* since its inception. They are, of course, the "backbone" of this volume and to them we offer, both for ourselves and for the field of school psychology, our deepest appreciation. Our respective universities, San Francisco State and Texas A&M, have also earned our most sincere appreciation. Thank you for providing an environment that allowed the long-term and concentrated effort that was necessary to produce a work of this scope. Finally, we would like to acknowledge the incredibly long list of colleagues, many of whom are authors in this volume, who have served to improve our thinking and our vision for the field. While it is simply not possible to list each of you, we want to acknowledge our gratitude for your friendship, expertise, professionalism, willingness to challenge us when necessary so that we could

continue to grow as psychologists, and devotion to our field. Two of these individuals played such foundational roles for us as our earliest mentors, however, that we would be remiss not to acknowledge them on an individual basis: Beeman N. Phillips and Alan S. Kaufman. Thank you for being who you are, setting such high standards for us to aim toward throughout our careers, and making monumental contributions to school psychology and all those we serve. We are in your debt.

In 1982, the first *Handbook of School Psychology* found its way into print. Now, more than a quarter century later, we proudly offer the fourth edition. For us, *The Handbook* series has been an ongoing labor of love. Few things either of us have done professionally have meant more to us. It is our ardent hope that each of the editions has, in its own way, contributed substantively to the growth and development of effective school psychological services across the nation. Although we must admit to some considerable level of bias in our opinion, we do believe that this volume reflects our best effort to date. Hopefully, you, our readers, will ultimately come to agree.

TERRY B. GUTKIN
CECIL R. REYNOLDS

REFERENCES

Burt, C. W., McCaig, L. F., & Rechtsteiner, E. A. (2007). Ambulatory medical care utilization estimates for 2005. *Advance data from vital and health statistics; no. 388*. Hyattsville, MD: National Center for Health Statistics.

Gutkin, T. B. (2009). Ecological school psychology: A personal opinion and a plea for change. In T. B. Gutkin & C. R. Reynolds (Eds.), *The handbook of school psychology* (4th ed.). New York: Wiley.

Reynolds, C. R. (1982). The problem of bias in psychological assessment. In C. R. Reynolds & T. B. Gutkin (Eds.), *The handbook of school psychology*. New York: Wiley.

Sheridan, S. M., & Gutkin, T. B. (2000). The ecology of school psychology: Examining and changing our paradigm for the 21st century. *School Psychology Review, 29*, 485–502.

U. S. Department of Health and Human Services. (1999). *Mental health: A report of the surgeon general*. Rockville, MD: U.S. Department of Health and Human Services.

U. S. Public Health Service. (2000). *Report of the Surgeon General's Conference on Children's Mental Health: A National Action Agenda*. Washington, DC: Department of Health and Human Services. www.ncbi.nlm.nih.gov/books/bv.fcgi?rid=hstat5.section.842

CONTENTS

THE SCIENTIFIC FOUNDATIONS OF SCHOOL PSYCHOLOGY

●

CHAPTER 1

ADVANCES IN QUANTITATIVE RESEARCH

TIMOTHY Z. KEITH
The University of Texas-Austin
MATTHEW R. REYNOLDS
University of Kansas

The purpose of this chapter is to provide an overview of advances in quantitative methods with relevance for school psychological research. Our intent is to provide a brief overview of such methods along with resources for additional study; many of the overviews include worked examples. Some of the methods we will discuss are not yet widely used in school psychological research, but are quite applicable to the questions asked by researchers. Other methods are more common, but are often not used fully.

We begin the overview with a review of some aspects of multiple regression that are less common, but that make it one of the most flexible and powerful statistical techniques. Multiple regression provides a nice segue into more complex methods, including multilevel modeling (MLM), and also structural equation modeling (SEM) using both measured and latent variables. The final topic for the chapter is latent growth curve modeling (LGM). LGM has enormous potential to answer important questions in school psychological research. In addition, it illustrates nicely the overlap between MLM and SEM, techniques that seem quite unrelated on their surface.

MULTIPLE REGRESSION

Multiple regression (MR) is familiar to most school psychological researchers, and its use is fairly common in research. Nevertheless, our experience suggests that many researchers are unaware of the full power and flexibility of the method. Here, we present a broad overview of the method, and present in slightly more depth the use of MR to test interactions.

Multiple regression is, in many ways, a near-direct implementation of the general linear model. As such, MR subsumes Analysis of Variance (ANOVA) and other methods that may be more familiar to many researchers. MR has advantages over ANOVA, however, especially for the analysis of nonexperimental data. ANOVA is generally conducted using categorical independent variables (e.g., treatment versus control), whereas most nonexperimental research involves continuous independent variables (e.g., level of academic motivation) or a mixture of categorical and continuous variables (e.g., sex and motivation). Suppose a researcher is interested in the effects of academic motivation on students' subsequent achievement. A common, but ill-advised, approach is to divide the motivation variable at the median (the infamous "median split") and analyze the data using ANOVA or a *t*-test. This approach is ill-advised because it discards variance in the independent variable which, in turn, results in a less-powerful statistical analysis (Cohen, 1983).

One major advantage of MR is that it naturally accommodates both categorical and continuous variables. In MR it is also easy to include multiple independent variables; it is not unusual to see reports of MR analyses with a dozen or more independent variables. Such analyses would quickly become unmanageable using ANOVA methods. Finally, whereas ANOVA methods are especially useful for the analysis of experimental research—when participants are assigned to one versus another experimental manipulation—MR can be used to analyze both experimental and nonexperimental research (Keith, 2006).

There are three major varieties of MR: simultaneous regression, sequential regression, and stepwise regression, with each variety serving somewhat different purposes. Stepwise regression, in which the computer program chooses the order of entry into the regression equation, should rarely be used; the results are "theoretical garbage" (Wolfle, 1980, p. 206). With simultaneous regression (also known as standard multiple regression or forced entry regression), all variables enter the regression equation at the same time, and interpretation often revolves around the unstandardized and standardized regression coefficients (b and β, respectively). With sequential (also known as hierarchical) regression, researchers add variables, either one at a time or in blocks, and generally focus on the change in variance explained (ΔR^2).

Researchers often use sequential regression in an effort to determine the *unique* influence of one or several variables on an outcome, and accomplish this purpose by entering each variable last in a series of sequential regressions. Many researchers seem unaware that the same information is obtainable through a single simultaneous regression, because the regression coefficients from simultaneous regression also provide estimates of the unique effect of each variable on the outcome. The statistical significance of the regression coefficients from a simultaneous regression is the same as the significance of the ΔR^2s from sequential regression when each variable is added last to the equation. It is also possible to request the semipartial correlations (also known as part correlations) as a part of the simultaneous regression output. The squared semipartial correlations (sr^2) are equal to the variance that would be explained by each variable if it were added last to the regression equation (i.e., ΔR^2). Researchers who use sequential regression often use the ΔR^2 as a measure of the relative "importance" of the variables testing in the MR. Darlington (1990) and Keith (2006) have argued, however, that $\sqrt{\Delta R^2}$ (or sr) is a better measure of such importance.

Despite their overlap, simultaneous and sequential MR do serve somewhat different purposes. We find it useful to think about MR results in figural, or path analytic form, such as shown in Figure 1.1. Simultaneous and sequential regression estimate different aspects of this model. Briefly, simultaneous regression estimates the direct effects (paths b and c) from this model. In contrast, sequential regression estimates the total effects in this model (to be more exact, the ΔR^2 estimates the *variance explained* by the total effects, not the total effects themselves). So, for

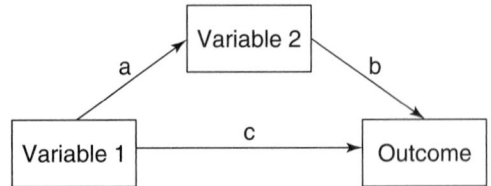

FIGURE 1.1 **Sequential versus simultaneous regression.**

example, if the model in Figure 1.1 were analyzed by first regressing Outcome on Variable 1 and then sequentially adding Variable 2, the ΔR^2 from the first step in this regression would represent the variance explained by the total effect of Variable 1 on the Outcome (total effect = the direct effect of Variable 1 on Outcome, plus the indirect effect of Variable 1 on Outcome through Variable 2). We hope it is obvious from this discussion that the order of entry in sequential regression is critical. That is, if the results are interpreted as suggesting the effect of one variable on another, then the variables need to be entered in the correct order, an order consistent with the true causal order.

At the same time, users of simultaneous regression underestimate, to some extent, the effect of one variable on another. A simultaneous regression of Outcome on Variable 1 and Variable 2 will provide estimates of path b and path c. As a result, simultaneous regression estimates the direct effect of Variable 1 on Outcome, but does not (without additional analysis) estimate the *indirect* effect of Variable 1 on Outcome through Variable 2 (path a times path b), nor does it estimate the total effect of Variable 1 on Outcome (direct plus indirect effect).

Mediation

This discussion of indirect and direct effects provides a useful transition into mediation in MR. Indirect effects are also referred to as mediated effects, and Variable 2 in Figure 1.1 could also be referred to as a mediator. School psychology researchers are becoming increasingly interested in issues of mediation, and for good reason. Understanding mediation can enrich the understanding of both experimental and nonexperimental findings. For example, by what mechanism does student motivation affect high school students' learning? One possibility is via the coursework that students take. Students who are more highly motivated take a more academic mix of high school courses, which in turn leads to higher achievement (Cool & Keith, 1991). By what mechanism does a treatment program reduce adolescent girls' depression? One possibility is by changing girls' mental schemata (Sander & McCarty, 2005; Stark et al., 2006). Understanding important mediators helps researchers to understand *how* a treatment has an effect.

Most researchers interested in mediation are familiar with the classic article by Baron and Kenny (1986). Many researchers seem unaware, however, that much progress has been made in understanding and testing mediation since that classic article was published (cf. MacKinnon, Lockwood, Hoffman, West, & Sheets, 2002; Shrout & Bolger, 2002). In particular, structural equation modeling (SEM) has become commonplace in the social sciences, and structural equation models (including path models) offer advantages for understanding and estimating mediated effects. Even those who use MR to test for mediation can benefit from an understanding of the SEM approach. For these reasons, we will postpone further discussion of mediation until the section on SEM.

Moderation

Although researchers routinely test for interactions when analyzing factorial experiments via ANOVA, it is less common to test for interactions in MR analyses. This difference is understandable for two reasons. First, interactions are relatively rare in nonexperimental research (Darlington, 1990), and MR is particularly useful for analyzing nonexperimental research. Second, testing for interactions in ANOVA often happens by default as a part of the statistical analysis, whereas testing for interactions requires a specific series of steps in MR (Aiken & West, 1991). Although less common, interaction testing in MR can answer important research questions.

Interactions answer whether the effects of an independent variable on an outcome vary depending on the values of another independent variable. Moderation is another term for interaction, and when a researcher reports that, for example, sex moderates the effect of self-concept on achievement, this is simply another way of saying that sex and self-concept interact in their effect on achievement. Cool and Keith (1991) examined the effects of a number of variables, including amount of academic coursework, on high school students' academic achievement. Although academic coursework affected achievement, it also

seems likely that the effects of academic coursework should vary depending on students' intellectual ability. That is, it seems likely that bright high school students would benefit from taking more academically challenging courses, but that such coursework would be less beneficial for low ability youth. Again, this is a question of moderation, or interaction: does ability *moderate* the effect of coursework on high school achievement?

The basic method for testing for interactions in MR first requires the creation of a new variable that is a crossproduct of the two variables that are to be tested for interaction. In the coursework and ability example, this would involve creating a crossproduct/interaction variable by multiplying the academic coursework variable by the intellectual ability variable. The crossproduct term (there may be more than one) is then entered sequentially after the original variables and any other independent variables; ΔR^2 is used to determine the statistical significance of the crossproduct/interaction. For interpretive purposes, it is generally beneficial to center any continuous interacting variables prior to multiplication. Thus for the coursework example, both variables (coursework and ability) would be centered; for the sex and self-concept example, only the self-concept variable would be centered prior to multiplying it times the sex variable. If a statistically significant interaction is found, graphing and other follow-ups can be used to understand better the nature of the interaction (Aiken & West, 1991; Keith, 2006).

The examples discussed briefly here illustrate that interactions can be tested with a categorical variable (sex) and a continuous variable, or with two continuous variables; two categorical variables can also be used. The ability to test interactions with continuous variables is an important advantage over ANOVA methods, which generally only consider categorical variables (e.g., treatment versus control) in interactions. The method is important in school psychology because there are several common research questions of interest in the field that involve the interaction of categorical and continuous variables. Tests of predictive bias in psychometric research and tests of aptitude-treatment interactions (ATIs) are two examples. ATIs are particularly relevant, because they are often incorrectly analyzed using median splits in ANOVA with a resulting loss of statistical power. Numerous examples are illustrated in more depth in Aiken and West (1991) and Keith (2006).

MULTILEVEL MODELING

A theme of this chapter is that all of the methods are in some way related to, or are extensions of, the general linear model (GLM). Multilevel modeling (MLM) is likewise a generalization of the general linear model, and a set of methods that include familiar ANOVA and regression techniques. MLM techniques, however, overcome some of the weaknesses of traditional regression and ANOVA approaches, providing researchers with more flexibility in testing research questions of interest.

Multilevel modeling, sometimes referred to as hierarchical linear modeling (HLM), random slopes modeling, or mixed modeling, is a set of modeling techniques used to test relations among variables that are structured in a hierarchical or nested manner. For example, students are nested in classrooms, which are nested in schools, which are nested in districts, and so on. Traditional statistical techniques have not adequately modeled these nested structures at their appropriate level, but MLM does (Raudenbush & Bryk, 2002). With the availability of programs such as HLM 6 (Raudenbush, Bryk, & Congdon, 2005), MLwiN (Rabash et al., 2000), Mplus (Muthén & Muthén, 1998–2007), and SAS PROC MIXED (Littell, Milliken, Stroup, & Wolfinger, 1996), MLM is becoming more popular among researchers in the social sciences.

MLM is of interest to social science researchers because it models clustering appropriately. One key assumption of most statistical analyses is that of the independence of observations. Meeting this assumption requires that all participants are drawn independently from the population. In the real world, however, participants are often clustered in groups. For example, graduate students in a math department tend to be more like each other than they are like students in a social work department; hence, there is clustering or dependency within departments. Typical regression methods do not account for this clustering, and as a result, run the risk of inflated standard errors and Type I error.

The fact that people are often clustered in groups is not a new revelation, and various methods have been used to take such clustering into account. One common method is to make comparisons at the group level rather than the individual level. For example, a researcher might aggregate individual test scores (Level 1) into higher level units such as mean scores from a math department and mean test scores from a social work department (Level 2). This method, however, results in losing valuable information about the data, unless of course everybody in the math department is identical to each other and everybody in the social work department is identical to each other. Because individuals do differ, comparisons at the group level result in a loss of information and a loss of power. The researcher would thus have to make a decision about whether to compare departments at the group level and lose power, compare students at the individual level and risk Type I error, or estimate them separately, which is cumbersome and does not allow for simultaneous estimations of effects. The advantage of MLM is that it makes use of estimation techniques that allow for the simultaneous estimation of group-level effects (accounting for dependency in the observations) and individual-level effects (so power is not lost). An example will help illustrate the method.

Example: Individual and School Effects on High School GPA
The Data

The data are from the National Education Longitudinal Study (see Keith, 2006 for numerous regression and SEM examples using these data). The data include 11,270 students from 836 schools. The variables Socioeconomic Status (SES, a composite of parent educational attainment, parent occupational status, and family income), Previous Achievement (an average of four short achievement tests administered in eighth grade), and Time Spent on Homework Out of School (tenth grade) will be used to explain student GPA (grade point average) in tenth grade. All analyses were performed with the HLM6 program (Raudenbush et al., 2005). A free student version of this program can be downloaded from www.ssicentral.com/hlm/downloads.html.

HLM software requires that the data be structured in a particular format so that there is a file containing a variable for each "level" of the model. Our model will have two levels, students at Level 1, and schools at Level 2, so in one file we have student-level variables and in the other file we have school-level variables. (For conceptual purposes it might be easier to think of the Level 1 model as the within-schools model and the Level 2 model as the between-schools model.) For the remainder of this example, we will use the term "student level" for Level 1 models and "school level" for Level 2 models. The student-level dataset contains the student variables SES, Previous Achievement, Homework, and GPA. The school-level dataset has the school variables School SES (average SES of a school), School Previous Achievement (average achievement of a school), and School Homework (average homework of a school). There is also a School ID variable in each data set. This variable links the student and school level models. In the student model there are 11,270 rows for 11,270 individual students, and each observation is associated with one of the 836 schools. In the school-level model there are 836 rows for 836 schools. Our general research question is: Are there both student-level and school-level effects on student GPA?

Fully Unconditional Model

The next step in MLM is to build the models. Note that it is often unnecessary to go through each of these steps as in this example, but building models in this fashion will make the relation of MLM to regression easier to follow. The first step is to estimate a "fully unconditional" model (Raudenbush & Bryk, 2002). The model is termed unconditional because it does not include explanatory variables at either the student or school level; the outcome is not "conditioned" on explanatory variables. This a baseline model that is compared to subsequent models.

The equations shown in Table 1.1 show the fully unconditional model as two equations and combined into a single equation. The overall outcome variable is GPA, which is the average GPA across all students and all schools. Y_{ij} represents the GPA for student i in school j. In the school model, β_{0j} represents the average GPA for school j. In the student model, GPA (Y_{ij}) is a function of the average GPA of an individual school (the intercept, β_{0j}) plus the student-level residual term (e_{ij}). However, as shown in the school model, a *school's* GPA (the intercept term from the student model, β_{0j}) is a function of the weighted average GPA of the all schools (grand mean, γ_{00}) plus the school level residual term (u_{0j}). In other words, the fully unconditional model simply says that a student's GPA is a function of the school mean GPA, plus or minus random variation at the school level, plus or minus random variation at the individual student level. In MLM models, the residual variance is separated into within- and between-school variance. If there is variability within the schools or between the schools, a researcher can add explanatory variables at the student level to explain the variability within schools and add explanatory variables at the school level to explain the variability between schools.

The results of the fully unconditional model are shown in Table 1.2 in the Fully Unconditional Model column. The results show that the mean GPA (γ_{00}) across all schools and students is 5.78. This mean is statistically significantly different from zero, but this is uninteresting because GPA is expected be greater than zero. Of interest, however, are the student (e_{ij}) and school (u_{0j}) level residual variance components (i.e., within-school and between-school variance). As shown in Table 1.2, the student level residual variance component is 1.95 and the school level residual variance component is .20. Both components are statistically significant.

These two residual variance components allow for the computation of the intraclass correlation, which tells us about the degree of clustering within groups. The intraclass correlation is simply the variability in GPA between schools divided by the total variability in GPA (between + within), or the proportion of variance that is at the school level. The intraclass coefficient for this model suggests that 9% of the total variation in the GPA scores is between schools. Or, if we were to randomly select two students from one school, their GPAs would correlate, on average, .09. Hence, there is some clustering or dependency within schools.

It is useful to specify a fully unconditional model as an initial step because the outcome variation can be separated into within- and between-school variation. Because explanatory variables are not included at either level in these models, all of the residual variance remains unexplained allowing researchers to determine whether there is substantial variability at both levels. In our example, although only 9% of the total variation in GPA is at the school level, it is statistically significant, and the validity of statistical inference may be affected if it is not modeled correctly. The

TABLE 1.1   **Equations for the MLM Fully Unconditional Model**

Student Level Equation	**School Level Equation**	**Combined Equation**
$Y_{ij} = \beta_{0j} + e_{ij}$	$\beta_{0j} = \gamma_{00} + u_{0j}$	$Y_{ij} = \gamma_{00} + u_{0j} + e_{ij}$

TABLE 1.2   MLM Results Explaining Student GPA as a Product of School-Level and Within-School SES, Previous Achievement, and Homework

Fixed Effects	Fully Unconditional Coefficients (se)	Means as Outcomes Coefficients (se)	Random-Coefficient Coefficients (se)	Means and Regression Coefficients as Outcomes Coefficients (se)	Final Model Coefficients (se)
Means (β_{0j})					
Intercept (γ_{00})	5.78 (.02)	5.75 (.02)	5.77 (.02)	5.75 (.02)	5.75 (.02)
School Previous Achievement (γ_{01})		.06 (.007)*		.06 (.005)*	.06 (.005)*
School Homework (γ_{02})		.13 (.03)*		.13 (.03)*	.12 (.03)*
School SES (γ_{03})		−.02 (.07)			
Previous Achievement Slopes (β_{1j})					
Intercept (γ_{10})			.08 (.001)*	.08 (.001)*	.08 (.001)*
School Previous Achievement (γ_{11})				.003 (.0007)*	.003 (.0005)*
School Homework (γ_{12})				−.008 (.003)*	−.009 (.003)*
School SES (γ_{13})				−.002 (.007)	
Homework Slopes (β_{2j})					
Intercept (γ_{20})			.08 (.01)*	.08 (.01)*	.08 (.01)*
School Previous Achievement (γ_{21})				.006 (.002)*	.004 (.001)*
School Homework (γ_{22})				−.002 (.01)	
School SES (γ_{23})				−.03 (.02)	
SES Slope (β_{3j})					
Intercept (γ_{30})			.21 (.02)*	.21 (.02)*	.21 (.02)*

TABLE 1.2 *(Continued)*

Random Effects	Variance Component	Variance Component	Variance Component	Variance Component	Variance Component
Student effects (e_{ij})	1.95 (1.40)	1.95 (1.40)*	1.34 (1.16)	1.34 (1.16)*	1.34 (1.16)*
School effects (u_{ij})					
Intercept (u_{0j})	.20 (.45)*	.09 (.30)	.24 (.49)*	.11 (.37)*	.13 (.37)*
Previous Achievement (u_{1j})			.0004 (.02)*	.0004 (.02)*	.0004 (.02)*
Homework (u_{2j})			.008 (.09)*	.007 (.09)*	.007 (.08)*
SES (u_{3j})			.02 (.000)		

*Note. * indicates statistical significance at the p < .05 level.*

next step is to add school-level explanatory variables to try to account for this variation between schools.

Means-As-Outcomes Model

The second model is referred to as a means-as-outcomes model (Raudenbush & Bryk, 2002). In this model, we try to explain the variation among the school level means. In our example, we will seek to explain the school-level residual variance from the fully unconditional model by adding the School Previous Achievement, School Homework, and School SES variables to the school level model. Each school mean is explained, in part, by School Previous Achievement, School Homework, and School SES. The multilevel equation for this model and subsequent models is shown in the appendix.[1]

In this model, the student-level model remains the same as in the fully unconditional model. In the school-level model, however, School Previous Achievement, School Homework, and School SES are added as explanatory variables to explain school GPA. Here, the school-level residual variance will be the between-school variance that remains after controlling for School Previous Achievement, School Homework, and School SES.

[1]We centered the student level variables around the group mean to keep all of the parameters interpretable, and all school level variables were centered about the grand mean. Space limitations preclude a discussion of the use of centering.

The results are displayed in Table 1.2 in the means as outcomes column, which shows the unstandardized regression coefficients and their standard errors. School SES was not statistically significant, meaning that school-level SES did not affect school GPA once School Previous Achievement and School Homework were controlled. School Previous Achievement and School Homework did, however, have a statistically significant effect on school GPA. In fact, School Previous Achievement and Homework explained 55% of the school-level variability among tenth grade school GPAs. This variance is calculated as the school residual variance from the fully unconditional model (essentially the "total" residual at the school level) minus the school residual variance from the means as outcome model, divided by the school-level residual variance from the fully unconditional model (.2–.09/.2). (Note that because we had an explanatory variable that was not significant we re-ran the analysis to figure out the proportion of variance explained by the two statistically significant variables). Comparisons of the intraclass correlation coefficients show that the correlation between two random GPA scores selected from a school is reduced from .09 to .04 after controlling for School Previous Achievement and School Homework.

It is worth reviewing what we just did. First, we separated out the variability of tenth grade GPA within schools from the variability of tenth grade GPA between schools. About 91% of the overall variation occurred within schools (i.e., at the student level); we have yet to try to account for this variation. We also found that about 9% of the overall variation occurred between schools (i.e., school level). School Previous Achievement and School Homework had statistically significant effects on school GPA and account for about 55% (of the 9%) of the variation in GPA at the school level. Of course we are interested in understanding more than just differences between school GPAs. Our interest is in explaining why schools *and* students have different GPAs. If we stopped here, it would be like comparing the math department with the social work department, excluding all of the within-department information. Therefore, subsequent models will include school- *and* student-level explanatory variables. We would not be modeling the data very well if we still had 91% of the variation in GPA scores left unaccounted!

Random-Coefficient Model

Before we begin with this model, we need to explain what a random coefficient is. Typically, when researchers perform regression analyses, the coefficients are fixed. That is, the coefficients represent a single estimate of the relation between the explanatory variable and the outcome variable across all students and schools. In MLM, we are concerned about different levels, so researchers are concerned about whether these coefficients vary across students *and* schools. As the title of this model suggests, the coefficients for the student-level variables will be free to vary across schools, like we allowed the school means to vary across schools in the unconditional model. In other words, the regression coefficient associated with homework for school 1 can be different from that found for school 2, which can be different from that found for school 3, and so on.

Figure 1.2 shows a graphic representation of what is happening. We selected 13 schools from our 836, and the lines in this figure represent separate regressions of GPA on Homework for each school. Note that on the y axis, the intercepts (the school GPAs) are not the same, they vary. It is this variability that we tried to explain in the means-as-outcomes model. If the school intercepts did not vary, then the lines would all cross the y axis at the same point. It is also easy to see that the steepness of the lines (or slopes) is not the same across schools. If they were, then all of the lines would be parallel to each other. Because we allowed the slopes (i.e., the regression

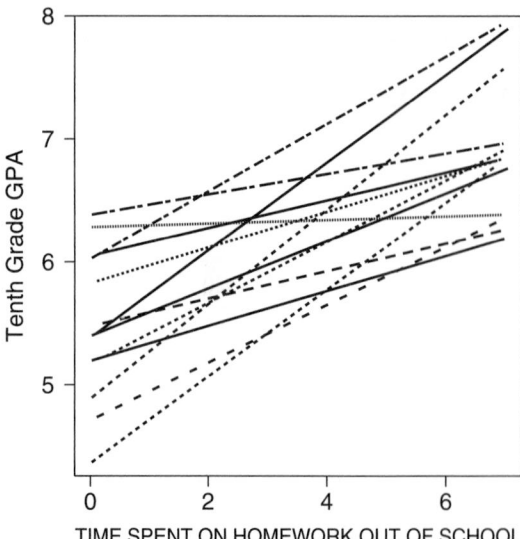

FIGURE 1.2 Regression lines for the effects of Homework on GPA for 13 different schools.

coefficients) to vary randomly across schools, they differ, and we will now try to explain this variability by including explanatory variables at the school level. Note that if we modeled the coefficients as fixed, then all of the lines would be parallel. If we modeled both the means (intercepts) and coefficients as fixed then we would just have one line that represents the relation between homework and GPA. (This latter type of model should sound familiar because that is what is modeled in a typical regression.) In the MLM example we have 836 schools, so we will have 836 individual regression equations with 836 regression coefficients associated with Homework, Previous Achievement, and SES. The variability of the coefficients about the average of each respective coefficient is captured in additional residual terms included at the school level for each coefficient.

Until now, we have been concerned only about differences in each school's GPA scores. Now, however, we are interested in determining, first, whether variables at the student level help explain GPA within schools, and second, if these relations vary across schools. Therefore in the student-level model we include the variables student Previous Achievement, Homework, and SES, and allow the relation between each of these variables with GPA to vary from school to school. The equation for this model is also shown in the appendix.

In the student-level model there are now three variables to explain GPA within schools. The residual term (e_{ij}) no longer captures the total within school variance; instead, it captures the within school variance that remains *after controlling for* Previous Achievement, Homework, and SES. Note that in the school-level model, a school-level residual term is included for each of the three explanatory variables (i.e., u_{1j}, u_{2j}, u_{3j}). If we had substantive reason to believe that any of these variables should *not* vary across schools, then we could model these as fixed by setting the school-level residual variance term to be zero (not allowing the coefficients to vary across schools, which is what is done typically in regression). For example, if theory suggested that there was no reason for the relation between Homework and GPA to vary across schools, we would fix the residual term, u_{2j}, to be zero for the Homework variable at the school level and the equation would be $\beta_{2j} = \gamma_{12} + 0$.

The column for the random-coefficients model in Table 1.2 shows that the student explanatory variables of Previous Achievement (β_{1j}), Homework (β_{2j}), and SES (β_{3j}), each had a statistically significant effect on within school GPA and thus will be included in subsequent models.

Next, to determine if there was significant variability in these effects across schools (that is, whether the slopes or regression coefficients differ across schools), we investigated whether the relation between Previous Achievement and GPA, and the relation between Homework and GPA, and the relation of SES and GPA varied among schools. This question is akin to asking whether schools interact with these variables in their effects on GPA, or whether schools moderate the effects of SES, Previous Achievement, and Homework on GPA. The table shows that the variance of the effects of SES on GPA *between* schools (u_{3j}) was not statistically significant. This means that the effect of student SES on GPA does not vary across the schools; SES had consistent effects for school 1 as school 2, and so on. Because SES effects did not vary across schools, in subsequent models we modeled SES as a fixed effect by fixing the school level residual variance term to zero. The effects of School Previous Achievement (u_{1j}) and School Homework (u_{2j}) on GPA, however, did vary across schools, so in subsequent models we will model these effects as random and include school-level variables to try to explain this variation.

So far we have analyzed three models. We know that school GPA varies across schools (9% of the total variation). School Previous Achievement and School Homework have a significant effect on school GPA, accounting for about 55% of the between school variation. We know that student SES, Homework, and Previous Achievement affect student GPA within schools. The effects of SES on GPA are consistent across schools; however, the effects of Previous Achievement and Homework are not consistent across the schools. Like we did when we tried to explain why GPA differed among schools by adding school-level explanatory variables, we now want to explain why the effects of Previous Achievement and Homework on GPA vary across schools by adding school-level explanatory variables.

Means and Regression Coefficients as Outcomes Model

The fourth model, which we will call the means and regression coefficients as outcomes model, is similar to the means as outcome model; it again includes School Previous Achievement and School Homework as explanatory variables for school GPA. Now, however, we also include school-level explanatory variables to try to explain why the relation between Previous Student Achievement and GPA and the relation between Homework and GPA varies across schools. Essentially, we are taking the regression coefficients from the student-level model and regressing them on school-level explanatory variables (Reise & Duan, 1999).

In this model, SES was modeled as a fixed effect because it did not vary across schools. Three school-level explanatory variables—School Previous Achievement, School Homework, and School SES—are included for each of the two random coefficients (Previous Achievement and Homework). The residual in the second school level equation, u_{1j}, now represents the between-school variation in the slopes of GPA on Previous Achievement, after controlling for School Previous Achievement, School Homework, and School SES. Note that any school-level explanatory variables can be included in the model. For example, other variables such as public versus Catholic schools, or urban versus rural location, could have been included in the model.

The results in Table 1.2 indicate that two school level variables, School Previous Achievement (γ_{11}) and School Homework (γ_{12}), moderate the relation between previous achievement and tenth grade GPA (β_{1j}). School SES (γ_{13}) is not significant so it will be deleted from subsequent models. The results also show that the School Previous Achievement (γ_{21}) moderates the relation between homework and tenth grade GPA (β_{2j}). School Homework (γ_{22}) and School SES (γ_{23}) were not significant in explaining variation in homework slopes, and will not be included in future models. The moderated relations between the school level variable and student level coefficient are referred to as a cross-level interactions.

Final Model

The fifth and final model is similar to the means and regression coefficients as outcomes model, but only includes variables that were statistically significant from the earlier models. The equations are shown in the appendix.

Previous Achievement, Homework, and SES are included as explanatory variables at the student level. At the school level, School Previous Achievement and School Homework are included to explain differences in school GPAs. We treat SES as a fixed effect by setting the school-level residual variance term to be zero, thus not allowing the SES coefficient to vary between schools. The coefficients for Previous Achievement and Homework, however, are free to vary across schools. The School Previous Achievement and School Homework variables are included to explain the variation in the previous achievement effects across schools. The School Previous Achievement variable is included at the school level to explain the variation in homework effects across schools. The results for the final model are shown in the final column of Table 1.2.

Interpretation of Final Model

With all of the variables and different levels included in MLM, the equations get messy and sometimes interpretation can get lost in the mess. Therefore, we will interpret these findings by focusing on answers to research questions related to this research. The interpretation shows some of the advantages of MLM over traditional regression (viz., interpretation at the appropriate level and not wasting information).

1. *Does any of the variation in tenth grade GPA occur between schools?* Yes, about 9% of the total variation in GPAs occurs between schools and 91% of the variation occurs within schools.

2. *Are there school-level variables that can explain the variation in GPA between schools?* Yes, School Previous Achievement and School Homework explain about 55% (of the 9%) of the between-school variation. This is a finding that would not be obtained in traditional regression.

3. *Do student-level variables affect GPA within schools?* Yes, Student Previous Achievement, Homework, and SES influence student GPA.

4. *Do the effects of previous achievement, homework, and SES vary across the 836 schools?* Yes, the effects of previous achievement and homework on tenth grade GPA vary across the schools. The effect of SES on tenth grade GPA does not vary across the schools.

5. *Do school-level variables help explain the differences in effects of previous achievement and homework across schools?* Yes, School Previous Achievement and School Homework explain some of the variation in the effects of previous achievement. Or stated differently, School Previous Achievement and School Homework moderate the effects of student previous achievement on GPA. Likewise, School Previous Achievement helps explain the variation between schools in the effects of homework on GPA. Or, School Previous Achievement moderates the effect of student homework on GPA.

This introduction has only discussed MLM as a method for dealing with nesting and school/organizational studies. MLM is also useful for answering questions about change (Singer & Willett, 2003) and for explaining variation in effects across studies (i.e., meta-analysis) (Hox, 2002). The application of MLM to studying change will be touched upon later in the growth modeling section of this chapter. The use of MLM for meta-analysis is a very appealing feature. The logic is similar to that presented here, except rather than having students nested within schools, in the meta-analytic framework, findings are nested within studies. Similar to adding school-level explanatory variables, in meta-analysis explanatory variables are included to explain varying effects across studies.

Again, this is only a cursory introduction to MLM. To learn about more about the basics as well as extensions, see Goldstein (2003), Hox (2002), Kreft and de Leeuw (1998), Raudenbush and Bryk (2002), or Snijders & Bosker (1999).

STRUCTURAL EQUATION MODELING[2]

We previously described MR as a close implementation of the general linear model. Likewise, structural equation modeling (SEM) can be considered a near-direct implementation of the multivariate general linear model. As such, SEM is a very general approach, one that subsumes many of the other statistical analyses common to the social sciences. With SEM, a researcher can use multiple independent variables to explain multiple dependent variables. When multiple measures of each construct are used in a *latent variable* SEM, unreliability and invalidity in the measures are taken into account, allowing the researchers to get closer to the construct level of true interest. Extensions of SEM also allow the analysis of latent categorical variables as well as multilevel models (e.g., Muthén & Muthén, 1998–2007).

In this chapter the term SEM will be used to refer to all types of structural equation modeling, with and without latent variables. The term *path analysis* will be used to refer to a subtype of SEM that uses only measured variables, whereas *latent variable SEM* will be used to refer to the subtype of SEM in which models include latent or unmeasured variables.

There are a number of computer programs available to conduct SEM, along with path analysis and confirmatory factor analysis. The first such program was LISREL (Jöreskog & Sörbom, 1996), an acronym for Linear Structural Relations; other common programs include EQS (Bentler, 1995) and Mplus (Muthén & Muthén, 1998–2007). Each program has its own unique features, advantages, and disadvantages. Mplus, for example, has sophisticated methods for dealing with categorical variables. We used the Amos (Analysis of Moment Structures) program (Arbuckle, 2006) to analyze the examples used in this chapter. Amos is probably the easiest SEM program to use, with graphic input for models and high quality graphic output (the SEM figures in this chapter are Amos input and output).

SEM with Measured Variables

The simplest form of SEM uses measured variables, and is often referred to as path analysis. An example will help illustrate the method and provide a comparison for more complex methods. Figure 1.3 shows a model designed to test the

influence of academic motivation and academic coursework on high school GPA. The data are from High School and Beyond (HSB), a nationally representative sample of high school sophomores and seniors from the 1980s. The example is drawn from Keith and Benson (1992), who focused on these and additional variables using longitudinal data from the sophomore cohort.

Family Background was a composite of parent education, parent occupational status, and family income. Ability was a measure of vocabulary knowledge. Academic Motivation was a composite of questions concerning students' school effort, school attitude, and academic aspirations. Coursework represented the number of academically-oriented courses in high school (coursework in the "New Basics"), and the Grades variable was students' high school GPA. The model is longitudinal: Family Background, Ability, and Motivation were measured in tenth grade, and Coursework and Grades were from students' transcripts at the end of high school.

The paths in the model represent the presumed effects of one variable on another. Effects may be direct, such as the effect of Motivation on Grades, or indirect, such as the effect of Motivation on Grades through Coursework, or both. Note that not all possible paths are drawn, so, for example, there is no path drawn from Family Background to Grades. This lack of a path means the researcher believes that there is no such effect; it is a strong statement, and is equivalent to drawing the path but constraining it to a value of zero. Because of this undrawn path, the model is "overidentified," meaning we have more information than we need to solve for the paths. As will be shown, there are advantages to having overidentified models. The curved line between Family Background and Ability represents the covariance (in the unstandardized solution) or correlation (standardized) between these two variables.

The small variables enclosed in ellipses are equivalent to the residuals from multiple regression, but are generally called *disturbances* (or sometimes errors) in SEM. Variables enclosed in circles or ellipses are, by convention, unmeasured variables, as opposed to the measured variables, enclosed in rectangles. The measured variables are just that; we have actual measures of Grades, Motivation, and so on, in our data set. Unmeasured, or latent, variables may seem a strange concept, but, in fact, we deal with them often, such as the residuals in MR, or the synthetic

---

[2]This section is adapted from Keith, 1999.

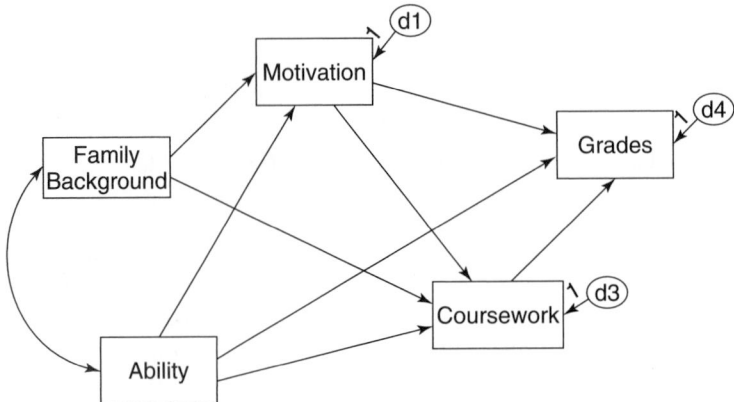

FIGURE 1.3 Initial path model of the effects of Motivation and Coursework on high school GPA.

variable analyzed in a repeated measures ANOVA. As will be shown, latent variables are often the most important variables in research. The paths from the disturbances to the corresponding measured variables are set to one. Latent variables have no inherent scale; setting this path to one simply sets the disturbances to have the same scale as the variable they are pointing to.

The model *could* be analyzed via multiple regression analysis. In that case, the standardized paths to Grades would be the βs from the simultaneous regression of Grades on Coursework, Motivation, and Ability; the paths to Coursework are the βs from the regression of Coursework on Motivation, Ability, and Family Background, and so on. There are, however, advantages to analyzing the model using a SEM program such as Amos or LISREL.

The standardized results of the analysis are shown in Figure 1.4. To the lower right of the figure are the fit statistics, providing information about the quality of the model. It would be possible to solve the model shown, by hand, via the original correlations among the variables in the model. One could also do the reverse: calculate the correlations from the paths shown in Figure 1.4. When a model is just-identified, meaning (loosely) that the number of correlations in the original matrix is equal to the number of paths and correlations estimated in the model[3], then the

original matrix and the matrix implied by the model will be identical. As noted above, however, this model is overidentified; with overidentified models, the actual matrix and the implied matrix will differ to some extent. The fit statistics shown in the lower right of Figure 1.4 use the extent of the similarity or difference in these two matrices to provide some feedback as to the plausibility of the model. For the present model, the fit indices suggest an excellent fit of the model to the data. What this means, and the different fit indices, will be discussed in a little more depth in the section on latent variable models. For now, simply understand that the ability to assess fit of overidentified models is a major advantage of analyzing such models using SEM programs.

The standardized results, shown in Figure 1.4, suggest that—given the accuracy of the model, and other things being equal—each *SD* unit change in Motivation will result in .22 *SD* change in GPA, and each *SD* unit change in academic Coursework will result in a .29 *SD* increase in Grades. The paths are statistically significant; with an *N* of 1,000, all the paths in the model are statistically significant. Thus further qualitative interpretation is also needed: Are these paths *important?* Standardized paths (and βs) may be thought of as similar to effect sizes in experimental research (Hoyle, 1995). One common rule of thumb is that a path less than .05 is too small to be considered *meaningful*, even if it is statistically significant. Keith suggested that for manipulable influences on learning, paths above .05 may be considered small but meaningful influences, paths above .10 may be considered as moderate

---

[3] This is an oversimplification of the rules of identification, but it will suffice for the present example. For more information about just-identified versus overidentified (and underidentified) models, see Kline (2005, chapter 5) or Keith (2006, chapter 10).

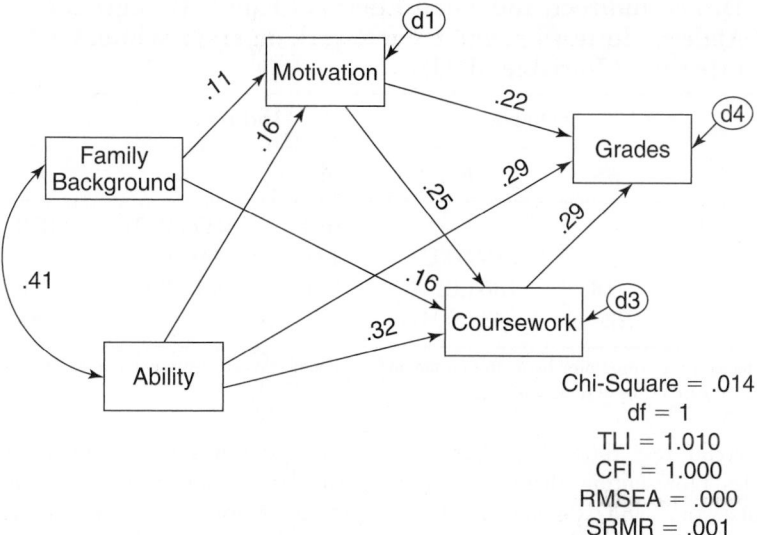

FIGURE 1.4   Standardized results: Effects of Motivation and Coursework on high school grades.

influences, and paths above .25 may be considered as large effects (2006, chapter 10). Using these rules of thumb, it appears that Coursework has a large effect on Grades; students who complete a more academic mix of coursework in high school learn more, as measured by Grades. Academic Motivation has a moderate effect on high school GPA; more motivated students achieve higher grades. Academic Ability also had a strong effect (.29) on GPA, an unsurprising finding: brighter students achieve higher grades.

Direct, Indirect, and Total Effects

The previous interpretation only focuses on *direct* effects. Inspection of the model also suggests the possibility of indirect effects, however. For example, in addition to affecting Grades directly, Motivation also affects Coursework (.25), which in turn affects Grades (.29). Students who are more highly motivated take a more academic mix of high school coursework, and that coursework, in turn, affects their learning (as measured by Grades). Such indirect effects are also important to evaluate, and are easily calculated by multiplying paths (and, if there is more than one indirect route, summing the products). There is only one indirect effect of Motivation on Grades—through Coursework—and the indirect effect is calculated as .25 x .29 = .07. It is also possible to calculate total effects by summing the direct

effects and indirect effects (.22 + .07 = .29). The process of multiplying and summing paths can get quite complex as one moves backward in the model—from proximal to distal influences—but all SEM programs can provide a table of total and indirect effects, both standardized (as calculated here) and unstandardized, as well as the statistical significance of these effects.

The ability to calculate all three types of effects is one of the advantages of analyzing measured-variable SEM models (path models) using dedicated SEM programs. Table 1.3 shows the direct, indirect, and total effects of each variable in the model on Grades. The effect of Coursework is completely direct, since there are no intervening variables between Coursework and Grades. In contrast, the effect of Family Background on Grades is completely indirect—through Motivation and Coursework—because there is no direct effect for Family Background on Grades. Ability has both direct effects and indirect effects, primarily through the coursework that students take.

The examination of indirect effects is an excellent method for examining possible mechanisms by which one variable influences another. We might wonder, for example, if one method by which Coursework affects Grades is by increasing homework demands or reducing other time-consuming activities, such as TV

TABLE 1.3   Direct, Indirect, and Total Effects of Family Background, Ability, Motivation, and Coursework on High School GPA (Measured Variable SEM)

Variable	Direct		Indirect		Total	
	β^a	b	β	b	β	b
Family Background	–	–	.078	.069 (.012)	.078	.069 (.012)
Ability	.291	.019 (.002)	.137	.009 (.001)	.428	.027 (.002)
Motivation	.218	.186 (.023)	.071	.061 (.009)	.290	.246 (.023)
Coursework	.287	.043 (.004)	–	–	.287	.043 (.004)

[a]Standardized coefficients are represented by β, and unstandardized coefficients are represented as b. Unstandardized coefficients are followed by the standard errors of those coefficients.

viewing. We could test those hypotheses by placing variables representing these constructs between Coursework and Grades (and, of course, measuring variables representing those constructs). If Homework and TV helped explain the effect of Coursework, if they were important *intervening* or *mediating* variables, then some of the direct effect of Coursework shown in Figure 1.4 would become indirect effect through Homework and TV Time. The *total* effect of Coursework on Grades, however, would remain unchanged. Thus the comparison of direct, indirect, and total effects is an excellent method for testing the importance of intervening variables.

Mediation

Of course another term for an intervening variable is a mediating variable, and SEM models and programs are an excellent way of testing for mediation. In the example from the previous paragraph, we were testing whether Homework and TV *mediated* the effect of Coursework on Grades. In Figure 1.4, Coursework is a partial mediator of the effect of Motivation on Grades, because Motivation has both direct and indirect effects on Grades. If, in contrast, the direct effect of Motivation on Grades was small (and not statistically significant), but the indirect effect meaningful, we might say that Coursework totally mediated the effect of Motivation on Grades. Some writers make a distinction between indirect effects and mediation (Holmbeck, 1997), but it is, in our opinion, an artificial distinction.

Return to Figure 1.1; to test for mediation in Figure 1.1, we would simply calculate the statistical significance of the indirect effect a*b. It is relatively easy to do this using multiple regression and what is know as the Soebel test, but it is even easier to do it using an SEM program. Even better,

some programs (e.g., Amos) use bootstrapping to calculate the statistical significance of the indirect effects, a more defensible method than the Soebel test (Preacher & Hayes, 2004). If the indirect effect was statistically significant, then Variable B mediates the effect of Variable A on the Outcome. Whether effect c was statistically significant would tell us whether this was complete or partial mediation. Kristopher Preacher's mediation web page is an excellent resource for those interested in the topic (http://www.quantpsy.org/).

Table 1.3 also shows the standard errors of the (unstandardized) direct, indirect, and total effects for the model shown in Figure 1.4. The column of indirect effects shows that the indirect effect of Motivation on Grades (through Coursework) was indeed statistically significant, meaning that Coursework was indeed a statistically significant mediator of the effect of Motivation on Grades.

Latent Variable SEM

Figure 1.5 shows a latent variable version of the motivation path model tested previously. The model is based on a different sample (the National Educational Longitudinal Study, NELS), and uses somewhat different measures than the previous model, but the two focus on similar questions (the example is drawn from Keith & Fine, 2005). Most of the variables in the previous analyses were composites of several measures. The Coursework variable in Figures 1.3 and 1.4, for example, was a sum of units of coursework across academic areas. In the latent variable model (Figure 1.5) these components are shown in rectangles. These variables are the *measured variables* (also know as manifest variables) in the latent variable analysis. The large variables shown in ellipses are the *latent variables* (or unmeasured variables) that are estimated from the measured variables. Unlike

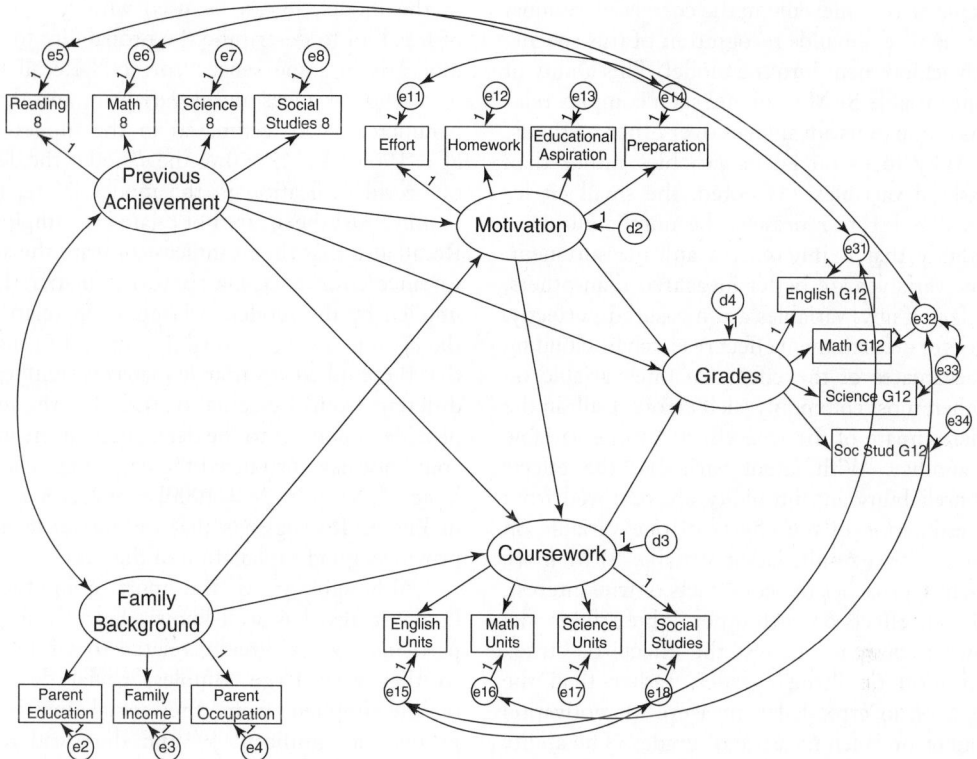

FIGURE 1.5 **A latent variable analysis of the effects of Motivation and Coursework on high school grades.**

the previous analysis, these variables are not composites, but are *factors* estimated from the measured variables.

The paths from the latent to measured variables constitute the *measurement model*, a joint confirmatory factor analysis of all of the latent variables; the numbers associated with those paths (in the subsequent figure) are factor loadings. The paths from one latent variable to another constitute the *structural model*, a path analysis of the latent variables. As before, the small circles labeled d1 through d4 are the disturbances; they may be considered the effects all other variables not included in the model on the latent variables. The small circles labeled e2 through e34 represent the combined unique (invalidity) and error (unreliability) variances of the measured variables. Like the disturbances, the errors can be thought of as all other influences on the measured variable besides the latent variable. For example, e6 represents all other influences on the eighth grade Math Achievement tests other than those from the construct general Previous Achievement. Those influences include error and specific math achievement.

As in the measured variable model, every latent variable has one path to a measured variable set to 1. The 1s beside the paths simply serve to set the scale to be the same as that of the variable to which the arrow points. The value of 1 for the path from Grades to English, for example, sets the scale of the latent Grades variable to be the same as that of the measured English Grades variable. Note that only one path from each latent variable is set to 1, and that for some latent variables, there is only one such path (the errors and disturbances). Once the unstandardized model has been estimated using these constrained values (the unstandardized or metric solution), all values in the model are restandardized (the standardized solution).

The model shown also includes curved lines among the errors of measurement. The curved lines between e5–e6 and e31–e32 represent correlations between the residuals of the eighth grade tests and the twelfth grade grades. It seems likely that math achievement test scores and later math grades will have more in common than the effect of general previous achievement on subsequent general GPA. That additional something, of course, is specific math achievement; the correlated residual from e6 to e32 builds recognition of this specific math achievement into the model. This ability of latent variable SEM to model such complex relations is one of its advantages over other methods.

Why focus on latent variables rather than measured variables? As noted, the small circles labeled as errors represent the unreliability and invalidity that is inherent in any measurement. Some variables are better measured than others, but few, if any, variables are measured perfectly. Errors of measurement affect research by clouding the estimates of the effects of one variable on another; most commonly such errors result in the underestimate of the true effects of one variable on another. With latent variables, the effects of unreliability and invalidity are removed from the estimation of the effects of one variable on another. As a result, latent variable SEM more closely approaches the constructs of true interest, and their effects on each other. Thus, the model shown is designed to test the effects of "true" motivation on "true" grades, rather than the effects of an error-laden measure of motivation on an error-laden measure of grades. The ability to examine the effects of variables on each other without the effects of error is a major advantage of latent variable SEM.

The model shown is overidentified. There are 19 measured variables in the model, and thus 171 parameters in the correlation matrix $\left(\frac{19 \times 18}{2}\right)$ and 190 in the variance/covariance matrix $\left(\frac{19 \times 20}{2}\right)$.[4] In comparison, only 54 parameters are estimated in the model: 23 paths (12 factor loadings and 8 paths from one latent variable to another), 8 correlations/covariances (e.g., between Family Background and Previous Achievement, and between several errors), and 24 variances (the errors, disturbances, and Family Background and Previous Achievement).

The estimated model is shown in Figure 1.6. Five fit indices are shown in the lower right of the figure, although there are dozens of possible indices from which to choose. Chi-Square (χ^2) is the most commonly reported index. It has the advantage of allowing a statistical test of the fit

of the model; it can be used with the degrees of freedom to determine the probability that the model is in some sense "correct." Recall there were 190 variances and covariances, and that 54 parameters were estimated in the model. The $df = 190 - 54 = 136$; thus the df index the degree of overidentification in the model. Note, then, that in SEM the df are not related to sample size. Recall also that the fit indices compare the actual variance/covariance matrix to the matrix that is implied by the model. A large χ^2 in relation to the df, and a small probability (p < .05) suggest that the implied covariance matrix is significantly different from the actual matrix, that the model provides a poor fit to the data, and that the model could not have produced the data. The relatively large χ^2 (χ^2 (χ^2 [136, N = 1000] = 362.219, p < .05) in Figure 1.6 suggests that the model does not provide a good explanation of the data.

Although χ^2 is the most ubiquitous fit index, it also has well-known shortcomings. In particular, χ^2 is directly related to sample size, so that with large samples, trivial deviations of the implied from the actual matrix will produce a significant χ^2 and thus lead to the rejection of a good model. With small samples, even badly misspecified models may produce insignificant χ^2s, thus leading to the acceptance of a poor model. A variety of other fit indices have been developed to deal with these and other problems; the ones shown in Figure 1.6 highlight different dimensions of fit (Tanaka, 1993). The Comparative Fit Index (CFI) and the Tucker-Lewis Index (TLI) compare the existing model to a null, or independence model, one in which the measured variables are assumed to be unrelated (although null models are the most common comparison, these indices can also be calculated with more restricted but substantive models). The CFI provides a population estimate of the improvement in fit over the null model; the TLI is relatively unaffected by sample size. For both indices, values approaching 1.0 suggest a better fit; common rules of thumb suggest that values over .95 represent a good fit of the model to the data (cf. Hu & Bentler, 1998, 1999).

Another problem with χ^2 and its associated probability is that p is the probability that a model fits *perfectly* in the population, even though most researchers would argue that a model is only designed to *approximate* reality. The Root Mean Square Error of Approximation (RMSEA) is designed to assess the approximate fit of a model. RMSEAs below .05 suggest a "close fit of

---

[4]We have gradually shifted from discussing correlations to covariances because most SEM programs are designed to analyze covariance, rather than correlation, matrices. Just recall that a correlation is nothing more than a standardized covariance, or, alternatively, a covariance is an unstandardized correlation.

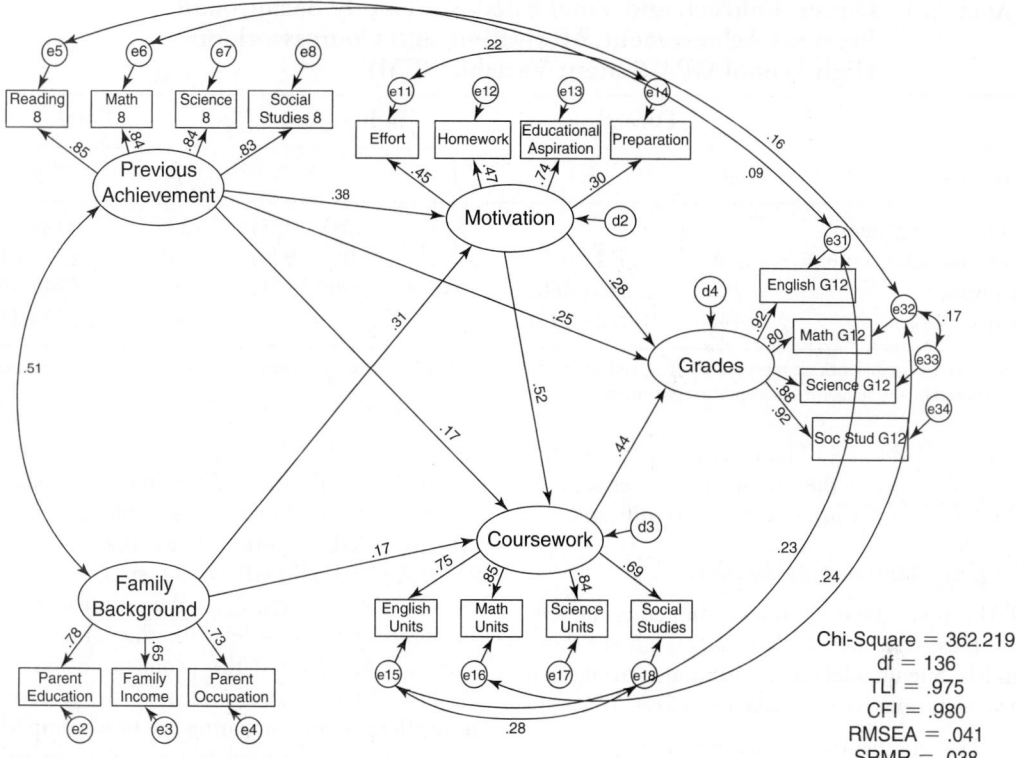

FIGURE 1.6   Standardized output for the latent variable SEM.

the model in relation to the degrees of freedom" (Browne & Cudeck, 1993, p. 144).

Recall that all fit indices compare the actual covariance matrix with the matrix implied by the model. The standardized root mean square residual (SRMR) is the standardized average of these differences. It thus represents the average difference between the actual correlations and those implied by the model. A common rule of thumb for the SRMR is that values less than .08 suggest a good fit of the model to the data. For simulation research supporting the rules of thumb referenced here, see Hu & Bentler (1998, 1999). All of the alternative fit indices suggest a good fit of the model to the data.

Given a good fit, the next step is the substantive interpretation of the model.[5] Perhaps the most interesting finding in Figure 1.6 is the path from Motivation to Grades ($\beta = .28$), suggesting that student's level of academic motivation has a powerful effect on their GPA, even after previous achievement and other background characteristics are controlled.

There are several other interesting interpretive aspects of the model. Motivation had a very strong effect on students' quantity of Coursework, as indexed by the number of units of coursework students completed in high school in four academic areas ($\beta = .52$). Coursework also had a powerful effect on Grades ($\beta = .44$). Thus the model suggests that students with higher levels of academic motivation take more academic courses in high school, and this coursework, in turn, leads to improvements in learning, as indexed by GPA. Stated differently, a portion of the effect of Motivation on Grades is *indirect* through Homework ($.52 \times .44 = .23$), or Coursework *mediates* the effect of Motivation on Grades. A summary of all direct, indirect, and total effects on Grades is

[5] In fact, the assessment of fit continues beyond that discussed here. Paths, factor loadings, R^2s, and other parameter estimates should be reasonable (e.g., no standardized paths > 1.0), and should be in the direction expected (e.g., a path expected to be positive should not be negative). If these expectations are not fulfilled, researchers should be suspicious of their findings. Examination of modification indices and standardized residuals (the actual matrix minus the implied matrix) are also useful in evaluating fit and in helping rectify a lack of fit.

TABLE 1.4 Direct, Indirect, and Total Effects of Family Background, Previous Achievement, Motivation, and Coursework on High School GPA (Latent Variable SEM)

Variable	Direct		Indirect		Total	
	β^a	b	β	b	β	b
Family Background	-	-	.235	.038 (.005)	.235	.038 (.005)
Previous Achievement	.246	.074 (.009)	.273	.083 (.009)	.519	.157 (.010)
Motivation	.280	2.516 (.460)	.230	2.068 (.341)	.509	4.584 (.509)
Coursework	.443	1.272 (.133)	-	-	.443	1.272 (.133)

[a]Standardized coefficients are represented by β, and unstandardized coefficients are represented as b. Unstandardized coefficients are followed by the standard errors of those coefficients.

shown in Table 1.4. The table also includes the standard errors of the unstandardized effects; all effects in the table are statistically significant.

Testing Alternative Models

SEM can also be used to test competing models, and thus test specific hypotheses about those models. Such model comparisons also strengthen the conclusions we can make from SEM research.

> The fact that one model fits the data reasonably well does not mean that there could not be other, different models that fit better. At best, a given model represents a tentative explanation of the data. The confidence with which one accepts such an explanation depends, in part, on whether other, rival explanations have been tested and found wanting (Loehlin, 2004, p. 61).

There is no path in Figure 1.6 from Family Background to Grades (or, alternatively, this path is constrained to a value of zero). Substantively, the model asserts that Family Background characteristics have no direct effect on subsequent GPA, but that they affect GPA only by affecting Previous Achievement, Motivation, and Coursework. The viability of these assertions can be tested by comparing the fit of that model with one in which the paths are estimated

(unconstrained). The fit of this less constrained model—called the direct effects model—is shown in Table 1.5. As shown in the table, this model also provided a good fit to the data (e.g., RMSEA = .041, SRMR = .037, etc.).

Of more interest is the comparison of the direct effects model with the initial model (Figure 1.6). Despite the problems listed with χ^2 as a "stand-alone" index of fit, it can be quite effective for comparing the fit of competing models. If the two models are nested, meaning that one model is a more constrained version of the other, then the *difference* between the two χ^2s (the χ^2 change, or $\Delta\chi^2$) is also distributed as χ^2 and can be used to determine whether the change in the model significantly improves or damages the fit. The direct effects model represents a relaxation of the initial model (one additional path was estimated), and thus both the χ^2 and the df will decrease. The question of interest is whether the decrease is statistically significant, a finding that would suggest that the relaxation in the model resulted in a statistically significant *improvement* in the fit of the model.

Information about change in χ^2 is shown in the third and fourth columns of the table. Freeing the extra path in the direct effects model resulted in a decrease in χ^2 of 2.007, along with one less degree of freedom. This value is statistically

TABLE 1.5 Fit Indices for the Latent Variable SEM of the Effects of Motivation and Coursework on GPA

Model	$\chi^2(df)$	$\Delta\chi^2(df)$	p	TLI	CFI	RMSEA	SRMR
Initial	362.219 (136)			.975	.980	.041	.038
Direct Effects	360.212 (135)	2.007 (1)	>.05	.975	.980	.041	.037
Fewer Correlated Errors	387.984 (138)	25.765 (2)	<.001	.972	.978	.043	.038
Total Mediation	396.676 (137)	34.457 (1)	<.001	.971	.977	.044	.040

insignificant ($p > .05$), suggesting that allowing this path to be estimated does not improve the fit of the model. Since parsimony is valued in science, and since the initial model fits as well as the direct effects model but is more parsimonious, we accept the initial model over the direct effects model. As a result, we would therefore conclude that Family Background characteristics indeed appear to affect Grades only indirectly, through Previous Achievement and Homework. The CFI, TLI, and similar indices are not as useful for comparing competing models (Hoyle & Panter, 1995), and they changed little from one model to the next.

The initial model makes another key assumption that could be tested: that the unique variances of the tests and grades are correlated. To test this assumption, we removed the correlated errors and re-estimated the model. The fit indices for this "fewer correlated errors" model are also shown in Table 1.5. This change in the model requires additional constraints on the model, and thus the χ^2 for the model (and the df) will both get larger (and the fit worse); the question, of course, is whether this change is statistically significant. As shown in the table, the change is indeed statistically significant ($\Delta\chi^2 = 25.765$ [2], $p < .001$); the model provided a worse fit to the data; the assumption of correlated errors of measurement for test scores and grades indeed appears viable.[6]

These two alternative models tested important assumptions about the initial model, but did not really test any substantive questions. One plausible, and theoretically interesting, question is the extent to which Coursework mediates the effect of Motivation on Grades. The model shown in Figure 1.6 suggests that Coursework *partially* mediates the effect, but it is possible that the mediation is total rather than partial. That is, perhaps motivation has no direct effect on students' grades, but rather that it affects grades *only* by affecting the coursework they take in high school. This possibility could be tested by removing the path from Motivation to Grades and comparing the fit of this model with the initial model. The fit indices for this "direct effects" model are also shown in Table 1.5. This change in the model required one

additional constraint (and thus resulted in one additional df), but resulted in a large and statistically significant increase in χ^2. There were, again, minor changes in the other fit indices. The comparison of models suggests that Motivation affects Grades both indirectly, through Coursework, and also directly. (Of course, with this univariate test, I would have come to the same conclusion by examining the z value associated with the path from Motivation to Grades in the Initial model: $z = 5.324, p < .001$).

More Complex Models

SEM programs can also model and estimate more complex hypotheses about the relations among constructs. We might suspect, for example, that Motivation and Coursework were causally related in a reciprocal fashion, so that more motivated students took more academic courses, and that more academic coursework, in turn, increased their motivation. This possibility could be tested in several ways. With some changes in the model, a nonrecursive version of the model could be tested, in which paths were drawn from Motivation to Coursework, and also from Coursework to Motivation. It may also be possible to compare nonequivalent models based on fit statistics, with one model having the path pointed in one direction and the other model with the path pointed in the opposite direction. Both of these methods require the structural model to be more overidentified than is the current model.[7] If, for example, we could find a variable that affected Motivation but not Coursework, and one that affected Coursework but not Motivation, these variables could be added to the model and either nonrecursive or nonequivalent models could be estimated. Another possibility for determining the reciprocal effects would be to estimate a longitudinal panel model, with Motivation and Coursework each measured repeatedly. These variations are discussed in more detail in Keith (2006) or Kline (2005).

We might also wonder whether the effects of motivation on grades—and indeed the entire model of motivation, coursework, and grades—is

---

[6]To summarize, the rule of thumb is that if $\Delta\chi^2$ is statistically significant, then one prefers the more complex, less parsimonious model. If $\Delta\chi^2$ is not statistically significant, then the more parsimonious model is preferred.

[7]If the path were reversed in the present model, the two models would be equivalent, meaning they could not be differentiated based on their fit. A nonrecursive version of the existing model (a model with paths drawn in both directions) would be underidentified, meaning it could not be estimated without additional constraints.

the same for boys and girls. Perhaps girls follow through on their intentions to work hard, so that their motivation has a stronger effect on their grades than for boys. Or perhaps boys gain more from each additional class they take, in which case the effect of Coursework on Grades might be stronger for boys than for girls. This type of question—is the *magnitude* of influence larger for one group versus another—is, in fact, a question of interaction or moderation. Does, for example, Gender interact with Motivation in its effects on Grades?

One obvious way to test for such interactions would be to analyze the model shown in Figure 1.5 separately for boys and girls and then examine the paths in the model to look for differences. A better alternative is the use of a multi-sample analysis, in which the model is fit to several groups simultaneously. Any or all aspects of the model can be specified as invariant across groups. So, for example, all paths and factor loadings might be specified as invariant for boys and girls, or only the path from Motivation to Grades might be specified as invariant (along with factor loadings). The fit for these various specifications can then be compared to determine whether the model differs significantly across groups and, if so, where those differences occur. Procedures for testing such multi-sample models are explicated in most standard SEM texts.

The SEM examples used here have focused on the estimation of variances, covariances, and effects (e.g., regression coefficients). It is also possible to estimate means and intercepts in such models, however. A confirmatory factor analysis, for example, can examine differences in latent means for boys and girls on the factors in the CFA. Girls may score higher on measures of reading, but do they score higher on "true" reading achievement (a latent variable)? SEM models with means can also be used to analyze the results of experimental research, with the latent variable advantage of cleansing the measures of unreliability and invalidity. Such analyses can also be used to examine and test some of the assumptions underlying more common analytic strategies for experimental research. Obviously, these topics are beyond the scope of this brief overview. For more information, see Hancock and Mueller (2006) or Kline (2005).

Summary of SEM Methods

One common criticism of quantitative research is that it is so reductionistic, and that it requires separating one or a few variables out of the system in which they naturally occur. We hope it is obvious that SEM methods are compatible with systems thinking and that structural models can allow sophisticated modeling of complex interrelations among variables. Latent variable SEM's ability to model complex structural *and measurement* relations adds another advantage over the measured variable approach. The ability to model reciprocal causation, correlated errors of measurement, and both direct and indirect effects makes latent variable SEM a powerful and flexible method of data analysis. This flexibility means that latent variable SEM can model and test the assumptions of other methods. The use of SEM has shown explosive growth in other areas of psychology; it should continue to experience similar growth in school psychology. School psychologists who conduct nonexperimental research should become familiar with the method because it provides a powerful, flexible, and theoretically driven method of analysis. Likewise, psychologists who read and consume research should become familiar with the method so that they can understand what they read and the strengths and weaknesses of the method. SEM can and should become an important method in school psychological research.

LATENT GROWTH CURVE MODELS

Latent growth curve models apply latent variable SEM methods to the study of growth, the influences *on* growth, and the effects *of* growth. Consider the graph shown in Figure 1.7. The figure shows 10 children's growth in reading achievement from Kindergarten through third grade (the data are from the Early Childhood Longitudinal Study). Each line represents the growth trajectory for an individual child. Latent growth modeling (LGM) uses these multiple time points to provide estimates of the *latent* aspects of growth in, in this case, children's reading skill, including children's "true" average level of *initial reading* (the intercept in a regression context), the extent to which individual children vary from the average initial level, the "true" *average rate of growth* (slope), and the variation in growth. Even more interesting, it is possible to study whether various influences affect the rate of growth and whether growth affects other possible outcomes. A brief example will illustrate the method.

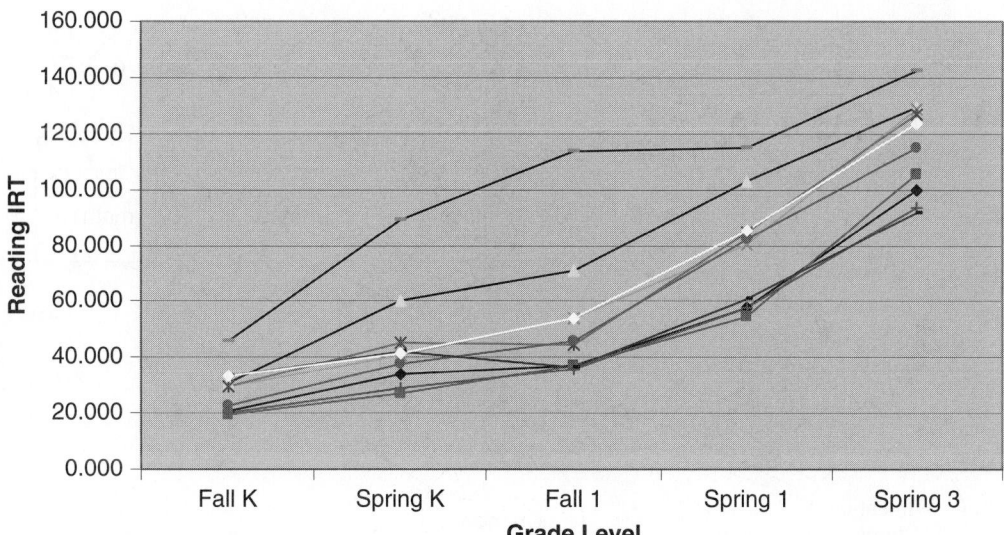

FIGURE 1.7 Growth in reading for 10 children from Kindergarten to third grade.

An Example

Muthén and Khoo (1998) illustrated LGM using math achievement data for four groups from the Longitudinal Study of American Youth (LSAY). Here we use math achievement data (the means, standard deviations, and correlations) from that article for a sample of 1331 girls in grades 7 (for the first time point) through 10 (the final time point).

LGM is often conducted in steps, first fitting the latent growth aspects of the model, and then adding influences or outcomes. This first step is often referred to as the unconditional model, and is analogous to the measurement model in SEM. The model in which influences on change are added is often referred to as the conditional model, and is in some ways analogous to the structural model in SEM. Figure 1.8 shows the initial specification of the unconditional model. The squares labeled math7 through math10 represent girls' scores on math test items drawn from the National Assessment of Educational Progress during the Fall of seventh, eighth, ninth, and tenth grades. Measures used in LGM need to be measured on the same metric, generally meaning that the same measure is administered repeatedly, or methods, such as IRT methods, are used to form a continuous scale from overlapping items. The latter method was used for these tests. Obviously, test scores cannot be standardized

within grade or age, or the growth characteristics of the data will be lost.

As in previous examples, the variables labeled E1 through E4 represent the errors of measurement for the math test scores. In the initial model we allowed these errors to correlate, with the assumption that the specific influences on a student's math score (other than initial status and growth) are likely to be similar for two adjacent time points.

The two latent variables affecting girls' scores on the math tests appear similar to factors in a standard CFA. The "factor loadings" from the factors to the time-dependent tests are fixed, however, rather than estimated. Fixing all of the loadings from the variable Initial Status to the math test scores to 1 forces this variable to represent the latent intercept, or the initial status of math achievement for these girls. The parameters to be estimated for this latent variable are the mean (the mean initial level of math) and the variability of that initial level of math achievement. The variable Change has factor loadings fixed at equal intervals, with the assumption that growth will be linear across the equal time intervals between each assessment. The approach used here is common, starting with zero and adding 1 for each assessment; the approach, in essence, shows the change in time, in years. Other approaches are

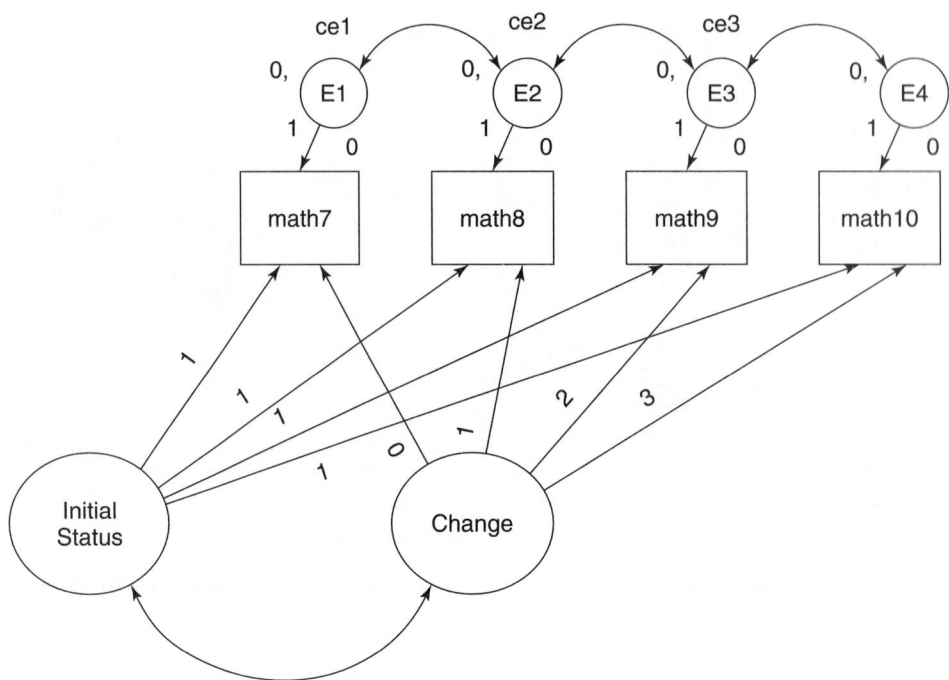

FIGURE 1.8 Initial latent growth model of math learning.

also possible (e.g., setting the loadings for the first and last assessment to zero and 1, or having the scale represent months between assessment). It is also possible to test whether growth is indeed linear by freeing some of these loadings, or to add other terms, such as quadratic growth, to test for possible curves in the growth line.

This initial model showed an adequate to good fit to the data (the relevant fit statistics are shown in Table 1.6), but inspection of other aspects of the model suggested possible changes. For the second model, a statistically insignificant error covariance was removed (set to zero), resulting in a small, statistically insignificant increase in χ^2. For the final unconditional model (Final Unconditional), the requirement for linear growth was relaxed. To do so, the first two loadings on the Change factor were constrained to zero and one, but the third and fourth loadings were free to vary.

The unstandardized results for the final unconditional model are shown in Figure 1.9. As shown in the figure (and the table), the model fit the data well, although there was only one degree of freedom for this model. More importantly, this model showed a statistically significant improvement in fit over the models that required linear growth ($\Delta\chi^2$ [2] = 12.429, $p < .01$ versus the second model), suggesting the need to relax the requirement of linear growth.

There are several interesting aspects to the output shown and the more detailed tabular output (not shown). The numbers next to the variables.[9] Initial Status and Change are their means and variances. Thus the average (latent) initial level of these girls on the math achievement test was 52.11. There was, however, statistically significant variation in girls' initial math performance (the variance of the initial

TABLE 1.6 Fit Indices for the Latent Growth Models of Math Learning

Model	$\chi^2(df)$	$\Delta\chi^2(df)$	p	TLI	CFI	RMSEA	SRMR
Initial Unconditional	12.820 (2)			.994	.998	.064	.0004
Unconditional 2	14.674 (3)	2.245 (1)	>.05	.995	.998	.054	.002
Final Unconditional	2.245 (1)	12.429 (2)	.002	.999	1.000	.031	.002
Conditional Model	21.849 (5)			.991	.997	.050	.010

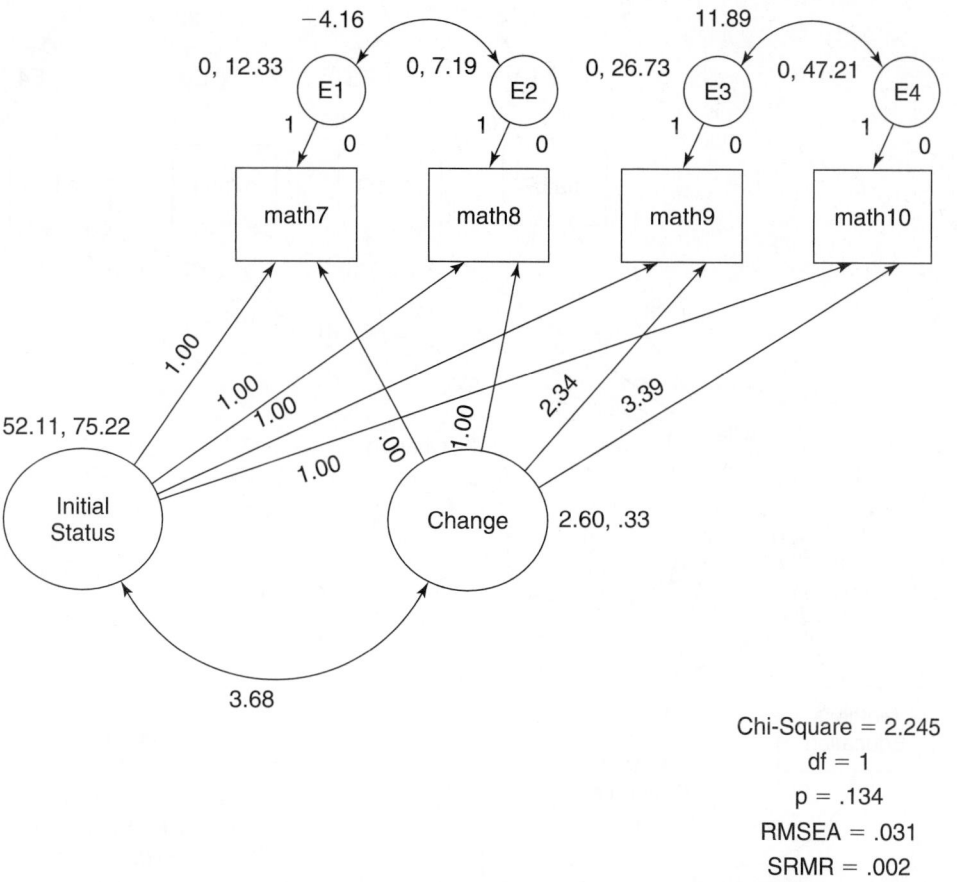

FIGURE 1.9 **Unstandardized solution for the final latent growth model.**

status variable, 75.22, was statistically significant, $p < .01$). The mean for the latent Change variable was 2.60, meaning that these girls' math achievement increased, on average, by 2.60 points per year. This value was statistically significant, meaning that this year-to-year increase is statistically significant. The loadings of the math tests on the Change latent variable suggest that growth was indeed nonlinear. The first two loadings set the scale for this variable; the third loading (2.34) shows a greater than expected growth from grades 8 to 9 for these girls, followed by approximately a one-year jump between ninth and tenth grades. As noted earlier, it would be possible to test more completely the nature of this curve by fitting additional latent Change variables (e.g., quadratic change). Finally, Initial Status and Change covaried positively (and statistically significantly), meaning that girls with higher initial level of math achievement also showed more growth than those with lower initial levels of achievement. The correlation (standardized covariance) between these two latent variables is not shown, but was .74, suggesting that the relation between initial status and growth is strong.

Conditional Model (Influences on Change)

These findings are interesting, but the conditional model shown in Figure 1.10 is even more interesting, in that it explores the variables that may *affect* both initial level of math achievement and growth in math achievement. The model shows the standardized findings. Included in this model are two family background variables that may affect such achievement: the mother's level of education and the financial resources of the family. For the model, the nonlinear aspects of growth from the final unconditional model were retained.

The fit of the model is adequate, but could likely be improved. Nevertheless, we will briefly interpret these findings. The results suggest that

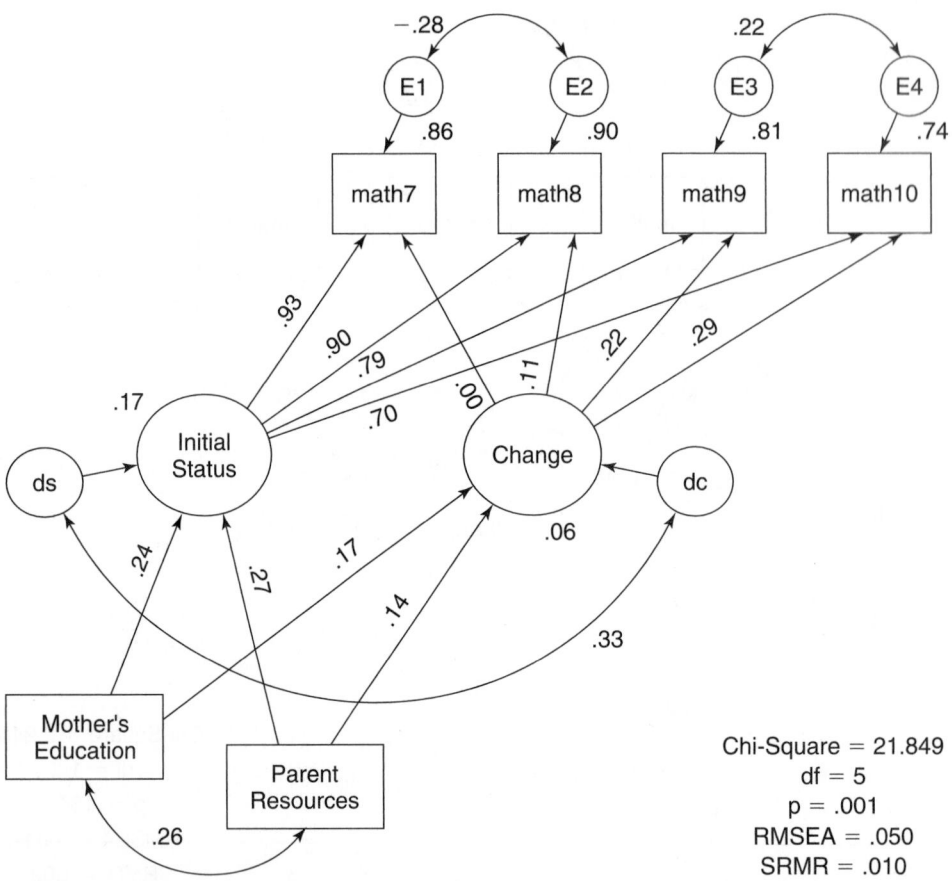

FIGURE 1.10 **Effects of Mother's Education and Parent Resources on growth in math learning (standardized estimates).**

Mother's Education had a strong effect on girls' initial math achievement (.24) and a moderate effect on their growth in math learning (.17); both effects were statistically significant. Girls with more educated mothers not only start seventh grade with higher math scores, but they improve at a faster rate than do girls with less educated mothers. The same pattern held for Family Resources as well: Girls from more advantaged backgrounds had higher initial scores (.27), on average, and grew in their math achievement at a faster rate (.14).

With the standardized output, the numbers next to the outcome variables (Initial Status, Change, Math7, etc.) are the squared multiple correlations. These findings suggest that the two family background variables account for 17% and 6%, respectively, of the variance in girls' initial math achievement and their growth in math achievement. The two latent growth variables, however, account for 74–90% of the variation in the grade-level math tests.

Variations of these models are also possible. As noted earlier, the fit of the model could be improved. For example, allowing Mother's Education to affect seventh grade Math achievement directly (in addition to indirectly through the latent Initial Status variable) would lead to a statistically significant improvement in fit. It would be possible to add additional explanatory variables. So, for example, some girls may have had a more conceptually-oriented math curriculum in elementary school. A variable representing elementary math curriculum might thus prove influential in subsequent math achievement and growth. It would also be possible to add outcome variables. So, for example, one could examine whether girls with faster growth in math perform better in subsequent science classes.

The applicability of LGM models to school psychological research should be obvious. With LGM researchers can examine the influences on growth in reading or other learning; psychopathology, such as depression in adolescence; risky behaviors, such as alcohol use; or personal characteristics, such as self-esteem. As noted earlier, it is also possible to use LGM to study the effects of these variables, and growth in those variables, on subsequent outcomes. The primary requirement is the measurement, on the same scale capable of measuring growth, at three points in time. Four points are even better, and all individuals should be measured at the same intervals.

MLM methods may also be used to analyze growth or change, and multilevel models can be "mapped" directly onto a latent growth model (Singer & Willett, 2003). With this approach, the individual time points are considered the level 1 model, with the individuals in the level 2 model. Advantages of MLM over SEM are that individuals need not have the same number of measurements and time intervals between measurements need not be constant across individuals. With SEM, however, it is possible to include multiple measures of constructs at each time point, thus allowing the advantages of latent variables. It is then possible to estimate intercepts and slopes of the latent variables (the curve-of-factors approach) or to estimate growth for each measure along with a second-order slope and intercept for all measures (the factor-of-curves approach). In general, SEM provides a much more flexible method that allows for the study of multiple relations among variables, even allowing for the study of simultaneous change of several domains over time. For example, student change in math and reading could be modeled simultaneously.

Causality

Even casual readers will have noticed our seemingly cavalier attitude toward the issue of causality. Although the methods illustrated here can all be used for the analysis of experimental data, their primary use is to analyze the results of nonexperimental research. Another term for nonexperimental research is, of course, correlational research, and everyone remembers the admonition from introductory statistics: don't infer causality from correlations. Yet such advice, "while well-intentioned... [is] grossly misleading" (Cohen & Cohen, 1983, p. 15). "In fact, with few exceptions, correlation does imply causation... A more accurate sound bite for introductory statistics would be that a simple correlation implies an *unresolved* causal structure" (Shipley, 2000, p. 3).

We do not have space to address this topic in depth in this chapter; our (Keith, 2005) and others' views (e.g., Mulaik, 1987; Pearl, 2000; Shipley, 2000) on the topic are explicated elsewhere. We will simply note that cautious conclusions about the effects of one variable on another are indeed possible using the methods outlined here. These methods are not magic, however, and sloppy thinking and bad theory will surely result in erroneous causal conclusions. It is imperative that users of such methods and consumers of nonexperimental research have a good understanding of the logical and empirical conditions needed to make a valid inference of causality. The references already cited may be a good place to start to develop this understanding.

Conclusion

The quantitative tools available to psychological researchers are becoming ever more sophisticated. Many of these tools have great potential to help answer some of the vexing problems facing school psychological researchers. New methods allow researchers the ability to model complex systems; to model children's behavior within classes and schools, or consultee's progress within consultants within models of consultation; to assess the effects of variables on one another without the messy overlay of errors of measurement; and to examine the effects on, and effects of, growth. These are incredibly flexible and powerful tools. We look forward to seeing the growth in these tools in school psychological research, and the fascinating questions they will be used to answer.

References

Aiken, L. S., & West, S. G. (1991). *Multiple regression: Testing and interpreting interactions*. Thousand Oaks, CA: Sage.

Arbuckle, J. L. (2006). *Amos 7.0 user's guide*. Chicago: SPSS.

Baron, R. M., & Kenny, D. A. (1986). The moderator-mediator variable distinction in social psychological research: Conceptual, strategic, and statistical considerations. *Journal of Personality and Social Psychology, 51*, 1173–1182.

Bentler, P. M. (1995). *EQS structural equations program manual*. Encino, CA: Multivariate Software.

Browne, M. W., & Cudeck, R. (1993). Alternative ways of assessing model fit. In K. A. Bollen & J. S. Long (Eds.), *Testing structural equation models* (pp. 136-162) Newbury Park, CA: Sage.

Cohen, J. (1983). The cost of dichotomization. *Applied Psychological Measurement, 7*, 249–253.

Cohen, J., & Cohen, P. (1983). *Applied multiple regression/correlation analysis for the behavioral sciences* (2nd ed.). Hillsdale, NJ: Erlbaum.

Cool, V. A., & Keith, T. Z. (1991). Testing a model of school learning: Direct and indirect effects on academic achievement. *Contemporary Educational Psychology, 16*(1), 28–44.

Darlington, R. B. (1990). *Regression and linear models*. New York: McGraw-Hill.

Goldstein, H. (2003). *Multilevel statistical models* (3rd ed.). New York: McGraw-Hill.

Hancock, G. R., & Mueller, R. O. (2006). *A second course in structural equation modeling*. Greenwich, CT: Information Age.

Holmbeck, G. N. (1997). Toward terminological, conceptual, and statistical clarity in the study of mediators and moderators: Examples from the child-clinical and pediatric psychology literature. *Journal of Consulting and Clinical Psychology, 65*, 599–610.

Hox, J. J. (2002). *Multilevel analysis: Techniques and applications*. Mahwah, NJ: Erlbaum.

Hoyle, R. H. (Ed.). (1995). *Structural equation modeling: Concepts, issues, and applications*. Thousand Oaks, CA: Sage.

Hu, L., & Bentler, P. M. (1998). Fit indices in covariance structure modeling: Sensitivity to underparameterized model misspecification. *Psychological Methods, 3*, 424–453.

Hu, L., & Bentler, P. M. (1999). Cutoff criteria for fit indexes in covariance structure analysis: Conventional criteria versus new alternatives. *Structural Equation Modeling, 6*, 1–55.

Jöreskog, K. G., & Sörbom, D. (1996). *LISREL 8 user's reference guide*. Lincolnwood, IL: Scientific Software.

Keith, T. Z. (2005, August). *Cause and correlation in school psychology*. Division 16 Senior Scientist Award Address, Annual Meeting of the American Psychological Association, Washington, DC.

Keith, T. Z. (1999). Structural equation modeling in school psychology. In C. R. Reynolds & T. B. Gutkin (Eds.), *The handbook of school psychology* (3rd ed., pp. 78–107). New York: Wiley.

Keith, T. Z. (2006). *Multiple regression and beyond*. Boston: Allyn and Bacon.

Keith, T. Z., & Benson, M. J. (1992). Effects of manipulable influences on high school grades across five ethnic groups. *Journal of Educational Research, 86*, 85–93.

Keith, T. Z., & Fine, J. G. (2005). Multicultural influences on school learning: Similarities and differences across groups. In C. L. Frisby & C. R. Reynolds (Eds.), *Handbook of multicultural school psychology* (pp. 457–482). New York: Wiley.

Kline, R. B. (2005). *Principles and practice of structural equation modeling* (2nd ed.). New York: Guilford.

Kreft, I. G. G., & de Leeuw, J. (1998). *Introducing multilevel modeling*. London: Sage.

Littell, R. C., Milliken, G. A., Stroup, W. W., & Wolfinger, R. D. (1996). *SAS system for mixed models*. Cary, NC: SAS Institute.

Loehlin, J. C. (2004). *Latent variable models: An introduction to factor, path, and structural analysis* (4th ed.). Hillsdale, NJ: Erlbaum.

MacKinnon, D. P., Lockwood, C. M., Hoffman, J. M., West, S. G., & Sheets, V. (2002). A comparison of methods to test mediation and other intervening variable effects. *Psychological Methods, 7*, 83–104.

Mulaik, S. A. (1987). Toward conception of causality applicable to experimentation and causal modeling. *Child Development, 58*, 18–32.

Muthén, B. O., & Khoo, S.-T. (1998). Longitudinal studies of achievement growth using latent variable modeling. *Learning & Individual Differences, 10*, 73–101.

Muthén, L. K., & Muthén, B. O. (1998–2007). *Mplus user's guide* (4th ed.). Los Angeles: Muthén & Muthén.

Pearl, J. (2000). *Causality: Models, reasoning, and inference*. New York: Cambridge University Press.

Preacher, K. J., & Hayes, A. F. (2004). SPSS and SAS procedures for estimating indirect effects in simple mediation models. *Behavior Research Methods, Instruments, and Computers, 36*, 717–731.

Rabash, J., Browne, W. J., Goldstein, H., Yang, M., Plewis, I., Healy, M., et al. (2000). *A user's guide to MLwiN (version 2.1)*. London: Institute of Education, University of London.

Raudenbush, S. W., & Bryk, A. S. (2002). *Hierarchical linear models: Applications and data analysis methods* (3rd ed.). Thousand Oaks, CA: Sage.

Raudenbush, S. W., Bryk, A. S., & Congdon, R. (2005). *HLM 6: Hierarchical linear and nonlinear modeling*. Chicago: Scientific Software.

Reise, S. P., & Duan, N. (1999). Multilevel modeling and its application in counseling psychology research. *The Counseling Psychologist, 27*, 528–551.

Sander, J. B., & McCarty, C. A. (2005). Youth depression in the family context: Familial risk factors and models of treatment. *Clinical Child and Family Psychology Review, 8*, 203–219.

Shipley, B. (2000). *Cause and correlation in biology*. Cambridge, UK: Cambridge University Press.

Shrout, P. E., & Bolger, N. (2002). Mediation in experimental and nonexperimental studies: New procedures and recommendations. *Psychological Methods, 7*, 442–445.

Singer, J. D., & Willett, J. B. (2003). *Applied longitudinal data analysis: Methods for studying change and event occurrence.* New York: Oxford University Press.

Snijders, T. A. B., & Bosker, R. J. (1999). *Multilevel analysis: An introduction to basic and advanced multilevel modeling.* London: Sage.

Stark, K. D., Hargrave, J., Sander, J. B., Custer, G., Schnoebelen, J., Simpson, J., et al. (2006). Treatment of childhood depression: The ACTION treatment program. In P. C. Kendall (Ed.), *Child and adolescent therapy.* New York: Guilford.

Tanaka, J. S. (1993). Multifaceted conceptions of fit in structural equation models. In K. S. Bollen & J. S. Long (Eds.), *Testing structural equation models* (pp. 10–39). Newbury Park, CA: Sage.

Wolfle, L. M. (1980). Strategies of path analysis. *American Educational Research Journal, 17*, 183–209.

APPENDIX

Means as Outcomes Model

Student Level: $Y_{ij} = \beta_{0j} + e_{ij}$

School Level: $\beta_{0j} = \gamma_{00} + \gamma_{01}$ (School Previous Achievement) $+ \gamma_{02}$ (School Homework) $+ \gamma_{03}$ (School SES) $+ u_{0j}$

Random Coefficient Model

Student Level: $Y_{ij} = \beta_{0j} + \beta_{1j}$ (Previous Achievement − Average Previous Achievement) $+ \beta_{2j}$ (Homework − Average Homework) $+ \beta_{3j}$ (SES − Average SES) $+ e_{ij}$

School Level: $\beta_{0j} = \gamma_{00} + u_{0j}$
$\beta_{1j} = \gamma_{01} + u_{1j}$
$\beta_{2j} = \gamma_{02} + u_{2j}$
$\beta_{3j} = \gamma_{03} + u_{3j}$

Means and Regression Coefficients as Outcomes Model

Student Level: $Y_{ij} = \beta_{0j} + \beta_{1j}$ (Previous Achievement − Average Previous Achievement) $+ \beta_{2j}$ (Homework − Average Homework) $+ \beta_{3j}$ (SES − Average SES) $+ e_{ij}$

School Level: $\beta_{0j} = \gamma_{00} + \gamma_{01}$ (School Previous Achievement) $+ \gamma_{02}$ (School Homework) $+ u_{0j}$
$\beta_{1j} = \gamma_{10} + \gamma_{11}$ (School Previous Achievement) $+ \gamma_{12}$ (School Homework) $+ \gamma_{13}$ (School SES) $+ u_{1j}$
$\beta_{2j} = \gamma_{20} + \gamma_{21}$ (School Previous Achievement) $+ \gamma_{22}$ (School Homework) $+ \gamma_{23}$ (School SES) $+ u_{2j}$
$\beta_{3j} = \gamma_{30} + 0$ (Fixed)

Final Model

Student Level: $Y_{ij} = \beta_{0j} + \beta_{1j}$ (Previous Achievement − Average Previous Achievement) $+ \beta_{2j}$ (Previous Homework − Average Previous Homework) $+ \beta_{3j}$ (SES − Average SES) $+ e_{ij}$

School Level: $\beta_{0j} = \gamma_{00} + \gamma_{01}$ (School Achievement) $+ \gamma_{02}$ (School Homework) $+ u_{0j}$
$\beta_{1j} = \gamma_{10} + \gamma_{11}$ (School Achievement) $+ \gamma_{12}$ (School Homework) $+ u_{1j}$
$\beta_{2j} = \gamma_{20} + \gamma_{21}$ (School Achievement) $+ u_{2j}$
$\beta_{3j} = \gamma_{30} + 0$ (Fixed)

CHAPTER 2

ADVANCES IN QUALITATIVE RESEARCH

BONNIE KAUL NASTASI
Tulane University

INTRODUCTION

Since the publication of the third edition of the *Handbook*, the field of school psychology has experienced a burgeoning interest in qualitative research as a tool for scientific inquiry paralleled by increasing recognition in psychology and other social sciences (e.g., anthropology, sociology, education) of the value of mixed-methods research for addressing real-world questions (Nastasi & Schensul, 2005). A major turning point in school psychology was the decision by the joint Division of School Psychology (Division 16) of the American Psychological Association (APA)—Society for the Study of School Psychology (SSSP) Task Force on Evidence-based Interventions in School Psychology[1] to appoint a subcommittee to develop criteria for reviewing the use of qualitative methods in intervention research and the subsequent publication of a special issue of *Journal of School Psychology* (2005, Volume 43, Issue 3) devoted to this topic. These events coincided with the publication by the National Institutes of Health (NIH, 1999) of guidelines for the inclusion of qualitative methods in health sciences research and the publication of the text *Qualitative Research in Psychology* (Camic, Rhodes, & Yardley, 2003) by APA.

Despite these recent events, much skepticism regarding the validity of qualitative research remains, often premised on the assumption that qualitative research methods are unsystematic and imprecise. Pursuing the long-standing qualitative versus quantitative debate seems counterproductive to advancing research in school psychology. Instead, the field is better served by focusing on identifying the most appropriate methods for addressing the major research questions facing school psychology science and practice. Underlying the discussion of qualitative research in this chapter is the assumption that science and practice are best served by a mixed-methods framework in which both qualitative and quantitative methods are valued and can be conducted with due attention to precision. Qualitative methods are viewed as an extension, rather than replacement, of data collection techniques germane to school psychologists (e.g., observation, interview, record review). One aim of this chapter is to reframe the less formalized components of data collection associated with psychological practice (e.g., interview) as a formal system of applied qualitative research, and in doing so, to facilitate narrowing the schism between intervention research and practice (Nastasi, 1998).

The purposes of this chapter are to:

1. Describe qualitative research, or naturalistic inquiry, and its application to school psychology research and practice.

2. Describe several approaches to qualitative research, with particular focus on ethnography and action research, which are distinctly relevant to culturally specific science-based practice.

3. Describe and illustrate the range of methods for data collection, analysis, and interpretation.

4. Describe the procedures for ensuring trustworthiness (i.e., reliability, validity, objectivity) of qualitative research findings and the criteria for evaluating qualitative research.

[1]Information on the efforts and outcomes of the joint Division of School Psychology (Division16) of the American Psychological Association—Society for the Study of School Psychology Task Force on Evidence-Based Interventions in School Psychology can be found in Stoiber and Kratochwill (2000), Kratochwill and Stoiber (2002a, 2002b), Nastasi and Schensul (2005), and Ingraham and Oka (2007).

5. Describe the application of qualitative methods in the context of a mixed-methods approach to informing science-based practice.

The chapter concludes with a discussion of future directions and implications for research, practice and professional preparation of school psychologists.

A review of the various texts in qualitative research[2] reveals a range of traditions or approaches to qualitative inquiry. These variations in part reflect the history and applications of qualitative research to various disciplines and theoretical paradigms (Creswell, 1998; Denzin & Lincoln, 2000). Qualitative research methods, with roots in sociology and anthropology, have been applied to the humanities, social sciences (e.g., psychology, education) and health sciences (e.g., nursing, public health). Further variations in traditions are reflected in application within particular theoretical paradigms or perspectives (e.g., postpositivism, interpretivism, constructivism, feminism, critical theory). Despite the variations, there are features and methods that characterize qualitative research and represent core elements. The primary focus of this chapter is application of qualitative research to school psychology research and practice. The core elements of qualitative research are provided as a framework for thinking about such applications. This chapter provides an introductory review of qualitative methods. Readers are encouraged to seek more detailed information about specific traditions, paradigms, and methods in the sources cited herein.

CHARACTERISTICS OF QUALITATIVE RESEARCH

Qualitative, or naturalistic inquiry, in psychology involves in-depth study of psychological phenomena within naturally occurring settings and/or

---

[2]Recommended texts on qualitative research methods from the fields of anthropology, sociology, education, and psychology include the following: Camic, Rhodes, and Yardley (2003), Creswell (1998), Denzin and Lincoln (2000), Lincoln and Guba (1985), Miles and Huberman (1994), Schensul and LeCompte (1999), Spradley (1979, 1980), Strauss and Corbin (1990), Wolcott (1994, 1999, 2001). Lincoln and Guba (1985) and Schensul, Schensul, and LeCompte (1999) provide excellent discussions of criteria for evaluating the quality or adequacy (trustworthiness; reliability and validity) of qualitative methods.

from the perspectives of the research participants. The primary goal of qualitative inquiry is to capture naturally occurring phenomena from the *emic* (insider's; research participant's) versus *etic* (outsider's; researcher's) perspective. Qualitative inquiry typically results in detailed idiographic representations. Furthermore, research designs are often considered to be emergent and data interpretation to be inductive. Lincoln and Guba (1985) identified several characteristics of naturalistic inquiry that distinguish it from more traditional quantitative approaches. In this section, the characteristics identified by Lincoln and Guba are described, with particular attention to school psychology applications.

Natural Setting

Based on the belief that psychological phenomena cannot be understood independent of context or ecology (Bronfenbrenner, 1989), qualitative research is conducted in real-life settings and research findings are considered to be context- and culture-bound. In addition, the contextual and cultural specificity of psychological phenomena limits generalization from one group, context, or culture to another, without additional data collection; and requires in-depth description of the conditions under which research is conducted. This perspective is consistent with ecological models of school psychological practice (Christenson & Conoley, 1992; Gutkin & Curtis, 1999; Nastasi, 1998, 2000; Power, 2000; Sheridan & Gutkin, 2000), which require understanding the reciprocal relationships of individuals and the multiple ecological systems (family, home, school) in which they operate, the relationships among these systems (e.g., home-school relationships), and the broader structural (organizational), social, historical, political and cultural influences. Effective application of ecological models requires in-depth understanding of context and culture which are consistent with the goals of qualitative inquiry.

Human Instrument

Because of the interpersonal nature of naturalistic inquiry, the researcher is viewed as the primary data collection instrument. Effective use of qualitative methods, such as participant observation or in-depth interviewing, depends on the researcher's skills in establishing relationships, gaining trust, and interacting with participants. Such skills are considered critical to school psychology practice as well, as exemplified in models of consultation (Gutkin & Curtis, 1999;

Ingraham, 2000; Nastasi, Varjas, Bernstein, & Jayasena, 2000; Rosenfield & Gravois, 1996; Sheridan, Kratochwill, & Bergan, 1996). The notion of human instrument also extends to the role of the researcher in the interpretation, application, and dissemination of findings. The inductive nature of data analysis is influenced by the researcher's theoretical perspective. The negotiation of outcomes that characterizes data interpretation relies on the researcher's capacity for interacting with representatives of the target population. Similarly, culturally appropriate and effective application and dissemination of findings depends on the researcher's knowledge of, and sensitivity to, participants.

Tacit Knowledge

In naturalistic inquiry, tacit (implicit) knowledge of the researcher is considered critical throughout the research process, yet also needs to be monitored and documented. The researcher's implicit knowledge is expected to influence question posing and data collection, analysis, and interpretation. To gauge this influence, researchers engage in an ongoing reflective process that involves making explicit one's theoretical perspective, knowledge, beliefs, and values; and examining the ways in which tacit knowledge guides one's thinking and actions during the research process. A common practice is the use of a reflective journal, in which the researcher makes explicit the interaction between tacit knowledge and the research process. Engaging in this introspective process is necessary if researchers are to use themselves as research instruments (Spradley, 1980). The reflective nature of inquiry is consistent with that of the school psychologist as reflective scientist-practitioner who continually explicates and evaluates his/her application of theory and research to practice (Nastasi, 1998).

Qualitative Methods

Key factors in the selection of instruments, or data collection methods, are utility and adaptability for capturing natural phenomena such as the real-life interactions between individuals. Unstructured or semi-structured observation and interview methods are more suited to naturalistic inquiry than highly structured standardized measures such as tests. The predominant use of qualitative methods such as narrative observation and in-depth interviewing does not preclude the use of quantitative methods such as standardized self- or other-report questionnaires. Adherence to a naturalistic paradigm, however, requires careful selection or development of culture/context-specific standardized instruments. Although participant observation, in-depth interviewing, and collection of artifacts or permanent products are the hallmarks of qualitative research, the methods are numerous. The variety of methods is presented in a later section.

Purposive Sampling

In qualitative inquiry, participants are selected with a specific purpose or focus determined by the researcher's questions. Rather than attempting to develop a normative perspective, the naturalistic researcher typically is interested in understanding the multiple manifestations of phenomena in reality and in detailing the particular in context. Thus, sampling is purposive, criterion-based (i.e., based on characteristics relevant to research questions), and context and culture specific. Qualitative studies, however, range from in-depth investigation of one or a few individuals (individual or multiple case studies) to attempts to represent the variation in a particular segment of the population. In addition, the emergent nature of the research design necessitates changes in sampling as the research progresses and the questions change. Schensul, Schensul, and LeCompte (1999) provide in-depth discussion of sampling strategies and issues related to varied questions and designs.

Inductive Data Analysis

The naturalistic researcher engages in a process of data analysis that involves generating meaning (i.e., *making sense;* Lincoln & Guba, 1985) from the data collected in the natural context. In contrast to the hypothetical-deductive tradition, qualitative research involves the generation of hypotheses and the emergence of a conceptual scheme (e.g., coding or categorization scheme) from the data. Inductive analysis of formative research data can facilitate the design of contextually or culturally relevant assessment and intervention techniques, thereby fostering acceptability and social validity. In addition, inductive analysis of data collected during implementation can enhance our understanding of how contextual factors influence intervention acceptability, integrity, and effectiveness.

In practice, analysis of qualitative data represents a continuum from inductive to deductive (Nastasi, 1999). At the inductive end of the continuum, researchers attempt to identify themes and patterns in the data that reflect the thinking of the participants, and avoid the intrusion of their own conceptions. Even in attempts to generate meaning from the data inductively, however, the researcher's focus and theoretical perspective are likely to influence the identification of themes or patterns. The explication of one's theory represents an attempt to make the researcher's influence clear. At the deductive end of the continuum, the researcher collects data using qualitative methods, but applies a preexisting conceptual (coding) scheme to data analysis. Thus, the participants' views and behaviors are interpreted from the researcher's (*etic*) perspective. Strict adherence to a preexisting scheme restricts the identification of culture-specific themes, and is contrary to the goal of portraying the participant's (*emic*) perspective. A preferable approach for achieving culture specificity is to extend or modify the preexisting scheme to reflect the experiences, thinking, and behavior of the informants, thus integrating etic and emic perspectives.

Grounded Theory

Consistent with an inductive approach to data analysis, naturalistic or qualitative inquiry is not driven by a priori theory. Instead, theory emerges empirically or is "grounded" in data, permitting the characterization of phenomena as they occur naturally (Lincoln & Guba, 1985; Strauss & Corbin, 1990). As noted in the preceding section, however, in practice data analysis is more likely to involve an integrated inductive and deductive approach.

Ethnography, one type of qualitative research, is focused on understanding culture from the perspective of its members (Spradley, 1979, 1980); thus a priori theory would limit the researcher's interpretive frame of reference, resulting in an etic perspective. Given the challenge faced by school psychologists of providing services to a culturally diverse population, grounded theory provides the mechanism for developing culture-specific theory, assessment tools and interventions.

Emergent Design

Given the open-ended nature of inquiry, the specific design and methodology of a naturalistic study evolves as a consequence of a recursive process of purposive sampling and data collection, inductive data analysis, and hypothesis generation and testing related to emerging grounded theory.

This process is repeated until redundancy of meaning (in data, constructs, and theory) occurs, also referred to as *data saturation*. The reliance on emergent design does not preclude the use of systematic procedures that guide the process. Indeed, the qualitative researcher is obligated to provide in-depth documentation of the research process and procedures, so that other investigators can track the steps from generating the research problem through case report (what Lincoln and Guba, 1985, refer to as an *audit trail*). Further, emergent design does not prohibit reliance on existing theory and research, but the researcher's preconceptions (i.e., tacit knowledge) must be made explicit initially and throughout the process.

Negotiated Outcomes

Negotiating outcomes refers to interactions between researcher and researched (participant) regarding the meaning or interpretation of data. Given that a primary focus of qualitative inquiry is to understand meaning as defined by the participants or members of the target culture, opportunities to present data and discuss the interpretation and eventual use of that data are valued and planned. The negotiation of data interpretation with participants is a way to guard against overreliance on a priori theory and to insure inclusion of grounded theory. The interactive process between researcher and participant is similar to the collaboration between consultant and consultee in school psychology practice, during which the partners consider available data and make decisions about interventions (e.g., Rosenfield & Gravois, 1996; Sheridan et al., 1996).

Case Study Reporting Mode

Consistent with the focus on in-depth contextualized understanding of the target phenomena, reporting of qualitative research is most appropriately done in a case study mode. *Case*, in this instance, can refer to an individual (e.g., student), context (e.g., classroom or family), or system (e.g., school building or district). The use of case study reporting is germane to the practice of psychologists within clinical and school settings.

The utility of research findings lies in their *transferability* (Lincoln & Guba's [1985] terminology) to other cases. Transferability is dependent on the depth or richness of description (i.e., *thick description;* Lincoln & Guba), which permits the consumer to determine the applicability to other persons and/or settings. In qualitative inquiry, the notion of transferability as the responsibility of the consumer (i.e., is this applicable or transferable to my context) is preferable to that of generalizability as the responsibility of the researcher (i.e., to what populations and contexts is this applicable). Furthermore, a case study reporting mode acknowledges the idiographic (versus nomothetic) focus of qualitative research. The use of thick description provides the level of detail necessary for practitioners to determine the extent to which assessment or intervention procedures and outcomes are relevant to particular settings. Moreover, the use of an idiographic perspective reflects recognition of the individual, cultural, and contextual specificity of applied practice (e.g., consultation, intervention), and may serve to bridge the often-cited gap between research and practice that results from trying to generalize population findings to individual cases.

Idiographic Interpretation

Acknowledging the particular and contextualized nature of their research findings, qualitative researchers restrict interpretation to the specific and guard against nomothetic interpretation. As noted in the preceding section, the extent to which research findings are useful to consumers depends on transferability to specific (similar) settings rather than generalizability across a wide range of settings. Idiographic interpretation also provides recognition of the complexity of psychological phenomena given the myriad personal and environmental factors that can influence functioning. Furthermore, idiographic interpretation is characteristic of applied work in school psychology.

Tentative Application

The idiographic nature of naturalistic inquiry requires that application to other individuals, groups, or contexts is done cautiously. Furthermore, decisions about transferability of qualitative findings are the responsibility of the consumer, not the researcher. Given the conditional nature of findings, it behooves interventionists to repeatedly test or evaluate the validity of evidence-based programs and strategies applied to different clientele. Such retesting is consistent with a data-based problem-solving approach that is the hallmark of school psychology practice.

Focus-Determined Boundaries

Decisions about the parameters of inquiry depend on the particular purpose or focus of the research, that is, the problem being researched. Even within a broad focus of understanding the culture from the perspective of its members, the researcher is likely to have a more specific purpose in mind (e.g., understanding how culture influences child-rearing practices). Similarly, the boundaries of data-based problem solving applied to school psychology practice are determined by specific concerns of professionals and/or specific needs and resources of stakeholders. The open-ended nature of qualitative inquiry and psychological practice requires continual return to definition of the problem. In both naturalistic inquiry and data-based problem solving, the specifics of problem definition are continually open to reformulation as more data are collected. In addition, as the processes are applied to new contexts or individuals, the questions and problem definitions change.

Special Criteria for Trustworthiness

Careful management and systematic analysis of qualitative data are essential for establishing data quality and trustworthiness of findings. Particularly given the researcher's role as a key instrument in data collection and analysis, adherence to procedures to ensure veracity or validity of findings is critical (Nastasi, Moore, & Varjas, 2004). Lincoln and Guba (1985) proposed four criteria of trustworthiness that parallel the traditional concepts of internal validity, external validity, reliability, and objectivity; and ten techniques that serve to regulate the data collection, analysis, and interpretation process of naturalistic inquiry. The Interdisciplinary Qualitative Research Subcommittee of the Task Force on Evidence-based Interventions in School Psychology (IQRS) also developed criteria for evaluating qualitative methods in intervention research (see Nastasi & Schensul, 2005).

In addition to the aforementioned criteria, several principles for trustworthy data transformation (i.e., description, analysis, interpretation; Wolcott, 1994) in school psychology research have been proposed (Nastasi et al., 2004).

1. *Data transformation is continuous.* The process of data collection, analysis, and interpretation is recursive. This is similar to the ongoing process of collecting, analyzing,

and interpreting data as the basis for reflective decision making in school psychology.

2. *Data collection, analysis and interpretation are guided by the researcher's (etic) perspective and the participants' (emic) perspectives.* The combined use of deductive and inductive coding, member checking (involving participants and/or stakeholders in interpretation of data) and peer debriefing (discussing findings with a neutral peer) can help researchers to monitor theoretical sensitivity (i.e., sensitivity to meaning in data, based on knowledge and experience; Strauss & Corbin, 1990) and ensure representation of emic and etic perspectives in study findings.

3. *Systematic documentation via audit trail is essential.* Meticulous recording of conditions and procedures can help to ensure dependability (reliability) and confirmability (objectivity) of findings (see Lincoln & Guba, 1985).

4. *Use both descriptive and inferential language when presenting findings.* Support key findings with exemplars and verbatim statements from the data, in much the same way that school psychologists support findings of psychological assessment with data from standardized measures.

5. *Take advantage of triangulation in data interpretation.* Make maximum use of data and interpretation based on multiple methods, sources, theories and investigators (i.e., *triangulation*, Lincoln & Guba, 1985). Base findings and inferences on multiple data sources.

6. *Seek confirming and disconfirming evidence related to data interpretation.* One of the strengths of qualitative research is the capacity for representing variation rather than central tendency. Accurate portrayal of variation and comprehensive understanding of key constructs are dependent on the identification of both typical and atypical cases.

7. *Tailor data interpretation to purpose and audience.* Be mindful of the research questions and potential application by consumers. Capitalize on the participatory process (with professional and lay partners) to ensure that findings meet the needs of intended and varied audiences.

8. *Ensure that data transformation is a participatory process.* Involve representatives of various stakeholders in data description, analysis, and interpretation.

Summary

Within the confines of the problem, naturalistic inquiry is conducted within a natural setting, with heavy reliance on the researcher (human) as the instrument of inquiry. Building on tacit knowledge (preconceptions based in scientific and personal knowledge) and using qualitative methods (e.g., observation, interviews), the researcher engages in the recursive process of purposive sampling and data collection, data analysis, and interpretation, and theory and hypothesis generation (grounded theory and emergent design). This process is repeated until redundancy in meaning (i.e., saturation) is reached. The resultant meaning is shared and negotiated with the research participants, leading to a case report of findings which are interpreted and applied with emphasis on the particulars of persons and contexts (i.e., idiographically interpreted and tentatively applied). The researcher takes care to establish trustworthiness of the process of inquiry and resultant findings. Given these characteristics, qualitative research provides a framework for engaging in disciplined investigations of psychological phenomena and school psychological practice. The characteristics of naturalistic inquiry described in this section are reflected across the various types or traditions of qualitative research described in the next section.

TYPES OF QUALITATIVE RESEARCH

The multiplicity of qualitative traditions or approaches that have developed across the social science disciplines precludes discussion of each. Creswell (1998), for example, identified over 25 traditions mentioned in qualitative research literature. Underlying this variety are several primary approaches or types of qualitative research, including biography, phenomenology, grounded theory, ethnography, case study, action research and participatory action research. Those with particular relevance to school psychology research and practice—*grounded theory, ethnography, case study*, and *participatory action research*—are described and illustrated in this section. Readers interested in biography (documentation of the life history of an individual; Denzin, 1989) or phenomenology (representation of meaning of experiences related to a particular phenomenon across individuals; Moustakas, 1994) are referred to the respective primary sources. In addition, Creswell (1998), Denzin and Lincoln (2000), and Camic, Rhodes and Yardley (2003) provide an overview of these and other approaches.

Grounded Theory

Grounded theory has its roots in sociology in the early work of Glaser and Strauss (1967) and the philosophical tradition of social interactionism (Blumer, 1969). The grounded theory approach involves the *inductive development of theory* through a systematic process of qualitative data collection, analysis and interpretation about a particular phenomenon (Strauss & Corbin, 1990). Grounded theory thus stands in stark contrast to the hypothetical-deductive method that characterizes experimental research in psychology, in which theory drives the research. Strauss and Corbin describe the underpinnings of grounded theory, stemming from social interactionist foundations, as follows:

> (a) the need to get out in the field, if one wants to understand what is going on; (b) the importance of theory, grounded in reality, to the development of a discipline; (c) the nature of experience ... as continually evolving; (d) the active role of persons in shaping the worlds they live in; (e) an emphasis on change and process, and the variability and complexity of life; and (f) the interrelationships among conditions, meaning, and action (pp. 24–25).

Furthermore, Henwood and Pidgeon (2003) characterize grounded theory from a constructivist framework, emphasizing the development of knowledge based on human interaction in context and the generation of theory by the researcher engaged in an ongoing interpretive interaction with data.

What most characterizes grounded theory methodologically is reliance on fieldwork (data collection in natural setting) and, more importantly, *interpretative analysis* (Henwood & Pidgeon, 2003; Stauss & Corbin, 1990). Data analysis and interpretation involve the application of the *constant comparative method*, a recursive process of generating and refining codes (categories) and connections among those categories from qualitative data until a point of theoretical *saturation* is reached (i.e., no new insights or knowledge is generated by additional cases, instances, data

sources). The steps in the process are (Strauss & Corbin): (a) *open coding* (identifying and labeling categories or concepts); (b) *axial coding* (identifying connections among categories); (c) *selective coding* (identifying core categories and connections among those); and (d) building conceptual models through development of a *conditional matrix* (representing actions in relationship to conditions and consequences).

As with other forms of qualitative research, engaging in grounded theory requires a *theoretical sensitivity* characterized by openness to constructs as reflected and defined in the data and the perspective of research participants, and continual reflection about preconceived or deductively derived understandings (Strauss & Corbin, 1990). Thus, acknowledging initially and monitoring one's theoretical perspective and empirically derived knowledge throughout the process of coding are critical to maintaining necessary scientific objectivity.

Ethnography

Ethnography, defined as the scientific description of people and their culture, dates back to fifteenth- and sixteenth-century interest in non-Western peoples and cultures following discovery of the so-called New World (Vidich & Lyman, 2000). This early interest in non-Western cultures predated the professionalization of ethnography and anthropology in the nineteenth century, with the advent of the comparative method of Auguste Compte (Vidich & Lyman) and work of Franz Boaz (father of American anthropology; Wolcott, 1999). Subsequent evolution of ethnography in the twentieth century was influenced by the fieldwork of Margaret Mead and Bronisław Malinowski in anthropology and the formalization of the participant observation method in sociology by William Foote Whyte at the University of Chicago in the twentieth century (Vidich & Lyman; Wolcott). During the twentieth century, ethnography was further transformed through integration of postpostivism, interpretivism, constructivism, critical theory, social network theory, and ecological theory into models of ethnography; and the evolution of applied ethnography (i.e., application of ethnographic methods to solving real-world problems; LeCompte & Schensul, 1999). Ethnography, as well as other forms of qualitative research, has come to influence more broadly the social and health sciences as reflected by work in education, public health and psychology.

Ethnography is characterized by its emphasis on *culture*, describing culture and understanding human behavior in the context of culture; and the emphasis on *emic* perspective, gaining an understanding of the phenomena being studied from the perspective of research participants or members of the respective culture. The primary methods of ethnography include *participant observation, in-depth interviewing* and *collection of artifacts* (products of the culture). These methods reflect the sources for understanding the human and cultural experience (Spradley, 1980, p. 5): "what people do, what people know, and the things that people make and use. When each of these are learned and shared by members of some group, we speak of them as *cultural behavior, cultural knowledge*, and *cultural artifacts*." Ethnography typically implies long-term immersion in the culture or context of interest, reflecting its roots in participation within a culture different from one's own for extended periods of multiple months and years. Such immersion is necessary for establishing rapport with informants, identifying consistencies and patterns in cultural practices, and exploring phenomena in sufficient depth to ensure accuracy of understanding.

Culture has been defined in a variety of ways. Spradley (1980) defined culture as "the acquired knowledge people use to interpret experience and generate behavior" (p. 6). Schaeffer (1998) defined culture as:

> an organic and dynamic whole which is concerned with the way people see and interpret the world, organize themselves, conduct their affairs, elevate and enrich life, and position themselves in the world . . . the complex interrelationships that comprise the domain of culture . . . the relationship of people to themselves; to each other; to the objects, artifacts and systems they create; to the particular culture in which they are embedded; to other cultures; to the natural environment; to the supernatural (p. 42).

Consistent with these conceptions and with an ecological perspective within school psychology, Nastasi et al. (2004) defined culture as:

> the beliefs, values, language, ideas, and behavioral norms shared by the members of the culture. Consistent with an ecological view, understanding the culture of the individuals requires consideration of not only their cultural experiences but also

their interpretations of those experiences. Appreciating a person's cultural background thus entails awareness of the myriad cultural experiences, interpretations of those experiences, and multiplicity of ecological contexts relevant to that person's life. Furthermore, the cultural diversity of any school or classroom necessitates consideration of both shared and unique cultural experiences of the students, teachers, and other relevant socializing agents (pp. 42–43).

The importance of ethnography to school psychology lies in the potential application to study of the individual within a cultural context, the study of cultural diversity within the multicultural context of schools and communities, and the analysis of individual-contextual relationships consistent with an ecological perspective. In addition, the relevance of ethnography to school psychology stems from the consistency of methods employed by the ethnographer and the practicing school psychologist, in particular the psychologist's use of observation, interviews, and permanent products (records, student work, etc.); and the emphasis on immersing oneself in the context for a period of time that is sufficient for identifying consistent patterns of behavior and understanding person-context dynamics.

Case Study

The case study approach involves in-depth examination and analysis of an individual "case." Although often used to characterize a focus on individual persons, Lincoln and Guba (1985) use case study to refer to the study of individual persons (e.g., individual student), programs (e.g., reading program, classroom), organizations or agencies (e.g., school), communities, societies, cultures, political or religious movements, or incidents (e.g., natural disaster, school shooting). Case study reporting is characterized by thick description (i.e., in-depth and detailed depiction of the individual and context) and designed to represent the emic perspective (Lincoln & Guba). Case studies can serve multiple purposes, for example, to portray a case for its own instrinsic merit (e.g., to document experiences following natural disaster), for instrumental reasons (e.g., to illustrate a particular issue or phenomenon) or to reflect collective experiences (e.g., through presentation of multiple case studies; Stake, 2000). Although case studies rely heavily on in-depth interviewing to capture the individual's perspective, they typically involve multiple methods (e.g., observation, record review, collection of artifacts). Case studies can take particular forms and represent distinct genres, such as narrative (story form; Murray, 2003) or portraiture (visual artistic representation; Davis, 2003). Moreover, Lincoln and Guba contend that *case study reporting* is the method of choice for all naturalistic inquiry.

School psychologists routinely employ case study methodology in conducting psycho-educational evaluations and consultation regarding individuals, classrooms or organizations. Consistent with such practice, case study research methods typically involve triangulation and can include both qualitative and quantitative data collection. The primary difference lies in the reliance on systematic analytic methods applied to qualitative data in case study research. Perhaps most closely associated with case study methods are single subject designs in school psychology. Despite the different philosophical and theoretical foundations (e.g., behavior theory) and primary reliance on quantitative data, single subject designs reflect a similar focus on analysis of individual cases for intrinsic, instrumental or collective purposes. Closer examination of case study approaches in qualitative research may serve to extend current research and applied methodologies in school psychology to include mixed qualitative-quantitative designs.

Participatory Action Research

The origins of participatory action research (PAR) have been attributed to the work of Kurt Lewin beginning in the 1940s (Fine et al., 2003; Stringer, 1996), efforts to bring about social change by liberation theologists and neo-Marxists of the 1970s and 1980s (e.g., work of Orlando Fals-Borda and Paulo Friere in Central and South America; Fine et al., 2003; Kemmis & McTaggart, 2000), and the community-based work of applied anthropologists such as Jean Schensul and Stephen Schensul beginning in the 1970s (Chambers, 2000; Schensul & Schensul, 1992). Consistent with its origins, PAR is characterized by: (a) *praxis or action research*, a recursive self-reflective process of theory, research, action/change and reflection; and (b) *participatory process*, involving key stakeholders (those with vested interests or resources such as research participants, community members, local agencies) as partners in the theory-research-action process (Greenwood, Whyte, & Harkavy, 1993; Kemmis & McTaggart, 2000; Nastasi, 1998; Nastasi et al., 2004; Schensul, 1998; Schensul & Schensul, 1992). The action research process involves the following steps: (a) use of existing theory and research to (b) generate research questions; (c) collecting and analyzing formative research data to (d) inform development of local or culture-specific theory, which then guides (e) culture-specific action (change efforts); and (f) research to evaluate the effectiveness of change efforts, the results of which subsequently (g) inform theory, research and practice (Nastasi et al., 2004). Consistent with its anthropological roots, PAR involves the use of mixed (qualitative and quantitative) research methodology. In addition to a self-reflective and recursive process, Kemmis and McTaggart (2000) describe PAR as (a) a social process (linking individual and social realms); (b) participatory (through active involvement of research participants in the research process); (c) practical and collaborative (brings people together to examine and solve social problems); (d) emancipatory (provides opportunities for social change); (e) critical (provides opportunities to challenge existing social structures); and (f) focused on transforming both theory and practice.

PAR provides "a systematic way to apply the scientific method of school psychology practice and to make explicit the integration of theory, research and practice" (Nastasi, 2000, p. 543). The participatory focus of PAR is consistent with collaborative models of school-based consultation (e.g., Christenson & Conoley, 1992; Rosenfield & Gravois, 1996; Sheridan et al., 1996). Most importantly, PAR provides the mechanism for extending the notion of the school psychologist as *scientist practitioner* (one who applies theory and research to practice) to that of *reflective practitioner* who engages in practice as a theory-research-action-reflection process (Nastasi, 1998).

QUALITATIVE RESEARCH METHODS

Despite the diversity in qualitative research approaches reflected in the preceding section, there are a common set of methods for collecting, analyzing and interpreting data. As noted above, the core methods are interviewing and observation. The full range of methods has most recently been described within the ethnographic research tradition (Schensul & LeCompte, 1999), and this range is reflected in the methods presented in this section. However, most of these methods can be applied across the traditions highlighted in this chapter. As is the case with any research, the application of methods is influenced by the theoretical and paradigmatic orientation of the researcher. Indeed, one's theoretical orientation influences the choice of research questions, target population, selection and application of data collection and analysis methods, and the interpretation of findings.

Data Collection

The core qualitative data collection methods are participant observation and in-depth interviewing (e.g., see Spradley, 1979, 1980), with the assumption that observing in the natural environment and exploring the experiences and perspectives of the research participants are essential to understanding psychological, cultural or social phenomena as they are experienced in real life. The range of qualitative data collection methods, however, extends beyond these traditional methods to include the following: key-informant interviews, focus group interviews, ethnographic surveys, elicitation techniques (freelist and pilesort), recording of fieldnotes, documentation through journals or logs, collecting artifacts or permanent products (e.g., school records, curriculum products), social networking and spatial mapping. Each of these is described briefly in this section. (For more detailed descriptions and illustrations of these methods see Schensul & LeCompte, 1999; Nastasi et al., 2004.)

Key-Informant Interview

Key-informant interviews are designed for gathering information from individuals who are considered knowledgeable about a particular topic, population, or context, and thus representative of key stakeholder groups. Stakeholders are defined as those individuals with either vested interests or potential resources relevant to addressing target issues; for example, in school-based research, key informants include teachers, parents, community members, community agency staff, students, school administrators. Key-informant interviews are conducted in an informal and unstructured manner with individuals or groups, and include both scheduled meetings (e.g., at weekly faculty meetings) and unplanned encounters (e.g., conversations with teachers in the hallway) with individuals or groups. They are particularly useful for facilitating entry into a new system or context, for assessing stakeholders' general perceptions about a target issue, for identifying key

issues or other key stakeholders, for exploring unintended outcomes of an intervention, or for gathering data "in the moment."

School psychologists are familiar with the information that can be obtained through informal interactions with teachers (e.g., in the hallway, lunchroom, playground), which can subsequently influence more formal data collection efforts. In day-to-day work, however, practitioners and researchers do not necessarily record the nature, content and outcome of such encounters. It is critical that researchers employ systematic methods for recording data from these informal contacts (whether planned or unplanned). Additionally, it is important that any decisions or insights resulting from these contacts are recorded. Ethnographers find it useful to designate a notebook (or laptop) for recording informal interactions, personal reactions, issues that require follow-up, and other noteworthy information (see subsequent section on field notes).

In-Depth Individual Interview

In-depth interviews are semistructured and focused on gathering data from individuals about specific topics related to the research question. Whereas key-informant interviews provide the opportunity to gather general impressions, in-depth interviews are used to investigate specific questions and confirm/disconfirm impressions generated during informal contacts. In-depth interviews are one of the primary methods for gathering data from individuals who represent the population of interest.

Conducting individual interviews is costly in terms of time and resources. Typical interviews last from 60 to 90 minutes, although they can be shorter or longer to accommodate the needs and capabilities of participants. Interviewee responses are recorded verbatim (in writing or audiotaped) for later analysis. Depending on the nature of the research questions and particular qualitative tradition, individuals may be interviewed over multiple sessions and/or extended periods of time. For example, case studies typically require multiple interview sessions. In addition, gathering reliable and valid data from in-depth interviews requires well-trained staff and ongoing monitoring/supervision. Furthermore, the recursive nature of qualitative data collection and analysis requires ongoing analysis, reflection and decision making on the part of the researchers. (This issue is discussed further in the subsequent data analysis section.)

The semistructured nature of in-depth interviews permits (a) standardization and comparison of responses across multiple interviewers, informants, stakeholder groups, and points in time; (b) in-depth exploration of topics; and (c) gathering of information expressed in the vernacular of the informants. Formulation of questions requires close attention to constructs of interest and potential bias resulting from the manner in which questions are posed and the researcher's reactions to interviewee responses. In-depth interview protocols typically include a set of open-ended questions specific to topics of interest, with specific probes (open or closed questions) designed to elicit elaboration or detail. Such interviews are consistent with those routinely conducted by school psychologists with teachers, parents and students to explore presenting concerns, contributing factors, and potential solutions. (For a more extensive discussion of in-depth interviews as a research method, see Schensul, Schensul, & LeCompte, 1999.)

Focused Group Interviews

Focus groups, or focused group interviews, are intended for gathering information about a specific (focused) topic from a group of individuals (Krueger, 1994; Morgan & Krueger, 1997; Schensul, 1999). Participants are asked to respond to questions as representatives of their stakeholder or peer group, and are not necessarily expected to reveal personal information. Informants can be asked to discuss and reach consensus in response to questions. Focus groups are an efficient way to gather information from a range of informants.

Group size and composition varies depending on population and issues being explored. Average group size is 8 to 10 members, but size can vary from 5 to 15 (Schensul, 1999). Although larger groups provide a broader range of perspectives, they may prevent full participation by all members. Smaller groups in contrast provide the opportunity to gather more in-depth information from participants. Groups can be conducted with homogeneous or heterogeneous representation. Conducting focus groups with representatives of a single stakeholder group (e.g., parents) provides the opportunity for open discussion of issues that may be controversial across different sectors (e.g., holding separate versus joint discussions about parent-teacher communication). In contrast, groups with representation across stakeholder groups provide opportunities to examine relationships among stakeholders (e.g., parents

and school staff) and the manner in which difficult issues are handled. Similarly, gender-specific groups may be preferable to mixed-gender groups for middle school students discussing reproductive health issues. Alternatively, mixed-gender groups might provide the context for exploring differences in perspectives about gender roles among adolescents.

Naturalistic/Participant Observation[3]

Naturalistic observations provide opportunities to document occurrences within real-life contexts (e.g., community, school playground, classroom, mental health clinic). The potential foci for observations are individual behaviors (verbal and nonverbal), interpersonal interactions (child-child, adult-child, etc.), activities or events, and static and dynamic contextual features (e.g., noise, light, equipment, materials, spatial arrangements, location). The observer's level of involvement and interaction with individuals within the setting can vary from that of passive observer to full participant.

Participant observation implies that the observer (researcher, data collector) has some degree of involvement in the activities within the context, for example, as member of the school staff. The assumption is that greater involvement permits more in-depth understanding of the activities, individuals, and culture. Additionally, as a legitimate member of the group/community, the observer's presence does not create an artificial situation. These advantages, however, must be weighed against difficulties related to balancing the roles of observer and participant, and potential bias created by immersion in the culture.

The recording of observations can take multiple forms, ranging from a full narrative or video recording to structured checklist or sampling procedure based on time or frequency (see Nastasi, 1999). The full narrative or video record provides an in-depth documentation of what occurs in the setting, and is particularly useful for capturing unanticipated occurrences or capturing a comprehensive rendering of the events. The primary advantage of a full narrative or video record is the permanence of the record that permits later analyses and member checking

---

[3] Suggested resources for observational methods in qualitative research include the following: Bakeman and Gottman (1986); Lofland and Lofland (1984); Nastasi (1999); Schensul, Schensul, and LeCompte (1999); Spradley (1980).

with participants (i.e., participants' review of their own tapes with the researcher, providing an opportunity to gather participant interpretation or additional data). The primary disadvantage is the time- and labor-intensive nature of recording, transcribing, and coding. In contrast, a structured approach (e.g., checklist) is more efficient, but requires clear delineation of the variables of interest and precludes subsequent exploration related to other variables from the same data base (e.g., tape or notes).

Observational techniques are commonplace for school psychologists and can range from unstructured narrative to highly structured time/event sampling. These techniques in practice are usually geared to exploring a concern about a particular student and thus tend to be used in a case study mode. Reliable and valid observations for research purposes require spending extended and multiple time periods to ensure identification of patterns or themes. As with in-depth interviewing, effective use of observational techniques requires training and monitoring of staff, and ongoing reflection and decision making about focus of data collection.

Ethnographic Survey

An ethnographic survey is a standardized self- or informant-report instrument (questionnaire, rating scale, checklist) designed for culture specificity based on formative research with the target population. The survey is designed to be completed in writing but also can be administered as a structured interview. Such instruments can be designed to assess knowledge, attitudes, beliefs, and behavior. The structure of ethnographic surveys parallels that of commonly used standardized psychological measures (e.g., self-, parent-, teacher-report instruments for assessing child adjustment, behavior functioning, attitudes, etc.). *The distinguishing feature of the ethnographic survey is its basis in ethnographic formative research.* Instead of relying on available instruments, program developers create their own tools to reflect the experiences and constructs that are relevant to the target population. This approach is particularly important for work with poorly investigated populations (e.g., specific minority groups, populations outside of the United States), or when investigating issues that have received minimal attention (e.g., use of club drugs by adolescents in United States). With the assistance of professionals with expertise in instrument development, program

planners can create culture-specific instruments and establish local norms. (For more information on ethnographically informed instruments, see Hitchcock et al., 2005; Nastasi, Hitchcock, Burkholder, Varjas, Sarkar, & Jayasena, 2007; Schensul, Schensul, & LeCompte, 1999.)

Elicitation Techniques: Freelist and Pilesort

Understanding shared meaning is a primary goal of ethnography. Elicitation techniques, such as freelists and pilesorts, are designed to gather information from members of a cultural group (e.g., society, community, segment of society, organization) in order to define *cultural domains*, that is, conceptual categories or shared meanings (Borgatti, 1999; Spradley, 1979). Borgatti makes an important distinction between elicitation and survey techniques: Whereas the purpose of a survey is to learn about the respondent's experiences or preferences (e.g., what symptoms of depression have you experienced), the purpose of elicitation is to learn what constitutes a domain or category (e.g., what are the symptoms of depression, from your perspective). The recommended sample size for freelists and pilesorts is 30, although the number necessary to establish culturally valid domains depends on the amount of variability across respondents (Borgatti). For example, high levels of consistency can be achieved with 20 individuals; alternatively, when substantial variability occurs, 60 respondents may be necessary before consistent responding can be achieved.

The *freelist technique*, similar to brainstorming, is used to elicit the elements of a domain by asking respondents in a semistructured interview format to list (in writing or orally) the items of a particular conceptual domain. An obvious alteration of the technique is to do freelisting or brainstorming in a focused group interview format. For example, to define the construct of adolescent stressors, one might ask a sample of adolescents to list all the situations that cause adolescent stress. To define the domain of school discipline problems, one might ask teachers to list all the student behaviors that they would include in the category of discipline problems. Using the lists, researchers identify those items listed most frequently across the sample of respondents; these items are then subjected to the pilesort technique.

The *pilesort technique* is designed to elicit the perceived relationships of items within a conceptual category, that is, similarities among items and basis for those distinctions. Informants are provided with a set of cards (e.g., index cards) with names or short descriptions representing elements of a particular domain (e.g., those generated via freelists) and asked to sort the items based on similarity (i.e., create piles by grouping similar items together). Instructions to guide sorting vary depending on the researcher's purpose. Respondents can be asked to sort in as many piles as they want, to sort into a specific number of piles, or to sort on some conceptual or perceptual basis. For example, individuals are provided with a list of behaviors representing displays of affection between people and asked to sort them (e.g., into three piles; on the basis of verbal versus nonverbal; or on the basis of type of relationship). The resulting piles are then used to distinguish, for example, affection based on type of relationship (e.g., with parent, peer, acquaintance, sexual partner, spouse). These distinctions are determined by the consistency (or consensus) of sorting across respondents. Respondents also can be asked to explain their rationale for sorting (e.g., why items were placed in particular piles). Software is available for the analysis (e.g., through hierarchical clustering and multidimensional scaling) of freelist and pilesort data (e.g., ANTHROPAC, Borgatti, 1996).

Fieldnotes

Fieldnotes provide a written record of observations and contacts within the field (real-life) setting (Schensul, Schensul, & LeCompte, 1999). Although fieldnotes can include the written narrative record of naturalistic observations and key informant interviews, the term is used here to refer to *informal and serendipitous observations and interview contacts* such as a conversation in the hallway with a teacher about how a classroom intervention is progressing, or an unplanned observation of students using target skills to resolve an argument in the cafeteria. A detailed accounting of the encounter (e.g., using descriptive, behavioral terms) is recorded, along with the researcher's impressions, questions, reflections, or considerations for follow-up. A designated notebook for recording fieldnotes is recommended. Typically, shorthand notes are recorded on-site, with subsequent transcription and elaboration as soon as possible (preferably within 24 hours; Schensul et al.).

Logs and Journals

Logs and journals are participant self-reports that provide written documentation of interactions,

activities, events and reflections of participants (Nastasi & Berg, 1999). *Logs* refer to structured forms (e.g., checklist or rating scale) for recording activities, events or interactions (e.g., teacher keeps record of instructional strategies, perceptions of the success of those, and modifications to the written curriculum for specific students). *Journals* are open-ended and personalized narrative accounts of thoughts, feelings, and behaviors (e.g., parents' daily narrative of feelings, thoughts and behaviors related to interactions with their child).

Nastasi et al. (2004) provide the following guidelines for using logs and journals as research tools in school and community settings:

1. Construct logs in checklist format with a minimal number of items, so they can be completed in a few minutes. Include space for comments.

2. Allow time in intervention or consultation sessions for completing logs; or negotiate specific time for completion on a daily basis.

3. Schedule regular times (e.g., weekly) for collecting completed logs and journals.

4. Use logs and journals in intervention and consultation settings to provide feedback, monitor progress, and identify needs for additional training or support.

5. Encourage participants to use logs and journals for reflection and self-evaluation.

6. Use logs and journals as components of multimethod, multisource data collection (e.g., use observations to confirm/disconfirm teacher logs of intervention implementation).

Artifacts or Permanent Products

Artifacts refer to *permanent products of a culture*, in this case, cultural products relevant to psychological phenomena of interest. They can include documents (e.g., government documents, diagnostic manuals, federal or state government regulations), records (e.g., student records, school academic rankings, official community statistics), media materials (e.g., news articles about drug use in the community, ads promoting alcohol consumption or smoking, public service announcements [PSAs] promoting screening for depression), and artistic products (e.g., music, literature, paintings) that reflect cultural beliefs, norms, and values. Many of these products provide important data about needs, resources, and perspectives relevant to cultural and social dimensions of psychological factors. For example, PSAs promoting screening for, and pharmacological treatment of, depression or social anxiety convey particular messages to the general community. Examining the extent to which these messages are accepted within, or reflect the views of, the local community or segment of the population provides critical information about the target culture (e.g., community perspectives can be gathered through other data collection methods such as participant observation or in-depth interviews). School records (e.g., suspensions, referrals for violence) are an important source of data to identify needs and to monitor the impact of current disciplinary policies and procedures. Government documents provide information about available resources (e.g., via informational materials), locally or nationally recognized needs (e.g., "school report cards" that reflect academic standing in the community or reports from the U. S. Surgeon General on the health and mental health of school-aged population), and parameters for providing care (e.g., state laws regarding access of adolescents to brief mental health counseling without parental consent). Finally, artistic products can be used to assess individual and cultural perspectives (e.g., lyrics to popular music as a reflection of teen culture).

Curriculum-based, or program-based, materials refer to the *permanent products of instructional or intervention programs*, those produced by either program staff (e.g., as intervention guides or protocols) or program recipients (e.g., reflecting their response to program activities). For example, the teacher's manual for a classroom-based violence prevention program reflects the goals, objectives, key messages, target skills, and activities embodied in the intervention (i.e., the planners' or stakeholders' intentions). Workbooks and other materials produced by students during an intervention can be used to portray student participation and progress towards skill development. These materials can be collected and subject to systematic analysis, for example, by coding student products for evidence of progress consistent with program goals. Program planners who intend to use student products of an intervention in this manner are advised to structure the materials for such use. Furthermore, developing materials with evaluation of participant progress in mind benefits both service providers and evaluators (e.g., can be used by teachers for monitoring and grading student progress).

Perhaps the best known artifacts among school psychologists are students' cumulative files, which yield information about behavioral and academic functioning through the course of a student's career. In addition, schools and districts maintain population (school or district level, respectively) records of indices such as discipline referrals, attendance, truancy, dropout, and incidence of violence. Although such archives can provide data for both formative and evaluative purposes, the consistency of record keeping may preclude reliable data collection. For example, the recording and definition of discipline referrals may vary across schools or time. Thus, it behooves program planners and evaluators to investigate the availability and reliability of archival school data before making decisions about their use, and, if necessary, to assist schools in establishing systematic procedures for recording data.

An example of the utility of media materials as data about cultural beliefs, values, and practices related to mental health issues comes from work in the country of Sri Lanka (Nastasi, Varjas, Sarkar, & Jayasena, 1998). During the formative research phase, national newspapers and other published materials were reviewed for information about cultural conceptions of mental health. A key concern was suicide, as the country had one of the highest suicide rates in the world. A review of newspapers revealed frequent publication of articles about suicide by ingesting pesticides (which were readily available for agricultural purposes). The articles, which occurred at least weekly and sometimes several times per week, portrayed the ingestion of pesticides in response to failed love affairs in a melodramatic manner (e.g., the rejected lover of a local police officer ingests pesticides and dies on the street in front of the police station). These stories provided important data about the portrayal of suicide, and the basis for further inquiry with key informants (e.g., psychiatrists, community members, adolescents, teachers). During this same period, the country's psychiatrists, in response to such media, advocated with government and news agencies to discontinue the publication of such articles out of concern for the messages that were being conveyed to the public. In this instance, media materials served as one source of information (in addition to interviews, focus groups, etc.) about social and cultural factors related to mental health.

Social Network Mapping

The study and depiction of social networks provides researchers and program planners with information about the *social ecology of target individuals*, either members of the culture under study or participants in a particular intervention. Social network mapping is a technique that permits graphic representation of interpersonal relationships in a variety of ways (for detailed description of ethnographic network data collection and analysis, see Trotter, 1999). Two network types, described by Trotter, are relevant to school psychology practice. *Ego-centered or personal networks* depict interpersonal relationships from the perspective of the individual (e.g., perceptions of relationships as stressful or supportive). *Full relational social networks* indicate interrelationships among all the members; these can include naturally occurring networks (e.g., peer network existing within school or community) or artificially contrived networks (e.g., created for the purpose of study or intervention). Social networks can be used to depict a wide range of topics such as the nature, strength, density, and types of relationships; roles, communication patterns, power and influence, and interpersonal distance; and segmentation (e.g., cliques) within a network. Network data are collected through a number of methods, including observation, interview, and structured network surveys. Software programs are available to assist in construction and analysis of social networks (ANTHROPAC, Borgatti, 1996; UCINET, Borgatti, Everett, & Freeman, 1992).

Spatial Mapping

The purpose of spatial mapping as an ethnographic method is to represent person-environment relationships in the target community (Cromley, 1999). The community is the location, or ecosystem, in which human behaviors and interactions of interest take place (e.g., school, neighborhood, classroom). Collection and mapping of spatial data can be used to address a variety of questions, such as the following: (a) Where do specific activities or events occur; for example, where do adolescents gather for entertainment (dancing, music, sports events, etc.)? (b) What are the locations of organizations of interest; for example, where are mental health centers located? (c) In what locations do target behaviors occur; for example, where do incidents of violence or sexual harassment occur in school, or where do incidents of drug trafficking occur in the neighborhood? (d) Where in the community does the target population live; for example, where do students from a particular school live? (e) How does

someone move about within a particular space; for example, what are the activity patterns within the community for a particular adolescent (i.e., tracking movement between home, school, friends' homes, neighborhood playground, and shopping mall in a typical week)? (f) What is the spatial arrangement of objects and people within a particular context; for example, what is the spatial arrangement of the classroom? (g) What is the flow of communication within a particular context; for example, how does communication flow during a mental health or instructional planning team meeting?

Spatial data can be collected through naturalistic observation, interviews, archival records review, logs, and surveys. Data management, representation, and analysis are facilitated through the use of computer-assisted mapping or graphics programs and data management systems, or geographic information systems (GIS; Maguire, Goodchild, & Rhind, 1999; see Cromley for more in-depth discussion of spatial data collection, mapping, and analysis). An example of spatial mapping as the basis for data-based decision making comes from a study of high school violence (Astor, Meyer, & Behre, 1999), in which researchers constructed maps based on student interviews to identify the locations, time of day, characteristics of perpetrators and victims, and contextual variables related to violent incidents on campus. Data were used to develop a comprehensive school plan for violence prevention and reduction. In similar ways, school psychologists could use spatial mapping to better understand bullying, development of cliques among adolescents, or interethnic social interactions.

Making Sense of Qualitative Data: Data Analysis and Interpretation

The task of organizing, analyzing, and interpreting qualitative data can be overwhelming. The open-ended nature of ethnographic data collection results in vast amounts of raw data, most frequently in the form of notes and text. Yet, the process of transforming data through description, analysis, and interpretation is fundamental to qualitative inquiry (Wolcott, 1994). Wolcott defines the components of the transformation process as follows:

> *Description* addresses the question, "What is going on here?" Data consist of observations made by the researcher and/or reported to the researcher by others. *Analysis* addresses

the identification of essential features and the systematic description of relationships among them—in short, how things work.... [When there are stated objectives, for example, in evaluative research] analysis also may be employed evaluatively to address questions of why the system is not working or how it might be made to work "better." *Interpretation* addresses processual questions of meanings and contexts: "[What] does it all mean?" "What is to be made of it all?" (p. 12)

Making sense of (or transforming) data depends on both the technical and conceptual skills of the researcher. Just as with data collection, the researcher also is the primary instrument for analysis and interpretation. This does not mean that the sense-making process is unsystematic. On the contrary, the generation of trustworthy findings (i.e., credible, dependable, transferable, and confirmable) requires meticulous and methodical management and transformation of the data. Furthermore, as noted by Camic et al. (2003), the scientific objectivity we seek may be illusive:

> No experiment, no research question, and certainly no interpretation of data can possibly be truly objective. The types of problems we are interested in, the questions we ask, the kind of data we collect, and the analyses we undertake all emanate from some context, be it socioeconomic, political, cultural, or personal. (p. 6)

A full treatment of data management, analysis, and interpretation procedures is beyond the scope of this chapter. In this, some general principles and guidelines are provided. Readers are encouraged to consult several excellent sources for more detailed discussions (LeCompte & Schensul, 1999; Miles & Huberman, 1994; Ryan & Bernard, 2000; Wolcott, 1994).

Data Management and Analysis

Data analysis, or coding of qualitative data, has several purposes. *Coding* reduces data to meaningful units or code categories, which can then be represented qualitatively (descriptively or through theme analysis) or quantitatively (e.g., frequency of particular codes). Coding can also serve to represent the emic perspective or "voice" of respondents. Results of data analysis can be used to represent both commonly shared perspectives and the range of voices. Particularly within the context of theory development, coding

can yield definitions of key constructs (e.g., definitions of stress and coping in different cultures) and assist researchers in determining the "boundaries" of construct definitions (i.e., identify inclusionary and exclusionary criteria). Finally, data analysis can facilitate development of culture-specific theory and/or culture-specific models for designing assessment tools or intervention programs (e.g., culturally sensitive tools to measure stress and coping; socially valid mental health promotion programs).

Management and analysis of qualitative data typically involves a systematic multistep process (Nastasi, 1999): (a) preparing the data, (b) making decisions about the coding process, (c) preparing reliable coders, (d) coding data, and (e) theme/pattern analysis.

Step 1. Data Preparation
All data are translated (when necessary), transcribed (e.g., transcription of audiotapes) and entered into the computer (e.g., textual processing program) for coding.[4]

Step 2. Decisions About Coding
Data analysis involves a process of building a conceptual framework based on coding of key constructs and then identifying themes and patterns to explain relationships among constructs. Coding of data can be approached inductively and/or deductively (Nastasi, 1999). One of the first decisions about coding involves identification of potential codes (definitions) that represent constructs or variables related to the theoretical-empirical foundations of the study. Coding can involve a deductive approach in which codes are theoretically or empirically driven, an inductive approach in which codes are derived from the data, or a combination of deduction and induction. *Deductive coding* involves application of preexisting theoretically or empirically derived codes (i.e., well-developed definitions of key constructs based on existing theory and research). Alternatively, *inductive coding* involves identification of codes (meaning units) as represented in or derived from the data (e.g., in grounded theory) and development of a new coding scheme. More

---

[4]Computer-based text search programs (e.g., *ATLAS.ti*, Scientific Software Development, 2004; *The Ethnograph*, Qualis Research Associates, 1998; *NVivo 7.0*, QSR International, 2006) can assist in the management, analysis and interpretation of data. Ultimately, however, data transformation is dependent on the technical and conceptual skills of the researcher.

often, coding involves a combination of deductive and inductive approaches, in which the researcher begins with the application of preexisting theoretically/empirically based major codes or constructs (e.g., depression or anxiety), and modifies the scheme through identification of additional codes (new categories or subcategories) to represent data that do not fit with preexisting construct definitions. For example, a researcher interested in stress and coping might initially code interview data collected from adolescents in Asia for instances of personal coping strategies that rely on the resources of the individual (e.g., problem solving, capacity for seeking social support; Lazarus & Folkman, 1984), but discover that adolescents in the target culture also engage in communal coping (collective attempts at adaptation, response to adversity, or goal accomplishment; Hobfoll, 2002). The evidence of strategies that are different would lead to identification of new types of coping and/or reformulation of our conceptions of coping. In summary, selecting or developing a coding scheme can involve adopting a preexisting scheme, modifying a preexisting scheme, or developing a new coding scheme. (For in-depth discussion and illustration of deductive and inductive approaches to coding, see Nastasi, 1999.)

Step 3. Preparing Reliable Coders

Ensuring reliable application of a coding scheme involves training coders, initially working toward an acceptable level of consistency or intercoder agreement, and then conducting periodic consistency checks throughout the coding process. The preparation of coders varies depending on the approach to coding (deductive, inductive or mixed; Nastasi, 1999). Regardless of the approach to coding, however, researchers initially need to ensure that coders are knowledgeable about appropriate ethical procedures, the study's research methodology, and theoretical and empirical underpinnings.

When using a deductive approach to coding (adopting a preexisting coding scheme), the researcher engages in a sequence of instruction with coders in the existing scheme (codes and code definitions), demonstration (through examples from earlier research or with a similar set or subset of a current data set), practice (coders apply codes to similar data sets or a current subset), and feedback (regarding accuracy of application; e.g., comparison with more experienced coders; Nastasi, 1999). This process continues until acceptable levels of intercoder agreement and

intracoder consistency are achieved (typically 85–90%, based on Cohen's kappa; Bakeman & Gottman, 1986).

Preparing coders in the context of an inductive or mixed deductive-inductive approach to coding (modifying or creating a new coding scheme) involves a more participatory approach, in which coders can become coresearchers. The sequence is described as follows (Nastasi, 1999):

Step 3.a. Coders learn about the research, the theoretical and empirical base, and the local culture and context. The coders must be sufficiently knowledgeable about the etic (researcher) and the emic (culture-specific) perspectives to ensure accurate representation of both. In the case of an inductive approach, researchers and coders must make explicit their biases in order to guard against etic interpretation of the participants' perspectives/meanings. In mixed inductive-deductive approach, the goal is an integrated etic-emic perspective that reflects both existing theory and research (as interpreted by the researcher) and the culturally based participant perspective.

Step 3.b. Researchers and coders work together to review transcribed data, discuss modification of existing codes or development of new codes, and identify exemplars of code categories. Discussion focuses on meaning (definition) of codes, distinctions among code categories and subcategories, and the boundaries of specific codes (i.e., inclusionary and exclusionary criteria, central versus peripheral aspects of the code category). A consensual process of discussion continues until the coding team (researcher and coders) reach agreement on codes, code definitions, and exemplars. This process typically involves a review of sufficient amounts of the data to ensure that variability across participants is represented and variations in meaning are represented in code categories.

Step 3.c. Coders independently apply the scheme to a particular subset of data, compare results of coding, and discuss points of disagreement. This process can result in further refinement of the coding scheme (e.g., clarifying meaning, adjusting boundaries, combining code categories, generating new codes). This process continues until coders establish an acceptable level of inter- and intracoder agreement as described above.

Step 4. Coding Data

Once acceptable agreement levels are reached, coders are ready to independently apply the coding scheme. When data are based on multiple sources (e.g., teachers, parents) or methods (e.g., observation, interview), each data set is coded independently (e.g., interview data are coded, then observation data are coded). Throughout the coding process, periodic checks are made to monitor application of the coding scheme, address any discrepancies that may arise across data sources and methods, and ensure intercoder and intracoder consistency. Typically a subset (e.g., 10%) of the files (randomly selected across types of data and time) is coded by at least two coders to determine overall levels of intercoder agreement (through computation of an agreement index; e.g., Cohen's kappa).

Step 5. Theme and Pattern Analysis

Coded data are reviewed and discussed among researchers and with representatives of stakeholder groups in order to identify themes and patterns, and develop or confirm conceptual models. This initial process of data interpretation involves (a) consideration of individual code categories and major constructs, (b) identification of consistent and variant themes within and between categories, and (c) development of a culture-specific conceptual model to fit the target population. For example, the process of developing a culture-specific theory of stress and coping would involve first identifying and defining types of stressors and coping strategies, and then identifying themes such as contextual variations in coping (e.g., coping with academic versus family stressors) or patterns related to gender (e.g., stressors specific to differing gender roles). The identified patterns are then reflected in development of new or modified conceptual models of stress and coping (e.g., see Nastasi et al., 2004; Nastasi et al., 1998).

Step 5 is also characterized by a recursive process of data analysis-interpretation in which preliminary interpretations can lead to further data collection to provide elaboration, confirmation/disconfirmation and validation of identified constructs, themes and patterns. For example, identification of contextual variations in response to stress can lead to additional data collection about relationships between context and use of individual and communal coping (e.g., expanding data collection to include response to environmental stressors such as natural disasters). The recursive data collection-analysis process continues until sufficient consistency and depth of understanding regarding key constructs and their relationships are reached, and additional data fail to yield further insights (referred to as data or theoretical saturation). Interpretative analysis is consistent with the constant comparative method of Strauss and Corbin (1990), described in the earlier section on grounded theory.

Finally, interpretative analysis also involves the presentation of data and preliminary interpretation to representatives of participant and other stakeholder groups, referred to as *member checking* (Lincoln & Guba, 1985). The purpose of member checking is to provide an opportunity to negotiate meaning with members of the target population and to ensure that the data and subsequent interpretation reflect the emic perspective. Inconsistencies between etic (researcher) and emic (participant) interpretations can lead to further data collection and analysis. The level of involvement of participants and stakeholders in data interpretation can vary from presenting findings and soliciting feedback (e.g., follow-up meetings or focus groups) to full involvement in the collection, analysis and interpretation of data that characterizes participatory approaches (e.g., PAR).

Data Interpretation and Transformation

Ultimately, interpretation and transformation of data into information that can inform science and practice is the responsibility of the researcher, and thus dependent on the researcher's knowledge and skill. Strauss and Corbin (1990) use the term *theoretical sensitivity* to refer to the personal quality of the researcher characterized by insight or awareness of meaning in data. In the case of school psychology, these insights are dependent on the ability to ascribe meaning which reflects knowledge of relevant theoretical and empirical foundations and their applications in practice (i.e., the etic perspective), understanding of the cultural background and experiences of the target population (emic perspective), ability to distinguish relevant from irrelevant information, and ability to integrate etic and emic perspectives into culture-specific concepts. Strauss and Corbin provide several suggestions for maintaining the necessary balance between science and creativity that characterizes theoretical sensitivity: (a) periodically stepping back and questioning the social validity of the data (i.e., do the data fit with the reality one is trying to represent?); (b) maintaining an attitude of skepticism regarding certainty of interpretations and conclusions, consistent with the notion of tentative (or provisional) application described in an earlier section; and (c) systematic application of research procedures to ensure appropriate scientific rigor. To this, one might add a fourth suggestion regarding the involvement of professional peers and stakeholders in analytic and interpretative discussions (peer debriefing and member checking, respectively; Lincoln & Guba, 1985). Finally, within the field of school psychology, transformation of data requires description, analysis, and interpretation that can inform theory, research and practice (e.g., development of assessment and intervention tools).

APPLICATIONS TO SCHOOL PSYCHOLOGY: MIXED-METHODS FRAMEWORK

As the Interdisciplinary Qualitative Research Subcommittee (IQRS)[5] of the Task Force on Evidence-Based Interventions in School Psychology undertook the task of identifying and explicating the criteria for evaluating qualitative research in school psychology, committee members were faced with a number of critical questions (Nastasi & Schensul, 2005). In addition to considering the potential contributions of qualitative methods to intervention research, the committee raised questions about the limitations of traditional intervention research that relied exclusively on quantitative designs, and proposed integration of qualitative and quantitative methods (i.e., a mixed-methods framework) within the *Procedural and Coding Manual for Review of Evidence-Based Interventions*

(Kratochwill & Stoiber, 2002b).[6] The outcome of Task Force discussions was the seamless integration of criteria related to quantitative and qualitative methods into a single coding manual which reflected a mixed-methods approach.

Nastasi and Schensul (2005) delineated the potential contributions of qualitative methods to intervention research in school psychology in an introduction to a special issue of the *Journal of School Psychology*, which was intended to summarize the work of the IQRS and illustrate the application of qualitative methods to facilitating evidence-based practice. Qualitative research methods can be applied to several stages of the intervention development process. First, qualitative methods applied to generative (basic) research can facilitate identification and definition of individual and social-cultural constructs related to the target concern (e.g., personal and social-cultural variables related to bullying). Second, qualitative research in formative phases of program development can serve to enhance the social and ecological validity of interventions, assist in the development of culture- and context-specific intervention programs, and aid in the identification of local needs and resources. Third, qualitative research in evaluation phases can serve to document program implementation and thus facilitate transfer and adaptation of evidence-based practices to new settings and populations through thick description, facilitate identification of core and adaptable components of interventions, evaluate ecological or contextual fit, and aid in the identification of manifestations of individual and ecological/systemic outcomes not captured by quantitative norm-referenced instruments. Thus, qualitative research, within a mixed-methods model, could help to address some of the limitations of traditional intervention research, such as limited attention to cultural and contextual factors and limited information about the challenges of implementation in real-life contexts.

---

[5]The members and respective disciplines of the IQRS included Bonnie Nastasi, cochair, School Psychology; Stephen Schensul, cochair, Anthropology; Doug Campbell, Educational Research; Denise DeZolt, School Psychology; David Fetterman, Anthropology; Karen Harris, Special Education/Educational Psychology; Evelyn Jacob, Anthropology; Colette Ingraham, School Psychology; Margaret LeCompte, Sociology; Joel Meyers, School Psychology; Evelyn Oka, School Psychology; Mittie Quinn, School Psychology; Jean J. Schensul, Anthropology; Cherie Tyler Balkcom, School Psychology; Stephen Truscott, School Psychology; Kristen Varjas, School Psychology; Harry Wolcott, Anthropology; Frank Worrell, School Psychology.

[6]The *Procedural and Coding Manual for Review of Evidence-Based Interventions* is currently being updated to reflect a mixed-methods framework with particular attention to criteria for ensuring sufficient attention to culture (discussion of the integration of cultural considerations can be found in Ingraham & Oka, 2007). For the most recent versions, contact Thomas R. Kratochwill, PhD, School Psychology Program, University of Wisconsin, Madison.

Nastasi and colleagues (Nastasi, Hitchcock, Burkholder, Sarkar, Varjas & Jayasena, 2007) present several mixed-methods designs[7] relevant to research in school psychology. These designs, based on current models of mixed-methods research (e.g., see Tashakkori & Teddlie, 2003), involve sequential, concurrent, and iterative combinations of qualitative and quantitative methods.[8] The designs are applicable to the varied research purposes that characterize multiyear applied research programs:

a. formative or basic research, Qual + Quan;
b. theory development and testing, Qual→/+ Quan →/+ Qual →/+ Quan, or Qual→ ←Quan;
c. instrument development and testing, Qual→/+ Quan →/+ Qual →/+ Quan, or Qual→ ←Quan;
d. program development/adaptation and evaluation, Qual→/+ Quan →/+ Qual →/+ Quan, or Qual→ ←Quan;
e. evaluation research, Qual + Quan; and
f. translation of evidence-based programs to other settings and populations (i.e., translational research); Qual→/+ Quan →/+ Qual →/+ Quan, or Qual→ ←Quan.

Such designs hold promise for addressing the aforementioned shortcomings of traditional intervention research and facilitating research-based practice in school psychology. Realizing this promise, however, requires examination of current models of research, practice and professional preparation, in the context of envisioning the future of school psychology.

---

[7] Comprehensive coverage of mixed-methods designs are beyond the scope of this chapter. Readers are referred to Tashakkori and Teddlie (2003) for detailed descriptions and illustrations of mixed qualitative-quantitative methodology. Nastasi, Moore, and Varjas (2004) illustrate a mixed-methods approach to multiyear applied research in school psychology.

[8] The following nomenclature has been used to characterize mixed methods designs (Nastasi, Hitchcock, Sarkar, Burkholder, Varjas, & Jayasena, 2007; Tashakkori & Teddlie, 2003):
Qual = Qualitative methods (*QUAL* denotes primary method; *Qual* denotes secondary method);
Quan = Quantitative methods (*QUAN* denotes primary method; *Quan* denotes secondary method);
→ = followed by [sequential design]; + = concurrent with [concurrent design]; →/+ = sequential or concurrent; → ← = recursive, interactive (subsumes both concurrent and sequential).

FUTURE DIRECTIONS: IMPLICATIONS FOR RESEARCH, PRACTICE AND PROFESSIONAL PREPARATION

What are the implications of the growing recognition of the value of qualitative research for school psychology? How might the increased use of qualitative research methods change the nature of school psychology research? What are the implications for enhancing evidence-based practice, fostering translation of research to practice, and informing psychological theory? And, what are the implications for school psychology training programs? This final section addresses these questions in the context of future school psychology research, practice and professional preparation.

School psychology, like much of psychology, has traditionally relied on quantitative research methods within positivistic and postpositivistic paradigms. The reliance on randomized controlled trials as the hallmark of social science research has guided the nature of research, conceptions of evidence-based practice, and graduate training in research methods. Deliberations among qualitative, quantitative and mixed-methods researchers on the Task Force on Evidence-Based Interventions in School Psychology resulted in an important decision: To move from separate coding manuals and criteria for quantitative and qualitative research toward an integration of criteria into a single coding manual (Kratochwill & Stoiber, 2002b; Ingraham & Oka, 2007; Nastasi & Schensul, 2005). Given the paradigmatic differences between qualitative and quantitative researchers (as noted in Lincoln & Guba, 1985; Teddlie & Tashakkori, 2003), the adoption of a mixed qualitative-quantitative perspective is a credit to the future-oriented thinking of the Task Force and reflects recognition of potential contributions of qualitative research methods to advancing evidence-based practice (Nastasi & Schensul, 2005). The availability of criteria for evaluating qualitative research in school psychology (see Nastasi & Schensul) can help to ensure the conduct of valid qualitative research and provide guidelines for review and publication of studies employing qualitative methods. Publication of qualitative research studies will depend on recognition of their value by journal editors, appointment of qualitative researchers to editorial review boards, and availability of models for presentation of qualitative research findings.

What are the implications of increased use of qualitative methods in school psychology? First, availability of qualitative research methods can influence research questions. Qualitative methods are particularly important for answering questions posed within an ecological or systems perspective; exploring cultural and contextual variations in psychological constructs; identifying contextual and cultural factors related to cognitive, academic, emotional, social and behavioral functioning; understanding the challenges of system-wide intervention programming and translating research to practice; conducting formative evaluation that involves systematic data-based modification of intervention programs and documents critical process variables; identifying unintended treatment outcomes; and contributing to the development of culture-specific psychological assessment and intervention methods informed by grounded theory. Second, qualitative research methodology provides a mechanism for integrating research and practice. The integration of characteristics of qualitative inquiry and methods into psychological assessment, consultation, and intervention can help to advance science-based practice. The application of qualitative data collection and analysis procedures and techniques for ensuring trustworthiness could enhance the reliability and validity of the more informal methods of psychological assessment (e.g., narrative observation and in-depth or key-informant interviewing). Finally, the systematic application of qualitative methods in research and practice could expand the knowledge base in school psychology, provide the mechanism to address current shortcomings of intervention research, and foster the integration of research and practice.

Resolving paradigmatic debates, establishing guidelines for conduct and evaluation of qualitative research, and providing outlets for dissemination of qualitative research findings are critical steps in broadening the available research tools in school psychology and enhancing the theoretical and empirical foundations of practice. Just as important, however, is the availability of training in qualitative methods. Opportunities for graduate and postdoctoral training will be critical for development of qualitative research skills among faculty, researchers and practitioners. Initially, questions about the depth and breadth of training will need to be addressed. Conducting valid qualitative research requires advanced preparation in data collection, analysis and interpretation. Preparing graduate students in both quantitative and qualitative methods will mean additional coursework and mentored experiences. Graduate program faculty will need to consider the implications of additional program requirements and necessary faculty expertise. Furthermore, the adoption of a mixed qualitative-quantitative research framework within graduate training will necessitate review and revision of the scope and sequence of research coursework. Ideally, a mixed-methods orientation needs to be introduced early in research training (e.g., in introductory research courses) rather than only at the advanced level (see Creswell, 2003; Creswell, Tashakkori, Jensen, & Shapley, 2003). In addition, models for mixed qualitative-quantitative methods training in school psychology are needed. (See Creswell et al., 2003 for guidelines and examples related to mixed-methods course development.)

A critical question for school psychology training programs is whether coursework in qualitative and mixed methods research should be required rather than optional or recommended. Do graduate training programs have the responsibility to prepare school psychologists as consumers and producers of quantitative, qualitative and mixed-methods research? The answer to this question has implications for the future of research, practice and professional preparation in school psychology. Moreover, decisions about what constitutes graduate training in research have repercussions for the participation and status of school psychology in the social sciences, and for the capacity of the profession to answer complex real-world questions.

References

Astor, R. A., Meyer, H. A., & Behre, W. J. (1999). Unowned places and times: Maps and interviews about violence in high schools. *American Educational Research Journal, 36*, 3–42.

Bakeman, R., & Gottman, J. M. (1986). *Observing interaction: An introduction to sequential analysis.* New York: Cambridge University Press.

Blumer, H. (1969). *Symbolic interactionism: Perspective and method.* Berkeley, CA: University of California Press.

Borgatti, S. P. (1996). *ANTHROPAC 4.0.* Natick, MA: Analytic Technologies.

Borgatti, S. P. (1999). Elicitation techniques for cultural domain analysis. In J. J. Schensul & M. D. LeCompte (Eds.), *Ethnographer's toolkit, Book 3: Enhanced ethnographic techniques: Audiovisual techniques, focused group interviews, and elicitation techniques.* (pp. 115–151). Walnut Creek, CA: AltaMira.

Borgatti, S. P., Everett, M. G., & Freeman, L. C. (1992). *UCINET IV Version 1.0.* Columbia, SC: Analytic Technologies.

Bronfenbrenner, U. (1989). Ecological systems theory. In R. Vasta (Ed.), *Annals of child development* (Vol. 6, pp. 187–249). Greenwich, CT: JAI Press.

Camic, P. M., Rhodes, J. E., & Yardley, L. (Eds.). (2003). *Qualitative research in psychology: Expanding perspectives in methodology and design.* Washington, DC: APA.

Chambers, E. (2000). Applied ethnography. In N. K. Denzin & Y. S. Lincoln (Eds.), *Handbook of qualitative research* (2nd ed.; pp. 851–869). Thousand Oaks, CA: Sage.

Christenson, S. L., & Conoley, J. C. (1992). (Eds.). *Home-school collaboration: Building a fundamental educational resource.* Silver Springs, MD: National Association of School Psychologists.

Creswell, J.W. (1998). *Qualitative inquiry and research design: Choosing among five traditions.* Thousand Oaks, CA: Sage.

Creswell, J. W. (2003). *Research design: Qualitative, quantitative, and mixed methods approaches.* Thousand Oaks, CA: Sage.

Creswell, J. W., Tashakkori, A., Jensen, K. D., & Shapley, K. L. (2003). Teaching mixed methods research: Practices, dilemmas, and challenges. In A. Tashakkori & C. Teddlie (Eds.), *Handbook of mixed methods in social and behavioral research* (pp. 619–638). Thousand Oaks, CA: Sage.

Cromley, E. K. (1999). Mapping spatial data. In J. J. Schensul & M. D. LeCompte (Eds.), *Mapping social networks, spatial data, and hidden populations. Ethnographer's toolkit, Book 4* (pp. 51–124). Walnut Creek, CA: AltaMira.

Davis, J. H. (2003). Balancing the whole: Portraiture as methodology. In P. M. Camic, J. E. Rhodes, & L. Yardley (Eds.), *Qualitative research in psychology: Expanding perspectives in methodology and design* (pp. 199–218). Washington, DC: APA.

Denzin, N. K. (1989). *Interpretive biography.* Thousand Oaks, CA: Sage.

Denzin, N. K., & Lincoln, Y. S. (Eds.). (2000). *Handbook of qualitative research* (2nd ed.). Thousand Oaks, CA: Sage.

Fine, M., Torre, M. E., Boudin, K., Bowen, I., Clark, J., Hylton, D., Martinez, M., Missy, et al. (2003). Participatory action research: From within and beyond prison bars. In P. M. Camic, J. E. Rhodes, & L. Yardley (Eds.), *Qualitative research in psychology: Expanding perspectives in methodology and design* (pp. 173–198). Washington, DC: APA.

Glaser, B., & Strauss, A. (1967). *The discovery of grounded theory.* Chicago: Aldine.

Greenwood, D. J., Whyte, W. F., & Harkavy, I. (1993). Participatory action research as a process and as a goal. *Human Relations, 46,* 175–192.

Gutkin, T. B., & Curtis, M. J. (1999). School-based consultation theory and practice: The art and science of indirect service delivery. In C. R. Reynolds & T. B. Gutkin (Eds.), *Handbook of School Psychology* (3rd ed., pp. 598–637). NY: Wiley.

Henwood, K., & Pidgeon, N. (2003). Grounded theory in psychological research. In P. M. Camic, J. E. Rhodes, & L. Yardley (Eds.), *Qualitative research in psychology: Expanding perspectives in methodology and design* (pp. 131–156). Washington, DC: APA.

Hitchcock, J. H., Nastasi, B. K., Dai, D. C., Newman, J., Jayasena, A., Bernstein-Moore, R., et al. (2005). Illustrating a mixed-method approach for identifying and validating culturally specific constructs. *Journal of School Psychology, 43*(3), 259–278.

Hobfoll, S. E. (2002). Alone together: Comparing communal versus individualistic resiliency. In E. Frydenberg (Ed.), *Beyond coping: Meeting goals, visions, and challenges* (pp. 63–82). Oxford, UK: Oxford University Press.

Ingraham, C. L. (2000). Consultation through a multicultural lens: Multicultural and cross-cultural consultation in schools. *School Psychology Review, 29,* 320–343.

Ingraham, C. L., & Oka, E. R. (2007). Multicultural issues in evidence-based interventions. *Journal of Applied School Psychology, 22,* 127–150.

Kemmis, S., & McTaggart, R. (2000). Participatory action research. In N. K. Denzin & Y. S. Lincoln (Eds.), *Handbook of qualitative research* (2nd ed.; pp. 567–606). Thousand Oaks, CA: Sage.

Kratochwill, T. R., & Stoiber, K. C. (2002a). Evidence-based interventions in school psychology: Conceptual foundations of the *Procedural and Coding Manual* of Division 16 and the Society for the Study of School Psychology Task Force. *School Psychology Quarterly, 17,* 341–389.

Kratochwill, T. R., & Stoiber, K. C. (2002b). *Procedural and coding manual for review of evidence-based interventions.* University of Wisconsin-Madison.

Krueger, R. A. (1994). *Focus groups: A practical guide for applied research* (2nd ed.). Thousand Oaks, CA: Sage.

Lazarus, R. S., & Folkman, S. (1984). *Stress, appraisal, and coping.* New York: Springer.

LeCompte, M. D., & Schensul, J. J. (1999). Designing and conducting ethnographic research. *Ethnographer's toolkit, Book 1.* Walnut Creek, CA: AltaMira.

Lincoln, Y. S., & Guba, E. G. (1985). *Naturalistic inquiry*. Thousand Oaks: CA. Sage.

Lofland, J., & Lofland, L. H. (1984). *Analyzing social settings: A guide to qualitative observation and analysis* (2nd ed.). Belmont, CA: Wadsworth.

Maguire, D. J., Goodchild, M. F., & Rhind, D. W. (Eds.). (1999). *Geographical information systems: Principles and applications*. Horlow, UK: Longman Scientific and Technical.

Miles, M. B., & Huberman, A. M. (1994). *Qualitative data analysis* (2nd ed.). Thousand Oaks, CA: Sage.

Morgan, D. L., & Krueger, R. A. (1997). *The focus group kit* (Volumes 1–6). Thousand Oaks, CA: Sage.

Moustakas, C. (1994). *Phenomenological research methods*. Thousand Oaks, CA: Sage.

Murray, M. (2003). Narrative psychology and narrative analysis. In P. M. Camic, J. E. Rhodes, & L. Yardley (Eds.), *Qualitative research in psychology: Expanding perspectives in methodology and design* (pp. 95–112). Washington, DC: APA.

Nastasi, B. K. (1998). A model for mental health programming in schools and communities. *School Psychology Review, 27*(2), 165–174.

Nastasi, B. K. (1999). Audiovisual methods in ethnography. In M. D. LeCompte & J. J. Schensul (Eds.), *Ethnographer's toolkit, Book 3: Enhanced ethnographic methods: Audiovisual techniques, focused group interviews, and elicitation techniques* (pp. 1–50). Walnut Creek, CA: AltaMira Press.

Nastasi, B. K. (2000). School psychologists as health care providers in the 21st century: Conceptual framework, professional identity, and professional practice. *School Psychology Review, 29*, 540–554.

Nastasi, B. K., & Berg, M. (1999). Using ethnography to strengthen and evaluate intervention programs. In J. J. Schensul & M. D. LeCompte (Eds.), *Ethnographer's toolkit, Book 7: Using ethnographic data: Interventions, public programming, and public policy* (pp. 1–56). Walnut Creek, CA: AltaMira Press.

Nastasi, B. K., Hitchcock, J. H., Burkholder, G., Varjas, K., Sarkar, S., & Jayasena, A. (2007). Assessing adolescents' understanding of and reactions to stress in different cultures: Results of a mixed-methods approach. *School Psychology International, 28*(2), 163–178.

Nastasi, B. K., Hitchcock, J., Sarkar, S., Burkholder, G., Varjas, K., & Jayasena, A. (2007). Mixed methods in intervention research: Theory to adaptation. *Journal of Mixed Methods Research, 1*, 164–182.

Nastasi, B. K., Moore, R. B., & Varjas, K. M. (2004). *School-based mental health services: Creating comprehensive and culturally specific programs*. Washington, DC: American Psychological Association.

Nastasi, B. K., & Schensul, S. L. (2005). Contributions of qualitative research to the validity of

intervention research. Special issue of *Journal of School Psychology, 43*(3), 177–195.

Nastasi, B. K., Varjas, K., Bernstein, R., & Jayasena, A. (2000). Conducting participatory culture-specific consultation: A global perspective on multicultural consultation. *School Psychology Review, 29*(3), 401–413.

Nastasi, B. K., Varjas, K., Sarkar, S., & Jayasena, A. (1998). Participatory model of mental health programming: Lessons learned from work in a developing country. *School Psychology Review, 27*, 260–276.

National Institutes of Health. (1999). *Qualitative methods in health services research: Opportunities and considerations in application and review*. Bethesda, MD: Office of Behavioral and Social Sciences Research, National Institutes of Health.

Power, T. J. (2000). Commentary. The school psychologist as community-focused, public health professional: Emerging challenges and implications for training. *School Psychology Review, 29*, 557–559.

Qualis Research Associates. (1998). *The Ethnograph v5.0* [Computer software]. Denver, CO: Author. www.qualisresearch.com

QSR International. (2006). *NVivo 7* [Computer software]. Doncaster, Victoria, Australia: QSR International Pty Ltd. www.qsrinternational.com

Rosenfield, S. A., & Gravois, T. A. (1996). *Instructional Consultation Teams: Collaborating for change*. New York: Guilford.

Ryan, G. W., & Bernard, H. R. (2000). Data management and analysis methods. In N. K. Denzin & Y. S. Lincoln (Eds.), *Handbook of qualitative research* (2nd ed.; pp. 769–802). Thousand Oaks, CA:

Schafer, P. (1998). *Culture: Beacon of the future*. Westport, CT: Praeger.

Schensul, J. J. (1998). Community-based risk prevention with urban youth. *School Psychology Review, 27*, 233–245.

Schensul, J. J. (1999). Focused group interviews. In J. J. Schensul & M. D. LeCompte (Eds.), *Ethnographer's toolkit, Book 3: Enhanced ethnographic techniques: Audiovisual techniques, focused group interviews, and elicitation techniques*. (pp. 51–114). Walnut Creek, CA: AltaMira.

Schensul, J. J., & LeCompte, M. D. (Eds.). (1999). *Ethnographer's toolkit* (Volumes 1 to 7). Walnut Creek, CA: AltaMira Press.

Schensul, J. J., & Schensul, S. L. (1992). Collaborative research: Methods of inquiry for social change. In M. D. LeCompte, W. L. Millroy, & J. Preissle (Eds.). *The handbook of qualitative research in education* (pp. 161–200). San Diego, CA: Academic.

Schensul, S. L., Schensul, J. J., & LeCompte, M.D. (1999). *Ethnographer's toolkit, Book 2: Essential ethnographic methods: Observations, interviews, and questionnaires*. Walnut Creek, CA: AltaMira.

Scientific Software Development. (2004). *ATLAS.ti 5* [Computer software]. Berlin, Germany: Author. www.atlasti.com

Sheridan, S. M., & Gutkin, T. B. (2000). The ecology of school psychology: Examining and changing our paradigm for the 21st century. *School Psychology Review, 29*, 485–502.

Sheridan, S. M., Kratochwill, T. R., & Bergan, J. R. (1996). *Conjoint behavioral consultation*. New York: Plenum.

Spradley, J. P. (1979). *The ethnographic interview*. NY: Holt, Rhinehart, Winston.

Spradley, J. P. (1980). *Participant observation*. NY: Holt, Rhinehart, Winston.

Stake, R. E. (2000). Case studies. In N. K. Denzin & Y. S. Lincoln (Eds.), *Handbook of qualitative research* (2nd ed.; pp. 435–454). Thousand Oaks, CA: Sage.

Stoiber, K. C., & Kratochwill, T. R. (2000). Empirically supported interventions and school psychology: Rationale and methodological issues—Part I. *School Psychology Quarterly, 15*, 75–105.

Strauss, A. and Corbin, J. (1990). *Basics of qualitative research: Grounded theory procedures and techniques*. Thousand Oaks, CA: Sage.

Stringer, E. T. (1996). *Action research: A handbook for practitioners*. Thousand Oaks, CA: Sage.

Tashakkori, A., & Teddlie, C. (Eds.). (2003). *Handbook of mixed methods in social and behavioral research*. Thousand Oaks, CA: Sage.

Teddlie, C. & Tashakkori, A. (2003). Major issues and controversies in the use of mixed methods in the social and behavioral sciences. In A. Tashakkori & C. Teddlie (Eds.), *Handbook of mixed methods in social and behavioral research* (pp. 3–50). Thousand Oaks, CA: Sage.

Trotter, R. T., III. (1999). Mapping spatial data. In J. J. Schensul & M. D. LeCompte (Eds.), *Ethnographer's toolkit, Book 4: Friends, relatives, and relevant others: Conducting ethnographic network studies*. (pp. 1–50). Walnut Creek, CA: AltaMira.

Vidich, A. J., & Lyman, S. M. (2000). Qualitative methods: Their history in sociology and anthropology. In N. K. Denzin & Y. S. Lincoln (Eds.), *Handbook of qualitative research* (2nd ed.; pp. 37–84). Thousand Oaks, CA: Sage.

Wolcott, H. F. (1994). *Transforming qualitative data: Description, analysis, and interpretation*. Thousand Oaks, CA: Sage.

Wolcott, H. F. (1999). *Ethnography: A way of seeing*. Walnut Creek, CA: AltaMira.

Wolcott, H. F. (2001). *Writing up qualitative research* (2nd ed.). Thousand Oaks, CA: Sage.

CHAPTER 3

ADVANCES IN SINGLE SUBJECT DESIGN

NANCY A. NEEF[1]
Ohio State University

Since its inception, a focal concern of school psychology has been the integration of research and practice. It is a sad reality, however, that many professional psychologists neither contribute to nor consume the research literature. The principal reasons cited for this reticence involve the perceived irrelevance or unrepresentativeness of research to "real life" situations encountered in practice (Phillips, 1999).

These concerns are long-standing, and in fact were the impetus for the development (if not the origination) of single subject designs. This chapter will consider the historical foundations for single subject designs from the beginnings of science and in the context of the rift—and attempts to remedy the rift—between research and practice (e.g., Kazdin, Kratochwill, & VandenBos, 1986). It will then describe characteristics and examples of single subject research designs. Advances will be illustrated with diverse arrangements that have been developed to investigate contextual factors that affect the generality of interventions—a topic of considerable interest to school psychologists. Finally, the chapter will consider the future of single subject research designs and their potential role in advancing practical, evidence-based interventions.

THE RISE AND FALL (AND RISE) OF THE SINGLE SUBJECT IN SCIENCE

Advances in single subject research can be understood in the context of their historical development. The focus on the study of individuals

can be traced to the very beginnings of science and medicine. Galen (ca. 129 to ca. 200), for example, used a form of a single subject reversal design (described later) to diagnose the cause of a patient's symptoms (see Brown, 2007). Indeed, many of the early advances in medicine made by luminaries such as Hippocrates (the "father of medicine"), Vesailius (credited with the first accurate knowledge of anatomy), Harvey (who discovered circulation), and others were based on repeated study of individual organisms.

Similarly, the origins of psychology and physiology as sciences in the mid-1800s were characterized by study of individual human behavior (Barlow & Hersen, 1984). Broca (1824–1880), for example, conducted a landmark study in a clinical extension of the extirpation of parts (a methodology in which brain function was mapped by systematically destroying parts of animals' brains and observing the effects on behavior). Broca's examination and subsequent autopsy of a man who could not speak intelligibly revealed a lesion on a part of the brain that Broca determined was the center for speech functions. The work was significant in demonstrating that the study of individuals could lead to important findings with wide generality.

At about the same time, the field of experimental psychology developed with Gustav Fechner's (1801–1887) use of repeated measures of individuals' responses to a stimulus presented at different intensities or locations (and examination of within-subject variability in responding across successive trials) in order to determine sensory thresholds. Fechner's methodology established a tradition in physiological psychology of studying individual organisms. In turn, this effort influenced the pioneering work of Hermann Ebbinghaus (1850–1909), who used repeated measures

[1]I am grateful to Alan W. McEvoy, Traci Cihon, and Laurice Joseph for their comments on an earlier draft of this chapter.

of individual performance over time as the foundation for studying memory (e.g., learning curve, the overlearning effect, forgetting over time). Similarly, Ivan Pavlov's (1849–1936) work on association and learning was based on the replicated study of individual organisms.

The focus on comparing large groups of individuals using statistical approaches and probability theory emerged with the work of Adolphe Quetelet (1796–1874), an astronomer widely regarded as the founder of the social sciences (Woolf, 1961). Quetelet observed that human traits such as height followed a normal distribution curve, and he saw the possibility of applying the calculus of probability as a means of estimating the ideals of human qualities. He viewed the average as the natural ideal and variations as errors, which could be accounted for using statistical techniques.

Comparisons of groups of individuals gained further prominence as interest in the measurement and testing of intelligence in the field of education emerged with the work of Francis Galton (1822–1911) and his development of the mathematical expression of correlation. It continued with Karl Pearson (1857–1936) who developed the concept of moments of distribution, the term "standard deviation," and the mathematics of sampling distributions. Galton and Pearson (who helped found the journal *Biometricka*) advanced the statistical methods of quantitative research used by psychologists in the construction of intelligence and mental tests. Alfred Binet's (1857–1911) interest, however, was in individual differences in mental performance, and he advocated for education for all children. He believed that intelligence testing was subject to variability and was not generalizable. Nevertheless, the Stanford-Binet scale was used in the United States to curtail the reproduction of "feeble-mindedness" in the eugenics movement.

Shortly thereafter, Ronald Fisher (1890–1962) introduced inferential statistics such as the analysis of variance. Fisher was a mathematician interested in genetics who chose a career as an agronomist for the opportunity to pursue independent research. His concern, similar to Quetelet's, was with the importance of the average. Agricultural interests are with variables such as soil treatments or plant varieties that produce better yields on the average than plots of land treated differently; in that context, the study of the individual plant is irrelevant. In addition, findings derived from particular plots

of land are relevant in agriculture only to the extent that they are generalizable to other plots of land that share similar characteristics (e.g., temperature, sunlight, rainfall, soil composition). Fisher therefore developed properties of statistical tests that allowed estimates of the applicability of data from a sample to a population having similar characteristics (induction or inference).

Between-group comparison designs and the statistical estimation approaches developed in basic fields of study came to dominate experimental psychology and, by extension, applied research as advocacy for the "scientist-practitioner" model began to emerge (Barlow, Hayes, & Nelson, 1984). With this influence, and some apocryphal claims of treatment effectiveness that arose from uncontrolled case studies in clinical psychology, interest in the study of single subjects declined by the 1950s.

Limitations of the group comparison approach, however, became evident with investigations involving clinically relevant problems. The most well known is the Cambridge-Somerville study (Powers & Witmer, 1951), which, together with subsequent replications (e.g., Barron & Leary, 1955), indicated that "counseling" for delinquents or potential delinquents did not yield any statistically significant differences relative to a matched control group. This created a rift between scientists, who disputed the effectiveness of psychotherapy (e.g., Eysenck, 1952), and clinicians, who disputed the research findings. A re-analysis of the data by Bergin (1966) revealed that some of the participants in the treatment group did in fact improve. Because others became worse, however, statistical averaging of the results produced no significant effect when compared to the control group.

This illustrates several related problems that led practitioners to question the relevance of group-comparison approaches for their needs. First, a risk of statistical averaging is that the average response may not represent any individual within the group. Similarly, unlike laboratory animals or crops, humans differ from one another in any number of important ways as a result of their individual histories and other variables (which also renders strictly homogenous and matched groupings impossible). Furthermore, whereas the practitioner's concern is with the individual, statistical significance does not provide information about the improvement of any participant who receives the intervention. Statistical averaging, therefore, can obscure individual responses to intervention that might lead to information on the conditions under which, and with whom, treatments are most likely to be effective. Quite simply, information important to the role of practitioners who seek to help individual clients cannot necessarily be gleaned from group-comparison designs.

Finally, because single post-tests often result in large differences between participants, the experimental intervention can have weak effects on performance but still produce average improvements that are statistically significant. Statistical significance is quite independent of clinical significance. Furthermore, numerous authors have argued that practitioners are (and should be) seeking interventions that are sufficiently powerful to be readily observed and detected without statistical transformation (e.g., Baer, 1977; Bergin & Strupp, 1972; Carver, 1978; Cronbach, 1975). As put bluntly by Stevens (1958), "Can no one recognize a decisive result without a significance test?" (p. 853).

While the research literature held little appeal for practitioners during this time, there were additional obstacles to practitioners conducting research in the context of the scientist-practitioner model. One was the need for large numbers of relatively homogeneous participants (or multisite studies to ensure a sufficiently large sample, which itself posed organizational challenges and expense). In addition, there were fundamental conflicts between research and practice. Prevailing research methodology required strict adherence to a treatment protocol without regard for—or even knowledge of—the participant's response until completion. This conflicted with treatment practices that involve ongoing monitoring of progress and adjustment to intervention strategies to achieve a beneficial outcome as quickly as possible. Furthermore, practitioners were understandably reluctant to withhold potentially effective treatments from individuals in control groups. Treatment effectiveness, it was thought, should not take a back seat to the need for methodological rigor. Little wonder that Barlow et al. (1984) reported that data during this time indicated the modal number of publications by practicing psychologists was zero.

The disaffection with a research approach that was ill suited to applied concerns led to a search for alternatives (for a description, see Barlow & Hersen, 1984). In the meantime, the pioneering work of B. F. Skinner (1904–1990) and his students and colleagues in the experimental analysis of behavior gained prominence. This group of psychologists at Harvard and Columbia had similarly encountered barriers associated with the predominant research methodology. The existing journals that seemed best suited for the subject matter of their work (e.g., the *Journal of Experimental Psychology*) generally were not favorably inclined toward an approach that stressed the behavior of individual organisms (Laties, 1987). Charles B. Ferster, a colleague of Skinner's, proposed and in 1958 became the founding editor of the *Journal of the Experimental Analysis of Behavior* which was and continues to be "primarily for the original publication of experiments relevant to the behavior of individual organisms."

Encouraged by its success, Murray Sidman and B. F. Skinner proposed a second journal that addressed concerns encountered in the practice of psychology. Founded in 1968, the *Journal of Applied Behavior Analysis* was established for "the original publication of reports of experimental research involving applications of the experimental analysis of behavior to problems of social importance." These developments heralded a renewed interest in the scientific study of the individual, and contributed to the development of single subject (also termed within-subject or single-case) research designs.

Single subject research became especially influential in special education. In the 1970s, the successes demonstrated with behavioral research contributed to increased recognition that individuals with developmental disabilities could benefit from educational programs. The passage of the Education of All Handicapped Children Act of 1975 (PL 94–142) included a mandate to develop individualized education programs, and this focus on individualization was consistent with a research emphasis on single organisms.

CHARACTERISTICS OF SINGLE SUBJECT RESEARCH DESIGNS

Single subject research is used to determine causal, or functional, relations between independent and dependent variables (for an overview of single subject research methodology, see Horner et al., 2005). The designs used in single subject research are a means of demonstrating that the events that constitute the independent variable are responsible for changes in the occurrence or nonoccurrence of an objectively measured behavior. As such, these designs are *experimental* rather than correlational or descriptive.

Single subject (or "within-subject") research design derives its name from the fact that the *individual subject is the unit of analysis*. Because the data for an individual subject can stand alone (at least for the purposes of demonstrating a functional relation), the designs can be (and often are) applied with small numbers of participants. For this reason, the designs are also sometimes referred to as small-*N* designs. The defining feature, however, is not the number of participants, but that each participant serves as his or her own control. Although it is possible for a study to include only one participant, some have involved more than 50 participants (e.g., Iwata et al., 1994; Neef et al., 2005). Experimental comparisons are between representative data that fully characterize each participant's behavior under each condition (rather than between single data samples for groups of participants who are exposed to only one condition or the other). Specifically, single subject research designs involve *experimental comparisons between extended data samples (repeated measures) with the same participants before (baseline) and during and/or after application of the independent variable*. Data are portrayed graphically so that the complete effects of each condition on the measured dimensions of the target behavior (termed "steady state") can be seen clearly through *direct visual examination* of changes in level, trend, or variability.

To demonstrate experimental control, *the effects of application of the independent variable on the participant's behavior must be replicated*. Single subject designs involve repeated demonstrations that manipulation of the independent variable is accompanied consistently by a change in the measured dimension of behavior relative to the participant's baseline pattern. Major threats to internal validity (i.e., passage of time, measurement effects, or extraneous variables to which the behavior change might otherwise be attributed) are ruled out in this way.

ADVANCES IN SINGLE SUBJECT RESEARCH DESIGNS

Single subject research designs involve the arrangement of conditions (schedules, independent variables) necessary for a convincing answer to an experimental question. Although they share certain characteristics (as described earlier), they are as limitless as experimental questions and may be as unique as a convincing answer to the question dictates.

Every experiment is unique ... In our search for new information we must be prepared at any point to alter our conception of what is desirable in experimental design. Nature does not yield its secrets easily, and each new problem of investigation requires its own techniques. Sometimes the appropriate techniques will be the same as those which have been employed elsewhere. Often the known methods will have to modified, and, on occasion, new principles of experimental design and procedure will have to be devised. There is no rule to inform an experimenter which of these eventualities he will meet. (Sidman, 1960, p. 214)

Given the potential for a wide number of variations in the arrangement of conditions, however, there has been an effort to classify single subject designs for the purpose of systematically evaluating research and coding evidence-based interventions in school psychology (see Gutkin, 2002). Shernoff, Kratochwill, and Stoiber (2002) describe a classification of single subject designs into four types based on an approach presented by Hayes, Barlow, and Nelson-Gray (1999) that encompasses both a scientist and practitioner framework:

(a) within-series designs (i.e., evaluating change in client measures within various phases, such as in an ABAB design); (b) between-series designs (i.e., evaluating change within a specific situation and across time in an alternating intervention design); (c) combined-series designs (i.e., making comparisons both within and between a data series, such as in a multiple baseline design across participants); and (d) mixed designs (i.e., our term to refer to a combination of single-participant and group designs or a combination of within-, between-, and combined series/multiple baseline designs) (p. 396).

This taxonomy characterizes the features of various arrangements in the development of single subject designs summarized below and detailed in numerous other sources (e.g., Hersen & Barlow, 1976; Iwata, Neef, Mace, & Vollmer, 2000; Johnston & Pennypacker, 1993; Kazdin, 1982; 1998; Kennedy, 2005; Kratochwill & Levin, 1992; Richards, Taylor, Ramasamy & Richards, 1999; Tawney & Gast, 1984).

Early Designs

When the experimental analysis of behavior emerged, the arrangement of conditions was in the form of schedules of reinforcement (e.g., multiple, mixed, concurrent) that did not require the addition of names for designs. With the subsequent extension to applied behavior analysis, Baer, Wolf, and Risley (1968) described and labeled two designs whose logic was similar to some of those schedules—the reversal and multiple baseline designs. The aforementioned characteristics of single subject experimental designs can be readily discerned in Baer et al.'s description of a reversal design:

> A behavior is measured, and the measure is examined over time until its stability is clear. Then, the experimental variable is applied. The behavior continues to be measured, to see if the variable will produce a behavior change. If it does, the experimental variable is discontinued or altered, to see if the behavioral change just brought about depends on it. If so, the behavioral change should be lost or diminished (thus the term "reversal"). The experimental variable then is applied again, to see if the behavioral change can be recovered. (p. 94)

In multiple baseline designs (which are commonly used when reversals of the behavior are either unlikely or undesirable), several different independent baselines are established. These can involve repeated measurement of different but related behaviors of the same participant (e.g., various academic behaviors) or of the same behavior in different settings (e.g., disruptions in several different classes). They can also involve repeated measurement of the same type of behavior across different participants. A multiple baseline across participants, however, differs from other single subject designs in that it requires more than one subject to demonstrate experimental control (i.e., it requires a comparison of data across/between subjects as well as within subjects). Following stable baseline performance, the independent variable is applied to the first behavior, setting, or participant. If there is a change (but not to the other baselines), it is applied to the second, and then to the third baseline, in sequential fashion. A reliable experimental effect is demonstrated by a change in the dependent variable only when the experimental variable is applied to it at the different points in time. Benjamin Franklin may have been among the first to use a multiple baseline across behaviors. He describes in his autobiography (1909) how he sought to develop 13 self-identified and defined "virtues" by addressing each one in a sequential

and cumulative manner while continuing to record his performance on all of them.

Extensions of multiple baseline designs developed. For example, the multiple probe design (Horner & Baer, 1978) emerged as an extension of the multiple baseline design with probe procedures to examine the effects of interventions to teach a sequence (chain) of responses. Instead of continuous measurement of each of the untreated baselines (as with multiple baseline designs), baseline measurement is repeated only when the response exposed to treatment has reached criterion levels. The design provides a valuable alternative when "continuous measurement during extended multiple baselines proves impractical, unnecessary, or reactive" (Horner & Baer, 1978 p. 196). Another design considered by Hartmann and Hall (1976) to be a variant of a multiple baseline is the changing criterion design, which was developed to evaluate the effectiveness of reinforcement-based treatments on a single behavior through gradual step-wise changes.

The multielement (Ulman & Sulzer-Azaroff, 1975) and closely related designs (e.g., alternating treatments design, Barlow & Hayes, 1979) are extensions of the reversal design. They differ in that the conditions being compared (e.g., baseline and intervention or two interventions) alternate rapidly (e.g., from one session to the next) rather than being implemented in sequential fashion. When unique stimuli are paired with each condition, the multielement design resembles a multiple schedule (Hersen & Barlow, 1976; Leitenberg, 1973). The design became attractive for use in educational settings for several reasons. First, it can be used with behaviors that may be expected to show some improvement in the absence of the experimental variable (such as with academic behaviors that increase over time, but not as rapidly as desired). With rapid and repeated reversals between conditions, an effect is evident if the behavior is consistently and considerably improved in one condition relative to the other. For the same reason, the arrangement is efficient; the rapid exposure to all conditions permits comparisons and detection of differences early on. Similarly, the design allows efficient comparison of different treatments because the rapid alternation between conditions minimizes the likelihood of sequence effects.

Design Variations

Design variations (typically combinations of the aforementioned designs) have continued to proliferate in response to unique needs. For example, Iwata et al. (1994) used a pairwise, test control design in functional analyses with some participants (presumably those for whom the rapid alternation of the four assessment conditions might have posed difficulties). It combines features of a multielement and reversal design by rapidly alternating two assessment conditions at a time in sequential fashion, with one assessment condition serving as the same comparison (control) across phases (e.g., attention versus play, demand versus play, alone versus play).

The sequential alternating treatments design (Wacker et al., 1990) is a variation that combines features of alternating treatments and multiple baseline designs. Two treatments are compared initially in an alternating treatments phase. The rapid alternation of two treatment conditions is extended across additional participants, settings, or tasks in a staggered manner as with a multiple baseline design. The alternating treatments phase (for each participant, setting, or task) can be followed by the sequential application of either or both treatments to evaluate changes associated with each independent variable in isolation. This arrangement may be especially well suited for situations in which a traditional no-treatment baseline is not feasible or practical.

Another variation is a parallel treatments design, which Gast and Wolery (1988) describe as similar to two superimposed, concurrently operating multiple probe designs. Specifically, two independent variables are simultaneously applied, each to a different data series, in a time-lagged fashion. It was developed as a means of comparing the relative effectiveness and efficiency of instructional procedures, such as prompting strategies, on the acquisition of new skills.

Developments in Single Subject Design

Descriptions of these different arrangements have usually been accompanied by labels, perhaps for the sake of convenience or to indicate their relation to other designs that have been named. This should not, however, suggest that any variation in arrangement must be codified with an accompanying set of "rules" to be followed in application. A risk of such misinterpretation is that experimental questions will be constrained by posing them in a manner to fit identified designs rather than posing whatever existing or novel arrangement is best suited for a convincing answer to an experimental question—akin to the tail wagging the dog. Baer, Wolf, and Risley (1987), Johnston and Pennypacker (1993), and Sidman (1960) are among those who have issued caveats against such tendencies.

The danger is exemplified by the rationale given for a series of articles on research methods in school psychology: "it seems likely that as our research methods continue to expand, so will the questions we ask of our research" (Keith, 1998, p. 503). In fact, advances are perhaps more likely when it is the other way around—as the questions we ask continue to expand, so will our research methods.

One example of this is the emergence of novel single subject experimental designs that could be used to address interaction effects and contextual factors, which are issues of increasing concern in school psychology. In fact, a number of authors have pointed to investigation of the contextual conditions that maximize, minimize, or mediate the effectiveness of interventions as an important direction in the analysis of their generality (Baer et al., 1987; Christenson, Carlson, & Valdez, 2002; Johnston, 1988; Kratochwill & Stoiber, 2002; Sidman, 1960; Stoiber, 2002; Van Houten, 1987). These conditions must be identified for a procedure to be optimally applied. To do so requires investigation of the *interaction* between two or more treatments and/or between two or more contextual parameters (to determine the differential effects of levels of a treatment variable in one context versus another).

Traditional uses of single subject designs, however, were not well suited to the study of interactions between variables necessary to determine the conditions affecting the generality and dependability of technologies (Hains & Baer, 1989). Nor have group designs offered an efficient methodology for the study of interactions (Cronbach, 1982). The prototypical group design is the 2 × 2 factorial, which is notoriously inefficient. Although some circumstances permit the use of more powerful data analytic techniques (multiple regression rather than analysis of variance), the study of complex or higher order interactions has generally required an enormous amount of data. Correlational methods provide a flexible but nonanalytic methodology for the study of complex interactions.

Historically, therefore, the study of treatment interactions (e.g., by persons, settings, and time) has had an uneasy status in social science methodology (Cook & Campbell, 1979). Treatment research generally has been dominated by the search for powerful *main effects*, with interactions regarded either "as unimportant, as a minor nuisance, or as food for *after*thought" (Cronbach, 1982, p. 149). The development of two novel single subject designs provided an alternative. These are described, along with illustrations of their use.

Superordinate Multielement Designs

In their simplest form, experimental questions concerning contextual issues ask whether particular variables affect behavior differently in context 1 than in context 2. The minimal requirements for investigating that question reliably would involve 16 conditions (e.g., at least two alternations of each of two variables in each of two contexts, replicated at least twice), which suggests the need for an efficient, fast-paced design (Baer et al., 1987). Hains and Baer (1989) proposed a superordinate multielement design for this purpose. By embedding a multielement design within a reversal design, treatment interactions and operative contextual controls can be examined relatively efficiently.

This type of arrangement is illustrated in a study by Northup et al. (1999). They evaluated the separate and interactive effects between common classroom contingencies and methylphenidate on disruptive and off-task behaviors, and on academic productivity, of children with a diagnosis of attention deficit hyperactivity disorder (ADHD). One of four classroom conditions (Variable 1) was in operation during each daily session: teacher reprimands (a disapproving statement contingent on the occurrence of a target misbehavior, e.g., "You need to stay in your seat"); brief nonexclusionary time-out contingent on the occurrence of a target misbehavior; no interaction (e.g., representing independent seat work situations); or alone (which also served as a control condition). Different staff members were assigned to each condition; this helped to make the conditions discriminable to the children, and best represented naturalistic situations in which different teachers may respond differently to student behavior, but each responds in a generally consistent manner. Each of the four conditions was repeated numerous times across successive days. On alternating days of each classroom condition, children received medication or a placebo (Variable 2). This enabled examination of the extent to which medication status (Variable 2) differentially affected children's behavior under each type of classroom condition (Variable 1).

Results indicated that medication had no effect on participants' high levels of off-task and disruptive behavior in the alone condition. However, medication (but not placebo) did produce substantial reductions in these behaviors with one or more of the other classroom contingencies for each participant. For three of the four participants, the exception was time-out, which produced zero or near-zero levels of misbehavior during both medication and placebo conditions. All children completed more problems with medication regardless of the classroom contingency, although the academic productivity of three of the children was differentially responsive to classroom conditions when they received the placebo. Northrup et al. conclude from these data "that active supervision and monitoring of children's behavior may be necessary to achieve the most beneficial medication effects, and that the addition of other behavioral consequences may further enhance MPH effects in some instances" (p. 47).

Another example of a superordinate multielement design to examine contextual factors is a study by Ferreri and Neef (2006). They examined a contextual factor that might differentially affect children's sensitivity to immediacy of reinforcement relative to other reinforcer dimensions. The question has implications for the assessment and treatment of impulsivity, a construct which can be defined as choices that produce immediate but smaller yields versus delayed reinforcers with higher yields. Because impulsivity is a defining characteristic of ADHD, additional comparisons were conducted for children with and without that diagnosis. This allowed examination of a subject variable as a second potential contextual factor.

The experimental task involved the selection and completion of math problems on a computer. Students could choose between two concurrently available sets of math problems at any point during the instructional session. Performance of math problems from one set resulted in immediate reinforcement. Performance of math problems from the other set resulted in delayed reinforcement. However, delayed reinforcers either were more preferred, delivered at a higher rate, or required less effort than the immediate reinforcer option. The computer recorded the percentage of problems selected and completed from one problem set versus the other. Thus, during each session, immediacy was compared to another (competing) reinforcer dimension using a concurrent schedule.

The three assessment conditions involving competing reinforcer dimensions (immediacy versus quality, rate, and effort, respectively) were alternated across sessions. This allowed determination of the extent to which reinforcer immediacy was more influential than the other reinforcer dimensions. For example, sensitivity to reinforcer delay was demonstrated by the student's consistent selection of problems from the set associated with immediate reinforcement even when those problems were more effortful or produced fewer or less preferred reinforcers than problems from the other set.

During alternate sessions for each of the three reinforcer dimension assessment conditions, one of two delay conditions was in effect. During delay to exchange (DE), choices were between problems that produced points exchangeable for prizes that were delivered immediately following the session versus the next day. For example, when assessing reinforcer immediacy versus effort in the DE condition, the student could choose at any point to complete difficult problems that produced points for prizes available immediately. Alternatively, the student could choose easy problems that produced points for prizes available the next day. During the delay to points (DP) condition, access to earned prizes was available immediately for both problem alternatives. However, information on the number of points earned was not available until the end of the session (as opposed to being signaled after completion of each problem). This approximated typical classroom conditions in which students turn in work which is then graded and returned.

Thus, alternation between two delay conditions (DE and DP) occurred within alternations between each of three reinforcer dimension assessment conditions (immediacy versus quality, rate and effort, respectively). (To minimize multiple treatment interference, each condition was associated with a distinct stimulus that clearly signaled the experimental condition in effect during a session.) The evaluation was conducted in this manner for students with and without a diagnosis of ADHD.

The design, then, allowed comparisons at four levels: (a) within-subject comparison of immediacy of reinforcement versus a competing dimension via concurrent schedules, (b) within-subject comparisons of the relative influence of each of the four reinforcer dimensions via a multielement design, (c) within-subject comparison of two delay conditions via a superordinate multielement design (permitting analysis of the extent to which delay to conditioned versus terminal reinforcers differentially influenced sensitivities to the reinforcer dimensions), and (d) between-subject comparisons of children with and without ADHD with respect to each of the above issues.

In general, the results indicated that point of delay was a contextual factor that influenced students' sensitivity to immediacy of reinforcement. Specifically, immediacy of the terminal reinforcer (access to prizes) was more likely to influence students' choices (relative to the other reinforcer dimensions) than immediacy of the conditioned reinforcer (point delivery). In fact, students rarely selected problems on the basis of reinforcer immediacy in the DP sessions. In contrast, most students' choices were influenced by immediacy of reinforcement in the DE sessions. Although there were individual differences in the relative influence of the different reinforcer dimensions, these were not associated with diagnostic status.

Within-Subject Latin Square Designs

Superordinate multielement designs offered an efficient means of examining treatment interactions and operative contextual controls. It is not well suited, however, to the analysis of some types of complex interactions, such as those involving treatment variables that are procedurally incompatible or in which the target behaviors are complex chains. Within-subject, repeated measures Latin square designs provided another alternative. With this design, each participant is exposed to two variables (V1 and V2) in each of two contexts (C1 and C2) in counterbalanced order (T1 versus T2).

The design is illustrated with a study that analyzed the role of the range of variation in training exemplars as a contextual variable influencing the effects of in vivo versus simulation training in producing generalized responding (Neef, Lensbower, Hockersmith, DePalma, & Gray, 1990). The question was relevant to the concerns of school personnel regarding classroom-based versus community-based instruction. The four participants received instruction on using washing machines and dryers. They first received single case instruction (using one machine), followed by general case instruction (using multiple machines which, when combined with the machine used for single case instruction, sampled the range of stimulus and response variations that might be encountered). In vivo training using actual appliances was used to teach one of the tasks (washing machine or dryer use) and simulated appliances were used to teach the other. In vivo and simulation training were counterbalanced across the two tasks for the two pairs of participants. Thus, two participants received in vivo single case training followed by in vivo general case training on dryers. At the same time, they received simulation single case training followed by simulation general case training on washing machines. The application of in vivo and simulation training to the two tasks was reversed for two other participants.

Probes were conducted with untrained washing machines and dryers following criterion on trained machines. Results showed that for both simulation and in-vivo paradigms, more errors on the steps of the task analysis were made after single case than after general case training. This suggests that generalization errors were affected by the range of training exemplars rather than by the use of simulated versus natural training stimuli.

THE FUTURE OF SINGLE SUBJECT RESEARCH DESIGNS: RISE OR FALL?

As intervention has assumed an increasingly prominent role in the activities—and preferred activities—of school psychologists (Reschly, 2000), there has been increasing concern with the effectiveness of interventions. Similarly, there has been concern with the extent to which research findings on the effectiveness of interventions affects practitioners' decisions (e.g., Gutkin, 1993; Kratochwill & Stoiber, 2002; Phillips, 1999; Stoiber, 2002). These concerns are reflected in the recent evidence-based practice movement. As illustrated by the aforementioned examples, single subject research designs offer an alternative that obviates the obstacles that have presumably accounted for the historical lack of influence of research on, or involvement in research by, practicing psychologists. Why, then, have single subject designs not exerted greater influence in the gap between science and practice?

One reason may be found in the aura of scientific respect that inferential statistical practices in basic research brought to the social sciences. As noted by Johnston and Pennypacker (1986), "The ensuing decades have seen the practice of designing experiments in accordance with the requirement of tests of statistical significance ossify into the methodological backbone of the social sciences" (p. 44). Psychologists have repeatedly expressed concern with the generalizability of randomized group designs to practice and school-based research (Christenson et al., 2002; Kazdin, 2000). Nevertheless, the tradition

has become so entrenched that it is referred to as "the gold standard," and any other experimental procedures often are erroneously labeled quasi-experimental (e.g., Keith, 1998).

Another reason may be rooted in misunderstandings of single subject research. The focus of this methodology on the individual as the unit of analysis may be misinterpreted as a preoccupation with internal validity to the exclusion of external validity, and as inappropriate for the search for interventions that have wide generality. Of course, if the data from a study do not represent true functional relations between the independent and dependent variable for each of the participants, the universality of those findings is irrelevant (i.e., without internal validity, external validity is moot). The generalizability of results from single subject research is determined through systematic replications in which subject, setting, or other variables that might modulate the effects of a procedure are manipulated across multiple studies.

Systematic replications across multiple studies as well as the emergence of designs for studying contextual factors within studies both contribute information about the "boundaries" of an intervention's effectiveness. Nevertheless, the contextual factors that can potentially influence the effectiveness and efficacy of interventions are limitless. As argued by Kratochwill and Stoiber (2002), practitioners themselves must therefore use these empirical methods "to facilitate an understanding of how beneficial a previously supported intervention will be when applied in a new school context or different situation" (p. 32).

Advances in school psychology are testament to the value of its use of multiple research methodologies matched to its multiple concerns. Continued advances in research methodology will depend on their ability to both inform and be informed by practice.

REFERENCES

Baer, D. M. (1977). "Perhaps it would be better not to know everything." *Journal of Applied Behavior Analysis, 10,* 167–172.

Baer, D. M., Wolf, M. M., & Risley, T. R. (1968). Some current dimensions of applied behavior analysis. *Journal of Applied Behavior Analysis, 1,* 91–97.

Baer, D. M., Wolf, M. M., & Risley, T. R. (1987). Some still current dimensions of applied behavior analysis. *Journal of Applied Behavior Analysis, 20,* 313–327.

Barlow, D. H., & Hayes, S. C. (1979). Alternating treatments design: One strategy for comparing the effects of two treatments in a single subject. *Journal of Applied Behavior Analysis, 12*, 199–210.

Barlow, D. H., Hayes, S. C., & Nelson, R. O. (1984). *The scientist practitioner: Research and accountability in clinical and educational settings.* New York: Pergamon.

Barlow, D. H., & Hersen, M. (1984). *Single case experimental designs: Strategies for studying behavior change* (2nd ed.). New York: Pergamon.

Barron, F., & Leary, T. (1955). Changes in psychoneurotic patients with and without psychotherapy. *Journal of Consulting Psychology, 19*, 239–245.

Bergin, A. E. (1966). Some implications of psychotherapy research for therapeutic practice. *Journal of Abnormal Psychology, 71*, 235–246.

Bergin, A. E., & Strupp, H. H. (1972). *Changing frontiers in the science of psychotherapy.* New York: Aldine.

Brown, R. T. (2007). Galen: Developer of the reversal design? *The Behavior Analyst, 30*, 31–35.

Carver, R. P. (1978). The case against statistical significance testing. *Harvard Educational Review, 48*, 378–399.

Christenson, S. L., Carlson, C., & Valdez, C. R. (2002). Evidence-based interventions in school psychology: Opportunities, challenges, and cautions. *School Psychology Quarterly, 17*, 466–474.

Cook, T. D., & Campbell, D. T. (1979). *Quasi-experimentation.* Boston, MA: Houghton Mifflin.

Cronbach, L. J. (1975). Beyond the two disciplines of scientific psychology. *American Psychologist, 30*, 116–127.

Cronbach, L. J. (1982). *Designing evaluations of educational and social programs.* San Francisco: Jossey-Bass.

Eysenck, H. J. (1952). The effects of psychotherapy: An evaluation. *Journal of Consulting Psychology, 16*, 319–324.

Ferreri, S. J. & Neef, N. A. (2006, May). *Impulsive choice as a function of point of reinforcer delay: Assessment and intervention.* Presentation at the Association for Behavior Analysis, Atlanta, GA.

Franklin, B. (1909). *The autobiography of Benjamin Franklin* (C. W. Eliot, Ed.). New York: Collier & Son.

Gast, D. L., & Wolery, M. (1988). Parallel treatments design: A nested single subject design for comparing instructional procedures. *Education and Treatment of Children, 11*, 271–284.

Gutkin, T. B. (1993). Conducting consultation research. In J. E. Zins, T. R. Kratochwill, & S. N. Elliott (Eds.), *Handbook of consultation services for children* (pp. 227–247). San Francisco: Jossey-Bass.

Gutkin, T. B. (2002). Evidence-based interventions in school psychology: State of the art and directions for the future. *School Psychology Quarterly, 17*, 339–340.

Hains, A. H., & Baer, D. M. (1989). Interaction effects in multielement designs: inevitable, desirable, and ignorable. *Journal of Applied Behavior Analysis, 22*, 57–69.

Hartmann, D. P., & Hall, R. V. (1976). The changing-criterion design. *Journal of Applied Behavior Analysis, 9*, 527–532.

Hayes, S. C., Barlow, D. H., & Nelson-Gray, R. O. (1999). *The scientist-practitioner: Research and accountability in the age of managed care.* Boston: Allyn & Bacon.

Hersen, M., & Barlow, D. H. (1976). *Single case experimental designs: Strategies for studying behavior change.* New York: Pergamon.

Horner, R. D., & Baer, D. M. (1978). Multiple-probe technique: A variation of the multiple baseline. *Journal of Applied Behavior Analysis, 11*, 189–196.

Horner, R. H., Carr, E. G., Halle, J., McGee, G., Odom, S., & Wolery, M. (2005). The use of single-subject research to identify evidence-based practice in special education. *Exceptional Children, 71*, 165–179.

Iwata, B. A., Neef, N. A., Mace, F. C., & Vollmer, T. R. (Eds.) (2000). *Methodological and conceptual issues in applied behavior analysis* (2nd ed.). Lawrence, KS: Society for the Experimental Analysis of Behavior.

Iwata, B. A., Pace, G. M., Dorsey, M. F., Zarcone, J. R., Vollmer, T. R., Smith, R. G., (1994). The functions of self-injurious behavior: An experimental-epidemiological analysis. *Journal of Applied Behavior Analysis, 27*, 215–240.

Johnston, J. (1988). Strategic and tactical limits of comparison studies. *The Behavior Analyst, 11*, 1–9.

Johnston, J. J. & Pennypacker, H. S. (1993). *Strategies and tactics of behavioral research* (2nd ed). Hillsdale, NJ: Lawrence Erlbaum.

Johnston, J. M., & Pennypacker, H. S. (1986). Pure versus quasi-behavioral research. In A. Poling & R. W. Fuqua (Eds.), *Research methods in applied behavior analysis: Issues and advances* (pp. 29–54). New York: Plenum.

Kazdin, A. E. (1982). *Single-case research designs: Methods for clinical and applied settings.* New York: Oxford University Press.

Kazdin, A. E. (1998). *Research design in clinical psychology* (3rd ed.). Boston: Allyn & Bacon.

Kazdin, A. E. (2000). *Psychotherapy for children and adolescents: Directions for research and practice.* New York: Oxford University Press.

Kazdin, A. E., Kratochwill, T. R., & VandenBos, G. (1986). Beyond clinical trials: Generalizing from research to practice. *Professional Psychology: Research and Practice, 3*, 391–398.

Keith, T. Z. (1998). Research methods in school psychology: An overview. *School Psychology Review, 17*, 502–520.

Kennedy, C. H. (2005). *Single case designs for educational research*. Boston: Pearson/Allyn & Bacon.

Kratochwill, T., & Levin, J. R. (1992). *Single-case research design and analysis: New directions for psychology and education*. Hillsdale, NJ: Lawrence Erlbaum.

Kratochwill, T. R., & Stoiber, K. C. (2002). Evidence-based interventions in school psychology: Conceptual foundations of the Procedural and Coding Manual of Division 16 and the Society for the Study of School Psychology Task Force. *School Psychology Quarterly, 17*, 341–389.

Laties, V. G. (1987). Society for the Experimental Analysis of Behavior—The first 30 years (1957–1987). *Journal of the Experimental Analysis of Behavior, 48*, 495–512.

Leitenberg, H. (1973). The use of single-case methodology in psychotherapy research. *Journal of Abnormal Psychology, 82*, 87–101.

Neef, N. A., Marckel J., Ferreri S. J., Bicard, D. F., Endo, S., Aman, M. G., (2005). Behavioral assessment of impulsivity: A comparison of children with and without attention deficit hyperactivity disorder. *Journal of Applied Behavior Analysis 38*, 23–37.

Neef, N. A., Lensbower, J., Hockersmith, I., DePalma, V., & Gray, K. (1990). In vivo versus simulation training: An interactional analysis of range and type of training exemplars. *Journal of Applied Behavior Analysis, 23*, 447–458.

Northup, J., Fusilier I., Swanson, V., Huete, J., Bruce, T., Freeland, J., (1999). Further analysis of the separate and interactive effects of methylphenidate and common classroom contingencies. *Journal of Applied Behavior Analysis, 32*, 35–50.

Phillips, B. N. (1999). Strengthening the links between science and practice: Reading, evaluating, and applying research in school psychology. In C. R. Reynolds & T. B. Gutkin (Eds.), *The handbook of school psychology* (3rd ed., pp. 56–77). New York: John Wiley.

Powers, E., & Witmer, H. (1951). *An experiment in the prevention of delinquency*. New York: Columbia University Press.

Reschly, D. J. (2000). The present and future status of school psychology in the United States. *School Psychology Review, 29*, 507–522.

Richards, S. B., Taylor, R., Ramasamy, R., & Richards, R. Y. (1999). *Single subject research: Applications in educational and clinical settings*. Belmont, CA: Wadsworth.

Shernoff, E. S., Kratochwill, T. R., & Stoiber, K. C. (2002). Evidence-based interventions in school psychology: An illustration of task force coding criteria using single-participant research design. *School Psychology Quarterly, 17*, 390–422.

Sidman, M. (1960). *Tactics of scientific research: Evaluating experimental data in psychology*. New York: Basic Books.

Stevens, S. S. (1958). Measurement, statistics and the schemapiric view. *Science, 161*, 849–856.

Stoiber, K. C. (2002). Revisiting efforts on constructing a knowledge base of evidence-based intervention within school psychology. *School Psychology Quarterly, 17*, 533–546.

Tawney, J. W., & Gast, D. L. (1984). *Single subject research in special education*. Columbus: Merrill.

Ulman, J. D., & Sulzer-Azaroff, B. (1975). Multi-element baseline design in educational research. In E. Ramp & G. Semb (Eds.), *Behavior analysis: Areas of research application* (pp. 359–376). Englewood Cliffs, NJ: Prentice-Hall.

Van Houten, R. (1987). Comparing treatment techniques: A cautionary note. *Journal of Applied Behavior Analysis, 20*, 109–110.

Wacker, D., McMahon, C., Steege, M., Berg, W., Sasso, G., & Melloy, K. (1990). Applications of a sequential alternating treatments design. *Journal of Applied Behavior Analysis, 23*, 333–339.

Woolf, H. (1961). *Quantification: A history of the meaning of measurement in the natural and social sciences*. Indianapolis: Bobbs-Merrill.

CHAPTER 4

THE CONTRIBUTIONS OF EDUCATIONAL PSYCHOLOGY TO SCHOOL PSYCHOLOGY

BRENDAN J. BARTLETT
Griffith University
STEPHEN N. ELLIOTT
Vanderbilt University

INTRODUCTION

Educational psychology is centrally about learning and the conditions that optimize outcomes for learners of all abilities and backgrounds. Subsumed within the field is an understanding of human development, instructional approaches, and methods for quantifying and evaluating both teaching and learning. In what follows, we assert prospective relevance in the contributions we have indicated from bodies of work in educational psychology. Actual relevance will follow rather than precede our readers' intelligent uses of the skill of spotting something likely to be relevant and evidence-based.

Berliner (2006) conceptualized the essential nature of educational psychology as "about using psychological concepts and methods for understanding the four commonplaces of education that philosopher Joseph Schwab (1973) first made popular: someone (a teacher, a parent, or technological device) teaches something (how to fix a bicycle, two column arithmetic with regrouping, the periodic table) to someone else (a student, novice, worker) in some setting (classroom, garden, assembly line)" (pp. 5–6). He indicated that problems in many previous attempts to support educators have had two predictable and related features. First, it has not been easy to do "good research" (Berliner, 2002) that accommodates the many individual differences that emerge when we ask questions about the highly specific characteristics of the *somebody* under study, and indeed about those of any of the commonplaces. The more the questions

are asked and such distinctions are included, the greater the complexity of design needed to provide robust, trustworthy research. Thus a second problematic feature is created in that much of our research approximates rather than reproduces the realities that practitioners see in their own enactments of Schwab's commonplaces. This presents practitioners with the dilemma of uncertainty about whether dialogue with educational psychologists about their needs for evidence-based assistance can and will be productive. Additionally, it concerns theorists and researchers who seek authentic problems for their research from practitioners because of a squeeze between the respective realities.

For practitioners, including school psychologists, overreliance on conclusions without proper attention to the qualities of the research that produced them, or underutilization of research because of disenchantment, are lost opportunities. In each case, the base for valuing the prospectivity of contributions is lost to a one-way perspective on the questions of current relevance and cyclical interaction and enhancement. The former seems to be problematic in the accessibility of information, and the perceived time and effort it takes to get it. For educational psychologists, there is a need to maintain rigor in building this corpus of data, to be aware of what it is that school psychology colleagues need to support their quests for excellence, and to have the flexibility and vision to bring both together.

Thus, we believe that school psychologists with the predisposition to locate helpful state-of-the-art facts and properly validated scientific interpretations (Winne & Alexander, 2006, p. xi) and who have the requisite skill and will to do so are likely to find that some of what is presented here will have immediate prospective appeal, while other aspects of the content may need time to transfer or seem not at all helpful. In either case, we intend only to convince school psychologists that they should visit educational psychology—its theories, its research, and its methods of inquiry—whenever they critically reflect on the conceptual basis of their work and seek to advance their understanding of learning-instruction interactions for the children they serve. We believe such effort will prove positive.

EDUCATIONAL PSYCHOLOGY: DEFINITION AND STRUCTURE

Derived from psychology and growing within it for more than a century, educational psychology is the application of psychology and psychological methods to the study of education (Zimmerman & Schunk, 2003). This general account has been given greater precision by others who have included a list of component areas as they see them. For example, Elliott, Kratochwill, Littlefield-Cook and Travers (2000) listed "*development, learning, motivation, instruction, assessment, and related issues that influence the interaction of teaching and learning*" (p. 2). However, this is a field that has expanded rapidly over the past half-century (Berliner & Calfee, 1996; Pressley & Roehrig, 2003; Winne & Alexander, 2006) and listing elements needs to be accompanied by cautions associated with this growth. For example, it intersects and shares many areas with other expressions of developmental science, such as sociology, language, and measurement, and with other fields of psychology, such as development, cognition and motivation. Perhaps this is why its contributions in the previous edition of the *Handbook of School Psychology* (Reynolds & Gutkin, 1999) are dispersed widely—principally but not exclusively across developmental psychology (Tharinger & Lambert, 1999), cognitive psychology (Alexander & Murphy, 1999), the psychology of individual differences (Kranzler, 1999) and biological psychology (Kalat & Wurm, 1999), notably concerning teaching and learning, and across developmental psychopathology (McConaughy & Achenbach, 1999) in relation to behavioral, emotional, and learning problems.

Despite its dispersion and overlap, educational psychology is generally well understood (Berliner, 2006; Berliner & Calfee, 1996; Pressley & Roehrig, 2003; Winne & Alexander, 2006). Its signage is planted firmly in the domains of *learning* and *instruction*, in what it is about us as people that we can and do learn, how learning happens and why, how teaching works to assist positive development in these processes, and how we know that people have learned. It also involves how we use knowledge as a design variable to deliberately engineer learning—manipulating it to learn how to bring creative and innovative dimensions to our thinking. Of course, *learning*, *instruction*, and *assessment* are inexorably linked, and if the kneebone-thighbone-tailbone metaphor is applied, the growing body of educational psychology work is defined by its underpinning range of interconnected and important subfields, very few of which belong to educational psychology alone.

As editors of the recently published, second edition of the *Handbook of Educational Psychology*, Alexander and Winne (2006) sought a definitive reference work as a source of background information for a ranging professional audience—as their predecessors, Berliner and Calfee (1996), had done with the first edition a decade earlier. Winne and Alexander gathered the field into 11 areas, noting an imprecision in boundaries and a likelihood that some areas would be found in constellations that formed other fields of psychology. The definitive 11 areas of educational psychology as they see it are: Foundations and the future of educational psychology; Learners' development; Individual differences; Cognition; Motivation; Content area teaching; Sociocultural perspectives on teaching and learning; Teachers and teaching; Instructional design; Teacher assessment; and, Modern perspectives on research methodologies, data and data analysis. Thus, the major and most recent great work of Division 15 (Educational Psychology) of the American Psychological Association has defined itself via a reference text based on the research and theory in these 11 areas. It is an important source for school psychologists whose interests align clearly with the areas or any subset of them. We have attempted to highlight many of the contributions from this tome, without pretending to have done so with the breadth and depth of coverage possible in the *Handbook's* volume of over 1000 pages. Apart from the *Handbook*, many individuals have defined the field in terms of significant areas of contribution. For example, Pressley and Roehrig's (2003) conceptualization presents a reasoned basis for accenting the field in other ways, notably to account for the high representation in published research in educational psychology of topics in cognition, motivation and individual differences. We refer throughout this chapter to these bodies of work.

We agree with the forward view of Bransford et al. (2006) that educational psychology is on the cusp of an era of synergy in its research. They imagined the coming years of research as likely to produce synergies that would "inform the design of learning environments that allow all students to succeed in the fast changing world of the 21st century" (p. 210). To help form the image, they explored major areas of research in implicit, informal and formal learning and advocated ways of drawing them together into an assisting focus. Others also have taken steps along this path (e.g., NRC, 2001, 2002, 2005) in the interest of seeing where in the convergence of related areas, the bodies of work may have more visible application. Together with our experiences in school psychology, this anticipation of greater synergy across the next decade has led us to an introduction and preferred structure under the broad headings, *learning* and *instruction*. We consider these two areas will connect where school psychologists are likely to search out helpful *state-of-the-art facts and properly validated scientific interpretations*. Given the current press in school psychology for multitiered delivery of instructional interventions designed to enhance learning and achievement, our focus on the core of educational psychology—learning and instruction—should highlight the relevance of educational psychology to the daily lives of school psychologists and the professional at large.

LEARNING

Learning is a change in a learner's knowledge (Mayer, 2001). It associates also with change in what we do, where "doing" has implied knowledge. But, there is great diversity in explanations of the phenomena of learning because of ripening theory about what "change" is and how it might be observed, about metaprocesses that guide thinking and doing in the acquisition and utilization of knowledge and about whether and how participatory practices and social factors complement individual processes in learning. Certainly, there are different types

of learning that happen in different contexts for different learners (Bransford et al., 2006). Some things we pick up naturally, like breathing and walking; others need lots of nurturing, like circular breathing to play a didgeridoo or walking in conformity with Olympic Games standards. The former are developmental, their growth a matter of maturity and typically inevitable, albeit with individual differences in when such things happen, and occasionally in whether they happen at all. The latter require learning. In behavioral, cognitive, and situational theories which we will outline later, learning is distinguished from what we gain through development, and in cognitive theory and cognitive-situative theory, metacognition has become a key tenet. Clearly, simple statements such as the one we have used to begin this subsection need elaboration to describe the richness and complexity of human learning as a phenomenon. Behavioral definitions that emphasized the relatively permanent changes in behavior resulting from practice have provided useful introductions to this richness and a springboard into later conceptualizations that encompass "mind," metaprocesses and social constructs which attempt to describe the complexity. Contemporary theories of learning speak of changes in the mind's structures and representations associated with knowledge as people learn, including the soft skills of metacognition that enable people to intelligently apply knowledge in generating new or further learning opportunities. Many speak also of the influence of situative factors that socialize learning.

In its review of contemporary theories, the National Research Council (NRC, 2001) noted that they "emphasize the way knowledge is represented, organized and processed in the mind" (p. 3). This involves cognition and its related constructs, particularly metacognition, a construct for knowing about cognition including the educationally significant skills of knowing what one knows and does not, and knowing how one might get to know. The NRC noted also an additional emphasis in contemporary theories given to "social and participatory practices that support knowing and understanding" (p. 3).

Thus it seems important for school psychologists searching out state-of-the-research definitions of learning to include the elements of (a) change, (b) its representation as knowledge, (c) the dynamic features of cognitive organizing and processing, and (d) social and participatory practices that support knowledge. But how does experience become represented as "knowledge in the mind" and when and where does this happen? A common explanation involves a theory of schema and schema activation.

A schema is a set of information and processes. It configures what one has available in long-term memory that might be brought forward to help make sense of new information or experience—or as Bransford et al. (2006) explain, on occasion to deliberately repress information in the interests of seeking innovation. Schemas are activated when a learner engages with the experience and interprets cues that help to establish, alter and refine the configuration. Such engagement ranges from not much at all, as in cases where a person appears inattentive, distracted or uninterested, to focused and sustained levels, where the person is involved in a careful and studied encounter with the experience. This is a process of ongoing construction and reconstruction of knowledge, not surprisingly referred to in learning theory as "constructivist" (Murphy & Mason, 2006; Piaget, 1954; Sinatra & Pintrich, 2003) in its generative role. Outcomes from an engagement may result in conceptual change with Piaget's theory (1954) of assimilation-accommodation setting a historical platform for what others later modeled as happening within such change.

Murphy and Mason (2006) provide an integrated account of several models to "help us understand that change is a process in which the interaction between emotions, appraisals, motivational aspects and cognition can be both facilitative and inhibitory" (p. 311). They add, "the notion of *intentionality* as a general mediator between 'internal' and 'external' factors implied in knowledge representations change (Vosniadou, 1999) is a further articulation of investigation in the field" (p. 311). Thus learners are more likely to succeed when they set out in their engagement to intentionally revise their knowledge structures (Murphy & Mason, 2006; Sinatra & Pintrich, 2003). Thus, having some background knowledge when accompanied by processes for selecting and applying it and a will to do so to change what is already known provides a basis for representing what one comes to learn and know from the interaction.

This theoretical notion underpins a principled relation between learning and instruction identified by the National Research Council (NRC, 1999, 2005, p. 1):

Students come to the classroom with preconceptions about how the world works. If their initial understanding is not engaged, they may fail to grasp the new concepts and information, or they may learn them for purposes of a test but revert to their preconceptions outside the classroom.

Educators seeking to help students engage their initial understandings will need to help first with establishing a sense of "learning" that indicates intentionally shifting position from a starting grid of what can be brought into working memory from long-term memory, how to do this, and how to do it while being aware of the many social and other conditions of the situation in which it is to be done. Greeno, Collins and Resnick (1996) described learning as moving along trajectories of expertise. This succinct statement carries the notions of *knowledge as actual and potential* (trajectories of expertise), *change* (moving along) and *individual difference* (with each learner having expertise and trajectory). We want to add two things that will help bring important determining conditions to mind. The first invites school psychologists to consider conclusions drawn by Ackerman and Lohman (2006) that "abilities" are both inputs and outcomes of good education and are at the heart of individual difference and education. Further, "those anxious to embrace a multidimensional view of educational outcomes might attend more to the measure of (individuals') organized systems of conceptual and factual knowledge in domains ... (and that) ... are more sensitive to instructional interventions" (Ackerman & Lohman, 2006, p. 156). The second point concerns knowledge for the Knowledge Age wherein it has commodity status that Bereiter and Scardamalia (2006) note is "a radical departure from how knowledge has traditionally been treated in both epistemology and education" and "where recent efforts (have been) to reshape teaching and instruction in response to perceived new needs arising from a shift from a manufacturing-based to a knowledge-based economy" (Drucker, 1994, p. 695). The reshaping involves teaching and instruction attending to strategies that enable knowledge to be deliberately called into the service of how to be generative as a learner—to have knowledge fit for the purposes of learning about how to learn.

Schools are places where children learn to learn—a description attributed to Ann Brown's perspective in her lifelong work to develop learning theory and its productive application (Palinsar, 2003). It is a positive view, and importantly so, as the research field has come to realize the significance of *meta* levels of learning and knowledge in the formation of robust learning strategies (Chen & Klahr, 1999; Kalat, 2005; Lorch & van den Broek, 1997; Meyer, Young & Bartlett, 1989; NRC, 1999, 2001, 2002, 2005). It is important for this realization to spread widely if more educators and community members are to advance the basis of our systems, policies and practices in education in informed and constructive ways. Such moves might include constructing deliberate opportunities where schools provide for students to *metalearn*, a process through which they learn about learning their knowledge structures strategically to generate changed knowledge for particular purposes. They might also include development and testing of models that teachers and others have and use to guide such learning, and assessment designed to determine what students have learned and how well. Having a theory of learning that includes metalearning, and knowledge of other theoretical positions, is especially critical for school psychologists whose work takes them into asking questions about students' learning and exploring possible interventions that are evidence-based and likely to enhance learning.

Writing on aspects of human learning that are particularly relevant to education, Bransford et al. (2006) indicated the huge challenge in bringing together different theories that traverse learning of different kinds in different settings and for different learners. Bransford and his colleagues integrated research and theory across three key areas: (1) implicit learning and the brain, (2) informal learning, and (3) formal learning. Each area will be well known by most school psychologists for particular implications suggested for practice. And each will have caused some to consider the relevance of the area, and perhaps, even of educational psychology. For example, Bransford et al. acknowledged that educators might ask about the first area, "What precisely are the advantages of knowing which brain regions are activated over time and how they are associated with behavioral changes? Will brain studies *really* alter what we do in schools?" (p. 212). They provided three good responses, noting that a mature science of learning will include explanations of when, how, and why learning occurs. The *when, how*, and *why*—and particularly the second and third—are better explained when their associated neural activity is known and the internal mechanisms that govern learning across ages and settings identified. Their second response was that because neural activity often precedes behavior, it offers a basis for educators to consider what it means to know and to learn. Third, they ventured that neural categorization may provide more precise ways for grouping educational strategies and policies to account for behaviors that appear similar, but are not.

Theoretical Perspectives That Have Contributed Significantly to Understanding Learning

There is a long history in educational psychology of research and theory regarding the nature of the human mind. Greeno, Pearson, and Schoenfeld (1996) suggested that four perspectives had been particularly significant, the *differential, behaviorist, cognitive,* and *situative* perspectives. Contemporary definitions of learning will track across some or all of the four. The National Research Council (NRC 2001) summarized the perspectives with particular focus on their contributions to testing and test development, an issue we take up in the final section of the chapter. However, they made the following key points about the recency and convergence of the perspectives that help pinpoint definitional issues:

1. The *cognitive* and the *situative* perspectives are most recent but the four perspectives have overlapped in their chronology and some theory has recognizable elements from more than one of them. So, they are not mutually exclusive; rather they have different emphases about knowing and learning with different implications for what should be assessed and how the assessment process should be transacted (see e.g., Greeno, Collins & Resnick, 1996; Greeno et al., 1996).

2. The *differential* perspective focuses mainly on individual differences in what people know and in their potential for learning. Its origins are in the mental testing movement of 100 years ago that attempted to match children with places available in Parisian schools (Binet & Simon, 1980) and in theories of intelligence that arose from patterns emerging in students' performance on tests. Elaborate statistical machinery was developed for determining the separate factors of intelligence (Carroll, 1993) that by and large, were considered to

be stable and separable from the processes and content of academic learning. In this view, it is the stable mental traits that are an aspect of knowledge, are measurable, and are a basis for differentiating individuals. The National Research Council (NRC 2001) did not present an explicit definition of learning to represent the perspective. In fact, they make it clear that the approach relied heavily on the notion of stable mental capabilities represented in patterns across test performances. However, it seems implicit to us that from the *differential* perspective, *learning is what people do deliberately to realize the potential represented in these patterns*. This interpretation is consistent with Greeno et al. (1996) who said, "The key feature of learning in the situative perspective is engaged participation with agency" (p. 2).

3. The *behaviorist* perspective is compatible with the differential perspective that preceded it and was still maturing as behaviorist researchers such as B. F. Skinner (1938) began describing stimulus-response systems in observable behaviors and rewarding and punitive conditions that shaped their strength. The stimulus-response systems and shaping are the essence of behaviorism. From a behavioral perspective, people learn by acquiring simple components of a skill through an accumulation of stimulus-response associations, then building this into more refined or elaborated ones by differentiating or combining them. Knowledge is what associations one forms, and *learning is the process by which one acquires those skills* (Thorndike, 1931).

4. *Cognitive* theories focus on how people develop structures of knowledge, including concepts associated with a subject matter or discipline and procedures for reasoning and solving problems. The field of cognitive psychology has focused on how knowledge is encoded, stored, organized in complex networks, and retrieved, and how different types of internal representations are created as people learn about a domain (NRC, 1999). Whereas differential and behavioral approaches concentrate on how much knowledge someone has, cognitive theory also emphasizes what type of knowledge someone has. From the *cognitive* perspective, knowledge is more than the accumulation of factual information and routine procedures;

it is an integration of information and procedures in ways that are useful for interpreting situations and solving problems. One basic tenet of cognitive theory is that *learning is an active construction of knowledge by connecting new information with prior knowledge*.

5. The *situative* perspective grew from concern with cognitive theory's nearly exclusive focus on individual thinking and learning. Instead of viewing thought as individual response to task structures and goals, the situative perspective is more oriented towards practical activity and context. Context refers to engagement in particular forms of practice and community. In this view *learning is a social practice and is contextually related as mediated activity. One learns to participate in the practices, goals and habits of mind of particular communities*. A community is any group that shares a purpose, for example, Division 15 of the American Psychological Association, a neighborhood poker club, or a school. Being part of the group mediates what and how one thinks and learns as one assumes knowledge and skills with cultural artifacts such as tools and language (Wertsch, 1998). Pellegrino, Chudowsky, and Glaser (2001) noted, "most current testing practices are not a good match with the situative perspective" (p. 64). This is because of a disjuncture between the real situations in which people perform and the abstract ways that traditional testing presents situations. In relation to its contribution to a definition of learning, the situational perspective underscores the importance of context, including social context, alongside accounting for the individual development of knowledge. (After NRC, 2001, p. 60–65)

This analysis further reveals an emphasis in contemporary theories of learning on *mind* and *situation* as core constructs. The mind is a hypothetical repository for knowledge—its acquisition and its management. It is a facility that coordinates the communicative coding and recoding of knowledge—typically through thinking, language or action, and includes capacity for affect and intentionality in its conceptual architecture and operation. The individual's capacity to be intentional when acting mindfully is affected by individual development and diversity, cognition, metacognition, opportunity, motivation, teaching, situational factors, and social participation. Learning is a particular representation of knowledge; it is knowledge newly organized in the mind as an outcome of a changing experience or thought.

While the notion of change is still an inherent marker for learning, the cognitive accounts we are now presenting speak to the "mind" behind such action, and particularly about the reorganization of mental and social systems as one does it—be it to establish some combinations of facts of a matter, facts of strategic processing, or in the case of cognitive-situative models, the preceding and facts of social participation. "Mind" is a hypothetical construct that has two major components—mental architecture such as memory and comprehension to provide a structure or model, and cognitive skills such as memorizing and comprehending to provide knowledge. Knowledge building is the key objective of learning in cognitive descriptions. Typically, it occurs in a process of construction where predisposing schema from our personal histories help us to "construct" memory and make sense about what we are seeking to acquire. This may be implicit, through action that is so automatic that we are unaware it has occurred or more or less explicit, where our metacognition and language enhance consciousness and description to some extent. We may be untutored in making the change, or guided through it as novices by someone more expert (e.g., by a parent, a teacher, a cooking coach). It may occur within formal settings for learning (such as schools where the agenda is education) or informal ones (such as homes where much learning occurs, but formal education usually is a minor part). And our motivation is very important. Intentionality about changing will focus our attention and engagement, power their retention throughout the learning experience, and help us make deep associations with what we learn and enhance its transferability.

Essentially, cognitive theories of learning are about the *know-how* to getting and using knowledge. They deal not just with the facts of knowledge, but also with ways that information and skills are brought together to help us interpret, analyze and respond to problems. Learning a mathematical formula, or a poem, will require a learner to accumulate factual information, to systematically integrate it with routines aligned with using it, and to test its transferability. Thus, cognitive views of instruction stretch well beyond the simple observation of behavioral shift as a student today recites a formula or a poem which seemingly he could not do yesterday. Rather, these views seek to establish both the observable and hidden conditions that made it so, and the extent to which it is incorporated into increasingly robust knowledge and know-how schemata.

Some theorists (e.g., Lave & Wenger, 1991) have helped us shift attention in our views of learning from knowledge-acquisition as an internal, individually situated cognitive process to include placing it in social relationships. Rather than concentrating on the cognition involved in learning, their emphasis is on the kinds of social engagements that will engender appropriate contexts for learning to happen. For example, students who learn "to do schooling" will be sensitive to the frameworks for operating successfully in a classroom involving peers, teacher, and school in common purposes. Those who do not or cannot learn the framework, or who choose not to participate, or whose potential contributions to reframing the practices of the classroom community are ignored, will be unsuccessful. Learning involves adjusting participation by identifying and adopting relevant practices in a community where members' shared knowledge and practices contribute to a common purpose—or creating such practices that are taken up by other members. The participation "refers not just to local events of engagement in certain activities with certain people, but to a more encompassing process of being active participants in the *practices* of social communities and constructing *identities* in relation to these communities" (Wenger, 1998, p. 4). Consequently, learning is seen as a process of social participation, which is influenced greatly by the nature of the situation in which a learner participates.

These theories are deeply rooted in the research traditions of cognition and social interaction. They permit us to conclude our section on definition with a view that learning occurs on a change trajectory that is different from maturation, and is reflected in knowledge newly organized in the mind as an outcome of a changing experience, and by the nature of the situation in which a learner participates in the experience.

Summary Implications of Learning Theory and Research

School psychologists who reflect on the science that has advanced what is known about learning may want to incorporate into their theories and approaches to professional interaction, five key elements from educational psychology. The first is the knowledge that contemporary theories about learning as change in knowledge reflect traditions of cognition and social participation. The second to fifth elements have to do with definitional features and combine into cautions that (a) learning as change observable in schools will usually be "observable" through language, and/or action, (b) the language and action themselves represent the representation of learning as knowledge in a learner's mind, (c) the dynamic features of the representations will have involved the learner in cognitive organizing and processing, and (d) social and participatory practices will have supported the learner's many decisions in recognizing, evaluating and responding to a learning opportunity. The authors consider the following to be particularly important in terms of evidence for its relevance in a changing world:

1. The changing conditions of teaching and learning in the Knowledge Age call for re-envisioning the teaching of academic skills and content, retention and transfer with greater deliberate attention to learning the generative skills of knowledge (Bereiter & Scardamalia, 2006; Wittrock, 1990, 1991). Bereiter and Scardamalia have distinguished between knowledge in belief mode where its acquisition equips learners to evaluate and decide between claims about the truth of things, and in design mode where its focus is generative. They stress the importance of both, and illustrate this in a depiction of movements a skilled trial lawyer might make between knowledge of the law (belief mode) and strategy in planning, looking for legal angles and conducting a case (design mode). It is not difficult to see similar balance in what successful students do as learners, yet how much of what is currently learned in formal education is knowledge in belief mode and what opportunities do students currently have to hone their awareness and skills in design mode? Bereiter and Scardamalia advocate educational environments being mindful that design mode is the principal form in knowledge-building enterprises (such as education, schools, classes, lessons, and learning events) and have detailed four methods to begin bringing appropriate learning opportunities into the academic curriculum. Their theory has far-reaching implications for what, where, how and when students will learn at a time when schools are part of community in transition to the Knowledge Age. We recommend that school psychologists consider the meanings of learning in an era of transition to the Knowledge Age, and the associated implications this has for instruction and assessment.

2. Metacognition is a determining factor in learning (NRC, 1999, 2001, 2005; Pressley & Harris, 2006). It has significant influence on how learners approach a learning task in such matters as whether or not to use cognitive strategies available to them. A "metacognitive" approach to instruction can help students to take control of their own learning by defining learning goals and actively monitoring their progress in achieving them (NRC, 2001). It can be taught (NRC, 1999, 2001). In applied settings, students have learned to be metacognitive about strategic behavior in relation to writing (Graham & Harris 2000; Harris & Graham, 1992), reading (Pressley, Johnson, Symons, McGoldrick & Kurita, 1989), and learning from text involving both reading and writing (Bartlett, Barton, & Turner, 1989). Pressley and Harris (2006) remind us that people are much more likely to continue using strategies they have learned if they know that the strategy has a positive impact when applied. It can be identified by think-aloud techniques as learners talk through their thinking about choosing, using, and evaluating the utility of strategies (Bereiter & Bird, 1985; Pressley & Harris, 2006). Such metacognitive knowledge is an orientation to remembering. Successful learners take it into a memory task (Nelson, 1996; NRC, 2001). It influences how well they comprehend and remember when learning from classroom texts (Meyer, et al., 1989), whether they can explain their learning strategies (Pressley & Harris, 2006) and whether they switch strategic behavior in the face of persisting challenge or lack of success (NRC, 2001). Accordingly, we recommend that school psychologists recognize that metacognition is a significant determining factor in learning, that its skills are learnable, and that its inclusion in operational understandings of learning is essential.

INSTRUCTION

Students are supposed to learn specified content, which must be clearly understood by both teachers and their students. When students don't know what is called for, their performance suffers. Likewise a teacher's effectiveness in the classroom can falter when the focus of instruction is unclear. What precisely do we want students to accomplish in a particular lesson, a unit, a course, and under what conditions? These concerns take us into the world of objectives and instructional design, an area central to educational psychology that impacts the practice of both teaching and school psychology interventions.

Learning Objectives

To achieve and maintain a higher level of instruction, educators and psychologists must continually decide exactly what students need to accomplish. Thus, educators are encouraged to formulate specific objectives that encompass their daily concerns and communicate with students what it is they are accountable to learn and under what conditions. If there is one indispensable guideline for formulating objectives, it is: be precise. Learning will improve because students will know exactly what is expected of them and, consequently, will understand the basis of feedback and a subsequent grade. In addition, the assessment of learning will be well served by this same precision.

In an excellent analysis of objectives, Bloom, Madaus, and Hastings (1981) noted that statements of educational objectives describe, in a relatively specific manner, what students should be able to produce or do, or what characteristics students should possess after the learning. An *instructional objective* is an intent communicated by a statement describing a proposed change in the learner: a statement of what the learner is to be able to do upon completion of the learning experience (Kim & Kellough, 1991). Thus an instructional objective requires a demonstrable behavioral change in the learner. Consequently, we can tell that learning has occurred only when we observe a change in behavior. Note the essential ingredients of this description: an objective is student-centered and involves learning outcomes and observable behavior. In other words, an instructional objective states what a student is expected to accomplish, the products of that learning (not the activities), and clearly defined student levels of performance.

Virtually every school psychologist has written or helped educators write measurable instructional objectives for students experiencing learning or behavior difficulties.

Benjamin Bloom is credited with devising a taxonomy of educational objectives that has widely influenced educational practices (Bloom, 1956). The main purpose of his taxonomy was to provide a classification of the goals of an educational system. There are three taxonomies (cognitive, affective, and psychomotor), however, the cognitive taxonomy has had a significant influence on educational practices. This taxonomy includes six levels:

> *Knowledge:* The recall of pertinent facts
> *Comprehension:* Understanding the meaning of what is presented
> *Application:* Use of ideas and rules
> *Analysis:* Separating a unit into its parts
> *Synthesis:* Constructing a whole from parts
> *Evaluation:* Making judgments

These six classes represent a hierarchical order of the different classes of objectives. The objectives of each class usually depend on the preceding classes. The great value of the taxonomy is its general application. Experts in curriculum construction can study it to refine the objectives of instruction in any school. Inexperienced educators and psychologists can turn to the taxonomy as a guide to the kinds of objectives for which students should be striving. Both expert and neophyte can profit by the wide range of test items that can be written based on these types of objectives to determine if students are actually achieving desired goals. The taxonomy, often referred to as Bloom's taxonomy, is a remarkably flexible tool. Not only does it offer reliable insights into the formation of acceptable objectives, but it also can be used as the basis for planning instruction, designing assessments, and evaluating types of learning.

Theoretical Perspectives That Have Contributed Significantly to Understanding Instruction

As many school psychologists know, Skinner is best known for his theoretical and applied work on operant learning, but during his lifetime he also contributed significantly to schooling and the technology of teaching. Specifically, he applied principles of operant conditioning to both learning and teaching, in a procedure called programmed instruction. Recall that Skinner believed teachers depend too heavily upon punishment while neglecting their use of positive reinforcement and antecedent control methods. Insisting that special techniques can arrange contingencies of reinforcement—resulting from the relationship between behavior and the consequences of that behavior—Skinner (1938) stated that teachers should be able to effectively control behavior. This assumption about contingency management is the basis of operant conditioning and one of the cornerstones of effective teaching and behavior management.

One of Skinner's favorite subjects was the teaching of arithmetic. In arithmetic, the primary behaviors of concern are speaking and writing figures, words, and signs. It is necessary to bring these responses under stimulus control. How do teachers accomplish this? According to Skinner, they should use reinforcers. Traditionally, this has meant reliance on negative consequences. Skinner noted that although yesterday's physical punishment is mostly gone, teachers still rely too much on sarcasm, ridicule, and low marks. So arithmetic, like most subjects, has become mired in a maze of dislike, anxiety, and ultimately, boredom. Improvement is possible, since there are general characteristics of teaching that, if practiced, cultivate both teaching and learning. For example, Skinner urged teachers to define the terminal behavior, that is, what students should be able to do after having been taught. Statements like "be a good citizen" are both inadequate and unworthy; they do not describe behavior. "Knowledge" is another deceptive goal of education. Students have learned something when they behave. That is, they respond to stimuli differently than they did before instruction. Students "know" when teachers can specifically identify their behavior; that is, teachers have taught them to behave in certain ways. What they know is what they do; therefore, according to Skinner teachers must objectively and concretely state their objectives.

Teachers must also solve the *problem of the first instance*. Once you have determined the terminal behavior, one must strengthen it by reinforcement. But you cannot reinforce what does not appear. The problem of the first instance means the need for pupils to exhibit some aspect of the desired behavior. One option is to induce it, as in physically taking a child's hand and guiding it to form letters or numbers. Another option is to have students imitate the teacher or some example of excellent work. Simply telling students what to

do and then reinforcing them when they do it is yet another possibility. Learning, however, does not occur because the teacher has primed the behavior; it occurs, according to Skinner, only when behavior is reinforced. The above examples illustrate only the first step in the process.

Skinner also stated that teachers should decide what they will use to prompt behavior. One reinforcement will hardly free a response from priming stimuli. When do you stop priming students? If you continue too long, you are inefficient; if you stop too soon, you may cause error. Use only as much as is necessary. For example, you may wish students to be able to identify the Midwestern states of the United States, their major cities, and their principal industries. You may begin by using maps and reading materials. Some cities may be near water and thus be port cities. Later, when students should know which cities do what, you may ask them to locate a city without using maps or texts. You thus have supplied various prompts as part of the original priming behavior.

Be sure that you program complex behavior. Priming and prompting evoke a behavior to be reinforced in the presence of required stimuli. Some behavior, however, is so complex that you cannot reinforce it as a unit. Educators must program (or structure) it, which does not mean teaching one thing at a time in an isolated manner and as a collection of responses. What a student does halfway through a program may not be a part of the terminal behavior. Small steps are needed to ensure constant reinforcement.

An instructional approach that reflects many of Skinner's instructional principles is the highly structured Bereiter-Englemann program, designed to prescribe teaching procedures for disadvantaged children and students at risk for school failure. Bereiter and Englemann (1966) stated that new teachers like to work with "ideas." Good teaching, however, employs much smaller and more intricate units than ideas; it involves specific information modules and specific techniques. Teaching is the interplay between information, pace, discipline, and rewards as they relate to curriculum (Bereiter & Englemann, 1966). Bereiter and Englemann devised several teaching strategies to use in an intensive preschool program for disadvantaged children. Nevertheless, their strategies have broad applicability. One suggestion is to be careful when you vary your presentation methods. Variations may confuse a learner. Excessive variation bothers and bewilders all children, who need to feel psychologically secure in the classroom. Still, youngsters, disadvantaged or not, must respond in a variety of situations and should be ready to respond to variation outside of the classroom. Although the authors' suggestion is pertinent, remember also to consider variation in relation to the readiness of students. Whatever educators do, they must give children sufficient time to respond. In their work, Bereiter and Englemann urged that a lesson's tempo be such that the youngster can respond thoughtfully. They also suggested that teachers use questions liberally. Questions are important because they help students attend to relevant cues. Teachers must consider the question's difficulty and ask if a student is capable of answering it. The value of questioning is clear from countless studies. Subjects tend to remember more about material on which they are questioned, and to retain it longer. The direct instructional effect of questioning is substantial. Bereiter and Englemann furnished several more suggestions that indicate the nature of their program: careful control of stimuli, judicious application of reinforcement, and assiduous avoidance of error. The Bereiter-Englemann program is an example of behavioral principles put to action. Work derived from the Bereiter-Englemann program has focused on curricular interventions and been applied to all students with great promise, especially with regard to higher-order thinking skills (Carnine, 1991).

Adapting Skinner's technology of teaching, while remaining faithful to the basic principles of operant conditioning, Susan Markle (1990; Tiemann & Markle, 1990) built her concept of "programed" (note the one "m") instruction around the principle of active responding (the student learns what the student does—Markle, 1990, p. 1). Although the original programed instruction movement enjoyed great initial success, Markle believes that too rigid adherence to these early views—small steps, heavy prompting, verbatim student responses to oft-repeated sentences—all contributed to criticism of the system as excessively sterile. Three programing principles, active responding, errorless learning, and immediate feedback, form the basis of Markle's model of instructional design and have also been influential in much of the intervention work that school psychologists undertake with students.

The Principle of Active Responding. Markle refers to meaningful responses that are covert, overt, psychomotor, or verbal as active responding. Note that active, overt responding provides rich opportunities for feedback and reinforcement, which is particularly important in the beginning stages of acquiring new knowledge or skills.

The Principle of Errorless Learning. The goal of instruction should be to reduce error as much as possible. If learners respond actively, they tend to remember the circumstances surrounding the learning: the teacher, the stimuli, the response, any feedback that was provided. If they give an incorrect response, what do they learn? They learn the error. Markle questioned the manner in which we treat error. If we tell a student "No, that's wrong," or make a red X on his or her paper, will the student suppress the mistake? No. The student will simply try some other response. However, nothing will have been done to reinforce the correct answers, in working toward errorless learning. If you say, "No, John, 9×7 is not 56; it's 63," then the student does not respond actively. Does it follow, then, that students should never be allowed to make mistakes? Not in this system. Errors serve many functions. They can be signals that instruction needs improvement; they are a reliable guide for diagnosis; they aid educators in shaping the final form of a program. There may also be good reasons for getting a mistake out in the open, such as diagnosing a lack of background information that is needed for a topic. Students should also be permitted to "mess around" with the subject matter, as in a lab or in simulated lab situations in computer-assisted instruction.

The Principle of Immediate Feedback. Markle linked the need for feedback to the manner in which the statement is framed. For example, there are instances in which feedback would add nothing to the learning. If I ask you what $2 + 2$ equals, you don't need me or the text to tell you that you are right. You have that information from your personal knowledge. Challenging situations, however, cause students to make more errors and learn less when feedback is lacking. Recent reviews of feedback continue to document how very important a role it plays in instruction and interventions that are effective in changing learner's knowledge and behavior (Hattie & Timperley, 2007).

The work of Robert Gagne, a leader in the field of instructional design for over three decades (Gagne & Briggs, 1979; Gagne & Driscoll, 1988; Gagne, Briggs, & Wager, 1988), provides another valuable perspective on instruction. Gagne's work was based upon his views of five learning outcomes: verbal information, intellectual skills, cognitive strategies, attitudes, and motor skills. According to Gagne, each of these five learning outcomes demands a different set of conditions for optimizing learning, retention, and transferability. The "optimal conditions" refer to a particular set of external events surrounding the learner: the instruction that students receive. Thus, the great value of Gagne's work is the close relationship between teaching and learning. In his view of teaching and learning, Gagne identified several instructional events that he believed helped students to learn meaningfully. First, you must *gain the attention of your students.* Instruction terminates immediately if attention falters. *Informing learners of the objective of the lesson* is another way of helping them focus their attention. What precisely is to be learned? Students should know the *criteria for mastery* and when they have achieved it. Gagne recommended that teachers *stimulate recall of prerequisite knowledge*, that is, appeal to students' prior knowledge. Students may need a simple reminder of previous learning, or they might require detailed help. This will help educators when they *present the stimulus material.* Use techniques that are as attractive and exciting as possible, whether verbal, demonstrative, or media-related. Make the material interesting and pertinent to facilitate attention and to spark inquiry. Educators may have to *provide learning guidance.* By this, Gagne meant you must ensure that students acquire the details involved in the learning objective; if a series of steps is needed for mastery, then students must know what these steps are and how to master them. Learn the geography; learn the history; finally, speculate about politics. This guidance in turn helps to *elicit the performance.* You cannot be certain that a student has learned unless he or she performs the behavior. Once students exhibit a response or performance, it is important that a teacher provides *appropriate feedback.* Good feedback means giving students accurate, detailed information about their performance, specifying what was done well and what needs improvement. Closely associated with providing feedback is assessing a student's performance. *Assessment of student performance* can occur in several ways.

A final step in creating optimal conditions for learning is to *enhance retention and transfer.* A teacher or psychologist simply cannot assume that students will automatically transfer their learning from one class or situation to another; instructional plans must make provisions for both review and the use of the material in novel situations.

Gagne believed that this nine-step model could function as a theory of learning and memory. It utilizes existing theory as a basis for designing instruction and attempts to include all types of learning outcomes that are typically of the objectives of instruction. Finally, the model provides an instructional basis for analyzing the interaction of internal events with external events; this makes the model applicable to instruction of many forms in a wide variety of settings, while simultaneously appealing to the individual differences of learners. We agree with Gagne, and therefore as a summary, provide the following checklist of key features that he believed created optimal learning conditions for most people.

1. Gain the attention of the learner.
2. Inform the learner of the learning objective and criteria determining mastery.
3. Stimulate recall of prerequisite knowledge that connects to information being taught.
4. Present the task or material to be learned in an interesting manner.
5. Provide learning guidance by pointing out details or major steps in learning the material.
6. Elicit a performance or demonstration of what the individual has learned.
7. Assess the performance of the student.
8. Provide the learner with specific feedback about performance.
9. Enhance retention and transfer of what has been a learned to a new situation or related subjects.

A close reading of this list and the points Gagne generated will reveal that we believe that assessment should precede feedback as opposed to following it. Good instructional assessment results in feedback to the learner and to the teacher. Other than this small difference in the sequencing of learning conditions, we believe Gagne's design of instruction is pedagogically sound and provides school psychologists a strong model of instruction to guide research and practice recommendations.

Adapting Instruction

Adapting instruction means attempting to "match the mix" between student aptitudes and the methods and materials used. A good example of this can be seen in the work of Bloom (1981), who identified several variables that influence the teaching-learning process, particularly time on task.

Time on Task

Time on task has always been recognized as a critical factor in learning, whether the term refers to years a subject appears in a curriculum, number of days in the school year, number of hours per day, or number of minutes per class. These are relatively fixed times, which tell us little about how much time students are actively engaged in learning. As Bloom observed, if one student is actively engaged 90% of the time while another is thus engaged only 30% of the time, we should not be surprised at their different achievement levels. As for teachers, studies of cues (what is to be learned), reinforcement (rewards for learning), and participation (active student engagement in learning) provide valuable clues as to just what teachers are doing with their time. What is most important to remember, however, is that time on task can be altered. Using Bloom's work as a basis, Gettinger (1990), a school psychologist, identified three aspects of learning time that could be increased. The first is the time used for instruction, the second is engaged time, and the third is productive learning time.

Cognitive Entry Behaviors

Bloom also believed that we must make a distinction between intelligence and cognitive entry behaviors. Although researchers repeatedly have demonstrated a link between intelligence and aptitude tests and later achievement, Bloom reasoned that these findings do not determine a student's potential for learning. Cognitive entry characteristics, which is knowledge essential for learning a particular subject (what we have referred to as "prior knowledge"), also show a close relationship with achievement and can be altered. These characteristics are subject to change because they contain specific content and skills that can be learned.

Use of Assessment

The purpose and uses of assessment are crucial according to Bloom, who favored formative testing and progress monitoring. While the customary use of classroom tests has been to measure a student's achievement at the completion of a block of work (summative evaluation), they have also been used to assess the quality of learning, as well as the quality of the learner. Formative assessment, on the other hand, is primarily intended to aid in the formation of learning by providing feedback about what has been learned and what still remains to be learned. Bloom believed that when assessments are used in this manner, the number of students who achieve mastery increases dramatically, chiefly because the necessary prerequisite skills have been identified for each student, student motivation intensifies, and more time is spent on tasks of central importance to learning.

Mastery Learning

Mastery learning is a key element in Bloom's work. Mastery learning is tied closely to the quality of instruction. Bloom began with the assumption that individual students need individual instruction to reach mastery, so teachers are challenged to adapt their teaching to individuals. In a classroom of 25 or 30 students to one teacher, this goal often remains elusive, reinforcing Bloom's idea that the quality of instruction must be considered in light of individual learners. This leads us to a student's ability to understand instruction. Do students understand what they are to learn and how they are to learn it? It is precisely here that student ability interacts with quality of instruction and curricular material. Since our schools are highly verbal places, ability to understand is linked to language ability and reading comprehension. Modifying instruction by using a variety of techniques—tutorial, group, text, and media—can benefit their comprehension. Do students show perseverance? How much time is a student willing to spend in learning? We know that student perseverance varies from subject to subject. Adapting instruction and using appropriate content has been shown to increase perseverance. Bloom emphasized the significance of perseverance by commenting on students' variability in the amount of time they are willing to spend on a task. Some students give up quickly on math problems, but will work indefinitely on faulty automobile engines. Bloom also believed that the key to increasing perseverance is appropriate design in instruction and learning materials. If aptitude determines the rate of learning, then the time allowed for learning can produce mastery. Bloom believed that some students spend as much as six times longer on homework than others—yet time spent on homework often has little relationship to final grades. Homework with the correct structure and conditions for learning, however, can be quite effective. The time spent on task can be altered by following mastery principles and allowing students the time they need to reach mastery in particular subjects. This in turn depends on aptitude, verbal ability, quality of instruction, and quality of help received outside of school.

If you are to help students achieve mastery of content taught, it is critical first to be certain what is meant by mastery, and then know when students reach it. Use formative assessment techniques as frequently as you think they are needed: divide a subject into meaningful sections, and then construct diagnostic tests to discover if students have mastered the material. You will then know where specific weaknesses lie and what steps need to be taken to overcome any difficulties. Not only has Bloom's work on mastery learning recommended itself for its obvious cognitive benefits, but students usually show an increased interest in subject matter, and, perhaps most important of all, an increased sense of self-worth. They do better on teacher-made tests, earn higher grades, and attain higher scores on standardized tests. Their retention and transfer of material learned under mastery learning conditions also improves substantially (Guskey, 1986).

Teachers also experience positive effects. When they see the improvement in students' learning, they gain a sense of professional renewal; they feel better about themselves and their work. Teachers using this approach tend to see learning as a cooperative venture in which their role is that of facilitators in helping their students reach the highest level of learning possible (Guskey, 1986).

Three interdependent variables, which can be phrased as questions, form the foundation of Bloom's integrated theory of learning and instruction. To what extent has a student learned the necessary prerequisites for the new learning to be attempted? To what extent can a student be motivated to engage in the learning process? To what extent is instruction appropriate to the learner? The theory addresses student characteristics, instruction, and learning outcomes. The student characteristics deemed to be most significant for learning are cognitive entry behaviors (the necessary prerequisite skills) and affective entry characteristics (motivation to

learn new material). Quality of instruction, as we have seen, refers to needed cues, practice, and reinforcement. Learning outcomes can be designated by level and type of achievement, rate of learning, and affective results. The three questions asked by Bloom, an educational psychologist, are very similar to those being asked by many school psychologists as they move forward with the implementation of response to intervention work.

Summary of Effective Instructional Theory and Research

So far in this chapter, we have examined several theoretical perspectives on learning and instruction. Each of them has something to offer educators and psychologists interested in enhancing the schooling of children. Effective instruction requires educators to have a wide range of activities and strategies in their repertoire for interacting with students. Although teachers can use different approaches, direct or indirect, to deliver instruction, effective teaching has several features in common. Specifically, the research suggests that effective teaching has a clear focus and explicit learning outcomes that students understand and are held accountable for learning. Well-written learning objectives provide teachers and students this type of focus. Second, instruction is delivered under conditions like those described by Gagne as optimal. That is, students' attention is under the control of the teacher, relationships or connections between what is being taught and their prior knowledge is established, material is presented in a manner that elicits active inquiry and interest, guidance is provided by the teacher as students interact with the new material or tasks, students are asked to respond to demonstrate what they are learning, and these responses are assessed and feedback is provided about the quality of the students' learning. Finally, review and practice follow over the course of several sessions to help facilitate retention of the new material and transfer to new situations or more complex problems. To accomplish this sequence of interactions with students and to enhance the effects of instruction, students often benefit from direct instruction in how to study and complete homework.

Much more could be written about instructional design and its role in advancing learning of students, but we assume a foundation case has been made that educational psychology and many of its leaders have much to offer psychologists working in schools. Let us summarize the contributions to learning and instruction we have discussed and also note a few more contributions from educational psychology that round out a picture of effective teaching for effective learning.

We believe there are at least 10 big ideas of effective teacher-student interactions that educational psychologists have developed and tested over the last 50 years. Many of these are at the center of the lives of school psychologists who consult with teachers to enhance the learning of all students by adapting learning environments (Elliott, DiPerna, & Shapiro, 2001).

1. ***Teachers communicate clear and high expectations for student learning.***
   - Learning goals and objectives are developed and prioritized according to (district and building) guidelines, selected or approved by teachers, sequenced to facilitate student learning, and organized or grouped into units or lessons.
   - Teachers set high standards for learning and let students know they are expected to meet them. Standards are set so they are both challenging and attainable.
   - All students are expected to attain the level of learning needed to be successful at the next level of education and are provided information about scoring criteria and grades before they start learning.

2. ***Classroom routines are smooth and efficient.***
   - Class starts on time and purposefully. The teacher has assignments or activities ready for students when they arrive.
   - Students are required to bring the materials they need to class each day.
   - Transitions between activities or classes are smooth and rapid.

3. ***Students are carefully oriented to lessons.***
   - Teachers help students get ready to learn by explaining lesson objectives in simple, everyday language and refer to them throughout lessons to maintain focus. Objectives may be posted or handed out to help students keep a sense of direction.
   - Students are challenged to learn, particularly at the start of difficult lessons. Students know in advance what's expected and are ready to learn.
   - The relationship of a current lesson to previous study is described. Students are reminded of key concepts or skills previously covered, thus connections are made between new material and students' prior knowledge. Students are encouraged to personalize learning by using information from their particular cultural backgrounds and lives outside of school to make connections with material they are studying in school.

4. ***Instruction is clear and developmentally appropriate.***
   - Lesson activities are reviewed; clear written and verbal directions are given; key points and instructions are repeated; and student understanding is checked. In effect, an advanced organizer is used at the outset of each lesson.
   - Presentations, such as lectures or demonstrations, are designed to communicate clearly to students; digressions are avoided.
   - Students have plenty of opportunity for guided and independent practice with new concepts and skills.
   - To check understanding, teachers ask clear questions and wait to make sure all students have a chance to respond. To ensure a high rate of student success, teachers select problems and other academic tasks that are well matched to lesson content and students' developmental levels. Seat work assignments also provide variety and challenge and opportunities for a teacher to monitor students' progress.

5. ***Instructional groups are based on instructional needs of students.***
   - When introducing new concepts and skills, teacher-led, whole-group instruction is most effective.
   - To maximize student learning, smaller groups are formed within the classroom as needed. Students are placed according to individual achievement levels based on subject matter assessments.
   - As achievement levels change, teachers review and adjust groups.

6. ***Learning progress is monitored frequently.***
   - Teachers frequently monitor student learning, both formally and informally.
   - Classroom assessments of student performance are aligned with learning objectives.
   - Teachers know and use sound test techniques to prepare valid, reliable assessment instruments.

- Routine assessment procedures simplify checking student progress. Students get results and constructive feedback quickly; reports to students are simple and clear; reports help students to understand and correct errors; and reports are tied to learning objectives.
- Teachers use assessment results not only to evaluate students but also for instructional diagnosis and to find out if their teaching methods are working.

7. *Review and reteach.*
   - New material is introduced as quickly as possible at the beginning of the year or course, with a minimum review or reteaching of previous content. Key prerequisite concepts and skills are reviewed thoroughly but quickly.
   - Teachers reteach priority lesson content until students demonstrate competence. Regular, focused reviews of key concepts and skills are used throughout the year to check on and strengthen student retention.
   - Computer software and peer tutors are often used effectively to facilitate meaningful and fun review sessions.

8. *Learning time must be increased.*
   - Teachers follow a system of priorities for using class time, allocating time for each subject or lesson. They use class time for learning and spend very little time on nonlearning activities after the first few days of class.
   - Teachers set and maintain a brisk pace for instruction that remains consistent with thorough learning. New objectives are introduced relatively quickly; clear start-and-stop cues help pace lessons according to specific time targets.
   - Students are provided frequent opportunities to respond during class presentations. Use of wait time by teachers after asking a question is important to encourage as many students as possible to think about an answer and to generate an answer.
   - Homework that students can complete successfully is assigned. It is typically in small increments and provides additional practice of content covered in class; work is checked and students are given prompt feedback. Homework extends the amount of learning time available.

9. *Personal interactions between teachers and students are positive.*
   - Teachers show students they care about them by paying attention to students' interests, problems, and accomplishments in social interactions both in and out of the classroom.
   - Students are allowed and encouraged to develop a sense of responsibility and self-reliance. Older students in particular are given opportunities to take responsibility for school-related matters and to participate in making decisions about important school issues.

10. *Incentives and rewards are used to promote excellence.*
   - Excellence is defined by objective standards and not by peer comparison. Systems are set up in the classroom for frequent and consistent rewards to students for academic achievement and excellent behavior. Rewards are appropriate to the developmental level of students.
   - Rewards are related to specific student achievements. Some rewards may be presented publicly, some should be immediately presented, while others are delayed to teach persistence. As students develop they are encouraged to set goals, evaluate their work, and to reward themselves.
   - Parents are told about their children's successes and are encouraged to help students keep working toward excellence.

RECOMMENDATIONS FOR SCHOOL PSYCHOLOGISTS TO GUIDE UTILIZATION OF EDUCATIONAL PSYCHOLOGY

School psychologists who engage with educational psychology to guide their pragmatic work and theorizing about schools and schooling practice will have a conceptual basis for describing their work and approach, and for considering probable, possible and preferred actions. As we have tried to illustrate in this chapter, educational psychologists interested in learning and instruction have provided a rich source of theories, methods, and principles to guide a significant portion of school psychologists' practices. Specifically, this knowledge from educational psychology enables school psychologists to better:

1. Consider the meanings of learning in an era of transition to the Knowledge Age, and the associated implications this has for instruction and assessment;

2. Understand that situation and social participation impact significantly on what "learning" means and can come to mean, and that learning and its process, quality, and outcomes are affected by individual development and diversity, cognition, metacognition, opportunity, motivation, and teaching;

3. Assess and describe the cognitive, metacognitive, social, cultural, and personal development of a child and bring this to bear (a) when accounting for his/her development as a strategic learner in current and past achievements, and how these achievements originated, and (b) in suggesting how to build within macro-educational environments the specific contexts within which the child is likely to flourish and grow—and to specify outcomes that will provide evidence of the child's growth;

4. Construct clear understandings of pedagogy and knowledge of how such understandings influence their views of what students and teachers come to learn, know and are skilled at doing;

5. Collaborate with teachers and parents in establishing learning environments conducive to a child's success as a learner;

6. Recognize and explain behavior within a theoretical framework that considers learning, instruction, assessment and related issues that impact on their interaction, and to connect outcomes and the psychology of educational events;

7. Use research-driven theory about learning and instruction when developing comprehensive assessment plans and methods for a child and to assist teachers and parents with accommodations for the child in relation to macro-environments; and

8. Conceptualize, describe, and measure social and academic performances of learners in varying learning environments.

Thus, educational psychology has much to offer school psychologists, ranging from theoretical models of learning and instruction to recommended practices for teaching and evaluating children's social and academic achievements. This assertion echoes a strong statement by editors of the *Handbook in Educational Psychology* that its content was intended to assist significant participants in the conduct and progression of education (such as school psychologists) "to advance their . . . engagements in education by enlarging and updating their work with state-of-the-art facts and properly validated scientific interpretations" (Winne & Alexander, 2006, p. xi). Additionally, educational psychology has much to gain for its own positive development if this chapter promotes dialogue through which school psychologists organize their practice to inform further research, theory building and productive interchange with educational psychology. This two-way street of mutual interchange across two important fields of psychology is important in adjusting to changing times affecting both fields. Where once it may have seemed good professional action to inform educational practice, including school psychology, with scientifically based research, there is now explicit demand to do so. The community of practice in education is faced with a significant contextual elaboration with reauthorization of the Elementary and Secondary Education Act (No Child Left Behind) and related press to employ evidence-based practice in schools (Shavelson and Towne, 2002). Our response has been mindful of this context and of opportunities to share the tools and language of our community of practice.

REFERENCES

Ackerman, P. L., & Lohman, D. F. (2006). Individual differences in cognitive function. In P. A. Alexander, & P. H. Winne (Eds.), *Handbook of educational pyschology* (2nd ed., pp. 139–162). Mahwah, NJ: Lawrence Erlbaum Associates.

Alexander, P. A., & Murphy, P. K. (1999). Learner profiles: Valuing individual differences within classroom communities. In P. L. Ackerman, P. C. Kyllonen, & R. D. Roberts (Eds.), *Learning and individual differences: Processes, traits and content determinants* (pp. 413–431). Washington, DC: American Psychological Association.

Alexander, P. A., & Winne, P. H. (Eds.). (2006). *Handbook of Educational Psychology* (2nd ed., pp. xi–xii). Mahwah, NJ: Lawrence Erlbaum Associates.

Bartlett, B. J., Barton, B., & Turner, A. (1989). *Knowing what and knowing how*. Melbourne: Nelson Educational.

Bereiter, C., & Bird, M. (1985). Use of thinking aloud in identification and teaching of reading comprehension strategies. *Cognition and Instruction*, *2*(2), 131–156.

Bereiter, C., & Englemann, S. (1966). *Teaching disadvantaged children in the preschool.* Englewood Cliffs, NJ: Prentice-Hall.

Bereiter, C., and Scardamalia, M. (2006). Education for the Knowledge Age: Design-centered models of teaching and instruction. In P. A. Alexander, & P. H. Winne (Eds.), *Handbook of educational psychology* (2nd ed., pp. 695–714). Mahwah, NJ: Lawrence Erlbaum Associates.

Berliner, D. C. (2002). Educational research: The hardest science of all. *Educational Researcher, 31*(8), 18–20.

Berliner, D. C. (2006). Educational psychology: Searching for essence throughout a century of influence. In P. A. Alexander & P. H. Winne (Eds.), *Handbook of educational psychology* (2nd ed., pp. 3–28). Mahwah, NJ: Lawrence Erlbaum Associates.

Berliner, D. C., & Calfee, R. C. (Eds.). (1996). *Handbook of educational psychology.* NY: Macmillan.

Binet, A., & Simon, T. (1980). *The development of intelligence in children.* Nashville, Tennessee: Williams Printing Company, 1980 [c1916] Edition.

Bloom, B. (1981). *All our children learning.* New York: McGraw-Hill.

Bloom, B. (Ed.). (1956). *Taxonomy of educational objectives. Handbook 1: Cognitive domain.* New York: McKay.

Bloom, B., Madaus, G., & Hastings, J. T. (1981). *Evaluation to improve learning.* New York: McGraw-Hill.

Bransford, J., Stevens, R., Schwartz, D., Meltzoff, A., Pea, R., Roschelle, J., et al. (2006). Learning theories and education: Toward a decade of synergy. In P. A. Alexander, & P. H. Winne (Eds.), *Handbook of educational psychology* (2nd ed., pp. 209–244). Mahwah, NJ: Lawrence Erlbaum Associates.

Carnine, D. (1991). Curricular interventions for teaching higher order thinking to all students: Introduction to the special series. *Journal of Learning Disabilities, 24*, 261–269.

Carroll, J. B. (1993). *Human cognitive abilities: A survey of factor-analytic studies.* New York: Cambridge University Press.

Chen, Z., & Klahr, D. (1999). All other things being equal: Acquisition and transfer of the control of variables strategy. *Child Development, 70*(5), 1098–1120.

Drucker, P. F. (1994). *The age of social transformation.* Atlantic Monthly, 53–80.

Elliott, S. N., DiPerna, J. C., & Shapiro, E. S. (2001). *AIMS: The Academic intervention monitoring system.* San Antonio: The Psychological Corporation.

Elliott, S. N., Kratochwill, T. R., Littlefield-Cook, J., & Travers, J. (2000). *Educational psychology: Effective teaching and learning interactions* (3rd ed.). Boston, MA: McGraw-Hill.

Gagne, R., & Briggs, L. (1979). *Principles of instructional design.* New York: Holt, Rinehart & Winston.

Gagne, R., Briggs, L., & Wager, W. (1988). *Principles of instructional design* (3rd ed.). New York: Holt, Rinehart & Winston.

Gagne, R., & Driscoll, M. (1988). *Essentials of learning for instruction* (2nd ed.). Englewood Cliffs, NJ: Prentice-Hall.

Gettinger, M. (1990). Best practices in increasing academic learning time. In A. Thomas & J. Grimes (Eds.), *Best practices in school psychology II* (pp. 393–405). Washington, DC: National Association of School Psychologists.

Graham, S., & Harris, K. R. (2000). The role of self-regulation and transcription skills in writing and writing development. *Educational Psychologist, 35,* 3–12.

Greeno, J. G., Collins, A., & Resnick, L. (1996). Cognition and learning. In R. Calfee & D. C. Berliner (Eds.), *Handbook of educational psychology* (pp. 15–46). NY: Macmillan.

Greeno, J. G., Pearson, P. D., & Schoenfeld, A. H. (1996). *Implications for NAEP of research on learning and cognition.* Report of a study commissioned by the National Academy of Education Panel on the NAEP Trial State Assessment, conducted by the Institute for Research on Learning. Stanford, CA: National Academy of Education.

Guskey, T. (1986). Bloom's mastery learning: A legacy of effectiveness. *Educational Horizons,* (Winter): pp. 80–86.

Harris, K. R., & Graham, S. (1992). Self-regulated strategy development: A part of the writing process. In M. Pressley, K. R. Harris, & J. T. Guthrie (Eds.), *Promoting academic competence and literacy in school* (pp. 277–309). NY: Academic Press.

Hattie, J., & Timperley, H. (2007). The power of feedback. *Review of Educational Research, 77* (1), 81–112.

Kalat, J. W. (2005). *Introduction to Psychology* (6th ed.). Belmont, CA: Wadsworth.

Kalat, J. W., & Wurm, T. (1999). Implications of recent research in biological psychology for school psychology. In Reynolds, C. R. & Gutkin, T. B. (Eds.), *The handbook of school psychology* (3rd ed., pp. 271–290). NY: John Wiley & Sons.

Kim, E., & Kellough, R. (1991). *A resource guide for secondary school teaching.* New York: Macmillan.

Kranzler, J. H. (1999). Current contributions of the psychology of individual differences to school psychology. In Reynolds, C.R., & Gutkin, T. B. (Eds.), *The handbook of school psychology* (3rd ed., pp. 223–246). NY: John Wiley & Sons.

Lave, J., & Wenger, E. (1991). *Situated learning: Legitimate peripheral participation.* New York: Cambridge University Press.

Lorch, R. F. Jr., & van den Broek, R. (1997). Understanding reading comprehension: Current and future contributions of cognitive science. *Contemporary Educational Psychology, 22,* 213–246.

Markle, S. (1990). *Designs for instructional designers* (2nd ed.). Champaign, IL: Stipes.

Mayer, R. E. (2001). Releasing the assault on science: The case for evidence-based reasoning in educational research. *Educational Researcher, 30*(7), 29–30.

McConaughy, S. H., & Achenbach, T. M. (1999). Contributions of developmental psychopathology to school psychology. In C. R. Reynolds & T. B. Gutkin (Eds.), *Handbook of school psychology* (3rd ed., pp. 247–270). New York: Wiley.

Meyer, B. J. F., Young, C. J., & Bartlett, B. J. (1989). *Memory improved: Reading and memory enhancement across the life span through strategic text structures.* Hillsdale, NJ: Lawrence Erlbaum Associates.

Murphy, P. K., & Mason, L. (2006). Changing knowledge and beliefs. In P. A. Alexander & P. H. Winne (Eds.), *Handbook of educational psychology* (2nd ed., pp. 305–326). Mahwah, NJ: Lawrence Erlbaum Associates.

National Research Council (1999). *Being fluent with information technology.* Washington DC: National Academies Press.

National Research Council (2001). *Knowing what students know: The science and design of educational assessment.* Washington DC: National Academies Press.

National Research Council (2002). *Learning and understanding: Improving advanced study of mathematics and science in US high schools.* Washington DC: National Academies Press.

National Research Council (2005). *How students learn: History, math and science in the classroom.* Washington DC: National Academies Press.

Nelson, R. C. (1996). *Memory-based recognition for 3-D objects.* Proceedings, ARPA Image Understanding Workshop, Palm Springs, CA, Feb 1996, pp. 1305–1310.

Palinsar, A. S. (2003). Ann Brown: Advancing a theoretical model of learning and instruction. In B. Zimmermann & D. Schunk (Eds.), *Educational psychology: A century of progress* (pp. 459–476). Mahwah, NJ: Lawrence Erlbaum Associates.

Pellegrino, J. W., Chudowsky, N., & Glaser, R. (2001). *Knowing what students know: The science and design of educational assessment.* Washington DC: National Academies Press.

Piaget, J. (1954). *The construction of reality in the child.* New York: Basic.

Pressley, M., & Harris, K. R. (2006). Cognitive strategies instruction: From basic research to classroom instruction. In P. A. Alexander & P. H. Winne (Eds.), *Handbook of educational psychology* (2nd ed., pp. 265–286). Mahwah, NJ: Lawrence Erlbaum Associates.

Pressley, M., Johnson, C. J., Symons, S., McGoldrick, J. A., & Kurita, J. A. (1989). Strategies that improve memory and comprehension of what is read. *Elementary School Journal, 90,* 3–32.

Pressley, M., & Roehrig, A. (2003). Educational psychology in the modern era: 1960 to the present. In B. Zimmermann & D. Schunk (Eds.), *Educational psychology: A century of progress* (pp. 333–366). Mahwah, NJ: Lawrence Erlbaum Associates.

Reynolds, C. R., & Gutkin, T. B. (Eds.) (1999). *The handbook of school psychology* (3rd ed.) NY: John Wiley & Sons.

Schwab, J. J. (1973). The Practical 3: Translation into curriculum. *School Review, 81,* 501–522.

Shavelson, R. J., & Towne, L. (Eds.) (2002). Scientific research in education. National Research Council, Committee on scientific principles for education research. Division of Behavioral and Social Sciences and Education. Washington DC: National Academy Press.

Sinatra, G. M., & Pintrich, P. R. (2003). The role of intentional conceptual change learning. In G. M. Sinatra & P. R. Pintrich. (Eds.), *Intentional conceptual change,* (pp. 1–18). Mahwah, NJ: Lawrence Erlbaum Associates.

Skinner, B. F. (1938). *The behavior of organisms.* NY: Appleton-Century-Crofts.

Tharinger, D. J., & Lambert, N. M. (1999). The application of developmental psychology to school psychology practice: Informing assessment, intervention, and prevention efforts. In C. R. Reynolds & T. B. Gutkin (Eds.), *Handbook of school psychology* (3rd ed., pp. 137–166). New York: Wiley.

Thorndike, E. L. (1931). *Human Learning,* New York, NY: The Century Company.

Tiemann, P., & Markle, S. (1990). *Analyzing instructional content: A guide to instruction and evaluation.* Champaign, IL: Stipes.

Vosniadou, S. (1999). Capturing and modelling the process of conceptual change. *Learning and Instruction, 4,* 45–69.

Wenger, E. (1998). *Communities of Practice.* Cambridge: Cambridge University Press.

Wertsch, J. V. (1998). *Mind as action.* NY: Oxford University Press.

Winne, P. H., & Alexander, P. A. (2006). Foreword. In P. A. Alexander, & P. H. Winne (Eds.), *Handbook of educational psychology* (2nd ed., pp. xi–xii). Mahwah, NJ: Lawrence Erlbaum Associates.

Wittrock, M. C. (1990). Generating processes of comprehension. *Educational Psychologist, 24*(4), 345–376.

Wittrock, M. C. (1991). Generative teaching of comprehension. *Elementary School Journal, 92,* 167–82.

Zimmerman, B.J., & Schunk, D.H. (Eds.) (2003). *Educational psychology: A century of contributions.* Mahwah, NJ: Lawrence Erlbaum Associates.

CHAPTER 5

CONTRIBUTIONS OF APPLIED BEHAVIOR ANALYSIS

EDWARD J. DALY III
University of Nebraska–Lincoln
BRIAN K. MARTENS
Syracuse University
CHRISTOPHER H. SKINNER
University of Tennessee
GEORGE H. NOELL
Louisiana State University

INTRODUCTION

As early as 1968, Sidney W. Bijou (1970) was able to make a unique offer to school psychologists in an invited address to the Division of School Psychologists of the American Psychological Association. In his address, he said,

> A small but rapidly growing group of psychologists can now offer educators (1) a set of concepts and principles derived entirely from the experimental analysis of behavior, (2) a methodology for the practical application of these concepts and principles, (3) a research method that deals with changes in individual behavior, and (4) a philosophy of science that says: "Look carefully to the relationships between observable environmental and behavioral events and their changes." (p. 70)

He was able to make this offer because the field of behavior analysis was already standing on the shoulders of some 40 years of experimental work for which sophisticated forms of experimental design (Sidman, 1960) and analysis (Bijou, Peterson, & Ault, 1968) had already been worked out. Considerable progress in the field has been made even since that time. The previous version of this chapter (Martens, Witt, Daly, & Vollmer, 1999) traces the history of this development in some detail, and need not be repeated here. In that chapter, Martens et al. defined the field in the following way: "Behavior analysis refers

to a set of strategies for selecting, implementing, and evaluating intervention programs based on the lawful principles of behavior" (p. 638). The purpose of this chapter is to present an updated and contemporary description of behavior analysis as it applies to educational settings. To this end, the chapter reviews behavior analytic research on the functional analysis and assessment of behavior, influencing students' choices in educational settings, academic responding, and treatment implementation.

FUNCTIONAL ANALYSIS AND ASSESSMENT

Stimulus Functions in the Natural Environment

Humans and nonhumans are able to physically sense many aspects of their environment, including both external (e.g., heat, sound) and internal (e.g., pressure, pain) stimuli. Based on experience, we learn which of these stimuli are important for our physical or emotional well-being and under what circumstances. When certain stimuli acquire the capacity to affect behavior, they are said to have a *stimulus function* (Pierce & Epling, 1995). Stimuli that follow behavior and increase its occurrence have a *reinforcement function*. Stimuli that are present before or during behavior and reliably predict when it will be reinforced have a *discriminative function*.

All reinforcing stimuli have a similar effect on behavior by making it more frequent, stereotyped, and efficient (Reynolds, 1975). Recognizing this fact, Skinner (1987) compared natural selection at a species level to operant selection at a behavioral level. Just as certain genetic variations of species are selected because of their survival value, certain variations of behavior are selected because of their reinforcement value. From this perspective, behaviors that occur frequently do so because they are functional (i.e., lead to reinforcement) in the situations in which they occur. Had these behaviors not led to reinforcement in the past (i.e., were extinguished), they would have likely been replaced with behaviors that did.

Despite their common function, reinforcing stimuli are idiosyncratic based on personal preferences for various items and activities (e.g., Berkowitz & Martens, 2001; Fisher et al., 1992) and even stimulus dimensions (e.g., quality, rate, and delay; Neef, Shade, & Miller, 1994). Moreover, reinforcing stimuli are conditional, meaning that the reinforcement of behavior always occurs in a broader context of other stimuli, some of which are correlated with reinforcer availability (discriminative function) and some of which are correlated with reinforcer effectiveness (establishing function) (Michael, 1993). The above discussion is important in efforts to identify and ultimately alter the reinforcing function of severe problem behavior for several reasons. First, although problem behavior may initially result from a variety of causes (e.g., physical illness, psychiatric disorder; Sturmey 1995), it may persist or even be strengthened by reinforcing consequences. Reinforcement functions, therefore, are sufficient but not necessary to cause or increase problem behavior and may also be sufficient but not necessary to reduce its occurrence over time. Second, because reinforcing stimuli and their dimensions vary across individuals and across situations within individuals, identifying reinforcement functions in the natural environment is a challenging task.

Development of Standard Functional Analysis Test Conditions
Test Conditions in Clinical and Institutional Settings

Early research by Lovaas and his colleagues (e.g., Lovaas & Simmons, 1969) and Carr and his colleagues (e.g., Carr, Newsom, & Binkoff, 1976) demonstrated that severe problem behavior in children was sensitive to the presentation of social-positive reinforcement in the form of attention as well as social-negative reinforcement via the removal of demands (Hanley, Iwata, & McCord, 2003). As such, these researchers showed that even high-rate problem behaviors like self-injury could be reduced and in some cases eliminated by altering their "function" or effect on the environment the child intended them to have. Drawing on these findings, Iwata, Dorsey, Slifer, Bauman, and Richman (1982/1994) first described a set of procedures for conducting a *functional analysis of behavior*. These procedures involved exposing children to a series of brief (e.g., 5 or 10 minutes) test and control conditions in a multielement format until clear differences in responding emerged. Each test condition was associated with its own establishing operation to increase the potency of the reinforcer being delivered (e.g., deprivation) and discriminative stimuli to signal which condition was in effect (e.g., a different therapist or room). More importantly, each test condition was designed to mimic and intensify a different reinforcement contingency potentially maintaining problem behavior in the natural environment. Depending on the condition, each occurrence of problem behavior was reinforced with attention, tangible items, or food as a test of social-positive reinforcement, with 30 seconds of escape from task demands as a test of social-negative reinforcement, or with the opportunity to continue engaging in behavior in the absence of social interaction as a test of automatic reinforcement (Iwata et al., 1982/1994). The test condition associated with the type of reinforcement the child had previously experienced and/or preferred for problem behavior in other settings was expected to produce higher rates of problem behavior during the functional analysis.

In the years following the study by Iwata et al. (1982/1994), functional analysis test conditions have become "the hallmark of behavioral assessment" in treating severe problem behavior (Hanley et al., 2003). In fact, Hanley et al. identified 277 published articles reporting a functional analysis of behavior through the year 2000. Of these studies, 70% involved children as participants, 91% involved individuals with developmental disabilities, and 65% were conducted in hospital, institution, or clinic settings. Approximately a third (31.4%) of the functional analyses reported in the literature were conducted in school settings. Of the 536 different individual data sets reported across the studies, over 95% found differentiated results or clear increases in problem behavior during one of the test conditions evaluated. In terms of function, 34.2% of problem behaviors were identified as being maintained by social-negative reinforcement, 35.4% of behaviors were maintained by social-positive reinforcement, and 15.8% were maintained by automatic reinforcement.

Test Conditions in School Settings

As suggested above, numerous functional analyses have been conducted in schools, and researchers have developed test conditions unique to this setting (Broussard & Northup, 1995, 1997; Northup et al., 1995). For example, Broussard and Northup (1997) evaluated teacher attention, peer attention, and escape as potential reinforcers for disruptive classroom behavior by four elementary-aged students. During the teacher attention condition, students were given easy work to complete and the teacher reminded the student to work quietly and stay seated contingent on disruptive behavior. Students were also given easy work to complete during the peer attention condition, but a student confederate was instructed to pay attention to the target student contingent on disruptive behavior. During the escape condition, students were given difficult work to complete and were placed in 30 second time-out contingent on disruptive behavior. Higher levels of disruptive classroom behavior were observed during the peer attention condition for all four students. Allowing students to earn time with a peer contingent on the absence of disruptive behavior (i.e., a differential reinforcement of other behavior or DRO procedure) reduced it to near zero levels.

Selecting Treatments Based on Functional Analysis Outcomes

Once the reinforcement contingency maintaining problem behavior has been identified through a functional analysis, it can be eliminated, reversed, or weakened through intervention (Martens et al., 1999). Extinction and functional communication training have been shown to be effective ways of eliminating reinforcement for problem behavior and therefore reducing its occurrence (Iwata et al., 1994; Wacker et al., 1990). Reversing the contingency maintaining problem behavior is typically accomplished through differential reinforcement of alternative (DRA), differential negative reinforcement of alternative (DNRA),

or differential reinforcement of other (DRO) behavior procedures (e.g., Broussard & Northup, 1997; Marcus & Vollmer, 1996). Reinforcement contingent on problem behavior can be weakened by providing the same reinforcer on a rich fixed-time schedule independent of behavior (i.e., noncontingent reinforcement) (e.g., Vollmer, Iwata, Zarcone, Smith, & Mazaleski, 1993) or by punishing occurrences of the behavior through procedures such as time-out or response cost.

Limitations of Functional Analysis Procedures

Although functional analysis has become a common assessment tool in a variety of settings, exactly how differentiated results should be interpreted remains somewhat unclear. When functional analyses are conducted by novel adults, in novel settings, or with novel tasks, the extent to which results are representative of reinforcement effects in the child's natural environment may be questionable (Hanley et al., 2003). On the one hand, increases that are observed in problem behavior may result from previous learning under similar conditions (i.e., stimulus generalization). This being the case, incorporating stimuli from the child's natural environment into functional analysis test conditions (e.g., classroom peers, teachers, similar work assignments) would likely increase the generalizability of findings (Hanley et al., 2003; Sasso et al., 1992). On the other hand, prolonged exposure to new contingencies of reinforcement during a functional analysis may increase problem behavior as a result of new learning (i.e., stimulus discrimination), preference for novel items used as reinforcers, or both.

Functional Behavior Assessment

The prevalence of functional analyses for self-injurious and aggressive behavior drew attention to the potential benefits of assessing the conditions surrounding *all* problem behavior. By extension, a variety of methods for conducting a *functional behavior assessment (FBA)* have been reported in the literature. FBA refers to a collection of procedures for describing antecedent-behavior-consequence relations in the natural environment in the absence of experimental manipulation (i.e., analysis) (Witt, Daly, & Noell, 2000). FBA makes use of both indirect and direct behavioral assessment methods in order to generate hypotheses about potential maintaining variables for problem behavior (Miltenberger, 2004). Indirect assessment methods used during an FBA typically include some version of a problem identification and analysis interview (Erchul & Martens, 2002), as well as informant report questionnaires like the Motivation Assessment Scale (Durand & Crimmins, 1988). Direct assessment methods include scatterplot observations relating behavior to antecedent conditions such as time of day or setting (Touchette, MacDonald, & Langer, 1985), narrative A-B-C recordings (Bijou, Peterson, & Ault, 1968), or sequential recordings of behavior and its consequences (e.g., Lalli, Browder, Mace, & Brown, 1993).

Federal Mandates and Best Practices in FBA

The Individuals with Disabilities Education Act Amendments of 1997 (IDEA '97) stipulated that school professionals conduct an FBA when students receiving special education services were (a) removed from school for over 10 days in a school year, (b) removed to an interim alternative educational setting for up to 45 calendar days due to weapons or drug charges, or (c) granted an alternative placement by a hearing officer as a result of engaging in behavior deemed dangerous to themselves or others (Drasgow & Yell, 2001). The 2004 reauthorization of IDEA in large part mirrored IDEA '97 regarding when an FBA was to be conducted, but made two additional stipulations. First, IDEA 2004 mandated that an FBA be conducted upon determining that a student's problem behavior was a manifestation of his or her disability. Second, the law required that an FBA be conducted when a student was removed to an interim setting for 45 school days rather than 45 calendar days as specified in IDEA '97.

There is currently a lack of consensus in the published literature regarding the necessary components of an FBA (Sterling-Turner, Robinson, & Wilczynski, 2001). In addition, there are few data available identifying particular procedures within an FBA that have been shown to accurately identify the functions of behavior (e.g., Lerman & Iwata, 1993; Mace & Lalli, 1991) or to maximize treatment outcomes (e.g., consultee verbal report versus systematic observation of behavior-consequence relations). In the absence of more extensive treatment validity data, a prototypical FBA sequence that is believed to reflect "best practices" by incorporating multiple data sources involves: (a) an operational definition of a target behavior; (b) indirect assessment methods including record reviews, teacher or student

interviews, and/or behavior rating scales; (c) direct observation of antecedents (e.g., events, times, situations) that occasion the occurrence and nonoccurrence of problem behavior; (d) direct observation of consequences for problem behavior; and (e) generation of hypotheses regarding potential maintaining variables (e.g., Drasgow & Yell, 2001; Sterling-Turner, Robinson, & Wilczynski 2001; Witt et al. 2000).

Collecting and Interpreting Observational Data During an FBA

As noted above, best practices in functional behavior assessment involve systematic observations of behavior and its consequences using event or interval recording (Eckert, Martens, & DiGennaro, 2005). Based on these data, consequences that reliably follow occurrences of problem behavior are viewed as potential reinforcers, whereas consequences that do not are ruled out. The ability of sequential observations of behavior and its consequences to identify functional reinforcers has been evaluated in previous research with mixed results (e.g., Mace & Lalli, 1991; Sasso et al., 1992).

Lerman and Iwata (1993) observed six adults with profound mental retardation for a total of 6 or 12 hours, and recorded sequences of self-injurious behavior (SIB) and staff responses using 10 second partial-interval recording. The proportion of each staff response that followed SIB as well as the proportion of SIB followed by each staff response were then computed and graphed separately across hours. Comparing these data to the results of standard functional analysis test conditions (Iwata et al., 1982/1994) revealed that the descriptive analyses often did not differentiate between attention or escape functions, whereas the functional analyses did. That is, conditional probabilities of staff responses given the occurrence of SIB tended to identify more potential reinforcers than were confirmed through experimental analyses. Similar results were obtained by Mace and Lalli (1991) who recorded events that were antecedent and subsequent to bizarre speech by an adult male with moderate mental retardation. Conditional probabilities of various staff responses given bizarre speech suggested both attention and escape functions. Subsequent experimental analyses, however, confirmed only the attention function.

Consistent results between descriptive and experimental analyses were obtained by Lalli et al. (1993) as well as Sasso et al. (1992) for children with profound mental retardation and autism, respectively, in school settings. However, these studies contained unique features that may have contributed to the congruent findings. For example, Lalli et al. used three additional assessment methods (i.e., teacher interview, scatterplot, narrative A-B-C recordings) prior to conducting the systematic observations in order to identify classroom activities associated with high rates of the target behaviors. In Sasso et al. (1992), functional analysis test conditions were designed to resemble classroom activities, and observations in the classroom were conducted during activities resembling the test conditions.

These findings suggest that systematic observations of problem behavior and its consequences under naturalistic conditions are limited in their ability to identify potential reinforcers. First, these data are descriptive in nature, whereas functional relations can only be identified with confidence through manipulation under controlled conditions (Sasso et al., 1992). Second, events in the natural environment may be observed to follow behavior infrequently (i.e., have a low conditional probability), yet still function as reinforcers. Conversely, consequences may have high conditional probabilities given the occurrence of behavior, but may not actually be contingent on behavior or function as reinforcers (Lerman & Iwata, 1993). Along these lines, Vollmer, Borrero, Wright, Camp, and Lalli (2001) distinguished between three classes of consequences, those that are *contiguous* with behavior, those that are *contingent* on behavior, and those that are *dependent* on behavior. Dependent consequences follow every instance of behavior but never occur in its absence, thereby exhibiting a perfect contingency. Contingent consequences occur more often following behavior than in its absence (i.e., show a positive contingency), whereas contiguous consequences may occur independent of behavior or favor its absence. Vollmer et al. suggested that these distinctions may be useful when conducting functional behavior assessments in that consequences may be contingent on behavior in varying degrees and still produce reinforcement effects.

Eckert et al. (2005) reported a procedure for displaying and interpreting sequential observation data that draws on mathematical definitions of contingency from the experimental operant literature. As described by Schwartz (1989), a contingent relation between behavior and a consequence can be defined mathematically from two conditional probabilities: (a) the probability of a consequence occurring given that behavior occurred (p[event/behavior]), and (b) the probability of a consequence occurring given that behavior did not occur (p[event/no behavior]). The first probability indicates the proportion of behavioral occurrences (or intervals of occurrence) that were followed by the consequence, and can be taken as an approximation of the reinforcement schedule for that behavior (e.g., 20% of occurrences = variable ratio 5 schedule). The second probability indicates the proportion of behavioral nonoccurrences that were followed by the same consequence, and represents the schedule of reinforcement for behavior other than the target (i.e., a DRO schedule).

When plotted together in coordinate space (the operant contingency space), these two conditional probabilities show whether a consequence is more likely to occur following behavior or its absence, thereby indicating degree of *contingency*. Results of the functional behavior assessment conducted by Eckert et al. (2005) showed that peer attention followed the off-task behavior of a 7-year-old boy on a rich schedule in both reading (.55) and math (.70) but rarely followed on-task behavior (.10 and .02, respectively). Peer attention, therefore, was shown to be contingent on off-task behavior and was hypothesized to be a potential reinforcer. Results of a brief experimental analysis in which peer and teacher attention were evaluated as treatments when provided for on-task behavior (i.e., DRA procedures) showed peer DRA to be the more effective alternative.

Limitations of FBA Procedures

Two primary limitations with school-based FBA procedures are that typical practices often fall woefully short of best practices and the inability of descriptive FBA procedures to identify functional reinforcers with accuracy. With respect to the first issue, Drasgow and Yell (2001) reviewed 14 due process hearings held at the state level between the time when IDEA '97 was enacted and August 2000. In these cases, parents contested the school districts' implementation of a mandated FBA. In 13 of the 14 cases, the hearing officer deemed the districts' implementation inadequate and ruled in favor of the parents. In 11 cases, the districts failed to conduct an FBA altogether, whereas in three cases the hearing officer determined that an inadequate FBA was conducted. These inadequate FBAs consisted of an interview with the student, a single, one-hour observation, and completion of a handwritten, fill-in-the-blank questionnaire. With respect to the second issue, data reviewed above suggest that FBA procedures tend to overidentify potential sources of reinforcement and perhaps should be followed up by a functional analysis of behavior as discussed earlier.

INFLUENCING STUDENTS' CHOICES IN EDUCATIONAL SETTINGS

From the Operant Chamber to the Classroom

In his operant chambers, B. F. Skinner (see Ferster & Skinner, 1957) investigated and established functional relationships between an organism's behavior (e.g., a bird pecking a key, a rat pressing a bar) and environmental consequences (e.g., delivery of food pellets). Within the experimental arrangement, one might conceptualize the organism's behavior within a choice paradigm. At any moment in time, the bird could choose to peck the key or choose to engage in numerous alternative competing behaviors (e.g., tuck its head under its wing). This line of investigation allowed B.F. Skinner to establish functional relationships between choices in behavior and their reinforcing consequences.

Applications to educational settings quickly become clear when one considers the classroom arrangement as a choice paradigm. For example, a student at his desk who is given an assignment has been placed in a continuous choice environment because at any given moment in time the student could choose to work on the assignment (e.g., like the bird pecking the key) or choose to engage in alternative behaviors like putting his head on his desk. Because few educational procedures will cause learning to occur unless students choose to engage in desired behaviors (e.g., completing assigned tasks), applications of choice research to education are important and relevant to what educators need to accomplish (Skinner, 1998; Skinner, Williams, & Neddenriep, 2004).

Herrnstein's (1961, 1970) basic research on competing schedules of reinforcement showed that merely considering contingencies for undesirable behaviors may not be sufficient when attempting to eliminate those behaviors. Herrnstein (1961) added another key to the chamber (thereby increasing the complexity of the environment) and measured the effects of competing schedules of reinforcement on key pecking.

Using these modified operant chambers Herrnstein found that he could make precise predictions of relative choice behavior (e.g., how often the bird would choose to peck one key relative to the other). His predictions, and later laboratory and applied research, were so precise that the basic principle governing behavior has come to be referred to as the matching *law* (Catania, 1998). Herrnstein showed that the probability of an organism choosing to engage in a specific behavior is functionally and mathematically related to the schedule of reinforcement for that behavior *relative* to the schedule of reinforcement for other behavior.

Returning to the student in the classroom, we can consider two choices: the choice to engage in assigned work and/or the choice to engage in disruptive behavior (e.g., leaving one's seat). Assuming that these two behaviors are incompatible, no physical restraints are used, and that the student can perform both behaviors, the student could choose to engage in either behavior at any given moment in time. Herrnstein's findings suggest that if we want to understand and influence the student's choices, we must consider the relative relationship between the two competing behaviors and their schedules of reinforcement. Thus, if the goal is to increase desired behaviors (e.g., engaging in assigned school work), we must not only consider reinforcement for engaging in assigned work, but also reinforcement for engaging in competing behaviors (e.g., leaving their seat). Similarly, if the goal is to decrease undesirable behaviors, success often may depend upon understanding the contingencies of reinforcement for those behaviors and the contingencies of reinforcement for competing behaviors (Myerson & Hale, 1994).

Variables Influencing Choice

It is beyond the scope of the current chapter to delineate all the mathematical models of choice developed by Herrnstein and others (see Myerson & Hale, 1994, and Billington & Ditommaso, 2003, for summaries). However, the precision provided via Herrnstein's formulas has allowed researchers to use the choice paradigm to identify four variables that can be manipulated to influence students' choices in the classroom (e.g., Martens & Houk, 1989). Three variables are related to contingencies of reinforcement and the final variable is effort required to complete competing behaviors. Each is reviewed in turn.

Characteristics of Contingencies of Reinforcement

The stronger the reinforcement contingencies, the more likely an organism will choose to engage in the contingent behavior (Neef, Mace, & Shade, 1993; Neef, Shade, & Miller, 1994). Three characteristics of reinforcement contingencies affect the likelihood of behavior. First, rate of reinforcement refers to how frequently reinforcement is delivered. If all else is held constant, students are more likely to choose to engage in the behavior that has yielded higher rates of reinforcement (Mace, McCurdy, & Quigley, 1990; Mace, Neef, Shade, & Mauro, 1996; Martens & Houk, 1989; Martens, Lochner, & Kelly, 1992). Second, immediacy of reinforcement refers to the delay between the target behavior and access to reinforcement. The briefer the delay, the more likely the organism will choose to engage in the behavior (Neef et al., 1993). Third, when all other conditions are equal, students are more likely to choose to engage in the behavior associated with higher-quality reinforcement (Neef et al., 1993; Neef, Mace, Shea, & Shade, 1992; Neef et al., 1994).

Response Effort

Response effort has also been shown to influence choice. If an organism has the choice of two competing behaviors with identical reinforcement (quality, rate, immediacy), the organism will be more likely to choose to engage in the behavior that requires less effort. Thus, if given a choice of two assignments with identical reinforcement for each assignment, students are more likely to choose the assignment that requires less effort (Billington & Skinner, 2002; Billington, Skinner, Hutchins, & Malone, 2004; Cates & Skinner, 2000; Cates et al., 1999).

Applying Choice Research to Classrooms

Most research on choice has involved the study of individual organisms. Although behavior takes place at the level of an individual organism, procedures designed to change student behavior are often applied to all students in the classroom. Thus, educators often employ independent group oriented contingencies in which students are given the same assignments and consequences for both desired (e.g., scoring 93% or higher is assigned a grade of "A") and undesired behaviors (fighting results in suspension). While such programs can

be effective and are seen as fair because each student's access to consequences is based solely on his or her own behavior (thus independent from classmates' behavior), in many instances uniform contingencies will not be effective for all students. Research on choice suggests why this is the case and how classroom contingencies can be structured to promote more optimal levels of appropriate student behavior (Skinner, Williams, & Neddenriep, 2004).

Strengthening Reinforcement Contingencies

As noted earlier, many reinforcers used to influence student choice behavior are idiosyncratic. Thus, what is a high-quality reinforcer for Joe may be a low-quality reinforcer or even a punishing stimulus for Sandy (Skinner, Cashwell, & Dunn, 1996). Additionally, within students reinforcer quality is not likely to be stable. For example, an opportunity to drink water (i.e., permission to go to the water fountain) is likely to be more reinforcing to Joe if he is thirsty. Because reinforcer quality is not stable across or within students, educators who want to reinforce desired behavior within their classrooms often find it difficult to identify reinforcers that can be applied to all students across time. A reward may increase the probability of one student engaging in a desired behavior, but may not have the same effect on a classmate's behavior.

Several strategies have been developed to address this concern. One strategy is to identify and deliver idiosyncratic, high-quality reinforcers to each student contingent upon desired behaviors meeting specified criteria. Another strategy is to use exchangeable reinforcers such as tokens and/or points and a pool of reinforcers. When students accumulate enough exchangeable reinforcers, they can then trade them in for desired reinforcers (Kazdin, 2001). While such procedures can work, and functional behavioral assessment procedures may assist with identifying idiosyncratic high quality reinforcers (Skinner et al., 2002), identifying and delivering specific reinforcers for each student is difficult and may require resources such as time and money that are often unavailable (Turco & Elliott, 1990).

Another strategy is to develop a pool of potential reinforcers and when student behavior meets the specified criterion for reinforcement, the reward is randomly selected. Such a procedure may be useful when all students receive access to rewards contingent upon a group-oriented criterion such as a class average (an interdependent group-oriented contingency). It may also be useful in cases in which all students in class receive access to rewards based on the behavior of a single student (a dependent group-oriented contingency). Delivering rewards to all, as opposed to some, students often takes less time and reduces the probability of students accessing rewards by stealing them from other students. When rewards are delivered to the entire class, as opposed to some class members and not others, educators can use activity rewards that may require few resources (e.g., listening to music during independent seat work, field trips, class being held outside). This strategy also overcomes difficulties associated with excluding some students from access to rewards. Finally, when an entire group receives access to rewards, additional social reinforcement may be provided as the group congratulates each other as they share the reward (Cashwell, Skinner, Dunn, & Lewis, 1998; Skinner et al., 2004).

When randomly selected reinforcers are used, it is not necessary that every reward in the pool be a high-quality reinforcer for each student. However, it is important that there be at least a couple of high-quality reinforcers for each student in the pool. To help ensure this occurs, educators can take suggestions from students for reinforcers. When doing so, it may be important to provide a variety of reinforcers, some which can be delivered immediately and some which may have to be delivered on a delayed schedule (Skinner, Cashwell & Dunn, 1996).

When reinforcers are clearly identified (e.g., exchangeable reinforcers), educators may find it easier to measure and control the rate of reinforcement for desired behavior and for competing behaviors. However, in many instances the reinforcement is subtle and not easily controlled. Immediate peer attention often serves to reinforce undesired disruptive behaviors. For example, consider the student who makes inappropriate verbal remarks that occasion immediate laughter from peers. While educators may often find it difficult to withdraw all attention for inappropriate behaviors (e.g., they often slip up when attempting to implement extinction), it can be even more difficult to control peer attention for inappropriate behaviors (Skinner et al., 2002). Fortunately, matching law research suggests that in order to decrease undesirable behaviors, one need not implement perfect extinction (i.e., withhold all reinforcement for desired behavior). Rather, educators can increase the probability of desired behavior by enhancing the rate of reinforcement for desired behaviors relative to the rate of reinforcement for undesired behavior (Skinner et al., 2004). Additionally, interdependent group contingencies that target peer attention can be applied to further reduce social reinforcement for undesired behaviors. For example, Sulzbacher and Houser (1968) reinforced the entire class contingent upon a decrease in both undesired behavior (i.e., displaying the naughty finger) and classmates responding to this behavior (e.g., tattling or commenting on a classmate who displayed the naughty finger).

In some instances reinforcement for undesired behavior can not be easily identified or controlled and is delivered at a higher rate and more immediately than reinforcement for desired behaviors. In these situations, it is still possible to increase the probability of desired behavior by reinforcing desired behaviors with higher-quality reinforcers (Mace et al., 1996; Neef et al., 1993). Furthermore, if these reinforcers are randomly selected from a menu of available reinforcers, it may not be necessary that all of these reinforcers be high quality for each student (Skinner et al., 2004).

Researchers also have been attempting to gain a better understanding of the variety of stimuli that can serve as a reinforcer. For example, if you enter almost any classroom and observe a teacher providing directions for the class to engage in an independent seatwork assignment (e.g., "Complete math problems 1–20 on page 18 of the workbook"), you are likely to see many students working on the assignment in the absence of any easily identifiable type of reinforcement. Using the matching law, Skinner (2002) found evidence which suggested that each completed problem may serve as a conditioned reinforcer. As students work on assignments, each complete discrete task serves as discriminative stimulus to move on to the next task as a part of an ongoing behavioral chain of behaviors. In some cases, completing the task also serves as a reinforcing stimulus that increases the probability of students choosing to engage in the academic tasks, as opposed to alternative behaviors (Skinner, 2002). Therefore, one way to increase student discrete task completion rates (and consequently the probability that students will choose to engage in assigned tasks) is to intersperse additional briefer discrete tasks among the assigned task (McCurdy, Skinner, Grantham, Watson, & Hindman, 2001; Skinner, 2002). Other procedures that may enhance discrete task completing rates include more rapid pacing during teacher-led recitations and using procedures such as explicit timing to enhance discrete task completion rates (Skinner, 2002).

Response Effort

Each of the above procedures for strengthening reinforcement can be used to address the problems related to response effort. As with reinforcer quality, response effort is likely to vary across and within students (Skinner, 1998). For example, a fluent reader may require little time and effort to complete a reading assignment with enough precision (e.g., 90% of the comprehension questions correct) to obtain a mild reinforcer (e.g., a gold star). However, the dysfluent reader sitting next to the fluent reader may have to expend much more time and effort to complete the same assignment with enough precision to obtain the gold star. If one assumes that the reinforcer is identical quality for each student for the sake of demonstration, choice research suggests that the dysfluent reader is less likely to choose to engage in the assigned reading because the effort required is not worth the quality of reinforcement (i.e., a gold star). Additionally, because the dysfluent reader requires more time to complete the task the rate of reinforcement is decreased. Finally, the dysfluent reader may be less likely to meet the performance criterion (e.g., 90%) for receiving reinforcement. Thus, research on choice suggests that the dysfluent reader is less likely to choose to do the assigned reading task and more likely to choose to engage in behaviors that require less effort and are more likely to be reinforced (Daly, Chafouleas, & Skinner, 2005).

This problem of effort is particularly salient in light of the fact that students who most need to engage in assigned tasks (i.e., those who are behind their classmates with respect to skill development) are (a) less likely to choose to do the assignment than those whose skills are more developed, and (b) more likely to engage in inappropriate behavior. This state of affairs causes a downward spiral as these students fall further and further behind their peers in their skill development. As new, more complex tasks are assigned in the classroom, these students may require even more time and effort to complete the task than their peers, making it even less likely that they will choose to

engage in these tasks for the same reinforcement contingencies, which further retards their skill development (Skinner, Pappas, & Davis, 2005). Matching law research suggests that enhancing the rate, immediacy, and quality of reinforcement for completing the instructional task would increase the probability of these students choosing to engage in the assigned, high-effort task. Nonetheless, many educators have been or are discouraged from reinforcing desired behaviors (e.g., see Kohn, 1999), which may have the unfortunate consequence of creating conditions for the emergence of escape/avoidance behaviors and perpetuating the regrettable downward spiral outlined earlier.

The Future of Choice Research

As researchers and practitioners begin to turn their attention toward procedures that reduce problem behavior by increasing desired behaviors (e.g., behaviors that cause learning), one would expect a resurgence of basic, applied, and application research of student behavior within a choice paradigm. Such research may have a significant impact on student learning and social behaviors by grasping the actual complexity of classrooms by further delineating the relationship between competing schedules of reinforcement and response effort. Additionally, as researchers gain a better understanding of reinforcers and the interaction between reinforcement contingencies and response effort, educators may become more effective at influencing student behavior in productive ways.

ACADEMIC RESPONDING

Public education is a massive enterprise that creates enormous demands for educators who attend to the educational and social needs of millions of students daily. As a result, educators tend to become highly pragmatic. In their pragmatism, they routinely perpetuate the logical fallacy of *affirming the consequent* by assuming that if a student is learning, the presumed principles underlying the teaching practices must be valid. Although logicians may cringe at this line of reasoning, practically speaking there is no harm in faulty deductive logic for students who are learning and growing at the expected pace. When students fail to progress academically and socially, however, educators are forced to scrutinize their teaching more carefully. For these students, the principles that are supposed to lend validity to the teaching practices have obviously broken down. Applied behavior analysis offers a unique, analytic perspective on learning and instruction that can prove useful to school psychologists who are often called upon to help identify what to do with students for whom current teaching routines are not working.

Within a behavior analytic framework, investigating why the student is not learning and what to do about it begins with tracking the trajectory of the student's responding. Student responding is not an end in and of itself, however. Student responding simply tells us what to do next. Englemann, Granzin, and Severson (1979) point out that, "The only valid way to draw conclusions about deficiencies involves first determining the degree to which the learner's performance is controlled by instruction" (p. 362). Nonetheless, student responding serves as the focal point for identifying why instructional practices are or are not effective. This section will provide a behavioral analysis of student academic responding by first tracking responding as it should progress through the curriculum and then describing instructional and/or motivational variables that can be directly manipulated to establish learning in the curriculum. The purpose is to illustrate a functional framework for analysis of and intervention with student responding based on empirically derived concepts.

Stimulus Control and Academic Responding

A behavior analytic paradigm views educators as working to either (a) accelerate the appearance of new, adaptive behavior for which the environment offers no more than a slim chance of shaping the behavior (e.g., reading), or (b) create adaptive repertoires of behavior which would be highly improbable without some direct intervention (e.g., doing differential calculus equations). Curriculum expectations drive what the behavior should be and outline the range of stimuli, demands, and activities to which students should be able to respond effectively and adaptively. Teachers accelerate or create adaptive behavior repertoires by influencing students' choices through the manipulation of instructional, task-related, and motivational variables. As noted in the earlier section, those choices (and hence student behavior) are controlled by consequences. However, new behavior begins to occur in the presence of stimuli that themselves are not consequences. Yet, they still end up exerting a

form of control over behavior. These stimuli are present at the time of the occurrence of behavior and should relate directly to curricular objectives. For example, students might be expected to learn to read a map in a geography lesson. Their responses to questions about direction, elevation, and terrain should occur as a function of what appears on the map as well as the consequences their behavior produces.

The basic learning process by which behavior occurs in the presence of antecedent stimuli is referred to as *stimulus control*. When students read words in a text, it is an indication that their behavior has come under the stimulus control of the configuration of letters, spaces, and punctuation marks. When students answer teacher questions (e.g., "Who was the second President of the United States?"), it is an indication that their responses have come under the stimulus control of critical information in the questions asked. Students write answers to math problems because the numbers and signs occasion responses that lead to a predictable mathematical outcome. Even elaborate behaviors (e.g., doing a science experiment) can be analyzed as a series of response chains governed by stimulus control (Lindsley, 1996). Stimulus control comes about as a result of differential reinforcement (Catania, 1998). When reinforcement is delivered contingent on the occurrence of the behavior in the presence of antecedent stimuli and withheld when critical antecedent stimuli do not occur, the behavior is much more likely to appear in appropriate situations (i.e., critical stimuli are present) and less likely to appear in other situations (i.e., critical stimuli are not present). These stimuli acquire control of behavior because of their association with effective consequences (Miltenberger, 2004). The curriculum therefore can be considered an outline of the stimulus-response relationships that students are supposed to acquire. In its most fundamental form, instruction can be considered as differential reinforcement applied to curricular materials. In this way, student responding serves as a diagnostic indicator of the degree to which instruction has effectively produced stimulus control.

Stimulus Generalization and Academic Responding

When one considers the range of stimulus-response relationships that need to be developed for a student to be successful within and beyond school, it becomes quickly apparent that the teacher would need at least several lifetimes to teach all possible stimulus-response relationships before sending students out into the world (Alessi, 1987). This is obviously not what happens. The many successful students whose teachers truncated the teaching of direct stimulus-response relationships at some point in time are a testimony to the fact that the effective teacher need not go to this extreme. This issue, however, raises the intriguing question of how students become able to generalize responding (i.e., the stimulus-response relationships) beyond what the teacher taught directly. One characteristic of stimulus control is that when behavior comes under the control of antecedent stimuli, the behavior is more likely to occur in the presence of other similar antecedent stimuli (Rilling, 1977). Indeed, *stimulus generalization* will not occur if stimulus control has not been established in the first place. The next question, however, is how behavior comes to be broadly and consistently generalizable beyond the stimulus-response relationships that were taught and/or other features of the training environment.

Stimulus generalization can occur in a variety of ways. The easiest form to detect is when the same behavior (e.g., reading a word in a text) occurs in different but similar contexts (i.e., the student correctly reads the newly learned word in different texts). Some forms of stimulus generalization, however, are more complex. Some behaviors are *component responses* that need to be incorporated into larger response repertoires—*composite skills* (Johnson & Layng, 1992). For example, writing numbers and doing simple math calculations (i.e., adding or subtracting) are two component responses of the larger composite skill of solving algebra problems (e.g., $3x - 2 = -2x + 5 + 4x + 8$).

Other behaviors may be barely recognizable from their original form, but equally critical to successful completion of composite skills. For example, verbalizing the correct sound for a phoneme (the smallest unit of speech) in the presence of a letter or letter combination is the smallest functional response in reading. The correct response needs to be made each and every time the letter/letter combination appears with other letters/letter combinations in words. To the inexperienced reader, those combinations are often not readily predictable and responding is difficult and laborious. Because

of its vital role in reading acquisition (Torgesen et al., 2001), however, phonemic responding is an important example of a *minimal response repertoire* (Alessi, 1987; Shahan & Chase, 2002; Skinner, 1957). Minimal response repertoires are functional because they contribute to producing a novel response (i.e., reading words in the presence of many different letter combinations) when they are done quickly, fluidly, and in combination with other responses. The isolated response in and of itself (i.e., saying a phoneme correctly) is hardly useful to the learner as an isolated response. Minimal response repertoires are functional when response strength reaches a point at which the learner can combine responses effectively when confronted with novel configurations of relevant stimuli.

Teaching as Establishing Stimulus Control and Generalization

When a student's behavior is under appropriate forms of stimulus control, there is a predictable functional relationship between environmental stimuli (i.e., antecedent and consequent stimuli) and student responding. In the classroom, student behavior appears to occur as a continuous chain of appropriate academic and task-related behaviors in response to assignments and teacher directions (Daly & Murdoch, 2000). Student responding becomes more complex as curricular tasks shift over time. The successful student's responding grows steadily both in terms of number of correct answers as well as breadth of types of correct answers, which should progressively "map on" to curricular objectives. When a student fails to progress in the curriculum as he or she should, there is a rupture in the relationship of environmental events to student behaviors. Curricular tasks do not occasion correct responses. Unfortunately, this rupture may create the conditions for less desirable behaviors to become functional (see the section on functional analysis). Nonetheless, the school psychologist may be called upon to help develop an intervention plan that establishes appropriate relationships between instructional demands and students' academic responding. In light of the analysis, what can be done to make teaching effective at establishing functional relationships (as defined by the curriculum)?

Direct Instruction

One of the most successful instructional approaches in education history is Direct

Instruction (DI). In a recent meta-analysis, Adams and Carnine (2003) found an average effect size of 0.93 for 17 studies of DI. When they examined variables like age, academic subject, type of test, and type of research design, the range of effect sizes was 0.73 to 1.31. To anyone familiar with the Follow Through Evaluation carried out by the U.S. Department of Education in the 1970s, these findings should come as no surprise. The Follow Through Evaluation was a massive longitudinal evaluation of a number of different instructional methods. DI's results were superior in every area to all of the other instructional methods (Gersten, Carnine, & White, 1984; Gersten, Woodward, & Darch, 1986). DI is especially relevant to the discussion here because it is grounded in principles of instruction that specifically target the development of stimulus control (Kinder & Carnine, 1991). The reader will recall that stimulus control comes about through differential reinforcement of responding. DI uses carefully designed curriculum materials and scripted instructional sequences to make antecedent stimuli clear and unambiguous and provide high levels of feedback in the form of error correction and praise for correct responding (Kinder & Carnine, 1991). Conditions for responding also are made clear through the careful selection of examples and nonexamples as the best exemplars of the teaching objective. DI requires demonstration of student mastery before the teacher moves on in the curriculum. Therefore, as an instructional program that is explicitly designed to promote stimulus control, DI should be a program of choice.

Learning Trials

When DI is not an option, school psychologists can step back to an analysis of instruction to determine what is missing or where there is a mismatch between academic responding and preparation for instruction, instructional materials, and/or delivery of instruction. In educational circles, the "learning trial" is a term often used for explaining how to produce stimulus control (Heward, 1994; Skinner, Fletcher, & Henington, 1996). The learning trial is based on the three-term contingency, which is comprised of an instructional antecedent (including both curricular stimuli and prompts to respond), a student response, and a consequence (reinforcement or corrective feedback). Therefore, the concept is synonymous with differential reinforcement. Heward (1994) describes the learning trial as "a basic unit of

analysis for examining teaching and learning from both the teacher's perspective (that is, an opportunity to teach) and the student's perspective (or an opportunity to learn)" (p. 284). Research on the number and rate of learning trials delivered by the teacher in the classroom has shown that learning trials have a significant effect on the amount of learning that occurs (Belfiore, Skinner, & Ferkis, 1995; Heward, 1994; Skinner, Fletcher, & Henington, 1996). When student responding to instructional exercises is problematic, practitioners are advised to examine whether complete learning trials are being delivered at an optimal rate (Skinner, Fletcher, & Henington, 1996).

Performance versus Skill Deficits

The utility of the learning trial as a unit of analysis is even greater when one considers two heuristics that have emerged in the research literature for guiding the diagnosis of instruction. Lentz (1988) described a distinction between performance deficits and skill deficits. In the case of a performance deficit, the necessary response repertoire exists. The problem is that the consequences for responding are not effective reinforcers for the appearance of the behavior. Student responding would occur if stronger or more desirable consequences for behavior existed. In the case of a skill deficit, the response repertoire is not strong enough for the individual to respond effectively, regardless of how strong or potentially effective the consequences are. For a skill deficit, the antecedent stimuli that are naturally present do not serve as effective prompts for the response to occur.

Distinguishing between a performance deficit and a skill deficit amounts to identifying whether emphasis needs to be given to the consequences (performance deficit) or antecedents to responding (skill deficit) in an intervention plan. This distinction has been shown to be useful in identifying individual differences in students' responsiveness to performance-based (i.e., programmed reinforcement) or skill-based (i.e., use of instruction) interventions (Duhon et al., 2004; Eckert, Ardoin, Daisey, & Scarola, 2000; Eckert, Ardoin, Daly, & Martens, 2002; Noell et al., 1998). In particular, Duhon et al.'s (2004) brief assessment procedures for generating hypotheses about skill versus performance deficits appear very promising. In this study, brief class-wide assessments were followed up with individualized assessments for a small group of students in the areas of math and writing. Two students were identified as having skill deficits and two students were identified as having performance deficits. Classroom applications of both types of interventions (alternated within a multielement experimental design) confirmed the hypotheses for all four students. Students with performance deficits showed superior performance in the reinforcement-based condition and students with skill deficits showed superior performance in the skill-based intervention condition. This study demonstrates the utility of tailoring interventions to students' needs according to skill or performance deficits.

When a skill deficit exists, effective consequences need to be paired more explicitly with effective response prompts to assure that responding occurs under the right conditions. Skill deficits can be analyzed even further through the use of the heuristic of the Instructional Hierarchy (IH; Haring & Eaton, 1978). The IH provides a conceptual outline for the types of response prompting and consequences that should occur as students progress toward skill mastery. To facilitate the initial appearance of accurate responses, modeling and error correction (involving consequent modeling and contingent response repetition) should be used by the teacher. Practice (i.e., frequent and repeated opportunities to respond) and reinforcement for rate should be used when responding is consistently accurate to promote response fluency. When skill fluency becomes the priority, performance feedback for rate of responding is also likely to be helpful. An examination of the reading intervention literature by Daly, Lentz, and Boyer (1996) revealed that patterns of effectiveness and ineffectiveness for intervention strategies across studies were predictable based on the IH according to the match between participants' skill level and instructional procedures used in the study. Furthermore, although there is some debate in the literature about what the causal mechanism is that makes fluency building strategies effective, there is a strong research base supporting its use (Binder, 1996; Doughty, Chase, & O'Shields, 2004).

Strategies for Establishing Stimulus Generalization

The other area in which students experience difficulty with academic responding is generalization. The teacher may observe that a student is inconsistent in his or her performance or that the student is not applying skills to new areas. For example, a student may be able to read words when they

are presented on flashcards, but not when they appear in text. In another case, a student may fail to use calculation skills correctly when presented with math word problems. In a seminal paper on generalization, Stokes and Baer (1977) organized the research on generalization into eight effective strategies that can be applied to improve the generality of behavior. (They also identified one ineffective strategy that is probably the most commonly used in research and practice—*train and hope*). These strategies have stood the test of time, as recent treatments of this topic in the literature (e.g., Alberto & Troutman, 2003; Miltenberger, 2004) continue to rely on the framework originally described by Stokes and Baer. Here, we will restrict ourselves to highlighting just several strategies that have been examined in the behavior analytic literature as means to improve students' generalized academic performance.

For stimulus generalization to occur, the teaching conditions should contain all the critical stimulus features necessary to occasion responding under natural, future conditions. For instance, if students learn to read words without learning to read them in connected text (the natural context for reading), they are less likely to read those words when they encounter them in texts (Skinner & Shapiro, 1989). Daly and Martens (1994) found that reading intervention strategies that include modeling and practice in text produced higher fluency rates in text than when modeling and practice were carried out with words presented in isolation. In general, it is best to teach in the natural context of use of the skill (Daly, Witt, Martens, & Dool, 1997).

Text difficulty level also has been shown to play a role in the degree to which students generalize. Daly, Martens, Kilmer, and Massie (1996) found greater generalized oral reading fluency increases when texts were at a better instructional match for participants' proficiency level. Participants were students who had severe reading fluency deficits. Students in the study read novel texts containing many of the same words faster when instruction was carried out in easier materials than in harder materials. Interestingly, Daly, Bonfiglio, Mattson, Persampieri, and Foreman-Yates (2005) found that participants in their study displayed greater generalized oral reading fluency in *harder* rather than in easier texts. The latter study, however, had participants whose fluency was much higher than the participants in the Daly, Martens, et al. study. The results of both studies, however, speak to the importance of tailoring instruction to an appropriate difficulty to maximize generalized reading effects.

Text difficulty level can be controlled *within* teaching sessions in a way that produces generalization as well. Martens et al. (2007) found generalized gains in oral reading fluency on untrained passages, phonological awareness, and passage comprehension when retention criteria were used. Students only progressed to more difficult passages when they could read instructional texts at a rate of 100 correctly read words per minute two days after training (and in the absence of practice on that passage for intervening days). Therefore, repeated practice with reading texts to fluency and retention criteria may help students generalize to other areas of reading as well.

Generalization of oral reading fluency has been investigated in the research literature through the manipulation of passage content. Investigators have created generalization texts that contain many of the same words as training texts but in a different order. As such, the generalization texts constitute different stories relative to the training texts, and the appearance of words in a different order creates novel stimulus conditions while retaining many of the words that were the target of instruction (making it a relatively sensitive measure of generalization effects). When a student improves his or her reading in a passage with high-word overlap as a function of instructional and/or motivational variables relative to other equal difficulty level but low-word overlap texts, generalization is demonstrated. Several studies have produced generalized effects by reinforcing instances of generalization following the application of instructional variables (i.e., modeling, practice, error correction, and performance feedback) to high-word overlap texts (Daly, Bonfiglio et al., 2005; Daly, Bonfiglio, Mattson, Persampieri, & Foreman-Yates, 2005; Daly, Murdoch, Lillenstein, Webber, & Lentz, 2002; Gortmaker, Daly, McCurdy, Persampieri, & Hergenrader, 2005; Persampieri, Gortmaker, Daly, Sheridan, and McCurdy, 2006). It is noteworthy that some participants respond to antecedent instruction only and do not require programmed contingencies for generalization to occur. A brief experimental analysis can help to sort out just which types of instructional and/or motivational strategies are needed for a particular student (Gortmaker et al., 2007).

One method for producing generalization is to teach skills that are generalizable. Stokes and Baer (1977) refer to this technique as training self-mediated generalization strategies. The earlier example of phoneme blending as minimal response repertoires represents a self-mediated generalization strategy in which a student's new behavioral repertoire (i.e., reading phonemes in novel arrangements in new words) increases his or her capacity to respond in ways that differ from the training conditions. A recent study demonstrated the superiority of bringing phonemes versus whole words under stimulus control for improving generalized word reading. Daly, Chafouleas, Persampieri, Bonfiglio, and LaFleur (2004) equated two conditions (phoneme training and whole-word training) for response opportunities, differential reinforcement, and degree of overlap in phonemes between trained words and generalization words. Assessment and reinforcement opportunities across conditions were made indiscriminable so that participants could not associate words with a particular condition and could only discriminate words based on textual properties of the stimuli. To measure generalization, participants were assessed for correct reading of unknown words while training was conducted with nonsense words that contained the phonemes from the unknown words. This arrangement allowed the experimenters to vary the stimulus conditions between training (nonsense words) and assessment (real words) while still having a sensitive measure of generalized performance.

The critical difference between the two conditions was the size of the response that was brought under stimulus control. In the phoneme blending condition, phonemes were trained. In the sight word condition, whole words were trained. During instruction, the letters corresponding to phonemes in unknown words were rearranged so that students learned to read a nonsense variant of each unknown word that contained all the same phonemes. Participants mastered many more words in the phoneme blending condition than in the sight word condition. The importance of phoneme blending and segmenting skills for becoming a proficient reader is undisputed (National Reading Panel, 2000). This study provides an explanatory mechanism for what makes the skill of phoneme blending and segmenting effective as a self-mediated generalization strategy.

APPLYING TREATMENT AND KNOWING THAT IT OCCURRED

Epistemological Traditions: How Do We Know?

One of the central challenges confronting professions such as medicine or school psychology is defining what constitutes knowledge in applied settings. In essence, what are the epistemological standards that must be met in order to assert that we know something? This is a natural extension of the challenges of developing epistemological standards for research. However, the challenge of extending research methodology and epistemology to referred individuals in practice is exceedingly complex, has received limited consideration in the professional literature, and can have grave consequences for the standards for care. One of the enduring challenges for practicing psychologists is the mismatch between the unit of analysis in much psychological research, groups, and the unit of analysis that is typical in practice, the individual. Although a traditional parametric study may demonstrate that a particular test has a specific factor structure for a large sample of individuals, there is no practical way to verify the accuracy of that factor structure for an individual (Gorsuch, 1983). Similarly, although research may demonstrate that strategy instruction is effective for groups of students (e.g., Pressley & Woloshyn, 1995), traditional group research design does not provide a method for evaluating whether or not strategy instruction is effective for a specific individual.

Extending knowledge gained within group research designs to individual cases has been based upon the assumption that findings demonstrated at the level of a group will generalize to individuals. Interestingly, relatively little consideration has commonly been given to individuals whose data do not fit the pattern of the group. Their results are commonly subsumed in the error term. This approach has the unfortunate effect of obscuring individual differences that may be meaningful, important, systematic, and ultimately inform effective treatment (Daly, Persampieri, McCurdy, & Gortmaker, 2005; Iwata et al., 1982/1994). Behavioral psychology and behavior analysis have provided alternative epistemological models that provide for the controlled analysis of the behavior of individuals. Critically, these models provide a link between basic research methodology and practice in which the unit of analysis, the individual, is matched across research

methodology and practice (Barlow & Hersen, 1984; Kazdin, 2001). Before examining the potential utility of behavior analytic epistemology within school psychology, the authors do wish to clarify a point to avoid creating a straw man either/or argument. The following is *not* intended as an argument that single subject designs have an exclusive grasp on truth or that they can even address all scientifically important questions. Rather, the authors argue that single subject methodologies are uniquely suited to meeting specific needs of school psychology as a discipline and a practice. The authors would suggest that in the context of practice, in particular, the single subject approaches that have characterized behavior analytic psychology are uniquely important because they provide the epistemological model that matches the level of analysis, the individual, to the common referral context in practice.

It can reasonably be argued that case management in practice revolves primarily around three issues: dependent variables (DV), independent variables (IV), and evaluation design. Although additional variables such as moderating or mediating variables may be important, it is the application of a treatment and the evaluation of its efficacy that is central to much case-centered work within school psychology and that is extensively represented in the emerging intervention-focused practices within education. In practice, moderating variables may infrequently be assessed, their importance to the individual may not be verifiable, and will frequently be unalterable. Behavior analytic psychology has made substantive contributions to the development of school psychology in the domains of dependent variables, independent variables, and evaluation designs.

Behavioral psychologists have a long tradition of emphasizing the direct measurement of concerns of interest rather than assessment of indirect indicators (Baer, Wolf, & Risley, 1968; Johnston & Pennypacker, 1993). For example, behavior analysts would suggest that if the referral concern is work completion, assessment should directly measure work completion rather than assessing the teachers' perception of work completion. Although that may seem intuitively obvious, it is worth noting that school psychology has an extensive tradition of measuring variables of interest indirectly through scales or tests and of measuring constructs rather than behaviors. Embedded within behavior analysis's extensive tradition of directly measuring the behaviors of interest is a considerable literature relevant to the technical characteristics of differing assessment methodologies and means of assessing the technical adequacy of specific measures (see Cooper, Heron, & Heward, 1987, or Cone, 1988). Although the practice of school psychology is likely to continue to exhibit some tension between assessing constructs such as intelligence versus behaviors such as words read per minute, the increasing emphasis upon consultation, intervention, and resistance to intervention increasingly calls for the direct measurement of behavior.

Typically within a problem-solving process, once the target concern has been identified (the DV), assessment data are used to identify an intervention that has a high probability of success (the IV). Previous sections of this chapter have given relatively extensive consideration to identifying IVs and as a result that issue will not be examined again here. Identification of the IV and DV should logically lead to consideration of how the effect of the IV upon the DV will be assessed: the evaluation design. Behavior analytic psychology has developed and described a number of evaluation methodologies that can be applied at the level of single individuals across differing contexts and types of concerns (see Barlow & Hersen, 1984, Cooper et al., 1987, or Kazdin, 2001). All single subject experimental designs will include the three elements of baseline logic. Space limitations preclude description of baseline logic, but interested readers might consult Cooper and colleagues for a very accessible description of baseline logic and single subject experimentation. Although it may not be possible to meet all the requirements of demonstrating experimental control within case work, approximations that provide for controlled case studies have also been extensively described in the sources above. These are particularly important given the evidence that continuous progress monitoring is beneficial to students (Stecker, Fuchs, & Fuchs, 2005) and the logical necessity of ongoing progress monitoring in the context of practices such as consultation or assessing resistance to intervention.

Treatment Plan Implementation

On its surface, it would seem that once the concern has been defined operationally (the DV), an appropriate intervention has been devised (the IV), and an assessment plan developed (the evaluation design), all of the key components

to effective intervention are in place. However, an emerging line of research spanning school psychology and behavior analysis suggests that this may not be the case (Noell, 2008). It appears that the entire process is in considerable danger of breaking down if attention is not directed to a very simple consideration: treatment plan implementation (TPI). In brief, considerable evidence exists that TPI can be exceedingly problematic in the absence of programmatic efforts to assure it occurs.

Concern regarding TPI emerged in the research literature notably with Peterson, Homer, and Wonderlich's (1982) discussion of a "curious double standard" (p. 478) regarding the specification and measurement of the independent and dependent variables. They argued that extensive standards had emerged to assure the veracity of DVs, but that little attention had been devoted to the accuracy of implementation of IVs. Behavioral researchers routinely provide operational definitions of dependent variables and reliability or observer agreement data for the measures employed. These standards have been extensively adopted in field-based psychological research to help control confounds that emerge in less controlled environments (Billingsley, White, & Munson, 1980). Interestingly, although Peterson and colleagues' seminal work contributed to a number of subsequent reviews and discussions regarding treatment integrity in the research literature, there was not an immediate focus upon treatment integrity in practice.

TPI in applied contexts recently has been an increasing focus of concern in the psychological treatment literature (e.g., Lentz & Daly, 1996; Mueller, Edwards, Trahant, 2003; Riley-Tillman & Chafouleas, 2003). This concern is particularly important for the treatment of children because those treatments that have the strongest empirical support also typically require some implementation by parents or teachers (e.g., Weiss & Weisz, 1995). Additionally, anecdotal and systematic observations from practice and research suggest that sustained accurate TPI may be relatively difficult to achieve (Foxx, 1996; Happe, 1982). Although much of the early research in this domain was based in part on the assumption that high treatment acceptability would lead to TPI, early research did not actually test this assumption directly and recent research data suggests that acceptability may not be sufficient to assure implementation (Noell et al., 2005).

Although the bulk of the research examining TPI in schools has focused upon the efficacy of performance feedback for enhancing and sustaining TPI, a few interesting studies have examined other issues. Two studies have suggested the importance of giving intervention providers implementation training that is relatively rigorous and includes practicing the intervention (Taylor & Miller, 1997; Sterling-Turner, Watson, Wildom, Watkins, & Little, 2001). However it is worth noting that issues with experimental design and external validity raise substantive concerns regarding the degree to which generalizable conclusions can be drawn from these studies. Also, the paucity of data in this area has not begun to address a likely reality: that intensive training may be needed for some interventions and for some treatment agents but not for others. Another study examining TPI investigated the extent to which adopting a collaborative versus a more directive approach in consultation would influence TPI (Wickstrom, Jones, LaFleur, & Witt, 1998). The notable findings of this study were that TPI was quite low and did not differ across the collaborative and directive groups.

The only variable with regard to TPI for which systematic research has been evident to date is the efficacy of performance feedback for increasing and sustaining TPI. Summarizing across studies, the fundamental conclusion is that providing teachers data-based feedback regarding their TPI and student outcomes has led to improved TPI (Noell, 2008). The initial studies in this area demonstrated the efficacy of performance feedback in improving TPI across diverse student populations (Jones, Wickstrom, & Friman, 1997; Martens, Hiralall, & Bradley, 1997; Mortenson & Witt, 1998; Witt, Noell, LaFleur, & Mortenson, 1997). These initial positive findings have been followed up with subsequent studies examining procedural variations and extending the research to more diverse referral concerns and interventions. For example, Noell, Witt, Gilbertson, Ranier, & Freeland (1997) demonstrated that performance feedback remained effective in the absence of the extensive in-vivo training that had characterized some of the previous research. Similarly, Mortenson and Witt (1998) extended the previous consultation, TPI, and performance feedback literature by examining the feedback schedule. They found weekly feedback to be effective, but less consistently so than daily feedback had been in previous studies.

Follow-up research also has examined the importance of specific components of performance feedback. Research has demonstrated that follow-up meetings that review objective data about implementation and child outcome are more effective than meetings that simply discuss the intervention with the teacher (Noell, Witt, LaFleur, Mortenson, Ranier, & LeVelle, 2000). Other findings suggest that reviewing time series graphs that depict implementation and child outcomes increases the effectiveness of performance feedback (Noell, Duhon, Gatti, & Connell, 2002). One of the interesting conceptual issues that has been raised regarding the use of performance feedback to sustain TPI has been the extent to which it is effective as the result of positive reinforcement, negative reinforcement, or prompting. A recent study designed to emphasize the negative reinforcement elements of performance feedback found that it remained effective when it resulted primarily in escape from additional consultation and training contacts (DiGennaro, Martens, & McIntyre, 2005).

Recent research also has extended this line of research to examine antecedent- as well as consequent-based strategies within a randomized field trial (Noell et al., 2005). The antecedent strategy was a package that included social influence and planning strategies drawn from the adult self-management literature. The performance feedback condition included a programmed procedure for fading performance feedback to once per week contacts. The control condition consisted of a brief weekly interview structured similar to a Problem Evaluation Interview. The key findings were that performance feedback was associated with superior TPI and child outcome in comparison to either of the other conditions, which did not differ. The data also suggested the need for additional research examining social influence strategies and self-management procedures. Teacher ratings of consultants and treatment acceptability were similar across conditions.

In summary, the literature examining the application of performance feedback to enhance TPI suggests at least four tenable conclusions. First, performance feedback regarding treatment implementation following consultation leads to improved TPI. Second, for common educational interventions, extensive training prior to TPI does not appear to be sufficient to sustain implementation and does not appear to be necessary for performance feedback to work.

This is not to suggest, however, that no training is needed or that extensive training would not be needed for interventions that are novel for the treatment agent. Third, review of objective data presented in a graph make follow-up meetings more effective. Finally, the phenomenon of problematic integrity and positive response to performance feedback is evident across interventions and referral concerns.

CONCLUSION

Bijou (1970) acknowledged that his offer was one that came from "a small minority" (p. 66) in the field of psychology. One thing that has not changed is that the work of behavior analysts continues to come from a small minority in the field. (However, we regret that because of page restrictions we were unable to cover all of the excellent work being done in the field at this time.) Another thing that has not changed is the content of the offer behavior analysts continue to make to school psychologists today. We trust that readers will see the continuity of objectives of this science of behavior in our sample of the state-of-the-art of behavior analysis research and practice in the schools. Though small in number, behavior analysts have remained true to their self-defined charge as they refine the analysis of independent and dependent variables at a unit of analysis that will always be relevant to educators—the individual.

REFERENCES

Adams, G., & Carnine, D. (2003). Direct instruction. In H. Lee Swanson, K. R. Harris, & S. Graham (Eds.), *Handbook of learning disabilities* (pp. 403–416). New York: The Guilford Press.

Alberto, P. A., & Troutman, A. C. (2003). *Applied behavior analysis for teachers* (6th ed.). Upper Saddle River, NJ: Merrill Prentice Hall.

Alessi, G. (1987). Generative strategies and teaching for generalization. *The Analysis of Verbal Behavior*, 5, 15–27.

Baer, D. M., Wolf, M. M., & Risley, T. R. (1968). Some current dimensions of applied behavior analysis. *Journal of Applied Behavior Analysis*, 1, 91–97.

Barlow, D. H., & Hersen, M. (1984). *Single case experimental designs* (2nd ed.). New York: Pergamon Press.

Belfiore, P. J., Skinner, C. H., & Ferkis, M. (1995). Effects of response and trial repetition on sight-word training for students with learning disabilities. *Journal of Applied Behavior Analysis*, 28, 347–348.

Berkowitz, M. J., & Martens, B. K. (2001). Assessing teachers' and students' preferences for school-based reinforcers: Agreement across methods and different effort requirements. *Journal of Developmental and Physical Disabilities*, 13, 373–387.

Bijou, S. W. (1970). What psychology has to offer education—now. *Journal of Applied Behavior Analysis*, 3, 65–71.

Bijou, S. W., Peterson, R. F., & Ault, M. H. (1968). A method to integrate descriptive and experimental field studies at the level of data and empirical concepts. *Journal of Applied Behavior Analysis*, 1, 175–191.

Billingsley, F., White, O. R., & Munson, R. (1980). Procedural reliability: A rationale and an example. *Behavioral Assessment*, 2, 229–241.

Billington, E. J., & Ditommaso, N. M. (2003). Demonstrations and applications of the matching law in education. *Journal of Behavioral Education*, 12, 91–104.

Billington, E. J., & Skinner, C. H. (2002). Getting students to choose to do more work: Evidence of the effectiveness of the interspersal procedure. *Journal of Behavioral Education*, 11, 105–116.

Billington, E. J., Skinner, C. H., Hutchins, H., & Malone, J. C. (2004). Varying problem effort and choice: Using the interspersal technique to influence choice towards more effortful assignments. *Journal of Behavioral Education*, 13, 193–207.

Binder, C. (1996). Behavioral fluency: Evolution of a new paradigm. *The Behavior Analyst*, 19, 163–197.

Broussard, C. D., & Northup, J. (1995). An approach to functional assessment and analysis of disruptive behavior in regular education classrooms. *School Psychology Quarterly*, 10, 151–164.

Broussard, C. D., & Northup, J. (1997). The use of functional analysis to develop peer interventions for disruptive classroom behavior. *School Psychology Quarterly*, 12, 65–76.

Carr, E. G., Newsom, C. D., & Binkoff, J. A. (1976). Stimulus control of self-destructive behavior in a psychotic child. *Journal of Abnormal Child Psychology*, 4, 139–153.

Cashwell, C. S., Skinner, C. H., Dunn, M., & Lewis, J. (1998). Group reward programs: A humanistic approach. *Humanistic Education and Development*, 37, 47–53.

Catania, A. C. (1998). *Learning* (4th ed.). Upper Saddle River, NJ: Prentice Hall.

Cates, G. L., & Skinner, C. H. (2000). Getting remedial mathematics students to prefer homework with 20% and 40% more problems: An investigation of the strength of the interspersing procedure. *Psychology in the Schools*, 37, 339–347.

Cates, G. L., & Skinner, C. H., Watkins, C. E., Rhymer, K. N., McNeill, B. S., & McCurdy, M. (1999). Effects of interspersing additional brief math problems on student performance and perception of math assignments: Getting students to prefer to do more work. *Journal of Behavioral Education, 9,* 177–193.

Cone, J. (1988). Psychometric considerations and the multiple models of behavioral assessment. In A. Bellack & M. Hersen (Eds.), *Behavioral assessment: A practical handbook* (2nd ed., pp. 42–66). New York: Pergamon.

Cooper, J. O., Heron, T. E., & Heward, W. L. (1987). *Applied behavior analysis.* Columbus, OH: Merrill Publishing Co.

Daly, E. J., III, Bonfiglio, C. M., Mattson, T., Persampieri, M., & Foreman-Yates, K. (2005). Refining the experimental analysis of academic skill deficits, Part I: An investigation of variables affecting generalized oral reading performance. *Journal of Applied Behavior Analysis, 38,* 485–498.

Daly, E. J., III, Bonfiglio, C. M., Mattson, T., Persampieri, M., & Yates, K. (2005). Refining the experimental analysis of academic skill deficits, Part I: An Investigation of variables affecting generalized oral reading performance. *Journal of Applied Behavior Analysis, 38,* 485–498.

Daly, E. J., III, Chafouleas, S. M., Persampieri, M., Bonfiglio, C. M., & LaFleur, K. (2004). Teaching phoneme segmenting and blending as critical early literacy skills: An experimental analysis of minimal textual repertoires. *Journal of Behavioral Education, 13,* 165–178.

Daly, E. J., Chafouleas, S., & Skinner, C. H. (2005). *Interventions for Reading Problems: Designing and Evaluating Effective Strategies.* New York: The Guilford Press.

Daly, E. J., III, Lentz, F. E., & Boyer, J. (1996). The instructional hierarchy: A conceptual model for understanding the effective components of reading interventions. *School Psychology Quarterly, 11,* 369–386.

Daly, E. J., III, & Martens, B. K. (1994). A comparison of three interventions for increasing oral reading performance: Application of the instructional hierarchy. *Journal of Applied Behavior Analysis, 27,* 459–469.

Daly, E. J., III, Martens, B. K., Kilmer, A., & Massie, D. (1996). The effects of instructional match and content overlap on generalized reading performance. *Journal of Applied Behavior Analysis, 29,* 507–518.

Daly, E. J., III, & Murdoch, A. (2000). Direct observation in the assessment of academic skill problems. In E. S. Shapiro & T. R. Kratochwill (Eds.), *Behavioral assessment in schools: Theory, research, and clinical foundations* (2nd ed., pp. 46–77). New York, NY: Guilford Publications.

Daly, E. J., III, Murdoch, A., Lillenstein, L., Webber, L., & Lentz, F. E. (2002). An examination of methods for testing treatments: Conducting experimental analyses of the effects of instructional components on oral reading fluency. *Education and Treatment of Children, 25,* 288–316.

Daly, E. J., III, Persampieri, M., McCurdy, M., & Gortmaker, V. (2005) Generating reading interventions through experimental analysis of academic skills: Demonstration and empirical evaluation. *School Psychology Review, 34,* 395–414.

Daly, E. J., III, Witt, J. C., Martens, B. K., & Dool, E. J. (1997). A model for conducting a functional analysis of academic performance problems. *School Psychology Review, 26,* 554–574.

DiGennaro, F. D., Martens, B. K., & McIntyre, L. L. (2005). Increasing treatment integrity through negative reinforcement: Effects on teacher and student behavior. *School Psychology Review. 34,* 220–231.

Doughty, S. S., Chase, P. N., & O'Shields, E. M. (2004). Effects of rate building on fluent performance: A review and commentary. *The Behavior Analyst, 27,* 7–23.

Drasgow, E., & Yell, M. L. (2001). Functional behavioral assessments: Legal requirements and challenges. *School Psychology Review, 30,* 239–251.

Duhon, G. J., Noell, G. H., Witt, J. C., Freeland, J. T., Dufrene, B. A., & Gilbertson, D. N. (2004). Identifying academic skills and performance deficits: The experimental analysis of brief assessments of academic skills. *School Psychology Review, 33,* 429–443.

Durand, V. M., & Crimmins, D. B. (1988). Identifying the variables maintaining self-injurious behavior. *Journal of Autism and Developmental Disorders, 18,* 99–117.

Eckert, T. L., Ardoin, S. P., Daisey, D. M., & Scarola, M. D. (2000). Empirically evaluating the effectiveness of reading interventions: The use of brief experimental analysis and single-case designs. *Psychology in the Schools, 37,* 463–474.

Eckert, T. L., Ardoin, S. P., Daly, E. J., III, & Martens, B. K. (2002). Improving oral reading fluency: An examination of the efficacy of combining skill-based and performance-based interventions. *Journal of Applied Behavior Analysis, 35,* 271–281.

Eckert, T. L., Martens, B. K., & DiGennaro, F. D. (2005). Describing antecedent-behavior-consequence relations using conditional probabilities and the general operant contingency space: A preliminary investigation. *School Psychology Review, 34,* 520–528.

Englemann, S., Granzin, A., & Severson, H. (1979). Diagnosing instruction. *The Journal of Special Education, 13,* 355–363.

Erchul, W. P., & Martens, B. K. (2002). *School consultation: Conceptual and empirical bases of practice* (2nd ed.). New York: Plenum.

Ferster, C. B., & Skinner, B. F. (1957). *Schedules of reinforcement*. Acton, MA: Copley Publishing Group.

Fisher, W., Piazza, C. C., Bowman, L. G., Hagopian, L. P., Owens, J. C., & Slevin, I. (1992). A comparison of two approaches for identifying reinforcers for persons with severe and profound disabilities. *Journal of Applied Behavior Analysis, 25*, 491–498.

Foxx, R. M. (1996). Twenty years of applied behavior analysis in treating the most severe problem behavior: Lessons learned. *The Behavior Analyst, 19*, 225–236.

Gersten, R., Carnine, D., & White, W. A. T. (1984). The pursuit of clarity: Direct instruction and applied behavior analysis. In W. L., Heward, T. E. Heron, D. S. Hill, & J. Trapp-Porter, *Focus on behavior analysis in education* (pp. 38–57). Columbus, OH: Charles E. Merrill Publishing Co.

Gersten, R., Woodward, J., & Darch, C. (1986). Direct-instruction: A research-based approach to curriculum design and teaching. *Exceptional Children, 53*, 17–31.

Gorsuch, R. L. (1983). *Factor analysis* (2nd ed.). Hillsdale, NJ: Lawrence Erlbaum.

Gortmaker, V. J., Daly, E. J., III, McCurdy, M., Persampieri, M. J., & Hergenrader, M. (2007). Improving reading outcomes for children with learning disabilities: Using brief experimental analysis to develop parent tutoring interventions. *Journal of Applied Behavior Analysis, 40*, 203–222.

Hanley, G. P., Iwata, B. A., & McCord, B. E. (2003). Functional analysis of problem behavior: A review. *Journal of Applied Behavior Analysis, 36*, 147–185.

Happe, D. (1982). Behavioral intervention: It doesn't do any good in your briefcase. In J. Grimes, (Ed.), *Psychological approaches to problems of children and adolescents* (pp. 15–41). Des Moines, IA: Iowa Department of Public Instruction.

Haring, N. G., & Eaton, M. D. (1978). Systematic instructional procedures: An instructional hierarchy. In Haring, N. G., Lovitt, T. C., Eaton, M. D., & Hansen, C. L. (Eds.), *The fourth R: Research in the classroom* (pp. 23–40). Columbus, OH: Merrill.

Herrnstein, R. (1961). Relative and absolute strength of response as a function of frequency of reinforcement. *Journal of Experimental Analysis of Behavior, 4*, 267–272.

Herrnstein, R. J. (1970). On the law of effect. *Journal of the Experimental Analysis of Behavior, 9*, 421–430.

Heward, W. L. (1994). Three "low-tech" strategies for increasing the frequency of active student response during group instruction. In R. Gardner III, D. M. Sainato, J. O. Cooper, T. E. Heron, W. L. Heward, J. W. Eshleman, & T. A. Grossi. (Eds.), *Behavior analysis in education: Focus on measurably superior instruction* (pp. 283–320). Pacific Grove, CA: Brooks/Cole Publishing Co.

Iwata, B. A., Dorsey, M. F., Slifer, K. J., Bauman, K. E., & Richman, G. S. (1982/1994). Toward a functional analysis of self-injury. *Journal of Applied Behavior Analysis, 27*, 197–209 (reprinted from *Analysis and Intervention in Developmental Disabilities, 2*, 1–20).

Iwata, B. A., Pace, G. M., Dorsey, M. F., Zarcone, J. R., Vollmer, T. R., Smith, R. G., et al. (1994). The functions of self-injurious behavior: An experimental-epidemiological analysis. *Journal of Applied Behavior Analysis, 27*, 215–240.

Johnson, K. R., & Layng, T. V. J. (1992). Breaking the structuralist barrier: Literacy and numeracy with fluency. *American Psychologist, 47*, 1475–1490.

Johnston, J. M., & Pennypacker, H. S. (1993). *Strategies and tactics of behavioral research*. Hillsdale, NJ: Lawrence Erlbaum Associates.

Jones, K. M., Wickstrom, K. F., & Friman, P. C. (1997). The effects of observational feedback on treatment integrity in school-based behavioral consultation. *School Psychology Quarterly, 12*, 316–326.

Kazdin, A. E., (2001). *Behavior modification in applied settings: 6th Edition*. Belmont, CA: Wadsworth.

Kinder, D., & Carnine, D. (1991). Direct instruction: What it is and what it is becoming. *Journal of Behavioral Education, 1*, 193–213.

Kohn, A. (1999). *Punished by rewards: The trouble with gold stars, incentive plans, A's, praise and other bribes*. Boston, Houghton Mifflin.

Lalli, J. S., Browder, D. M., Mace, F. C., & Brown, D. K. (1993). Teacher use of descriptive analysis data to implement interventions to decrease students' problem behavior. *Journal of Applied Behavior Analysis, 26*, 227–238.

Lentz, F. E. (1988) Effective reading interventions in the regular classroom. In J. L. Graden, J. Zins, & M. J. Curtis (Eds.), *Alternative educational delivery systems: Enhancing instructional options for all students* (pp. 351–370). Washington, DC: The National Association of School Psychologists.

Lentz, F. E., & Daly, E. J., III. (1996). Is the behavior of academic change agents controlled metaphysically? An analysis of the behavior of those who change behavior. *School Psychology Quarterly, 11*, 337–352.

Lerman, D. C., & Iwata, B. A. (1993). Descriptive and experimental analyses of variables maintaining self-injurious behavior. *Journal of Applied Behavior Analysis, 26*, 293–319.

Lindsley, O. R. (1996). Is fluency free-operant response-response chaining? *The Behavior Analyst, 19*, 211–224.

Lovaas, O. I., & Simmons, J. Q. (1969). Manipulation of self-destruction in three retarded children. *Journal of Applied Behavior Analysis, 2,* 143–157.

Mace, F. C., & Lalli, J. S. (1991). Linking descriptive and experimental analyses in the treatment of bizarre speech. *Journal of Applied Behavior Analysis, 24,* 553–562.

Mace, F. C., McCurdy, B., & Quigley, E. A. (1990). The collateral effect of reward predicted by matching theory. *Journal of Applied Behavior Analysis, 23,* 197–205.

Mace, F. C., Neef, N. A., Shade, D., & Mauro, B. C. (1996). Effects of problem difficulty and reinforcer quality on time allocated to concurrent arithmetic problems. *Journal of Applied Behavior Analysis, 29,* 11–24.

Marcus, B.A., & Vollmer, T.R. (1996). Combining noncontingent reinforcement and differential reinforcement schedules as treatment for aberrant behavior. *Journal of Applied Behavior Analysis, 29,* 43–51.

Martens, B. K., Eckert, T. L., Begeny, J. C., Lewandowski, L. J., DiGennaro, F. D., Montarello, S. A., et al. (2007). Effects of a fluency-building program on the reading performance of low-achieving second and third grade students. *Journal of Behavioral Education, 16,* 39–54.

Martens, B. K., Hiralall, A. S., & Bradley, T. A. (1997). A note to teacher: Improving student behavior through goal setting and feedback. *School Psychology Quarterly, 12,* 33–41.

Martens, B. K., & Houk, J. L. (1989). The application of Herrnstein's law of effect to disruptive and on-task behavior of a retarded adolescent girl. *Journal of the Experimental Analysis of Behavior, 51,* 17–27.

Martens, B. K., Lochner, D. G., & Kelly, S. Q. (1992). The effects of variable-interval reinforcement on academic engagement: A demonstration of matching theory. *Journal of Applied Behavior Analysis, 25,* 143–151.

Martens, B. K., Witt, J. C., Daly, E. J., III, & Vollmer, T. R. (1999). Behavior analysis: Theory and practice in educational settings. In C. R. Reynolds & T. B. Gutkin (Eds.), *The handbook of school psychology* (3rd ed., pp. 638–663). New York, NY: John Wiley & Sons.

McCurdy, M., Skinner, C. H., Grantham, K., Watson, T. S., & Hindman, P. M. (2001). Increasing on-task behavior in an elementary student during mathematics seat-work by interspersing additional brief problems. *School Psychology Review, 30,* 23–32.

Michael, J. (1993). Establishing operations. *The Behavior Analyst, 16,* 191–206.

Miltenberger, R. G. (2004). *Behavior modification: Principles and procedures* (3rd ed.). Belmont, CA: Wadsworth/Thomson Learning.

Mortenson, B. P., & Witt, J. C. (1998). The use of weekly performance feedback to increase teacher implementation of a prereferral academic intervention. *School Psychology Review, 27,* 613–627.

Mueller, M. M., Edwards, R. P., & Trahant, D. (2003). Translating multiple assessment techniques into an intervention selection model for classrooms. *Journal of Applied Behavior Analysis, 36,* 563–573.

Myerson, J., & Hale, S. (1994). Practical implications of the matching law. *Journal of Applied Behavior Analysis, 17,* 367–380.

National Reading Panel (2000). *Teaching children to read: An evidence-based assessment of the scientific research literature on reading and its implications for reading instruction* Available online: www.nichd.nih.gov/publications/nrp/smallbook.htm

Neef, N. A., Mace, F. C., & Shade, D. (1993). Impulsivity in students with serious emotional disturbance: The interactive effects of reinforcer rate, delay, and quality. *Journal of Applied Behavior Analysis, 26,* 37–52.

Neef, N. A., Mace, F. C., Shea, M. C., & Shade, D. (1992). Effects of reinforcer rate and reinforcer quality on time allocation: Extension of matching theory to educational settings. *Journal of Applied Behavior Analysis, 25,* 691–699.

Neef, N. A., Shade, D., & Miller, M. S. (1994). Assessing the influential dimensions of reinforcers on choice in students with serious emotional disturbance. *Journal of Applied Behavior Analysis, 27,* 575–583.

Noell, G. H. (2008). Research examining the relationships among consultation process, treatment integrity, and outcomes. In W. P. Erchul & S. M. Sheridan (Eds.), *Handbook of research in school consultation* (pp. 323–341). New York, NY: Lawrence Erlbaum Associates.

Noell, G. H., Duhon, G. J., Gatti, S. L., & Connell, J. E. (2002). Consultation, follow-up, and behavior management intervention implementation in general education. *School Psychology Review, 31,* 217–234.

Noell, G. H., Witt, J. C., Gilbertson, D. N., Ranier, D. D., & Freeland, J. T. (1997). Increasing teacher intervention implementation in general education settings through consultation and performance feedback. *School Psychology Quarterly, 12,* 77–88.

Noell, G. H., Witt, J. C., LaFleur, L. H., Mortenson, B. P., Ranier, D. D., & LeVelle, J. (2000). A comparison of two follow-up strategies to increase teacher intervention implementation in general education following consultation. *Journal of Applied Behavior Analysis, 33,* 271–284.

Noell, G. H., Witt, J. C., Slider, N. J., Connell, J. E., Gatti, S. L., Williams, K. L., et al., (2005). Treatment implementation following behavioral consultation in schools: A comparison of three follow-up strategies. *School Psychology Review, 34,* 87–106.

Northup, J., Broussard, C., Jones, K., George, T., Vollmer, T. R., & Herring, M. (1995). The differential effects of teacher and peer attention on the disruptive classroom behavior of three children with a diagnosis of attention deficit hyperactivity disorder. *Journal of Applied Behavior Analysis, 28,* 227–228.

Persampieri, M., Gortmaker, V., Daly, E. J., III, Sheridan, S. M., & McCurdy, M. (2006). Promoting parent use of empirically supported reading interventions: Two experimental investigations of child outcomes. *Behavioral Interventions, 21,* 31–57.

Peterson, L., Homer, A. L., & Wonderlich, S. A. (1982). The integrity of independent variables in behavior analysis. *Journal of Applied Behavior Analysis, 15,* 477–492.

Pierce, W. D., & Epling, W. F. (1995). *Behavior analysis and learning.* Englewood Cliffs, NJ: Prentice–Hall.

Pressley, M. E., & Woloshyn, V. E. (1995). *Cognitive strategy instruction that really improves children's academic performance. Cognitive strategy training series* (2nd ed.). Cambridge, MA: Brookline Books.

Reynolds, G. S. (1975). *A primer of operant conditioning.* Glenview, IL: Scott Foresman.

Riley-Tillman, T. C., & Chafouleas, S. M. (2003). Using interventions that exist in the natural environment to increase treatment integrity and social influence in consultation. *Journal of Educational & Psychological Consultation, 14,* 139–156.

Rilling, M. (1977). Stimulus control and inhibitory processes. In W. K. Honig & J. E. R. Staddon (Eds.), *Handbook of operant behavior* (pp. 432–480). Englewood Cliffs, NJ: Prentice-Hall, Inc.

Sasso, G. M., Reimers, T. M., Cooper, L. J., Wacker, D., Berg, W., Steege, M., et al. (1992). Use of descriptive and experimental analyses to identify the functional properties of aberrant behavior in school settings. *Journal of Applied Behavior Analysis, 25,* 809–821.

Schwartz, B. (1989). *Psychology of learning and behavior.* New York: W.W. Norton & Co.

Shahan, T. A., & Chase, P. N. (2002). Novelty, stimulus control, and operant variability. *The Behavior Analyst, 25,* 175–190.

Sidman, M. (1960). *Tactics of scientific research: Evaluating experimental data in psychology.* New York: Basic Books.

Skinner, B. F. (1957). *Verbal behavior.* Acton, MA: Copley Publishing Group.

Skinner, B. F. (1987). Whatever happened to psychology as the science of behavior? *American Psychologist, 42,* 780–786.

Skinner, C. H. (1998). Preventing academic skills deficits. In T. S. Watson & F. Gresham (Eds.), *Handbook of child behavior therapy: Ecological considerations in assessment, treatment, and evaluation* (pp. 61–83). New York: Plenum.

Skinner, C. H. (2002). An empirical analysis of interspersal research: Evidence, implications and applications of the discrete task completion hypothesis. *Journal of School Psychology, 40,* 347–368.

Skinner, C. H., Cashwell, C., & Dunn, M. (1996). Independent and interdependent group contingencies: Smoothing the rough waters. *Special Services in the Schools, 12,* 61–78.

Skinner, C. H., Fletcher, P. A., & Henington, C. (1996). Increasing learning rates by increasing student response rates: A summary of research. *School Psychology Quarterly, 11,* 313–325.

Skinner, C. H., Pappas, D. N., & Davis, K. A. (2005). Enhancing academic engagement: Providing opportunities for responding and influencing students to choose to respond. *Psychology in the Schools, 42,* 389–403.

Skinner, C. H., & Shapiro, E. S. (1989). A comparison of taped-words and drill interventions on reading fluency in adolescents with behavior disorders. *Education and Treatment of Children, 12,* 123–133.

Skinner, C. H., Waterson, H. J., Bryant, D. R., Bryant, R. J., Collins, P. M., Hill, C. J., et al. (2002). Team problem solving based on research, functional behavioral assessment data, teacher acceptability, and Jim Carey's interview. *Proven Practices: Prevention & Remediation Solutions for Schools, 4,* 56–64.

Skinner, C. H., Williams, R. L., & Neddenriep, C. E. (2004). Using interdependent group-oriented reinforcement to enhance academic performance in general education classrooms. *School Psychology Review, 33,* 384–397.

Stecker, P. M., Fuchs, L. S., & Fuchs, D. (2005). Using curriculum-based measurement to improve student achievement: Review of research. *Psychology in the Schools, 42,* 795–819.

Sterling-Turner, H. E., Robinson, S. L., & Wilczynski, S. M. (2001). Functional assessment of distracting and disruptive behaviors in the school setting. *School Psychology Review, 30,* 211–226.

Sterling-Turner, H. E., Watson, T. S., Wildmon, M., Watkins, C., & Little, E. (2001). Investigating the relationship between training type and treatment integrity. *School Psychology Quarterly, 16,* 56–67.

Stokes, T. F., & Baer, D. M. (1977). An implicit technology of generalization. *Journal of Applied Behavior Analysis, 10,* 349–367.

Sturmey, P. (1995). Diagnostic-based pharmacological treatment of behavior disorders in persons with developmental disabilities: A review and a decision-making typology. *Research in Developmental Disabilities, 16,* 235–252.

Sulzbacher, S. I., & Houser, J. E. (1968). A tactic to eliminate disruptive behaviors in the classroom: Group contingent consequences. *American Journal of Mental Deficiency, 73,* 88–90.

Taylor, J. & Miller, M. (1997). When timeout works some of the time: The importance of treatment integrity and functional assessment. *School Psychology Quarterly, 12,* 4–22.

Torgesen, J. K., Alexander, A. W., Wagner, R. K., Rashotte, C. A., Voeller, K. K. S., & Conway, T. (2001). Intensive remedial instruction for children with severe reading disabilities: Immediate and long-term outcomes from two instructional approaches. *Journal of Learning Disabilities, 34,* 33–58.

Touchette, P. E., MacDonald, R. F., & Langer, S. N. (1985). A scatter plot for identifying stimulus control of problem behavior. *Journal of Applied Behavior Analysis, 18,* 343–351.

Turco, T. L., & Elliott, S. N. (1990). Acceptability and effectiveness of group contingencies for improving spelling achievement. *Journal of School Psychology, 28,* 27–37.

Vollmer, T. R., Borrero, J. C., Wright, C. S., Van Camp, C., & Lalli, J. S. (2001). Identifying possible contingencies during descriptive analyses of severe behavior disorders. *Journal of Applied Behavior Analysis, 34,* 269–287.

Vollmer, T. R., Iwata, B. A., Zarcone, J. R., Smith, R. G., & Mazaleski, J. L. (1993). The role of attention in the treatment of attention-maintained self-injurious behavior: Noncontingent reinforcement and differential reinforcement of other behavior. *Journal of Applied Behavior Analysis, 26,* 9–21.

Wacker, D. P., Steege, M. W., Northup, J., Sasso, G., Berg, W., Reimers, T., et al. (1990). A component analysis of functional communication training across three topographies of severe behavior problems. *Journal of Applied Behavior Analysis, 23,* 417–429.

Weiss, B., & Weisz, J. R. (1995). Relative effectiveness of behavioral versus nonbehavioral child psychotherapy. *Journal of Consulting and Clinical Psychology, 63,* 317–320.

Wickstrom, K. F., Jones, K. M., LaFleur, L. H., & Witt, J. C. (1998). An analysis of treatment integrity in school-based consultation. *School Psychology Quarterly, 13,* 141–154.

Witt, J. C., Daly, E. M., & Noell, G. (2000). *Functional Assessments: A step-by-step guide to solving academic and behavior problems.* Longmont, CO: Sopris West.

Witt, J. C., Noell, G. H., LaFleur, L. H., & Mortenson, B. P. (1997). Teacher usage of interventions in general education: Measurement and analysis of the independent variable. *Journal of Applied Behavior Analysis, 30,* 693–696.

CHAPTER 6

SCHOOL PSYCHOLOGY AND DEVELOPMENTAL PSYCHOLOGY: MOVING FROM PROGRAMS TO PROCESSES[1]

ROBERT C. PIANTA
University of Virginia

School psychology and developmental psychology have a long, but somewhat mixed record of association. The theories of development that undergird much of the understanding of human behavior clearly have had a role in the applications of psychological science in the schools. But tracing the link between what we know about development and the practice of school psychology is not at all easy. One reason for this is that school psychology has been a profession dominated by technique rather than theory. For good reason, school psychologists want to solve pressing problems in schools, whether they involve identifying disability, consulting on classroom management, or helping students learn to read. The school psychology research literature, as a consequence of this focus on technique, has for the most part been about discriminating the value of one technical approach to problems from another. Much less attention has

[1]The work reported herein was supported in part by support to the National Center for Early Development and Learning under the Educational Research and Development Centers Program, PR/Award No. R307A60004, as administered by the Office of Educational Research and Improvement, U.S. Department of Education. It was also supported by the National Institute of Child Health and Human Development (NICHD) Study of Early Child Care (U10-HD25449) and NICHD R21-43750. The contents do not necessarily represent the positions or policies of the Office of Educational Research and Improvement, the U.S. Department of Education, or the NICHD, and endorsement by the federal government should not be assumed.

been paid to understanding the mechanisms that explain why a given technique should or should not work, and mechanism is in large part the focus of developmental psychology. Over the long haul, this cleaving of a focus on mechanism from attention to technique has eroded the extent to which research and practice in school psychology is rooted in knowledge about the various circumstances under which children change and grow, and the contextual conditions that optimize or prevent such growth. In some ways, the starting point for school psychology has been the technical issues in solving educational problems. A complementary approach to solving problems in schools is to start from an understanding of developmental processes and mechanisms. Neither is sufficient: to focus on technique at the expense of mechanism can stifle scientifically based progress supporting progressively more sophisticated and effective techniques; to focus on mechanism at the expense of application can create knowledge divorced from practical realities.

Of course approaching problem solving in education from both sides, technique and mechanism, is probably most desirable. In the present chapter, I frame this link between school psychology and development psychology as a movement from programs to processes; that is, in order for practitioners to be best equipped to address the needs of children and teachers in schools, knowledge about developmental processes may be a "tool" as or more useful than the latest technique. I will try to illustrate this by examples from the study of adolescent development and implications for approaches to actions in classrooms that can enhance the value of experiences in those settings for adolescent development. Prior to this illustrative discussion, the chapter provides an overview of broad issues related to linking school and developmental psychology. This progression from basic knowledge about development to interventions in schools designed to promote development, is illustrative of the more general movement from a focus on program and technique to process and mechanism that I am suggesting can be helpful to the field of school psychology.

CONCEPTUAL LINKAGE OF SCHOOL AND DEVELOPMENTAL PSYCHOLOGY

This chapter is being written at a time in which there is increasing recognition that understanding the nature and course of development is linked both with our understanding of schooling's effects on development, and renewed interest in applying those understandings to creating solutions that work for children. In the last two decades, with the rise of contextualism in developmental science (Cicchetti & Aber, 1998; Lerner, 1998) and the focus on positive development in community settings (Connell, Kubisch, Schorr, & Weiss, 1995), schools have become of great interest to developmentalists (e.g., www.cfchildren.org). Extensive developmentally informed programs of research on schooling and its effects have been reported in the last 10 to 15 years (e.g., Alexander & Entwisle, 1988; Eccles & Roeser, 1998; Ladd & Burgess, 1999; Morrison & Connor, 2002; Ramey et al., 2000; Stevenson & Lee, 1990). From the school psychology side of the relationship, it is abundantly clear that the major publication outlets for original research in the field have included a greater number of articles focused on developmental processes and theories (e.g., Gifford-Smith & Brownell, 2003), and that cross-fertilization of knowledge, ideas, and research methods, is active and ongoing.

Schools are *designed* to intentionally and strategically direct the nature and course of development. Development is the focus of schooling and school psychologists most often become engaged in the link between schooling and development when the output of this interaction of context (school) and process (development) is not acceptable to teachers, students, or parents. Solving this problem is, in part, the job of the school psychologist. The best solutions have

to be grounded in both the most up-to-date understanding of how development has been and could be shaped by experiences in school, and how to apply that knowledge in an efficient and effective manner that solves problems.

Rutter and Maughan (2002) conclude their recent summary of 30 years of research on schooling and development by identifying a set of knowledge gaps that prevent successful solutions to the problems of school failure: 1) the need for solid evidence on factors related to changing failing schools, including attention to contextual features (such as community attitudes), resources (intake mix), teacher recruitment, finances, and leadership; 2) the need for knowledge on peer processes and influences within schools; 3) the lack of attention to characteristics of schools that matter for social, behavioral, and self-efficacy outcomes; 4) the need to know how schools foster motivation and citizenship; and 5) the profound lack of knowledge related to how different experiences in schools affect children differently based on their pattern of strengths and limitations, and how and why children respond so differently to the school environment.

These questions chart a research agenda that melds school psychology's interests in solutions with a developmental framework or paradigm for conducting that research. Although these knowledge gaps, identified by developmental scientists, could easily have been among those listed by school superintendents, they reflect developmental psychology's interest in contexts and processes; in individual differences as well as normative growth; in multiple domains of functioning; and in multilayered systems co-acting across time. I have argued elsewhere (Pianta, 2006b) that school psychologists and developmental psychologists share the same *development in context* paradigm, and that both fields would benefit from more strategic and systematic exploitation of that mutual interest.

Educators and developmental psychologists have made great headway in identifying key ingredients of school settings that, when systematically altered, can provide supports for children's academic and social outcomes (Brophy, 2004; Greenberg, Domitrovich, & Bumbarger, 2001; Hamre & Pianta, 2005). This knowledge has spawned an assortment of intervention packages, programs, and techniques developed to address students' needs. Similarly, the field of school psychology, and applied psychology more generally, has embarked on an effort to identify, catalog, and disseminate knowledge about intervention techniques that have been demonstrated empirically to show benefits for children (Kratochwill & Stoiber, 2002). In the area of assessment, increasing attention is being paid to integrating techniques and tools traditionally included in school psychologists' portfolios (e.g., tests of decontextualized abilities and traits) with measurement procedures more closely tied to school performance (e.g., standards assessments, functional behavioral analysis, response-to-intervention). In each of these examples, we see a closer connection between programs and techniques on the one hand, and the processes and mechanisms that support the use of those techniques, on the other. In the academic arena this progression is evident in the shifting of attention over the last decade from a search for evidence-based curricula, to a focus on processes related to implementation of curricula, to recent calls for research on teacher training mechanisms that support high-quality implementation (Institute of Education Sciences [IES], 2004a). This movement from program to process is not a simple repackaging of old ideas, but a foundational shift in focus and effort. This shift is best illustrated by recent work in preventive intervention and the informant-based assessments that are described below.

The "Problem" of Implementation Variation

In conclusions drawn from their comprehensive review of school-age (and mostly school-based) prevention efforts, Greenberg et al. (2001) noted the need to focus attention on qualities of the school environment that moderate intervention effects and account for the high levels of interindividual variability in response to standardized clinical trial interventions. Understanding, and ultimately harnessing, factors related to program or practice *implementation* (another term for interindividual variability) is a serious challenge to developmental psychopathologists' intervention and prevention work. Large amounts of accrued evidence suggest that even the most well-described, manualized, standardized, scientifically based programs are enacted in practice in ways that vary widely from child to child or classroom to classroom (e.g., Greenberg et al., 2001). This phenomenon could be responded to as a source of error in evaluation studies, as an obstacle to delivering mental health resources to children, or as an aspect of the context into which interventions are being inserted that warrants attention in its own right. This latter response is consistent with the movement from programs to processes

that has occurred in some domains of academic achievement in relation to renewed attention to identifying the specific processes by which teacher education experiences eventually produce academic achievement (IES, 2004a). There is a growing recognition that educational techniques and mechanisms are two sides of the same coin (IES, 2004a).

Consistent with this view, Rones and Hoagwood (2000) conclude there is so little exploration in technique-focused clinical trial research of the quality of, and factors related to, implementation, that it greatly impedes the provision of supportive services to children precisely because variation in implementation involves attention to process and mechanism. Roeser, Eccles, and Sameroff (2000) extend the linkage between developmental studies and education even further when arguing, with respect to understanding middle-school effects, that the need is for research "linking the study of adolescents' experience, motivation, and behavior in school with the study of their teachers' experience, motivation, and behavior at school" (p. 466). Such a perspective directly addresses the interindividual variability observed in standardized clinical trial interventions by making variation in psychological and behavioral processes a legitimate focus of study. This interface is where developmental and school psychology meet.

To extend this point it can be argued that the lack of a process-focused research agenda related to socioemotional adaptation in schools is in part responsible for the often-reported conclusion from reviews of intervention and prevention programs that implementation processes account for significant variation in the efficacy of such efforts (Greenberg et al., 2001; Rones & Hoagwood, 2000). Greenberg et al. (2001), in their comprehensive review of programs for preventing mental disorders in children, conclude that if programs found effective in clinical trials are to go to "scale" then one of the key steps will be to identify implementation mechanisms responsible for both effective and ineffective results. In this sense, variation in implementation of effective interventions (the bane of the technically focused) is of paramount importance for the light it sheds on developmental-contextual mechanisms responsible for effects (and lack of effects).

A Multilevel Framework Guiding Developmental Analysis of School Settings

One of the more serious conceptual impediments to a fuller realization of the mutual benefits of school and developmental psychology is the tendency toward dichotomization that divides these disciplines (Sameroff, 2000) into a research-practice polarity. This divide of territory, knowledge, and technical expertise is not helpful to solving the problems that Rutter and Maughan (2002) so aptly described.

Pianta (2006b) has presented an integrative developmental-contextualist framework consistent with the type of multilevel model of development in context that is a well-accepted feature of developmental psychology (Bronfenbrenner & Morris, 1998). In this conceptualization, the basic processes and mechanisms in which development progresses (e.g., in mastery, motivation, relationships, identity) are threaded through and continuous with experiences that stimulate these processes in a range of settings (e.g., schools, families, peer groups) in such a way that development is continuous across settings rather than bounded by settings. To put it more simply, processes of affiliation and autonomy, so important in peer groups, are activated and shaped by experiences in the neighborhood and the classroom that operate not independently of one another, but in concert, to shape the stance and rules that will guide the way a child forms relationships (Sroufe, Egeland, Carlson, & Collins, 2005). To understand (and change) behavior with peer relationships in one setting (e.g., school) it is necessary to understand how developmental processes related to affiliation and autonomy operate normatively, and for a given child, in other settings.

This emphasis on continuity of processes *across* settings in contrast to process as *bounded within* settings opens up ways to examine and test aspects of the general ecological-developmental model in schools. For example, in developmental research focused on family adaptation or family effects, child-parent relationships and interactions, parents' psychological attributes and development, sibling relationships, and peer relations are modeled as part of the ecology. In school settings, processes related to teacher-child relationships and interactions, classroom social and instructional qualities, collaborative grouping of peers, and peer status are also proximal agents of change that likely involve many of the same mechanisms as the corresponding family-based proximal processes (e.g., Gambone, Klem, & Connell, 2002), but have yet to be examined with this cross-validation of general principles in mind.

To elaborate, instead of positing that relational mechanisms and processes that occur between parents and children in home settings are separate or somehow different from relational processes that may be activated toward adults in child care or school settings, this conceptualization posits that developmental processes are activated and developmentally meaningful across ecologies. To continue, the processes by which self-regulation mechanisms develop and function have been widely studied in relation to family effects and patterns of adaptation in family settings. Similarly, normative biobehavioral processes related to temperament, stress-reactivity, and pubertal development, having received considerable attention related to developmental antecedents and sequelae in family settings. But biobehavioral development and self-regulatory processes are also relevant in relation to understanding school adaptation and school effects (Quas, Murowchick, Bensadoun, & Boyce, 2002; Watamura, Donzella, Alwin, & Gunnar, 2003). For example, cortisol levels vary with prior experience in families (Quas et al., 2002) but also appear related to experiences during the school (or child care) day (Watamura et al., 2003) and interact with the peer network and quality of child-teacher relationship in classroom settings (Little & Kobak, 2003). In an elegant example of studying developmental mechanisms in school settings, Little and Kobak (2003) examined cortisol secretion of students in special education classrooms for children with emotional disturbances as a function of the quality of their relationship with the teacher. High levels of secretion were evident for these students, on average, indicating the stressful nature of the setting. However, the students sharing a close, emotionally supportive relationship with the teacher, showed significantly lower levels of cortisol than did their classmates. In this research, studying in classroom settings, a normative developmental process usually attended to in laboratory or family-based work, revealed mechanisms nearly identical to those uncovered by research done in family settings.

Classrooms reflect proximal-process experiences of children that include: engaging and appropriate instruction, opportunities for problem solving, systematic use of feedback on one's performance-guided instruction, opportunities and support for peer relations and friendships, and classroom management in which behavioral expectations are stated clearly and enforced consistently (see Evertson & Weinstein, 2006), as well as relationships with teachers and peers and status within peer networks (e.g., Gifford-Smith &

Brownell, 2003; Good & Brophy, 1986; Pianta, Steinberg, & Rollins, 1995). The kind of instructional and social interactions with adults that occur in classroom settings have reliable and detectable effects on children's achievement and social competence (e.g., Howes et al., 2008; Meyer, Wardrop, Hastings, & Linn, 1993; Morrison & Connor, 2002; NICHD ECCRN, 2002, 2004; Peisner-Feinberg & Burchinal, 1997). Likewise, interactions with peers within schools are also predictive of a range of social, psychological, and academic outcomes (Gifford-Smith & Brownell, 2003). Mining this rich vein of knowledge from both the school psychology perspective on identifying and solving problems and the developmental psychology focus on theory and mechanism, can only enhance the interests of both.

ADOLESCENT DEVELOPMENT AND SCHOOL PSYCHOLOGY: A SERIES OF TRANSLATIONS

Adolescence is a challenge to school psychologists and is an area of recent advances in developmental psychology that make it a prime starting point for illustrating the potential linkages between the two. Creating middle school and high school settings that appropriately respond to and enhance the development of the wide range of students enrolled is perhaps one of the most daunting prospects facing educators in the next decade of school reform. A good place to begin will be the knowledge of adolescent development emerging from developmental psychology. In this section I will outline this work briefly and describe a series of translational steps linking developmental science and educational practice: the first a link from basic science to a developmentally informed view of school settings; and the second that links the developmental understanding of school settings to practices that enhance the potential value of those settings.

Step One: What Do We Know about Development in Adolescence?

As children move from late childhood into early and middle adolescence they experience biological, cognitive, social-cognitive, and emotional changes that require renegotiation of autonomy and relatedness in the family (Collins, Gleason, & Sesma, 1997; Holmbeck, Paiakoff, & Brooks-Gunn, 1995), that stimulate changes in peer relationships and coping with peer pressures (Hogue & Steinberg, 1995; Windle &

Davies, 1999), and that precipitate the development of sexual friendships and romantic relationships (Connolly & Johnson, 1996; Neeman, Hubbard, & Masten, 1995). Moreover, the developmental changes of this period lead to new opportunities for social engagement outside of family relationships and for developing a sense of one's own efficacy in a broader world. Relevant to these developments is work on civic engagement (Eccles & Barber, 1999; Killen & Horn, 2000), religiosity (Furstenberg & Hughes, 1995; King, Elder, & Whitbeck, 1997), work orientation (Larson, 2000), and future orientation (Nurmi, 1991). Broadly speaking, psychosocial functioning in adolescence can be characterized in terms of two arenas: (a) functioning in interpersonal relationships in family, peer, and extrafamilial settings, and (b) features of individual socioemotional development involving relations to institutions, goals, and self. Socioemotional development during adolescence is marked by the emergence and consolidation of the youth's connections and relations to community institutions, as well as the youth's own goals and values. In some discussions, this set of outcomes is referred to as "positive youth development" (Larson, 2000) and marks a view of adolescence as a period of opportunity in contrast to one of stress and pathology (Steinberg & Morris, 2001).

To better understand adolescent cognitive development, we must view it within the contexts in which the adolescent grows up and seek to understand "how these contexts are changing and how these changes are changing the nature of adolescence" (Steinberg, 2002, p. xv). Wigfield, Eccles, and Pintrich (1996) note that this growing emphasis on contextual models of development offers potentially important and exciting insights in psychological and educational theory. Important changes occur in children's thinking as they progress through adolescence. At a descriptive level, the most striking changes include the increasing ability to think more abstractly and hypothetically, to employ more sophisticated information-processing strategies, to consider multiple dimensions of a problem, and to reflect on one's self and on complicated problems (Keating, 1990, 2004). Increasingly, individuals encounter more challenging academic tasks that require the use of varied and sophisticated learning strategies and higher-order cognitive processes. Work in brain imaging (Giedd et al., 1999), neuropsychological assessment (Luciana & Nelson, 2000, 2002; Luciana, Sullivan, & Nelson,

2001), and small-scale longitudinal studies (e.g., Demetriou, Christou, Spanoudis, & Platsidou, 2002), points toward a central role of the prefrontal cortex and of executive function in adolescent cognitive development. Attention, planning, reasoning, memory, and other strategic cognitive processes of executive function undergird virtually all learning.

These processes of memory, planning/decision making, and attention are in turn regulated by brain developments in the prefrontal cortex (Keating, 2004; Luciana et al., 2001). Strategic cognitive processes also are likely to predict acquisition of academic skills. Like attention, planning and problem solving are essential for success in many domains of human functioning, for example, mathematics and writing (Bruer, 1993). Spatial working memory also is important to the demands of adolescent learning and information processing (Petrides & Milner, 1982). There is a convergence of evidence from research on reasoning, basic processing, decision making, and neuroimaging that it is the integration of basic cognitive elements into a system of executive functions under increasingly conscious control that is the hallmark of adolescent cognition, rather than any single cognitive "driver" of such change (Keating, 2004).

Academic performance in school is a potent predictor of functioning in later life, including school dropout and delinquency (Cairns & Cairns, 1994; Moffitt & Caspi, 2001), as well as college and later job performance (Steinberg, Brown, & Dornbusch, 1996). Patterns of academic interests diversify and individualize to shape intellectual and social adjustment (Roeser & Eccles, 1998), and academic trajectories become more canalized, partly shaping friendship patterns and extracurricular activities (Eccles, Early, Fraser, Belansky, & McCarthy, 1997). Often it is the interaction of pubertal changes with contextual and experiential factors (e.g., the transition to middle school) that influence academic achievement (Lerner & Jovanovic, 1999). Keating (1990) notes that increases in achievement slow during adolescence, but that a number of factors in school settings can promote gains, such as facilitated experiences in using cognitive skills. Yet, observational research in middle schools has shown that cognitive processing demands are often lower than in elementary school classrooms and this factor could account for disengagement and decreases in achievement (Eccles et al., 1993).

In Eccles' theory of adolescent achievement motivation, two constructs are central: Beliefs about one's competence, and values attached to achievement (Eccles et al., 1997). Young people's perceptions of their abilities and the value they attach to achievement are important determiners of school achievement, as well as being related to other motivational variables, such as enjoyment and interest (MacIver, Stipek, & Daniels, 1991). Parents' perceptions of their children's academic abilities have a direct influence on their children's self-perceptions, and in turn children's valuing of achievement is a mediator of performance (Holloway, 1986; Jacobs & Eccles, 1992; Parsons, Adler, & Kaczala, 1982). Children tend to confirm parents' expectations of their school performance regardless of the measured academic potential of the child (Alexander & Entwisle, 1988; Jacobs, 1991). Academic self-efficacy as well as achievement values also are related to students' experiences in school (Ferguson & Dorman, 2001; Pintrich, Roeser, & DeGroot, 1994). Based on extensive research, Eccles, Lord, and Roeser (1996) call for "studies of different developmental trajectories in achievement-related characteristics and their relation to school performance and choice" (pp. 155–156).

Poor adjustment in adolescence often is expressed as a mix of aggressive and antisocial behavior as well as signs of depressed mood and social anxiety—more generally referred to as externalizing and internalizing problems. These are often reflections of normal development, as adolescents cope with increased freedom and responsibility, more choices, decisions about the future, peer pressures, and the biological changes of puberty (Siegel & Scovill, 2000). For some adolescents, however, internalizing (anxiety, depression) and/or externalizing (aggression, antisocial behavior, delinquency) problems represent the continuation of earlier patterns of poor adjustment. For still others, the onset of problems in adolescence may be harbingers of more chronic problems that will continue into adulthood. Rates of both internalizing and externalizing problems have been found to increase in adolescence (Cohen et al., 1993; Moffitt, Caspi, Rutter, & Silva, 2001).

To many, the very term adolescence connotes the biological changes that take place during puberty, and no study of adolescence, especially when set in a longitudinal framework, would be complete without consideration of pubertal processes. Although the sequence of pubertal changes is predictable, pubertal timing is extremely variable (Largo & Prader, 1983a, 1983b; Marshall & Tanner, 1969, 1970). The normal range of onset is ages 8 to 14 in females and ages 9 to 15 in males, although physical maturation takes place at younger ages in African American children, especially girls, than European American children (Herman-Giddens, Slora, Wasserman, & Bourdony, 1997; Kipke, 1999). Indeed, the timing of puberty can be altered by stress, socioeconomic status, environmental toxins, nutrition and diet, exercise, amount of fat and body weight, and the presence of chronic illness. Family, peer group, and neighborhood factors influence pubertal timing, though their role remains unclear (Crockett & Petersen, 1993; Susman, Dorn & Schiefelbein, 2003). For example, family conflict accelerates the onset of menarche (Graber, Brooks-Gunn, & Warren, 1995; Moffitt, Caspi, Belsky, & Silva, 1992; Surbey, 1989), as do stepfather presence and dyadic stress in the parent-child relationship (Ellis & Garber, 2000). Also, the positive quality of early father involvement plays a role in regulating the timing of menarche, although the exact mechanisms remain unknown (Ellis, McFadyen-Ketchum, Dodge, Pettit, & Bates, 1999). Other work also highlights the potentially influential role of positive features of family relationships in influencing the timing of girls' puberty (Graber & Brooks-Gunn, 1999).

A substantial body of evidence suggests that variations in the age of onset of puberty may have developmental and behavioral conse-quences during adolescence and even beyond (Graber, Brooks-Gunn & Petersen, 1996; Graber, Lewinsohn, Seeley, & Brooks-Gunn, 1997; Mon-temayor, Adams & Gullotta, 1990; Wigfield et al., 1996). A growing literature suggests that the early onset of puberty poses risks for girls' development (e.g., Caspi, Lynam, Moffitt, & Silva, 1993; Dick, Rose, Kaprio, & Viken, 2000; Flannery, Rowe, & Gulley, 1993; Ge, Conger, & Elder, 1996; Ge, Brody, Conger, Simons, & Murry, 2002; Ge et al., 2003; Stattin & Magnusson, 1990). Early maturers tend to be shorter and heavier; have higher rates of conduct disorders; have lower self-esteem and higher rates of depression, eating disorders, and suicide (Kipke, 1999); and, in Sweden, were found to obtain less education and marry earlier than later-maturing girls (Magnusson, 1988; Stattin & Magnusson, 1990).

Of note in the discussion above is that most of the citations are of work published in the last 15 years—in no other area of developmental science has progress been so rapid as in adolescence. Translating this information into practices relevant for school psychologists' efforts

to solve problems in schools has been slow relative to the need for this information. For example, a recent National Governor's Association meeting called for the redesign of high school education, predicated in part on intersecting pressures. These include the perception that the returns to increased achievement from standards-based reform may be limited, the exceptional levels of variability in performance through high school and evidence that gaps in math and science are increasing, and the business community's call for a workforce that is better trained in life skills and work habits as well as technical expertise. The recent advances in basic knowledge about development have something to say about how reform can be accomplished and directed. The most mature knowledge base is centered on developmentally informed views of motivational processes in classroom settings, which will be the focus of the "translation" described next.

Step Two: Developmentally Informed Views of Classrooms Supporting Positive Adolescent Outcomes

Increasingly research on the social development of both normal and at-risk youths suggests ways of understanding adolescent social development and motivation that can inform educational practices and the very nature of the classroom as a behavior setting for youth. Below, this knowledge is described in relation to three features of classrooms supports (Pianta, 1999) for adolescents' levels of motivation within the classroom setting. These are based on recent research in several areas of adolescent psychosocial development that have focused on adolescents' needs to achieve a sense of connection within settings that also promote a sense of autonomy and competence (Allen, Hauser, Bell, & O'Connor, 1994; Allen, Kuperminc, Philliber, & Herre, 1994; Allen et al., 2002; Ryan & Deci, 2000). This suggests that an adolescent's motivation in any setting will partly depend on the extent to which the setting provides supports for *relatedness*, *autonomy*, and *competence* within that setting.

As a behavior setting, the classroom runs on two primary types of relationships: that between the student and the teacher, and the relationship of the students with one another. Adolescents *live* for their social relationships. Indeed, lack of relationships to others in school is one of the single best predictors of the propensity to drop out of school (Cairns, Cairns, & Neckerman,

1989; Lee & Burkam, 2003). Yet, the quality of these relationships is frequently an afterthought in battles over curricula, testing, school structure, and funding.

Positive relationships with adults are perhaps the single key ingredient in promoting positive youth development. The link between parental relationship quality and youth development is so well-established as to be a truism (Allen, Moore, Kuperminc, & Bell, 1998; Sroufe et al., 2005; Steinberg, 2001). Teacher-student relationship quality has received far less attention, yet teachers often spend *more* time interacting with adolescents each day than do parents (even when teaching students only for a single subject). Collectively, secondary school teachers provide the greatest exposure to adult influence that most adolescents experience in their daily lives. When teachers make modest efforts to form a personal connection with their adolescent students—such that the student feels known—they can dramatically enhance student motivation in school and emotional functioning outside of school (Roeser, Eccles, & Sameroff, 1998; Skinner, Zimmer-Gembeck, & Connell, 1998). Consistent with this idea, a recent phone survey found adolescents reporting that they would learn a great deal more if they felt their teachers cared about them personally (Public Agenda, 1997). Not surprisingly, at-risk adolescents report that a close and supportive relationship with a teacher is a key feature distinguishing those who succeed in school from those who do not (Resnick et al., 1997). Pianta, Hamre, and Stuhlman (2003), in their comprehensive review of the literature on the nature and significance of student-teacher relationships, conclude that for adolescents the dimension of closeness, connection, and affiliation afford them a sense of being known in the school and is a critical feature of these relationships in terms of developmental salience, even more so than relational conflict. Most secondary students, unfortunately, do not feel their teachers cared about them personally (Resnick et al., 1997).

The secondary school classroom can be an alienating and isolating setting not just for students but for teachers as well. Presumably, secondary school teachers enter their profession with some degree of affinity for working with and interacting with adolescents. Yet, for every 10 new teachers entering the profession each year, two or three will have become discouraged and changed professions within one year. The motivation of these teachers is in turn likely to be highly influenced by the quality of their classroom interactions with youth. Teachers, of course, experience the same needs for connection, competence, and autonomy as do the youth they teach (Deci, 1989). Yet, the nature of the classroom is such that it is often highly isolating for teachers. No one other than adolescents—or the occasional administrator in a position to judge their performance—is ever likely to be able to observe and interact with a teacher about what goes on within his/her classroom. Breaking down the isolation experienced by secondary school teachers—both by making interactions with students more positive and by building in *meaningful* and nonjudgmental peer interactions that are closely linked to what occurs within classrooms—potentially can bring about major changes in teacher motivation and development as well.

Building a healthy, academically and personally supportive relationship with students is certainly not an impossible task—some teachers do it instinctively—and it is a task that typically brings gratifications to teachers that more than makes up for the energy it may require of them. But for many teachers, structuring their classroom in ways to facilitate the development of healthy relationship with students will take a conscious effort and some guidance (Pianta, 1999; 2006a). One facet of the translation of science to practice being discussed is to focus upon turning the classroom setting into a *purposefully socially engaging environment* that motivates students and teachers to work toward and attain mutually satisfying competence goals. This begins with knowledge about the nature and consequences of everyday instructional and social interactions through which successful teachers establish a productive and satisfying interpersonal climate, and then seek to enhance the value of these interactions for promoting relationships. Hamre and Pianta (2005) recently demonstrated the powerful effects of everyday instructional and social interactions with teachers to close achievement gaps.

Focus groups of recent high school graduates have found that, when asked to think of the characteristics of their best teachers in high school, youths very frequently mentioned individuals who had taken *small extra steps* that showed they cared about students as individuals. Such behaviors are embedded in everyday interactions, but are often *strategic practices guided by knowledge of development*. These steps did not involve the kind of massive, unsustainable efforts sometimes heroically depicted in films, but rather were events as isolated as one-time conversations lasting 20 to 30 minutes at a critical point, or small gestures or jokes in the hallways outside of class that set up a cascading, self-sustaining cycle in which increasingly engaged students can energize and support teachers' energy and efforts, which in turn can further bolster student motivation (Eccles et al., 1993).

In addition to the teacher-youth relationship, peer interactions have tremendous potential as motivational forces for adolescents (Hartup & Stevens, 1997; Seidman et al., 2001), though it has long been recognized that these influences are frequently not toward positive academic outcomes (Bishop, Bishop, Gelbwasser, Green, & Zuckerman, 2003; Coleman, 1961). Nonetheless, evidence also suggests that peer processes can be built into classroom interactions in productive ways, both large and small, *if* a conscious, thoughtful effort is made in this regard (Crosnoe, Cavanagh, & Elder, 2003). Research now demonstrates that the power of these interactions can be directed toward (or away) from academic purposes depending on the structure of the classroom (Berndt & Keefe, 1996). The traditional competitive organization of the classroom—with more energetic, able, or assertive students receiving most of the attention and rewards—has long been known to potentially create a "reverse peer culture" in which those who excel are seen as making life relatively harder for the rest of the class (Coleman, 1961). In addition, the extent to which teachers routinely use differential treatment of students and competitive techniques in classrooms has been linked not only to poorer academic attitudes but also to lower student self-esteem (Roeser & Eccles, 1998). In contrast, more cooperative methods, particularly those which in some way reward students for the learning of *all* students within their group, have been consistently found to increase levels of student engagement and achievement (Slavin, 1996). The extremes of either style, of course, rarely occur within classroom settings, but significant gradations between these two styles clearly exist and suggest opportunities to increase the extent to which peers become positive motivating forces within the classroom setting.

Establishing a sense of autonomy is by far the most pressing concern of most adolescents. Teens are engaged by challenges that are within reach and that also provide a sense of self-efficacy and control (Bandura, Barbaranelli, Caprara,

& Pastorelli, 1996; Eccles et al., 1993); these are experiences that offer challenges viewed as adult-like but for which appropriate scaffolding and support must be provided. One of the most tragically avoidable errors that secondary school teachers make is to assume that youth pushes for autonomy and self-expression are negative forces to be countered rather than positive energy to be harnessed. This basic misunderstanding of adolescent development (one of many promoted in most teacher education courses and reinforced by school policies) then takes form in highly controlling and punitive classroom and school settings, and through instruction that is highly teacher-driven and discouraging of exploration and curiosity. This mismatch of classroom and development, driven by a profound misunderstanding of teens, results in schools narrowing, rather than expanding, the "space" in which can be created zones of proximal development for youth.

Teens intrinsically seek to control their environments, but in almost all circumstances they do so in ways that nevertheless attend to relevant environmental constraints. Thus, a teen might argue endlessly, rudely, and even viciously with a parent over a seemingly minor issue of parental versus teen control—where the teen senses some possibility of the argument paying off. Teens want autonomy, desperately, but they are more than capable of recognizing structural limits to their autonomy and control, and seeking autonomy within those structures. They also are highly motivated by their own developing competence—as it offers the promise of greater future autonomy. The key then, is to direct teens' autonomy/control strivings in ways that develop their confidence while maintaining clear environmental controls.

The extent to which the classroom as a setting provides a structure that allows student effort to be quickly recognized and rewarded may be one of the single most important features in harnessing student autonomy strivings. Highly proximate goals tend to best maximize student motivation (Bandura & Schunk, 1981). Perhaps the most powerful example of this effect is seen in the almost ridiculously high levels of motivation provided by the second-by-second (but otherwise superficial and meaningless) reinforcement of video games. Youths will literally spend hours transfixed by moving dots on a computer screen—provided those dots are sufficiently responsive to their own inputs. Contrast this proximate motivation with the very long-delayed reinforcement provided by school programs that may enhance career potential many years in the future. Effective teachers bridge this gap through instruction that provides highly proximal goals manifest in a minute-by-minute way within the classroom (i.e., attention and concentration are scaffolded/supported by high-quality instruction and involvement is rewarded by active engagement in meaningful activities), and when homework is directly linked to learning (by being relevant and providing immediate consequences for completion versus noncompletion). This then engages the "video-game effect" in which settings that are highly contingent and meaningful in the very short term can elicit high levels of motivation and effort, and appears to be the exact opposite of what occurs in many middle and high school classrooms (Eccles et al., 1993).

The degree to which a student's effort in the classroom setting immediately "matters" to that student (i.e., it affects something that the student cares about, at least to some extent) is fundamental to motivation. The normal variation in classroom feedback/responsiveness is tremendous (NICHD ECCRN, 2005). These range from classrooms where teachers lecture as a monologue for 45 minutes and return graded papers only several weeks after they are turned in, to classrooms where students are asked to participate in thoughtful ways on a minute-by-minute basis that rapidly detects flagging attention or comprehension, and in which assignments are graded and feedback provided almost instantly to students. Observations of fifth grade classrooms, for example, demonstrate that the average student interacts with their teacher fewer than four times during a given one-hour period (NICHD ECCRN, 2005), a rate that is not conducive to building systems of interaction that serve as regulatory mechanisms with respect to students' affective, motivational, or learning-related experience and behavior (Pianta, 1999). Teachers can also support student competence development by having high expectations within their classrooms. Research to date suggests that the degree of the "academic press" within the classroom has effects on achievement even over and above relational supports (Phillips, 1997). Similarly, high teacher expectations for students have been found to predict achievement scores, particularly for more at-risk students (Madon, Jussim, & Eccles, 1997).

Teachers also have many opportunities to provide adolescents with meaningful choices in classrooms in ways that do not threaten teacher authority, but do not always recognize these opportunities or their importance to adolescent motivation. Supporting student autonomy does not mean giving up teacher control; on the contrary, autonomy can be supported by giving students choices of partners for group projects, types of projects to perform, and so on (Allen, Kuperminc et al., 1994; Anderman & Midgley, 1998). Students who are making choices are, by definition, not passive, but must to some degree become engaged in the learning process (Deci, 1991). The fundamental challenge to teachers in this regard to is to understand adolescents' developmental push for autonomy so that they can then seek to guide and direct it.

Relevance is the criteria by which adolescents will judge adults' efforts to have input into their lives—its salience is the byproduct of cognitive and social processes described earlier. Bronfenbrenner (1979) has eloquently described the importance youth attach to whether what occurs in a setting, such as a classroom, is actually linked to what happens in other important settings beyond it. Too often, the high school curriculum and the rationales behind it are taken as a "given" without recognition that these rationales need to be made clear to each new generation of students. Evidence suggests that drawing even tangential connections between what occurs within high school and the larger "real world" can transform student behavior. For example, involving students in significant, real-world, voluntary community service and then discussing it within the classroom in an ongoing way has been found to reduce failure rates by 50% in randomly controlled trials, with similarly profound effects upon other behaviors in youths' lives as well (Allen, Philliber, Herrling, & Kuperminc, 1997). Centuries ago, late adolescents were commanding armies and running countries (Barzun, 2000); centuries later an ever more competent generation of adolescents is confined to a classroom for hours a day with little vision of how what occurs within that classroom relates to the larger world which most find so fascinating.

On a smaller scale, teachers may increase the relevance of the classroom by making repeated, explicit ties between curricular material and real-world applications and engaging peer group processes in learning (given peer groups' intrinsic meaningfulness to youth). The key factor here is that the real-world connections must be made in ways that are meaningful *as perceived by the student*. Stating that principles of trigonometry can be used to determine the length of a ladder may be of little interest or relevance to a student who has never cared much about the length of ladders and can't easily imagine this being important to his/her future. On a different scale, connecting school work to actual careers in meaningful ways (e.g., describing how trigonometry gets used in designing jet fighter planes and GPS systems, exposing students to professionals working in these fields) can dramatically enhance motivation.

In short, the transformation of and increasing interconnections among basic cognitive, interpersonal, biological, and intrapersonal processes during adolescence can inform an understanding of how educational settings and resources intersect with those processes. For the most part these intersections are accidental, and often are driven by outdated views of adolescence or the organizational and institutional constraints and agendas of the educational setting. Successful school settings will demonstrate a deep understanding of and responsiveness to development—in this case, secondary schools in which the school and classroom settings provide support for the role(s) that relationships, autonomy/competence, and relevance play as primary drivers for youth.

Step Three: Solving Problems Using a Developmentally Informed Lens

In general terms, the next step in the translational process being discussed is to design practices that draw from a developmentally informed view of the educational setting (in the present case, classrooms). At this stage it is important to recognize that an exceptionally large number of interventions or practices can be imagined or implemented using such a lens. One way of approaching the organization of this universe of possibilities is to divide them into those potential solutions that are add-on programs (e.g., motivational programs in health class), or those that engage the typical everyday interactions in schools and seek to enhance the carrying capacity of those interactions for promoting development. For example, the frequently mentioned change to later start times for secondary schools is one approach to knowledge about the sleep cycles of adolescents and their relation to educationally relevant capacities such as attending to and processing information. The following discussion presents an approach to improving the motivational capacity of classrooms for promoting achievement and is presented in more detail in Allen and Pianta (2006).

The practical approach to increasing capacity in secondary classroom settings described by Allen and Pianta (2006) emphasizes two key features in terms of their suitability for addressing "capacity" problems in secondary classroom settings. First, it is based on a fundamental premise that interactions between teachers and youth are the key medium through which motivation is created, and thus the capacity of these interactions is critically dependent on teachers. As such the approach uses regular training and coaching sessions as the primary contacts with teachers that provide them with support and feedback to increase the level of available "social resources" in the classroom. This support and feedback is explicitly geared toward giving secondary school teachers (who enter the profession at least in part because they *like* working with youths) a way to make their relationships with adolescents far more mutually engaging and motivating. Teachers are likely to be far more motivated when their workplace consists of more engaged and motivated youth, and thus more willing to devote both time and emotional energy in developing their classroom environments. From this perspective, the intervention addresses the long-recognized, inherent, and chronic "resource crisis" in schools by recognizing that high school classrooms frequently contain vast, untapped (i.e., wasted) *human* resources seen as ennui on the part of both students and teachers (Sarason, 1982). *Both* teachers and students become far more engaged and energetic when the classroom can be structured so as to allow them to relate to one another successfully. These changes not only improve the academic outcomes of these settings—their primary purpose—but also may alter students' broader levels of well-being as well (Opdenakker & Damme, 2000; Roeser et al., 2000).

The second central feature of this approach is an objective framework for understanding and organizing the dimensions of student-teacher social and instructional interactions that are the focus of the support to teachers. In short, the practical value of support to teachers must be anchored on a validated, objective, standardized lens for gauging the developmental value of classrooms—this is one place where technical principles must be superimposed on knowledge of developmental mechanisms. In fact, Pianta (2005) has argued that validated, objective, standardized observational assessment of classroom interactions is the key to teacher professional development aimed at improving classroom effects on development. Thus the second key feature of the approach described by Allen and Pianta (2006) is that the feedback and support provided to teachers is *directly* tied to validated standardized observational systems that are shown to assess aspects of teachers' social and instructional interactions that predict growth in student performance (Pianta, La Paro, & Hamre, 2004). The vocabulary used to describe teacher-student interactions is based on this standardized, validated, developmentally informed system for assessing interaction processes in classrooms.

It is not foreign for school psychologists to rely on such process-focused assessment systems to inform problem-solving practices, although even some approaches that appear process-focused (such as Curriculum-Based Measurement, or response-to-intervention) are not anchored or implemented in real-time measurement of everyday learning and social interactions. The approach described by Allen and Pianta (2006) trains and supports teachers to rely on descriptions of the dimensions of classroom interaction presented in the Classroom Assessment Scoring System (CLASS; Pianta et al., 2004). The detailed descriptions of scale points on those dimensions are used to provide feedback to teachers about how they interact in their own classroom. Because the CLASS is one of the most current and widely used standardized assessments of social and instructional interactions in classrooms (and is designed to capture precisely those aspects of classroom interactions known to be resources for adolescent engagement and motivation), it functions as the "target" for teachers' interactions with students and the "content" of the work done in providing feedback and support to teachers to increase classroom capacity. In the Allen and Pianta (2006) approach, the CLASS functions as the "hinge" that intersects basic knowledge of development with solutions for practical problems in actual settings because it assesses how development occurs in those settings.

CONCLUSIONS

In closing, it is clear that school psychology and developmental psychology have in common a focus on understanding how and under what conditions experiences in school influence developmental processes and outcomes for children and youth. Although these fields differentially emphasize a focus on theory and understanding on the one hand, and technical concerns related to application and problem solving on the other, finding ways to systematically translate knowledge and expertise across diverse professional needs and foci is of tremendous importance to both fields. This chapter presented a way of thinking about the translation of knowledge and expertise in the form of links from developmental theory and school psychology techniques to developmentally informed understandings of schooling processes. It is this intersecting interface of these two fields, focusing on understanding and improving the ways that schooling processes shape development in that context, that is likely to be a very fruitful area of research in the coming decades.

REFERENCES

Alexander, K. L., & Entwisle, D. R. (1988). Achievement in the first 2 years of school: Patterns and processes. *Monographs of the Society for Research in Child Development*, *53*(2), (Serial No. 231).

Allen, J. P., Hauser, S. T., Bell, K. L., & O'Connor, T. G. (1994). Longitudinal assessment of autonomy and relatedness in adolescent-family interactions as predictors of adolescent ego development and self-esteem. *Child Development*, *65*, 179–194.

Allen, J. P., Kuperminc, G., Philliber, S., & Herre, K. (1994). Programmatic prevention of adolescent problem behaviors: The role of autonomy, relatedness, and volunteer service in the teen outreach program. *American Journal of Community Psychology*, *22*, 617–638.

Allen, J. P., Marsh, P., McFarland, C., McElhaney, K. B., Land, D. J., Jodl, K. M., et al. (2002). Attachment and autonomy as predictors of the development of social skills and delinquency during midadolescence. *Journal of Consulting & Clinical Psychology*, *70*, 56–66.

Allen, J. P., Moore, C., Kuperminc, G., & Bell, K. (1998). Attachment and adolescent psychosocial functioning. *Child Development*, *69*, 1406–1419.

Allen, J. P., Philliber, S., Herrling, S., & Kuperminc, G. P. (1997). Preventing teen pregnancy and academic failure: Experimental evaluation of a developmentally based approach. *Child Development*, *68*, 729–742.

Allen, J. P., & Pianta, R. C. (2006). *Intervention RFP proposal: Recasting the secondary school classroom as a context for positive youth development*. Submitted grant proposal, University of Virginia, Charlottesville.

Anderman, L. H., & Midgley, C. (1998). Motivation and middle school students. *ERIC Digest*, *EDO-PS-98-5*.

Bandura, A., & Schunk, D. H. (1981). Cultivating competence, self-efficacy and intrinsic interest through proximal self-motivation. *Journal of Personality and Social Psychology, 41,* 586–598.

Bandura, A., Barbaranelli, C., Caprara, G. V., & Pastorelli, C. (1996). Multifaceted impact of self-efficacy beliefs on academic functioning. *Child Development, 67,* 1206–1222.

Barzun, J. (2000). *From dawn to decadence: 500 years of western cultural life 1500 to the present.* London: HarperCollins.

Berndt, T. J., & Keefe, K. (1996). Friends' influence on school adjustment: A motivational analysis. In J. Juvonen & K. R. Wentzel (Eds.), *Social motivation: Understanding children's school adjustment. Cambridge studies in social and emotional development* (pp. 248–278). New York: Cambridge University Press.

Bishop, J., Bishop, M., Gelbwasser, L., Green, S., & Zuckerman, A. (2003). Nerds and freaks: A theory of student culture and norms. In D. Ravitch (Ed.), *Brookings papers on education policy: 2003.* Washington, DC: Brookings Institution Press.

Bronfenbrenner, U. (1979). *The ecology of human development: Experiments by nature and design.* Cambridge, MA: Harvard University Press.

Bronfenbrenner, U., & Morris, P. A. (1998). The ecology of developmental processes. In W. Damon & R. M. Lerner (Eds.), *Handbook of child psychology: Vol. 1. Theoretical models of human development* (5 ed., pp. 993–1029). New York: John Wiley & Sons.

Brophy, J. (2004). *Teaching. Educational Practices Series 1. International Academy of Education, Internationala Bureau of Education.* Lausanne, Switzerland: PCL.

Bruer, J. (1993). *Schools for thought: A science of learning in the classroom.* Cambridge, MA. MIT Press.

Cairns, B. D., & Cairns, R. B. (1994). *Lifelines and risks. Pathways of youth in our time.* Hemstead, NY: Harvester Wheatsheaf.

Cairns, R. B., Cairns, B. D., & Neckerman, H. J. (1989). Early school dropout: Configurations and determinants. *Child Development, 60,* 1437–1452.

Caspi, A., Lynam, D., Moffitt, T., & Silva, P. (1993). Unraveling girls' delinquency: Biological, dispositional and contextual contributions to adolescent misbehavior. *Developmental Psychology, 36,* 180–189.

Cicchetti, D., & Aber, J. L. (1998). Editorial: Contextualism and developmental psycho-pathology. *Development and Psychopathology, 10,* 137–141.

Cohen, P., Cohen, J., Kasen, S., Velez, C. N., Hartmark, C., Johnson, J., et al. (1993). An epidemiological study of disorders in late childhood and adolescence: I. Age- and gender-specific prevalence. *Journal of Child Psychology and Psychiatry, 34,* 851–868.

Coleman, J. S. (1961). *The adolescent society: The social life of the teenager and its impact on education.* New York: Free Press.

Collins, W. A., Gleason, T., & Sesma, A. (1997). Internalization, autonomy, and relationships: Development during adolescence. In J. E. Grusec & L. Kuczynski (Eds.) *Parenting and children's internalization of values: A handbook of contemporary theory* (pp. 78–99). New York: Wiley.

Connell, J. P., Kubisch, A., Schorr, L. B., & Weiss, C. (1995). *New approaches to evaluating community initiatives: Concepts, methods and contexts.* Washington, DC: Aspen Institute.

Connolly, J. A. & Johnson, A. M. (1996). Adolescents' romantic relationships and the structure and quality of their close interpersonal ties. *Personal Relationships, 3,* 185–195.

Crockett, L., & Petersen, A. (1993). Adolescent development: Health risks and opportunities for health promotion. In S. Millstein, A. Petersen & E. Nightingale (Eds.), *Promoting the health of adolescents* (pp. 33–87). NY: Oxford University Press.

Crosnoe, R., Cavanagh, S., & Elder, G. H., Jr. (2003). Adolescent friendships as academic resources: The intersection of friendship, race, and school disadvantage. *Sociological Perspectives, 46,* 331–352.

Deci, E. L. (1989). Self-determination in a work organization. *Journal of Applied Psychology, 74,* 580.

Deci, E. L. (1991). Motivation and education: The self-determination perspective. *Educational Psychologist, 26,* 325.

Demetriou, A., Christou, C., Spanoudis, G., & Platsidou, M. (2002). The development of mental processing: Efficiency, working memory, and thinking. *Monographs of the Society for Research in Child Development, 67*(1, Serial No. 268).

Dick, D., Rose, R., Kaprio, J., & Viken, R. (2000). Pubertal timing and substance use: Associations between and within families across late adolescence. *Developmental Psychology, 36,* 180–189.

Eccles, J. S., & Barber, B. L. (1999). Student council, volunteering, basketball, or marching band: What kind of extracurricular involvement matters? *Journal of Adolescent Research, 14,* 10–43.

Eccles, J. S., Early, D., Fraser, K., Belansky, E., & McCarthy, K. (1997). The relation of connection, regulation, and support for autonomy in the context of family, school, and peer group to successful adolescent development. *Journal of Adolescent Research, 12,* 263–286.

Eccles, J. S., Lord, S., & Roeser, R. W. (1996). Round holes, square pegs, rocky roads, and sore feet: A discussion of stage-environment fir theory applied to families and school. In D. Cicchetti & S. L. Toth (Eds), *Rochester symposium on developmental psychopathology: Vol. VII. Adolescence: Opportunities and challenges* (pp. 47–92). Rochester, NY: University of Rochester Press.

Eccles, J. S., Midgley, C., Wigfield, A., Buchanan, C. M., Reuman, D., Flanagan, C., et al. (1993). Development during adolescence: The impact of stage-environment fit on young adolescents' experiences in schools and in families. *American Psychologist, 48*, 90–101.

Eccles, J. S., & Roeser, R. W. (1998). School and community influences on human development. In M. H. Bornstein & M. E. Lamb (Eds), *Developmental psychology: An advanced textbook* (4th ed., pp. 503–554). Mahwah, NJ: Erlbaum.

Ellis, B. J., & Garber, J. (2000). Psychosocial antecedents of variation in girls' pubertal timing: Maternal depression, stepfather presence, and marital and family stress. *Child Development, 71*, 485–501.

Ellis, B., McFadyen-Ketchum, S., Dodge, K., Pettit, G., & Bates, J. (1999). Quality of early family relationships and individual differences in the timing of pubertal maturation in girls. *Journal of Personality and Social Psychology, 77*, 387–401.

Evertson, C. M., & Weinstein, C. S. (Eds.). (2006). *The handbook of classroom management: Research, practice, & contemporary issues*. Mahwah, NJ: Lawrence Erlbaum.

Ferguson, J. M. & Dorman, J. P. (2001). Psychosocial classroom environment and academic efficacy in Canadian high school mathematics classes. *Alberta Journal of Educational Research, 47*, 276–279.

Flannery, D. J., Rowe, D. C., & Gulley, B. L. (1993). Impact of pubertal status, timing and age on adolescent sexual experience and delinquency. *Journal of Adolescent Research, 8*, 21–40.

Furstenberg, F. F., & Hughes, M. E. (1995). Social capital and successful development among at-risk youth. *Journal of Marriage and the Family, 57*, 580–592.

Gambone, M. A., Klem, A. M., & Connell, J. P. (2002). *Finding out what matters for youth: Testing key links in a community action framework for youth development*. Philadelphia: Youth Development Strategies, Inc.

Ge, X., Brody, G., Conger, R., Simons, R., & Murry, V. (2002). Contextual amplification of pubertal transition effects on deviant peer affiliation and externalizing behavior problems among African American children. *Developmental Psychology, 38*, 42–54.

Ge, X., Conger, R. D., and Elder, G. H. (1996). Coming of age too early: pubertal influences on girls' vulnerability to psychological distress. *Child Development, 67*, 3386–3400.

Ge, X., Kim, I. J., Brody, G. H., Conger, R. D., Simons, R. L., Gibbons, F. X., & Cutrona, C. E. (2003). It's about timing and change: Pubertal transition effects on symptoms of major depression among African American youths. *Developmental Psychology, 39*, 430–439.

Giedd, J. N., Blumenthal, J., Jeffries, N. O., Castellanos, F. X., Liu, H., Zijdenbos, A., Paus, T., Evans, A. C., & Rapoport, J. L. (1999). Brain development during childhood and adolescence: A longitudinal MRI study. *Nature Neuroscience, 2*, 861–863.

Gifford-Smith, M. E., & Brownell, C. A. (Eds.). (2003). Childhood peer relationships: Social acceptance, friendships, and peer networks [Target issue]. *Journal of School Psychology, 41*(4).

Good, T. L., & Brophy, J. E. (1986). School effects. In M. Wittrock (Ed.), *Third handbook of research on teaching* (pp. 570–602). New York: Macmillan.

Graber, J., & Brooks-Gunn, J. (1999, April). Antecedents of age at menarche. Paper presented at the biennial meeting of the Society for Research in Child Development, Albuquerque, NM.

Graber, J. A., Brooks-Gunn, J., & Petersen, A. C. (Eds.) (1996). *Transitions through adolescence: Interpersonal domains and context*. Hillsdale, NJ: Erlbaum.

Graber, J., Brooks-Gunn, J., & Warren, M. (1995). The antecedents of menarcheal age: Heredity, family environment, and stressful life events. *Child Development, 66*, 346–359.

Graber, J. A., Lewinsohn, P. M., Seeley, J. R., & Brooks-Gunn, J. (1997). Is psychopathology associated with the timing of pubertal development? *Journal of the American Academy of Child and Adolescent Psychiatry, 36*, 1768–1776.

Greenberg, M. T., Domitrovich, C., & Bumbarger, B. (2001). The prevention of mental disorders in school-aged children: Current state of the field [Special issue]. *Prevention and Treatment, 4*.

Hamre, B. K., & Pianta, R. C. (2005). Can instructional and emotional support in the first grade classroom make a difference for children at risk of school failure? *Child Development, 76*, 949–967.

Hartup, W. W., & Stevens, N. (1997). Friendships and adaptation in the life course. *Psychological Bulletin, 121*, 355–370.

Herman-Giddens, M., Slora, E., Wasserman, C., & Bourdony, M. (1997). Secondary sex characteristics and menses in young girls seen in office practices. *Pediatrics, 99*, 505–512.

Hogue, A., & Steinberg, L. (1995). Homophily of internalised distress in adolescent peer groups. *Developmental Psychology, 31*, 897–906.

Holloway, S. D. (1986). The relationship of mothers' beliefs to children's mathematics achievement: Some effects of sex differences. *Merrill-Palmer-Quarterly, 32*, 231–250.

Holmbeck, G. N., Paikoff, R. L., & Brooks-Gunn, J. (1995). Parenting adolescents. In M. Bornstein (Ed.) *Handbook of parenting: Children and parenting* (Vol.1, pp. 91–118) Hillsdale, NJ: Erlbaum.

Howes, C., Burchinal, M., Pianta, R., Bryant, D., Early, D., Clifford, R., & Barbarin, O. (2008). Ready to learn? Children's pre-academic achievement in pre-kindergarten programs. *Early Childhood Research Quarterly, 23,* 27–50.

Institute of Education Sciences, U.S. Department of Education. (2004a). www.ed.gov/programs/edresearch/applicant.html

Jacobs, J. E. (1991). Influence of gender stereotypes on parent and child mathematics attitudes. *Journal of Educational Psychology, 83,* 518–527.

Jacobs, J. E., & Eccles, J. S. (1992). The impact of mothers' gender-role stereotypic beliefs on mothers' and children's ability perceptions. *Journal of Personality and Social Psychology, 63,* 932–944.

Keating, D. P. (2004). Cognitive and brain development. In R. Lerner & L. Steinberg (Eds.), *Handbook of adolescent psychology* (pp. 45–84). New York: Wiley & Sons.

Keating, D. P. (1990). Adolescent thinking. In S. Feldman, & G. Elliott (Eds), *At the threshold: The developing adolescent* (pp. 54–89). Cambridge, MA: Harvard University Press.

Killen, M., & Horn, S. S. (2000). Facilitating children's development about morality, community, and autonomy: A case for service-learning experiences. In W. van Haaften, T. Wren & A. Tellings (Eds.), *Moral sensibilities and education: The schoolchild* (Vol. II, pp. 89–113). Bemmel: The Netherlands.

King, V., Elder, G. H., & Whitbeck, L. B. (1997). Religious involvement among rural youth: An ecological and life-course perspective. *Journal of Research on Adolescence, 7,* 431–456.

Kipke, M. (Ed.) (1999). *Adolescent development and the biology of puberty.* books.nap.edu/html/ado_dev_bio_pub/

Kratochwill, T. R., & Stoiber, K. C. (2002). Evidence-based interventions in school psychology: conceptual foundations of the Procedural and Coding Manual of Division 16 and the Society for the Study of School Psychology Task Force. *School Psychology Quarterly, 17,* 341–389.

Ladd, G. W., & Burgess, K. B. (1999). Charting the relationship trajectories of aggressive, withdrawn, and aggressive/withdrawn children during early grade school. *Child Development, 70,* 910–929.

Largo, R. H., & Prader, A. (1983a). Pubertal development in Swiss boys. *Paediatrica Acta, 38,* 211–228.

Largo, R. H., & Prader, A. (1983b). Pubertal development in Swiss girls. *Paediatrica Acta, 38,* 229–243.

Larson, R. W. (2000). Toward a psychology of positive youth development. *American Psychologist, 55,* 170–183.

Lee, V. E., & Burkam, D. T. (2003). Dropping out of high school: The role of school organization and structure. *American Educational Research Journal, 40,* 353–393.

Lerner, R. M. (1998). Theories of human development: Contemporary perspectives. In W. Damon & R. M. Lerner (Eds), *Handbook of child psychology: Vol. 1. Theoretical models of human development* (5th ed., pp. 1–24). New York: Wiley.

Lerner, R. M., & Jovanovic, J. (1999). *Cognitive and moral development and academic achievement in adolescence.* NY: Garland.

Little, M., & Kobak, R. (2003). Emotional security with teachers and children's stress reactivity: A comparison of special education and regular classrooms. *Journal of Clinical Child and Adolescent Psychology, 32,* 127–138.

Luciana, M. & Nelson, C. A. (2000). Neuro-developmental assessment of cognitive function using the Cambridge Neuropsychological Testing Automated Battery (CANTAB): Validation and future goals. In M. Ernst & J. Rumsey (Eds.), *The foundation and future of functional neuroimaging in child psychiatry* (pp. 379–397). Cambridge, England: Cambridge University Press.

Luciana, M. & Nelson, C. A. (2002). Assessment of neuropsychological function through use of the Cambridge Neuropsychological Testing Automated Battery: Performance in 4- to 12-year-old children. *Developmental Neuropsychology, 22,* 595–624.

Luciana, M., Sullivan, J., & Nelson, C. A. (2001). Associations between phenylalanine-to-tyrosine ratios and performance on tests of neuropsychological function in adolescents treated early and continuously for phenylketonuria. *Child Development, 72,* 1637–1652.

MacIver, D., Stipek, D., & Daniels, D. (1991). Explaining within semester changes in student effort in junior high school and senior high school courses. *Journal of Educational Psychology, 83,* 361–371.

Madon, S., Jussim, L., & Eccles, J. (1997). In search of the powerful self-fulfilling prophecy. *Journal of Personality and Social Psychology,* 791–809.

Magnusson, D. (1988). *Individual development from an international perspective.* Hillsdale, NJ: Erlbaum.

Marshall, W. A., & Tanner, J. M. (1969). Variations in pattern of pubertal changes in girls. *Archives of Disease in Childhood, 44,* 291–303.

Marshall, W. A., & Tanner, J. M. (1970). Variations in the pattern of pubertal changes in boys. *Archives of Disease in Childhood, 45,* 13–23.

Meyer, L. A., Wardrop, J. L., Hastings, C. N., & Linn, R. L. (1993). Effects of ability and settings on kindergarteners' reading performance. *Journal of Educational Research, 86,* 142–160.

Moffitt, T. E., & Caspi, A. (2001). Childhood predictors differentiate life-course persistent and adolescence limited antisocial pathways among males and females. *Development and Psychopathology, Special Issue, 13*, 2355–2375.

Moffitt, T. E., Caspi, A., Belsky, J., & Silva, P. A. (1992). Childhood experience and the onset of menarche: A test of a sociobiological model. *Child Development, 63*, 47–58.

Moffitt, T. E., Caspi, A., Rutter, M., & Silva, P. A. (2001). *Sex differences in antisocial behaviour.* Cambridge, UK: Cambridge University Press.

Montemayor, R., Adams, G. R., & Gullotta, T. P. (Eds.). (1990). *From childhood to adolescence: A transitional period?* Newbury Park, CA: Sage Publications, Inc.

Morrison, F. J., & Connor, C. M. (2002). Understanding schooling effects on early literacy: A working research strategy. *Journal of School Psychology, 40*, 493–500.

Neeman, J., Hubbard, J. & Masten, A. (1995). The changing importance of romantic relationship involvement to competence from late childhood to late adolescence. *Development and Psychopathology, 7*, 727–750.

NICHD Early Child Care Research Network. (2002). Child care structure process outcome: direct and indirect effects of child care quality on young children's development. *Psychological Science, 13*, 199–206.

NICHD Early Child Care Research Network. (2004). Does class size in first grade relate to children's academic and social performance or observed classroom processes? *Developmental Psychology, 40*, 651–664.

NICHD Early Child Care Research Network. (2005). A day in third grade: A large-scale study of classroom quality and teacher and student behavior. *The Elementary School Journal, 105*, 305–323.

Nurmi, J. (1991). How do adolescents see their future? A review of the development of future orientation and planning. *Developmental Review, 11*, 1–59.

Opdenakker, M.-C., & Van Damme, J. (2000). The importance of identifying levels in multilevel analysis: An illustration of the effects of ignoring the top or intermediate levels in school effectiveness research. *School Effectiveness and School Improvements, 11*, 103–130.

Parsons, J. E., Adler, T. F., & Kaczala, C. M. (1982). Socialization of achievement attitudes and beliefs: Parental influences. *Child-Development, 53*, 310–321.

Peisner-Feinberg, E. S., & Burchinal, M. R. (1997). Relations between preschool children's child care experiences and concurrent development: The cost, quality, and outcomes study. *Merrill-Palmer Quarterly, 43*, 451–477.

Petrides, M., & Milner, B. (1982). Deficits in subject-ordered tasks after frontal and temporal-lobe lesions in man. *Neuropsychologia, 220*, 249–262.

Phillips, M. (1997). What makes schools effective? A comparison of the relationships of communitarian climate and academic climate to mathematics achievement and attendance during middle school. *American Educational Research Journal, 34*, 633.

Pianta, R. C. (1999). *Enhancing relationships between children and teachers.* Washington, D.C.: American Psychological Association.

Pianta, R. (2005). Standardized observation and professional development: A focus on individualized implementation and practices. In M. Zaslow and I. Martinez-Beck (Eds.), *Critical issues in early childhood professional development* (pp. 231–254). Baltimore, Paul H. Brookes Publishing.

Pianta, R. (2006a). *Professional development interventions to support effective teaching.* Manuscript in preparation. University of Virginia, Charlottesville.

Pianta, R. (2006b). Schools, schooling, and developmental psychopathology. In D. Cicchetti & D. Cohen (Eds.), *Developmental Psychopathology, Volume 1: Theory and Method* (pp. 494–529). Hoboken, NJ: John Wiley & Sons, Inc.

Pianta, R. C., Hamre, B., & Stuhlman, M. (2003). Relationships between teachers and children. In W. Reynolds & G. Miller (Eds.), *Educational psychology* (Vol. 7, pp. 199–234). Hoboken, NJ: Wiley & Sons, Inc.

Pianta, R. C., La Paro, K. M., & Hamre, B. K. (2004). *Classroom Assessment Scoring System [CLASS].* Unpublished measure, University of Virginia.

Pianta, R. C., Steinberg, M. S., & Rollins, K. B. (1995). The first two years of school: Teacher-child relationships and deflections in children's classroom adjustment. *Development and Psychopathology, 7*, 295–312.

Pintrich, P. R., Roeser, R. W., & DeGroot, E. A. M. (1994). Classroom and individual differences in early adolescents' motivation and self-regulated learning. *Journal of Early Adolescence, 14*, 139–161.

Public Agenda. (1997). *Getting by: What American teenagers really think about their schools.* New York: Author.

Quas, J. A., Murowchick, E., Bensadoun, J., & Boyce, W. T. (2002). Predictors of children's cortisol activation during the transition to kindergarten. *Journal of Developmental & Behavioral Pediatrics, 23*, 304–313.

Ramey, C. T., Campbell, F. A., Burchinal, M., Skinner, M. L., Gardner, D. M., & Ramey, S. L. (2000). Persistent effects of early childhood education on high-risk children and their mothers. *Applied Developmental Science, 4*, 2–14.

Resnick, M. D., Bearman, P. S., Blum, R. W., Bauman, K., Harris, K. M., Jones, J., et al. (1997). Protecting adolescents from harm: Findings from the National Longitudinal Study of Adolescent

Health. *Journal of the American Medical Association*, *278*, 823–832.

Roeser, R. W. & Eccles, J. S. (1998). Adolescents perception of middle school: Relation to longitudinal changes in academic and psychological adjustment. *Journal on Research on Adolescence*, *8*, 123–158.

Roeser, R. W., Eccles, J. S., & Sameroff, A. J. (1998). Academic and emotional functioning in early adolescence: Longitudinal relations, patterns, and prediction by experience in middle school. *Development and Psychopathology*, *10*, 321–352.

Roeser, R. W., Eccles, J. S., & Sameroff, A. J. (2000). School as a context of early adolescents' academic and social-emotional development: A summary of research findings. *Elementary School Journal*, *100*, 443–471.

Rones, M., & Hoagwood, K. (2000). School-based mental health services: A research review. *Clinical Child and Family Psychology Review*, *3*, 223–241.

Rutter, M., & Maughan, B. (2002). School effectiveness findings, 1979–2002. *Journal of School Psychology*, *40*, 451–475.

Ryan, R. M., & Deci, E. L. (2000). Self-determination theory and the facilitation of intrinsic motivation, social development, and well-being. *American Psychologist*, *55*, 68–78.

Sameroff, A. J. (2000). Developmental systems and psychopathology. *Development and Psychopathology*, *12*, 297–312.

Sarason, S. B. (1982). *The culture of the school and the problem of change* (2nd ed.). Boston: Allyn and Bacon.

Seidman, E., Chesir, D., Friedman, J. L., Yoshikawa, H., Aber, J. L., Allen, L., et al. (2001). *The risk and protective functions of perceived family and peer microsystems among urban adolescents in poverty*. Manuscript submitted for publication, New York University.

Siegel, A. W. & Scovill, L. C. (2000). Problem behavior: The double symptom of adolescence. *Development and Psychopathology*, *12*, 763–794.

Skinner, E. A., Zimmer-Gembeck, M. J., & Connell, J. P. (1998). Individual differences and the development of perceived control. *Monographs of the Society for Research in Child Development*, *63*(2–3).

Slavin, R. E. (1996). Research on cooperative learning and achievement: What we know, what we need to know. *Contemporary Educational Psychology*, *21*, 43–69.

Sroufe, L. A., Egeland, B., Carlson, E. A., & Collins, W. A. (2005). *The development of the person: The Minnesota study of risk and adaptation from birth to adulthood*. New York: The Guilford Press.

Stattin, H., & Magnusson, D. (1990). *Pubertal maturation in female development*. Hillsdale, NJ: Erlbaum.

Steinberg, L. (2001). We know some things: Parent-adolescent relationships in retrospect and prospect. *Journal of Research on Adolescence*, *11*, 1–19.

Steinberg, L. (2002). *Adolescence*. (6th ed.) New York: McGraw Hill.

Steinberg, L., Brown, B. B., & Dornbusch, S. M. (1996). *Beyond the classroom: Why school reform has failed and what parents need to do*. New York: Simon and Schuster.

Steinberg, L., & Morris, A. S. (2001). Adolescent development. *Annual Review of Psychology*, *52*, 83–110.

Stevenson, H. W., & Lee, S. Y. (1990). Contexts of achievement: A study of American, Chinese, and Japanese children. *Monographs of the Society for Research in Child Development*, *55* (1–2, Serial No. 221).

Surbey, M. (1989). Family composition, stress, and the timing of human menarche. In F. Bercovitch & T. Zeigler (Eds.), *The socioendocrinology of primate reproduction*. New York: Liss.

Susman, E. J., Dorn, L. D., & Schiefelbein, V. (2003). Puberty, sexuality, and health. In R. M. Lerner, M. A. Easterbrooks & J. Mistry (Eds.), *The comprehensive handbook of psychology: Developmental psychology* (Vol. 6). New York: Wiley.

Watamura, S. E., Donzella, B., Alwin, J., & Gunnar, M. R. (2003). Morning to afternoon increases in cortisol concentrations for infants and toddlers at child care: Age differences and behavioral correlates. *Child Development*, *74*, 1006–1020.

Wigfield, A., Eccles, J. S., & Pintrich, P. R. (1996). Development between the ages of 11 and 25. In D. C. Berliner & R. C. Calfee (Eds.), *Handbook of educational psychology* (pp. 148–185). New York: Macmillan.

Windle, M., & Davies, P. T. (1999). Depression and heavy alcohol use among adolescents: Concurrent and prospective relations. *Development and Psychopathology*, *11*, 823–844.

CHAPTER 7

CONTRIBUTIONS OF COGNITIVE PSYCHOLOGY TO SCHOOL PSYCHOLOGY

GREGORY SCHRAW
University of Nevada–Las Vegas
PETER REYNOLDS
Clark County School District

This chapter provides an introduction to contemporary cognitive psychology and principles that apply to learning, instruction, and school psychology. Cognitive psychology encompasses a large variety of topics such as memory, models of knowledge representation, and the interface between neurology and learning. In this chapter, we focus on educational aspects of cognitive psychology that are of special importance for understanding a highly successful learner. This chapter is divided into five sections. The first section summarizes the information processing model (IPM) that has served as a model of learning and instruction for half a century. Section 2 considers how knowledge is represented and organized in long-term memory. We provide a taxonomy of different kinds of knowledge and describe two organization frameworks, *schemata* and *scripts*, that facilitate memory and learning. Section 3 focuses on the role of beliefs and motivation in the learning process, and the role that demonstration and modeling play in increasing positive self-beliefs. Section 4 provides a framework for understanding the key components of learning and their inter-relationships. Section 5 summarizes six principles of effective learners and briefly describes ways to promote the development of these characteristics.

THE INFORMATION PROCESSING MODEL

Cognitive psychology focuses on human thought and cognition. To do so, researchers developed the information processing model (IPM) in the early 1950s, which has been used as the modal model of cognition since that time. The IPM consists of three main components: sensory memory, working memory, and long term memory (see Figure 7.1). Sensory and working memory enables us to manage limited amounts of incoming information during initial processing, whereas long-term memory serves as a permanent repository for knowledge. We use the information processing model as a metaphor for successful learning because it is well supported by research and provides a well-articulated means for describing the main cognitive structures (i.e., memory systems) and processes (i.e., strategies) in the learning cycle.

Sensory memory processes incoming sensory information for very brief periods of time, usually on the order of one-half to three seconds. The amount of information held at any given moment in sensory memory is limited to five to seven discrete elements such as letters of the alphabet or pictures of human faces. Thus, if a person viewed 10 letters for one second, it is unlikely that more than five to seven of those letters would be remembered.

The main purpose of sensory memory is to screen incoming stimuli and process only those stimuli that are most relevant at the present time. For example, imagine that you are driving on a busy freeway in heavy traffic. Visual and auditory stimuli bombard you constantly. To maximize efficiency and safety, you process only information that is relevant to safe driving. Thus, you would attend to road conditions, but not buildings you pass as you drive. Similarly, you would attend to

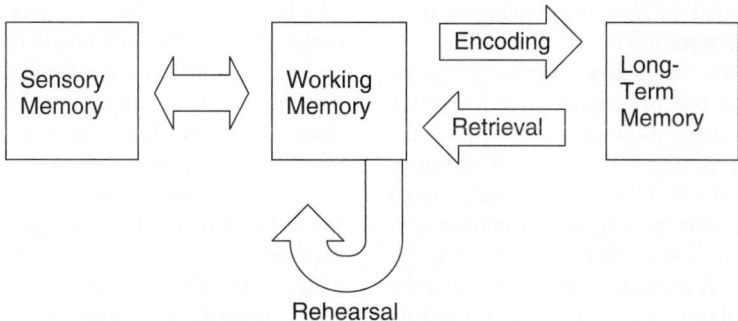

FIGURE 7.1   The Information Processing Model.

sounds of other cars, but not to music from the radio or one passenger's casual conversation to another passenger.

Several useful terms have been developed to explain efficient cognitive processing in sensory memory. One term is *limited attentional resources*, which refers to the highly limited nature of information processing (Anderson, 2000; Neath, 1998). All individuals experience severe limitations on how much mental activity they can engage in due to limited cognitive resources (Kane & Engle, 2002). By analogy, an engine capable of 12 horsepower has limited resources compared to an engine of 200 horsepower. Although humans differ with respect to available cognitive resources, all learners experience severe limitations regardless of their skill and ability level. Often, differences between one learner and another are not due to the amount of resources, but how efficiently those resources are used.

Another key term is *automaticity*, which refers to being able to perform a task very quickly and efficiently due to repeated practice (Stanovich, 2003). Automated activities usually require few cognitive resources; thus, even a complex skill such as driving a car at 75 miles per hour can seem effortless. Effective information processing in sensory memory requires a high degree of automaticity with regard to recognition of familiar stimuli such as spoken or printed words, faces, sounds, etc.

A third key term is *selective processing*, which refers to the act of intentionally focusing one's limited cognitive resources on stimuli that are most relevant to the task at hand. For example, when driving in snow, one might allocate more of one's limited cognitive resources to watching the center line in the highway than one would allocate on a clear summer day. In contrast, on an extremely windy day, one would pay little

attention to the whereabouts of the center line, but pay special attention for flying debris that could cause an accident. In essence, selective processing enables learners to be optimally efficient by putting all of their cognitive eggs in one basket. It is no coincidence that highly effective learners succeed because they identify what is most important to learn and allocate little attention to other information.

The notion of limited attentional capacity, automaticity, and selective processing apply to working memory as well. Working memory is a term that is used to refer to a multicomponent temporary memory system where information is assigned meaning, linked to other information, and essential mental operations such as inferences are performed. A number of different models of working memory have been proposed (Shah & Miyake, 1999). However, the three-component model developed by Baddeley (1998, 2001) is the most common.

Baddeley's (2001) model of working memory consists of three components, including the *executive control system, articulatory loop, and visual-spatial sketch pad*. The role of the executive control system is to select incoming information, determine how to best process that information, subsequently transfer the processed information to long-term memory or choose to delete that information from the memory system altogether (e.g., a no-longer-needed telephone number). The role of the articulatory loop is to maintain and further process verbal information. The role of the visual-spatial sketch pad is analogous to the articulatory loop in that it maintains and further processes nonverbal and visual information. Information is lost quickly from working memory (i.e., 5–15 seconds) unless some type of mental rehearsal occurs. Barring rehearsal (e.g., repeating a telephone number), information is either forwarded to long-term memory or is deleted from the system.

Baddeley's model makes several critical assumptions about the processing of information in working memory. One is that each of the three subsystems possesses its own pool of limited cognitive resources. This means that, under normal information processing circumstances, each subsystem performs work without taxing the other subsystem. A second assumption is that the executive control system regulates the articulatory loop and visual-spatial sketch pad.

Unlike sensory and working memory, long-term memory is not constrained by capacity or duration of attention limitations. The role of long-term memory is to provide a seemingly unlimited repository for all the facts and knowledge in memory. Most researchers believe that long-term memory is capable of holding millions of pieces of information for very long periods of time (Anderson, 2000). A great deal of thought and research has gone into identifying two key aspects of long term memory: (a) what types of information are represented, and (b) how information is organized. These two questions are addressed in the next section of this chapter. For present purposes, there is universal agreement that qualitatively different types of information exist in long-term memory and that information must be organized, and therefore quickly accessible, to be of practical use to learners.

Figure 7.1 shows that working memory and long-term memory are connected by *encoding* and *retrieval* processes. Encoding refers to a large number of strategies that move information from temporary store in working memory to long-term memory. Examples include organization, inferencing, and elaboration strategies, which we discuss later. Retrieval refers to processes that enable individuals to search memory and retrieve information for active processing in working memory. Both encoding and retrieval greatly facilitate learning when information in long-term memory is organized for easy access.

A comparison of the three components of the IPM indicates that both sensory and working memory are relatively short term in nature (see Table 7.1). The main role is to screen incoming information, assign meaning, and relate individual units of information to other units. In contrast, the main role of long-term memory is to serve as a highly organized permanent storage system. Sensory and working memory process few pieces of information within a short time frame. Automaticity of processing and selective allocation of limited cognitive resources greatly increases the efficiency of information processing. Long-term memory is assumed to be more or less permanent and unlimited in terms of capacity. The main processing constraint on long-term memory is the individual's ability to quickly encode and retrieve information using an efficient organizational system.

The information processing model provides a conceptual model that explains the different functions and constraints on human memory. The IPM also has had a major impact on instructional theory and practice. Sweller and Chandler (1994) developed *cognitive load theory* to explain how different instructional and learner constraints affect optimal information processing. The crux of their argument is that each task imposes some degree of cognitive load, which must be met either by available cognitive resources or learned strategies such as selective attention and automaticity. Reducing cognitive load enables

TABLE 7.1   A Comparison of Sensory, Working, and Long-Term Memory

Type of Memory	Purpose	Capacity	Duration of Retention
Sensory Memory	Provides initial screening and processing of incoming stimuli.	3 to 7 discrete units	0.5 to 3 seconds
Working Memory	Assigns meaning to stimuli and links individual pieces of information into larger units. Enables learner to construct meaning and perform visual-spatial mental operations.	7 to 9 units of information	5 to 15 seconds without rehearsal
Long-Term memory	Provides a permanent repository for different types of knowledge	Infinite	Permanent

individuals to learn with less overall mental effort. Cognitive load theory has been especially helpful in terms of planning instruction and developing learning materials. Others researchers such as Mayer and Moreno (2003) have developed frameworks to increase learning by systematically reducing cognitive load through better design of learning materials and more strategic use of limited resources by students.

Summary

The information processing model postulates a three-component model of information processing. The IPM is consistent with empirical findings and provides an excellent framework for understanding principles of effective learning, which we consider later in this chapter. Sensory and working memory are limited with respect to capacity and duration, whereas long term memory is more or less unlimited. Information processing is increased due to automaticity and selectivity. Encoding and retrieval of information in long term memory is increased due to efficient organizational strategies.

THE REPRESENTATION AND ORGANIZATION OF KNOWLEDGE IN LONG-TERM MEMORY

This section focuses on two issues. The first issue is what types of knowledge are represented in long-term memory. We consider three generic types, commonly referred to as declarative, procedural, and self-regulatory knowledge. The second issue is how knowledge is organized in long term memory. We focus on the role of schemata and scripts as organizational aids to encoding and retrieving knowledge from memory.

A Taxonomy of Knowledge

Each adult stores a huge amount of knowledge in long-term memory. Different types of knowledge serve different purposes, yet all are important and necessary for effective learning (Schraw, 2006). This section focuses on three main types of knowledge and subtypes within each of the three main categories shown in Figure 7.2. Declarative knowledge refers to the facts and concepts. Procedural knowledge refers to how to do things. Self-regulatory knowledge refers to knowledge we have about ourselves as learners, what we know, and how to control our learning. All three types of knowledge are important. However, even a large amount of declarative and procedural knowledge, without self-regulatory knowledge to support it, does little to help us survive and adapt successfully (Zeidner, Boekaerts, & Pintrich, 2000; Zimmerman, 2000).

Declarative Knowledge

Declarative knowledge is a broad category that includes facts, concepts, and the relationships between concepts that lead to an integrated conceptual understanding of a domain of knowledge. Declarative knowledge includes thousands of facts such as the names of colors, numbers, coins, trees, and so forth. Concepts consist of two or more units of factual information that are used to understand a broader phenomenon such as human rights or social justice. Often concepts are phenomena we can describe abstractly, such as freedom or happiness, even though these phenomena do not exist in the physical world. Declarative knowledge also includes integrated conceptual knowledge that is sometimes referred to as *structural knowledge* or *mental models* (Halpern, 2003). The information in Figure 7.2 provides an example of structural knowledge in

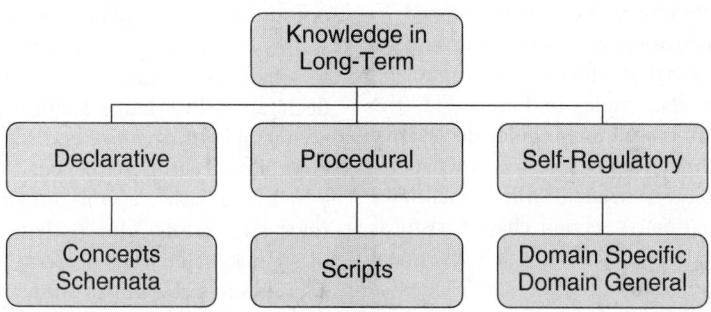

FIGURE 7.2   **Knowledge in Long-Term Memory.**

which facts and concepts are interrelated into a single conceptual model.

One of the most important organizational units in memory is the *schema*, which refers to an organized body of information about some distinct domain of knowledge. For example, every adult has a "car schema" in which information about different types of cars is organized. A car schema could be organized in several ways using either the cost of the car or size of the car to generate subcategories. If I asked you to name a luxury car, you quickly could name cars such as Rolls Royce or Jaguar as examples. Most other people who share the same knowledge would have it organized in a similar way as well.

A schema is extremely useful, even essential, for several reasons. One reason is that it enables us to organize a large amount of information into an integrated body of knowledge in an efficient manner. In essence, a schema can be likened to a file drawer in a file cabinet. The file cabinet might contain many drawers, each containing different types of information. When we need to find a particular type of information, we go to the drawer it is filed in. A second reason is that a schema greatly facilitates encoding and retrieving individual pieces of information from memory in a manner that reduces cognitive demand on memory (Sweller, van Merrienboer, & Pass, 1998). Each schema contains *slots* for specific types of information. For example, if you told me that you drive a Volkswagen Beetle, it would be possible to quickly file that information in a slot subsumed under compact foreign cars in my car schema, remembering that information retrieval later would be facilitated by going directly to the slot in memory where it is stored. A third reason is that a schema can be activated to support thinking and problem solving. Skilled readers, for instance, use organized knowledge in a schema to make predictions when they read, to fill in missing information in a text, to form plausible hypotheses, and to interpret events in a story.

How is information in a schema arranged? One characteristic is that information is organized hierarchically. For example, in Figure 7.2, the concept "schema" is subsumed under declarative knowledge. A schema can be entered at whatever level of specificity is needed, which facilitates access to information. A second characteristic is that a schema can be connected to other schemata; thus, searching memory to find one particular piece of information may make it easier to find another piece of related information.

There are probably thousands of schemata in most adults' memory. We simply could not organize all that we know effectively without something like an integrated collection of schemata. Unfortunately, schemata also may create problems because they enable us to generate inferences consistent with what we already know, even though that inference may not be justified in every case. For example, people may recall events that never happened because those events are consistent with information in memory. A large number of studies have demonstrated that people make constructive and reconstructive errors when remembering events because they generate inferences consistent with their knowledge in schemata in memory. These types of errors are quite common in eyewitness testimony (Neath, 1998).

Procedural Knowledge

Procedural knowledge is knowledge about how to do things, ranging from simple action sequences such as buttering toast, to complex actions such as writing a dissertation or flying an airplane. Most adults possess an enormous amount of procedural knowledge, which enables them to perform complex activities such as driving a car easily because those procedures are automated through practice. Although there are many different types of action sequences, there are three sequences of special importance: complex scripted actions, algorithms, and heuristics. Scripts are extended action sequences stored as single entities in memory.

Scripts

Scripts refer to extended action sequences and plans that are stored in memory as single units of knowledge (Bruning, Schraw, Norby & Ronning, 2004). Each person possesses thousands of scripts for getting dressed, driving a car, dining at restaurants, and social interactions that save us enormous amounts of time because we can activate scripts intact from memory. Scripts are analogous to schemata. Whereas schemata help us organize declarative knowledge about a topic or domain, scripts help us organize and remember steps in a complicated action sequence.

There are several important advantages regarding scripts. One is that a large repertoire of scripts enable us to perform many of our daily activities in a straightforward, automated manner without expending a great deal of thought or effort to do so. For example, most of us wake up, shower, eat, brush our teeth, and drive to work without ever giving any of these activities much thought. Instead, as we perform these scripted activities automatically, we plan other nonroutine daily activities such as when to schedule a doctor's appointment, service the car, and arrange our schedules to accommodate family needs, travel, and other pressing business. In a nutshell, scripts save us an incredible amount of time and effort.

A second advantage of scripted behavior is that it allows us eventually to perform activities that initially appear to be beyond the normal range of performance for most people. For example, with extended practice, chess experts can play several games simultaneously while blindfolded, doctors perform complicated surgeries, and performing artists reach amazing levels of technical proficiency.

A third advantage of scripts is that they enable us to predict what is likely to happen in the future. For example, an experienced salesperson possesses a "closing the deal" script which enables her to sequence her sales pitch, monitor whether the pitch is working, and steer her client toward accepting the deal. Or consider an "argument script" you may have with a sibling, spouse, or parent. Sometimes key words or events in the script occur that trigger ensuing events, such as an outburst or verbal threat, that you wish to avoid. Scripts may be very helpful in helping us negotiate interpersonal communications. For example, most adults possess some type of "interview" script that can be used when being interviewed for a new job.

Scripts have their downside too. Because so much of what we do in life is scripted, it is possible that we make choices and decisions in a scripted manner that leads to a state of mindlessness at times. Perhaps you have had the experience of meeting a casual acquaintance in public and engaging in a highly scripted conversation, only to realize later how empty and "scripted" the conversation was. Scripts can also lead to biased reactions to people or automated responses rather than critical evaluation of arguments.

Scripts frequently work to our advantage. They enable us to perform complicated activities with relative ease. Adults possess a wide variety of scripts. One type of script that is especially important in learning is a general problem-solving script shown in Figure 7.3. This script suggests that there is a general logical sequence to follow when solving a problem, which includes identifying the nature of the problem, developing an internal or external representation of the problem, selecting the most appropriate solution strategy and evaluating the solution (Pretz, Naples, & Sternberg, 2003). Figure 7.3 also reveals the role that expert schemata play in problem solving by eliminating the problem representation stage because experts have solved similar problems many times before. Research indicates that experts construct a schema in memory, which enables them to categorize different types of problems and solution strategies, and in turn, quickly match an appropriate strategy to the problem (Halpern, 2003).

Self-Regulatory Knowledge

Self-regulatory knowledge is knowledge about how to regulate our memory, thought, and learning (Schunk & Zimmerman, 2006). Declarative and procedural knowledge alone are not sufficient to be an adaptive learner. In addition, we must possess knowledge about ourselves as learners and about the skills we need to learn effectively. Self-regulatory knowledge can be divided into two types, including domain specific knowledge

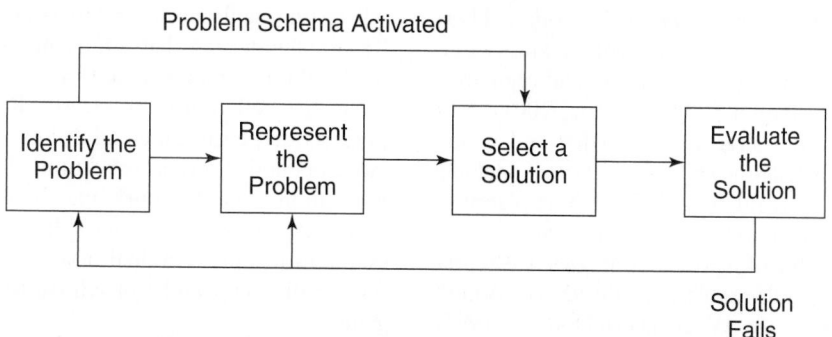

FIGURE 7.3 **The Problem Solving Process.**

and domain general knowledge (Alexander, 2003). The former is knowledge we possess about ourselves with regard to a domain such as mathematics or a subdomain such as geometry. In contrast, the latter includes general knowledge such as learning strategies that enable us to adapt and self-regulate across all domains.

Domain Specific Knowledge

Domain specific knowledge refers to knowledge that is encapsulated with a particular domain of learning such as mathematics, history, literature. Sometimes domain specific knowledge is referred to as *topic knowledge*, although this term suggests knowledge about a specific topic such as geometry within a broader domain such as mathematics. Domain specific knowledge is extremely important in the development of expertise and skilled problem solving (Ericsson, 2003). Cognitive psychologists once believed that is possible to capture the knowledge of experts through interviews and observation, and in turn, help novices become experts quickly. Instead, researchers discovered that experts become experts slowly through years of hard work, deliberate practice, and guidance from other experts. Most experts have deep knowledge in one domain, yet shallow knowledge in other domains, due in large part to the amount of time they invest in developing expertise in their chosen domain. Expertise in one domain usually does not transfer spontaneously to other domains, although it can be facilitated through direct instruction and analogical cues which help the learner understand the relationship between two different problems (Bassock, 2003).

Domain General Knowledge

Domain general knowledge refers to knowledge that is equally useful to learners across domains and topics. Domain general knowledge often is referred to as *metacognitive knowledge*. There are two main types of metacognitive knowledge, including knowledge of cognition and regulation of cognition (Kuhn, 1999; Schraw, 2001). The former includes strategy knowledge and conditional knowledge, while the latter includes knowledge of regulatory skills such as planning, monitoring, and evaluation of learning.

Knowledge of learning strategies is essential for effective self-regulation (Butler & Winne, 1995; Pressley & Wharton-McDonald, 1997). Skilled learners possess a wide variety of strategies, but research suggests that self-regulated learners rely in large part on a relatively small repertoire of general strategies used in a flexible way. These include identifying main ideas, drawing plausible inferences, slowing down for important information, skipping unimportant information, and summarizing in words or by creating graphic organizers. Reviews by Hattie, Biggs, and Purdie (1996) and Rosenshine, Meister, and Chapman (1996) support the following four claims regarding strategy instruction:

1. Strategy instruction typically is moderately to highly successful.
2. Strategy instruction appears to be most helpful for younger and underachieving students.
3. Programs that combine several interrelated strategies are more effective than those that include only one strategy. An interrelated repertoire of four or five strategies seems optimal.
4. Strategy interventions are more effective when they teach conditional knowledge.

Conditional knowledge refers to knowing why, when, and where to use a particular strategy. Individuals with a high degree of conditional knowledge are better able to identify the demands of a specific learning situation and, in turn, select strategies that are most appropriate for that situation (Schraw, 2001).

Regulation of cognition refers to knowledge about how to self-regulate one's learning. Three essential skills include planning, monitoring, and evaluating one's learning. Planning involves the selection of appropriate strategies and the allocation of resources. Planning includes goal setting, activating relevant background knowledge, and budgeting time. Previous research suggests that experts are more self-regulated compared to novices largely due to effective planning, particularly global planning that occurs prior to beginning a task. Monitoring includes self-testing skills necessary to control learning. Research indicates that adults monitor at both the local (i.e., an individual test item) and global levels (i.e., all items on a test). Research also suggests that even skilled adult learners are poor monitors under certain conditions (Kuhn, 1999). Evaluation refers to appraising the products and regulatory processes of one's learning. Typical examples include reevaluating one's goals, revising predictions, and consolidating intellectual gains.

Domain general knowledge is late developing and often implicit in nature. Adults tend to have more knowledge about their own cognition and are better able to describe that knowledge than children and adolescents. However, many adults cannot explain their expert knowledge and performance and often fail to spontaneously transfer domain specific knowledge to a new setting. Indeed, much of the domain general that learners possess may be tacit in nature and acquired implicitly without conscious awareness.

Summary

Long-term memory serves as repository for all our knowledge. The organization of information in memory is complex, and continues to be debated, but there is general agreement that information falls into one of three categories. Declarative knowledge is factual or conceptual in nature; procedural knowledge is performative and action based in nature; self-regulatory is executive in nature in that it better enables learners to mange their learning and achievement. Much of the information in long-term memory is organized into schemata or scripts. Information that is not organized is more difficult to access, encode, and retrieve.

MOTIVATION AND LEARNING

Knowledge and strategies are not enough to foster truly effective learning. Students need to be motivated as well, both inside and outside the classroom (Anderman & Wolters, 2006; Perry, Turner, & Meyer, 2006). Indeed, self-regulated learning theorists have distinguished between the *skill* and the *will* components of learning. Skill components refer to a body of organized declarative and procedural knowledge in long-term memory, a flexible repertoire of learning strategies, and the metacognitive awareness to use them effectively. In contrast, will refers to the desire to engage and persist in an activity until one gains competence or mastery. Although the skill and will components are inseparable, motivational aspects of the will component may determine whether students engage and persist in an activity long enough to acquire essential knowledge and strategies.

Cognitive and social psychologists have explored a variety of motivational variables over the past three decades. We focus on the role of self-efficacy, attributions, and goal orientations due to the sophistication of current theories and a long-standing empirical research base. In addition, each of these variables is known to have a strong effect on effective learning. Each type of motivation is assumed to work in conjunction with other motivational variables, even though we describe them individually.

Self-efficacy refers to the degree to which an individual is confident that he or she can perform a specific task or accomplish a specific goal (Bandura, 1997). Self-efficacy is extremely important for self-regulated learning because it affects the extent to which learners engage and persist at a challenging task. Previous research indicates that students with higher self-efficacy are more likely to engage in a difficult task and more likely to persist at a task even in the face of initial failures compared to low-efficacy students (Pajares, 1997). Higher levels of self-efficacy are related positively to school achievement and self-esteem. The trends observed with respect to student self-efficacy also generalize to teachers and even schools. Teachers with higher levels of teaching self-efficacy, for example, set higher goals and standards, give more autonomy to students, and help students reach higher levels of achievement than do teachers with lower levels of self-efficacy (Goddard, Hoy & Hoy, 2000; Woolfolk Hoy & Burke-Spero, 2005; Woolfolk Hoy, Davis, & Pape, 2006).

Self-efficacy is affected by a number of variables, but especially vicarious learning and modeling. Vicarious learning occurs when individuals learn by observing others perform a skill or discuss a topic. Vicarious learning is advantageous to learners because they are not expected to perform the task, and therefore experience less anxiety, and also can focus all of their resources on observing experts. Modeling occurs when learners learn intentionally from other individuals such as teachers and students. Modeling typically includes the teacher breaking a complex task into manageable parts and asking students to demonstrate each part separately in sequence. Bandura (1997) proposed that modeling is effective because it raises expectations that a new skill can be acquired, in addition to providing a great deal of knowledge about the skill. Peer models are usually the most effective because they are more similar to the learner than a teacher or expert. Indeed, self-efficacy is most likely to increase when a student observes a model of similar ability level.

There are two main ways to increase students' self-efficacy. One is to use both expert (e.g., teacher) and nonexpert (e.g., student peer) models. Research demonstrates that models improve cognitive skills and self-efficacy. The second is to provide as much informational feedback to students as possible. Feedback should indicate not only whether the skill was performed acceptably, but provide as much information as possible about how to improve subsequent performance. Given detailed feedback, performance and self-efficacy can increase even after students experience initial difficulty performing a skill.

Attributions refer to causal explanations of events that happen in our lives. For example, two students may do poorly on a test. One student may attribute her poor performance to bad luck, while the other student attributes her poor performance to lack of effort. These attributions provide very different explanations of the same event. Attribution theory states that it is not an event per se that affects us, but our interpretation of that event.

Weiner (1986) proposed that attributions vary along three dimensions. The first is *locus of control*, which defines the cause of an outcome as either internal or external to the individual. Mood and emotions are examples of internal causes, whereas teachers are external causes. A second dimension is *stability*, which pertains to whether an attributional cause is permanent or temporary. Ability is stable, whereas effort tends to be less stable. A third dimension is *controllability*, which refers to whether an event is under the student's control or is uncontrollable. Controllable causes of academic success include effort and strategy use, whereas uncontrollable causes include luck or task difficulty.

Researchers have considered the separate effects of locus of control, stability, and controllability; however, of greater importance is how the three dimensions contribute simultaneously. Internal-controllable-stable causes such as effort promote positive academic responses, whereas external-uncontrollable-unstable causes such as luck produce frustration or undermine academic confidence. Weiner (1986) reported that internal, controllable causes such as strategy use promote positive affective responses, whereas internal, uncontrollable causes such as ability may create negative emotions such as shame and guilt.

Fortunately, students may be helped to change negative attributional responses through observation and training. A review of the attributional retraining literature found that the majority of attribution retraining programs are successful. Successful programs included the following three components: (1) individuals are taught to identify desirable behaviors such as effort and strategy use, (2) attributions that support positive behaviors are evaluated, and (3) favorable attributional responses are rewarded. Overall, the attributional retraining literature provides evidence that individuals can learn to make more adaptive attributional responses that improve motivation and achievement-related behaviors such as effort, help seeking, and persistence.

Goal orientations refer to beliefs about ability and how these beliefs affect learning. Dweck and Leggett (1988) proposed that learners adopt either performance goals or learning goals based on personal beliefs about the stability of intelligence. Students who believe that intelligence is fixed and unchangeable adopt performance goals, in which they seek to *prove* their competence in academic settings. Those who believe that intelligence is malleable and changeable adopt learning goals, in which they seek to *improve* their competence. A number of studies suggest that students who adopt learning goals are more adaptive and satisfied than students who adopt performance goals. Learning-oriented students typically achieve more because they seek challenge, persist, use strategies, attribute success to effort, and demonstrate positive responses to periodic failure. In contrast, performance-oriented students often adopt maladaptive response patterns characterized by avoidance of challenge, quitting after initial failure, use of inappropriate strategies, helplessness, and attributing success to uncontrollable causes such as ability and luck.

Learning and performance-oriented students differ with respect to academic self-efficacy and self-regulated learning. Students with learning goals report higher levels of self-efficacy, which in turn, is related to higher levels of academic achievement. Learning-oriented students also appear to have better relationships with their teachers and consider teachers to be more important than effort, ability, or strategy use. Surprisingly, however, learning-oriented students did not attribute their failure to teachers, whereas performance-oriented students did!

Bruning et al. (2004) have suggested a number of ways to foster adaptive goals. One is to promote a flexible attitude about the role of ability. Students should be encouraged to make the most of their existing ability rather than focus on how much ability they have compared to other students. Second, teachers and parents should concentrate on rewarding effort. Third, teachers should stress that mistakes are a normal part of learning and are best dealt with by persistence, help seeking, and strategy use.

Summary

Motivation is a necessary component of effective learning that complements knowledge and strategies. Many aspects of motivation are important. Three types of motivation that are especially important are self-efficacy, attributions, and goal orientations. High self-efficacy, internal attributions based on effort and strategy use, and mastery goals which motivate students to improve have been linked to effective learning. Students who are characterized by these beliefs are more likely to engage and persist in difficult learning tasks.

Components of Effective Learning

Thus far we have reviewed key ideas from cognitive psychology. In this section, we provide a schematic model of how major components of learning fit together. Figure 7.4 shows a schematic of the Interactive Compensatory Model of Learning (ICML) described by Schraw, Brooks and Crippen (2005). We developed the ICML for two reasons. The first reason was to discuss the likely interrelationships among key components of learning such as cognitive ability, knowledge, self-regulation, motivation, and learning. The arrows indicate relationships between components. The second reason was to provide a framework for thinking about the types of intervention that teachers and school psychologists often want to implement. We use the ICML here to briefly discuss different types

of interventions and the likely effectiveness of these interventions.

As shown in Figure 7.4, the ICML includes five components: cognitive abilities, an organized knowledge base, metacognitive skills, a flexible repertoire of learning strategies, and motivational beliefs. We define these components as follows:

- Cognitive abilities refer to a general capacity to learn. This component includes aspects of working memory such as speed and capacity, as well as intellectual ability, which some researchers have linked to working memory.
- The organized knowledge base refers to an individual's domain specific and domain general knowledge in long term memory. This knowledge enables individuals to think, reason, and solve problems effectively.
- Metacognition includes knowledge about oneself, the conditions of learning within a particular content, comprehension monitoring, and the ability to regulate one's learning.
- The strategies component refers to a repertoire of procedures that enable learners to solve specific problems.
- Motivation refers to a variety of beliefs about one's learning goals and performance.

We assume that each component contributes directly or indirectly to learning. For example, cognitive abilities may affect learning directly by providing more speed or capacity in working memory. Cognitive abilities may also indirectly affect learning by helping students acquire knowledge and self-regulation skills. In the subsections that follow, we discuss the likelihood that instruction can change the component of interest,

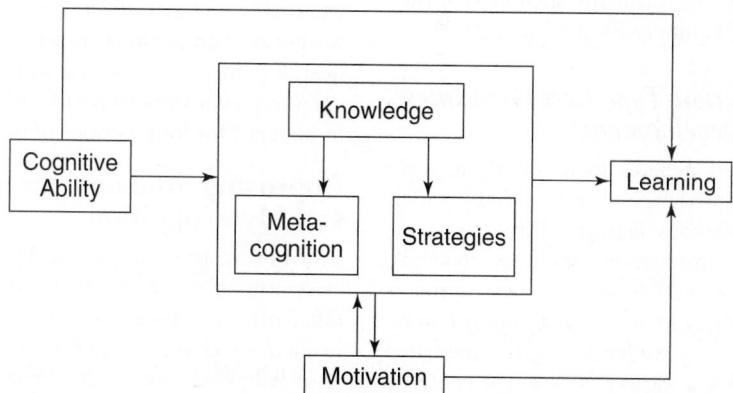

Figure 7.4   Schematic Representation of the Interactive Compensatory Model of Learning (ICML).

and the extent to which changing that component might benefit the student.

Improving Students' Cognitive Ability

Debate continues regarding the extent to which teachers or environmental factors such as peers or cooperative groups can change cognitive ability. Virtually everyone agrees that few short-term changes are possible, even if it is possible to change ability over a longer period. Some researchers believe that memory capacity can be changed through effective instruction (Ericsson, 2005). However, cognitive ability generally is assumed to be stable and difficult to change due to instructional interventions (Kane & Engle, 2002).

Improving Students' Knowledge

Classroom instruction increases knowledge and improves learning in many ways. The debate is not so much whether knowledge is changeable, but how to change knowledge most effectively in a limited amount of time and in ways that promote deeper conceptual understanding. Three general questions arise concerning changing knowledge.

What Kind of Knowledge Does One Want to Develop?

Factual knowledge can be changed in a matter of weeks with well-organized instruction, whereas a broad conceptual understanding of a domain may take years to develop. Effective instruction consists of modeling procedural skills, helping novices understand the conceptual relationships within a domain, and mentors demonstrating skilled thinking and problem solving (Pressley & Harris, 2006; White & Frederiksen, 2005).

What Instruction Type Best Facilitates Knowledge Development?

Most educational debates focus on three main instructional approaches: direct, socially mediated, and autonomous learning (Bruning et al., 2004). Direct instruction includes teacher-led classrooms as well as learning environments such as laboratories in which procedural knowledge is modeled for students. Socially mediated learning includes a variety of student-centered approaches such as cooperative learning, in which a small group of students works together with minimal assistance from teachers. Students can

and do work autonomously, independent of teachers and other students. Computer assisted instruction usually involves autonomous learning.

All three approaches can be effective and are not mutually exclusive. We advocate a blend of all three approaches. Direct instruction enables teachers to convey a large body of knowledge quickly and efficiently to students. A primary advantage to direct instruction is modeling by an expert. Teachers model in many ways. Most important, they model ways of thinking. Teachers should make every effort to make their thinking explicit to students in order to promote self-regulatory skills. Socially mediated learning helps students use knowledge to solve problems, and to modify that knowledge to fit new problems. Autonomous learning helps students reflect on new ways to apply that knowledge.

Which Instructional Practices Best Promote Deeper Learning and Expertise?

Research suggests it takes about five to ten years, or 10,000 hours, to become an "expert." For example, training a physician from the beginning of medical school to the end of a three-year residency program takes seven years and nearly 20,000 hours. One reason expertise develops so slowly is that much of the declarative and procedural knowledge needed to master a domain is acquired tacitly over a long period. Evidence suggests that much of our knowledge is acquired tacitly even when we receive a great deal of formal training in a domain (Alexander, 2003; Ericsson, 2005). Because of this, even highly skilled experts often find it difficult to describe what it is they know about a body of knowledge and, consequently, may be poor decision makers when forced to reflect on their knowledge. Successful instructional practices for developing deep learning and expertise will both require and encourage students to remain positively engaged in material for long periods of time.

Improving Students' Strategies and Metacognition

Strategy instruction is ideally suited for the classroom because it can be done quickly and efficiently compared to the time and effort needed to change cognitive ability and expert knowledge (Pressley & Wharton-McDonald, 1997). We distinguish between general and specific strategies. General strategies usually are domain-independent heuristics and are described by terms such as help seeking, summarizing, para-phrasing, and positive self-talk. Specific strategies are usually domain-dependent, such as using the Pythagorean theory in trigonometry or strategies to balance chemical equations in a chemistry class.

Experts recommend strategy instruction before, during, and after the main learning episode. Strategies that occur before learning include setting goals, determining how much information to learn, deciding how this infor-mation relates to what one already knows, and anticipating how the information-to-be-learned will be used. Strategies needed during learning include identifying important information, pre-dicting, monitoring, analyzing, and interpreting. Strategies used after learning include reviewing, organizing, and reflecting. Good strategy users possess some degree of competence in each of these areas.

Improving Students' Motivation to Learn

Many studies suggest that motivational beliefs are highly malleable (Alderman, 1999). Changes occur for several reasons, including student awareness, teacher modeling of adaptive beliefs, and changes in classroom processes such as eval-uation and grading.

Promote Students' Self-Efficacy

One way to increase motivation is to improve students' self-efficacy. Self-efficacy refers to the degree to which a student feels capable of achieving a specific goal. Self-efficacy is affected by self-assessments, performance-based feedback, and environmental cues (Bandura, 1997). Increase students' awareness of the self-efficacy concept. Emphasize the positive consequences of high efficacy by describing how efficacy develops and deteriorates, and promote positive efficacy messages in the classroom. Peer and teacher modeling also increase self-efficacy. In many settings, peer models are most effective because they are judged to be most similar to students. Behavioral and environmental feedback are two of the most important influences on self-efficacy. Feedback is most effective when it relates perfor-mance outcomes to activities that cause those outcomes.

Encourage Mastery Orientations in Students

Previous research has distinguished between mastery and performance goals. Mastery goals are characterized by the desire to improve one's competence. Performance goals are characterized by the desire to prove one's competence. Students with mastery goal orientations are more focused on learning, demonstrate more effort, have higher levels of self-efficacy, and perform better than students with performance goal orientations. Dweck and Leggett (1988) suggest that goal orientations are due to attitudes about the changeability of cognitive ability. This is really important for chemistry teachers. We are thought to be teaching content that is "hard," and that access to the content is controlled by one's ability. While this certainly is partly true, it most often is overrated. Help students develop strong mastery orientations.

A mastery goal orientation is promoted when instruction focuses on mastery learning. Mastery learning, where learners are expected to continue studying material until they are able to demonstrate that they know the material, has an excellent basis in research. Short of tutoring or mentoring, mastery learning has the strongest research support of any known teaching strategy. Stress that mistakes are a normal (and healthy) part of learning. Everyone makes mistakes when learning something new. How teachers respond to these mistakes sends a powerful message to students. When mistakes are viewed positively, receive corrective attention, and are used to provide feedback to students, students learn more than when mistakes are viewed in a negative light.

Six Characteristics of Effective Learners

All students are different, yet it is fair to say that all successful students share a core set of academic characteristics. Sternberg (2001) pro-vides an excellent summary of five characteristics, including a large, organized schematic network of knowledge; choosing efficiently from a large repertoire of useful strategies; quickly construct-ing detailed integrated mental models of a prob-lem; performing skills in a highly automated fashion; and carefully monitoring the difficulty of problems and one's ability to solve problems. To this list, we add the characteristic of being highly motivated and able to persist in a difficult task even when a student experiences temporary fail-ure. Each of these characteristics is linked closely to one or more components of the ICML.

Highly effective learners possess a great deal of organized knowledge within a particular domain such as reading, mathematics, or science. They also possess general problem solving and critical thinking scripts that enable them to perform well across different domains. It is important to note that it may take years to acquire a sufficient knowledge base to perform like an expert or even at an emerging-expert level. There is no easy path to expertise except sustained effort and coaching from other skilled students and teachers (Ericsson, 2005). One of the best ways to promote the acquisition and development of expertise is through collaborative work with peers who are slightly above the level of their mentors.

All effective learners draw from a repertoire of learning strategies in a flexible manner. Good learners use a wide variety of strategies; however, there are three general strategies that all effective learners use in most situations. These include *organization, inferencing,* and *elaboration.* Organization refers to how information is sorted and arranged in long-term memory. Information that is related to what one already knows is easier to encode and retrieve than isolated information. In some cases, individuals already possess well-organized knowledge with empty slots that can be filled easily with new information. Activating existing knowledge prior to instruction, or providing a visual diagram of how information is organized, is one of the best ways to facilitate learning new information.

Elaboration refers to our ability to embellish new information by linking it to information in long-term memory. Elaboration can occur at a shallow or deep level. Shallow elaboration often is referred to as maintenance rehearsal. For example, students may memorize the Great Lakes by repeating them over and over. In contrast, students could engage in several types of elaborative rehearsal such as creating an acronym (e.g., HOMES: Huron, Ontario, Michigan, Erie, and Superior), or by constructing a mental image based on a map. Students could encode this information even more deeply by associating different lakes with different colors. For example, Lake Ontario could be remembered as orange, while Lake Michigan is remembered as magenta.

Inferencing refers to our ability to infer new information from existing knowledge and information. Inferencing is crucial to self-regulated learning because it enables us to go beyond what we know, constructing what we need to know to perform at a higher level of proficiency. The role of inference generation has been studied extensively by cognitive

psychologists, particularly as it pertains to reading. Researchers know that self-regulated readers combine facts and main ideas in a text into themes that are never stated explicitly, but are essential for comprehension.

Effective learners also possess mental models of the activity they are engaged in. This is perhaps one of the most difficult skills to teach to novices, but can be facilitated greatly through teacher and peer discussions and modeling. Effective instruction provides an overview of the mental model of an activity before students engage in the activity. For example, students benefit from a discussion of the problem solving model shown in Figure 7.3 before solving problems. Similarly, providing a template for writing a report or critique is helpful prior to instruction. The basic script the first author uses for writing the introduction of an experimental research report includes the following seven steps:

Step 1. Introduce the problem

Step 2. Provide a theoretical framework for the research by summarizing current research

Step 3. State the main purpose of the research

Step 4. State two competing hypotheses

Step 5. Provide clear definitions of the constructs (e.g., self-efficacy) discussed in the research

Step 6. Make data-based predictions of what you expect your results to be

Step 7. Summarize the overall purpose of the research

Each of these steps includes detailed substeps that clarify how to accomplish each step. For example, under Step 2, one could discuss with students two main strategies for creating a theoretical framework that one could refer to as the *theory comparison* and *thematic summary* approaches that differ in their appropriateness, depending on the current state of existing research literature. The point of this activity is twofold. First, the script provides an integrated, systematic approach to the writing process. Second, the script forces students to plan and evaluate their research explicitly.

As discussed earlier, automaticity is an important aspect of effective learning for two reasons. One is that it frees up limited resources that can be used for other activities such as drawing inferences and connecting new information to existing information in memory. Second, being automated makes it easier to selectively allocate limited resources to information that is most relevant to the task at hand. Unfortunately, there is no easy road to automaticity other than sustained, regular practice.

Monitoring one's learning is necessary to identify and correct errors. Many students prior to age 10 find it difficult to monitor effectively, and even older students and adults experience difficulties (Kuhn, 1999). Direct instruction in monitoring one's learning is extremely helpful, coupled with peer modeling and discussion. Sternberg (2001) argues that comprehension monitoring should be part of all instructional activities, even with younger students, in order to provide an opportunity for these skills to develop.

Lastly, motivation is crucial. Teaching students sophisticated strategies and providing them with well-organized conceptual models of a domain may go for naught if students are unwillingly to use the strategies and knowledge they possess. Two of the most effective ways to increase student motivation is through peer modeling and teacher modeling expectations (Alderman, 1999). Peer modeling is effective because students who cannot yet perform a certain task acquire efficacy from observing a similar student perform the task. In essence, students come to believe that they can learn to perform a task by working strategically and being persistent. Teacher expectations are important as well. Teachers who model and promote mastery orientations in their classroom by supporting engagement and persistence, and downplaying the role of temporary failures, can facilitate achievement over time.

Summary

Effective learners share the six academic characteristics described above. All of these characteristics are necessary to some degree for a learner to be successful. Each of these skills can be taught by teachers and successfully modeled in the classroom by students and teachers. In contrast, we argue that failure to learn is due to lack of some or all of the skills described above. We believe that all students, regardless of ability levels, can make substantial improvement if given the opportunity to acquire necessary knowledge and master essential skills such as flexible strategy use and comprehension monitoring. Once combined, knowledge, self-regulatory skills, and student motivation enable most students to be successful.

REFERENCES

Alderman, M. K. (1999). *Motivation for achievement: Possibilities of teaching and learning*. Mahwah, NJ: Erlbaum.

Alexander, P. A. (2003). The development of expertise: The journey from acclimation to proficiency. *Educational Researcher, 32*, 10–14.

Anderman, E. M., & Wolters, C. A. (2006). Goals, values, and affect: Influences on student motivation. In P. A. Alexander & P. H. Winne (Eds.), *Handbook of educational psychology* (2nd ed., pp. 369–390). Mahwah, NJ: Erlbaum.

Anderson, J. R. (2000). *Cognitive psychology and its implication* (5th ed.). New York, NY: Worth Publishers.

Baddeley, A. D. (1998). *Human memory: Theory and practice*. Boston, MA: Allyn and Bacon.

Baddeley, A. D. (2001). Is working memory still working? *American Psychologist, 56*, 851–864.

Bandura, A. (1997). *Self-efficacy: The exercise of control.* New York: Freeman.

Bassock, M. (2003). Analogical transfer in problem solving. In J. E. Davidson & R. J. Sternberg (Eds.), *The psychology of problem solving* (pp. 343–369). Cambridge, England: Cambridge University Press.

Bruning, R. H., Schraw, G. J., Norby, M. M., & Ronning, R. R. (2004). *Cognitive psychology and instruction* (4th ed.). Upper Saddle River, NJ: Pearson Education, Inc.

Butler, D. L., and Winne, P. H. (1995). Feedback and self-regulated learning: A theoretical synthesis. *Review of Educational Research* Vol. 65, 245–281.

Dweck, C. S., & Leggett, E. S. (1988). A social-cognitive approach to motivation and personality. *Psychological Review, 95*, 256–273. This review article presents Dweck and Leggett's influential theory in a highly readable fashion.

Ericsson, K. A. (2003). The acquisition of expert performance as problem solving: Construction and modification of mediating mechanisms through deliberate practice. In J. E. Davidson and R. J. Sternberg (Eds.), *The psychology of problem solving* (pp. 31–83). Cambridge, England: Cambridge University Press.

Ericsson, K. A. (2005). An interview with K. Anders Ericsson. *Educational Psychology Review, 17*, 389–412.

Goddard, R. D., Hoy, W. K., & Hoy, A. W. (2000). Collective teacher efficacy: Its meaning, measure and impact on student achievement. *American Educational Research Journal, 37*, 479–507.

Halpern, D. F. (2003). *Thought and knowledge: An introduction to critical thinking* (4th ed.). Mahwah, NJ: Erlbaum.

Hattie, J., Biggs, J., & Purdie, N. (1996). Effects of learning skills interventions on student learning: A meta-analysis. *Review of Educational Research, 66*, 99–136.

Kane, M. J., & Engle, R. W. (2002). The role of prefrontal cortex in working memory capacity, executive attention, and general fluid intelligence: An individual differences perspective. *Psychonomic Bulletin & Review, 9*, 637–671.

Kuhn, D. (1999). A developmental model of critical thinking. *Educational Researcher, 28*, 16–25.

Mayer, R. E. & Moreno, R. (2003). Nine ways to reduce cognitive load in multimedia learning. *Educational Psychologist, 38*, 43–53.

Neath, I. (1998). *Human memory: An introduction to research, data, and theory*. Pacific Grove, CA: Brooks/Cole Publishing.

Pajares, F. (1997). Current directions in self-efficacy research. In M. Maehr & P. R. Pintrich (Eds.), *Advances in motivation and achievement* (Vol. 10, pp. 1–49). Greenwich, CT: JAI Press.

Perry, N. E., Turner, J. C., & Meyer, D. K. (2006). Classrooms as contexts for motivating learning. In P. A. Alexander & P. H. Winne (Eds.), *Handbook of educational psychology* (2nd ed., pp. 327–348). Mahwah, NJ: Erlbaum.

Pressley, M., & Harris, K. R. (2006). Cognitive strategy instruction: From basic research to classroom instructions. In P. A. Alexander & P. H. Winne (Eds.), *Handbook of educational psychology* (2nd ed., pp. 265–287). Mahwah, NJ: Erlbaum.

Pressley, M., & Wharton-McDonald, R. (1997). Skilled comprehension and its development through instruction. *School Psychology Review, 26*, 448–466.

Pretz, J. E., Naples, A. J., & Sternberg, R. J. (2003). Recognizing, defining, and representing problems. In J. E. Davidson and R. J. Sternberg (Eds.), *The psychology of problem solving* (pp. 3–30). Cambridge, England: Cambridge University Press.

Rosenshine, B., Meister, C., & Chapman, S. (1996). Teaching students to generate questions: A review of the intervention studies. *Review of Educational Research, 66*, 181–221.

Schraw, G. (2001). Promoting general metacognitive awareness. In H. J. Hartman (Ed.), *Metacognition in learning and instruction: Theory, research and practice* (pp. 3–16). London, England: Kluwer Academic Publishers.

Schraw, G. (2006). Knowledge: Structures and processes. In P. Alexander & P. Winne (Eds.), *Handbook of educational psychology* (2nd ed., pp. 245–264). San Diego: Academic Press.

Schraw, G., Brooks, D. W., & Crippen, K. J. (2005). Using an interactive compensatory model of learning to improve teaching. *Journal of Chemical Education, 82*, 637–640.

Schunk, D. H., & Zimmerman, B. J. (2006). Competence and control beliefs: Distinguishing means and ends. In P. A. Alexander & P. H. Winne (Eds.), *Handbook of educational psychology* (2nd ed., pp. 349–368). Mahwah, NJ: Erlbaum.

Shah, P., & Miyake, A. (1999). Models of working memory. In A. Miyake & P. Shah (Eds.), *Models of working memory: Mechanisms of active maintenance and executive control* (pp. 1–25). Cambridge, England: Cambridge University Press.

Stanovich, K. E. (2003). The fundamental computational biases of human cognition: Heuristics that (sometimes) impair decision making and problem solving. In J. E. Davidson & R. J. Sternberg (Eds.), *The psychology of problem solving* (pp. 291–342). Cambridge, England: Cambridge University Press.

Sternberg, R. J. (2001). Metacognition, abilities, and developing expertise: What makes an expert student? In H. J. Hartman (Ed.), *Metacognition in learning and instruction: Theory, research, and practice* (pp. 247–260). Dordrecht, Netherlands: Kluwer Academic Publishers.

Sweller, J., & Chandler, P. (1994). Why some material is difficult to learn. *Cognition and Instruction, 12*, 185–253.

Sweller, J., van Merrienboer, J. J. G., & Pass, F. (1998). Cognitive architecture and instructional design. *Educational Psychology Review, 10*, 251–296.

Weiner, B. (1986). *An attributional theory of motivation and emotion*. New York: Springer-Verlag.

White, B., & Frederiksen, J. R. (2005). A theoretical framework and approach for fostering metacognitive development. *Educational Psychologist, 40*, 211–223.

Woolfolk Hoy, A. & Burke-Spero, R. (2005). Changes in teacher efficacy during the early years of teaching: A comparison of four measures. *Teaching and Teacher Education, 21*, 457–471.

Woolfolk Hoy, A., Davis, H., & Pape, S. J. (2006). Teacher knowledge and beliefs. In P. A. Alexander & P. H. Winne (Eds.), *Handbook of educational psychology* (2nd ed., pp. 715–737). Mahwah, NJ: Erlbaum.

Zeidner, M., Boekaerts, M., & Pintrich, P. R. (2000). Self-regulation: Directions and challenges for future research. In M. Boekaerts, P. R. Pintrich, & M. Zeidner (Eds.), *Handbook of self-regulation* (pp. 13–39). San Diego, CA: Academic Press.

Zimmerman, B. J. (2000). Attaining self-regulation: A social cognitive perspective. In M. Boekaerts, P. R. Pintrich, & M. Zeidner (Eds.), *Handbook of self-regulation* (pp. 13–39). San Diego, CA: Academic Press.

CHAPTER 8

CONTRIBUTIONS OF SOCIAL PSYCHOLOGY
TO SCHOOL PSYCHOLOGY

FREDERIC J. MEDWAY AND THOMAS P. CAFFERTY
University of South Carolina

In what is considered the first experiment in modern social psychology, Triplett (1897) asked school children in Indiana to wind fishing line on a reel and found that those who did so in the presence of other children did so faster than did those who wound reels by themselves. This study ushered in more than 100 years of controlled research in social psychology, established the central role of social influence as a key psychological topic, and set the stage for social psychology's contributions to clinical and school psychology (Kowalski & Leary, 2003; Medway & Cafferty, 1992). In this chapter we consider the parameters of social psychology, briefly review both historical developments and contemporary research emphases, and discuss selected topics of particular relevance for school psychologists emphasizing both classic readings and contemporary literature.

THE FIELD OF SOCIAL PSYCHOLOGY

What is Social Psychology?

Allport (1985) defined social psychology as studying how an individual's thoughts, feelings, and behavior are influenced by the actual or implied presence of others, and this definition continues to be used today (e.g., Aronson, Wilson, & Akert, 2005). Much of contemporary social psychology focuses on the following topics of study (Smith & Mackie, 2007; Tesser & Bau, 2002): (a) social cognition, (b) attitudes, (c) attribution (including motivational and interpersonal issues), (d) the self, (e) interpersonal influence, (f) intergroup relations and stereotypes, (g) prosocial and antisocial behavior, (h) culture

and evolution, and (i) interpersonal relationships. Because of historical and social influences the affinities of social psychologists are continually changing; currently, there is more interest on ingroup-outgroup phenomenon and biological influences than in past years. Social psychologists have also led the way in studies of methodological issues of human subject research including demand characteristics, placebo effects, research ethics, and internal and external validity. Social psychological research has led to the development of the aligned fields of organization development, program evaluation, and marketing research. There are currently 4500 members of the Society for Personality and Social Psychology (see www.spsp.org). Most social psychologists teach and do research in higher education settings. While most of these are employed in psychology departments, many others are employed in diverse higher education disciplines such as business, law, medicine, public health, and education. Others are employed in government settings and nonprofit organizations addressing program evaluation, conflict prevention and resolution, and environmental concerns. And finally, many are employed as private consultants, researchers, and strategists.

The Development of Contemporary Social Psychology

Interest in understanding human social behavior can be traced back nearly 2500 years, first to philosophers such as Plato (427–347 BC) and Aristotle (384–322 BC), then to evolutionary and instinct theorists, later to sociologists and experimental psychologists (primarily) within the Gestalt tradition, and most recently to collaborations between social psychologists and others in related disciplines (see reviews by Allport, 1985; Jones, 1985; Medway, 1992). The early roots of social psychology were strongly influenced by the Darwinian revolution and views that human behavior was instinctual. Later on, when social psychology and sociology were less distinct than today, there emerged the idea that group and crowd behavior is more than the sum of individual behavior (Durkheim, 1951; LeBon, 1896). Following this was the emergence of psychological theories of learning and conditioning as advanced by Thorndike, Watson, and Pavlov who proposed that human behavior did not depend on instinctual processes; as a result instinct and sociological views of human behavior fell out of favor (Berntson & Cacioppo, 2000). However, recent years have seen a reemergence of interest in both biological and sociological influences as research paradigms focus on behavioral neuroscience and the self.

Emergence of Social Psychology

Social psychology as a distinct discipline began to emerge in the latter half of the 1890s. Wilhelm Wundt (1832–1921) pursued interests in language, custom, and social organization and would direct the dissertation of Lightner Witmer (1867–1956), considered the founder of clinical and school psychology. Witmer considered both pedagogy and sociology as important to examining and treating children's learning problems. In 1908 the first social psychology textbook, *An Introduction to Social Psychology*, was published (McDougall, 1908). During the 1920s and 1930s social psychology was distinctly an applied field, and there was a focus on integrating social psychology and abnormal psychology; there was research interest in understanding the absorption of immigrants into American society, the rise of juvenile gangs, and the nature of social group relations. This time period also witnessed the first use of groups for therapeutic purposes. Social workers led the way in demonstrating that recreational groups and clubs could be formed for character building, and psychotherapists further demonstrated early and important ways that groups could be helpful in modifying behavior (Reid, 1981). Social psychologists like Jacob Moreno (1889–1974) using sociometry (cf. Zettergren, 2005) not only studied the social networks among children in schools but pioneered the techniques of psychotherapeutic role playing. Moreno was greatly influenced by the writings of John Dewey who, at the time, broadened the purpose of education to include not only the transmission of information but the development of leadership, cooperation, and interpersonal relations, all important topics within the relatively new field of social psychology. Nevertheless, starting in the 1930s, social psychology took on a distinct experimental flavor by focusing on trying to understand social behavior by studying it in lab settings, a movement attributed to Sherif (1936) who effectively used this method to study the development of social norms. This movement resulted in a separation of the previously aligned fields of social psychology and sociology.

Social psychology received a significant boost in its development during the period of and immediately following World War II (see Cartwright, 1979; Jones, 1985) due to new technical advances in attitude measurement (e.g., Thurstone, Likert) and the immigration of European psychologists, such as Fritz Heider, Solomon Asch, and Kurt Lewin, who came to America to escape Germany's religious persecution. Lewin's work, serving as the foundation for the group dynamics movement, was directly tied to the war effort (Lewin, 1947). Further, social psychology research on communication and attitude change was seen as useful in countering German propaganda and helping the country understand why certain types of leaders can rise to power.

Between World War II and the late 1950s, social psychology was dominated by the study of attitude change, group dynamics, and conformity. The two major theoretical orientations were behavioral psychology (e.g., Hovland, Janis, & Kelley, 1953) and the Gestalt approach. The latter, originating with Heider and Lewin, was subsequently advanced by Festinger, Kelley, and Thibaut, and ultimately led to two popular theories: cognitive dissonance and attribution. The last 20 years have witnessed the domination of the field by the cognitive perspective (Fiske & Taylor, 1991), the merging of social psychology with clinical and health psychology (Snyder, Tennen, Affleck, & Cheavens, 2000), a reemergence of small group research (McGrath, Arrow, & Berdahl, 2000), a new interest in ethnic and sexual stereotyping (Madon et al., 2001), and attempts to apply social psychology to understanding the current state of society in light of threats of terrorism following the destruction of the World Trade Center in 2001 (Pyszczynski, Solomon, & Greenberg, 2002).

ATTITUDES AND ATTITUDE CHANGE

The study of attitudes has long held a major position in the field of social psychology. Indeed, at one time attitude issues virtually defined the field (Allport, 1935; Jones, 1998). Although this is no longer the case, attitude research remains a popular topic of study, in part because there are a number of unresolved theoretical issues, but also because the field is so important to so many areas of applied psychology (Ajzen, 2001; Crano & Prislin, 2006; Eagly & Chaiken, 1993, 1998; Petty & Wegener, 1998). The literature on attitudes of greatest relevance for school psychology involve (a) the definition of attitude(s), (b) techniques for measuring them, (c) strategies for changing them, and (d) understanding their impact on actual behavior. The current standard in the field of attitude theory is the volume by Eagly and Chaiken (1993), although McGuire's earlier (1985) review also contains useful historical, theoretical, and empirical material.

Definition of Attitudes

Upon even a brief acquaintance with the attitude literature, one becomes aware of differences and ambiguities in the definition of the term "attitude." At present, most researchers in the area have adopted the definition offered by Eagly and Chaiken (1993) of attitude as "a psychological tendency that is expressed by evaluating a particular entity with some degree of favor or disfavor" (p. 1). The key terms in this definition are "tendency" and "evaluating." The use of the term "tendency" reflects a view that an attitude is an internal process, and thus not directly accessible to measurement. When it is expressed, such expression takes the form of an evaluative response that can be measured. The response may involve one or more of three components: affect, cognition, or behavior.

Perhaps the most significant recent development in the area of attitudes has been the distinction between implicit and explicit attitudes (Ajzen, 2001; Crano & Prislin, 2006; Gawronski & Bodenhausen, 2006; Rydell & McConnell, 2006). Explicit attitudes are the consciously held attitudes that respondents report via traditional attitude scales. They are defined as the product of controlled consideration of the attitude object. On the other hand, implicit attitudes are automatic and perhaps unconscious evaluative reactions to the attitude object. They are measured through

reaction time tasks or primed semantic association tasks. The implication of this distinction is that one may actually hold multiple attitudes toward the same attitude object, and that these attitudes may be inconsistent. A further implication is that it is possible to achieve change on an implicit or explicit attitude without parallel change on the other.

Attitude Measurement

The discussion of the definition of attitudes in the preceding section suggests that attitudes may be measured in a variety of ways. Techniques have been developed for assessing attitudes via physiological measurement, measures of cognitive processes, and behavioral indicators (Cafferty, 1992; Himmelfarb, 1993). By far the favored means of measuring explicit attitudes, and the one typically used by school psychologists, is the self-report scale. From a practical point of view, there are two related concerns that are usually raised about such scales. The first is whether an adequate scale exists to measure some given attitude of interest. The second is the method of constructing such a scale if one does not exist.

With respect to the first concern, most attitude scales in use have been devised for purposes of a specific study, and—unlike the situation for other scales used by school psychologists—there is no easily accessible source for them. However, some popular scales in general use have been collected and critiqued in volumes by Robinson, Shaver, and Wrightsman (1991, 1999) and Shaw and Wright (1967). With respect to the second concern, there are several types of scale construction techniques. Each technique has been derived from a different definition of attitude and a different set of scaling assumptions. Each produces a quantitative index of the degree of favorable or unfavorable evaluation of an attitude object. Guidelines for the construction and evaluation of attitude scales are contained in a number of sources, including Fishbein (1967), Mueller (1986), Rossi, Wright, and Anderson (1983), and Summers (1970).

Attitude Change

Perhaps the earliest program of research on attitude change was that initiated by Hovland during World War II and incorporated into the Yale Persuasive Communications Program. A basic premise of the program was that an attitude was a learned response. A persuasive communication was an attempt to change that response. Thus, a successful persuasive communication would necessarily contain some factors that provided an incentive to change (Hovland, Janis, & Kelley, 1953). Hovland felt that these factors could be conveniently grouped into categories that had been recognized as the components of successful argumentation since antiquity, namely, the source (or communicator), the message (or communication), and the audience. He and his colleagues systematically varied aspects of each of these components and measured the impact on the dependent variables of attention, comprehension, and yielding to the message. While the list of components has been expanded to include factors such as those related to the medium of the communication and the list of dependent variables has become more highly articulated (McGuire, 1985), many of the early findings remain quite robust. For instance, effective communicators are those who are seen as trustworthy and having expertise by their audience. These are, for example, characteristics of effective and respected classroom teachers. Message effectiveness is often a function of both the message construction and the audience to whom it is delivered. For example, the same communicator and message that are effective for adults may not be effective at all for a student audience.

A second strategy for change is based on the view that humans seek cognitive consistency in their transactions with the world. This view underlies cognitive dissonance theory (Festinger, 1957). According to this view, attitude change occurs when one encounters inconsistencies in one's cognitions. The cognitions themselves may refer to behavior or to beliefs. One of the most powerful antecedents of attitude change is a perceived inconsistency between one's behavior and the beliefs salient to that behavior. One brings about attitude change, then, by arranging the environment so as to create an inconsistency in cognitions for the target. This conceptualization has been applied directly to clinical practice by Brehm (1976), Hughes (1983), and Sandoval (2003). These authors have suggested that in working with clients and consultees, psychologists should ask these individuals to freely choose courses of action that are theoretically presumed to increase dissonance and thus result in greater behavioral compliance with therapy or consultation suggestions.

The models of change reviewed above both suggest a general single mechanism (incentive or inconsistency reduction) underlying the process of attitude change. The literature suggests, however, that these single process models seem to predict change well in some contexts but not in others. To account for this variance in the findings, some researchers have more recently proposed dual process models (Ajzen, 2001; Crano & Prislin, 2006). The most prominent of these is the Elaboration-Likelihood model proposed by Petty and Cacioppo (1981). Basic to the model is the proposition that attitudes may be changed through either of two mental routes, *central* or *peripheral*. Which route is taken depends on the degree to which a persuasive message is cognitively elaborated by the recipient. If the recipient is motivated and capable of elaborating or thinking about the message, it will be processed via the central route. Change is difficult to bring about through the central route because the person is likely to marshal his or her cognitive resources to defend the existing position. However, once change is achieved, it is relatively long-lasting, since it involves cognitive restructuring. If, on the other hand, the recipient is either unmotivated or incapable of elaborating or thinking about the message, it will be processed via the peripheral route. Change achieved through the peripheral route is of relatively short duration and is relatively superficial. Petty and Cacioppo have noted that these routes are not mutually exclusive, and that both are usually operating to some extent in most persuasive communications. The model's strength is that it specifies the factors that determine choice of central or peripheral route and the conditions under which change is likely to occur once a route is activated. Andrews and Gutkin (1994) applied the Elaboration-Likelihood model to an analysis of the factors involved in teacher acceptance of a psychological evaluation whose findings disagreed with teachers' initial preference.

One important class of theories of attitude change that is receiving renewed attention in the literature are those based on the notion that attitudes may fulfill a variety of functions, and that different attitudes (or the same attitude among different people) might fulfill different functions (Maio & Olson, 2000). The primary import of this treatment of functions is that to change an attitude one must know what function(s) it fulfills. Trying to change an attitude that is based on one function by an appeal that is constructed around an assumed other function is likely to be unsuccessful. Chassin, Presson, Sherman, and Curran (1992) demonstrated the importance of this approach for school psychologists in their evaluation of efforts to change drug abuse patterns in adolescents.

Attitudes and Behavior

Most attitude research has been conducted assuming that an attitude has some implication for behavior, but a variety of studies demonstrate that the relationship between the two is not particularly strong (see Wicker, 1969). Partly in response to these concerns, Fishbein and Ajzen have suggested some modifications to traditional views of the attitude-behavior relationship that have proven very useful to researchers (1974, 1975; Ajzen & Fishbein, 1980). These modifications have taken the form of two models: the Theory of Reasoned Action (TRA) and the Theory of Planned Behavior (TPB).

Perhaps the most important modification suggested in the TRA was the suggestion that the relationship between attitudes and behavior is mediated by behavioral intentions, which are dispositions to act toward an object in favorable or unfavorable ways. Intentions, in turn, are determined by an individual's (a) attitude toward the behavior and (b) perception of subjective norms regarding the behavior and motivation to comply with them. For example, a child may have a positive attitude toward studying math, but the behavioral intention may be influenced by what he or she perceives as his or her friends' view of studying and by how important peer influence is to him or her. One factor lacking in the TRA concerned the perceived level of control one had over the behavior in question. The TPB adds consideration of perceived control to the prediction of intentions. Recent research on the TPB has revealed that behavior is closely, but not perfectly, related to behavioral intentions, a finding that has stimulated further research on a variety of situational or temporal constraints that may thwart intended behavior.

The approach of Fishbein and Ajzen to the attitude-behavior question rests on consideration of methodological and other factors for improving prediction. An alternative approach derived from recent work in social cognition suggests that not all attitudes are equally predictive of behavior and that the same attitude may be differentially predictive of behavior over time. This approach suggests that attitudes that are readily *accessible* are better predictors of behavior than those attitudes that are less accessible (Fazio, 1989). Accessibility refers roughly to the ease with which an attitude comes to mind in a situation calling for behavior toward an attitude object. The work of Fazio and his colleagues suggests that factors that increase accessibility will increase the correspondence between an attitude and a related behavior. Some of these factors include direct experience with the attitude object, and priming of the attitude by some prior exposure. Thus a teacher who has worked with disabled students is likely to show greater attitude-behavior correspondence on issues involving student disability than a teacher who has not directly worked with such students.

PERSON PERCEPTION

One of the core research areas within social psychology for more than 50 years has been the area of person perception. This refers to the study of how people form impressions, judgments, beliefs, and opinions about others, both others' temporary states and others' enduring and stable dispositions and traits. The study of the ways in which people come to know one another has recently been named *ordinary personology* (Gilbert, 1998), which is an attempt to integrate the traditional literature with advances in attribution theory—the study of how individuals assign causation and how they act on this information (Ross & Nisbett, 1991; Trope, 1986). Attribution theory began with Fritz Heider's (1958) seminal writings. Heider noted that, when faced with deciding the reasons for a person's behavior, ordinary people typically choose a cause that lies within the person (leading to an internal attribution) or outside the person in the environment (leading to an external attribution). For example, a teacher may perceive a child's test grade to reflect the student's ability or effort (internal causes) or the test characteristics (external causes). Heider's work was particularly influential because it led to the development of other theories focusing on more narrowly defined attributional processes. These included the classic work of Jones and Davis (1965), describing the conditions under which individuals attribute intentions and dispositions to others (the theory of correspondent inferences), and Kelley's (1967) paper claiming that ordinary people use the same tools as scientists in making causal judgments, i.e., consistency, distinctiveness, and consensus (theory of covariation).

By the early 1970s most attribution theorists discarded the belief that attribution was exclusively a rational process based on informational cues and discussed how biases or distortions influence causal reasoning about others (Jones & Nisbett, 1971). One of these biases, known as ego-defensive or egocentric attribution, holds that individuals are motivated to view the world in such a way that their self-image is enhanced or protected from threat. According to this view, people generally see themselves as the causes of positive events but deny personal responsibility for negative events (Pronin, Lin, & Ross, 2002); individuals also may believe that good things are more likely to happen to themselves and bad things are less likely to happen to themselves than to others (Weinstein & Klein, 1996). A second bias known as the "fundamental attribution error" is the tendency for people to underestimate the impact of situational causes and overestimate the influence of internal dispositional factors in others' behavior, particularly in comparison to their own behavior. Such tendencies have been studied in numerous clinical settings relevant to school psychologists, including marital attributions (Gordon, Friedman, Miller, & Gaertner, 2005) and maternal attributions for child behavior and its links to discipline practices (Snarr, Strassberg, & Smith-Slep, 2003). Nevertheless, the prevailing view of person perception continues to be based primarily on information processing models (Trope & Higgins, 1993). The newest attribution models suggest that much of attribution and behavior categorization occurs automatically and favors dispositional over situational causes. Given time and opportunity for reflection, perceivers more fully consider these attributions and adjust them to give added emphasis to situational causes.

These writings reviewed above represent the major papers describing the general process of causal attribution. In addition to these, there have been several attribution models for specific types of events (domain specific attributions). Three of these extensions of attribution theory hold particular relevance for school psychology and have generated considerable research. They are briefly summarized below: attributional models of achievement behavior (Levesque & Lowe, 1992; Weiner 1972), research on extrinsic-intrinsic motivation, and Abramson's (Abramson, Seligman, & Teasdale, 1978) reformulated attributional model of learned helplessness.

Achievement-Related Attributions

Weiner (1972) developed an influential attribution theory analysis of achievement behavior that expanded Heider's internal-external attribution dimensions to include the dimensions of stability (stable or variable) and controllability (potentially controllable or not). This analysis explicates why individuals approach or avoid achievement-related tasks, how they make judgments about achievement outcomes, and how this subsequently affects their affect, expectations, and future behavior. Weiner gives most emphasis to the locus of causality and stability dimensions and notes that people normally ascribe the causes of their achievement behavior to one of four causes: their ability, their effort or motivation, the ease or difficulty of the task, or luck. There are several excellent updates of Weiner's work that will be particularly useful for school psychologists and educators. Levesque and Lowe (1992) summarized the research on attributional antecedents, and reviewed the relevant research on students' self-attributions as well as teacher attributions for student behavior.

Levesque and Lowe discussed attributions based on class or reference group information such as race, gender, and social class and attributions based on specific outcome performance or performance pattern. Regarding the latter, high achievers tend to attribute success to ability and failure to lack of effort whereas low achievers tend to attribute failure to lack of ability, which lowers their expectations for future performance, increases negative affect such as disappointment, and decreases future task persistence. Similarly, Reyna (2000) reviewed how stereotypes convey attributional information to teachers and children themselves. Work on students' cross-cultural attributions was offered by Armbrister, McCallum, and Lee (2002). In addition, Graham (1991) reviewed how attributions affect emotional reactions in the classroom, the provision of help to others, peer acceptance and rejection, and specifically the attributions of African American students. Particularly important to school psychologists is research on how teachers assign causation for student learning and how student outcomes and attributions affect teachers' emotions and behavior. In particular, if teachers' perceive that a child's difficulties are due to lack of effort the teacher may be more critical of the child and angry than if the child's difficulties are attributed to lack of ability (Georgiou, Christou, Stravrinides & Panaoura, 2002; Medway, 1979).

Extrinsic versus Intrinsic Motivation

Deci and colleagues (e.g., Deci, Koestner, & Ryan, 2001) have argued that people seek personal autonomy and thus prefer intrinsic rather than extrinsic reasons or motives to engage in a behavior. A classic finding in social psychology is that promising an extrinsic reward for engaging in an interesting activity (one in which there already is high intrinsic motivation) serves to undermine that motivation (the overjustification effect). This finding is particularly strong for school-aged children (Deci, Ryan, & Koestner, 2001). Students reportedly enjoy learning less when taught by demanding and controlling teachers (Grolnick & Ryan, 1987) and when taught by paid compared to volunteer teachers (Wild, Enzle, & Hawkins, 1992). An interesting model of high school dropout behavior based on intrinsic-extrinsic motivation theory was proposed by Vallerand, Fortier, and Guay (1997). In the home, strong relationships have been found between cognitive stimulation by parents and children's intrinsic academic motivation (Gottfried, Fleming, & Gottfried, 1998).

Cognitive Diathesis-Stress Model of Depression

According to the Cognitive Diathesis-Stress model of depression, individuals are likely to be depressed when (a) they experience a stressful event and (b) have a general style of interpreting that event to aspects of the self. One such model of depression is the reformulated learned helplessness and learned hopelessness model of depression of Abramson and colleagues (Abramson, et al., 1978; Abramson, Metalsky, & Alloy, 1989). This model holds that people who attribute a negative life event to stable, global, and internal causes are more likely to suffer depression than those with a less negative explanatory style. Peterson (1992) has argued that learned helplessness can be recognized by three criteria: maladaptive passivity, uncontrollability, and beliefs that personal responses and outcomes are independent. Although several studies do show an attribution-behavior link, the phenomenon appears more complex than initially proposed (Hill & Larsen, 1992). Peterson (1992) also noted that uncontrollability beliefs can be modified and passivity reduced by: (a) restructuring the learning environment so that there are clear rewards based on student effort, (b) using cognitive therapy to change from negative to positive explanatory style, (c) by adopting attribution retraining (McCormick & Pressley, 2006), and (d) by changing the attributions that caregivers pass on to their children.

Applications of Attribution Theory to Consultation and Therapy

Particularly relevant to school psychology are attribution theory applications to school-based interventions. Early studies (Martin & Curtis, 1981; Smith & Lyon, 1986) demonstrated tendencies for school-based consultants to hold consultees responsible for negative consultation outcomes. Other studies have found little relationship between teachers' attributions about children and their desire to seek consultation (Hughes, Barker, Kemenoff, & Hart, 1993) and use instructional practices (Bibou-Nakou, Kiosseoglou, & Stogiannidou, 2000). A second area is the impact of attributions on client change in therapy. Sandoval and Davis (1992) described how many therapy models aim to increase clients' sense of internal causation rather than relying on tendencies to externalize blame.

SOCIAL COGNITION

A key topic in social psychology is social cognition, which is defined as how people think about their social behavior and that of others (Fiske & Taylor, 1991). Research has shown that impressions of others are formed quickly, automatically, and without much conscious thought. This is done through the use of schemas that help organize information about the social world, access it, and use existing information to respond to new information. Schemas allow one to go beyond the social information given in a specific instance and generate hypotheses and additional items of information that may have important implications for behavior toward a social object. Understanding schemas is particularly relevant to school psychology because schemas are invoked whenever judgments are made about social groups. These groups may include students with special education labels, individuals differing in race, gender, or ability level, or members of certain social groups such as gangs. Schemas may serve to focus attention on only certain aspects of a child's behavior that are expected within the schema, and structure the interpretation of that behavior in ways that are consistent with the schema. And it may influence the kind of behavior displayed toward the child in such a way that behavior consistent with the schema is elicited from the child. Thus, labeling a child mildly retarded may initiate an event schema or expected sequence of behaviors pertaining to how the child might handle a challenging school task. To the extent that the child's performance matches the schema, the use of the schema is validated. Perhaps more important, the existence of the schema may lead the perceiver to overlook important but not necessarily dramatic departures, thus maintaining the original and possibly incorrect judgment.

Nisbett and Ross (1980) contended that people have developed a variety of cognitive strategies to deal with the potentially overwhelming amount of information to which they are exposed. These strategies serve to filter out unnecessary information and frequently result in efficient and speedy judgments. Priming refers to the process by which recent experiences or observations increase the accessibility of a certain schema. The perseverance effect refers to the finding that people may persist in certain beliefs (i.e., maintain the schema) even when new data discredits the schema. A related phenomenon is the illusory correlation which refers to the perception of an association when none actually exist (Chapman & Chapman, 1969).

INTERPERSONAL ATTRACTION

Social psychologists have had a longstanding interest in what attracts people to one another, how intimate relationships develop, and the consequences of the failure to develop meaningful relationships (Bersheid & Regan, 2005; Moreno, 1934). There are several classic theories of attraction. These include cognitive consistency theories that hold that we like those who like us (also known as reciprocal liking, e.g., Kubitschek & Hallinan, 1998) and reinforcement theories that hold that we like people who reward us in some way (Kelley & Thibaut, 1978). In the last two decades social psychologists have also studied intense emotions and moods related to relationship functioning such as loneliness (Johnson, Rose, & Russell, 1992) and depression (Tennen, Hall, & Affleck, 1995). Much of this research follows the cognitive model and stresses attributions, expectations, and schema.

Three factors have been found to be especially important in influencing attraction in initial and brief encounters. These are the physical attractiveness of the other, the similarity of the other to the individual, and to a lesser extent, social contact. Across race, sex, age, and social class physically attractive people are liked more (and seen as more popular and outgoing) than less attrac-

tive people. Of particular importance to school psychologists are studies indicating a relationship between children's popularity and attractiveness (Boyatzis, Baloff, & Durieux, 1998; Davison & McCabe, 2006) and studies showing that teachers give attractive children better evaluations, more opportunities to perform, and treat them less harshly when they transgress (Berscheid & Regan, 2005). Second, research clearly shows that people are drawn to similar others (Byrne, 1997). This basic notion has numerous implications for school psychologists, ranging from understanding the cohesion of groups of similar racial makeup to understanding why males tend to be referred for behavior problems by teachers, especially female teachers. Third, research demonstrates that social conduct, familiarity, and physical proximity (the propinquity effect) increase liking and attraction. The more exposure people have toward others, in the absence of negative interactions, the greater the attraction. The social contact hypothesis underlies many social experiments designed to reduce prejudice and stereotyping, starting with school integration in the 1950s (Clark & Clark, 1965; Cook, 1984; Stephan, 1978), to the deinstitutionalization of the mentally ill, to the mainstreaming/inclusion movements for special needs children (Carter, Hughes, Guth, & Copeland, 2005).

In recent years attachment theory has been widely used to explain interpersonal attraction, friendship and peer relationships, and the reactions of adults and children separated from caretakers and loved ones (Bartholomew & Perlman, 1994; Pietromonaco & Barrett, 1997). According to the original formulation of attachment theory by Bowlby (1980) and its extension to adult relationships (Hazan & Shaver, 1994), young children form cognitive (working) models of their primary caregivers (such as parents). These working models influence not only reactions and relationships in childhood but extend well beyond this developmental period and subsequently impact interpersonal relationships well into the adult years. When attachment to parents is secure (as compared to anxious-ambivalent or avoidant), children will want to maintain these relationships and the emotional closeness over time and distance (Ainsworth, 1991; Hazan & Shaver, 1994). When attachment to parents is insecure, adolescents are more likely to report loneliness, anxiety, depression, and lack of self-confidence (Cooper, Shaver, & Collins, 1998; Shaver & Clark, 1994).

GROUP INFLUENCES AND DYNAMICS

A group is defined as two or more people who interact, influence each other, and are interdependent as to their needs and goals. The early work in the field of social psychology focused on groups with incompatible goals (e.g., Deutsch, 1968) and groups in conflict (Sherif, Harvey, White, Hood, & Sherif, 1961). For example, Sherif et al. (1961) in a classic study showed that intergroup hostility can be overcome when competing groups are faced with an external challenge that requires cooperation to meet that challenge. There are numerous aspects of group study that have relevance to school psychology. These include the study of how norms are formed and perceived, how social and gender roles develop, how groups develop cohesiveness, the nature of cooperation (e.g., Parks, Sanna, & Berel, 2001), and how the presence of others influences individual behavior—the original research area in social psychology (e.g., Dion, 2000; see also the journal *Group Dynamics: Theory, Research, and Practice* published by the American Psychological Association).

There are several aspects of group dynamics that are particularly important for school psychologists. One important contribution of this literature is its role in understanding the origins and consequences of prejudice and discrimination. Prejudice refers to an attitude toward members of another group based solely on their membership in that group, while discrimination refers to behaviors based on that attitude. According to Tajfel's (1978) social identity theory, identification with one's own group enhances personal identity and causes one to elevate the ingroup and denigrate the outgroup (Ellemers, Spears, & Doosje, 2002). Cameron, Alvarez, Ruble, and Fuglini (2001) noted that a positive bias toward their own familiar group underlies children's prejudice.

Another group dynamics principle with relevance for understanding prejudice is the contact hypothesis, which, in its simplest form, holds that intergroup contact can reduce prejudice and bias (Pettigrew, 2005). A reformulated hypothesis suggests that the effect of increased intergroup contact depends on the social context (e.g., cooperative activity), the nature of contact activity (e.g., interacting), and the (equal) status of the participants (Amir, 1998). The contact hypothesis has been applied in the so-called "jigsaw" classroom to increase racial harmony in children. Well-known

social psychologist Eliot Aronson, one of the developers of the method, describes the approach and its results on his website (www.jigsaw.org). Aronson clearly makes the case for the approach as a means of teaching tolerance in light of the series of school shootings the country has witnessed, particularly the 1999 school shooting in Columbine. A second body of work derived from the contact hypothesis has been the research on cooperative learning techniques (Bohlmeyer & Burke, 1987; Slavin, 1996) and involves two approaches. The first, student-teams-achievement-division (STAD), involves multiracial peer teaching in small groups or teams. The teams gain by improvement of members each at their own level, thus enhancing cooperation among team members. The second technique, teams-games-tournaments (TGT), also involves multiracial peer teaching, but achievement is assessed in tournaments among students of comparable achievement levels. Cooperative learning techniques and other interventions to reduce racism and prejudice in children (Aboud & Levy, 2000) have been widely adopted in schools nationwide, and increasingly school psychologists are playing a role in the delivery of this instructional activity (Bramlett, 1994).

There is also recent interest in the effects of racism, discrimination, and prejudice on the discriminated group. Some have held that just the threat of prejudice may be enough to be disruptive. Social psychologist Claude Steele (e.g., Steele, Spencer, & Aronson, 2002) has argued that in situations where a negative stereotype exists, the stereotyped group may be at risk of confirming it both to themselves and others. The phenomenon is termed "stereotyped threat." Steele has argued that for African American students the sheer act of taking a scholastic or achievement test may raise a threat of being stereotyped and that the stereotype threat may, by directing attention away from task demands, undermine performance. The implications of Steele's work for school psychology were addressed by Jordan and Lovett (2007) in a recent paper. Their paper is an excellent extension of social psychology to school psychology.

Besides the area of prejudice and discrimination, another important implication of the group dynamics literature for school psychology is research on group decision making. Group behavior processes have taken on particular importance for school psychologists since the late 1980s as school psychologists now make decisions and judgments, often within special education contexts, as part of multidisciplinary, collaborative teams. These teams, composed of diverse members—psychologists, teachers, student family members, and even, if of age, students themselves—are faced with the challenge of reaching consensus on educational decisions about the student's future educational programming (Gutkin & Curtis, 1999). Indeed the issue of team decision making is one of the few in which basic social psychological principles have been directly applied to the day-to-day functioning of school psychologists in such a way that the research base has clear practical implications (Gutkin & Nemeth, 1997). Gutkin and Nemeth (1997) reviewed several basic social psychological research areas, including group decision making, the role of majorities and minorities in groups, group polarization, and group norms, all of which have an impact on the decisions of school-based teams. This paper is one of the most direct connections of social psychology to school psychology in the literature.

Aggression and Violence

Aggression may be defined as behavior with the intention to injure another person. The aggressive act may be primarily a means toward some other end (e.g., a child hitting to get a toy or attention). This is known as *instrumental* aggression. Or, the aggression may be the end in itself (e.g., a child striking another with the sole intent to harm). This is known as *hostile* aggression. Social psychologists, while acknowledging the role of biologically based instincts as a cause of human aggression, generally agree that a human's capacity to inhibit aggression or display it depends on a complex interplay of social situations and cues (Berkowitz, 1993). There are several excellent overviews of the social psychology of aggression (Buss & Duntley, 2006; Krahe, 2001).

Beyond instinctual causes of aggression, social psychologists have offered several theories that attempt to account for aggressive behavior. These include the classic frustration-aggression hypothesis (Miller, 1941) and Bandura's (1965) social learning theory. The latter theory holds that there are certain antecedent or situational conditions that lead to emotional arousal that may, because of observational learning, reinforcement, or personality characteristics, lead to aggression or some alternative response. There are several antecedents that trigger emotional arousal. These include sex-role training that encourages boys

to be more aggressive than girls, the presence of others that results in groups exhibiting more aggression than individuals alone, aggressive cues such as knives and guns, and characteristics of the target of aggression such as their gender and potential for retaliation. Some types of people are especially likely to be attacked, such as the handicapped and unattractive (Zebrowitz & Lee, 1999). Further, it has been found that unpleasant environmental conditions, such as heat, crowding, and invasions of personal space, can trigger aggression. According to social learning theory, the major conditions intervening between a potentially aggressive stimulus and aggressive response are (a) the degree of emotional arousal (Schacter, 1964), and (b) the reinforcement expected for oneself or given to another for an aggressive act. This model also holds that arousal (or anger) may eventuate in several outcomes besides aggression depending on a variety of factors associated with the individual and situation.

Media Influences

Readers of this chapter are well familiar with numerous examples of violent media images that appear to lead to calamitous outcomes. One is the often-cited connection between John Hinkley, Jr.'s identification with a character in the movie "Taxi Driver" and his subsequent attempt to assassinate President Ronald Reagan in March 1981. Hinkley claimed he watched this movie 15 times. Since then, many other examples come to mind. The 1994 movie "Natural Born Killers" by director Oliver Stone allegedly provided the impetus for two eighteen-year olds from Oklahoma to go on a killing spree; Stone's alleged culpability for the murders was argued in a case that went all the way to the Supreme Court. Following the Columbine shootings, the parents of the victims sued several video game companies for $5 billion for their alleged responsibility. Killers Eric Harris and Dylan Klebold maintained a website devoted to the video game "Doom" and it was argued that the game helped blur the adolescents' ability to distinguish reality from fantasy. The trench coats worn by Harris and Klebold have been said by some to be inspired by the film "The Matrix." And most recently, writers have speculated that Virginia Tech shooter Cho Seung-Hui may have been influenced by a violent South Korean film "Oldboy." Today, the conversations are more about which media are the most violent and affect kids the most;

children online argue for their favorite violent images, and there is little disagreement that children are attentive to these images. Beyond the headlines there is now overwhelming evidence that exposure to violent images, in television and movies, in songs, in video games, and to some extent on the Internet, is associated with aggressive behavior. Given the complexity of this topic the reader is referred to an excellent summary of this work by Anderson et al. (2003). The authors argue that the evidence is unequivocal and that the effects are found in terms of both short-term and long-term influences, especially when the viewers are preschool or young children who have difficulty judging intentionality and motive. Nevertheless, as Morrison, Furlong, and Morrison (1994) pointed out several years ago, the topics of aggression, violence, and related issues such as vandalism and victimization (excluding bullying) have not traditionally been discussed in the school psychology literature with few exceptions (Bernthal & Medway, 2005). Indeed, in some recent introductory texts (Merrell, Ervin, & Gimpel, 2006) there is no coverage at all, and there remains a need for school psychologists, particularly in the wake of high-profile school and university violence incidents, to take an active role in preventing and reducing violence in the schools—violence among children and violence against children by older individuals (see Hyman & Perone, 1998). This can include working with children to modify viewing habits or their interpretation of violent events, reducing those conditions that reinforce aggression, supporting national organizations and local PTAs that seek to reduce media violence, and assisting families to teach children the value of prosocial rather than antisocial and aggressive behavior.

Violence Against Women

Several social psychological theories, including social learning theory, cognitive psychology ("sexual scripts"), attachment theory, and social exchange theory, have been used to understand violence against women—a problem that has been of growing concern to society in the last 20 years. For example, regarding sexual scripts, significant numbers of adolescents believe that when a woman says "no," she may mean "yes." Gelles (1999) proposed a social psychological model that attempts to account for domestic violence with regard to family organization and structure, intimate partner interactions, and cultural norms and attitudes. Sonkin and Dutton (2003) have

proposed a model that seeks to understand domestic violence and treat batterers based on attachment theory's internal working models of self and other. And others, using social exchange theory, have argued that abuse occurs when the rewards (including control over the partner) outweigh the costs (Hampton, Vandergriff-Avery, & Kim, 1999). Social psychologists also have applied their theories to studying the impact of pornography on individuals, and the impact of alcohol as a factor that reduces the inclination not to aggress (Aronson et al., 2005).

ORGANIZATIONAL BEHAVIOR

In accordance with our definition of social psychology, most of the contributions to school psychology discussed thus far have applied to relatively simple social situations and interactions (e.g., student-teacher, teacher-psychologist, and student-student). The school in which these situations and interactions occur, however, is a complex formal organization that to some extent determines and is affected by the interactions that take place. Organizational theory and research is a rapidly expanding interdisciplinary enterprise (Pfeffer, 1985, 1998), and a review of this literature is not within the scope of the present chapter. However, social psychologists have contributed a perspective and a research tradition to some aspects of the field and continue to do so, particularly at the level of individual behavior in the organization.

Leadership

One important tradition originated in the work of Lewin and his associates on leadership in groups (Lewin, Lippett, & White, 1939). Appropriately, this work was largely conducted in schools, with teachers serving in the role of leaders for their classes. The most famous of these studies concerned the role of the leader in creating a "climate" for the group. Autocratic, democratic, and laissez-faire styles of supervision were employed to create a so-called "climate" in which the groups of students worked. Demonstrating that the democratic climate proved superior on overall criteria of performance ushered in a period of active research on leader behavior which received a considerable boost during World War II, with a focus on the training of effective leaders in military situations.

Subsequent work by Lewin's students and colleagues clarified the dimensions of leader behavior and established the validity of the socioemotional versus task distinction in leader orientations (Stogdill, 1974). After a period of research on characteristics of effective leaders, this tradition culminated in Fiedler's development of the contingency theory of leadership effectiveness. According to Fiedler (1964), there is no one most effective leader across all situations. Instead, situations can be characterized as favorable or unfavorable to the leader based on characteristics such as the structure of the task, the preexisting leader-member relations, and the position power of the leader. For situations characterized as very favorable or unfavorable to the leader, those who are relatively task oriented are likely to prove most effective, whereas for situations between the extremes, those who are relatively human relations oriented are likely to prove most effective. Research derived from this theory has provided partial support and identified areas needing modification. Vroom and Jago (2007) review some of the suggested alternatives, including their own contingency model.

Such contingency notions have important implications for the school environment, in terms of both principal-teacher and teacher-class interactions. The suggestion from this literature is that whether a given principal or teacher will be effective in their leadership position depends not only on their personal styles and resources, but on the nature of the environment in which such styles and resources are enacted.

Group Dynamics and Processes

A second research tradition developed by Lewin (1947, 1951) involves the study of group dynamics, the forces that develop in groups to encourage participation and change in their members, as well as commitment to group decisions. The first major study in this area was Lewin's project to change the shopping habits of Midwestern homemakers to buy less desirable cuts of meat. Lewin first analyzed the forces on the homemakers influencing their current purchase decisions. He then set about to change these forces by a variety of discussion techniques, finding that active participation in discussion and group commitment brought about the greatest reported change. The power of group discussion to change behavior and the effectiveness of participatory management became cornerstones of the group dynamics movement as established by Lewin.

Ironically, Lewin's techniques of participatory management and group-work decision were adopted by the Japanese and, in recent years, exported back to the United States (Ross & Nisbett, 1991). One form of participatory management, Quality Circles, has been shown to produce positive effects on workers in industrial and business settings. Quality Circles refer to small groups of workers who perform similar organizational tasks. These groups meet to identify and solve work-related problems, and recommend solutions to management. The Quality Circle approach has been used successfully with teams of school psychologists (Maher & Kruger, 1992) and appears to be an important, although as yet underutilized, method for enhancing the delivery of a full range of psychological services.

Performance Appraisal

A more recent area where interests of social psychologists intersect with those of large organizations involves the process of performance appraisal, which refers to the periodic evaluation of an employee's job performance (Arvey & Murphy, 1998). Organizations use these appraisals to make decisions about raises, promotions, transfers, remedial training, or termination. Performance appraisals usually involve rating scales of traits or behaviors relevant to the position being evaluated, so there has been a long-standing concern about their reliability and validity (Landy & Farr, 1980). Efforts to improve relatively poor reliability centered initially on the scales themselves, with efforts to incorporate more specific behavioral descriptors into the scales. Later emphasis was placed on the training of raters to avoid common errors in the rating process (Landy & Farr, 1980; Williams & Williams, 1992). Both of these approaches, which produced improved, but far from ideal, ratings, assumed that the problems were mainly mechanical in nature. Work in social cognition, however, suggests that various rating problems may be the result of inherent information processing strategies that work quite well in most social contexts (Srull, 1983). The social cognition approach is derived from the recognition that performance appraisals are usually made from memory, and that they cover activities of the subordinate over a relatively long period of time (e.g., a year or 6 months). Under such conditions, a variety of factors that are now of interest to those in social cognition may play an important role in the appraisal process. For instance, general impressions of the subordinate may be formed early, based on salient behavior and various stereotype expectations. The early general impression forms the basis for a schema that in turn directs behavior toward the subordinate and information processing of the subordinate's behavior. Later appraisal of the subordinate is based on recall of information in the context of the schema. That recall of information may be biased in a number of ways; for example, information consistent with the schema may be more readily recalled than schema-inconsistent information, or negative information may be recalled more readily than positive information (DeNisi, Cafferty, & Meglino, 1984).

Williams and Williams (1992) have reviewed this area as it applies to the school psychologist as both rater and ratee for work performance in educational settings. They point out that, in this climate of increased accountability and expanded accreditation requirements, the area of performance appraisal research has much to offer school psychologists.

CONCLUDING REMARKS

The purpose of this chapter was to provide a look at classic and contemporary social psychology and its implications and applications to school psychology. Social psychology as a vibrant research field is roughly 100 years old (if we date from publication of the first textbook), although most of the field's contributions have only been in the last 50 years. As noted over the years, social psychology has made significant contributions to our understanding of human behavior, both within lab and applied settings (although the research participant base has been, in recent years, predominately college undergraduates). Today's social psychologists are concerned with understanding major life challenges—violence, prosocial behavior, prejudice and discrimination, social attraction and social influence, and the interplay of environments and psychophysiology, to name but a few. Clearly, all these topics should be of interest to school psychologists.

Although we have argued in the past that coursework in social psychology should be part of the basic training of all school psychologists and others have argued for extensions of social psychology to school psychology (Gutkin, 1996), to date, the promise of integrating the two fields has yet to be fully realized. Indeed, only a handful of papers thoroughly review a particular social psychology topic and apply it, through example, to school psychology. While this connection of the two fields may be arguably stronger, the application of social psychology to broader educational issues has been realized, as evidenced by a journal specifically designed for this purpose that has been published for over 10 years (*Social Psychology of Education: An International Journal* from Springer Publications). Clearly, social psychology provides both school practitioners and school researchers with relevant theories and methodological tools. It is hoped that through this overview readers will be intrigued with advances in social psychology in recent years and begin to apply social psychology to understanding the social interactions that occur within schools and educational settings.

REFERENCES

Aboud, F. E., & Levy, S. R. (2000). Interventions to reduce prejudice and discrimination in children and adolescents. In S. Oskamp (Ed.), *Reducing prejudice and discrimination* (pp. 269–293). Mahwah, NJ: Erlbaum.

Abramson, L. Y., Seligman, M. E. P., & Teasdale, J. D. (1978). Learned helplessness in humans: Critique and reformulation. *Journal of Abnormal Psychology*, *87*, 49–75.

Abramson, L. Y., Metalsky, G. I., & Alloy, L. B. (1989). The hopelessness theory of depression: Does the research test the theory? In L. Y. Abramson (Ed.), *Social cognition and clinical psychology: A synthesis* (pp. 33–65). New York: Guilford Press.

Ainsworth, M. D. S. (1991). Attachments and other affectional bonds across the life cycle. In C. M. Parkes, J. Stevenson-Hinde, & P. Marris (Eds.), *Attachment across the life cycle* (pp. 33–51). London: Routledge.

Ajzen, I. (2001). Nature and operation of attitudes. *Annual Review of Psychology*, *52*, 27–58.

Ajzen, I., & Fishbein, M. (1980). *Understanding attitudes and predicting social behavior*. Englewood Cliffs, NJ: Prentice-Hall.

Allport, G. W. (1935). Attitudes. In C. Murchison (Ed.), *Handbook of social psychology* (pp. 798–844). Worcester, MA: Clark University Press.

Allport, G. W. (1985). The historical background of social psychology. In G. Lindzey & E. Aronson (Eds.), *The handbook of social psychology* (3rd ed., Vol. *1*, pp. 1–46). Hillsdale, NJ: Erlbaum.

Amir, Y. (1998). Contact hypothesis in ethnic relations. In E. Weiner (Ed.), *The handbook of interethnic coexistence* (pp. 162–181). New York: Continuum Publishing.

Anderson, C. A., Berkowitz, L., Donnerstein, E., Huesmann, L. R., Johnson, J. D., Linz, D., et al., (2003). The influence of media violence on youth.

Psychological Science in the Public Interest,
4, 81–110.

Andrews, L. W., & Gutkin, T. B. (1994). Influencing attitudes regarding special class placement using a psychoeducational report: An investigation of the Elaboration Likelihood Model. *Journal of School Psychology, 32*, 321–337.

Armbrister, R. C., McCallum, R. S., & Lee, H. D. (2002). A cross cultural comparison of student social attributions. *Psychology in the Schools, 39*, 39–49.

Aronson, E., Wilson, T. D., & Akert, R. M. (2005). *Social psychology* (5th ed.). Upper Saddle River, NJ: Pearson Education.

Arvey, R. D. & Murphy, K. R. (1998). Performance evaluation in work settings. *Annual Review of Psychology, 49*, 141–168.

Bandura, A. (1965). Vicarious processes: A case of no-trial learning. In L. Berkowitz (Ed.), *Advances in experimental social psychology* (Vol. 2, pp. 301–329). New York: Academic Press.

Bartholomew, K., & Perlman, D. (1994). *Attachment processes in adulthood*. London: Jessica Kingsley.

Berkowitz, L. (1993). *Aggression: Its causes, consequences, and control*. New York: McGraw-Hill.

Bernthal, M. B., & Medway, F. J. (2005). An initial exploration into the psychological implications of adolescents' involvement with professional wrestling. *School Psychology International, 26*, 224–242.

Berntson, G. G., & Cacioppo, J. T. (2000). Psychobiology and social psychology: Past, present, and future. *Personality and Social Psychology Bulletin, 4*, 3–15.

Berscheid, E., & Regan, P. C. (2005). *The psychology of interpersonal relationships*. New York: Prentice-Hall.

Bibou-Nakou, I., Kiosseoglou, G., & Stogiannidou, A. (2000). Elementary teachers' perceptions regarding school behavior problems: Implications for school psychological services. *Psychology in the Schools, 37*, 123–134.

Bohlmeyer, E. M., & Burke, J. P. (1987). Selecting cooperative learning techniques: A consultative strategy guide. *School Psychology Review, 16*, 36–49.

Bowlby, J. (1980). *Attachment and loss: Vol. III. Loss.* New York: Basic Books.

Boyatzis, C. J., Baloff, P., & Durieux, C. (1998). Effects of perceived attractiveness and academic success on early adolescent peer popularity. *Journal of Genetic Psychology, 159*, 337–344.

Bramlett, R. K. (1994). Implementing cooperative learning: A field study evaluating issues for school-based consultants. *Journal of School Psychology, 32*, 67–84.

Brehm, S. S. (1976). *The application of social psychology to clinical practice*. New York: Wiley.

Buss, D. M., & Duntley, J. D. (2006). The evolution of aggression. In M. Schaller, J. A. Simpson, & D. T. Kendrick (Eds.), *Evolution and social psychology: Frontiers of social psychology* (pp. 263–285). Madison, CT: Psychosocial Press.

Byrne, D. (1997). An overview (and underview) of research and theory within the attraction paradigm. *Journal of Social and Personal Relationships, 14*, 417–431.

Cafferty, T. P. (1992). Measuring and changing attitudes in educational contexts. In F. J. Medway and T. P. Cafferty (Eds.), *School psychology: A social psychological perspective* (pp. 25–46). Hillsdale, NJ: Erlbaum.

Cameron, J. A., Alvarez, J. M., Ruble, D. N., & Fuglini, A. J. (2001). Children's lay theories about ingroups and outgroups: Reconceptualizing research on prejudice. *Personality and Social Psychology Review, 5*, 118–128.

Carter, E. W., Hughes, C., Guth, C. B., & Copeland, S. R. (2005). Factors influencing social interaction among high school students with intellectual disabilities and their general education peers. *American Journal of Mental Retardation, 110*, 366–377.

Cartwright, D. (1979). Contemporary social psychology in historical perspective. *Social Psychology Quarterly, 42*, 82–93.

Chapman, L. J., & Chapman, J. P. (1969). Illusory correlation as an obstacle to the use of valid psychodiagnostic signs. *Journal of Abnormal Psychology, 74*, 271–280.

Chassin, L., Presson, C. C., Sherman, S. J., & Curran, P. J. (1992). Social psychological factors in adolescent substance use and abuse. In F. J. Medway and T. P. Cafferty (Eds.), *School psychology: A social psychological perspective*. Hillsdale, NJ: Erlbaum.

Clark, K. B., & Clark, M. P. (1965). Racial identification and preference in Negro children. In H. Proshansky & B. Seidenberg (Eds.), *Basic studies in social psychology* (pp. 308–317). New York: Holt, Rinehart and Winston.

Cook, S. W. (1984). The 1954 social science statement and school desegregation: A reply to Gerard. *American Psychologist, 39*, 819–832.

Cooper, M. L., Shaver, P. R., & Collins, N. L. (1998). Attachment styles, emotion regulation, and adjustment in adolescence. *Journal of Personality and Social Psychology, 74*, 1380–1397.

Crano, W. D., & Prislin, R. (2006). Attitudes and persuasion. *Annual Review of Psychology, 57*, 345–374.

Davison, T. E., & McCabe. M. P. (2006). Adolescent body image and psychosocial functioning. *Journal of Social Psychology, 146*, 15–30.

Deci, E. L., Koestner, R., & Ryan, R. M. (2001). Extrinsic rewards and intrinsic motivation in education: Reconsidered once again. *Review of Educational Research, 71,* 1–27.

DeNisi, A. S., Cafferty, T. P., & Meglino, B. M. (1984). A cognitive view of the performance appraisal process: A model and research propositions. *Organizational Behavior and Human Performance, 33,* 360–396.

Dion, K. L. (2000). Group cohesion: From "fields of forces" to multidimensional construct. *Group Dynamics, 4,* 7–26.

Deutsch, M. (1968). The effects of cooperation and competition upon group process. In D. Cartwright & A. Zander (Eds.), *Group dynamics* (3rd ed., pp. 461–482). New York: Harper & Row.

Durkheim, E. (1951). *Suicide.* Glencoe, IL: Free Press.

Eagly, A. H., & Chaiken, S. (1993). *The psychology of attitudes.* Fort Worth, TX: Harcourt Brace Jovanovich.

Eagly, A. H., & Chaiken, S. (1998). Attitude structure and function. In D. T. Gilbert, S. T. Fiske, & G. Lindsey (Eds.), *The handbook of social psychology* (4th ed., Vol. *1,* pp. 269–322). New York: McGraw-Hill.

Ellemers, N., Spears, R., & Doosje, B. (2002). Self and social identity. *Annual Review of Psychology, 53,* 161–186.

Fazio, R. H. (1989). On the power and functionality of attitudes: The role of attitude accessibility. In A. R. Pratkanis, S. J. Breckler, & A. G. Greenwald, (Eds.), *Attitude structure and function* (pp. 153–179). Hillsdale, NJ: Erlbaum.

Festinger, L. (1957). *A theory of cognitive dissonance.* Stanford, CA: Stanford University Press.

Fiedler, F. E. (1964). A contingency model of leadership effectiveness. In L. Berkowitz (Ed.), *Advances in experimental social psychology* (Vol. *1,* pp. 150–190). New York: Academic Press.

Fishbein, M. (Ed.). (1967). *Readings in attitude theory and measurement.* New York: Wiley.

Fishbein, M., & Ajzen, I. (1974). Attitudes toward objects as predictors of single and multiple behavioral criteria. *Psychological Review, 81,* 59–74.

Fishbein, M., & Ajzen, I. (1975). *Belief, attitude, intention, and behavior: An introduction to theory and research.* Reading, MA: Addison-Wesley.

Fiske, S. T., & Taylor, S. E. (1991). *Social cognition* (2nd ed.). New York: McGraw-Hill.

Gawronski, B., & Bodenhausen, G. V. (2006). Associative and propositional processes in evaluation: An integrative review of implicit and explicit attitude change. *Psychological Bulletin, 132,* 692–731.

Gelles, R. J. (1999). Family violence. In R. L. Hampton (Ed.), *Family violence, 2nd edition: Prevention and treatment* (pp. 1–32). Thousand Oaks, CA: Sage.

Georgiou, S., Christou, C., Stravrinides, P., & Panaoura, G. (2002). Teacher attributions of student failure and teacher behaviour toward the failing student. *Psychology in the Schools, 39,* 583–595.

Gilbert, D. T. (1998). Ordinary personology. In D. T. Gilbert, S. T. Fiske, & G. Lindzey (Eds.), *The handbook of social psychology* (4th ed., pp. 89–150). New York: McGraw-Hill.

Gordon, K. C., Friedman, M. A., Miller, I. W., & Gaertner, L. (2005). Marital attributions as moderators of the marital discord-depression link. *Journal of Social and Clinical Psychology, 24,* 876–893.

Gottfried, A. E., Fleming, J. S., & Gottfried, A. W. (1998). Role of cognitively stimulating home environment in children's academic intrinsic motivation: A longitudinal study. *Child Development, 69,* 1448–1460.

Graham, S. (1991). A review of attribution theory in achievement contexts. *Educational Psychology Review, 3,* 5–39.

Grolnick, W. S., & Ryan, R. M. (1987). Autonomy in children's learning: An experimental and individual difference investigation. *Journal of Personality and Social Psychology, 52,* 890–898.

Gutkin, T. B. (1996). Special issue. *Journal of School Psychology.*

Gutkin, T.B., & Curtis, M.J. (1999). School-based consultation theory and practice: The art and science of indirect service delivery. In C.R. Reynolds & T.B. Gutkin (Eds.), *The handbook of school psychology* (3rd ed., pp. 598–637). New York: Wiley.

Gutkin, T. B., & Nemeth, C. (1997). Selected factors impacting decision making in prereferral intervention and other school-based teams: Exploring the intersection between school and social psychology. *Journal of School Psychology, 35,* 195–216.

Hampton, R. L., Vandergriff-Avery, M., & Kim, J. (1999). Understanding the origins and incidence of spousal abuse in North America. In T. P. Gullotta & S. J. McElhaney (Eds.), *Violence in homes and communities: Prevention, intervention, and treatment* (pp. 39–70). Thousand Oaks, CA: Sage.

Hazan, C., & Shaver, P. R. (1994). Deeper into attachment theory. *Psychological Inquiry, 5,* 68–79.

Heider, F. (1958). *The psychology of interpersonal relations.* New York: Wiley.

Hill, K. J., & Larson, L. M. (1992). Attributional style in the reformulated learned helplessness model of depression: Cognitive processes and measurement implications. *Cognitive Therapy and Research, 16,* 83–94.

Himmelfarb, S. (1993). The measurement of attitudes. In A. H. Eagly and S. Chaiken, *The psychology of attitudes* (pp. 23–87). Fort Worth, TX: Harcourt Brace Jovanovich.

Hovland, C. I., Janis, I. L., & Kelley, H. H. (1953). *Communication and persuasion*. New Haven, CT: Yale University Press.

Hughes, J. N. (1983). The application of cognitive dissonance to consultation. *Journal of School Psychology, 21*, 349–357.

Hughes, J. N., Barker, D., Kemenoff, S., & Hart, M. (1993). Problem ownership, causal attributions, and self-efficacy as predictors of teachers' referral decisions. *Journal of Educational and Psychological Consultation, 4*, 369–384.

Hyman, I. A., & Perone, D. C. (1998). The other side of school violence—Educator policies and practices that may contribute to student misbehavior. *Journal of School Psychology, 36*, 7–27.

Johnson, R. A., Rose, J., & Russell, D. W. (1992). Loneliness and interpersonal relationships across the school years. In F. J. Medway & T. P. Cafferty (Eds.), *School psychology: A social psychological perspective* (pp. 377–396). Hillsdale, NJ: Erlbaum.

Jones, E. E. (1985). Major developments in social psychology during the past five decades. In G. Lindzey & E. Aronson (eds.), *Handbook of social psychology* (3rd ed., Vol. *1*, pp. 47–108). New York: Random House.

Jones, E. E. (1998). Major developments in five decades of social psychology. In D. T. Gilbert, S. T. Fiske, & G. Lindsey (Eds.), *The handbook of social psychology* (4th ed., Vol. *1*, pp. 3–57). New York: McGraw-Hill.

Jones, E. E., & Davis, K. E. (1965). From acts to dispositions: The attribution process in person perception. In L. Berkowitz (Ed.), *Advances in experimental social psychology* (Vol. 2, pp. 219–266). New York: Academic Press.

Jones, E. E., & Nisbett, R. E. (1971). *The actor and the observer: Divergent perceptions of behavior*. Morristown, NJ: General Learning Press.

Jordan, A. H., & Lovett, B. J. (2007). Stereotype threat and test performance: A primer for school psychologists. *Journal of School Psychology, 45*, 45–59.

Kelley, H. H. (1967). Attribution in social psychology. In D. Levine (Ed.), *Nebraska symposium on motivation* (pp. 192–238). Lincoln: University of Nebraska Press.

Kelley, H. H., & Thibaut, J. W. (1978). *Interpersonal relations: A theory of independence*. New York: Wiley.

Kowalski, R. M., & Leary, M. R. (2003). *The interface of social and clinical psychology*. London: Psychology Press.

Krahe, B. (2001). *The social psychology of aggression*. New York: Psychology Press.

Kubitschek, W. N., & Hallinan, M. T. (1998). Tracking and students' friendships. *Social Psychology Quarterly, 61*, 1–15.

Landy, F. S., & Farr, J. L. (1980). Performance rating. *Psychological Bulletin, 87*, 72–107.

Le Bon, G. (1896). *The crowd*. London: T. Fisher Unwin.

Levesque, M. J., & Lowe, C. A. (1992). The importance of attributions and expectancies in understanding academic behavior. In F. J. Medway & T. P. Cafferty (Eds.), *School psychology: A social psychological perspective* (pp. 47–81). Hillsdale, NJ: Erlbaum.

Lewin, K. (1947). Group decision and social change. In T. M. Newcomb & E. L. Hartley (Eds.), *Readings in social psychology* (pp. 330–344). New York: Henry Holt.

Lewin, K. (1951). Psychological ecology. In D. Cartwright (Ed.), *Field theory in social science* (pp. 170–187). New York: Harper & Row.

Lewin, K., Lippett, R., & White, R. K. (1939). Patterns of aggressive behavior in experimentally created "social climates." *Journal of Social Psychology, 10*, 271–299.

Madon, S., Guyll, M., Aboufadel, K., Montiel, E., Smith, A., Palumbo, P., & Jussim, L. (2001). Ethnic and national stereotypes: The Princeton Trilogy revisited and revised. *Personality and Social Psychology Bulletin, 27*, 996–1010.

Maher, C. A., & Kruger, L. J. (1992). The Quality Circle approach and school psychological services: Description and application. *Special Services in the Schools, 6*, 129–154.

Maio, G. R., & Olson, J. M. (Eds.) (2000). *Why we evaluate: Functions of attitudes*. Mahwah, NJ: Erlbaum.

Martin, R. P., & Curtis, M. (1981). Consultant's perceptions of causality for success and failure of consultation. *Professional Psychology, 12*, 671–676.

McCormick, C. B., & Pressley, M. (2006). *Child and adolescent development for educators*. New York: Guilford Press.

McDougall, W. (1908). *An introduction to social psychology*. London: Methuen.

McGrath, J. E., Arrow, H., & Berdahl, J. L. (2000). The study of groups: Past, present, and future. *Personality and Social Psychology Review, 4*, 95–105.

McGuire, W. J. (1985). Attitudes and attitude change. In G. Lindzey & E. Aronson (Eds.), *The handbook of social psychology* (3rd ed., Vol. 2, pp. 233–346). Hillsdale, NJ: Erlbaum.

Medway, F. J. (1979). Causal attributions for school-related problems: Teacher perceptions and teacher feedback. *Journal of Educational Psychology, 71*, 809–819.

Medway, F. J. (1992). Rapprochement of social psychology and school psychology: A historical analysis. In F. J. Medway & T. P. Cafferty (Eds.),

School psychology: A social psychological perspective (pp. 5–23). Hillsdale, NJ: Erlbaum.

Medway, F. J. & Cafferty, T. P. (1992). (Eds.). *School psychology: A social psychological perspective.* Hillsdale, NJ: Erlbaum.

Merrill, K. W., Erwin, R. A., & Gimpel, G. A. (2006). *School psychology for the 21st century.* New York: Guilford Press.

Miller, N. E. (1941). The frustration-aggression hypothesis. *Psychological Review, 48,* 337–342.

Moreno, J. L. (1934). *Who shall survive?* (Monograph No. 58). Washington, DC: Nervous and Mental Disease Publishing.

Morrison, G. M., Furlong, M. J., & Morrison, R. L. (1994). School violence to school safety: Reframing the issue for school psychologists. *School Psychology Review, 23,* 236–256.

Mueller, D. J. (1986). *Measuring social attitudes: A handbook for researchers and practitioners.* New York: Teachers College Press.

Nisbett, R. E., & Ross, L. (1980). *Human inference: Strategies and shortcomings in social judgment.* Englewood Cliffs, NJ: Prentice Hall.

Parks, C. D., Sanna, L. J., & Berel, S. R. (2001). Actions of similar others as inducements to cooperate in social dilemmas. *Personality and Social Psychology Bulletin, 27,* 345–354.

Peterson, C. (1992). Learned helplessness and school problems. In F. J. Medway & T. P. Cafferty (Eds.), *School psychology: A social psychological perspective* (pp. 359–376). Hillsdale, NJ: Erlbaum.

Pettigrew, T. F. (2005). Allport's intergroup contact hypothesis: Its history and influence. In Dovidio, J. F., Glick, P., & Rudman, L. A. (Eds.), *On the nature of prejudice: Fifty years after Allport* (pp. 262–277). Malden, MA: Blackwell.

Petty, R. E., & Cacioppo, J. T. (1981). *Attitudes and persuasion: Classic and contemporary approaches.* Dubuque, IA: Wm. C. Brown.

Petty, R. E., & Wegener, D. T. (1998). Attitude change: Multiple roles for persuasion variables. In D. T. Gilbert, S. T. Fiske, & G. Lindsey (Eds.), *The handbook of social psychology* (4th ed., Vol. *1,* pp. 323–390). New York: McGraw-Hill.

Pfeffer, J. (1985). Organizations and organization theory. In G. Lindzey & E. Aronson (Eds.), *The handbook of social psychology* (3rd ed., Vol. *1,* pp. 379–440). Hillsdale, NJ: Erlbaum.

Pfeffer, J. (1998). Understanding organizations: Concepts and controversies. In D. T. Gilbert, S. T. Fiske, & G. Lindsey (Eds.), *The handbook of social psychology* (4th ed., Vol. 2, pp. 733–777). New York: McGraw-Hill.

Pietromonaco, P. R., & Barrett, L. F. (1997). Working models of attachment and daily social interactions. *Journal of Personality and Social Psychology, 73,* 1409–1423.

Pronin, E., Lin, D. Y., & Ross, L. (2002). The bias blind spot: Perceptions of bias in self versus others. *Personality and Social Psychology Bulletin, 28,* 369–381.

Pyszczynski, T. A., Solomon, S., & Greenberg, J. (2002). *In the wake of 9/11: The psychology of terror.* Washington, DC: American Psychological Association.

Reid, K. E. (1981). *From character building to social treatment: The history and use of groups in social work.* Westport, CT: Greenwood Press.

Reyna, C. (2000). Lazy, dumb, or industrious: When stereotypes convey attribution information in the classroom. *Educational Psychology Review, 12,* 85–110.

Robinson, J. P., Shaver, P. R., & Wrightsman, L. S. (1991). *Measures of personality and social psychological attitudes, Vol. 1.* San Diego, CA: Academic Press.

Robinson, J. P., Shaver, P. R. & Wrightsman, L. S. (1999). *Measures of political attitudes, Vol. 2. Measures of social psychological attitudes.* San Diego, CA: Academic Press.

Ross, L., & Nisbett, R. E. (1991). The person and the situation. *Perspectives of social psychology.* New York: McGraw-Hill.

Rossi, P. H., Wright, J. D., & Anderson, A. B. (Eds.). (1983). *Handbook of survey research.* New York: Academic Press.

Rydell, R. R. & McConnell, A. R. (2006). Understanding implicit and explicit attitude change: A systems of reasoning analysis. *Journal of Personality and Social Psychology, 91,* 995–1008.

Sandoval, J. (2003). Constructing conceptual change in consultee-centered consultation. *Journal of Educational and Psychological Consultation. 14,* 251–261.

Sandoval, J. J., & Davis, J. M. (1992). Applications of social psychology to school counseling and therapy. In F. J. Medway & T. P. Cafferty (Eds.), *School psychology: Asocial psychological perspective* (pp. 245–268). Hillsdale, NJ: Erlbaum.

Schachter, S. (1964). The interaction of cognitive and physiological determinants of emotional state. In L. Berkowitz (Ed.), *Advances in experimental social psychology* (Vol. *1,* pp. 49–80). New York: Academic Press.

Shaver, P. R., & Clark, C. (1994). The psychodynamics of adult romantic attachment. In J. M. Masling & R. F. Bornstein (Eds.), *Empirical perspectives on object relations theory. Empirical studies of psychoanalytic theories* (Vol. *5,* pp. 105–156). Washington, DC: American Psychological Association.

Shaw, M. E., & Wright, J. M. (1967). *Scales for the measurement of attitudes.* New York: McGraw-Hill.

Sherif, M. (1936). *The psychology of social norms.* New York: Harper.

Sherif, M., Harvey, O. J., White, B. J., Hood, W. R., & Sherif, C. W. (1961). *Intergroup conflict and cooperation: The Robbers' Cave experiment.* Normal: University of Oklahoma Book Exchange.

Slavin, R. E. (1996). Research on cooperative learning and achievement. *Contemporary Educational Psychology, 21,* 43–69.

Smith, D. K., & Lyon, M. A. (1986). School psychologists' attributions for success and failure in consultations with parents and teachers. *Professional Psychology: Research and Practice, 17,* 205–209.

Smith, E. R., & Mackie, D. M. (2007). *Social psychology* (3rd ed.). New York: Psychology Press.

Snarr, J. D., Strassberg, Z., & Smith-Slep, A. M. (2003). Making faces: Testing the relation between child behavior problems and mothers' interpretations of child emotional expressions. *Journal of Abnormal Child Psychology, 31,* 371–380.

Snyder, C. R., Tennen, H., Affleck, G., & Cheavens, J. (2000). Social, personality, clinical, and health psychology tributaries: The merging of a scholarly "river of dreams." *Personality and Social Psychology Review, 4,* 16–29.

Sonkin, D., & Dutton, D. (2003). Treating assaultive men from an attachment perspective. *Journal of Aggression, Maltreatment, and Trauma, 7,* 105–133.

Srull, T. K. (1983). Organizational and retrieval processes in person memory: An examination of processing objectives, presentation format, and the possible role of self-generated retrieval cues. *Journal of Personality and Social Psychology, 44,* 1157–1170.

Steele, C. M., Spencer, S. J., & Aronson, J. (2002). Contending with group image: The psychology of stereotype and social identity threat. In M. P. Zanna (Ed.), *Advances in experimental social psychology.* (Vol. 34, pp. 379–440). New York: Academic Press.

Stephan, W. G. (1978). School desegregation: An evaluation of predictions made in Brown v. Board of Education. *Psychological Bulletin, 85,* 215–238.

Stogdill, R. (1974). *Handbook of leadership: A survey of theory and research.* New York: Free Press.

Summers, G. E. (Ed.). (1970). *Attitude measurement.* Skokie, IL: Rand McNally.

Tajfel, H. (1978). *Differentiation between social groups.* London: Academic Press.

Tennen, H., Hall, J. A., & Affleck, G. (1995). Depression research methodologies in the *Journal of Personality and Social Psychology*: A review and

critique. *Journal of Personality and Social Psychology, 68,* 870–884.

Tesser. A., & Bau, J. J. (2002). Social psychology: Who we are and what we do. *Personality and Social Psychology Bulletin, 6,* 72–85.

Triplett, N. (1897). The dynamogenic factors in pacemaking and competition. *American Journal of Psychology, 9,* 507–533.

Trope, Y. (1986). Identification and inferential processes in dispositional attribution. *Psychological Bulletin, 93,* 239–257.

Trope, Y., & Higgins, E. T. (1993). The what, when, and how of dispositional inference: New answers and new questions. *Personality and Social Psychology Bulletin, 19,* 493–500.

Vallerand, R. J., Fortier, M. S., & Guay, F. (1997). Self-determination and persistence in a real-life setting: Toward a motivational model of the high school dropout. *Journal of Personality and Social Psychology, 72,* 1161–1176.

Vroom, V. H. & Jago, A. G. (2007). The role of situation in leadership. *American Psychologist, 62,* 17–24.

Weiner, B. (1972). Attribution theory, achievement motivation, and the educational process. *Review of Educational Research, 42,* 203–215.

Weinstein, N. D., & Klein, W. M. (1996). Unrealistic optimism: Present and future. *Journal of Social and Clinical Psychology, 15,* 1–8.

Wicker, A. (1969). Attitudes versus actions: The relationship of verbal and overt behavioral responses to attitude objects. *Journal of Social Issues, 25,* 41–78.

Wild, T. C., Enzle, M. E., & Hawkins, W. L. (1992). Effects of perceived extrinsic versus intrinsic teacher motivation on student reactions to skill acquisition. *Personality and Social Psychology Bulletin, 18,* 245–251.

Williams, K. J., & Williams, G. (1992). Applications of social psychology to school employee evaluation and appraisal. In F. J. Medway and T. P. Cafferty (Eds.), *School psychology: A social psychological perspective* (pp. 333–354). Hillsdale, NJ: Erlbaum.

Zebrowitz, L., & Lee, S. Y. (1999). Appearance, stereotype-incongruent behavior, and social relationships. *Personality and Social Psychology Bulletin, 25,* 570–585.

Zettergren, P. (2005). Childhood peer status as predictor of midadolescence peer situation and social adjustment. *Psychology in the Schools, 42,* 745–757.

CHAPTER 9

CONTRIBUTIONS OF BIOLOGICAL PSYCHOLOGY

JAMES W. KALAT AND JOHN C. BEGENY
North Carolina State University

Research in biological psychology has accelerated in recent decades, and many generalizations that once seemed secure have become outdated. For example, if you took a course in biological psychology or behavioral neuroscience, you probably learned that the action potential of a neuron begins in the axon hillock—the bulge where the soma adjoins the axon. In 2005, researchers reported an exception to that rule: In the Purkinje cells of the cerebellum, action potentials begin at the first node of Ranvier, not at the axon hillock (Clark, Monsivais, Branco, London, & Häuser, 2005). If you haven't been diligently keeping up with the neuroscience literature, that bit of information may have escaped your attention. Now that you know it, how will it affect your practice of school psychology? Our guess is, not at all. Some of the progress in neuroscience is important for you to know, but much of it is tangential at best.

In this chapter we focus on topics that seem more relevant to school psychology. In each major section we describe a possible scenario that school psychologists may face when practicing in school settings, and then provide information that school psychologists may find useful within the context of that scenario. Admittedly, some of the scenarios will occur infrequently; however, each is intended as an example in which biology and neuroscience can help inform the school psychologist.

We also present two appendices that school psychologists may find valuable as a reference. The first outlines symptoms and syndromes known to have major biological influences. The second lists a few drugs and related terms that school psychologists might want to know when conversing with physicians or parents.

ASSESSMENT METHODS IN HUMAN NEUROANATOMY

As a school psychologist, you are working in an elementary school where a student is scheduled to receive a brain scan to diagnose a possible tumor or epilepsy. Another child may undergo a brain scan to shed light on severe learning difficulties accompanied by uncontrollable emotional outbursts. In both cases, the parents are curious: What is this brain scan, anyway? How does it work? What can we tell from it? The child's teacher wants to be able to discuss the results with the physician. In meeting with the child's parents and teachers, you want to provide at least a general overview about different brain scan methodologies, their procedures, the types of information they can provide, and the possible ramifications of the assessment for the child. Your goal is to provide parents or teachers with enough information to make them feel more comfortable and knowledgeable about the procedures, before they talk with the physician.

One of the older methods is computerized axial tomography, better known as a CT or CAT scan. A physician uses a needle to inject a dye into someone's blood to increase contrast in the image, places the person's head into a scanner, and passes X-rays through the head. Detectors on the other side record the X-rays and relay information to a computer. As the CT scanner slowly rotates through 180 degrees, the computer forms an image of the entire brain. A CT scan shows anatomical structures; it does not indicate activity levels. It is useful for detecting and locating tumors or any kind of brain damage. The entire procedure usually lasts only a few minutes, rarely more than 30, and produces no pain other than the prick of the needle. The person is awake throughout. Although the procedure exposes the brain to X-rays, the associated risk is small for a single exposure, with increasing risk after repeated exposures.

A newer method, magnetic resonance imaging (MRI), is also useful for examining brain structure (Warach, 1995). MRI uses the fact that any atom with an odd-numbered atomic weight has an axis of rotation. Hydrogen, with an atomic weight of one, is the most abundant element in the human body—as well as the universe—and MRIs are usually set to measure water, which contains hydrogen atoms. The person's head is placed within a powerful magnet, about 25,000 times as strong as the earth's magnetic field, aligning the axes of rotation of all the hydrogen atoms in the brain. Then a brief radio frequency field tilts all these axes. Turning off the radio field frees the atoms to release electromagnetic energy as they return to their original axis. MRI devices measure that energy and feed it into a computer that constructs an image of the brain, showing details smaller than a millimeter in diameter. Typically, an MRI session lasts 15–45 minutes. So far as we know, the procedure poses no health risk, unless someone has a piece of metal in the body area exposed to the magnetic field. (The metal could overheat.) However, the procedure is unsuitable for use with anyone who is unable or unwilling to lie motionless in a narrow, loud apparatus.

A variant of this procedure is functional magnetic resonance imaging (fMRI). (The f in fMRI is always lowercase; try to avoid using it at the start of a sentence.) Ordinary MRI, which attends to water molecules, provides excellent detail for static structures but shows no changes over time, because the brain has almost no net movement of water. With fMRI, researchers alter the settings to record responses of hemoglobin, the blood protein that binds oxygen. The binding or removal of oxygen changes hemoglobin's paramagnetic properties—that is, its response to a magnetic field (Detre & Floyd, 2001). Because neurons that increase their activity also increase their oxygen consumption (Mukamel et al., 2005), fMRI detects the relative activity levels in various brain areas. An fMRI image has a spatial resolution of 1 or 2 mm (almost as good as standard MRI) and

temporal resolution of 1 or 2 seconds. You may also encounter the term BOLD, an abbreviation for blood oxygen level dependent contrast. BOLD is a type of fMRI.

Positron-emission tomography (PET) records brain activity in a different way. First the investigator radioactively labels a chemical, such as glucose, and injects it into the person's blood. Glucose, almost the brain's only fuel, enters mainly the most active brain areas. In variations of this technique, investigators radioactively label amino acids, drugs with affinity for particular receptors, or other chemicals. In any case, when the radioactively labeled chemical decays, it releases a positron, which immediately reacts with an electron to emit two gamma rays in exactly opposite directions. Detectors surrounding the head detect these rays and identify a spot halfway between them as the point of origin. A computer determines the amount of radioactivity coming from each area, indicating which areas are most active or which ones most abundantly bind the chemical that was used (Phelps & Mazziotta, 1985). A typical PET session includes about a 1-hour wait after the injection, and then 30 to 40 minutes in the scanner. PET provides detailed information, but it does require exposing the body to a small amount of radioactivity. As with CAT scans, the risk associated with a single exposure is low, but repeated exposures increase the risk. A variant of PET is regional cerebral blood flow (rCBF); the method is slightly different but the principles are similar.

Unfortunately, interpreting the results of an fMRI or PET scan is often problematic. Suppose, for example, a particular brain area is important for a given type of learning. During a task requiring that type of learning, someone who fails to learn will show decreased activity in this brain area, but so will someone who has already learned it, or someone who learns so easily that the brain exerts little effort (Puttemans, Wenderoth, & Swinnen, 2005; Pesenti et al., 2001). That is, the results can be ambiguous if interpreted out of the context of everything else one knows about a person. We assume that individuals certified to administer the techniques know the limitations; however, school psychologists and parents benefit by knowing the limitations as well.

Visit www.radiologyinfo.org for more information on brain scan techniques.

AGE, DEVELOPMENT, AND BRAIN PLASTICITY

Do people have "critical periods" or "windows of opportunity" for certain kinds of learning? Some of the early work of Konrad Lorenz on imprinting in birds implied that (a) certain experiences strongly influence animals only during relatively brief and well-defined periods early in life, and (b) the experiences during those critical periods are permanent and irreversible (Bruer, 2001; Lorenz, 1937). Research on birdsong learning pointed the same direction. Males of certain species have to learn their song; a male raised in isolation from his species develops only a poor approximation. Early studies indicated that a male could learn the song only if exposed to it during a limited period early in life, such as age 10–50 days, depending on species. Hearing the song when he was younger or older had no effect. However, that research used a design of letting a young bird hear only tape-recorded songs. Later studies with live tutors found that a bird could learn well beyond age 50 days, and can even modify his dialect from year to year (Baptista & Petrinovich, 1984; Marler & Peters, 1987, 1988). Further work in other fields ranging from imprinting to sensory systems of the cerebral cortex confirmed that critical periods are seldom either brief or tightly defined (Horton, 2001; Lichtman, 2001), and experiences after the supposed critical period can in many cases modify the results (Bailey, Bruer, Symons, & Lichtman, 2001; Bateson, 1983; Colombo, 1982).

Nevertheless, authorities sometimes still suggest that specific, well-defined critical periods exist in certain domains of human development. For instance, some reports suggest the foundations for learning, social development, and emotional control must be established from birth to age 3 (Begley, 1996; Carnegie Corporation, 1994) or from birth to age 6 or 12 (Carnegie Corporation, 1996; Shore, 1997). Educators have suggested that certain kinds of learning are restricted to critical periods from age 3 to 10 (Sousa, 1998; Wolfe & Brandt, 1998).

Misinterpretations of early intervention research may have led to such proposals. Bruer (2001) notes that popular press and policy literature often cite two large early intervention studies (i.e., the North Carolina Abecedarian Project and the Infant Health Program and Development Study) in arguing "that there is a sensitive period from birth to age 3 years during which childhood intervention programs are particularly effective" (p. 22). According to Bruer, the misinterpretations of these studies are then used to advocate that "age 3 is too late to permanently and irreversibly rewire children's brains" (p. 22). In fact, these studies do not speak directly to any notions of critical or sensitive periods of learning. Interventions that begin earlier last longer, so the results of many studies confound age of onset with duration of intervention. Furthermore, in some cases very early intervention is clearly not best, depending on the skill or system in question. For example, it is fruitless, and potentially harmful, to try to teach something that is developmentally inappropriate (e.g., teaching a 1-year-old letters of the alphabet). Accordingly, school psychologists, teachers, and parents need to be aware of different developmental milestones in order to know when it is appropriate to teach certain skills (Bailey & Symons, 2001). In the following sections, we consider research on two examples of critical or sensitive periods: language learning and visual development.

Language Development

What about language learning? Are people predisposed to learn language best during a sensitive period early in life? Imagine the following scenario. As a school psychologist in an affluent school district with mostly upper-middle class, English-speaking students, you enter school one day to find that two new students (one elementary-aged, and one high school-aged) have entered the school district as a result of moving in with a relative who has lived in the area for the past six months. You have little information about these students, except that they are refugees from a country with a long history of civil war. As a result, the students have been transient since birth and have received no formal schooling. Part of your role is to work with the teachers to ensure a more successful transition into each child's respective school. Teachers want more information from you and the school's speech pathologist about the children's capacity for learning English, and would like to know whether the older of the two students will need more intensive language intervention than the younger child.

Children go through a clear transition when they become capable of learning language. Most 1-year-olds can say only a few words, if any. By age 1 1/2, they are adding to their vocabulary at a rate of almost one word per waking hour, and they continue at that rate for the next few years

(Carey, 1978). Thus, language acquisition has a minimum age, but does it have a maximum also?

The strongest evidence of a sensitive or critical period for language development comes from studies of children who are deaf. If they do not learn to read lips, and if no one teaches them a sign language, they invent one of their own and try to teach it to their parents. As they grow older, the system becomes increasingly complex (Goldin-Meadow & Mylander, 1998). However, if the adults fail or refuse to learn the child's sign language, the child abandons the effort. If the adults continue trying to teach the child to read lips, and the child continues to fail, eventually the adults concede and begin teaching sign language. However, if they do not initiate that teaching until the child is, say, 12 years old, the child progresses slowly and never catches up with those who began learning sign language earlier (Harley & Wang, 1997; Mayberry, Lock, & Kazmi, 2002). Evidently someone who does not learn language in early childhood does not completely get the idea later.

In the case of immigrant students, however, the question is not how well they can learn a first language, but how well they can learn a second one. In general, youth is an advantage for learning a second language, although only in certain regards. Adults memorize the vocabulary of a second language more rapidly than children, but children are quicker to master the pronunciation and unfamiliar points of grammar. For example, most Chinese adults trying to learn English are persistently baffled by the distinction between *a* and *the*, because Chinese has no such distinction. Even children who grow up in a bilingual neighborhood have an advantage at later mastering the other language, even if they paid little attention to it during childhood (Au, Knightly, Jun, & Oh, 2002). However, the evidence does not support the idea of a distinct end to a critical period or sensitive period for second-language learning. Researchers examined English proficiency among immigrants to the United States from Chinese- and Spanish-speaking countries. On the average, the younger someone was at the time of immigration, the greater that person's English proficiency ten years later. However, the decline was steady over age, with no sign of a sharp drop at any age. For example, 10-year-olds learned English better than 20-year-olds, 20-year-olds better than 40-year-olds, and 40-year-olds better than 60-year-olds (Hakuta, Bialystok, & Wiley,

2003). The overall conclusion: Early experience is more effective than later experience, but the decline is gradual.

Experience and the Visual Cortex

Another apparent case of a critical period, and a subject of extensive research, is the ability of visual experience to modify the properties of the visual cortex. The mammalian visual system matures to a certain point automatically. However, research pioneered by David Hubel and Torsten Wiesel, beginning in the 1950s, demonstrated that visual experience during a sensitive period early in life sustains and fine-tunes the connections from the eyes to the cerebral cortex. For example, kittens ordinarily open their eyes for the first time at age 9 or 10 days. If one eye is kept closed for the next 4 to 6 weeks, the visual cortex becomes unresponsive to that eye, and the kitten becomes functionally blind to it (Rittenhouse, Shouval, Paradiso, & Bear, 1999; Wiesel, 1982; Wiesel & Hubel, 1963). In contrast, if both eyes are kept shut early in life, the cortex remains somewhat responsive to both eyes, though progressively more sluggish in its responses (Crair, Gillespie, & Stryker, 1998). Evidently the loss of response to a closed eye results from competition by the open eye; if neither eye is open, neither is fully displaced.

In other research a kitten sees with its left eye one day, right eye the next day, and so forth. Therefore both eyes are stimulated about equally, but never at the same time. Alternatively, both eyes can be kept open at all times, but because of weak or damaged eye muscles, the kitten cannot focus both eyes in the same direction. That is, the kitten has strabismus (or strabismic amblyopia), like some children. As a result, almost every neuron in the visual cortex gradually restricts its response to one eye or the other, unlike the usual pattern of responding to parts of both eyes. The kitten therefore loses stereoscopic depth perception (Blake & Hirsch, 1975; Hubel & Wiesel, 1965).

Consider some further examples of distorted early visual experience. If a kitten sees through goggles with horizontal lines painted on them, the cells in its visual cortex become responsive only to horizontal lines (Stryker & Sherk, 1975; Stryker, Sherk, Leventhal, & Hirsch, 1978). In one experiment, kittens spent their early life in an environment illuminated only by a strobe light that flashed for 10 microseconds eight times per second. These kittens lost their ability to detect visual motion, although they retained their ability to respond to stationary visual stimuli (Cynader & Chernenko, 1976).

Altered experiences affect the adult cortex also, but less extensively. For example, when an adult mammal is trained to respond to some stimulus, its visual neurons increase their response to that stimulus and decrease it to others (Dragoi, Rivadulla, & Sur, 2001; Schoups, Vogels, Qian, & Orban, 2001). However, these changes are much smaller than those demonstrable at earlier stages of development.

Similar processes occur in humans, although the duration of the sensitive period is ill defined. For example, children with "lazy eye" (amblyopia) fail to attend to the vision in one eye. Putting a patch over the dominant eye forces the child to increase attention to the ignored eye, and early intervention is more effective than later intervention. However, researchers have found no sharp dividing line for when intervention is too late; it simply becomes less and less effective at later ages (Lewis & Maurer, 2005). When infants have dense cataracts on the lenses of their eyes, vision recovers better if the cataracts are removed early. However, the sensitive period is much longer for some aspects of vision, such as acuity, than for others, such as motion detection (Lewis & Maurer, 2005). Someone who had cataracts removed before age 6 months develops seemingly normal vision in most regards, but careful testing shows subtle deficits on complex tasks, such as the ability to discriminate between two similar faces (Le Grand, Mondloch, Maurer, & Brent, 2001, 2003). In a few cases, cataracts remained from early childhood until beyond age 40. Even then, experience enabled the person to make partial, gradual improvements in vision (Fine, Smallman, Doyle, & MacLeod, 2002; Fine et al., 2003).

All of these studies establish the importance of early experience, because early distortions of experience produce more serious and more lasting effects than similar distortions later in life. However, the boundaries of the sensitive period are by no means sharp; the effects of experience decline gradually as development proceeds, and experience continues to modify the cortex in subtle ways even during adulthood.

The mechanism of cortical change, and therefore of the sensitive period, depends on interactions between excitatory and inhibitory neurotransmitters. Strengthening one set of synapses almost always comes at the expense of inhibiting others (Royer & Paré, 2003). The ability to alter the strength of one synapse versus another begins when neurons begin releasing GABA, the brain's most abundant inhibitory transmitter (Fagiolini & Hensch, 2000). The sensitive period begins to close when the brain starts producing certain chemicals that inhibit axons from forming new branches (or "sprouts"). The sensitive period is long for certain functions such as acuity or binocular interactions because the adjustments require only local rearrangements of synapses. It is shorter for functions such as motion detection that require integration of information across greater distances (Tagawa, Kanold, Majdan, & Shatz, 2005). That is, an alteration of visual motion detection would require axons to grow over substantial distances. In short, research ranging from birdsong to language and the visual cortex indicates that early experience is generally more effective than later experience, but adjustments are not limited to a restricted period of time.

EARLY ENRICHMENT AND IMPAIRMENT

Closely related to the concept of early sensitive periods is that of early enrichment. Working as a school psychologist in an elementary school, you are asked to evaluate a first-grade student whose parents are convinced is gifted. Beyond seeking an evaluation of academic giftedness, they also want to know what types of early enrichment activities will help their child to excel and what effects that enrichment might have.

Let us first consider attempts to use general enrichment to improve brain functioning. Some well-known studies on laboratory animals documented the benefits of an enriched environment—improved performance on various tests of learning and memory, a thicker cerebral cortex, wider dendritic branching, and finer tuning of cortical cells so that they respond more precisely to the details of sensory stimuli (Greenough, 1975; Polley, Kvasnák, & Frostig, 2004; Rosenzweig & Bennett, 1996). However, in each of these studies the enriched environment was "enriched" relative to a very impoverished baseline, which for laboratory rats is a small gray cage. The enriched environment was simply a larger cage, with a few other rats in it and some pieces of junk to explore. Much of the benefit of the enriched environment came from the fact that the animals could move around more, and it is possible to get comparable brain benefits by adding a running wheel to a small, isolated cage (Rhodes et al., 2003; van Praag, Kempermann, & Gage, 2000). That is, the enrichment worked partly or largely by increasing blood flow to the brain. To date, researchers have not demonstrated additional brain enhancement from still greater enrichment of the environment.

In 1993, researchers reported that listening to a Mozart sonata before performing a spatial reasoning task improved students' performance (Rauscher, Shaw, & Ky, 1993). They speculated that the patterns of Mozart's compositions imposed a rhythm onto the synapses that was optimal for performance. If reliable, that finding would be an exciting demonstration of general, though perhaps temporary, enhancement of overall brain activity. Unfortunately, the results have been hard to replicate. To the extent that listening to Mozart's works is helpful at all, the benefit is apparently due to relaxation, as one can get the same small benefit by listening to anything else that one considers pleasant (Chabris, 1999; Nantais & Schellenberg, 1999; Steele, Bass, & Crook, 1999; Thompson, Schellenberg, & Husain, 2001).

Whereas it is difficult to demonstrate general enhancement of brain function, general impairment is easy. From prenatal life through early childhood, the brain is highly vulnerable. As Lewis Wolpert (1991, p. 12) said, "It is not birth, marriage, or death, but gastrulation, which is truly the important time of your life." (Gastrulation is an early stage of embryological development.) In other words, a small impairment of early development can produce huge problems later.

Challenges that produce only mild, temporary problems for an adult are hazardous in early development. Examples include malnutrition, toxic chemicals (such as lead), and exposure to drugs. Thyroid deficiency or low blood glucose in prenatal life or infancy can lead to mental retardation, whereas it produces only lethargy in adults (Nelson et al., 2000). Children of mothers who smoked cigarettes during pregnancy are at increased risk for attention-deficit/hyperactivity disorder, impairments of the immune system, and other problems (Brennan, Grekin, & Mednick, 1999; Fergusson, Woodward, & Horwood, 1998; Finette, O'Neill, Vacek, & Albertini, 1998; Milberger, Biederman, Faraone, Chen, & Jones, 1996; Slotkin, 1998).

Adults and children easily tolerate fever, but elevated body temperature impairs neuronal proliferation and development in a fetus (Laburn, 1996). Research suggests that the probability of schizophrenia is slightly enhanced among children of women who had influenza or other infections during the second trimester of pregnancy, thereby exposing the fetus to increased temperature (Adams, Kendell, Hare, & Munk-Jørgensen, 1993; Brown et al., 2001, 2004; Buka et al., 2001).

Drinking alcohol during pregnancy exposes infants to the risk of fetal alcohol syndrome, characterized by attention problems, hyperactivity, impulsiveness, facial abnormalities, and some degree of mental retardation. The mechanisms behind this syndrome are now largely understood. During prenatal development, the nervous system forms far more neurons than will survive to birth, and still more die in infancy. This loss of cells is a normal process, called apoptosis (a-po-TOE-sis), by which the nervous system weeds out neurons that fail to form effective connections. Alcohol impairs release of the brain's main excitatory neurotransmitter, glutamate, while facilitating activity of its main inhibitory transmitter, GABA. Consequently, many neurons receive much less net excitation than normal, and they react as if they had failed to form normal connections. That is, they die (Ikonomidou et al., 2000). Theoretically, the same risk should apply if a pregnant woman takes other drugs that inhibit synaptic activity, including tranquilizers.

Research on specific types of enrichment have converged in a remarkable way: According to research in cognitive psychology, expertise in any area, ranging from chess to violin to athletics, requires about ten years of concentrated practice. Researchers have further concluded that expertise produces effects restricted to the area of specialization. For example, an expert chess player excels over all others at chess, but may be no better than average on any other kind of intellectual task (Ericsson & Charness, 1994). Brain research supports a parallel conclusion: Prolonged practice of a particular intellectual activity changes specific brain areas to facilitate the practiced activity. In this regard, exercising your brain is unlike exercising a muscle: Exercising a muscle increases the size and strength of the muscle, thereby enhancing performance on a wide variety of tasks that use this muscle. Exercising the brain, however, shifts synapses around. Learning Latin, for example, improves the ability to learn similar languages, but it doesn't help someone learn to solve mathematical equations.

Several research groups have examined the brains of people who spent years playing musical instruments. Although no one has conducted longitudinal studies to examine how an individual's brain changes during years of musical training, the assumption is that large differences between the brains of musicians and nonmusicians are probably the result of training, not the cause of it. Brain scan studies have found that part of the right hemisphere's temporal cortex—an area associated with hearing—is significantly larger in professional musicians than in nonmusicians, and responds about twice as strongly to pure tones (Schneider et al., 2002). A study of professional keyboard players found thicker than average gray matter in several brain areas, especially those related to hand control and vision (Gaser & Schlaug, 2003). A study of people who play stringed instruments examined the postcentral gyrus, in the parietal lobe, which is the main target for the sense of touch. For these people, a larger than normal percentage of the postcentral gyrus was devoted to sensations from the fingers of the left hand, which they use to control the strings (Elbert, Pantev, Wienbruch, Rockstroh, & Taub, 1995). The amount of cortex devoted to the fingers correlated strongly with the number of years of practice.

Reorganization of the cortex is presumably beneficial, as a rule. It increases the brain's ability to detect fine differences in sensation, such as the touch sensations in the fingers controlling violin strings. However, it is possible for the reorganization to go too far. In some professional musicians, the representation of each finger in the cortex continues expanding until it largely overlaps the representation of each neighboring finger. At that point, the person has difficulty distinguishing the feeling of one finger from another. The result is known as focal hand dystonia, or informally as "musician's cramp," which can end a career. Similarly, some typists experience writer's cramp. Physicians have long assumed that the problem was in the hand itself, but current research indicates that the problem lies largely in the sensory areas of the thalamus and cerebral cortex (Byl, McKenzie, & Nagarajan, 2000; Elbert et al., 1998; Lenz & Byl, 1999; Sanger, Pascual-Leone, Tarsy, & Schlaug, 2001).

Even greater brain organization is demonstrable among people who are blind from birth or infancy. People blind since infancy outperform sighted people on many tests of tactile discrimination, as we might expect. The more surprising result is that performance of tactile tasks activates the occipital cortex in blind people, according to brain scans (Burton et al., 2002; Sadato et al., 1996). For sighted people, only visual cues excite the occipital cortex. Evidently, prolonged absence of visual input during early development enabled axons representing tactile stimulation to take over much of this area.

Research indicates that verbal information also invades the occipital cortex of blind people. For blind people, and not sighted people, performance of verbal tasks activates the occipital cortex, and the amount of occipital cortex activation correlates significantly with performance on the task (Amedi, Raz, Pianka, Malach, & Zohary, 2003; Amedi, Floel, Knecht, Zohary, & Cohen, 2004). On the average, blind people outperform sighted people on verbal tasks to a small but statistically reliable degree, presumably because of the wider brain response to verbal tasks.

In summary, the brain is more plastic early in life, when experiences can alter its structure and connections to a remarkable extent. However, the decline in plasticity over age is gradual, with no sharp transition indicating the end of any sensitive period. Furthermore, most effects of experience can be described as modifications to improve performance on the particular kinds of tasks the individual has practiced.

BIOLOGY OF SOCIAL AND EMOTIONAL BEHAVIOR

Excessive displays of emotion are a common problem in everyday classroom management. Unfortunately, most biological research on emotion has focused more on brain damage that impairs emotion than on conditions that exaggerate it. Although a parent's, teacher's, and school psychologist's first approach to addressing a child's behavior problems should probably rely on effective contingency management and teaching relevant skills, we provide a foundation for considering social and emotional behavior from a biological perspective. The following scenario illustrates an instance where additional knowledge about the biology of social emotional behavior may have some benefit.

A fourth-grade student in your school has just exhibited his sixth seriously aggressive outburst in four months, this time attempting to stab another student in the back with a sharp pencil. The student is already in a self-contained classroom for students with emotional/behavioral disorders and the more "typical" consequences for this type of behavior (i.e., suspension) have already been exhausted. You have conducted a thorough functional behavior assessment, and teachers have implemented powerful behavior management interventions with high degrees of integrity, without apparent benefit. Before taking further action, school administrators want to gather a more thorough understanding of the possible biological components. Although the parents expressed hesitance to possible medication, the educators feel that providing more information about the possible biological causes might make the parents more amenable.

The Amygdala

A key area for emotion is the amygdala, a small structure within the temporal lobe of the brain. Activity in the amygdala increases when people look at emotion-arousing pictures, such as guns or snakes (Hariri, Mattay, Tessitore, Fera, & Weinberger, 2003). It also increases when people look at photographs of people showing emotional expressions, such as fear and anger. The amount of response depends on the amount of processing needed to understand the expression. For example, people usually find it easier to understand someone's expression of fear when that person is looking to the side than when he or she is looking directly at the viewer (Adams & Kleck, 2005). A fear expression to the side indicates danger *over there*. A fear expression directed at the viewer is more confusing. ("Is that person afraid of *me*?") However, the amygdala responds more strongly to a fearful expression directed at the viewer than one directed to the side (Adams, Gordon, Baird, Ambady, & Kleck, 2003). Presumably the amygdala responds more strongly to the direct view precisely because it is more difficult to process.

In most studies, the amygdala has shown little response to happy faces. One possible explanation is that the amygdala may be more specialized to detect negative than positive emotions. However, another possibility is that smiles, being easy to understand, usually evoke little effort at processing. Extraverted people show larger amygdala responses to happy faces than do most other people, perhaps because they react more strongly, processing the implications of a smile more fully (Canli, Sivers, Whitfield, Gotlib, & Gabrieli, 2002). Still another possible explanation is that research has evaluated responses to happy faces in comparison to responses to neutral faces,

which, because of their ambiguity, evoke a certain amount of emotional processing. The results indicate that people feeling strong anxiety react to neutral faces as if they were slightly unpleasant or threatening (Somerville, Kim, Johnstone, Alexander, & Whalen, 2004).

The amygdala responds rapidly to an emotional stimulus, sometimes even when the viewer is not attending to that stimulus and cannot report it afterward. For example, if an angry or frightened face flashes briefly on the screen while the viewer is attending to something else, the amygdala nevertheless responds, as indicated by both brain scans and autonomic responses such as sweating and heart rate (Kubota et al., 2000; Vuilleumier, Armony, Driver, & Dolan, 2001; Williams, Morris, McGlone, Abbott, & Mattingley, 2004). Evidently the brain is specialized to make rapid emotional responses to potential threats, separately from conscious attention. Conceivably, this process could be responsible for what people call "gut feelings."

People with a rare genetic disorder called Urbach-Wiethe disease accumulate calcium in the amygdala, producing damage there. Such people say they continue to feel emotions, but they are impaired at various aspects of emotional processing. For example, when in need of help, they approach people almost randomly, instead of trying to find people who act friendly (Adolphs, Tranel, & Damasio, 1998). Also, unlike other people, when they hear a narrative or view a series of photographs, they are no more likely to remember the emotionally arousing items than the more mundane ones (Adolphs, Tranel, & Buchanan, 2005).

They also have difficulty recognizing facial expressions of emotion, especially fear, in drawings and photographs (Adolphs, Baron-Cohen, & Tranel, 2002; Boucsein, Weniger, Mursch, Steinhoff, & Irle, 2001). However, the reason is surprising: One woman with bilateral damage to her amygdala focused almost exclusively on the nose and mouth of any photo, whereas the eyes express fear more strongly than the rest of the face. When researchers urged her to look at the eyes, she quickly identified the expression as indicating fear (Adolphs, Gosselin, et al., 2005).

People differ in their emotional reactivity; might some of that difference relate to variation in the amygdala? The studies of Jerome Kagan and his colleagues found that most people retain a certain temperament from infancy onward. According to a longitudinal study, infants with an "inhibited" temperament, who are shy and easily frightened, develop into young adults who show an enhanced amygdala response to the sight of any unfamiliar face (Schwartz, Wright, Shin, Kagan, & Rauch, 2003). Part of this variance in amygdala response has been traced to genetic influences, including one gene that influences reuptake of the neurotransmitter serotonin in the amygdala (Flint, 2004; Hariri et al., 2002). Undoubtedly, for the practicing school psychologist who aims to improve a student's social and/or emotional behavior, evaluating and manipulating a student's educational environment and teaching the student appropriate behaviors will be more useful and more feasible than assessing the student's biological structure; however, the aforementioned research sheds an interesting light on the multiple factors that can influence social and emotional behavior.

The Prefrontal Cortex

The prefrontal cortex, which is among the slowest areas of the brain to reach maturity, regulates activity in many other brain areas, including the amygdala and the nucleus accumbens, an area in the ventral forebrain that is essential to the effects of sex, addictive drugs, and most if not all other types of reinforcement. For example, one theory about addiction is that it depends on a change in the input from the prefrontal cortex to the nucleus accumbens, such that only the strongest stimuli—addictive drugs—can now stimulate the nucleus accumbens, instead of the wide variety of natural reinforcements that are usually effective (Kalivas, Volkow, & Seamans, 2005).

According to Antonio Damasio (1994), people with damage to certain parts of the prefrontal cortex are especially impaired at considering the emotional consequences of possible decisions. That is, they can calculate the probable outcomes of various possible decisions, but they don't immediately imagine how one outcome would make them feel good and another would make them feel bad. The result is a series of bad decisions.

Prefrontal cortex early in life can produce even more profound effects. In a case study investigating this topic, two children who incurred damage to the prefrontal cortex during infancy had lifelong problems of theft, deception, lack of guilt feelings, and severe difficulty relating to other people (Anderson, Bechara, Damasio, Tranel, & Damasio, 1999). Although one should be cautious in making generalizations from

this case study, it does add at least some additional information about the possible role of the prefrontal cortex in individuals' behavioral regulation.

INDIVIDUAL DIFFERENCES

You have found that a child's IQ falls nearly two standard deviations below the mean. You have discussed the implications of this with the parents and teacher and have identified strategies and recommendations for the home and the classroom to help the child academically. Alluding to a recent television program they saw, the child's parents ask whether instructional recommendations will even benefit their child, as the child's head circumference has always been measured below the third percentile. In essence, they suspect that their child's IQ is lower than average because of his small head and brain. Confident that your recommendations will, in fact, help the child, you want to help the parents understand the relationship between brain size and IQ with the hope that this will increase their likelihood of following your recommendations.

The general organization of the brain—in terms of the relative locations of various areas, what they do, and the type of connections among them—are strikingly similar across individuals, and indeed to a large extent across all vertebrate species. The chemicals used as neurotransmitters are the same, with only minor exceptions, not only across all vertebrates but throughout the animal kingdom. However, quantitative differences among brains are fairly large. Does overall brain size correlate with intelligence? For theoretical reasons we should not expect much of a relationship. For analogy, people's skills in tennis or basketball have little relationship to muscle size. Furthermore, studies over more than the last hundred years have failed to find any distinctive feature in the brains of the great and the eminent (Burrell, 2004).

However, whenever research fails to find a significant correlation between two variables, a possible explanation is that one or both were measured poorly. Today, modern methods such as MRI can measure brain volume with reasonable accuracy in living people, enabling researchers to correlate those measurements with IQ scores or other objective measurements in a reasonable sample of people. These studies have not answered the question, but at least they have raised our confusion to a higher level.

Two studies using these methods found about a .3 correlation between IQ scores and brain volume in general, or gray matter (neuron cell bodies) in particular (Frangou, Chitins, & Williams, 2004; Willerman, Schultz, Rutledge, & Bigler, 1991). However, another study failed to find a significant relationship, using the superior procedure of comparing children to their own siblings (Schoenemann, Budinger, Sarich, & Wang, 2000). Twin studies have found stronger correlations between monozygotic than dizygotic twins for both IQ and brain volume, especially volume of the subcortical areas (Pennington et al., 2000; Posthuma et al., 2002). Because the volume of one twin's brain correlates with the other twin's IQ, especially for monozygotic twins, researchers concluded that the same genes that affect brain size also affect IQ (Pennington et al., 2000). Researchers have identified several genes that affect both IQ and brain size (Pezawas et al., 2004; Zhang, 2003). However, none of these effects were large enough to make confident predictions about individuals.

A serious theoretical problem is that, on the average, men have larger brains than women, despite equal IQ scores. A possible resolution to this contradiction is that on the average, women have deeper gyri (indentations) in the surface of the brain, and as a result men and women have virtually equal amounts of gray matter; men have more white matter, which is composed of axons (Allen, Damasio, Grabowski, Bruss, & Zhang, 2003; Luders et al., 2004). So the pattern of results may be coherent, if intelligence depends more on gray matter than white matter. However, there are reasons to question that assumption as well, because the difference between human brains and chimpanzee or gorilla brains consists mostly of increased white matter in humans (Schoenemann, Sheehan, & Glotzer, 2005).

A more fruitful strategy may be to abandon the search for brain correlates of something as broad as overall intelligence, and instead examine more specific functions. For example, consider the optic nerve, which conveys information from the eyes to the thalamus and other parts of the brain. Even among healthy, normal people the number of axons in the optic nerve varies threefold. Those with more axons also have more neurons in the visual cortex (Andrews, Halpern, & Purves, 1997; Stevens, 2001). Compared to other people, they can detect fainter lights and briefer flashes of light. They also detect slighter or more rapid changes in visual stimuli (Halpern, Andrews, & Purves,

1999). That is, two people might both have "20-20" vision and nevertheless differ sharply in their ability to perceive details.

Are people who are disadvantaged with regard to vision at a similar disadvantage for other functions? Or do people who are weak in one system compensate by being strong in another? The data do not consistently support either hypothesis. The amount of gray matter in a given brain area correlates only moderately with the amount in other areas, as a rule, and some pairs of areas have low negative correlations (Mechelli, Friston, Frackowiak, & Price, 2005). Although we are skeptical of labeling children as "visual learners" or "auditory learners," it is nevertheless true that children differ in the relative amount of brain area devoted to various sensory systems.

TERMINOLOGY THAT FAMILIES AND TEACHERS MAY NEED TO KNOW

Finally, we conclude with a reference section, listing terms that you, the teachers in your school, or the families you deal with might want to know:

Symptoms and Syndromes

absence seizure. Type of epilepsy in which people have brief periods, less than a minute, when they stare blankly without talking or moving; then they do something without any apparent purpose.

amblyopia (lazy eye). Reduced vision resulting from disuse of one eye, usually associated with failure of the two eyes to point in the same direction.

anomia. Difficulty recalling the names of objects.

aphasia. Severe language impairment.

attention-deficit/hyperactivity disorder (ADHD). Condition marked by excesses of impulsiveness, activity, and shifts of attention.

bipolar disorder. Condition in which a person alternates between the two poles of mania and depression.

Broca's aphasia. See nonfluent aphasia.

bulimia nervosa. Condition characterized by alternation between dieting and overeating.

cataplexy. Attack of muscle weakness while a person remains awake.

closed head injury. Sharp blow to the head resulting from a fall, an automobile or motorcycle accident, an assault, or other trauma that does not puncture the brain.

conductive deafness (middle-ear deafness). Hearing loss that occurs if the bones of the middle ear fail to transmit sound waves properly to the cochlea.

congenital adrenal hyperplasia (CAH). Condition in which the adrenal glands secrete high amounts of steroid hormones during prenatal and early postnatal life, resulting in partial masculinization of genetic females.

Down syndrome. Condition marked by mental retardation, caused by an extra copy of chromosome 21.

edema. Accumulation of fluid.

fetal alcohol syndrome. Condition resulting from prenatal exposure to alcohol and marked by decreased alertness, hyperactivity, varying degrees of mental retardation, motor problems, heart defects, and facial abnormalities.

fluent aphasia (Wernicke's aphasia). Condition marked by poor language comprehension and great difficulty remembering the names of objects.

fragile X syndrome. Impaired speech, cognitive impairments, and autistic-like social impairments, caused by a break in the X chromosome.

Huntington's disease. Inherited disorder characterized initially by jerky arm movements and facial twitches and later by tremors, writhing movements, and psychological symptoms, including depression, memory impairment, hallucinations, and delusions.

inner-ear (nerve) deafness. See nerve deafness.

middle-ear (conductive) deafness. See conductive deafness.

narcolepsy. Condition characterized by unexpected periods of sleepiness during the day.

nerve deafness (inner-ear deafness). Hearing loss that results from damage to the cochlea, the hair cells, or the auditory nerve.

night terror. Experience of intense anxiety during sleep from which a person awakens screaming in terror.

nonfluent aphasia (Broca's aphasia). Condition marked by loss of fluent speech and impaired use and understanding of prepositions, word endings, and other grammatical devices.

phenylketonuria (PKU). Inherited inability to metabolize phenylalanine, leading to mental retardation unless the afflicted person stays on a strict low-phenylalanine diet throughout childhood.

Prader-Willi syndrome. Excessive appetite and moderate cognitive impairment, related to deletion of part of chromosome 15.

prosopagnosia. Impaired ability to recognize or identify faces.

Rasmussen's encephalopathy. Rare condition in which an autoimmune disorder attacks first the glia and then the neurons of one or the other hemisphere of the brain.

Rett syndrome. Condition virtually limited to girls, in which dendrites shrink, leading to loss of speech, motor skills, and social interactions.

sleep apnea. Inability to breathe while sleeping.

strabismus. Condition in which the two eyes point in different directions.

tardive dyskinesia. Side effect of neuroleptic drugs characterized by tremors and other involuntary movements.

tinnitus. Frequent or constant ringing in the ears.

type I alcoholism. Generally less severe type of alcohol abuse with a gradual onset and only a weak genetic predisposition; occurs about equally in men and women.

type II alcoholism. Indicated by severe alcohol abuse with a strong genetic basis and rapid onset early in life; much more common in men.

visual agnosia. Impaired ability to identify visual objects despite otherwise satisfactory vision.

Wernicke's aphasia. See fluent aphasia.

Williams syndrome. Type of mental retardation in which the person has good language skills in spite of extremely limited abilities in other regards.

Drugs, Neurotransmitters, and Related Terms

agonist. Drug that mimics or increases the effects of a neurotransmitter.

amphetamine. Stimulant drug that increases the release of dopamine.

antagonist. Drug that blocks the effects of a neurotransmitter.

antipsychotic. Drug that relieves schizophrenia.

atypical antidepressants. Miscellaneous group of drugs with antidepressant effects but only mild side effects.

atypical antipsychotics. Drugs that alleviate schizophrenia without producing movement disorders; in many cases relieve negative as well as positive symptoms.

barbiturates. Class of drugs sometimes used as anxiety reducers.

benzodiazepines. Class of widely used anti-anxiety drugs.

butyrophenones. Class of antipsychotic drugs that includes haloperidol.

catecholamines. Compounds such as dopamine, norepinephrine, and epinephrine that contain both catechol and an amine (NH_2).

chlorpromazine (Thorazine). First drug found to relieve the positive symptoms of schizophrenia.

cocaine. Stimulant drug that increases the stimulation of dopamine synapses by blocking the reuptake of dopamine by the presynaptic neuron.

endorphins. Category of chemicals the body produces that stimulate the same receptors as do opiates.

insulin. Pancreatic hormone that facilitates the entry of glucose into the cells.

L-dopa. Chemical precursor of dopamine and other catecholamines.

methylphenidate (Ritalin). Stimulant drug that increases the stimulation of dopamine synapses by blocking the reuptake of dopamine by the presynaptic neuron.

monoamine oxidase inhibitor (MAOI). Drug that blocks the enzyme monoamine oxidase (MAO), a presynaptic terminal enzyme that metabolizes catecholamines and serotonin into inactive forms.

neuroleptic. Drug that relieves schizophrenia.

neurotransmitters. Chemicals released by neurons that affect other neurons. Important examples include glutamate (the most abundant excitatory neurotransmitter), GABA (the most abundant inhibitory neurotransmitter), acetylcholine, dopamine, norepinephrine, and serotonin.

second-generation antipsychotics. Drugs that alleviate schizophrenia without producing movement disorders; in many cases relieve negative as well as positive symptoms.

selective serotonin reuptake inhibitor (SSRI). Drug that blocks the reuptake of serotonin into the presynaptic terminal.

thorazine (chlorpromazine). See chlorpromazine.

tricyclic. Drug that prevents the presynaptic neuron that releases serotonin or catecholamine molecules from reabsorbing them.

REFERENCES

Adams, R. B. Jr., Gordon, H. L., Baird, A. A., Ambady, N., & Kleck, R. E. (2003). Effects of gaze on amygdala sensitivity to anger and fear faces. *Science, 300,* 1536.

Adams, R. B. Jr., & Kleck, R. E. (2005). Effects of direct and averted gaze on the perception of facially communicated emotion. *Emotion, 5,* 3–11.

Adams, W., Kendell, R. E., Hare, E. H., Munk-Jørgensen, P. (1993). Epidemiological evidence that maternal influenza contributes to the aetiology of schizophrenia. *British Journal of Psychiatry, 163,* 522–534.

Adolphs, R., Baron-Cohen, S., & Tranel, D. (2002). Impaired recognition of social emotions following amygdala damage. *Journal of Cognitive Neuroscience, 14,* 1264–1274.

Adolphs, R., Gosselin, F., Buchanan, T. W., Tranel, D., Schyns, P., & Damasio, A. R. (2005). A mechanism for impaired fear recognition after amygdala damage. *Nature, 433,* 68–72.

Adolphs, R., Tranel, D., & Buchanan, T. W. (2005). Amygdala damage impairs emotional memory for gist but not details of complex stimuli. *Nature Neuroscience, 8,* 512–518.

Adolphs, R., Tranel, D., & Damasio, A. R. (1998). The human amygdala in social judgment. *Nature, 393,* 470–474.

Allen, J. S., Damasio, H., Grabowski, T. J., Bruss, J., & Zhang, W. (2003). Sexual dimorphism and asymmetries in the gray-white composition of the human cerebrum. *NeuroImage, 18,* 880–894.

Amedi, A., Floel, A., Knecht, S., Zohary, E., & Cohen, L. G. (2004). Transcranial magnetic stimulation of the occipital pole interferes with verbal processing in blind subjects. *Nature Neuroscience, 7,* 1266–1270.

Amedi, A., Raz, N., Pianka, P., Malach, R., & Zohary, E. (2003). Early "visual" cortex activation correlates with superior verbal memory performance in the blind. *Nature Neuroscience, 6,* 758–766.

Anderson, S. W., Bechara, A., Damasio, H., Tranel, D., & Damasio, A. R. (1999). Impairment of social and moral behavior related to early damage in human prefrontal cortex. *Nature Neuroscience, 2,* 1032–1037.

Andrews, T. J., Halpern, S. D., & Purves, D. (1997). Correlated size variation in human visual cortex, lateral geniculate nucleus, and optic tract. *Journal of Neuroscience, 17,* 2859–2868.

Au, T. K., Knightly, L. M., Jun, S.-A., & Oh, J. W. (2002). Overhearing a language during childhood. *Psychological Science, 13,* 238–243.

Bailey, D. B., Bruer, J. T., Symons, F. J., & Lichtman, J. W. (2001). *Critical thinking about critical periods.* Baltimore, MD: Paul H. Brookes.

Bailey, D. B., & Symons, F. J. (2001). Critical periods: Reflections and future directions. In D. Bailey, J. Bruer, F. Symons, & J. Lichtman (Eds.), *Critical thinking about critical periods* (pp. 289–292). Baltimore, MD: Paul H. Brookes.

Baptista, L. F., & Petrinovich, L. (1984). Social interaction, sensitive phases and the song template hypothesis in the white-crowned sparrow. *Animal Behaviour, 32,* 172–181.

Bateson, P. (1983). Sensitive periods in behavioral development. *Archives of Disease in Childhood, 58,* 85–86.

Begley, S. (1996, February 19). Your child's brain. *Newsweek,* 55–62.

Blake, R., & Hirsch, H. V. B. (1975). Deficits in binocular depth perception in cats after alternating monocular deprivation. *Science, 190,* 1114–1116.

Boucsein, K., Weniger, G., Mursch, K., Steinhoff, B. J., & Irle, E. (2001). Amygdala lesion in temporal lobe epilepsy subjects impairs associative learning of emotional facial expressions. *Neuropsychologia, 39,* 231–236.

Brennan, P. A., Grekin, E. R., & Mednick, S. A. (1999). Maternal smoking during pregnancy and adult male criminal outcomes. *Archives of General Psychiatry, 56,* 215–219.

Brown, A. S., Begg, M. D., Gravenstein, S., Schaefer, C. A., Wyatt, R. J., Bresnahan, M., et al. (2004). Serologic evidence of prenatal influenza in the etiology of schizophrenia. *Archives of General Psychiatry, 61,* 774–780.

Brown, A. S., Cohen, P., Harkavy-Friedman, J., Babulas, V., Malaspina, D., Gorman, J. M., et al. (2001). Prenatal rubella, premorbid abnormalities, and adult schizophrenia. *Biological Psychiatry, 49,* 473–486.

Bruer, J. T. (2001). A critical and sensitive period primer. In D. Bailey, J. Bruer, F. Symons, & J. Lichtman (Eds.), *Critical thinking about critical periods* (pp. 3–26). Baltimore, MD: Paul H. Brookes.

Buka, S. L., Tsuang, M. T., Torrey, E. F., Klebanoff, M. A., Bernstein, D., & Yolken, R. H. (2001). Maternal infections and subsequent psychosis among offspring. *Archives of General Psychiatry, 58,* 1032–1037.

Burrell, B. (2004). *Postcards from the brain museum.* New York: Broadway Books.

Burton, H., Snyder, A. Z., Conturo, T. E., Akbudak, E., Ollinger, J. M., & Raichle, M. E. (2002). Adaptive changes in early and late blind: A fMRI study of Braille reading. *Journal of Neurophysiology, 87,* 589–607.

Byl, N. N., McKenzie, A., & Nagarajan, S. S. (2000). Differences in somatosensory hand organization in a healthy flutist and a flutist with focal hand dystonia. *Journal of Hand Therapy, 13,* 302–309.

Canli, T., Sivers, H., Whitfield, S. L., Gotlib, I. H., & Gabrieli, J. d. E. (2002). Amygdala response to happy faces as a function of extraversion. *Science, 296,* 2191.

Carey, S. (1978). The child as word learner. In M. Halle, J. Bresnan, & G. A. Miller (Eds.), *Linguistic theory and psychological reality* (pp. 264–293). Cambridge, MA: MIT Press.

Carnegie Corporation of New York. (1994). *Starting points: Meeting the needs of our youngest children.* New York: Author.

Carnegie Corporation of New York. (1996). *Years of promise: A comprehensive learning strategy for America's children.* New York: Author.

Chabris, C. F. (1999). Prelude or requiem for the "Mozart effect"? *Nature, 400,* 826–827.

Clark, B. A., Monsivais, P., Branco, T., London, M., & Häuser, M. (2005). The site of action potential initiation in cerebellar Purkinje neurons. *Nature Neuroscience, 8,* 137–139.

Colombo, J. (1982). The critical period concept: Research, methodology, and theoretical issues. *Psychological Bulletin, 9,* 260–275.

Crair, M. C., Gillespie, D. C., & Stryker, M. P. (1998). The role of visual experience in the development of columns in cat visual cortex. *Science, 279,* 566–570.

Cynader, M., & Chernenko, G. (1976). Abolition of direction selectivity in the visual cortex of the cat. *Science, 193,* 504–505.

Damasio, A. R. (1994). *Descartes' error.* New York: Putnam & Sons.

Detre, J. A., & Floyd, T. F. (2001). Functional MRI and its applications to the clinical neurosciences. *Neuroscientist, 7,* 64–79.

Dragoi, V., Rivadulla, C., & Sur, M. (2001). Foci of orientation plasticity in visual cortex. *Nature, 411,* 80–86.

Elbert, T., Candia, V., Altenmüller, E., Rau, H., Sterr, A., Rockstroh, B., et al. (1998). Alteration of digital representations in somatosensory cortex in focal hand dystonia. *Neuroreport, 9,* 3571–3575.

Elbert, T., Pantev, C., Wienbruch, C., Rockstroh, B., & Taub, E. (1995). Increased cortical representation of the fingers of the left hand in string players. *Science, 270,* 305–307.

Ericsson, K. A., & Charness, N. (1994). Expert performance: Its structure and acquisition. *American Psychologist, 49,* 725–747.

Fagiolini, M., & Hensch, T. K. (2000). Inhibitory threshold for critical-period activation in primary visual cortex. *Nature, 404,* 183–186.

Fergusson, D. M., Woodward, L. J., & Horwood, J. (1998). Maternal smoking during pregnancy and psychiatric adjustment in late adolescence. *Archives of General Psychiatry, 55,* 721–727.

Fine, I., Smallman, H. S., Doyle, P., & MacLeod, D. I. A. (2002). Visual function before and after the removal of bilateral congenital cataracts in adulthood. *Vision Research, 42,* 191–210.

Fine, I. Wade, A. R., Brewer, A. A., May, M. G., Goodman, D. F., Boynton, G. M., et al. (2003). Long-term deprivation affects visual perception and cortex. *Nature Neuroscience, 6,* 915–916.

Finette, B. A., O'Neill, J. P., Vacek, P. M., & Albertini, R. J. (1998). Gene mutations with characteristic deletions in cord blood T lymphocytes associated with passive maternal exposure to tobacco smoke. *Nature Medicine, 4,* 1144–1151.

Flint, J. (2004). The genetic basis of neuroticism. *Neuroscience and Biobehavioral Reviews, 28,* 307–316.

Frangou, S., Chitins, X., & Williams, S. C. R. (2004). Mapping IQ and gray matter density in healthy young people. *NeuroImage, 23,* 800–805.

Gaser, C., & Schlaug, G. (2003). Brain structures differ between musicians and non-musicians. *Journal of Neuroscience, 23,* 9240–9245.

Goldin-Meadow, S., & Mylander, C. (1998). Spontaneous sign systems created by deaf children in two cultures. *Nature, 391,* 279–281.

Greenough, W. T. (1975). Experiential modification of the developing brain. *American Scientist, 63,* 37–46.

Hakuta, K., Bialystok, E., & Wiley, E. (2003). Critical evidence: A test of the critical-period hypothesis for second-language acquisition. *Psychological Science, 14,* 31–38.

Halpern, S. D., Andrews, T. J., & Purves, D. (1999). Interindividual variation in human visual performance. *Journal of Cognitive Neuroscience, 11,* 521–534.

Hariri, A. R., Mattay, V. S., Tessitore, A., Fera, F., & Weinberger, D. R. (2003). Neocortical modulation of the amygdala response to fearful stimuli. *Biological Psychiatry, 53,* 494–501.

Hariri, A. R., Mattay, V. S., Tessitore, A., Kolachana, B., Fera, F., Goldman, D., et al. (2002). Serotonin transporter genetic variation and the response of the human amygdala. *Science, 297,* 400–403.

Harley, B., & Wang, W. (1997). The critical period hypothesis: Where are we now? In A. M. B. deGroot & J. F. Knoll (Eds.), *Tutorials in bilingualism* (pp. 19–51). Mahwah, NJ: Erlbaum.

Horton, J. C. (2001). Critical periods in the development of the visual system. In D. Bailey, J. Bruer, F. Symons, & J. Lichtman (Eds.), *Critical thinking about critical periods* (pp. 27–44). Baltimore, MD: Paul H. Brookes.

Hubel, D., & Wiesel, T. N. (1965). Binocular interaction in striate cortex of kittens reared with artificial squint. *Journal of Neurophysiology, 28,* 1041–159.

Ikonomidou, C., Bittigau, P., Ishimaru, M. J., Wozniak, D. F., Koch, C., Genz, K., et al. (2000). Ethanol-induced apoptotic neurodegeneration and fetal alcohol syndrome. *Science, 287,* 1056–1060.

Kalivas, P. W., Volkow, N., & Seamans, J. (2005). Unmanageable motivation in addiction: A pathology in prefrontal-accumbens glutamate transmission. *Neuron, 45,* 647–650.

Kubota, Y., Sato, W., Murai, T., Toichi, M., Ikeda, A., & Sengoku, A. (2000). Emotional cognition without awareness after unilateral temporal lobectomy in humans. *Journal of Neuroscience, 20,* RC97, 1–5.

Laburn, H. P. (1996). How does the fetus cope with thermal challenges? *News in Physiological Sciences, 11,* 96–100.

Le Grand, R., Mondloch, C. J., Maurer, D., & Brent, H. P. (2001). Early visual experience and face processing. *Nature, 410,* 890.

Le Grand, R., Mondloch, C. J., Maurer, D., & Brent, H. P. (2003). Expert face processing requires visual input to the right hemisphere during infancy. *Nature Neuroscience, 6,* 1108–1112.

Lenz, F. A., & Byl, N. N. (1999). Reorganization in the cutaneous core of the human thalamic principal somatic sensory nucleus (ventral caudal) in patients with dystonia. *Journal of Neurophysiology, 82,* 3204–3212.

Lewis, T. L., & Maurer, D. (2005). Multiple sensitive periods in human visual development: Evidence from visually deprived children. *Developmental Psychobiology, 46,* 163–183.

Lichtman, J. W. (2001). Developmental neurobiology overview: Synapses, circuits, and plasticity. In D. Bailey, J. Bruer, F. Symons, & J. Lichtman (Eds.), *Critical thinking about critical periods.* (pp. 27–44). Baltimore, MD: Paul H. Brookes.

Lorenz, K. (1937). The companion in the bird's world. *The Auk, 54,* 245–273.

Luders, E., Narr, K. L., Thompson, P. M., Rex, D. E., Jancke, L., Steinmetz, H., et al. (2004). Gender differences in cortical complexity. *Nature Neuroscience, 7,* 799–800.

Marler, P., & Peters, S. (1987). A sensitive period for song acquisition in the song sparrow, *Melospiza melodia:* A case of age-limited learning. *Ethology, 76,* 89–100.

Marler, P., & Peters, S. (1988). Sensitive periods for song acquisition from tape recordings and live tutors in the swamp sparrow, *Melospiza georgiana*. *Ethology*, *77*, 76–84.

Mayberry, R. I., Lock, E., & Kazmi, H. (2002). Linguistic ability and early language exposure. *Nature*, *415*, 1026–1029.

Mechelli, A., Friston, K. J., Frackowiak, R. S., & Price, C. J. (2005). Structural covariance in the human cortex. *Journal of Neuroscience*, *25*, 8303–8310.

Milberger, S., Biederman, J., Faraone, S. V., Chen, L., & Jones, J. (1996). Is maternal smoking during pregnancy a risk factor for attention deficit hyperactivity disorder in children? *American Journal of Psychiatry*, *153*, 1138–1142.

Mukamel, R., Gelbard, H., Arieli, A., Hasson, U., Fried, I., & Malach, R. (2005). Coupling between neuronal firing, field potentials, and fMRI in human auditory cortex. *Science*, *309*, 951–954.

Nantais, K. M., & Schellenberg, E. G. (1999). The Mozart effect: An artifact of preference. *Psychological Science*, *10*, 370–373.

Nelson, C. A., Wewerka, S., Thomas, K. M., Tribby-Walbridge, S., deRegnier, R., & Georgieff, M. (2000). Neurocognitive sequelae of infants of diabetic mothers. *Behavioral Neuroscience*, *114*, 950–956.

Pennington, B. F., Filipek, P. A., Lefly, D., Chhabildas, N., Kennedy, D. N., Simon, J. H., et al. (2000). A twin MRI study of size variations in the human brain. *Journal of Cognitive Neuroscience*, *12*, 223–232.

Pesenti, M., Zago, L., Crivello, F., Mellet, E., Samson, D., Duroux, B., et al. (2001). Mental calculation in a prodigy is sustained by right prefrontal and medial temporal areas. *Nature Neuroscience*, *4*, 103–107.

Pezawas, L., Verchinski, B. A., Mattay, V. S., Callicott, J. H., Kolachana, B. S., Straub, et al. (2004). The brain-derived neurotrophic factor val66met polymorphism and variation in human cortical morphology. *Journal of Neuroscience*, *24*, 10099–10102.

Phelps, M. E., & Mazziotta, J. C. (1985). Positron emission tomography: Human brain function and biochemistry. *Science*, *228*, 799–809.

Polley, D. B., Kvasnák, E., & Frostig, R. D. (2004). Naturalistic experience transforms sensory maps in the adult cortex of caged animals. *Nature*, *429*, 67–71.

Posthuma, D., De Geus, E. J. C., Baaré, W. F. C., Pol, H. E. H., Kahn, R. S., & Boomsma, D. I. (2002). The association between brain volume and intelligence is of genetic origin. *Nature Neuroscience*, *5*, 83–84.

Puttemans, V., Wenderoth, N., & Swinnen, S. P. (2005). Changes in brain activity during the acquisition of a multifrequency bimanual coordination task: From the cognitive stage to advanced levels of automaticity. *Journal of Neuroscience*, *25*, 4270–4278.

Rauscher, F. H., Shaw, G. L., & Ky, K. N. (1993). Music and spatial task performance. *Nature*, *365*, 611.

Rhodes, J. S., van Praag, H., Jeffrey, S., Girard, I., Mitchell, G. S., Garland, T. Jr., et al. (2003). Exercise increases hippocampal neurogenesis to high levels but does not improve spatial learning in mice bred for increased voluntary wheel running. *Behavioral Neuroscience*, *117*, 1006–1016.

Rittenhouse, C. D., Shouval, H. Z., Paradiso, M. A., & Bear, M. F. (1999). Monocular deprivation induces homosynaptic long-term depression in visual cortex. *Nature*, *397*, 347–350.

Rosenzweig, M. R., & Bennett, E. L. (1996). Psychobiology of plasticity: Effects of training and experience on brain and behavior. *Behavioural Brain Research*, *78*, 57–65.

Royer, S., & Paré, D. (2003). Conservation of total synaptic weight through balanced synaptic depression and potentiation. *Nature*, *422*, 518–522.

Sadato, N., Pascual-Leone, A., Grafman, J., Ibañez, V., Deiber, M.-P., Dold, G., & Hallett, M. (1996). Activation of the primary visual cortex by Braille reading in blind subjects. *Nature*, *380*, 526–528.

Sanger, T. D., Pascual-Leone, A., Tarsy, D., & Schlaug, G. (2001). Nonlinear sensory cortex response to simultaneous tactile stimuli in writer's cramp. *Movement Disorders*, *17*, 105–111.

Schneider, P., Scherg, M., Dosch, G., Specht, H. J., Gutschalk, A., & Rupp. A. (2002). Morphology of Heschl's gyrus reflects enhanced activation in the auditory cortex of musicians. *Nature Neuroscience*, *5*, 688–694.

Schoenemann, P. T., Budinger, T. F., Sarich, V. M., & Wang, W. S.-Y. (2000). Brain size does not predict general cognitive ability within families. *Proceedings of the National Academy of Sciences (U.S.A.)*, *97*, 4932–4937.

Schoenemann, P. T., Sheehan, M. J., & Glotzer, L. D. (2005). Prefrontal white matter volume is disproportionately larger in humans than in other primates. *Nature Neuroscience*, *8*, 242–252.

Schoups, A., Vogels, R., Qian, N. & Orban, G. (2001). Practicing orientation identification improves orientation coding in V1 neurons. *Nature*, *412*, 549–553.

Schwartz, C. E., Wright, C. I., Shin, L. M., Kagan, J., & Rauch, S. L. (2003). Inhibited and uninhibited infants "grown up": Adult amygdalar response to novelty. *Science*, *300*, 1952–1953.

Shore, R. (1997). *Rethinking the brain: New insights into early development*. New York: Families and Work Institute.

Slotkin, T. A. (1998). Fetal nicotine or cocaine exposure: Which is worse? *Journal of Pharmacology and Experimental Therapeutics*, *285*, 931–945.

Somerville, L. H., Kim, H., Johnstone, T., Alexander, A. L., & Whalen, P. J. (2004). Human amygdala responses during presentation of happy and neutral faces: Correlations with state anxiety. *Biological Psychology, 55,* 897–903.

Sousa, D. A. (1998, December 16). Is the fuss about brain research justified? *Education Week.*

Steele, K. M., Bass, K. E., & Crook, M. D. (1999). The mystery of the Mozart effect: Failure to replicate. *Psychological Science, 10,* 366–369.

Stevens, C. F. (2001). An evolutionary scaling law for the primate visual system and its basis in cortical function. *Nature, 411,* 193–195.

Stryker, M. P., & Sherk, H. (1975). Modification of cortical orientation selectivity in the cat by restricted visual experience: A reexamination. *Science, 190,* 904–906.

Stryker, M. P., Sherk, H., Leventhal, A. G., & Hirsch, H. V. B. (1978). Physiological consequences for the cat's visual cortex of effectively restricting early visual experience with oriented contours. *Journal of Neurophysiology, 41,* 896–909.

Tagawa, Y., Kanold, P. O., Majdan, M., & Shatz, C. J. (2005). Multiple periods of functional ocular dominance plasticity in mouse visual cortex. *Nature Neuroscience, 8,* 380–388.

Thompson, W. F., Schellenberg, E. G., & Husain, G. (2001). Arousal, mood, and the Mozart effect. *Psychological Science, 12,* 248–251.

van Praag, H., Kempermann, G., & Gage, F. H. (2000). Neural consequences of environmental enrichment. *Nature Reviews Neuroscience, 1,* 191–198.

Vuilleumier, P., Armony, J. L., Driver, J., & Dolan, R. J. (2001). Effects of attention and emotion on face processing in the human brain: An event-related fMRI study. *Neuron, 30,* 829–841.

Warach, S. (1995). Mapping brain pathophysiology and higher cortical function with magnetic resonance imaging. *Neuroscientist, 1,* 221–235.

Wiesel, T. N. (1982). Postnatal development of the visual cortex and the influence of the environment. *Nature, 299,* 583–591.

Wiesel T. N., & Hubel, D. (1963). Single-cell responses in striate cortex of kittens deprived of vision in one eye. *Journal of Neurophysiology, 26,* 1003–1017.

Willerman, L., Schultz, R., Rutledge, J. N., & Bigler, E. D. (1991). In vivo brain size and intelligence. *Intelligence, 15,* 223–228.

Williams, M. A., Morris, A. P., McGlone, F., Abbott, D. F., & Mattingley, J. B. (2004). Amygdala responses to fearful and happy facial expressions under conditions of binocular suppression. *Journal of Neuroscience, 24,* 2898–2904.

Wolfe, P. & Brandt, R. (1998). What do we know from brain research? *Educational Leadership, 56,* 8–13.

Wolpert, L. (1991). *The triumph of the embryo.* Oxford, UK: Oxford University Press.

Zhang, J. (2003). Evolution of the human *ASPM* gene, a major determinant of brain size. *Genetics, 165,* 2063–2070.

CHAPTER 10

CONTRIBUTIONS OF DEVELOPMENTAL PSYCHOPATHOLOGY TO SCHOOL PSYCHOLOGY[1]

JOHN E. LOCHMAN, CAROLINE L. BOXMEYER AND NICOLE P. POWELL
The University of Alabama

Developmental psychopathology is a relatively young field, with the first textbook so titled appearing in 1974 (Achenbach, 1974). In the subsequent 30 years, the benefits of using a developmental psychopathology approach have been increasingly recognized by the scientific community and, as reviewed later in this chapter, research on the causative factors and treatment of childhood mental health issues such as conduct problems and depression has been advanced and expanded under a developmental psychopathology framework.

The need for a developmental psychopathology approach arose out of growing recognition of the limitations of traditional developmental and psychological perspectives (Rutter & Sroufe, 2000). At the same time, emerging research demonstrated that developmental pathways were complex and dynamic, involving both individual and environmental factors (Rutter & Sroufe, 2000). An inclusive framework that allowed examination of a multitude of factors on developmental processes was needed to integrate the growing bodies of information from diverse disciplines such as sociology, biology, and epidemiology. By taking a developmental psychopathology perspective, clinicians and researchers attempt to understand the processes by which behaviors, both normative and atypical, arise and are maintained.

Various authors have defined key features of developmental psychopathology. These include:

(1) an integrative nature; (2) an understanding of causal processes; (3) the role of development; and (4) continuities between normality and pathology.

Luthar, Burrack, Cicchetti, and Weisz (1997) emphasize the integrative nature of developmental psychopathology. This integration takes several forms, including the application of traditional developmental theory to the study of psychopathological processes, as well as the application of knowledge from psychopathology to inform and expand our understanding of normal development. The former approach might involve application of a classic developmental theory, such as Piaget's, to understanding the origins of an individual's maladaptive behavior. In the latter approach, the study of a developmental problem, such as a learning disability, can clarify typical developmental processes (e.g., how children learn to read) as well as elucidating individual factors that may place a child at risk (e.g., lack of environmental stimulation) or provide protection against problem development (e.g., early intervention).

Because a main goal of developmental psychopathology is to provide a comprehensive understanding of human development across the life span, the field must encompass information from disciplines beyond human development and clinical psychology/psychiatry. Toward this goal, it incorporates knowledge from the social sciences, natural sciences, medicine, and education and attempts to integrate this information within a developmental framework.

Developmental psychopathology is concerned with the question of how causal processes operate to result in a given outcome (Rutter & Sroufe, 2000). Questions of nature versus nurture and of the relative contributions of genetic and

[1] The preparation of this chapter was supported by grants provided by the National Institute of Drug Abuse (DA08453; DA16135), the Centers for Disease Control and Prevention (R49\CCR418569), and WT Grant Foundation.

environmental factors are considered under the umbrella of causal processes. Research conducted from a developmental psychopathology perspective has helped to demonstrate the complex interactions of genes and environment in normal and abnormal behavioral variations (Plomin & Rutter, 1998). In the study of causal processes, the developmental psychopathology approach also incorporates the principles of equifinality (i.e., the same outcome through different pathways) and multifinality (i.e., different outcomes through the same pathway). Equifinality can be exemplified by mental retardation, which may occur from genetic, environmental, or psychosocial causes, or any combination of these. The principle of multifinality can be demonstrated through children's reactions to a large-scale traumatic event, such as a devastating hurricane or tornado; some children will develop internalizing symptoms (e.g., anxiety, withdrawal) as a result, others will develop externalizing problems (e.g., aggression, defiance), while a resilient subgroup may show no emotional or behavioral sequelae at all.

Knowledge of normative developmental processes and behaviors corresponding to different developmental levels is imperative to understanding maladaptive behaviors and disorders (Essau & Petermann, 1997; Sroufe & Rutter, 1984). At the most basic level, problems can be identified by making contrasts between expected abilities at a given stage of development and an individual's actual functioning (Edelbrock, 1984). For example, physical aggression is common among preschoolers, but steadily declines with age to become almost nonexistent by the end of adolescence (Bongers, Koot, Van der Ende, & Verhulst, 2004). In a developmental psychopathology perspective, the *processes* involved in development are also crucial considerations. For example, the influences of genetic and environmental factors must be analyzed in the context of ongoing developmental processes within the individual (Rutter & Sroufe, 2000).

The concept of continuity across development is also important in the developmental psychopathology perspective (e.g., Essau & Petermann, 1997; Rutter & Sroufe, 2000). Development can be understood as continuous, but dynamic and changing over the life span (Essau & Petermann, 1997). A central assumption is that developmental processes are linked across time and that developmental events at one stage are related to those at later stages. For example, young children who are aggressive are more likely to also

be aggressive during later childhood and adolescence (Kellam, Ling, Merisca, Brown, & Ialongo, 1998). Discontinuities in typical and disordered behavior are also highlighted within developmental psychopathology. For example, conduct problems in a preschool-age child may be manifested in destruction of toys and stubbornness, while conduct problems in an adolescent may consist of bullying or theft. Further, children's aggression is related not only to later disruptive behaviors, but also to substance abuse and delinquency (e.g., Lochman & Wayland, 1994; Nagin & Tremblay, 1999).

To illustrate how developmental psychopathology research has shaped our understanding of causative risk factors for childhood mental health problems and provided a sound empirical basis for assessment and intervention, we will describe current models of risk for two common childhood problems, conduct problems and depression, and highlight the ways in which school psychologists can employ assessment and intervention procedures to treat and prevent these problems.

DEVELOPMENTAL MODELS OF CONDUCT PROBLEMS AND OF DEPRESSION

Developmental models of various forms of psychopathology can serve as the foundation for new interventions by identifying the active mechanisms which could be the targets of the intervention (Lochman, 2006). Although therapeutic breakthroughs are more likely to occur when theory is emphasized in treatment research (Jensen, 1999), there had been a long-standing neglect of theory and of empirical tests of theory in child and adolescent psychotherapy research until recent years (Kazdin, 1999). A thriving science of intervention requires reciprocal and lively interaction between empiricism and theory (Hughes, 2000).

Thus, intervention programs should be based on clear, well-articulated models for the development and maintenance of particular problem behaviors (Conduct Problems Prevention Research Group, 1992), and model-related research and theory should be emphasized in the development of new interventions (Lochman, 2000). The conceptual, assessment and intervention models should all be well integrated. Conceptual models should identify potentially mutable deficits (in the child or in the child's social contexts) associated with the specific disorder, and these deficits should become the targets for assessment and intervention.

Conduct Problems

As an example of the use of research findings to form a contextual social-cognitive model which serves as the basis of our Coping Power program (Lochman & Wells, 2002a), empirically identified risk factors which predict children's antisocial behavior were examined (Coie & Dodge, 1998; Hawkins, Catalano & Miller, 1992; Loeber & Farrington, 2001; Pennington, 2002). These risk factors can be conceptualized as falling within five categories: biological and temperamental child factors, family context, neighborhood context, peer context, and later-emerging child factors involving their social cognitive processes and emotional regulation.

With regard to biological and temperamental child factors, some prenatal factors such as maternal exposure to alcohol, methadone, cocaine, and cigarette smoke and severe nutritional deficiencies (Brennan, Grekin, & Mednick, 1999; Delaney-Black, et al., 2000; Kelly, Davis, & Henschke, 2000; Rasanen et al., 1999) have been found to have direct effects on child aggression. However, it is more commonly found that aggression is the result of interactions between child risk factors and environmental factors, in diathesis-stress models (Masten, Best, & Garmezy, 1990). Thus, risk factors such as birth complications, genes, cortisol reactivity, testosterone, abnormal serotonin levels and temperament all contribute to children's conduct problems, but only when environmental factors such as harsh parenting or low socioeconomic status (SES) are present (Arseneault, Tremblay, Boulerice, & Saucier, 2002; Coon, Carey, Corley, & Fulker, 1992; Dabbs & Morris, 1990; Raine, Brennan, & Mednick, 1997; Scarpa, Bowser, Fikretoglu, Romero, & Wilson, 1999). For example, some male children have been found to have a gene that expresses only low levels of MAOA (monoamine oxidase A) enzyme. MAOA metabolizes and gets rid of excess neurotransmitters. Low MAOA leads to violent behavior, but only if children were maltreated—an indicator of diathesis-stress (Caspi et al., 2002). Similarly, birth complications, including pre-eclampsia, umbilical cord collapse, forceps delivery and fetal hypoxia, increase the risk of later violence among children, but only when the infants subsequently experience adverse

family environments or maternal rejection (Arseneault et al., 2002; Raine et al., 1997).

A child's developmental course is set within the child's social ecology, and an ecological framework is required (Lochman, 2004). Risk factors in the child's family, neighborhood and peer groups can have key influences on children's aggression behavior. Children's aggression has been linked to family background factors such as parent criminality, substance use and depression (Barry, Dunlap, Cotton, Lochman, & Wells, 2005; Loeber, Farrington, Stouthamer-Loeber, Moffitt, & Caspi 1998), low SES and poverty (Sampson & Laub, 1993), stressful life events (Barry et al., 2005; Guerra, Huesmann, Tolan, VanAcker, & Eron, 1995), single and teenage parenthood (Blum, Boyle, & Offord 1988; Nagin, Pogarsky, & Farrington, 1997), and insecure, disorganized attachment (Shaw, Owens, Vondra, & Keenan, 1996). All of these family factors intercorrelate, especially with SES (Luthar, 1999), and they can impact child behavior through their effect on parenting processes.

Parenting processes linked to children's aggression (e.g. Lochman, 2006; Patterson, Reid & Dishion, 1992; Shaw, Keenan, & Vondra, 1994) include: (1) nonresponsive parenting at age 1, with pacing and consistency of parent responses not meeting children's needs, (2) coercive, escalating cycles of harsh parental nattering and child noncompliance, starting in the toddler years, especially for children with difficult temperaments, (3) harsh, inconsistent discipline, (4) unclear directions and commands, (5) lack of warmth and involvement, and (6) lack of parental supervision and monitoring, as children approach adolescence. Weiss, Dodge, Bates, and Pettit (1992) found that ratings of the severity of parental discipline were positively correlated with teacher ratings of aggression and behavior problems. In addition to higher aggression ratings, children experiencing harsh discipline practices exhibited poorer social information processing even when controlling for the possible effects of socioeconomic status, marital discord, and child temperament. It is important to note that although such parenting factors are associated with childhood aggression, child temperament and behavior also affect parenting behavior (Fite, Colder, Lochman, & Wells, 2006), and these relations are bidirectional.

At the community context level, high neighborhood crime rates and low social cohesion have been found to predict disruptive behavior in children (Majumder, Moss, & Murrelle, 1998; Maughan, 2001). Neighborhood effects begin to create heightened risk during middle childhood (Ingoldsby & Shaw, 2002), as children become more independent in moving around their community. Children are also affected by risk factors within their schools and classrooms. The overall aggressiveness of students in a classroom has been found to increase the aggressiveness of target children's behavior (Barth, Dunlap, Dane, Lochman, & Wells, 2004).

By elementary school, aggressive behavior can lead to peer rejection, although the relation is bidirectional (Coie, Dodge, & Kupersmidt, 1990). Peer rejection predicts a variety of negative outcomes, including delinquency, school dropout, internalizing problems, adolescent pregnancy, and drug and alcohol use. Particularly high rates of antisocial outcomes are evident for children who are both aggressive and rejected by their peer group (Coie, Lochman, Terry, & Hyman, 1992). Peer rejection from the broad peer group can set the stage for involvement with deviant peers, which is itself a critical peer risk factor by adolescence.

These early child risk factors and contextual risk factors lead to later emerging child risk factors involving their social cognitive processes and emotional regulation abilities. Based on children's temperament and biological dispositions, and on children's contextual experiences from their family, peers and community, they begin to form stable patterns of processing social information (Dodge, Laird, Lochman, Zelli, & Conduct Problems Prevention Research Group, 2002) and of regulating their emotions. Aggressive children have difficulty managing their anger expression, and they have characteristic social information processing deficits (Crick & Dodge, 1994; Lochman, Whidby, & FitzGerald, 2000) including: (1) cue encoding difficulties, by excessively recalling hostile social cues (Gouze, 1987), (2) hostile attributional biases, and distorted perceptions of self and other in peer conflict situations (Lochman & Dodge, 1994, 1998), (3) nonaffiliative, dominance-oriented social goals (Lochman, Wayland, & White, 1993), (4) less competent problem solutions, with fewer verbal assertion, compromise and bargaining solutions and more action-oriented and aggressive solutions (Dunn, Lochman, & Colder, 1997; Lochman & Dodge, 1994; Pepler, Craig, & Roberts, 1998), (5) expectations that aggressive solutions will work and higher regard for aggressive solutions

(Crick & Werner, 1998; Lochman & Dodge, 1994), which can lead to recursive effects on subsequent deviant processing of social cues (Zelli, Dodge, Lochman, Laird, & Conduct Problems Prevention Research Group, 1999), and (6) poor enactment of solutions, due to weak social skills (Dodge, Pettit, McClaskey, & Brown, 1986). The encoding and attributional biases tend to be more prominent in reactively aggressive children than in proactively aggressive children (Dodge, Lochman, Harnish, Bates, & Pettit, 1997). Deficient beliefs at the fifth stage of information processing, when they make decisions to act, are especially characteristic for children with proactive aggressive behavior patterns (Dodge et al., 1997) and for youth who have callous-unemotional traits consistent with early phases of psychopathy (Pardini, Lochman, & Frick, 2003).

Schemas have been proposed to have a significant impact on the information processing steps within the contextual social-cognitive model underlying cognitive-behavioral interventions with aggressive children (Lochman, Magee, & Pardini, 2003; Lochman & Wells, 2004). Schemas can involve children's expectations and beliefs of others (Lochman et al., 2003) and of themselves, including their self esteem and narcissism (Barry, Thompson, Barry, Lochman, Adler, & Hill, 2007). Early in the information processing sequence, when the individual is perceiving and interpreting new social cues, schemas can have a clear direct effect by narrowing the child's attention to certain aspects of the social cue array (e.g., Lochman, Nelson, & Sims, 1981). A child who believes it is essential to be in control of others and who expects that others will try to dominate him or her, often in aversive ways, will attend particularly to verbal and nonverbal signals about someone else's control efforts, easily missing accompanying signs of the other person's friendliness, or attempts to negotiate. Schemas can also have indirect effects on information processing through the influence of schemas on children's expectations for their own behavior and for others' behavior in specific situations. Lochman & Dodge (1998) found that aggressive boys' perceptions of their own aggressive behavior were primarily affected by their expectations prior to an interaction, while nonaggressive boys relied more on their actual behavior during interactions to form their perceptions.

The contextual social-cognitive model (Lochman & Wells, 2002a) which is derived from these research findings, indicates that certain family and community background factors (neighborhood problems; maternal depression; low social support; marital conflict; low SES) have both a direct effect on children's aggressive behaviors, and an indirect effect, through their influence on key mediational processes (parenting practices; children's social cognition and emotional regulation; children's peer relations). This model can then lead to intervention which is designed to change these specific mutable, mediating risk factors, and thereby reduce children's aggressive behaviors, and their subsequent delinquent and substance-abusing behavior (Lochman & Wells, 2002a, 2002b, 2003, 2004). The intervention goals would be expected to follow directly from the mediational processes in the developmental model derived from research on the risk factors.

Depression

A developmental model accounting for the emergence and maintenance of depression in children and adolescents is driven by etiological research on biological, cognitive and interpersonal factors that are associated with depression (Garber & Horowitz, 2002). Most conceptual frameworks for understanding depression in childhood are downward extensions of models used to account for adult depression, although some child-specific models related to how children react to others' perceptions of their competence have been proposed (Cole, 1991).

With regard to biological factors implicated in childhood depression, behavioral genetic studies have provided evidence for both genetic and environmental effects on childhood depression. Twin studies have found greater concordance for identical twins than fraternal twins, indicating moderate levels of heritability that are consistent with estimates found for adults (McGuffin, Katz, Watkins, & Rutherford, 1996). Adoption study designs, which are better able to disentangle shared and nonshared environmental effects, have found less contribution for genetic effects (e.g., Eley, Deater-Deckard, Fombonne, Fulker, & Plomin, 1998). Overall, research indicates that vulnerability to depression has some genetic component. Although the mechanism of risk is not yet clear, it is likely that genetic factors have an effect on neurobiological or cognitive mechanisms (Garber & Horowitz, 2002).

Neurobiological research in childhood depression has examined psychoneuroendocrinology, neurotransmitters, and functional and anatomical brain differences (Garber & Horowitz, 2002). With regard to psychoneuroendocrinology, hypothalamic-pituitary-adrenal (HPA) axis research has found that evening hypersecretion of cortisol (Dahl et al., 1991; Goodyer, Herbert, & Altham, 1998) has been linked to severity and stability of depression symptoms, although developmental changes in the HPA axis have led to inconsistent findings on other aspects of cortisol response. Another method for examining HPA axis functioning is through growth hormone (GH), and GH appears to be a vulnerability marker for depression. Children of depressed parents have blunted GH response following administration of growth hormone releasing hormone (GHRH) (Birmaher et al., 1999). With regard to neurotransmitters, serotonergic system dysregulation has been noted in childhood depression (Emslie et al., 1997), evident in blunted cortisol response following administration of L-5-hydroxytryptophan (L-5HTP) (Birmaher et al., 1997). In terms of brain anatomy, little research has been conducted with children, but infants and children at risk for depression have been found to have hypoactivation of the left frontal cortex (Jones, Field, Fox, Lundy, & Davalos, 1997; Tomarken, Simien, & Garber, 1994).

The presence of stressful life events predicts children's later levels of depressive symptoms in longitudinal studies (Little & Garber, 2000), and the first onset of depressive disorders (Monroe, Rohde, Seeley, & Lewinsohn, 1999). Stressful life events related to disappointments, loss, or interpersonal conflict are particularly related to children's depression (Monroe et al., 1999), especially when the child is highly oriented to social contact (Little & Garber, 2000).

Cognitive theories of depression assume that depressed individuals have more negative beliefs about themselves and their future, and make global, stable and internal attributions for negative events. Research on the cognitive characteristics of depressed children and adolescents have found distortions in their depressogenic attributions, self-evaluation, hopelessness, and perceptions of past and present events (Gladstone & Kaslow, 1995; Kendall & Lochman, 1994). Depressed children have similar causal attributions for both positive and negative events, hence displaying depressogenic attributions (Kaslow, Rehm, Pollack, & Siegel, 1988), and they have a more external locus of control (Mullins, Siegel, & Hodges, 1985). Curry and Craighead (1990) found that inpatient depressed adolescents had particular difficulties in their cognitions about positive events, as they attributed the cause of positive events to external, unstable and specific causes. Depressed children also have been found to have poor perceptions of their competence (Kendall & Lochman, 1994), but in longitudinal studies, the relation between perceived competence and depression appears to be bidirectional, with low perceived competence leading to depression and vice versa (Hoffman, Cole, Martin, Tram, & Seroczynski, 2000). In the last decade, research has supported the notion that negative cognitions affect children's depression largely through diathesis-stress models, rather than as simple isolated causal factors. Children who have negative attributions or perceptions of their self-worth have increasing depression over time if they have also experienced important stressors (e.g., low grades, peer rejection, school transitions) (Hilsman & Garber, 1995). The effect of negative cognitions on subsequent depression becomes more apparent as children become older. Negative attributions about the cause of events is more predictive of depression among eighth graders than among third graders (Nolen-Hoeksema, Girgus, & Seligman, 1992), indicating the importance of taking a developmental perspective in understanding the cognitive factors contributing to depression.

Children's interpersonal relations are also linked to their depression. On the one hand, family and peer environments can create negative schemas about self and others, which make the child vulnerable to depression. Parents of depressed children have been found to be rejecting and controlling (Garber, 2000; Stein et al., 2000), and the children are often rejected by their peers (Kistner, Balthazor, Risi, & Burton, 1999; Rudolph, Hammen, & Burge, 1994), and these negative social patterns precede escalating depression. On the other hand, children's reactions to these environments can trigger negative recurring and reciprocal interactions with others, resulting in more rejection and depression (Barber, 1996; Rueter, Scaramella, Wallace, & Conger, 1999). A transactional model best describes the relation between depressed children and their social environment (Garber & Horowitz, 2002).

Based on these findings, important goals of an intervention for childhood depression would be to influence these mutable cognitive, interpersonal, and familial processes which mediate depressive symptoms. The assessment process can also shape the intervention goals by determining not just the presence and severity of depressive symptoms, but also by determining which mediating risk factors are present, particularly those that are contributing most strongly.

DEVELOPMENTAL PSYCHOPATHOLOGY AND ASSESSMENT

Given the broad scope encompassed by a developmental psychopathology perspective, assessment conducted within this framework is necessarily comprehensive in nature. As such, important goals will include: evaluation of multiple domains of functioning, collection of information from multiple sources, and application of multiple assessment methods. For example, a clinician will want to include measures of social, emotional, and behavioral functioning when a child suspected of having a learning disability is referred for psychoeducational assessment. The additional measures may help to elucidate associated features involved in the development and maintenance of the child's learning problems. Multi-informant techniques are important in evaluating the consistency of behaviors. For example, to qualify for a diagnosis of attention-deficit/hyperactivity disorder (ADHD), the DSM-IV (American Psychiatric Association, 2000) requires impairment from symptoms in at least two settings which, for most children, will include home and school. In this case, using multiple informants is likely to yield the most accurate information, with parents reporting on home behavior and teachers providing information about the child's behavior at school. It is also important to use comprehensive, multi-informant methods in assessing conduct problems and depression; however, evaluators will want to consider that youths are generally better reporters of their own internalizing mood states, while parents and teachers tend to report behavior problems more accurately (Cantwell, Lewinsohn, Rhode, & Seely, 1996; Herjanic & Reich, 1997). Finally, every individual assessment tool and type of assessment tool has its own set of benefits and limitations; drawing from the various types of assessment methods will help to elucidate consistencies in behavior and minimize limiting features of each measure. Five main types of assessment measures commonly used as part of a comprehensive assessment battery include: (1) rating scales, (2) diagnostic interviews, (3) observation techniques, (4) cognitive assessment, and (5) peer-referenced assessment.

Rating scales may be broad in scope, assessing a range of internalizing, externalizing, and adaptive behaviors (e.g., Reynolds & Kamphaus, 2004), or narrowly focused, specifically assessing a certain behavior or construct of interest (e.g., Reynolds & Richmond, 1978; Kovacs, 1992). Both types of rating scales offer ease of administration and time efficiency as advantages for use; both also provide normative data, allowing an individual respondent's information to be compared to other children of similar demographic status (Lochman, Barry, Powell, Boxmeyer, & Holmes 2008). In addition, both types of rating scales often offer alternate versions for parents, teachers, and youth self-report, streamlining the interpretation of data from multiple sources. Unique advantages of broadband rating scales include the ability to assess for infrequent behaviors and to screen for comorbid problems. As a consequence of their efficiency, rating scales are limited in the information they can provide and often do not cover symptoms in depth or provide information on important associated features (Lochman et al., 2008).

Structured *diagnostic interviews*, such as the DISC-IV (Shaffer, Fisher, Lucas, Dulcan, & Schwab-Stone, 2000) address some of the limitations associated with rating scales. Diagnostic interview schedules are detailed and comprehensive, assessing for factors such as age of onset, frequency, and severity of symptoms. However, the interviews are cumbersome, time-consuming, and often require specialized training.

Through the use of *direct observation*, mental health professionals have the opportunity to experience a child's behavior firsthand, reducing the effects of informant bias. Through direct observation clinicians can gather information about the antecedents and consequences of behaviors, as well as observing for associated features and comorbid problems. Observation systems are available as part of several comprehensive assessment packages, including the Child Behavior Checklist (Achenbach, 1991) and the BASC-2. Observation methods, however, are often time-consuming, do not offer normative information, and may require specialized training.

Cognitive assessment includes measures of intellectual ability, academic achievement, language skills, and executive processing. Such measures provide normative information, and the resulting information on the child's cognitive developmental level is an important starting point for evaluation of other areas of functioning (e.g., social, emotional, behavioral). These types of assessment methods are generally individually administered and are time-consuming. In addition, they require specialized training in administration and interpretation.

In a *peer-referenced assessment*, a group of children provide information on the social status of a target child (i.e., sociometric assessment). Typically, ratings include variables such as "fights," "leader," "like most," and "like least." Though parents and teachers often provide information on children's social status, they may lack awareness of the subtleties of students' interpersonal relations; information obtained from peers themselves is more likely to accurately capture a child's true social standing. Drawbacks of sociometric methods include the need for access to a group of peers, including parental consent for participation, the length of time required for administration, and the potential for students to share their responses among themselves in a manner that is hurtful to unpopular students.

Mash and Terdal (1997) have identified several important considerations in assessment as related to developmental psychopathology, including (1) the rapid and uneven nature of developmental change in children; (2) the principles of plasticity and modifiability in relation to environmental influences; and (3) age and gender considerations.

Consideration of the rapid and uneven nature of developmental change is relevant in determining whether a child's presentation is significantly different from expected behavior patterns and in making prognostic inferences from assessment information. It is important to consider normative information and to realize that behaviors that are typical at one stage of development (e.g., bedwetting in toddlers) are inappropriate at other stages of development (e.g., bedwetting in later childhood and adolescence). In addition, problems identified at one stage of development will not necessarily predict similar problems as children mature (Garber, 1984). Although certain constructs do demonstrate stability over time (e.g., IQ, temperament) clinicians need to be sensitive to the tendency for children, particularly at very young ages, to show sudden and large changes in developmental status; therefore, prognoses are best stated tentatively.

Plasticity and modifiability refer to children's susceptibility to change based on environmental influences (Mash & Terdal, 1997). More so than in older individuals, children's behavior and neurological structure and functioning can be altered through their experiences. Environmental influences are therefore important considerations in assessment of causal factors, as well as in informing treatment recommendations.

Finally, age and gender are important factors to consider in planning for assessment. These features are not only important in determining normative information, but also in deciding upon assessment methods to employ (Mash & Terdal, 1997). For example, children's ability to provide valid and reliable self-report information varies as a function of age-related cognitive and linguistic abilities. Clinicians also need to consider the role of gender when interpreting assessment information. The frequency and expression of certain behaviors vary according to gender, as do the implications of certain behaviors for a child's functioning (e.g., boys' physical aggression may be more likely to be tolerated by parents and teachers than that of girls).

DEVELOPMENTAL PSYCHOPATHOLOGY AND INTERVENTION

Developmental psychopathology research provides a critical foundation for crafting therapeutic interventions that are based on well-articulated empirical models of the onset and maintenance of particular problem behaviors. Interventions designed from a developmental psychopathology perspective seek to target malleable risk and protective factors that have been causally linked to specific emotional, behavioral, and learning problems in children. Particular emphasis is placed on prevention and early intervention to help at-risk children remain in the normative range or to modify their developmental trajectory toward more adaptive functioning as early as possible. To illustrate how developmentally based interventions address key risk and protective factors across multiple domains, we will describe evidence-based interventions for the two forms of psychopathology highlighted above, conduct problems and depression.

Treatment of Conduct Problems

Parent behavior training programs and child-directed cognitive behavioral interventions that address key contextual and social cognitive mediational processes described above have been found to produce significant behavioral improvements in children with conduct problems (Brestan & Eyberg, 1998; Lochman & Salekin, 2003; Smith, Lochman, & Daunic, 2005). Several of these evidence-based interventions are available for implementation by school mental health professionals (Hibbs & Jensen, 2005; Kazdin & Weisz, 2003). Parent behavior training programs focus on improving caregiver involvement with children and reducing poor parenting practices such as inconsistent limit setting, unclear expectations for behavior, deficient monitoring, few rewards for positive behavior, harsh and inconsistent punishment, and lack of parental involvement in activities with children (Lochman, 2000). Cognitive behavioral interventions with children focus on remediating the distorted or deficient social cognitive processes underlying their intra- and interpersonal difficulties (i.e., biases in their attributions about the intentions of others and expectations about the consequences of aggressive versus verbal problem-solving strategies). Multicomponent interventions that combine both parent behavior training and child-directed cognitive behavioral intervention consistently produce stronger therapeutic effects and better maintenance of improvements over time than do interventions that focus on either the child or parent alone (Lochman & Salekin, 2003). Moreover, multicomponent preventive interventions that target children in the at-risk rather than disordered range can significantly improve children's developmental trajectories toward more adaptive functioning (Lochman & Wells, 2004). Coping Power is one such program, and will be described to illustrate the structure and skills taught in a school-based intervention designed to address key mediational processes in children with conduct problems.

Coping Power Program

The contextual social-cognitive model was used as a conceptual framework in the development of the Coping Power program. Coping Power draws upon many of the operant learning techniques of well-established parent behavior training programs, while also incorporating novel techniques that target malleable, child-level social-cognitive risk factors. Coping Power includes a 34-session child component and a coordinated 16-session parent component. Both components are delivered in a small group format across 16 to 18 months. Intervention topics and activities are outlined in session-by-session treatment manuals (Lochman, Wells, & Lenhart, 2008; Wells, Lochman, & Lenhart, 2008).

Coping Power was originally designed to be implemented with fourth to sixth grade children, but has been successfully adapted for younger and older children. The program can be implemented by school psychologists, guidance counselors, and related school personnel as well as by mental health clinicians in clinic settings. Teacher and classroom curricula are also available. Efficacy and effectiveness studies indicate that Coping Power produces lower rates of delinquent behavior and substance use, both post-intervention and at a one-year follow-up, in comparison to a randomly assigned control condition (Lochman & Wells, 2003, 2004), and lower self-reported substance use, reduced proactive aggression, improved social competence, and greater teacher-rated behavioral improvement at the end of intervention, in comparison to children who had not received Coping Power (Lochman & Wells, 2002b). The follow-up effects on delinquency and substance use are mediated by program-induced changes in children's attributional biases, outcome expectations for aggression, internal locus of control, and parents' consistency in their use of discipline (Lochman & Wells, 2002a).

The *Coping Power Child Component* has a number of intervention foci designed to enhance children's coping and social problem-solving skills. The initial sessions are devoted to establishing group rules, introducing a system for contingent reinforcement of prosocial behavior, and setting personal behavioral goals. Next, students are taught techniques for coping with anger arousal, including coping self-statements, relaxation, and distraction. Major focus is then placed on teaching effective social problem-solving skills. Intervention activities teach students to identify problems and to consider others' perspectives using both pictured and actual social problem situations. Students practice generating alternative solutions to social problems and proactively consider the consequences of each potential solution. Next, the students view modeling videotapes of children becoming aware of physiological arousal when angry, using self-statements ("Stop! Think! What should I do?"), and employing the complete set of problem-solving skills to enact effective solutions. To reinforce their public commitment to effective problem solving, the students finish this module by creating their own videotape modeling effective social problem-solving skills. The remaining child sessions focus on enhancing social skills, including active practice of methods for entering new peer groups and joining positive peer networks; resisting peer pressure; and academic and organizational skills. Adjunct individual sessions are held monthly to monitor and reinforce children's attainment of classroom and social behavior goals (e.g., avoiding fights with peers; resisting peer pressure) as well as to address specific attributional biases and social problem-solving deficiencies that children have had in recent social conflicts with peers, teachers, or parents.

The *Coping Power Parent Component* is derived from social learning theory–based parent training programs developed and evaluated by prominent clinician-researchers in the field of child aggression (Patterson, Reid, Jones, & Conger, 1975). Over the course of the Coping Power parent program, parents learn skills for (a) identifying specific prosocial and problem target behaviors in their children; (b) rewarding appropriate child behaviors and ignoring attention-seeking behaviors; (c) giving effective instructions and establishing age-appropriate rules and expectations for their children in the home; (d) applying effective consequences to negative child behaviors; (e) managing child behavior outside the home; and (f) establishing ongoing family communication structures in the home (such as weekly family meetings). In addition to these "standard" parenting skills, parents also learn additional skills that support the social-cognitive and problem-solving skills that their children are learning in the Coping Power Child Component. These parent skills are introduced at the same time that the respective child skills are introduced, so that parents and children can work together on what they are learning at home. For example, parents learn to set up homework support structures and to reinforce organizational skills around homework completion as the children are learning study and organizational skills. Parents learn to apply the problem-solving model to family problems so that the skills the children are learning will be prompted and reinforced in the family context. A final section of the Coping Power parent component includes sessions on stress management for parents. This segment aims to help parents learn to remain calm and in control during stressful or irritating disciplinary interactions with their children.

Treatment of Depression

Youth-directed cognitive behavioral interventions that address the cognitive, interpersonal, and familial risk factors for depression described above have proven to be effective in reducing depression symptoms in clinically (Brent et al., 1997; Lewinsohn, Clarke, Hops, & Andrews, 1990) and non-clinically (e.g., Stark, 1990) depressed children and adolescents. Interpersonal psychotherapy, which conceptualizes depression symptoms within the interpersonal context and focuses on identifying and altering maladaptive interpersonal patterns, has also been shown to effectively treat depression in adolescents (Mufson, Weissman, Moreau, & Garfinkel, 1999; Rosello & Bernal, 1999). Intervention with individuals from youths' primary environments (i.e., parents, family, school) is also seen as essential for reinforcing children's use of coping skills and development of new adaptive schemas outside the therapy setting, as well as for altering contextual factors that contribute to the onset and maintenance of their depressive symptoms (e.g., limited social support, conflictual and punitive family milieu, parental psychopathology). However, while multicomponent cognitive behavioral interventions that include parent training components produce significant reductions in depression symptoms and significant improvements in remission rates, research has yet to demonstrate enhanced effects of multicomponent or family-based interventions over and above child-only interventions for youths with depressive disorders (for review, see Stark, Sander, Yancy, Bronik, & Hoke, 2000).

ACTION Treatment Program

The ACTION program is a cognitive behavioral intervention program for childhood depression with child, parent, and teacher/school consultation components (Stark, 1990; Stark et al., 2000). The developers of the ACTION program have published a therapist manual that describes the intervention in a session-by-session format (Stark & Kendall, 1996) as well as an accompanying child workbook (Stark et al., 1996).

The *Child Component of the ACTION Program* offers 30 sessions with intervention strategies designed to target specific cognitive, affective, and interpersonal disturbances that underlie children's depressive symptoms. To teach children to use their thoughts and mood as cues to engage in coping activities, therapists progressively lead children through intervention modules on affective education, problem solving, emotion regulation, cognitive restructuring, assertiveness training, self-evaluation/self-improvement, and programming for generalization of skills. Interactive games and activities are first used to provide children with a vocabulary for describing their affective experiences and for therapists to demonstrate empathic understanding of the children's emotional experiences. Pleasant events scheduling (including activities likely to lead to a sense of mastery) is then used to boost children's mood and establish the link between their thoughts, actions, and emotions. Children are then taught to adopt a problem-solving approach to managing negative mood states and reducing stressors. Through interactive modeling and rehearsal activities using hypothetical and real-life problem situations, children learn to generate and enact effective coping strategies such as adaptive self-statements, relaxation, distraction, social interaction, exercise, and other pleasurable activities. Modifying children's maladaptive cognitions is a central focus of the intervention; however this is not emphasized until children develop a range of effective coping skills, which generally occurs midway through the program. During this module, children are taught to become "thought detectives" who identify maladaptive thoughts and schemas (i.e., "I am no good"; "No one loves me") and learn to generate alternative interpretations (i.e., "There are things I am good at and things I am not so good at, just like everyone else"; "Dad loves me, he just shows it in his own way"). Children are taught to conduct behavioral experiments that provide contradictory evidence for existing maladaptive schemas and supporting evidence for new, more adaptive schemas. The last portion of the child component focuses on improving children's self-perceptions and facilitating the transfer of their new skills to other settings.

The *Parent Component of the ACTION Program* is implemented at the same time as the child component and is designed to create more positive family environments in which children's gains can be fostered and maintained. Parents are taught to use positive behavior management procedures similar to those described for the Coping Power program to reinforce positive affect and behavior in their children. Specific emphasis is placed on parents' participation in pleasurable activities with their children and increased provision of praise and decreased criticism of their child. Parents are taught similar strategies for coping with negative mood states as the children. This intervention component has dual aims, to help parents model and reinforce the use of adaptive coping skills for their children and to decrease the likelihood that they will direct harsh verbal attacks toward their children when they become emotionally aroused. Finally, parents are taught empathic listening skills to help them create more validating environments for their children.

IMPLICATIONS FOR SCHOOL PSYCHOLOGY

Developmental psychopathology provides an inclusive framework for understanding the complex and dynamic processes that shape children's behavior as they develop. This is illustrated in the description of the individual, familial and contextual characteristics that interact to determine whether children develop conduct problems or depression. Equally rich models are available for other common mental health and learning problems in children (Cicchetti & Cohen, 2006). By taking a developmental psychopathology perspective, school psychologists will be best able to understand the causative risk and protective factors for mental health and learning problems in children. In turn, this will arm school psychologists with a sound empirical basis for assessing and intervening with students in need.

REFERENCES

Achenbach, T. M. (1974). *Developmental psycho-pathology*. New York: Ronald Press.

Achenbach, T. M. (1991). *Integrative guide for the 1991 CBCL/4-18, YSR and TRF profiles*. Burlington: University of Vermont, Department of Psychiatry.

American Psychiatric Association. (2000). *Diagnostic and statistical manual of mental disorders* (4th ed., Text Revision). Washington, DC: American Psychiatric Press.

Arseneault, L., Tremblay, R.E., Boulerice, B., & Saucier, J.F. (2002). Obstetric complications and adolescent violent behaviors: Testing two developmental pathways. *Child Development, 73*, 496–508.

Barber, B. K. (1996). Parental psychological control: Revisiting a neglected construct. *Child Development, 67*, 3296–3319.

Barry, T. D., Dunlap, S. T., Cotton, S. J., Lochman, J. E., & Wells, K. C. (2005). The influence of maternal stress and distress on disruptive behavior problems in children. *Journal of the American*

Academy of Child and Adolescent Psychiatry, 44, 265–273.

Barry, T. D., Thompson, A., Barry, C. T., Lochman, J. E., Adler, K., & Hill, K. 2007. The importance of narcissism in predicting proactive and reactive aggression in moderately to highly aggressive children. *Aggressive Behavior, 33*, 185–197.

Barth, J. M., Dunlap, S. T., Dane, H., Lochman, J. E., & Wells, K. C. (2004). Classroom environment influences on aggression, peer relations, and academic focus. *Journal of School Psychology, 42*, 115–133.

Birmaher, B., Dahl, R. E., Williamson, D. E., Perel, J. M., Brent, D. A., Axelson, D. A., et al. (1999). *Growth hormone secretion in children and adolescents at high risk for major depressive disorder*. Paper presented at the Child and Adolescent Consortium, Western Psychiatric Institute and Clinic, Pittsburgh, PA.

Birmaher, B., Kaufman, J., Brent, D. A., Dahl, R.E., Perel, J. M., Al-Shabbout, M., et al. (1997). Neuroendocrine response to 5-hydroxy-l-tryptophan in prepubertal children at high risk of major depressive disorder. *Archives of General Psychiatry, 54*, 1113–1119.

Blum, H., Boyle, M., & Offord, D. R. (1988). Single-parent families: Child psychiatric disorder and school performance. *Journal of the American Academy of Child and Adolescent Psychiatry, 27*, 214–219.

Bongers, I. L., Koot, H. M., Van der Ende, J., & Verhulst, F. C. (2004). Developmental trajectories of externalizing behaviors in childhood and adolescence. *Child Development, 75*, 1523–1537.

Brennan, P. A., Grekin, E. R., & Mednick, S. A. (1999). Maternal smoking during pregnancy and adult male criminal outcomes. *Archives of General Psychiatry, 56*, 215–219.

Brent, D. A., Holder, D., Kolko, D., Birmaher, B., Baugher, M., Roth, C., et al. (1997). A clinical psychotherapy trial for adolescent depression comparing cognitive, family, and supportive therapy. *Archives of General Psychiatry, 54*, 877–885.

Brestan, E. V., & Eyberg, S. M. (1998). Effective psychosocial treatments of conduct-disordered children and adolescents: 29 years, 82 studies, and 5,272 kids. *Journal of Clinical Child Psychology, 27*, 180–189.

Cantwell, D. P., Lewinsohn, P. M., Rhode, P., & Seely, J. (1996). Correspondence between adolescent report and parent report of psychiatric diagnostic data. *Journal of the American Academy of Child and Adolescent Psychiatry, 36*, 610–619.

Caspi, A., McClay, J., Moffitt, T., Mill, J., Martin, J., Craig, I. W., et al. (2002). Role of genotype in the cycle of violence in maltreated children. *Science, 297*, 851–854.

Cicchetti, D., & Cohen, D. J. (2006). *Developmental Psychopathology* (2nd Ed.). New York: Wiley.

Coie, J. D., & Dodge, K. A. (1998). Aggression and antisocial behavior. In N. Eisenberg (Ed.) & W. Damon (Series Ed.). *Handbook of child psychology: Volume 3. Social, emotional and personality development* (5th ed., pp. 779–862). New York: Wiley.

Coie, J. D., Dodge, K. A., & Kupersmidt, J. (1990). Peer group behavior and social status. In S. Asher & J. Coie (Eds.), *Peer rejection in childhood* (pp. 17–59). New York: Cambridge University Press.

Coie, J. D., Lochman, J. E., Terry, R. & Hyman, C. (1992). Predicting early adolescent disorders from childhood aggression and peer rejection. *Journal of Consulting and Clinical Psychology, 60*, 783–792.

Cole, D. A. (1991). Preliminary support for a competency-based model of depression in children. *Journal of Abnormal Psychology, 100*, 181–190.

Conduct Problems Prevention Research Group (1992). A developmental and clinical model for the prevention of conduct disorder: The Fast Track Program. *Development and Psychopathology, 4*, 509–527.

Coon, H., Carey, G., Corley, R., & Fulker, D. W. (1992). Identifying children in the Colorado adoption project at risk for conduct disorder. *Journal of the American Academy of Child and Adolescent Psychiatry, 31*, 503–511.

Crick, N. R., & Dodge, K. A. (1994). A review and reformulation of social information-processing mechanisms in children's social adjustment. *Psychological Bulletin, 115*, 74–101.

Crick, N. R., & Werner, N. E. (1998). Response decision processes in relational and overt aggression. *Child Development, 69*, 1630–1639.

Curry, J. F., & Craighead, W. E. (1990). Attributional style in clinically depressed and conduct disordered adolescents. *Journal of Consulting and Clinical Psychology, 58*, 109–116.

Dabbs, J. M., & Morris, R. (1990). Testosterone, social class, and antisocial behavior in a sample of 4,462 men. *Psychological Science, 1*, 209–211.

Dahl, R. E., Ryan, N. D., Puig-Antich, J., Nguyen, N. A., Al-Shabbout, M., Meyer, V. A., et al. (1991). 24-hour cortisol measures in adolescents with major depression: A controlled study. *Biological Psychiatry, 30*, 25–36.

Delaney-Black, V., Covington, C., Templin, T., Ager, J., Nordstrom-Klee, B., Martier, S., et al. (2000). Teacher-assessed behavior of children prenatally exposed to cocaine. *Pediatrics, 106*, 782–791.

Dodge, K. A., Laird, R., Lochman, J. E., Zelli, A., & the Conduct Problems Prevention Research Group (2002). Multi-dimensional latent construct analysis of children's social information processing patterns: Correlations with aggressive behavior problems. *Psychological Assessment, 14*, 60–73.

Dodge, K. A., Lochman, J. E., Harnish, J. D., Bates, J. E., & Pettit, G. S. (1997). Reactive and proactive aggression in school children and psychiatrically impaired chronically assaultive youth. *Journal of Abnormal Psychology, 106*, 37–51.

Dodge, K. A., Pettit, G. S., McClaskey, C. L., & Brown, M. M. (1986). Social competence in children. *Monographs of the Society for Research in Child Development, 51*, 1–85.

Dunn, S. E., Lochman, J. E., & Colder, C. R. (1997). Social problem-solving skills in boys with conduct and oppositional disorders. *Aggressive Behavior, 23*, 457–469.

Edelbrock, C. (1984). Developmental considerations. In T. Ollendick & M. Hersen (Eds.), *Child behavioral assessment: Principles and procedures* (pp. 20–37). Elmsford, NY: Pergamon Press.

Eley, T. C., Deater-Deckard, K., Fombonne, E., Fulker, D. W., & Plomin, R. (1998). An adoption study of depressive symptoms in middle childhood. *Journal of Child Psychology and Psychiatry, 39*, 337–345.

Emslie, G. J., Rush, A. J., Weinberg, W. A., Kowatch, R. A., Hughes, C. W., Carnody, T., et al. (1997). A double-blind, randomized, placebo-controlled trial of fluoxetine in children and adolescents with depression. *Archives of General Psychiatry, 54*, 1031–1037.

Essau, C. A., & Petermann, F. (1997). *Developmental psychopathology: Epidemiology, diagnostics, and treatment*. Amsterdam, The Netherlands: Harwood Academic Publishers.

Fite, P. J., Colder, C. R., Lochman, J. E., & Wells, K. C. (2006). The mutual influence of parenting and boys' externalizing behavior problems. *Journal of Applied Developmental Psychology, 27*, 151–164.

Garber, J. (1984). Classification of child psychopathology: A developmental perspective. *Child Development, 55*, 30–48.

Garber, J. (2000). Development and depression. In A. J. Sameroff, M. Lewis, & S. M. Miller (Eds), *Handbook of developmental psychopathology* (2nd ed., pp. 467–490). Dordrecht, The Netherlands: Kluwer Academic Publishers.

Garber, J., & Horowitz, J. J. (2002). Depression in children. In I. H. Gotlib & C. L. Hammen (Eds.), *Handbook of depression* (pp. 510–540). New York: Guilford.

Gladstone, T. R. G., & Kaslow, N. J. (1995). Depression and attributions in children and adolescents: A meta-analytic review. *Journal of Abnormal Child Psychology, 23*, 597–606.

Goodyer, I. M., Herbert, J., & Altham, P. E. (1998). Adrenal steroid secretion and major depression in 8- to 16-year-olds: III. Influence of cortisol/DHEA ratio at presentation on subsequent rates of disappointing life events and persistent major depression. *Psychological Medicine, 28,* 265–273.

Gouze, K. R. (1987). Attention and social problem solving as correlates of aggression in preschool males. *Journal of Abnormal Child Psychology, 15,* 181–197.

Guerra, N. G., Huesmann, L. R., Tolan, P. H., VanAcker, R., & Eron, L. D. (1995). Stressful events and individual beliefs as correlates of economic disadvantage and aggression among urban children. *Journal of Consulting and Clinical Psychology, 63,* 513–528.

Hawkins, J. D., Catalano, R. F., & Miller, J. Y. (1992). Risk and protective factors for alcohol and other drug problems in adolescence and early adulthood: Implications for substance abuse prevention. *Psychological Bulletin, 112,* 64–105.

Herjanic, B., & Reich, W. (1997). Development of a structured psychiatric interview for children: Agreement between child and parent on individual symptoms. *Journal of Abnormal Child Psychology, 25,* 21–31.

Hibbs, E. D., & Jensen, P. S. (2005). *Psychosocial treatments for child and adolescent disorders: Empirically based strategies for clinical practice* (2nd Ed.) Washington, DC: American Psychological Association.

Hilsman, R., & Garber, J. (1995). A test of the cognitive diathesis-stress model of depression in children: Academic stressors, attributional style, perceived competence, and control. *Journal of Personality and Social Psychology, 69,* 370–380.

Hoffman, K. B., Cole, D. A., Martin, J. M., Tram, J., & Serocynski, A. D. (2000). Are the discrepancies between self- and others' appraisals of competence predictive or reflective of depressive symptoms in children and adolescents: A longitudinal study, Part II. *Journal of Abnormal Psychology, 109,* 651–662.

Hughes, J. H. (2000). The essential role of theory in the science of teaching children: Beyond empirically supported treatments. *Journal of School Psychology, 38,* 301–330.

Ingoldsby, E. M., & Shaw, D. S. (2002). Neighborhood contextual factors and early-starting antisocial pathways. *Clinical Child and Family Psychology Review, 5,* 21–55.

Jensen, P. S. (1999). Links among theory, research, and practice: Cornerstones of clinical scientific progress. *Journal of Clinical Child Psychology, 28,* 553–557.

Jones, N. A., Field, T., Fox, N. A., Lundy, B., & Davalos, M. (1997). EEG activation in 1-month-old infants of depressed mothers. *Development and Psychopathology, 9,* 491–505.

Kaslow, N. J., Rehm, L. P., Pollack, S. L., & Siegel, A. W. (1988). Attributional style and self-control behavior in depressed and nondepressed children and their parents. *Journal of Abnormal Child Psychology, 16,* 163–175.

Kazdin, A. E. (1999). Current (lack of) status of theory in child and adolescent psychotherapy research. *Journal of Clinical Child Psychology, 28,* 533–543.

Kazdin, A. E. & Weisz, J. R. (2003). *Evidence-based psychotherapies for children and adolescents.* New York: Guilford.

Kellam, S. G., Ling, X., Merisca, R., Brown, C. H., & Ialongo, N. (1998). The effect of the level of aggression in the first grade classroom on the course and malleability of aggressive behavior into middle school. *Development and Psychopathology, 10,* 165–185.

Kelly, J. J., Davis, P. O., & Henschke, P. N. (2000). The drug epidemic: Effects on newborn infants and health resource consumption at a tertiary perinatal centre. *Pediatric Child Health, 36,* 262–264.

Kendall, P. C. & Lochman, J. E. (1994). Cognitive-behavioral therapies. In M. Rutter, L. Hersov, & E. Taylor (Eds.), *Child and adolescent psychiatry: Modern approaches* (3rd Ed.) Oxford, England: Blackwell Scientific Publications.

Kistner, J., Balthazor, M., Risi, S., & Burton, C. (1999). Predicting dysphoria in adolescence from actual and perceived peer acceptance in childhood. *Journal of Clinical Child Psychology, 28,* 94–104.

Kovacs, M. (1992). *Children's Depression Inventory (CDI).* New York: Multi-Health Systems.

Lewinsohn, P. M., Clarke, G., Hops, H., & Andrews, J. (1990). Cognitive-behavioral treatment for depressed adolescents. *Behavior Therapy, 21,* 385–401.

Little, S. A., & Garber, J. (2000). Interpersonal and achievement orientations and specific hassles predicting depressive and aggressive symptoms in children. *Cognitive Therapy and Research, 24,* 651–671.

Lochman, J. E. (2000). Theory and empiricism in intervention research: A dialectic to be avoided. *Journal of School Psychology, 38,* 359–368.

Lochman, J. E. (2004). Contextual factors in risk and prevention research. *Merrill Palmer Quarterly, 50,* 311–325.

Lochman, J. E. (2006). Translation of research into interventions. *International Journal of Behavioral Development, 31,* 31–38.

Lochman, J. E., Barry, T. D., Powell, N. R., Boxmeyer, C., & Holmes, K. (2008). Externalizing conditions. In M. L. Wolraich, D. D. Drotar, P. H. Dworkin, & E. C. Perrin (Eds.), *Developmental and Behavioral Pediatrics.* Philadelphia: Mosby, Inc.

Lochman, J. E., Boxmeyer, C. L., & Jackson, M. F. (2007). School-based intervention for youth antisocial behavior: The Coping Power Program.

Advances in School-Based Mental Health, Vol. 2., Kingston, NJ: Civil Research Institute.

Lochman, J. E., & Dodge, K. A. (1994). Social-cognitive processes of severely violent, moderately aggressive, and nonaggressive boys. *Journal of Consulting & Clinical Psychology, 62*, 366–374.

Lochman, J. E., & Dodge, K. A. (1998). Distorted perceptions in dyadic interactions of aggressive and nonaggressive boys: Effects of prior expectations, context, and boys' age. *Development & Psychopathology, 10*, 495–512.

Lochman, J. E., Magee, T. N., & Pardini, D. (2003). Cognitive behavioral interventions for children with conduct problems. In M. Reinecke & D. Clark (Eds.), *Cognitive therapy over the lifespan: Theory, research and practice* (pp. 441–476). Cambridge, UK: Cambridge University Press.

Lochman, J. E., Nelson, W. M. III, & Sims, J. P. (1981). A cognitive behavioral program for use with aggressive children. *Journal of Clinical Child Psychology, 10*, 146–148.

Lochman, J. E., & Salekin, R.T. (2003). Prevention and intervention with aggressive and disruptive children: Next steps in behavioral intervention research. *Behavior Therapy, 34*, 413–419.

Lochman, J. E., & Wayland, K. K. (1994). Aggression, social acceptance, and race as predictors of negative adolescent outcomes. *Journal of the American Academy of Child and Adolescent Psychiatry, 33*, 1026–1035.

Lochman, J. E., Wayland, K. K., & White, K. J. (1993). Social goals: Relationship to adolescent adjustment and to social problem solving. *Journal of Abnormal Child Psychology, 21*, 135–151.

Lochman, J. E., & Wells, K. C. (2002a). Contextual social-cognitive mediators and child outcome: A test of the theoretical model in the Coping Power Program. *Development and Psychopathology, 14*, 971–993.

Lochman, J. E., & Wells, K. C. (2002b). The Coping Power Program at the middle school transition: Universal and indicated prevention effects. *Psychology of Addictive Behaviors, 16*, S40–S54.

Lochman, J. E., & Wells, K. C. (2003). Effectiveness study of Coping Power and classroom intervention with aggressive children: Outcomes at a one-year follow-up. *Behavior Therapy, 34*, 493–515.

Lochman, J. E., & Wells, K. C. (2004). The Coping Power program for preadolescent aggressive boys and their parents: Outcome effects at the one-year follow-up. *Journal of Consulting and Clinical Psychology, 72*, 571–578.

Lochman, J. E., Wells, K. C., & Lenhart, L. (2008). *Coping power: Child group facilitator's guide..* New York: Oxford University Press.

Lochman, J. E., Whidby, J. M., & FitzGerald, D. P. (2000). Cognitive-behavioral assessment and treatment with aggressive children. In P. C.

Kendall (Ed.), *Child and adolescent therapy: Cognitive-behavioral procedures*, (2nd ed., pp. 31–87). New York: Guilford.

Loeber, R., & Stouthamer-Loeber, M., (1998). Development of juvenile aggression and violence: Some common misconceptions and controversies. *American Psychologist, 53*, 242–259.

Loeber, R., & Farrington, D. P. (2001). The significance of child delinquency. In R. Loeber & D. P. Farrington (Eds.), *Child delinquents: Development, intervention, and service needs* (pp. 1–22). Thousand Oaks, CA: Sage.

Loeber, R., Farrington, D. P., Stouthamer-Loeber, M., Moffitt, T. E., & Caspi, A. (1998). The development of male offending: Key findings from the first decade of the Pittsburgh Youth Study. *Studies on Crime & Crime Prevention, 7*, 141–171.

Luthar, S. S. (1999). *Children in poverty: Risk and protective factors in adjustment.* Thousand Oaks, CA: Sage.

Luthar, S. S., Burack, J. A., Cicchetti, D., & Weisz, J. R. (1997). *Developmental psychopathology: Perspectives on adjustment, risk, and disorder.* Cambridge, UK: Cambridge University Press.

Majumder, P. P., Moss, H. B., & Murrelle, L. (1998). Familial and nonfamilial factors in the prediction of disruptive behaviors in boys at risk for substance abuse. *Journal of Child Psychology and Psychiatry, 39*, 203–213.

Mash, E. J., & Terdal, L. G. (1997). Assessment of child and family disturbance: A behavioral-systems approach. In E. J. Mash & L. G. Terdal (Eds.). *Assessment of childhood disorders* (3rd ed., pp. 3–68). New York: Guilford Press.

Masten, A. S., Best, K. M., & Garmezy, N. (1990). Resilience and development: Contributions from the study of children who overcome adversity. *Development and Psychopathology, 2*, 425–444.

Maughan, B. (2001). Conduct disorder in context. In J. Hill & B. Maughan (Eds.), *Conduct disorders in childhood and adolescence* (pp. 169–201). Cambridge, UK: Cambridge University Press.

McGuffin, P., Katz, R., Watkins, S., & Rutherford, J. (1996). A hospital-based twin registry study of the heritability of DSM-IV unipolar depression. *Archives of General Psychiatry, 53*, 129–136.

Monroe, S. M., Rohde, P., Seeley, J. R., & Lewinsohn, P. M. (1999). Life events and depression in adolescence: Relationship loss as a prospective risk factor for first onset of major depressive disorder. *Journal of Abnormal Psychology, 108*, 606–614.

Mufson, L., Weissman, M. M., Moreau, D., & Garfinkel, R. (1999). Efficacy of interpersonal psychotherapy for depressed adolescents. *Archives of General Psychiatry, 56*, 573–579.

Mullins, L. L., Siegel, L. J., & Hodges, K. (1985). Cognitive problem-solving and life event correlates of depressive symptoms in children. *Journal of Abnormal Child Psychology, 13*, 305–314.

Nagin, D., Pogarsky, G., & Farrington, D. (1997). Adolescent mothers and the criminal behavior of their children. *Law and Society, 31,* 137–162.

Nagin, D., & Tremblay, R. E. (1999). Trajectories of boys' physical aggression, opposition, and hyperactivity on the path to physically violent and nonviolent juvenile delinquency. *Child Development, 70,* 1181–1196.

Nolen-Hoeksema, S., Girgus, J. S., & Seligman, M. E. (1992). Predictors and consequences of childhood depressive symptoms: A 5-year longitudinal study. *Journal of Abnormal Psychology, 101,* 405–422.

Pardini, D. A., Lochman, J. E., & Frick, P. J. (2003). Callous/unemotional traits and social cognitive processes in adjudicated youth. *Journal of the American Academy of Child and Adolescent Psychiatry, 42,* 364–371.

Patterson, G. R., Reid, J. B., & Dishion T. J. (1992). *Antisocial boys.* Eugene, OR: Castalia.

Patterson, G. R., Reid, J. B., Jones, R. R., & Conger, R. E. (1975). *A social learning approach, Vol. 1. Families with aggressive children.* Eugene, OR: Castalia.

Pennington, B. F. (2002). *The development of psychopathology: Nature and nurture.* New York: Guilford.

Pepler, D. J., Craig, W. M., & Roberts, W. I. (1998). Observations of aggressive and nonaggressive children on the school playground. *Merrill-Palmer Quarterly, 44,* 55–76.

Plomin, R., & Rutter, M. (1998). Child development, molecular genetics, and what to do with genes once they are found. *Child Development, 69,* 1223–1242.

Raine, A., Brennan, P., & Mednick, S. A. (1997). Interactions between birth complications and early maternal rejection in predisposing individuals to adult violence: Specificity to serious, early onset violence. *American Journal of Psychiatry, 154,* 1265–1271.

Rasanen, P., Hakko, H., Isobarmi, M., Hodgins, S., Jarvelin, M. R., & Tiihonen, J. (1999). Maternal smoking during pregnancy and risk of criminal behavior among male offspring in the northern Finland 1996 birth cohort. *American Journal of Psychiatry, 156,* 857–862.

Reynolds, C. R., & Kamphaus, R. W. (2004). *Behavior assessment system for children* (2nd Ed.) Circle Pines, MN: AGS Publishing.

Reynolds, C. R., & Richmond, B. O. (1978). What I think and feel: A revised measure of children's manifest anxiety. *Journal of Abnormal Psychology, 6,* 271–280.

Rosello, J., & Bernal, G. (1999). The efficacy of cognitive-behavioral and interpersonal treatments for depression in Puerto Rican adolescents. *Journal of Consulting and Clinical Psychology, 67,* 734–745.

Rudolph, K. D., Hammen, C., & Burge, D. (1994). Interpersonal functioning and depressive symptoms in childhood: Addressing the issues of specificity and comorbidity. *Journal of Abnormal Child Psychology, 22,* 355–371.

Rueter, M. A., Scaramella, L., Wallace, L. E., & Conger, R. D. (1999). First onset of depressive or anxiety disorders predicted by the longitudinal course of internalizing symptoms and parent-adolescent disagreements. *Archives of General Psychiatry, 56,* 726–732.

Rutter, M., & Sroufe, L. A. (2000). Developmental psychopathology: Concepts and challenges. *Development and Psychopathology, 12,* 265–296.

Sampson, J. H., & Laub, R. J. (1993). *Crime in the making: Pathways and turning points through life.* Cambridge, MA: Harvard University Press.

Scarpa, A., Bowser, F. M., Fikretoglu, D., Romero, N., & Wilson, J. W. (1999). Effects of community violence II: Interactions with psychophysiologic functioning. *Psychophysiology, 36* (Supplement), 102.

Shaffer, D., Fisher, R., Lucas, C. R., Dulcan, M., & Schwab-Stone, M. E. (2000). NIMH Diagnostic Interview Schedule for Children—Version IV (NIMH DISC-IV): Description, differences from previous versions and reliability of some common diagnoses. *Journal of the American Academy of Child and Adolescent Psychiatry, 39,* 28–38.

Shaw, D. S., Keenan, K., & Vondra, J. I. (1994). Developmental precursors of externalizing behavior: Ages 1 to 3. *Developmental Psychology, 30,* 355–364.

Shaw, D. S., Owens, E. B., Vondra, J. I., & Keenan, K. (1996). Early risk factors and pathways in the development of early disruptive behavior problems. *Development and Psychopathology, 8,* 679–699.

Smith, S. W., Lochman, J. E., & Daunic, A. P. (2005). Managing aggression using cognitive-behavioral interventions: State of the practice and future directions. *Behavior Disorders, 30,* 227–240.

Sroufe, L. A., & Rutter, M. (1984). The domain of developmental psychopathology. *Child Development, 55,* 17–29.

Stark, K. D. (1990). *Childhood depression: School-based intervention.* New York: Guilford Press.

Stark, K. D., & Kendall, P. C. (1996). *Treating depressed children: Therapist manual for "Action."* Ardmore, PA: Workbook Publishing.

Stark, K. D., Kendall, P. C., McCarthy, M., Stafford, M., Barron, R., & Thomeer, M. (1996). *ACTION: A workbook for overcoming depression.* Ardmore, PA: Workbook Publishing.

Stark, K. D., Sander, J. B., Yancy, M. G., Bronik, M. D., & Hoke, J. A. (2000). Treatment of depression in childhood and adolescence: Cognitive-behavioral procedures for the individual and family. In P. C. Kendall (Ed.), *Child and adolescent therapy: Cognitive-behavioral procedures* (2nd ed., pp. 173–234). New York: Guilford Press.

Stein, D., Williamson, D. E., Birmaher, B., Brent, D. A., Kaufman, J., Dahl, R. E., et al. (2000). Parent-child bonding and family functioning in depressed children and children at high risk and low risk for future depression. *Journal of the American Academy of Child & Adolescent Psychiatry, 39,* 1387–1395.

Tomarken, A. J., Simien, C., & Garber, J. (1994). Resting frontal brain asymmetry discriminates adolescent children of depressed mothers from low risk controls. *Psychophysiology, 3,* S97–S98.

Weiss, B., Dodge, K. A., Bates, J. E., & Pettit, G. S. (1992). Some consequences of early harsh discipline: Child aggression and maladaptive social information processing style. *Child Development, 63,* 1321–1335.

Wells, K. C., Lochman, J. E., & Lenhart, L. (2008). *Coping power: Parent group facilitator's guide.* New York: Oxford University Press.

Zelli, A., Dodge, K. A., Lochman, J. E., Laird, R. D., & the Conduct Problems Prevention Research Group (1999). The distinction between beliefs legitimizing aggression and deviant processing of social cues: Testing measurement validity and the hypothesis that biased processing mediates the effects of beliefs on aggression. *Journal of Personality and Social Psychology, 77,* 150–166.

PSYCHOLOGICAL AND EDUCATIONAL ASSESSMENT

•

CHAPTER 11

ROLES OF DIAGNOSIS AND CLASSIFICATION
IN SCHOOL PSYCHOLOGY

ERIN DOWDY
University of California–Santa Barbara
KRISTEN L. MAYS AND RANDY W. KAMPHAUS
Georgia State University
CECIL R. REYNOLDS
Texas A&M University

The field of psychology has been grappling with the issue of classification for decades (Achenbach, 1998, 2001). While practitioners, researchers, and educators agree about the importance of classification for a variety of reasons, including enhanced communication among professionals, ease of description, the necessity of valid taxonomies for grouping individuals for research, and the ability to differentiate individuals (Scotti & Morris, 2000; Blashfield, 1998; Cantwell, 1996), consensus on the optimal way to classify individuals has not been achieved. Despite this lack of agreement, psychologists frequently engage in the practice of diagnosing and classifying individuals. In fact, the classification of children's problems and strengths has long been, and is likely to remain, a central function of school psychology. School psychologists are often expected to provide diagnostic and classification services for the children, families, schools, and community members that they serve. Although classifying individuals might be an expected duty, school psychologists can provide these services in a meaningful way that facilitates treatment planning and leads to improved outcomes. The direct link that is often made from classification to service delivery highlights the importance of this role for school psychologists.

The interest and importance of classification does not end solely with those individuals receiving services. Parents, teachers, pediatricians, school administrators, policy makers, and a myriad of others have a vested interest in the accurate diagnoses and classification of these disorders. For example, parents may want to better understand their child's difficulties, while teachers may need to know how to teach children presenting with a cluster of symptoms more effectively. Additionally, pediatricians may want to ensure that they are medically managing a child's symptoms appropriately, while policy makers may need to plan for systemic reform of the special education system based on how children are classified for services. Classification is an important tool that psychologists frequently use that can benefit not only the individuals who are classified but a variety of other individuals as well. The necessity for accurate classification is vital for both scientific progress and the effective treatment of individuals. It is imperative that school psychologists understand the many issues involved in the classification and diagnosis of children.

First, school psychologists should recognize that the terms and processes involved in classification and diagnosis are not entirely interchangeable. While it is human nature to group or classify things according to some order, this process is not always diagnostic. For example, while it is not uncommon for school psychologists to categorize students as "overachievers," "athletes," or "musicians," these are not considered diagnoses per se.

In general, the term classification represents the overarching process of ordering individuals according to a general set of rules, whereas the term diagnosis is reserved for a more restrictive, formal process of classification according to a specific medical (or medical-like) diagnostic system (e.g., Diagnostic and Statistical Manual of Mental Disorders (DSM-IV-TR); American Psychiatric Association, 2000). Within schools, psychologists generally use the term classification to reflect the process of assigning individuals to the more general special education categories and the term diagnosis to reflect the process of classifying students according to the more specific DSM-IV-TR diagnostic categories.

Classification and diagnosis can vary in terms of the amount and utility of the information that they require. Consider, for instance, the differing amounts of information needed to classify a child as eligible for special education as opposed to making a diagnosis according to a more specific system, such as the DSM-IV-TR. While the determination of eligibility for participation in a school-based, federally reimbursed program for children with an emotional behavior disorder is a form of classification, it is arguably less precise than a medical diagnosis, which provides a detailed picture of the development and nature of the particular type of emotional or behavioral disorder. For example, a child who meets the criteria for classification as a student with an emotional behavioral disorder may additionally meet a more specified set of criteria for major depressive disorder, anxiety disorder, or conduct disorder, all of which vary dramatically in their etiology, course, and prognosis. Although the classification of an emotional behavioral disorder for special education eligibility purposes may be accomplished more easily than the precise classification of major depressive disorder, the latter form of classification leads more readily to specified interventions or treatments. Unfortunately, in some school settings, the classification process ends after eligibility determination and thus, an indepth conceptualization of intraindividual child problems is not achieved. For example, severe attention problems in school that are associated with a substance abuse disorder would be treated very differently than would be the case for attention problems attributable to ADHD. Unfortunately, all too often, school professionals do not make such an important distinction in diagnosis or treatment.

This chapter highlights selected issues of diagnosis that were chosen with one primary objective: to familiarize school psychologists in training with historical, treatment-related, and other diagnostic issues commonly faced by school (and other) psychologists. Knowledge of these issues is central to a school psychologist's ability to develop an adequate long-term perspective on diagnostic issues. This perspective allows the psychologist to incorporate and respond to new diagnostic knowledge in a more sophisticated manner.

USES OF DIAGNOSTIC SYSTEMS

Diagnostic systems continue to be used for a variety of reasons and serve many scientific and clinical objectives. This next section will discuss the utility of classification systems for: enhanced communication, differentiation among individuals, efficient delivery of services, determining service need, facilitation of research and clinical practice, and financial reimbursement. School psychologists will likely employ classification systems for many of these distinct purposes. Furthermore, through an increased awareness of the potential benefits and limitations of classification, school psychologists can utilize classification systems more effectively and become cognizant of how their own classification practices can impact both clients and future research.

Enhanced Communication

A primary purpose for classification is enhanced communication among a variety of professionals (Blashfield, 1998; Scotti & Morris, 2000). Classification allows for a common nomenclature which enables clinicians and researchers to discuss and share information easily. For example, two psychologists working at different schools can easily discuss their success in working with children with anxiety without having to discuss all of the specific anxiety symptoms. However, the ease with which individuals can share and discuss information will be impacted by both the novelty and specificity of the term. A term that is quite new, recently revised, or ill-researched will carry with it less of a common understanding, whereas a familiar, long-standing, well-researched term will enhance communication to a higher degree. For instance, because of a long history of classification work, psychologists have a relatively consistent understanding of a specific case of mental retardation. If a student is being transferred to a new school system with a classification of "mild mental retardation," the receiving school psychologist will have an adequate understanding of the intellectual and adaptive difficulties that this student will face. On the other hand, the consistency of our understanding of the classification of "social maladjustment" is not universal at the time of this writing. As a result, the school psychologist receiving a student with a classification of social maladjustment will have a weaker understanding of the specific abilities and limitations of that particular student. The specificity of the term being used will also enhance communication to varying degrees. For instance, some of the language used in educational systems, such as "emotional behavior disorder," conveys less specific information than a diagnosis of major depressive disorder.

Sample Case—Enhancing Communication

Jorge is a five-year-old male who is entering kindergarten in the fall. His preschool director has sent a letter to his new school, describing Jorge's behavior during the previous year. In this letter the director described Jorge as a child with many behavior problems including setting fires, biting other children, and fighting. The director also indicated that Jorge experienced poor peer relationships and some academic delays. A diagnosis was not included in his records.

In this case, the detailed information about specific behavior problems is helpful in that, prior to personal observation and potentially difficult classroom disruption, the psychologist has a basis for the development of needed assessment and intervention plans. However, by not including a diagnosis, the director omitted a crucial piece of information. According to a psychologist who has assessed Jorge during the previous year, Jorge's development was normal until a few months before being placed in preschool. At that time, he witnessed his mother being shot in an attempted carjacking. The psychologist diagnosed Jorge with a post-traumatic stress disorder (PTSD). Knowledge of this diagnosis and historical information would almost certainly affect the receiving psychologist's conceptualization of this case. Without knowledge of this diagnosis, the psychologist may have initially thought that Jorge was displaying early evidence of a disruptive behavior disorder with a likely chronic course. The diagnosis of PTSD, however,

communicates a different kind of information that relates to Jorge's special needs and dictates a radically different form of intervention as well as prognosis.

If a diagnostic category is highly valid, then knowledge of the diagnosis is more likely to communicate accurate information. A related purpose of classification is that it provides a description of a patient's cluster of symptoms (Blashfield, 1998). Individuals are classified, or placed into groups based on their similarities; classification, therefore, indicates that individuals with similar diagnoses should have similar symptom profiles (Lorr, 1966) and past characteristics (Kagan, 1997). Patients with similar diagnoses would also be readily distinguishable from patients with differing diagnoses (Everitt, 1974). For example, a student classified as having a specific learning disability will likely present differently than a student classified as having severe orthopedic impairment.

Consider the following example, which highlights the importance of using precise terms to describe a patient's symptomology. A school psychologist may describe a child as shy, which is a relatively imprecise term and not a diagnostic label. This description of the child will communicate little information about this child to another psychologist who becomes involved in the child's treatment. When asked, the psychologist may then say that the child is anxious. This description may communicate some additional information about the child's behavior, but we do not yet know if "anxious" is a symptom or a diagnosis. If, however, the psychologist goes on to say that the child has recently been diagnosed with separation anxiety disorder, early onset, the second psychologist may be able to make more specific predictions about the child's behavior. Based on this diagnosis, the new psychologist will be more likely to observe parent and child interactions closely and consider family-based interventions.

Efficient Delivery of Services

The ability to easily communicate and share information as a function of classification thereby ensures more efficient delivery of services (Kamphaus & Frick, 1996). Again, consider the example of a student being transferred to a new school system. Knowledge of the previous classification will allow the receiving school psychologist to anticipate how to best accommodate and serve the new student. A child who arrives at a new school district with the classification of "gifted" is going to create different expectations for service planning than a child who enters with a diagnosis of dementia subsequent to traumatic brain injury.

Labels can, of course, be used to stigmatize a child and result in the delivery of inappropriate or inferior services. The use of a formal, codified system of diagnosis such as the DSM-IV-TR (APA, 2000), or the system of diagnosis in the Individuals with Disabilities Education Improvement Act (IDEIA; the reauthorization of the Individuals with Disabilities Education Act) belies the often informal, derogatory labeling that may occur among less informed teachers or other school personnel. Given the most common characteristics of a diagnosis of major depressive disorder among children, a teacher unaware of the child's formal classification may be prone to calling the student lazy, disinterested, irritable, or worse. However, a formal diagnosis of a depressive disorder would be less derogatory and more accurate. A considerable body of literature (e.g., see Reynolds, 1979), indicates that such informal labeling of children is frequent in educational settings and is most often inaccurate and pejorative.

Determining Service Need

In addition to enhancing communication and providing a clinical description of an individual, classification systems are the most well-developed procedure for determining the need for services. As noted previously, service delivery is often triggered immediately by the classification of a child as eligible for special education. For example, once the child is deemed eligible due to Other Health Impairment (OHI), an individualized education plan (IEP) is developed to specify which services the child should receive. Classification schemes may also be used in determining the parameters of treatment, such as the treatment's intensity and/or duration. For instance, a student classified as having autistic-like characteristics might receive more intensive services, and for a longer period of time, than a student classified as having a specific learning disability. Formal diagnostic systems will likely continue to be used for placement decisions until decision-making systems with better validity, reliability, and practicality are designed.

Sometimes attempts at improving diagnosis and identification of students with disabilities leads to increased subjectivity, learning disabilities

being a prime example. IDEIA allows for movement away from the traditional discrepancy-based model of identification towards a "process that determines if the child responds to scientific, research-based intervention" (IDEIA, 2004, 20 USC §§ 1,400). However, there is very little consensus on how schools currently classify children with learning disabilities and determine their need for more intensive services. The ways in which children are classified as having learning disabilities will undoubtedly influence the determination of service need. For example, if a student is deemed eligible for services due to his failure to respond to specified interventions, then the next logical step would be to determine that he needs additional remediation and intervention services. However, this change in classification may allow for more service delivery prior to classification as eligible for special education services. Regardless of the classification method used for determining a student's specific learning disability, the act of classifying a child should assist in determining what services are needed and provide information regarding the intensity and duration of treatment. As of yet, the use of the so-called response-to-intervention (RTI) model has not clarified the diagnostic process for learning disability determination and leaves great latitude to each educational agency to determine just what constitutes a failure to respond to interventions. This, in turn, leads to difficult situations where diagnosis is situational, but still deemed to represent a disability (e.g., see Reynolds, 2008, for a more detailed discussion).

Sample Case—Determining Service Need

Marta is a 15-year-old high school sophomore who has a lengthy history of academic underachievement. She is frequently cited by teachers for failure to work up to her potential. Consequently, she has always had passing, but few high, grades. She occasionally shows evidence of her academic potential during class discussions and question sessions, when she verbally displays keen insights and an extraordinary memory. If a test is based exclusively on class notes, she does well. In direct contrast, if performance on the test is based on homework assignments, she does poorly. She has seen her high school counselor, who reports that Marta is often sad because of family problems. She is also nervous and somewhat shy. Parent conferences resulted in a referral to her family physician, who did not identify the presence of any significant mental health problems. One day, however, Marta's mother called her homeroom teacher to report that Marta had been hospitalized in a general hospital psychiatric unit for observation because of suicidal threats. The hospital staff completed an evaluation that resulted in the DSM-IV-TR diagnosis of major depression, recurrent and severe.

Because of this diagnosis, school personnel will probably treat Marta differently upon her return to school. First, the diagnosis may or may not make her eligible for special education services, although she would probably receive or be considered for them as her educational performance was negatively impacted. She may be required to meet regularly with the school counselor or psychologist to ensure that she is receiving adequate counseling for school problems associated with her depression. She may also receive additional interventions to improve her homework completion. The purpose of this case is to highlight how the same behaviors can be viewed differently and trigger additional services when provided with classification information. In Marta's case, the school viewed her ongoing depressive behaviors as significant once a diagnostic label was applied. Her eligibility for services, that was heretofore considered unnecessary, was now given appropriate consideration solely due to the addition of a diagnostic label.

Facilitate Research and Clinical Practice

Classification systems also facilitate research and clinical practice, lending further support for the utility of classification systems (Clark, Watson, & Reynolds, 1995; Kamphaus & Frick, 1996). Classification systems allow for organization of the common nomenclature, which aids in the retrieval of information. Specifically, researchers and clinicians can retrieve information for the purpose of interpretation, clinical decision making, and statistical reporting (Scotti & Morris, 2000). A simple literature review on conduct disorder provides a school psychologist with a wealth of information to assist in accurate classification and in clinical decision making regarding effective treatments. The use of classification systems also provides insight into the identification of risk or adjustment status (Kagan, 1997). Namely, with a certain diagnosis, it should be more possible to predict the course of the disorder and track individual developmental pathways (Richters, 1997). Through a literature review a school psychologist might discern that a child

with an earlier onset of conduct disorder would be at higher risk for later problems than a child with later onset (Moffitt, Caspi, Harrington, & Milne, 2002).

Classification should aid in the prediction of effective treatment approaches and interventions (Lewczyk, Garland, Hurlburt, Geanty, & Hough, 2003; Scotti & Morris, 2000), lead to better understanding of symptoms and causes of disorders, and allow for the differentiation of individuals by etiology (Cantwell, 1996). This implies that classification should help guide research and practice for the prevention and treatment of disorders and serve as a concept formation system that may be used to develop theories of psychopathology (Blashfield, 1998). If each case is evaluated with idiosyncratic methods and classified accordingly, a research base cannot be developed as efficiently. Again, mental retardation serves as an excellent example. As a result of comorbidity research, we now know from the American Association on Intellectual and Developmental Disabilities (AAIDD), formerly the American Association on Mental Retardation (AAMR), that children with a diagnosis of mental retardation are at higher risk (20% to 35%) for other mental health problems than children who do not have this disability (15% to 19%). These children are at increased risk for schizophrenia, personality disorders, depression, ADHD, and other mental health problems. A variety of studies have found that the prevalence of psychopathology is nearly four times higher in individuals with mental retardation than in the general population (Masi, 1998; Szymanski & King, 1999; Rush, Bowman, Eidman, Toole, & Mortenson, 2004). Dykens and Hodapp (2001) indicated that as a general rule of thumb, approximately 25% of individuals with mental retardation will have significant psychiatric problems. These findings have led to the prescription that all children with this diagnosis should receive a thorough social-emotional evaluation to ensure that they are not also suffering the ill effects of a significant mental health condition (AAMR, 1992). These comorbidity findings also suggest that psychologists should engage in preventive interventions for children who have been diagnosed with mental retardation.

Similarly, it is now clear that children with a diagnosis of ADHD are at a higher risk for developing an anxiety disorder at a later point in development (Last, 1993). The diagnosis of

ADHD encourages the clinician to be vigilant for additional problems that may not be anticipated if based merely on conventional wisdom. Subsequently, because of findings in other areas of educationally handicapping conditions, such as learning disabilities, orthopedic impairments, and the like, IDEIA legislation now requires a behavioral assessment as part of every school-based determination of student disability. If research is to guide practice, there must be a direct link between the two. Diagnoses provide ways to access research and enlighten practice.

Sample Case—Applying Research Findings

Ivan, a 12-year-old male, was referred for placement in a special education program. He was evaluated on two occasions prior to this referral and was determined to not qualify for special education services at either time. Although he has below-average academic achievement, the test scores found were not low enough to warrant classification into special education. He also showed evidence of hyperactivity and attention problems in previous evaluations, but the symptoms were thought to be subsyndromal. His adjustment to school at that time was poor; he was failing all of his middle school classes, and teachers did not feel that he had the academic competencies to perform the regular curriculum adequately. In addition, teachers noted that his behavior was immature for his age, and he was considered a social outcast. He had difficulty sitting still in class and paying sufficient attention to lectures. His parents noted deteriorating behavior at home and an increasingly negative attitude toward school.

Upon reevaluation, Ivan was found to have significant impairments in cognitive development and adaptive behavior that warranted a diagnosis of mild mental retardation. This diagnosis also triggered a thorough social-emotional assessment consistent with AAIDD guidelines. As a result of further diagnostic work, Ivan was found to meet and exceed diagnostic criteria for ADHD-combined type. The presence of ADHD had previously been overlooked, and his behavior problems were erroneously attributed to global developmental delay (American Association on Mental Retardation, 1992). Consequently, Ivan responded favorably to pharmacological treatment, which resulted in better adaptation in the classroom and improved work output.

Financial Reimbursement

A final practical use of classification systems involves financial reimbursement for services (Scotti & Morris, 2000). Managed care organizations frequently only provide payment for services in those cases in which formal diagnoses are made, and commonly base the amount of allowable services dependent on the severity of the disorder and the subsequent need for services (Scotti & Morris, 2000). By using a common classification nomenclature, service providers can more readily receive reimbursement for the services they render. While school psychologists might not be readily confronted with issues such as reimbursement for services, they are, however, frequently required to classify a child in order to render them eligible to receive services at all. Additional reasons for diagnostic systems remain, such as for their use in advocacy and administrative ease. Apparently, there are enough incentives to use diagnostic systems that they continue to propagate and change form.

These sample cases are intended to show that diagnostic systems exist for many reasons, such as enhancing communication among professionals, description of symptomology, identifying service needs, conducting research and basing practice on research findings, and financial reimbursement. Each goal indicates the pressing need for accurate classification models. Accurate classification for school-age children is particularly critical, as the developmental courses or pathways of children are likely to influence subsequent outcomes (Jimerson, Coffino, & Sroufe, 2007; Sroufe, Egeland, Carlson, & Collins, 2005). Insight into children's adjustment and risk status (Kagan, 1997), tracking developmental pathways (Richters, 1997), differentiating individuals by etiology (Cantwell, 1996), and predicting effective treatment approaches (Scotti & Morris, 2000) are among the most salient reasons that accurate classification in school-age children is important. Psychologists should use diagnostic systems with adequate understanding of their stated objectives and ensure that the diagnostic systems that they are using are appropriate for the fulfillment of those objectives.

CLASSIFICATION SYSTEMS

There are a number of classification systems frequently used in the field of psychology. The classification systems associated with the

2004 reauthorization of the Individuals with Disabilities Education Act (IDEIA, P.L. 108-446) and the DSM-IV-TR (APA, 2000) have had the most substantial influence on the daily diagnostic work of psychologists who practice with school-aged children. While school psychologists will most frequently work within IDEIA and DSM classification systems, they should also be aware of other laws, such as Section 504 of the Rehabilitation Act of 1974 and the Americans with Disabilities Act (ADA). Additional publications, such as the American Association on Mental Retardation's (AAMR; 1992) publication *Mental Retardation: Definition, Classification, and Systems of Support*, also provide classification information.

The Diagnostic and Statistical Manual of Mental Disorders

The modern practice of diagnosis traces its roots to European physicians of the 1600s. The work of Sydenham, Griesenger, and Kraepelin provided the foundation for the development of current diagnostic systems (Kamphaus, Morgan, Cox, & Powell, 1995). Before this era, mental disorders were often thought to be the result of supernatural phenomena, and the mentally ill were treated with scorn, fear, and torture. An early function of diagnosis was to disabuse society of such notions by linking diagnoses to specific, natural (disease) phenomena.

The ancestor of the well-known modern version of the DSM-IV-TR (APA, 2000) was published in 1893. This publication was intended to serve the medical community worldwide; hence, it was entitled the International Classification of Causes of Death (Kamphaus et al., 1995). This manual was the foundation for the modern International Statistical Classification of Disease, Injuries, and Causes of Death (ICD). Despite efforts to create a medical classification system that could be used internationally, differing diagnostic systems (although many of them have some similarity to the ICD) have been used in Egypt, China, and France, among other countries. The ICD system, currently on its tenth version, however, includes an extensive compilation of mental disorders.

The DSM-IV, published in 1994, is currently the most widely used method of psychiatric classification in the United States (Beutler & Malik, 2002). A text revision (TR) in 2000 produced few changes. The first DSM was published in 1952 by the American Psychiatric Association (APA) and included three main categories of psychopathology: mental deficiency, functional disorders, and organic brain symptoms. In 1968, the DSM was revised to include eleven major diagnostic categories (DSM-II), and was the first time that diagnostic criteria for children and adolescents appeared. These criteria appeared in a short section entitled *Disorders of Childhood and Adolescence* (Kamphaus & Frick, 1996). In 1980, the third edition introduced a multiaxial system, the inclusion of explicit criteria, and removed unsubstantiated theoretical inferences (Scotti & Morris, 2000). The DSM-III expanded the section for children and adolescents further under the heading *Disorders Usually Evident in Infancy, Childhood, or Adolescence*. This edition provided additional diagnoses with more descriptive information for each category (Kamphaus & Frick, 1996). Subsequently, the third, revised edition (DSM-III-R) placed ADHD and conduct disorder under the heading *Disruptive Behavior Disorders*, and provided some research evidence for their differentiation. The DSM-III-R emphasized empirical literature and the DSM-IV continued with this emphasis on empirical findings (Scotti & Morris, 2000). The DSM-IV reportedly made modest improvements in the reliability and validity of several diagnostic categories, but reliability estimates for many disorders of childhood and adolescence remain in question (Langenbucher & Nathan, 2006). See Table 11.1 for a summary of DSM diagnoses particularly relevant to children and adolescents.

The DSM-IV filled the gaps in the ICD by providing a comprehensive classification of mental disorders (Kamphaus et al., 1995). Moreover, the latest version of the DSM attempted, for the first time, to provide scientific support for its diagnostic criteria. Much of the work in previous editions was based on "expert" judgment and other rational (nonempirical) methods. The DSM-IV used the following methods to develop many of its classifications (Widiger, Frances, Pincus, Davis, & First, 1991):

- *Literature reviews.* Comprehensive reviews of psychopathology and related research literatures were sought or created in order to advise the work of committees. This process was more systematic than depending on the memories of committee members for a "review of the literature."
- *Data reanalyses.* Some existing large data sets were reanalyzed in order to refine diagnostic criteria. These data sets were

TABLE 11.1 Summary of DSM-IV Axes I and II Diagnoses Relevant to Children and Adolescents[1]

Intellectual	Mental retardation
Learning	Mathematics disorder
	Disorder of written expression
	Reading disorder
Language and speech	Expressive language disorder
	Mixed receptive-expressive
	Language disorder
	Phonological disorder
	Stuttering
	Selective mutism
Motor skills	Developmental coordination disorder
Pervasive developmental	Autistic disorder
	Rhett's disorder
	Childhood disintegrative disorder
	Asperger's disorder
Behavioral	Attention-deficit/Hyperactivity disorder
	Oppositional defiant disorder
	Conduct disorder
	Adjustment disorder with disturbance of conduct
Emotional (anxiety)	Separation anxiety disorder
	Generalized anxiety disorder
	Panic disorder
	Agoraphobia
	Social phobia
	Obsessive compulsive disorder
	Post-traumatic stress disorder
	Adjustment disorder with anxious mood
Emotional (mood)	Major depression*
	Dysthymia*
	Bipolar disorder (I & II)*
	Cyclothymia*
	Adjustment disorder with depressed mood*
Identity	Gender identity disorder of childhood
	Reactive attachment disorder of infancy or early childhood
Physical (eating)	Anorexia nervosa*
	Bulimia nervosa*
	Pica
	Rumination disorder
Physical (motor)	Tourette's disorder
	Chronic motor or vocal tic disorder
	Transient tic disorder
	Stereotypic movement disorder
Physical (elimination)	Encopresis
	Enuresis
Physical (somatic)	Somatization disorder*
	Conversion disorder*
	Pain disorder*
	Hypochondriasis*
	Body dysmorphic disorder*
	Adjustment disorder with physical complaints
Psychosis	Schizophrenia*
Substance-related disorders	Alcohol (amphetamine, cannabis, etc.) dependence*

[1]We are responsible, not the DSM-IV, for the selection of disorders "most relevant" to children and adolescents and the way they are grouped.
*Denotes disorders that have the same criteria for children and adults.
Adapted from Box 3.3 of Kamphaus & Frick (1996) with permission.

used in an iterative fashion for testing the applicability of proposed diagnostic criteria.

• *Field trials.* These data collection efforts were used for testing the reliability and validity of proposed diagnostic categories. A substantial field trial was conducted in order to develop diagnostic criteria for disruptive behavior disorders (Lahey, Applegate, Barkley, & Garfikel, 1994).

DSM-IV-TR Diagnostic Criteria for ADHD

The ADHD criteria of the DSM-IV provide a useful example of the modern status of the DSM system because they are based on extensive research (Lahey et al., 1994). The minimum age for the onset of behaviors for ADHD to be diagnosed is seven years old; impairment must be observed in two or more settings that affect the person's life functioning in some manner for a minimum of six months. In the DSM-IV-TR, two symptom lists yield three subtypes relative to hyperactive symptomatology.

The first type—ADHD, predominantly inattentive type—refers to difficulty in sustaining attention, following and completing instructions, ignoring important stimuli, and organizing. Furthermore, inattention is marked by frequent forgetfulness, loss of necessary items to complete tasks, and failure to give adequate attention to detail. The problems of attention are isolated from hyperactive or impulsive symptoms.

The second type—ADHD, predominantly hyperactive-impulsive type—focuses on the presence of hyperactive and/or impulsive behaviors without problems of inattention. The associated behaviors include fidgeting, inappropriate movement in the classroom or other settings, excessive talking, constant energy, and difficulty in participating in quiet activities. The impulsive symptoms focus on behaviors that exhibit poor impulse control and impatience, especially in activities that require taking turns.

The third type is a combination of the two previous types, with the expression of at least six symptoms identified as being representative of inattention and hyperactivity-impulsivity. This combination is referred to as attention deficit/hyperactivity disorder, combined type.

Modern research has allowed the DSM system to make great strides in its psychometric sophistication (Kamphaus & Frick, 1996). At the same time, even the best diagnostic system is characterized by unwanted imperfections, much

in the same way that psychological tests cannot avoid some amount of error variance. Moreover, even the most sophisticated diagnostic systems are prone to misapplication by poorly trained professionals (Cantwell, 1996; Reynolds, 1992).

The preplanning for DSM-V began in 1999 and is now significantly underway. A major focus of the newest revision of the DSM is to incorporate a comprehensive review of empirical data. Empirical research is sought to allow for, and improve upon, diagnostic decision making. Furthermore, international collaboration is sought to increase the likelihood of the development of a unified DSM/ICD system for classification. The publication of the DSM-V is tentatively planned for release in 2011 and will hopefully provide improvements upon this popular classification method.

The Individuals with Disabilities Education Improvement Act

It would be simplistic to suggest that the exclusive purpose of the Individuals with Disabilities Education Act (IDEA; PL 101-476) was to promulgate a new diagnostic nosology. The intention of the Act was to serve children with special needs in the public school system, rather than in residential or other settings. However, the Act resulted in the development of a system equivalent to a diagnostic system. Under IDEA, students may be classified as eligible for special education services if they meet criteria for one of thirteen disabilities. However, it can readily be seen that the IDEA classification has not benefited from continuous improvement.

Nevertheless, this classification system remains the most popular in U.S. school systems (Kamphaus & Frick, 1996). The categories for severe emotional disturbance, specific learning disabilities, and other conditions (see Table 11.2) are used to determine eligibility for special education and related services. Because of this use, the IDEA classification scheme is more widely used in schools than the DSM-IV-TR. Similar to the DSM-IV-TR classification, in which symptoms must be present *and* there must be impairment in some life functioning or clinically significant distress, IDEA classification has a two-part approach. Under IDEA, a student must first be found to have a disability and then, by reason of this disability, a student must be found to require special education services (McLaughlin, et al., 2006).

Unfortunately, public schools are using this classification system (in sometimes slightly varied

TABLE 11.2 Sample Special Education Eligibility Classifications from the Individuals with Disabilities Education Act

1. The term "children with disabilities" means children with mental retardation, hearing impairments including deafness, speech or language impairments, visual impairments including blindness, serious emotional disturbance, orthopedic impairments, autism, traumatic brain injury, other health impairments, or specific learning disabilities.

2. The term "children with specific learning disabilities" means those children who have a disorder in one or more of the basic psychological processes involved in understanding or in using language, spoken or written, which disorder may manifest itself in imperfect ability to listen, think, speak, read, write, spell, or do mathematical calculations. Such disorders include such conditions as perceptual disabilities, brain injury, minimal brain dysfunction, dyslexia, and developmental aphasia. Such term does not include children who have learning problems which are primarily the result of visual, hearing, or motor disabilities, of mental retardation, of emotional disturbance, or of environmental, cultural, or economic disadvantage. (Section 5[b][4])

3. The term "seriously emotionally disturbed" means a condition exhibiting one or more of the following characteristics over a long period of time and to a marked degree, which adversely affects educational performance:

   a. An inability to learn which cannot be explained by intellectual, sensory, or health factors;
   b. An inability to build or maintain satisfactory relationships with peers and teachers;
   c. Inappropriate types of behavior or feelings under normal circumstances;
   d. A general pervasive mood of unhappiness/depression; or
   e. A tendency to develop physical symptoms or fears associated with personal or school problems.

   The term includes children who are schizophrenic (or autistic). The term does not include children who are socially maladjusted, unless it is determined that they are socially disturbed. (U.S. Department of Health, Education, and Welfare, 1977, p. 42478)

4. The term "autism" means a developmental disability significantly affecting verbal and nonverbal communication and social interaction, generally evident before age three, that adversely affects educational performance. Characteristics of autism—irregularities and impairments in communication, engagement in repetitive activities and stereotyped movements, resistance to environmental change or change in daily routines, and unusual responses to sensory experiences. (U.S. Department of Education, 1991, p. 41271).

forms) in the absence of empirical support. The IDEA diagnostic system has been roundly criticized for its limited conceptualization of severe emotional disturbance (Bower, 1982; Forness & Knitzer, 1992). A quick review of Table 11.2 gives the immediate impression that the IDEA nosology is not so well developed as the most recent edition of the DSM. It appears that researchers in child psychopathology have devoted most of their energies to improving the DSM, leaving the IDEA to suffer continuing neglect. In fact, newer, multivariate approaches to child classification are currently receiving more research attention than the IDEA nosology.

The IDEA has not undergone any significant revisions. When reauthorized in 2004, and renamed the Individuals with Disabilities Education Improvement Act (IDEIA), many of the evaluation procedures and eligibility determinations remained the same and few notable changes were made. Most relevant to the discussion of classification was perhaps the change indicating that local education agencies, when determining whether a child has a specific learning disability, "shall not be required to take into consideration whether a child has a severe discrepancy between achievement and intellectual ability" (IDEIA, 2004, § 614(b)(6)(A)). This indicates that school systems, if they so choose, can use a system that determines if the child responds to intervention to assist in classifying children under the category of specific learning disability. This has direct impact on school psychologists' assessments for, and classifications of, children under this category.

The IDEIA nosology, more concerned with establishing eligibility for services, does not seek the diagnostic specificity of the IDC-10 or DSM-IV-TR that is required to link specific interventions to diagnoses. The IDEIA's only links are to categories of placement in special education, requiring a comprehensive assessment that leads to the development of IEPs (individualized educational plans) where interventions are specified. More detailed diagnoses, such as those suggested in the DSM-IV-TR and similar systems, are required at the IEP stage, whereas more limited diagnostic decisions (i.e., eligible or not eligible for services in the schools) are all that are required in the initial classification stage in the schools. Failure to understand the simple distinction between diagnosis as an eligibility decision and a more refined, detailed diagnosis for developing treatment plans has led some (see, most prominently, Gresham & Gansle, 1992) to the simplistic conclusion that detailed diagnostic systems such as the DSM-IV-TR are irrelevant to practice in school psychology. Obviously, we disagree, for reasons noted throughout this chapter and elsewhere (see e.g., Reynolds, 1992).

CATEGORICAL, DIMENSIONAL, AND PERSON-ORIENTED APPROACHES TO CLASSIFICATION

School psychologists should be aware of the growing consensus that current diagnostic systems, such as the DSM-IV-TR and IDEIA, have lagged behind the increase in knowledge about psychopathology and classification (Beutler & Malik, 2002; Houts, 2002; Helzer & Hudziak, 2000; Jablensky, 1999). A primary concern with current classification systems is the overreliance on the use of purely categorical methods. Categorical systems, such as the DSM-IV-TR and IDEIA, use rules to determine membership in a specific category (Blashfield, 1998). These systems are essentially dichotomous in nature: A child is classified as either having a disability (IDEIA) or a mental disorder (DSM-IV-TR) or not. A parent may legitimately ask classification-related questions that cannot be answered by using categorical systems. For example, a parent may ask, "I was told that my child may have a mild case of ADHD; is that true?" This question is difficult to answer because most categorical systems do not classify disorders on a continuum (although there are exceptions, such as the classification of levels of depression). Similarly, ranking along a continuum on a particular construct is inherently more informative. Height provides yet another example

of the desirability of dimensional approaches to classification. When we are told that someone is tall, we are likely to have a follow-up question: "How tall?"

There seems to be a lack of "goodness of fit" between current categorical classification systems and "clinical reality" (Jablensky, 1999), as verified by empirical findings. Evidence suggests that there are not true or clinically meaningful qualitative points where individuals should be categorically separated, or "diagnosed" (Sroufe, 1997; Widiger, 1992), supporting the need for dimensional methods. Throughout the scientific literature evidence exists suggesting that symptoms of hyperactivity/impulsivity, inattention, conduct problems, depression, and anxiety occur along a continuum, or show evidence of quantitative differences (Deater-Deckard, Reiss, Hetherington, & Plomin, 1997; Fergusson & Horwood, 1995; Hudziak, Wadsworth, Heath, & Achenbach, 1999; Nease, Volk, & Cass, 1999).

Dimensional approaches to classification assume that behavior does not occur dichotomously, but rather along a continuum. Descriptive variables are collected and combined with other correlated variables to form a dimension, which summarizes information about the descriptive variables into an abstract, higher-order variable (Blashfield, 1998). Grouping behaviors by constructs (or dimensions) allows for the classification of all children on a particular dimension or several dimensions of behavior (Meehl, 1995). A dimensional approach allows the clinician to classify the full range of behavior for all children evaluated, much in the way we measure the constructs of height, weight, intelligence, anxiety, and so on, both in and out of the school. For example, using a dimensional approach to classification, a school psychologist might gather information regarding a student's internalizing difficulties using a rating scale. This dimensional approach allows for the inclusion of information about the severity of the problems and the psychologist would have information about which areas are the most problematic, which could guide the initial focus of treatment. However, if he/she had used a categorical approach, this information about severity would not have been included.

Dimensional approaches can have greater predictive validity than categorical methods (Fergusson & Horwood, 1995), measure comorbidity more precisely (Caron & Rutter, 1991), and represent categorical disorders like borderline personality disorder with greater accuracy (Garb, 1996).

When quantitative symptoms are artificially converted to a dichotomous, categorical scale, reliable and valid information is often lost (Widiger, 1992). Reliability and validity are increased by using a set of scores examined through factor analysis and other statistical approaches (Arend, Lavigne, Rosenbaum, Binns, & Christoffel, 1996), and by not arbitrarily forming dichotomous variables from continuous variables (Westen, Heim, Morrison, Patterson, & Campbell, 2002). However, dimensional methods still focus on variables of interest and produce a system that is less parsimonious than a categorical system of classification (Helzer & Hudziak, 2000).

Person-oriented, or multivariate, methods of classification attempt to blend categorical and dimensional methods by producing a categorical classification system through the use of dimensional scales. The resulting typology is a different type of categorical classification system that encompasses a full range of dimensionally scaled variables. Additionally, person-oriented approaches have been proposed due to their strength in emphasizing the individual as a whole, not just a linear combination of variables (Bergman & Magnusson, 1997). This person-oriented approach to a typology of behavior is conducive to a better understanding of the complexity and range of child behaviors (Meehl, 1995; Speece & Cooper, 1991) and provides consistency with psychological theoretical models of psychological systems development (Gottlieb, 2000; Waddington, 1971). Multivariate behavior typologies, derived through cluster analytic techniques, are gaining wider acceptance as models of classification due to evidence supporting the relative superiority of multivariate methods in explaining the complex interactions, correlates, and comorbidities in children (van Lier, Verhulst, van der Ende, & Crijnen, 2003; Greenberg, Speltz, DeKlyen, & Jones, 2001). Children who may be healthy or below diagnostic thresholds can also be incorporated into these classification systems, which allow for the use of large, representative samples to more adequately study the full range of child behavior (Kamphaus, Huberty, DiStefano, & Petoskey, 1997).

Cluster analytic and factor analytic methods have been used most frequently in efforts to develop person-oriented classification schemes for behavior, often to subtype clinical, referral, and national samples of children. The early work of Edelbrock & Achenbach (1980) reflects an attempt to develop a classification system using dimensional information. Their initial cluster study produced groups of children who were assigned such labels as depressed, somatic complaints, schizoid, hyperactive, delinquent, aggressive, and so on. Curry and Thompson (1985) used the Missouri Children's Behavior Checklist (MCBC) to cluster-analyze small clinical and referral samples. The identified seven clusters in this study are: inhibited-nonaggressive, low social skills, behavior problem–free, mildly aggressive, aggressive-active, aggressive-inhibited, and undifferentiated disturbance. Achenbach, Howell, McConaughy, and Stanger (1995) identified new clusters for a national sample, including: strange, irresponsible, and shows off, when using the Young Adult Behavior Checklist and Young Adult Self-Report.

McDermott and Weiss (1995) studied classroom behavioral "styles" for a representative national sample. Their study of teachers' ratings of behavior (i.e., the Adjustment Scales of Children and Adolescents) produced 22 clusters (styles) of behavior that ranged from absence of behavior problems to clinical (presumably diagnosable) significance. They classified 77% of the sample as either well or marginally adjusted. Approximately 21% were classified as at risk or seriously maladjusted.

Finally, Kamphaus, Huberty, DiStefano, and Petoskey (1997) completed a cluster analysis of the national norming sample of the Teacher Rating Scales–Child (TRS–C) of the Behavior Assessment System for Children (BASC, Reynolds & Kamphaus, 1992). They also identified seven clusters as a viable solution based on the BASC TRS–C dimensions, including well adapted, average, disruptive behavior problems, learning problems, physical complaints and worry, severe psychopathology, and mildly disruptive. This seven-cluster solution was subsequently replicated across samples in the U.S. population (Kamphaus et al., 1997), a U.S. urban and rural sample (DiStefano, Kamphaus, Horne, & Winsor 2003), and a sample in Medellin, Colombia (Kamphaus & DiStefano, 2001). Furthermore, results of a study by DiStefano, et al. (2003) indicated that this seven-cluster solution can be replicated by independent cluster analysis, cross classification among grouping procedures, and through relationships between disciplinary actions and cluster memberships.

Preliminary research evidence suggests that behavior typologies created by these multivariate techniques show evidence of external replication (DiStefano, et al., 2003), stability (Mattison & Spitznagel, 1999), replication across samples and instruments (Kamphaus et al., 1997; DiStefano et al., 2003; Kamphaus & DiStefano, 2001), and predictive validity (Flanagan, Bierman, & Kam, 2003; Toshiaki, Awaji, Nakazato, & Sumita, 1995; Fergusson & Horwood, 1995). Theoretically, classification systems including dimensional information offer practitioners a classification choice. They may choose among classifications based on comparison, categorically based diagnostic criteria, or an empirically derived syndrome of behaviors based on dimensional methods. Person-oriented, multivariate methods, however, have not yet emerged as serious alternatives for diagnostic practice. At the present time, they serve primarily as research tools that may eventually affect child classification.

While the advantages of person-oriented methods of classification appear to be promising, distinct disadvantages of this method remain. It has been suggested that the real-world applicability of clusters is limited because it involves a complex process to assign individuals to cluster membership. Additionally, classification systems derived from cluster analysis have not yet provided a sufficiently substantial amount of information about their clinical and predictive value (Speece, 1995; Mattison & Spitznagel, 1999). The utility of clusters to inform clinicians about the future behavior of individuals is unknown (Blanchard, Morgenstern, Morgan, Labouvie, & Bux, 2003), and it remains unclear if person-oriented methods are superior to dimensional methods when predicting behavioral outcomes (Dowdy & Kamphaus, 2007). These studies highlight the need for further examination on the predictive validity of clusters of individuals. Moreover, Cantwell (1996) noted additional problems with dimensional studies. Cluster analytic methods, for example, are more likely to identify relatively common forms of maladjustment, whereas rare disorders will probably go undetected. In addition, dimensional approaches do not easily allow the application of etiology or other qualitative considerations to the diagnostic process. Accordingly, Cantwell suggests that eventually some combination of categorical and dimensional approaches to classification will best capture the full range of children's behavior.

Meehl (see e.g., 1954) has argued convincingly that actuarial rules applied to diagnosis—such as in the development of clusters of syndromes that depict diagnostic entities—are more accurate than clinical impressions or single logistical approaches; his arguments are supported by decades of research (see e.g., Dawes, 1988). Although psychologists have been remarkably resistant to actuarial modeling of diagnosis and the use of empirical classification systems, we are moving ever so slowly in this direction (see e.g., Faust & Ackley, 1998; Kleinmuntz, 1990; Reynolds, 1998).

EFFECTS OF DIAGNOSIS

The inherent error in diagnosis has led some to recoil at the perceived hegemony of the DSM-IV-TR. Critics assail the scientific evidence that supports some or all of the diagnostic categories as dubious. For example, Kovacs (1996) concluded, "The DSM-IV is not an enumeration of scientifically validated 'nervous and mental disorders' (whatever those are), but is in reality a disguised set of moral, highly culture-bound descriptions about those behaviors that are to be tolerated and those that are the stigmatized and extinguished" (p. 19).

Helmchen (1994) also took issue with the value of current medical diagnostic systems, concluding that they are of limited utility:

> At best, they currently may (1) serve to organize epidemiological data for administrative use in service planning as a framework for specific treatment; (2) regulate in some cases the financing of treatment, care and service use (e.g., in Alzheimer's disease); and (3) be used for each specific diagnosis as a key to knowledge, an instrument to organize and document the individual evaluation, and a challenge for decision making (p. 224).

Yet another criticism has been leveled by Beutler and Harwood (1995), who suggest that medical diagnostic systems are typically not linked to treatment. It is probably often the case, they argue, that a diagnosis merely indicates that there is a need for treatment or intervention, nothing more and nothing less. This is particularly true of the IDEIA system for classifying a child with a disability. Unfortunately, children can be deemed eligible for special education services with little information provided to parents or teachers on how best to intervene. Furthermore, in today's litigious society, school psychologists can become overly cautious about the recommendations provided in psychoeducational reports and fail to provide any meaningful information regarding treatment planning.

The rejection of formal logical-deductive diagnostic systems has led some to propose what they deem functional classification systems. However, such proposed systems, to date, have been overly simplistic and ignore the many different presentations seen by clinicians in the schools and elsewhere. Gresham and Gansle (1992), in their arguments against the relevance of the DSM series, propose a four-group classification scheme for all of childhood psychopathology, which they suggest would be more related to treatment. Such systems do not lead to specific interventions, despite claims by their advocators, and lack even heuristic value in such simplified forms (Reynolds, 1992). The clinician often must follow the diagnostic process by using other quantitative and qualitative assessment procedures to design interventions. Low incidence disorders and other matters related to the tremendously disproportionate incidence of various disorders, as well as resulting statistical compromises, prevent the development of purely empirical classification systems. We are bound to use a combination of clinical, logical-deductive, actuarial methods in developing and applying diagnostic schemes (see e.g., Reynolds, 1998).

Other problems are associated with any classification system. The DSM-IV-TR and other diagnostic systems are categorical at their essence, which leads unerringly to an oversimplification of psychological phenomena. As noted previously, psychological constructs are often best represented as dimensional (anxiety, hyperactivity, etc.) rather than categorical (Kamphaus et al., 1997).

Categorical classification has many effects, not the least of which is the potential to overlook children with significant problems who nearly meet diagnostic criteria. Many children do not receive the mental health services that they need, in part due to the inadequate methods of classification currently in use. Children are often classified into groups that receive services only after they exhibit significant impairment. This "wait-to-fail" treatment approach could result from current classification systems that fail to identify subsyndromal psychopathology (Cantwell, 1996) or current risk status. These cases of subclinical problems are sometimes associated with significant adjustment difficulties (Cantwell, 1996). The diagnoses of mental retardation or of gifted represent this problem of categorical classification well. For example, consider how a child with an overall intelligence composite of 130 is admitted to a gifted enrichment program, while a child with a composite of 124 is not. It is not likely that the first child has a substantially better academic trajectory than the second child.

Categorical classification can also pose problems in behavioral and other assessments in which decisions are made about who receives treatment, for what duration, and so on. Clinicians may, for example, use behavioral assessment to determine when to cease treatment, such as social skills training. This decision can be made inappropriately by using rigid cut scores. Children with identical behavioral measures of social skills may have very different levels of adaptation, depending on their familial or school milieu. Hence, categorical special education or mental health diagnostic systems are often accompanied by the problem of forcing dimensional phenomena into a categorical framework. Other than not making decisions about treatment, eligibility for services, or other important decisions, the only option is to avoid inappropriately rigid uses of categorical systems. This objective can be accomplished in part by merging dimensional and categorical approaches as much as possible (Kamphaus & Frick, 1996).

ASSESSMENT VERSUS DIAGNOSIS AND CLASSIFICATION

Classification is only one of the objectives of assessment. Others may include treatment planning, political advocacy, program evaluation, and research (Keough, 1994). The objectives of the evaluation must be delineated at the outset of the assessment protocol as this decision affects test (assessment method) selection, scheduling, and virtually all other aspects of the assessment process. It is imperative that school psychologists fully understand the reasons for referral so that the steps taken are most appropriate.

Referral questions may be more or less suited to various objectives and assessment procedures.

Some sample assessment questions and objectives may include the following:

Question	Assessment Objective
1. Does my child have ADHD?	Diagnosis
2. Will my child outgrow his depression?	Diagnosis and prognosis
3. Is my daughter getting better?	Treatment evaluation
4. What can I do to help her stop avoiding school?	Treatment planning
5. Will schizophrenia keep her from going to college?	Prognosis
6. Can he get extra time when taking the SAT?	Diagnosis and eligibility
7. Did he get his anxiety problems from me?	Etiology
8. Why is his behavior management program not working?	Treatment evaluation
9. Does she also have a reading disability?	Diagnosis and comorbidity

Adept psychologists will be mindful of the multiple purposes of the assessment to ensure that the battery of tests and procedures utilized can answer the primary questions of interest. Moreover, classification is only one assessment purpose, and it should not be established as the ultimate one. One the one hand, classification may actually be, in some cases, orthogonal to the necessary assessment process for treatment planning or other objectives. On the other hand, classification may have implications for treatment, depending on the results of research related to particular diagnoses.

DIAGNOSIS AND TREATMENT

Much of the developmental psychopathology research to date is aimed at measuring psychological constructs with increased validity (Kamphaus & Frick, 1996). A diagnosis, therefore, may also serve as a construct in that it represents a tool for classification. Research on children who fit the diagnosis may, in turn, produce implications

for treatment, prevention, prediction of outcomes, and so on. This form of psychopathology research, however, differs from research aimed exclusively at establishing an inextricable link between classification and treatment. In other words, child psychopathology research is similar to medical research in that the creation of a diagnosis does not lead inextricably to cures, as is the case for acquired immune deficiency syndrome (AIDS). The creation of an accurate AIDS diagnosis (construct) simply allows research of the disorder to progress at a faster rate, including research into treatment. In similar fashion, the delineation of ADHD subtypes in the DSM-IV-TR simply provide diagnostic categories that can be studied in more effective manners. As a consequence, we now know that children with ADHD, combined type, tend to be more socially rejected, impulsive, and at greater risk for conduct problems. Children with ADHD, primary inattentive type, are quite different: they may be more reticent, perhaps drowsy, and respond well to low doses of stimulant medication (Kamphaus & Frick, 1996). None of these treatment-relevant findings, however, would be available to clinicians without the initial creation of the constructs of subtypes.

It is probably true that child psychopathology research that is based on diagnostic groups is not ideally suited to the development of specific treatment regimens for each diagnosis. Even well-refined diagnostic categories are useful only for stating probabilities (Helmchen, 1994). It is not true that all children with ADHD, primary inattentive type, will respond well to low doses of stimulant medication. This treatment suggestion is merely a probability statement, which suggests to the physician a promising intervention. As Helmchen notes, "in other words, the more individualized the treatment goal, the less useful the psychiatric diagnosis is, and vice versa" (p. 218).

The process of classification is helpful to the extent that the classification itself has some validity. It thus allows us to think like psychologists. Specifically, classification schemes, whether psychiatric, educational, or behavioral in origin, give psychologists ready access to a burgeoning research literature. It is by accessing this literature that we have the opportunity to apply science to practice, as psychologists are trained to do (Stricker, 1997). Following the process of classification, school psychologists have access to a wealth of information as to what treatments might be most efficacious for that child. Frequently trained as science practitioners, school psychologists should also be adept at providing these invaluable treatments to children and determining if they meet desired goals. Therefore, classification is truly helpful to the extent that school psychologists use information wisely to properly plan treatments and interventions. This should not be simply stated as, "The child should receive special education services." This oversimplification does not take into account information on the effects of special education or information on the specific type of services that could benefit the student most. Meta-analyses of special education placement (with data sets for as many as 27,000 students) have not only shown relatively small effect sizes, but also shown that many effects are negative, which suggests that for some children placement in special education might actually be harmful (Kavale & Forness, 1999). However, other well-researched student interventions (such as behavior modification and peer tutoring) have shown positive and substantial effect sizes (Kavale & Forness, 1999). Therefore, it is incumbent upon school psychologists, when qualifying a child for special education services, to provide additional information about specific treatments that might be beneficial for the student. As previously stated, a goal of classification should be to facilitate clinical practice, including providing information for treatment planning.

FUTURE OF DIAGNOSTIC PRACTICE IN SCHOOL PSYCHOLOGY

It is likely that continual progress will be made to improve current diagnostic systems. Furthermore, future innovations in diagnostic systems will probably be more incremental than radical. In the interim, the astute clinician has to deal with the problems of using categorical systems for determining eligibility for specialized treatments by teaching others how to use these systems in an enlightened fashion.

There are, however, continuing demands for school psychologists to move beyond the role of solely classifying and placing children. Sheridan and Gutkin (2000) proposed that school psychologists are the most highly trained mental health experts in the schools and therefore should be engaged in a variety of roles within the school system including prevention, promoting wellness, changing ecological systems that impact the lives of children, facilitating change in educator's

behaviors, and establishing connections with families. They also indicated that there should be a shift away from primarily focusing attention on the identification and measurement of problems. The implications of IDEIA further highlight the importance of providing early intervention and prevention services, an additional role for school psychologists. However, a primary role of school psychologists will likely continue to be providing accurate classification and diagnostic services for the children they serve. It will become increasingly important to accurately classify children not only for special education services, but also according to risk status so that children will appropriately receive prevention, early intervention, and/or treatment services.

Problems in psychological classification research may be solved by combining current categorical methods with dimensional approaches (Kamphaus & Frick, 1996) and extending the results through logical-deductive methods for disorders of very low incidence (Aicardi syndrome, Soto's syndrome, and the like). Most current diagnostic systems have been based on a medical, often nonempirical tradition. Psychologists are still in the early stages of building person-oriented assessment systems that are based on multivariate statistical models including dimensional information. These models may push the field forward, although other problems in determining the role of etiology in diagnosis remain (Cantwell, 1996).

We would also do well to remember that diagnoses per se are not likely to inform our important treatment decisions. Accurate classification can only provide the foundation necessary for research, which in turn may reveal treatment-related findings that can be applied only by highly trained professionals. Just as an inept automobile mechanic prevents an accurate diagnosis of a car's problems, so, too, the most valid diagnosis system is of dubious value in the hands of the unskilled clinician.

REFERENCES

Achenbach, T. (1998). Diagnosis, assessment, taxonomy, and case formulations. In T. Ollendick and M. Hersen (Eds.). *Handbook of Child Psychopathology* (3rd ed., pp. 63–87). New York: Plenum Press.

Achenbach, T. (2001). Challenges and benefits of assessment, diagnosis, and taxonomy for clinical practice and research. *Australian and New Zealand Journal of Psychiatry*, 35(3), 263–271.

Achenbach, T. M., Howell, C. T., McConaughy, S. H., & Stanger, C. (1995). Six-year predictors of problems in a national sample: III. Transitions to young adult syndromes. *Journal of the American Academy of Child and Adolescent Psychiatry, 34,* 658–669.

American Association on Mental Retardation. (1992). *Mental retardation: Definition, classification, and systems of supports* (9th ed.). Washington, DC: American Association on Mental Retardation.

American Association on Mental Retardation AD Hoc Committee on Terminology and Classification. (2002). *Mental retardation: Definition, classification, and systems of supports* (10th Ed.). Washington DC: American Association on Mental Retardation.

American Psychiatric Association. (2000). *Diagnostic and statistical manual of mental disorders* (4th ed., text rev.). Washington, DC: Author.

Arend, R., Lavigne, J. V., Rosenbaum, D., Binns, J. J., & Christoffel, K. K. (1996). Relation between taxonomic and quantitative diagnostic systems in preschool children: Emphasis on disruptive disorders. *Journal of Clinical Child Psychology, 25*(4), 388–397.

Bergman, L. R., & Magnusson, D. (1997). A person-oriented approach in research on developmental psychopathology. *Development and Psychopathology, 9*(2), 291–319.

Blanchard, K. A., Morgenstern, J., Morgan, T. J., Labouvie, E., & Bux, D. A. (2003). Motivational subtypes and continuous measures of readiness for change: Concurrent and predictive validity. *Psychology of Addictive Behaviors, 17*(1), 56–65.

Blashfield, R. K. (1998). Diagnostic models and systems. In A. A. Bellack, M. Hersen, & C. R. Reynolds (Eds.), *Comprehensive clinical psychology: Vol. 4. Assessment.* New York: Elsevier Science.

Bower, E. M. (1982). Severe emotional disturbance: Public policy and research. *Psychology in the Schools, 19,* 55–60.

Beutler, L. E., & Harwood, T. M. (1995). How to assess clients in pretreatment planning. In J. N. Butcher (Ed.), *Clinical personality assessment practical approaches* (pp. 59–77). New York: Oxford University Press.

Beutler, L. E. & Malik, M. L. (2002). *Rethinking the DSM: A psychological perspective.* Washington, DC: American Psychological Association.

Cantwell, D. P. (1996). Classification of child and adolescent psychopathology. *Journal of Child Psychology and Psychiatry, 37,* 3–12.

Caron, C., & Rutter, M. (1991). Comorbidity in child psychopathology: Concepts, issues, and research strategies. *Journal of Child Psychology and Psychiatry and Allied Disciplines, 32,* 1063–1080.

Clark, L. A., Watson, D., & Reynolds, W. S. (1995). Diagnosis and classification of psychopathology: Challenges to the current system and future directions. *Annual Review of Psychology, 46,* 121.

Curry, J. F., & Thompson, R. J. (1985). Patterns of behavioral disturbance in developmentally disabled and categorically referred children: A cluster analytic approach. *Journal of Pediatric Psychology, 10,* 151–167.

Dawes, R. M. (1988). You can't systematize human judgment: Dyslexia. In Dowie, J. & Elstein, A. S., *Professional Judgment: A Reader in Clinical Decision Making* (pp. 150–162). New York, NY: Cambridge University Press.

Deater-Deckard, K., Reiss, D., Hetherington, E. M., & Plomin, R. (1997). Dimensions and disorders of adolescent adjustment: A quantitative genetic analysis of unselected samples and selected extremes. *Journal of Child Psychology and Psychiatry, 38*(5), 515–535.

Distefano, C., Kamphaus, R. W., Horne, A. M., & Winsor, A. P. (2003). Behavioral adjustment in the U. S. elementary school: Cross-validation of a person-oriented typology of risk. *Journal of Psychoeducational Assessment, 21,* 338–357.

Dowdy, E., & Kamphaus, R.W. (2007). A comparison of classification methods for use in predicting school-based outcomes. *The California School Psychologist, 12,* 119–130.

Dykens, E. M. & Hodapp, R. M. (2001). Research in mental retardation: Toward an etiological approach. *Journal of Child Psychology and Psychiatry and Allied Disciplines, 42,* 49–71.

Edelbrock, C., & Achenback, T. M. (1980). A typology of child behavior profile patterns: Distribution and correlates for disturbed children aged 6–16. *Journal of Abnormal Child Psychology, 8,* 441–470.

Everitt, B.S. (1974). *Cluster analysis.* New York: Halstead Press.

Faust, D., & Ackley, M. (1998). Did you think it was gonna be easy? Some methodological suggestions for the investigation and development of malingering detection techniques. In C. R. Reynolds (Ed.), *Detection of malingering during head injury litigation.* New York: Plenum.

Fergusson, D. M., & Horwood, J. (1995). Predictive validity of categorically and dimensionally scored measures of disruptive childhood behaviors. *Journal of Clinical Child and Adolescent Psychology, 32,* 396–407.

Flanagan, K. S., Bierman, K. L., & Kam, C. M. (2003). Identifying at-risk children at school entry: The usefulness of multibehavioral problem profiles. *Journal of Clinical Child and Adolescent Psychology, 32,* 396–407.

Forness, S. R., & Knitzer, J. (1992). A new proposed definition and terminology to replace "serious emotional disturbance" in the individuals with disabilities act. *School Psychology Review, 21,* 12–20.

Garb, H. N. (1996). Taxometrics and the revision of diagnostic criteria. *American Psychologist, 51*, 553–554.

Gottlieb, G. (2000). Understanding genetic activity within a holistic framework. In L. R. Bergman, R. B. Cairns, L. G. Nilsson, & L. Nested (Eds.), *Developmental science and the holistic approach* (pp. 180–201). Mahwah, NJ: Erlbaum.

Greenberg, M. T., Speltz, M. L., DeKlyen, M., & Jones, K. (2001). Correlates of clinic referral for early conduct problems: Variable- and person-oriented approaches. *Development and Psychopathology, 13*, 255–276.

Gresham, F. M., & Gansle, K. A. (1992). Misguided assumptions of DSM-III-R: Implication for school psychological practice. *School Psychology Quarterly, 7*, 79–95.

Helmchen, H. H. (1994). The validity of diagnostic systems for treatment. In J. E. Mezzich, Y. Honda, & M. C. Kastrup (Eds.), *Psychiatric diagnosis, a world perspective* (217–227). New York: Springer-Verlag.

Helzer, J. E., & Hudziak, J. J. (2000). *Defining psychopathology in the twenty-first century: DSM-V and beyond.* Washington, DC: American Psychiatric Association.

Houts, A. C. (2002). Discovery, invention, and the expansion of the modern diagnostic and statistical manuals of mental disorders. In J. E. Helzer & J. J. Hudziak (Eds.), *Defining psychopathology in the twenty-first century: DSM-V and beyond.* Washington, DC: American Psychiatric Association.

Hudziak, J. J., Wadsworth, M. E., Heath, A. C., & Achenbach, T. M. (1999). Latent class analysis of child behavior checklist attention problems. *Journal of American Academy of Child and Adolescent Psychiatry, 38*(8), 985–991.

Individuals with Disabilities Education Improvement Act of 2004, Pub. L. No. 108–446.

Jablensky, A. (1999). The nature of psychiatric classification: Issues beyond ICD-10 and DSM-IV. *Australian and New Zealand Journal of Psychiatry, 33*, 137–144.

Jimerson, S. R., Coffino, B., & Sroufe, L. A. (2007). Building school-based interventions on attachment theory and research, *Journal of Early Childhood and Infant Psychology, 3*, 79–94.

Kagan, J. (1997). Conceptualizing psychopathology: the importance of developmental profiles. *Development and Psychopathology, 9*, 321–334.

Kamphaus, R. W., & DiStefano, C. (2001). Evaluación multidimensional de la psicopatología infantil. *Revista de Neurpsicología, Neuropsyqiatría y Neurociencias, 3*(1), 85–98.

Kamphaus, R. W., & Frick, J. P. (1996). *Clinical assessment of child and adolescent personality behavior.* Needham Heights, MA: Allyn & Bacon.

Kamphaus, R. W., Huberty, C., J., Distefano, C., & Petoskey, M. D. (1997). A typology of teacher rated child behavior for a national U.S. sample. *Journal of Abnormal Child Psychology, 25*, 453–463.

Kamphaus, R. W., Morgan, A. W., Cox, M. R., & Powell, R. M. (1995). Personality and intelligence in the psychodiagnostic process: The emergence of diagnostic schedules. In D. H. Saklofske and M. Zeidner (Eds.), *International handbook of personality and intelligence* (525–544). New York: Plenum.

Kavale, K. A., & Forness, S. R. (1999). *Efficacy of special education and related services.* Washington, DC: American Association on Mental Retardation.

Keough, B. K. (1994). A matrix of decision points in the measurement of learning disabilities. In G. R. Lyon (Ed.), *Frames of reference for the assessment of learning disabilities: New views on measurement issues* (15–26). Baltimore, MD: Paul H. Brookes.

Kleinmuntz, B. (1990). Why we still use our heads instead of the formulas: toward an integrative approach. *Psychological Bulletin, 107*, 296–310.

Kovacs, A. L. (1996, Winter). We have met the enemy and he is us! *AAP Advance, 6*, 18.

Lahey, B. B., Applegate, B., Barkley, R. A., & Garfikel, B. (1994). DSM-IV field trials for oppositional defiant disorder and conduct disorder in children and adolescents. *American Journal of Psychiatry, 151*(8), 1163–1171.

Langenbucher, J., & Nathan, P. E. (2006). *Diagnosis and classification.* Hoboken, NJ, US: John Wiley & Sons Inc.

Last, C. G. (1993). *Conclusions and future directions.* In C. G. Last (Ed.), *Anxiety across the lifespan: A developmental perspective* (204–213). New York: Springer.

Lewczyk, C. M., Garland, A. F., Hurlburt, M. S., Gearity, J., & Hough, R. L. (2003). Comparing DISC-IV and clinician diagnoses among youths receiving public mental health services. *Journal of American Academy of Child and Adolescent Psychiatry, 42*(3), 349.

Lorr, M. (1966). *Explorations in typing psychotics.* New York: Pergamon.

Masi, G. (1998). Psychiatric illness in mentally retarded adolescents: Clinical features. *Adolescence, 33*(130), 425–434.

Mattison, R. E., & Spitznagel, E. L. (1999). Long-term stability of child behavior checklist profile types in a child psychiatric clinic population. *Journal of the American Academy of Child and Adolescent Psychiatry, 38*, 700–707.

McDermott, P. A., & Weiss, R. V. (1995). A normative typology of health, subclinical, and clinical behavior styles among American children and adolescents. *Psychological Assessment, 7*, 162–170.

McLaughlin, M. J., Dyson, A., Nagle, K., Thurlow, M., Rouse, M., & Hardman, M. (2006). Cross-cultural perspectives on the classification of children with disabilities: Part II. implementing classification systems in schools. *The Journal of Special Education, 40*(1), 46–58.

Meehl, P. E. (1995). Bootstraps taxometrics: Solving the classification problems in psychopathology. *American Psychologist, 50*, 266–275.

Meehl, P. E. (1954). *Clinical versus statistical prediction: A theoretical analysis and a review of the evidence.* Minneapolis, MN: University of Minnesota Press.

Moffitt, T. E., Caspi, A., Harrington, H., & Milne, B. J. (2002). Males on the life course- persistent and adolescence-limited antisocial pathways: Follow-up at age 26 years. *Development and Psychopathology, 14*, 179–207.

Nease, D. E., Volk, R. J., & Cass, A. R. (1999). Investigation of a severity-based classification of mood and anxiety symptoms in primary care patients. *Journal of the American Board of Family Practice, 12*(1), 21–31.

Reynolds, C. R. (1979). Should we screen preschoolers? *Contemporary Educational Psychology, 4*, 175–181.

Reynolds, C. R. (1992). Misguided epistemological shifting, misdirected misology, and dogma in diagnosis. *School Psychology Quarterly, 7*, 96–99.

Reynolds, C. R. (1998). Common sense, clinicians, and actuarialism in the detection of malingering during head injury litigation. In C. R. Reynolds (Ed.), *Detection of malingering during head injury litigation*. New York: Plenum.

Reynolds, C. R. (2008). RTI, neuroscience, and sense: Chaos in the diagnosis and treatment of learning disabilities. In E. Fletcher-Janzen and C. R. Reynolds (Eds.), *Neuropsychological Perspectives on Learning Disabilities in the Era of RTI* (pp. 14–27). New Jersey: John Wiley & Sons.

Reynolds, C. R., & Kamphaus, R. W. (1992). *Behavior assessment system for children: Manual*. Circle Pines, MN: American Guidance Service.

Richters, J. E. (1997). The Hubble hypothesis and the developmentalists' dilemma. *Development and Psychopathology, 9*(2), 193–229.

Rush, K. S., Bowman, L. G., Eidman, S. L., Toole, L. M., & Mortenson, B. P. (2004). Assessing psychopathology in individuals with developmental disabilities. *Behavior modification, 28*(5), 621–637.

Scotti, J. R., & Morris, T. L. (2000). Diagnosis and classification. In M. Hersen & R. T. Ammerman (Eds.), *Advanced abnormal child psychology* (2nd ed., pp. 15–32). Mahwah, NJ: Erlbaum.

Sheridan, S. M., & Gutkin, T. B. (2000). The ecology of school psychology: Examining and changing our paradigm for the 21st century. *School Psychology Review, 29*(4), 485–501.

Speece, D.L. (1995). Cluster analysis in perspective. *Exceptionality, 5*(1), 31–44.

Speece, D. L., & Cooper, D. H. (1991). Retreat, regroup, or advance? An agenda for empirical classification research in learning disabilities. In L. V. Feagans, E. J., Short, & L. J. Meltzer (Eds.), *Subtypes of learning disabilities: Theoretical perspectives and research* (pp. 33–52). Hillsdale, NJ: Erlbaum.

Sroufe, L. A. (1997). Psychopathology as an outcome of development. *Development and Pyschopathology, 9*(2), 251–268.

Sroufe, L. A., Egeland, B., Carlson, E. A., & Collins, W. A. (2005). *The development of the person: The Minnesota study of risk and adaptation from birth to adulthood*. New York: Guilford Press.

Stricker, G. (1997). Are science and practice commensurable? *American Psychologist, 52*, 442–448.

Szymanski, L., & King, B. H. (1999). Practice parameters for the assessment and treatment of children, adolescents, and adults with mental retardation and comorbid mental disorders. *Journal of the American Academy of Child and Adolescent Psychiatry, 38*(Suppl.), S5–S31.

Toshiaki, F., Awaji, R., Nakazato, H., & Sumita, Y. (1995). Predictive validity of subtypes of chronic affective disorders derived by cluster analysis. *Acta Psychiatrica Scandinavica, 91*, 379–385.

van Lier, P. A. C., Verhulst, F. C., van der Ende, J., & Crijnen, A. A. M. (2003). Classes of disruptive behavior in a sample of young elementary school children. *Journal of Child Psychology and Psychiatry and Applied Disciplines, 44*, 377–387.

Waddington, C. H. (1971). Concepts of development. In L. R. Aronson, E. Shaw, & E. Tobach (Eds.), *Biopsychology of Development* (pp. 17–23). New York: Academic Press.

Westen, D., Heim, A. K., Morrison, K., Patterson, M., & Campbell, L. (2002). Simplifying diagnosis using a prototype-matching approach: Implication for the next edition of the *DSM*. In L. Beutler & Malik (Eds.), *Rethinking the* DSM: *Psychological perspectives* (pp. 221–250). Washington, DC: American Psychological Association.

Widiger, T.A. (1992). Categorical versus dimensional classification: Implications from and for research. *Journal of Personality Disorders, 6*(4), 287–300.

Widiger, T. A., Frances, A. J., Pincus, H. A., Davis, W. W., & First, M. B. (1991). Toward an empirical classification for the DSM-IV. *Journal of Abnormal Psychology, 100*, 280–288.

CHAPTER 12

ERRORS IN DIAGNOSTIC DECISION MAKING AND CLINICAL JUDGMENT

MARLEY W. WATKINS
Arizona State University

Paradoxically, humans simultaneously attain extraordinary achievements and commit remarkable errors. Humans have walked on the moon, and died in the fiery ruins of space shuttles. Humans have extracted energy from atoms, and created a radioactive wasteland surrounding Chernobyl. Olympic athletes perform feats of strength and balance, but tourists stumble over guard rails and plummet into the Grand Canyon. Cognitive psychologists have speculated that this coincident capacity for attainment and error are "two sides of the same cognitive 'balance sheet' [where] each entry on the asset side carries a corresponding debit" (Reason, 1990, p. 2). For example, the lack of higher-level cognitive control during automatic performances allows smooth, highly integrated behavior but is vulnerable to distraction or preoccupation.

Given that errors are inevitable, it is crucial to identify when and how they might occur so that palliative action can be taken. Although there is no generally accepted taxonomy of error, Reason (1990) has articulated a tripartite generic error-modeling system that may be applied to school psychology.

GENERIC ERROR-MODELING SYSTEM

Skill-Based Errors

Behavior at the skill level is "primarily a way of dealing with routine and nonproblematic activities in familiar situations" (Reason, 1990, p. 56). Once learned, these behaviors are relatively automatic and do not rely on higher-level cognitive control nor on problem-solving processes. Errors are likely to be *slips* and *lapses* due to inattention, interference, and distraction. Among trained school psychologists, skill-based errors are likely to occur during such overlearned professional activities as administration and scoring of tests. Research has, in fact, found an alarming number of scoring errors on intelligence tests (Slate, Jones, Coulter, & Covert, 1992) as well as objective personality tests (Allard & Faust, 2000).

Rule-Based Errors

When problem solving, people learn to combine information for greater mental efficiency and to develop complex sets of if-then rules with utility in particular situations. This allows the problem solver to quickly abstract the pertinent details of a situation and automatically apply prototypical strategies that have previously been effective in similar situations. These cognitive rules can be complex. For example, expert medical diagnosticians recognize meaningful patterns that allow them to identify diseases and quickly access mental models for treatment of each disease (Ericsson, 2004).

Rules formed in this manner are not necessarily the most efficient and can go astray in a variety of ways. Initially, there are basic information processing limitations. People have a short-term memory capacity of 7 (± 2) bits of information and are inaccurate when attempting to interpret the interaction of more than 3 or 4 variables (Halford, Baker, McCredden, & Bain, 2005). For example, attempts to verify the complex nonlinear configural rules claimed by clinicians have consistently found that simple linear models are equally accurate (Ruscio, 2003; Sandavol, 1998). Ultimately, the problem solver may attend to noninformative aspects of a situation, ignore or discount other important signs, persist in using a familiar but ineffectual rule, apply the wrong rule, employ rules inconsistently, and so on (McDermott, 1981). Children, for instance, often misapply rules when solving subtraction problems, revealing a systematic misunderstanding of borrowing (Reason, 1990). Likewise, a clinician may automatically, but incorrectly, diagnose learning disabilities when observing depressed Arithmetic, Coding, Information, and Digit Span subtest scores on a Wechsler scale (Watkins, 2003).

Knowledge-Based Errors

When confronted with a problem, humans prefer to search for and apply a rule-based solution. However, they revert to knowledge-based reasoning in novel situations or when available rules are not sufficient. Errors at this level arise from resource limitations and incomplete or incorrect knowledge.

SUBOPTIMAL DECISIONS BY PSYCHOLOGISTS

School psychologists are often called on to make difficult decisions with incomplete and uncertain data in complex environments: classification decisions, placement decisions, intervention decisions, and many others. Unfortunately, it has been well documented that school psychologists exhibit inconsistency and inaccuracy in their professional decisions (Algozzine & Ysseldyke, 1981; Aspel, Willis, & Faust, 1998; Barnett, 1988; Brown & Jackson, 1992; Davidow & Levinson, 1993; Dawes, 1994; Della Toffalo & Pedersen, 2005; deMesquita, 1992; Fagley, 1988; Fagley, Miller, & Jones, 1999; Gnys, Willis, & Faust, 1995; Huebner, 1989; Johnson, 1980; Kennedy, Willis, & Faust, 1997; Kirk & Hsieh, 2004; Macmann & Barnett, 1999; McDermott, 1980, 1981; Ysseldyke, Algozzine, Regan, & McGue, 1981).

Flawed decision making has also been found among clinical psychologists and psychiatrists. When diagnosing psychopathology, psychologists and psychiatrists have demonstrated weak interrater agreement, made errors of both under- and overidentification, and been unduly influenced by the race or gender of the client (Clark & Harrington, 1999; Faust, 1986; Garb, 1997, 1998; Garb & Boyle, 2003; Garb & Lutz, 2001). For example, "normal individuals have been misdiagnosed as brain damaged in about one out of every three cases" by neuropsychologists (Wedding & Faust, 1989, p. 241).

Psychologists have also been found to be unreliable and inaccurate in assigning children to the most appropriate level of care (Bickman, Karver, & Schut, 1997), have demonstrated low agreement when determining the function of school refusal behaviors among children (Daleiden, Chorpita, Kollins, & Drabman, 1999), and disagreed when composing case formulations for treatment of depression (Persons & Bertagnolli, 1999). Clinician agreement and accuracy on length of treatment and treatment recommendations have also been negative (Allen, Coyne, & Logure, 1990; Garb, 1998, 2005; Strauss, Chassin, & Lock, 1995).

Given this bleak record, it is not surprising that statistical prediction rules have consistently outperformed subjectively derived clinical predictions (Dawes, Faust, & Meehl, 1989; Grove & Meehl, 1996) and that experienced clinicians are no more accurate than novices in many clinical judgment tasks (Garb, 1998). In recognition of this dismal situation, Meehl (1973), in his "Why I Do Not Attend Case Conferences," scathingly satirized psychological decision making.

SUBOPTIMAL DECISIONS BY OTHER PROFESSIONALS

Evidence of decision-making inconstancy is not restricted to psychologists. The agreement of psychiatrists on diagnoses made in routine clinical practice and diagnoses based on semistructured interviews has been found to be poor (Shear et al., 2000). Similarly, agreement by physicians on psychotropic medication prescriptions, surgical procedures, and mammogram interpretation has been variable (Beam, Layde, & Sullivan, 1996; Dunn et al., 2005; Pappadopulos, et al., 2002). Large-scale studies of hospitalized patients have estimated that preventable medical errors annually account for 44,000 to 98,000 deaths in the United States (Leape, 1994). In agreement, autopsy studies have found high rates (35% to 40%) of erroneous diagnoses (Anderson, Hill, & Key, 1989). A meta-analysis of the reliability and validity of child protective agency caseworker decisions about allegations of child sexual abuse estimated that there are "at least 25,000 erroneous substantiation [of child sexual abuse] decisions (false positives and false negatives) per year by CPS case workers" (Herman, 2005, p. 105). Punitive monetary awards and unjust verdicts have been traced to inaccurate jury decisions (Colwell, 2005; Hastie, Schkade, & Payne, 1999). Dramatically, faulty analysis of data from space shuttle launches by NASA engineers failed to detect the o-ring malfunction caused by cold temperatures that destroyed the *Challenger* (Dawes, 2001).

SUBOPTIMAL DECISIONS ARE UNIVERSAL AND SYSTEMATIC

In fact, research has conclusively demonstrated that *all* human decision making is susceptible to incomplete data gathering, cognitive shortcuts, errors, and biases (Arkes, 1991; Baron, 1994; Dawes, 2001; Foster & Huber, 1997; Gilovich, Griffin, & Kahneman, 2002; Nickerson, 2004; Nisbett & Ross, 1980; Plous, 1993; Reason, 1990). Whereas early conceptions of decision making were based on the fundamental belief that humans are rational, Simon (1955), who won a Nobel Prize in Economics in 1978 for his work, recognized that people do not make normatively accurate, optimal decisions because of their incomplete access to information and limited computational and predictive abilities. Instead, humans simplify the parameters of the situation, approximate the computations needed for a decision, and arrive at a satisfactory, although not necessarily optimal, decision.

Following Simon's observations, Tversky and Kahneman (1974) demonstrated that when making judgments under uncertainty people are likely to use a wide variety of nonnormative information processing techniques. These judgmental heuristics, cognitive shortcuts, or cognitive rules of thumb (Kahneman & Tversky, 1996) often yield decisions that are close approximations to optimal, but in circumstances that require logical analysis and an understanding of abstract relationships they can result in systematic biases (Baron, 1994). Kahneman's work on human judgment and decision making under uncertainty was recognized with the Nobel Prize in Economics in 2002.

Piattelli-Palmarini (1994) has referred to these heuristics and biases as *cognitive illusions* and compared them to the classical visual illusions described by experimental psychologists. For example, the vertical and horizontal lines at the top of Figure 12.1 are exactly the same length. Likewise, the two horizontal lines found at the bottom of Figure 12.1 are of equal length. Based on the limitations of human vision, a wide variety of visual illusions have been demonstrated (Robinson, 1998).

Similarly, a variety of cognitive illusions can be illustrated (see Plous, 1993 for multiple

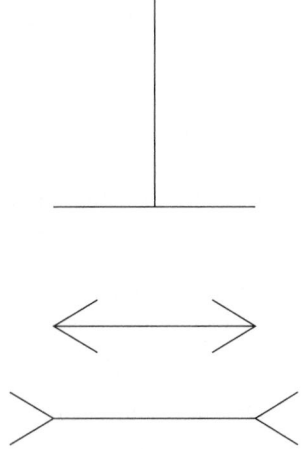

FIGURE 12.1   Visual illusions.

examples). For instance: *Each of the cards in Figure 12.2 has a number on one side and a letter on the other. Someone asserts that "if a card has a vowel on one side, it has an even number on the other side." Which of the cards should you turn over to decide whether this person is lying?* Most research participants, including psychologists, elected to look at the hidden sides of cards E and 2 in an attempt to confirm the cooccurrence of vowels and even numbers (Evans & Wason, 1976). However, the observation of an odd number on the reverse of card E or a vowel on the reverse of card 5 would more efficiently refute the statement (Plous, 1993).

A second cognitive illusion is illustrated by this diagnostic problem: *The probability of colorectal cancer is 0.3%. If a person has colorectal cancer, the probability that a hemoccult test will show a positive result is 50%. If a person does not have colorectal cancer, the probability of a positive hemoccult test is 3%. Considering only this information, what is the probability that a person who has a positive hemoccult test actually has colorectal cancer?* Many people think the correct answer is around 50%. Alarmingly, when 24 physicians were tested, only one gave the correct answer of 5% (Gigerenzer & Edwards, 2003).

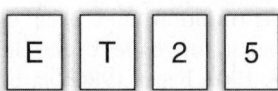

FIGURE 12.2   Given four cards, participants are asked to test the rule that, "if a card has a vowel on one side, it has an even number on the other."

COMMON COGNITIVE HEURISTICS, BIASES, OR ILLUSIONS

The perceptual illusion illustrated in Figure 12.1 persists even after using a ruler to measure the line segments. The only resolution is to use a ruler and remain confident in reason over the senses. Following this principle, a safe pilot will rely on flight instruments over fallible visuo-perceptual cues when flying in darkness. Analogous to the good pilot, the good psychologist recognizes that intuitive cognitive cues might be satisfactory in most situations but potentially misleading when making cognitively complex decisions under uncertainty. Although Croskerry (2003) identified more than 30 cognitive rules of thumb in medicine, the following cognitive heuristics, biases, confusions, and illusions are especially pertinent for school psychology.

Representativeness

According to Tversky and Kahneman (1974), people often answer probabilistic questions by relying on "the degree to which A is representative of B, that is, by the degree to which A resembles B" (p. 1124). For example, consider Steve, a man who has been described as "very shy and withdrawn, invariably helpful, but with little interest in people, or in the world of reality. A meek and tidy soul, he has a need for order and structure, and a passion for detail" (Tversky & Kahneman, 1974, p. 1124). When people were asked to select Steve's probable occupation (i.e., farmer, salesman, pilot, librarian, or physician), they tended to choose librarian because the description of Steve was most *representative* of, or similar to, their stereotype of a librarian.

In diagnostic decision making, the representativeness heuristic seems to cause psychologists to discount formal diagnostic criteria in favor of a comparison of how similar the client is to the stereotypical or prototypical client with that diagnosis (Garb, 1996). Stereotypes and prototypes are partially based on clinicians' experiences, so they differ from one clinician to another and from published diagnostic criteria. Representativeness often corresponds to likelihood, so it can yield accurate results. The problem with relying on representativeness is that other relevant factors can be ignored or discounted, leading to error (Tracey & Rounds, 1999). These factors are discussed further.

Insensitivity to Prior Probabilities

The base rate, or prior probability, of a disorder or outcome has no effect on representativeness, but should have a major influence on the calculation of an accurate probability estimate. In the case of Steve, the base rate of occupations in the population can allow a more accurate prediction of whether he is, for example, a librarian or a salesman. After all, if salesmen are much more common than librarians then, absent other pertinent information, it is more rational to assign Steve to the salesman category. Interestingly, Tversky and Kahneman (1974) found that people only ignored base rates in the absence of other information. In contrast, they relied on representativeness rather than base rates when supplementary information was available. In most clinical situations, psychologists will have obtained considerable information about clients and, thus, are likely to discount or ignore base rates in favor of representativeness (Kennedy et al., 1997). Accordingly, their diagnoses tend to be subjective comparisons of the match between client symptoms and prototypical diagnostic categories (Garb, 1997). The ramifications of base rate neglect in psychodiagnostic decisions were first described by Meehl and Rosen (1955).

Misperception of Regression

In his 1877 investigation of inheritance, Sir Francis Galton found that tall parents had, on average, children who were shorter than them and short parents had, on average, children who were taller than them (Barnett, van der Pols, & Dobson, 2004). Called *regression to the mean* by Galton, this statistical phenomenon has since been found in a wide variety of situations where people are selected based upon an extreme score or characteristic. For example, a person who scored very low on one examination is likely to score somewhat higher (closer to the mean) on a second examination because extreme scores contain error that will not be repeated on a subsequent test. The problem is that "people do not develop correct intuitions about this phenomenon. First they do not expect regression in many contexts where it is bound to occur. Second, when they recognize the occurrence of regression, they often invent spurious causal explanations for it" (Tversky & Kahneman, 1974, p. 1126).

The tendency to overlook or misattribute regression effects can lead to pernicious outcomes. For example, Tversky and Kahneman (1974) described a situation where flight school instructors erroneously concluded that it was harmful to praise student pilots for outstanding performance. Nonregressive predictions are also likely to be dangerous when "measures designed to stem a 'crisis' (a sudden increase in crime, disease, or bankruptcies, or a sudden decrease in sales, rainfall, or Olympic gold medal winners) will, on the average, seem to have greater impact than there actually has been" (Nisbett & Ross, 1980, p. 163). Other detrimental outcomes of nonregressive judgments have been described by Barnett et al. (2004), Bland and Altman (1994), Glutting and McDermott (1990), and Sandoval (1998).

Misconceptions about Chance

To render realistic probability estimates, an accurate understanding of how chance operates is necessary. Unfortunately, there are a variety of common misconceptions about chance.

Gambler's Fallacy

People think that chance is a self-correcting process so that deviations in one direction will cause offsetting deviations in the opposite direction to restore the balance (Tversky & Kahneman, 1993). Most famously, this results in the *gambler's fallacy*, the belief that a run of bad, or good, luck will soon be followed by the opposite. Thus, after a long run of red on the roulette wheel, most people believe that black is due. Likewise, if a series of coin tosses has resulted in consecutive heads, many people expect a tail to appear on the next toss. However, each spin of the wheel or toss of the coin is independent and, thus, each outcome is also independent.

Conjunction Fallacy

People tend to believe that the conjunction of two events is more, rather than less, probable than one of the events alone (Fantino, 1998). This, of course, violates the basic principle of probability (Dawes, 1993). For example, research participants were told that "Linda is 31 years old, single, outspoken, and very bright. She majored in philosophy. As a student, she was deeply concerned with issues of discrimination and social justice" (Kahneman & Tversky, 1996, p. 583). Participants were then asked whether it was more likely that Linda was a (a) bank teller or (b) bank teller active in the feminist movement. Logic dictates that being both a bank teller *and* an active feminist is less likely than being either a feminist *or* a bank teller. Participants in many

studies, however, chose the incorrect conjunctive response. This violates probability principles but is consistent with a bias toward representativeness.

Illusory Correlation

People are not very good at distinguishing random from nonrandom outcomes and are poor judges of correlation (Baron, 1994). Studies have consistently found that people see patterns in random data and, as a consequence, have a tendency to overinterpret chance events (Gnys et al., 1995; Plous, 1993). A classic example in psychology is the *illusory correlation* phenomenon described by Chapman and Chapman (1967), who demonstrated that people associated features of projective drawings (e.g., large or unusual eyes) with diagnostic labels (e.g., suspiciousness) because of the apparent similarity, or representativeness, of the sign and symptom when, in fact, no such correlation existed. These faulty associations are strikingly similar to the shared clinical stereotypes held by many psychologists about human figure drawings and inkblots and are a prime example of how "we convince ourselves that we know all manner of stuff that just isn't so" (Paulos, 1998, p. 27).

Insensitivity to Sample Size

The size of the sample drawn from a population should have a major influence on estimates of the accuracy with which that sample represents the population. Small samples are likely to be variant whereas large samples are less likely to stray from population parameters. In statistics, this is called the law of *large* numbers. It appears that people believe small samples to be more representative of the population than sampling theory would suggest. For instance, when asked the probability of obtaining an average height greater than six feet in samples of 1000, 100, and 10, participants rendered the same value for all three samples (Tversky & Kahneman, 1974). This tendency to regard a sample, regardless of its size, as representative of a population has been called the law of *small* numbers (Tversky & Kahneman, 1971) and has been shown to result in exaggerated confidence in the validity of conclusions based on small samples. For example, clinicians may think a small sample of child behavior (e.g., during a three-hour testing session) generalizes to the classroom and home even though research has shown this to be an unwarranted assumption (Glutting, Youngstrom, Oakland, & Watkins, 1996). Similarly, the behavior of a small, unrepresentative group of children encountered during prior clinical experiences will be overgeneralized.

The reliance on small, idiosyncratic clinical samples can result in the *clinician's illusion* (Cohen & Cohen, 1984), where clinicians and researchers hold disparate beliefs about the long-term prognosis for a disorder. The clinician samples from the population currently suffering from the disorder and thereby obtains cases that are biased toward long duration. In contrast, research samples more nearly approximate a population sample composed of cases with all possible durations and severities.

Pseudodiagnosticity

When tasked with the estimation of the relationship between two variables based on information in 2×2 contingency tables (e.g., positive or negative scores on a test versus presence or absence of a disorder), people tend to place undue emphasis on the cell that represents positive test scores in the presence of a disorder and pay insufficient attention to the three other cells (Doherty, Mynatt, Tweney, & Schiavo, 1979). In the contingency table illustrated in Figure 12.3, people will disproportionately focus on the *Yes-Positive* cell. However, all four cells must be examined to accurately judge the strength of the relationship (Schustack & Sternber, 1981). Failing to do so systematically biases the estimate upward, potentially leading to the conclusion that a strong relationship exists when it does not (Nickerson, 2004).

Inverse Probabilities

Insensitivity to prior probabilities and other misperceptions about chance contribute to a persistent difficulty in distinguishing conditional probabilities. For example, the probability of being a chronic smoker *conditional* on (given) a diagnosis of lung cancer is about .90, but the probability of having lung cancer *conditional* on (given) smoking is only around .10 (Dawes, 2001). Thus, many lung cancer patients are smokers but only a small minority of smokers will succumb to lung cancer. If the purpose of an analysis is to predict behavior, inverse probabilities will usually be systematic overestimates (Dawes, 1993). These results are predicated on the theorems of Thomas Bayes, an eighteenth-century British cleric (for a full explication and formulae, see Nickerson, 2004).

Within the context of medical and psychological tests, the probability of a positive test result given the presence of the disorder is known as the *sensitivity* of the test. The probability of the presence of the disorder given the positive test result is known as the *positive predictive power* of the test. Other conditional probabilities are *specificity*, which is the probability that the test is negative given that the disorder is absent, and *negative predictive power*, which is the probability that the disorder is absent given that the test is negative. These outcomes are illustrated in Figure 12.3 and described in Table 12.1. Psychologists are usually asked to predict membership in a diagnostic category given a positive test score and

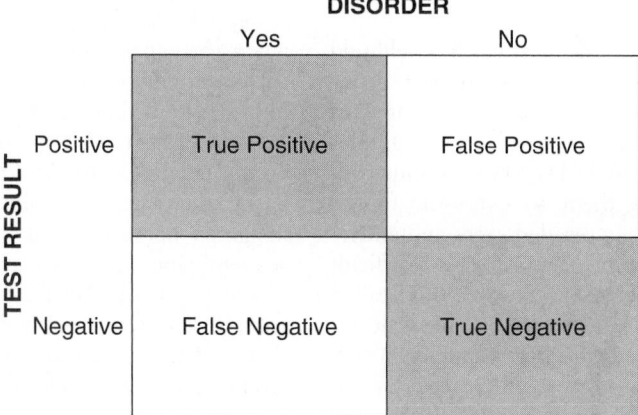

FIGURE 12.3   Contingency table or matrix of possible outcomes when a test is used to diagnose a disorder.[1]

[1]True positives are those with the disorder who test positive. True negatives are those without the disorder who test negative. False negatives are those with the disorder but the test falsely indicates the condition is not present. False positives are those without the disorder but the test falsely indicates the condition is present.

TABLE 12.1   Diagnostic Statistics

Statistic	Description	Calculation[1]
Sensitivity	Given that a person has the target disorder, the probability of obtaining a positive test score.	$TP \div (TP + FN)$
Specificity	Given that a person does *not* have the target disorder, the probability of obtaining a negative test score.	$TN \div (TN + FP)$
Positive Predictive Power	Given that a person obtains a positive test score, the probability of that person having the target disorder.	$TP \div (TP + FP)$
Negative Predictive Power	Given that a person obtains a negative test score, the probability of that person *not* having the target disorder.	$TN \div (TN + FN)$
Overall Correct Classification	Hit rate. Proportion of people with *and* without the target disorder who were correctly classified by the test.	$(TP + TN) \div (TP + TN + FP + FN)$
Area Under the Curve (AUC)	Probability that a person randomly selected from the group with the disorder will have a higher score on the test than a randomly selected person from the group that does not have the disorder.	

[1] TP = true positive, FN = false negative, TN = true negative, and FP = false positive.

are rarely charged with predicting a positive test score given a particular diagnosis. Thus, the positive predictive power of the test is usually the statistic of interest, depending on the purpose of testing. Nevertheless, an understanding of the relationships between the diagnostic statistics in Table 12.1 is critical to appropriate application of tests in psychology and medicine (Galanter & Patel, 2005).

Availability

Rather than laboriously calculating the likelihood of an event or outcome from appropriate prior probabilities, people often make a judgment based on how easily they can bring examples or occurrences to mind (Tversky & Kahneman, 1974). This causes them to overestimate the probability of an easily recalled event and underestimate the probability of an ordinary or difficult to recall event. Events are more easily recalled if they are vivid, salient, visualizable, recent, imaginable, and explainable. For example, "which is a more likely cause of death in the United States—being killed by falling airplane parts or by a shark?" (Plous, 1993, p. 121). Most people think sharks are the greatest risk, whereas falling airplane parts are actually more likely. Shark attacks are easy to visualize and receive considerable media attention, which makes them

easier to bring to mind. Availability also comes into play when people are faced with a choice between vivid personal testimonials versus "pallid, abstract, or statistical information" (Plous, 1993, p. 126). When considering the purchase of a new car, for example, emotional stories of a friend's lemon can outweigh the comprehensive statistical data published by *Consumer Reports*.

Research has also shown that thinking about or explaining a future event can lead to its increased availability in memory. For instance, when participants were asked to generate explanations for hypothetical future events and later judged the likelihood of those events, increased likelihood estimates for the previously explained events resulted (Hirt & Markman, 1995). Similarly, the extent to which physicians simply imagined being exposed to HIV at work subsequently increased their estimate of actual risk of exposure (Heath, Acklin, & Wiley, 1991). Likewise, illnesses particularly difficult to treat, those that received media attention, and recent conference topics were judged to be more common by physicians than they actually are (Galanter & Patel, 2005). In psychology, extreme cases from a clinician's unrepresentative sample of clients are especially memorable because they are vivid and salient, which partially explains why clinicians rely on their own experience over "pallid, abstract, [and] statistical" (Plous, 1993, p. 126) research reports (Tracey & Rounds, 1999). Likewise, preferred theories and preconceptions are readily available in memory and exert a powerful influence.

Anchoring and Adjustment

In many situations, people make estimates by starting with an initial value that is then adjusted, based on computations or further evidence, to arrive at a final solution. Unfortunately, these adjustments are often insufficient. As described by Piattelli-Palmarini (1994), "we always remain anchored to our original opinion, and we correct that view only starting from that same opinion" (p. 127). A demonstration of this bias was provided by Tversky and Kahneman (1974) who asked two groups of people to estimate the percentage of African countries in the United Nations. Before that, however, both groups had spun a roulette wheel to obtain a random comparison number. The first group randomly began with 10 and the second group with 65. Their subsequent estimates of the percentage of African countries in the UN were 25 and 45, respectively. These results have been replicated in more realistic situations. For example, real estate agents were shown to be anchored to initial listing prices (Northcraft & Neale, 1987). As summarized by Plous (1993, p. 151), "the effects of anchoring are pervasive and extremely robust.... People adjust insufficiently from anchor values, regardless of whether the judgment concerns the chances of nuclear war, the value of a house, or any number of other topics."

The adjustment and anchoring heuristics may become influential when school psychologists are provided with initial information about referrals. For example, "referral information, or previous test data may be available that may unduly affect the ultimate outcome of an assessment by providing a different 'starting point' in a way analogous to the anchoring of numerical predictors" (Fagley, 1988, p. 317). This supposition has been supported by several studies (deMesquita, 1992; Della Toffalo & Pedersen, 2005; McCoy, 1976; Ysseldyke et al., 1981).

Framing

Scores of studies have demonstrated that people view positive outcomes as more probable than negative outcomes (Plous, 1993). For example, Rosenhan and Messick (1966) asked participants to predict the probability of drawing cards

from a deck containing cards stamped with smiling or frowning faces. People consistently underestimated the probability of obtaining a card with a frowning face and overestimated the probability of drawing a card with a smiling face. Likewise, people unrealistically expect their personal outcomes to exceed those of other people or objective indicators (Carroll, Sweeny, & Shepperd, 2006). For instance, students rated themselves more likely than others to experience positive life events and less likely to experience negative life events (Weinstein, 1980), smokers overestimated the probability that they would quit smoking in the coming year (Weinstein, Slovic, & Gibson, 2004), and student teachers believed they would experience less difficulty than the average beginning teacher during their first year of teaching (Weinstein, 1988). This *optimistic* bias might be salient when school psychologists consider the advisability of intervention or placement options.

However, framing effects are more complex than a simple preference for positive outcomes. Tversky and Kahneman (1981) argued that people evaluate outcomes in context: positive framing (describing options in terms of gains) leads people to be risk averse and choose certain gain over potential loss, whereas negative framing (describing options in terms of losses) causes people to accept risk to avoid certain loss. Thus, different ways of presenting the same information can result in diametrically different decisions. In one study, for example, participants were presented two sets of data and asked to make two separate choices. First, would they prefer (a) a sure gain of $75 or (b) a 75% chance to win $100 and a 25% chance to gain nothing. Second, would they prefer (c) a sure loss of $75 or (d) a 75% chance to lose $100 and a 25% chance to lose nothing. In the first choice, 84% of the participants chose the first alternative (a sure gain). In contrast, 88% of the participants chose to gamble against a sure loss in the second scenario. As expected, people were risk averse when gains were at stake, but chose risk when losses were at issue.

It has been discovered that the way medical procedures are framed (mortality versus survival) has a powerful effect on patient and physician choices (Armstrong, Schwartz, Fitzgerald, Putt, & Ubel, 2002), and the way bets are framed (winning versus losing) profoundly affects gamblers (Nickerson, 2004). Framing effects have also been observed in school psychology. Fagley et al. (1999) provided doctoral school psychology students with positively and negatively framed choices on dropout prevention programs, smoking prevention programs, mainstreaming versus special education placements, and so on. As expected, more risky choices were made in response to negatively framed decision problems.

Hindsight Bias

Probability estimation can also be distorted by hindsight bias (Fischhoff, 1975), where people who know the outcome of an event will posthoc overestimate the probability of that outcome. This is analogous to Monday morning quarterbacking, where many people are confident that they could have predicted the outcome of Sunday's football game. However, this is an overestimate of their actual prognostication abilities. In part, this *illusion of learning* stems from an inability to imagine an alternative outcome (i.e., availability heuristic). Unfortunately, people seem to be relatively insensitive to the operation of hindsight bias and it may cause them to become more confident of their decisions because the actual outcomes seemed so obvious and preordained. For example, hindsight knowledge of a diagnosis might result in an overinflated belief that one would have been able to make the diagnosis with accuracy (Wedding & Faust, 1989). Hindsight bias could also cause clinicians to remember successful predictions of client behavior and forget or ignore unsuccessful predictions (Gibbs & Gambrill, 1996).

Fundamental Attribution Error

There is a robust, ubiquitous tendency of people to (a) attribute the behavior of others to enduring and consistent dispositions (i.e., personal traits) rather than the particular situation, and (b) attribute their own behavior to the demands of the situation instead of personal traits (Kahneman & Tversky, 1996). Thus, people will attribute success to their own efforts, intelligence, and perspicacity and failure to bad luck and circumstances beyond their control. For instance, one study found that 97.3% of student problems were attributed by teachers to internal student traits and home causes (Christenson, Ysseldyke, Wang, & Algozzine, 1983). Another study found that all student learning problems were attributed by school psychologists to student or family deficiencies and none to school deficits (Alessi, 1988). In clinical practice, the fundamental attribution error "results in blaming the client, rather than identifying and altering environmental events related to problems" (Gibbs & Gambrill, 1996, p. 132).

Overconfidence

Possibly because of fundamental attributions and other cognitive biases, people often express extreme confidence in highly fallible judgments (Smith & Dumont, 2002). In fact, "judgments produced in decision environments such as psychodiagnosis, which are by nature complex and ambiguous, appear to be most vulnerable to overconfidence" (Smith & Dumont, 1997, p. 342). Surprisingly, research has shown that confidence is directly related to the *number* of decisions made, irrespective of the *accuracy* of those decisions (Arkes, Hackett, & Boehm, 1989). Thus, professionals may become more confident with experience but not more accurate (Dunning, Heath, & Suls, 2004). Because of this overly positive view of themselves and their decisions, individuals tend to think their own behavior is typical of others and to assume that most people would have made the same decision as themselves (the *false consensus effect*). Overconfidence can impart a false sense of security and overconfident individuals may be less likely to objectively evaluate their own performance. Physicians, nurses, police officers, and psychologists have been shown to exhibit unwarranted confidence in their professional decisions (Baumann, Deber, & Thompson, 1991; Garb & Schramke, 1996; Kassin & Gudjonsson, 2004).

Confirmation Bias

It has repeatedly been found that people prefer confirmatory to disconfirmatory strategies and, accordingly, selectively seek and interpret evidence supportive of their prior beliefs or hypotheses and ignore or discount nonsupportive evidence (Nickerson, 1998). Typically, a preliminary hypothesis is quickly formed and then support for that initial position becomes the salient activity. As described by Baron (1994, p. 302), "this is what makes us into lawyers, hired by our own earlier views to defend them against all accusations, rather than detectives seeking the truth itself."

Confirmation bias does not operate alone—it is confounded with other cognitive heuristics, biases, and misperceptions. Representativeness, hindsight bias, fundamental attributions, and availability, among other phenomena, operate in the formulation of initial hypotheses. Research has demonstrated that counselors, jurors, lawyers, physicians, police officers, and psychologists develop preliminary hypotheses very quickly and inadequately revise them based on subsequent information (Colwell, 2005; Haverkamp, 1993; Kassin & Gudjonsson, 2004; Lopez, 1989; Meehl, 1960). For example, psychologists arrived at problem formulations within the first few clinical sessions, and failed to reformulate them during the subsequent 24 sessions (Meehl, 1960). This combination of hastily formed diagnoses and resistance to reasonable competing alternatives was the most common cognitive cause of diagnostic errors made by internists (Graber, Franklin, & Gordon, 2005).

Resistance to revision of initial hypotheses arises from several sources. First, people seek the information they expect to find, assuming that their hypotheses are correct. Accordingly, they will disproportionately emphasize the *Yes-Positive* cell (pseudodiagnosticity) of Figure 12.3 and fail to fully consider the diagnostic information contained in the other three cells. They will also favor positive tests, as illustrated in Figure 12.2. Third, they will ignore base rates, misinterpret regression effects, overgeneralize from small samples of behavior or clients, find explanations for chance occurrences, frame the problem in positive terms, and so forth. Fourth, information acquired early in the decision-making process will be given more weight than information acquired later. This *primacy effect* will prematurely terminate the revision process. Finally, even if initial hypotheses are revised, those adjustments will be insufficient because they were anchored to early, inaccurate estimates.

Once expectations have been confirmed, individuals become increasingly overconfident. They consistently focus on evidence that affirms their accuracy and disregard contrary data. Because of this heightened confidence, a false sense of security ensues. In this flattering light, individuals assume that most people would have made the same decision as them and consequently see no need to objectively evaluate their own performance. Through these intertwined mechanisms, people develop high levels of confidence in their decisions regardless of the objective merit of those decisions.

INTERVENTIONS

Although the variety and scope of human errors have been extensively investigated, interventions to decrease errors have not received commensurate attention. Few interventions have been investigated and even fewer have been found effective. Within that context, the following recommendations are proffered to improve diagnostic decision making and clinical judgment in school psychology.

Understand Cognitive Heuristics

School psychologists must become familiar with cognitive biases and heuristics on the assumption that such awareness will reduce the influence of those cognitive biases and heuristics. Although not sufficient, knowledge is necessary. The comprehensive treatments of Nickerson (2004) and Plous (1993), as well as direct instruction via classes and continuing education programs may be informative (Croskerry, 2003; Davidow & Levinson, 1993; Lilienfeld, Lynn, & Lohr, 2003).

Check for Errors

School psychologists must also recognize their vulnerability to skill-based errors, especially when administering and scoring tests. Such errors are indefensible. Scoring and administration errors can be ameliorated by careful use of checklists and guidelines that provide immediate corrective feedback (Moon, Fantuzzo, & Gorsuch, 1986). Computer-based scoring may also be beneficially employed.

Acknowledge Limitations

School psychologists must acknowledge that they are prey to the same sensory and cognitive limitations as other professionals. Meehl (1973) wrote, "it is absurd, as well as arrogant, to pretend that acquiring a PhD somehow minimizes me from the errors of sampling, perception, recording, retention, retrieval, and inference to which the human mind is suspect" (p. 278). Even the visual judgment of graphed data in single-case research designs by expert behavioral analysts has been found to be unreliable (Kromrey & Foster-Johnson, 1996). Understanding these limitations will be especially important as school psychologists increasingly utilize single-case design methodology for decision making within response-to-intervention approaches promulgated by special education laws. In terms of information processing, this means that configural complexity, limits of memory, and so on are especially relevant. Therefore, psychologists should use checklists, flowcharts, notes, practice guidelines, computer programs, standardized work processes, and other aids to reduce reliance on memory and minimize the influence of other cognitive biases (Galanter & Patel, 2005).

Become a Self-Directed, Lifelong Learner

School psychologists must become "informed students of the professional literature, capable of assessing, understanding, and applying the quality of evidence therein" (Gill & Pratt, 2005, p. 95). This includes knowledge of assessment and intervention practices, as well as of measurement and statistical principles. Good intentions, without knowledge, do not assure beneficial results. Quite the opposite, harm can occur: iatrogenic effects have been observed with well-intentioned crisis intervention and adolescent conduct disorder programs (Bootzin & Bailey, 2005; Gambrill, 2005). Professional practice extends for decades after initial preparation, and the half life of scientific knowledge is steadily decreasing (Rutter & Yule, 2002). One study estimated that college exposes professionals to only about one-sixth of the knowledge they will need during their careers (Tenopir & King, 1997). Consequently, it is imperative that school psychologists manage their own learning. The increasing availability of electronic documents and search engines may be useful tools for such self-directed, lifelong learning.

Avoid Overconfidence

Although comforting, overconfidence in complex professional judgments is unwarranted. Research has taught us that we are likely to attribute success to our own astuteness, but failure to bad luck and environmental circumstances. In contrast, we are likely to attribute the behavior of others to enduring dispositions. Consequently, *our* decisions will appear ineluctably reasonable to *us*. This is especially true in hindsight, where it can seem as if the decision was so obvious that most other clinicians would have inevitably arrived at the same conclusion. Ironically, the very processes that generate overconfidence may operate to shield a person from recognizing the limits of their competence. As noted by Kruger and Dunning (1999), the deficits in metacognitive skills that allowed an *illusion of validity* to develop are implicated in the inability to recognize a discrepancy between behavior and belief. However, appropriate feedback and training appear to diminish overconfidence (Baumann et al., 1991; Smith & Dumont, 1997).

Experience is not Necessarily Expertise

Unfortunately, the overconfident perception of competence can be exacerbated by experience. "More experienced clinicians are more confident of their judgments than are novices, even though the judgments are no less accurate" (Tracey & Rounds, 1999, p. 125). Although experience can be valuable, it generally does not produce expertise unless acquired under specific conditions. Most importantly, expert performance only develops after about 10 years of deliberate practice with feedback (Ericsson & Charness, 1994). This has been seen in diverse fields, including chess, music, medicine, and athletics (Ericsson, 2004). For example, chess grandmasters had studied about five times more than average chess tournament players by their tenth year of play (Charness, Tuffiash, Krampe, Reingold, & Vasyukova, 2005). Without deliberate practice, 10 years of experience "may lead to nothing more than learning to make the same mistakes with increasing confidence" (Skrabanek & McCormick, 1990, p. 28) or may have no more value than one year of experience, repeated ten times. This may be one explanation for the ineffectiveness of typical clinical services (Bickman, 1999).

Consequently, school psychologists must not assume, absent empirical evidence, that their experience equates to competence (Dawes, 1994; Garb & Boyle, 2003). Clinicians cannot achieve expertise without extensive deliberate practice. Deliberate practice requires immediate corrective feedback. Clinicians do not usually receive adequate feedback about their decisions and, consequently, have trouble learning from their experiences (Bickman, 1999). Although constrained by the clinical arena, psychologists must collect data on the accuracy of their decisions (Stricker, 2006) and must learn from their mistakes (Popper, 1992). Proactive attention to evaluative data is crucial to the development of professional expertise. Objective competence is infinitely preferable to overconfidence and wishful thinking.

Use Decision Aids and Actuarial Methods

McDermott (1981) found that school psychologists' decisions were affected by inconsistent decision rules, theoretical orientations, weighing of diagnostic cues, and diagnostic styles. These inconsistencies arise, at least partially, from the fallibility of human information processing. Decision aids such as checklists will help reduce inconsistency in some situations. Another powerful remedy can be found in actuarial methods, which have consistently been found superior to clinical judgment (Dawes et al., 1989). Actuarial methods depend on mechanical or statistical prediction whereas clinical methods rely on subjective, impressionistic judgment. Critically, the information used for prediction, whether actuarial or clinical, can be of any type. The task is, "given a data set (e.g., life history facts, interview ratings, ability test scores, MMPI profiles, nurses' notes), how is one to put these various facts (or first-order inferences) together to arrive at a prediction about the individual" (Grove & Meehl, 1996, p. 299). It is not the nature of the data, but how the data are combined, mechanically or clinically, that produces superior results (Baron, 1994). For example, case managers' clinical judgment regarding home treatment visits needed by aggressive and disruptive children was inferior to a linear combination of six rating items assessing parental functioning rendered by those same clinicians (Bierman, Nix, Murphy, & Maples, 2006). Accordingly, spurious arguments against actuarial methods should be rejected (Grove & Meehl, 1996) and actuarial methods applied whenever possible.

Use Reliable, Valid Tools

It is a truism that the ability of school psychologists is limited by the reliability and validity of the tools they employ (Palmiter, 2004). As illustrated by Frazier and Youngstrom (2006), reliance on instruments with solid reliability and validity evidence is integral to evidence-based diagnosis and evidence-based testing (Mash & Hunsley, 2005; McFall, 2005). School psychologists might profitably emulate this approach. Further, given that judgments are inordinately influenced by information obtained early in the diagnostic process, it is advisable to begin that process with the most valid three or four nonredundant pieces of data (Wedding & Faust, 1989).

Use Bayesian Reasoning

Bayesian reasoning entails being aware of base rates as well as avoiding inverse probabilities and pseudodiagnosticity. Unfortunately, people do not intuitively grasp Bayesian methods and have considerable difficulty applying them correctly even after professional training (Gigerenzer, 2002). For example, problems similar to the previously presented colorectal cancer example were solved by only 5% to 17% of physicians (Gigerenzer, 2002). Although people tend to do better with natural frequencies than with probabilities or percentages, decision aids such as computer programs are probably the best solution to this natural human weakness. Software solutions for calculating Bayesian statistics are freely available at www.public.asu.edu/~mwwatkin.

Do Not Confuse Classical Validity with Diagnostic Utility

Relatedly, school psychologists should not confuse classical validity methods with diagnostic statistics (Wiggins, 1988). Average group score differences indicate that *groups* can be discriminated. This classical validity approach cannot be uncritically extended to conclude that mean group differences are distinctive enough to differentiate among *individuals*. Figure 12.4 illustrates this dilemma. It displays hypothetical score distributions of children from regular and exceptional student populations. Group mean differences are clearly discernable, but the overlap between distributions makes it difficult to accurately identify group membership for those individuals within the overlapping distributions. Group separation is necessary but not sufficient for accurate decisions about individuals.

Unfortunately, errors in assigning individuals to normal or disabled groups are unavoidable given the imperfect tools and taxonomies available to psychologists (Zarin & Earls, 1993). The relative proportion of correct and incorrect diagnostic decisions depends on the cut score used. In Figure 12.4, for example, X1 represents a low cut score and X2 a high cut score. With a low cut score, there are a large number of false positive and a small number of false negative decisions. With a high cut score, there are a large number of false negative and a small number of false positive decisions. Beyond cut scores, the accuracy of diagnostic decisions is dependent on the base rate or prevalence of the particular disability in the population being assessed (Meehl & Rosen, 1955).

In contrast, by systematically using all possible cut scores of a diagnostic test and graphing true positive against false positive decision rates for each cut score, the full range of that test's diagnostic utility can be displayed (McFall & Treat, 1999; Swets, Dawes, & Monahan, 2000). Designated the receiver operating characteristic

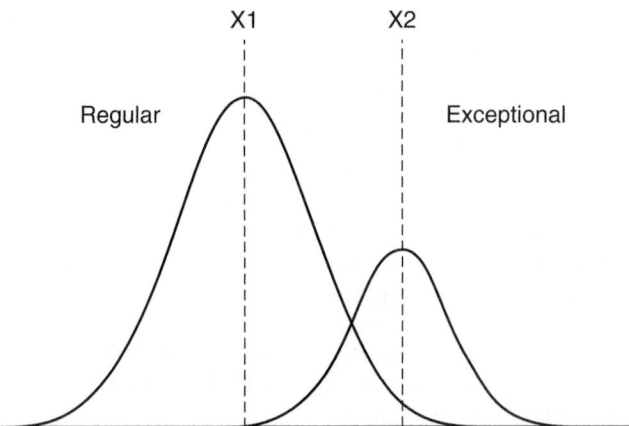

FIGURE 12.4 Hypothetical test score distributions for regular and exceptional student populations with two cut points (X1 and X2).

(ROC), this procedure is not confounded by cut scores or prevalence rates. Consequently, ROC curves are "the state-of-the-art method for describing the diagnostic accuracy of a test" (Weinstein, Obuchowski, & Lieber, 2005, p. 16) and are "recognized widely as the most meaningful approach to quantify the accuracy of diagnostic information and diagnostic decisions" (Metz & Pan, 1999, p. 1).

The area under the ROC curve (AUC) provides an accuracy index of the test. AUC values can range from 0.5 to 1.0. An AUC value of 0.5 signifies that no discrimination exists. In this case, the ROC curve lies on the main diagonal of the graph and the diagnostic system is functioning at the level of chance. In contrast, an AUC value of 1.0 denotes perfect discrimination. The AUC also has an intuitive meaning: If one person is randomly selected from the nondisordered population and one from the disordered population, the AUC is the probability of distinguishing between those two individuals with the test.

Two illustrative ROC curves are presented in Figures 12.5 and 12.6. In Figure 12.5, Verbal and Performance IQ score differences on the Wechsler Intelligence Scale for Children–Third Edition (WISC-III; Wechsler, 1991) were compared between 1,153 children with learning disabilities and the 2,200 children in the WISC-III normative sample. Figure 12.6 displays the ROC curve for the Overreactivity Scale of the Adjustment Scales for Children and Adolescents (ASCA; McDermott, Marston, & Stott, 1993) for 21 children with emotional disabilities compared to 1,056 children in the ASCA normative sample.

The AUCs were .57 and .94, respectively, for Figures 12.5 and 12.6. AUC values of 0.5 to 0.7 indicate low test accuracy, 0.7 to 0.9 indicate moderate test accuracy, and 0.9 to 1.0 indicate high test accuracy (Swets, 1988). In this example, Verbal-Performance IQ score differences were not useful in identifying children with learning disabilities but ASCA Overreactivity scores were extremely accurate in distinguishing children with emotional disabilities. Accordingly, school psychologists should routinely use diagnostic statistics, including the ROC and its AUC, when considering the accuracy of diagnostic information. Software solutions for ROC curves are freely available at www.rad.jhmi.edu/jeng/javarad/roc/JROCFITi.html and www.public.asu.edu/~mwwatkin.

Rely on a Scientific Approach

Adopt and adhere to a scientific approach when making professional decisions (Dawes, 1995; Hayes, Barlow, & Nelson-Gray, 1999; McFall, 1991, 2000). Unfortunately, scientific reasoning does not come naturally: it demands critical thinking, tolerance of ambiguity, skepticism, openness to criticism, and acceptance of fallibility (Baron, 1994; Cromer, 1993; Wilson, 1995). Science does not confuse reasoning with rationalizing, nor beliefs with facts. Instead, science is a self-correcting process of objective investigation and logical inquiry used to accumulate a reliable body of knowledge (Gibbs & Gambrill, 1996).

It is often assumed that hypothetico-deductive reasoning in psychological practice is analogous to scientific reasoning. That is, formulation of diagnostic hypotheses that guide

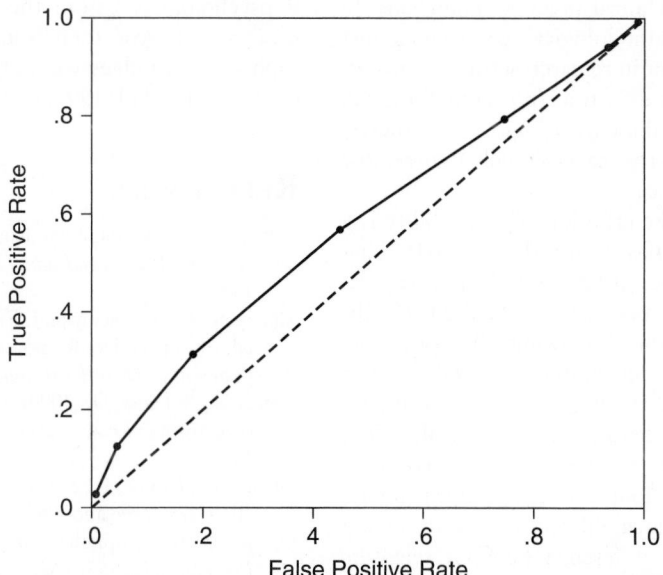

FIGURE 12.5 **ROC curve of Verbal-Performance IQ score differences on the Wechsler Intelligence Scale for Children–Third Edition (WISC-III) for 1,153 children with learning disabilities and the 2,200 children in the WISC-III normative sample.**

subsequent data gathering that, in turn, either supports or fails to support the proposed hypotheses. For example, Lichtenberger (2006, p. 27) suggested that "a hypothesis...can be confirmed with one piece of supplementary data, but two pieces of confirmatory data are preferable. If one

or more pieces of data contradict the hypothesis, then that hypothesis may not be valid for that client." Hypothetico-deductive strategies work in science because they are public and can be tested and refuted by other researchers but "the idealized process often goes astray" (Aspel et al.,

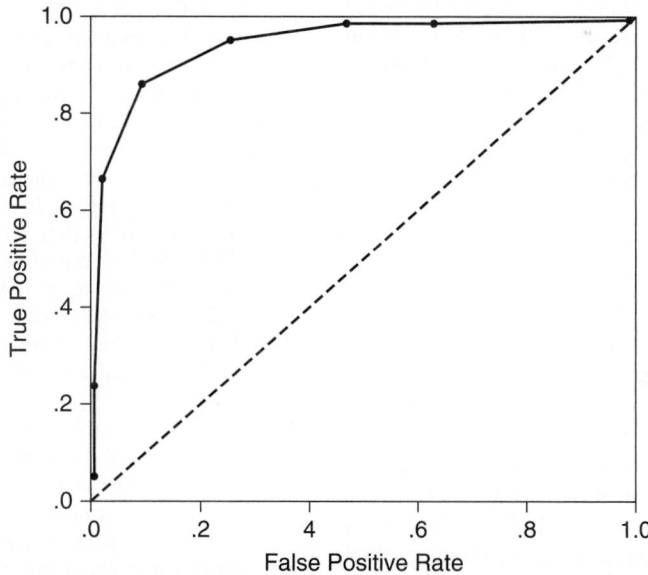

FIGURE 12.6 **ROC curve of the Overreactivity Scale of the Adjustment Scales for Children and Adolescents (ASCA) for 21 children with emotional disabilities compared to 1,056 children in the ASCA normative sample.**

1998, p. 138) in clinical practice. Clinicians do not apply the methodological controls against bias that are present in research settings. Further, clinical hypotheses are private (no competitors will attempt to refute the psychologist's hypotheses) and are, therefore, exceptionally vulnerable to confirmation bias.

In contrast, the criterion of falsifiability is a hallmark of scientific inquiry (Platt, 1964). That is, theories are scientific only if they can be subjected to tests that can refute them (Gibbs & Gambrill, 1996). Following this principle, clinicians must actively search for *disconfirmatory* evidence to reduce the influence of confirmatory bias (Arkes, 1991; Faust, 1986; Sandoval, 1998). "Always look first for that which disconfirms your beliefs; then look for that which supports them. Look with equal diligence for both. Doing so will make the difference between scientific honesty and artfully supported propaganda" (Gibbs, 2003, p. 89). An even better strategy may be to formulate plausible competing hypotheses and actively search for disconfirmatory evidence (Croskerry, 2003; Hirt & Markman, 1995; Plous, 1993; Tracey & Rounds, 1999; Wedding & Faust, 1989). This *competing hypothesis strategy* is preferable to the hypothetico-deductive strategy in clinical practice.

Reliance on science (both as a problem-solving process and as a reliable body of knowledge) is central to evidence-based practice, empirically supported practice, and science-based psychology (Gambrill, 2005; Gibbs & Gambrill, 1996; Lilienfeld & O'Donohue, 2006; Lonigan, Elbert, & Johnson, 1998; McFall, 1991; Stricker, 2006; USDOE, 2003). As with evidence-based assessment, school psychologists might beneficially incorporate these approaches into their professional practice.

Conclusion

Almost 300 years ago, Alexander Pope reminded us that to err is human. Nevertheless, it is the moral, ethical, and legal obligation of psychologists to err as little as possible in their diagnostic decision making and clinical judgments (Gambrill, 2005; Hummel, 1999; McFall, 2000; Meehl, 1973; Poortinga & Soudijn, 2003; Popper, 1992). Lawyers and judges are increasingly aware of scientific method and are being trained to adjudicate complex scientific disputes (Federal Judicial Center, 2000; Foster & Huber, 1997). Consequently,

if psychologists ignore their duty to minimize professional error, then "some smart lawyers and sophisticated judges will either discipline or discredit us" (Meehl, 1997, p. 98).

References

Alessi, G. (1988). Diagnosis diagnosed: A systemic reaction. *Professional School Psychology, 3*, 145–151.

Algozzine, B., & Ysseldyke, J. E. (1981). Special education services for normal children: Better safe than sorry? *Exceptional Children, 48*, 238–243.

Allard, G., & Faust, D. (2000). Errors in scoring objective personality tests. *Assessment, 7*, 119–129.

Allen, J. G., Coyne, L., & Logure, A. M. (1990). Do clinicians agree about who needs extended psychiatric hospitalization? *Comprehensive Psychiatry, 31*, 355–362.

Anderson, R. E., Hill, R. B., & Key, C. R. (1989). The sensitivity and specificity of clinical diagnostics during five decades: Toward an understanding of necessary fallibility. *Journal of the American Medical Association, 261*, 1610–1617.

Arkes, H. R. (1991). Costs and benefits of judgment errors: Implications for debiasing. *Psychological Bulletin, 110*, 486–498.

Arkes, H. R., Hackett, C., & Boehm, L. (1989). The generality of the relation between familiarity and judged validity. *Journal of Behavioral Decision Making, 2*, 81–94.

Armstrong, K., Schwartz, J. S., Fitzgerald, G., Putt, M., & Ubel, P. A. (2002). Effect of framing as gain versus loss on understanding and hypothetical treatment choices: Survival and mortality curves. *Medical Decision Making, 22*, 76–83.

Aspel, A. D., Willis, W. G., & Faust, D. (1998). School psychologists' diagnostic decision-making processes: Objective-subjective discrepancies. *Journal of School Psychology, 36*, 137–149.

Barnett, A. G., van der Pols, J. C., & Dobson, A. J. (2004). Regression to the mean: What it is and how to deal with it. *International Journal of Epidemiology, 34*, 215–220.

Barnett, D. W. (1988). Professional judgment: A critical appraisal. *School Psychology Review, 17*, 658–672.

Baron, J. (1994). *Thinking and deciding* (2nd ed.). NY: Cambridge University Press.

Baumann, A. O., Deber, R. B., & Thompson, G. G. (1991). Overconfidence among physicians and nurses: The 'micro-certainty, macro-uncertainty' phenomenon. *Social Science in Medicine, 32*, 167–174.

Beam, C. A., Layde, P. M., & Sullivan, D. C. (1996). Variability in the interpretation of screening mammograms by U.S. radiologists: Findings from a national sample. *Archives of Internal Medicine*, *156*, 209–213.

Bickman, L. (1999). Practice makes perfect and other myths about mental health services. *American Psychologist, 54*, 965–978.

Bickman, L., Karver, M. S., & Schut, J. A. (1997). Clinician reliability and accuracy in judging appropriate level of care. *Journal of Consulting and Clinical Psychology, 65*, 515–520.

Bierman, K. L., Nix, R. L., Murphy, S. A., & Maples, J. J. (2006). Examining clinical judgment in an adaptive intervention design: The Fast Track program. *Journal of Consulting and Clinical Psychology, 74*, 468–481.

Bland, J. M., & Altman, D. G. (1994). Some examples of regression towards the mean. *British Medical Journal, 309*, 780.

Bootzin, R. R., & Bailey, E. T. (2005). Understanding placebo, nocebo, and iatrogenic treatment effects. *Journal of Clinical Psychology, 61*, 871–880.

Brown, R. T., & Jackson, L. A. (1992). Ex-Huming an old issue. *Journal of School Psychology, 30*, 215–221.

Carroll, P., Sweeny, K., & Shepperd, J. A. (2006). Forsaking optimism. *Review of General Psychology, 10*, 56–73.

Chapman, L. J., & Chapman, J. P. (1967). Genesis of popular but erroneous psychodiagnostic observations. *Journal of Abnormal Psychology, 72*, 193–204.

Charness, N., Tuffiash, M., Krampe, R., Reingold, E., & Vasyukova, E. (2005). The role of deliberate practice in chess expertise. *Applied Cognitive Psychology, 19*, 151–165.

Christenson, S., Ysseldyke, J. E., Wang, J. J., & Algozzine, B. (1983). Teachers' attributions for problems that result in referral for psychoeducational evaluation. *Journal of Educational Research, 76*, 174–180.

Clark, A., & Harrington, R. (1999). On diagnosing rare disorders rarely: Appropriate use of screening instruments. *Journal of Child Psychology and Psychiatry, 40*, 287–290.

Cohen, P., & Cohen, J. (1984). The clinician's illusion. *Archives of General Psychiatry, 41*, 1178–1182.

Colwell, L. H. (2005). Cognitive heuristics in the context of legal decision making. *American Journal of Forensic Psychology, 23*(2), 17–41.

Cromer, A. (1993). *Uncommon sense: The heretical nature of science*. NY: Oxford University Press.

Croskerry, P. (2003). The importance of cognitive errors in diagnosis and strategies to minimize them. *Academic Medicine, 78*, 775–780.

Daleiden, E. L., Chorpita, B. F., Kollins, S. H., & Drabman, R. S. (1999). Factors affecting the reliability of clinical judgments about the function of children's school-refusal behavior. *Journal of Clinical Child Psychology, 28*, 396–406.

Davidow, J., & Levinson, E. M. (1993). Heuristic principles and cognitive bias in decision making: Implications for assessment in school psychology. *Psychology in the Schools, 30*, 351–361.

Dawes, R. M. (1993). Prediction of the future versus an understanding of the past: A basic asymmetry. *American Journal of Psychology, 106*, 1–24.

Dawes, R. M. (1994). *House of cards: Psychology and psychotherapy built on myth*. NY: Free Press.

Dawes, R. M. (1995). Standards of practice. In S. C. Hayes, V. M. Follette, R. M. Dawes, & K. E. Grady (Eds.), *Scientific standards of psychological practice: Issues and recommendations* (pp. 31–43). Reno, NV: Context Press.

Dawes, R. M. (2001). *Everyday irrationality: How pseudo-scientists, lunatics, and the rest of us systematically fail to think rationally*. Boulder, CO: Westview Press.

Dawes, R. M., Faust, D., & Meehl, P. E. (1989). Clinical versus actuarial judgment. *Science, 243*, 1668–1674.

Della Toffalo, D. A., & Pedersen, J. A. (2005). The effect of a psychiatric diagnosis on school psychologists' special education eligibility decisions regarding emotional disturbance. *Journal of Emotional and Behavioral Disorders, 13*, 53–60.

deMesquita, P. (1992). Diagnostic problem solving of school psychologists: Scientific method or guesswork? *Journal of School Psychology, 30*, 269–291.

Doherty, M. E., Mynatt, C. R., Tweney, R. D., & Schiavo, M. D. (1979). Pseudodiagnosticity. *Acta Psychologica, 43*, 111–121.

Dunn, W. R., Schackman, B. R., Walsh, C., Lyman, S., Jones, E. C., Warren, R. F., & Marx, R. G. (2005). Variation in orthopaedic surgeons' perceptions about the indications for rotator cuff surgery. *Journal of Bone and Joint Surgery, 87*, 1978–1984.

Dunning, D., Heath, C., & Suls, J. M. (2004). Flawed self-assessment: Implications for health, education, and the workplace. *Psychological Science in the Public Interest, 5*, 69–106.

Ericsson, K. A. (2004). Deliberate practice and the acquisition and maintenance of expert performance in medicine and related domains. *Academic Medicine, 79*(10), S70–S81.

Ericsson, K. A., & Charness, N. (1994). Expert performance: Its structure and acquisition. *American Psychologist, 49*, 725–747.

Evans, J., & Wason, P. C. (1976). Rationalization in a reasoning task. *British Journal of Psychology, 67*, 486–497.

Fagley, N. S. (1988). Judgmental heuristics: Implications for the decision making of school psychologists. *School Psychology Review, 17*, 311–321.

Fagley, N. S., Miller, P. M., & Jones, R. N. (1999). The effect of positive or negative frame on the choices of students in school psychology and educational administration. *School Psychology Quarterly, 14*, 148–162.

Fantino, E. (1998). Judgment and decision making: Behavioral approaches. *The Behavior Analyst, 21*, 203–218.

Faust, D. (1986). Research on human judgment and its application to clinical practice. *Professional Psychology: Research and Practice, 17*, 420–430.

Federal Judicial Center. (2000). *Reference manual on scientific evidence* (2nd ed.). Washington, DC: Author.

Fischhoff, B. (1975). Hindsight ≠ foresight: The effects of outcome knowledge on judgment under uncertainty. *Journal of Experimental Psychology: Human Perception and Performance, 1*, 288–299.

Foster, K. R., & Huber, P. W. (1997). *Judging science: Scientific knowledge and the federal courts.* Cambridge, MA: MIT Press.

Frazier, T. W., & Youngstrom, E. A. (2006). Evidence-based assessment of attention-deficit/ hyperactivity disorder: Using multiple sources of information. *Journal of the American Academy of Child and Adolescent Psychiatry, 45*, 614–620.

Galanter, C. A., & Patel, V. L. (2005). Medical decision making: A selective review for child psychiatrists and psychologists. *Journal of Child Psychology and Psychiatry, 46*, 675–689.

Gambrill, E. (2005). *Critical thinking in clinical practice: Improving the quality of judgments and decisions* (2nd ed.). Hoboken, NJ: Wiley.

Garb, H. N. (1996). The representativeness and past-behaviors heuristics in clinical judgment. *Professional Psychology: Research and Practice, 27*, 272–277.

Garb, H. N. (1997). Race bias, social class bias, and gender bias in clinical judgment. *Clinical Psychology: Science and Practice, 4*, 99–120.

Garb, H. N. (1998). *Studying the clinician: Judgment research and psychological assessment.* Washington, DC: American Psychological Association.

Garb, H. N. (2005). Clinical judgment and decision making. *Annual Review of Clinical Psychology, 1*, 67–89.

Garb, H. N., & Boyle, P. A. (2003). Understanding why some clinicians use pseudoscientific methods: Findings from research on clinical judgment. In S. O. Lilienfeld, S. J. Lynn, & J. M. Lohr (Eds.), *Science and pseudoscience in clinical psychology* (pp. 17–38). New York: Guilford.

Garb, H. N., & Lutz, C. (2001). Cognitive complexity and the validity of clinicians' judgments. *Assessment, 8*, 111–115.

Garb, H. N., & Schramke, C. J. (1996). Judgment research and neuropsychological assessment: A narrative review and meta-analyses. *Psychological Bulletin, 120*, 140–153.

Gibbs, L. E. (2003). *Evidence-based practice for the helping professions: A practical guide with integrated multimedia.* Pacific Grove, CA: Brooks/Cole.

Gibbs, L., & Gambrill, E. (1996). *Critical thinking for social workers: Exercises for the helping professions.* Thousand Oaks, CA: Pine Forge Press.

Gigerenzer, G. (2002). *Calculated risks: How to know when numbers deceive you.* New York: Simon & Schuster.

Gigerenzer, G., & Edwards, A. (2003). Simple tools for understanding risks: From innumeracy to insight. *British Medical Journal, 327*, 741–744.

Gill, K. J., & Pratt, C. W. (2005). Clinical decision making and the evidence-based practitioner. In R. E. Drake, M. R. Merrens, & D. W. Lynde (Eds.), *Evidence-based mental health practice: A textbook* (pp. 95–122). New York: W. W. Norton.

Gilovich, T., Griffin, D., & Kahneman, D. (2002). *Heuristics and biases: The psychology of intuitive judgment.* New York: Cambridge University Press.

Glutting, J. J., & McDermott, P. A. (1990). Principles and problems in learning potential. In C. R. Reynolds & R. W. Kamphaus (Eds.), *Handbook of psychological and educational assessment: 1. Intelligence and achievement* (pp. 296–347). New York: Guilford Press.

Glutting, J. J., Youngstrom, E. A., Oakland, T., & Watkins, M. W. (1996). Situational specificity and generality of test behaviors for samples of normal and referred children. *School Psychology Review, 25*, 94–107.

Gnys, J. A., Willis, W. G., & Faust, D. (1995). School psychologists' diagnoses of learning disabilities: A study of illusory correlation. *Journal of School Psychology, 33*, 59–73.

Graber, M. L., Franklin, N., & Gordon, R. (2005). Diagnostic error in internal medicine. *Archives of Internal Medicine, 165*, 1493–1499.

Grove, W. M., & Meehl, P. E. (1996). Comparative efficiency of informal (subjective, impressionistic) and formal (mechanical, algorithmic) prediction procedures: The clinical-statistical controversy. *Psychology, Public Policy, and Law, 2*, 293–323.

Halford, G. S., Baker, R., McCredden, J. E., & Bain, J. D. (2005). How many variables can humans process? *Psychological Science, 16*, 70–76.

Hastie, R., Schkade, D. A., & Payne, J. W. (1999). Juror judgments in civil cases: Hindsight effects on judgments of liability for punitive damages. *Law and Human Behavior, 23*, 597–614.

Haverkamp, B. E. (1993). Confirmatory bias in hypothesis testing for client-identified and counselor identified self-generated hypotheses. *Journal of Counseling Psychology, 40*, 303–315.

Hayes, S. C., Barlow, D. H., & Nelson-Gray, R. O. (1999). *The scientist-practitioner: Research and accountability in the age of managed care* (2nd ed.). Boston: Allyn and Bacon.

Heath, L., Acklin, M., & Wiley, K. (1991). Cognitive heuristics and AIDS risk assessment among physicians. *Journal of Applied Social Psychology, 21,* 1859–1867.

Herman, S. (2005). Improving decision making in forensic child sexual abuse evaluations. *Law and Human Behavior, 29,* 87–120.

Hirt, E. R., & Markman, K. D. (1995). Multiple explanation: A consider-an-alternative strategy for debiasing judgments. *Journal of Personality and Social Psychology, 69,* 1069–1086.

Huebner, E. S. (1989). Errors in decision-making: A comparison of school psychologists' inter-pretations of grade equivalents, percentiles, and deviation IQs. *School Psychology Review, 18,* 51–55.

Hummel, T. J. (1999). The usefulness of tests in clinical decisions. In J. W. Lichtenberg & R. K. Goodyear (Eds.), *Scientist-practitioner perspectives on test interpretation* (pp. 59–112). Boston: Allyn and Bacon.

Johnson, V. M. (1980). Analysis of factors influencing special educational placement decisions. *Journal of School Psychology, 18,* 191–202.

Kahneman, D., & Tversky, A. (1996). On the reality of cognitive illusions. *Psychological Review, 103,* 582–591.

Kassin, S. M., & Gudjonsson, G. H. (2004). The psychology of confessions: A review of the literature and issues. *Psychological Science in the Public Interest, 5,* 33–67.

Kennedy, M. L., Willis, W. G., & Faust, D. (1997). The base-rate fallacy in school psychology. *Journal of Psychoeducational Assessment, 15,* 292–307.

Kirk, S. A., & Hsieh, D. K. (2004). Diagnostic consistency in assessing conduct disorder: An experiment on the effect of social context. *American Journal of Orthopsychiatry, 74,* 43–55.

Kromrey, J. D., & Foster-Johnson, L. (1996). Determining the efficacy of intervention: The use of effect sizes for data analysis in single-subject research. *Journal of Experimental Education, 65,* 73–93.

Kruger, J., & Dunning, D. (1999). Unskilled and unaware of it: How difficulties in recognizing one's own incompetence lead to inflated self-assessments. *Journal of Personality and Social Psychology, 77,* 112–1134.

Leape, L. L. (1994). Error in medicine. *Journal of the American Medical Association, 272,* 1851–1857.

Lichtenberger, E. O. (2006). Computer utilization and clinical judgment in psychological assessment reports. *Journal of Clinical Psychology, 62,* 19–32.

Lilienfeld, S. O., Lynn, S. J., & Lohr, J. M. (2003). *Science and pseudoscience in clinical psychology.* New York: Guilford.

Lilienfeld, S. O., & O'Donohue, W. T. (2006). What are the great ideas of clinical science and why do we need them? *The General Psychologist, 41*(2), 15–18.

Lonigan, C., Elbert, J. C., & Johnson, S. B. (1998). Empirically supported psychosocial interventions for children: An overview. *Journal of Clinical Child Psychology, 27,* 138–145.

Lopez, S. R. (1989). Patient variable biases in clinical judgment: Conceptual overview and methodological considerations. *Psychological Bulletin, 106,* 184–203.

Macmann, G. M., & Barnett, D. W. (1999). Diagnostic decision making in school psychology: Understanding and coping with uncertainty. In C. R. Reynolds & T. B. Gutkin (Eds.), *Handbook of school psychology* (3rd ed., pp. 519–548). New York: Wiley.

Mash, E. J., & Hunsley, J. (2005). Evidence-based assessment of child and adolescent disorders: Issues and challenges. *Journal of Clinical Child and Adolescent Psychology, 34,* 362–379.

McCoy, S. A. (1976). Clinical judgments of normal childhood behavior. *Journal of Consulting and Clinical Psychology, 44,* 710–714.

McDermott, P. A. (1980). Congruence and typology of diagnoses in school psychology: An empirical study. *Psychology in the Schools, 17,* 12–24.

McDermott, P. A. (1981). Sources of error in psychoeducational diagnosis of children. *Journal of School Psychology, 19,* 31–44.

McDermott, P. A., Marston, N. C., & Stott, D. H. (1993). *Adjustment scales for children and adolescents.* Philadelphia, PA: Edumetric and Clinical Science.

McFall, R. M. (1991). Manifesto for a science of clinical psychology. *The Clinical Psychologist, 44* (6), 75–88.

McFall, R. M. (2000). Elaborate reflections on a simple manifesto. *Applied & Preventive Psychology, 9,* 5–21.

McFall, R. M. (2005). Theory and utility—Key themes in evidence-based assessment: Comment on the special section. *Psychological Assessment, 17,* 312–323.

McFall, R. M., & Treat, T. A. (1999). Quantifying the information value of clinical assessments with signal detection theory. *Annual Review of Psychology, 50,* 215–241.

Meehl, P. E. (1960). The cognitive activity of the clinician. *American Psychologist, 15,* 19–27.

Meehl, P. E. (1973). Why I do not attend case conferences. In P. E. Meehl, *Psychodiagnosis: Selected papers* (pp. 225–302). Minneapolis: University of Minnesota Press.

Meehl, P. E. (1997). Credentialed persons, credentialed knowledge. *Clinical Psychology: Science and Practice, 4,* 91–98.

Meehl, P. E., & Rosen, A. (1955). Antecedent probability and the efficiency of psychometric signs, patterns, or cutting scores. *Psychological Bulletin, 52,* 194–216.

Metz, C. E., & Pan, X. (1999). "Proper" binormal ROC curves: Theory and maximum-likelihood estimation. *Journal of Mathematical Psychology, 43,* 1–33.

Moon, G. W., Fantuzzo, J. W., & Gorsuch, R. L. (1986). Teaching WAIS-R administration skills: Comparison of the mastery model to other existing clinical training modalities. *Professional Psychology: Research and Practice, 17,* 31–35.

Nickerson, R. S. (1998). Confirmation bias: A ubiquitous phenomenon in many guises. *Review of General Psychology, 2,* 175–220.

Nickerson, R. S. (2004). *Cognition and chance: The psychology of probabilistic reasoning.* Mahwah, NJ: Erlbaum.

Nisbett, R., & Ross, L. (1980). *Human inference: Strategies and short-comings of social judgment.* Englewood Cliffs, NJ: Prentice Hall.

Northcraft, G. B., & Neale, M. A. (1987). Experts, amateurs, and real estate: An anchoring-and-adjustment perspective on property pricing decisions. *Organizational Behavior and Human Decision Processes, 39,* 84–97.

Palmiter, D. J. (2004). A survey of the assessment practices of child and adolescent clinicians. *American Journal of Orthopsychiatry, 74,* 122–128.

Pappadopulos, E., Jensen, P. S., Schur, S. B., MacIntyre, J. C., Ketner, S. Van Orden, K., et al. (2002). 'Real world' atypical antipsychotic prescribing practices in public child and adolescent inpatient settings. *Schizophrenia Bulletin, 28,* 111–121.

Paulos, J. A. (1998). *Once upon a number: The hidden mathematical logic of stories.* New York: Basic Books.

Persons, J. B., & Bertagnolli, A. (1999). Interrater reliability of cognitive-behavioral case formulations of depression: A replication. *Cognitive Therapy and Research, 23,* 271–283.

Piattelli-Palmarini, M. (1994). *Inevitable illusions: How mistakes of reason rule our minds.* New York: Wiley.

Platt, J. R. (1964). Strong inference. *Science, 146,* 347–352.

Plous, S. (1993). *The psychology of judgment and decision making.* New York: McGraw-Hill.

Poortinga, Y. H., & Soudijn, K. A. (2003). Ethical principles of the psychology profession and professional competencies. In W. O'Donohue & K. Ferguson (Eds.), *Handbook of professional ethics for psychologists: Issues, questions, and controversies* (pp. 67–80). Thousand Oaks, CA: Sage.

Popper, K. (1992). *In search of a better world: Lectures and essays from thirty years.* New York: Routledge.

Reason, J. (1990). *Human error.* New York: Cambridge University Press.

Robinson, J. O. (1998). *The psychology of visual illusion.* Mineola, NY: Dover Publications.

Rosenhan, D. L., & Messick, S. (1966). Affect and expectation. *Journal of Personality and Social Psychology, 3,* 38–44.

Ruscio, J. (2003). Holistic judgment in clinical practice. *Scientific Review of Mental Health Practice, 2,* 49–60.

Rutter, M., & Yule, W. (2002). *Child and adolescent psychiatry* (4th ed.). Malden, MA: Blackwell Science.

Sandoval, J. (1998). Critical thinking in test interpretation. In J. Sandoval, C. L. Frisby, K. F. Geisinger, J. D. Scheuneman, & J. R. Grenier (Eds.), *Test interpretation and diversity: Achieving equity in assessment* (pp. 31–49). Washington, DC: American Psychological Association.

Schustack, M. W., & Sternber, R. J. (1981). Evaluation of evidence in causal inference. *Journal of Experimental Psychology: General, 110,* 101–120.

Shear, M. K., Greeno, C., Kang, J., Ludewig, D., Frank, E., Swartz, M. D., & Hanekamp, M. (2000). Diagnosis of nonpsychotic patients in community clinics. *American Journal of Psychiatry, 157,* 581–587.

Simon, H. A. (1955). A behavioral model of rational choice. *Quarterly Journal of Economics, 69,* 99–118.

Skrabanek, P., & McCormick, J. (1990). *Follies and fallacies in medicine.* Buffalo, NY: Prometheus Books.

Slate, J. R., Jones, C. H., Coulter, C., & Covert, T. L. (1992). Practitioners' administration and scoring of the WISC-R: Evidence that we do err. *Journal of School Psychology, 30,* 77–82.

Smith, D., & Dumont, F. (1997). Eliminating overconfidence in psychodiagnosis: Strategies for training and practice. *Clinical Psychology: Science and Practice, 4,* 335–345.

Smith, J. D., & Dumont, F. (2002). Confidence in psychodiagnosis: What makes us so sure? *Clinical Psychology and Psychotherapy, 9,* 292–298.

Strauss, G., Chassin, M., & Lock, J. (1995). Can experts agree when to hospitalize adolescents? *Journal of the American Academy of Child and Adolescent Psychiatry, 34,* 418–424.

Stricker, G. (2006). The local clinical scientist, evidence-based practice, and personality assessment. *Journal of Personality Assessment, 86,* 4–9.

Swets, J. A. (1988). Measuring the accuracy of diagnostic systems. *Science, 240,* 1285–1293.

Swets, J. A., Dawes, R. M., & Monahan, J. (2000). Psychological science can improve diagnostic decisions. *Psychological Science in the Public Interest, 1,* 1–26.

Tenopir, C., & King, D. W. (1997). Trends in scientific scholarly publishing in the United

States. *Journal of Scholarly Publishing, 28,* 135–170.

Tracey, T. J., & Rounds, J. (1999). Inference and attribution errors in test interpretation. In J. W. Lichtenberg & R. K. Goodyear (Eds.), *Scientist-practitioner perspectives on test interpretation* (pp. 113–131). Boston: Allyn and Bacon.

Tversky, A., & Kahneman, D. (1971). Belief in the law of small numbers. *Psychological Bulletin, 76,* 105–110.

Tversky, A., & Kahneman, D. (1974). Judgment under uncertainty: Heuristics and biases. *Science, 185,* 1124–1131.

Tversky, A., & Kahneman, D. (1981). The framing of decisions and the psychology of choice. *Science, 211,* 453–458.

Tversky, A., & Kahneman, D. (1993). Belief in the law of small numbers. In G. Keren & C. Lewis (Eds.), *A handbook for data analysis in the behavioral sciences: Methodological issues* (pp. 341–349). Hillsdale, NJ: Erlbaum.

United States Department of Education. (2003). *Identifying and implementing educational practices supported by rigorous evidence: A user friendly guide.* Retrieved March 1, 2006, from www.ed.gov/rschstat/research/pubs/rigorousevid/index.html.

Watkins, M. W. (2003). IQ subtest analysis: Clinical acumen or clinical illusion? *Scientific Review of Mental Health Practice, 2,* 118–141.

Wechsler, D. (1991). *Wechsler intelligence scale for children—Third edition.* San Antonio, TX: The Psychological Corporation.

Wedding, D., & Faust, D. (1989). Clinical judgment and decision making in neuropsychology. *Archives of Clinical Neuropsychology, 4,* 233–265.

Weinstein, C. S. (1988). Preservice teachers' expectations about the first year of teaching. *Teaching and Teacher Education, 4,* 31–40.

Weinstein, N. D. (1980). Unrealistic optimism about future life events. *Journal of Personality and Social Psychology, 39,* 806–820.

Weinstein, N. D., Slovic, P., & Gibson, G. (2004). Accuracy and optimism in smokers' beliefs about quitting. *Nicotine and Tobacco Research, 6,* 375–380.

Weinstein, S., Obuchowski, N. A., & Lieber, M. L. (2005). Clinical evaluation of diagnostic tests. *American Journal of Roentgenology, 184,* 14–19.

Wiggins, J. S. (1988). *Personality and prediction: Principles of personality assessment.* Malabar, FL: Krieger Publishing Company.

Wilson, E. O. (1995). Science and ideology. *Academic Questions, 8*(3), 73–81.

Ysseldyke, J. E., Algozzine, B., Regan, R., & McGue, M. (1981). The influence of test scores and naturally occurring pupil characteristics on psychoeducational decision making with children. *Journal of School Psychology, 19,* 167–177.

Zarin, D. A., & Earls, F. (1993). Diagnostic decision making in psychiatry. *American Journal of Psychiatry, 150,* 197–206.

CHAPTER 13

ASSESSMENT OF INTELLIGENCE AND ACHIEVEMENT

RANDY W. KAMPHAUS[1]
Georgia State University

Knowledge of intelligence theory, intelligence testing, and academic achievement testing is foundational for school psychology, and for all of psychology. A little historical foundation is necessary to put the intelligence testing, and later academic achievement testing, breakthroughs into perspective. (Kamphaus, Rowe, Winsor, & Kim, 2005)

Interest in the formal measurement of human individual differences traces its roots to Chinese society where civil service examinations were in use as long as 3,000 years ago (DuBois, 1970). The concept of individual differences in human performance was mentioned by great thinkers as diverse as Socrates, Plato, Mohammedan rulers, and Charles Darwin (French & Hale, 1990).

An early intelligence test, described by Sir Anthony Fitzherbert, was published in 1534. This test was intended to differentiate between the "idiot" and the "lunatic." This diagnostic differentiation was an important one for experts interested in the humane treatment of individuals with mental retardation. The insane or mentally ill were submitted to torture and institutionalization without rehabilitation, whereas hope was held out for the successful treatment of individuals with mental retardation, with education and training (Kamphaus, forthcoming). In effect, it took nearly 400 years for Binet and Simon (1905) to achieve this diagnostic differentiation and usher in a new area in services for individuals with mental retardation. Fitzherbert (1534) described his crude measure of intelligence as follows (as cited by Pintner, 1923):

> And he who shall be said to be a sot and idiot from his birth, is such a person who cannot

account or number 20 pence, nor can tell who was his father or mother, nor how old he is, etc., so as it may appear that he hath no understanding of reason what shall be for his profit, nor what for his loss. But if hath such understanding, that he know and understand his letters, and do read by teaching or information of another man, then it seemeth that he is not a sot nor a natural idiot. (p. 6)

The eventual breakthrough test was long anticipated and welcomed with enthusiasm. Goddard (1912) optimistically predicted that the 1905 Binet-Simon "scale would one day take a place in history of science beside Darwin's theory of evolution and Mendel's laws of heredity" (p. 326). This sentiment remains strong in the community of scientists a century later (Lubinski, 2004). Furthermore, the research and development work surrounding intelligence testing still impacts psychological practice and scientific work a century later. Thanks to intelligence testing we have the principle of standardized assessment procedure; a concept borrowed from Wundt's laboratory by James McKeen Cattell when he sought to create his first intelligence test at Columbia College (now Columbia University; Wissler, 1901), the creation of academic achievement tests in the 1920s by E. L. Thorndike, and concerns raised about response-to-intervention approaches to classification based on the failed history of test-teach-test models that were popular in intelligence testing in the 1960s and 1970s. Entering the search term "intelligence test" in Google on 2 March, 2008 yielded 14.6 million "hits," providing ample testimony to the enduring importance of this scientific and technical breakthrough. Given that the general public has often equated the term IQ with intelligence testing, a search using this term yielded an astounding 90.8 million hits on this

---

[1] The author has a potential for conflict of interest with several tests discussed in this chapter including service as project director for the original K-ABC, and coauthor of the RIAS.

same date. By comparison, the search term "individualized educational plan" yielded 5.2 million hits, and this procedure is required daily practice in schools in the United States. It is difficult to argue that intelligence testing has little impact on psychology.

These trends beg the question as to why intelligence testing became popular and endures in the face of legal challenges, public unpopularity, and active opposition. Among other things, the scientific support for the tests has been unwavering despite innumerable attempts to discount it. This chapter will focus on these data since they have been and should continue to be the foundation upon which intelligence and achievement testing should thrive or be discarded. This chapter cannot capture the rich 3,000, 400, 100, or even 50 year history of individual differences assessment research. With apologies to the myriad theories, tests, and issues related to intelligence and achievement testing, this work will focus on enduring scientific threads of evidence that are likely to continue to guide this assessment field for the foreseeable future.

MATURE TECHNOLOGIES

Intelligence and academic achievement tests are both relatively "mature" technologies, in the sense that all major tests available measure the same core constructs with practically equivalent evidence of validity for the inferences offered. Virtually every intelligence test does a good job of measuring the core constructs of interest, namely general intelligence "*g*," verbal, and spatial cognitive abilities (see Table 13.1). All major survey level achievement test batteries used by school systems measure the same academic constructs of reading/literacy, mathematics, and other subjects, and all mathematics tests measure the same knowledge and skills including fractions, proportions, estimation, statistics and probability, and so forth. Although these tests are published by different publishers, use different author and consulting teams, use different stimulus materials, have different administration times and product costs, their similarities far outweigh their differences. This construct assessment "parity," however, is recognized in the case of other widely used mature technologies, but not appreciated in assessment in the social sciences. In psychology, for example, one will often encounter articles and opinion pieces claiming clear superiority for this test or another, and inferiority for other tests.

There is ample evidence that some social science assessment instruments, those that fall into the intelligence test and achievement test classes, are interchangeable for many assessment purposes due to product or technological maturity.

This concept of technological maturity is best communicated by medical assessment metaphor. Intelligence tests are mature in the same sense that Magnetic Resonance Imaging (MRI) scanners all work on the same basic principles regardless of their manufacturer. When most patients enter into medical assessment they typically do not consider the brand of instrument used to assess them; they would never consider asking the brand of MRI, for example, because they had read a review suggesting that one manufacturer's model may be better than another. In fact, most consumers may not be aware that there is a substantial array of manufacturers of MRIs, including General Electric, Hitachi, Siemens, Philips, and Fonar (as of 2 March, 2008). Metaphorically speaking one could easily list the WISC-IV, Stanford-Binet V, K-ABC II, Woodcock-Johnson Cognitive, RIAS, and DAS II.

This premise, however, requires support from a variety of data sources, which will be offered in later sections of this chapter. Primarily, the maturation of the intelligence testing technology was made possible by the emergence of unifying theories of cognitive abilities based on hundreds of factor analytic studies of various tests—both experimental and commercial.

"*g*" THEORY

Intelligence test development and intelligence theory developed relatively independently, with the former often preceding the latter (Kamphaus, forthcoming). Concurrently with the development of practical tests, Charles Spearman's (1927) theory of general intelligence has become the most influential. As is the case with most innovations, Spearman's theoretical breakthrough was simultaneously simple and insightful. He made the critical observation that various cognitive tests always correlated positively with one another (Carroll, 1993), a property of intelligence test subtests to this day. One need merely review the intercorrelation matrices included in all intelligence test manuals to see these positive correlations or "positive manifold" at work, where all subtests correlate positively with coefficients as high as .70 or greater not unusual. This positive manifold suggested to Spearman that performance

TABLE 13.1 Three Statum Theory (Carroll, 1993) Cognitive Abilities Hypothesized to be Assessed by Popular Intelligence Tests

	General Intelligence	Fluid Intelligence	Crystalized Intelligence	Memory & Learning	Broad Visual Perception	Broad Aud Perception	Broad Retr Ability	Broad Cog Speediness	Processing Speed
WISC-IV									
FS	X								
VCI			X						
PRI		X			X				
WMI				X					
PSI								X	
RIAS									
CIX	X								
VIX			X						
NIX					X				
CMX				X					
KABC-II									
FCI	X								
Gsm				X					
Gv					X				
Glr							X		
Gf		X							
Gc			X						
S-Binet 5									
FSIQ	X								
VIQ			X						
NVIQ					X				
FR		X							
KN			X						
QR		X							
VS					X				
WM				X					
WJ III									
Gc			X						
Glr							X		
Gv					X				
Ga						X			
Gf		X							
Gs								X	X
Gsm				X					
DAS-II									
VA			X						
NVA		X							
SA					X				
WM				X					
PS									X
SR									
SNC									
GCA	X								

Source: Kamphaus, forthcoming.

on cognitive tests was in large part determined by a common *general intelligence* or "*g*" that causes all cognitive tests to correlate.

The availability of early factor analytic techniques in the 1940s and 1950s allowed a more sophisticated test of Spearman's theory by testing the hypothesis that most of the variance of a cognitive test was determined by a single underlying *g* latent trait (the term "latent" is used to denote the fact that the construct cannot be observed, as is the case with vision, hearing, anxiety, depression, etc.). If, on the other hand, *g* was not influential in determining performance on a set of cognitive tests, several factors (i.e. latent traits) would be necessary to account for the reliable variance in a cognitive test. Using typical intelligence test subtests as examples, *g* theory would predict that performance on a vocabulary knowledge test would be determined primarily by a) shared variance between cognitive tests or *g*, or by b) unique variance or variance that is specific "*s*" to a test. Hundreds of factor analytic studies have shown that *g* theory is correct. Vocabulary tests are "*g* saturated" in that most of the reliable variance in a vocabulary subtest is attributable to *g* (general intelligence) and secondarily to "*s*" (a specific ability or skill such as vocabulary knowledge) (Carroll, 1993; Kamphaus, forthcoming). Up to this point this central premise of *g* theory remains incontrovertible. As one of the most respected and eminent psychologists of the twentieth century, Paul Meehl (1998), strongly (perhaps stridently) summarized the support for *g* theory;

> Development of more sophisticated factor analytic methods than Spearman or Thurstone makes it clear that there is a *g* factor that is manifested in either omnibus IQ tests or elementary cognitive tasks, that it is strongly hereditary, and that its influence permeates all areas of competence in human life.... A century of research—more than that if we start with Galton—has resulted in a triumph of scientific psychology, the footdraggers being either uninformed, deficient in quantitative reasoning, or impaired by political correctness.

All modern intelligence tests measure general intelligence as defined by producing a first factor (or component since principal components analysis is often used to identify *g*) that accounts for the largest proportion of variance in an intelligence test battery. Factor analytic studies

of the WISC-IV and Binet V are typical in this regard. Watkins (2006), for example, used the Schmid and Leiman orthogonalization procedure to assess the amount of variance explained by the FSIQ and four first-order factor scores of the WISC-IV. The results indicated that the FSIQ factor accounted for 38.3% of the total variance and 71.3% of the common variance. Consistent with Spearman's original theory the FSIQ factor explained more variance within each of the 10 subtests than did any other factor score. Each subtest had considerable unique variance, which, combined with the influence of the FSIQ factor, explained more variance than did any of the first-order factors. Watkins (2006) concluded that *g* as measured by the FSIQ accounted for the majority of the variance in the WISC-IV, and should be favored over the first-order factors in the test interpretation process.

In a factor analytic study of the Binet V, DiStefano and Dombrowski (2006) utilized both exploratory and confirmatory factor analytic methods to identify the number of factors present in the Binet V in order to better guide interpretation of the scale. As the Binet V manual reported only confirmatory factor analyses, which often results in overfactoring as will be demonstrated later, the authors sought to apply alternative methods in order to provide a fuller understanding of the latent traits measured the instrument. Exploratory and confirmatory factor analyses were conducted separately for five age groups. The confirmatory factor analyses tested four models: unidimensional or *g*, two-factor (verbal, nonverbal), five-factor (based on the CHC theory), and a four-factor model (Knowledge, Abstract Visual Reasoning, Quantitative Reasoning, and Memory) based on the results of their exploratory factor analyses and previous editions of the Stanford-Binet.

The results of the exploratory factor analyses indicated that the unidimensional model (*g*) accounted for 46% of the variance across age groups and produced the highest factor loadings for the subtests. On the other hand, the younger age groups (2–5 years and 6–10 years) showed evidence in support of a two-factor model, measuring verbal and nonverbal (spatial) intelligence. No support was found for additional factors. The results of the confirmatory factor analysis produced similar findings, suggesting that the *g* or unidimensional model was the best overall model regardless of age group. The five-factor model had slightly better fit indices for the youngest age group (2–5 years); however, the authors found that in the face of such similar fit indices, parsimony should favor the one factor model. For the remaining four age groups, the unidimensional model was the best fit. DiStefano and Dombrowski (2006) concluded that, regardless of age group and type of factor analysis used, the *g* model was the most representative of intelligence as measured by the Binet V.

If all major intelligence tests measure *g* first and foremost, then the next logical question is the degree to which this is the same *g*. An analogous question is whether or not the Philips and GE MRIs measure the same constructs. A study by Johnson, Bouchard, Krueger, McGue, and Gottesman (2004) provided evidence that the measurement of *g* is relatively independent of the intelligence test used. They hypothesized that if, in fact, the one true measure of intelligence is *g*, then an individual's score for *g* across cognitive assessment batteries should be the same. To measure their hypothesis, Johnson et al. used preexisting data from the Minnesota Study of Twins Reared Apart (MSTRA) sample. A total of 436 individuals (multiples themselves, spouses of multiples, and other family members) were evaluated with three cognitive ability tests, as well as a substantial range of other psychological and physical examinations.

The three cognitive ability tests administered were the Comprehensive Ability Battery (CAB), the Hawaii Battery, including Raven's Progressive Matrices (HB), and the Wechsler Adult Intelligence Scale (WAIS). In order to reduce redundancy and mitigate the claim that, of course, scores on the same subtests would produce the same results, only those subtests that measured different constructs in different ways were administered to the participants. Also, some tests from the Educational Testing Service Kit of Factor Referenced Cognitive Tests were added to the HB to provide a more thorough evaluation of abilities. The result of these modifications was that 14 tests were administered as part of the CAB, 17 from the HB, and 7 from the WAIS. No two subtests directly overlapped in terms of task demands.

Factor analysis was then performed to determine the number of distinct factors that comprised each test battery. The authors settled on a five-factor solution including Numerical Reasoning, Figural Reasoning, Perceptual Reasoning, Fluency, Memory, and Verbal. A five-factor solution was also found to be the best fit for the

HB including Logical Reasoning, Spatial, Fluency, Visual Memory, and Patterns. The WAIS was found to consist of three factors—Verbal Comprehension, Freedom from Distraction, and Perceptual Organization. The correlations among the *g* factors derived from the three batteries confirmed the primary hypothesis in that they ranged from .99 to 1.00. These findings provide a strong test of the durability of measurement of the *g* construct, and the premise offered earlier in this chapter that intelligence tests have become commodities in that while they offer different features, their measurement of the most important intelligence construct is virtually identical.

But one could and should question the findings cited previously because modern intelligence tests purport to measure an increasing number of latent traits with improved precision. An answer to this question is provided by a comprehensive study by Frazier and Youngstrom (2007), where they examined the factor structure of most major tests of intelligence using minimum average partial (MAP) analysis and Horn's parallel analysis (HPA). They investigated tests dating from 1949 to those currently in use. The purpose of their study was to identify the number of factors per test using MAP and HPA, and compare that number to the number of factors purportedly measured by each test. This study provided convincing results indicating that the number of factors identified through HPA and MAP analyses were significantly less than the number of purported factors, supporting the hypothesis that overfactoring is indeed occurring. Also, there was a significant increase in purported number of factors measured from past to current tests. Finally, while test length increased marginally, the number of purported factors increased exponentially.

Frazier and Youngstrom proposed several possible causal factors for overfactoring. First, they suggested that increasingly complex theories of intelligence, those with a hierarchical order and multiple strata, for example, may be driving test authors to try to measure these additional abilities. Second, they point to test publishers and their desire to provide more clinically useful instruments. The authors also suggest that the publishers are including measures of additional factors, which may not be clinically useful, to appeal to researchers. Publishers are also driven to continually provide new versions of tests that are bigger and better (i.e. measure more constructs) than previous tests. Third, they proposed that overfactoring may be occurring due to the application of "liberal" statistical criteria and theoretically driven statistical methods associated with PCA, CFA, and EFA that can lead to the retention of too many factors. In order to remedy the growing problem of overfactoring, Frazier and Youngstrom recommended either increasing test length to measure the additional purported abilities or simply measuring g with a brief measure of ability. Furthermore, they recommended that if publishers choose to increase test length, they should increase the number of subtests per factor, to four in some cases, to increase internal consistency reliability to an acceptable level. This thorough analysis of factor analytic procedures as applied to intelligence test development has many implications, including providing indirect evidence in support of the presence of an ubiquitous g factor across tests and general intelligence theory.

Detracting from the g construct is the inability of scientists to determine its exact nature. Supporters of g theory counter that, even in sciences considered more advanced, the nature of constructs measured by "tests" remains a source of debate and continued scientific inquiry. Although the thermometer is considered quite useful for daily life because if its ability to measure ambient temperature, competing theories of temperature remain. As has been the case with intellectual assessment, the last three centuries of temperature theory have been characterized by controversy, change, and competition among theories and methods (Chang, 2004).

Intelligence theory development remains as vigorous and controversial as ever. Carroll's (1993) Three Stratum Theory has become the most important unifying theory currently available, because 1) it incorporates general intelligence into the model while at the same time accounting for the influence of specific cognitive abilities, 2) it is based on over 400 separate factor analyses conducted for the purposes of writing his book, and 3) his findings are in general agreement with thousands of other prior investigations. Other popular models, such as the "Cattell-Horn" model as it has been called (McGrew, 2005) include virtually identical second order factors and similar specific abilities, but they eschew the existence of an overarching general intelligence. With this consideration in mind, Carroll's theory is a better fit to the data.

John B. Carroll's tome represents one of the most ambitious undertakings in the history of factor analytic research. Carroll (1993) gathered hundreds of sets of correlational data for cognitive tests, both experimental and clinical, and reanalyzed the data using factor analysis. This compilation of factor analytic findings is of such breadth and depth that no distillation of his findings will suffice, including that which follows. There is no substitute for reading the text in its entirety.

In its simplest form the three stratum theory derives from data, not the clinical or theoretical musings of Dr. Carroll. The data utilized to generate the theory are the results of hundreds of hierarchical factor analyses that yielded three "strata" of factors. The first "narrow" stratum consists of factors that measure relatively discrete cognitive abilities such as Piagetian reasoning, lexical knowledge, spelling ability, visual memory, spatial scanning, speech sound discrimination, ideational fluency, rate of test taking, and simple reaction time.

The second "broad" stratum in the hierarchy represents measures of traits that are combinations of stratum I measures. The stratum II construct of crystallized intelligence, for example, is produced by measuring first-stratum traits such as tests of language development, verbal language comprehension, and lexical knowledge. The complete list of second-stratum traits hypothesized by Carroll includes fluid intelligence, crystallized intelligence, general memory and learning, broad visual perception, broad auditory perception, broad retrieval ability, broad cognitive speediness, processing speed (i.e., reaction time decision speed) (See Table 13.1). He found equivocal evidence for the existence of a quantitative reasoning ability factor. Carroll's theory has proved influential if one considers its impact on the structure of modern intelligence tests.

The important message communicated by the data in Table 13.1 is that all major modern tests measure general intelligence, crystallized, spatial, and memory abilities to some extent, and most measure fluid abilities. Differentiation begins to occur with the remaining abilities in stratum II, abilities that are less highly correlated with general intelligence, academic achievement, and important life outcomes. And, it could very well be that these latter factors are not actually measured well on modern intelligence tests (Frazier & Youngstrom, 2007).

An example of the continuing vigorous debate in intelligence test theory is provided by Johnson and Bouchard (2005), who conducted a factor analytic study of the structure of adult intelligence. They evaluated three models of human intelligence. Model 1 was the fluid (Gf)–crystallized (Gc) model made popular by Cattell and Horn. Model 2 was the four strata Vernon model (1950), which consists of g, v:ed (verbal-educational) and k:m (spatial-mechanical), broad abilities, and narrow abilities. The third model compared was Carroll's three stratum model.

The results from the MISTRA study were used (same data set cited earlier), with scores from the CAB, HB, and WAIS serving as intelligence measures. Maximum likelihood confirmatory factor analysis was performed to determine which of the above models offered the best fit. For model 1 (Gf–Gc), there was a 0.85 correlation between the two third-stratum factors (fluid and school) that the authors suggested served as evidence for a g factor. The second model (Vernon), had a 0.76 correlation between v:ed and k:m, also suggesting the presence of a g factor. This model also had distinguishable second and third stratum factors, ranging from 0.29 (number) to 0.97 (verbal). Finally, the third model (Carroll) had a 1.00, and, therefore, indistinguishable correlation between the third stratum factor of g and the second stratum factor of fluid intelligence.

The authors suggested that the Gf–Gc and Carroll models were essentially the same, with g adding little to the models. They determined that the Vernon model was the best, but was still lacking in fit. They added a memory factor to the model and shifted around subtests on the CAB and came up with a verbal-perceptual-memory model that fit their hypotheses best. Then they added a mental rotation factor, moved the memory factor under perceptual, and came up with a verbal-perceptual-image rotation (VPR) model that had the best fit. The final VPR model had high correlations between each of the second strata factors and g (0.96 verbal, 0.99 perceptual, and 0.97 image rotation). The correlations ranged among the third strata factors and the second from 0.27 (number) to 1.00 (image rotation).

And so goes the ongoing debate among theoretical models of intelligence. Such a rich scientific tradition requires more space than can be allocated in a single book chapter. This chapter has merely highlighted a few of the most important theories that have guided test development as shown in Table 13.1. It is up to the individual psychologist to decide which test to use for an individual child or adolescent. There is now, however, a preponderance of scientific evidence to suggest that if one is interested in assessing g, the theoretical model of an intelligence test is not a major consideration. Furthermore, other measurement properties of popular intelligence tests vary little by scale, as shown in Table 13.2. Basic internal consistency coefficients are highly similar across scale. Thus, the choice of intelligence test rests more on nontheoretical or practical considerations such as test format, length, cost, child friendliness, and similar matters.

TEST SCORE INTERPRETATION

Intelligence test score interpretation was straightforward for the first 50 years of test existence, prior to World War II. Up to that point all major tests yielded a single overall score and most called it an "intelligence quotient" or IQ. In most cases this score was a "ratio IQ" based on the formula IQ = mental age/chronological age × 100 until the use of the interval scale standard score (versus the ordinal scale ratio IQ score) was popularized by the Wechsler Bellevue in the 1930s. Thus there was considerable innovation occurring about the time of the Second World War, including innovation in test interpretation. The leading Wechsler clinical research team of the day was at the Menninger Clinic in Topeka, Kansas, where Rapaport, Gil, and Schafer worked with adult clinical inpatient populations. Based on their extensive and careful review of Wechsler Bellevue results for these populations they proposed that part scores (or subtest scores and item scores in some cases) yielded more clinical diagnostic information than the overall IQ score (measure of g). They proposed further that various configurations of part or subtest scores were of specific diagnostic or prescriptive value. This latter approach has come to be known as the process of "profile analysis." This interpretive breakthrough was made possible by the unique structure of the Wechsler scales, which provided part (e.g. Performance IQ and Verbal IQ) and subtest scores for the first time on a major test of intelligence. The Wechsler scale stood in stark contrast to the Binet scale, which offered only one overall IQ score and was the most popular of the day. If one were buying a commodity it could be said that the new Wechsler scale provided more interpretive "value" because this range of scores could be combined in numerous ways to create more "clinical" information for the benefit of adult psychiatric patients. The efforts of this team were reported in a 1944–1945 encyclopedic volume listing the score patterns and individual item response patterns of various diagnostic groups from schizophrenia, to depression,

TABLE 13.2a   Internal Consistency Coefficients for Popular Intelligence
Tests

	Reliability Coefficients				Reliability Coefficients	
WISC-IV			**WJ III**			
FS	0.97		G*c*		0.95	
VCI	0.94		G*lr*		0.88	
PRI	0.92		G*v*		0.81	
WMI	0.92		G*a*		0.91	
PSI	0.88		G*f*		0.95	
			G*s*		0.93	
RIAS			G*sm*		0.88	
CIX	0.96		**Bayley**			
VIX	0.94		Lang		0.93	
NIX	0.95		Cog		0.91	
CMX	0.95		**DAS-II**		Early Years	School Age
			VA		0.90	0.89
KABC-II	ages 3–6	ages 7–18	NVA		0.89	0.92
FCI	0.96	0.97	SA		0.95	0.95
G*sm*	0.91	0.89	SNC		0.95	0.96
G*v*	0.92	0.88	GCA		0.95	0.96
G*lr*	0.91	0.93	**WAIS-III**			
G*f*		0.88	FSIQ		0.98	
G*c*	0.90	0.92	VIQ		0.97	
			PIQ		0.94	
S-Binet 5			VCI		0.96	
FSIQ	0.98		POI		0.93	
VIQ	0.96		WMI		0.94	
NVIQ	0.95		PSI		0.88	
FR	0.86		**WPPSI-III**			
KN	0.89		FSIQ		0.96	
QR	0.87		VIQ		0.95	
VS	0.88		PIQ		0.93	
WM	0.84		GLC		0.93	
			PSQ		0.89	

to mania samples. Rapaport et al. (1945–1946) observed that "Every subtest score—especially the relationship of very subtest score to the other subtest scores—has a multitude of determinants" (p. 106).

While this volume served as the interpretation volume of choice for generations of clinical psychologists through the 1970s, problems were cited with the configural intepretation (i.e. profile) approach from its earliest days. These problems were blamed on the Wechsler-Bellevue itself by suggesting that the subtests were too highly correlated with one another, thus making profiles less able to differentiate clearly between diagnostic groups. There is, however, an alternative explanation; that *g* is a parsimonious explanation for the

totality of intelligence test performance for most individuals being tested. As was cited in the previous section the "problem" of positive intercorrelations between subtests has never been solved.

A landmark study by McDermott, Fantuzzo, and Glutting (1990) proposed just this alternative view. They proposed, 45 years after Rapaport and colleagues, that the meaning of the vast majority of profiles of subtest and composite scores on intelligence tests do not reflect important meaning about an individual's intellectual development. On the contrary, these profiles are primarily reflective of error variance. McDermott et al. (1990) cautioned against the use of ipsative comparisons (the comparison of each of an individual's subtest scores to her average subtest score to create a

TABLE 13.2b

Test-Retest Stability

	N	Test 1 M (SD)	Test 2 M (SD)	Gain	Correlation adj
KABC-II (MPI)					
3–5 yrs	60	100.7 (15.5)	106.6 (16.3)	5.9	0.86
7–12 yrs	82	99.8 (16.2)	111.7 (18.7)	11.9	0.89
13–18 yrs	61	101.8 (13.7)	113.1 (18.4)	11.3	0.91
KABC-II (FCI)					
3–5 yrs	60	100.1 (15.6)	105.4 (16.7)	5.3	0.90
7–12 yrs	82	99.6 (16)	109.9 (18.5)	10.3	0.91
13–18 yrs	61	101.3 (13.7)	111.6 (17.8)	10.3	0.94
WISC-IV (FSIQ)					
6–7 yrs		99.0 (13.0)	108.2 (13.8)	9.2	0.92
8–9 yrs		99.4 (11.2)	105.5 (11.6)	6.1	0.91
10–11 yrs		100.9 (10.4)	106.5 (11.1)	5.6	0.93
12–13 yrs		101.4 (11.1)	105.6 (11.6)	5.2	0.96
14–16 yrs		103.1 (12.6)	107.4 (14.1)	4.3	0.93
All Ages	243	101 (11.7)	106.6 (12.5)	5.6	0.93
RIAS (CIX)					
3–4 yrs	33	99.64 (14.39)	101.45 (17.17)	1.84	0.78
5–8 yrs	22	100.79 (16.39)	104.64 (17.94)	4.35	0.92
9–12 yrs	16	103.57 (17.26)	110.00 (18.53)	6.43	0.97
13–82 yrs	15	106.20 (12.14)	107.18 (10.51)	0.98	0.93
Binet 5 (FSIQ)					
2–5 yrs	96	99.7 (11.75)	102.61 (12.89)	2.91	0.95
6–20 yrs	87	101.99 (12.67)	105.94 (13.19)	3.95	0.93
21–59 yrs	81	105.59 (12.69)	109.02 (13.01)	3.43	0.93
60+ yrs	92	101.63 (13.97)	103.83 (14.86)	2.2	0.95
Bayley (Lang)					
2–4 Months	50	99.9 (14.2)	103.5 (14.2)	3.6	0.77
9–13 Months	50	100.8 (14.3)	102.8 (14.1)	2	0.85
19–26 Months	49	97.7 (9.3)	98.9 (10.6)	1.2	0.88
33–42 Months	47	102.9 (10.2)	104.7 (11.6)	1.8	0.94
Bayley (Cog)**					
2–4 Months	50	9.6 (3.5)	10.9 (3.0)	1.3	0.71
9–13 Months	50	10.3 (2.9)	11.4 (3.0)	1.1	0.77
19–26 Months	49	9.4 (2.3)	10.1 (2.5)	0.7	0.86
33–42 Months	47	10.8 (3.0)	11.5 (3.2)	0.7	0.86
DAS-II (GCA)					
3:6–4:11 yrs	109	101.0 (15.9)	106.2 (16.8)	5.2	0.91
5:0–8:11 yrs	107	101.5 (12.1)	106.4 (13.5)	4.9	0.91
School Age	147	101.0 (12.5)	106.2 (13.9)	5.2	0.94
All Ages	363	101.2 (13.5)	106.3 (14.7)	5.1	0.92
WAIS-III (FSIQ)					
16–29 yrs	100	101.7 (11.7)	107.4 (12.4)	5.7	0.95
30–54 yrs	102	99.6 (14.3)	104.7 (15.7)	5.1	0.96
55–74 yrs	104	99.0 (14.3)	102.9 (15.0)	3.9	0.97
75–89 yrs	88	99.0 (14.1)	102.2 (16.3)	3.2	0.96
WPPSI-III (FSIQ)					
2:6–3:11		99.0 (14.7)	102.4 (13.7)	3.4	0.92
4:0–5:5		103.4 (9.5)	109.8 (9.2)	6.4	0.92
5:6–7:3		99.0 (12.7)	104.5 (13.5)	5.5	0.92
All ages	157	99.9 (12.7)	105.1 (12.9)	5.2	0.92

*WJ III reports correlations in lieu of mean scores.

**Bayley Cognitive scores are reported with a mean of 10 and a standard deviation of 3.

Source: Kamphaus, forthcoming.

profile) because ipsatization removes common variance (i.e., g) from all scores. The resulting profile has less predictive accuracy and less score stability than the conventional norm-referenced subtest scores. They demonstrated further that it is also impossible to compare ipsatized scores across individuals because each is altered by a different amount (the individual's personal average). Finally, they observed that ipsatized scores do not have meaning for directing intervention or treatment because they must sum to zero because of the arithmetic process utilized. In other words, if one area of "weakness" is identified through ipsative comparison, and that specific area is improved, it must come at the expense of an area of "strength" to continue to sum to zero.

McDermott et al. (1990) also found flaws with many studies of profile analysis that attempted to identify profiles unique to diagnostic groups. They pointed out that groups that have the same or similar diagnoses may not be homogeneous categories, and, therefore, any resulting profile for the group may not be reflective of the whole group. Essentially it is tautological to both use ipsative comparisons to form diagnostic groups and then find profiles that define these same diagnostic groups. Researchers would be in a better position to claim to have discovered a unique diagnostic profile only if they are comparing it to a null hypothesis (e.g., a commonplace profile in a population of children).

This controversial proposal for a paradigm change in intelligence test interpretation has subsequently been supported by empirical findings. The composite score produced by intelligence tests, the measure of g, has been shown to be stable over the course of development (Moffitt, Caspi, Harkness, & Silva, 1993). In fact, Moffitt et al. (1993) demonstrated that the popular alternative to the composite score, the profile of scores represented by a variety of intelligence test subtests, was unstable when analyzing data from a large longitudinal study of change. Watkins and Canivez (2004) produced identical findings. Their study examined the temporal stability of WISC-III subtest scores. Using a large sample of 579 children tested twice, they compared IQ, composite, and ipsatized scores for each child across testing sessions. Like prior findings they found that overall intelligence test composite scores were stable across testing, as well as providing consistent classification of special education classification status. In direct contrast the temporal stability of strengths and weaknesses

(profiles produced via ipsatization) was at chance levels. Study participants were tested at differing test-retest intervals (.5–6 years) and when interval length was examined, the results for profiles remained insignificant. This paradigm shift has certainly been challenged, although with less than effective outcomes.

Consider an oft-cited study by Fiorello, Hale, McGrath, Ryan, and Quinn (2002). This study used regression commonality analysis to try to identify the proportion of variance in FSIQ scores that was predicted by unique contributions of variables, as opposed to common or shared variance of variables. Scores from 873 children from the WISC-III–WIAT linking standardization sample data were utilized. An additional 47 children from a learning disabled (LD) sample and 51 from an ADHD sample were added to the overall sample. The profiles of each child were examined and the sample was divided into variable (n = 707) or flat (n = 166) profile groups based on variability in index scores on the WISC-III. The criteria for the variable profile group was one or more index score that was statistically significant from the others. Unique and shared variance estimates of FSIQ were calculated for each participant and compared across subgroups. Their results confirmed the a priori hypothesis in that the FSIQ variance in the flat profile group was 89% shared. The authors thus concluded that interpreting the FSIQ as a general measure of ability for this group was acceptable based upon the high proportion of shared variance. For the variable profile group, 36% of the variance was shared, 61% was unique, and g accounted for only 2% of shared variance. Similarly, the LD and ADHD groups revealed that g accounted for only 3% and 2% of shared variance respectively. The authors of this study argue against interpretation of FSIQ only for the majority of the sample and maintain that profile analysis is needed to ensure that FSIQ accurately reflects one's ability.

Dana and Dawes (2007) situate their understanding of this debate in methodological considerations and prior research on the validity of clinical inferences made by psychologists. They concluded:

> We are not optimistic that any of these approaches will establish the validity of profile interpretations. Following our earlier arguments about linear combinations, a linear regression using subcomponents would unlikely make reliably better

predictions than FSIQ alone because FSIQ is a linear combination of the subcomponents. Of course, this argument does not rule out the possibility that configurations of subtests or indices could provide incremental validity over FSIQ. We note, however, that it is notoriously difficult to quantify (and thus test) what is meant by "configural," and that complex models rarely outpredict simple linear models (Dawes, 1979). Until such time as this sort of positive evidence exists, it appears that clinicians should continue, as McDermott, Fantuzzo, and Glutting (1990) suggest, to "just say no" to subtest analysis.

A further consideration is the nature of evidence available in this debate. McDermott et al. (1990) and Fiorello et al. (2002) provide evidence based on measurement methods that "estimate" proportions and other variables of interest. It could be argued that the longitudinal studies of Moffit et al. (1993) and Watkins and Canivez (2004) provide direct tests of the longer and long-term stability of profiles of intelligence test scores. Findings such as these make it difficult for practicing psychologists to have faith in the reliability of interpretations of test score profiles when the profiles themselves change from one testing session to the next.

CONTENT VALIDITY AND ACHIEVEMENT TESTING

Up to this point in this chapter and in most of the extant psychological assessment literature, one is concerned with the assessment of "latent traits" of human abilities. They are referred to as "latent" for a singular reason, because they cannot be observed or palpated. Examples of latent traits include anxiety, intelligence, spatial ability, and vision—yes, vision. Although it sounds implausible, "vision" cannot be "seen," and is only inferred from test score results. Consider, for example, the ubiquitous Snellen Chart used to screen for vision problems as cited by Carroll (1993). The Snellen Chart does not even "look" like a vision test. In fact, to a four or five year old child it is not a test of vision but rather is a test of English language letter recognition skills—a variant of a reading test. As it turns out the content, or "content validity," of a test of a latent trait is not very important as exemplified by the Snellen Chart. The determination of whether the Snellen Chart, or the Block Design or Vocabulary

subtests, is a good measure of its intended latent trait is based on the logical network of evidence gathered to support its test score inferences, consistent with the peer-developed guidelines provided in the *Standards for Educational and Psychological Testing* (AERA, APA, NCME, 1999). If frequency of test use is any indication, the Snellen Chart is considered by opthalmologists to be a good screening measure of the latent trait of visual acuity.

The distinction between test content and validity for the assessment of a latent trait is a subtle and challenging one. It defies the typical human intuition that the content of a test item should be crucial for determining the validity of test score inferences. It is as challenging as and not unlike the counterintuitive but well-supported principle of negative reinforcement, as any instructor of an introduction to psychology or educational psychology course can attest.

There is, however, one testing domain where content validity is crucial, and that is the assessment of academic achievement domains. R. L. Thorndike contrasted academic achievement testing with latent trait assessment by referring to it as "domain mastery" assessment. Content validity is crucial in achievement testing as elucidated by Thorndike (1982).

> The fruitfulness of the orientation in terms of domain mastery depends on the possibility of defining a domain clearly and incisively, so that the range of performances that lie within the domain can be fully specified and agreed on. It should then be possible to sample tasks from that domain in such a way that the complete domain is adequately represented and inferences about completeness of mastery of the domain are a reasonable possibility. The approach really applies only to aspects of school achievement. (p. 2)

A further distinction between latent trait and domain mastery assessment lies in the assumptions regarding test performance. Changes in domain mastery test performance are presumed to be affected by teaching and schooling, whereas latent trait test performance is presumed to be less amenable to mild or short-term factors. Latent traits are often, although not always presumed to be stable over time, particularly short periods of time.

If an examiner seeks to measure domain mastery then the selection of test content should be, as Thorndike suggests, "incisive." Given that many psychologists are not academic domain specialists, content experts or expert opinion as expressed through international or national standards are often used to specify a content blueprint. The blueprint for the KeyMath-3 Diagnostic Assessment (DA) for example, specifies the following skill areas for elementary and middle school mathematics based on U.S. national standards.[2]

- Numeration
- Algebra
- Geometry
- Measurement
- Data Analysis and Probability
- Mental Computation and Estimation
- Addition and Subtraction
- Multiplication and Division
- Foundations of Problem Solving
- Applied Problem Solving

Because of the existence of this content blueprint, the meaning of derived scores from the KeyMath subtests and composite subtests is clearer with regard to domain mastery. Furthermore, a lack of mastery leads directly to content areas that should become the focus of instruction.

Roughly speaking, academic achievement measures may be separated into two types; those seeking to assess student progress, or formative assessments, and those that assess knowledge and skills acquired, or summative assessments (Gronlund, 2003). Sample achievement assessments used by psychologists that may be formative include curriculum-based measures and multi-level survey achievement batteries. Summative assessments may include individually administered diagnostic or survey achievement tests.

Curriculum-Based Measurement

CBM assessments of academic achievement are intended to be both formative and brief, and designed to determine whether or not a child is making adequate academic progress (Jiban & Deno, 2007). Measures are typically in the form of one-minute "probes" designed for reading and mathematics assessment. Reading probes may be as simple as requiring a child to read aloud for one minute while word reading accuracy and fluency are scored. In this type of assessment test, content sampling is limited and of lesser importance since summative assessment is of lesser interest. Assessment results, produced quarterly or even weekly, are used to determine the need for a course change in intervention, not to guide the type of intervention per se since content is inadequate to make such decisions. Thus the ability of curriculum-based measures to predict comprehensive summative measures of achievement is of high interest. Jiban and Deno (2007) addressed this question by assessing the criterion-related validity evidence for three one-minute curriculum-based measurements (CBM) for predicting third (n = 35) and fifth (n = 49) graders' performance on a state criterion-referenced test of mathematics achievement. The CBM probes included a basic mathematics facts measure and a "cloze" measure of mathematics achievement (i.e., fill in the blank). A one minute silent reading measure served as the third CBM. The results revealed that the one-minute measures were not adequate predictors of criterion performance measures of summative achievement, thus calling into question the utility of the traditional one-minute CBMs as indicators of the need to modify classroom instruction for an individual child. Significant criterion-related validity coefficients were obtained when one-minute measures were aggregated over time to produce two-minute CBMs.

The majority of CBM research has been conducted in the area of reading, in grades 2 through 5 in U.S. classrooms, and for the purposes of achievement progress monitoring (Wayman, Wallace, Wiley, Tichá, & Espin, 2007). The research evidence in support of the use of CBM within these parameters is strong in that numerous replications, extensions, and even a few longitudinal studies have been conducted.

The record for CBM outside these parameters is less clear, which is likely simply due to the relative youth of the CBM technology. A decade or two of research will be needed to close the many research gaps and build an adequate evidentiary base. Recently, the use of CBM has been extended beyond its original focus in that CBM methods are now utilized or advertised for use as summative measures of achievement that may be used for classification/diagnostic purposes, where

---

[2] Subtests are grouped into three areas: Basic Concepts (conceptual knowledge), Operations, (computational skills), and Applications (problem solving). Item content reflects the content and process standards described in the National Council of Teachers of Mathematics's (NCTM's) *Principles and Standards for School Mathematics* (NCTM, 2002–2004).

an individual's slope of change over time is utilized to make important decisions about a child's status. The evidentiary basis for this new purpose of CBM is slight. Wayman et al. (2007) provide a thorough discussion of the research agenda needed to provide evidence that CBM is useful for classification or diagnostic purposes.

> The validity of the measures for these new purposes has yet to be established. There is little known, relatively speaking, about the technical characteristics of the slopes produced by CBM measures. For example, what is the best method for determining validity and reliability of the slope? How many data points are needed to obtain a reliable and valid slope? Does this number differ with the age of the student, the material used, or the equivalency of "parallel"passages? How do we establish parallel passages? There is also little known about normative or ambitious rates of performance and growth. For example, how much growth should be expected from students at different age and performance levels? Should national norms be developed? If so, must standard sets of materials be developed for this purpose? Finally, little is known about teachers' understanding of CBM progress data and the thinking processes teachers use as they interpret and use data for decision making. For example, how accurate are teachers at interpreting CBM data? How long does it take them to learn how to interpret and use CBM data? How easy is it for teachers to connect progress-monitoring data to instructional decisions, and are there methods to enhance their ability to tie data and instruction together? We believe that areas must be explored if CBM is to be used as a part of a decision-making process related to determining the need for special education services. (p. 116)

Multilevel Survey Achievement Batteries

These broad-based measures of academic achievement are well known as summative measures of academic achievement, whether they are designed for this purpose or not. They are comprehensive and lengthy, taking several hours of testing time per child (See Table 13.3 for an example of test content of the Iowa Tests of Basic Skills), and

modern measures are designed to be summative, formative, and to assess a student's progress from grade to grade.

In fact, the scaling of these measures is particularly well suited to tracking progress over time because of the availability of developmental norms or "scaled" scores. These scores are based on Item Response Theory measurement technology (Suen, 1990) where item difficulty and a person's ability are estimated and modeled in order to create a developmental norm that remedies many of the problems associated with older developmental norms such as age and grade equivalent scores. Grade and age equivalents are known to have a crucial weakness; unequal units between points on their scale, thus rendering them useless for estimating growth over time (Kamphaus, forthcoming). On the contrary, IRT scores are developmental norms with equal units along their scale. Their interpretation, however, is not intuitive as is the case for grade equivalents, and their scaling is not equivalent across tests as is the case for the standard scores yielded by many intelligence tests that have a common mean of 100 and standard deviation of 15. An example will help clarify the interpretation of IRT scaled scores and help the reader become comfortable with their scaling, which includes larger numerical values than is typical for derived scores. Brian obtained the grade equivalents and scaled scores shown below:

Grade

	First	Second	Third	Fourth
Grade Equivalent	1.7	2.7	3.7	4.7
Scaled Score	240	260	280	300

Based on scaled score results it could be said that Brian is progressing at about the same rate from year to year, a statement that can only be made since scaled scores have equal units along the scale. On the other hand, one cannot conclude that Brian is making the same gains every year based on grade equivalents because of their unequal scale units. A corollary characteristic of scaled scores is that they are less useful for making comparisons across subtests or composites. If a child, for example, obtains a scaled score of 392 in mathematics and 377 in reading, it does not necessarily follow that he or she is better in mathematics than in reading.

Generally speaking, survey achievement measures have utilized more advanced statistical

TABLE 13.3   Content Description of the Iowa Tests of Basic Skills Levels 5–8 (Primary Grades) (March, 2008)

The descriptions below are brief summaries of the content and skills measured by the separate tests. In addition to these tests, a Practice Page, which consists of six questions covering several test areas, precedes the first test in the Levels 5 and 6 booklets.

Vocabulary. At Levels 5 and 6, the Vocabulary test measures listening vocabulary. Students hear a word, and sometimes they also hear the word used in a sentence. Then they choose one of three pictorial response options. The Vocabulary test at Levels 7 and 8 measures reading vocabulary. For each question, a pictorial or written stimulus is followed by a set of written responses. Approximately equal numbers of nouns, verbs, and modifiers are tested at all levels.

Word Analysis. The questions on the Word Analysis test assess how well students can recognize letters and letter-sound relationships. No written words are used at Level 5, but in subsequent levels, both pictures and words are used as stimuli and response choices.

Reading Comprehension. There is no Reading Comprehension test in the Level 5 Battery, and the one in the Level 6 Battery allows several options. The Reading test presents students with a variety of tasks, which progressively require more independence in reading as the test level increases. The tasks in Levels 6–8 include using print, context, and picture cues to identify unfamiliar words; completing sentences that tell about a picture by choosing a word for filling in a blank; and answering multiple-choice questions after reading a brief story. The questions associated with pictures and stories often ask students to make inferences or to generalize about what they have read.

Listening. In the Listening test, short oral scenarios are presented, and then one or more multiple-choice questions are read. Since all response options are pictorial, the scores from this test do not depend on students' reading abilities. Like the Reading Comprehension test, the Listening test requires students to demonstrate both literal and inferential understanding. Students' abilities to follow directions, understand sequences, and predict outcomes are also measured.

Language. The Language tests of Levels 5 and 6 measure students' abilities to understand linguistic relationships—how language is used to express ideas. These are developmental language skills that include aural language usage and word classification tasks. Questions are presented orally by the teacher, and students choose from a set of pictorial responses. For Levels 7 and 8, a major portion of the test deals with skills in spelling, capitalization, punctuation, and skills in usage and expression in writing. For these tasks, the questions and response choices are read by the teacher as students read silently. A separate score is provided for spelling.

Mathematics. The Mathematics test at Levels 5 and 6 consists of questions measuring beginning math concepts, problem solving, and math operations. Areas covered include numeration, number systems, geometry, measurement, and the use of addition and subtraction in word problems. Questions are presented orally, and response options are pictures or numerals. In the Levels 7 and 8 batteries, there are separate tests for Math Concepts, Math Problem Solving, and Math Computation. The Math Concepts test deals with numeration and number systems, whole numbers, geometry, measurement, fractions, currency, and number sentences. The Math Problem Solving test has two parts. In the first, students solve brief word problems; in the second part, they interpret information presented in graphs and tables. The Math Computation test presents addition and subtraction problems. One section of it is timed so that information about students' rates of work on computation can be obtained.

Social Studies. Only the Levels 7 and 8 batteries contain a Social Studies test. The questions on this test measure objectives of the social studies curriculum that are not measured elsewhere in the *ITBS* tests. All questions are presented orally, and all response options are pictorial. The content of the questions is taken from the areas of geography, history, government, economics, sociology, and the other social sciences.

Science. Like the Social Studies test, the Science test is included in only the Levels 7 and 8 batteries. Its content focuses on aspects of the science curriculum that are not measured on other tests in the battery. The knowledge and skills measured by the Science test questions come from the areas of life science, earth and space sciences, and physical sciences. Considerable emphasis is also given to the nature of science—the methods and process skills used in science.

Sources of Information. Only the Levels 7 and 8 batteries contain a Sources of Information test. The questions are read aloud by the teacher, and students choose answers from among words or short phrases that they read themselves. The main skills measured are alphabetizing, using a picture dictionary, using a table of contents, and using maps to determine location, direction, and distance.

www.education.uiowa.edu/itp/itbs/itbs_about_5-8.htm; reprinted with permission.

methods than clinical measures of intelligence and academic achievement. They were used in the 1960s to work out advanced cross-grade and age equating techniques, item bias detection methods, and later, IRT item selection and test construction and scaling methods. Consequently, the scores yielded by these measures may be quite valuable for clinical assessment purposes in psychology, particularly for corroborating, clarifying, or contradicting findings from clinical assessment measures. If, for example, a child is found to have below-average academic achievement in mathematics on a clinical and CBM measure but demonstrated average performance on a survey achievement battery, the survey battery, based on measurement properties alone, would be considered the most accurate summative assessment until proven otherwise (Kamphaus, forthcoming).

Clinical Tests of Achievement

Clinical, or individually administered comprehensive and screening measures of academic achievement, may also be either summative or formative. Screening measures, such as those that assess only a few constructs such as spelling, word reading, and mathematics achievement and use only a few items per subtest to do so (e.g., 50 to 70 items or less), are more likely to be useful for formative interpretation, because individual subtests do not have strong evidence of content validity to support inferences. There are still other clinical measures that have detailed content blueprints for their subtests, which allow for extensive error analyses that may be used to plan instruction for a student (e.g., KeyMath-2 DA cited earlier). Users of clinical tests are advised to study the content blueprint for a clinical subtest of achievement to determine whether or not the test is most useful for summative (strong content blueprint), formative, or both interpretive purposes.

Clinical achievement measures have commonly been used as part of the special education assessment and classification processes, often in conjunction with an intelligence test among other assessment methods. In fact, the notion of an "ability-achievement" discrepancy became synonymous with the identification of a specific learning disability (Kamphaus, forthcoming). The ability-achievement discrepancy model of learning disability diagnosis has fallen into disfavor and is rapidly being replaced by both response to intervention and assessment of core deficit models of learning disabilities (Brueggemann,

Kamphaus, & Dombrowski, in press). These latter models, sometimes referred to as functional impairment models, do not require a discrepancy between any two measures to identify a learning disability because of the problems inherent in profile analysis cited earlier. Instead, the focus is on the mere presence of an achievement deficit as indicated by below average achievement test scores. While too complex to be fully developed in this chapter, this approach to learning disability diagnosis places new emphasis on the presence of content validity evidence in support of any summative measures of academic achievement that are utilized to make the diagnostic decision. In this newer model of learning disability diagnosis, the clinical achievement measure of academic achievement is not a contributor to the diagnostic decision but is the primary arbiter of the decision, thus placing considerable responsibility for amassing validity evidence with the test developers, and careful test selection on the part of psychologists or other users.

CONCLUSIONS

Intelligence and academic achievement testing technologies are advancing at impressive rates yet most of the tillable acreage remains to be plowed. On the one hand, intelligence and achievement testing are among the few "knowns" of school psychology practice because of the decades and centuries of research supporting and defining their use. There is considerable research that identifies the parameters of their use; that is, the purposes for which these measures are not well suited. For example, their near-term benefits for treatment, rehabilitation, and intervention planning are not clear.

In this sense, these measures are like MRI, EKG, EEG, Snellen Charts, behavior rating scales, and measures of height and weight in that they measure constructs with considerable fidelity, but their relationship to cures for heart disease, cancer, weight problems, or visual limitations is indirect. Intelligence and achievement measures contribute to the development of "cures" and prevention indirectly by improving their measurement of constructs. The ability of achievement measures to assess various measures of phonological skills, for example, has some import for the design of early intervention programs for children with reading problems but, of greater impact, this discovery has substantially altered the definition of a reading disability and produced a paradigm shift in reading disability diagnosis (Brueggemann, Kamphaus, & Dombrowski, forthcoming). These improvements, in turn, provide information necessary to conduct better research, which, in turn, produces breakthroughs in intervention. Progress is linked to better definition and measurement of constructs on many fronts.

REFERENCES

American Educational Research Association, American Psychological Association, and National Council on Measurement in Education. (1999). *Standards for educational and psychological testing.* Washington, DC: Author.

Binet, A., & Simon, T. (1905). New methods for the diagnosis of the intellectual level of subnormals. *L'Anne'e Psychologique, 11,* 191–244.

Brueggemann, A. E., Kamphaus, R. W., & Dombrowski, S. (forthcoming). An impairment model of learning disability diagnosis. *Professional Psychology: Research and Practice.*

Carroll, J. B. (1993). *Human cognitive abilities: A survey of factor analytic studies.* New York: Cambridge University Press.

Chang, H. (2004). *Inventing Temperature: Measurement and Scientific Progress.* Oxford University Press: London

Dana, J., & Dawes, R. (2007). Comment on Fiorello et al., "Interpreting Intelligence Test Results for Children with Disabilities: Is Global Intelligence Relevant?" *Applied Neuropsychology, 14,* 21–25.

Dawes, R. M. (1979). The robust beauty of improper linear models in decision making. *American Psychologist, 34,* 571–582.

DiStefano, C., & Dombrowski, S. C. (2006). Investigating the theoretical structure of the Stanford-Binet–fifth edition. *Journal of Psychoeducational Assessment, 24,* 123–136.

DuBois, P. H. (1970). *A history of psychological testing.* Boston: Allyn & Bacon.

Fiorello, C. A., Hale, J. B., McGrath, M., Ryan, K., & Quinn, S. (2002). IQ interpretation for children with flat and variable test profiles. *Learning and Individual Differences, 13,* 115–125.

Frazier, T. W. & Youngstrom, E. A. (2007). Historical increase in the number of factors measured by commercial tests of cognitive ability: Are we overfactoring? *Intelligence, 35,* 169–182.

French, J. L., & Hale, R. L. (1990). A history of the development of psychological and educational testing. In C. R. Reynolds & R. W. Kamphaus (Eds.), *Handbook of psychological and educational assessment of children* (pp. 3–28). New York: Guilford.

Goddard, H. H. (1912). Echelle metrique de lintelligence de Binet-Simon. *Annee psychol., 18,* 288–326.

Gronlund, N. E. (2003). *Assessment of student achievement* (7th Ed.). Boston, MA: Allyn & Bacon.

Jiban, C. L., & Deno, S. L. (2007). Using math and reading curriculum-based measurements to predict state mathematics test performance: Are simple one-minute measures technically adequate? *Assessment for Effective Intervention, 32,* 78–89.

Johnson, W. & Bouchard, T. J., Jr. (2005). The structure of human intelligence: It is verbal, perceptual, and image rotation (VPR), not fluid and crystallized. *Intelligence, 33,* 393–416.

Johnson, W., Bouchard, T. J., Jr., Krueger, R. F., McGue, M., & Gottesman, I. I. (2004). Just one *g*: Consistent results from three test batteries. *Intelligence, 32,* 95–107.

Lubinski, D. (2004). Introduction to the special section on cognitive abilities: 100 years after Spearman's (1904) "general intelligence," objectively determined and measured. *Journal of Personality and Social Psychology, 86,* 96–111.

Kamphaus, R. W. (in press). *Clinical assessment of child and adolescent intelligence—3rd Edition.* New York: Springer.

Kamphaus, R. W., Rowe, E. W., Winsor, A. P., & Kim, S. (2005). A history of intelligence test interpretation. In D. Flanagan & P. Harrison, (Eds.), *Contemporary intellectual assessment* (3rd ed., pp. 23–38). New York: The Guilford Press.

McDermott, P. A., Fantuzzo, J. W., & Glutting, J. J. (1990). Just say no to subtest analysis: A critique on Wechsler theory and practice. *Journal of Psychoeducational Assessment, 8,* 290–302.

McGrew, K. S. (2005). The Cattell-Horn-Carroll Theory of Cognitive Abilities: Past, present, and future. In D. Flanagan & P. Harrison (Eds.), *Contemporary intellectual assessment* (3rd ed., pp. 23–38). New York: The Guilford Press.

Meehl, P. E. (1998, May 23). *The power of quantitative thinking.* Speech delivered upon receipt of the James McKeen Cattell Fellow award at the meeting of the American Psychological Society, Washington, D.C.

Moffitt, T. E., Caspi, A., Harkness, A. R., & Silva, P. A. (1993). The natural history of change in intellectual performance: Who changes? How much? Is it meaningful? *Journal of Child Psychology and Psychiatry, 34,* 455–506.

National Council of Teachers of Mathematics (2002–2004). *Principles and Standards for school Mathematics.* Author

Pintner, R. (1923). *Intelligence testing.* New York: Henry Holt and Company.

Rapaport, D., Gill, M., & Schafer, R. (1945–1946). *Diagnostic psychological testing* (2 vols.). Chicago: Year Book Publishers.

Suen, H. K. (1990). *Principles of test theories.* Hillsdale, N.J.: Lawrence Earlbaum.

Spearman, C. (1927). *The abilities of man*. New York: Macmillan.

Thorndike, R. L. (1982). *Applied Psychometrics*. Boston, MA: Houghton Mifflin.

Watkins, M. W. (2006). Orthogonal higher order structure of the Wechsler Intelligence Scale for Children–fourth edition. *Psychological Assessment*, *18*, 123–125.

Watkins, M. W. & Canivez, G. L. (2004). Temporal stability of WISC-III subtest composite: Strengths and weaknesses. *Psychological Assessment*, *16*, 133–138.

Wayman, M. M., Wallace, T., Wiley, H. I., Tichá, R., & Espin, C. A. (2007). Literature synthesis on curriculum-based measurement in reading. *The Journal of Special Education*, *41*, 85–120.

Wissler, C. (1901). The correlation of mental and physical tests. *Psychological Review Monograph Supplement*, *3*(6), pp. 1–62.

CHAPTER 14

PRESCHOOL ASSESSMENT

PATTI L. HARRISON
The University of Alabama

Assessment has long been emphasized as one of the primary professional services of school psychologists, and preschool assessment has been an integral part of school psychology practice. Ysseldyke et al. (2006) placed assessent within a comprehensive model of data-based decision making and accountability and recommended that data-based decision making should permeate every aspect of school psychology. Key characteristics of data-based decision making that have relevance for preschool assessment are listed below and are integrated throughout the present chapter:

- Application of systematic processes to define problems and collect data for making valid decisions and implementing effective services for young children
- Use of varied models and methods of assessment, including norm-referenced tools, direct observations of behaviors, family interviews, and other techniques
- Collection of data regarding young children's cognitive, academic, social, developmental, and other characteristics
- Evaluation of factors in home, school, and community environments that can interact with young children's characteristics and impact their development and competence
- Focus on data collection that results in effective prevention and intervention services and promotes young children's development and competence
- Use of data to monitor progress in and outcomes of services and plan further services for young children, including services needed for children's transitions from early childhood programs to elementary school programs

Data-based decision making and its implications for effective services for young children have received renewed emphasis in school psychology during recent years. For example, Dawson et al. (2004) described the outcomes of the 2002 conference on the future of school psychology, and preschool assessment practices align well with the conference outcomes. The conference concluded that school psychology practice must focus on prevention and early intervention, and that school psychologists should promote systems for early identification of problems and provision of evidence-based, early intervention services that prevent growth of these problems. In addition, the conference outcomes stressed that school psychology must reduce its emphasis on traditional individual assessment practices that primarily focus on diagnoses and eligibility and place greater emphasis on assessment linked to intervention and accountability.

The purpose of this chapter is to describe preschool assessment practices that may be integrated into school psychologists' data-based decision making for preschool children and lead to early identification, intervention, and prevention of problems. The use of preschool assessment for eligibility for special education is summarized. A more recent emphasis on appropriate preschool assessment for young children in general education and intervention programs is described. Purposes and guidelines for preschool assessment are provided. Selected assessment methods, including norm-referenced and authentic techniques, are presented.

LEGISLATION AND POLICY RELATED TO PRESCHOOL ASSESSMENT

Traditional preschool assessment activities by school psychologists have been promoted by legislation for special education services for young children and their families. However in recent years, preschool assessment has seen increased importance in general education and early intervention programs for young children. As described in this section of the chapter, preschool assessment increasingly has been characterized by its links to prevention and intervention and its role in promoting accountability for program effectiveness.

Special Education

Assessment of preschool children by school psychologists has been greatly influenced by legislation for special education. Ford and Dahinten (2005) and Prasse (2002) described the components of special education legislation from the 1970s through 1990s that had a significant impact on services for preschool children. P. L. 94-142, the Education for All Handicapped Children Act of 1975, mandated a free and appropriate education for all children with disabilities between the ages of 3 and 21. However, the act allowed states to choose whether they were going to serve preschool children, and most states chose to focus their special education programs on services for school-age children. P. L. 94–142 established a number of requirements for appropriate assessment practices for children with disabilities that continue to be applied in more current legislation. The 1986 amendments of the Education for All Handicapped Children Act, P. L. 99–457, required that all preschool children with disabilities must be served. In addition, P. L. 99–457 included provisions for serving infants and toddlers. In 1990 with P.L. 101–476, Congress amended the act and retitled it the Individual with Disabilities Education Act (IDEA).

The amendments to IDEA in 1997 (P.L. 105–17) represented a number of changes in special education, particularly for preschool children. Part B of IDEA '97 included an emphasis on developmental delay and noted that a "child with a disability" aged 3 through 9 years could include a child experiencing developmental delays. A developmental delay could be identified in one or more areas, including physical development, cognitive development, communication development, social or emotional development, and adaptive development. In IDEA '97, the age range for children that could be classified as having a developmental delay was expanded from previous legislation, from children ages 3 through 5 years to children ages 3 through 9 years. In addition, IDEA '97 included provisions to allow states to use developmental delay as well as specific disability categories (e.g., mental retardation, learning disability) for children ages 3 through 9.

Part C of IDEA '97 also provided services for infants and toddlers with disabilities through multidisciplinary state agencies. An infant or toddler receiving services could be one with a developmental delay, with a condition having a high probability of resulting in a development delay, or, at-risk children, at the discretion of states. Part C also emphasized smooth, effective transition services for children participating in early intervention programs under Part C into preschool programs under Part B.

Since 1997, a number of coordinated efforts by professional associations, parent groups, and policy makers criticized requirements of special education legislation and current state practices concerning special education. One of most notable critiques of special education was found in the President's Commission on Excellence in Special Education (2002). The commission found that IDEA generally provided children with access to special education and also promoted basic safeguards. However, the commission concluded that current special education legislation focused on compliance more than on effective instruction. The commission noted that the system resulted in a model of waiting for children to fail in order to receive special education services, but encouraged few practices of early identification of problems or prevention and intervention techniques using research-based approaches.

The President's Commission had a number of recommendations with relevance for young children. The commission strongly recommended the implementation of research-based, early identification and intervention programs to serve children with learning and behavioral problems at an earlier age and indicated that special education funds should be used for prereferral services. The commission recommended the implementation of effective and reliable screening of young children to identify those who may be at risk for later academic and behavioral problems, including those that may be later referred and placed in special education. Further, the commission recommended that IDEA should create a more seamless system of early intervention services for infants/toddlers, preschoolers, and school age children.

The most recent reauthorization of IDEA, the Individuals with Disabilities Education Improvement Act of 2004 (P. L. 108–446) attempted to respond to the criticisms of special education. IDEA 2004, Part B, retained many components of previous IDEA legislation for preschool and school-age children, such as allowing identification of developmental delay for children ages 3 through 9 in one or more developmental areas, including physical, cognitive, communication, social or emotional, or adaptive. IDEA 2004 also continued to include Part C for infants or toddlers with disabilities who need early intervention services because of developmental delays, have diagnosed physical or mental problems with a high probability of resulting in developmental delay, or, at states' discretion, are children who are at risk.

However, a major change with IDEA 2004 was the greater emphasis on early interventions. Under IDEA 2004, school districts may use up to 15% of their federal funds for early intervention services. The early intervention services may be composed of evaluations, services, and supports, including scientifically based literacy instruction. Early intervention services may include students in grades K–12, but there is a particular emphasis on students in grades K–3. Furthermore, early intervention services are intended for children who need instructional support to succeed in a general education environment but have not been identified as needing special education. IDEA 2004 placed greater emphasis on transition services from Part C programs for infants and toddlers to Part B programs for preschool children. In addition, Part C of IDEA 2004 identified the importance of interventions based on scientifically based research and interventions for preliteracy and language skills.

Earlier versions of IDEA had a number of requirements for appropriate assessment practices that continue to be part of IDEA 2004. Assessments must be administered in the student's native language or other mode of communication and must be validated for their uses. Assessments must include a variety of tools and strategies to gather functional and developmental information, including information from parents and information related to children's progress in the

general education curriculum. For preschool children, assessment information should be related to their involvement and participation in developmentally appropriate activities. Assessment tools must include those that assess educational need and not merely instruments that include a single general intelligence quotient, and no procedure may be used as the only criterion for determining that a child has a disability. Assessment must be comprehensive and directly relevant for identifying special education and other services needs of children.

As a result of IDEA, state special education policies for serving preschool children with disabilities have expanded in recent years. In 2007, Danaher reported that a total of 50 of 51 states included a unique category for preschool children within their disability categories, with 37 states using developmental delay or a similar term. Danaher also investigated the eligibility criteria used by states for their disability classifications for young children and found that 44 states used quantitative criteria. A total of 39 states use norm-referenced criteria, with 36 states using 2 standard deviations below the mean in at least one developmental area, or 1.5 standard deviations below the mean in two development areas, as the criterion for developmental delay or similar classification. A total of 18 states used percent of delay, with 16 states using percent of delay of 20 to 33 percent in one or two areas as the criterion for the disability category. In addition, 14 states permitted eligibility based on factors such as clinical or professional judgment, in lieu of quantitative test scores.

Increasing numbers of preschool children are receiving special education services. The Office of Special Education and Rehabilitative Services, U.S. Department of Education (2003), in its 25th annual report to Congress on IDEA, noted that since 1991 the number of children ages 3 through 5 who received services under Part B of IDEA increased steadily. As of December 1, 2001, 5.2% of the total population of 3- through 5-year-old children living in the 50 states and the District of Columbia were receiving services.

General Education and Early Intervention

School psychologists' assessment activities with preschool children have emphasized eligibility for special education programs. However, IDEA 2004 promoted an increased focus on assessment for instruction, intervention, and accountability.

Similarly, recent years have seen an increased focus on assessment in general education programs through legislation and policy for young children. "Current practices of assessing young children have evolved from a legacy of questionable practices and objectionable uses to a search for ways to assess young children appropriately that contribute to accountability for external audiences and improving programs and instruction" (Mashburn & Henry, 2004, p. 16).

For example, the Head Start program has a long history of comprehensive and high quality early childhood services designed to foster healthy development in low-income children. Head Start's new National Reporting System is another indication of the increasing interest in assessing the development of young children (U.S. Department of Health and Human Services, 2003). The Head Start assessment focuses on literacy, language, and numeracy indicators.

As noted by Mashburn and Henry (2004), assessment practices for young children in general education began to change significantly in the late 1980s when the National Education Goals were adopted by Congress and the states. Goal 1, that every child will start school ready to learn, acknowledged the early childhood period as one to prepare young children with the prerequisites skills for academic success. The National Education Goals Panel was a body of federal and state officials created in 1990 to assess and report state and national progress toward achieving the National Education Goals. Shepard, Kagan, and Wurtz (1998) developed recommendations for early childhood assessment to guide policy and practice related to Goal 1; four general categories of assessment purposes were developed for the National Education Goals Panel:

- Assessment should promote children's learning and development and should be integrated with curriculum and instruction.
- Screening and referral should be used with young children to identify health or learning problems. The use of screening tests should be monitored, given the potential misuse of cognitive tests.
- Assessment should monitor trends and evaluate services. However, it should be noted that assessments for young children are not reliable enough for uses outside the classroom.
- Assessment of academic achievement should be used for accountability of individual students, teachers, and schools. Although testing for high-stakes decisions for individual children should not occur before the end of third grade, instructional assessments to support student learning should occur throughout all grades.

Kochanoff, Newcombe, Hirsh-Pasek, and Weinraub (2003) and Sekino and Fantuzzo (2005) noted that one of the major reasons for increases in preschool assessment in general education was the passage of the No Child Left Behind Act. The No Child Left Behind (NCLB) Act of 2001 (P.L. 107-100) focused on improving student achievement through educational programs demonstrated as effective in scientific research. No Child Left Behind emphasized accountability, and assessments are used in each state to measure what children have learned.

Reading programs are important components of No Child Left Behind for young children. Kadlic and Lesiak (2003) provided support for the increased emphasis on early reading programs. They noted that 68% of low-income fourth graders have limited reading proficiency and there is 90% probability that poor readers in first grade will be poor readers in fourth grade. Furthermore, they emphasized that most reading problems can be prevented through effective programs in preschool and the early grades.

No Child Left Behind supports scientifically based reading instruction programs in the early grades under the Reading First program and in preschool under the Early Reading First program. Both Reading First and Early Reading First require use of assessments to identify children who may be at risk for reading failure, and to monitor children's progress. In Reading First, students are taught the following five skills identified by research as critical to early reading success: phonemic awareness, phonics, fluency, vocabulary, and comprehension.

The Early Reading First program of No Child Left Behind supports preschools, especially those serving low-income families, that provide children with foundational skills. Early Reading First provides funds to enhance early language, cognitive, and reading development skills through strategies based on scientific research. Additional goals of Early Reading First include provision of high-quality language and print-rich environments and implementation of scientifically supported language and literacy activities related to oral language, phonological awareness, print awareness, and alphabet knowledge.

In addition to programs funded through No Child Left Behind, recent public policy and practices have emphasized early intervention programs for young children. A number of early intervention programs have been implemented and expanded in recent years. Research has supported that early intervention services can have positive and long-term benefits for children's development and functioning, and can be cost effective by reducing the need for later services such as special education. Donovan and Cross (2002) concluded that early intervention programs can produce modest to large effects (effect sizes of 0.2 to over 1.0 standard deviation) on children's cognitive and social development, and that program quality is a key factor related to these effects. Larger effect sizes were found when programs were of good quality, included interventions that began early and continued for a longer duration, and provided more hours of service delivery. Children and their parents who participated actively and regularly demonstrated the greatest benefits.

The NICHD Early Childcare Research Network (2005) investigated associations between early child care and children's functioning. Higher-quality child care was related to better math, reading, and memory. Gilliam and Zigler (2000) found that early intervention programs for preschool children were associated with later, positive outcomes for children, including better school attendance and lower rates of grade retention. Magnuson, Meyers, Ruhn, and Waldfogel (2004), using data from the Early Childhood Longitudinal Study, found that children who attended a center or preschool program performed better on reading and math assessments, even when family background and other factors were controlled, and that the better performance continued into first grade. Furthermore, the researchers found that the positive effects were largest for children from disadvantaged backgrounds.

However, Donovan and Cross (2002) noted that practices in early childhood programs are often insufficient to provide systematic prevention and that programs may serve only a small percentage of children who are eligible or high risk. Similarly, Magnuson and Waldfogel (2005) investigated African American, Caucasian, and Hispanic children's differing experiences

in early childhood education and examined implications of different preschool experiences for school readiness. They found race and ethnic differences in both the percentage of children enrolled in preschool and the quality of care in early childhood programs. African American children were more likely to attend preschool than Caucasian children, but were more likely to participate in lower-quality programs. Hispanic children attended preschool less than Caucasian children. The researchers concluded that increases in Hispanic and Caucasian children's enrollment in preschool, alone or in combination with improvements in quality, may impact school readiness.

Many states have recognized the importance of preschool programs in promoting school readiness and reducing later learning problems, especially for children with social or economic risks (Mashburn & Henry, 2004). Magnuson and Waldfogel (2005) reported that, although state funding for prekindergarten programs varies, it increased 250% since 1990, to about $1.9 million in 2002. Most state programs focus on disadvantaged 3- and 4-year-old children. However, only 14% of 4-year-old children were enrolled in public prekindergarten programs in school districts in 2002. In addition, quality indicators suggested that many of these prekindergarten programs provided relatively high-quality services.

PURPOSES AND GUIDELINES FOR PRESCHOOL ASSESSMENT

The Early Childhood Research Institute on Measuring Growth and Development (1998) provided a comprehensive definition of preschool assessment: "Assessment is the process of gathering information for the purpose of making decisions. Developmental assessment in early childhood is designed to gain information about a child's skills and capabilities as well as of the environments that provide the contexts for learning in order to make decisions that will support the development of the child" (p. 2). This section of the chapter describes the purposes of preschool assessment when used in traditional special education eligibility decisions and when used in interventions. The section concludes with a compilation of preschool assessment guidelines from major policy documents and position statements of professional associations.

Assessment for Eligibility

As noted in the previous section, school psychology practices in preschool assessment have traditionally been defined by requirements for special education eligibility. Nagle (2000), Losardo and Notari-Syvereson (2001) and Lerner, Lowenthal, and Egan (1998) identified broad stages of assessment within a general model of special education service delivery for preschool children with disabilities and other problems.

- *Stage 1: Case finding.* The initial stage of special education service delivery, also known as "child find," includes procedures to locate young children and their families who might be eligibile for and benefit from special education. Case finding may include assisting parents in determining that their child may have a developmental problem or making parents aware of the availability of services.
- *Stage 2: Screening.* Screening is typically a brief evaluation to determine if children potentially have problems. Screening may consist of interviews, observations, or admininisration of brief norm-referenced tools and may result in a referral for more comprehensive diagnostic evaluations.
- *Stage 3: Diagnostic assessment.* Diagnostic assessment is a comprehensive and intensive evaluation including interviews, observations, case history, norm-referenced assessment, and other procedures. The assessment typically is conducted by a multidisciplinary team. The goals of diagnostic assessment include identifying strengths and weaknesses of children and families, evaluating the nature and severity of the problem, and determining eligibility for special education services.
- *Stage 4: Planning of programs and interventions.* For children who are eligibile for special education services, results of diagnostic and additional assessments are used to develop goals and interventions for programs.
- *Stage 5: Program monitoring.* After special education programs are implemented, continous monitoring is implemented to evaluate children's progress in the intervention program. Program monitoring may include observations, curriculum-based measures, rating scales, parent interviews, and other techniques. Assessment information focuses on identifying skills that children are or are not mastering.
- *Stage 6: Program evaluation.* Program evaluation emphasizes evaluation of children's attainment of intervention goals, identification of needs and changes for intervention programs, and planning new goals and interventions.

Although the steps listed above have been used widely in a traditional and comprehensive model for special education for preschool children, these steps have been criticized. The Early Childhood Research Institute on Measuring Growth and Development (1998) noted that the traditional stages of assessment are fragmented and have a number of limitations. One limitation is a lack of linkage across the assessment steps, resulting in a nonintegrated assessment system. Specifically, assessments used in the diagnostic assessment stage are often focused on special education eligibility criteria and not on identifying needs and goals for instruction and interventions. A second limitation is the model's failure to promote establishment of long-term goals for children. Although the steps summarized earlier include program monitoring to determine if children are mastering needed skills, the assessment often focuses on immediate skills and not on repeated measures of progress toward long-term outcomes. The third limitation of the traditional assessment model is its lack of theoretical frameworks for decision making.

Assessment for Intervention

Due to recent changes in legislation and policy related to both special education and general education and the recognition of the benefits of early childhood education and intervention, current preschool assessment practices emphasize integrated assessment and intervention services for young children. Meisels and Atkins-Burnett (2000) noted, "Perhaps the most significant change to take place in early childhood assessment in recent years concerns the *fusion* of assessment and intervention" (p. 249). Meisels and Atkins-Burnett emphasized widely recognized principles of preschool assessment: The value of assessment is its relationship to interventions, assessment must be viewed as a first step in implementing interventions, and assessment must be used to evaluate progress throughout an intervention.

Neisworth and Bagnato (1996) identified treatment utility as an important component for preschool assessment practices. They described the following criteria for treatment utility: (a) assessment results should be beneficial to children, (b) assessment results should provide information to help teachers and parents, (c) assessment should be based on goals and objectives of the curriculum, (d) assessment should result in identification of feasible goals and objectives for intervention, and (e) assessment should contribute to evaluating success of the intervention.

The Early Childhood Research Institute on Measuring Growth and Development (1998) suggested that assessment should be incorporated into a problem-solving, linked-systems model that integrates assessment with intervention and evaluation. In the model, assessment activities focus on identifying baselines of children's skills, as well as how to implement interventions and the expected outcomes of the interventions. Interventions, in turn, provide the framework for further assessment, evaluating progress, and revising the intervention as needed. The assessment model proposed by the Early Childhood Research Institute on Measuring Growth and Development is described as using practices that are convergent and ecobehavioral and that target continuous performance monitoring. In the linked-systems model of the Research Institute, the traditional steps of assessment described in the previous section of the chapter are replaced with the following steps:

- **Step 1: Identify.** The first step involves identification of children, including those with deficits in developmental skills or who may be at risk for school difficulties.
- **Step 2: Validate.** In the second step, children's skills are evaluated to determine if they are severe or persistent enough to warrant intervention.
- **Step 3: Explore.** The third step includes exploration of types of intervention and environmental modifications that may promote children's development. Step 3 also includes exploration of the intervention objectives, skills that should be the focus of intervention, and instructional techniques.
- **Step 4: Evaluate.** During implementation of intervention, the fourth step requires monitoring of progress to determine improvement in children's skills and effectiveness of the intervention.
- **Step 5: Resolve.** The fifth step includes an evaluation of children's status to determine if they continue to have developmental skill deficits or continue to be at risk for developing school-related problems.

General Guidelines for Assessment Practices

Meisels and Atkins-Burnett (2000) summarized the need to use sound professional practices in early childhood assessment: "Early childhood assessment is a field in transition. Dominated from its inception by psychometric models and measurement strategies used with older children and adults, it is only now beginning to forge a methodology that is unique to very young children" (p. 231). Recognizing that assessment of preschool children requires principles and techniques to address the varied and unique assessment methodologies that should be used with young children, numerous professional associations, policy groups, and others have developed guidelines for preschool assessment. The following guidelines represent an integration of positions and recommendations from the Division for Early Childhood Council for Exceptional Children (2001); Epstein, Schweinhart, DeBruin-Parecki, and Robin (2004); National Association for the Education of Young Children and the National Association of Early Childhood Specialists in State Departments of Education (2003); National Association of School Psychologists (NASP; 2005); Shepard et al. (1998); and Southern Early Childhood Association (2000).

1. *Preschool assessment should include evaluation of skills in multiple developmental, behavioral, and academic domains that are relevant for the preschool period.* Preschool assessment must be based on sound principles of child growth and development and on a foundation of typical development during the early childhood period. Assessment must consider the whole child, multiple domains and skills, and the interdependence of developmental domains. Assessment must include current skills, as well as emerging skills. Traditionally, preschool assessment has emphasized developmental domains, including language, social, cognitive, physical/motor, sensory, health, and adaptive domains. Due to an increased focus on early literacy and readiness skills for academic learning, preschool assessment should also include preacademic and academic domains such as phonological awareness, alphabetic principle, print awareness, and numeracy. Assessment must

recognize the integration of young children's emotional and cognitive capabilities, in order to better understand their organizing skills and functioning.

2. *Assessment techniques should be child-centered and responsive to the diverse needs and characteristics of young children.* Preschool assessment procedures cannot rely on techniques that may be more appropriate with older students. Preschool children are characterized by wide variability in maturation, unique developmental and behavioral characteristics, and fluctuations in skills. Assessment procedures must be appropriate for the age and other characteristics of preschool children, in terms of both content and data collection methods. Assessment methods must recognize that preschool children need familiar contexts to demonstrate their abilities while being evaluated. Examiners must anticipate and respond to differences in the following characteristics among children and often in the same child at different points in time: activity level, wariness of strangers, reactions to testing situations, motivation, fatigue, restlessness, fear and anxiety, stress, temperament, attention span, and distractibility. Assessment procedures must be culturally sensitive and linguistically appropriate and recognize that, all assessments involve some components of language and culture.

The National Association for the Education of Young Children (2005) developed specific recommendations about assessment practices for young English language learners. The association noted that great emphasis must be given to aligning assessment procedures with children's specific cultural and linguistic characteristics. However, they also noted that current assessment tools have limited application for English language learners, development of additional and better assessment tools is greatly needed.

3. *Parents must be an integral and collaborative component of the assessment of their preschool children.* Assessment procedures for preschool children should recognize that parents are a significant source of assessment information and are both an audience and user of the assessment results; preschool assessment and intervention must be viewed as collaboration between parents and professionals. Preschool assessment should center on children in their family systems and home environments, and recognize the importance of both in young children's development. Preschool assessment must be family-centered; family functioning, resources, priorities, and concerns should drive the data collection and decision-making process.

4. *Preschool assessment techniques should be authentic and should assess children's behavior and skills within their natural environments.* To the greatest extent possible, preschool assessment should focus on children while they are engaged in their typical daily activities and in their natural settings. In addition, data collection should assess children's typical routines and should also assess the environmental contexts in which children must demonstrate specific skills and behaviors. Evaluation of children's responses to people, objects, events, and settings assists in determining if children's strengths and weaknesses are pervasive. Formal standardized testing of young children has a number of limitations, and authentic assessment should be an important component of decision making for young children.

5. *Preschool assessment should be functional and yield meaningful information for understanding children's needs.* Assessment should be beneficial for preschool children and lead to improved knowledge about their strengths and needs. Assessment should be tailored to a specific purpose and should be valid for that purpose; it should have developmental and educational significance and provide information that is meaningful and applicable for meeting the needs of children and families and identifying relevant components for services. Assessment should have consequential validity, predict later competence, and be sensitive to individual changes in development and skills. Importantly, assessment should be viewed as the first step in intervention and must be useful for planning and implementing interventions, monitoring progress during intervention, and evaluating intervention outcomes; it must lead to improved curriculum and instructional practices for preschool children. Assessment must be linked to long-term outcomes for children as a result of intervention.

6. *Preschool assessment must employ multiple informants and methods.* No single source of information, no single informant, or no

single assessment method should be used as the only, or even primary, component of preschool assessment. Assessment should utilize information from parents, teachers, caregivers, and other individuals who know the preschool child and his or her behavior in multiple environments. Use of multiple informants and sources of information yields a comprehensive understanding of children's behavior and skills across the multiple contexts and settings in which they must function. Young children's capabilities cannot be evaluated adequately through a single type of assessment procedure, and assessment for young children must integrate a variety of techniques, including direct observations and interviews.

7. *Preschool assessment must be ongoing and continuous.* To an even greater extent than is true for older children, young children's capabilities cannot be assessed adequately through measures at limited points in time. Preschool children's behavior is characterized by great variation across time and contexts, and, thus, assessment data must be collected across multiple points over time to provide the most comprehensive evaluation of children's growth, development, behavioral change, and response to intervention.

8. *The technical adequacy of preschool assessment techniques must be carefully evaluated, and technical limitations must be recognized and addressed.* Preschool assessment instruments, as with instruments for older children, must be evaluated to determine that they are in compliance with professional technical criteria and accepted psychometric standards. Professionals must ensure that assessments are as valid and reliable as possible for the specific child being assessed, and any limitations in technical quality must be recognized when using the assessment results for decision making. The reliability and validity of sources of assessment information, including parents and teachers, must be evaluated, and limitations must be addressed. Preschool assessment methods must also demonstrate ease of use and scoring in order to provide efficient use.

9. *Professionals engaged in preschool assessment must have comprehensive training and necessary professional skills for working with young children and families.* Professionals in multidisciplinary teams that assess preschool children must have the background, knowledge, interpersonal skills, and professional expertise required for valid assessment of young children. They should have knowledge of typical and atypical development, family and cultural backgrounds, and linguistic diversity. Professionals who conduct assessment with preschool children and their families must be good observers and careful listeners. They must be skilled in techniques for interacting with children and families and must be able to control environmental factors that can impact assessment situations. Professionals must ensure that assessments are well planned and used appropriately and that all professional standards for preschool assessment are addressed.

10. *Preschool assessment must be understandable for all possible audiences.* Preschool assessment practices must recognize that assessment results must be understood by an increasing large number of stakeholders (e.g., parents, teachers, administrators, other professionals), policy makers, and many others. Professionals must ensure that the uses and results of preschool assessment are communicated effectively to all audiences and must prevent misunderstanding, inaccurate perceptions, and misuses of preschool assessment.

ASSESSMENT METHODS

Preschool assessment practices include a variety of methods, techniques, domains, and sources of information. In this section, norm-referenced and authentic methods are summarized. Selected techniques for specific types of assessment are described and include cognitive assessment, behavior rating scales, academic and literacy skills, observation, family assessment, and screening.

Norm-Referenced and Authentic Assessment

Norm-Referenced Assessment Issues

Although standardized, norm-referenced assessment of preschool children remains an important activity of school psychologists, traditional norm-referenced methods for preschool assessment have been the subject of much controversy and debate. It is widely recognized that norm-referenced approaches have a number of limitations for use with preschool children. Position statements by professional organizations, such as the Division for Early Childhood Council for Exceptional Children (2001) and National Association of School Psychologists (2005) encourage professionals to use caution with traditional preschool tests and other standardized, norm-referenced assessment methods because they are less accurate and predictive for younger children, in comparison to standardized, norm-referenced assessments used for school-age children.

A number of characteristics of preschool children impact the usefulness of traditional assessments for decision making. The National Association of School Psychologists (2005) noted that young children have little test-taking experience, short attention spans, and rapid and variable development. Nagle (2000) and Losardo and Notari-Syvereson (2001) elaborated several important factors that are related to the development and behavior of preschool children and that can impact test performance and professional decision making based on scores from traditional norm-referenced instruments. School psychologists' use of traditional standardized assessments requires careful evaluation and consideration of these characteristics during each assessment situation and consideration of these characteristics when interpreting scores.

- Development of young children is complex, and there is great variability across children in what is considered to be "typical development." Preschool development demonstrates uneven growth across domains. For example, motor skills may develop more rapidly than language skills for a young child, while another child exhibits the opposite pattern.
- Preschool children exhibit unpredictable fluctuations in their behavior and factors such as fatigue, motivation, and anxiety about being with a stranger in an unfamiliar testing room can impact children's performance. Behavior of preschool children is characterized by instability. For example, a young child may demonstrate quite different behaviors from one day to the next—or even within the same hour.
- Situational variables such as the climate of the assessment settings and noise and other distractions can impact young children's responses in a testing situation.
- Preschool children have great variations in their experience. For example, some preschool children may have less exposure to

print materials, drawing, counting, and other preacademic activities than other preschool children.

Psychometric characteristics of many norm-referenced preschool instruments are impacted by these characteristics of preschool children. Bracken (1987, 1988, 2000) developed a set of criteria for evaluating the technical properties of traditional norm-referenced preschool assessment instruments:

- Test floors indicate the extent to which tests provide meaningful information about preschool children at low levels of functioning. Bracken recommended that, at minimum, tests should yield scores down to at least two standard deviations below the mean (e.g., at least 70 on a standard score scale with a mean of 100 and standard deviation of 15). He suggested that many preschool instruments have inadequate test floors for preschool children with lower functioning, especially for children younger than 4 years of age.
- Test ceilings indicate the extent to which tests provide meaningful information about preschool children at high levels of functioning. Although most preschool instruments are used to evaluate children with learning and behavior problems, rather than high functioning, Bracken recommended that adequate test ceilings should result in scores at least two standard deviations above the mean.
- Item gradients indicate the steepness of tests' standard scores in relation to raw scores. Tests with adequate item gradients result in comparable changes in standard scores with incremental changes in raw scores and do not, for example, have significant standard score increases in correspondence to a 1- or 2-point increase or decrease in raw scores. Bracken recommended that a raw score change of one point should not result in a standard score change of more than 1/3 standard deviation.
- Reliability refers to the proportion of test score variability that is due to true variance versus error variance. Areas of reliability important in preschool assessment include internal consistency, test-retest reliability (stability), and, for some instruments, interrater reliability. Bracken suggested that preschool instruments should demonstrate total test reliability coefficients of at least .90,

with composite reliabilities and average subtest reliabilities of .80 or higher.

- Validity comprises a variety of investigations to support the extent to which the instrument can be used for its intended purpose and for accurate decision making about preschool children. For example, validity for preschool assessments should support their use in predicting later academic performance or determining children who may have developmental delays or disabilities.

- Normative data for preschool instruments must address the significant growth and development during the early years of life. Bracken concluded that norms tables for preschool ages should be available in increments of no more than three months. Furthermore, Bracken noted that the age of norms and period of time in which a test is standardized are important factors, and that the most recent instruments should be used.

Bracken (2000) summarized the issues related to traditional, norm-referenced assessment of preschool children in terms of *construct relevance*. Construct relevance refers to the extent to which assessment results provide a valid measure of the construct in question (e.g., intelligence, language, social skills, etc.) and limit the role of construct-irrelevant variables such as child characteristics (e.g., fatigue, motivation, behavior) and technical limitations of instruments. Appropriate assessment practices of school psychologists require that they evaluate the construct-relevant and construct-irrelevant variables when interpreting test performance and using results in important decision-making activities for young children.

Bracken's criteria for preschool assessments have been applied in critical reviews of cognitive tests (Bracken, 1987; Bradley-Johnson, 2001; Flanagan & Alfonzo, 1995; Ford & Dahinten, 2005), social and behavioral assessments (Bracken, Keith, & Walker, 1994; Demaray, Ruffalo, & Carlson, 1995; Floyd & Bose, 2003), and preschool screening instruments (Emmons & Alfonso, 2005), among others. For example, one of the most recent applications of Bracken's technical criteria was by Bradley-Johnson and Durmusoglu (2005) for test floors and item gradients for reading and math tests used with young children. They reviewed commonly used reading and math tests for children aged 4 through 7 years and found that few of these tests had adequate floors

at the lower ages at which their norms begin. Most of the reading tests had adequate item gradients, compared to only one-third of the math tests.

Authentic Techniques

Losardo and Notari-Syvereson (2001) cited a number of limitations of traditional, norm-referenced assessment approaches with preschool children. Norm-referenced tests may not adequately assess the complex and holist nature of development of young children and may not assess all types of behavior. Norm-referenced instruments may not address variations in preschool children's behavior across different contexts or the influences of family and social-cultural factors on children's development. However, one of the most frequently cited limitations of traditional, norm-referenced assessment instruments for preschool children is their failure to provide information relevant for planning interventions and instruction (Bagnato, 2005; Barnett, Bell, & Gilkey, 1999; Neisworth & Bagnato, 1996). Authentic assessment techniques have been characterized as controlling for the many limitations of norm-referenced techniques, while providing more application for interventions with young children.

Puckett and Black (2000) defined authentic assessment as "the process of observing, recording, and otherwise documenting the work that children do and how they do it as a basis for educational decisions that affect individual learners.... Authentic assessment provides continuous, qualitative information that can be used by the teacher to guide the instruction of individuals" (p. 7). Authentic assessments include multiple sources of information, multiple assessment approaches, are conducted in multiple settings, and are conducted continuously over time. Authentic techniques may include observations, curriculum-based assessment, analysis of work samples, checklists, anecdotal records, performance assessment, portfolio assessment, and other techniques. Losardo and Notari-Syvereson (2001) suggested that authentic assessment can include embedded approaches, which include nonstructured and structured observations of children within natural contexts, and mediated approaches, which include analysis of children's responsiveness to instruction.

Instead of reliance on only standardized, norm-referenced assessment techniques, preschool assessment guidelines stress that a holistic process is necessary to provide a comprehensive understanding of children and family needs and that the process should include authentic data collection techniques. Several features of authentic, performance assessment are relevant for preschool assessment (Division of Early Childhood Council for Exceptional Children, 2001; Meisels & Atkins-Burnett, 2000; NASP, 2005). Authentic data collection does not focus on isolated skills, but is characterized as a method for evaluating elements of development and learning that traditional norm-referenced assessment may not do well. Authentic assessment is an integrated method of documenting typical behaviors and routines within natural environments and typical responses of children to adults, peers, objects, and events in those environments. Authentic techniques help to determine that possible delays are real and pervasive in a natural context, instead of demonstrated in an artificial testing situation. In addition, authentic data collection also evaluates environments that have substantial influences on development, including family systems, home environments, and school environments. Importantly, ongoing authentic assessment, by assessing the learning of children and the environments in which learning is occurring, provides a method for data collection during intervention and information about effects of the intervention.

A number of different applications for using authentic assessment with preschool children have been described. For example, Barnett et al. (1999) recommended intervention-based assessment, which includes analysis of child, environmental, and instructional variables; direct assessment of children and their behavior in their environments; and collection of information from parents. The Early Childhood Research Institute for Measuring Growth and Development (1998) suggested exploring solutions assessment, which includes evaluation of program features, curriculum-based assessment, ecobehavioral assessment, and evaluation of intervention implementation.

Selected Assessment Techniques
Cognitive Assessment

Probably the most controversial aspect of preschool assessment has been the use of intelligence tests. In 1992, Neisworth and Bagnato expressed opposition to the continued use of intelligence testing in early intervention for young children and highlighted concerns about reliability, prediction, standardized administration procedures, professional acceptability, valid use

in decision making, and consistency with special education legislation for young children.

The controversy was illustrated in a debate in *School Psychology Quarterly* in 1994. Bagnato and Neisworth (1994) presented survey results of school psychologists' cognitive assessment practices with infants, toddlers, and preschoolers. Respondents reported that results of tests of intelligence for young children were unusable 50% of the time and described concerns about form, content, and function of the tests. Respondents also suggested that early cognitive assessment did not address important goals for determining early intervention for young children. Bagnato and Neisworth concluded that infant and preschool cognitive testing should be discontinued and that state laws requiring cognitive tests for admission to special programs should be eliminated. They suggested that early cognition should be redefined as functional, everyday problem-solving skills rather than responses to intelligence tests. They urged the use of alternative assessment techniques that are team based, multidimensional, focused on curriculum, functional, and ecological.

In response to Bagnato and Neisworth (1994), Bracken (1994) concurred that intelligence tests are less technically adequate especially for children younger than 4 years of age and that restrictive special education mandates requiring intelligence tests for young children are inappropriate. However, he argued that, when used by well-trained professionals, intelligence tests can be appropriately incorporated into assessment of young children, along with alternative assessment techniques. Gyurke (1994) suggested that use of cognitive tests and alternative techniques should be guided by the goals of assessment and careful consideration of the assessment methods to address the goals, recognizing that all assessment methods have limitations that should be considered in decision making. Bracken and Gyurke both emphasized that the multiple sources and multiple methods of collecting information should be used in preschool assessment and that no single assessment method can answer all assessment questions.

A number of researchers have evaluated the technical properties of intelligence tests according to criteria first established by Bracken (1987, 1988). Bracken (1987), Flanagan and Alfonso (1995), and Alfonso and Flanagan (1999) concluded that many norm-referenced cognitive tests for young children have a number of psychometric problems, including poor item gradients as well as inadequate subtest, scale, and total test floors. However, the researchers noted that improvements in technical quality were apparent in recently developed cognitive tests, and tests for children age 4 years and older generally were more psychometrically sound than those for younger children.

In the most recent review of technical characteristics of cognitive tests used with preschool children, Ford and Dahinten (2005) reviewed the Bayley Scales of Infant Development–II, Mullen Scales of Early Learning, Wechsler Preschool and Primary Scale of Intelligence–III, Differential Ability Scales, Stanford Binet–Fifth Edition, Woodcock Johnson–III, Kaufman Assessment Battery for Children–II, Leiter International Performance Scale–Revised, and NEPSY: A Developmental Neuropsychological Assessment. They concluded that newer versions of cognitive tests appear to be addressing some of the psychometric limitations of previous versions, especially in the areas of test floors and item gradients. Ford and Dahinten identified a recent trend toward more developmentally relevant and technically sound cognitive assessment for preschool children.

Ford and Dahinten (2005) noted that several of the newer cognitive tests for preschool children also include recent theoretical frameworks for understanding cognitive abilities, including the Cattell-Horn-Carroll (CHC) model. Using a sample of 4- and 5-year old preschool children, Tusing and Ford (2004) conducted a factor analysis of cognitive test scores based on CHC model. The researchers identified ability factors of crystallized intelligence, long range memory, short term memory, auditory processing, and nonverbal ability and suggested that the CHC theoretical framework will enhance practices in preschool cognitive assessment.

Although recent preschool cognitive tests demonstrate improved technical qualities, concerns about technical properties of cognitive tests used with infants and toddlers continue. Bradley-Johnson (2001) conducted an analysis of psychometric properties of cognitive tests used with infant and toddlers, including the Battelle Developmental Inventory, Bayley Scales of Infant Development–Second Edition, Cognitive Abilities Scale, Leiter International Performance Scale–Revised, Mullen Scales of Early Learning, and Stanford-Binet–Fourth Edition. Bradley-Johnson found that all instruments generally had adequate internal consistency.

However, few had adequate test-retest reliability and almost all tests demonstrated inadequate floors. A number of tests had steep item gradients, which may impact the tests' sensitivity to differences in children's performance.

Social-Behavior Rating Scale Assessment

Standardized rating scales are often used in assessment of preschoolers. Rating scales may assess social-emotional functioning, social skills, adaptive behavior, and problem behaviors. Although rating scales have limitations, they may contribute to preschool assessment in a number of ways (Harrison & Raineri, 2006). Most rating scales for preschool children utilize one or more informants (e.g., parent, teacher, caregiver, etc.) as respondents to the scale. Use of multiple informants provides information about children, their environments, and interactions between the children and significant people in their environments. Use of third-party informants to rating scales also allows important individuals, such as parents and teachers, to participate in the assessment process for young children. Rating scales provide information about children's behavior in different environments (e.g., home, school, community) in which they function and, thus, focus on behavior in naturalistic settings. Rating scale items focus on children's specific behaviors and functional skills related to home, family, and school factors and may have implications for interventions for preschool children. Finally, norm-referenced scores from rating scales result in a standardized developmental reference for children's behavior and skills.

However, rating scale assessments may have a number of limitations. Rating scales of social, emotional, behavioral, and adaptive skills may fail to take into account a variety of factors necessary to obtain comprehensive information about preschool children's functioning. Rating scales generally provide only a sampling of target skills but do not sample all possible behaviors; rating scale items may be limited only to skills that can be assessed reliably through a rating scale or questionnaire completed by an informant. Furthermore, rating scales are not direct assessments of children's behaviors and do not assess many environmental conditions and contexts surrounding behavior, including antecedents and consequences of children's specific responses.

Rating scales are dependent on the ratings obtained from third party informants and may present biases or inaccuracies when informants have insufficient knowledge abut children's daily activities. Informants' perceptions may vary due to different expectations for appropriate behavior in home, school, or other settings. Research generally has found low correlations between parent and teacher ratings and ratings between two parents. For example, Walker and Bracken (1996) investigated inter-parent agreement on four preschool behavior rating scales and found low to moderate correlations between parents across all four instruments. It is important to take into account these limitations of standardized behavior rating scales when interpreting data and making decisions. Because rating scales have a number of limitations, they should be supplemented with authentic assessment techniques, including direct assessment, naturalist observations, and interviews to obtain additional information about children's strengths and limitations.

Several studies have applied Bracken's (1987, 1988) psychometric criteria to behavior rating scales. Bracken et al. 1994 investigated the psychometric qualities of 13 preschool third-party measures of social-emotional functioning. The instruments included the Behavior Assessment System for Children, Burks Behavior Rating Scales, Child Behavior Checklist, Louisville Behavior Checklist, Personality Inventory for Children, Preschool Behavior Questionnaire, Preschool and Kindergarten Behavior Scales, Social Skills Rating System, Temperament Assessment Battery for Children, Vineland Adaptive Behavior Scales, and Walker Problem Behavior Identification Checklist. Bracken et al. evaluated standardization sample, internal consistency, stability, interrater reliability, test floor and ceiling, item gradients, and validity. Although no instrument met all technical criteria, several of the instruments met most of them, especially the most recent scales.

Floyd and Bose (2003) focused on scales specifically designed to assess emotional disturbance of school age children, including the Behavior Evaluation Scale–2: Home and School Versions; Behavior Disorders Identification Scale, Second Edition: Home and School Versions; Devereux Behavior Rating Scale–School Form; Emotional and Behavior Problem Scale, Second Edition: Home and School Versions; Scale for Assessing Emotional Disturbance; and Social-Emotional Dimension Scale. Although all instruments had adequate test floors and ceilings, as well as item gradients, all instruments had technical limitations with at least two other technical properties.

Demaray et al. (1995) completed a review of six published rating scales used to assess the social skills of preschool and school-aged children, including the School Social Behavior Scales, Social Skills Rating System, Waksman Social Skills Rating Scale, Walker-McConnell Scale of Social Competence and School, School Social Skills Rating Scale, and Social Behavior Assessment Inventory. They reviewed content, standardization samples, norms, scores, and other psychometric properties and concluded that most scales had several technical limitations.

Academic Skills, School Readiness, and Early Literacy

One of the most recent areas emphasized for preschool assessment is assessment of factors related to school readiness, especially early literacy skills and readiness for academics. As noted earlier in this chapter, federal programs such as No Child Left Behind, Reading First, and Early Reading First are promoting increased use of preschool assessments related to early literacy. In addition, Part B (preschool and school age) and Part C (infants and toddlers) of IDEA 2004 both emphasize early literacy skills.

In spite of increased emphasis in federal policy on school readiness, states are just beginning to develop practices for academic readiness assessment. Saluja, Scott-Little, and Clifford (2000) surveyed state departments of education and found that there were few consistent state regulations in how school readiness is assessed. Children's age was the only consistent criterion across all states as an indicator of readiness for school. Only 13 states conducted statewide assessment for children entering kindergarten, although an additional five states required school districts to conduct assessments and allowed school districts to determine their own assessment methods. Twenty-six states did not require readiness assessments, but allowed local districts to do so, and 16 states had initiatives in place to plan statewide readiness assessment systems.

Scarpati and Silver (1999) identified two different perspectives for assessment of school readiness for preschool children. Traditionally, readiness measures have focused on processes, such as cognitive skills, that are believed to provide an underlying foundation for academic skills that will be encountered in schools. More recently, assessment of school readiness has placed increased emphasis on direct evaluation of behaviors, skills, and knowledge that are considered as prerequisites to academic skills. For example, academic readiness assessment may focus on direct assessment of print awareness, alphabetic knowledge, and other specific prerequisites for reading. As a result of significant national focus on early literacy interventions, recent assessment of school readiness has emphasized ongoing and continuous authentic and curriculum-based techniques. Kochanoff et al. (2003) described the outcomes of the Temple University Conference on Preschool Assessment, and identified a number of preacademic and academic factors that should be assessed for preschool children, including vocabulary, concept of a word, print awareness, phonemic awareness, alphabet, relations of letters and sounds, counting, enumeration, mental number line, addition, and subtraction.

One of the most widely used direct measures of early literacy skills is the Dynamic Indicators of Basic Early Literacy Skills (DIBELS; Good, Gruba, & Kaminski, 2002). The DIBELS is used by school districts around the country to assess early literacy skills of children in kindergarten through third grade. The brief assessments are administered to all students three times per year to determine individual student progress toward meeting benchmarks. In addition, percentages of children in classrooms, schools, and school districts that meet benchmarks are used for evaluations of programs such as Reading First. The DIBELS measures were designed to assess major factors of early literacy, including phonological awareness, alphabetic principle, and fluency with connected text. Specific DIBELS measures for kindergarten and first grade children include initial sounds fluency, letter naming fluency, phoneme segmentation fluency, nonsense word fluency, and oral reading fluency. Preschool assessments are described as individual growth indicators and include picture naming, alliteration, and rhyming (Missall & McConnell, 2004).

In addition to direct assessment of preacademic and academic skills, assessment of children's social-emotional skills needed for an academic learning environment also is recommended. Kochanoff et al. (2003) suggested that social and emotional skills, including regulatory behavior, prosocial behavior, behavior problems, and temperament, should be assessed directly routinely for information about preschool children's behavioral readiness for academic learning. Similarly, McWayne, Fantuzzo, and McDermott (2004) identified a number of preschool competencies needed for academic success, including general classroom competence (literacy, numeracy, motor skills, and social skills), specific approaches to learning (persistence, attention, motivation, and responses to instruction), and interpersonal classroom behavior problems (children's interactions with peers during play, difficulty with interpersonal aspects of the classroom learning process). Blom-Hoffman, Dwyer, Clarke, and Power (2002) described important skills of children and instructional process variables that should be assessed for early literacy programs: instructional outcomes, including alphabet recognition and phonological skills; academic learning time; amount of instruction; social validity of the instruction; procedural integrity; and family involvement.

Teacher judgments are often used in assessment of young children's school readiness. Rimm-Kaufman, Pianta, and Cox (2000), using a national sample, found that kindergarten teachers estimated that approximately one-sixth of their students have adjustment problems. Their findings suggested that kindergarten teachers perceive a fairly high rate of problems that may interfere with kindergarten children's potential for classroom success. Mashburn and Henry (2004) investigated the validity of preschool and kindergarten teachers' ratings of children's skills in following areas: kindergarten readiness, academic skills, and communication skills. When they compared teacher ratings with direct assessments, they found that teacher ratings generally were more highly related to direct assessments of basic academic skills and less related to direct assessments of problem-solving and vocabulary. Importantly, the researchers found that teachers with more education rated children more consistently with direct assessments of skills. Similarly, they found that teacher ratings reliably predicted student learning in kindergarten to third grade in the areas of language, literacy, and mathematical thinking.

Observational Techniques

Observational techniques are an important component of preschool assessment and can increase information about children's strengths and limitations in natural contexts. Structured and semistructured naturalistic observations focus on direct and systematic observation of preschool children in settings, such as classrooms, homes, and playgrounds. Behavioral observations of preschool children provide opportunities for assessing behaviors in a variety of settings and situations (Knoff, Stollar, Johnson, & Chenneville, 1999) and yield a fund of information about children's activities. Observations allow professionals to evaluate, first-hand, children's responses to the situational demands in their environments. For example, children can be observed in interactions with younger versus older peers. Children's interactions with parents and teachers can be compared. Environmental characteristics may be assessed to identify factors that may prevent children from responding in one situation but not in another. Continuous observations of children's responses to interventions can be examined to monitor the effectiveness of a particular intervention.

In addition to nonstructured and semistructured behavioral observation methods, a number of structured observational techniques are used with preschool children. For example, Brown, Odom, and Holcombe (1996) described the System for Observation of Children's Social Interactions that includes observations and coding systems for behavioral strategies, complimentary statements, gestural communications, physical assistance, play noises, social goals, and success of interactions. Sekino and Fantuzzo (2005) described the Child Observation Record, in which teachers rate cognitive, coordinated movement, and social engagement dimensions. Wakschlag et al. (2005) offered a diagnostic observational tool, the Disruptive Behavior Diagnostic Observation Schedule, that provides distinctions between normative and atypical behavior, integration of behavioral dimensions of children's behavior, observations within and outside of parent-child interactions, and use of tasks to elicit behaviors.

Play assessment has received focus as an observational technique for evaluating preschool children. Athanasiou (2000) and Ross (2002) suggested that play assessment can be used to observe cognitive, social-behavioral, language, and motor domains. Play assessment may include unstructured, naturalistic observations. Play assessment may be structured by observers using specific toys, situations, or interactions. Observations of children's play may be conducted in clinical settings, home, and preschool classrooms and may be conducted with children interacting with parents, peers, and teachers.

However, several limitations of play assessment are recognized, including limited data to support reliability and validity and a qualitative focus that may not address criteria for eligibility decisions.

One of the most widely used models of play assessment is transdisciplinary play-based assessment (Linder, Holm, & Walsh, 1999). In the transdisciplinary model, assessment is conducted by teams of professionals from several disciplines and parents while children are engaging in structured and free play situations. A number of advantages are cited for this model, including the involvement of both professionals and parents and a flexible approach.

Myers, McBride, and Peterson (1996) compared the social validity of transdisciplinary, play-based assessment by randomly assigning young children to either a multidisciplinary, standardized assessment or a transdisciplinary play-based assessment. The researchers collected data about parent and staff perceptions, time factors, utility of reports, and parent and staff consistency in judgment-based ratings. The play-based assessments were reported to take less time to complete, in comparison to standardized assessments. Additionally, play assessments were congruent with developmental ratings.

Kelly-Vance and Ryalls (2005) also addressed systematic procedures for play assessment and noted technical limitations with play assessment techniques, including the variation in procedures and methods of coding child behaviors. They developed a set of standardized procedures for play assessment, and a coding scheme with an empirical foundation and found high interobserver reliability for the assessment. Kelly-Vance, Ryalls, and Glover (2002) explored the use of play assessment with young children and found that children's play primarily consisted of exploratory play, pretend play, and problem solving. However, the authors recommend that more research is needed before play assessment can be used routinely in early childhood assessment.

Family Assessment

The importance of family involvement in the assessment of preschoolers is widely recognized. Boudreau (2005) described a number of important characteristics of family assessment. Family assessment may evaluate parents' knowledge about their children. Further, family assessment may provide information about children's behaviors across time and in different contexts. Parent reports may reduce potential difficulties associated with formal assessment, including children's lack of familiarity with examiners and the stressful framework of a testing situation. Although a number of techniques may be used for family assessment, Krauss (2000) suggested that most are informal, nonstandardized, and flexible. However, Krauss noted that little research has investigated a relationship between family assessment and service outcomes, and that professionals in early childcare programs generally are not well trained in conducting family assessments. Davis and Gettinger (1995) found that parents preferred a self-report measure combined with a structured interview in comparison to either used alone.

A family focus in assessment is important for evaluating a variety of characteristics related to family impact on child functioning, planning intervention implementation, and determination of outcomes. Kalesnik (1999) and Krauss (2000) suggested that family assessment may evaluate factors such as roles, responsibilities, stressors, strengths, resources, supports, and needs. However, most family assessment focuses on needs from the service delivery system and adjusting to a child's disability. Bailey, McWilliam, and Darkes (1998) emphasized the importance of a family-centered approach in planning and evaluating early interventions, and suggested that attainment of family outcomes should be assessed in the following areas: (a) perceptions of the current impact of early intervention on children and their families, (b) views about professionals and the service delivery system, (c) perceptions of how programs may assist families in helping their children, (d) evaluations of early intervention outcomes for strengthening families, and (e) views of future impacts of early intervention services.

Another focus of family assessment is parent-child interactions. Kelly and Barnard (2000) described the importance of assessing parent-child interactions and their implications for interventions. They identified several important interaction factors to assess, including attachment, regulation, reading of cues, and using play and teaching for learning. They noted that standardized observational measures to evaluate interactions may not be used widely in early intervention programs and that additional research is needed to identify components of improvement in parent child interactions that have the greatest outcomes for children.

More recent approaches in family assessment recognize the current emphasis on assessing young children's early literacy skills. For example, Boudreau (2005) used a parent questionnaire in the assessment of literacy skills of preschool children with language impairments Parent reports were compared to formal measures of early literacy, and results demonstrated a strong relationship between the two assessment techniques.

Screening

Historically, preschool and kindergarten screening has been utilized to initially identify potential children who may be at risk for developmental, learning, and behavior problems and who may need special services to achieve their potential. During traditional screening, brief norm-referenced measures of development are administered to large groups of children and selected children are referred for more comprehensive assessment before a decision is made about eligibility for special services. Gredler (1997) and Thurlow and Gilman (1999) provided several characteristics of traditional preschool and kindergarten screening. Screening provides global information with limited samples of behavior and is conducted on a probability basis to select children most likely to be at risk. Screening assists in planning further, more comprehensive assessment but does not yield diagnostic information or a final decision about special services. Domains assessed for children during screening include, for example, cognitive, language, motor, health, and social areas. Finally, a decision-theory model is applied to preschool screening in which agreement between screening outcomes and comprehensive assessment outcomes are evaluated. Validity of a screening instrument is typically evaluated in terms of sensitivity (percentage of true positives identified by the instrument) and specificity (percentage of true negatives identified by the instrument).

Preschool and kindergarten screening has been applied widely by school districts across the country. For example, Costenbader, Rohrer, and DiFonzo (2000) investigated practices for screening new enrollees for kindergarten in New York State. Most respondents (95%) reported that screening was conducted but on an individual school district basis. In 45% of the districts, professionals spent more than 30 minutes in screening procedures with each child. On average, 3.58 professionals participated in screening procedures in each district.

Barnett, Macmann, and Carey (1992) identified questionable techniques of traditional preschool screening. Although they noted that screening is used as a less costly procedure that can be delivered to a larger segment of the population, they suggested that screening may be used because of traditions in school practices rather than consideration of costs, benefits, and error rates of the procedures. As with other norm-referenced techniques used in preschool assessment, traditional, norm-referenced preschool screeners may be characterized by technical limitations in reliability, validity, norms, test floors, and item gradients. Furthermore, because they are brief, they may assess only very limited samples of skills and behavior and may not provide direct assessment of academic or pre-academic skills and behaviors important for learning. Emmons and Alfonso (2005) evaluated the technical characteristics of five standardized screening batteries, including the Brigance Screens, Developmental Indicators for the Assessment of Learning–Third Edition, Early Screening Inventory–Revised, Early Screening Profiles, and FirstSTEP. They based their review on technical characteristics identified by Bracken 1987, 1988. Although they discovered variation in technical information presented in the test manuals, they found that the instruments generally had adequate reliability. However, sensitivity and specificity data for the instruments resulted in varying percentages of children accurately identified as at risk or not at risk.

Due to limitations of traditional, norm-referenced screening batteries and increased national emphasis on early intervention in both special and general education, new approaches to screening have included more direct and authentic techniques. For example, an increased focus on early literacy is seen in preschool and kindergarten screening. Invernizzi, Justice, and Landrum (2004) described a statewide, screening effort to assess core literacy components by developing the Phonological Awareness and Literacy Screening–Kindergarten, which was used in Virginia. Justice, Invernizzi, & Geller (2005) found that criterion-referenced early literacy tasks used in statewide screening effectively discriminated between 4- and 5-year-old children. Molfese, Molfese, and Modglin (2004) examined a new screening tool (Get Ready to Read) for assessing early reading skills of 3- and 4-year-old children. They found that vocabulary and phonological-sensitive scores from the screener correlated with cognitive assessments.

In recent years, preschool and kindergarten screening also has included more extensive assessment of social-emotional and school competence factors. Miller et al. (2003) used brief functional screenings for children from low-income families that were at risk for difficult transitions to preschool. Functional screenings, including classroom observations, were conducted in naturalistic settings and focused on areas relevant for successful transition, including social and emotional skills and cognitive and language abilities. The researchers found that the brief functional screening predicted outcomes over a one year period. Agostin and Bain (1997) found that cooperation and self-control, in addition to receptive language and visual memory, predicted academic outcomes and grade promotion or retention in the early school years.

CONCLUSIONS

School psychologists must be prepared for the increasing focus on assessment for special education, general education, and early intervention services for preschool children, especially in the areas of early literacy, reading, and academic competence. Legislation and policy has provided clear mandates that education for young children must include identification of potential problems that interfere with school success and must emphasize provision of effective early intervention for these problems. School psychologists must be leaders in using assessment that has clear links to identifying problems, planning interventions, monitoring children's progress during intervention, and providing accountability for intervention services. Although norm-referenced techniques have demonstrated technical improvements in recent years and will continue to be used to provide a developmental, standardized reference for evaluating preschool children, direct and authentic assessment of preacademic and academic skills, in addition to social and behavioral factors related to school competence, will be a major part of preschool service activities of school psychologists. As assessment experts, school psychologists will remain key members of multidisciplinary teams that evaluate preschool children and plan interventions. In addition, they will serve as consultants for teacher, parents, administrators, policy makers, and others in integrating assessment with intervention and using assessment results to evaluate children, interventions, and programs.

REFERENCES

Agostin, T. M., & Bain, S. K. (1997). Predicting early school success with developmental and social skills screeners. *Psychology in the Schools, 34,* 219–228.

Alfonso, V. C., & Flanagan, D. P. (1999). Assessment of cognitive functioning in preschoolers. In E. V. Nuttall, I. Romero, & J. Kalesnik (Eds.), *Assessing and screening preschoolers: Psychological and educational dimensions* (2nd ed., pp. 186–217). Needham Heights, MA: Allyn & Bacon.

Athanasiou, M. S. (2000). Play-based approaches to preschool assessment. In B. A. Bracken (ed.), *The psychoeducational assessment of preschool children* (3rd ed., pp. 412–427). Needham Heights, MA: Allyn & Bacon.

Bagnato, S. J. (2005). The authentic alternative for assessment in early intervention: An emerging evidence-based practice. *Journal of Early Intervention, 28,* 17–22.

Bagnato, S. J., & Neisworth, J. T. (1994). A national study of the social and treatment "invalidity" of intelligence testing for early intervention. *School Psychology Quarterly, 9,* 81–101.

Bailey, D. B., McWilliam, R. A., & Darkes, L. A. (1998). Family outcomes in early intervention: a framework for program evaluation and efficacy research individualized family service plans. *Exceptional Children, 64,* 313–329.

Barnett, D. W., Bell, S. H., & Gilkey, C. M. (1999). The promise of meaningful eligibility determination: Functional intervention-based multifactored preschool evaluation. *Journal of Special Education, 33,* 112–124.

Barnett, D. W., Macmann, G. M., & Carey, K. T. (1992). Early intervention and the assessment of developmental skills: Challenges and directions. *Topics in Early Childhood Special Education, 12,* 21–43.

Blom-Hoffman, J., Dwyer, J. F., Clarke, A. T., & Power, T. J. (2002, November). Evaluating intervention outcomes: Strategies for conducting outcome evaluations of early intervention literacy programs. *Communiqué, 31*(3), 34–35.

Boudreau, D. (2005). Use of a parent questionnaire in emergent and early literacy assessment of preschool children. *Language, Speech & Hearing Services in Schools, 36,* 33–48.

Bracken, B. A. (1987). Limitations of preschool instruments and standards for minimal levels of technical adequacy. *Journal of Psychoeducational Assessment, 4,* 313–326.

Bracken, B. A. (1988). Ten psychometric reasons why similar tests produce dissimilar results. *Journal of School Psychology, 26,* 155–166.

Bracken, B. A. (1994). Advocating for effective preschool practices: A comment on Bagnato and Neisworth. *School Psychology Quarterly, 9,* 103–108.

Bracken, B. A. (2000). Maximizing construct relevant assessment: The optimal preschool testing situation. In B. A. Bracken (Ed.), *The psychoeducational assessment of preschool children* (3rd ed., pp. 33–44). Needham Heights, MA: Allyn & Bacon.

Bracken, B. A., Keith, L. K., & Walker, K. C. (1994). Assessment of preschool behavior and social-emotional functioning: A review of thirteen third-party instruments. *Rehabilitation and Exceptionality, 1,* 331–346.

Bradley-Johnson, S. (2001). Cognitive assessment for the youngest children: A critical review of tests. *Journal of Psychoeducational Assessment, 19,* 19–44.

Bradley-Johnson, S., & Durmusoglu, G. (2005). Evaluation of floors and item gradients for reading and math tests for young children. *Journal of Psychoeducational Assessment, 23,* 262–278.

Brown, W. H., Odom, S. L., & Holcombe, A. (1996). Observational assessment of young children's social behavior with peers. *Early Childhood Research Quarterly, 11,* 19–40.

Costenbader, V., Rohrer, A. M., & DiFonzo, N. (2000). Kindergarten screening: A survey of current practice. *Psychology in the Schools, 35,* 323–332.

Danaher, J. (2007). *Eligibility policies and practices under Part B of IDEA* (NECTAC Notes, No. 24). Chapel Hill: University of North Carolina Chapel Hill, FPG Child Development Institute, National Early Childhood Technical Assistance Center. Retrieved January 12, 2008 from www.nectac.org/~pdfs/pubs/nnotes24.pdf.

Dawson, M., Cummings, J., Harrison, P. L., Short, R., Gorin, S., Palomares, R. (2004). The 2002 multi-site conference on the future of school psychology: Next steps. *School Psychology Review, 33,* 115–125.

Davis, S. K. & Gettinger, M. (1995). Family-focused assessment for identifying family resources and concerns: Parent preferences, assessment information, and evaluation accross three methods. *Journal of School Psychology, 33,* 99–121.

Demaray, M. K., Ruffalo, S. L., & Carlson, J. (1995). Social skills assessment: A comparative evaluation of six published rating scales. *School Psychology Review, 24,* 648–671.

Division for Early Childhood, Council for Exceptional Children (2001). *Concept paper on developmental delay as an eligibility category.* Missoula, MT: Author. Retrieved January 12, 2008, from www.dec-sped.org/pdf/positionpapers/ConceptPaper_DevDelay.pdf.

Donovan, M. S., & Cross, C. T. (Eds.) (2002). *Minority students in special and gifted education.* Washington, DC: National Research Council.

Early Childhood Research Institute on Measuring Growth and Development (1998). *Theoretical foundations of the Early Childhood Research Institute* on *Measuring Growth and Development: An early childhood problem solving model* (Technical Report 6). Minneapolis: University of Minnesota. Retrieved January 12, 2008 from cehd.umn.edu/ceed/projects/ecri/ecrirpt6.pdf

Emmons, M. R.., & Alfonso, V. C. (2005). A critical review of the technical characteristics of current preschool screening batteries. *Journal of Psychoeducational Assessment, 23,* 111–127.

Epstein, A., Schweinhart, L., DeBruin-Parecki, A., & Robin, K. (2004). Preschool assessment: A guide to developing a balanced approach. *Preschool Policy Matters, 7,* 1–12. Retrieved January 12, 2008 from 72.14.205.104/search?q=cache:PnMJsny K8EsJ:nieer.org/resources/policybriefs/7.pdf+ Preschool+assessment:+A+guide+to+ developing+a+balanced+approach&hl=en& ct=clnk&cd=1&gl=us.

Flanagan, D. P., & Alfonso, V. C. (1995). A critical review of the technical characteristics of new and recently revised intelligence tests for preschool children. *Journal of Psychoeducational Assessment, 13,* 66–90.

Floyd, R. J., & Bose, J. E. (2003). Behavior rating scales for assessment of emotional disturbance: A critical review of measurement characteristics. *Journal of Psychoeducational Assessment, 21,* 43–78.

Ford, L., & Dahinten, V. S. (2005). Use of intelligence tests in the assessment of preschoolers. In D. P. Flanagan & P. L. Harrison (Eds.), *Contemporary intellectual assessment: Theories, tests, and issues* (2nd ed., pp. 487–503). New York: Guilford.

Gilliam, W. S., & Zigler, E. F. (2000). A critical meta-analysis of all evaluations of state funded preschool from 1977 to 1998: Implications for policy, service delivery and program evaluation. *Early Childhood Research Quarterly, 15,* 441–473.

Good, R. H, Gruba, J., & Kaminski, R. A. (2002) Best practices in using Dynamic Indicators of Basic Early Literacy Skills (DIBELS) in an outcomes-driven model. In A. Thomas and J. Grimes (Eds.), *Best Practices in School Psychology IV* (pp. 699–720). Bethesda, MD: National Association of School Psychologists.

Gredler, G. (1997). Issues in early childhood screening and assessment. *Psychology in the Schools, 34.* 98–106.

Gyurke, J. S. (1994). A reply to Bagnato and Neisworth: Intelligent versus intelligence testing of preschoolers. *School Psychology Quarterly, 9,* 109–112.

Harrison, P. L., & Raineri, G. 2006. Assessment of adaptive behavior. In B. A. Bracken & R. Nagle (Eds.), *Psychoeducational assessment of preschool children* (4th ed. pp. 195–218). Mahwah, NH: Lawrence Erlbaum.

Invernizzi, M., Justice, L., & Landrum, T. J. (2004). Early literacy screening in kindergarten: Widespread implementation in Virginia. *Journal of Literacy Research, 36,* 479–500.

Justice, L. M., Invernizzi, M., & Geller, K. (2005). Descriptive-developmental performance of at-risk preschoolers on early literacy tasks. *Reading Psychology, 26,* 1–25.

Kadlic, M., & Lesiak, M. A., (2003, February). *Early reading and scientifically based research: Implications for practice in early childhood education programs.* National Association of State Title I Directors Conference, Washington, DC. Retrieved January 12, 2008 from www.ed.gov/admins/lead/read/ ereadingsbr03/ecreading03.ppt.

Kalesnik, J. (1999). Family assessment. In E. V. Nuttall, I. Romero, & Kalesnik, J. (Eds.), *Assessing and screening preschoolers* (2nd ed., pp. 112–125). Needham Heights: Allyn & Bacon.

Kelly, J. F., & Barnard, K. E. (2000). Assessment of parent-child interaction: Implications for early intervention. In J. P. Shonkoff & S. J. Meisels (Eds.), *Handbook of early childhood intervention* (2nd ed; pp. 258–289). New York: Cambridge University Press.

Kelly-Vance, L., & Ryalls, B. O. (2005). A systematic, reliable approach to play assessment in preschoolers. *School Psychology International, 26,* 398–412.

Kelly-Vance, L., Ryalls, B. O., & Glover, K. G. (2002). The use of play assessment to evaluate cognitive skills of two and three year old children. *School Psychology International, 23,* 169–185.

Knoff, H. M., Stollar, S. A., Johnson, J. J., & Chenneville, T. A. (1999). Assessment of social-emotional functioning and adaptive behavior. In E. V. Nuttall, I. Romero, & J. Kalesnik (Eds.), *Assessing and screening preschoolers* (2nd ed., pp. 126–160). Needham Heights, MA: Allyn & Bacon.

Kochanoff, A., Newcombe, N., Hirsh-Pasek, K., & Weinraub, M. (2003). *Using science to inform preschool assessment: A summary report of the Temple University Forum on Preschool Assessment.* Philadelphia, PA: Temple University Center for Improving Resources in Children's Lives. Retrieved January 12, 2008 from www.temple .edu/psychology/FacultyWebs/Weinraub/Links/ CIRCL_PreSchAssesmt%20Final%20report%20 paper%2010-03.pdf.

Krauss, M. W., (2000). Family assessment within early intervention programs. In J. P. Shonkoff & S. J. Meisels (Eds.), *Handbook of early childhood intervention* (2nd ed; pp. 290–308). New York: Cambridge University Press.

Lerner, J., Lowenthal, B., & Egan, R. (1998). *Preschool children with special needs: Children at-risk, children with disabilities.* Needham Heights, MA: Allyn & Bacon.

Linder, T. W., Holm, C. W., & Walsh, K. A. (1999). Transdisciplinary play-based assessment. In E. V.

Nuttall, I. Romero, & J. Kalesnik (Eds.), *Assessing and Screening Preschoolers*. (2nd ed. pp. 161–185). Needhan Heights, MA: Allyn & Bacon.

Losardo, A., & Notari-Syvereson, A. (2001) *Alternative approaches in assessing young children*. Baltimore: Paul H. Brookes.

Magnuson, K. A., Meyers, M. K., Ruhm, C. J., & Waldfogel, J. 2004. Inequality in preschool education and school readiness. *American Educational Research Journal, 41*, 115–157.

Magnuson, K. A., & Waldfogel, J. (2005). Early childhood care and education: Effects on ethnic and racial gaps in school readiness. *The Future of Children, 15*, 169–196.

Mashburn, A. J., & Henry, G. T. (2004). Assessing school readiness: Validity and bias in preschool and kindergarten teachers' ratings. *Educational Measurement: Issues and Practice, 23*, 16–30.

McWayne, C. M., Fantuzzo, J. W., & McDermott, P. A. (2004). Preschool competency in context: An investigation of the unique contribution of child competencies to early academic success. *Developmental Psychology, 40*, 633–645.

Meisels, S. J., & Atkins-Burnett, S. (2000). The elements of early childhood assessment. In J. P. Shonkoff & S. J. Meisels (Eds.), *Handbook of early childhood intervention* (2nd ed; pp. 231–257). New York: Cambridge University Press.

Miller, A. L., Gouley, K. K., Shields, A., Dickstein, S., Seifer, R., Magee, K. D., & Fox, C. (2003). Brief functional screening for transition difficulties prior to enrollment predicts socio-emotional competence and school adjustment in head start preschoolers. *Early Child Development & Care, 173*, 681–698.

Missall, K. N., & McConnell, S. R. (2004). *Psychometric characteristics of individual growth and development indicators: Picture naming, rhyming, and alliteration*. Minneapolis: University of Minnesota Center for Early Education and Development. Retrieved January 12, 2008 from ggg.umn.edu/techreports/ecri_report8.html.

Molfese, V. J., Molfese, D. L., & Modglin, A. T. (2004). Screening early reading skills in preschool children: Get ready to read. *Journal of Psychoeducational Assessment, 22*, 136–150.

Myers, C. L., McBride, S. L., & Peterson, C. A. (1996). Trandisciplinary play-based assessment in early childhood special education: An examination of social validity. *Topics in Early Childhood Special Education, 16*, 102–126.

Nagle, R. J. (2000). Issues in preschool assessment. In B. Bracken (Ed.), *The psychoeducational assessment of preschool children* (3rd ed., pp. 19–32). Needham Heights, MA: Allyn & Bacon.

National Association for the Education of Young Children (2005). *Screening and assessment of young English-language learners*. Washington DC: Author. Retrieved January 12, 2008 from www.naeyc.org/about/positions/ELL_Supplement.asp.

National Association for the Education of Young Children and National Association of Early Childhood Specialists in State Departments of Education (2003). *Early childhood curriculum, assessment, and program evaluation—Building an effective, accountable system in programs for children birth through age 8*. Washington, DC: Author. Retrieved January 12, 2008 from www.naeyc.org/about/positions/pdf/pscape.pdf.

National Association of School Psychologists. (2005). *Position statement on early childhood assessment*. Bethesda, MD: Author. Retrieved January 12, 2008 from www.nasponline.org/about_nasp/pospaper_eca.aspx.

Neisworth, J. T., & Bagnato, S. J. (1992). The case against intelligence testing in early intervention. *Topics in Early Childhood Special Education, 12*, 1–20.

Neisworth, J. T., & Bagnato, S. J. (1996). Assessment for early intervention: Emerging themes and practices. In S. L. Odom & M. E. McLean (Eds.), *Early intervention/early childhood special education: Recommended practices* (pp. 23–58). Austin, TX: Pro-Ed.

NICHD Early Childcare Research Network. (2005). Early child care and children's development in the primary grades: Follow-up results from the NICHD study of early child care. *American Educational Research Journal, 42*, 537–570.

Office of Special Education and Rehabilitative Services, U.S. Department of Education. (2003). *The 25th annual report to congress on the implementation of the Individuals with Disabilities Education Act*. Washington, DC: Author. Retrieved January 12, 2008 from www.ed.gov/about/reports/annual/osep/2003/index.html.

Prasse, D. P. (2002). Best practices in school psychology and the law. In A. Thomas and J. Grimes (Eds.) *Best practices in school psychology IV* (pp. 57–75). Bethesda, MD: National Association of School Psychologists.

President's Commission on Excellence in Special Education. (2002). *A new era: Revitalizing special education for children and their families*. Washington, DC: U.S. Department of Education Office of Special Education and Rehabilitative Services. Retrieved January 12, 2008 from www.ed.gov/inits/commissionsboards/whspecialeducation/reports/index.html.

Puckett, M. B., & Black, J. K. (2000). *Authentic assessment of the young child: Celebrating development and learning*. Upper Saddle River, NJ: Prentice-Hall.

Rimm-Kaufman, S., Pianta, R. C., & Cox, M. (2000). Teachers' judgments of problems in the transition to school. *Early Childhood Research Quarterly, 15*, 147–166.

Ross, R. P. (2002). Best practices in the use of play for assessment and intervention with young children. In A. Thomas and J. Grimes (Eds.), *Best practices in school psychology IV*. Bethesda, MD: National Association of School Psychologists.

Saluja, G., Scott-Little, C. & Clifford, R. M. (2000). Readiness for school: A survey of state policies and definitions. *Early Childhood Research and Practice*, 2. Accessed January 12, 2008 from ecrp.uiuc.edu/v2n2/saluja.html.

Scarpati, S., & Silver, P. G. (1999). Readiness for academic achievement in preschool children. In E. V. Nuttall, I. Romero, & J. Kalesnik (Eds.), *Assessing and screening preschoolers: Psychological and educational dimensions* (2nd ed., pp. 262–280). Needham Heights, MA: Allyn & Bacon.

Sekino, Y., & Fantuzzo, J. (2005). Validity of the Child Observation Record: An investigation of the relationship between core dimensions and social-emotional and cognitive outcomes for Head Start children. *Journal of Psychoeducational Assessment*, 23, 242–261.

Shepard, L., Kagan, S. L., & Wurtz, E. (Eds.) (1998). *Principles and recommendations for early childhood assessments*. Washington DC: National Education Goals Panel. Retrieved January 12, 2008 from govinfo.library.unt.edu/negp/Reports/prinrec.pdf.

Southern Early Childhood Association. (2000). *Assessing development and learning in young children*. Little Rock, AR: Author. Retrieved January 12, 2008 from www.southernearlychildhood.org/position_assessment.html.

Thurlow, M. L., & Gilman, C. (1999) Issues and practices in the screening of preschool children. In E. V. Nuttall, I. Romero, & J. Kalesnik (Eds.), *Assessing and screening preschoolers: Psychological and educational dimensions* (2nd ed., pp. 72–93). Needham Heights, MA: Allyn & Bacon.

Tusing, M. E., & Ford, L. (2004). Examining preschool cognitive abilities using a CHC framework. *International Journal of Testing*, 4, 21–114.

U.S. Department of Health and Human Services (2003). Head Start child outcomes—Setting the context for the National Reporting System. *Head Start Bulletin*, 76. Retrieved January 12, 2008 from www.headstartinfo.org/publications/hsbulletin76/cont_76.htm.

Wakschlag, L., Leventhal, B., Briggs-Gowan, M., Danis, B., Keenan, K., Hill, C., et al. (2005). Defining the "disruptive" in preschool behavior: What diagnostic observation can teach us. *Clinical Child and Family Psychology Review*, 8, 183–201.

Walker, K. C., & Bracken, B. A. (1996). Inter-parent agreement on four preschool behavior rating scales: Effects of parent and child gender. *Psychology in the Schools*, 33. 273–281.

Ysseldyke, J., Burns, M., Dawson, P., Kelley, B., Morrison, D., Ortiz, S., et al. (2006). *School psychology: A blueprint for training and practice III*. Bethesda, MD: National Association of School Psychologists.

CHAPTER 15

CHILDREN'S KNOWLEDGE OF BASIC CONCEPTS: AN ESSENTIAL COMPONENT OF DIRECTION FOLLOWING AND PROBLEM SOLVING[1]

ANN E. BOEHM
Columbia University

Basic concepts include such concepts as *top* and *bottom*, *more* and *less*, and *begin* and *end*. All involve a child's ability to make relational decisions about persons, things, and events (Boehm, 1971, 1976, 1982, 1986a, b, c; 2001a, b). They help children describe objects, quantities, and experiences; order events; give directions; and express ideas and feelings. They are integral aspects of language development and of early learning in reading and mathematics. Basic concepts are also essential for making comparisons and classifying and serve as building blocks for more complex concepts and problem solving. However, basic relational concepts are difficult for many children, since they have no constant referent or imagery set (Boehm, 1976, 1982; deVilliers & deVilliers, 1978). The group with the *most* people in one situation may have the *fewest* in another; the *tallest* animal in one group may be the *shortest* in another. Many basic concepts describe positions that are reversible: For instance, the object on *top* of one pile may be placed at the *bottom* of a different pile; the *first* car in one line may be the *last* in another. Children with early learning problems, such as delay in language development or in understanding basic concepts such as these, are at risk for experiencing school problems (Boehm, 1971, 1986a, b, c, 2001a, b; Bracken, 1986, 2002,

2006a, b; Lichtenstein & Ireton, 1984; Wiig & Semel, 1976).

The first section of this chapter focuses on factors that contribute to the development and use of basic concepts in varying direction formats among children during their early school years. A multiple-step assessment approach is presented that combines observation, standardized testing procedures, and interview techniques (strategy probes) to reveal the strategies young children use to answer questions focused on basic relational concepts. The strategy probes can be used to expand upon the results gained from both norm-referenced and criterion-referenced approaches across tasks to inform intervention. The second section begins to explore essential components of direction following.

THE IMPORTANCE OF BASIC CONCEPTS TO LEARNING

The importance of concepts to learning has been well documented in both the developmental and educational literature. Indeed, concepts are widely viewed as essential components of thinking. Concepts are used across all cultures to describe or explain objects and events, to communicate with others, and to organize experiences. It follows that concepts are also an important part of a child's preschool and primary school experience and that educators are concerned about assessing children's concept understanding. A rich literature exists regarding some functions served by concepts and

---

[1]This chapter is an extension of the chapter, "Assessment of Children's Knowledge of Basic Concepts" that first appeared in the C. R. Reynolds and R. W. Kamphaus (Eds.), *Handbook of Psychological and Educational Assessment of Children: Intelligence and Achievement*. (1990). New York: The Guilford Press.

some features of their development, including the following:

- They are symbolic in nature (Vinacke, 1951) and help individuals organize their thinking and experience (Ausubel, 1968; Klausmeirer, 1976, 1992; Siegler, 1988, 1998)
- Their acquisition is facilitated through language and relies on the comprehension of language (Bruner, 1964; deVilliers & deVilliers, 1978; Gentner & Lowenstein, 2002; Klausmeier, 1971, 1992; Vygotsky, 1962, 1978)
- Levels of concept attainment change with development from early childhood through adolescence (Gagné, 1985; Klausmeier, 1971, 1992; Piaget, 1970)
- Their acquisition is related to conditions in the learner, everyday experience, and the context in which they are used (Boehm, 1986b, 1990, 2000; French & Nelson, 1985; Klausmeier, 1971; Marcus, Cooper, & Sweller, 1996; Vinacke, 1951)
- They are building blocks for problem solving and thinking (Boehm, 1976; Gentner & Loewenstein, 2002; Kagan, 1966; Klausmeier, 1976; Siegler, 1988, 1998)

The range of concepts that children are likely to encounter during early schooling is broad and includes objects, colors, sizes, shapes, numbers, qualities of objects and events, relationships between objects and events, and sequences in space or time. Emotional and affective expressions and personal relationships all involve concepts as well. The focus of this chapter is on relational concepts, referred to hereafter as "basic concepts" and their importance to following directions and problem solving.

The Role of Basic Concepts in Verbal Interchanges

Both teachers and parents use a wide range of basic concepts in their verbal interchanges with children. And, many directions used during early instruction contain multiple concepts. Kaplan (1979) and Kaplan and White (1980), for example, reviewed a sample of 1,417 oral directions given by teachers from kindergarten to third grade. These directions were analyzed for (1) the number of behaviors needed to follow (execute) the direction, and (2) the number of qualifiers that set conditions on the response. Of these directions, 71% were found to have no more than one behavior and one qualifier. But the other 29% contained two or more behaviors and/or qualifiers. Of the terms defined by Kaplan and White as qualifiers, 41% were also identified (Boehm, 1971) as basic relational concepts.

The use of basic relational concepts by preschool teachers in their spoken exchanges with 3- and 4-year-old children was studied (Boehm, Classon, & Kelly, 1986). Teachers, who were unaware of the specific purpose of the study, recorded these samples of their spoken interactions with children over a 1-hour period. A wide range (n = 62) of relational concept terms was used by two teachers of 3-year-olds and four teachers of 4-year-olds in two classroom settings (nursery and urban day care).

Curricular materials presented to young children also are likely to include a large number of relational concepts. For example, basic concepts are essential for success related to early reading such as children's book knowledge (*front-back* of books; *top-bottom* of pages), comprehension of stories (what happened *before-after* another event), and phonemic awareness (words that have the same *beginning, ending* sound). Basic concepts are also part of a child's informal mathematical knowledge when they enter preschool and are essential for understanding size, quantity, time, and word problems (e.g., from a first grade text—"the number is greater than 7 and less than 10 and has 2 parts that are equal").

The Role of Basic Concepts to Achievement, Testing, and Children with Special Needs

Since basic concepts are an integral part of teachers' oral directions and appear frequently in curricular materials across subject matter areas, it is not surprising that basic concept knowledge contributes to school achievement. This relationship has been supported across studies both in the mainland United States (Beech, 1981; Bracken, 1998; Brown, 1976; Estes, Harris, Moers, & Woodrich, 1976; Levin, Henderson, Levin, & Hoffer, 1975; Moers & Harris, 1978; Piersel & McAndrews, 1982; Steinbauer & Heller, 1978; Steinert, 1979), England (Smith, 1986), Mainland China (Zhou, Peverly, Boehm, & Lin, 2000), Puerto Rico (Bracken & Fouad, 1987; Nason, 1986; Preddy, Boehm, & Shepherd, 1984) and Venezuela (Bracken et al., 1990).

The importance of basic relational concepts has been demonstrated in a number of other ways of particular concern for school psychologists, including (1) their inclusion in the procedural directions of intelligence tests (Bracken, 1986; Flanagan, Alfonso, Kaminer, & Rader, 1995; Kaufman, 1978; McGrew & Flanagan, 1998) and achievement tests (Cummings & Nelson, 1980); and (2) their difficulty for populations with special needs, such as Native Americans (Mickelson & Galloway, 1973), the hearing impaired (Bracken & Cato, 1986; Brown, 1976; Davis, 1974; Dickie, 1980), the blind (Caton, 1976, 1977), the learning disabled (DiNapoli, Kagedan-Kage, & Boehm, 1980; Kavale, 1982), the educable mentally retarded (Chin, 1976; Fazlo, Johnston, & Brandi, 1993: Nelson & Cummings, 1981), and children with deviant development of syntax (Spector, 1977, 1979). These findings underscore the importance for school psychologists to determine whether or not children understand the terms included in the oral administrative directions of commonly used tests. McGrew and Flanagan (1998), for example, reviewed the basic concepts included in five widely used measures of intelligence at ages 3, 4, and 5: the Differential Assessment Scale, (DAS; Elliot, 1990), Kaufman Assessment Battery for Children, (KABC; Kaufman & Kaufman, 1983), Wechsler Preschool and Primary Scale of Intelligence–Revised, (WPPSI-R; Wechsler, 1989), Woodcock-Johnson Psycho-educational Battery–Revised, (WJ-R; Woodcock and Johnson, 1989), and the Stanford-Binet-IV, (SB-IV; Roid, 2003). They found that few basic concepts were used at these age levels in directions to the K-ABC (3) and WJ-R (10). Considerably more were included on the DAS (22), SB-IV (22), and the WPPSI-R (32). Some subtests were particularly laden with these concepts, suggesting that obtained scores must be used with great caution. Later revisions of some of these tests have not taken account of this caution. Thus, it is important to assess children's knowledge of those basic concepts used, teach them, if necessary, prior to administering tests such as these, and review the results of tests with a heavy basic concept load cautiously (Kaufman, 1978). McGrew and Flanagan (1998) also caution that the extensive language demands of intelligence batteries can place individuals at an unfair disadvantage, such as those with limited hearing, language disabilities, or learners of English as a second language.

Basic Concepts and Thinking Skills

Basic concepts are also important to the development of thinking skills (Boehm, 1976, 1984, 1986a, b, c, 2000; Siegler, 1996, 1998) and help children acquire knowledge. Learning relational terms is important to the development of abstract thought (i.e., to notice relations and reason about relations across contexts, activities that take considerable time for many children). As Gentner and Loewenstein (2002) detail, the process of making comparisons helps children see commonalities between objects and situations and helps them grasp their representation at a more abstract level. These researchers also demonstrate that adult labeling of relevant spatial relationships facilitates task performance and matching new examples with stored knowledge.

As children progress through the early grades, concepts often are used in combination with other concepts, such as the direction "Mark *all* the pictures that *begin* with the same sound." Transcriptions of first-grade teachers' oral directions (Kaplan, 1979) revealed that they often used more than one relational concept in a direction. Thirty-four percent of the directions in their study contained two or more concepts from the Boehm Test of Basic Concepts (1971), their antonyms or synonyms, or simpler relational concepts. In order to encode and follow directions such as those containing several relational concepts, many processes are involved. To be successful, children need to do the following:

- Listen to the direction, pay attention to and encode the spoken elements, and recognize the words that name concepts
- Scan pictorial representations or collections of objects
- Be familiar with the object or situations presented (i.e., have the schemas or mental representations of these objects and events)
- Remember critical components
- Select the relevant elements and information (i.e., match new exemplars with stored knowledge)
- Know each basic concept individually and retrieve it from long-term memory
- Coordinate and act upon multiple components of information
- Be able to identify multiple members of a class as triggered by the terms *all* or *every*

The assessor needs to identify which of these processes might be influencing a child's performance and use this information to inform intervention.

Furthermore, increasing levels of abstraction may apply to the same concept, from simple to complex. For example, a box may be the *same* color, size, or shape as another box, or it may be the *same* in respect to all of these attributes. Children need to learn how to combine concepts and to use them for comparing and classifying things. For example, a child who is able to point to the *widest* block in a picture may not be able to point to the block that is "*wider* than one, but not the *widest*." Some concepts, such as *right* and *left*, have more components of meaning (cross-laterality) that take considerable time to master. The kinds of problems children encounter, the errors they make, and the strategies they use are as important as their successes in planning intervention.

This lengthy introduction has been presented to highlight both the complexity of concept learning and the importance of basic concepts to learning and problem solving. If basic concepts are also basic building blocks of learning, their assessment needs to occur early, during a child's preschool and primary school experience and along with or prior to other tests used with young children. It can be expected that normally progressing children will be familiar in some context with most basic concepts by the time they enter first grade, but not necessarily use them to comply with more complex directions or as tools of thinking.

A MULTIPLE-STEP MODEL FOR ASSESSING BASIC CONCEPTS

Given the importance and complexity of relational concepts, I believe assessors need to engage in a multiple-step concept assessment procedure that includes the following:

1. Standardized tests that survey a broad array of relational concepts early during the year in pre-kindergarten, kindergarten, and grade one to provide feedback to teachers, parents, and therapists regarding a broad range of concepts children are familiar with or need to learn.

2. Review of successes and the types of errors made during testing to identify patterns among individual children or the class as a whole.

3. Interviews that focus on the strategies and styles a young child uses to arrive at answers

of a sample of items responded to correctly and incorrectly, as well as the child's linguistic repertoire. This step is often omitted in time-limited testing situations but needs to be incorporated into standard procedures.

4. Mini-teaching experiences to help determine how ready the child is to acquire a concept and the type of adult support that is needed.

5. Observation over time in natural contexts such as the classroom of a child's spontaneous expressive use of the target concepts and/or correct use of these concepts in response to a teacher's or parent's directions.

6. Observation of generalized use of basic concepts across the contexts of *time*, *space*, and *quantity* important to early literacy activities in reading, writing, and mathematics. Concepts such as *before* and *after* have spatial, quantitative, and temporal meanings that are not learned at the same time.

7. Observation of basic concept use across different direction formats (as will be described later in this chapter).

The multiple-step assessment procedure recommended incorporates the positive features of testing, error analysis, observation, and clinical interviewing. At the same time, this approach involves converging measures and has increased ecological validity, which has been cited by Ysseldyke and Thurlow (1984) as an essential concern for assessors that will lead to targeted instructional activities. This procedure can also be of help in setting appropriate benchmarks to document progress. A critical issue is the use of concepts across contexts and in different direction formats. French and Nelson (1985), for example, studied young children's productive use of temporal and causal terms by requesting children to respond to queries concerning six familiar events that had a clear organized structure, with a specific goal ("e.g., buying food, making cookies"; p. 6). Children aged 2 years, 11 months to 5 years, 6 months were asked to tell what happened when they engaged in particular activities such as "going to a restaurant or when getting dressed" (p. 6). Contrasting with the majority of the available research data, French and Nelson's findings indicated that very young children do understand and produce temporal logical relationships. Based on these findings, the authors noted the limitations of production tasks for the assessment of children's understanding of the "range of application of a term" (p. 7). However, because a concept term may have been acquired for a particular context, it may be context-bound. With development, children's use of concepts will become *decontextualized*. Therefore, children's understanding of a term cannot be generalized to the full adult meaning of the term and must be considered in relation to the context of its use. According to French and Nelson, the context of an item is more likely to have a negative effect on tests of receptive knowledge than on measures of production, given a familiar event such as a birthday party. This same limitation relating to context applies to any receptive test and points to the need for converging methods, including both comprehension and production measures.

Formal Testing of Basic Concepts

Testing of young children's repertoire of basic concepts is a challenge for most early childhood educators since it is not possible to explore the range and depth of a child's basic concept understanding from a single test or task or for the teacher to observe all children's use of a large range of concepts early on during the school year to help inform instruction. As discussed above, the forms of basic concept assessment can range from informal observation to standardized tests. Standardized tests, in turn, can range in comprehensiveness from brief screening devices that include a small number of basic concepts such as the Early Screening Inventory–Revised (Meisels, Marsden, Wiske, & Henderson, 1997) and the AGS Early Screening Profiles (Harrison, 1990) to longer tests covering a large number of concepts such as the Boehm Test of Basic Concepts–3 (Boehm 2001a,b) and the Bracken Basic Concept Scale Third Edition-Receptive (Bracken, 2006a). The results from tests for which norms have been collected can provide information to the assessor regarding a child's performance relative to that of other children of the same age, grade, or geographic area. The test can be used as part of a battery to predict readiness or preparedness for instruction or help to identify children at possible future "risk." Criterion-referenced use of results can be made from some measures by considering a child's understanding of a specific concept or content area in addition to the total score. Although the results from criterion-referenced interpretations of tests can lead to behavioral objectives and recommendations for classroom instruction, they do not address a number of critical issues such as (a) how a child solves a problem, (b) how the child is best taught, and (c) what accounts for a child's failures (Lidz, 1983, 1992, 2003). By analyzing a child's errors with basic concepts (Boehm, 1982, 1986a, 1990, 2000), the assessor can begin to formulate hypotheses to guide learning activities that can be shared with the teacher, parent, and therapist.

Another consideration when assessing basic concepts is the increasing number of children for whom English is their second language. As was pointed out by Erickson and Inglesias (1989), it is important to assess all of a child's languages, even when one is dominant, in order to determine communication competence and develop educational plans. These authors present a case study of a Spanish-dominant child who was administered both the Spanish and English versions of the Boehm Test of Basic Concepts–Revised (BTBC-R; Boehm, 1986a). Her performance on each version was 3 standard deviations below the mean. However, when the number of individual concepts that she knew across both versions was tabulated, her performance was slightly above the mean. This information helps highlight where the issue is, concept understanding versus knowledge of English, and has important implications for assessment and instructional planning.

Screening tests used with young children include a small sample of basic concepts. In general the basis for which concepts are included is not detailed. Other tests, such as the Developmental Tasks for Kindergarten Readiness–II (DTKR-II; Lesiak & Lesiak, 1994), the Test of Early Mathematics Ability, 3rd edition (Ginsburg & Baroody, 2003) and the Sequential Assessment of Mathematics Inventories (SAMI; Reisman & Hutchinson, 1985) include subtests that assess selected basic concepts. Many individually administered tests that assess language functioning at the preschool level also include a subtest that measures basic concepts. Among these are the Preschool Language Scale–4 (Zimmerman, Steiner, & Pond, 2002), the CELF-Preschool: Revised (Wiig, Secord, & Semel, 2004) and the Test of Language Development–Primary, Third Edition (TOLD-P:3, Newcomer & Hammill, 1997). Many of these tests, however, cannot be administered by the teacher. Four tests that include a large number of basic relational concepts that can be administered by the teacher include the Boehm Test of Basic Concepts–3 (BTBC-3; Boehm, 2001a) the Boehm Test of Basic Concepts–3 Preschool (BTBC-3 Preschool; Boehm, 2001b), the Bracken Basic Concept Scale–Third Edition: Receptive (Bracken, 2006a), and the Bracken School Readiness Assessment (2002). A brief overview of these tests follows.

1. The BTBC-3 is a group-administered test for children in kindergarten through second grade that surveys understanding of 50 relational concepts of spatial position, size, direction, quantity, sequence, and time, for the purpose of instructional planning. Two forms, E and F, allowing pre- and post-testing, and a Spanish version and norms are available. A special feature of this test is that each item is *repeated two times* to lessen the memory load and give children the opportunity to look at the pictorial representations and focus attention on the target concept. Scores include a total score and item scores, which serve as the major basis of interpretation. Percentile ranks and standard scores are presented for the total score. Norms are presented by grade, and time of year (fall, spring). The normative sample for Forms E and F included 2,866 and 2,348 children in the fall and 3,189 and 2,196 in the spring, representative of national characteristics. The child Record Form includes a section summarizing the child's performance on all items that can be given to the parent, along with suggested activities. A section is provided for the teacher that can be placed in the child's folder for observing the use of concepts across the contexts of "Following Teacher Directions and Classroom Activities," "Mathematics and Science," and "Reading" (highlighting the concepts to be observed in each of these areas), and "Using Concepts as Thinking Tools." Suggestions for intervention are provided in the manual and the *Boehm Resource Guide for Basic Concept Teaching* (1976). An *Applications Booklet* (1986c) is detailed later in this chapter.

2. The BTBC-3 Preschool represents a downward extension of the BTBC-3 and assesses understanding of 26 basic concepts among children 3 years 0 months through 3 years 11 months and 26 concepts at ages 4.0 to 5 years 11 months. Thirteen of these concepts are common to both age groups. A picture easel is presented, and children, who are individually tested, point to their response. A unique feature of this test is that two items are included per concept, allowing assessors to identify concepts that children know, do not know,

or that are emerging. Scores include the total score, percentile ranks, standard scores, and item scores. Age norms based on a sample of 660 children are presented in 6-month age bands. A Spanish version and norms are available. A number of items overlap with those included on the BTBC-3. Support materials, as with the BTBC-3, include a Parent Report Form and a Teacher Observation Across Contexts Form with the response booklet. Instructional activities are suggested in the manual and the *Boehm Resource Guide for Basic Concept Teaching* (1976)(revision in process).

3. The Bracken Basic Concept Scale–Third Edition: Receptive (2006a) (replaces the Bracken Basic Concept Scale–Revised, 1998) is an individually administered scale testing 308 educational concepts among children 2 years 6 months through 7 years 11 months. The test includes concepts in 11 categorical areas: Colors, Letters, Numbers/Counting, Sizes, Comparisons, Shapes, Direction/Position, Self-Social Awareness, Texture/Material, Quantity, and Time/Sequence. A picture easel is presented and the child points to one of four pictures in response to each item. One form and a Spanish edition with limited norms are available. The scale consists of two instruments: the full diagnostic test, and a screening test, the School Readiness Composite (SRC) that consists of the first 6 subtests. These first six subtests (Colors, Letters, Numbers/Counting, Sizes, Comparisons, and Shapes) are available separately in the Bracken School Readiness Assessment (2002). Items are arranged hierarchically by difficulty level within each category. The raw score on the SRC is used to determine the start point for subtests 7–11 for which a basal level as well as a ceiling level need to be determined. This approach assumes knowledge of concepts below the basal level. Thus users can identify which of the 11 categories are areas of strength or weakness. Scores include the percent of mastery in each of the 11 areas, along with subtest and composite percentile ranks, standard scores by age, and concept age equivalents. Support materials include a suggested Parent/Teacher Conference Form provided in the manual appendix and instructional suggestions in the manual and the Bracken Concept Development Program (1986). Bracken (2006b) has also developed the Bracken Basic

Concept Scale: Expressive, which is not reviewed in this chapter.

Each test has its own strengths and limitations, depending on the purposes of the user. Whatever the purpose of the user, however, it is important to realize that within the 20 to 30 minutes normally allotted for testing basic concepts, no one test can ever measure the extent of a child's concept understanding; test results must be considered only as a starting point for interpretation. The BTBC-3 is group administered by the teacher so that a summary of a child's performance across many concepts is provided, in relation to that of the class as a whole, providing useful information for instruction. The Bracken is helpful for summarizing an individual child's performance across concept areas. It is essential, however, that individuals who provide intervention, such as the speech-language specialist, educational specialist, and teacher also observe children's generalized concept use over space, time, and quantity contexts. It should not be surprising to teachers and assessors that different tasks and different representations of objects tap different aspects of a child's understanding, and that learning concepts such as "*more*" and "*less*" is not an all-or-none affair. Spector (1979), for example, has pointed to a number of possible reasons for difficulty on the BTBC items—concerns that apply to other tests as well. These include a) the inability to focus on key words in the directions, b) the length and complexity of the direction, c) deficits in spatial perception, d) lack of knowledge or confusion regarding the concept label, e) relatively high level of abstraction required, difficulty with polar concepts such as *high* and *low*, and f) poor auditory memory for sentences. Most of these issues apply to all orally presented tests.

Another concern centers on the small sample of items on most tests used with young children. Since many concepts or areas need to be covered, often only a few basic concepts are sampled, or only one item is included to cover a concept area. An exception is the BTBC Preschool-3 described in this chapter that includes two items per concept and the BTBC-3 that covers 50 basic concepts and includes two forms. The Bracken covers 308 concepts across 11 categories. This test, however, employs basal and ceiling limits that narrows down the number of concepts assessed. Whether they are norm-referenced or criterion-referenced, the scores that result can serve only as a starting point for interpretation. Assessors play the key role.

USING OUTCOMES TO PLAN INTERVENTION

When considering the results of tests, a first step is to review a child's responses and consider questions such as: "To what extent are the child's errors due to item presentation such as familiarity with the picture used or the multiple-choice format?" Assessors may also review errors to raise hypotheses about the child's misconceptions. For example, did the child choose the *opposite* of the target concept, *overinclude* additional objects, or respond only to *part of* the instruction? In order to establish a basis for reviewing errors, it is necessary to explore the developmental literature in memory, language and concept acquisition. This review may help identify typical stumbling blocks children encounter or errors that they make, which in turn contributes to the error analysis step of test interpretation and leads to intervention.

Reviewing How Relational Concepts Develop as a Basis for Error Analysis

Between the ages of 2 and 6, children demonstrate significant growth in their ability to use relational terms in their day-to-day interactions in language and to respond to questions and requests. Studies of concept attainment in general indicate that the child moves from being able to apply concepts generally in concrete situations to being able to apply them precisely at increasing levels of abstraction. According to Clark (1983) and as demonstrated by French & Nelson (1985), as early as age $2\frac{1}{2}$ to 3, children can understand some relational terms in the same way as adults do. Children as young as 3 can accurately express temporal order (Brown, 1976). By the time children are 6, most have extensive knowledge of most relational terms, at least at their simpler levels of application (Boehm, 1966, 1982). But, as indicated earlier, a child's ability to apply a concept is dependent on the context in which it is used and the ability of the child to access that concept. An extensive literature traces the acquisition of individual relational concepts in children aged 2 through 6 (see, e.g., Brown, 1976; Carey, 1978; Carni & French, 1984; Clark, 1983; French & Nelson, 1985; Harris & Strommen, 1971; Johnston & Slobin, 1979; Kuczaj & Maratos, 1975; Richards, 1982). The results of studies such as these indicate that (a) errors decrease in type and frequency with age, (b) concept terms (such as *right* and *left*) vary in their linguistic complexity and difficulty, (c) task requirements, such as the number of objects in a display or whether the child needs to point to something, demonstrate a concept relationship, tell stories about pictures, or describe named events, all affect the difficulty of a concept, and (d) the context of a concept (spatial, quantitative, or temporal, or comprehending the order of the alphabet) affects its difficulty. A number of relevant issues are addressed by French and Nelson (1985) in their book *Young Children's Knowledge of Relational Terms*. These researchers present an analysis of temporal and causal structure of a small set of relational terms (including *before*, *after*, and *first*) used by preschool children in the course of describing familiar events such as "making cookies." These researchers found that young children used relational terms in the course of describing familiar events and that they used these terms correctly. However, comprehension of some terms may appear to lag behind production, since the context of comprehension measures is more likely to be unfamiliar to the child. Thus, the seeming disparity between comprehension and production may be accounted for by context. Extralinguistic knowledge (children's event knowledge) and general event representations (those for which children already have mental representations) are important to the learning of relational terms. Assessment, therefore, needs to incorporate information gained from both production and comprehension tasks; it also needs to take into account a child's event knowledge, as well as his or her ability to apply concepts to both familiar and unfamiliar events. This *decontextualized* use of concepts is the ultimate goal of concept learning and has important implications for intervention.

An error analysis, based on a review of the literature on basic concept development, can serve as a starting point for program planning by targeting concepts for instruction and by suggesting possible reasons for difficulty. But an error analysis alone does not yield the reason for a child's misunderstanding. Assessors need both to observe and to interview children in order to gain this information. By analyzing the kinds of errors children make, assessors can begin to trace the stages of concept development. Elsewhere (Boehm, 1976, 2000, 2001a, b), I have suggested activities to be considered in the development of individual basic concepts that can be incorporated into instructional planning. A "Teacher Observation of Concepts Across Contexts" form is a part of the Boehm-3.

Systematic observation of basic concept use across situations is a necessary next step. These include the child's responsive understanding of concepts across contexts and curricular areas, productive use of concept terms to describe everyday events, answer questions, and to meet personal needs, and use of concepts at more complex level (in combination with other concepts, to make comparisons, to classify or order, and to solve complex problems). Although observing the child across activities provides important insight into his or her behavior, it does not necessarily indicate why a child responds in a particular way.

Strategy Interviews

Process-oriented assessment, observing methods children use to solve problems, is particularly relevant (Lidz, 1983, 1992). Piaget's (1929) technique focused on such observation, and the research of Piaget and others (Flavell, 1970; Ginsburg, 1986, 1997) has furthered our understanding of how children think and develop. Through presenting novel tasks, Piaget was able to identify important developmental stages of critical thinking. The clinical interview was an essential part of his procedure. According to Ginsburg (1986, p. 246), the clinical interview serves three distinguishable purposes: It "aims at discovering cognitive activities; specifying them with precision; and evaluating levels of competence." Piaget's clinical interview procedure has important implications for strategy assessment. What this term refers to is a set of activities that probe children's responses without suggesting answers. The assessor uses language suitable for the child's level of understanding and modifies wording until the child understands what the task involves. This step requires only an additional 10 minutes of time and can yield invaluable information that allows assessors to refine their hypotheses (such as questions regarding attention, memory, language, the testing situation, lack of exposure, and the child's cognitive processes) and to plan more appropriate interventions. The strategy interview may also be viewed as a form of convergent measure of basic concept understanding and draws on the work of cognitive psychology that seeks to understand how the individual processes information in learning situations (e.g., Davidson, 1996; Gentner & Lowenstein, 2002; Myers & Lytle, 1986; Marcus et al., 1996). A workable next step following testing, then, is that of interviewing the child.

Given time to respond and with appropriate probes young children can provide reasons for many of their responses. (Ginsburg, 1997, in his text *Entering Children's Minds*, provides excellent examples of strategy interviewing in the area of mathematical thinking.) An example follows to illustrate the approach.

A boy who was 6 years, 5 months old and attended an urban kindergarten program was administered the BTBC-R During April of the school year. The child performed at the 70th percentile. The next day the child and his assessor worked together again so as to understand how he had arrived at his answers. A strategy interview was conducted with some of the items he had answered correctly and a number of items he had responded to incorrectly, with a dialogue such as the following after repeating the question for item 36 ("Look at the tree and the houses. Point to the *third* house from the tree") that he responded to incorrectly:

Q: Tell me what I asked you to figure out here?

A: The third house from the tree.

Q: How did you figure out your answer?

A: There are two houses from the tree.

Q: How did you know your answer was right?

A: Because that one is next to the tree (the house he had selected)

Q: Tell me more about why you chose that?

A: Because that one is a road house and that tree is next to the house.

Q: Why wasn't this one right (pointing)?

A: Because that one is on the left.

The interview helped establish that he remembered the question and that his incorrect response was not a guess. Rather, his responses illustrated that he was not able to apply the concept "third." He also was familiar with concept "left."

Another example is with a girl who was 3 years, 5 months old, attended an urban day care center, and was administered the Boehm-3: Preschool. The child appeared to enjoy the task, but performed at the 20th percentile. Her attention was good, and she spontaneously named and counted objects included on the picture cards. She demonstrated the inconsistency typical of many 3-year-olds by answering correctly only one of the two items per concept measuring the relational term "tallest." Later in the morning, the child and her assessor worked together again so as

to understand how she arrived at her answers. A strategy interview was conducted with some of the items she had answered correctly and a number of items she had responded to incorrectly, with a dialogue such as the following, after repeating question 48 for an item answered incorrectly.

Q: How did you know your answer was right?

A: Because this is right (pointing) and this isn't (pointing).

Q: Why wasn't this one right (pointing)?

A: Because it's the biggest.

Q: How did you know it was the tallest?

A: I told you already, it's little.

The girl selected the "shortest" of four animals and then volunteered that it was the "littlest." She had refined the concept of "little." But, she confused "shortest" and "tallest." On other items she talked about each item choice.

With other items, assessors might use probes such as these:

> "How did you know it wasn't (pointing to another choice)?"
> "Where is the [target object]?"
> "Tell me about the picture."
> "How would you tell a little kid to figure out the answer?"
> "You know, someone else told me that this one was the shortest (pointing to tallest). Was that person right?"

The strategy probe then continues, with each question contingent on the child's previous response until the assessor has a picture of how the child arrived at his or her answer. Children's schematic knowledge often helps them explain their response. Although some children first respond to some questions with answers such as "I guessed" or "Because I'm smart," further probing, and a little patience on the part of the assessor, generally reveals a good deal more.

My colleagues and I have been collecting videotapes of this type of exchange in day care centers serving children from low-income families and with children in kindergarten through grade 3, and have used these tapes in meetings with the teachers and parents. If videotaping is not feasible, audiotaping is a possible alternative. The 10–15 extra minutes involved are well worth the effort. The children are easily engaged and have demonstrated a considerable range of concept language and important problem-solving strategies. A number of points useful for teachers in developing instruction become clear, such as (1) a child's use of related concepts that may be appropriate synonyms, or related but less precise terms; (2) use of other number, size, and object concept terms; (3) useful strategies for eliminating inappropriate choices; (4) consistent errors; (5) the robustness of a response (does the child want to change immediately with a probe?); and (6) the wealth of language and understanding the child possesses. It becomes much clearer when a child does know a concept, when he or she confuses a concept with its antonym, when the concept is just emerging and unstable, and when the child is ready to learn the concept then and there, as well as the amount of adult support needed.

Children can self-correct, refocus attention, gain insight, or hold steadfastly to their original response. With some children, we need to reassure them that we are not trying to trick them, but are just trying to understand how they figured out their answers. Strategy interviewing takes considerable patience—children pause, give many "ums," and then can come up the correct response.

Strategy assessment is related to, but not identical to, dynamic assessment procedures (Lidz, 1992) that uses a "test-teach-test" format to assess a child's zone of potential development through gains the child makes when optimal teaching strategies are used. Dynamic assessment procedures provide extensive information regarding the conditions that facilitate learning; they also require a considerable investment of time. The purpose of the strategy assessment proposed here is not to assess a child's zone of potential development, but to provide assessors with a wealth of information based on a small investment of time. The outcomes can be used to develop intervention goals.

Mini-Teaching

If time permits, the assessor may wish to teach one or two basic concepts that the child has missed, using the objects. This is particularly important if a child has been assessed to ensure they know concepts used in the directions of an intelligence test. The examiner breaks the task apart and presents tasks in a step-by-step manner. For example, for the concept "middle," the examiner may have the child name the colors and then move the three blocks or cars used into different orders. Then the assessor identifies the color of the block in the middle and asks the child to move and name other blocks in the middle

position. Finally, the assessor can represent the test item to see whether there is any transfer. The idea here is to see whether the child can respond to the concept with minimal teaching. Some children pick up the concept immediately suggesting lack of prior exposure to the term; others comprehend one aspect of a concept, such as being able to move cars *near* and *far* from each other, but are not yet able to catch on to the comparative position *nearest*. The skill of the assessor in presenting tasks systematically to identify what a child knows is crucial here. This interchange, however, often reveals alternate concept terms understood by the child, good attention, ability to follow simple directions, and understanding of easier concepts.

The outcome of the multiple-step assessment procedure described in this part of the chapter can be used for instructional planning, for increasing understanding of a child's unique response styles, and as the basis for parent and teacher workshops. In this context, a child's test score or percentile does not need to assume undue importance. The strategy component of the assessment process needs to be the major focus of attention, to be followed by brief teaching interventions. As suggested earlier, these activities need to be followed by observation over time, to determine a child's ability to use concepts in the context of the classroom at increasing levels of complexity. The steps involved in comprehensive assessment of basic concepts are summarized in Table 15.1.

ISSUES RELATED TO USING BASIC CONCEPTS ACROSS DIFFERENT DIRECTION FORMATS

Teachers consistently state that children's direction following is an important educational objective and is one of the major reasons for referral of a child. Surprisingly, little current research focuses on direction following. Although many early childhood tests have items to identify children who can follow two or three step directions (i.e., "Pick up the big box and put it on the table"), these do not identify the source of the child's difficulty. As indicated in the Kaplan and White (1980) study referred to earlier in this chapter, the *number of behaviors and qualifiers* included greatly increases the difficulty of the direction. In a related study, Kaplan (1979) developed a task called "The Directions Game," which systematically varied the number of behaviors and qualifiers in directions. This task was administered to 36 children at each grade

TABLE 15.1   Steps in Comprehensive Assessment of Basic Concepts

Step	Assessor Role
1. Formal test administered using standardized procedure (Session 1)	Observe/record child's: • Response pattern • Attention to task • Spontaneous verbalizations
2. Review of responses	Review child's errors; compare with developmental information regarding individual concepts
3. Strategy interview (Session 2)	Interview to determine: • Child's knowledge of related concepts • How child eliminates options • Concept words used by child
4. Mini-teaching experience (Session 2)	Present brief examples using concrete materials: • Does child catch on immediately to concept? • Does child learn a component of the idea taught? • Can child generalize to a second example?
5. Ongoing observation (over time)	Observe and record examples. Does child use concept: • Across tasks in reading and mathematics? • In both spatial and temporal contexts? • In combination with other concepts? • As a tool of thinking? • In tasks involving multiple-step directions?

level from kindergarten to fifth grade. The results indicated that with increasing age, children were able to execute increasingly complex directions. Young children in particular had much difficulty following directions containing more than one or two behavior (procedural) steps and with more than one qualifier. There was a strong relationship ($r = .71$) between concept mastery as measured by the BTBC and following directions. Relational concepts frequently serve as qualifiers and, adding a qualifier to a direction may reduce the number of behaviors that are executed correctly (Kaplan, 1979). In a reanalysis of Kaplan's transcripts we found that teachers in kindergarten, first, and second grade used 33 of the 50 terms assessed by the BTBC directly in their oral directions as well as antonyms, synonyms, and comparative forms of these terms (Preddy, Kaplan, & Boehm, 1980). One out of every two of these teacher directions contained at least one BTBC term plus many "easier" concepts such as *under, across,* and *down.*

Working memory capacity plays a critical role in direction following and directions that exceed this capacity may hamper learning (Sweller, 1994). Engle, Carullo, and Collins (1991), for example, examined the role of working memory capacity in following directions in subjects from first, third, and sixth grade using word span test, sentence word span test, a directions task adapted from the test given by Kaplan and White (1980), and a grade-appropriate comprehension test. Results indicated a significant increase in word span from first to sixth grade. The correlations between simple word span and comprehension were all significant across the three grade levels. Performance on the Directions Game task was significantly related to performance on the comprehension task for all three age groups. At the first grade level simple word span did not predict the Directions Game score, but sentence span did. The reverse was true for third graders. Both span tasks predicted performance at the sixth grade level. These findings indicate that the memory demands of directions need to be a central concern for assessors and teachers. The processes that children use to encode and retrieve information, such as rehearsal and grouping, also need to be explored. The work of Case, Kurland, and Goldberg (1982) documents that processes children use become more efficient during childhood.

We (Zhou and Boehm) have been investigating children's ability to follow directions represented in different direction formats typically used by teachers, using the Boehm Test of Basic Concepts–Revised Applications (1986). This task consists of 26 items in the following types of formats: (a) choose an object with one or more qualifying attributes (e.g. "the shortest flower between two tall flowers"); (b) choose all objects with one or two qualifying attributes (e.g., "Mark all the arrows that are wide and pointing up"); (c) choose pictures showing equal numbers of objects, (e.g., "Mark the pictures that have an equal number of stars"); (d) understand comparatives involving intermediate positions (e.g., "Mark the tree that is taller than one but shorter than another"); (e) place objects or scenes in temporal order (e.g., "Find the picture to keep the story in order"); and (f) follow a series of commands (e.g., "Begin at the left. Make an X on the first square. Skip a square and make an X on the next square"). A comparison of the performance of first and second grade children in Beijing, China with those in the standardization group was conducted (Zhou & Boehm, 2004). The findings revealed both similarities as well as differences across cultures in children's ability to apply relational concepts across directions types. For example, while *"tall"* and *"short"* are concepts mastered by most children at the preschool level, identifying a tree *"taller than one but shorter than another"* continues to be difficult for first grade children (71% of first grade children passing the item in the United States and 76% in China). Both groups followed directions with either two or three attributes equally well. However, the level of conceptual complexity of a particular concept and the number of behavioral steps contained in a direction affected performance for both groups. For example, both American and Chinese first and second grade children had great difficulty with *left-right* perspective taking ("Mark the *right back* leg of the horse"). The Chinese children, however, performed significantly better than their American peers on directions that contained *right* and *left* in relation to objects. Nearly all of the

Chinese children could apply the concept of *equal* at the end of first grade, but less than 66% of American children were successful. Both American and Chinese children had difficulty following multistep directions. These findings have led to our interest in the strategies children use to follow directions.

In our current work on strategy interviewing using the *Applications* tasks and the Boehm-3 we (Zhou and Boehm, in process) have identified successful strategies such as (a) the child spontaneously repeating the question, (b) targeting in and eliminating options, (c) using their left and right hand as a reference point, (d) using their own internal representations (i.e., "Because I looked at my left and right and small and big. And I was measuring in my head"), (e) verbalizing and walking through each step of the direction, (f) breaking the task down, (g) emphasizing key words in the direction, and (h) spontaneously explaining their answer. Less successful strategies included (a) confusing the concept term with its opposite, (b) focusing in or attending to one part of the question only, such as the first part (primacy) or last part (recency), (c) focusing in on an irrelevant aspect of the question (such as the physical layout of groups of stars when the task required identifying equal numbers) and (d) focusing in on an emotional aspect of the picture not related to the question. A large number of children have been interviewed and we are in the process of coding strategy use to better inform intervention.

Moving From Assessment to Intervention

Overall, the findings indicate that children who have had special instruction in basic concepts at the preschool level (Armour-Thomas, 1984; Blai, 1973; Fisher & Braine, 1981; Levin et al., 1975; Seifert & Schwartz, 1991) and primary school levels (Moers & Harris, 1978; Nason, 1986) have made gains both in their concept understanding and on standardized tests of achievement. An extensive research literature has been devoted to identifying successful strategies for grouping, presenting, and teaching concepts. Reviews by Clark (1971), Tennyson and Cocchiarella (1986), and Tennyson and Park (1980) are particularly relevant, as is the work of Gagné (1985) and Klausmeier 1976, 1992. Strategies particularly relevant to teaching basic relational concepts are presented elsewhere (Boehm, 1976, 1986a, 2001a, b). These strategies include the following:

(a) present and label multiple familiar concrete examples of one member of the concept pair, followed by multiple examples of its opposite, (b) present and label examples where both members of the pair are illustrated, (c) request the child to use the concept label throughout these tasks, (d) request children to identify the relation with respect to other familiar objects in their environment, and (e) provide immediate feedback to children about the correctness of their responses (Boehm, 2001a, b). Another strategy is to provide additional similar activities when concepts (such as *more* and *less* or *before* and *after)* are applied to temporal, spatial, and quantitative contexts. The next steps involve activities in which concepts are used in directions that increase in length and complexity and as tools of thinking (such as for classification, ordering, and class inclusion).

The use of concepts across contexts requires considerable practice, and some concepts such as *right* and *left* are particularly difficult to generalize across tasks. Siegler (1989) points out that even young children often use diverse strategies to solve a given class of problems and are able to adapt these strategies as the demands of the task change. A programmatic line of research by Siegler shows that children use multiple strategies on a wide variety of educational tasks over a short period of time. Identifying the strategies that children use across problem types, as was demonstrated by the difficulties children continue to have in first and second grade using the BTBC-R: Applications is particularly relevant. The directions incorporated into this task are typical of those required in the classroom. Children who do not apply these concepts may have difficulty in following teacher directions, resulting in possible inattention and other behavior problems (Glutting, Kelly, Boehm, & Burnett, 1989) or learning problems. Such directions are also essential to the tasks involved in reading and mathematical problem solving.

Only a small research literature has been devoted to direction following in general. Specific aspects of direction following, however, have been identified in the research literature (which is beyond the scope of this chapter to review in depth). A possible framework is suggested next for drawing upon this research literature and related concerns. The first step is to consider the task variables involved in directions in relationship to child variables. The next step is to consider assessor variables and outcomes as summarized in Table 15.2. A review of these variables needs to be an integral component of assessment.

SUMMARY

This chapter has highlighted both the complexity of basic concept acquisition and the importance of basic relational concepts to learning and to complying with teachers' oral directions and instructional activities. They are important building blocks of learning and thinking. They need to be assessed early during a child's preschool and primary school experience. Basic concept assessment can play an important role in adjusting instruction to meet a child's needs. Such assessment can help one to (1) gain an understanding of a child's overall repertoire of basic concepts; (2) pinpoint concepts that are understood, that are partially understood, or that need to be developed; (3) identify strategies a child uses to approach a problem and the kinds of errors made; and (4) translate results into intervention.

A comprehensive assessment model of basic concepts is detailed which involves a number of steps to be carried out throughout the school year. These steps include (1) standardized testing of a large number of relational concepts, (2) review of errors based on findings in the research literature, (3) strategy interviews, (4) a brief teaching sample, and (5) systematic observation across contexts over time. The assessor uses language suitable for the child's level of understanding and modifies wording until the child understands what the task involves. These steps lead to intervention activities to ensure that students are able to generalize concepts across contexts and at increasing levels of complexity.

The school psychologist can help by (a) listening to teacher directions and helping them present shorter directions, emphasize key words, pause between segments of longer directions, and teach needed concepts; (b) providing help to individual students moving systematically from concrete applications of basic concepts to more complex directions, with ample practice while engaging in everyday activities; and (c) reviewing the concept load of directions and word problems in the instructional materials presented to the child to make sure he or she grasps the essential concepts and can break down tasks as needed. It is particularly important to identify children's reasoning strategies and help them to use effective strategies (such as repeating the question to self, walking through the tasks step by step, eliminating

TABLE 15.2 Assessor Variables and Outcomes

Direction Task Variables	Task Variables That Can Influence Outcomes
• Knowledge of individual concepts that vary in level of difficulty • The number of behaviors to be complied with and the number of qualifiers involved in following directions • The linguistic difficulty of the direction such as order of mention of tasks to be followed • Inclusion of negative qualifiers • Concepts used across contexts (spatial, temporal, quantitative) • Concepts used in different problem formats and at increasing levels of complexity such as integrating time, distance, and speed)	• Directions repeated as part of regular administrative procedures • Cultural appropriateness of task representations • Directions presented in child's home language • The syntactic complexity of the direction • The use of negative qualifiers • Order of mention corresponds to order of occurrence ("Before you come to the table wash your hands" versus "Wash your hands before you come to the table")

Child Variables	Assessor Variables
• Focused attention • Working memory • Processing speed • Cognitive and language skills • Language or dialect spoken • Vision and hearing status • Physical well-being (cold; blocked ears) • Partial knowledge, emerging skills • Use of efficient strategies relevant to different classes to tasks	• Gains child's attention • Pace of presentation of directions and emphasis placed on key words • Strategy interview conducted • Review of errors • Mini-teach providing contextual supports as needed • Develops activities to teach concepts and effective strategies for problem solving • Provides needed adult supports such as praise and walking child through the task

incorrect options, thinking of familiar words or situations, and other back-up strategies) to solve problems that incorporate concepts at increasing levels of complexity, such as the integration of time, speed, and distance concepts.

REFERENCES

Armour-Thomas, E. (1984). *Microcomputer teaching concepts: Types of computer feedback in learning of relational concepts at kindergarten level.* Unpublished doctoral dissertation, Teachers College, Columbia University.

Ausubel, D. P. (1968). *Educational psychology: A cognitive view.* New York: Holt, Rinehart & Winston.

Beech, M. A. (1981). Concurrent validity of the Boehm Test of Basic Concepts. *Learning Disability Quarterly, 4,* 53–60.

Blai, B. (1973). Concept learning-mastery in Harcum Junior College Laboratory Nursery School/Kindergarten. *Psychology, 10*(2), 35–36.

Boehm, A. E. (1966). *The development of comparative concepts in primary school children.* Unpublished doctoral dissertation, Columbia University.

Boehm, A. E. (1971). *Boehm Test of Basic Concepts.* New York: Psychological Corporation.

Boehm, A. E. (1976). *Boehm resource guide for basic concept teaching.* New York: Psychological Corporation.

Boehm, A. E. (1982). Assessment of basic concepts. In D. Paget & B. A. Bracken (Eds.), *The psychoeducational assessment of preschool children* (pp. 145–161). New York: Grune & Stratton.

Boehm, A. E. (1984). *Assessing and teaching basic concepts and thinking skills.* Paper presented at the

Conference on Early Childhood Education, New York, NY.

Boehm, A. E. (1986a). *Boehm Test of Basic Concepts–Revised*. San Antonio, TX: The Psychological Corporation.

Boehm, A. E. (1986b). *Boehm Test of Basic Concepts–Preschool Version* San Antonio, TX: The Psychological Corporation.

Boehm, A. E. (1986c). *Boehm Test of Basic Concepts–Revised: Applications*. San Antonio, TX: The Psychological Corporation.

Boehm, A. E. (1990). Assessment of children's knowledge of basic concepts. In C. R. Reynolds & R. W. Kamphaus (Eds.), *Handbook of psychological and educational assessment of children: Intelligence and achievement* (pp. 654–670). New York: Guilford.

Boehm, A. E. (2000). Assessment of basic relational concepts. In B. A. Bracken (Ed.), *The psychological assessment of preschool children* (3rd ed., pp. 186–203). Needham Heights, MA: Allyn & Bacon.

Boehm. A. E. (2001a). *Boehm Test of Basic Concepts-3* San Antonio, TX: The Psychological Corporation.

Boehm, A. E. (2001b). *Boehm test of Basic Concepts–3: Preschool*. San Antonio, TX: The Psychological Corporation.

Boehm, A. E., Classon, B., & Kelly, M. (1986). *Preschool teachers' spoken use of basic concepts*. Unpublished manuscript, Teachers College, Columbia University.

Bracken, B. A. (1986). *Bracken Concept Development Program*. San Antonio, TX: PsychCorp.

Bracken, B. A. (1998). *Bracken Basic Concept Scale–Revised*. San Antonio, TX: The Psychological Corporation.

Bracken, B. A. (2002). *Bracken School Readiness Assessment*. San Antonio, TX: PsychCorp.

Bracken, B. A. (2006a). *Bracken Basic Concept Scale-Third Edition.: Receptive*. San Antonio, TX: PsychCorp.

Bracken, B. A. (2006b). *Bracken Basic Concept Scale: Expressive*. San Antonio, TX: PsychCorp.

Bracken, B. A. (1986). Incidence of basic concepts in the directions of five commonly used American tests of intelligence. *School Psychology International*, 7, 1–10.

Bracken, B. A., Barona, A., Bauermeister, J. J., Howell, K. K., Poggioli, L., & Puente, A. (1990). Multinational validation of the Spanish Bracken Basic Concept Scale for cross-cultural assessments. *Journal of School Psychology*, 28(4), 325–341.

Bracken, B. A., & Cato, L. A. (1986). Rate of conceptual development among deaf preschool and primary children as compared to a matched group of nonhearing impaired children. *Psychology in the Schools*, 23, 95–99.

Bracken, B. A. & Fouad, N. (1987). Spanish translation and validation of the Bracken Basic Concept Scale. *School Psychology Review*, 16(1), 94–102.

Brown, D. (1976). Validation of the Boehm Test of Basic Concepts (Doctoral dissertation, University of Wisconsin, 1976). *Dissertation Abstracts International*, 36, 4338A.

Bruner, J. S. (1964). The course of cognitive growth. *American Psychologist*, 19, 1–15.

Carey, S. (1978). The child as word learner. In M. Halle, J. Bresnan, & G. Miller (Eds.), *Linguistic theory and psychological reality* (pp. 264–291). Cambridge, MA: MIT Press.

Carni, E., & French, L. A. (1984). The acquisition of *before* and *after* reconsidered: What Develops? *Journal of Experimental Child Psychology*, 37, 394–403.

Case, R., Kurland, D. M., & Goldberg, J. (1982). Operational efficiency and the growth of short-term memory span. *Journal of Experimental Child Psychology*, 33(3), 386–404.

Caton, H. (1976). *The tactile test of basic concepts*. Louisville, KY: American Printing House for the Blind.

Caton, H. (1977). The development and evaluation of a tactile analogue to the Boehm Test of Basic Concepts, Form A. *Journal of Visual Impairment and Blindness*, 71, 382–386.

Chin, J. (1976). The development of basic relational concepts in educable mentally retarded children (Doctoral dissertation, Teachers College, Columbia University). *Dissertation Abstracts International*, 36, 4338A.

Clark, D. C. (1971). Teaching concepts in the classroom: a set of teaching prescriptions derived from experimental research [Monograph]. *Journal of Educational Psychology*, 62, 253–278.

Clark, E. (1983). Meanings and concepts. In P. H. Flavell & E. M. Markman (Eds.), *Handbook of child psychology: Vol. 3. Cognitive development* (4th ed., pp. 787–840). New York: Wiley.

Cummings, J. A., & Nelson, R. B. (1980). Basic concepts in oral directions of group achievement tests. *Journal of Educational Research*, 73, 259–261.

Davidson, D. (1996). The role of schemata in children's memory. In H. W. Reese (Ed.), *Advances in child development and behavior* (Vol. 26, pp. 35–58). San Diego: Academic Press.

Davis, J. (1974). Performance of young learning impaired children on a test of basic concepts. *Journal of Speech and Hearing Research*, 17, 342–351.

deVilliers, J. G., & deVilliers, P. A. (1978). *Language acquisition*. Cambridge, MA: Harvard University Press.

Dickie, D. C. (1980). Performance of severely and profoundly hearing impaired children on aural/oral and total communication presentations of the Boehm Test of Basic Concepts (Doctoral dissertation, Michigan State University). *Dissertation Abstracts International, 40,* 6227A–6228A.

DiNapoli, N., Kagedan-Kage, S. M., Boehm, A. E. (1980). Basic concept acquisition in learning-disabled children. (ERIC Document Reproduction Service No. ED 240 781).

Elliott, C. D. (1990). *Differential Ability Scales.* San Antonio, TX: The Psychological Corporation.

Engle, R. W., Carullo, J. J. & Collins, K. W. (1991). Individual differences in working memory for comprehension and following directions. *Journal of Educational Research, 84*(5), 253–262.

Erickson, J. G., & Inglesias, A. (1989). Assessment of communication disorders in non-English proficient children. In O. Taylor (Ed.), *Nature of communication disorders in culturally and linguistically diverse populations* (pp. 181–217). San Diego, CA: College Hill Press.

Estes, G., Harris, J., Moers, F., & Woodrich, D. (1976). Predictive validity of the Boehm Test of Basic Concepts for achievement in first grade. *Educational and Psychological Measurement, 36,* 1031–1035.

Fazlo, B. B., Johnston, J. R., & Brandi, L. (1993). Relation between mental age and vocabulary development among children with mild mental retardation. *American Journal on Mental Retardation, 97,* 541–546.

Fisher, C. B., & Braine, L. G. (1981). Children's left-right concepts: Generalization across figure and location. *Child Development, 52,* 451–456.

Flanagan, D., Alfonso, V. C., Kaminer, T., & Rader, D. E. (1995). Incidence of basic concepts in the directions of new and recently revised American intelligence tests for preschool children. *School Psychology International, 16,* 345–364.

Flavell, J. H. (1970). Concept development. In P. H. Mussen (Ed.), *Carmichael's manual of child psychology* (3rd ed., pp. 983–1059). New York: Wiley.

French, L. A., & Nelson, K. (1985). *Young children's knowledge of relational terms: Some ifs, ors, or buts.* New York: Springer–Verlag.

Gagné R. M. (1985). *The conditions of learning* (4th ed.). New York: Holt, Rinehart & Winston.

Gentner, D., & Loewenstein, J. (2002). Relational language and relational thought. In E. Amsel & J. P. Byrnes (Eds.), *Language, literacy, and cognitive development: The development and consequences of symbolic communication* (pp. 87–120). Mahwah, NJ: Lawrence Erlbaum Associates.

Ginsburg, H. P. (1986). Academic diagnosis. In J. Valsiner (Ed.), *The individual subject and scientific psychology* (pp. 235–260). New York: Plenum Press.

Ginsburg, H. P. (1997). *Entering children's minds.* New York: Teachers College Press.

Ginsburg, H. P., & Baroody, A. (2003) *Test of Early Mathematics Ability* (3rd ed.). Austin, TX: Pro-Ed.

Glutting, J. J., Kelly, M. S., Boehm, A. E., & Burnett, T. R. (1989) Stability and predictive validity of the Boehm Test of Basic Concepts–Revised among black kindergarteners. *Journal of School Psychology, 27,* 365–371.

Harris, L., & Strommen, E. (1971). The role of front-back features in children's "front, back, and beside" placement of objects. *Merrill Palmer Quarterly, 18,* 259–271.

Harrison, P. L. (1990). *AGS Early Screening Profiles.* Circle Pines, MN: American Guidance Service.

Johnston, J. R., & Slobin, D. I. (1979). The development of locative expressions in English, Italian, Serbo-Croatian and Turkish. *Journal of Child Language, 6,* 529–545.

Kagan, J. A. (1966). A developmental approach to cognitive growth. In H. J. Klausmeier & C. W. Harris (Eds.), *Analysis of concept learning* (pp. 97–116). New York: Academic Press.

Kaplan, C. H. (1979). *A developmental analysis of children's direction following behavior in grades K–5.* Unpublished doctoral dissertation, Columbia University.

Kaplan, C. H., & White, M. A. (1980). Children's direction-following behavior in grades K–5. *Journal of Educational Research, 74,* 43–48.

Kaufman, A. (1978). The importance of basic concepts in individual assessment of preschool children. *Journal of School Psychology, 16,* 207–211.

Kaufman, A. S., & Kaufman, N. L. (1983). *Kaufman Ability Battery for Children.* Circle Pines, MN: American Guidance Service.

Kavale, K. A. (1982). A comparison of learning disabled and normal children on the Boehm Test of Basic Concepts. *Journal of Learning Disabilities, 15,* 160–161.

Klausmeier, H. J. (1971). Cognitive operations in concept learning. *Educational Psychologist, 9,* 1–8.

Klausmeier, H. J. (1976). Conceptual development during the school years. In J. R. Levin & K. K. Allen (Eds.), *Cognitive learning in children* (pp. 5–29). New York: Academic Press.

Klausmeier, H. J. (1992). Concept learning and concept teaching. *Educational Psychologist, 27,* 267–286.

Kuczaj, S., & Maratos, M. (1975). On the acquisition of front, back, and side. *Child Development, 46,* 202–210.

Lesiak, W. J., & Lesiak, J. L. (1994). *Developmental Tasks for Kindergarten Readiness–II.* Brandon, VT: Clinical Psychology Publishing Company.

Levin, J. R., Henderson, B., Levin, A. M., & Hoffer, G. L. (1975). Measuring knowledge of basic concepts by disadvantaged preschoolers. *Psychology in the Schools, 12,* 132–139.

Lichtenstein, R., & Ireton, H. (1984). *Preschool screening.* New York: Grune & Stratton.

Lidz, C. S. (1983). Issues in assessing preschool children. In K. D. Paget & B. A. Bracken (Eds.), *The psychoeducational assessment of preschool children* (pp. 17–27). New York: Grime & Stratton.

Lidz, C. S. (1992). *Practitioner's guide to dynamic assessment*. New York: The Guilford Press.

Lidz, C. S. (2003). *Early childhood assessment*. Hoboken, NJ: John Wiley & Sons

Marcus, N., Cooper, M., & Sweller, J. (1996). Understanding instructions. *Journal of Educational Psychology, 88*, 49–63.

McGrew, K. S., & Flanagan, D. P. (1998). *The intelligence tests desk reference (ITDR)*. Needham Heights, MA: Allen & Bacon.

Meisels, S. J., Marsden, D. B., Wiske, M. S., & Henderson, L. W. (1997). *Early Screening Inventory-Revised*. Ann Arbor, MI: Rebus.

Mickelson, N. I., & Galloway, C. G. (1973). Verbal concepts of Indian and non-Indian school beginners. *Journal of Educational Research, 67*, 55–56.

Moers, F., & Harris, J. (1978). Instruction in basic concepts and first grade achievement. *Psychology in the Schools, 15*, 84–86.

Myers, J., & Lytle, S. (1986). Assessment of the learning process. *Exceptional Children, 53*, 138–144.

Nason, F. O. (1986). *Systematic instruction of basic relational concepts: Effects on the acquisition of concept knowledge and of language and mathematics achievement of Puerto Rican first graders from low income families*. Unpublished doctoral dissertation, Teachers College, Columbia University.

Nelson, R. B., & Cummings, J. A. (1981). Basic concept attainment of educably mentally handicapped children: Implications for teaching concepts. *Education and Training of the Mentally Retarded, 16*, 303–306.

Newcomer, P. L., & Hammill, D. D. (1997). *Test of Language Development-Primary*. Austin, TX: Pro-Ed.

Piaget, J. (1929). *The child's conception of the world*. New York: Harcourt Brace.

Piaget, J. (1970). Piaget's theory. In P. H. Mussen (Ed.), *Carmichael's manual of child psychology* (3rd ed., pp. 703–732). New York: Wiley.

Piersel, N. C., & McAndrews, T. (1982). Concept acquisition and school progress: An examination of the Boehm Test of Basic Concepts. *Psychological Reports, 50*, 783–786.

Preddy, D., Boehm, A. E., & Shepherd, M. J. (1984). PBCB: A norming of the Spanish translation of the Boehm Test of Basic Concepts. *Journal of School Psychology, 22*, 407–413.

Preddy, D., Kaplan, C., & Boehm, A. E. (1980). *How important are basic concepts to instruction? Validation of Boehm Test of Basic Concepts*. Unpublished manuscript, Teachers College, Columbia University, New York.

Reisman, F. K., & Hutchinson, T. A. (1985). *Sequential Assessment of Mathematics Inventories*. Columbus, OH: Charles E. Merrill.

Richards, M. M. (1982). Empiricism and learning to mean. In S. Kuczaj (Ed.), *Language development: Vol. 1. Syntax and semantics* (pp. 365–396). Hillside, NJ: Erlhaum.

Roid, G. H. (2003). *Stanford Binet Intelligence Scales*, Fifth Edition. Itasca, IL: Riverside Publishing.

Seifert, H., & Schwartz, I. (1991). Treatment effectiveness of large group instruction with Head Start students. *Language, Speech, and Hearing Services in Schools, 22*, 60–64.

Siegler, R. S. (1988). Individual differences in strategy choices: Good students, not-so-good students, and perfectionists. *Child Development, 59*, 833–851.

Siegler, R. S. (1989). Hazards of mental chronometry: An example from children's subtraction. *Journal of Educational Psychology. 81*(4), 497–506.

Siegler, R. S. (1996). *The emerging mind: The process of change in children's thinking*. New York: Oxford University Press.

Siegler, R. S. (1998). *Children's thinking* (3rd ed.). Upper Saddle River, NJ: Prentice Hall.

Smith E. F. (1986). The validity of the Boehm Test of Basic Concepts. *British Journal of Educational Psychology, 56*, 332–344.

Spector, C. C. (1977). *Concept comprehension of normal kindergarten children with deviant syntactic development*. Unpublished doctoral dissertation, New York University.

Spector, C. C. (1979). The Boehm Test of Basic Concepts: Exploring the test results for cognitive deficits. *Journal of Learning Disabilities, 12*, 564–567.

Steinbauer, E., & Heller, M. S. (1978). The Boehm Test of Basic Concepts as a predictor of academic achievement in grades 2 and 3. *Psychology in the Schools, 15*, 357–360.

Steinert, M. C. (1979). Construct and criterion-related validity of the Boehm Test of Basic Concepts (Doctoral dissertation, Kent State University, 1978). *Dissertation Abstracts International, 39*, 7147A.

Sweller, J. (1994). Cognitive load theory, learning difficulty and instructional design. *Learning and Instruction, 4*, 295–312.

Tennyson, R. D., & Cocchiarella, M. J. (1986). An empirically based instructional design theory for teaching concepts. *Review of Educational Research, 86*, 40–71.

Tennyson, R. D., & Park, O. (1980). The teaching of concepts: A review of instructional design research literature. *Review of Educational Research, 50*, 55–70.

Vinacke, E. W. (1951). The investigation of concept formation. *Psychological Bulletin, 48*, 1–31.

Vygotsky, L. S. (1962). *Thought and language*. Cambridge, MA: MIT Press.

Vygotsky, L. S. (1978). *Mind in society: The development of higher psychological processes*. Cambridge, MA: Harvard University Press.

Wechsler, D. (1989). *Wechsler Preschool and Primary Scale of Intelligence–Revised*. San Antonio, TX: Psychcorp.

Wiig, E., & Semel, E. (1976). *Learning disabilities in children and adolescents*. Columbus, OH: Charles E. Merrill.

Wiig, E. H., Secord, W. A., & Semel, E. (2004). *CELF–Preschool*, 2nd ed. San Antonio, TX: PsychCorp.

Woodcock, R. W., and Johnson, M. B. (1989). *Woodcock-Johnson Psycho-Educational Battery-Revised*. Chicago: Riverside Publishing.

Ysseldyke, J. E., & Thurlow, M. L. (1984). Assessment practices in special education: Adequacy and appropriateness. *Educational Psychologist, 19*, 123–136.

Zhou, Z., & Boehm, A. E. (2004). American and Chinese children's understanding of basic relational concepts in directions. *Psychology in the Schools, 41*, 261–272.

Zhou, Z., Peverly, S. T., Boehm, A. E., & Lin, C. D. (1998). *The role of instruction in children's understanding of distance, time, and speed interrelations*. Poster presented at the 106th Annual Convention of the American Psychological Association. San Francisco, CA.

Zhou, Z., Peverly, S. T., Boehm, A. E., & Lin, C. D. (2000). American and Chinese children's understanding of distance, time, and speed interrelations. *Cognitive Development, 15*, 215–240.

Zimmerman, I. L., Steiner, V. G., & Pond, R. E. (2002). *Preschool Language Scale–4*. San Antonio, TX: Harcourt Assessment Inc.

CHAPTER 16

ASSESSMENT OF PERSONALITY
AND ADJUSTMENT

CEDAR W. O'DONNELL AND PAUL J. FRICK[1]
University of New Orleans

INTRODUCTION

Maria is 14 years old. She has been sent to the school psychologist at the request of the principal. Maria has been skipping classes and her grades have dropped significantly over the last few months. She has recently received detentions for being tardy, being disruptive in the classroom, and smoking on the school grounds. Maria also has few friends at school and was suspended on one occasion for a verbal argument and fight with another girl. Maria's mother was recently rehospitalized for a chronic illness and Maria's stepfather has indicated that he is scheduled to undergo a major surgery in the very near future.

The psychologist who sees Maria will need to evaluate how well she is coping with the many challenges she is currently facing. For example, Maria is coping with normal developmental demands of adolescence—gaining autonomy from her parents, getting along with peers, performing well in school, establishing her self-identity, and regulating her emotions. Further, she is experiencing several significant additional stressors at home concerning her parents' health. How does one determine whether Maria's psychological resources are able to cope with these demands, or whether she will need additional mental health services to overcome the emotional and behavioral difficulties she is experiencing?

As this example of Maria illustrates, assessing the personality and adjustment of children and adolescents involves more than simply being able to administer a number of different tests. To adequately interpret these tests, one must understand the normal developmental processes that are operating on children at a given age. By doing so, one can understand the unique stressors being experienced by the child and how these stressors influence the child's adjustment by interacting with individual strengths, vulnerabilities, and unique life experiences. Furthermore, many children who are having problems in adjustment often have problems in other important areas, spanning the child's behavioral, emotional, and social functioning (Frick & Kimonis, 2005). Therefore, assessments typically need to be comprehensive and cover a number of adjustment areas in order to ensure that all potential areas in need of services are adequately considered. Finally, research has made it clear that one cannot adequately understand a child's emotional, behavioral, or social functioning without understanding the influence of the child's many important social contexts, including the influences of family, peers, school, neighborhood, and cultural group (Sameroff, Peck, & Eccles, 2004). Therefore, assessments must not only consider the child's individual strengths and vulnerabilities but also how they interact with his or her context to influence his or her adjustment.

Clearly, this makes the assessment process a very complicated one and providing a thorough discussion of each of these issues would be beyond the scope of a single chapter (see Kamphaus & Frick, 2005; Mash & Terdal,

---

[1] Requests for reprints should be sent to Paul J. Frick, Department of Psychology, University of New Orleans, 2001 Geology & Psychology Building, New Orleans, LA 70148. Email: pfrick@uno.edu.

1997 for more extended discussions). However, these important issues guide the content and structure of this chapter and we start by discussing several definitional issues that differentiate among some interrelated concepts related to the development of personality. Specifically, we discuss the commonalities and distinctions among the constructs of temperament, personality, and psychopathology. This discussion is critical for understanding the differences and similarities among some of the common measures used to assess children's personality. We then discuss several important considerations for understanding a child or adolescent's social context, and how to integrate this understanding into the assessment of his or her personality and adjustment. These general discussions provide the context for our selected review of some commonly used methods for assessing children's personality and adjustment. Finally, we discuss how these issues related to the development of personality and the available assessment methods can be integrated to provide an evidence-based (i.e., based on the most current psychological research) assessment of some of the most common types of adjustment problems experienced by children and adolescents in the school setting.

TEMPERAMENT, PERSONALITY, AND PSYCHOPATHOLOGY

Temperament generally refers to biologically based individual differences in a child's pattern of emotional and cognitive responses to his or her environment that are evident from very early in life (Kagan & Fox, 2006). While there are a number of different classification systems for defining temperament dimensions (see Frick, 2004a for a review), most classification systems focus on individual differences in the child's emotionality, such as the child's pattern of emotional reactivity and ability to regulate this reactivity (Goldsmith, 1996; Rothbart & Jones, 1998). Emotional reactivity refers to individual differences in the child's typical emotional experience and can vary in the valence (e.g., anger, sadness, happiness), intensity, and threshold (i.e., how easy it is to elicit the emotion) of the child's emotion (Rubin, Coplan, Fox, & Calkins, 1995). Emotional regulation focuses on the processes that the child learns to modulate his or her emotional experience such as approach, avoidance, and attention control (Morris, Silk, & Steinberg, 2002).

Personality is typically seen as including a wider range of stable and enduring individual differences in how a child feels, thinks, and behaves (Caspi & Shiner, 2006). While these traits by definition show some continuity across time, research has consistently shown that personality traits in children and adolescents are less stable then they are in adults (Roberts & DelVecchio, 2000). Importantly, a child's temperament makes him or her more or less likely to develop certain personality traits. For example, young children who show a temperament characterized by high levels of emotional reactivity to unfamiliar people and novel stimuli are more likely to show avoidant and socially anxious traits (i.e., high neuroticism) later in development (Kagan & Snidman, 2004; Schwarz, Snidman, & Kagan, 1999). Like temperament, there are a number of different methods for distinguishing among different personality dimensions, although there is growing support for the "Big Five" dimensions that include: extraversion (many interpersonal interactions and high in positive emotionality), neuroticism (prone to psychological distress), conscientiousness (degree of organization and persistence), agreeableness (compassionate and concerned towards others), and openness (appreciation for experience and exploration of the unfamiliar; McCrae & Costa, 1999; Saucier & Goldberg, 2001).

Psychopathology refers to emotions and behaviors that are maladaptive and cause problems in a child's social or academic functioning (Frick & Silverthorn, 2001). From this definition, it is clear that psychopathology shares aspects of both temperament (e.g., emotional responses) and personality (e.g., behavioral and social functioning). This overlap of constructs has led to several different views as to how psychopathology, temperament, and personality are related to each other and how they diverge (Frick, 2004a). For some, the difference is quantitative, with psychopathology representing extremes of temperament and personality (e.g., anxiety disorders being extreme levels of negative emotionality and neuroticism; Clark, Watson, & Mineka, 1994). For others, the difference is qualitative, with certain temperaments and personality dimensions serving as risk factors for the development of psychopathology (Beauchaine, 2001; Lahey & Waldman, 2003).

Despite the unresolved nature of this distinction, it is clear that the concepts of temperament, personality, and psychopathology are all important for understanding a child's adjustment at school and in other contexts. For example, as discussed in more detail later in the chapter, children with conduct problems represent a significant concern for school personnel (Frick, 2004b) and there is evidence that there are distinct subgroups of children with conduct problems, who can be defined by their different temperaments (Frick & Morris, 2004). Further, again discussed in more detail below, children with problems in one area of adjustment will often also show problems in other areas. One potential reason that has been proposed for this high degree of "comorbidity" is that the co-occurring problems may be due to common temperamental or common personality risk factors. For example, problems in emotional regulation have been proposed as one possible reason for the associations among depression, anxiety, and oppositional-defiant behaviors (Caspi & Shiner, 2006).

Unfortunately, the content of most of the assessment instruments that are reviewed in this chapter do not adequately distinguish among psychopathology, personality and temperament dimensions (Lahey & Waldman, 2003; Lemery, Essex, & Smider, 2002). Therefore, it is often left to assessors to interpret the resulting information in a way that attempts to disentangle the unique temperamental or personality risk factors that may differentiate within students who have the same problems in adjustment, or uncover common personality dimensions underlying different problems in adjustment.

CONTEXTUAL INFLUENCES ON CHILD PERSONALITY AND ADJUSTMENT

Traditionally, personality assessment has largely focused on assessing individual differences in the child's emotions and behaviors, whether they are viewed as temperament, personality, or psychopathology. However, it has become increasingly clear that it is impossible to adequately understand children's personality and adjustment without also considering the child's family, peer, school, community, and cultural context. The importance of contextual factors is supported by evidence that the child's context can play a major role in the development and maintenance of adjustment problems (Sameroff et al., 2004). However, it is also important to recognize that children's behavioral difficulties can have a negative impact on their home (Lytton,

1990) and school (Frick, 2004b) environments. In either case, an adequate understanding of the child's personality and adjustment requires information on the many important contexts which can influence and be influenced by the child's personal characteristics.

The importance of understanding the transactional nature between the child and his or her context is illustrated by the developmental concept of "goodness-of-fit." Thomas and Chess (1977) noted that whether a child's temperament leads to problematic outcomes can depend on the goodness-of-fit, or the match, between the child's temperament and the contextual demands placed on the child. For example, Kochanska (1993, 1995) has suggested that certain forms of discipline may be more or less effective for children in helping them to learn to internalize rules from parents and teachers, depending on their temperamental styles.

In addition, the child's context is also important for understanding the assessment information obtained on the child's personality and adjustment. Specifically, there is a substantial body of literature indicating that ratings of a child's personality and behavior in different contexts (e.g., school and home) are only modestly correlated (Achenbach, McConaughy, & Howell, 1987; De Los Reyes & Kazdin, 2005). For example, in their meta-analysis of over 119 studies, Achenbach et al. (1987) reported that the average correlation in ratings of children's adjustment between informants who see the child in different settings (e.g., parents and teachers) was $r = .28$. In short, these modest correlations suggest that when collecting assessment information from multiple sources, it is quite likely that the different sources will give very different views of the child's personality and adjustment. Kamphaus and Frick (2005) provide recommendations for integrating information across sources. Their recommendations include trying to explain discrepancies across sources by understanding characteristics of the various contexts that may have either influenced the child's behavior in that context (e.g., an unstructured classroom without clear rules or methods of enforcement), or influenced an informant's ratings of the child's behavior (e.g., parental adjustment problems).

One particular contextual influence that deserves special note is the child's cultural context. Unfortunately, many measures used to assess child personality and adjustment have not been adequately tested to determine if their validity for various interpretations in the school context are comparable across ethnic groups (Kamphaus & Frick, 2005). Achenbach, Rescorla, and Ivanova (2005) provide a comprehensive review of both the consistencies and sources of variation in the ratings of child and adolescent psychopathology across various cultures. They note several important issues for interpreting assessment information for ethnically diverse children. First, these authors emphasize the need to recognize that variations within cultural groups on measures of personality are often much larger then variations across cultural groups, making it important to understand the specific characteristics and experiences of the child and his or her family. Second, it is important to understand the unique sources of support (e.g., strong extended family support) and unique sources of stress (e.g., exposure to systematic discrimination) within the child's cultural context that may influence a child's adjustment. This includes the child and family's level of acculturation or identification with the dominant culture. Third, it is important to understand cultural differences in how personality and mental health is viewed by different cultures to understand how assessment measures may be interpreted by the child and family and how best to communicate the findings to them in a way that will foster collaborative efforts for intervention.

DEVELOPMENTAL CHANGES AND PERSONALITY ASSESSMENT

As noted previously, the long-term stability of measures of personality are much lower in children and adolescents than in adults (Roberts & DelVecchio, 2000). This lack of stability is likely related to the many rapid changes in cognitive, emotional, social, and biological maturation that children and adolescents experience. These developmental changes have a number of important implications for assessing personality. First, it is important that strong "trait-like" interpretations not be made when interpreting personality measures because of the fairly substantial changes that can occur in the child's personality and behavior across development. Second, it is important that assessment batteries include measures that allow for normative interpretations, which compare the child's personality and behavior to other students of approximately the same developmental level (Kamphaus & Frick, 2005). As a result, a critical

issue in evaluating the assessment techniques used to assess children and adolescent's personality and adjustment is the adequacy of the norms that are available to enhance the interpretation of the scores.

Third, the child's age and developmental level can influence the choice of the optimal methods for assessment. For example, Kamphaus and Frick (2005) summarize research suggesting that the reliability and validity of children's self-report on structured assessment techniques is often modest before age 9 but tends to increase with age. This finding has led to several innovative methods for obtaining self-report information in young children, such as the Dominic-R (Valla, Bergeron, & Smolla, 2000) that uses pictorial stimuli, rather than questions, to obtain information from the child. Kamphaus and Frick (2005) also review research suggesting that the reliability and validity of parent and teacher report often decrease across development, especially as the child enters adolescence. During adolescence parents may have less complete knowledge of the child's emotions and behaviors, and the child spends less time with any single teacher. As recommended by these authors, it is still often desirable to have multiple sources of information on the child's personality and adjustment at all ages. However, the type of assessment information that is emphasized and given more weight when making decisions on intervention, especially when the information is discrepant across sources, may change across development.

METHODS OF ASSESSMENT

This need for multiple sources of information relates to a broader issue in the assessment of children's personality and adjustment. That is, an adequate assessment needs to include multiple methods of assessment. This goes beyond simply needing multiple informants on behavior ratings scales. It is also important to include multiple methods of assessment to adequately understand a student's personality and adjustment. Like the differences noted across informants, the correlations for traits and behaviors across methods also is quite modest and rarely exceeds correlations of about .30, such as between parent or teacher ratings of inattention and laboratory measures of attention (Barkley, 1991) or between self-report and clinician ratings of personality in adolescents (Lee, Vincent, Hart, & Corrado, 2003). Therefore, assessors are still left with difficult decisions concerning how to interpret differences in findings across methods. Such decisions can be guided by recognizing the strengths and limitations of the various methods that are available for assessing children and adolescent personality and adjustment.

Rating Scale Systems

Standardized rating scales have long played a prominent role in the assessment of children's personality and psychological adjustment (Frick & Kamphaus, 2001). The importance placed on rating scales can be traced to several different sources. One source is the long history of using self-report inventories to assess personality dimensions in adults (e.g., Hathaway & McKinley, 1942). Having adults rate their attitudes, emotions, and behaviors using a standardized format (e.g., standard questions, standard response format) results in very reliable information that can be collected in a time-efficient manner. Both the reliability and time efficiency of these ratings enable them to be used widely in research, thus allowing for the validity of these ratings in predicting clinically important criteria (e.g., degree of impairment, need for special education services) to be tested. Also, the ease of administration allows standardized rating scales to be given to large samples of individuals in a community. Thus, rating scales often provide some of the best normative data on a student's personality and adjustment. And finally, there are now a number of ratings scales that allow for information to be collected across multiple informants (e.g., parent, child, and teacher) in a standardized and consistent manner that helps in assessing areas of consistency and inconsistency in a child's adjustment across various settings and across multiple informants' perspectives.

Based on these strengths, behavior rating scales are indispensable in the assessment of student's personality and adjustment. However, standardized rating scales also possess a number of limitations as well. One of the key limitations of standardized ratings is that they assess a rater's *perceptions* of their own personality or other's attitudes, emotions, and behaviors. As such, these perceptions can be influenced by a host of factors such as intentional or unintentional biases, imperfect knowledge of a child's behavior, inaccuracies in perceptions due to immaturity, and differences in raters' standards for judging the severity of behavior. A second

limitation is that there are substantial variations in how rating scales are constructed, leading to substantial variability in how psychological constructs are assessed across the scales. For example, items on subscales assessing "attention problems" may vary greatly across different ratings scales (see for example Achenbach & Rescorla, 2004; Reynolds & Kamphaus, 2004) and may differ from diagnostic definitions used to define psychopathology (American Psychiatric Association, 2000). Finally, while rating scales often have data on large standardization samples, which allow for the conversion of raw scores to norm-referenced scores (e.g., T-scores), the size and composition of the standardization samples can vary greatly across scales.

Given the space limitations for this chapter, a comprehensive review of available ratings scale systems is not possible. However, we have chosen three commercially available rating scales systems to serve as examples of the types of systems available and to illustrate some of the important issues involved in evaluating them for use in the assessment of children and adolescents.

Achenbach System of Empirically Based Assessment (ASEBA; Achenbach & Rescorla, 2001)

Description

The ASEBA is the name given to the system of assessment instruments including the Child Behavior Checklist (CBCL). The CBCL has a long and prominent history for assessing children's emotional and behavioral functioning (Achenbach & Edelbrock, 1978) and may be one of the most widely used rating scale systems reviewed in this chapter. Most notably it has been extensively used, not only in the United States, but there are currently translations of the ASEBA in 69 languages and published reports of the use of the ASEBA in 62 countries (Achenbach & Rescorla, 2001). The original CBCL was a parent rating scale that was quickly expanded into analogous teacher (CBCL-TRF) and youth self-report (YSR) scales to promote multi-informant assessments. In fact, one of the hallmarks of the ASEBA system has been its focus on promoting a multi-informant and multimethod assessment of children's adjustment. For example, the current ASEBA system includes a Direct Observation Form, described in more detail in a later section, and a semistructured interview of the child, the Semi-Structured Clinical Interview for Children and Adolescents.

The rating scale components of the ASEBA include forms for preschool ages (1.5–5 years; Achenbach & Rescorla, 2000), school ages (6–18 years; Achenbach & Rescorla, 2001), as well as for younger (19–59 years) and older (60–90+ years) adults (Achenbach & Rescorla, 2004). The most widely used and most extensively validated of these scales are the parent report CBCL for children ages 4–18, the teacher report CBCL-TRF for children ages 5–18 and the YSR for ages 11–18. The content of the 113 items across the three assessment formats is identical, as are the subscales, all of which greatly facilitates interpreting information across different raters. All CBCL items are rated as being "Not True," "Somewhat True or Sometimes True," or "Very True or Often True." Thus, each form takes about 10 to 15 minutes. There are both hand-scoring and computer-scoring options available. The computer-scoring system is particularly helpful for converting raw scores to norm-referenced scores appropriate for the child's age and gender and for providing cross-informant and cross-method comparison across the components of the ASEBA system.

The items on the child and adolescent rating scales components of the ASEBA system provide a broad coverage of internalizing behavior (e.g., anxiety, depression, and somatic complaints), externalizing behavior (antisocial behavior, aggression, oppositional), social behavior problems, and attention problems. The scoring results in a Total Problems Scores, that provides the most global assessment of the child's adjustment across all problem areas, and it provides externalizing and internalizing composites. There are additionally eight narrow band scales that provide norm-referenced scores for more specific problem areas. New in the more recent revisions of the ASEBA is the ability to determine six scales that are designed to have item content corresponding to some of the major categories of childhood psychopathology (American Psychiatric Association, 2000).

Summary of Psychometric Properties

The normative samples collected for the various school-aged rating scale components of the ASEBA are generally quite extensive and representative of the 48 contiguous United States for socioeconomic status (SES), ethnicity, region, and urban-suburban-rural residence (Achenbach & Rescorla, 2001). Importantly, the samples generally excluded children if they had been referred for mental health or special education services within the past year, making them normal samples rather than normative samples. However, the large samples allows for norm-referenced scores that can be age and gender specific. These extensive normative samples also provided extensive factor support for the various ASEBA scales and the factor structure has been replicated extensively, not only in the United States but in many different countries (Achenbach et al., 2005). Also, these studies have provided strong support for the reliability of both the global composites and, with only a few exceptions, the narrow band scales as well (Achenbach & Rescorla, 2001). Finally, the extensive research on the ratings scale component of the ASEBA have provided strong support for the validity of the scales in differentiating children with adjustment problems from normal developing children, with the most support being found for broad internalizing and externalizing scales and the narrow band composites focusing on conduct problems (i.e., the Aggressive Behavior and Rule Breaking scales; Frick & Kamphaus, 2001). Importantly, there is less data available on the newer scales designed to approximate the criteria from the Diagnostic and Statistical Manual of Mental Disorders-Fourth Edition-Text Revision. (DSM-IV-TR; American Psychiatric Association, 2000).

Overall Evaluation

The ASEBA system is a time-efficient method of assessing a range of emotional and behavioral problems that provides norm-referenced scores to which one can confidently compare a child's scores to others of the same gender and similar age. Its multiple components and computer software all promote a multi-informant and multimethod assessment of a student's adjustment. Further, its wide use in research has provided a wealth of data on the reliability and validity of its scales. Most specifically, the time-efficient nature of the ASEBA scales and the extensive validation of the internalizing and externalizing composites make these scales a very useful method of screening children for emotional and/or behavioral difficulties.

The primary limitations in the ASEBA scales involve the narrow band scales. The content, by being broad in coverage, sometimes does not allow for adequate assessments of some specific domains that may be important for some evaluations of children and adolescents. For example, there is no separate depression scale or a scale assessing hyperactivity. Further, the sole reliance on factor analysis in developing scales led to some heterogeneity in the content of some of the narrow band scales (Kamphaus & Frick, 2005). For example, the Attention Problems scales on the parent and teacher scales include items related to attention (e.g., can't concentrate, can't pay attention for long), as well as items such as "acts too young for his/her age" and "nervous or high strung" that are not specific to inattention. This scale heterogeneity needs to be considered when interpreting the narrow band scales. And finally, the new DSM-IV-TR scales have not been extensively validated currently and, because they were limited to existing scale items, do not always provide a very extensive coverage of DSM-IV-TR criteria.

Behavior Assessment System for Children-2 (BASC-2; Reynolds & Kamphaus, 2004)

Description

The BASC system of scales is a relative newcomer compared to the ASEBA system. It was originally published in 1993 (Reynolds & Kamphaus, 1993) with the second edition, the BASC-2 (Reynolds & Kamphaus, 2004) published 10 years later. Like the ASEBA, the BASC-2 rating scales provide a multi-informant assessment of a wide range of emotional and behavioral problems across childhood and adolescence. The Self-Report of Personality (SRP) has a form for children ages 8 to 11, for adolescents ages 12 to 21, and for college students ages 18 to 25. The Parent Rating Scales (PRS) and Teacher Rating Scales (TRS) have three formats; one for preschool children (2–5 years), a second for elementary school children (6–11 years), and a third for middle/high school children (12–21 years). Although the SRP includes some True/False items, the majority of the behavioral descriptors on the BASC-2 scales are rated on a four-point scale, ranging from "Never" to "Almost Always." Also like the ASEBA, the BASC-2 has several assessment formats in addition to their ratings scales. The BASC-2 also includes a semistructured interview to collect background information on the child, Structured Developmental History (SDH), and a system for observing a student's behavior in the classroom, the Student Observation System (SOS). Both of these components of the BASC-2 are described in more detail below.

The content of the BASC-2 is quite comprehensive, covering the major types of adjustment problems experienced by students (e.g., anxiety, depression, conduct problems, hyperactivity). Also, the BASC-2 assesses a number of adaptive skills, such as social skills, leadership, study skills, and self-reliance. The BASC-2 also includes a number of validity scales designed to assess possible response sets (e.g., attempts to provide overly positive or overly negative ratings). While such validity scales are fairly common in many self-report inventories, their inclusion on the parent and teacher ratings is somewhat unique. This more expanded content adds to the BASC-2 lengths with the teacher rating scales having between 100 and 139 items, the parenting rating scales having between 134 and 160 items, and the self-report scales having between 139 and 185 items. As a result, it takes between 15 and 20 minutes to complete the BASC-2. The content of the teacher and parent versions of the BASC-2 are fairly similar, with the main difference being that teachers also rate behaviors indicative of learning problems and study skills. The content of the SRP, however, is quite different. For example, the child does not rate his or her own level of conduct problems but instead provides more extended coverage of the child's attitudes (e.g., attitudes toward parents and teachers), his or her self-concept (e.g., self-esteem and sense of inadequacy), and his or her social relationships.

Summary of Psychometric Properties

There are both English and Spanish versions of the BASC and there are both hand-scoring and computer-scoring formats that allow for easy calculation of norm-referenced scores (T-scores and percentile ranks) to aid in interpreting the scales. These scores are based on very large samples of children (ranging from n = 3,400 for the SRP to n = 4,800 for the PRS) spanning 375 testing sites across the United States and Canada. The sampling procedures were designed to ensure an adequate representation of ethnic minorities and the sample is based on U.S. population estimates obtained from the March 2001 *Current Population Survey* (Reynolds & Kamphaus, 2004).

The manual for the BASC-2 provides evidence for various types of reliability (e.g., internal consistency, test-retest reliability, and interrater reliability) for the BASC-2 subscales. The manual of the BASC-2 provides factor analytic support for the construct validity of the scales as well, and provides correlations between the BASC-2 scales and several other commonly used rating scales. Also, while the scale content was guided by factor analyses, rational decisions were also made to ensure that the content of the BASC-2 scales were somewhat homogeneous and correspond to current conceptualizations of most constructs. Furthermore, tests of concurrent validity indicate that groups of children with preexisting clinical diagnoses tend to have distinct BASC-2 profiles (Reynolds & Kamphaus, 2004).

Overall Evaluation

The BASC-2 scales cover the major domains of behavioral and emotional functioning, as well as assessing many aspects of adaptive behavior (adaptability, leadership, social skills, and study skills). The content of the BASC-2 seems to reflect current conceptualizations of childhood psychopathology in many important respects, such as including separate anxiety and depression scales and including separate hyperactivity and attention scales. The BASC-2 scales were developed to have fairly homogenous item content on the subscales which greatly facilitates interpretation of scale scores. Also, the BASC-2 includes validity indices for all ages and informants. The BASC-2 PRS and TRS versions have a preschool version for children ages 2 to 5, an age group often not included in many other rating scales and the self-report version was standardized to a younger age (i.e., age 8) than many other scales. Finally, the BASC-2 has a large nationwide normative sample allowing an assessor to make confidently many norm-referenced interpretations. However, with the expanded content, the BASC-2 is longer than many other rating scales. Also, because the BASC-2 was published fairly recently, there is less research on the validity of its scales.

Conners Rating Scales (CRS; Conners, 1997)

Description

The Conners Rating Scale was originally developed to assess the effectiveness of medication trials for hyperactive children (Conners, 1969). The 10-item Conners Global Index (CGI; formerly called the Hyperactivity Index) remains one of the best validated measures for this purpose. The most recent version of the CRS published by Multi-Health Systems in 1997 has parent and teacher versions for assessing children and adolescents ages 3 through 17 and a self-report version for ages 12 through 17. Each report format has both long (ranging

from 59 to 87 items) and short (ranging from 27 to 28 items) forms. Items on the CRS are rated on a 0 ("Not true at all") to 3 ("Very much true") scale. The item content and scale structure is fairly similar for the parent and teacher versions. Both versions assess both externalizing (oppositional, hyperactivity) and internalizing behaviors (anxious-shy, perfectionism), and they assess social problems and behaviors indicative of learning difficulties. The adolescent self-report version of the CRS includes scales assessing the adolescent's perception of family functioning and the presence of anger control problems. The content of the CRS is fairly reflective of current conceptualizations of childhood emotional and behavior problems and the method of scale construction.

Summary of Psychometric Properties

The CRS has both hand-scoring and computer-scoring formats that allow for easy calculation of norm-referenced scores. This normative sample consisted of children from 45 states and 10 provinces throughout the United States and Canada, ranging in size from 3,394 for the adolescent report formats to 1,973 for the teacher formats. The manual is unclear about how individuals of different ethnicities and socioeconomic status are represented in the normative samples. Internal consistency coefficients for the CRS subscales in the standardization sample were uniformly high (generally above .80). Further support for the reliability of the scales comes from test-retest reliability (6–8 weeks) in a sample of 50 children and adolescents, in which the only scales showing somewhat low test-retest reliability were the Anxious-Shy scale from parent report ($r = .47$) and the Cognitive Problems scale from teacher report ($r = .47$). Evidence for the factor structure of all versions of the CRS is also provided in its manual and it is quite impressive. However, other evidence for the validity of the subscales is not extensively provided in the manual, although it is available in independent research studies (e.g., Kumar & Steer, 2003).

Overall Evaluation

The revised CRS content closely corresponds to current conceptualizations of childhood psychopathology and the Conners Global Index (CGI; formerly the Hyperactivity Index) is one of the best validated measures for assessing medication response in children with attention-deficit/hyperactivity disorder (ADHD).

Further, the availability of several short forms is very useful as time-efficient screenings of mental problems and for repeated assessments (e.g., pre-and postintervention assessments) of the same student. Also, the method of scale formation led to scales with fairly homogeneous item content and there is good correspondence across scales on the parent and teacher versions, which facilitates comparisons in a multi-informant assessment. However, only oppositional types of conduct problems are assessed and not more serious conduct problems (e.g., stealing, lying, and vandalism). Also, there is fairly minimal coverage of depression items, especially on parent and teacher versions, and there is no assessment of attention difficulties on the main forms of the CRS. Also, the CRS normative sample, although large and geographically diverse, has unclear representation of ethnic minorities.

Interviews

Historically, one of the main methods for assessing both children and adults in many applied settings was through direct face-to-face interviews with the assessor determining what questions to ask and how to follow up on responses provided by the child or other informant. This approach had many advantages because it allowed the assessor to adjust the questions to the age, educational level, and cultural background of the person being assessed. Further, it allowed for questions to be tailored to the unique situation of the person being assessed. This method is still important in most assessment situations to obtain background information that is unique to the child, such as information on the child's family background and caretaking arrangements, developmental history, medical history, educational history, and history of previous mental health interventions. Most assessments involve collecting this information in a way that is unique to the assessor or the setting in which the assessment is being conducted. However, the BASC-2 includes a Structured Developmental History (SDH; Reynolds & Kamphaus, 2004) that provides a more standard format for collecting this type of background information.

While the interview format offers maximum flexibility to the assessor in developing questions based on the needs of the individual being assessed, it also relies on the clinician's theoretical orientation and expertise to determine what questions are asked and how the answers are to be interpreted. As a result, the flexibility of this format must be balanced by the unreliability often associated with such an unstructured assessment format (McClellan & Werry, 2000). Thus, over the past several decades there have been several structured interview schedules developed to assess children's and adolescent's adjustment in more standardized ways (Loney & Frick, 2003).

Structured diagnostic interviews consist of an explicit set of questions that the assessor asks the child or adolescent or his or her primary caretaker. They also include explicit guidelines on how a child's responses are to be scored. These interviews are generally structured around stem questions (e.g., Have you been involved in many physical fights?) followed by a series of follow-up or contingency questions to define relevant parameters such as frequency (e.g., How many fights have you been in the past year?), severity (e.g., Have you ever used a weapon in a fight?), duration (e.g., When was the first time you got in trouble for fighting?), and impairment (e.g., Has fighting caused problems for you at school, home, or with kids your age?). Due to the stem and follow-up format, the length of time that it takes to administer a diagnostic interview is heavily dependent on the number of problems being experienced by the child, with most interviews taking between 60 and 90 minutes to administer. While contingent questioning adds to the difficulty in administering many of these interviews, many of the commonly used schedules now have computer-administered versions that provides the interviewer with the appropriate questions to ask based on previous responses (Loney & Frick, 2003).

The content of most structured interview schedules have been based on the diagnostic criteria from the *Diagnostic and Statistical Manual of Mental Disorders* (DSM-IV-TR; American Psychiatric Association, 2000). Also, these interviews often do not have formats to obtain teacher information, both of which limit their usefulness somewhat in many school settings where formal psychiatric diagnoses are not the goal of most assessments. However, they do have characteristics that make them useful in some school-based assessments, especially for assessing students who may have serious behavioral or emotional difficulties. First, most interview schedules provide standard questions that assess the age at which a child's behavioral difficulties began to emerge and how long they have caused problems for the child, which could be critical in treatment planning for some children with behavior problems (Frick, 2004b). It also allows for the assessment of the temporal ordering of a child's problems, such as whether the child's behavioral problems predated his emotional difficulties, which could suggest that the emotional distress is secondary to the problems caused by the behavior problems. This temporal ordering could have important implications for what problems are the initial targets of intervention. Finally, unlike rating scales that often focus on how a child's adjustment compares to that of other children, structured interviews often focus on how impairing the problems are for the child in the classroom, with peers, and at home.

Behavioral Observations

A third major method of assessing a child's or adolescent's personality and adjustment is through direct behavioral observations of the child, either in his or her natural environment (e.g., classroom, playground, home) or in a controlled setting (e.g., playroom in a clinic; Skinner, Freeland, & Shapiro, 2003). The major advantage of behavioral observations is that, unlike behavior ratings scales or interviews, observations are not filtered through the perceptions of others. Also, direct observations allow for the assessment of environmental factors that can be producing, maintaining, or exacerbating the student's behavior, such as determining how teachers and other students respond to the child's behavior in ways that may not be readily apparent to those involved in these interactions.

While these advantages of behavioral observations make them an important component of many assessments of children's behavior, they also have several limitations. For example, it is often very time consuming to train observers to conduct observations in a standard and reliable manner. As a result, there are few observations systems that have been used on large normative samples that allow one to compare the behavior of the child being observed to other children of the same age or sex. Further, the presence of an observer can influence children's behavior, termed the "reactivity" of the observation, which can reduce the validity of the observations (Harris & Lahey, 1982). Also, it is sometimes difficult to obtain an adequate sample of behavior that ensures the behavior being observed is representative of the child's typical behavior. It is also difficult to obtain observations of internal events like attitudes, thoughts, and emotions that are critical in the assessment of a student's personality.

Due to these limitations, assessments of children's personality and adjustment should never rely solely on behavioral observations but observations may play an important part of a multi method assessment battery. To aid in this multi method battery, several of the rating scales systems reviewed previously include observational systems designed to be used in conjunction with parents, teachers, and self-report ratings. For example, the BASC-2 (Reynolds & Kamphaus, 2004) includes a Student Observation System (SOS) in which children's behavior in the classroom can be observed using a momentary time-sampling procedure. The SOS specifies 65 behaviors that are common in classrooms settings and includes both adaptive (e.g., follows directions; returns material used in class) and maladaptive (e.g., fidgets in seats, teases others) behaviors. The observation period involves 15 minutes in the classroom and this period is divided into 30 intervals of 30 seconds each. The child's behavior is observed for 3 seconds at the end of each interval and the observer marks all behaviors on scoring sheet that were observed during this time window.

A similar observational system can be used as part of the ASEBA assessment system. The Direct Observation Form (DOF; Achenbach & Rescorla, 2004) was designed to observe students, ages 5 to 14, for 10-minute periods in the classroom. Following this period, the observer writes a narrative of the child's behavior and rates 96 behaviors on a 4-point scale (0 = behavior was not observed, through 3 = definite occurrence of behavior with severe intensity or for greater than 3 minutes duration). Like the rating scale companions on the ASEBA, these ratings can be summed into Total Problem, Internalizing, and Externalizing behavior composites.

Projective Techniques

There is no type of assessment that has engendered as much controversy as projective techniques. Traditionally, these techniques have been some of the most commonly used assessment methods for assessing the personality of children and adolescents (Tuma & Pratt, 1982), although their popularity has declined somewhat in recent years, especially for school psychologists (Kamphaus, Petoskey, & Rowe, 2000). However, for some, projective testing remains synonymous with personality testing and provides some of the richest sources of information on the child's intrapsychic processes (Weiner, 1999). For others, projective techniques often don't meet basic psychometric standards and their use can detract from the assessment process (Lilienfeld, Wood, & Garb, 2000).

Most projective techniques were originally based on the projective hypothesis that states when persons are presented with an ambiguous stimuli (e.g., an ink blot; an ambiguous picture), "there is the tendency for people to interpret the stimuli in conformity with their past experiences and present wants" (Murray, 1943, p. 1). Thus, the projective test was a way to gain a window into a person's motivations and desires, of which the person may not be aware or be able to report through direct questioning. Also, most early methods of interpreting these techniques were not structured or systematic, relying on the assessor's experience and expertise to focus on the most important aspects of the person's response to the stimuli in the interpretation (Rabin, 1986).

Over the past several decades there have been several trends away from these traditional uses of the projective tests. For example, many projective techniques have tried to reduce the level of inference involved in traditional techniques by providing stimuli that are less ambiguous and designed to tap specific emotional or social content. For example, the Roberts Apperception Test for Children Second Edition (McArthur & Roberts, 1982) is a projective storytelling technique designed to have the child tell a story about cards containing pictures, which are designed specifically to elicit certain themes (e.g., a picture of a child doing homework designed to elicit themes related to attitudes towards school). Similarly, there are sentence completion tests in which a child is provided an incomplete sentence (e.g., "My teacher is _____") and the child is asked to complete the sentence (for a review of different sentence completion techniques see Holaday, Smith, & Sherry, 2000). The content of these sentences, like the pictures of the Roberts Apperception Test, are explicitly designed to have the child express his or her feelings about certain topics. As a final example, the Kinetic Family Drawing technique asks the child to "draw a picture of everyone in your family, including you, doing something" (Burns & Kaufman, 1970, p. 5). The child is asked to describe the people in the picture and what they are doing and it is explicitly designed to help the child express feelings about his or her family in a nonthreatening way.

The second trend away from traditional uses of the projective techniques is the development of standardized methods of administering and scoring the techniques. Two notable examples are the explicit scoring instructions accompanying the Roberts Apperception Test for Children (McArthur & Roberts, 1982) and the Exner Comprehensive System (ECS; Exner & Weiner, 1995) that was developed to standardize the scoring of the Rorschach inkblot test. This explicit scoring has resulted in these procedures providing scores that are reliable and has led to the collection of normative samples (Allen & Hollifield, 2003), although the adequacy of these norms has been questioned (Bell & Nagle, 1999; Hunsley & Di Guilio, 2001). Also, many of the scores derived from these systems have not always been highly correlated with other objective measures of child adjustment. For example, measures of social adjustment and depression from the Rorschach scored by the ECS were not significantly correlated with a rating scale measure of social skills and depression in a sample of children and adolescents (Stredny & Ball, 2005).

The lack of adequate norms and the failure of many of the scores to correlate with objective behavioral criteria are probably the two biggest limitations in the usefulness of many of the available projective techniques for assessments conducted by school psychologists. Further, how to translate the findings from these techniques directly into school-based interventions is not always clear (Kamphaus et al., 2000). Thus, while projective techniques often provide a vehicle for establishing rapport with children and provide methods for having children begin to discuss important and sometimes distressing information in a nonthreatening and indirect manner, their other limitations and the time necessary to administer and score the techniques in the standardized manner necessary to obtain reliable scores likely preclude the use of these techniques in many school-based assessments.

EVIDENCE-BASED ASSESSMENT OF CHILDHOOD PSYCHOPATHOLOGY

In this chapter, we started with a summary of some key points from research on the normal development of personality and their implications for assessing children and adolescents. This was followed by a brief summary and evaluation of some of the major techniques used to obtain information on children's personality and adjustment. In this section, we attempt to integrate information from these two sections with research on the most common types of adjustment problems that children may experience in the school setting to provide evidence-based guidelines for assessing students (Kamphaus & Frick, 2005; Mash & Hunsley, 2005). Although we at times use diagnostic terms in this discussion, these guidelines are important even in instances when a formal diagnosis is not the goal of assessment. That is, the behaviors associated with these diagnostic categories are often a primary reason for referral to school psychologists. And though, in the interest of space we have limited our discussion to a few select types of problems that likely lead to the largest numbers of referrals for services in the school setting, similar guidelines have been developed for less typical forms of psychopathology such as bipolar disorder (Youngstrom, Findling, Youngstrom, & Calabrese, 2005) and autistic spectrum disorders (Ozonoff, Goodlin-Jones, & Solomon, 2005).

Assessing Attention-Deficit/ Hyperactivity Disorder (ADHD)

ADHD is one of the most common forms of psychopathology found in children, with prevalence rates ranging from 2% to 9% of school-aged children (American Academy of Child and Adolescent Psychiatry, 1997). Although there has been some debate over the years as to the best way to define the core symptoms of the disorder (Frick & Lahey, 1991), most current classification systems focus on two primary symptom dimensions: inattention/disorganization (e.g., difficulty completing tasks such as schoolwork; easily distracted; makes careless mistakes) and impulsivity-hyperactivity (e.g., difficulty waiting turn; being excessively fidgety and restless; difficulty playing quietly; American Psychiatric Association, 2000). Children with this disorder can have different patterns of these behaviors, with the majority showing both inattention/disorganization and impulsivity/hyperactivity (combined type) and others showing the former symptoms only (predominantly inattentive type) or the later symptoms only (predominantly hyperactive-impulsive type).

Although the diagnosis of ADHD does not itself typically qualify children for special education services under the Individuals with Disabilities Education Act (IDEA), many children with ADHD have other problems in their learning or emotional functioning that would warrant special education services (Kamphaus & Frick, 2005). Also, it is generally accepted that ADHD qualifies as a handicap under Section 504 of the Rehabilitation Act Amendments of 1973, requiring academic accommodations be made for children with this disorder. Irrespective of the statutory requirements, the behaviors exhibited by children with ADHD clearly can have a major effect on the child's functioning in the school setting, such as making it difficult to complete schoolwork, causing significant disruptions in the classroom, and often leading to significant problems in the child's peer relationships (DuPaul & Stoner, 2003). While research on this disorder is quite extensive (see Barkley, 1997; Hinshaw, 1994 for reviews), there are a few pieces of research that have specific and important implications for guiding assessments of students with ADHD (Pelham, Fabian, & Massetti, 2005).

The first implication is that it is critical to assess several dimensions on which the behavior of children with ADHD can be differentiated from normative inattentive, impulsive, and overactive behaviors. First, the level of these behaviors in children with ADHD is often more extreme than is found in other children (Lahey et al., 1994) and this is often best assessed through behavior rating scales that can compare the child's level of behavior to norms or structured interviews that can determine if the level of symptoms crosses a diagnostic threshold. Second, it is critical to assess the level and degree of impairment that are associated with these symptoms (Pelham et al., 2005). As noted previously, children with ADHD often have significant problems in their academic and social adjustment that can be assessed by behavior ratings scales, observations of the child in academic and social settings, and through samples of the child's academic work. Third, the behaviors associated with ADHD are not transient reactions to some specific event and are often evident very early in life (Lahey et al., 1994). Thus, it is important to assess the duration of the child's problems through structured or unstructured interviews and through records of the child's adjustment over time. Fourth, although the severity of a child's behavior may vary somewhat across situations due to differing demands across situations for sustained attention (e.g., structured classroom versus recess), the behavior problems of children with ADHD are often present in many different settings with similar demands

(Barkley, 1997). Thus, it is important to obtain assessments of the child's behavior, either through ratings scales or observations, across multiple settings.

The second implication from research is that children with ADHD have higher rates of conduct problems, emotional problems and low self-esteem, learning problems, and social difficulties than other students (Barkley, 1997; Hinshaw, 1994). Further, many of these secondary or comorbid problems are often important targets of treatment. Thus, assessments cannot focus solely on the core symptoms of the disorder itself but must at least screen for other behavioral, emotional, and learning problems that may be displayed by children with ADHD. This initial screening is often best accomplished by behavior ratings scales to assess a wide range of areas of adjustment. Specific areas of concern uncovered by this screening can be the focus of more in-depth assessments with interviews, behavioral observations, and/or standardized academic tests (Pelham et al., 2005).

Assessing Conduct Problems

Conduct problems constitute a broad spectrum of "acting out" behaviors, ranging from relatively minor oppositional behaviors such as yelling and temper tantrums to more serious forms of antisocial behavior such as aggression, physical destructiveness, and stealing. There have been a number of methods used to try to divide conduct problems into important subtypes (see Frick & Ellis, 1999; Frick & Marsee, 2006 for reviews). For example, DSM-IV-TR (American Psychiatric Association, 2000) has diagnostic categories of oppositional defiant disorder (ODD) and conduct disorder (CD). ODD is a pattern of negativistic (e.g., deliberately doing things that annoy other people, blaming others for own mistakes), disobedient (e.g., defying or not complying with grownups' rules or requests), and angry behaviors (e.g., losing temper). CD consists of more severe antisocial and aggressive behavior that involves serious violations of others' rights (e.g., aggression, property destruction, theft) or deviations from major age-appropriate norms (e.g., truancy, running away from home). Other systems of classification have attempted to divide conduct problems into those that involve direct confrontation of others (e.g., oppositional behavior, aggression) and those that are covert and nonconfrontational in nature (e.g., lying, stealing; Frick et al., 1993). Still other

methods have distinguished between aggressive and nonaggressive forms of conduct problems and, even more specifically, into different patterns of aggression. For example, retaliatory, hostile, or reactive aggression is aggression that is a defensive reaction to a perceived threat and is characterized by anger and hostility (Crick & Dodge, 1996). Premeditated, proactive, or instrumental aggression is behavior used for personal gain or to influence and coerce others (bullying and dominance; Poulin & Boivin, 2000).

Based on this research, one implication for the assessment of children with conduct problems is the need to assess the number, types, and severity of the conduct problems carefully and thoroughly. Also, it is critical to assess the level of impairment that the conduct problems are causing for the child or adolescent (e.g., school suspensions, police contacts, peer rejection) and the danger that the child's behavior presents to his or her teachers and classmates (Frick, 2004b). This assessment can be done through interviews with the parents, youth, and teacher; behavior rating scales; and behavioral observations (McMahon & Frick, 2005).

Like ADHD, children with conduct problems often have a number of problems in adjustment in addition to their behavioral difficulties which also necessitate a comprehensive assessment (Frick, 1998). In addition, research has suggested that conduct problems result from a complex interaction of multiple causal factors (Dodge & Petit, 2003; Raine, 2002). These include biological, emotional, and cognitive factors within the child; and factors within the child's social context involving his or her family, peers, and broader social ecology (e.g., neighborhood, community). An extended discussion of the many ways in which these factors may interact to place a child at risk for conduct problems is beyond the scope of this chapter (see Frick & Dickens, 2006). However, the possible presence of these many risk factors highlights the need to assess dimensions within the child, as well as the child's social context, to understand adequately the development of his or her behavior problems and to design appropriate interventions (Frick, 2001).

One final area of research has focused on the different causal pathways through which youths may develop conduct problems. Each causal pathway involves a different constellation of risk factors and each involves somewhat different causal processes (Frick & Dickens, 2006). Currently, the most widely accepted model distinguishes between children who begin showing severe conduct problems prior to adolescence and those whose onset of severe conduct problems coincides with the onset of puberty (for a review see Moffitt, 2003). Specifically, children in the childhood-onset group show more severe and more aggressive conduct problems in childhood and adolescence and are more likely to continue to show antisocial and criminal behavior into adulthood (Moffitt & Caspi, 2001). Also, these children show more of the dispositional (e.g., temperamental risk, low intelligence) and contextual (e.g., family dysfunction) risk factors suggesting a more serious and characterological disturbance (Moffitt & Caspi, 2001). Further, within this childhood-onset group there is a subgroup of children who also show high levels of callous and unemotional (CU) traits (e.g., lacking empathy and guilt), who seem to show a more severe and aggressive pattern of conduct problems (Frick & Dickens, 2006), and who also exhibit a distinct temperamental style (Frick & Morris, 2004). That is, children with CU traits tend to show a lack of emotional responsiveness to cues of dangerousness or distress in others, whereas those childhood-onset children without these traits often are highly emotional and are more likely to have problems in their verbal intelligence (Frick & Morris, 2004). This research is critical in the understanding of and development of assessments for children and adolescents with conduct problems. All of these factors suggest that assessments of conduct problems need to determine the history of the child's behavior problems through structured or unstructured interviews. Assessments also should consider the child's emotional and cognitive functioning to determine which of these developmental pathways may best explain the development of a child's behavioral difficulties (McMahon & Frick, 2005).

Assessing Anxiety

While behavioral problems like ADHD and conduct problems often are the difficulties that most commonly lead to a student's referral for services, there is some evidence that problems of anxiety may be just as prevalent in school-aged children (Costello, Mustillo, Erkanli, Keeler, & Angold, 2003). While anxious children often don't cause the same level of disruptions in the classroom as children with behavior problems, there is evidence to suggest that anxiety can impair a child's academic and social functioning and place

the child at risk for future problems in adjustment (Morris & March, 2004). Thus, screening of children for anxiety using time-efficient behavior ratings scales is often an important endeavor to ensure that students with emotional difficulties are not overlooked in the classroom (Silverman & Ollendick, 2005).

For children and adolescents who show indications of significant levels of anxiety, it is important to identify and quantify the type of anxiety, its severity, and the degree of impairment associated with the emotional disturbance (Silverman & Ollendick, 2005). That is, anxiety can range from very discrete fears (specific phobia) to more generalized forms in which the anxiety is not focused on any single type of stimuli (generalized anxiety disorder). It can also vary according to the source of the worries, such as separation from parents (separation anxiety) or evaluation fears in social situations (social phobia). There is substantial research suggesting that some level of anxiety and fear is normal in children and adolescents, and that certain types of fears are more common at specific ages (Silverman & Ollendick, 1999). Therefore, it is critical that ratings scales that allow for a comparison of a child's level of anxiety to other children of the same age be part of the assessment, and it is important that assessments focus on the degree of impairment that is associated with the child's level of anxiety, such as the effect of the anxiety on the child's school performance or attendance (Silverman & Albano, 1996).

An additional recommendation made by Silverman and Ollendick (2005) in assessing childhood anxiety is the need to identify controlling and maintaining factors related to the child's anxious behavior. For example, there is evidence that some children may have temperamental predispositions to anxiety which may make them more likely to react negatively to threatening situations (Kagan & Snidman, 2004; Schwarz et al., 1999). Further, anxious children are more likely to show cognitive styles in which they view more things as threatening and they underestimate their ability to cope with them (Weems, Berman, & Silverman, 2001). There has also been research to suggest that anxious children often have others in their environment, such as parents and teachers, that inadvertently reinforce their anxious behavior by being overprotective and allowing them to avoid aversive events due to their anxiety (Manassis, Hudson, & Webb, 2004). Thus, all of these temperamental, cognitive, and contextual factors need to be assessed through rating scales, interviews, and behavioral observations in order to intervene effectively for students who are showing extreme levels of anxiety.

Assessing Depression

While severe levels of depression are relatively rare prior to puberty, the rate increases dramatically in adolescence (Garber & Kaminski, 2000). In adolescents, it is important to differentiate clinical levels of depression from normal adolescent moodiness (Arnett, 1999). Also, prior to adolescence, it is important to disentangle low self-esteem that can sometimes accompany behavior problems from depressive disorders. To do this, there are a number of norm-referenced ratings scales focusing specifically on depression that can be used to compare the severity of a student's self-reported mood to others of the same age (Klein, Dougherty, & Olino, 2005). Also, clinical depressed mood is usually accompanied by other signs of severity, such as loss of interest or pleasure in activities, weight loss, sleep disturbance, loss of energy, difficulty concentrating, and thoughts of death (American Psychiatric Association, 2000). Many of these clinical indicators can be assessed using rating scales or with interviews.

To be diagnosed with major depression, the episode has to last at least 2 weeks (American Psychiatric Association, 2000). However, children and adolescents who become clinically depressed often have episodes that last 7 to 8 months (Birmaher, Arbelaez, & Brent, 2002). Chronic depression can have very devastating effects on the child's academic and social functioning (Garber & Horowitz, 2002). For example, depressed adolescents have been shown to have higher rates of school drop out and unplanned pregnancy (Waslick, Kandel, & Kakaouros, 2002). Also, depression in youth has been associated with increased risk for suicide and substance abuse (Klein et al., 2005). Thus it is critical that assessments determine the length of time that the student has been depressed and the types and level of impairments that have resulted from the depression.

Like anxiety, depression has been associated with a particular cognitive style that can play a role in the onset and maintenance of depression and, as a result, is an important target of intervention. For example, depressed youth show a tendency to attribute success to unstable and temporary factors (e.g., luck) and failure to stable and permanent factors (e.g., lack of intelligence; Kaslow, Adamson, & Collins, 2000). Similarly, Klein et al. (2005) noted the importance of assessing the number and severity of negative life events experienced by the depressed youth because of their association with the onset and persistence of depressive symptoms. These authors also recommend assessing whether there is a family history of depression, given evidence that such a history also is a risk factor for more severe forms of depression.

SUMMARY AND CONCLUSIONS

In this chapter, we have attempted to illustrate that to adequately assess Maria, the girl in the case example at the start of the chapter, is not a simple process. First, it requires that the assessor be able to integrate several types of research, including research on normal development of personality, research on specific methods of assessment, and research on specific problems in adjustment in order to design an appropriate assessment battery. As noted in the various sections of this chapter, each of these areas of research provides important information as to the areas in need of assessment, the most appropriate methods to obtain the information, and the scientific basis for interpreting the information to provide the most appropriate services for Maria.

Second, any single method of assessment has both strengths and limitations in the information it provides. Thus, a second level of complexity involved in the assessment process is the need to include multiple methods of assessment to take advantage of the unique perspective each method provides and to overcome their specific limitations. Further, these methods must allow for the assessment of the student in different contexts, given that a child's behavior can be very different across situations. This need for a multimethod assessment across situations increases the time spent in administration of tests, but also complicates the interpretation of the information obtained by requiring the assessor to integrate information across various sources. Unfortunately, while the need for such comprehensive assessments is a standard recommendation in the assessment of children's personality and adjustment, there are relatively few explicit guidelines provided to help in the process of integrating information across sources (see Kamphaus & Frick, 2005 for such guidelines).

Third, and further increasing the comprehensiveness of the assessment, is the need to screen across multiple areas of adjustment, given that children and adolescents who have problems in one area often have co-occurring problems in other areas. Further, because the same problem can have multiple causes, an adequate assessment must consider the host of risk factors that could play a causal or maintaining role in the child's problems in adjustment, including both factors within the child (e.g., temperament; cognitive style) and factors within his social context (e.g., peer relationships; family background). Finally, many problems in adjustment can result in varying levels of impairment in the child's academic, social, and home adjustment. This necessitates assessing not only the child's adjustment but also the potential areas of impairment that can be negatively impacted by the problems in adjustment.

Obviously, all of the necessary information to conduct such complex assessments would be beyond the scope of a single chapter. However, our goal was to highlight some of the most critical issues involved in the assessment of children and adolescents' personality and adjustment. More importantly, we hoped to promote an evidence-based approach to this process, one that is well grounded in the most current psychological research. While such an approach does make the process complex, it is critical given the importance of assessment for providing the most effective services for children and adolescents with emotional or behavioral difficulties (Frick, 2000). Many important decisions that can have a major impact on the child's future adjustment are made from these assessments. As a result, it is imperative that these decisions are based on the most advanced technology available so that students, like Maria, will have the best chance of obtaining the services that they need.

REFERENCES

Achenbach, T. M., & Edelbrock, C. (1978). The classification of child psychopathology: A review and analysis of empirical efforts. *Psychological Bulletin, 85*, 1275–1301.

Achenbach, T. M., McConaughy, S. H., & Howell, C. T. (1987). Child/adolescent behavioral and emotional problems: Implications of cross-informant correlations for situational specificity. *Psychological Bulletin, 101*(2), 213–232.

Achenbach, T. M., & Rescorla, L. A. (2000). *Manual for the ASEBA Preschool Forms & Profiles*. Burlington, VT: University of Vermont.

Achenbach, T. M., & Rescorla, L. A. (2001). *Manual for the ASEBA School-Age Forms & Profiles*. Burlington, VT: University of Vermont.

Achenbach, T. M., & Rescorla, L. A. (2004). The Achenbach System of Empirically Based Assessment (ASEBA) for Ages 1.5 to 18 Years. In Maruish, M. E. (Ed.), *The use of psychological testing for treatment planning and outcomes assessment: Volume 2: Instruments for children and adolescents* (3rd ed., pp. 179–213). Mahwah, NJ: Lawrence Erlbaum Associates, Publishers.

Achenbach, T. M., Rescorla, L. A., & Ivanova, M. Y. (2005). International cross-cultural consistencies and variations in child and adolescent psychopathology. In Frisby, C. L. & Reynolds, C. R. (Eds.), *Comprehensive handbook of multicultural school psychology* (pp. 674–709). Hoboken, NJ: John Wiley & Sons, Inc.

Allen, J. C. & Hollifield, J. (2003). Using the Rorschach with children and adolescents: The Exner Comprehensive System. In C. R. Reynolds & R.W. Kamphaus (Eds.), *Handbook of psychological and educational assessment of children: Personality, behavior, and context* (2nd ed., pp. 182–197). New York: Guilford.

American Academy of Child and Adolescent Psychiatry. (1997). Practice parameters for the psychiatric assessment of children and adolescents. *Journal of the American Academy of Child & Adolescent Psychiatry, 36*, 4S–20S.

American Psychiatric Association. (2000). *Diagnostic and Statistical Manual of Mental Disorders, Fourth Edition, Text Revision*. Washington, DC: Author.

Arnett, J. J. (1999). Adolescent storm and stress, reconsidered. *American Psychologist, 54*(5), 317–326.

Barkley, R. A. (1991). The ecological validity of laboratory and analogue assessment methods of ADHD symptoms. *Journal of Abnormal Child Psychology, 19*(2), 149–178.

Barkley, R. A. (1997). Behavioral inhibition, sustained attention, and executive functions: Constructing a unifying theory of ADHD. *Psychological Bulletin, 121*, 65–94.

Beauchaine, T. P., (2001). Vagal tone, development, and Gray's motivational theory: Toward an integrated model of autonomic nervous system functioning in psychopathology. *Development and Psychopathology, 3*(2), 183–214.

Bell, N. L., & Nagle, R. J. (1999). Interpretive issues with the Roberts Apperception Test for Children: Limitations of the standardization group. *Psychology in the Schools, 36*(4), 277–283.

Birmaher, B., Arbelaez, C., & Brent, D. (2002). Course and outcome of child and adolescent major depressive disorder. *Child and Adolescent Psychiatric Clinics of North America, 11*(3), 619–638.

Burns, R. C., & Kaufman, S. (1970). *Kinetic family drawings (K-F-D): An introduction to understanding children through kinetic drawings*. Oxford, England: Brunner/Mazel.

Caspi, A., & Shiner, R. L. (2006). Personality development. In W. Damon, R.M. Lerner, & N. Eisenberg (Eds.) *Handbook of Child Psychology, Vol. 3: Social, Emotional, and Personality Development*, 6th Ed. (pp. 300–365). New York, NY: Wiley & Sons.

Clark, L. A., Watson, D., & Mineka, S. (1994). Temperament, personality, and the mood and anxiety disorders. *Journal of Abnormal Psychology*, *103*, 103–116.

Conners, C. K. (1969). Dextroamphetamine sulfate in children with learning disorders: Effects on perception, learning, and achievement. *Archives of General Psychiatry, 21*(2), 182–190.

Conners, C. K. (1997). *Conners' Rating Scales*. Toronto, ON: Multi-Health Systems Inc.

Costello, E. J., Mustillo, S., Erkanli, A., Keeler, G., & Angold, A. (2003). Prevalence and development of psychiatric disorders in childhood and adolescence. *Archives of General Psychiatry, 60*, 837–844.

Crick, N. R., & Dodge, K. A. (1996). Social information-processing mechanisms in reactive and proactive aggression. *Child Development, 67*, 993–1002.

De Los Reyes, A., & Kazdin, A. E. (2005). Informant discrepancies in the assessment of childhood psychopathology: A critical review, theoretical framework, and recommendations for further study. *Psychological Bulletin, 131*, 483–509.

Dodge, K. A., & Pettit, G. S. (2003). A biopsychosocial model of the development of chronic conduct problems in adolescence. *Developmental Psychology, 39*, 349–371.

DuPaul, G. J., & Stoner, G. (2003). *ADHD in the schools: Assessment and intervention strategies* (2nd ed.) New York, NY: Guilford Press.

Exner, J. E., & Weiner, I. B. (1995). *The Rorschach: A comprehensive system (Vol. 3): Assessment of children and adolescents* (2nd ed.). New York, NY: Wiley.

Frick, P. J. (1998). *Conduct disorders and severe antisocial behavior*. New York: Plenum.

Frick, P. J. (2000). Laboratory and performance-based measures of childhood disorders: Introduction to the special section. *Journal of Clinical Child Psychology, 29*, 475–478.

Frick, P. J. (2001). Effective interventions for children and adolescents with conduct disorder. *The Canadian Journal of Psychiatry, 46*, 26–37.

Frick, P. J. (2004a). Integrating research on temperament and childhood psychopathology: Its pitfalls and promise. *Journal of Clinical Child and Adolescent Psychology, 33*(1), 2–7.

Frick, P. J. (2004b). Developmental pathways to conduct disorder: Implications for servicing youth who show severe aggressive and antisocial behavior. *Psychology in the Schools, 41*, 823–834.

Frick, P. J., & Dickens, C. (2006). Current perspectives on conduct disorder. *Current Psychiatry Reports, 8*(1), 59–72.

Frick, P. J., & Ellis, M. L. (1999). Callous-unemotional traits and subtypes of conduct disorder. *Clinical Child and Family Psychology Review, 2*, 149–168.

Frick, P. J., & Kamphaus, R. W. (2001). Behavior rating scales in the assessment of children's behavioral and emotional problems. In C. E. Walker & M. C. Roberts (Eds.), *Handbook of clinical child psychology* (3rd ed., pp. 190–204). New York: Wiley.

Frick, P. J. & Kimonis, E. R. (2005). Externalizing disorders of childhood and adolescence. In J. E. Maddux & B. A. Winstead, (Eds.), *Psychopathology: Foundations for a contemporary understanding* (pp. 325–351). Mahwah, NJ: Lawrence Erlbaum Associates.

Frick, P. J., & Lahey, B. B. (1991). The nature and characteristics of attention-deficit hyperactivity disorder. *School Psychology Review, 20*(2), 163–173.

Frick, P. J., Lahey, B. B., Loeber, R., Tannenbaum, L., Van Horn, Y., Christ, M.A.C., et al. (1993). Oppositional defiant disorder and conduct disorder: A meta-analytic review of factor analyses and cross-validation in a clinic sample. *Clinical Psychology Review, 13*(4), 319–340.

Frick, P. J., & Marsee, M. A. (2006). Psychopathic traits and developmental pathways to antisocial behavior in youth. In C. J. Patrick (Ed.), *Handbook of Psychopathy* (pp. 355–374). New York, NY: Guilford Press.

Frick, P. J., & Morris, A. S. (2004). Temperament and Developmental Pathways to Conduct Problems. *Journal of Clinical Child and Adolescent Psychology, 33*(1), 54–68.

Frick, P. J., & Silverthorn, P. (2001). Psychopathology in children. In P. B. Sutker & H. E. Adams, (Eds.), *Comprehensive handbook of psychopathology* (3rd ed., pp. 881–920). New York, NY: Kluwer Academic/Plenum Publishers.

Garber, J. & Horowitz, J. L. (2002). Depression in children. In I. H. Gotlib & C. L. Hammen, (Eds.), *Handbook of depression* (pp. 510–540). New York, NY: Guilford Press.

Garber, J. & Kaminski, K. M. (2000). Laboratory and performance-based measures of depression in children and adolescents. *Journal of Clinical Child Psychology, 29*(4), 509–525.

Goldsmith, H. H. (1996). Studying temperament via construction of the Toddler Behavior Assessment Questionnaire. *Child Development, 67*, 218–235.

Harris, F. C., & Lahey, B. B. (1982). Subject reactivity in direct observational assessment: A review and critical analysis. *Clinical Psychology Review, 2*(4), 523–538.

Hathaway, S. R. & McKinley, J. C. (1942). *The Minnesota Multiphasic Personality Schedule*. Minneapolis, MN: University of Minnesota Press.

Hinshaw, S. P. (1994). *Attention deficits and hyperactivity in children*. Thousand Oaks, CA: Sage Publications, Inc.

Holaday, M., Smith, D. A., & Sherry, A. (2000). Sentence completion tests: A review of the literature and results of a survey of members of the Society for Personal Assessment. *Journal of Personality Assessment, 74*, 371–383.

Hunsley, J. & Di Giulio, G. (2001). Norms, norming, and clinical assessment. *Clinical Psychology: Science and Practice, 8*, 378–382.

Kagan, J., & Fox, N. (2006). Biology, culture, and temperamental biases. In W. Damon, R.M. Lerner, & N. Eisenberg (Eds.) *Handbook of Child Psychology, Vol. 3: Social, Emotional, and Personality Development* (6th ed.). New York, NY: Wiley & Sons.

Kagan, J., & Snidman, N. (2004). *The long shadow of temperament*. Cambridge, MA: Harvard University Press.

Kamphaus, R. W. & Frick, P. J. (2005). *Clinical assessment of child and adolescent personality and behavior* (2nd ed). New York, NY: Springer Science and Business Media.

Kamphaus, R. W., Petoskey, M. D., & Rowe, E. W. (2000). Current trends in psychological testing of children. *Professional Psychology: Research and Practice, 31*, 155–164.

Kaslow, N. J., Adamson, L. B., & Collins, M. H. (2000). A developmental psychopathology perspective on the cognitive components of child and adolescent depression. In Sameroff, A. J., Lewis, M., & Miller, S. M. (Eds.), *Handbook of developmental psychopathology* (2nd ed., pp. 491–510). Dordrecht, Netherlands: Kluwer Academic Publishers.

Klein, D. N., Dougherty, L. R., & Olino, T. M. (2005). Toward Guidelines for Evidence-Based Assessment of Depression in Children and Adolescents. *Journal of Clinical Child and Adolescent Psychology, 34*(3), 412–432.

Kochanska, G. (1993). Toward a synthesis of parental socialization and child temperament in early development of conscience. *Child Development, 64*(2), 325–347.

Kochanska, G. (1995). Children's temperament, mother's discipline, and security of attachment: Multiple pathways to emerging internalization. *Child Development, 66*(3), 597–615.

Kumar, G. & Steer, R. A. (2003). Factorial validity of the Conners' Parent Rating Scale–Revised: Short Form with psychiatric outpatients. *Journal of Personality Assessment, 80*(3), 252–259.

Lahey, B. B., Applegate, B., McBurnett, K., Biederman, J., Greenhill, L., Hynd, G. W., et al. (1994). DMS-IV field trials for attention deficit hyperactivity disorder in children and adolescents. *American Journal of Psychiatry, 151*(11), 1673–1685.

Lahey, B. B. & Waldman, I. D. (2003). A developmental propensity model of the origins of conduct problems during childhood and adolescence. In B. B. Lahey, T. E. Moffitt, & A. Caspi (Eds.), *Causes of Conduct Disorder and Juvenile Delinquency* (pp. 76–117), New York, NY: Guilford Press.

Lee, Z., Vincent, G. M., Hart, S. D., & Corrado, R. R. (2003). The validity of the Antisocial Process Screening Device as a self-report measure of psychopathy in adolescent offenders. *Behavioral Sciences & the Law, 21*(6), 771–786.

Lemery, K. S., Essex, M. J., & Smider, N. A. (2003). Revealing the relation between temperament and behavior problem symptoms by eliminating measurement confounding: Expert ratings and factor analyses. *Child Development, 73*, 867–882.

Lilienfeld, S. O., Wood, J. M., & Garb, H. N. (2000). The scientific status of projective techniques. *Psychological Science in the Public Interest, 2*, 27–66.

Loney, B. R., & Frick, P. J. (2003). Structured diagnostic interviewing. In C. R. Reynolds & R. W. Kamphaus, (Eds.), *Handbook of psychological and educational assessment of children: Personality, behavior, and context* (2nd ed., pp. 235–247). New York, NY: Guilford Press.

Lytton, H. (1990). Child and parent effects in boys' conduct disorder: A reinterpretation. *Developmental Psychology, 26*(5), 683–697.

Manassis, K., Hudson, J. L., & Webb, A. (2004). Beyond behavioral inhibition: Etiological factors in childhood anxiety. *Cognitive and Behavioral Practice, 11*, 3–12.

Mash, E. J., & Hunsley, J. (2005). Evidence-based assessment of child and adolescent disorders: Issues and challenges. *Journal of Clinical Child and Adolescent Psychology, 34*(3), 362–379.

Mash, E. J., & Terdal, L. G. (1997). *Assessment of childhood disorders* (3rd ed.). New York, NY: Guilford Press.

McArthur, D. S., & Roberts, G. E. (1982). *Roberts Apperception Test for Children: Manual*. Los Angeles, CA: Western Psychological Services.

McClellan, J. M., & Werry, J. S. (2000). Introduction-research psychiatric diagnostic interviews for children and adolescents. *Journal for American Academy of Child and Adolescent Psychiatry, 39*(1), 19–27.

McCrae, R. R., & Costa, P. T. (1999). A five-factor theory of personality. In L. A. Pervin & O. P. John (Eds.), *Handbook of personality: Theory and research* (pp. 139–153). New York: Guilford Press.

McMahon, R. J. & Frick, P. J. (2005). Evidence-Based Assessment of Conduct Problems in Children and Adolescents. *Journal of Clinical Child and Adolescent Psychology, 34*(3), 477–505.

Moffitt, T. E. (2003). Life-course persistent and adolescence-limited antisocial behavior: A 10-year research review and research agenda. In Lahey, B. B. Moffitt, T. E., & Caspi, A. (Eds.), *Causes of conduct disorder and juvenile delinquency* (pp. 49–75). New York: Guilford.

Moffitt, T. E., & Caspi, A. (2001). Childhood predictors differentiate life-course persistent and adolescence-limited antisocial pathways among males and females. *Development and Psychopathology,* 355–375.

Morris, T. L. & March, J. S. (2004). *Anxiety disorders in children and adolescents* (2nd ed.). New York, NY: Guilford Press.

Morris, A. S., Silk, J. S., & Steinberg, L., (2002). Temperamental vulnerability and negative parenting as interacting of child adjustment. *Journal of Marriage and Family, 64*(2), 461–471.

Murray, H. A. (1943). *Thematic Apperception Test.* Cambridge, MA: Harvard University Press.

Ozonoff, S., Goodlin-Jones, B. L., & Solomon, M. (2005). Evidence-based assessment of autism spectrum disorders in children and adolescents. *Journal of Clinical Child and Adolescent Psychology, 34,* 523–540.

Pelham, W. E., Fabiano, G. A., Massetti, G. M. (2005). Evidence-based assessment of Attention Deficit Hyperactivity Disorder in children and adolescents. *Journal of Clinical Child and Adolescent Psychology, 34*(3), 449–476.

Poulin, F. & Boivin, M. (2000). The role of proactive and reactive aggression in the formation and development of boys' friendships. *Developmental Psychology, 36*(2), 233–240.

Rabin, A. I. (1986). Concerning projective techniques. In A. I. Rabin (Ed.) *Projective techniques for adolescents and children* (pp. 3–13). New York, NY: Springer.

Raine, A. (2002). Biosocial studies of antisocial and violent behavior in children and adults: A review. *Journal of Abnormal Child Psychology, 30,* 311–326.

Reynolds, C. R. & Kamphaus, R. W. (1993). *Behavior assessment system for children (BASC).* Bloomington, MN: Pearson Assessments.

Reynolds, C. R., & Kamphaus, R. W. (2004). *Behavior Assessment System for Children–2 (BASC-2).* Bloomington, MN: Pearson Assessments.

Roberts, B. W. & DelVecchio, W. F. (2000). The rank-order consistency of personality traits from childhood to old age: A quantitative review of longitudinal studies. *Psychological Bulletin, 126*(1), 3–25.

Rothbart, M. K. & Jones, L. B. (1998). Temperament, self-regulation, and education. *School Psychology Review, 27,* 479–491.

Rubin, K. H., Coplan, R. J., Fox, N. A., & Calkins, S. D. (1995). Emotionality, emotion regulation, and preschoolers' social adaptation. *Development and Psychopathology, 7,* 49–62.

Sameroff, A. J., Peck, S. C., & Eccles, J. S. (2004). Changing ecological determinants of conduct problems from early adolescence to early adulthood. *Development and Psychopathology, 16,* 873–896.

Saucier, G., & Goldberg, L. R. (2001). Lexical studies of indigenous personality factors: Premises, products, and prospects. *Journal of Personality, 69,* 847–880.

Schwarz, C. E., Snidman, N., & Kagan, J. (1999). Adolescent social anxiety and outcome of inhibited temperament in childhood. *Journal of the American Academy of Child and Adolescent Psychiatry, 38,* 1008–1015.

Silverman, W. K., & Albano, A. M. (1996). *Anxiety Disorders Interview Schedule for DSM–IV: Child and Parent Interview Schedule.* San Antonio, TX: The Psychological Corporation.

Silverman, W. K., & Ollendick, T. H. (1999). *Developmental issues in the clinical treatment of children.* Needham Heights, MA: Allyn & Bacon.

Silverman, W. K., & Ollendick, T. H. (2005). Evidence-Based Assessment of Anxiety and Its Disorders in Children and Adolescents. *Journal of Clinical Child and Adolescent Psychology, 34*(3), 380–411.

Skinner, C. H., Freeland, J. T., & Shapiro, E. S. (2003). Procedural issues associated with behavioral assessment of children. In C.R. Reynolds & R.W. Kamphaus (Eds.), *Handbook of psychological and educational assessment of children: Personality, behavior, and context* (2nd ed., pp. 30–47). New York, NY, US: Guilford Press.

Stredny, R. V., & Ball, J. D. (2005). The utility of the Rorschach Coping Deficit Index as a measure of depression and social skills deficits in children and adolescents. *Assessment, 12,* 295–302.

Thomas, A., & Chess, S. (1977). *Temperament and development.* New York, NY: Brunner/Mazel.

Tuma, J. M. & Pratt, J. M. (1982). Clinical child psychology practice and training: A survey. *Journal of Clinical Child Psychology, 11*(1), 27–34.

Valla, J., Bergeron, L., & Smolla, N. (2000). The Dominic–R: A pictorial interview for 6- to 11-year-old children. *Journal of the American Academy of Child & Adolescent Psychiatry, 39*(1), 85–93.

Waslick, B. D., Kandel, R., & Kakouros, A. (2002). Depression in children and adolescents: An overview. In D. Shaffer & B. D. Waslick, (Eds.), *The many faces of depression*

in children and adolescents (pp. 1–36).
Washington, DC: American Psychiatric
Publishing, Inc.

Weems, C. F., Berman, S. L., & Silverman, W. K.
(2001). Cognitive errors in youth with anxiety
disorders: The linkages between negative
cognitive errors and anxious symptoms. *Cognitive
Therapy and Research*, 25, 559–575.

Weiner, I. B. (1999). What the Rorschach can do for
you: Incremental validity in clinical applications.
Assessment, 6, 327–339.

Youngstrom, E. A., Findling, R. L., Youngstrom,
J. K., & Calabrese, J. R. (2005). Toward an
evidence-based assessment of pediatric bipolar
disorder. *Journal of Clinical Child and Adolescent
Psychology*, 34(3), 433–448.

CHAPTER 17

NEUROPSYCHOLOGICAL ASSESSMENTS IN THE SCHOOL

JOAN W. MAYFIELD
Our Children's House at Baylor
CECIL R. REYNOLDS
Texas A&M University
ELAINE FLETCHER-JANZEN
Private Practice

The use of neuropsychological principles and their accompanying assessment approaches in the schools is not a new endeavor, but has been present for decades, although hardly a part of mainstream school psychology. In 1981, the *School Psychology Review* was one of the first journals to address the concept of bringing neuropsychology into the school systems (Hynd, 1981). At that time, doctoral students in school psychology were only beginning to venture into clinical neuropsychology as part of their internship or postdoctoral programs. The first edition of this *Handbook of School Psychology* (Reynolds & Gutkin, 1982) contained a chapter on neuropsychological assessment by one of the pioneers of pediatric neuropsychology, Lawrence Hartlage. Now there are numerous school psychology programs in various parts of the country that have strands or specific specializations in the area of clinical neuropsychology (see Hynd & Reynolds, 2005, for a detailed history of the development of neuropsychology in school psychological practice). Neuropsychology played a key role in early conceptualizations of special education programs early in the twentieth century, but fell from favor during the age of behaviorism and because of the failures of such programs as perceptual-motor based training and other deficit-centered programs (e.g., Reynolds & Hickman, 1987) to improve academic performance in children with disabilities. The reincorporation of neuropsychology into the schools was spurred by several factors, most notably a resurgence of interest in the biological bases of behavior near the time of the passage of PL 94–142 (Education for All Handicapped Children Act of 1975) and the various reauthorizations and revisions of PL 94–142, typically known as the Individuals with Disability Education Acts (IDEA), which in the 1990s included traumatic brain injury to children as a required category of special education services. With the passage of these laws, school psychologists have been challenged with the opportunity of diagnosing children with learning differences viewed as neurologically based disorders. Handbooks of "School Neuropsychology" have become available (e.g., D'Amato, Fletcher-Janzen, & Reynolds, 2005), and students trained primarily in school psychology but with additional training and experience in neuropsychology are more and more finding their way into employment in nontraditional settings for school psychologists, including medical-surgical hospitals, medical schools, and rehabilitation facilities.

At the same time, the entire field of neuropsychological assessment has rapidly matured since the early empirical work of Ralph M. Reitan (1955) and other important contributors too numerous to mention here (please see Fitzhugh-Bell, 1997, for a review of the early history of clinical neuropsychology). The usefulness of neuropsychological assessment techniques in diagnosis and in the design of rehabilitation and related treatments has been recognized officially by the American Academy of Neurology (AAN) in an official report of its Therapeutics and Technology Assessment Subcommittee (American Academy of Neurology, 1996). Traditionally, the major contribution of clinical neuropsychology was the evaluation and diagnosis of brain injury and other forms of central nervous system dysfunction. There are, however, multiple other uses of neuropsychological tests that have been developed and refined over more than five decades of research on clinical neuropsychology. These include both contributions to diagnosis (e.g., Reitan & Wolfson, 2000, 2001; Reynolds, 2001) and to rehabilitation (e.g., Bennett, 2001). More recently, the use of neuropsychological tests for explicit diagnosis of the presence or absence of central nervous system (CNS) damage has declined due to advances in neuroimaging techniques; however, a rise in the application of neuropsychological measures for determining the functional deficits and related functional implications of CNS damage or dysfunction has increased as neuroimaging reveals damage heretofore unseen. Functional assessment of potential deficits and an evaluation of the implications of such findings are necessary through neuropsychological testing because neuroimaging methods cannot specify the true functional implications of any visualized abnormality or injury. For the latter, functional neuropsychological testing is required and is most often conducted by clinical neuropsychologists, clinical and school psychologists with additional specialized training in neuropsychology, and by speech and language pathologists with such specialized training as well as certain other professionals who may have obtained necessary specialized training (e.g., occupational therapists). Such large government programs as Medicare, Social Security, and CHAMPUS reimburse appropriately credentialed professionals and clinicians for clinical neuropsychological assessment, and the American Medical Association (2001) assigns unique billing codes for neuropsychological testing. The entire discipline of neuropsychology has grown tremendously, especially since the establishment of its key professional organizations, such as the International Neuropsychological Society (INS), and the National Academy of Neuropsychology (NAN), The Reitan Society, and the availability of board certification through the American Board of Professional Psychology, as well as other peer review boards such as the American Board of Professional Neuropsychology and the American Board of Pediatric Neuropsychology for those principally interested in children.

Clinical neuropsychological testing produces findings and conclusions that are used in a wide variety of settings such as medical, educational, and legal arenas, and by a variety of professionals, primarily clinical neuropsychologists, but also neurologists, psychiatrists, pediatricians, clinical, counseling, school, educational, rehabilitation, and pediatric psychologists, occupational therapists, speech and language professionals, physical therapists, life care planners, vocational rehabilitation experts, and others interested in assessment of brain-behavior relationships and the functional implications of CNS impairment. In addition to the diagnosis of brain impairment or dysfunction, neuropsychological testing also is used in the design of cognitive and physical rehabilitation programs, monitoring medical treatment outcomes and medication effects, and in the evaluation of other disorders as diverse as attention-deficit/hyperactivity disorder, learning disabilities, addictive disorders, speech and language disorders, traumatic brain injury, and dementia.

This chapter provides an overview and guidance to the neuropsychological assessment of children, focusing on conducting these assessments in school, as opposed to other clinical settings. While assessment using a neuropsychological paradigm and tests that are commonly thought of as neuropsychological in nature form but one component of the far broader discipline of neuropsychology, it is a critical component both historically and in contemporary neuropsychology, and one that can advance our ability to assist many children with disabilities in school settings. School psychologists who have additional advanced training in neuropsychology are in a particularly good position to provide neuropsychological assessments and related services to children for a variety of reasons, not the least of which is their concomitant knowledge of schools and school systems as well as the educational needs of children with disabilities, the meeting of which will greatly enhance their lives as adults.

Children in general have always posed special problems in clinical assessment and evaluation due principally to the diversity of their behavior and the rapid changes in development inherent to the childhood and adolescent years but that occur at such different rates for individual children. Infancy and childhood are the times of the greatest (and most rapid) breadth and depth of change in the human lifetime. Children who are developing normally or with mild levels of disability can be difficult to assess accurately, for reasons related to the maturity of their language development, motor development, social skills, and attention, concentration, and memory skills. As the extent of any disability increases, accurate assessment becomes more challenging. School psychologists are trained to evaluate children with a host of disabilities and unique characteristics, and the addition of a neuropsychological paradigm from which to draw additional information and perspectives on interventions seems a logical outgrowth of the school psychologist's training and the increasing knowledge base of the importance of our biology, and especially brain function, on a variety of crucial life outcomes.

Historically, neuropsychological evaluations were conducted with adults with known brain damage or injury, to determine localization of lesions or injury. Additionally, neuropsychologists are often asked to provide information concerning prognosis for recovery, functional ability, and course of treatment. The practice of neuropsychology has broadened to include the need to clarify conditions when brain damage or CNS compromise has not been identified; in these cases, evaluations provide additional information for differential diagnoses, which result in more effective treatment planning. As neuropsychologists gained more knowledge about brain-behavior relationships, they applied their knowledge to adults without known brain damage. After this, they turned their attention to problems of earlier development, which ultimately provided an understanding of brain-behavior functioning in children (Reitan & Wolfson, 1974). As medical advances continue and the incidences of neurologically impaired children enter the classroom, it will be increasingly important for school psychologists to have an understanding of neurologically based disorders.

WHAT IS NEUROPSYCHOLOGY?

Neuropsychology is the study of brain-behavior relationships. It requires acceptance of the idea that the brain, working as an interdependent, systemic network, controls and is all-inclusively responsible for behavior. Although this premise seems simple enough now, radical behavioral psychology in the 1960s and early 1970s ignored the brain, leading some to espouse the view that the brain was irrelevant to learning and behavior. As such, neuropsychology provides an alternative paradigm for viewing as well as collecting assessment data and for organizing assessments and the reporting of assessments. Neuropsychological paradigms will not be the

best paradigms for every assessment issue or outcome, but we know of no single paradigm that is best to apply to all children who sit before us—we need multiple paradigms to best account for the myriad of children we see. The neuropsychological paradigm for organizing assessments and interpreting and presenting the results of an assessment is a strong one for many cases we will see. It is also important to understand up front that neuropsychological assessment is not a simple product—a "neuropsychological report" for instance, though reports of the neuropsychological assessment should always be generated. Neuropsychological assessment done well and properly is a process driven by a way of thinking about children's development and behavior and relating it to brain function.

However, neuropsychologists examine the relationship between brain functioning and behavior through using tests that tap specific domains of functioning and that tend to have greater specificity than tests commonly used in more general clinical or school-based assessments, in addition to tests commonly used by school psychologists, typically assessing much more specific domains than those that are represented on general tests of intelligence, such as attention, memory, forgetting, sensory functions, constructional praxis, and motor skills (Farmer & Peterson, 1995; Reitan & Wolfson, 1985). This state of practice has lead some to conclude that neuropsychology is principally a specialized set of assessment devices. Neuropsychology is not a set of specialized tests, but again is a way of thinking about test data from a brain-behavior perspective. In this sense there are no tests that are specifically neuropsychological tests—rather, all tests are neuropsychological tests when viewed from the perspective that the brain is responsible for behavior and that test scores represent samples of behavior (e.g., see Reynolds, Livingston, & Willson, 2006). Neuropsychological approaches dictate that behavior samples be viewed from the perspective of the brain systems involved in producing the behavior, coupled with in-depth knowledge of the child's history and current life circumstances.

A neurologist looks at the anatomical construction of the brain. Working in conjunction with neurologists, neuropsychologists are able to determine the functional sequelae of CNS dysfunction. Neurologists use advanced neuroimaging techniques, including magnetic resonance imaging (MRI), positron emission topography

(PET), and single-photon emission computed topography (SPECT) of brain regions. Working in conjunction with neurologists, neuropsychologists focus on behavior and cognition in order to offer educational help and remediation strategies to family members, vocational specialists, and counselors. Clinical neuropsychologists deal with a variety of issues as family members seek to understand the cognitive and psychological needs of students who are coping with neurological deficits or dysfunction. Family members frequently want to know what they can do to provide the optimal environment to help their loved one return to their prior level of functioning after an injury to the brain, an illness that causes brain damage, or how to facilitate the optimal development of a child with a brain that has deviated from normal developmental trajectories. They seek to understand the specific deficits. On the basis of a person's medical, family, and developmental history, as well as the specific behavioral and vocational concerns, a neuropsychological assessment is designed and conducted. Importantly, neuropsychology is not a set of techniques. Rather, it is a way of thinking about behavior, often expressed as test scores; it is a paradigm for understanding behavior.

The Luria Model

To have an understanding of neuropsychology, and to develop skills in the interpretation of neuropsychological data, considerable training is required and is detailed in a variety of sources (e.g., see D'Amato et al., 2005). We find that one of the most clinically or practically useful models of brain function to apply when interpreting neuropsychological test data, especially with an eye on rehabilitation and related interventions, is the functional anatomical model of Alexander R. Luria, a Russian neuropsychologist, who was a major figure in the development of the scientific discipline of neuropsychology. His many publications (see especially 1966a, 1966b, and 1973) provide key understandings of the neuropsychological basis of intelligence and the workings of the brain as related to behavior. His theory of higher cortical functioning brought him international acclaim. He posited that the frontal lobes played a major role in intelligence, and the more the frontal lobes have been studied over the past several decades, the more important the functions of the frontal lobes and related executive systems have become in understanding brain-behavior relationships. Luria described mental processes in terms of two sharply defined

groups, "simultaneous" and "successive," based on the earlier works of Sechenov (1863/1965). Simultaneous processing indicates the synthesis of successive elements into simultaneous spatial schemes, while successive processing means the synthesis of separate elements into successive series. The original Kaufman Assessment Battery for Children (Kaufman & Kaufman, 1983) was developed on this model and was designed and standardized for use with children ages 2 1/2 years through 12 1/2 years. Scores are provided for a Sequential Processing Scale and the Simultaneous Processing Scale, which are summed together to provide a Mental Processing Composite. In this instrument, the Sequential Processing subtests emphasizes the arrangement of stimuli in sequential or serial order for successful problem solving. The Simultaneous Processing scale involves spatial, analogical and organizational abilities (Kaufman & Kaufman, 1983).

Luria (1966a, 1966b) divided the brain into three blocks. The first block is comprised of the brainstem, including the reticular formation, the midbrain, pons, and medulla. This portion of the brain is responsible for regulating levels of consciousness, arousal, and the overall tone of the cortex. The second block consists of the parietal, occipital, and temporal lobes, which are frequently referred to as the association areas of the cortex. This portion of the brain is responsible for receiving and encoding sensory input, and subsequently preparing this information for use by other areas of the brain as well as integrating information from these sometimes disparate areas. Block 2 is essentially receptive, however, and does not generate behavior as we understand it. The third block of the brain is comprised of the remaining area of the cortex anterior to the central sulcus and the sensory-motor strip, principally the frontal lobes. This section of the brain is responsible for the self-regulation of behavior, including such constraints as attention, planning and execution of behavior, and other operations referred to as "executive functioning." The frontal lobes are generative, that is, they are expressive and cause other brain areas to act in specific ways, in addition to formulating and controlling the execution of plans for behavior. It should be noted that these three blocks do not function independently of each other, and that a weakness in any part of the brain may impair functioning in other areas (Languis & Miller, 1992; Reynolds, 1981). Luria's model supports strength-centered intervention models, where the clinician focuses on intact complex functional systems of the brain which can be used for habilitation and to facilitate learning, rather than focusing on remediating dysfunctional or damaged brain functioning (Riccio & Reynolds, 1998). A detailed understanding of Luria's model is beyond the scope of the present chapter, but it is necessary to achieve an understanding of behavior samples as implicating brain function accurately (see Luria's cited works above as well as Reynolds, 1981, and Reynolds & French, 2005, for more detailed explanations).

Particularly relevant to this task are several key Lurian concepts, the complex functional system and the concept of the brain as a dynamic functional system. Luria gives credit for developing the notion of the brain as a dynamic functional system to Hughlings Jackson, an English physician, who lived in the nineteenth century. Luria (1964) noted that the higher cognitive processes were formed as a function of the process of communication and represent "*complex functional systems* based on jointly working zones of the brain cortex" (pp. 11–12). Luria goes on to state, "It becomes completely understandable that a higher (mental) function may suffer as a result of the destruction of *any link which is a part of the structure of a complex functional system* and ... may be disturbed even when the centres differ greatly in localization" (pp. 11–12). In addition, Luria postulated that, "when one or another link has been lost, the whole functional system will be disturbed in a particular way, and symptoms of disturbance of one or another higher (mental) function will have a *completely different structure, depending on the location of the damage*" (pp. 11–12). An example of a simple complex functional system would be speaking aloud a word printed on a card. To accomplish such a seemingly simple tasks requires that the instruction to read and say the word be understood (a task of the left temporal regions in most people), the seeing and interpretation of the written stimuli (the occipital regions), and the formulation of a plan for speaking the word and its execution (distinct portions of the frontal regions including the motor strip). All of these brain regions must coordinate successfully to achieve the goal of speaking aloud a printed word. This coordination represents a complex functional system. The concept of dynamic localization of function comes into play clinically when the examinee fails to complete this task—depending

upon the type or nature of the mistakes made when trying to execute the task, the breakdown in the brain systems under examination can be discerned (assuming one has sufficient training in functional neuroanatomy, developmental psychopathology, and assessment). Damage to any of the regions of the brain noted above can prevent the examinee from reading a printed word aloud correctly, but the reason for the inability to perform the task correctly will differ considerable depending upon which link in this coordinated chain of events is defective. It is the task of the neuropsychological examination to discover and catalog in an integrated manner the various complex functional systems of the brain relevant to the referral issues, and provide an appraisal of their functional integrity, all with an eye clearly on facilitating development and rehabilitation where required. In different settings, this process and the components of the neuropsychological examination that receive emphasis will differ.

SCHOOL-BASED NEUROPSYCHOLOGICAL EVALUATIONS

How does the practice of a school neuropsychologist differ from a child clinical neuropsychologist? Just as clinical psychology and school psychology differ in populations served, treatment goals, and place of practice, so do their neuropsychology counterparts. Table 17.1 summarizes some of the ways that the practice of neuropsychology differs in clinical versus school settings.

In general, the school neuropsychologist always has an educational goal in mind. The entire assessment process has a focus about how it can help the child meet the demands of everyday living in the classroom and school environment, from both cognitive and purely academic perspectives to the day-to-day behavioral demands of such a structured setting. This approach keeps in mind that a child's quality of life is much influenced by academic and social and behavioral successes in school. Therefore, an accurate statement of the child's neuropsychological status and how that translates into learning becomes the basis for the assessment. Interventions based on the neuropsychological assessment are designed, carried out, supervised, and evaluated by the school neuropsychologist working in tandem with an educational team. In addition, the relationship with the child and the team may go on for the child's entire school career. The school

TABLE 17.1 Summary of Differences Between Practice Parameters of School and Clinical Child Neuropsychological Assessment

Area of Specialty	School	Clinical
Outcome Agenda	Ecological validity of school neuropsychological assessment.	Diagnosis, recommendations, and possible short-term management/intermittent consultation.
Neuropsychological Assessment	Educationally focused.	Outpatient: Clinically focused, diagnosis/report and sometimes short-term follow-up.
	Inclusion of academic and achievement measures.	Inpatient: Clinically focused, initial diagnosis, short-term treatment goals, master treatment plan evaluation, discharge preparation.
	Primarily academic/educational interventions, with behavior management programming as necessary for behavioral and emotional sequelae of any CNS dysfunction or damage.	
	Evaluated by sustained and evidence-based gains in classroom.	
Informants for the Assessment	Parents, teachers, school personnel, physicians, community members, siblings, school nurse, school counselor, social worker, office staff, librarian, support staff.	Parents, school reports, consulting physicians.
Prior Personal Knowledge of Child	None or can be up to years.	Usually none.
Clinician's Relationship with Parents	Ongoing and indefinite (through age 21).	For the period of assessment and possible follow-up.
Clinician's Relationships with Consulting Physicians	Ongoing.	Ongoing.
Clinician's Relationship with Child	Ongoing or as needed (through age 21).	Time limited for assessment and focused treatment.
Clinician's Relationship with Teacher	Consultative and ongoing.	Little or no contact.
Clinician's Relationship with Treatment Team	Can be supervisory, consultative, or direct care provider.	Outpatient clinician: typically none or limited, but some provide therapy and consultation services on a longer term basis.
	Long term.	Inpatient: time limited treatment team member.
Clinician's Responsibility for Ongoing Medication Monitoring	Frequent and long term.	Infrequent and short term.

neuropsychologist, therefore, has the potential to have a long-term relationship with every child with whom he or she works. In fact, this is common since most students placed in special education programs remain in these programs for many years.

Long-term professional relationships allow the school neuropsychologist to have a unique clinical perspective. School neuropsychologists have opportunities to follow children to determine whether diagnostic formulations were correct, especially when the course of a disorder is expected to resolve, stabilize, or worsen (McCaffrey, Palav, O'Bryant, & Labarge, 2003). They witness the children growing up and meeting developmental milestones, sometimes watching them grow into disabilities, sometimes watching them overcome and outgrow disabilities, and more importantly, helping children and their teachers and families prevent negative outcomes that so often occur with children who have neuropsychological deficits. In comparison, clinical neuropsychologists have much shorter and clinically intense windows of opportunity with their clients that oftentimes ends with a diagnosis and written recommendations (McCaffrey et al., 2003).

The school neuropsychologist also has to rely on consultation skills to create change through other school personnel and parents. For the most part, the majority of school psychologists spend the bulk of their professional time assessing children. Therefore, others who do not have training in neuropsychology must deliver the services that will create good outcomes. Clinical psychologists in inpatient settings share direct-care therapeutic duties with other qualified personnel who generally have smaller caseloads than staff in the public schools. In outpatient settings, clinical psychologists are often restricted to working with just the family, as school consultations are many times not funded by insurance, and sheer distance limits how much supervision of treatment that can occur by a non-employee of the school district.

School neuropsychologists are much more likely to have extended personal contact with informants (D'Amato, Rothlisberg, & Leu Work, 1999). Over the years, the school psychologist forms close professional relationships with teachers and other personnel. The school psychologist knows the classroom climate from experience, and he or she knows the structure and expectations in a given classroom. Indeed, the school psychologist may know a child very well before

he or she is even referred. Clinical psychologists, on the other hand, are much less likely to have these kinds of relationships with school personnel, and their fund of knowledge about the child, the personnel who work with the child on a daily basis, and the limits of that setting. Having a deep understanding and familiarity of the child's daily living and the personnel who will be recruited to help the child simply creates better chances for treatment success and accountability (D'Amato et al., 1999). The objective verification of the latter statement, however, needs to be evaluated as the practice of school neuropsychology grows.

Why is a discussion of the differences between the practice of child neuropsychology in the schools and clinical settings related to the topic of neuropsychological assessment? The goals of school neuropsychological assessment and the competencies that a school neuropsychologist must have are related by the shift in perspective demanded by the setting of service delivery. To achieve positive outcomes, the school neuropsychologist has to handle assessment and group process in a real-world setting. It is clinical child neuropsychology "without walls."

The educational team brings the referral; the team has vital information that provides a large portion of the assessment information; the team has to formulate and buy into the intervention/treatment plan; the team has to carry out the plan; and, the team has to evaluate the plan. The school neuropsychologist is the only team member who has the training and expertise to lead the team in directions that are specific to the neuropsychological needs of the individual child. Therefore, the diagnosis must be accurate, but the assessment is ongoing. The process of neuropsychological assessment in the schools does not end when a diagnosis is made as it often does in clinical settings. It ends when a positive, evidence-based outcome is documented for some time in the classroom.

ASSESSMENT APPROACHES IN NEUROPSYCHOLOGY

Historically, assessment approaches in child neuropsychology have centered on the battery and the process approaches (Batchelor & Dean, 1996; Fennell, 1994, 2002) that reflect the early medical model settings. In recent years, there has been a tendency for these models to be expanded into less medically oriented settings, and ecological aspects have been included into the models of assessment (e.g., Bigler, Nussbaum, & Foley, 1997; Fennell, 2002; Teeter & Semrud-Clikeman, 1997). For example, Teeter and Semrud-Clikeman (1997) use a transactional model with a basic premise that because "the child's biobehavioral status acts and is acted on by the environment, it is important that this assessment evaluate home, school, and community functioning as well as neuropsychological performance" (p.103).

Fixed and Flexible Batteries

Some neuropsychologists prefer the fixed battery approach where the decision about which tests to administer is determined a priori. Standardized batteries such as the *Luria-Nebraska Children's Battery* (Golden, 1986), and the *Halstead-Reitan Neuropsychological Test Batteries for Children* (Reitan & Wolfson, 1985) fit well into this approach. These batteries have been shown to be quite effective in detecting the presence, lateralization, and localization of brain dysfunction (Bauer, 1994).

Others prefer a flexible approach to assessment where instruments are chosen depending on the presenting issues or suspected pathologies and are sometimes based on a short screening battery. The flexible battery approach is an "experiment-in-evolution" and the course of the battery changes as the "early data returns" are obtained (Bauer, 1994, p. 263). Both approaches have advantages and disadvantages (Bauer, 1994; Kamphaus, 2001; Russell, 1994; Teeter & Semrud-Clikeman, 1997), and the clinician has to determine which approach is best for the setting within which they are practicing, and/or the populations involved.

In the end, the job of the clinician is to answer the referral question. Sometimes the question can be answered in the context of a fixed approach to the assessment and sometimes hypotheses need to be tested by bringing in other tests to satisfy lingering questions. Indeed, it has been argued that there is really no substantial difference between the fixed or flexible approaches (Bauer, 1994) and there is essentially no data suggesting superiority of one over the other with regard to clinical outcomes (Kamphaus, 2001).

One bright point in the use of any battery is that the field of psychometrics is advancing and more reliable and valid instruments geared towards neuropsychological constructs with children are available and affordable (e.g., Reynolds, 2002; Reynolds & Voress, 2007). These tests will hopefully increase predictive validity and provide compensation for tests that historically have been downward extensions of adult tests, and batteries that had little or no reliability data (Batchelor & Dean, 1996; Hartlage & Williams, 1990).

Process Approach

Very much a qualitative approach to assessment, the process approach uses an initial set of tests to sample different domains of functioning. The child's performance on these tests is then analyzed from a quantitative and qualitative perspective to aid in the formation of hypotheses that will be tested further (Lezak, 1995). Based in the Lurian tradition (Bauer, 1994; Kamphaus, 2001; Kolb & Whishaw, 1990), observations about how a test is solved (or not solved) are considered to be more important than reporting success or failure of the task (Bauer, 1994). The limits of performance are tested in the process approach and then the treatment plan is formed (Teeter & Semrud-Clikeman, 1997). This approach melds quantitative and qualitative data and individual cases wander or vary on a continuum between the two methods of data collection (Batchelor & Dean, 1996; Kaplan, 1998).

A process-oriented approach may be suited for the school setting because it relies on clinical observations in standardized and experimental situations. The school neuropsychologist has the luxury of forming hypotheses of pathology and compensatory skills and seeing how they relate to everyday functioning in the real world. The school neuropsychologist has, if you will, a working laboratory in the classroom within which to test hypotheses that emerge from the assessment. However, our collective experience is that the qualitative approach is very difficult to implement accurately without substantial supervised experience in its application as well as much actual experience with known neurologic patients having well-documented lesion sites and types. More purely standardized tests are easier to learn and to interpret accurately.

Ecological/Treatment Models

There have been many models for neuropsychological assessment in the past that have had a clinical or medical focus. Today, assessment models take on much more of a developmental, adaptive, and child-oriented treatment focus (Yeates & Taylor, 1998). For example, Rourke, Bakker, Fisk, and Strang (1983) created the "preliminary developmental neuropsychological remediation/habilitation model" which was later revised and is now called the Treatment-Oriented Model.

This model accommodates the continuing relationship between neuropsychological assessment and intervention during the course of treatment.

Teeter and Semrud-Clikeman (1997) have a similar model emphasizing a more ecological and transactional focus that includes:

> (1) a description of the neuropsychological correlates of the disorder; (2) identification of behavioral characteristics of various childhood disorders; (3) takes into consideration moderator variables such as family, school, and community interactions; and (4) determines how the existing neuropsychological constraints interact with the child's coping ability and developmental changes that occur at various ages. (p. 104)

Fennell (1994) has used more of a patient-centered approach where the emphasis is on the isolation of the specific neuropsychological mechanism that underlies a particular behavior disorder. Taylor and Fletcher (1990) propose the biobehavioral approach that recognizes four types of variables present in the assessment: (1) presenting complaint; (2) cognitive and psychosocial characteristics; (3) environmental, sociocultural, and historical variables; and (4) biologic and genetic variables.

Regardless of the assessment approach taken by the school neuropsychologist, the most common neuropsychological batteries and approaches will need to be supplemented in specific ways, depending upon the referral questions posed. The following general guidelines should nevertheless prove useful and are derived from a variety of sources, including our own practices and experiences with many varied disability populations, the general teachings of Lawrence C. Hartlage, and other specific sources, in particular, Rourke, Bakker, Fisk, and Strang (1983).

1. All (or at Least a Significant Majority) of an Examinee's Relevant Cognitive Skills or Higher-Order Information-Processing Skills Should be Assessed

This will often involve an assessment of general intellectual level (*g*) via a comprehensive IQ test, such as a Wechsler Scale, the Reynolds Intellectual Assessment Scales, or another measure that provides information on both verbal and nonverbal intellectual domains. Measurement of the efficiency of mental processing as assessed by strong measures of *g* is essential to provide a baseline for interpreting all other aspects of the assessment process. Assessment of basic academic skills (including reading, writing, spelling, and math) will be necessary, along with tests such as the Test of Memory and Learning-Second Edition (TOMAL-2; Reynolds & Voress, 2007), which also have the advantage of including performance-based measures of attention and concentration. Problems with memory, attention/concentration, and new learning are the most common of all complaints following CNS compromise and are frequently associated with more chronic neurodevelopmental disorders (e.g., learning disability, attention-deficit/hyperactivity disorder [ADHD]).

2. Testing Should Sample the Relative Efficiency of the Right and Left Hemispheres of the Brain

Asymmetries of performance are of interest on their own, but different brain systems are involved in each hemisphere, and these have differing implications for treatment. Even in a diffuse injury such as anoxia, it is possible to find greater impairment in one portion of an individual's brain than in another. Specific neuropsychological tests like those of Halstead-Reitan Neuropsychological Battery (HRB) are useful here, along with measures of verbal and nonverbal memory processes. The various Wechsler scales do not have scales that correspond well to right versus left hemispheric localization (we think most likely due to the ease of application of verbal encoding as a problem-solving strategy on some of Wechsler's performance tasks), and memory tasks as well as language, sequencing, and spatial tasks of various sorts are useful.

3. Testing Should Sample both Anterior and Posterior Regions of Cortical Function

The anterior portion of the brain is generative and regulatory, whereas the posterior region is principally receptive. Deficits and their nature in these systems will have a great impact on treatment choices. Many common tests, such as tests of receptive (posterior) and expressive (anterior) vocabulary, may be applied here, along with a systematic and thorough sensory perceptual examination and certain specific tests of motor function. Measures such as trail-making tests (e. g., Reynolds, 2002) and set-shifting (e. g., Heaton, 1981; Reynolds & Horton, 2006) and fluency (Reynolds & Horton, 2006) along with measures of behavioral control are particularly useful in assessing the integrity of frontal or anterior regions of the brain. In conjunction with point 2 above, this allows for evaluation of the integrity of the four major quadrants of the neocortex: right anterior, right posterior, left anterior, and left posterior.

4. Testing Should Determine the Presence of Specific Deficits

Any specific functional problems a child is experiencing must be determined and assessed. In addition to such problems being of importance in the assessment of children with neurodevelopmental disorders, traumatic brain injury (TBI), stroke, and even some toxins can produce very specific changes in neocortical function that are addressed best by the neuropsychological assessment. Similarly, certain transplant patients will display specific patterns of deficits as well. Neuropsychological tests tend to be less g-loaded as a group and to have greater specificity of measurement than many common psychological tests. Noting areas of specific deficits is important in both diagnosis and treatment planning.

5. Assessment Should Determine the Acuteness versus the Chronicity of any Problems or Weaknesses Found

The "age" of a problem is important to diagnosis and to treatment planning. When a thorough history is combined with the pattern of test results obtained, it is possible, with reasonable accuracy, to distinguish chronic neurodevelopmental disorders such as dyslexia or ADHD from new, acute problems resulting from trauma, stroke, or disease. Particular care must be taken in developing a thorough, documented history when such a determination is made. Rehabilitation and habilitation approaches take differing routes in the design of intervention and treatment strategies, depending upon the acuteness or chronicity of the problems evidenced. As people with neurodevelopmental disorders age, symptoms will wax and wane as well, and distinguishing new from old symptoms is important when treatment recommendations are being made.

6. Testing Should Locate Intact Complex Functional Systems

The brain functions as a series of interdependent, systemic networks Luria (1964) referred to as "complex functional systems." Multiple systems are affected by CNS problems, but some systems are almost always spared except in the most extreme cases. It is imperative in the assessment process to locate strengths and intact systems that can be used to overcome the problems the person is experiencing. Treatment following CNS compromise involves habilitation and rehabilitation, with the understanding that some organic deficits will represent permanently impaired systems. As the brain consists of complex, interdependent networks of systems that produce behavior, the ability to ascertain intact systems is crucial to enhancing the probability of designing successful treatment. Identification of intact systems also suggests the potential for a positive outcome, as opposed to fostering low expectations and fatalistic tendencies on identification of brain damage or dysfunction. Even in the case of chronic neurodevelopmental disorders, the location of strengths in cognitive as well as behavioral domains is key to developing intervention programs based on teaching methods that are driven by student characteristics as opposed to other factors.

7. Testing Should Assess Affect, Personality, and Behavior

Neuropsychologists sometimes ignore their roots in psychology and focus on assessing the neural substrates of a problem. However, CNS compromise will result in changes in affect, personality, and behavior. Some of these changes will be transient and some will be permanent. Some of these changes will be direct (i.e., the results of CNS compromise at the cellular and systemic levels), and others will be indirect (i.e., reactions to loss or changes in function, or to how others respond to and interact with the individual). A thorough history, including times of onset of problem behaviors, can assist in determination of direct versus indirect effects. Such behavioral changes will also require intervention, and intervention will not necessarily be the same if the changes noted are direct versus indirect or if premorbid behavior problems were evident. School psychologists many times do not assess behavior and personality when evaluating a referral associated more commonly with cognitive issues such as learning disabilities and intellectual impairments. However, students with a learning disability, as well as students with mental retardation and a host of other chronic neurodevelopmental problems, frequently have comorbid behavioral and emotional disorders (e.g., see Fletcher-Janzen & Reynolds, 2003). Additionally, assessment of behavioral and emotional status provides key information about the integrity of some very important brain systems, particularly the executive functions of the frontal regions that are heavily responsible for self-regulation of behavior and affect.

8. Test Results Should be Presented in Ways that are Useful in a School Environment, not Just to Acute Care or Intensive Rehabilitation Facilities, or to Physicians

This should go without saying but our personal experiences argue otherwise. While the ability to communicate to school professionals effectively is a strength for most school psychologists, at times those who receive training and supervision in neuropsychology after obtaining their school psychology degree will write reports that are more appropriate for medical settings. A review of the primary distinctions in school-based versus medically-based neuropsychological assessment practice given in Table 17.1 should highlight the need to communicate and to recommend programs that are feasible in a school environment and readily understood by those who must implement such interventions.

HISTORY AND CONTEXT ARE CRUCIAL TO NEUROPSYCHOLOGICAL ASSESSMENT

We have chosen to emphasize history and context in this chapter because our many years of experience tell us that a detailed history and/or contextual analysis is the foundation of a successful neuropsychological assessment/intervention. In addition, our experience tells us that history and context are elements of assessment (of any kind) that are seldom obtained in school-based evaluations. We wish to promote enhancement of history taking and understanding of context as components of the school neuropsychological examination in a formal but expedient manner. The elements of history taking and context examined in this section are not exhaustive, but illustrative of the breadth and depth of knowledge needed by the clinician to provide an adequate foundation on which to base the neuropsychological assessment and resultant recommendations for intervention and follow-up.

File Reviews

Children's referrals come with varying amounts of history. A file review looks for patterns in information, omissions of information, conflicting information, previous test results, clues to premorbid functioning (Vanderploeg, 1994), and clues as to when and how the child's problems began and took hold. Following is a list of items that would be of particular interest to a school neuropsychologist during a file review:

Absences from School

Lack of exposure to the school curriculum may be responsible for some low scores on achievement tests and social or adaptive tests. Many children with chronic illness or severe injuries from accidents may miss a great deal of the school year and, therefore, not evidence academic skills that would be age appropriate. While this factor may not influence neuropsychological tests results per se, it will affect how those results are interpreted. The interventions for children with lack of exposure to the curriculum are different than for those who have neuropsychological deficits who do not miss school. Simply put, the school neuropsychologist seeks to find out why low achievement scores are present and exposure to the curriculum is a very good place to start.

History of Chronic Illness

A large part of differential diagnosis for children with chronic illness is weighing the neuropsychological effects of the disorder, the effects of medications for the disorder (positive and negative), the existence of secondary or comorbid effects of the disorder (e.g., depression), expectations of family and teachers regarding stereotypes associated with the disorder, quality and duration of medical attention, and exposure to the curriculum. Even with a detailed file, this is difficult at best. The interventions, however, for each of the above effects by themselves or together are different and, therefore, they need to be identified as much as possible. The clinician needs to mark questions about the disorder for future use during the history taking with the family.

Evidence of Events that Could Have Induced Psychological Trauma

The neuropsychological detective waits for diagnostic cues. Often times, the file review will note an event with no mention of its severity or the reaction to the event. For example, the file may note that the child was in an automobile accident where a family member in the car died, but there will be no mention of any injuries sustained, psychological trauma incurred, or follow-up treatment. Other times, the file review will note multiple moves, major life changes, and other stressors known to evoke adjustment problems. Again, the clinician needs to make notes for further questioning about these events during history taking with the family.

Evidence of Events that Could be Reflective of Neurotoxin Exposure

An unfortunate characteristic of neurotoxic exposure in children is that it is often unidentified especially if the exposure did not cause an emergency room visit as with an accidental overdose of medicine, for example. Therefore the clinician needs to be alert for negative symptoms that happen suddenly, or if a sibling exhibits the same symptoms, or symptoms occurring after a move to a new home. Notes in the file that suggest normal early development and then a change in behavior and skill levels should be investigated for many obvious reasons including neurotoxin exposure.

Prior Assessments

The file review often provides previous assessment results. More often than not, the previous school assessments will deal more with the psychoeducational aspects of special education eligibility rather than neuropsychological assessments. The former assessments are helpful indicators of how the child has functioned in the past, how the child responded to individual testing, and what recommendations were offered and implemented. The clinician should note if the prior referral question was the same as the present question and how previous school systems coped with the child's deficits and strengths.

Developmental/Medical History Taken with Caregivers

It is imperative that the school neuropsychologist conduct a thorough history of the child with the primary caregivers. However, the history-taking process in neuropsychological assessment is often much more diagnostic, prescriptive and influenced by medical references. In addition, young children have smaller "repertoires of objectively measurable behaviors" (Hartlage & Williams, 1990, p. 47). Therefore, developmental indices that can be documented by other means are crucial for creating a comprehensive diagnostic picture. Berg, Franzen, and Wedding (1987) suggest that

> A careful history is the most powerful weapon in the arsenal of every clinician, whether generalist of specialist. Brain-behavior relations are extremely complex and involve many different moderator variables, such as age, level of premorbid functioning, and amount of education. Without knowledge of values for these moderator variables, it is virtually impossible to interpret even specialized, sophisticated test results. (p. 47)

This statement takes on more emphasis when working with children and adolescents because estimates of premorbid functioning often rely on subjective accounts from caregivers about dynamic developmental processes (Baron & Gioia, 1998), despite the availability and increased accuracy of empirical methods.

Teeter and Semrud-Clikeman (1997) have suggested that the history is important for several reasons: identifying risk factors during pregnancy and delivery that have been associated with neurodevelopmental disorders; uncovering previous head trauma and/or other health factors; determining the presence of similar or related disorders in other family members or hereditary linkages that might be helpful for understanding the etiology of a particular disorder; determining the nature and extent of the developmental correlates of the child's problem; and determining the presence of coexisting disorders that affect long-term outcomes.

During the history-taking session it is possible to forge a relationship with the family that will maximize cooperation and provide a stakehold in the assessment process. It is a good opportunity to show the family that the clinician cares about the child and that their input is important. It is an opportunity to form a trusting relationship where information that ordinarily may remain hidden comes to light. The treatment process really begins with the initial contact with the family and there may be some opportunities to correct misconceptions about the child's condition and even mismanagement of illnesses and other conditions that might be exacerbating the issues at hand.

It is important for the clinician to determine if there are any socioeconomic issues facing the family that have affected the child to date or may get in the way of appropriate treatment in the future. Families from lower socioeconomic groups may not have access to health care and may have difficulty prioritizing the needs of the child with the needs of the family. If there are socioeconomic obstacles to treatment, the clinician needs to include these variables into the treatment plans.

There are many fine examples of background interviews and structured histories available on the market (e.g., the Structured Developmental History, Reynolds & Kamphaus, 2004; also see Swaiman, 1999). Table 17.2 shows some of the elements that neurologists use in a history taking. Most of the time, the clinicians use the form with which they are most comfortable. Some use established forms like those of Reynolds and Kamphaus (2004) and others prefer to establish their own. Clinician-designed forms have the advantage of reflecting the information needed for special settings and populations.

Long before any objective neuropsychological tests enter the assessment process, the clinician investigates any data that is related to central nervous system (CNS) functioning. Most of the time the history will be negative for telling CNS events. However, when the conversation proceeds from one developmental period to another, or from one story to another, the clinician has to be aware of when to probe and when to move on to other topics. All of this information claims the clinician's attention and becomes magnified or recedes depending on how it fits into the diagnostic picture. The history-taking session should not be viewed as a "netting operation with data to be subsequently sorted" (Swaiman, 1999, p. 10); it should be a system where data are synthesized as they are collected and then used to change the direction, breadth, and depth of questions. Differential diagnosis hypotheses should be pretty well formed by the time the clinician starts to use the objective test portion of the assessment. The information from the referral question, file review, and the developmental history creates hypotheses and questions that objective testing can help answer.

Neurologists follow a similar history-taking sequence as they organize incoming information to help with differential diagnosis. Of course, neurologists work from the medical model, but it is not uncommon for neuropsychologists and neurologists to work hand in hand, and it is important to know how neurologists regard history taking. Swaiman (1999) explains:

> The chief complaint should trigger the process of differential diagnosis in the examiner's thinking, which begins as a listing of the disease conditions that could cause the chief complaint at the child's age. The following three specific questions should be answered, if possible, in the history of the present illness: (1) Is the process acute or insidious? (3) Is it focal or generalized? And (3) Is it progressive or static? The order in which disease findings develop and the precise time of onset of symptoms and signs may be critical factors in the process of accurate diagnosis. The presence of repeated episodes or associate phenomena should be determined. Detailed questions should be asked of the caregivers and child to elucidate the facts. (p. 1)

The neurologist wants to know if the chief complaint is acute or insidious because the way that a condition manifests in terms of time can help diagnosis which systems are involved. For example, degenerative diseases symptoms progress over weeks or months whereas infectious diseases may reach highest levels within a day to several days. The neurologist also wants to know if the symptoms manifest in a focal, multifocal, or generalized way. This knowledge helps in understanding where a problem might be located in the brain. In addition, knowing if the condition is progressive or static is gained from the history taking and usually takes the form of finding out that the child can no longer perform some developmental milestones that were previously marked. Conditions that are static or that improve spontaneously are sometimes the result of traumatic or anoxic episodes, acute toxicity, or resolving infection (Hartlage & Williams, 1990; Swaiman, 1999).

The school neuropsychologist has to go outside of the familiar research disciplines to be aware of the breadth and depth of possible factors that can affect a child's neuropsychological functioning. It is not possible, in the context of this chapter, to describe each element of the history taking in detail. However, some descriptions of the different areas of history taking may provide some insight into why we ask the questions and what we can do with the answers.

TABLE 17.2 Typical Neurological History-Taking List

Adapted from Swaiman, (1999).

- Family history of illness
- Family history of perception about illness
- Family current health
  Siblings
  Extended family
- Genetic illnesses in family
- Prenatal
  Medications taken by mother
  Substances taken by mother (alcohol, tobacco, other)
  Illnesses during pregnancy
  Stressors during pregnancy
  Prenatal care
- Labor & Delivery
  Breech or unusual position
  Forceps used
  Delay in respiration or cry
  APGAR score
  Oxygen administered?
  Type of anesthesia employed for mother
- Newborn Period
  Jaundice
  Cyanosis
  Infections
  Seizures
  Anemia

Medications administered
Home from hospital in _____ days
- Development
  Smiled
  First words
  Put words together "bye-bye"
  Complete sentences
  Rolled over
  Sat without support
  Pulled to standing
  Walked around furniture
  Walked unassisted
- Illnesses
  Hospitalizations
  Operations
  Injuries
  Accidental poisonings
  History of being knocked out, unconscious
  History of convulsions/seizures
  History of ear infections
  History of sleep disturbances
  History of somatic complaints
- Other
  Eating habits
  Sudden changes in development
  Early traumatic events
  Hearing screening results
  Vision screening results

Adapted from Fletcher-Janzen (2005). Copyright John Wiley and Sons, with permission of the copyright holder.

Reason for Referral

Initially children are referred to a school psychologist because of learning or behavioral problems. Parents may seek a diagnosis of Learning Disabled or ADHD as they see their children struggling in school. Parents may voice concern about their inability to cope with their child's problems at home and at school because of "hyper-ness" or "inability to sit still." Many times the child's learning difficulties are not explained by a simple discrepancy between their intellectual functioning and their academic abilities. The school psychologist with training in neuropsychology seeks to look at the testing results and apply that clinical competence to add to his or her already acquired professional knowledge.

Oftentimes, teachers and parents are unable to define a specific referral question. Their primary concern is related to an inability to function in the classroom. Teachers are often unprepared to address these difficulties and do not understand the specific learning problems of children with brain dysfunction. No two learning disabilities or brain dysfunctions are exactly the same. Two children may present with the same diagnosis or brain injury and still require different modifications in the classroom based on their individual learning strengths and weaknesses. Parents as well as teachers are looking for answers—ways to teach their children and to provide appropriate educational opportunities. A neuropsychological evaluation helps to furnish that information; it provides data for answering the question "So what do we do now?" after a diagnosis has been made. The information gained from a neuropsychological evaluation enables the school psychologist to make recommendations concerning attention, learning and memory, intellectual functioning, cognitive strengths and weaknesses, problem-solving abilities, and so forth to the parents and the educators.

Once the reason for referral has been reviewed and refined, understanding the child's history and the current context of the child's life are crucial. There are many areas to assess in taking a history and not all require the in-depth evaluation or information gathering to be noted below—sometimes a "no" from the parent is sufficient to move on.

Family History of Illness

Finding a family history of a particular disorder or disease sets the diagnostic journey for the clinician, and it is important to couch questions in terms that are easily understood by the family. On the other hand, the clinician needs to be alert to language used by the family and help them define conditions. For example, symptoms may be described by the family in less specific names such as "fainting spells," "nervous breakdown" and these terms need to be clarified and documented (Swaiman, 1999). On the other hand, the clinician may have to use less medical terms to help the family understand what types of illnesses are being investigated. In general, the most important fact is to determine if the child in question suffers from any problems that are shared with other family members and if the information suggests alternate neuropsychological interpretations (Hartlage & Williams, 1990).

History Positive for Problems with Attention

Attention is not a pure brain function. It is really a group of processes dependent on many other brain functions and it is very difficult to define (Light, et al., 1996). Light et al. define attention as "a flexible state of cognitive alertness directed toward stimuli over time and in the face of competing stimuli associated with a task-appropriate response" (p. 273).

The diagnosis of attentional problems is established on the positive history for inattention, impulsivity, and hyperactivity (Barkley, 2003; Shaywitz, Fletcher, & Shaywitz, 1999). There are several interrelated components of attention: arousal, sustained attention/vigilance, selective/divided attention, and shifting/alternating attention (Barkley, 2003; Light et al., 1996). It might be possible when taking a history to help the family delineate different aspects of attention by asking questions about functional behaviors associated with attention. For example, instead of asking if the child exhibits sustained attention or vigilance it might be more appropriate to couch the question as "Does he start his homework and then stay with it until it is finished?" or "Does she concentrate on her homework even if her favorite song comes on the radio?"

During history taking it is important to note if the family has a realistic expectation of attentional capacity in the child. Many behaviors that are considered to be inattentive at one age may be perfectly normal for a younger child (Shaywitz et al. 1999). Inattention is also highly comorbid with brain injury, neurotoxic effects; learning disabilities, and psychiatric disorders, therefore, the clinician needs to make sure that previous diagnoses of ADHD or a layperson diagnosis of ADHD does not color the interview process by preconceived notions of what ADHD is or is not.

History Positive for Ear Infections/Hearing Problems

There are many genetic, congenital, and acquired reasons for hearing loss in children and the single most important variable related to education is age of onset. The ramifications of language and cultural development differ greatly for children who experience hearing loss prelingually because they are not able to experience the usual course of language development.

One diagnostic area that provides some work for the school neuropsychologist is the investigation of intermittent hearing loss in children who have experienced repeated otitis media. Otitis media is responsible for more reading problems than any other physical illness. The research literature, for many years, has suggested that chronic conditions, regardless of onset, can also significantly interfere with language/speech acquisition (Rapin, 1999).

A detailed history should be taken for those children positive for repeated ear infections. The clinician should take note as to the frequency, intensity, duration, and treatment history. In addition, the clinician should ask about concomitant behaviors that might signal hearing loss. For example, the child not responding when his or her name is called, ignoring verbal/social cues, or having trouble with beginning phonological awareness skills.

Rapin (1999) suggests "the mere suspicion of hearing loss in such children requires prompt, definitive assessment of hearing and middle ear function with physiologic testing, without wasting time on repeated and unreliable behavioral tests" (p. 87). This is good advice because there are so many varying degrees of hearing loss that have different consequences, and the technology to definitively evaluate hearing loss is readily available even within most school districts.

Clinicians should note that some children are able to pass hearing screenings in the school because they may have sloping hearing losses that are common and affect higher tones to a much greater degree than lower frequencies. Activities and tests that measure lower frequencies will not catch the subtle high frequency losses and the child might appear quite normal. Screening may also miss fluctuating hearing loss resulting from chronic middle ear effusion that can last for weeks after an ear infection (Rapin, 1999).

History Positive for Vision Problems

Vision disorders are the fourth most common disability among children in the United States. As many as 2–5% of preschool children are estimated to have impaired vision. Despite the prevalence of vision disorders, however, there is not a set of universally accepted standardized guidelines for vision screening in the public schools. In addition, vision screening conducted in the United States varies by state and geographic region. Although as many as 94% of children aged birth to 17 years in the US have access to a ongoing source of health care, studies estimate that only 21% of all preschool children are screened for vision problems and only 14% receive a comprehensive vision exam (American Academy of Pediatrics, 2003).

Many school vision screenings are limited to visual acuity measures and are inadequate because they do not address visual efficiency problems such as near focus, near point convergence, tracking saccades and pursuits, and other diseases of the eye (Swaiman, 1999). These fine eye movements make up a large portion of the visual sensory motor components needed for reading. Any child that is referred with reading problems should be evaluated regarding the oculomotor movements that he or she makes when reading (American Academy of Pediatrics, 2003). There are some behavioral indicators associated with visual efficiency problems; children with near point convergence problems,

for example, have trouble getting both eyes to focus on the same point, especially in close-up activities. Behaviors that are common to this problem are covering one eye during visually taxing activities, complaining of double vision, complaining of headaches, and other behaviors that reflect severe eyestrain. On the other hand, children with tracking problems tend to lose their place when they are reading, skip lines, and have problems with reading comprehension because of the missed or mixed-up text.

School psychologists and neuropsychologists can obtain training from eye-care professionals to perform basic screenings for visual efficiency disorders, and the results should be carefully evaluated against behavioral indicators and reading test results. Currently, there is no data to suggest that visual efficiency disorders are revealed by visual processing or visual-motor subtests commonly found on ability batteries or any other standardized measures of visual processing. As with any other salient information in the school neuropsychological history taking, a small piece of accurate information can inform the differential diagnosis and change the whole course of the assessment and intervention. There is growing evidence that visual efficiency problems are currently going undetected, are not causes for referrals when they are detected, are not included in school vision screenings, are not mentioned in school psychology training programs, and can be major sources of reading problems in children. School neuropsychologists, therefore, need to seek training in the field of vision disorders to enhance their diagnostic abilities with children referred for academic problems.

History Positive for Febrile Seizures

Febrile seizures are seizures in association with fever in the absence of a CNS infection or acute electrolyte imbalance in children older than 1 month of age without a history of prior afebrile seizures. Physicians can only make the diagnosis of a febrile seizure if other causes have been ruled out. On the whole febrile seizures are benign and very few signal the beginning of epilepsy or other neurologic disorder.

Febrile seizures occur in the United States in 2–4% of the population, with the peak incidence at 18 months of age (American Academy of Pediatrics, 1996). The risk factors for recurrent febrile seizures are: family history of febrile seizures, younger than 18 months of age, height of temperature and duration of fever. Between 2%

and 10% of children who have febrile seizures will go on to develop epilepsy, and the risk factors for this relationship are: neurodevelopmental abnormality, complex febrile seizure, family history of epilepsy, and duration of fever.

In general, if the developmental history of the child is positive for febrile seizures, it may be appropriate for the clinician to dig a little deeper as to the details of the frequency, duration, and medical management of the seizures. The risk of febrile seizures developing into epilepsy or being indicative of neurologic disease is small but neuropsychologists often deal with small brain factors that can have large behavioral effects.

History Positive for Afebrile Seizures or Epilepsy

School neuropsychologists will rarely be involved in helping diagnose epilepsy. Involvement is usually for purposes of establishing a baseline or for evaluation of neurocognitive and neurobehavioral status (Hartlage & Williams, 1990). Epilepsy is diagnosed after a child has had two or more seizures that are not related to a concurrent illness such as brain injury, fever, or drug intoxications. The definition of epilepsy allows for a large variety of disorders because the age of onset, etiology, severity, comorbid diagnoses, medication management, and prognosis vary widely. Issues associated with the negative cognitive, social, and emotional sequelae of antiepileptic medications are also added to the management of epilepsy, yielding a general call for neuropsychologists to be involved in cases of epilepsy right from the beginning of treatment.

Differential diagnosis of seizure disorders is difficult and in many cases cannot stand on the results of an EEG or imaging results alone (Camfield & Camfield, 1999). Reflexive seizures resulting from vasodepressor syncope or cyanotic breath-holding are easily misinterpreted as epilepsy; and disorders such as tic disorder, migraines, vertigo, night terrors, sleep walking, self-stimulatory behaviors, cardiac dysrhythmias, startle disease, and temper tantrums with amnesia for the rage event are commonly mistaken for seizure activity (Camfield & Camfield, 1999).

The school neuropsychologist cannot diagnose epilepsy, but he or she can be of considerable help to physicians who are in the process of making a diagnosis. A detailed history of seizure-like behaviors and a thorough knowledge of the child's medical history with current observations can help with differential diagnosis. For those children who are referred with a known seizure disorder, the school neuropsychologist can help with the treatment goal of minimal medication side effects with little or no seizure activity. This goal is difficult to reach and is made much easier by the services of a professional who is trained to document brain-behavior activities.

History Positive for Sleep Disorders

Sleep disorders in childhood are often age dependent and related to the child's physical, emotional, and neurologic development. Questions about sleep history should include information about bedtime, sleep onset, duration of nighttime sleep, morning awakening, daytime behavior/naps and general concerns. This may help the clinician decide if the sleep problem fits into the differential diagnosis of dyssomnia, those disorders associated with initiating and/or maintaining sleep or producing excessive daytime sleepiness. The parasomnias are phenomena associated with arousal, partial arousal, and sleep state transition. The third group includes sleep problems associated with medical or psychiatric disorders (American Sleep Disorders Association, 1990). The relationship between sleep interruption and deprivation and its negative effects on social, emotional, and academic functioning has long been established, and the examination of the sleep habits of any child or adolescent is well worth the time and effort.

History Positive for Headaches

Serious neurological disorders are uncommon causes of headaches. Various conditions such as tumors, brain abscesses, hypertension, vasculitis, subdural hematoma, and hemorrhage do, however, create headaches (Rothner, 1999). Common headaches that are the primary disorder are called migraine, tension, or cluster, and are classified using the temporal pattern of the headache plotted against the severity of the headache. There are five patterns that can be identified: acute, acute recurrent, chronic progressive, chronic nonprogressive, and mixed (Rothner, 1999).

Questions that are asked by the clinician during the history taking should attempt to denote if the headaches are acute or chronic, static or progressive, or run in the family, just to get a general idea of the scope and severity of the headache episodes. Of course, the proper diagnosis of a significant history of headaches needs to be checked out by a medical professional.

History Positive for Traumatic Brain Injury

The incidence of pediatric brain injury is high and all episodes of loss of consciousness, concussions, contusions, lacerations, and hematomas concerning the brain should be investigated in detail by the school neuropsychologist. The most common sequelae of brain injury are attention and memory problems, which makes TBI of special concern in the schools.

Linking neurologic sequelae to sports injuries or other incidents common to active children and adolescents (falls, bicycle accidents) is difficult. Symptoms of mild brain injury or concussion vary widely and may include, dizziness, headaches, irritability, memory problems, and impaired concentration lasting from days to months (Teeter & Semrud-Clikeman, 1997). These types of symptoms may have serious behavioral consequences for social relationships and academic performance but are simply not recognized by many professionals in the public schools.

Any intimation that the child in question has sustained a concussion, mild brain injury, or moderate to severe brain injury should be investigated at length by the school neuropsychologist. The exact circumstances and date of the injury should be ascertained. The course of immediate and then ongoing treatment should be documented. In addition, questions about post injury symptoms are essential.

History of Hypoxic-Ischemic Injury of the Brain

Children with a positive history for near drowning, electric shock, severe acute asthma, airway obstruction, aspiration or cardiac arrest may have sequelae of oxygen deprivation and incidents should be investigated. The brain damage resulting from hypoxic-ischemic episodes is represented by cell necrosis and programmed cell death especially in the hippocampus and cortical layers III and V. Five minutes of oxygen deprivation will create cell death within 48 to 72 hours (Perkin & Ashwall, 1999). Neuropsychological deficits after oxygen deprivation of this nature vary widely and are related to the length of deprivation and type of treatment received during the emergency.

Special attention should be paid to learners with asthma, which is a condition that is on the increase. Hypoxic episodes for young children with asthma are not uncommon. They create loss of consciousness and cyanosis related to mild brain damage. Indeed, severe asthma attacks are the leading cause for pediatric hospitalizations and school absenteeism. In addition, from the school neuropsychological point of view, there is always the impact of lack of exposure to the curriculum (because of excessive medical absences) further compounding differential diagnosis. The morbidity and mortality rates are climbing for asthma. Mortality is associated with lack of proper diagnosis of asthma severity and lack of adequate treatment due to limited funds for access (Perkin & Ashwall, 1999). Therefore, careful attention should be paid to the family's history of access to health care during the history taking. The clinician should also pay attention to the history of how the disease has been medically treated, and screen for side effects of medications such as: growth delay, cognitive deficits, nervousness, nausea, hyperactivity, drowsiness, and problems with visual and tactile motor tasks.

History Positive for Poisoning/Neurotoxin Exposure

Children are more likely at risk than adults for neurotoxic exposure to many substances (Hartman, 1995). Human neurotoxic damage can occur directly from toxic injury to the neuron, and/or indirectly insofar as injury to other body systems (e.g., pulmonary, renal) produces secondary neuronal damage with consequent neuropsychological dysfunction (Tarter, Edwards, & Van Thiel, 1988, cited in Hartman, 1995).

There are so many different sources of toxins it is difficult to summarize possible sources of neurotoxins with children. Industrial toxins range from localized sources such as industrial factory emissions near a child's home to household items such as pesticides, solvents, and cleaning items. Biologic agents can range from tobacco products to flowers, plants, and venom from snakes; medications are also a common source of neurotoxins with children. Younger children may copy adults taking medications and ingest inappropriate substances, may ingest accidental overdoses from caregivers, may simply like the taste of some medications and drink or eat them without parent knowledge, or have access to medications that do not have child-locks. Teenagers are much more likely to ingest toxic substances in suicide attempts or through substance abuse. Common suicide methods include exhaust inhalation, overdose on medications, and substances with alcohol ingestion.

Any history that is positive for toxin exposure presents a unique problem for the school neuropsychologist because it will require finding out exactly what the substance was, age at exposure, short-term reaction to exposure, long-term reaction to exposure, and establishment of level of monitoring required. This profile is highly individualized and substance specific. The clinician may be required to research information about the toxin and consult with medical personnel for clarification.

The history surrounding a neurotoxic event (and other acquired brain injuries) also has to focus on premorbid functioning, which in the case of children, is compounded by natural physical, cognitive, social, emotional, and academic development. Children are "moving targets" concerning assessment, and the school neuropsychologist has to weigh natural development, subclinical symptoms becoming visible, a child "growing into" disabilities caused by toxic substances, and possible medical treatment effects.

Behavioral toxicology batteries for children have received comparatively little attention in the research literature (Hartman, 1995). General core batteries that cover all areas of neuropsychological functioning should be administered so that important areas of functioning are not unwittingly left out. The clinician should also keep in mind that nonverbal abilities tend to be differentially more affected by common neurotoxins and, therefore, the choice of neuropsychological tests (either from a fixed or flexible battery) should load heavily on nonverbal ability assessment (Hartman, 1995).

TRAUMATIC BRAIN INJURY IN THE SCHOOLS

Perhaps the need for school neuropsychological services are best illustrated in the assessment and treatment of children and adolescents with brain injuries. Traumatic brain injury (TBI) is the most common cause of acquired injury in children. More and more children are entering the classroom with significant cognitive and behavioral deficits. Children who sustain traumatic brain injuries have impaired functioning in many areas including neurologic and endocrine, neuromuscular and orthopedic, neurocognitive, and neuropsychiatric (Guthrie, Mast, Richards, McQuaid, & Pavlakis, 1999). The extent of these deficits is not fully understood or evident immediately following the injury. Even

after acute hospitalization and rehabilitation, it is difficult to know the child's recovery process. Although the word "recovery" is used frequently during the healing process, the implication may be better expressed with the word "improvement." With "recovery" linked to a "return to normal," parents may develop unrealistic hopes (Lezak, 1986). Immediately following the injury, parents are focused on whether the child will live and they may be unable to think about any subsequent physical, motor, cognitive, and behavioral deficits that may result from an injury. Additionally, there is little information about the recovery process or the time required to recover. Moreover, when information is provided in the acute setting, parents often are unable to hear or understand what is being said to them. All they know is that they want "their child back."

However, when the child enters an educational environment, many factors affect the way the child learns and behaves. Children who have obvious physical deficits associated with their traumatic brain injury are most easily understood, and accommodations are readily provided. When a child enters the classroom in a wheelchair or with a walker, we as educators are quickly reminded that the child has sustained injuries. In contrast, when children are seemingly age-appropriate (walking and talking with no obvious physical deficits), it is easy to assume that they have made a complete recovery and require no academic or behavioral assistance. If the child had a cast on his or her head, that would serve as a reminder that the child will require modification, academically and behaviorally, for some time.

The learning deficits observed in a child who has sustained a neurological insult may be subtle. Because the child's brain is maturing and continuing to change, it is often difficult to determine if the deficits are a result of a developmental lag or a dysfunction of the central nervous system. Understanding of the neuropsychological development of a child may help the school psychologist in the selection of appropriate testing instruments, the interpretation of the results, and the implementation of appropriate recommendations. "By integrating neuropsychological insights into a more comprehensive conceptualization of the challenges of functioning in a school setting, school psychologists may supplement their methods for understanding children and improve the provision of services to children" (Berson, 1990).

Children are entering the school system from a post-hospital setting and continue to require extensive modifications as they remain in acute phase of recovery. Continued monitoring of their recovery and cognitive strengths and weaknesses is essential as their cognitive condition continually changes.

A significant proportion of children who suffer a brain injury are at risk for impairments in the developmental process. A wide range of factors interacts to determine the extent and nature of impairments following brain injuries in children. The type and severity of injury sustained are closely related to outcome (Lowenthal, 1998). Developmental issues, including age at injury and pre-injury abilities also have been found to impact ongoing development post-injury (Anderson & Moore, 1995; Taylor & Alden, 1997). Children sustaining early injuries may present with similar patterns of impairment, but have poorer outcomes than do children sustaining their injuries later in childhood (Anderson & Moore, 1995; Wrightson, McGinn, & Gronwall, 1995). As a child matures and societal demands increase in complexity, problems with cognition and executive function may emerge (Guthrie et al., 1999). The full extent of the effects of brain injury in children may not be realized for some time because the long-term consequences may involve impairments in planning, execution of personal goals, and social behavior.

The brain injury sustained by a child occurs concurrently with development and may create an incomplete collection of abilities (Brazzelli, Colombo, Della Sala, & Spinnler, 1994). When a child suffers a brain injury, damaged brain cells cannot regenerate or repair themselves; however, new neural connections can form between the intact areas of the brain. These new connections allow areas of the developing brain to take over the functions of the injured brain cells (Lowenthal, 1998). However, this reorganization of brain functions usually results in a cost to the child's overall cognitive capacity. For example, past research indicated that the young child's right hemisphere can assume the language functions of the damaged dominant left hemisphere (Keefe, Feldman & Holland, 1989). Other studies, however, reported that general language functioning is compromised in young children when the right hemisphere has to take over language development (Hemphill et al., 1994). Adverse effects of brain injury often are not apparent in young children because there are limited cognitive skills established at a young age. However, as infants and toddlers mature, delays

are more evident and children may "grow into" their deficits with new impairments emerging as expected developmental gains are not achieved (Bannich, Cohen-Levine, Kim, & Huttenlocher, 1990; Dennis, Wilkinson, Koski, & Humphreys, 1995).

In young school-age children who sustain a brain injury, impairments are most evident in areas of nonverbal functioning, attention, memory, and learning. Postinjury performance IQ scores, which involve nonverbal functioning, visuomotor ability, and processing speed are a more sensitive correlate of severity of injury than verbal IQs (Max et al., 1998). Perceptual difficulties may persist for many of these children. Following a traumatic brain injury, children may have difficulties with spatial concepts and often have difficulty navigating around the hospital, school, and neighborhood (Guthrie et al., 1999). School-age children who suffer a brain injury often exhibit problems with attention that hinder new learning in the classroom. Anderson and colleagues (1997) found that children who had moderate to severe brain injury displayed greater impairment in sustained and divided attention, whereas focused attention was relatively intact. In the areas of memory and learning, children with brain injuries often retain older, overlearned information; however, they have problems with encoding, storing, and retrieving novel information (Reid & Kelly, 1993).

Slower recovery on motor and visual-spatial tasks has been found in younger adolescents than with older adolescents who experienced a similar head injury (Thompson et al., 1994). Repeated neuropsychological assessment of motor, visual-spatial, and somatosensory skills revealed that younger children with severe injuries recovered slower than not only older children with similar injuries, but also children of the same age with milder head injuries. This research supports the belief that neurological development continues until at least 12 years of age, and that the frontal lobes are the last neurological structure to mature at around 12 to 14 years (Lord-Maes & Obrzut, 1997). As children with brain injuries mature and cognitive demands increase, executive functioning skill deficits emerge and may include problems with: (1) planning and organization, (2) initiating tasks and/or inhibiting behavior, (3) concept formation, (4) cognitive flexibility, and (6) problem-solving (Lowenthal, 1998; Rutter, 1982).

Further information about school-based neuropsychological services for traumatic brain injury can be found in Semrud-Clikeman, Kutz, and Strassner, 2005 and Stanford forthcoming.

BASES FOR EDUCATIONAL MODIFICATIONS

One of the primary reasons for conducting an evaluation is not to determine "what has been impaired," but rather to determine "what has been spared." Educations and parents supply numerous examples of what the child is unable to do. "He cannot follow instructions," "She can't remember anything," "He cannot read." Very seldom does a referral source approach an evaluation with a list of the activities or skills that the child is able to accomplish with ease and proficiency. But whether or not the source realizes it at the time of the referral, such a list contains the very information that is urgently needed for the child to move forward in the educational process. It is essential that we teach to the child's strengths instead of his or her weaknesses. As pointed out by Reynolds (1981), teaching to a child's weaknesses focuses on brain areas that are damaged or dysfunctional. When teaching methods focus on cortical areas that are not intact, the child's potential for failure is increased, and this is harmful to the child. Reynolds (1981) also points out that research on these remedial practices (referred to as "deficit-centered models" of remediation) has found them to be ineffective.

In contrast, teaching to a child's strengths has a number of advantages. This method may be especially helpful for children who are resistant to focused remediation of weaknesses (Rourke et al., 1983). When self-confidence is low or when a failure syndrome emerges as a result of frustration, a strength-centered approach should be adopted. Second, teaching to the child's strengths may reduce the possibility of the child's falling farther and farther below peers in academic areas. Finally, Luria (1973) suggested that recovery of function following cortical damage can be achieved "by the replacement of the lost cerebral link by another which is still intact" (p. 55). "For example, a child with an impaired auditory system could be taught to differentiate simple sounds using visual or nonverbal images" (Teeter & Semrud-Clikeman, 1997, p. 364). More details on strength-centered models of remediation may be found in Reynolds and Hickman (1987).

After the neuropsychologist makes his or her assessment and recommendations, the school personnel and the parents hold a multidisciplinary team meeting. The purposes of this meeting are to make appropriate modifications in the classroom that will enable the child to reach his or her academic potential, and to develop an individualized educational plan (IEP) for the child. In many cases, the educational modifications that teachers are currently using in their regular classrooms (e.g., small groups, modified assignments, individualized instructions) are the only modifications needed. Cohen (1991) suggests developing active learning situations, slowing down, assuring that lesson tasks address the appropriate deficits, teaching the process of the activity, teaching students to become more independent, and developing strategies that can be used in various situations. In other cases, the needed modifications include scheduling or placement issues that involve much more than the regular classroom setting. Placement options include the regular classroom, with no provision or support in the classroom; modified regular education, which could include a lighter course load or special tutorial sessions; a collapsed or half-day schedule; or special education services ranging from part-time to full-time. Class size may also be a consideration. Homebound or residential education programming may be yet another option. Fatigue is common during recovery from a head injury or stroke, and a schedule that allows for a structured rest time may also be a needed option (Cohen, 1991).

SCHOOL PSYCHOLOGIST WITH A SPECIALTY IN NEUROPSYCHOLOGY

School psychologists play an important part in the school system and are faced with a number of challenges. Children enter the school system with a wide variety of central nervous system related deficits ranging from low birth weight, in-utero anomalies, to traumatic brain injury. As the advances in medical technology continue to improve, the number of children with acquired or congenital anomalies entering the school setting will increase, and the school psychologist is presented with more children who need assistance and support services. Many of these children will require continued support to ensure quality of life and appropriate transition into adulthood.

Although school psychologists do not necessarily have training in neuropsychology, many have begun to acquire knowledge in the area. Many graduate programs now have specialized classes in neuropsychology. The annual conferences of NASP (National Association of School Psychologists) and APA Division of School Psychologists have responded to the requests of their members and are offering courses in this area. It has become patently clear to many that the knowledge base of most school psychologists needs to be expanded into incorporating principles of neuropsychological assessment and intervention into everyday practice. The incorporation of neuropsychological assessment principles requires extensive learning on the part of the clinician about the history of neuropsychology, neuropsychological models of brain function, assessment approaches, broad and specific measures of brain function, superior history taking skills, and advanced knowledge about diverse conditions such as epilepsy, neurotoxicology, rare/orphan diseases, traumatic brain injury, developmental disorders, and learning disabilities. In fact, the list of areas of specialized knowledge are limitless and, therefore, require school psychologists who not only wish to learn the basic principles of brain-behavior relationships, but also school psychologists who continue to pursue neuropsychological knowledge with vigor for as long as they practice.

The school psychologist with the appropriate training in brain-behavior relationships has the advantage of being able to monitor a child's progress and observe the child in a variety of settings. No other professional has the opportunity to view the way the child functions in real-life situations with a variety of people. With an understanding of the dynamics of the school, the psychologist is able to observe a child with neuropsychological difficulties in his or her day-to-day structured environment, monitor progress, and provide interventions that are feasible and consistent with the child's needs. Neuropsychology practiced in any venue requires the utmost conviction and dedication to translating research about the brain into remedial treatment of the brain. Perhaps the practice of neuropsychology in the schools has the potential to create an ecologically sound model of intervention that translates research into the classroom and beyond.

REFERENCES

American Academy of Neurology (1996). Assessment: Neuropsychological testing of adults; Considerations for neurologists. *Neurology, 47,* 592–599.

American Academy of Pediatrics (2003). Policy statement: Eye examination in infants, children, and young adults by pediatricians. *Pediatrics, 111,* 902–907.

American Academy of Pediatrics (1996). Provisional committee on quality improvement. Practice parameter: The neurodiagnostic evaluation of the child with a simple febrile seizure. *Pediatrics, 97,* 769.

American Sleep Disorders Association (1990). *The international classification of sleep disorders.* Lawrence, Kansas: Allen Press.

American Medical Association (2001). *Current procedural terminology.* Washington, DC: Author.

Anderson, V. A., & Moore, C. (1995). Age at injury as a predictor of outcome following pediatric head injury. *Child Neuropsychology, 1,* 187–202.

Anderson, V. A., Morse, S. A., Klug, G., et al. (1997). Predicting recovery from head injury in young children: A prospective analysis. *Journal of International Neuropsychology Society, 3,* 568–580.

Bannich, M. T., Cohen-Levine, S., Kim, H., & Huttenlocher, P. (1990). The effect of developmental factors on IQ in hemiplegic children. *Neuropsychologia, 28,* 35–47.

Barkley, R. A. (2003). Attention-deficit/hyperactivity disorder. In E. J. Mash & R. A. Barkley (Eds.), *Child psychopathology* (pp. 75–145). New York: Guilford.

Baron, I. S., & Gioia, G. A. (1998). Neuropsychology of infants and young children. In G. Goldstein, P. D. Nussbaum, & S. R. Beers (Eds.), *Neuropsychology* (pp. 9–29). New York: Plenum.

Batchelor, E. S., & Dean, R. S. (1996). *Pediatric neuropsychology.* Needham Heights, MA: Allyn & Bacon.

Bauer, R. M. (1994). The flexible battery approach to neuropsychological assessment. In R. D. Vanderploeg (Ed.), *Clinician's guide to neuropsychological assessment* (pp. 259–290). Hillsdale, New Jersey: Lawrence Erlbaum Associates.

Bennett, T. L. (2001). Neuropsychological evaluation in rehabilitation planning and evaluation of functional skills. *Archives of Clinical Neuropsychology, 16*(3), 237–253.

Berg, R., Franzen, M., & Wedding, D. (1987). *Screening for brain impairment: A manual for mental health practice.* New York: Springer.

Berson, I. R. (1990). *Neuropsychology in the schools: Implications for school psychology.* Paper presented at the University of Toledo (ERIC Document Reproduction Service No. ED334471).

Bigler, E. D., Nussbaum, N., & Foley, H. (1997). Child neuropsychology in the private medical practice. In C. R. Reynolds & E. Fletcher-Janzen (Eds.), *The handbook of clinical child neuropsychology* (2nd. ed., pp. 725–742). New York: Kluwer/Plenum.

Brazzelli, M., Colombo, N., Della Sala, S., & Spinnler, H. (1994). Spared and impaired cognitive abilities after bilateral frontal damage. *Cortex, 30*(1), 27–51.

Camfield, P. R., & Camfield, C. S. (1999). Pediatric epilepsy: an overview. In K. E. Swaiman & S. Ashwal (Eds.), *Pediatric neurology* (pp. 629–646). St. Louis, MO: Mosby.

Cohen, S. B. (1991). Adapting educational programs for students with head injuries. *Journal of Head Trauma Rehabilitation, 6*(1), 47–55.

D'Amato, R., Fletcher-Janzen, E., & Reynolds, C. R. (Eds.) (2005). *The handbook of school neuropsychology.* NY: John Wiley & Sons.

D'Amato, R. C., Rothlisberg, B. A., & Leu Work, P. H. (1999). Neuropsychological assessment for intervention. In C. R. Reynolds & T. B. Gutkin (Eds.), *Handbook of school psychology* (3rd ed., pp. 452–475). New York: Wiley.

Dennis, M., Wilkinson, M., Koski, L., & Humphreys, R. P. (1995). Attention deficits in the long term after childhood head injury. In S. Broman & M. E. Michel (Eds.), *Traumatic head injury in children* (pp. 165–187). New York: Oxford University Press.

Farmer, J. E., & Peterson L. (1995). Pediatric traumatic brain injury: Promoting successful school reentry. *School Psychology Review, 24*(2), 230–243.

Fennell, E. B. (1994). Issues in child neuropsychological assessment. In R. D. Vanderploeg (Ed.), *Clinician's guide to neuropsychological assessment* (pp. 113–163). Hillsdale, New Jersey: Lawrence Erlbaum.

Fennell, E. B. (2002). Ethical issues in pediatric neuropsychology. In S. S. Bush & M. L. Drexler (Eds.), *Ethical issues in clinical neuropsychology* (pp. 75–86). Lisse, The Netherlands: Swets & Zeitlinger.

Fitzhugh-Bell, K. (1997). Historical antecedents of clinical neuropsychology. In A.M. Horton, D. Wedding, & J. Webster (Eds.), *The neuropsychology handbook* (pp. 67–90). New York: Springer.

Fletcher-Janzen, E. (2005). The school neuropsychological examination. In R. D'Amato, E. Fletcher-Janzen, and C. R. Reynolds (Eds.), *The handbook of school neuropsychology* (pp. 172–212). NY: John Wiley & Sons.

Fletcher-Janzen, E. & Reynolds, C. R. (Eds.) (2003). *Childhood disorders diagnostic desk reference.* NY: John Wiley and Sons.

Golden, C. J. (1986). *The Luria-Nebraska Neuropsychological Battery: Children's revision.* Los Angeles: Western Psychological Services.

Guthrie, E., Mast, J., Richards, P., McQuaid, M., & Pavlakis, S. (1999). Traumatic brain injury in children and adolescents. *Neurological Disorders: Development and behavioral sequelae, 8*(4), 807–826.

Hartlage, L. C., & Williams, B. L. (1990). Neuropsychological assessment in the childhood and adolescent years. In A. MacNeill Horton (Ed.), *Neuropsychology across the life-span: Assessment and treatment* (pp. 44–63). New York: Springer.

Hartman, D. E. (1995). *Neuropsychological toxicology: Identification and assessment of human neurotoxic syndromes.* 2nd ed. New York: Plenum.

Heaton, R. (1981). *Wisconsin card sorting test.* Odessa, FL: Psychological Assessment Resources.

Hemphill, L., Feldman, H. M., Camp, L., Griffin, T. M., Miranda, A. B., & Wolf, D. P. (1994). Developmental changes in narrative and non-narrative discourse in children with and without brain injury. *Journal of Communicative Disorders, 27,* 91–106.

Hynd, G. W. (1981). Rebuttal to the critical commentary on neuropsychology in the schools. *School Psychology Review, 10*(3), 389–393.

Hynd, G. W., & Reynolds, C. R. (2005). School neuropsychology: The evolution of a specialty in school psychology. In R. D'Amato, E. Fletcher-Janzen, and C. R. Reynolds (Eds.), *The handbook of school neuropsychology* (pp. 3–14). NY: John Wiley & Sons.

Kamphaus, R. W. (2001). *Clinical assessment of child and adolescent intelligence.* Needham Heights, MA: Allyn & Bacon.

Kaplan, E. (1998). A process approach to neuropsychological assessment. In T. Boll & B. K. Bryant (Eds.), *Clinical neuropsychology and brain function: Research, measurement, and practice* (pp. 125–167). Washington DC: American Psychological Association.

Kaufman, A. S., & Kaufman, N. L. (1983). *Administration and scoring manual for the Kaufman Assessment Battery for Children.* Circle Pines, MN: American Guidance Service.

Keefe, K. A., Feldman, H. M., & Holland, A. L. (1989). Lexical learning and learning abilities in preschoolers with perinatal brain injury. *Journal of Speech and Hearing Disorders, 54,* 395–402.

Kolb, B., & Whishaw, I. Q. (1990). *Fundamentals of human neuropsychology* (3rd. ed.). New York: W. H. Freeman.

Languis, M. L., & Miller, D. C. (1992). Luria's theory of brain functioning: A model for research in cognitive psychophysiology. *Educational Psychologist, 27,* 493–511.

Lezak, M. D. (1995). *Neuropsychological assessment* (3rd ed.). New York: Oxford University Press.

Lezak, M. D. (1986). Psychological implications of traumatic brain damage for the patient's family. *Rehabilitation Psychology, 3*(4), 241–250.

Light, R., Satz, P., Asarnow, R. F., Lewis, R., Ribbler, A., & Neumann, E. (1996). Disorders of attention. In E. S. Batchelor & R. S. Dean (Eds.), *Pediatric neuropsychology* (pp. 269–302). Needham Heights, MA: Allyn & Bacon.

Lord-Maes, J., & Obrzut, J. E. (1997). Neuro-psychological consequences of traumatic brain injury in children and adolescents. In E. D. Bigler & E. Clark (Eds.), *Childhood traumatic brain injury: Diagnosis, assessment and intervention* (pp. 101–114). Austin, TX: Pro-Ed.

Lowenthal, B. (1998). Traumatic brain injury in early childhood: Developmental effects and interventions. *The Transdisciplinary Journal, 8*(4), 377–388.

Luria, A. R. (1964). Neuropsychology in the local diagnosis of brain damage. *Cortex, 1*, 3–18.

Luria, A. R. (1966a). *Human brain and psychological processes*. New York: Harper & Row.

Luria, A. R. (1966b). *Higher cortical functions in man*. NY: Basic Books.

Luria, A. R. (1973). *The working brain*. London: Penguin.

Max, J. E., Lindgren, S. D., Knutson, C., Pearson, C. S., Ibrig, D., & Welborn, A. (1998). Child and adolescent traumatic brain injury: Correlates of injury severity. *Brain Injury, 12*(1), 31–40.

McCaffrey, R. J., Palav, A. A., O'Bryant, S. E., & Labarge, A. S. (2003). *Practitioner's guide to symptom base rates in clinical neuropsychology*. New York: Kluwer/Plenum.

Perkin, R. M., & Ashwall, S. (1999). Hypoxic-ischemic encephalopathy in infants and older children. In K. E. Swaiman & S. Ashwal (Eds.), *Pediatric neurology* (pp. 915–944). St. Louis, MO: Mosby.

Rapin, I. (1999). Hearing impairment. In K. E. Swaiman & S. Ashwal, (Eds.). *Pediatric neurology* (pp. 77–94). St. Louis, MO: Mosby.

Reid, D., & Kelly, M. (1993). Wechsler Memory Scale-Revised in closed head injury. *Journal of Clinical Psychology, 49*, 245–254.

Reitan, R. M. (1955). The relation of the Trail Making Test to organic brain damage. *Journal of Consulting Psychology, 19*, 393–394.

Reitan, R. M., & Wolfson, D. (1974). *Clinical neuropsychology: Current status and applications*. Washington, DC: Winston.

Reitan, R. M., & Wolfson, D. (1985). *The Halstead-Reitan Neuropsychological Battery. Theory and clinical interpretation*. Tucson, AZ: Neuropsychological Press.

Reitan, R. M., & Wolfson, D. (2001). Critical evaluation of "Assessment: Neuropsychological Testing of Adults." *Archives of Clinical Neuropsychology, 16*(3), 215–226.

Reitan, R. M., & Wolfson, D. (2000). *Mild head injury: Intellectual, cognitive, and emotional consequences*. Tucson, AZ: Neuropsychology Press.

Reynolds, C. R. (1981). The neuropsychological basis of intelligence. In G. Hynd & J. Obrzut (Eds.), *Neuropsychological assessment and the school-aged child* (pp. 87–124). New York: Grune & Stratton.

Reynolds, C.R. (2001). Commentary on the American Academy of Neurology Report on Neuropsychological Assessment. *Archives of Clinical Neuropsychology, 16*(3), 199–200.

Reynolds, C. R. (2002). *Comprehensive trail-making test*. Austin, TX: Pro-Ed.

Reynolds, C. R., & French, C. L. (2005). The brain as a dynamic organ of information processing and learning. In R. D'Amato, E. Fletcher-Janzen, and C. R. Reynolds (Eds.), *The Handbook of school neuropsychology* (pp. 86–119). NY: John Wiley & Sons.

Reynolds, C. R., & Gutkin, T. B. (Eds.) (1982). *The handbook of school psychology*. NY: John Wiley and Sons.

Reynolds, C. R., & Hickman, J. A. (1987). Remediation, deficit-centered models of. In C. R. Reynolds & L. Mann (Eds.), *Encyclopedia of special education* (pp. 1339–1342). New York: Wiley-Interscience.

Reynolds, C. R., & Horton, A. M. (2006). *Test of verbal conceptualization and fluency*. Austin, TX: Pro-Ed.

Reynolds, C. R., & Kamphaus, R. W. (2004). *The Behavior Assesment Scale for Children*–second edition. Circle Pines, MN: AGS.

Reynolds, C. R., Livingston, R. A., & Willson, V. L. (2006). *Measurement and assessment in education*. Boston: Allyn & Bacon.

Reynolds, C. R., & Voress, J. (2007). *Test of Memory and Learning*, second edition. Austin, TX: Pro-Ed.

Riccio, C. A., & Reynolds, C. R. (1998). Neuropsychological assessment of children. In M. Hersen & A. Bellack (Series Eds.) & C. R. Reynolds (Vol. Ed.), *Comprehensive clinical psychology: Vol. 4. Assessment* (pp. 267–302). New York: Elsevier Science.

Rothner, A. D. (1999). Headaches. In K. E. Swaiman & S. Ashwal, (Eds.), *Pediatric neurology* (pp. 747–758). St. Louis, MO: Mosby.

Rourke, B. P., Bakker, D. J., Fisk, J. L., & Strang, J. D. (1983). *Child neuropsychology*. New York: Guilford Press.

Russell, E. W. (1994). The cognitive-metric fixed battery approach to neuropsychological assessment. In R. D. Vanderploeg (Ed.), *Clinician's guide to neuropsychological assessment* (pp. 259–290). Hillsdale, NJ: Lawrence Erlbaum.

Rutter, M. (1982). Syndromes attributed to "minimal brain dysfunction" in childhood. *American Journal of Psychiatry, 139*(1), 21–33.

Sechenov, I. (1965). *Reflex of the brain*. Cambridge, MA: MIT Press. (Original work published 1863).

Semrud-Clikeman, M., Kutz, A. & Strassner, E. (2005). Providing neuropsychological services to students with learning disabilities. In R. D'Amato, E. Fletcher-Janzen, & C. R. Reynolds (Eds.), *The Handbook of School Neuropsychology* (pp. 425–444). NY: John Wiley & Sons.

Shaywitz, B. A., Fletcher, J. M., & Shaywitz, S. E. (1999). Attention-deficit/hyperactivity disorder.

In K. E. Swaiman & S. Ashwal, (Eds.), *Pediatric neurology* (pp. 585–597). St. Louis, MO: Mosby.

Stanford, L. (in press). Pediatric brain injury: Mechanisms and amelioration. In C.R. Reynolds & E. Fletcher-Janzen (Eds.), *Handbook of clinical child neuropsychology*. New York: Springer.

Swaiman, K. F. (1999). Neurologic examination of the older child. In K. E. Swaiman & S. Ashwal, (Eds.), *Pediatric neurology* (pp. 676–691). St. Louis, MO: Mosby.

Taylor, H. G., & Alden, J. (1997). Age-related differences in outcomes following childhood brain insults: An introduction and overview. *Journal of the International Neuropsychological Society, 3*(6), 555–567.

Taylor, H. G., & Fletcher, J. M. (1990). Neuropsychological assessment of children. In G. Goldstein & M. Hersen (Eds.), *Handbook of psychological assessment* (pp. 239–401). New York: Pergamon Press.

Teeter, P. A., & Semrud-Clikeman, M. (1997). *Child neuropsychology: Assessment and intervention for neurodevelopmental disorders*. Needham Heights, MA: Allyn & Bacon.

Thompson, N. M., Francis, D. J., Steubing, K. K., Flecther, J. M., Ewing-Cobbs, I., Miner, M. E. et al. (1994). Motor, visual-spatial, and somatosensory skills after closed head injury in children and adolescents: A study of change. *Neuropsychology, 8*(3), 333–342.

Vanderploeg, R. D. (1994). Estimating premorbid level of functioning. In R.D. Vanderploeg (Ed.), *Clinician's guide to neuropsychological assessment* (pp. 43–68). Hillsdale, NJ: Lawrence Erlbaum.

Wrightson, P., McGinn, V., & Gronwall, D. (1995). Mild head injury in preschool children: Evidence that it can be associated with persisting cognitive defects. *Journal of Neurology, Neurosurgery, and Psychiatry, 59*, 375–380.

Yeates, K. O., & Taylor, G. (1998). Neuropsychological assessment of older children. In G. Goldstein, P. D. Nussbaum, & S. Beers (Eds.), *Neuropsychology* (pp. 35–61). New York: Plenum.

CHAPTER 18

THE PROBLEM OF BIAS

IN PSYCHOLOGICAL ASSESSMENT[1]

CECIL R. REYNOLDS
Texas A&M University
PATRICIA A. LOWE
University of Kansas

In God we trust, all others must have data.
                                    Unknown

The issues of bias in psychological testing have been a source of intense and recurring social controversy throughout the history of mental measurement. In England, Burt (1921) raised the issue early in the last century. The first investigation into cultural bias, however, can be traced to Binet, originating around 1910 in France (Binet & Simon, 1916/1973), and to Stern (1914) shortly thereafter. Discussions pertaining to test bias are frequently accompanied by polemic debate, decrying the use of mental tests with any minority group members since ethnic minorities have not been exposed to the cultural and environmental circumstances and values of the so-called White middle class. Intertwined within the general issues of bias in tests, one finds the more specific question of whether intelligence tests should be used for educational purposes. Although scientific and societal discussions about differences among groups on measures of cognitive or intellectual functioning in no way fully encompass the broader topic of bias in mental measurement, there is little doubt that the so-called IQ controversy has received the lion's share of public scrutiny over the years. It has been the subject of numerous

publications in the more popular press (see Gould, 1981; Herrnstein & Murray, 1994; Jensen, 1980), and court actions and legislation have addressed the use of IQ tests in schools and industry. Court challenges to the use of tests with minorities in educational and vocational settings alike, based on claims of cultural bias, are a common occurrence, despite their limited success.

From Binet to Jensen, many professionals have addressed the problem, with varying and inconsistent outcomes. Unlike the pervasive and polemical nature-nurture argument, the bias issue was until the 1970s largely restricted to the professional literature, except for a few early discussions in the popular press (e.g., Freeman, 1923; Lippmann, 1923a, 1923b). Of some interest is the fact that one of the psychologists who initially raised the question was Cyril Burt (1921), who even in the 1920s, was concerned about the extent to which environmental and motivational factors affected performance on intelligence tests. Within the last 40 years, however, questions of cultural test bias have burst forth as a major problem far beyond the bounds of scholarly academic debate. The debate over bias has raged in both the professional and the popular press for decades (e.g., Brooks, 1997; Fine, 1975). Entangled in the larger issues of individual liberties, civil rights and social justice, the bias issue has become a focal point for psychologists, sociologists, politicians, and the public. Increasingly, the issue has become a political and legal one, as reflected in numerous court cases and passage in the state of New York (and consideration elsewhere) of what is

---

[1]Portions of this chapter are based in part on a variety of previous works, including Reynolds (1982a, 1982b, 1983, 1995, 2000), Reynolds and Brown (1984), Reynolds and Carson (2005), Reynolds and Kaiser (1990), and Reynolds, Lowe, and Saenz (1999).

popularly known as truth-in-testing legislation. The magnitude—and the uncertainty—of the controversy and its outcome are shown in two highly publicized federal district court cases. The answer in trial courts to the question "Are the tests used for pupil assignment to classes for the educable mentally retarded biased against cultural and ethnic minorities?" was yes in California (*Larry P. et al. v. Wilson Riles et al., 1979*) and no in Illinois (PASE, 1980).

The word *bias* has several meanings, not all of which are kept distinct, and researchers and the public do not always know which meaning is being professed. In relation to the present issue, *bias* defined as "partiality toward a point of view or prejudice" and *bias* defined as "a statistical term referring to a constant error in the estimation of some value" (direction as opposed to random error) frequently becomes coalesced. If the latter meaning did not have the excess baggage of the former, the issue of bias in mental testing would be far less controversial and emotional. However, as indicated in the *Oxford English Dictionary*, *bias* defined as "partiality or prejudice" can be traced at least to the sixteenth century and clearly antedates the statistical meaning. Nevertheless, the discussion of bias in psychological testing as a *scientific* issue should concern only the statistical meaning: whether or not there is systematic error in the measurement of a psychological attribute as a function of membership in one or another cultural or racial subgroup (Reynolds, 1982a, 1982b). This definition, elaborated more technically as required later, will be followed throughout this chapter.

THE CONTROVERSY OVER BIAS IN PSYCHOLOGICAL TESTING: WHAT IT IS AND WHAT IT IS NOT

Systematic group differences on standardized intelligence and aptitude tests occur as a function of socioeconomic level, race or ethnic background, and other demographic variables throughout the various countries of the world. Differences between African Americans and Whites on IQ measures in the United States have received extensive investigation over the past 100 years. Jensen (1980), Shuey (1966), Tyler (1965), and Willerman (1979) have reviewed the preponderance of these studies and newer works provide few to no new insights. Results have not changed fundamentally in the last century and few such studies have been published since the early 1980s. Although the results occasionally differ slightly, depending on the age groups under consideration, random samples of African Americans and Whites show a mean difference of about 1 standard deviation, with the mean score of Whites consistently exceeding that of African Americans. The differences have persisted at relatively constant levels for quite some time and under a variety of methods of investigation.

When a number of demographic variables are taken into account (most notably socioeconomic status), the size of the mean difference between African Americans and Whites in the United States reduces to .5 to .7 standard deviations (e.g., Jensen, 1980; Kaufman, 1973; Kaufman & Kaufman, 1973; Reynolds & Gutkin, 1981) but is robust in its appearance. However, not all studies of racial and ethnic group differences on ability tests show higher levels of performance by Whites. Although not as thoroughly researched as African American–White groups, Asian groups have been shown to perform consistently as well as or better than White groups (Pintner, 1931; Tyler, 1965; Willerman, 1979). Depending on the specific aspect of intelligence under investigation, other racial and ethnic groups show performance at or above the performance level of White groups. There have been arguments over whether any racial differences in intelligence are real or even researchable (e.g., Schoenfeld, 1974), but the reliability across studies is very high, even when relying on self-identification of race, and the existence of the differences is now generally accepted. It should always be kept in mind, however, that the overlap among the distributions of intelligence test scores for the different races is much greater than the degree of differences between the various groups. There is always more within-group variability than between-group variability in performance on psychological tests, whether one considers race, ethnicity, gender, or socioeconomic status (SES). The differences are, nevertheless, real ones and are unquestionably complex (e.g., Reynolds & Jensen, 1983).

The issue at hand is the explanation of these group differences. It should be emphasized that both the lower scores of some groups and the higher scores of others need to be explained, although not necessarily, of course, in the same way. The problem was clearly stated by Eells in his classic study of cultural differences (Eells, Davis, Havighurst, Herrick, & Tyler, 1951): "Do the higher test scores of the children from high socioeconomic backgrounds reflect genuine superiority in inherited, or genetic, equipment? Or do the high scores result from a superior environment which has brought about real superiority of the child's 'intelligence'? Or do they reflect a bias in the test materials and not any important differences in the children at all?" (p. 4). Eells et al. also concisely summarized cultural test bias as it applied to differences in SES:

> If (a) the children from different social-status levels have different kinds of experiences and have experiences with different types of material, and if (b) the intelligence tests contain a disproportionate amount of material drawn from the cultural experiences with which pupils from the higher social-status levels are more familiar, one would expect (c) that children from the higher social-status levels would show higher IQs than those from the lower levels. This argument tends to conclude that the observed differences in pupil IQs are artifacts dependent upon the specific content of the test items and do not reflect accurately any important underlying ability in the pupils. (p. 4)

Eells was aware that his descriptions were oversimplifications and that it was unlikely that any one of the three factors alone could explain all of the observed group differences. Loehlin, Lindzey, and Spuhler (1975) concluded that all three factors were probably involved in racial differences in intelligence, as have a myriad of other researchers (e.g., Bouchard & Segal, 1985; Flynn, 1991). In its present, more complex form, the hypothesis of test bias itself considers factors other than culture-loaded items. But the basics of Eells' summary of the hypothesis still hold: group differences stem from characteristics of the test or from aspects of test administration; that is, because mental tests are based largely on middle-class, White values and knowledge, standard interpretations are more valid for those groups and are biased against other groups to the extent that they deviate from those values and knowledge bases.

This position has been reframed slightly over the years, principally by Mercer (1979b), who argued that the lower scores of ethnic minorities on aptitude measures can be traced to the Anglocentrism (degree of adherence to White, middle-class value systems) of aptitude measures. Mercer developed an entire system of assessments

designed to provide complex demographic corrections to IQs obtained by ethnic minorities that had the effect of equating these groups' mean scores on IQ measures. (This system, known as the System of Multicultural Pluralistic Assessment [SOMPA; Mercer, 1979a], was quite popular for several years in the late 1970s and early 1980s, but rapidly lost popularity, and it is rarely used today because of its conceptual and psychometric inadequacies.) Lonner (1985) discusses similar issues under the rubric of cultural isomorphism in testing and assessment. Helms (1994) makes similar criticisms of ability tests, rejects most psychometric research on these issues, and posits (quite similar to Mercer's position) that it is the Eurocentric nature of aptitude tests that produce artifactual differences in mean levels of performance across ethnic lines, focusing especially on the performance of African Americans. Helms (1992) asserts that implicit biological or environmental philosophical perspectives used to explain differences in cognitive ability in test performance across racial and ethnic groups are based on deficient conceptualizations of culture and that neither perspective provides useful information about the cultural equivalence (meaning) of test scores across racial or ethnic groups. Racial and ethnic groups are culturally, socially, and cognitively different from members of the dominant culture. Therefore, the examination of cultural equivalence in standard cognitive ability tests is needed. In all of these conceptual models, which are essentially contemporaneous (most even with arguments of Burt as early as 1921), ethnic and other group differences in mean levels of performance on aptitude measures are seen to result from flawed psychometric methodology and not from actual differences in aptitude (see also Harrington, 1975, 1976).

Harrington (1975, 1976) has taken a quite different, experimentally oriented approach to the issue of test bias. In earlier research, Harrington (1968a, 1968b) raised the issue of representation in the test development sample from a slightly different perspective. The small actual number of minority children in the standardization sample is unable to exert any significant impact on the item analysis data, and the content of the test subsequently becomes biased against groups with less than minority representation. Although this argument is no longer new, Harrington's (1975, 1976) subsequent approach was quite interesting and innovative. He began by creating experimental populations with varying proportions of minority composition (group membership was defined on a genetic basis). For his experimental populations, he used six species of rats from genetically homogeneous groups. He then set out to develop six intelligence tests, using African American and/or White Hebb-Williams types of mazes. Items that showed the greatest item-total correlations within each population were retained for the "IQ" test for that population.

Significant positive correlations occurred between the group mean on any individual test and the degree of group representation in the population used to develop the test. Harrington (1975, 1976) concluded that the greater the proportional representation of a homogeneous group in the test base population (the test development sample), the higher the mean score of the group on the test derived on that population. From further analysis of the data set, Harrington concluded that it is not possible for a test that was developed and normed on a White majority to have equivalent predictive validity with African Americans or any other minority group. Harrington's comments on predictive validity are particularly crucial since, as will be seen, most definitions of test bias rely heavily on the differential prediction of some specific criterion (e.g., Anastasi, 1976; Bartlett & O'Leary, 1969; Reynolds, 1995).

While Harrington's (1975, 1976) results are impressive and seem to call into question certain basic psychometric assumptions underlying test construction (particularly as they apply to the development of intelligence tests), his generalizations fail on three major points. First, intelligence and other aptitude tests have most often been shown to have equivalent predictive validity across racial groupings in a variety of circumstances with a rather diverse set of criterion measures. Second, well-documented findings that Japanese Americans, Chinese Americans, and Jewish Americans typically score as well or better than Whites on traditional intelligence tests and tests of some specific aptitudes (Gross, 1967; Majoribanks, 1972; Tyler, 1965; Willerman, 1979) are entirely contradictory to Harrington's (1975, 1976) results, given their proportionately small representation in the test development population of such instruments. Third, Harrington's theory of minority-majority group score differences cannot account for different patterns of cognitive performance between minority groups (Bogen, DeZure, Tenhouten, & March, 1972; Dean, 1979; Dershowitz & Frankel, 1975; Reynolds, McBride, & Gibson, 1979;

Vance, Hankins, & McGee, 1979, Willerman, 1979).

As described, this hypothesis reduces to one of differential validity. The hypothesis of differential validity for mental tests states that tests measure intelligence more accurately and make valid predictions about the level of intellectual functioning for individuals from the groups on which the tests are mainly based than for those from other groups. Artifactually low scores on an aptitude test could lead to pupils' misassignment to educational programs and unfair denial of admission to college, graduate school, or other programs or occupations in which such test scores are an important decision-making component. This is the issue over which most legal cases have been fought. Furthermore, there would be dramatic implications for whole areas of psychological research and practice if, on the one hand, the test-bias hypothesis is correct; the principal research of the last century in the psychology of human differences would have to be dismissed as confounded and largely artifactual because much of the work is based on standard psychometric theory and testing technology. The result would be major upheavals in the practice of applied psychology, as the foundations of clinical, school, counseling, and industrial psychology are strongly tied to the basic academic field of individual differences. The issue, then, is crucial not only to the science of psychology but also to practice (Lonner, 1985; Reynolds, 1980c). On the other hand, if the test-bias hypothesis is incorrect, group differences are not attributable to the tests and must be due to one or to some combination of factors mentioned by Eells et al. (1951). That group differences in test scores reflect real group differences in ability should be admitted as a possibility, and one that calls for scientific study.

The controversy over test bias should not be confused with that over the etiology (beyond the test itself) of any obtained group differences in test scores (see Reynolds & Kaiser, 1990, for review). Unfortunately, it has often been inferred that measured differences themselves indicate genetic differences and, therefore, the genetically based intellectual inferiority of some groups. Jensen has consistently argued since 1969 that mental tests measure, to a greater or lesser extent, the intellectual factor g, which has a large genetic component, and that group differences in mental test scores may then reflect group differences in g. Unless one reads Jensen's statements carefully, it is easy to overlook the many qualifications that he makes regarding these differences and conclusions and his contention that other factors do make significant contributions, albeit lesser ones, to intellectual development.

Jensen or anyone else's position on the genetic basis of actual group differences should be seen as irrelevant to the issue of test bias. However controversial, etiology is a separate issue. It would be tragic to accept the test-bias hypothesis as true if it is, in fact, false. In that case, measured differences would be seen as not real, and children might be denied access to compensatory or remedial programs or to another educational environment best suited to them. Furthermore, research on the basis of group differences would be stifled, as would implementation of programs designed to remediate any deficiencies. The most advantageous position for the true White racist and bigot would be to *favor* the test-bias hypothesis. Acceptance of it *inappropriately* would eventually result in inappropriate pupil assignment, less adaptive education for some groups, and less implementation of long-range programs to raise intellectual performance. Inappropriate confirmation of the test-bias hypothesis would appear to maintain, not break down, the poverty cycle (Birch & Gussow, 1970).

The controversy also does not involve the blatantly inappropriate administration and use of mental tests. The administration of a test in English to an individual for whom English is a second language and whose English language skills are poor is inexcusable, regardless of any bias in the tests themselves. It is of obvious importance that tests are administered by skilled and sensitive professionals who are aware of the factors that may artifactually lower an individual's scores. Considering the use of tests to assign pupils to special education classes or other programs, a question needs to be asked: what would one use instead? Teachers' recommendations are notoriously less reliable and less valid than standardized test scores. Whether special education programs are of adequate quality to meet the needs of children is an important educational question but distinct from the test-bias one.

The controversy over the use of mental tests is complicated further by the fact that resolution of the test-bias question in either direction will not resolve the problem of the role of nonintellective factors that may influence the test scores of *individuals* from any ethnic group. Regardless of any group differences, it is individuals who are tested and whose scores may or may not be accurate. Similarly, it is individuals who are assigned to classes, chosen for universities, placed in jobs or vocations, and accepted or rejected. As indicated by Wechsler (1975) and others, nonintellectual factors, informational content, and emotional-motivational conditions may be reflected in performance on mental tests. The extent to which these factors influence individual as opposed to group performance is difficult to determine. Perhaps with more sophisticated multivariate designs, we will be better able to identify individuals with characteristics that are likely to have an adverse effect on their performance on mental tests. Outside of the major thrust of the issue of bias against groups, potential bias against individuals is a serious problem itself and merits research and analysis. Sternberg (1980), also concerned about individual performance, observed that research on bias has concentrated on "status variables" such as ethnicity rather than on "functional variables" such as cognitive styles and motivation.

THE NATURE OF PSYCHOLOGICAL TESTING ADDS TO THE CONTROVERSY

The question of bias in mental testing arises largely because of the nature of psychological processes and their measurement (Reynolds & Brown, 1984). Psychological processes, by definition internal and not directly subject to observation or measurement, must be inferred from behavior. Theoretically, in the classic discussion by MacCorquodale and Meehl (1948), a psychological process has the status of an intervening variable if it is used only as a component of a system that has no properties beyond those that operationally define it, but it has the status of a hypothetical construct if it is thought actually to exist and have properties beyond the defining ones. A historical example of a hypothetical construct is a *gene*, which has meaning beyond its use to describe the cross-generational transmission of characteristics. Intelligence, from its treatment in the professional literature, has the status of a hypothetical construct, as does personality.

It is difficult to determine one-to-one relationships among observable events in the environment, the behavior of an organism, and the hypothesized underlying mediational processes. Many classic controversies over theories of learning have revolved around constructs such as expectancy, habit, and inhibition (Goldstein, Krantz, & Rains, 1965; Hilgard & Bower, 1975; Kimble, 1961). Disputes among different camps in learning have been polemical and of long duration. Indeed, there are still disputes about the nature and the number of processes such as emotion and motivation (Bolles, 1975; Mandler, 1975). One of the major areas of disagreement has been over the measurement of psychological processes. It should be expected that intelligence, as one of the most complex psychological processes, involves definitional and measurement disputes that are difficult to resolve.

Assessment of intelligence, like that of many other psychological processes in humans, is accomplished by standard psychometric procedures that are the focus of the bias issue. These procedures, described in detail in general assessments texts (e.g., Reynolds, Livingston, & Willson, 2006), are only briefly summarized here in relation to the issue of bias. The problems specific to validity are discussed in a separate section.

Similar procedures are used in the development of any standardized psychological test. First, a large number of items are developed that for theoretical or practical reasons are thought to measure the construct of interest. Through a series of statistical steps, those items that best measure the construct in a unitary manner are selected for inclusion in the final test battery. The test is then administered to a sample, which should be chosen to represent all aspects of the population on whom the test will be used. Normative scales based on the scores of the standardization sample then serve as the reference for the interpretation of scores of individuals tested thereafter. Thus, as has been pointed out numerous times, an individual's score is meaningful only in relation to the norms and is a relative, not an absolute, measure. Charges of a bias frequently arise from the position that the test is more appropriate for the groups heavily represented in the standardization sample. Whether bias does, in fact, result from this procedure is one of the specific questions that must be empirically addressed.

Intelligence is measured by psychological tests on an interval scale of measurement. Interval scales of measurement have no true zero point and are thus entirely relativistic. To define an interval scale, one begins at the midpoint (usually the mean) of a distribution and measures toward the two ends of the score distribution. Interval scales derived from one test are not directly comparable to interval scales derived from another test and must be compared through regression methods. These added levels of complexity in how the hypothetical construct of intelligence must be measured and compared across tests, and their abstruseness to the media and even most of the intelligencia, increases the level of controversy over bias. The issues surrounding scales of measurement and their implications for score interpretation are not well understood by most clinicians or other psychologists outside of the measurement field.

There are few charges of bias of any kind for physical measures that are on absolute scales, especially ratio scales. Group differences in height, as an extreme example, are not attributed by anyone we know of to any kind of cultural test bias. There is no question about the validity of measures of the height or weight of anyone in any culture. Nor is there any question about one's ability to make cross-cultural comparisons of these absolute measures, even though many of these variables, such as height, weight, and blood pressure, are clearly subject to genetic and environmental interactions.

The whole issue of cultural bias arises because of the procedures involved in the development and application of psychological tests. Psychological tests measure traits that are not directly observable, that are subject to differences in definition, and that are measurable only on a relative scale. From this perspective, the question of cultural bias in mental testing is a subset—obviously of major importance—of the problems of uncertainty and of other possible biases in psychological testing in general. Bias may exist not only in aptitude and achievement tests but in other types of psychological tests as well, including personality and vocational tests, behavior rating scales, and even observational instruments and curriculum-based assessment approaches. Making the problem of bias in mental testing even more complex is the fact that not all tests are of the same quality. There is a tendency for critics and defenders alike to overgeneralize across tests, lumping virtually all tests together under the heading "mental tests" or "intelligence tests." Professional opinions of mental tests vary considerably, and some of the most used tests are not well respected by psychometricians. Thus, unfortunately, the question of bias must eventually be answered on a virtually test-by-test basis.

MINORITY OBJECTIONS TO STANDARDIZED PSYCHOLOGICAL TESTING

In 1969, the Association of Black Psychologists (ABP) adopted the following official policy on educational and psychological testing:

> The Association of Black Psychologists fully supports those parents who have chosen to defend their rights by refusing to allow their children and themselves to be subjected to achievement, intelligence, aptitude and performance tests which have been and are being used to a) label African American people as uneducable, b) place African American children in "special" classes and schools, c) perpetuate inferior education in African Americans, d) assign African American children to educational tracks, e) deny African American students higher education opportunities, and f) destroy positive growth and development of African American people.

Since 1968, the ABP has sought a moratorium on the use of all psychological and educational tests with the culturally different (Samuda, 1975; Williams, Dotson, Dow, & Williams, 1980, have provided a more detailed history of these efforts). The ABP carried its call for a moratorium to other professional organizations in psychology and education. In direct response, the Board of Directors of the American Psychological Association (APA) requested its Board of Scientific Affairs to appoint a group to study the use of psychological and educational tests with disadvantaged students. The committee's report (Cleary, Humphreys, Kendrick, & Wesman, 1975) was subsequently published in an official journal of the APA, *American Psychologist*.

Subsequent to the ABP's policy statement, other groups have adopted policy statements on testing: the National Association for the Advancement of Colored People (NAACP), the National Education Association (NEA), the National Association of Elementary School Principals (NAESP), the American Personnel and Guidance Association (APGA), and others (Williams et al., 1980). The APGA called for the Association for Measurement and Evaluation in Guidance (AMEG), a sister organization, to develop a position paper as well.

The NAACP, at its annual meeting in 1974, adopted a more detailed resolution, demanded a moratorium on standardized testing of minority groups, and called on the ABP to assert leadership in aiding the College Entrance Examination Board (CEEB) to develop standardized tests that have been corrected for cultural bias and fairly measure the amount of knowledge retained by students regardless of his or her individual background. Later that year, the Committee on Testing of the ABP issued a position paper on the testing of African Americans that described their intent as well as their position:

1. To encourage, support and to bring action against *all* institutions, organizations and agencies who continue to use present psychometric instruments in the psychological assessment of African American people;

2. To continue efforts to bring about a cessation of the use of standard psychometric instruments on African American people until culturally specific tests are made available;

3. To establish a national policy that in effect gives African American people and other minorities the right to demand that psychological assessment be administered, interpreted, and supervised by competent psychological assessors of their own ethnic background;

4. To work toward and encourage efforts to remove from the records of all African American students and African American employees data obtained from performance on past and currently used standard psychometric, achievement, employment, general aptitude and mental ability tests;

5. To establish a national policy that demands the appropriate proportional representation of competent African American psychologists on all committees and agencies responsible for the evaluation and selection of tests used in the assessment of African American people;

6. To establish a national policy that demands that all persons engaged in the evaluation, selection and placement of African American people undergo extensive training so they may better relate to the African American experience;

7. To demand that all African American students improperly diagnosed and placed into special education classes be returned to regular class programs;

8. To encourage and support all suits against any public or private agency for the exclusion, improper classification, and the denial

of advancement opportunities to African American people based on performance tests.

The statements by these various organizations *assume* that bias is present in tests and that what is needed is its removal. These assumptions continue in the work of Helms (1992), Mercer (1979b), Padilla (1988), and others (e.g., Guilford Press, 1997).

WHAT ARE POSSIBLE SOURCES OF BIAS?

African American and other minority psychologists have raised many potentially legitimate objections to the use of educational and psychological tests with minorities. Unfortunately, these objections are frequently stated as facts on rational rather than empirical grounds (e.g., Chambers, Barron, & Sprecher, 1980; Council for Exceptional Children, 1978; Dana, 1996; Helms, 1992; Hilliard, 1979). The most frequently stated problems fall into one of the following categories:

1. *Inappropriate content.* African Americans and other minorities have not been exposed to the material in the test questions or other stimulus materials. The tests are geared primarily toward the majority class's homes, vocabulary, and values. Different value systems among cultures may produce cognitively equivalent answers, which are scored as incorrect because of prejudicial value judgments, not differences in ability (Bond, 1987; Butler-Omololu Doster & Lahey, 1984).

2. *Inappropriate standardization samples.* Ethnic minorities are underrepresented in standardization samples used in the collection of normative reference data. Proportionate sampling with stratification by ethnicity is the herald for standardization samples for tests and is done to enhance the accuracy of parameter estimations for scaling purposes. Thus, although represented proportionately, ethnic minorities may appear in test standardization samples in small absolute numbers, and this may bias item selection (e.g., Harrington, 1975, 1976) and also fails to have any impact of significance from these ethnic groups on the tests themselves (Greenlaw & Jensen, 1996). In earlier years, it was not unusual for standardization samples to be all White (e.g., the Stanford-Binet

Intelligence Scale [SB], Terman & Merrill, 1937; and the Wechsler Intelligence Scale for Children [WISC], Wechsler, 1949).

3. *Examiners' and language bias.* Because most psychologists in the United States are White and speak only standard English, they may intimidate African Americans and other ethnic minorities. They are also unable to communicate accurately with minority children—to the point of being intimidating and insensitive to ethnic pronunciation of words on the test. Lower test scores for minorities, then, may reflect only this intimidation and difficulty in the communication process, not lower ability (Clarizio, 1982; Emerling, 1990; Isern, 1986).

4. *Inequitable social consequences.* As a result of bias in educational and psychological tests, minority group members, already at a disadvantage in the educational and vocational markets because of past discrimination and being thought unable to learn, are disproportionately relegated to dead-end educational tracks. Labeling effects also fall under this category (Chipman, Marshall, & Scott, 1991; Payne & Payne, 1991).

5. *Measurement of different constructs.* Related to point 1, this position asserts the tests measure different attributes when used with children from other than the majority culture, the culture on which the tests are largely based, and thus are not valid measures of minority intelligence or personality.

6. *Differential predictive validity.* Although tests may accurately predict a variety of outcomes for members of the majority culture, they do not predict successfully any relevant behavior for minority group members. Furthermore, there are objections to the use of the standard criteria against which tests are validated with minority cultural groups. For example, scholastic or academic attainment levels in White, middle-class schools are themselves considered by a variety of African American psychologists to be biased as criteria (see discussion in Reynolds, 1982a, pp. 179–180).

7. *Qualitatively distinct minority and majority aptitude and personality.* Championed by Helms (1992), this position would lead to the conclusion that ethnic minorities and the majority culture are so different as to require

different conceptualizations of ability and of personality. Helms, for example, argues the potential existence of a "White *g*" factor that is separate from an "African *g*" (p. 1090), which would necessitate separate tests for these groups.

Contrary to the situation of the late 1960s and 1970s, when the current controversies resurfaced after some decades of simmering, research has examined these areas of potential bias in assessment. Except for the still unresolved issue of labeling effects, the least amount of research is available on the long-term social consequences of testing, although there are some limited (but aging) data (e.g., Lambert, 1979). Both of these problems are aspects of testing in general and are not limited to minorities. The problem of the social consequences of educational tracking is frequently lumped with the issue of test bias and in fact, many of the issues of test bias are discussed in the *Standards for Educational and Psychological Testing* (American Educational Research Association [AERA], APA, & National Council on Measurement in Education [NCME], 1999) under the general rubric of validity evidence related to the consequences of test use (with little discussion of the consequences of making decisions in the absence of test use). Those issues, however, are separate. Educational tracking and special education should be treated as problems of education, not assessment.

MEAN SCORE DIFFERENCES AS TEST BIAS

A popular lay view has been that differences in mean levels of scoring on cognitive, achievement, or personality tests among groups constitute bias in tests; however, such differences alone are clearly not evidence of bias. A number of writers in the professional literature have also taken this position (Abebimpe, Gigandet, & Harris, 1979; Chinn, 1979; Guilford Press, 1997; Hilliard, 1979; Jackson, 1975; Mercer, 1976; Padilla, 1988; Williams, 1974; Wright & Isenstein, 1977/1978). Those who support this definition of test bias correctly state that there is no valid a priori scientific reason to believe that intellectual or other cognitive performance levels should differ across race. It is the inference that tests demonstrating such differences are inherently biased, because in reality there can be no differences, that is fallacious. Just as there

is no a priori basis for deciding that differences exist, there is no a priori basis for deciding that differences do not exist. From the standpoint of the objective methods of science, a priori or premature acceptance of either hypothesis (differences exist versus differences do not exist) is untenable. As stated by Thorndike (1971), "The presence (or absence) of differences in mean score between groups, or of differences in variability, tells us nothing directly about fairness" (p. 64). Some adherents of the "mean score differences as bias" viewpoint also require that the distribution of test scores in each population or subgroup be identical before one can assume that the test is fair: "Regardless of the purpose of a test, or its validity for that purpose, a test should result in distributions that are statistically equivalent across the groups tested in order for it to be considered nondiscriminatory for those groups" (Alley & Foster, 1978, p. 2). Portraying a test as biased regardless of its purpose or validity is psychometrically naïve. Mean score differences and unequivalent distributions have been the most uniformly rejected of all criteria examined by sophisticated psychometricians in investigating the problems of a bias in assessment. Ethnic group differences in mental test scores are among the best-documented phenomena in psychology, and they have persisted over time at relatively constant levels (Gottfredson, 2005; Reynolds & Gutkin, 1980, 1981).

Jensen (1980) sees the "mean score differences as bias" position as exemplary of the egalitarian fallacy, which contends that all human populations are in fact identical on all mental traits or abilities, that is, any differences in any aspect of the distribution of mental test scores indicate that something is wrong with the test itself. Such an assumption is totally scientifically unwarranted. There are simply too many examples of specific abilities and even sensory capacities that have been shown to differ unmistakably across human populations. The result of the egalitarian assumption, then, is to remove the investigation of population differences in ability from the realm of scientific inquiry. Logically followed, this fallacy leads to other untenable conclusions as well. Torrance (1980), an adherent of the cultural bias hypothesis, pointed out that the disadvantaged African American children in the United States occasionally earn higher scores on creativity tests—and therefore have more creative ability—than many White children because their environment has forced them to learn to "make do" with less and with simpler objects. The egalitarian assumption would hold that this is not true, rather that the content of creativity tests is biased against White or high SES children. At its extreme, the egalitarian fallacy would argue against any genetic influence on intelligence even within groups, seeing all variation as environmental, in the tradition of tabula rasa (see also Nichols, 1978).

The attachment of minorities to the "mean score differences as bias" definition is probably related to the nature-nurture controversy at some level. Certainly, data that reflect racial differences on various aptitude measures have been interpreted to indicate support for a hypothesis of genetic differences in intelligence and to imply that one race is superior to another. However, as discussed previously, the so-called nature-nurture issue is not an inextricable component of bias investigation. Assertions about the relative impact of genetic factors on group ability levels step into a separate arena of scientific inquiry, with differing bodies of knowledge and methods of research. It is enough to say that in the arena of bias investigation, mean differences on aptitude, achievement, or personality measures among selected groups are not evidence per se that the measures are biased.

Culture-free Tests, Culture Loading, and Culture Bias

A third area of bias investigation that has been confusing in both the professional (e.g., Alley & Foster, 1978; Chinn, 1979) and the lay literature has been the interpretation of culture loading and culture bias. A test can be culture loaded without being culturally biased. Culture loading refers to the degree of cultural specificity present in the test or individual items of the test. Certainly, the greater the cultural specificity of a test item, the greater the likelihood of the item being biased when it is used with individuals from other cultures. The test item "Who was the first president of the United States?" is a culture-loaded item. However, the item is general enough to be considered useful with school-aged children who have been attending school since first grade in the United States. The cultural specificity of the item is too great, however, to allow the item to be used on an aptitude measure of 10-year-old children from other countries (although it might qualify as an appropriate item on a test of achievement in American history). Virtually all tests in current use are bound in

some way by their cultural specificity. Culture loading must be viewed on a continuum from general (defining a culture in a broad, liberal sense) to specific (defining a culture in narrow, highly distinctive terms).

A variety of attempts have been made to develop a culture-free (sometimes referred to as a culture-fair) intelligence test (Cattell, 1979). However, the reliability and validity of these tests are uniformly inadequate from a psychometric perspective (Anastasi, 1982; Ebel, 1979). The difficulty in developing a culture-free measure of intelligence lies in making the test irrelevant to intellectual behavior in the culture under study. Intelligent behavior is defined in large part on the basis of behavior judged to be of value to the survival and improvement of the culture and the individuals in it. A test that is culture-blind, then, cannot be expected to predict intelligent behavior in a variety of culture settings. Once a test has been developed in a culture (a culture-loaded test), generalizability to other cultures or subcultures within the dominant societal framework becomes a matter for empirical investigation, and tests should not be interpreted consistently across cultures without demonstrative evidence for the validity of inferences to be drawn from them.

Jensen (1980) admonishes that when one is investigating the psychometric properties of culture-loaded tests across differing societies or cultures, one cannot assume that simple inspection of the content will determine which tests or items are biased against those cultures or societies not represented in the tests or item content. Tests or items that exhibit characteristic of being culturally loaded cannot be determined to be biased with any degree of certainty unless objective statistical inspection is completed. Jensen refers to the mistaken notion that anyone can judge tests and/or items as being "culturally unfair" on superficial inspection as the "culture-bound fallacy." The issue of item bias is revisited in some detail later in this chapter.

The Examiner-Examinee Relationship

In evaluative situations, many individuals believe examiners from the majority culture depress test scores of minority children (Sattler, 2001). However, this belief runs contrary to the empirical evidence (Gerken, 1978; Sattler & Gwynne, 1982) and is viewed as one of the leading myths in psychology (Sattler & Gwynne, 1982). Many psychologists have uncritically accepted this myth as fact and have allowed it to guide their thinking and practice.

Research refutes the myth that racial differences in the examiner-examinee relationship depress test scores of minority children (Sattler, 2001). Sattler and Gwynne (1982) reviewed 27 studies on the effects of the examiner's race on children and youths' tests scores on a variety of cognitive measures. Children and adolescents in these studies were in grades preschool through 12 and were from largely urban areas, representing the major geographic regions throughout the United States. In 25 of the 29 published studies, no significant relationship was found between the race of the examiner (i.e., African American or White) and African American and White examinees' test scores. The four studies that did report significant differences in the examiner-examinee relationship were found to be lacking in methodological rigor, including inappropriate statistical designs—such as the lack of comparison groups and external criteria to evaluate the validity of various procedures—and statistical tests. These findings suggest that White examiners have little or no influence on the test score performance of African American children and youth.

Likewise, evidence suggests that White examiners have little or no influence on the test score performance of Hispanic American children (Sattler, 2001). Gerken (1978) conducted a study on racial differences in the examiner-examinee relationship with a group of Hispanic American children, ages 4 to 6. The children in this study were administered either the Wechsler Preschool and Primary Scale of Intelligence (WPPSI; Wechsler, 1967) or the Leiter International Performance Scale (LIPS; Leiter, 1948). Gerken found that the examiner's ethnicity (i.e., White or Hispanic American) and linguistic skills (monolingual or bilingual) did not have a significant effect on the children's test scores. Based on the results of these studies, racial differences in the examiner-examinee relationship does not appear to contribute substantially to lower test score performance of minority children (Sattler, 2001).

Although depressed test scores of minority children are not likely to be associated with racial differences in the examiner-examinee relationship, examiners need to keep in mind the ethnicity of the examinees. Examiners need to be *competent* in the administration and interpretation of test results with minority children. Language and dialectical differences need to be addressed, and selection of appropriate tests and proper test administration are required. During the assessment process, examiners need to establish rapport and identify any *nuances* in the evaluative situation that may invalidate test score performance in their work with children and adolescents from the minority as well as the majority culture (Suzuki, Meller, & Ponterotto, 1996). The examiner's competency is the critical issue in test administration and interpretation, not racial differences in examiner-examinee relationships, and is best addressed by rigorous academic and clinical training.

The Question of Labeling Effects

The relative impact of placing a label on a person's behavior or developmental status has also been a hotly discussed issue in the field of psychometrics in general and bias investigation in particular. The issue undoubtedly has been a byproduct of the practice of using intellectual measures for the determination of mental retardation. Although the question of labeling effects is a viable and important one, it requires consideration in bias research only in much the same way as does the ongoing debate of the nature-nurture question. As the concept of consequential validity grows, this issue will likewise grow in importance. However, there are some important considerations concerning bias in referral for services, diagnosis, and labeling that no interested student of the diagnostic process in psychology can afford to ignore.

Rosenthal (1976) is the researcher most closely associated with the influence of labeling on teachers' and parents' perceptions of a child's ability and potential. Even though his early studies had many methodological and statistical difficulties, labeling effects have been shown in some subsequent experimental studies (Critchley, 1979; Foster & Ysseldyke, 1976; Jacobs, 1978) but not in others (MacMillan, Jones, & Aloia, 1974; McCoy, 1976). However, these studies have generally been of a short-term nature and have usually been conducted under quite artificial circumstances. Typically, participants are asked to rate the behavior or degree of pathology of a child seen on videotape. Categorical labels for the child are systematically varied while the observed behaviors remain constant. The demand characteristics of such a design are substantial. Long-term effects of labeling and special education placement in real-life situations have been examined less vigorously. Comparisons of the effects of formal diagnostic labels with the informal, often cursory, personal labeling process that occurs between teachers and children over the course of a school year, and which is subsequently passed on to the next grade in the teachers' lounge (Dworkin & Dworkin, 1979), need to be made. Although Reynolds (1982b) called for this research decades ago, this important question has not been addressed. The strict behaviorist position (Ross, 1974, 1976) also contends that formal diagnostic procedures are unnecessary and potentially harmful because of labeling effects. However, whether or not the application of formal labels has detrimental effects remains an open question now, much as it did at the conclusion of a monumental effort to address these important questions throughout the United States in the mid-1970s (Hobbs, 1975).

From the standpoint of cultural *test* bias, the question of labeling children or not labeling children is moot. Cultural test bias is concerned with the accuracy of such labels across some nominal grouping system (typically race, gender, and SES have been the variables of interest). It is a question of whether race, gender, or any other demographic variable influences the diagnostic process or the placement of a child in special programs, independent of the child's cognitive, emotional, and behavioral status. Several well-designed studies have investigated the influences of race and SES on the class placement recommendations of school and clinical psychologists (i.e., bias in test interpretation) and these have been summarized in Reynolds, Lowe, and Saenz (1999). Little has been added to the literature since that time and their conclusions remain appropriate and are summarized below.

These studies reviewed therein indicate that the demographic variables of race and SES do not, independent of other pupil characteristics, influence or bias psychologists' diagnostic or placement behavior in a manner that would cause African Americans or lower-SES children to be labeled inaccurately or placed inappropriately or in disproportionate numbers in special education programs. The empirical evidence, rather, argues in the opposite direction. In the United States, African American and low-SES children are *less* likely to be recommended for special education classes than their White or higher-SES peers with similar cognitive, behavioral, and emotional characteristics. The data simply do not support Williams' (1970) and others' (e.g., Guilford Press, 1997; Padilla, 1988) charges that ethnic minority children are placed in special education programs on the basis of race or test bias against African Americans. The disproportionate representation of minorities in special education programs historically can be accounted for by the disproportionately higher incidence of referrals among minority student populations.

The Nature-Nurture Issue

While Bond (1981) observes that there has been a strong pull by professionals and the lay public alike to formulate conclusions regarding the relative impact of genetic and environmental factors on test performance, determining which conclusions are most acceptable can be more a matter of doctrine than of science (Gottfredson, 1994). Bond points out that one reason bias research and intelligence testing has remained so vital a social issue is the pervasive discussions pertaining to race differences and intelligence. He asks the reader to consider this statement: "Test results indicate that White students, on average, achieve higher levels of competence in most academic subjects than African American students, on average" (p. 56). The statement, viewed objectively, merely addresses a presumed result of past academic achievement and does not provide an etiology for observed differences. However, consider this: "Test results indicate that White students as a group possess greater aptitude for academic work than African American students as a group" (p. 56). The seemingly minor change in language quickly elevates the statement into the realm of genetic or innate superiority of one group and, understandably, triggers a decidedly emotional response.

The investigation of test bias can proceed unabated without paying attention to the nature-nuture question. That is not to say that the relative impact of endowment and experience on human intellectual development is not a viable issue in the scientific arena. It is, but it is also burdened with inadequate methodology at present for convincing conclusions to be made. Jensen (1980) notes that data obtained from all test scores are measures of phenotypic and not genotypic expression. The idea of phenotype in scientific terminology refers to the detectable expression of the interaction of both genotype and the environment, which ultimately constitute the characteristics of an organism. Consequently, investigation of test bias is, by nature, investigation of possible bias in the measure of phenotypes. If bias is not found in a purely statistical sense in a test, conclusions drawn about genetic differences between and among groups using the "nonbiased" measure are, simply put, another issue with a plethora of complicating factors.

THE PROBLEM OF DEFINITION

The definition of test bias has produced considerable continuing debate among measurement and assessment experts (Angoff, 1976; Bernal, 1975; Cleary et al., 1975; Cole & Moss, 1989; Cronbach, 1976; Darlington, 1978; Einhorn & Bass, 1971; Flaugher, 1978; Gordon, 1984; Gross & Su, 1975; Helms, 1992; Humphreys, 1973; Hunter & Schmidt, 1976, 1978; Linn, 1976; McNemar, 1975; Moreland, 1995; Novick & Peterson, 1976; Reschly, 1980; Reynolds, 1978, 1982b, 1995; Reynolds & Brown, 1984; Reynolds & Carson, 2005; Sawyer, Cole & Cole, 1976; Schmidt & Hunter, 1974; Thorndike, 1971). Although the resulting debate has generated a number of selection models with which to examine bias, they tend to focus on the decision-making system and not on the test itself. The various selection models are discussed at some length in Hunter and Schmidt (1976), Hunter, Schmidt, and Rauschenberger (1984), Jensen (1980), and Ramsey (1979). The choice of a decision-making system (especially a system for educational decision making) must ultimately be a societal one; as such, it will depend to a large extent on the value systems and goals of the society. Thus, before a model for test use in selection can be chosen, it must be decided whether the ultimate goal is equality of opportunity, equality of outcome, or representative equality (these concepts are discussed in more detail in Nichols, 1978).

Equality of opportunity is a competitive model in which selection is based on ability. As more eloquently stated by Lewontin (1970), under equality of opportunity "true merit . . . will be the criterion of men's earthly reward" (p. 92). Equality of outcome is a selection model based on ability deficits. Compensatory and remedial programs are typically constructed on the basis of the equality-of-outcome model. Children of low ability or children believed to be at high risk for academic failure are selected

for remedial, compensatory, or other special educational programs. In a strictly predictive sense, tests are used in a similar manner in both of these models. However, in equality of opportunity, selection is based on the prediction of a high level of criterion performance; in equality of outcome, selection is determined by the prediction of failure or a preselected low level of criterion performance. Interestingly, it is the failure of compensatory and remedial education, bilingual education, and similar special programs to bring the disadvantaged learner to "average" levels of performance that has continued the charges of test bias now in vogue.

The model of representative equality also relies on selection, but selection that is proportionate to numerical representation of subgroups in the population under consideration. Representative equality is typically thought to be independent of the level of ability in each group; however, models can be constructed that select from each subgroup the desired proportion of individuals (1) according to the relative ability level of the group, (2) independent of group ability, or (3) according to some decision rule between these two positions. Even under the conditions of representative equality, it is imperative to employ a selection device (test) that will rank-order individuals within groups in a reliable and valid manner. The best way to ensure fair selection in any of these models is to employ tests that are equally reliable and equally valid for all groups concerned. The tests should also be the most reliable and most valid for all groups under consideration. The question of test bias per se, then, becomes a question of test validity. Test use (i.e., fairness) may be defined as biased or nonbiased only by the societal value system; at present, this value system in the United States is leaning strongly toward some variant of the representative equality selection model. As noted, all models are facilitated by the use of a nonbiased test. That is, the use of a test with equivalent cross-group validities allows the most parsimonious selection model, greatly simplifying the creation and application of the selection model that has been chosen.

This leads to the essential definitional component of test bias. Test bias refers in a global sense to *systematic* error in the estimation of some "true" value for a group of individuals. The key word here is *systematic*; all measures contain error and in all cultural settings, but this error is assumed to be random unless shown to be otherwise.

Bias investigation is a statistical inquiry that does not concern itself with culture loading, labeling effects, or test use or test fairness. Concerning the last of these, Jensen (1980) comments, "Unbiased tests can be used unfairly and biased tests can be used fairly. Therefore, the concepts of bias and unfairness should be kept distinct . . . [A] number of different, and often mutually contradictory, criteria for fairness have been proposed, and no amount of statistical or psychometric reasoning per se can possibly settle any arguments as to which is best" (pp. 375–376).

There are three types of validity as traditionally conceived: content, construct, and predictive (or criterion-related). Test bias may exist in any or all of these categories of validity. Although no category is completely independent of any other category, each is discussed separately here for clarity and convenience. (All true evidence of validity is as likely as not to be construct validity, and other, more detailed divisions, including this one, are for convenience of discussion). Frequently encountered in bias research are the terms *differential validity* and *single-group validity*. The latter refers to the phenomenon of a score interpretation being valid for one group but not another. Differential validity refers to a condition in which an interpretation is valid for all groups concerned, but the degree of validity varies as a function of group membership. Although these terms have been most often applied to predictive or criterion-related validity (validity coefficients are then examined for significance and compared across groups), the concepts of single-group and differential validity are equally applicable to content and construct validity.

RESEARCH STRATEGIES AND RESULTS

The methodologies available for research into cultural bias in tests grew rapidly in numbers and sophistication in the 1980s and 1990s. Extensive reviews of the methodologies used for research into cultural test bias are available in Camilli and Shepard (1994), Jensen (1980), Reynolds (1982b, 1995, 2000), Reynolds and Brown (1984), and Reynolds et al. (1999). We review the most popular methods used and examples of these methods to examine cultural bias in tests. The sections are organized primarily by methodology in each content area of research (i.e., research into content, construct, and predictive validity). We have retained these essential

headings rather than adopt the new rubric of the 1999 (AERA, APA, NCME) *Standards for Educational and Psychological Tests*, because the majority of the research has been done using these terms and the changes in language, while important, may yet lead to some confusion. The traditional tripartite conceptualization of validity seems best for organizing this discussion as well.

Bias in Content Validity

The earliest work in cultural test bias focused on the content of items on a test. Lower scores on items of a test by ethnic minority children in comparison to ethnic majority children suggest the possibility of cultural bias at the item level. Reynolds (2000) identified three types of problems that may lead individuals to believe that one or more items on a test are biased: (1) the items ask for information that an ethnic minority or a disadvantaged individual has not had an equal opportunity to learn; (2) the scoring of the items is improper because the test's author has arbitrarily decided on the correct answers, and an ethnic minority or a disadvantaged individual is inappropriately penalized for giving answers that would be correct in his or her own culture but not in the author's culture; and/or (3) the wording of the questions is unfamiliar, and an ethnic minority or a disadvantaged individual who may "know" the correct answers may not be able to respond because he or she does not understand the questions. Each of these problems have the same basic empirical result: the items become more difficult for ethnic minority children, and these children will respond differently to the biased items than ethnic majority children even when these two groups of children have the same standing on the construct of interest.

One popular method to identify content bias at the item level is to examine item difficulties across all ethnic groups of interest. A difficult item or a group of difficult items for any ethnic group will be eliminated from a test because of potential bias. Detection of a difficult item or group of difficult items is indicated when differences in the rank order of the item difficulties occurs across groups. When there are such differences, the potential for bias at the item level exists. Although examination of item difficulties is a common method to identify biased items, other methods have been developed to detect cultural bias at the item level. A discussion of these methods follows.

Analysis of Variance

Analysis of Variance (ANOVA) and other related procedures were once widely used to detect cultural bias at the item level. Until the late 1980s, ANOVA was the most popular empirical approach (Camilli & Shepard, 1987). When an ANOVA is performed to examine content bias at the item level, test developers or researchers are interested in whether the group by item interaction is significant. A significant group by item interaction indicates that the items are not uniform across cultural groups (i.e., the relative differences in item difficulty across ethnic groups for each item on the test are not the same) and suggests that the items are biased. Earlier researchers and test developers hoped the ANOVA procedure would be able to identify a group of items of similar content that were biased and these items, then, would be eliminated and not used in future test development (Flaugher, 1978). However, very little similarity among the items determined to be biased has been found. No one has been able to identify those characteristics of an item that cause it to be biased. It seems that poorly written, sloppy, and ambiguous items tend to be identified as biased with greater frequency than those items typically encountered in a well-constructed, standardized instrument. The variable at issue, then, may be the item reliability. Item reliabilities are typically not large, and poorly written or ambiguous test items may have reliabilities near zero. These items may be identified with greater frequency as being biased than items with high reliabilities. However, these items with low reliabilities may not be biased but are simply ambiguous or poorly written (Reynolds, 2000). Informal inventories and locally derived tests are much more likely to be biased than professionally written, standardized tests, which have been scrutinized for bias in the items and whose item characteristics are known.

The ANOVA methodology is appealing conceptually but has some significant problems, even though it was the dominant methodological approach to the issue of item bias through the 1980s. Camilli and Shepard (1994) provide an algebraic demonstration for why the ANOVA procedure should not be used to detect item bias. Using contrived data, Camilli and Shepard found that the ANOVA method often fails to identify some items as biased as well as identifies other items as biased that are not. Camilli and Shepard concluded based on their findings that the ANOVA method should no longer be used to detect cultural bias at the item level.

Item Response Theory

Based on their thorough and compelling analyses of methods for detecting biased items, Camilli and Shepard (1994) recommend methods derived from item response theory (IRT) to detect item bias. IRT is the most common method to detect item bias in current use (Reynolds, 2000). The goal of IRT is to determine the degree to which items function differently across groups. The degree to which items do function differently across groups has come to be known as differential item functioning (DIF). Once these items that function differently across groups are identified, a logical analysis is conducted to determine why these items are relatively more difficult for one or more groups. Based on the analysis, a subset of DIF items are identified as biased and are eliminated from a test. Significant DIFs do not necessarily mean that particular items are biased. Biased items are determined according to the *interpretation* of the items within a coherent and substantive framework about their relevancy to the construct being measured. In other words, if items tap traits irrelevant to the intended construct, as determined through careful judgment and additional empirical investigation, these items are considered to be biased. For example, if baseball is the topic of a reading passage on the reading comprehension section of the verbal portion of a college entrance exam, and items relating to baseball on the reading comprehension section produce significant DIFs when comparing males and females, further analyses would need to be conducted to determine if these items were measuring reading comprehension or tapping some other trait, such as prior knowledge about baseball. Through careful deliberations and further empirical study, if it is found that these items are tapping the examinees' knowledge about baseball instead of reading comprehension, these items would be labeled as biased and would be removed from the test.

IRT is primarily concerned with the probability of a particular response to a test item as a function of the examinee's relative position on the latent trait. The IRT's principal conceptual unit, the item characteristic curve (ICC), represents this relationship. The ICC is determined by three parameters, a, b, and c. The

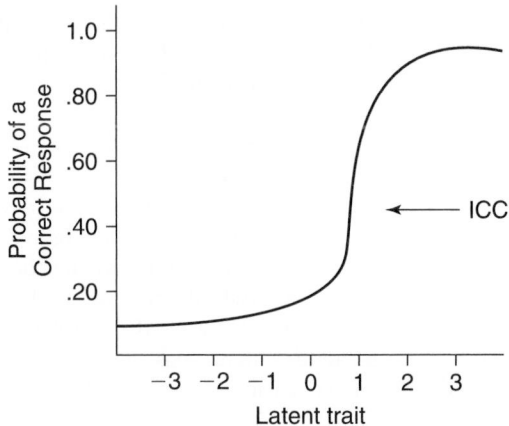

FIGURE 18.1 An item characteristic curve (ICC).

a parameter represents the discrimination power of an item (i.e., how well an item distinguishes examinees who score high from those who score low on the latent trait). Discrimination corresponds to the slope of the ICC. The *b* parameter represents the difficulty of an item and is measured in the same scale units as the latent trait. The *b* parameter is located along the latent trait scale at the point where the probability of a correct response is equal to $(1 + c)/2$. The *c* parameter, the guessing parameter, represents the lower asymptote of the ICC. These three parameters determine the shape of the ICC. Diagrammatic representation of one group's ICC for one item is depicted in Figure 18.1.

Different IRT models are derived from estimates of these three different parameters. As Embertson and Reise (2000) note, there are unidimensional and multidimensional models with one, two, or three parameters. The three-parameter (3P) model consists of three parameter estimates and is a commonly used IRT model, especially with multiple-choice items. However, large sample sizes are required to develop reliable and valid 3P models. A two-parameter (2P) model and one-parameter (1P), or Rasch, model also exist. The Rasch model is another IRT model widely used in testing. The selection of an appropriate IRT model is critical, as failure to use an adequate model will lead to inaccurate estimates of item parameters and decrease the utility of IRT techniques. Computer programs are available for estimating item and latent parameters, such as LOGIST and BILOG, using joint maximum likelihood

(JML) or marginal maximum likelihood (MML) techniques, respectively.

In applying IRT to DIF, the ICCs of two different groups (groups A and B) are compared on the same item. Conceptually, the ICCs for the two groups are plotted on the same scale, and the area between the two ICCs is measured to determine the degree of DIF. The area between the two ICCs, for group A and group B, DIF, is depicted in Figure 18.2. Different statistical procedures have been developed to measure DIF. If the DIF index is significant, further analysis of the item as well as other items with significant DIFs is needed to determine if they are biased.

Two techniques have been developed for equating the item parameter estimates across groups, the anchor-test method and separate-test method. The latter requires running the IRT analyses separately for each group and then transforming the parameter estimates so they can be placed on a common scale. This method involves explicit equating. McGrew and Woodcock (2001) provide an example of the use of explicit equating when the authors used IRT methods to determine whether items functioned differently across race (White-non-White), ethnicity (Hispanic/non-Hispanic), and gender (male/female) on the Woodcock-Johnson-III-Tests of Achievement (WJ-III-Tests of Achievement; Woodcock, McGrew, & Mather, 2001a) and Woodcock-Johnson-III-Tests of Cognitive Abilities (WJ-III-Tests of Cognitive Abilities; Woodcock, McGrew, & Mather, 2001b). The authors

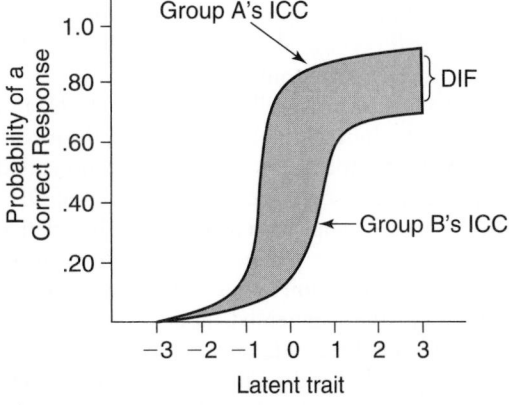

FIGURE 18.2 A visual representation of DIF. DIF is the shaded region between group A and group B's item characteristic curves (ICCs).

conducted DIF analyses using the Rasch IRT model. DIF analyses were performed on the items on the Comprehension-Knowledge test of the WJ-III-Tests of Cognitive Abilities and the Academic Knowledge test of the WJ-III-Tests of Achievement. Five of the items on these tests were identified as displaying significant DIFs. One of these five items was eventually dropped because it displayed significant DIF and was identified as problematic in separate bias reviews conducted by content experts.

The anchor-test method, a more implicit equating approach recommended by Camilli and Shepard (1994), requires that estimated parameters for both groups be simultaneously equated during a single computer estimation run using MML. During the computer run, all items except the item of interest, known as the anchor item, are constrained. This procedure is repeated for each item on the test so that biased items will not spoil the estimation of the examinee's latent trait.

To determine the degree of DIF, an IRT method for measuring the size of the area or differential performance of the two groups on a test is needed. The IRT measures of DIF include simple area indexes, b parameter difference indexes, pseudo-IRT indexes, and probability difference indexes. According to Camilli and Shepard (1994), probability difference indexes are the preferred methods because these methods have more stability and power and have outperformed the other measures in DIF detection. Once the degree of DIF is measured, an IRT statistical test such as the test of b differences, item drift method, Lord's chi-square, bootstrap and jackknife methods, or model comparison measures is performed to determine whether DIF is statistically significant.

According to Camilli and Shepard (1994) and Thissen, Steinberg, and Wainer (1993), the model comparison procedures are the recommended approaches to use to test for significance of DIF. In the model comparison procedures, the relative fit of the compact model (which assumes all of the estimated parameters for all groups are the same) and the augmented model (which allows one, two, or three estimated parameters to vary) are compared. Based on the comparison, an item fit statistic is calculated. If the item fit statistic is significant, significant DIF exists for that one item. This procedure is repeated for all items on the test. Once this procedure is completed, those items with significant DIFs undergo further

empirical study and deliberation to determine if they are biased. If the items are determined to be biased, they are removed from the test. Bracken and McCallum (1998b) used item fit statistics to identify possible items for inclusion on the Universal Nonverbal Intelligence Test (UNIT; Bracken & McCallum, 1998a). Although the type of item fit statistic used was not specified, item fit statistics were calculated in relation to the total sample and specific cultural subsamples.

The IRT methods are the preferred techniques to detect item bias because they provide the most sensitive tests for DIF and they produce generalizable results. However, IRT methods do have their drawbacks that may limit their usefulness. These methods require large samples for testing model fit, resources, time, and computer programming expertise. As a result, contingency table (CT) approaches, using nonparametric methods, for detecting DIF are often used in applied test development contexts.

In comparison to the IRT methods, CT approaches correspond closely to the visual inspection of the area between the ICC curves (Camilli & Shepard, 1994). The CT methods for testing DIF include logistic regression, summed chi-square, and Mantel-Haenszel chi-square. The Mantel-Haenszel technique for testing DIF has been used in the test development of many cognitive measures, including the Cognitive Assessment System (CAS, Naglieri & Das, 1997a) and the Stanford-Binet Intelligence Scales–Fifth Edition (SB5, Roid, 2003a). Naglieri and Das (1997b) applied the Mantel-Haenszel technique to the items included in all of the subtests that measure successive and simultaneous processing, with the exception of one subtest. Naglieri and Das tested for DIF across gender (male, female), race (African American, White), and ethnicity (Hispanic, non-Hispanic). Significant DIFs were reported for less than 5% of the items. The authors removed all of these items from the CAS. The Mantel-Haenszel technique was also applied to the items on the SB5. Roid (2003b) tested for DIF across gender (male, female), race (African American, White), and ethnicity (Hispanic, non-Hispanic). Of the more than 400 standardization items on the SB5, only five items were dropped from the test due to significant DIFs. Both the CT and IRT methods have their advantages; however, the decision whether to use one or the other often boils down to sample size.

The IRT models, such as those used to detect DIF, are conceptually similar to other models, such as ANOVA. The IRT models to detect DIF are primarily superior to previous methods because they are less sample-dependent, and they allow one to estimate multiple item statistics more precisely than a technique like ANOVA. Using the item characteristic curves, DIF more accurately and readily detects when the probability of a particular response changes as a function of some nominal variable (e.g., gender or ethnicity) for individuals with the same relative standing on the latent trait assessed.

Partial Correlation

The partial correlation procedure was developed independently by Stricker (1982) and Reynolds, Willson, and Chatman (1985). The partial correlation procedure allows one to test for differences between groups by determining the amount of variation in the observed scores not due to the total score. In this method, a partial correlation is calculated between the item score and a demographic variable (e.g., gender or ethnicity), partialling out the correlation between the demographic variable and total score. The total score is held constant across the nominal groups of interest in this method and any significant difference noted is used to identify a potentially biased item. When partial correlations have been calculated to detect item bias, no systematic bias in measures of intelligence and related aptitudes has been found (Reynolds et al., 1999).

Reynolds and Kamphaus (2003b) used the partial correlation method to screen for potentially biased items on the Reynolds Intellectual Assessment Scales (RIAS; Reynolds & Kamphaus, 2003a). Reynolds and Kamphaus computed partial correlations between the observed scores and each demographic variable, (i.e., gender, race, and ethnicity), partialling out the correlation between subtest total scores and each demographic variable of interest in separate analyses. Partial correlations were calculated and comparisons were made between males and females, African Americans and Hispanics, African Americans and Whites, and Hispanics and non-Hispanics. Reynolds and Kamphaus also examined item bias across gender and ethnicity by age groups using the partial correlation procedure. In applying this procedure, the authors were able to determine whether a developmental interaction (i.e., a gender by age

or an ethnicity by age interaction) was present. The authors detected several potentially biased items at different age levels, especially between non-Hispanics and Hispanics, using this method. Had the partial correlation method not been applied by age group to the items on the RIAS, these items may never have been detected. All potentially biased items using the partial correlation procedure were eliminated from the test.

Bracken and McCallum (1998b) also used the partial correlation method to detect potentially biased items in the development of the UNIT. Demographic variables examined in their analyses were gender, race, and ethnicity. Results of the partial correlational analyses revealed that no more than 2.25% of the variance of an item was associated with a nominal variable of interest. Based on these results, Bracken and McCallum concluded that overall the items on the UNIT were not significantly related to gender, race, or ethnicity.

Multiple-Choice Items and Attractiveness of Distractors

With multiple-choice tests, another level of complexity is added to the examination of content bias. With a multiple-choice question, three or four distractors are typically given, in addition to the correct response. Distractors may be examined for their attractiveness (the relative frequency with which they are chosen) across groups. When distractors are found to be disproportionately attractive for members of any particular group, the item may be defined as biased. When items are constructed to have an equal distribution of responses to each distractor for the total test population, chi-square can be used to examine the distribution of choices for each distractor for each group (Burrill, 1975).

Jensen (1976) investigated the distribution of wrong responses for two multiple-choice intelligence tests, the Peabody Picture Vocabulary Test (PPVT; Dunn, 1959) and Raven's Progressive Matrices (Raven, 1960). These two tests were individually administered to 600 White and 400 African American children between the ages of 6 and 12. The analysis of incorrect responses for the PPVT indicated that the errors were distributed in a nonrandom fashion across the distractors for a large number of items. However, no racial bias in response patterns occurred because the disproportionate choice of distractors followed the same pattern for African Americans and Whites. On the Raven, African Americans made different types of errors than Whites, but only on a small number of items. Jensen followed up on these items and compared the African American response pattern to the response pattern of White children at a variety of age levels. For every item showing differences in African American–White response patterns, the African American response patterns could be duplicated by the response patterns of Whites approximately two years younger than African Americans.

Veale and Foreman (1983) have advocated inspecting multiple-choice tests for bias in distractor or "foil" response distribution as a means of refining tests *before* they are finalized for public use. They note that there are many instances in which unbiased external criteria (such as achievement or ability) or culturally valid tests are not readily accessible for detecting bias in the measure under study. They add that inspection of incorrect responses to distractor items can often lead to greater insight into cultural bias in any given question than would inspection of the percentage of correct responses across groups. Veale and Foreman provide the statistical analyses for their "overpull probability model," along with the procedures for measuring cultural variation and diagramming the source of bias in any given item.

P Decrements

Jensen (1976) pursued another approach to the identification of biased items. According to Jensen, if a test contains items that are disproportionately more difficult for one group of examinees than another, the correlation of P decrements between adjacent items will be low for the two groups. (A P decrement is the difference in the difficulty index, P, from one item of a test to the next item. Typically, power tests such as tests of aptitude and achievement are arranged in ascending order of difficulty). Jensen (1974, 1976) also contends that if a test contains biased items, the correlation between the rank order of item difficulties for one group with another will be low.

This method has proved popular with some test publishers who want to look at the items on a test as a group, despite the fact that this approach may be overly sensitive. Using the Detroit Tests of Learning Aptitude (DTLA–3; Hammill, 1991a), Hammill (1991b) reported

correlations of P decrements of .90 or above for all subtests (with most above .95). Similar results have been reported for other aptitude measures. On the 14 subtests of the Test of Memory and Learning (TOMAL; Reynolds & Bigler, 1994a), Reynolds and Bigler (1994b) reported correlations across P decrements by gender and ethnicity. All correlations across P decrements were above .90 (with most above .95).

Expert Approaches

A common practice in recent years has been to have expert reviewers evaluate items for new psychological and educational tests for potential bias, offensiveness, or perceived content validity. This approach was used in development of the Kaufman Assessment Battery for Children–Second Edition (K-ABC-II; Kaufman & Kaufman, 2004), the RIAS, the SB5, the UNIT, and a number of other contemporary tests. The practice typically involves asking expert reviewers to evaluate the items with emphasis on content validity and to review the experience of examiners in the administration of the test. In the test development of the SB5, individuals from diverse backgrounds (i.e., different racial, linguistic, and religious backgrounds) served as expert reviewers and these reviewers evaluated items on the SB5 for their content validity and offensiveness in relation to their own social group. Five ethnic, racial, and linguistic groups (i.e., African American, Alaskan Native, American Indian, Asian, Hispanic, and White), five religious groups (i.e., Buddhist, Christian, Jewish, Hindu, and Muslim), two groups with special needs (deafness or hearing impaired and a general category), and gender (male and female) were represented among the expert reviewers. The reviewers' comments were used to select, revise, or delete items for inclusion in the SB5 (Roid, 2003b).

Although expert approaches have been used in the development of tests, scientific data does not support the position that expert reviewers—upon surface inspection—can detect the degree to which any given item will function differentially across groups (Camilli & Shepard, 1994; McGurk, 1951; Reynolds, 2000). Several researchers (Jensen, 1976; Miele, 1979) have shown that expert reviewers are unable to identify culturally biased items in the item review process. However, expert reviewers continue to be used in the item review process in the development of tests even without empirical support. The question is *why*. Those who support the continued use of expert reviewers in the item review process see it as a means of gaining greater rapport with the public. As pointed out by Sandoval and Mille (1979), "Public opinion, whether it is supported by empirical findings, or based on emotion, can serve as an obstacle to the use of a measurement instrument" (p. 7). The elimination of items that are offensive or otherwise objectionable to any substantive segment of the population for whom the test is intended seems an appropriate action that may aid in the public's acceptance of new and better psychological assessment tools. However, the expert approach should not be allowed to supplant the use of more sophisticated analyses in the determination of biased items. The expert approach should serve as a supplemental procedure, and items identified through this method can be eliminated when a) some interrater agreement between the expert reviewers can be obtained and b) a psychometrically equivalent (or better) item can replace the offensive item when the intent of the item is kept intact (Reynolds, 2000).

Bias in Construct Validity

Construct validity refers to "a judgment about the appropriateness of inferences drawn from tests scores regarding individual standings" on a specified construct or trait (Cohen & Swerdlik, 1999, p. 197). No single method has been developed for the accurate determination of the construct validity of educational and psychological tests. Defining bias in construct validity thus requires a general statement that can be researched from a variety of viewpoints with a broad range of methodologies. Reynolds (1982a) offered a definition of bias in relation to construct validity that allows investigations from different perspectives, using a broad range of methods, stating that "bias exists in regard to construct validity when a test is shown to measure different hypothetical traits (i.e., psychological constructs) for one group than another or to measure the same trait but with differing degrees of accuracy" (p. 194). Reynolds (2000) notes the importance of investigating bias in educational and psychological tests. If bias is present in our major measurement tools, then much of the research on group differences of the twentieth century would need to be discarded because the findings of the research would be confounded and some of the major

theories in education and psychology would need to be abandoned because they would not be accurate or relevant.

As befits the concept of construct validity, many different methods have been employed to examine existing tests for potential bias. One of the most popular and most important group of empirical approaches to investigating construct validity is factor analysis (Anastasi, 1988; Cronbach, 1990).

Factor Analytic Methods

Factor analysis is a family of empirical approaches that identifies clusters of test items or clusters of subtests of psychological or educational tests that correlate highly with one another but less so or not at all with other items or subtests. Factor analysis allows one to determine patterns of interrelationships of performance among groups of individuals. For example, if several subtests of an intelligence scale are most salient on the same factor and if a group of individuals score high on one of these subtests, it would also be expected that this group of individuals would score high on the other subtests that are highly salient on the same factor. Psychologists attempt to determine, through a review of the test content and correlates of performance on the factor in question, what psychological trait underlies performance; or, in a more hypothesis-testing approach, they will make predictions concerning the pattern of factor coefficients.

Although researchers do not necessarily agree that the results of factor analysis speak to the innateness of the abilities being measured by an instrument, consistent factor analytic results across populations do provide strong evidence that whatever is being measured by the instrument is being measured in the same manner and is, in fact, the same construct within each group. The information derived from comparative factor analysis across populations is directly relevant to the use of educational and psychological tests in diagnosis and other decision-making functions. For psychologists to make consistent interpretations of test score data, they must be certain that a test measures the same variable across populations.

Two basic approaches, exploratory and confirmatory factor analytic approaches, have been used to compare factor analytic results across populations. Exploratory factor analysis is the more popular of the two approaches and addresses the issue of the degree of similarity of the latent structure of a test across nominal groups of interest. In contrast, confirmatory factor analysis determines whether there is a statistically significant difference in the results of the factor analysis across nominal groups of interest. With confirmatory factor analysis, researchers are interested in determining how different the latent structure is across groups. However, for interpretation of test scores, the exploratory factor analytic approach may be of more value and relevance than the confirmatory factor analytic approach because the use of large sample sizes with the confirmatory factor analytic approach may yield statistically significant differences, when in reality the differences reported are trivial. This leads to the entire argument about statistical significance testing and the role of effect sizes, which will not be covered in this chapter. In comparing the usefulness of these two approaches, the exploratory factor analytic approach has more importance to the practical application of tests to diagnosis, whereas the confirmatory factor analytic approach may be more important in hypothesis-testing research. Several methods for testing for statistically significant differences and for examining similarities across groups have been developed. A discussion of these methods follows.

Methods for Assessing Similarities of the Latent Structure Across Groups

A number of techniques have been developed to measure the similarity of factors across groups. The techniques include the Pearson correlation coefficient, coefficient of congruence, factor score comparison, and salient variable similarity index. When large sample sizes are used, these techniques produce similar results (Reynolds & Harding, 1983). However, when only small sample sizes are available, the use of more than one method is recommended because of the possible effects of sampling error (Reynolds & Harding, 1983). Each of these techniques has its advantages and disadvantages, and some of these techniques have proven to be more satisfactory than others.

The two most common methods of determining factorial similarity or factorial invariance involve the direct comparison of factor coefficients across groups. The two primary techniques for this comparison are (1) the calculation of a coefficient of congruence (Harman, 1976) between the factor coefficients of the pairs of corresponding factors for two groups and (2) the simple calculation of a Pearson product-moment correlation coefficient between the factor coefficients of the corresponding factors. Although the latter technique was used with some frequency in the past, it is no longer recommended because in the comparison of factor coefficients of the pairs of matched factors across groups certain assumptions that underlie the Pearson r may be violated (i.e., linearity and normality) and transformation of the factor coefficients to Fisher zs before computing the Pearson r statistic does not correct the problem (Cattell, 1978; Reynolds, 2000).

As mentioned, the coefficient of congruence is a common method used to determine whether the pairs of corresponding factors on a measure are similar across groups. To determine the coefficient of congruence between a pair of corresponding factors for two groups (e.g., males and females) on a measure, factor coefficients for the males and females on each item are multiplied together and summed, and then divided by the square root of the factor coefficients for the males squared and summed times the factor coefficients for the females squared and summed. A coefficient of congruence value of .90 or above indicates, although arbitrarily, that the pair of corresponding factors is similar across groups (Cattell, 1978; Harman, 1976, Mulaik, 1972).

There are two potential limitations associated with the use of the coefficient of congruence. The first potential limitation is whether the coefficient of congruence should be computed using factor coefficients derived from orthogonal rotation procedures to examine the pair of matched factors on a measure across groups of interest. The second potential limitation is the use of the coefficient of congruence index when the variances across groups of interest are not equal. Reynolds (2000) reported that these potential limitations may attenuate the value of the coefficient of congruence. However, attenuation of the value of the coefficient of congruence would actually reduce the risk of overinterpreting the results.

Another method of assessing the similarity of pairs of corresponding factors across groups is the salient variable similarity index (Cattell, 1978). Unlike the coefficient of congruence, which is a parametric statistic, the salient variable similarity index is a nonparametric statistic and is often used to supplement the interpretation of the coefficient of congruence. The computation of the salient variable similarity index in addition to the coefficient of congruence is often performed because the salient variable similarity index is not affected by factor size or nonequivalent variance-covariance matrices (Reynolds & Paget, 1981). To calculate the salient variable similarity index, the pairs of matched factors' factor coefficients are classified as either being salient or nonsalient and positive or negative (based on the sign of the variable's factor coefficient). Salience or nonsalience for a factor coefficient is determined by the cutoff value chosen. Cattell (1978) recommended a cutoff value of ± .10 as the threshold of salience, so any factor coefficient with an absolute value of .10 or higher would be classified as being salient. Although Reynolds (2000) agreed that a threshold of salience of ± .10 is appropriate for personality measures, he believed this threshold of salience was too liberal for cognitive measures, which have higher internal consistency reliabilities and a strong general factor, *g*. Reynolds recommended a threshold of salience of ± .15 up to ± .25 for cognitive measures. Once a factor coefficient is determined to be positively or negatively salient or not salient, it is paired with the factor coefficient of the comparison group on each variable (e.g., item) of a factor, then the pairings are entered into a matrix (see Table 18.1).

After all pairings for a factor are recorded (a simple frequency count) in the matrix, then the numbers are inserted into the salient variable similarity index formula. The formula for the salient variable similarity index (*s*) follows:

$$s = \frac{f_{11} + f_{33} - f_{13} - f_{31}}{f_{11} + f_{33} + f_{13} + f_{31} + \frac{f_{11} + f_{33} - f_{13} - f_{31}}{2}}$$

Salient variable similarity index values range from −1.00 to +1.00. The closer the salient variable similarity index value is to +1.00, the more similar the matched factors are across the groups of interest. In contrast, a negative salient variable similarity index value is a strong indicator of bias, barring no error in the calculation of the salient variable similarity index and the use of well-developed scales (Reynolds, 2000). Cattell (1978) provides tables for determining whether a salient variable similarity index value is statistically significant.

Lowe and Lee (2008) computed the coefficient of congruence and salient variable similarity index values for pairs of corresponding factors across gender on the Test Anxiety Inventory for Children and Adolescents (TAICA; Lowe & Lee, 2004). The TAICA is a 45-item multidimensional self-report measure of test anxiety for elementary and secondary school students in grades 4 through 12. The TAICA is based on the most recent conceptualizations of the test anxiety construct (see Friedman & Bendas-Jacob, 1997; Hodapp, 1996; Stöber, 2004; Zeidner, 1998). The TAICA consists of a Total Test Anxiety scale, Performance Enhancement/Facilitation Anxiety scale, Lie scale, and four debilitating test anxiety subscales (Cognitive Obstruction/Inattention, Physiological Hyperarousal, Social Humiliation, and Worry). Coefficient of congruence values ranged from .93 for the Cognitive Obstruction/Inattention subscale to .99 for the Performance Enhancement/Facilitation Anxiety scale and Total Test Anxiety scale, and all salient variable similarity index values were statistically significant for the six-factor promax solution. Based on these findings, the authors concluded that the latent structure of the TAICA was invariant across gender.

In addition to gender, Reynolds and Kamphaus (2003b) examined the similarity of the factor structure across race on the RIAS. Reynolds and Kamphaus computed coefficient of

TABLE 18.1 **Salient Variable Similarity Index Matrix**

Factor for Group A	Factor for Group B		
	Positive Salient Factor Coefficient	**Nonsalient Factor Coefficient**	**Negative Salient Factor Coefficient**
Positive salient factor coefficient	f_{11}	f_{12}	f_{13}
Nonsalient factor coefficient	f_{21}	f_{22}	f_{23}
Negative salient factor coefficient	f_{31}	f_{32}	f_{33}

Source: Adapted from formulas given in R. B. Cattell (1978, p. 257).

congruence and salient variable similarity index values separately by gender (male, female) and race (African American, White) for multiple solutions on the RIAS. The authors reported coefficient of congruence values of .98 to .99 across gender and race on the RIAS. In addition, all salient variable similarity index values were statistically significant across gender and race. Based on these findings, Reynolds and Kamphaus concluded that the factor structure of the RIAS was invariant across groups.

Reynolds (2002b) also addressed the issue of factorial invariance on the Comprehensive Trail-Making Test (CTMT; Reynolds, 2002a) across gender (male, female) and race/ethnicity (African American, European–American, and Hispanic). The CTMT consists of five visual scanning, search and sequencing tasks. Performance on these tasks are influenced by visual scanning, search and sequencing skills as well as an individual's attention, concentration, cognitive flexibility, and resistance to distraction. Exploratory factor analyses were performed separately for males and females and for the three racial/ethnic groups. The same factor extraction methods and rotational procedures were used with the subgroups as had been used with the total sample. Two factors, a simple sequencing factor and a complex sequencing factor, emerged from the factor analysis performed for each of the subgroups. Coefficient of congruence and salient variable similarity index values were computed separately for the corresponding factors across gender and across race/ethnicity. Coefficient of congruence and salient variable similarity index values reported suggested high degrees of factorial similarity across gender and race/ethnicity.

Lowe and Reynolds (2005, 2006) examined the factor structure of two personality measures, the Adult Manifest Anxiety Scale–College Version (AMAS-C; Reynolds, Richmond, & Lowe, 2003a) and the Adult Manifest Anxiety Scale–Elderly Version (AMAS-E; Reynolds, Richmond, & Lowe, 2003b) across gender to determine whether test bias existed. The AMAS-C and AMAS-E are upward extensions of the Revised Children's Manifest Anxiety Scale (RCMAS; Reynolds & Richmond, 1978). The AMAS-C and AMAS-E assess chronic, manifest anxiety in the college student and older adult populations, respectively. The AMAS-C consists of four anxiety subscales (Physiological Anxiety, Social Concern/Stress, Test Anxiety, and Worry/Oversensitivity) and a Lie scale, whereas the AMAS-E consists of three anxiety subscales (Fear of Aging, Physiological

Anxiety, and Worry/Oversensitivity) and a Lie scale. In addition to the anxiety subscales and the Lie scale, both the AMAS-C and AMAS-E have a Total Anxiety scale (Reynolds, Richmond, & Lowe, 2003c). Lowe and Reynolds factor analyzed separately the responses of the total sample and the male and female subsamples on both versions of the AMAS and then calculated coefficient of congruence and salient variable similarity index values for the pairs of corresponding factors for each measure across gender. Coefficient of congruence values for the AMAS-C and AMAS-E ranged from .91 to .98 (Lowe & Reynolds, 2005) and from .91 to .99 (Lowe & Reynolds, 2006), respectively. In addition, all salient variable similarity index values for the AMAS-C and AMAS-E were statistically significant (Lowe & Reynolds, 2005, 2006). The authors concluded that the AMAS-C and AMAS-E were invariant across gender.

Another method for examining the similarity of the factor structure across groups of interest involves the use of factor score comparisons (Katzenmeyer & Stenner, 1977). In factor score comparisons, the Pearson r statistic is computed between the factor scores of the combined groups of interest and each separate group of interest. The factor scores are composite scores and these scores are obtained by summing an individual's weighted scores for each item, subtest, or scale on a factor. The weights are directly related to the factor coefficients. Pearson correlation coefficients are then examined to determine whether the factor structure is invariant across groups. According to Reynolds (2000), factor score comparisons have not been used extensively. However, Reynolds believes this technique is a good method to use to examine the similarity of the factors across groups of interest.

A few technical issues need to be highlighted in conducting test bias research with exploratory factor analytic techniques. The first technical issue has to do with small sample sizes. Samples of less than 200 individuals for each group or a variable ratio of less than 10:1 may produce large standard errors of correlations of variables with factors. Under these circumstances, the magnitude of the standard errors needs to be examined and more than one factorial similarity index should be computed before bias in a test is assumed because the factorial similarity indices fall below the criterion cutoff value or level of significance. The second technical issue has to do with the number of factor extraction methods to use in studies of bias. Reynolds (2000) states there are many competing views and suggest one of two options. The first option is to select a factor extraction method (e.g., eigenvalues greater than one rule, use of scree plots, or preferred theory of the investigator) and apply it to the majority group when factor analyzing the majority group's responses. Then apply this method to the minority group and compare the pairs of matched factors on the measure across groups of interest using one or more factorial similarity indices to determine whether test bias exists. The second and preferred option, because it produces more stable results, is to select a factor extraction method and apply it to the combined sample when factor analyzing the combined sample's responses. Then apply the same factor extraction method when factor analyzing separately the responses of each group and compare the pairs of corresponding factors on the measure across groups using one or more similarity indices to determine whether bias exists.

Methods for Assessing Differences in the Latent Structure Across Groups

Unlike exploratory factor analysis, confirmatory factor analysis addresses the issue of how different the latent structure of a measure is across groups. The method of confirmatory factor analysis, originally developed by Jöreskog (1969, 1971), allows for simultaneous model fitting of the hypothesized factor structure across multiple groups. Goodness-of-fit statistics such as chi-square (χ^2), comparative fit index (CFI), and root mean square error of approximation (RMSEA) are calculated across the factor analytic results of two or more groups to check for invariance of the model. Goodness-of-fit statistics calculated provide information on the fit of the model across groups of interest. If the goodness-of-fit statistics suggest a lack of fit of the model across groups, test bias may be present. Confirmatory factor analytic computational methods are quite complex and a full treatment of this method is beyond the scope of this chapter. Although this approach has not been used extensively in the area of test bias yet, studies are beginning to appear in the literature.

McGrew and Woodcock (2001) conducted three multiple group confirmatory factor analyses (CFAs) comparing females and males, Hispanics and non-Hispanics, and Whites and non-Whites on the broad factors of the WJ-III. McGrew

and Woodcock were interested in determining whether the factor model based on the work of Horn and Cattell (see Horn, 1988) and Carroll (1993) was invariant across groups. According to Carroll (1998), the Cattell-Horn-Carroll model is highly similar across gender and race. McGrew and Woodcock (2001) conducted the CFAs and reported root mean square of error approximation (RMSEA) values between .039 and .042. These values suggest that the WJ-III factor model is invariant across the cultural groups studied.

Bracken and McCallum (1998b) applied the multiple group confirmatory factor analysis procedure in their examination of the UNIT across different groups, including females, males, African Americans, and Hispanics. The factor structure of Whites was presumed to have been examined earlier when the factor structure of the entire sample was evaluated. The authors reported RMSEA values and 12 additional fit statistics for each group based on three different models examined. The three different models examined were a one-factor model, a memory-reasoning model, and a symbolic-nonsymbolic model. Results suggested that the one-factor model was invariant across groups.

Jensen's (1980) chi-square method is another technique for evaluating significant differences between factors of a measure across two groups. The chi-square method involves converting all the factor coefficients on each factor on the measure to Fisher z scores for the two groups. Then the factor coefficients for one group are paired with the factor coefficients for the other group by variable. Next, the difference between paired z scores is determined. These differences are squared and then summed. Finally, this value is divided by the standard error of measurement of the difference in the factor coefficients. The standard error of measurement of the difference in the factor coefficients is determined by the following formula

$$\sqrt{(1/N_1 - 3) + (1/N_2 - 3)}$$

where N_1 represents the number of subjects in Group 1 and N_2 is the number of individuals in Group 2. The statistic obtained will be distributed as a chi-square with one degree of freedom.

Another method to assess cultural group differences is to examine the correlation matrices of the groups (see Jensen, 1980). Although there is no direct statistical test to investigate the equivalence of correlation matrices across groups, Jensen's (1980) chi-square method (mentioned above) may be applied to give one an approximation of the difference between the matrices of the two groups. In this test of significance, the correlations of the two matrices are transformed to Fisher zs. Then the correlations of one matrix are paired with the correlations of the other matrix. Next, the paired correlations are squared separately and then a difference is obtained for each pair of the correlations. Finally, the differences are squared and summed and a mean of the squared differences is calculated. This value represents the numerator. The numerator is then divided by the standard error of measurement of the difference between correlations. The formula for the standard error of measurement of the difference between correlations is as follows

$$\sqrt{(1/N_1 - 3) + (1/N_2 - 3)}$$

where N_1 represents the number of participants in Group 1 and N_2 is the number of individuals in Group 2. The statistic as mentioned above is a chi-square statistic with one degree of freedom. Jensen suggests that the alpha level for this statistical analysis be set at .01, so the results will not be overinterpreted. In addition to examining differences between correlation matrices of cultural groups, researchers may wish to investigate differences in covariance matrices across cultural groups. However, caution needs to be exercised when researchers examine these differences in large samples, as statistically significant differences found between the variances in the covariance matrices across cultural groups may be trivial.

Roid (2003b) used Jensen's chi-square method to examine differences in the correlation matrices across racial/ethnic groups. Roid's random sample of examinees was from the standardization sample of the SB5 and consisted of 443 African Americans, 129 Asians, 447 Hispanics, and 450 Whites. The 10 verbal and nonverbal subtests of the SB5 were correlated for each of the groups. Then, the correlations from the correlation matrix of the majority (i.e., White) group were compared to the correlations from the correlation matrix of each of the minority groups. Jensen's chi-square method was performed for each group comparison. No chi-square values were statistically significant at the .01 level. Thus, equivalence of correlation matrices across

cultural groups included in Roid's study was established.

Reliability Methods to Examine Construct Bias

As is appropriate for studies of construct validity, comparative factor analysis has not been the only method of determining whether single-group or differential validity exists. Another group of techniques to investigate construct bias is the use of reliability methods including internal consistency reliability, test-retest reliability, and alternate forms reliability.

Internal Consistency Reliability

A comparison of the reliability estimates of internal consistency across groups is one method to investigate construct bias. Internal consistency reliability refers to the degree to which the items on a scale or subscale are all measuring a similar construct. To be unbiased in construct validity, internal consistency reliability estimates should be approximately equal across groups. This characteristic has been investigated with males, females, African Americans, Hispanics, and Whites on a number of popular aptitude tests.

Reynolds and Kamphaus (2003b) calculated coefficient alphas separately by gender and age and by race and age for the different subtests on the RIAS. Coefficient alphas ranged from .84 to .98 and from .85 to .97 for females and males, respectively, on the different subtests of the RIAS. Coefficient alphas for African Americans and Whites ranged from .70 to .99 and .83 to .98, respectively, on the different subtests. Reynolds and Kamphaus then used the Feldt technique (1969) to determine whether the coefficient alphas on the different subtests were statistically significantly different from each other across gender and race. The Feldt calculation (see formula below) involves dividing the largest error variance (1-alpha) or $(1-r_{xx})$ for the groups being compared on a particular subtest or scale by the smallest error variance (1-alpha) or $(1-r_{xx})$ for the groups being compared on the same subtest or scale. This analysis yields an F-value. Once an F-value is obtained, it is compared to the critical F-value, which is determined by the degrees of freedom in the numerator (N_1-1) and denominator (N_2-1). F-values exceeding the critical F-value are statistically significantly different and these differences suggest the presence of test bias. The equation for the Feldt technique is as follows:

$$F = \frac{1\text{-alpha}_1}{1\text{-alpha}_2}$$

Reynolds and Kamphaus (2003b) found no significant differences across gender and race on the different subtests of the RIAS using the Feldt technique with Bonferroni corrections, suggesting homogeneity of test content across gender and race on the RIAS.

Roid (2003b) also compared the reliability estimates of internal consistency across groups to investigate construct bias on the SB5. Roid calculated coefficient alphas for African Americans, Hispanics, and Whites by two age groups (ages 6 to 10 and ages 11 to 16) and used the Feldt technique to determine whether there were any significant differences on the verbal and nonverbal scales of the SB5. Coefficient alphas ranged from .73 to .90 across race/ethnicity on the verbal and nonverbal scales of the SB5. Feldt's statistic was calculated and no significant differences in the comparisons made between majority and minority groups were found, with the exception of one comparison between Hispanics and Whites, ages 6 to 10, on the verbal subtests. The one significant difference noted on the verbal subtests favored Hispanics.

Bracken and McCallum (1998b) compared internal consistency reliability estimates across cultural groups using the split-half method corrected with the Spearman-Brown formula to investigate construct bias on the subtests and scales of the UNIT. Bracken and McCallum calculated reliability estimates for females, males, African Americans, and Hispanics. It should be noted that reliability estimates for the total sample had been computed earlier across the different subtests and scales of the UNIT. Bracken and McCallum reported scale reliability coefficients corrected with the formula for reliability of linear combinations (Nunnally, 1978) and another set of scale reliability coefficients corrected with Gulliksen and Wilks' (1950) formula to account for age restriction or expansion. Overall, Bracken and McCallum did not find evidence to suggest bias on the UNIT.

Although not an aptitude test, Reynolds (2002b) examined internal consistency estimates across gender and race/ethnicity to determine whether construct bias was present on the CTMT. Reynolds computed coefficient alphas separately by gender (male, female) and race/ethnicity (African American, European American, Hispanic) for the five different trail-making tasks and the composite index on the CTMT. Coefficient alphas ranged from .70 to .93 and from .71 to .93 for females and males, respectively, on the different trail-making tasks and the composite index. Coefficient alphas for African Americans, European Americans, and Hispanics ranged from .76 to .93, .70 to .93, and .73 to .92, respectively, on the different trail-making tasks and the composite index. Reynolds then used the Feldt technique to test for significance of the difference of these reliability estimates and found no significant differences across gender and race/ethnicity. However, Reynolds did report that the CTMT scores were slightly more reliable for African Americans and Hispanics than European Americans.

Test-Retest Reliability

Another method to use to investigate the existence of construct bias in reliability estimates of a measure across groups is test-retest reliability. In the test-retest reliability method, differences in the test-retest correlations across groups are examined. To determine whether there is a significant difference between the test-retest correlations across groups, a Z statistic is calculated. The Z statistic is computed by transforming the test-retest correlations into Fisher zs. The Fisher zs of one group (z_1) is subtracted from the Fisher zs of the other group (z_2) and summed. Then the summed difference in the Fisher zs between the two groups is divided by the standard error of the difference between the Fisher zs (i.e., the square root of 1 divided by N_1-3 plus 1 divided by N_2-3 where N_1 and N_2 are the sample sizes of Groups 1 and 2, respectively). Finally, a table of the normal curve may be used to determine whether the Z-value obtained is significant. The formula for the Z statistic follows:

$$Z = \sum z_{1-z2} / \sqrt{(1/N_1 - 3 + 1/N_2 - 3)}$$

When a significant difference between the test-retest correlations is found, the results should be interpreted with caution. The difference between test-retest correlations may indicate the existence of test bias or it may be due to other factors such as practice effects on cognitive measures or instability in a trait examined on a personality measure across time.

Alternate Forms Reliability

The Z statistic may also be applied to alternate forms reliability correlations to determine the existence of test bias across groups. To compute the Z statistic, the groups of interest take both forms of the measure or test and Pearson *r* statistics are calculated between the scores of each group on both forms. Then, the correlations obtained are transformed to Fisher zs and the same procedures are followed to compute the Z statistic as described above. The alternate forms reliability method is more likely to be used when coefficient alpha or Kuder-Richardson 20 (KR_{20}), a special case of coefficient alpha when responses on a measure are recorded on a dichotomous scale, are not possible or inappropriate to compute.

Other Methods to Assess Construct Bias

Other methods (e.g., multitrait-multimethod validation, comparative item selection, kinship correlation and difference, and correlation of raw scores with age) have been developed and some of these methods have been used to determine the construct validity of popular psychometric instruments across groups. Because intelligence is considered a developmental phenomenon, the correlation of raw scores with age has been viewed as one measure of construct validity for intelligence tests. Reynolds and Kamphaus (2003b) examined developmental trends on the RIAS for children and adolescents, ages 3 to 18, across gender (male, female) and race/ethnicity (African American, Hispanic, White). Reynolds and Kamphaus computed correlations between age and raw score for each subtest for the total sample, male and female subsamples, and the three racial/ethnic subsamples. Reynolds and Kamphaus found that none of the correlations between age and raw scores differed significantly across groups for any of the subtests. The actual differences reported between the correlations for each subtest for all groups were relatively small, with the largest absolute difference of .06 being noted. Overall, these results provide support for the developmental nature of the latent constructs of the RIAS subtests across gender and race/ethnicity.

Construct validity of a large number of popular psychometric assessment instruments has been investigated across race/ethnicity and gender with minority and majority children

and adolescents and with a divergent set of methodologies (see Reynolds, 2000, for a review of methodologies). All roads have led to Rome: No consistent evidence of bias in construct validity has been found with any of the many measures investigated. This leads to the conclusion that psychological tests (especially aptitude tests) function in essentially the same manner; test materials are perceived and reacted to in a similar manner, and tests measure the same construct with equivalent accuracy for African Americans, Hispanics, Whites, and other American minorities of both genders. Single-group validity and differential validity have not been found and probably do not exist in well-constructed and well-standardized psychological and educational tests.

Bias in Predictive or Criterion-Related Validity

Evaluating bias in predictive validity of educational and psychological tests is less closely related to the evaluation of group intelligence test score differences than to the evaluation of individual test scores in a more absolute sense. This is especially true for aptitude (as opposed to diagnostic) tests, in which the primary purpose of administration is the prediction of some specific future outcome or behavior. Internal analyses of bias (such as in content and construct validity) are less confounded than analyses of bias in predictive validity, however, because of the potential problems in bias in the criterion measure. Predictive validity is also strongly influenced by the reliability of criterion measures, which frequently are poor. The degree of relationship between a predictor and a criterion is restricted as a function of the square root of the product of the reliabilities of the two variables.

Arriving at a consensual definition of bias in predictive validity is also a difficult task. Yet, from the standpoint of the practical applications of aptitude and intelligence tests, predictive validity is the most crucial form of validity in relation to test bias. Cleary et al. (1975) provide a definition, although slightly rephrased here, of test bias with regard to predictive validity:

> A test is considered biased with respect to predictive validity if the inference drawn from the test score is not made with the smallest feasible random error or if there is constant error in an inference or prediction as a function of membership in a particular group. (p.17)

Examination of Bias in Prediction

The evaluation of bias in prediction under Cleary et al.'s (1975) definition (the regression definition) is quite straightforward. With simple regression, prediction takes the form of $\hat{Y}_i = aX_i + b$, where a is the regression coefficient and b is a constant. When this equation is graphed (forming a regression line), a represents the slope of the regression line and b the Y intercept. Since our definition of fairness in predictive validity requires errors in prediction to be independent of group membership, the regression line formed for any pair of variables must be the same for each group for whom predictions are to be made. Whenever the slope or the intercept differs significantly across groups, there is bias in prediction if one attempts to use a regression equation based on the combined groups. When the regression equation for two (or more) groups is equivalent, prediction is the same for all groups. This condition is referred to variously as homogeneity of regression across groups, simultaneous regression, or fairness in prediction. Homogeneity of regression across groups is illustrated in Figure 18.3. In this case, the single regression equation is appropriate with all groups, any errors in prediction being random with respect to group membership (i.e., residuals uncorrelated with group membership). When homogeneity of regression does not occur, separate regression equations

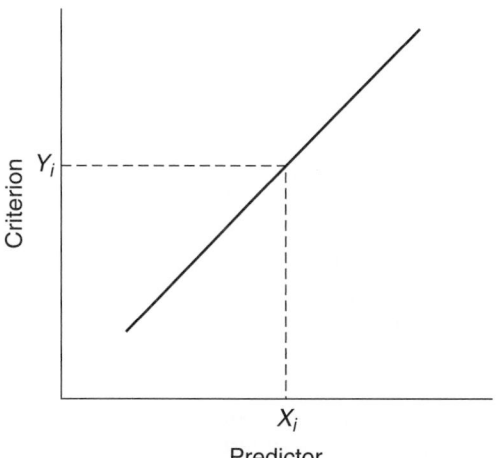

FIGURE 18.3 Equal slopes and intercepts result in homogeneity of regression that causes the regression lines for group a, group b, and the combined group c to be identical.

must be used for each group for fairness in prediction to occur.

In actual clinical practice, regression equations are seldom generated for the prediction of future performance. Instead, some arbitrary or perhaps statistically derived cutoff score is determined, below which failure is predicted. For school performance, IQs that are 2 or more standard deviations below the test mean are used to infer a high probability of failure in the regular classroom if special assistance is not provided for the student in question. Essentially, then, clinicians are establishing mental prediction equations that are assumed to be equivalent across race, gender, and so on. Although these mental equations cannot be readily tested across groups, the actual form of criterion prediction can be compared across groups in several ways. Errors in prediction must be independent of group membership. If regression equations are equal, this condition is met. To test the hypothesis of simultaneous regression, slopes and intercepts must both be compared. An alternative method is the direct examination of residuals through an ANOVA or similar design (Reynolds, 1980a).

Potthoff (1966) has described a useful technique that allows one to test simultaneously the equivalence of regression coefficients and intercepts across K independent groups with a single F ratio (the Potthoff equations may also be found in Reynolds, 1982b). (In addition, Portthoff's method is included in some of the most common statistical software packages, including SAS and SPSS). If a significant F results, the researcher may then test the slopes and intercepts separately for information about which value differs. When homogeneity of regression does not occur, three basic conditions may result: (1) intercept constants differ, (2) regression coefficients (slopes) differ, or (3) slopes and intercepts differ. These conditions are depicted pictorially in Figures 18.4, 18.5, and 18.6, respectively.

The regression coefficient is related to the correlation coefficient between the two variables and is one measure of the strength of that relationship. When intercepts differ and regression coefficients do not, a situation such as that shown in Figure 18.4 results. Relative accuracy of prediction is the same for the two groups (*a* and *b*); yet, the use of a regression derived by combining the two groups results in bias that works against the group with the higher mean criterion score. Because the slope of the

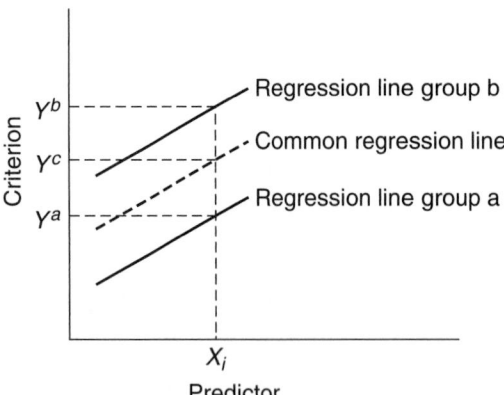

FIGURE 18.4 Equal slopes with differing intercepts result in parallel regression lines and a constant bias in prediction.

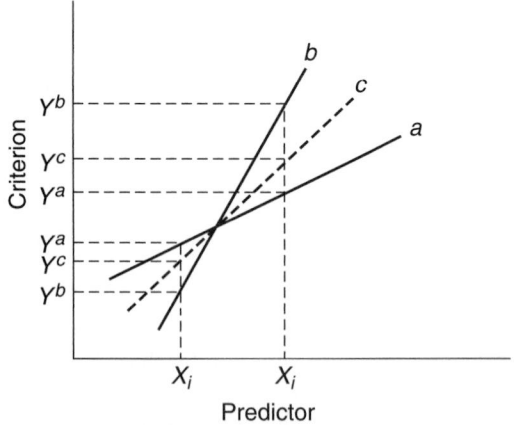

FIGURE 18.6 Differing slopes and intercepts result in the complex condition where the amount and the direction of the bias are a function of the distance of an individual's score from the origin.

regression line is the same for all groups, the degree of error in prediction remains constant and does not fluctuate as a function of an individual's score on the independent variable. That is, regardless of the group b member's score on the predictor, the degree of underprediction in performance on the criterion is the same. As illustrated in Figure 18.4, the use of the common score of Y^c for a score of X overestimates how well members of group a will perform and underestimates the criterion performance of members of group b.

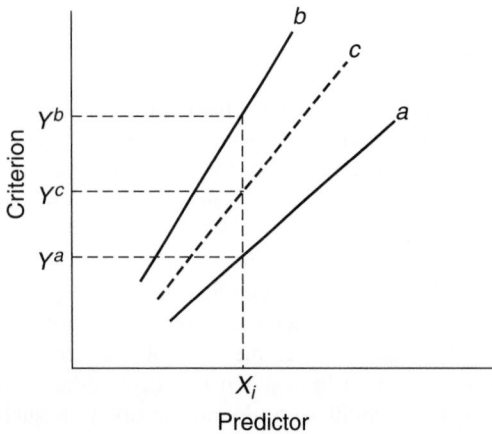

FIGURE 18.5 Equal intercepts and differing slopes result in nonparallel regression lines with the degree of bias dependent on the distance of the individual's score (x_i) from the origin.

In Figure 18.5, nonparallel regression lines illustrate the case in which intercepts are constant across groups but the slope of the line is different for each. Here, too, the performance of the group with the higher mean criterion score is typically underpredicted when a common regression equation is applied. The amount of bias in prediction that results from using the common regression line is the distance of the score from the mean. The most difficult, complex case of bias is represented in Figure 18.6. Here we see the result of significant differences in slopes and intercepts. Not only does the amount of bias in prediction accruing from the use of a common equation vary in this instance, but also the actual direction of bias can reverse, depending on the location of the individual's score in the distribution of the independent variable. Only in the case of Figure 18.6 do members of the group with the lower mean criterion score run the risk of having their performance on the criterion variable underpredicted by the application of a common regression equation.

A considerable body of literature has developed about the differential predictive validity of tests across gender, race, and ethnicity. Studies examining the predictive validity of scores of current measures of intelligence follow.

In the development of the SB5, Roid (2003b) investigated the predictive validity of the SB5 scores with a sample of 472 individuals.

Roid examined gender (female, male), racial (African American, White), and ethnic (Hispanic, non-Hispanic) differences of the SB5 Full Scale IQ scores in predicting scale/composite scores of the WJ-III-Tests of Achievement. Roid looked specifically at the Basic Reading Skills, Reading Comprehension, Math Calculation Skills, Math Reasoning, Broad Math, Written Expression, and Academic Applications scores. Equivalence of regression slopes across gender, race, and ethnicity was found. For the intercepts, no significant differences between groups were reported, with the exception of two significant differences in intercepts based on gender on the WJ-III Reading Comprehension and Written Expression scales. However, Roid reviewed the data and other considerations and came to the conclusion that the SB5 Full Scale IQ was probably not biased in the prediction of academic achievement scores across gender.

Naglieri and Das (1997b) examined the predictive validity of the CAS scores of children across gender, race, and ethnicity. Naglieri and Das' goal was to determine whether the CAS scores predicted achievement as measured by the Woodcock-Johnson Psychoeducational Battery–Revised (WJ-R; Woodcock & Johnson, 1989) Skills cluster scores across the different gender, racial and ethnic groups. Naglieri and Das first matched each of the three samples (female/male, African American/White, and Hispanic/non-Hispanic) on the CAS standard scores and then the test developers examined the equivalence of the regression slopes across the different groups. Results revealed no statistically significant differences in regression slopes across gender, race, and ethnicity.

Bracken and McCallum (1998b) conducted a predictive validity study with the UNIT. Bracken and McCallum examined the differences in the regression slopes by gender (female, male), race (African American, White), and a gender-by-race interaction. The UNIT Full Scale IQ scores served as the predictor variable and the scores of an academic achievement test served as the criterion variable in these analyses. Bracken and McCallum found no significant differences in the regression slopes based on gender, race, or a gender by race interaction.

The Use of One or More Predictor and/or Criterion Variables

Occasionally, practitioners and researchers are interested in using more than one variable

to predict a criterion, one variable to predict several criterion variables, or multiple predictors to predict multiple criterion variables. Several methods are available to detect bias in these cases. An extension of Potthoff's (1966) single-test method or a method recommended by Reynolds (1980b), which involves the use of residual (error) terms, may be used to predict a criterion based on one or more predictor variables. The former method is a more complicated approach to use because it is difficult to estimate exact probability levels, thus increasing the likelihood of Type I errors. In contrast, the latter method is a less complicated approach to use. Criterion scores for all individuals are predicted based on the total sample. Residual scores (i.e., the difference between the observed score and predicted score for each individual) are then computed. Finally, an ANOVA is performed with the standardized residual scores serving as the dependent variable and group membership serving as the independent variable. Results obtained from the ANOVA suggest no test bias when nonsignificant findings are reported.

The use of one predictor variable to predict more than one criterion variable may be accomplished by carrying out separate tests of bias for each criterion variable and adjusting the alpha level to reduce the probability of a Type I error in these analyses. Reynolds (2000) suggests this approach may be used when the number of criterion variables does not go beyond three variables. For more than three criterion variables, Porthoff (1966) provides equations necessary to conduct multivariate tests to detect test bias. However, when researchers or practitioners are interested in examining multiple predictors and multiple criterion variables for test bias, canonical correlation analysis would be the appropriate method to use.

Path Analysis

Keith and Reynolds (1990) have suggested the use of path analysis as an alternative model for assessing bias in predictive validity. In such a path model, ability would be proposed to predict achievement, and group membership would be assessed as a moderator variable. Diagrammatic representations of biased and unbiased models are shown in Figures 18.7, 18.8, and 18.9.

Figure 18.7 shows a path model of nonbias in which the scores on an intelligence test serve as the predictor variable and the scores on an achievement test serve as the criterion.

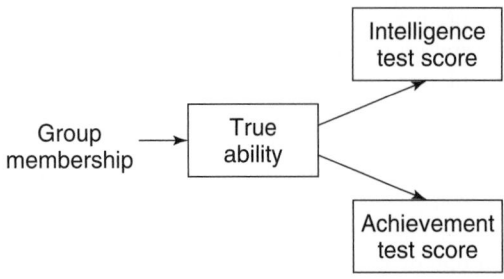

FIGURE 18.7 A path model of nonbias. Group membership affects intelligence test scores or achievement test scores indirectly through true ability.

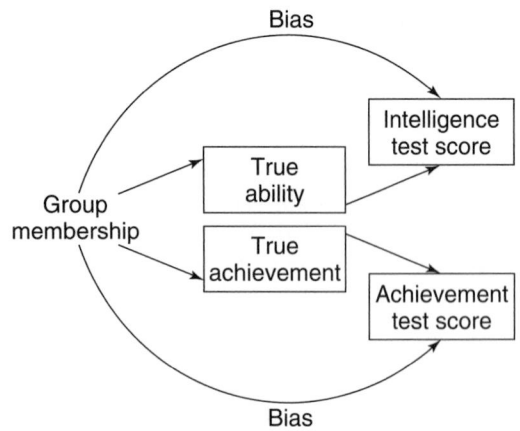

FIGURE 18.9 A more complete path model of bias. Group membership affects intelligence test scores directly producing conditions in which the intelligence test and achievement test are biased.

Group membership is the dichotomous bias variable, coded 0 for all individuals who are members of one group (e.g., the minority group or males) and 1 for all members who make up the other group (e.g., the majority group or females). The true ability variable is the latent trait or factor. In the nonbiased model, group membership affects intelligence test scores and achievement test scores only through true ability, the latent trait. In contrast, Figure 18.8 shows a path model of bias in which group membership affects not only true ability but also intelligence test scores independent of true ability. In other words, the path that connects group membership to intelligence test scores (i.e., the relationship between group membership and intelligence test scores) deviates from 0. The extent to which the path deviates from 0 indicates that the intelligence test is considered biased and errors of measurement are associated with group membership (Keith & Reynolds, 1990).

The path model of bias depicted in Figure 18.8 is probably not an accurate or a realistic diagrammatic representation, as the direct effect of group membership on true achievement has not been included. That is, group membership affects achievement test scores directly through true achievement, a latent trait variable, or indirectly through true ability. Bias occurs when group membership affects intelligence test scores independent of true ability, as well as when group membership affects achievement test scores independent of true achievement. In other words, the path directly connecting group membership to intelligence test scores and/or the path directly linking group membership to achievement test scores deviate from 0. The extent to which these paths deviate from 0 provide evidence that the intelligence test and/or achievement test is biased and the errors of measurement are related to group membership. Figure 18.9 illustrates this more complete path model of bias (Keith & Reynolds, 1990).

An example of a path model of bias that affects achievement test scores occurs when one group of high school students completes more academic coursework than another group of high school students. The coursework variable would affect achievement test scores directly. The direct path between group membership and achievement test scores would deviate from 0, and evidence of bias would be present (Keith & Reynolds, 1990).

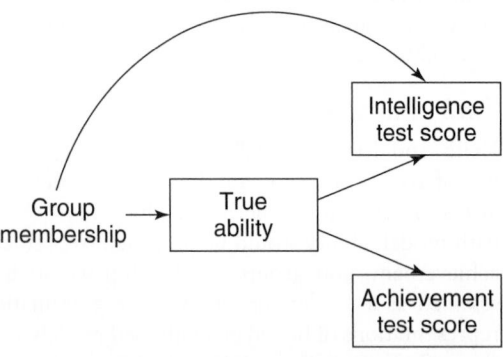

FIGURE 18.8 A path model of bias. Group membership affects intelligence test scores directly producing a condition in which the intelligence test is biased.

As noted, bias in prediction exists when group membership affects measured ability *independent* of true ability and/or when group membership affects measured achievement *independent* of true achievement; that is, errors of measurement in testing of ability and/or achievement would be correlated with group membership.

Equivalence of Validity Coefficients

Equivalence of validity coefficients between groups would be another method to assess bias in prediction. This method involves the calculation of validity coefficients (i.e., correlations between a test score and a criterion variable) for the groups of interest followed by a test of significance (see Z statistic formula presented earlier in this chapter) to determine whether a significant difference exists in the coefficients of the two groups. Depending on the reason for the study (to test theory or to examine practice), adjustments may be made in the validity coefficients such as correcting for unreliability or restriction of range before the test of significance is performed. Each validity coefficient used in studies to test theory, including theories of test bias, should be divided by the square root of the product of the reliability coefficients of the group of interest on each measure before the test of significance is conducted. A significant difference reported after the test of significance is performed would suggest the presence of test bias in prediction.

Standard Errors of Estimate

Differences in the standard error of estimate across groups may suggest the presence of test bias. The standard error of estimate is defined as the standard deviation of the residuals (i.e., error term remaining after prediction of the criterion variable from the predictor variable). The group with the largest standard error of estimate squared or variance of the standard error of estimate is divided by the group with the smallest standard error of estimate squared. The difference yields an F *ratio* with $N_{\text{largest group}}$ -2 degrees of freedom in the numerator and $N_{\text{smallest group}}$ -2 degrees of freedom in the denominator.

Diagnostic Utility

Test authors are increasingly including information in their manuals on the accuracy of classification based on test scores across different special education populations (see Roid, 2003b). This approach may also be applied to the examination of test bias across gender, race, and ethnicity.

There are two methods to examine test bias in the determination of accurate classification. The first method is a comparison of sensitivity and specificity rates across gender, race, and/or ethnic groups. Sensitivity is defined as the proportion of true positives divided by the sum of false negatives and true positives. Sensitivity refers to the probability that group membership will be accurately predicted when individuals of the group are present. On the other hand, specificity is defined as the proportion of true negatives divided by the sum of true negatives and false positives. Specificity refers to the probability of detecting the absence of group membership for individuals who are not members of the group. Sensitivity and specificity rates may be compared across groups of interests using one of several z-tests that test for significance of the difference between two proportions. Significant differences in sensitivity and/or specificity rates suggest the presence of test bias. Besides examining sensitivity and specificity rates, a comparison of logistic regression models may be used to predict group membership across gender and ethnic/racial groups. The logistic regression model is a direct extension of Potthoff's (1966) model discussed earlier in the chapter.

For bias in predictive validity, the empirical evidence suggests conclusions similar to those for bias in content and construct validity. There is no strong evidence to support contentions of differential or single-group validity. Bias occurs infrequently and with no apparently observable pattern, except when instruments of poor reliability and high specificity of test content are examined. When bias occurs, it is most often in the direction of favoring low-SES, disadvantaged, ethnic minority children or other low-scoring groups. Clearly, bias in predictive validity cannot account for the disproportionate number of minority group children diagnosed and placed in programs for children with disabilities.

CULTURAL EQUIVALENCE AS A FUTURE APPROACH?

As mentioned earlier in this chapter, Helms (1992) asserted that the implicit biological or environmental philosophical perspectives used to explain differences in cognitive ability test performance across racial and ethnic groups were based on deficient conceptualizations of culture. Neither perspective, according to Helms, provides useful information about cultural equivalence (meaning) of test scores across racial or ethnic groups.

Helms (1992) claims that racial differences in IQ test performance are due to cultural bias in the tests. Although her claim may have some merit and future research in bias assessment will continue, as it has in the past, to address the cultural variable, Helm's underlying logic runs counter to the empirical evidence. She suggests that African Americans or other visible racial or ethnic groups are culturally, socially, and cognitively different from members of the dominant culture. However, research shows that IQ tests appear to measure the same psychological characteristics in African Americans or other racial or ethnic groups and Whites (Rowe, 1994).

Nevertheless, Helms (1992) and Bentancourt and Lopez's (1993) calls to address the cultural variable to a greater extent than has been done in the past may or may not be *the wave of the future in bias assessment research*. However, if Helms' position prevails, and it has not though she continues to champion this view, the examination of the cultural equivalence of existing and future standardized cognitive ability tests across seven dimensions will be required (Butcher, 1982): (1) functional equivalence (the extent to which test scores have the same meaning across different cultural groups), (2) conceptual equivalence (whether test items have the same familiarity and meaning in different racial groups), (3) linguistic equivalence (whether the tests have the same linguistic meaning to different groups), (4) psychometric equivalence (the extent to which the tests measure the same thing across groups), (5) testing condition equivalence (whether groups are equally familiar with testing procedures and view testing as means of assessing ability) (6) contextual equivalence (the extent to which the cognitive ability to be assessed is evaluated similarly in different contexts in which people function), and (7) sampling equivalence (the idea that comparable samples of each cultural group are available at the test development, validation, and interpretation stages).

Helms (1992) recommends six areas for future research in test development to address the cultural equivalence issue: (1) development of measures for determining interracial cultural dependence and levels of acculturation and assimilation in test items, (2) modification of existing test content to include items that reflect cultural diversity, (3) examination of wrong answers, (4) incorporation of cognitive psychology

into interactive modes of assessment, (5) utilization of theories to examine environmental content of criteria, and (6) separate racial group norms for existing tests. Helms' recommendations to address, investigate, and possibly control the culture of cognitive ability tests may or may not prove to be beneficial. She suggests that the field proceed with caution in the interpretation of test results until psychometricians develop more diverse methodologies to address the culture issue.

Much of this has in fact been done. Virtually every area noted in the preceding paragraph has been addressed in the literature review in this chapter. Psychometricians have been working diligently, but all of the answers are not yet in. If Helms (1992) were calling for continued research into these areas, such a call would have our support, but to dismiss the many studies that are addressing these issues is improper. Helms *coins* new terms for what she believes needs to be done, but her definitions reveal constructs that have been researched for many years. Cronbach and Drenth (1972) provided a book-length treatment of many of these issues that is decades old.

Cross-Cultural Testing When Adaptation is Required

When a test is translated from one language to another, the research findings discussed thus far do not hold. It is inappropriate to simply translate a test and apply it in a different linguistic culture. A test needs to be adapted. Test adaptation is a much broader concept than the "more popular and frequently used term test translation" (Hambleton, 2005, p. 4). Test translation is simply one of the many steps in the test adaptation process. Test adaptation "includes all the activities from deciding whether or not a test could measure the same construct in a different language and culture, to selecting translators, to deciding on appropriate accommodations to be made in preparing a test for use in a second language, to adapting the test and checking its equivalence in the adapted form" (Hambleton, 2005, p. 4).

Beginning with the Binet-Simon Scales (Binet & Simon, 1905), the adaptation of educational and psychological tests from one language or culture to another has become common practice. Despite the long history, few psychologists are familiar with the proper methods for conducting test adaptations and establishing score equivalence (Hambleton & Kanjee, 1995). Judgmental and statistical methods and procedures for adapting tests are available, which focus on identifying nonequivalent items. When these methods and procedures are used, the validity of the adapted tests increases (Hambleton & Kanjee, 1995).

Psychological or educational tests are adapted for many reasons. The three most common reasons for adapting a test are: 1) it allows individuals to be assessed in their own language; 2) it facilitates international and national comparative studies across language and cultural groups; and 3) it reduces the time and costs associated with the development of new tests. There are other reasons for adapting tests, but these are the three most common and are at the heart of the cross-cultural testing movement.

Although adapting tests over the last century has been a common practice, the field of cross-cultural assessment is relatively new. Currently its major thrust revolves around the development and use of guidelines for adapting tests (Hambleton, 2005; Hambleton & Li, 2005), ways to interpret and use cross-cultural and cross-national data (Hambleton & Kanjee, 1994; Poortinga & Malpass, 1986), and methods and procedures for establishing equivalence of test items and ultimately test scores (Ellis, 1991; Hambleton, 1993; van de Vijver & Poortinga, 1991), much of which predates Helms' (1992) contention that no such study has been undertaken.

Establishment of the equivalence of test items is the most central issue in cross-cultural or cross-national research (Poortinga, 1983). Test items are considered to be equivalent when members of each group—that is, members from different language and/or cultural groups—with the same score on the construct measured by the test have the same probability of selecting the correct answer on the latent trait item (Hambleton & Kanjee, 1994).

Judgmental and statistical designs (data collection designs) are used to establish item equivalence. Judgmental designs are based on an individual or group's decision concerning the degree of each item's translation equivalence. Two of the most common judgmental designs are forward translation and backward translation (Hambleton, 2005). In forward translation, one or more translators adapt the measure from the original, called the source, to the target language or culture. The source and target versions are then assessed by another individual or group of

translators to determine their equivalency. If the versions are not equivalent, changes are made to the target version of the test. Sometimes an additional step is added when an individual, not necessarily a translator, will edit the target version of the test to make the language on the test smoother (i.e., less choppy). In backward translation, one or more translators adapt the instrument from the source to the target language or culture, and then another translator or a group of translators retranslate the test items back to the source language or culture. The original and the back-translated versions of the test are then assessed to determine whether they are equivalent. The backward translation design is the most popular of the judgmental designs (Hambleton, 2005). Judgmental designs provide good preliminary checks or item translation equivalence, but additional checks are needed, such as statistical methods like DIF.

In addition to judgmental designs, there are three data collection designs to assess the equivalency of the items and the factor structure. The three data collection designs are: 1) bilingual examiners take the source and target versions of a test; 2) source and target monolinguals take the source and target versions of the test, respectively, and 3) source monolinguals take the source and backward translation of the test (Hambleton, 2005). These three different data collection designs differ in the characteristics of the samples who take the tests and the version (i.e., source, target, and/or back-adapted version) of the test taken. Once testing has been completed, specific analytical procedures are selected such as factor analysis to determine equivalence of the factor structure on the different versions of the test or item response theory, logistic regression, and Mantel-Haenszel procedure to detect DIF. If DIF is significant, further analyses of the significant DIF items are needed to determine whether the items are biased or language and/or cultural equivalency has not been obtained.

In the field of cross-cultural testing, equivalence of test items has been a major methodological concern as the need for multilanguage versions of cognitive, academic achievement, and personality tests and cross-cultural research continues to grow (Hambleton, 2005). Because of this growth, the International Test Commission (ITC), consisting of a committee of international scholars, developed and published in 2002 a set of guidelines to assist researchers and practitioners in the adaptation of educational and psychological tests for use in other cultures and languages (Hambleton & Li, 2005). The guidelines are organized into four sections: cultural context, instrument development and adaptation, administration, and documentation or score interpretation. The context guidelines address concerns about construct equivalence in the target group(s) of interest. The instrument development and adaptation category provides information on the process of adapting a measure such as selection of translators, judgmental and statistical designs, and statistical tests needed to examine test score equivalency. The administration guidelines address ways to administer the test. The documentation and score interpretation category addresses the need for researchers to document the adaptation process and to establish the validity of adapted tests. A review of the ITC guidelines are found in Hambleton (2005) and Hambleton and Li (2005).

The importance of addressing test item and score equivalence and of the ITC guidelines for adapting educational and psychological tests is highlighted in a study that examined the relationship between level of acculturation and performance on the Halstead-Reitan Neuropsychological Battery (HRNB; Reitan & Wolfson, 1985) test with Hispanics (Arnold, Montgomery, Castaneda, & Longoria, 1994). Arnold and colleagues reported that the level of acculturation affected several tests found on the HRNB, including the Tactual Performance Test (TPT), the Seashore Rhythm Test (SRT), and the Halstead Category Test (HCT). These results raise questions about the validity of existing norms with Hispanics. Arnold et al. suggest that acculturation measures should accompany neuropsychological evaluations of Hispanics until the specificity and sensitivity of existing neuropsychological tests are better understood. Moreover, the authors suggest greater interpretative caution when assessing Hispanics who have not been acculturated or exhibit low levels of acculturation.

In contrast, the findings from a study of 47 Lao children, ranging in age from 5 to 12, suggest that cognitive and neuropsychological measures can be adapted so that they can effectively tap basic and universal brain-behavior traits (Boivin et al., 1996). The Lao children completed the Kaufman Assessment Battery for Children (K-ABC; Kaufman & Kaufman, 1983), the TPT, and the computerized Test of Variables of Attention (TOVA; Greenberg, 1988–1999). The TPT performance was found to be related to nutritional development; the K-ABC performance was sensitive to parental education and home environment; and the TOVA performance was associated with attention, K-ABC global performance, and TPT memory.

Boivin et al.'s (1996) study suggests that tests can be adapted for use with groups from other cultures; however, the problems in adapting tests across cultures are difficult and present challenges to the field of psychometrics. Contrary to Helms' (1992) view, psychologists have been confronting these issues for many years. Cronbach and Drenth (1972) have provided a book-length treatment of these problems and various experiences with proposed solutions to the cross-cultural adaptation of psychological tests in some 30 nations throughout the world. The various contributors describe both the strengths and limitations of adapting tests cross-culturally, providing perspectives from such diverse disciplines as psychometrics, cognitive and developmental psychology, and anthropology. More recent guidelines can be found in Hambleton, Merenda, and Spielberger (2005).

There is little question that the issue of bias in intelligence testing is an important one with strong historical precedence in the social sciences and, ultimately, formidable social consequences. Because the history of mental measurement has been closely wed from the outset to societal needs and expectations, testing in all forms has remained in the limelight, subjected to the crucible of social inspection, review, and (at times) condemnation in various cultures throughout the world. However, the fact that tests and measures of human aptitude and achievement continue to be employed in most modern cultures (and were more than 2000 years ago in some cultures) indicates strongly that the practice has value, despite the recurring storms of criticism over the years. The ongoing controversy related to test bias and the "fair" use of measures undoubtedly will remain with the social sciences for at least as long as we entangle the nature-nurture question with these issues and affirm differences between and among groups in mean performance on standardized tests. Numerous scholars in the field of psychometrics have been attempting to separate the nature-nurture issue and data on mean score differences from the more orderly, empirically driven specialty of bias investigation, but the separation will undoubtedly not be a clean one. A sharp distinction has developed between the popular press and scientific literature about the interpretation of mental measurement research. The former all too often engenders beliefs that biased measures are put into use for socially pernicious purposes (e.g., psychology and education) often accused of courting political, social, and professional ideologies, and it appears to have created confusion in public opinion about the possibility of "fair" testing, to say the least. The latter—reported in this chapter—has been demonstrating through a body of data that the contention that tests are culturally biased is not supported at present, at least in cultures with a common language and some degree of common experience. In any event, societal scrutiny and ongoing sentiment about testing have without question forced the psychometric community to refine its definition of bias further, to inspect practices in the construction of nonbiased measures, and to develop statistical procedures to detect bias when it is occurring. We can argue whether the social sciences have from the outset overstepped their bounds in implementing testing for social purposes before adequate data and methods were developed, but the resulting advancements in bias technology in response to ongoing public inspection are undeniable.

Data from the empirical end of bias investigation do suggest several guidelines to ensure equitable assessment: (1) investigation of possible referral source bias, as there is evidence that persons are not always referred to services on the basis of impartial, objective rationales; (2) inspection of test developers' data for completed evidence that sound statistical analyses for bias across groups to be evaluated with the measure; (3) assessment with the most reliable measure available, and (4) assessment of multiple abilities with multiple methods. In other words, psychologists need to view multiple sources of accurately derived data before making decisions about individuals. We may hope that this is not too far afield from what has actually been occurring in the practice of psychological assessment, although one continues to hear isolated stories of grossly incompetent diagnostic decisions. This does not mean that psychologists should be blind to a person's environmental background. Information about the home, community, and other environmental circumstances must be evaluated in the individualized decision-making process. Exactly how this may be done is addressed in other chapters and volumes of this work. Neither, however, can the psychologist ignore the fact that low-IQ, disadvantaged children from

ethnic minority groups are just as likely to fail academically as are majority, middle-class, low-IQ children, provided that their environmental circumstances remain constant. Indeed, it is the purpose of the assessment process to beat the prediction—to provide insight into hypotheses for environmental interventions that will prevent the predicted failure.

A philosophical perspective that is emerging in the bias literature requires test developers not only to demonstrate whether their measures have differential content, construct, and predictive validity across groups *before* publication but also to incorporate in some form content analyses by interested groups to ensure that offensive materials are omitted. Although there are no sound empirical data to suggest that persons can determine bias upon surface inspection, the synergistic relationship between test use and pure psychometrics must be acknowledged and accommodated in orderly fashion before tests gain greater acceptance in society. Ideally, a clear consensus on fairness (and steps taken to reach this end) is needed between those persons with more subjective concerns and those interested in gathering objective bias data during and after test construction. Accommodation along this line will ultimately ensure that all parties interested in any given test believe that the measure in question is nonbiased, and that the steps taken to achieve fairness can be held up to public scrutiny without reservation. Given the significant and reliable methods developed over the last several decades in bias research, it is untenable at this point to abandon statistical analyses in favor of armchair determination of bias. Test authors and publishers need to demonstrate factorial invariance across all groups for whom the test is designed to make the instrument more readily interpretable. Comparisons of predictive validity across race, ethnicity, and gender during the test development phase are also needed. Contrary to the state of test development practices as recently as the 1990s, evaluations of bias in tests has become far more commonplace among the major publishing houses (e.g., see Reynolds & Carson, 2005), but still many tests are published with little or no attention to objective, psychometric studies of test bias. Bias research in personality testing must be expanded. Little has been done, and this represents a major weakness in the literature. Only recently have publishers begun to give appropriate attention to this problem. Researchers in personality and psychodiagnostics must move ahead in this area of concern.

REFERENCES

Abebimpe, V. R., Gigandet, J., & Harris, E. (1979). MMPI diagnosis of Black psychiatric patients. *American Journal of Psychiatry, 136*, 85–87.

Alley, G., & Foster, R. (1978). Nondiscriminatory testing of minority and exceptional children. *Focus on Exceptional Children, 9*, 1–14.

American Educational Research Association, American Psychological Association, & National Council on Measurement in Education. (1999). *Standards for educational and psychological testing*. Washington, DC: AERA.

Anastasi, A. (1976). *Psychological testing* (4th ed.). New York: Macmillan.

Anastasi, A. (1982). *Psychological testing* (5th ed.). New York: Macmillan.

Anastasi, A. (1988). *Psychological testing* (6th ed.). New York: Macmillan.

Angoff, W. H. (1976). Group membership as a predictor variable: A comment on McNemar. *American Psychologist, 31*, 612.

Arnold, B., Montgomery, G., Castaneda, I., & Longoria, R. (1994). Acculturation and performance of Hispanics on selected Halstead-Reitan neuropsychological tests. *Assessment, 1*, 239–248.

Bartlett, C. J., & O'Leary, B. S. (1969). A differential prediction model to moderate the effect of heterogeneous groups on personnel selection. *Personnel Psychology, 22*, 1–18.

Bentancourt, H., & Lopez, S. R. (1993). The study of culture, ethnicity, and race in American psychology. *American Psychologist, 48*, 629–637.

Bernal, E. M. (1975). A response to "educational uses of tests with disadvantaged students." *American Psychologist, 30*, 93–95.

Binet, A., & Simon, T. (1905). Methods nouvelles pour le diagnostic du nivea intellectual des anormaux. *L'Ann Ce Psychologique, 11*, 191–244.

Binet, A., & Simon, T. (1916/1973). *The development of intelligence in children*. New York: Arno.

Birch, H. G., & Gussow, J. D. (1970). *Disadvantaged children: Health, nutrition, and school failure*. New York: Grune & Stratton.

Bogen, J. E., DeZure, R., Tenhouten, N., & March, J. (1972). The other side of the brain: IV. The a/p ratio. *Bulletin of the Los Angeles Neurological Society, 37*, 771–778.

Boivin, M., Chounramany, C., Giordani, B., Xaisida, S., Choulamountry, L., Pholsena, P., et al., (1996). Validating a cognitive ability testing protocol with Lao children for community development applications. *Neuropsychology, 10*, 1–12.

Bolles, R. C. (1975). *Theory of motivation* (2nd ed.). New York: Harper & Row.

Bond, L. (1981). Bias in mental tests. In B. F. Green (Ed.), *Issues in testing: Coaching, disclosure, and ethnic bias*. San Francisco: Jossey-Bass.

Bond, L. (1987). The golden rule settlement: A minority perspective. *Educational Measurement Issues and Practice, 6*, 23–25.

Bouchard, T. J., & Segal, N. L. (1985). Environment and IQ. In B. Wilman (Ed.), *Handbook of intelligence* (pp. 391–464). New York: Wiley-Interscience.

Bracken, B. A., & McCallum, R. S. (1998a). *Universal Nonverbal Intelligence Test*. Itasca, IL: Riverside.

Bracken, B. A., & McCallum, R. S. (1998b). *Universal Nonverbal Intelligence Test: Examiner's manual*. Itasca, IL: Riverside.

Brooks, P. (1997, October 15). TAAS unfair to minorities, lawsuit claims. *Austin American Statesman*, p. A1.

Burrill, L. E. (1975). *Statistical evidence of potential bias in items and tests assessing current educational status*. Paper presented at the Annual Meeting of the Southeastern Conference on Measurement in Education, New Orleans.

Burt, C. (1921). *Mental and scholastic tests*. London: P. S. King.

Butcher, J. N. (1982). Cross-cultural research methods in clinical psychology. In P. C. Kendall & J. N. Butcher (Eds.), *Black children: Social educational and parental environments* (pp. 33–51). Beverly Hills, CA: Sage.

Butler-Omololu, C., Doster, J., & Lahey, B. (1984). Some implications for intelligence test construction and administration with children of different racial groups. *Journal of Black Psychology, 10*, 63–75.

Camilli, G., & Shepard, L. A. (1987). The inadequacy of ANOVA for detecting test bias. *Journal of Educational Statistics, 12*, 87–99.

Camilli, G., & Shepard, L. A. (1994). *Methods for identifying biased tests items*. Thousand Oaks, CA: Sage.

Carroll, J. B. (1993). *Human cognitive abilities: A survey of factor-analytic studies*. New York: Cambridge University Press.

Carroll, J. B. (1998). Human cognitive abilities: A critique. In J. J. McArdle & R. W. Woodcock (Eds.), *Human cognitive abilities: A survey of factor-analytic studies*. New York: Cambridge University Press.

Cattell, R. B. (1978). *The scientific use of factor analysis in behavioral and life sciences*. New York: Plenum.

Cattell, R. B. (1979). Are culture fair intelligence tests possible and necessary? *Journal of Research and Development in Education, 12*, 3–13.

Chambers, J. S., Barron, F., & Sprecher, J. W. (1980). Identifying gifted Mexican-American students. *Gifted Child Quarterly, 24*, 123–128.

Chinn, P. C. (1979). The exceptional minority child: Issues and some answers. *Exceptional Children, 46*, 532–536.

Chipman, S., Marshall, S., & Scott, P. (1991). Content effect on word-problem performance: A possible source of test bias? *American Educational Research Journal, 28*, 897–915.

Clarizio, H. (1982). Intellectual assessment of Hispanic children. *Psychology in the Schools, 19*, 61–71.

Cleary, T. A., Humphreys, L. G., Kendrick, S. A., & Wesman, A. (1975). Educational uses of tests with disadvantaged students. *American Psychologist, 30*, 15–41.

Cohen, R. J., & Swerdlik, M. E. (1999). *Psychological testing and assessment: An introduction to tests and measurement* (4th ed.). Mountain View, CA: Mayfield Publishing Company.

Cole, N. S., & Moss, P. (1989). Bias in test use. In R. Linn (Ed.), *Educational measurement* (3rd ed.; pp. 201–219). New York: Macmillan.

Council for Exceptional Children (1978). Minorities position policy statements. *Exceptional Children, 45*, 57–64.

Critchley, D. L. (1979). The adverse influence of psychiatric diagnostic labels on the observation of child behavior. *American Journal of Orthopsychiatry, 49*, 157–160.

Cronbach, L. J. (1976). Equity in selection—where psychometrics and political philosophy meet. *Journal of Educational Measurement, 13*, 31–42.

Cronbach, L. J. (1990). *Essentials of psychological testing* (5th ed.). New York: Harper & Row.

Cronbach, L. J., & Drenth, P. J. D. (Eds.). (1972). *Mental tests and cultural adaptation*. The Hague: Mouton.

Dana, R. H. (1996). Culturally competent assessment practices in the United States. *Journal of Personality Assessment, 66*, 472–487.

Darlington, R. B. (1978). Cultural test bias: Comments on Hunter and Schmidt. *Psychological Bulletin, 85*, 673–674.

Dean, R. S. (1979, September). *WISC-R factor structure for Anglo and Hispanic children*. Paper presented at the Annual Meeting of the American Psychological Association, New York.

Dershowitz, Z., & Frankel, Y. (1975). Jewish culture and the WISC and WAIS test patterns. *Journal of Consulting and Clinical Psychology, 43*, 126–134.

Dunn, L. (1959). *Peabody Picture Vocabulary Test*. Circle Pines, MN: American Guidance Services.

Dworkin, N., & Dworkin, Y. (1979). The legacy of Pygmalion in the classroom. *Phi Delta Kappan, 61*, 712–715.

Ebel, R. L., (1979). Intelligence: A skeptical view. *Journal of Research and Development in Education, 12*, 14–21.

Eells, K., Davis, A., Havighurst, R. J., Herrick, V. E., & Tyler, R. W. (1951). *Intelligence and cultural differences: A study of cultural learning and problem-solving*. Chicago: University of Chicago Press.

Einhorn, H. J., & Bass, A. R. (1971). Methodological considerations relevant to discrimination in employment testing. *Psychological Bulletin, 75*, 261–269.

Ellis, B. B. (1991). Item response theory: A tool for assessing the equivalence of translated tests. *Bulletin of the International Test Commission, 18*, 33–51.

Embertson, S. E., & Reise, S. P. (2000). *Item response theory for psychologists*. Mahwah, NJ: Erlbaum.

Emerling, F. (1990). An investigation of test bias in nonverbal cognitive measures for two ethnic groups, *Journal of Psychoeducational Assessment, 8*, 34–41.

Feldt, L. S. (1969). A test of the hypothesis that Cronbach's alpha or Kuder-Richardson twenty is the same for two tests. *Psychometrika, 34*, 363–373.

Fine, B. (1975). *The stranglehold of the IQ*. Garden City, NY: Doubleday.

Flaugher, R. L. (1978). The many definitions of test bias. *American Psychologist, 33*, 671–679.

Flynn, J. R. (1991). *Asian-Americans: Achievement beyond IQ*. Hillsdale, NJ: Erlbaum.

Foster, G., & Ysseldyke, J. (1976). Expectancy and halo effects as a result of artificially induced teacher bias. *Contemporary Educational Psychology, 1*, 37–45.

Freeman, F. N. (1923). A referendum of psychologists. *Century Illustrated Magazine, 107*, 237–245.

Friedman, I. A., & Bendas-Jacob, O. (1997). Measuring perceived test anxiety in adolescents: A self-report scale. *Educational and Psychological Measurement, 57*, 1035–1046.

Gerken, K. C. (1978). Performance of Mexican-American children on intelligence test. *Exceptional Children, 44*, 438–443.

Goldstein, H., Krantz, D. L., & Rains, J. D. (Eds.). (1965). *Controversial issues in learning*. New York: Appleton-Century-Crofts.

Gordon, R. A. (1984). Digits backward and the Mercer-Kamin law: An empirical response to Mercer's treatment of internal validity of IQ tests. In C. R. Reynolds & R. T. Brown (Eds.), *Perspectives on bias in mental testing*. New York: Plenum.

Gottfredson, L. (1994). Egalitarian fiction and collective fraud. *Society, 31*, 53–59.

Gottfredson, L. (2005). Implications of cognitive differences for schooling within diverse societies. In C. Frisby and C. Reynolds (Eds.), *The comprehensive handbook of multicultural school psychology* (pp. 517–554). NY: John Wiley and Sons.

Gould, S. J. (1981). *The mismeasure of man*. New York: Norton.

Greenberg, L. M. (1988–1999). *The Test of Variables of Attention*. Los Alamitos, CA: Universal Attention Disorders.

Greenlaw, R., & Jensen, S. (1996). Race norming and Civil Rights Act of 1991. *Public Personnel Management, 25,* 13–24.

Gross, A. L., & Su, W. (1975). Defining a "fair" or "unbiased" selection model. *Journal of Applied Psychology, 60,* 345–351.

Gross, M. (1967). *Learning readiness in two Jewish groups.* New York: Center for Urban Education.

Guilford Press. (1997). Culturally sensitive assessment: Paying attention to cultural orientation. *Child Assessment News, 6,* 8–12.

Gulliksen, H., & Wilks, S. S. (1950). Regression tests for several samples. *Psychometrika, 15,* 91–114.

Hambleton, R. K. (1993). Translating achievement tests for use in cross-national studies. *European Journal of Psychological Assessment, 9,* 54–65.

Hambleton, R. K. (2005). Issues, designs, and technical guidelines for adapting tests into multiple languages and cultures. In R. K. Hambleton, P. F. Merenda, & C. D. Spielberger (Eds.), *Adapting educational and psychological tests for cross-cultural assessment* (pp. 3–38). Mahwah, NJ: Lawrence Erlbaum.

Hambleton, R. K., & Kanjee, A. (1994). Enhancing the validity of cross-cultural studies: Improvements in instrument translation methods. In T. Husen & T. Postlewaite (Eds.), *International encyclopedia of education* (2nd ed.). Oxford: Pergamon.

Hambleton, R. K., & Kanjee, A. (1995). Increasing the validity of cross-cultural assessments: Use of improved methods for adaptations. *European Journal of Psychological Assessment, 11,* 147–157.

Hambleton, R. K., & Li, S. (2005). Translation and adaptation issues and methods for educational and psychological tests. In C. L. Frisby & C. R. Reynolds (Eds.), *Comprehensive handbook of multicultural school psychology* (pp. 881–903). New York: John Wiley & Sons.

Hambleton, R. K., Merenda, P. F., & Spielberger, C. D. (Eds.) (2005). *Adapting educational and psychological tests for cross-cultural assessment.* Mahwah, NJ: Lawrence Erlbaum.

Hammill, D. (1991a). *Detroit Tests of Learning Aptitude* (3rd ed.). Austin, TX: Pro-Ed.

Hammill, D. (1991b). *Detroit Tests of Learning Aptitude* (3rd ed.): *Manual.* Austin, TX: Pro-Ed.

Harman, H. (1976). *Modern factor analysis* (2nd ed.). Chicago: University of Chicago Press.

Harrington, G. M. (1968a). Genetic-environmental interaction in "intelligence": I. Biometric genetic analysis of maze performance of Rattus norvegicus. *Developmental Psychobiology, 1,* 211–218.

Harrington, G. M. (1968b). Genetic-environmental interaction in "intelligence": II. Models of behavior, components of variance, and research strategy. *Developmental Psychobiology, 1,* 245–253.

Harrington, G. M. (1975). Intelligence tests may favor the majority groups in a population. *Nature, 258,* 708–709.

Harrington, G. M. (1976, September). *Minority test bias as a psychometric artifact: The experimental evidence.* Paper presented at the Annual Meeting of the American Psychological Association, Washington, DC.

Helms, J. E. (1992). Why is there no study of cultural equivalence in standardized cognitive ability testing? *American Psychologist, 47,* 1083–1101.

Helms, J. E. (1994). The conceptualization of racial identity and other "racial" constructs. In E. Trickett, R. Watts, & D. Birman (Eds.), *Human diversity* (pp. 285–311). San Francisco, CA: Jossey-Bass.

Herrnstein, R. J., & Murray, C. (1994). *The bell curve.* New York: Free Press.

Hilgard, E. R., & Bower, G. H. (1975). *Theories of learning* (4th ed.). Englewood Cliffs, NJ: Prentice Hall.

Hilliard, A. G. (1979). Standardization and cultural bias as impediments to the scientific study and validation of "intelligence." *Journal of Research and Development in Education, 12,* 47–58.

Hobbs, N. (1975). *The futures of children.* San Francisco: Jossey-Bass.

Hodapp, V. (1996). The TAI-G: A multidimensional approach to the assessment of test anxiety. In C. Schwarzer, & M. Zeidner (Eds.), *Stress anxiety, and coping in academic settings* (pp. 95–130). Tubingen, Germany: Francke-Verlag.

Horn, J. L. (1988). Thinking about abilities. In J. R. Nesselroade & R. B. Cattell (Eds.), *Handbook of multivariate psychology* (pp. 645–685). New York: Academic

Humphreys, L. G. (1973). Statistical definitions of test validity for minority groups. *Journal of Applied Psychology, 58,* 1–4.

Hunter, J. E., & Schmidt, F. L. (1976). Critical analysis of the statistical and ethnical implications of various definitions of test bias. *Psychological Bulletin, 83,* 1053–1071.

Hunter, J. E., & Schmidt, F. L. (1978). Bias in defining test bias: Reply to Darlington. *Psychological Bulletin, 85,* 675–676.

Hunter, J. E., Schmidt, F. L., & Rauschenberger, J. (1984). Methodological, statistical, and ethical issues in the study of bias in psychological tests. In C. R. Reynolds & R. T. Brown (Eds.), *Perspectives on bias in mental testing.* New York: Plenum.

Isern, M. (1986). An investigation of bias in tests of writing ability for bilingual Hispanic college students. Doctoral dissertation, University of Miami. *Dissertation Abstracts International, 47,* 2135A.

Jackson, G. D. (1975). Another psychological view from the Association of Black Psychologists. *American Psychologist, 30,* 88–93.

Jacobs, W. R. (1978). The effect of the learning disability label on classroom teachers' ability objectively to observe and interpret child behaviors. *Learning Disability Quarterly, 1*, 50–55.

Jensen, A. R. (1974). How biased are culturally loaded tests? *Genetic Psychology Monographs, 90*, 185–224.

Jensen, A. R. (1976). Test biased and construct validity. *Phi Delta Kappan, 58*, 340–346.

Jensen, A. R. (1980). *Bias in mental testing*. New York: Free Press.

Jöreskog, K. (1969). A general approach to confirmatory maximum likelihood factor analysis. *Psychometrika, 34*, 183–202.

Jöreskog, K. (1971). Simultaneous factor analysis in several populations, *Psychometrika, 30*, 409–426.

Katzenmeyer, W. G., & Stenner, A. J. (1977). Estimation of the invariance of factor structures across race and sex with implications for hypothesis testing. *Educational and Psychological Measurement, 37*, 111–119.

Kaufman, A. S. (1973). Comparison of the performance of matched groups of Black children and White children on the Wechsler Preschool and Primary Scale of Intelligence. *Journal of Consulting and Clinical Psychology, 41*, 186–191.

Kaufman, A. S., & Kaufman, N. L. (1973). Black-White differences on the McCarthy Scales of Children's Abilities. *Journal of School Psychology, 11*, 196–206.

Kaufman, A. S., & Kaufman, N. L. (1983). *Kaufman Assessment Battery for Children*. Circle Pines, MN: American Guidance Service.

Kaufman, A. S., & Kaufman, N. L. (2004). *Kaufman Assessment Battery for Children* (2nd ed.). Circle Pines, MN: American Guidance Service.

Keith, T. Z., & Reynolds, C. R. (1990). Measurement and design issues in child assessment research. In C. R. Reynolds & R. W. Kamphaus (Eds.), *Handbook of psychological and educational assessment of children*. New York: Guilford.

Kimble, G. A. (1961). *Hilgard and Marquis' conditioning and learning* (2nd ed.). New York: Appleton-Century-Crofts.

Lambert, N. M. (1979, October). *Adaptive behavior assessment and its implications for educational programming*. Paper presented to the Fourth Annual Midwestern Conference on Psychology in the Schools, Boys Town, Nebraska.

Larry P. et al. v. Wilson Riles et al. (1979, October). C 71 2270. U.S. District Court for the Northern District of California, slip opinion.

Leiter, R. G. (1948). *Leiter International Performance Scale*. Chicago, IL: Stoelting.

Lewontin, R. C. (1970). Race and intelligence. *Bulletin of Atomic Scientists, 26*, 2–8.

Linn, R. L. (1976). In search of fair selection procedures. *Journal of Educational Measurement, 13*, 53–58.

Lippmann, W. (1923a). A judgment of the tests. *New Republic, 34*, 322–323.

Lippmann, W. (1923b). Mr. Burt and the intelligence tests. *New Republic, 34*, 263–264.

Loehlin, J. C., Lindzey, G., & Spuhler, J. N. (1975). *Race differences in intelligence*. San Francisco: Freeman.

Lonner, W. J. (1985). Issues in testing and assessment in cross-cultural counseling. *The Counseling Psychologist, 13*, 599–614.

Lowe, P. A., & Lee, S. W. (2004). *The Test Anxiety Inventory for Children and Adolescents*. Lawrence, KS: University of Kansas.

Lowe, P. A., & Lee, S. W. (2008). Factor structure of the Test Anxiety Inventory for Children and Adolescents (TAICA) scores across gender among students in elementary and secondary school settings. *Journal of Psychoeducational Assessment, 26*, 231–246.

Lowe, P. A., & Reynolds, C. R. (2005). Factor structure of the AMAS-C scores across gender among students in collegiate settings. *Educational and Psychological Measurement, 65*, 687–708.

Lowe, P. A., & Reynolds, C. R. (2006). Examination of the psychometric properties of the Adult Manifest Anxiety Scale-Elderly Version (AMAS-E) scores. *Educational and Psychological Measurement, 66*, 93–115.

MacCorquodale, K., & Meehl, P. E. (1948). On a distinction between hypothetical constructs and intervening variables. *Psychological Review, 55*, 95–107.

MacMillan, D. L., Jones, R. L., & Aloia, G. F. (1974). The mentally retarded label: A theoretical analysis and review of research. *American Journal of Mental Deficiency, 79*, 241–261.

Mandler, G. (1975). *Mind and emotion*. New York: Wiley.

Marjoribanks, K. (1972). Ethnic and environmental influences on mental abilities. *American Journal of Sociology, 78*, 323–337.

McCoy, S. A. (1976). Clinical judgments of normal childhood behaviors. *Journal of Consulting and Clinical Psychology, 44*, 710–714.

McGrew, K. S., & Woodcock, R. W. (2001). *Technical manual: Woodcock-Johnson III*. Itasca, IL: Riverside.

McGurk, F. V. J. (1951). *Comparison of the performance of Negro and White high school seniors on cultural and noncultural psychological test questions*. Washington, DC: Catholic University of America Press.

McNemar, Q. (1975). On so-called test bias. *American Psychologist, 30*, 848–851.

Mercer, J. R. (1976, August). *Cultural diversity, mental retardation, and assessment: The case for nonlabeling*. Paper presented to the Fourth International Congress of the International Association for the Scientific Study of Mental Retardation, Washington, DC.

Mercer, J. R. (1979a). *System of Multicultural Pluralistic Assessment*. San Antonio, TX: The Psychological Corporation.

Mercer, J. R. (1979b). *System of Multicultural Pluralistic Assessment: Conceptual and technical manual*. San Antonio, TX: The Psychological Corporation.

Miele, F. (1979). Cultural bias in the WISC. *Intelligence*, 3, 149–164.

Moreland, K. L. (1995). Persistent issues in multicultural assessment of social and emotional functioning. In L. A. Suzuki, P. J. Meller, & J. G. Ponterrotto (Eds.), *Handbook of multicultural assessment: Clinical psychological and educational applications*. San Francisco: Jossey-Bass.

Mulaik, S. A. (1972). *The foundation of factor analysis*. New York: McGraw-Hill.

Naglieri, J. A., & Das, J. P. (1997a). *The Cognitive Assessment System*. Itasca, IL: Riverside.

Naglieri, J. A., & Das, J. P. (1997b). *The Cognitive Assessment System: Interpretive handbook*. Itasca, IL: Riverside.

Nichols, R. C. (1978). Policy implications of the IQ controversy. In L. S. Schulman (Ed.), *Review of research in education* (Vol. 6). Itasca, IL: Peacock.

Novick, M. R., & Petersen, N. S. (1976). Towards equalizing educational and employment opportunity. *Journal of Educational Measurement*, 13, 77–88.

Nunnally, J. C. (1978). *Psychometric theory*. New York: McGraw-Hill.

Padilla, A. M. (1988). Early psychological assessment of Mexican-American children. *Journal of the History of the Behavioral Sciences*, 24, 113–115.

PASE (parents in action special education) *et al* v. *Hannon et al* (1980, July). No. 74C 3586. U.S. District Court for the Northern District of Illinois, Eastern Division, slip opinion.

Payne, B., & Payne, D. (1991). The ability of teachers to identify academically at-risk elementary students. *Journal of Research in Childhood Education*, 5, 116–126.

Pitner, R. (1931). *Intelligence testing*. New York: Holt, Rinehart & Winston.

Poortinga, Y. H. (1983). Psychometric approaches to intergroup comparison: The problem of equivalence. In S. H. Irvine & J. W. Berry (Eds.), *Human assessment and cross-cultural factors* (pp. 237–258). New York: Plenum.

Poortinga, Y. H., & Malpass, R. S. (1986). Making inferences from cross-cultural data. In W. J. Lonner & J. W. Berry (Eds.), *Field methods in cross-cultural psychology* (pp. 17–46). Beverly Hills, CA: Sage.

Potthoff, R. F. (1966). *Statistical aspects of the problem of biases in psychological tests*. Institute of Statistics Mimeo Series No. 479. Chapel Hill: University of North Carolina.

Ramsey, R. T. (1979). *The testing manual: A guide to test administration and use*. Pittsburgh: Author.

Raven, J. C. (1960). *Raven's Progressive Matrices*. New York: The Psychological Corporation.

Reitan, R. M., & Wolfson, D. (1985). *The Halstead-Reitan Neuropsychological Test Battery: Theory and clinical interpretation*. Tucson, AZ: Neuropsychology Press.

Reschly, D. J. (1980). Concepts of bias in assessment and WISC-R research with minorities. In H. Vance & F. Wallbrown (Eds.), *WISC-R: Research and interpretation*. Washington, DC: National Association of School Psychologists.

Reynolds, C. R. (1978). *Differential validity of several preschool assessment instruments for Blacks, Whites, males, and females*. Doctoral dissertation, University of Georgia, Athens.

Reynolds, C. R. (1980a). An examination for test bias in preschool battery across race and sex. *Journal of Educational Measurement*, 17, 137–146.

Reynolds, C. R. (1980b). Differential construct validity of intelligence as popularly measured: Correlation of age and raw scores on the WISC-R for Blacks, Whites, males and females. *Intelligence: A Multidisciplinary Journal*, 4, 371–379.

Reynolds, C. R. (1980c). In support of "Bias in Mental Testing" and scientific inquiry. *The Behavioral and Brain Sciences*, 3, 352.

Reynolds, C. R. (1982a). Construct and predictive bias. In R. A. Berk (Ed.), *Handbook of methods for detecting test bias*. Baltimore, MD: Johns Hopkins University Press.

Reynolds, C. R. (1982b). The problem of bias in psychological assessment. In C. R. Reynolds & T. B. Gutkin (Eds.), *The handbook of school psychology* (pp. 178–208). New York: Wiley.

Reynolds, C. R. (1995). Test bias in the assessment of intelligence and personality. In D. Saklofske & M. Zeidner (Eds.), *International handbook of personality and intelligence* (pp. 545–576). New York: Plenum.

Reynolds, C. R. (2000). Methods for detecting and evaluating cultural bias in neuropsychological tests. In E. Fletcher-Janzen, T. L. Strickland, & C. R. Reynolds (Eds.), *Handbook of cross-cultural neuropsychology* (pp. 249–285). New York: Kluwer Academic.

Reynolds, C. R. (2002a). *Comprehensive Trail-Making Test*. Austin, TX: Pro-Ed.

Reynolds, C. R. (2002b). *Comprehensive Trail-Making Test: Examiner manual*. Austin, TX: Pro-Ed.

Reynolds, C. R., & Bigler, E. D. (1994a). *Test of Memory and Learning*. Austin, TX: Pro-Ed.

Reynolds, C. R., & Bigler, E. D. (1994b). *Test of Memory and Learning: Manual*. Austin, TX: Pro-Ed.

Reynolds, C. R. & Brown, R. T. (1984). Bias in mental testing: An introduction to the issues. In C. R. Reynolds & R. T. Brown (Eds.), *Perspectives on bias in mental testing* (pp. 1–39). New York: Plenum.

Reynolds, C. R., & Carson, A. D. (2005). Methods for assessing cultural bias in tests. In C. L. Frisby and C. R. Reynolds (Eds.), *The comprehensive handbook of multicultural school psychology* (pp. 795–823). NY: John Wiley and Sons.

Reynolds, C. R., & Gutkin, T. B. (1980, September). *WISC-R performance of Blacks and Whites matched on four demographic variables*. Paper presented at the Annual Meeting of the American Psychological Association, Montreal.

Reynolds, C. R., & Gutkin, T. B. (1981). A multivariate comparison of the intellectual performance of Blacks and Whites matched on four demographic variables. *Personality and Individual Differences, 2,* 175–180.

Reynolds, C. R., & Harding, R. E. (1983). Outcome in two large sample studies of factorial similarity under six methods of comparison. *Educational and Psychological Measurement, 43,* 723–728.

Reynolds, C. R., & Jensen, A. R. (1983, September). *Patterns of intellectual performance among Blacks and Whites matched on "g."* Paper presented at the Annual Meeting of the American Psychological Association, Montreal.

Reynolds, C. R., & Kaiser, S. (1990). Test bias in psychological assessment. In T. B. Gutkin & C. R. Reynolds (Eds.), *The handbook of school psychology* (2nd ed., pp. 487–525). New York: Wiley.

Reynolds, C. R., & Kamphaus, R. W. (2003a). *Reynolds Intellectual Assessment Scales.* Lutz, FL: Psychological Assessment Resources.

Reynolds, C. R., & Kamphaus, R. W. (2003b). *Reynolds Intellectual Assessment Scales and the Reynolds Intellectual Screening Test: Professional manual.* Lutz, FL: Psychological Assessment Resources.

Reynolds, C. R., Livingston, R. L., & Willson, V. (2006). *Measurement and assessment in the classroom.* Boston: Allyn & Bacon.

Reynolds, C. R., Lowe, P. A., & Saenz, A. (1999). The problem of bias in psychological assessment. In C. R. Reynolds & T. B. Gutkin (Eds.), *The handbook of school psychology* (3rd ed., pp. 549–595). New York: Wiley.

Reynolds, C. R., McBride, R. D., & Gibson, L. J. (1979, March). *Black-White IQ discrepancies may be related to differences in hemisphericity.* Paper presented at the Annual Meeting of the National Association of School Psychologists, San Diego.

Reynolds, C. R., & Paget, K. (1981). Factor analysis of the Revised Manifest Anxiety Scale for Blacks, Whites, males, and females with a national normative sample. *Journal of Consulting and Clinical Psychology, 49,* 349–352.

Reynolds, C. R., & Richmond, B. O. (1978). *The Revised Children's Manifest Anxiety Scale.* Los Angeles, CA: Western Psychological Services.

Reynolds, C. R., Richmond, B. O., & Lowe, P. A. (2003a). *The Adult Manifest Anxiety Scale–College Version (AMAS-C).* Los Angeles, CA: Western Psychological Services.

Reynolds, C. R., Richmond, B. O., & Lowe, P. A. (2003b). *The Adult Manifest Anxiety Scale–Elderly Version (AMAS-E).* Los Angeles, CA: Western Psychological Services.

Reynolds, C. R., Richmond, B. O., & Lowe, P. A. (2003c). *The Adult Manifest Anxiety Scales (AMAS) manual.* Los Angeles, CA: Western Psychological Services.

Reynolds, C. R., Willson, V. L., & Chatman, S. P. (1985). Regression analyses of bias on the Kaufman Assessment Battery for Children. *Journal of School Psychology, 23,* 195–204.

Roid, G. H. (2003a). *Stanford-Binet Intelligence Scales, Fifth Edition.* Itasca, IL: Riverside.

Roid, G. H. (2003b). *Stanford-Binet Intelligence Scales, Fifth Edition: Technical manual.* Itasca, IL: Riverside.

Rosenthal, R. (1976). *Experimenter effects in behavioral research.* New York: Halstead.

Ross, A. O. (1974). A clinical child psychologist "examines" retarded children. In G. J. Williams & S. Gordon (Eds.), *Clinical child psychology: Current trends and future perspectives* (p. 545). New York: Behavioral Publications.

Ross, A. O. (1976). *Psychological aspects of learning abilities and reading disorders.* New York: McGraw-Hill.

Rowe, D. (1994). No more than skin deep. *American Psychologist, 49,* 215–216.

Samuda, A. J. (1975). *Psychological testing of American minorities: Issues and consequences.* New York: Dodd, Mead.

Sandoval, J., & Mille, M. (1979). *Accuracy judgments of WISC-R item difficulty for minority groups.* Paper presented at the Annual Meeting of the American Psychological Association, New York.

Sattler, J. M. (2001). *Assessment of children* (4th ed.). San Diego: Author.

Sattler, J. M., & Gwynne, J. (1982). White examiners generally do not impede the intelligence test performance of Black children: To debunk a myth. *Journal of Consulting and Clinical Psychology, 50,* 196–208.

Sawyer, R. L., Cole, N. S., & Cole, J. W. (1976). Utilities and the issue of fairness in a decision theoretic model for selection. *Journal of Educational Measurement, 13,* 59–76.

Schmidt, F. L., & Hunter, J. E. (1974). Racial and ethnic bias in psychological tests: Divergent implications of two definitions of test bias. *American Psychologist, 29,* 1–8.

Schoenfeld, W. N. (1974). Notes on a bit of psychological nonsense: "Race differences in intelligence." *Psychological Record, 24,* 17–32.

Shuey, A. M. (1966). *The testing of Negro intelligence* (2nd ed.). New York: Social Science Press.

Stern, W. (1914). *The psychological methods of testing intelligence*. Baltimore, MD: Warwick & York.

Sternberg, R. J. (1980). Intelligence and test bias: Art and science. *Behavioral and Brain Sciences, 3*, 353–354.

Stöber, J. (2004). Dimensions of test anxiety: Relations to ways of coping with pre-exam anxiety and uncertainty. *Anxiety, Stress, and Coping, 17*, 213–226.

Stricker, L. J. (1982). Identifying test items that perform differentially in population subgroups: A partial correlation index. *Applied Psychological Measurement, 6*, 261–273.

Suzuki, L. A., Meller, P. J., & Ponterotto, J. G. (1996). Multicultural assessment: Present trends and future directions. In L. A. Suzuki, P. J. Meller, & J. G. Ponterotto (Eds.), *Handbook of multicultural assessment: Clinical, psychological, and educational applications*. San Francisco: Jossey-Bass.

Terman, L. M., & Merrill, M. A. (1937). *Measuring intelligence: A guide to the administration of the new revised Stanford-Binet tests of intelligence*. Boston: Houghton Mifflin.

Thissen, D., Steinberg, L., & Wainer, H. (1993). Detection of differential item functioning using the parameters of item response models. In P. W. Holland & H. Wainer (Eds.), *Differential item functioning: Theory and practice* (pp. 67–113). Hillsdale, NJ: Erlbaum.

Thorndike, R. L. (1971). Concepts of culture-fairness. *Journal of Educational Measurement, 8*, 63–70.

Torrance, E. P. (1980). Psychology of gifted children and youth. In W. M. Cruickshank (Ed.), *Psychology of exceptional children and youth*. Englewood Cliffs, NJ: Prentice Hall.

Tyler, L. E. (1965). *The psychology of human differences*. New York: Appleton-Century-Crofts.

Vance, H. B., Hankins, N., & McGee, H. (1979). A preliminary study of Black and White differences on the Wechsler Intelligence Scale for Children. *Journal of Clinical Psychology, 35*, 815–819.

van de Vijver, F., & Poortinga, Y. H. (1991). Culture-free measurement in the history of cross-cultural psychology. *Bulletin of the International Test Commission, 18*, 72–87.

Veale, J. R., & Foreman, D. F. (1983). Assessing cultural bias using foil response data: Cultural variation. *Journal of Educational Measurement, 20*, 249–258.

Wechsler, D. (1949). *The Wechsler Intelligence Scale for Children*. New York: The Psychological Corporation.

Wechsler, D. (1967). *Wechsler Preschool and Primary Scale of Intelligence*. New York: The Psychological Corporation.

Wechsler, D. (1975). Intelligence defined and undefined: A relativistic appraisal. *American Psychologist, 30*, 135–139.

Willerman, L. (1979). *The psychology of individual and group differences*. San Francisco: Freeman.

Williams, R. L. (1970). Danger: Testing and dehumanizing Black children. *Clinical Child Psychology Newsletter, 9*, 5–6.

Williams, R. L. (1974). From dehumanizing to Black intellectual genocide: A rejoinder. In G. J. Williams & S. Gordon (Eds.), *Clinical child psychology: Current practices and future perspectives*. New York: Behavioral Publications.

Williams, R. L., Dotson, W., Dow, P., & Williams, W. S. (1980). The war against testing: A current status report. *Journal of Negro Education, 49*, 263–273.

Woodcock, R. W., & Johnson, M. B. (1989). *Woodcock-Johnson Psychoeducational Battery—Revised*. Itasca, IL: Riverside.

Woodcock, R. W., McGrew, K. S., & Mather, N. (2001a). *Woodcock-Johnson-III-Tests of Achievement*. Itasaca, IL: Riverside.

Woodcock, R. W., McGrew, K. S., & Mather, N. (2001b). *Woodcock-Johnson-III-Tests of Cognitive Abilities*. Itasaca, IL: Riverside.

Wright, B. J., & Isenstein, V. R. (1977/1978). Psychological tests and minorities. DHEW Publication No. (ADM) 78-482. Rockville, MD: National Institutes of Mental Health.

Zeidner, M. (1998). *Test anxiety: The state of the art*. New York: Plenum.

CHAPTER 19

BEHAVIORAL ASSESSMENT

TIMOTHY R. VOLLMER
University of Florida

CLAIRE C. ST. PETER PIPKIN
West Virginia University

JORGE R. REYES
Westfield State College

KIMBERLY N. SLOMAN
Rutgers University

INTRODUCTION

Behavioral assessment is a form of evaluation based upon the notion that behavior displayed by individuals is, at least in part, learned. Therefore, problematic behavior that has been learned previously can be unlearned, and desirable behavior that has not yet been learned can be taught. An assumption of a behavioral assessment is that features of the social or nonsocial environment make behavior more or less likely to occur. In fact, numerous studies have shown that behavior problems can be maintained by social positive reinforcement (such as attention), social negative reinforcement (such as escape or avoidance of instructional demands), or automatic positive or negative reinforcement (i.e., reinforcement that is produced independent of the social environment) (Derby et al., 1994; Iwata, Dorsey, Slifer, Bauman & Richman, 1982/1994; Hanley, Iwata, & McCord, 2003; Kurtz et al., 2003; Northup et al., 1991; Rapp, Miltenberger, Galensky, Ellingson, & Long, 1999). One task of the psychologist or behavior analyst is to identify pertinent environmental antecedents (events that occur before behavior) and consequences (events that occur as a result of behavior). By identifying important antecedents and consequences, the environment can be arranged to reduce the probability of behavior problems or to increase the probability of desirable behavior. Without the information obtained in a behavioral assessment, behavioral interventions and environmental modifications involve a great degree of guesswork.

It is important to note that behavioral assessments are not unique to school settings. Such assessments have been implemented in diverse settings such as the workplace, athletic fields, residential facilities, and homes, among many others. Further, behavioral assessments have been used to evaluate the behavior of a wide range of individuals across different groups, such as workers, athletes, adults with mental retardation, families, and so on. Of course, this chapter will focus on behavioral assessment methods that are particularly pertinent to school-age children (i.e., students), both with and without developmental disabilities. The chapter will *not* focus on behavioral interventions, as that is covered elsewhere in this volume.

One unique feature of behavioral assessments, then, is that the general approach is not necessarily population specific. Thus, the methods described in this chapter (descriptive assessments, functional analyses, and reinforcer/preference assessments) are potentially applicable to groups of students ranging from typically developing children in regular education classrooms to children with profound developmental disabilities. Of course, idiosyncratic modifications to assessment formats must be made in order to appropriately serve the student being assessed. For example, a reinforcer assessment with a typically developing verbal child may involve a verbal questionnaire whereas a reinforcer assessment for a child with profound developmental disabilities who does not speak might involve pointing instead of talking. Further, the items or activities tested as possible reinforcers are very likely to be different for children with and without disabilities, or children of various ages.

Similarly, the behavioral assessment approach is not oriented toward any particular form of behavior problem. Thus, the general methods described in this chapter are potentially applicable to fighting at recess time and to severe self-injurious behavior. Again, however, the person conducting the evaluation must identify which components of a behavioral assessment are most suitable for the problem behavior in question. For example, if fighting on the playground happens once per month, it is unlikely that an analog functional analysis would be useful because an analog functional analysis requires that the behavior is observed rather frequently and can be reproduced by arranging the environment in particular ways. In that case, a detailed descriptive assessment might be more appropriate (possibly involving teacher interviews, direct observation of social interactions at recess time, and so on). If severe self-injurious behavior is occurring several times per minute, then a highly controlled analog functional analysis is a viable option to go along with a detailed descriptive assessment.

The first section of the chapter will cover descriptive assessments methods, including indirect (e.g., interview) and direct (e.g., observation) methods. Generally speaking, descriptive methods are designed to identify the problem behavior and possible replacement behavior, establish baseline levels of occurrence, and possibly to construct hypotheses about the operant function of behavior. Although dozens if not hundreds of checklists, scales, and interview formats have been developed, the focus here will be on indirect assessments designed to identify relevant antecedent and consequent events.

The second section will cover functional analysis methods. Generally speaking, functional analysis methods involve the intentional manipulation of variables hypothesized to maintain problem behavior, suppress appropriate behavior, or both. Because descriptive methods can only identify correlations between behavior and environmental events, functional analyses are useful because they provide an evaluation of causal relations between environmental and behavioral events. Information from a functional analysis is used to directly link assessment outcomes to intervention. For example, if a functional analysis shows that classroom disruptive behavior is inadvertently reinforced by teacher attention, the teacher could minimize attention when problem behavior occurs and maximize attention when

appropriate classroom participation occurs (i.e., differential reinforcement).

The third section covers reinforcer (or "stimulus preference") assessments. Sometimes behavioral interventions require the identification of powerful reinforcers, which may include stimulus events (e.g., presentation of a "treat") or activity events (e.g., extended recess time). Preference assessments are potentially useful either when a functional analysis cannot be conducted (i.e., in order to override, via reinforcement, whatever contingencies might be maintaining problem behavior) or when powerful reinforcers must be identified as a feature of an individual or classroom-wide intervention (e.g., in the development of token systems).

DESCRIPTIVE ASSESSMENTS

Indirect Assessments

In contrast to direct observation, indirect assessments rely on reports from informants including parents, teachers, caregivers, or students. Informants are generally asked questions about possible antecedents to and consequences of problem behavior. Indirect assessments include methods such as record reviews, structured interviews (e.g. O'Neil, Horner, Albin, Storey, & Sprague, 1997), questionnaires (e.g. Lewis, Scott, & Sugai, 1994), checklists (e.g. Achenbach, 1991), and rating scales (e.g. Durand & Crimmins, 1988; Weiseler, Hanson, Chamberlain, & Thompson, 1985). Table 19.1 includes a short list of some commonly used indirect assessment checklists and

TABLE 19.1 Commonly Used Indirect Assessment Methods

Motivational Assessment Scale (MAS)	Durand & Crimmins (1988)
Child Behavior Checklist (CBCL)	Achenbach (1991)
Problem Behavior Questionaire (PBQ)	Lewis, Scott, & Sugai (1994)
Questions About Behavioral Function (QABF)	Matson & Vollmer (1995)
Functional Analysis Screening Tool (FAST)	Iwata & DeLeon (1996)
Functional Assessment Interview (FAI)	O'Neill et al. (1997)

questionnaires. Information gathered from these assessments may assist in developing treatments or informing more direct assessments (e.g., descriptive or experimental analyses).

The primary limitation of indirect assessments is that verbal reports do not always match actual events. This problem has proven especially true when people are asked to conjecture about the possible reasons that problem behavior occurs. Nonetheless, there are certain advantages of indirect assessments. One, the time expenditure can be minimal. If no useful information is obtained, little time is lost. Two, indirect assessments can open up an initial dialogue between the psychologist or behavior analyst and care providers, including teachers. Three, indirect assessments can prove useful in constructing operational definitions of problematic behavior. Four, indirect assessments can help identify variables that are possibly idiosyncratic to an individual. For example, Borrero, Vollmer, and Borrero (2004) observed low rates of aggression during the course of an inpatient functional analysis for a previously maltreated boy who displayed severe aggression. Following an interview with the boy's adoptive mother, Borrero et al. found that a specific type of instruction evoked aggression and they were able to use this information to construct a more effective assessment and treatment.

Over the past few decades, numerous variations of indirect assessment questionnaires and rating scales have been developed. In recent years, a prominent approach has been to ask questions examining several possible sources of reinforcement for problem behavior, including social attention, access to items or activities (tangibles), escape from tasks or instructional activity, escape from other people, and automatic or sensory reinforcement (automatic reinforcement merely refers to reinforcement that is not socially mediated; see Vaughan & Michael, 1982). Most of the relatively recent questionnaires have also stressed identification of the antecedent events for problem behavior. For example, the Motivational Assessment Scale (MAS) by Durand and Crimmins (1988) includes questions such as, "Would the behavior occur if no one was around?" Questions such as these are aimed at identifying behavior that may be maintained by automatic reinforcement. Other questions include, "Does the behavior occur following a request to perform a difficult task?" and, "Does the behavior occur when you stop attending to the person?" Affirmative answers to these questions may indicate that behavior is reinforced by escape from demands or social attention, respectively.

The reliability of indirect assessments has sometimes been evaluated by comparing the results of indirect assessments across independent informants. Among indirect assessments aimed at identifying the operant function of problem behavior, the aforementioned MAS (Durand & Crimmins, 1988) is perhaps the most empirically evaluated scale or checklist. Evaluations of this assessment method have yielded mixed results (e.g., Durand & Crimmins; Andorfer, Miltenberger, Woster, Rortvedt, & Gaffaney, 1992; Zarcone, Rodgers, Iwata, Rourke, & Dorsey, 1991). For example, Durand and Crimmins conducted an examination of the reliability of the MAS by comparing two independent informants' reports and found high interrater reliability. However, correlations were not conducted with each individual response so it is not clear whether the raters agreed on specific questions. Zarcone et al. evaluated the point-by-point correspondence of responses to specific questions on the MAS. Results showed little correlation between the two independent assessment ratings.

Reliability in indirect assessments is a tricky issue when the operant function of behavior is in question. It is possible in some cases that the behavior problem serves different functions in the presence of different people. Thus, both informants could be accurate but low interrater reliability would be obtained. Also, it is not uncommon that the operant function of behavior might change over time (Lerman, Iwata, Smith, Zarcone, & Vollmer, 1994). Thus, the same informant could be accurate at different points in time but with different responses. In such cases, low test-retest reliability would be obtained.

Validity evaluations have been conducted by comparing indirect assessment outcomes to functional analyses. These evaluations also have yielded mixed results (e.g., Andorfer et al., 1992; Toogood & Timlin, 1996). For example, Andorfer et al. (1992) compared results from both the MAS and structured interviews (O'Neill, Horner, Albin, Storey, & Sprague, 1990) to experimental (functional) analyses. The functions obtained from caregiver interviews matched the functions obtained in the experimental analyses. However, there was less consistency between experimental analyses and the MAS. Thus, the results indicated that some indirect methods may yield more valid results than others. However, the comparison was limited to only two indirect assessment methods.

Therefore, evaluations of other indirect methods are needed.

To summarize, indirect assessments have inherent shortcomings. Mainly they rely on verbal report, which may be unreliable in many circumstances. Also, verbal informants frequently describe correlated events, but correlated events do not necessarily equate to functionally related events (St. Peter et al., 2005). Nonetheless, as stated previously, there are some inherent advantages to the approach, such as ease of implementation and brevity. Can the inherent advantages and disadvantages be reconciled? Probably the most important consideration in that regard is that indirect assessments should not be used as a sole source of information about problematic behavior. Further, several steps can be taken to improve the validity of indirect assessments. For instance, interviews could be conducted only with caregivers who have extensive experience with the behavior or individual being assessed (Miltenberger, 1998). Additionally, structured interviews or questionnaires may be more useful than open-ended questions to caregivers or clients (Iwata, Vollmer, & Zarcone, 1990). Structured interviews may restrict the verbal reports to more objective descriptions of the target behavior.

Thus, with some caveats, indirect assessments can be used as an adjunct to more objective approaches, such as direct observation and functional analysis. Also, indirect assessments may provide an alternative assessment approach when direct assessment methods are inappropriate or impossible. For example, it would be ethically inappropriate to conduct an experimental analysis of certain problematic sexual behavior, such as unwanted touching of others, or dangerous behavior, such as knife wielding. Yet, obtaining at least *some* information via indirect assessment about the possible function of such behavior is clearly advantageous in developing interventions. Finally, indirect assessments may be especially useful for extremely low-rate behavior. Some behavior may occur too infrequently to be reliably observed directly in its natural context or in an analog assessment.

Direct Observation

Direct descriptive observations involve examining the target behavior in a natural (or at least naturalistic) context, with no experimental manipulation of environmental variables. Prior to beginning direct observation, the analyst must operationally define the target behavior and possible antecedent and consequent events, select observation times, and identify methods for organizing and evaluating the data (Bijou, Peterson, & Ault, 1968). Unlike indirect assessments, direct descriptive observation does not rely on verbal report. Like indirect assessments, however, one inherent limitation is that resulting data are correlational. In this section, four variations of direct descriptive observation will be described: Antecedent-behavior-consequence (ABC) assessments, scatter plots, frequency or interval data collection, and structured descriptive analysis.

The ABC method involves directly observing and recording each instance of the target behavior. In addition, each time the target behavior occurs, events that immediately preceded (antecedent) and immediately followed (consequence) the behavior are recorded. In addition to comparisons described previously, Andorfer et al. (1992) compared results from ABC assessments to results of structured caregiver interviews and to experimental (functional) analyses for five children. Results showed that the hypothesized functions from the ABC assessment corresponded with both the interviews and experimental analyses. In addition, several studies have used ABC assessments to form effective hypothesis-based interventions for problem behavior (e.g., Bird, Dores, Moniz, & Robinson, 1989; Smith, 1985). The ease of implementing the ABC assessment method may vary. For instance, some ABC assessments require the data collector to simply fill out a prearranged checklist of events when the response occurs (e.g., O'Neill et al., 1990). Other ABC assessments require a narrative account of events preceding and following the response (e.g., Groden, 1989).

One limitation of the ABC assessment method is that recording by inexperienced observers may lead to subjective rather than objective accounts of behavior. For example, inexperienced informants may be inclined to speculate on unobservable or poorly defined events (e.g., "having a bad day") rather than observable environmental events (e.g., "Jim was asked to erase the blackboard"). In addition, the ABC method generally focuses only on immediately preceding and subsequent events. Thus, more remote variables affecting behavior may be overlooked. In part to circumvent some of these limitations, Groden (1989) and Pyles and Bailey (1990) developed more detailed ABC checklists. The more detailed ABC checklists limit the types of events that are included in order to provide more objective definitions of behavior and environmental events. In addition, the more detailed ABC forms include space to record remote variables, such as a possibly relevant event that occurred earlier in the day (Groeden, 1989).

Another limitation of the ABC recording method is that events are only recorded when the target behavior occurs. For example, one might ascertain from ABC data that the probability of problem behavior preceded by an instructional demand is .4, but one cannot ascertain the probability of problem behavior given an instructional demand (because instructional demands are only reported if they are followed by problem behavior). These limitations of ABC recording, coupled with the more general limitation of descriptive observation (i.e., correlation not causation) suggest that the approach should not be used as a stand-alone assessment. However, the advantages of getting information about antecedents and consequences suggest that ABC recording methods can be a useful component of a more comprehensive assessment.

Touchette, MacDonald, and Langer (1985) developed a second direct observation method to identify variables affecting target behavior, using a scatter plot analysis. The scatter plot is composed of a chart divided into intervals (e.g., 30 minutes) across successive days (usually one week or one month is depicted on one page, with columns representing the time intervals throughout one day). Each interval in which no instances of target behavior occur is left blank. Each interval in which target behavior occurs is marked (for example, with a hatch mark). If several instances of behavior occur in the interval, the entire interval box is filled in. Overall, this system of marking intervals creates a visual representation of when behavior has and has not occurred. The purpose of the scatter plot is to identify specific times of day, days of the week, or weeks of the month when the target behavior is most likely to occur. These times may be associated with other events such as presence or absence of certain people, items, or activities. Touchette et al. found that, for two participants, there were clear temporal patterns of responding and each time period was correlated with certain events (e.g., presence of therapy aide, vocational activity). The information from these analyses was then used to establish treatments that resulted in decreases in problem behavior for the participants.

For example, data from the scatter plot indicated that one participant's aggression was correlated with group classes. The participant's schedule was revised, group classes were eliminated, and aggression was reduced to low levels.

Presumably due to the ease of implementation, the scatter plot approach is now widely used in classrooms, homes and residential facilities. However, it should be noted that recent studies have brought into question the utility of the scatter plot method in the assessment of problem behavior. For example, Kahng et al. (1998) conducted scatter plot analyses for 15 individuals. Results showed no clear temporal patterns of responding for any of the participants. There are several possible reasons for these findings. One, it is possible that there was a lack of consistency in the individual's schedule and, therefore, no patterns could be observed. Thus, scatter plot analyses may be less effective in identifying temporal patterns of problem behavior for individuals who have variable schedules. Two, it is possible that the recording interval (30 minutes) was too large and thus failed to detect subtle changes in the environment that may have occasioned problem behavior. Three, the large recording interval may be insensitive to changes in extremely high-rate behavior (such as behavior that at some points in the day occurs 3 times per 30 minutes and at other times occurs 60 times per 30 minutes; both 30-minute intervals would be scored the same). Despite possible limitations of the scatter plot, its relative ease of implementation makes it a reasonable candidate for an initial component of a behavioral assessment. At the very least, the scatter plot would provide a rough estimate of the baseline levels of behavior.

Bijou et al. (1968) detailed a more general variation of direct descriptive assessment that is commonly used in research today. The approach involves recording behavior and relevant events through frequency or interval recording procedures. Frequency and interval recording methods are amenable to a wide variety of data analysis techniques. Several studies have evaluated conditional probabilities of behavior-environment relations to formulate hypotheses of behavioral function (e.g., Lerman & Iwata, 1993; Mace & Lalli, 1991; Vollmer, Borrero, Wright, Van Camp, & Lalli, 2001). For example, antecedent events may be evaluated by dividing the number of observation intervals containing the antecedent and the response by the total number of intervals containing the

TABLE 19.2 Examples of Conditional Probability Calculations

Conditional probability of aggression given instructional delivery:

$$\frac{\text{\# of intervals of containing instructional demand and aggression}}{\text{\# of intervals containing instructional demand}} = \frac{8}{10} = .8$$

Conditional probability of attention given aggression:

$$\frac{\text{\# of intervals of containing aggression and attention}}{\text{\# of intervals containing aggression}} = \frac{5}{10} = .5$$

antecedent event (e.g., Mace & Lalli). Similarly, consequent events may be evaluated by dividing the number of intervals containing problem behavior and a particular consequent event by the number of intervals containing problem behavior. Table 19.2 shows some hypothetical examples of conditional probability calculations. The upper calculation is an example of an antecedent evaluation. The lower calculation is an example of a consequences evaluation.

In the upper calculation in Table 19.2, there is a high probability of aggression given instructional demands (.8). Thus, one hypothesis derived from the data may be that aggression is maintained by negative reinforcement in the form of escape from instructional demands. The second calculation shows essentially that attention follows problem behavior half of the time. This may lead to a hypothesis that problem behavior is reinforced by attention (possibly reinforced on a variable ratio schedule). Again, as with all descriptive methods, this sort of analysis is inherently limited insofar as it is merely correlational, in the same sense that the event "bless you" is highly correlated with the behavior of sneezing (but "bless you" is not a reinforcer for the sneeze). As an example of the correlation problem, St. Peter et al. (2005) recently reported nearly perfect correlations between problem behavior and attention even in cases when a functional analysis showed that attention did not reinforce problem behavior. Another limitation with conditional probability analyses is that the unconditional (background) probability of possibly reinforcing events (such as attention, escape, etc. that occurs independently of behavior) is not considered. Thus, it is possible, for example, that attention occurs so frequently that a probability of .5 (as in the Table 19.2 example) represents no change in attention levels or even represents a reduction in the ongoing probability of attention (e.g., if the background probability were, say, .75).

In part to address this latter limitation, Vollmer et al. (2001) evaluated a method of comparing the conditional probability of events to the unconditional or background probability of the same events. They suggested that if the conditional probability was higher than the unconditional probability, this indicates a possible "positive" contingency. For example, if the conditional probability of a tangible item delivery given aggression was .5 and the unconditional probability of tangible item delivery was .05, it is possible that aggression is reinforced by tangible items because the behavior is associated with an increased probability of tangible item delivery. There is at least a sufficient condition for reinforcement. On the other hand, if the conditional probability of tangible item delivery given aggression is .5, and the unconditional probability is .7, the hypothesis that aggression is reinforced by item delivery is less tenable because the behavior is actually associated with a decreased probability of obtaining tangible items (this is a "negative contingency").

Direct observation using frequency or interval recording has been compared with the outcome of a functional analysis. For example, Mace and Lalli (1991) conducted descriptive and experimental analyses for one participant who engaged in bizarre speech. The results from the descriptive analysis showed that the behavior was preceded by both task presentation and periods of low attention. These results suggested that the participant's bizarre speech was maintained both by positive reinforcement in the form of attention and negative reinforcement in the form of task removal. However, the experimental analysis results showed that the participant's bizarre speech was maintained only by attention, and was not negatively reinforced. A similar study by Lerman and Iwata (1993) also compared descriptive and experimental analyses outcomes. Results of the experimental analysis did not match the results of the descriptive assessments for five of the six participants. The results from these studies and others indicate that descriptive assessments often fail to discriminate social positive from social negative reinforcement of behavior. This limitation could result in the development of treatments that are contraindicated for problem behavior (Mace & Lalli; Lerman & Iwata). For example, a treatment for escape-maintained behavior in which a therapist continually provides instructions could reinforce attention-maintained behavior.

A fourth approach to direct descriptive observation is a sort of hybrid between a descriptive and a functional analysis, known as a "structured descriptive assessment" (SDA, e.g., Anderson & Long, 2002; Freeman, Anderson, & Scotti, 2000). In an SDA, antecedent events are "scripted," in the sense that care providers are asked to present specific antecedent events such as instruction delivery or low attention levels. In contrast, consequences for problem behavior are not scripted, in order to observe naturally occurring events that might function as reinforcement. Freeman et al. (2000) compared SDA with typical descriptive analysis methods and analog functional analysis for two participants. The comparison showed that the results from the SDA and analog functional analysis yielded similar hypotheses about behavioral function. Additionally, the SDA allowed more direct observation of relevant environmental events (e.g., specific antecedents and consequences) than did typical descriptive analyses. However, the study included only two participants, and no treatment evaluations were conducted based on the results of the SDA. Thus, further evaluations of this methodology are necessary to determine the generality and clinical validity of the approach.

To summarize, because they are primarily correlational, descriptive assessments are probably most useful as an adjunct to a functional analysis if the goal is to identify cause and effect relations between behavior and the environment. However, it is possible that in some cases effective behavioral interventions could be developed based on descriptive information alone. Best practice is probably that several descriptive assessments methods might be used in conjunction to gain as much information about the problem behavior as possible. Almost certainly, any behavioral assessment should include some sort of initial interview (indirect assessment) coupled with some kind of data collection by care providers or teachers (e.g., ABC forms or scatter plots, or both), followed by or in parallel with direct observation by a professional psychologist or behavioral analyst. In no case should a mere interview or an isolated use of ABC forms or scatter plots serve as a sole source of information.

FUNCTIONAL ANALYSIS

Although functional analysis can refer to any experimental analysis of behavior, in the realm of behavioral assessment the term has recently been used to refer to a specific set of procedures designed to identify the operant function of problematic behavior. Most of the published work in this area has involved participants with developmental disabilities. The procedures were initially developed as an assessment for behavior problems displayed by children with developmental disabilities, so it makes sense that much of the work would continue with that population. However, functional analyses and functional analysis logic are viable with diverse populations, as has been exemplified in recent research (for a review, see Ellis and Magee, 2004).

The most commonly used functional analysis procedures were initially described by Iwata et al. (1982/1994). Numerous variations (e.g., brief functional analysis; Derby et al., 1992), extensions (e.g., functional analysis of precursor behavior; Smith & Churchill, 2002), and alternative methods (e.g., Carr & Durand, 1985) have subsequently emerged. Typical functional analysis procedures involve providing brief access to a potential reinforcer following problem behavior. If rates of problem behavior increase in conditions when a particular stimulus or event is provided relative to other conditions, the effect suggests that the tested stimulus or event is in fact a reinforcer. Because independent variables (possible reinforcers) are presented and withdrawn strategically in an experimental fashion, this approach differs from the descriptive assessment approaches previously described.

Although it may seem counterintuitive to intentionally provide reinforcers following problem behavior, the rationale is that identification of the variables maintaining problem behavior will ultimately improve the intervention. One might consider the arrangement to be similar to an allergy test, in which a patient is briefly exposed to possible allergens in order to identify the best possible course of treatment. The exposure to the allergen is an analog to natural exposure the patient might experience in the environment outside of the physician's clinic. Indeed, functional analysis procedures are designed to serve as analogs to the types of reinforcers that probably follow problem behavior in the student's everyday environment. For example, teachers or caregivers may attend to a student following problem behavior (e.g., reprimands), or they may terminate an instructional activity following problem behavior.

The intentional reinforcement of problem behavior (for the purposes of functional analysis) may be best reserved for situations when a student can be pulled out of class for the assessment. Otherwise, teachers may not find the procedure acceptable because reinforcing problem behavior in the classroom is likely to disrupt the academic environment, even if temporarily. Pulling a student out from class has the advantage of isolating suspected variables, but has the disadvantage of reducing assessment external validity. If a functional analysis is implemented in the context of a classroom, it may be more viable to either deliver reinforcers following appropriate behavior (thus testing for a reinforcement effect) or to withhold suspected reinforcers for problem behavior (thus testing for an extinction effect).

Several "test conditions" are commonly included in a functional analysis, with each condition associated with the delivery of a particular potential reinforcer. Most often, the conditions are rapidly alternated with each other in an experimental design known as a multielement format (Sidman, 1960), although other experimental designs have been used (e.g., Vollmer, Iwata, Duncan, & Lerman, 1993). Rates of responding in each test condition are compared with each other and to rates of responding during a control condition. During the control condition, motivation to engage in problem behavior is attenuated by providing free access to potential reinforcers. For example, preferred items are available, an adult interacts with the student in a friendly way, and no demands are presented. When rates of responding are elevated in a test condition in comparison to the control condition, a potential reinforcer for problem behavior has been identified.

Testing for Social Positive Reinforcement

Social attention is one of the most frequent consequences of problem behavior in natural environments (Thomas, Presland, Grant, & Glynn, 1978; Thompson & Iwata, 2001). In a typical attention condition, the student has access to preferred items or activities while the therapist works or engages in other activities that do not involve the participant. When the student engages in the targeted problem behavior, the therapist turns to the student and provides a brief period of attention. If this procedure is used in the classroom, it is possible that the teacher might provide attention following some appropriate behavior, withhold suspected reinforcement for problem behavior, or both. The form of the attention can be chosen based on the forms of attention that are most prevalent in the student's natural environment. These forms of attention could include reprimands (e.g., "Don't do that"), statements of concern (e.g., "Are you feeling okay?"), or touching, such as soothing motions like those intended to calm the student. Increases in problem behavior during the attention condition relative to other test conditions and relative to the control condition suggest that the student's behavior is reinforced by access to attention.

Figure 19.1 shows four graphs depicting hypothetical outcomes of functional analyses. Although hypothetical, the graphs are very similar to common outcomes seen in our research and research in other applied laboratories. For all panels in the figure, the rate or percentage of responding is along the y-axis, and consecutive functional analysis sessions are plotted along the x-axis. Each data path depicts responding in one of the functional analysis conditions. The upper panel of the figure shows the hypothetical results of a functional analysis in which the highest rates of problem behavior occurred in the attention condition. In this case, rates of self-injury were consistently greater in the attention condition (depicted by the closed triangles) than in the play, escape, or tangible conditions.

A second possible type of positive reinforcement involves tangible items such as food, toys, drinks, objects, and so on. Parents and teachers sometimes give tangible items to a child in an effort to calm or appease him or her. The effects of tangible items as reinforcement have been reported frequently in the literature (e.g., Iwata et al., 1994; Marcus & Vollmer, 1996; Mueller, Wilczynski, Moore, Fusilier, & Trahant, 2001). Tangible conditions are usually included in a functional analysis only when access to tangible items seems to be a common consequence for that particular student, based on descriptive observations. For example, Vollmer, Ringdahl,

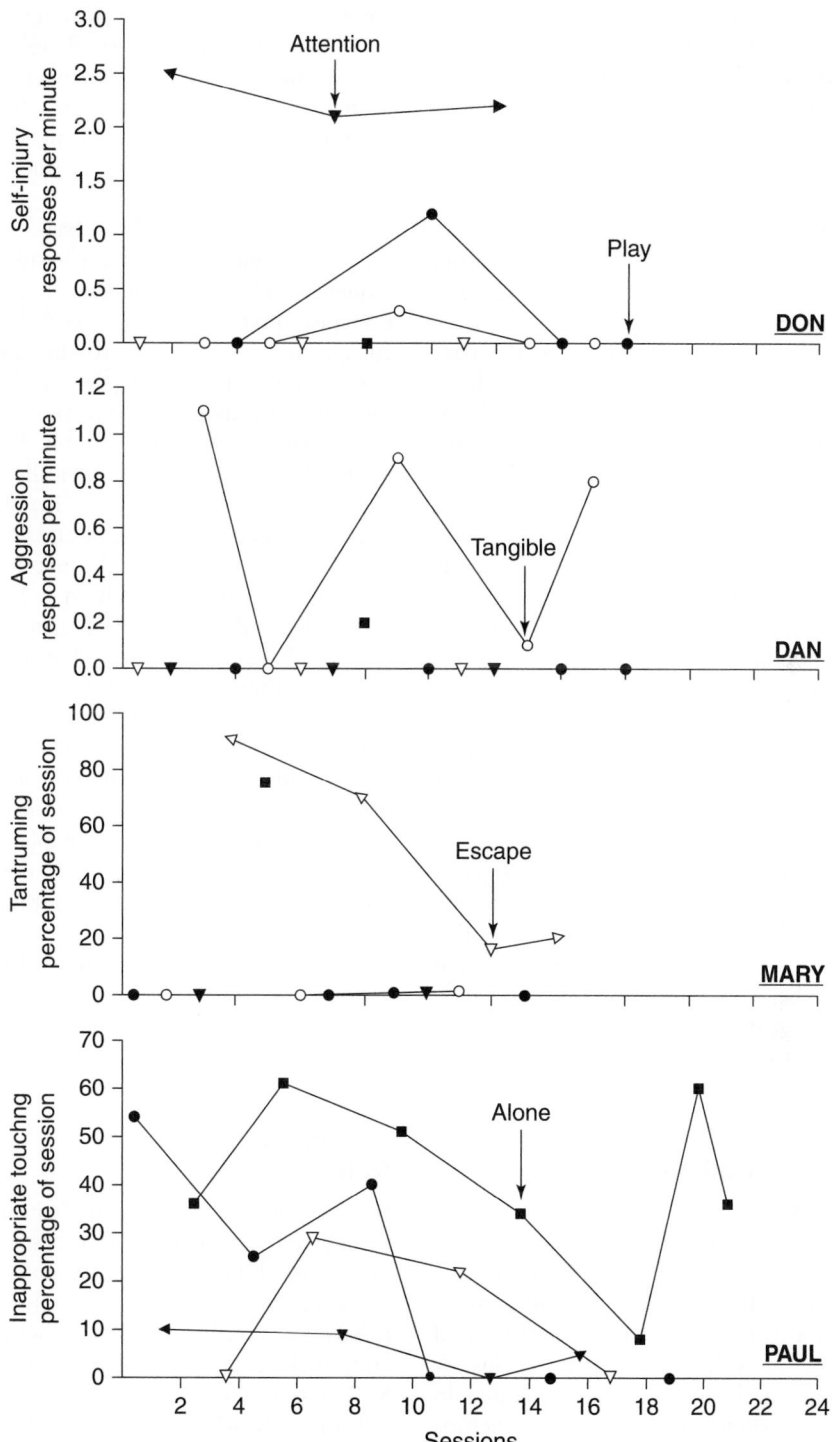

FIGURE 19.1 Hypothetical functional analysis outcomes. For all of the panels, the attention condition is represented by the closed triangles, the tangible condition is represented by the open circles, the escape condition is represented by the open triangles, the alone condition is represented by the closed squares, and the play condition is represented by the closed circles. (Upper Panel) Functional analysis outcome for self-injury. (Upper Middle Panel) Functional analysis outcomes for aggression. (Lower Middle Panel) Functional analysis outcome for tantrums. (Lower Panel) Functional analysis outcome for screaming.

Roane, and Marcus (1997) reported a case of an adolescent girl with developmental disabilities who carried around magazines most of the day. When an adult tried to remove the magazines from the girl's hands, she became aggressive and the magazines were returned to her as if to "calm her down."

The tangible condition of a functional analysis tests for the possible reinforcing effects of access to items or activities. During tangible conditions, the therapist restricts access to items while otherwise attending to the participant on some response-independent basis (i.e., regardless of the occurrence of problem behavior). When the targeted problem behavior occurs, the therapist provides brief (e.g., 30-second) access to the items before again restricting access. This process is repeated throughout the session. If rates of responding are higher in the tangible condition than rates in the other test conditions or rates in the control condition, it suggests that the problem behavior is reinforced by access to items or activities. If the assessment is conducted in a classroom context, the teacher might deliver tangible items following appropriate behavior (to test for a reinforcement effect) or might withhold tangible items following problem behavior (to test for an extinction effect). The second panel of Figure 19.1 shows the hypothetical results of a functional analysis of aggression. In this case, higher rates of aggression were observed when that behavior produced access to tangible items than in any other condition, suggesting that aggression was reinforced by access to tangible items.

Testing for Social Negative Reinforcement

The escape condition (sometimes called a "demand" condition) tests for negative reinforcement of problem behavior. The type of demand and format of demand presentation varies based on what the individual encounters in his or her environment. Demand situations tested in the literature include various activities such as self-care demands, academic demands, daily living demands, social interaction, and so on. Choosing the demand context can have important implications for the outcome of the analysis; Broussard and Northup (1995), for example, observed much higher rates of problem behavior when difficult academic materials were used in the demand

condition than when easy materials were used. To help strengthen external validity of the assessment, therapists should take particular care to match the demand used in the functional analysis to demands typically presented to the student in the classroom or other naturalistic settings.

During a functional analysis, demands are usually presented using a three-step prompting sequence. During three-step prompting, the therapist first provides a verbal request to engage in the activity. If the student does not comply following the verbal request, the therapist models completion of the task. If the student does not comply following the model, the therapist may physically guide completion of the task. Compliance at any stage of the sequence results in brief praise, and usually restarts the prompting sequence at the first step. Instances of problem behavior result in a brief removal of the demands and demand materials. If more problem behavior is observed in this condition than in other test conditions or in the play condition, it suggests that the student's behavior is maintained by escape from demand situations (i.e., negative reinforcement). If escape is tested in the classroom context, the teacher might provide escape following compliance (testing for a reinforcement effect) or might withhold escape following problem behavior (testing for an extinction effect).

The third panel of Figure 19.1 shows the hypothetical results of a functional analysis of tantrums. Tantrums occurred at high levels in the escape condition compared to other conditions.

Testing for Automatic Reinforcement

In some instances, problem behavior may be maintained independent of the social environment. For children with developmental disabilities and autism, automatically reinforced problem behavior can include stereotypic behavior such as body rocking or hand flapping (Rapp, Vollmer, St. Peter, Dozier, & Cotnoir, 2004), and some self-injurious behavior (Iwata et al., 1982/1994). For children in general, various problematic forms of behavior can be maintained by automatic reinforcement. For example, Rapp et al. (1999) showed that trichotillomania (hair pulling) was automatically reinforced for one participant. Other examples of common automatically reinforced behavior include thumb sucking (Stricker,

Miltenberger, Garlinghouse, Deaver, & Anderson, 2001), nail biting (Long, Miltenberger, Ellingson, & Ott, 1999) and at times common classroom disruptive behavior such as running around the room, screaming, or climbing. Assessment and treatment of behavior that persists independently of social reinforcers may be especially challenging because it may be more difficult to precisely identify the reinforcer, and the therapist may have little or no control over reinforcer delivery.

An alone or no-consequence condition may be included in a functional analysis to test whether the behavior persists independent of social reinforcement. During this condition, the student may be left alone in a room (and observed through a one-way observation window) or may be in the room with other individuals who provide no programmed consequences for the problem behavior (in cases when observation windows are not available). Because nothing in the external social environment is changing following problem behavior, high rates of behavior in this condition would suggest that the behavior itself produces some reinforcing consequence independent of the social environment (i.e., it is automatically reinforced).

The fourth panel of Figure 19.1 shows the hypothetical functional analysis results for screaming. In this case, screaming occurred in several of the conditions, but the most consistent rates of responding were observed in the alone condition. These results suggest that screaming may be maintained by automatic reinforcement.

Considerations When Conducting Functional Analyses in Schools

Conducting functional analyses in school settings can require special considerations. A few will be discussed briefly in this section. One, it could be argued that the entire academic context resembles a demand context and, therefore, academic activity should be superimposed upon all test conditions. Two, it is possible that problem behavior is reinforced by events not commonly tested or easily controlled in a functional analysis, such as peer attention. Three, many of the problematic forms of behavior seen in schools are not especially suited to a standard functional analysis because they may occur infrequently (such as an occasional but dangerous fight) or may occur covertly (such as stealing). Four, school personnel are extremely busy and often they are underresourced and,

hence, do not have sufficient time to complete a complex analysis.

The School as a "Demand" Context

During typical functional analysis procedures, demands are presented only during the escape condition; the other conditions are free of demands. This is done intentionally in order to isolate the effects of demands and escape from demands as possible variables influencing problematic behavior. In classroom situations, however, demands may be present to some degree across a wide range of situations. Therefore, it is possible that demands interact with other variables to influence problem behavior in academic contexts.

Carr and Durand (1985) simulated the academic context in an assessment of problem behavior by incorporating demands into attention and play conditions. The experimenters incorporated easy tasks (tasks that could be completed with 100% accuracy) into the control and attention conditions of a functional analysis and difficult tasks (tasks that were typically completed with only 25% accuracy) into a demand-type condition. An additional modification was that no reinforcers were provided following problem behavior. Although the procedures may more closely simulate an academic environment (in comparison to other conditions of a functional analysis), the absence of a test for reinforcement effects is a limitation of the approach.

Broussard and Northup (1995) also conducted functional analyses that included demands during attention and control conditions. Like Carr and Durand's (1985) procedures, task difficulty was varied across conditions such that the attention and control conditions were associated with easy tasks while the escape condition was associated with a more difficult task. Unlike Carr and Durand's procedures, Broussard and Northup also manipulated possibly reinforcing events such as attention and escape. Similarly, in other studies, attention has been incorporated into escape conditions such that the consequence for problem behavior in the escape condition includes both a break from the task and attention from an adult (Mueller, Sterling-Turner, & Moore, 2005). This combination of consequences was included because it was frequently observed in the classroom, and resulted in higher rates of problem behavior than did contingent attention or escape alone.

In short, the conditions typically used in a functional analysis need not be considered "fixed" in relation to how demands or academic activities are presented. The best approach would appear to be as follows: (a) identify the typical context and consequences for problem behavior seen in the classroom environment, and (b) incorporate those contexts and consequences into a functional analysis. If the typical consequence for problem behavior includes multiple variables (e.g., contains both attention and escape), then those consequences could be tested in combination and independently.

Other Possible Forms of Reinforcement

It is possible that the form of reinforcement maintaining problematic behavior in school settings is unique to the school setting, at least in some cases. Some examples include peer attention, teacher (not just any adult) attention, and escape from the classroom context (rather than merely escape from isolated instructions).

In part to address the concern about alternative forms of reinforcement, Broussard and Northup (1997) conducted functional analyses in regular classroom settings and included one condition in which problem behavior resulted in peer attention. The teacher attention and escape conditions were conducted while the participant was seated 3 meters from the other students in the classroom, facing away from them. During the teacher attention condition, the participants were asked to work quietly on mastered work. Any instances of problem behavior resulted in a verbal reminder to work from the teacher. During the escape condition, the participants were asked to complete difficult work (previously completed at 50% accuracy or less). Participants were put in a 30-second "time-out," moved away from the work, the teacher, and the other students, contingent on problem behavior. During the peer attention condition, a peer confederate was identified as the participant's "helper," and was instructed to remind the participant to keep working if problem behavior occurred. The experimenters showed that clear functional analysis results were obtained for all of the participants: disruptive behavior was maintained by peer attention instead of adult attention. The results of the functional analyses allowed the experimenters to develop a peer-based intervention program that was effective in decreasing disruptive behavior.

Conducting functional analyses in classrooms may allow incorporation of not only classroom specific reinforcers, like peer attention, but also typical antecedents occurring in the students' everyday environment (Umbriet, 1995). Particular features of demand presentation, such as particular facial expressions or a tone of voice, may be especially likely to evoke problem behavior. Or, demands may be aversive only in the presence of peers, such as when a student is called upon to answer a question aloud. To be sure, there is a trade-off when using the classroom environment as a context for the functional analysis: a degree of control is lost because hypothesized variables cannot be easily manipulated. For example, during a teacher attention condition, a peer might laugh at problem behavior. Thus, the advantages associated with external validity must be weighed against the advantages of isolating variables. Some combination (e.g., using both approaches in difficult cases) may eventually prove to be most effective.

Low-Rate and Covert Problem Behavior

One potential limitation of functional analysis procedures is with the assessment of problem behavior that occurs at low rates, such as with fighting that occurs once per month. One possible way of assessing low-rate problem behavior is through an assessment of precursor behavior (Smith & Churchill, 2002). For example, if some higher-rate precursor behavior, such as complaining, reliably occurs before the low-rate response, such as aggression, then a functional analysis can be conducted targeting the precursor behavior. Unfortunately, not all low-rate responses are associated with predictable precursors. Another possibility is to create a larger window of time in which to evaluate reinforcement contingencies (such as an "attention" week). However, this approach may be time consuming and impractical.

As for covert behavior, an indirect assessment may be more suitable than a functional analysis because one would not see the behavior in a functional analysis, but other individuals in the environment might be able to identify the context in which behavior has occurred in the past. However, this approach is somewhat unappealing because of the shortcomings of indirect assessments discussed previously. Another, possibly more objective, solution is to measure response products as an assessment component (e.g., number of items stolen; Maglieri, DeLeon,

Rodriguez-Catter, & Sevin, 2000; Switzer, Deal, & Bailey, 1977). Thus, although an observer might not see the behavior as it occurs, permanent products of the behavior can be measured as an assessment component. Also, Himle, Miltenberger, Flessner, and Gatheridge (2004) presented an interesting methodology to discretely observe children playing with guns. Although gun play per se is hopefully not available to children in most schools, the general methodology could be adapted to evaluate behavior such as stealing, or talking to strangers (e.g., Poche, Brouwer, & Swearingen, 1981).

Time and Resource Limitations

Another potential problem with conducting functional analyses in a school setting is time constraints. For example, students or therapists may only be available for limited time periods. Because of time constraints, many school professionals have chosen to use indirect assessment methods (discussed previously in this chapter). However, indirect assessments are not the only option when time and space constraints are an issue—additional modifications of standard functional analysis procedures have been developed to address time limitations.

One way to address possible time constraints is the use of brief functional analysis procedures (Cooper, Wacker, Sasso, Reimers, & Donn, 1990; Cooper et al., 1992; Derby et al., 1992; Harding, Wacker, Cooper, Millard, & Jensen-Kovalan, 1994; Northup et al., 1991). Northup et al. used brief functional analyses in an outpatient clinic in which each participant was available for only a 90-minute period. The procedures were similar to those outlined by Iwata et al. (1982/1994), but each condition was presented only once or twice, depending on the reinforcers thought to maintain the problem behavior. Using this approach, a student who engages in problem behavior hypothesized to be maintained by attention might be exposed to one control session, one alone session, one escape session, and two attention sessions. In addition, a "contingency reversal" is often used to test the effects of the hypothesized reinforcer on some alternative, desirable behavior. In a summary study on this approach, Derby et al. were able to identify the function of the problem behavior in 76% of cases.

To get as much information as possible from a brief assessment, minute-by-minute response frequencies can be plotted graphically. Vollmer, Iwata, Zarcone, Smith, and Mazaleski (1993), for example, showed one case in which responding increased dramatically at the beginning of sessions that followed an attention session, but responding declined as the session continued. This outcome suggested that the behavior was reinforced by attention and the burst of responding in subsequent sessions was an extinction burst. This pattern would not have been noticed using overall session rates of the problem behavior. Vollmer, Marcus, Ringdahl, and Roane (1995) showed that functional analysis outcomes can sometimes be clear after just a very few sessions when minute-by-minute data analysis is used. Thus, there may be no need to prolong the assessment in some cases.

Another potential resource-related concern is a lack of specialized or trained staff to conduct the analyses. In fact, the need for highly trained staff has been cited as a major limitation of functional analysis procedures (Freeman et al., 2000). Fortunately, research has shown that not only can functional analysis procedures remain effective when implemented in a naturalistic setting, but that teachers and caregivers can be trained to conduct the analysis in a short period of time (e.g., Cooper et al., 1990; Moore et al., 2002; Wallace, Doney, Mintz-Resudek, & Tarbox, 2004). Training teachers or caregivers to implement functional analysis procedures may increase the utility of these procedures because inclusion of specialized staff would be unnecessary.

Thus, although time and personnel constraints are legitimate issues in school settings, the use of brief assessments and assessments conducted during the flow of natural classroom activity may minimize this problem. Nonetheless, briefer assessments conducted by relatively less trained individuals are probably not ideal and these approaches probably should be avoided in the most dangerous circumstances.

Summary

Recent research suggests that functional analysis can be a useful tool for the identification of reinforcers that maintain problem behavior. Functional analysis procedures seem reasonably effective even when implemented using brief assessments and natural "therapists," such as teachers and caregivers. Despite the proven utility of these methods, much research remains to be done. For example, the problem of low-rate or covert behavior has not yet been sufficiently addressed, although promising approaches have been proposed. Also, more research is warranted on the incorporation of functional analyses into the classroom, and for the use of functional analyses with typically developing students.

PREFERENCE ASSESSMENTS

The majority of behavioral treatment programs revolve around reducing problem behavior and increasing appropriate behavior through the use of reinforcement. As expressed in the preceding sections of this chapter, the reinforcers maintaining problem behavior are often identified via descriptive assessment and functional analysis. Once identified, the reinforcers can be withheld when problem behavior occurs and delivered contingent on appropriate behavior (differential reinforcement) or response independently (noncontingent reinforcement). However, at times it is difficult to identify or withhold reinforcers for problem behavior. Hence, other powerful reinforcers must be identified. Also, sometimes the goal of a behavioral intervention involves behavioral acquisition and does not involve behavior reduction. Therefore, conducting an assessment of an individual's preference for preferred items or activities is an important component of many behavioral assessments. The rationale for formally assessing an individual's preference for items or activities is that preferred items have been shown to function as more powerful reinforcers when compared to items selected at random (e.g., Piazza, Fisher, Hagopian, Bowman, & Toole, 1996).

Various methods have been developed to identify potential reinforcers. This process typically involves at least two components. One, items or activities are selected in a preference test. Two, the items or activities are made contingent on some task in order to test for a reinforcement effect. Comparisons are usually made between performance on the task when high- and low-preference items are used as reinforcers, and relatively higher levels of task engagement for one of the items is indicative of reinforcer strength.

Preference Assessment Methods

One commonly used technique to identify reinforcers involves the use of surveys and questionnaires administered to either the client or student. Oddly, preferences based on open-ended surveys or questionnaires often do not predict subsequent reinforcer efficacy (Northup, George,

Jones, Broussard, & Vollmer, 1996). This is odd because it would seem reasonable to assume that people could accurately report what they like. In an early example of this methodology, Cautela and Kastenbaum (1967) developed a survey entitled the Reinforcement Survey Schedule (RSS). The purpose of the survey was to identify potential reinforcers based on categories such as stimuli that are easily presentable (e.g., food), activities that could not be presented easily (e.g., sports), and social situations (e.g., talking with a friend). An open section was included so that the participant could describe items or activities that he or she thinks about either 5, 10, 15, or 20 times a day. Within each category, participants were instructed to respond on a scale in terms of "liking" from "not at all" to "much" and "very much." The study involved college students and juvenile offenders. The outcomes of this survey showed that participants' responding across the categories and response scales was generally undifferentiated, but a degree of differentiation was noted in some categories depending upon the particular population examined. Overall, the survey did not produce very robust effects and, furthermore, items identified as preferred were never tested as reinforcers.

Another type of survey, developed by Fantuzzo, Rohrbeck, Hightower, and Work (1991), was an attempt to determine preferences for items typically delivered as rewards in elementary school classrooms. This survey, labeled the Child Reinforcement Survey (CRS), consisted of 36 items in four categories: edible, tangible, activities, and social. The items included on the survey were chosen based on teacher ratings of their appropriateness for use in school settings. Children were asked, on an individual basis, to rate how much they liked a particular item within given parameters (i.e., a little, a lot, etc.) and teachers were also asked about the types and frequency of rewards used in the classroom. Results showed that items in the social category were generally most preferred, followed by items in the activity category and the tangible category. More importantly, items frequently used by teachers did not match student preference as measured by the survey. Additionally, the reinforcing function of the preferred items was not assessed.

Northup, Jones, Broussard, and George (1995) compared a variety of preference assessment formats with children diagnosed with attention-deficit/hyperactivity disorder (ADHD), including a "child nomination" phase in which the participants were asked to label their favorite items. A second phase involved covertly observing the children in a room with the items used in the assessments while measuring the percentage of time spent playing with each item. A final phase involved making each rated item contingent on a particular task (to test for reinforcement effects). The results indicated that the child nomination assessment method had poor predictive validity and would likely have little treatment utility. Other studies investigating reinforcer surveys have shown similar outcomes, essentially finding that verbal report outcomes are no better than chance at predicting reinforcer efficacy (Northup, 2000; Northup et al., 1996).

Studies in which caregivers have been asked to identify preferred items for their students or clients also have yielded mixed outcomes (e.g., Green et al., 1988). However, at least one study has demonstrated the potential utility of including caregiver opinions as one component of the assessment process. Fisher, Piazza, Bowman, and Amari (1996) compared the results of preference assessments using standard sets of stimuli taken from other studies to stimuli chosen by caregivers through the use of a structured interview entitled the Reinforcer Assessment for Individuals with Severe Disabilities (RAISD). Caregivers were asked to rank both sets of stimuli and results showed that the items ranked highest, chosen through the interview, were slightly more likely to function as reinforcers than the highly ranked stimuli from the standard set. Fisher et al. cautioned, however, that the difference was very minor. Collectively, the outcomes of caregiver nomination studies show that sole reliance on caregiver opinions to rank reinforcers from a standard set of stimuli is insufficient (e.g., Green, Reid, Canipe, & Gardner, 1991), but asking caregivers to rank stimuli that are determined through structured interviews may have some utility.

Alternatives to the use of verbal report measures in reinforcer identification involve taking direct measures of behavior. One of the earliest procedures to assess preference in this way was developed by Pace, Ivanic, Edwards, Iwata, and Page (1985). Pace et al. presented a variety of items, one at a time, and measured simply whether the participant approached an item. If an approach response occurred, access to that item was allowed for a brief period of time. The results showed that the procedure was effective in differentiating

between preferred items (those approached on a high percentage of trials) and nonpreferred items (those rarely or never approached). Furthermore, when preferred stimuli were made contingent on a target response, higher rates of responding were obtained than when nonpreferred stimuli were made contingent on the same response (i.e., a reinforcement effect).

The single-stimulus presentation procedure developed by Pace et al. (1985) represented an improvement over indirect assessments such as caregiver interviews for the same reason that functional analysis is an improvement over indirect assessments of problematic behavior: a reinforcement effect is actually demonstrated empirically. One limitation of the single-stimulus presentation procedure, however, is that some individuals tend to approach virtually any item as an exploratory response (e.g., Paclawskyj & Vollmer, 1995). Thus, it is difficult to "rank" the array of stimuli in order of preference. Fisher, Piazza, Bowman, Hagopian, Owens, and Slevin (1992) proposed an alternative preference assessment methodology in which pairs of items are presented concurrently and participants can select one of the items (this was originally called "forced choice," but because the choice is not actually forced, the procedure is now usually called "paired choice"). Each of the items chosen for the assessment is paired with every other item in a randomized order. The pairs of items are presented to the participant and a choice is measured as an approach response to one of the items. Attempts to select both of the items are blocked, and failure to select one of the items results in a sampling of each item followed by another choice period. If an item is selected, the participant is allowed access to the item for a brief period of time. One major advantage of this approach in comparison to the single-stimulus presentation is that it allows for a more distinct ranking of items from most to least preferred.

Fisher et al. (1992) compared the results of the paired-choice procedure with the Pace et al. (1985) single-stimulus procedure. One of the most important findings was that the single-stimulus approach procedure identified more of the items as preferred than did the paired-choice procedure. Also, many of the items identified as preferred in the single-stimulus procedure were identified as low to moderately preferred on the paired-choice procedure. Finally, items identified as highly preferred on both assessments were associated with higher rates of responding (i.e., a stronger reinforcement effect) when compared to items ranked high on only the single-stimulus procedure. Therefore, the outcomes of the Fisher et al. procedure proved to be more effective in *differentially* identifying reinforcers.

A further development in preference assessment methodology involved an extension of the paired presentation format. Windsor, Piché, and Locke (1994) presented an array of items together in a group as opposed to presenting items in pairs. Each item for the preference assessment was presented during every trial, for a total of ten trials, and the location of each item was randomized. Selection of an item was measured by an approach response or actual contact with the item and was followed by access to the item. After a selection was made, all of the items were presented again in the ensuing trial. Comparisons between this multiple stimulus (MS) format and the paired-choice format have shown that both procedures tend to identify the same items as most preferred. However, each format is associated with some distinct advantages and disadvantages. One of the primary advantages to the MS format is that it can be administered in approximately half the time it takes to administer the paired-choice format (Windsor et al.). Furthermore, in Windsor's study, the paired-choice format also resulted in more consistent outcomes across repeated administrations. However, the paired-choice format allows for a more distinct ranking of items in that the most preferred items may not always be presented in a given trial and a choice between potentially less preferred items is required.

DeLeon and Iwata (1996) attempted to combine the most beneficial aspects of the paired-choice and MS formats. Items were presented in a MS format as in the procedure described by Windsor et al. (1994). However, when an item was selected it was removed from the subsequent presentations on subsequent trials. Because choices between less preferred stimuli are ultimately required, this manipulation allows for a more distinct ranking of stimuli as in the paired-choice procedure. DeLeon and Iwata labeled this procedure "multiple stimulus without replacement (MSWO)" and distinguished it from the procedure developed by Windsor et al., which was essentially a MS *with replacement* format.

In order to determine the utility of the MSWO format, DeLeon and Iwata (1996) compared its outcomes to the outcomes of both the MS format and the paired-choice format.

In general, all of the assessments identified the same stimulus as the most preferred. Across repeated administrations, however, the MSWO and paired-choice formats provided the most consistent preference rankings. Both the MSWO and MS formats required less than half the time needed for the paired-choice format, but the MS format reliably took the least amount of time to implement. Even though the MSWO format required more time than the MS format, the increased consistency of rank-ordered stimuli produced by the MSWO assessment offers a high degree of utility for practical application.

In an analysis of reinforcer strength, DeLeon and Iwata (1996) made comparisons between items that had never been selected in the MS assessment, but had been selected at some level during the MSWO and paired-choice arrangements. The purpose of such a comparison was to determine if the MS procedure failed to identify some potential reinforcers, and whether or not those same items, if identified by the MSWO procedures and the paired-choice procedures, had a reinforcement effect. Results indicated that even those stimuli never selected during the MS (but selected during the MSWO and paired choice) produced a reinforcement effect when made contingent on responding. Thus, the MS procedure identified high-preference items, but the MSWO and paired-choice formats identified a wider range of potentially reinforcing items.

As an extension of the MS procedure, Roane, Vollmer, Ringdahl, and Marcus (1998) investigated the use of a brief preference assessment format. This procedure involved a free-operant format in which individuals had brief (5-minute) access to an array of stimuli during the entire assessment. The participant could engage with any of the items at any point in time, and none of the stimuli were removed during the assessment period. Evaluations of this procedure showed that the stimuli identified in the brief assessment functioned as reinforcers for an operant response. Furthermore, when compared to a paired-choice format, the brief assessment had some advantages, such as reduced implementation time. The brief assessment also produced lower rates of problem behavior because the stimuli were never removed during an assessment (in the paired choice approach, some participants began to engage in problem behavior when preferred items were withdrawn). One disadvantage to the brief procedure, however, is that it does not consistently produce a rank order of stimuli because the most preferred item stays available throughout. A second disadvantage is that large amounts of consumable items, such as food and beverages, can be consumed even in a 5-minute period.

The aforementioned preference assessments involve intentional manipulations of the environment and reinforcer presentations. Further, they tend to rely on the notion that some stimulus event will function as a reinforcer (as opposed to some activity serving as a reinforcer). An alternative strategy involves collecting descriptive data on naturally occurring response allocation. According to the Premack Principle (Premack, 1958), access to high-probability behavior can be used to reinforce low-probability behavior. This effect has been demonstrated numerous times, with various populations of students (Andrews, 1970; McIntire, 1963; Wasik, 1970; Yawkey & Le Penna Griffith, 1974). An example would be if a student is observed to read comic books for about 120 minutes per day if given free access but engages in math work only 2 minutes per day, access to comic books could be made contingent on working for greater durations on math.

A refinement of the Premack Principle is the Response Deprivation approach (Allison & Timberlake, 1974; Klatt & Morris, 2001; Konarski, Crowell, Johnson, & Whitman, 1982). This approach differs from the Premack Principle in that even access to low-probability behavior (in addition to access to high-probability behavior) can function as a reinforcer, when access to the (low or high) probability behavior is restricted below baseline levels. An example of the Response Deprivation approach would be if a student is observed to chat with other students for approximately 5% of the day (relatively low-probability behavior) and engages in desk work approximately 78% of the day (relatively high-probability behavior), higher allocations of desk work could be reinforced with access to chatting if chatting is restricted below the 5% level. In other words, chatting is established as a potent reinforcer if and only if it is restricted below the levels observed during baseline (descriptive) observations.

Miscellaneous Considerations

There are a variety of issues that arise with the use of preference assessments. One relates to the robustness of the reinforcement effects generated by stimuli identified as highly preferred. Typical preference assessment formats require a very low-effort response (e.g., approach) to identify preferred stimuli. Given this arrangement, it is not clear whether a stimulus identified under a low-effort response will reinforce responses of a higher effort. For example, you might reach out and interact with a radio if it were placed in front of you, but that does not mean you would mow your neighbor's lawn to gain access to a radio. Tustin (1994) evaluated the rate of responding for concurrently available stimuli under increasing response requirements for three adults with developmental disabilities. Results showed that the response rates for both stimuli were similar under low-response requirements. When response effort increased (i.e., more responses were required to access the reinforcers), participants responded to one of the stimuli more than the other. In other words, when more effort was required to obtain both reinforcers, preference for one of the reinforcers emerged. Other studies have reported similar results (e.g., DeLeon, Iwata, Goh, & Worsdell, 1997; Roane, Lerman, & Vorndran, 2001; Taravella, Lerman, Contrucci, & Roane, 2000) and point to the fact that while a less preferred stimulus may function as a reinforcer for a low-effort response, it may not be effective for more effortful responses.

A second issue involving preference assessment methodology concerns the use of food. In general, the items used in a preference assessment consist of either food items (e.g., Windsor, et al., 1994), or some combination of food and leisure/activity items (e.g., Fisher et al., 1992; Green et al., (1988); Northup et al., 1996; Pace et al., 1985). The inclusion of food within an assessment, however, may present some limitations. According to DeLeon, Iwata, and Roscoe (1997), individuals with developmental disabilities disproportionately select food items in comparison to leisure items or activities. The potential problems with this arrangement are: (a) it may be difficult to assess preference for non-food items when food items are present, and (b) the use of food as a reinforcer may not be appropriate in all settings (e.g., classroom settings) or for all people (e.g., a person with a health or weight problem). DeLeon et al. investigated this issue by comparing preference for leisure items presented with and without food. They showed that when presented with food items, leisure items were ranked low. When presented alone, many of the leisure items were ranked high in preference.

Furthermore, in subsequent tests of reinforcer efficacy, high-prefernce leisure items maintained high rates of responding.

A third issue is that studies have focused on *stimulus* preferences as opposed to *activity* preferences. Access to activities is frequently used as a reinforcer in school settings, so assessments should be designed to accommodate this possibility. Assessment of preferred activities involves similar methodologies as stimulus preference assessments. However, on occasion some modifications are needed during the assessment process. For example, with adults with developmental disabilities as participants, Hanley, Iwata, and Lindberg (1999) assessed preference for activities such as playing basketball and riding a bicycle. Instead of using the actual activities, the assessment involved the use of pictorial representations. Results showed that selection between pictures yielded differential preferences, but only when the selection was followed by a period of access to the actual activity.

Other types of activity preference assessments have involved the use of response-restriction (RR) procedures (e.g., Green & Striefel, 1988; Hanley, Iwata, Lindberg, & Conners, 2003). These assessments typically involve observing individuals engaging in particular activities and measuring how they allocate the majority of time. As the assessment progresses, some of the activities are taken away on subsequent trials and the individual has fewer options from which to choose (Hanley et al.). The advantage of this format is ease of implementation, similar to that offered by the MS format discussed previously. The RR procedures also creates a rank order of preferred activities.

A fourth issue relates to the potential difficulty of having all stimuli or activities available during the assessment. In part to address this problem, Higbee, Carr, and Harrison (1999) used pictorial representations of stimuli. Pictures may be easier than tangible stimuli to present during an assessment and they could be more efficient if there is no time required for item consumption or manipulation (Higbee et al.). Another development that has potential advantages is the use of verbal formats, in which participants are asked to state which items they prefer in a paired-choice format (i.e., would you rather have "X" or "Y"). Notice that this approach differs from more traditional reinforcer surveys and questionnaires (such as those described previously). Still, preference

assessment studies that have investigated verbal formats have reported mixed results. For example, Northup et al. (1996) compared verbal and picture formats and showed differences in preference rankings as a function of the assessment format. Also, when compared to assessments conducted with actual items, Higbee et al. also reported differences between item rankings with the use of pictures. A study by Cohen-Almeida, Graff, and Ahearn (2000), however, compared assessment outcomes using a verbal choice format and actual items and reported high correspondence between the assessment formats for both high- and low-preference items. Given the potential benefits of using pictures or verbal report measures in preference assessments, more research is needed to determine the conditions under which such formats can be used effectively.

Summary

Stimulus preference assessments are an important component to a behavioral assessment. For individuals with developmental disabilities, the most promising format seems to be a variation of MS. If there is no need to identify multiple reinforcers, then a brief assessment format should suffice (e.g., Roane et al., 1998). If multiple reinforcers are needed, then the MSWO arrangement is probably most useful. These same arrangements may be useful with typically developing children, and there is some promising research to show that choice formats can be effective in written or verbal formats. However, a limitation of preference assessment research has been that relatively few studies have included students without disabilities.

CONCLUSION

Three general categories of behavioral assessment were discussed, including descriptive assessment, functional analysis, and reinforcer assessment. Descriptive assessments are useful in the initial gathering of information and when a functional analysis is not feasible. However, because of limitations related to verbal reporting and correlation, no single type of descriptive assessment is recommended as a stand-alone assessment procedure. Functional analyses are useful when there is a need to identify cause-and-effect relations between behavior and environmental events. However, not all problem behavior seen in schools is amenable to a functional analysis. Reinforcer assessments are useful when there is a need to identify powerful reinforcers for behavioral interventions, skill acquisition, or classroom-wide procedures (such as token systems). However, more research is needed to evaluate the potency of identified reinforcers under conditions of greater response requirements, such as those seen in classrooms. A thorough behavioral assessment is likely to include components or features of all three of these general assessment categories. The prepared school psychologist will adopt the procedures as necessary to suit his or her clientele.

REFERENCES

Achenbach, T. M. (1991). *Manual for the Child Behavior Checklist/4-18 and 1991 Profile*. Burlington, VT: University of Vermont, Department of Psychiatry.

Allison, J. & Timberlake, W. (1974). Instrumental and contingent saccharin licking in rats: Response deprivation and reinforcement. *Learning and Motivation*, *5*, 231–247.

Anderson, C. M., & Long, E. S. (2002). Use of a structured descriptive assessment methodology to identify variables affecting problem behavior. *Journal of Applied Behavior Analysis*, *35*, 137–154.

Andorfer, R., Miltenberger, R., Woster, S., Rortvedt, A., & Gaffaney, T. (1992). In-home functional assessment and treatment of challenging behavior. Unpublished master's thesis, North Dakota State University.

Andrews, H. B. (1970). The systematic use of the Premack Principle in modifying classroom behaviors. *Child Study Journal*, *1*, 74–79.

Bijou, S., Peterson, R., & Ault, M. (1968). A method to integrate descriptive and experimental field studies at the level of data and empirical concepts. *Journal of Applied Behavior Analysis*, *1*, 175–191.

Bird, F., Dores, P. A., Moniz, D., & Robinson, J. (1989). Reducing severe aggression and self-injurious behavior with functional communication training. *American Journal on Mental Retardation*, *94*, 37–48.

Borrero, C. S. W., Vollmer, T. R., & Borrero, J. C. (2004). Combining descriptive and functional analysis logic to evaluate idiosyncratic variables maintaining aggression. *Behavioral Interventions*, *19*, 247–162.

Broussard, C., & Northup, J. (1995). An approach to functional assessment and analysis of disruptive behavior in regular education classrooms. *School Psychology Quarterly*, *10*, 151–164.

Broussard, C., & Northup, J. (1997). The use of functional analysis to develop peer interventions for disruptive classroom behavior. *School Psychology Quarterly*, *12*, 65–76.

Carr, E. G., & Durand, V. M. (1985). Reducing problem behavior through functional communication training. *Journal of Applied Behavior Analysis*, *18*, 111–126.

Cautela, J. R. & Kastenbaum, R. (1967). A reinforcement survey schedule for use in therapy, training, and research. *Psychological Reports*, *20*, 1115–1130.

Cohen-Almeida, D., Graff, R. B., & Ahearn, W. H. (2000). A comparison of verbal and tangible stimulus preference assessments. *Journal of Applied Behavior Analysis*, *33*, 329–334.

Cooper, L., Wacker, D., Sasso, G., Reimers, T., & Donn, L. (1990). Using parents as therapists to assess the appropriate behavior of their children: Application to a tertiary diagnostic clinic. *Journal of Applied Behavior Analysis*, *23*, 285–296.

Cooper, L., Wacker, D., Thursby, D., Plagmann, L., Harding, J., Millard, T., & Derby, M. (1992). Analysis of the effects of task preferences, task demands, and adult attention on child behavior in outpatient and classroom settings. *Journal of Applied Behavior Analysis*, *25*, 823–840.

DeLeon, I. G. & Iwata, B. A. (1996). Evaluation of a multiple-stimulus presentation format for assessing reinforcer preferences. *Journal of Applied Behavior Analysis*, *29*, 519–533.

DeLeon, I. G., Iwata, B. A., Goh, H., & Worsdell, A. S. (1997). Emergence of reinforcer preference as a function of schedule requirements and stimulus similarity. *Journal of Applied Behavior Analysis*, *30*, 439–449.

DeLeon, I. G., Iwata, B. A., & Roscoe, E. M. (1997). Displacement of leisure reinforcers by food during preference assessments. *Journal of Applied Behavior Analysis*, *30*, 475–484.

Derby, K. M., Wacker, D. P., Peck, S., Sasso, G., DeRaad, A., Asmus, J., & Ulrich, S. (1994). Functional analysis of separate topographies of aberrant behavior. *Journal of Applied Behavior Analysis*, *27*, 267–278.

Derby, K. M., Wacker, D. P., Sasso, G., Steege, M., Northup, J., Cigrand, K., & Asmus, J. (1992). Brief functional assessment techniques to evaluate aberrant behavior in an outpatient setting: A summary of 79 cases. *Journal of Applied Behavior Analysis*, *25*, 713–721.

Durand, V. M. & Crimmins, D. B. (1988). Identifying the variables maintaining self-injurious behavior. *Journal of Autism and Developmental Disorders*, *18*, 99–117.

Ellis, J., & Magee, S. (2004). Modifications to basic functional analysis procedures in school settings: A selective review. *Behavioral Interventions*, *19*, 205–228.

Fantuzzo, J. W., Rohrbeck, C. A., Hightower, A. D., & Work, W. C. (1991). Teachers' use and children's preferences of rewards in elementary school. *Psychology in the Schools*, *28*, 175–181.

Fisher, W. W., Piazza, C. C., Bowman, L. G., & Amari, A. (1996). Integrating caregiver report with a systematic choice assessment to enhance reinforcer identification. *American Journal on Mental Retardation, 101*, 15–25.

Fisher, W., Piazza, C. C., Bowman, L. G., Hagopian, L. P., Owens, J. C., & Slevin, I. (1992). A comparison of two approaches for identifying reinforcers for persons with severe and profound disabilities. *Journal of Applied Behavior Analysis, 25*, 491–498.

Freeman, K. A., Anderson, C. M., & Scotti, J. R. (2000). A structured descriptive methodology: Increasing agreement between descriptive and experimental analyses. *Education & Training in Mental Retardation & Developmental Disabilities, 31*, 55–66.

Green, C. W., Reid, D. H., Canipe, V. S., & Gardner, S. M. (1991). A comprehensive evaluation of reinforcer identification processes for persons with profound multiple handicaps. *Journal of Applied Behavior Analysis, 24*, 537–552.

Green, C. W., Reid, D. H., White, L. K., Halford, R. C., Brittain, D. P., & Gardner, S. M. (1988). Identifying reinforcers for persons with profound handicaps: Staff opinion versus systematic assessment of preferences. *Journal of Applied Behavior Analysis, 21*, 31–43.

Green, G., & Striefel, S. (1988). Response restriction and substitution with autistic children. *Journal of the Experimental Analysis of Behavior, 50*, 21–32.

Groden, G. (1989). A guide for conducting a comprehensive behavioral analysis of a target behavior. *Journal of Behavior Therapy and Experimental Psychology, 20*, 163–169.

Hanley, G. P., Iwata, B. A., & Lindberg, J. S. (1999). Analysis of activity preferences as a function of differential consequences. *Journal of Applied Behavior Analysis, 32*, 419–435.

Hanley, G. P., Iwata, B. A., Lindberg, J. S., & Conners, J. (2003). Response-restriction analysis: I. Assessment of activity preferences. *Journal of Applied Behavior Analysis, 36*, 47–58.

Hanley, G. P., Iwata, B. A., & McCord, B. E. (2003). Functional analysis of problem behavior: A review. *Journal of Applied Behavior Analysis, 36*, 147–185.

Harding, J., Wacker, D. P., Cooper, L. J., Millard, T., & Jensen-Kovalan, P. (1994). Brief hierarchical assessment of potential treatment components with children in a outpatient clinic. *Journal of Applied Behavior Analysis, 27*, 279–289.

Higbee, T. S., Carr, J. E., & Harrison, C. D. (1999). The effects of pictorial versus tangible stimuli in stimulus-preference assessments. *Research in Developmental Disabilities, 20*, 63–72.

Himle, M. B., Miltenberger, R. G., Flessner, C., & Gatheridge, B. (2004). Teaching safety skills to children to prevent gun play. *Journal of Applied Behavior Analysis, 37*, 1–9.

Iwata, B., & DeLeon, I. (1996). *The functional analysis screening tool.* Gainesville, FL: The Florida Center on Self-Injury, University of Florida.

Iwata, B. A., Dorsey, M. F., Slifer, K. J., Bauman, K. E., & Richman, G. S. (1994). Toward a functional analysis of self-injury. *Journal of Applied Behavior Analysis, 27*, 197–209 (Reprinted from *Analysis and Intervention in Developmental Disabilities, 2*, 3–20, 1982).

Iwata, B. A., Pace, G. M., Dorsey, M. F., Zarcone, J. R., Vollmer, T. R., Smith, R. G., et al. (1994). The functions of self-injurious behavior: An experimental-epidemiological analysis. *Journal of Applied Behavior Analysis, 27*, 215–240.

Iwata, B. A., Vollmer, T. R., & Zarcone, J. R. (1990). The experimental (functional) analysis of behavior disorders: Methodology, applications, and limitations. In A. C. Repp & N. N. Singh (Eds.), *Perspectives on the use of non-aversive and aversive interventions for persons with developmental disabilities* (pp. 301–330). Sycamore, IL: Sycamore Publishing.

Kahng, S., Iwata, B. A., Fischer, S. M., Page, T. J., Treadwell, K. R. H., Williams, D. E., & Smith, R. G. (1998). Temporal distributions of problem behavior based on scatter plot analyses. *Journal of Applied Behavior Analysis, 31*, 593–604.

Klatt, K. P., & Morris, E. K. (2001). The Premack Principle, response deprivation, and establishing operations. *Behavior Analyst, 24*, 173–180.

Konarski, E. A., Crowell, C. R., Johnson, M. R., & Whitman, T. L. (1982). Response deprivation, reinforcement, and instrumental academic performance in an EMR classroom. *Behavior Therapy, 13*, 94–102.

Kurtz, P. F., Chin, M. D., Huete, J. M., Tarbox, R. S. F., O'Connor, J. T., Paclawskyj, T. R., & Rush, K. S. (2003). Functional analysis and treatment of self-injurious behavior in young children: A summary of 30 cases. *Journal of Applied Behavior Analysis, 36*, 205–219.

Lerman, D. C., & Iwata, B. A. (1993). Descriptive and experimental analyses of variables maintaining self-injurious behavior. *Journal of Applied Behavior Analysis, 26*, 293–319.

Lerman, D. C., Iwata, B. A., Smith, R. G., Zarcone, J. R., & Vollmer, T. R. (1994). Transfer of behavioral function as a contributing factor in treatment relapse. *Journal of Applied Behavior Analysis, 27*, 357–370.

Lewis, T. J., Scott, T. M., & Sugai, G. (1994). The problem behavior questionnaire: A teacher-based instrument to develop functional hypotheses of problem behavior in general education classrooms. *Diagnostique, 19*, 103–115.

Long, E. S., Miltenberger, R. G., Ellingson, S. A., & Ott, S. M. (1999). Augmenting simplified habit reversal in the treatment of oral-digital habits exhibited by individuals with mental retardation.

Journal of Applied Behavior Analysis, 32, 353–365.

Mace, F. C., & Lalli, J. S. (1991). Linking descriptive and experimental analyses in the treatment of aberrant behavior. *Journal of Applied Behavior Analysis, 24,* 553–562.

Maglieri, K. A., DeLeon, I. G., Rodriguez-Catter, V., & Sevin, B. M. (2000). Treatment of covert food stealing in an individual with Prader-Willi syndrome. *Journal of Applied Behavior Analysis, 33,* 615–618.

Marcus, B. A., & Vollmer, T. R. (1996). Combining noncontingent reinforcement and differential reinforcement schedules as treatment for aberrant behavior. *Journal of Applied Behavior Analysis, 29,* 43–51.

Matson, J. L., & Vollmer, T. R. (1995). *User's guide: Questions About Behavioral Function (QABF).* Baton Rouge, LA.: Scientific Publishers, Inc.

McIntire, R. W. (1963). Reinforcement and verbal learning: A test of the Premack hypothesis. *Psychological Reports, 12,* 99–102.

Miltenberger, R. G. (1998). Methods for assessing antecedent influences on challenging behaviors. In J. K. Luiselli & M. J. Cameron (Eds.), *Antecedent control: Innovative approaches for behavioral support.* Baltimore, MA: Paul H. Brookes Publishing Co.

Moore, J. W., Edwards, R. P., Sterling-Turner, H. E., Riley, J., DuBard, M., & McGeorge, A. (2002). Teacher acquisition of functional analysis methodology. *Journal of Applied Behavior Analysis, 35,* 73–77.

Mueller, M. M., Sterling-Turner, H. E., & Moore, J. W. (2005). Towards developing a classroom-based functional analysis condition to assess escape-to-attention as a variable maintaining problem behavior. *School Psychology Review, 34,* 425–431.

Mueller, M. M., Wilczynski, S. M., Moore, J. W., Fusilier, I., & Trahant, D. (2001). Antecedent manipulations in a tangible condition: The effects of stimulus preference on aggression. *Journal of Applied Behavior Analysis, 34,* 237–240.

Northup, J. (2000). Further evaluation of the accuracy of reinforcer surveys: A systematic replication. *Journal of Applied Behavior Analysis, 33,* 335–338.

Northup, J., George, T., Jones, K., Broussard, C., & Vollmer, T. R. (1996). A comparison of reinforcer assessment methods: The utility of verbal and pictorial choice procedures. *Journal of Applied Behavior Analysis, 29,* 201–212.

Northup, J., Jones, K., Broussard, C., & George, T. (1995). A preliminary comparison of reinforcer assessment methods for children with attention deficit hyperactivity disorder. *Journal of Applied Behavior Analysis, 28,* 99–100.

Northup, J., Wacker, D. P., Sasso, G., Steege, M., Cigrand, C., Cook, J., et al. (1991). A brief functional analysis of aggressive and alternative behavior on an outclinic setting. *Journal of Applied Behavior Analysis, 24,* 509–521.

O'Neill, R. E., Horner, R. H., Albin, R. W., Storey, K., & Sprague, J. R. (1990). *Functional analysis of problem behavior: A practical guide.* Sycamore, IL: Sycamore Press.

O'Neill, R. E., Horner, R. H., Albin, R. W., Storey, K., & Sprague, J. R. (1997). *Functional assessment and program development for behavior problems.* Pacific Grove, CA: Brooks/Cole.

Pace, G. M., Ivanic, M. T., Edwards, G. L., Iwata, B. A., & Page, T. J. (1985). Assessment of stimulus preference and reinforcer value with profoundly retarded individuals. *Journal of Applied Behavior Analysis, 18,* 249–255.

Paclawskyj, T. R., & Vollmer, T. R. (1995). Reinforcer assessment for children with developmental disabilities and visual impairments. *Journal of Applied Behavior Analysis, 28,* 219–224.

Poche, C., Brouwer, R., & Swearingen, M. (1981). Teaching self-protection to young children. *Journal of Applied Behavior Analysis, 14,* 169–176.

Piazza, C. C., Fisher, W. W., Hagopian, L. P., Bowman, L. G., & Toole, L. (1996). Using a choice assessment to predict reinforcer effectiveness. *Journal of Applied Behavior Analysis, 29,* 1–9.

Premack, D. (1958). Toward empirical behavior laws: I. Positive reinforcement. *Psychological Review, 66,* 219–233.

Pyles, D. A. M. & Bailey, J. S. (1990). Diagnosing severe behavior problems. In A. C. Repp & N. N. Singh (Eds.). *Perspectives on the use of nonaversive and aversive interventions for persons with developmental disabilities* (pp. 381–401). Sycamore, IL: Sycamore Publishing.

Rapp, J. T., Miltenberger, R. G., Galensky, T. L., Ellingson, S. A., & Long, E. S. (1999). A functional analysis of hair pulling. *Journal of Applied Behavior Analysis, 32,* 329–337.

Rapp, J. T., Vollmer, T. R., St. Peter, C., Dozier, C. L., & Cotnoir, N. M. (2004). Analysis of response allocation in individuals with multiple forms of stereotyped behavior. *Journal of Applied Behavior Analysis, 37,* 481–501.

Roane, H. S., Lerman, D. C., & Vorndran, C. M. (2001). Assessing reinforcers under progressive schedule requirements. *Journal of Applied Behavior Analysis,* 145–167.

Roane, H. S., Vollmer, T. R., Ringdahl, J. E., & Marcus, B. A. (1998). Evaluation of a brief stimulus preference assessment. *Journal of Applied Behavior Analysis, 31,* 605–620.

Sidman, M. (1960). Tactics of scientific research. New York: Basic Books.

Smith, M. D. (1985). Managing the aggressive and self-injurious behavior of adults disabled by autism. *Journal of the Association for Persons with Severe Handicaps, 10,* 228–232.

Smith, R. G., & Churchill, R. M. (2002). Identification of environmental determinants of behavior disorders through functional analysis of precursor behaviors. *Journal of Applied Behavior Analysis, 35,* 125–136.

St. Peter, C. C., Vollmer, T. R., Bourret, J. C., Borrero, C. S. W., Sloman, K. N., & Rapp, J. T. (2005). On the role of attention in naturally occurring matching relations. *Journal of Applied Behavior Analysis, 38,* 429–443.

Stricker, J. M., Miltenberger, R. G., Garlinghouse, M. A., Deaver, C. M., & Anderson, C. A. (2001). Evaluation of an awareness enhancement device for the treatment of thumb sucking in children. *Journal of Applied Behavior Analysis, 34,* 77–80.

Switzer, E. B., Deal, T. E., & Bailey, J. S. (1977). The reduction of stealing in second graders using a group contingency. *Journal of Applied Behavior Analysis, 10,* 267–272.

Taravella, C. C., Lerman, D. C., Contrucci, S. A., Roane, H. S. (2000). Further evaluation of low-ranked items in stimulus-choice preference assessments. *Journal of Applied Behavior Analysis, 33,* 105–108.

Thomas, J. D., Presland, I. E., Grant, M. D., & Glynn, T. L. (1978) Natural rates of teacher approval and disapproval in grade 7 classrooms. *Journal of Applied Behavior Analysis, 11,* 91–94.

Thompson, R. H., & Iwata, B. A. (2001). A descriptive analysis of social consequences following problem behavior. *Journal of Applied Behavior Analysis, 34,* 169–178.

Toogood, S., & Timlin, K. (1996). The functional assessment of challenging behaviour: A comparison of informant-based, experimental, and descriptive methods. *Journal of Applied Research in Intellectual Disabilities, 9,* 206–222.

Touchette, P. E., MacDonald, R. F., & Langer, S. N. (1985). A scatter plot for identifying stimulus control of problem behavior. *Journal of Applied Behavior Analysis, 18,* 343–351.

Tustin, R. D. (1994). Preference for reinforcers under varying schedule arrangements: A behavioral economic analysis. *Journal of Applied Behavior Analysis, 27,* 597–606.

Umbriet, J. (1995). Functional assessment and intervention in a regular classroom setting for the disruptive behavior of students with Attention Deficit Hyperactivity Disorder. *Behavioral Disorders, 20,* 267–278.

Vaughn, M. E., & Michael, J. (1982). Automatic reinforcement: An important but ignored concept. *Behaviorism, 10,* 217–227.

Vollmer, T. R., Borrero, J. C., Wright, C. S., Van Camp, C., & Lalli, J. S. (2001). Identifying possible contingencies during descriptive analyses of severe behavior disorders. *Journal of Applied Behavior Analysis, 34,* 269–287.

Vollmer, T. R., Iwata, B. A., Duncan, B. A., & Lerman, D. C. (1993). Within-session patterns of self-injury as indicators of behavioral function. *Research in Developmental Disabilities, 14,* 479–492.

Vollmer, T. R., Iwata, B. A., Zarcone, J. R., Smith, R. G., & Mazaleski, J. L. (1993). The role of attention in the treatment of attention-maintained self-injurious behavior: Noncontingent reinforcement and differential reinforcement of other behavior. *Journal of Applied Behavior Analysis, 26,* 9–21.

Vollmer, T. R., Marcus, B. A., Ringdahl, J. E., & Roane, H. S. (1995). Progressing from brief to extended experimental analyses in the evaluation of aberrant behavior. *Journal of Applied Behavior Analysis, 28,* 561–576.

Vollmer, T. R., Ringdahl, J. E., Roane, H. S., & Marcus, B. A. (1997). Negative side effects of noncontingent reinforcement. *Journal of Applied Behavior Analysis, 30,* 161–164.

Wallace, M. D., Doney, J. K., Mintz-Resudek, C. M., & Tarbox, R. S. F. (2004). Training educators to implement functional analyses. *Journal of Applied Behavior Analysis, 37,* 89–92.

Wasik, B. H. (1970). The application of Premack's generalization on reinforcement to the management of classroom behavior. *Journal of Experimental Child Psychology, 10,* 33–43.

Weisler, N. A., Hanson, R. H., Chamberlain, T. P., & Thompson, T. (1985). Functional taxonomy of stereotypic and self-injurious behavior. *Mental Retardation, 23,* 230–234.

Windsor, J., Piché, L. M., & Locke, P. A. (1994). Preference testing: A comparison of two presentation methods. *Research in Developmental Disabilities, 15,* 439–455.

Yawkey, T. D. & Le Penna Griffith, D. (1974). The effects of the Premack principle on affective behaviors of young children. *Child Study Journal, 4,* 59–70.

Zarcone, J. R., Rodgers, T. A., Iwata, B. A., Rourke, D. A., & Dorsey, M. F. (1991). Reliability analysis of the motivational assessment scale: A failure to replicate. *Research in Developmental Disabilities, 12,* 349–360.

CHAPTER 20

CURRICULUM-BASED ASSESSMENT

JOHN M. HINTZE
University of Massachusetts at Amherst

Since their introduction to the field over twenty years ago (Tucker, 1985), the use of curriculum-based assessment procedures have increased steadily and are now part of nearly all school psychologists' training and practice. Originally conceived as an alternative to more traditional published norm-referenced tests, curriculum-based assessment has demonstrated itself to be a highly desirable practice for assessing academic skill problems as judged by school psychologists and general and special education teachers (Eckert, Shapiro, & Lutz, 1995; Elliott & Fuchs, 1997; Shapiro & Eckert, 1994). Curriculum-based assessment (CBA) can be defined as any set of measurement activities that uses "direct observation and recording of a student's performance in the local curriculum as a basis for gathering information to make instructional decisions" (Deno, 1987, p. 41).

CURRICULUM-BASED ASSESSMENT: OVERVIEW AND RATIONALE

In thinking about CBA, Lentz and Shapiro (1986) identified a core set of assumptions that serve as key components to academic assessment methodologies that are considered to be curriculum based.

1. *An assessment of academic skills must reflect how the behavior appears in the natural environment.* An evaluation of academic skills problems must help the evaluator understand the nature of the problem that is occurring in the classroom under typical instructional arrangements. If the child is removed from the classroom and evaluated in a small, quiet, nondistracting room (as might be typical during an

individual psychoeducational assessment) and the child's behavior in that setting differs from the behavior in the typical instructional environment, the teacher will probably not consider the results of the evaluation useful for instructional programming. Also, if the conditions of the assessment process include formats that are substantially different from the way in which teachers typically conduct evaluations of academic behavior (e.g., multiple or forced-choice tests), the outcomes of the assessment may partially reflect the format for assessment rather than the student's skills themselves. The methods used for conducting an assessment need to be a direct reflection of the behaviors commonly seen in the classroom.

2. *What is tested should be what is taught.* A problem often noted with many norm-referenced tests is the lack of overlap between what is being taught in the curriculum and the content of the items on the tests (Bell, Lentz, & Graden, 1992; Good & Salvia, 1988; Jenkins & Pany, 1978; Martens, Steele, Massie, & Diskin, 1995; Shapiro & Derr, 1987). A critical component in a more authentic and content-valid assessment is that the assessment process must indicate to an evaluator exactly what has and has not been learned from the instructional process.

3. *The primary purpose of an assessment is to develop interventions and solve problems.* Although assessments of academic skills can serve multiple purposes, the primary reason for an individual evaluation must be to develop more effective interventions to remediate deficient skill areas. Assessment methods that are designed specifically to inform the evaluator of potential remediation

strategies should therefore be the primary methods used to conduct evaluations of academic skills problems.

4. ***Assessment should be capable of providing ongoing evaluation of progress.*** It is not enough for assessment methods to inform evaluators of the current status of students' progress. Because the assessments are designed to assist in the development of instructional strategies, evaluation of the effectiveness of these strategies must be a critical component of the assessment process. Methods selected to evaluate academic progress must be capable of reflecting change in the student's performance of academic skills. Thus measures must be sensitive to small units of change, must be able to be repeated frequently, and must have high degrees of acceptability to teachers.

5. ***Measures should be primarily idiographic as opposed to nomothetic.*** If the primary purpose of the assessment process is to develop and monitor intervention strategies, the measurement tools must be idiographic. Such idiographic, within-student assessment is critical if one is to determine whether the student is progressing as compared to his or her past performance. Nomothetic measures, those whose primary focus is in between- or across-student comparisons, are important but can only reflect outcomes at a specific moment in time.

6. ***Assessment methods should reflect both skill and performance problems.*** Academic skill problems are simply not a reflection of the inner learning capacities of students. The structure of the academic environment can play a significant role in shaping the success or failure of a student's performance (Heller, Holtzman, & Messick, 1982; Lentz & Shapiro, 1986; Ysseldyke & Christenson, 1993). Any assessment of academic skill problems must be able to divide the problems between those that are primarily skill and those that are primarily performance deficits (Daly, Martens, Dool, & Hintze, 1998; Duhon et al., 2004; Eckert, Ardoin, Daly, & Martens, 2002).

7. ***Measures should be capable of a wide range of uses, including screening, determining eligibility for special education, setting goals, evaluating programs, and developing interventions.*** Although the primary purpose for

an academic assessment should be to help inform modifications in instruction, such assessment should also be able to serve multiple outcomes and be used in making a variety of assessment decisions.

While CBA approaches are not the only assessment methodologies that adhere to these assumptions, the problem with many published norm-referenced tests is that they fall short in meeting many of these desirable criteria.

For example, Jenkins and Pany (1978) and Shapiro and Derr (1987) examined the extent to which published norm-referenced tests overlapped with content which was taught in a number of common reading curricula, and the assessments that go along with those curricula, in grades 1 through 5. In doing so the researchers assumed that a hypothetical student at each grade level had mastered all the words that were explicitly taught in each of the curricula and cross-referenced those words to a number of commercially available norm-referenced tests. Results indicated that the scores that would be obtained at each grade level varied significantly as a function of the curriculum that was used to derive the standard score on the norm-referenced test. For example, if the student were taught in curriculum A he/she may receive a standard score of 93, whereas if they were taught in curriculum B he/she would be expected to receive a standard score of 79. The difference in standard scores reflects the differences in the words that are explicitly taught in each of the curriculum. Overall, Jenkins and Pany (1978) and Shapiro and Derr (1987) found very little overlap between what was taught and what was ultimately tested on commercially available norm-referenced tests. Moreover, the degree of overlap varied significantly across tests and curricula, suggesting that quite different decisions would be reached on the same hypothetical child as a function of what curriculum he/she was taught and the test that was used to assess his/her reading skills.

Similarly, Good and Salvia (1988) and Bell et al. (1992) found that test performance could be reliably predicted as a function of the overlap between a reading curriculum and what was required on norm-referenced tests of reading. In examining the performance of actual students in grades 1 through 5, results of these studies once again showed significant differences in the standard scores obtained from commonly used norm-referenced tests of reading. For example, students in one district obtained average standard scores on the Woodcock Reading Mastery Test–Revised (Woodcock, 1987) that were a full standard deviation greater than the average standard score that was obtained on the Wide Range Achievement Test–Revised (WRAT; Wilkinson, 1993). Collectively the results of these studies suggest that what most norm-referenced tests are assessing is students' ability to transfer learned knowledge to untaught items on a test. Although at times such assessment questions may be of primary importance, the problems brought about by poor curriculum/test overlap threaten the content validity of such tests for assessing what a child has learned in the classroom and an evaluation of their progress across time. Clearly if these latter assessment questions are of primary importance, evaluators need tests that are tightly tied to the curriculum that is taught in the classroom and are available in multiple alternate forms to adequately assess learning over time.

A second problem associated with many available norm-referenced tests lies in their relevance for planning and improving students' instructional planning. Thurlow and Ysseldyke (1982) examined this point by asking 200 school psychologists and special education teachers how instructionally useful they found published norm-referenced tests. Given a list of commonly administered tests, including the Wechsler Intelligence Scale for Children–Revised (WISC-R; Wechsler, 1974), Bender Visual Motor Gestalt Test (BVMGT; Koppitz, 1963), and the WRAT, 100 school psychologists rated such measures with respect to their utility for instructional planning. Seventy-two percent of the school psychologists reported that the WISC-R was helpful, 64% endorsed the BVMGT, and 80% endorsed the WRAT as aiding in instructional planning. Comparatively, when 100 special education teachers were asked to evaluate the same list of tests, only 10% considered the BVMGT as instructionally relevant, 30% rated the WISC-R as useful, and 10% indicated that the WRAT contributed to developing effective instructional plans. In another study Mirkin, Deno, Tindal, and Kuehnle (1982) found that when teachers used CBA measures for at least four months, over 90% indicated that the results obtained from CBAs were useful for instructional planning, developing goals and objectives, and for making formative decisions as to when to change instructional strategies.

A third concern with typical norm-referenced assessment techniques is their reliance on test items that measure skills indirectly. Frequently, such tests utilize response formats such as selection-type responses (e.g., matching, pointing to, elimination) or multiple-choice response and rarely ask the student to perform the behavior of concern as it would occur in the classroom. The advantage of such response formats is in their ease of scoring, time efficiency, and good interscorer reliability (Popham, 2004). The primary disadvantage, however, is that they provide little or no information on why a student earns a particular score (Marston, 1989).

Fourth, contributing to the limitations of the selection-type responses is the absence of considering fluency of response. Although most published norm-referenced tests do an excellent job of measuring the acquisition of response, few consider the importance of fluency of responding. While acquisition is an important stage in the instructional hierarchy of learning (Haring, Lovitt, Eason, & Hansen, 1978), fluency is the critical foundation skill that leads to adequate transfer and generalization of learning. Children who work slowly, despite being accurate, have not actually mastered a skill and would be at a distinct disadvantage compared to those students whose performance is both accurate and fluent (White & Haring, 1980).

Finally, most norm-referenced tests are not available in multiple forms that would allow for the ongoing monitoring of progress over time. Because of this, evaluators have commonly relied on the pre-post test design for the purpose of measuring change in student learning. Such an approach is problematic for a number of reasons. One, norm-referenced tests have been developed with the explicit purpose of measuring between-individual nomothetic differences and were not designed to measure change in within-individual idiographic performance over time and are often insensitive to student growth. Marston, Fuchs, and Deno (1986) demonstrated this point in a comparison of CBA procedures to norm-referenced achievement tests. Over a 16-week period, students grew significantly on the CBA measures and showed little growth on the norm-referenced measures. Moreover, teacher judgment of student growth was more highly correlated with CBA scores than with norm-referenced scores. Second, norm-referenced achievement tests fail to capture student progress accurately because of the types of scores that they use most frequently (e.g., age and/or grade equivalents, standard scores, percentiles). While such scores provide some indication of a student's relative standing, they provide little or no information about what the child can and cannot do. Third, the reliability of measuring student pre-post gain is psychometrically dubious. Because the difference scores of such tests tend to be unstable, making decisions regarding student improvement proves difficult. Finally, because they are available in limited forms, the frequency with which norm-referenced tests can be administered is problematic. While such measures provide adequate summative information, their use in a formative assessment format is highly questionable.

In contrast, CBA approaches have been developed with specific design features aimed at overcoming some of the challenges posed by norm-referenced tests. First, CBA partially overcomes the problems associated with test-text overlap because students are assessed directly on materials and behaviors that they are expected to learn in their classrooms. In creating materials, CBAs pay particular attention to creating assessment tasks and soliciting behaviors that are highly similar to those expected in the classroom. Since the ability to read fluently, spell words correctly, and solve mathematics problems accurately is expected in the classroom, these behaviors are directly assessed in a CBA. Second, as a result of increased content validity, CBAs are directly linked to instructional objectives. Areas of student performance weaknesses suggest direct targets for intervention. Third, although they share features of classroom-based informal assessment, CBAs have been shown to provide reliable and valid measures of students' performance in reading (Deno, 1985; Deno, Mirkin, & Chiang, 1982), spelling (Marston, 1989), writing (Gansle, Noell, VanDerHeyden, Naquin, & Slider, 2002; Gansle et al., 2004), and mathematics (Christ, Johnson-Gros, & Hintze, 2005; Fuchs, Compton, & Fuchs, 2005; Hintze, Christ, & Keller, 2002; Seethaler & Fuchs, 2005). Fourth, because CBAs are developed with alternate forms and are quick and easy to administer they can be used repeatedly over time to monitor progress and make formative instructional decisions. Importantly, CBAs have been found to be highly sensitive to student change toward both short- and long-term instructional objectives (Deno, 1985; Hintze &

Christ, 2004; Hintze, Daly, & Shapiro, 1998; Hintze, Owen, Shapiro, & Daly, 2000; Shinn, 1989). Fifth, although developed primarily as an idiographic assessment strategy, CBA has been found to be highly efficient in screening, early intervention, program evaluation, and making between-student comparisons (Hasbrouck & Tindal, 1992; Hintze & Silberglitt, 2005; Shinn, 1988; Silberglitt & Hintze, 2005). Data collected at the local level can assist schools in setting district-wide goals and individual student goals, in making between-school comparisons within districts, and in facilitating eligibility decisions (Elliott & Fuchs, 1997; Shinn, Habedank, Rodden-Nord, & Knutson, 1993).

CBA MODELS

Although the term CBA has been frequently used to characterize a particular form of assessment, it actually represents a number of diverse assessment practices (Hintze, Christ, & Methe, 2006). Shinn, Rosenfield, and Knutson (1989) identified at least four different models of CBA that have been presented in the professional literature: (a) CBA for Instructional Design (CBA-ID), as proposed by Gickling and associates (Gickling & Havertape, 1981; Gickling, Shane, & Croskery, 1989; Gickling & Thompson, 1985); (b) Criterion-Referenced CBA (CR-CBA), as proposed by Blankenship (1985) and Idol, Nevin, and Paolucci-Whitcomb (1999); (c) Curriculum-Based Evaluation (CBE), as proposed by Howell (1986; Howell & Nolet, 2000); and (d) Curriculum-Based Measurement (CBM), as proposed by Deno and colleagues (Deno, 1985, 1986; Fuchs, Deno, & Mirkin, 1984; Shinn, 1989).

Although each of these models are similar in the sense that they develop assessment materials that mirror the types of instructional activities and behaviors that would be expected in a typical classroom, they differ with respect to the manner in which instructional activities and learner behaviors are sampled and considered for inclusion in the assessment process. More broad-based general approaches to CBA consider all the instructional objectives and learner behaviors of an academic construct that would be expected within a school year. After considering all possible learning components, items and/or tasks are selected randomly for inclusion in assessment. For example, in developing a more general CBA in the area of spelling the evaluator would sample from all the words that a student would be expected to master during the entire academic year. In doing so, the evaluator would likely sample from across a broad spectrum of skills (e.g., blends, vowel teams, final vowels, irregular words, digraphs) and be able to assess a student's skill development toward these generalized outcomes (Fuchs & Deno, 1991). The purpose of this type of assessment is to be able to evaluate students' skill development across the entire curriculum.

Comparatively, other assessment situations call for assessment of a student's abilities on a very specific set of academic skills. Rather than being interested in assessing general performance across a broad array of skills or an entire curriculum sequence, such assessment is primarily interested in determining the extent to which a student has mastered specific skills that are explicitly taught within the curriculum in a sequential fashion. Such an approach breaks down the global curricular outcomes into a set of specific subskills which are then ordered sequentially as short-term instructional objectives (Fuchs & Deno, 1991). In comparison to the more general approach, where all possible skills could be included as part of a CBA, specific forms of CBA are developed with a very specific instructional objective and/or learner behavior in mind. Again, using the example of spelling, rather than create CBAs that have all possible skills included, specific CBA

forms would assess a very specific aspect of the curriculum (e.g., spelling words ending with a silent *e*). Here, all CBA items would contain the same specific skill and a student's performance would be judged relative to his or her mastery performance on the specific skill. Such specific forms of CBA rely on a mastery measurement approach, where small domains of test items and mastery criteria are specified for each subskill. These criterion-referenced items are designed to produce student performance data that are required for inferring mastery of the subtasks embedded in the curricular objectives (Fuchs & Deno, 1991).

In considering these two approaches to developing CBAs, Fuchs and Deno (1991) organized the various approaches into two distinct forms of assessment. Figure 20.1 categorizes the four main instructionally relevant CBA approaches by the manner in which the assessments are constructed and interpreted. As illustrated by the figure, CBA can be thought of as an "umbrella" term under which many different forms of CBA fall. At subsequent levels CBAs are organized into two groups on the basis of whether they better represent a form of *specific subskill mastery measurement* or *general outcome measurement*.

As can be seen by the figure, most forms of CBA rely on the features associated with specific subskill mastery measurement. This approach

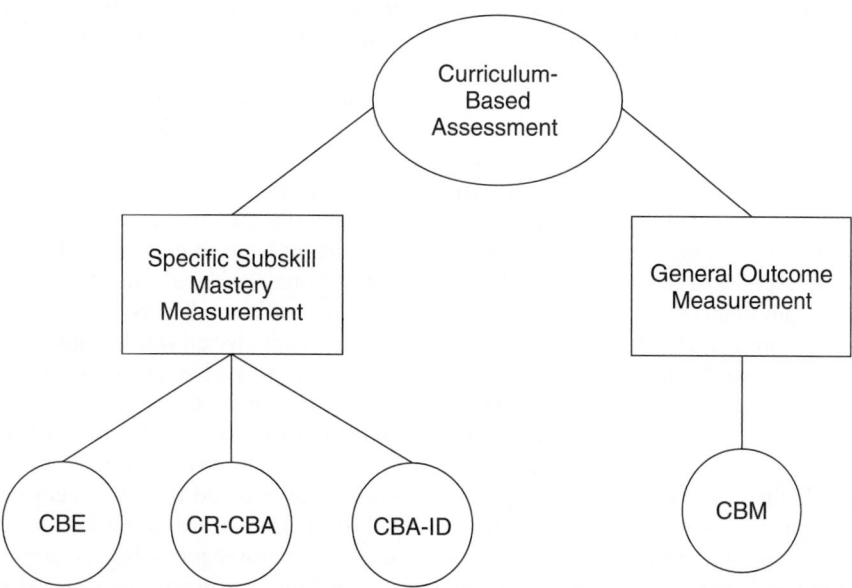

Figure 20.1 **Organizational chart of different models of curriculum-based assessment.**

divides yearly curricular outcomes into sets of subskills that are then ordered as short-term instructional objectives from which assessment material is developed. Comparatively, general outcome measurement relies on assessment of proficiency on global skills and behaviors toward which the entire year-long curriculum is directed. For the most part, the tasks that make up general outcome measurement are of average difficulty. This is in direct comparsion to specific subskill mastery measurement, where instructional hierarchies are specific to each CBA.

Specific Subskill Mastery Measurement Models

CBA-ID

Developed by Gickling and colleagues (Gickling & Havertape, 1981; Gickling et al., 1989; Gickling & Thompson, 1985), CBA-ID is defined as "a system for determining the instructional needs of a student based upon the student's ongoing performance within existing course content in order to deliver instruction as effectively and efficiently as possible" (Gickling et al., 1989, pp. 344–345). In doing so, CBA-ID is based on four basis principles (Gickling & Rosenfield, 1995). First, CBA-ID aligns assessment practices with that which is being taught in the classroom. Because curriculum serves as the natural context for assessment, teachers are able to assess both the performance of their students and the effectiveness of classroom instruction with materials that they use for teaching.

Second, CBA-ID begins with a thorough assessment of what the student currently knows, and then attempts to determine specific areas of skill deficit or weakness. Doing so maximizes instructional on-task time and minimizes the fragmentation of learning where students are asked to act in response to curricular materials that have excessive amounts of unknown information (Gickling & Rosenfield, 1995).

Third, since students exhibiting learning problems often experience a mismatch between what they are currently able to do and what is being asked of them, CBA-ID places a high priority on eliminating the instructional gap by determining the appropriate fit or instructional match. This is accomplished by keeping task variability and task demand within appropriate levels of challenge and modifying the pace of instruction to match a student's learning rate.

In practice, the instructional match is defined as those learning tasks where a student can respond independently (i.e., without teacher support) with 93% to 97% accuracy, and with support (i.e., under teacher direction) with 70% to 85% accuracy. These ratios are fundamental to applying CBA-ID, as they serve as guidelines for assessing what a student's entry skills are and form the basis for modifying task difficulty (i.e., identifying appropriate difficulty levels within a curriculum in which student learning and progress can be optimized).

Fourth, CBA-ID is predicated on mastery learning such that students maintain high rates of success and benefit from appropriately matched instruction. This is in contrast to more common instructional practices whereby all students are taught with the same instructional materials and at the same pace. Doing so almost ensures that some students will be unable to conform to singular teaching practices. As such, the goal of assessment is to identify appropriate "comfort" levels of instruction.

Conducting a CBA-ID

CBA-ID involves a four step process (Gickling & Rosenfield, 1995). Using reading as an example, in Step 1, the evaluator selects a passage for the student to read (in other content areas the process would begin with a mathematics worksheet, list of spelling words, sample of word problems, etc.). The initial assessment material is usually drawn from material in which the student is currently being instructed, although other material can be used to start with based on the student's level of reading skill. The process begins with attempting to identify the student's entry-level skills with respect to prior knowledge, vocabulary, comprehension, and reading rate. To do so, the evaluator may initially discuss the nature of the story with the student by examining the title, looking at the illustrations associated with the story, and so on. Next, a word search is conducted by having the student read selected words from the passage that the student should know. This process continues for about 2 or 3 minutes or until approximately 20 to 30 words have been surveyed. If five or more words are produced incorrectly, then an easier passage is selected and the assessment begins again. If five or fewer words are noted incorrectly, the assessment moves on to the next step.

In Step 2, the student is asked to read the passage selection aloud to assess how the student interacts with the text. The evaluator notes errors and calculates an oral reading fluency rate (i.e., words read correctly per minute). Once the entire passage is read, the evaluator engages in dialogue with the student in an effort to ascertain a general level of reading comprehension.

In Step 3, information from Step 1 and Step 2 are used to match a student's skill level with instruction. Tentative hypotheses regarding the level of teacher support and instructional level or "comfort" zone are made, keeping in mind the independent and instructional ratios noted previously. Lastly, in Step 4, instructional material is chosen and instruction continues. Continuous monitoring provides feedback regarding changing instructional needs, and formative decisions are made on the basis of ongoing assessment.

CR-CBA

CR-CBA reflects "the practice of obtaining direct and frequent measures of a student's performance on a series of sequentially arranged objectives from the curriculum that is used in the classroom" (Blankenship & Lilly, 1981, p. 81). Similar to other forms of CBA, the primary purpose of CR-CBA is to determine what curricular and instructional materials are most appropriate for enhancing learning. Conducting a CR-CBA again follows a basic stepwise process (Idol et al., 1999). Using multiple forms, items are selected from the curriculum or are independently developed to match the curriculum that is being taught. Items are then ordered by difficulty and combined within a single test and administered to the student. Following this, two more forms of the same test, containing similar items and ordering as the first test, are constructed and administered on Days 2 and 3. In administering the CR-CBA, the evaluator attempts to assess student skill across several levels of the curriculum and determine the nature and type of learning skills that are deficient. Typically, acceptable performance is established locally using normative sampling procedures by taking samples of average and acceptable student performance in general education classes and determining a mastery criterion. CR-CBAs can be used in their entirety, or sections of the learning hierarchy may be given over time. Even if an entire CR-CBA is given initially, the evaluator may use it later as a means of assessing student gains. If this second option is chosen, it is recommended that several alternate-form CR-CBAs be developed as a means of controlling for practice effects or memory of test items.

Conducting a CR-CBA

As with CBA-ID, the major reason for conducting a CR-CBA is to determine the instructional level at which a student is performing. Using reading again as an example, the evaluator uses CR-CBA much like an informal reading inventory would be used with repeated assessment across days (for a detailed account of the process, see Idol et al., 1999). Specifically, reading assessments are created by selecting 100-word passages from the beginning, middle, and end of a reading series for a given grade level. Once constructed, the student is assessed on three separate days with nine different 100-word passages (i.e., nine passages total—three each from the beginning, middle, and end of the graded reading curriculum). The student reads each passage aloud and the examiner notes the occurrence of the following errors: omissions, substitutions, additions, repetitions, self-corrections, and pauses. The amount of time (in seconds) that it took the student to read the 100-word passage is recorded. An *accuracy* score is calculated by noting the percentage of words read correctly across the entire 100-word passage (e.g., if the student read the 100-word passage with four errors, *accuracy* would be 96%). In addition, *rate* (words read correct per minute, or *wcpm*) is determined by multiplying the *accuracy* score by 60 and dividing this product by the total number of seconds it took the student to read the 100-word passage (e.g., if it took the student 95 seconds to read the entire 100-word passage with 96% accuracy, the wcpm score would be 61 [rounded]). After each passage is read the examiner also asks the student six comprehension questions: two *text-explicit* questions that are test dependent (i.e., the answers are explicitly found in the passage or illustration); two *text-implicit* questions, whose answers are based upon two or more nonexplicitly connected details of the passage and/or illustration; and two *script-implicit* questions, whose answers require integration of prior knowledge and one or more details of the passage and/or illustration. These procedures are repeated on each of three days of assessment, scores are summarized (i.e., accuracy, rate, and comprehension), and student performance is compared to mastery criteria and instructional decisions are made (see Idol et al., 1999).

CBE

Developed by Howell (1986; Howell & Nolet, 2000), CBE is based on a task-analytic model where the curriculum is conceptualized as a maze of interrelated and occasionally isolated tasks (Howell, 1986). What a student should be taught at any particular time is determined by where the student is in relation to the interrelated tasks (Howell & Nolet, 2000). The examiner's goal then is to identify which tasks the student is ready to learn as a function of his or her present level of educational performance.

In considering what to teach, all learning activities are conceptualized as being composed of subtasks and strategies. Subtasks involve declarative knowledge (e.g., facts, vocabulary) that students need to know and apply to complete a learning activity. Strategies correspond to procedural knowledge and are represented by the rules, procedures, and algorithms that students must follow to combine subtasks successfully. Strategies from different learning activities can be combined into different and more complex operations or divided into task-specific strategies—procedures that a student must follow within a narrowly defined domain to achieve a particular end (e.g., a long-division problem). In addition, general strategies are identified and represented by those general problem-solving skills that underlie a wide variety of student learning. Because nearly all academic instruction involves elements of each, good diagnostic assessment must sample skills from all domains. If a student is missing a subtask component, he or she is missing one of the essential building blocks of the task. If a student is missing a strategy component, he or she may have all the subtasks necessary to succeed with the learning objective, but not know how to put them together meaningfully.

Conducting a CBE

A CBE begins by assessing the student's general whereabouts in the curriculum. This is accomplished through the use of a survey-level assessment that samples from a wide range of skills within a curricular domain (e.g., reading). Once a survey-level assessment is completed, the examiner begins diagnostic assessment following a task analytic procedure using skill-specific procedures (e.g., assessing words with specific consonant blends, digraph patterns, silent-*e* endings).

Continuing with the example of reading, a CBE assessment would begin with a survey-level assessment designed to sample student behavior across the broad range of reading skills. Such

an assessment might include decoding tasks, comprehension tasks, and vocabulary tasks. If a student's reading skills were weak at this level, skill-specific diagnostic assessment would likely be indicated and focus on such areas as early reading skills (e.g., preliminary print knowledge, book and page conventions, word boundaries and length, letter names, segmenting, rhyming, blending), rereading (e.g., assessing whether a student's fluency increases with repeated practice), error analysis (e.g., mispronunciations, insertions, omissions, hesitations, repetitions, monitoring of punctuation, intonation), assisted self-monitoring (e.g., examiner taps the table every time an error is made, student then attempts to self-correct the error), and an evaluation of phonics (e.g., letter sounds, sight words, blending). Although the process of survey-level and specific-level assessment remains the same, the tasks vary for each CBE academic area. Howell and Nolet (2000) developed task analytic procedures for reading comprehension, decoding, language, written expression, mathematics, social skills, and task-related skills (e.g., vocabulary, study and test-taking skills). CBE and survey level assessment can be facilitated through the use of the *Multilevel Academic Skills Inventory* (MASI; Howell, Zucker, & Moorehead, 2000).

General Outcome Measurement Models
CBM

Developed by Deno and colleagues (Deno, 1985; Fuchs et al., 1984, Shinn, 1989), CBM is a set of standardized measurement procedures that can be used to quantify student performance in the basic academic skill areas of reading, spelling, mathematic, and written expression. As a general outcome measurement approach, CBM differs from previously reviewed specific subskill mastery measurement CBA approaches in a number of important ways (Fuchs & Deno, 1991). First, unlike mastery measurement approaches, CBM focuses on broad, long-term objectives rather than short-term mastery objectives. As opposed to assessing specific skills along a specified continuum, CBM uses a long-term goal structure whereby the assessment process throughout the assessment period focuses on the same continuous performance objectives. This focus on broad goals of the curriculum is in sharp contrast to specific subskill mastery measurement approaches where the assessment material changes with each new short-term objective. Second, because it focuses on broad aspects of the curriculum, CBM allows for the assessment of retention and generalization of learning. As a result, CBM scores represent performance across current instructional objectives as well as those representing past and future instructional targets. Third, CBM uses a standardized approach in specifying the material that should be sampled during assessments as well as the administration, scoring, and summarizing of information gathered from CBMs. Because of this, CBM allows for the comparison of scores across students as well as within students across time.

In comparison to specific subskill mastery measurement methods, where the approach to assessment and the manner in which information is gathered across skill domains is quite diverse, CBM uses a select number of standardized and validated measures of student performance in the basic academic skill areas (for an example of such measures, see www.aimsweb.com). For example, in reading, students read aloud from controlled graded reading material for 1 minute with the number of words read correctly during that time serving as the basic unit of datum. In addition, maze, a multiple-choice reading technique, also can be used to assess reading comprehension. Although CBM appears similar to other CBA approaches, CBM differs in that it focuses on a limited number of test strategies, items are drawn from across the curriculum, and the basic unit of analysis focuses on fluency (i.e., a combination of accuracy and speed) as the behavior of interest. These properties allow CBM measures to function as *dynamic indicators* of basic academic skills. The procedures are dynamic in the sense that they are designed to be sensitive to short-term effects of instruction and responsive to change over time. Moreover, the measures have been purposively designed to serve as an *indicator* of key academic behaviors in the sense that they have been validated to be strong correlates of key behaviors indicative of overall performance in an academic area.

Conducting a CBM Assessment

As with CBE, CBM begins the assessment process with a survey-level assessment. Here, however, the survey-level assessment involves the summative assessment of a student's skills at a variety of difficulty levels with the goal of determining what level of material the student

has mastered, what level is instructional, and what level appears frustrational. Once these levels have been determined, progress monitoring procedures are used within a formative assessment strategy to assess student growth over time in response to some instructional modification. In doing so, CBM uses a long-term goal level strategy for progress monitoring—frequently assessing a student's growth and responsiveness to material that reflects one year's worth of growth.

Using reading again as an example, the survey-level assessment would begin by administering three equivalent reading passages from the grade level at which the student is currently placed. The student is asked to read each passage aloud while the examiner follows along noting errors. At the end of 1 minute, the student is asked to stop reading, and the examiner quickly scores the reading passage for the number of words read correctly per minute. Once all three reading passages are administered and scored, the median number of words read correctly across the three passages is noted and compared to expectations for that particular grade level (see www.aimsweb.com for ranges of typical expected performance by grade and time of academic year). The survey-level assessment then proceeds with the examiner moving up and/or down grade levels until three placement standards are determined (e.g., mastery, instructional, frustrational). Generally, the highest level at which the student reads at an instructional rate indicates where instruction would be most profitable.

Following the survey-level assessment and the designing of intervention, CBM is used formatively to monitor the progress of reading skills over time using CBM progress-monitoring material that is selected from long-term goal-level material (i.e., material that represents where the student should be in one year's time). Developing CBM progress monitoring material are administered and scored in the same manner as during survey-level assessment with the exception that only one 1-minute sample of reading be collected during each progress monitoring session (i.e., only one reading probe is administered rather than three). Typically student progress is monitored at least weekly (or more frequently if time allows), data are graphed (see Shinn, 1989), and decisions are made with respect to the amount of growth observed over time. Growth over time is usually indexed using ordinary least squares regression, although easier methods can also be used (e.g., split-middle techniques; Tawney & Gast, 1984).

Case Example

The following case illustration demonstrates how features of both specific subskill mastery and general outcome measurement can be combined in a model of individual student evaluation that comprehensively addresses the needs for diagnostic instructional information, instructional planning, and the measurement of student growth and response to instruction over time.

Jake was a second grade student who came to the attention of general education teachers following a routine benchmark reading assessment conducted in the fall of the academic year. The school's benchmark assessment consisted of using CBM general outcome procedures whereby all students read three CBM reading passages from the grade in which they were currently placed. At that time, Jake was found to be reading about 15 words correct per minute in grade 2 material, which placed him at or around the 10th percentile relative to other second grade students. As a result of his performance on the benchmark assessment, a member of the school's instructional support team continued with a survey-level assessment of Jake's oral reading fluency skills. In doing so, the examiner moved down the curriculum and administered three grade 1 reading passages and summarized Jake's performance with the median score across the three passages. Jake's median score on the three grade 1 passages was 20, which placed him at or around the 75th percentile when compared to first grade students who had read the same passages. The results of the survey-level assessment suggested that with equal access to instructional opportunities within the general education setting, Jake's progress thus far was substantially below that of typically developing peers and standards for oral reading fluency development, and would require formal reading intervention efforts.

Following the survey-level assessment, specific level CBE assessment procedures were used diagnostically in an attempt to isolate those reading subskills that might be possible targets for intervention. To do so, a series of word lists were generated to assess very specific phonetic elements of reading that should have been mastered by the end of first grade. The following specific phonetic elements were assessed: short and long vowels (e.g., CVC and CVCe words), open syllables

(e.g., basic, he, iris, old, unit), consonant-le words (e.g., little, gentle), r-controlled vowels (e.g., star, fork, curl), vowel digraphs (e.g., pie, food, soup), diphthongs (e.g., toy, how, out), and consonant blends (e.g., st, gr, fl, nd, ld). Results indicted that while Jake could accurately and fluently identify basic sight words, he experienced difficulties implementing word attack skills to unknown words. More specifically, while Jake seemed to be able to have no difficulties with consonant blends, he experienced considerable difficulty with vowels, particularly in differentiating between long and short vowels and their variations.

Over the next six weeks, Jake received individualized instruction with the targeted phonetic skills as well as with reading fluency. Supplemental instruction was provided in 20-minute intervals three to four times per week by a reading specialist. In addition, Jake's general education teacher and parents provided daily practice in reading text that was controlled for difficulty and included frequent opportunities to practice the target skills.

In addition to the intervention noted above, Jake's response to intervention was assessed using both CBE word lists and grade 2 CBM progress monitoring reading passages. The CBE word lists were comprised of randomly selected words that were representative of the phonetic difficulties evidenced during the CBE. The CBM progress monitoring materials were represented by second grade connected text reading passages, and were used to assess improvements in reading fluency and the generalized benefits of the targeted intervention. Second grade reading passages were selected to monitor progress as this represented the long-term goal for Jake (i.e., to have him reading comfortably in second grade material by the end of the year). The results of the CBE subskill progress monitoring evidenced a steady rate of improvement from a beginning level of 4 correctly read words per minute (with 20% accuracy) to 21 correctly read words per minute (with 91% accuracy). In addition, results of CBM progress monitoring indicated that Jake had made consistent generalized improvement in fluent reading in second grade reading passages after six weeks of intervention. Importantly, these improvements were maintained at the next school-wide benchmarking period where Jake was reading 48 words correct per minute, which placed him just below the 50th percentile when compared to other second grade students (see Figure 20.2).

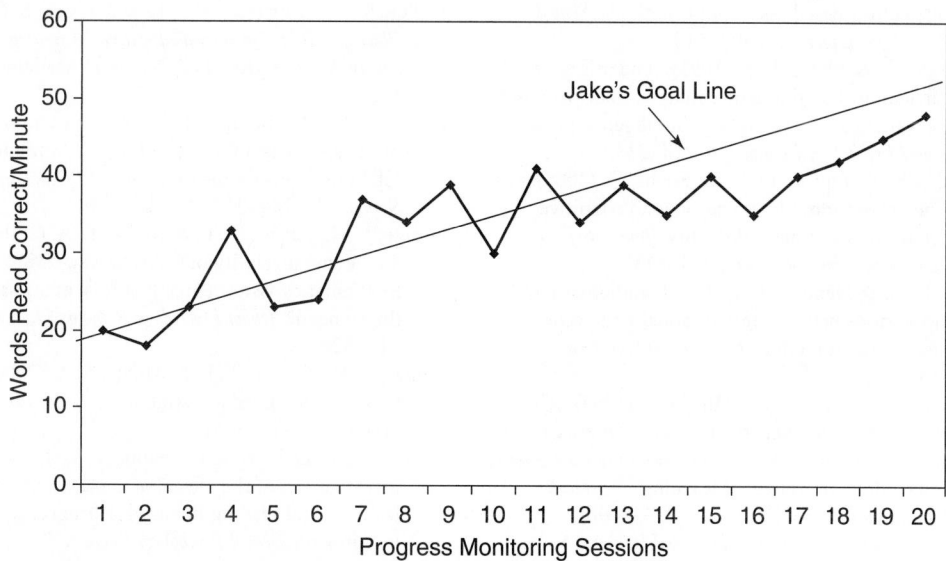

FIGURE 20.2 CBM progress monitoring chart.

SUMMARY AND CONCLUSIONS

CBA procedures have become a frequently used set of tools in the assessment of student academic functioning and achievement. Practitioners, however, are encouraged to carefully consider their assessment questions when choosing among the various techniques. Specific subskill mastery measurement techniques are very well suited for use in planning instructions and determining interventions. General outcome measures on the other hand are extremely valuable in the monitoring of interventions and student response to instruction. By combining procedures from both models, practitioners can develop a comprehensive approach to academic assessment that addresses both diagnostic and formative assessment needs.

REFERENCES

Bell, P. F., Lentz, F. E., & Graden, J. L. (1992). Effects of curriculum-test overlap on standardized test scores: Identifying systematic confounds in educational decision making. *School Psychology Review, 21,* 644–655.

Blankenship, C. S. (1985). Using curriculum-based assessment data to make instructional decisions. *Exceptional Children, 52,* 233–238.

Blankenship, C. S., & Lilly, S. (1981). *Mainstreaming students with learning and behavior problems: Techniques for the classroom teacher.* New York: Holt, Rinehart, & Winston.

Christ, T. J., Johnson-Gros, K. N., & Hintze, J. M. (2005). An examination of the reliability of the digit correct fluency metric in making mathematics calculations decisions. *Psychology in the Schools, 42,* 615–622.

Daly, E. J., Martens, B. K., Dool, E. J., & Hintze, J. M. (1998). Using brief functional analysis to select interventions for oral reading. *Journal of Behavioral Education, 8,* 203–218.

Deno, S. L. (1985). Curriculum-based measurement: The emerging alternative. *Exceptional Children, 52,* 219–232.

Deno, S. L. (1986). Formative evaluation of individual student programs: A new role for school psychologists. *School Psychology Review, 15,* 358–374.

Deno, S. L. (1987). Curriculum-based measurement. *Teaching Exceptional Children, 20,* 41.

Deno, S. L., Mirkin, P., & Chiang, B. (1982). Identifying valid measures of reading. *Exceptional Children, 49,* 36–45.

Duhon, G. J., Noell, G. H., Witt, J. C., Freeland, J. T., Dufiene, B. A., & Gilbertson, D. N. (2004). Identifying academic skills and performance deficits: The experimental analysis of brief assessments of academic skills. *School Psychology Review, 33,* 429–443.

Eckert, T. L., Ardoin, S. P., Daly, E. J., & Martens, B. K. (2002). Improving oral reading fluency: A brief experimental analysis of combining an antecedent intervention with consequences. *Journal of Applied Behavior Analysis, 35,* 271–281.

Eckert, T. L., Shapiro, E. S., & Lutz, J. G. (1995). Teachers' ratings of the acceptability of curriculum-based assessment methods. *School Psychology Review, 24*, 499–510.

Elliott, S. N., & Fuchs, L. S. (1997). The utility of curriculum-based measurement and performance assessment as alternatives to intelligence tests. *School Psychology Review, 26*, 224–233.

Fuchs, L. S., Compton, D. L., & Fuchs, D. (2005). The prevention, identification, and cognitive determinants of math difficulty. *Journal of Educational Psychology, 97*, 493–513.

Fuchs, L. S., & Deno, S. L. (1991). Paradigmatic distinctions between instructionally relevant measurement models. *Exceptional Children, 57*, 488–500.

Fuchs, L. S., Deno, S. L., & Mirkin, P. (1984). The effects of frequent curriculum-based measurement and evaluation on pedagogy, student achievement, and student awareness of learning. *American Educational Research Journal, 21*, 449–460.

Gansle, K. A., Noell, G. H., VanDerHeyden, A. M., Naquin, G. M., & Slider, N. J. (2002). Moving beyond total words written: The reliability, criterion validity, and time cost of alternate measures for curriculum-based measurement in writing. *School Psychology Review, 31*, 477–497.

Gansle, K. A., Noell, G. H., VanDerHeyden, A. M., Slider, N. J., Hoffpauir, L. D., Whitmarsh, E. L. et al. (2004). An examination of the criterion validity and sensitivity to brief intervention of alternate curriculum-based measures of writing skills. *Psychology in the Schools, 41*, 291–300.

Gickling, E. E., & Havertape, S. (1981). *Curriculum-based assessment (CBA)*. Minneapolis, MN: School Psychology Inservice Training Network.

Gickling, E. E., & Rosenfield, S. (1995). Best practices in curriculum-based assessment. In A. Thomas & J. Grimes (Eds.), *Best Practices in School Psychology III* (pp. 587–595). Washington, DC: National Association of School Psychologists.

Gickling, E. E., Shane, R. L., & Croskery, K. M. (1989). Developing math skills in low-achieving high school students. *School Psychology Review, 18*, 344–355.

Gickling, E. E., & Thompson, V. P. (1985). A personal view of curriculum-based assessment. *Exceptional Children, 52*, 205–218.

Good, R. H., & Salvia, J. (1988). Curriculum bias in published, norm-referenced reading tests: Demonstrable effects. *School Psychology Review, 17*, 51–60.

Hasbrouck, J. E., & Tindal, G. (1992). Curriculum-based oral reading fluency norms for students in grades 2 through 5. *Teaching Exceptional Children, 24*(3), 41–44.

Haring, N. G., Lovitt, T. C., Eaton, M. D., & Hansen, C. L. (1978). *The fourth R: Research in the classroom*. Columbus, OH: Merrill.

Heller, K. A., Holtzman, W. H., & Messick, S. (1982). *Placing children in special education: A strategy for equity*. Washington, DC: National Academy Press.

Hintze, J. M., & Christ, T. J. (2004). An examination of variability as a function of passage variance in CBM progress monitoring. *School Psychology Review, 33*, 204–217.

Hintze, J. M., Christ, T. J., & Keller, L. A. (2002). The generalizability of CBM survey-level mathematics assessments: Just how many samples do we need? *School Psychology Review, 31*, 514–528.

Hintze, J. M., Christ, T. J., & Methe, S. A. (2006). Curriculum-based assessment. *Psychology in the Schools, 43*, 45–56.

Hintze, J. M., Daly, E. J., & Shapiro E.S. (1998). An investigation of the effects of passage difficulty level on oral reading fluency for progress monitoring. *School Psychology Review, 27*, 433–445.

Hintze, J. M., Owen, S. V., Shapiro E.S., & Daly, E. J. (2000). Generalizability of oral reading fluency measures: Application of G theory to curriculum-based measurement. *School Psychology Quarterly, 15*, 52–68.

Hintze, J. M., & Silberglitt, B. (2005). A longitudinal examination of the diagnostic accuracy and predictive validity of R-CBM and high stakes testing. *School Psychology Review, 34*, 372–386.

Howell, K. W. (1986). Direct assessment of academic performance. *School Psychology Review, 15*, 324–335.

Howell, K. W., & Nolet, V. (2000). *Curriculum-based evaluation: Teaching and decision making* (3rd ed.) Belmont, CA: Wadsworth.

Howell, K. W., Zucker, S. H., & Moorehead, M. K. (2000). *Multilevel academic skills inventory*. Bellingham, WA: Western Washington University, Applied Research and Developmental Center.

Idol, L., Nevin, A., & Paolucci-Whitcomb, P. (1999). *Models of curriculum-based assessment: A blueprint for learning*. Austin, TX: Pro-Ed.

Jenkins, J. R., & Pany, D. (1978). Standardized achievement tests: How useful for special education? *Exceptional Children, 44*, 448–453.

Koppitz, E. M. (1963). *The Bender Gestalt Test for Young Children*. New York: Grune and Stratton.

Lentz, F. E., & Shapiro E.S. (1986). Functional assessment of the academic environment. *School Psychology Review, 15*, 346–357.

Marston, D. (1989). Curriculum-based measurement: What is it and why do it? In M.R. Shinn (Ed.), *Curriculum-based measurement: Assessing special children* (pp. 18–78). New York: Guilford.

Marston, D., Fuchs, L. S., & Deno, S. L. (1986). Measuring pupil progress: A comparison of standardized achievement tests and curriculum-related measures. *Diagnostique, 11,* 77–90.

Martens, B. K., Steele, E. S., Massie, D. R., & Diskin, M. J. (1995). Curriculum bias in standardized tests of reading decoding. *Journal of School Psychology, 33,* 287–296.

Mirkin, P., Deno, S. L., Tindal, G., & Kuehnle, K. (1982). Frequency of measurement and data utilization as factors in standardized behavioral assessment of academic skill. *Journal of Behavioral Assessment, 4,* 361–370.

Popham, W. J. (2004). *Classroom assessment: What teachers need to know.* Boston, MA: Pearson Education.

Seethaler, P. M., & Fuchs, L. S. (2005). A drop in the bucket: Randomized controlled trials testing reading and math interventions. *Learning Disabilities Research and Practice, 20,* 98–102.

Shapiro E.S., & Derr, T. F. (1987). An examination of overlap between reading curricula and standardized achievement tests. *The Journal of Special Education, 21,* 59–67.

Shapiro E.S., & Eckert, T. L. (1994). Acceptability of curriculum-based assessment by school psychologists. *Journal of School Psychology, 32,* 167–184.

Shinn, M. R. (1988). Development of curriculum-based local norms for use in special education decision-making. *School Psychology Review, 17,* 61–80.

Shinn, M. R. (1989). *Curriculum-based measurement: Assessing special children.* New York: Guilford.

Shinn, M. R., Habedank, L., Rodden-Nord, L., & Knutson, N. (1993). Using curriculum-based measurement to identify potential candidates for reintegration into general education. *The Journal of Special Education, 27,* 202–221.

Shinn, M. R., Rosenfield, S., & Knutson, N. (1989). Curriculum-based assessment: A comparison of models. *School Psychology Review, 18,* 299–316.

Silberglitt, B., & Hintze, J. M. (2005). Formative assessment using CBM-R cut scores to track progress toward success on state-mandated achievement tests: A comparison of methods. *Journal of Psychoeducational Assessment, 23,* 304–325.

Tawney, J. W., & Gast, D. L. (1984). *Single-subject research in special education.* Boston: Houghton Mifflin.

Thurlow, M. L., & Ysseldyke, J. E. (1982). Instructional planning: Information collected by school psychologists vs. information considered useful by teachers. *Journal of School Psychology, 20,* 3–10.

Tucker, J. A. (1985). Curriculum-based assessment: An introduction [Special issue]. *Exceptional Children, 52.*

Wechsler, D. (1974). *Manual for the Wecsler Intelligence Scale for Children–Revised.* New York: Psychological Corporation.

White, O. R., & Haring, N. G. (1980). *Exceptional teaching.* Columbus, OH: Merrill.

Wilkinson, G. S. (1993). *Wide Range Achievement Test–3* (3rd ed.) Wilmington, DE: Wide Range.

Woodcock, R. W. (1987). *Woodcock Reading Mastery Tests–Revised.* Circle Pines, MN: American Guidance Service.

Ysseldyke, J. E., & Christenson, S. (1993). *TIES-II, The Instructional Environment System II.* Longmont, CO: Sopris West.

CHAPTER 21

FUNCTIONAL ASSESSMENT OF INSTRUCTIONAL ENVIRONMENTS FOR THE PURPOSE OF MAKING DATA-DRIVEN INSTRUCTIONAL DECISIONS

JIM YSSELDYKE AND MATTHEW BURNS
University of Minnesota, Twin Cities

Data-Driven Decision Making and Accountability is one of the primary domains of competence listed in the *Blueprint for Training and Practice III* (Ysseldyke et al. 2006). In that document it is argued that "School psychologists should be good problem solvers who collect information that aids in understanding problems, make decisions about appropriate interventions, assess educational outcomes, and help others become accountable for the decisions they make" (p. 34). School psychologists typically have been well trained in person-centered assessment of abilities, as well as in assessing the extent to which students have acquired specific academic and functional skills. A new focus, advocated for quite some time, is now articulated in provisions of the reauthorized Individuals with Disabilities Educational Improvement Act (IDEA) and No Child Left Behind (NCLB). That focus is on using evidenced-based instructional practices in teaching all students, including students with disabilities.

It is common in our profession to think about evidence-based instruction narrowly; professionals look to adopt instructional *programs* that publishers, authors, or sanctioning websites (What Works Clearinghouse, National Center on Student Progress Monitoring) indicate are evidence based. Having an evidence-based instructional program available and even implementing the program is not enough. It is critical to implement programs with high intervention integrity (fidelity of treatment) and in so doing to apply well-confirmed principles, strategies and tactics of effective instruction.

So, how do we know the extent to which evidence-based instructional practices are in place? How do we assess the extent to which a student's academic difficulties may be due to inadequate or inappropriate instruction? When we apply a Response-to-Intervention model, and consider the extent to which students fail to profit from evidence-based instruction, how do we know whether effective instruction is occurring? In this chapter we argue that a comprehensive assessment always includes conceptually coherent and instructionally sensitive assessments. We describe the functional assessment of academic environments for the purposes of (a) identifying the extent to which effective instruction is occurring for individual students, and (b) creating successful learning environments for those individual students. We describe recent developments in legislation, research, practice, and instrument development.

We describe specific ways to gather and use information on effective instruction of individual learners. These individuals learn in specific instructional contexts or environments. These include, but are not limited to, classrooms and schools. Rather, we like to think of school contexts, home contexts, and the contexts created by home-school partnerships. We describe the current evidence base in instruction, the support for the current movement, arguments for an ecological or ecobehavioral perspective, and a functional framework for applying best practices. We then describe ways to collect information that will enhance the planning, management, delivery, and evaluation of instruction, and relate this to the efforts of school psychologists to create successful learning environments for all students. We close with consideration of a set of important issues that we need to resolve to move forward.

THE CURRENT MOVEMENT IN INSTRUCTION

New adjectives increasingly are being used to describe desired instructional practices: terms like results-oriented, evidence-based, research-based, data-based, data-driven, and empirically-derived. There is a major attempt to shift from practices thought to be or shown to be ineffective (Bateman, 1990; Mann, 1979; Kavale & Forness, 2000) to practices supported by evidence, most often defined as based on the results of findings of randomized controlled experiments.

Over the past two decades assessment practices in U.S. schools have shifted from those characterized by what Sarason and Doris (1979) called a child deviance or child pathology orientation to what typically is labeled a problem-solving orientation (Batsche, et al., 2005; Reschly & Ysseldyke, 1995, 2002; Tilly, 2002; Tilly, Reschly & Grimes, 1999). This resulting shift is twofold: one of *orientation* (from child pathology to problem solving, reciprocal determinism, and creation of successful learning environments), and one of *process* (collection of information on how changes in intervention are functionally related to intervention success in everyday instructional environments).

Since publication in 1999 of the third edition of the *Handbook of School Psychology* (Reynolds & Gutkin, 1999) several factors, singly and in interaction, have served as an impetus for new directions in assessment for the purpose of planning instructional interventions. The first has been a general push for accountability in society at large. The second has been a set of federal laws, rules, regulations and/or guidelines. When Congress reauthorized the Individuals with Disabilities Education Act (IDEA) in 1997 it added a set of accountability provisions. The third factor has been a shift in the training and practice of school psychologists.

Calls for accountability permeate our evaluations of corporate practices, CEO practices, truth in advertising, professional sports, public schools and colleges and universities. The term "accountability" has been used in a twofold way to push for integrity and for a focus on results.

Business and professional leaders are to lead organizations that produce high-level results, and they are to do so without lying or cheating about the results. Schools are held accountable for both excellence *and* equity. They are to achieve high standards (excellence) and they are to achieve this for all students, including those who are severely disabled or who are English language learners.

The Federal NCLB law included a provision that school personnel are to employ evidence-based instructional practices with students and the 1997 reauthorization of IDEA mandated that states report annually on the performance and progress of all students, including students with disabilities. This provision was reiterated in the 2004 reauthorization of the IDEA, and that law included an option for school personnel to make decisions about eligibility for special education services based on data on student response to evidence-based instruction.

One final push is unique to the profession of school psychology. The third edition of the *Blueprint for Training and Practice in School Psychology* included a competence domain entitled Data-Based Decision Making and Accountability, and suggested that school psychologists should have skills necessary to make data-based instructional and accountability decisions.

SUPPORT FOR THE CURRENT MOVEMENT

Sheridan and Gutkin (2000) described anomalies in school psychology that necessitated a paradigm shift in the field. For example, many traditional assessment approaches in school psychology address student-centered pathology, but meeting the unique educational and mental health needs of children "almost always requires us to influence the behaviors of people other than, or in addition to, referred children themselves" (Sheridan & Gutkin, 2000, p. 486). Thus, a disconnect between current and best practices facilitated the focusing on ecological systems in which the child lives and learns.

To fully understand the child, we must examine the home, school, community, and culture in which the child lives (Bronfenbrenner, 1986). Moreover, a review of various assessment models in school psychology found that each generally lacks ecological validity because it does not adequately represent real-life situations, does not use stimuli that are relevant to daily classroom activity, and does not require student responses that are representative of the construct being assessed (Dean, Burns, Grialou, & Varro, 2006).

Perhaps many of the current assessment practices lack ecological relevance because they are designed to provide data that inform a student-centered deficit model of instruction and remediation. There is a long history of attempts to improve student academic skills through remediation of child-centered deficits, the cumulative results of which have only negligible to small effects (Kavale & Forness, 2000). This compares to strong mean effect sizes associated with environmental changes and contextual instruction such as direct instruction ($d = .84$), mnemonic strategies ($d = 1.62$), and behavioral analyses ($d = .93$). Moreover, effective instructional methodology significantly reduces the influence of individual differences such as intelligence (MacQuarrie, Tucker, Burns, & Hartman, 2002).

WHY AN ECOLOGICAL PERSPECTIVE IS NEEDED

Perhaps the difficulties students in schools face are different than previous generations, or perhaps the educational system has become so complex that it too must be examined when analyzing problems. Regardless, an ecological approach allows for a more comprehensive and in-depth analysis of skills and deficits than does an individual psychological approach. As such, an ecological approach was suggested as the most effective method to address several problems including suicide prevention (Ayyash-Abdo, 2002), bullying prevention (Swearer & Doll, 2001), preventing depression among children (Herman, Merrell, Reinke, & Tucker, 2004), community violence (Overstreet & Mazza, 2003), and school violence (Baker, 1998). Moreover, and perhaps more importantly, the aforementioned ecological interventions were actually prevention efforts, which suggests a more preventative role for school psychologists. Research has consistently demonstrated the effectiveness of preventative approaches for enhancing both behavioral and academic outcomes (Greenberg et al., 2003). Sheridan and Gutkin (2000) claimed that "changing the ecological systems that pervade the lives of children (e.g., schools, families, communities) provides us with the only meaningful route to prevention and must be among our very highest priorities as a field" (p. 490).

The ecological prevention approach provides a specific framework for examining academic deficits and providing systemic interventions. For example, the instructional triangle, proposed by Gravois, Rosenfield, and Gickling (1999), includes the student, instruction, and task/environment; the interactions between which are potential sources for student difficulty. Most educators focus only on the student point of the triangle and assume that is where difficulties occur. However, task/environmental issues could include difficulty level, sequencing of examples during instruction, activity level, and pacing (VanDerHeyden & Burns, 2005), any one of which could also be a related to student problems. When curricular materials are modified to match the skill level of the student, enhanced learning occurs. Thus, an ecological perspective allows for more systemic thinking and interventions, which is a critical aspect of school psychology.

From an assessment perspective, ecological validity can be best assured with environmental assessments. Such assessments are focused on identifying the extent to which effective instruction is occurring for individual students in multiple environmental contexts (classrooms, homes, and as a result of home-school partnerships). Ecologically valid assessments are ones that represent the real-life situation, are relevant to daily classroom activities, and utilize natural responses that represent the construct being assessed (Dean et al., 2006). Therefore, assessing the instructional environment should focus on observations of the classroom activity and sample the instructional process. The reliability of data from an instructional environment assessment would need to be determined, but ecological validity seems likely.

PAST INSTRUCTIONAL ENVIRONMENTAL ASSESSMENT MODELS

Although environmental assessment does not deny the importance of previous learning and other historical factors, the primary emphasis is on the interaction among the student, the task, and the environment in which instruction occurs. Assessment of the educational environment is an important piece of the complex puzzle of exploring what deficits and excesses exist and what role they play in creating the problem behavior. There has always been recognition that assessment of the environment is necessary and important, but the focus of most evaluations has been on assessing the student rather than the instructional context. Before there were formalized methods of collecting information on instructional environments, a variety of assessment approaches were used by school psychologists.

Observation

Direct observations of student behavior is a common (Wilson & Reschly, 1996) and increasingly prevalent (Reschly, 2003) assessment technique among school psychologists that may be the most direct approach to data collection in the educational environment to assess classroom ecology. Typically, this involves systematic observation of behavior in the setting where the problem behavior is exhibited. However, observations could involve either a narrative and subjective assessment of what was seen or heard, or systematically observing a specific and operationalized behavior with measures such as its frequency, duration, magnitude, or latency. Although direct observation of students and classrooms will probably always remain a critical aspect of an instructional environment assessment, systematic direct observations demonstrated adequate interrater agreement, but questionable reliability and generalizability (Hintze & Matthews, 2004).

Several observation systems have been published and are currently available. Some commonly used examples include the Academic Engaged Time Code of the Systematic Screening for Behavior Disorders (AET-SSBD; Walker & Severson, 1992), the Behavioral Observation of Students in Schools (BOSS; Shapiro, 2004), the Direct Observation Form (DOF; Achenbach, 1986) and the Student Observation System of the Behavioral Assessment System for Children (SOS; Reynolds & Kamphaus, 2004). A review of seven such coding systems found sufficient psychometric properties for all but the SOS to recommend use of them within a multimethod assessment model (Volpe, DiPerna, Hintze & Shapiro, 2005). However, valid observations are dependent on well defined behavior, generalizability of the target behavior, high interobserver agreement, appropriate coding and unbiased observations (Merrell, 2007).

Teacher Interview and Rating Scales

Teachers have been a primary source of information for a long time. Information from interviews has typically been used to identify the target behavior is and how it is impending learning and/or classroom instruction. The product is descriptive data, the quality of which depends heavily on the knowledge of the person being interviewed. Rating scales are used to more objectively describe learning and/or behavior deficiencies as witnessed in the classroom and home. The Vineland Adaptive Behavior Scale-2 (Sparrow, Cicchetti & Balla, 2005) is an example of a formal interview, whereas examples of rating scales include the Child Behavior Checklist (Achenbach, 1985, 1991), the Behavior Evaluation Scale (McCarney & Leigh, 1990), and the Systematic Screening for Behavior Disorders (Walker & Severson, 1992).

Teacher ratings of student behavior are positively correlated with academic achievement, academic competence and social skills (Crosby & French, 2002; Hoge & Coladarci, 1989). Moreover, teacher interviews are frequently used and rated as helpful during assessments of English language learners (Ochoa, Riccio, Jimenez, de Alba, & Sines, 2004). However, these interviews and rating scales do not provide an objective framework for the social and psychological context in which the child functions (Saracho, 1991).

Climate Inventories

Several formal measures are available to assess a broad range of skills, feelings, and attitudes that students display in the classroom (Burns, Vance, Szadokierski, & Stockwell, 2006; Krug, Ahadi, & Scott, 1991; Maehr & Ames, 1988; Braskamp & Maehr, 1988). Most scales involve input from teachers, parents, and administrators to assess perceptions of how caring and supportive the school climate is. Previous research supported the reliability and validity of data from these scales (Burns et al., 2006; Worrell, 2000), but as of yet little research has been conducted on the inventories.

Teacher-Student Interactions

The assessment of teacher-student interaction has been used to identify the quantity and quality of the exchange. The *Flanders Interaction Analysis* (FIE) provides a framework for analyzing class interactions by observing teacher-student verbal behavior (Flanders, 1970). The FIA focuses on discovering relationships between a teacher's behavior and a student's growth. It allows the observer to draw conclusions about the classroom climate and make inferences about the communications strategies used in the classroom. More recently, scholars have used observations of student-teacher interactions as assessments of classroom climate (Kagan, 1990).

Parent Interview and Social History

Interviewing a parent or guardian is an attempt to uncover family, medical, birth, and developmental milestones that may be contributing to in-school learning and behavior. Parents are often interviewed and/or asked to complete checklists that target their perception of the student's problem in the home. Although unstructured interviews of parents may have questionable psychometric properties, social history information has significantly differentiated children with emotional disorders from those with conduct disorders when no other psychometric data could (Steinhausen & Reitzle, 1996). However, one of the difficulties with this approach is that a parent or guardian's definition or perception of the problem is often different from that of the school or classroom teacher. Thus, it is important to aggregate data from different sources.

A FRAMEWORK FOR INSTRUCTION AND ASSESSMENT OF INSTRUCTIONAL ENVIRONMENTS

Educators talk about the need to identify the extent to which effective instruction is occurring for individual students. But, how should we go about gathering data on effective instruction? Most research on effective instruction has been conducted with students in general education settings, is correlational in nature, reports results of group studies, and uses global measures of achievement as the central measure of educational results, efficacy, or effectiveness. Several researchers have produced descriptions or lists of components of effective instruction. Sometimes they describe effective instruction in general, broad ways (Astleitner, 2005; Marzano, Pickering & Pollock, 2001; Reith & Evertson, 1988; Stevens & Rosenshine, 1982; VanDerHeyden & Burns, 2005). In other instances they describe components of effective instruction in specific content areas such as reading or math (Englert, 1984; Good & Brophy, 1984; Taylor, Pearson, Peterson & Rodriguez, 2005; Vaughn, 2007).

Those who identify components of effective instruction do so at varying levels of specificity, and while some focus only on academic aspects, others focus on socio-emotional factors that determine the effectiveness of instruction. Rosenshine and his colleagues (Rosenshine, 1983;

Rosenshine & Stevens, 1986) identified six components of effective instruction: (a) daily review; (b) presentation of new content and skills; (c) initial practice, with much teacher-pupil interaction and an 80% success rate; (d) feedback and correctives; (e) independent practice for mastery and automaticity; and (f) weekly and monthly reviews, reteaching concepts and skills if necessary. Rosenshine (1983) indicated that instruction is more effective if it is structured, briskly paced, proceeds in small steps, includes detailed and redundant instructions and many concrete examples, provides students with many opportunities to make overt responses, includes the teacher's monitoring of performance, and emphasizes overlearning. Good and Brophy (1984), and Blair (1984) also identified several general factors related to effective instruction and improved academic performance. Among these were students' opportunity to learn, active teaching, high rates of students' engagement, efficient use of instructional time, varied and flexible grouping patterns, rapid progress through the curriculum, teaching to mastery, placement of students at appropriate instructional levels, clearly defined goals and objectives, and the presence of a well-organized, academically focused, pleasant learning environment.

Astleitner (2005) highlighted motivational and emotional factors in addition to the kinds of factors identified by Rosenshine, Good and Brophy, and others. Astleitner listed the following components: (a) opportunity for students to reflect on their learning, (b) cognitive, motivational, and emotional supports for learning, (c) focusing on student strengths, (d) contextual variation, (e) stimulation of higher order thinking and problem solving, (f) student skill in identifying, constructing and evaluating arguments, (g) self-regulated learning, (h) interest stimulation, (i) efficiency, (j) positive as opposed to negative thinking and feeling, (k) respect along with responsibility, and use of self-instructional learning materials.

Ysseldyke and Christenson (1987) identified common elements of effective teaching programs and identified two factors, structure and interaction. The instructional structure is teacher directed, academically focused, and follows a demonstrate-prompt-practice instructional sequence. Clear lesson explanations, supervised guided practice, sufficient independent practice (classroom and homework), and evaluation of student performance are provided. Monitoring occurs at all points throughout the instructional sequence. A high degree of teacher-student inter-action is maintained by teacher questioning and student responding patterns, and by providing students with informative feedback. Students are provided many opportunities to respond; cues and prompts are provided to increase accuracy of responses. Students work toward mastery of skills. Highly structured, interactive instruction has resulted in greater achievement gains and active participation (academic engaged time) for students.

VanDerHeyden and Burns (2005) described strategies that, when applied correctly, were shown to produce growth for children of diverse backgrounds and in diverse settings. They described effective management of instruction as consisting of management of instructional planning, student responding, instructional con-sequences, and individual learning problems.

Vaughn, Gersten and Chard (2000) summa-rized research syntheses on instructional prac-tices that lead to improved reading outcomes for students with disabilities. They identified three critical factors that strongly affect student learn-ing regardless of content area: 1) control of task difficulty, 2) teaching in small (six or less) interac-tive groups, and 3) directed response questioning: encouraging students to "think aloud" about what they are working on. Additional effective instruc-tional strategies they identified for specific content areas included extended practice with feedback, breaking tasks into component parts (task analysis) while fading prompts and cues, use of technol-ogy, provision of guided feedback, and use of interventions that taught self-questioning strate-gies such as comprehension monitoring and text structuring.

In describing components of effective instruction Algozzine and Ysseldyke (1992) proposed a specific framework. This was later refined by Algozzine, Ysseldyke and Elliott (1997) and used by them to construct a set of *Strategies and Tactics for Effective Instruction*. The framework also was used by Ysseldyke & Christenson to refine *The Instructional Environment System* (TIES; Ysseldyke & Christenson, 1987) and to develop *The Instructional Environment System II* (TIES II; Ysseldyke & Christenson, 1993). More recently, Ysseldyke and Christenson (2002) used the Algozzine-Ysseldyke framework as the structured organizer for the *Functional Assessment of Academic Behavior* (FAAB). This framework, illustrated in Table 21.1 includes four

components of effective instruction: planning, managing, delivering, and evaluating. For each component Algozzine, Ysseldyke and Elliott (1997) identified a set of evidence-based principles of effective instruction. For example, in planning instruction, one must decide what to teach, decide how to teach, and communicate realistic expectations to the student. Specific strategies and tactics for implementing principles of effective instruction were devised and published (Algozzine et al., 1997). The Algozzine-Ysseldyke Model of Effective Instruction is shown in Table 21.2. Shown are four components of effective instruction, evidence-based principles for each of the components, and specific strategies for implementing the principles. We describe the components and major principles of effective instruction in the sections that follow.

Planning Instruction

Instructional results are better when instruction is planned. Planning involves making decisions about what to teach, how to teach, and the communication of realistic expectations. It is important to assess the extent to which instruction has been planned adequately and appropriately for individual students.

Deciding What to Teach

In making decisions about what to teach, educa-tional professionals must accurately assess student characteristics (e.g., skill levels, motivation), task characteristics (e.g., sequence, cognitive demands) and classroom characteristics (e.g., instructional groupings, materials). It is important to achieve a match between a student's level of skill devel-opment and the level of instruction. Assessors accomplish this by measuring students' entry-level cognitive and affective behaviors. Effective teach-ers are aware of what skills their students have mastered and achieve an appropriate match both on initial tasks and on the modifications they make as instruction proceeds. Daly, Martens, Kilmer and Massie (1996) showed that instructional out-comes (reading accuracy and fluency) were better when instruction was matched to student's skill levels and when assessment materials were sim-ilar to those used during instruction. Moreover, previous research also found that children who read passages that were matched to their individ-ual skill level, using curriculum-based assessment, demonstrated increased time on task (Treptow,

TABLE 21.1 Functional Assessment of Academic Behavior (FAAB)

Instructional Support for Learning Components for FAAB

Instructional Planning: Decisions are made about what to teach and how to teach the student. Realistic expectations are communicated to the student.

- *Instructional Match.* The student's needs are assessed accurately, and instruction is matched appropriately to the results of the instructional diagnosis.
- *Instructional Expectations.* There are realistic, yet high, expectations for both the amount and accuracy of work to be completed by the student, and these are communicated clearly to the student.

Instructional Managing: Effective instruction requires managing the complex mix of instructional tasks and student behaviors that are part of every classroom interaction. This means making decisions that control and support the orderly flow of instruction. To do this, teachers make decisions about classroom rules and procedures, as well as how to handle disruptions, how to organize classroom time and space to be most productive, and how to keep classrooms warm, positive, and accepting places for the student with different learning preferences and performances.

- *Classroom Environment.* The classroom management techniques used are effective for the student; there is a positive, supportive classroom atmosphere; and time is used productively.

Instructional Delivering: Decisions are made about how to present information, as well as how to monitor and adjust presentations to accommodate individual differences and enhance the learning of the student.

- *Instructional Presentation.* Instruction is presented in a clear and effective manner; the directions contain sufficient information for the student to understand the kinds of behaviors or skills that are to be demonstrated; and the student's understanding is checked.
- *Cognitive Emphasis.* Thinking skills and learning strategies for completing assignments are communicated explicitly to the student.
- *Motivational Strategies.* Effective strategies for heightening student interest and effort are used with the student.
- *Relevant Practice.* The student is given adequate opportunity to practice with appropriate materials and a high success rate. Classroom tasks are clearly important to achieving instructional goals.
- *Informed Feedback.* The student receives relatively immediate and specific information on his/her performance or behavior; when the student makes mistakes, correction is provided.

Instructional Evaluating: Effective instruction requires evaluating. Some evaluation activities occur during the process of instruction (i.e., when teachers gather data during instruction and use those data to make instructional decisions). Other evaluation activities occur at the end of instruction (e.g., when the teacher administers a test to determine whether a student has met instructional goals).

- *Academic Engaged Time.* The student is actively engaged in responding to academic content; the teacher monitors the extent to which the student is actively engaged and redirects the student when the student is unengaged.
- *Adaptive Instruction.* The curriculum is modified within reason to accommodate the student's unique and specific instructional needs.
- *Progress Evaluation.* There is direct, frequent measurement of the student's progress toward completion of instructional objectives; data on the student's performance and progress are used to plan future instruction.
- *Student Understanding.* The student demonstrates an accurate understanding of what is to be done and how it is to be done in the classroom.

TABLE 21.1 (*Continued*)

Home Support for Learning Components for FAAB

Home Expectations and Attributions: High, realistic expectations about schoolwork are communicated to the child, and the value of effort and working hard in school is emphasized.

Discipline Orientation: There is an authoritative, not permissive nor authoritarian, approach to discipline, and the child is monitored and supervised by the parents.

Home-affective Environment: The parent-child relationship is characterized by a healthy connectedness; it is generally positive and supportive.

Parent Participation: There is an educative home environment, and others participate in the child's schooling and learning, at home and/or at school.

Structure for Learning: Organization and daily routines facilitate the completion of schoolwork and support for the child's academic learning.

Home-School Support for Learning Components for FAAB

Shared Standards and Expectations: The level of expected performance held by key adults for the student is congruent across home and school, and reflects a belief that the student can learn.

Consistent Structure: The overall routine and monitoring provided by key adults for the student have been discussed and are congruent across home and school.

Cross-setting Opportunity to Learn: The variety of learning options available to the youth during school hours and outside of school time (i.e., home and community) supports the student's learning.

Mutual Support: The guidance provided by, the communication between, and the interest shown by adults to facilitate student progress in school is effective. It is what adults do on an ongoing basis to help the student learn and achieve.

Positive, Trusting Relationships: The amount of warmth and friendliness; praise and recognition; and the degree to which the adult-youth relationship is positive and respectful. It includes how adults in the home, in the school, and in the community work together to help the student be a learner.

Modeling: Parents and teachers demonstrate desired behaviors and commitment and value toward learning and working hard in their daily lives to the student.

Source: Ysseldyke, J. & Christenson, S. (2002).

Burns, McComas 2007) and an increased rate of reading growth over a period of 12 weeks (Burns, 2007).

In deciding what to teach, it is important also to analyze task variables. Engaging in task analysis and examining specifically the psychological demands of classroom tasks assists diagnostic and instructional personnel in designing effective instructional units. In addition, it is important to take into account the ways in which classrooms are organized. Physical space, peer interactions, and instructional grouping arrangements affect a teacher's planning (Squires, Huitt, & Segars, 1984). Those who assess instructional environments experienced by individual students will have to examine the ways in which instruction is planned for the student.

Deciding How to Teach

Knowing ahead of time how to teach is difficult. Teaching is an experimental process. The best way to decide how to teach is to teach and to gather data on the kinds of things that do and do not work. This does not mean that instructional planning is blind; experience provides a basis for knowing what works, and the professional literature is filled with guidelines for instruction (Taylor, Peterson, Pearson & Rodriquez, 2002; Wittrock, 1985). Based on information available for students in their classes, effective teachers set instructional goals and performance standards. They select instructional methods, including grouping structures and pace, and materials to help them achieve their goals. Effective teachers also utilize monitoring procedures that will help

TABLE 21.2   The Algozzine–Ysseldyke Model of Effective Instruction

Component	Principle	Strategy
Planning Instruction	Decide What to Teach	Assess skill levels to identify gaps between actual and expected level of performance; establish logical sequences of instruction; consider contextual variables.
	Decide How to Teach	Set instructional goals, establish performance standards; choose instructional methods and materials; establish grouping structures; pace instruction appropriately; monitor students' performance and use performance to plan instruction.
	Communicate Realistic Expectations	Teach goals, objectives, and standards; teach students to be active, involved learners; teach students consequences of performance.
Managing Instruction	Prepare for Instruction	Set classroom rules; communicate classroom rules; teach rule compliance; handle disruptions efficiently; communicate consequences of behavior; teach students to manage their own behavior.
	Use Time Productively	Establish routines and procedures; organize physical space; give task directions; keep transitions short; allocate time to academic activities; maintain academic focus.
	Establish Positive Classroom Environment	Make classrooms pleasant, friendly places; accept individual differences; keep interactions positive; establish supportive, cooperative environment; make students respond and participate.
Delivering Instruction	Present Instruction	For Presenting Content: Gain students' attention; review prior skills or lessons; provide organized, relevant lessons; maintain students' attention; interact positively with students. For Teaching Thinking Skills: Model thinking skills; teach fact-finding skills; teach divergent thinking; teach learning strategies. For Motivating Students: Show enthusiasm and interest; help students value schoolwork; use rewards effectively; consider level and student interest. For Providing Relevant Practice: Develop automaticity; vary opportunities for practice; use seatwork effectively; provide students with help; use relevant tasks and varied materials; assign the right amount of work; vary methods during practice.

TABLE 21.2 *(Continued)*

Component	Principle	Strategy
	Monitor Instruction	For Providing Feedback: Give immediate, frequent, explicit feedback; provide specific praise and encouragement; model correct performance; provide prompts and cues; check student understanding. For Keeping Students Actively Involved: Monitor performance regularly; monitor performance during practice; use peers to provide instruction; provide opportunities for success; limit opportunities for failure; monitor engagement rates.
	Adjust Instruction	Adjust lessons to meet student needs; provide many instructional options; adjust pace.
Evaluating Instruction	Monitor Student Understanding	Check understanding of directions; check process understanding; monitor success rate.
	Monitor Engaged Time	Check student participation; teach students to monitor their own participation.
	Maintain Records of Student Progress	Teach students to chart their own progress; regularly inform students of performance; maintain records of student performance.
	Use Data to Make Decisions	Use data on student progress to decide when more services are warranted; use student progress to make teaching decisions; use student progress to make decisions about when to change service delivery.

Source: Reprinted with permission from Algozzine, B., Ysseldyke, J., & Elliott, J. (1997).

them decide the extent to which students are achieving goals. School psychologists can work collaboratively with teachers to identify the best way to present desired content, but must be aware of alternative ways of doing so.

Communicating Realistic Expectations

Good and Brophy (1984), Edmonds (1979), and Kagan (1992) have written about the importance of setting high but realistic expectations for all students. Their research indicates that high academic expectations and students' accountability for meeting them are necessary parts of effective instruction. Students do better when they are expected to perform well and when their performance is monitored and reported on. The work of Anderson (1985) and Kagan indicates that teachers' expectations for success must be communicated clearly to the student. If unstated by the teacher, students' understandings of goals and expectations may be mistaken. Clear communication of high, realistic expectations is an integral part of learning and effective instruction. In assessing students, it is important to consider the expectations that others hold for their performance and the extent to which those expectations are communicated effectively.

Managing Instruction

Instructional outcomes are enhanced when classrooms and instruction are effectively organized. Few of us are comfortable in unstructured and chaotic situations, particularly in the classroom. Most students function better in orderly environments and with organized instruction. Cothran, Kulinna and Garrahy (2003) interviewed students and asked them what kinds of classroom management practices work best. Students reported two: the setting of clear expectations and consequences for student behavior, and building positive relationships.

Effective instruction requires managing the complex mix of instructional tasks and student behaviors that are part of every classroom. Effective classrooms are those in which there is a cooperative, pleasant atmosphere, as well as structure and order, and students are accepted and assisted in completing academic work successfully (Doyle, 1985). There are three principles of effective instructional management: (1) preparing for instruction, (2) using time productively, and (3) establishing a positive classroom environment.

Preparing for Instruction

Outcomes for students are enhanced when their teachers set rules early in the year, communicate them to the students, teach students the consequences of behavior, handle disruptions effectively (often followed by reteaching), teach consistently, and teach students to manage their own behavior. It is possible to go into classrooms, observe instruction, interview students, or interview teachers to ascertain the extent to which each of thee factors is present for an individual student.

In addition to long-term preparatory activities, teachers that immediately prepare students for instruction see enhanced student learning as well. Preteaching activities in reading include any method with which the student is provided an opportunity to read or listen to a passage before receiving instruction (Rose, 1984). Preteaching reading material before completing a reading assignment consistently led to better fluency and understanding (Rose, 1984; Rousseau & Tam, 1991; Salend & Nowak, 1988; Weinstein & Cooke, 1992). Moreover, preteaching unknown key words to children identified as learning disabled in reading led to significant gains in fluency, but comprehension more than doubled from a short intervention (Burns, Dean, & Foley, 2004). Thus, preteaching activities prepare the student for instruction and allow for more effective and efficient teaching.

Using Time Productively

The concept of time on task has driven instruction for some time. Grounded in the idea that students need ample opportunities to respond to academic and other classroom tasks, time-management strategies have become central concerns for effective teachers. Well-managed instructional environments involve well-established routines and procedures, organized physical space, short transitions between activities, few interruptions that

break the flow of classroom activities and academic, task-oriented focus, and allocation of sufficient time to academic activities (Ysseldyke & Algozzine, 1995). Effective classes are those in which time is conserved by planning activities and tasks to fit learning materials (Evertson & Harris, 1992).

When time is used productively, this maximizes the amounts of time students spend actively engaged in learning and minimizes the time spent on activities not related to learning. It is possible to gather data on the extent to which time is used productively for individual students.

Establishing a Positive Classroom Environment

Most students perform better and are more motivated when teachers interact positively with them and are supportive and helpful during learning activities. Effective teachers carefully assess the learning atmosphere in their classrooms; they "read" their students and strive to make the classroom a comfortable and supportive environment. An overriding goal in classrooms is positive interaction that fosters active student responding.

Delivering Instruction

Teaching is the systematic presentation of content assumed necessary for mastery of the subject matter. Good teaching does not happen by accident. It involves strategic planning of what to teach and the effective management of classrooms and instruction. It also involves carefully planned delivery of instruction that is focused on specific academic tasks and content areas of appropriate curricula. Algozzine and Ysseldyke (1992) identified seven principles of effective instructional delivery: (a) instruction is presented in effective ways, (b) students are motivated, (c) thinking skills are taught, (d) students are given relevant practice, (e) feedback is provided, (f) students are actively involved, and (g) instruction is modified on the basis of information on pupils' performance.

Effectively Presenting Instruction

There are empirically demonstrated effective ways to present instruction: getting students' attention, reviewing earlier lessons or skills, discussing the goals of instruction, making lessons relevant, maintaining students' attention, being enthusiastic, being organized, pacing briskly, interacting positively, communicating instructional goals and intentions, and checking that students understand what they are to do. These effective methods for presenting instruction have been incorporated into several model teaching programs including the active teaching model (Good & Grouws, 1979), the exemplary center for reading instruction (Reid, 1986, 1997), direct instruction (Adams & Carnine, 2003; Becker, Engelmann, Carnine, & Rhine, 1981), and mastery learning (Bloom, 1976; Gentile & Lalley, 2003).

Teaching Thinking Skills

An effective way to teach thinking skills is to model thinking skills. It is important to model "how to think" when instructing students in reading comprehension (Duffy, Roehler, & Rackliffe, 1985). Thinking skills are also taught by teaching fact-finding skills, divergent thinking skills, and learning strategies. Most studies of effective instruction contend that the thinking skills used in completing assignments should also be explained to students (Taylor, Peterson, Marx & Chein, 2005). It is important for teachers to check often the extent to which students understand what it is they are supposed to do.

Motivating Students

The importance of motivation for learning is undisputed in the educational and psychological literature. Instructional psychology includes the use of motivational strategies as a principle of learning, and a relationship between achievement and motivation is consistently demonstrated (Brophy, 1983; Newby, 1991). Students learn better when they are motivated. Teachers motivate students by making instruction relevant to the student's background, showing enthusiasm and interest when they present information, rewarding students on an intermittent schedule, providing an appropriate level of challenge given the child's individual skill level, and making students believe they can do the work they are assigned.

Providing Relevant Practice

There must be ample amounts of two kinds of practice—controlled (guided) or independent (seatwork or homework)—to optimize students' achievement, and the tasks should be relevant to instructional goals. Variety is important; lack of it increases boredom and potential behavior problems. Providing guided practice and independent practice, both with corrective feedback, is a desirable and monumental task (Algozzine & Ysseldyke, 2006). Even when teachers find time and creative ways to provide

students relevant practice on facts, concepts, and strategies, they often contend that staying with that practice until mastery has occurred is difficult. However, several effective drill models exist (Burns, 2005; Cooke & Reichard, 1996; MacQuarrie et al., 2002; Shapiro, 2004) that can be used to effectively deliver high repetition for individual students.

In addition to how the information is rehearsed, it is also critical that students be assigned the right amount of work so as not to overload their individual capacity. This involves a judgment made by taking into account students' characteristics, level of skill development, and past academic performance. The size of practice sets, or the number of items rehearsed, can be reliably determined by noting the number of previous items retained or by noticing student errors (Burns, 2001).

Providing Feedback

It is essential that students receive information about the quality of their performance and the extent to which they are performing in accordance with expectations (Bloom, 1985). Good teachers give students immediate, frequent, explicit feedback on their performance and behavior (Algozzine & Ysseldyke, 2006). The most effective feedback gives students increased opportunity to respond, and error-correction procedures increased reading achievement for elementary students (Reid, 1986). These procedures provided feedback in the form of cues and prompts to guide the student to the correct answer. Effective teachers maintain an atmosphere of openness and support when providing feedback, and they strive to minimize the extent to which their responses are viewed as judgmental (Algozzine et al., 1997).

Keeping Students Actively Involved

Academically engaged time is a moderate predictor of students' achievement. (Strategies that teachers use to keep students actively engaged include clear communication of goals, monitoring of students' performance, immediate and academically oriented feedback, carefully sequenced materials and tasks, appropriate pacing, use of reinforcement and praise). Allocation of sufficient time for instruction is appropriate for individual students, but it is important to look at the extent to which they are actively engaged in responding to instruction. Cognitive engagement is critical, though more difficult to assess (Taylor, Pearson, Peterson & Rodriquez,

2005). Assessment of active engagement is usually accomplished by direct observation of behavior in the classroom, but the observable behavior may not actually represent the level of substantive engagement.

Modifying or Adapting Instruction

Effective teachers make adjustments in the instructional content and approaches they use with individual students as a result of information gathered on performance. The number of options available for adapting instruction, the teacher's willingness to implement modifications, and the consistency with which modifications are used are all factors that affect adaptive instruction. Effective teachers adapt instruction by changing goals, materials, teaching methods, or task demands.

Evaluating Instruction

Evaluation is the process by which those responsible for instructing students decide whether the approaches, methods, and materials they are using are effective. It is on this basis that instructional personnel decide to refer students. Two kinds of instructional evaluation are used: (a) formative evaluation, or evaluation that occurs during instruction and is designed to provide data on progress, and (b) summative evaluation, or evaluation that occurs at the end of instruction to see whether pupils have achieved the desired outcomes. Algozzine et al. (1997) identified five principles for evaluating instruction: monitoring students' understanding, monitoring engaged time, monitoring students' activity and maintaining their records, and using data to make decisions. Assessors should document the extent to which each of these factors occurs for individual students.

Monitoring Students' Understanding

Students' perceptions of what they are to do are not always congruent with teachers' expectations and intentions (Winne & Marx, 1982). Teachers' goals must be explicitly stated, as students do not always automatically identify them. Assessors need to examine the extent to which students understand what teachers expect them to do and the process they need to go through to complete classroom assignments, as well as the methods being used by instructors to check students' success rate.

Monitoring Engaged Time

Students who are actively engaged learn more in school. Engaged time increases when instruction is paced appropriately, goals are communicated, immediate feedback is given, sequencing is appropriate, and so on. In other words, engaged time is directly related to other aspects of effective instruction. Greenwood, Carta, Kamps and Delquadri (1995) demonstrated the importance of engaged time and developed a methodology (*Ecobehavioral Assessment System Software*) for assessing it.

Monitoring Students' Activity and Maintaining Performance Records

It is important that teachers monitor pupils' performance and success rate rates and keep records of them. Record keeping can be informal or formal, but teachers should be able to indicate the extent to which students are making progress. In addition, assessors can examine the ways in which teachers have taught students to monitor their own progress.

Using Data to Make Instructional Decisions

Effective teachers use data on students' performance to make decisions about when to refer students for evaluation, to make teaching changes, and to decide when to discontinue provision of special or remedial services. Salvia and Ysseldyke (2007) described the kinds of decisions teachers make and provided detailed information on the ways in which assessment information may be used. The practice of data-driven decision making is fundamental to the practice of school psychology (Ysseldyke et al., 2006).

WHAT ARE THE HOME FACTORS THAT DETERMINE EDUCATIONAL OUTCOMES?

Ysseldyke and Christenson (2002) identified five factors in the home that support or negate what is occurring instructionally in classrooms: (a) expectations and attributions, (b) discipline orientation, (c) affective environment, (d) parental participation, and (e) structure for learning. Education takes place in both the home and the school, and it is important to take each into account.

Expectations and Attributions

Academic achievement is consistently correlated with high but realistic parental expectations. For example, we know that when parental expectations and actual performance are at similar levels, students perform better on cognitive tasks (Scott-Jones, 1984). The effects of parental expectations and attributions can also be indirect. They may influence parental behavior and also affect the extent to which parents participate in schooling. These, in turn, can affect pupils' achievement in that the relationship between parents' expectations and children's achievement was stronger than the relationships between parental behaviors and children's achievement (Halle, Kurtz-Costes & Mahoney, 1997).

Discipline Orientation

Researchers have demonstrated that specific parental discipline patterns are correlated with students' high achievement (Dornbusch, Ritter, Leiderman, 1987; Steinberg, Elmen, & Mounts, 1989). Authoritative discipline is superior to permissive or authoritarian discipline; overcontrol and undercontrol are correlated negatively with academic outcomes.

Affective Environment

Academic outcomes are usually better in situations in which parents accept children's strengths and weaknesses, nurture children, encourage them, get involved in their activities, and are emotionally responsive to their needs. Thus, a positive parent-child relationship is generally related to academic success (Ysseldyke & Christenson, 1993).

Parental Participation

Parental involvement in children's schooling at home and in school is correlated highly with positive academic outcomes and with diminished behavior problems (Fantuzzo, McWayne, Perry & Childs, 2004; Henderson, 1989). Also, students achieve more when there is a match between home and school concerning rules and expectations.

Structure for Learning

Structure includes both organization of the home environment and manipulation of that environment to support learning. Academic outcomes are better when parents provide opportunities for students to complete homework, give some assistance with school work, and monitor other activities so that students can be involved in learning.

Home-School Collaboration

Family-school partnerships are a viable and critical way to increase the opportunities and supports for all students to enhance their learning progress (Christenson, 2003; Ysseldyke & Christenson, 2002). Ysseldyke and Christenson (2002) developed a methodology for assessing the extent to which those factors are present in students' environments. In this section we provide a quick overview of the factors identified by Ysseldyke and Christenson.

Educational outcomes are enhanced when the level of expected performance held by key adults for the student is congruent across home and school, and reflects a belief that the student can learn. Moreover, professionals and parents can and should develop common goals for learning and behavior, as well as effective communication (Christenson & Sheridan, 2001). One aspect of effective communication includes overall routines and methods of monitoring (including who does it) that are agreed upon by key adults for the student, that have been discussed with the student, and are congruent across home and school.

There should also be ample opportunity to learn both in school and at home. The variety of learning options available to the youth during school hours and outside of school time (i.e., home and community) supports a student's learning outcomes. However, mutual instructional and emotional support from their teachers and parents is also critical. The guidance provided by, the communication between, and the interest shown by adults to facilitate student progress in school is effective. It is what adults do on an ongoing basis to help the student learn and achieve.

The amount of warmth and friendliness, praise and recognition, and the degree to which the adult-youth relationship is positive and respectful support and enhance student outcomes. This factor includes how adults in the home, in the school, and in the community work together to help the student be a learner. The quality of parent-teacher interactions was a better predictor of trust than the frequency of interactions, and parent trust at the high school level was significantly correlated with school performance as measured by credits earned, grade point average (GPA), and attendance (Adams & Christenson, 2000).

Finally, students need good instructional models. When parents and teachers demonstrate desired behaviors and commitment and value toward learning and working hard in their daily lives to the student, student performance is enhanced (Christenson, 2003).

How Should We Assess Educational Environments?

We have argued that assessment of instructional environments is important and necessary in designing effective instructional programs for students, and we have shown that there is a solid and extensive knowledge base on effective instruction. In short, we know that we ought to take these factors into account, and we know what to assess. But how do we do so in practice? What methods can be used to assess instructional environments?

Salvia, Ysseldyke, & Bolt (2007; in press) indicate that when a student experiences difficulty in school, two related and complementary types of assessment should be performed. First, the instruction a student has received is assessed to ascertain whether the student's difficulties stem from inappropriate curriculum or instruction. This approach has its roots in the work of Englemann, Granzin, and Severson (1979) who recommended a process they called instructional diagnosis, one designed "to determine aspects of instruction that are inadequate to find out precisely how they are inadequate, and to imply what must be done to correct their inadequacy" (p. 361). Englemann, Granzin, and Severson were focused on interactions between learners and learning tasks, and their assessments typically involved analyzing complex tasks into component parts, assessing learner skill development, and diagnosing the extent to which the learner had the skills to perform the complex task. Teaching consisted of providing students with skills, and integration of skills to enable learners to perform complex tasks.

In addition to the aforementioned assessments associated with instructional diagnosis, the assessment of instructional environments is also important (Ysseldyke & Christenson, 2002). In this section we focus on assessing instructional environments, and in *doing so, instructional challenge typically is assessed* by looking at the extent to which instruction is matched appropriately to student skill level.

There are six primary ways to gather data about instructional environments including direct observation, interviews, ratings or checklists, curriculum-based assessment and measurement, portfolios, and functional analysis or ecobehavioral assessment. We briefly describe each of these data collection methods, and we then conclude this chapter with illustrations of current instrumentation.

Observation

Observation may be either formal or informal. In formal observation, the factors to be observed are decided ahead of time, and the frequency, duration, or magnitude of their occurrence is recorded. Informal observation, in contrast, involves visiting classrooms and recording behaviors and events as they happen. Observation may be quantitative or qualitative. Quantitative observation is distinguished by five characteristics: "(a) the goal of observation is to measure (for example, count) specific behaviors; (b) the behaviors being observed have been precisely defined previously; (c) before observation, procedures for gathering objective and replicable information about the behavior are developed; (d) the times and places for observation are carefully selected and specified; and (e) the ways in which behavior will be quantified are specified prior to observation" (Salvia & Ysseldyke, 2004, p. 189). Qualitative approaches to observation are characterized by watching or listening and drawing inferences about the presence or absence of known characteristics. An observer could gather data informally on each of the instructional, home, and home-school components by knowing what to look for and observing classroom and home learning settings. Observation is the preferred method of assessing social and many academic behaviors.

Interviews

Assessment information often is collected by interviewing. When gathering data about instructional environments there usually are three sources of interview data: interviews of students, educational professionals (typically teachers and paraprofessionals), and parents/caregivers. When students are interviewed, they typically are asked to reveal common behaviors in which they engage or to identify inner feelings. When applied to assessment of instructional environments, students would be asked to describe or rate the nature of the instruction they receive including designation of approaches that work best with them; or they might be asked to show an interviewer how they did an assignment or how they know what to do when they complete an assignment before their classmates are finished.

Teacher interviews typically are designed to ascertain the kinds of instructional approaches that have been attempted with the student and the extent to which those approaches are effective. Data collected through interviews of parents/caregivers typically consist of questions about the nature of the instructional environment at home (time or structure for doing work; what parents/caregivers communicate about instruction) or questions about the kinds of approaches that parents/caregivers have found do and do not work with the child.

Rating Scales or Checklists

Checklists and rating scales are common tools and differ in their response formats. Checklists often use yes-or-no responses. For example a checklist for instructional management techniques might include teacher-directed, guided practice; independent practice; self-monitoring; or cooperative learning formats. Any or all of these could be checked by the respondent. Rating scales are generally qualitative in nature because typically respondents rank opinions or types of behaviors within some range of response. For example, in written expressive language subtests, ratings might indicate superior to average, below average, or deficient, based on writing samples of different students.

Curriculum-Based Assessment and Measurement

Frustration with norm-referenced assessments of academic achievement led to the development of several alternative assessment models. Two approaches particularly relevant to the assessment of an instructional environment were curriculum-based assessment (CBA; Gickling & Havertape, 1981) and curriculum-based measurement (CBM; Deno, 1985). CBA assesses "instructional needs of a student based upon the ongoing performance within the existing course content in order to deliver instruction as effectively as possible" (Gickling, Shane, & Croskery, 1989, pp. 344–345), whereas CBM assesses the effectiveness of instruction/intervention with fluency metrics (Burns, MacQuarrie, & Campbell, 1999). Both use frequent, short, and repeated measures, and involve product-type responses such as oral reading (Shinn, Rosenfield & Knutson, 1989). Moreover, adequate data exist for both to suggest the data are sufficiently reliable and valid for instructional decision making (Burns, 2004; Marston, 1989).

Although CBA and CBM are quite similar in appearance, fundamental differences exist (Burns et al., 1999). From an instructional environment perspective, the goal of CBA is instructional planning rather than measuring intervention

effectiveness, in that CBA data are used to identify appropriate instructional material and specific interventions (Burns et al., 1999). Moreover, CBA addresses the planning, managing and delivery phases of instruction, but CBM assesses instructional effectiveness (Burns, Dean, & Klar, 2004). Therefore, the two approaches used together provide data that can assess the appropriateness of the instructional material for the individual student while examining if the individual child is sufficiently responding to the instruction (Burns et al., 2004). Research has consistently found that each of these approaches led to enhanced student learning (Burns, 2007; Cundari & Suppa, 1988; Gickling & Armstrong, 1978), and the two in concert resulted in a particularly effective assessment to intervention model (Burns, 2002).

Portfolios

The use of portfolios in schools is one attempt to provide more relevant assessment to enhance instructional decision making and the evaluation of students' progress. Portfolios are purposeful collections of work that compile multiple samples of student performance through an extended time period to demonstrate effort, progress, and achievement (Paulson, Paulson, & Meyer, 1991; Taylor & Nolen, 2005).

Portfolio assessment evolved from the authentic assessment movement of the 1980s, in which professionals in education and other fields desired an assessment model that was more closely related to actual learning tasks and job requirements (Alper et al., 2001). Thus, they could be a particularly relevant assessment of academic achievement within an instructional environmental model. Several different models of portfolio assessment have been introduced and deciding which to use should be based on the purpose of the assessment. Although the profession is far from reaching a consensus about what constitutes a portfolio, recent research found a reliability coefficient of .91 and sufficient evidence for valid decisions from the data as long as scoring is based on specific and objective rubrics (Burns & Haight, 2005).

Functional Analysis or Ecobehavioral Assessment

A rapidly developing area in the field of assessing instructional environments, specifically applied to behavior analysis, is ecobehavioral analysis, the observation of functional relationships or interactions between the student's behavior and its ecological contexts. Ecobehavioral assessment takes into consideration the importance of situation or contextual factors. This approach is used to identify interactions among students' behavior, teachers' behavior, time allocated to instruction, physical grouping structures, types of tasks, and instructional content. Ecobehavioral assessment enables educators to identify natural instructional conditions associated with academic success, behavioral competence, or challenging behaviors. It also provides a means to gather data on the opportunity to learn, an important component of Carroll's (1963) model of school learning.

ASSESSMENT METHODS AND INSTRUMENTS

There are several kinds of instruments and methodologies used to gather data on instructional environments and on the extent to which effective instruction is occurring for individual students.

The *Instructional Priority System* (IPS) is a brief but thorough qualitative rating scale that bases students' instructional needs on expectations and demands of the instructional environment (Welch & Link, 1991). Specifically, the IPS is used to gather information from the special educator, student, and content area teacher to (a) clarify teachers' expectations and classroom demands, (b) determine the degree to which the student is able to meet identified classroom expectations and demands, (c) identify areas in which students are having problems, and (d) decide which problem to address first.

The *Analysis of Classroom and Instructional Demands* (ACID; West, 1999) is an inventory designed to identify and describe the demands of the instructional environment. A teacher or observer rates the target student's ability to meet instructional expectations. The ACID test rates nine areas of students' behavior in the context of the instructional environment: classroom rules, instructional content, presentation, assignment completion, group work, instructional materials, study skills, test taking, and grading procedures.

The checklists (IPS and ACID) have in common the fact that they do not specifically assess the components of effective instruction, and they do not enable drawing functional relationships between contextual factors and student academic performance. A quantitative, computer-enhanced assessment system was developed by Greenwood, Carta, Delquadri, Arreaga-Mayer, Utley and their colleagues at Juniper Gardens Children's Center at the University of Kansas for the purpose of gathering information on functional relationships or interactions between multiple aspects of student behavior, teacher behavior, instructional content, and contextual factors. The first version of ecobehavioral assessment was a paper-and-pencil coding system developed by Stanley & Greenwood (1981) and was called the *Code for Instructional Structure and Student Academic Response* (CISSAR). The CISSAR eventually evolved into a laptop computer observational system. The taxonomy for the current CISSAR is shown in Figure 21.1. This system allows assessors to categorize ecobehavioral events into students' and teachers' behaviors, as well as to consider the ecology of the classroom. Using momentary time sampling, behaviors are recorded over the entire school day. The frequency of occurrence and the interactions among behaviors and environmental stimuli are analyzed.

Increasingly, ecobehavioral assessment is being used to develop and validate specific instructional procedures, develop a number of approaches to the reduction of challenging behaviors, improve understanding of the components of effective instruction (including the identification of instructional risk factors), and provide a better understanding of how the quality of instructional implementation affects student outcomes (Greenwood, Carta, & Atwater, 1991; Greenwood, Abbott & Tapia, 2003). Ecobehavioral assessment is one way to gather data on the opportunity to learn, an important component of Carroll's Model of School Learning and the Algozzine-Ysseldyke Model of Effective Instruction.

CISSAR uses momentary time sampling (10-second intervals) over the entire school day. Observers record the ecology (specific activity, task used to control instruction, and class structure), teacher behavior (teacher position and actions), and student behavior (academic responses, competing responses, and task-management responses). After observational data have been recorded, the assessor can determine the frequency of occurrence of specific behaviors and the interactions among behaviors and environmental stimuli.

Three derivatives of CISSAR have been developed since the late 1980s. One of these, *Ecobehavioral System for Complex Assessments of Preschool Environments* (ESCAPE), was developed for use with preschool children. Another, mainstream version of CISSAR (MS-CISSAR), was designed to be used in observations of students with disabilities in general education

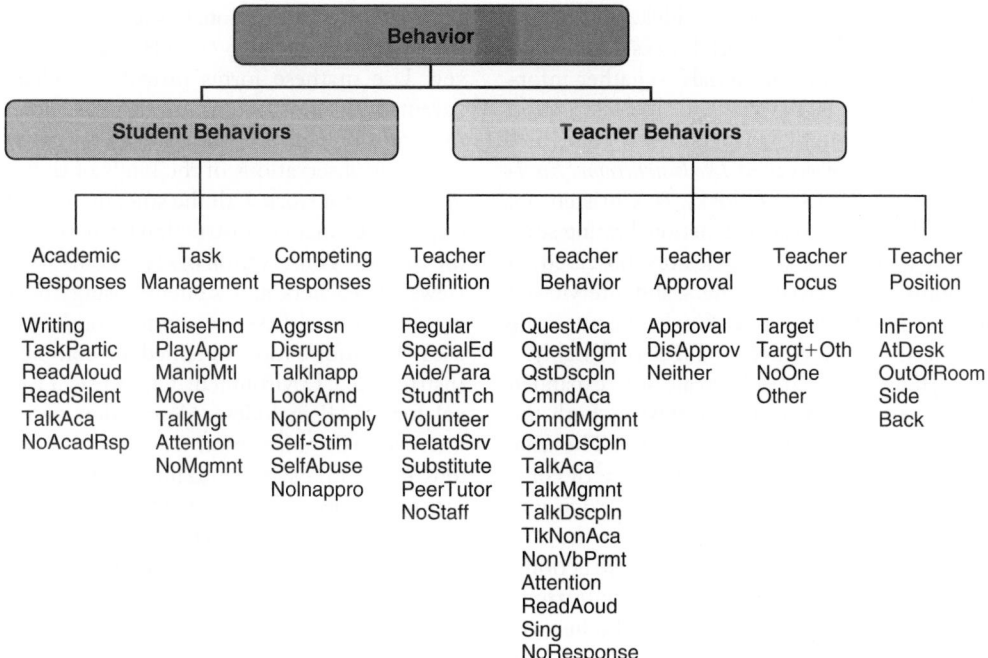

FIGURE 21.1   MS-CISSAR taxonomy.

classes. (The MS-CISSAR taxonomy is shown in Figure 21.1.) The third, *Ecobehavioral System for the Contextual Recording of Interactional Bilingual Environments* (ESCRIBE; Arreaga-Mayer, Carta & Tapia, 1992) is designed for ecobehavioral assessment of bilingual students and classes for English language learners. The four derivative ecobehavioral-assessment systems (CISSAR, ESCAPE, ESCRIBE, and MS-CISSAR) have been combined in a new software program, *Ecobehavioral Assessment System Software* (EBASS; Greenwood, Carta, Kamps, & Delquadri, 1995).

EBASS is a software system that enables school personnel to conduct systematic classroom observational assessments using laptop, notebook, or hand-held computers. EBASS was designed specifically for school psychologists, but it may be used by other professionals responsible for assessment, teacher training, and program evaluation activities, including instructional staff in general and special education. Typical applications include assessments of individual students for the purpose of planning instructional interventions, evaluating individual pupil progress, and evaluating educational programs. Computerization allows computer-assisted training in instrument use, calibration of reliability checks, instrument modification (each of the three measures can be downsized into shorter measures), simple and complex data analyses, caseload management, and database capabilities.

The classroom observer decides which observational instrument is appropriate (ESCAPE, CISSAR, or MS-CISSAR) and goes into classrooms with a portable computer to gather data in 10-second intervals. The training package available with EBASS is used for teaching observers what to look for and how to code behaviors. The training system is self-instructional and includes short lessons, classroom video examples, computer exercises with feedback, and observational practice. It takes about 8 to 10 hours to learn any of the three instruments, and additional time is needed for practice in data collection. Reports from an observation may consist of percentage occurrence for all events or probabilities of student behavior given specific arrangements of the classroom ecology. These latter probabilities are called "conditional probabilities." The computer can generate reports based on a single observation, on observations sequenced by time of observation, and on observations pooled over time. The professional who uses EBASS is able to give the teacher information on academic engaged time, the occurrence of inappropriate behavior, and the occurrence of task-management responses. The strength of EBASS is that it provides precise information on the frequency of occurrence of specific kinds of behaviors (such as writing, playing inappropriately, waiting, and engaging in disruptive behavior) and on the kinds of contextual factors associated with the occurrence of each of the behaviors.

Over the past 20 years Ysseldyke and Christenson have developed a set of devices designed to enable educational professionals to gather information on the extent to which effective instruction is occurring for individual students. The first device developed was called *The Instructional Environment Scale* (TIES; Ysseldyke & Christenson, 1987). TIES included an instructional rating scale that was completed after assessors observed in classrooms, interviewed teachers, and interviewed students. The Instructional Environment Scale was revised and published as TIES II (Ysseldyke & Christenson, 1993). The scale was expanded to enable assessment in the context of both the classroom and the home environments. The scale took into account not only the presence of components of effective instruction in the classroom and home but also their importance to the student's performance in school. The 12 instructional components and five home-support-for-learning components were nearly identical to the instructional and home components described earlier in this chapter.

In 2002 Ysseldyke and Christenson revised TIES-II and published the revision as the *Functional Assessment of Academic Behavior* (FAAB; Ysseldyke & Christenson). Using information gained from interviews with the students, teachers, and parents helps formulate interventions options. In addition, structured classroom observations are preplanned with the teacher and observers to understand the learning goals and objectives prior to the observation. Thus, the observation can be recorded in the context of classroom expectations. FAAB is used to help professionals gather essential information on 12 instructional environment components, five home-support-for-learning components, and six home-school-support-for-learning components. The components on which data are collected are listed and defined briefly in Table 21.1. FAAB is a flexible system that allows professionals to select the data-collection tools they will use. Among the tools available for use are four required forms (The Instructional Environment Checklist annotated or nonannotated form, Instructional Needs Checklist, a survey of Parental Experience with Their Child's Learning and Schoolwork, and an Intervention Documentation Record) and four optional forms (Observation Record, Student Interview Record, Teacher Interview Record, and Parent Interview Record).

Users of FAAB typically start their assessment of the instructional environment for an individual student by asking the student's teacher to complete the Instructional Needs Checklist and the parent/caregiver to complete the Parent survey. Use of these forms provides teachers and parents with an opportunity to share their perspectives on the nature of the student's performance and their observations of the kinds of things that do and do not work with the student. The second step in assessment of instructional environments is the assessor's observation of classrooms and interviews of teachers and students using the forms provided. Once these are completed, the assessor uses the information obtained to complete the Instructional Environment Checklist. The manual for FAAB includes a description of how an instructional intervention team can use the various forms in a systematic intervention planning process. It also includes an extensive set of interventions that may be selected and implemented to meet student needs in specific components.

CONCLUSIONS

Learning happens when the learning environment is modified to facilitate an appropriate response from the student. School psychology has a rich history and tradition of assessing students in order to identify causes of academic and behavioral difficulties and to develop interventions. Recently the focus has shifted to the belief that the initial focal point for efforts to close the gap between actual and desired student performance is to apply principles of effective instruction. Doing so requires knowledge of the principles, and systematic identification of the extent to which the learner is getting an opportunity to learn and is being engaged actively in learning. It requires identification of the extent to which evidence-based components of effective instruction (as they occur in classrooms, homes, and the partnership between classrooms and homes) are present in students' environments. A major shift is taking place in the practice of school psychologists, a shift away from a child-centered deficit model to an ecological model in which as much time and energy are devoted to assessing the instructional environment as to assessing the student. The focus of assessment is on intervention planning, and intervention begins with making changes in the nature of instruction.

This focus on assessing instructional environments is becoming more prevalent for four major reasons: (a) multiple factors affect academic outcomes, (b) learning does not occur in a vacuum, (c) there are limits to assessing a learner, and (d) to put content into consultation. In the past, assessment of instructional environment has been limited to observation, interaction analyses, and interviews. There is an extensive knowledge based on the instructional factors that influence academic outcomes, as well as on the home factors that also interact to influence outcomes.

Until recently there were no systematic methodologies for assessing instructional environments. Several alternative approaches are now available that build on the previous technologies. We described some recently developed instruments to assess instructional environments. The success of these approaches depends on several alterable variables that are in direct control of those who choose to implement them.

The emphasis on directly assessing changeable environmental variables stems from a long and rich history in applied behavior analysis. As such, there are many studies that support the instructional utility of these data. However, reliability data for most of these instructional environment assessments, including FAAB, are lacking. Future researchers should consider evaluating the interobserver agreement of the various components of the assessments. Validity of decisions made from the data could be inferred from previous applied behavior analysis studies that focused on classroom environments, but explicit investigation of these tools is also mostly lacking. It would be somewhat difficult to adequately study this question, using randomized controlled trials, because the level of experimental control needed would be almost impossible to achieve within an applied setting. Having said that, researchers could examine student outcomes before and after using FAAB data with a multiple-baseline design using classrooms as the participants. Other designs could also address the question with varying degrees of causal validity and all could probably make an important contribution to the assessment-to-intervention literature.

Over the years, education has created the refer-test-place and the dual system monsters. It is now time to tame them. The past practice of assessing students has been not only familiar but comfortable. Accountability has been minimal or protected by a smoke screen of bureaucracy. Too long we have rested on historical, testimonial, and cash-validated practices. The band wagons have come and gone, yet many children are not benefiting from the instruction they receive. Now is as good a time as ever to explore proactively, to introduce building-based teams, and to use effective methods of assessing instructional environments for the good of all learners.

REFERENCES

Achenbach, T. M. (1985). *Child behavior checklist.* Burlington, VT: University of Vermont, Department of Psychiatry.

Achenbach, T. M. (1986). *The direct observation form (DOF).* Burlington, VT: University of Vermont, Department of Psychiatry.

Achenbach, T. M. (1991). *Teacher's report form.* Burlington, VT: University of Vermont, Department of Psychiatry.

Adams, G. & Carnine, D. (2003). Direct instruction. In L. Swanson, K. Harris, & S. Graham, (Eds.), *Handbook of Learning Disabilities.* New York: Guilford Press, pp. 403–416.

Adams, K. & Christenson, S. L. (2000). Trust and the family-school relationship: Examination of parent-teacher differences in elementary and secondary grades. *Journal of School Psychology, 38*(5), 477–497.

Algozzine, B. A. & Ysseldyke, J. E. (1992). *Strategies and tactics for effective instruction.* Longmont, CO: Sopris West.

Algozzine, B. A. & Ysseldyke, J. E. (2006). *Effective instruction: A practical approach to special education for every teacher.* Thousand Oaks, CA: Corwin Press.

Algozzine, B. A. & Ysseldyke, J. E. & Elliott, J. (1997). *Strategies and tactics for effective instruction* 2nd ed. Longmont, CO: Sopris West.

Alper, S., Ryndak, D. L. & Schloss, C. N. (2001). *Alternative assessment of students with disabilities in inclusive settings.* Needham Heights, MA: Allyn and Bacon.

Anderson, L. M. (1985). What are students doing when they do all that seatwork? In C. W. Fisher & D. C. Berliner, (Eds.), *Perspectives on instructional time.* New York: Longman, pp. 189–202.

Arreaga-Mayer, C., Carta, J. & Tapia, Y. (1992). *ESCRIBE: Ecobehavioral system for the contextual recording of interactional bilingual environments.* Kansas City, KS: Juniper Gardens Children's Project, University of Kansas.

Astleitner, H. (2005). Principles of effective instruction: General standards for teachers and instructional designers. *Journal of Instructional Psychology, 32,* 3–8.

Ayyash-Abdo, H. (2002). Adolescent suicide: An ecological approach. *Psychology in the Schools, 39,* 459–475.

Baker, J. A. (1998). Are we missing the forest for the trees? Considering the social context of school violence. *Journal of School Psychology, 36,* 29–44.

Bateman, B. (1990). *Academic child abuse: By the study group, International Institute for Advocacy for School Children.* Eugene, OR: International Institute for Advocacy for School Children.

Batsche, G., Elliott, J., Graden, J. L., Grimes, J., Kovaleski, J. F., Prasse, D., et al. (2005). *Response to intervention: Policy considerations and implementation.* Alexandria, VA: National Association of State Directors of Special Education.

Becker, W., Englemann, S., Carnine, D. et al. (1981). The direct instruction model. In R. Rhine (Ed.), Encouraging change in America's schools: A decade of experimentation, (pp. 45–83). New York: Academic Press.

Blair, T. R. (1984). Teacher effectiveness: The know-how to improve student learning. *The Reading Teacher, 38*, 138–142.

Bloom, B. (1976). *Human characteristics and student learning.* New York: McGraw-Hill.

Braskamp, L. A., & Maehr, M. L. (1988). *Instructional Climate Inventory: Form S.* Champaign, IL: MetriTech, Inc.

Bronfenbrenner, U. (1986). Ecology of the family as a context for human development: Research perspectives. *Developmental Psychology, 22*, 723–742.

Brophy, J. (1983). Classroom organization and management. *The Elementary School Journal, 83*, 254–285.

Burns, M. K. (2001). Measuring acquisition and retention rates with curriculum-based assessment. *Journal of Psychoeducational Assessment, 19*, 148–157.

Burns, M. K. (2004). Using curriculum-based assessment in the consultative process: A review of three levels of research. *Journal of Educational and Psychological Consultation, 15*, 63–78.

Burns, M. K. (2005). Using incremental rehearsal to practice multiplication facts with children identified as learning disabled in mathematics computation. *Education and Treatment of Children, 28*, 237–249.

Burns, M. K. (2007). Using curriculum-based assessment to match instruction and skill: Implications for response to intervention. *School Psychology Quarterly, 22*, 297–313.

Burns, M. K., Dean, V. J., & Foley, S. (2004). Preteaching unknown key words with incremental rehearsal to improve reading fluency and comprehension with children identified as reading disabled. *Journal of School Psychology, 42*, 303–314.

Burns, M. K., Dean, V. J., & Klar, S. (2004). Using curriculum-based assessment in the responsiveness to intervention diagnostic model for learning disabilities. *Assessment for Effective Intervention, 29*(3), 47–56.

Burns, M. K., & Haight, S. L. (2005). Psychometric properties and instructional utility of assessing special education teacher candidate knowledge with portfolios. *Teacher Education and Special Education, 28*, 185–194.

Burns, M. K., Vance, D., Szadokierski, I., & Stockwell, C. (2006). Student needs survey: A psychometrically sound measure of the five basic needs. *International Journal of Reality Therapy, 25*(2), 4–8.

Burns, M. K., MacQuarrie, L. L., & Campbell, D. T. (1999). The difference between curriculum-based assessment and curriculum-based measurement: A focus on purpose and result. *Communiqué, 27*(6), 18–19.

Carroll, J. (1963). A model of school learning. *Teachers College Record, 64*, 723–733.

Cundari, L. A., & Suppa, R. J. (1988). The potential uses of curriculum-based assessment for decision making in special education. *Exceptional Child, 35*, 143–154.

Christenson, S. (2003). The family-school partnership: An opportunity to promote the learning competence of all students. *School Psychology Quarterly, 18*(4), 454–482.

Christenson, S. L. & Sheridan, S. M. (2001). *Schools and families: Creating essential connections for learning.* New York: Guilford Press.

Cooke, N. L., Reichard, S. M. (1996). The effects of different interspersal drill ratios on acquisition and generalization of multiplication and division facts. *Education & Treatment of Children, 19*, 124–142.

Cothran, D. J., Kulinna, P. H. & Garrahy, D. S. (2003). This is kind of giving the secret away. . .": Students perspectives on effective class management. *Teaching and Teacher Education, 19*, 435–444.

Crosby, E. G., & French, J. L. (2002). Psychometric data for teacher judgments regarding the learning behaviors of primary grade children. *Psychology in the Schools, 39*, 235–244.

Daly, E. J., Martens, B. K., Kilmer, A. & Massie, D. R. (1996). The effects of instructional match and content overlap on generalized reading performance. *Journal of Applied Behavior Analysis, 29*(4), 507–518.

Dean, V. J., Burns, M. K., Grialou, T., & Varro, P. J. (2006). Comparison of ecological validity of learning disabilities diagnostic models. *Psychology in the Schools, 43*, 157–168.

Deno, S. L. (1985). Curriculum-based measurement: The emerging alternative. *Exceptional Children, 52*, 219–232.

Dornbusch, S. M., Ritter, P. L., Leiderman, P. H. et al. (1987). The relation of parenting style to adolescent school performance. *Child Development, 58*, 1244–1257.

Doyle, W. (1985). Classroom organization and management. In M. C. Wittrock (Ed), *Handbook of research on teaching* (3rd edition, pp. 392–431). New York: MacMillan,.

Duffy, G. G. Roehler, L. R. & Rackliffe, G. (1985). *Qualitative differences in teachers' instructional talk as they influence student awareness of lesson content.* Paper presented at the American Educational Research Association Conference, Chicago.

Edmonds, R. R. (1979). Some schools work and more can. *Social Policy, 9*, 28–32.

Englemann, S., Granzin, A. & Severson, H. (1979). Diagnosing instruction. *Journal of Special Education, 13*, 355–365.

Englert, C. (1984). Effective direct instruction practices in special education settings. *Remedial and Special Education, 5*(2), 38–47.

Evertson, C. M., & Harris, A. H. (1992). What we know about managing classrooms. *Educational Leadership, 49,* 74–78.

Fantuzzo, J., McWayne, C., Perry, M. S., & Childs, S. (2004). Multiple dimensions of family involvement and their relationships to behavioral and learning competencies for urban, low-income children. *School Psychology Review, 33*(4), 467–480.

Flanders, N. A. (1970) *Analyzing teaching behaviour.* Reading, MA: Addison-Wesley.

Gentile, J. R. & Lalley, J. P. (2003). *Standards and mastery learning: Aligning teaching and assessment so all children can learn.* Thousand Oaks, CA: Corwin Press.

Gickling, E. E., & Armstrong, D. L. (1978). Levels of instructional difficulty as related to on-task behavior, task completion, and comprehension. *Journal of Learning Disability, 11,* 559–566.

Gickling, E. E. & Havertape, S. (1981). *Curriculum-based assessment (CBA).* Minneapolis, MN: School Psychology Inservice Training Network.

Gickling, E. E., Shane, R. L., & Croskery, K. M. (1989). Developing math skills in low-achieving high school students through curriculum-based assessment. *School Psychology Review, 18,* 344–356.

Good, T. & Brophy, J. (1984) *Looking in classrooms.* New York: Harper & Row.

Good, T. & Grouws, D. A. (1979). The Missouri mathematics effectiveness project: An experimental study in fourth grade classrooms. *Journal of Educational Psychology, 71,* 355–362.

Gravois, T., Rosenfield, S., & Gickling, E. (1999). *Instructional consultation teams: Training manual.* College Park: University of Maryland, Instructional Consultation Lab.

Greenberg, M. T., Weissberg, R. P., Utne O'Brien, M., Zins, J. E., Fredericks, L., Resnik, H., & Elias, M. J. (2003). Enhancing school-based prevention and youth development through coordinated social, emotional, and academic learning. *American Psychologist, 58,* 466–474.

Greenwood, C. R., Carta, J. J., & Atwater, J. (1991). Ecobehavioral analysis in the classroom: Review and implications. *Journal of Behavioral Education, 1,* 59–77.

Greenwood, C. R., Carta, J. J., Kamps, D., & Arreaga-Mayer, C. (1990). Ecobehavioral analysis of classroom instruction. In S. R. Schroeder (Ed.), *Ecobehavioral analysis and developmental disabilities: The twenty-first century* (pp. 33–63). New York: Springer-Verlag.

Greenwood, C. R., Carta, J. J., Kamps, D., & Delquadri, J. (1995). *Ecobehavioral Assessment System Software.* Kansas City, KS: Juniper Gardens Children's Center.

Greenwood, C. R., Abbott, M., & Tapia, Y. (2003) Ecobehavioral strategies: Observing, measuring and analyzing behavior and reading interventions for inclusion. In S. Vaughn & K. L. Briggs (Eds.), *Reading in the classroom: Systems for observing teaching and learning,* Baltimore: Brookes.

Halle, T. G., Kurtz-Costes, B. & Mahoney, J. L. (1997). Family influences on school achievement in low-income, African American children. *Journal of Educational Psychology, 89,* 527–537.

Henderson, A. T. (1989). *The evidence continues to grow: Parent involvement improves student achievement.* Columbia, MD: National Committee for Citizens in Education.

Herman, K. C., Merrell, K. W., Reinke, W. M., & Tucker, C. M. (2004). The role of school psychology in preventing depression. *Psychology in the Schools, 41,* 763–775.

Hintze, J. M. & Matthews, W. J. (2004). The generalizability of systematic direct observations across time and setting: A preliminary investigation of the psychometrics of behavioral observations. *School Psychology Review, 33,* 258–270.

Hoge, R. D., & Coladarci, T. (1989). Teacher-based judgments of academic achievement: A review of literature. *Review of Educational Research, 59,* 297–313.

Kagan, D. M. (1992). Implications of research on teacher beliefs. *Educational Psychologist, 27*(1), 65–90.

Kagan, D. M. (1990). How schools alienate students at risk: A model for examining proximal classroom variables. *Educational Psychologist, 25,* 105–125.

Kavale, K. A. & Forness, S. R. (2000). Policy decisions in special education: The role of meta-analysis. In R. Gersten, E. P. Schiller, & S. Vaughn (Eds.), *Contemporary special education research: Synthesis of the knowledge base on critical instructional issues* (pp. 281–326). Mahway, NJ: Lawrence Erlbaum Associates.

Krug, S. E., Ahadi, S. A., & Scott, C. K. (1991). Current issues and research findings in the study of school leadership. In P. Thurston & P. Zodiates (Eds.), *Advances in educational administration* (Vol. 2, pp. 241–260). Greenwich, CT: JAI.

MacQuarrie, L. L., Tucker, J. A., Burns, M. K., & Hartman, B. (2002). Comparison of retention rates using traditional, Drill Sandwich, and Incremental Rehearsal flashcard methods. *School Psychology Review, 31,* 584–595.

Maehr, M. L., & Ames, R. (1988). *Instructional leadership inventory.* Champaign, IL: MetriTech.

Mann, L. (1979). On the trail of process. New York: Grune & Stratton.

Marston, D. B. (1989). A curriculum-based measurement approach to assessing academic performance: What it is and why do it. In M. R. Shinn (Ed.), *Curriculum-based measurement: Assessing special children* (pp. 18–78). New York: Guilford Press.

Marzano, R. J., Pickering, D. J., & Pollock, J. E. (2001). *Classroom instruction that works: Research-based strategies for increasing student achievement.* Alexandria, VA: Association for Supervision and Curriculum Development.

McCarney, S. & Leigh, J. E. (1990). *Behavior evaluation scale-2.* Columbus, OH: Hawthorne Educational Services.

Merrell, K. W. (2007). *Behavioral, social, and emotional assessment of children (3rd ed.).* New York, NY: Routledge.

Newby, T. J. (1991). Classrooms motivation: Strategies of first-year teachers. *Journal of Educational Psychology, 83,* 195–200.

Ochoa, S. H., Riccio, C., Jimenez, S., de Alba, R. G., & Sines, M. (2004). Psychological assessment of English language learners and/or bilingual students: An investigation of school psychologists' current practice. *Journal of Psychoeducational Assessment, 22,* 185–208.

Overstreet, S., & Mazza J. (2003). An ecological-transactional understanding of community violence: Theoretical perspectives. *School Psychology Quarterly, 18,* 66–87.

Paulson, F. L., Paulson, P. R., & Meyer, C. A. (1991). What makes a portfolio? *Educational Leadership, 48*(5), 60–63.

Reid, E. (1986). *The reader newsletter.* Salt Lake City, UT: Exemplary Center for Reading Instruction.

Reid, E. (1997). *The reader newsletter.* Salt Lake City, UT: Exemplary Center for Reading Instruction.

Reid, E. R. (1997). Exemplary Center for Reading Instruction (ECRI). *Behavior and Social Issues, 7*(1), 19–24.

Reith, H. & Evertson, C. (1988). Variables related to the effective instruction of difficult-to-teach children. *Focus on Exceptional Children, 20,* 2–7.

Reschly, D. & Ysseldyke, J. E. (1995). The paradigm shift in school psychology. In A. Thomas & J. Grimes (Eds.), *Best practices in school psychology III.* Washington, DC: National Association of School Psychologists.

Reschly, D. & Ysseldyke, J. E. (2002). Paradigm shift: The past is not the future. In A. Thomas & J. Grimes (Eds.). *Best Practices in School Psychology IV.* Bethesda, MD: National Association of School Psychologists.

Reschly, D. J. (2003, December). *What if LD identification changed to reflect research findings?: Consequences of LD identification changes.* Paper presented at the Responsiveness-to-Intervention Symposium, Kansas City, MO.

Reynolds, C. & Kamphaus, R. (2004). *Student Observation System of the Behavioral assessment system for children–2nd ed.* Circle Pines, MN: Pearson.

Reynolds, C. R. & Gutkin, T. B. (Eds.). (1999). *The Handbook of School Psychology.* (3rd ed.). New York: J. Wiley & Sons.

Rose, T. L. (1984). The effects of previewing on retarded learners' oral reading. *Education and Training of the Mentally Retarded, 19,* 49–53.

Rosenshine, B. (1983) Teaching functions in instructional programs. *The Elementary School Journal, 83,* 335–351.

Rosenshine, B. & Stevens, R. (1986). Teaching functions. In M.C. Wittrock (Ed.), *Handbook of research on teaching (3rd edition)* (pp. 376–391). New York: MacMillan.

Rousseau, M. K., & Yung Tam, B. K. (1991). The efficacaty of previewing and discussion of key words on the oral reading proficiency of bilingual learners with speech and langauge impairments. *Education and Treatment of Children, 14,* 199–209.

Salend, S. J., & Nowak, M. R. (1988). Effects of peer-previweing on LD students oral reading skills. *Learning Disability Quarterly, 10,* 47–53.

Salvia, J., & Ysseldyke, J. (2004). *Assessment in special and inclusive education (9th edition).* Boston: Houghton-Mifflin.

Salvia, J., Ysseldyke, J. & Bolt, S. (2007). *Assessment in special and inclusive education (10th edition).* Boston: Houghton-Mifflin.

Saracho, O. N. (1991). Teacher expectations of students' performance: A review of the research. *Early Childhood Development and Care, 76,* 27–41.

Sarason, S. B. & Doris, J. (1979). *Educational handicap, public policy, and social history.* New York: Free Press.

Scott-Jones (1984). Family influences on cognitive developmental and school achievement. *Review of Research in Education, 11,* 259–304.

Shapiro, E. (2004). *Behavioral observation of students in schools.* San Antonio, TX: Pearson.

Shapiro, E. S. (2004). *Academic skills problems: Direct assessment and intervention (3rd Ed.).* New York: Guilford Press.

Sheridan, S. M., & Gutkin, T. B. (2000). The ecology of school psychology: Examining and changing out paradigm for the 21st century. *School Psychology Review, 29,* 485–502.

Shinn, M. R., Rosenfield, S., & Knutson, N. (1989). Curriculum-based assessment: A comparison of models. *School Psychology Review, 18,* 299–316.

Sparrow, S., Cicchetti, D. & Balla, D. (2005). *Vineland adaptive behavior scales (2nd edition).* Circle Pines, MN: Pearson.

Squires, D. A., Huitt, W. G. & Segars, J. K. (1984). *Effective schools and classrooms: A research-based perspective.* Alexandria, VA: Association for Supervision and Curriculum Development.

Stanley, S. O., & Greenwood, C. R. (1981). *CISSAR: Code for instructional structure and student academic response: Observer's manual.* Kansas City, KS: Juniper Gardens Children's Project, Bureau of Child Research, University of Kansas.

Steinberg, L., Elmen, J. D., & Mounts, N. S. (1989). Authoritative parenting, psychosocial maturity, and academic success among adolescents. *Child Development, 60,* 1424–1436.

Steinhausen, H. C. & Reitzle, M. (1996). The validity of mixed disorders of conduct and emotions in children and adolescents: A research note. *Journal of Child Psychology and Psychiatry, 37*, 339–343.

Stevens, R. & Rosenshine, B. (1982) Advances in research on teaching. *Exceptional Education Quarterly, 2*(1), 1–9.

Swearer, S. M., & Doll, B. (2001). Bullying in schools: An ecological framework. In R. A. Geffner, M. Loring, & C. Young (Eds.) *Bullying behavior: Current issues, research, and intervention* (pp. 7–23). Binghamton, NY: Haworth Maltreatment and Trauma Press.

Taylor, C. S., & Nolen, S. B. (2005). *Classroom assessment: Supporting teaching and learning in real classrooms.* Upper Saddle River, NJ: Pearson Education.

Taylor, B. M. Peterson, D. S., Marx, M. & Chein M. (2005). *Scaling up a reading reform in high-poverty schools.* Paper presented at the third Guy Bond Memorial Conference on Reading. St. Paul, MN: University of Minnesota Center for Research on Reading.

Taylor, B. M., Pearson, P. D., Peterson, D.S., & Rodriquez, M. (2005). Reading growth in high-poverty classrooms: The influence of teacher practices that encourage cognitive engagement in literacy learning. *Elementary School Journal, 104*, 3–28.

Taylor, B. M., Peterson, D. S., Pearson, P. D., & Rodriquez, M. (2002). Looking inside classrooms: Reflecting on the "how" as well as the "what" in effective reading instruction. *The Reading Teacher, 56*, 70–79.

Tilly, W. D. III. (2002). School psychology as a problem solving enterprise. In A. Thomas & J. Grimes (Eds.), *Best practices in school psychology IV* (pp. 25–36). Bethesda, MD: National Association of School Psychologists.

Tilly, W. D. III., Reschly, D. J., & Grimes, J. P. (1999). Disability determination in problem solving systems: Conceptual foundations and critical components. In D. J. Rschly, W. D. Tilly III, & J. P. Grimes (Eds.), *Special education in transition: Functional assessment and noncategorical programming.* Longmont, CO: Sopris West.

Treptow, M. A., Burns, M. K., & McComas, J. J. (2007). Reading at the frustration, instructional, and independent levels: Effects on student time on task and comprehension. *School Psychology Review, 36*, 159–166.

VanDerHeyden, A. M., & Burns, M. K. (2005). Effective instruction for at-risk minority populations. In C. L. Frisby & C. R. Reynolds (Eds.) *Comprehensive handbook of multicultural school psychology.* Hoboken, NJ: John Wiley & Sons

Vaughn, S., Wanzek, J., & Fletcher, J. M. (2007). Multiple tiers of intervention: A framework for prevention and identification of students with reading/learning disabilities. In B. M. Taylor & J. E. Ysseldyke (Eds.), *Effective instruction for struggling readers, K-6* (pp. 173–195). New York: Teacher's College Press.

Vaughn, S., Gersten, R., & Chard, D. (2000). The underlying message in LD intervention research. *Council for Exceptional Children, 67*, 99–114.

Volpe, R. J., DiPerna, J. C., Hintze, J. M., & Shapiro, E. S. (2005). Observing students in the classroom settings: A review of seven coding systems. *School Psychology Review, 34*, 454–474.

Walker, H. & Severson, H. (1992). *Systematic screening for behavior disorders (2nd edition).* Longmont, CO: Sopris West.

Weinstein, G., & Cooke, N. L. (1992). The effects of two repeated reading interventions on generalization of fluency. *Learning Disability Quarterly, 15*, 21–28.

Welch, M. & Link, D. (1991). The instructional priority system: A method for assessing the educational environment. *Intervention in School and Clinic, 14*, 121–132.

West, F. (1999). Making effective instructional decisions in inclusive settings. In T. P. Lombardi (Ed.) *Inclusion: Policy and practice* (pp. 35–42). Bloomington, IN: Phi Delta Kappa Educational Foundation.

Wilson, M. S., & Reschly, D. J. (1996). Assessment in school psychology training and practice. *School Psychology Review, 25*, 9–23.

Winne, P. H. & Marx, R. W. (1982). Students' and teachers' views of thinking processes for classroom learning. *Elementary School Journal, 82*, 493–518.

Wittrock, M. C. (1985). *Handbook of research on teaching (3rd ed.).* New York: MacMillan.

Worrell, F. C. (2000). The reliability and validity of the instructional climate-inventory—student form. *Psychology in the Schools, 37*, 291–298.

Ysseldyke, J. E. & Algozzine, B. A. (1995). *Special education: A practical approach for teachers.* Boston: Houghton-Mifflin.

Ysseldyke, J. E. & Christenson, S. (1993). *The instructional environment system—II.* Longmont, CO: Sopris West.

Ysseldyke, J. E. & Christenson, S. L. (1987) *The instructional environment scale: A comprehensive methodology for assessing an individual student's instruction.* Austin, TX: Pro Ed.

Ysseldyke, J. E. & Christenson, S. L. (2002). *The functional assessment of academic behavior.* Longmont, CO: Sopris West.

Ysseldyke, J. E., Burns, M. K., Dawson, M., Kelly, B., Morrison, D., Ortiz, S., et al. (2006). *School Psychology: A blueprint for the training and practice in school psychology III.* Bethesda, MD: National Association of School Psychologists.

CHAPTER 22

RESPONSE TO INTERVENTION

DANIEL J. RESCHLY
Vanderbilt University
MELISSA K. BERGSTROM
Southern Illinois University–Edwardsville

Response to intervention (RTI) is a data-based process to establish, implement, and evaluate interventions that are designed to improve human services outcomes. RTI as a system depends on a graduated series of interventions, called tiers, that vary by intervention intensity and measurement precision. Services are provided based on empirically validated interventions, revised as needed through progress monitoring and formative evaluation, and evaluated through comparing results to goals. RTI applications in educational settings and implications for school psychological services and roles are emphasized in this chapter. Essential RTI features and issues are discussed including critical components, theory and research foundations, implementation through multiple educational tiers involving general, remedial, and special education, disability identification, system change processes, and preparation/continuing education of professionals.

RTI CRITICAL COMPONENTS

The RTI term has become popular and sometimes misused. General consensus exists around the following essential RTI components and processes (Barbour, 2002; Batsche et al., 2005; Marston, 2002; Tilly, 2008; VanDerHayden, Witt, & Gilbertson, 2006; Vaughn & Roberts, 2007).

1. Delivery of interventions through a system with multiple tiers that vary in intensity of intervention and measurement precision. Although three tiers are typically used, some RTI systems use four or even five tiers. In this chapter a three-tier model is discussed.

2. Identification of overall goals and specific objectives based on priorities established in educational, family, and community systems. Goals most often originate in federal, state, and local standards for academic achievement and local standards for behavior and emotional regulation.

3. Periodic universal screening of all students is used to assess curricular and instructional effectiveness and individual risk status using measures related to socially valid outcomes such as state and local achievement standards.

4. Determination of student academic, behavioral, and emotional regulation needs in relation to socially validated priorities including identification of significant differences between current and desired levels of performance. Gaps in expected and actual performance levels are the focus of RTI interventions.

5. RTI interventions are based on selection of empirically validated interventions in the domains of academics, behavior, and emotional regulation, matched to student needs, and implemented over a sufficient period of time with good treatment fidelity to achieve goals. These generally effective interventions typically are based on experimental studies comparing treatments or on results from multiple single subject studies.

6. Frequent progress monitoring is used with appropriate measures, results compared to developmental benchmarks and goals, graphing of results against goals, and formative evaluation decision rules specifying changes in interventions (if results do not meet goals) or raising goals (if results exceed goals). Individual progress monitoring is essential because generally effective

interventions based on research are not always effective for individual classrooms or children.

7. RTI models differ in the breadth with which they are used in educational decision making. Some models only address what are described later as Tiers I and II. The comprehensive model described in this chapter uses RTI results to determine decisions about student needs, intensity of instruction, frequency of measurement, changes in instruction/interventions, disability diagnosis and special education eligibility, progress in special education, and continuation, revision, or cessation of special education service(s).

8. Evaluation of individuals, classrooms, and schools is based in RTI data including decisions about curriculum and instructional procedures.

Implications

A major implication of RTI is the need to reallocate resources. In most states educational budget increases above inflation and student growth are unlikely in the foreseeable future. Implementing RTI, however, requires establishment of services not currently available in most schools such as universal screening for academic and behavioral problems. The necessary resources will have to come from existing sources. The largest school expenditures are for professional personnel and implementing RTI will require that current personnel, including school psychologists, adopt different practices. The basis for the reallocation of time should be a clear-eyed assessment of which current practices are and are not empirically connected to improved outcomes. Those that are should be continued and enhanced. Those that are not should be reduced or eliminated in favor of more effective practices. We will point out areas where we see potential reallocation of resources.

Problem Solving (PS) and RTI

The terms RTI and problem solving (PS) are sometimes used interchangeably. To sharpen the focus on both, we define RTI as a system of tiered interventions that relies heavily on PS processes at each level. PS refers to a strategy that proceeds through stages typically involving behavioral definitions of concerns, collection of baseline data, determination of goals using developmental standards and norms, analysis of conditions related to the behavior(s) of concern (including prior knowledge), selection of empirically validated interventions matched to problems, implementation of interventions with good fidelity, progress monitoring in relation to goals, formative evaluation, and evaluation of success against goals (see later discussion of behavioral consultation) (Bergan, 1977; Bergan & Kratochwill, 1990; Upah & Tilly, 2002). PS interventions may be instructional, behavioral, or both. For example, we see standard protocol reading interventions (Vaughn & Roberts, 2007) as an application of PS principles. Further, most students with educational performance problems need both academic (perhaps through standard protocol tutoring) and behavioral interventions (likely through PS).

PS is pragmatic, data based, atheoretical, and self-correcting. In practice interventions are selected, implemented, continued, modified, or discontinued based on results. Decisions are based on data. The theoretical basis for PS interventions is eclectic and pragmatic, in that the only criteria for the selection of an intervention are data to document that it works with a specific kind of problem and that the intervention is within ethical boundaries. In practice, behavioral approaches are applied more frequently to educational and behavioral problems than other approaches because more data exists to support the former (Kavale, 2005, 2007; Reschly, 2004).

Interventions from other perspectives are used if they are empirically validated. For example, some cognitively based interventions are empirically validated (Harris, Graham, & Mason, 2006; Swanson & Hoskyn, 1998). A typical characteristic of these interventions is a focus on specific academic skill development and explicit instruction. Reading comprehension instructional routines that direct attention and expectations to specific components of reading passages are effective (Kavale, 2005). Although the reading comprehension teaching routines are not strictly behavioral, they are perfectly acceptable in PS because they are empirically validated. Many other popular cognitive interventions have little or no empirical support (Kavale, 2007). The key feature of PS interventions is empirical support, not theoretical origins.

PS is self-correcting in that interventions that are not working are modified or discontinued, perhaps the most fundamental idea of all. Ineffective interventions are changed as soon as reliable data indicate insufficient growth in competencies. Changes in interventions are based on decision rules that specify the strategy for determining when revisions should be considered.

Brief History of RTI

Although PS models and methods were developed several decades ago and applied to a wide array of human problems (Bergan, 1977; Deno & Mirkin, 1977), the term response to intervention (RTI) emerged in the late 1990s to early 2000s to describe multitiered reading (Lyon et al., 2001; Vaughn, Linan-Thompson, & Hickman, 2003) and behavior (Horner & Sugai, 2000) interventions. The concept, however, is ancient. We tell our students the story that RTI was invented by a cave woman very early in human history as she tried out different cooking methods and ingredients and, depending on results, either continued, modified, or discontinued specific practices. This hypothetical woman *discovered* the essential processes used in modern PS and RTI. Some wonder, "Where was her husband in all of this?" We believe he was lost in the woods because he refused to ask directions.

Although the tongue-in-cheek explanation above should not be taken seriously, it is obvious that humans used RTI principles throughout history to improve many conditions and practices. Learning from results is fundamental to human adaptation. What is new today in educational system RTI applications are the solid scientific foundations for academic and behavioral interventions, improved measurement precision, formal decision rules, and policy and legal supports. Each is discussed later in the chapter.

RTI FOUNDATIONS IN RESEARCH, POLICY, AND LAW

RTI rests on a foundation of research on assessment and interventions that increases the probability of good outcomes for children and youth in general and special education. The research foundations increasingly influenced policy development in the late 1990s to early 2000s which, in turn, influenced legal requirements in the early- and mid-2000s. The progression from research to policy to legal requirements is discussed in this section.

Research Foundations

RTI is based on research foundations (Griffiths, Parson, Burns, VanDerHeyden, & Tilly, 2007),

particularly knowledge bases from applied behavior analysis, instructional science, behavior assessment, and behavioral consultation/PS. Each is discussed briefly, citing sources for more in-depth study.

Applied Behavior Analysis

The development of applied behavior analysis (ABA) over the last 50 years profoundly influenced modern PS and response to intervention (Bandura, 1969; Sulzer-Azaroff & Mayer, 1991; Witt, Elliott, & Gresham, 1988). ABA principles and strategies have significant effects on improving a wide range of academic, social, and emotional regulation outcomes across a variety of settings including schools (Kavale, 2005, 2007). Further elaborations on traditional ABA principles have led to more focused interventions through experimental analyses of behavior to test hypotheses about the causes of behavior (O'Neill et al., 1997; Tilly, Knoster, & Ikeda, 2000), systematic applications to broad populations (Walker, Colvin, & Ramsey, 1995; Walker et al., 1996), and system-wide school interventions designed to prevent and, when necessary, treat behavioral problems (Horner & Sugai, 2000; Sugai et al., 2000). Multiple examples of successful ABA applications in schools and school psychology practice exist (Shinn, Stoner, & Walker, 2002). RTI absent ABA foundations likely would not exist.

Behavior Assessment, Curriculum-Based Measurement, and Formative Evaluation

Behavior assessment and intervention procedures developed in the 1960s and 1970s markedly influenced the development of direct links between assessment and intervention over broad domains of human functioning. Procedures to precisely measure observable social behaviors emerged first, leading to highly effective interventions to improve appropriate prosocial behaviors in schools, homes, and community settings such as engaged time in academic settings (Bandura, 1969; Barrish, Saunders, & Wolf, 1969). Continued progress in the development of behavior assessment procedures further enriches the foundations for RTI today (Shapiro & Kratochwill, 2000).

Curriculum-based measurement (CBM) is critical to RTI applications. CBM originated in application of behavior assessment methods to academic skills (Deno, Mirkin, & Shinn, 1979;

Deno & Mirkin, 1977). The common features of behavior assessment and CBM measures are: (a) direct measurement of the behavior/academic skill of interest in natural settings, (b) efficient measures that are brief, inexpensive, and repeatable over short time intervals, (c) sensitive to small increments of growth in the behavior/academic skill, (d) high reliability (consistency and stability), and (e) validity in the sense of relationships to socially valid outcomes such as overall achievement in a subject such as reading (Deno, 1985; Germann & Tindal, 1985).

Many studies reporting impressive results on the reliability and validity of CBM measures are available in the literature (Fuchs & Fuchs, 1986, 2004). Reliabilities of CBM reading measures typically are in the high .80s to mid .90s over multiple studies. CBM reading correlations with standardized achievement test reading measures and passing rates on high-stakes state accountability tests typically are in the range of .7 to .9, depending on the test and time interval between the measures. In addition to these highly desirable technical characteristics, CBM measures are efficient, inexpensive, and accurate in determining the short- and long-term outcomes of interventions.

The most frequently used CBM measure currently is oral reading fluency, typically involving brief timed samples (1 to 3 minutes) of oral reading using passages with carefully controlled difficulty levels. Multiple parallel forms of passages at each grade level are used to enable assessment of progress at different intervals (weekly, monthly) depending on the intensity of the intervention. Over the past 5–7 years several widely available and easily applied CBM measures have been developed. The most prominent currently are the Dynamic Indicators of Basic Early Literacy Skills (DIBELS; Good & Kaminski, 2003) and AIMSweb developed by Germann and colleagues (AIMSweb, 2007). DIBELS includes measures of oral reading fluency and reading comprehension. AIMSweb includes CBMs in oral reading fluency, reading comprehension, numeracy, math computation, and writing. Other curriculum-based measures exist, often tied to specific curricula. These measures are reviewed at www.studentprogress.org/default.asp. Use of CBM with formative evaluation produces significant improvement in academic skills (see effect sizes below).

RTI Foundations in Principles of Learning and Instruction

Throughout the twentieth century intense debates were devoted to the foundations of school curricula and instructional methods. These debates continue with as much emotion as ever, sometimes featuring extreme positions that seem to ignore the best interests of children and youth.

A fundamental principle sometimes ignored is the interaction between level of prior knowledge and need for explicit, complete instruction. The irrefutable principle is that learners with low levels of prior knowledge need more complete, explicit instruction (Chall, 2000). Learners with higher levels of prior, relevant knowledge can profit from less complete instruction because they can use prior relevant knowledge to efficiently learn new competencies. Consider learning computer software that is new to you. If you have a lot of prior knowledge with the specific computer platform and with software in general, you will almost undoubtedly learn the new software with a minimum of guidance and practice. If prior knowledge in this area is less well developed (like that of the senior author), more explicit instruction will be needed with multiple examples and guided exercises to learn essential skills (perhaps Microsoft Excel for Dummies). The difference is not the overall ability of the learner per se, although we would not deny such effects, but rather the level of prior knowledge (Chall, 2000; Mayer, 2004).

Findings regarding pure discovery versus varying degrees of explicit instruction are unequivocal. Guided, teacher-led instructional approaches varying from implicitly organized instruction (for persons with a high level of prior knowledge) to direct, explicit instruction are more effective. This has been a consistent finding for a century (Chall, 2000). Pure discovery is less effective than guided instruction regardless of the level of student prior knowledge and ability. Mayer (2004) concluded, "The debate about discovery has been replayed many times in education, but each time, the research evidence has favored a guided approach to learning" (p. 18).

RTI often is focused on improving results for struggling learners (see later discussion). Instruction for these learners is unequivocally more effective if it incorporates explicit and direct procedures. Discovery approaches are less effective with struggling learners because of the absence of sufficient, relevant prior knowledge.

Meta-Analysis Findings

Decisions about interventions in RTI systems are guided by the results of multiple studies with largely consistent results, especially meta-analyses. Meta-analysis is a statistical method to summarize the results of many studies on a specific program or intervention. The meta-analytic statistic is the *effect size* which is a z-score with a mean of 0 (indicating no effect) and a standard deviation of 1. The effect size is typically computed for each study by the simple formula of the treatment group mean minus the control group mean divided by the pooled standard deviation. These effect sizes are then averaged across studies (sometimes weighted for specific factors or presented separately for studies varying in methodology). Effect sizes can be negative or positive depending on whether the treatment group did better or worse than the control group. Although there are many factors that should be considered in determining the effect size magnitude that makes a meaningful difference, effect sizes above +0.5 generally are considered significant in evaluating human services programs or interventions.

RTI systems emphasize instructional and behavioral programs and interventions that have empirically validated significant benefits to children and youth. Results of meta-analysis examinations are valuable in making choices about what does and does not work with different kinds of learners and educational problems. Kavale and colleagues have presented meta-analysis results on instructional and behavioral interventions for at least 20 years (Kavale, 1990, 2005, 2007; Kavale & Forness, 1999) (See Table 22.1).

Key findings from meta-analysis studies of programs and interventions support the use of applied behavior analysis (Kavale, 2005, 2007), direct, systematic, and explicit instruction, PS (Kavale 2005), and behavior assessment (CBM is a form of behavioral assessment) with graphing against goals, formative evaluation decision rules for making changes in interventions or goals, and positive reinforcement for effort and gains (Fuchs & Fuchs, 1986; Kavale 2007). Explicit instructional routines also produce significant benefits to children and youth in key areas such as reading, mathematics, and writing (Baker, Gersten, & Lee, 2002; Gersten & Baker, 2001; Gersten, Fuchs, Williams, & Baker, 2001; Harris, Graham, & Mason, 2006). Learning strategies, a more cognitively based array of interventions, also are effective when applied through specific instructional routines at the middle and high school levels for learning subject matter (science, social studies) (Harris et al., 2006; Swanson & Deshler, 2003; Swanson, Hoskyn, & Lee, 1999).

Direct Instruction

Direct instruction involves teaching methods that rely on complete instruction (all elements of

TABLE 22.1 **Summary of Meta-Analysis Results on Effective Instruction and Behavioral Interventions[1]**

Instruction/Intervention	Effect Size in SD Units
Applied behavior analysis re: social behaviors such as disruptive classroom behavior (many specific techniques are included) (Kavale & Forness, 1999)	+0.9 to 1.0
Frequent curriculum-based measurement: graph results against goals with formative evaluation decision rules that lead to decisions to maintain current interventions, increase goals, or improve the instruction along with positive reinforcement for effort and gains (Fuchs & Fuchs, 1986; Kavale & Forness, 1999)	+0.7 to 1.0
Explicit instruction, direct instruction, and PS processes (many specific techniques are included) (Kavale, 2005; Kavale & Forness (1999)	+0.7 to 1.5
Comprehension strategies (explicit instructional routines) (Gersten et al., 2001)	+1.0
Interventions in math (Baker et al., 2002)	+0.6 to 1.1
Interventions in writing (Gersten & Baker, 2001; Graham & Harris, 2006)	+0.5 to 0.8
Learning strategies such as study skills in content areas applied with middle and high school students with achievement problems (Swanson, Hoskyn, & Lee, 1999)	+0.5 to 1.0

[1]The results in this table are by no means exhaustive. Instruction and interventions for students with learning and behavior problems were emphasized in the results summarized.

the task are taught), precise specification of the skills required for complex competencies and explicit teaching of each skill, building fluency with each skill, rapid pacing, individual and group response methods, frequent responding with immediate feedback, and reinforcement contingencies to maintain motivation (Coyne, Kame'enui, & Carnine, 2007). The degree of directness or explicitness is determined by learner outcomes. Failure to master key competencies leads to further task analysis, greater explicitness, further practice, and responding with feedback. Mastery of key competencies leads to a faster pace and less explicitness.

Several models of direct instruction exist that vary on degree of explicitness and application to different content areas (Coyne et al., 2007; Snow, Burns, & Griffin, 1998). Vaughn, Gersten, and Chard (2000) reviewed a large number of studies on instructional practices and reported that the direct and explicit methods that are effective for students with at-risk characteristics and educational disabilities also are effective with general education students. An instructional method often used in direct instruction procedures with varying degrees of explicitness involves the sequence of: (a) teacher models the skill, (b) students and teacher produce the skill simultaneously, (c) students produce the skill independently with feedback, (d) student practices the skill to automaticity, and (e) skill is integrated with prior competencies (Vaughn et al., 2000). The teacher modeling with student responding can be implemented flexibly according to the degree to which students need explicit instruction.

Reading

Advances in the understanding of effective methods to teach reading are fundamental to most RTI applications (National Reading Panel, 2000; Snow et al., 1998). Improved reading is critical to improving results and accomplishing the goals in federal and state accountability legislation. Recent National Assessment of Educational Progress (NAEP) findings indicate that current reading levels are inadequate to meet national and state educational goals, especially for some minority group students (NAEP, 2007). Reading levels at the fourth grade by group appear in Figure 22.1. Reading levels for all groups need to be improved to support higher order learning in advanced subject matter at later grade levels. Depending on group, proportions reading at a below basic level varies from 23% to 54%. Moreover, high proportions of African American (54%), Latino/a (51%), and Native American Indian (49%) children were reading at a below basic level.

Reading at a below basic level in fourth grade has several important implications (Snow et al., 1998). First, expectations to "read to learn" increase in fourth grade and accelerate

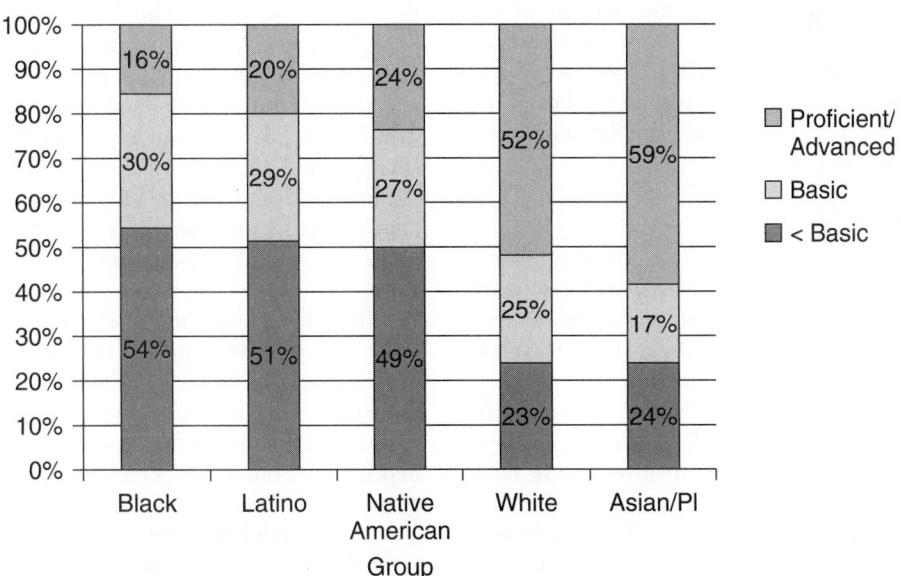

FIGURE 22.1   NAEP 2007 Fourth Grade Reading Results by Race/Ethnicity.

through subsequent school grades, contributing to increasing achievement gaps for below basic readers. Second, the vast majority (about 80%) of students reading below basic levels at fourth grade will be poor readers at age 18 and beyond. Third, poor reading skills increase risk for a variety of poor outcomes including failure to pass demanding classes, development of and referral for behavior problems, special education placement, noncompletion of high school, and constricted postsecondary education and employment opportunities. Fourth, approximately 70% to 80% of student referrals to special education implicate reading problems as the first or second priority (Fletcher et al., 2002). Clearly, reading is a critical, gateway competence that markedly influences subsequent educational and career opportunities for most students.

A broad consensus now exists supporting the importance of instruction in five reading content areas, phonemic awareness, phonics, fluency, vocabulary, and comprehension (National Reading Panel, 2000; Snow et al., 1998; Torgesen, 2002; Torgesen et al., 1999). Less consensus, but strong research evidence supports the importance of reading instruction that is direct, explicit, and systematic (Denton, Vaughn, & Fletcher, 2003; Torgesen, 2002; Vaughn et al., 2003; Vaughn & Roberts, 2007) along with universal screening at early school grades and progress monitoring (Deno, 1985; Fuchs & Fuchs, 1986, 2004; Good, Simmons, & Kame'enui, 2001; Kavale, 2007). Implementation of scientifically based reading instruction (SBRI) reduces the number of students reading below basic levels by significant percentages (Lyon et al., 2001; Torgesen, 2002). Unfortunately, large gaps exist in teacher preparation and practice regarding implementation of SBRI (see later discussion).

Learning Strategies

Learning strategy instruction in the context of learning academic subjects such as math, social studies, and science improves the achievement of all learners including students at risk for poor educational outcomes and students with disabilities (SWD) (Kavale, 2007; Swanson & Deshler, 2003; Swanson & Hoskyn, 1998). Learning strategies involve a wide range of instructional practices that assist students in focusing on relevant aspects of academic content, directing attention, self-regulation of attention and effort, study skills, and so on. Learning strategies instruction is particularly effective

at the middle school through postsecondary educational levels.

Consultation Methods for PS

Consultation has been emphasized in discussions of school psychology roles for at least 50 years (Cutts, 1955). Bergan and colleagues (Bergan, 1977; Bergan, Curry, Currin, Haberman, & Nicholson, 1973; Bergan & Kratochwill, 1990; Sheridan, Kratochwill, & Bergan, 1996) established consultation processes to carry out the essential steps of PS. The stages of PS are accomplished through structured interviews and the implementation of interventions with progress monitoring. The structured interviews generally involve questions that direct consultee attention to PS and statements that review and confirm consultee decisions. The use of consultation interviewing strategies increases the involvement of teachers or parents in all intervention decisions, enhances the acceptability of interventions, and guides the discussion toward the development of essential features of PS (behavioral definition, baseline data).

Research on behavioral consultation reveals high rates of success IF the necessary stages are implemented with good fidelity (See Table 22.2). Early research indicated that if the PS stages were accomplished, particularly problem identification and data collection (Bergan & Tombari, 1976; Tombari & Bergan, 1978) high success in accomplishing goals and resolving problems was attained. Other researchers demonstrated the importance of behavioral consultation training (Kratochwill, Van Someren, & Sheridan, 1989; McDougall, Reschly, & Corkery, 1988) and the relationship of good fidelity in implementing the PS stages and intervention outcomes (Flugum & Reschly, 1994; Telzrow, McNamara, Hollinger, 2000; Upah & Tilly, 2002). Some evidence supports the effectiveness of scripted, simplified behavioral consultation (Fuchs & Fuchs, 1989).

Behavioral consultation strategies markedly assist school psychologists and others in the implementation of PS principles and RTI processes. This approach creates a natural way of interacting with teachers and parents that leads to productive outcomes. Teachers and parents are nearly always highly satisfied with interventions created through behavioral consultation because, at least in part, a collaborative relationship is established with distributed power and careful active listening processes.

TABLE 22.2   Stages of Behavioral Consultation Problem Solving

Problem Identification Stage

Define the concern in objective, behavioral terms

Estimate current strength of the behavior

Tentatively identify setting and expectations

Agree on method and procedures to collect baseline data

Problem Analysis Stage

Review baseline data and establish goals

Analyze conditions (including prior knowledge)

Development of intervention strategy(ies) and tactics

Agreements for continued data collection and fidelity checks

Intervention Implementation Stage

Support for intervention provided

Intervention implemented with good fidelity including fidelity checks

Progress monitoring with changes made as indicated by data and decision rules

Intervention Evaluation

Review and evaluate results against goals

Continue, modify, discontinue intervention

Consider other problems

Decisions made about additional interventions and services

Sources: Bergan, 1977; Bergan & Kratochwill, 1990.

Policy Foundations for RTI

Concerns about persistent problems in PreK–12 education led to several policy analyses in the late 1990s to early 2000s and, in turn, to changes in legal requirements that supported PS and RTI processes. The persistent problems, described in more detail in Reschly (2008), included:

- Low achievement levels in basic areas such as reading (see prior discussion), large inequalities across groups in educational outcomes, and low relative performance in international achievement comparisons (*Learning for Tomorrow's World*, 2003)
- Expensive education programs with equivocal results, e.g., Title I and special education (Lyon et al., 2001)
- Disconnected and inefficient programs intended for similar populations, often the same children

- Disconnected eligibility, treatment, and program evaluation practices, including assessment procedures and disability diagnoses that have little or no treatment applications
- Failure to implement empirically validated curricula and interventions in academic and behavioral domains

Major policy analyses related to these problems in the late 1990s and early 2000s set the stage for legal requirements fostering the implementation of RTI processes. The policy recommendations were markedly influenced by the research foundations discussed in the previous section. The policy statements originated from diverse influences and agencies (*A New Era: Revitalizing Special Education for Children and their Families*, 2002; Bradley, Danielson, & Hallahan, 2002 (see especially the LD Researchers recommendations, pp. 791–804); Donovan & Cross, 2002; Lyon et al., 2001; National Reading Panel, 2000; Snow et al., 1998), but yielded highly similar findings (See Table 22.3). Perhaps the overriding themes in the policy analyses were accountability and demands for improved results through better implementation of empirically validated practices.

Legal Foundations of RTI

It might be argued that the RTI critical components described in this chapter always were consistent with the intent of the original Education of the Handicapped Act (EHA; 1975/1977), reauthorized in 1991, 1997, and 2004 as the Individuals with Disabilities Education Act (IDEA). The original intent of the EHA legislation, that is, a strong emphasis on improving results for SWD, was not realized until Congress significantly changed the focus of federal general and special education legislation beginning in the 1990s. The Elementary and Secondary Education Act reauthorizations in 1995 and 2002 (named the No Child Left Behind Act NCLB in 2002) and reauthorization of IDEA changed the federal focus from the *processes* of how services were delivered to the *results* of the programs.

The policy developments just discussed were the foundations for the changes from processes to results. From 1977 through 1997 it is accurate to observe that federal and state monitoring of programs for SWD rarely if ever addressed results. Rather, the focus was almost entirely on processes like how the referral was done, when and how parental consent was obtained and documented,

TABLE 22.3 Recommendations in Policy Analyses (1998–2002)

Greater accountability for results	All
Prevention through early universal screening and early intervention	All, see especially Snow et al. (1998) and Donovan & Cross (2002)
Multiple tiers of intervention	All, see especially Donovan & Cross (2002)
PS, empirically validated interventions in academic and behavior domains	All
Greater integration of educational systems (general, remedial, and special education), more permeable boundaries between systems	All, but especially *A New Era*, (2002)
Eliminate IQ-achievement discrepancy in learning disabilities identification	All, see especially Lyon et al. (2001) and Cross & Donovan (2002)
Reading instruction based on five components plus explicit instruction and progress monitoring	All, see especially Lyon et al. (2001) and National Reading Panel (2000)

the components of the preplacement evaluation, who decided about eligibility and on what bases, how and who formulated the individual education program, and whether the special education services were delivered. The emphasis in the education of SWD was on access and process, not results. The shift from *processes* to *results* through legislation demanding accountability for results profoundly affects current educational services in general and special education as well as, increasingly, the roles of school psychologists.

No Child Left Behind Legislation

Prominent NCLB priorities in Section 1001 include, *(2) "meeting the educational needs of low-achieving children in our Nation's highest-poverty schools, limited English proficient children, migratory children, **children with disabilities**, Indian children, neglected or delinquent children, and young children in need of reading assistance; and (3) closing the achievement gap between high- and low-performing children, especially the achievement gaps between minority and nonminority students, and between disadvantaged children and their more advantaged peers"* (NCLB, 2002, Section 1001, emphasis added).

Specific NCLB (2002) provisions that fostered the development of RTI systems are: (a) frequent assessment of results, (b) accountability for results including annual yearly progress, (c) endorsement of instruction and interventions drawn from research, (d) reading instruction in the five major components of reading, (e) prevention and early identification-early treatment for students with achievement deficits, and (f) public reports of achievement and other outcomes disaggregated by race/ethnicity, poverty (eligible

for free or reduced cost school lunch), English language status, and disability. The latter placed much greater emphasis on the achievement of SWD since a district can be sanctioned even to the point of being regarded as a "failing" district if SWD did not meet NCLB goals for achievement and other outcomes.

Congress aligned IDEA 2004 closely with NCLB regarding reporting requirements, highly qualified teacher provisions, and research foundations for interventions (e. g., see 34 C.F.R. 300.35). Specific IDEA legal requirements fostering RTI are discussed in a later section on identification of specific learning disabilities (SLD).

MULTIPLE TIERS OF INTERVENTION, ASSESSMENT, AND DECISION MAKING

RTI multitiered systems are organized around levels of instruction or intervention that are matched to the needs of students (see Figure 22.2). The goal is the improved performance of all students. Each tier represents a specific level of intervention intensity and measurement precision. The basic principle is: the greater the needs of a student, the more intense the intervention.

Student performance is evaluated against academic and behavioral benchmarks. The academic benchmarks are not equivalent to classroom, school, or national means or medians; rather, they are connected to passing rates on state high-stakes tests. Behavioral benchmarks and goals are largely locally determined. Significant individual or group variations from typical behaviors of peers, or expectations that interfere with positive learning and developmental

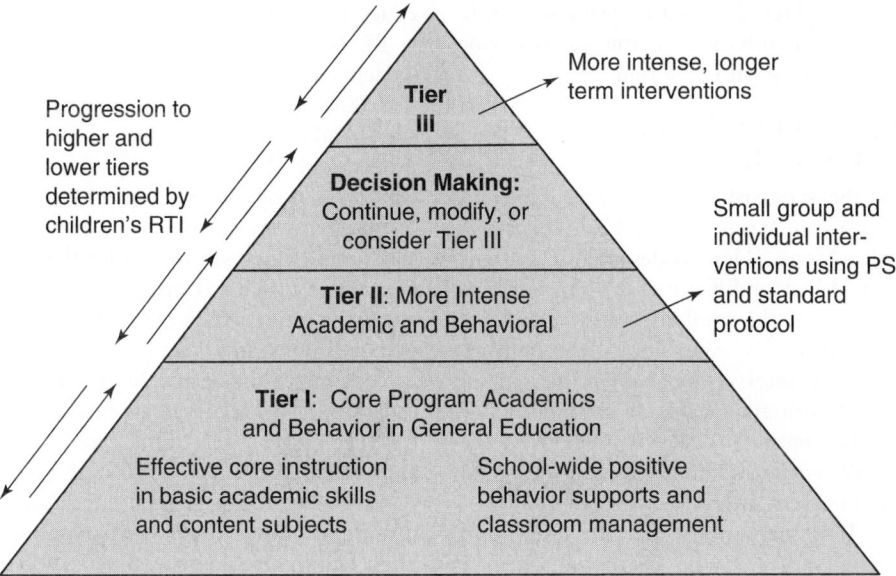

FIGURE 22.2 MultiTiered Interventions Varying in Intensity and Measurement Precision.

trajectories, are the focus of behavioral and emotional regulation interventions.

RTI System Variations

RTI systems generally implement the eight critical components described in the first section of this chapter, but system variations exist in terminology, relative emphasis on PS and standard protocol procedures, number of tiers, and disability identification practices. Good examples of comprehensive models exist in some states: Iowa (Ikeda, Tilly, Stumme, Volmer, & Allison, 1996; Tilly, 2008), Illinois (www.illinoisaspire.org/), Ohio (Graden, Stollar, & Poth, 2007), Idaho (Nunn & McMahon, 2000) and Florida (Batsche, Curtis, Dorman, Castillo, & Porter (2007) and many districts, for example, Minneapolis (Marston, 2002) and Horry County, South Carolina (Barbour, 2002). All states are currently developing RTI implementation plans subsequent to the RTI Summit sponsored by the U.S. Department of Education Offices of Elementary and Secondary Education and Special Education Programs (www.rtisummit.org).

Prevention and Early Identification-Early Intervention

Tiered systems subscribe to the old adage "An ounce of prevention is worth a pound of cure." In fact, prevention is the most economical and humane method known to human sciences professionals. Prevention and early identification–early intervention reduce the prevalence and severity of significant achievement and behavior problems (Donovan & Cross, 2002; Snow et al., 1998; Torgesen 2002; Torgesen et al., 1999; Walker, Colvin, & Ramsey, 1995). When problems do emerge, the intent is to implement effective interventions before problems become more severe and too difficult to resolve in general education settings. For example, multiple studies demonstrate the effectiveness of identifying potential reading problems as early as kindergarten and intervening at ages 5–7 before the problems become severe. A National Research Council Panel (Donovan & Cross, 2002) concluded, *"There is substantial evidence with regard to both behavior and achievement that early identification and intervention is more effective than later identification and intervention"* (p. 6). Walker et al. (1995) made the same point regarding aggressive behavior, *"If antisocial behavior is not changed by the end of grade 3, it should be treated as a chronic condition much like diabetes. That is, it cannot be cured, but can be managed with the appropriate supports and continuing intervention"* (p. 6).

Academic performance and behavior are inextricably connected (Hinshaw, 1992; Nelson, Benner, Lane, & Smith, 2004; Torgesen, 2002). Academic success or failure both influences and is influenced by behavior. Effective, challenging instruction also influences and is influenced by behavior. Tiered systems promote early intervention into both the academic and behavior problems occurring with children.

Description of the Tiers (see Figure 22.2)

Tier I is the standard or core curriculum and behavior program; it is universal, that is, it is delivered to all students. Tier I is designed to prevent learning and behavior difficulties through effective instructional and behavioral interventions and, for those who fall below expectations, the delivery of more intense interventions *within* the general education classroom. Tier II is considered for students who continue to perform below expectations, with even more intense teacher-designed classroom interventions.

Tier II interventions are designed and implemented either in the classroom or in a combination of the general education classroom and pull-out, small group tutoring sessions. The purpose of Tier II is to resolve learning and behavioral difficulties and to keep the student in the general education program without the need for more intense programming. Tier II also serves as a diagnostic process to determine if more intensive Tier III interventions are needed.

Tier III intensive treatments are delivered to students who do not make sufficient progress in Tier II to meet benchmarks and who are likely to require longer term (one year or more), sustained, intense interventions. Tier III may or may NOT involve special education. For many students needing relatively long-term Tier III intervention, special education is inappropriate because the specially designed instruction and related services provided through special education do not match the nature of the student's problem(s).

Differences Between the Tiers

Although the three tiers are linked to one another, they are different in several important ways. The primary differences are in the number of students participating at each tier, the intensity of student needs, the intensity of instruction/intervention, and the precision of measuring student progress.

Proportions of Students

All students participate in Tier I academic and behavioral programs. The kind and degree of participation varies according to the needs of students, but as the President's Commission on Excellence in Special Education concluded, "Consider children with disabilities as general education children first" (*A New Era*, 2002, p. 8). In an RTI system it is expected that all students are involved with general education and that 80% to 85% of all students meet national, state, and local benchmarks and developmental expectations through participation in the general education program without additional supports or interventions outside of the general education classroom. Much smaller proportions of students participate in Tier II programs (10% to 15% at any given time) involving typically 10 to 20 weeks of more intense intervention (see later discussion). In contrast to the relatively time-limited Tier II interventions, Tier III interventions are expected to continue for a year or more and should involve approximately 10% to 12% of all students. RTI systems depend on general education programs that are successful for the vast majority of students. High failure rates in general education leading to excessive use of Tier II and III interventions place unsustainable financial pressures on most school districts.

Degree of Need

The second difference among students at different tiers is intensity of need, defined by the student's rate of progress and the gap between benchmark expectations and current performance. The greater the gap between performance and rate of progress, the greater the student's need.

Intensity of Intervention

Intervention intensity varies across tiers, defined by conditions such as the size of the instructional group, the amount of time devoted to instruction in a specific area, the degree and precision with which instructional objectives are analyzed in terms of prerequisite skills, the degree of explicitness of the intervention, the frequency of feedback about performance, and the use of incentives to increase and sustain motivation. Generally, the greater the student's need, the greater the intensity required to achieve progress toward benchmark standards.

Measurement Frequency and Precision

Measurement frequency and precision increase across the tiers. For example, all students initially are screened for academic and behavioral problems in Tier I (prevention). Progress toward meeting benchmark expectations is assessed perhaps three times per year. This amount of assessment is adequate for students who are performing academically and behaviorally at or above benchmarks. For students who are performing below benchmarks, however, the initial response is to provide more instructional opportunities in the general education classroom and to increase the measurement of progress to perhaps once or twice per month. If intensified instruction within the general education classroom is not sufficient to move the student to benchmark levels, then Tier II likely will be considered. In Tier II, progress monitoring typically is increased to once per week or more, depending on the primary concerns and the intervention goals and objectives.

In good multitier systems, there is symmetry between tiers, student needs, instructional/intervention intensity, and measurement precision. Increases or decreases in any component produce increases or decreases in the others. Data-based decision making in multitiered systems enhances efficient and effective resource utilization.

Tier I: Universal or Core Program

Tier I involves all students. At Tier I, effective instruction in academics and behavior is expected, although it is not always achieved (Batsche et al., 2007; Vaughn & Roberts, 2007). The vast majority of students (80% to 85%) should be on course to meet state and local benchmark standards in an effective Tier I classroom, school, district, or state. If the Tier I instructional and behavior programs do not meet the 80% to 85% performance level, changes in the general education academic and behavior curriculum and instruction likely are needed.

The kinds of decisions that are made at Tier I about individuals and instructional programs are depicted in Figure 22.3. Actual data from two kindergarten classrooms in the same school building serving the same population of students (100% eligible for free/reduced cost school lunch and 99% African American) are shown in Figure 22.3. The first kindergarten teacher is achieving dramatically better results than the second on a widely used early measure of literacy, initial sound fluency (AIMSweb, 2007; Good & Kaminski, 2003). This measure is related to likelihood of reading competently at the end of third grade and is useful for identifying students below benchmarks who need early additional assistance in general education to prevent reading problems.

The first teacher has 21 students. All but four of the students are at or above the benchmark of

25 sounds correct per minute, that is, 81% of the students are at or above the benchmark. Based on these results in an RTI system, the conclusion is that the core reading program is successful. Given a successful core program, the next step is to identify students below the benchmark. The four students below the benchmark all look a bit different. Student numbers 1 and 18 represent the greatest concerns because both are well below the benchmark and both show slow rates of progress. Both likely would be placed in Tier II for more intensive interventions. Students 2 and 11 also are below the benchmark, but both made considerable progress and likely will respond to more intense instruction within the general education classroom. Progress monitoring for students 2 and 11 should be increased to perhaps twice per month to determine if they are responding to the more intense within-classroom instruction.

The second classroom represented in Figure 22.3 is a very different situation. Here only 2 of 17 students are at the benchmark of 25 sounds per minute and 2 additional students are approaching the benchmark. Even with a slightly liberal interpretation of the benchmark, 13 of 17 students are below the benchmark, that is, only 23% are close to or above the benchmark. In this case the core program of curriculum and instruction is inadequate. Additional resources to improve student performance and continuing education for the teacher in the second classroom were deployed to improve results. A key point is that class-wide progress monitoring identified problems early before the deficits became more severe and persistent and when intervention success is more likely. RTI results at Tier I should be applied to classrooms, schools, and districts, not just individuals.

In many RTI systems, teachers and others (principal, reading specialists) periodically review data from all students in all classrooms at a specific grade level. The discussion focuses on the results for all children in each classroom and on individual students. Teachers assist each other in improving overall results and share ideas about how to achieve better results for students below benchmarks.

The Tier I behavior program applies the same principles. First, effective school-wide positive behavior supports are expected along with effective classroom organization and behavior management (Horner & Sugai, 2000; Sugai et al., 2000). Both have significant influences on

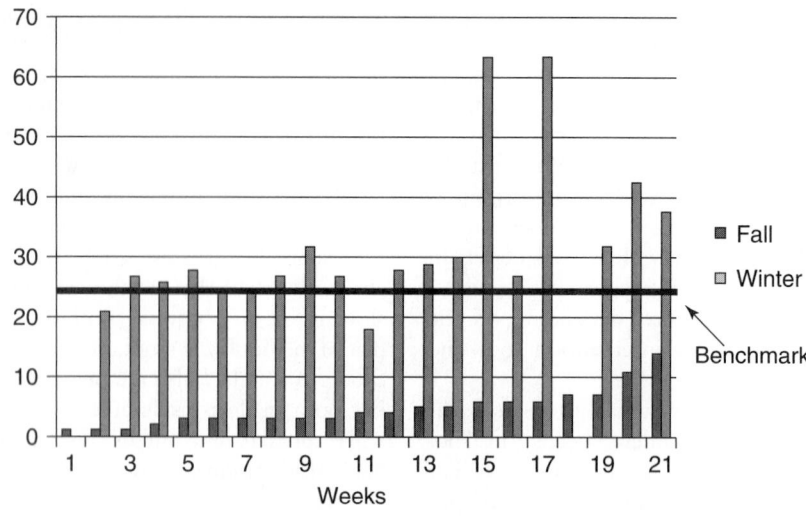

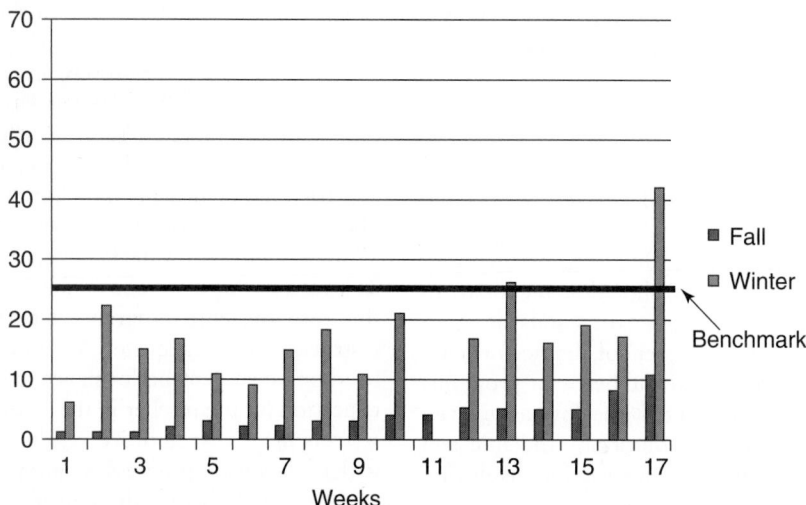

FIGURE 22.3   Initial Sound Fluency: Two Kindergarten Classrooms, Fall to Winter.

the frequency of behaviors that interfere with achievement and the learning environment for all children (Greer-Chase, Rhodes, & Kellam, 2002; Kellam, Xiange, Merisca, Brown, & Ialongo, 1998).

In addition to the core behavior program, all children should be screened for problem behaviors using simple, cost effective methods (Walker et al, 1995). Screening is especially important with aggressive behaviors, but other domains also should be considered including disruptive classroom behavior and social isolation. Behaviors are regarded as problems in these domains only if they deviate significantly from typical behaviors of peers and interfere with normal learning and social development.

Tier II: Strategic Interventions–Secondary Prevention

Some students do not respond sufficiently to even the most effective Tier I instruction and curricula. For perhaps 10% to 15% of students with greater needs, a second level of intense intervention is established. The second tier is delivered within the general education program and is part of early identification–early intervention with academic and behavior problems.

Tier II interventions are delivered in a variety of ways, depending on whether a student's needs are academic, behavioral, or both and on the nature of the interventions. Two approaches are prominent in the literature and practice,

PS and standard protocol (Burns, Appleton, & Stehouwer, 2005). Some erroneously suggest a dichotomy, or an either-or relationship, between these two options. In fact, both are used in many individual cases depending on student needs.

PS

The major features of PS were discussed in an earlier section. The PS methods are applied at Tier II to develop individual and, in some cases, small group interventions delivered in general education around academic and/or behavioral concerns. PS interventions often are delivered through behavioral consultation (Bergan, 1977; Bergan & Kratochwill, 1990). Data-based decision making is emphasized.

Standard Protocol

Standard protocol interventions focusing on academic skill growth are a second general kind of Tier II intervention (Torgesen, 2002; Torgesen et al., 1999; Vaughn et al., 2003). Standard protocol interventions are delivered in groups of about 3 to 5 children because research on tutorial interventions indicates that small group interventions are just as effective as individual interventions (Elbaum, Vaughn, Hughes, & Moody, 2000). Standard protocol interventions are most often used in reading. In the Vaughn et al. (2003) approach the intervention was delivered daily over approximately 20 weeks in 35 minute pull-out sessions. Each of the five critical components of reading was taught each day with greater emphasis on weak areas. SBRI principles were implemented including instruction that is systematic and explicit with frequent student responding and feedback (National Reading Panel, 2000; Snow et al., 1998). Progress monitoring and graphing of individual student progress against goals was done at least once per week with formative evaluation rules applied. A significant proportion of the poor readers included in the Vaughn et al. (2003) standard protocol intervention made sufficient gains to remain in general education without further support, thus very likely improving overall achievement in the school and reducing the need for expensive special education programming.

PS or Standard Protocol?

This is a false dichotomy. First, both approaches achieve strongly positive results in research trials and in practice situations (Burns et al., 2005). The Burns et al. meta-analysis indicated a median effect size of +1.1 across 24 studies for both approaches to Tier II interventions. It also is important to note that effect sizes varied from +6.71 to +0.18, suggesting that simply adopting RTI tiers is not sufficient. The interventions in the tiers must be empirically validated, implemented with good fidelity, and revised as needed through formative evaluation procedures.

For many students both standard protocol and PS interventions are needed. The standard protocol intervention may be the most efficient and effective means to address the academic problem while PS is the most effective means to address off-task, disruptive behaviors that interfere with learning in the general education classroom and in small-group tutorial sessions. Most standard protocol reading interventions now include a point system with back-up reinforcers to improve task engagement, because in previous studies with equivocal results behavior often interfered with efficient learning and improved progress (Torgesen et al., 1999, Vaughn et al., 2003). Moreover, PS to address disruptive and off-task behavior in the general education classroom is essential to generalization of achievement gains from the tutorial sessions.

Figures 22.4 and 22.5 illustrate the intervention and data-based processes used in Tier II in example cases of students with reading problems. In Figure 22.4 a successful Tier II intervention is depicted leading to the decision to return the child to general education with no additional or supplemental interventions. An unsuccessful intervention is depicted in Figure 22.5.

In both Figures 22.4 and 22.5 hypothetical children with reading difficulties in the first grade are depicted. The students are in a school that has adopted an RTI system including universal screening of all children using age-appropriate curriculum-based measures in reading. Both children were below benchmark levels in the spring of kindergarten and the fall of first grade. Additional classroom interventions were implemented for both and progress monitoring was increased to twice per month during the fall semester. Despite the greater instructional intensity and more frequent progress monitoring with formative evaluation in the general education classroom, the children were significantly below the winter first grade benchmark in oral reading fluency. The first student also had lower rates of on-task behavior and engaged in a moderate level of disruptive behavior. No behavior issues were reported for the second student.

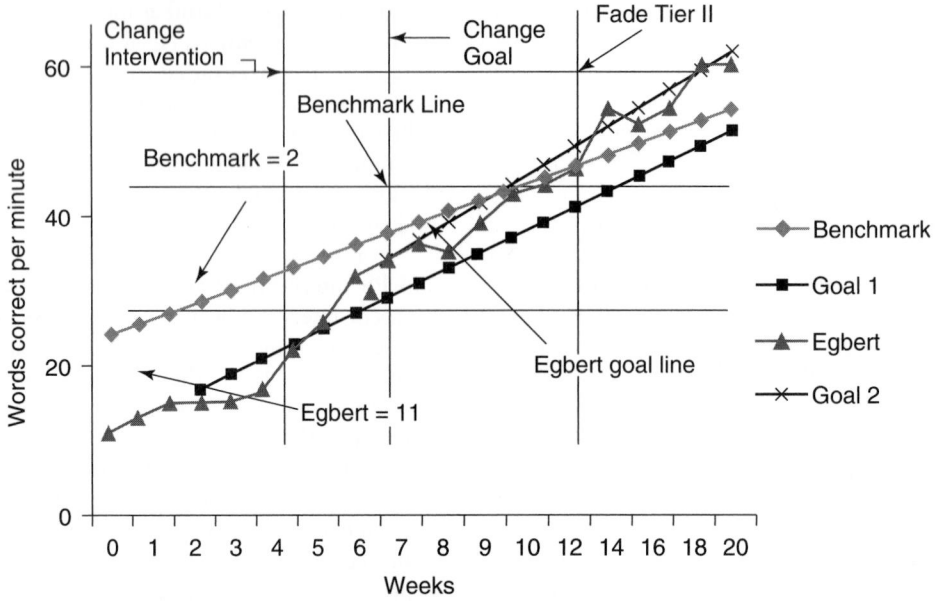

FIGURE 22.4   Successful Tier II Reading Intervention.

An individual graph was established for the first student (see Figure 22.4). The essential features of the graph were the ordinate reflecting levels of oral reading fluency and the abscissa representing time in weeks. A line is entered on the graph representing the benchmark level in oral reading fluency for students in the middle of first grade to early second grade (20 weeks). The initial level is 24 words correct per minute. The slope of the benchmark line is based on the average rate of growth for first grade students of 1.5 words correct per week. The goal for the student is set at an ambitious growth level of 2 words correct per week, which allows the student to reach the benchmark level after 20 weeks. The rationale is that the student is receiving the more intense

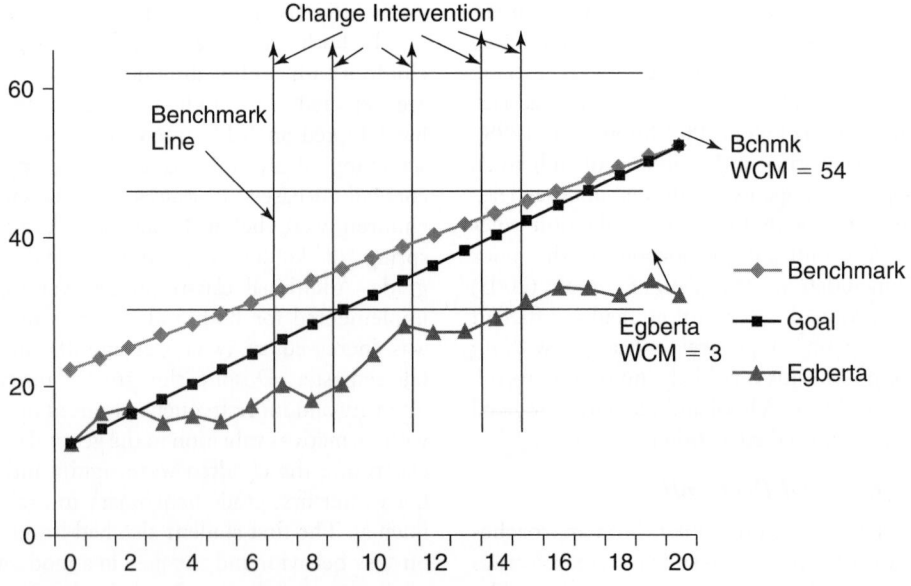

FIGURE 22.5   Unsuccessful Tier II Reading Intervention.

Tier II intervention that will, if effective, produce a more rapid growth rate.

The student is then placed in a Tier II standard protocol reading intervention with behavior intervention to increase task engagement and reduce disruptive behavior in the general education classroom and tutorial sessions. The graph for the first student, *Egbert*, shows the following. First, the initial growth over the first 2 weeks of intervention meets the goal of 1.5 words correct growth per week. Results over the next 3 weeks do not meet the goal. Applying the formative evaluation rule of making changes in interventions that produce insufficient results over 2 or 3 data points, the intervention is changed to better meet the child's needs and to improve the results. The change is indicated by the vertical line at week 5.

Instruction and behavior intervention continue as does progress monitoring. Over the next 4 weeks the rate of progress meets the goal, then exceeds the goal for 3 consecutive weeks. Again applying the formative evaluation decision making rules of making changes if the results either fail to meet or exceed the goal for 3 weeks, the goal now is increased from 2 to 2.5 words correct per week, a new goal line is established, and a vertical line is entered at week 9 to signify a change in the goal. Instruction and behavior intervention continue.

By week 16 the results indicate that the child has caught up to the benchmark in terms of level of performance and rate of progress. At this point the Tier II intervention is reduced in intensity through fewer sessions per week with progress monitoring continued through the 20th week. The child's progress continues over the next 4 weeks after which the Tier II intervention is discontinued. The behavior plan also is reduced in intensity; however, weekly progress monitoring is continued for at least another 4 weeks to ensure that progress continues at benchmark rates.

A second Tier II intervention with insufficient results is depicted in Figure 22.5 (*Egberta*). Intervention changes were made at weeks 5, 8, 12, 15, and 18. The child makes progress (growth rate of approximately 1 word correct per week), but not at a rate to catch-up with the benchmark. Based on these results, there is a significant gap in level of performance and rate of progress. Tier III is considered when students likely need intense instruction and significantly more time to reach benchmarks based on the rate of progress achieved in Tier II.

Decision Making at Tier II

Decisions are made based on the results obtained through the Tier II intervention(s). The decision choices are,

1. *Discontinuation* and return to the general education classroom full-time if the results meet benchmarks,
2. *Discontinuation* and consider Tier III because the results were insufficient to meet benchmarks,
3. *Continuation* of the intervention for a few more weeks because the results are approaching benchmarks levels and a few more weeks likely will be sufficient to meet benchmarks, or
4. *Modification and continuation* of the intervention (adding some instructional or behavior change element if results are approaching the benchmark).

Tier III: Intensive, Long-Term Intervention

Tier III is reserved for those students who do not respond sufficiently to Tier II and who likely need long-term intensive intervention. In some cases Tier III involves continuation of the same level of resources over a longer time period (anticipated to be a year or more) and/or the utilization of additional resources. Progress monitoring at least weekly against goals and formative evaluation decision rules are applied in Tier III. Placement criteria in Tier III always should be accompanied by exit criteria defining the level of progress (usually stated in terms of state benchmarks and/or behavioral expectations) that will trigger movement to lower tiers.

Contrary to some misconceptions, Tier III does not exclusively involve special education. Special education eligibility and programming may or may not be involved with Tier III. First, some Tier III students need more intensive interventions, but NOT the specially designed instruction that is the hallmark of special education. For example, many children and youth with internalizing problems do not need special education in order to reach academic benchmarks, but do need mental health services to improve emotional regulation competencies. For some students with intense and persistent needs, other general education programs may be available and more appropriate. Special education will be considered for many, but not all students with intense and persistent learning and/or behavior problems.

Special Education Eligibility in RTI

Information from Tiers I and II is essential, but not sufficient, to meet the legal requirements to determine special education eligibility. If special education is considered subsequent to Tier II, a comprehensive evaluation is required that meets the legal standards established in state rules and IDEA (2004, 2006). The principal legal requirements concerning special education eligibility determination established in IDEA and adopted by states appear at 34 C.F.R. 300.301 through 34 C.F.R. 300.306 in the section, *Evaluations and Reevaluations*. All school psychologists should be intimately familiar with these requirements. Many of the requirements appeared first in the EHA (1975/1977) and have not changed over the last 30 years.

The legal requirements just cited establish a two-pronged criteria for special education eligibility that should have equal weight in decision making.

- First, an educational disability must be diagnosed using classification criteria established by the state education agency (SEA). States must serve the children and youth represented in the 13 disability categories described in IDEA at 34 C.F.R. 300.8, but SEAs have wide discretion in determining the number of disability categories, the names of the categories, and the classification criteria (Reschly & Hosp, 2004).
- Second, the disability, if one exists, must cause adverse impact on the child's education and the child must need special education, that is, specially designed instruction and, if necessary to provide an appropriate education, related services as well.

Both criteria are equally important. There are children who have a disability, but do not need special education and some children who need special education but do not meet the classification criteria for a disability.

RTI results are relevant to several of the critical IDEA (2004, 2006) evaluation and reevaluation requirements concerning the assessment procedures at 34 C.F.R. 300 including (quoted directly or slightly paraphrased), (a) full and individual evaluation (300.301a), (b) use of a variety of assessment tools and strategies to gather relevant functional, developmental, and academic information

(300.304b), (c) for eligible children, the content of the IEP and specification of the involvement with and progress in the general education curriculum (300.304b.1.ii), (d) assessments tailored to assess specific areas of educational need, (e) current classroom-based, local or state assessments (300.305a.1.ii), and (f) present levels of academic achievement and related developmental needs (300.305.a.2.i.B).

The essential role of effective instruction in the general education classroom and Tier II before eligibility determination is further emphasized in legal provisions at 34 C.F.R. 300.306 *forbidding* the determination that the child is eligible if the determinant factor in eligibility is "*lack of appropriate instruction in reading, including the essential components of reading instruction* (as defined in the No Child Left Behind Act of 2002) (see prior discussion of reading), or *lack of appropriate instruction in math*, or *limited English proficiency*. These requirements focus attention on the content of the general education curriculum (does it provide instruction in the five reading content areas) and the appropriateness of the instruction. The curriculum content and instructional appropriateness might logically be interpreted as the degree to which children are on course to meet benchmark expectations, a critical Tier I question in RTI. If more than 25% of students are not on course to meet benchmarks, it is logical to implicate the quality of the curriculum and instruction as contributing significantly to the low achievement.

Comprehensive Evaluation

Students considered for special education are entitled to a full and individual, comprehensive evaluation that identifies educational and behavioral needs. A critical regulation unchanged since EHA (1997) 1977 specifies, "*The child is assessed in all areas related to the suspected disability including, if appropriate, health, vision, hearing, social and emotional status, general intelligence, academic performance, communication status, and motor abilities*" [(34 C.F.R. 300.304(b)(4)].

This and other regulations suggest that extensive information over multiple domains should be gathered and considered in determining disability eligibility, educational needs, and special education placement. Significantly, this legal requirement allows professional judgment about the domains to be assessed. The regulation does not say to assess in all the areas listed; rather, it has the qualification, *if appropriate*. The requirement should be interpreted as requiring consideration of many domains (perhaps 12 or more) through screening followed by, when appropriate, in-depth assessment within specific domains (Reschly 2005, 2008). If screening suggests the possibility of an educationally related deficit in the domain, then in-depth assessment is required. If screening indicates a low probability of an educationally related deficit, then in-depth assessment is wasteful and irrelevant to the goals of the evaluation.

Eligibility evaluations will vary by state special education system characteristics, especially the use of noncategorical identification for high-incidence disabilities (Tilly, Reschly, & Grimes, 1999). To date, most states continue to use categorical eligibility (Reschly & Hosp, 2004). The 12 domains in which screening should occur for all children and youth are health, vision, hearing, general intellectual functioning, reading, math, written language, adaptive behavior, communication, behavior, emotional regulation, and motor. In-depth assessment is needed only in those domains in which screening indicates possible educationally related deficits. This approach is illustrated in Table 22.4 for 4 of the 12 domains.

For example, the school entrance physical examination, teacher observations, and nurse records and notes are sufficient for nearly all children to screen for an educationally related health deficit. However, consider the situation

TABLE 22.4 Comprehensive Evaluation through Screening to In-Depth Assessment[1]

Domain	Screening Information. Is there a potential deficit?	In-Depth Assessment	Outcome
Health Status	Physical exam records. Teacher and nurse observations. Possible deficit? If no, stop. If yes, proceed to in-depth assessment	Medical evaluation. If deficit(s) identified, consider medical treatment and educational implications	Special Education eligibility and placement if needed
Reading	Group achievement tests, daily work, teacher records. If no, stop. If yes, proceed to in-depth assessment	Formal and informal diagnostic reading assessments, CBM in reading to determine progress	Tier II interventions and possible special education and placement
Adaptive Behavior	Teacher and parent observations and interview with brief screening measures. If no, stop. If yes, proceed to in-depth assessment	Formal adaptive behavior measures supplemented by systematic observations and skills/competencies analysis	Adaptive behavior interventions, Consider MR eligibility and special education eligibility
Intelligence	Achievement test results, teacher observations, adaptive behavior screening results. If no evidence of MR, stop. If MR possible, proceed to in depth assessment	Administration of a comprehensive test of general intellectual functioning, interpreted appropriately	Determination of MR eligibility on the intelligence dimension. Consideration of special education eligibility and placement

[1]Four domains are listed from the array of 12 or domains in which screening should occur followed by, if appropriate, in-depth assessment.

of a child observed by the teacher to have higher rates than most children of needing to go to the restroom, being thirsty, and variations in energy level. These are signs of a possible diabetic condition. The screening information just described is not, of course, sufficient for a diagnosis. Given this screening information, an in-depth assessment is needed through a specialized medical evaluation. Similar reasoning applies to all other areas. For example, consider a child referred due to behavior issues for whom school records and teacher classroom ratings indicate reading at or above national age norms. This student does not, of course, need an in-depth, diagnostic reading assessment. Screening first, followed by in-depth assessment as needed, is the basis for good educational decisions and consistent with federal IDEA legal requirements.

The traditional practice of administering an individual general intellectual functioning measure to nearly all referred children must be reconsidered (Fletcher, Coulter, Reschly, & Vaughn, 2004; Fletcher, Lyon, Fuchs, & Barnes, 2007; Fletcher & Reschly, 2005; Reschly, 2004). First, RTI will be allowed by states as a means to determine specific learning disability (SLD) eligibility (see later discussion). If IQ-achievement discrepancy and cognitive processing are replaced by RTI, the next issue is the need for assessment of general intellectual functioning in disability determination. If RTI is used in a categorical disability system, all students should be *screened* for significant, educationally related deficits in general intellectual functioning through examination of group achievement test results, samples of academic work, and teacher ratings. If the information from these sources suggests possible intellectual functioning at a significantly subaverage level, then and only then are traditional measures of intellectual functioning relevant to educational decision making. The traditional intelligence tests and the largely parallel current tests of hypothetical cognitive processes are useful in these circumstances to rule out mild mental retardation as a disability and as an exclusion factor in the diagnosis of SLD. Adoption of RTI and PS in the identification of disabilities, especially SLD, should reduce IQ testing in schools by about 90% (Marston, 2002, Reschly, 2005). Special issues and legal requirements specific to SLD are discussed in the following section.

Specific Learning Disabilities: Legal Requirements and Eligibility in RTI Systems

IDEA (2004, 2006) established RTI as one of the acceptable methods to diagnose specific learning disabilities (SLD) and as a prerequisite to referral for SLD. Legal requirements concerning SLD are especially relevant to this discussion because of the central role school psychologists play in SLD identification and the high prevalence of SLD (accounting for about half of all children diagnosed with disabilities in educational settings). SLD is unique among the categories of disability in that it is the only category for which classification criteria are established in federal law. For the other 12 IDEA disability categories, conceptual definitions are established at 34 C.F.R. 300.8, but no classification criteria appear with the conceptual definitions or elsewhere in the law.

SLD classification criteria were included in the initial EHA (1975/1977) and remained unchanged until 2004. SLD was and is treated differently due to Congressional concerns about uncontrolled SLD prevalence rates and large variations across states in the diagnosis of SLD (see Reschly & Hosp, 2004 for a review).

From 1975 to 2004 the federal SLD classification criteria were: (a) low achievement in at least one of seven designated areas, (b) severe discrepancy between intellectual ability and achievement in one of the designated areas, and (c) elimination of other causes of poor achievement such as another educational disability or cultural factors. The results of evaluations conducted by school psychologists were crucial to each of the three SLD criteria.

Current Federal SLD Criteria

The federal SLD criteria were changed significantly in IDEA (2004, 2006) (see Table 22.5). Minor changes were made through adding an eighth achievement area (reading fluency), clarifying that the achievement had below age and/or state mandated standards for achievement thereby solidifying the requirement of below age or grade level achievement, and indirectly allowing greater flexibility to states in SLD classification. The largest changes were: (a) elimination of the mandatory severe ability-achievement discrepancy, b) replacing it with two alternatives (RTI or pattern of strengths and weaknesses), and (c) addition of a fourth prong, ruling out poor

TABLE 22.5   IDEA (2004, 2006) SLD Classification Criteria

C. F. R. 300.307(a)	a) "General. *A State must adopt, consistent with §300.309, criteria for determining whether a child has a specific learning disability as defined in §300.8(c)(10). In addition, the criteria adopted by the State.*"
C. F. R. 300.307(a)1–3	"*(1) Must not require the use of a severe discrepancy between intellectual ability and achievement for determining whether a child has a specific learning disability, as defined in §300.8(c)(10);* *(2) Must permit the use of a process based on the child's response to scientific, research-based intervention; and* *(3) May permit the use of other alternative research-based procedures for determining whether a child has a specific learning disability, as defined in §300.8(c)(10).*"
C. F. R. 300.309(a)1 Classification Criteria	1. Low achievement, that is, "*The child does not achieve adequately for the child's age or to meet State-approved grade-level standards in one or more of the following areas, when provided with learning experiences and instruction appropriate for the child's age or State-approved grade–level standards,*" then 8 achievement areas are listed.
C. F. R. 300.309(a)2 Classification Criteria	2. RTI OR Pattern of Strengths and Weaknesses: "*(i) The child does not make sufficient progress to meet age or State-approved grade-level standards in one or more of the areas identified in paragraph (a)(1) of this section when* **using a process based on the child's response to scientific, research-based intervention**" (emphasis added). *or* *(ii) The child exhibits a pattern of strengths and weaknesses in performance, achievement, or both, relative to age, State-approved grade-level standards, or intellectual development, that is determined by the group to be relevant to the identification of a specific learning disability, using appropriate assessments, consistent with §§300.304 and 300.305.*"
C. F. R. 300.309(a)3 Classification Criteria	3. Exclusion Factors. *The group determines that its findings . . . are not primarily the result of* "*(i) A visual, hearing, or motor disability; (ii) Mental retardation; (iii) Emotional disturbance; (iv) Cultural factors; (v) Environmental or economic disadvantage; or (vi) Limited English proficiency.*"
C. F. R. 300.309(b)1–2 Classification Criteria	4. Rule out poor instruction with RTI. "*(1) Data that demonstrate that prior to, or as a part of, the referral process, the child was provided appropriate instruction in regular education settings, delivered by qualified personnel; and (2) Data-based documentation of repeated assessments of achievement at reasonable intervals, reflecting formal assessment of student progress during instruction, which was provided to the child's parents.*"

instruction and requiring what we interpret to mean RTI including progress monitoring (34 C.F.R. 300.309.b, 1–2) (See Table 22.5). Current federal SLD classification essentially requires RTI prior to or during a referral and allows RTI data to be used as a major component of SLD identification.

The reasons for the elimination of the ability-achievement discrepancy are not reviewed extensively here (see for example, Fletcher et al., 2002; Gresham, 2002; Reschly, 2005). To summarize briefly, the ability-achievement discrepancy,

according to several studies replicated by different authors, was unreliable, invalid, and caused harm through delaying treatment to age 10 or 11. Although a few SLD scholars continue to advocate for continuation of the ability-achievement discrepancy as part of SLD eligibility (Kavale, 2002), an overwhelming body of research supports its discontinuation.

SLD eligibility using PS and RTI is based on multiple criteria as follows: (a) significant differences in *level* of performance compared to academic and behavioral benchmarks despite multiple high quality interventions implemented with good fidelity and adjusted using formative evaluation procedures, (b) low *rate* of skill acquisition given the conditions in "a" above, (c) documented adverse impact on the educational program and documented needs for special education, and (d) application of the exclusion factors cited in Table 22.5. Prevention, early identification-early treatment, and close connections between general, remedial, and special education are fostered by the PS and RTI eligibility determination procedures along with enhanced probability of effective special education programs.

SLD Eligibility: RTI or Pattern of Strengths and Weaknesses

Significant disagreements exist within school psychology regarding the SLD eligibility criteria. There is broad consensus that RTI processes are required prior to or during referral for eligibility determination; however, what happens after referral is very much in dispute (Fletcher & Reschly, 2005; Hale, Naglieri, Kaufman, & Kavale, 2004). We support the point of view that RTI should be a comprehensive, system-wide process that guides eligibility determination in SLD and other disability categories (Fletcher & Reschly). Our position is based on the high priority we place on achieving better outcomes at all levels of intervention and the importance of using RTI information from general education in the design, implementation, and evaluation of special education programs for SLD.

The alternative advocated primarily by those associated with standardized testing and traditional views of SLD is that RTI should be used in general education, but once an eligibility evaluation commences, traditional intellectual and measures of hypothetical cognitive processes should be used as the primary basis for the comprehensive evaluation in SLD (Hale, Naglieri, Kaufman, & Kavale, 2004). According to advocates of the traditional assessment approach, RTI methods should be applied in general education. Once Tiers I and II turn out to be insufficient, then another approach should be used to identify the (presumed) causes of the learning problem and to suggest more effective treatments. The problem with these contentions is that no evidence exists to support the assumed connection between hypothetical cognitive processes strengths and weakness and improved instruction or enhanced achievement growth in any area of achievement. The focus

on intellectual ability and hypothetical cognitive processes is consistent with the tradition definition of SLD that appears at 34 C.F.R. 300.8; however, the processing part of that definition has been entirely ignored in federal SLD classification criteria since 1977 *because* of the absence of data supporting links between hypothetical cognitive processes and improved SLD identification, interventions, and outcomes. Absent evidence documenting those links and benefits to children, we continue to be highly skeptical of the usefulness *to children* of assessing hypothetical cognitive processes as part of SLD identification.

Decisions regarding the nature of the comprehensive evaluation with students who may be identified as SLD will have a profound impact on the kind of practice established by school psychologists and the integration of diagnosis with treatment. The basic options are practice focused on interventions through PS versus practice based on making inferences about the causes of learning problems based on hypothetical cognitive processes and continuation of the traditional refer-test-place model of school psychology services (Sheridan & Gutkin, 2000). Although the latter approach represents less change and may be preferred by many because of that alone, the information collected regarding hypothetical processes does NOT translate into more effective programs for students with learning problems, nor does it improve or limit SLD identification. To date, no research on hypothetical cognitive processes validates their use to identify SLD, prescribe instructional methods, or to determine intervention content or goals (Gresham, 2002; Kavale, 2007; Reschly, 2005). Absent research evidence confirming benefits to children, we urge avoidance of hypothetical cognitive processes in school psychology evaluations of students with learning challenges.

Moreover, focusing on strengths and weaknesses using hypothetical cognitive processes likely will make nearly all children with learning problems eligible for SLD diagnosis on that criterion because, statistically, scatter or subtest variations are the most common feature of human performance across a wide variety of psychometric measures. These variations are not more common among children with learning problems, a fact established several decades ago (Fuchs, Fuchs, Tindal, & Deno, 1986; Hallahan & Kauffman, 1977). If the "pattern of strengths and weaknesses" part of the federal SLD criteria is emphasized, we can predict with near certainty that nearly all students with learning problems will meet that part of the SLD classification criteria. The reason is the ubiquity of subtest and scale variations that almost guarantees a sufficient pattern of strengths and weaknesses to be judged by a team to be consistent with SLD. Scatter is normal (Kaufman, 1976). It occurs very frequently with normal children across a battery of tests. Therefore, it cannot be a unique or identifying feature of a phenomenon that occurs relatively infrequently, such as SLD.

RTI in Special Education

Several studies confirm that the special education programs delivered to children in the most commonly identified high-incidence disability categories (SLD, emotional/behavior disorders [E/BD], other health impaired [a proxy in most states for attention-deficit/hyperactivity disorder] and mild mental retardation) typically do not implement research-based academic instruction and behavior interventions leading to equivocal results (Forness, Kavale, Blum, & Lloyd, 1997). In a recent evaluation study of 900 randomly selected complete case files of children in special education conducted by the senior author for a court action on special education services, only 11 graphs showing progress monitoring and formative evaluation procedures appeared. No practitioner to whom these results have been presented has expressed surprise. All confirm that progress monitoring and formative evaluation are rare in special education.

RTI implementation in special education programs has the promise of producing closer connections between empirically validated instruction and interventions and enhanced results for SWD. Unfortunately, despite the extensive and detailed IDEA requirements for the content of individualized education programs, there is no IEP requirement for progress monitoring and formative evaluation. In our view that is an egregious flaw in IDEA (2004, 2006).

RTI has the potential for sharpening the focus of special education programs toward adoption of the most effective interventions to improve academic and behavioral competencies. There is a long way to go in this regard, but recent legal changes establish the conditions for a much closer overall connection between general and special education as well as specific connections between RTI-based eligibility evaluations and special education goals, content, interventions, and outcomes.

CHALLENGES IN THE IMPLEMENTATION OF RTI

Implementation of RTI involves system change. Such changes are difficult and time consuming. Fundamental changes are required in how teachers, school psychologists, and other professionals think about learning and behavior problems. The traditional thought processes of focusing first on remote and unchangeable background factors (home factors, poverty, etc.) or potential internal child deficits in terms of hypothetical emotional states or cognitive processes must change to a focus on effective interventions. Focusing on relatively unchangeable characteristics of the child's background or presumed internal attributes interferes with effective PS and the development of effective interventions. RTI requires a focus on what can be changed in the environment to produce better outcomes, not unchangeable environmental or internal attribute conditions. This shift is difficult for persons trained in traditional models.

Personnel Preparation and Continuing Education Needs

All well-implemented RTI systems known to the authors involved significant continuing education opportunities for practicing professionals including teachers and school psychologists (Reschly & Grimes, 1991; Nunn & McMahon, 2000). Some teachers and school psychologists are well prepared for the RTI system changes. Many are not. Effective continuing education is expensive and time consuming. Absent critical competencies, RTI systems simply do not work.

Changes in professional preparation of teachers, school psychologists, and other professionals also are critical to successful RTI implementation. Current school psychology programs vary significantly in the quality of graduate education concerning RTI. Some do an excellent job. Many do not. For example, in most programs today more emphasis is placed on standardized tests assessing hypothetical intellectual and cognitive processes than on intervention-oriented assessment, and academic and behavioral change principles.

Improved teacher education also is critical. Two recent studies indicate that both general education elementary teachers and special education teachers for high-incidence disabilities typically are not prepared to implement SBRI principles (five critical content areas of reading plus explicit, systematic instruction, universal screening, and progress monitoring with formative evaluation) (Reschly, Holdheide, Smartt, & Oliver, 2007; Walsh, Glaser, & Wilcox, 2006). Effective reading instruction is one of the critical components of an RTI system that produces better results for all children.

Treatment Integrity

Ensuring treatment integrity in an RTI system is an enormous challenge. RTI systems will not achieve the intended results of improved achievement and behavior competencies absent implementation of the multiple tiers and components as they are designed and intended to be implemented. Intervention or treatment fidelity is a significant issue across multiple disciplines including education, psychology, and medicine. For example, studies examining SLD identification using traditional SLD classification criteria reveal that 25% to 50% of students do not meet the state classification criteria (Gresham, MacMillan, & Bocian, 1998; Kavale & Reese, 1992; McLeskey & Waldron, 1991). Treatment fidelity is a persistent issue in education settings and in the work of school psychologists.

Regardless of the system adopted in educational systems, treatment integrity will be a challenge requiring effort, time, and resources. The relevant question is what system should be adopted and resources committed to ensuring treatment integrity. Our clear preference is to devote those resources to an RTI system that is supported by research, policy, and legal requirements. We note that recent research and practice advances provide improved methods to prompt and produce greater treatment fidelity (Noell, Duhon, Gatti, & Connell, 2002).

SUMMARY

RTI implementation should be seen as a system change, shifting the focus from processes and inputs to improved results in achievement, behavior, and emotional regulation. RTI systems vary, but typically share common elements. Perhaps the most fundamental is a commitment to improved results and data-based decision making. Making decisions based on results along with commitments to precise and frequent assessment of progress and implementation of research-based interventions form the core of RTI. These commitments have enormous potential for improving results and creating the intervention-oriented, effective school psychology envisioned over the last half-century.

REFERENCES

AIMSweb (2007). San Antonio, TX: Psychological Corporation.

A New Era: Revitalizing Special Education for Children and their Families. (2002). Report of the Presidents Commission on Excellence in Special Education. Washington, DC: U.S. Department of Education.

Baker, S., Gersten, R., & Lee, D. (2002). A synthesis of empirical research on teaching mathematics to low-achieving students. *Elementary School Journal*, *103*(1), 51–73.

Bandura, A. (1969). *Principles of behavior modification*. New York: Holt, Rinehart, & Winston.

Barbour, B. (2002). Best practices in promoting educational reform at a school district level. In A. Thomas and J. Grimes (Eds.), *Best practices in school psychology* (4th ed. pp. 293–300). Bethesda, MD: National Association of School Psychologists.

Barrish, H. H., Saunders, M., & Wolf, M. M. (1969). Good behavior game: Effects of individual contingencies for group consequences on disruptive behavior in a classroom. *Journal of Applied Behavior Analysis*, *2*, 119–124.

Batsche, G. M., Curtis, M. J., Dorman, C., Castillo, J. M., & Porter, L. J. (2007). The Florida problem-solving/response to intervention model: Implementing a statewide initiative. In S. Jimerson, M. Burns, & A. VanDerHeyden (Eds.), *Handbook of response to intervention: The science and practice of assessment and intervention* (pp. 378–395). New York, N.Y: Springer.

Batsche, G., Elliott, J., Graden, J. L., Grimes, J., Kovaleski, J. F., Prasse, D., et al. (2005). *Response to intervention*. Alexandria, VA: National Association of State Directors of Special Education.

Bergan, J. R. (1977). *Behavioral consultation*. Columbus, OH: Charles E. Merrill.

Bergan, J. R., Curry, D. R., Currin, S., Haberman, K., & Nicholson, E. (1973). *Tucson early education psychological services*. Tucson: Arizona Center for Educational Research and Development, College of Education, University of Arizona.

Bergan, J. R., & Kratochwill, T. R. (1990). *Behavioral consultation and therapy*. New York: Plenum.

Bradley, R., Danielson, L., & Hallahan, D. P. (Eds.) (2002). *Identification of learning disabilities: Research to practice*. Mahwah, NJ: Lawrence Erlbaum.

Burns, M. K., Appleton, J. J., & Stehouwer, J. D. (2005). Meta-analytic review of responsiveness-to-intervention research:

Examining field-based and research implemented. *Journal of Psychoeducational Assessment, 23,* 381–394.

Chall, J. S. (2000). *The academic achievement challenge: What really works in the classroom.* New York: Guilford.

Cutts, N. E. (1955). *School psychology at mid-century.* Washington DC: American Pychological Association.

Coyne, M. D., Kame'enui, E. J., & Carnine, D. W. (2007). *Effective teaching strategies that accommodate diverse learners* (3rd ed.). Columbus, OH: Merrill Publishing Company.

Deno, S. L. (1985). Curriculum-based measurement: The emerging alternative. *Exceptional Children, 52,* 219–232.

Deno, S., Mirkin, P., & Shinn, M. (1979). *Behavioral perspectives on the assessment of learning disabled children.* Minneapolis, MN: Institute for Research on Learning Disabilities, University of Minnesota. ERIC ED 185769

Deno, S. L., & Mirkin, P. K. (1977). *Data-based program modification: A manual.* Minneapolis: Leadership Training Institute for Special Education, University of Minnesota. ERIC ED 144270.

Denton, C. A., Vaughn, S., & Fletcher, J. M. (2003). Bringing research-based practice in reading intervention to scale. *Learning Disabilities, 18,* 201–211.

Donovan, M. S., & Cross, C. T. (2002). *Minority students in special and gifted education.* Washington, DC: National Academy Press.

Education of All Handicapped Children Act of 1975, 20 U.S.C. § 1400 et seq. (statute); 34 CFR 300 (regulations published in 1977).

Elbaum, B., Vaughn, S., Hughes, M. T., & Moody, S. W. (2000). How effective are one-to-one tutoring programs in reading for elementary students at risk for reading failure? A meta-analysis of the intervention research. *Journal of Educational Psychology, 92,* 605–619.

Fletcher, J. M., Coulter, W. A., Reschly, D. J., Vaughn, S. (2004). Alternative approaches to the definition and identification of learning disabilities: Some questions and answers. *Annals of Dyslexia, 54,* 304–331.

Fletcher, J. M., Lyon, G. R., Barnes, M., Stuebing, K. K., Francis, D. J., Olson, R. K., & Shaywitz, S. E. (2002). Classification of Learning Disabilities: An evidence-based evaluation. In R. Bradley, L. Danielson, & D. P. Hallahan (Eds.), *Identification of learning disabilities: Research to practice* (pp. 185–250). Mahwah, NJ: Lawrence Erlbaum.

Fletcher, J. M., Lyon, G. R., Fuchs, L. S., & Barnes, M. A. (2007). *Learning disabilities: From identification to intervention.* New York: Guilford.

Fletcher, J. M., & Reschly, D. J. (2005). Changing procedures for identifying learning disabilities: The danger of perpetuating old ideas. *The School Psychologist, 59*(1), 10–15.

Forness, S. R., Kavale, K. A., Blum, I., & Lloyd, J. W. (1997). Mega-analysis of meta-analyses: What works in special education and related services. *Teaching Exceptional Children, 29*(6), 4–9.

Fuchs, D., Fuchs, L. S., Tindal, G., & Deno, S. L. (1986). Performance instability of learning disabled, emotionally handicapped, and nonhandicapped children. *Learning Disability Quarterly, 9,* 84–88.

Fuchs, L. S., & Fuchs, D. (1986). Effects of systematic formative evaluation: A meta-analysis. *Exceptional Children, 53,* 199–208.

Fuchs, L. S., & Fuchs, D. (2004). Determining adequate yearly progress from kindergarten through grade 6 with curriculum-based measurement. *Assessment for Effective Instruction, 29*(4), 25–38.

Germann, G., & Tindal, G. (1985). An application of curriculum-based assessment: The use of direct and repeated measurement. *Exceptional Children, 52,* 244–265.

Gersten, R., & Baker, S. (2001). Teaching expressive writing to students with learning disabilities: A meta-analysis. *Elementary School Journal, 101,* 251–272.

Gersten, R., Fuchs, L. S., Williams, J. P., & Baker, S. (2001). Teaching reading comprehension strategies to students with learning disabilities: A review of the research. *Review of Educational Research, 71,* 279–320.

Good, R. H., & Kaminski, R. A. (2003). *Dynamic indicators of early basic literacy skills.* Longmont, CO: Sopris West.

Good, R. H., Simmons, D., & Kame'enui, E. (2001). The importance and decision-making utility of a continuum of fluency-based indicators of foundational reading skills for third-grade high-stakes outcomes. *Scientific Studies of Reading, 5,* 257–288.

Graden, J. L., Stollar, S. A., & Poth, R. L. (2007). The Ohio Integrated Systems Model: Overview and lessons learned. In S. R. Jimerson, M. K. Burns, & A. Van Der Heyden (Eds.), *Handbook of response to intervention: The science and practice of assessment and intervention* (pp. 290–301). New York: Springer.

Graham, S., & Harris, K. R. (2006). Explicitly teaching struggling writers (and their classmates) strategies for mastering the writing process. *Intervention in School and Clinic, 41,* 290–294.

Greer-Chase, M., Rhodes, W. A., & Kellam, S. G. (2002). Why the prevention of aggressive disruptive behaviors in middle school must begin in elementary school. *The Clearing House, 75*(5), 242–245.

Gresham, F. M. (2002). Responsiveness to intervention: An alternative approach to the identification of learning disabilities. In R. Bradley, L. Danielson, & D. P. Hallahan (Eds.), *Identification of learning disabilities: Research to practice* (pp. 467–519). Mahwah, NJ: Lawrence Erlbaum.

Gresham, F. M., MacMillan, D. L., & Bocian, K. M. (1998). Agreement between school study team decisions and authoritative definitions in classification of students at risk for mild disabilities. *School Psychology Quarterly, 13,* 181–191.

Griffiths, A.-J., Parson, L. B., Burns, M. K., VanDerHeyden, A., & Tilly, W. D. (2007). *Response to intervention: Research to practice.* Alexandria, VA: National Associaiton of State Directors of Special Education.

Hale, J. G., Naglieri, J. A., Kaufman, A. S., & Kavale, K. A. (2004). Specific learning disability classification in the new Individuals with Disabilities Education Act: The danger of good ideas. *The School Psychologist, 58*(1), 6–13.

Hale, J. G., Kaufman, A. S., Naglieri, J. A., & Kavale, K. A. (2006). Implementing IDEA: Integrating response to intervention and cognitive assessment methods. *Psychology in the Schools, 43,* 753–770.

Hallahan, D. & Kauffman, J. (1977). Labels, categories, behaviors: ED, LD, and EMR reconsidered. *Journal of Special Education, 11,* 139–149.

Harris, K. R., Graham, S., & Mason, L. H. (2006). Improving the writing, knowledge, and motivation of struggling writers: Effects of self-regulated strategy development with and without peer support. *American Educational Research Journal, 43,* 295–340.

Hinshaw, S. P. (1992). Externalizing behavior problems and academic underachievement in childhood and adolescence: Causal relationships and underlying mechanisms. *Psychological Bulletin, 111,* 127–155.

Horner, R. H., & Sugai, G. (2000). School-wide behavior support: An emerging initiative (special issue). *Journal of Positive Behavioral Interventions, 2,* 231–233.

Ikeda, M. J., Tilly, W. D. III., Stumme, J., Volmer, L., & Allison, R. (1996). Agency-wide implementation of problem solving consultation: Foundations, current implementation, and future directions. *School Psychology Quarterly, 11,* 228–243.

Individuals with Disabilities Education Act (1997, 2004 2006). 20 U. S. C. 1400 et. Seq. (Statute). 34C.F.R. 300 (Regulations).

Kaufman, A. (1976). A new approach to interpretation of test scatter on the WISC-R. *Journal of Learning Disabilities, 9,* 160–168.

Kavale, K. (1990) The effectiveness of special education. In T. B. Gutkin & C. R. Reynolds (Eds.), *The handbook of school psychology* (2nd ed., pp. 868–898). New York: Wiley.

Kavale, K. A. (2002). Discrepancy models in the identification of learning disability. In R. Bradley, L. Danielson, & D. P. Hallahan, (Eds.), *Identification of learning disabilities: Research to practice* (pp. 369–426). Mahwah, NJ: Lawrence Erlbaum.

Kavale, K. A. (2005). Effective intervention for students with specific learning disability: The nature of special education. *Learning Disabilities, 13,* 127–138.

Kavale, K. A. (2007). Quantitative research synthesis: Meta-analysis of research on meeting special educational needs. In L. Florian (Ed.), *The Sage handbook of special education* (pp. 207–221). London: Sage Publications.

Kavale, K. A., & Forness, S. R. (1999). Effectiveness of special education. In C. R. Reynolds & T. B. Gutkin (Eds.), *The handbook of school psychology* (3rd ed., pp. 984–1024). New York: Wiley.

Kavale, K. A., & Reese, J. H. (1992). The character of learning disabilities: An Iowa profile. *Learning Disability Quarterly, 15,* 74–94.

Kellam, S. G., Xiange, L., Merisca, R., Brown, C. H., & Ialongo, N. (1998). The effect of level of aggression in the first grade classroom on the course and malleability of aggressive behavior into middle school. *Development and Psychopathology, 10,* 165–185.

Learning for Tomorrow's World (2003). Paris: United Nations, Office of Economic Cooperation and Development, Programme for International Student Assessment.

Lyon, G. R, Fletcher, J. M., Shaywitz, S. E., Shaywitz, B. A., Wood, F. B., Schulte, A., & Olson, R. (2001). Rethinking learning disabilities. In C. E. Finn, Jr., A. J. Rotherham, & C. R. Hokanson, Jr. (Eds.), *Rethinking special education for a new century* (pp. 259–287). Washington DC: Thomas B. Fordham Foundation and Progressive Policy Institute.

Marston, D. (2002). A functional and intervention-based assessment approach to establishing discrepancy for students with learning disabilities. In R. Bradley, L. Danielson, & D. P. Hallahan (Eds.) *Identification of learning disabilities: Research to practice* (pp. 437–447). Mahwah, NJ: Lawrence Erlbaum.

Mayer, R. E. (2004). Should there be a three-strikes rule against pure discovery learning: The case for guided instruction. *American Psychologist, 59,* 14–19.

McCleskey, J., & Waldron, N. (1991). Identifying students with learning disabilities: The effect of implementing state guidelines. *Journal of Learning Disabilities, 24,* 501–506.

National Assessment of Educational Progress (2007). *The Nation's Report Card: Reading.* Washington DC: U.S. Department of Education, National Center for Educational Statistics.

National Reading Panel (2000). *Report of the National Reading Panel: Teaching children to read: An evidence-based assessment of the scientific research literature on reading and its implications for reading instruction.* Washington, DC: National Institute of Child Health and Human Development. www.nichd.nih.gov/publications/nrp/smallbook.pdf.

Nelson, J. R., Benner, G. J., Lane, K., & Smith, B. W. (2004). An investigation of the academic achievement of K–12 students with emotional and behavioral disorders in public school settings. *Exceptional Children, 71,* 59–73.

No Child Left Behind Act of 2001, Pub. L. No. 107–110, 115 Stat. 1425 (2002).

Noell, G. H, Duhon, G. J, Gatti, S. L, & Connell, J. E. (2002). Consultation, follow-up, and implementation of behavior management interventions in general education. *School Psychology Review, 31,* 217–234

Nunn, G. D., & McMahon, K. R. (2000). IDEAL problem solving using a collaborative effort for special needs and at-risk students. *Education, 121*(2), 305–312.

O'Neill, R. E., Horner, R. H., Albin, R. W., Sprague, J. R., Storey, K., & Newton, J. S. (1997). *Functional assessment and program development for problem behavior.* New York: Brooks/Cole Publishing Company.

Reschly, D. J. (2004). Paradigm shift, outcomes criteria, and behavioral interventions: Foundations for the future of school psychology. *School Psychology Review, 33,* 408–416.

Reschly, D. J. (2005). LD identification: primary intervention, secondary intervention, then what? *Journal of Learning Disabilities, 38,* 510–515.

Reschly, D. J. (2008). School psychology paradigm and beyond. In A. Thomas & J. Grimes (Eds.), *Best practices in school psychology V* (pp. 3–15). Bethesda, MD: National Association of School Psychologists.

Reschly, D. J., & Grimes, J. P. (1991). State department and university cooperation: Evaluation of continuing education in consultation and curriculum based assessment. *School Psychology Review, 20,* 519–526.

Reschly, D. J., Holdheide, L. R., Smartt, S. M., & Oliver, S. M. (2007). *Evaluation of LBS-1 Teacher Preparation in Inclusive Practices, Reading, and Classroom Organization—Behavior Management.* Springfield, IL: Illinois State Board of Educaiton.

Reschly, D. J., & Hosp, J. L. (2004). State SLD policies and practices. *Learning Disability Quarterly, 27,* 197–213.

Shapiro, E. S., & Kratochwill, T. R. (Eds.). (2000). *Behavioral assessment in schools: Theory, research, and clinical applications* (2nd ed.). New York: Guilford Press.

Sheridan, S. M., & Gutkin, T. B. (2000). The ecology of school psychology: Changing our paradigm for the 21st century. *School Psychology Review, 29,* 485–502.

Sheridan, S. M., Kratochwill, T. R., & Bergan, J. (1996). *Conjoint behavioral consultation: A procedural manual.* New York: Plenum.

Shinn, M. R., Stoner, G., & Walker, H. M. (2002). *Interventions for academic and behavioral problems II: Preventive and remedial approaches.* Bethesda, MD: National Association of School Psychologists.

Snow, C. E., Burns, M. S. & Griffin, P. (Eds.) (1998). *Preventing reading difficulties in young children.* Washington DC: National Academy Press.

Sugai, G., Horner, R. H., Dunlap, G., Hieneman, M., Lewis, T. J., Nelson, C. M., et al. (2000). Applying positive behavioral support and functional behavioral assessment in the schools. *Journal of Positive Behavioral Interventions, 2,* 131–143.

Sulzer-Azaroff, B., & Mayer, G. R. (1991). *Behavior analysis for lasting change.* Fort Worth, TX: Holt, Rinehart, Winston.

Swanson, H. L., & Deshler, D. (2003). Instructing adolescents with learning disabilities: Converting a meta-analysis to practice. *Journal of Learning Disabilities, 36,* 124–135.

Swanson, H. L., & Hoskyn, M. (1998). Experimental intervention research on students with learning disabilities: A meta-analysis of treatment outcomes. *Review of Educational Research, 68,* 277–321.

Swanson, H. L., Hoskyn, M., and Lee, C. (1999). *Interventions for students with learning disabilities: A meta-analysis of treatment outcomes.* New York: Guilford.

Tilly, W. D. III (2008). The evolution of school psychology to science-based practice. In A. Thomas & J. Grimes (Eds.), *Best practices in school psychology V* (pp. 17–36). Bethesda, MD: National Association of School Psychologists.

Tilly, W. D. III, Knoster, T. P., & Ikeda, M. J. (2000). Functional behavioral assessment: Strategies for behavioral support. In C. F. Telzrow & M. Tankersley (Eds.), *IDEA amendments of 1997: Practice guidelines for school-based teams* (pp. 151–198). Bethesda, MD: National Association of School Psychologists.

Tilly, W. D. III., Reschly, D. J., & Grimes, J. P. (1999). Disability determination in problem solving systems: Conceptual foundations and critical components. In D. J. Reschly,

W. D. Tilly III., & J. P. Grimes (Eds.), *Special education in transition: Functional assessment and noncategorical programming* (pp. 285–321). Longmont, CO: Sopris West.

Torgesen, J. K. (2002). The prevention of reading difficulties. *Journal of School Psychology, 40,* 7–26.

Torgesen, J. K., Wagner, R. K., Rashotte, C. A., Rose, E., Lindamood, P., Conway, T., & Garban, C. (1999). Preventing reading failure in young children with phonological processing disabilities: Group and individual responses to instruction. *Journal of Educational Psychology, 91,* 579–593.

Upah, K. R. F., & Tilly, W. D. III (2002). Designing, implementing and evaluating quality interventions. In A. Thomas and J. Grimes (Eds.), *Best practices in school psychology* (4th ed., pp. 483–501). Bethesda, MD: National Association of School Psychologists.

VanDerHayden, A. M., Witt, J. C., & Gilbertson, D. (2006). A multi-year evaluation of the effects of a response to intervention (RTI) model on identification of children for special education. *Journal of Special Education, 45,* 225–256.

Vaughn, S., Gersten, R., & Chard, D. J. (2000). The underlying message in LD intervention research: Findings from research syntheses. *Exceptional Children, 67,* 99–114.

Vaughn, S., Linan-Thompson, S., & Hickman, P. (2003). Response to instruction as a means of identifying students with reading/learning disabilities. *Exceptional Children, 69,* 391–409.

Vaughn, S., & Roberts, G. (2007). Secondary interventions in reading: Providing additional instruction for students at risk. *Teaching Exceptional Children, 39*(5), 40–46.

Walker, H. M., Colvin, G., & Ramsey, E. (1995). *Antisocial behavior in school: Strategies and best practices.* Pacific Grove, CA: Brooks/Cole.

Walker, H. M., Horner, R. H., Sugai, G., Bullis, M., Sprague, J. R., Bricker, D., et al. (1996). Integrated approaches to preventing antisocial behavior patterns among school-age children and youth. *Journal of Emotional and Behavioral Disorders, 4,* 194–209.

Walsh, K., Glaser, D., & Wilcox, D. D. (2006). *What education schools aren't teaching about reading and what elementary teachers aren't learning.* Washington DC: National Center on Teacher Quality (see www.nctq.org).

Witt, J. C., Elliott, S. N., & Gresham, F. M. (1988). *The handbook of behavior therapy in education.* New York: Guilford.

INTERVENTION:
FOCUS ON CHILDREN

●

CHAPTER 23

ECOLOGICAL SCHOOL PSYCHOLOGY: A PERSONAL OPINION AND A PLEA FOR CHANGE

TERRY B. GUTKIN[1]
San Francisco State University

"All is not well in school psychology." Those were the opening words I used along with Jane Conoley in 1990 to characterize the status of school psychology at that point in time. Today, in 2009, there is reason for both optimism and pessimism in this regard. In the intervening 19 years, school psychology has started down a long road, the end of which we will surely not see in my lifetime, and maybe not even in the lifetime of our most junior colleagues. Still, it is my personal opinion that we have at least started moving in some very productive directions. We have struggled with growing success against the inertia of history and tradition that has too often weighed us down. Evidence of real progress is discernable in areas such as empirically based interventions (Kratochwill et al., this volume), effective teaching (Doll, LeClair, & Kurien, this volume; Gettinger & Stoiber, this volume), classroom intervention (Cowan & Sheridan, this volume; Pressley et al., this volume; Reisman, this volume), data-based instructional decision making (Ysseldyke & Burns, this volume), prevention and early intervention (Durlak, this volume), fostering resilience in children and youth (Masten & Motti-Stefanidi, this volume), consultation and coordination of services with school personnel (Gravois, Groff, & Rosenfield, this volume; Gutkin & Curtis, this volume) and families (Buerkle, Whitehouse & Christenson, this volume), response to intervention methodologies (Jimerson, Burns, & VanDerHeyden, 2007; Reschly & Bergstrom,

this volume), and meaningful systemic and organizational change (Meyers, Meyers, Proctor, & Graybill, this volume), to name but a few domains. Nonetheless, the gap Jane Conoley and I noted in 1990, between the potential of our field and the day-to-day realities facing the overwhelming majority of practicing school psychologists, remains wide indeed, far too wide for any of us to rest on our laurels. It is perhaps worth reiterating a bit more of what we wrote 19 years ago.

> Many (perhaps most) school psychologists view the profession as having achieved but a shadow of its potential. Visions of what school psychology should be and could be are not congruent with the reality of what school psychology has come to be. (p. 203)

The struggle for school psychology to move forward has been both long and hard. Many have written extensively and eloquently before, and I am confident that others will continue to do so long after this chapter is gathering dust on library bookshelves.

My objectives for this chapter are modest, but at the same time bold. On the one hand, I aspire to be but one of many voices addressing our collective professional future. Progress will emerge only if there is continuing exploration and debate among a critical mass of school psychologists who choose to articulate a coherent vision for our field. On the other hand, I seek in this chapter to be provocative and "say what needs saying."

My primary goals are threefold. First, I wish to challenge the traditional and longstanding adherence to a medical model view of human

[1] I would like to acknowledge and thank Michael J. Curtis for his important contributions in reviewing and providing feedback for this chapter.

behavior and psychological dysfunction among professional psychologists in general and school psychologists in particular. Despite many strong opinions to the contrary (e.g., Graden, 2004; Meyers, Meyers, & Grogg, 2004; Reschly, 2008; Reschly & Ysseldyke, 2002; Sheridan & Gutkin, 2000), this paradigm remains so omnipresent, both in society and among a large majority of professional psychologists (and psychiatrists), that it is reminiscent of the problem facing fish who fail to discern that they are surrounded by water. My intent in this chapter is to call attention to the problems and "warts" that are inextricably linked to medical model psychological services, highlighting how that model stands as a barrier to progress. Second, I will attempt to communicate an alternative and more constructive model for school psychology, namely one that is based on ecological understandings of human behavior. This theoretical perspective dates back to the writings of Kurt Lewin (1951), Urie Bronfenbrenner (1979), Roger Barker (1965, 1968), Rudolf Moos (1973), and Albert Bandura (1978), among many others, and offers a superior foundation on which to anchor psychological services in general and school psychological services in particular. Third, I will attempt to translate the ecological model into the day-to-day professional practices that might flow from it were this orientation to emerge as the dominant conceptual basis underlying school psychological services. How would ecological school psychology differ from traditional medical model practice, and how might this alternative model bring our field significantly closer to bridging the longstanding gap between actual and ideal practice that has been noted by so many throughout our history (e.g., Brown, Holcombe & Bolen, 2006; Hosp & Reschly, 2002; Levinson, 1990; Meacham & Peckham, 1978; VanVoorhis & Levinson, 2006)?

Prior to deconstructing the medical model, it is important to consider why this analysis is so vital. Stated as tersely as possible, (a) the medical model serves as the conceptual foundation upon which traditional psychological and school psychological services are based, and (b) these traditional approaches to service delivery are failing both our society and our schools terribly.

AMERICA'S MENTAL HEALTH AND EDUCATION PANDEMICS

Evidence of a national pandemic relating to both the mental and educational health of our nation is everywhere to be found. There seems to be little, if any, doubt that our current models of care are seriously broken and that systemic change is needed. The following is but a sampling of the evidence supporting this conclusion.

In a recent nationally representative survey of approximately 10,000 individuals, the National Comorbidity Survey Replication (NCSR), it was reported that over the course of their lifetime nearly half of our national population (approximately 150 million people) will develop a diagnosable, DSM-IV (American Psychiatric Association, 1994) mental disorder (Kessler, Berglund, Demler, Jin, & Walters, 2005). In any given year, more than 25% of Americans (approximately 75 million people) could be diagnosed, with approximately 60% of these people suffering from ailments that are either moderate or serious in nature and a large percentage having two or more identifiable conditions (Kessler, Chiu, Demler & Walters, 2005). Of those experiencing mental illnesses in any given year, nearly 60% will receive no treatment during that year, and many of those who do receive services will do so from providers with inadequate mental health training (Wang, Lane, Olfson, Pincus, Wells, & Kessler, 2005). Complementing these results are findings that for those with lifetime disabilities the median time gap between the onset of a disorder and the receipt of treatment ranges from 6 to 23 years, depending on the nature of the diagnosis (Wang, Berglund, Olfson, Pincus, Wells & Kessler, 2005). Essentially confirming this state of affairs, Norcross (2006) summarized the results of the WHO World Mental Health Survey Consortium (2004) and reported that:

> The statistics on professionally treated mental disorders are compelling. Approximately 85% of Americans will not receive health care treatment for their diagnosable mental or substance-abuse disorder within a year. In fact, more than 70% of them will never receive specialized mental health care. (p. 683)

In summarizing the NCSR data, Wang, Lane et al. (2005) concluded that "most people with mental disorders in the United States remain either untreated or poorly treated" (p. 629). Above and beyond pain and suffering, this translates into a staggering cost of nearly $220 billion per year for our nation in treatment expenditures and lost economic output, third only to cancer and coronary disease (DeVol & Bedroussian, 2007). The director of the National Institute of Mental Health, Thomas Insel, characterizes data such as these as indicative of "a systemic and unacceptable failure in the provision of [mental health] care" in the United States (Insel & Fenton, 2005, p. 590).

Unfortunately, the situation appears to be no better when it comes to America's children and youth. As noted in the opening sentence of the summary of the Report of the Surgeon General's Conference on Children's Mental Health (U. S. Public Health Service, 2000), "the nation is facing a public crisis in mental healthcare for infants, children and adolescents." Garbarino (1995) writes, "The mere act of living in our society today is dangerous to the health and well-being of children and adolescents ... the social world of children, the social context in which they grow up, has become poisonous to their development" (p. ix, 4).

Statistics abound detailing the threats facing young people. Data presented by Sheridan and Gutkin (2000) and Crockett (2003) are representative of these findings, a small sampling of which includes the following.

- Three million teenagers struggle with depression
- 19% of high school aged students who completed the 2001 Youth Risk Behavior Surveillance System from the Centers for Disease Control and Prevention seriously considered suicide at some point in the prior year
- Only 36% of youth at risk for suicide during the past year received mental health services
- One in every four girls and seven boys has been sexually abused before the age of 18
- Millions of children start school not ready to learn
- 17% of youth between the ages of 12 and 17 reportedly carried weapons
- 50% of adolescents are at moderate to high risk for mental health problems
- Every day 1500 students drop out of school

Other sources of child- and youth-based statistics are equally concerning. Mental Health America, for example, reports on its website (www1.nmha.org/children/prevent/stats.cfm) that at any given time approximately 20% of young people (approximately 8–13 million individuals) are affected by a mental health problem, between 500,000–1,000,000 youths attempt suicide each year, and that only about one-third of children and youth needing assistance with mental health problems are getting the help they need. Contemporary research suggests that the frequencies of a wide array of significant psychological dysfunctions (e.g., learning disabilities, autism spectrum disorders, bipolar disorders, major depression, substance abuse, suicide, eating disorders) are increasing, some quite rapidly (e.g., Blader & Carlson, 2007; Prosser & McArdle, 1996; Raphael & Lacey, 1994; Scruggs & Mastropieri, 2002; Sweeney & Hoffman, 2004). The Surgeon General (U. S. Department of Health and Human Services, 1999), who issued a comprehensive report on the nation's mental health, concluded "there are approximately 6 to 9 million children and adolescents in the United States with serious emotional disturbances" (p. 179). The "foremost finding [of this report] is that most children in need of mental health services do not get them" (p.180).

These statistics, and a myriad of other supporting evidence not cited in this chapter due to space limitations, are sobering. One gets the sense of being in a sinking boat, in which the water is pouring in faster than we can bail it out. We are in a worsening crisis, and if there is to be any hope of making real progress the response of our profession must go far beyond simply doing more of the same. It is (and has been for quite a while) time for a fundamental re-examination of the foundational assumptions on which our professional services are built. A central thesis of this chapter is that our collective failure to respond adequately to the mental health and education pandemics described above results in large part from the implementation of services premised on the medical model, which provides practitioners, researchers, and university trainers alike with a flawed understanding of (a) human behavior, and (b) treatment provision.

THE MEDICAL MODEL: A PARADIGM THAT HAS OUTLIVED ITS USEFULNESS

The central defining and most problematic features of the medical model as it is applied to the field of psychology in general, and school psychology in particular, are (a) analogizing psychological problems to medical illnesses, and (b) focusing attention on internal client pathologies while largely ignoring external environmental variables (Albee & Joffe, 2004).

Regarding the former, unwanted human behavior is conceptualized as emanating from mental diseases that are internal to the individual, much as physical problems result from inner physiological disorders. The focus on interior pathologies is clearly evident in the introduction to the American Psychiatric Association's *Diagnostic and Statistical Manual* (DSM-IV) (1994), which defines "mental disorder ... [as] a manifestation of a behavioral, psychological, or biological dysfunction *in the individual* [italics added]" (pp. xxi–xxii). In terms of the latter characteristic, environmental and contextual stimuli are relegated to relatively minor roles in relationship to the internal disease states from which patients/clients are believed to suffer. For school psychologists, this overreliance on what occurs "inside" children at the expense of considering what goes on in the multiple environments that surround them is a crucial error with profound implications for our profession and the services we deliver.

For the purposes of this chapter, analysis of the medical model will center on problems related to its (a) underlying conceptual assumptions, (b) efficacy, and (c) practicality.

Conceptual Problems

"Mental Illness," Unlike Medical Disease, Is Largely Defined by Its Environmental Context

Treating psychological dysfunction as a medical disease suggests a level of independence from environmental variables that is not warranted (Albee & Joffe, 2004). Medical disorders are always medical disorders regardless of the situational contexts in which they occur. To put it simplistically, lung cancer is always a disease independent of the circumstances surrounding its appearance. Medical illnesses are context-independent. The same cannot be said for the preponderance of "mental illnesses." *Whether a human behavior, thought or feeling is considered a mental disorder depends to a large extent on the context of values, norms, human expectations, ethics, morals, laws, politics, religious beliefs, economics, history, mores, and so forth in which it becomes manifest* (Albee & Joffe, 2004; Szasz, 1960). The status of human psychological functioning as a disease entity is, with only a few exceptions, context-dependent, that is, it is a reflection of human culture.

Past, present and potential future examples of the context-dependent nature of mental disorders abound and only space limitations prevent a very long list of illustrations from being presented.

Gazing backwards in time we find drapetomania, a medical/psychiatric diagnosis put forth in 1851 (Cartwright, 1851; White, 2002). At the time drapetomania was thought to be a mental disease afflicting American slaves, causing them to flee captivity. Although ludicrous by contemporary standards, the racist social norms of the day made it easy for a slave-owning society to conceptualize runaway slaves as mentally ill. After all, if slaves were less than fully human and thus incapable of sustaining themselves without the assistance of slave owners, why would slaves try to escape from the safe and secure environment of slavery into probable self-destruction unless they were mentally ill?

In more contemporary times, we find an array of issues pertaining to homosexuality. Once deemed by the American Psychiatric Association to be a mental disorder, it has, since the publication of the DSM III (American Psychiatric Association, 1980), been declassified and is no longer considered to be a "mental illness." Although there is no absolute proof that can be offered, logic and a recounting of the political process behind the decision making suggests that the recent view of homosexuality as "normal" reflects a change in the culture of Western and American societal norms rather than any scientific discovery that homosexuality is not actually a "disease" (Greenberg, 1997). It is instructive to point out, however, that given today's ongoing political strife surrounding gay-lesbian-bisexual-transgender (GLBT) lifestyles and behaviors, it would not be too difficult to imagine circumstances (e.g., Western culture pervasively returned to "traditional family values") under which homosexuality could be reclassified as a mental disorder. Alternatively, if political and cultural trends continue to progress in the direction of gay rights, it would not be surprising to find homophobia enshrined as a mental illness in the future. In essence, whether GLBT individuals, or those who are intolerant of such persons, are considered to be "mentally ill" always has been, and will continue to be, determined primarily by sociocultural rather than medical facts.

Looking to the future, it is not too difficult to envision how cultural controversies could be converted into "mental illnesses." Abortion provides one of many possible examples. For the sake of discussion, let's assume that over the course of the next 50 years the "pro-life" view of abortion becomes the dominant mindset in our society.

Through this lens, abortion would be perceived as murder and those who had abortions might logically be considered to be suffering from a mental illness. The mental illness metaphor would provide our culture with at least one explanation for why women might voluntarily "murder" their own unborn children. Continuing along this line of thought, doctors who performed hundreds or thousands of abortions for money and vocational fulfillment might be construed as socio- or psychopaths. They would appear to a "pro-life" society as serial killers with no grasp of the irrationality of their deeds and no sense of remorse for their actions.

Shifting specifically to children, schools, and the field of school psychology, the influence of context on determinations of psychopathology is no less evident. Having lived for extensive periods of time in New York City, Lincoln, Nebraska, and San Francisco, it is patently obvious to me that behaviors diagnosed as "abnormal" in one environment might be viewed as "normal" in another. Thresholds for referrals, diagnoses and placements pertaining to conduct disorder, attention deficit hyperactivity disorder (ADHD), emotional disturbance, learning disabilities, and so forth likely vary dramatically depending on the demographic and socioeconomic characteristics of school districts, and the tolerance levels and resources of individual primary caregivers (e.g., teachers, parents) who work and live in those school districts. Research done in this area has shown, for example, how the interpretation of diagnostic criteria can differ from state to state, city to city, and district to district (e.g., Coutinho & Oswald, 1998; Lester & Kelman, 1997; Oswald, Coutinho, & Best, 2001; Scruggs & Mastropieri, 2002; Singer, Palfrey, Butler, & Walker, 1989; Skiba, Grizzle, & Minke, 1994).

"Mental Illness" Is Often Created or Facilitated by External Environments Rather than Internal Diseases

Another element of the context-dependent nature of psychological dysfunction is that *in many instances it is precisely the environmental context that either creates or facilitates the creation of "mental illnesses."* Viewing a person's problems as a context-independent, internal disease opens the door to blaming the victim and overlooking potential intervention opportunities directed toward causal variables in the environment.

Slavery once again provides an easy historical example of how this flawed mechanism can work.

Slaves were systematically denied access to formal education and then were subsequently viewed as intellectually inferior. By conceptualizing the problem as an internal characteristic of the slaves (a context-independent explanation) rather than the result of a dysfunctional and inhumane system (a context-dependent perspective), society was able to divert attention away from the injustices of the day and failed to appreciate the cognitive abilities of the slave population. Although the fallacy of this logic is clear today, it nonetheless highlights the role of the internal pathology metaphor in drawing attention away from causal environmental variables, even when the role of those variables should have been obvious to anyone who would have taken even a superficial glance at them.

The 1950s reveal a parallel, although less extreme, example of the same phenomenon, namely the "depressed housewife" (Friedan, 1963). At that point in American history, women were relegated primarily to being housewives, secretaries, teachers, nurses, airline stewardesses, librarians, and so on. Those who had alternative career aspirations were stifled and prevented from living out their dreams. Not surprisingly, many of these women may have become "depressed" (e.g., Krause, 1983; McMullen & Stoppard, 2006; Repetti & Crosby, 1984). From a medical model perspective, they were suffering from context-independent, medical disorders. With hindsight, however, we might hypothesize that much of their problem was a function of an environmental context that facilitated the emergence of their "illness." Failing to see the context-dependent nature of this psychological problem is to miss its very essence (e.g., Ballou & Brown, 2002; Caplan, 1992; Stoppard & McMullen, 2003; Unger, 2001).

Although the problems of today are different, this underlying criticism of medical model conceptualizations of human suffering remains the same. Bulimia and anorexia provide good contemporary exemplars. Can it be a coincidence that the dramatic rise of these serious problem behaviors mirrors the shift in our culture toward a standard of female beauty that is based on extreme thinness? Logic, the research literature (e.g., Halliwell & Harvey, 2006; Raphael & Lacey, 1994; Stice, 1994; Tolman, Impett, & Tracy, 2006), and the work of leading therapists (e.g., Pipher, 1995) suggest otherwise. Medical model views that focus almost exclusively on the context-independent internal pathologies of anorexia and bulimia victims miss the point of how external societal forces contribute to the development of eating disorders. Recent analyses of cultural contexts associated with suicidal behavior among racial minority adolescents effectively make the same point (Goldston, Molock, Whitbeck, Murakami, Zayas, & Hall, 2008). Failing to grasp these relationships will prevent mental health professionals from meaningfully reducing these problems on a societal basis, even though we may achieve success with individual clients.

Parallel arguments can be made regarding depression and anxiety. Based on the ever increasing number of antidepression and antianxiety medications being sold to people of all ages, these "mental illnesses" appear to be on their way to becoming virtually omnipresent in our society. A very recent report from the Centers for Disease Control and Prevention, for example, indicates that antidepressants are now the most frequently prescribed category of medications in the nation (Burt, McCaig, & Rechtsteiner, 2007). Should this be understood as a massive failure of DNA and biological functioning in America's adults, adolescents and children? Should the growing levels of psychological distress be attributed to an increasing presence of internal medical pathologies that are plaguing our nation's population? I think not. Essentially, psychosocial stressors have become increasingly potent and pervasive in our society for ever-growing numbers of people, and this environmental and cultural shift ultimately translates into increasing incidence of psychological problems, including depression, anxiety and a large number of other psychopathologies (e.g., Albee, 1992, 2005; Rusk & Rusk, 2007; Wargo, 2007). A medical model view focusing on context-independent disease entities is not going to be very helpful if one's intent is to slow down and reverse the spread of depression and anxiety among Americans.

More specific to school psychology is the issue of academic failure. Based on medical model logic, when academic progress is sufficiently slow, students are diagnosed with one of a variety of pathological conditions (e.g., learning disabilities, ADHD, emotional disturbance, mental retardation). This is done even though I suspect that virtually every practicing school psychologist knows that very often many of the causes for current or historical student learning problems (particularly for the mildly handicapped) lie with factors originating in problematic school, home, community and other relevant surrounding

environments. Yet, driven by the medical model, it is the student we identify as "diseased" rather than diagnosing the confluence of environmental forces that surround and interact with students.

The recent Hurricane Katrina disaster provides a good example. Masses of children in New Orleans were uprooted from their normal lives and thrown into traumatic and sometimes life-threatening circumstances. Many lost parents, siblings, or friends. Others were separated from their families and forced to move to previously unknown cities and entirely new school, community and social contexts. For those not impacted directly by Katrina, it is hard to even imagine the level of psychological distress inflicted on the children of New Orleans. Beyond question, upon returning to school (some in a devastated New Orleans and others in entirely new parts of the country) many of these children experienced learning problems. Are we to understand these learning problems as the result of internal, medical pathologies that are independent of environmental conditions? Of course, that would be ludicrous as the environment was so clearly and so deeply involved in the creation of these problems. And yet many of these very children, whose educational burden has been so dramatically increased by external environmental events, have been assessed and diagnosed by school psychologists as disturbed, disabled, or mentally ill in one way or another. The DSM (American Psychiatric Association, 1994) and IDEIA (Individuals with Disabilities Education Improvement Act) (U. S. Department of Education, 2006) diagnoses we affix to these students serve to tell everyone that it is not society, it's institutions, or environmental contextual variables that have negatively impacted these children. Rather, it is the children themselves who are not "normal."

A less dramatic but nonetheless illuminating example comes from a personal work experience in an urban, lower SES (socioeconomic status) school in which approximately 85% of the students were reading below grade level. The principal instructed me, as the school psychologist, to test as many of these students as possible because he believed that the preponderance of these poor readers were, in fact, learning disabled. My response was to suggest that a more reasonable course of action might be to consider revising the reading curriculum for the school so that more effective instructional practices were instituted. The difference in our reactions to the conditions we both observed was that the principal attributed students' reading problems to medical model, context-independent, internal pathologies, and I viewed them as resulting largely from student interactions with an instructional environment that failed to meet their needs.

Medicalizing Human Behavior Is Not an Effective Way to Conceptualize Psychological Dysfunction, Despite the Central Role Played by Biology

Despite the fact that it is becoming increasingly popular to medicalize psychological dysfunction, a closer analysis suggests that this may not be a helpful way to view "mental illness" (e.g., Kutchins & Kirk, 1997; Wyatt & Midkiff, 2006). Much of the drive to employ the medical model emerges from a growing body of scientific information indicating that there are, in fact, biological factors that underlie many behaviors considered to be psychopathological (e.g., López-Ibor, Gaebel & Maj, 2002; Zorumski & Rubin, 2005). Although appealing, this observation is not a compelling reason to adopt a medical model orientation in clinical practice.

In the final analysis, humans are biological beings and thus "biological mechanisms underlie all behavior" (Breedlove, Rosenzweig & Watson, 2007, p. 7). As biological science progresses and grows in sophistication, a rapidly growing list of both positive and negative human behaviors with noteworthy biological factors is going to emerge (Ratey & Johnson, 1997). To date, in addition to various psychopathologies, this includes "normal" behavior (Shrivastava & Rao, 1997) and positive traits such as happiness (Cardoso, 2007); empathy, sympathy, altruism, and prosocial behavior (Hastings, Zahn-Waxler, & McShane, 2006); humor (Fry, 1994); creativity (Pfenninger & Shubik, 2001); and artistic expression (Zaidel, 2005), to name a few. Should the existence of biological underpinnings for these behaviors lead us as psychologists to treat these phenomena as medical in nature? Should the emerging movements in positive psychology and mental health promotion (e.g., Keyes, 2007; Seligman, Steen, & Park, 2005) be focused primarily on internal, biological and neuropsychological variables? I would argue that this would be entirely inappropriate.

By itself, the fact that undesirable human behaviors have a basis in biology does not justify invoking the medical model as a framework for either understanding or treating "mental illnesses." To do so is to be entrapped by the fundamental attribution error, in which negative behaviors of others are inappropriately attributed to internal variables while the causal impact of external factors are largely ignored (Jones & Harris, 1967).

A few examples will hopefully illuminate this fallacy. For the sake of discussion, let's assume that sexual attraction to members of one's own gender is almost exclusively a function of biology. Although it is not yet known whether this is true, I suspect that few would be surprised if a biological link to human homosexuality were unearthed at some point in the not-too-distant future, especially in light of recent findings of a sexuality gene in fruit flies that controls homo- versus heterosexual behavior (Grosjean, Grillet, Augustin, Ferveur, & Featherstone, 2007). Even if a strong genetic, hormonal, biochemical or neurological connection to human homosexuality was discovered, however, it would shed no light on whether human homosexuality is (or is not) a "mental illness." If a substantive physiological link with human sexual orientation were established irrefutably, would mental health professionals be compelled to reclassify homosexuality as a disease simply because it was proven to be biologically based? Of course that would not be the case. On the opposite side of the coin, if it were determined scientifically that suicidal tendencies had virtually no biological basis whatsoever, that is, they were found to result almost entirely from environmental factors, would that make suicidal ideation or suicide attempts less of a "mental illness"? That would also be an illogical conclusion which few, if any, mental health specialists would reach.

The bottom line is that determining that various problematic human behaviors, thoughts or feelings are impacted by one's biology does not logically mean that these phenomena should be conceptualized or treated as "mental illnesses" and addressed via context-independent, medical model services. One does not imply the other. First, regardless of whether particular behaviors have biological components, the decision as to whether various forms of human functioning are viewed as a "mental illness" is determined, as argued earlier, primarily by criteria that are cultural and value-based. Second, even though psychological functioning is affected by biological factors, an approach focusing almost exclusively on internal, intrapersonal variables is inappropriate in light of the fact (as detailed subsequently in this chapter) that environmental variables exert powerful causal influence as well (e.g.,

Bandura, 1986a; Barker, 1968; Bronfenbrenner, 1979; Cowan & Sheridan, this volume; Doll et al. this volume; Gettinger & Stoiber, this volume; Skinner, 1953).

Without doubt there are some diagnoses in which biological causation is very evident and powerful. Traumatic brain injury, severe autism, and severe/profound mental retardation would be among these. Using conditions such as these to justify the use of the medical model as the foundational and overarching conceptual tool for all psychological services, however, is to allow the "tail to wag the dog." Clearly, the overwhelming preponderance of clients being served by psychology and school psychology practitioners do not include those for whom biological mechanisms are as palpable as they are in these specific situations. As such, we ought not to allow this handful of lower-frequency diagnoses to dictate the manner in which we approach our work in general. The "dog" should "wag the tail," not vice versa.

Beyond this, it is noteworthy that even for those diagnosed with traumatic brain injury, severe autism, and severe/profound mental retardation, environmental rather than internal medical interventions are often the most successful treatment modalities (e.g., Bregman, Zager, & Gerdtz, 2005; Gurdin, Huber, & Cochran, 2005; Matson, Bamburg, & Smalls, 1997). Thus, even when working with clients who are clearly suffering from biologically based dysfunction, analysis of relevant environmental factors must still receive significant attention from psychologists, contrary to the principle thrust of the medical model directing our attention almost exclusively toward the internal pathologies of clients.

Finally, it is critical to understand that the relationship between biology (e.g., brain functioning, genetics, biochemistry) and the environment is interactive in nature; a metaphorical "two-way street." The medical model is deeply flawed because it highlights only one of these directions, namely the influence of internal bodily processes on behavior. It fails to address the equally important effect of behavior and environment on one's biology. Evidence for this latter set of relationships, however, is everywhere to be found (Breedlove et al., 2007; Rusk & Rusk, 2007; U. S. Department of Health and Human Services, 1999). Fundamental internal physiological reactions to external environmental events, such as stress responses, sexual arousal and sleep patterns, reflect the impact of environments on biological functioning with great clarity. Pianta (this volume)

discusses how factors such as socioeconomic status, family conflict, peer group and neighborhood factors, exercise, and so forth all influence the timing of puberty onset in adolescents. In relationship specifically to mental health issues, posttraumatic stress disorder (PTSD) provides an excellent illustration of this bidirectional principle. While it is generally accepted that PTSD reflects a cascade of biological events (Everly & Lating, 2004; Vasterling & Brewin, 2005), it is also clear that these internal physiological reactions are set in motion by exposure to one or more environmentally based traumas (e.g., Delahanty & Nugent, 2006). The same can be said for depression. Although a manifestation of various internal biochemical states, it can be set off by a series of distressing external environmental events (e.g., Kaufman & Charney, 2001; Smolin, Klein, & Levy, 2007; van Praag, de Kloet, & van Os, 2004). Even in the area of genetics,

> there is a growing recognition by biologists that the environment determines which genes are expressed and how they are expressed. Although biological processes are the essential mechanisms mediating all physical and psychological functioning, micro- and macro-environments determine which of these genes are being turned on or off, from conception until death. (Rusk & Rusk, 2007, pp. 4–5)

Building on this line of research, Walker and Tessner (2008) present a detailed analysis of how gene-environment interactions play an important role in the development of schizophrenia.

When focusing on school-aged children, the "two-way street" between internal and external variables is equally evident. For example, given that effective teaching and classroom structures lead to better learning and academic achievement (Doll et al., this volume; Gettinger & Stoiber, this volume), it is hard indeed to comprehend how these environmental manipulations would not also translate into biochemical and neurological effects for students as they take in new information and develop cognitive skills for learning more effectively and efficiently in the future. Pellegrini (1995) critically analyzes ADHD, arguing that traditional conceptualizations based on unidirectional influences of biology on behavior are inaccurate as evidence suggests an interactive relationship between internal mechanisms and the environment. And what of students who become addicted to legal (e.g., cigarettes, alcohol) or illegal (e.g., methamphetamines) substances as a result of peer influence and exposure to the drug culture? This is yet a further and very obvious demonstration of how the environment can dramatically impact the biology of children and youth.

Understanding the reciprocal and dynamic relationship between the environment and internal biological states highlights the fallacy of relying on the medical model to guide professional practice, as this traditional approach directs the preponderance of school psychologists' time and energy toward the assessment and diagnosis of internal pathologies while largely ignoring potentially crucial environmental variables.

Curing "Mental Illness" Is Not the Best Way to Engender Mental Health

Historically, the near-exclusive focus of the medical model has been on ridding clients of internally based mental illnesses. Recently, however, it has become increasingly clear that even if psychologists and psychiatrists were to be successful at curing all psychological diseases (which, in light of the mental health pandemic documented earlier, is very far beyond our reach as of this point in time), this would not necessarily result in people who are psychologically healthy. Stated succinctly, mental health has come to be viewed as more than the mere absence of mental illness. It is an "entity" unto itself. This more modern sense of mental health focuses primarily on promoting positive and healthy psychological behaviors rather than just curing those that are dysfunctional and unhealthy (e.g., Huebner & Gilman, 2003; Keyes, 2007). This growing zeitgeist is reflected clearly in contemporary literatures pertaining to positive mental health (Clonan, Chafouleas, & McDougal, 2004; Seligman et al., 2005), flow (Schmidt, Shernoff, & Csikszentmihalyi, 2007), and resilience (Masten & Motti-Stefanidi, this volume), to name a few areas of ongoing research and theory development.

As such, one of the largest conceptual problems with the medical model is that it "misses the mark" and is not sufficiently ambitious. If generating positive mental health is a goal for psychology in general and school psychology in particular, and I would argue vigorously that it most certainly should be, then the medical model is not the vehicle for helping us "get from here to there." Creating and facilitating positive mental health is going to require systemic and proactive change in a broad array of societal environments (most definitely including schools). The medical

model is inherently inadequate for this task as it is inescapably reactive in nature (coming into play subsequent to the emergence of psychopathology) and overly focused on a "psychology of the individual" rather than systems (Sarason, 1981, p. 827). Employing a pathology-based model as the primary "default option" for mental health services in the twenty-first century constrains the potential of psychologists (including school psychologists) to promote positive mental health by diverting virtually all of our attention away from this goal and toward curing "mental illness."

Efficacy Problems

As suggested by the mental health and education pandemics described previously, our current service delivery systems, based on the medical model, are not adequately efficacious. In fact, they are seriously broken and in need of substantive repair. For the purposes of this chapter, analyses of this point center on (a) a critique of historical and contemporary diagnostic systems emerging from the medical model, (b) inadequate treatment outcomes following traditional school psychological service provision, and (c) the disconnect between assessment information gathered under the medical model and the nature of information needed for effective treatment.

Systems of Diagnosis

The most prominent elements of school psychologists' job roles, both historically and in contemporary practice, are assessment and diagnostic services (Reschly & Ysseldyke, 2002). The dominance and power of the medical model in these arenas are amply illustrated by two simple questions. Who/what gets assessed? Who/what gets diagnosed? In both instances, it is individual students and their presumed internal pathologies. This, of course, is not an accident, coincidence, or happenstance. It is a logical outgrowth of utilizing the medical model to guide school psychological practice. Relevant environments in which students function (e.g., classrooms, schools, communities, homes) and the adults who control these environments (e.g., teachers, principals, community leaders, parents) are generally given a "pass," as they are not overtly conceptualized in the medical model as major contributors to the problem at hand. Given the central role often played by environmental factors (Bandura, 1986a; Barker, 1968; Bronfenbrenner, 1979; Cowan & Sheridan, this volume; Doll et al., this volume; Gettinger & Stoiber, this volume; Skinner, 1953) in creating and/or sustaining student dysfunction, however, it should come as no surprise that many of the intervention plans generated by traditional school psychological practice often lack sufficient efficacy.

Above and beyond the tunnel vision described above, it is important to note that the medical model diagnostic systems employed most frequently by school psychologists (those promulgated by IDEIA [U. S. Department of Education, 2006] and the DSM series [American Psychiatric Association, 1980, 1994]) are often problematic in terms of fundamental psychometric properties such as reliability and validity. Longstanding difficulties in these areas have been well documented by others (Davidow & Levinson, 1993; Macmann & Barnett, 1999; Sarbin, 1997; Watkins, this volume). Space limitations prevent anything other than a cursory review in this chapter.

One of the most interesting "defenses" of traditional medical model assessment and diagnosis comes from Matarazzo (1990). He writes:

> Therefore, in regard to the critical issue that the validity of DSM-III-type differential diagnoses has not be been adequately established ... my belief [is] that currently there is no body of research that indicates that psychological assessment across the whole domain is valid or is other than clinical art. However ... I include ... the equally relevant opinion that in this regard psychology is little different than engineering, medicine, or other professions. (p. 1015)

Matarazzo's summary of research pertaining to psychological assessment and diagnosis, however, provides little reassurance of the scientific quality of these processes, and unintentionally only serves to raise significant concerns about diagnostic systems in professions such as medicine.

Underscoring Matarazzo's (1990) conclusions are limitations of categorical diagnostic systems noted in the DSM itself.

> In DSM-IV, there is no assumption that each category of mental disorder is a completely discrete entity with absolute boundaries dividing it from other mental disorders *or from no mental disorder* [italics added]. ... The clinician using DSM-IV should therefore consider that individuals sharing a diagnosis are likely to be heterogeneous *even in regard to the defining features of the diagnosis* [italics added]. (American Psychiatric Association, 1994, p. xxii)

In light of these characteristics of the premiere medical model diagnostic system, the lack of interclinician reliability and the absence of strong evidence of scientific validity is somewhat predictable.

Closely examining current criteria for some of the more common medical model diagnoses serves to further clarify why reliability and validity have proven to be such vexing problems. The IDEIA (U. S. Department of Education, 2006) diagnosis for Emotional Disturbance (ED) (see Table 23.1), for example, is replete with ambiguity regarding pivotal components of the diagnosis. The following terms drawn directly from the ED diagnostic criteria are open to a myriad of interpretations by practitioners and researchers alike: (a) "a long period of time,"

TABLE 23.1   **Individuals with Disabilities Education Improvement Act (IDEIA) Definition of Emotional Disturbance**

The term "emotional disturbance" means a condition exhibiting one or more of the following characteristics over a long period of time and to a marked degree, which adversely affects educational performance:

a.   An inability to learn which cannot be explained by intellectual, sensory, or health factors;
b.   An inability to build or maintain satisfactory relationships with peers and teachers;
c.   Inappropriate types of behavior or feelings under normal circumstances;
d.   A general pervasive mood of unhappiness/depression; or
e.   A tendency to develop physical symptoms or fears associated with personal or school problems.

The term includes children who are schizophrenic (or autistic). The term does not include children who are socially maladjusted, unless it is determined that they are socially disturbed.

Reprinted from U. S. Department of Health, 2006, p. 46756.

(b) "to a marked degree," (c) "satisfactory interpersonal relationships," (d) "inappropriate types of behavior or feelings," and (e) "under normal circumstances." The crowning point of confusion, however, can be found in the last section of the ED definition, which suffers from (a) defining a term by referring to itself, and (b) broad ranging disagreement from state to state regarding the existence and definition of "social maladjustment" (Skiba et al., 1994).

The diagnostic criteria for ADHD, drawn from DSM-IV (American Psychiatric Association, 1994), fares only slightly better. For example, ADHD is not supposed to be "diagnosed if the symptoms are better accounted for by another mental disorder (e.g., Mood Disorder, Anxiety Disorder, Dissociative Disorder, Personality Disorder ...)" (p. 83); however, no clear procedures for distinguishing ADHD from these other diagnostic categories (each of which is an umbrella term for more specific disorders) is provided in the DSM. Furthermore, to be diagnosed with ADHD, clients must show six of nine listed symptoms for inattention or six of nine listed symptoms of hyperactivity/impulsivity. The requirement of six rather than some other number of symptoms seems entirely arbitrary. To my knowledge, there is no existing research or theory validating the requirement for precisely six or more of the nine listed symptoms in the DSM. Beyond that, virtually every one of these symptoms lacks any operational definition (e.g., "does not *seem to* [italics added] listen when spoken to directly" [p. 84]) and would thus appear vulnerable to broadly divergent understandings by clinicians. This problem is seriously exacerbated by the fact that each of these symptoms employs the descriptor "often," but no definition of this term is provided (see Reid & Maag, 1994, for a discussion of this problem with behavior rating scales). One other ambiguity, among many others that are not being discussed, is the requirement of documenting "clear evidence of clinically significant impairment in social, academic, or occupational functioning" (p. 84). Again, no operational definitions are provided and this mandated expression of ADHD would seem to be open to interpretation in a wide variety of ways.

The psychometric shortcomings associated with medical model diagnostic systems are evident throughout the psychology literature. Attempting to summarize some of these, Widiger and Trull (2007) recently wrote the following.

There are many failures of the existing DSM-IV-TR diagnostic categories, including excessive diagnostic comorbidity, inadequate coverage, arbitrary and unstable boundaries with normal psychological functioning, heterogeneity among persons sharing the same categorical diagnosis, and [an] inadequate scientific base. (p. 72)

Consistent with this conclusion, Watkins (Chapter 12) characterizes the quality of clinical and diagnostic decision making by psychologists as "suboptimal ... bleak ... [and] dismal".

Specific to the practice of school psychology, the research literature shows that the reliability and validity of diagnoses are often severely limited. For example, Ward, Ward, and Clark (1991) and Gresham, MacMillan, and Bocian (1998) found that school-based teams frequently misdiagnose referred cases. Aspel, Willis, and Faust (1998) reported that "discrepancies between objective and subjective cue use during diagnostic decision-making in school psychology are likely to be highly incompatible with diagnostic accuracy" (p. 147). Singer et al. (1989) investigated the congruence of diagnoses across five different school districts around the nation and found low levels of agreement for the ED, MR, and LD categories. McDermott (1980) assessed reliability of diagnoses among school psychology practitioners, doctoral interns, and students and found levels of agreement that barely exceeded chance in all three groups. Regarding learning disabilities in particular, (a) Gresham (2002) reported that from 52% to 70% percent of students identified as learning disabled fail to meet federal and/or state requirements for this diagnosis; (b) Reschly and Hosp (2004), who studied the definitions of learning disabilities across states, concluded that "enormous variability in SEA [state education agency] SLD [specific learning disability] requirements produces significant differences in what SLD means, depending on the location of the child's residence" (p. 209); (c) Epps, McGue and Ysseldyke (1982) found very low rates of inter-rater agreement regarding the diagnosis of learning disabilities; and (d) Bus (1989) discovered substantial disagreement pertaining to diagnosis and treatment recommendations for students with reading and spelling disabilities. The findings of these empirical studies are consistent with contemporary theoretical analyses that raise serious questions about the reliability and validity of historical and contemporary approaches to diagnosing SLD (Dean, Burns & Grialou, 2006; Fletcher, Denton, & Francis, 2005). For referred students suspected of emotional disturbance, Tharinger, Laurent and Best (1986) found only a 37% level of diagnostic agreement between decisions based on criteria from PL 94–142, DSM III (American Psychiatric Association, 1980), and the Child Behavior Checklist (Achenbach & Edelbrock, 1983). Significant diagnostic problems in the areas of ADHD (e.g., Amador-Campos, Forns-Santacana & Guàrdia-Olmos, 2006; Mandal, Olmi & Wilczynski, 1999; Reid & Maag, 1994; Wolraich, Lambert & Bickman, 2004) and mental retardation (e.g., Macmann & Barnett, 1993) have also been published.

Treatment Outcomes

The ultimate measure of any approach to service delivery is the effectiveness of treatment outcomes. In the case of medical model approaches relevant to the professional practice of school psychology, the efficacy of special education services is critical as diagnosis and placement in special education programs are the predominant outcomes resulting from traditional school psychological services (Reschly & Ysseldyke, 2002). As reported by Kavale and Forness (1999), however, comprehensive meta-analyses suggest that results do "not paint an optimistic picture" (p. 1003). They go on to report that special education "interventions demonstrated effects that primarily ranged from negligible to small and, at best, *medium* [italics in original], ... [and] the obtained ESs [effect sizes] are not eloquent testimony to the efficacy of practices that have almost come to define special education" (p. 1003). As to the impact of placing children experiencing academic and behavioral difficulties into special education placements, which is a major (if not primary) outcome of traditional school psychological services, meta-analyses reveal that the grand effect size is −0.12. This indicates results that are best interpreted as ranging between making no difference to achieving slightly negative outcomes.

Perhaps of even greater concern is the relative absence of systematic results suggesting that diagnostic findings reported by school psychologists practicing in accordance with the medical model have important implications for intervention, regardless of whether those interventions take place in either special or general education settings. To justify traditional school psychological practices that focus almost exclusively

on determining the nature of pathologies and mental illnesses afflicting referred students, there ought to be clear evidence of treatment validity demonstrating that information of this nature is necessary, or at least helpful, to the development of effective treatment plans. Such evidence, however, is either rare or nonexistent. There is little if any research suggesting that students with particular diagnoses benefit uniquely and systematically from particular types of treatment. That is, knowing a student's medical model diagnosis provides practitioners with precious little scientifically based information about how to assist that child with whatever challenges face him/her. This is of such great concern because there would seem to be only very limited clinical (as opposed to research) value to diagnosis if it does not significantly inform treatment choices. To frame the issue in simplistic medical terms, what would be the point of determining that a patient suffers from a brain tumor versus a broken arm if there were not validated, differential treatments (VDTs) for brain tumors and broken arms? Although some school psychology diagnostic systems purport to produce VDTs (historically referred to as aptitude-treatment interactions [ATIs]), the evidence for this is thin at best (see, for example, Cronbach, 1975; Good, Vollmer, Creek, Katz & Chowdhri, 1993; Gresham & Gansle, 1992; Gresham & Witt, 1997; Reschly & Ysseldyke, 2002). After presenting a scholarly, balanced and thorough analysis of the strengths and weaknesses of diagnostic and classification systems in school psychology, Dowdy, Mays, Kamphaus and Reynolds (Chapter 11) state in their concluding paragraph that "we would all do well to remember that diagnoses per se are not likely to inform our important treatment decisions."

Significantly, the lack of treatment validity is not at all limited to school psychology, but rather characterizes clinical and professional psychology practice in general. Widiger and Trull (2007), after reviewing research pertaining to contemporary medical model, diagnostic systems state the following.

> The intention of this information is to help the clinician determine which particular mental disorder is present, the identification of which would hopefully indicate the presence of a specific pathology and suggest a specific treatment. It is evident, however, that DSM-IV-TR routinely fails in this goal. (p. 72)

Disconnect Between Assessment Information Gathered and Treatment Information Needed

One of the most serious problems associated with the medical model is that it directs school psychologists away from gathering crucial treatment information during assessment processes. Specifically, because of the near-exclusive focus on internal diseases, practitioners concentrate data gathering on the search for IDEIA- (U. S. Department of Education, 2006) or DSM- (American Psychiatric Association, 1994) type pathologies but do little to assess the nature of the environmental contexts within which referred students function. In point of fact, however, the treatments provided in school psychology overwhelmingly involve environmental manipulations of one sort or another (e.g., changes in class placement, modification of teaching approaches and behavior management strategies, curriculum revisions, alterations of classroom/home structures and routines) and knowing a student's IDEIA or DSM diagnosis tells us very little about how to accomplish these environmental changes successfully. As noted previously, ATIs/VDTs associated with diagnostic categories and student pathologies are few and far between. That is, knowing that a student, for example, is learning disabled tells us almost nothing about how to educate and work with that student. Developing effective school-, home-, or community-based treatment plans requires detailed information about teachers and the classroom environments in which they work, parents and the nature of the home environments in which they live, and community leaders and the array of community programs they offer. The medical model directs school psychologists away from these sorts of information and towards the administration of tests designed to determine the nature of students' cognitive functioning, achievement, aptitude, perceptual-motor skills, personality, psychopathology, and so forth. The end result is a major disconnect between the types of data school psychologists gather during assessment processes and the types of information school psychologists need to create efficacious treatment plans. It is an approach that inadvertently encourages the development of weak and ineffective interventions.

Practicality Problems

Beyond issues pertaining to underlying conceptual assumptions and an inadequate body of evidence supporting its efficacy, the medical model also suffers from problems that make it highly impractical. Two specific topics will be addressed: (a) insufficient focus on prevention services, and (b) creating personpower shortages by disempowering mental health paraprofessionals.

Insufficient Focus on Prevention Services

One of the major reasons we face the mental health and education pandemics described earlier is because professional resources are directed almost exclusively toward treating rather than preventing human dysfunction (Albee, 2005). This stance is congruent with and emerges from the traditional approach to medical service delivery, in which most physicians do not provide services to people until they become sick enough to be diagnosed with an illness. Following this model, traditionally oriented school psychologists also direct the overwhelming bulk of their service efforts towards students who have "achieved" diagnosable levels of dysfunction. Our field could learn, however, from the children's story of Humpty Dumpty, which tells us that "all the king's horses and all the king's men, couldn't put Humpty Dumpty back together again." Given the weak efficacy data presented previously in this chapter, it simply makes no sense for school psychologists to postpone the provision of services until students are in deep enough trouble to be diagnosed. Our professional focus ought to be directed toward keeping Humpty Dumpty up on the proverbial wall rather than trying to figure out how to put him "back together again" after he falls.

Essentially, neither school psychology nor any other branch of psychological services will ever be able to treat its way out of the pandemics we currently face. George Albee (1999) observed that "no mass disorder has ever been eliminated by treating one person at a time" (p. 133). Many decades ago, Bower (1969) also suggested that trying to meet the nation's mental health needs by relying primarily on remediation strategies "is about as effective as trying to turn back the Mississippi at New Orleans" (p. 113). Nothing has changed in this regard. In fact, as documented earlier in this chapter, matters have simply gotten worse as the number of people with serious mental health and educational challenges continues to grow. Although we may be able to provide high-quality psychological services to a small number of privileged clients who have adequate access to treatment, attempting to serve the general population in this manner is an act of futility.

As shown by innumerable examples from the field of medicine, prevention is always superior to remediation because it is far less debilitating for the client and ultimately it is substantially cheaper as well. Here are a few obvious examples of this truism: (a) using seat belts is better than trying to piece human bodies back together following serious car accidents, (b) brushing your teeth and flossing is superior to periodontic surgery, (c) teaching people not to smoke is more humane than providing chemotherapy for lung cancer, and (d) facilitating exercise and appropriate diets leads to healthier outcomes than treating morbid obesity, diabetes, and heart disease. As Conoley and Gutkin (1995) argued, it is better to drain the swamp than treat those suffering from malaria.

The superiority of prevention is so patently obvious that it would not even be worth mentioning if it were not for the fact that traditional school psychology practice seems yoked entirely to remediation services. Even today, when there is clear and growing interest in response to intervention methodologies (Jimerson et al., 2007; Reschly & Bergstrom, this volume), many (probably most) school psychologists have yet to consider how these processes might be applied proactively and universally to students, preferring instead to see their role as beginning only after special education referrals are initiated.

For the purposes of this chapter it is important to point out that a significant part (certainly not all) of the reason for focusing so heavily on remediation at the expense of prevention is the dominance of the medical model in our field. Viewing our professional mission as the diagnosis and treatment of internal student pathologies (e.g., IDEIA educational disabilities, DSM mental illnesses) leads almost inescapably to this result. Continuing to function in this manner, however, will all but guarantee falling further and further behind in our efforts to address America's mental health and education pandemics. This is particularly disheartening in light of a large body of research evidence showing that prevention services are effective (Durlak, this volume) and growing documentation indicating that they deliver considerable cost benefits as well (Bagley & Pritchard, 1998; Cohen, 1998; Foster & Jones, 2005; Spoth, Guyll, & Day, 2002).

Personpower Shortages for Providing Mental Health Services

Another byproduct of relying on the medical model to undergird psychological services in general and school psychological services in particular is the creation of permanent shortages of treatment personnel. This was predicted long ago and more recently reaffirmed by Albee (1968, 1990), who both foresaw this problem and explained how it resulted from the use of medical explanations to address psychological problems.

> It is so simple. The explanatory model dictates the kind of professional manpower needed. . . . I suggest that as psychologists we have played the illness game . . . long enough. The rules of the illness game are such that there will never be enough professional people available to provide care except to selected members of the middle and upper classes. (Albee, 1968, pp. 318, 319)

In other words, the more we view psychological problems as the result of medical *illnesses* and *diseases*, the more our society is likely to restrict the provision of mental health treatment services to "doctors" (those with MD, PhD, PsyD, and EdD degrees).

This, of course, is reflected in the psychology licensure laws throughout our nation, which generally require doctoral degrees to provide psychological services, and is currently being played out in the American Psychological Association's recommendation to drop the exemption clause for nondoctoral school psychologists from its model licensure act (www.kasp.org/documents/APAMLA.ppt). The problem clearly pointed out by Albee (1968), however, is that by taking this position we are creating an unavoidable personpower crisis. There simply are not (and never will be) enough "doctors" to serve all the victims of the mental health pandemic. This fact is exacerbated by the serious personnel shortage that currently is facing school psychology and projected to continue through at least 2020, during which "doctoral-level school psychologists will very likely represent a disproportionate segment of the projected shortage" (Curtis, Hunley, & Grier, 2004, p. 439).

In defense of the medical model, the logic behind requiring "doctors" to treat "mental illness" seems sound enough. One might argue that this level of advanced training is necessary in order to protect the public. To do otherwise would lead to ineffective and potentially harmful services.

As alluring as this reasoning appears to be, however, it does not stand up to close scrutiny. Let's begin in medicine, where arguing that an MD degree is necessary for all medical procedures is clearly an untenable position. Paramedics, people who have been trained to administer the Heimlich maneuver and/or CPR, patients taught to self-administer injections, and members of the general public buying home cardiac difibrulators, among many other examples, all speak clearly to this point. In fact, perhaps the two most powerful and impactful medical interventions of all time do not require either a medical degree or any medical training at all. Specifically, I would suggest that more people have been saved from medical illnesses and death thanks to public sanitation and washing one's hands with soap than any other medical procedure in history. Would it be good public policy to limit the practice of these or any of the other aforementioned interventions only to medical doctors? Obviously, the answer is a resounding "no." Doing so would result in countless people being unserved and underserved (much like what we have now in the area of mental health).

In passing, it is worth noting the irony in psychology's advocacy for "doctoral only" treatment in licensing laws. Are not the arguments behind these proposals the very same ones used by psychiatrists for the last 50–60 years in their attempt to prevent doctoral psychologists from providing patients with psychotherapy unless under the supervision of physicians (Bernard, 1981; Kiesler & Pallak, 1980; "Brief of American Psychological Association," 1980) and, more recently, with prescriptions for psychoactive medications (DeLeon, Folen, & Jennings, 1991)? The underlying logic appears similar, if not identical. Mental illness is an internal, biological, pathology and therefore only those who are medical doctors are qualified to treat patients safely and effectively.

In my opinion, the psychiatrists were always wrong in their efforts to restrict psychologists from providing treatment services, and the doctoral-only advocates among psychologists are wrong now. There is much that can be done effectively by those without doctoral degrees. For one thing, there is virtually no existing evidence that a doctorate is needed to provide efficacious psychological or mental health services. In fact, quite the opposite appears to be case. Christensen and Jacobson (1994) conducted a comprehensive literature review and concluded that the "evidence strongly suggests that under many if not most conditions, paraprofessionals ... perform as well as or better than professionally trained psychotherapists" (p. 10). Focusing specifically on psychotherapy with adolescents, a meta-analysis conducted by Weisz, Weiss, and Han (1995) reported that, in general, "paraprofessionals produced larger overall treatment effects than professional therapists or students" (p. 450), although better outcomes were reported for professionals with a few specific client groups. Even self-help materials and self-help groups have been found to be effective. Norcross (2006) indicated that "the effect sizes of self-help versus formal treatment typically show that they are almost, but not quite, as effective as therapist-assisted interventions within the same studies" (p. 684). Continuing this trend, a number of other literature reviews have confirmed that paraprofessionals are effective treatment providers for a wide array of problems and client groups, and often are equally or more effective than professional therapists (Berman & Norton, 1985; Bright, Baker, & Neimeyer, 1999; Hattie, Sharpley, & Rogers, 1984; Nielsen, 1995).

In terms of treatments specific to school and family environments, there is little doubt that mental health paraprofessionals have the potential to implement a wide array of important educational and mental health programs (Buerkle et al., this volume; Cowen & Sheridan, this volume). Although sometimes suffering from limitations related to research design, numerous studies document broad-ranging and clinically meaningful outcomes using parent and family-based interventions (Carlson & Christenson, 2005). Work in the area of conjoint behavioral consultation, focusing on both teachers and parents, has been particularly encouraging (e.g., Guli, 2005; Sheridan, Eagle, & Doll, 2006), as have been innumerable behavioral intervention studies (e.g., Cooper, Heron, & Heward, 2007; Zirpoli, 2005). A meta-analysis of play therapy conducted by Bratton, Ray, Rhine and Jones (2005) found that although all treatment providers were effective, "the mean effect size of parent-conducted play therapy ... was significantly greater than the mean effect size of play therapy treatment provided by a mental health professional" (p. 381). Even more intriguing is the idea that children and adolescents can themselves be taught important psychological intervention skills (e.g., Alvord & Grados, 2005;

Kraag, Zeegers, Kok, Hosman, & Abu-Saad, 2006; Polsgrove & Smith, 2004).

Essentially, by conceptualizing psychological dysfunction as a medical problem, the medical model has facilitated the creation of a severe shortage of treatment personnel by unnecessarily disempowering all those without doctoral training, despite consistent empirical evidence that they have excellent potential as treatment providers. In 1969 George Miller articulated an alternative vision in his Presidential Address to the American Psychological Association. He wrote that psychology's responsibility to society "is less to assume the role of experts and try to apply psychology ... than to give it away to people ... and that includes everyone" (p. 1071). Building on Miller's thoughts, Christensen and Jacobson (1994) concluded their literature review on paraprofessional therapists as follows.

> The research summarized in this article suggests that the psychology that is given away ... through paraprofessional, self-administered, and mutual-support group treatment may be as effective for some problems as the professional psychology that is sold. A second body of research summarizing the current prevalence of psychological disorder and the available resources to provide treatment suggests that if psychology is not given away, most people in need will not get it.... The first body of research encourages us in our efforts to give psychology away. The second body of research demands it. (p. 13)

Summary

The thrust of the prior analyses has been to contend that the medical model has truly outlived its usefulness. Suffering from conceptual, efficacy and practicality problems that are major in scope, the medical model not only fails to assist school psychology's progress toward more advanced levels of service delivery, it actually serves as an impediment. For decades, leading school psychologists have called for dramatic changes in research, training, and practice (e.g., Bardon, 1983; Cummings, Harrison, & Dawson, 2004; D'Amato, Sheridan, Phelps, & Lopez, 2003–2004b; Gutkin & Conoley, 1990; Reschly, 2008; Reschly & Ysseldyke, 2002; Sheridan & Gutkin, 2000; Ysseldyke et al., 2006). Moving beyond the medical model is one essential step in reaching these goals.

THE ECOLOGICAL MODEL: A SUPERIOR FOUNDATION ON WHICH TO BUILD SCHOOL PSYCHOLOGICAL SERVICES

The central point of this chapter is to advocate for replacing the medical model "default option" in school psychology with an ecological perspective. Thus far in this chapter I have argued that the former stands in the way of progress in our field. From this point forward I wish to make the case that the latter provides an outstanding platform for the purposes of more effectively understanding human behavior, treating psychological dysfunction, and promoting psychological health. If adopted fully, it could provide a platform from which we may be able to successfully address the mental health and education pandemics described earlier.

Core Elements of Ecological Psychology

The central idea underlying ecological psychology is that human behavior is a function of complex interactions between the characteristics of individuals and the environments in which they function. Neither the former nor the latter provide adequate explanatory power in isolation from each other. Unlike the medical model, which focuses primarily on context-independent disease states to frame psychological problems, the ecological approach is premised on the idea that "context counts." That is, both positive (psychologically healthy) and negative (psychologically unhealthy) human behaviors result from the interplay of individuals interacting with their surroundings. From an ecological perspective, the point is not that internal, biological states and characteristics are unimportant. Clearly, as discussed earlier, they play a significant role in all human experience. Any argument to the contrary seems naïve given our current understanding of neuro- and physiological psychology (e.g., Breedlove et al., 2007). Rather, the defining conceptual issue of ecological theory is that knowing about internal, biological states is not sufficient in and of itself, as these phenomena always find expression as they interact with external environments. It is this interaction, between internal states and external environments, which must be the fundamental unit of analysis for psychologists.

Once our professional "lens" becomes focused on person-environment interactions, other crucial insights emerge rather quickly. For one thing, it is clear that these interactions occur at multiple levels. In his classic work, Urie Bronfenbrenner (1979) identified micro- (i.e., immediate systems in which a person participates directly, such as a classroom), meso- (i.e., interactions among micro-systems, such as the relationship between home and school settings), exo- (i.e., more distal systems in which a person might not participate directly but which nonetheless exert a meaningful influence on that person, such as decisions made by a school board) and macro- (i.e., broad, distal systems, such as national culture or religion) environments. Bronfenbrenner's work and that of other ecological theorists (e.g., Bandura, 1978, 1986a; Barker, 1965, 1968; Bronfenbrenner & Morris, 2006; Chess & Thomas, 1999; Cicchetti & Toth, 1997; Conyne & Cook, 2004; Lewin, 1951; Moos, 1973, 2002; Morse, 1993; Pianta, 1999; Stormshak & Dishion, 2002; Swartz & Martin, 1997) present a view of person-environment interactions that are pervasive, powerful, and reciprocal "living systems" with each element in the ecosystem continually affecting the others in an ongoing and dynamic manner.

The following brief example reflects an ecosystem in action.

> A national economic recession (macro-system) results in a local school board deciding to cut costs by increasing its student-teacher ratio (exo-system). Bobby is a fourth grade student in this school district. Since entering school he has had to struggle somewhat with academics and a variety of mild behavior problems, but he has been able to progress successfully despite these challenges. Bobby's fourth grade teacher, Ms. Smith, who cares deeply about him (micro-system) has a number of additional difficult students transferred into to her class from a school in the district that was closed due to budget cuts (meso-system). Ms. Smith's professional life is further complicated by the school district (exo-system) listing her school as one that is not making adequate yearly progress (AYP) according to the guidelines stipulated by No Child Left Behind (macro-system). The principal of the school begins to place considerable pressure on all of the teachers to bring up the school's test scores (meso-system). Ms. Smith is no longer able to devote as much personal time to Bobby

and he begins to fall progressively further behind academically (micro-system). Bobby's harried teacher eventually refers him for special education services (micro-system). He is diagnosed as learning disabled and placed part-time in a resource program with a teacher who has little patience for his "needy" behaviors (micro-system). For Bobby, failure experiences in school become increasingly prevalent and by the end of the fourth grade he "turns off" to learning and begins to escalate his acting out in a variety of ways at home (micro-system) and school (micro-system). As the next academic year begins, the district budget crisis worsens (exo-system) resulting in progressively higher student-teacher ratios throughout the school district (meso-system) and at Bobby's school (micro-system). The resource teacher informs Bobby's fifth grade teacher that he is a difficult student who needs stern discipline (meso-system). The fifth grade teacher puts Bobby's parents on notice that she will not tolerate his "disruptive and disrespectful" behaviors (meso-system). This leads to increasing pressure at home from his parents to "straighten up and fly right" (micro-system) and ultimately a change in his relationship patterns at school resulting in a new, less academically oriented circle of friends (micro-system). As the fifth grade ends, Bobby is moving on to middle school with poor basic academic skills, a "bad attitude," and a preference for peers who see little value in education.

Although oversimplified, there is nothing extraordinary about this scenario. Most importantly, it shows how events at all levels of Bobby's ecosystem interact with each other and ultimately affect his life in profound ways.

Two additional fundamental elements of ecological theory are demonstrated clearly in the preceding example. First, is the concept of "fit," "match," or "congruence" that occurs (or fails to occur) between: (a) an individual's pattern of personal strengths and weaknesses, and (b) the demands and expectations of relevant environments. Apter and Conoley (1984) capture this idea as follows.

> Disturbance is not viewed as a disease located within the body of the child but, rather, as discordance (a lack of balance) in the system. . . . Discordance may be defined

as a disparity between an individual's abilities and the demands or expectations of the environment—"failure to match" between child and system. (pp. 89, 91)

Bobby's initial success with Ms. Smith, as well as with his prior teachers, followed by subsequent failures with Ms. Smith, and his resource and fifth grade teachers illustrates this point. From an ecological perspective, the problem was not that Bobby was "sick," it was that he was unable to adapt successfully to the changing environments in which he found himself on a day-to-day basis. Second, as suggested by the "ecological" metaphor, modifying any element of interlocking human systems reverberates throughout the ecosystem changing both people and environments. As discussed below, this concept has major implications for designing interventions in that it suggests that change can be brought about by modifying either the individual or the environment.

Advantages of the Ecological Model

There are a number of advantages that might be hypothesized as resulting from employing ecological rather than medical model approaches in school psychology. Several of these are discussed below.

Providing a More Accurate Picture of "Reality"

Perhaps the most fundamental benefit of ecological thinking is that it provides a more accurate view of human functioning. With the possible exception of the most severe aspects of psychopathology, people are best understood by considering them in context rather than in isolation from their natural environments. The objective reality is that micro-, meso-, exo-, and macro-systems routinely exert a substantive influence on almost all human behavior (Albee, 1992). This is true for the overwhelming majority of children and youth, regardless of whether they are "normal" or have disabilities.

Conceptualizing school psychological questions in terms of person-environment interactions leads to a richer array of relevant data than can be gathered by limiting our consideration to the nature of internal student pathologies. If nothing else, it forces school psychologists to get out of the "testing cubical" to immerse themselves in the classroom, school, home, community, and other environments in which students live. It is hard to see how this would not lead to higher quality data

and a more complete understanding of presenting problems.

Gaining Access to a More Extensive Array of Intervention Options

By including Bronfenbrenner's (1979) multiple environmental levels in the conceptualization of human functioning, the ecological model dramatically expands the array of intervention foci available to practitioners. In addition to interventions directed toward student pathologies, modifying micro-, meso-, exo-, and/or macro-environments also become viable approaches. The ecological perspective suggests that changing *either* the person or the environment has the potential to bring about clinically important alterations to the person-environment interaction. In the example of Bobby discussed earlier, the medical model would point school psychologists largely to person-centered interventions such as special class placement, counseling/psychotherapy, and/or medication. The ecological model, however, significantly increases the array of possible intervention targets. In this case the school psychologist might have intervened with Ms. Smith (the fourth grade teacher), the resource teacher, the fifth grade teacher, the middle school to which he was transferring, Bobby's parents, or Bobby's peer group. Theoretically, intervention could also have been directed toward the local school board in the form of organization development consultation (see Meyers et al., this volume), or even Congress by supporting groups such as APA and NASP as they lobby for a change in the No Child Left Behind law (Sheridan & Gutkin, 2000). The central point, as illustrated by the example of Bobby, is that encompassing both persons and environments allows ecologically oriented school psychologists to select from a much larger group of treatment targets and interventions.

Focusing on the Most Malleable Intervention Targets

Although not always the case, it is generally easier to make significant modifications to educational environments than to longstanding, characterological traits of individual students. A simple example should suffice to make this point. Assume for the sake of discussion, that Sally, a third grade student in Mr. Green's class, has a low average level of intelligence and is failing to make adequate academic progress in school as a result. To correct this situation, either Sally's level of intelligence can be raised so that she can function more effectively in Mr. Green's class or the nature of Mr. Green's class can be changed to more effectively meet Sally's educational needs. Clearly, the latter is the easier and more achievable option. Given that environments are typically more malleable than individual traits or pathologies, it only makes sense to concentrate most of our professional efforts on environmental change. By highlighting the central role played by environment, the ecological model helps school psychologists apply their assessment and intervention efforts accordingly, thus potentially maximizing the impact of their services.

Parenthetically, I suspect that few school psychologists reading this chapter would argue that it would be better to focus our energies on raising Sally's IQ than on modifying Mr. Green's class environment, and yet most school psychologists spend most of their time meticulously gathering detailed information on student-centered variables such as IQ while learning vastly less about the micro-, meso-, exo-, and macro-environments that surround children. What is the reason for this apparent discrepancy? In addition to ill-founded beliefs in the existence of ATIs/VDTs (e.g., Cronbach, 1975; Reschly & Ysseldyke, 2002) and other important elements in the "ecology of school psychology" (Sheridan & Gutkin 2000, p. 496), I would suggest that the dominance of the medical model plays a major role. If, in fact, school psychologists conceptualized their work in terms of person-environment interactions rather than treating internal pathologies, they would be far less likely to fall into this "trap."

Successfully Addressing the "Paradox of School Psychology"

A crucial premise underlying the argument for ecologically oriented approaches to school psychology is the "Paradox of School Psychology" (Gutkin & Conoley, 1990), which postulates that "to serve children effectively school psychologists must, first and foremost, concentrate their attention and professional expertise on adults" (p. 212). The decisive key to being able to help young people is not our ability to "cure" their psychological "diseases," it is our skill at facilitating the effective functioning of the various ecologies in which they live, learn, and develop. The crucial "players" in schools, homes and communities are adults such as teachers, parents and community leaders. Any thought of systematically improving the lives of large numbers of children, be it in the areas of mental

health or education, without working successfully with and through such people is, to put it bluntly, ludicrous. What could be more obvious? The key to providing children with an effective education is teachers. The key to socializing and raising psychologically healthy children is parents. Regardless of how insightful and expert school psychologists might be, they cannot really make very much of a difference for young people without the competent assistance and cooperation of adults such as these.

Extrapolating from the "Paradox of School Psychology" (Gutkin & Conoley, 1990) it should be obvious that the robust engagement of teachers, parents, and other relevant adults in the delivery of school psychological services is central to achieving success (Buerkle et al., this volume; Gutkin & Curtis, this volume). Making this happen requires an approach that empowers mental health paraprofessionals and increases their sense of self-efficacy in relationship to school-, home- and community-based services, as research clearly shows that efficacy perceptions are powerfully and positively related to meaningful, sustained and voluntary participation in challenging activities (Bandura, 1977, 1986b, 2000). Couching school psychological services in terms of internal, biological, and psychopathological disease states, however, has the very real potential of disempowering teachers, parents and community leaders by lowering their perceptions of self-efficacy since the overwhelming majority of these people have limited or no training in psychology, psychiatry, neurology, medicine, and so on. Upon hearing that a student is suffering from neurological deficits or an "emotional disturbance," for example, it would be easy for many crucial adults in that student's environment to "check out," assuming that they cannot possibly be of significant assistance. The perceptions of teachers, for instance, which may or may not be verbalized publicly, might go something like this: "How can they expect me to work with and teach these children? Their brains don't work properly. They need to be seen by a psychiatrist or a specialist of some sort. There's nothing that I can really do. It's not my job to work with 'crazy' kids." This is consistent with research by Bergan, Byrnes, and Kratochwill (1979), who demonstrated the negative influence that medical model verbal cues can have on teacher expectancies for a student. Placing educational and mental health problems within a medical model framework likely encourages feelings of impotence, resentment, disengagement, and passivity by teachers and other important adults in the lives of children. Effective treatment under these circumstances is difficult.

The ecological model, on the other hand, frames presenting problems in terms of person-environment interactions, thus opening up the very real possibility of achieving meaningful change via environmental manipulations. Unlike addressing internal dysfunction, creating environmental change is something that can be accomplished successfully by virtually everyone. Within a classroom setting, for example, potential targets for environmental change include, but are not at all limited to, curriculum, pedagogical approach, behavior management, seating arrangements, scheduling, instructional format, reinforcement and punishment contingencies, classroom rules and procedures, parental involvement, and student responsibilities and privileges. Each of these, and the nearly limitless array of other potential environmental manipulations that could be initiated, are an integral part of teaching and what it is that teachers already do day-in and day-out as a routine part of their job (for discussion of a broad array of classroom-based strategies for dealing with academic as well as behavioral student issues, see Sections 3 and 4 of this volume). A similar list, of course, could be drawn up for parents and the role of parenting.

By employing person-environment mismatch rather than medical model pathology as the metaphor for conceptualizing student-related problems, the teachers, parents and other relevant adults in students' lives should have a substantially easier time understanding how (a) they can successfully contribute to the design and implementation of effective intervention plans, and (b) why their active engagement with this process is so vital to achieving success. The ecological model should thus empower primary caregivers in children's lives, raise their sense of efficacy in this regard, and ultimately allow us to effectively address the "Paradox of School Psychology." (Gutkin & Conoley, 1990).

Creating Supportive Environments Facilitates the Potential for Longer Lasting Change

If one accepts the seemingly obvious idea that environmental factors play a significant role in human behavior, then it should be obvious that building supportive environments is crucial to achieving long-term positive outcomes for children (e.g., Baker, 2006; Baker, Dilly, Aupperlee,

& Patil, 2003; Barth, Dunlap, Dane, Lochman, & Wells, 2004). Consider the following metaphorical example.

> John's home is on fire and he is rescued after receiving multiple serious burns. John is taken to a burn center where he is treated successfully. Once the burns are cured, John is returned to his home. Unfortunately, his house is still on fire.

Although lacking in subtlety, this story captures the problem of medical model approaches that focus exclusively on "curing" victims while largely ignoring their dysfunctional environmental surroundings. "Curing" internal pathologies and then returning children to unchanged environments that either created or supported the creation of these pathologies in the first place would seem to be an act of futility that invites recidivism and poor generalization (e.g., Cooper et al., 2007; Stokes & Osnes, 1989). When translated into school psychological parlance, this means that classroom, school, home, and community environments must be intervention foci if there is to be serious hope that advances resulting from treating children are to be long lasting (Durlak, this volume; Weissberg & Greenberg, 1998). As suggested by the "Paradox of School Psychology" (Gutkin & Conoley, 1990), it means that we must bring about change in the primary care givers (e.g., teachers, parents, community leaders) who "stay behind" in the natural environment of young people after school psychologists have left and moved on to subsequent cases. This is unlikely to happen systematically, however, until school psychologists replace their medical model orientation with an ecological perspective.

Tackling the Mental Health and Education Pandemics: Creating Effective Prevention Services

As detailed earlier in this chapter, one of the major contributors to the pandemics facing America's children and youth is our excessive reliance on remediation rather than prevention services. This fuels our mental health and education pandemics because it is not possible to remedy problems as rapidly as they are created, and thus we continue to fall further behind with each passing year. Increasing our focus on the delivery of prevention services is a vital key to solving this dilemma as it creates opportunities to stop problems before they happen and/or intervene early on to avoid full-blown crises.

As detailed by Durlak (Chapter 42) in his review of meta-analyses covering over 1600 studies and more than 150,000 children, we know that prevention services are effective. He writes, "there is strong empirical support for the value of school-based prevention in reducing the rate of many different types of problems that include both internalizing and externalizing difficulties (e.g., anxiety, depression, conduct problems, aggression, school suspensions), poor academic achievement, and drug use." Numerous others agree with this important conclusion (e.g., Greenberg et al., 2003).

Durlak (this volume) also highlights how the ecological model provides much of the theoretical foundation on which prevention services are built. Ecological thinking is highly valuable in this regard because it directs our attention to the "two general strategies evident in most effective [prevention] programs … skill building and environmental—organizational change" (Greenberg et al., 2003, p. 469). It is noteworthy that both of these directions are discussed as foundational in *Blueprint III* (Ysseldyke et al., 2006).

Taking the latter point first, it should be obvious that ecological perspectives help us understand and intervene with essential environmental phenomena, such as those that are manifest in school, home and community settings. Changing relevant environments leads to prevention by creating ecological contexts that facilitate and support healthy and effective human functioning, both in the areas of mental health and education. As one simple example, the creation of effective schools and classrooms leads to better academic achievement, which, in turn, leads to greater psychological health, which, in turn, leads to ongoing high academic achievement (e.g., Stoep, Weiss, & Kuo, 2003; Strein, Hoagwood, & Cohn, 2003).

Regarding the former point, the ecological model is also central to client skill building. Recall that those employing this approach consider both the environment *and* the person. Unlike the medical model, however, which focuses on people in terms of alleviating their internal mental diseases, the ecological model is directed primarily toward competence promotion. The goal is to create an educational process that helps people develop the capacity to successfully navigate the environments in which they live, creating a functional match between environmental demands and personal abilities (e.g., Apter & Conoley, 1984; Chess & Thomas, 1999; Conyne & Cook, 2004; Kuperminc, Leadbeater, &

Blatt, 2001; Pianta, 1999; Reynolds, Gutkin, Elliott, & Witt, 1984). Work by Botvin (2000), building drug resistance skills among adolescents, demonstrates how competence promotion can lead to prevention by helping students to cope more effectively with challenging environments that encourage substance abuse.

When attempting to address our nation's mental health and education pandemics by creating effective prevention services, it seems very clear that employing the medical model to treat "sick" people is not the best route to achieving these goals (Albee & Joffe, 2004). The ecological approach would appear to be superior on both a theoretical and an empirical basis.

Tackling the Mental Health and Education Pandemics: Addressing the Personpower Shortage

The lack of sufficient numbers of treatment providers, as discussed earlier in this chapter, is a second major factor contributing to the extant pandemics in our nation. Basically, by preventing potentially effective service providers from providing services, the medical model exacerbates the number of people who go without necessary treatment (Albee, 1968; Christensen & Jacobson, 1994). This leads to increased numbers of unserved people becoming even more dysfunctional and thus further overwhelming our systems of care.

To combat this problem we must empower all those who might be able to provide effective psychological services by giving psychology away to as many mental health paraprofessionals as possible, as argued eloquently by Miller (1969). The ecological model uniquely creates an opportunity to do just that by articulating how meaningful behavioral and personological change can be brought about via environmental specialists, including teachers and parents, who can be taught to effectively execute appropriate environmental modifications and thus reduce the numbers of those who receive either inadequate or no services (Christensen & Jacobson, 1994). This would dramatically and directly help to solve the mental health and education pandemics we currently face.

Summary

In the preceding section I have argued vigorously that the field of school psychology and the clients we value so highly would be best served by a paradigm shift toward an ecological orientation.

There are numerous advantages to doing so, and these advantages can never be realized without changing the status quo. The traditional medical model provides us with the wrong sets of tools to accomplish our most important missions. The numbers of young people facing serious and debilitating problems related to their education and mental health speaks powerfully to the need for change. The ecological model provides a framework that could be employed to transform the very foundations of our field and dramatically alter the way we "do business."

PROFESSIONAL IMPLICATIONS

I turn now to a discussion of the professional implications of shifting the dominant paradigm in school psychology away from the medical model and toward an ecological orientation, the ramifications of which are substantial.

Re-Framing Services Within an "Education" Metaphor

Overarching all the specific and concrete professional changes that flow from adopting an ecological approach to school psychology is a reframing of our guiding metaphor from medicine to education. While the medical model is all about *curing*, the ecological model is all about *teaching*. Creating functional person-environment interactions is, first and foremost, an educational process premised fundamentally on helping people *learn* how to: (a) function more effectively in their day-to-day environments, and (b) adapt environments to meet the needs of those they serve. When viewed ecologically, psychological problems are less about internal diseases than they are about skill deficits and settings that do not serve their constituents effectively. Decades ago, Hans Strupp (1978), a renowned psychotherapist, called attention to the idea of "therapeutic learning" (p. 123) and how "psychotherapy is not a form of medical treatment.... If analogies are called for, an educational or parenting model is more appropriate" (p. 128). Of even greater relevance to this point is the classic writing of Jack Bardon (1983), who argued forcefully some 25 years ago that the future of school psychology rests with its ability to reinvent itself by viewing its traditional mental health agendas through an educational lens.

Systematic desensitization (Masters, Burish, Hollon & Rimm, 1987; Wolpe, 1968), a well-established and empirically supported intervention, can be employed to demonstrate

how psychological interventions are often, at root, educational rather than medical in nature. The active ingredients of systematic desensitization are *teaching* clients how to: (a) achieve deep muscle relaxation, (b) generate calming and positive self-talk, (c) establish a fear hierarchy, and (d) attain deep muscle relaxation and positive self-talk while progressing through their fear hierarchy (either cognitively or in-vivo). In essence, clients are *learning* how to cope effectively with stressful situations and environments that previously led to feelings of panic and anxiety. There is no "disease" being "cured" by systematic desensitization. The essence of the therapeutic process is educational in nature.

Shifting Away From Diagnostic to Intervention and Consultation Services

The most important change in professional functioning that would result from organizing school psychological services around ecological rather than medical-model thinking would be an epic move away from diagnosis and toward intervention and consultation. The traditional, long-standing fixation with seeking to identify internal student pathologies would be mitigated dramatically. Personological variables would be of interest *only* if there was reason to believe they had significant implications for intervention design. To date, however, as has been noted previously in this chapter, few ATIs/VDTs have been clearly identified despite decades of searching and the promulgation of seemingly endless numbers of hypotheses (Cronbach, 1975; Reschly & Ysseldyke, 2002).

Prior to proceeding with this analysis, it is important to clarify that since the individual is a major component of person-environment interactions, it is certainly possible that future research will identify internal traits with strong ATI/VDT characteristics. If such traits were to be identified, they would be worthy diagnostic targets in an ecological model. Having acknowledged this, however, it is equally important to note that I am doubtful that such traits will ever emerge in meaningful numbers. My pessimism stems from basic ecological thinking, which suggests that the impacts of individual characteristics are always mediated by their interaction with environmental variables. As such, it would be reasonable to expect that the best treatment approach for two students exhibiting the exact same profile of cognitive, neuropsychological, personality, and other patterns might be entirely different based on a vast array of variables, including, but not limited to, the following: (a) the personality of their teachers; (b) the interpersonal relationship between these students and their teachers; (c) their teachers' pedagogical philosophy, strengths, and weaknesses; (d) job satisfaction, professional motivation, and perceptions of teaching self-efficacy for their teachers; (e) their teachers' relationship with colleagues, team leaders, and/or their school principal, and the pedagogical preferences of these individuals; (f) curriculum options made available to the teachers by their respective school districts; (g) student-teacher ratios in their respective classrooms; (h) the availability of teacher and/or parent aides to support instruction and behavior management in each classroom; (i) peer group interactions in the respective classrooms, schools and communities, including levels of substance abuse, violence, achievement motivation, and other factors; (j) interactional patterns and philosophical agreements/disagreements between each student's parents and his/her teacher; (k) interactional patterns between each student and his/her parents; and (l) interactional patterns with siblings; and so forth. When viewed against this matrix of numerous and powerful factors, it is clear that internal student characteristics are but one piece of the "puzzle" and thus are unlikely to be determinative of the best intervention approach for students in and of themselves.

When functioning within an ecological perspective, the primary goal for school psychologists is to address dysfunctional person-environment interactions. Two global approaches are prevalent, both of which are educational in nature, focus on "giving psychology away" (Miller, 1969), and can be applied to achieve both remedial and preventive outcomes (in contrast to the medical model, which focuses almost exclusively on the former).

The first approach involves direct intervention, teaching students skills designed to promote their psychological and academic competence (Durlak, Chapter 42; Masten & Motti-Stefanidi, Chapter 33). Exemplifying this is the work of Alvord and Grados (2005), who detail the enhancement of children's resilience by helping them learn effective coping strategies (e.g., problem solving, how to express their feelings, optimistic thinking, relaxation and self-control techniques) that can be employed in advance of or in response to a myriad of intra- and extra-personal stresses faced throughout the life

cycle. Other examples abound, including skill training in areas such as social competence (e.g., McNamara, 2002), prevention of sexual abuse (Mace, 2000), anger management (e.g., Larson, 2005), problem solving (Frauenknecht & Black, 2004), drug and alcohol refusal (e.g., Botvin, 2000; Goldstein, 1989), studying and test taking (e.g., Gleason, Archer, & Colvin, 2002), and coping with bullies (Sheridan, Warnes, & Dowd, 2004). Even when referred to as "therapy" (Stark, Hargrave, Gerber, Fisher, & Hamilton, Chapter 29), these direct interventions remain ecological in nature as long as their core purpose is to improve the ability of students to meet relevant environmental demands and expectations rather than "curing mental illnesses."

The second approach involves indirect intervention, commonly referred to as consultation (Gutkin & Curtis, Chapter 28). The focus here is on impacting students via the adults who control the environments that surround them, as per the "Paradox of School Psychology" (Gutkin & Conoley, 1990). Rather than "giving psychology away" (Miller, 1969) to students per se, school psychologists work with teachers, parents, community leaders and other relevant adults who are in a position to support and facilitate academic, behavioral, and affective growth in students by making important changes in school, home and community settings. This includes consultation directed toward: (a) micro-environments, addressing issues such as effective teaching (e.g., Rosenfield, 1987), behavior management (e.g., Bergan & Kratochwill, 1990), and parenting (Sheridan, 1993); (b) meso-environments, designed to facilitate effective coordination of services, such as cross-disciplinary teaming (e.g., Gravois et al., this volume) and home-school coordination (e.g., Sheridan, Kratochwill, & Bergan, 1996); and (c) exo- and macro-environments, utilizing organization development methodologies (e.g., Meyers et al., Chapter 43). Although occurring at widely divergent levels, the underlying idea of indirect service is the same in all instances. As per the ecological model, person-environment interactions are altered by implementing clinically meaningful environmental change.

Incorporating Case-Based Formative Evaluation

Underlying most school psychological services premised on the ecological model is a necessary and fundamental transformation of practice toward case-based formative evaluation, also referred to as "short-run empiricism" (Cronbach, 1975, p. 126), "data-based decision making" (Ysseldyke et al., 2006, p. 17) and an "experimenting school society" (Stoner & Green, 1992, p. 159). In the medical model, client diagnoses are relied upon by clinicians to direct them to appropriate treatment choices, such as when physicians prescribe insulin for patients with diabetes and cholesterol-lowering medications for those with heart disease. As detailed earlier, however, few, if any, ATIs/VDTs exist in school psychology and thus internal pathology diagnoses are of little or no value for the purposes of treatment selection (e.g., Reschly & Ysseldyke, 2002). Instead, ecologically based school psychologists rely on conducting client-specific mini-experiments. As assessments of person-environment interactions are completed, intervention choice is determined by a combination of problem solving (Gutkin & Curtis, Chapter 28), research on empirically supported interventions (Kratochwill et al., Chapter 24), and clinical judgment. Subsequently, given the absence of ATIs/VDTs and the presence of meta-analytic evidence supporting formative evaluation (Fuchs & Fuchs, 1986), practitioners collect and analyze ongoing outcome data to ascertain whether selected treatments have been effective. Positive results imply successful response to intervention and the opportunity to continue with treatment as is. Negative results indicate the need to revise or change the intervention, using the formative evaluation data that have already been gathered as input for the next iteration of the treatment selection process. These professional job roles stand in sharp contrast to those that typify medical model services, in which school psychologists spend the bulk of their time conducting pathology-focused assessments, writing psychological reports and attending meetings to determine special education eligibility for students (Reschly & Ysseldyke, 2002). Parenthetically, in the opinion of the author, the typical failure of school psychologists using the medical model to reconsider formal psychological treatment recommendations more frequently than once every three years when special education reevaluations are conducted is a profound shortcoming of traditional job roles.

Prereferral Intervention Teams and Response to Intervention Services

Although both prereferral intervention teams (PRI) (also commonly referred to as intervention assistance teams) (Graden, 1989; Graden, Casey, & Christenson, 1985; Kovaleski, 2002) and response to intervention methodologies (RTI) (Jimerson et al., 2007; Reschly & Bergstrom, Chapter 22) were developed initially as part of medical model diagnostic services, both are consistent with and have evolved into approaches that clearly reflect ecological thinking and practice. PRI and RTI were each designed to assist in traditional diagnostic processes by identifying students who are potential false positives in the special education diagnostic process, i.e., those who appear to have disabilities, but who are not actually in need of special education services. The essence of both methodologies is to adapt school, classroom, and home environments to best meet the needs of referred students to determine if they can be served effectively in general education settings. PRI and RTI are thus both based on the concept of modifying student-environment interactions for the purposes of developing an effective fit whenever that is possible, and thus are inherently ecological in nature (Curtis, Zins, & Graden, 1987; Reschly, Coolong-Chaffin, Christenson, & Gutkin, 2007).

For the purposes of this chapter, PRI and RTI are particularly noteworthy because each (a) is growing in importance and becoming more commonplace in school systems throughout the nation, with the former being required or recommended in 69% and 86% of states, respectively (Truscott, Cohen, & Sams, 2005), and the latter being permissible in all states for all school systems under federal law (IDEIA—U. S. Department of Education, 2006); (b) was created in response to systemic failures of traditional, medical model services; (c) leads to new professional roles for school psychologists; (d) employs a case-based formative evaluation process; (e) appears to be highly effective when executed properly (Burns & Symington, 2002; Jimerson et al., 2007; Reschly & Bergstrom, Chapter 22); and (f) reflects the evolution of traditional school psychological service delivery towards an ecological framework. As Bob Dylan suggested so many decades ago, at least in this respect the times do, indeed, appear to be changing.

Moving Toward a Public Health Agenda

Moving practice towards a public health model is one of the most significant ideas to surface in decades regarding the continuing evolution of our field, and it would have profound implications for school psychologists' professional roles. Growing out of the consultation, prevention, and systems change literatures, there has been a recent and well-deserved spate of interest in this concept, including several key publications (e.g., Albee, 1998; Graden, 2004; Meyers et al., 2004; Nastasi, 2004; Strein et al., 2003; Ysseldyke et al., 2006), a special journal issue (Pianta, 2003), the 2002 Future of School Psychology Conference (D'Amato et al., 2003, 2004a, b), professional newspaper articles (e.g., Desrochers, 2006) and the Surgeon General's report on mental health (U. S. Department of Health and Human Services, 1999). Of direct importance for this chapter is the explicit recognition in many of these documents that ecological psychology provides the theoretical foundation on which most public health models and services are built.

Propelling the public health agenda forward for school psychologists are two pivotal insights. First, there is a growing recognition that few, if any, other service delivery approaches have as much potential to reduce the mental health and education pandemics detailed earlier in this chapter. By directing professional practice toward populations and institutions rather individual clients, and by focusing our energies on the creation of environments that prevent the emergence of problems and facilitate the promotion of competence, public health methodologies offer a unique platform on which to build a powerful future.

Second, among all other mental health professions, school psychology is best positioned to create and implement public health programs. The ideal target population for such work is children and youth, as they have had the least time to establish or solidify unhealthy behavior patterns and are the most malleable of all potential client groups for the purposes of prevention and competence promotion. Additionally, Kessler, Berglund et al. (2005) report in the National Comorbidity Survey Replication project that since half of all lifetime diagnosable mental disorders begin by age 14, "interventions aimed at prevention or early treatment need to focus on youth" (p. 593). Schools, of course, not only provide school psychologists with universal access to young people, but do so over an extended period of time and during vital developmental periods. Unlike mental health clinics, hospitals, agencies, and private practice offices, schools are part of the "real world" in which children live rather than serving only as short-term, "artificial" treatment environments. This makes schools a superior site for public health intervention. Services in schools are also free and nonthreatening to the public at large, and provide school psychologists with innumerable avenues for interacting with and influencing the most important people in the lives of children, specifically teachers, parents, and peers. Additionally, the very core of every school's mission, namely the provision of education, is widely believed to be causally and reciprocally related to positive mental health, with each supporting and reinforcing the other (Strein et al., 2003). When school psychologists help educational institutions teach students more effectively, they are, in essence, already engaging in a public health intervention. Finally, as practitioners of "applied educational psychology" (Bardon, 1983, p. 194), school psychologists have a more sophisticated understanding of teaching and learning processes than any other mental health professional. This is crucial because so many public health endeavors are founded on educational processes (e.g., teaching parents to employ authoritative rather than authoritarian or laissez-faire parenting styles, teaching adolescents to use effective problem-solving techniques when faced with a crisis, teaching educators how to manage children's behavior without having to rely excessively on punishment and demeaning tactics).

In summary, with public health approaches being one of the most important means by which our nation might successfully address its mental health and education pandemics, school psychology resides at the very nexus of factors that have the potential to facilitate this work. We have unparalleled access to the very best possible client population. We are employed in the very best possible setting to design and implement public health projects for that population. Our training and experience give us the very best possible knowledge base for carrying out these roles. The stage is set. Without embracing an ecological orientation, however, this is all very unlikely to happen.

Summary

Choosing between ecological and medical model approaches to school psychological service delivery has profound implications for the professional functions of school psychologists. Many of the most important differences between these two approaches were detailed in this section, although this discussion is far from exhaustive. Essentially, retaining a medical model orientation serves to support long-standing assessment and diagnostic activities that historically have characterized our field, making meaningful role transformation difficult (perhaps impossible) to achieve. If, in fact, focusing on internal student pathologies is the key to effective school psychological services, then there would seem to be little need for systemic change. On the other hand, turning to ecological conceptualizations of human behavior and student functioning, emphasizing person-environment interaction, opens the door to far greater emphases on intervention, consultation, case-based formative evaluation, prevention, and public health job roles, among others. If, as strongly suggested by the 2002 Future of School Psychology Conference (D'Amato et al., 2003, 2004a, b; Cummings et al., 2004), these are directions in which we would like our field to move, transitioning toward ecological understandings of our professional work would be a major step in the right direction.

CONCLUSIONS AND LOOKING TOWARD THE FUTURE

Like all powerful and dominant scientific paradigms (Kuhn, 1970), the medical model directs, shapes, and constrains the thought processes and ideas of those who use it. When you are a hammer, everything looks like a nail. Of course, in this metaphor, nailing things down would be perfectly fine as long as the challenges at hand did not require screwdrivers, wrenches, and pliers. In school psychology, the extant mental health and educational pandemics argue persuasively that we are in need of new "tools." More of the same is not the answer. The medical model is critically flawed. Continuing to use it as we have will lead to a continuation of the past; too many serious mental health and educational problems, and vastly too few effective solutions or service providers to carry them out.

The need for change could not be more apparent. Replacing the medical model with an ecological alternative would meaningfully change how we conceptualize both the problems we face and the solutions we offer. It would be a watershed event in the history of our field.

Looking beyond this to the future, however, it is clear that creating the profession envisioned at the 2002 Future of School Psychology Conference (D'Amato et al., 2003, 2004a, b; Cummings et al., 2004) will require more (much more) than just reorienting our collective theoretical underpinnings. Wide arrays of additional actions are going to be required including (but not at all limited to) changing (a) professional training programs, (b) research foci, (c) school administrator understandings of school psychological services, (d) family and community conceptualizations of mental illness, and (d) federal and state legislation specifying funding patterns and service delivery mandates. Sheridan and Gutkin (2000) referred to these challenges as grappling with "the ecology of school psychology" (p. 496). None of this will be easy and none of this will occur quickly. The central point of this chapter, however, is to contend that if we fail to purposefully reorient our field away from the medical model and toward ecological perspectives, none of this will be possible.

Time will tell whether the "plea for change" that has been presented will ultimately be heeded and brought to fruition. Doing so will take many years, if not decades, to accomplish. Even more importantly, it will require many school psychologists with a strong and compelling vision of what is, what could be, and what ought to be. Hopefully, this chapter has, in some way, contributed to creating and supporting that vision. If, as a reader, you are hoping to experience this change during the course of your professional career but wonder who among us is going to make it happen, I close by invoking a line used throughout the generations by children on the playground . . . "tag, you're it."

REFERENCES

Achenbach, T. M., & Edelbrock, C. S. (1983). *Manual for the child behavior checklist and revised child behavior profile*. Burlington, VT: Queens City Printers.

Albee, G. W. (1968). Conceptual models and manpower requirements in psychology. *American Psychologist, 23*, 317–320.

Albee, G. W. (1990). The futility of psychotherapy, *Journal of Mind and Behavior, 11*, 369–384.

Albee, G. W. (1992). Powerlessness, politics, and prevention: The community mental health approach. In S. Staub & P. Green (Eds.), *Psychology and social responsibility: Facing global challenges* (pp. 211–220). New York: University Press.

Albee, G. W. (1998). Fifty years of clinical psychology: Selling our soul to the devil. *Applied & Preventive Psychology, 7*, 189–194.

Albee, G. W. (1999). Prevention, not treatment, is the only hope. *Counselling Psychology Quarterly, 12*, 133–146.

Albee, G. W. (2005). Call to revolution in the prevention of emotional disorders. *Ethical Human Psychology and Psychiatry: An International Journal of Critical Inquiry, 7*, 37–44.

Albee, G. W., & Joffe, J. M. (2004). Mental illness is NOT "an illness like any other." *Journal of Primary Prevention, 24*, 419–436.

Alvord, M. K., & Grados, J. J. (2005). Enhancing resilience in children: A proactive approach. *Professional Psychology: Research and Practice, 36*, 238–245.

American Psychiatric Association. (1980). *Diagnostic and statistical manual of mental disorders* (3rd ed.). Washington, DC: Author.

American Psychiatric Association. (1994). *Diagnostic and statistical manual of mental disorders* (4th ed.). Washington, DC: Author.

Amador-Campos, J. A., Forns-Santacana, M., & Guàrdia-Olmos, J. (2006). DSM-IV Attention Deficit Hyperactivity Disorder symptoms: Agreement between informants in prevalence and factor structure at different ages. *Journal of Psychopathology and Behavioral Assessment, 28*, 23–32.

Apter, S. J., & Conoley, J. C. (1984). *Childhood behavior disorders and emotional disturbance: An introduction to teaching troubled children*. Englewood Cliffs, NJ: Prentice-Hall.

Aspel, A. D., Willis, W. G., & Faust, D. (1998). School psychologists' diagnostic decision-making processes: Objective-subjective discrepancies. *Journal of School Psychology, 36*, 137–149.

Bagley, C., & Pritchard, C. (1998). The billion dollar costs of troubled youth: Prospects for cost-effective prevention and treatment. *International Journal of Adolescence and Youth, 7*, 211–225.

Baker, J. A. (2006). Contributions of teacher-child relationships to positive school adjustment during elementary school. *Journal of School Psychology, 44*, 211–229.

Baker, J. A., Dilly, L. J., Aupperlee, J. L., & Patil, S. A. (2003). The developmental context of school satisfaction: Schools as psychologically healthy environments. *School Psychology Quarterly, 18*, 206–221.

Ballou, M., & Brown, L. S. (2002). *Rethinking mental health and disorder: Feminist perspectives*. New York: Guilford.

Bandura, A. (1977). Self-efficacy: Toward a unifying theory of behavioral change. *Psychological Review, 84*, 191–215.

Bandura, A. (1978). The self-system in reciprocal determinism. *American Psychologist, 33*, 344–358.

Bandura, A. (1986a). *Social foundations of thought and action: A social cognitive theory*. Englewood Cliffs, NJ: Prentice-Hall.

Bandura, A. (1986b). The explanatory and predictive scope of self-efficacy theory. *Journal of Social & Clinical Psychology, 4*, 359–373.

Bandura, A. (2000). Self-efficacy: The foundation of agency. In W. J. Perrig & A. Grob (Eds.), *Control of human behavior, mental processes, and consciousness: Essays in honor of the 60th birthday of August Flammer* (pp. 17–33). Mahwah, NJ: Erlbaum.

Bardon, J. I., (1983). Psychology applied to education: A specialty in search of an identity. *American Psychologist, 38*, 185–196.

Barker, R. G. (1965). Explorations in ecological psychology. *American Psychologist, 20*, 1–14.

Barker, R. G. (1968). *Ecological psychology*. Stanford, CA: Stanford University Press.

Barth, J. M., Dunlap, S. T., Dane, H., Lochman, J. E., & Wells, K. C. (2004). Classroom environment influences on aggression, peer relations, and academic focus. *Journal of School Psychology, 42*, 115–133.

Bergan, J. R., Byrnes, I. M., & Kratochwill, T. R. (1979). Effects of behavioral and medical models of consultation on teacher expectancies and instruction of a hypothetical child. *Journal of School Psychology, 17*, 306–316.

Bergan, J. R., & Kratochwill, T. R. (1990). *Behavioral consultation and therapy*. New York: Plenum.

Berman, J. S., & Norton, N. C. (1985). Does professional training make a therapist more effective? *Psychological Bulletin, 98*, 401–407.

Bernard, J. L. (1981). Analysis of the blues decision: Milestone or way station? *American Psychologist, 36*, 429–431.

Blader, J. C., & Carlson, G. A. (2007). Increased rates of bipolar disorder diagnoses among U.S. child, adolescent, and adult inpatients: 1996–2004. *Biological Psychiatry, 62*, 107–114.

Botvin, G. J. (2000). Preventing drug abuse in schools: Social and competence enhancement approaches targeting individual-level etiologic factors. *Addictive Behaviors, 25*, 887–897.

Bower, E. M. (1969). *Early identification of emotionally handicapped children in school* (2nd ed.). Oxford, England: Charles C Thomas.

Bratton, S. C., Ray, D., Rhine, T., & Jones, L. (2005). The efficacy of play therapy with children: A meta-analytic review of treatment outcomes. *Professional Psychology: Research and Practice, 36*, 376–390.

Breedlove, S. M., Rosenzweig, M. R. & Watson, N. V. (2007). *Biological psychology: An introduction to behavioral, cognitive, and clinical neuroscience* (5th ed.). Sunderland, MA: Sinauer Associates.

Bregman, J. D., Zager, D., & Gerdtz, J. (2005). Behavioral interventions. In F. R. Volkmar, R. Paul, A. Klin, & D. Cohen (Eds.), *Handbook of autism and pervasive developmental disorders: Vol. 2: Assessment, interventions, and policy* (3rd ed., pp. 897–924). Hoboken, NJ: Wiley.

Brief of American Psychological Association as Amicus Curiae: Virginia Academy of Clinical Psychologists, et al., Appellants, v. Blue Shield of Virginia, et al., Appellees. (1980) *American Psychologist*, *35*, 1028–1043.

Bright, J. I., Baker, K. D., & Neimeyer, R. A. (1999). Professional and paraprofessional group treatments for depression: A comparison of cognitive-behavioral and mutual support interventions. *Journal of Consulting and Clinical Psychology*, *67*, 491–501.

Bronfenbrenner, U. (1979). *The ecology of human development*. Cambridge, MA: Harvard University Press.

Bronfenbrenner, U., & Morris, P. A. (2006). The bioecological model of human development. In R. M. Lerner & W. Damon (Eds.), *Handbook of child psychology: Vol. 1, Theoretical models of human development* (6th ed., pp. 793–828). Hoboken, NJ: Wiley.

Brown, M. B., Holcombe, D. C., & Bolen, L. M. (2006). Role function and job satisfaction of school psychologists practicing in an expanded role model. *Psychological Reports*, *98*, 486–496.

Burns, M. K., & Symington, T. (2002), A meta-analysis of prereferral intervention teams: Student and systemic outcomes. *Journal of School Psychology*, *40*, 437–447.

Burt, C. W., McCaig, L. F., & Rechtsteiner, E. A. (2007). Ambulatory medical care utilization estimates for 2005. *Advance data from vital and health statistics* (no. 388). Hyattsville, MD: National Center for Health Statistics.

Bus, A. G. (1989). How are recommendations concerning reading and spelling disabilities arrived at and why do experts disagree? *Psychology in the Schools*, *26*, 54–61.

Caplan, P. J. (1992). Driving us crazy: How oppression damages women's mental health and what we can do about it. *Women & Therapy*, *12*, 5–28.

Cardoso, S. H. (2007). Hardwired for happiness. In C. A. Read (Ed.), *Cerebrum 2007: Emerging ideas in brain science* (pp. 169–184). Washington, DC: Dana Press.

Carlson, C., & Christenson, S. L. (2005). Evidence-based parent and family interventions in school psychology. *School Psychology Quarterly* [special issue], *20*(4).

Cartwright, S. A. (1851). Report on the diseases and physical peculiarities of the Negro race. In E. D. Pellegrini, A. L. Caplan, J. J. McCartney, & D. A. Sisti (Eds.), (2004), *Health, disease, and illness: Concepts in medicine* (pp. 28–37). Washington DC: Georgetown University Press.

Chess, S., & Thomas, A. (1999). *Goodness of fit: Clinical applications from infancy through adult life*. Philadelphia, PA: Brunner/Mazel.

Christensen, A., & Jacobson, N. S. (1994). Who (or what) can do psychotherapy: The status and challenge of nonprofessional therapists. *Psychological Science*, *5*, 8–14.

Cicchetti, D., & Toth, S. L. (1997). Transactional ecological systems in developmental psychopathology. In S. S. Luthar, J. A. Burack, D. Cicchetti, & J. R. Weisz (Eds.), *Developmental psychopathology: Perspectives on adjustment, risk, and disorder*. New York: Cambridge University Press.

Clonan, S. M., Chafouleas, S. M., & McDougal, J. (2004). Positive psychology goes to school: Are we there yet? *Psychology in the Schools*, *41*, 101–110.

Cohen, M. A. (1998). The monetary value of saving a high-risk youth. *Journal of Quantitative Criminology*, *14*, 5–33.

Conoley, J. C., & Gutkin, T. B. (1995). Why didn't—why doesn't—school psychology realize its promise? *Journal of School Psychology*, *33*, 209–217.

Conyne, R. K., & Cook, E. P. (Eds.). (2004). *Ecological counseling: An innovative approach to conceptualizing person-environment interaction*. American Counseling Association: Alexandria, VA.

Cooper, J. O., Heron, T. E., & Heward, W. L. (2007). *Applied behavior analysis* (2nd ed.). Upper Saddle River, New Jersey: Prentice Hall.

Coutinho, M. J., & Oswald, D. P. (1998). Understanding identification, placement and school completion rates for children with disabilities: The influence of economic, demographic and educational variables. In T. E. Scruggs & M. A. Mastropieri (Eds.), *Advances in learning and behavioral disabilities* (Vol. *12*, pp. 43–78). San Diego, CA: Elsevier Science/JAI Press.

Crockett, D. (2003). Critical issues children face in 2000. *School Psychology Quarterly*, *18*, 446–453.

Cronbach, L. J. (1975). Beyond two disciplines of scientific psychology. *American Psychologist*, *30*, 116–127.

Cummings, J. A., Harrison, P. L., & Dawson, M. M. (2004). The 2002 Conference on the Future of School Psychology: Implications for consultation, intervention and prevention services. *Journal of Educational and Psychological Consultation*, *15*, 239–256.

Curtis, M. J., Hunley, S. A., & Grier. J. E. (2004). The status of school psychology: Implications of a major personnel shortage. *Psychology in the Schools*, *41*(4), 431–442

Curtis, M. J., Zins, J. E., & Graden, J. L. (1987). Prereferral intervention programs: Enhancing student performance in regular education settings. In C. A. Maher & J. E. Zins (Eds.), *Psychoeducational interventions in the schools: Methods and procedures for enhancing student competence* (pp. 7–25). Elmsford, NY: Pergamon.

D'Amato, R. C., Sheridan, S. M., & Phelps, L., Lopez, E. C. (Eds.). (2003). Psychology in the Schools, School Psychology Review, School Psychology

Quarterly, and Journal of Educational and Psychological Consultation editors collaborate to chart school psychology's past, present, and "futures." *School Psychology Quarterly* [Special issue], *18*(4).

D'Amato, R. C., Sheridan, S. M., Phelps, L., & Lopez, E. C. (Eds.). (2004a). Psychology in the Schools, School Psychology Review, School Psychology Quarterly, and Journal of Educational and Psychological Consultation editors collaborate to chart school psychology's past, present, and "futures." *Journal of Educational and Psychological Consultation* [Special issue], *15*(3–4).

D'Amato, R. C., Sheridan, S. M., Phelps, L., & Lopez, E. C. (Eds.). (2004a, b). Psychology in the Schools, School Psychology Review, School Psychology Quarterly, and Journal of Educational and Psychological Consultation editors collaborate to chart school psychology's past, present, and "futures." *School Psychology Review* [Special issue], *33*(1).

Davidow, J., & Levinson, E. M. (1993). Heuristic principles and cognitive bias in decision making: Implications for assessment in school psychology. *Psychology in the Schools, 30,* 351–361.

Dean, V. J., Burns, M. K., & Grialou, T. (2006). Comparison of ecological validity of learning disabilities diagnostic models. *Psychology in the Schools, 43,* 157–168.

Delahanty, D. L., & Nugent, N. R. (2006). Predicting PTSD Prospectively Based on Prior Trauma History and Immediate Biological Responses. In R. Yehuda (Ed.), *Psychobiology of posttraumatic stress disorders: A decade of progress* (Vol. *1071,* pp. 27–40). Malden, MA: Blackwell Publishing.

DeLeon, P. H., Folen, R. A. & Jennings, F. L. (1991). The case for prescription privileges: A logical evolution of professional practice. *Journal of Clinical Child Psychology, 20,* 254–267.

Desrochers, J. E. (2006, March). Prevention and the future of school psychology: A public health model of practice. *Communiqué, 34*(6), 34.

DeVol, R., & Bedroussian, A. (2007). *An unhealthy America: The economic burden of chronic disease.* Santa Monica, CA: Milken Institute. www .milkeninstitute.org/pdf/ES_ResearchFindings .pdf

Dowdy, E., Mays, K. L., Kamphaus, R. W., & Reynolds, C. R. (this volume). Roles of diagnosis and classification in school psychology. In T. B. Gutkin & C. R. Reynolds (Eds.), *The handbook of school psychology* (4th ed.). New York: Wiley.

Epps, S., McGue, M., & Ysseldyke, J. E. (1982). Interjudge agreement in classifying students as learning disabled. *Psychology in the Schools, 19,* 209–220.

Everly, G. S., Jr., & Lating, J. M. (2004). Biological foundations of posttraumatic stress disorder. In G. S. Everly Jr. & J. M. Lating (Eds.),

Personality-guided therapy for posttraumatic stress disorder (pp. 53–67). Washington, DC: American Psychological Association.

Fletcher, J. M., Denton, C., & Francis, D. J. (2005). Validity of alternative approaches for the identification of learning disabilities: Operationalizing unexpected underachievement. *Journal of Learning Disabilities, 38,* 545–552.

Foster, E. M., & Jones, D. E. (2005). The high costs of aggression: Public expenditures resulting from conduct disorder. *American Journal of Public Health, 95,* 1767–1772.

Frauenknecht, M., & Black, D. R. (2004). Problem-Solving Training for Children and Adolescents. In E. C. Chang, T. J. D'Zurilla, & L. J. Sanna (Eds.), *Social problem solving: Theory, research, and training* (pp. 153–170). Washington, DC: American Psychological Association.

Friedan, B. (1963). *The feminine mystique.* Oxford, England: Norton.

Fry, W. F. (1994). The biology of humor. *Humor: International Journal of Humor Research, 7,* 111–126.

Fuchs, L. S., & Fuchs, D. (1986). Effects of systematic formative evaluation: A meta-analysis. *Exceptional Children, 53,* 199–208.

Garbarino, J. (1995). *Raising children in a socially toxic environment.* San Francisco: Jossey-Bass.

Gleason, M. M., Archer, A. L., & Colvin, G. (2002). Interventions for improving study skills. In M. A. Shinn, H. W. Walker, & G. Stoner (Eds.), *Interventions for academic and behavior problems II: Preventive and remedial approaches* (pp. 651–680). Bethesda, MD: National Association of School Psychologists.

Goldstein, A. P. (1989). Refusal skills: Learning to be positively negative. *Journal of Drug Education, 19,* 271–283.

Goldston, D. B., Molock, S. D., Whitbeck, L. B., Murakami, J. L., Zayas, L. H., & Hall, G. C. N. (2008). Cultural considerations in adolescent suicide prevention and psychosocial treatment. *American Psychologist, 63,* 14–31.

Good, R. H., III, Vollmer, M., Creek, R. J., Katz, L., & Chowdhri, S. (1993). Treatment utility of the Kaufman Assessment Battery for Children: Effects of matching instruction and student processing strength. *School Psychology Review, 22,* 8–26.

Graden, J. L. (1989). Redefining 'prereferral' intervention as intervention assistance: Collaboration between general and special education. *Exceptional Children, 56,* 227–231.

Graden, J. L. (2004). Arguments for change to consultation, prevention, and intervention: Will school psychology ever achieve this promise? *Journal of Educational and Psychological Consultation, 15,* 345–359.

Graden, J. L., Casey, A. & Christenson, S. L. (1985). Implementing a prereferral intervention system:

I. The model. *Exceptional Children*, *51*, 377–384.

Greenberg, G. (1997). Right answers, wrong reasons: Revisiting the deletion of homosexuality from the DSM. *Review of General Psychology*, *1*, 256–270.

Greenberg, M. T., Weissberg, R. P., O'Brien, M. U., Zins, J. E., Fredericks, L., Resnik, H., & Elias, M. J. (2003). *American Psychologist*, *58*, 466–474.

Gresham, F. M. (2002). Responsiveness to intervention: an alternative approach to the identification of learning disabilities. In R. Bradley, L. Danielson, & D. P. Hallahan (Eds.), *Identification of learning disabilities: Research to practice* (pp. 467–519). Mahwah, NJ: Erlbaum.

Gresham, F. M., & Gansle, K. A. (1992). Misguided assumptions of SDM-III-R: Implications for school psychological practice. *School Psychology Quarterly*, *7*, 79–95.

Gresham, F. M., MacMillan, D. L., & Bocian, K. M. (1998). Agreement between school study team decisions and authoritative definitions in classification of students at risk for mild disabilities. *School Psychology Quarterly*, *13*, 181–191.

Gresham, F. M., & Witt, J. C. (1997). Utility of intelligence tests for treatment planning, classification, and placement decisions: Recent empirical findings and future directions. *School Psychology Quarterly*, *12*, 249–267.

Grosjean, Y., Grillet, M., Augustin, H., Ferveur, J., & Featherstone, D. E. (2007). A glial amino-acid transporter controls synapse strength and courtship in Drosophila. *Nature Neuroscience*, *11*, 54–61.

Guli, L. A. (2005). Evidence-based parent consultation with school-related outcomes. *School Psychology Quarterly*, *20*, 455–472.

Gurdin, L. S., Huber, S. A., & Cochran, C. R. (2005). A critical analysis of data-based studies examining behavioral interventions with children and adolescents with brain injuries. *Behavioral Interventions*, *20*, 3–16.

Gutkin, T. B., & Conoley, J. C. (1990). Reconceptualizing school psychology from a service delivery perspective: Implications for practice, training, and research. *Journal of School Psychology*, *28*, 203–223.

Halliwell, E., & Harvey, M. (2006). Examination of a sociocultural model of disordered eating among male and female adolescents. *British Journal of Health Psychology*, *11*, 235–248.

Hastings, P. D. Zahn-Waxler, C., & McShane, K. (2006). We are, by nature, moral creatures: Biological bases of concern for others. In M. Killen & J. G. Smetana (Eds.), *Handbook of moral development* (pp. 483–516). Mahwah, NJ: Erlbaum.

Hattie, J. A., Sharpley, C. F., & Rogers, H. J. (1984). Comparative effectiveness of professional and paraprofessional helpers. *Psychological Bulletin*, *95*, 534–541.

Hosp, J. L., & Reschly, D. J. (2002). Regional differences in school psychology practice. *School Psychology Review*, *31*, 11–29.

Huebner, E. S., & Gilman, R., (2003). Toward a focus on positive psychology in school psychology. *School Psychology Quarterly*, *18*, 99–102.

Insel, T. R., & Fenton, W. S. (2005). Psychiatric epidemiology: It's not just about counting anymore. *Archives of General Psychiatry*, *62*, 590–592.

Jimerson, S. R., Burns, M. K., & VanDerHeyden, A. M. (Eds.). (2007). *Handbook of response to intervention: The science and practice of assessment and intervention*. Springer: New York.

Jones, E. E., & Harris, V. A. (1967). The attribution of attitudes. *Journal of Experimental Social Psychology*, *3*, 1–24.

Kaufman, J., & Charney, D. (2001). Effects of early stress on brain structure and function: Implications for understanding the relationship between child maltreatment and depression. *Development and Psychopathology*, *13*, 451–471.

Kavale, K. A., & Forness, S. R. (1999). Effectiveness of special education. In C. R. Reynolds & T. B. Gutkin (Eds.), *The handbook of school psychology* (3rd ed., pp. 984–1024). New York: Wiley.

Kessler, R. C., Berglund, P., Demler, O., Jin, R., & Walters, E. E. (2005). Lifetime prevalence and age-of-onset distributions of DSM-IV disorders in the National Comorbidity Survey Replication. *Archives of General Psychiatry*, *62*, 593–602.

Kessler, R. C., Chiu, W. T., Demler, O., & Walters, E. E. (2005). Prevalence, severity, and comorbidity of 12-month DSM-IV disorders in the National Comorbidity Survey Replication. *Archives of General Psychiatry*, *62*, 617–627.

Keyes, C. L. M. (2007). Promoting and protecting mental health as flourishing. *American Psychologist*, *62*, 95–108.

Kiesler, C. A. & Pallak, M. S. (1980). The Virginia blues. *American Psychologist*, *35*, 953–954.

Kovaleski, J. F. (2002). Best Practices in Operating Pre-Referral Intervention Teams. In A. Thomas & J. Grimes (Eds.), *Best practices in school psychology IV* (pp. 645–655). Washington, DC: National Association of School Psychologists.

Kraag, G., Zeegers, M. P., Kok, G. Hosman, C., & Abu-Saad, H. H. (2006). School programs targeting stress management in children and adolescents: A meta-analysis. *Journal of School Psychology*, *44*, 449–472.

Krause, N. (1983). Conflicting sex-role expectations, housework dissatisfaction, and depressive symptoms among full-time housewives. *Sex Roles*, *9*, 1115–1125

Kuhn, T. S. (1970). *The structure of scientific revolutions* (2nd ed.). Chicago: The University of Chicago Press.

Kuperminc, G. P., Leadbeater, B. J., & Blatt, S. J. (2001). School social climate and individuals differences in vulnerability to psychopathology among middle school students. *Journal of School Psychology, 39,* 141–159.

Kutchins, H., & Kirk, S. A. (1997). *Making us crazy: DSM: The psychiatric bible and the creation of mental disorders.* New York: Free Press.

Larson, J. (2005). *Think first: Addressing aggressive behavior in secondary schools.* New York: Guilford.

Lester, G., & Kelman, M. (1997). State disparities in the diagnosis and placement of pupils with learning disabilities. *Journal of Learning Disabilities, 30,* 599–607.

Levinson, E. M. (1990). Actual/desired role functioning, perceived control over role functioning, and job satisfaction among school psychologists. *Psychology in the Schools, 27,* 64–74.

Lewin, K. (1951). *Field theory in the social sciences.* Harper & Row: New York.

López-Ibor, J. J., Gaebel, W., & Maj, M. (2002). *Psychiatry as a neuroscience.* New York: Wiley.

Mace, P. G. (2000). What works in prevention of child sexual abuse: Child-focused prevention techniques. In M. P. Kluger, G. Alexander, & P. A. Curtis (Eds.), *What works in child welfare* (pp. 75–85). Washington, DC: Child Welfare League of America.

Macmann, G. M., & Barnett, D. W. (1999). Diagnostic decision making in school psychology: Understanding and coping with uncertainty. In C. R. Reynolds & T. B. Gutkin (Eds.), *The handbook of school psychology* (3rd ed., pp. 519–548). New York: Wiley.

Mandal, R. L., Olmi, D. J., & Wilczynski, S. M. (1999). Behavior rating scales: Concordance between multiple informants in the diagnosis of attention-deficit/hyperactivity disorder. *Journal of Attention Disorders, 3,* 97–103.

Masters, J. C., Burish, T. G., Hollon, S. D., & Rimm, D. C. (1987). *Behavior therapy: Techniques and empirical findings.* Orlando, FL: Harcourt.

Matson, J. L., Bamburg, J., & Smalls, Y. (1997). Evaluating behavioral techniques in training individuals with severe and profound mental retardation to use functional independent living skills. *Behavior Modification, 21,* 533–544.

Matarazzo. J. D. (1990). Psychological assessment versus psychological testing: Validation from Binet to the school, clinic, and courtroom. *American Psychologist, 45,* 999–1017.

McDermott, P. A. (1980). Congruence and typology of diagnoses in school psychology: An empirical study. *Psychology in the Schools, 17,* 12–24.

McMullen, L. M., & Stoppard, J. M. (2006). Women and depression: A case study of the influence of feminism in Canadian psychology. *Feminism & Psychology, 16,* 273–288.

McNamara, K. (2002). Best practices in promotion of social competence in the schools. In A. Thomas & J. Grimes (Eds.), *Best practices in school psychology IV* (pp. 911–927). Bethesda, MD: National Association of School Psychologists.

Meacham, M. L. & Peckham, P. D (1978). School psychologists at three-quarters century: Congruence between training, practice, preferred role and competence. *Journal of School Psychology, 16,* 195–206.

Meyers, J., Meyers, A. B., & Grogg, K. (2004). Prevention through consultation: A model to guide future developments in the field of school psychology. *Journal of Educational and Psychological Consultation, 15,* 257–276.

Miller, G. A. (1969). Psychology as a means of promoting human welfare. *American Psychologist, 24,* 1063–1075.

Moos, R. H. (1973). Conceptualizations of human environments. *American Psychologist, 28,* 652–665.

Moos, R. H. (2002). 2001 Invited Address: The mystery of human context and coping: An unraveling of clues. *American Journal of Community Psychology, 30,* 67–88.

Morse, W. C. (1993). Ecological approaches. In T. R. Kratochwill & R. J. Morris (Eds.), *The handbook of psychotherapy with children and adolescents* (pp. 320–355). Needham Heights, MA: Allyn & Bacon.

Nastasi, B. K. (2004). Meeting the challenges of the future: Integrating public health and public education for mental health promotion: *Journal of Educational and Psychological Consultation, 15,* 295–312.

Nielsen, B. A. (1995). Paraprofessionals: They can be competent, and there is more good news. *Journal of Psychological Practice, 1,* 133–140.

Norcross, J. C. (2006). Integrating self-help into psychotherapy: 16 practical suggestions. *Professional Psychology: Research and Practice, 37,* 683–693.

Oswald, D. P., Coutinho, M. J., & Best, A. M. (2001). Impact of sociodemographic characteristics on the identification rates of minority students as having mental retardation. *Mental Retardation, 39,* 351–367.

Pellegrini, A. D. (1995). A developmental contextualist critique of Attention Deficit Hyperactivity Disorder. *Educational Researcher, 24,* 13–19.

Pfenninger, K. H., & Shubik, V. R. (2001). *The origins of creativity.* New York: Oxford University Press.

Pianta, R. C. (1999). *Enhancing relationships between children and teachers.* Washington, DC: American Psychological Association, 1999.

Pianta, R. C. (Ed.). (2003). School psychology: A public health framework. *Journal of School Psychology* [Special issue], *41*(1).

Pipher, M. (1995). *Hunger pains: The modern woman's tragic quest for thinness.* New York: Ballantine Books.

Polsgrove, L., & Smith, S. W. (2004). Informed practice in teaching self-control to children with emotional and behavioral disorders. In R. B. Rutherford, M. M. Quinn and S. R. Mathur (Eds.), *Handbook of research in emotional and behavioral disorders* (pp. 399–425). New York: Guilford Press.

Prosser, J., & McArdle, P. (1996). The changing mental health of children and adolescents: Evidence for a deterioration? *Psychological Medicine, 26,* 715–725.

Raphael, F. J., & Lacey, J. H. (1994). The aetiology of eating disorders: A hypothesis of the interplay between social, cultural and biological factors. *European Eating Disorders Review, 2,* 143–154.

Ratey, J. J., & Johnson, C. (1997). *Shadow syndromes.* New York: Pantheon Books.

Reid, R., & Maag, J. W. (1994). How many fidgets in a Pretty Much: A critique of behavior rating scales for identifying students with ADHD. *Journal of School Psychology, 32,* 339–354.

Repetti, R. L., & Crosby, F. (1984). Gender and depression: Exploring the adult-role explanation. *Journal of Social & Clinical Psychology, 2,* 57–70.

Reschly, D. J. (2008). School psychology paradigm shift and beyond. In A. Thomas & J. Grimes (Eds.), *Best practices in school psychology V* (pp. 3–16). Bethesda, MD: National Association of School Psychologists.

Reschly, A. L., Coolong-Chaffin, M., Christenson, S. L., & Gutkin, T. B. (2007). Contextual influences and response to intervention: Critical issues and strategies. In S. R. Jimerson, M. K. Burns, & A. M. VanDerHeyden (Eds.), *Handbook of response to intervention: The science and practice of assessment and intervention* (pp. 148–160). New York: Springer.

Reschly, D. J., & Hosp, J. L. (2004). State SLD identification policies and practices. *Learning Disability Quarterly, 27,* 197–213.

Reschly, D. J., & Ysseldyke, J. E. (2002). Paradigm shift: The past is not the future. In A. Thomas & J. Grimes (Eds.), *Best practices in school psychology IV* (pp. 3–20). Bethesda, MD: National Association of School Psychologists.

Reynolds, C. R., Gutkin, T. B., Elliott, S. N., & Witt, J. C. (1984). *School psychology: Essentials of theory and practice.* New York: Wiley.

Rosenfield, S. A. (1987). *Instructional consultation.* Hillsdale, NJ: Erlbaum.

Rusk, T. N., & Rusk, N. (2007). Not by genes alone: New hope for prevention. *Bulletin of the Menninger Clinic, 71,* 1–21.

Sarason, S. B. (1981). An asocial psychology and a misdirected clinical psychology. *American Psychologist, 36,* 827–836.

Sarbin, T. R. (1997). On the futility of psychiatric diagnostic manuals (DSMs) and the return of personal agency. *Applied & Preventive Psychology, 6,* 233–243.

Schmidt, J. A., Shernoff, D. J., & Csikszentmihalyi, M. (2007). Individual and situational factors related to the experience of flow in adolescence: A multilevel approach. In A. D. Ong and M. van Dulmen (Eds.), *Oxford handbook of methods in positive psychology* New York: Oxford University Press.

Scruggs, T. E., & Mastropieri, M. A. (2002). On babies and bathwater: Addressing the problems of identification of learning disabilities. *Learning Disability Quarterly, 25,* 155–168.

Seligman, M. E. P., Steen, T. A., & Park, N. (2005). Positive psychology progress: empirical validation of interventions. *American Psychologist, 60*(5), 410–421.

Sheridan, S. M. (1993). Models for working with parents. In J. E. Zins, T. R. Kratochwill, & S. N. Elliott (Eds.), *Handbook of consultation services for children: Applications in educational and clinical settings* (pp. 110–133). San Francisco, CA: Jossey-Bass.

Sheridan, S. M., Eagle, J. W., & Doll, B. (2006). An examination of the efficacy of conjoint behavioral consultation with diverse clients. *School Psychology Quarterly, 21,* 396–417.

Sheridan, S. M., & Gutkin, T. B. (2000). The ecology of school psychology: Examining and changing our paradigm for the 21st century. *School Psychology Review, 29,* 485–502.

Sheridan, S. M., Kratochwill, T. R., & Bergan, J. R. (1996). *Conjoint behavioral consultation: A procedural manual.* New York: Plenum.

Sheridan, S. M., Warnes, E. D. & Dowd, S. (2004). Home-school collaboration and bullying: An ecological approach to increase social competence in children and youth. In D. L. Espelage & S. M. Swearer (Eds.), *Bullying in American schools: A social-ecological perspective on prevention and intervention* (pp. 245–268). Mahwah, NJ: Erlbaum.

Shrivastava, A. K., & Rao, S. (1997). Brain, mind, and behaviour—Culture and environmental perspective. *International Medical Journal, 4,* 145–148.

Singer, J. D., Palfrey, J. S., Butler, J. A., & Walker, D. K. (1989). Variation in special education classification across school districts: How does where you live affect what you are labeled? *American Educational Research Journal, 26,* 261–281.

Skiba, R., Grizzle, K., & Minke, K. M. (1994). Opening the floodgates? The social maladjustment exclusions and state SED prevalence rates. *Journal of School Psychology, 32*, 267–282.

Skinner, B. F. (1953). *Science and human behavior.* Oxford, England: Macmillan.

Smolin, B., Klein, E., & Levy, Y. (2007). Major depression as a disorder of serotonin resistance: Inference from diabetes mellitus type II. *International Journal of Neuropsychopharmacology, 10*, 839–850.

Spoth, R. L., Guyll, M., & Day, S. X. (2002). Universal family-focused interventions in alcohol-use disorder prevention: Cost-effectiveness and cost-benefit analyses of two interventions. *Journal of Studies on Alcohol, 63*, 219–228.

Stice, E. (1994). Review of the evidence for a sociocultural model of bulimia nervosa and an exploration of the mechanisms of action. *Clinical Psychology Review, 14*, 633–661.

Stoep, A. V., Weiss, N. S., & Kuo, E. S. (2003). What proportion of failure to complete secondary school in the US population is attributable to adolescent psychiatric disorder? *Journal of Behavioral Health Services & Research, 30*, 119–124.

Stokes, T. F., & Osnes, P. G. (1989). An operant pursuit of generalization. *Behavior Therapy, 20*, 337–355.

Stoner, G., & Green, S. K. (1992). Reconsidering the scientist-practitioner model for school psychology practice. *School Psychology Review, 21*, 155–166.

Stoppard, J. M., & McMullen, L. M. (2003). *Situating sadness: Women and depression in social context.* New York: New York University Press.

Stormshak, E. A., & Dishion, T. J. (2002). An ecological approach to child and family clinical and counseling psychology. *Clinical Child and Family Psychology Review, 5*, 197–215.

Strein, W., Hoagwood, K., & Cohn, A. (2003). School psychology: A public health perspective I. Prevention, populations, and, systems change. *Journal of School Psychology, 41*, 23–38.

Strupp, H. H. (1978). Psychotherapy: Research, practice, and public policy (How to avoid dead ends). *American Psychologist, 41*, 120–130.

Swartz, J. L., & Martin, W. E., Jr. (1997). *Applied ecological psychology for schools within communities: Assessment and intervention.* Mahwah, NJ: Erlbaum.

Sweeney, D. P., & Hoffman, C. D. (2004). Research in autism spectrum disorders. In R. B. Rutherford, M. M. Quinn, & S. R. Mathur (Eds.), *Handbook of research in emotional and behavioral disorders* (pp. 302–317). New York: Guilford.

Szasz, T. S. (1960). The myth of mental illness. *American Psychologist, 15*, 113–118.

Tharinger, D. J., Laurent, J. & Best, L. R. (1986). Classification of children referred for emotional and behavioral problems: A comparison of PL 94–142 SED criteria, DSM III, and the CBCL system. *Journal of School Psychology, 24*, 111–121.

Tolman, D. L., Impett, E. A., & Tracy, A. J. (2006). Looking good, sounding good: Femininity ideology and adolescent girls' mental health. *Psychology of Women Quarterly, 30*, 85–95.

Truscott, S. D., Cohen, C. E., & Sams, D. P. (2005). The current state(s) of prereferral intervention teams: A report from two national surveys. *Remedial and Special Education, 26*, 130–140.

Unger, R. K. (2001). *Handbook of the psychology of women and gender.* Hoboken, NJ: Wiley.

U. S. Department of Education. (2006). Assistance to states for the education of children with disabilities and preschool grants for children with disabilities; Final rule. *Federal Register, 71*(156), 46540–46845.

U. S. Department of Health and Human Services. (1999). *Mental health: A report of the surgeon general.* Rockville, MD: U.S. Department of Health and Human Services.

U. S. Public Health Service. (2000). *Report of the Surgeon General's Conference on Children's Mental Health: A national action agenda.* Washington, DC: Department of Health and Human Services. www.ncbi.nlm.nih.gov/books/bv.fcgi?rid=hstat5 .section.842

van Praag, H. M., de Kloet, E. R., & van Os, J. (2004). *Stress, the brain and depression.* New York: Cambridge University Press.

VanVoorhis, R. W., & Levinson, E. M. (2006). Job satisfaction among school psychologists: A meta-analysis. *School Psychology Quarterly, 21* 77–90.

Vasterling, J. J., & Brewin, C. R. (2005). *Neuropsychology of PTSD: Biological, cognitive, and clinical perspectives.* New York: Guilford.

Walker, E., & Tessner, K. (2008). Schizophrenia. *Perspectives on Psychological Science, 3*, 30–37.

Wang, P. S., Berglund, P., Olfson, M., Pincus, H. A., Wells, K. B., & Kessler, R. C. (2005). Failure and delay in initial treatment contact after first onset of mental disorders in the National Comorbidity Survey Replication. *Archives of General Psychiatry, 62*, 603–613.

Wang, P. S., Lane, M., Olfson, M., Pincus, H. A., Wells, K. B., & Kessler, R. C. (2005). Twelve-month use of mental health services in the United States: Results from the National Comorbidity Survey Replication. *Archives of General Psychiatry, 62*, 629–640.

Ward, S. B., Ward, T. J. Jr., & Clark, H. T. III. (1991). Classification congruence among school psychologists and its relationship to type of referral question and professional experience. *Journal of School Psychology, 29*, 89–108.

Wargo, E. (2007). Understanding the have-knots: The role of stress in just about everything. *Observer, 20*(11), 18–23.

Weissberg, R. P., & Greenberg, M. T. (1998). School and community competence-enhancement and prevention programs. In W. Damon (Series Editor) and I. E. Siegel & L. A. Renninger (Vol. Eds.), *Handbook of child psychology: Vol. 4. Child psychology in practice* (5th ed., pp. 877–954). New York: Wiley.

Weisz, J. R., Weiss, B. & Han, S. S. (1995). Effects of psychotherapy with children and adolescents revisited: A meta-analysis of treatment outcome studies. *Psychological Bulletin, 117*, 450–468.

White, K. (2002). *An introduction to the sociology of health and illness*. Thousand Oaks, CA: Sage Publications.

WHO World Mental Health Survey Consortium. (2004). Prevalence, severity, and unmet need for treatment of mental disorders in the World Health Organization world mental health surveys. *Journal of the American Medical Association, 291*, 2581–2590.

Widiger, T. A., & Trull, T. J. (2007). Plate tectonics in the classification of personality disorder: Shifting to a dimensional model. *American Psychologist, 62*, 71–83.

Wolpe, J. (1968). Psychotherapy by reciprocal inhibition. *Conditional Reflex, 3*, 234–240.

Wolraich, M. L., Lambert, E. W., & Bickman, L. (2004). Assessing the impact of parent and teacher agreement on diagnosing Attention-Deficit Hyperactivity Disorder. *Journal of Developmental & Behavioral Pediatrics, 25*, 41–47.

Wyatt, W. J., & Midkiff, D. M. (2006). Biological psychiatry: A practice in search of a science. *Behavior and Social Issues, 15*, 132–151.

Ysseldyke, J., Morrison, D., Burns, M., Ortiz, S., Dawson, P., Rosenfield, S. Brenna, K., & Telzrow, C. (2006). *School psychology: A blueprint for training and practice III*. Bethesda, MD: National Association of School Psychologists.

Zaidel, D. W. (2005). *Neuropsychology of art: Neurological, cognitive, and evolutionary perspectives*. New York: Psychology Press.

Zirpoli, T. J. (2005). *Behavior management applications for teachers* (4th ed.). Upper Saddle River, NJ: Pearson, Merrill, Prentice Hall.

Zorumski, C. F., & Rubin, E. H. (2005). *Psychopathology in the genome and neuroscience era*. Washington, DC: American Psychiatric Publishing.

CHAPTER 24

Evidence-Based Interventions and Practices in School Psychology: Challenges and Opportunities for the Profession[1]

THOMAS R. KRATOCHWILL
University of Wisconsin–Madison

KIMBERLY EATON HOAGWOOD, JESSICA MASS LEVITT, SERENE OLIN, AND LISA HUNTER ROMANELLI
Columbia University

JENNIFER L. FRANK
Vanderbilt University

NOA SAKA
Hebrew University of Jerusalem

Across the nation, the goal of finding evidence to support professional practice in schools is motivated by a search for an answer to the question of "what works?" In the United States, both Congress and the U.S. Department of Education are hopeful that increasing the quality of education research and encouraging the application of this knowledge in practice will increase the quality of academic and behavioral intervention programs to which children attending public schools are exposed.

This complicated process of creating and applying research-based knowledge to practice, known as *evidence-based practice* (EBP),

has stimulated the production of countless books, scholarly articles, monographs, and websites. Entire journals, such as the *Journal of Evidence-Based Practice in Schools*, now exist for the purpose of promoting EBP in educational settings. Evidence-based practice might be described as a "movement" within the field of school psychology, resulting in organized efforts to identify, disseminate, and promote the adoption of practices with demonstrated efficacy and effectiveness. It has been embraced by professional organizations representing the field. Many of the core principles of EBP have been integrated into many of the ethical codes and principles of practice governing the delivery of psychological services in schools as well.

We are by no means alone. EBP has been endorsed by individuals and associations representing the fields of medicine and psychiatry (Evidence-Based Medicine Working Group,

---

[1] In this chapter we use the term "intervention" to refer to a wide range of prevention, treatment, educational or service programs that are typically used in clinical or educational settings. We also use the terms intervention and treatment interchangeably.

1992; Sackett, Straus, Richardson, Rosenberg, & Haynes, 2000), speech and language pathology (American Speech-Language and Audiology Association, 2001; Reilly, Perry, Douglas, & Oates, 2001); clinical psychology, social work (Gambrill, 1999); rehabilitation psychology (Johnston, Sherer, & Whyte, 2006); occupational therapy (Law & Baum, 1998), nursing (Melnyk, Fineout-Overholt, Stone, & Ackerman, 2000), health promotion and prevention science (Simnett, Perkins, & Wright, 1999). Endorsing the principles of EBP signifies reaffirmation of a profession's commitment to developing a scientific knowledge base, and signals the expectation that important professional and practice-related decisions be based on evidence derived from scientific research. Some groups, such as the American Speech-Language-Hearing Association (ASHA), have even implemented standards for clinical certification that require applicants "demonstrate knowledge of processes used in research and the integration of research principles into evidence-based clinical practice" (ASHA, 2001, p. 6).

All things considered, it is somewhat ironic that there is fairly limited empirical support for the underlying assumption that implementation of EBP will necessarily improve service delivery, reduce costs, or improve access to services. Very few studies have been undertaken to identify how best to integrate EBP into routine practice, or whether implementation of EBP will necessarily lead to the types of positive outcomes that have been obtained under carefully controlled, "laboratory type" research conditions. For example, it is unknown if or how preservice training in EBP will assist students in becoming more effective practitioners. These are all hypotheses that remain untested and questions the field has only begun to address.

In this chapter, we discuss arguments in support of the hypothesis that research on implementation of EBP in school settings does indeed have the potential to enhance the quality and efficiency of school-based psychological services. Although there are many questions that remain unanswered with regards to EBP, we would argue that the products and practices associated with EBP hold the potential to improve a variety of practical and scientific issues currently facing the field. Realizing the vision of improved student outcomes through implementation of EBP is likely to require significant changes in how the field organizes,

examines, and translates scientific information into action and how practice assimilates and shapes scientific knowledge. It will require clarification of our understanding of what is acceptable evidence, and the development of new training paradigms for current and future school psychologists. It will likely require expansion of the professional role school psychologists occupy within the larger educational and mental health service delivery system. In the concluding section of this chapter, we explore these necessary changes in greater depth and examine areas of progress and current challenges facing the field. This chapter is an overview of some of the major issues raised in previous publications by us and others (see for example, Hoagwood, Burns, Kiser, Ringeisen, & Schoenwald, 2001; Hoagwood & Johnson, 2003; Kratochwill, 2006; Kratochwill & Hoagwood, 2006; Kratochwill & Shernoff, 2003; Kratochwill & Stoiber, 2002; Stoiber & Kratochwill, 2000; White & Kratochwill, 2005; Weisz et al., 2000; 2004; 2005). Readers are referred to publications cited herein for elaboration on the issues raised in this chapter.

EVIDENCE-BASED PRACTICE: CORE CONSTRUCTS AND ISSUES

The EBP movement is best understood as a part of a much larger cultural phenomenon that reflects an increasing trend in public policy towards enhanced accountability and demands for efficiency among helping professions with claims to specialized knowledge. Shaping this movement are legal and political changes including the passage of the No Child Left Behind Act of 2001 and the Individuals with Disabilities Education Improvement Act of 2004.

Current federal legislation emanating from the U.S. Department of Education in the No Child Left Behind (NCLB; 2001) and the Individuals With Disabilities Improvement Education Act (IDEA, 2004) emphasize the importance of using intervention procedures (spanning instructional and behavioral domains) that are based on strong scientific support and merit whenever possible (Kratochwill, Clements, & Kalymon, 2007). For example, NCLB requires that programs and practices be based on scientific research. The term "scientifically based research" is defined as research that involves the application of rigorous, systematic and objective procedures to obtain reliable and valid knowledge relevant to education activities and programs. To be considered "research based" the research must: (1) involve systematic, empirical methods that draw on observation or experiment; (2) involve rigorous data analyses that are adequate to test the stated hypotheses and justify the general conclusions drawn; (3) rely on measurements or observational methods that provide reliable and valid data across evaluators and observers, across multiple measurements and observations, and across studies by the same or different investigators; (4) are evaluated using experimental or quasi-experimental designs; (5) provide sufficient detail to clarify and allow for replication, or offer the opportunity to build systematically on their findings; and (6) have been accepted by a peer-reviewed journal or by a panel of independent experts through a comparably rigorous, objective, and scientific review.

Similarly, IDEA 2004 allows states to use a process to determine disability status based on responsiveness to intervention, defined as the change in behavior or performance as a function of an intervention. Rather than focusing on the discrepancy between actual and expected achievement based on group standardized test scores, response to intervention (RTI) examines discrepancy in terms of pre- and postintervention levels of performance. The core features of RTI include: (1) evidence-based instruction and curricular materials; (2) ongoing classroom-based performance monitoring; (3) universal screening; (4) implementation of evidence-based interventions; (5) progress monitoring to document intervention effectiveness; and (6) fidelity documentation. Considered together, the scope and depth of this legislation will surely encourage, if not force, the application of EBP in school psychology (Kratochwill, 2006).

What is Evidence-Based Practice?

Although inspired by large-scale professional and legal accountability measures, EBP has no universally agreed upon operational definition (Dunst, Trivette, & Cutspec, 2002). One of the earliest and most commonly cited definitions of EBP comes to us from the field of medicine in which it has been defined as "conscientious, explicit and judicious use of current best evidence in making decisions about the care of individual patients" (Sackett, Rosenberg, Gray, Haynes, & Richardson, 1996, p. 71). More recently, this definition has been extended to include the integration of clinical expertise and values with the best research evidence available (Institute

of Medicine, 2001; Sackett, Straus, Richardson, Rosenberg, & Haynes, 2000). By clinical expertise, Sackett et al. (2000) referred to advanced clinical skills used to assess, diagnose and treat disorders; and by patient preferences and values, they meant the full inclusion of the patient in the analysis of the likelihood of benefit and risk. The American Psychological Association (APA) adopted a similar definition in its policy statement which defined EBP as "the integration of the best available research with clinical expertise in the context of patient characteristics, culture, values and preferences" (Presidential Task Force on Evidence-Based Practice, 2005, p. 1).

Although commonalities exist, it is important to keep in mind that subtle yet important differences are emerging in how various professions have begun to define this construct. Table 24.1 provides a sampling of definitions and major dissemination initiatives undertaken by various professional groups that might work in related or supplemental service provider groups working in school settings. As Table 24.1 illustrates, there are both common and conceptually distinct elements in how each profession defines and operationalizes its EBP. For example, all definitions recognize the value of empirical evidence in guiding decision making; however, differences are common in how "evidence" is defined. Some definitions explicitly require the application of the "best" or most rigorous research evidence available, while others simply require that research be used to inform a theory of action that can be tested and validated within the context of professional practice.

Likewise, all professions recognize the need to consider context and factors related to the client or practice setting to varying degrees. However, important differences exist with regards to the specific contextual or client-based factors that should be considered. Some definitions emphasize the need to consider specific client-related factors such as culture or values, while others take into account organizational context, cost, and other factors related to transportability.

In terms of dissemination to the field, approaches have varied widely as well. Some professional groups including divisions of the American Psychological Association have developed specific study coding criteria for grading the quality of research evidence within their respective fields (Chambless & Hollon, 1998; Kratochwill & Stoiber, 2002), while other professions (e.g., early childhood) propose utilizing functional or theory-driven criteria derived

TABLE 24.1 Variations on the Term Evidence-Based Practice Across Professions and Major Intervention Dissemination Initiatives

Profession	Source	Definition	Examples of Major Initiatives
Medicine	Institute of Medicine	"Conscientious, explicit, and judicious use of current best evidence in making decisions about the care of individual patients. The practice of evidence-based medicine means integrating individual clinical expertise with the best available external clinical evidence from systematic research."	Cochrane Collaboration National Guideline Clearinghouse
Psychology	APA	"Evidence-based practice in psychology (EBPP) is the integration of the best available research with clinical expertise in the context of patient characteristics, culture and preferences."	APA Division 12 Task Force APA Division 16 Task Force
Social Work	McNeece & Thyer (2004)	"Evidence-based practice can be defined as the integration of the best research evidence with clinical expertise and client values in making practice decisions."	
Occupational Therapy	Bennett & Bennett (2000)	"The process of evidence-based practice is essentially the same in occupational therapy as it is for other health disciplines. Differences in its application arise from differing practice domains and theoretical models used."	CATS reviews Program Evaluation Guidelines & Qualitative/Quantitative Research Review Guides
Speech, Language, Hearing and Audiology	ASHA	"Evidence-based practice refers to an approach in which current, high-quality research evidence is integrated with practitioner expertise and client preferences and values into the process of making clinical decisions."	Criteria and Practice Standards and Guidelines
Early Childhood	Dunst, Tivette & Cutspec (2002)	"Evidence-based practices are informed by research in which the characteristics and consequences of environmental variables are empirically established and the relationship directly informs what a practitioner can do to produce a desired outcome."	DEC Recommended Practices Center for Evidence-Based Practices
Reading/ Literacy	International Reading Association	"To be described as 'evidence based,' an instructional program or collection of practices should have been tested and shown to have a record of success. That is, reliable, trustworthy, and valid evidence indicates that when that program or set of practices is used, children can be expected to make adequate gains in reading achievement. 'Research-based instruction' is sometimes used to convey the same meaning."	Teaching Reading Well Synthesis

from various research sources in order to justify practice-related decisions (Dunst et al., 2002). Some groups including federal agencies (i.e., Substance Abuse and Mental Health Service Administration's (SAMHSA) National Registry of Effective Practices) have undertaken formal dissemination of EBP; however the rigor of the review process adopted by these groups has varied widely.

What is an Evidence-Based Intervention (EBI)?

Just as there is no universally agreed upon operational definition of "evidence-based practice," definitions of EBIs have varied as well. EBP assumes the presence of a coherent body of scientific knowledge relevant to a range of service practices, and is designed to allow for the prediction of the impact of a particular type of intervention, treatment or service on a particular student, client or system process. An evidence-based intervention (EBI) is the term more commonly used in the clinical and school psychology literatures (see Kratochwill & Stoiber, 2001 for a review of distinctions in terminology) to refer to interventions or programs that meet criteria designated by a task force or professional group based on experimental research support. Typically these criteria are used to code the quality of a variety of quantitative between-group and single-participant research designs—although there are exceptions to this general perspective.

Criteria developed to assess evidence quality, or establish an "evidence base" are created to answer substantive questions related to the summative knowledge regarding the overall effectiveness of a given program or practice (West, King, Carey, Lohr, McKoy, & Lux, 2002). Such reviews generally take into account three interrelated dimensions of: (1) the quality of basic research in a given area (e.g., design, conduct and analysis has minimized selection, measurement and confounding biases), (2) the quantity of that research (e.g., magnitude of treatment effect, number of studies, sample size across studies), and (3) the consistency of findings across multiple studies (e.g., similar findings reported using similar and different designs). Accordingly, evidence derived from high-quality individual studies is necessary, but insufficient, for establishing an evidence base. Considerations related to the quantity and consistency of evidence must also be taken into account. Thus, EBIs are treatments that have been subjected to systematic

review and existing evidence graded in terms of general research quality, quantity, and consistency to obtain a general rating of scientific credibility.

What Is an Intervention?

Although an intervention's designation of "evidence based" is ultimately determined by the specific criteria and review process applied, not all school-based interventions are equally suited for such review. One limitation may stem from the general lack of research evidence regarding a particular intervention or practice. However, another (perhaps related) difficulty arises in the review of interventions that are difficult to operationalize or are, by definition, highly individualized and thus subject to change. Although we can describe the features and core components of various interventions and treatment programs, we have very few generic or universal models useful for describing and comparing intervention processes and outcomes derived from different theoretical bases or whose components may be difficult to define. Such models or conceptual schemes may prove very useful. For example, we have argued elsewhere (Frank & Kratochwill, 2008) that operationalizing the active intervention components of a consultation process is difficult because of the (a) lack of specificity about the goal and intervention targets that the consultation is targeting, (b) lack of specificity about the necessary and sufficient intervention inputs (e.g., assessment information and resources), (c) conceptual and experimental overlap between the process and content of consultation, and (d) difficulty controlling for the mediator and moderator variables that impact the effectiveness of interventions delivered through consultation.

Many of the same challenges are present in studies of individual or group school-based interventions as well. The lack of a general framework for defining the features of school-based EBP presents practical challenges in terms of making cross-intervention comparisons, and empirical challenges in the selection of appropriate controls and comparisons within the context of research studies.

Consider the following: What might a school-based intervention *placebo* consist of? What sorts of inert but necessary procedural elements must be in place to deliver the "active ingredients" of an intervention and how are they best controlled? Out of all of the many actions that can be undertaken within the context of an intervention, what *really* matters in term of eliciting a treatment effect and to what degree? Knowledge of what *really* matters, and the process through which a treatment effect is elicited, is important for clinicians interested in predicting whether a specific intervention is likely to be effective in treating the issues presented by a *specific* child in a *specific* context. Knowing what *really* matters is also important to the concept of intervention fidelity, which requires practitioners to actively monitor the implementation of those intervention variables responsible for evoking treatment effects to rule out possible threats to validity.

In the absence of a common definition of a school-based intervention, for the purposes of this chapter, we consider an intervention to be the systematic use of a technique, program or practice designed to improve learning or behavior in specific areas of student need. Applying this definition, an intervention includes: (1) specific and measurable outcomes for academic, social and/or behavioral functioning; (2) a well-defined plan identifying participants, timelines, frequency, and scope of interventions; (3) precise methods for monitoring progress at designated intervals; (4) evidence-based or scientifically supported practices implemented consistently with their design and purpose; and (5) an explicit link to educational decision making. These attributes would apply to both academic and behavioral interventions delivered at the system, group, or individual level in school settings. Thus, EBIs are simply interventions which can be described and compared in relation to these characteristics, relevant research subjected to systematic review, and supporting evidence rated along a continuum of scientific credibility.

Figure 24.1 provides an overview of a generic framework that could be used to organize and describe the essential intervention components of a hypothetical school-based drug prevention program using the definition above. As Figure 24.1 illustrates, the essential intervention components identified by the program theory can be subsumed under an even broader intervention logic model defined in terms of inputs, outputs, and outcomes. The relationship between these inputs, outputs, and outcomes in turn represent the intervention or program theory to be tested within the context of experimental research.

Other reasonable organizational schemes *could*, and probably *should*, be considered. However, the benefits of having a widely generalizable model describing the essential features of relevance to the implementation of a school-based

intervention could be quite beneficial in terms of facilitating communication, identifying essential and adaptable intervention components and processes, assigning costs to various features of an intervention, and organizing information in such a way as to facilitate comparison. Ultimately, how this model is defined could have important implications for how the field evolves with regards to how we organize, develop, investigate, adapt, and disseminate EBI information.

GOALS OF THE EVIDENCE-BASED PRACTICE MOVEMENT AND ITS MEANING FOR SCHOOL PSYCHOLOGY

Today we take it for granted that the practices of most of modern medicine are grounded in scientific knowledge derived from basic research. However, if we define scientific knowledge as knowledge derived from true experiments (referred to as Randomized Clinical Trial or RCTs in medicine) or quasi-experiments that address the threats to validity in other than randomized clinical trials (Campbell & Stanley, 1963), then this has not always been the case. Historians of science point to several important events in the history of medicine that contributed to the popularization of EBP. One is the Flexner Report (Millenson, 1997), which created a blueprint for medical education based on a rigorous scientific curriculum. The second is development of the Randomized-Control Trial design and successful application of efficacy results in the treatment of tuberculosis (Millenson, 1997). As studies of this sort began to expand, a third major turning point was the establishment of the FDA and related governmental organizations with the mission of testing the safety and effectiveness of medical interventions developed within the context of such scientific studies. The fourth is the emergence of the use of meta-analysis as a tool to distill and synthesize research studies to determine a general estimate of treatment effect across studies with divergent findings (Glass, 1976; Kazdin, 2005; Weisz et al., 2004). Fifth is the establishment of the Cochrane Collaborative (www.cochrane.org) as a structure to facilitate dissemination of synthesized evidence-based information into the field. Finally, the emergence of practice guidelines as a strategy to disseminate profession-wide consensus on how to approach the assessment and treatment of various problems, and application of these guidelines in training and

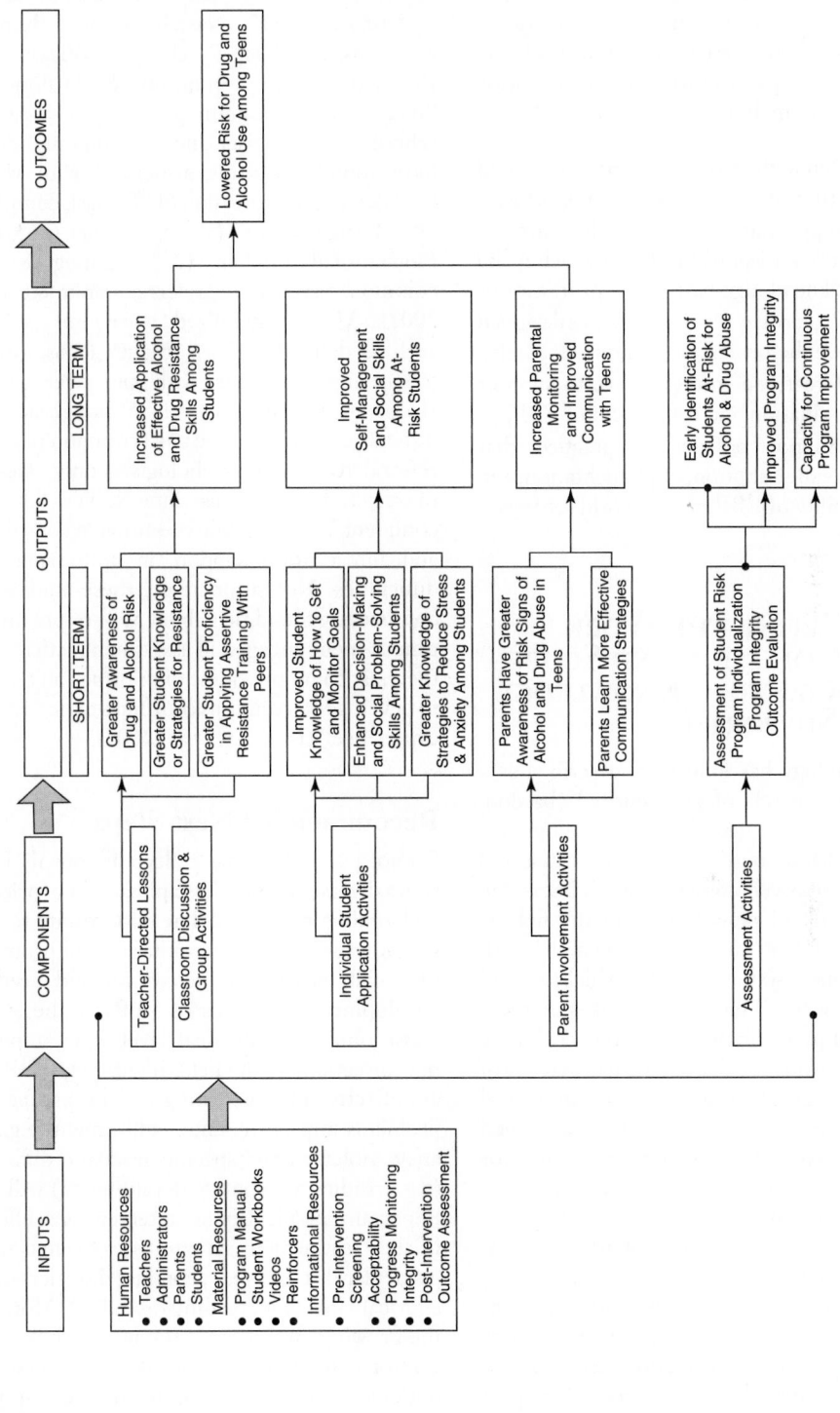

INPUTS

COMPONENTS

OUTPUTS

OUTCOMES

Human Resources
Teachers
Administrators
Parents
Students
Material Resources
Program Manual
Student Workbooks
Videos
Reinforcers
Informational Resources
Pre-Intervention
Screening
Acceptability
Progress Monitoring
Integrity
Post-Intervention
Outcome Assessment

Teacher-Directed Lessons

Classroom Discussion & Group Activities

Individual Student Application Activities

Parent Involvement Activities

Assessment Activities

SHORT TERM

Greater Awareness of Drug and Alcohol Risk

Greater Student Knowledge or Strategies for Resistance

Greater Student Proficiency in Applying Assertive Resistance Training With Peers

Improved Student Knowledge of How to Set and Monitor Goals

Enhanced Decision-Making and Social Problem-Solving Skills Among Students

Greater Knowledge of Strategies to Reduce Stress & Anxiety Among Students

Parents Have Greater Awareness of Risk Signs of Alcohol and Drug Abuse in Teens

Parents Learn More Effective Communication Strategies

Assessment of Student Risk
Program Individualization
Program Integrity
Outcome Evalution

LONG TERM

Increased Application of Effective Alcohol and Drug Resistance Skills Among Students

Improved Self-Management and Social Skills Among At-Risk Students

Increased Parental Monitoring and Improved Communication with Teens

Early Identification of Students At-Risk for Alcohol & Drug Abuse

Improved Program Integrity

Capacity for Continuous Program Improvement

Lowered Risk for Drug and Alcohol Use Among Teens

FIGURE 24.1 Sample logic model of a drug prevention program.

practice is the sixth and final stage of this process (White & Kratochwill, 2005).

What will it take to bring EBP to the field of school psychology? If we begin with the model of EBP implementation as it occurred in medicine, the essential steps towards profession-wide adoption seem to include the following:

Step 1: Define the work of the profession and the scientific knowledge base to support it;

Step 2: Support and coordinate the efforts of organizations responsible for advancing the scientific knowledge base of the profession;

Step 3: Promote a research agenda designed to improve the professional knowledge base;

Step 4: Create an infrastructure to support the dissemination and refinement of EBP;

Step 5: Support policies and practices that encourage the adoption, implementation, and sustainability of EBP in real-world settings.

STEP 1: DEFINE THE WORK OF THE PROFESSION AND SCOPE OF THE SCIENTIFIC KNOWLEDGE BASE TO SUPPORT IT

School psychology has long been described as a profession "in search of an identity" (Bardon, 1983). Part of the problem in finding this identity is related to the highly contextualized nature of school psychology practice. That is, the day-to-day work of practitioners in the field is highly dependent on the broader mental health and educational system within which school psychologists work. This context makes defining what a school psychologist is, and the work they do, challenging indeed. The day-to-day practice of school psychologists is far more heavily influenced by federal and state role definitions than their clinical psychology counterparts. Thus, for evidence-based practice to be viable, an important activity will be to clarify and operationalize the critical roles and activities of psychologists working in school settings, determine their most critical information needs, and important contextual variables impacting practice. A better understanding of the information needs of the ultimate "consumers" of products to support EBP (e.g., practice guidelines, intervention and assessment tools) is important for establishing priorities in terms of research, dissemination, and related objectives described below.

Various surveys of school psychologists' time spent in various work activities have been conducted over the past two decades (Benson & Hughes, 1985; Nastasi, Varjas, Bernstein, & Pluymert, 1998; Reschley & Wilson, 1995; Bramlett, Murphy, Johnson, & Wallingsford, 2002). Surveys examining the types of referrals school psychologists most commonly receive have found problems associated with reading (57%), written expression (43%), task completion (39%), mathematics (39%), conduct (26%), and motivational problems (24%) among the most common reasons for referral (Bramlett et al., 2002). More generalized behavioral problems such as defiance (17%), truancy (8%), violence (6%), and problems with peer relationships (16%) are prevalent as well. Although academic difficulties constitute the most common reason for referral to school psychologists, only one-third of respondents in this same survey felt "very confident" in their ability to provide consultation and intervention support in addressing these difficulties. Not surprisingly, these studies have consistently found that about 50% of practitioner time is spent engaged in assessment activities and the most common source of information relied on to develop interventions continues to be "personal experience" (Bramlett et al., 2002).

Recommended Next Steps

School psychology has reflected from its inception a diverse and multidisciplinary set of priorities and guiding principles. The opportunity to move beyond testing and consultation to promotion of social, emotional, behavioral and academic development by means of EBPs at the system, classroom, and individual level is an important new direction for the field. Identifying EBPs that are effective in remediating general psychosocial problems impacting school adjustment (e.g., truancy, violence) and specific academic difficulties (e.g., reading vocabulary development) will be as important as identifying interventions effective in the treatment of symptoms associated with a particular disorder (e.g., conduct disorder) or categorical label (e.g., reading disability). Moreover, the growing awareness of the importance of prevention and multitiered and systemic intervention options in schools means it will be important to identify effective programs and interventions that treat the proximal and distal causes of academic and behavioral problems most prevalent in school settings and to target both academic and emotional/behavioral outcomes (Hoagwood et al., 2001).

This new expanded definition of the appropriate targets and contexts of intervention has the potential to enhance individual change processes for students, teachers, families and other stakeholders, and can improve schools as systems. However, it will be critical to establish priorities and focus on the review and dissemination of EBP and related information that school psychologists *want* and *need*. Additional research surrounding the information needs of school psychologists working in different contexts and capacities would greatly support this effort.

STEP 2: SUPPORT AND COORDINATE THE EFFORTS OF ORGANIZATIONS RESPONSIBLE FOR ADVANCING THE SCIENTIFIC KNOWLEDGE BASE OF THE PROFESSION

In the absence of a Food and Drug Administration (FDA) to regulate the provision of school-based mental health services, a variety of organizations and institutions have taken it upon themselves to synthesize and grade the quality or extent of evidence in support of various school-based prevention and intervention programs. Table 24.2 provides a sampling of some of the major organizations who have pursued the task of reviewing and disseminating school-based prevention and intervention programs, and this list continues to grow with time. Although the activities of these organizations may be well intentioned, their activities are somewhat anarchic and can be a source of confusion to consumers looking for an "authoritative source" of evidence-based recommendations. Today, a significant challenge facing the field lies not only in determining *what works* and for *whom*, but what works *according to* whom.

Numerous professional groups and task forces use somewhat different criteria to designate an intervention or program as "evidence based." These different designations have presented several challenges for practitioners intending to adopt evidence-based programs (Kratochwill & Hoagwood, 2006). For example, the What Works Clearinghouse (WWC) has traditionally relied on between-group randomized trial methodology and high-quality quasi-experimental studies

for evidence review, thereby limiting the knowledge base in an intervention domain to intervention procedures and programs tested using these methodologies. Although such stringent screening standards favor research with a high degree of internal validity, evidence derived from correlational research is excluded from consideration despite the fact that such evidence can provide tentative support for intervention effectiveness when approaches to analysis such as causal modeling are applied (Thompson, Diamond, McWilliam, Snyder, & Snyder, 2003).

Moreover, not all evidence considered in the review and rating of intervention programs conducted by the WWC has been subjected to peer review and published in a scholarly journal. A recent review of evidence used by the WWC workgroup to identify effective early reading intervention programs found that less than half of the articles that met WWC methodological screening standards had actually been published in a peer reviewed scholarly journal (Frank, Albers, Kratochwill, & Roach, in press). Of those, approximately one-quarter of the supporting evidence had been conducted by the program or curriculum developers themselves, thus reflecting a long-standing challenge in the field in terms of obtaining high-quality, independent studies of effective programs and practices. Again, the empirical and practical implications of basing evidence ratings on evidence derived from dissertations, working papers, or evaluation reports as opposed to peer-reviewed articles is not entirely clear.

Finally, the frequency with which new evidence is integrated and used to update intervention ratings varies as well. Although the evidence used to identify effective programs and practices should be cumulative, and thus subject to some degree of change over time, the procedures adopted by various organizations in terms of how to integrate new research and update ratings over time is not always transparent. Also, some organizations do not feature programs and practices for which there is no support. Although it might be implied that if one's program is not listed, it does not have the support of the organization, this is not always necessarily the case.

Areas of Progress

In the field of school psychology, the Task Force on Evidence-Based Interventions in School Psychology was formed in 1999 with a charter to assist the profession in developing and promoting

TABLE 24.2   Organizations Conducting Reviews of School-Based Prevention and Intervention Programs

Organization or Agency	Mission	Relevance for School-Based Practices	Major Review & Dissemination Initiatives	Methods
Institute for Educational Sciences	To provide rigorous evidence on which to ground education practice and policy	Academic and behavioral	What Works Clearinghouse	Systematic review
Campbell Collaboration	Help people make well-informed decisions about the effects of interventions in the social, behavioral and educational arenas	Academic & behavioral intervention, instruction, remediation, treatment programs in education	Reviews of Interventions and Policy Evaluations, Social, Psychological, Education, and Criminological Trials Registry	Systematic review & meta-analysis
Coalition for Evidence-Based Policy	[provide] policymakers and practitioners with clear, actionable information on what works, as demonstrated in scientifically valid studies, that they can use to improve the lives of the people they serve	Academic and behavioral early childhood practices, K–12 academic and behavioral interventions, substance abuse, mental health, violence prevention, and school-based health programs	Social Programs that Work Website	Review of RCT evidence
Office of English Language Acquisition, U.S. Department of Education	Overseeing the implementation of programs and development of more effective practices to support the learning and development of English language learners (ELLs)	Academic programs for English Language Learners	National Clearinghouse for English Acquisition and Instructional Educational Programs (NCELA)	Systematic review
Center for Academic and Social Emotional Learning (CASEL)	To establish social and emotional learning (SEL) as an essential part of education	Social and emotional learning programs and interventions	Safe and Sound: An Educational Leader's Guide to SEL Programs	Systematic review

the adoption of EBIs among school psychologists (for overview see Kratochwill & Stoiber, 2000; Kratochwill & Shernoff, 2003, 2004; Stoiber & Kratochwill, 2000, 2001). The Task Force was supported by APA Division 16 of the American Psychological Association (APA) and the Society for the Study of School Psychology (SSSP) and received official endorsement by the National Association of School Psychologists (NASP).

The Task Force began with the development of a *Procedural and Coding Manual for Evidence-Based Interventions in School Psychology* (2003; hereafter called the *Manual*). The basis for development of the *Manual* was to take into account a broader array of contextual and content issues than what was currently available in the *Procedural and Coding Manual* developed by the Clinical Psychology Task Force (see Weisz & Hawley, 2001). The goal of the *Manual* was to provide a template for reviewing studies relevant to intervention research in school psychology and to serve as a guideline for graduate training of new

generations of intervention researchers within the profession of school psychology. The conceptual, philosophical, and methodological features of the *Manual* have been reviewed by Kratochwill and Stoiber (2002) and most recently, through the efforts of the Cultural Diversity Committee and the Qualitative Committee of the Task Force, further developments and refinements have been made in the content of the *Manual*. Table 24.3 provides an overview of the domains currently addressed by Task Force Criteria, Table 24.4 a listing of review articles that have utilized Task Force criteria, and Table 24.5 an example of how coding criteria could be applied to analyze the strength of evidence of home-school collaboration interventions.

Recommended Next Steps

Although some work has begun in terms of coding and reviewing studies, there is still much to be done. The extent to which the *Manual* will be used in the future will obviously depend on the efforts of individual researchers to pursue

TABLE 24.3   Summary of Group-Based Design Studies

Indicator	Overall Evidence Rating NNR = No Numerical Rating or 0–3	Description of Evidence Strong Promising Weak No/Limited Evidence or Descriptive Ratings
General Characteristics		
General Study Characteristics		
General Design Characteristics		
Data Analysis		
Type of Program		
Stage of Program		
Concurrent/Historical Intervention Exposure		
Key Features		
Research Methodology		
Measurement		
Comparison Group		
Primary/Secondary Outcomes are Statistically Significant		
Cultural Significance		
Educational/Clinical Significance		
External Intervention Components		
Durability/Generalization		
Identifiable Intervention Components		
Implementation Fidelity		
Replication		
Site of Implementation		

TABLE 24.4   Review Articles That Have Used the Task Force on Evidence-Based Interventions in School Psychology

Author(s)	Citation
Prevatt, F., & Kelly, F. D. (2005)	Dropping out of school: A review of intervention programs. *Journal of School Psychology, 41*, 377–395.
Lehr, C. A., Hansen, A., Sinclair, M. F., & Christenson, S. L. (2003)	Moving beyond dropout towards school completion: An integrative review of data-based interventions. *School Psychology Review, 32*, 342–364.
Bates, S. L. (2005)	Evidence-based family-school interventions with preschool children. *School Psychology Quarterly, 20*, 352–370.
Fishel, M., & Ramirez, L. (2005)	Evidence-based parent involvement interventions with school-aged children. *School Psychology Quarterly, 20*, 371–402.
Valdez, C. R., Carlson, C., & Zanger, D. (2005)	Evidence-based parent training and family interventions for school behavior change. *School Psychology Quarterly, 20*, 403–433.
Hoard, D., & Shepard, K. N. (2005)	Parent education as parent-centered prevention: A review of school-related outcomes. *School Psychology Quarterly, 20*, 434–454.
Guli, L. A. (2005)	Evidence-based parent consultation with school-related outcomes. *School Psychology Quarterly, 20*, 455–472.
Cox, D. D. (2005)	Evidence-based interventions using home-school collaboration. *School Psychology Quarterly, 20*, 473–497.

the systematic review of research pertaining to a given intervention, recommendations from journal editors that authors utilize coding criteria within the context of systematic reviews, and strength of competition from organizations that currently code school-based prevention and intervention research. One way professional organizations contribute to the identification and dissemination of EBPs is by supporting the publication of systematic reviews utilizing Task Force Criteria in peer-reviewed journals. For example, *Psychiatric Services*, a journal of the American Psychiatric Association, has included a special section, "Focusing on Evidence-Based Practices," in its issues. The production of these articles usually depends on the initiative of individual scientists. Under the editorship of Terry B. Gutkin, a special section of the journal *School Psychology Quarterly* was formed and devoted to EBIs. Unfortunately, this section was not continued. As developments have occurred in various applications of the *Manual*, several recommendations for how the process might be improved, the challenges involved in using the *Manual*, and the limitations of the *Manual* have been forthcoming (see for example, Kelly & Prevatt, 2005; Kratochwill & Hoagwood, 2006).

Future work dedicated to refining and field testing the *Manual* is recommended.

Coordination and cooperation among groups with an investment in advancing evidence-based practices in schools is another strategy to address the multiplicity of criteria and competing recommendations of existing groups and task forces conducting systematic reviews of intervention programs. It is important to bear in mind that there are no universally agreed upon standards for how to measure or compare the degrees of scientific credibility. Evidence is a multidimensional construct with many levels of relevance, and in some cases irrelevance, to the practice of school psychology. Evidence can also be described in terms of both quality and quantity (West et al., 2002), and questions regarding what is or is not relevant to our assessment of evidence and how much evidence is "enough" to establish credibility are fundamental questions facing the field today.

The criteria developed by the Division 16 Task Force have evolved over time to include the analysis of evidence in support of the cultural significance, educational and clinical significance, and durability and generalizability of treatment effects over time. While these criteria are likely to continue to evolve over time, a key question facing

TABLE 24.5   Methodological Features of Home-School Collaboration Studies[1]

	S1	S2	S3	S4	S5	S6	S7	S8	S9	S10	S11	S12	S13	S14	S15	S16	S17	S18
Random assignment	1	1	0	1	1	1	0	0	1	1	0	0	1	1	0	0	0	0
Appropriate unit of analysis	1	1	1	1	1	1	1	na	1	1	na	na	1	1	1	1	na	na
Family-wise error rate controlled	0	0	1	1	0	1	0	na	1	1	na	na	1	na	na	1	na	na
Sufficiently large N	1	1	1	0	0	1	1	na	1	1	na	na	1	1	1	1	na	na
Reliable outcome measures	1	1	0	1	0	1	1	0	0	1	0	1	1	1	1	1	1	1
Multiple assessment methods	1	1	1	1	1	1	1	1	1	1	0	1	1	1	0	1	1	1
Measures obtained from multiple sources	1	1	1	1	1	1	1	1	1	1	0	1	1	1	0	1	1	1
Validity of measures reported	1	0	0	1	0	0	0	0	0	1	0	1	1	1	0	0	0	0
Control or comparison group	1	1	1	1	1	1	1	0	1	1	0	0	1	1	0	1	0	0
Counterbalancing of change agents	0	0	0	na	na	na	0	na	0	na	na	na	1	1	0	0	na	na
Group equivalence established	1	1	1	1	1	1	1	na	0	1	0	na	1	1	0	1	1	0
Equivalent mortality with low attrition	1	1	0	1	0	0	0	na	1	1	1	1	1	1	0	1	1	1
Effect size reported	0	0	0	1	0	0	0	0	0	1	0	0	1	0	0	1	0	0
Null findings reported	na	1	1	1	0	1	1	1	1	1	1	1	0	1				
Educational/clinical significance of change assessed	1	1	1	1	1	1	1	1	1	1	1	1	1	1	1	1	1	1
Program components documented	1	1	1	1	1	1	1	1	1	1	1	1	1	1	1	1	1	1
Identifiable components linked to primary outcomes	1	1	1	1	0	0	0	1	1	1	1	1	1	1	0	1	1	0
Interventions were manualized	0	1	0	1	1	0	0	0	1	1	0	0	1	1	0	1	0	0
TOTAL	13	13	11	16	10	12	10	6	12	17	6	9	18	16	6	15	8	8

[1]S = study; 1 = methodological features was present; 0 = methodological feature was absent, unknown, or uncodable; na = methodological feature was not applicable.
Source: Cox (2005).

the field is: What do we want or need *evidence of* with regards to school-based interventions? It is possible to summarize the extent of evidence for a variety of relevant features including efficacy, cost-effectiveness, acceptability, cultural sensitivity, and real-world effectiveness, just to name a few. However, the process of identifying EBIs will require much greater knowledge about what *really* matters—what explains a meaningful and significant source of variation in intervention outcomes and what the necessary and sufficient features of school-based interventions really are.

In light of competing ideas with regards to the important study features that should be included in such reviews, one first step could be to conduct research comparing the practical implications of utilizing different criteria, and the consequences of those differences with regards to selecting and adopting various evidence-based programs and practices. Meta-analytic research might also be conducted in which the various criteria are compared in terms of their contribution to the overall effect size of outcomes in intervention research. For example, randomization, blinding to condition, or the use of standardized versus curriculum-based measures may be a significant moderator of effect within some types of intervention programs, but not others. Such a strategy could provide an empirical, rather than simply a conceptual, basis for including various criteria in rating of evidence for various prevention and intervention practices.

Finally, to address the issue of confusion regarding distinctions between programs that lack support, and those that simply have insufficient support or have not yet been subject to review, it may be worthwhile to undertake the significant task of creating a comprehensive repository of intervention information derived from multiple sources (Kratochwill, 2007). A similar process was undertaken by the Hawaii Task Force on Evidence-Based Practices (Chorpita, Yim, Donkervoet, Arensdorf, Amundsen, McGee et al., 2002).

STEP 3: PROMOTE A STRATEGIC RESEARCH AGENDA DESIGNED TO IMPROVE THE PROFESSIONAL KNOWLEDGE BASE

A variety of research approaches can be used to generate knowledge in the profession. Effectiveness research addresses the validity of inter-vention approaches in real-world settings; process-outcome research investigates the mechanisms of change; meta-analysis research analyzes the size of effects based on syntheses of multiple studies; health service system research examines public health issues, utilization acceptance, cost and cost offsets; and qualitative research describes meaning and inductively builds hypotheses and theories. School psychology research also lends itself well to single-case designs, which are useful for tracking client progress over time.

To date, EBP movement has relied mostly on experimental methodologies to establish the knowledge base for effective practice. Efficacy and effectiveness research have been identified as two types of studies that fall along a methodological continua (Hoagwood, Hibbs, Brent, & Jensen, 1995). Efficacy studies tend to be studies that are conducted in tightly controlled settings and under conditions that typically depart from routine clinical practice. Effectiveness studies on the other hand tend to be conducted in more typical "real world" settings that are characterized by having a diverse set of clients, therapists, service delivery, and context characteristics. The vast majority of EBIs have been tested in efficacy-type studies and therefore major concerns have been raised about the generalizability of these findings to routine practice settings (Hoagwood et al., 1995, Westen, Novotny, & Thompson-Brenner, 2004).

As we have noted previously, the consequence of the almost unilateral emphasis on a single methodological approach is that some of the complicated issues involving the integration of EBP into routine practice settings have not yet been examined. For example, contextual issues such as characteristics of the setting, of the practitioners delivering an intervention, of the structural or fiscal incentives or disincentives, and of the work environment or organizational context are often not assessed at all. Therefore, very limited information is available about the many contextual issues that may have a direct bearing on the adoption, implementation, and sustainability of interventions in practice settings. The consequence of not focusing on contextual variables is that there is almost no evidence base to guide implementation of EBPs into educational and mental health service systems. This state of affairs is not a function of the RCT design itself, but rather a function of the lack of concerted research attention to implementation issues (Kratochwill & Hoagwood, 2006).

Recommended Next Steps

A considerable amount of conceptual work has been done in recent years to identify models for advancing research designed to directly impact practice. One promising framework, developed by Chorpita (2003), organizes studies of EBPs at various stages of dissemination (see also Kratochwill, 2006). Chorpita's approach and corresponding methodological features can help researchers and practitioners understand better how interventions can be effectively transported and disseminated in applied settings and the various conceptual variables that need to be considered in this research. Moreover, qualitative investigation procedures and methodologies can be applied to facilitate the understanding of the features of research that need to be addressed in applied settings (see Brantlinger, Jiminez, Klingner, Pugach, & Richardson, 2005; Chorpita, 2003; Nelson & Quintana, 2005 for further information on the range of methodologies that can be used to develop EBPs).

Secondly, to advance EBP, researchers should consider a broader range of studies assessing the implementation factors that impede or facilitate the uptake of EBIs. In addition to experimental designs, it will also be important to consider a range of methodological tactics to understand the challenges in implementing interventions in practice settings. Although experimental methodology as reflected in both randomized group and single-case research design can make a very important contribution to efficacy and effectiveness studies, a full range of methodologies will be needed to build a comprehensive knowledge base on how EBIs can be transported to applied settings.

Expanded Conceptualization of Efficacy and Effectiveness

In any discussion of interventions it is now important to move beyond simplistic dichotomies such as efficacy or effectiveness and instead consider the feasibility, utility, effectiveness, and relevance of interventions as they are delivered and adapted in local communities. Although at this point there is a large body of evidence for the efficacy of specific interventions, and a growing body of evidence for the effectiveness of broader interventions, there has been almost no attention paid to the important issues of change processes and what accounts for change at multiple levels of implementation. For example, in addition to accounting for the efficacy of specific factors, it is incumbent on researchers to also account for the possible placebo, or non-specific factors that are typically unaccounted for by treatment research designs. For example, in a review of 52 studies conducted between 1995 and 2004 that met scientific criteria for EBPs in the psychosocial treatment literature, very few studies systematically examined whether the presumed active therapeutic ingredients of the therapy actually accounted for therapeutic change (Jensen, Weersing, Hoagwood, & Goldman, 2005). This review concluded that many child psychotherapy trials have not adequately controlled for non-specific factors, such as attention and treatment intensity, and they have failed to examine potential mediators of change. Other researchers have suggested that only a small percentage of treatment effects are accounted for by technique, while 50% can be accounted for by the therapist (Beutler, 2004; Lambert & Barley, 2002). Although the definition of therapist effects is complex, there is no doubt that the interaction of a skilled therapist with effective techniques is important.

Similarly, it is important to understand the potential contributions of therapeutic alliance, empathy, expectancy, and motivation to the changes that occur in intervention research. Unfortunately, the mechanisms producing a good alliance remain vague despite many attempts to help clarify this issue (Horvath & Bedi, 2002; Okiishi, Lambert, Nielson, & Ogles, 2003). However, some studies have suggested that a positive alliance leads to better treatment compliance (Blackwell, 1997), which suggests that the more powerful the alliance, the greater the benefit from treatment. The reverse is also possible, with stronger treatment change processes leading to improved alliance.

Studies of change processes and factors affecting implementation of EBPs are also needed at more macro levels, including organizational, environmental, and systemic levels. A handful of researchers in children's mental health services are beginning to target these processes (e.g., MacArthur Foundation's Youth Research Network), and the study of the contextual factors that improve the adoption, implementation, and sustained use of EBP in schools is a ripe area for future studies.

Expanded Use of Single-Case Research

Although clinical and school task forces have embraced a broader range of methodologies (e.g., both the clinical and school psychology task forces code single case-research design as part of their evidence base), it is only more recently that educational researchers have seriously considered the use of single-case research designs to establish the scientific basis for educational practices (see Horner, Carr, Halle, McGee, Odom, & Wolery, 2005). *Systematic* information obtained with individuals in clinical practice can greatly contribute to the knowledge base. *Systematic* assessment and accumulation of cases can yield new insights even when experimental designs cannot be used. Over time, as cases accumulate, analyses can identify client characteristics that may influence the outcome and course of change in treatment among individuals with different types of problems.

Expanded Assessment of Treatment Process Variables

When well-designed psychological treatments are matched to specific forms of psychological pathology, robust effects are apparent. Although some have suggested that all treatments are equally effective (Wampold, 2001), other analyses have suggested otherwise (Beutler, 2002; Crits-Christoph, 1997). Therefore, in addition to the measurement of client functioning, measurement of treatment processes is important as well. The specific types of processes used and features of those processes typically dictate the focus of assessment. To the extent that these processes vary with treatment implementation, their assessment is very useful in determining what factors were responsible (or not responsible) for the changes observed.

A recent development in treatment outcome literature is referred to as "patient-oriented" research (Howard, Moras, Brill, Martinovich, & Lutz, 1996; Lambert et al., 2003). The key to patient-oriented research is ongoing assessment and monitoring of individual clients from the beginning to the end of intervention, and the use of information to chart progress and make decisions about treatments. Unlike RCTs, patient-oriented research does not involve an extensive battery of pre- and posttreatment assessments. Therapists typically conduct multiple assessments and use brief measures at each session to capture functioning in diverse domains. Patient-oriented research provides a methodology that could nicely complement training and could help practitioners become more interested in systematic evaluation of the interventions they provide. Process research should be included into

clinical trials. Well-controlled RCTs are necessary, but they are not sufficient to elucidate the mechanisms of action underlying a therapeutic effect.

Study Different Trajectories of Change

It is important to monitor intervention effects in an ongoing way to make decisions about continuing, terminating, or altering interventions treatments on the basis of client response. Some clients may make rapid changes quite early in treatment, so-called sudden therapeutic gains (DeRubeis, Tang, Gelfand, & Feeley, 2000); while others do not make expected changes and do not respond to treatment, so-called signal alarm cases (Lambert et al., 2003). Of course, change may occur in some areas but not in others, and change may occur at different rates in the different areas. Systematic evaluation permits finer delineation of therapeutic changes than would be possible with more global clinical judgments and unsystematic assessments. Grouped analyses across treatments and conditions that ignore important interactions are at risk of clouding potential interactive benefits.

STEP 4: CREATE AN INFRASTRUCTURE TO SUPPORT THE DISSEMINATION AND REFINEMENT OF EVIDENCE-BASED PRACTICES

In general, school psychologists are well prepared for the new changes EBPs may require because of a common background in statistics, measurement, and assessment. Nonetheless, importing research-based practices into school psychological services requires more than simply the existence of a robust general knowledge base. In fact, a range of system issues immediately come into play when new programs—whether evidence-based or not—are considered for integration into routine school settings. These system issues include professional development, structural factors (e.g., governance and regulatory issues), fiscal or budgetary factors, aspects of the organizational context (e.g., the culture and climate of provider environments), and linkage across systems. Unfortunately, few studies have yet been undertaken to examine the impact of system variables on the adoption of EBPs.

Scientific inattention to systems change has been further hampered by the lack of a unified theoretical base with which to understand the processes of change (Silverman, Kurtines, &

Hoagwood, 2004). Although the children's mental health movement has been importantly guided by the systems of care framework first enunciated by Stroul and Friedman (1988) and by the landmark study of Knitzer (Unclaimed Children, 1982), current national, state, and local attention to the implementation of EBP in children's mental health has brought into sharp relief the absence of an integrated theoretical framework with which to understand implementation and dissemination processes.

These system obstacles become apparent when individuals not affiliated with the development and testing of a particular intervention design strategy attempt to take that model to scale (Torrey et al., 2001; Torrey et al., 2002). Although several groups of intervention developers have produced similar multilevel approaches to the problem of taking an effective model to scale (e.g., Schoenwald, Halliday-Boykins, & Henggeler, 2003), the methods to do so have been largely idiosyncratic and informed as much by field experience as by theory or research on implementation processes.

An initiative of the Research-to-Practice Committee of the Task Force on Evidence-Based Interventions is focused on identification of contextual factors that have a bearing on the transportability of programs and procedures into schools. This project involves structured interviews with 26 intervention developers whose programs have been implemented in schools and whose models have been scientifically examined in multiple rigorous trials. This project is based on the assumption that choosing to adopt an EBP does not automatically guarantee its successful implementation. Various factors related to funding, technical assistance, training and supervision on the one hand, and school climate, characteristics, ideology, funding sources, policies and previous experiences with program adoption may all be crucial for implementing and sustaining an EBP. As sites vary in key implementation variables—organizational capacity, key staff, leadership, program support, and so forth—deficits in any of these areas may undermine program effectiveness, despite its proven efficacy in clinical trials.

Studies examining the actual content of instruction in graduate school and preparedness of practicing school psychologists for implementing EBPs has yielded disappointing results (e.g., Frank, Kumke, & Kratochwill, 2008; Kratochwill & Shernoff, 2004; Shernoff, Kratochwill, & Stoiber, 2003). For example, Shernoff et al. (2003) found that most graduate school programs in school psychology are not adequately preparing their students in EBPs. Many trainers of school psychologists have not had supervised training in many of the EBIs that are currently being recommended for school practice. School psychology practitioners are inadequately prepared for EBP (see Frank et al., 2008; Kratochwill, 2006 for more detailed discussion).

Recommended Next Steps

Design High-Quality Professional Development Programs

Professional development in prevention and intervention practices is an area that has been given minimal attention in the EBP movement (Kratochwill, Volpiansky, Clements, & Ball, 2008). Even if large numbers of effective programs were available, it is a major challenge to provide the profession with the education and training necessary to ensure the adoption and implementation of these practices. Generally, there is a lack of skill and funding needed for dissemination of prevention and intervention programs, and incentives for acquiring new skills in evidence-based prevention and intervention (Weisz et al., 2005).

An increasingly important option is to promote training institutes in EBP at national conferences. For example, the Task Force has been engaged in training sessions at state and national school psychology meetings. However, this agenda needs to be expanded to other professional education fields such as administrators and general education teachers. Ultimately, however, one-shot workshops will not do justice to the training and supervision that is needed for effective implementation of EBP. Mentorship and supervision in training are critical to facilitate the integrity of program implementation.

Expand Professional Training Options

Another important option is to place more reliance on technology and, specifically, web-based courses and distance education technology to facilitate applied and clinical training in EBPs (Kratochwill, 2007). For example, a network of compressed video training options across graduate training programs in clinical and school psychology as well as education could be quite useful. These options could facilitate applied and clinical training, and disseminate important areas of knowledge across training programs that do not have expertise among their faculty in a particular area.

Enhance Manualized Intervention Options

Intervention manuals can help ensure that therapists or practitioners are using appropriate techniques to intervene with a given disorder or problem. Manuals and manualized treatments are tools and guidelines for practitioners, not fixed unalterable packages (Sackett et al., 1996). A treatment manual is meant to serve as a tool that provides clinicians with both the basic psychological principles that will help most clients with a specific problem and a combination of techniques that are provided to accomplish those principles (Craske, Barlow & Meadows, 2000). There are, of course, times that these techniques do not work and the treatment plan needs to be adjusted. Moreover, clinicians must be able to deal expertly with the complications that may arise in the course of treatment. Training, supervision, and guided practice are all necessary conditions for this outcome to happen. Treatment manuals should all be utilized in a way that includes expert supervision to maximize the benefits of their use. Therapists also need to learn how to incorporate aspects of treatment not articulated in the manual (Abramowitz, Huppert, Cohen, Tolin, & Cahill, 2002) and to understand and clarify this unwritten knowledge.

Research priorities over the next decade will include examination of types of training approaches and strategies that improve practitioner uptake. Researchers who are developing EBPs are encouraged to include and test a range of strategies for self-instructional learning within the program/modules that are being developed for use in practice. Such strategies as manualized treatments accompanied by instructional guides or, possibly, video training options for these interventions should be encouraged as individuals develop this material for future dissemination.

Develop Professional Practice Guidelines

One possible option is to disseminate EBPs in applied and clinical settings in the form of practice guidelines (White & Kratochwill, 2005). Practice guidelines define a range of empirically supported practices, which incorporate diagnosis, assessment, intervention, and related intervention information. Faced with spiraling costs and inadequacies in health care quality, many health care agencies are adopting EBPs and accompanying accountability systems (Barlow, 1996; Institute of Medicine, 2001). A range of "best practice algorithms" and "clinical practice guidelines" have been created and embraced by professional associations (White & Kratochwill, 2005) and in some instances professionals who apply such guidelines reap various advantages such as increased referrals, differential reimbursements, or exemptions from malpractice liability in increasing numbers of states (Barlow, Levitt, & Bufka, 1999). In anticipation of the need to evaluate the adequacy of these guidelines for psychological practice, APA created a task force to develop criteria for their evaluation (APA, 1996; 2000a). The criteria generated from this task force are presented in Table 24.6.

Create a Centralized Information Dissemination Clearinghouse

To manage the problem of dissemination, it may be useful to create a national clearinghouse to help manage databases across various organizations (Kratochwill, 2007). The purpose of a national clearinghouse would be to list all of the evidence-based criteria from various organizations and cast the various evidence-based interventions and practices along the continuum of methodological, conceptual, and statistical criteria that have been established by these groups, including practice guidelines. Practitioners could then select interventions from among the groups based on a clear articulation of these coding criteria for purposes of defining future practice.

STEP 5: SUPPORT POLICIES AND PRACTICES THAT ENCOURAGE THE ADOPTION, IMPLEMENTATION, AND SUSTAINABILITY OF EVIDENCE-BASED PRACTICES IN REAL-WORLD SETTINGS

The President's New Freedom Commission on Mental Health (2003) recommended that the nation "advance evidence-based practices using dissemination and demonstration projects and create a public-private partnership to guide their implementation and improve and expand the workforce by providing evidence-based mental health services and supports" (p. 25). Substantial resources have been devoted to programs aimed at increasing practitioner adoption of EBPs. For example, a major joint initiative of the National Institute of Mental Health (NIMH)

TABLE 24.6   Criteria Established by American Psychological Association for Evaluating Treatment Guidelines

Treatment Efficacy Criteria	1. Guidelines should be based on broad and careful consideration of the relevant empirical literature. 2. Recommendations on specific interventions should take into consideration the level of methodological rigor and clinical sophistication of the research supporting the intervention. 3. Recommendations on specific interventions should take into consideration the treatment consideration to which the interventions have been compared. 4. Guidelines should consider available evidence regarding patient-treatment matching. 5. Guidelines should specify the outcomes the intervention is intended to produce and the evidence should be provided for each outcome.
Clinical Utility Criteria	6. Guidelines should reflect the breadth of patient variables that may influence the clinical utility of the intervention. 7. Guidelines should take into account data on how differences between individual health care professionals may effect the efficacy of the treatment. 8. Guidelines should take into account information pertaining to the setting in which the treatment is offered. 9. Guidelines should take into account data on treatment robustness. 10. Guidelines should take into account the intervention's level of acceptability to the patients who are to receive the service.

Source: From "Criteria for Evaluating Treatment Guidelines", by the American Psychological Association (2002). *American Psychologist, 57,* pp. 1054–057.

and the Substance Abuse and Mental Health Services Administration (SAMHSA) focuses on promoting and supporting the implementation of evidence-based mental health treatment practices in state mental health systems. An important set of studies are beginning to be undertaken to examine how, whether, and to what extent system factors (e.g., structural, regulatory, fiscal, organizational) affect implementation of EBPs (e.g., the MacArthur Foundation Youth Mental Health Research Network, J. Weisz, PI). One of these studies—the Clinic Systems Project (CSP)—is examining issues surrounding the adoption of new clinical practices in a national sample of almost 200 child-serving mental health clinics (Schoenwald et al., 2008). The findings from these studies will help guide treatment developers, policy makers, and practitioners in understanding how best to fit specific practices into larger organizational and systems contexts, including schools. A national survey of family advocacy, support and education organizations linked to the child-serving clinics identified a set of strategies and supports that families deem critical to improving delivery of effective practices for children (Hoagwood et al., 2008). One

approach that actively links parent coordinators or advisors to clinical case management teams (called the Parent Empowerment Program) is being examined by Hoagwood, Jensen, and colleagues to assess its impact on the adoption of EBPs within a state mental health system (Hoagwood et al., 2008).

In addition, important work by Schoenwald and her associates (Schoenwald et al., 2003; Glisson & Schoenwald, 2006) and Glisson (Hemmelgarn, Glisson, & James 2006) has identified the importance of fidelity to treatment models and the impact of organizational context on adherence to model fidelity. These studies are helping elucidate the larger system issues that affect the uptake of EBPs into routine service settings.

Funding for collaborative efficacy and effectiveness research also illustrates the increased recognition of the need to advance knowledge about the generalizability of efficacious interventions and the importance of connecting research to practice settings. For example, SAMHSA established the National Child Traumatic Stress Network specifically to develop and disseminate EBIs to treat trauma-related distress and impairment in children and families. Part of the center's funding is specifically allocated to collaboration with other centers. This collaboration ensures that all treatment development centers are in communication with the clinical service centers, have access to research expertise, and have the ability to provide feedback and influence treatment adaptations and refinements.

Recommended Next Steps

Support Creative and Collaborative Policy Models

Several national leadership organizations (National Implementation Research Network; Child Evidence-Based Practices Consortium for States (Bruns & Hoagwood, 2005) and Commissioner-led initiatives within states (e.g., New York, California, Ohio, New Mexico, Hawaii) have begun to plan collaborative research and practice activities examining the implementation of EBPs within large state systems. These planning groups reflect multistakeholder input, including family advocates, scientists, practitioners, and policy makers.

In addition, alternatives to a top-down model of EBP policy implementation are also being examined (Daleiden, Chorpita, Donkervoet, Arensdorf, & Brogan, 2006; Garland et al., 2004, 2006; Hodges & Wotring, 2004; Southam-Gerow, Ringeisen, & Sherrill, 2006). These approaches are creating learning communities within typical practice settings—encouraging these settings to become empirically driven centers for both delivering services and examining the impact of routine practice on outcomes. Such normalization of research-based approaches to practice can demystify the scientific enterprise and create services that can be constantly evaluated, refined, and improved. This approach also encourages the construction of locally relevant evidence and creates a context for empiricism within routine service settings, leading ultimately, one hopes, to improvements in the quality of services provided.

Create Sustainable Research-to-Practice Networks

Research-to-practice networks should be established to further evaluate techniques and disseminate them into clinical processes while simultaneously informing future research (Borkovec, 2004; Borkovec, Echemendia, Ragusea, & Ruiz, 2001). It is important to establish these networks as formal connections to other professions and dissemination networks. Also, collaborative practitioner-researcher networks, such as the Pennsylvania Practice Research Network (Borkovec et al., 2001), show promise for the further development of effectiveness research in natural settings. Other large-scale efforts for the implementation of EBP have been funded by the National Institute of Drug Abuse in its clinical trials network initiative and by various state governments (e.g., Chorpita et al., 2002). With sufficient technology and coordination, the potential surely exists to begin to build an infrastructure in which school psychologists working in academic settings pursue the hard work necessary to pose reasonable hypotheses regarding "what works," listen closely to the field to learn *if* these hypotheses were confirmed, and partner with practitioners to gain insight as to *why*.

PROMISE AND POTENTIAL PITFALLS OF EVIDENCE-BASED PRACTICE

School psychology, with its historical focus on science as a partner to practice, is well positioned to help facilitate the transfer of EBPs to school settings. We need to maintain a watchful eye on both the misuse of science and the misuse of practice not supported by evidence. School psychologists can play a vital role in integrating evidence-based academic and mental health services into schools, as they are ideally suited to assist school administrators and teachers through consultation and support about selection of appropriate evidence-based screening and assessment, intervention, and outcome evaluation procedures. The capacity for professionals to live up to these responsibilities is important to maintain the health and relevance of our role in modern school settings. The following quote by Freidson (1970) is instructive:

> The professional is an expert because (s)he (sic) is thought to possess some special knowledge unavailable to laymen who have not gone through his special course of professional training. This special professional knowledge may not be demonstrably and consistently efficacious, but it is the best available to the times, and it is taught to all members of the profession in order to prepare them for the proper performance of their work. (p. 338)

When a profession cannot reliably predict what an individual practitioner will *do* or *how they will do it*, public demand for increased professional and personal accountability is only natural. Although individuals may choose to decide which profession is best suited and able to solve their problem, once that decision is made, trust and power are placed in the professional to resolve that problem using methods that are effective, ethical, and appropriate. When individual practitioners fail to live up to those expectations, they lose the trust of their clients and may be sanctioned by representatives within their profession. When entire professions fail to live up to those expectations, they begin to lose the trust of the public, and may be sanctioned through political and legal mandates which are intended to be the voice of the people.

Significant state and national policy initiatives are currently focused on more closely aligning science and practice and attending to these issues. These initiatives present unique opportunities for linking scientific developments on effective interventions and practices for children to organizational system and policy reform. The availability of a growing research base on effective interventions and practices offers an opportunity to tap into a reservoir of scientifically based strategies, and to test their applicability within locally based school psychological services. However, limitations to the evidence base, as well as limitations to the connectedness of EBPs to issues of real-world implementation in schools, suggest that new models for crossing the boundaries between research and practice are sorely needed.

Although the EBP movement is well underway with considerable progress, numerous challenges are present as well. In this chapter we offered our perspectives on some "next steps" that can be taken in research and professional practice. The science-to-practice translational activities in school psychology are complex, but aligning our profession with developments in other fields—most notably services and systems research, organizational behavior, implementation and dissemination studies, and clinical efficacy and effectiveness research—are likely to yield fruitful partnerships for both significant scientific advancement and for practical utility in better serving the educational and psychological needs of children and families.

REFERENCES

Abramowitz, J. S., Huppert, J. D., Cohen, A. B., Tolin, D. F., & Cahill, S. P. (2002). Religious obsessions and compulsions in a non-clinical sample: The Penn Inventory of Scrupulosity (PIOS). *Behaviour Research and Therapy, 40,* 824–838.

American Psychological Association. (2002). Criteria for evaluating treatment guidelines. *American Psychologist, 57,* 1054–1057.

American Psychological Association (1996). *Guidelines and principles for accreditation of programs in professional psychology.* Washington DC: Author.

American Speech-Language-Hearing Association Ad Hoc Committee on Reading and Written Language Disorders (2001). *Roles and responsibilities of speech-language pathologists with respect to reading and writing in children and adolescents.* Retrieved August 10, 2007 from www.asha.org/docs/html/ps2001-00104.html.

Bardon, J. I. (1983). Psychology applied to education: A specialty in search of an identity. *American Psychologist, 38,* 185–196.

Barlow, D. H. (1996). Health care policy, psychotherapy research, and the future of psychotherapy. *American Psychologist, 51,* 1050–1058.

Barlow, D. H, Levitt, J. T, & Bufka, L. F. (1999). The dissemination of empirically supported treatments: A view to the future. *Behaviour Research and Therapy, 37*(1), S147–S162.

Bates, S. L. (2005). Evidence-based family-school interventions with preschool children. *School Psychology Quarterly, 20*(4), 352–370.

Bennett, S., & Bennett, J. W. (2000). The process of evidence-based practice in occupational therapy: Informing clinical decisions. *Australian Occupational Therapy Journal, 47,* 171–180.

Benson, A. J., & Hughes, J. (1985). Perceptions of role definition processes in school psychology: A national survey. *School Psychology Review, 14,* 64–74.

Beutler, L. E. (2002). The dodo bird is extinct. *Clinical Psychology: Science and Practice, 9*(1), 30–34.

Beutler, L.E. (2004). The empirically supported treatments movement: A scientist-practitioner's response. *Clinical Psychology: Science and Practice, 11*(3), 225–229.

Blackwell, B. (Ed.). (1997). *Treatment compliance and the therapeutic alliance.* Amsterdam: Harwood Academic Publishers.

Borkovec, T. D. (2004). Research in training clinics and practice research networks: A route to the integration of science and practice. *Clinical Psychology: Science and Practice, 11*(2), 211–215.

Borkovec, T. D, Echemendia, R. J, Ragusea, S. A, & Ruiz, M. (2001). The Pennsylvania Practice Research Network and future possibilities for clinically meaningful and scientifically rigorous psychotherapy effectiveness research. *Clinical Psychology: Science and Practice, 8*(2), 155–167.

Brantlinger, E., Jimenez, R., Klingner, J., Pugach, M., & Richardson, V. (2005). Qualitative studies in special education. *Council for Exceptional Children, 71*(2), 195–207.

Bramlett, R. K., Murphy, J. J., Johnson, J., & Wallingsford, L. (2002). Contemporary practices in school psychology: A national survey of roles and referral problems. *Psychology in the Schools, 39,* 327–335.

Burns, B. J. & Hoagwood, K. (2005). Evidence-based practice, part II: Effecting change. *Child & Adolescent Psychiatric Clinics of North America, 14*(2), xv–xvii.

Campbell, D. T., & Stanley, J. C. (1963). *Experimental and quasi-experimental designs for research.* Chicago: Rand McNally.

Chambless, D. L., & Hollon, S. D. (1998). Defining empirically supported therapies. *Journal of Consulting and Clinical Psychology, 66,* 7–18.

Chorpita, B. F. (2003). The frontier of evidence-based practice. In A. F. Kazdin & J. R. Weisz (Eds.), *Evidence-based psychotherapies for children and adolescents* (pp. 42–59). New York: Guilford Press.

Chorpita, B. F., Yim, L. M., Donkervoet, J. C., Arensdorf, A., Amundsen, M. J., McGee, C., et al. (2002). Toward large-scale implementation of empirically supported treatments for children: A review and observations by the Hawaii Empirical Basis to Services Task Force. *Clinical Psychology: Science and Practice, 9*(2), 165–190.

Cox, D. D. (2005). Evidence-based interventions using home-school collaboration. *School Psychology Quarterly, 20*(4), 473–497.

Craske, M. G., Barlow, D. H., & Meadows, E. (2000). *Mastery of your anxiety and panic: Therapist guide for anxiety, panic, and agoraphobia (MAP-3).* Boulder, CO: Gaywind Publications.

Crits-Christoph, P. (1997). Limitations of the dodo bird verdict and the role of clinical trials in psychotherapy research: Comment on Wampold et al. (1997). *Psychological Bulletin, 122*(3), 216–220.

Daleiden, E. L., Chorpita, B. F., Donkervoet, C. A., Arensdorf, A. M., & Brogan, M. (2006). Getting better at getting them better: Health outcomes and evidence-based practice within a system of care. *Journal of the American Academy of Child and Adolescent Psychiatry, 45,* 749–756.

DeRubeis, R. J., Tang, T. Z., Gelfand, L. A., & Feeley, M. (2000). Recent findings concerning the processes and outcomes of cognitive therapy for depression. In S. L. Johnson, A. M. Hayes, T. M. Field, N. Schneiderman, & P. M. McCabe (Eds.), *Stress, coping, and depression* (pp. 223–240). Mahwah, NJ: Lawrence Erlbaum Associates Publishers.

Dunst, C. J., Trivette, C. M., & Cutspec, P. A. (2002). Toward an operational definition of evidence-based practice. Centerscope: Evidence-based approaches in Early Childhood Development, 1(1). Retrieved August 19, 2003 from www.evidencebasedpractices.org/ centerscope/centerscopevol1no1.pdf.

Evidence-Based Medicine Working Group (1992). Evidence-based medicine: A new approach to teaching the practice of medicine. *JAMA, 268,* 2420–2425.

Fishel, M., & Ramirez, L. (2005). Evidence-based parent involvement interventions with school-aged children. *School Psychology Quarterly, 20*(4), 371–402.

Frank, J. L., Albers, C. A., Kratochwill, T. R., & Roach, A. T. (2008). Cost analysis in educational decision making: Approaches, procedures and case examples. *Journal of Evidence-Based Practice in Schools.*

Frank, J. L., & Kratochwill, T. R. (2008). School-based problem-solving consultation: Plotting a new course for evidence-based research and practice in consultation. In W. P. Erchul & S. M. Sherican (Eds.), *Handbook of research in school consultation: Empirical foundations for the field.* New York: Erlbaum.

Frank, J., Kumke, P., & Kratochwill, T. R. (2008). *School psychologists' use and awareness of treatment guidelines: Present and future.* Manuscript submitted for publication.

Freidson, E. (1970). *Profession of medicine: A study of the sociology of applied knowledge.* New York: Dodd, Mead.

Gambrill, E. (1999). Evidence-based clinical behavior analysis, evidence-based medicine and the Cochrane collaboration. *Journal of Behavior Therapy and Experimental Psychiatry, 30*(1), 1–14.

Garland, A. F., Lewczyk-Boxmeyer, C. M., Gabayan, E. N., & Hawley, K. M. (2004). Multiple stakeholder agreement on desired outcomes for adolescents' mental health services. *Psychiatric Services, 55*(6), 671–676.

Garland, A. F., Hurlburt, M. S., Hawley, K. M. (2006). Examining psychotherapy processes in a services research context. *Clinical Psychology: Science and Practice, 13,* 30–46.

Glass, G. V (1976). Primary, secondary, and meta-analysis of research. *Educational Researcher, 5,* 3–8.

Glisson, C., & Schoenwald, S. (2006). An organizational and community development strategy for implementing evidence-based children's mental health treatments. *Mental Health Services Research.*

Guli, L. A. (2005). Evidence-based parent consultation with school-related outcomes. *School Psychology Quarterly, 20*(4), 455–472.

Hemmelgarn, A. L, Glisson, C., & James, L. R. (2006). Organizational Culture and Climate: Implications for services and interventions research. *Clinical Psychology: Science and Practice, 13*(1), 73–89.

Hoagwood, K., Burns, B. J., Kiser, L., Ringeisen, H., & Schoenwald, S. K. (2001). Evidence-based practice in child and adolescent mental health services. *Psychiatric Services 52*(9) 1179–1189.

Hoagwood, K., Green, E., Kelleher, K., Schoenwald, S., Rolls-Reutz, J., Landsverk, J., Glisson, C., & Mayberg, S. (2008) Research Network on Youth Mental Health. Family advocacy, support and education in children's mental health: Results of a national survey. *Administration & Policy in Mental Health. 35*(1–2) 73–83.

Hoagwood, K., Hibbs, T., Brent, D, Jensen, P. (1995). Efficacy and effectiveness in studies of child and adolescent psychotherapy. *Journal of Consulting & Clinical Psychology, 63*(5), 683–687.

Hoagwood, K., & Johnson, J. (2003). School psychology: A public health framework: I. From evidence-based practices to evidence-based policies. *Journal of School Psychology 41*, 3–21.

Hoard, D., & Shepard, K. N. (2005). Parent education as parent-centered prevention: A review of school-related outcomes. *School Psychology Quarterly, 20*(4), 434–454.

Hodges K., & Wotring, J. (2004). The role of monitoring outcomes in initiating implementation of evidence-based treatments at the state level. *Psychiatric Services, 55*(4), 396–400.

Horner, R. H., Carr, E. G., Halle, J., McGee, G., Odom, S., & Wolery, M. (2005). The use of single-subject research to identify evidence-based practice in special education. *Exceptional Children, 71*(2), 165–179.

Horvath, A. O., & Bedi, R. P. (2002). The alliance. In J. Norcross (Ed.), *Psychotherapy relationships that work: Therapist contributions and responsiveness to patients* (pp. 37–69). New York: Oxford University Press.

Howard, L. I., Moras, K., Brill, P. L., Martinovich, Z., & Lutz, W. (1996). Efficacy, effectiveness, and patient progress. *American Psychologist, 51*, 1059–1064.

Individuals with Disabilities Education Improvement Act of 2004, P.L. 108–446, 20 U.S.C. § 601(c).

International Reading Association. *Teaching Reading Well: A synthesis of the International Reading Association's research on teacher preparation for reading*. International Reading Association. Newark, DE.

Institute of Medicine. (2001). *Crossing the quality chasm: A new health system for the 21st century*. Washington, DC: National Academy Press.

Jensen, P. S., Weersing, R., Hoagwood, K. E., & Goldman, E. (2005). What is the evidence for evidence-based treatments? A hard look at our soft underbelly. *Mental Health Services Research*, 7(1), 53–74.

Johnston, M. V. P., Sherer, M. P., & Whyte, J. M. D. P. (2006). Applying Evidence Standards to Rehabilitation Research. *American Journal of Physical Medicine & Rehabilitation, 85*, 292–309.

Kazdin, A. E. (2005). Evidence-based assessment for children and adolescents: issues in measurement development and clinical application. *Journal of Clinical Child and Adolescent Psychology, 34*, 548–558.

Kelly, F. D., & Prevatt, F. (2005). Evaluating evidence-based interventions in schools. *Journal of Evidence-Based Practices for Schools, 6*(2), 165–185.

Knitzer, J. 1982. *Unclaimed Children: The Failure of Public Responsibility to Children and Adolescents in Need of Mental Health Services*. Washington, D.C.: Children's Defense Fund.

Kratochwill, T. R. (2006). Evidence-based interventions and practices in school psychology: The scientific basis of the profession. In R. F. Subotnik & H. J. Walberg (Eds.), *The scientific basis of educational productivity* (pp. 229–267). Information Age Publishing, 62, 826–843.

Kratochwill, T. R. (2007). Preparing psychologists for evidence-based practice: Lessons learned and challenges ahead. *American Psychologist, 62*, 826–843.

Kratochwill, T. R., Clements, M. A., & Kalymon, K. M. (2007). Response to intervention: Conceptual and methodological issues in implementation. In S. R. Jimerson, M. K. Burns, & A. M. VanderHeyden (Eds.), *The handbook of response to intervention: The science and practice of assessment and intervention* (pp. 22–52). New York: Springer, Inc.

Kratochwill, T. R., & Hoagwood, K. E. (2006). Evidence-based interventions and system change: Concepts, methods and challenges in implementing evidence-based practices in children's mental health. *Child and Family Policy and Practice Review, 2*, 12–16.

Kratochwill, T. R., & Shernoff, E. S. (2003). Evidence-based practice: Promoting evidence-based intervention in school psychology. *School Psychology Quarterly, 18*, 389–408.

Kratochwill, T. R., & Shernoff, E. S. (2004). Evidence-based practice: Promoting evidence-based interventions in school psychology. *School Psychology Review, 33*(1), 34–48.

Kratochwill, T. R., & Stoiber, K. C. (2000). Empirically supported interventions in school psychology: Conceptual and practice issues—part II. *School Psychology Quarterly, 15*, 233–253.

Kratochwill, T. R., & Stoiber, K. C. (2001). Empirically supported interventions and school psychology: Conceptual and practices issues—part II. *School Psychology Quarterly*, *15*, 233–253.

Kratochwill, T. R., & Stoiber, K. C. (2002). Evidence-based interventions in school psychology: Conceptual foundations of the procedural and coding manual of Division 16 and the Society for the Study of School Psychology Task Force. *School Psychology Quarterly*, *17*, 341–389.

Kratochwill, T. R., Volpiansky, P., Clements, M. C., & Ball, C. (2008), Professional development in implementing and sustaining multi-tier prevention models: Implications for response-to-intervention. *School Psychology Review*, *36*, 618–631.

Lambert, M. J., & Barley, D. E. (2002). Research summary on the therapeutic relationship and psychotherapy outcome. In J. C. Norcross (Ed.), *Psychotherapy relationships that work: Therapist contributions and responsiveness to patients* (pp. 17–32). New York, NY: Oxford University Press.

Lambert, M. J, Whipple, J. L., Hawkins, E. J., Vermeersch, D. A., Nielsen, S. L., & Smart, D. W. (2003). Is it time for clinicians to routinely track patient outcome? A meta-analysis. *Clinical Psychology: Science and Practice*, *10*(3), 288–301.

Law, M., & Baum, C. (1998). Evidence-based occupational therapy. *Canadian Journal of Occupational Therapy*, *65*, 131–135.

Lehr, C. A., Hansen, A., Sinclair, M. F., & Christenson, S. L. (2003). Moving beyond dropout towards school completion: An integrative review of data-based interventions. *School Psychology Review*, *32*, 342–364.

McNeece, C. A. & Thyer, B. A. (2004). Evidence-based practice and social work. *Journal of Evidence-Based Social Work*, *1*(1), 7–23.

Melnyk, B. M., Fineout-Overholt, E., Stone, P., & Ackerman M. (2000). Evidence-based practice: The past, the present, and recommendations for the millennium. *Pediatric Nursing*, *26*, 77–80.

Millenson, M. L. (1997). *Demanding medical excellence: Doctors and accountability in the information age*. Chicago: University of Chicago Press.

Nastasi, B. K., Varjas, K., Bernstein, R., & Pluymert, K. (1998). Mental health programming and the role of school psychologists. *School Psychology Review*, *27*, 217–232.

Nelson, M. L., & Quintana, S. M. (2005). Qualitative clinical research with children and adolescents. *Journal of Clinical Child and Adolescent Psychology*, *34*, 344–356.

NCLB (2001). No Child Left Behind Act. P.L. No. 107–110, 115 Stat. 1425 (2002).

Okiishi, J., Lambert, M. J., Nielsen, S. L., & Ogles, B. M. (2003). Waiting for supershrink: An empirical analysis of therapist effects. *Clinical Psychology & Psychotherapy*, *10*(6), 361–373.

President's New Freedom Commission on Mental Health. (2003). *Achieving the promise: Transforming mental health care in America*. Rockville, MD: U.S. Department of Health and Human Services.

Presidential Task Force on Evidence-Based Practice of the American Psychological Association (2005). Report of the 2005 Presidential Task Force on Evidence-Based Practice American Psychological Association. Accessed April 4, 2006 from www.apa.org/practice/ebpreport.pdf.

Prevatt, F., & Kelly, D. F. (2005). Evidence-based interventions in school psychology. *Journal of Evidence-based Practices of Schools*, *6*, 165–185.

Reschly, D. J., & Wilson, M. S. (1995). School psychology practitioners and faculty: 1986 to 1991–92: Trends in demographics, roles, satisfaction, and system reform. *School Psychology Review*, *24*, 62–80.

Reilly, S., Perry, A., Douglas, J., & Oates, J. (2001). *Evidence-based practice in speech pathology*. London: Whurr.

Sackett, D. L., Rosenberg, W. M., Gray, J. A., Haynes, R. B., & Richardson, W. S. (1996). Evidence-based medicine: What it is and what it isn't. *British Medical Journal*, *312*, 71–72.

Sackett, D. L., Straus, S. E., Richardson, W. S., Rosenberg, W., & Haynes, R. B. (2000). *Evidence-based medicine: How to practice and teach EBM* (2nd ed.). London: Churchll Livingstone.

Schoenwald, S. K., Chapman, J. E., Kellecher, K., Hoagwood, K. E., Landsverk, J., Stevens, J., Glisson, C., Rools-Reutz, J., and The Research Network on Youth Mental Health. (2008). A Survey of the Infrastructure for Children's Mental Health Services: Implications for the Implementation of Empirically Supported Treatments (ESTs). *Administration and Policy in Mental Health and Mental Health Services Research*, *35*, 84–97.

Schoenwald, S. K., Halliday-Boykins, C. A., & Henggeler, S. W. (2003). Client-level predictors of adherence to MST in community service settings. *Family Process*, *42*(3), 345–359.

Shernoff, E. S., Kratochwill, T. R., & Stoiber, K. C. (2003). Training in evidence-based interventions: What are school psychology programs teaching? *Journal of School Psychology*, *41*, 467–483.

Silverman, W. K., Kurtines, W. M., & Hoagwood, K. (2004). Research progress on effectiveness, transportability, and dissemination of empirically supported treatments: Integrating theory and research. *Clinical Psychology: Science and Practice*, *11*(3), 295–299.

Simnett, I., Perkins, E. R., & Wright, L. (Eds.). (1999). *Evidence-based health promotion*. New York: Wiley.

Southam-Gerow, M. A., Ringeisen, H. L., & Sherrill, J. T. (2006). Integrating interventions and services research: Progress and prospects. *Clinical Psychology: Science and Practice*, *13*(1), 1–8.

Stoiber, K. C., & Kratochwill, T. R. (2000). Empirically supported interventions and school psychology: Rationale and methodological issues: Part I. *School Psychology Quarterly, 15*, 75–105.

Stroul, B. A., & Friedman, R. M. (1988). Caring for severely emotionally disturbed children and youth. Putting principles into practice. *Children Today 17*(4), 15–17.

Task Force on Evidence-Based Interventions in School Psychology. (2003). *Procedural and coding manual for review of evidence-based interventions*. Retrieved February 6, 2004, from www.sp-ebi.org/_workingfiles/EBImanual1.pdf.

Thompson, B., Diamond, K. E., McWilliam, R., Snyder, P., & Snyder, S. W. (2003). Evaluating the quality of evidence from correlational research for evidence-based practice. *Exceptional Children, 71*(2), 181–194.

Torrey, W. C., Drake, R. E., Cohen, M., Fox, L. B., Lynde, D., Gorman, P., & Wyzik, P. (2002). The challenge of implementing and sustaining integrated dual disorders treatment programs. *Community Mental Health Journal, 38*(6), 507–521.

Torrey, W. C., Drake, R. E., Dixon, L., Burns, B. J., Flynn, L., Rush, A. J. et al. (2001). Implementing evidence-based practices for persons with severe mental illnesses. *Psychiatric Services, 52*(1), 45–50.

Valdez, C. R., Carlson, C., & Zanger, D. (2005). Evidence-based parent training and family interventions for school behavior change. *School Psychology Quarterly, 20*(4), 403–433.

Wampold, B. E. (2001). *The great psychotherapy debate: Models, methods, and findings*. Mahwah, NJ: Lawrence Erlbaum.

Weisz, J. R., & Hawley, K. M. (2001). *Procedural and coding manual for identification of beneficial treatments (Draft 4)*. Washington DC: American Psychological Association, Society for Clinical Psychology Division 12 Committee on Science and Practice.

Weisz, J. R., Hawley, K. M., & Doss, A. J. (2004). Empirically tested psychotherapies for youth internalizing and externalizing problems and disorders. *Child and Adolescent Psychiatric Clinics of North America, 13*, 729–815.

Weisz, J. R., Hawley, K. M., Pilkonis, P. A., Woody, S. R., & Follette, W. C. (2000). Stressing the (other) three Rs in the search for empirically supported treatments: Review procedures, research quality, relevance to practice and the public interest. *Clinical Psychology: Science and Practice, 7*(3), 243–258.

Weisz, J. R., Sandler, I. N., Durlak, J. A., & Anton, B. S. (2005). Promoting and protecting youth mental health through evidence-based prevention and treatment. *American Psychologist, 60*, 628–648.

West, S., King, V., Carey, T., Lohr, K., McKoy, N., & Lux, L. (2002). *Systems to Rate Strength of Evidence* (AHRQ Publication No. 02-E016). Rockville, MD: AHRQ.

Westen, D., Novotny, C. M., & Thompson-Brenner, H. (2004). The Empirical Status of Empirically Supported Psychotherapies: Assumptions, Findings, and Reporting in Controlled Clinical Trials. *Psychological Bulletin, 130*, 631–663.

White, J. L., & Kratochwill, T. R. (2005). Practice guidelines in school psychology: Issues and directions for evidence-based interventions in practice and training. *Journal of School Psychology, 43*, 99–115.

CHAPTER 25

WORKING WITH STRUGGLING READERS: WHY WE MUST GET BEYOND THE SIMPLE VIEW OF READING AND VISIONS OF HOW IT MIGHT BE DONE

MICHAEL PRESSLEY, NELL K. DUKE, LAUREN FINGERET, YONGHAN PARK,
KELLY REFFITT, LINDSEY MOHAN, AND STEPHANIE COLLINS
Michigan State University

IRENE W. GASKINS
Benchmark School

JULIET L. HALLADAY
University of Vermont

KATHERINE R. HILDEN
Radford University

SHENGLAN ZHANG
Winona State University

LISA M. RAPHAEL
SEDL

JULIA REYNOLDS
Aquinas College

DEBORAH GOLOS
Utah State University

KATHRYN L. SOLIC
University of Tennessee

Our assignment was to write about "working with students with reading problems." This is a huge topic, with many volumes written on the diagnosis and educational remediation of students who are struggling to learn to read (e.g., including one by the first author, Pressley, 2006). That said, without a doubt, there is one feature common to most reading interventions, one approach that has received more researcher and public attention than any other: the preponderance of struggling readers in America who experience intervention for difficulties in learning to read experience some form of phonics instruction. This reflects the fact that phonics instruction has existed for at least two millennia (see chapter 1 in Pressley, Allington, Wharton-McDonald, Block, & Morrow, 2001). It also reflects that for the past half-century, researchers and others have made the case repeatedly and prominently for the effectiveness (indeed, superiority) of phonics to other forms of beginning reading instruction, in particular for struggling readers. (e.g., Adams,

1990; Chall, 1967; Flesch, 1955; National Reading Panel, 2000). Of course, there often is a sensibility to opting for a form of remediation that focuses on teaching students how to read the words, for the most frequent symptom of reading disability that results in intervention is that a child fails to learn how to read words during the primary grade years. Often, such students are only able to read a very few words after several years of teaching in kindergarten, grade 1, grade 2, and perhaps even grade 3.

Although the specifics of the phonics intervention the child experiences can vary, the approaches enjoying the most scientific support involve intense teaching of basic sound-, letter-, and word-level skills, perhaps for a sustained period of time (see Pressley, 2006, chapter 5). There may be efforts first to develop phonemic awareness, which is awareness that words are composed of sounds blended together, a competency that many struggling readers lack (e.g., Adams, 1990; Blachman, 2000; Pennington, Groisser, & Welsh, 1993; Stanovich, 1986, 1988), a competency that predicts early reading achievement (e.g., Badian, 2001; Bowey, 1995, 2002; Goswami, 2002; Hulme et al., 2002; Muter, Hulme, Snowling, & Stevenson, 2004; McBride-Chang & Kail, 2002; Näslund & Schneider, 1996; Speece, Ritchey, Cooper, Roth, & Schatschneider, 2004; Storch & Whitehurst, 2002; Stuart & Masterson, 1992; Torgesen & Burgess, 1998; Wesseling & Reitsma, 2001; Windfuhr & Snowling, 2001). Phonemic awareness is developed through games and exercises requiring the child to reflect on the sounds of words (e.g., What would *pam* sound like with the /p/ sound missing? Let's tap the sounds in *catch*). Such experiences, in fact, improve students' subsequent learning to read words (see the meta-analyses in the National Reading Panel, 2000; Ehri et al., 2001).

Efforts to develop phonemic awareness should be accompanied and are typically followed by intense phonics instruction, which includes teaching letter-sound associations, including the common individual sounds and digraphs defined by letter combinations. This will be in anticipation of intense practice in sounding out words, with students typically learning how to sound out words by blending the component sounds defined by the word's letters and letter combinations. Such instruction involves much repetition, often including the reading of contrived texts that repeat words and word patterns (e.g., Fat Pat and a rat sat on a mat). Such intense instruction does, in

fact, make a small impact on learning how to recognize words, something established in many true experiments (Camilli, Vargas, & Yurecko, 2003; Ehri, Nune, Stahl, & Willows, 2001). Phonics instruction has a small, positive effect on comprehension (National Reading Panel, 2000, chapter 4).

An exceptionally important recent finding is that even several years of such remediation with struggling readers does not necessarily produce fluent readers (see Torgesen, 2004). Because fluency in reading words facilitates comprehension (e.g., LaBerge & Samuels, 1974), that phonics instruction does not produce fluency in struggling readers may help explain why phonics instruction has only a small impact on comprehension, which we view as the competency that must be improved if reading instruction is to be considered to have worked well.

It should not be surprising that, as we write this chapter, we are frustrated with the overattention to sound-, letter-, and word-level processing that characterizes instruction for many struggling readers, given the evidence that progress often boils down to a little progress in learning how to sound out words and only small improvement in comprehension. This is not to say we believe phonics instruction is not necessary for many struggling readers, but that it is not sufficient.

Although the traditions and research cited until this point go far in explaining the popularity of phonics in the contemporary schoolplace, among psychologists, theory also plays a very large part with respect to instructional decision making. One theory, in particular, has played a prominent role in psychologists' thinking about reading intervention and the centrality of phonics with respect to remediation: The theory is known as the simple view of reading. We believe that an important step in moving on to more complete interventions that might have greater impact on struggling readers is to come to a less simple view of reading that motivates a less simple view of reading instructional intervention. The chapter will build to that, culminating in a discussion of the nature of effective literacy instruction, when it is observed, including in a school that is an existence proof that less simple instruction can be delivered to students with severe challenges in learning to read, instruction that produces more impressive outcomes than observed with only intense phonics instruction for such readers (Torgesen, 2004).

Recognizing the central role of theoretical frameworks in the design and development of instruction and instructional interventions, we make a case in this chapter for overturning a theory of reading and reading intervention that is prominent among psychologists in favor of a more complex theory, one that motivates longer-term and more complex reading intervention with struggling beginning readers. We do so by highlighting several inadequacies of the simple view of reading, a theoretical perspective which inspires the overattention to word-level instructional approaches, and then by examining a more complex and effective interventional program that follows from a less simple view of reading. First we consider how the simple view model and its component constructs fail to account for the influence of development and for a variety of individual difference variables and reading tasks that are significant to reading comprehension. Second, we consider how the kinds of instruction inspired by the simple view model fails to meet the reading performance demands of current policy mandates, including state standards and the Reading First policy. Third, we consider how the simple view model fails to inspire the kind of research necessary for productive movement toward understanding the efficacy of instructional interventions on multiple levels. At each point we will also consider how a less simple theoretical lens may better contribute to inspiring the complexity of instruction each shortcoming demands. Finally, we turn our attention to examining a highly effective interventional program, with our intention to highlight the less simple theory in which it is situated and from which it has been developed and refined.

Such an essay provides a vehicle at least for touching on some of the most relevant research on reading intervention that should be on the minds of psychologists, as well as some current policy issues. Along the way, there will be consideration of a range of interventions, from the conceptually simple (i.e., several years of intense phonics and related skills instruction) to the more conceptually complex (e.g., comprehensive reading programs) to the very conceptually complex (i.e., years of schooling aimed at developing the full panorama of reading competencies). We warn readers in advance, however, that our view is that there is much more research needed on reading intervention before there can be certain conclusions about how best to remediate students. That is, we offer more hypotheses here than certain conclusions, hypotheses that are credible, however, because they are grounded in data.

THE SIMPLE AND LESS SIMPLE VIEW OF READING

The simple view of reading is that reading comprehension is a function of two processes—decoding (which includes being able to say the printed word and retrieve its meaning) and linguistic comprehension (often operationalized and termed *listening comprehension*), and that all other influences on reading comprehension work through these two subprocesses (e.g., Gough & Tunmer, 1986). Gough's group (e.g., Hoover & Gough, 1990) was able to generate some evidence that they considered to be in favor of the perspective. For example, in English-Spanish bilingual children, they found that both decoding and listening comprehension skills were predictive of reading comprehension. Consistent with how they believed decoding and listening comprehension determine reading comprehension, they found that the product of decoding and listening comprehension significantly increased prediction of reading comprehension over the linear sum of decoding and listening comprehension skill. They interpreted a negative correlation between decoding and listening comprehension skills, especially for poor readers, to be consistent with their position. And, they reported some regression model data that seemed consistent with their position. In short, Gough and his colleagues believed there was quite a bit of support in the data they explored for the position that reading comprehension is a function of decoding and linguistic comprehension.

A variety of other researchers continued the work on the relationship between decoding, listening comprehension, and reading comprehension—although usually without studying other variables, with increasing support for the simple view and especially the version of the simple view that included the decoding-listening comprehension multiplicative component (e.g., Dreyer & Katz, 1992; Marx & Jungmann, 2000; Savage, 2001). Yes, some papers differed in the variation of the formulation that best predicted reading comprehension, for example, (decoding + listening comprehension) + (decoding × listening comprehension) or (decoding + listening comprehension)/2 or the square root of decoding × listening comprehension) (Chen & Vellutino, 1997; Carver, 1993, 1998), but, the bottom line was that those researching the simple view found much to favor formulations involving decoding and listening comprehension as predictive of reading comprehension (Joshi & Aaron, 2000).

The simple view of reading has been and continues to be highly influential in the field of reading research. For example, according to the Web of Science Citation Index, from 2000 through 2007, Gough and Tunmer (1986) was cited 117 times and Hoover and Gough (1990) was cited 91 times. Authors citing this work most often did so in the context of accepting or operating on the basic assumption that reading comprehension is indeed accounted for by decoding and listening comprehension (e.g., Catts & Hogan, 2003; Storch & Whitehurst, 2002). There are several reasons, however, to suspect the simple view does not adequately explain individual differences in reading performance in ways that permit the development of school-based interventions that will have positive impact on all struggling readers with respect to the many demands put on them. The focus in this section is to review briefly the work on individual differences that, in part, motivates moving on to a more complex theory of reading comprehension and intervention to produce readers who can read with understanding.

The Importance of the Simple View Components Varies with Development

Those concerned with the simple view of reading comprehension certainly are more interested in beginning reading than more mature reading, with many of those most strongly identified with the position (e.g., Gough and Tunmer) emphasizing the development of decoding skills as key in reading development. Recent work by Scott Paris and his associates (Paris, Carpenter, Paris, & Hamilton, 2005) suggests that the simple view may be much more a model of beginning than more mature reading. In particular, they have found that oral reading fluency correlates more highly with reading comprehension in the early primary grades than later in the elementary years, and with reading of the kinds of texts that occur in the early primary years compared to texts read in the later elementary years. Catts, Hogan, and Adlof (2005) provided data even more forcefully making the case that the relationship between decoding, listening comprehension, and reading comprehension is not that simple with respect to development. Rather, individual differences in decoding are decreasingly predictive of reading comprehension going from the primary to the middle school years, whereas

individual differences in listening comprehension increasingly predict reading comprehension as children mature from the primary grades to middle school. Yes, the components favored by simple view advocates are in the equation throughout elementary and middle school, but their weighting very much changes, something not well explicated in the classic simple view of reading.

Individual Differences Not Taken Into Account by the Simple View (or Not Taken Into Account Completely Enough)

There are many individual differences either ignored or not given sufficient attention by those advocating the simple view. Here is a sampler of the evidence:

Unexplained Poor Comprehension

If the simple view is correct, then those who can decode well and have good listening comprehension skills should have good reading comprehension. Catts, Hogan, Adlof, and Barth (2003), however, found 13.9% of second graders, 15.7% of fourth graders, and 23.5% of eighth graders who are poor comprehenders do not show a deficit in either listening comprehension or word recognition (which they operationalized through both a word attack and word identification task, both measures of decoding). This is a significant portion of readers.

Low General Intelligence

According to the simple view of reading, there are three types of poor comprehenders: Those who do not decode well, those who do not have good listening comprehension, and those who have neither good decoding nor good listening comprehension. The third category is often referred to as garden-variety poor readers. In addition to decoding and listening comprehension difficulties, however, garden-variety poor readers typically have many other intellectual deficiencies, expressed summarily as below-average IQ (e.g., Catts, Hogan, & Fey, 2003). The simple view at the least misses the bigger picture for these readers, and, in any case, has little to say about the reading problems of students with low general intelligence, with reading problems frequent among those with low intelligence, and low intelligence students common in many school populations.

Working Memory

Working memory is the consciousness where active processing of material takes place, with its most salient characteristic being its limited capacity—people can hold only a relatively few pieces of information in mind at once (e.g., Baddeley, 1976). There is growing evidence in normally achieving readers that greater working memory capacity is associated with better comprehension and memory of text (e.g., Baddeley, Logie, & Nimmo-Smith, 1985; Bayliss, Jarrold, Baddeley, & Leigh, 2005; Crain & Shankweiler, 1988; Daneman & Carpenter, 1980, 1983; Just & Carpenter, 1992; Perfetti & Goldman, 1976; Perfetti & Lesgold, 1977; Seigneuric, Ehrlich, Oakhill, & Yuill, 2000), over and above the variance in reading comprehension explained by differences in decoding and general verbal skills, which, especially relevant to the simple view, include listening comprehension (see especially Cain, Oakhill, & Bryant, 2004). In addition, the ability to manage information in working memory—keeping goal-relevant ideas in mind and suppressing less-relevant ones—also seems to be related to reading comprehension ability (Carretti, Cornoldi, De Beni, & Palladino, 2004; Carretti, Cornoldi, De Beni, & Romanò, 2005).

One possibility, consistent with the simple view, is that individual differences in working memory boil down to individual differences in language abilities, with poorer language abilities making it more difficult to hold and juggle text in working memory, functionally reducing working memory capacity, and accounting for correlations between working memory capacity as measured with linguistic tasks and reading comprehension (see Perfetti, Landi, & Oakhill, 2005). Our view, however, is that until that possibility is established more clearly through research, there is reason to continue to explore how both working memory capacity and the ability to manage content in working memory are individual differences that matter in reading comprehension, with the possibility that working memory skills are at least partially independent of language skills.

Effortful versus Fluent Decoding

There is no distinction in the simple view model between decoding with effort and decoding with automaticity (i.e., fast and relatively effortless, automatic reading of words—what is often referred to as fluent word reading). At least since LaBerge and Samuels (1974), there has been an understanding that word reading fluency matters with respect to comprehension, that effortful word recognition consumes cognitive resources that otherwise would be devoted to comprehending what was read, and, thus, undermines comprehension (Eldredge, 2005). For normally developing readers, there is a natural progression from effortful word recognition to fluent reading of words (e.g., Chall, 1996; Ehri, 1995), with the simple view not illuminating the dynamics of reading comprehension during the effortful versus fluent stages.

Rapid Automatized Naming

Given that retrieval of meaning gets explicit reference in the simple view, it is especially notable that there might be individual differences in retrieval processes that impact reading. Despite the mention, however, such differences are mostly ignored in work on the simple view relative to differences in how well readers can say the printed word at all. The idea that there might be differences in lexical retrieval speed that contribute to reading differences is more than a quarter-century old. Thus, Denckla and Rudel (1972) noted that some poor first grade readers exhibited long latencies between perceiving colors and saying the names of the colors. Based on this finding, the researchers designed a series of four Rapid Automatized Naming (RAN) tasks to measure naming speed—naming of colors, objects, letters, and numbers (Denckla & Rudel, 1972, 1974). These tasks measure visual-verbal processing speed by presenting subjects with a sequence of visual stimuli and asking them to verbally name each item as quickly as possible. There now exists a considerable body of evidence that RAN is related to reading ability (Aaron, Joshi, & Williams, 1999; Bowers & Newby-Clark, 2002; Compton, 2003; Denckla, 1999; Denckla & Rudel, 1972, 1974; Joshi & Aaron, 2000; Wolf, Bally, & Morris, 1986). What has also become clear from a variety of analyses, however, is that individual differences in RAN are not easily interpretable as individual differences in lexical retrieval skills (Bowey, 2005). For example, individual differences in RAN might reflect individual differences in general processing speed (e.g., Kail & Hall, 1994), at least in part (Compton, 2003). Also, RAN tasks, even ones that do not involve processing alphabetic or numerical symbols (e.g., color & object naming), involve mental decoding processes not unlike those involved in the fluent recognition of words (i.e., decoding of items—objects, colors, letters, numbers—as single units, analogous to how a fluent reader processes words as whole units; e.g., Compton, 2003). If so, what proportion of the individual differences in RAN performance are due to recognition of the whole objects per se versus retrieval of the names of the objects is impossible to gauge based on present data (Compton, 2003; Fawcett & Nicolson, 1994; Nicolson & Fawcett, 1994). All that said, despite the fact that the exact processing differences reflected in naming speed differences remain debatable, we emphasize here that naming speed differences matter in reading comprehension (Wolf et al., 1986) and above and beyond decoding and listening comprehension. When students are matched for decoding and listening comprehension skills, those with faster naming speeds have better reading comprehension (Aaron et al., 1999; Joshi & Aaron, 2000).

A position known as the "double deficit" hypothesis points to the importance of considering naming speed in reading—that readers with deficit phonological abilities *and* slow naming speed should be weaker readers than those with a phonological deficit or naming speed deficit alone (Wolf & Bowers, 1999). Although support for this position is equivocal (see Schatschneider, Carlson, Francis, Foorman, & Fletcher, 2002; Schatschneider, Fletcher, Francis, Carlson, & Foorman, 2004; Vukovic, Wilson, & Nash, 2004), the prominence of the hypothesis makes clear that naming speed should be an individual differences variable that is considered as part of a full study of capable and not-so-capable reading comprehension.

Of course, it has been recognized for a long time that one way to be a poor reader is to be accurate in reading words but slow in doing so (Lovett, 1984). Thus, this call for attention to speed of processing during reading is really a call for greater attention to a variable that has been hypothesized to be a determinant of reading skill for longer than the simple view has been with us. Moreover, the conceptualization of RAN has been around long enough that there are more than 20 correlations between RAN and comprehension in the literature, with the average correlation being about .46 (Swanson, Trainin, Necoechea, & Hammill, 2003). In short, there's enough evidence of connection between RAN and comprehension in the literature to justify more attention to the variable than it receives when absorbed in simply being able to say the printed word, as it is in the simple view.

Meaning Selection

Many words have more than one meaning. For example, the word *rock*, can refer to those big brown objects in the mountains or to a diamond. Good readers make use of the semantic context for a word to determine its meaning (i.e., they use the sentence, paragraph, and passage meaning cues to determine the correct meaning), basically suppressing other potential meanings for the word (e.g., concluding the rock is a diamond in the sentence, "The gentleman presented his lady friend with a *rock*"; Gernsbacher, 1990). If an ambiguous word is encountered before semantic clues that narrow its meaning (e.g., the *rock* was in the jeweler's case), the skilled reader probably activates its range of meanings, focusing on the correct meaning when the supporting semantic clues are encountered (e.g., Kintsch, 1994; Swinney, 1979). Yes, the skilled reader decodes the target word (as well as the other words in these sentences) and the reader comprehends the semantic context as part of understanding the decoded word. But, understanding the decoded word involves processes over and above word recognition and understanding the context: It involves sorting through the various possible meanings of the word, and poor comprehenders seem not to be as good at this as good comprehenders (e.g., Gernsbacher, 1990).

The perspective just described differs considerably from Hoover and Gough's (1990) conception of word recognition. According to Hoover and Gough, the reader either sounds out or automatically recognizes the word and then *retrieves* its meaning. What Gernsbacher and Kintsch emphasize, however, is that what is critical is not just retrieving word meanings from long-term memory but selecting the correct meaning and suppressing incorrect meanings. Yes, those identifying with the simple view have recognized for a very long time that to understand what a word means requires considering its semantic context (e.g., Gough, 1983, 1984), but this processing just does not get much attention in the simple view compared to recognizing the word, with individual differences in such selection and suppression simply not addressed. This seems an important oversight, for good readers clearly juggle phonological and semantic cues and seem to do so better than poor readers (see especially Cartwright, 2002).

World Knowledge

Human beings possess knowledge about the world, with a great deal of theorizing about how such knowledge impacts reading comprehension as well as substantial empirical support for the conclusion that possessing prior knowledge related to the topic of a text favorably impacts reading comprehension (Anderson & Pearson, 1984; Dochy, Siegers, & Buehl, 1999; Shapiro, 2004). For example, the facts in a text are remembered better if a reader possesses knowledge that can be connected to those facts (e.g., Fincher-Kiefer, Post, Greene, & Voss, 1988; Pressley, Symons, McDaniel, Snyder, & Turnure, 1988; Schneider, Korkel, & Weinert, 1989). Readers with extensive prior knowledge about a topic can often spot the organization of ideas in text and use that organization to understand the text (e.g., Caillies, Denhière, & Kintsch, 2002). In addition, a reader with high prior knowledge related to a text is in a better position than a reader with low prior knowledge to make sense of poorly constructed text about a topic (McNamara, Kintsch, Songer, & Kintsch, 1996). If a reader is reading about a familiar topic, she or he is more likely to monitor whether what is being read makes sense (Vosniadou, Pearson, & Rogers, 1988). The reader with high prior knowledge is also in a better position to recognize content being sought in a reading when it is encountered than the reader with low prior knowledge (Symons & Pressley, 1993). In short, prior knowledge impacts readers' attention as they read, permitting inferences and connections (e.g., between ideas in the text and the reader's prior knowledge) and enhances memory of what is read, as posited by Anderson and Pearson (1984).

Given the long and rich literature on the importance of prior knowledge in reading comprehension, it seems unlikely that advocates of the simple view would deny the effect of prior knowledge on reading comprehension. However, they would argue that the effect works through listening comprehension, with listening comprehension including automatic connections to relevant prior knowledge. They could point to the fact that prior knowledge has been shown to impact listening comprehension (e.g., in first graders in Hare & Devine, 1983), but that does not preclude additional impact of prior knowledge on less automatic, consciously deployed processes (e.g., enabling deliberate attempts to look for ideas in a text one does not already know, enabling deliberate attempts to make sense of

poorly organized text on a topic familiar to the reader). In fact, often, automatic connecting of prior knowledge to ideas in text is much less extensive than the connecting that can occur when a reader is prompted to make efforts to understand the relationship between an idea in the text and prior knowledge (Pressley, Wood et al., 1992). The degree of prior knowledge related to the content of a text being read by a reader is an individual difference variable that has to be in a complete theory of reading comprehension, with the expectation that sometimes it impacts the kinds of automatic processes that can occur as one listens to the stream of text being read and other times it impacts more controlled text-dependent processes (e.g., identification of text structure) that are over and above what occurs during listening.

Vocabulary

An important part of knowledge is vocabulary. People with larger vocabularies tend to comprehend better (e.g., Cunningham & Stanovich, 1997; Davis, 1944, 1968; Singer, 1965; Spearitt, 1972; Thurstone, 1946). From the simple view perspective, what greater vocabulary does is improve listening comprehension skill. Although we could hope for more data, the experimental data that do exist permit the conclusion that increasing a reader's vocabulary through instruction, in fact, causes improved reading comprehension (e.g., Beck, Perfetti, & McKeown, 1982; Carlo et al., 2004; McKeown, Beck, Omanson, & Perfetti, 1983; for reviews, see Stahl & Fairbanks, 1986, and Wixson, 1986). That vocabulary seems to be a factor that can be isolated from other aspects of comprehension seems reason enough to us at least to think more about differences in vocabulary knowledge in a complete theory of reading comprehension than is the case for the simple view. We particularly note that the differences between conditions in these studies could not have been due to differences with respect to the listening comprehension skills of participants (i.e., random assignment to conditions should have assured equivalent general listening comprehension skills in the two conditions).

Passive versus Active Reading

Reading can be passive, basically reading a text from first word to last and listening to oneself read. With easy texts, such passive reading often works. That is, simply listening to oneself read is all that is required to comprehend easy text, consistent with the simple view.

Alternatively, reading can be active and often needs to be in order to make sense of complicated texts. That is, skilled readers often go beyond (and need to go beyond) passive listening comprehension, doing much more than simply reading the words and listening to oneself reading. Thinking aloud has proven to be one of the most illuminating methodologies with respect to the conscious processes used by readers to understand text (see Pressley & Afflerbach, 1995).

When skilled readers read, they are very active before, during, and after reading in the service of getting meaning from text. Before reading, they often skim a text, for example, looking for the parts of text most relevant to their purpose. They make predictions about what might be in the text. As they read the text, readers can decide to read linearly from beginning to end or to read selectively or skim or read very carefully. They can pause and reflect or take notes. They notice whether their predictions were correct. They look for important ideas in the text. They ask themselves questions (e.g., Why is the author making such a big deal of this point?), and they notice when the text addresses such questions. As reading proceeds, there is a lot of inference making, especially by good comprehenders (Brown & Brewer, 1996; Cain, Oakhill, Barnes, Bryant, 2001; Laing & Kamhi, 2002), with such inferencing probably a causal factor in comprehension (see McGee & Johnson, 2003). For example, good readers infer the referents for pronouns, the meanings of unfamiliar words, connections between ideas in text and the reader's world or personal knowledge, characteristics of the author, characteristics of the characters (in fiction), and conclusions that are implied but not stated. Some of the inferences are clearly personalized interpretations of the text, for example, visual images representing the characters, settings, and the actions. There is much integrating of information in the text, with readers noting big ideas and their relationship to details and smaller ideas. The active reader does a lot of juggling of the ideas in text as part of making inferences. See Pressley and Afflerbach (1995) for a detailed catalog of the many types of inferences good readers make as they read.

The skilled reader also monitors much (Baker, 1984; Garner, 1980; Hacker, 1997)—for example, characteristics of the text (e.g., Is it relevant to the reader's purpose? Is it easy or difficult to read?) and whether the reading is making sense (i.e., Am I understanding the text?). On the basis of such monitoring, the reader may adjust reading, for example, reading more slowly or rereading, if text is not being comprehended, skimming a text if it is covering familiar ideas, or looking ahead to see if there is information that might be more informative in a later section of the text. Good readers also are very evaluative, noticing whether they like a text, or whether they agree or disagree with the ideas in it. After reading, meaning making can continue. The reader can think additionally about some of the ideas in the text, review selectively parts of the text, or intentionally construct a summary capturing important ideas or ones especially pertinent to the reader's purpose (again, Pressley & Afflerbach, 1995, reviewed in detail the monitoring, evaluation, and reflective activities of good readers).

All of this processing matters. In fact, there is voluminous evidence that engaging in the strategic comprehension processes used by skilled readers—making predictions, making connections, asking questions, constructing mental images, creating summaries—in fact increases comprehension and memory of text, with much of the relevant data produced in well-controlled true experiments (e.g., for reviews, see National Reading Panel, 2000; Pressley, 2000). The passive listening comprehension processing implied by the simple view of reading is closer to what occurred in the control conditions of these studies. A complete view of reading must take into account the comprehension strategies employed by readers.

In summary, being able to decode words and then understand what has been decoded are important, with individual differences both in students' decoding and listening comprehension that contribute to differences in reading comprehension (i.e., there is some merit in the simple view). Being able to decode and possessing good listening comprehension probably are not sufficient to produce reading comprehension, however, for some students who can decode and understand what they hear but still not good readers. Something must be undermining these students' reading comprehension. In fact, there are a variety of individual differences variables that probably contribute to whether and how well one can read. Some may not be easily remediated, including generally low intelligence, slow processing of verbal materials, and limited working memory capacity. Hence, little more will be said about these in the chapter.

Other individual differences probably can be impacted by intervention and experience, beginning with decoding skill and reading of words more generally: fluency can be impacted somewhat (National Reading Panel, 2000, chapter 3; Stahl, 2004). Students can learn comprehension strategies, and development of world knowledge (including vocabulary) depends greatly on exposure to information. Thus, interventions aimed at fluency, comprehension strategies, vocabulary, and other world knowledge will be considered additionally as the chapter proceeds, but not before expanding a bit about an additional way of thinking about the inadequacy of the simple view as a guide to contemporary reading instruction and remediation.

Nontraditional Reading Tasks

Even if the simple view of reading explains comprehension during traditional reading of traditional texts, especially easy ones, it cannot explain other types of reading tasks and reading of other types of texts.

Skimming

In skimming readers are seeking meaning, but hope to construct meaning more quickly than with general reading. There is no direct correlate of skimming in listening comprehension. One can, of course, only partially listen to what someone has to say, but the overall time of listening is not faster, as it is when skimming in reading. One could listen to a tape set on a faster speed, but all the language on the tape will still be heard on some level, so it is not as intentionally selective as is skimming in reading. Fundamentally, the nature of written text is such that it seems skimming is far more in the reader's control than listening is in the listener's control, though this is an empirical question. How can the simple view, which seems premised on reading every word and listening to every word read, capture skimming?

Text Search and Navigation

Often text, especially informational text, is read for the purpose of finding particular information, with the reader certainly not reading every word of the text. Such searching has been studied, with readers' use of tables of content, indexes, headings, and other text features critical in guiding the search (e.g., Guthrie, 1988; Symons,

MacLatchy-Gaudet, Stone, & Reynolds, 2001). Such picking and choosing of what to read does not have an obvious correspondence to listening comprehension.

Those subscribing to the simple view might argue that this kind of text search is not about comprehension (see Guthrie, 1988). Such navigating and searching of some texts is so much what using these texts are about, however, that the study of reading comprehension is incomplete if it cannot account for the meaning construction that occurs during text search. Intelligent search of text is far more than decoding some words and listening for their meaning—it involves many decisions about where to look next as well as decisions about when the search goal has been met (i.e., that the information sought has been found or that all the information likely to be in this source has been uncovered).

Comprehending Illustrated Texts

Another problem with the simple view perspective is that many texts are more than just words. Whether the illustrations in a storybook, the photographs in a medical textbook, charts and graphs in a newspaper, or the cover of a novel, illustrations are part of many of the texts that we read, and they impact comprehension. There have been many experimental studies of the effects of illustrations on text comprehension, typically involving readers experiencing the same text with or without illustrations. A variety of effects of illustrations on comprehension have been documented (for reviews, see Carney & Levin, 2002, and Levin, Anglin, & Carney, 1987). For example, sometimes illustrations repeat information in text, with the increased comprehension and memory of text easily interpretable within dual-coding theory—the accompanying illustration increases the probability that the reader will code the information mentioned in text and depicted in the illustration both verbally and visually (see Sadoski & Paivio, 2001). In informational text, diagrams can organize spatial components that can only be described linearly in text, and, thus, increase understanding about how components in a system relate to one another. How illustrations can be adapted to impact comprehension in various ways, and why they do, is an area of extensive contemporary research (see Gyselink & Tardieu, 1999). As we browse contemporary bookstores that are filled with lavishly illustrated reference books, we cannot miss the limitation of a simple model of comprehension that does not address completely the comprehension processes that occur during reading of illustrated text.

Hypertext Comprehension

Hypertext is becoming a prevalent form of information presentation (Goldman, 1996). One of the features of hypertext is the nonlinear presentation of information. Readers are provided with great control over the selection of information units (Conklin, 1986; Esperet, 1996). The abundance of choices in the hypertext environment means that readers have many decisions to make about what to read and how to access it (Kim & Hirtle, 1995; Patterson, 2000). The reading process involves selecting search terms, reading and clicking links—a continuous cycle of information evaluation, selection, and processing (Schmar-Dobler, 2003). Navigation or searching is absolutely integral to hypertext reading, to construction of meaning in hypertext environments—so much so that it is very difficult to think about what comprehension of hypertext would be without these processes. And again, there is really no direct correlate of hypertext comprehension in listening comprehension; the simple view is inadequate for dealing with comprehension of this form of text.

Hypertext also underscores the point regarding the omission of comprehension of illustrations in the simple view. Hypertext often contains many nonword components, including a wide variety or illustrations or graphics, as well as video clips, music, animation, and so on; in fact this is part of what seems to attract readers to this type of text (Slatin, 1991). In order to comprehend this text successfully, readers must be able to comprehend all of these media, not only separately but as a whole. It is difficult to imagine how one could separate the comprehension of the word component of these texts from the other components, and in any case it is difficult to imagine why one would try to do so. The need to account for the new forms of reading required by these texts is part of the impetus behind the growing new literacies movement (e.g., Leu, Kinzer, Coiro, & Cammack, 2004).

Hypertext also reinforces the need to assign a greater role for prior knowledge in a model of reading comprehension than occurs in the simple view. Readers' prior knowledge in the nonlinear reading environment is more important than in any other reading environments because, among other things, prior knowledge helps to lessen the likelihood of disorientation, a common phenomenon in hypertext reading (Calisir

& Gurel, 2003; Lawless, Brown, Mills & Mayall, 2003; McDonald & Stevenson, 1996, 1998; Potelle & Rouet, 2003). A reader's prior knowledge of the navigational features of hypertext also plays a critical role in its comprehension (Coiro & Dobler, 2007).

Summary

Reading at the beginning of the twenty-first century often is not processing the words on book pages filled only with words. The simple view cannot explain comprehension of lavishly illustrated books or their Internet counterparts, many-layered hypertexts. Skilled readers skim and search such texts, as well as traditional texts, as part of meaning-making, with such processes not easily understood within the simple view of reading. The education of readers cannot be just about teaching students how to read words on a page given the reading processes and text tasks expected in contemporary society, with those expectations taken up next.

The Standards Perspective on Reading Achievement

In the past decade, U.S. states have been adopting standards with respect to reading, detailed expectations about what they expect of a student at each level of schooling (see the achieve.org site for the standards of many states). At the kindergarten level, mastery of prereading skills are expected, for example acquisition of phonemic awareness, the alphabetic principle—that sounds are mapped by letters in words—the alphabet and letter-sound mappings. Kindergarten students begin to read words. They also recognize that words have meanings and are expected to know the meanings of many frequently encountered words. With advancing age, students are expected to be able read words both in and out of meaningful contexts (i.e., alone or in sentences and paragraphs), and they are expected to read words with increasing fluency, with the number of words recognized and understood increasing with advancing grade level.

More than being able to read and understand words, students are expected to be able to read and understand entire texts, including both narrative and informational texts. This includes becoming familiar with many different genres, literature representing a variety of cultures and U.S. subcultures, and particular authors and topics that are covered in texts frequently encountered in elementary school (e.g., familiarity with U.S. history as portrayed in historical narratives and informational texts; familiarity with the elementary science ideas conveyed in informational texts targeted at elementary students, from topics such as monarch butterflies and their life cycles to magnets and electricity). Students are expected to learn common narrative and expository text structures and to make use of such knowledge to understand the texts they are reading. In addition, the states expect students to acquire understanding of many, many subtleties of English language usage as they learn to read diverse texts, from how dialogue is used to convey ideas to how text signals (e.g., headers, bold print, italics, accompanying illustrations and captions) are used to convey meaning.

Students are expected to become active comprehenders, making many connections between their knowledge of the world (including text worlds) and ideas in texts being read. They are expected to be active in the ways skilled comprehenders are active, making predictions, generating questions while reading, constructing images representing the ideas expressed in text, constructing summaries, and making interpretations and evaluations of texts (i.e., they are expected to become appropriately critical, able to reflect on and recognize the strengths and weaknesses of texts as well as the personal stances of the authors). Moreover, the expectation is that students will be so active on their own, without teacher prompting, knowing when they need to be especially active (e.g., when tackling a difficult text that probably has layers of meaning) and being active on those occasions. They are expected to monitor their reading, being aware of when they are understanding text and when they are not and making appropriate shifts in reading when text is not being understood (e.g., trying different strategies).

Many state reading standards go beyond the purely cognitive, beyond expectations about students learning how to read. There is also the expectation that reading instruction will develop a desire to read and the habit of reading (i.e., a positive reading attitude and motivation to read), as well as develop various stances towards reading, including aesthetic, information-seeking, and critical.

In summary, the nation has decided that much achievement is expected as part of a student's reading education. Those many components are not sufficiently addressed by instruction inspired by the simple view, a point elaborated in concluding this section.

Summary: The Simple View and the Instruction/Research It Inspires versus The Less Simple View and the Instruction/Research It Inspires

The instruction inspired by the simple view is even simpler than the model demands. The simple view of reading comprehension specifies reading comprehension as a function of decoding and listening comprehension. Even so, the instruction inspired by the simple view often boils down to sound-, letter-, and word-level skills aimed at developing skill in decoding words (i.e., phonics). The listening comprehension side of the simple view is often given little instructional attention by many who invoke the simple view. This is despite the fact that the evidence is overwhelming that early language problems predict later reading problems (Scarborough, 2001), including connections between language disorders and comprehension problems (e.g., Catts, 1993; Catts, Fey, Tomblin, & Zhang, 2002; Catts, Fey, Zhang, & Tomblin, 1999; Kamhi & Catts, 2005; Nation, 2001). With the exception of the work on phonemic awareness, there is very little study of the effects of interventions intended to stimulate language development on reading. We join others (e.g., Catts et al., 1999) in urging that serious study of the effects of long-term linguistic enrichment on reading achievement be studied, expecting that might lead to insights about how to increase reading comprehension in students.

The less simple view of reading comprehension differs from the simple view in a number of ways. First, although the less simple view recognizes that being able to decode the words is important in reading, especially at the beginning stages, the less simple view is explicit that there is more to reading than decoding the words and listening to oneself read. Thus, at the word level, good readers can recognize words automatically without expending much mental capacity to do so, permitting attention to the meaning of what is being read (LaBerge & Samuels, 1974)—they can read fluently. The less simple view also specifies that there may be some very strong limits with respect to potential reading achievement because of inherent ability limitations. Low general intelligence, slow processing of verbal materials, and lack of as much mental capacity as possessed by others to hold and juggle information consciously may all limit the extent to which one can become a good reader, one who reads demanding materials with high comprehension.

Typically, most reading occurs in context, with the less simple view more complete about how reading of words is impacted by context. According to the less simple view, the good reader pays attention to context cues, which may aid in identifying the word (e.g., permitting the correct reading of *bow*, depending on whether the context is a concert or an archery competition) and permits zeroing in on the intended meaning of the word decoded. Many words have several meanings, and good readers with their extensive vocabulary knowledge often know several meanings for words, although with each encounter of a word in context they focus their attention on the meaning that makes sense in the reading context. In doing so, the good reader is not distracted by the other meanings of the words decoded, something that occurs in some poor readers, undermining their comprehension (e.g., Gernsbacher, 1990; Williams, 1993). That is, according to the less simple view of reading, the reader skillfully juggles the multiple cuing systems that are involved in the complete act of reading and understanding a word (Adams, 1998; Cartwright, 2002): the reader decodes words using their knowledge of phonics and sight words they have acquired, and activates the meanings associated with the read words, but attends to and processes only those meanings consistent with the context clues as part of reading the text.

According to the less simple view of reading, the good reader is anything but passive, listening to one's own reading, but rather is actively connecting ideas in text to prior knowledge, and, while doing so, making predictions about ideas to come, raising questions, constructing mental images representing ideas in text, monitoring when confused and seeking clarifications, and constructing summaries, interpretations, and evaluations. Good readers are skillful skimmers of text and searchers for particular information, doing so with traditional narrative and informational texts (and a variety of genres within these two general text types), texts that are accompanied with informative illustrations, and new types of text, such as hypertext. Good readers skillfully understand and make use of many text and print conventions.

So, what are the instructional implications of the less simple model? As is the case for the simple view, there is endorsement of teaching decoding skills. The less simple view recognizes that teaching students how to sound out words is not enough for high reading comprehension: Decoding instruction and reading experiences must be sufficient to move the reader to the point of fluent word recognition, with an important vehicle for that being much practice reading (Stahl, 2004), consistent with the general perspective that much good comes from extensive reading—increased fluency, increased vocabulary, increased world knowledge, and so on (see Stanovich, 1986). More than imply that rich oral language experiences are necessary for developing language comprehension skills, the broad range of language arts instruction called for by the less simple view includes many language-rich experiences with written as well as oral tasks. Thus, what is read matters according to the less simple view, for texts filled with information that is important for people to know (e.g., social studies, science, literary themes) are a vehicle for developing the world knowledge that is so critical for understanding the texts encountered in school and an ever-demanding real world (Anderson & Pearson, 1984). Such rich texts are filled with vocabulary, not only providing opportunity for exposure to new vocabulary but also opportunities for students to learn how to learn vocabulary from context (e.g., Fukkink & de Glopper, 1998). Student readers should be taught to analyze sentence, paragraph, and larger text contexts for cues to the meanings of newly encountered vocabulary, with such encounters very important (Sternberg, 1987), probably playing a larger role in vocabulary acquisition than direct teaching of vocabulary, although a strong case can be made for such teaching as well (see Pressley, 2006, chapter 7). Beyond figuring out the meanings of unfamiliar words based on context clues, more generally, readers should be taught to be anything but passive as they read text, to do far more than simply listen to themselves read, they should be taught to use the comprehension strategies used by good readers (see Pressley, 2000). Although there has been much less research on how to teach students to search documents and make best use of the information in them (e.g., tables of contents, titles, section headers, pictures and captions, accompanying figures), including hypertext, there will be more work in the near future on the strategies students can be taught to search and learn from various types of documents (e.g., Goodman, 2003; Graesser, McNamara, & VanLehn, 2005). Perhaps the hallmark of the less simple instructional model is that students should be taught to engage texts actively, thinking hard about the ideas in them and juggling those ideas to come to understandings that are not immediately apparent on first reading or even repeated passive reading. Finally, given a less simple view of reading, teachers should do everything possible to motivate students to read (see Pressley, Dolezal et al., (2003), for a compendia of the many ways teachers can do so), for readers who are motivated to read will read (i.e., motivation to read accounts well for the total amount of reading a child does; Wang & Guthrie, 2004).

We have already made the point that instruction consistent with the simple model (i.e., intense phonics) is common with severely struggling readers. Much of the remainder of this chapter will make the point that the choice of the less simple model is realistic for such readers, that it can occur in real educational settings, although there may need to be a great deal of support for it to happen. First, however, we want to make the point that what is happening in the United States right now with respect to the federal government's program intended to promote reading achievement in populations at risk for reading failure, Reading First, starkly concretizes that either instruction more consistent with the simple model or instruction consistent with the less simple model is possible for students who very much need help if their success in learning to read is to be assured.

READING FIRST

The No Child Left Behind (NCLB) legislation makes provisions for funds to promote reading achievement during the primary grades in schools enrolling students at high risk of reading failure (i.e., students living in poverty, enrolled in schools that have a track record of underachievement with respect to beginning reading). The law provides funding for professional development and reading education materials for eligible schools, with the proviso that the professional development and materials must promote evidence-based instruction, specifically including five factors specified by the National Reading Panel (2000) as promoting beginning reading achievement: Reading First schools must provide instruction to (1) promote phonemic awareness, (2) teach phonics, (3) provide experiences that promote fluency in students (e.g., teacher-guided reading and rereading of texts with struggling readers; see Pressley, 2006, chapter 6, for a review; also National Reading Panel, 2000, chapter 3), (4) teach vocabulary (see Pressley, 2006, chapter 7, for a review of techniques that enjoy research

support, as well as discussion of the evidence that teaching vocabulary improves children's reading comprehension; also, National Reading Panel, chapter 4), and (5) teach students to use the repertoire of comprehension strategies used by good readers, beginning with teacher-explanation and modeling of the strategies and continuing with teacher scaffolded student practice of the strategies continuing over the elementary school years (see Pressley, 2006, chapter 9; also National Reading Panel, chapter 4; and Pressley, 2000).

Unfortunately, as of the time this Chapter was written, Reading First is a very underanalyzed program, so that what goes on in Reading First schools is anything but certain. That said, we have informally visited enough such settings to be confident that phonemic awareness and phonics consistently receive great attention in these settings. And, as is the case in many American elementary schools everywhere (see Pressley, Wharton-McDonald, Hampston, & Echevarria, 1998; Taylor, Pearson, Clark, & Walpole, 2000), there is not much attention to comprehension strategies instruction, and certainly not the type of instruction that is likely to lead to the long-term, self-regulated use of the comprehension strategies employed by the best readers (see Pressley et al., 1992, for detail about how such instruction is provided).

More positively, some Reading First schools provide more comprehensive reading instruction, attending in greater depth to not only phonemic awareness, phonics, and fluency, but also to vocabulary and comprehension strategies instruction as mandated by Reading First. They might do so through extensive professional development and faculty development of a program tailored to the needs and interests of the teachers and children in the school, or, more often, they do it by buying a comprehensive reading instructional program developed by a publisher. For such programs to make it in the marketplace, they must meet state reading standards, which means they have to cover the much broader waterfront of competencies that states require of reading programs (reviewed earlier). When we visit these schools, there definitely is a feeling of greater instructional balance, with the instruction less simple and more complete, reflecting that a less simple view of reading is driving such programs.

A great frustration with Reading First as of the time this chapter was written is the limited evaluation of the program. A few state web sites offer uncontrolled pre- to post–Reading

First data, documenting that performance on reading tests has improved a little in Reading First schools. Unfortunately, however, we know of no well-controlled experimental evaluation of the Reading First program (the evaluation funded by the federal government, which was to be released after this chapter was written, is not a controlled, randomized experiment; see www.mdrc.org/project_28_65.html). With respect to the more comprehensive programs that can be purchased with Reading First funds, there exist no well-controlled experimental evaluations of these programs (either in Reading First schools or other settings), although we are aware of such studies that are now underway, so there is reason to be optimistic for a better basis for evaluating such programs in the foreseeable future.

We hope for more, however. If well-controlled evaluations of both Reading First type instruction driven by the simple view and instruction driven by the less simple view can be generated, it should be possible to begin to determine whether the simple view is adequate for driving beginning reading instruction for at-risk readers or more complete instruction is needed. Of course, comprehensive evaluations will tap a broad range of reading competencies, and our suspicion is that the broader the range of competencies tapped, the more apparent the advantage of more complete instruction will be. We emphasize, however, that Reading First is intended to prevent reading problems among those at risk for reading failure. Whatever works with such populations probably will be less than what is required to solve the reading problems of the most disabled of readers. Recent work, taken up next, suggests that for those readers, instruction consistent with the less simple model can produce better than the very limited gains produced by intense phonics alone, which often results in readers who can sound out words but not do so fluently and who remain far behind agemates with respect to reading achievement (Torgesen, 2004).

A LIGHTHOUSE INTERVENTION FOR STUDENTS WITH SEVERE READING DISABILITIES AS A SOURCE OF READING INSTRUCTIONAL THEORY: BENCHMARK SCHOOL

For the past decade, a group of researchers led by Pressley has been documenting effective teaching of elementary reading, studying teachers who succeed with their students and teachers who do not, and more recently, studying whole schools that produce high reading achievement relative to otherwise comparable schools (e.g., Bogner, Raphael, & Pressley, 2002; Dolezal, Welsh, Pressley, & Vincent, 2003; Knapp & Associates, 1995; Morrow, Tracey, Woo, & Pressley, 1999; Mosenthal, Lipson, Torncello, Russ, & Mekkelsen, 2004; Pressley, Allington, Wharton-McDonald, Block, & Morrow, 2001; Pressley, Dolezal et al., 2003; Pressley, Mohan, Raphael & Fingeret, 2007; Pressley, Raphael, Gallagher, & DiBella, 2004; Pressley, Roehrig et al., 2003; Pressley, Wharton-McDonald, & Mistretta, 1998; Pressley, Wharton-McDonald, Raphael, Bogner, & Roehrig, 2001; Taylor et al., 2000; Wharton-McDonald, Pressley, & Hampston, 1998). In a nutshell, we have found instruction that is anything but consistent with the simple view model in effective classrooms and schools, basically observing teaching and experiences that are intended to stimulate the entire range of reading competencies covered in the most extensive of state standards.

Given how informative the study of effective teachers and schools was with respect to the reading education of students in regular education settings, we decided that such an approach might be similarly illuminating with respect to the education of the most struggling of beginning readers. Thus, we studied through extensive observations, document analyses, and interviews a school that has an exceptional track record with respect to the education of students who fail to learn to read during their first few years of regular education. The goal was to construct a theory grounded in data (Strauss & Corbin, 1998) about how the school produces reading achievement in its students, a theory that can be evaluated subsequently to determine the potential generality of the approach taken by the school.

Benchmark School located outside Philadelphia is an elementary and middle school, with most students first enrolling when they are 7 to 9 years of age, coming to the school with severe reading problems. The students come from a range of socioeconomic backgrounds, have normal to superior general intelligence, although their reading performances tend to be quite low (e.g., a recent cohort averaged about the 34th percentile at entrance on a standardized test). When they depart the school four to seven years later, their reading performances are much stronger, for example, at the 77th percentile for the same recent cohort. Children who entered Benchmark at high risk for long-term school failure emerge to enroll in demanding suburban high schools, with virtually all Benchmark graduates going on to complete high school and then postsecondary education.

The first point to make here with respect to the school is that remediating these children's academic problems took four to seven years, which is considerably greater than the most long-term phonics instruction that have been studied, which were two-to three-year interventions (Torgesen, 2004).

The instruction provided at the school is multifaceted from the very first day of student matriculation. Consistent with the simple view, there is intense attention to teaching the students how to read words, with such instruction continuing for all of the elementary years. The students in particular learn strategies for sounding out words. However, they also learn strategies for spelling words, composing, and comprehending. There is a great deal of teaching of vocabulary. There is much reading as part of reading class, in content area classes, and as homework. Much of the reading in science and social studies is in the service of developing knowledge that can mediate future reading comprehension, with students also receiving a great deal of instruction about how to use what they know already to understand new ideas encountered in text. Content instruction includes teaching of note-taking, study, and test-preparation strategies. Whenever students are reading, they are encouraged to monitor whether they are understanding what they read, just as they are taught to monitor whether what they are writing makes sense, and whether they know what they are expected to know for a test.

We emphasize that Benchmark students are taught to be active thinkers as they read. They learn to size up text before they read it, predicting on the basis of pictures, headers, tables of contents, and other text features. As they read, they associate ideas in text to what they already know. They construct images representing the ideas in text, ask questions and look for answers, and construct personalized summaries of the ideas in text. If they are reading to learn or are preparing for a project, they may take notes. Benchmark students learn how to process all types of texts, illustrated and not illustrated, in printed books and on web sites. Benchmark students learn to read carefully, but they also learn how to skim and how to find

particular information in text. The reading that Benchmark students learn to do is not simple nor captured by the simple view.

Benchmark instruction takes years, in part because a student who has failed to learn to read in the first few years of school is substantially behind agemates. It takes awhile to catch up. More than that, however, years of instruction permit opportunities to teach students how to deal with the ever-more complex texts that they encounter with advancing grade in school. That is, in the primary grades, students learn how to comprehend simple stories and informational texts. In the later years, students are provided explicit instruction in strategies for understanding much longer texts (e.g., novels) and much practice in coming to understand topics by finding a variety of informative texts, selectively reading the various texts, and constructing integrative understandings across the texts. That is, during the first few years of Benchmark, students do read many of the fairly easy-to-understand texts that those advocating the simple view seemed to have in mind; with advancing age levels the texts are much less simple, with simply listening to oneself read a sure formula for not understanding or for misunderstanding the texts.

A final reason that a Benchmark education takes awhile is that several years of reading failure is psychologically devastating. Students who fail to learn to read come to believe they are stupid and have very low academic self-esteem (e.g., Pearl, Bryant, & Donahue, 1980). Much of a Benchmark education is about convincing students that they can learn to read and be good students by exerting efforts, in particular efforts directed through the strategies used by good readers, writers, and thinkers (Borkowski, Carr, Rellinger, & Pressley, 1990), the strategies they are taught at Benchmark. Such understanding can only be produced through years of academic success that is mediated by use of the strategies learned, with explicit efforts to make salient that success occurred because of the strategic efforts.

Thus, the grounded theory (Strauss & Corbin, 1998) that emerged from the study was that Benchmark School produces achievement in students at very great risk of long-term school failure, especially reading failure, by intensively teaching reading skills including phonics, but much more is taught as well. Benchmark students are also educated to understand that intellectually, and, as readers, they are largely what they do—If they read texts the way that skilled readers read text, they are more likely to get something out of the reading than if they read passively, that is, if they decoded text and only listened to themselves read, if they read in a fashion consistent with the simple view of reading. Over years of schooling, students have opportunities to practice the skills they are learning with many different types of texts and tasks involving texts (e.g., using texts to locate material to include in reports, using texts to take notes in anticipation of a test), with extensive reading of texts that improve students' knowledge of the world in ways that are likely to improve their comprehension in the future.

Many Benchmark students emerge reading pretty much as agemates read, but not all Benchmark students achieve that feat. Even the Benchmark elementary and middle school experience is not sufficient to make fluent readers of some Benchmark students, although the proportion in this category is low. Then, there is the occasional student who simply cannot learn how to read words. In such cases, the school emphasizes strategies that permit the student to circumvent their difficulty as much as possible. Thus, for students who remain dysfluent, one strategy is to encourage them to read easier texts. For example, if they are studying a particular topic in social studies, there are often easier texts available than the ones assigned to the class, with these easier texts covering many of the most important ideas in the texts assigned to all students. For students who cannot read at all, or perhaps do so slowly so that reading takes a prohibitive amount of time, they are taught to make use of recorded texts and various kinds of technology supports. That is, the school teaches students how to get the information from texts that they need, rather than to be stopped dead in their tracks when they are assigned texts that are difficult or impossible for them to read. Of course, the instruction of such strategies also fits nowhere in instruction consistent with the simple view of reading.

Beyond the study at Benchmark, our group has collected data in two other school settings that provide data affirming the Benchmark approach of teaching decoding strategies intensively to struggling readers, but doing so in the context of a curriculum that teaches the many competencies of literacy and does so intensely and with a deep concern for motivation (Pressley, Mohan, Raphael, & Fingeret, 2007; Reffitt & Pressley, 2007). Both of the other schools studied produce very high language arts achievement, as measured by state and standardized tests, relative to

schools serving comparable populations and with comparable resources. Both schools, nonetheless, have their share of struggling readers. In both schools, the most struggling readers receive additional skills instruction, including instruction aimed at promoting phonemic awareness, word recognition, and reading fluency. More than that, however, the struggling students in these normally achieving schools are taught comprehension strategies explicitly (as well as other literacy strategies, such as for writing and oral communication) and practice their reading with many types of texts, most of which have the potential to contribute to increasing worthwhile world knowledge. They also learn to find information in text through skimming and other search tactics. Consistent with Benchmark, reading instruction occurs much of the school day across content instruction, with the language arts skills and strategies instruction of each year connecting with the instruction of the next year. Even so, sound-, letter-, and word-level skills instruction is more salient in the primary years, yielding to much more emphasis on extensive, diverse, and demanding reading in the upper grades, including demands for much more reflection on the ideas in text with each increasing year. Consistent with Benchmark, students requiring support receive it for the long term, with some students receiving intense skills and other literacy instruction for the entire time they are in the elementary schools we have been studying.

Thus, the hypothesis that emerges from the work on effective classrooms (see especially, Pressley, Allington et al., 2001, chapter 3) and schools is that struggling beginning readers should receive intense skills instruction but in the context of instruction covering the full range of literacy competencies that American elementary students are expected to achieve. Because the hypothesis includes the belief that such instruction occurs over years (i.e., beginning in kindergarten and grade 1 and continuing through all of the elementary years at least), we are not optimistic that a fully randomized true experiment will ever be conducted to evaluate it. We do think that some quasi-experiments are possible, which would involve matching students on their reading achievements at the outset, students who differ in the instruction they receive. If the hypothesis advanced here is correct, then initially struggling students who receive years of intense skills and other literacy instruction should achieve at a much higher level with respect to reading by the end of their elementary and/or middle school experience than students receiving less intense and complete instruction, which we know typifies many classrooms in American elementary schools (see Pressley, Allington et al., 2001). This hypothesis deserves the resources required for the half dozen or more years that will be required to explore it (i.e., it will require at least a half dozen years to follow even one cohort of students). It especially deserves testing since the instruction we have observed at Benchmark and the other two effective schools is, in fact, very complete relative to the expectations for language arts instruction that have emerged in the United States in the last decade (see achieve.org).

SUMMARY

The simple view of reading comprehension is that reading comprehension depends on decoding text and listening to what has been decoded. If a person can decode and understand the language they hear, they should be able to read with comprehension. If they cannot learn to read, the culprit is either lack of decoding skills, oral language comprehension difficulties, or both. To date, the

---

TABLE 25.1   The Less Simple View of Reading

Sound- (e.g., phonemic awareness), letter- (e.g., alphabet recognition and knowledge of letter-sound associations), and word-level skills (i.e., phonics skills) contribute to skill in decoding printed words.

Language comprehension abilities contribute to understanding what is read.

Reading is affected by general intelligence. Readers who have difficulty reading because of low intelligence may lack decoding and language comprehension skills, but they lack many other competencies as well that may contribute to their inability to read.

Much of reading occurs in working memory, and, hence, greater working memory is associated with greater reading achievement.

Speed of processing verbal material matters, with those who can process verbal materials more rapidly more likely to read well than those who process relatively slowly.

Speed of processing with respect to reading words especially matters: fluent reading of words leads to better comprehension than effortful sounding out of words.

Text comprehension depends on knowing the meanings of the words in text, and, hence, readers with an extensive vocabulary are more likely to comprehend text than those with less extensive vocabulary knowledge.

An essential comprehension skill is understanding the meaning of each word relative to its context, focusing on the meaning of a multi-meaning word that is consistent with context and suppressing other meanings. Not doing so can undermine reading comprehension and achievement.

Text comprehension depends on knowledge of the world related to the ideas in the text, with readers who possess relevant prior knowledge more likely to comprehend well than those who do not. Those who read many information-rich texts will have more complete world knowledge than those who do not.

Text comprehension depends on active processing of text—more than listening to it, but previewing text, responding to the text with predictions about what might be in the text, associations to other knowledge, construction of mental images depicting information conveyed in the text, asking questions and looking for answers, monitoring reading (e.,g., noticing when text being read is understood and when it is not), seeking clarification when confused, and coming to summaries and interpretations.

Reading is not simply word-for-word decoding of text, but often is very selective, as when a reader skims or looks for specific information.

Reading occurs not only in texts that are just printed words but with texts that convey meaning through words and other symbols (e.g., pictures), with mixed-symbol texts, and texts that are not intended to be read completely or from beginning to end, increasingly prevalent in the world.

Motivation to read matters. As is the case for just about every human competency, if practice does not make perfect, it probably makes faster and better (see Annett, 1989). Readers who elect to read more will likely read better, with reading more depending on the student being motivated to read and deciding to read rather than do other activities.

TABLE 25.2   Instruction According to the Less Simple View of Reading

Teach phonemic awareness, alphabetics, and phonics, including more intensively to struggling readers.

Encourage reading and much rereading, with struggling readers receiving many lessons during which they read and reread texts with teachers, receiving feedback and instruction as they do so.

Teach students vocabulary that they need to know and teach students how to figure out the meanings of vocabulary encountered in context, encouraging them to do so consistently.

Encourage reading of texts filled with worthwhile knowledge, including the science, social studies, and literary content contemporary students are expected to know.

Teach students to process text actively, to preview text, predict what might be in a text based on what has been encountered thus far, connect what they know already to ideas encountered in text, construct images depicting ideas conveyed by text, ask questions and seek answers as text is read, monitor when reading is going well and when there is a need to clarify (and then do so), summarize, interpret, and continue to reflect on the ideas in text.

Teach students how to skim texts for the big ideas and how to search texts for specific information being sought.

Provide experiences with many different types of texts, including hypertexts, and teach students to use all the resources in a text to construct meaning, rather than just reading the printed words when text affords other symbolic experiences and information conveyed through nonverbal media.

Do all possible to make reading motivating, with Pressley, Dolezal et al. (2003) cataloguing the many possibilities that are supported broadly by research and occur regularly in language arts achievement-producing classrooms and schools (Bogner et al., 2002; Dolezal et al., 2003).

---

simple view theory and related positions, even ones that posit that other factors impact reading (e.g., Adams, 1990; Chall, 1967), seem to inspire primarily sound-, letter-, and word-level interventions for struggling readers and those who are at risk for reading failure.

The less simple view of reading is summarized in Table 25.1. The instructional perspective that follows from it is that intensive and extensive instruction aimed at all of the competencies in Table 25.1 may be what is required to obtain maximally favorable outcomes with readers who initially struggle to learn to read, with Table 25.2 a summary of the instructional elements that should be substantially included as part of reading instruction according to the simple view.

A meta-message many take from the simple view is that remediating struggling readers can be done relatively inexpensively, with one component—phonics and associated sound-, letter-, and word-recognition skills the focus. Consistent with dated stage perspectives on reading acquisition (e.g., Chall, 1996), such decoding instruction is considered to be at the heart of learning to read. In contrast, the less simple view makes clear that teaching reading, especially to struggling readers, is multicomponential and long term.

Beyond learning to decode words, readers must learn to read words fluently, experience years of rich text environments, learn much vocabulary along the way, learn how to abstract meaning from a range of text (i.e., from the meanings of individual, unfamiliar words to the gist and interpretive understandings of very large texts), which means learning the many strategies used by the most sophisticated readers to make sense of text. Readers have to learn how to read word by word, but also how to skim and find specific pieces of information. The modern reader is confronted with many, many different types of texts that have to be negotiated, with the research community only now figuring out how to teach students to navigate worlds such as hypertexts. And, if the sheer volume of the task is not daunting enough, such complex and long-term instruction must be done in ways that motivate students. That there are classrooms and schools where this happens is an existence proof that such instruction is possible. Whether more teachers and schools can learn how to teach this way is an empirical question that should be a high focus of research and policy in the near future, as part of evaluating the full impact of such less simple instruction on student readers.

REFERENCES

Aaron, P. G., Joshi, R. M., & Williams, K. A. (1999). Not all reading disabilities are alike. *Journal of Learning Disabilities, 32*, 120–137.

Adams, M. J. (1990). *Beginning to read*. Cambridge, MA: Harvard University Press.

Adams, M. J. (1998). The three-cueing system. In J. Osborn & F. Lehr (Eds.), *Literacy for all: Issues in teaching and learning* (pp. 73–99). New York, NY, US: Guilford Press.

Anderson, R. C., & Pearson, P. D. (1984). A schema-theoretic view of basic processes in reading comprehension. In P. D. Pearson, R. Barr, M. L. Kamil, & P. Mosenthal (Eds.), *Handbook of reading research* (pp. 255–291). New York: Longman.

Annett, J. (1989). *Training in transferable skills*. Wanwick University, Coventry.

Baddeley, D. A. (1976). *The psychology of memory*. New York: Basic Books, Inc.

Baddeley, A., Logie, R., & Nimmo-Smith, I. (1985). Components of fluent reading. *Journal of Memory and Language, 24*, 119–131.

Badian, N. A. (2001). Phonological and orthographic processing: Their roles in reading prediction. *Annals of Dyslexia, 51*, 179–202.

Baker, L. (1984). Spontaneous versus instructed use of multiple standards for evaluating comprehension: Effects of age, reading proficiency, and type of standard. *Journal of Experimental Child Psychology, 38*, 289–311.

Bayliss, D. M., Jarrold, C., Baddeley, A. D., & Leigh, E. (2005). Differential constraints on the working memory and reading abilities of individuals with learning difficulties and typically developing children. *Journal of Experimental Child Psychology, 92*, 76–99.

Beck, I. L., Perfetti, C. A., & McKeown, M. G. (1982). Effects of long-term vocabulary instruction on lexical access and reading comprehension. *Journal of Educational Psychology, 74*, 506–521.

Blachman, B. A. (2000). Phonological awareness. In M. L. Kamil, P. B. Mosenthal, P. D. Pearson, & R. Barr (Eds.), *Handbook of reading research* (Vol. 3, pp. 483–502). Mahwah, NJ: Erlbaum.

Bogner, K., Raphael, L. M., & Pressley, M. (2002). How grade 1 teachers motivate literate activity by their students. *Scientific Studies of Reading, 6*, 135–165.

Borkowski, J. G., Carr, M., Rellinger, E. A., & Pressley, M. (1990). Self-regulated strategy use: Interdependence of metacognition, attributions, and self-esteem. In B. F. Jones (Ed.), *Dimensions of thinking: Review of research* (pp. 53–92). Hillsdale NJ: Erlbaum & Associates.

Bowers, P. G., & Newby-Clark, E. (2002). The role of naming speed within a model of reading acquisition. *Reading and Writing: An Interdisciplinary Journal, 15*, 109–126.

Bowey, J. A. (1995). Socioeconomic status differences in preschool phonological sensitivity and first-grade reading achievement. *Journal of Educational Psychology, 87*, 476–487.

Bowey, J. A. (2002). Reflections on onset-rime and phoneme sensitivity as predictors of beginning word reading. *Journal of Experimental Child Psychology, 82*, 29–40.

Bowey, J. A. (2005). Predicting individual differences in learning to read. In M. J. Snowling & C. Hulme (Eds.), *The science of reading: A handbook* (pp. 155–172). Malden, MA: Blackwell.

Brown, P. M., & Brewer, L. C. (1996). Cognitive processes of deaf and hearing skilled and less skilled readers. *Journal of Deaf Studies & Deaf Education, 1*, 263–270.

Caillies, S., Denhière, G., & Kintsch, W. (2002). The effect of prior knowledge on understanding from text: Evidence from primed recognition. *European Journal of Cognitive Psychology, 14*, 267–286.

Cain, K., Oakhill, J., Barnes, M. A., & Bryant, P. E. (2001). Comprehension skill, inference-making ability, and the relation to knowledge. *Memory & Cognition, 29*, 850–859.

Cain, K., Oakhill, J., & Bryant, P. (2004). Children's reading comprehension ability: Concurrent prediction by working memory, verbal ability, and component skills. *Journal of Educational Psychology, 96*, 31–42.

Calisir, F., & Gurel, Z. (2003). Influence of text structure and prior knowledge of the learner on reading comprehension, browsing and perceived control. *Computers in Human Behavior, 19*, 135–145.

Camilli, G., Vargas, S., & Yurecko, M. (2003). Teaching children to read: The fragile link between science and federal education policy. *Education Policy Analysis Archives, 11*.

Carlo, M. S., August, D., McLaughlin, B., Snow, C. E., Dressler, C., Lippman, D. N., et al. (2004). Closing the gap: Addressing the vocabulary needs of English-language learners in bilingual and mainstream classrooms. *Reading Research Quarterly, 39*, 188–215.

Carney, R. N., & Levin, J. R. (2002). Pictorial illustrations still improve students' learning from text. *Educational Psychology Review, 14*(1), 5–26.

Carretti, B., Cornoldi, C., De Beni, R., & Palladino, P. (2004). What happens to information to be suppressed in working-memory tasks? Short and long term effects. *Quarterly Journal of Experimental Psychology A: Human Experimental Psychology, 57*, 1059–1084.

Carretti, B., Cornoldi, C., De Beni, R., & Romanò, M. (2005). Updating in working memory: A comparison of good and poor comprehenders.

Journal of Experimental Child Psychology, 91, 45–66.

Cartwright, K. B. (2002). Cognitive development and reading: The relation of reading-specific multiple classification skill to reading comprehension in elementary school children. *Journal of Educational Psychology, 94,* 56–63.

Carver, R. P. (1993). Merging the simple view of reading with rauding theory. *Journal of Reading Behavior, 25,* 439–455.

Carver, R. P. (1998). Predicting reading level in grades 1 to 6 from listening level and decoding level: Testing theory relevant to the simple view of reading. *Reading and Writing: An Interdisciplinary Journal, 10,* 121–154.

Catts H. W. (1993). The relationship between speech-language impairments and reading disabilities. *Journal of Speech & Hearing Research, 36,* 948–958.

Catts, H. W., Fey, M. E., Tomblin, J. B., & Zhang, X. (2002). A longitudinal investigation of reading outcomes in children with language impairments. *Journal of Speech, Language, Hearing Research, 45,* 1142–1157.

Catts, H. W., Fey, M. E., Zhang, X., & Tomblin, J. B. (1999). Language basis of reading and reading disabilities: Evidence from a longitudinal investigation. *Scientific Studies of Reading, 3,* 331–361.

Catts, H. W., & Hogan, T. P. (2003). Language basis of reading disabilities and implications for early identification and remediation. *Reading Psychology, 24,* 223–246.

Catts, H. W., Hogan, T. P., & Adlof, S. M. (2005). Developmental changes in reading and reading disabilities. In H. W. Catts & A. G. Kamhi (Eds.), *The connections between language and reading disabilities.* Mahwah, NJ: Lawrence Erlbaum Associates.

Catts, H. W., Hogan, T. P., Adlof, S. M., & Barth, A. E. (2003). *The simple view of reading: Changes over time.* Paper presented at the annual meeting of the Society for the Scientific Study of Reading, Boulder, CO.

Catts, H. W., Hogan, T. P., & Fey, M. E. (2003). Subgrouping poor readers on the basis of individual differences in reading-related abilities. *Journal of Learning Disabilities, 36,* 151–164.

Chall, J. S. (1967). *Learning to read: The great debate.* New York: McGraw-Hill.

Chall, J. S. (1996). *Stages of reading development* (2nd ed.). Fort Worth, TX: Harcourt-Brace.

Chen, R. S., & Vellutino, F. R. (1997). Prediction of reading ability: A cross-validation study of the simple view of reading. *Journal of Literacy Research, 29,* 1–24.

Coiro, J., & Dobler, E. (2007). Exploring the online reading comprehension strategies used by sixth-grade skilled readers to search for and locate information on the Internet. *Reading Research Quarterly, 42,* 214–257.

Compton, D. L. (2003). Modeling the relationship between growth in rapid naming speed and growth in decoding skill in first-grade children. *Journal of Educational Psychology, 95,* 225–239.

Conklin, J. (1986). A survey. *Proceedings of the Conference on Computer-Supported Cooperative Work,* Austin, TX, 3–5

Crain, S., & Shankweiler, D. (1988). Syntactic complexity and reading acquisition. In A. Davison & G. M. Green (Eds.), *Linguistic complexity and text comprehension: Readability issues reconsidered.* Hillsdale, NJ: Lawrence Erlbaum Associates.

Cunningham, A. E., & Stanovich, K. E. (1997). Early reading acquisition and its relation to reading experience and ability 10 years later. *Developmental Psychology, 33,* 934–945.

Daneman, M., & Carpenter, P. A. (1980). Individual differences in working memory and reading. *Journal of Verbal Learning & Verbal Behavior, 19,* 450–466.

Daneman, M., & Carpenter, P. A. (1983). Individual differences in integrating information between and within sentences. *Journal of Experimental Psychology: Learning, Memory, and Cognition, 9,* 561–584.

Davis, F. B. (1944). Fundamental factors in reading comprehension. *Psychometrica, 9,* 185–197.

Davis, F. B. (1968). Research in comprehension in reading. *Reading Research Quarterly, 3,* 499–545.

Denckla, M. B. (1999). History and significance of rapid automatized naming. *Annals of Dyslexia, 49,* 29–42.

Denckla, M. B., & Rudel, R. G. (1972). Color-naming in dyslexic boys. *Cortex, 8,* 164–176.

Denckla, M. B., & Rudel, R. G. (1974). Rapid "Automatized" Naming of pictured objects, colors, letters, and numbers by normal children. *Cortex, 10,* 186–202.

Dochy, F., Segers, M., & Buehl, M. M. (1999). The relation between assessment practices and outcomes of studies: The case of research on prior knowledge. *Review of Educational Research, 69,* 145–186.

Dolezal, S. E., Welsh, L. M., Pressley, M., & Vincent, M. (2003). How nine third-grade teachers motivate student academic engagement. *Elementary School Journal, 103,* 239–267.

Dreyer, L. G., & Katz, L. (1992). An examination of "the simple view of reading." *Yearbook of the National Reading Conference, 41,* 169–175.

Ehri, L. C. (1995). Phases of development in learning to read words by sight. *Journal of Research in Reading, 18,* 116–125.

Ehri, L. C., Nunes, S. R., Stahl, S. A., & Willows, D. M. (2001). Systematic phonics instruction helps students learn to read: Evidence from the National Reading Panel's meta-analysis. *Review of Educational Research*, 71, 393–448.

Ehri, L. C., Nunes, S. R., Willows, D. M., Schuster, B. V., Yaghoub-Zadeh, Z., & Shanahan, T. (2001). Phonemic awareness instruction helps children learn to read: Evidence from the National Reading Panel's meta-analysis. *Reading Research Quarterly*, 36, 250–287.

Eldredge, J. L. (2005). Foundations of fluency: An exploration. *Reading Psychology*, 26, 161–181.

Esperet, E. (1996). Notes on Hypertext, Cognition and Language. In J. Rouet, J. J. Levonen, A. Dillon & R. J. Spiro (Eds.), *Hypertext and cognition* (pp. 149–156) Mahwah, NJ: Lawrence Erlbaum Associates.

Fawcett, A. J., & Nicolson, R. I. (1994). Naming speed in children with dyslexia. *Journal of Learning Disabilities*, 27, 641–646.

Fincher-Kiefer, R., Post, T. A., Greene, T. R., & Voss, J. F. (1988). On the role of prior knowledge and task demands in the processing of text. *Journal of Memory & Language*, 27, 416–428.

Flesch, R. (1955). *Why Johnny can't read*. New York: Harper and Row.

Fukkink, R. G., & de Glopper, K. (1998). Effects of instruction in deriving word meaning from context: A meta-analysis. *Review of Educational Research*, 68, 450–469.

Garner, R. (1980). Monitoring of understanding: An investigation of good and poor readers' awareness of induced miscomprehension of text. *Journal of Reading Behavior*, 12, 5–63.

Gernsbacher, M. A. (1990). *Language comprehension as structure building*. Hillsdale, NJ: Erlbaum.

Goldman, S. J. (1996) Reading, writing and learning in hypermedia environments. In H. van Oostendorp & S. de Mul (Eds.), *Cognitive Aspects of Electronic Text Processing* (pp. 7–42). Norwood, NJ: Ablex Publishing.

Goodman, S. (2003). *Teaching youth media: A Critical Guide to Literacy*. Video Production. New York: Teachers College Press.

Goswami, U. (2002). In the beginning was the rhyme? A reflection on Hulme, Hatcher, Nation, Brown, Adams, and Stuart (2002). *Journal of Experimental Child Psychology*, 82, 47–57.

Gough, P. B. (1983). Context, form, and interaction. In K. Rayner (Ed.), *Eye movements in reading* (pp. 203–211). New York: Academic Press.

Gough, P. B. (1984). Word recognition. In P. D. Pearson, R. Barr, M. L. Kamil, & P. Mosenthal (Eds.), *Handbook of reading research* (pp. 225–254). White Plains, NY: Longman.

Gough, P. B., & Tunmer, W. E. (1986). Decoding, reading, and reading disability. *Remedial and Special Education*, 7, 6–10.

Graesser, A. C., McNamara, D. S., & VanLehn, K. (2005). Scaffolding deep comprehension strategies through Point&Query, AutoTutor, and iSTART. *Educational Psychologist*, 40, 225–234.

Guthrie, J. T. (1988). Locating information in documents: Examination of a cognitive model. *Reading Research Quarterly*, 23, 178–199.

Gyselinck V., & Tardieu, H. (1999). The role of illustration in text comprehension: what, when, for whom, and why? In S. R. Goldman & H. van Oostendorp (Eds.), *The construction of mental representation during reading* (pp. 195–218). Mahwah, NJ: Lawrence Erlbaum Associates.

Hacker, D. J. (1997). Comprehension monitoring of written discourse across early-to-middle adolescence. *Reading and Writing*, 9, 207–240.

Hare, V. C., & Devine, D. A. (1983). Topical knowledge and topical interest predictors of listening comprehension. *Journal of Educational Research*, 76, 157–160.

Honig, B., Diamond, L., & Gutlohn, L. (2000). *Teaching reading sourcebook for kindergarten through eighth grade*. Novato CA: Arena Press.

Hoover, W. A., & Gough, P. B. (1990). The simple view of reading. *Reading and Writing: An Interdisciplinary Journal*, 2, 127–160.

Hulme, C., Hatcher, P. J., Nation, K., Brown, A., Adams, J., & Stuart, G. (2002). Phoneme awareness is a better predictor of early reading skill than onset-rime awareness. *Journal of Experimental Child Psychology*, 82, 2–28.

Joshi, R. M., & Aaron, P. G. (2000). The component model of reading: Simple view of reading made a little more complex. *Reading Psychology*, 21, 85–97.

Just, M. A., & Carpenter, P. A. (1992). A capacity theory of comprehension: Individual differences in working memory. *Psychological Review*, 99, 122–149.

Kail, R. V., & Hall, L. K. (1994). Processing speed, naming speed, and reading. *Developmental Psychology*, 30, 949–954.

Kamhi, A. G., & Catts, H. W. (2005). Language and reading: Convergences and divergences. In H. W. Catts & A. G. Kamhi (Eds.), *Language and reading disabilities* (2nd ed., pp. 1–25). Boston: Pearson.

Kim, H, & Hirtle, S. C. (1995). Spatial metaphors and disorientation in hypertext browsing. *Behaviour and Information Technology*, 14, 239–250.

Kintsch, W. (1994). Text comprehension, memory, and learning. *American Psychologist*, 49, 294–303.

Knapp, M. S. and Associates (1995). *Teaching for meaning in high poverty schools*. New York: Teachers College Press.

LaBerge, D., & Samuels, S. J. (1974). Toward a theory of automatic information processing in reading. *Cognitive Psychology*, 6, 293–323.

Laing, S. P., & Kamhi, A. G. (2002). The use of think-aloud protocols to compare inferencing abilities in average and below-average readers. *Journal of Learning Disabilities, 35,* 436–447.

Lawless, K. A., Brown, S. W., Mills, R., & Mayall, H. J. (2003). Knowledge, interest, recall and navigation: A look at hypertext processing. *Journal of Literacy Research, 35,* 911–934.

Leu, D. J., Jr., Kinzer, C. K., Coiro, J., & Cammack, D. (2004). Toward a theory of new literacies emerging from the Internet and other information and communication tecnologies. In R. B. Ruddell & N. Unrau (Eds.), *Theoretical models and processes of reading* (5th ed., pp. 1568–1611). Newark, DE: International Reading Association.

Levin, J. R., Anglin, G. J., & Carney, R. N. (1987). On empirically validating functions of pictures in prose. In D. M. Willows & H. A. Houghton (Eds.), *The psychology of illustration* (Vol. 1, pp. 51–85). New York: Springer-Verlag.

Lovett, M. W. (1984). The search for subtypes of specific reading disability: Reflections from a cognitive perspective. *Annals of Dyslexia, 34,* 155–178.

McBride-Chang, C., & Kail, R. V. (2002). Cross-cultural similarities in the predictors of reading acquisition. *Child Development, 73,* 1392–1407.

McCardle, P., & Chhabra, V. (Eds.) (2004). *The voice of evidence in reading research.* Baltimore: Brookes.

McDonald, S., & Stevenson, R. (1996). Disorientation in hypertext: The effects of three text structures on navigation performance. *Applied Ergonomics, 27,* 61–68.

McDonald, S., & Stevenson, R. (1998). Effects of text structure and prior knowledge of the learner on navigation in hypertext. *Human Factors, 40,* 18–27.

McGee, A., & Johnson, H. (2003). The effect of inference training on skilled and less skilled comprehenders. *Educational Psychology, 23,* 49–59.

McKeown, M. G., Beck, I. L., Omanson, R. C., & Perfetti, C. A. (1983). The effects of long-term vocabulary instruction on reading comprehension: A replication. *Journal of Reading Behavior, 15,* 3–18.

McNamara, D. S., Kintsch, E., Songer, N. B., & Kintsch, W. (1996). Are good texts always better? Text coherence, background knowledge, and levels of understanding in learning from text. *Cognition and Instruction, 14,* 1–43.

Marx, H., & Jungmann, T. (2000). Abhèangigkeit der Entwicklung des Leseverstehens von Hèorverstehen und grundlegenden Lesefertigkeiten im Grundschulalter: Eine Prèufung des Simple View of Reading-Ansatzes [Dependency of reading comprehension development on listening and basic reading skills: An examination of the Simple View of Reading]. *Zeitschrift fèur Entwicklungspsychologie und Pèadagogische Psychologie, 32,* 81–93.

Morrow, L. M., Tracey, D. H., Woo, D. G., & Pressley, M. (1999). Characteristics of exemplary first-grade literacy instruction. *Reading Teacher, 52,* 462–476.

Mosenthal, J., Lipson, M., Torncello, S., Russ, B., & Mekkelsen, J. (2004). Contexts and practices of six schools successful in obtaining reading achievement. *Elementary School Journal, 104,* 343–367.

Muter, V., Hulme, C., Snowling, M. J., & Stevenson, J. (2004). Phonemes, rimes, vocabulary, and grammatical skills as foundations of early reading development: Evidence from a longitudinal study. *Developmental Psychology, 40,* 665–681.

Näslund, J. C., & Schneider, W. (1996). Kindergarten letter knowledge, phonological skills, and memory processes: Relative effects on early literacy. *Journal of Experimental Child Psychology, 62,* 30–59.

Nation, K. (2001). Reading and language in children: Exposing hidden deficits. *The Psychologist, 14,* 238–242.

National Reading Panel (2000). *Teaching children to read: An evidence-based assessment of the scientific research literature on reading and its implication for reading instruction—Reports of the subgroups.* Washington, DC: National Institute of Child Health and Development.

Nicolson, R. I., & Fawcett, A. J. (1994). Reaction times and dyslexia. *Quarterly Journal of Experimental Psychology, 47,* 29–48.

Paris, S. G., Carpenter, R. D., Paris, A. H., & Hamilton, E. E. (2005). Spurious and genuine correlates of children's reading comprehension. In S. G. Paris & S. A. Stahl (Eds.), *Children's reading comprehension and assessment.* Mahwah, NJ: Lawrence Erlbaum Associates.

Patterson, N. G. (2000). Hypertext and the changing roles of readers. *English Journal, 90,* 74–80.

Pearl, R., Bryan, T., & Donahue, M. (1980). Learning disabled children's attributions for success and failure. *Learning Disability Quarterly, 3,* 3–9.

Pennington, B. F., Groisser, D., & Welsh, M. C. (1993). Contrasting cognitive deficits in attention deficit hyperactivity disorder versus reading disability. *Developmental Psychology, 29,* 511–523.

Perfetti, C. A., & Goldman, S. R. (1976). Discourse memory and reading comprehension skill. *Journal of Verbal Learning & Verbal Behavior, 15,* 33–42.

Perfetti, C. A., Landi, N., & Oakhill, J. (2005). The acquisition of reading comprehension skill. In M. J. Snowling & C. Hulme (Eds.), *The science of reading: A handbook* (pp. 227–247). Malden, MA: Blackwell.

Perfetti, C. A., & Lesgold, A. M. (1977). *Coding and comprehension in skilled reading and implications for reading instruction.* Washington, DC: National Institute of Education.

Potelle, H., & Rouet, J. (2003). Effects of content representation and readers' prior knowledge on the comprehension of hypertext. *International Journal of Human-Computer Studies, 58,* 327–345.

Pressley, M. (2000). What should comprehension instruction be the instruction of? In M. L. Kamil, P. B. Mosenthal, P. D. Pearson & R. Barr (Eds.), *Handbook of reading research (Vol. III).* Mahwah, NJ: Lawrence Erlbaum Associates.

Pressley, M. (2006). *Reading instruction that works: The case for balanced teaching,* 3rd edition. New York: Guilford.

Pressley, M., & Afflerbach, P. (1995). *Verbal protocols of reading: The nature of constructively responsive reading.* Hillsdale, NJ: Lawrence Erlbaum Associates.

Pressley, M., Allington, R., Wharton-McDonald, R., Block, C. C., & Morrow, L.M. (2001). *Learning to read: Lessons from exemplary first grades.* New York: Guilford.

Pressley, M., Dolezal, S. E., Raphael, L. M., Mohan, L., Roehrig, A.D., & Bogner, K. (2003). *Motivating primary-grade students.* New York: Guilford.

Pressley, M., El-Dinary, P. B., Gaskins, I., Schuder, T., Bergman, J., Almasi, L., & Brown, R. (1992). Beyond direct explanation: Transactional instruction of reading comprehension strategies. *Elementary School Journal, 92,* 511–554.

Pressley, M., Mohan, L., Raphael, L. M., & Fingeret, L. (2007). How does Bennett Woods Elementary School produce such high reading and writing achievement? *Journal of Educational Psychology, 99*(2), 221–240.

Pressley, M., Raphael, L., Gallagher, J. D., & DiBella, J. (2004). Providence-St. Mel School: How a school that works for African-American students works. *Journal of Educational Psychology, 96,* 216–235.

Pressley, M., Roehrig, A., Raphael, L., Dolezal, S., Bohn, K., Mohan, L., Wharton-McDonald, R., & Bogner, K. (2003). Teaching processes in elementary and secondary education. In W. M. Reynolds & G. E. Miller (Eds.), *Comprehensive handbook of psychology. Volume 7: Educational Psychology* (pp. 153–175). New York: John Wiley & Sons.

Pressley, M., Symons, S., McDaniel, M. A., Snyder, B. L., & Turnure, J. E. (1988). Elaborative interrogation facilitates acquisition of confusing facts. *Journal of Educational Psychology, 80,* 268–278.

Pressley, M., Wharton-McDonald, R., Hampston, J. M., & Echevarria, M. (1998). The nature of literacy instruction in ten grade-4 and -5 classrooms in upstate New York. *Scientific Studies of Reading, 2,* 159–191.

Pressley, M., Wharton-McDonald, R., & Mistretta, J. (1998). Effective beginning literacy instruction: Dialectical, scaffolded, and contextualized. In J. L. Metsala & L. C. Ehri (Eds.), *Word recognition in beginning literacy* (pp. 357–373). Mahwah NJ: Erlbaum Associates.

Pressley, M., Wharton-McDonald, R., Raphael, L. M., Bogner, K., & Roehrig, A. D. (2001). Exemplary first grade teaching. In B. M. Taylor & P. D. Pearson (Eds.), *Teaching Reading: Effective Schools and Accomplished Teachers* (pp. 73–88). Mahwah NJ: Erlbaum & Associates.

Pressley, M., Wood, E., Woloshyn, V. E., Martin, V., King, A., & Menke, D. (1992). Encouraging mindful use of prior knowledge: Attempting to construct explanatory answers facilitates learning. *Educational Psychologist, 27,* 91–110.

Reffitt, K., & Pressley, M. (2007, April). *Effective literacy instruction in a rural school district: How do they do it?* Presentation to the Annual Conference of the American Educational Research Association (AERA), Chicago, IL.

Sadoski, M., & Paivio, A. (2001). *Imagery and text: A dual coding theory of reading and writing.* Mahwah, NJ: Lawrence Erlbaum Associates.

Savage, R. (2001). The 'simple view' of reading: Some evidence and possible implications. *Educational Psychology in Practice, 17,* 17–33.

Scarborough, H. S. (2001). Connecting early language and literacy to later reading (dis)abilities: Evidence, theory, and practice. In S. B. Neuman & D. K. Dickinson (Eds.), *Handbook of early literacy research* (pp. 97–110). New York: Guilford Press.

Schatschneider, C., Carlson, C. D., Francis, D. J., Foorman, B. R., & Fletcher, J. M. (2002). Relationship of rapid automatized naming and phonological awareness in early reading development: Implications for the double-deficit hypothesis. *Journal of Learning Disabilities, 35,* 245–256.

Schatschneider, C., Fletcher, J. M., Francis, D. J., Carlson, C. D., & Foorman, B. R. (2004). Kindergarten prediction of reading skills: A longitudinal comparative analysis. *Journal of Educational Psychology, 96,* 265–282.

Schmar-Dobler, E. (2003, December). *Building a bridge: An exploration of the reading strategies used for internet reading.* Paper presented at the annual meeting of the National Reading Conference. Scottsdale, AZ.

Schneider, W., Korkel, J., & Weinert, F. E. (1989). Domain-specific knowledge and memory performance: A comparison of high- and low-aptitude children. *Journal of Educational Psychology, 81,* 306–312.

Seigneuric, A., Ehrlich, M. F., Oakhill, J. V., & Yuill, N. M. (2000). Working memory resources and children's reading comprehension. *Reading and Writing, 13*, 81–103.

Shapiro, A. M. (2004). How including prior knowledge as a subject variable may change outcomes of learning research. *American Educational Research Journal, 41*, 159–189.

Singer, H. A. (1965). A developmental model of speed of reading in grades 3 through 6. *Reading Research Quarterly, 1*, 29–49.

Slatin, J. (1991). Reading hypertext: Order and coherence in a new medium. In P. Delaney & G. P. Landow (Eds.), *Hypermedia and literary studies* (pp. 153–170). Cambridge, MA: MIT press.

Spearitt, D. (1972). Identification of subskills of reading comprehension by maximum likelihood factor analysis. *Reading Research Quarterly, 8*, 92–111.

Speece, D. L., Ritchey, K. D., Cooper, D. H., Roth, F. P., & Schatschneider, C. (2004). Growth in early reading skills from kindergarten to third grade. *Contemporary Educational Psychology, 29*, 312–332.

Stahl, S. A. (2004). What do we know about fluency? Findings of the National Reading Panel. In P. McCardle & V. Chhabra (Eds.), *The voice of evidence in reading research* (pp. 187–211). Baltimore: Brookes Publishing Co.

Stahl, S. A., & Fairbanks, M. M. (1986) The effects of vocabulary instruction: A model-based meta-analysis. *Review of Educational Research, 56*, 72–110.

Stanovich, K. E. (1986). Matthew effects in reading: Some consequences of individual differences in the acquisition of literacy. *Reading Research Quarterly, 21*, 360–406.

Stanovich, K. E. (1988). The right and wrong places to look for the cognitive locus of reading disability. *Annals of Dyslexia, 38*, 154–157.

Sternberg, R. J. (1987). Most vocabulary is learned from context. In M. G. McKeown & M. E. Curtis (Eds.), *The nature of vocabulary acquisition* (pp. 89–105). Hillsdale, NJ, England: Lawrence Erlbaum Associates, Inc.

Storch, S. A., & Whitehurst, G. J. (2002). Oral language and code-related precursors to reading: Evidence from a longitudinal structural model. *Developmental Psychology, 38*, 934–947.

Strauss, A., & Corbin, J. (1998). *Basics of qualitative research: Grounded theory procedures and techniques* (2nd ed.) Newbury Park, CA: Sage.

Stuart, M., & Masterson, J. (1992). Patterns of reading and spelling in 10–year-old children related to prereading phonological abilities. *Journal of Experimental Child Psychology, 54*, 168–187.

Swanson, H. L., Trainin, G., Necoechea, D. M., & Hammill, D. D. (2003). Rapid naming, phonological awareness, and reading: A meta-analysis of the correlation evidence. *Review of Educational Research, 73*, 407–440.

Swinney, D. A. (1979). Lexical access during sentence comprehension: (Re)consideration of context effects. *Journal of Verbal Learning and Verbal Behavior, 18*, 645–659.

Symons, S., MacLatchy-Gaudet, H., Stone, T. D., & Reynolds, P. L. (2001). Strategy instruction for elementary students searching informational text. *Scientific Studies of Reading, 5*, 1–33.

Symons, S., & Pressley, M. (1993). Prior knowledge affects text search success and extraction of information. *Reading Research Quarterly, 28*, 250–261.

Taylor, B. M., Pearson, P. D., Clark, K., & Walpole, S. (2000). Effective schools and accomplished teachers: Lessons about primary-grade reading instruction in low-income schools. *Elementary School Journal, 101*, 121–165.

Thurstone, L. L. (1946). A note on a reanalysis of Davis' reading texts. *Psychometrica, 11*, 185–188.

Torgesen, J. K. (2004). Lessons learning from research on interventions for students who have difficulties learning to read. In P. McCardle & V. Chhabra (Eds.), *The voice of evidence in reading research* (pp. 355–382). Baltimore: Paul Brookes Publishing.

Torgesen, J. K., & Burgess, S. R. (1998). Consistency of reading-related phonological processes throughout early childhood. In J. Metsala & L. Ehri (Eds.), *Word recognition in beginning reading* (pp. 161–188). Mahwah, NJ: Erlbaum.

Vosniadou, S., Pearson, P. D., & Rogers, T. (1988). What causes children's failures to detect consistencies in text? Representation versus comparison difficulties. *Journal of Educational Psychology, 80*, 27–39.

Vukovic, R. K., Wilson, A. M., & Nash, K. K. (2004). Naming speed deficits in adults with reading disabilities: A test of the double-deficit hypothesis. *Journal of Learning Disabilities, 37*, 440–450.

Wang, J. H. Y., & Guthrie, J. T. (2004). Modeling the effects of intrinsic motivation, extrinsic motivation, amount of reading, and past reading achievement on text comprehension between U.S. and Chinese students. *Reading Research Quarterly, 39*, 162–186.

Wesseling, R., & Reitsma, P. (2001). Preschool phonological representations and development of reading skills. *Annals of Dyslexia, 51*, 203–229.

Wharton-McDonald, R., Pressley, M., & Hampston, J. M. (1998). Outstanding literacy instruction in first grade: Teacher practices and student achievement. *Elementary School Journal, 99*, 101–128.

Williams, J. P. (1993). Comprehension of students with and without learning disabilities: Identification of narrative themes and idiosyncratic text representations. *Journal of Educational Psychology, 85*, 631–641.

Windfuhr, K. L., & Snowling, M. J. (2001). The relationship between paired associate learning and phonological skills in normally developing readers. *Journal of Experimental Child Psychology, 80*, 160–173.

Wixson, K. K. (1986). Vocabulary instruction and children's comprehension of basal stories. *Reading Research Quarterly, 21*, 317–329.

Wolf, M., Bally, H., & Morris, R. (1986). Automaticity, retrieval processes, and reading: A longitudinal study in average and impaired readers. *Child Development, 57*, 988–1000.

Wolf, M., & Bowers, P. G. (1999). The double-deficit hypothesis for the developmental dyslexias. *Journal of Educational Psychology, 91*, 415–438.

CHAPTER 26

WORKING WITH CHILDREN WITH MATH PROBLEMS

FREDRICKA K. REISMAN
Drexel University

This chapter considers seven factors that affect mathematics learning in children, with a special emphasis on children identified as learning disabled. The seven factors are:

i. Mathematics content and processes relating to learning disabilities,
ii. Creativity,
iii. Math anxiety,
iv. Students' perceptions of self-efficacy,
v. Quality of mathematics instruction,
vi. Intervention theories (e.g., Feuerstein's Mediated Learning, Reisman's Heuristic Diagnostic Teaching and Generic Influences on learning), and
vii. National and state mathematics standards and assessments.

i. MATHEMATICS CONTENT AND PROCESSES RELATING TO LEARNING DISABILITIES

Mathematics learning problems are referred to as dyscalculia, a collection of symptoms interfering with learning mathematics content dealing with time, money, measurement, temperature, volume, speed, place value, computation with whole numbers, fractions and decimals. Children (about 6%) having problems with math experience difficulty in developing number concepts (e.g., cardinality, or the "how much-ness" of a group), number relationships (e.g., one-to-one correspondence, greater/less-than/equivalence), operations on numbers (e.g., addition, multiplication, subtraction, division), and solving word problems.

What processes underlie dyscalculia? They include: following sequential directions, spatial orientation/space organization, pattern recognition, visualization, inductive and deductive think-

ing, and estimating (e.g., predicting quantitative relationships such as "If I owe $4.73 what is the smallest bill I need? One dollar? Five dollars? Ten dollars?"). These processes act as "anchors" for mathematics ideas and serve to focus instruction. The degree of onset and severity to which these prerequisite skills are or are not developed, directly affect mathematics learning. Table 26.1 presents a framework for connecting mathematics learning disabilities, learning outcomes, and suggestions for bridging these through instruction. Creative problem identification and problem solving will be an integrative component of this chapter.

ii. CREATIVITY

Many terms represent creativity, such as original, thinking out of the box, usefully relevant, influential, innovative, fluent, flexible, divergent, open, resists premature closure, tolerates ambiguity, risk taker, and courageous. There is a logical interaction among learning mathematics creatively (Torrance & Reisman, 2002 a, b; Reisman & Torrance, 2003), learning to cope with and circumvent dyscalculia, and teachers who use their own creativity in their teaching. Creative teachers can accommodate those with math learning problems by breaking out of traditional curriculum sequences of instruction (e.g., teach time to the minute first instead of last; see Reisman, 1972, 2008a); create new instructional approaches to place value and computation of signed numbers using counting boards (see Torrance & Reisman, 2002a); identify covert trouble spots in learning mathematics such as interpreting bar graphs or solving word problems; and estimation (see Reisman & Kauffman, 1980; Reisman, & Payne 1987).

TABLE 26.1 Math Learning Disability, Learning Outcome, Pedagogy

Mathematics Learning Disability	Mathematics Learning Outcome	Instructional Suggestion
Does not relate cardinality as the value of the final number representing the quantity of items in the counted set	Find the cardinality (how much ness) of a group of objects Relate number words and numerals to cardinality Recognize that numbers can be decomposed into smaller numbers or combined to create larger numbers (underlies subtraction and addition) Recognize and use one-one correspondence. One and only one word (e.g., "one," "two") is assigned to each counted object (encipherment)	Engage the learner in abstract thinking whereby if cardinality is the goal, given objects with different color, size, texture, shape, or function, the child ignores color, size, texture, shape, or function of the objects in two or more equivalent groups and states the number property (both groups have the same number). Use concrete objects (e.g., blocks, toys, fruit) that can be sorted. Begin with two equivalent groups with the same objects, then add a third group with a change in physical characteristics (perhaps the first two groups were comprised of three red blocks (same shape, thickness, size); the third group added might consist of two red blocks and a blue block (change one attribute—color). Add a fourth group of three where a different shape is added (perhaps a yellow triangle or pentagon block). Continue in this manner until the only attribute which is the same across all equivalent groups is their number property (three ness). The student states, "All groups have the same number; all groups have three."
Language processing problems include inability to follow sequential directions—sequencing (including reading numbers out of sequence, substitutions, reversals, omissions and doing operations backwards), organizing detailed information, remembering specific facts and formulas for completing their mathematical calculations	State ordinality of an object in a series using the words *first, second, third, . . .* State verbally and in writing words and their correct sequence ("one, two, three "), as well as the associated Arabic numbers and sequence (i.e., 1, 2, 3, . . .)	Use concrete objects (e.g., blocks, toys, students, chairs) that can be ordered spatially in sequence; order objects on some characteristic (e.g., size, color hue, thickness, number of sides). Ask children to count a series of objects and then ask them "How many are there?" Many young children with math problems have difficulties with tasks that involve ordinality and believe that only adjacent items can be counted, suggesting that they understand counting as a fixed, mechanical activity. Use role play with a puppet who counts wrong sometimes and correct at other times (i.e., employs one—one correspondence) and have the child tell if the count was correct or not and explain why. When the teacher explains why or why not the puppet is correct he or she is employing a modeling technique described by Feuerstein using careful and accurate language.

Slow the pace of delivery and maintain normal timing of phrases. The "chunking" of verbal information is important when asking questions, giving directions, presenting concepts, and offering explanations.

Avoid elaborations as they confuse rather than help this type of learner.

Demonstrate directionality and spatial orientation skills

Visual spatial confusion includes acquiring spatial orientation/space organization/direction, easily disoriented (including left/right orientation), trouble reading graphs

Use cueing (e.g., larger size, different color, velvet cut-outs) to focus attention on the operational sign as children sometimes mix up the + and x. They also need cues to help them in sequencing the steps in complex operations.

Pictures and diagrams can be confusing, so these should not be used when trying to teach or clarify concepts. In fact, this group of children is specifically in need of coaching in picture interpretation, diagram and graph reading, and nonverbal social cues.

Anchor verbal experiences with materials that can be felt, seen, and moved around as they are talked about. For example, students of this type may be better able to learn to identify triangles by holding a triangular block and saying to them, "A triangle has three sides. When we draw it, it has three connected lines."

When children have difficulty organizing their written work on a page, have them use graph paper.

Difficulty with temporal relations

Read, interpret, and follow schedules, tell and keep track of time, and sequence past and future events.

Teach telling time to the minute first, not last as counting is learned by ones initially, not by 30's or 15's or 5's or fractions (e.g., quarter, half, etc.). Early on focus only on time after the minute (e.g., 35 minutes after 2 o'clock, 60 minutes after the hour is the same as zero minutes after the next hour) before involving reversal of thinking (e.g., ten minutes before 2 o'clock).

TABLE 26.1 (*Continued*)

Mathematics Learning Disability	Mathematics Learning Outcome	Instructional Suggestion
Unusually high anxiety	Students employ cognitive monitoring and visualization to calm down	Teacher models talking aloud (e.g., I can do this, I remember what this means, I know what the problem is asking for). Instead of being asked to memorize $7 + 8 = 15$? ask, "How do you remember that $7 + 8 = 15$?" A strategy might be that $7 + 7 = 14$, so $7 + 8 = 15$. Use strategies that foster self reliance and diminish the need for meaningless memorization. Math anxious students often will take risks if their fears are acknowledged and support is provided.
Poor memory; many learning disabled students have persistent trouble "memorizing" basic number facts in all four operations despite adequate understanding	Stating and computing basic facts (e.g., $9 + 2 = 11$, $11 - 2 = 9$, $3 \times 9 = 27$, $27 \div 9 = 3$) automatically without use of a crutch (e.g., counting fingers, tally marks, etc.)	Do not hold students back "until they know their facts" but allow use of a calculator so they can focus on problem solving. Use distributed practice (e.g., two 15-minute sessions per day, few numbers of facts to be mastered at one time, frequent practice using the commutative property e.g., $3 + 8$ and $8 + 3$, 2×9 and 9×2). Poor memory relates to need for repetition. Present small amounts of material to be learned, incorporate redundancy and rehearsal strategies, employ frequency to develop number-word-object associations.
Needs more practice than peers	Demonstrates acquisition of knowledge given sufficient practice	Principles for Designing Practice Activities: 1. Avoid memory overload by assigning manageable amounts of homework. 2. Build retention by providing review within a day or two of the initial learning of difficult skills, and by providing supervised practice to prevent students from practicing misconceptions and "misrules." 3. Connect new learning to what the student knows. 4. Practice easier knowledge and skills before teaching and practicing more complex content. 5. Require fluent responses. 6. Ensure that skills to be practiced can be completed independently with high levels of success.

A great deal can be done in classroom settings to encourage creativity for the gifted as well as for those with learning disabilities. Unfortunately, classroom environments often stifle instead of enhance students' creativity. Teachers usually feel comfortable with the *ideal student* (Whitelaw, 2007; Torrance, 1963) profiled as "polite, punctual, and conventional ... courteous, follow assignments" (Runco, 2007, p. 178). This is not the profile of one with learning disabilities.

Recent research suggests that nonverbal tasks like the Figural Battery of the Torrance Tests of Creative Thinking (TTCT) (Torrance, 1974) are better assessments of creativity—especially for those with limited verbal skills. A study of all seventh, ninth, and tenth graders in a low socioeconomic, poor-performing school district in Pennsylvania found that the majority of students scored in the bottom quartile on the TTCT-Verbal (similar results on the Terranova achievement test), while these same students scored in the 75th–95th percentile on the TTCT-Figural (Reisman, Bach et al., 2002). Since many learning disabilities (LD) are language based, a figural approach to assessing creative strengths rather than the TTCT-Verbal battery makes sense.

In addition to being sensitive to students' creative strengths, teachers should avoid what Davis (1999) called possible *squelchers*; namely, statements such as: *This is the way to solve this problem; Listen to what I say as I solve this equation—do it my way; Look for cue words in problems such as more or less than* ... Identifying, valuing, and using one's creativity (teachers' students', and parents') is becoming recognized as a powerful pedagogy for providing a more accepting and divergent environment for learners.

iii. MATH ANXIETY

Math anxiety has been an issue for a long time (Tobias, 1990, 1993). Some anxiety is good and in fact required for getting energy and motivation up for a test or other challenge. Peak performance occurs when anxiety optimally alerts the body to respond. However, if anxiety continues to increase too much, it interferes with performance and can even act as a block. Students with test anxiety often describe their minds as going blank. Therefore, the goal is to help students reduce anxiety to a facilitative level rather than be at an inhibiting level.

Math-anxious students may complain of nervousness, inability to concentrate on problems, mind going blank, and even illness when confronted with a math test. A negative relationship between math anxiety and math achievement has been found across all grade levels, kindergarten through college (Betz, 1978; Ma, 1999). Research suggests various ways that teachers can prevent and reduce math anxiety: designing better teaching practices (Steele and Arth, 1998), creating a comfortable atmosphere (Jackson and Leffingwell, 1999; Steele and Arth, 1998), providing encouragement (Godby, 1997; Jackson and Leffingwell, 1999), using alternative assessment (NCTM, 1989; Steele and Arth, 1998), and exhibiting a better understanding of learning styles (Fiore, 1999; Fotoples, 2000).

A variety of techniques that can help reduce math anxiety include not requiring oral responses, having students engage in team test taking, slowing instruction, and providing peer coaching. Encouraging manipulatives to represent mathematical concepts and allowing calculators help. Use alternative assessments such as oral questioning, teacher observation, student demonstration, small group discussion, keeping logs, retesting on missed test items, group and individual projects, performance tasks and portfolios, and most importantly, showing enthusiasm about mathematics. Additional strategies for teachers include presenting clear explanations, frequent reviews, giving partial credit, and reviewing specific concepts and computations for exams.

iv. STUDENTS' PERCEPTIONS OF SELF-EFFICACY

Students rushed into math remediation very often experience expectation of failure and its accompanying low self-efficacy and feelings of inadequacy (low self-esteem) as mathematics learners. Often they find themselves in this situation as a result of poor instruction (Engelmann & Carnine, 1982; Kameenui & Simmons, 1990) which when coupled with typical learning disabilities leads to a domino effect of continuous failure in math performance. Bandura 1986, 1993 distinguished between *self-esteem* and *self-efficacy*. Self-esteem relates to a person's sense of self-worth, whereas self-efficacy relates to a person's perception of their ability to reach a goal.

Pajares and Miller's (1994) study of self-efficacy and mathematics found that when instruction is effective (i.e., when students master specified outcomes), performance is enhanced and an accurate and positive perception of self-efficacy results. On the other hand, ineffective instruction leads to poor performance and a pessimistic approximation of self-efficacy. Thus, students' perceptions of their self-efficacy initially stem from past math success and failure often resulting from inept instruction. These low expectations frequently result in low-achieving students not even attempting to learn or persevere in acquiring mathematical concepts and skills.

v. Quality of Mathematics Instruction

Quality of mathematics instruction is dependent first of all on the teacher's content knowledge. However, research assessing teachers' knowledge of mathematics consistently reveals that their content knowledge in mathematics is weak, especially in the elementary grades (Reisman, 1992; Narramore, 1968; Glennon, 1948). This situation brings into question the pervasiveness of the concept of *remediation* as an approach that permeates the special needs education practice and which places the cause of poor mathematics performance by students squarely on their learning disability or special need. This is a deficit philosophy which stems from the medical model of *diagnose, prescribe, remediate*. However, very often the need for a *remedy* is misplaced; rather, the need is for *re-mediation*, to use Feuerstein's (1980) notion of mediated learning discussed in the next section. The students are not ill as in the need for a remedy to cure; they require creative instruction which circumvents their learning disability while incorporating pedagogy that provides modeling of thinking and plays into their learning strengths. The theories of Feuerstein and Reisman discussed in the next section facilitate development of quality mathematics teaching.

Research on high school students having math problems has general applicability to elementary and middle grades as well. For example, Carpenter (1985) pointed out that severe deficits in mathematics achievement are persistent and several researchers found that secondary students with LD continue to make progress in learning more complex mathematical concepts and skills; however, their progress is very gradual (Cawley, Fitzmaurice, Shaw, Kahn, & Bates, 1979; Cawley & Miller, 1989). McLeod and Armstrong (1982) surveyed junior high, middle school, and high school math teachers regarding mathematics achievement and concluded that skill deficits in basic computation and numera-

tion were pervasive, including basic operations, percentages, decimals, measurement, and the language of mathematics. Algozzine, O'shea, Crews, and Stoddard (1987) noted that students with LD consistently scored higher on items requiring the factual, exact use of arithmetic skills than on items requiring applications of concepts. Similarly, Carpenter, Matthews, Linquist, and Silver (1984) and Hasselbring, and Bransford (1988) reported that when students in the elementary grades fail to acquire skills in operations and applications of mathematics, they are hindered in development of higher-level mathematics skills.

There are varied opinions about what comprises quality instruction; frequently, beliefs and convictions play more significant roles than solid research results. Proponents of current efforts to reform mathematics education believe that if the quality of instruction is to be improved, then many educators will have to dramatically change their perspectives on how mathematics should be taught, e.g., Feuerstein's approach described below in comparison to the emphasis on constructivism.

Constructivism is a theory that had become increasingly popular in the mathematics education reform movement. Its assumption (which stems from Piaget's work) is that knowledge is created by the learner through active engagement in the process of assimilating information and accommodating cognitively to the new knowledge (Cobb, 1994a, 1994b; Driver, Asoko, Leach, Mortimer, & Scott, 1994; Gadanidis, 1994; Harris & Graham, 1994; Poplin, 1988; Pressley, Harris, & Marks, 1992) rather than being transmitted from teacher to learner. Thus, the learner constructs knowledge.

Reid, Kurkjian, and Carruthers (1994) and Carnine (1992) acknowledged that the constructivist perspective, though intuitively appealing, is currently unsupported by empirical research and is logically inadequate for the task of teaching adolescents with LD. The premise that secondary students with LD will construct their own knowledge about important mathematical concepts, skills, and relationships, or that in the absence of specific instruction or prompting they will learn how or when to apply what they have learned, is unsupported by empirical investigations.

vi. Intervention Theories

Reueven Feuerstein concentrated on how children learn, building upon and modifying Piaget's ideas.

Feuerstein started working with children after World War II. He was a student of Piaget after the end of the war, and then migrated to Israel. He worked with students who others gave up on, especially those with Down syndrome. Ironically, one of Feuerstein's grandchildren has Down syndrome. The fundamental premises of Feuerstein's theory consider the brain as modifiable, as a network of interconnections (cognitive structures). For some there may be missing or ill-developed cognitive structures, but these deficient cognitive structures may be corrected through mediated experiences, and when the corrections occur they are permanent.

Feuerstein has an exercise called "Organizing the Dots" which involves imposing a structure on a seemingly meaningless random distribution of dots. The exercise calls for the student to find one square and two right triangles in each distribution, by connecting the dots. Finding the shapes in the first two frame distributions is relatively straightforward, but the problems quickly became more difficult as the geometric shapes are more embedded among many dots. Some problem-solving techniques involve looking for the four dots that made the square first. Students discuss what conditions a square had to meet (e.g., equal sides with right angles). Another approach is to look at a dot on the outside of the distribution and check to see if it is the corner of the square. If not, move to the next dot on the outside, and so forth around the distribution. Many of Reisman's generic influences on learning discussed below come into play in successful performance of the dot activity.

Feuerstein developed an assessment method which he calls the "Learning Potential Assessment Device" (LPAD). It is a series of tasks designed to identify those aspects of learning in which the learner is equipped to improve. Using the LPAD, the mediator assesses the difficulties of the learner. Based on the results, the mediator and learner then work together to devise strategies for improvement.

LPAD is a method for assessing the propensity of a student to learn. It differs in both method and philosophy from conventional psychological testing. In conventional psychometrics, the purpose is to obtain an "objective" measure of the students' attainments. In a typical test, the person administering the test is supposed to be passive, giving only a standardized set of instructions and conducting the test in a standardized way. The focus of LPAD is on process and continuous improvement. In the LPAD approach students are given various kinds of puzzles to solve; and they are observed by the assessor who studies not what they do, but rather how they do it. Given a problem to solve, the learner's activities are examined with respect to three phases: 1. Input phase—the taking in of information, 2. Elaboration phase—the analysis of the information, the production of new information and new questions, and 3. Output phase—the production of a result. Note the similarity to the creative problem-solving process (identifying the *real* problem, generating possible solutions, selecting and trying a solution, and evaluating the result) as well as Reisman's Heuristic Diagnostic Teaching model discussed below.

For each phase Feuerstein identified a set of "cognitive deficiencies". There are eight commonly found difficulties during input; for example, blurred and sweeping perception; unplanned, impulsive and unsystematic exploratory behavior; and lack of, or impaired receptive verbal tools that affect discrimination (e.g., objects, events and relationships are not labeled).

Tests are given and the observer is taught to recognize when one or more of these cognitive deficiencies is observed. The mediator then develops exercises and activities to alleviate the deficiency as in Feuerstein's LPAD. For example, suppose that unplanned, impulsive and unsystematic exploratory behavior is thought to be present. One of the reasons people will engage in a random approach to solving their problem is that they do not have a clear view of the problem; that is, the learner does not have a clear goal. Without a clear goal, the learner does not know what he or she is trying to do and cannot fashion a plan to do it. Thus, the mediator models planning behavior for the learner.

Table 26.2 shows a series of thinking skills and a comparison of unproductive and improved performance. These thinking skills underlie a series of assessment instruments devised by Feuerstein. The Feuerstein Instrumental Enrichment program (www.umanitoba.ca/unevoc/conference/papers/getz.pdf) contains more than 500 pages of paper and pencil exercises divided into 15 assessment instruments including the following:

- *Nonverbal instruments* are Organization of Dots, Analytic Perception, and Illustrations
- *Instruments that have limited vocabulary* and may therefore require teacher assistance in reading the directions are Orientation in

TABLE 26.2   **Instrumental Enrichment and Mediated Learning Experience: Thinking Skills Improvement**

Thinking Skills	Unproductive Performance	Improved Performance
Able to find relationships between objects or events	Does not understand relationships including spatial and temporal; solves problems by trial and error	Uses a planned problem solving approach
Able to organize data into categories	Cannot group objects by attributes	Can classify by a given attribute
Able to compare and contrast	Does not look for relationships	Can make connections between like and unlike phenomena
Able to divide a whole into its parts as well as integrate (joining parts into a whole)	Does not see interrelationships, differences, and distinctions; can't see the whole from its parts	Uses cognitive strategies (see generic cognitive influences below) for differentiation and integration
Ability to resist impulsivity when encountering tasks	Comes to premature closure regarding listening to instructions	Reflects before acting
Uses language with precision	Language not precise; does not follow instructions	Seeks clarification of instructions

Space I–III, Comparisons, Family Relations, Numerical Progression, and Syllogisms

• *Instruments that need independent reading and comprehension skills* are Categorization, Instructions, Temporal Relations, Transitive Relations, and Representational Stencil Designs

The fundamental theory underlying mediated learning is that cognitive functions appear as a result of mediation and they are associated with real changes in neural connections. Feuerstein refers to very fundamental cognitive functions out of which thinking skills are built. They may be absent because parents did not help the child acquire them, or because of brain damage or illness, because of alcohol or drugs. Feuerstein listed 50 mediation strategies including: mediated focusing, selection of stimuli, imitation, repetition, reinforcement and reward, verbal stimulation, recall of short-and long-term memory. Others include mediation of assuming responsibility, of shared responsibility, of cause-and-effect relationships, of discrimination and sequencing, of spatial and temporal orientation; mediated fostering of a sense of completion; mediation of directing attention, of deductive and inductive reasoning, of developing inferential thinking, of problem-solving strategies, and mediation of systematic exploration (Feuerstein, 1980).

Mediation differs from ordinary teaching in a number of ways. In mediated learning the mediator pays very close attention to how the learner is learning and administers various tests to ascertain which functions may be absent. One of the tests involves a matrix of four figures. Only three of the figures are shown and the task is for the learner to select from among a set of six or more possible shapes, of which one logically will fit into the missing space. They differ in shape, color, number of elements, size, line thickness, and so on. When a youngster would pick out one of the possibilities, Feuerstein would note how he used his eyes. Did he just pick out the first one he saw? Did he look at all of them carefully before picking one? When he picked out the correct one, Feuerstein would ask him what was wrong with another one. If the boy said, "It is green," Feuerstein would say, "It is the wrong color, isn't it?" If the boy persisted in saying, "green," Feuerstein would not let it pass but would insist that the boy use the word "color." Color is a concept at a higher level of abstraction and Feuerstein's theory says that one of the cognitive deficiencies is lack of vocabulary. If a person does not have a vocabulary that includes names of classifications, that person will not be able to reason about elements of a class. Dr. Feuerstein, therefore, insisted on the students saying "size" and not just "bigger", on saying "shape" instead of "circle" or "square". The first two of Reisman's Generic Influences on Learning presented below also acknowledge the importance of vocabulary and symbols on abstract learning.

A pedagogy that has many of the features of Feuerstein's mediated instruction is *direct instruction*, a set of procedures for actively involving students in academic learning (Christenson, Ysseldyke, & Thurlow, 1989; Rosenshine, 1976; Rosenshine & Stevens, 1986). Direct instruction is teacher-led and characterized by (a) explicit performance expectations, (b) systematic prompting, (c) structured practice, (d) monitoring of achievement, and (e) reinforcement and corrective feedback. Furthermore, research indicates that direct instruction has been effective when used to teach math skills to older students with LD (e.g., Perkins & Cullinan, 1985; Rivera & Smith, 1988).

Generic Influences on Learning

In addition to knowing the content to be taught, these interventions focus on another aspect of quality instruction: knowing the learner. Here Reisman and Payne, 1987; Reisman 2008a has incorporated the notion of *Generic Influences on Learning* (Table 26.3) as a tool for profiling a student's strengths and weaknesses in various domains: cognitive including creative strengths, social, emotional, physical/sensory, and psychomotor. To learn correct conceptualizations, students must be taught which attributes are relevant and which are irrelevant. The major cognitive generic influence involved in the examples below (dealing with abstracting the concept of thickness of blocks and of needing to ignore irrelevant cue words) would be ability to attend to salient aspects of a situation. "Ability to attend to salient aspects of a situation" refers to the ability to notice the important and most relevant aspect(s) or attribute(s) of a situation and simultaneously disregard extraneous cues; the ability to attend to detail and to differentiate the essential from the nonessential (e.g., to select the attribute of thickness of blocks when given blocks of various color, shape, size, and thickness when asked to pick out the thinnest blocks—as shown in Figure 26.1).

Another illustration of not attending to salient features is the frequent use of cue words in story problems (Carpenter, Matthews, Linquist, & Silver, 1984; Nesher, 1976; Wright, 1968). Although these words frequently appear in story problems and supposedly indicate the correct operation, they often are not relevant and indeed

FIGURE 26.1   Attribute Blocks.

misleading to the solution of the problem. Unfortunately, many low-achieving students learn to depend on cue words instead of attending to the more critical information presented in the problem such as *what is wanted, what is given*, and based on this, *what operation is appropriate*. Often what appear as cues end up as inhibitors to arriving at the solution. For example, in the problem: *"How many more blocks does Jane walk than John if Jane walks 12 and John walks 9?"* This actually is a comparison subtraction problem but the key word *more* leads students to add.

This generic influence of attending to salient features of a situation also is key in Piaget's conservation tasks where perceptual aspects of a task lead the nonconserver to the wrong answer. For example, in the conservation of number task (Figure 26.2) where the child is shown two parallel linear groups with six objects (coins, raisins, blocks, etc.) in each group, once it is agreed that there is the same number of objects in each group (example A), one group is spread out (example B). The conserver notices that although more space is now taken up, nothing was added or taken away and therefore the number stays the same. The nonconserver will claim that there are more in the stretched out group. A variation of this task is to keep the endpoints the same but insert more objects (as shown in example C). The non conserver will say the two rows have the same number of objects as they are focusing on the

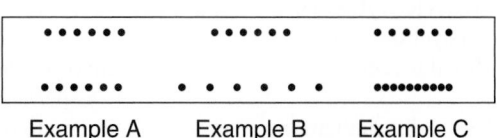

Example A   Example B   Example C

FIGURE 26.2   Piaget's Conservation of Number Task.

TABLE 26.3 Generic Influences on Learning

Generic Influence Cognitive	Description
Ability to learn symbol systems and arbitrary associations	Refers to communication of thoughts through a conventional system of signs or symbols that simultaneously are understood by the sender and the receiver.
Size of vocabulary compared to peers	Refers to the number of words a student understands and uses as well as the number of different meanings and nuances for a given word.
Ability to form relationships, concepts, and generalizations	Refers to the psychological nature of the content that is being learned. For example, constructing one-to-one correspondence is forming a relationship; abstracting the number property (three from a set of three objects forms a concept); and putting two or more concepts together into some kind of relationship forms a generalization (e.g., combine the concepts two and three into an addition relationship).
Use of problem-solving strategies	Refers to a systematic organized approach to tasks as compared to those who flounder randomly, never moving beyond a trial and error approach.
Ability to make decisions and judgments	Involves recognizing salient aspects of a situation, using important information given, being aware of missing information, abstracting essential from nonessential details, evaluating relationships embedded in a situation, and making choices among alternatives.
Ability to draw inferences, conclusions, and hypothesize	Involves generating a set of possible alternatives, dealing with future ideas, and making judgments according to a set of criteria.
Ability in general to abstract and to cope with complexity	Includes classifying objects or ideas, finding logical relationships or analogies, performing simple operations of logical deductions, and using similes and metaphors.
Creativity	Includes originality, fluency, and flexibility of ideas generated; resistance to premature closure (i.e., keep an open mind), elaboration (both verbal and figural), risk taking, humor, courage . . .
Rate and amount of learning compared to age peers	Refers to the length of time taken to learn a given amount of material in relationship to other members of a similar age group.
Speed of learning related to specific content	Involves consideration of a student's strengths and weaknesses in particular learning tasks such as verbal comprehension (e.g., reading and listening), perceptual organization (e.g., puzzles, geometry, spelling), numerical reasoning (e.g., mathematics).
Ability to retain information	Refers to tasks that utilize memory such as repeating digits, obeying simple commands, role counting, or naming the days of the week.
Need for repetition	Refers to the amount of practice necessary for mastery.
Facility with verbal skills	Involve tasks such as comprehending and producing written and spoken words and sentences.
Generic Influence Psychomotor	
Visual perception	Involves the child's understanding the world through visual experience—through what he or she sees.
Visual discrimination	Refers to the ability to perceive the difference between two similar visual symbols (e.g., + and ×, − and ÷, 6 and 9, 3 and E).
Visual field dependence/field independence	Refers to the ability to separate figure from the background (i.e., to screen out irrelevant visual stimuli).

TABLE 26.3 *(Continued)*

Generic Influence Cognitive	Description
Visual form constancy	Involves the ability to recognize a visual stimulus when it appears in different spatial positions on is slightly different forms (e.g., the digit 5 placed around the classroom in different size of color representations).
Visual-sequential memory	Involves the ability to process or recall a series of visual stimuli in sequential memory (e.g. saying alphabet of digits 0–9 in a counting order)
Auditory perception	Involves the child's understanding the world through auditory experience—through what he or she hears.
Auditory discrimination	Refers to the ability to perceive the difference between two similar auditory symbols (e.g., child with a problem in this area might draw hair instead of a chair, or child gets in instead of on a box).
Auditory field dependence/field independence	Refers to the ability to screen out irrelevant auditory stimuli and focus upon the primary auditory message (e.g., child with a problem in this area cannot concentrate on what the teacher is saying in the classroom because of noises outside).
Auditory form constancy	Is the ability to recognize sounds spoken by different people or presented in different environments (e.g., recognizing the sound of a train on a recording, understanding language when spoken with a dialect different from what the student is accustomed to).
Auditory-sequential memory	Involves the ability to process or recall a series of auditory events in order (e.g., repeat telephone number, retell a story, name the days of the week in order).
Ability to form rules (phonological, morphological, syntactical, semantic)	Involves interpretation and expression of combinations of sounds inflectional endings, word order, and word meaning.
Generic Influence Physical and Sensory	
Physical impairments	Include cardiac conditions, diabetes, epilepsy, rheumatic fever, cerebral palsy, muscular dystrophy, etc.
Low vitality and fatigue	May result from chronic medical problems and from effects of medication.
Sensory limitation	Includes blindness and hearing and speech impairment.
Generic Influence Emotional	
Feeling afraid, anxious, frustrated, joyous, angry, surprised	Involve conscious experience that can be communicated to another person.
Becoming overly upset, moody, sad, happy	Represent extremes of emotion that one learns to control under normative development.
Generic Influence Social	
Rules of conduct, moral codes values, customs	Involve being able to relate well to peers and adults.
Modeling other's behavior	Can be positive if acceptable behavior is modeled.
Being aware of cues in the environment	Involves knowing when to quiet down, when to speak up, responding appropriately to others behavior.
Relating to and interacting with other people	Includes cooperation and consideration.
Using diplomacy	Includes tactfulness.
Understanding another's point of view and empathizing	Includes having an emotional as well as a cognitive view of another's needs.

distance between the two endpoints instead of the number of objects.

Secondary students must learn to deal with complex notations, operations, and problem-solving strategies. Complexity is sometimes related to the level of abstraction the student must deal with; it may also be related to understanding the relationships between associated concepts. These situations involve several cognitive generic influences on learning. Additional generic factors that affect learning (and in particular learning by youngsters with special educational needs) include psychomotor, emotional, social, physical and sensory.

Instruction should be designed in light of where a student falls on continua that represent extremes of each generic influence. For example, as a result of diagnostic observation on the part of the instructor, does the student demonstrate ability to cope with complexity with ease, average, with difficulty, not at all? Therefore, to what extent must a problem be broken into parts or simplified to lessen the complexity? Does the youngster notice salient aspects of situations or is cueing necessary?

Heuristic Diagnostic Teaching

Reisman & Kauffman (1980) talk about *heuristic diagnostic teaching* as a pedagogy. Heuristic diagnostic teaching is the opposite of the linear medical model of diagnose-prescribe-remediate. Instead, heuristic diagnostic teaching is a continuous feedback model that allows for ongoing modification where content knowledge and the appropriate pedagogy are synthesized into a system of and use of reflective techniques such as metacognition to enhance performance. Metacognition is being aware of and evaluating one's own thinking during learning. Research shows that metacognition is an effective heuristic.

Heuristic diagnostic teaching requires that teachers understand learners as whole persons—not just as mathematics students. Instructors must be aware of and take into consideration such things as socioeconomic status, gender, ethnicity, culture, motivation, and language facility. Teaching diagnostically involves the following: a) recognizing generic learner characteristics or influences on learning including learning and engagement styles, b) having in-depth command of the content to be taught, c) assessing where students' learning gaps occur, and d) using a repertoire of instructional strategies appropriate to the learner's characteristics and the content to be taught.

Students learn in many ways—by seeing and hearing, reflecting and acting, reasoning logically and intuitively, memorizing and visualizing. Teaching methods also vary. Some instructors lecture, others demonstrate or discuss; some focus on rules and others on examples; some emphasize memory and others understanding. How much a given student learns in a class is governed in part by that student's native ability and prior preparation, but also by the compatibility of his or her characteristic approach to learning and the instructor's characteristic approach to teaching.

Learning Styles

The ways in which an individual characteristically acquires, retains, and retrieves information are collectively termed the individual's *learning style*. Over 30 learning style assessment instruments have been developed in the past three decades (Guild & Garger, 1985). Table 26.4 shows how Sternberg & Grigorenko (1997) characterized "learning styles" as individual preferences for how to learn.

Engagement Styles

Engagement styles also need to be considered, and they are different from learning styles. Engagement styles in this context involve responding to instruction. Early studies relied upon *time-on-task* in assessing student engagement (e.g., Fisher et al., 1980; McIntyre, Copenhaver, Byrd, & Norris, 1983; Brophy, 1983). More recently, however, at least two other definitions have emerged (Nystrand & Gamoran, 1992). One focuses on the learner's willingness to participate in routine school activities, class attendance and participation, and handing in homework and other assignments; the other spotlights cognitive and affective evidence of student engagement. Skinner & Belmont (1993) proposed that engagement refers to the intensity and emotional quality of children's involvement in initiating and carrying out learning activities. Children who are engaged show sustained involvement in learning activities. They demonstrate positive emotions such as enthusiasm, optimism, curiosity, and interest. The opposite of engagement is disaffection. Disaffected children are passive, do not try hard, and give up easily in the face of challenges, appear bored, depressed, anxious, or even angry; they can be withdrawn and are sometimes rebellious towards teachers and classmates. Mathematics related thinking

TABLE 26.4   **Summary of Learning Styles**

Learning Style	Dichotomy	Proponent	Characteristics
Sensing	Intuitive	Jung (1971)	*Sensing* involves observing, gathering data through the senses (concrete and methodical); *intuition* involves indirect perception by way of the subconscious—accessing memory, speculating, imagining (abstract and imaginative).
Visual	Verbal	Dunn, Dunn, & Price (1978)	*Visual learners* prefer that information be presented visually—in pictures, diagrams, flow charts, time lines, films, and demonstrations—rather than in spoken or written words. *Verbal learners* prefer spoken or written explanations to visual presentations.
Active	Reflective	Kolb (1984)	*Active learners* learn well in situations that enable them to do something physical; *reflective learners* learn well in situations that provide them with opportunities to think about the information being presented.
Sequential	Global	Oxford (1990)	*Sequential learners* absorb information and acquire understanding of material in small connected chunks; *global learners* take in information in seemingly unconnected fragments and achieve understanding in large holistic leaps.
Inductive	Deductive	Glaser (1984)	*Induction* is a reasoning progression that proceeds from particulars (observations, measurements, data) to generalities (rules, laws, theories). *Deduction* proceeds in the opposite direction where one starts with axioms, principles, or rules, deduces consequences, and formulates applications.

processes that involve engagement are presented in Table 26.5.

Practice

Another flaw in instruction, especially for students having problems with math, is a lack of systematic practice once a concept is learned. Practice is the consolidation phase of learning and should follow activities involving inquiry, manipulation with concrete objects that are the physical representation of a math idea, and creative problem solving.

Practice activities are essential components of mathematics instructional programs. Students with LD will generally need more practice and practice that is better designed than students without LD, if they are to achieve adequate levels of fluency and retention (Carnine, 1989; Garnett, 1998). Practice should motivate students' attentiveness to the practice activity which is as crucial as time spent on the practice. Distributed practice such as two 15-minute daily sessions, rather than an hour session every other day is suggested. Also, helpful practice consists of the commutative property for addition and multiplication (e.g., $3 + 2 = 5$ and $2 + 3 = 5$; $4 \times 2 = 8$ and $2 \times 4 = 8$) and inverses (e.g., $8 \div 4 = 2$ and $8 \div 2 = 4$) where students keep track of how many and which facts are mastered and how many more there are to go by filling in grids as the shown in Table 26.6 (Reisman, 2008a). A grid comprised of the basic addition facts 6–9, as in the Addition/Subtraction grid, show which facts need further study. Thus, a student may fill in the majority of cells in the grid correctly and then need to focus on learning only those missed. The next grid would include only those facts missed.

Table 26.7 shows a multiplication/division grid that not only provides practice but also is a vehicle for discovering patterns (e.g., square numbers—4, 16, 25, etc.; the multiplicative identity—1; the role of zero in multiplication,

TABLE 26.5 Mathematics Thinking Processes and Illustrations of Each

Thinking Process	Illustration
Applying what was learned	Students demonstrate and deepen their understanding of basic mathematics knowledge and skills through contextual learning in such settings as sports, classroom store, concrete measurements, music and art, etc.
Solving problems	Recognize and investigate problems; formulate and propose solutions supported by explanation. Solving problems is at the heart of "doing mathematics," i.e., apply knowledge of numbers, symbols, operations, measurement, algebraic approaches, geometric concepts and relationships, and data analysis.
Express and interpret information	The ability to shift between verbal, graphical, numerical and symbolic modes of representing a problem.
Represent information, using technology	Technology provides a means to carry out operations with speed and accuracy; to display, store and retrieve information and results; and to explore and extend knowledge. The technology of paper and pencil is appropriate in many mathematical situations. In many other situations, calculators or computers are required to find answers or create images.
Applying individual knowledge and skills while working on teams	Working in teams allows students to share ideas, to develop and coordinate group approaches to problems, and to share and learn from each other in communicating findings.
Making connections	Mathematics provides a language for expressing ideas across disciplines, while, at the same time, providing connections linking number and operation, measurement, geometry, data and algebra within mathematics itself.

TABLE 26.6 Selected Basic Facts Addition Grid

+	6	7	8	9
6		13	14	15
7	13		15	16
8	14	15		17
9	15	16	17	

and the inverse relation between multiplication and division). This grid, in addition to serving as a nice practice activity, also allows LD students to exercise their creativity in discovering patterns within the grid.

Assessing Mathematics Disability

Use of interviews and assessment instruments serve for noting details in how the learner processes information, problem solves, and feels about mathematics. A mathematics interview should include the use of manipulatives (i.e., coins, base-ten blocks, Cuisenaire rods, place value charts, clock face, etc.). A calculator is an important tool and can be used to uncover the difference between comprehension and computation difficulties. The interview should reveal a full range of mathematical thinking including computation, making predictions based upon patterns, sorting, copying complex figures involving spatial relationships, and attitudes about math and one's competence in doing math. Note whether the child talks to him or herself, whether they use aids such as drawings, do they salivate profusely as the perceived pressure increases, do they move around or sit still in their chair, do they become flushed, do they persevere or give up? These observations yield information concerning how to individualize mathematics instruction.

vii. NATIONAL AND STATE MATHEMATICS STANDARDS AND ASSESSMENTS

The spotlight on mathematics standards and assessment was triggered by the politically motivated and extremely controversial legislation entitled No Child Left Behind (NCLB) Act of 2001. The following excerpt from the website

TABLE 26.7   **Basic Multiplication/Division Facts Grid**

×/÷	0	1	2	3	4	5	6	7	8	9
0	**0**		**0**			**0**				
1		**1**	2			5				
2	0	**2**	**4**	6	8	10	12	14	16	18
3			6	**9**		15				
4			8		**16**	20				
5	0	**5**	10	15	20	**25**	30	35	40	45
6			12			30	**36**			
7			14			35		**49**		
8			16			40	48		**64**	
9			18			45				**81**

homepage for No Child Left Behind, which is the revised Elementary and Secondary Education Act, explains the substance of the law:

> The law sets deadlines for states to expand the scope and frequency of student testing, revamp their accountability systems and guarantee that every teacher is qualified in their subject area. NCLB requires states to make demonstrable annual progress in raising the percentage of students proficient in reading and math, and in narrowing the test-score gap between advantaged and disadvantaged students.

The premier framework for national mathematics standards were those presented by the National Council of Teachers of Mathematics (NCTM) entitled *Curriculum and Evaluation Standards for School Mathematics* (1989). States incorporated these NCTM standards into their mathematics curriculum as did some textbook and test publishers.

Simultaneously, educators have come to the conclusion that traditional standardized achievement testing does not provide adequate information for solving instructional problems, and that a greater emphasis should be placed on data from functional or curriculum-based measurements (Reschly, 1992). Assessments that use the various mathematics standards as the structure satisfy this emphasis. A grades 1 through 2 Diagnostic Mathematics Assessment (DMA) (Reisman, 2008, 2008a, 2009) which is structured on the overlapping mathematics standards of three state, one national, and one international mathematics assessment, as well as The NCTM Focal Points (which suggest a focus on only three topics at grades K–8), is representative of mathematics standards used throughout the United States. The standards that were common across the NCTM, NAEP, Pennsylvania, Illinois, and California (and the NCTM Focal Points) form the framework of objectives that underlie the DMA items. Also incorporated are items that require the test taker to use their creativity. Following in Tables 26.8 and 26.9 are selected examples from the grades 1 and 2 Diagnostic Mathematics Assessment (DMA). The grade-level goals are as follows:

Goal: By the end of grade 1, students understand and use the concept of "ones" and "tens" in the place value number system. Students add and subtract small numbers with ease. They measure with simple units and locate objects in space. They describe data and analyze and solve simple problem situations.

Goal: By the end of second grade, students deepen their understanding of place value and their understanding of and skill with addition, subtraction, multiplication, and division of whole numbers. Students estimate, measure, and describe objects in space. They use patterns to help solve problems. They represent number relationships and conduct simple probability experiments.

SUMMARY

This chapter has presented factors that affect mathematics learning in terms of math content and pedagogy, creativity, math anxiety, self-efficacy, quality of mathematics instruction, intervention theories, and national and state mathematics standards and assessments. Strategies for enhancing practice were presented. Additional methods for circumventing math problems include helping students to visualize math

TABLE 26.8 Grade 1 DMA Overlap Standards

Strand	Standard	Objective	Sample Item
NS: Number Sense	NS1. Students understand and use numbers up to 100	NS1.1. Count, read, and write whole numbers to 100.	Mark the number of buttons on the calculator by filling in the circle under it. 6 9 3 5 ○ ○ ○ ○
	NS2. Students demonstrate the meaning of addition and subtraction and use these operations to solve problems	NS2.1. Know the addition facts (sums to 20) and the corresponding subtraction facts and commit them to memory.	Mark the sum for 3 + 4 *by* filling in the circle under it. 6 7 8 9 ○ ○ ○ ○
	NS3. Students use estimation strategies in computation and problem solving that involve numbers that use the ones, tens, and hundreds places	NS3.1. Make reasonable estimates when comparing larger or smaller numbers.	Mark the estimate for spending four dollars and ninety-five cents by filling in the circle under it. $4.00 $5.00 $4.25 $4.50 ○ ○ ○ ○
AF: Algebra and Functions	AF1. Students use number sentences with operational symbols and expressions to solve problem	AF1.1.Write and solve number sentences from problem situations that express relationships involving addition and subtraction.	Mark how to solve this problem by filling in the circle under it. Nan has three dogs. Barbara has two dogs. How many more dogs does Nan have? 3−?=5 3+?=5 5+3=? 3−2=1 ○ ○ ○ ○

Strand	Standard	Sub-standard	Test Item
MG: Measurement and Geometry	MG1. Students use direct comparison and nonstandard units to describe the measurements of objects		Mark the smallest box by filling in the circle under it.
STAT: Statistics, Data Analysis, and Probability	STAT1. Students organize, represent, and compare data by category on simple graphs and charts	STAT1.1 Sort objects and data by common attributes and describe the categories.	Mark the picture of the *fastest transportation* by filling in the circle under it.
MR: Mathematical Reasoning	MR1. Students make decisions about how to set up a problem	MR1.2 Use tools, such as manipulatives or sketches, to model problems.	Mark the best way to solve word problems by filling in the circle under it. read aloud / draw what the problem says / ask your teacher / ask a friend
		MR1.1 Determine the approach, materials, and strategies to be used.	
	MR2. Students solve problems and justify their reasoning	MR2.1 Select the best representation of a problem.	Mark the best drawing to model the problem by filling in the circle under it. Mary had three cats and Sally had two. How many cats did both girls have?

TABLE 26.9   Grade 2 DMA Overlap Standards

Strand	Standard	Objective	Sample Item
Number Sense	NS1.0 Students understand place value concepts of whole numbers	NS1.2 Compare and order whole numbers to 10,000.	Mark the correct statement by filling in the circle under it. 6<4 79>70 99999<10,000 999<100 o o o o
	NS2.0 Students calculate and solve problems involving addition, subtraction, multiplication, and division	NS2.3 Use the inverse relationship of addition and subtraction to compute and check results. NS2.9 Solve one- and two-step problems involving whole numbers, fractions and decimals using addition, subtraction, multiplication and division.	Mark how you could use a problem below to check for the following problem by filling in the circle under it. 68 − 41 = 27 68+27 41−27 27+41 68+41 o o o o David and Tom shared 12 cookies. David ate 1/3 of the cookies and Tom ate 1/4 of the cookies. How many cookies did they eat in all? Mark how many cookies both students ate by filling in the circle under it. 7 15 1/7 1/12 o o o o
Algebra and Functions	AF1.0 Students select appropriate symbols, operations and properties to represent, describe, simplify, and solve simple number relationships	AF1.3 Select appropriate operational and relational symbols to make an expression true (e.g., 4 __ 3 = 12, what operation symbol goes in the blank?).	Mark the sign for *seven is less than eight* by filling in the circle under it. ≤ # ≠ < o o o o
Measurement and Geometry	MG1.0 Students choose and use appropriate units and measurement tools to quantify the properties of objects	MG1.3 Find the perimeter of a polygon with integer sides.	Mark the perimeter of the following shape that has sides which measure 3, 5, and 8 by filling in the circle under it. Remember there are 4 sides. 19 16 24 21 13 o o o o o

| | MG2.0 Students describe and compare the attributes of plane and solid geometric figures and use their understanding to show relationships and solve problems | MG2.1 Identify, describe, and classify polygons (including pentagons, hexagons, and octagons). | Mark the *hexagon* by filling in the circle under it.

○ ○ ○ ○ |
| Statistics, Data Analysis, and Probability | STAT1.0 Students conduct simple probability experiments by determining the number of possible outcomes and make simple predictions | 1.1 Identify whether common events are certain, likely, unlikely, or improbable. | A bag of marbles contains 3 green, 5 red, 8 blue, and 7 yellow marbles. If you pick one marble without looking, mark which is the least likely color you would pick by filling in the circle under it.

green   red   blue   yellow
○ |
| Mathematical Reasoning | MR1.0 Students make decisions about how to approach problem | MR1.1 Analyze problems by identifying relationships, distinguishing relevant from irrelevant information, sequencing and prioritizing information, and observing patterns. | Mark how to solve this problem by filling in the circle under it.
Keesha left her home and walked 3 miles and stopped to rest. Then she walked 5 miles more. How many more miles does she have to walk to reach her grandmother's house which is 12 miles from her home?

Add   Subtract   Add and Subtract   Add and divide
○   ○   ○   ○ |

565

problems by drawing; giving extra time for students to process any visual information in a picture, chart, or graph, using visual and auditory examples; using real-life situations that make problems functional and applicable to everyday life; performing math problems on graph paper to keep the numbers in line; using uncluttered worksheets to avoid too much visual information; using rhythm or music to help students memorize; using distributive practice; and encouraging students to track their progress (e.g., what they know and what they need to learn).

There may be more learning disabled students in a math class than is appreciated. Signs may include reading numbers backwards, problem telling time, difficulty remembering basic facts, algorithms, and equations, and difficulty forming concepts. It is important to make sure that the cause of math problems are recognized—are they related to generic influences on learning, engagement styles, low self-efficacy, inadequate instruction, or a combination of these forces? The heuristic diagnostic teaching approach helps focus on cause while Feuerstein's mediated learning provides some ideas on instruction. The challenges for the student having problems learning mathematics include questioning when he or she does not understand something until they do "get it," knowing that just because a parent or other relative was not a good math student doesn't mean it's hereditary, and seeking out someone (e.g., teacher, friend, relative) who can help.

REFERENCES

Algozzine, B., O'Shea, D. J., Crews, W. B., & Stoddard, K. (1987). Analysis of mathematics competence of learning disabled adolescents. *Journal of Special Education, 21*, 97–107.

Bandura, A. (1986). *Social foundations of thought and action: A social cognitive theory*. Englewoods Cliffs, NJ: Prentice Hall.

Bandura, A. (1993). *Perceived self-efficacy in cognitive development and functioning*. Lawrence Erlbaum Associates, Inc.

Betz, N. (1978). Prevalence, distribution, and correlates of math anxiety in college students. *Journal of Counseling Psychology, 25*(5), 441–48.

Brophy, J. (1983). Conceptualizing student motivation. *Educational Psychologist, 18*, 200–215.

Carnine, D. (1989). Designing practice activities. *Journal of Learning Disabilities, 22*, 603–607.

Carnine, D. (1992). Expanding the notion of teachers' rights: Access to tools that work. *Journal of Applied Behavior Analysis, 25*, 13–19.

Carpenter, R. L. (1985). Mathematics instruction in resource rooms. *Learning Disability Quarterly, 8*, 95–100.

Carpenter, T. P., Matthews, W., Linquist, M. M., & Silver, E. A. (1984). Achievement in mathematics: Results from the national assessment. *Elementary School Journal, 84*, 485–495.

Cawley, J. F., Fitzmaurice, A. M., Shaw, R., Kahn, H., & Bates, H., III. (1979). LD youth and mathematics: A review of characteristics. *Learning Disability Quarterly, 2*(1), 29–44.

Cawley, J. F., & Miller, J. H. (1989). Crosssectional comparisons of the mathematical performance of children with learning disabilities: Are we on the right track toward comprehensive programming? *Journal of Learning Disabilities, 22*, 250–259.

Christenson, S. L., Ysseldyke, J. E., & Thurlow, M. (1989). Critical instructional factors for students with mild handicaps: An integrative review. *Remedial and Special Education, 10*(5), 21–31.

Cobb, P. (1994a). Constructivism in mathematics and science education. *Educational Researcher, 23*(7), 4.

Cobb, P. (1994b). Where is the mind? Constructivist and sociocultural perspectives on mathematical development. *Educational Researcher, 23*(7), 13–20.

Davis, G. (1999). Barriers to creativity and creative attitudes. In M. A. Runco & S. Pritzker (Eds.), *Encyclopedia of creativity* (pp. 165–174). San Diego: CA: Academic Press.

Driver, R., Asoko, H., Leach, J., Mortimer, E., & Scott, P. (1994). Constructing scientific knowledge in the classroom. *Educational Researcher, 23*(7), 512.

Dunn, R, Dunn, K. & Price, G. E. (1978). *Learning Style Inventory*. Lawrence, KS: Price Systems.

Eduction Commission of the States (2001). The No Child Left Behind (NCLB) Act of 2001. http://nc1b2.ecs.org/Projects Centers (accessed June 26, 2008).

Engelmann, S., & Carnine, D. (1982). *Theory of instruction: Principles and applications*. New York: Irvington.

Feuerstein, R. (1980). *Instrumental enrichment*. Baltimore: University Park Press.

Fiore, G. (1999). Math-abused students: Are we prepared to teach them? *Mathematics Teacher, 92*(5), 403–407.

Fisher, C., Berliner, D., Filby, N., Marliave, R., Cahen, L., & Dishaw, M. (1980). Teaching behaviours, academic learning time, and student achievement: An overview. In C. Denham & A. Lieberman (Eds.), *Time to learn*. Washington, D.C.: National Institute of Education.

Fotoples, R. (2000). Overcoming math anxiety. *Kappa Delta Pi Record, 35*(4), 149–51.

Garnett, K. (1998). *Math Learning Disabilities*. Arlington, VA: Journal of Council for Exceptional Children. www.ldonline.org/article/5896.

Gadanidis, G. (1994). Deconstructing constructivism. *Mathematics Teacher, 87*(2), 91–97.

Glaser, R. E. (1984) "Education and Thinking: The Role of Knowledge. *American Psychologist, 39*, 93–104.

Glennon, V. J. (1948). *A Study of the Growth and Mastery of Certain Basic Mathematical Understandings on Seven Educational Levels.* Ed.D. Unphblished dissertation, Harvard University.

Godby, C. (1997). *Mathematics anxiety and the underprepared student.* (Report No. JC 990 063). TN: Middle Tennessee State University (ERIC Document Reproduction Service No. ED 426 734).

Guild, P., & Garger, S. (1985). *Marching to different drummers.* Alexandria, VA: Association for Supervision and Curriculum Development.

Harris, K. R., & Graham, S. (1994). Constructivism: Principles, paradigms, and integration. *Journal of Special Education, 28*, 233–247.

Hasselbring, T. S., Goin, L. T., & Bransford, J. D. (1988). Developing math automaticity in learning handicapped children: The role of computerized drill and practice. *Focus on Exceptional Children, 20*(6), 1–7.

Jackson, C., & Leffingwell, R. (1999). The role of instructors in creating math anxiety in students from kindergarten through college. *Mathematics Teacher, 92*(7), 583–587 (ERIC Document Reproduction Service No. ED 431 628).

Jung, C. G. (1971). *Psychological Types.* London: Routledge & Kegan Paul. (Collected Works of C. G. Jung, Vol. 6).

Kameenui, E. J., & Simmons, D. C. (1990). *Designing instructional strategies: The prevention of academic problems.* Columbus, OH: Merrill.

Kolb, D. A. (1984) *Experiential Learning: Experience as the Source of Learning and Development.* Upper Saddle River, New Jersey: Prentice Hall.

Ma, X. (1999). A meta-analysis of the relationship between anxiety toward mathematics and Achievement in mathematics. *Journal for Research in Mathematics Education, 30*(5). 520–40.

McIntyre, D. J., Copenhaver, R. W., Byrd, D. M., & Norris, W. R. (1983). A study of engaged student behaviour within classroom activities during mathematics class. *Journal of Educational Research, 77*(1), 55–59.

McLeod, T. M. & Armstrong, S. E., (1982). Learning disabilities in mathematics: Skill deficits and remedial approaches at the intermediate and secondary level. *Learning Disability Quarterly, 5*(3), 305–311.

Naramore, V. (1968). *Cognitive Continuity: A Study of the Secondary School Teachers' Knowledge of the Field Properties of Mathematical Systems. Dissertation Abstracts.* Syracuse University.

National Council of Teachers of Mathematics (NCTM) (1995). *Assessment Standards for School Mathematics.* Reston, Va: National Council of Teachers of Mathematics.

Nesher, P. (1976). Three determinants of difficulty in verbal arithmetic problems. *Educational Studies in Mathematics, 7*, 369–388.

Nystrand, M., & Gamoran, A. (1992). Instructional discourse and student engagement. In D. H. Schunk & J. Meece (Eds.), *Student Perceptions in the Classroom* (pp. 149–179). Hillsdale, NJ: Lawrence Erlbaum.

Oxford, R. L. (1990) *Language learning strategies: What every teacher should know.* New York: Newbury House/Harper & Row.

Pajares, F., & Miller, M. D. (1994). Role of self-efficacy and self-concept beliefs in mathematical problem solving: A path analysis. *Journal of Educational Psychology, 86*, 193–203.

Perkins, V., & Cullinan, D. (1985). Effects of direct instruction for fraction skills. *Education and Treatment of Children, 8*, 41–50.

Poplin, M. S. (1988). Holistic/constructivist principles of the teaching/learning process: Implications for the field of learning disabilities. *Journal of Learning Disabilities, 21*, 401–416.

Pressley, M., Harris, K. R., & Marks, M. R. (1992). But good strategy instructors are constructivists! *Educational Psychology Review, 4*, 331.

Reschly, D. J. (1992). Special education decision making and functional/behavioral assessment. In W. Stainback & S. Stainback (Eds.), *Controversial issues confronting special education: Divergent perspectives* (pp. 127–138). Boston: Allyn & Bacon.

Reid, D. K., Kurkjian, C., & Carruthers, S. S. (1994). Special education teachers interpret constructivist teaching. *Remedial and Special Education, 15*, 267–280.

Reisman, F. K. (1972). An Evaluative Study of Cognitive Acceleration in Mathematics in the Early School Years. *ERIC Reports*, Educational Resources Information Center, Washington, D.C.: Document #062207.

Reisman, F. K. (1992). Massive intervention in elementary and middle school mathematics instruction. *Teacher Education in an Era of Global Change.* Arlington, VA: International Council on Education for Teaching (ICET).

Reisman, F.K. (2008). *Diagnostic Mathematics Assessment (DMA) Grade One.* Bensenville, Ill.: Scholastic Testing Service.

Reisman, F.K. (2008a). *Diagnostic Mathematics Assessment (DMA) Grades One & Two: Manual for Instructional Suggestions.* Bensenville, Ill.: Scholastic Testing Service.

Reisman, F.K. (2009). *Diagnostic Mathematics Assessment (DMA) Grade Two.* Bensenville, Ill.: Scholastic Testing Service.

Reisman, F.K., Bach, C. N., Auth, P. C., Batastini, S., Clark, S., Gigli, R. W., Keiser, L. J., Nessler, C. N., & Whitelaw, L. (2002). The future of creativity. In A. G. Aleinkov (Ed.), *Creativity Stems from Divergent Chaotic Crisis (DC²)* pp. 91–112. Bensenville, Ill: Scholastic Testing Service, Inc.,

Reisman, F. K. and Kauffman, S. H. (1980). *Teaching Mathematics to Children with Special Needs.* Columbus, OH: Charles E. Merrill.

Reisman, F. K. and Payne, B. D. (1987). *Elementary education: A basic text.* Columbus, Ohio: Charles E. Merrill.

Reisman, F. K. and Torrance, E. P. (2003). *Learning and using primes, fractions and decimals creatively.* Bensenville, IL: Scholastic Testing Service.

Rivera, D., & Smith, D. D. (1988). Using a demonstration strategy to teach midschool students with learning disabilities how to compute long division. *Journal of Learning Disabilities, 21,* 77–81.

Rosenshine, B. (1976). Classroom instruction. In N. L. Gage (Ed.), *The psychology of teaching methods.* Chicago: University of Chicago Press.

Rosenshine, B., & Stevens, R. (1986). Teaching functions. In M. C. Whittrock (Ed.), *Handbook of research on teaching* (3rd ed., pp. 376–391).

Runco, M. A. (2007). Contrarianism. In M.A. Runco & S. Pritzker, (Eds.), *Encyclopedia of Creativity.* Amsterdam, The Netherlands: Elsevier.

Skinner, E. A & Belmont, M. J. (1993). Motivation in the classroom: Reciprocal effects of teacher behaviour and student engagement across the school year. *Journal of Educational Psychology, 85*(4), 571–581.

Steele, E. & Arth, A. (1998). Lowering anxiety in the math curriculum. *Education Digest, 63*(7), 18–24.

Sternberg, R. J. & Grigorenko, E. L. (1997). Are Cognitive Styles Still in Style? *American Psychologist, 52,* 1997.

Tobias, S. (1990). Math anxiety: An update. *NACADA Journal, 10*(1), 47–50.

Tobias, S. (1993). *Overcoming Math Anxiety.* New York: W. W. Norton.

Torrance, E. P. (1963). The creative personality and the ideal pupil. *Teacher college record, 65,* 220–226.

Torrance, E. P. (1974). *Torrance tests of creative thinking.* Bensenville, IL: Scholastic Testing Service.

Torrance, E. P. and Reisman, F. K. (2000a). *Learning to use place value creatively.* Bensenville, IL: Scholastic Testing Service.

Torrance, E. P. and Reisman, F. K. (2000b). *Learning to solve mathematics word problems creatively.* Bensenville, IL: Scholastic Testing Service.

Whitelaw, L. A. (2007). *An evaluative study of teacher creativity, use of the heuristic diagnostic teaching process and student mathematics performance.* Unpublished Doctoral dissertation, Drexel University.

Wright, J. P. (1968). A study of children's performance on verbally stated problems containing word clues and omitting them. *Dissertation Abstracts International, 29,* 1770B.

CHAPTER 27

EVIDENCE-BASED APPROACHES TO WORKING WITH CHILDREN WITH DISRUPTIVE BEHAVIOR

RICHARD J. COWAN
Kent State University

SUSAN M. SHERIDAN
University of Nebraska–Lincoln

The education of children is perhaps one of the most complex challenges faced by educators, parents and community partners. In addition to helping ensure that children are successful in academic content areas (e.g., reading, mathematics, written communication, science, government, health, art), the educational system has been assigned the role of teaching children to "use their minds such that they are prepared for responsible citizenship, further learning, and productive employment" (*Goals 2000: Educate America Act*, 1994, H.R. 1804, Sec. 102). The school setting is viewed as a place for educating children about the core academic curriculum, for socializing children, and for helping children overcome challenging behavior so they are able to maximize their learning within the educational setting and grow up to be responsible, productive citizens. Educating children involves teaching and reinforcing specific academic, social and behavioral skills and providing children with multiple opportunities to use these skills in applied settings (Alberto & Troutman, 2006). The education of children also relies on careful manipulation of the environment, including the application of strategies to enhance learning while simultaneously controlling disruptive behaviors that may hinder one or more child's academic success. Structuring the learning environment to maximize learning for all students is a goal shared by parents and educators alike (Christenson & Sheridan, 2001; Ysseldyke & Christenson, 2002).

There are two major pieces of legislation that govern the education of children within the public school system: the Individuals with Disabilities Education Improvement Act (IDEA, 2004), and No Child Left Behind (NCLB, 2002). The Individuals with Disabilities Education Improvement Act outlines the obligation of educators and related professionals to intervene regarding behaviors that are disruptive to the education of either the student receiving special education services (i.e., a child identified as having a specific disability), or his/her peers in the classroom. In addition, IDEA outlines the eligibility criteria for 13 distinct disability categories. Although disruptive behaviors may be associated with any of the specific disability categories, the following categories are most likely to be associated with behaviors that interfere with the educational process: mental retardation, emotional disturbance, autism, traumatic brain injury, other health impairment (e.g., attention-deficit/hyperactivity disorder), specific learning disabilities, and developmental delay. Of these categories, emotional disturbance (ED; also referred to as severe emotional disturbance, or SED) is most often cited as linked to behavioral excesses (i.e., disruptive behaviors) and deficits (i.e., failure to gain meaningful social relationships) that interfere with learning. No Child Left Behind, derived from Goals 2000, mandates that public schools provide data regarding the academic progress of all students, including children with and without specific disabilities.

A complete review of IDEA and NCLB is beyond the scope and purpose of this chapter; however, these federal laws are described here because they (a) contain language about enhancing the overall quality of education for students, and (b) have been interpreted to reflect account-ability regarding both academic and behavioral performance. In addition, these laws build on the foundation of objectives identified in Goals 2000: Educate America Act (1994). Upon consideration of these major legislative acts, it is clear that the educational system is responsible for *all* children, and that educators must effectively intervene with challenging behaviors that interfere with or impair a student's ability to experience academic success. This is applicable to children identified as having a specific disability (e.g., children with autism or students designated as emotionally disturbed) as well as children who do not receive special education and related services.

Although this chapter could be structured to describe the application of behavior modification strategies to children with specific disability categories, it does not take that format; rather, it is written to provide an overview of evidence-based approaches to behavior change that are applicable to any child demonstrating behaviors that are impeding his or her academic success. The strategies reviewed here may be implemented for an individual child at the prereferral or posteligibility stage of service delivery; alternatively, they may be implemented at a universal (or primary) level to enhance learning for all students and prevent problem behaviors from further disrupting the educational process. This chapter begins with the definition and brief history of applied behavior analysis (ABA) within the educational system. Here we review the major components and assumptions of ABA as well as provide an overview of its application to behavior in schools. Next we consider positive behavior supports as delivered through universal, targeted and intensive levels of preventive intervention. This discussion is followed by a literature review focusing on evidence-based interventions to enhance positive behaviors and decrease disruptive behaviors in school. The chapter concludes with a discussion of some essential issues related to the behavior modification process.

DEFINITION AND HISTORY OF APPLIED BEHAVIOR ANALYSIS

Definition of Applied Behavior Analysis

Applied behavior analysis (ABA) is a systematic approach to behavior change that involves

observing a behavior, selecting an intervention grounded in behavioral principles, implementing the intervention within a socially relevant setting, and evaluating its impact on the target behavior. Of all the approaches used by educators to address behaviors that interfere with learning, those grounded in applied behavior analysis are considered to have the greatest theoretical and empirical support (Maag, 1999). The ABA approach is *applied* in that it is concerned with behaviors deemed socially valid (i.e., viewed as important by others; Wolf, 1978) as they occur in criterion settings; it is *behavioral* as it focuses on the systematic observation of specific, discrete, observable behaviors over time; and it is *analytic* in that it is concerned with the practice of establishing systematic control of behavior over time such that observed changes in the target behavior may be attributed to the application of a specific, controlled intervention (i.e., independent variable) over time (Baer, Wolf, & Risley, 1968, 1987). The ABA interventionist develops hypotheses regarding the cause of a behavior, systematically manipulates the environment to change those conditions surrounding the behavior (i.e., antecedents and consequences), and allows the data to guide the behavior change process.

Antecedent manipulation is a core feature of ABA. Unfortunately, much of the behavioral literature focuses primarily on the manipulation of consequences to promote behavior change. Perhaps this is because ABA is grounded in the operant conditioning paradigm (see discussion below), which emphasizes the influence of consequences on subsequent behavior. If interventionists rely solely on consequential manipulation, they miss out on multiple opportunities to guide and shape behavior through "setting up" conditions under which the desired behavior is likely to occur. Furthermore, once the desired behavior occurs in part due to antecedent manipulation (e.g., prompting), this provides an opportunity to reinforce the desired behavior, thus further enhancing the likelihood of recurrence. Within the ABA framework, new or replacement behaviors are promoted through providing opportunities to practice the desired behavior (i.e., implementing antecedent strategies such as prompting and coaching) and following the demonstration of behavior with immediate reinforcement (i.e., behavior change is influenced through both antecedent and consequential manipulation). As applied to disruptive behavior, ABA promotes behavior change through changing the environment such that the disruptive behavior is less likely to occur (i.e., antecedent manipulation) and if it occurs, the behavior is followed by the consequence of punishment. Hence, it is critical for school-based practitioners to recognize that ABA considers both antecedent and consequential manipulations in behavior change, and to tap the power of antecedent controls to prevent disruptive behaviors from occurring as well as to enhance desired behavior.

As indicated above, many interventions implemented through ABA methodology are derived from the operant conditioning paradigm (Alberto & Troutman, 2006; Martens, Witt, Daly, & Vollmer, 1999). An assumption of *operant conditioning* is that all behavior—both desirable and undesirable—is learned, and that behavior changes as the result of the consequence of that behavior. Specifically, when a behavior is followed by something perceived as pleasant by the individual, it is more likely to recur; alternatively, when a behavior is followed by something perceived as unpleasant by the individual, it is less likely to recur. When the former occurs, reinforcement is in effect; when the latter occurs, punishment is in effect. Consequences for behavior are classified as either reinforcement or punishment, based on their impact on subsequent behavior. What is reinforcing for one student may be punishing for another, and vice versa. The operant conditioning paradigm is grounded in the assumption that although interventionists are capable of changing others' behavior through the intentional application of reinforcement or punishment (i.e., *intervention*), a significant proportion of learning (i.e., *conditioning*) is the result of unintentional consequences (Alberto & Troutman, 2006). For example, a student may learn to swear in class and disrupt others daily during his least favorite subject if he/she is regularly sent to the principal's office and thus allowed to escape the task he/she finds undesirable. Alternative behaviors may be taught to replace disruptive behaviors through the intentional application of functionally related consequences. For example, in the scenario just described where the student's disruptive behavior was conditioned and maintained through negative reinforcement, an ABA-based intervention would allow the child to escape the required task contingent upon completion of a portion of the assignment rather than as a result of disruptive behavior. If the child increased his/her on-task behavior to escape additional work, negative

reinforcement would be in effect. Escape is a powerful motivator for many children.

In addition to considering the influence of reinforcement on behavior, it is important to consider how punishment affects subsequent behavior. Punishment occurs when there is an observed decrease in the disruptive behavior following a consequence perceived by the individual to be unpleasant (Alberto & Troutman, 2006). Punishment may be either additive (e.g., giving a child more work as a consequence for disruptive behavior) or reductive (e.g., taking away privileges following a disruptive behavior). Although interventionists may intentionally change disruptive behavior through the controlled, systematic application of punishment as an intervention, many disruptive behaviors are learned through the unintentional punishment of desired behaviors (Alberto & Troutman, 2006). For example, if students are punished for raising their hands to get their teacher's attention (i.e., they are told to keep working independently until the end of the instructional period), they are likely to seek an alternative means of getting their teacher's attention (e.g., verbally disrupting the class); if this behavior results in reinforcement (i.e., the teacher answers their questions), they are likely to talk out instead of raising their hand the next time they desire assistance. An ABA-based intervention would be to respond favorably to hand-raising and ignore talking out. Other operant principles that influence behavior include extinction (i.e., behavior is ignored), prompting, and modeling (i.e., behavior is conditioned by the child observing someone else being reinforced for the behavior) (Martens et al., 1999; Miltenberger, 2003). Some disruptive behaviors are related to skill deficits (i.e., the child has not learned a more appropriate behavior that leads to the desired consequence). In terms of planning intervention, skill deficits are qualitatively different from performance deficits. Whereas the functional intervention for skill deficits is to teach the child a positive replacement skill, the functional intervention for performance deficits is to enhance motivation by manipulating antecedent and/or consequential conditions.

Applied behavior analysis relies heavily on functional behavioral assessment (FBA), which involves gathering information to develop hypotheses about what may be causing or maintaining a behavior (Crone & Horner, 2003; Watson & Steege, 2003). FBA information is gathered through various methods, including permanent product review, interviews with teachers and/or parents, rating scales, and observations, with observations being the most reliable and objective source of information (Watson & Steege, 2003). When developing hypotheses, there are essentially two categories to consider: positive reinforcement (the individual is receiving something positive as a consequence for a behavior; e.g., attention, access to tangibles, food, or preferred activities); and negative reinforcement (the student gets out of something aversive as a consequence for a behavior; e.g., escaping or avoiding an undesirable task or demand) (Crone & Horner, 2003; Watson & Steege, 2003). Although power, revenge, and control are often described as functions of disruptive behavior, because these elements may not be objectively observed and systematically manipulated, they are not part of the ABA approach to intervention (Watson & Steege, 2003).

Interventions implemented through ABA are geared toward changing the environment so the undesirable behavior no longer results in the consequence desired by the student (e.g., reinforcement), with the guiding hypothesis that once the desired consequence is no longer obtained, the problem behavior will recur with less frequency, intensity, and/or duration (Maag, 1999). In addition, the environment is changed such that an alternative behavior results in reinforcement, thus increasing the likelihood of the desirable behavior while simultaneously decreasing the likelihood of the disruptive behavior (Tilly, Knoster, & Ikeda, 2000). Interventions implemented through ABA also consider the influence of punishment on behavior. As indicated earlier, many desired behaviors are unintentionally punished. Through the intentional use of reinforcement, desired behaviors may be systematically enhanced through ABA. Furthermore, through the use of additive or reductive punishment, disruptive behaviors may be decreased or extinguished.

Information gleaned through FBA also lends to antecedent strategies. For example, following a comprehensive FBA an educator might manipulate the environment such that it "captures" the desired behavior by creating an environment containing those conditions under which the student is most likely to achieve success. This might include teaching addition or subtraction utilizing manipulative objects for visual learners, or allowing a "high energy" student to engage in a motor task (e.g., walking to

the office to run an errand) just prior to instruction in a challenging content area. There are a variety of evidence-based antecedent approaches that increase the likelihood of success; these strategies are reviewed in a subsequent section.

History of Applied Behavior Analysis in Education

The fields of education and psychology have a long history of incorporating ABA into educational programming and behavior modification for children within educational settings (Baer, Wolf, & Risley, 1987; Martens et al., 1999). Experimental research involving the principles underlying applied behavior analysis dates back to the work of B.F. Skinner in the 1930s whereby he systematically manipulated variables in a controlled environment (i.e., the "Skinner box") to examine the effects of such manipulations on subsequent animal behavior. This *operant conditioning* technology (i.e., the investigation of the effect of specific consequences on subsequent behaviors; Kazdin, 1982) continued to be scientifically investigated throughout the 1940s and 1950s and was moved out of the laboratory and into applied settings throughout the 1960s and 1970s (Kazdin, 1982; Martens et al., 1999). Once this technology was moved into naturalistic applications with human research participants, the fields of education and psychology began to develop a comprehensive research literature focusing on evidence-based behavioral interventions for use with students demonstrating disruptive behaviors in applied settings (Baer, Wolf, & Risley, 1968, 1987; Martens et al., 1999). The term *applied behavior analysis* (Baer, Wolf, & Risley, 1968) was coined to capture the applied nature of experimental methodology that emerged during this time period. The majority of evidence-based interventions used in the classroom today were developed between the 1970s and 1990s. To date, there are thousands of studies demonstrating the efficacy of behavioral interventions as delivered through ABA for individuals demonstrating behavioral deficits or excesses. In addition, it has been argued that as compared to nonbehavioral approaches to intervention, behavioral interventions are the strongest interventions for children and adolescents (e.g., Weisz, Weiss, Alicke, & Klotz, 1987; Weisz, Weiss, Han, Granger, & Morton, 1995). Next we consider the various levels through which school-based behavioral intervention may be delivered.

Behavioral Support through Universal, Targeted, and Intensive Interventions

In most school settings, 80–85% of students respond appropriately to general behavioral and disciplinary methods that are implemented consistently and effectively (Lewis & Sugai, 1999). An additional 10–15% of students do not respond to these universal approaches and require more focused, sometimes intensive programs that are individualized to meet unique and idiosyncratic needs. Positive behavioral support (PBS; Sugai et al., 1999) is an intervention approach that addresses the needs of all students by supporting both the comprehensive needs of school systems, and the individualized needs of students who require additional attention. PBS relies on positive behavioral interventions and systems change to achieve important, socially valid outcomes for children. It integrates behavioral science, practical interventions, socially significant foci, and a systems perspective to support positive behavioral functioning. Strategies inherent in many interventions implemented within the context of PBS include environmental restructuring, curricular changes, antecedent control, behavioral consequences, the application of functional behavioral assessments, and data-based decision making (Sugai et al., 1999).

Positive behavioral support is operationalized through a three-tier behavioral support system that incorporates (a) *universal intervention programs* delivered in school- or classwide systems, which are generally effective for the majority of students whom exhibit mild or no behavioral concerns; (b) *targeted interventions* aimed at approximately 10–15% of students for whom the universal behavioral approach was insufficient to remediate problematic behavioral patterns; and (c) *intensive intervention programs* for approximately 1–7% of students whose chronic behavioral problems require individualized functional assessment and intervention planning given their lack of responsiveness to more global, less intrusive behavioral programming (Walker et al., 1996). The three-tier model is depicted in Figure 27.1.

The three-tier framework is founded on the premise that schools are positioned to effectively prevent the development of violent or antisocial behavioral patterns in the majority of students. It is argued that a well-developed and effectively implemented universal behavioral and social support program will address the majority of concerns that may arise. As interventions become more intensive, they require additional time, effort, and resources. For example, they require variations of functional behavioral assessments to ascertain environmental conditions that support or maintain inappropriate behavioral patterns, and individualized interventions to alter the child's behaviors within the context of the school, classroom, or other settings. Examples of universal, targeted, and intensive interventions are presented below.

Universal Interventions

Universal programs, sometimes referred to as primary prevention programs, implemented at the level of entire groups of students are focused on *preventing* the development of antisocial, negative behaviors in children. Universal structures within the "host environment" (i.e., the entire school) promote a learning climate characterized by the delivery of evidence-based practices and norms for positive behaviors (Sugai et al., 1999). A fairly substantial research base has identified several strategies that promote positive schoolwide discipline and behavioral management. Among the strategies most typically associated with universal prevention programs are (a) classwide social skills training with opportunities to learn and practice prosocial interpersonal and self-control skills; (b) effective instruction, including academic and curricular restructuring and adaptation; (c) rules and expectations regarding behavior that are clear, consistent, and enforced; (d) behaviorally based interventions; and (e) early screening and identification of students with antisocial behavioral patterns (Sprague, Sugai, & Walker, 1998; Walker, Colvin, & Ramsey, 1995).

The Effective Behavioral Support (EBS; Sprague et al., 1998; Sugai & Horner, 1994) model is an example of a universal prevention program. It is a multiple system, whole-school approach with several essential features. First, both problem behaviors and appropriate, positive alternatives are defined for all students and staff. Second, students are taught alternate behaviors directly and given assistance to acquire necessary replacement skills. Third, incentives and motivational systems are put into place, encouraging students to engage in appropriate replacement behaviors. Staff members at participating schools engage in training, coaching, and other supportive practices to ensure that the adults responsible for implementing and maintaining the program acquire the necessary skills, and to promote schoolwide capacity for

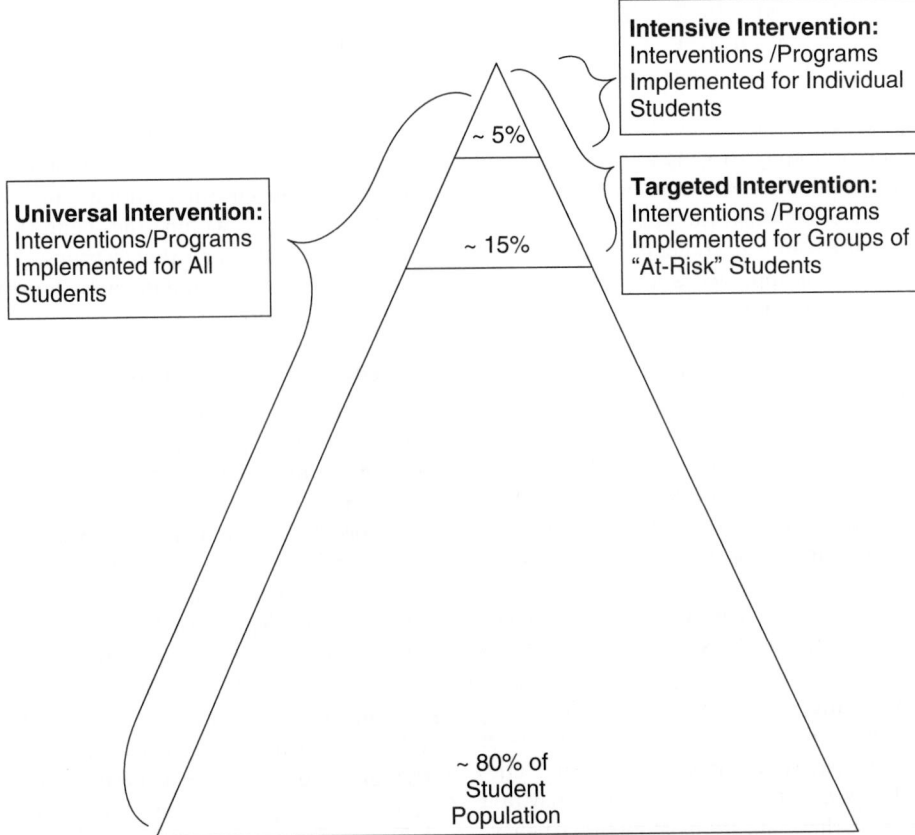

FIGURE 27.1 **Three-tier Model Adapted from OSEP Technical Assistance Center on Positive Behavioral Interventions and Supports (n.d.).**

delivery of the program with integrity. Finally, systems for measuring and monitoring the effectiveness of the EBS program are established and implemented (Sprague et al., 2001).

Sprague et al. (2001) described the application of a universal intervention package comprised of EBS and the Second Step violence prevention program (Committee for Children, 1997), which has been shown to increase higher order social skills in elementary age children and decrease aggressive behavior on the playground (Grossman et al., 1997). The schoolwide intervention was intended to improve the safety and social behaviors of students by providing effective educational services, behavioral supports, and social skills training to all students in participating schools. Four main intervention strategies were used: formal training and technical assistance; a consistent system of behavioral enforcement, monitoring and positive reinforcement; data-based feedback to schools; and the delivery of the Second Step violence prevention curriculum via structured social skills

lessons. After one year of intervention, greater reductions in office referrals were noted for intervention schools as compared to control schools. Furthermore, improved social skill knowledge was evident in students who participated in the universal prevention program compared to students in control schools, and school personnel reported improved operation of the school and motivation to continue in subsequent years. It should be noted that the authors used quasi-experimental procedures (i.e., treatment and control groups were not randomly assigned, nor were they matched on any variables), and the primary outcome measure was comprised of nonspecific outcomes (i.e., office referrals) rather than direct assessments of behavioral change.

Targeted Interventions

Targeted interventions, or those designed as secondary prevention programs, are intended to support students who are not responding to universal interventions. They are more intensive than universal programs and are focused on students at risk for developing serious behavioral problems. In general, interventions at the targeted level involve small groups of students and may teach new, prosocial skills as alternatives to problem behaviors; involve basic environmental manipulations; or deliver simple, individualized interventions in a flexible manner. They involve a simple assessment to identify the function of a problem behavior (i.e., a functional behavioral assessment; FBA) and the development of nonintrusive intervention plans focused on the identified function. Functional behavioral assessment (Crone & Horner, 2003) involves defining the challenging behavior and identifying predictors and consequences of the behavior, often through a brief teacher interview. Targeted interventions are nonintrusive and focus on specific behavioral concerns. They typically manifest several key features. Specifically, they (a) are continuously available to the student; (b) require little effort by teachers; (c) are consistent with other schoolwide efforts; (d) are implemented by all staff within a school; (e) are flexible and based on functional or behavioral assessments; and (f) require continuous monitoring to assess student responsiveness to the program (OSEP Technical Assistance Center on Positive Behavioral Interventions and Supports, n.d.).

One example of a targeted intervention is the Behavioral Education Program (BEP; Crone, Horner, & Hawken, 2004). The BEP (also known as the "check in/check out" system) provides the student with immediate feedback on his or her behavior through the use of teacher ratings on a daily progress report and increased positive adult attention contingent on appropriate social behaviors. The student "checks in" with an adult before school, "checks out" with an adult after school, and engages with teachers through periodic checks and ratings throughout the school day. In addition, back-up reinforcers are earned if the student meets predetermined behavioral goals. Daily progress reports are brought home for review by parents, who sign off on the form before the student returns it to school the following day.

Hawken and Horner (2003) evaluated the effects of the BEP system using a multiple baseline across participant design. The study identified for inclusion six students who received at least five office discipline referrals and were nominated by instructional staff. Of these six students, four completed the study. Measures of both problem behaviors and academic engagement were collected to test the effects of the intervention. The authors found a modest relationship between implementation of the intervention and reduction in problem behaviors, with the most notable effect seen in the reduction of variability of problem behaviors. Likewise, increases in mean levels of academic engagement were noted for all students. Social validity measures assessing acceptability of the intervention by teachers, parents and students yielded mixed results.

Intensive Interventions

Despite the general desirability and promising support for universal and targeted interventions, it remains the case that a small percentage of students fail to respond to these interventions and require intensive, individualized services. Such services are often delivered in the context of behavioral consultation with specialists, teachers, and whenever possible, parents responsible for the systematic identification, analysis, treatment, and evaluation of problem behaviors. Behavioral consultation (BC) is an indirect problem-solving and decision-making model wherein a consultant works with a consultee (typically a teacher or parent) to address behavioral, social, or academic concerns of a child for whom they are responsible (Kratochwill & Bergan, 1990). Within the framework of a three-tier model, BC serves as a process by which intensive interventions are delivered. BC adheres to a four-stage problem-solving process with specific interviewing objectives at each stage (e.g., establish goals for change, analyze antecedents and consequences). Behavioral assessment methods, treatment technologies, and evaluation strategies are used within the four-stage process.

Behavioral consultation has a rich tradition as a systematic, data-based problem-solving and decision-making model with decades of empirical support (see Martens & DiGennaro, 2007; Medway & Updyke, 1985; Sheridan, Welch, & Orme, 1996). Since its inception (Bergan, 1977), variations of the model have emerged (e.g., problem-solving consultation; Gutkin & Curtis, 1990). Among the most noteworthy is conjoint behavioral consultation (CBC; Sheridan & Kratochwill, 2008; Sheridan, Kratochwill, & Bergan, 1996), which focuses on addressing learning and behavioral concerns as they are manifested across systems and contexts. The stagewise progression of BC and CBC are highly similar; thus, the discussion will proceed with a focus on CBC, recognizing the high degree of overlap with other individual applications of BC.

In CBC, parents, teachers, and other caregivers engage in a structured problem-solving process with a consultant to address the needs of children collaboratively across settings. Parents, teachers, and other supportive adults work together to share in the identification of needs for children and to develop, implement, and evaluate interventions to address those needs. All stages of consultation are conducted with parents and teachers together, in a simultaneous (rather than parallel) manner (Sheridan & Kratochwill, 2008; Sheridan et al., 1996). By joining parents, teachers, and other relevant caregivers and supportive adults in the decision-making process, attention is focused on the child's behaviors as they are manifested in individual and interacting systems over contextual and temporal bases (i.e., across settings and time).

The BC and CBC process consists of four stages implemented in a collaborative, dynamic manner (see Figure 27.2). These stages are (a) conjoint needs (problem) identification, (b) conjoint needs (problem) analysis, (c) plan implementation, and (d) conjoint plan evaluation (Sheridan & Kratochwill, 2008; Sheridan, Kratochwill et al., 1996). Procedures for implementing consultation are similar across behavioral and conjoint behavioral consultation, with an added emphasis on cross-setting assessment and intervention in CBC, as well as attention to relationships among primary caregivers (parents and teachers) and cross-systemic influences (home and school) in the conjoint model. Whereas a detailed discussion of these stages is beyond the scope of this chapter, we identify the primary objectives of each stage below. For more detailed information, the interested reader is referred to Kratochwill and Bergan (1990), Sheridan and Kratochwill (2008), and Sheridan, Kratochwill et al. (1996).

The first stage of BC and CBC is conjoint needs/problem identification. The main objectives include prioritizing needs, specifying and defining target concerns, and establishing procedures for collecting baseline data across the home, school and other natural settings. The second stage of BC and CBC is conjoint problem analysis. In this stage, parents and teachers evaluate the baseline data, decide upon behavioral goals for the child, and conduct a functional assessment. Upon completion of a functional assessment, data-based, ecological

hypotheses about what may be motivating a target concern (e.g., attention, escape from an undesired event or task, lack of information or skill) are used to collaboratively develop an appropriate intervention. The third stage of BC/CBC is plan implementation. During this stage, parents and teachers implement the intervention procedures in the home and school settings, supporting implementation across settings. This stage does not involve a structured interview; however, the consultant remains in close contact with parents and teachers (e.g., phone calls and personal visits) throughout implementation of the intervention to provide support, ensure understanding of the plan, offer assistance, reinforce parent and teachers' intervention efforts, and determine the need for any immediate plan modifications.

The final stage of BC/CBC is conjoint plan evaluation. During this stage, consultants, parents and teachers examine the behavioral data collected to evaluate the effects of the intervention and determine if the goals of consultation have been met across the home and school settings. Additional assessments are also warranted, such as assessment of goals and social validity. Maintenance interviews are often desirable several weeks following the final plan evaluation interview to assure continued performance in the positive direction. These interviews are important to evaluate the ongoing progress being made, and determine whether recycling through any problem-solving steps is warranted. Importantly, methods and procedures for continuing conjoint problem-solving or shared decision-making among parents and teachers can be discussed to encourage continued collaboration and partnering across home and school contexts.

Regardless of the level of intervention (i.e., universal, targeted, or intensive), it is critical that educators and interventionists acknowledge that there exists different levels of support for a variety of categories and specific forms of interventions. Essentially, there are three categories of interventions, those that have (a) been empirically supported, (b) not yet been either empirically supported or refuted, and (c) been empirically refuted (T.B. Gutkin, personal communication, March 13, 2007). It is in their best interest for school-based practitioners to select from research-validated interventions whenever possible. For those conditions under which research-based interventions are not accessible, practitioners might have to implement interventions that have been neither empirically

BC/CBC Stage: BC/CBC Process:

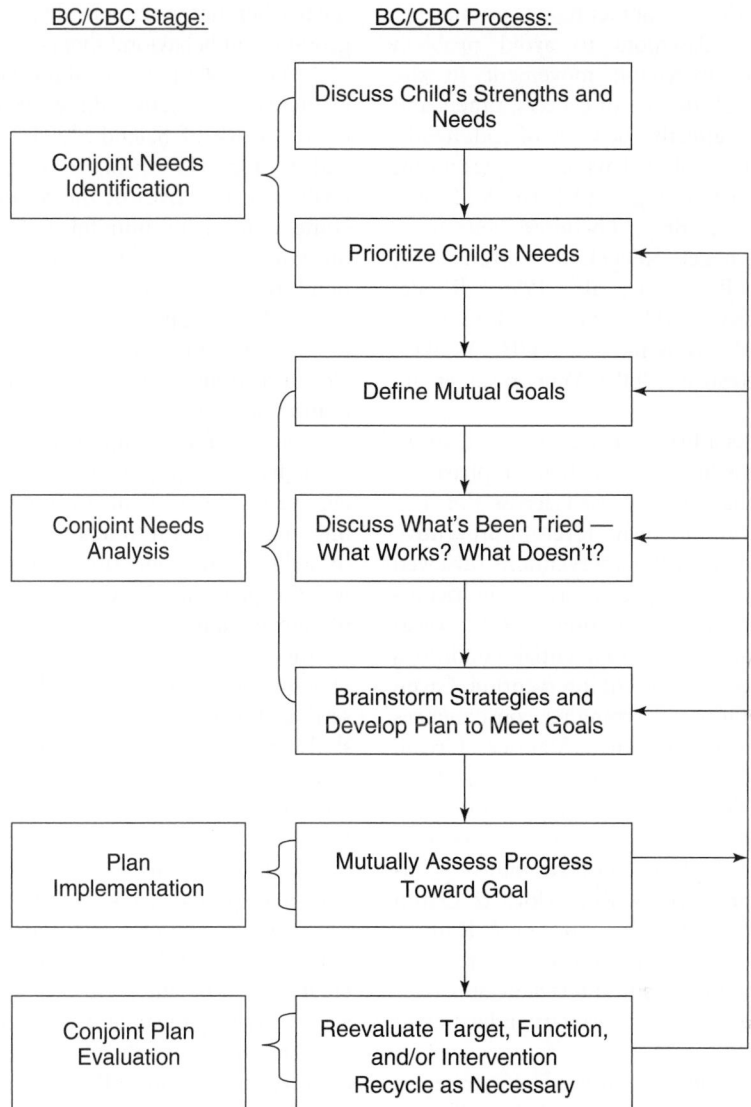

FIGURE 27.2   Collaborative Problem-Solving Framework.

supported nor refuted. Perhaps the most critical guideline is that practitioners avoid at all times those interventions that have been empirically refuted and/or deemed primarily harmful to students.

When operating within an ABA approach, it may be in the team's best interest to consider both antecedent- and consequence-based methods for behavior change. Next we consider interventions for which there exists some research to support application in educational settings for a variety of students. Because both antecedent and consequent strategies are relevant for ABA-based prevention and intervention, we have organized the following sections under these broad categories.

EVIDENCE-BASED ANTECEDENT STRATEGIES

Within the context of applied behavior analysis, antecedent strategies are those environmental manipulations that "set the stage" for success in criterion settings (Alberto & Troutman, 2006). Antecedent strategies may be used to either (a) modify existing disruptive behaviors, or (b) facilitate effective instruction while simultaneously preventing disruptive behaviors (i.e., universal design or primary prevention). Multiple exemplars of antecedent strategies have proven effective in applied research, including public posting of classroom rules, proximity control, behavioral momentum, prompting, setting up the classroom to avoid problem behaviors (e.g., managing movement in the classroom through the use of centers, timers and visual supports), effective delivery of commands, verbal reminders of behavioral expectations, and self-governed strategies (Alberto & Troutman, 2006; Kehle, Bray, Theodore, Jenson, & Clark, 2000; Koegel, Koegel, & Carter, 1999; Maag, 1999; Reavis et al., 1996; Rhode, Jenson, & Reavis, 1993; Sugai, Horner, & Gresham, 2002; Miltenberger, 2003; Walker, Ramsey, & Gresham, 2004; Wilczynski et al., 2003).

Following is a brief overview of some applications from this literature, with an emphasis on interventions that may be used across the universal, targeted and intensive levels of preventive intervention. Many of the interventions reviewed below were proven effective as part of a multicomponent approach to intervention; in some cases both antecedent and consequential conditions were manipulated as a part of intervention. Given the reported efficacy of arranging consequences to increase desired behavior (Maurice, Green, & Luce, 1996), combined with evidence from meta-analyses demonstrating that multicomponent interventions result in stronger behavioral outcomes than single component interventions (Kavale, Mathur, Forness, Rutherford & Quinn 1997; Mathur, Kavale, Quinn, Forness, & Rutherford, 1998), it is likely that future research will continue to combine both antecedent and consequential manipulations as primary independent variables.

Our discussion of antecedent strategies begins with a brief discussion of the effective use of direct instruction. The effective teaching literature is rich with evidence-based interventions to prevent disruptive behaviors in the classroom. This topic is critical, given that the response-to-intervention model dominating the fields of education and school psychology assumes that primary prevention is grounded in evidence-based instructional strategies (Fuchs, Mock, Morgan, & Young, 2003). That is, targeted and intensive interventions are warranted only when the student fails to respond to universally applied, evidence-based teaching and/or behavior management strategies (Gresham, 2004). Perhaps one of the most important aspects of educational programming is the effective use of direct instruction (Maag, 1999). When used appropriately, direct instruction maximizes learning as

the teacher incorporates evidence-based strategies grounded in behavioral theory.

Maag (1999) identified the following 10 core elements of effective direct instruction, based on the work of Salend (1994) and Mastropieri and Scruggs (1994): (a) start by explaining the goals and objectives of the lesson; (b) sequence content in a meaningful manner (i.e., build on a hierarchy of skills, recognizing that skills build on one another); (c) review and check knowledge regarding all prerequisite skills; (d) deliver content information clearly; (e) give clear directions, explanations of tasks, and relevant examples; (f) provide sufficient guided practice; (g) check for comprehension; (h) provide immediate, specific feedback; (i) allow the child to engage in independent practice; and (j) conduct ongoing evaluation to determine the child's level of skills acquisition. Although these procedures were originally used to describe proactive teaching of curriculum, they may easily be adapted as the core elements used to teach students effective behavioral skills within the educational setting. For example, borrowing from the social skills literature, direct instruction, modeling, role playing, and providing immediate feedback are among the most common interventions for effective social skills intervention (Jones, Sheridan, & Binns, 1993). This approach to teaching specific skills may be combined with other antecedent strategies and/or consequential strategies (e.g., token economies, contracting) to create powerful interventions that may be used across a variety of students and settings.

Precision commands (i.e., the effective delivery of commands; Rhode et al., 1993), public posting of rules (i.e., prompting), and teacher movement are all evidence-based antecedent strategies for preventing and targeting disruptive behavior in both disabled and nondisabled students (Kehle et al., 2000). For example, in a study involving general education students who demonstrated high baseline levels of disruptive classroom behaviors, De Martini-Scully, Bray, & Kehle (2000) had a classroom teacher explain classroom rules to students and publicly display the rules (i.e., a visual prompt). In addition, the teacher was instructed to move around the classroom while teaching (i.e., proximity control, another antecedent strategy) and use precision commands. Because these antecedent strategies were used in a treatment package also consisting of behavioral contracting, a token economy system, and response cost, it is difficult to determine the relative contribution of public posting of rules and teacher movement. However, during the second treatment phase of the combined multiple baseline/reversal design—a phase during which the token economy and response cost components were eliminated—the intervention demonstrated a continued desired effect on the target behaviors (i.e., a decrease in disruptive behaviors). Similar outcomes have been reported in related studies including a variety of student populations (e.g., Johnson, Stoner, & Green, 1996; Mottram, Bray, Kehle, Broudy, & Jenson, 2002; Musser, Bray, Kehle, & Jenson, 2001). This line of inquiry demonstrates how preventive strategies may be easily incorporated into the general education setting, which has the potential to foster success in all students while simultaneously preventing disruptive behaviors.

As indicated above, prompting is a well-established antecedent strategy. There are a variety of prompting techniques that may be used to elicit desired behaviors in the instructional environment: gestural (e.g., pointing to the appropriate response or toward a visual cue depicting the appropriate response); graduated time delay (i.e., starting with an immediate prompt and gradually increasing the wait time); modeling (live or video); physical (e.g., guiding hand-over-hand); visual; position (e.g., placing the target item closer to the student than other nonrelevant stimuli); verbal; and within-stimulus (e.g., a feature is exaggerated to increase the likelihood that a student will select the appropriate response) (Alberto & Troutman, 2006; Wilczynski et al., 2003). In general, prompts are first introduced to help the student achieve success in an applied setting and then systematically faded until the student independently demonstrates the target behavior across conditions.

Script-fading (Krantz & McClannahan, 1993) is a unique application of prompting that has developed into a distinctive line of inquiry. This approach involves first introducing written scripts into naturalistic settings to increase social interactions in children with autism and then systematically fading the scripts through using smaller font and/or fading the clarity of the text. This approach has proven effective, been modified to include pictorial and auditory prompts, and replicated in subsequent research (e.g., Krantz & McClannahan, 1998; Sarakoff, Taylor, & Poulson, 2001). In addition to applications with individuals with autism, prompting has proven effective in multiple studies involving individuals who are developmentally delayed and individuals with low cognitive functioning (Alberto & Troutman, 2006; Rathvon, 2003).

Also related to the treatment of autism, Koegel and colleagues developed Pivotal Response Training (PRT; Koegel et al., 1999), an intervention that relies heavily on antecedent strategies. Pivotal behaviors are those "behaviors that are central to wide areas of functioning such that a change in the pivotal behavior will produce improvement across a number of behaviors" (Koegel et al., 1999, p. 577). The idea of targeting pivotal or "king-pin" behaviors (Rhode et al., 1993) is applicable to a variety of students—not just students with autism—and may be used to guide universal, targeted and intensive level intervention. According to Koegel et al., pivotal behaviors include responding to multiple cues, motivation, self-management, and self-initiations. Motivation has received much attention in the literature as an antecedent strategy. PRT incorporates motivation into learning by presenting the student with preferred toys and activities to be used as learning tools, to enhance the likelihood of their initial engagement in the learning process. Once the learning trial ends, the student is given access to the preferred item, thus incorporating a naturalistic reinforcer into each learning trial. In addition, PRT incorporates motivation into learning by interspersing maintenance trials (i.e., mastered tasks) with learning trials focusing on emerging skills. This latter approach is grounded in behavioral momentum theory, which hypothesizes that if a student builds momentum through positive learning trials, she/he is likely to continue with this momentum into more challenging and/or less desirable tasks (Alberto & Troutman, 2006; Ardoin, Martens, & Wolfe, 1999).

Behavioral momentum has also proven effective to increase compliance in the general education classroom. Specifically, Ardoin, Martens, and Wolfe (1999) investigated the effectiveness of using a series of high-probability commands (i.e., instructions likely to be followed by students) followed immediately by a low-probability command to increase compliance. Ardoin et al. reported that this intervention effectively increased compliance during transition times in the general education classroom. Behavioral momentum in applied contexts has received much attention in the intervention literature. Readers are referred to Banda, Neisworth, and Lee (2003) for a review of this literature.

EVIDENCE-BASED CONSEQUENTIAL STRATEGIES

The operant conditioning paradigm from which ABA is derived relies heavily on consequential manipulations to change behavior in applied settings. There is an extensive literature on the effectiveness of a variety of reinforcement- and punishment-based interventions. For example, positive reinforcement, verbal praise, token reinforcers, contracting, group contingency procedures, negative reinforcement, differential reinforcement, response cost procedures, extinction, and overcorrection have all proven effective in the behavior modification literature (Alberto & Troutman, 2006; Maag, 1999; Miltenberger, 1993; Rhode et al., 1993). In general, reinforcement-based techniques are used to enhance desired behaviors and punishment-based techniques are used to decrease disruptive behaviors. There are a variety of negative outcomes and side effects associated with the use of punishment, including the potential for learned helplessness, emotional reaction, increased aggression (especially in cases where physical punishment is administered), response substitution (e.g., replacing one inappropriate or undesired behavior for another, such as biting with hitting), and failure to teach the appropriate replacement behavior (Newsome, Favell, & Rincover, 1983). Given that the use of punishment may be associated with such side effects, it is recommended that interventionists (a) begin with positive interventions, and when necessary (b) select the least aversive punishment strategy, carefully monitoring for and eliminating potential side effects (Newsome et al., 1983). Because reinforcement- and punishment-based strategies are commonly combined into multicomponent packages, interventions are generally categorized into those that increase behavior and those that decrease behavior. Following is a brief review of this literature.

Using Consequences to Increase Behavior

Positive reinforcement is one of the most widely supported consequential interventions to date. When used immediately following a behavior and when it is contingent on a specific behavior level or goal, positive reinforcement can be a very powerful intervention. Positive reinforcement may come in the form of attention (e.g., descriptive praise), materials (e.g., favorite toys, stickers), edibles (including food and drinks),

and/or activities (e.g., access to the computer). Rhode et al. (1993) offer the following guidelines when implementing reinforcement (referred to as the IFEED-AV Rules): reinforce the student *I*mmediately following the desired behavior; reinforce the student as *F*requently as possible; be *E*nthusiastic when delivering praise and other reinforcers; make *E*ye contact when delivering reinforcement; *D*escribe the behavior being rewarded; build *A*nticipation through reminding students of available rewards; and incorporate *V*ariety into reinforcement. There exists an extensive literature to support the use of positive reinforcement in the classroom setting. Two specific applications have received much attention and are reviewed next because of their potential for use at the universal, targeted and intensive levels of intervention: verbal praise and token reinforcement. This discussion is followed by a brief overview of negative reinforcement and contracting.

Verbal praise has long been identified as an effective means of reinforcing desired behaviors in the classroom. Stemming from research in the 1960s and 1970s (e.g., Hay, Hay, & Nelson, 1977), verbal praise continues to be a widely researched consequential intervention. For example, in a recent study, Matheson and Shriver (2005) investigated the effectiveness of an intervention consisting of both effective commands and contingent praise on the compliance rate of two students in a general education classroom setting. Results indicated that effective commands increased compliance; however, compliance rates further increased when contingent praise was added. Despite its extensive research support, praise is perhaps one of the most underutilized reinforcement strategies in the classroom setting (Rhode et al., 1993). This is unfortunate, given its reported effectiveness and adaptability for use in universal, targeted and intensive interventions. To promote a positive climate that clearly communicates behavioral expectations to all students, it is recommended that teachers provide positive praise at a much higher rate than reprimands. Specifically, a 4:1 ratio (i.e., four positive statements for every reprimand or redirect) is recommended in the classroom (Girls and Boys Town, 2005). It has also been argued that although verbal praise may be effective for many school-aged children, older children (i.e., middle- and high-school-aged students) may find public acknowledgement embarrassing, thus resulting in a decrease in desired behavior (i.e., praise becomes a form of punishment) (Bowen, Jenson, & Clarke, 2004). This emphasizes the importance of monitoring behavior change as a means of determining whether a consequence is indeed a reinforcer.

Token reinforcers have been used to teach multiple types of skills (e.g., academic, social, vocational) across a variety of settings (e.g., general education, self-contained, and resource classrooms) (Rathvon, 2003). In practice, this approach involves using a token (e.g., poker chip, coupon) as a consequence for positive behaviors (e.g., remaining on task, praising peers); this token is later exchanged for a back-up reinforcer with more value to the student (e.g., free time on the computer, candy, toys). Token reinforcers have proven effective in both individual and group-based applications. Interventionists may select from three types of classroom-based contingencies: independent, dependent and interdependent (Kehle et al., 2000). With independent contingency systems, all students are held to the same criteria and each student's access to rewards is independently determined. With dependent contingency systems, rewards are contingent on the performance of one student or a small group of students. Interdependent group contingencies involve multiple groups where members of groups are treated as individuals with regard to access to rewards. Interventionists should select the format that best meets the characteristics of the classroom in which the intervention is implemented (Kehle et al., 2000).

Negative reinforcement is another intervention that may be used to increase the probability of a desired behavior. This strategy involves the removal of an aversive stimulus contingent on an acceptable level of an appropriate behavior. A common example of negative reinforcement involves escaping or avoiding an undesired activity or assignment. In a unique application of negative reinforcement to increase academic performance, Doyle, Jenson, Clark, & Gates (1999) implemented an intervention whereby students earned dot-shaped stickers for the accurate completion of math worksheet problems. Specifically, students earned one sticker per two problems they completed accurately, with no limit as to how many stickers they could earn. Once the stickers were earned, students placed them over math problems on future assignments, thus escaping work contingent on accurately completing math problems. Results indicated that students increased both their work completion and accuracy rates.

Contracting is another evidence-based intervention that may be used to increase behavior. Contracts have proven effective for both low-frequency behaviors to be increased (e.g., cooperation) and high-frequency behaviors to be decreased (e.g., physical aggression), across a variety of students and settings (Ruth, 1996). Rhode et al. (1993) suggest that the following components help define an effective contract: (a) there is agreement between the teacher and the student (i.e., the student is actively involved in contract development); (b) there is a formal exchange between behavior and reward; (c) a specific goal is determined; (d) a specific reward is identified (which may include a bonus for exceptional behavior); and (e) a clearly operationalized behavior is predetermined. There are multiple studies that have included contracts in conjunction with skill-building interventions (e.g., direct instruction, reinforcement) to improve behavior in applied settings. For example, De Martini-Scully et al. (2000) and Musser et al. (2001) used contracting as part of a multicomponent intervention described earlier to decrease disruptive behaviors in the classroom.

Using Consequences to Decrease Behavior

Response cost is a well-documented intervention used to decrease disruptive behaviors. Response cost involves taking away a token as a consequence for disruptive behavior (e.g., violating a classroom rule). When used as part of a token economy system, tokens are earned for positive behaviors (token reinforcement) and taken away for disruptive behaviors or rule violations (response cost). Often used as part of a comprehensive treatment package, response cost has proven effective in reducing disruptive behaviors in children with specific disabilities, including attention-deficit hyperactivity disorder (e.g., McGoey & DuPaul, 2000), autism (e.g., Pelios, MacDuff, & Axelrod, 2003), and behavior disorder (e.g., Musser et al., 2001). Response cost may also be effective with general education students (Rathvon, 2003).

Differential reinforcement is a unique intervention that incorporates reinforcement, either (a) for a behavior that is topographically incompatible with the behavior to be reduced, (b) for a more appropriate alternative to the behavior to be reduced, (c) when the behavior is not present for predetermined period of time, or (d) when a behavior occurs at a lower rate than previously observed (Alberto & Troutman, 2006; Maag, 1999). These forms of differential reinforcement are referred to as differential reinforcement of incompatible behavior (DRI), differential reinforcement of an alternative behavior (DRA), differential reinforcement of the omission of behavior (DRO), or differential reinforcement of lower rates of behavior (DRL), respectively. Because this intervention uses the application of both reinforcement to increase appropriate behavior and ignoring (i.e., punishment) to decrease disruptive behavior and because it may eliminate as much as 95% of students' disruptive behavior in applied settings, it is generally a well-received intervention (Maag, 1999). Differential reinforcement has been applied to a variety of behaviors (e.g., off-task behavior, out-of seat behavior, disruptive behavior) in both special education and general education settings (Alberto & Troutman, 2006; Maag, 1999). All forms of differential reinforcement (i.e., DRI, DRA, DRO, and DRL) are evidence-based interventions that have a long history of research to support their effectiveness (Alberto & Troutman, 2006; Maag, 1999).

Additional evidence-based reductive techniques include extinction (e.g., systematic, planned ignoring), overcorrection, and time-out from positive reinforcement. Extinction involves ignoring behavior that previously resulted in attention. Although it can be a powerful intervention, it is hard for many to implement because there is often an extinction burst immediately following its application (i.e., the behavior escalates before it decreases) (Alberto & Troutman, 2006). Overcorrection involves the student practicing a desired alternative behavior as a consequence for demonstrating an undesirable behavior (e.g., if the student throws a paper on the floor, she may be expected to pick it up as well as all other papers on the floor). Time-out from positive reinforcement involves removing the student from access to "time in" (i.e., a desired work setting or positive attention) as a consequence for a disruptive behavior. One form of time-out—*exclusionary time-out*—involves removing the student from a desired setting; another form of time out—*nonexclusionary time-out*—involves having the child remain in the setting while the student is denied access to reinforcers in that setting (Alberto & Troutman, 2006). It is critical to remember that these forms of time-out are only effective once "time in" has been established in the criterion setting. That is, sufficient reinforcers must be in

place in the criterion setting such that removing the child from access to reinforcement is indeed punitive. Removing a child from an environment lacking attention and other features the child deems desirable may be just what he/she is seeking when engaged in disruptive behavior (i.e., in this case, "time-out" is not time out from reinforcement; rather, the child may be trying to earn escape from a setting he/she deems punishing). Furthermore, reductive techniques may result in negative side effects, and they are often implemented either without integrity or without regard to the function of the behavior (Maag, 1999; Newsome, Favell, & Rincover, 1983). It is recommended that reductive techniques be implemented with caution, and used only when deemed necessary. Indeed, there are many alternatives designed to teach students appropriate alternative behaviors (i.e., teaching students what *to* do rather than merely what *not* to do).

ISSUES RELEVANT TO THE BEHAVIOR MODIFICATION PROCESS

Identifying and Measuring Behavior

Regardless of whether the behavior modification process is applied to an individual student or a group of students, the first step is to identify a socially valid *target behavior* (Kazdin, 1982). Socially valid behaviors are those deemed important by the consumer (Wolf, 1978). It is critical to consider input from key stakeholders at all levels (e.g., teachers, related services personnel, administrators), as doing so may enhance their motivation to follow through with intervention and progress monitoring (Sugai et al., 1999). Once priorities are established, the primary concern is defined operationally in terms that are clear, measurable, and manageable. Seminal research has demonstrated the importance of clear, operational definitions in behavioral consultation and its positive relationship to effective outcomes (Bergan & Tombari, 1976).

Once the team has identified and clearly operationalized the target behavior, a behavioral observation system is selected. Essentially, there are two categories of general behavior observation strategies: permanent product review and direct observation (Alberto & Troutman, 2006). Permanent product review is valid only when (a) the behavior of interest results in a change in the environment, (b) only that behavior can result in the change in the environment, and (c) the behavior of interest always results in the same change in the environment (Alberto & Troutman, 2006). When these conditions are not satisfied, direct observation is warranted. There are four general types of *direct observation* systems: event recording (tallying the number of times a behavior occurs), duration recording (recording the time the student is engaged in a specific behavior), latency recording (recording the time that transpires between the delivery of a request and the initiation of the child's behavioral response), and interval recording (recording the occurrence of behavior within a specific time interval).

As applied to measuring academic behaviors, school psychologists and educators have come to rely on curriculum-based measurement (CBM; Shinn, 1989). CBM is a set of standard, simple, short-duration fluency measures of readings, mathematical computations, and written expression (Shinn, 1989, 1998). The unit of analysis is typically words read correct per minute for reading; number of digits correct per minute for mathematical computation; and number of words written per three minutes for written expression (Shapiro, 2004). Typically, schools collect data across all students and use the average performance level within each grade level and domain as a representative unit of academic achievement. This system may be used at both the individual and group levels. Whereas CBM is often used to measure academic behaviors over time, a similar system has been developed to monitor disruptive behaviors at the schoolwide level: Schoolwide Information System (SWIS, n.d.). The primary unit of analysis for SWIS is the number of office referrals. This system provides information about the number of discipline events reported to the office, the types of problems occurring (e.g., inappropriate verbal language, physical contact, noncompliance, harassment, bullying), the students being referred, the locations of problem behaviors, and the times of day when the disruptive behaviors occur (SWIS, n.d.). As with the CBM information systems, SWIS allows educators to make informed decisions about school-based interventions as applied to multiple students.

Developing a Valid Intervention

Conducting a functional assessment is perhaps the most important step in selecting a valid intervention. The process of gathering information to develop hypotheses regarding the function(s) of behavior allows interventionists to select evidence-based interventions for condition-specific behaviors, thus eliminating the use of interventions not directly linked to the underlying function of a particular behavior. The steps of a basic functional assessment coincide with the acronym "VAIL" (Validate, Assess, Interpret-Link to intervention; Witt, Daly, & Noell, 2000). In the validation step, behavioral interventionists gather and interpret data to determine whether a problem exists to the extent that warrants further evaluation. The second step is assessment, which involves gathering information about the student and his or her behaviors or performance. The interpret-link step entails interpretation of the data and linking the results of the assessment to an appropriate intervention (Witt et al., 2000). The functional behavioral assessment process is dynamic and may be adapted to fit within the context of either individual- or group-focused intervention; Crone and Horner (2003) offer models for both applications.

Another essential consideration when developing an intervention is the social validity of the procedures themselves (Kazdin, 1982; Wolf, 1978). It may be argued that the most efficacious intervention in existence is only as strong as the rigor with which it is implemented. That is, if the intervention is not implemented, its impact on the target behavior cannot be determined. Although there are many variables related to whether an intervention results in a desired outcome, the school psychology literature emphasizes the following: treatment acceptability, treatment integrity (or intervention fidelity), and treatment effectiveness (Eckert & Hintze, 2000). Treatment acceptability is defined as "judgments about the treatment procedures by nonprofessionals, lay persons, clients and other potential consumers of treatment regarding whether treatments are appropriate, fair, reasonable, and intrusive, and whether treatments meet with conventional notions about what treatments should be" (Kazdin, 1982, p. 259). Witt and Elliott (1985) hypothesize that treatment acceptability leads to treatment integrity (i.e., the degree to which the intervention is implemented as intended; Yeaton & Sechrest, 1981), which supports favorable outcomes (i.e., treatment effectiveness). That is, if teachers and other treatment agents find an intervention to be acceptable, they are more likely to implement the intervention with integrity. Assuming the behavioral intervention is responsible for any observed change in behavior, treatment integrity may be a necessary prerequisite to positive intervention outcomes (Telzrow & Beebe, 2002; Witt & Elliott, 1985).

There are many factors hypothesized to impact treatment acceptability and treatment integrity, including level of knowledge about the intervention, perceived effectiveness, costs associated with implementation, time necessary for implementation, type of treatment (teachers report a preference for positive interventions over negative interventions), complexity of the intervention, problem severity (i.e., more complex problems are generally perceived to warrant more complex interventions), and treatment side effects (Eckert & Hintze, 2000; Reimers, Wacker, & Koeppl, 1987; Witt & Elliott, 1985). It has also been hypothesized that a goodness-of-fit between the intervention and the treatment setting is an important consideration when developing an intervention (Dietrich, 1999; Eckert & Hintze, 2000; Lentz, Allen, & Ehrhardt, 1996). Although there are multiple studies investigating those factors hypothesized to impact treatment acceptability, the majority involve analog conditions whereby participants rate contrived interventions as opposed to applied conditions within naturalistic settings (Cowan & Sheridan, 2003; Eckert & Hintze, 2000). In addition, the complexity of the relationship between treatment acceptability and treatment integrity makes it challenging to investigate the relationship between these variables in applied settings (Cowan & Sheridan, 2003). Although many of the variables maintain face validity and may have some evidence to support their impact on treatment acceptability and/or integrity, more research is needed to guide practitioners in this domain.

Enhancing and Monitoring Treatment Integrity

Treatment integrity reflects and influences the reliability, validity and efficacy of an intervention (Moncher & Prinz, 1991). To demonstrate a functional relationship between the independent and dependent variables, it is necessary to monitor both participant behavior and treatment integrity (Gresham, MacMillan, Beebe-Frankenberger, & Bocian, 2000). An important role for the practicing school psychologist is to seek ways to monitor and enhance treatment integrity throughout the intervention process. Treatment integrity may be monitored via direct and/or indirect methods (Gresham et al., 2000). Whereas direct assessment involves either direct

observation or permanent product review, indirect assessment involves various techniques such as self-reports, rating scales, and treatment checklists. In general, direct approaches are more reliable than indirect approaches because they are more objective than self-report measures or checklists (Gresham et al., 2000; Wicksrom et al., 1998). It is recommended that direct measures be used as primary treatment integrity data, with indirect measures providing supplemental information (Gresham et al., 2000; Telzrow & Beebe, 2000). It is also recommended that treatment integrity be considered throughout treatment implementation.

As related to enhancing treatment integrity, interventionists may use intervention scripts or training manuals to convey specific procedural components (Martens et al., 1999; Telzrow & Beebe, 2002). The use of training scripts may increase the acceptability of an intervention (Ehrhardt et al., 1996), and their use has been associated with positive outcomes for children in applied research (Ehrhardt et al., 1996; Hirallal & Martens, 1998). In addition, treatment integrity may be enhanced by the use of direct instruction, modeling, role playing, and practice with feedback (Martens et al., 1999). There is an emerging line of research to support these related procedures as a means of increasing observed treatment integrity (e.g., Hirallal & Martens, 1998). Another mechanism that may be used to assist with treatment fidelity is the use of treatment integrity checklists, which not only serve as cues for interventionists but also provide a means of maintaining a record of treatment implementation (Telzrow & Beebe, 2002).

Using Progress Monitoring to Determine the Effectiveness of Interventions

Regardless of whether an intervention is linked to a particular line of research or part of a student's educational programming, it is critical that ongoing progress monitoring drive the intervention process. At both the prereferral and posteligibility phase, *IDEA* mandates that progress monitoring be used to determine whether or not educational programming is helping the student achieve academic success. In addition, *NCLB* mandates that schools monitor the progress of all students, including those with and without specific disabilities. Time series analysis is perhaps the most logical approach to progress monitoring. The primary unit of analysis may be the metric derived from one or more of the permanent product or direct observation systems described earlier, or the result of a standardized progress monitoring system designed to monitor either academic (e.g., CBM) or behavioral (e.g., SWIS) performance as described earlier, converted to a simple line graph.

Grounded within the tradition of ABA, there are several well-established means of assessing whether a particular intervention is producing a meaningful change in the target behavior level. Specifically, interventionists may consider the following indicators: mean levels comparison, data stability (within and across phases), trend analysis, percent nonoverlapping data, and effect size (Busk & Serlin, 1992; Kazdin, 1982; Parker et al., 2005; Scruggs, Mastropieri, & Casto, 1987; Tawney & Gast, 1984). For the purposes of determining overall effectiveness, time series data points on a graph may represent either (a) a single student, or (b) a larger group of students (e.g., group averages, data points across a random sample of students). Following is a brief review of indicators of treatment efficacy.

Mean levels comparison involves comparing the mean baseline level of performance with the mean intervention or treatment level of performance. If the mean changes in the hypothesized direction, the interventionist has gathered some evidence of efficacy (assuming control of extraneous variables). *Data stability* is another measure of intervention effectiveness that may be used to make decisions regarding both (a) when to begin intervention, and (b) whether or not the intervention is influencing the target behavior. Generally speaking, baseline data should be stable and flat (i.e., no strong trends present) prior to implementing an intervention; however, this is rarely the case in applied research (Parker et al., 2005). The standard deviation within each phase may also be used as a measure of data stability. Stability is critical because if baseline data are variable, it is difficult to say with certainty what pattern is likely to result without intervention. In cases where intervention implementation is warranted due to the seriousness of the target behavior (e.g., hitting), the interventionist may implement the intervention soon after baseline begins. In this case, if the data become more stable during the intervention phase (as compared to baseline), this may be interpreted to indicate that the intervention results in more predictable behavior patterns (i.e., the intervention demonstrates

control over the dependent variable, which provides data to support efficacy). *Trend analysis* is another important measure of overall behavior change. Trend analysis entails developing a trend line to both (a) determine during baseline what pattern is likely to emerge without intervention, and (b) compare trend lines across the baseline and treatment phases to determine the overall effectiveness of the intervention.

Percent nonoverlapping data (PND; Scruggs et al., 1987) concerns investigating the degree to which treatment phase data overlap with the baseline data. Specifically, the interventionist determines the range of baseline data points and then calculates the percent of treatment phase data that fall within the baseline data range. Using the PND metric, higher levels of nonoverlapping data indicate more meaningful change in behavior patterns. Specifically, when PND is between 75% and 100%, the intervention is deemed effective; when PND is between 50% and 75%, the intervention is deemed moderately effective; and PND below 50% indicates little to no effectiveness (Kavale et al., 1997; Mathur et al., 1998). Whereas PND is helpful in determining whether or not there is an observed change in behavior level, it fails to provide information about the relative magnitude of the behavior change.

For many reasons, including the desire to interpret and report data more clearly and objectively, school-based researchers have adopted more traditional statistical procedures in small-N research (e.g., calculating *effect sizes*) (Busk & Serlin, 1992; Parker et al., 2005). These procedures are often used in combination with visual analysis procedures commonly associated with small-N research (e.g., trend and stability analysis). Although calculating effect sizes in applied research remains somewhat controversial, it has been argued that when used with caution as a supplementary technique, reporting effect sizes may be helpful to research-practitioners seeking a means of identifying and building support for evidence-based interventions (Busk & Serlin, 1992; Parker et al., 2005). One of the most common procedures is referred to as the "standardized mean difference" (Parker et al., 2005). Derived from the principles used in applying effect size calculation to meta-analyses of group designs (e.g., Cohen, 1988; Glass, 1976), the calculation of effect sizes for meta-analyses (or replications) of single subject research designs entails subtracting the intervention mean from the baseline mean and dividing that number by the baseline standard deviation. This converts the data to a metric of standard deviation units whereby an effect size of. 20 is considered small, an effect size of. 50 is deemed moderate, and an effect size of. 80 is interpreted as highly effective (Cohen, 1988). Despite its recent popularity, this technique should be approached with caution. Specifically, because these procedures were developed for studies with greater statistical power to control for chance error, their use in single subject research may result in inflated effect size scores that are difficult to interpret (e.g., effect size = 6). Research-practitioners are encouraged to consider the strengths and limitations of their population size and research design, select from a variety of alternative methods available in the published literature, and interpret results conservatively (Parker et al., 2005)

Generalization Considerations

Generalization is concerned with the application of newly acquired skills to novel settings, individuals, tasks, and times. This construct has received much attention in the literature, especially with regard to social skills intervention (Gresham, 2003). It is of particular interest when intervention takes place in an analog setting (i.e., learning takes place in a setting other than the criterion setting), as opposed to naturalistic settings (i.e., where the child is expected to perform the skill). However, whenever a new skill is being taught, generalization training should be incorporated from the beginning of intervention (Sheridan, Hungelmann, & Maughan, 1999). Unfortunately, several research studies fail to incorporate training procedures or monitoring systems to develop and assess generalization (Gresham, 1997). Many researchers rely on a "train and hope" approach to intervention (Stokes & Baer, 1977) wherein they *train* an individual in one setting and *hope* the skill transfers to novel conditions. An alternative to the "train and hope" paradigm is to systematically arrange intervention so generalization is more likely to occur (Stokes & Baer, 1977).

There is widespread agreement that generalization will not occur unless there are specific procedures implemented to enhance the likelihood of generalization (Cowan & Allen, 2007). Although a number of strategies have been proposed for promoting generalization, they may be grouped into the following three general approaches: using natural consequences, training diversely, and incorporating mediators (Stokes &

Osnes, 1989). The use of natural consequences stems from the acknowledgement that desired behaviors are more likely to generalize when educators use reinforcing consequences that occur naturally and do not require artificial programming. Training diversely involves employing natural variations during training (i.e., using a variety of stimuli across multiple settings). Incorporating mediators involves using stimuli in training that will also be present in applied settings. Regardless of the level of intervention (i.e., individualized or group based) and/or educational placement of the student(s), it is imperative that interventionists look for ways to ascertain that newly acquired skills are being taught, practiced and reinforced in naturalistic settings (Cowan & Allen, 2007).

Challenges associated with generalization of skills taught in artificial treatment settings (e.g., "pull-out" social skills groups) or under highly controlled analogue situations have led some researchers to focus on intervening in natural settings (i.e., natural learning environments; Bruder & Dunst, 2000; Sheridan et al., 1999). Natural learning environments provide frequent opportunities for students to witness desired behaviors as modeled by competent peers, opportunities for reinforcement for appropriate behaviors (Cripe & Venn, 1997), and opportunities for generalized teaching. Strategies for training in natural environments include prompts, elaborations, and modeling by adults or peers (Brown, McEvoy & Bishop, 1991). Parents, educators, and other individuals in the natural environments can be taught to identify naturalistic teaching opportunities during routine activities at any community-based setting within which the child regularly functions (Cowan & Allen, 2007).

Conclusions

Driven both by parents' and teachers' desire to enhance learning for all students and by federal legislation, the joint mission of preventing and responding to disruptive behaviors in schools has become paramount in the education of children. Applied behavior analysis has achieved and maintained the status of being the most promising and evidence-based approach to behavior modification across settings. The field of school psychology has long recognized the importance of early intervention and prevention, as evidenced by multiple publications rich with references to universal, targeted and intensive level preventive intervention.

Scientist-practitioners have enriched the practice of school psychology by investigating systematic, controlled procedures for expanding ABA technology from intensive into universal and targeted level applications. In addition, scholars continue to investigate procedures for measuring both (a) student behavior change, and (b) consumer satisfaction (i.e., social validity) in response to student- and setting-specific intervention. Although ABA interventionists have a rich literature from which to seek guidance, there remains a need for additional research to guide practice, especially with regard to universal and targeted level applications. Given both (a) the ever-increasing demand for accountability in both general and special education, and (b) the fact that the broad-ranging needs of children continue to challenge educators and parents alike, the need for additional research continues to be a priority for scientist-practitioners in the schools.

References

Alberto, P. A., & Troutman, A. C. (2006). *Applied behavior analysis for teachers* (7th ed.). Upper Saddle River, NJ: Merrill Prentice Hall.

Ardoin, S., Martens, B., & Wolfe, L. (1999). Using high-probability instruction sequences with fading to increase student compliance during transitions. *Journal of Applied Behavior Analysis, 32*, 339–351.

Baer, D. M., Wolf, M. M., & Risley, T. R. (1968). Some current dimensions of applied behavior analysis. *Journal of Applied Behavior Analysis, 1*, 91–97.

Baer, D. M., Wolf, M. M., & Risley, T. R. (1987). Some still current dimensions of applied behavior analysis. *Journal of Applied Behavior Analysis, 20*, 313–327.

Banda, D. R., Neisworth, J. T., & Lee, D. L. (2003). High-probability sequences and young children: Enhancing compliance. *Child and Family Behavior Therapy, 25*, 17–29.

Bergan, J. R. (1977). *Behavioral consultation*. Columbus, OH: Merrill.

Bergan, J. R., & Tombari, M. L. (1976). Consultant skill and efficacy and the implementation and outcome of consultation. *Journal of School Psychology, 14*, 3–14.

Bowen, J., Jenson, W. R., & Clark, E. (2004). *School-based interventions for students with behavior problems*. New York: Kluwer Academic/Plenum Publishers.

Brown, W. H., McEvoy, M. A., & Bishop, N. (1991). Incidental teaching of social behaviors: A naturalistic approach for promoting young children's peer interactions. *Teaching Exceptional Children, 24*, 35–38.

Bruder, M. B., & Dunst, C. (2000). Expanding learning opportunities for infants and toddlers in natural environments. *Zero to Three, 20*(3), 34–36.

Busk, P. L., & Serlin, R. C. (1992). Meta-analysis for single-case research. In T. R. Kratochwill & J. R. Levin (Eds.), *Single-case research design and analysis: New directions for psychology and education* (pp. 187–212). Hillsdale, NJ: Lawrence Erlbaum Associates.

Christenson, S. L., & Sheridan, S. M. (2001). *School and families: Creating essential connections for learning*. New York: Guilford Press.

Cohen, J. (1988). *Statistical power analysis for the behavioral sciences* (2nd ed.). Hillsdale, NJ: Erlbaum.

Committee for Children (1997). *Second Step violence prevention program*. Seattle, WA: Author.

Cowan, R. J., & Allen, K. D. (2007). Using naturalistic procedures to enhance learning in individuals with autism: A focus on generalized teaching in the school setting. *Psychology in the Schools, 44*, 701–716.

Cowan, R. J., & Sheridan, S. M. (2003). Investigating the acceptability of behavioral interventions in applied conjoint behavioral consultation: Moving from analog conditions to naturalistic settings. *School Psychology Review, 18*, 1–21.

Cripe, J., & Venn, M. (1997). Family-guided routines for early intervention services. *Young Exceptional Children, 1*(1), 18–26.

Crone, D. A., & Horner, R. H. (2003). *Building positive behavior support systems in schools*. New York: Guilford Press.

Crone, D., Horner, R., & Hawken, L. (2004). *Responding to problem behavior in schools: The Behavior Education Program*. New York: Guilford Press.

De Martini-Scully, D., Bray, M. A., & Kehle, T. J. (2000). A packaged intervention to reduce disruptive behaviors in general education students. *Psychology in the Schools, 37*, 149–156.

Dietrich, R. (1999). Increasing treatment fidelity by matching interventions to contextual variables within the educational setting. *School Psychology Review, 28*, 608–620.

Doyle, P. D., Jenson, W. R., Clark, E., & Gates, G. (1999). Free time and dots as negative reinforcement to improve academic completion and accuracy for mildly disabled students. *Proven Practice, 2*, 10–15.

Eckert, T. L., & Hintze, J. (2000). Behavioral conceptions and applications of acceptability: Issues related to service delivery and research methodology. *School Psychology Quarterly, 15*, 123–148.

Ehrhardt, K.E., Barnett, D.W., Lentz, F.E., Stollar, S. A., & Reifin, L. H. (1996). Innovative methodology in ecological consultation: Use of scripts to promote treatment acceptability and integrity. *School Psychology Quarterly, 11,* 149–168.

Fuchs, D., Mock, D., Morgan, P. L., & Young, C. L. (2003). Responsiveness-to-intervention: Definitions, evidence, and implications for the learning disabilities construct. *Learning Disabilities Research and Practice, 18,* 157–171.

Girls and Boys Town. (2005). Girls and Boys Town Education Model fidelity and effects on academic engagement, suspension rates, and academic performance of Hartford Public Schools elementary school students. Boys Town, NE: Author.

Glass, G. (1976). Primary, secondary, and meta-analysis of research. *Educational Research 5,* 3–8.

Goals 2000: Educate America Act. (1994, March 31). Pub. Law 103–227.

Gresham, F. M. (1997). Social competence in children with behavior disorders: Where we've been, where we are, and where we should go. *Education and Treatment of Children, 20,* 233–249.

Gresham, F. M. (2003). Teaching social skills to high-risk children and youth: Preventive and remedial strategies. In M. R. Shinn, H. M. Walker, & G. Stoner (Eds.), *Interventions for academic and behavior problems II: Preventive and remedial approaches* (pp. 403–432). Bethesda, MD: National Association of School Psychologists.

Gresham, F. M. (2004). Current status and future directions of school-based behavioral interventions. *School Psychology Review, 33,* 326–343.

Gresham, F. M., MacMillan, D. L., Beebe-Frankenberger, M. E., & Bocian, K. M. (2000). Treatment integrity in learning disabilities intervention research: Do we really know how treatments are implemented? *Learning Disabilities Research & Practice, 15,* 198–205.

Grossman, D. C., Neckerman, H. J., Koepsell, T. D., Liu, P., Asher, K. N., Beland, K., et al. (1997). Effectiveness of a violence prevention curriculum among children in elementary school: A randomized control trial. *Journal of the American Medical Association, 277,* 1605–1611.

Gutkin, T. B., & Curtis, M. J. (1990). School-based consultation: Theory, techniques, and research. In T. B. Gutkin & C. R. Reynolds (Eds.), *The handbook of school psychology* (2nd ed., pp. 577–611). New York: Wiley.

Hawken, L. S., & Horner, R. H. (2003). Evaluation of a targeted intervention within a schoolwide system of behavior support. *Journal of Behavioral Education, 12,* 225–240.

Hay, W. M., Hay, L. R., & Nelson, R. O. (1977). Direct and collateral changes in on-task and academic behavior resulting from on-task versus academic contingencies. *Behavior Therapy, 8,* 431–441.

Hirallal, A. S., & Martens, B. K. (1998). Teaching classroom management skills to preschool teachers: The effects of scripted instructional sequences on teacher and student behavior. *School Psychology Quarterly, 13,* 94–115.

Individuals with Disabilities Education Improvement Act Amendments of 2004. (2004, December). Pub. Law 108–446.

Johnson, T. J., Stoner, G., & Green, S. K. (1996). Demonstrating the experimenting society model with classwide behavior management interventions. *School Psychology Review, 25,* 199–214.

Jones, R. N., Sheridan, S. M., & Binns, W. R. (1993). Schoolwide social skills training: Providing preventive services to students at risk. *School Psychology Quarterly, 8,* 57–80.

Kavale, K. A., Mathur, S. R., Forness, S. R., Rutherford, R. B., & Quinn, M. M. (1997). Effectiveness of social skills training for students with behavior disorders: A meta-analysis. *Advances in Learning and Behavioral Disabilities, 11,* 1–26.

Kazdin, A. E. (1982). *Single-case research designs: Methods for clinical and applied settings.* New York: Oxford University Press.

Kehle, T. J., Bray, M. A., Theodore, L. A., Jenson, W. R., & Clark, E. (2000). A multi-component intervention designed to reduce disruptive classroom behavior. *Psychology in the Schools, 37,* 475–481.

Koegel, R. L., Koegel, L. K., & Carter, C. M. (1999). Pivotal teaching interactions for children with autism. *School Psychology Review, 28,* 576–594.

Krantz, P. J., & McClannahan, L. E. (1993). Teaching children with autism to initiate to peers: Effects of a script-fading procedure. *Journal of Applied Behavior Analysis, 26,* 121–132.

Krantz, P. J., & McClannahan, L. E. (1998). Social interaction skills for children with autism: A script-fading procedure for beginning readers. *Journal of Applied Behavior Analysis, 31,* 191–202.

Kratochwill, T. R., & Bergan, J. R. (1990). *Behavioral consultation: An individual guide.* New York: Plenum Press.

Lentz, F. E., Allen, S. J., & Ehrhardt, K. E. (1996). The conceptual elements of strong interventions in school settings. *School Psychology Quarterly, 11,* 118–136.

Lewis, T. J., & Sugai, G. (1999). Effective behavior support: A systems approach to proactive school-wide management. *Effective School Practices, 17*(4), 47–53.

Maag, J. W. (1999). *Behavior management: From theoretical implications to practical applications.* San Diego, CA: Singular Publishing Group.

Martens, B. K., & DiGennaro, F. D. (2007). Behavioral consultation. In W. P. Erchul & S. M. Sheridan (Eds.), *Handbook of research in school* consultation: Empirical foundations for the field. Hillsdale, NJ: Lawrence Erlbaum.

Martens, B. K., Witt, J. C., Daly, E. J., III, & Vollmer, T. R. (1999). Behavior analysis: Theory and practice in educational settings. In C. R. Reynolds & T. B. Gutkin (Eds.), *The handbook of school psychology* (3rd ed., pp. 638–663). New York: John Wiley & Sons.

Mastropieri, M. A., & Scruggs, T. E. (1994). *Effective instruction for special education* (2nd ed.). Austin, TX: PRO-ED.

Matheson, A. S., & Shriver, M. D. (2005). Training teachers to give effective commands: Effects on student compliance and academic behaviors. *School Psychology Review, 34,* 202–219.

Mathur, S. R., Kavale, K. A., Quinn, M. M., Forness, S. R., & Rutherford, R. B. (1998). Social skills interventions for students with emotional or behavioral disorders: A meta-analysis of the single-subject research. *Behavioral Disorders, 23,* 149–152.

Maurice, C., Green, G., & Luce, S. C. (Eds.) (1996). *Behavioral intervention for young children with autism.* Austin, TX: PRO-ED.

McGoey, K. E., & DuPaul, G. J. (2000). Token reinforcement and response cost procedures: Reducing the disruptive behavior of preschool children with attention-deficit hyperactivity disorder. *School Psychology Quarterly, 15,* 330–343.

Medway, F. J, & Updyke, J. F. (1985). Meta-analysis of consultation outcome studies. *American Journal of Community Psychology, 13,* 489–505.

Miltenberger, R. G. (2003). *Behavior modification: Principles and procedures* (3rd ed.). Belmont, CA: Wadsworth/Thomson Learning.

Moncher, F. & Prinz, R. (1991). Treatment fidelity in outcome studies. *Clinical Psychology Review, 11,* 247–266.

Mottram, L., Bray, M. A., Kehle, T. J., Broudy, M., & Jenson, W. R. (2002). A classroom- based intervention to reduce disruptive behaviors. *Journal of Applied School Psychology, 19,* 65–74.

Musser, E. H., Bray, M. A., Kehle, T. J., & Jenson, W. R. (2001). Reducing disruptive behavior in students with social and emotional disorders. *School Psychology Review, 30,* 294–304.

Newsom, C., Favell, J., & Rincover, A. (1983). The side effects of punishment. In J. Apsche & S. Axelrod (Eds.), *Punishment: Its effects on human behavior* (pp. 285–316). New York: Academic Press.

No Child Left Behind. (2002, January). Pub. Law 107–110.

OSEP Technical Assistance Center on Positive Behavioral Interventions and Supports (PBIS) (n.d.). *Overview of tertiary intervention.* Retrieved June 1, 2006, from www.pbis.org/tertiary Prevention

Parker, R. I., Brossart, D. F., Vannest, K. J., Long, J. R., De-Alba, R. G., Baugh, F. G., et al. (2005). Effect sizes in single case research: How large is large? *School Psychology Review, 34,* 116–132.

Pelios, L. V., MacDuff, G. S., & Axelrod, S. (2003). The effects of a treatment package in establishing independent academic work skills in children with autism. *Education and Treatment of Children, 26*(1), 1–21.

Rathvon, N. (2003). *Effective school interventions: Strategies for enhancing academic achievement and social competence.* New York: Guilford.

Reavis, H. K., Sweeten, M. T., Jenson, W. R., Morgan, D. P., Andrews, D. J., & Fister, S. (1996). *Best practices: Behavioral and educational strategies for teachers.* Longmont, CO: Sopris West.

Reimers, T. M., Wacker, D. P., & Koeppl, G. (1987). Acceptability of behavioral interventions: A review of the literature. *School Psychology Review, 16,* 212–227.

Rhode, G., Jenson, W. R., & Reavis, H. K. (1993). *The tough kid book.* Longmont, CO: Sopris West.

Ruth, W. J. (1996). Goal setting and behavior contracting for students with emotional and behavioral difficulties: Analysis of daily, weekly and total goal attainment. *Psychology in the Schools, 33,* 153–158.

Salend, S. J. (1994). *Effective mainstreaming: Creating inclusive classrooms* (2nd ed.). New York: MacMillon.

Sarokoff, R. A., Taylor, B. A., & Poulson, C. L. (2001). Teaching children with autism to engage in conversational exchanges: Script-fading with embedded textual stimuli. *Journal of Applied Behavior Analysis, 34,* 81–84.

School-wide Information System: What is SWIS? Retrieved June 1, 2006 from www.swis.org/index.php?p=overview;q=1

Scruggs, T. E., Mastriopieri, M. A., & Casto, G. (1987). The quantitative synthesis of single-subject research: Methodology and validation. *Remedial and Special Education, 8,* 24–33.

Shapiro, E. (2004). *Academic skills problems: Direct assessment and intervention* (3rd ed.). New York: Guilford Press.

Sheridan, S. M., Hungelmann, A., & Maughan, D. (1999). A contextualized framework for social skills assessment, intervention, and generalization. *School Psychology Review, 28,* 84–103.

Sheridan, S. M., & Kratochwill, T. R. (2008). *Conjoint behavioral consultation: Promoting family-school connections and interventions.* New York: Springer.

Sheridan, S. M., Kratochwill, T. R., & Bergan, J. R. (1996). *Conjoint behavioral consultation: A procedural manual.* New York: Plenum.

Sheridan, S. M., Welch, M., & Orme, S. (1996). Is consultation effective? A review of outcome research. *Remedial and Special Education*, 17, 341–354.

Shinn, M. R. (1989). Identifying and defining academic problems: CBM screening and eligibility procedures. In M. R. Shinn (Ed.), *Curriculum based measurement: Assessing special children* (pp. 90–129). New York: The Guilford Press.

Shinn, M. R. (1998). *Advanced applications of curriculum-based measurement.* New York: Guilford Press.

Sprague, J. R., Sugai, G., & Walker, H. (1998). Antisocial behavior in schools. In S. Watson & F. M. Gresham (Eds.), *Handbook of child behavior therapy* (pp. 451–474). New York: Springer.

Sprague, J., Walker, H., Golly, A., White, K., Myers, D. R., & Shannon, T. (2001). Translating research into effective practice: The effects of a universal staff and student intervention on indicators of discipline and school safety. *Education and Treatment of Children*, 24, 495–511.

Stokes, T. F., & Baer, D. M. (1977). An implicit technology of generalization. *Journal of Applied Behavior Analysis*, 10, 349–367.

Stokes, T. F., & Osnes, P. G. (1989). An operant pursuit of generalization. *Behavior Therapy*, 20, 337–355.

Sugai, G., & Horner, R. H. (1994). Including students with severe behavior problems in general education settings: Assumptions, challenges, and solutions. *Oregon Conference Monograph*, 6, 102–120.

Sugai, G., Horner, R. H., & Gresham, F. M. (2002). Behaviorally effective school environments. In M. R. Shinn, H. M. Walker, & G. Stoner (Eds.), *Interventions for academic and behavior problems II: Preventive and remedial approaches* (pp. 315–341). Bethesda, MD: National Association of School Psychologists.

Sugai, G., Horner, R. H., Dunlap, G., Hieneman, M., Lewis, T. J., Nelson, C. M., et al. (1999). *Applying positive behavioral support and functional behavioral assessment in schools.* Washington, DC: OSEP Center on Positive Behavioral Interventions and Supports.

Tawney, J. W., & Gast, D. L. (1984). *Single subject research in special education.* Columbus, OH: Charles E. Merrill Publishing Co.

Telzrow, C. F. & Beebe, J. J. (2002). Best practices in facilitating intervention adherence and integrity. In A. Thomas & J. Grimes (Eds.), *Best Practices IV* (Ch. 34). Bethesda MD: National Association of School Psychologists.

Tilly, W. D., Knoster, T., & Ikeda, M. J. (2000). Functional behavioral assessment: Strategies for positive behavior support. In C. Telzrow & M. Tankersley (Eds.), *IDEA Implementation* (pp. 135–189). Washington, DC: National Association of School Psychologists.

Walker, H. M., Colvin, G., & Ramsey, E. (1995). *Antisocial behavior in school: Strategies and best practices.* Belmont, CA: Brookes/Cole.

Walker, H. M., Horner, R. H., Sugai, G., Bullis, M., Sprague, J. R., Bricker, D., & Kaufman, M. J. (1996). Integrated approaches to prevention anti-social behavior patterns among school-age children and youth. *Journal of Emotional and Behavioral Disorders*, 4, 194–209.

Walker, H. M., Ramsey, E., & Gresham, F. M. (2004). *Antisocial behavior in school: Evidence- based practices* (2nd ed.). Belmont, CA: Wadsworth/Thomson Learning.

Watson, T.S., & Steege, M.W., (2003). *Conducting school-based functional behavioral assessments.* New York: Guilford Press.

Weisz, J. R., Weiss, B., Alicke, M. D., & Klotz, M. L. (1987). Effectiveness of psychotherapy with children and adolescents: A meta-analysis for clinicians. *Journal of Consulting and Clinical Psychology*, 55, 542–549.

Weisz, J. R., Weiss, B., Han, S. S., Granger, D. A., & Morton, T. (1995). Effects of psychotherapy with children and adolescents revisited: A meta-analysis of treatment outcome studies. *Psychological Bulletin*, 117, 450–468.

Wickstrom, K. F., Jones, K. M., LaFleur, L. H., & Witt, J. C. (1998). An analysis of treatment integrity in school-based behavioral consultation. *School Psychology Quarterly*, 13, 141–54.

Wilczynski, S. M., Cowan, R. J., Wolf, K., Vauce, T., Lewis, L. J., Hayes, A., et al. (2003). Project BEST-CASE: A model for structuring an intensive early childhood intervention program for children with autistic spectrum disorder. *Proven Practice*, 5, 23–36.

Witt, J. C., Daly, E., & Noell, G. (2000). *Functional assessments: A step-by-step guide to solving academic and behavior problems.* Longmont, CO: Sopris-West.

Witt, J. C., & Elliott, S. N. (1985). Acceptability of classroom intervention strategies. In T. R. Kratochwill (Ed.), *Advances in school psychology* (Vol. 4, pp. 251–288). Hillsdale, NJ: Lawrence Erlbaum.

Wolf, M. M. (1978). Social validity: The case for subjective measurement or how applied behavior analysis is finding its heart. *Journal of Applied Behavior Analysis*, 11, 203–214.

Yeaton, W. H., & Sechrest, L. (1981). Critical dimensions in the choice and maintenance of successful treatment: Strength, integrity, and effectiveness. *Journal of Consulting and Clinical Psychology*, 49, 156–167.

Ysseldyke, J. & Christenson, S. (2002). *Functional assessment of academic behavior: Creating essential learning environments.* Longmont, CO: Sopris West.

CHAPTER 28

SCHOOL-BASED CONSULTATION: THE SCIENCE AND PRACTICE OF INDIRECT SERVICE DELIVERY

TERRY B. GUTKIN
San Francisco State University
MICHAEL J. CURTIS
University of South Florida

Over the last several decades, school-based consultation has continued to emerge as one of the professional activities most preferred by school psychologists, often being ranked by practitioners as the most desired role and almost always viewed as a job function in which they would like to engage more often (e.g., Bahr, 1996; Cummings, Harrison, & Dawson, 2004; Fisher, Jenkins, & Crumbley, 1986; Meacham & Peckham, 1978; Roberts & Rust, 1994; Sheridan & Walker, 1999; Sheridan, Welch, & Orme, 1996; VanVoorhis & Levinson, 2006). Since the publication of this chapter in the first edition of the *Handbook of School Psychology* (Gutkin & Curtis, 1982), a continuing stream of books, book chapters, and journal miniseries have appeared at an increasing rate, attesting to the central role of school-based consultation in the professional practice of school psychology (Bergan & Kratochwill, 1990; Bernard & DiGiuseppe, 1994; Brown, Pryzwansky, & Schulte, 2006; Caplan & Caplan, 1993; Cole & Siegel, 2003; Conoley & Conoley, 1992; Costenbader, Swartz, & Petrix, 1992; Dinkmeyer & Carlson, 2007; Dougherty, 2005; Erchul, 1993a, 2003; Erchul & Martens, 2002; Erchul & Sheridan, 2007; Gutkin, 1997; Kampwirth, 2006; Kratochwill & Bergan, 1990; Kratochwill, Elliott, & Callan-Stoiber, 2002; Kratochwill, Elliott, & Carrington Rotto, 1995; Lambert, Hylander, & Sandoval, 2004; Levinson, 1990; Marks, 1995; Nastasi, 2006; Noell, 1996; Parsons & Kahn, 2005; Rosenfield, 1987, 2002; Rosenfield & Gravois, 1996; Sheridan, 1997; Sheridan, Kratochwill, & Bergan, 1996; Zins & Erchul, 1995; 2002; Zins, Kratochwill, & Elliott, 1993b; Zins

& Ponti, 1990). The initiation of the *Journal of Education and Psychological Consultation* in 1990, a refereed journal devoted entirely to consultation theory, research, and practice, is further evidence of the expanding interest of school psychologists and other human service professionals in consultation. Consistent with the positive attitudes toward consultation reflected in these and other publications has been a growing number of literature reviews and meta-analyses indicating that school-based consultation is an effective means of service delivery (Guli, 2005; Kratochwill, Elliott & Busse, 1995; Mannino & Shore, 1975; Medway, 1979, 1982; Medway & Updyke, 1985; Sheridan, Eagle, Cowan, & Mickelson, 2001; Sheridan, Eagle, & Doll, 2006; Sheridan et al. 1996).

Although the remainder of this chapter is devoted primarily to the examination of school-based consultation services from the perspective of school psychologists, it is important to note that school psychologists are not alone in their support for this approach to service delivery in educational as well as community settings. For example, special educators (e.g., Idol, Nevin, & Paolucci-Whitcomb, 1994; Zins & Heron, 1996), mental health professionals (Crothers, Hughes, & Morine, 2008; Sears, Rudisill, & Mason-Sears, 2006), counselors (e.g., Conyne & Cook, 2004; Duncan, 1995; Lusky & Hayes, 2001; Otwell & Mullis, 1997; Randolph & Mitchell, 1995), community psychologists (e.g., O'Hearn & Gatz, 1996), psychiatrists (Bostic & Bagnell, 2001; "Practice Parameter," 2005; Rappaport, 2001; Walter, 2001), and speech pathologists (Centeno & Eng, 2005; Secord, 1990), among others, also appear to view these services as vital. Above and beyond these individual professional groups, there is clear evidence that entire school districts, agencies, state departments of education, and national professional organizations are implementing and/or promoting consultation as a core element in student services delivery (American School Counselor Association, 2005; Bush et al., 1989; Canter, 1991; Connecticut State Department of Education, 2004; Council for the Accreditation of Counseling and Related Educational Programs, 2001; Council on Social Work Education, 2001; Cummings et al., 2004; D'Amato, Sheridan, & Phelps, 2003, 2004; Franklin & Duley, 1991, 2002; Givens-Ogle, Christ, & Idol, 1991; House & McInerney, 1996; Ikeda, Tilly, Stumme, Volmer, & Allison, 1996; National Association of School Psychologists [NASP], 2000; Tindal, Shinn, Walz, & Germann, 1987; Ysseldyke et al., 1997; Ysseldyke et al., 2006). Work on school-based consultation in international settings is also appearing in the literature with increasing frequency (e.g., Annan, 2005; Bozic, 2004; Duch, 2005; Gillies, 2000; Hatzichristou, 2003; Larney, 2003; Moreno & Torrego, 1999; Nastasi, Varjas, Bernstein, & Jayasena, 2000; Nastasi, Varjas, & Schensul, 2000; O'Brien & Miller, 2005; Pérez-Gonzalez, García-Ros, & Gómez-Artiga, 2004; Sinha, Kishore, & Thakur, 2003).

IMPORTANCE OF CONSULTATION FOR SCHOOL PSYCHOLOGICAL SERVICES

The Paradox of School Psychology

The ability of school psychologists to serve children has always been, and probably always will be, mediated to a large extent by their ability to function effectively as consultants. While consultation services have always been valued highly by both school psychologists and the consumers of school psychological services (Gutkin & Curtis, 1982), recent events have served to underscore even further the centrality of this approach. With each passing year, consultation seems to grow in importance as a foundational role for the profession (Ysseldyke et al., 2006).

The critical importance of consultation for school psychologists lies in what Gutkin and Conoley (1990) termed the "Paradox of School Psychology." That is, "to serve children effectively school psychologists must, first and foremost, concentrate their attention and professional expertise on adults" (p. 212). Although not intuitively obvious, the impact of school psychologists on children is typically a function of actions taken (or not taken) by adults other than school psychologists in the school and home environments of children (Sheridan & Gutkin, 2000). In earlier times, many believed that the school psychologist's job was complete after correctly diagnosing a child's problem(s) and/or designing an efficacious intervention for a referred child. Today, such a belief would be considered naïve (Witt, 1990b).

Gutkin and Conoley (1990) provide the following example to illustrate the nature of the "Paradox of School Psychology."

Consider the hypothetical case of a third grade child who is referred to a school psychologist because of academic difficulties. The school psychologist is highly sophisticated regarding academic dysfunctions of third graders and does a superior job of assessing and diagnosing the child's difficulties. In addition to isolating and correctly diagnosing the specific psychoeducational deficits exhibited by the referred child, the psychologist also develops a set of insightful treatment recommendations centering on the initiation of a system of contingent positive reinforcement for appropriate academic behavior in the child's regular classroom. The psychologist communicates her or his expertise and ideas for intervention to the classroom teacher via a detailed written report and a multidisciplinary team meeting. Although the stage is set for effective treatment to occur, no such outcome ever comes to pass ... because the child's teacher, who has to implement the psychologist's plan, believes that behavior modification is tantamount to bribery (a belief that is not uncommon among teachers [Grieger, 1977]). The final results of the school psychologist's efforts in this hypothetical (but not at all unusual) case are (a) a high-quality assessment of the referred child, (b) an accurate diagnosis of the referred child's problems, (c) the development of an effective treatment plan for the referred child, but (d) no meaningful psychological service provided to the referred child. (pp. 210–211)

In other words, the expertise of the school psychologist was of no benefit to the child. As per the "Paradox of School Psychology," the ability of this school psychologist to deliver meaningful assistance to this student hinged directly on his or her ability to consult effectively with the teacher, going beyond both the diagnosis of the child's problems and written recommendations for intervention.

Given the "Paradox of School Psychology," interpersonal influence with adults should be viewed as a key to successful school psychological services for children (Gutkin, 1997). And while consultation clearly is not the only means by which school psychologists can exert influence on the lives of children through significant adults, it would seem to hold more promise than either assessment (Andrews & Gutkin, 1994) or child-focused therapy services "given its unique emphasis on long-term, face-to-face, collaborative relationships between school psychologists and relevant third-party adults" (Gutkin & Conoley, 1990, p. 211).

Shifting Paradigm

There has been significant change in the educational context for the practice of school psychology over the last three decades (Cobb, 1990; Graden, Zins, Curtis, & Cobb, 1988; Reschly & Ysseldyke, 1995, 2002). Major paradigm shifts have occurred during that time for both general and special education, as well as for school psychology (Gutkin, Chapter 23; Reschly, 2008; Sheridan & Gutkin, 2000).

Following a long history of services to students with disabilities through segregated pull-out special education programs or their exclusion from public education altogether, the passage of the Education for All Handicapped Children Act (PL 94–142) in the mid-1970s launched an emphasis on the inclusion of students with special needs in mainstream and general education environments. This movement has continued to gain momentum as a national priority largely in response to (1) meta-analyses indicating that segregated, pull-out placements are not typically superior to the maintenance of children in mainstream settings (Carlberg & Kavale, 1980; Kavale, 2005; Kavale & Forness, 1999; Wang & Baker, 1986); (2) research indicating that special education placements often provide educational programs that are pedagogically indistinguishable from what is offered in general education (Epps & Tindal, 1987; Ysseldyke,

Christenson, & Thurlow, 1989); (3) data documenting the disproportional representation of minority students in special education programs (National Research Council, 2002); (4) evidence of rapidly increasing costs of educating children with disabilities in non-mainstream environments (President's Commission on Excellence in Special Education, 2002; Ysseldyke, Algozzine, & Thurlow, 1992); (5) federal mandates for education in the least restrictive environment, initiated by the Education for All Handicapped Children Act (PL 94-142) and continued through subsequent reauthorizations, including the Individuals with Disabilities Education Act (IDEA, PL 101-476) and the Individuals with Disabilities Education Improvement Act (IDEIA, PL 108-446); (6) federal, state, and professional guidelines for approaches such as prereferral intervention (Truscott, Cohen, & Sams, 2005) and response to intervention (Reschly & Bergstrom, Chapter 22; Jimerson, Burns, & VanDerHeyden, 2007); (7) growing disillusionment by school psychologists (e.g. Gutkin & Tieger, 1979; Ysseldyke et al., 1984) and other powerful groups of educators (National Association of State Boards of Education, 1992; National Association of State Directors of Special Education, 2005) with categorical approaches to special education services; and (8) research supportive of inclusive practices for a broad range of children with disabilities (Farrell, Jimerson, Howes, & Davies, Chapter 38; Hollowood, Salisbury, Rainforth, & Palombaro, 1994; Janney, Snell, Beers & Raynes, 1995; Salisbury, Evans & Palombaro, 1997; Shinn, Powell-Smith, & Good, 1996).

To promote the inclusion of students with disabilities, schools have relied on two primary strategies, both of which are premised on the delivery of consultation services by school psychologists and other educational specialists. First, students with disabilities in segregated, special education programs are returned to general education classrooms to the maximum extent possible. Given that many of these children still have significant needs relating to academic performance and behavior, the general education teachers who work with them are typically in need of substantial support and assistance (Curtis & Meyers, 1988; Gravois, Groff, & Rosenfield, Chapter 37; Scruggs & Mastropieri, 1996; Ysseldyke & Burns, Chapter 21; Zins, Curtis, Graden, & Ponti, 1988). School districts that have documented successful programs for reintegrating children with disabilities into general education have relied very heavily on consultation and collaborative services as a primary vehicle for providing this support (e.g., Bush et al., 1989; Canter, 1991; Franklin & Duley, 1991; Givens-Ogle et al., 1991; Janney et al., 1995; Shapiro, Miller, & Sawka, 1999; Wilkinson, 2005).

A second strategy intended to support the movement toward inclusive education initially was termed *prereferral intervention*. However, for many teachers, this term created a belief that the associated process simply represented procedural obstacles that had to be cleared before referring a child for a suspected disability, rather than a process to address the student's needs (Kovaleski, 2002). To address this issue, the term *intervention assistance* was proposed (Zins, Curtis, Graden, & Ponti, 1988). The latter term is more likely to convey a message of support for teachers in their attempts to respond to children's needs. As detailed by Graden, Casey, and Christenson (1985) in one of the earlier descriptions of this approach, the process involves joint problem solving by teachers and educational specialists for the purposes of designing and implementing effective educational programs in mainstream settings for children who are experiencing significant academic and behavioral problems. The goal of this approach is to prevent children from being removed unnecessarily from general education environments. Currently, intervention processes prior to special education assessment and/or placement are required or recommended in 69% and 86% of states, respectively (Truscott et al., 2005).

Growing interest in prevention and intervention, as well as continued concerns about categorical special education services, particularly for students with mild disabilities, have led to even stronger mandates for change in both general and special education through the passage of federal legislation such as the No Child Left Behind Act (NCLB) and the Individuals with Disabilities Educational Improvement Act (IDEIA). The requirements of this legislation have been largely responsible for the emergence of a national movement for school reform based on the implementation of a problem solving/response to intervention (PS/RTI) model for addressing the needs of all students. Reschly and Bergstrom (this volume) note that although the terms problem solving and response to intervention (RTI) are sometimes used interchangeably, RTI refers to a tiered system for the delivery of empirically based interventions of varying intensity that employs a data-based problem-solving process.

To encourage and support state departments of education in efforts to move toward the implementation of a PS/RTI model, the National Association of State Directors of Special Education has published two documents, *Response to Intervention: Policy Considerations and Implementation* (2005) and *Response to Intervention: Research for Practice* (2007). In addition, the *Handbook of Response to Intervention: The Science and Practice of Assessment and Intervention* (Jimerson et al., 2007) addresses a range of issues relating to foundations of problem-solving and response to intervention strategies, data-based decision making, research-based prevention and intervention strategies, and implementation issues. It is apparent that a PS/RTI model is not only consistent with, but in fact dependent on, the delivery of effective consultation services by school psychologists and other educational specialists for successful implementation.

To be successful within the context of a PS/RTI model, school psychologists must have expertise in at least two areas: (a) evidence-based practices and interventions (EBI's) (Kratochwill et al., this volume), and (b) consultee-centered and small group consultative problem solving procedures. (Since the implementation of a PS/RTI model represents major organizational change in most schools, there also is both a need and an opportunity for school psychologists to engage in system-level consultation—see Curtis, Castillo, & Cohen, 2008 and Meyers, Meyers, Proctor & Graybill, this volume, for a discussion of the role of school psychologists in organizational/systems change). Consequently, school psychologists must have at least fundamental familiarity with research on effective instructional practices (see Doll, LeClair, & Kurien, Chapter 36; Gettinger & Stoiber, Chapter 35; Pressley et al., Chapter 25; Reisman, Chapter 26), classroom management strategies (Daly, Martens, Skinner, & Noell, Chapter 5; Cowan, & Sheridan, Chapter 27), and effective teaming (Gravois, Groff & Rosenfield, Chapter 37).

Consultation is essential to each of the developments discussed above. Consultation services provide school psychologists with a mechanism by which they can positively affect the educational and psychological development of all children, rather than just those with disabilities. The opportunity to provide services to *all* children has been articulated as a major goal for the profession since the Thayer Conference in 1954 (Cutts, 1955) and continues to be reflected in the most contemporary statements of professional standards (e.g., NASP, 2000) and role definitions (e.g., Thomas & Grimes, 2008). To accomplish this goal, school psychologists strive to "give psychology away" (Miller, 1969, p. 1071) through consultation services to those persons who have the most intensive daily contact with the broadest range of children (e.g., teachers). By enhancing the psychological, educational, and mental health skills of consultees such as teachers, school psychologists can indirectly benefit the lives of innumerable children.

Clearly, consultation is a crucial component of the school psychologist's professional role, and this has been recognized in virtually (if not, literally) every major professional document that addresses comprehensive school psychological services (e.g., Ysseldyke et al., 2006). Proceeding within this context, we turn now to a delineation of the core characteristics of consultation services that undergird the interactions between consultants and consultees. Specifically, we examine those central philosophical and operational components that we perceive to make up the basic foundations of consultation theory and practice.

CORE CHARACTERISTCS OF SCHOOL-BASED CONSULTATIVE SERVICES

Consultation is a complex and sophisticated set of service delivery methodologies. And although there are numerous consultation models from which the practitioner can choose (three of the more prominent models are described below), these models are bound together by a set of essential characteristics and assumptions that constitute the core of all consultation services. These core elements are the defining features of consultation that serve both to unify the various consultation models and to set them apart from other approaches to service delivery, such as psychotherapy.

The discussion that follows details those core characteristics that have both significant historical roots (e.g., Bergan, 1977; Caplan, 1970; Schein, 1969) and broad contemporary acceptance (e.g., Bergan & Kratochwill, 1990; Caplan & Caplan, 1993; Conoley & Conoley, 1992; Gutkin, 1996a), emerging from theories that hold diverse orientations. Although widely accepted, these core elements are not without controversy, and many authors have noted the need to continuously re-examine and revise these assumptions in response to emerging theoretical and empirical

information (e.g., Erchul, 1999; Gresham & Noell, 1993; Gutkin, 1993b; Noell & Witt, 1996; Schulte & Osborne, 2003; Witt, 1990a).

An Overarching Definition

Despite the broad and growing interest in consultative approaches among educators, school psychologists, and other health service providers, there remains considerable confusion regarding what constitutes consultation per se. Part of the problem is the term *consultation* itself, which is used in so many contexts and in reference to so many different types of service relationships that for some it has almost become devoid of meaning. Decades ago Barry (1970) observed, "Today almost everyone is a consultant. Every program has consultants. Sometimes it seems as if there are more consultants than consultees!" (p. 363). This statement remains quite accurate more than 35 years after it was made.

Although there is no single definition of consultation with universal support, we continue to find Medway's definition (1979) to be both succinct and accurate. As such, it is used for the purposes of this chapter. Specifically, Medway defines consultation as a process of "collaborative problem-solving between a mental health specialist (the consultant) and one or more persons (the consultees) who are responsible for providing some form of psychological assistance to another (the client)" (p. 276).

Indirect Service Delivery

Indirect service is the single most definitive characteristic of consultation. In the more traditional system of direct service delivery, the psychologist's primary contact is with a client (or patient) who receives services directly from the psychologist. Psychotherapy and counseling are common exemplars of direct services. Psychologists who work from an indirect service delivery model, however, interact primarily with other professionals and caregivers (consultees) who work directly with clients. In the indirect model, psychologists do not provide services directly to clients themselves. In school-based consultation, school psychologists frequently function as the consultant, teachers or parents as the consultees, and students as clients. Of course, other alignments are possible. That is, other professionals may serve as either the consultant or consultee, and the client could be anyone associated with the school (e.g., principal, team leaders, teacher aides). Regardless of the specific case, however, when functioning as a consultant, psychologists provide indirect services to one or more clients by working through one or more consultees who have direct and continuing contact with clients. These relationships are illustrated in Figure 28.1.

The indirect service concept should not be mistakenly assumed to imply that consultants are prohibited from having any direct contact with clients as they provide consultation services (Noell & Witt, 1996). The crucial issue is not whether consultants interact directly with clients, but rather that treatment services are ultimately delivered to clients as a result of the consultation process and are implemented by one or more consultees instead of by the consultant. Seen from this perspective, it is clear that psychologists' assessment activities, be they traditional (e.g., norm-referenced testing) or nontraditional (e.g., curriculum-based assessment) in nature, should not be viewed as antithetical to consultation processes, as long as they facilitate the provision of treatment interventions by consultees (Gutkin & Conoley, 1990).

Focus of Consultation

The primary focus of consultation interactions is the provision of services to one or more clients. That is, consultants interact with consultees to improve the educational and psychological circumstances of clients. Whereas success at improving the lives of clients (e.g., children) will often simultaneously lighten the burden of consultees (e.g., teachers and parents), this is a byproduct (albeit one that is very positive) rather than the central purpose of consultative interactions. In consultation, unlike psychotherapy, the personal needs of the consultee are a legitimate focus only to the extent that these personal needs have an impact on a client. Thus, while it would be entirely

appropriate to consult with teachers about methods for controlling their anger toward students, it would be inappropriate to consult with these same teachers about reducing angry outbursts directed toward their spouses. Although circumstances can sometimes make it difficult to distinguish between consultation and psychotherapeutic services, consultants must remain vigilant to avoid dual relationships (i.e., serving as a consultant and a psychotherapist to the same individual), in accordance with our codes of ethics (APA, 2002). Consultation should remain focused first and foremost on the provision of services to clients, not on the provision of psychotherapeutic services to consultees.

Multicultural Considerations

Given the increasing diversity among the parents, students and professionals in today's schools, it is essential that consultation services are delivered in a manner that reflects cultural awareness, sensitivity and responsiveness. Minority students make up 42.6% of the student population in American schools and many of these students speak a language other than English as their primary language (U. S. Department of Education, 2006). The NCLB (2002) requires states to submit yearly reports in which data are disaggregated, enabling an examination of performance for students in different groups, including race/ethnicity, free and reduced lunch, and English language learners. Students of color, those from low SES households, and those for whom English is a second language represent a disproportionately high percentage of struggling learners (National Research Council, 2002). National professional organizations directly relevant to school psychology emphasize the importance of culturally responsive practices (APA, 2002; NASP, 2000). Moreover, given the

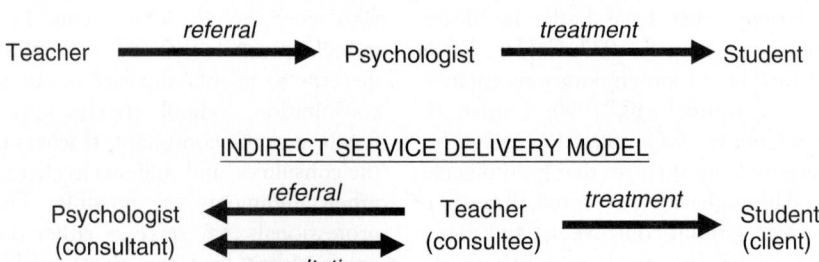

FIGURE 28.1 Direct and Indirect Service Delivery Models.

limited representation of persons of color within the field of school psychology (Curtis, et al., 2008), the attainment of multicultural competence becomes paramount among school psychologists in providing appropriate and effective services to an increasingly diverse student population.

Ingraham and Meyers (2000) note that, although "the consultation literature offers some excellent models for delivering preventive, problem-solving, and indirect psychological services in schools and for researching the efficacy of school consultation services... (it) does not yet provide adequate conceptual or applied models for guiding research and practice concerning school-based consultation with differing cultural populations" (p. 315). A fairly recent issue of *School Psychology Review* (Ingraham & Meyers, 2000) devoted to "Multicultural and Cross-Cultural Consultation in the Schools" included a review of relevant literature, a discussion of many issues relating to this important area, and recommendations to guide culturally competent practice.

Tarver Behring and Ingraham (1998) posited that *multicultural consultation* requires the consultant to adapt "the consultation services to address the needs and cultural values of the consultee, the client, or both" (p. 58). We believe that a comprehensive framework proposed by Ingraham (2000) would be helpful in furthering understanding of multicultural consultation, associated areas for professional development, and multicultural consultation practice. The framework that she proposes includes five components to facilitate understanding of the influence of culture on consultation: (1) Domains

of Consultant Learning and Development, (2) Domains of Consultee Learning and Development, (3) Cultural Variations in the Consultation Constellation, (4) Contextual and Power Influences, and (5) Hypothesized Methods for Supporting Consultee and Client Success. Citing references to support each, she identifies eight domains for "consultant learning and development," which we believe would be helpful in guiding the school psychologist's pursuit of multicultural consultative competence (see Table 28.1).

Recognizing that consultation is based on a triadic relationship that includes a consultant, consultee(s) and client(s), Ingraham (2000) also discusses *cross-cultural consultation* (i.e., when consultation occurs across cultures) in terms of potential variations in culture among the three participant roles. She identifies specific issues that must be considered relating to each of the four possible cultural combinations: (1) Consultant and Consultee—Same, Client—Different; (2) Consultant and Client—Same, Consultee—Different; (3) Consultant—Different, Consultee and Client—Same; and (4) Consultant, Consultee and Client—All Different. Ingraham suggests that a fifth variation can exist in which all three consultation participants share a minority culture that is different from that of the larger context in which they function. While we concur with the issues she raises specific to this particular combination, we would also argue that the potential influence of contextual variables must be considered in all cases with regard to culture, regardless of the cultural similarities or differences of the consultant, consultee(s), and client(s).

TABLE 28.1   Domains for Consultant Learning and Development

1. Understanding one's own culture
2. Understanding the impact(s) of one's own culture on others
3. Respecting and valuing other cultures
4. Understanding individual differences within cultural groups and the multiple cultural identities prevalent in many individuals
5. (a) Cross-cultural communication and (b) Multicultural consultation approaches for developing and maintaining rapport throughout consultation
6. Understanding cultural saliency and how to build bridges across salient differences
7. Understanding the cultural context for consultation (dominant culture, culture of the school or community)
8. Multicultural consultation and interventions appropriate for the consultee(s) and client(s) (Ingraham, 2000, p. 328).

Although much of the work to date in the area of multicultural consultation has been theoretical in nature (e.g., Duncan, 1995; Ramirez, Lepage, & Kratochwill, 1998), there are some noteworthy exceptions. Naumann, Gutkin, and Sandoval (1996), for example, found no significant effects when evaluating whether consultant or client race impacted consultee perceptions of intervention acceptability or consultant credibility. These findings must be interpreted cautiously, however, given the analog nature of this investigation and findings by Rogers (1998) in another analog study in which race and the use of race-sensitive versus race-blind verbalizations were found to impact perceptions of consultant competence and multicultural sensitivity. Ingraham (2003), who conducted a qualitative study of three ethnically diverse consultants employing multicultural consultee-centered consultation in cases with hypothesized cultural elements comprising the presenting problem, also suggested that diversity issues can play a role in successful versus unsuccessful consultation cases. Recent field-based clinical research evaluating the impact of conjoint behavioral consultation using clients exhibiting varying degrees of diversity revealed strong, positive home- and school-based outcomes across all client groups (Sheridan et al., 2006). Gravois and Rosenfield (2006), likewise, reported dramatic decreases in the number of minority children referred to and placed in special education following intervention by instructional consultation teams. These results, in conjunction with the work of Nastasi and her colleagues (Nastasi, Varjas, & Schensul, 2000; Nastasi et al., 2000), who reported on successful cross-cultural consultation in Sri Lanka, are both intriguing and encouraging, suggesting that multicultural consultation services can be provided effectively across national and international cultural groups.

Goals of Consultation

All consultation models have a dual set of goals. One goal is to provide remedial services for clients' presenting problems while another goal is to improve the functioning of consultees so they can prevent and/or respond more effectively to similar problems in the future. The degree of emphasis placed on each of these goals varies across consultation models, but both goals should always be present in the consultant's mind as she or he works with a consultee.

Remediation

The remedial goals of consultation services are rather straightforward. Typically, children (clients) are referred to school psychologists (consultants) because teachers or parents (consultees) are experiencing academic and/or behavioral difficulties that they have been unable to resolve on their own. The consultant's role is to work with one or more consultees to develop effective interventions. Success is determined by assessing whether the referred problem is resolved or has been improved to everyone's satisfaction.

Most available consultation research addresses remedial rather than preventive goals. That is, the bulk of the consultation literature examines whether consultants were able to bring about behavioral and attitudinal changes in consultees and clients in response to presenting problems. Although this body of research has been criticized on methodological grounds and for its lack of specific directions for practitioners (Fuchs, Fuchs, Dulan, Roberts, & Fernstrom, 1992; Gresham & Kendell, 1987; Gutkin 1993b; Hughes, 1994; Medway, 1982; Meyers, Pitt, Gaughan, & Friedman, 1978; Pryzwansky, 1986), there is consensus that school-based consultation services are effective from a remedial perspective. For example, reviewing the consultation research literature from 1985 to 1995, Sheridan, Welch, and Orme (1996) reported positive outcomes in 76% of published studies, which was remarkably similar to the earlier findings of Mannino and Shore (1975) and Medway (1979)—78% and 76% positive outcomes, respectively. Employing meta-analyses, Medway and Updyke (1985) documented effect sizes of .55 for consultees and .39 for clients, indicating that "consultees showed improvements greater than 71% and clients showed improvements greater than 66% of untreated comparable groups" (p. 489). Another meta-analysis by Kratochwill, Elliott, and Busse (1995) of changes in individual clients over time reported an overall effect size of .95, indicating that the average client moved from the 50th percentile before treatment to roughly the 83rd percentile following intervention. Parenthetically, this latter finding is equivalent to the effect sizes typically reported in contemporary psychotherapy outcome research (Lambert & Bergin, 1994). Most recently Sheridan, et al., (2001, 2006) reported large meta-analytic effect sizes (ES > 1.0) for both school and home behavior change when conjoint behavioral consultation was employed with a total of 125 cases.

Prevention

While the prevention goals of consultation are a bit less obvious at first glance, they are every bit as significant. In fact, when viewed from a public health perspective (Meyers, Meyers, & Grogg, 2004; Nastasi, 2004; Strein, Hoagwood & Cohn, 2003), one could make a strong case that the prevention outcomes of consultation are substantially more important in the long term than are those related to remediation (Conoley & Gutkin, 1995).

Within the context of consultation services, prevention is most frequently conceptualized as consultants' efforts to "give psychology away" (Miller, 1969, p. 1071) to consultees. That is, as consultees learn new ways of remediating presenting problems, it is hoped and expected that they may also be able to apply newly acquired content and process knowledge and skills to clients' problems that arise in the future, thus nipping new problems in the bud (secondary prevention) or preventing them from occurring in the first place (primary prevention).

On the content side, if a teacher learns how to work effectively with, for example, a child's acting-out behaviors through consultation with a school psychologist, he or she may be able to apply these same behavior management techniques to other students, either now or in the future, and thus reduce and/or prevent the appearance of other discipline problems. Supportive research findings include the following: (a) dramatic decreases in student referral rates following consultation (Burns & Symington, 2002; Fuchs, Fuchs, & Bahr, 1990; Graden, Casey, & Bonstrom, 1985; Gravois & Rosenfield, 2006; Gutkin, Henning-Stout, & Piersel, 1988; Henning-Stout, Lucas, and McCary, 1993; Nelson, Smith, Taylor, Dodd, & Reavis, 1991; Ponti, Zins, and Graden, 1988; Rosenfield, 1992); (b) generalization of client's gains and/or enhanced consultee content skills (Carrington Rotto & Kratochwill, 1994; Freeland, 2003; Gutkin, 1980, 1986; Gutkin, Singer, & Brown, 1980; Jason & Ferone, 1978; Hundert, 2007; Meyers, 1975; Peck, Killen, & Baumgart, 1989; Ray, Skinner, & Watson, 1999; Riley-Tillman & Eckert, 2001; Watkins-Emonet, 2001); and (c) empirical evaluations of long-standing prevention programs based largely on consultation methodologies (e.g., Cowen & Hightower, 1990; Durlak, Chapter 12; Hightower, Johnson, & Haffey, 1995).

In terms of process, consultation is intended to also help consultees become better problem solvers. With a large body of research suggesting that even young children can be taught problem-solving skills through modeling (e.g., Johnson, Gutkin, & Plake, 1992), it seems quite reasonable to assume that consultation interactions can be utilized by consultants to enhance the problem-solving skills of consultees (Brown & Schulte, 1987; Gutkin, 1993a). To date, a number of studies suggest that consultees' process skills can, in fact, be improved by exposure to consultation, the modeling of consultation, or consultation training (Anderson, Kratochwill, & Bergan, 1986; Cleven & Gutkin, 1988; Curtis & Metz, 1986; Curtis & Watson, 1980; Curtis & Zins, 1988; Gravois, Knotek, & Babinski, 2002; Jefferson, 2001; Kratochwill, VanSomeren, & Sheridan, 1989; Lepage, Kratochwill, & Elliott, 2004; McDougall, Reschly, & Corkery, 1988; Revels & Gutkin, 1983; Watson & Kramer, 1995; Zins & Ponti, 1996). Although some negative findings have been reported (Robbins & Gutkin, 1994) and it is clear that additional research is needed in this area (Noell & Witt, 1996), there appears to be sound empirical reason for cautious optimism (Kratochwill, Bergan, Sheridan, & Elliott, 1998).

Consultant-Consultee Relationship

Much as the therapist-client relationship is thought to be crucial to the process of psychotherapy (Cormier & Cormier, 1991), the consultant-consultee relationship is viewed as pivotal to effective consultation. Although initially given less attention by those who were focused primarily on the technology of a client's behavior change, it is becoming increasingly clear to consultation advocates of all persuasions that the person-to-person relationships established during the course of consultation mediate the effectiveness of consultation services (Conoley & Conoley, 1992; Gutkin, 1999; Kratochwill, Elliott, & Callan-Stoiber, 2002; Rosenfield, 1991; Zins & Erchul, 2002).

The "Paradox of School Psychology" concept (Gutkin & Conoley, 1990) discussed earlier in this chapter and/or a review of Figure 28.1 makes it abundantly clear why the consultant-consultee relationship is so crucial. Quite simply, the consultee always comes between the consultant and the client. Without the cooperation of the consultee, the consultant is powerless to provide assistance to the client. Consequently, consultants will probably be successful only to the extent that they are able to elicit the cooperation of consultees in the execution of treatment programs. While not the sole determinant of this phenomenon, the nature of the consultant-consultee relationship is undoubtedly one major factor influencing whether a consultee adopts a resistant or a cooperative approach to the consultation process and the intervention plans that result.

The following dimensions of consultant-consultee relationships are thought to be particularly important to the success of consultation services. Although not an exhaustive list, these factors do communicate collectively the intended "spirit" of the consultation process. They are also quite consistent with theory and research emerging from the psychotherapy literature, indicating that therapists are more likely to succeed with their clients when these clients perceive their therapists as high on trustworthiness, attractiveness, and expertness (Beutler, Machado, & Neufeldt, 1994).

Coordinate Power Status

Perhaps the most common and long-standing assumption about consultant-consultee relationships is that they should be collegial and collaborative rather than hierarchical and coercive (Bergan, 1977; Caplan, 1970; Meyers, 1973). Prior to consultation, the dominant relationship metaphors in psychological services were doctor-patient and superior-subordinate. Neither, however, is believed to be suitable for consultation.

A doctor-patient relationship is clearly not appropriate because the consultee is not the consultant's patient. The consultee is neither sick nor seeking assistance with a personal problem. Rather, consultation is designed to assist consultees as they examine alternative ways to interact with and serve their clients.

Likewise, superior-subordinate relationships are deemed to be inappropriate. First and foremost, they do not reflect the realities that confront school psychologists or other educational professionals who function as consultants. Whereas Captain Picard may have been able to gain cooperation and compliance from his Star Trek crew simply by commanding them to "Make it so," few if any school psychologists will ever find themselves in this position vis-à-vis the consultees with whom they work (e.g., teachers, parents, principals). Although schools may have a formal organizational chart, implying that some individuals are in superordinate positions, few successful schools function by having those at the top of the organizational chart issue orders and commands to those beneath them (Davis & Thomas, 1989;

Schmuck, 1990). Schools are inherently different from either military or corporate environments; consequently different decision-making and relationship styles are necessary.

Coordinate power status is thought to be appropriate for relationships between consultants and consultees. The most essential element of such a relationship is shared and equal power in the decision-making process. That is, neither consultants nor consultees should be making unilateral decisions against the wishes of their consulting partners. This means that a consultee must be allowed to accept or reject ideas put forth by a consulting school psychologist, based on that consultee's perception of the merit and/or appropriateness of the ideas, rather than being pressured into acceptance because the consultant "ordered" the consultee to "Make it so."

Having noted what is meant by coordinate power status, we must also note what is not meant by this term, for it is subject to misinterpretation without some further explanation. Coordinate power status does *not* mean that consultants and consultees have equivalent or the same bodies of knowledge, for they do not. Whereas psychologists, teachers, parents, and others each have knowledge that is important for the success of a consultation interaction, it is not the same knowledge. In fact, it is these very differences that make the consultation relationship so potentially powerful, as different perspectives and knowledge bases are integrated and synthesized to produce solutions that would not have been evident to either the consultant or consultee working in isolation (Tyler, Pargament, & Gatz, 1983).

Also, coordinate power status does *not* mean that consultants and consultees function in the same way during consultation interactions (Gutkin, 1999; Schulte & Osborne, 2003; Sheridan, 1992). Research (Erchul, 1987; Erchul & Chewning, 1990; Erchul, Covington, Hughes, & Meyers, 1995; Erchul, Hughes, Meyers, Hickman, & Braden, 1992; Gutkin, 1996b; Martens, Erchul, & Witt, 1992; Witt, Erchul, McKee, Pardue, & Wickstrom, 1991) suggests strongly that consultants and consultees behave quite differently as they consult with each other. The most consistent finding to emerge from this growing body of research is that consultants tend to ask more questions than consultees, whereas consultees tend to talk more than consultants, especially during the problem identification process.

Some have interpreted these data to suggest that the need for consultant-consultee collaboration is little more than a myth in the context of school-based consultation (e.g., Erchul & Martens, 1997; Witt, 1990a). We disagree vigorously with this conclusion (see Gutkin, 1999, for an extensive review of this body of research). The finding that consultants are, in some ways, more directive than consultees during the consultation process does *not* suggest the absence of collaboration. Gutkin argues that consultants can be *both* directive and collaborative at the same time, for *directiveness* and *collaboration* are not opposites. The opposite of *collaboration* is *coercion*. Consultants who suggest topics and issues to explore with their consultees while accepting that consultees may either accept or reject their ideas are, in fact, being both directive and collaborative. There are no indications in any of the research conducted to date suggesting that an effective consultant "tells the consultee what to do" (Erchul & Martens, 1997, p. 23; see Deno, 1975, for an interesting case study and Erchul, Sheridan, Ryan, Grisson, Killough & Mettler, 1999, for an analysis pertaining to conjoint behavioral consultation) or that school psychologists should behave like "Conan the Consultant" (Erchul, 1992, p. 364).

It is precisely this lack of empirical support for a hierarchical power relationship between the consultant and consultee that leads us to reaffirm the long-standing conclusion that school-based consultation is conducted more effectively within a collaborative context. While other researchers (e.g., Erchul, 1992; Erchul & Martens, 1997) continue to prefer descriptors such as *cooperation* and *teamwork* rather than *collaboration* to describe the consultation enterprise, our primary point is that a "rose by any other name would smell just as sweet." Regardless of what term we use, there appears to be a research-based consensus that noncoercive, coordinate power relationships are more facilitative of effective school-based consultation.

Voluntary Participation

As might be surmised from the concept of coordinate power relationships, consultation has always been conceptualized as a voluntary activity (e.g., Reschly, 1976; Zins, Kratochwill, & Elliott, 1993a). Much as is true for involuntary psychotherapy, trying to pressure a consultee into consultation makes it very difficult to achieve a successful outcome. Although school authorities can mandate that a teacher interact with a psychologist about a particular problem, they have few (if any) ways to ensure that this interaction will

be productive. Given the nature of consultative activities, it is quite easy for either party to sabotage the effort when he or she has a hidden agenda to do so. When forced to consult, teachers may wish to "prove" the ineffectiveness of the consultant's ideas.

Especially subtle and problematic are those instances in which a teacher is required by his or her principal to work with a psychologist but, to save face, the psychologist is never overtly informed of the mandatory nature of the interaction. In these circumstances, consultants may experience significant reactance and resistance from their consultees, and successful consultation may be difficult to achieve (Cautili, 2006; Gonzalez, Nelson, & Gutkin, 2004; Gorges, Elliott & Kettler, 2004; Gutkin & Hickman, 1990; Hughes & Falk, 1981; Piersel & Gutkin, 1983; Wickstrom & Witt, 1993).

Consistent with the voluntary nature of consultation, it is desirable that case initiation ideally should come from the consultee rather than the consultant. Initiation by the consultee is thought to be beneficial because it suggests that the consultee recognizes the existence of a problem and is motivated to take action. Reality, of course, is not always congruent with theoretical ideals (Harris & Cancelli, 1991). In actual practice, school psychologists may find that they must initiate contact, often at the request of principals, intervention assistance teams, or parents. For example, if a school has implemented a PS/RTI service delivery model, the requirement for data-based validation of effective classroom management and instructional effectiveness for all students might indicate that such conditions are not present in a particular classroom and could result in a request by the principal for consultative services. The critical issue, however, is not so much who initiates the consulting relationship, but the nature of the relationship once initiated. In the above example, it would be helpful for all involved, including the school psychologist, to focus on working collaboratively with the teacher and others to establish a classroom environment that is effective both academically and behaviorally, rather than focusing on shortcomings of the teacher.

Confidentiality of Communication

While there has always been a strong consensus that confidentiality is an essential element of consultation relationships (Conoley & Conoley, 1992; Parsons & Kahn, 2005; Zins et al.,

1993a), there has been virtually no empirical study of this important assumption (see Nowell & Spruill, 1993, and Woods & McNamara, 1980, for exceptions pertaining to psychotherapy). Nevertheless, the logic of maintaining confidentiality with consultees seems compelling and congruent with important standards of professional ethics (APA, 2002; Hughes, 1986; NASP, 2000). To be successful in consultation, consultees have to feel free to communicate with consultants in an open and honest manner. It is highly unlikely that they would do so, exposing their professional weaknesses, personal concerns, and so on, if they perceived that this information might be leaked to other people in the school or community. Without trust in the consultant, consultees would probably feel the need to focus only on safe topics, steering clear of controversial and potentially embarrassing facts and opinions. Doing so, however, could render the consultation process impotent.

Not all information can be or should be kept confidential, however. Consultants frequently have to make subtle judgment calls, balancing the confidentiality rights of consultees with the rights of society, school officials, and parents to be informed about the education and treatment of children. At the extreme are suspected cases of child abuse; threats of violence against a reasonably identifiable victim as per the Tarasoff case (Fischer & Sorenson, 1996; Jacob-Timm & Hartshorne, 1994); and the commission of felonies, in which psychologists have the legal responsibility to report information to the proper authorities (e.g., child protective service agencies, local police) in most states. Even in those states with protections of privileged communication that apply to psychologists, it strikes us as unlikely that a consultee (as opposed to a patient or client) could invoke that privilege. As such, consultants could probably be compelled to break confidentiality in a court of law.

Of course, most consultations are not nearly so dramatic, and the legitimacy of maintaining confidentially is less problematic. But even in routine cases, not all information should be or can be kept confidential. For example, the fact that a psychologist is consulting with a teacher about a particular child may be part of an intervention assistance plan or an Individualized Educational Program (IEP). In such instances, both the existence and goals of this consultation relationship would probably be known, in advance, to the intervention assistance or IEP team. Likewise, principals, parents, and others would seem to have a legitimate right to know if a psychologist was consulting with a teacher about a particular child and the nature of the problem being addressed (e.g., the child is having difficulty in adding three-digit numbers and completing homework assignments). Although sharing information such as this would rarely be a problem, it would be important for consultants to maintain confidentiality about sensitive issues that arose during consultation sessions (e.g., personal feelings, professional inadequacies of the consultee).

Given the complexity of confidentiality decisions, it is important for consultants to discuss with consultees and other key members of an organization the nature and limits of confidentiality before entering into any consultation relationships, as per our ethics codes (APA, 2002; Hughes, 1986; NASP, 2000). Of equal importance, there should be a consensus between the consultant and the consultee at all points during a consultation relationship about which aspects of this relationship are public and which are confidential.

Encouraging Active Participation by Consultees During Consultation

To whatever extent it is possible, consultants should encourage active participation by consultees throughout the consultation process. Consultees' involvement during consultation is thought to (a) facilitate the collection of broad-ranging assessment data, as consultees typically have a unique and in-depth view of clients' behaviors in relevant environments, such as the school and home (Gresham, MacMillan, & Bocian, 1997; Pyle, 1977); (b) provide consultants with an opportunity to assess and develop treatments in response to the professional perspectives and "biases" of the consultee, which may prove to be crucial information when packaging interventions to make them more attractive and ecologically friendly for the consultee (Conoley, Conoley, Ivey, & Scheel, 1991; Gutkin, 1997; Martens & Witt, 1988b; Riley-Tillman & Chafouleas, 2003; Witt & Martens, 1988); (c) enhance consultees "ownership" of interventions, thus increasing the likelihood that they will carry out a treatment as planned (Meichenbaum & Turk, 1987; Reinking, Livesay, & Kohl, 1978; Rosenfield, 1991); (d) generally expand the opportunity for consultants and consultees to provide each other with corrective feedback, helping both members of the consultation dyad stay on track throughout the entire process; and (e) increase the opportunities to "give psychology away" (Miller, 1969, p. 1071) to consultees as more "teachable moments" are created during the consultation process.

Despite the apparent advantages of having consultees actively engaged in the consultative problem-solving process, the extent to which most teachers wish to participate actively remains clouded. On the positive side, there are long-standing indications that teachers prefer consultation to more traditional and passive forms of service delivery by school psychologists (e.g., Babcock & Pryzwansky, 1983; Gutkin, 1980; Gutkin & Curtis, 1982; Kutsick, Gutkin, & Witt, 1991) and are actively involved during actual consultation sessions (Conoley, Conoley, & Gumm, 1992; Gutkin 1996b, 1999; Martens et al., 1992). On the negative side, there are also long-standing indications that consultees may sometimes just be going through the motions, particularly in regard to prereferral intervention (e.g., Burns, Vanderwood, & Ruby, 2005; Flugum & Reschly, 1994; Lambert, 1976; Meyers, Valentino, Meyers, Boretti, & Brent 1996; Wilson, Gutkin, Hagen, & Oats, 1998). As noted above, it has been suggested that the term *prereferral intervention* itself may have contributed to expectations by teachers that this process is merely an administrative hurdle that must be cleared for a child to be considered for a different placement, typically a special education class. As of this date, we are forced to reiterate our conclusion from the previous edition pertaining to this crucial issue. Specifically, "We do not know just how much the 'typical' teacher is predisposed to be an active participant in consultative interactions and ... such inclinations probably vary with the specifics of particular circumstances" (Gutkin & Curtis, 1999, p. 607).

Perhaps the best tact for contemporary school psychologies is to worry less about whether teachers do or do not wish to be active consultation participants—for it appears that the answer to that question is highly variable—and concentrate more on how we might increase their involvement in working with difficult-to-teach children, in general, and in consultation, in particular. With these goals in mind, Bandura's (1993) work on self-efficacy would seem to be especially important, as persons with high self-efficacy perceptions

> set themselves challenging goals and maintain strong commitment to them. They maintain a task-diagnostic focus that guides effective performance. They heighten and

sustain their effort in the face of failure. They attribute failure to insufficient effort or deficient knowledge and skills that are acquirable. They quickly recover their sense of efficacy after failures or setbacks. They approach threatening situations with assurance that they can exercise control over them. (pp. 144–145)

Research specific to teaching seems to confirm Bandura's hypotheses pertaining to heightened levels of self-efficacy and teachers' persistence in the face of difficult problems (e.g., Gibson & Dembo, 1984; Gorrell & Capron, 1990; Hughes, 1992; Hughes, Barker, Kemenoff, & Hart, 1993; Meijer & Foster, 1988; Podell & Soodak, 1993; Sachs, 1988; Smylie, 1988; Woolfolk & Hoy, 1990). Recent works by Skaalvik and Skaalvik (2007) and Gibbs (2007) are especially interesting as the former authors report "a particularly strong correlation between teacher self-efficacy and teacher burnout" (p. 620) and the latter provides theoretical analyses of teachers' perceptions of efficacy and their willingness to engage in inclusive education.

Building on Bandura's (1993) work and the suggestions of Brown and Schulte (1987), Gutkin and Ajchenbaum (1984) and Gutkin and Hickman (1988) found a positive relationship between teachers' perceptions of control over presenting problems and their preferences for consultative versus referral services. DeForest and Hughes (1992) also reported a positive relationship between teaching self-efficacy, and teachers' ratings of consultants and the acceptability of interventions. However, even in those studies in which heightened self-efficacy was not related to increased preferences for consultation per se (e.g., Hughes et al., 1993), a positive relationship between efficacy and willingness to persist with difficult instructional tasks emerged. As such, increasing teachers' self-efficacy appears to be a worthy goal for school-based consultants (Hughes, Grossman, & Barker, 1990).

Although still few in number, there are some reports of successfully increasing teachers' self-efficacy and these may provide consultants with useful tools for accomplishing this goal. Ponti and Curtis (1984), for instance, found a significant increase in teacher's generalized expectations for success in dealing with students' problems after only three weeks of interactions with high-skilled consultants. Wehmann, Zins, and Curtis (1989) reported that teachers' expectations for successful problem resolution increased significantly following 10 weeks of school psychological consultation. Likewise, Gutkin et al. (1980) discovered that teachers perceived a broad range of common school problems as less severe after receiving 14 weeks of consultation services in comparison to a control group that had no access to consultants. Focusing on enhancing teachers' confidence and knowledge about classroom interventions, Gutkin and Hickman (1988) and Hagen, Gutkin, Wilson, and Oats (1998) were able to raise in-service and preservice teachers' perceptions of self-efficacy and, in the former study, increase teachers' preferences for consultation versus referral services as well. These studies suggest that increasing the content and process skills of consultees in classroom interventions and consultation interactions (which, as described earlier in this chapter, has been done successfully in the past) might also result in increased efficacy perceptions by teachers. Finally, research by Bergan, Byrnes, and Kratochwill (1979) and Tombari and Bergan (1978) indicate that teachers are more likely to experience a positive sense of efficacy when classroom problems are framed in behavioral rather than medical-model terms. These findings are presumably the result of feeling some reasonable sense of control over classroom environmental variables but little control over students' internal pathological traits.

Intervention Processes and Products

Assessment

To develop interventions that will benefit clients, it is necessary to conduct a thorough assessment. That is, interventions should be based on the gathering of relevant information and data (Reschly, 2008; Tilly, 2008), not simply the consultant's or consultee's intuitions and opinions. Given the vast array of assessment techniques that are available, a multitude of approaches could be employed. While it is not possible to specify what should be done in all circumstances within the limited confines of this chapter, some overarching guidance can be provided.

First, assessment processes should be congruent with one's underlying assumptions about the nature of human behavior. As suggested by Gutkin (Chapter 23) and Reynolds, Gutkin, Elliott, and Witt (1984), the ecological and reciprocal determinism models proposed by Bronfenbrenner (1979) and Bandura (1978), respectively,

provide the most effective conceptual foundations on which to base consultation. From these points of view, a student's individual characteristics, behavior, and surrounding micro-, meso-, exo-, and macro-environment are all seen as having continuous, mutual, and reciprocal influences on one another. As such, the assessments of individual, behavioral, and/or environmental characteristics are all viewed as legitimate foci. Beyond this, however, the ecological and reciprocal determinism perspectives direct us to pay particular attention to the *interaction* among individual, behavioral, and environmental variables.

In light of this, consultants should rely primarily (but not exclusively) on assessments of clients' behavior in the natural environment, where the interaction of individual, behavioral, and environmental variables are easiest to observe. Thus, functional analyses of behavior, classroom observations, portfolio assessment, empiric assessment, and curriculum- and performance-based assessment methods (e.g., Beavers, Kratochwill, & Braden, 2004; Burns, 2004; Cowan & Sheridan; Chapter 27; Daly, Martens, Skinner, & Noell, Chapter 5; Hintze, Chapter 20; Vollmer, St. Peter Pipkin, Reyes, & Sloman, Chapter 19; Ysseldyke & Burns, Chapter 21) are employed more frequently than are norm-referenced measures as they permit consultants and consultees to assess the interaction among these factors more readily. Likewise, teacher and parent interviews are a major source of assessment data. By "living" with their students and children in the natural environment day-in and day-out, month-in and month-out, both parents and teachers are in a unique position to analyze individual, behavioral, and environmental interactions over a sustained period of time and under a wide variety of conditions. It is important to note, however, that even in those instances when consultees' observations are less than completely accurate, these data will be critical because the subjective perceptions of consultees will probably influence their behavior toward clients, as well as their willingness to implement interventions (Conoley et al., 1991).

A second useful guideline in conducting assessments is that they should be designed to answer relevant questions. If, as is generally the case, the focus of consultation is on developing a school- or home-based intervention, the assessment process should be such that resulting information contributes to resolving important issues in intervention and treatment. Data that assist only with the identification of a special education diagnosis (e.g., learning disabilities) are of limited utility within this context. Once again, assessment methods that focus on the intersection of individual characteristics, behavior, and the environment are most likely to shed important new light on how best to develop effective interventions. Thus, for example, learning from direct observation what environmental stimuli lead to appropriate and inappropriate learning behaviors for a child will typically be of much greater significance to consultation processes than will discovering through an intelligence test whether that child is or is not mildly mentally retarded.

Finally, assessments should be conducted in a way that secures useful information without unnecessarily disrupting the natural environment in which the assessment takes place. In classrooms, this means that data-gathering procedures involving teachers should require no more time and training on their part than is absolutely necessary. Observational procedures, for example, should be designed so they are simple to learn and easy to conduct. There are numerous possibilities—for example, having teachers move a coin from their left to their right pockets as a way to conduct frequency counts, engaging children in self-monitoring of problem behaviors, or focusing on permanent products produced by clients whenever possible (Shapiro, 1987). Involving consultees in a thorough discussion of data collection procedures is probably the best way to ensure that assessment processes will provide necessary information in a manner that is acceptable to the consultee, without being unnecessarily cumbersome or disruptive to the natural environment.

Interventions

Subsequent to conducting an assessment, the focus of consultation shifts to the design of interventions. Fortunately, there is nearly a limitless array of intervention strategies from which to choose (e.g., Buerkle, Whitehouse, & Christenson, Chapter 30; Cowan & Sheridan, Chapter 27; Pressley et al., Chapter 25; Reisman, Chapter 26; Shinn, Walker, & Stoner 2002; Stark, Hargrave, Gerber, Fisher, & Hamilton, Chapter 29; Stroud & Reynolds, Chapter 34; Thomas & Grimes, 2002, 2008; Wittrock, 1986), and there is likely to be a multitude of approaches that could be used effectively with any given case. Despite this, however, designing a successful consultative intervention is often a complex and difficult task. The following are among the issues to consider when developing an intervention plan within the context of a consultation relationship.

Has the intervention been shown to be effective (Kratochwill et al., Chapter 24)? Consistent with a scientist-practitioner model for professional practice, empirical knowledge should form the basis for selecting a treatment strategy. The research literature should be consulted to determine the efficacy of an intervention before implementation decisions are made. Doing so will help consultants and consultees avoid treatments for which there is no relevant research or there has been a demonstrated lack of success. Of course, as every practitioner knows, there is usually not a one-to-one correspondence between formal research studies and the specifics of a presenting case (Bardon, 1987; Stoner & Green, 1992). By reading the research literature critically, however, it should be possible to make a reasoned and informed judgment about whether the findings of one or more studies are applicable to the specifics of a particular problem.

Although important, the efficacy of a treatment is not sufficient, in and of itself, to achieve a successful consultation intervention. A number of other critical factors must be considered. Specifically, since the treatment plans developed during consultation will be implemented by the consultee, it is essential to consider those aspects of the treatment plan that might determine whether the intervention is acceptable to the consultee. Efficacy is only one of those factors (Gutkin, 1993c; Martens & Witt, 1988a; Witt, 1990b). Although a comprehensive review of the treatment acceptability literature is beyond the scope of this chapter (the interested reader is referred to Elliott, 1988; Nastasi & Truscott, 2000; and Reimers, Wacker, & Koeppl, 1987), its importance cannot be overstated because it is unlikely that a consultee will implement any treatment that she or he does not find acceptable. As noted by Gutkin and Curtis (1981) more than two decades ago, "Once the door to the classroom is closed, there is little that any of the educational specialists can do to ensure the occurrence of any event that the teacher does not want to occur.... We must recognize that if a teacher decides that a remedial program is inappropriate, it is highly unlikely that the plan will ever be implemented. This would be true regardless of the actual quality of the particular program" (pp. 220–221). Thus, to be successful, consultants and consultees must design interventions that satisfy a number of important criteria, above and beyond the documented effectiveness of those interventions (Lentz & Daly, 1996).

1. It would seem to be important to develop interventions that consultees believe themselves to be capable of doing. Based on a broad array of self-efficacy and locus of control research reported earlier in this chapter, consultants should not expect consultees to carry through on interventions that they do not believe they can do. It is generally believed that focusing on the ecological rather than psychopathological elements of presenting problems will help consultees achieve a sense of competence and enhanced self-efficacy (Bergan et al., 1979; Gutkin, Chapter 23; Tombari & Bergan, 1978).

2. Beyond the perception of self-competence by consultees, success will hinge to a large extent on whether consultees are, in fact, able to execute an intervention correctly, that is, with high treatment integrity (Gresham, 1989). Although extensive research with a broad array of intervention techniques makes it clear that mental health paraprofessionals (e.g., teachers and parents) are quite capable of implementing educational and psychological treatments effectively (e.g., Christensen & Jacobson, 1994; Gutkin, Chapter 23), this capability should not be taken for granted (McIntyre, Gresham, & DiGennaro, 2007; Wilkinson, 2006). Horror stories of inappropriately executed interventions are not uncommon, such as one teacher we know who implemented a timeout program by placing a kindergarten child into a small, isolated space for five hours a day for an entire week. Recent work suggests that direct training, performance feedback, and intervention scripts may increase consultees' treatment integrity when implementing various intervention techniques (Allen & Blackston, 2003; Ehrhardt, Barnett, Lentz, Stollar, & Reifin, 1996; Hagermoser Sanetti, Luiselli, & Handler, 2007; Jones, Wickstrom, & Friman, 1997; Noell, Witt, Gilbertson, Ranier, & Freeland, 1997; Noell, Witt, LaFleur, Mortenson, Ranier, & LeVelle, 2000; Resetar, Noell, & Pellegrin, 2006; Sterling-Turner, Watson, & Moore, 2002; Telzrow & Beebe, 2002; Watson & Robinson, 1996).

3. Consultees must perceive an intervention to be congruent with their legitimate professional responsibilities before they are likely to carry it through. One of the major sources of resistance to consulting psychologists who strive to implement legal mandates and professional guidelines, such as least restrictive environment programming, prereferral interventions (Truscott, Cohen, & Sams, 2005), and inclusion (Farrell et al., Chapter 38), is the perception by many general education teachers that the education of children with disabilities in general education settings is simply not their job (Graden, Zins, Curtis, & Cobb, 1988; Stainback & Stainback, 1988). From their point of view, working with children who have special needs is the responsibility of specialists, such as resource teachers, special educators, school psychologists, counselors, and speech therapists. To consult successfully under these circumstances, consultants must work with consultees to develop interventions that are considered legitimate to the consultee. As noted earlier, framing children's problems in environmental rather than pathological terms may help with this dilemma (Bergan et al., 1979; Gutkin, Chapter 23, Tombari & Bergan, 1978), as teachers are more likely to perceive manipulations of the educational environment than internal psychological and psychiatric diseases to be within their normal job role.

4. Interventions are more likely to be implemented by a consultee if they are congruent with the consultee's perceptions of the problem. As demonstrated by Witt, Moe, Gutkin, and Andrews (1984), the terms used to describe an intervention to a teacher can substantively affect his or her evaluation of that intervention. Along similar lines, research by Conoley et al. (1991) indicates that consultants can increase the acceptability of treatment recommendations simply by matching the rationale for them to the perceptions expressed by their consultees. Thus, consultants should attempt to frame interventions that emerge from consultation in terms that are compatible with the worldviews of their consultees. It would appear that the way in which interventions are presented to consultees may prove to be as important as the operational specifics of the interventions themselves.

5. Interventions are more likely to be implemented by a consultee if they fit easily into the natural ecology in which the consultee must carry out the plan (Gutkin, 1993c;

Lentz, Allen, & Ehrhardt, 1996; Lentz & Daly, 1996). Treatments that are incompatible with the manner in which consultees manage their environments are likely to be rejected or implemented incorrectly. Teachers who depend exclusively on large-group instruction, for example, are unlikely to utilize individualized techniques even if these interventions have been shown to be efficacious. To be successful with such consultees, consultants should focus their energies on developing intervention strategies that can be implemented within the context of large-group instruction. Building on existing behavioral regularities and taking advantage of the existing strengths of consultees are effective strategies for enhancing the probabilities for successful consultation outcomes (Martens & Witt, 1988b; Witt & Martens, 1988).

Although not an exhaustive discussion by any means, the above points serve to communicate how important it is for consultants to think more deeply about the interventions they might recommend to consultees than simply assessing whether an intervention has been demonstrated by research to be effective. Interventions must not only have been demonstrated to be efficacious in general but also to work well for the particular consultee, client, and environmental context in which the presenting problem occurs (Kratochwill et al., Chapter 24).

Short-Term Follow-Up

Short-term follow-up (ranging from a day to a few weeks) is an essential element of consultation services. This need stems from the reality that regardless of how thorough and comprehensive our assessment might be, we are unable to know in advance whether our intervention recommendations will resolve presenting problems effectively (e.g., Stoner & Green, 1992). For both children and adults, there are few documented relationships between taxonomies of formal diagnoses and empirically validated interventions (Good, Vollmer, Creek, Katz & Chowdhri, 1993; Gresham & Gansle, 1992; Gresham, & Witt, 1997; Reschly & Ysseldyke, 2002; Widiger & Trull, 2007). Thus, mechanisms for corrective feedback must be built into all consultation services. Even those intervention plans in which we are most confident should be implemented with the expectation that follow-up will be required to determine

if refinement or replacement of the original treatment program will be necessary and to assess if treatments were implemented with sufficient integrity (Noell et al., 2000). To be effective, school-based consultation must be an iterative process. A meta-analysis by Fuchs and Fuchs (1986) provides empirical support for incorporating systematic formative evaluation procedures into the consultation process.

The concept of follow-up, including evaluation of intervention effectiveness leading to continuation, adjustment, or abandonment of that intervention, is fundamental to a PS/RTI model. The core of that model is based on the intent to continue data-based evaluation of intervention effectiveness until acceptable results are attained (i.e., a satisfactory response to intervention is realized). This is another illustration of the compatibility between consultation services and the use of a PS/RTI framework for service delivery. Each of the aspects of follow-up discussed below is as important to PS/RTI as it is to consultation.

There are numerous other reasons why follow-up contacts with consultees are thought to be so important. To quote an old and wise adage, "There are many slips twixt the cup and the lip." First, ideas that sound simple during the course of consultation may, in fact, require skills that the consultee does not possess to an adequate degree. Often, the consultee does not become aware of this fact until actually attempting to implement the strategy in question. At this point, it may become painfully clear to the consultee that he or she does not really know how to carry out the treatment that was agreed on. For example, a teacher who has always depended on punishment for class control may agree to institute a program of contingent social reinforcement for a child but have considerable difficulty because it runs counter to already well-ingrained teaching habits and requires skills that he or she does not have. Follow-up is needed in such cases to monitor implementation and either revise the treatment or assist the consultee in acquiring the necessary skills (Ehrhardt et al., 1996; Watson & Robinson, 1996).

Second, the consultee may realize after attempting to implement a program that he or she lacks one or more prerequisite resources. Many psychoeducational interventions are complex and require a variety of materials and support in order to be administered effectively. Individualized instruction is perhaps one of the best examples. A teacher who attempts to implement such a program may be stymied by a lack of time to carry out the intervention, inadequate access to necessary curricular materials, the absence of a paraprofessional, an excessively large number of other children in the classroom (many of whom also need considerable personal attention), or any of a wide variety of other similar problems. Follow-up contacts provide the consultant with an opportunity to work with the consultee either to secure necessary resources or to redesign the intervention so that it can be carried out effectively without the aid of such supports.

Third, there is evidence to indicate that teachers are often so busy that they are not aware of the nature of their own interactions with children (Martin & Keller, 1976). Jackson (1968), for example, reported that teachers may engage in up to 1,000 interpersonal interchanges per day, a pace at which it is very difficult to recall accurately the details of each interaction. When this is the case, teachers may improperly implement interventions because of a lack of awareness of their own classroom behavior. In these cases, follow-up observations by a consultant, coupled with performance feedback to the teacher (Ehrhardt et al., 1996; Watson & Robinson, 1996), will be critical to increase treatment integrity and thus the probable success of the intervention (Gresham, 1989).

Fourth, as discussed previously, treatments need to be compatible with the natural ecology of a classroom if they are to succeed over a protracted period of time (Gutkin, 1993c; Lentz et al., 1996; Lentz & Daly, 1996; Martens & Witt, 1988b; Witt & Martens, 1988). When trying to implement an agreed-upon treatment plan, teachers may discover that it does not fit easily into the pedagogical structure they have established for their classroom. In these instances, it is unlikely that consultees would modify their instructional or disciplinary approaches for their entire class just to meet the needs of a single, difficult-to-teach student. In all likelihood, these consultees will simply discard the intervention, even though they had agreed to it previously during consultation sessions. Follow-up consultation sessions provide consultants with an opportunity to address this dilemma by either assisting in the refinement of treatments, helping consultees to be more flexible and individualized in the approaches they take with their class, or perhaps even facilitating a broad-based change in a consultee's teaching style.

Fifth, the consultant's reinforcement of the consultee is also critical during that period of time

after the intervention has been initiated and before treatment success or failure is evident. In those instances when interventions do not bring about the desired results, the consultant needs to be around to share the responsibility and frustration, provide support, and join the consultee in starting over. Given the lack of clear diagnosis-treatment relationships (e.g., Good, Vollmer, Creek, Katz & Chowdhri, 1993; Gresham & Gansle, 1992; Gresham & Witt, 1997; Reschly & Ysseldyke, 2002; Widiger & Trull, 2007), unsuccessful outcomes are bound to occur despite everyone's best efforts and intentions. In fact, it may be important for the consultant to alert the consultee beforehand to this reality in order to reduce the likelihood of unrealistic expectations for instant cures. Follow-up permits the consultant to help the consultee learn to take a lack of satisfactory results in stride and to use information resulting from an unsuccessful program as input for the generation of a new intervention.

Sixth, when treatment proves to be successful, someone should provide reinforcement to the consultee for a job well done. As Sarason, Levine, Goldenberg, Cherlin, and Bennett (1966) point out, "teaching is a lonely profession" (p. 74) and teachers typically go without overt reinforcement from adults (e.g., colleagues, support specialists, supervisors, administrators) when everything is going well. This tends to sap consultees' motivation for handling future problems. During follow-up, consultants are in an excellent position to provide reinforcement to consultees for their successes and, perhaps of equal importance, to receive some reinforcement for their own work.

Last, follow-up facilitates the professional growth of both the consultee and the consultant. Recalling that all consultation interactions have both remedial and preventative goals, follow-up contacts give consultants an opportunity to review effective interventions with consultees and to determine the underlying reasons for a program's success. There is considerable potential for learning in this process for both consultees and consultants, and this knowledge can be used by either party for dealing with similar cases encountered in the future.

Consultant and Consultee Responsibilities

First and foremost, consultants are responsible for the process elements of consultation interactions. As detailed by Dunst and Trivette (1988), the help offered by human service providers such as consultants can be either helpful, leading consultees to increased perceptions of self-efficacy, empowerment, and independence, or harmful, resulting in the opposite outcomes. It is the responsibility of consultants to create a service delivery context that supports and encourages consultees' growth and development as consultative assistance is provided. The relationship elements described earlier are believed to facilitate these outcomes, as are open, affiliative, and supportive styles of communication (e.g., attentive, genuine, empathetic, high in positive regard, and effective listening) with consultees (Cormier & Cormier, 1991; Ivey, 1994; Kratochwill, Elliott, & Callan-Stoiber, 2002; Kurpius & Rozecki, 1993; Maitland, Fine, & Tracy, 1985; Rosenfield, 1991; Sheridan, Meegan, & Eagle, 2002; Zins & Erchul, 2002).

Consultants are also responsible for the integrity of the problem-solving processes that are employed during consultation interactions. More often than not, consultees will have little previous training in the art and science of problem solving per se. Thus, consultants must not only be cognizant of the content being discussed during consultation sessions but also monitor the problem-solving process. When the process goes off track (e.g., when a consultee tries to rush ahead with generating solutions before a problem has been defined adequately), it is the responsibility of the consultant to direct the interaction in more productive directions. Curtis and Van Wagener (1988) demonstrated that, despite very positive ratings of the consultation process by both consultant and consultee, the process can lack adherence to a structured problem-solving process and result in the absence of specific strategies to assist the student in the classroom. While historically there has been some sense that focusing solely on consultation processes might be a sufficient contribution by consultants (e.g., Schien, 1969), we believe this is unlikely to be adequate in and of itself in most schools.

In addition to the process obligations of the consultant, both the consultant and consultee are responsible for bringing their content expertise to bear on presenting problems. As professionals, each should draw on the science and practice knowledge of their respective fields (e.g., psychology, education) during consultative interactions. Even parents, who would not be considered to be professionals in the strict sense of the term, have important content expertise to contribute in terms of the dynamics of day-to-day life in their own family and the history of behavior exhibited by their child in the home or other settings (Sheridan, Kratochwill, & Bergan, 1996). As noted earlier, it is the mixing, integrating, and synthesizing of these distinct bodies of knowledge and information brought to the consultation relationship by consultants and consultees alike that makes consultation such a powerful tool.

Given the indirect service delivery nature of consultation, consultees are responsible for taking action based on treatment plans that emerge from interactions with consultants. While this does not rule out some intervention strategies that would involve consultants in providing direct service to clients, such instances clearly would be the exception rather than the rule. School psychologists can not move into either the classroom or the home to provide services on a long-term, ongoing basis. The ultimate responsibility for implementing interventions in schools and homes clearly will fall to persons such as teachers and parents, that is, consultees. This underscores further how important it is for the consultee to believe in the treatment plan and to have a sense of ownership of it (Dunst & Trivette, 1988).

That consultees have the primary responsibility for intervention implementation, of course, does not rule out the role of consultants as role models and providers of feedback. Thus, when appropriate, given the specifics of a particular case, and when invited to do so, psychologists could enter the classroom or the home to provide demonstrations for and feedback to consultees (Ehrhardt et al., 1996; Watson & Robinson, 1996). Providing consultees with support services such as these should dramatically increase the probability that interventions would be implemented as they were intended, that is, with high treatment integrity (Gresham, 1989).

As noted earlier, consultees also have the primary responsibility for initiating the consultation relationship. Whereas principals or multidisciplinary and intervention assistance teams may sometimes assign a consultant to a consultee, it is thought to be best when consultees approach consultants rather than vice versa. Given the nature of the consultation relationship, it would be easy to get off on the wrong foot if consultees were to work with a consultant because they had been ordered to do so by some external authority. At the very least, it seems important that ongoing consultation interactions be based on voluntary participation by the consultee, regardless of who initiates the first contact.

Finally, both consultants and consultees are responsible for the successes and failures of the interventions they jointly design for clients. Both parties should share in the "glory" of positive outcomes and both should feel obligated to improve on strategies that produced less than desired results.

Entry Processes

Given the substantive differences between consultation and the traditional roles of school psychologists (e.g., assessment, psychotherapy/counseling), many consultation theorists (e.g., Conoley & Conoley, 1992; Fullan, Miles, & Taylor, 1980; Meyers, 2002) believe that offering consultation services within a new organization should begin with an entry process. The purpose and goals of such entry processes are numerous.

For example, there is a need for school personnel to develop an understanding of the consultation process. Thus consultants need a way to communicate the core characteristics described in this chapter to potential consultees, as well as to persons in influential positions, typically starting with the building principal (Marks, 1995). In some instances, a written contract may be helpful for specifying "fees, obligations, times, acceptable activities, time limits, and so on" (Conoley & Conoley, 1992, p. 81). Subsequent interactions should involve assistant principals, team leaders, specialists, and so on. Eventually, the consultant should have the opportunity to meet with the entire school faculty to explain the consultation model. The goal for all these meetings is to clarify proactively the nature of consultation services that will be offered and help school personnel see the advantages that these services might hold for them and their students.

A second goal for an entry process is to allow potential consultees to get to know the consultant as a person. Given that the success of consultation services will hinge to a considerable degree on the consultant's ability to establish a facilitative relationship with consultees (Gutkin, 1999; Kratochwill, Elliott, & Callan-Stoiber, 2002) and communicate her or his unique process and content skills (Knoff, Hines, & Kromrey, 1995; Stenger, Tollefson, & Fine, 1992), it is important to start building these perceptions at the earliest possible opportunity. As suggested by psychotherapy research (Beutler et al., 1994), consultants should strive to communicate their expertness, attractiveness, and trustworthiness to potential consultees. By establishing these relationships, consultants can quickly gain the confidence of school personnel and come to be viewed as one of "us" rather than one of "them."

Third, it is very important for the consultant to get to know individual consultees, the organizational structure within which they work, and the school climate (Marks, 1995). Before consulting with teachers, for example, it is helpful if consultants can get a feel for how the teachers in a particular building teach and how they conceptualize their role as teachers. In this way, consultants are able to present ideas and concepts that match and mesh easily with the natural ecologies in a school building (Conoley et al., 1991; Martens & Witt, 1988b; Witt & Martens, 1988). Also, it is important to identify political hot spots in a school as quickly as possible to avoid being caught unintentionally in a conflict among school personnel.

With all of this information in hand, consultants and consultees can jointly determine exactly how consultation services should be provided in their building. Referred to in the research literature as mutual adaptation (McLaughlin, 1976), this is an empirically validated way to increase the adoption of innovations by school organizations. Rather than informing schools that they must implement the consultation model in one particular manner (i.e., the consultant's way), it is much more effective to negotiate implementation procedures with the host organization, even if this means less than full implementation of the model initially.

Despite broad support among theorists for an entry process, there has been precious little research specifically focused on this topic (see Martens, Lewandowski, & Houk, 1989, and Robinson, Cameron, & Raethel, 1985, for exceptions). And while it is reasonable to extrapolate conclusions from other bodies of work (e.g., the adoption of innovations and treatment acceptability literatures), this is a poor substitute for research on the entry process per se. As noted by Gutkin (1993b), empirical work in this area is among the most pressing contemporary agendas for school-based consultants.

MODELS OF SCHOOL-BASED CONSULTATION

Over the last half century or so, a considerable number of differing consultation models have emerged in the school psychology literature. Although each of these models shares the core characteristics detailed earlier in this chapter, each is also different enough in orientation and operation to warrant independent examination. What follows is a brief review of the three major consultation models employed by school psychologists: (1) ecological consultation, (2) mental health consultation, and (3) organizational consultation.

Ecological Consultation
A Word About Terminology

With each new version of this chapter our thinking has evolved somewhat about how best to name this form of consultation. In our original work (Gutkin & Curtis, 1982), we distinguished between problem-solving and behavioral consultation and treated them as two separate models. Eight years later (Gutkin & Curtis, 1990), we shifted our terminology after becoming convinced that there were many commonalities between the problem-solving and behavioral approaches and neither title captured the essence of the model being discussed. Thus, we renamed and integrated these two approaches into one model and called it ecological consultation. In the third edition of this chapter (Gutkin & Curtis, 1999), we introduced a new title, ecobehavioral consultation. Our goal at the time was to embed the strong empirical tradition of behavioral psychology within an ecological framework without losing the systemic elements of ecological thinking (Gutkin, 1993c). At the time we thought that adopting, "an ecobehavioral orientation toward consultation allows us to have our cake and eat it too" (p. 616). With perfect hindsight, however, it appears we were only partially successful. Although the "eco" half of "ecobehavioral" has emerged in a number of consultation publications (e.g., Annan, 2005; Jeltova & Fish, 2005; Nastasi, 2006; Rosenfield, 2002; Sheridan, Clarke, & Knoche, 2006; Sheridan, Warnes, & Dowd, 2004), it has been dwarfed by a focus on more narrowly construed behavioral consultation methods in the preponderance of the contemporary literature. With new emergent thinking on this matter (Gutkin, this volume) and the hope of underscoring the significance of mutual and reciprocal systemic interactions between micro-, meso-, exo- and macro-environments in school-based consultation, we are reverting back to the title "ecological consultation" for the purposes of this chapter.

Operationalizing the Ecological Consultation Model

Drawing on ecological (e.g., Bandura, 1978; Barker, 1965, 1968; Bronfenbrenner, 1979; Christenson, Abery, & Weinberg, 1986; Cicchetti & Toth, 1997; Lewin, 1951; Moos, 1973; Morse, 1993; Pianta, 1999; Swartz & Martin, 1997), ecobehavioral (Greenwood, Carta, & Atwater, 1991; Morris & Midgley, 1990; Rogers-Warren & Warren, 1977; Willems, 1974) and behavioral (Cooper, Heron, & Heward, 2007; Skinner, 1953) theory and research, as well as empirically validated interventions (Kratochwill et al., this volume), ecological consultants work with their consultees to identify and manipulate relevant person-environment relationships to improve, eliminate, and/or prevent identified problems. For school psychologists who are using this approach, presenting problems typically center around academic and/or behavioral difficulties that result from dysfunctional interactions among children, teachers, peers, parents, siblings, school administrators, and others in school, home, and community environments.

To develop effective interventions for identified problems, the ecological consultant facilitates movement of the consultee through one or more forms of structured problem solving. While there are many different problem-solving processes from which to choose, most are highly similar to one another (Gutkin & Curtis, 1990). Bergan's (1977) four-step sequence has received the most attention in the school psychology literature, and very detailed operational descriptions have been presented in a number of books, book chapters, and training manuals (e.g., Bergan & Kratochwill, 1990; Kratochwill & Bergan, 1990; Kratochwill, Elliott, & Carrington Rotto, 1995; Sheridan, Kratochwill, & Bergan, 1996). A highly congruent seven-step model proposed by Gutkin and Curtis 1982, 1990, based on the work of Osborn (1963) and D'Zurilla and Goldfried (1971), has also been used frequently in both school psychology research and practice (Bush et al., 1989; Henning-Stout & Conoley, 1988), as have other variations on these problem-solving sequences (e.g., Goodwin & Coates, 1976; Jayanthi & Friend, 1992; Maitland et al., 1985).

Step 1 of Bergan's (1977) problem-solving process is *problem identification*, in which the consultant and consultee delineate a clearly defined statement of the presenting problem. Although, to the novice, this may sound like the easiest step of the process, experienced consultants recognize that problem definition is usually complicated by the fact that problems occur in interconnected clusters rather than in isolation and may be clouded by consultees' affective reactions (e.g., frustration, anger, anxiety). Teasing out the central problem from the background noise can be quite complex. Some criteria for selecting and isolating target behaviors are deciding which are (a) most important to address, (b) easiest to fix, (c) most distressing to the consultee or other relevant people in the client's ecosystem, or (d) most impactful in that resolving this one behavior may result in the muting or disappearance of other problem behaviors. Early research suggests that successful completion of the problem identification stage is closely related to the efficacy of the entire consultation process (Bergan & Tombari, 1976).

A useful problem definition is one that is stated in concrete, descriptive, behavioral terms so that it is both directly observable and amenable to quantification. Lambert's (1976) study of elementary school teachers, however, led her to conclude that teachers experience considerable difficulty when trying to specify pupils' problems in this manner. She found that teachers tended to report students' problems with general and vague statements (e.g., the child is poorly motivated, the student has low ability) rather than in terms that have clear implications for "operational changes in classroom practice" (p. 516). More recent research by Wilson et al. (1998) reinforces this perception. Coolahan (1991) also found that teachers made many "inferential" statements in describing students' problems, although consultants' verbalizations resulted in increased numbers of validation and specification statements by these same consultees. Other research also suggests that teachers exposed to highly skilled consultants through direct interaction, modeling, or instruction significantly improve their problem clarification skills (Cleven & Gutkin, 1988; Curtis & Watson, 1980; Zins & Ponti, 1996).

One of the consultant's first tasks, therefore, is to help consultees arrive at a concrete, behavioral definition of a problem. One means for doing this is simply to ask for further specification of vague problem statements. For example, if a consultee states that Johnny has "a bad attitude toward school," the consultant could ask, "Can you be more specific?" or "What behaviors lead you to say that he has a bad attitude?" or "The last time you found yourself realizing that Johnny had a bad attitude toward school, what was he actually doing at that moment?" Often a series of questions such as these can lead to a useful clarification of the problem. Giving the consultee sufficient space to express her or his thoughts may be another effective vehicle. It is hoped that as a consultee expresses his or her perceptions, more and more operational specificity will arise.

Often consultees are unable to provide a clear behavioral definition of a problem because they are trying to describe too many problems at once. Both experience and research (Caron & Rutter, 1991; Dietz & Montague, 2006; Mash & Dozois, 1996; Saxe, Cross, & Silverman, 1988; Widiger & Trull, 2007) tell us that comorbidity is common in that children typically have multiple rather than singular difficulties. Social adjustment problems, for example, often occur concomitantly with academic difficulties and family dysfunction. The range of difficulties with children is often so broad that a specific behavioral definition of the problem may be very difficult to develop. In such instances, the consultant should help the consultee divide the overall problem into its component parts, rank each of the specific components, and work towards a behavioral definition for the problem that the consultee decides to address first. This procedure should help consultees reduce the complexity of presenting problems so that they can avoid being overwhelmed and work more effectively toward the development of a useful problem statement.

A frequent error made by consulting psychologists during problem identification is to assume that a consultee's first verbalization of a problem statement reflects the consultee's major concern. Although never researched directly, it is our experience that initial problem statements by consultees often serve, either intentionally or unintentionally, to mask their real concern. In some instances, they may need to establish a strong sense of trust in a consultant before revealing highly sensitive information. In presenting a safe problem, consultees may be testing the consultant. The consultant's ability to execute an effective entry process and maintain a nonevaluative stance should increase the probability that the consultee will eventually reveal problems that are both more substantive and more sensitive. In other instances, consultees may be experiencing so many problems that they are genuinely confused about what constitutes the essential versus the peripheral elements of the situation. In these cases, the consultant's listening skills and ability to help consultees discuss and establish priorities for the component parts of the problem situation will be important.

Once an effective problem definition has been agreed on, it is important to focus on the collection of baseline data and the development of realistic, short-term (three-to-six week) goals. This will allow the consultant and consultee to judge accurately whether their treatment plans are working satisfactorily soon after they are implemented. This step is highly congruent with data-based decision making processes employed by prereferral intervention teams and RTI methodologies (Kovaleski, 2002; Reschly & Bergstrom, Chapter 22; Ysseldyke & Burns, Chapter 21).

Step 2 is *problem analysis*. This is the assessment and treatment generation phase of the consultation process. The primary goals are to develop and assess hypotheses pertaining to why the target behaviors are occurring and to work up a set of intervention plans that are likely to produce desired outcomes.

Proximal environmental antecedents and consequences that surround target behaviors are typically analyzed in great detail at this point (Daly et al., Chapter 5). Interactions among the behaviors, distal environments, and individual characteristics of all involved must also be considered to understand more fully the client's ecosystem (Gutkin, 1993c, this volume). When conducting problem analysis assessments, it is important to identify client and ecosystem resources that might be incorporated into treatment plans (e.g., the student is highly motivated to improve and has strong peer relationships; the parents have a positive history with the teacher and are highly motivated to support treatment plans in whatever way they can; the school and community have relevant after-school programs), as well as focusing on problematic phenomena.

The generation of intervention plans should flow naturally from the problem definition process and the ecological assessment data that have been collected. Brainstorming is thought to be an effective mechanism for these purposes. Specifically, the consultant and consultee should engage in a freewheeling generation of as many potential intervention strategies as possible, while refraining at this point from criticizing or praising each other's ideas. Research (e.g., D'Zurilla & Goldfried, 1971; Heppner, 1978; Jayanthi & Friend, 1992) suggests that criticism (either positive or negative) will reduce the number

of ideas, and that the larger the number of brainstormed ideas there are to choose among, the higher the probability of finding optimal and high quality solutions. Once a sufficient number of potential ideas have arisen, the consultant and consultee should review the list of alternatives to determine which are acceptable to the consultee and most likely to meet the needs of the client.

Step 3 is *plan implementation*. Treatments and interventions designed in step 2 are now put into action by the consultee (and others, when appropriate), and data are collected and analyzed (Shinn, 1995) to determine their impact. Given the complexity of relationships between attitudes and behaviors (e.g., Petty, Heesacker, & Hughes, 1997) and the subtleties of treatment compliance and integrity (Gresham, 1989; Gutkin & Conoley, 1990; Meichenbaum & Turk, 1987; Witt, 1990b), consultants should never assume that a consultee's good intentions and verbal agreements to implement a particular treatment program will be carried out as intended. As discussed earlier, follow-up contact is crucial.

To increase the probabilities that appropriate action will be taken by consultees, consultants should design interventions that are highly compatible with the natural ecosystems in which they are to be implemented (Martens & Witt, 1988a, 1988b; Witt & Martens, 1988). Thus, for example, proposed consultative interventions should build on the existing strengths of consultees, rather than focusing on the remediation of deficits, and take advantage of existing resources, rather than depending on the intrusion of new resources into an ecosystem.

When consultees fail to implement agreed-upon intervention plans, consultants should assume (at least initially) that there are legitimate reasons for this decision rather than leaping to the conclusion that the consultee is resistant, incompetent, or a "three-toed sloth" (Witt, 1990a, p. 369). The ecologies in which most consultees function are complex, unpredictable, uncontrollable in many ways, and often pressure-packed. Implementing treatment plans for difficult-to-teach children may often be secondary to meeting the needs of other children in the classroom, principal's demands, parental pressures, excessive numbers of team meetings, a demanding (and, perhaps, unreasonable) team leader, unexpected emergencies, and so on. In our opinion, attributing a consultee's failure to act on treatment recommendations to resistance is less likely to result in meaningful and positive change in consultee behavior than attempting to understand and assist with the demands and pressures placed on a consultee by the ecosystem in which she or he functions (Conoley, 1994).

The fourth and final step is *treatment evaluation*. At this point the consultant and consultee determine jointly whether the implemented intervention was successful. Baseline data and short-term goals developed during problem identification, assessment data collected during problem analysis, and treatment data collected during plan implementation are crucial in making this judgment. At the extremes, the consultant and consultee may conclude that the intervention was (a) a resounding success and that the consultation relationship for this particular problem can now be terminated, or (b) a total failure and that the consultation relationship should either be continued or terminated, according to the perceptions of both participants that subsequent interactions will lead to more substantive and positive outcomes. More often than not, however, the outcome falls somewhere between these two extremes, and the consultant and consultee both perceive the need for additional refinements and adjustments in the intervention program. Returning to the problem identification, problem analysis, and/or plan implementation steps, and relying on processes of data-based decision making (Reschly & Bergstrom, Chapter 22; Ysseldyke & Burns, Chapter 21), should facilitate the attainment of this goal.

Mental Health Consultation

As the first consultation model to be articulated in detail, the term *mental health consultation* has sometimes been taken as a generic phrase for all consultation models (Meyers, Parsons, & Martin, 1979). Our use of this term is much more restricted and reflects primarily the work of Gerald Caplan (Caplan, 1970; Caplan & Caplan, 1993). Caplan's impact on mental health consultation has been so significant, in fact, that recently others have begun to publish books and chapters focusing solely on the history of his work (Erchul, 1993a).

Although Caplan's mental health consultation has a great deal in common with the ecological approach (most of the core characteristics of school-based consultation were first articulated by him in 1970), there are enough unique aspects to warrant its presentation as a distinct model. In particular, since Caplan and many of the earlier theoreticians were psychoanalytically oriented

psychiatrists, the early literature often focused on such topics as ego state, pre- and subconscious motivations, penis envy, castration fears, and so forth. In this regard, mental health consultation is quite disparate from the more extrapersonal, situationally oriented perspectives of ecological approaches.

In both his early and more recent writings, Caplan (1970; Caplan & Caplan, 1993) discusses four overlapping types of mental health consultation: (1) client-centered case consultation, (2) consultee-centered case consultation, (3) program-centered administrative consultation, and (4) consultee-centered administrative consultation. These approaches differ according to whether the primary goal of consultation is prevention or remediation and whether the focus of consultation is on individual cases or programs. Most school psychologists consider consultee-centered case consultation to be the centerpiece of Caplan's contributions and thus it receives more detailed analysis here.

Consultee-centered case consultation, in which the primary goal is prevention and the focus is on individual cases, is described by Caplan and Caplan (1993) as follows:

> The consultant's primary focus is on elucidating and remedying the shortcomings in the consultee's professional functioning. The discussion is mainly restricted to clarifying the details of the client's situation to increase the consultee's cognitive grasp and emotional mastery of the issues involved in caring for him. This is likely to lead to an improvement in the consultee's professional planning and action, and hopefully to improvement in the client. But in consultee-centered consultation, improvement in the client is a side effect, welcome though it may be; the primary goal is to improve the consultee's capacity to function effectively in this category of case, in order to benefit many similar clients in the future. Because of the educational emphasis, the consultant uses the discussion of the current case situation not primarily to understand the client but to understand and remedy the consultee's work difficulties. (p. 101)

There are several subtle but significant differences between ecological consultation, on the one hand, and consultee-centered case consultation, on the other. In the former, the consultant works with the consultee to delineate the causes of a client's presenting problems, as well as potential solutions. In the latter, a consultant is only indirectly interested in the causes for and solutions of the client's presenting problem. Instead, the primary focus is on determining why the consultee is having difficulties with a particular case and resolving these difficulties so that he or she can handle the client's problem independently. For example, under the ecological consultation methodology, a consultant might work with a consultee to determine why a particular child is continuously hostile to his or her teacher and peers. The outcome would typically be a series of planned interventions designed to reduce the occurrence of the child's problem behaviors. In consultee-centered case consultation, however, the consultant's main concern would be neither on the causes of the child's behavior nor on potential solutions for this problem. Rather, the consultant would be interested in determining why the consultee cannot handle this particular problem more effectively and implementing strategies to improve the consultee's professional functioning in such situations.

Throughout his writings, Caplan (1970; Caplan & Caplan, 1993) has postulated four reasons for consultee-centered case consultation. First, consultees might lack professional knowledge pertaining to a particular problem. Second, consultees might lack necessary professional skills. That is, even though they know what they need to do for a client, they lack the ability to carry it out. Third, consultees might lack sufficient self-confidence. In these instances, consultees would not be lacking either knowledge or skills but would be held back because they didn't fully trust themselves to intervene effectively with the client. Fourth, consultees might lack sufficient professional objectivity. That is, they find themselves unable to resolve a presenting problem because they have become emotionally involved in a case and have lost their professional distance. Caplan and Caplan (1993) describe this lack of professional objectivity as follows.

> The consultee is either too close or too distant from actors in the client's life drama, and is not able to perceive them accurately enough to carry out his task. Personal subjective factors in the consultee cloud his judgment, so that in this current case he behaves less effectively than is usual for him and thus is not able to utilize his existing

knowledge and skills. By the time he comes for consultation, this situation is usually aggravated by his feelings of frustration at the impasse in the case, by a feeling of professional failure, and a consequent lowering of self-esteem, all of which add to his loss of professional poise. (p. 107)

In early writings, Caplan (1970) discounts the relative importance of consultees' lack of knowledge, skill, and self-confidence, assuming that most consultees in need of consultee-centered case consultation were experiencing a lack objectivity: "in a well-organized institution or agency in which there is an effective personnel system, administrative control, and a well-developed supervisory network, most cases that present themselves . . . fall into this fourth [lack of objectivity] category" (p. 131). In the second edition (Gutkin & Curtis, 1990), we questioned the logic of this assumption in reference to schools, wondering whether they are typically characterized by "an effective personnel system, administrative control, and a well-developed supervisory network," and also noting that existing empirical evidence (Gutkin, 1981) was not consistent with Caplan's assumptions. More recently, Caplan appears to be ambivalent about this issue, indicating in an interview with Erchul (1993b) that "most of the cases that come from consultation are cases where the consultee has difficulties because of lack of knowledge or lack of skill" (p. 65) but, in Caplan and Caplan (1993), that "most cases of consultee-centered case consultation fall into this last [lack of objectivity] category" (p. 107).

It is clear that Caplan's work in this area (Caplan, 1970; Caplan and Caplan, 1993) represents a major contribution to the consultation literature. In his writings he details five reasons why a consultee might suffer from a lack of objectivity: (1) direct personal involvement of the consultee with the client, (2) simple identification of the consultee with the client, (3) transference of consultee experiences and psychic difficulties onto the client's case, (4) characterological distortions of perception and behavior on the part of the consultee in regard to the client, and (5) theme interference. Because the last of these causes is a concept that Caplan stresses so heavily and one with which most school psychologists are not familiar, theme interference requires some additional explanation:

> The theme is a continuing representation of an unsolved problem or a defeat; it carries a negative emotional tone of rankling failure.

It also has a quality of repetition compulsion. This usually takes a syllogistic form, involving an inevitable link between two items or statements. Statement A denotes a particular situation or condition that was characteristic of the original unsolved problem. Statement B denotes the unpleasant outcome. The syllogism takes the form "All A inevitably lead to B." The implication is that whenever the person finds himself involved in situation or condition A, he is fated to suffer B; also, that this generalization applies universally, that everyone who is involved in A inevitably suffers B.... For instance, if statement A (initial category) is "A person who masturbates excessively" and Statement B (inevitable outcome) is "His nervous system will be damaged and his intelligence will be blunted," the syllogism take the form of "*All* people who masturbate excessively damage their nervous system and blunt their intelligence." This theme may be a sequel to guilt-ridden conflicts over masturbation in the professional worker's childhood or adolescence, and represents a foreboding that one day in the future a punishing nemesis will inevitably strike. When, for whatever reason, the defenses against this old conflict weaken, the situation is ripe.... The consultee unconsciously selects a client from his caseload and fits him into the initial category of "a person who masturbates excessively." This then arouses the expectations that "his nervous system will inevitably be damaged and his intelligence blunted." The worker becomes very upset by this foreboding and attempts to stave off the expected doom.... These preventive efforts are usually panicky and inconsistent, and a realization of their obvious ineffectiveness confirms the consultee's certainty that the expected doom can not be prevented despite all his efforts. Unconsciously, his consolation is that this time the catastrophe will occur to a client and not to himself. (Caplan & Caplan, 1993, pp. 122–124)

Caplan (1970; Caplan & Caplan, 1993) proposes several techniques to reduce theme interference. One strategy is to unlink the presenting problem from the theme by convincing the consultee that the client does not fit into the initial category. For example, if the theme is "all children who are not sufficiently disciplined by their parents will grow up without self-control and thus lead unproductive lives as adults," the consultant could attempt to show the consultee that in the current case the client is adequately disciplined by his or her parents. If successful with this intervention, the consultee would unlink the client from the theme and return to his or her normal professional efficiency. Although unlinking may resolve the presenting problem, Caplan argues against using this tactic because it leaves the consultee's theme intact. The situation has been resolved for a specific client, but the generalized bias remains. In place of unlinking, Caplan (Caplan & Caplan, 1993) proposes strategies for the reduction of theme interference, all of which are intended to weaken a consultee's theme and thus enable the consultee to cope effectively with the presenting problem and future problems of a similar nature.

> The goal of the consultant's intervention is to invalidate the obligatory link between the two categories that express the theme. The consultant accepts and supports the displacement of the theme onto the client's case and the definition of it as a test case by concurring with the initial category in all its details that are personally meaningful to the consultee. The consultant then engages the consultee in a joint examination of the link between the initial category and the outcome category and helps the consultee realize that this outcome is not inevitable. Since the syllogism says that the connection is inevitable, if we can demonstrate that on even one occasion *in an authentic test case* that meets all the consultee's unconscious requirements the connection between the categories does not hold, we will dissipate or weaken the theme. (pp. 139–140)

Caplan suggests four specific theme inference reduction techniques, all of which reflect his general approach. The first of these strategies is called "verbal focus on the client." In this approach, the consultant verbally examines the presenting problem with the consultee and "demonstrates that although the inevitable outcome is one logical possibility, there are other possibilities too; and the evidence indicates that one or more of these is more probable than the doom that the consultee envisages" (Caplan & Caplan, 1993, p. 140). The second approach is called "verbal focus on an alternate object—the parable," in which the consultant directs discussion away from the client's situation and onto a case that is superficially as different as possible from the presenting case but which retains the essential elements of the theme. The third tactic is termed "nonverbal focus on the case." The essence of this technique is for the consultant to remain calm and relaxed, thus non-verbally signaling that the expected inevitable outcome and the negative consequences associated with it are rather unlikely. Caplan hypothesizes that this method will work only if the consultant successfully communicates to the consultee that she or he "truly understands the danger in the case [so that the consultee will not] believe that the consultant's relaxed behavior means that he does not understand what is likely to happen to the client, or does not care" (pp. 152–153). Caplan's fourth intervention is "nonverbal focus on the consultation relationship." He hypothesizes that consultees will often express themes in the way they relate to the consultant and that the consultant can invalidate these themes by purposefully acting in ways that are congruent with the initial category but then failing to behave in a manner that is consistent with the inevitable outcome.

Building on Caplan's (1970; Caplan & Caplan, 1993) work, Bernard and DiGiuseppe (1994) have proposed a model they call rational-emotive consultation (REC). Like Caplan, they suggest that irrational thinking by consultees may play a major factor in many consultation problems. Unlike Caplan, however, they employ a rational-emotive (Ellis, 1963) rather than a psychodynamic framework to understand and intervene with this phenomenon. Whereas Caplan recommends dealing indirectly with inappropriate emotion through theme interference reduction, Bernard and DiGiuseppe suggest a more confrontational approach, in which the irrational thoughts of a consultee are challenged directly.

To date, although mental health consultation has been a long-standing tool for school-based consultants and REC seems quite promising, there has been a paucity of empirical research into these models. In 1987, Gresham and Kendell concluded after reviewing the consultation literature that "there is no empirical support for the hypothesis that theme interference (Caplan, 1970) seriously impedes consultees' professional objectivity nor is there empirical support for the techniques suggested by Caplan (1970) to reduce theme interference" (p. 311). Unfortunately, little seems to have changed in this regard, and it is clear that a focused and systematic program of empirical research is needed to advance the theory and practice of these approaches.

Organizational and Systems Consultation

Unlike either ecological or mental health consultation, both of which focus primarily on the problems of individuals, the client in organizational and systems consultation is typically a group within an organization or an entire organizational system itself (for a discussion of the role of school psychologists in organizational consultation, see Meyers, Meyers, Proctor & Graybill, this volume). In discussing system-level consultation, Curtis, Castillo and Cohen (2008) provide examples in which school psychologists could be engaged in such efforts at several different levels (e.g., classroom, grade, building, district). Going a step further, Grimes and Tilly (1996) discuss their experiences in working toward systemic changes on a statewide basis. Given that school psychologists frequently practice within groups (e.g., intervention assistance, IEP, and multidisciplinary teams) and are typically situated in community organizational settings (e.g., schools, community mental health centers, hospitals, residential facilities), the ability to address group, organizational, and system problems would seem to be crucial to the profession (Curtis, Castillo & Cohen, 2008; Forman, 1995; Gutkin & Conoley, 1990; Gutkin & Nemeth, 1997; Meyers et al., this volume; Sheridan & Gutkin, 2000; Ysseldyke et al., 2006). The working assumption underlying school-based organizational and systems consultation is that "healthy" educational and psychological experiences for children and teachers alike are more likely to occur in "healthy" organizations and systemic contexts (Davis & Thomas, 1989; Schmuck, 1990; Snapp, Hickman, & Conoley, 1990).

Historically, changing schools at the organizational and systems level has been a major goal for school psychologists (Reynolds et al., 1984). In Bardon and Bennett's (1974) classic book, entitled *School Psychology*, for example, serving as a systems change agent was conceptualized as the highest level of functioning. Likewise, consultation pertaining to organizational issues has long been recognized as a major role for school-based consultants (e.g., Meyers, 1973). With recent growing emphases on school reform and innovation, including movement to a PS/RTI model, contemporary school psychologists appear to be more interested than ever in focusing on consultation services that promote organizational and system-wide change (Castillo, Cohen, & Curtis, 2007; Curtis, Castillo & Cohen, 2008; Curtis & Stollar, 2002; Elliott & Witt, 1986; Graden, Zins, & Curtis, 1988; Gutkin, this volume; Henning-Stout & Conoley, 1988; Knoff, 1995; Knoff & Curtis, 1996; Meyers et al., Chapter 43; Plas, 1986; Ponti et al., 1988; Schmuck, 1990; Snapp et al., 1990; Ysseldyke et al., 2006; Zins & Ponti, 1990).

Theoretical Bases and Empirically Validated Approaches

To provide organizational and systems consultation services, school psychologists draw on a broad array of theoretical perspectives, ranging from those that are widely applicable to all organizational systems, for example, force field analysis (Lewin, 1951) and general systems theory (von Bertalanffy, 1968), to those that were developed specifically for human service organizations like schools, for example, domain theory (Dappen & Gutkin, 1986; Kouzes & Mico, 1979). Although a considerable number of specific operational models have been articulated (e.g., Knoff, 1995; Maher & Illback, 1985), four interrelated elements seem to emerge as crucial components of successful organizational/systems consultation.

First, mutual adaptation emerged from a comprehensive Rand Corporation review of 293 local organizational change projects carried out under four federal programs in 18 different states (McLaughlin, 1976, 1990). Specifically, it was found that implementation success in schools hinged to a substantial degree on the extent to which local school personnel were able to shape and mold innovations to make them fit into the local ecology of their communities, school districts, and classrooms (see Meyers, 2002, for a cross-cultural case study illustrating this point). McLaughlin (1990) reported that for effective change programs, "local variability is the rule; uniformity is the exception" (p. 13). Parenthetically, these findings appear to be contrary to the research and theory reported earlier regarding the use of scripts and direct consultation methods, in which highly prescriptive behaviors by consultants were deemed to facilitate treatment implementation (Ehrhardt et al., 1996; Watson & Robinson, 1996). In light of mutual adaptation, however, it is our suspicion that scripts would probably be most effective when consultees are given sufficient elbow room to adapt them to

local conditions as necessary. This is, of course, an empirical question and one that should be addressed through research rather than armchair theorizing. Nevertheless, based on contemporary empirical analyses, it does appear that mutual adaptation is an essential ingredient of consultation at the organizational and systems level. Consultants must learn how to work collaboratively with local school personnel in shaping and reformulating systemic change efforts rather than expecting to dictate the wholesale adoption of prefabricated packages. This point is reinforced by Curtis and Stollar (1995), who emphasize the need to design change strategies that respond to the uniqueness of each system. Janney et al. (1995) provide an example of these processes in action, as five school districts in Virginia set out to increase the integration of students with moderate and severe handicaps into general education classes.

The second concept is the involvement of all primary stakeholders in all aspects of the change process. The literature identifies this principle as fundamental to any successful change program. Curtis, Castillo and Cohen (2008) see the failure to involve classroom teachers as a major reason that efforts to implement intervention assistance programs encounter resistance and are often unsuccessful:

> Typically, the discussions, planning, and even implementation have involved seemingly everyone *but* classroom teachers. Principals, special education personnel, school psychologists, and other related services professionals then "inform" teachers about the new procedures. Confusion and frustration result when teachers do not participate regardless of the good intentions of the change agents.... They [teachers] should be meaningfully involved in every aspect of such change efforts, beginning with initial discussions regarding *potential* change and continuing through implementation. (p. 893)

Needless to say, parents represent another primary stakeholder group that is largely ignored in many school-based change efforts.

The third element is the endorsement of change efforts by relevant system administrators. Although bottom-up planning, such as mutual adaptation, seems to be crucial in organizational change, it is widely believed that there is a simultaneous need for top-down sanctioning and support (e.g., Curtis, Castillo & Cohen,

2008; Henning-Stout & Conoley, 1988; Knoff, 1995; Schrag, 1996; Villa, Thousand, Meyers, & Nevin, 1996). Studies by Broughton and Hester (1993), Ponti et al. (1988), Janney et al. (1995), and McLaughlin (1990), among others, support this assumption. Although it would appear that administrative and upper-management support for change in no way ensures its success, its absence may substantially increase the chances for failure.

Finally, the literature has long suggested the need for a coherent system of collaborative problem solving (e.g., Schmuck, Runkel, Arends, & Arends, 1977). Given the complexity and multivariate nature of organizational and systems consultation, it would be very easy for consultants and consultees alike to get overwhelmed and confused without a structured road map for approaching target problems. Exemplifying one such road map is the model proposed by Curtis, Castillo and Cohen (2008):

> **Step 1.** Describe the problem to be addressed as concretely and in as much detail as possible.
>
> **Step 2.** Analyze the specific issue chosen in terms of factors that might help in reducing or eliminating the problem (resources), as well as factors that might serve as barriers to its resolution.
>
> **Step 3.** Select *one* barrier identified in Step 2 that is important in terms of preventing resolution of the problem defined in Step 1.
>
> **Step 4.** By focusing on only the one obstacle selected in Step 3 the team should brainstorm strategies that might be used to reduce or eliminate that specific barrier.
>
> **Step 5.** Design multiple action plans to guide the implementation of the systems intervention(s) for the purpose of reducing or eliminating only the barrier identified in Step 3.
>
> **Step 6.** Develop a plan for following up with each action plan/intervention that explains how implementation will be monitored as well as how support will be provided to the person responsible, if needed.
>
> **Step 7.** Develop a detailed plan that explains how data will be collected to evaluate progress at two different levels: (a) reduction or elimination of the barrier identified in Step 3, and (b) progress toward attainment of the desired outcome of the problem-solving effort identified in Step 1.
>
> **Step 8.** Describe the process and timeline for using data collected through Step 7 to decide if satisfactory progress is being made toward reduction/elimination of the barrier and attainment of the desired outcome of problem solving as well as next steps in the problem-solving process. (pp. 414–415)

Note that although the words differ from the problem-solving steps described earlier for ecological consultation, which is employed primarily with individual cases, this suggested sequence is quite similar from a functional point of view. Curtis, Castillo and Cohen (2008) provide examples of the use of this sequence at both a micro- and a macro-level for the implementation of a PS/RTI model in an elementary school setting.

Targets for Organizational and Systems Consultation

Without a doubt, an enormous range of important issues can be addressed by organizational and systems consultation, for example, program evaluation, diffusion of innovations, organizational conflict, group norms, group process, role expectations, leadership, group decision making, intra- and intergroup communication, group problem solving, and school-community relationships (Knoff & Curtis, 1996; Owens, 1987; Romualdi & Sandoval, 1995; Sarason, 1982; Schein, 1969; Schmuck et al., 1977; Snapp et al., 1990; Thomas & Grimes, 2008). Several case studies have already been presented in the research literature, such as Ponti et al. (1988), Rosenfield (1992), Curtis and Metz (1986), Hertz-Lazarowitz and Od-Cohen (1992), and Snapp et al. (1990).

Beyond these published reports, however, the need for increased organizational consultation activities by school psychologists seems clear. Consider, for example, the growing epidemic of violence in our nation's schools (Goldstein, Harootunian, & Conoley, 1994). There seems to be little or no attention to this issue until children commit serious acts of violence. Then schools respond by (a) assessing the offenders to determine if they are seriously emotionally disturbed, (b) consulting with the individual teachers and parents of the offenders to develop remedial programs for them, and/or (c) placing the offending student into psychotherapy. A superior alternative to any of these approaches might be to initiate a proactive organizational consultation process with school administrators, teachers, and community leaders to develop violence prevention programs (Hyman, 1997).

Along similar lines, one of us worked as a psychologist in a school in which 85% of the students were reading below grade level. Once becoming aware of these dismal data, the principal suggested that the school psychologist begin testing a very long list of students who were below grade level to determine who was handicapped. The school psychologist suggested to the principal that instead he would like to start an organizational consultation project with the school's team leaders and the district's reading specialists to redesign the reading curriculum.

A final example centers around the fact that although virtually all important special education decisions are made in team meetings of one sort or another, relatively few school personnel ever receive formal training of any kind in group processes, dynamics, or problem-solving methodologies. The result is that many team meetings are dysfunctional, and something less than the best decisions often are made for difficult-to-teach and referred children (Flugum & Reschly, 1994; Gravois, Groff, & Rosenfield, this volume; Gutkin & Nemeth, 1997; Meyers et al., 1996; Wilson et al., 1998; Ysseldyke, 1987). Obviously, working with or consulting about individual students will not lead to effective solutions for this type of problem. Intervention at the organizational and systems level will be required. It is also important to note that until systemic impediments such as these are removed, it will be difficult for school personnel to make high-quality decisions for the students who are in need of school psychological or related support services.

CONCLUDING COMMENTS

Consultation has always been viewed as a major role for school psychologists (Bardon & Bennett, 1974). Based on contemporary thinking, as evidenced in Blueprint III (Ysseldyke et al., 2006) and the 2002 Future of School Psychology Conference (Cummings et al., 2004; D'Amato et al., 2003, 2004) among many other sources, it would appear that its centrality is continuing to increase. Above and beyond its own independent benefits, the "Paradox of School Psychology" (Gutkin & Conoley, 1990, p. 212, discussed at the beginning of this chapter) suggests that consultation services undergird and strengthen the impact of virtually all other professional activities performed by school psychologists. Assessment results in and of themselves, for example, are unlikely to produce positive educational and psychological

changes for children unless they are followed up by effective consultative interactions with significant adults in children's lives, such as teachers and parents. Likewise, the impact of individual therapy with children can be enhanced through coordination of services with those adults who populate the daily worlds of children. Finally, consultation holds unique potential for achieving effective prevention (Durlak, this volume) and public health (Gutkin, this volume; Strein et al., 2003) outcomes by creating opportunities to "give psychology away" (Miller, 1969, p. 1071) to those non-psychologists who are in a position to use psychological information for the benefit of children (Christensen & Jacobson, 1994). Given the mental health and education pandemics that are extant in our nation today (Gutkin, Chapter 23), few priorities would seem to be more important for our field or the young people we serve.

REFERENCES

Allen, S. J., & Blackston, A. R. (2003). Training preservice teachers in collaborative problem solving: An investigation of the impact on teacher and student behavior change in real-world settings. *School Psychology Quarterly, 18,* 22–51.

American Psychological Association. (2002). Ethical principles of psychologists and code of conduct. Washington, DC: Author. Available from www.apa.org/ethics/code2002.html.

American School Counselor Association (2005). *The ASCA national model: A framework for school counseling programs* (2nd ed.). Alexandria, VA: Author

Anderson, T. K., Kratochwill, T. R., & Bergan, J. R. (1986). Training teachers in behavioral consultation and therapy: An analysis of verbal behaviors. *Journal of School Psychology, 24,* 229–241.

Andrews, L. W., & Gutkin, T. B. (1994). Influencing attitudes regarding special class placement via a psychoeducational report: An investigation of the elaboration likelihood model. *Journal of School Psychology, 32,* 321–337.

Annan, J. (2005). Situational analysis: A framework for evidence-based practice. *School Psychology International, 26,* 131–146.

Babcock, N. L., & Pryzwansky, W. B. (1983). Models of consultation: Preferences of educational professionals at five stages of service. *Journal of School Psychology, 21,* 359–366.

Bahr, M. W. (1996). Are school psychologists reform-minded? *Psychology in the Schools, 33,* 295–307.

Bandura, A. (1978). The self-system in reciprocal determinism. *American Psychologist, 33,* 344–358.

Bandura, A. (1993). Perceived self-efficacy in cognitive development and functioning. *Educational Psychologist, 28,* 117–148.

Bardon, J. I. (1987). The translation of research into practice into school psychology. *School Psychology Review, 16,* 317–328.

Bardon, J. I., & Bennett, V. C. (1974). *School psychology.* Englewood Cliffs, NJ: Prentice Hall.

Barker, R. G. (1965). Explorations in ecological psychology. *American Psychologist, 20,* 1–14.

Barker, R. G. (1968). *Ecological psychology.* Stanford, CA: Stanford University Press.

Barry, J. R. (1970). Criteria in The evaluation of consultation. *Professional Psychology, 1,* 363–366.

Beavers, K. F., Kratochwill, T. R., & Braden, J. P. (2004). Treatment utility of functional versus empiric assessment with consultation for reading problems. *School Psychology Quarterly, 19,* 29–49.

Bergan, J. R. (1977). *Behavioral consultation.* Columbus, OH: Merrill.

Bergan, J. R., Byrnes, I. M., & Kratochwill, T. R. (1979). Effects of behavioral and medical models of consultation on teacher expectancies and instruction of a hypothetical child. *Journal of School Psychology, 17,* 306–316.

Bergan, J. R., & Kratochwill, T. R. (1990). *Behavioral consultation and therapy.* New York: Plenum.

Bergan, J. R., & Tombari, M. L. (1976). Consultant skill and efficiency and the implementation and outcomes of consultation. *Journal of School Psychology, 14,* 3–14.

Bernard, M. E., & DiGiuseppe, R. (Eds.). (1994). *Rational-emotive consultation in applied settings.* Hillsdale, NJ: Erlbaum.

Beutler, L. E., Machado, P. P. P., & Neufeldt, S. A. (1994). Therapist variables. In A. E. Bergin & S. L. Garfield (Eds.), *Handbook of psychotherapy and behavior change* (4th ed., pp. 229–269). New York: Wiley.

Bostic, J. Q., & Bagnell, A. (2001). Psychiatric school consultation: An organizing framework and empowering techniques. *Child and Adolescent Psychiatry Clinics of North America, 10,* 1–12.

Bozic, N. (2004). Using letters to support consultative work in schools. *Educational Psychology in Practice, 20,* 291–302.

Bronfenbrenner, U. (1979). *The ecology of human development.* Cambridge, MA: Harvard University Press.

Broughton, S. F., & Hester, J. R. (1993). Effects of administrative and community support on teacher acceptance of classroom interventions. *Journal of Educational and Psychological Consultation, 4,* 169–177.

Brown, D., Pryzwansky, W. B., & Schulte, A. C. (2006). *Psychological consultation and collaboration: Introduction to theory and practice* (6th ed.). Boston, MA: Allyn & Bacon.

Brown, D., & Schulte, A. C. (1987). A social learning model of consultation. *Professional Psychology: Research and Practice, 18,* 283–287.

Burns, M. K. (2004). Using curriculum-based assessment in consultation: A review of three levels of research. *Journal of Educational and Psychological Consultation, 15,* 63–78.

Burns, M. K., & Symington, T. (2002). A meta-analysis of prereferral intervention teams: Student and systemic outcomes. *Journal of School Psychology, 40,* 437–447.

Burns, M. K., Vanderwood, M. L., & Ruby, S. (2005). Evaluating the readiness of pre-referral intervention teams for use in a problem solving model. *School Psychology Quarterly, 20,* 89–105.

Bush, K. J., Carter, D. W., Dickerson, C., Evans, G., Martin, F., Raskind, L. T., & Thomas, A. (1989). Gwinnett County: Changing its service delivery in response to population growth. *Professional School Psychology, 4,* 189–200.

Canter, A. S. (1991). Effective psychological services for all students: A data-based model of service delivery. In G. Stoner, M. R. Shinn, & H. M. Walker (Eds.), *Interventions for achievement and behavior problems* (pp. 49–78). Silver Spring, MD: National Association of School Psychologists.

Caplan, G. (1970). *The theory and practice of mental health consultation.* New York: Basic Books.

Caplan, G., & Caplan, R. B. (1993). *Mental health consultation and collaboration.* San Francisco: Jossey-Bass.

Carlberg, C., & Kavale, K. (1980). The efficacy of special versus regular class placement for exceptional children: A meta-analysis. *Journal of Special Education, 14,* 295–309.

Caron, C., & Rutter, M. (1991). Comorbidity in child psychopathology: Concepts, issues, and research strategies. *Journal of Child Psychology and Psychiatry, 32,* 1063–1080.

Carrington Rotto, P., & Kratochwill, T. R. (1994). Behavioral consultation with parents: Using competency-based training to modify child noncompliance. *School Psychology Review, 23,* 669–693.

Castillo, J. M., Cohen, R. M., & Curtis, M. J. (2007). Evaluating intervention outcomes: A problem solving/response to intervention model as systems-level change. *Communiqué, 35*(8).

Cautili, J. (2006). Resistance is not futile: An experimental analogue of 'resistance' effects on the consultant's therapeutic behavior in the treatment of disruptive students. *Dissertation Abstracts International: Section B: The Sciences and Engineering, 67*(1-B), 523.

Centeno, J. G., & Eng, N. (2005). Bilingual speech-language pathology consultants in culturally diverse schools: Considerations on theoretically-based consultee engagement. *Journal of Educational and Psychological Consultation, 16,* 333–347.

Christensen, A., & Jacobson, N. S. (1994). Who (or what) can do psychotherapy: The status and challenge of nonprofessional therapies. *Psychological Science, 5,* 8–14.

Christenson, S., Abery, B., & Weinberg, R. A. (1986). An alternative model for the delivery of psychological services in the school community. In S. N. Elliott & J. C. Witt (Eds.), *The delivery of psychological services in schools: Concepts, processes, and issues* (pp. 349–391). Hillsdale, NJ: Erlbaum.

Cicchetti, D., & Toth, S. L. (1997). Transactional ecological systems in developmental psychopathology. In S. S. Luthar, J. A. Burack, D. Cicchetti, & J. R. Weisz (Eds.), *Developmental psychopathology: Perspectives on adjustment, risk, and disorder.* New York: Cambridge University Press.

Cleven, C. A., & Gutkin, T. B. (1988). Cognitive modeling of consultation processes: A means for improving consultees' problem definition skills. *Journal of School Psychology, 26,* 379–389.

Cobb, C. T. (1990). School psychology in the 1980s and 1990s: A context for change and definition. In T. Gutkin & J. Grimes (Eds.), *The handbook of school psychology,* (2nd ed. pp. 21–31). New York: John Wiley & Sons.

Cole, E., & Siegel, J. A. (Eds.). (2003). *Effective consultation in school psychology* (2nd ed.) Ashland, OH: Hogrefe & Huber.

Connecticut State Department of Education (2004). *Guidelines for the practice of school psychology.* Hartford, CT: Author.

Conoley, C. W., Conoley, J. C., & Gumm, W. B., II. (1992). Effects of consultee problem presentation and consultant training on consultant problem definition. *Journal of Counseling and Development, 71,* 60–62.

Conoley, C. W., Conoley, J. C., Ivey, D. C., & Scheel, M. J. (1991). Enhancing consultation by matching the consultee's perspectives. *Journal of Counseling and Development, 69,* 546–549.

Conoley, J. C. (1994, December). *Resistance to consultation. Communiqué,* pp. 26–28.

Conoley, J. C., & Conoley, C. W. (1992). *School consultation: Practice and training* (2nd ed.). New York: Pergamon.

Conoley, J. C., & Gutkin, T. B. (1995). Why didn't—Why doesn't—school psychology realize its promise? *Journal of School Psychology, 33,* 209–217.

Conyne, R. K., & Cook, E. P. (2004). *Ecological counseling: An innovative approach to conceptualizing person-environment interaction.* Alexandria, VA: American Counseling Association.

Coolahan, S. M. (1991). *An analysis of consultation verbal behavior during problem identification interviews.* Unpublished doctoral dissertation, University of Cincinnati.

Cooper, J. O., Heron, T. E., & Heward, W. L. (2007). *Applied behavior analysis* (2nd ed.). Upper Saddle River, NJ: Pearson/Merrill Prentice-Hall.

Cormier, W. H., & Cormier, L. S. (1991). *Interviewing strategies for helpers: Fundamental skills and cognitive behavioral interventions* (3rd ed.). Pacific Grove, CA: Brooks/Cole.

Costenbader, V., Swartz, J., & Petrix, L. (1992). Consultation in the schools: The relationship between preservice training, perception of consultative skills, and actual time spent in consultation. *School Psychology Review, 21,* 95–108.

Council for the Accreditation of Counseling and Related Educational Programs (2001). *2001 Standards.* http://www.cacrep.org/2001Standards.html

Council on Social Work Education (2001). *Educational Policy and Accreditation Standards.* http://www.cswe.org/CSWE/accreditation/

Cowen, E. L., & Hightower, A. D. (1990). The Primary Mental Health Project: Alternative approaches in school-based preventive intervention. In T. B. Gutkin & C. R. Reynolds (Eds.), *The handbook of school psychology* (2nd ed., pp. 775–795). New York: Wiley.

Crothers, L., Hughes, T., & Morine, K. (2008). *Cases in school-based consultation: A resource for school psychologists, school counselors, special educators, and other mental health professionals.* New York: Routledge.

Cummings, J. A., Harrison, P. L., & Dawson, M. M. (2004). The 2002 Conference on the Future of School Psychology: Implications for consultation, intervention and prevention services. *Journal of Educational and Psychological Consultation, 15,* 239–256.

Curtis, M. J., Castillo, J. M., & Cohen, R. (2008). Best practices in system-level change. In A. Thomas & J. Grimes (Eds.). *Best practices in school psychology-V* (pp. 887–901). Bethesda, MD: National Association of School Psychologists.

Curtis, M. J., Lopez, A. D., Castillo, J. M., Batsche, G. M., Minch, D., & Smith, J. C. (2008). The status of school psychology: Demographic characteristics, employment conditions, professional practices, and continuing professional development. *Communiqué, 36*(5), 27–29.

Curtis, M. J., & Metz, L. W. (1986). System level intervention in a school for handicapped children. *School Psychology Review, 15,* 510–518.

Curtis, M. J., & Meyers, J. (1988). Consultation: A foundation for alternative services in schools. In J. Graden, J. Zins, & M. Curtis (Eds.), *Alternative educational delivery systems: Enhancing instructional options for all students* (pp. 35–48). Washington, DC: National Association of School Psychologists.

Curtis, M. J., & Stollar, S. A. (1995). Best practices in system-level consultation and organizational change. In A. Thomas & J. Grimes (Eds.), *Best practices in school psychology III* (pp. 51–58). Washington, DC: National Association of School Psychologists.

Curtis, M. J., & Stollar, S. A. (2002). Best practices in system-level change. In A. Thomas & J. Grimes (Eds.), *Best practices in school psychology IV* (pp. 223–234). Bethesda, MD: National Association of School Psychologists.

Curtis, M. J., & Van Wagener, E. (1988, April). *An analysis of failed consultation.* Paper presented at the annual meeting of the National Association of School Psychologists, Chicago, IL.

Curtis, M. J., & Watson, K. L. (1980). Changes in consultee problem clarification skills following consultation. *Journal of School Psychology, 18,* 210–221.

Curtis, M. J., & Zins, J. E. (1988). Effects of training in consultation and instructor feedback on acquisition of consultation skills. *Journal of School Psychology, 26,* 185–190.

Cutts, N. E. (Ed.). (1955). *School psychologists at mid-century.* Washington, DC: American Psychological Association.

D'Amato, R. C., Sheridan, S. M., & Phelps, L. (Eds.). (2003). Psychology in the Schools, School Psychology Review, School Psychology Quarterly, and Journal of Educational and Psychological Consultation editors collaborate to chart school psychology's past, present, and "futures." *School Psychology Quarterly* [Special issue], *18*(4).

D'Amato, R. C., Sheridan, S. M., & Phelps, L. (Eds.). (2004). Psychology in the Schools, School Psychology Review, School Psychology Quarterly, and Journal of Educational and Psychological Consultation editors collaborate to chart school psychology's past, present, and "futures." *School Psychology Review* [Special issue], *33*(1).

Dappen, L. D., & Gutkin, T. B. (1986). Domain Theory: Examining the validity of an organizational theory with public school personnel. *Professional School Psychology, 1,* 257–265.

Davis, G. A., & Thomas, M. A. (1989). *Effective schools and effective teachers.* Boston: Allyn & Bacon.

DeForest, P. A., & Hughes, J. N. (1992). Effect of teacher involvement and teacher self-efficacy on ratings of consultant effectiveness and intervention acceptability. *Journal of Educational and Psychological Consultation, 3,* 301–316.

Deno, S. (1975). Brad and Mrs. E.: A consulting problem in which student behavior change is the focus. In C. A. Parker (Ed.), *Psychological consultation: Helping teachers meet special needs* (pp. 11–16). Reston, VA: Council for Exceptional Children.

Dietz, S., & Montague, M. (2006). Attention deficit hyperactivity disorder comorbid with emotional and behavioral disorders and learning disabilities in adolescents. *Exceptionality, 14,* 19–33.

Dinkmeyer, Jr., D., & Carlson, J. (2007). *Consultation: Creating school-based interventions* (3rd ed.). New York: Routledge.

Dougherty, A. M. (2005). *Psychological consultation and collaboration in school and community settings* (4th ed.). Belmont, CA: Brooks/Cole.

Duch, H. (2005). Consultation in international development: The case of early childhood in Maldives. *School Psychology International, 26,* 178–191.

Duncan, C. F. (1995). Cross-cultural school consultation. In C. C. Lee (Ed.), *Counseling for diversity: A guide for school counselors and related professionals* (pp. 129–141). Needham Heights, MA: Allyn & Bacon.

Dunst, C. J., & Trivette, C. M. (1988). Helping, helpfulness, and harm. In J. C. Witt, S. N. Elliott, & F. M. Gresham (Eds.), *The handbook of behavior therapy in education* (pp. 343–376). New York: Plenum.

D'Zurilla, T. J., & Goldfried, M. R. (1971). Problem solving and behavior modification. *Journal of Abnormal Psychology, 78,* 107–126.

Ehrhardt, K. E., Barnett, D. W., Lentz, F. E., Jr., Stollar, S. A., & Reifin, L. H. (1996). Innovative methodology in ecological consultation: Use of scripts to promote treatment acceptability and integrity. *School Psychology Quarterly, 11,* 149–168.

Elliott, S. N. (1988). Acceptability of behavioral treatments: Review of variables that influence treatment selection. *Professional Psychology: Research and Practice, 19,* 68–80.

Elliott, S. N., & Witt, J. C. (Eds.). (1986). *The delivery of psychological services in schools: Concepts, processes, and issues.* Hillsdale, NJ: Erlbaum.

Ellis, A. (1963). *Rational-emotive psychotherapy.* New York: Institute for Rational-Emotive Therapy.

Epps, S., & Tindal, G. (1987). The effectiveness of differential programming in serving students with mild handicaps: Placement options and instructional programming. In M. C. Wang, M. Reynolds, & H. J. Walberg (Eds.), *Handbook of special education: Research & practice* (Vol. 1, pp. 213–248). New York: Pergamon.

Erchul, W. P. (1987). A relational communication analysis of control in school consultation. *Professional School Psychology, 2,* 113–124.

Erchul, W. P. (1992). On dominance, cooperation, teamwork, and collaboration in school-based consultation. *Journal of Educational and Psychological Consultation, 3,* 363–366.

Erchul, W. P. (Ed.). (1993a). *Consultation in community, school, and organizational practice: Gerald Caplan's contributions to professional psychology*. Washington, DC: Taylor & Francis.

Erchul, W. P. (1993b). Reflections on mental health consultation: An interview with Gerald Caplan. In W. P. Erchul (Ed.), *Consultation in community, school, and organizational practice: Gerald Caplan's contributions to professional psychology* (pp. 57–72). Washington, DC: Taylor & Francis.

Erchul, W. P. (1999). Two steps forward, one step back: Collaboration in school-based consultation. *Journal of School Psychology, 37*, 191–203.

Erchul, W. P. (Ed.). (2003). Communication and interpersonal processes in consultation. *Journal of Educational and Psychological Consultation* [Special issue], *14*(2).

Erchul, W. P., & Chewning, T. G. (1990). Behavioral consultation from a request-centered relational communication perspective. *School Psychology Quarterly, 5*, 1–20.

Erchul, W. P., Covington, C. G., Hughes, J. N., & Meyers, J. (1995). Further explorations of request-centered relational communication within school consultation. *School Psychology Review, 24*, 621–632.

Erchul, W. P., Hughes, J. N., Meyers, J., Hickman, J. A., & Braden, J. P. (1992). Dyadic agreement concerning the consultation process and its relationship to outcome. *Journal of Educational and Psychological Consultation, 3*, 119–132.

Erchul, W. P., & Martens, B. K. (1997). *School consultation: Conceptual and empirical bases of practice*. New York: Plenum.

Erchul, W. P., & Martens, B. K. (2002). *School consultation: Conceptual and empirical bases of practice* (2nd ed.). New York: Plenum.

Erchul, W. P. & Sheridan, S. M. (2007). *Handbook of research in school consultation: Empirical foundations for the field* (pp. 89–114). New York: Lawrence Erlbaum Associates.

Erchul, W. P., Sheridan, S. M., Ryan, D. A., Grisson, P. F., Killough, C. E., & Mettler, D. W. (1999). Patterns of relational communication in conjoint behavioral consultation. *School Psychology Quarterly, 14*, 121–147.

Fisher, G. L., Jenkins, S. J., & Crumbley, J. D. (1986). A replication of a survey of school psychologists: Congruence between training, practice, preferred role, and competence. *Psychology in the Schools, 23*, 271–279.

Fischer, L., & Sorenson, G. P. (1996). *School law for counselors, psychologists, and social workers* (3rd ed.). White Plains, NY: Longman.

Flugum, K. R., & Reschly, D. J. (1994). Prereferral interventions: Quality indices and outcomes. *Journal of School Psychology, 32*, 1–14.

Forman, S. G. (1995). Organizational factors and consultation outcome. *Journal of Educational and Psychological Consultation, 6*, 191–195.

Franklin, M. R., Jr., & Duley, S. M. (1991). Psychological services in Amphitheater School District. *School Psychology Quarterly, 6*, 66–80.

Franklin, M. R., Jr., & Duley, S. M. (2002). Best practices in planning school psychology service delivery programs: An update. In A. Thomas & J. Grimes (Eds.), *Best practices in school psychology-IV* (pp. 145–158). Washington, DC: National Association of School Psychologists.

Freeland, J. T. (2003). Analyzing the effects of Direct Behavioral Consultation on teachers: Generalization of skills across settings. *Dissertation Abstracts International Section A: Humanities and Social Sciences, 63* (10-A), 3471.

Fuchs, D., Fuchs, L. S., & Bahr, M. W. (1990). Mainstream assistance teams: A scientific basis for the art of consultation. *Exceptional Children, 57*, 128–139.

Fuchs, D., Fuchs, L. S., Dulan, J., Roberts, H., & Fernstrom, P. (1992). Where is the research on consultation effectiveness? *Journal of Educational and Psychological Consultation, 3*, 151–174.

Fuchs, L. S., & Fuchs, D. (1986). Effects of systematic formative evaluation: A meta-analysis. *Exceptional Children, 53*, 199–208.

Fullan, M., Miles, M. B., & Taylor, G. (1980). Organization development in schools: The state of the art. *Review of Educational Research, 50*, 121–183.

Gibbs, S. (2007). Teacher perceptions of efficacy: Beliefs that may support inclusion or segregation. *Educational and Child Psychology, 24*, 47–53.

Gibson, S., & Dembo, M. H. (1984). Teacher efficacy: A construct validation. *Journal of Educational Psychology, 76*, 569–582.

Gillies, E. (2000). Developing consultation partnerships. *Educational Psychology in Practice, 16*, 31–37.

Givens-Ogle, L., Christ, B. A., & Idol, L. (1991). Collaborative consultation: The San Juan Unified School District Project. *Journal of Educational and Psychological Consultation, 2*, 267–284.

Goldstein, A. P., Harootunian, B., & Conoley, J. C. (1994). *Student aggression: Prevention, management, and replacement training*. New York: Guilford.

Gonzalez, J. E., Nelson, J. R., & Gutkin, T. B. (2004). Teacher resistance to school-based consultation with school psychologists: A survey of teacher perceptions. *Journal of Emotional and Behavioral Disorders, 12*, 30–37.

Good, R. H., III, Vollmer, M., Creek, R. J., Katz, L., & Chowdhri, S. (1993). Treatment utility of the Kaufman Assessment Battery for Children: Effects of matching instruction and student processing strength. *School Psychology Review, 22*, 8–26.

Goodwin, D. L., & Coates, T. J. (1976). *Helping students help themselves*. Englewood Cliffs, NJ: Prentice Hall.

Gorges, T., Elliott, S. N., & Kettler, R. J. (2004). Resistance: Experienced and novice consultants' interpretations and strategies for addressing it in behavioral consultation interviews. *Journal of School Psychology, 19,* 1–32.

Gorrell, J., & Capron, E. (1990). Cognitive modeling and self-efficacy: Effects on preservice teachers' learning of teaching strategies. *Journal of Teacher Education, 41,* 15–22.

Graden, J. L., Casey, A., & Bonstrom, O. (1985). Implementing a prereferral intervention system: Part II. The data. *Exceptional Children, 51,* 487–496.

Graden, J. L., Casey, A., & Christenson, S. L. (1985). Implementing a prereferral intervention system: Part I. The model. *Exceptional Children, 51,* 377–384.

Graden, J. L., Zins, J. E., & Curtis, M. J. (1988). *Alternative educational delivery systems: Enhancing instructional options for all students.* Washington, DC: National Association of School Psychologists.

Graden, J. L., Zins, J. E., Curtis, M. J., & Cobb, C. T. (1988). The need for alternatives in educational services. In J. L. Graden, J. E. Zins, & M. J. Curtis (Eds.), *Alternative educational delivery systems: Enhancing instructional options for all students* (pp. 3–15). Washington, DC: National Association of School Psychologists.

Gravois, T. A., Knotek, S., & Babinski, L. M. (2002). Educating practitioners as consultants: Development and implementation of the Instructional Consultation Team Consortium. *Journal of Educational and Psychological Consultation, 13,* 113–132.

Gravois, T. A., & Rosenfield, S. A. (2006). Impact of instructional consultation teams on the disproportionate referral and placement of minority students in special education. *Remedial and Special Education, 27,* 42–52.

Greenwood, C. R., Carta, J. J., & Atwater, J. (1991). Ecobehavioral analysis in the classroom: Review and implications. *Journal of Behavioral Education, 1,* 59–77.

Gresham, F. M. (1989). Assessment of treatment integrity in school consultation and prereferral intervention. *School Psychology Review, 18,* 37–50.

Gresham, F. M., & Gansle, K. A. (1992). Misguided assumptions of DSM-III-R: Implications for school psychological practice. *School Psychology Quarterly, 7,* 79–95.

Gresham, F. M., & Kendell, G. K. (1987). School consultation research: Methodological critique and future research directions. *School Psychology Review, 16,* 306–316.

Gresham, F. M., MacMillan, D. L., & Bocian, K. M. (1997). Teachers as "tests": Differential validity of teacher judgments in identifying students at risk for learning difficulties. *School Psychology Review, 26,* 47–60.

Gresham, F. M., Noell, G. H. (1993). Methods for documenting the effectiveness of consultation: A critical analysis. In J. E. Zins, T. R. Kratochwill, & S. N. Elliott (Eds.), *The handbook of consultation services for children* (pp. 249–273). San Francisco: Jossey-Bass.

Gresham, F. M., & Witt, J. C. (1997). Utility of intelligence tests for treatment planning, classification, and placement decisions: Recent empirical findings and future directions. *School Psychology Quarterly, 12,* 249–267.

Grieger, R. M. (1977). Teacher attitudes as a variable in behavior modification consultation. In J. Meyers, R. Martin, & I. Hyman (Eds.), *School consultation: Readings about preventive techniques for pupil personnel workers* (pp. 137–148). Springfield, IL: Thomas.

Grimes, J., & Tilly, W. D., III. (1996). Policy and process: Means to lasting educational change. *School Psychology Review, 25,* 465–476.

Guli, L. A. (2005). Evidence-based parent consultation with school-related outcomes. *School Psychology Quarterly, 20,* 455–472.

Gutkin, T. B. (1980). Teacher perceptions of consultation services provided by school psychologists. *Professional Psychology, 11,* 637–642.

Gutkin, T. B. (1981). Relative frequency of consultee lack of knowledge, skill, confidence, and objectivity in school settings. *Journal of School Psychology, 19,* 57–61.

Gutkin, T. B. (1986). Consultees' perceptions of variables relating to the outcomes of school-based consultation interactions. *School Psychology Review, 15,* 375–382.

Gutkin, T. B. (1993a). Cognitive modeling: A means for achieving prevention in school-based consultation. *Journal of Educational and Psychological Consultation, 4,* 179–183.

Gutkin, T. B. (1993b). Conducting consultation research. In J. E. Zins, T. R. Kratochwill, & S. N. Elliott (Eds.), *Handbook of consultation for children: Applications in educational and clinical settings* (pp. 227–248). San Francisco: Jossey-Bass.

Gutkin, T. B. (1993c). Moving from behavioral to ecobehavioral consultation: What's in a name. *Journal of Educational and Psychological Consultation, 4,* 95–99.

Gutkin, T. B. (1996a). Core elements of consultation service delivery for special service personnel. *Remedial and Special Education, 17,* 333–340.

Gutkin, T. B. (1996b). Patterns of consultant and consultee verbalizations: Examining communication leadership during initial consultation interviews. *Journal of School Psychology, 34,* 199–219.

Gutkin, T. B. (Ed.). (1997). Social psychology and consultation. *Journal of School Psychology* [Special section]. *35*(2).

Gutkin, T. B. (1999). Collaborative versus directive/prescriptive/expert school-based consultation: Reviewing and resolving a false dichotomy. *Journal of School Psychology, 37*, 161–190.

Gutkin, T. B., & Ajchenbaum, M. (1984). Teachers' perceptions of control and preferences for consultative services. *Professional Psychology: Research and Practice, 15*, 565–570.

Gutkin, T. B., & Conoley, J. C. (1990). Reconceptualizing school psychology from a service delivery perspective: Implications for practice, training, and research. *Journal of School Psychology, 28*, 203–223.

Gutkin, T. B., & Curtis, M. J. (1981). School-based consultation: The indirect service delivery concept. In M. J. Curtis & J. E. Zins (Eds.), *The theory and practice of school consultation* (pp. 219–226). Springfield, IL: Thomas.

Gutkin, T. B., & Curtis, M. J. (1982). School-based consultation: Theory and techniques. In C. R. Reynolds & T. B. Gutkin (Eds.), *The handbook of school psychology* (pp. 796–828). New York: Wiley.

Gutkin, T.B., & Curtis, M. J. (1990). School-based consultation: Theory, techniques, and research. In T. B. Gutkin & C. R. Reynolds (Eds.), *The handbook of school psychology* (2nd ed., pp. 577–611). New York: Wiley.

Gutkin, T. B., & Curtis, M. J. (1999). School-based consultation theory and practice: The art and science of indirect service delivery. In C.R. Reynolds & T.B. Gutkin (Eds.), *The handbook of school psychology* (3rd ed., pp. 598–637). New York: Wiley.

Gutkin, T. B., Henning-Stout, M., & Piersel, W. C. (1988). Impact of a district-wide behavioral consultation prereferral intervention service on patterns of school psychological service delivery. *Professional School Psychology, 3*, 301–308.

Gutkin, T. B., & Hickman, J. A. (1988). Teachers' perceptions of control over presenting problems and resulting preferences for consultation versus referral services. *Journal of school Psychology, 26*, 395–398.

Gutkin, T. B., & Hickman, J. A. (1990). Relationship of consultant, consultee, and organizational characteristics to consultee resistance to school-based consultation: An empirical analysis. *Journal of Educational and Psychological Consultation, 1*, 111–122.

Gutkin, T. B., & Nemeth, C. (1997). Selected factors impacting decision making in prereferral intervention and other school-based teams: Exploring the intersection between school and social psychology. *Journal of School Psychology, 35*, 195–216.

Gutkin, T. B., Singer, J. H., & Brown, R. (1980). Teacher reactions to school-based consultation services: A multivariate analysis. *Journal of School Psychology, 18*, 126–134.

Gutkin, T. B., & Tieger, A. G. (1979). Funding patterns for exceptional children: Current approaches and suggested alternatives. *Professional Psychology, 10*, 670–680.

Hagen, K. M., Gutkin, T. B., Wilson, C. P., & Oats, R. B. (1998). Using vicarious experience and verbal persuasion to enhance self-efficacy in preservice teachers: "Priming the pump" for consultation. *School Psychology Quarterly 13*(2), 169–178.

Hagermoser Sanetti, L. M., Luiselli, J. K., & Handler, M. W. (2007). Effects of verbal and graphic performance feedback on behavior support plan implementation in a public elementary school. *Behavior Modification, 31*, 454–465.

Harris, A. M., & Cancelli, A. A. (1991). Teachers as volunteer consultees: Enthusiastic, willing, or resistant participants? *Journal of Educational and Psychological Consultation, 2*, 217–238.

Hatzichristou, C. (2003). Psychological consultation in the school context. *Psychology: The Journal of the Hellenic Psychological Society, 10*, 343–361.

Henning-Stout, M., & Conoley, J. C. (1988). Influencing program change at the district level. In J. L. Graden, J. E. Zins, & M. J. Curtis (Eds.), *Alternative educational delivery, Systems: Enhancing instructional options for all students* (pp. 411–490). Washington, DC: National Association of School Psychologists.

Henning-Stout, M., Lucas, D. A. & McCary, V. L. (1993). Alternative instruction in the regular classroom: A case illustration and evaluation. *School Psychology Review, 22*, 81–97.

Heppner, P. P. (1978). A review of the problem-solving literature and its relationship to the counseling process. *Journal of Counseling Psychology, 25*, 366–375.

Hertz-Lazarowitz, R., Od-Cohen, M. (1992). The school psychologist as a facilitator of a community-wide project to enhance positive learning climate in elementary schools. *Psychology in the Schools, 29*, 348–358.

Hightower, A. D., Johnson, D., & Haffey, W. G. (1995). Best practices in adopting a prevention program. In A. Thomas & J. Grimes (Eds.), *Best practices in school psychology-III* (pp. 311–323). Washington, DC: National Association of School Psychologists.

Hollowood, T. M., Salisbury, C. L., Rainforth, B., & Palombaro, M. M. (1994). Use of instructional time in classrooms serving students with and without severe disabilities. *Exceptional Children, 61*, 242–253.

House, J. E., & McInerney, W. F. (1996). The school assistance center: An alternative model for the delivery of school psychological services. *School Psychology International, 17,* 115–124.

Hughes, J. N. (1986). Ethical issues in school consultation. *School Psychology Review, 15,* 489–499.

Hughes, J. N. (1992). Social psychology foundations of consultation. In F. J. Medway & T. P. Cafferty (Eds.), *School psychology: A social psychological perspective* (pp. 269–303). Hillsdale, NJ: Erlbaum.

Hughes, J. N. (1994). Back to basics: Does consultation work? *Journal of Educational and Psychological Consultation, 5,* 77–84.

Hughes, J. N., Barker, D., Kemenoff, S., & Hart, M. (1993). Problem ownership, causal attributions, and self-efficacy as predictors of teachers' referral decisions. *Journal of Educational and Psychological Consultation, 4,* 369–384.

Hughes, J. N., & Falk, R. S. (1981). Resistance, reactance, and consultation. *Journal of School Psychology, 19,* 134–142.

Hughes, J. N., Grossman, P., & Barker, D. (1990). Teachers' expectancies, participation in consultation, and perceptions of consultant helpfulness. *School Psychology Quarterly, 5,* 167–179.

Hundert, J. P. (2007). Training classroom and resource preschool teachers to develop inclusive class interventions for children with disabilities: Generalization to new intervention targets. *Journal of Positive Behavior Interventions, 9,* 159–173.

Hyman, I. A. (1997). *School discipline and school violence: The teacher variance approach.* Boston: Allyn & Bacon.

Idol, L., Nevin, A., & Paolucci-Whitcomb, P. (1994). *Collaborative consultation* (2nd ed.). Austin, TX: Pro-Ed.

Ikeda, M. J., Tilly, W. D., III, Stumme, J., Volmer, L., & Allison, R. (1996). Agency-wide implementation of problem solving consultation: Foundations, current implementation, and future directions. *School Psychology Quarterly, 11,* 228–243.

Ingraham, C. L. (2000). Consultation through a multicultural lens: Multicultural and cross-cultural consultation in schools. *School Psychology Review, 29,* 320–343.

Ingraham, C. L. (2003). Multicultural consultee-centered consultation: When novice consultants explore cultural hypotheses with experienced teacher consultees. *Journal of Educational and Psychological Consultation, 14,* 329–362.

Ingraham, C. L., & Meyers, J. (2000). Introduction to multicultural and cross-cultural consultation in schools: Cultural diversity issues in school consultation. *School Psychology Review, 29*(3), 315–319.

Ivey, A. E. (1994). *Intentional interviewing and counseling: Facilitating client development in a multicultural society* (3rd ed.). Pacific Grove, CA: Brooks/Cole.

Jackson, P. W. (1968). *Life in classrooms.* New York: Holt, Rinehart & Winston.

Jacob-Timm, S., & Hartshorne, T. (1994). *Ethics and law for school psychologists* (2nd ed.). Brandon, VT: Clinical Psychology Publishing.

Janney, R. E., Snell, M. E., Beers, M. K., & Raynes, M. (1995). Integrating students with moderate and severe disabilities into general education classes. *Exceptional Children, 61,* 425–439.

Jason, L. A., & Ferone, L. (1978). Behavioral versus process consultation interventions in school settings. *American Journal of Community Psychology, 6,* 531–543.

Jayanthi, M., & Friend, M. (1992). Interpersonal problem solving: A selective literature review to guide practice. *Journal of Educational and Psychological Consultation, 3,* 39–53.

Jefferson, G. L. (2001). An evaluation of the generalized effects of training teachers of young children to use functional assessment in combination with behavioral consultation to remediate problematic classroom behaviors. *Dissertation Abstracts International: Section B: The Sciences and Engineering, 62*(6-B), 2948.

Jeltova, I., & Fish, M. C. (2005). Creating school environments responsive to gay, lesbian, bisexual, and transgender families: Traditional and systemic approaches for consultation. *Journal of Educational and Psychological Consultation, 16,* 17–33.

Jimerson, S. R., Burns, M. K., & VanDerHeyden, A.M. (2007). *Handbook of response to intervention: The science and practice of assessment and intervention.* New York: Springer.

Johnson, K. M., Gutkin, T. B., & Plake, B. S. (1992). The use of modeling to enhance children's interrogative strategies. *Journal of School Psychology, 29,* 81–88.

Jones, K. M., Wickstrom, K. F., & Friman, P. C. (1997). The effects of observational feedback on treatment integrity in school-based behavioral consultation. *School Psychology Quarterly, 12,* 316–326.

Kampwirth, T. J. (2006). *Collaborative consultation in the schools: Effective practices for students with learning and behavioral problems* (3rd ed). Columbus, OH: Pearson.

Kavale, K. A. (2005). Effective intervention for students with specific learning disabilities: The nature of special education. *Learning disabilities: A Multidisciplinary Journal, 13*(4), 127–138.

Kavale, K. A., & Forness, S. R. (1999). History, rhetoric, and reality. *Remedial and Special Education, 21*(5), 279–296.

Knoff, H. M. (1995). Best practices in facilitating school-based organizational change and strategic planning. In A. Thomas & J. Grimes (Eds.), *Best practices in school psychology III* (pp. 239–252).

Washington, DC: National Association of School Psychologists.

Knoff, H. M., & Curtis, M. J. (Eds.). (1996). Organizational change and school reform. *School Psychology Review* [Special series], *25*(4).

Knoff, H. M., Hines, C. V., & Kromrey, J. D. (1995). Finalizing the consultant effectiveness scale: An analysis and validation of the characteristics of effective consultants. *School Psychology Review, 24,* 480–496.

Kouzes, J., & Mico, P. (1979). Domain Theory: An introduction to organizational behavior in human services organizations. *Journal of Applied Behavioral Science, 15,* 449–469.

Kovaleski, J. F. (2002). Best practices in operating pre-referral intervention teams. In A. Thomas & J. Grimes (Eds.), *Best practices in school psychology IV* (pp. 645–655). Washington, DC: National Association of School Psychologists.

Kratochwill, T. R., & Bergan, J. R. (1990). *Behavioral consultation in applied settings: an individual guide.* New York: Plenum.

Kratochwill, T. R., Bergan, J. R., Sheridan, S. M., & Elliott, S. N. (1998). Assumptions of behavioral consultation: After all is said and done more has been done than said. *School Psychology Quarterly, 13*(1), 63–80.

Kratochwill, T. R., Elliott, S. N., & Busse, R. T. (1995). Behavior consultation: A five-year evaluation of consultant and client outcomes. *School Psychology Quarterly, 10,* 87–117.

Kratochwill, T. R., Elliott, S. N., & Callan-Stoiber, K. (2002). Best practices in school-based problem-solving consultation. In A. Thomas & J. Grimes (Eds.), *Best practices in school psychology IV* (pp. 583–608). Washington, DC: National Association of School Psychologists.

Kratochwill, T. R., Elliott, S. N., & Carrington Rotto, P. (1995). Best practices in school-based behavioral consultation. In A. Thomas & J. Grimes (Eds.), *Best practices in school psychology III* (pp. 519–537). Washington, DC: National Association of School Psychologists.

Kratochwill, T. R., VanSomeren, K. R., & Sheridan, S. M. (1989). Training behavioral consultants: A competency-based model to teach interview skills. *Professional School Psychology, 4,* 41–58.

Kurpius, D. J., & Rozecki, T. G. (1993). Strategies for improving interpersonal communication. In J. E. Zins, T. R. Kratochwill, & S. N. Elliott (Eds.), *Handbook of consultation services for children: Applications in educational and clinical settings* (pp. 137–158). San Francisco: Jossey-Bass.

Kutsick, K. A., Gutkin, T. B., & Witt, J. C. (1991). The impact of treatment development process, intervention type, and problem severity on treatment acceptability as judged by classroom teachers. *Psychology in the Schools, 28,* 325–331.

Lambert, M. J., & Bergin, A. E. (1994). The effectiveness of psychotherapy. In A. E. Bergin & S. L. Garfield (Eds.), *Handbook of psychotherapy and behavior change* (4th ed., pp. 143–189). New York: Wiley.

Lambert, N. M. (1976). Children's problems and classroom interventions from the perspective of classroom teachers. *Professional Psychology, 7,* 507–517.

Lambert, N. M., Hylander, I., & Sandoval, J. H. (Eds.). (2004). *Consultee-centered consultation: Improving the quality of professional services in schools and community organizations.* Mahwah, New Jersey: Lawrence Erlbaum Associates, Publishers.

Larney, R. (2003). School-based consultation in the United Kingdom: Principles, practice and effectiveness. *School Psychology International, 24,* 5–19.

Lentz, F. E., Allen, S. J., & Ehrhardt, K. E. (1996). The conceptual elements of strong interventions in school settings. *School Psychology Quarterly, 11,* 118–136.

Lentz, F. E., Jr., & Daly, E. J., III. (1996). Is the behavior of academic change agents controlled metaphysically? An analysis of the behavior of those who change behavior. *School Psychology Quarterly, 11,* 337–352.

Lepage, K., Kratochwill, T. R., & Elliott, S. N. (2004). Competency-based behavior consultation training: An evaluation of consultant outcomes, treatment effects, and consumer satisfaction. *School Psychology Quarterly, 19,* 1–28.

Levinson, E. M. (1990). Actual/desired role functioning, perceived control over role functioning, and job satisfaction among school psychologists. *Psychology in the Schools, 27,* 64–74.

Lewin, K. (1951). *Field theory in social science: Selected theoretical papers.* New York: Harper.

Lusky, M. B., & Hayes, R. L. (2001). Collaborative consultation and program evaluation. *Journal of Counseling and Development, 79,* 26–38.

Maher, C. A., & Illback, R. J. (1985). Implementing school psychological service programs: Description and application of the DURABLE approach. *Journal of School Psychology, 23,* 81–89.

Maitland, R. E., Fine, M. J., & Tracy, D. B. (1985). The effects of an interpersonally based problem-solving process on consultation outcomes. *Journal of School Psychology, 23,* 337–345.

Mannino, F., & Shore, M. (1975). The effects of consultation: A review of empirical studies. *American Journal of Community Psychology, 3,* 1–21.

Marks, E. S. (1995). *Entry strategies for school consultation.* New York: Guilford.

Martens, B. K., Erchul, W. P., & Witt, J. C. (1992). Quantifying verbal interactions in school-based consultation: A comparison of four coding schemes. *School Psychology Review, 21,* 109–124.

Martens, B. K., Lewandowski, L. J., & Houk, J. L. (1989). The effects of entry information on the consultation process. *School Psychology Review, 18,* 225–234.

Martens, B. K., & Witt, J. C. (1988a). On the ecological validity of behavior modification. In J. C. Witt, S. N. Elliott, & F. M. Gresham (Eds.), *Handbook of behavior therapy in education* (pp. 325–341). New York: Plenum.

Martens, B. K., & Witt, J. C. (1988b). Expanding to the scope of behavioral consultation: A systems approach to classroom behavior change. *Professional School Psychology, 3,* 271–281.

Martin, R. P., & Keller, A. (1976). Teacher awareness of classroom dyadic interactions. *Journal of School Psychology, 14,* 47–55.

Mash, E. J., & Dozois, D. J. A. (1996). Child psychopathology: A developmental-systems perspective. In E. J. Mash & R. A. Barley (Eds.), *Child Psychopathology* (pp. 3–60). New York: Guilford.

McDougall, L. M., Reschly, D. J., & Corkery, J. M. (1988). Changes in referral interviews with teachers after behavioral consultation training. *Journal of School Psychology, 26,* 225–232.

McIntyre, L. L., Gresham, F. M., & DiGennaro, F. D. (2007). Treatment integrity of school-based interventions with children in the Journal of Applied Behavior Analyses 1991–2005. *Journal of Applied Behavior Analysis, 40,* 659–672.

McLaughlin, M. W. (1976). Implementation as mutual adaptation: Change in classroom organization. *Teachers College Record, 77,* 339–351.

McLaughlin, M. W. (1990). The Rand change agent study revisited: Macro perspectives and micro realities. *Educational Researcher, 18*(9), 11–16.

Meacham, M. L., & Peckham, P. D. (1978). School psychologists at three-quarters century: Congruence between training, practice, preferred role and competence. *Journal of School Psychology, 16,* 195–206.

Medway, F. J. (1979). How effective is school consultation: A review of recent research. *Journal of School Psychology, 17,* 275–282.

Medway, F. J. (1982). School consultation research: Past trends and future directions. *Professional Psychology, 13,* 422–430.

Medway, F. J., & Updyke, J. F. (1985). Meta-analysis of consultation outcome studies. *American Journal of Community Psychology, 13,* 489–504.

Meichenbaum, D., & Turk, D. C. (1987). *Facilitating treatment adherence: A practitioner's guidebook.* New York: Plenum.

Meijer, C. J. W., & Foster, S. F. (1988). The effect of teacher self-efficacy on referral chance. *The Journal of Special Education, 22,* 378–385.

Meyers, B. (2002). The contract negotiation stage of a school-based, cross-cultural organizational consultation: A case study. *Journal of Educational and Psychological Consultation, 13,* 151–183.

Meyers, B., Valentino, C. T., Meyers, J., Boretti, M., Brent, D. (1996). Implementing prereferral intervention teams as an approach to school-based consultation in an urban school system. *Journal of Eductional and Psychological Consultation, 7,* 119–149.

Meyers, J. (1973). A consultation model for school psychological services. *Journal of School Psychology, 11,* 5–15.

Meyers, J. (1975). Consultee-centered consultation with a teacher as a technique in behavior management. *American Journal of Community Psychology, 3,* 111–121.

Meyers, J., Meyers, A. B., & Grogg, K. (2004). Prevention through consultation: A model to guide future developments in the field of school psychology. *Journal of Educational and Psychological Consultation, 15,* 257–276.

Meyers, J., Parsons, R. D., & Martin, R. (1979). *Mental health consultation in the schools.* San Francisco: Jossey-Bass.

Meyers, J., Pitt, N. W., Gaughan, E. J., & Friedman, M. P. (1978). A research model for consultation with teachers. *Journal of School Psychology, 16,* 137–145.

Miller, G. A. (1969). Psychology as a means of promoting human welfare. *American Psychologist, 24,* 1063–1075.

Moos, R. H. (1973). Conceptualizations of human environments. *American Psychologist, 28,* 652–665.

Moreno, J. M., & Torrego, J. C. (1999). Fostering PRO social behavior in the Spanish school system: A whole school approach. *Emotional and Behavioural Difficulties, 4,* 23–31.

Morris, E. K., & Midgley, B. D. (1990). Some historical and conceptual foundations of ecobehavioral analysis. In S. Schroeder (Ed.), *Ecobehavioral analysis and developmental disabilities: The twenty-first century* (pp. 1–32). New York: Springer-Verlag.

Morse, W. C. (1993). Ecological approaches. In T. R. Kratochwill & R. J. Morris (Eds.), *Handbook of psychotherapy with children and adolescents* (pp. 320–355). Boston: Longwood.

Nastasi, B. K. (2004). Meeting the challenges of the future: Integrating public health and public education for mental health promotion. *Journal of Educational and Psychological Consultation, 15,* 295–312.

Nastasi, B. K. (2006). Multicultural issues in school psychology practice: Introduction. *Journal of Applied School Psychology, 22,* 1–11.

Nastasi, B. K., & Truscott, S. D. (2000). Acceptability research in school psychology: Current trends and future directions. *School Psychology Quarterly, 15,* 117–122.

Nastasi, B. K., Varjas, K., Bernstein, R., & Jayasena, A. (2000). Conducting participatory culture-specific consultation: A global perspective on multicultural consultation. *School Psychology Review, 29*, 401–413.

Nastasi, B. K., Varjas, K., & Schensul, S. L. (2000). The Participatory Intervention Model: A framework for conceptualizing and promoting intervention acceptability. *School Psychology Quarterly, 15*, 207–232.

National Association of School Psychologists (2000). Guidelines for the provision of school psychological services. In *Professional conduct manual* (pp. 38–60). Bethesda, MD: Author.

National Association of State Boards of Education. (1992). *Winners all: A call for inclusive schools.* Alexandria, VA: Author.

National Association of State Directors of Special Education (2005). *Response to intervention: Policy considerations and implementation.* Alexandria, VA: National Association of State Directors of Special Education, Inc.

National Association of State Directors of Special Education (2007). *Response to Intervention: Research for Practice.* Alexandria, VA: National Association of State Directors of Special Education, Inc.

National Research Council (U.S.) Committee on Minority Representation in Special Education; Donovan, M. S. & Cross, C. T. (Eds.). (2002). *Minority students in special and gifted education.* Washington, DC: National Academy Press.

Naumann, W. C., Gutkin, T. B., & Sandoval, S. R. (1996). The impact of consultant race and student race on perceptions of consultant effectiveness and intervention acceptability. *Journal of Educational and Psychological Consultation, 7*, 151–160.

Nelson, J. R., Smith, D. J., Taylor, L., Dodd, J. M., & Reavis, K. (1991). Prereferral intervention: A review of the research. *Education and Treatment of Children, 14*, 243–253.

No Child Left Behind Act, U.S.C 115 STAT. 1426 (2002). Retrieved January 5, 2007 from http://ed.gov/nclb/landing.html.

Noell, G. H. (Ed.). (1996). New directions in behavioral consultation. *School Psychology Quarterly* [Special issue], *11*(3).

Noell, G. H., & Witt, J. C. (1996). A critical evaluation of five fundamental assumptions underlying behavioral consultation. *School Psychology Quarterly, 11*, 189–203.

Noell, G. H., Witt, J. C., Gilbertson, D. N., Ranier, D. D., & Freeland, J. T. (1997). Increasing teacher intervention implementation in general education settings through consultation and performance feedback. *School Psychology Quarterly, 12*, 77–88.

Noell, G. H., Witt, J. C., LaFleur, L. H., Mortenson, B. P., Ranier, D. D. & LeVelle, J. (2000). Increasing intervention implementation in general education following consultation: A comparison of two follow-up strategies. *Journal of Applied Behavior Analysis, 33*, 271–284.

Nowell, D., & Spruill, J. (1993). If it's not absolutely confidential, will information be disclosed? *Professional Psychology: Research and Practice, 24*, 367–369.

Osborn, A. F. (1963). *Applied imagination* (3rd ed.). New York: Scribner.

O'Brien, L., & Miller, A. (2005). Challenging behaviour: Analysing teacher language in a school-based consultation within the discursive action model. *Educational and Child Psychology, 22*, 62–73.

O'Hearn, T. C., & Gatz, M. (1996). The educational pyramid: A model for community intervention. *Applied & Preventive Psychology, 5*, 127–134.

Otwell, P. S., & Mullis, F. (1997). Counselor-led staff development: An efficient approach to teacher consultation. *Professional School Counseling, 1*, 25–30.

Owens, R. G. (1987). *Organizational behavior in education* (3rd ed.). Englewood Cliffs, NJ: Prentice Hall.

Parsons, R. D., & Kahn, W. J. (2005). *The school counselor as consultant: An integrated model for school-based consultation.* Belmont, CA: Thomson.

Peck, C. A., Killen, C. C., & Baumgart, D. (1989). Increasing implementation of special education instruction in mainstream preschools: Direct and generalized effects of nondirective consultation. *Journal of Applied Behavior Analysis, 22*, 197–210.

Pérez-Gonzalez, F., García-Ros, R., & Gómez-Artiga, A. (2004). A survey of teacher perceptions of the school psychologist's skills in the consultation process. *School Psychology International, 25*, 30–41.

Petty, R. E., Heesacker, M., & Hughes, J. N. (1997). The elaboration likelihood model: Implications for the practice of school psychology. *Journal of School Psychology, 35*, 107–136.

Pianta, R. C. (1999). *Enhancing relationships between children and teachers.* Washington, DC: American Psychological Association, 1999.

Piersel, W. C., & Gutkin, T. B. (1983). Resistance to school-based consultation: A behavioral analysis of the problem. *Psychology in the Schools, 20*, 311–320.

Plas, J. M. (1986). *Systems psychology in the schools.* New York: Pergamon.

Podell, D. M., & Soodak, L. C. (1993). Teacher efficacy and bias in special education referrals. *Journal of Educational Research, 86*, 247–253.

Ponti, C. R., & Curtis, M. J. (1984, August). *Effects of consultation on teachers' attributions for children's school problems.* Paper presented at the Annual Meeting of the American Psychological Association, Toronto.

Ponti, C. R., Zins, J. E., & Graden, J. L. (1988). Implementing a consultation-based service delivery system to decrease referrals for special education: A case study of organizational considerations. *School Psychology Review, 17,* 89–100.

Practice parameter for psychiatric consultation to schools. (2005). *Journal of the American Academy of Child and Adolescent Psychiatry, 44,* 1068–1084.

President's Commission on Excellence in Special Education. (2002). *A new era: Revitalizing special education for children and their families.* Washington, DC: U. S. Department of Education.

Pryzwansky, W. B. (1986). Indirect service delivery: Considerations for future research in consultation. *School Psychology Review, 15,* 479–488.

Pyle, R. R. (1977). Mental health consultation: Helping teachers help themselves. *Professional Psychology, 8,* 192–198.

Ramirez, S. Z., Lepage, K. M., & Kratochwill, T. R. (1998). Multicultural issues in school-based consultation: Conceptual and research considerations. *Journal of School Psychology, 36,* 479–509.

Randolph, D. L., & Mitchell, M. M. (1995). A survey of consultation articles in key counseling journals, 1967–1991. *Journal of Educational and Psychological Consultation, 6,* 83–94.

Rappaport, N. (2001). Psychiatric consultation to school-based health centers: Lessons learned in an emerging field. *Journal of the American Academy of Child and Adolescent Psychiatry, 40,* 1473–1475.

Ray, K. P., Skinner, C. H., & Watson, T. S. (1999). Transferring stimulus control via momentum to increase compliance in a student with autism: A demonstration of collaborative consultation. *School Psychology Review, 28,* 622–628.

Reimers, T. M., Wacker, D. P., & Koeppl, G. (1987). Acceptability of behavioral interventions: A review of the literature. *School Psychology Review, 16,* 212–227.

Reinking, R. H., Livesay, G., & Kohl, M. (1978). The effects of consultation style on consultee productivity. *American Journal of Community Psychology, 6,* 283–290.

Reschly, D. J. (1976). School psychology consultation: "Frenzied, faddish, or fundamental?" *Journal of School Psychology, 14,* 105–113.

Reschly, D. J. (2008). School psychology paradigm shift and beyond. In A. Thomas & J. Grimes (Eds.), *Best Practices in School Psychology V* (pp. 3–16). Bethesda, MD: National Association of School Psychologists.

Reschly, D. J., & Ysseldyke, J. E. (2002). Paradigm shift: The past is not the future. In A. Thomas & J. Grimes (Eds.), *Best practices in school psychology IV* (pp. 3–20). Bethesda, MD: National Association of School Psychologists.

Resetar, J. L., Noell, G. H., & Pellegrin, A. L. (2006). Teaching parents to use research-supported systematic strategies to tutor their children

in reading. *School Psychology Quarterly, 21,* 241–261.

Revels, O. H., & Gutkin, T. B. (1983). Effects of symbolic modeling procedures and model status on brainstorming behavior. *Journal of School Psychology, 21,* 311–318.

Reynolds, C. R., Gutkin, T. B., Elliott, S. N., & Witt, W. C. (1984). *School psychology: Essentials of theory and practice.* New York: Wiley.

Riley-Tillman, T. C., & Chafouleas, S. M. (2003). Using interventions that exist in the natural environment to increase treatment integrity and social influence in consultation. *Journal of Educational and Psychological Consultation, 14,* 139–156.

Riley-Tillman, T. C., & Eckert, T. L. (2001). Generalization programming and school-based consultation: An examination of consultees' generalization of consultation-related skills. *Journal of Educational and Psychological Consultation, 12,* 217–241.

Robbins, J. R., & Gutkin, T. B. (1994). Consultee and client remedial and preventive outcomes following consultation: Some mixed empirical results and directions for future research. *Journal of Educational and Psychological Consultation, 5,* 149–167.

Roberts, A. H., & Rust, J. O. (1994). Role and function of school psychologists, 1992–93: a comparative study. *Psychology in the Schools, 31,* 113–119.

Robinson, V. M. J., Cameron, M. M., & Raethel, A. M. (1985). Negotiation of a consultative role for school psychologists: A case study. *Journal of School Psychology, 23,* 43–49.

Rogers, M. R. (1998). The influence of race and consultant verbal behavior on perceptions of consultant competence and multicultural sensitivity. *School Psychology Quarterly, 13,* 265–280.

Rogers-Warren, A., & Warren, S. F. (Eds.). (1977). *Ecological perspectives in behavior analysis.* Baltimore, MD: University Park Press.

Romualdi, V., & Sandoval, J. (1995). Comprehensive school-linked services. Implications for school psychologists. *Psychology in the Schools, 32,* 306–317.

Rosenfield, S. A. (1987). *Instructional consultation.* Hillsdale, NJ: Erlbaum.

Rosenfield, S. A. (1991). The relationship variable in behavioral consultation. *Journal of Behavioral Education, 1,* 329–336.

Rosenfield, S. A. (1992). Developing school-based consultation teams: A design for organizational change. *School Psychology Quarterly, 7,* 27–46.

Rosenfield, S. A. (2002). Best practices in instructional consultation. In A. Thomas & J. Grimes (Eds.), *Best practices in school psychology-IV* (pp. 609–623). Bethesda, MD: National Association of School Psychologists.

Rosenfield, S., & Gravois, T. (1996). *Instructional consultation teams*. New York: Guilford Press.

Sachs, J. (1988). Teacher preparation, teacher self-efficacy and the regular education initiative. *Education and Training in Mental Retardation, 23*, 327–332.

Salisbury, C. L., Evans, I. M., & Palombaro, M. M. (1997). Collaborative problem-solving to promote the inclusion of young children with significant disabilities in primary grades. *Exceptional Children, 63*, 195–209.

Sarason, S. B. (1982). *The culture of the school and the problem of change* (2nd ed.). Boston: Allyn & Bacon.

Sarason, S. B., Levine, M., Goldenberg, I. I., Cherlin, D. L., & Bennett, E. (1966). *Psychology in community settings*. New York: Wiley.

Saxe, L., Cross, T., & Silverman, N. (1988). Children's mental health: The gap between what we know and what we do. *American Psychologist, 43*, 800–807.

Schein, E. H. (1969). *Process consultation: Its role in organization development*. Reading, MA: Addison-Wesley.

Schmuck, R. (1990). Organization development in schools: Contemporary concepts and practices. In T. B. Gutkin & C. R. Reynolds (Eds.), *The handbook of school psychology* (2nd ed., pp. 899–919). New York: Wiley.

Schmuck, R. A., Runkel, P. J. Arends, J. H., & Arends, R. I. (1977). *The second handbook of organization development in schools*. Palo Alto, CA: Mayfield.

Schrag, J. A. (1996). Systems change leading to better integration of services for students with special needs. *School Psychology Review, 25*, 489–495.

Schulte, A. C., & Osborne, S. S. (2003). When assumptive worlds collide: A review of definitions of collaboration in consultation. *Journal of Educational and Psychological Consultation, 14*, 109–138.

Scruggs, T. E., & Mastropieri, M. A. (1996). Teacher perceptions of mainstreaming/inclusion, 1958–1995: A research synthesis. *Exceptional Children, 63*, 59–74.

Sears, R., Rudisill, J., & Mason-Sears, C. (2006). *Consultation skills for mental health professionals*. Hoboken, NJ: Wiley.

Secord, W. A. (Ed.). (1990). *Best practices in school speech-language pathology—Collaborative programs in the schools: Concepts, models, and procedures*. San Antonio, TX: Psychological Corp.

Shapiro, E. S. (1987). *Behavioral assessment in school psychology*. Hillsdale, NJ: Erlbaum.

Shapiro, E. S., Miller, D. N., & Sawka, K. (1999). Facilitating the inclusion of students with EBD into general education classrooms. *Journal of Emotional and Behavioral Disorders, 7*, 83–93.

Sheridan, S. M. (1992). What do we mean when we say "collaboration"? *Journal of Educational and Psychological Consultation, 3*, 89–92.

Sheridan, S. M. (1997). Conceptual and empirical bases of conjoint behavioral consultation. *School Psychology Quarterly, 12*, 119–133.

Sheridan, S. M., Clarke, B. L., & Knoche, L. L. (2006). The effects of conjoint behavioral consultation in early childhood settings. *Early Education and Development, 17*, 593–617.

Sheridan, S. M., Eagle, J. W., Cowan, R. J., & Mickelson, W. (2001). The effects of conjoint behavioral consultation results of a 4-year investigation. *Journal of School Psychology, 39*, 361–385.

Sheridan, S. M., Eagle, J. W., & Doll, B. (2006). An examination of the efficacy of conjoint behavioral consultation with diverse clients. *School Psychology Quarterly, 21*, 396–417.

Sheridan, S. M., & Gutkin, T. B. (2000). The ecology of school psychology: Examining and changing our paradigm for the 21st century. *School Psychology Review, 29*, 485–502.

Sheridan, S. M., Kratochwill, T. R., & Bergan, J. R. (1996). *Conjoint behavioral consultation*. New York: Plenum.

Sheridan, S. M., Meegan, S. P., & Eagle, J. W. (2002). Assessing the social context in initial conjoint behavioral consultation interviews: An exploratory analysis investigating processes and outcomes. *School Psychology Quarterly, 17*, 299–324.

Sheridan, S. M., & Walker, D. (1999). Social skills in context: Considerations for assessment, intervention, and generalization. In C. R. Reynolds & T. B. Gutkin (Eds.), *The handbook of school psychology* (3rd ed., pp. 686–708). Wiley. New York.

Sheridan, S. M., Warnes, E. D., & Dowd, S. (2004). Home-school collaboration and bullying: An ecological approach to increase social competence in children and youth. In D. L. Espelage & S. M. Swearer (Eds.), *Bullying in American schools: A social-ecological perspective on prevention and intervention* (pp. 245–268). Mahwah, NJ: Erlbaum.

Sheridan, S. M., Welch, M., & Orme, S. F. (1996). Is consultation effective? A review of outcome research. *Remedial and Special Education, 17*, 341–354.

Shinn, M. R. (1995). Best practices in curriculum-based measurement and its use in a problem-solving model. In A. Thomas & J. Grimes (Eds.), *Best practices in school psychology III* (pp. 547–567). Washington, DC: National Association of School Psychologists.

Shinn M. R., Powell-Smith, K. A., & Good, R. H., III (1996). Evaluating the effects of responsible reintegration into general education for students with mild disabilities on a case-by-case basis. *School Psychology Review, 25,* 519–539.

Shinn, M. R., Walker, H. M. & Stoner, G. (2002). *Interventions for academic and behavior problems II: Preventive and remedial approaches.* Bethesda, MD: National Association of School Psychologists.

Sinha, V. K., Kishore, M. T., & Thakur, A. (2003). A school mental health program in India. *Journal of the American Academy of Child & Adolescent Psychiatry, 42,* 624.

Skaalvik, E. M. & Skaalvik, S. (2007). Dimensions of teacher self-efficacy and relations with strain factors, perceived collective teacher efficacy, and teacher burnout. *Journal of Educational Psychology, 99,* 611–625.

Skinner, B. F. (1953). *Science and human behavior.* New York: Macmillan.

Smylie, M. A. (1988). The enhancement function of staff development: Organizational and psychological antecedents to individual teacher change. *American Educational Research Journal, 25,* 1–30.

Snapp, M., Hickman, J. A., & Conoley, J. C. (1990). Systems interventions in school settings: Case studies. In T. B. Gutkin & C. R. Reynolds (Eds.), *The handbook of school psychology* (2nd ed., pp. 920–934). New York: Wiley.

Stainback, S., & Stainback, W. (1988). Changes needed to strengthen regular education. In J. L. Graden, J. E. Zins, & M. J. Curtis (Eds.), *Alternative educational delivery systems: Enhancing instructional options for all students* (pp. 17–32). Washington, DC: National Association of School Psychologists.

Stenger, M. K., Tollefson, N., & Fine, M. J. (1992). Variables that distinguish elementary teachers who participate in school-based consultation from those who do not. *School Psychology Quarterly, 7,* 271–284.

Sterling-Turner, H. E., Watson, T. S., & Moore, J. W. (2002). The effects of direct training and treatment integrity on treatment outcomes in school consultation. *School Psychology Quarterly, 17,* 47–77.

Stoner, G., & Green, S. K. (1992). Reconsidering the scientist-practitioner model for school psychology practice. *School Psychology Review, 21,* 155–166.

Strein, W., Hoagwood, K., & Cohn, A. (2003). School psychology: A public health perspective I. Prevention, populations, and, systems change. *Journal of School Psychology, 41,* 23–28.

Swartz, J. L., & Martin, W. E., Jr. (1997). *Applied ecological psychology for schools within communities: Assessment and intervention.* Mahwah, NJ: Erlbaum.

Tarver Behring, S., & Ingraham, C. L. (1998). Culture as a central component to consultation: A call to the field. *Journal of Educational and Psychological Consultation, 9*(1), 57–72.

Telzrow, C. F., & Beebe, J. J. (2002). Best practices in facilitating intervention adherence and integrity. In A. Thomas & J. Grimes (Eds.), *Best practices in school psychology IV.* Bethesda, MD: National Association of School Psychologists.

Thomas, A., & Grimes, J. (Eds.). (2002). *Best practices in school psychology IV.* Bethesda, MD: National Association of School Psychologists.

Thomas, A., & Grimes, J. (Eds.). (2008). *Best practices in school psychology V.* Bethesda, MD: National Association of School Psychologists.

Tilly, W. D. (2008). The evolution of school psychology to science-based practice. In A. Thomas & J. Grimes (Eds.), *Best practices in school psychology V* (pp. 17–36). Bethesda, MD, National Association of School Psychologists.

Tindal, G., Shinn, M., Walz, L., & Germann, G. (1987). Mainstream consultation in secondary settings: The Pine County model. *The Journal of Special Education, 21,* 94–106.

Tombari, M. L., & Bergan, J. R. (1978). Consultant cues and teacher verbalizations, judgments, and expectancies concerning children's adjustment problems. *Journal of School Psychology, 16,* 212–219.

Truscott, S. D., Cohen, C. E., & Sams, D. P. (2005). The current state(s) of prereferral intervention teams: A report from two national surveys. *Remedial and Special Education, 26,* 130–140.

Tyler, F. B., Pargament, K. I., & Gatz, M. (1983). The resource collaborator role: A model for interactions involving psychologists. *American Psychologist, 38,* 388–398.

U.S. Department of Education, National Center for Educational Statistics (2006). *The condition of education, 2006,* NCES 2006–071, Washington, DC: U.S. Government Printing Office.

VanVoorhis, R. W., & Levinson, E. M. (2006). Job satisfaction among school psychologists: A meta-analysis. *School Psychology Quarterly, 21,* 77–90.

Villa, R. A., Thousand, J. S., Meyers, H., & Nevin, A. (1996). Teacher and administrator perceptions of heterogeneous education. *Exceptional Children, 63,* 29–45.

von Bertalanffy, L. (1968). *General systems theory.* New York: Braziller.

Walter, H. J. (2001). School-based prevention of problem behaviors. *Child and Adolescent Psychiatric Clinics of North America, 10,* 117–127.

Wang, M. C., & Baker, E. T. (1986). Mainstreaming programs: Design features and effects. *Journal of Special Education, 19,* 503–523.

Watkins-Emonet, C. E. (2001). Evaluating the teaching components of direct behavioral consultation on skill acquisition and generalization in Head Start classrooms.

Dissertation Abstracts International: Section B: The Sciences and Engineering, 61 (10-B), 5547.

Watson, T. S., & Kramer, J. J. (1995). Teaching problem solving skills to teachers-in-training: An analogue experimental analysis of three methods. *Journal of Behavioral Education, 5,* 281–293.

Watson, T. S., & Robinson, S. L. (1996). Direct behavioral consultation: An alternative to traditional behavioral consultation. *School Psychology Quarterly, 11,* 267–278.

Wehmann, B., Zins, J. E., & Curtis, M. J. (1989, March). *Effects of consultation on teachers' perceptions of children's problems.* Paper presented at The Annual Meeting of The National Association of School Psychologists, Boston.

Wickstrom, K. F., & Witt, J. C. (1993). Resistance within school-based consultation. In J. E. Zins, T. R. Kratochwill, & S. N. Elliott (Eds.), *Handbook of consultation services for children: Applications in educational and clinical settings* (pp. 159–178). San Francisco: Jossey-Bass.

Widiger, T. A., & Trull, T. J. (2007). Plate tectonics in the classification of personality disorder: Shifting to a dimensional model. *American Psychologist, 62,* 71–83.

Wilkinson, L. A. (2005). Supporting the inclusion of a student with Asperger Syndrome: A case study using conjoint behavioural consultation and self-management. *Educational Psychology in Practice, 21,* 307–326.

Wilkinson, L. A. (2006). Monitoring treatment integrity: An alternative to the 'Consult and Hope' strategy in school-based behavioural consultation. *School Psychology International, 27,* 426–438.

Willems, E. P. (1974). Behavioral technology and behavioral ecology. *Journal of Applied Behavior Analysis, 7,* 151–165.

Wilson, C. P., Gutkin, T. B., Hagen, K. M., & Oats, R. G. (1998). General education teachers' knowledge and self-reported use of classroom interventions for working with difficult-to-teach students: Implications for consultation, prereferral intervention and inclusive services. *School Psychology Quarterly, 13,* 45–62.

Witt, J. C. (1990a). Collaboration in school-based consultation: Myth in need of data. *Journal of Educational and Psychological Consultation, 1,* 367–370.

Witt, J. C. (1990b). Complaining, pre-Copernican thought and the univariate linear mind: Questions for school-based behavioral consultation research. *School Psychology Review, 19,* 367–377.

Witt, J. C., Erchul, W. P., McKee, W. T., Pardue, M. M., & Wickstrom, K. F. (1991). Conversational control in school-based consultation: The relationship between consultant and consultee topic determination and consultation outcome. *Journal of Educational and Psychological Consultation, 2,* 101–116.

Witt, J. C. & Martens, B. K. (1988). Problems with problem-solving consultation: A re-analysis of assumptions, methods, and goals. *School Psychology Review, 17,* 211–226.

Witt, J. C., Moe, G., Gutkin, T. B., & Andrews, L. (1984). The effect of saying the same thing in different ways: The problem of language and jargon in school-based consultation. *Journal of School Psychology, 22,* 361–367.

Wittrock, M. C. (Ed.). (1986). *Handbook of research on teaching* (3rd ed.). New York: Macmillan.

Woods, K. M., & McNamara, J. R. (1980). Confidentiality: Its effect on interviewee behavior. *Professional Psychology, 11,* 714–721.

Woolfolk, A. E., & Hoy, W. K. (1990). Prospective teachers' sense of efficacy and beliefs about control. *Journal of Educational Psychology, 82,* 81–91.

Ysseldyke, J. E. (1987). Classification of handicapped students. In M. C. Wang, M. Reynolds, & H. J. Walberg (Eds.), *Handbook of special education: Research & practice* (Vol. 1, pp. 253–271). New York: Pergamon.

Ysseldyke, J. E., Algozzine, B., & Thurlow, M. L. (1992). *Critical issues in special education* (2nd ed.). Boston: Houghton Mifflin.

Ysseldyke, J. E., Burns, M. K., Dawson, M., Kelley, B., Morrison, D., Ortiz, S., Rosenfield, S., & Telzrow, C. (2006). *School Psychology: A blueprint for the future of training and practice III.* Bethesda, MD: National Association of School Psychologists.

Ysseldyke, J. E., Christenson, S. L., & Thurlow, M. L. (1989). Are different kinds of instructional tasks used by different categories of students in different settings? *School Psychology Review, 18,* 98–111.

Ysseldyke, J., Dawson, P., Lehr, C., Reschly, D., Reynolds, M., & Telzrow, C. (1997). *School psychology: A blueprint for training and practice-II.* Bethesda, MD: National Association of School Psychologists.

Ysseldyke, J. E., Reynolds, M. C., Weinberg, R. A., Bardon, H., Heaston, P., Hines, L., Ramage, J., Rosenfield, S., Schakel, J., & Taylor, J. (1984). *School psychology: A blueprint for training and practice.* Minneapolis, MN: National School Psychology Inservice Training Network.

Zins, J. E., Curtis, M. J., Graden, J. L., & Ponti, C. R. (1988). *Helping students succeed in the regular classroom: A guide for developing intervention assistance programs.* San Francisco: Jossey-Bass.

Zins, J. E., & Erchul, W. P. (1995). School consultation. In A. Thomas & J. Grimes (Eds.), *Best practices in school psychology-III* (pp. 609–623). Washington, DC: National Association of School Psychologists.

Zins, J. E., & Erchul, W. P. (2002). Best practices in school consultation. In A. Thomas & J. Grimes (Eds.), *Best practices in school psychology-IV* (pp. 625–644). Washington, DC: National Association of School Psychologists.

Zins, J. E., & Heron, T. E. (Eds.). (1996). Current practices, unresolved issues, and future directions in consultation. *Remedial and Special Education* [Special issue], *17*(6).

Zins, J. E., Kratochwill, T. R., & Elliott, S. N. (1993a). Current status of the field. In J. E. Zins, T. R. Kratochwill, & S. N. Elliott (Eds.), *Handbook of consultation services for children: Applications in educational and clinical settings* (pp. 1–12). San Francisco: Jossey-Bass.

Zins, J. E., Kratochwill, T. R., & Elliott, S. N. (1993b). *Handbook of consultation services for children: Applications in educational and clinical settings.* San Francisco: Jossey-Bass.

Zins, J. E., & Ponti, C. R. (1990). Strategies to facilitate the implementation, organization, and operation of system-wide consultation programs. *Journal of Educational and Psychological Consultation, 1,* 205–218.

Zins, J. E., & Ponti, C. R. (1996). The influence of direct training in problem solving on consultee problem clarification skills and attributions. *Remedial and Special Education, 17,* 370–376.

Chapter 29

Conducting Evidence-Based Interventions in the Schools

Kevin D. Stark, Jennifer Hargrave, Bradley Gerber, Melissa Fisher
and Amy Hamilton
University of Texas at Austin

Mental Health Needs of Children

The mental health needs of children far outweigh the opportunities for services (Costello, Egger, & Angold, 2005). As many as 14–20% of school-aged children develop mental health concerns within a 12-month period (Sawyer et al., 2001; Briggs-Cowan, Horwitz, & McCue 2000; U.S. Department of Health and Human Services, 1999). In a school of 1000 students, approximately 180 to 220 children would be expected to meet criteria for a diagnosable psychiatric disorder (Doll, 1996). Of these children, approximately three-quarters are not receiving the services they need (Costello, Messer, Bird, Cohen, & Reinherz, 1998; Leaf et al., 1996; Sawyer et al., 2001, National Institute of Mental Health, 2001; see Hoagwood & Johnson, 2003). The majority of children (70–80%) who need mental health services and are fortunate enough to receive them are provided with services in the schools (Burns et al., 1995). Furthermore, for the majority of these children, school personnel are the sole providers of services.

While schools are charged with the role of educating children, it is paramount to realize that the academic success of children is dependent upon the development of social and emotional competencies (Elias, Zins, Graczyk, & Weissberg, 2003). Children's mental health concerns effect their achievement, probability of graduating, social functioning (Capaldi & Stoolmiller, 1999; Fergusson & Woodward, 2002; Riley, Ensminger, Green, & Kang, 1998), likelihood of abusing substances, and their health, and puts them at risk for self-destructive behaviors (Bardone et al., 1998; Capaldi & Stoolmiller, 1999; Weissman et al., 1999). In addition, children's emotional disturbances affect their teachers and the other students in their classrooms. They also create a burden for their caregivers in terms of lost time from work and for their families in terms of lost income (Hinshaw et al., cited in Hoagwood & Johnson, 2003).

Youth with psychiatric disorders, relative to those that don't have them, have lower educational outcomes and more difficulty with employment in the future. For example, seventh graders' social and emotional skills and behaviors are related to academic achievement in tenth grade even after controlling for demographic factors and academic achievement in fourth grade (Fleming et al., 2005). Adolescents who met diagnostic criteria for depression between 14 and 16 years of age have a higher risk of experiencing school failure, are less likely to participate in higher educational opportunities, and are more likely to experience recurrent unemployment between the ages of 16 and 21 (Fergusson & Woodward, 2002). Similarly, Weissman et al. (1999) followed depressed and nondepressed adolescents into adulthood, and their results indicated that the depressed group had lower educational attainment and missed more work as a result of mental health issues. The academic achievement and future employment of children who experience comorbid anxiety and depression also is lower than that of children without psychological disorders (Last & Hansen, 1997). Middle school boys with conduct problems are less likely to graduate from high school, attend college, attain a job, or keep a driver's license (Capaldi & Stoolmiller, 1999).

Mental health issues place children at increased risk for social difficulties. Riley et al. (1998) studied youths 11–17 years old and found that the children who had psychiatric disorders were not as likely as children without a disorder to be well accepted by peers or to participate in extracurricular activities. More specifically, boys with psychiatric disorders are more likely to have poor relationships with friends, family, and peers, and girls with disorders had more trouble with appropriate behaviors and communication skills. Boys who report depressive symptoms in middle school, not even full-blown depressive disorders, have been found to experience more negative peer relationships during twelfth grade (Capaldi & Stoolmiller, 1999). Adolescents who experience a recurrent course of depression between the ages of 12 and 18 are more likely to have significant impairment in their relationships with friends and in their overall life satisfaction (Rao et al., 1995). Depressed adolescents report more social difficulties across work, family, and other settings in general as adults (Weissman et al., 1999).

Substance use and dependence is another area in which children and adolescents with psychiatric disorders seem to struggle. For example, a survey of over 22,000 adolescents between the ages of 12 and 17 revealed that of those who had experienced a major depressive episode in the past year, 38% had used illicit drugs over the previous 12 months, 19.8% experienced illicit drug or alcohol dependence, and 5.3% reported daily use of cigarettes (Office of Applied Studies, 2006). In contrast, 18% of adolescents who did not report an episode of depression used illicit drugs in the past year, 6.9% experienced drug or alcohol dependence, and 2.5% used cigarettes daily. In addition, among adolescents who reported alcohol or drug dependence, 21.7% had experienced a major depressive episode in the past year. Fergusson and Woodward (2002) also reported that depressed adolescents have a greater risk of experiencing substance dependence in the future. Similar results have been reported for girls with conduct disorder (Bardone et al., 1998). Girls experiencing conduct disorder at 15 are more likely to meet criteria for a substance dependence disorder at 21, and 15-year-old girls with comorbid depression or conduct disorder are more likely to experience tobacco dependence

when they are 21. Conduct problems in middle school boys also are related to increased substance use in twelfth grade (Capaldi & Stoolmiller, 1999).

Early pregnancy and negative health outcomes in adulthood are related to early psychiatric problems. Girls with conduct disorder have more sexual partners, are more likely to contract a sexually transmitted disease, and are more likely to experience pregnancy compared to girls without disorders (Bardone et al.,1998). In addition, girls with conduct disorder, depression, or an anxiety disorder are more likely to experience medical problems at 21 years of age. Middle school boys with conduct problems are more likely to cause a pregnancy and experience early fatherhood at 18–21 years old (Capaldi & Stoolmiller, 1999). Adolescents with depressive disorders also are more likely to experience early parenthood (Fergusson & Woodward, 2002).

Children and adolescents with depression are also at risk for suicidal behaviors in adulthood. Out of the follow-up group in Weissman et al.'s (1999) study, which included 73 adults who were depressed as adolescents, 50.6% had made a suicide attempt before the follow-up assessment and 22% had made multiple suicide attempts. Seven of their original group of 91 adolescents had committed suicide. Fergusson and Woodward's (2002) results also suggested that the adolescents in their study that met criteria for depression were more likely to display suicidal behaviors between 16 and 21 years of age.

SCHOOL AS A POINT OF DELIVERY OF THERAPY

Burns et al. (1995) posit that improving mental health services for children can be accomplished through increasing the availability of these services in the schools. Relative to other mental health settings, children are more likely to use school-based services (Anglin, Naylor, & Kaplan, 1996; Earls, Robins, Stiffman, & Powell, 1989). Providing services in the schools reduces transportation issues, and may reduce the stigma associated with visiting a hospital or outpatient clinic. Furthermore, it eliminates financial barriers, and it reduces the burden on the parents to miss work to take their child to his or her appointments. Moreover, when a good relationship exists between school staff and the child and his or her caregivers, trust is already established which can facilitate acceptance of, and compliance with, therapy. School-based services reach families that are not familiar with therapy services conducted in the medical community. When conducting group therapy, an advantage to school-based services is that group cohesion can develop quickly as the students already know each other and often come from the same communities. When this occurs, valuable time usually spent building rapport between new group members can be applied to skills training or other therapeutic endeavors. Since the children attend the same school and often live within the same neighborhood, the opportunity to establish friendships and socialize outside of group is greater.

School-based therapists have the advantage of ready access to multiple informants as well as additional change agents. Teachers and other staff members provide useful information about the child's ability level, current behaviors, mood, and peer interactions which helps the therapist to obtain the whole picture of the child's functioning. This information is often missing in clinic-based interventions. In addition, teachers and other school staff can be involved in treatment by supporting the generalization of the skills that were taught within the sessions, following a behavior management plan, or helping the child to see evidence that supports a new, more adaptive belief. Group members are also able to provide information they witness in school to help support or dispute the accuracy of other group members' distorted thoughts and beliefs. Evidence provided by peers is a powerful tool for restructuring distorted thoughts and maladaptive beliefs. Group members are also able to bring problems to therapy in real time, as these often take place during the school day. They may have just experienced an argument with a friend, a break-up, peer teasing, or received a bad grade. Therapists are able to take these events and intervene in the moment. Additionally school staff can help by monitoring a child's safety.

Nastasi, Varjas, Bernstein, and Pluymert (1998) note the importance of increasing the role of school psychologists in providing mental health services. School psychologists are in a unique position to identify children with mental health needs and to provide them with necessary services (Doll, 1996). The need for direct mental health services for children, the many advantages to conducting therapy in the schools, and the growing body of child therapy effectiveness studies (Burns, Hoagwood, & Mrazek, 1999)

solidifies the importance of the role of therapist for school psychologists.

SCHOOL PSYCHOLOGIST AS THERAPIST

While Stoiber and Kratochwill (2000) have stated that the sine qua non of school psychologists is intervention, the role of school psychologists is varied, multidimensional, and dominated by engagement in special education activities. School psychologists attempt to balance time between assessment, direct intervention, consultation, and research/evaluation. Of these responsibilities, psycho-educational assessment consumes the largest portion, approximately half of the average workload (Reschly, 2000). This imbalance appears to be largest in public schools, with private and nonschool settings reporting a smaller percentage of time spent conducting psycho-educational assessments. It appears directly related to the role of the Individuals with Disabilities Education Act (IDEA) and funding through special education for many school psychologists (Reschly, 2000). As a result, school psychologists spend most of their time with students in special education, leaving little time for therapy-related activities or involvement with children outside of this classification process. Thus, when school psychologists are conducting therapy, students who have received the special education classification of Severely Emotionally Disturbed (SED) are likely to be the recipients. Youngsters that have been classified as SED are the most severely impaired clients of any youth within any mental health system (Garland et al., 2001). Consequently, they may be the most complex cases and those that require the most skilled therapists and effective interventions possible. Another central issue facing school psychologists in attempting to deliver direct interventions is the ratio of students to school psychologists, which is approximately 1874:1 (Lund, Reschly, & Martin, 1998). This large ratio, combined with the need to evaluate and reevaluate students for special education, leaves inadequate time for fulfilling students' needs for therapy. Thus, school psychologists need to be as effective as possible in the least amount of time so that they can serve as many students as possible.

The majority perspective of school psychologists is that they would like to see a reduction in time spent completing assessment activities in order to increase their work in other areas including individual and group therapy (Watkins, Crosby, & Pearson, 2001). Administrators and teachers would also like to see an increase in therapy services provided by school psychologists (Watkins, Crosby, & Pearson, 2001). However, school personnel would like this accomplished without a reduction in assessment activities. Results have varied in regard to the amount of time school psychologists spend engaged in the delivery of therapy services. Bramlett, Murphy, Johnson, and Wallingsford (2002) found that school psychologists spend only 3 hours per week providing therapy. However, others have reported that school psychologists typically spend 8 hours per week engaged in therapy (Prout, Alexander, Fletcher, Memis, & Miller, 1993). School psychologists serve an average of 17 students per week, within approximately 10 sessions, with an average session length of 30–40 minutes (Prout et al., 1993).

Research indicates that a relationship exists between the amount of training that school psychologists complete in therapy and the amount of therapy they conduct in practice. School psychologists who complete more training and supervised experience in therapy spend more time conducting therapy in practice (Pryzwansky, Harris, & Jackson, 1984). School psychologists who matriculate through doctoral training complete an average of approximately two (Brown & Minke, 1986) to three (Minke & Brown, 1996) courses in individual therapy, a course in group therapy, and additional training in behavioral interventions (Minke & Brown, 1996). In addition to completing relevant didactic coursework, school psychologists complete an average of 642 (Minke & Brown, 1996) to 845 (Romans, Boswell, Carlozzi, & Ferguson, 1995) hours of supervised practicum work.

While there has been a paucity of research on the therapeutic practices of school psychologists, when they identify a particular approach to therapy, they state that they are likely to use cognitive-behavioral and behavioral procedures (Pryzwansky et al., 1984). These findings are consistent with other research that has reported that when psychologists are asked which theoretical approach they follow in their applied practice, the most common response is cognitive behavioral therapy (Prout et al., 1993). However, it is important to note that most practitioners state that they don't follow any particular theoretical approach; instead their therapeutic practices are characterized by an eclectic mix of cognitive,

behavioral and psychodynamic procedures. Thus, in general psychologists do not adhere to any single theoretical approach to therapy. These results suggest that psychologists in general do not employ evidence-based interventions. Further evidence of this state of affairs is the abundance of research that indicates that practitioners tend to believe that research does not apply to their practice so they do not incorporate research findings into their work with clients (Goldfried & Wolfe, 1996).

Most of the evidence-based interventions come from the genre of cognitive behavioral therapy (CBT). It is commonly believed that CBT is a relatively easy therapeutic approach to implement. In reality, it is a complex approach to clinical practice that requires a sound understanding of its theoretical tenets (which in and of itself is complex as CBT is a general label for a broad range of theoretical approaches to therapy that share a number of common core principles). A theoretical understanding is necessary for developing a conceptualization of each case. This case conceptualization is the road map that guides treatment (Stark et al., in press). It helps the therapist to choose the core beliefs, intermediate beliefs, and automatic thoughts that are going to be targeted for change, as well as the coping, interpersonal, emotion regulation, problem-solving, and other behavioral skills that are going to be taught. The conceptualization also guides the therapist's choice of environmental targets for intervention. In addition to a theoretical understanding of CBT in general, a cognitive behavioral therapist would be aware of the relevant research on the nature of the disorder to be treated and of the outcome research that identifies effective intervention strategies both for the child and his or her caregivers. All of this information is integrated with the individual's assessment data to develop a conceptualization of each case and to develop an individualized treatment plan for the child and the significant environments in which he or she functions.

Based on our experiences with the ACTION treatment, it appears as though CBT is more effective when it is driven by an accurate case conceptualization. In addition, CBT is most effective when the case conceptualization and thus the intervention strategies chosen and the process of implementation are based on a thorough understanding of the disorder being treated. A portion of this background work has been completed for therapists when they choose to follow treatment manuals that have been proven to be efficacious as many of these manuals have been developed by experts on the target disorder. However, in order to be maximally effective in the delivery of the intervention, the therapist must be able to conceptualize the cases and thus individualize treatment and deliver treatment in an engaging fashion while addressing the child's specific maladaptive core beliefs and deficits in problem solving, emotion regulation, and other skills that are critically important for healthy functioning. In addition, to be successful at conducting CBT the therapist has to be aware of, and skillful at, all of the nonspecific and interpersonal aspects of therapy.

The extent to which school psychologists are trained and supervised in the use of CBT for specific disorders is not known. Furthermore, among school psychologists who state that they use CBT, the extent to which they follow evidence-based protocols in their therapeutic work is not known. Unfortunately, school psychologists are just as likely as their peers from other psychological disciplines to disregard research on evidence-based practices (Kratochwill & Stoiber, 2000). Thus, they are not likely to employ evidence-based protocols. This is unfortunate as meta-analytic research indicates that following a more structured treatment protocol is associated with more effective interventions (Weisz et al., 1995). Furthermore, a commitment to evaluating, understanding and disseminating empirically supported interventions could be a way to promote changes in practice (Stoiber & Kratochwill, 2000), and more specifically, to promote the role of school psychologist as therapist.

EFFICACY OF COMMUNITY-BASED CHILD THERAPY

If school psychologists in general follow the treatment practices of other child therapists, they would use an eclectic mix of cognitive, behavioral, psychodynamic, and other procedures (Addis & Krasnow, 2000). Weisz (2000, p. 837) states that "most of the 2.5 million American children seen in clinical practice each year receive interventions that have never been tested in a clinical trial." There is no evidence to support the efficacy of this approach to child psychotherapy (Bickman, Noser, & Summerfelt, 1999). Furthermore, it appears as though this form of child psychotherapy is no more effective than no treatment at all (Andrade, Lambert, & Bickman, 2000).

Treatment as usual in the community does not appear to be as effective as treatment delivered within a research protocol. Weersing and Weisz (2002) for example report that depressed youth who received treatment through a research protocol relative to those that received treatment in a community mental health center (CMHC) improved very quickly and their scores were significantly better than those for the CMHC sample immediately following treatment. Furthermore, at posttreatment depressed youth who received CBT reported enough improvement in depressive symptoms that their scores fell near those of a normative sample. This significant difference between youth who received CBT and those that received treatment as usual through the CMHC held through one- and three-month follow-up assessments. In comparison, youth who received the eclectic treatment in the CMHC showed a trajectory of change that was similar to participants in the research protocols that had not received treatment due to random assignment to a waiting list. For CMHC youth, change occurred at a slow rate. In fact, their rate of improvement was longer than that for the youth who received CBT, and it was twice as slow as youth who did not receive treatment. It took the CMHC sample a year to catch up to the youth who received CBT. It appears as though the eclectic treatment produced no more improvement in depressive symptoms than that which occurs due to the natural passing of time.

It could be argued that the failure to find any evidence for the effectiveness of traditional child therapy is due to the limited number of sessions that the youngsters received in the CMHC and due to a failure to assess the change that is likely to accrue over longer periods of time from more insight-oriented treatments. Weiss, Catron, and Harris (2000) addressed this issue in a study of the effectiveness of traditional child therapy that included an open-ended treatment protocol, and tracking the youngsters' internalizing and externalizing symptoms over a two-year follow-up period. Overall, results provided little to no support for the effectiveness of traditional child psychotherapy. Children who were experiencing elevated symptoms of internalizing or externalizing disorders self-reported no more change than did students who received tutoring over this same period of time. Overall, it is evident that there is no evidence for the efficacy of eclectic interventions.

Given the lack of evidence for the efficacy of traditional child psychotherapy, the severity of children served, the overwhelming numbers of children who need services, and the limited amount of time to provide needed services, it is especially important for school psychologists to provide the students they serve with evidence-based interventions. Moreover, it is necessary to maximize the efficacy of their interventions so that they can achieve maximum gains in the least amount of time. Unfortunately, as Hoagwood and Johnson (2003) note, a gap exists between research-based practices and the delivery of such services in the schools. No research base exists for guiding the successful implementation and dissemination of evidence based-practices to settings outside of research labs (Weisz, Donenberg, Weiss, & Han, 1995). A need exists for identifying barriers to real world implementation of research-supported treatments (Connor-Smith & Weisz, 2003; Kazdin & Kendall, 1998). In the following sections, an attempt is made to describe the authors' experience with implementing and evaluating the effectiveness of an evidence-based intervention in the public schools for one of the more common mental health concerns among youth. With funding from the National Institute of Mental Health (NIMH), the authors have been delivering and evaluating the effectiveness of the ACTION treatment program for pre- and early adolescent girls who are experiencing depressive disorders. Our experiences over the past five years with delivering this intervention in the schools along with suggestions for how to avoid and overcome impediments will be described in the hope that it will facilitate the delivery of other evidence-based treatments in the schools. An attempt is made to provide suggestions for accomplishing this.

DESCRIPTION OF THE ACTION PROJECT

The research project we have been conducting that serves as the basis for the following sections of this chapter will be briefly described to create a context for understanding the possible genesis of the impediments to delivering an evidence-based treatment that we have identified. The overall objective of the study was to evaluate the relative efficacy of CBT with and without a parent-training component for the treatment of 9- to 13-year-old girls who are depressed. The investigation was conducted in the schools from 2002 to 2007. Participants were identified through a multiple-gate screening

and identification procedure (Reynolds, 1986). Permission letters describing the study were sent home to parents of all of the girls from grades 4 to 7 in the participating schools. Girls who received permission and assented to participate in the study (47%) completed the Children's Depression Inventory (CDI; Kovacs, 1992). If they scored at least 16, they were interviewed the same day with a Diagnostic and Statistical Manual (DSM) symptom interview. If they reported symptoms of a depressive disorder on the symptom interview, their primary caregiver was called to discuss assessment results and they were informed that another permission letter for conducting a semi-structured diagnostic interview would be sent home with their daughter. The girls who received permission and assented were interviewed with the Present Episode version of the Schedule for Affective Disorders and Schizophrenia for School-Aged Children (Ambrosini & Dixon, 2000) within 2 weeks of completing the screening measures. Parent consent letters for participation in further pretreatment assessment and random assignment to one of the three treatment conditions were sent home with the children who received a diagnosis of a depressive disorder. Children who received permission and assented along with their primary caregiver completed a battery of measures that assessed depression, cognition, and family functioning using multiple measures and multiple methods. Subsequently, the girls were randomly assigned to either CBT, CBT + Parent Training, or a minimal contact control condition. Immediately following treatment and annually thereafter, the participants and their primary caregiver were interviewed with the Kiddie-Schedule for Affective Disorders & Schizophrenia (K-SADS) and they once again completed the battery of outcome measures. In addition, each semester following treatment until the end of the study, the girls participated in three booster sessions.

The ACTION program is prototypical of CBT for depressed youth. The primary components are appropriate for males and females and for children and adolescents. However, by design the activities, coping skills, and illustrations in the treatment materials are specific to girls between 9 and 13 years old. It is a group treatment that follows a structured therapist's manual (Stark et al., 2006a) and workbook (Stark et al., 2006b). Each of the 20 group and two individual meetings lasts approximately 60 minutes and is conducted twice a week for 11 weeks. The treatment is designed to be fun and engaging while teaching the youngsters a variety of skills that are applied to their depressive symptoms, interpersonal difficulties, and other stressors. The skills are taught to the girls through didactic presentations and activities, they are rehearsed during in-session activities, and they are applied through therapeutic homework.

To make the intervention developmentally appropriate, activities are experiential in nature. When the girls are taught a therapeutic concept or skill, they actually experience its benefits within the session. Activities are used to build the rationale for treatment and for teaching the children how to use the therapeutic skills and strategies. Similarly, when a therapeutic skill is introduced, the girls complete an activity so that they can change their thinking. Experiencing the benefits of the treatment strategies combats their pessimism, increases treatment credibility, and provides them with a sense of personal efficacy. Application of skills outside of meetings is critical for successful treatment. Thus, skill application is monitored and recorded through completion of therapeutic homework, and homework completion is encouraged through an in-session reward system.

The treatment program is based on a self-regulation model in which youngsters use skills to achieve and maintain a pleasant mood, or they use a change in mood or negative thoughts as a sign to engage in coping, problem solving and/or cognitive restructuring. The girls are taught to use the "3B's" (Brain, Body, and Behavior) to identify their emotional experiences. By paying attention to the thoughts in their heads, the reactions of their bodies, and their own behavior, the girls are better aware of their own emotions and over the course of therapy they become more aware of changes in their emotions, and more skilled at using the changes as cues to engage in coping, problem solving, or cognitive restructuring. Activities completed within the meetings and as homework help the girls to become more aware of their personal experiences and the links between their thoughts, behaviors, and emotions.

Depressed youth often experience undesirable situations that are not within their control and thus cannot be changed by them. In such situations, the children can take action to improve their mood and other depressive symptoms through coping skills that are taught and applied during the first nine meetings. Participants experience the benefits of using coping skills within session and they are encouraged to use these skills outside of meetings through self-monitoring and recording their use.

Some undesirable situations that occur within the lives of depressed youth can be changed or managed, and are within the girls' control. The girls are taught a five-step problem-solving procedure to change undesirable situations and thus to reduce distress and the accompanying emotional upset. Over time, the therapist helps the girls apply problem solving to promote desirable change in their lives. By the middle of treatment, the youngsters typically are proficient at using coping and problem solving skills and this enables them to focus on identifying and changing negative thoughts.

Depressed youth are taught to recognize and then evaluate negative thoughts using a number of cognitive restructuring strategies. A variety of within-session activities and therapeutic homework exercises are used to teach youngsters to be "thought judges" who evaluate the validity of their negative thoughts using two questions: (1) What is another way of looking at it? (2) What is the evidence? If their negative thought is realistic and reflects a situation that can be changed, then the youngster is encouraged to use problem solving to develop and follow a plan that produces improvement. If the situation is real but cannot be changed, then a coping strategy is used to manage her reaction to the situation.

Since children are developing critical beliefs and self-regulatory strategies from their interactions with significant others, the ACTION program includes a parent training component. This component was designed to create a more positive family environment that facilitates the development of adaptive core beliefs, and effective coping and problem-solving skills. The parent-training component consists of eight group meetings and two individual family meetings completed over the 11 weeks that the girls are engaged in their group treatment. An attempt is made to help the caregivers and their daughters experience the benefits of the treatment strategies within the meetings as a means of increasing the likelihood that they would apply the skills to their everyday lives. The parent-training component has two broad objectives: (1) create a positive family environment that encourages adaptive behavior, and the development of emotion regulation, problem solving skills, and healthy core beliefs; and (2) help the parents to acquire and use the same skills that the children are learning. To create the positive family environment parents are taught (1) to use positive behavior management strategies and to reduce their use of punitive strategies, (2) family problem solving, (3) communication skills, (4) conflict resolution skills, and (5) how their behavior impacts their child's thinking and belief system. Children are present during half of the meetings.

IMPLEMENTATION OF AN EVIDENCE-BASED INTERVENTION: THREATS AND SOLUTIONS

Evidence-based interventions have been developed for a variety of childhood disorders (See Table 29.1). These interventions have demonstrated their efficacy within research laboratories, but they have not yet been transported to applied settings such as schools. For these interventions to be effective and useful, they must demonstrate efficacy in real-world settings. While implementing the ACTION treatment program in two school districts that included 11 elementary schools and 6 middle schools over the past five years, we have encountered a number of threats to the valid implementation of the intervention. Some of these threats are common to therapy in general while others may be specific to an evidence-based intervention.

To successfully transport an evidence-based intervention to another setting it is necessary to follow the same procedures that were used when it was implemented during clinical trials. Alterations of the standardized procedures may result in a reduction in, or loss of, efficacy. Thus, the length of treatment in terms of total number of sessions and the number of weeks during which treatment is completed, length of meetings, spacing and ordering of sessions, all have to be completed in the standardized fashion. There are numerous threats to these aspects of treatment.

Gaining Support for Intervention Services

A basic impediment to conducting therapy is a lack of support from school administrators and staff. While administrators and teachers would like school psychologists to conduct more therapy, they want this to occur without a reduction in student achievement and without any cost to them in terms of increased workloads or hassles. So,

at the most basic level the first impediment to conducting an evidence-based intervention is lack of support from administration and staff. We were outsiders, so we may have had to take more steps than a school psychologist who is working within the school district, but we did a number of things to secure support from administrators and staff.

We started by obtaining support for the intervention from the superintendents of the two school districts where the treatment study was conducted. Fortunately, both superintendents understood the importance of providing therapy for depressed youth and valued such services. As one of the superintendents stated, "Our students' emotional needs have to be met before they can achieve up to their potentials." Since our therapists were not being paid by the school districts, they also saw the advantages of receiving countless hours of state-of-the-art intervention services for their students at no cost to their constituents. We also found that the superintendents appreciated receiving information about the prevalence and impact of depression on students, parents, and classrooms. We helped them to understand that the students' performance on statewide tests, their attendance (tied to amount of state funding received), and parental support in general were likely to improve following successful treatment. After receiving support from the superintendents, the principal investigator (PI) met with them on an annual basis to provide information on how the intervention program was going in terms of number of participants served and reactions to the program. This regular contact seemed to help maintain support for the intervention. While it isn't something that we as school psychologists find to be tasteful, nor are we provided with training in how to best do it, it is important for our profession to complete some public relations work in which we provide administrators with information about the good work that we do. We seem to assume that they automatically know and value what we do, but in reality there are so many misperceptions about psychology, that many administrators hold misperceptions about what we do, how we do it, and how effective we are.

Despite having superintendent support, therapists can have difficulty gaining access to individual school campuses and classrooms. Both superintendents were very clear that while they supported the treatment program, their principals would make the decision about whether their campuses would participate. Regardless of the

TABLE 29.1   Empirically Supported Treatments for Children
and Adolescents

	Well-established efficacy	Probably efficacious
ADHD	Behavioral parent training	Social skills training with generalization components
	Behavioral modification in classroom	Summer treatment programs
Anxiety Disorders*	none	Cognitive behavioral therapy
		Cognitive behavioral therapy plus family anxiety management
		Modeling
		In vivo exposure
		Relaxation training
		Reinforced practice
ODD and CD	Parent training based on living with children	Anger control training with stress inoculation (adolescents)
	Videotape-modeling parent training	Assertiveness training (adolescents)
		Multisystemic therapy (adolescents)
		Rational emotive therapy (adolescents)
		Problem-solving skills training (school age)
		Anger coping therapy (school age)
		Delinquency prevention program (preschool age)
		Parent-child interaction therapy (preschool age)
		Time out plus signal seat training (preschool age)
		Parent training program (preschool age)
Encopresis	Behavior modification	none
Enuresis	Behavior modification	none
Depression**	Interpersonal therapy	Coping with depression course with skills training (adolescents)
		Cognitive behavioral therapy (children)
Obesity	none	Behavior therapy
Phobias	Participant modeling	Cognitive behavioral therapy
	Reinforced practice	Filmed modeling
		Imaginal desensitization
		In vivo desensitization
		Live modeling
Pervasive Developmental Disorders	Contingency management for undesired behaviors	none

*Anxiety Disorders includes Separation Anxiety, Generalized Anxiety, and Social Phobia.
**Depression includes Major Depression, Dysthymic Disorder, and Adjustment Disorder.
Data from Chambless & Ollendick (2001) and Society of Clinical Child and Adolescent Psychology & the Network on Youth Mental Health (2007).

circumstances, having the support of principals is crucial as they are the ultimate gatekeepers at the campus level and they set the tone for the teachers in their schools. In addition, they can be helpful when a teacher becomes obstructionistic. Principals also bear the brunt of parental disgruntlement when a problem arises. Obtaining support from the principals was initially obtained by asking the superintendent from each school district to introduce the PI to the principals at the start of one of their monthly meetings. In addition to introducing the psychologist, the superintendent was asked to state his or her support for the intervention program. Subsequently, the psychologist provided the principals with a description of the impact of depression on youth and the treatment program that was going to be provided. The description of the impact of depression tapped into their sincere concern for the total welfare of their students and the description of the treatment program helped to alleviate fears that we were going to be implementing some sort of therapy that was an embarrassment and difficult to present to, or defend when dealing with, parents. Rather, CBT makes intuitive sense and the principals could see the benefits to all students of learning how to reduce stress and improve mood through acquiring coping skills, problem solving, and more realistic and positive ways of thinking. They commonly joked about wanting to participate in the programs themselves. Given the very high rate of depression among adults, many of the administrators knew someone who was depressed and they were aware of its devastating impact. Since depressive disorders among children are more severe and of longer duration than adult variants, they were sympathetic to the treatment needs of these youngsters (Jensen, Ryan, & Prien, 1992).

The ACTION program was initially provided to girls between the ages of 9 and 13; however, these girls continued to receive booster sessions for up to four and a half years, so some of the girls received services through high school. At the middle and high school levels, the principals were interested in hearing about how treating depression could reduce school violence, suicidal behavior, and vandalism. At all grade levels, the fact that the intervention had an evidence base and that we could predict that approximately 70% of the girls were going to improve helped as the principals could see that the time away from classes was going to be of benefit for most of the girls. Overall, it is important to provide the principals with complete information about the treatment program so that they can address all parental inquiries. Principals do not want to be asked a question about their school that they cannot answer. If they are uninformed and cannot answer a question, they are embarrassed and their leadership is brought into question. Thus, they need to be fully informed.

Teacher support is necessary for the smooth implementation of the intervention on a day-to-day basis. Teachers have to allow their students to leave class to attend meetings, provide instruction that was missed, and provide the students with any assignments that were given while they were out of the classroom. If the teachers are not approached before the intervention, therapists run the risk of teachers feeling forced into participating and permitting their students to miss instruction time. They can react in a less-than-helpful fashion by giving the student a zero on a test, quiz, or assignment that was missed while the child was attending therapy meetings. The teacher might not provide instruction over the class material that was missed or the teacher may purposely fail to inform the child about an assignment that was given while the child was attending therapy.

To obtain support from teachers, we have found that it is useful for the principal to introduce the psychologist and state his or her support for the services to be provided during a weekly or biweekly faculty meeting. Once again, a description of how the intervention services will impact the child, teacher and the other students is useful for gaining support. A number of the teachers (1 in 5) will have experienced a depressive episode during their lifetime, and others may have a significant other or family member who is depressed, so they are well aware of the devastating impact of the disorder. Consequently, they often are sympathetic to the children's need for therapy. It also is useful to describe the intervention program as the teachers will receive inquiries from parents and the teacher will want to be able to describe the program to these parents. Furthermore, if they express their support for the intervention, then parents are more likely to give their permission for participation.

Hassles

Unfortunately, inherent to conducting therapy in the schools is an increase in the probability that something is going to happen that would be considered to be a hassle by an administrator. It is part of working with an unhealthy population. For example, as children begin to trust their therapist they reveal abuse, neglect, parental substance abuse, and family violence. These situations lead to calls to Child Protective Services, which often leads to phone calls and visits from angry parents. Children may reveal mental health crises such as suicidal and homicidal intent, substance abuse, delusions and hallucinations. These mental health crises may lead to a recommendation for psychiatric consultation or hospitalization. When this happens, parents may become upset with the school psychologist and contact the principal. If the parents do not follow through and take care of their child's mental health crisis, the school psychologist may have to report the parent to social services for neglecting their child's health needs which once again can lead to angry parents. The principal has to be on board and prepared for such situations. In other instances, a child who needs mental health services may have a parent who also has mental health needs. The act of providing therapy for their child can elicit or invite unusual behaviors from the parent that are directed at school personnel. Ultimately, this involves the principal. A good practice is to keep the principal informed of all contacts with social services, the reasons for the reports, and all future actions that are likely to occur. It also is helpful to inform the principal of angry, or potentially antagonistic parents and the possible reasons for the upset.

Time Constraints

Evidence-based interventions are time limited, but they still require a lot of time to complete. If treatment is delivered during normal school hours, this results in time away from the classroom that naturally leads to concerns about a reduction in academic achievement for participants. For example, girls who participated in ACTION spent at least 22 hours engaged in treatment activities outside of the classroom. They also missed classes to complete pre- and posttreatment measures. While it would be possible to provide the intervention after or before school, doing so adds to the length of the school psychologist's workday and it decreases the probability that the children will regularly attend meetings. One of the advantages to conducting therapy in the schools is that the students enjoy the change in routine of going to therapy meetings rather than class. In addition, if treatment is conducted before or after school, transportation issues become a problem and reduce attendance.

When treatment is conducted during school hours, administrators and staff would like the intervention to be as short as possible so as to minimize time away from the classroom. Because this would pose a threat to the validity of the intervention, it is not possible to reduce the length of treatment. Thus, it is important to educate administrators and staff ahead of time about the realities of the duration of treatment. When following the treatment manual for an evidence-based intervention, the manual will be comprised of a set number of meetings. Typically, the interventions consist of 16 to 22 sessions. However, the meetings in the manuals are designed with the ideal client, session, rate of skill acquisition, and rate of progress in mind. They also typically include more material than can be completed within one meeting. So, it is important to let teachers and administrators know that the intervention could take two to four meetings longer than the manual indicates. The pace and number of meetings will actually vary dependent on the intellectual ability, degree of insight, introspective ability, emotional intelligence, amount of time that the child spends thinking about the treatment between meetings, the extent to which the child applies the skills to every day life, and the number of therapeutic homework assignments the child completes. Even when we prepare teachers ahead of time, we have found that some teachers still become less forgiving about the child missing class as treatment progresses.

To try to minimize the impact of missing class, we have done a number of things. We do everything possible to *not* work with students while they are in core courses. Thus, we typically work with students during "specials" or electives. We alternate or rotate meeting times so that no single class is missed regularly. Teachers are consulted when setting meeting times to minimize the disturbance to the classroom and to learning. It also prevents the therapist from wasting travel time going to meet a student and then the student is out on a field trip, taking a test, and so forth. The therapist keeps the teachers informed about the skills being taught each week and why they are important. Teachers appear to be more open to students missing class when they know that the students are acquiring an important skill. All of the initial communication is completed in person as this is more personal and enables the therapist to establish a relationship with the teacher. The therapist also asks the teacher for his or her preference for future communication (e.g., in person, notes, or email).

Since teachers are doing a lot to facilitate treatment such as reminding the child that it is time to go to the meeting, informing the child about assignments that were given, and providing instruction that was missed, it is important for the therapist to regularly express appreciation to the teacher for his or her support. Teachers especially appreciate it when the therapist leaves treats in their lounge with a note of appreciation.

School Climate

School climate varies across campuses, even within the same school district. Sometimes a principal will enthusiastically commit to interventions, but therapists will find that they have walked into a negative school climate where a distrusting relationship exists between students/parents, teachers, and school administration. We have found that this mistrust transfers into the therapy group where the students may not trust the therapist and/or one another. When this occurs, it is helpful to spend more time developing a therapeutic alliance with clients or more cohesion among group members. We also have found that it is helpful to openly discuss the concerns about trust, and the therapist's commitment to maintaining confidentiality. Of course, the limits of confidentiality are discussed too.

Meeting Space

Most schools are overcrowded and short on physical space. Often school district personnel such as speech therapists, school psychologists, and social workers have difficulty finding space to provide their services. These space limitations can adversely impact an evidence-based intervention by creating an uncomfortable space or an environment that doesn't provide the clients with privacy. Consequently, they fail to disclose therapeutically relevant information or they don't come to meetings out of fear that other students will see them meeting with the therapist or with other students of lower social status. School personnel are helpful and willing to find acceptable space, but therapists have to be prepared to work in small or less than desirable places and adapt to weekly changes. These changes cut into therapy time as the student isn't sure where to meet, so the therapist has to locate the student and then walk back to the meeting room. Once again, any loss of meeting time is a threat to the standardized administration of the treatment. Some schools will not be viable intervention sites because there is no acceptable space available for conducting group or individual therapy.

Training

The field of psychology in general is moving to an evidence-based model. Entire states (e.g., Hawaii, New York) are providing their mental health workers with training in evidence-based interventions. Insurance companies are requiring psychologists to demonstrate that they are following an evidence-based intervention to receive approval for therapy services. As noted earlier, it behooves school psychology to join or take the lead in this endeavor. Training in evidence-based interventions should be part of the core curriculum for all training programs. It will require a minimum of a two-year supervised intervention practicum that focuses on teaching the theory and methods that characterize evidence-based interventions. While a two-year sequence sounds like a lot of training, as noted in an earlier section it is consistent with the norm for the amount of therapy training that students in PhD programs receive.

As an example of the extent of training required for being able to competently deliver an evidence-based treatment, the therapists for the ACTION program had completed at least one year of supervised practicum experience in CBT, participated in a semester of didactic training in the implementation of the ACTION intervention, observed a senior therapist implement the treatment through completion, co-led an ACTION group along with a senior therapist, and then independently implemented the intervention with intense supervision. During the entire year and a half of training and as long as they ran a treatment group, they attended group supervision meetings led by the PI. Despite all of this training, based on their in-session performance, it wasn't until they independently conducted their third therapy group that they were truly competent. However, as a result of their experiences with the depression intervention, they were able to more quickly learn other evidence-based interventions.

How much training in evidence-based interventions is necessary for school psychologists who already are in practice? There isn't a simple answer to this question. It would in part depend on the amount of training that they had in evidence-based interventions during graduate training and the year of internship. Most practitioners will have to acquire their training from workshops. Typically, this involves attending a one-day training in which the intervention is described and some role-playing of treatment strategies takes place. Oftentimes, a therapist's manual is provided to the participants, but it is important to note that these manuals cannot be delivered in a simple step-by-step or cookbook fashion, and attending a one-day workshop is not adequate training to implement the manual at an acceptable level. One day of training provides the participants with knowledge about and some understanding of the intervention. The attendee becomes familiar with the treatment program, but not proficient at implementing it. There are many subtle aspects to successfully implementing these treatments. To become truly effective, attendees would have to receive continued training and supervision as they try to implement the intervention over the ensuing six months to a year. Otherwise, after a short period of using the new treatment strategies, the therapist drifts back to his or her old, more comfortable procedures. In response to this tendency, some of the new approaches to training in evidence-based interventions have included a one- or two-day training followed by a year of expert supervision. In some training models, an additional half-day or one-day workshop is completed after six months of implementing the intervention. During this follow-up training, the therapists learn more advanced skills and they have an opportunity to ask questions about their experiences implementing the intervention. The regular supervision meetings, typically conducted over the phone with an expert, keep the trainee moving forward with implementing the intervention as it was designed, and it allows the trainee to ask questions as they arise so that he or she doesn't become frustrated and revert back to prior comfortable procedures. It also enables the supervisor to provide the trainee with encouragement and support as he or she learns the new skills. In some instances, for example the Beck Institute, trainees are provided with even more intense experiences over a year including four weekend workshops and weekly individual supervision that includes feedback on therapy tapes. Thus, it appears as though the common model of continued education that is used for training psychologists in new skills is inadequate. A more intense and longer model appears to be more effective.

Parental Involvement

A number of the evidence-based interventions including the ACTION program include a parent education, training, or therapy component. Thus, parental participation is necessary for a valid delivery of the intervention. Securing a commitment for involvement from parents and getting them motivated to participate in treatment can be problematic. Furthermore, once they are engaged in the treatment program, a number of threats to the standardized delivery of the treatment may occur.

Unlike clinical trials where the parents are aware that their child has an emotional concern and bring him or her to the clinic with the hope and expectation that securing services will lead to improvement in their child's functioning, when parents are contacted by a school psychologist it may be the first time that they are informed that their child is experiencing emotional difficulties. Similarly, for most of the parents who participated in ACTION, the first contact they had with project staff was a phone call informing them that their daughter had an elevated score on the CDI and endorsed symptoms of depression on the DSM interview. Thus, in clinical trials, parents are soliciting help and are likely to be more motivated and more likely to participate in the treatment program. In contrast, when parents are informed that their child is having some difficulties and they are invited to participate in the treatment, they may not be as motivated. The impact of this difference in the method used to gain parental involvement in treatment is not known. It could contribute to parents not attending meetings, failing to engage in the meetings, failing to incorporate the therapy into their family life, failing to apply the skills outside of the meetings, and failing to complete therapeutic homework. Approximately 30% of the parents who were invited to participate in the ACTION program did not participate in the parent training.

Sometimes parents would state a priori that we had permission to work with their daughter but they would be unable to participate because they worked multiple jobs and just did not have any free time. In other cases, they stated that they would not be able to attend parent meetings because they had to provide transportation to extracurricular activities for their other children. Other parents initially agreed to participate but they didn't attend any of the meetings and they would not answer the therapist's phone calls.

While there isn't any way to know why they didn't participate, it is suspected that some chose not to participate because they thought that if they did, it was admitting that they had done something wrong that led to their child's depression. In other cases, participation was difficult because it meant that they were going to be seen in public meeting with the therapist. This was potentially embarrassing for parents who maintained a high public profile. Other parents may have believed that their child had the problem and thus she was the one who needed to be in therapy and not them. Still others may not have believed that therapy was of any benefit so they didn't attend. Based on information from personnel at school, some parents may not have attended meetings because they may have been worried that family secrets such as substance abuse would be revealed.

We did a number of things to maximize parental participation and attendance. First, we tried to have the therapist for the school complete all correspondence with the parent after the initial phone contact. The therapist worked to establish rapport and a therapeutic relationship with the parent(s) during these phone calls and meetings. The therapists arranged a meeting to give the parents in-person feedback on the results of the diagnostic interviews. Subsequently, the therapists organized and attended a meeting in the evening in which the parents gathered to complete the pretreatment measures. After treatment was underway, if the group meetings were held over or close to the dinner hour, we provided them with dinner and when the meetings were held at other times, we provided snacks and soft drinks. We always provided free childcare and transportation if needed. We also went out of our way to be flexible to arrange the meetings to fit with the parents' schedules. The therapists always called the parents the night before a meeting to remind them of the day and time of the meeting. Most parents appeared to enjoy the meetings and stated that they did. In fact, one parent stated that the meetings were the highlight of her week as she was able to talk with other adults, not have to prepare a meal and clean up afterwards, but have a free dinner, and have someone else take care of her children for a while. Parents' failure to attend the meetings also sent their daughters an unwanted message that may have supported their core beliefs of worthlessness or unlovability. If you hold the belief that no one loves you, you are in a group of girls and the other girls' parents attend the meetings that are designed to help them

and your parents don't, their failure to attend is going to confirm the belief that they really don't love you. Likewise, if you hold the belief that you are worthless and your parents fail to attend the meetings because they have other things to do such as take siblings to extracurricular activities, this is going to be evidence that supports the belief that you are worthless. Thus, failure of parents to attend may in fact have a deleterious impact on their child's functioning that goes beyond the failure to acquire important parenting skills.

Something that often is not clear from manualized treatments and the related outcome research is who should attend the meetings. Is the program designed with both parents in mind? Is it desirable to have one parent attend the meetings and then share the information with the other parent? Is it okay if the parents alternate who attends the meetings? What do you do when parents are divorced and the child shares time with both of them? What do you do if there are additional stepparents in the picture? We believe that it is helpful to have all of the child's primary environments designed to facilitate the use of the skills the girls are acquiring and to be more positive and supportive in general. Our policy is to try to include as many parents and stepparents as possible as long as they can work together in an amicable fashion. While we tried to get both parents to participate in the training, more often than not only mothers attended the meetings. Parents were informed that this would be okay, but it was surprising how many people chose this option. When the parents were divorced, if the noncustodial parent had lost his or her parental rights, they were not contacted nor invited to participate in treatment. If the noncustodial parent continued to maintain parental rights, the therapist would discuss with the custodial parent the importance of also involving the noncustodial parent in the treatment process. The custodial parent was asked if he or she thought that the two parents could work together as a team or at least interact with each other amicably. If they thought that they could, then the therapist would invite the noncustodial parent to attend meetings. Typically they would decline, but in a few instances we had both the custodial and noncustodial parents attending the meetings. In other cases, the noncustodial parent and his or her new spouse would attend the meetings. While rare, it was possible to have the mother, stepfather, father, and stepmother all attending meetings. If it was apparent that the parents could not withhold their hostility towards one another, we would set ground rules for the meetings. Usually, this was adequate.

PROCEDURES FOR MAXIMIZING THE EFFECTIVENESS OF TREATMENT

School psychologists typically provide services to children who have qualified for special education under the handicapping condition of SED. As noted earlier, these are the children who are experiencing the most severe psychological disorders (Garland et al., 2001). They may in fact be more severely impaired than the children who participated in the original clinical trials that have been used to establish the efficacy of the treatment. More severely impaired youth may require a more intense intervention, or at least one that maximizes the likelihood that it will be effective. What are the variables that maximize treatment efficacy? Some research has tried to focus on identifying factors that work better for individuals with certain characteristics, as these factors moderate treatment efficacy (meaning they interact with treatment to predict treatment outcome). Other research has examined the mechanisms of CBT that produce change as these mechanisms are mediators and theoretically account for the intervention effects. Unfortunately, this research has failed to consistently identify any moderators or mediators of treatment outcome for depressed youth. Thus, we are left to conjecture about the variables that may be focused on to maximize efficacy.

Characteristics of the therapist appear to play a significant role in therapy outcome (Kazdin, Bass, Ayers, & Rodgers, 1990). These therapist qualities are necessary but not sufficient for producing change (Beck, Rush, Shaw, & Emery, 1979). A meta-analysis of child treatment studies demonstrates the importance of the child-therapist relationship (Shirk & Karver, 2003). Existence of a good therapeutic relationship along with the identification of common goals, comprise the therapeutic alliance. The presence of a good working alliance may encourage the client to engage in therapeutic activities in session. Some of the important qualities of the therapist include warmth, accurate empathy, and genuineness (Beck et al., 1979). The therapeutic relationship is built through establishing trust, rapport, establishment of a collaborative context, and the child viewing the therapist as a helper (Shirk & Karver, 2006).

Kendall suggests that treatment efficacy is enhanced when the therapist is guided by theory (Kendall, 2006). As noted earlier, this represents a training issue and highlights the importance of providing extensive training in the theories that form the foundation of the evidence-based interventions. It also appears to be important to tie the theory to the intervention and to explain this relationship to the client. In other words, it is helpful within treatment to explain in developmentally sensitive terms how the intervention is going to help the child client. Taking this one step further, Stark et al. (in press) note the importance of theory guiding case conceptualization and of the conceptualization guiding the therapist through implementation of the intervention. The conceptualization helps the therapist to identify information that is important to attend to, it helps the therapist to recognize the critical targets for change within the child and the significant environments within which that child functions, and it helps the therapist to prioritize his or her work.

One of the better predictors of treatment outcome is the extent to which the child is engaged in treatment. Engagement can be maximized for youth by providing them with developmentally sensitive and gender-specific treatment materials. For example, the language used, the concepts discussed, and so on would vary according to the child's developmental level. Similarly, the issues discussed and possibly targeted for change would vary depending upon the age and gender of the child. A therapist might focus more on interpersonal conflict when working with an adolescent girl while the focus might be on personal competence for an adolescent boy. In the ACTION program the therapeutic activities were designed to be developmentally sensitive and gender specific. An overarching design feature to the ACTION program is that the therapeutic concepts being taught to the children are illustrated through an experiential activity rather than taught to the children through a didactic presentation. Thus the children actually experienced within the session the benefits of the therapeutic strategies. For example, when the group members are feeling down, the therapist illustrates the impact of the coping strategy of doing something fun and distracting by first getting a mood rating for each girl and then taking the girls outside to play with hoola hoops followed by another mood rating. Inevitably, their moods would be elevated by a few minutes of having fun.

An oft-forgotten variable in conducting therapy with children and adolescents is that they don't know how to be good clients. In other words, they don't know what they are supposed to do to maximize treatment gains. Children often think that they can be passive recipients of therapy and that they don't have to do anything beyond being present with the therapist to get better. As part of the ACTION program, the therapists systematically shape the participants' behavior and relevant cognitions to help them to maximize what they get out of treatment. The therapists reinforce the children for attending, asking questions, raising problems and concerns, sharing thoughts and feelings, completing therapeutic homework, thinking about treatment between sessions, looking within themselves to identify maladaptive thoughts, behaviors, and emotions, and so forth. In addition, since the intervention is delivered within a group format, the child's interpersonal behavior is shaped to enhance group cohesion and an overall sense of safety and support. The therapists will use praise within the sessions as the children exhibit desirable behaviors and they will highlight specific behaviors during the "catch the positive" activity completed near the end of every meeting.

Another developmental difference that has not been adequately discussed in the literature is the spacing of therapy meetings for children. Given their tendency to forget very quickly critical events, it is beneficial for children to meet twice a week with the therapist. When we piloted the ACTION treatment, we discovered that when we switched from a twice weekly meeting format midway through treatment to a weekly meeting format, the degree to which the girls were engaged in therapy and the likelihood that they would apply the skills to their daily lives decreased. Thus, we switched back to twice-a-week meetings and their engagement once again improved. Given the time constraints faced by school psychologists, twice-weekly meetings make it even more difficult for us to provide effective therapy in the schools. Perhaps we are caught in a conundrum. To help administrators and parents to recognize the importance of investing more time in therapy it is necessary to provide the students with effective treatments. To be able to provide effective interventions, more time is needed than may be available.

Treatment manuals are designed with a prototypical depressed child, anxious child, child with a conduct disorder or other disorders in mind. The treatment manual has to be brought to life with the individual child client in mind. This is easier when the therapist develops and follows a case conceptualization. Treatment manuals have activities, points of discussion, and other suggestions for each meeting. However, these examples are used to illustrate what might be done to teach a specific skill or therapeutic concept. The therapist is much more effective when he or she uses what the child brings to each meeting as the context in which to teach the child a skill and how to apply it, or about a therapeutic concept such as the relationship between thinking and feeling. In order to make the intervention relevant, real, and truly useful for the child, the treatment has to be individualized.

While research into the moderators of treatment efficacy has not suggested that including parents in treatment adds to the efficacy of psychotherapy for depression, it may be an important adjunct to the treatment of anxiety disorders and is critical for the treatment of externalizing disorders. It makes intuitive sense that systematically changing the child's primary environment would increase the efficacy of the intervention and maximize the chances of producing a change that will be maintained. In addition, parents can help their children to apply the things that they are learning in therapy meetings. Thus, they help the children to experience the benefits of treatment over longer periods of time and across environments.

SUMMARY AND CONCLUSIONS

An unfulfilled need exists for the delivery of therapy services in the schools. School psychologists, as well as the administrators and teachers in their schools, would like more time spent providing therapy for students. However, demands to meet the other needs of special education students is, in part, responsible for limiting the amount of time spent conducting therapy. The amount of therapy that school psychologists deliver also is related to the amount of relevant training and supervision they have had. It has been suggested that if school psychologists delivered evidence-based interventions, thus, more effective interventions, administrators would be more likely to make therapy a priority. It behooves the field of school psychology to emphasize evidence-based interventions in university training programs and for practicing school psychologists to receive continuing education in evidence-based interventions. Research indicates that typical community-based interventions are no more effective than the change that occurs due to the passing of time. In contrast, evidence-based interventions produce more changes and the changes that occur are achieved more quickly.

While it would be advantageous for school psychologists to adopt an evidence-based approach to therapy, there have not been any reports of how to transport an evidence-based intervention from the laboratory to the school setting. The ACTION treatment program for depressed girls is an evidence-based intervention that is designed for the schools. While we implemented this treatment program in the schools over five years with approximately 160 depressed youth, a number of potential impediments to implementing the intervention as designed were encountered. As we encountered the impediments we developed procedures for minimizing or eliminating the problems. The most common impediments that were encountered included (1) failure to obtain administrators' and staff support for therapy services, (2) principals' need to be informed, (3) unexpected and expected hassles for administrators and staff, (4) time constraints, (5) expecting too much from teachers, (6) school climate that was characterized by mistrust, (7) lack of or inappropriate space for therapy, (8) lack of training of school psychologists, (9) difficulty getting parents involved in treatment.

School psychologists spend most of their time working with students who receive special education services including students who qualify as SED. These youth are the most severely impaired children that enter the mental health system. Thus, it is imperative that the school psychologists are aware of variables that can maximize the efficacy of their interventions. The following variables were discussed: (1) the child-therapist relationship, (2) the treatment is guided by theory, (3) a theory-based case conceptualization guides treatment, (4) the therapy is engaging, (5) the participants are taught how to be good clients, (6) the manual is delivered in a flexible fashion, (7) the meetings with children are held twice a week, and (8) the parents are encouraged to be involved in treatment.

REFERENCES

Addis, M. E., & Krasnow, A. D. (2000). A national survey of practicing psychologists' attitudes toward psychotherapy treatment manuals. *Journal of Consulting and Clinical Psychology, 68*(2), 331–339.

Ambrosini, P. J., & Dixon, J. F. (2000). *Schedule for affective disorders & schizophrenia for school age children (6–18 years)—Kiddie-SADS (KSADS) (present state and lifetime version) K-SADS-IVR (Revision of K-SADS-IIIR)*. Unpublished manuscript. Eastern Pennsylvania Psychiatric Institute, Philadelphia, PA.

Andrade, A. R., Lambert, E. W., & Bickman, L. (2000). Dose effect in psychotherapy: Outcomes associated with negligible treatment. *Journal of the American Academy of Child and Adolescent Psychiatry, 39*(2), 161–168.

Anglin, T. M., Naylor, K. E., & Kaplan, D. W. (1996). Comprehensive school-based health care: High school students' use of medical, mental health, and substance abuse services. *Pediatrics, 97,* 318–330.

Bardone, A. M., Moffitt, T. E., Caspi, A., Dickson, N., Stanton, W. R., & Silva, P. A. (1998). Adult physical health outcomes of adolescent girls with conduct disorder, depression, and anxiety [Electronic Version]. *Journal of the American Academy of Child and Adolescent Psychiatry. 37*(6), 594–601.

Beck, A. T., Rush, A. J., Shaw, B. F., & Emery, G. (1979). *Cognitive therapy of depression*. New York: Guilford Press.

Bickman, L., Noser, K., & Summerfelt, W. T. (1999). Long-term effects of a system of care on children and adolescents. *Journal of Behavioral Health Services & Research, 26*(2), 185–202.

Bramlett, R. K., Murphy, J. J., Johnson, J., & Wallingsford, L. (2002). Contemporary practices in school psychology: A national survey of roles and referral problems. *Psychology in the Schools, 39*(3), 327–335.

Briggs-Gowan, M. J., Horwitz, S. M., & McCue, S. (2000). Mental health in pediatric settings: Distribution of factors related to service use. *Journal of the American Academy of Child and Adolescent Psychiatry, 39*(7), 841–849.

Brown, D. T., & Minke, K. M. (1986). School psychology graduate training: A comprehensive analysis. *American Psychologist, 41*(12), 1328–1338.

Burns, B. J., Costello, E. J., Angold, A., Tweed, D., Stangl, D., Farmer, E. M. Z., et al. (1995). Children's mental health services use across service sectors. *Health Affairs, 14*(3), 147–159.

Burns, B. J., Hoagwood, K., & Mrazek, P. J. (1999). Effective treatment for mental disorders in children and adolescents. *Clinical Child and Family Psychology Review, 2*(4), 199–254.

Capaldi, D. M., & Stoolmiller, M. (1999). Co-occurrence of conduct problems and depressive symptoms in early adolescent boys: III. Prediction to young-adult adjustment [Electronic Version]. *Development and Psychopathology, 11,* 59–84.

Chambless, D. L., & Ollendick, T. H. (2001). Empirically supported psychological interventions: Controversies and evidence. *Annual Review of Psychology, 52*, 685–716.

Connor-Smith, J. K, & Weisz, J. R. (2003). Applying treatment outcome research in clinical practice: Techniques for adapting interventions to the real world. *Child and Adolescent Mental Health, 8*, 3–10.

Costello, E. J., Egger, H., & Angold, A. (2005). 10-year research update review: The epidemiology of child and adolescent psychiatric disorders: I. Methods and public health burden. *Journal of the American Academy of Child and Adolescent Psychiatry, 44*(10), 972–986.

Costello, E. J., Messer, S. C., Bird, H. R., Cohen, P., & Reinherz, H. Z. (1998). The prevalence of serious emotional disturbance: A re-analysis of community studies. *Journal of Child and Family Studies, 7*(4), 411–432.

Doll, B. (1996). Prevalence of psychiatric disorders in children and youth: An agenda for advocacy by school psychology. *School Psychology Quarterly, 11*(1), 20–46.

Earls, F., Robins, L. N., Stiffman, A. R. & Powell, J. (1989). Comprehensive health care for high-risk adolescents: An evaluation study. *American Journal of Public Health, 79*, 999–1005.

Elias, M. J., Zins, J. E., Graczyk, P. A., & Weissberg, R. P. (2003). Implementation, sustainability, and scaling up of social-emotional and academic innovations in public schools. *School Psychology Review, 32*(3), 303–319.

Fergusson, D. M., & Woodward, L. J. (2002). Mental health, educational, and social role outcomes of adolescents with depression [Electronic Version]. *Archives of General Psychiatry, 59*, 225–231.

Fleming, C. B., Haggerty, K. P., Catalano, R. F., Harachi, T. W., Mazza, J. J., & Gruman, D. H. (2005). Do social and behavioral characteristics targeted by preventive interventions predict standardized test scores and grades? [Electronic Version]. *Journal of School Health, 75*(9), 342–349.

Garland, A. F., Hough, R. L., McCabe, K. M., Yeh, M., Wood, P. A., & Aarons, G. A. (2001). Prevalence of psychiatric disorders in youths across five sectors of care. *Journal of the American Academy of Child and Adolescent Psychiatry, 40*(4), 409–418.

Goldfried, M. R., & Wolfe, B. E. (1996). Psychotherapy practice and research: Repairing a strained alliance. *American Psychologist, 51*, 1007–1016.

Hoagwood, K., & Johnson, J. (2003). School psychology: A public health framework I. From evidenced-based practices to evidenced-based policies. *Journal of School Psychology, 41*(1), 3–21.

Jensen, P. S., Ryan, N. D. & Prien, R. (1992). Psychopharmacology of child and adolescent major depression: Present status and future directions. *Journal of Child and Adolescent Psychopharmacology, 2*, 31–45.

Kazdin, A. E., Bass, D., Ayers, W. A., & Rodgers, A. (1990). Empirical and clinical focus of child and adolescent psychotherapy research. *Journal of Consulting and Clinical Psychology, 58*(6), 729–740.

Kazdin, A. E., & Kendall, P. C. (1998). Current progress and future plans for developing effective treatments: Comments and perspectives. *Journal of Clinical Child Psychology, 27*, 217–226.

Kendall, P. C. (2006). Guiding theory for therapy with children and adolescents. In P.C. Kendall (Ed.), *Child and Adolescent Therapy: Cognitive-Behavioral Procedures* (pp. 3–30). New York, NY: Guilford Press.

Kovacs, M. (1992). *Children's depression inventory (CDI) manual*. North Tonawanda, NY: Multi-Health Systems, Inc.

Kratochwill, T. C., & Stoiber, K. C. (2000). Empirically-supported interventions and school psychology: Conceptual and practical issues: Part II. *School Psychology Quarterly, 15*, 233–253.

Last, C. G., & Hansen, C. (1997). Anxious children in adulthood: A prospective study of adjustment [Electronic Version]. *Journal of the American Academy of Child and Adolescent Psychiatry, 36*(5), 645–652.

Leaf, P. J., Alegria, M., Cohen, P., Goodman, S. H., Horwitz, S. M., Hoven, C.W., et al. (1996). Mental health service use in the community and schools: Results from the four-community MECA study. *Journal of the Academy of Child and Adolescent Psychiatry, 35*, 889–897.

Lund, A. R., Reschly, D. J., & Martin, L. M. (1998). School psychology personnel needs: Correlates of current patterns and historical trends. *School Psychology Review, 27*(1), 106–120.

Minke, K. M., & Brown, D. T. (1996). Preparing psychologists to work with children: A comparison of curricula in child-clinical and school psychology programs. *Professional Psychology: Research and Practice, 27*(6), 631–634.

Nastasi, B. K., Varjas, K., Bernstein, R., & Pluymert, K. (1998). Mental health programming and the role of school psychologists. *School Psychology Review, 27*(2), 217–232.

National Institute of Mental Health. (2001). *Blueprint for change: research on child and adolescent mental health*. Retrieved June 7, 2007 from www.nimh.nih.gov/childhp/councildesc.cfm.

Office of Applied Studies. (2006). Results from the 2005 national survey on drug use and health: National findings. Retrieved June 6, 2007 from oas.samhsa.gov/NSDUH/2k5NSDUH/2k5results.htm.

Prout, H. T., Alexander, S. P., Fletcher, C. E., Memis, J. P., & Miller, D. W. (1993). Counseling and psychotherapy services provided by school psychologists: An analysis of patterns and in practice. *Journal of School Psychology, 31*(2), 309–316.

Pryzwansky, W. B., Harris, J. F., & Jackson, J. H. (1984). Therapy/counseling practices of urban school psychologists. *Professional Psychology: Research and Practice, 15*(3), 396–404.

Rao, U., Ryan, N. D., Birmaher, B., Dahl, R. E., Williamson, D. E., Kaufman, J., et al. (1995). Unipolar depression in adolescents: Clinical outcome in adulthood. *Journal of the American Academy of Child and Adolescent Psychiatry, 34*(5), 566–578.

Reschly, D. J. (2000). The present and future status of school psychology in the United States. *School Psychology Review, 29*(4), 507–522.

Reynolds, W. M. (1986). A model for screening and the identification of depressed children and adolescents in school settings. *Professional School Psychology, 1*(2), 117–129.

Riley, A. W., Ensminger, M. E., Green, B., & Kang, M. (1998). Social role functioning by adolescents with psychiatric disorders. *Journal of the American Academy of Child and Adolescent Psychiatry, 37*(6), 620–628.

Romans, J. S. C., Boswell, D. L., Carlozzi, A. F., & Ferguson, D. B. (1995). Training and supervision practices in clinical, counseling, and school psychology programs. *Professional Psychology: Research and Practice, 26*(4), 407–412.

Sawyer, M. G., Arney, F. M., Baghurst, P. A., Clark, J. J., Graetz, B. W., Kosky, R. J., et al. (2001). The mental health of young people in Australia: Key findings from the child and adolescent component of the national survey of mental health and well-being. *Australian and New Zealand Journal of Psychiatry, 35*(6), 806–814.

Shirk, S. R., & Karver, M. (2003). Prediction of treatment outcome from relationship variables in child and adolescent therapy: A meta-analytic review. *Journal of Consulting and Clinical Psychology, 71*(3), 452–464.

Shirk, S. R., & Karver, M. (2006). Process issues in cognitive-behavioral therapy for youth. In P. C. Kendall (Ed.), *Child and Adolescent Therapy: Cognitive-Behavioral Procedures* (pp. 465–491). New York, NY: Guilford Press.

Society of Clinical Child and Adolescent Psychology & the Network on Youth Mental Health. (2007). *Evidenced-based treatments for children and adolescents*. Retrieved June 8, 2007 from www.effectivechildtherapy.com.

Stark, K. D., Hargrave, J., Hersh, B., Greenberg, M., Herren, J., & Fisher, M. (In press). Treatment of youth depression: The ACTION program. In J. R. Z. Abela & B. L. Hankin (Eds.), *Child and adolescent depression: Causes, treatment and prevention*. New York: Guilford Press.

Stark, K. D., Simpson, J., Schnoebelen, S., Glenn, R., Hargrave, J., & Molnar, J. (2006a). *ACTION Workbook*. Ardmore, PA: Workbook Publishing.

Stark, K. D., Schnoebelen, S., Simpson, J., Hargrave, J., Molnar, J., & Glenn, R. (2006b). *Treating depressed children: Therapist manual for ACTION*. Ardmore, PA: Workbook Publishing.

Stoiber, K. C., & Kratochwill, T. R. (2000). Empirically-supported interventions and school psychology: Rationale and methodological issues: Part I. *School Psychology Quarterly, 15*, 75–105.

U.S. Department of Health and Human Services. (1999). *Mental health: A report of the Surgeon General*. Rockville, MD. Author.

Watkins, M. W., Crosby, E. G., & Pearson, J. L. (2001). Role of the school psychologist: perceptions of school staff. *School Psychology International, 22*(1), 64–73.

Weersing, V. R., & Weisz, J. R. (2002). Community clinic treatment of depressed youth: Benchmarking usual care against CBT clinical trials. *Journal of Consulting and Clinical Psychology, 70*, 299–310.

Weiss, B., Catron, T., & Harris, V. (2000). A 2-year follow-up of the effectiveness of traditional child psychotherapy. *Journal of Consulting and Clinical Psychology, 68*(6), 1094–1101.

Weissman, M. M, Wolk, S., Goldstein, R. B., Moreau, D., Adams, P., Greenwald, S., et al. (1999). Depressed adolescents grown up. *Journal of the American Medical Association, 281*(18), 1707–1713.

Weisz, J. R. (2000). Agenda for child and adolescent psychotherapy research: On the need to put science into practice. *Archives of General Psychiatry, 57*, 837–838.

Weisz, J. R., Donenberg, G. R., Han, S. S., & Weiss, B. (1995). Bridging the gap between laboratory and clinic in child and adolescent psychotherapy. *Journal of Consulting and Clinical Psychology, 63*, 688–701.

Weisz, J. R., Weiss, B., Han, S. S., Granger, D. A., & Morton, T. (1995). Effects of psychotherapy with children and adolescents revisited: A meta-analysis of treatment outcome studies. *Psychological Bulletin, 117*, 450–468.

CHAPTER 30

PARTNERING WITH FAMILIES
FOR EDUCATIONAL SUCCESS

KARLA BUERKLE, ELIZABETH M. WHITEHOUSE AND SANDRA L. CHRISTENSON
University of Minnesota, Twin Cities

INTRODUCTION

Partnering with families is salient for children's educational success. Clear evidence of the reciprocal influences of home and school on learning provides a framework for what we believe is a necessary paradigm shift in working with families (Christenson, 2004; Comer, Haynes, Joyner, & Ben-Avie, 1996). Engaging families in children's learning is no longer simply desirable; rather, families are necessary partners in helping youth reach their academic potential (Pianta & Walsh, 1996). As children's primary socialization environments, home and school are key foundations for learning and healthy development, and effective partnerships between these two settings are essential.

Partnering with families becomes critical to school success when we consider that children spend 9% of their time breathing school air and the remaining 91% of their time from birth to age 18 outside of school hours (Walberg, 1984). The impact of out-of-school time can no longer be ignored for performance in school. The passage of the No Child Left Behind (NCLB) Act requires school accountability for the improvement of all students, including those with disabilities, English Language Learners (ELL), and those living in poverty, homeless, or highly mobile (U.S. Department of Education, 2001). How students are socialized as learners differentiates high- and low-performing ethnically diverse students (Bempechat, Graham, & Jimenez, 1999); mediates attendance, which predicts achievement for highly mobile students (Buerkle, 1997); and impacts attendance and school completion rates for students with and without disabilities (Christenson & Havsy, 2004; Lehr, Sinclair, & Christenson,

2004; Sinclair, Christenson, & Thurlow, 2005). Considering the 3 Rs—students', parents', and educators' rights, roles, and responsibilities—is integral to conceptualizing family-school connections that promote learning outcomes. The family-school relationship is the foundation for clarifying rights, defining and negotiating roles, and sharing responsibility for consistent messages and support across environments to optimize students' learning. If families remain uninvolved, educators can continue to provide information on children's learning, invite parents to partner, and access resources for students and the family. Schools steeped in a partnership approach may have the best chance to meet the challenge of creating a culture of success for all students.

In this chapter, we provide the scientific basis for partnering with families and a framework for partnering to enhance students' educational success. Our mesosystemic orientation emphasizes the unique contributions that families and schools bring to partnerships, as we believe a productive partnership can take many forms. The partnership cannot, therefore, be prescribed or static; rather it must be flexible and responsive (Christenson & Sheridan, 2001). Building a strong foundation relies on culturally relevant and personally meaningful relationships among stakeholders—students, families, and educators—and clearly defining shared goals, shared contributions, and shared accountability (Fantuzzo, Tighe, & Childs, 2000). We promote our conceptual framework for developing effective partnerships based on a systems-ecological perspective, as this not only allows responsiveness to individual families' needs, but also best utilizes the strengths of school psychologists as systems consultants. Okagaki's (2001) model of minority children's school achievement is relevant as it underscores a systemic orientation; specifically, how the form and perceived function of the school, the family's cultural norms and beliefs about education and development, and the characteristics of the child interact to foster students' academic identity. These concepts are theorized to contribute to outcomes for motivation to learn and school performance. Finally, we view the primary goal of school-family partnerships as not simply to involve families, but rather to enhance learning opportunities, educational progress, and school success for students in four domains: academic, social, emotional, and behavioral (Christenson & Sheridan, 2001). Ideally, partnering with parents to enhance child outcomes is viewed with a preventive, solution-oriented focus that creates conditions to facilitate student learning and constructive relationships over time, because learning and behavioral difficulties for students, as school psychologists know, do not go away with one family-school problem-solving session.

RATIONALE FOR PARTNERING WITH FAMILIES

Historical Background

The evolution of families' roles in supporting children and youth in schooling has undergone much transformation. Originally evoked by historical change, education went from a privilege enjoyed by few to availability among the masses. As schooling became more mainstream, the education system needed to adjust to meet growing needs. Children came to school with a variety of abilities, from disparate environments and circumstances, and with differing expectations for their school experiences. Families, also, varied in their view of schooling. Value placed on education influenced attendance, work completion, and quality of work. Some families integrated schooling into their lives by fostering connections between book learning and day-to-day experiences, while others saw schools as responsible for their children from eight to three o'clock and left schools to their job of teaching, preferring to be left to their job of parenting.

Several key theorists have provided a foundation for the evolution of separate responsibilities for home and school, from parent involvement in education to partnership with families. Epstein (1987) described "spheres of influence" as overlapping or not to illustrate models of separate or shared responsibilities for students. The nature of the interaction may change based on grade level and student, family, or school need. A separate responsibility approach is more likely to involve a division of labor between home and school. She argued there is no pure school or pure family time, as children and adolescents demonstrate behaviors across settings regardless of the overlap present in their home-school situation. Bronfenbrenner (1986) articulated his well-known theory of "nested connections" between children's environments and multiple influences on children's development. Specifically, the home-school relationship is a significant factor for learning, as are separate or consistent influences from home and school environments. Finally, Coleman (1987) contended that the home and school provide different and critical inputs to children's success in school. He described the home as teaching children the value of schooling, the importance of effort, and a positive sense of self. Input from school allows new learning opportunities and demands, and rewards performance. According to Coleman, the interaction between home and school leads to differential socialization outcomes. Schools do make a difference for children; however, they do not have an equal effect on children. Coleman also noted that there is greater variation in family resources than school resources for children's learning.

A growing awareness of family influences on children's educational success, including school readiness, developmental progress, motivation to learn, and school completion, spurred a dramatic increase in family involvement in education (Berger, 1991). Researchers found fertile ground when exploring the impact of family factors on children's development and learning. The importance of involving families in children's education to improve success became well documented (Christenson & Buerkle, 1999; Henderson & Berla, 1994).

While schools' connections with families have improved, some families' and children's needs have become increasingly difficult to meet. Currently, the dramatic changes in family structure and function, the influx of immigrant students and corresponding rise in non-English-speaking children and families, the culturally diverse student population, and high mobility and poverty rates in many schools are challenging successful parent engagement with children's learning (Bempechat et al., 1999; Liontos, 1992). Continuing on our path to improving every student's educational success requires another shift in our thinking—the development of ongoing, dynamic partnerships among educators, students, and their families.

Empirical Evidence for Benefit of Partnerships

The effect of family and home influences on student performance in school is undisputed. There is a multitude of evidence supporting family involvement in education for promoting children's competencies across academic, social, behavioral, and emotional domains (for a complete review, see Christenson & Buerkle, 1999). Although the role of family in promoting student performance in school and better developmental outcomes is agreed upon, much of the empirical data base is correlational, showing significant, positive findings in the .40 to .70 range (Christenson & Peterson, 1998).

Family Involvement in Schooling Promotes Children's Competencies

Family involvement in schooling has been associated with many and varied benefits for students, including improvement in grades, test scores, attitude toward schoolwork, completion of homework, self-esteem, academic perseverance, and participation in classroom activities. Benefits for students also have included fewer placements in special education, greater enrollment in postsecondary education programs, higher attendance rates, lower dropout rates, fewer suspensions, realization of exceptional talents, and a higher probability of avoiding high-risk behavior in adolescents (Christenson & Sheridan, 2001; Henderson & Mapp, 2002). The correlations across studies are significant, positive, and moderate; strength for the database comes from the fact that the findings converge in a similar direction. Because of the correlational nature of the database, we can conclude only that parents facilitate, but do not determine, their children's level of success.

Home Influences Are Significant Correlates of Student Performance Across Domains

Student achievement in academic, social, and behavioral domains may be positively influenced by specific home practices. For example, three factors that are under parental control explained nearly 90% of the variance in mean achievement in 37 states and the District of Columbia: attendance, variety of reading materials in the home, and amount of television viewing (Barton & Coley, 1992). Intuitively, family involvement in specific educational practices would help raise children's academic performance, as homework help, communication with teachers, and increased presence in children's schools and classrooms all strengthen a focus on learning along with practice skills. For example, Heller and Fantuzzo (1993) found that combining parent involvement with peer tutoring in mathematics showed the greatest achievement in math scores, better work habits, and higher levels of motivation. In addition to raising children's confidence with peers and in the classroom, high levels of satisfaction were reported by parents, teachers, and children.

Social competence often predicts successful adaptation and functioning in school, and family factors impact the development of children's social competencies such as interpersonal skills, coping styles, motivation, and values (Coleman, 1987; Saunders & Green, 1993). School-based research done by Reynolds (1989) has demonstrated the positive impact of family involvement on social/emotional maturity (e.g., readiness to learn, work completion, rule following, working well with others) and motivation to learn. Based on longitudinal study results, the researchers asserted that parents' satisfaction with schools and expectations for success were strongly related to children's social and academic competence (Reynolds, Mavrogenes, Hagemann, & Bezruczko, 1993).

Behavioral competence is a given for a successful student; when children exhibit noncompliance or disruptive behavior, their relationships with both peers and teachers suffer and academic success is much harder to attain. Within a framework of shared responsibility, Sheridan and colleagues developed a partnership model between parents and teachers using collaborative problem solving to address behavioral concerns. The conjoint behavioral consultation evidence-based model utilizes a consultant to help home and school solve behavioral problems that interfere with school functioning (Sheridan & Kratochwill, 1992). For children with diagnoses of behavioral disorders such as attention deficit hyperactivity disorder (ADHD), conduct disorder (CD), and oppositional defiant disorder (ODD), family-based interventions such as family therapy and behavior management training have shown positive effects on school adjustment and in redirecting students to success in school (Barkley, Guevremont, Anastopoulos, & Fletcher, 1992; Reid & Patterson, 1989; Webster-Stratton &

Hammond, 1990). When parents, teachers, and students communicate, meet, and plan together, fewer behavioral problems and improved school experiences result (Webster-Stratton, 1993).

Parent Engagement with Children's Learning Has Clear Benefits

Evidence of benefits for key stakeholders—students, parents, and teachers—are a very positive sign for establishing the necessary conditions for creating partnerships. Benefits for teachers include recognition from parents for better interpersonal and teaching skills, higher ratings of performance from principals, and greater job satisfaction. It has been shown that parents experience an increased sense of self-efficacy, better understanding of school policies and practices, heightened appreciation of their role in their children's education, improved communication with their children, and more support from school personnel (Christenson & Sheridan, 2001). We also know that benefits for stakeholders vary as a function of the ways parents and teachers connect. For example, Epstein (1995) has shown that ways to help families establish home learning environments was associated with better attendance for students, increased teacher awareness of parental challenges, and more parental respect for teachers. Activities that develop parent leaders and include parents in school decisions have been associated with increased student awareness of family representation in decisions, higher parent ownership of policy changes, and greater teacher awareness of parental perspectives for policy development and decisions. The most evidence for improving student achievement and behavior exists for programs that enhance home support for learning, an important finding given the finite resources in schools. Edwards (2004) has referred to these efforts as making positive "strategic connections" to children's learning.

The Distinction Between Family Status and Process Variables Is Critical to Enhance Student Outcomes

This knowledge is helpful to target NCLB requirements. We know that process variables—what families do—have a stronger impact on educational success than status variables—who families are. Families bolster children's achievement when they provide a positive educational experience through strong, consistent values about the importance of education; demonstrate a willingness to help children and intervene at school; and become

involved. These types of process actions predict up to 60% of the variance in achievement, whereas status variables of family structure and social class predict up to 25% of achievement variance (Kellaghan, Sloane, Alvarez, & Bloom, 1993). This distinction helps explain that there are high performing low-income students in our schools, and it illustrates how increasing home support for learning is an alterable variable through responsive interventions.

Positive, Specific Actions by Families Are Identifiable

This curriculum of the home (Christenson & Buerkle, 1999), comprised of specific actions or identifiable patterns of family life, supports school performance. Although there is a long laundry list of discrete supportive family actions, there is no consensus about the prescription for the precise way families facilitate student learning. Clark (1983) demonstrated the seminal nature of both parent attitudes (e.g., "I expect you to do well in school") and parent behaviors (e.g., "I will communicate with your teachers and support your learning"). While there are several ways for families to support children's learning, interest is typically at a thematic level. For example, home support for learning programs could be designed with a focus on ways parents *structure* (e.g., priority given to schoolwork, consistent monitoring of how time is spent), *support* (e.g., parental responsibility for assisting, modeling learning by reading and using math, expression of encouragement), *set expectations* (e.g., use of effort and ability attributions, interest in and establishment of standards for schoolwork), and *provide an enriching environment* (e.g., frequent dialogue, opportunities for good language habits, and reading with children). One study identified parent expectations, talking about schoolwork, providing learning materials, and learning opportunities outside of school as the most influential family actions (Peng & Lee, 1992). Explanatory variables for the academic achievement of adolescents from diverse ethnic groups include parental attitudes and expectations plus student perception of parental expectations (Patrikakou, 1997), along with parental monitoring and supervision (Dornbusch & Ritter, 1992).

The Power of Out-of-School Time for Student Performance in School Cannot be Ignored

For example, low income, high achieving students in grades K–12 in urban districts were involved, on average, 25 hours per week in constructive learning activities, activities that involved thinking and supportive guidance from an adult or peer (Clark, 1990). In a large longitudinal study of students in the Baltimore Schools, Alexander, Entwisle, and Olson (2001) have shown that low-income children made comparable grade equivalent gains in reading and math during the school year as did middle-income children. Differences in overall student achievement were explained as a seasonal effect, where the summer experiential learning and home resources afforded to middle-income children contributed. Very sobering was their finding that the gap in achievement between the low- and middle-income students widened across school years, due to significant differences in out-of-school learning time. The Harvard Family Research Project (2006) described "complementary learning" as the conceptual framework for their focus addressing the achievement gap. Complementary learning refers to a linked network of supports beyond school that work toward consistent learning and developmental outcomes for children. Linked supports include families, school programs, community institutions, and out-of-school programs and activities, with functions changing over time as the child matures. Their research series "Family Involvement Makes a Difference" provides evidence and policy recommendations for working with children of all ages. Finally, partnering with families needs to begin early—preferably prior to kindergarten enrollment. Hart and Risley (1995) observed parent-child interaction in 42 families who differed in terms of income. They found that children ages 1–3 in professional families heard 2,150 words per hour, whereas children in working-class (1,250) and welfare (620) families were exposed to many less words. The cumulative language experience by age 3 differed in amount and kind; these differences were significantly correlated with children's reading/language performance at ages 9–10.

The Intensity of Family Involvement Is Especially Critical to Strengthen Student Achievement for Diverse Families

Encouraging family involvement at home and with supportive school professionals involves building relationships and connecting families with needed training and resources. According to the research synthesis on diverse families, defined as families from varying backgrounds in three categories: racial or ethnic, culture (including language), and socioeconomic status, all families hold high aspirations and concerns for their children's school success (Boethel, 2003). However, there is collective evidence to suggest that diverse families define involvement broadly, encompassing efforts to support the well-being of the whole child rather than only academic achievement, which teachers emphasize. Also, nonwhite families and, to a lesser extent, low-income families tend to play a more limited role at school in favor of more involvement at home when compared to white, "mainstream" families. Diverse families tend to seldom initiate contact with school professionals and are unquestioning of white middle-class schools.

Mattingly, Prislin, McKenzie, Rodriquez, and Kayzar (2002) found that most intervention programs focused on changing parent behavior and home support for learning rather than changing teacher practices or school structures. In contrast, Boethel (2003) strongly advocated for both building relationships among schools, communities, and families and helping families strengthen student achievement. With respect to the latter, it is essential to understand that the depth of involvement at home for diverse families may be less. For example, low-income families irrespective of racial, ethnic, or cultural background, strive to support their children's learning, however their levels of involvement are lower than those of families who do not live in poverty. The intensity of parent-child interaction from birth paired with limited knowledge of how to foster early literacy for many families creates stark differences in children's vocabulary and experiences at kindergarten entrance. Closing this preexisting condition demands a more intense outreach to many families. Hence, Boethel recommended the following strategies: "provide families with training and resources to support early literacy, help families use specific communication and monitoring strategies to support their children's learning, encourage and support students' involvement in a range of school- and community-sponsored extracurricular and after-school activities, and help low-income families obtain supports and services they need to keep themselves safe, healthy, and well fed" (pp. 74–75).

The Results of Family-School Interventions are Showing Positive Gains for Students' Learning and Development

While only recently synthesized, reviews of methodologically sound research have established gains. Although the review by Mattingly et al. (2002) found limited evidence for the effect of parent involvement programs, primarily due to poor methodological rigor and differences in terminology, others have found the involvement of parents in early intervention/prevention programs to be beneficial. In fact, some programs were considered to be well-established or probably efficacious treatment approaches when specific criteria were used (Shepard & Carlson, 2003).

The scientific base that supports the use of parent and family interventions that are implemented in schools or coordinated with school settings and demonstrate a change in the school-related behaviors and learning problems of children and youth has been examined (Carlson & Christenson, 2005). Reviews were conducted in six domains: parent education, parent involvement, parent consultation, family-school collaboration/partnership, family systems therapy and parent training, and early childhood family-focused interventions. Over 100 intervention studies were found and coded using the criteria of the Evidence-Based Interventions in School Psychology Task Force (Division 16 and Society for the Study of School Psychology Task Force, 2003). The most effective program components were home-school collaborative interventions that emphasized dialogue about educational programming and two-way communication/monitoring of children's school performance, parent education programs that targeted specific behaviors to be learned, parent involvement strategies that underscored the role of parents as tutors and focus on a single academic area, and parent consultation about child-specific concerns. It is noteworthy that the effective components are illustrative of a systemic orientation, viewing parents/families and educators as both essential and in a dynamic relationship for impacting child outcomes in school. The authors concluded that the components—especially dialogue and two-way communication with monitoring—identified partnership variables worthy of attention for future intervention efforts.

Evidence Exists for Creating Partnerships Universally or Having a Schoolwide Philosophy for the Importance of Family-School Connections for Children's Learning

Schoolwide programs aim to promote children's learning and development across all domains by partnering with all parents. Schoolwide programs that are comprehensive, well planned, and provide

parental options have demonstrated that: a) the more extensive the involvement, the higher the achievement, and b) children the farthest behind make the greatest gains (Comer et al., 1996). For example, Comer's School Development Program (SDP) targets collaborative problem solving, decision by consensus, and regular meetings for the entire school community. Children improved their behavior (e.g., less suspensions, punishments, and absences), attitudes, participation, and achievement, and showed increases in self-concepts. Parents and students reported significantly more positive assessments of their classrooms and school climate. Comer and his colleagues concluded that programs that address attitudes, philosophy, structure, and day-to-day practices show improvement in achievement consistent with middle-class schools. Dauber and Epstein (1993) demonstrated that programs are stronger when teachers agree about family involvement practices, concluded that parents need consistency across school years, and reported parents would spend more time on activities if given guidance. Finally, Edwards (2004) reported on gains in literacy for elementary students when the home-school reading programs were implemented at the school level, sensitive to grade-level concerns, and made a strategic connection with parents that emphasized realistic reinforcement of the reading curriculum.

The Curriculum of the Home Creates Habits of Learning that Enhance Teachers' Effectiveness and Can be Implemented with Parents Across SES Levels

As noted by Redding (2000), the home's influence on academic learning is significant; however, the quality and quantity of classroom instruction and the child's own characteristics are of equal or perhaps greater significance. The notion is that we do not want to emphasize the family's contribution to the learning equation and forgive weaknesses in the instructional program at school. And yet, ignoring gains that can be made by the family's contribution limits the overall potential effectiveness of the school. Teachers are integral to the success of school-family partnerships. The more parents perceived teachers as valuing their contributions, keeping them informed of their child's strengths and weaknesses, and providing them with suggestions, the higher parental engagement in children's learning in urban settings (Patrikakou & Weissberg, 2000).

Continuity Across Home and School About Children's Learning Is an Important Protective Factor

Consensus and consistency in the partnership between home and school strengthens a positive, pro-education message. The relationship between home and school can function as either a protective factor or a risk factor for students' learning (Christenson & Sheridan, 2001). As a protective factor, families are active partners, supportive, and involved. As a protective factor, educators invite families, inform families, and include families in decisions; they support families when they need information about how schools function or how to assist their children's learning progress. For a significant number of students, however, discontinuity between home and school is a risk factor, particularly with respect to expectations, value placed on learning, and communication patterns (Pianta & Walsh, 1996). Consistency across environments significantly impacts educational outcomes, yet is often minimized in interventions. If students receive competing messages from home and school, the effectiveness of either is compromised (Hansen, 1986; Hess & Holloway, 1984). This becomes particularly risky when considering other influences such as negative peer pressure or mass-media images.

Congruence across settings affects student achievement; therefore a focus on creating consistent messages and conditions that promote student success offers much promise. According to Chall (2000), "The processes and characteristics that enhance academic achievement are essentially the same—whether found in the home or in the school" (p. 159). Although this may seem initially to be an intriguing statement, the home predictors of school learning—work habits of the home, academic guidance and support, stimulation to explore and discuss ideas and events, language environment, and academic aspirations and expectations (Kellaghan et al., 1993)—are similar to school factors that enhance achievement. Also, benefits of school-family partnerships for learning outcomes that are vital to effective assessment and intervention efforts, albeit less described in the literature, have been described (Christenson & Sheridan, 2001). The benefits focus on conditions that facilitate the partnership which include: enhancing communication and coordination between parents and educators, continuity in programs and approaches across family and school contexts, shared ownership and commitment to educational goals, increased understanding of the complexities of the child and his/her situation, and pooling of resources to increase the range and quality of solutions, diversity in expertise, and integrity of educational programs.

Christenson and Peterson (1998) examined the influence of family, school, and community systems on children's learning. The available database, however, was primarily cross-sectional; the researchers examined over 200 studies of family, school, or community influences on positive indicators of school success, such as improved academic performance, attendance, self-esteem, and motivation to learn; fewer suspensions; and increased classroom participation. A major conclusion of this review was that there is evidence for a common set of contextual influences important for learning regardless of the child's immediate microsystem (i.e., home or school setting). They identified six factors that reflect the complementary nature of family-school-community roles for children's school success: Standards and Expectations, Structure, Opportunity to Learn, Support, Climate and Relationships, and Modeling (Christenson & Anderson, 2002). Remarkable similarity in the contextual influences that enhanced student learning emerged as a result of examining studies from family, school, and community literature simultaneously. For example, structure was evident when families established a routine that included priority for schoolwork and the classroom maintained an academic, task-oriented focus. Or evidence existed for opportunity to learn in home and school contexts when students were involved in constructive learning activities after school and the amount of academic learning time during school was high.

The ecological validity of the factors was assessed by gathering student perspectives. Consistent and inconsistent learners (as nominated by teachers) differed in their ratings of the importance of the factors for their learning success as well as the number of examples generated for each factor. Consistent learners rated the importance of each factor higher than inconsistent learners; the home and school experiences described by consistent learners were more frequent, systematic, and clearly more evident across grade levels than were those described by inconsistent learners, suggesting a cumulative effect of family and school learning environments for students' academic competence (Christenson & Anderson, 2002).

These factors underscore that student learning is not influenced exclusively by teachers or the 6.25 hours per day students spend in school. Rather, student learning is a shared responsibility where teachers are responsible for the formal education and instruction and parents are responsible for the informal education and instruction (i.e., valuing education, homework support). While different, both roles are essential to optimal learning conditions for students. In sum, the factors suggest conditions that increase the likelihood that students will be more successful in school. Because there are many ways for these factors to be reinforced at home, in school, and within the community, there is not one prescription for supporting learners. Rather, the critical variables are the degree to which children's family and school systems are learning environments, and complementary roles, not symmetrical roles, are created among families, schools, and communities. This is more difficult for some family-school connections.

Estranged Families

Families, like students, come to school in very different places with respect to learning. Parents, regardless of their educational status, income level, or ethnic background, report wanting their children to be successful in school. However, parents are often uncertain about their roles in schooling and how to best help children with schoolwork, and they desire more information about school policies and practices and child-specific developmental issues (Christenson, Hurley, Sheridan, & Fenstermacher, 1997). Significant challenges reaching uninvolved families center around different expectations for schooling, dissimilar goals, and mismatched communication patterns. If differences are not recognized and addressed, the communication gap widens and students are forced to deal with increasingly separate and discrepant messages from their two primary socialization contexts (National Association of School Psychologists [NASP], 2005).

Open communication is critical to better understand and respect others' perspectives. Rather than making an informed choice, parents may lack critical information about education. For example, Delgado-Gaitan (1991) noted that the difference between involved and uninvolved families is that involved family members are aware they have a critical role in their children's education. In other situations, parents are often not used as a resource until problems become so embedded they are difficult to eradicate (Procidano & Fisher, 1992). Instead of seeking parental advice or feedback in problem solving,

educators may make decisions on their own, believing that a parent they do not see or hear from is not a helpful resource. Parents feel disconnected and blame educators for their child's difficulties.

When schools change the ways they reach out to families, value others' perspectives, and seek involvement by parents in problem solving and decision making, families become more engaged in their children's education (Christenson, 2004; Dauber & Epstein, 1993). Thus, finding alternative ways to connect with disengaged or disenfranchised parents is essential to enhance the success of all students. A significant subset of parents have not had a positive, personal school experience and are less likely to feel comfortable in schools; therefore, they are less likely to partner, without support, with educators. The already high and increasing percentage of families with a single parent as head of household or with both parents working limits the physical involvement many parents have at school and time spent on school issues at home. The large number of new immigrants in the American school system highlights the critical need for information on schooling and the important role of parents in educational success. The loss of cultural and social capital in the lives of students already struggling with an unfamiliar or unfriendly education system is a significant burden to overcome. Cultural capital refers to the support and strength families gain from their cultural group or background, including the amount and quality of information available to the group about how schools function and how to help their children in school (Lareau, 1987). Social capital is quality support that youth gain from important adults in their lives, which is often represented by the amount of child-adult interaction around personal and academic matters; this is highly impacted by changes in family demographics such as divorce rates, dual and full-time working parents, and less community cohesion (Coleman, 1987). This is no small issue, as success in school depends in part on support, opportunity to learn, and resources available to the child (Pianta & Walsh, 1996).

There are many ways that school psychologists and other educators can reach out to disenfranchised or uninvolved families. As Edwards (1992) noted, empowering parents is crucial, and power can refer to the resources parents have that are recognized by the school. Empowerment involves mutual respect, critical reflection, caring, and group participation through which people lacking an equal share of valued resources gain greater access to and control over resources. Critical elements include inclusion in decision making.

Kohl, Lengua, and McMahon (2000) noted that the quality of parental involvement in school had not been integrated into most current definitions. However, the quality of the parent-teacher relationship has been more strongly associated with child outcomes than simply the amount of contact in which they engage (Kohl, Weissberg, Reynolds, & Kasprow, 1994). Thus, their model focuses on the quality of the relationship between parent and teacher, the teacher's perception of the parent's value of education, and the parent's satisfaction with the child's school. It has become apparent that family involvement in education is a multifaceted idea that includes a variety of behaviors and attitudes.

Overall goals of promoting consistency and helping parents learn how best to help their children in school requires thinking broadly. Mesosystemic thinking highlights the autonomous nature of the two primary microsystems in children's lives—home and school—and the challenge for connecting in constructive ways. A productive relationship can take many forms, and the value of developing partnerships, with an active role also for students, around shared goals, shared contributions, and shared accountability cannot be overestimated.

A focus on process is necessary to take us to the next step. What kind of relationship do the partners want, what will it take to get there, and how will the partnership grow and develop over time? The evidence is clear—vital, effective partnerships between key stakeholders in students' lives promote achievement and the growth of competencies for children and youth in social, behavioral, emotional, and academic domains.

A PROCESS FOR THE PATHWAY TO PARTNERSHIP

The four A's (Christenson & Sheridan, 2001)—Approach, Attitudes, Atmosphere, and Actions—represent a process for constructing quality family-school connections for children's learning. The process, which is illustrated in Figure 30.1, consists of prerequisite conditions and actions. Prerequisite conditions set a tone for partnership, namely, a) the approach adopted toward the role of families; b) the degree to which constructive attitudes between families and educators exist; and c) the atmosphere present for interaction between families and educators in their particular school context. There must be coherence across the prerequisite conditions to create the pathway to partnership, which is reflected in the core actions. Putting actions in place prior to

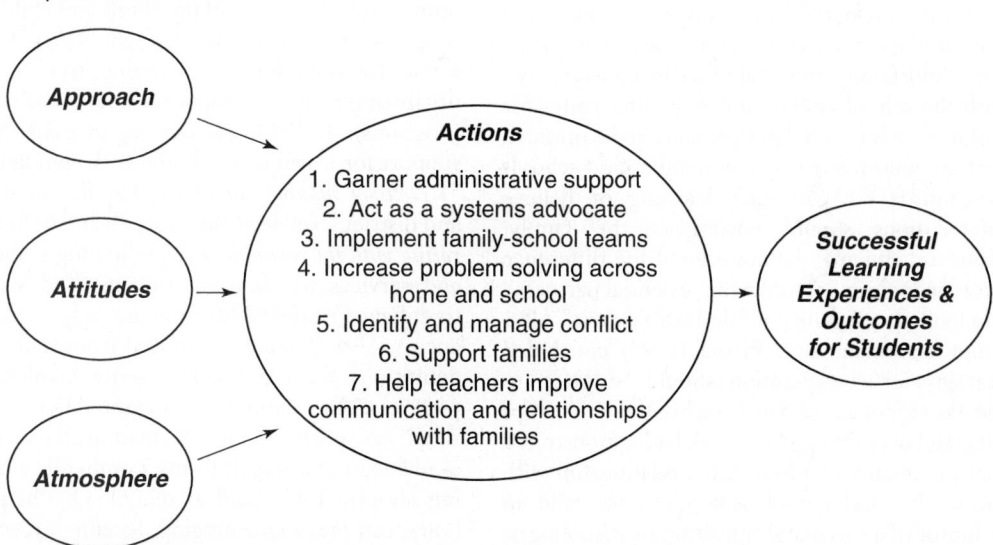

Prerequisite Conditions:
These 3 A's must be in place for Actions to be accepted and effective

Approach

Attitudes

Atmosphere

Actions
1. Garner administrative support
2. Act as a systems advocate
3. Implement family-school teams
4. Increase problem solving across home and school
5. Identify and manage conflict
6. Support families
7. Help teachers improve communication and relationships with families

Successful Learning Experiences & Outcomes for Students

FIGURE 30.1 The four A's: Developing pathways to partnerships.

ensuring the solidarity of the prerequisite conditions can result in limited success.

Approach

Approach refers to the framework for interaction with families. Fundamental to the philosophy personified in family and school as partners is a belief in shared responsibility for and shared goals in educating and socializing children. From a collective responsibility perspective, the product of education—learning—is not produced by schools, but by students with the help of parents, educators, peers, and community professionals who support learners (Seeley, 1985). Thus, students learn because of what students do, but students "do" because of a supportive network between home and school.

Systems-ecological theory provides the framework for organizing the reciprocal influences between home and school. It helps to think about home *and* school together and avoid thinking of separate responsibilities to be completed at home *or* school. When students are having trouble, a systems thinker never debates whether the cause is at home or school or elsewhere. Rather, contributing factors from all environments, instead of causes, are most relevant. Because both facilitate the child's learning, both contribute to the child's level of academic performance. Thus, efforts are directed to home and school with the goal of helping the whole system work better for encouraging and supporting the child's progress.

Pianta and Walsh (1996) described a necessary belief system for educators, one where educators understand that children develop and learn in the context of the family, and *that* system (i.e., child/family) must interface in a positive way with the school system and schooling issues for children's educational performance to be optimal. Not all educators recognize families and schools as contexts for children's learning or believe interventions should encompass the family. However, this may be considered the difference between looking at families as "essential partners" and looking at families as "desirable extras." Also, Rimm-Kaufmann and Pianta (1999) concluded that greater consideration should be given to the development of family-school relationships early and over time. Their work has demonstrated that the quality of the parent's relationship with the teacher and school personnel is as valid an indicator of a successful transition to schooling as the child's competence in kindergarten. In fact, the quality of this relationship predicts later school success, particularly where discontinuity between the systems is present.

An advocate of systems theory and systems intervention for children and youth, Garbarino (1982) aptly notes that support for children's development is represented by "connections that occur whenever individuals (e.g., parents, teachers) or systems (e.g., schools, churches, families) have ongoing contact with each other that is organized around concern for the welfare of the child" (p. 125). Therefore, it is important to establish an approach in which the significance of families for children's school performance is clear, and meaningful roles and shared responsibilities are defined explicitly (and sometimes negotiated) for families and educators with respect to fostering educational success. In comprehensive programs, family involvement is an integral part of what the school does to enhance learning opportunities and educational progress for students. To create an overall partnership philosophy, many schools have benefited from the work of Dr. Joyce Epstein, the National Parent-Teacher Association (PTA), or conceptualization of co-roles advocated by the U.S. Department of Education for urban schools (Moles, 1993). Particularly noteworthy is the potential of varied parental roles.

Noted researcher Joyce Epstein (1995) delineated six types of school-family partnerships, underscoring that families can and do participate both at school and at home. Her types include: 1) *Parenting* (assisting families with parenting skills, helping parents understand child and adolescent development); 2) *Communicating* (two-way communication about school programs and children's progress between home and school); 3) *Volunteering* (school efforts in recruiting, training, and organizing families to support students and school programs); 4) *Enhancing learning at home* (home support for learning and homework completion); 5) *Decision making* (involving families in school and district level decision making); and 6) *Collaborating with the community* (coordinating resources and services to families, students, and schools to enhance students' learning and school experiences). Also, Epstein has moved from traditional definitions for the various family involvement practices. For example, she suggested that "workshop" can mean making information about a topic available in a variety of forms, not merely a meeting about a topic held at school. Or "help" at home can mean encouraging, listening, reacting, monitoring and discussing schoolwork, not only "teaching" school subjects.

The *National Standards for Parent/Family Involvement Programs* (National PTA, 1998) mirror Epstein's partnership types. According to the National PTA, effective involvement of parents requires understanding the four key roles (teachers/nurturers, communicators/advisors, supporters/learners, and collaborators/decision makers) parents play in comprehensive and inclusive parent involvement programs. Similarly, Moles (1993) described varied roles for families and school personnel: cocommunicators, cosupporters, colearners, coteachers, and codecision makers. Particularly noteworthy about the conceptualization of these roles is that the labels (e.g., cocommunicator) were deliberately selected to facilitate and encourage a shared responsibility approach for children's learning. Thus, the tone for the relationship is set by the choice of language. Also, this conceptualization identifies roles for parents or educators within the family-school relationship. The roles are arranged as a pyramid with cocommunicators at the base, followed by cosupporters, colearners, and coteachers with codecision makers at the top. Each subsequent role requires more active participation, commitment, and skill; thus, they are likely to engage fewer individuals. It is assumed that all families and educators are involved as cocommunicators, and fewer are occupied as codecision makers. Clearly, there are a variety of ways for parents to participate and different levels of commitment required. This provides a concrete way of thinking about how all families can be involved in some way, a way that is sensitive to their needs or family circumstances.

In sum, constructive family-school collaboration is an approach, not merely an activity. The intersection of family and school is considered vital for children's learning, and the emphasis is placed on the quality of the relationship rather than roles or specific activities to be executed by home or school. An often missing piece is the explicit acknowledgment, particularly in school attitudes and actions that parents are essential partners. Adopting an approach that recognizes the significance of families and the contributions of schools for children's learning and engagement with school provides a necessary framework for constructive partnerships.

Attitudes

Attitudes refer to the values and perceptions that both parents and educators hold about family-school relationships. Collaboration, which involves both equality—the willingness to listen

to, respect, and learn from one another, and parity—the blending of knowledge, skills, and ideas to enhance the relationship and outcomes for children, must be embraced as a central mode of operating in constructive partnerships. Thus, families and schools "share joint responsibilities and rights, are seen as equals, and can jointly contribute to the process" (Vosler-Hunter, 1989, p. 15). According to Christenson and Sheridan (2001, p. 98), specific behaviors characterize this collaborative process: "Listening to one another's perspective; viewing differences as strengths; focusing on mutual interests; sharing information to co-construct understandings; respecting the skills and knowledge of each other by asking for opinions and ideas; planning together and making decisions that address the needs of parents, teachers, and students; refraining from finding fault (i.e., there are no problematic individuals; rather a problematic situation that requires our attention); and celebrating 'our' successes."

Attitudes about the value of the partnership must be held by both parents and educators. A set of basic beliefs that represent attitudes necessary for the formation of effective partnerships are summarized in Table 30.1. As a corollary, partnerships thrive when parents and educators are aware of and systematically strive to resolve attitudes that create barriers to the partnership (see Table 30.2). Inherent in this analysis of attitudes is the importance expressing confidence that partnering will benefit the student's learning outcomes, requesting parental knowledge and assistance to address a concern, encouraging a role for parents, and engaging in perspective taking. Using the golden rule as a guideline, Canter and Canter (1991) suggest a practical practice for educators. They can ask: If I had a child in school, what specific information would I want to hear from the teacher at the beginning of the year? How and when would I want to be approached about a problem? How would I want to be spoken to? Listened to? Would I like to hear from the teacher when my child is doing well or only when there is a problem?

Constructive attitudes set the stage for keeping the focus how parents and educators can work together to address a concern or shared goal for the student. Perspective taking and win-win attitudes stand out as important for connecting with parents. A helpful nonjudgmental attitude is to assume that parents are doing the best they can. It also helps not to engage in an "archeological trip" on the family by bringing up past behaviors

TABLE 30.1   **Attitudes Necessary for Positive, Productive
Home-School Relations**

School Attitudes

- Families are potential facilitators, not determinants of children's educational success.
- Families must be recognized for their essential role in influencing student success.
- Home support for learning helps to differentiate high and low achievers.
- Families across income levels support their children's education, although in different ways.
- Outreach to families is essential. Families need information about children, school policies and practices, and what they can do to assist their children as learners.
- Open and clear communication with parents is needed.
- Assumptions about families build walls. Judgments about families and students must be suspended.

Family Attitudes

- Schools provide a context where support and guidance for learning are established. Schools are places where individual students can grow and develop, not just groups of students.
- Schools bear the essential responsibility for establishing a climate that allows families to partake in the educational development of their child.
- There are several ways that a home environment can support learning.
- Interest in and valuing school activities is an important way for parents to show support for children's education.
- Schools need information about how they can best support a child's unique development.
- Assumptions about schools and teachers build walls. Judgments about schools and teachers must be suspended.
- Clear, honest communication with teachers and school personnel is needed.
- Parents have a responsibility to play a role in their child's development and to support their children's learning.

Source: From Christenson, S. L., & Sheridan, S. M. (2001) .

TABLE 30.2   **Attitudes that Produce Barriers to the Establishment
of Effective Relationships**

- Partial resistance toward increasing home/school cooperation.
- Assumptions made about others that are based on specific labels or structural characteristics.
- Stereotypic views of people, events, conditions, or actions that are not descriptive of behavior, but portray a causal orientation.
- Assumption that parents and teachers must hold identical values and expectations.
- Failure to view differences as a strength.
- Limiting impressions of child to observations in only one environment.
- Lack of belief in a partnership orientation to enhance student learning/development influences interactions.
- A blaming and labeling attitude that permeates the home/school atmosphere.
- A win-lose rather than a win-win attitude in the presence of conflict.
- Tendencies to personalize anger-provoking behaviors by the other individual.
- Lack of perspective taking or empathizing with the other person.
- Failure to recognize the importance of preserving the family/school relationship.

Source: From Christenson, S. L., & Sheridan, S. M. (2001).

(Weiss & Edwards, 1992). Families and children are at different points with respect to their connection to schooling and learning, and some families are dealing with unique situations that make it difficult for them to be involved and available. Constructive school-family partnerships are fostered when educators accommodate parents by beginning where they are, not where educators think parents should or could be. As family members and school personnel work together to identify shared goals for learning and negotiate roles that family members can take to support their child's academic progress, school personnel must be "willing to learn about a family's uniqueness but also learn with and from them" (Christenson & Sheridan, 2001, p. 78). Emphasizing this win-win orientation helps to circumvent blame and finger pointing when students are having learning and behavioral difficulties in school. Educators portray this sort of attitude when they state a desire to work toward resolution, avoid making attributions for problems (e.g., student is unmotivated or lacks home support), discuss what can be done at home and school to achieve goals for the student, and use nonblaming interactions. Techniques for blocking blame have been developed by Howard Weiss and are presented in Table 30.3.

Attitudes are among the most salient and powerful precursors to healthy partnerships with parents. The attitudes parents and educators hold about each other set the stage for an atmosphere conducive for quality interaction.

Atmosphere

An additional prerequisite for a constructive partnership to enhance children's learning and school experiences is the atmosphere or climate for interaction between families and educators. An atmosphere that is open, trusting, and inviting provides an important, supportive infrastructure within which attitudes can be shared and actions implemented. Two particularly noteworthy characteristics of a school's atmosphere are the frequency and quality of interactions among its participants (i.e., communication), and feelings of trust and respect existing within the school community (Haynes et al., 1996). Schools want parents to be engaged with their children's learning, but their engagement depends on parents being *invited, informed* (and educators being informed by), and *included,* especially for families with low cultural capital. Sound educational practice focuses on ways to address three primary barriers for parent engagement: (a) negotiating meaningful and viable roles for families; (b) enhancing parental self-efficacy;

and (c) making regular invitations for parents to partner, invitations that are explicitly tied to their children's school success (Hoover-Dempsey & Sandler, 1997).

To establish an atmosphere that is comfortable, friendly and approachable for all families, it is crucial for educators to consider how the school climate is welcoming for and inclusive of input from all families. Parents' perceptions of their abilities to assist in their child's development, and in the attainment of important educational goals, may be partly a function of the degree to which parents identify the school as open and approachable. Of utmost importance is the school's willingness to include parents and be responsive to parental input and desires with respect to children's learning experiences. Successful partnership-oriented schools find ways to ensure parents have access (i.e., parental right to inclusion in decision making processes), voice (i.e., feeling of parents that they were heard and listened to at all points in the process), and ownership (i.e., parents agree with and are contributing to any action plan affecting them and their child) (Comer et al., 1996; Osher, 1997).

When family members feel welcome and wanted at school, and know what their role is or can be, generally they will be better able to participate meaningfully and actively in the education of their children. Importantly, when family members recognize the school as a place (and schooling as a process) in which they belong, and the meaningful role they play, they increase their beliefs that their efforts make a difference for their child (Delgado-Gaitan, 1991). Parents' connection to schools is enhanced with invitations to partner, clearly articulated benefits for their involvement, and options for being engaged with their children's learning.

Relationships and interaction variables are critically important to parents in determining welcoming school environments (Windram, Godber, Hurley, & Christenson, 2001). Of 27 choices, a sample of ethnically diverse parents in a large Midwestern urban school district indicated that their "top 10" variables for contributing to a welcoming environment were: 1) experience talking with their child's teacher, 2) the relationship between their child and his/her teacher, 3) meetings with school personnel to address concerns, 4), the overall "feeling" in their child's class, 5) the overall "feeling" in their child's school, 6) the relationship between families and teachers, 7) parent-teacher conferences, 8) cleanliness of the school, 9) initial contact when

TABLE 30.3   Techniques for Blocking Blame

Direct Blocking: Signaling that the purpose of the interaction is not to blame but to solve a problem. Example:

- Student: *Johnny always starts the fights—it's not my fault.*
- Teacher: *We're not here to find out who's to blame but to figure out how you and Johnny can get your work done instead of fighting.*

Reframing: Providing an alternate point of view about a set of facts which gives the facts a more positive, productive meaning. Example:

- Teacher: *These parents drive me nuts—all they're concerned about is whether their child is going to get into the top class. It starts in pre-kindergarten.*
- Teacher: *It sounds as if they're trying to be an advocate for their child's education and get them started off on the right track.*

Probing: Eliciting additional information to clarify the context leading to the blaming. Example:

- Student: *The teacher always picks on me.*
- Teacher: *I certainly don't intend to pick on you, David. What do you see me doing that makes you think I'm picking on you? Give me some examples.*

Refocusing: A statement that redirects the discussion from a nonproductive or nonessential area to an area relevant to helping the student. Example:

- Parent: *Jose did great last year with Ms. Johnson. We think that Ms. Williams is just not as good a teacher.*
- Guidance Counselor: *I can see that you're very concerned that Jose has a good year this year, too.*

Illustrating: Giving concrete examples of areas of concern. *Example:*

- Parent: *He doesn't act that way at home. You just don't know how to deal with him.*
- Teacher: *What I've observed is that Johnny acts that way when he is with his friends. They enjoy talking with each other so much that they don't seem to be able to stop when it's time to get down to work.*

Validating: Recognizing the validity of another's perception or efforts. Example:

- Parent: *I know Jane needs me to spend more time with her—maybe I should quit going to school.*
- Principal: *I can understand your concern about spending time with Jane, but your going to school is also a positive role model for her. Let's see if there are other ways you could be helpful to her.*

Agreeing: Confirming someone's perception of a situation. *Example:*

- Teacher: *It really drives me nuts when people come in and think they can just take over the classroom.*
- Parent: *It would drive me nuts, too, if I thought someone was trying to take over something that I was responsible for.*

Source: Training handout reprinted with permission from Howard M. Weiss, Center for Family-School Collaboration, Ackerman Institute for the Family, New York, NY.

families first enter the school, and 10) how differences of opinion or conflict are handled.

A positive atmosphere that promotes partnerships around learning is built on a foundation of trust. According to Davies (1991), trust is the "essential lubrication for more serious intervention" (p. 378). Many families who are reluctant to participate in school activities or communicate with school personnel may have a history of negative interactions with school, whether due to a specific personal experience or a long-held familial belief. School personnel must work through mistrust by using personalized and persistent efforts to contact families, social events that promote the opportunity to find friendly faces in the crowd, frequent efforts to invite all families to school functions and activities, and a welcoming school climate. Parent-teacher trust in urban and suburban schools for students with and without disabilities, however, is somewhat sobering with respect to teacher trust of parents. Adams and Christenson (2000) found that teacher trust of parents was significantly lower than parental trust of teachers. This finding has recently been replicated in British schools (Dunsmuir, Frederickson, & Lang, 2004). Given that educators are responsible for making partnerships a priority and for reaching out to families, one can only speculate how teacher mistrust may affect family-school interactions.

Persistent efforts such as frequent letters home and good news phone calls convey the message that the school personnel wish to work with the family and share the successes of the child. School personnel may need to visit families in a comfortable or neutral environment (e.g., the family's home, a coffee shop) before families feel welcome at school. Practices such as making sure the child is well known by at least one staff member help to create a positive atmosphere which is conducive to partnership. Physical factors such as bulletin boards with current school-family reading support activities and information parents can take with them as they walk through the hallways indicates the school's value of learning and encourages parents to partner with them around academic achievement. Also, the use

of family-centered principles, which appear in Table 30.4, have been found to be successful in building partnerships in early intervention (McWilliam, Tocci, & Harbin, 1998) and for families alienated from the schooling process (Sinclair, Christenson, Lehr, & Anderson, 2003).

Although the responsibility to communicate openly and honestly is the responsibility of educators and parents (Epstein, 1995), most researchers believe it is the role of educators to set the stage for honest, open, two-way communication. For example, Christenson and Sheridan (2001) identified several guidelines for effective school-based communication practices: a) strive for a positive orientation rather than a deficit-based or crisis orientation (e.g., invite and incorporate parent reactions to policies and practices, contact parents at the first sign of a concern); b) consider tone as well as content of communications (e.g., reframe language from problems to goals for the student); c) develop and publicize regular, reliable, varied two-way communication systems (e.g., system-wide assignment notebooks and partnership agreements, handbooks and newsletters, "Thursday folders" including relevant home and

TABLE 30.4 Dimensions of Family-Centered Practices

- Family Orientation: Opening the Door
  A willingness to orient services to the whole family, rather than just to the child. Providers must establish enough trust with parents to be able to ask them about their own concerns.
- Positiveness: Thinking the Best of Families
  Positiveness is a philosophy of thinking the best about parents without passing judgment. Similar to "unconditional positive regard." Characterized by a belief in parents' abilities, a nonjudgmental mindset, an optimistic view of children's development, and an enthusiasm for working with families.
- Sensitivity: In the Parents' Shoes
  An ability to recognize and understand families' concerns, needs, and priorities. It is the idea of putting oneself in the parent's position in order to anticipate how families might feel as opposed to prejudging families or thinking for them.
- Responsiveness: Doing Whatever Needs to Be Done
  Two forms of responsiveness include paying attention and taking action when parents express a need (e.g., for information, for support) or complaint. Incorporates an individualized and flexible approach to service provision.
- Friendliness: Treating Parents as Friends
  Being a "professional friend" entails developing a reciprocal relationship, building trust, taking time to talk to parents about their concerns, listening to parents, encouraging them, offering practical help, and conveying caring for both parents and the child.
- Child and Community Skills: Being a Resource
  This dimension includes child level skills (e.g., having knowledge about helping children become engaged with school and learning) and community level skills (awareness of economic/cultural climate, familiarity with community resources, and a willingness to collaborate).

Source: Adapted from McWilliam, R.A., Tocci, L., & Harbin, G.L. (1998).

school information, telephone tree, and electronic technology); d) emphasize a "win-win" orientation, rather than placing blame (e.g., discuss and focus on mutual goals and interests, use words such as "we," "us," and "our," versus "you," "I," "yours," and "mine."); e) keep the focus of communication on the child's performance (e.g., bi-directional communications regarding classroom activities, progress, suggested activities for parents, shared parent-educator monitoring system); f) ensure that parents have needed information to support children's educational progress (e.g., orientation and curriculum nights, parent support groups, progress reports and practical suggestions); g) create formal and informal opportunities to communicate and build trust between home and school (e.g., multicultural potlucks, grade-level bagel breakfasts, family fun nights, principal's hour); and h) underscore all communication with a shared responsibility between families and schools. With respect to the latter guideline, Weiss and Edwards (1992) recommended that an underlying goal of communication is "to provide consistent messages to families that the school will work with them in a collaborative way to promote the educational success of the student" (p. 235). Accordingly, all communications should strive to convey at least three consistent themes to families: the desire to develop a working partnership with families, the crucial nature of family input for children's educational progress, and the importance of working together to identify a mutually advantageous solution in light of problems. The probability that parents will be more involved is higher when optimistic and realistic messages are conveyed to parents about children's educational progress (Canter & Canter, 1991). In sum, communication should be oriented toward ways to improve child's school success, link parents' goals for their child's education to classroom tasks, and link parents' efforts to child performance (Christenson, 2004).

An atmosphere that facilitates partnerships is characterized by trust, effective communication, and a mutual problem-solving orientation. The physical as well as psychological messages conveyed through the school's climate can serve to augment or restrain parental engagement with children's learning.

Actions

Approach, attitudes, and atmosphere are the backdrop for the actions that are carried out. Actions are purposefully distinguished from activities,

because actions focus on the family-school relationship or connection for children's school performance, whereas activities represent a narrow focus on a strategy or tactic to involve families in education. Actions are oriented toward building shared responsibility for educational outcomes by maximizing the congruence between students' in- and out-of-school learning time.

An immediate way to enhance shared responsibility is to identify traditional ways families and educators connect (e.g., orientation/back-to-school night, conferences, volunteering), and to alter the existing structure to build in more broad and shared responsibilities for parents, teachers, and students. For example, parent-teacher conferences traditionally are one-way communication with a high percentage of time spent in "teacher talk" focusing on student evaluation. Furthermore, the systemic orientation is absent because students infrequently attend. Newer conference strategies include student-led conferences and information sharing across home and school with respect to goals, tasks, expectations, and ideas for interventions (Christenson & Sheridan, 2001). Parent-teacher-student partnership agreements represent another way; a variation would be to lay out the roles and responsibilities of parents, teachers, and students to reach IEP goals. Christenson and Sheridan identified school-based practices that highlight shared responsibility for educational outcomes and are consistent with two tenets of effective school-family partnerships: 1) Parents are their children's first teachers and have a lifelong influence on their values, attitudes, and aspirations; and 2) Children's optimal learning success requires congruence between what is taught at school and values matched at home.

School psychologists are in a unique leadership role that provides opportunity combined with responsibility to develop partnerships with families to ensure optimal conditions of success for students. As systems thinkers and advocates, school psychologists work with the knowledge that children are largely influenced by their environments—both in school and out. Relationships with important others in their lives impact their beliefs and values, their skill building, their knowledge, and their level of motivation and effort, all of which has a strong connection to educational success.

Leading a paradigm shift in working with families as partners for educational success is challenging. To better meet this challenge, we offer seven broad actions for school psychologists, all of

TABLE 30.5 School Psychologists' Actions to Enhance Family-School Connections for Children's Learning

Action	Description	Example
Garner administrative support	Provide information and training to school personnel on working as partners	Develop district- and school-based policies for working with parents as partners
Act as a systems advocate	Provide information on the benefits of school-family partnerships for student learning	Identify current home-school connections and alter to build in responsibility for parents, educators, and students
Implement family-school team	Focus on collaboration and shared decision making for congruent messages about school and non-blaming problem solving	Create team with key stakeholders; overrepresent parents for a critical mass. Clarify needs-driven or referral-oriented purpose
Increase problem solving across home and school	Develop solution-oriented approach to build consensus, resolve concerns	Use team-based problem solving: (a) introductions (b) collaborative brainstorming (c) joint selection of immediate concern (d) solution implementation
Identify and manage conflict	Encourage perspective sharing in accepting environment and moderate conflict resolution	Agree on common goal and work toward solution by exploring alternatives
Support families	Foster positive home learning environments	Work with family to provide opportunities for constructive learning activities out of school
Help teachers improve communication and relationships with families	Create positive communication channels with families; be persistent and opportunistic	Start with positive message and convey desire to work together to help child succeed

Source: Adapted from Christenson, S. L., & Sheridan, S. M. (2001).

which focus on fostering the interface of home and school and originally were articulated by Christenson and Sheridan (2001). The actions, which are presented in Table 30.5, help to set the stage for student success. Embedded in these broad actions are the "Seven P's" of school-family partnerships: priority, planned, proactive, positive, personalized, practical, and program (Patrikakou & Weissberg, 1999; see Table 30.6).

Garner Administrative Support

Although educators traditionally value parent involvement, many lack training on how to work with parents as partners. The National Association of School Psychologists (NASP) has underscored "working with families as partners" in their most recent position statement (2005) and as an identified goal for research and training from the 2002 Invitational Conference: The Future of School Psychology, calling for school psychologists to be leaders in securing support for school-family partnerships. School principals in particular often set the tone for how their buildings work with families. They will play a key role in making partnerships a priority in the school. Securing administrative support may encompass, among other actions, sharing information on the significant role played by family, home, and school influences on learning, and the importance of in- and out-of-school time for children's school success. Schools effective in making partnerships a priority

TABLE 30.6 The Seven P's of Family-School Partnerships

Seven P's Philosophy	Description
Priority	Establish a family-school partnering policy that permeates the entire school building.
Planned	Partnerships require an intensive effort, including a thorough needs assessment.
Proactive	Regular, consistent contact starting at the beginning of the year. Schools need to be persistent in inviting, informing, and including families.
Positive	Have contact with families to report good news and maintain a solution-oriented focus.
Personalized	Give families specific information about their own children, and attempt to meet at locations and times convenient for the individual family.
Practical	Provide families with specific and simple strategies to help their children succeed in school.
Program	Systematically evaluate family-school programs, and utilize family feedback.

Source: Adapted from Patrikakou, E. N., & Weissberg, R. P. (1999).

have established a school-family partnering policy, ensured that a partnership tone is infused into the school building, provided training to school personnel about how to work as partners, provided resources for reaching out to families, recognized the accomplishments of parents and educators for improving educational outcomes, selected the types of partnerships that are important for the school context, and understood the breadth of roles parents can play (Comer et al., 1996). School psychologists can share ideas on making the school climate more welcoming to all families and illustrate constructive attitudes for working with families such as a nonblaming stance, strength-based orientation, and team approach to problem solving, to provide a roadmap to administrative leadership in developing school-based or even district-wide policies for working with parents as equal partners in school success (Christenson & Sheridan, 2001).

Act as a Systems Advocate

Research has shown that parents want to do what is best for their children's education and, if given specific opportunities and information about what they can do, provide significant support for their child's learning. This support comes in a variety of forms; the role of the school psychologist focuses on reducing traditional barriers to parent involvement and strengthening home-school relationships to provide opportunity for partnering and support (Christenson & Sheridan, 2001). This kind of system change is

long term and focuses on process-related actions rather than targeted activities. Before system change can occur, a school demographic profile might be conducted to get to know families better and collect information in order to be more responsive to children's needs (Edwards 2004). This information can include socioeconomic status of families, racial and ethnic groups represented, types of residences families live in, services provided by the community, and favorite hangouts.

A relationship-based approach for supporting learning relies on a foundation of trust and communication to promote the notion of shared responsibility, which requires systems thinking about connections between a student, family, and the larger community. For example, a traditional approach to back-to-school night is an allotted time period on one evening where parents are welcomed by the principal and follow a schedule in their child's class. A systems oriented partnership approach may offer multiple times for visiting the classroom to accommodate parents' schedules or may ask parents to bring their child with them so goals can be developed together and students play an active and ongoing role in evaluating progress; similarly, school psychologists can ensure that parents are active participants in our assessment and intervention practices (Christenson & Sheridan, 2001).

The acronym DURABLE helps to frame a seven-phase action-oriented approach for implementing new services within a school (Maher & Illback, 1985): (a) *Discussing* takes place with relevant individuals or groups and occurs prior to any change; (b) *Understanding* is concerned with readiness of the school community; (c) *Reinforcing* provides acknowledgement to staff for carrying out their program roles and responsibilities; (d) *Acquiring* refers to readiness of conditions necessary for program implementation; (e) *Building* describes cooperative relationships between change agent and individuals implementing the program; (f) *Learning* is for activities helpful for individuals responsible for carrying out procedures; and (g) *Evaluating* consists of reflecting on program implementation and goal attainment.

Implement Family-School Teams

Many schools have found that planning for and sustaining effective school-family partnerships is best facilitated by a family-school action team. The team establishes a tone of shared responsibility for the partnership; namely that both family and school are essential for optimal learning outcomes. The team reinforces that "we" (not "you" or "I") can address mutual concerns about children's learning progress and together "we" can provide improved learning outcomes and experiences for students. Teams convey the attitude that parents and educators have equal power and influence in decisions that are made on behalf of students. Leaders in promoting parents as valued and active participants, Joyce Epstein and James Comer have developed models of successful collaboration between parents and educators. Epstein (1995) describes a process of partnering through the development of an action team to design six partnership practices whereas the Comer model relies on the goal of consensus through School Planning and Management Teams (Comer et al., 1996).

In some schools, the team provides the opportunity to address the social and physical distance between families and school personnel, which can be quite large. Families and educators, who often feel like strangers, far too often interact only when there is a problem, and far too often try to resolve the problem without first developing a foundational relationship. The saying "the shortest distance between two strangers is a story" is appropriate—both home and school need to share their story about issues, concerns, observations of children, effect of interventions, and suggestions for improving the family-school connection and children's learning.

When creating a family-school team, an initial, important consideration is who serves on the team. There is general agreement that a team should be comprised of key stakeholders with respect to children's learning. Therefore, teams may include teachers from different grade levels, parents with children in different grade levels, an administrator, possibly a member from the community at large, and others central to the school's work with families. Although team membership may be based on parent and teacher interest or parent interest and teacher assignment, it is most appropriate to select members in a way to attain the broadest representation of parent and educator perspectives. Parents from different ethnic and social class backgrounds, parents with different educational and skill levels, parents whose children are performing with varied academic success, and parents who are more and less involved at school are examples of categories of "voices" to be considered for participation. Finally, overrepresenting parents, particularly in urban areas, is an efficient way to maintain a "critical mass" of parents available to attend regularly scheduled team meetings.

One of the roles of the family-school team might be program monitoring. School-family partnerships can be improved as long as they are systematically evaluated, and effectiveness of the strategies used are considered (Patrikakou & Weissberg, 1999). Members of the team can obtain feedback from school staff and parents with regard to what is working and what is not, and then brainstorm new approaches for what is not effective. Monitoring is important for examining individual student progress and family-school relationships as well. As Epstein (1995) has pointed out, family-school teams can also delve into exploring which families are being systematically excluded with current outreach strategies. She has suggested that educators ask: In your school, who are the parents who are the hardest to reach? How might more parents, different parents, or all parents be involved and better informed about school programs and their children's progress? Think of each grade level and consider families where both parents work, where there is a single parent who works during the day, those who cannot read, those who cannot speak English well, young parents, and other "hard-to-reach" families.

Increase Problem Solving Across Home and School

Home-school problem-solving models are based on four common principles that allow for structure and reciprocal support to be operationalized. Principles include (1) joint responsibility for solving problems, (2) child is central, (3) open and direct conflict management, and (4) a focus on solutions (Christenson & Hirsch, 1998), all of which empower parents to become meaningful and active participants in their child's education. When family competencies are assumed and different viewpoints acknowledged, perspective sharing can bring about creative solutions based on shared responsibility and accountability. Problem-solving models such as conjoint behavioral consultation (CBC), developed by Sheridan and colleagues, and solution-oriented family-school consultation, developed by Carlson and colleagues, apply systems principles while focusing on participants' strengths, growth-producing actions, and solutions (Carlson, Hickman, & Horton, 1992; Sheridan, Kratochwill, & Bergan, 1996).

Identify and Manage Conflict

Partnerships lead to increased interaction between family members and educators. A benefit of more contact is greater opportunities for different ideas and perspectives to be shared, an outcome to be expected based on the diverse ways with which individuals approach life. Along with varied perspectives and approaches, however, comes conflict. Although conflict is often viewed negatively, as an interference to goal attainment (Friend & Cook, 1992), we instead offer conflict or conflictual situations as opportunities for educational partners to explore differences in goals, priorities, expectations. When addressed constructively, conflict resolution strengthens student-parent-educator partnerships (Christenson & Sheridan, 2001).

If communication about school problems is an issue, it is important that school staff have the confidence to address it right away. Canter and Canter (1991) describe a system with which to communicate about students in a positive manner: begin with a statement of concern, describe specific behaviors, describe steps taken to resolve the issue, get parental input, present a plan to the parent, express concern, and inform parents about follow-up contact. However, it should be noted that communication regarding positive student behavior should be a fundamental aspect of contact with parents. If these exchanges have been made, discussions of problem behavior will likely go more smoothly, largely because home-school trust has been built.

Support Families

Given that over 90% of students' time is spent outside of school, fostering positive home learning environments is integral to educational success. However, it is critical to differentiate home support for learning strategies and supporting families (Christenson & Sheridan, 2001). One issue is that education and schooling must be made a salient focus in many homes. For some families, education and schoolwork get "lost," whether due to excessive family and work demands, previous negative interactions with school personnel, or negative personal school experience. Equally important to sharing effective home support for learning strategies is supporting families to sustain their engagement with their children's learning. Families do not need to be fixed—they need to be supported in their efforts to educate their children in ways they see fit.

We support families when we deliver a clear, unambiguous message about the benefits of the partnership and the essential nature of the parental role for children's learning. Many parents need an explicit invitation to partner. Using the established empirical base for family involvement, we can explain that children perform most optimally in school when instructional, home, and home-school support for learning exists (Ysseldyke & Christenson, 2002). Should parents choose not to participate, educators can explain they will do their part at school; however, they can also make it clear that they believe this is only part of the equation for optimal school success (Christenson, 2004; Christenson & Buerkle, 1999). In these situations, repeating this message while providing ongoing opportunities for parents to partner is critical for some parents to become engaged.

We support families when we meet families where they are and when we strive to understand their perspectives, desires, and needs. Reaching out to parents by finding out what they desire to be actively engaged in their children's learning is critical. We want to set the expectation for parental engagement, but we should be wary of dictating how parents might best participate. We support families to enhance learning at home when we find a way to affirm all parents' participation. Affirming parents' roles and giving them options helps educators be responsive to specific situational demands. The classification of parental roles by Scott-Jones (1995) is very helpful. She has suggested that parents can enhance learning at home and performance in school by valuing, mentoring, helping, and doing; note that doing is not necessarily linked to child learning. Similarly, the distinction between academic and motivational home support for learning is highly relevant (Bempechat, 1998). We would be wise to rethink the traditional role for parents of assisting with and reinforcing academic work (i.e., academic support), and to consider also how parents help by developing *habits of learning* (i.e., motivational support). Bempechat (1998) has called cogently for parents and teachers to make education and learning a priority, arguing that motivational support for learning (encouraging student effort, reinforcing the value of learning, persisting in the face of challenge, structuring time for studying) is critical to socialize students as learners. Supporting families to enhance learning at home requires nothing less than attending to the process for creating productive relationships.

We support families when we individualize information on successful home and classroom learning environments (Ysseldyke & Christenson, 2002). A key is to find what works for a particular child and his/her family. The intensity and frequency with which the home environment is a learning environment must be considered. For example, if parents cannot help due to specific circumstances (e.g., working two jobs), a supportive strategy is to identify with the parents an individual who serves as a contact with the school and supports the student's learning after school hours. Finally, thinking of our connecting with parents across levels and in a nonpejorative way is helpful for the partnership. We want to focus on the kinds of supports parents would find helpful to assist

their children's learning. Parental needs vary; perhaps there are parents who need information (i.e., information only), need attention to unique situational demands/circumstances in the family context (i.e., information + attention), and need support on an ongoing basis (i.e., information + attention + support). Thus, personal contact about specific information about how to assist the child's out-of-school learning time will work for some parents. Others will need information plus learning resources. Still others will need information, resources and case management—ongoing weekly communication. As families need varying levels of support, practical and specific suggestions can be made at three levels, from universal to selected, to indicated, with continuity across home and school increasingly important (see Figure 30.2). As educators, school psychologists might focus on the top of the pyramid in order to close the achievement gap. Some strategies to reach families with the highest need include providing tangible resources to support learning at home (e.g., books, learning packets), making personal resources available like school contacts and home visits, and offering ongoing support through parent support groups or a case manager.

Helping Teachers Improve Communication and Relationships with Parents

Every parent wants their child to succeed and every educator has the same goal for their students. One of the ways to engage families is through proactive and persistent communication. By taking opportunities for optimistic communication with families and encouraging teachers

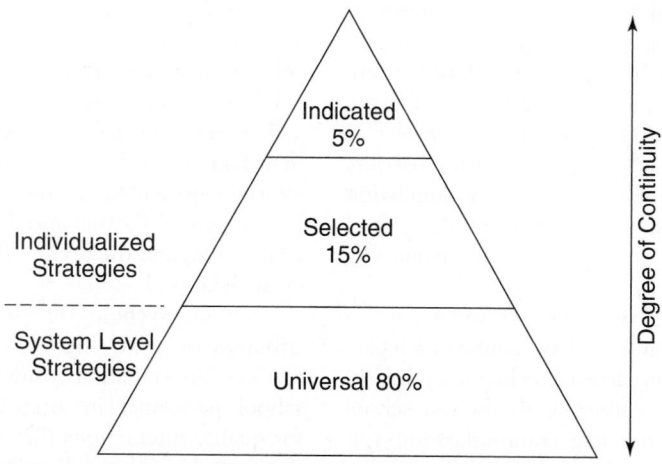

FIGURE 30.2   Three Levels of Support.

to do the same, school psychologists establish a constructive working relationship with families who may have experienced only negative interactions with schools. Messages to be communicated include the school's desire to partner with families and the crucial nature of their input for their children's school success. Schools can facilitate trust building activities centered around education to get to know families, and disseminate information to those who cannot attend. Perhaps the most important aspect of improving communication to build partnerships is to consistently invite, inform, and include parents.

When families learn what they can do, receive information on academic and motivational support for learning, and know the importance of consistent messages between home and school for learning, relationships among students, families, and educators become a strong foundation for partnering together for educational success (Bempechat, 1998). Effective communication helps parents view their children as learners, enhances parental beliefs that they can be helpful and make a difference, and enhances parents' comfort level at schools and with educational issues (Weiss & Edwards, 1992).

Barriers to Partnerships

Reducing barriers to school-family partnerships is essential. While issues and barriers for families have often been overemphasized in the literature, in reality there are barriers for families, educators, and the family-school relationship. Some of these issues are structural while others are psychological (Christenson, 2004). For families, structural issues can be lack of information, childcare and transportation, and cultural differences, while psychological barriers include feelings of inadequacy and lack of responsiveness to needs. For educators, some concerns are lack of funding or training, doubts about the abilities of families to address their child's school needs, and fear of conflict. Finally, examples of relationship barriers consist of limited time, lack of a communication system, limited use of perspective taking, and failure to recognize the importance of the ongoing partnership.

According to Chavkin (1993), some ways to reduce barriers include: (a) have contact with parents before children/adolescents begin school; (b) have contact with parents early in the school year; (c) establish ongoing communication systems that include good news as well as sharing of concerns with a way to dialogue and share

resources to address concerns; (d) use two-way communication formats: telephone, home visits, assignment/communication notebook, community liaisons; and (e) focus on the knowledge and interests of individual families.

To build healthy partnerships, partners must understand each other's concerns and recognize the constraints of each system. Further, all parties must make an effort to systematically remove barriers, using various strengths to overcome limitations. Additionally, though structural matters are more often discussed, psychological issues are critical and must not be ignored.

There are some families that we will not be able to reach, some that will continue to believe education is the school's responsibility, and others that simply will not respond. Although we cannot force families to be involved in their children's education, we have the responsibility to keep inviting families to participate and let them know that their children will not have as much success without their involvement. Our goal is to communicate the message that parents and educators are essential partners in education.

CONCLUDING REMARKS

Given the scientific findings for the effect of the home environment and school-family connections on children's school performance, partnering with families to promote children's learning is warranted. We know that the greatest gains are made when we develop quality relationships with students and families, when learning opportunities out of school are increased, and when we improve our consistency across home and school by sending congruent messages about the importance of school and learning. Creating a systemic orientation for improving academic, social, behavioral, and emotional learning outcomes for children in grades K–12 should be placed front and center, especially for estranged learners and their families. In fact, this is occurring in relevant efforts represented by the Futures Conference Home-School Partnership Task Force (Sheridan et al., 2006) and the revised *Blueprint for Training* (Ysseldyke et al., 2006).

School psychologists can make a unique contribution by providing both direct and indirect services. As systems consultants, they can assist school personnel in attending to the process for quality interactions that were represented by the four A's. This will ensure that our schools are implementing a schoolwide philosophy about the value of and ways to connect with families. In contrast to this universal approach, school psychologists can also make a unique contribution by becoming directly involved with families, particularly those who need individualized support strategies (e.g., resources, case management, ongoing consultation). In doing so, they will work with approximately 20% of the students and families, those who fall at the selected or indicated level of service delivery (see Figure 30.2).

Organizing strategies and activities with families according to the universal, selected and indicated levels of service delivery helps to make school-family partnerships a priority, stresses a schoolwide philosophy, and uses the finite resources in schools efficiently. Furthermore, school psychologists can focus on improving academic, social, and emotional outcomes for students by developing home support for learning programs with teachers, maximizing the assessment-to-intervention link through coordinated home-school interventions, and supporting families as interventions are implemented. Given our knowledge base and as we work at the selected and indicated levels, we can deliver an explicit message about shared responsibility for educational outcomes, affirm a role for all parents by showing and guiding how they can make a difference, expect parents to be engaged, provide several options and allow parents to select, provide information about the child's progress and ways parents can assist, and reemphasize the desire to partner should parents still be disengaged. Reaching disengaged and disenfranchised families requires building trust through persistence and focusing on relationships (Sinclair et al., 2003).

School psychologists are in a pivotal position to "raise the bar" for meaningful dialogue and participation among school and family members. Raising the bar for student achievement depends on no less than maximizing out-of-school learning time and bringing congruence to the value of education through school-family partnerships (Patrikakou, Weissberg, Redding, & Walberg, 2005).

REFERENCES

Adams, K., & Christenson, S. L. (2000) Trust and the family-school relationship: Examination of parent-teacher differences in elementary and secondary grades. *Journal of School Psychology, 38*(5), 477–497.

Alexander, K. L., Entwisle, D. R., & Olson, L. S. (2001). Schools, achievement, and inequality: A seasonal perspective. *Educational Evaluation and Policy Analysis, 23*, 171–191.

Barkley, R. A., Guevremont, D. C., Anastopoulos, A. D., & Fletcher, K. E. (1992). A comparison of three family therapy programs for treating family conflicts in adolescents with attention-deficit hyperactivity disorder. *Journal of Consulting and Clinical Psychology, 60*(3), 450–462.

Barton, P. E., & Coley, R. J. (1992). *American's smallest school: The family*. Princeton, NJ: Educational Testing Service, Policy Information Report.

Bempechat, J. (1998). *Against the odds: How "at-risk" students exceed expectations*. San Francisco: Jossey-Bass.

Bempechat, J., Graham, S. E., & Jimenez, N. V. (1999). The socialization of achievement in poor and minority students: A comparative study. *Journal of Cross-Cultural Psychology, 30*(2), 139–158.

Berger, E. A. (1991). Parent involvement: Yesterday and today. *The Elementary School Journal, 91*(3), 209–220.

Boethel, M. (2003). *Diversity: School, family, & community connections*. Austin, TX: Southwest Educational Development Laboratory.

Bronfenbrenner, U. (1986). Alienation & the four worlds of childhood. *Phi Delta Kappan*, 430–436.

Buerkle, K. (1997). Mobile children and families: Qualitative and quantitative explorations of the meaning and impact of residential mobility and school changes. Doctoral dissertation, University of Minnesota, 1997. *Dissertation Abstracts International, 58*(6), 2067.

Canter, L., & Canter, M. (1991). *Parents on your side: A comprehensive parent involvement program for teachers*. Santa Monica, CA: Lee Canter & Associates, PO Box 2113, Santa Monica, CA 90407-2113.

Carlson, C., & Christenson, S. L. (Eds.). (2005). Evidence-based parent and family interventions in school psychology [Special issue]. *School Psychology Quarterly, 20*(4).

Carlson, C. I., Hickman, J., & Horton, C. B. (1992). From blame to solutions: Solution-oriented family-school consultation. In S. L. Christenson & J. C. Conoley (Eds.), *Home-school collaboration: Enhancing children's academic and social competence* (pp. 193–213). Silver Spring, MD: National Association of School Psychologists.

Chall, J. S. (2000). *The academic achievement challenge: What really works in the classroom?* New York: Guilford Press.

Chavkin, N. F. (Ed.). (1993). *Families and schools in a pluralistic society*. Albany: State University of New York Press.

Christenson, S. L. (2004). The family-school partnership: An opportunity to promote the learning competence of all students. *School Psychology Review, 33*(1), 83–104.

Christenson, S. L., & Anderson, A. R. (2002). Commentary: The centrality of the learning context for students' academic enabler skills. *School Psychology Review, 31*(3), 378–393.

Christenson, S. L., & Buerkle, K. (1999). Families as educational partners for children's school success: Suggestions for school psychologists. In C. R. Reynolds & T. B. Gutkin (Eds.), *Handbook of school psychology* (pp. 709–744). New York: Wiley.

Christenson, S. L., & Havsy, L. H. (2004). Family-school-peer relationships: Significance for social, emotional, and academic learning. In J. E. Zins, R. P. Weissberg, M. C. Wang, & H. J. Walberg (Eds.), *Building academic success on social and emotional learning: What does the research say?* (pp. 59–75). New York: Teachers College Press.

Christenson, S. L., & Hirsch, J. (1998). Facilitating partnerships and conflict resolution between families and schools. In K. C. Stoiber & T. Kratochwill (Eds.), *Handbook of group interventions for children and families* (pp. 307–344). Boston: Allyn & Bacon.

Christenson, S. L., Hurley, C. M., Sheridan, S. M., & Fenstermacher, K. (1997). Parents' and school psychologists' perspectives on parent involvement activities. *School Psychology Review, 26,* 111–130.

Christenson, S. L., & Peterson, C. J. (1998). *Family, school, and community influences on children's learning: A literature review.* Parents as Teachers Project (formerly Live and Learn Project). Minneapolis, MN: University of Minnesota Extension Service.

Christenson, S. L., & Sheridan, S. M. (2001). *School and families: Creating essential connections for learning.* New York: Guilford Press.

Clark, R. M. (1983). *Family life and school achievement.* Chicago: University of Chicago Press.

Clark, R. M. (1990). Why disadvantaged students succeed: What happens outside school is critical. *Public Welfare,* 17–23.

Coleman, J. (1987). Families and schools. *Educational Researcher,* August–September, 32–38.

Comer, J. P., Haynes, N. M., Joyner, E. T., & Ben-Avie, M. (1996). *Rallying the whole village: The Comer process for reforming education.* New York: Teachers College Press.

Dauber, S. L., & Epstein, J. L. (1993). Parents' attitudes and practices of involvement in inner city elementary and middle schools. In N. F. Chavkin (Eds.), *Families and schools in a pluralistic society* (pp. 53–72). Albany: State University of New York Press.

Davies, D. (1991). Schools reaching out: Family, school, and community partnerships for student success. *Phi Delta Kappan, 72*(5), 376–382.

Delgado-Gaitan, C. (1991). Involving parents in the schools: A process of empowerment. *American Journal of Education, 100*(1), 20–46.

Division 16 and Society for the Study of School Psychology Task Force (2003). *Procedural and Coding Manual for Evidence Based Interventions.* Retrieved April 9, 2007, from www.sp-ebi.org/documents/workingfiles/EBImanual1.pdf.

Dornbusch, S. M., & Ritter, P. L. (1992). Home-school processes in diverse ethnic groups, social classes, and family structures. In S. L. Christenson & J. C. Conoley (Eds.), *Home-school collaboration: Enhancing children's academic and social competence* (pp. 111–126). Silver Spring, MD: National Association of School Psychologists.

Dunsmuir, S., Frederickson, N., & Lang, J. (2004). Building home-school trust. *Educational and Child Psychology, 21*(4), 109–128.

Edwards, P. A. (1992). Strategies and techniques for establishing home-school partnerships with minority parents. In A. Barona & E. Garcia (Eds.), *Children at risk: Poverty, minority status, and other issues in educational equity* (pp. 217–236). Silver Spring, MD: National Association of School Psychologists.

Edwards, P. A. (2004). *Children's literacy development: Making it happen through school, family, and community involvement.* Boston: Pearson Education, Inc.

Epstein, J. L. (1987). Toward a theory of family-school connections: Teacher practices and parent involvement. In K. Hurrelmann, F. Kaufmann, & F. Losel (Eds.), *Social interaction: Potential and constraints* (pp. 121–136). New York: deGruyter.

Epstein, J. L. (1995). School/family/community partnerships: Caring for the children we share. *Phi Delta Kappan, 76,* 701–712.

Fantuzzo, J., Tighe, E., & Childs, S. (2000). Family involvement questionnaire: A multivariate assessment of family participation in early childhood education. *Journal of Educational Psychology, 92*(2), 367–376.

Friend, M., & Cook, L. (1992). *Interactions: Collaboration skills for school professionals.* New York: Longman.

Garbarino, J. (1982). *Children and families in the social environment.* New York: Aldine.

Hansen, D. A. (1986). Family-school articulations: The effects of interaction rule mismatch. *American Educational Research Journal, 23*(4), 643–659.

Hart, B., & Risley, T. R. (1995). *Meaningful difference in the everyday experience of young American children.* Baltimore, MD: Paul H. Brookes.

Harvard Family Research Project (2006). *Complementary learning.* Retrieved May 15, 2007, from www.gse.harvard.edu/hfrp/projects/complementary-learning.html.

Haynes, N. M., Ben-Avie, M., Squires, D. A., Howley, J. P., Negron, E. N., & Corbin, J. N. (1996). It takes a village: The SDP school. In J. P. Comer, N. M. Haynes, E. T. Joyner, & M. Ben-Avie (Eds.), *Rallying the whole village: The Comer Process for reforming education* (pp. 42–71). New York: Teacher's College Press.

Heller, L. R., & Fantuzzo, J. W. (1993). Reciprocal peer tutoring and parent partnership: Does parent involvement make a difference? *School Psychology Review, 22*(3), 517–534.

Henderson, A. T., & Berla, N. (Eds.). (1994). *A new generation of evidence: The family is critical to student achievement.* Washington, DC: National Committee for Citizens in Education.

Henderson, A. T., & Mapp, K. L. (2002). *A new wave of evidence: The impact of school, family, and community connections on student achievement.* Austin, TX: Southwest Educational Development Laboratory.

Hess, R. D., & Holloway, S. D. (1984). Family and schools as educational institutions. In R. D. Parke, R. M. Emde, H. P. McAdoo, & G. P. Sackett (Eds.), *Review of Child Development Research: Volume 7. The Family* (pp. 179–222). Chicago: University of Chicago Press.

Hoover-Dempsey, K. V., & Sandler, H. M. (1997). Why do parents become involved in their children's education? *Review of Educational Research, 67,* 3–42.

Kellaghan, T., Sloane, K., Alvarez, B., & Bloom, B. S. (1993). *The home environment and school learning: Promoting parental involvement in the education of children.* San Francisco: Jossey-Bass.

Kohl, G. O., Lengua, L. J. & McMahon, R. J. (2000). Parent involvement in school: Conceptualizing multiple dimensions and their relations with family and demographic risk factors. *Journal of School Psychology, 38*(6), 501–523.

Kohl, G. K., Weissberg, R. P., Reynolds, A. J., & Kasprow, W. J. (1994, August). *Teacher perceptions of parent involvement in urban elementary schools: Sociodemographic and school adjustment correlates.* Paper presented at the annual meeting of the American Psychological Association, Los Angeles, CA.

Lareau, A. (1987). Social class differences in family school relationships: The importance of cultural capital. *Sociology of Education, 60,* 73–85.

Lehr, C. A., Sinclair, M. F., & Christenson, S. L. (2004). Addressing student engagement and truancy prevention during the elementary years: A replication study of the Check & Connect model. *Journal of Education for Students Placed At-Risk, 9*(3), 279–301.

Liontos, L. B. (1992). *At-risk families and schools: Becoming partners.* Eugene, OR: ERIC Clearinghouse on Educational Management, College of Education, University of Oregon.

Maher, C. A., & Illback, R. J. (1985). Implementing school psychological service programs:

Description and application of the DURABLE approach. *Journal of School Psychology, 23*(1), 81–89.

Mattingly, D. J., Prislin, R., McKenzie, T. L., Rodriquez, J. L., & Kayzar, B. (2002). Evaluating evaluations: The case of parent involvement programs. *Review of Educational Research, 72*(4), 549–576.

McWilliam, R. A., Tocci, L., & Harbin, G. L. (1998). Family-centered services: Service providers' discourse and behavior. *Topics in Early Childhood Special Education, 18,* 206–221.

Moles, O. (1993). Collaboration between schools and disadvantaged parents: Obstacles and openings. In N. Chavkin (Ed.), *Families and schools in a pluralistic society* (pp. 21–49). Albany, NY: State University of New York Press.

National Association of School Psychologists (NASP). (2005, April). Position statement on home-school collaboration: Establishing partnerships to enhance educational outcomes. Retrieved February 21, 2006, from www.nasponline.org/ information/pospaper_hsc.html.

National PTA. (1998). *National standards for parent/family involvement programs.* Chicago: Author.

Okagaki, L. (2001). Triarchic model of minority children's school achievement. *Educational Psychologist, 36*(1), 9–20.

Osher, T. (July 1997). IDEA Reauthorized—role for families enhanced. *Claiming Children,* 1–8.

Patrikakou, E. N. (1997). A model of parental attitudes and the academic achievement of adolescents. *Journal of Research and Development in Education, 31*(1), 7–26.

Patrikakou, E. N., & Weissberg, R. P. (1999, February 3). Seven P's to promote school-family partnership efforts. *Education Week,* pp. 34, 36.

Patrikakou, E. N., & Weissberg, R. P. (2000). Parents' perceptions of teacher outreach and parent involvement in children's education. *Journal of Prevention & Intervention in the Community, 20*(1–2), 103–119.

Patrikakou, E. N., Weissberg, R. P., Redding, S., & Walberg, H. J. (2005). *School-family partnerships for children's success.* New York: Teacher's College Press.

Peng, S. S., & Lee, R. M. (1992, April). Home variables, parent-child activities, and academic achievement: A study of 1988 eighth graders. Paper presented at the annual meeting of the American Educational Research Association, San Francisco.

Pianta, R., & Walsh, D. B. (1996). *High-risk children in schools: Constructing sustaining relationships.* New York: Routledge.

Procidano, M. E., & Fisher, C. B. (Eds.) (1992). *Contemporary families: A handbook for school professionals.* New York: Teachers College Press.

Redding, S. (2000). *Parents and learning*. Educational Practices Series–2. Brussels, Belgium: International Academy of Education; Geneva, Switzerland, International Bureau of Education.

Reid, J. B., & Patterson, G. R. (1989). Early prevention and intervention with conduct problems: A social interactional model for the integration of research and practice. In G. Stoner, M. R. Shinn, & H. M. Walker (Eds.), *Interventions for achievement and behavior problems* (pp. 715–739). Silver Spring, MD: National Association of School Psychologists.

Reynolds, A. J. (1989). *A structural model of first-grade outcomes for an urban, low socioeconomic black population* (ERIC: Reproduction Document Service). Paper presented at the Annual Meeting of the American Educational Research Association, San Francisco.

Reynolds, A. J., Mavrogenes, N. A., Hagemann, M., & Bezruczko, N. (1993). *Schools, families, and children: Sixth year results from the Longitudinal Study of Children at Risk*. Chicago: Chicago Public Schools, Department of Research, Evaluation, and Planning.

Rimm-Kaufmann, S. E., & Pianta, R. C. (1999). Patterns of family-school contact in preschool and kindergarten. *School Psychology Review, 28*(3), 426–438.

Saunders, S. A., & Green, V. (1993). Evaluating the social competence of young children: A review of the literature. *Early Child Development and Care, 87*, 39–46.

Scott-Jones, D. (1995). Parent-child interactions and school achievement. In B. A. Ryan, G. R. Adams, T. P. Gullotta, R. P. Weissberg, & R. L. Hampton (Eds.), *The family-school connection: Theory, research, and practice* (pp. 75–107). Thousand Oaks, CA: Sage.

Seeley, D. S. (1985). *Education through partnership*. Washington, DC: American Enterprise Institute for Public Policy Research.

Shepard, J., & Carlson, J. S. (2003). An empirical evaluation of school-based prevention programs that involve parents. *Psychology in the Schools, 40*(6), 641–656.

Sheridan, S. M., Garbacz, S. A., Rohlk, A. M., Woods, K. E., & Members of the Futures Task Force on Family-School Partnerships. (2006). Futures Task Force on Family-School Partnerships: The time really *is* now. *Communique, 34*(5), 12–14.

Sheridan, S. M., & Kratochwill, T. R. (1992). Behavioral parent-teacher consultation: Conceptual and research considerations. *Journal of School Psychology, 30*(2), 117–139.

Sheridan, S. M., Kratochwill, T. R., & Bergan, J. R. (1996). *Conjoint behavioral consultation: A procedural manual*. New York: Plenum.

Sinclair, M. F., Christenson, S. L., Lehr, C. A., & Anderson, A. R. (2003). Facilitating student engagement: Lessons learned from Check & Connect longitudinal studies. *The California School Psychologist, 8*(1), 29–42.

Sinclair, M. F., Christenson, S. L., & Thurlow, M. L. (2005). Promoting school completion of urban secondary youth with emotional or behavioral disabilities. *Exceptional Children, 71*(4), 465–482.

U.S. Department of Education. (2001). *No Child Left Behind Act*. Retrieved February 21, 2006 from www.ed.gov/nclb/landing.jhtml?src=pb.

Vosler-Hunter, R. W. (1989). *Changing roles, changing relationships: Parent and professional collaboration on behalf of children with emotional disabilities*. Portland, OR: Portland State University, Research and Training Center on Family Support and Children's Mental Health.

Walberg, H. J. (1984). Families as partners in educational productivity. *Phi Delta Kappan, 65*, 397–400.

Webster-Stratton, C. (1993). Strategies for helping early school-aged children with oppositional defiant and conduct disorders: The importance of home-school partnerships. *School Psychology Review, 22*(3), 437–457.

Webster-Stratton, C., & Hammond, M. (1990). Predictors of treatment outcome in parent training for families with conduct problem children. *Behavior Therapy, 21*(3), 319–337.

Weiss, H. M., & Edwards, M. E. (1992). The family-school collaboration project: Systemic interventions for school improvement. In S. L. Christenson & J. C. Conoley (Eds.), *Home-school collaboration: Enhancing children's academic and social competence* (pp. 215–243). Silver Spring, MD: National Association of School Psychologists.

Windram, H., Godber, Y., Hurley, C., & Christenson, S. L. (2001, August). Diverse parent perspectives of welcoming school environments. Paper presented at the meeting of the American Psychological Association, San Francisco.

Ysseldyke, J. E., Burns, M. K., Dawson, M., Kelly, B., Morrison, D., Ortiz, S., Rosenfield, S., & Telzrow, C. (2006). *School Psychology: A blueprint for the future of training and practice III*. Bethesda, MD: National Association of School Psychologists.

Ysseldyke, J. E., & Christenson, S. L. (2002). *FAAB: Functional assessment of academic behavior: Creating successful learning environments*. Longmont, CO: Sopris West.

CHAPTER 31

PSYCHOPHARMACOLOGY IN SCHOOL-AGE CHILDREN

RONALD T. BROWN AND DOLORES M. ZYGMONT
Temple University

INTRODUCTION

There has been an increasing recognition of psychiatric disorders among children and adolescents (Riddle, Kastelic, & Frosch, 2001), and these disorders are different from that of their older adult counterparts. As a result, significant research efforts have emerged to establish evidenced-based treatment of this population. The mental health care system has, to some extent, relied on pharmacological approaches, partly as an attempt at cost containment and partly because of the limited availability of those trained in psychotherapy with children. The result has been a considerable body of research on the central nervous system. Researchers have examined neurotransmitters and the association of these neurotransmitters to specific psychiatric disorders. Moreover, radiographic assessments, including magnetic resonance imaging and positron emission tomography, have made it possible to identify specific markers in the brain associated with specific psychiatric disorders. It is now possible to manage a variety of mental illnesses pharmacologically.

Concerns about the potential overuse of pharmacotherapy for pediatric populations (echoed in the lay press) has resulted in several collaborative investigations, including those initiated by the National Institutes of Mental Health (NIMH). It is our contention, however, that research pertaining to pediatric psychopharmacology has not kept pace with clinical practice and in this chapter we highlight particular psychiatric disorders in need of investigation.

The change in prescriptive practices also has expanded the scope of practice of school personnel. For example, one study found that up to 65% of all referrals for attention-deficit/hyperactivity disorder (ADHD) came from school personnel (Snider, Frankenberg & Aspenson, 2000). Teachers are in a prime position to observe the behavioral and academic effects of various pharmacological interventions. School nurses administer psychotropic medications to children and adolescents and are therefore in an ideal position to evaluate these children for adverse side effects. More important, school psychologists can collaborate with providers, teachers, school nurses, parents, and children to assess the effectiveness of psychotropic agents. This change in practice is supported by up to 77% of school psychologists (Kubiszyn & Carlson, 1995).

Further, there has been recent legislation that has delineated specific parameters for medication administration in school settings. For example, the Individuals with Disabilities Education Act (1997) established parameters for children with disabilities receiving special education (Leubbert, Malone, & Rieser, 2000). Despite the increasing use of psychotropic agents in the school-age population, efforts are underway in some states to limit the recommendations school psychologists may suggest to caregivers of children and adolescents, including the use of psychotropic medications (National Association of School Psychologists, 2004). The Child Medication Safety Act (2004) limits school psychologists' scope of practice and curtails the ability of caregivers of children and adolescents to discuss the use of psychotropic agents.

The role of school psychologists is especially important with the increase in pharmacotherapy among school-age children. School psychologists can identify children who may be potential candidates for pharmacotherapy, educate caregivers about pharmacotherapy, and monitor the effects of psychotropic medications on behavior and learning (Phelps, Brown, & Power, 2002).

Regardless of legislation, school psychologists need information regarding psychotropic agents commonly prescribed for school-aged children.

FUNDAMENTALS OF PEDIATRIC PSYCHOPHARMACOLOGY

Psychopharmacology is the branch of pharmacology that examines the effects of psychotropic medications on the central nervous system (CNS) and their effects on behavior and cognition (Poling, Gadow, & Cleary, 1991). Psychotropic medications are prescribed for a variety of psychiatric disorders and include antidepressants, stimulants, mood stabilizers, and anxiolytic agents. Psychotropic agents are used with children and adolescents based on symptoms the prescribing care provider wishes to ameliorate. For example, a child is withdrawn and tearful and diagnosed with depression. When antidepressants are prescribed, they are deemed effective if the tearfulness and withdrawn behavior are eliminated. If a psychotropic medication is deemed effective for a particular disorder, it is "indicated" for that disorder. If a medication worsens a preexisting disorder or interacts with other medications, it is "contraindicated" for specific conditions (Werry & Aman, 1999).

Medications are assigned a generic name based on their chemical composition and a copyrighted trade name by the manufacturer.[1] There is usually no difference in the effectiveness between generic and trade brands of psychotropic agents. Generic medications are usually less costly than trade-name medications, hence many third-party providers (i.e., insurance plans) require the provider to prescribe the generic brand of the medication.

Psychotropic medications achieve their effect by affecting the CNS. When the medication is administered, it is absorbed into the circulatory system and carried to the brain, where it begins to exert its effect. First, the drug binds with a specific targeted receptor. Electrochemical changes release the drug from the receptor cite where it exerts its desired effect. Typically the drug alters the transmission of nerve impulses so that information is either unable to be transmitted or is subsequently received. This is achieved by either altering the availability of the neurotransmitter required for impulse transmission or altering the cell membrane. The terms *affinity* and *specificity* describe the binding strength between the drug and the receptor site and the amount of drug needed to saturate the receptors and achieve a therapeutic effect. A drug has high affinity and specificity if the amount of drug needed to achieve a desired therapeutic effect (and receptor saturation) is small (see Werry & Aman, 1999).

In most cases, the lower the dose of the medication, the less likely adverse side effects will occur. Adverse side effects may be mild, moderate, or severe. Mild adverse side effects are often transient and usually do not interfere with functioning. Severe adverse side effects may be life threatening. It is important to note that not all significant adverse effects are known when a medication is approved by the Food and Drug Administration (FDA). Therefore, careful follow-up of children and adolescents receiving psychotropic medications is important. For example, reports of an increase in suicidal ideation with the use of some selective serotonin reuptake inhibitors have prompted the FDA to warn against the use of these agents with children and adolescents. This has had a significant impact on the prescribing practices of many health care providers. It is also important to use multiple sources of information to determine adverse side effects. The child should be questioned, as well as the child's caregiver(s), teacher(s), school nurse, and other individuals who come in contact with the child on a regular basis.

In this chapter we review the various psychotropic medications prescribed for psychiatric disorders commonly diagnosed among children and adolescents. We have used the nosology employed in the *Diagnostic and Statistical Manual–IV* (DSM-IV) (American Psychiatric Association [APA], 2000). We have employed the schema of externalizing and internalizing disorders. *Externalizing disorders* include ADHD, conduct disorder (CD), and oppositional defiant disorder (ODD).[2] *Internalizing disorders* include anxiety disorders and mood disorders. Finally, schizophrenia and other *psychotic disorders* are reviewed with *pervasive developmental disorders*.

---

[1] In accepted pharmaceutical practice the generic name begins with a lowercase letter (e.g., methylphenidate) and the trade name begins with an uppercase letter (e.g., Ritalin). In this chapter, we use the generic name.

[2] Because there is significant comorbidity of ADHD and tic disorders, Tourette's syndrome is reviewed with externalizing disorders.

EXTERNALIZING DISORDERS

Attention-Deficit/Hyperactivity Disorder (ADHD)

ADHD is a neurobiological disorder that manifests as a persistent pattern of inattention and hyperactivity-impulsivity more frequent and severe than typically observed in individuals at comparable levels of development (APA, 1994; Barkley, 2005). The disorder is one of the most prevalent in child psychiatry and has been heavily researched. In fact, it has been suggested that ADHD is a chronic health condition and should be managed by primary care providers as a chronic illness (American Academy of Pediatrics, 2001b).

ADHD is a disease with a discrete pathophysiology and potentially multiple etiologies, some of which may be anatomical and some of which may be a dysfunction of the neurotransmitter (Madras, Miller, & Fischman, 2005; Rappley, 2005). Although a complete understanding of the CNS dysfunction of individuals with ADHD is still in its infancy, work by Biederman (2005) and Volkow, Wang, Fowler, and Ding (2005) has added to our comprehension of the role of neurotransmitters (i.e., epinephrine, dopamine) in the CNS of these individuals. Despite these recent developments, much of what is known about the pharmacology of individuals with ADHD is in behavioral pharmacology, where the goal of treatment is to manage specific symptoms of the disorder.

Pharmacotherapy

Stimulant medications employed to manage symptoms associated with ADHD are classified as *symthomimetic agents* that excite the CNS. Stimulants have an affinity to dopamine and norepinephrine at the synapse level within the central cortex, and inhibit the reuptake of dopamine at the level of the synapse (Madras et al., 2005). Table 31.1 identifies stimulants used to manage the symptoms of ADHD, the major neurochemical alterations that result from each stimulant, and their peak effect.

It has been estimated that 80% or more of children with ADHD are successfully managed; the most commonly employed stimulants include methylphenidate or amphetamine (Dopheide, 2005; Greenhill, Haperin, & Abikoff, 1999; McGough, 2005; Rappley, 2005). The majority of studies have demonstrated that stimulants improve core symptoms of ADHD at least in the short term (see American Academy of Pediatrics,

2001a, b; Brown, Arnstein, & Simerly, 2005; Brown & Sammons, 2002).

A significant body of evidence attests to the efficacy of methylphenidate in the management of ADHD (American Academy of Pediatrics Subcommittee on ADHD; 2001). The majority of investigations have been conducted with school-age children. Methylphenidate has been demonstrated to improve a number of domains in the short term, although the strongest effects sizes have been demonstrated among measures of attention, distractibility, impulsivity, and observable classroom behavior, although only modest effect sizes have been reported for academic achievement (McMaster University Evidence-Based Practice Center, 1999). In general, stimulants have been demonstrated to enhance cognition, including attention and memory, as well as complex problem-solving tasks (Baldwin et al., 2004; Chelonis et al., 2002). Performance on cognitive tasks has been demonstrated to be linearly related to dose of stimulants (McCracken et al., 2003), and cognition and behavior have generally responded to similar doses. Although no one cognitive task has been demonstrated to predict response to stimulant medication, performance on academic tasks has been most sensitive to the effects of stimulant medication (McCracken et al., 2003). Findings from the McMaster University Evidence-Based Practice Center (1999) noted few differences among methylphenidate, dextroamphetamine, and pemoline. Moreover, studies comparing different formulations of the same drug revealed no significant formulation effects. In general, however, findings suggest that combined stimulant drug therapy and psychotherapy are not necessarily superior to medication alone, at least when focusing on specific ADHD symptoms.

The NIMH Collaborative Multisite Multimodal Treatment Study of Children with ADHD (MTA) (Jensen et al., 1999; MTA, 1999a; Taylor, 1999) addressed the issue of the relative efficacy of pharmacotherapy and other nonpharmacological therapies either alone or in combination. Participants included 579 children with ADHD (combined type) who were assigned randomly to one of four treatment groups: (1) state-of-the-art medication management, (2) intensive behavioral interventions, (3) a combination of the two aforementioned interventions, and (4) a community treatment control group who received "usual care" (most frequently pharmacotherapy). Findings revealed improvements over time, with the medication management and the combined

TABLE 31.1 Pharmacology of Stimulant Medications: Primary Treatment for ADHD

Drug	Action	Onset	Peak effect	Duration	Dose*
Methylphenidate	blocks reuptake of Norepinephrine and Dopamine				
Short acting		30–60 min	1.5–2.5 hours	3–5 hours	
Ritalin					5–20 mg BID or TID
Metadate					↓
Methylin					↓
Focalin (combined with amphetamine)					2.5–10 mg BID or TID
Intermediate acting		30–60 min		3–8 hours	
Ritalin SR					20–40 mg QID
Metadate ER					↓
Methylin ER					↓
Long acting		30–60 min		8–12 hours	
Concerta					18–54 mg QD
Metadate CD					20–60 mg QD
Amphetamine	increases release of Norepinephrine and Dopamine				
Short acting		30–60 min	2–3 hours	4–6 hours	
Dexadrine					5–15 mg BID; 5–10 mg TID
Dextrostat					↓
Adderall					10–30 mg QD; 5–15 mg BID
Intermediate				6–8 hours	
Dexedrine Spansules					10–30 mg QD
Long acting				8–12 hours	
Adderall XR					10–30 mg QD
Pemoline (Cylert)	influences DA receptors	2–3 weeks	2–4 hours	12–24 hours	56.25–75 mg QD

*QD = every day; BID = twice a day; TID = three times a day; QID = four times a day.

intervention associated with greater improvement than either intensive behavioral intervention employed alone or the community treatment control group (Jensen et al., 1999; MTA, 1999a; Taylor, 1999). It should be noted, however, that only those families who were assigned to the combined treatment group demonstrated consistently greater benefits than those families in the community treatment group when examining other functional outcomes (e.g., disruptive behavior, parent-child relationships, social skills) (Conners et al., 2001; Jensen et al., 1999; MTA, 1999b; Taylor, 1999). Moreover, children with ADHD who had comorbid anxiety disorders responded well in treatment groups that included the intensive behavioral intervention (Jensen et al., 2001; March et al., 2000).

A major component of the intensive behavioral intervention arm of the MTA Cooperative Group study was the summer treatment program. Pelham et al. (2000) evaluated 117 children participating in a summer camp–like program at three of the MTA Cooperative Group sites. Half of the children were assigned randomly to the behavior intervention alone group, whereas the remaining half was assigned to the combined treatment group. Children in the program who also were medicated demonstrated a better response to treatment, including rule following, good sportsmanship, peer negative nominations, and summer program teacher ratings of ADHD symptoms. Nonetheless, children responded similarly to treatment regardless of medication status on the majority of other measures.

The majority of stimulant medications are now available in short-, intermediate-, and long-acting forms (each form has a progressively longer duration of action). The advantage of these longer-term actions is that the medication may be administered less frequently throughout the course of the day; some stimulants can be administered only once per day. The clinical efficacy of stimulant drug therapies on behavioral symptoms of the three forms is generally comparable (Barkley, Connor, & Kwasnik, 2000; Faraone et al., 2002; Pliszka, Browne, Olvera, & Wynne, 2000), thereby making the longer-acting agents more desirable for children and adolescents, who typically do not wish to have to take medication during the school day (due to embarrassment at having to leave the classroom to receive medication) or ingest medication in front of peers. Moreover, another related advantage of once-daily dosing is that adherence to the prescribed regimen also is enhanced (Greevich, Rowane, Marcellino, & Sullivan-Hurst, 2001). Another advantage of the longer-acting formulations is that unlike the shorter-acting agents, the longer-acting agents continue to be effective after school. Some children evidence a "rebound effect" to stimulant medication. Specifically, when the effect of stimulant medication dissipates, there is a significant increase in motor activity (Greenhill et al., 1999). Long-term acting agents diminish this rebound effect. Further, because short-acting stimulants have been demonstrated to affect sleep—the last dose of medication is typically administered at the end of the day or during dinner—another advantage of the long-acting agents is that they exert their effects throughout the day. There is some evidence, however, that long-acting stimulants may not be as effective early in the morning (James et al., 2001).

It has been demonstrated that response to stimulant medication is frequently variable; many children and adolescents respond differently according to the dose (Greenhill et al., 1999). A child typically begins at the lowest possible dose and medication is titrated at weekly or biweekly intervals. Target behaviors include classroom or caregiver ratings of attention and concentration, overactivity, and impulsivity. For example, one frequently used stimulant medication, methylphenidate (Ritalin), is typically initiated at a dose of 5 mg on a twice daily basis. After a week or two, and based on specific ratings of attention, concentration, or academic productivity, the dose is increased from 5 to 10 mg. After another week, the medication may be increased again by 5 to 10 mg increments. Target behaviors are assessed, as are adverse effects that may be associated with the medication. When the target behaviors are achieved with the lowest possible dose, the titration ceases. Typically, if a successful response is not achieved, the practitioner might consider an alternative stimulant medication, such as dextroamphetamine (Pliszka et al., 2000) and the titration process begins anew. Thus, careful monitoring of stimulant drug effects and ongoing titration of the medication are necessary to determine whether the child or adolescent is a "responder" to the medication. If the child does not respond to one stimulant, the chances are good that the child will respond to another.

In an investigation of adolescents receiving methylphenidate, findings revealed that when the adolescents were involved in a well-controlled behavioral intervention, the best results were achieved at lower doses of the medication. Moreover, findings revealed that higher doses of medication had no additional benefit on behavioral or academic performance and could result in a number of adverse effects (Smith et al., 1998).

The monitoring of stimulant medication typically is based on data provided from multiple informants across settings (James et al., 2001). It also is necessary to monitor adverse effects and for any change in dosage to be communicated among all individuals who are responsible for the care of the child, including teachers or school nurses. Such communication is necessary so that these individuals can observe and report changes in behavior, peer relationships, and academic performance, each of which may be influenced by medication effects.

According to the literature, the most frequently encountered adverse effects associated with stimulant medication include appetite suppression, sleep disturbances, headaches, motor tics, abdominal pain, irritability, nausea, and fatigue (for review, see Brown et al., 2005). In general, many of the adverse effects associated with stimulant medications appear to be minimal, of short duration, and responsive to dosage and timing of medications. Moreover, few differences in adverse effects have been found among the various stimulants, including methylphenidate, dextroamphetamine, and pemoline (for review, see Brown et al., 2005).

One condition for which stimulant drug therapy may be contraindicated is Tourette's syndrome (TS) or motor or vocal tics. Although some research has cast doubt on the association between stimulant drug therapy and TS (see Arnstein & Brown, 2005; Brown & Ievers, 1999), others have cautioned that stimulants may precipitate motor and vocal tics, particularly where there is a family history of TS or tics (Greenhill et al., 1999; Rappley, 2005). Thus, if tics emerge in response to stimulant drug therapy or if there is a history of TS in the child or in the family, the practitioner may wish to consider alternatives to stimulants.

Alternative Pharmacotherapies

Tricyclic antidepressants (American Academy of Pediatrics Subcommittee of ADHD, 2001; Dopheide, 2005) are considered an alternative treatment for the management of symptoms associated with ADHD. Some studies have compared the efficacy of tricyclic antidepressant medication versus placebo in managing the symptoms associated with ADHD. Six studies have examined the effects of desipramine (Biederman et al., 1989, 1993; Donnelly, McGilloway, Mays, & Kerr, 1996; Gualtieri, Keenan, & Chandler, 1991; Rapport, Carlson, Kelly, & Petaki, 1993; Singer et al., 1995; Wilens et al., 1996) and all revealed improvements for children taking desipramine when compared to placebo. Some studies have examined the efficacy of imipramine (Gualtieri & Evans, 1988) and have generally reported inconsistent findings, with improved performance on some tasks and behavior measures but not on others. Although data have suggested their efficacy, tricyclic antidepressants pose a significant risk of cardiac toxicities and as a result these drugs are only employed in rare circumstances and under careful supervision. More research needs to be conducted with these pharmacotherapies to determine the role—and safety—of these agents in the management of ADHD.

Bupropion, an atypical antidepressant, has demonstrated some promise in the management of ADHD, although the risk of adverse effects is considerably greater than that of stimulants (Rappley, 2005). The most common adverse side effects are sedation, tics, and seizures.

Some experts contend that atomoxetine is the first alternative medication that should be employed in the management of children who fail to respond to stimulants (Dopheide, 2005). Atomoxetine is a nonstimulant medication approved by the FDA for the management of ADHD in children and adolescents (Kratochvil, Vaughan, Harrington, & Burke, 2003). It is a selective inhibitor of the presynaptic norepinephrine transporter in the CNS. Atomoxetine increases both norepinephrine and dopamine levels, especially in the prefrontal cortex. In a two-month, randomized placebo-controlled trial in children and adolescents ranging in age from 8 to 18 years, atomoxetine was found to demonstrate a significant reduction in core ADHD symptoms and to enhance social and family functioning compared to placebo (Michelson et al., 2001). In a 10-week randomized open-label trial, atomoxetine was compared to methylphenidate. Findings revealed significant improvements in attention, overactivity, and impulsivity for both medications when assessed by parents and clinicians. Adverse side effects were similar and included appetite suppression and initial weight loss; with the exception of atomoxetine which does not cause or worsen insomnia, in the early phase it can result in drowsiness (Kratochvil et al., 2002). Further, atomoxetine therapy was associated with small, albeit statistically significant, increases in blood pressure in children, adolescents, and adults (Wernicke et al., 2003). Blood pressure and pulse tended to increase early in therapy and returned to baseline following discontinuation of medication. No significant differences between atomoxetine and placebo were found on electrocardiograms.

Another class of medications employed in the management of ADHD and overactivity are the alpha-adrenergic agonists, which pose considerable risks for cardiac adverse effects, particularly because these agents were originally designed to decrease blood pressure and tachycardia. They are, therefore, recommended as an adjunct treatment for insomnia in the child with ADHD (Dopheide, 2005). Because the alpha-adrenergics lower blood pressure, it is necessary that adherence be carefully monitored; abrupt cessation of the medication may result in serious adverse effects.

Conduct Disorder (CD) and Oppositional Defiant Disorder (ODD)

Children or adolescents are diagnosed with conduct disorder (CD) if they repeatedly demonstrate behavior that violates the rights of others or is contrary to social mores for the child's age group (APA, 2000). Within the 12 months preceding the diagnosis, the child or adolescent must demonstrate aggression toward people or animals, destruction of property, deceitfulness or theft, and/or serious violations of rules. Moreover, the aggressive behavior must also impair academic or social functioning. Despite behaviors indicating remorse, children and adolescents with CD frequently experience no guilt or little remorse at the consequences of their behavior.

Oppositional defiant disorder (ODD) is manifested by a pattern of negative, hostile, and defiant behavior that is demonstrated by the frequent presence of at least four of the following over a period of at least six months: loss of temper, arguments with adults, defiance of adult rules or requests, deliberately annoys people, blames others for the misbehavior, easily annoyed by others, is angry and resentful, and is spiteful or vindictive. Again, the behavior must significantly affect academic and social functioning.

Pharmacotherapy

Pharmacotherapy is directed at controlling the aggression that may be present in CD and ODD. Aggression is frequently symptomatic of CD and hence many clinical trials have focused on aggression as a primary dependent variable. Kaplan & Hussain (1995) reviewed the results of several clinical trials that demonstrated the efficacy of traditional neuroleptics, including chlorpromazine and haloperidol, as well as lithium (a mood stabilizer) and propanolol (a beta-blocker) for managing aggressive behavior in children and adolescents. Riddle et al. (1999) reviewed clinical trials demonstrating the efficacy of propanolol, clonidine, and guanfacine, the latter two being alpha-adrenergics, in the management of aggressive behavior in children and adolescents.

Much of the recent research has been focused on the efficacy of atypical neuroleptic agents for the management of aggressive behavior. In a double-blind pilot study, low doses of risperidone, an atypical neuroleptic, were found to significantly reduce aggressive behavior relative to placebo in children with CD (Findling et al., 2000). Sandor

and Stephens (2000) obtained similar findings in a retrospective review of medical records of children with TS where aggressive behavior was managed with risperidone (Croonberghs et al., 2005). Sandor & Stephens (2000) found a 78% reduction in aggressive behaviors. An open-trial (Croonberghs et al., 2005) examined the long-term efficacy of risperidone for the management of aggression in children and adolescents. A reduction in aggressive behavior was revealed with minimal adverse side effects. The investigators concluded that risperidone is effective for the management of aggressive behavior in children and adolescents.

Given the comorbidity of ADHD and conduct disorders coupled with the fact that both disorders are included under the nosology of disruptive behavior disorders of childhood (APA, 1994), it is of interest whether children with conduct disorders and ODD respond to stimulants similarly to their peers with ADHD. However, few studies have examined the effects of stimulants on children with CD or ODD when these disorders occur without ADHD. There is support for the effects of stimulants on disruptive and aggressive behaviors (Connor, Glatt, Lopez, Jackson, & Melloni, 2002). Some studies have shown that antisocial behaviors in school-age children (e.g., stealing and fighting) can be reduced by stimulant treatment (Hinshaw, Heller, & McHale, 1992; Klein et al., 1997). Gerardin, Cohen, Mazet, & Flament (2002) reported that treatment with methylphenidate improved some CD symptoms, even in the absence of ADHD. Klein et al. (1997) investigated the effects of stimulants on CD in children. The participants were administered methylphenidate (up to a total of 60 mg/day) or a placebo for a period of five weeks. Parent, teacher, and clinician ratings were employed as dependent measures, as well as direct observations of classroom behavior. The majority of the sample had comorbidity, with two-thirds of the participants also meeting the criteria for ADHD. Findings revealed that ratings of antisocial behaviors specific to CD were significantly diminished with the use of stimulants. Moreover, the magnitude of the methylphenidate effects suggested meaningful clinical benefits, including diminished symptoms of oppositional defiant behavior and CD. The investigators conclude that stimulants have a positive, albeit short-term, effect on children and adolescents with CD. Although the majority of the sample had comorbidity of ADHD, because of the improvements in conduct-related symptoms, the investigators suggest that the effects of the methylphenidate are independent of ADHD-symptom severity.

Stimulants have been shown to be effective in reducing aggression, primarily in children with CD when comorbid with ADHD. However, there is little research on children with disruptive behavior disorders without ADHD (i.e., without comorbidity) when compared with placebo, and no psychotropic medications have been approved specifically for the treatment of ODD (Kaplan et al., 2004). Moreover, stimulants have yet to show significant effects on covert antisocial behaviors, such as lying or cheating (Gilligan & Lee, 2004). Therefore, it has been suggested that for pure conduct or ODD, the first-line treatment for these disorders should be behavioral and psychosocial interventions, with pharmacotherapy considered as an augmentation only when aggression and/or impulsivity are marked and persistent (Kutcher et al., 2004). Conversely, for children with ADHD with comorbid CD, evidence suggests that psychosocial intervention combined with pharmacotherapy is the treatment of choice (Kutcher et al., 2004).

Tic Disorders

Tics are sudden rapid, recurrent, and involuntary motor movements or vocalizations (APA, 2000). Tics can be simple, involving a limited number of muscles or sounds (e.g., eye blinking, nose wrinkling, facial grimacing, grunting) or complex, involving multiple muscle groups or the utterance of full sentences (e.g., jumping, stomping, squatting). Complex motor tics also may involve a sudden sexual gesture (copropraxia) or the imitation of the actions of another person (echopraxia), whereas complex verbal tics may be demonstrated by the repetition of the last word or phrase heard (echolalia) or the sudden verbalization of socially unacceptable words or phrases (coprolalia). A tic disorder may be a comorbid condition of ADHD or be exacerbated by the stimulant agents used in the management of ADHD. According to the DSM-IV there are four diagnostic categories of tic disorders: Tourette's syndrome (TS), chronic motor or vocal tic disorder, transient tic disorder, and tic disorder not otherwise specified (APA, 2000).

Pharmacotherapy

The management of tic disorders in children and adolescents is aimed at decreasing the severity and frequency of the tic manifestation. Alpha-adrenergic agonist agents (e.g., clonidine and guanfacine) are antihypertensive agents used in the management of tic disorder. The effectiveness of the alpha agonists is believed to be related to the suppression of noradrenergic hormone secretion, which decreases activity, heart rate, and blood pressure (Riddle et al., 1999). The reduction of noradrenergic hormones to manage tic disorders is consistent with the suggestion that tics are a mechanism to relieve increased internal pressure (APA, 2000). The data from multiple clinical trials (for review see Kaplan & Hussain, 1995; Riddle et al., 1999) suggest equivocal efficacy for the use of alpha-adrenergic agonists for the management of tic disorders.

Neuroleptic agents, particularly traditional agents (e.g., haloperidol, pimozide), have demonstrated efficacy in the management of tic disorders (Kaplan et al., 1995). As indicated in our review of the use of neuroleptic agents for psychotic disorders (below), the significant adverse side-effect profile with traditional neuroleptics makes them a less than desirable choice as the first-line agent for the management of tic disorders.

One randomized, double-blind crossover trial compared the efficacy of risperidone relative to pimozide in reducing the number and severity of tics (Gilbert, Batterson, Sethuraman, & Salee, 2004). Children were assigned randomly to either the resperidone/pimozide sequence or the pimozide/respiridone sequence of the trial. After four weeks, there was a 42% reduction in the frequency and severity of tics with respiridone versus a 16% reduction with pimozide. The researchers concluded that risperidone is superior to pimozide for tic reduction but is associated with a larger weight gain.

In one placebo-controlled clinical trial examined the efficacy of risperidone relative to placebo in the management of TS (Scahill, Leckman, Schultz, Katsovich, & Peterson, 2003), the clinician evaluator reported a 32% reduction in the severity of the tics versus 7% for placebo. Findings revealed a decrease of 35% in the severity of tics versus 2% for placebo. The investigators concluded that respiridone is an effective agent for the management of TS with a significantly reduced adverse risk profile.

Many children with TS experience additional neurobehavioral problems including inattention, overactivity, and impulsivity. Tic disorders and TS are frequently accompanied by other conditions; the most frequent comorbid condition is

ADHD (about 50% of patients with TS have accompanying ADHD) (Burd, 1995).

Treatment of comorbid ADHD has been controversial because of reports that stimulants hasten the onset or exacerbate the severity of tics in some patients (Kurlan, 1997; Sverd, Gadow, Nolan, Sprafkin, & Ezor, 1992). Given this concern, greater efforts have been undertaken to examine the effects of stimulants in ADHD children with comorbid tic disorders.

Gadow, Sverd, Sprafkin, Nolan, & Ezor, (1995) conducted a prospective, follow-up open trial that examined the effects of long-term treatment with methylphenidate therapy for ADHD symptoms and motor and vocal tics among prepubertal children with ADHD and chronic multiple tic disorder (the majority of children qualified for a diagnosis of TS). Children included in this study had participated in an earlier eight-week, double-blind, placebo-controlled trial. Findings from group data provided no evidence to support the notion that motor or vocal tics changed in frequency or severity during methylphenidate maintenance therapy compared with diagnostic or initial double-blind placebo evaluations. Moreover, behavioral improvements demonstrated during the acute drug trial were sustained at the follow-up evaluation. Gadow et al. (1995) suggest that long-term treatment with methylphenidate seems to be safe and effective for the management of ADHD symptoms in many (but not necessarily all) children with mild to moderate tic disorder. However, Gadow et al. (1995) caution that clinical monitoring should always be the standard of care to rule out the possibility of drug-induced tic exacerbation in children with comorbid ADHD.

Castellanos et al. (1997) examined the effects of stimulants (methylphenidate or dextroamphetamine) and dose response on tic severity for the management of boys with ADHD and comorbid TS. Results indicated that a substantial minority of the comorbid participants had consistent exacerbation of tics on stimulants. Despite this concern, however, it should be noted that the majority of boys evidenced improvement in symptoms associated with ADHD with no real exacerbation of tics. Overall, treatment with methylphenidate was better tolerated than dextroamphetamine therapy in children with TS. This investigation is important as it is one of the few studies to compare specific types of stimulants in a controlled clinical trial for children with TS.

The Tourette's Syndrome Study Group (2002) conducted a randomized double-blind, placebo controlled trial with a 16-week follow-up period on the effects of clonidine and methylphenidate for the treatment for 136 children with ADHD. Methylphenidate compared to placebo resulted in beneficial effects for ADHD symptoms as assessed by teacher ratings of ADHD symptoms; however, the greatest benefit was observed with combined clonidine and MPH. Results also revealed that the combined treatment of clonidine and methylphenidate was most effective in diminishing tic severity (75% of the children showed improvement) and enhancing overall global functioning. Findings also revealed that methylphenidate alone was effective in diminishing tic severity and decreasing functional impairments. Tics were not found to be substantially worse in the active medication group versus the placebo group; however, the study failed to address the relationship between dose of methylphenidate and the emergence of tics (Goldberg, 2002). Findings from this study and those of Law and Schachar's (1999) study are potentially important as clinicians may take comfort in the fact that treatment with methylphenidate does not cause or exacerbate tics (Tourette's Syndrome Study Group, 2002). Nonetheless, studies are needed to examine dose response associations between specific doses of stimulants (e.g., high versus low doses) and the emergence of tics.

In summary, recent studies have suggested that stimulants are an effective and safe intervention for children with ADHD who have comorbid tic disorders. However if, after assessment, the practitioner elects a trial of stimulants, caution should be the standard, together with ongoing monitoring regarding adverse effects including the emergence or exacerbation of tics. Additional studies are needed to examine the risks and benefits of stimulants in children and adolescents with TS or a family history of TS, as well as dose-response relationships that could connect the emergence of tics to specific stimulant doses.

INTERNALIZING DISORDERS

Internalizing disorders include anxiety disorders and mood disorders (i.e., depressive disorders, bipolar disorders) and we review recent developments in pharmacotherapy for each of these disorders.

Anxiety Disorders

Anxiety disorders are among one of the most prevalent mental health related diagnoses in children and adolescents (Yorbik & Birmaher, 2003). Yet clinical trials examining the safety and efficacy of pharmacologic agents in the management of anxiety disorders in the pediatric population are only now increasing in frequency. The risk associated with anxiety disorders in children and adolescents is significant and includes substance abuse, poor academic performance, poor social skills, inadequate social relationships, and other psychiatric comorbidity (e.g., depression, ADHD), and specific anxiety disorders (e.g., post-traumatic stress disorder, phobias) (Layne, Bernstein, Egan, & Kushner, 2003).

There are several types of anxiety disorders that may be experienced by children and adolescents. Anxiety disorders are characterized by excessive worry and fear. The origin of the worry or fear may differ, as does the overt manifestation and response to treatment (APA, 1994).

Separation anxiety disorder can begin as early as 6 years of age and is characterized by excessive distress at the possibility of separation from familiar persons or environments. The diagnosis is made when the symptoms persist for approximately four weeks.

Generalized anxiety disorder (GAD) is characterized by excessive worrying about activities or events. The worrying occurs most days and that lasts for more than six months (APA, 2000). Children and adolescents with GAD are typically perfectionists who may redo a task multiple times because they are dissatisfied with the outcome.

Panic disorder is present when a child or adolescent experiences multiple panic attacks and is consistently concerned about the possibility of experiencing another panic attack (APA, 2000). The life of the child or adolescent with panic disorder is consumed with worry and apprehension over when the next panic attack will occur and the consequences of the panic attack. In one investigation, the prevalence rate of panic attack was found to be 8.7% in a sample of adolescents (Hayward, Wilson, Lagle, Killen, & Taylor, 2004).

Selective mutism is characterized by lack of speech in specific situations despite an ability to speak otherwise. This goes beyond the normal shyness or hesitancy to speak experienced by many children in novel situations. The diagnosis of selective mutism is made when the inability to speak extends beyond one year (APA, 2000).

Social phobia (SP) is characterized by an excessive or abnormal fear of a readily identifiable situation or object that sustains for at least six months (APA, 2000). Although adolescents or adults can understand that their fear and anxiety may be out of proportion to the actual danger posed by the object or situation, children are unable to recognize this particular paradox, much like a specific phobia.

Social anxiety disorder (SAD) is more prevalent among females than among men; the peak occurrence among both genders occurs among children between 11 and 15 years (Cottraux, 2005).

Obsessive-compulsive disorder (OCD) is characterized by persistent obsessions and or compulsions so severe as to impose themselves on all aspects of the individual's life. *Obsessions* are defined as ideas or thoughts that persistently intrude into the thoughts and are associated with significant anxiety, worry, and distress. *Compulsions*, in contrast, are repetitive behaviors that serve to externalize the internal distress (APA, 2000). For children and adolescents, the repetitive behaviors may include any type of activity, including washing hands or checking the light switch a specific number of times.

Finally, *post-traumatic stress disorder* (PTSD) develops following direct exposure to a threatening situation or event (APA, 2000). The symptoms should be present for a period of at least one month following exposure to the traumatic event to qualify for a diagnosis of PTSD.

Pharmacologic Agents

Until recently, pharmacologic management of anxiety disorders in children and adolescents had not been well researched in pediatric populations (Williams & Miller, 2003). Similar to the pharmacologic management of depression, adult studies were primarily employed to guide the pharmacological management of children and adolescents. In the past, the pharmacologic agents of choice for the management of various anxiety disorders were benzodiazepines and tricyclic antidepressants. The use of each of these agents presents unique concerns, which are discussed below.

Benzodiazepines

Benzodiazepines are the primary pharmacologic agents used in the management of anxiety disorders classified as anxiolytics. They decrease anxiety by increasing transmission of the neurotransmitter GABA (aminobutyric acid), which provides an inhibitory effect on the arousal state induced by anxiety (Morgan, Krystal, & Southwick, 2003). The mechanisms of action associated with this agent are consistent across all benzodiazepines; the major differences among the agents within the class of benzodiazepines are the timing of peak effects and the duration of action. As noted above, although the benzodiazepines have historically been recommended as the first-line treatment for anxiety disorders, they recently have been supplanted by SSRIs (Cloos, 2005; Williams & Miller, 2003; Yorbik & Birmaher, 2003). Despite efforts to change practice patterns to reflect the recommendation of SSRIs as a first-line choice for the management of anxiety disorders, many providers still continue to prescribe benzodiazepines for children and adolescents with anxiety disorders (Bruce et al., 2003).

Most of the controlled clinical trials of benzodiazepines have been conducted on adults and their results have been extrapolated for use with children and adolescents. Reviews by Yorbik and Birmaher (2003) and Riddle et al. (1999) show that studies of benzodiazepines for management of anxiety have demonstrated mixed results.

Benzodiazepines have been associated with behavioral and motor toxicities in children and adolescents that may include symptoms such as ataxia, loss of motor control, or disinhibition of behavior. Children who develop disinhibition syndrome are likely to display irritability, tantrums, and aggression, whereas adolescents may exhibit irritability and behavioral outbursts (Riddle et al., 1999). Obviously, such symptoms can adversely affect interpersonal relationships with family, friends, and teachers. It also is important to note that there is a significant risk of abuse with the use of benzodiazepines (Basile, Lippa, & Skolnick, 2004; Kilic, Curran, Noshirvani, Marks, & Basoglu, 1999; Williams & Miller, 2003), particularly among the adolescent population (Riddle et al., 1999). For these reasons, utmost caution should be taken in prescribing these agents for children and adolescents.

Selective Serotonin Reuptake Inhibitors

The Selective Serotonin Reuptake Inhibitors (SSRIs) are currently the most widely researched pharmacologic agents for the treatment of anxiety disorders. In a 15-year follow-up of patients with panic disorder, the use of SSRIs increased to 27% whereas the use of tricyclic antidepressants and benzodiazepines significantly decreased (Andersch & Hetta, 2003). Although SSRIs are classified as antidepressants, their efficacy has been documented for several anxiety disorders. Morgan et al. (2003) postulate that stress elevates glutamate levels in the brain, which cause the typical stress response of hyperarousal and excitation. Through an increase in serotonin at the level of the synapse, GABA is increased, which enhances the inhibitory response.

The efficacy and safety of fluoxetine for the management of anxiety disorders in children and adolescents has been examined in several randomized clinical trials. When employed for the management of generalized anxiety disorder (GAD), separation anxiety disorder (SAD), or social phobia (SP), fluoxetine was demonstrated to be more effective than placebo. Birmaher et al. (2003) concluded that children who received fluoxetine demonstrated improvement relative to the placebo dose by the fourth week of the trial. At the end of the 12-week trial, over 60% of the children who were treated with the active agent reported anxiety symptoms being either "very much improved" or "improved" when compared to the placebo treated group, where only 35% of the sample reported a decrease in anxiety symptoms. When the results for each discrete anxiety disorder were examined, the researchers concluded that when children and adolescents with GAD or SPs are managed with fluoxetine, there is a significant improvement in clinical outcomes (76% and 67% respectively) relative to placebo. There was no significant difference between the fluoxetine and placebo groups for the children diagnosed with SAD. Of the children who reported a significant improvement in anxiety symptoms, half of the sample continued to have at least three symptoms of anxiety. The data were interpreted to suggest that fluoxetine may be effective for the relief of some symptoms of anxiety disorders, although conclusions with regard to remission of symptoms must be demonstrated through additional research.

Sertraline was compared with cognitive behavior therapy (CBT) for the management of children and adolescents with OCD (March, Foa et al., 2004). This was a 12-week clinical trial that consisted of four arms: sertraline alone, CBT alone, sertraline plus CBT, and placebo. The three active treatment arms were significantly more effective than placebo. However, the group receiving active treatment with CBT plus sertraline reported a 53.6% remission rate over either CBT alone (39.3% remission rate) or sertraline alone (21.4% remission rate). Based on these data, the investigators concluded that children and adolescents with OCD should begin treatment with CBT alone or CBT plus sertraline. The data indicate that pharmacologic agents alone may not be sufficient in the management of OCD for children and adolescents.

Fluvoxamine was compared to placebo for efficacy and safety in the management of anxiety disorders in children and adolescents, including SP, SAD, and GAD (Walkup et al., 2001). There was a 76% response in the group receiving active fluvoxamine versus a placebo response of 29%. Moreover, there was a marked decrease in symptoms associated with anxiety by the third week of the trial that persisted until the sixth week of the study. Thus, fluvoxamine is an effective pharmacotherapy in the treatment of anxiety disorders in the pediatric population.

Tricyclic Antidepressants

The use of tricyclic antidepressants in the management of anxiety disorders has been based primarily on research conducted with adult patients. Because the adverse side-effect profile of tricyclic antidepressants is significant and potentially lethal, including the possibility of cardiac toxicity, their use has fallen into disfavor. For this reason, tricyclics are currently reserved for use as a second or third-line agent only for children and adolescents who have failed trials with SSRIs or as a supplement to SSRI management.

A review of randomized clinical trials (Yorbik & Birmaher, 2003) demonstrated equivocal results for the use of tricyclics in the pediatric population. The five studies reviewed involved either clomipramine or imipramine as the active pharmacological agent. Findings from three of the studies demonstrated that the active agent and placebo exerted generally similar effects. Two of the studies demonstrated increased efficacy for active pharmacotherapy, one of which involved the addition of CBT. However, the degree of treatment effect due to pharmacotherapy versus psychotherapy is unclear.

There have been significant advances in the number of randomized clinical trials designed to determine the safety and efficacy of pharmacologic agents for the management of anxiety disorders in children and adolescents. Because of their favorable side-effect profile, most of the trials have included SSRIs. The research to date is promising with regard to efficacy and safety. Nevertheless, there continues to be a gap between evidenced-based practice and the widely prescribed use of pharmacologic agents with pediatric populations.

Depression

It is now recognized that depression affects children as young as 5 years of age. It is believed that up to 2% of children and 6% of adolescents qualify for a diagnosis of major depressive disorder (Cheung, Emslie, Mayes 2005), with higher rates of the disorder occurring among adolescent females. Moreover, it has been suggested that almost half of adolescents with depression will have a recurrence during adulthood (Olfson, Gameroff, Marcus, & Waslick, 2003). Despite this rate of occurrence, it is estimated that only 1% of children and adolescents with depression are being appropriately treated (Olfson et al., 2003). Depression in children and adolescents that remains untreated has an adverse side effect on functional outcomes, including academic performance and relationships with peers and family members, including parents and authority figures. If not appropriately managed, the negative sequelae associated with depression can extend into adulthood and affect adult relationships and employment as well as increasing the risk for substance abuse (Apter, Kronenberg, & Brent, 2005). There is evidence suggesting a genetic component to the disorder (Kovacs, Devlin, Pollock, Richards, & Mukerji, 1997; Todd, Neuman, Geller, Fox, & Hickok, 1993).

To qualify for a diagnosis of depression, the child or adolescent must experience one or more depressive episodes each lasting at least two weeks. The depressed mood must be accompanied by at least four additional symptoms that are of new onset or markedly worse than noted on previous occasions (APA, 2000). In some cases, rather than experiencing sadness, the child or adolescent may complain of somatic symptoms with no findings of physiologic abnormalities on physical examination. The child or adolescent may report an inability to enjoy activities that were previously enjoyed (anhedonia) or may withdraw from social situations. Children and adolescents may experience a change in appetite that ranges from an increase, decrease, or craving of sweets. In some cases, children may be unable to achieve the expected weight gains for their height and age. Complaints of sleep disturbances are not uncommon. Children and adolescent may have difficulty falling asleep or awaken early and be unable to fall back to sleep. Further, some children and adolescents may also have profound feelings of worthlessness or feelings of guilt over minor past events. Moreover, some children and adolescents may have difficulty concentrating or making decisions. Finally, depressed youths may have suicidal ideations.

Pharmacotherapy

In the past, treatment of depression in children was approached similarly to that of adults (Fetner & Geller, 1992). Results of clinical trials demonstrating the efficacy of pharmacologic agents in adults were applied to children on the assumption that they were equally applicable. This practice ignored the fact that the pharmacokinetics of antidepressants are vastly different due to a considerably increased metabolism in pediatric populations relative to adults. This difference affects pediatric dosage requirements, dosing intervals, elimination rates, and physiologic and behavioral responses of children to psychotropic medications (Birmaher, Ryan, Williamson, Brent, & Kaufman, 1996). There is now a concerted effort in the research community to conduct clinical trials that are targeted toward determining the efficacy and safety of antidepressants for children and adolescents.

There have been recent reports of an increased number of attempted and successful suicides among adolescents treated with antidepressants (Caballero & Nahata, 2005). As a result of these incidents, the FDA now requires that a "black box warning" be placed on all antidepressant prescriptions, specifically warning of the increased risk of suicide that may be associated with the treatment of children and adolescents on antidepressant medication (Krishnan, 2005). Although such actions have, to some extent, resulted in a decrease of the prescribing of antidepressant agents in the pediatric population, there is still widespread use of these agents with children and (especially) adolescents (Ringold, 2005).

There are four classifications of antidepressant medications available at this time that are employed with children and adolescents: selective serotonin reuptake inhibitors (SSRIs), tricyclic antidepressants (tricyclics), atypical antidepressants (atypicals), and monoamine oxidase inhibitors (MAOIs). Because of the minimal adverse side-effect profile of SSRIs, they have become the most widely prescribed antidepressants (Caballero & Nahata, 2005; Murray, deVries, & Wong, 2004). Tricyclic antidepressants, formerly the most widely employed antidepressants prior to SSRIs, are now the second-line

treatment for depression due to the frequency of adverse side effects associated with their use, some of which exert particularly deleterious effects on the cardiovascular system (Caballero & Nahata, 2005). Atypical antidepressants are the third-line treatment employed in this population due, in part, to the paucity of research data with regard to efficacy and safety in children and adolescents. Finally, monoamine oxidase inhibitors (MAOIs) are rarely used in children because of the dietary modifications required when administering these agents. These agents are typically used when children fail to respond to SSRIs and tricyclics.

Selective Serotonin Reuptake Inhibitors (SSRIs)

SSRIs have been widely available since 1990 and their use for management of depression in pediatric groups increased steadily since their introduction. Prior to the availability of SSRIs, antidepressants were used infrequently for the management of depressive symptoms among children and adolescents (Olfson et al., 2003). In a survey of insured clients between 1998 and 2002, SSRIs were reportedly responsible for a 9.2% annual increase in the use of antidepressant medications (Delate, Gelenberg, Simmons, & Motheral, 2004). In comparison to other psychotropic agents available, SSRIs are an attractive alternative for the management of depression in pediatric populations because they are well tolerated and have minimal adverse effects (American Academy of Child & Adolescent Psychiatry, 1998). Nonetheless, there are still questions regarding their long-term efficacy and safety in children and adolescents.

There have been few clinical trials of SSRIs involving children and adolescents, although there have more studies in recent years. After clinical reports of an increase in suicidality with SSRIs, both the FDA and the British Medicines and Health Care Products Regulatory Agency (MHRA) performed a meta-analysis of the existing clinical trials on antidepressant medication use in children and adolescents. The MHRA concluded that because of a lack of evidence on efficacy, antidepressants are contraindicated in children less than 18 years (Whittington, Kendall, & Pilling, 2005). The FDA examined the same studies and concluded that the only pharmacologic agent with documented efficacy and safety in children and adolescents with depression is fluoxetine (Caballero & Nahata, 2005).

In open trials of SSRIs, where participants were aware if they were receiving active medication versus placebo, investigators reported a positive response rate to pharmacotherapy ranging from 70 to 90% (Colle, Belair, DiFeo, Weiss, & LaRoache, 1994; Jain, Birmaher, Garcia, Al-Shabbout, & Ryan, 1992). Nonetheless, despite these encouraging data, because the studies were open clinical trials, it is difficult to ascertain whether the positive response is due to the drug or a placebo effect. Additional controlled clinical trials are needed in pediatric populations to further evaluate the efficacy of fluoxetine. Until further data are forthcoming, the practitioner must be judicious in prescribing these agents.

A number of randomized controlled clinical trials have been conducted to evaluate the efficacy and safety of other SSRIs in children and adolescents. Jureidini, Doecke, Mansfield, Haby, Menkes, and Tonkin (2004) performed a meta-analysis of seven randomized clinical trials of various SSRIs [i.e., fluoxetine (n = 3), paroxetine (n = 1), sertraline (n = 2) and venlafaxine (n = 1)]. When the data from the studies were collapsed, the measure of effect size was 0.26 (considered to be a generally small effect size). The conclusion was that there is no major clinical benefit to these drugs. A randomized clinical trial with paroxetine conducted by Keller et al. (2001) provided data that indicated a 63% positive response rate to the active medication versus a 46% response to placebo. Wagner, Ambrosini et al. (2003) examined the efficacy and safety of sertraline and found a 69% positive response rate versus a 59% response for placebo. In both of these investigations, the conclusion was that the active medication is efficacious in treating depression in children and adolescents, despite the small differences in response rate between placebo and active medication.

A major question that has been the focus of much research is whether antidepressants are more efficacious than traditional psychotherapy for the management of children and adolescents with depression. In a seminal investigation, the Treatment for Adolescents with Depression Study (March, Silva et al., 2004), the relative efficacy of fluoxetine and CBT was examined. CBT has demonstrated efficacy in the management of depression. Participants included 439 patients between the ages of 12 and 17. The investigation consisted of four arms: fluoxetine alone, CBT alone, fluoxetine plus CBT, and placebo. Adolescents participated in the investigation for three months. Findings revealed that fluoxetine plus CBT demonstrated the greatest efficacy when compared to placebo alone. When fluoxetine alone was compared with fluoxetine plus CBT, the combined treatment was superior to the fluoxetine alone arm. The findings from this investigation are important as they demonstrate that psychotherapy (i.e., CBT) is an important adjunct to pharmacotherapy in the management of depression in adolescents.

Tricyclic Antidepressants

Prior to the introduction of SSRIs, the use of tricyclic antidepressants for the management of childhood and adolescent depression was based primarily on the success of their use with adults. However, in randomized clinical trials tricyclics have been demonstrated to be no more effective in treating depression in this age group than placebo (for review, see Birmaher et al., 1996; Ryan & Varma, 1998). Although the lack of effect may be associated with study design, populations studied, or dosing, Ryan and Varma (1998) suggest that the ineffectiveness of tricyclic antidepressants is likely based on their mechanism of action. Tricyclics block the reuptake of norepinephrine, a noradrenergic neurotransmitter. It is hypothesized that their ineffectiveness in children and adolescents may in part be a function of the immaturity of the noradrenergic system in pediatric populations. Although there has been a marked reduction in the use of tricyclics, they still continue to be prescribed even in the face of suboptimal efficacy for depression and the increased likelihood of treatment noncompliance due to their numerous adverse effects (Murray et al., 2004).

The frequency and severity of adverse side effects associated with tricyclics has resulted in many individuals ceasing treatment early, before beneficial effects can be observed (Birmaher et al., 1996). Of greatest concern in the pediatric population is the potential for toxic cardiac-related adverse side effects (Wilens et al., 1996). Another adverse cardiac effect is postural orthostatic hypotension, a condition where there is a rapid drop in blood pressure, which can lead to dizziness, as a result of a sudden change in position. There also have been reports of an increase in both systolic and diastolic blood pressure as a result of tricyclics. The most potentially lethal cardiac effect of tricyclic antidepressants is the prolongation of the cardiac cycle, which can lead to a lethal cardiac dysrhythmia. In their review of relevant studies, Wilens et al. (1996) found that at "normal" doses and serum blood levels there are mild increases in blood pressure, heart rate, and prolonged cardiac conduction. Because these cardiac effects are more pronounced with exercise, children and adolescents receiving tricyclic antidepressants should be carefully monitored during recess or physical education activities. Because higher doses and concomitant serum blood levels exacerbate these effects, utmost caution should be exercised in titrating doses upward.

Atypical Antidepressants

Atypical antidepressants (i.e., bupropion, nefazodone, trazodone, mirtazapine, venlafaxine) are grouped together because of their differing, and in some cases, uncertain mechanisms of action. Each of these pharmacotherapies affects the availability of norepinephrine at the synaptic cleft. As with tricyclics, the presumed lack of maturity of the noradrenergic system in pediatric populations may contribute to the lack of efficacy of these agents. Additional research in this area is necessary, including controlled clinical trials that can examine the efficacy and safety of these agents.

Venlafaxine is unique among atypical antidepressants because it inhibits the reuptake of both norepinephrine and serotonin. Reportedly effective for depression that is resistant to the more typical antidepressants in adults (Emslie, Walkup, Pliszka, & Ernst, 1999), there is one investigation of children where the treatment effect with venlafaxine was found to be similar to placebo (Mandocki, Tapia, Tapia, Sumner, & Parker, 1997). Two investigations of children and adolescents (Wagner, 2005) reported no advantage of active medication relative to placebo. Thus, the efficacy of venlafaxine in the management of depression in children and adolescents has yet to be demonstrated.

Bupropion inhibits the reuptake of both dopamine and norepinephrine (Goodnick, Dominguez, DeVane, & Bowden, 1998; Horst & Preskorn, 1998). Few studies have examined the efficacy of bupropion for the management of depressive symptoms in children and adolescents. An open trial of the effectiveness of bupropion-SR (sustained release) in the management of adolescent depression was conducted over an eight-week period. The data revealed a positive response rate of over 70% for both clinicians and patients. The investigators concluded that bupropion-SR may be an effective agent in the management of adolescent depression (Glod, Lynch, Flyn, Berkowitz, & Baldessarini, 2003). Another open label study examined the use of bupropion for symptom management of both depressive disorder and ADHD. The data revealed an overall response rate of 88% to bupropion for relief from depressive symptoms and a 63% response rate for management of symptoms related to ADHD. The investigators concluded that bupropion may be an effective agent for management of ADHD with comorbid depressive symptoms (Davis et al., 2001).

Monoamine Oxidase Inhibitors (MAOIs)

MAOIs (e.g., phenelzine, isocarboxasid, tranylcypromine) prevent the breakdown of the neurotransmitters by preventing the release of the enzyme monoamine oxidase. When an individual receiving an MAOI ingests any food containing the amino acid tyramine, due to the lack of the enzyme monoamine oxidase, tyramine cannot be broken down thereby potentiating an interaction with the neurotransmitters, thus causing a hypertensive crisis (Emslie et al., 1999). Because tyramine is prevalent in many foods consumed by children, such as cheeses and yogurt, MAOIs are rarely prescribed to children and adolescents (Brown & Sammons, 2002). There are new MAOIs available that have a different mechanism of action than those currently approved by the FDA. An advantage of these newer agents is that they do not carry the same risk of hypertensive crisis. Although these agents have been approved for use in Europe, they are not yet available in the United States (Emslie et al., 1999). Traditional MAOIs frequently result in significant sedation in children and adolescents. This is especially noteworthy because academic performance may be negatively affected. In a recent review of the extant literature, Wagner (2005) observed that no studies can be located on the use of the currently available MAOIs in the treatment of depression for children and adolescents. In the absence of such data, the clinician must be especially judicious in prescribing any of these agents for children and adolescents.

Bipolar Disorder

Bipolar disorder is a mood disorder characterized by alternating depressed and manic moods. The clinical presentation is similar between the adult and pediatric populations; children, however, often present with multiple comorbid diagnoses, the most frequent of which is ADHD (Ryan, Bhatara, & Perel, 1999). It is particularly troublesome when bipolar disorder is diagnosed in adolescents who present with rapid cycling (i.e., four or more episodes within a year). Rapid cycling bipolar disorder makes pharmacologic management difficult (Kafantaris, Coletti, Dicker, Padula, & Kane, 2003) and approximately 75% of children and adolescents with rapid cycling bipolar disorder are unresponsive to lithium, the first choice for the pharmacologic management of bipolar disorder (Calabrese et al., 2005).

Pharmacotherapy

As with the majority of other pharmacologic agents reviewed in this chapter, the use of mood stabilizers in children and adolescents historically has been based on clinical trials with adult populations. Although clinical trials with children and adolescents are increasing in frequency, they are still insufficient to establish safety and efficacy in children and adolescents. According to the APA (1994), the first-line agents of choice for the management of mania in children and adolescents are lithium and valproic acid (an anticonvulsant agent). Antipsychotic agents may be used to reduce the psychotic symptoms that may occur with mania or to decrease aggressive behavior. They should not be used in the long term as they have no anti-manic properties and pose a significant risk of adverse side effects. According to Cookson (2001), this recommendation is not currently reflected in clinical practice, where use of antipsychotic agents in the management of bipolar disorder continues at a high pitch.

Lithium

Since the mid-1970s, the only approved treatment available for the management of bipolar disorder has been lithium. Although the exact mechanism of action of lithium is uncertain, there is evidence to suggest that lithium affects neurochemical transmission within the brain (Belmaker, 2004). Neuroimaging studies have demonstrated that individuals with bipolar disorder may lose gray matter within the brain, whereas lithium has been shown to increase the amount of gray matter. This suggests a neuroprotective effect of lithium on the CNS (Sassi et al., 2002).

Kafantaris et al. (2003) conducted an open trial examining the efficacy of lithium for the management of acute mania in adolescents. More than one-half of the adolescents in the study had at least a 50% reduction in manic symptoms. Suicidal ideation also was decreased by 82%. These researchers did not find a response to lithium in the adolescents with major depressive disorder.

Geddes, Burgess, Hawton, Jamison, & Goodwin, (2004) reviewed five randomized clinical trials to determine the efficacy of lithium in the management of bipolar disorder. Based on their review, they found a difference in the rate of new episodes of mood disturbances for those receiving treatment with lithium relative to placebo (40% relapse rate versus 60%, respectively). Of interest is that the difference was more pronounced with the manic episode than with the depressive episode. Another review of 12 clinical trials was conducted to determine the efficacy of lithium in management of bipolar disorder (Poolsup, Po, & de Oliveira, 2000). Conclusions are that lithium was more effective than placebo in reducing symptoms of mania. In studies comparing lithium to the neuroleptic agents, lithium has been found to be more effective than the chlorpromazine and as effective as haloperidol. Lithium also was as effective as the anticonvulsants valproate and carbamazepine. Additional study is needed with all of these pharmacologic agents, particularly in the pediatric population because the pharmacodynamics are different for adults than for children and may affect the ability of lithium to prevent a relapse.

Lithium is available in two forms. Lithium carbonate comes in pill form; lithium citrate is an elixir (liquid). Equivalent doses and duration of effect are typically achievable when the child or adolescent switches between the pill and elixir forms (Reischer & Pfeffer, 1996). As noted above, however, children and adolescents have a more rapid metabolic rate than adults, suggesting that the duration of effect may differ in pill versus elixir form because of differing absorption rates and metabolism. Reischer and Pfeffer (1996) recommend that when changing from liquid to pill, the practitioner should begin at the lower dose and titrate upward gradually until the desired target behaviors are achieved.

Lithium frequently produces side effects of such severity that many patients often discontinue the medication prematurely (Bowden, 2004; Calabrese et al., 2005). The most commonly reported reasons for discontinuing lithium are associated cognitive changes experienced by the child or adolescent during the course of therapy, including poor verbal memory, inability to concentrate, and, for some, even loss of creativity. Moreover, there are reports of slowed psychomotor speed (Pachet & Wisniewski, 2003). These changes have significant repercussions both for the academic performance of children and adolescents as well as peer relationships. There also are long-term implications for nonadherence with lithium therapy. If symptoms recur each time there is cessation of lithium, there is evidence to suggest that the neuropsychological effects of lithium cessation are cumulative (Geddes et al., 2004).

Anticonvulsants

Approximately 20% of individuals do not respond to lithium therapy and for this reason, alternate psychotropics may be needed (Poolsup, Po, & de Oliveira, 2000). Anticonvulsants are believed to exert their effect on the same neurochemical pathways as lithium (Belmaker, 2004; Brunello, 2002). Carbamazepine and valproic acid are the primary anticonvulsants used in the management of bipolar disorder in children and adolescents. Divalproate, a derivative of valproic acid, and approved by the FDA for use with bipolar disorder in 1995, has been found to be effective in the management of both the manic and depressive episodes in bipolar disorder (Bowden, 2004) as well as mixed-type bipolar disorders (Ryan et al., 1999). Carbamazepine has been used as a mood stabilizer since the 1970s (Cookson, 2001), although there is insufficient evidence of its efficacy. Lamotrigine, gabapentin, and topiramate also have been used to manage the symptoms of bipolar disorder, although more clinical trials are needed to examine their efficacy and safety in children and adolescents (Licht, Vestergaard, Kessing, Larsen, & Thomsen, 2003).

There have been few clinical trials examining the efficacy and safety of anticonvulsants in the management of bipolar disorder. Until the approval of divalproate, the use of carbamazapine was not approved by the FDA for use in the management of bipolar disorder in children and adolescents. As a result, there are few data concerning the efficacy of divalproate in the management of bipolar disorder in children and adolescents.

Although the risk of adverse effects is less for anticonvulsants compared to lithium, there are still significant adverse effects associated with the anticonvulsants. Children and adolescents should begin the anticonvulsant agent at a low dose and the dose should be gradually increased until target symptoms are controlled or until adverse side effects present (Licht et al., 2003).

The risk of suicidal ideation or active suicide attempts are increased during the acute manic phase of bipolar disorder. Goodwin et al. (2003) compared the suicide risk of adolescents and adults 14 years and older, all of whom were managed with either lithium or divalproex. Findings revealed that the risk for suicidal ideation was almost three times greater for those managed with divalproex. The data are inconsistent with those of Yerevanian, Kock, and Mintz (2003) who found no difference in the suicide risk for those managed with divalproex versus lithium. The question of suicide risk with any psychotropic agent requires systematic investigation.

There has been an increase in the number of randomized clinical trials examining the safety and efficacy of pharmacologic agents for the management of bipolar disease in children and adolescents, but more are needed. Despite the lack of an evidence base, clinicians continue to prescribe pharmacologic agents that have not been studied in the pediatric population or that are not recommended as a first-line treatment. Greater research efforts are needed, particularly research that addresses the effect of the various agents on symptoms as well as functional impairments experienced by children and adolescents with bipolar disorder.

SCHIZOPHRENIA AND OTHER PSYCHOTIC DISORDERS

Psychotic disorders are characterized by symptoms including hallucinations, delusions, disorganized speech, and disorganized or catatonic behavior. There are several different psychotic disorders, many of which are diagnosed based on a comparison with schizophrenia (APA, 2000).

Schizophrenia is the prototypical psychotic disorder. It typically begins in adolescence or young adulthood (Freedman, 2003). The symptoms of schizophrenia are classified as "positive symptoms" when they represent a distortion of normal functioning: a distortion in thought content (delusions), perceptions (hallucinations), language and thought process (disorganized speech), and self-monitoring of behavior (grossly disorganized or catatonic). "Negative symptoms" of schizophrenia reflect a loss or decline in normal functioning: a restricted range of emotional expression (flat affect), decreased fluency in thought and speech (alogia), and a decreased ability to participate in goal-directed behavior (avolition).

According to the APA (2000), schizophrenia is characterized by the presence of any two of the following symptoms: delusions, hallucinations, disorganized speech, disorganized or catatonic behavior, or negative symptoms, including flat affect, alogia, and avolition. These symptoms are present for the better portion of a month in addition to at least a six-month period of other cognitive or behavioral symptoms, including unusual perceptions, inferential thinking, language or communication difficulties, lack of attention or drive, and flat affect. The diagnosis of schizophrenia is made independent of other medical or psychiatric diagnoses.

Pharmacotherapy

Neuroleptic agents are used in the management of symptoms of schizophrenia and other psychotic symptoms in children and adolescents, despite the fact that many have not been approved for use in pediatric populations. There are currently two classes of neuroleptic agents: traditional and atypical neuroleptics.

Until the 1990s, traditional neuroleptics were the only agents available for the management of schizophrenia and were considered the most effective in controlling the positive symptoms (Armenteros, Whitaker, Welikson, Stedge, & Gorman, 1997). There is, however, little empirical evidence to support the use of these agents in children and adolescents and what little evidence is available has been derived from studies of adult populations (Malone, Sheikh, & Zito, 1999). The first traditional neuroleptic agent is chlorpromazine (Thorazine), followed by increasingly more potent agents such as haloperidol (Haldol) (Freedman, 2003). A significant portion of children and adolescents with schizophrenia who are managed with traditional neuroleptics do not respond to these agents (Kumra et al., 1996; Turetz et al., 1997). For this reason, and coupled with the significant adverse side-effect profile of traditional neuroleptics, research efforts have focused on the development of a new class of agents with increased efficacy and less severe adverse events.

Atypical neuroleptic agents control both the positive and negative symptoms of schizophrenia (Armenteros et al., 1997; Kumra et al., 1996; Lemmens, Brecher, & Van Baelen, 1999) and are replacing traditional agents as the first-line agent in the management of schizophrenia, aggression, psychosis, and TS (Jefferson, Markowitz, & Brewerton, 1998; Malone et al., 1999). Clozapine, the first atypical neuroleptic agent, is more effective than traditional neuroleptic agents

(Frazier et al., 2003), but has potentially serious adverse side effects. Additional atypical neuroleptic agents (e.g., risperidone, quetiapine, ziprasidone, aripiprazole) appear to exhibit a similar mechanism of action to traditional neuroleptics but with a reduced adverse side-effect profile (Freedman, 2003).

An open trial examined the efficacy of clozapine in the management of individuals with treatment-resistant schizophrenia (Turetz, Mozes Toren, Chernauzan, & Yoran-Hegesh, 1997). All outcome measures were improved with a 50% reduction in scores. The most profound improvement occurred early in the trial with sustained improvement throughout the eighth week of the clinical trial. The researchers conclude that use of clozapine early in the diagnosis of schizophrenia may decrease some of the long-term functional impairments observed in schizophrenia.

The development of significant adverse side effects in neuroleptic agents appears to be linearly related to dosage: as the dose increases, the development of adverse events concomitantly increases (Lemmens et al., 1999). It is therefore recommended that children and adolescents be started on the lowest possible dose to manage symptoms without the development of adverse side effects. In general, the dose of a neuroleptic agent should be increased incrementally at approximately one week intervals until symptoms abate or significant adverse side effects develop. The provider should be aware that the maximum response may not be necessarily evident for up to nine months of treatment (Kumra et al., 1996).

Adverse side effects associated with neuroleptic agents appear to be more common in children than for adults (Frazier et al., 2003). This has significant implications for patients diagnosed with schizophrenia or psychotic disorder at an early age, and thus may require treatment with a neuroleptic agent for an extended period of time.

There are significant concerns regarding adverse side effects associated with long-term use of these neuroleptic agents. Of particular concern for patients taking traditional neuroleptics are *extrapyramidal symptoms* (Turetz et al., 1997), which are associated with motor movements (e.g., chorea type of movements, athetosis, tremors similar to Parkinson's disease). Extrapyramidal symptoms develop in the majority of patients treated with typical neuroleptic agents (reports range from 75% [Armenteros et al., 1997] to 90% [Lemmens et al., 1999]) with symptoms of such severity that treatment with anti-Parkinsonian agents is frequently indicated.

Tardive dyskinesia is another adverse motor effect that may develop in as many as 20% of patients (Lemmens et al., 1999) following administration of traditional neuroleptic agents. It is primarily manifested in involuntary oral-facial movements but also may involve the trunk, fingers, and toes. These motor effects have a deleterious impact on the long-term functional outcome of those who are treated with these agents. Although most reports indicate that tardive dyskinesia is the result of long-term treatment with traditional neuroleptics, there is evidence that tardive dyskinesia may develop as soon as three months following the initiation of treatment (Turetz et al., 1997). Withdrawal of the causative neuroleptic agent may eliminate the symptoms but there have been cases where the tardive dyskinesia persists despite the removal of the causative agent.

Neuroleptic malignant syndrome is a potentially fatal side effect of all traditional neuroleptic agents, although the exact incidence with atypical neuroleptic agents is uncertain (Mann & Campbell, 2001). Neuroleptic malignant syndrome can develop within 24 hours of initiating a neuroleptic agent, with most incidences occurring within one month of the initial dose. More than three-fourths of the patients with neuroleptic malignant syndrome experience mental status changes, elevated heart and respiratory rates, profuse diaphoresis (sweating), labile blood pressure, incontinence, muscle rigidity, and tremors. There also is a temperature elevation that can be high enough to cause brain damage if the temperature is not immediately lowered. Neuroleptic malignant syndrome is a medical emergency and the child or adolescent must be hospitalized.

The risk of extrapyramidal symptoms, tardive dyskinesia, and neuroleptic malignant syndrome is believed to decrease with the use of atypical neuroleptic agents (Frazier et al., 2003; Lemmens et al., 1999; Pollak & Zbuk, 2000; Tandon, 2003). Atypical neuroleptic agents, however, only have been available for the management of schizophrenia in children and adolescents for a relatively brief period of time. Moreover, randomized clinical trials with large pediatric populations have only recently been conducted to determine the safety and efficacy of these agents. Anecdotal reports indicate that although the risk for these adverse side effects is decreased with atypical neuroleptic agents, they are not completely eliminated with either traditional or atypical neuroleptics. Health-care providers should be aware that major risks still exist for patients being managed with atypical agents.

With the administration of atypical neuroleptic agents weight gain is a particular concern with pediatric populations. Safer (2004) found that weight gain was more pronounced in preadolescent youths who were managed with atypical neuroleptic agents. Further, there is some evidence that the amount of weight gain is directly associated with the dose of the neuroleptic agent (Frazier et al., 2003). Prepubescence is a difficult time developmentally and children desire to be similar in appearance to their peers. A significant weight gain can cause the child to stop taking the neuroleptic agent and result in an exacerbation in symptoms. There also is an association between obesity that results from the weight gain and the development of fat deposits in the liver. Landau and Martin (1998) have raised the question as to whether the elevation in hepatic enzymes seen in patients managed with neuroleptic agents is actually associated with the fat deposits rather than the direct intervention of the neuroleptic on the function of the liver. Regardless, the provider must be especially cautious in administering any neuroleptic agent to children and adolescents due to the potential of adverse side effects.

Despite an increase in research related to the use of neuroleptic agents for the management of schizophrenia in pediatric populations, there is a paucity of randomized clinical trials supporting a firm evidence base concerning efficacy and safety. Anecdotal reports, open trials, and controlled clinical trials provide the mainstay of evidence for the continued use of neuroleptic agents, in particular atypical neuroleptics; as such, only when the benefits of managing psychotic symptoms outweigh the potential risk of deleterious side effects should neuroleptics be used with children and adolescents. Despite clinical evidence of efficacy, randomized clinical trials are needed in pediatric populations.

PERVASIVE DEVELOPMENTAL DISORDERS

Pervasive developmental disorders are usually evident within the first several years of life and are frequently associated with some degree of mental retardation (APA, 2000). There are several diagnoses grouped within the pervasive developmental disorder framework (e.g., autistic disorder, Asperger's disorder, Rett's disorder, childhood disintegration disorder); however, they are all characterized by a severe impairment of social interaction skills, communication skills, or the presence of stereotypical behavior. With the exception of Asperger's syndrome, the other pervasive developmental disorders often may be associated with mental retardation.

Pharmacotherapy

Several clinical trials have examined the efficacy of risperidone in the management of the symptoms of pervasive developmental disorder, particularly aggression and stereotypical behaviors. Clinical trials have demonstrated that risperidone is effective for the management of aggression and stereotypical behaviors but does not affect social interaction (Arnold et al., 2003; Malone, Maislin, Choudhury, Gifford, & Delaney, 2002; McDougle et al., 2005; McCracken & Research Units on Pediatric Psychopharmacology Autism Network, 2002; Research Unit on Pediatric Psychopharmacology Autism Network, 2005).

SUMMARY AND CONCLUSION

The review of literature in this chapter underscores the significant research conducted over the past several years with regard to pharmacological treatments in pediatric populations. There is no doubt that there has been an increase in the use of psychotropic medications with children and adolescents and this has been a major concern to children's caregivers, teachers, and pediatricians. This increase has been partly due to changes in health-care delivery in this country as well as reduced availability of mental health services. Thus, many pediatricians have been faced with the challenge of managing psychiatric disorders that previously were delegated to mental health professionals. Pediatricians sometimes find they have insufficient training in this new role as a gatekeeper of psychological services.

The psychotropic agents that have received the most attention are the stimulants that have been the first-line choice to manage problems associated with attention and concentration among children and adolescents. Although the recent investigation of the integration of pharmacological and behavioral treatments seems to be a step in the right direction, there are a number of questions that have not yet been addressed by this multisite investigation. These questions include

the long-term safety of the stimulants in pediatric populations and the best order of sequencing of treatments (i.e., medication first or behavioral treatments first). Although psychopharmacological research continues with investigations of internalizing disorders, we believe that research has not kept pace with the clinical use of these agents among children and adolescents. Much more research will need to be conducted concerning the combination of therapies for the management of major depression and anxiety disorders in children and adolescents. In addition to the aforementioned question of safety, it is also of concern how these pharmacotherapies may interact with other behavioral therapies, including cognitive behavior therapy. Finally, the use of neuroleptic agents among children and adolescents with developmental disabilities is of concern, particularly regarding the long-term safety of these agents with these special populations.

What has been most striking in our review of this literature is the dearth of research to guide clinical practice that is based primarily on pediatric populations. Although some National Institute of Mental Health multisite clinical trials have been useful in delineating practice guidelines, again, research has not kept pace with the widespread use of these agents. Given budget cuts for funding of clinical trials, we do not expect this state of affairs to improve much over the next several years. Clearly, policy needs to be developed that mandates careful research through controlled clinical trials prior to endorsing a psychotropic agent as safe and effective for pediatric populations. Such policy will need to emanate from federal guidelines at the congressional level.

It is anticipated that school psychologists will be able to assist in these research endeavors through their training in measurement and research design. More important, it is anticipated that school psychologists will be able to assist pediatricians, family practice physicians, and child psychiatrists in the assessment of these medications. Issues to be determined include:

- the efficacy of learning and behavior in the classroom and the home;
- the safety of these agents by evaluating adverse effects through the systematic collection of quantitative data; and finally,
- the development of rating scales that quantify adverse effects.

Thus, given their training in research, clinical assessment, and analyzing the clinical literature, we hope that school psychologists will contribute to pediatric psychopharmacology by documenting the efficacy of pharmacological agents on various outcomes and across various settings through research and evidenced-based practice. We hope this will ultimately enhance the quality of life for children and adolescents with psychiatric disorders and the lives of their families.

REFERENCES

American Academy of Child & Adolescent Psychiatry. (1998). Practice parameters for the assessment and treatment of children and adolescents with depressive disorders. *Journal of the American Academy of Child & Adolescent Psychiatry 37* (*supplement*), 63S–83S.

American Academy of Pediatrics. (2001a). Clinical practice guideline: Diagnosis and evaluation of a child with Attention-Deficit/Hyperactivity Disorder. *Pediatrics, 105,* 1158–1170.

American Academy of Pediatrics. (2001b). Clinical practice guideline: Treatment of the school-aged child with Attention-Deficit/Hyperactivity Disorder. *Pediatrics, 105,* 1033–1038.

American Academy of Pediatrics Subcommittee on ADHD & Committee of Quality Improvement. (2001). Clinical practice guideline: treatment of the school aged child with Attention Deficit Hyperactivity Disorder. *Pediatrics, 108,* 1033–1044.

American Psychiatric Association. [APA] (1994). Practice Guideline for the treatment of patients with bipolar disorder. *American Journal of Psychiatry, 151* (s12), 1–36.

American Psychiatric Association. [APA] (2000). *Diagnostic and Statistical Manual of Mental Disorders* (4th ed. Text Revision). Washington, DC: Author.

Andersch, S., & Hetta, J. (2003). A 15-year follow-up study of patients with panic disorder. *European Psychiatry, 18,* 401–408.

Apter, A., Kronenberg, S., & Brent, D. (2005). Turning darkness into light. *European Child & Adolescent Psychiatry, 14,* 113–116.

Armenteros, J. L., Whitaker, A. H., Welikson, M., Stedge, D. J., & Gorman, J. (1997). Risperidone in adolescents with schizophrenia: An open pilot study. *Journal of Child & Adolescent Psychiatry, 36,* 694–700.

Arnold, L. E., Vitiello, B., McDougle, C., Scahill, L., Shah, B., et al. (2003). Parent-defined target symptoms respond to risperidone in RUPP autism study: Customer approach to clinical trials. *Journal of the American Academy of Child & Adolescent Psychiatry, 42,* 1443–1450.

Arnstein, L., & Brown, R. T. (2005). Gilles de la Tourette's Syndrome. In C. R. Reynolds & S. Goldstein (Eds.), *Handbook of neurodevelopmental and genetic disorders in adults.* New York: Guilford Press.

Baldwin, R., Chelonis, J. J., Flake, R. A., Edwards, M. C., Field, C. R., Meaaux, J. B., et al. (2004). Effect of methylphenidate in children with Attention Deficit/Hyperactivity Disorder. *Experimental & Clinical Psychopharmacology 12,* 57–64.

Barkley, R. A. (2005). *Taking charge of ADHD: The complete, authoritative guide for parents* (3rd ed.). New York: Guilford Press.

Barkley, R. A., Connor, D. F., & Kwasnik, D. (2000). Challenges to determining drug responding in an outpatient clinical setting: Comparing Adderall and methylphenidate in adolescents with ADHD. *Journal of Attention Disorders, 4,* 102–113.

Basile, A. S., Lippa, A. S., & Skolnick, P. (2004). Anxioselective anxiolytics: Can less be more? *European Journal of Pharmacology, 500,* 441–451.

Belmaker, R. H. (2004). Medical progress: Bipolar disorder. *New England Journal of Medicine, 351,* 476–486.

Biederman, J., Baldessarini, R. J., Wright, V., Knee, D., & Harmatz, J. S. (1989). A double-blind placebo controlled study of desipramine in the treatment of ADD: I, Efficacy. *Journal of the American Academy of Child & Adolescent Psychiatry, 28,* 777–784.

Biederman, J., Baldessarini, R. J., Wright, V., Keenan, K., & Faraone, S. (1993). A double-blind placebo controlled study of desipramine in the treatment of ADD: III. Lack of impact of comorbidity and family history factors in clinical response. *Journal of the American Academy of Child & Adolescent Psychiatry, 32,* 199–204.

Biederman, J. (2005). Attention-Deficit/Hyperactivity Disorder: A selective overview. *Biological Psychiatry, 57,* 1215–1220.

Birmaher, B., Axelson, D. A., Monk, K., Kalas, C., Clark, D. B., Ehman, M., et al. (2003). Fluoxetine for the treatment of childhood anxiety disorders. *Journal of American Academy of Child & Adolescent Psychiatry, 42,* 415–423.

Birmaher, B., Ryan, N. D., Williamson, D. E., Brent, D. A., & Kaufman, J. (1996). Childhood and adolescent depression: A review of the past 10 years. Part II. *Journal of the American Academy of Child & Adolescent Psychiatry, 35,* 1575–1583.

Bowden, C. (2004). The effectiveness of divalproate in all forms of mania and the broader bipolar spectrum: Many questions, few answers. *Journal of Affective Disorders, 79* (S1), 9–14.

Brown, R. T., Arnstein, L., & Simerly, E. (2005). *Medications for children: A guide for the practitioner.* New York: Guilford Press.

Brown, R. T., & Ievers, C. E. (1999). Giles de la Tourette's syndrome. In S. Goldstein

& C. R. Reynolds (Eds.), *Handbook of neurodevelopmental and genetic disorders in children* (pp. 185–215). New York: Guilford.

Brown, R. T., & Sammons, M. (2002). Pediatric psychopharmacology: A review of new developments and recent research. *Professional Psychology: Research & Practice, 33,* 135–147.

Bruce, S. E., Vasile, R. G., Goisman, R. M., Salzman, C., Spencer, M., Machan, J. T., et al. (2003). Are benzodiazepines still the medication of choice for patients with panic disorder with or without agoraphobia? *American Journal of Psychiatry, 160,* 1432–1438.

Brunello, N. (2002). Mood stabilizers: Protecting the mood . . . protecting the brain. *Journal of Affective Disorders, 79* (s1), 15–20.

Burd, L. (1995). *Children with Tourette Syndrome: A handbook for parents and teachers.* Grand Forks, ND: Jessica Kingsley.

Caballero, J., & Nahata, M. (2005). Selective serotonin re-uptake inhibitors and suicidal ideation and behavior in children. *American Journal of Health System Pharmacy, 62,* 864–867.

Calabrese, J. R., Rapport, D. J., Youngstrom, D., Jackson, S, Bilali, S., & Findling, R. I. (2005). New data on the use of lithium, divalproate, and lamotrigine in rapid cycling bipolar disorder. *European Psychiatry, 20,* 92–95.

Castellanos, F. X., Giedd, J. N., Elia, J., Marsh, W. L., Ritchie, G. F., Hamburger, S. D., et al. (1997). Controlled stimulant treatment of ADHD and comorbid Tourette's Syndrome: Effects of stimulant and dose. *Journal of the American Academy of Child & Adolescent Psychiatry, 36,* 589–596.

Chelonis, J. J., Edwards, M. C., Schulz, E. G., Baldwin, R., Blake, D. J., Wenger, A., et al. (2002). Stimulant medication improves recognition memory in children diagnosed with Attention Deficit/Hyperactivity Disorder. *Experimental & Clinical Psychopharmacology, 10,* 400–407.

Cheung, A. H., Emslie, G. J., & Mayes, T. L. (2005). Review of the efficacy and safety of antidepressants in youth depression. *Journal of Child Psychology & Psychiatry, 46,* 735–754.

Cloos, J-M. (2005). The treatment of panic disorder. *Current Opinion in Psychiatry, 18,* 45–50.

Colle, L. M., Belair, J. F., DiFeo, M., Weiss, J., & LaRoache, C. (1994). Extended open-label fluoxetine treatment of adolescents with major depression. *Journal of Child & Adolescent Psychopharmacology 4,* 225–232.

Connor, D. F., Glatt, S. J., Lopez, I. D., Jackson, D., & Melloni, R. H., Jr. (2002). Psychopharmacology and aggression. I: A meta-analysis of stimulant effects on overt/covert aggression-related behaviors in ADHD. *Journal of the American Academy of Child & Adolescent Psychiatry, 41,* 253–261.

Connors, C. K., Epstein, J. N., March, J. S., Angold, A., Wells, K. C., Klaraic, J., et al. (2001). Multimodal treatment of ADHD in the MTA: An alternative outcome analysis. *Journal of the American Academy of Child & Adolescent Psychiatry, 40,* 159–167.

Cookson, J. (2001). Use of antipsychotic drugs and lithium in mania. *British Journal of Psychiatry, 178* (S41), s148–s156.

Cottraux, J. (2005). Recent developments in research and treatment for social phobia (social anxiety disorder). *Current Opinion in Psychiatry, 18,* 51–54.

Croonberghs, J., Fegert, J. M., Findling, R. L., De Smedt, G., Van Dongen, S., & Risperidone Disruptive Behavior Study Group. (2005). Risperidone in children with disruptive behavior disorders and subaverage intelligence: A 1-year, open-label study of 504 patients. *Journal of the American Academy of Child & Adolescent Psychiatry, 44,* 64–72.

Davis, W. B., Bentivoglio, P., Racusin, R., Brown, K. M., Bostic, J. Q., & Wiley, L. (2001). Bupropion sustained release in adolescents with comorbid Attention-Deficit/Hyperactivity Disorder and depression. *Journal of the American Academy of Child & Adolescent Psychiatry, 40,* 307–314.

Delate, T., Gelenberg, A. J., Simmons, V. A., & Motheral, B. R. (2004). Trends in the use of antidepressants in a national sample of commercially insured pediatric patients, 1998 to 2002. *Psychiatric Services 55,* 387–391. Retrieved August 30, 2005, from psychservices .psychiatryonline.org/cgi/content/abstract/ 55/4/387.

Donnelly, M., McGilloway, S., Mays, N., & Kerr, P. (1996). Long-stay patients with mental health problems and learning difficulties: Selection and preparation for community living. *International Journal of Rehabilitation Research, 19,* 175–179.

Dopheide, J. A. (2005). ASHP therapeutic position statement on the appropriate use of medications in the treatment of Attention Deficit/Hyperactivity Disorder in pediatric patients. *American Journal of Pharmacology, 62,* 1502–1509.

Emslie, G. J., Walkup, J. T., Pliszka, S. R., & Ernst, M. (1999). Nontricylcic antidepressants: Current trends in children and adolescents. *Journal of the American Academy of Child & Adolescent Psychiatry, 38,* 517–528.

Faraone, S. V., Short, E. J., Biederman, J., Findling, R. L., Roe, C., & Manos, M. J. (2002). Efficacy of Adderall and methylphenidate in Attention Deficit Hyperactivity Disorder: A drug-placebo and drug-drug response curve analysis of a naturalistic study. *International Journal of Neuropsychopharmacology, 5,* 121–129.

Fetner, H. H., & Geller, B. (1992). Lithium and tricyclic antidepressants. *Psychiatric Clinics of North America, 15,* 223–241.

Findling, R. L., McNamara, N. K., Branicky, L. A., Schluchter, M. D., Lemon, E., & Blumer, J. L. (2000). A double-blind pilot study of risperidone in the treatment of conduct disorder. *Journal of the American Academy of Child & Adolescent Psychiatry*, *39*, 509–516.

Frazier, J. A., Cohen, L. G., Jacobsen, L., Grothe, D., Flood, J., et al. (2003). Clozapine pharmacokinetics in children and adolescents with childhood-onset schizophrenia. *Journal of Clinical Psychopharmacology*, *23*, 87–91.

Freedman, R. (2003). Drug therapy: Schizophrenia. *New England Journal of Medicine*, *349*, 1738–1749.

Gadow, K. D., Sverd, J., Sprafkin, J., Nolan, E. E., & Ezor, S. N. (1995). Efficacy of methylphenidate for Attention-Deficit Hyperactivity Disorder in children with tic disorder. *Archives of General Psychiatry*, *52*, 444–455.

Geddes, J. R., Burgess, S., Hawton, K., Jamison, K., & Goodwin, G. (2004). Long-term lithium therapy for bipolar disorder: Systematic review and meta-analysis of randomized controlled trials. *American Journal of Psychiatry*, *161*, 217–222.

Gerardin, P., Cohen D., Mazet P., & Flament, M. F. (2002). Drug treatment of conduct disorder in young people. *European Neuropsychopharmacology*, *12*, 361–370.

Gilbert, D. L., Batterson, J. R., Sethuraman, G., & Sallee, F. R. (2004). Tic reduction with risperidone versus pimozide in a randomized, double-blind, crossover trial. *Journal of the American Academy of Child & Adolescent Psychiatry*, *43*, 206–214.

Gilligan, J., & Lee, B. (2004). The psychopharmacologic treatment of violent youth. *Annals of the New York Academy of Sciences*, *1036*, 356–381.

Glod, C. A., Lynch, A., Flynn, E., Berkowitz, C., & Baldessarini, R. J. (2003). Open trial of bupropion SR in adolescent major depression. *Journal of Child & Adolescent Psychiatric Nursing*, *16*, 123–30.

Goodnick, P. J., Domingues, R. A., DeVane, C. L., & Bowden, C. L. (1998). Bupuropion slow release response in depression: Diagnosis and biochemistry. *Biological Psychiatry*, *44*, 629–632.

Goodwin, F. K., Fireman, B., Simon G., Hunkeler, E., Lee, J., & Revicki, D. (2003). Suicide risk in bipolar disorder during treatment with lithium and divalproex. *Journal of the American Medical Association*, *290*, 1467–1473.

Greevich, S., Rowane, W. A., Marcellino, B., & Sullivan-Hurst, S. (2001). Retrospective comparison of Adderall and methylphenidate in the treatment of Attention Deficit Hyperactivity Disorder. *Journal of Child & Adolescent Psychopharmacology*, *11*, 35–41.

Greenhill, L. L., Halperin, J. M., & Abikoff, H. (1999). Stimulant Medications. *Journal of the American Academy of Child & Adolescent Psychiatry*, *38*, 503–512.

Gualtieri, C. T., & Evans, R. W. (1988). Stimulant treatment for the neurobehavioral sequelae of traumatic brain injury. *Brain Injury*, *2*, 273–290.

Gualtieri, C. T., Keenan, P. A., & Chandler, M. (1991). Clinical and neuropsychological effects of desipramine in children with Attention Deficit Hyperactivity Disorder. *Journal of Clinical Psychopharmacology*, *11*, 155–159.

Hayward, C., Wilson, K. A., Lagle, K., Killen, K., & Taylor, C. B. (2004). Parent- reported predictors of adolescent panic attacks. *Journal of the American Academy of Child & Adolescent Psychiatry*, *43*, 613–620.

Hinshaw, S. P., Heller, T., & McHale, J. P. (1992). Covert antisocial behavior in boys with Attention-Deficit Hyperactivity Disorder: External validation and effects of methylphenidate. *Journal of Consulting and Clinical Psychology*, *60*, 274–281.

Horst, W. D., & Preskorn, S. H. (1998). Mechanisms of action and clinical characteristics of three atypical antidepressants: Venlafaxine, nefazodone, bupropion. *Journal of Affective Disorders*, *51*, 237–254.

Jain, U., Birmaher, B., Garcia, M., Al-Shabbout, M., & Ryan, N. (1992). Fluoxetine in children and adolescents with mood disorders: a chart review of efficacy and adverse effects. *Journal of Child & Adolescent Psychopharmacology 2*, 259–265.

James, R. S., Sharp, W. S., Bastain, T. M., Lee, P. P., James, M., Czarnolewski, M., et al. (2001). Double-blind, placebo-controlled study of single-dose amphetamine formulations in ADHD. *Journal of the American Academy of Child & Adolescent Psychiatry*, *40*, 1268–1276.

Jefferson, A. M., Markowitz, J. S., & Brewerton, T. D. (1998). Atypical antipsychotics. *Journal of Child & Adolescent Psychiatry*, *37*, 1243–1244.

Jensen, P. S., Bhatara, V. S., Vitiello, B., Hoagwood, K., Feil, M., & Burke, L. B. (1999). Psychoactive medication prescribing practices for U.S. children: Gaps between research and clinical practice. *Journal of the American Academy of Child & Adolescent Psychiatry*, *38*, 557–565.

Jensen, P. S., Hinshaw, S. P., Kraemer, H. C., Lenora, N., Newcorn, J. H., Abikoff, H. B., et al. (2001). ADHD comorbidity findings from the MTA study: Comparing comorbid subgroups. *Journal of the American Academy of Child & Adolescent Psychiatry*, *40*, 147–158.

Jureidini, J. N., Doecke, C. J., Mansfield, P. R., Haby, M. M., Menkes, D. B., & Tonkin, A. L. (2004). *British Medical Journal*, *328*, 879–883.

Kafantaris, V., Coletti, D. J., Dicker, R., Padula, G., & Kane, J. (2003). Lithium treatment of acute mania in adolescents: A large open trial. *Journal of the*

American Academy of Child & Adolescent Psychiatry, 41, 1038–1045.

Kaplan, S., Heiligenstein, J., West, S., Busner, J., Harder, D., Dittman, R., et al. (2004). Efficacy and safety of atomoxetine in childhood Attention-Deficit/Hyperactivity Disorder with comorbid oppositional defiant disorder. *Journal of Attention Disorders, 8*, 45–52.

Kaplan, C. A., & Hussain, S. (1995). Use of drugs in child and adolescent psychiatry. *British Journal of Psychiatry, 166*, 291–298.

Keller, M. B., Ryan, N. D., Strober, M., Klein, M., Kutcher, S. P., et al. (2001). Efficacy of paroxetine in the treatment of adolescent major depression: A randomized, controlled trial. *Journal of the American Academy of Child & Adolescent Psychiatry, 40*, 762–772.

Kilic, C., Curran, H. V., Noshirvani, H., Marks, I. M., & Basoglu, M. (1999). Long-term effects of alprazolam on memory: A 3.5 year follow-up of agoraphobia/panic patients. *Psychological Medicine, 29*, 225–231.

Klein, R. G., Abikoff, H., Klass, E., Ganeles, D., Seese, L. M., & Pollack, S. (1997). Clinical efficacy of methylphenidate in conduct disorder with and without Attention Deficit Hyperactivity Disorder. *Archives of General Psychiatry, 54*, 1073–1080.

Kovacs, M., Devlin, B., Pollock, M., Richards, C., & Mukerji, P. (1997). A controlled family history study of childhood-onset depressive disorder. *Archives of General Psychiatry 54*, 613–623.

Kratochvil, C. J., Heiligenstein, J. H., Dittmann, R., Spencer, T. J., Biederman, J., et al. (2002). Atomoxetine and methylphenidate treatment in children with ADHD: A prospective, randomized, open-label trial. *Journal of the American Academy of Child & Adolescent Psychiatry, 41*, 776–84.

Kratochvil, C. J., Vaughan, B. S., Harrington, M. J., & Burke, W. J. (2003). Atomoxetine: a selective noradrenaline reuptake inhibitor for the treatment of Attention-Deficit/Hyperactivity Disorder. *Expert Opinion on Pharmacotherapy, 4*, 1165–1174.

Krishnan, K. R. R. (2005). Through the looking glass: Risk perception (Commentary). *Biologic Psychiatry, 57*, 1477–1478.

Kubiszyn, T., & Carlson, C. I. (1995). School psychologists' attitudes toward an expanded health care role: Psychopharmacology and prescription privileges. *School Psychology Quarterly, 10*, 247–270.

Kumra, S., Frazier, J. A., Jacobsen, L. K., McKenna, K., Gordon, C. T., et al. (1996). Childhood-onset schizophrenia: A double-blind clozapine-haloperidol comparison. *Archives of General Psychiatry, 53*, 1090–1097.

Kurlan, R. (1997). Tourette syndrome: Treatment of tics. *Neurologic Clinics, 15*, 403–409.

Kutcher, S., Aman, M., Brooks, S. J., Buitelaar, J., van Daalen, E., Fegert, J., et al. (2004). International consensus statement on Attention-Deficit/Hyperactivity Disorder (ADHD) and disruptive behaviour disorders (DBDs): Clinical implications and treatment practice suggestions. *European Journal of Neuropsychopharmacology, 14*, 11–28.

Landau, J., & Martin, A. (1998). Is liver function monitoring warranted during risperidone treatment? *Journal of Child & Adolescent Psychiatry, 37*, 1007–1008.

Law, S. F., & Schachar, R. J. (1999). Do typical clinical doses of methylphenidate cause tics in children treated for Attention-Deficit Hyperactivity Disorder? *Journal of the American Academy of Child & Adolescent Psychiatry, 38*, 944–951.

Layne, A. E., Bernstein, G. A., Egan, E. A., & Kushner, M. G. (2003). Predictors of treatment response in anxious-depressed adolescents with school refusal. *Journal of the American Academy of Child & Adolescent Psychiatry, 42*, 319–326.

Lemmens, P., Brecher, M., & Van Baelen, B. (1999). A combined analysis of double-blind studies with risperidone vs. placebo and other antipsychotic agents: Factors associated with extrapyramidal symptoms. *Acta Psychiatrica Scandanavica, 99*, 160–170.

Leubbert, J. E., Malone, R. P., & Rieser, L. (2000). Disability law and the administration of psychotropic medication in the school setting. *Psychiatric Services, 51*, 1369–1370.

Licht, R. W., Vestergaard, P., Kessing, L. V., Larsen, J. K., & Thomsen, P. H. (2003). Psychopharmacological treatment with lithium and antiepiletic drugs: Suggested guidelines from the Danish Psychiatric Association and the Child & Adolescent Psychiatric Association in Denmark. *Acta Psychiatrica Scandinavica, 108* (s149), 1–22.

Madras, B. K., Miller, G. M., & Fischman, A. J. (2005). The dopamine transported and Attention Deficit/Hyperactivity Disorder. *Biological Psychiatry, 57*, 1397–1409.

Malone, R. P., Sheikh, R., & Zito, J. M. (1999). Novel antipsychotic medications in the treatment of children and adolescents. *Psychiatric Services, 50*, 171–174.

Malone, R. P., Maislin, G., Choudhury, M., Gifford, C., & Delaney, M. A. (2002). Risperidone treatment in children and adolescents with autism: Short- and long-term safety and effectiveness. *Journal of the American Academy of Child & Adolescent Psychiatry, 41*, 140–147.

Mandoki, W., Tapia, M. R., Tapia, M. A., Sumner, G. S., & Parker, J. L. (1997). Venlafaxine in the treatment of children and adolescents with major depression. *Psychopharmacology Bulletin, 33*, 149–154.

Mann, S. C., & Campbell, E. C. (2001). Neuroleptic Malignant Syndrome. *Adverse Drug Reaction Bulletin, 209,* 799–802.

March, J. S., Foa, E., Gammon, P., Chrisman, A., Curry, J., et al. (2004). Cognitive-behavioral therapy, sertraline, and their combination for children and adolescents with Obsessive-Compulsive Disorder: The pediatric OCD treatment study (POTS) randomized control trial. *Journal of the American Medical Association, 292,* 1969–1976.

March, J., Silva, S., Petrycki, S., Wells, K., Fairbank, J., Burns, B., et al. (2004). Fluoxetine, cognitive-behavioral therapy, and their combination for adolescents with depression: Treatment for adolescents with depression study (TADS) Randomized Controlled Trial. *Journal of the American Medical Association, 292,* 807–820.

March, J. S., Swanson, J. M., Arnold, L. E., Hoza, B., Conners, C. K., Hinshaw, S. P., et al. (2000). Anxiety as a predictor and outcome variable in the multimodal treatment study of children with ADHD (MTA). *Journal of Abnormal Child Psychology, 28,* 527–541.

McCracken, J. T., & Research Units on Pediatric Psychopharmacology Autism Network. (2002). Risperidone in children with autism and serious behavioral problems. *New England Journal of Medicine, 347,* 314–321.

McCracken, J. T., Biederman, J., Greenhill, L. L., Swanson, J. M., McGough, J. J., Spencer, T. J., et al. (2003). Analog classroom assessment of a once-daily mixed amphetamine formulation, SLI381 (Adderall XR), in children with ADHD. *Journal of the American Academy of Child & Adolescent Psychiatry, 42,* 673–683.

McDougle, C. J., Scahill, L., Aman, M. G., McCracken, J. T., Tierney, E., et al. (2005). Risperidone for the core symptom domains of autism: Results from the study by the Autism Network of the Research Units on Pediatric Psychopharmacology. *American Journal of Psychiatry, 162,* 1142–1148.

McGough, J. J. (2005). Attention-Deficit/Hyperactivity Disorder pharmocogenics. *Biological Psychiatry 57,* 1367–1373.

McMaster University Evidence-Based Practice Center. (1999). Treatment of Attention-Deficit Hyperactivity Disorder. *Evidence report/technology assessment no. 11,* AHCPR Publication No. 99-E018. Rockville, MD: Agency for Health Care Policy & Research.

Michelson, D., Faries, D., Wernicke, J., Kelsey, D., Kendrick, K., Sallee, F. R., et al. (2001). Atomoxetine in the treatment of children and adolescents with Attention-Deficit/Hyperactivity Disorder: A randomized, placebo-controlled, dose-response study. *Pediatrics, 108,* E83.

Morgan, C. A., Krystal, J. H., & Southwick, S. M. (2003). Toward early pharmacological posttraumatic stress intervention. *Biological Psychiatry, 53,* 834–843.

Multimodal Treatment Study of Children with ADHD Cooperative Group. (1999a). A 14-month randomized clinical trial of treatment strategies for Attention-Deficit Hyperactivity Disorder (ADHD). *Archives of General Psychiatry, 56,* 1073–1086.

Multimodal Treatment Study of Children with ADHD Cooperative Group. (1999b). Moderators and mediators of treatment response for children with Attention-Deficit/Hyperactivity Disorder: The multimodal treatment study of children with Attention-Deficit/Hyperactivity Disorder. *Archives of General Psychiatry, 56,* 1088–1096.

Murray, M. L., de Vries, C. S., & Wong, I. C. K. (2004). A drug utilization study of antidepressants in children and adolescents using the General Practice Research Database. *Archives of Disease in Childhood, 89,* 1098–1102.

National Association of School Psychologists. (2004). *IDEA reauthorization timeline: Implications for ongoing advocacy.* Bethesda, MD: Author.

Olfson, M., Gameroff, M. J., Marcus, S. C., & Waslick, B. D. (2003). Outpatient treatment of child and adolescent depression in the United States. *Archives of General Psychiatry 60,* 1236–1242.

Pachet, A. K., & Wisniewski, A. M. (2003). The effects of lithium on cognition: A updated review. *Psychopharmacology 179,* 225–234.

Pelham, W. E., Gnagy, E. M., Greiner, A. R., Hoza, B., Hinshaw, S. P., & Swanson, J. M., et al. (2000). Behavioral versus behavioral and pharmacological treatment in ADHD children attending a summer treatment program. *Journal of Abnormal Child Psychology, 28,* 507–526.

Phelps, L., Brown, R. T., & Power, T. (2002). *Pediatric psychopharmacology: Combining medical and psychosocial intervention.* Washington, DC: American Psychological Association.

Pliszka, S. R., Browne, R. G., Olvera, R. L., & Wynne, S. K. (2000). A double-blind, placebo-controlled study of Adderall and methylphenidate in the treatment of Attention Deficit/Hyperactivity Disorder. *Journal of the American Academy of Child & Adolescent Psychiatry, 39,* 619–626.

Poling, A., Gadow, K. D., & Cleary, J. (1991). *Drug therapy for behavior disorders: An introduction.* New York: Pergamon Press.

Pollak, P. T., & Zbuk, K. (2000). Quetiapine fumarate overdose: Clinical and pharmacokinetic lessons from extreme conditions. *Clinical Pharmacology & Therapeutics, 68,* 92–97.

Poolsup, N., Po, A. L., & de Oliveira, I. R. (2000). Systematic overview of lithium treatment in acute mania. *Journal of Clinical Pharmacy & Therapeutics, 25,* 139–156.

Rappley, M. D. (2005). Attention Deficit-Hyperactivity Disorder. *New England Journal of Medicine, 352,* 165–173.

Rapport, M. D., Carlson, G. A., Kelly, K. L., & Petaki, C. (1993). Methylphenidate and desipramine in hospitalized children: I, Separate and combined effects on cognitive function. *Journal of the American Academy of Child & Adolescent Psychiatry, 32,* 333–342.

Reischer, H., & Pfeffer, C. (1996). Lithium pharmacokinetics. *Journal of the American Academy of Child & Adolescent Psychiatry, 35,* 130–131.

Research Unit on Pediatric Psychopharmacology Autism Network. (2005). Risperidone treatment of autistic disorder: Longer-term benefits and blinded discontinuation after six months. *American Journal of Psychiatry, 162,* 1361–1369.

Riddle, M. A., Bernstein, G. A., Cook, E. H., Leohard, H. L., March, J. S., & Swanson, J. M. (1999). Anxiolytics, adrenergic agents, and naltrexone. *Journal of Child & Adolescent Psychiatry, 38,* 546–556.

Riddle, M. A., Kastelic, E. A. & Frosch, E. (2001). Pediatric psychopharmacology. *Journal of Child Psychology and Psychiatry. 42,* 73–90.

Ringold, S. (2005). Antidepressant warning focuses attention on unmet need for child psychiatrists. *Journal of the American Medical Association, 293,* 537–538.

Ryan, N. D., Bhatara, V. S., & Perel, J. M. (1999). Mood stabilizers in children and adolescents. *Journal of the American Academy of Child & Adolescent Psychiatry, 38,* 529–536.

Ryan, N. D., & Varma, D. (1998). Child and adolescent mood disorders—experience with serotonin-based therapies. *Biological Psychiatry, 44,* 336–340.

Safer, D. J. (2004). A comparison of risperidone-induced weight gain across the age span. *Journal of Clinical Pharmacology, 24,* 429–436.

Sandor, P., & Stephens, R. J. (2000). Risperidone treatment of aggressive behavior in children with Tourette Syndrome. *Journal of Clinical Psychopharmacology, 20,* 10–712.

Sassi, R. B., Nicoletti, M., Brambilla, P., Mallinger, A. G., Frank, E., et al. (2002). Increased gray matter volume in lithium treated bipolar disorder patients. *Neuroscience Letters, 329,* 243–245.

Scahill, L., Leckman, J. F., Schultz, R. T., Katsovich, L., & Peterson, B. S. (2003). A placebo-controlled trial of risperidone in Tourette's Syndrome. *Neurology, 60,* 1130–1135.

Singer, H. S., Brown, J., Quaskey, S., Rosenberg, L. A., Mellitis, E. D., & Denckla, M. B. (1995). The treatment of Attention-Deficit Hyperactivity Disorder in Tourette's Syndrome: A double-blind placebo-controlled study with clonidine and desipramine. *Pediatrics, 95,* 74–81.

Smith, B. H., Pelham, W. E., Evans, S., Gnagy, E., Molina, B., Bukstein, O., et al. (1998). Dosage effects of methylphenidate on the social behavior of adolescents diagnosed with Attention-Deficit Hyperactivity Disorder. *Experimental & Clinical Psychopharmacology, 6,* 187–202.

Snider, V., Frankenberg, W., & Aspenson, M. (2000). The relationship between learning disabilities and Attention Deficit Hyperactivity Disorder: A national survey. *Developmental Disabilities Bulletin, 28,* 18–37.

Sverd, J., Gadow, K. D., Nolan, E. E., Sprafkin, J., & Ezor, S. N. (1992). Methylphenidate in hyperactive boys with comorbid tic disorder. *Advances in Neurology, 58,* 271–281.

Tandon, R. (2003). Improvement without impairment: A review of clinical data for quetiapine in the treatment of schizophrenia. *Journal of Clinical Psychopharmacology, 23* (S1), S15–S20.

Taylor, E. (1999). Developmental neuropsychology of attention deficit and impulsiveness. *Development and Psychopathology, 11,* 607–628.

Todd, R. D., Neuman, R., Geller, B., Fox, L. W., & Hickok, J. (1993). Genetic studies of affective disorders: Should we be starting with childhood onset probands? *Journal of the American Academy of Childhood & Adolescent Psychiatry 32,* 1164–1171.

Tourette's Syndrome Study Group. (2002). Treatment of ADHD in children with tics: A randomized controlled trial. *Neurology, 58,* 527–536.

Turetz, M., Mozes, T., Toren, P., Chernauzan, N., & Yoran-Hegesh, R. (1997). An open trial of clozapine in neuroleptic-resistant childhood-onset schizophrenia. *British Journal of Psychiatry, 170,* 507–510.

Volkow, N. D., Wang, G-J., Fowler, J. S., & Ding, Y-S. (2005). Imaging the effects of methyl-phenidate on brain dopamine: New model on its therapeutic actions for Attention Deficit/Hyperactivity Disorder. *Biological Psychiatry 57,* 1410–1415.

Wagner, K. D. (2005). Pharmacotherapy for major depression in children and adolescents. *Progress in Neuro-Psychopharmacology & Biological Psychiatry 29,* 819–826.

Wagner, K. D., Ambrosini, P., Rynn, M., Wohlberg, C., Yang, R., Greenbaum, M. S., et al. (2003). Efficacy of sertraline in the treatment of children and adolescents with major depressive disorder: Two randomized controlled trial. *Journal of the American Medical Association, 290,* 1033–1041.

Walkup, J. T., Labellarte, M. J., Riddle, M. A., Pine, D. S., Greenhill, L., et al. (2001). Fluvoxamine for the treatment of anxiety disorders in children and adolescents. *New England Journal of Medicine, 344,* 1279–1285.

Wernicke, J. F., Faries, D., Girod, D., Brown, J., Gao, H., Kelsey, D., et al. (2003). Cardiovascular effects of atomoxetine in children, adolescents, and adults. *Drug Safety, 26,* 729–40.

Werry, J. S., & Aman, M. G. (Eds). (1999). *Practitioner's guide to psychoactive drugs for children and adolescents* (2nd ed.). New York: Plenum Press.

Whittington, C. J., Kendall, T., & Pilling, S. (2005). Are the SSRIs and atypical antidepressants safe and effective for children and adolescents? *Current Opinion in Psychiatry, 18,* 21–25.

Wilens, T. E., Biederman, J., Baldessarini, R. J., Geller, B., Schleifer, D., Spencer, T. J., et al. (1996). Cardiovascular effects of therapeutic doses of tricyclic antidepressants in children and adolescents. *Journal of the American Academy of Child & Adolescent Psychiatry, 35,* 1491–1501.

Williams, T. P., & Miller, B. D. (2003). Pharmacologic management of anxiety disorders in children and adolescents. *Current Opinion in Pediatrics 15,* 483–490.

Yerevanian, B. I., Kock, R. J., & Mintz, J. (2003). Lithium, anticonvulsants and suicidal behavior in bipolar disorder. *Journal of Affective Disorders, 73,* 223–228.

Yorbik, O., & Birmaher, B. (2003). Pharmacologic treatment of anxiety disorders in children and adolescents. *Bulletin of Clinical Pharmacology, 13,* 133–141.

CHAPTER 32

PEDIATRIC SCHOOL PSYCHOLOGY: FUTURE DIRECTIONS FOR TRAINING SCHOOL PSYCHOLOGISTS[1]

EDWARD S. SHAPIRO
Lehigh University
JESSICA BLOM-HOFFMAN
Northeastern University
JENNIFER A. MAUTONE
Children's Hospital of Philadelphia

In the early 1990's, the United States began a significant shift in attention toward the health of our children and youth. *Healthy People 2000* (U.S. Department of Health & Human Services, 1991) was a national policy statement which showed that there were substantial unmet health needs among children and adolescents, concerns that placed large numbers of these children at high risk for the development of chronic, lifelong health problems. Most importantly, the document set forth over 300 objectives related to prevention of health problems across the American population. Although *Healthy People 2000* was focused broadly across all American age groups, it set our nation on the path of recognizing that the schools could indeed play a very critical role in facilitating the health of our children. Schools had historically been looked upon as major potential contributors to health promotion, particularly through efforts to establish in-school or school-linked health centers (e.g., Fothergill & Ballard, 1998; Reynolds, 1999). However, with *Healthy People 2000*, the energies of the entire

health care community were focused on the real possibility of support from the highest level of policy makers and stakeholders.

Embedded across many of the priority areas of *Healthy People 2000* were specific and focused objectives related to health and health education within the schools, such as improving healthy eating, reducing tobacco, alcohol and drug use, increasing nonviolent conflict resolution, and preventing injuries, HIV, and other sexually transmitted diseases. In addition, attention was given to improving immunization laws for preschool age children and the quality of health education curricula. These objectives were focused across pre-K to twelfth grade.

At the same time that our nation was turning its attention toward improving the health of our population, our schools had already been the focus of policy study that raised serious alarms about the quality of the educational experience. *A Nation at Risk* (National Commission on Excellence in Education, 1983) provided the context for recognizing that the outcomes in American public schools were unacceptable. Indeed, the report resulted in very significant reform movements to alter the school experiences of children, in both academics and behavior. Follow-up reports such as *Beyond Rhetoric* (National Commission on Children, 1991), and *Raising Standards for American Children* (National Council on Education and Testing, 1992), began suggesting solutions toward the alarms raised in the earlier report. Under the

[1] This chapter was supported by grant H325D06008 from the U.S. Department of Education to Lehigh University and the first author and 5K23HD047480 to Northeastern University and the second author. The opinions expressed in this chapter are solely the views of the authors and do not represent the position of the U.S. Department of Education or the National Institutes of Health.

administration of President George H. Bush in 1989, through the work of the National Education Summit, the National Education Goals Panel was established, which put in place a set of national goals focused on performance outcomes that can guide states and local educational groups toward policy and reform initiatives.

In a series of critical articles, Talley and Short recognized the parallels between the developing efforts in health and school reform (Short & Talley, 1997; Talley & Short, 1995). These same issues were also brought forward by Kolbe, Collins, and Cortese (1997) who saw the need for serious reform of school health programs requiring a joint effort between educators and health providers. The powerful and persuasive attention that these writers brought to the psychological community offered a launching point for the potential need for school personnel who had the knowledge and experience to bridge the gap between the school and health communities. Indeed, it was the thought-provoking nature of Talley, Short, Kolbe, Dreyfus, the policy makers, legislators, and many other writers through the late 1980s and mid-1990s that laid the foundation for what has become to be known as *pediatric school psychology*.

INITIAL CONCEPTUALIZATION

The initial conceptualization of this specialization of school psychology was first discussed by Power, DuPaul, Shapiro, and Parrish (1995). The rationale for the specialization was built on the reports of the links between chronic health problems of children and later outcomes as adults. Power et al. (1995) noted that while there were areas of psychology whose emphasis was on the healthy development of children, such as pediatric psychology or child clinical psychology, those disciplines focused primarily on the psychological issues surrounding the presence of serious health problems and illnesses among children and adolescents, rather than on the potential impact that such illnesses might have on school functioning. Typically, pediatric psychologists did not spend much of their training on understanding the dynamics, ecology, and focused issues within school settings. Likewise, school psychologists rarely were trained to fully understand how children's health problems related to school problems.

As psychology in general shifted toward a more ecological perspective for children and youth (e.g., Sameroff, Seifer, & Burke, 1997), effective strategies for prevention and intervention would require a knowledge base that crossed the boundaries between the educational and health systems. Multiple authors called for school psychology to adopt a training perspective that recognized the interaction of school, health, family, and community in achieving effective service delivery to children with health problems (Power, DuPaul, Shapiro, & Kazak, 2003; Shapiro, & Manz, 2003). Power et al. (1995) envisioned the training of a new type of school psychologist, one who served as an effective communicator between health and school communities but truly understood the school environment and had sufficient knowledge and experience in working within the medical community. The term "pediatric school psychologist" was selected to represent individuals with this type of hybrid training between pediatric and school psychology, as an appropriate way to express the importance, value, and effort to link these two areas of development. At the same time, a key to the pediatric school psychologist as conceptualized by Power et al. (1995) was the fact that although trained to understand and interact within the medical community, the individual's heart and soul remained within the school setting. Thus, the outreach was from the school toward the medical community.

In its original conceptualization, Power et al. (1995) described several roles for pediatric school psychologists. One role involved serving as a child advocate by working between the health and school communities. Individuals who are knowledgeable about health disorders can serve in a capacity to educate and inform school personnel about the potential links between the medical condition of the child and its impact on school performance. Another role involved the facilitation of medication monitoring. Students with medical conditions often take medications, yet health providers do not receive sufficient empirical feedback on the impact of the medications in school (Volpe, Heicke, & Guerasko-Moore, 2005). Typically, such feedback is limited to parent and/or child report to the health provider, with little empirical documentation of the impact these medications have on children's behavioral, academic and social functioning. The pediatric school psychologist was envisioned as someone with the expertise to develop and implement a plan for medication monitoring and to provide feedback to medical providers about medication effects.

Other roles for the pediatric school psychologist included providing collaborative communication between schools and health providers.

Being conversant in medical and school environments, these trained professionals could offer two-way communication between these entities. Further, the pediatric school psychologist was viewed as someone who would be involved in the development of prevention programs within school settings. The critical component that made these professionals unique was the presence of a high level of understanding of health providers' perspectives while also understanding the school culture and the intersection of effective programming.

RATIONALE FOR PEDIATRIC SCHOOL PSYCHOLOGY

The primary responsibility of schools is to educate students. Historically, however, a major function of schools has been to promote health (Kolbe et al., 1997). The relationship between health and learning is very important, and was recognized as such in the Health Security Act of 1994. Simply stated, when children's health and mental health needs are not met, their ability to learn and function in school is compromised. Students frequently engage in risky, unhealthy behaviors (Eaton et al., 2006), which can impact learning and academic achievement in negative ways. Many of these risky behaviors are amenable to change (Kolbe et al., 1997). As such, efforts to promote health and wellness and to decrease risky behaviors in the institution that touches nearly all American children and adolescents, the schools, are critical (Short & Talley, 1997). To be most effective, educational and health care services should be provided in an integrated manner (Short & Talley, 1997). Indeed, school-based health centers, a service delivery model designed to enhance access to and coordination of care (Short & Talley, 1997), and comprehensive school health programs (Allensworth, 1997) are examples of these efforts.

In addition to school professionals' involvement with health promotion and prevention efforts, there also is a clear need for school-based intervention related to chronic illness. It has been estimated that up to 15% of children and adolescents will be diagnosed with some type of chronic illness before they reach 18 years of age (Brown & Anderson, 1999). As medical technology improves and children survive these chronic illnesses more frequently, there is an increasing need for empirically supported interventions to address the cognitive, social, and behavioral development of these children (Roberts, Mitchell, & McNeal, 2003).

Given that children with chronic illnesses increasingly return to school, it is likely that they will require school-based supports. Pediatric school psychologists are well situated to contribute to the coordination of care for these children.

In the decades since the passage of the Education of the Handicapped Act of 1975, roles and functions of school psychologists have expanded to focus on early intervention to ameliorate early signs of social-emotional and academic difficulties, health and wellness promotion, and family-school collaboration. Training in these areas is central to pediatric school psychology. More recently, the three-tiered public health model of service delivery has been applied to schools to expand their capacity to meet the needs of children (e.g., Hoagwood & Johnson, 2003; Merrell, Buchanan, & Tran, 2006). School psychologists and their special education colleagues have been making steady progress in applying the three-tiered public health model of service delivery to the school setting to reduce and prevent behavioral and academic difficulties. School Wide Positive Behavior Support (SWPBS) is an exemplary school-based application of the public health model (Sugai & Horner, 2006) wherein the intensity of interventions to promote prosocial behaviors and to prevent challenging behaviors are delivered along a continuum depending on students' needs. Services are delivered to all students in large groups, to smaller groups of students who need additional help, and to individual students who require even more intensive intervention. This prevention-focused service delivery perspective is markedly different from school psychology's historic tradition of intervening with children after a problem developed or reached a significant magnitude. Yet this prevention-focused perspective is necessary for school psychologists to maximize their impact on the wellbeing of children.

Indeed, the import of a prevention and wellness promotion focus for all students has been highlighted recently by leaders in the field of school psychology. Examples include discussion at the 2002 Futures Conference (Harrison, Cummings, Dawson, Short, Gorin, & Palomares, 2004), a focus on training graduate students in these areas as outlined in the third edition of *School Psychology: A Blueprint for Training and Practice* (Ysseldyke et al., 2006), the prevention-oriented theme of the 2006 Annual Convention of the National Association of School Psychologists, *Prevention is an Intervention*, and the organization of *Best Practices in School Psychology V* (Thomas &

Grimes, 2008) around problem solving and the three-tiered public health model. Further, a clear link between school psychology practice and a public health model of prevention has been suggested as a model for conducting doctoral training in school psychology (Hoagwood & Johnson, 2003; Nastasi, 2004; Strein, Hoagwood, & Cohn, 2003).

Pediatric school psychology recognizes the need for school psychologists to focus their efforts on school-based health promotion for all children, to understand the multiple layers of factors that influence child development, including the bidirectional relationships among internal child characteristics and family, school, and community systems when developing interventions, and to work effectively across family, school and community settings in service delivery. With their broad training in both school and health care systems, pediatric school psychologists work with children and families in school and community settings, are partners in school-based health promotion, and can address the needs of children with medical conditions that put them at risk for social-emotional and learning difficulties.

CURRENT EFFORTS IN TRAINING AND RESEARCH

Training pediatric school psychologists includes specific coursework, practica, and research

emphases to develop the required competencies to function in this emerging role. Given the need for school psychologists who are able to work collaboratively across family, school, community, and health care systems, training models have been developed to prepare individuals to act as liaisons between family members, school staff, and health care providers. For example, the training program at Lehigh University developed the model illustrated in Table 32.1. The training program includes specialized coursework (e.g., health psychology, pharmacology) and unique practicum training opportunities (e.g., placements that include both school- and hospital-based training experiences) which are completed during students' final two years of preinternship training. The coursework follows the development of foundational skills during the first two years of training in all aspects of professional psychology including developmental psychopathology, ethics, assessment, intervention, and consultation.

Practicum during the final two years includes requirements that integrate school and medical settings. For example, students might complete practicum training in primary care and specialty pediatrics clinics. Within these settings, students work collaboratively with primary care physicians, pediatricians, and families to link the child's medical and health providers with schools (e.g., Mautone, Heick, & Clarke, 2007). Within the school setting, these students are engaged in both

TABLE 32.1 Highlights of Coursework, Practica, and Research Experiences of Students in the Lehigh University Pediatric School Psychology Training Program

Coursework (last two years)	Practica (last two years)	Research
Yearlong seminars:	Three full days per week:	Examples of research projects:
• Intervention for those with health problems	• Integrated between medical and school settings	• Evaluating a school-based asthma prevention program
• Health promotion and comprehensive school health programs	• Urban environments	• Establishing and evaluating a school-based program to improve healthy eating
• Grant writing	• Focus on students with health and health-related problems	• Establishing and evaluating a school-based medication adherence program
• Prevention science for students with health problems	• Focus on students at risk for developing emotional/behavior disorders	• Establishing and evaluating a school reentry program for students hospitalized for chronic health problems
• Neuropharmacology		
• Organizational management		
• Multicultural perspective in service delivery		

typical practica experiences for developing school psychologists such as conducting academic and behavioral assessments, consulting with teachers and other school staff, meeting with families, and providing collaborative interaction with agencies outside of schools to support students at risk or with emotional and/or behavioral needs as well as practica experiences that are specific to pediatric school psychology as described above. The portion of field work in the medical setting might also involve practica on inpatient units, such as pediatric oncology programs where students would assist with school reentry and coordination of care with community-based providers when the child returns home after treatment. The objective of this type of training is to produce graduates who have a unique understanding of the school environment and the educational implications of chronic illnesses, such as cancer, and are well trained to act as the liaison between the hospital-based treatment team, the family, the child's school, and any community-based providers who are involved in the child's care. Table 32.2 shows the nature of some of the many practica experiences reported by students who have completed the pediatric school psychology subspecialization at Lehigh University. The table also illustrates how someone trained from a pediatric school psychology perspective might conceptualize the reason for referral, and the actions they might take toward solving the problem.

As a specialization within school psychology, pediatric school psychology is still in its infancy. Clearly, research and program development in this area are necessary. Therefore, pediatric school psychology students also need to receive specific training and support related to grant writing, intervention design, and program evaluation. Training programs might require completion of one or more independent research projects related to pediatric school psychology (i.e., projects that relate to the health, educational, or social-emotional needs of students).

Over the past few decades there has been a significant increase in health-related articles that have been published in the school psychology literature. Wodrich and Schmitt (2003) examined this trend from 1981 to 2001 and found over 220 pediatric-related articles published in five of the leading school psychology journals during this period. These articles included a combination of review articles and empirical investigations. The topics of the articles addressed:

(a) a broad range of pediatric conditions; (b) attention-deficit/hyperactivity disorder in particular (e.g., collaboration with medical providers and medication-related roles); and (c) professional scope and practice role issues. Recently, *Psychology in the Schools* published an entire issue dedicated to providing school practitioners with information about school-based health promotion. The special issue included articles on wellness promotion, healthy eating promotion, school-based health centers, prevention of sexually transmitted infections, promoting success among students with specific chronic diseases, and helping children transition from the hospital back into the school setting (Walcott et al., 2008). In addition to the increased presence of health-related articles in peer reviewed school psychology journals, since 2003 pediatric school psychology articles have been published regularly in the National Association of School Psychologists' *Communiqué*. Additional publications from the National Association of School Psychologists, such as *Children's Needs III* (Bear & Minke, 2006), *Best Practices V* (Thomas & Grimes, 2008), and *Helping Children at Home and School: Handouts for Families and Educators* (Canter, Paige, Roth, Romero, & Carroll, 2004) have included information related to the intersection between children's physical, mental, academic, and social/emotional wellbeing. These examples illustrate the emerging presence of health-related scholarship in the school psychology literature.

PROMOTING HEALTHY EATING BEHAVIORS: AN ILLUSTRATION OF PEDIATRIC SCHOOL PSYCHOLOGY RESEARCH

One example of school-based health promotion research is the line of investigation currently being pursued by the second author (JBH). This line of inquiry demonstrates how school psychologists can apply their knowledge and skills related to behavior change, child development, school ecology, family-school involvement, and interdisciplinary team work to address a major public health problem: Childhood obesity. Over the past few decades childhood obesity (also termed childhood overweight) has reached epidemic proportions in the United States (Centers for Disease Control and Prevention, 2007a). Biology, behavior, environment, culture and socioeconomic status all contribute to body

TABLE 32.2 Pediatric School Psychology (PSP) Clinical and Research Illustrations

Presenting Issue	PSP Lens	PSP Roles

Child with cancer is ready to transition back to school.	• PSP has training in oncology unit and school settings and understands:
	  • how some forms of cancer and subsequent treatments can affect cognition;
	  • family systems issues that can facilitate or impede school reentry;
	  • how peers may respond to child's return to school.
		• PSP assesses the student's academic skills to ensure an appropriate instructional match.
		• PSP works with the child, caregivers, and teachers to facilitate a transition plan that is sensitive to the child's social, emotional, and academic needs.
		• PSP collaborates with the hospital neuropsychologist and medical providers to incorporate assessment results into the school plan and to understand how medications may impact school functioning.

School district is concerned about the epidemic rates of overweight in students.	• PSP recognizes that:
	  • overweight is a public health issue and can be prevented through comprehensive behavior change strategies;
	  • school is only one setting where children function and effective strategies will require collaboration with families and communities.
		• PSP works with the school district to develop comprehensive wellness policies that address students' access to physical activity and the sale of foods that are high in sugar and fat during and after school hours.
		• PSP helps curriculum committee select evidenced-based health programs.
		• PSP helps staff identify nonfood fundraisers.

An adolescent with HIV/AIDS is having difficulty adhering to his medication regimen and is experiencing significant difficulty in school.	• PSP understands:
	  • the complex challenges associated with adherence to medical regimens;
	  • interventions aimed to increase adherence;
	  • potential psychosocial and neurocognitive impact of HIV/AIDS as it relates to functioning;
	  • issues of confidentiality and disclosure in school and medical settings.
		• PSP explores factors surrounding adherence and works with the adolescent, his family and/or friends (who are aware of his status) to develop a plan to increase adherence by addressing barriers.
		• Being sensitive to confidentiality issues, the PSP works with school staff on the adherence plan and the student's school schedule.
		• PSP collaborates with school personnel to assess the impact of HIV on the student's cognition and school functioning.

Student returns to school with traumatic brain injury (TBI) and is displaying problem behaviors.	• PSP understands:
	  • the trajectory of rehabilitation and TBI through training in hospital and school-based rehabilitation services;
	  • special accommodations and support services for school reentry.
		• PSP reviews the student's neuropsychological evaluation.
		• PSP facilitates appropriate school reentry services and team meetings.
		• PSP ensures appropriate services are provided and follow up care is received.

weight, and obesity results when people eat too many calories and are not physically active enough (Centers for Disease Control and Prevention, 2007b). School-based obesity prevention efforts can be far reaching. Given that most children and adolescents attend school and eat meals in this setting, schools can play an important role in helping students achieve a healthy body weight and develop lifelong health behaviors (Institute of Medicine, 2007).

As a result of the current obesity epidemic, the Child Nutrition and WIC Reauthorization Act of 2004 mandated that all school districts participating in a federal school meals program establish a local school wellness policy by the start of the 2006–2007 school year. At a minimum the law requires that wellness policies include goals for nutrition education and physical activity, nutrition guidelines for all food sold in school, plans to evaluate the policy goals, and community involvement. Additional areas of wellness promotion, which are consistent with coordinated school health programs such as mental health and staff wellness promotion (Centers for Disease Control and Prevention, 2007c), can be incorporated into school districts' wellness policies. There are multiple ways that pediatric school psychologists can participate in these efforts, including helping districts implement and evaluate their wellness policies. The following example demonstrates how a pediatric school psychologist is helping two elementary schools in Boston to meet the goals of their district's wellness policy.

Following completion of the pediatric school psychology subspecialization in the school psychology program at Lehigh University and a postdoctoral fellowship at the Children's Hospital of Philadelphia, both of which involved training in school and hospital settings, the second author is now the principal investigator on a federal grant, which is funded to design, implement and evaluate a multicomponent, school-based nutrition program for kindergarten through third grade students. The health promotion program, designed to help children increase their consumption of fruit and vegetables, is grounded in social learning theory and involves key members of the school community (e.g., teachers and lunch aides) and parents who participate in the design and implementation of the program (see Blom-Hoffman, 2008).

This multiyear, multicomponent program includes components that are implemented by school staff and parents in the classroom, lunchroom, and at home. The program involves school-based interdisciplinary collaboration among a school psychologist, nutritionists, school nurses, teachers, and administrators. In addition, there is a strong family-school program emphasis. In the classroom, students receive CD-ROM-based nutrition education. In the lunchroom, lunch aides "catch" students eating fruit and vegetables and give them a sticker and verbal praise contingent on a bite of these foods. School-wide announcements are made each morning about the fruit or vegetable being served that day in the school lunch. Family-school activities include a series of interactive children's books assigned as homework and the development of a school fruit and vegetable cookbook that is used as healthy fundraiser (Blom-Hoffman, Wilcox, Dunn, Leff & Power, 2007).

Preliminary data indicate the program has been implemented with integrity and is perceived by key stakeholders as acceptable and feasible (Blom-Hoffman, 2008; Blom-Hoffman, Franko, Thompson, Power, & Stallings, 2007). The program has resulted in improved student knowledge. More importantly, the program has resulted in increased levels of students' fruit and vegetable consumption in the school lunch with a more pronounced and enduring effect on fruit relative to vegetable consumption (Blom-Hoffman, Franko et al., in press).

Despite these encouraging program evaluation results, implementation of this line of research has been challenging. The most significant challenges related to conducting this type of work have included issues related to obtaining informed consent from parents who may be skeptical about the role of research in their children's school (Blom-Hoffman, Leff, Franko, Beakley & Power, 2007), school-based fundraisers (i.e., bake sales and candy sales) that contradict health promotion messages, yet serve an important function in the school, and the ability of teachers to incorporate health education into the curriculum, given other high-priority academic areas. An additional challenge is related to economic factors that make it difficult for many schools to serve fresh fruits and vegetables on a frequent basis. There are complex societal factors that underlie the obesity epidemic (Pollan, 2006); however, schools can serve as healthful environments for students and staff, and pediatric school psychologists can assist in these efforts.

PEDIATRIC SCHOOL PSYCHOLOGISTS IN PRIMARY CARE: A SECOND RESEARCH ILLUSTRATION

Another example of pediatric school psychology-related research is the ADHD in Primary Care project at the Children's Hospital of Philadelphia. The ADHD in Primary Care project is a hospital-funded model demonstration project aimed at developing integrated and comprehensive services for children with ADHD. Many effective unisystemic interventions (e.g., family behavior therapy, school-based interventions) have been identified to address impairment related to ADHD symptoms (e.g., Anastopoulous, Shelton, DuPaul, & Guevremont, 1993; Jitendra et al., 2007; McMahon & Forehand, 2003); however, commonly employed unisystemic interventions focus primarily on change in one system. Few programs emphasize change across both the home and school environments. Given that children with ADHD experience impairment in multiple settings, it is important that interventions focus on change across systems. In addition, schools and primary care practices are the primary sites for service delivery for children with ADHD; however, these two systems frequently face significant challenges related to coordination of care.

One of the primary goals of the ADHD in Primary Care Project was to identify the perceptions of primary care providers (PCPs) about their roles and challenges related to the diagnosis and treatment of ADHD. To that end, a needs assessment was conducted with the primary care physicians throughout the hospital's network ($n = 180$ PCPs). Results indicated that PCPs believe it is highly appropriate for them to have a role in the diagnosis and treatment of ADHD; however, they experience particular challenges related to working with schools to obtain diagnostic and treatment effectiveness data (i.e., medication monitoring). In addition, PCPs feel they need additional support related to providing nonmedication treatments for ADHD (e.g., behavioral interventions), and challenges are significantly greater for PCPs working in urban versus suburban settings (Power, Mautone, Manz, Frye, & Blum, 2008).

An additional goal of the ADHD in Primary Care Project was to develop a model of integrated services across the home, school, and primary care systems (Power, DuPaul et al., 2003). Partnering to Achieve School Success (PASS) is currently

being developed by the ADHD in Primary Care team at The Children's Hospital of Philadelphia to address some of the challenges related to coordination of care for children with ADHD. This intervention is an approach to service delivery that focuses on promoting partnerships between families, schools, and PCPs based in urban primary care practices to address the behavioral and academic needs of children with or at risk for ADHD and comorbid conditions. In the PASS model, a clinician (i.e., pediatric school psychologist) works in partnership with families, PCPs, and school staff to promote family engagement in treatment, progress toward treatment plan goals, and collaboration across the family, school, and health-care systems (Power, Jones, Mautone, & Blum, forthcoming). To be maximally effective, the clinician must have a solid understanding of family systems, health-care practices, and school ecology. Pediatric school psychologists are ideally suited to fill this role.

To address home- and school-based concerns, the PASS program includes the following components: (a) Engagement and Progress Monitoring, with a primary focus on developing and maintaining a collaborative relationship with the family to foster engagement in treatment; (b) Brief Family Intervention to address home-based behavioral goals that may be responsive to targeted, brief treatment; (c) Family-School Conjoint Behavioral Consultation (CBC) to address school-based behavioral and academic targets; (d) Medication Management (in cases where medication is warranted and acceptable to the family); (e) Psychological Evaluation to identify comorbid conditions; and (f) Crisis Intervention to assist families in dealing with unforeseen stressors, when necessary. Motivational interviewing strategies are employed throughout the intervention to promote families' readiness, willingness, and ability to become actively engaged in the intervention (Dishion & Stormshak, 2007; Miller & Rollnick, 2002).

Pilot data indicate that PASS is a feasible and acceptable program for children and families coping with ADHD. Service utilization data for children in kindergarten through grade 6 who had received at least two months of intervention were analyzed ($N = 18$). All of the children met criteria for ADHD. The majority of the children were male (78%), African American (94%), students in public schools (67%), and on Medicaid (about 80%). Mean age of the sample was 9.6 years ($SD = 2.3$), and families were involved in intervention for an average of 5.2 months ($SD =$ 2.0). Mean number of face-to-face sessions with families was 5.2, and the mean number of contact hours with families was 8.7. Approximately 89% of participating families received the Brief Family Intervention module, 78% received the Family-School Conjoint Behavioral Consultation module, 22% completed an evaluation, and 28% required Crisis Intervention. Only three families (17%) participated in the medication management module of PASS, which involved education about medication and careful monitoring of medication effects. However, a total of 50% of the participants were on medication at some point during the intervention. Anecdotal reports from PCPs and families indicate that providers and family members consider PASS to be a beneficial intervention for urban families coping with ADHD (Power, Jones et al., forthcoming).

Although pilot data indicate that PASS is a feasible and acceptable intervention, there have been several challenges related to program development and implementation, including keeping families and teachers engaged in the treatment and creating a standardized model of care across participants (Power, Jones et al., forthcoming). PASS clinicians make consistent efforts to maintain contact with families; however, at times it is difficult to develop and maintain relationships with urban low-income families who are coping with multiple stressors. In addition, in order to develop a collaborative, trusting relationship with families, PASS clinicians must be aware of cultural differences with respect to various treatment options (e.g., medication). In order to keep families interested and engaged in treatment, PASS clinicians must respect families' beliefs and values with respect to treatment components while providing appropriate education and treatment for the child and family.

In addition, when the care plan includes school-based goals, PASS clinicians assist the family in developing a collaborative relationship with the child's teacher and other school staff members. In most cases, PASS participants attend urban schools that are often underresourced, and teachers and school staff members may have limited time to devote to intervention plan development and implementation. Pediatric school psychologists, who have an understanding of school ecology and school-based intervention development and evaluation, would be well-suited to assist in the development of school-based plans that are effective and acceptable to all members of the treatment team.

ROLES FOR PEDIATRIC SCHOOL PSYCHOLOGISTS

Surveys of physicians and health care providers have demonstrated the needs for psychologists with the types of skills described above. Three reported surveys illustrate the potential role that pediatric school psychologists can play. Shapiro et al. (2006) surveyed pediatricians and family practitioners regarding the value of the type of services that school psychologists trained in pediatric school psychology can offer to their medical practice. The survey asked a convenience sample of 54 physicians and/or residents in family practice or pediatrics from two regional training hospitals to rate the degree to which professionals who are trained to work with their practices and communicate with schools would: (a) help with implementing recommendations for schools from physicians, (b) understand the needs of schools, (c) work with families on health promotion, and (d) discuss the impact of healthy behavior on school performance. The survey also asked whether the physicians currently had individuals in their practice who were engaged in these tasks and if so, how satisfied they were with the outcomes of these services.

Results from the survey found that over 70% of all respondents indicated that an individual who engaged in activities linking schools and health systems practices would be very valuable to their practice. At the same time, 60–80% of all respondents indicated that they did not have anyone in their practices focused on linkages to schools and that when they did, it was typically an individual who was trained as a school psychologist.

A second survey of primary care physicians specifically related to ADHD highlights the need for pediatric school psychologists. The ADHD Questionnaire for PCPs (AQ-PCP) is a 24-item scale designed to assess primary care pediatricians' (PCP) views about the extent to which clinical activities related to the assessment and treatment of ADHD are appropriate and feasible in primary care settings (Power, Mautone et al., 2008). Items were rated on a 4 point scale (1 = not at all; 4 = very much) for appropriateness and feasibility. To identify the perceptions of PCPs, the AQ-PCP was administered to 180 providers in 27 practices affiliated with a hospital in a large city in the Northeast (23 practices are located in suburban settings serving families with primarily private insurance and 4 are in urban settings serving families who are eligible for Medicaid).

Participants rated each of the 24 items twice: once to indicate the perceived appropriateness of the clinical activity given sufficient time and resources, and a second time to indicate the feasibility of the activity in their actual practice.

An exploratory factor analysis of ratings of the appropriateness of activities related to managing ADHD identified four domains of clinical practice: (a) assessing ADHD, (b) providing mental health care, (c) recommending and monitoring FDA-approved medications for ADHD, and (d) recommending non-FDA-approved medications for ADHD. Mean ratings indicated that PCPs believe it is highly appropriate for them to have a role in the management of ADHD (i.e., assessment and medication monitoring); however, they face significant challenges related to communication with schools (e.g., obtaining rating scales from teachers). These challenges are greater for providers working in urban low-income settings than for those serving families with private insurance. The results highlighted the need for practice-based resources to coordinate school communication and collaboration with mental health providers, particularly in urban practices.

Blevins, Magee, Sheridan, Woods, and Magee (2007) reported the outcomes of a survey of 31 graduates of APA-accredited school psychology programs that provide specialized training in pediatric school psychology. Results of the survey indicated that 86% of graduates had been in the field for 6 years or less reflecting the relatively recent addition of this type of training within doctoral programs in school psychology. The distribution of where these individuals were employed showed that 32% were in school settings, 23% in hospital settings, and 16% as university faculty. However, a total of 10% were employed in medical clinics and 3% in school-based health clinics, two potential employment options for graduates with training in pediatric school psychology. When asked about their specific practices in which they engaged, the highest rated frequency of activities reflected the roles typical of school psychologists (i.e., behavioral intervention adherence, behavioral consultation, assisting with academic support for students, and parent training), probably most related to the nature of functioning primarily in school settings. Those activities more likely to occur in medically related settings (such as medication management, medication treatment adherence, and pain management) were the least indicated by the participants. It is important to

note that the survey did not break down the roles specifically for the part of the sample who were not engaged in school settings.

CHALLENGES FOR THE FUTURE

Despite the identified need for psychologists trained in pediatric school psychology, the acceptance and employment of such individuals within school settings has not at this time been fully realized. One of the difficulties comes from role definition of school psychologists within school settings. Historically, the role of school psychologists has been transforming in many ways. Efforts to move away from the more traditional role of conducting evaluations for special education eligibility has been a long-time discussion in the professional literature (e.g., Merrell, Ervin, & Gimpel, 2006; Sheridan & D'Amato, 2003). Emerging roles for school psychologists have especially called for increased prevention efforts (e.g., Braden, DiMarino-Linnen, & Good, 2001; Graden, 2004; Meyers, Meyers, & Grogg, 2004).

Although these calls for transforming the role of school psychologists toward prevention are well intentioned, they are highly dependent on how resources in schools are actually allocated. Over the past decade, there has been a substantial and needed attention to students' academic outcomes. In particular, efforts to reform schools, increase accountability for school professionals, and focus on developing literacy in young children have dominated the attention of schools. These efforts are not surprising and are very much needed, given that the development of reading performance in young children can often serve as the foundation for success or failure throughout the entire school experience. At the same time, the attention devoted toward improving academics clearly affects resource allocations that can impact the efforts aimed at the mental and physical health needs of children and youth.

Perhaps one piece of indirect evidence related to resource allocation has been the emerging crisis related to childhood obesity (e.g., Blom-Hoffman, George, & Franko, 2006; Story, Kaphingst, & French, 2006). Resources allocated toward improving the nutrition and eating habits of children have nowhere equaled the energies placed into improving their academics. Until substantial shifts in public policy and attention to outcomes in schools beyond academics become high priorities, the reallocation of school psychology personnel to roles similar to those of pediatric school psychologists may be difficult to attain.

Another challenge for the future is related to the development of training programs devoted to pediatric school psychology. Although pediatric psychologists trained in health-care settings may be potential candidates to provide services within school settings, the typical training sequences for these students do not involve an understanding of school-based service delivery (Lescano, Plante, & Spirito, 2004). Likewise, because typical school psychologists are not provided opportunities for training in health-care settings, gaining employment within health-care settings as school psychologists is somewhat limited. As a result, there is a need for preservice training programs to organize and deliver models of training that offer students the knowledge, experience, and competence to function across health-care and school settings. Over the past decade, very few programs of this nature have emerged (e.g., Lehigh University, University of South Florida, University of Nebraska–Lincoln, University of Wisconsin–Madison, University of Wisconsin–Milwaukee, and East Carolina University have models or partial components of their school psychology training programs in this area). Likewise, finding internship sites that are receptive to accepting students trained in pediatric school psychology where the roles and functions of these students are consistent with their training remains a challenge.

Finally, acceptance of pediatric school psychology within the related subdiscipline of pediatric psychology is essential for this subarea of school psychology to thrive into the future. Recognition of the importance of training across settings to provide psychological service for children with medical needs is still in its early stages (Brown, 2004; Power, Shapiro, & DuPaul, 1998, 2003). Indeed, Blevins et al. (2007) in their survey also found that the greatest reported challenge by graduates of programs in pediatric school psychology was the reported misunderstanding of their role and/or lack of support in their employment setting, particularly the schools. One opportunity to increase both the acceptance of the subspecialty of pediatric school psychology within and outside of the school psychology profession, as well as potentially influence resource allocation in schools and medical settings to include these professionals, could come with providing more postdoctoral opportunities where individuals trained in a pediatric school psychology model can gain critical

experience. Across the graduates of the training program at Lehigh University, three individuals were successful in landing postdoctoral employment in health-related, school-focused services all within health-care settings. However, finding opportunities for training in providing pediatric school psychology based in schools are far less available. Perhaps developing more training sites devoted to pediatric school psychology within schools would offer the needed change agent to alter school practice and resource allocation.

Despite the challenges, the emerging subspecialty of pediatric school psychology offers a chance for school psychologists to move toward expanding their role in prevention and health promotion. Such a role is fully consistent with where school psychology as a profession sees itself heading in the twenty-first century.

REFERENCES

Allensworth, D. D. (1997). *Schools and our nation's health investment.* Washington, DC: National Academy Press.

Anastopoulos, A. D., Shelton, T., DuPaul, G. J., & Guevremont, D. C. (1993). Parent training for attention deficit hyperactivity disorder: Its impact on parent functioning. *Journal of Abnormal Child Psychology, 21,* 581–596.

Bear, G. G., & Minke, K. M. (Eds.) (2006). *Children's Needs III: Development, Prevention, and Intervention.* Bethesda, MD: National Association of School Psychologists.

Blevins, C. A., Magee, K. L., Sheridan, S. M., Woods, K. E., & Magee, H. E. (2007, August). The emerging discipline of pediatric school psychology: Roles, benefits, and challenges. Presented at the American Psychological Association, San Francisco.

Blom-Hoffman, J. (2008). Promoting fruit and vegetable consumption in multi-culturally diverse, urban schools. *Psychology in the Schools, 45,* 16–27.

Blom-Hoffman, J. Franko, D. L., Thompson, D. R., Power, T. J., & Stallings, V. A. (2007). Increasing children's fruit and vegetable consumption in school lunch: Longitudinal behavioral effects of a fruit and vegetable promotion program. Unpublished manuscript.

Blom-Hoffman, J., George, J, B. E., & Franko, D. L. (2006). Childhood overweight. In G. Bear & K. Minke (Eds.), *Children's needs III: Development, prevention, and intervention* (989–1000). Washington, DC: National Association of School Psychologists.

Blom-Hoffman, J., Leff, S. S., Franko, D. L., Weinstein, E., Beakley, K. & Power, T. J. (in press). Using a multi-component, partnership-based approach to improve participation rates in school-based research. *School Mental Health.*

Blom-Hoffman, J., Wilcox, K. R., Dunn, L., Leff, S. S., & Power, T. J. (2007). Family involvement in school-based health promotion: Bringing nutrition information home. Unpublished manuscript.

Braden, J. S., DiMarrino-Linnen, E., & Good, T. L. (2001). Schools, society, and school psychologists: History and future directions. *Journal of School Psychology, 39*, 203–219.

Brown, R. T. (Ed.) (2004). *Handbook of pediatric psychology in school settings.* Mauwah, NJ: Lawrence Erlbaum Associates.

Brown, R. T., & Anderson, D. L. (1999). Cognition in chronically ill children. In R. T. Brown (Ed.), *Cognitive aspects of chronic illness in children* (pp. 1–11). New York: Guilford.

Canter, A. S., Paige, L. Z., Roth, M. D., Romero, I., & Carroll, S. A. (Eds.) (2004). *Helping children at home and school II: Handouts for families and educators.* Bethesda, MD: National Association of School Psychologists.

Centers for Disease Control and Prevention (2007a). Prevalence of overweight among children and adolescents: United States, 2003–2004. Retrieved October 6, 2007 from www.cdc.gov/nchs/products/pubs/pubd/hestats/overweight/overwght_child_03.htm.

Centers for Disease Control and Prevention (2007b). Overweight and obesity: Contributing factors. Retrieved October 6, 2007 from www.cdc.gov/nccdphp/dnpa/obesity/contributing_factors.htm.

Centers for Disease Control and Prevention (2007c). Coordinated School Health Program. Retrieved October 6, 2007 from www.cdc.gov/Healthy Youth/CSHP/.

Dishion, T. J., & Stormshak, E. A. (2007). Intervening in children's lives: An ecological, family-centered approach to mental health care. Washington, DC: American Psychological Association.

Eaton, D. K., Kann, L., Kinchen, S., Ross, J., Hawkins, J., Harris, W. A., et al. (2006). *Youth risk behavior surveillance—2005.* MMWR: Survelliance summaries. Atlanta, GA: Center for Disease Control.

Fothergill, K., & Ballard, E. (1998). The school-linked health center: A promising model of community-based care for adolescents. *Journal of Adolescent Health, 23* 27–36.

Graden, J. L. (2004). Arguments for change to consultation, prevention, and intervention: Will school psychology ever achieve this promise? *Journal of Educational & Psychological Consultation, 15*, 345–359.

Harrison, P. L., Cummings, J. A., Dawson, M., S., Gorin, S., & Palomares, R. (2004). Responding to the needs of children, families, and schools: The 2002 multisite conference on the future of school psychology. *School Psychology Review, 33*, 12–33.

Hoagwood, K., & Johnson, J. (2003). School psychology: A public health framework I. From evidence-based practices to evidence-based policies. *Journal of School Psychology, 41*, 3–21.

Institute of Medicine (2007). *Nutrition standards for foods in schools.* Washington DC: The National Academies Press.

Jitendra, A. K., DuPaul, G. J., Volpe, R. J., Tresco, K. E., Vile Junod, R. E., Lutz, J. G., et al. (2007). Consultation-based academic intervention for children with Attention Deficit Hyperactivity Disorder: School functioning outcomes. *School Psychology Review, 36*, 217–236.

Kolbe, L. J., Collins, J., & Cortese, P. (1997). Building the capacity of schools to improve the health of the nation: A call for assistance from psychologists. *American Psychologist, 52*, 256–265.

Lescano, C., Plante, W., & Spirito, A. (2004). Training in the delivery of pediatric psychology services in school systems. In R. T. Brown (Ed.), *Handbook of pediatric psychology in school settings* (pp. 701–712). Mahwah, NJ: Lawrence Erlbaum Associates.

Mautone, J. A., Heick, P. F., & Clarke, A. T. (2007, August). Models for linking schools and primary care in assessing ADHD. Paper presented at the annual meeting of the American Psychological Association, San Francisco, CA.

McMahon, R. J., & Forehand, R. L. (2003). *Helping the Noncompliant Child: Family-Based Treatment for Oppositional Behavior* (2nd ed.). New York: Guilford Press.

Merrell, K. W., Buchanan, R., & Tran, O. K. (2006). Relational aggression in children and adolescents: A review with implications for school settings. *Psychology in the Schools, 43*, 345–360.

Merrell, K. W., Ervin, R. A., & Gimpel, G. A. (2006). *School psychology for the 21st century: Foundations and practices.* New York: Guilford Press.

Meyers, J., Meyers, A., & Grogg, K. (2004). Prevention through consultation: A model to guide future developments in the field of school psychology. *Journal of Educational & Psychological Consultation, 15*, 257–276.

Miller, W. R., & Rollnick, S. (2002). *Motivational Interviewing: Preparing People for Change* (2nd ed.). New York: Guilford Press.

Nastasi, B. K. (2004). Meeting the challenges of the future: Integrating public health and public education for mental health promotion. *Journal of Educational & Psychological Consultation, 15*, 295–312.

National Commission on Children (1991). *Beyond Rhetoric: A New American Agenda for Children and Families. Final Report of the National Commission on Children.* Washington, DC: U.S. Government Printing Office.

National Commission on Excellence in Education. (1983). *A nation at risk: The imperative for educational reform*. Washington, DC: U.S. Government Printing Office.

National Council on Education and Testing (1992). *Raising Standards for American Education. A Report to Congress, the Secretary of Education, the National Education Goals Panel, and the American People*. Washington, DC: U.S. Government Printing Office.

Pollan, M. (2006). *The omnivore's dilemma: A natural history of four meals*. New York, NY: Penguin.

Power T. J., DuPaul, G. J., Shapiro, E. S., & Kazak, A. (2003). *Promoting children's health: Integrating school, family, and community*. New York: Guilford Press.

Power, T. J., DuPaul, G. J., Shapiro, E. S., & Parrish, J. (1995). Pediatric school psychology: The emergence of a subspecialty. *School Psychology Review, 24*, 244–257.

Power, T. J., Jones, H. A., Mautone, J. A., & Blum, N. J. (forthcoming). Early intervention for attention and behavior problems in urban contexts. In B. Doll (Ed.), *Handbook of Youth Prevention Science*, New York: Routledge.

Power, T. J., Mautone, J. A., Manz, P. H., Frye, L., & Blum, N. J. (2008). Managing ADHD in primary care: A systematic analysis of roles and challenges. *Pediatrics, 121*, electronic pages 65–72.

Power, T. J., Shapiro, E. S., & DuPaul, G. J. (1998). Role of the school-based professional in health-related services. In L. Phelps (Ed.), *Health-related disorders in children and adolescents: A guidebook for understanding and educating* (pp. 15–26). Washington, DC: American Psychological Association.

Power, T. J., Shapiro, E. S., & DuPaul, G. J. (2003). Preparing psychologists to link systems of care in managing and preventing children's health problems. *Journal of Pediatric Psychology, 28*, 147–155.

Reynolds, A. J. (1999). Educational success in high-risk settings: Contributions of the Chicago Longitudinal study. *Journal of School Psychology, 37*, 345–354.

Roberts, M. C., Mitchell, M. C., & McNeal, R. (2003). The evolving field of pediatric psychology: Critical issues and future challenges. In M. C. Roberts (Ed.), *Handbook of Pediatric Psychology* (3rd ed., pp. 3–18). New York: Guilford.

Sameroff, A. J., Seifer, R., & Burke, W. T. (1997). Environmental perspectives on adaptation during childhood and adolescence. In S. S. Luthar, J. A. Burack, D. Cicchetti, & J. E. Weisz (Eds.), *Developmental Psychopathology: Perspectives on adjustment, risk, and disorder* (pp. 507–526). Cambridge, U.K.: Cambridge University Press.

Shapiro, E. S., & Manz, P. H. (2003). Collaborating with schools in the provision of pediatric psychological services. In R. T. Brown (Ed.), *Handbook of pediatric psychology in school settings*

(pp. 49–64). Mahwah, NJ: Lawrence Erlbaum Associates.

Shapiro, E. S., DuPaul, G. J., Power, T. J., Barrett, C., Freeman, T., Hodges, J., & Stein, R. (2006). A survey of pediatrician and family practice physicians perspectives on pediatric school psychology. Lehigh University, unpublished manuscript.

Sheridan, S. M., & D'Amato, R. C. (Eds.) (2003). Partnering to chart our futures: School psychology review and school psychology quarterly combined issue on the multisite conference on the future of school psychology. *School Psychology Quarterly, 18*, 352–357.

Short, R. J., & Talley, R. C. (1997). Rethinking psychology and the schools: Implications of recent national policy. *American Psychologist, 52*, 234–240.

Story, M., Kaphingst, K. M., & French, S. (2006). The role of schools in obesity prevention. *The Future of Children: Special Issue Childhood Obesity, 16*, 109–142.

Strein, W., Hoagwood, K., & Cohn, A. (2003). School psychology: A public health perspective I. Prevention, populations, and systems change. *Journal of School Psychology, 41*, 23–38.

Sugai, G., & Horner, R. R. (2006). A promising approach for expanding and sustaining school-wide positive behavior support. *School Psychology Review, 35*, 245–255.

Talley, R. C., & Short, R. J. (1995). *School health: Psychology's role. A report to the nation*. Washington, DC: American Psychological Association.

Thomas, A., & Grimes, J. (Eds.) (2008). *Best practices in school psychology V*. Washington, DC: National Association of School Psychologists.

U.S. Dept. of Health & Human Services (1991). *Healthy people 2000:* National Health Promotion and Disease Prevention Objectives (1991). Washington, DC: U.S. Department of Health and Human Services.

Volpe, R. J., Heick, P., & Guerasko-Moore, D. (2005). An agile behavioral model for monitoring the effects of stimulant medication in school settings. *Psychology in the Schools, 42*(5), 509–523.

Walcott, C. M., Chafouleas, S. M., McDougal, J. L., Miller, D. N., Riley-Tillman, T. C., Blom-Hoffman, J., et al. (2008). School-based health promotion: An introduction to the practitioner's edition. *Psychology in the Schools, 45*, 1–4.

Wodrich, D. L., & Schmitt, A. J. (2003). Pediatric topics in the school psychology literature: Publications since 1981. *Journal of School Psychology, 41*, 131–141.

Ysseldyke, J., Burns, M., Dawson, M., Kelley, B., Morrison, D., Ortiz, S., et al. (2006). *School Psychology: A blueprint for training and practice III*. Washington, DC: National Association of School Psychologists.

CHAPTER 33

UNDERSTANDING AND PROMOTING RESILIENCE IN CHILDREN: PROMOTIVE AND PROTECTIVE PROCESSES IN SCHOOLS[1]

ANN S. MASTEN
University of Minnesota
FROSSO MOTTI-STEFANIDI
University of Athens

Four decades of research on resilience in children have yielded important clues to understanding and promoting positive adaptation among children at risk from adverse circumstances (Luthar, 2006; Masten, 2007c; Masten & Gewirtz, 2006). Findings implicate the school context in many of the processes that reduce or ameliorate risk, promote positive development, and prevent problems in child development. Moreover, since most children attend school in many societies, this context affords important opportunities to facilitate resilience (Doll, Zucker, & Brehm, 2006; Pianta, 2006).

In this chapter, we examine findings from the research on resilience in children for clues to the role schools may play in fostering resilience. The chapter has four sections. In the first section, we describe the meaning and scope of resilience as studied in children. In the second section, we highlight convergent findings on resilience from diverse investigations pertinent to school-age children. In section three, we describe several of the key protective systems implicated by these findings and how they may work in a school context. In section four, we describe a framework for promoting resilience among school children. In conclusion, we discuss exciting new developments in resilience research and the potential for a new generation of preventive interventions engaging schools in a broader effort to promote competence and resilience in development.

THE MEANING OF RESILIENCE IN CHILDREN

Resilience is a very broad idea referring to patterns of positive adaptation in a system (Masten, 2007c). Thus, resilience can be considered at many levels, from the perspective of an individual, a family, a school, a community, or an ecosystem. In the developmental sciences, resilience generally refers to a pattern of positive adaptation following exposure to risk or adversity (Masten, 2001; Wright & Masten, 2005). Resilience is an inference about a child's life pattern involving judgments about two critical components: how well a child is doing in life and exposure to significant risk or adversity.

In terms of the first judgment, whether one is simply thinking of a case example of a resilient

[1] Support for the preparation of this chapter was provided by a grant from the European Social Fund and Greek National Resources (EPEAEK II-PYTHAGORAS) to the second author, which has facilitated the collaboration of the authors and their students, and a Distinguished McKnight University Professorship to the first author. The authors also express their deep appreciation to the faculty and students of the Project Competence Studies of Risk and Resilience in Minnesota and the Athena Studies of Resilient Adaptation (AStRA) in Greece for their many contributions to theoretical and empirical work of the authors. The authors give a special thanks to Jelena Obradović and Vassilis Pavlopoulos.

person or setting out to conduct systematic research on resilience in a school full of children, criteria are required for judging or evaluating successful adaptation. Investigators must make these criteria explicit and different scientists may not agree on how to define "doing OK in life." Developmental scientists often define success in life according to how well a child is doing in relation to *competence in developmental tasks*, described below. By whatever criteria, however, simply doing well is not sufficient to meet the definition of resilience, which also requires some kind of serious threat to adaptation or development.

The second judgment concerns the past or present condition of adversity exposure, a judgment that something has threatened the viability of the system. Investigators have studied many kinds of potential threats or risk factors, including premature birth, death or divorce of parents, maltreatment, living in a war zone, natural disasters, poverty, violence in the neighborhood, and accumulations of such experiences over time. A risk factor or cumulative risk gradient refers to the presence of conditions where evidence indicates a higher than usual probability of some undesirable outcome. Developmental scientists often define risks in terms of conditions or attributes that regularly forecast problems in developmental task achievement or that predict behavioral problems, emotional distress, or mental disorders.

Competence in Developmental Tasks: Judging Positive Adaptation in Developmental Context

It could be argued that one of the most important contributions of the behavioral resilience researchers was their focus on the development of competence and how to assess it (Masten & Obradović, 2006). Pioneers of resilience research, including Norman Garmezy, Lois Murphy, Arnold Sameroff, and Emmy Werner, emphasized the importance of positive perspectives on development and assessments of positive adaptation (Masten & Reed, 2002). In developmental research on resilience in children, positive adaptation has included subjective well-being, as well as competence in age-salient developmental tasks, reflecting a psychological perspective on the dual nature of adaptation in a living system: good internal functioning (versus distress or misery) and good functioning in the environment (versus maladaptive

functioning) (Masten, Burt, & Coatsworth, 2006).

In the Project Competence studies, initiated by Norman Garmezy, and subsequently directed by the first author, the definition and assessment of competence in age-salient developmental tasks have played a central role in the research agenda (Masten & Powell, 2003). In this research tradition, resilience has been defined in terms of how well a child is doing with respect to what is expected for children in this context of development, history, culture and situation. Competence is defined as *effective performance in age-salient developmental tasks*. These investigators, including the first author, did not disregard internal well-being, of interest in its own right, but they focused on the observable benchmarks of making one's way in the world.

The concept of developmental tasks has a long history in science, as well as ancient origins in biological and cultural evolution (see Masten, Burt, & Coatsworth, 2006). For millennia, children have been expected to learn to walk and talk and eventually to take on adult roles in their societies. In modern times, children also are expected in many cultures to attend school and learn the requisite skills for adult roles, to get along with other children, and to follow the rules of classroom and society. These developmental task expectations change as children develop, just as the expectations for learning and behavior change in a school classroom. Adolescents are expected to follow rules without constant supervision and to develop deeper friendships than young children. As children move toward adulthood, they usually are expected to learn work skills and engage in romantic relationships, and eventually to form families of their own. These expectations, conceptualized as developmental tasks, serve as benchmarks for how well development (in a particular context of history and culture) is proceeding. Adults and other stakeholders have learned over time that significant problems with achieving expected behaviors in these core task domains often signal trouble ahead. Concomitantly, meeting these task expectations serves as a harbinger of future success, because these achievements appear to serve as a sturdy platform on which subsequent development is constructed.

In societies such as the United States, functioning effectively in the school context plays a central role in meeting developmental task expectations. Academic achievement, getting along with children in school, and following school rules for conduct are important developmental tasks for school-age children in many societies.

Some investigators combine internal and external success in their definitions of resilience, requiring happiness (or the absence of significant internal distress and symptoms) plus doing well in developmental task domains such as academic and social achievement. This is a topic of some debate (Masten, 2007a; Masten & Gewirtz, 2006). In either case, however, it is clearly possible to be successful in developmental tasks in society and unhappy, or failing in many domains while happy. In other words, internal and external aspects of adaptation show some independence. Nonetheless, extreme dysfunction within a living system, or maladaptation of a system in its environment is likely to undermine all aspects of adaptation. A child who is extremely weak from a viral infection is unlikely to function well at school or with peers; similarly, a child who is failing every developmental expectation in a family or community is unlikely to be happy unless the child is blissfully unaware of these failures or actively rejecting or rebelling against community standards.

Still other investigators define resilience in terms of psychopathology, with "good adaptation" referring to the absence of symptoms or disorder, taking a page from the medical model of mental health and illness. Most developmental scientists and school psychologists, however, emphasize a positive definition of doing well over the life course, involving more than the absence of problems.

Life Events and Cumulative Risks: Judging Adversity Exposure

A child who is doing well in the developmental tasks of his or her culture might be described as competent or successful or well adjusted, but that child would not be judged "resilient" without exposure to significant adversity. Many kinds of adversity exposure have been studied in the resilience literature, as noted previously in this chapter, ranging from individual catastrophes, such as loss of parents or rape, to massive catastrophes, such as hurricanes or war. Whatever the adversity, however, the level of exposure must be high enough to pose a real threat to adjustment or development. Resilience does not refer to handling the minor bumps on the road of life, but to withstanding or recovering from the kind of situations that have the potential

to disrupt development or destabilize the whole system.

Risky situations can be defined empirically or by judgment. There are some well-established "risk factors" that consistently have shown statistical predictive power in forecasting significantly higher rates of particular problems or broad maladaptation in populations of children. These risk factors may also co-occur and cumulative risk indices often show even greater (or broader) predictive validity than single risk factors (Obradović, Shaffer, & Masten, in press; Sameroff, 2006). Examples of risk factors and correlated outcomes include low birth weight for learning problems, child abuse for behavioral and emotional problems, malnutrition for physical and cognitive development, or a combination of all three risks for multiple problems in development. Individual children may have a unique configuration of adversity exposure that nearly any set of judges would agree constitute high adversity exposure (e.g., a child has been reared in a dangerous home and neighborhood, exposed to violence and drugs, kidnapped by a parent, and then abandoned).

Over the years, a wide variety of risks have been studied in the search for understanding resilience. In recent years, great attention has been given to the meaning of risk and also to whether there are differential effects of particular risks for particular outcomes. Composite risk indices are often powerful global predictors, but they tend to obscure the processes involved. Helena Kraemer and her colleagues have delineated a more precise definition of risk factors, in an effort to discriminate correlates of undesirable outcomes from clear antecedent predictors and causal risk factors (Kraemer et al., 1997; Kraemer, Stice, Kazdin, Offord, & Kupfer, 2001). By their standards for terminology, for example, a risk factor must be clearly antecedent in time to the outcome of interest it predicts. This seemingly straightforward standard is not easy to establish for many risk factors in child development because it is often difficult to identify the starting point for a problem in behavior. Many "risk factors" in the literature are actually correlates that were measured earlier in time than the "outcomes" they predict, but it is not known with certainty when the problem actually began.

The most compelling evidence for establishing a causal risk factor in resilience research is a randomized experiment. A randomly assigned group of children is exposed to an intervention designed to prevent, eliminate, reduce, or counteract the risk factor in question; this intervention convincingly results in both a change of risk and a more favorable outcome for the children in the intervention group as compared to the children randomly assigned to the alternative group. Similar strategies can be used to show that adding something to the lives of children can offset or ameliorate the effects of adversity.

THE SHORT LIST OF CLUES TO PROMOTIVE AND PROTECTIVE PROCESSES

Resilience researchers are searching for explanations of how some people "make it" while others have trouble in the aftermath of adversity, with the practical goal of using this knowledge to promote better outcomes among children who might not make it without some help. Thus, investigators also have studied potential candidates for "what makes a difference." These factors are often called "assets," "promotive factors," "resources" or "protective factors" (Masten & Gewirtz, 2006; Wright & Masten, 2005).

Assets, promotive factors, and resources all refer to attributes of a person or environment associated with better outcomes across most levels of adversity exposure. These qualities, such as good parenting and good nutrition, are generally good for development. In many cases, these qualities are the positive end of a bipolar attribute, where the negative end (e.g., "bad parenting") is associated with negative outcomes, although it is conceivable for a factor to function only in a positive way.

Protective factors have a special role when risk or adversity is high, over and above whatever generally positive effects they may have. Like the human immune system, or the airbag in an automobile, these factors provide special protection under specific hazardous conditions. Protective factors appear to *moderate* the impact of adversity. Effective teachers, for example, may be good for learning outcomes for all children, but prove to be particularly important for children growing up in very disadvantaged homes.

There are also negative and bipolar moderators that encompass the possibility of vulnerability effects, where effects of a threat are *increased* by the presence of the moderator. Some children, for example, may be more vulnerable or more resistant to the effects of an adverse experience, such as maltreatment, although often it is not

clear whether a moderator is operating to increase vulnerability, protection, or both, depending on the level or degree of the moderating condition. For example, resilience studies have implicated individual differences in temperament (among younger children) or personality (among older youth) as moderators of an adversity response (Luthar, 2006; Masten & Powell, 2003). However, it is not usually clear whether observed statistical interaction effects are the result of children who are susceptible to negative emotions, often referred to as "stress reactive," or children who are protected by their "easygoing" disposition, or both. Moreover, Boyce has recently proposed that stress reactivity may actually reflect a general "sensitivity to context" which may produce exceptionally positive outcomes in favorable environments as well as poor outcomes in negative settings (Boyce, 2007; Boyce & Ellis, 2005). In this case, it is the particular combination of individual disposition and context that matters, reflecting a truly joint effect. Whatever their character, such interaction effects are assumed to reflect underlying processes that need to be explicated.

When researchers focus exclusively on high-risk samples, where all the children have experienced significant adversity, it is not possible to differentiate a promotive from a protective factor. This situation has led to some confusion, so it is important to keep in mind that establishing a protective effect requires evidence that something different is happening under high-adversity conditions as compared to low-adversity conditions. Nonetheless, there are situations where a low-adversity comparison group is not available and there is good reason to surmise that protection has occurred. Disasters of massive scale, such as hurricanes and wars, overwhelm many systems; recovery suggests the operation of restorative and protective processes, probably at many levels (Masten & Obradović, 2007).

Predictors of Resilience in Children

Given the diversity of situations studied and methodologies employed, there has been rather remarkable consistency in the findings emerging from resilience research (Masten, 2001). Earlier lists of what appeared to matter, initially compiled by pioneers in resilience research (Garmezy, 1985), have much in common with recently compiled lists of promotive or protective factors (Wright & Masten, 2005). This observation led the first author to describe a "short list" of

TABLE 33.1   Short List of Commonly Reported Predictors of Resilience in Children

Within the child

Good intellectual functioning and problem-solving skills; intelligence
Self-regulation skills; abilities to control or direct one's attention or actions
Self-efficacy; positive views of one's own capabilities; motivation to achieve
Positive outlook on life; beliefs that life has meaning
Attributes and talents appealing or attractive in society

Within the family context

Close relationships with parenting adults who provide warmth, high expectations, support, and structure
Connections to extended family and family-like adults who are competent and caring
Parents involved in child's education
Faith and religious affiliations
Socioeconomic advantages

Within the community

Attending effective schools
Friendships with prosocial peers
Communities with opportunities and support for children and families
Cultures that provide positive standards, rituals, relationships, and community support

---

predictors associated with resilience, a list that has changed very little in content over the years (Masten, 2007c; Masten & Reed, 2002). Table 33.1 provides a list of these commonly reported promotive/protective factors.

Many nuances are glossed over in such a list. Promotive or protective factors associated with resilience undoubtedly vary in their functional significance for individuals, for people of different ages, genders, or cultures, and in terms of their potency for particular outcomes. Moreover, the same influence can have a protective effect in regard to one outcome and a vulnerability effect with respect to another domain of functioning. A child with a shy personality growing up in a bad neighborhood, for example, could be less likely to follow the risk-taking crowd (a protective factor for delinquency) and yet more likely to develop anxiety symptoms. Age variations are also important. Protective factors related to agency or romantic relationships would be more important in older youth than in preschoolers. Nonetheless, the consistency of potential promotive or protective factors that turn up on these lists across many years and studies suggests the possibility of important underlying systems at work.

Masten (2001) proposed that there are fundamental human adaptive systems for development that may account for much of the observed resilience in children. Examples are shown in

Table 33.2. When such systems develop and operate normally, children have considerable capacity for resilience. Masten argued that it is when such fundamental systems are damaged or destroyed (which can happen as a result of diverse catastrophes), or when they fail to develop normally (something is wrong in the organism, the family, or the community) that adversity poses the greatest threats to children and their future development. "Ordinary magic" refers to the power of these basic systems to enable a child to endure or recover from adversity; much of the resilience observed in children appears to result from adaptive capacity that has evolved in biological and cultural evolution for adaptation and the protection of development (Masten, 2001).

TABLE 33.2   Adaptive Systems Implicated by Resilience Research

Attachment
Learning and cognitive systems
Mastery motivation system
Stress response systems
Self-regulation systems
Family system
School system
Peer system
Cultural and societal systems

COMPETENCE-PROMOTING AND PROTECTIVE SYSTEMS

In this section, we focus on promotive and protective systems most closely associated with individual resilience in children, from the level of child to the level of school and community systems. Many studies have hinted at the significance of these systems for children, which have been studied in many ways across many levels of analysis and disciplines. Other chapters of this volume address many of these same influences in diverse ways. The scope of our discussion is necessarily limited to a focus on systems most central to the goals of this chapter.

Attachment

Many have noted the importance of attachment relationships for resilience over the years (Garmezy, 1985; Luthar, 2006; Masten & Gewirtz, 2006; Rutter, 1979). Early in development, relationships with parenting adults play a key role in adaptation to adversity, as well as in general development (Gunnar, 2006; Masten & Gewirtz, 2006; Sroufe, Egeland, Carlson, & Collins, 2005). Parents undoubtedly function in many ways to protect children, ranging from the feelings of security the proximity of an attachment figure can afford, widely known as a "secure base," to the proactive behaviors of pulling a child back from danger, finding food and medical care after a disaster, training children to beware of dangerous situations, and comforting a child after a major loss or disappointment.

Parents not only promote and protect adaptive behavior, they also play a vital role in development itself, because many of the key adaptive systems that will enable children to adapt later in life, including their brain development, self-control systems, and capacity for relating to others, are influenced by early parent actions and interactions with the child. In recent years, for example, there has been great interest in the role of parent-child interactions in shaping behavioral self-control skills and the "effortful control" of attention (Rothbart & Bates, 2006), two key aspects of "self-regulation" that have been implicated as moderators of resilience.

Effective parents, defined and assessed in diverse ways, have been broadly implicated in the school success of high-risk, as well as low-risk children. Parents influence their children's academic outcomes through their involvement in school (e.g., Grolnick, Benjet, Kurowski &

Apostoleris, 1997; Gutman, Sameroff & Eccles, 2002; Raffaele & Knoff, 1999). Parental involvement is not a unidimensional construct, but instead refers to a number of different ways in which parents can support their children's education. Examples include participating in the school building, providing support through home-based activities, and following the child's educational progress. Among children living in a homeless shelter, those who have involved parents (who convey the importance of school and ensure that children go to school and do their homework despite the current situation) are more likely to behave well and to learn well at school (Miliotis, Sesma, & Masten, 1999). Furthermore, parental involvement has been positively related to school achievement of poor urban youth (e.g., Gutman & McLoyd, 2000).

Siblings and extended family also provide important relationships for children that may play a critical role in resilience, particularly when primary caregivers are unable to serve protective functions. Eventually, adults outside the family, in the form of teachers, mentors, friends, and romantic partners, become important for the individual's attachment network of relationships and also for resilience. In her recent, comprehensive review of the literature, Luthar (2006) concluded: "The first take-home message is this: Resilience rests, fundamentally, on relationships" (p. 780).

Relationships, of course, are multifaceted and complex patterns of interaction over time. Thus, it is conceivable that different aspects of important relationships, such as those observed among family members, could serve different roles in facilitating resilience, although differential roles are rarely studied. At the same time, these roles could vary for children of different cultural backgrounds and different community contexts. "Authoritative parenting" (Baumrind, 1973), which is associated with competence and resilience in numerous studies (Masten & Shaffer, 2006), is a higher-order description of relationships characterized by closeness and warmth, structure and age-appropriate discipline, and high expectations for child competence shared by parent and child. Differential validity data suggest that the closeness/warmth dimension of parent-child relationships is more strongly associated with social competence, while structure and expectations are more associated with rule-abiding conduct and school achievement (Clarke-Stewart & Dunn, 2006). In a recent study of adolescent students, consistent discipline (related to achievement for high-risk and low-risk youth) had particular significance for the achievement of African American adolescents living in risky environments (Gutman, Sameroff & Eccles, 2002).

One of the most important aspects of the school context for resilience is the potential for positive relationships with competence-promoting adults who inspire, support, open doors, and in many other ways provide a secure base and proactive protection for children who may lack such resources at home. Administrators, teachers, and coaches are often mentioned in autobiographical accounts of high-risk youth who manage to succeed. Teachers are often listed among the most supportive people in the lives of children (Pianta, 2006). Studies of teacher-child relationships corroborate the importance of these relationships for student motivation and well-being (Eccles & Roeser, 1999). A study of middle school students (Reddy, Rhodes, & Mulhall, 2003) found that changes in perceived support predicted changes in psychological adjustment (depressed mood and self-esteem). Furthermore, interventions designed to promote relationships of children with adults at school, such as the Primary Mental Health Project (Cowen et al., 1996), are effective methods of preventing problems and promoting success in school. Pianta (2006) emphasized that there are two distinct aspects to teacher-child relationships, with possibly differential significance: instructional support, which predicts achievement, and emotional support, which predicts social competence. The differential significance of these two teacher-child relationship dimensions may be analogous to the distinct roles played by two dimensions of parent-child relationships—structure/expectations versus warmth/closeness—that were noted above.

Learning and Problem-Solving Systems

Schools also have been given a major role in shaping the learning and problem-solving skills of the developing human brain, a key aspect of "human capital" investment in modern societies. As children move from the preschool years into the school years, the shared burden of shaping and developing human capital in children shifts in emphasis from home to school, although parents continue to play an important supporting role.

Many studies of resilience implicate some aspect of high level cognitive functioning or problem-solving skills, measured by various tests of information processing ability or knowledge. Since intelligence has been defined as the mental activity associated with positive and purposeful adaptation (Sternberg, 1985), it is not surprising that IQ test scores and numerous other indices of cognitive problem-solving capacity are among the most robust correlates and predictors of resilience in children.

Measures of intellectual ability, of course, are strongly associated with learning and general competence in academic contexts. Thus it would not be surprising to find that intellectual abilities are associated with better competence at school across all levels of adversity, indicating a main effect or promotive factor. In addition, however, intellectual skills as measured by IQ-type measures—along with good quality parenting—have shown the most consistent protective effects in the literature on resilience, suggesting an added benefit for children growing up under disadvantaged or risky circumstances; in other words, for children who experience adversity, IQ seems to matter more than usual (Luthar, 2006; Masten et al., 1999).

Performing well on tests of intellectual functioning requires integrated skills related to multiple aspects of higher cognition, motivation, and cooperation. A child who has difficulty paying attention, or is not motivated to perform well, or resists testing, is not going to perform as well as a motivated and engaged child who concentrates well. Thus, the strong associations of IQ with resilience may be related in part to the array of cognitive, motivational, and personality characteristics and aptitudes that often accompany strong cognitive skills. In particular, the capacity to control one's attention and behavior are crucial, and these may be important aspects of the functional significance of IQ test performance for competence and resilience.

Contemporary human information processing also encompasses effective utilization of auxiliary systems, such as computers. As informational technologies expand, the learning capacities of the human brain increasingly depend on electronic tools, both at home and at school. Thus, children must learn how to use these tools effectively in their problem solving. To date, resilience research has not focused much attention on the promotive or protective effects of computer-related information processing systems in child development.

Self-Control Systems of Attention and Action

One of the hallmarks of human behavior is the capacity of human individuals to control and direct their own behavior to achieve goals. It was noted early in the resilience literature that adaptive school-aged children had good attention skills and self-control of emotions or behavior, while maladaptive children showed poor concentration, impulsive behavior, or some variation of stress-reactive emotionality (Garmezy & Rutter, 1983; Werner & Smith, 1982). In recent years, this broad domain of behavior has been studied under the rubric of "self-regulation," temperament, or personality, and specific components such as "effortful control" (Rothbart & Bates, 2006; Rueda, Posner, & Rothbart, 2004).

An array of broad and specific self-regulation skills have been associated with better school success in community samples and also in studies of high-risk children, although the latter studies are less common (Eisenberg, Champion, & Vaughan, 2007; Masten & Coatsworth, 1998; Rothbart & Bates, 2006). Naturally occurring improvements in self-regulation skills forecasted academic achievement in disadvantaged kindergartners in one recent study (Blair & Razza, 2007). There is also provocative new evidence suggesting that effortful control skills can be improved through intervention, which raises the possibility of intervention designs to promote school success through improving attention and inhibitory control skills (Diamond, Barnett, Thomas, & Munro, 2007; Rueda, Rothbart, McCandless, Saccomanno, & Posner, 2005). Greenberg and colleagues have argued persuasively that some of the well-established preventive interventions that target behavior in school, such as the PATHS curriculum, work by altering self-regulation systems (Greenberg, Riggs, & Blair, 2007). Diamond and her collaborators (Diamond et al., 2007) recently demonstrated the promising effects of the "Tools of the Mind" curriculum on executive function in preschoolers in a compelling experiment with randomized assignment of classrooms to alternative curricula.

Self-Efficacy and the Reward Systems for Mastery and Adaptation

Robert White argued in his seminal article, "Motivation Reconsidered: The Concept of Competence," that humans and animals are motivated to adapt to the environment as a result of natural selection (White, 1959). Over the years, the motivation to adapt in children has been discussed in terms of "mastery motivation," "intrinsic motivation," "self-efficacy" and "pleasure in mastery" (Masten, Burt, & Coatsworth, 2006). All of these concepts assume that successful adaptation has a feedback system whereby perceived success provides feelings of pleasure in mastery, which in turn leads to positive expectations about one's capabilities and reinforces the motivation to adapt in the future. The reward systems driving adaptation provide the engine for human agency.

Self-efficacy beliefs have been described as correlates, mediators and moderators of adversity (Bandura, 1997). From this perspective, adversity has some of its damaging consequences by undermining confidence in the self. Competent and resilient young people have more positive beliefs about their effectiveness and more persistence in the context of adversity. Individuals with lower self-efficacy are less likely to persist and therefore less likely to succeed (Bandura, 1997; Bandura, Barbaranelli, Caprara, & Pastorelli, 2001). Success yields greater confidence about one's own efficacy and confidence yields greater motivation and persistence in future adaptation. Concomitantly, failure could yield less self-confidence and people who don't believe they can do anything to influence what happens may lose the motivation to make an effort.

The mastery motivation system is powerful, but can be extinguished by experiences that teach children they have no control over what happens in the world. The negative complement of self-efficacy concepts can be found in theories of learned helplessness, where a lost sense of efficacy is likely to produce decreases in agency (Abramson, Seligman, & Teasdale, 1978). Clinical depression is associated with "turned off" reward systems for agency. Clinicians have noted that it is difficult to help a child who has lost the sense that his or her own behavior makes any difference for achieving desired goals. Child neglect or maltreatment, including multiple foster care placements, could lead to the suppression of this system, as could disasters that destroy a whole community. Adults, too, can lose their sense of agency and self-efficacy as a result of depression, disaster, torture, or loss. Rekindling the mastery motivation systems in children and the adults in their world can be an important step in moving a child toward achievement or recovery.

School is an important context for cultivating self-efficacy (Wigfield, Eccles, & Rodriguez, 1998). As children develop cognitive competencies and acquire knowledge and problem-solving skills, they also develop beliefs in their own cognitive capabilities. Their beliefs may be influenced directly by experienced success or failure, which can be facilitated by adults. Beliefs may also be influenced by how the individual interprets experiences, as well as by the interpretations of influential adults. Thus, teachers who interpret student successes and failures in relation to their ability or effort may influence the self-efficacy beliefs of their students (Bandura, 1997).

All effective teachers probably engage the mastery motivation system, consciously or unconsciously, in their work with children, as do effective clinicians and coaches. However, different strategies would be necessary for different children. For example, very young children can be provided with enough support to guarantee success and still be convinced easily that they did it on their own. The same strategy would backfire with most adolescents, who need to experience real accomplishments that meet the exacting expectations of themselves and their peers. Similarly, in communities following disaster, adolescents can be engaged in meaningful rebuilding efforts as a strategy for returning hope for the future and engaging the mastery motivation system to promote recovery (Pine, Costello, & Masten, 2005).

School Systems

Effective schools and positive school experiences have been implicated in numerous studies of resilience (Condly, 2006; Luthar, 2006; Masten, Best, & Garmezy, 1990; Rutter & Maughan, 2002; Wang & Gordon, 1994). Research on school effectiveness has parallels to studies of family effectiveness, in that research implicates qualities similar to "authoritative parenting" styles, combining high expectations, orderly structure, and warm relationships among staff and students.

The role of schools in resilience can be considered much more broadly, however. Good teachers, like good parents, function directly as promotive and protective factors in the lives of high-risk children, while at the same time they nurture the child's capacity for self-promotion and self-protection. The school context provides many opportunities to engage and nurture the adaptive systems implicated by the short list

discussed previously. Schools are designed to foster human capital in many societies, and, at the same time, afford many opportunities for children to gain social capital through relationships with competent and nurturing adults. Schools contain many possibilities for positive relationships with adult role models and mentors, as well as opportunities to experience pleasure in mastery, learn new skills that build self-efficacy, and reward systems that reinforce the mastery motivation system. Schools may also provide basic needs for very disadvantaged children, including food and health care.

Studies that examine the effect of school experiences on children's mental health and development need to consider the structural and dynamic nature of these complex systems, the role of school culture and climate, layers of interaction and relationship, and other factors, yet few have done so (Pianta, 2006). The school context has levels of structural and process features that interact with development to influence growth and adaptation of individual children. The classroom, the most proximal school microsystem for the child, is one of multiple levels that are embedded in each other and mutually influential, including classroom, school building, school district, larger community, and national-level organizations (Eccles, 2004; Masten, 2003). Eccles and Roeser (1999) argued that the regulatory processes (organizational, social and instructional) characterizing schools are interrelated across these hierarchically ordered levels and change as children move through the school grades and affect children's development. Understanding how schools affect children's adaptation and development requires, therefore, the simultaneous study of change both at the individual and the institutional levels.

Pianta (2006) has delineated a comprehensive contextualist framework for understanding how schools influence development, drawing on developmental and ecological systems theory and integrating school processes with other interrelated contexts and processes that shape human development in and among the family, school, peers, and community/neighborhood. From this perspective, processes (structural, proximal, psychological, biobehavioral) that affect child outcome are continuous across settings and are not bounded within them. Structural characteristics of the school context, such as class size and per-pupil expenditure, may influence or regulate proximal processes such as child-teacher relationships or peer relations, which in turn influence or regulate psychological processes such as emotion/self-regulation, beliefs, or academic achievement, which then interacts with biobehavioral processes such as stress reactivity. Integrated theory and research addressing such multilevel dynamics are a challenging but exciting characteristic of the growing edge of developmental science (Masten, 2007b).

Cultural Systems

The lives of children are also deeply embedded in cultural systems, characterized by a wide variety of traditions, rituals, and practices that have been passed on from generation to generation, often with the explicit or implicit intention of promoting positive adaptation, educating the next generation, or protecting the group. Cultural protective and promotive influences were neglected in early studies of resilience, although culture (religion in particular) was implicated from the outset in many reports about resilience (Wright & Masten, 2005). In a recent volume on spirituality and development, religion and spiritual beliefs are analyzed from the perspective of resilience (Crawford, Wright, & Masten, 2006). The authors examine how religious practices work to engage many of the same fundamental systems discussed above, including self-regulation (through meditation or prayer, as well as rules or expectations for conduct) and attachment relationships (with spiritual figures and religious leaders, and other members of the religious community). There is much to be learned about the many possible ways that cultural practices enhance or interfere with resilience.

Cultural practices may also support or hinder the functional roles of school in resilience. Some cultures revere teachers and learning, while others do not. Cultural subgroups in a community or even in a school may value or devalue the importance of school achievement. An interesting study on academic achievement and peer influences found that the math achievement of African American adolescents at varying levels of risk was moderated by the degree to which their peers supported achievement (Gutman, Sameroff, & Eccles, 2002). Supportive peers were particularly important at high-risk levels, suggesting a protective influence.

Immigrant children, who are at risk for adjustment problems with respect to salient developmental issues (Motti-Stefanidi et al., 2008a), have to deal both with the stressful processes inherent in immigration and with the normative developmental challenges that all children face. The same processes, such as self-efficacy, internal locus of control, and parental involvement that are promotive of all children's adaptation and development, are associated with positive school adaptation in immigrant children (Motti-Stefanidi, Pavlopoulos, Dalla, Obradović, & Masten, 2006). However, acculturation strategies also play an important role in the quality of adaptation of immigrant adolescents (Berry, 1997). Berry, Phinney, Sam, and Vedder (2006) have distinguished between immigrant children's psychological adaptation, which refers to personal well-being and good mental health, and sociocultural adaptation, which refers to the child's social competence in managing their daily life in an intercultural setting. It has been proposed that orientation toward the ethnic culture may be a better predictor of psychological adaptation, whereas orientation toward the national (or majority) culture would be a better predictor of sociocultural adaptation (Oppedal, Roysamb, & Sam, 2004; Ward, Bochner, & Furnham, 2001), and these hypotheses have been partially corroborated (Berry et al., 2006; Motti-Stefanidi, Pavlopoulos, Obradović & Masten, 2008b).

PROMOTING RESILIENCE IN CHILDREN: A FRAMEWORK FOR PRACTICE AND POLICY

Basic research on naturally occurring resilience in children held the promise from the outset of informing interventions to purposefully enhance children's chances for success. At the same time, prevention science was also emerging, and the findings from interventions focused on promoting positive adaptation among children at risk for problems generally have proven to be highly congruent with findings from the basic empirical literature on resilience (Luthar, 2006; Masten, 2007a; Masten, Burt, & Coartsworth, 2006; Wright & Masten, 2005). In recent years, interventions have been explicitly designed to promote resilience by engaging or enhancing promotive or protective effects. Randomized trials to test these interventions represent a powerful test of resilience theory or models. Wright and Masten (2005) described these efforts as the "third wave" of resilience research.

Most of the interventions to promote competence among high-risk children of school age have included school-based components, often including some kind of mentoring or adult-child interaction, tutoring, after-school activities, and activities engaging families; and/or home-school communications and related activities designed to boost school engagement, enhance the quality of adult and peer relationships available to a child, increase motivation, boost learning, and so on. (Cicchetti, Rappaport, Sandler, & Weissberg, 2000; Luthar, 2006; Nation et al., 2003; Weissberg, Kumpfer, & Seligman, 2003). Successful programs often take a comprehensive approach of combining multiple components to create a synergistic effect among protective/promotive processes, reflecting dynamic models of how interrelated systems actually work to shape development. Schools are a central connecting point among many of the systems that shape child development (Masten, 2003; Pianta, 2006).

Resilience-Based Frameworks for Practice

The study of resilience in children has revolutionized thinking about how to prevent and ameliorate problems in children at risk, providing a useful framework to guide practice and policy. Masten delineated four key elements of a resilience framework for practice in terms of four Ms: Mission, Models, Measures, and Methods (Masten, 2007a; Masten & Powell, 2003; Masten & Reed, 2002). Recent developments in resilience research implicate a fifth M, for multiple systems and multiple levels of analysis.

Mission: Frame Positive Goals

A resilience framework for practice or policy begins with a positive statement of objectives or mission. This seemingly simple step reflects a transformation in practice from deficit-based and symptom-focused/illness models to strength-based and competence-focused/healthy development models. The articulation of positive objectives serves multiple purposes. Positive goals are consistent with the accumulating evidence that competence promotion strategies are effective means for preventing problems, interrupting developmental cascades into trouble, and augmenting treatment for mental disorders (Masten, Burt, & Coatsworth, 2006). Programs to promote academic success, graduation, leadership, or talent development are less stigmatizing

and more appealing to stakeholders, including youth and their parents, than programs to prevent drug abuse, pregnancy, violence, mental illness, school drop-out, or academic failure. Positive goals appear to promote the assessment and attainment of progress toward positive outcomes, and may have a motivating influence on staff. Such benefits have been reported internationally following the adoption of the Looking after Children (LAC) program for children in care of the state (Masten, 2006). The LAC system exemplifies a positive intervention model, with a positive motto ("good parenting—good outcomes") and mission statements framed in positive terms ("designed to improve the parenting experience of children looked after by welfare agencies"). Explicit goals for each child in the system are framed in terms of progress in "seven developmental dimensions of well-being." The task for a team in setting goals with a young person has a different tone when they are reviewing plans for progress in seven positively described domains of behavior rather than documenting current symptoms and how much symptoms have risen or declined.

Schools typically have the advantage of a positive charge from society. All too often, however, the objectives of programs for children at risk for school problems or already in trouble have been framed in terms of reducing problems or risks for dropping out or other failures rather than proactively targeting positive progress and achievement goals. The concept of "prevention" has been criticized for just this reason, in that it highlights the prevention of problems rather than the promotion of successes, although the aims of most prevention programs have broadened over the years to encompass positive goals (Masten, Burt, & Coatsworth, 2006). Evidence-based interventions that work in schools to promote competence and reduce problems often frame positive goals. Similarly, effective schools for high-risk populations of children stay focused on positive outcomes (see Chapter 36).

Focusing on positive objectives does not mean that problems or risk factors are ignored. While there are compelling reasons to focus on positive objectives, it does not make sense to build a beautiful new school on a field where land mines have not been removed, or to focus solely on a tutor in school for a child who has untreated medical problems or inadequate nutrition, or to ignore untreated major depression or neglect to focus on academic achievement at school.

Models: Include Positive as Well as Negative Influences

One of the most important contributions of the resilience research was in adding positive processes into models of developmental task achievement and intervention with children at risk for problems. Understanding risk and vulnerability processes leading to bad outcomes provides a very limited perspective on all of the potential processes for achievement and positive developmental outcomes or changing the odds for positive adaptation. The pioneers in resilience research understood the importance of learning how positive outcomes arise in children at risk for poor outcomes. Over the years, numerous models for resilience have been delineated (Garmezy, Masten, & Tellegen, 1984; Luthar, Cicchetti, & Becker, 2000; Masten, 1989, 2001; Masten & Reed, 2002). What distinguishes these models from many that came before is the inclusion of positive as well as negative components, such as assets, promotive factors, protective processes, and the like. In some cases, this is achieved by highlighting the bidirectional nature of dimensions that matter for children (good and poor parenting, better and worse attentional skills, safer and more dangerous environments). The action may occur all along a continuum of variation. However, some of the influences added into the picture in resilience models extended beyond the opposite end of risk or vulnerability factors. Opportunities to develop specific talents, leadership training, mentoring programs, and crisis response teams for students are built on promotive and protective models that describe actively positive processes.

Resilience models also highlighted the reality of high-risk young people who were functioning much better than one might expect based on the number of risk factors piled up in their lives. Risk gradients, plotting the general odds for poor outcomes by level of cumulative risk did not capture their reality. These "off the gradient" children, succeeding in the context of high odds for maladaptation, were singled out for study as living clues to what makes a difference (Masten & Obradović, 2006). Similarly, young people whose lives showed unexpected turns in positive directions inspired greater attention to the ideas of windows of opportunity for positive change (Masten, Obradović, & Burt, 2006).

The result has been more comprehensive models of child development in hazardous circumstances. Concomitantly, resilience models have facilitated improvements in measurement and creative advances in interventions designed to foster positive outcomes or change.

Measures: Assess the Positive as Well as the Negative

Positive goals and processes required attention to positive domains of functioning and positive measures of outcome and progress. In the early years of resilience research, extensive work was needed to develop more assessment tools for monitoring progress in age-salient developmental tasks, positive adaptation, and so forth. Achievement domains were in better shape from an assessment perspective than positive behavioral domains such as prosocial behavior. To this day, there are better validated measures of symptoms and behavior problems than positive development. An important contribution of the positively framed LAC model has been the development of assessment tools to monitor progress in the seven developmental domains of well being included in this framework; tools were developed and standardized to assess health, education, identity, family and social relationships, social presentation, emotional and behavioral development, and self-care skills among children in care (Flynn, Ghazal, Legault, Vandermeulen, & Petrick, 2004). One of the most interesting benefits of this tool development was its effects on systems of care: the requirements to assess these domains regularly and to keep a comprehensive "Assessment and Action Record" have facilitated positive system change (Flynn, Dudding, & Barber, 2006). Attention and thereby resources were focused on positive goals and progress, and systems were evaluated by measurable positive goal attainment. Children's own perspectives on positive goals and their satisfaction with programs were highlighted as well. In short, these tools support and encourage "good practice" based on research.

Methods: Reduce Risks, Add Resources, and/or Mobilize Adaptive Systems

Resilience models and perspectives draw attention to different strategies for intervention, targeting risks, resources, or adaptive systems. Theoretically, the likelihood of a particular positive outcome can be increased in a population of children in multiple ways: (a) by reducing their exposure to damaging risks; (b) by increasing or enhancing the quality or availability of resources; and (c) by protecting, restoring, or mobilizing the power of key assets or protective systems. Schools play a vital role in the implementation of these strategies because children spend so much time in this context and because many of the resources and protective systems for human development are nurtured, provided, or connected in the school context. Increasingly, resources for children and their families are co-located in schools or in close proximity, and programs designed to enhance protections for children take place in schools. These efforts take many forms, including tutors, mentors, after-school activities, health check-ups, reading programs, and meals.

Multiple Components, Systems, and Levels of Analysis

The fifth *M* stands for *multiple*: multifaceted interventions for multiply caused and complex problems, engaging multiple systems in solutions, and considering systems at multiple levels of analysis. One of the first lessons learned from the study of children at risk for problems was that children rarely face one, isolated threat to development. Rather, risks typically come in bundles or cumulate over time; multiple-risk situations are more common than the experience of one risk. This not only led investigators to study cumulative risks and risk gradients, but also to consider combined strategies for addressing multiple-risk situations. "Cumulative protection for cumulative risk" was an important theme arising from early research on risk and resilience (Masten, 1999; Wyman, Sandler, Wolchik, & Nelson, 2000; Yoshikawa, 1994) and many of the evidenced-based preventive intervention programs have a multiple-component approach, including Head Start (Zigler & Muenchow, 1992), FAST Track (Conduct Problems Prevention Research Group, 1992), and the Seattle Social Development Project (Hawkins et al., 1992).

Resilience is firmly grounded in a developmental systems theory, where an individual child is viewed as a living system, continually interacting with the systems of family, peer groups, schools, community, and other systems in which the child's life is embedded. At the same time, the child's functioning is influenced by the internal operation of many systems that comprise the living organism, from molecules to central nervous system, all interconnected in the dynamics of living. From this perspective, there are many potential levels for intervention that could be considered, from cells (e.g., medicine or nutrition)

to schools (e.g., teaching, sports, counseling by a school psychologist) to society (e.g., social policies about education, media messages).

In contemporary prevention research, it is increasingly common for intervention designs to consider combining strategies not only across systems, but also across levels, attempting to engage the dynamics of system coaction in the service of positive change. This trend is evident in school-based preventive interventions (Pianta, 2006). For example, the PATHS curriculum (Greenberg, Kusche, Cook, & Quamma, 1995), an effective preventive intervention program for school-aged children, has evolved to target neural systems believed to underlie self-control of attention and behavior, along with classroom behavior, classroom functioning, and whole-school functioning (Greenberg et al., 2007). Interventions to prevent the development of antisocial behavior also now target deliberately multiple system levels, including the individual child, the family, the peer group, and the classroom or school (Dishion & Patterson, 2006).

Combining multiple strategies in interventions to promote positive adaptation in children is also highly congruent with Bronfenbrenner's (1979) concept of the mesosystem. Such interventions are designed to create a synergistic effect by engaging multiple systems in the process of change in a coordinated way. Moreover, interventions can be designed to target the systems with the most leverage at a particular time in development. Prevention programs for young adolescents, for example, are much more likely to engage the power of peer influence for change than an intervention for infants or toddlers. Similarly, interventions for school-aged children typically attempt to engage school-based influences in the processes for change, as well as mesosystem influences such as home-school relationships or community-school connections.

CONCLUSIONS AND CAUTIONS

The past four decades of research on resilience in children has yielded important concepts and clues about positive adaptation and development in difficult circumstances. Schools appear to be integrally involved in the meaning and processes of resilience and evidence suggests that a resilience-based approach could enhance efforts to promote positive development in school contexts among disadvantaged or traumatized children.

Nonetheless, it is important to underscore the limitations of the work to date on resilience, and the potential pitfalls in this approach. First, as already noted, there is the danger of ignoring risks, vulnerabilities, and problems in the lives of children, many of which are preventable. It is far more difficult to help a child after damaging exposure to adversity, in many cases, than to prevent the exposure from happening in the first place. Premature birth provides a classic example. There are also circumstances so terrible that no child can be resilient and the situation must be changed for resilience to emerge. It is important to remember that no child is invulnerable. Second, there is a pernicious and persistent tendency to locate the causes and responsibility for resilience *in the child*, despite the overwhelming evidence that resilience emerges from the dynamic interplay of child and context, with much of the protection arising in relationships and context, rather than something within the child (Luthar, 2006; Pianta & Walsh, 1998; Riley & Masten, 2005). The latest version of this tendency has manifested in the notion of the resilient brain or protective genes, when it is the complex interplay of person or gene and environment at many levels that eventually manifests as a pattern of resilience in a person's life (Cicchetti & Curtis, 2006; Masten & Obradović, 2006). Third, though the broad conclusions about *what matters* show striking consistency, little is actually known about *how resilience works*, at multiple levels of analysis, for different processes, children and context. In other words, there remains much to be learned about the processes of naturally occurring resilience and also how to intervene successfully to create resilience where it would not naturally occur. There have been few experimental tests of resilience processes to date. Fourth, there remains little work on resilience in some of the key systems assumed to matter in child development, particularly protective systems embedded in culture, including the culture of schools and the cultures of the people involved in schools, and in the developmental interplay of genes with environment at many levels. Finally, there is very limited research integrating resilience processes across system levels (from cells to societies) or species.

There have been three major waves of resilience research: the first was characterized by descriptive research, which yielded the short list; the second is focused on processes, with much work remaining; and the third wave is comprised of research to apply and test resilience models through intervention (Wright & Masten, 2005). A fourth wave is rising on the horizon (Masten, 2007c), heralded by the New York Academy of Sciences conference on "Resilience in Children," held in February, 2006 (Lester, Masten, & McEwen, 2006). Investigators are attempting to forge a more comprehensive understanding of resilience in children by integrating biological, neuroscience, behavioral, and social-contextual approaches.

Future resilience research holds exciting possibilities for creating, repairing or "reprogramming" fundamental systems for adaptive and healthy development, which will require the talents and collaboration of multiple stakeholders, scientists, and practitioners. Professionals concerned with learning and development in the school context are likely to play instrumental roles in formulating, translating, testing, implementing, and reformulating these evolving and emerging models of resilience.

REFERENCES

Abramson, L. Y., Seligman, M. E. P., & Teasdale, J. D. (1978). Learned helplessness in humans: critique and reformulation. *Journal of Abnormal Psychology*, 87, 49–74.

Bandura, A. (1997). *Self-Efficacy: The excercise of control*. New York: Freeman and Company.

Bandura, A., Barbaranelli, C., Caprara, G. V., & Pastorelli, C. (2001). Self-efficacy beliefs as shapers of children's aspirations and career trajectories. *Child Development, 72*(1), 187–206.

Baumrind, D. (1973). The development of instrumental competence through socialization. In A. D. Pick (Ed.), *Minnesota symposium on child psychology* (Vol. 7, pp. 3–46). Minneapolis: University of Minnesota Press.

Berry, J. W. (1997). Immigration, acculturation, and adaptation. *Applied Psychology: An International Review, 46*(1), 5–68.

Berry, J. W., Phinney, J. S., Sam, D. L., & Vedder, V. (2006). *Immigrant youth in cultural transition: Acculturation, identity and adaptation across national contexts*. Mahwah NJ: Erlbaum.

Blair, C., & Razza, R. P. (2007). Relating effortful control, executive functioning, and false belief understanding to emerging math and literacy ability in kindergarten. *Child Development, 78* 647–663.

Boyce, W. T. (2007). A biology of misfortune: Stress reactivity, social context, and the ontogeny of psychopathology in everyday life. In A. S. Masten (Ed.), *Multilevel dynamics in developmental psychopathology: Pathways to the future. The*

Minnesota Symposia on Child Psychology (Vol. *34*, pp. 45–82). Mahwah, NJ: Erlbaum.

Boyce, W. T., & Ellis, B. J. (2005). Biological sensitivity to context: A. An evolutionary-developmental theory of the origins and functions of stress reactivity. *Development and Psychopathology, 17*, 271–301.

Bronfenbrenner, U. (1979). *The ecology of human development: Experiments by nature and design.* Cambridge, MA: Harvard University Press.

Cicchetti, D., & Curtis, W. J. (2006). The developing brain and neural plasticity: Implications for normality, psychopathology, and resilience. In D. Cicchetti & D. J. Cohen (Eds.), *Developmental psychopathology: Vol. 2. Developmental neuroscience* (2nd ed., pp. 1–64). Hoboken, NJ: Wiley.

Cicchetti, D., Rappaport, J., Sandler, I., & Weissberg, R. P. (Eds.). (2000). *The promotion of wellness in children and adolescents.* Washington, DC: CWLA Press.

Clarke-Stewart, A., & Dunn, J. (Eds.). (2006). *Families count: Effects on child and adolescent development.* New York: Cambridge University Press.

Condly, S. J. (2006). Resilience in children: A review of literature with implications for educators. *Urban Education, 41*(3), 211–236.

Conduct Problems Prevention Research Group. (1992). A developmental and clinical model for the prevention of conduct disorder: The FAST Track Program. *Development and Psychopathology, 4*, 509–527.

Cowen, E. L., Hightower, A. D., Pedro-Carroll, J. L., Work, W. C., Wyman, P. A., & Haffey, W. G. (1996). *School-based prevention for children at risk: The Primary Mental Health Project.* Washington, DC: American Psychological Association.

Crawford, E., Wright, M. O. D., & Masten, A. S. (2006). Resilience and spirituality in youth. In P. L. Benson, E. C. Roehlkepartain, P. E. King, & L. Wagener (Eds.), *The handbook of spiritual development in childhood and adolescence* (pp. 355–370). Newbury Park, CA: Sage.

Diamond, A., Barnett, W. S., Thomas, J., & Munro, S. (2007). Preschool program improves cognitive control. *Science, 318*, 1387–1388.

Dishion, T. J., & Patterson, G. R. (2006). The development and ecology of antisocial behavior in children and adolescents. In D. Cicchetti & D. J. Cohen (Eds.), *Developmental psychopathology: Vol. 3. Risk, disorder, and adaptation* (pp. 503–541). New York: Wiley.

Doll, B., Zucker, S., & Brehm, K. (2006). *Resilient classroom: Creating health environments for learning.* New York: Guilford.

Eccles, J. (2004). Schools, motivation, and stage-environment fit. In R. M. Lerner & L. Steinberg (Eds.), *Handbook of Adolescent Psychology* (2nd ed., pp. 125–148). Hoboken NJ: Wiley.

Eccles, J. S., & Roeser, R. W. (1999). School and community influences on human development. In M. H. Bornstein & M. E. Lamb (Eds.), *Developmental psychology: An advanced textbook* (4th ed., pp. 503–554). Mahwah, NJ: Lawrence Erlbaum Associates.

Eisenberg, N., Champion, C., & Vaughan, J. (2007). Effortful control and its socioemotional consequences. In J. J. Gross (Ed.), *Handbook of emotion regulation.* New York: Guilford.

Flynn, R. J., Dudding, P. M., & Barber, J. G. (Eds.). (2006). *Promoting resilience in development: A general framework for systems of care.* Ottawa: University of Ottawa Press.

Flynn, R. J., Ghazal, H., Legault, L., Vandermeulen, G., & Petrick, S. (2004). Use of population measures and norms to identify resilient outcomes in young people in care: an exploratory study. *Child and Family Social Work, 9*, 65–79.

Garmezy, N. (1985). Stress-resistant children: The search for protective factors. In J. E. Stevenson (Ed.), *Recent research in developmental psychopathology: Journal of Child Psychology and Psychiatry Book Supplement #4* (pp. 213–233). Oxford: Pergamon Press.

Garmezy, N., Masten, A. S., & Tellegen, A. (1984). The study of stress and competence in children: A building block for developmental psychology. *Child Development, 55*, 97–111.

Garmezy, N., & Rutter, M. (1983). *Stress, coping and development in children.* New York: McGraw-Hill.

Greenberg, M. T., Kusche, C. A., Cook, E. T., & Quamma, J. P. (1995). Promoting emotional competence in school-aged children: The effects of the PATHS curriculum. *Development and Psychopathology, 7*, 117–136.

Greenberg, M. T., Riggs, N. R., & Blair, C. (2007). The role of preventive interventions in enhancing neurocognitive functioning and promoting competence in adolescence. In D. Romer & E. Walker (Eds.), *Adolescent psychopathology and the developing brain: Integrating brain and prevention science* (pp. 441–462). New York: Oxford University Press.

Grolnick, W. S., Benjet, C., Kurowski, C. O., & Apostoleris, N. H. (1997). Predictors of parent involvement in children's schooling. *Journal of Educational Psychology, 89*(3), 538–548.

Gunnar, M. (2006). Social regulation of stress in early child development. In K. McCartney & D. Phillips (Eds.), *Blackwelll handbook of early childhood development* (pp. 106–125). Malden, MA: Blackwell.

Gutman, L. M. & McLoyd, V. C. (2000). Parents' management of their children's education within the home, at school, and in the community: An examination of high-risk African American families. *Urban Review, 32* 1–24.

Gutman, L. M., Sameroff, A. J., & Eccles, J. S. (2002). The academic achievement of African American students during early adolescence: An examination of multiple risk, promotive, and protective factors. *American Journal of Community Psychology, 30*, 367–399.

Hawkins, J. D., Catalano, R. F., Morrison, D. M., O'Donnell, J., Abbott, R. D., & Day, L. E. (1992). The Seattle Social Development Project: Effects of the first four years on protective factors and problem behavior. In J. McCord & R. E. Tremblay (Eds.), *Preventing antisocial behavior: Interventions from birth through adolescence* (pp. 139–161). New York: Guilford Press.

Kraemer, H. C., Kazdin, A. E., Offord, D., Kessler, R. C., Jensen, P. S., & Kupfer, D. (1997). Coming to terms with the terms of risk. *Archives of General Psychiatry, 54*, 337–343.

Kraemer, H. C., Stice, E., Kazdin, A., Offord, D., & Kupfer, D. (2001). How do risk factors work together? Mediators, moderators, and independent, overlapping, and proxy risk factors. *American Journal of Psychiatry, 158*, 848–856.

Lester, B. M., Masten, A. S., & McEwen, B. S. (Eds.) (2006). *Resilience in Children*. Vol. 1094, New York Academy of Sciences.

Luthar, S. S. (2006). Resilience in development: A synthesis of research across five decades. In D. Cicchetti & D. J. Cohen (Eds.), *Developmental psychopathology, Vol. 3: Risk, disorder, and adaptation* (2nd ed., pp.). New York: Wiley.

Luthar, S., Cicchetti, D., & Becker, B. (2000). The construct of resilience: A critical evaluation and guidelines for future work. *Child Development, 71*(3), 543–562.

Masten, A. S. (1989). Resilience in development: Implications of the study of successful adaptation for developmental psychopathology. In D. Cicchetti (Ed.), *The emergence of a discipline: Rochester Symposium on Developmental Psychopathology* (Vol. 1, pp. 261–294). Hillsdale, NJ: Lawrence Erlbaum Associates, Inc.

Masten, A. S. (1999). Commentary: The promise and perils of resilience research as a guide to preventive interventions. In M. D. Glantz & J. L. Johnson (Eds.), *Resilience and development: Positive life adaptations. Longitudinal research in the social and behavioral sciences* (pp. 251–257). New York, NY: Kluwer Academic/Plenum Publishers.

Masten, A. S. (2001). Ordinary magic: Resilience processes in development. *American Psychologist, 56*(3), 227–238.

Masten, A. S. (2003). Commentary: Developmental psychopathology as a unifying context for mental health and education models, research, and practice in schools. *School Psychology Review, 32*(2), 170–174.

Masten, A. S. (2006). Promoting resilience in development: A general framework for systems of care. In R. J. Flynn, P. M. Dudding & J. G. Barber (Eds.), *Promoting resilience in child welfare* (pp. 3–17). Ottawa: University of Ottawa Press.

Masten, A. S. (2007a). Competence, resilience and development in adolescence: Clues for prevention science. In D. Romer & E. Walker (Eds.), *Adolescent psychopathology and the developing brain: Integrating brain and prevention science*. New York: Oxford University Press.

Masten, A. S. (Ed.). (2007b). *Multilevel dynamics in developmental psychopathology*. Mahwah, NJ: Erlbaum.

Masten, A. S. (2007c). Resilience in developing systems: Progress and promise as the fourth wave rises. *Development and Psychopathology, 19* 921–930.

Masten, A. S., Best, K. M., & Garmezy, N. (1990). Resilience and development: Contributions from the study of children who overcome adversity. *Development and Psychopathology, 2,* 425–444.

Masten, A. S., Burt, K. B., & Coatsworth, J. D. (2006). Competence and psychopathology in development. In D. Cicchetti & D. Cohen (Eds.), *Developmental psychopathology, Vol. 3. Risk, disorder and psychopathology* (2nd ed., pp. 696–738). New York: Wiley.

Masten, A. S., & Coatsworth, J. D. (1998). The development of competence in favorable and unfavorable environments: Lessons from research on successful children. *American Psychologist, 53*(2), 205–220.

Masten, A. S., & Gewirtz, A. H. (2006). Vulnerability and resilience in early child development. In K. McCartney & D. A. Phillips (Eds.), *Handbook of early childhood development* (pp. 22–43): Blackwell.

Masten, A. S., Hubbard, J. J., Gest, S. D., Tellegen, A., Garmezy, N., & Ramirez, M. L. (1999). Competence in the context of adversity: Pathways to resilience and maladaptation from childhood to late adolescence. *Development and Psychopathology, 11*, 143–169.

Masten, A. S., & Obradović, J. (2006). Competence and resilience in development. *Annals of the New York Academy of Sciences, 1094* 13–27.

Masten, A. S., & Obradović, J. (2007). Disaster preparation and recovery: Lessons from research on resilience in human development. *Ecology and Society, 13(1)*: 9 [on line] URL: http://www.ecologyandsociety.org/vol13/iss1/art9/

Masten, A. S., Obradović, J., & Burt, K. B. (2006). Resilience in emerging adulthood: Developmental perspectives on continuity and transformation. In J. J. Arnett & J. L. Tanner (Eds.), *Emerging adults in America: Coming of age in the 21st century* (pp. 173–190). Washington, DC: American Psychological Association Press.

Masten, A. S., & Powell, J. L. (2003). A resilience framework for research, policy, and practice. In S. Luthar (Ed.), *Resilience and vulnerability: Adaptation in the context of childhood adversities* (pp. 1–25). New York: Cambridge University Press.

Masten, A. S., & Reed, M.-G. J. (2002). Resilience in development. In C. R. Snyder & S. J. Lopez (Eds.), *Handbook of positive psychology* (pp. 74–88). London: Oxford University Press.

Masten, A. S., & Shaffer, A. (2006). How families matter in child development: Reflections from research on risk and resilience. In C.-S. A. & J. Dunn (Eds.), *Families count: Effects on child and adolescent development* (pp. 5–25). New York: Cambridge University Press.

Miliotis, D., Sesma, A., Jr., & Masten, A. S. (1999). Parenting as a protective process for school success in children from homeless families. *Early Education and Development, 10*(2), 111–133.

Motti-Stefanidi, F., Pavlopoulos, V., Dalla, M., Obradović, J., & Masten, A. S. (2006, July). *Risk, resources and academic resilience in Albanian immigrant and native Greek adolscents.* Paper presented at the eighteenth International Congress of Cross-Cultural Psychology, Spetses, Greece.

Motti-Stefanidi, F., Pavlopoulos, V., Obradović, J., Dalla, M., Takis, N., Papathanasiou, A., & Masten, A. S. (2008a). Immigration as a risk factor for adoelscent adaptation in Greek urban schools. *European Journal of Developmental Psychology, 5*, 235–261.

Motti-Stefanidi, F., Pavlopoulos, V., Obradović, J., & Masten, A. S. (2008b). Acculturation and adaptation of Pontian Greeks and Albanian Adolescents in Greek urban schools. *International Journal of Psychology, 43*, 45–58.

Nation, M., Crusto, C., Wandersman, A., Kumpfer, K. L., Seybolt, d., Morrissey-Kane, E., et al. (2003). What works in prevention: Principles of effective prevention programs. *American Psychologist, 58*, 449–456.

Obradović, J., Shaffer, A., & Masten, A. S. (in press). Risk in developmental psychopathology: Progress and future directions. In L. C. Mayes & M. Lewis (Eds.), *The environment of human development: A handbook of theory and measurement.* New York: Cambridge University Press.

Oppedal, B., Roysamb, E., & Sam, D. L. (2004). The effect of acculturation and social support on change in mental health among young immigrants. *International Journal of Behavioral Development, 28*, 481–494.

Pianta, R. C. (2006). Schools, schooling, and developmental psychopathology. In D. Ciccheti & D. J. Cohen (Eds.), *Developmental psychopathology: Vol. 1. Theory and method* (2nd ed., pp. 494–529). Hoboken, NJ: Wiley.

Pianta, R. C., & Walsh, D. J. (1998). Applying the construct of resilience in schools: Cautions from a developmental systems perspective. *School Psychology Review, 27*, 407–417.

Pine, D. S., Costello, J., & Masten, A. S. (2005). Trauma, proximity, and developmental psychopathology: The effects of war and terrorism on children. *Neuropsychopharmacology, 30*, 1781–1792.

Raffaele, L.M., & Knoff, H.M. (1999). Improving home-school collaboration with disadvantaged families: Organizational principles, perspectives, and approaches. *The School Psychology Review, 28*(3), 448–466.

Reddy, R., Rhodes, J. E., & Mulhall, P. (2003). The influence of teacher support on student adjustment in the middle school years: A latent growth curve study. *Development and Psychopathology, 15*, 119–138.

Riley, J. M., & Masten, A. S. (2005). Resilience in context. In R. Peter, R. McMahon & B. Leadbeater (Eds.), *Resilience in children, families, communities: linking context to practice and policy* (pp. 13–25). New York: Kluwer Academic/Plenum.

Rothbart, M. K., & Bates, J. E. (2006). Temperament in children's development. In W. Damon, R. Lerner & N. Eisenberg (Eds.), *Handbook of child development: Vol 3. Social, emotional and personality development* (6th ed.; pp. 99–166). Hoboken, NJ: Wiley.

Rueda, M. R., Posner, M. I., & Rothbart, M. K. (2004). Attentional control and self-regulation. In R. F. Baumeister & K. D. Vohs (Eds.), *Handbook of self-regulation: Research, theory, and applications* (pp. 283–300). New York: Guilford.

Rueda, M. R., Rothbart, M. K., McCandless, B. D., Saccomanno, L., & Posner, M. I. (2005). Training, maturation, and genetic influences on the development of executive attention. *Proceedings of the National Academy of Sciences, 102*, 14931–14936.

Rutter, M. (1979). Protective factors in children's responses to stress and disadvantage. *Annals of the Academy of Medicine, Singapore, 8*, 324–338.

Rutter, M., & Maughan, B. (2002). School effectiveness findings, 1979–2002. *Journal of School Psychology, 40*, 451–475.

Sameroff, A. (2006). Identifying risk and protective factors for healthy child development. In A. Clarke-Stewart & J. Dunn (Eds.), *Families count: Effects on child and adolescent development* (pp. 53–76). Cambridge: Cambridge University Press.

Sroufe, L. A., Egeland, B., Carlson, E. A., & Collins, B. E. (2005). *The development of the person:*

The Minnesota Study of Risk and Adaptation from Birth to Adulthood. New York: Guilford.

Sternberg, R. J. (1985). *Beyond IQ: A triarchic theory of human intelligence*. New York: Cambridge University Press.

Wang, M. C., & Gordon, E. W. (1994). *Educational resilience in inner-city America: Challenges and prospects*. Hillsdale, NJ: Lawrence Erlbaum Associates.

Ward, C., Bochner, S., & Furnham, A. (2001). *The psychology of culture shock* (2nd ed.). Hove, UK: Routledge.

Weissberg, R. P., Kumpfer, K. L., & Seligman, M. E. P. (2003). Prevention that works for children and youth: An introduction. *American Psychologist, 58*(6/7), 425–432.

Werner, E. E., & Smith, R. S. (1982). *Vulnerable but invincible: A study of resilient children*. New York: McGraw-Hill.

White, R. W. (1959). Motivation reconsidered: The concept of competence. *Psychological Review, 66*, 297–333.

Wigfield, A., Eccles, J. S., & Rodriguez, D. (1998). The development of children's motivation in school contexts. *Review of Research in Education, 23*, 73–118.

Wright, M. O. D., & Masten, A. S. (2005). Resilience processes in development: Fostering positive adaptation in the context of adversity. In S. Goldstein & R. Brooks (Eds.), *Handbook of resilience in children* (pp. 17–37). New York: Kluwer Academic/Plenum.

Wyman, P. A., Sandler, I., Wolchik, S., & Nelson, K. (2000). Resilience as cumulative competence promotion and stress protection: Theory and intervention. In D. Cicchetti, J. Rappaport, I. Sandler, & R. P. Weissberg (Eds.), *The promotion of wellness in children and adolescents* (pp. 133–184). Thousand Oaks, CA: Sage Publications.

Yoshikawa, H. (1994). Prevention as cumulative protection: Effects of early family support and education on chronic delinquency and its risks. *Psychological Bulletin, 115*, 28–54.

Zigler, E., & Muenchow, S. (1992). *Head Start: The inside story of America's most successful educational experiment*. New York: Basic Books.

CHAPTER 34

ASSESSMENT OF LEARNING STRATEGIES AND RELATED CONSTRUCTS IN CHILDREN AND ADOLESCENTS

KATHY STROUD
Carrollton-Farmers Branch Independent School District
CECIL R. REYNOLDS
Texas A&M University

Few will argue that one of the greatest accomplishments of childhood is the acquisition of a meaningful education. Success in school is dependent on numerous factors, many of which are not fully controllable or easily identified. It is important to identify variables that we can affect to improve learning. Among these, the development and use of efficient learning and study strategies can be critical to academic success. Research during the last 30 years has shown that children and adolescents who are active participants and strategic in their learning perform at higher academic levels than their peers. Increasing demands to assess academic performance through state testing and response-to-intervention programs have left educators and school psychologists searching for ways to incorporate and assess learning strategies that improve test scores. To date, however, several obstacles have hindered our understanding and assessment of these strategies.

Perhaps the most basic difficulty in the assessment of learning strategies has been the lack of a consensual definition and the use of several different terms for similar or identical constructs. Learning strategies may be defined as "the purposeful behaviors of a learner that are intended to facilitate the acquisition and processing of information" (Stroud & Reynolds, 2006, p. 2). Learning strategies differ from learning styles, described as "characteristic cognitive, affective, and physiological behaviors that serve as relatively stable indicators of how learners perceive, interact with, and respond to the learning environment" (Keefe, 1979, p. 4). Schmeck (1988) looked at learning styles in comparison with learning strategies, writing that learning styles indicated a tendency to use a certain repertoire of strategies

for learning. Learning styles (which is a far more controversial area than that of learning strategies) may be more dependent on the preferences of the learner and are often not purposeful in the sense of being under conscious control; learning strategies, on the other hand, are more universal and necessary in their ability to improve learning.

The terms study strategies or skills are often used interchangeably with learning strategies. For example, Gall, Gall, Jacobsen, and Bullock (1990) acknowledged the similarity of their definition of study skills to that of learning strategies, but they stated that they prefer the term study skills because of its popular use with educators. Educators even distinguish between the terms study skills and study strategies, asserting that study skills are specific steps in a task, while study strategies are a more global approach to a learning task (Gettinger & Siebert, 2002). Study strategies, however, appear to refer to a specific subset of behaviors that facilitate learning of presented material whereas learning strategies would encompass approaches to many aspects of learning (i.e., reading comprehension, writing, note taking). Cognitive strategies on the other hand appear to encompass the learning and study strategies used in the school learning environment as well as more global strategies used in work or home environments. A related term, metacognitive strategy, is a strategy designed to "monitor cognitive progress" (Garner, 1988, p. 63). Despite the use of cognitive strategies outside the academic setting as well, cognitive strategies and learning strategies have come to be used almost synonymously in the literature in recent years.

Garner (1988) described several characteristics necessary to be considered strategic. First, strategic behavior is considered to be a sequence of activities. It is important to consider strategic behavior as a group of smaller behaviors rather than one event when examining the differences between groups. Secondly, strategic behavior can be controlled by the learner. Next, a strategy must be flexible and used based on its level of effectiveness in a given situation. Metacognitive strategies monitor and direct this flexibility of use.

THEORETICAL PERSPECTIVES

While much research on cognitive learning strategies exists and numerous remedial programs have been developed, few researchers have proposed theoretical models for cognitive strategies as they relate to other variables that influence learning. Weinstein and Mayer (1986) developed a taxonomy of learning strategies that included the following categories: rehearsal, elaboration, organization, comprehension monitoring, and affective strategies. Rehearsal, elaboration, and organization each involve specific techniques that are used to promote organizing and learning information. Comprehension monitoring involves the learner's metacognitive awareness of learning and ability to control the use of strategies (Weinstein, Husman, & Dierking, 2000). Affective strategies are used to "help focus the learner's attention and maintain the learner's motivation" (Weinstein et al., 2000, p. 732). As Weinstein et al. (2000) asserted, this model makes clear the notion that strategies do not exist in isolation. Rather, they are intertwined with other factors, including motivation and metacognition. Weinstein and colleagues have since expanded their view of cognitive strategies to provide a more comprehensive model. Weinstein's "model of strategic learning has at its core the learner: a unique individual who brings to each learning situation a critical set of variables, including his or her personality, prior knowledge, and school achievement history" (Weinstein et al., 2000, p. 733). This model includes three components: skills, will, and self-regulation. The skill component encompasses the learner's knowledge about himself/herself as a learner, characteristics of the academic task, learning strategies, prior knowledge, and learning content as well as skills in the use of learning strategies, identifying important information, reading and listening comprehension, listening and note taking, study and test-taking skills, and reasoning (Weinstein, 1994). The will component includes the following: development and use of goals, academic motiva-

tion, affect regarding learning, beliefs, volition, and a positive mindset toward learning. Finally, self-regulation in the context of strategic learning involves time management, concentration, monitoring comprehension, a systematic approach to learning and accomplishing academic tasks, coping with academic stress, and managing motivation (Weinstein, 1994).

While Weinstein's theory of learning strategies subsumes self-regulated learning, theories of self-regulation likewise encompass learning strategies. Theories of self-regulated learning have the same origins in cognitive psychology as learning strategies. Self-regulated learners are strategic and goal oriented in their approach to learning tasks. They monitor and adapt their learning according to the situation at hand. They rely on intrinsic self-control of the situation rather than merely reacting to external controls (Purdie, Hattie, & Douglas, 1996). Zimmerman (1998) described the learning process as occurring in three cycling phases: forethought, performance or volitional control, and self-reflection. Each of these phases is, in turn, divided into subprocesses. Forethought includes setting goals, strategic planning, self-efficacy beliefs, goal orientation, and intrinsic interest. The performance phase involves attention focusing, self-instruction, and self-monitoring. Finally, self-reflection is characterized by self-evaluation regarding performance, attributions for success/failure, positive or negative self-reactions, and appropriate adaptation (Zimmerman, 1998). According to their performance in each of these domains, learners have been described as skilled or nonskilled learners, differing significantly in their approach to learning tasks. For example, in the forethought phase, Zimmerman cited Pintrich and DeGroot (1990), who suggested that skilled self-regulators more often had a mastery orientation, or an intrinsic desire to improve their ability while nonskilled learners typically demonstrated a performance orientation, or learning in response to threatened evaluation. Other differences suggested in this phase include nonspecific distal goals versus specific hierarchical goals, low self-efficacy versus high self-efficacy, and disinterested attitude versus interested orientation. Zimmerman also identified key differences in unskilled versus skilled performers in the performance phase, including unfocused or divided focus versus a focus on performance, use of ineffective (handicapping) strategies versus self-instruction or strategic learning, and monitoring of outcome versus monitoring of success. Finally, self-reflection for skilled learners involves self-evaluation which leads to appropriate attributions for strategies used. Consequently, this creates positive self-reactions and an adaptive approach to subsequent tasks and differing situations (Zimmerman, 1998).

Winne and Hadwin (1998) also have proposed a model of self-regulated learning. Their model depicts self-regulated learning as an event with four phases. First, the task must be defined. Second, a student sets goals and devises a strategy for achieving them. Next, tactics and strategies are used. Finally, the fourth phase allows the student to monitor, evaluate, and make changes as needed.

Measurement of self-regulated learning has taken many forms. Winne and Perry (2000) reviewed measures according to their measurement of self-regulated learning as an aptitude and as an event, finding that self-regulated learning is most often measured as an aptitude by self-report measures. Two measures commonly used are the Learning and Study Strategies Inventory (LASSI; Weinstein, Schulte, & Palmer, 1987) and Motivated Strategies for Learning Questionnaire (MSLQ; Pintrich, Smith, Garcia, & McKeachie, 1991; Winne & Perry, 2000). Other methods of measuring self-regulated learning as an aptitude include structured interviews and teacher judgments. Researchers have measured learning as an event by using think-aloud procedures, error detection tasks, trace methodologies, and observations. A summary of theoretical perspectives can be found in Table 34.1.

Specific Populations in Need of Learning Strategies

While students of all abilities can and do benefit academically from becoming strategic in their learning (e.g., Gall et al., 1990; Weinstein & Hume, 1998; Faber, Morris, & Lieberman, 2000), and the routine teaching of learning strategies in regular education classrooms may well provide some inoculation from academic deficiencies (i.e., prevention) for some significant number of children, children with special needs or circumstances may require particular attention. Many children with disabilities have been argued to possess poor or inefficient skills when it comes to knowing how to learn, and it is knowing how to learn that is at the root of learning strategies. Although few controlled studies exist, several researchers have asserted the need for specific educational interventions related to learning strategies with children who are survivors of childhood cancer

TABLE 34.1 Theoretical Models for Learning Strategies and Self-Regulated Learning

Learning Strategies

Weinstein & Mayer (1986)
  Rehearsal
  Elaboration
  Organization
  Comprehension Monitoring
  Affective Strategies

Weinstein (1994)
Model of Strategic Learning:
  Skills
  Will
  Self-Regulation

Self-Regulated Learning

Zimmerman (1998)
3 cycling phases of learning:
  Forethought
  Performance or Volitional control
  Self-Reflection

Winne & Hadwin (1998)
4 phases of learning:
  Define the task
  Set goals and devise a strategy
  Use tactics and strategies
  Monitor, evaluate, and make changes

(Jannoun & Chessells, 1987) and also children with a traumatic brain injury. They advocate for what is termed cognitive strategy training, or "learning how to learn" (Powers, Vanetta, Noll, Cool, & Stehbens, 1995). Similar recommendations have been made for children with attention-deficit/hyperactivity disorder (ADHD) (DuPaul & Stoner, 1994), learning disorders (Scruggs & Mastropieri, 2000), and other psychiatric disorders (Brackney & Karabenick, 1995). Neuropsychological deficits can be wide-ranging, depending on the nature of the illness or injury. Therefore, accurate assessment of learning and study strategies is necessary to determine the nature of the deficits a child may have as well as strengths that may be used. This is particularly important for children and adolescents who may be receiving special services and whose time for intervention within the school is limited.

Students with a learning disability comprise approximately 7% of the current academic population and include more than 50% of the special education population (U.S. Department of Education, 1999). It is clear that students with learning disabilities differ in their use of learning strategies as compared to their normal achieving peers. Students with learning disabilities display significant problems with memory on academic tasks (Scruggs & Mastropieri, 2000). They can benefit greatly from instruction in test-taking skills, including mnemonic strategies (Scruggs & Mastropieri, 2000). Reading comprehension strategies instruction has also helped to improved understanding of science and social studies texts (Bakken, Mastropieri, & Scruggs, 1997). It has been the subject of debate in the literature whether such differences are due to a lack of knowledge of appropriate strategies, failure to use those strategies, or inefficient use of strategies. Depending on the task at hand, all three may be an issue for a given student. Given that these students have typically experienced failure in at least one area of academic achievement, factors including test anxiety (Glanz, 1994), motivation, and self-efficacy may also impact the use of strategies by students with a learning disability.

LEARNING STRATEGIES AND RELATED CONSTRUCTS

The study of learning strategies encompasses numerous topics. The most common topics in the literature include academic motivation (Schunk, 1991; Pajares & Urdan, 2002), note taking and listening skills (Hughes & Suritsky, 1994; Bygrave, 1994), time management (Britton & Tesser, 1991), test anxiety (Cassady & Johnson, 2002), research strategies (Quarton, 2003), concentration/attention (Reynolds & Shirey, 1988; Rabiner & Coie, 2000), organizational techniques (Ho & McMurtrie, 1991; Shapiro, DuPaul, & Bradley-Klug, 1998), test-taking strategies (Scruggs & Mastropieri, 1992), study strategies (Sweidel, 1996), and reading and comprehension strategies (Gersten, Fuchs, Williams, & Baker, 2001). Other theoretical frameworks of learning strategies and their components are helpful for continued research and insight into the nuances of learning. However, the above-mentioned constructs provide concrete, distinct areas that can be targeted for direct and indirect teaching in different classroom settings. Proficiency in these areas has broad academic implications and may increase achievement in most, if not all, subject areas. The relationship of each of these topics to academic achievement has been empirically

supported. Therefore, all of these topics must be considered in order to better understand the development and selective use of cognitive strategies. A brief description of each construct as it relates to learning and study strategies follows.

Study Strategies

Gettinger and Seibert (2002) pointed out four aspects of studying that make it a unique academic task. First, it is skillful. It requires instruction for acquiring and retaining important information. Studying is also a purposeful or intentional task that requires effort. Next, unlike the classroom where much learning takes place as a group or with some sort of social interaction, studying is an individual process that is highly dependent on the characteristics of the student. Fourth, studying relies heavily on self-regulation or monitoring.

When studying, students need to be able to develop a strategy and apply it, as well as identify important information, make associations when learning, use a variety of resources when a concept is not understood, and use strategies for memory and encoding. Students receive an enormous amount of academic information. Being able to select and arrange information according to a valid hierarchy is crucial to developing effective study strategies. Having a systematic, strategic approach to studying is important to learning as well. Students perform better academically when strategies for learning and study are taught (e.g., Alexander & Murphy, 1999; Paris & Winegrad, 1990). Teaching methods for organizing information from different sources such as class notes, textbooks, and worksheets or homework, as well as memory aids should be included in general learning strategies approaches. Such rehearsal, elaboration, and organizational strategies are essential for acquiring and using information in a meaningful way and can be taught in a group or individual setting (e.g., Weinstein & Hume, 1998).

Study strategies would primarily include those used to aid in storing and retrieving information. Mnemonics are helpful tools for remembering information or necessary steps for other types of learning, particularly for special populations such as students with behavioral and emotional difficulties (Mastropieri & Scruggs, 1998). They are essential for transferring information from working memory to long-term memory, the main goal of studying (Goll, 2004). Three types include letter (i.e., acronyms and acrostics), keyword (relating new material to a familiar word that can be visualized to help remember the new information), and pegword (ordered information is connected using rhyme and pictures; Kleinheksel & Summy, 2003) mnemonics.

Reading Comprehension Strategies

Automating reading as a skill and increasing reading comprehension is critical to achievement in numerous academic subjects. Yet, through classroom observations, Durkin (1979) asserted that less than 1% of instructional time in reading was used for actual instruction in comprehension. Samuels (1989) stated that reading is an "active goal-directed problem-solving process in which the reader's task is to construct meaning from information contained in the text." (p. 3).

In addition to recognizing text structure, students with learning disabilities have difficulties related to poor vocabulary knowledge, limited background knowledge, poor reading fluency, and poor task persistence (Gersten et al., 2001). Researchers have also studied the effects of working memory on reading comprehension. It appears that, while poor comprehenders do not demonstrate differences on short term memory measures, they do have significantly lower performance on working memory measures (De Beni & Palladino, 2000). De Beni and Palladino demonstrated that students with poor comprehension made more intrusion errors than their peers. Their recall of irrelevant information was, in fact, better than their recall of relevant information. Intrusion errors were a predictor of reading comprehension performance one year later.

Paris, Lipson, and Wixson (1983) proposed three types of knowledge necessary for effective reading strategy use. First, declarative knowledge is considered to be the characteristics or concepts of the task at hand. Procedural knowledge is the learner's understanding of how to execute the skill. Finally, conditional knowledge is the reader's concept of when and under what conditions to apply a strategy. In addition to these types of knowledge, Baker and Brown (1984) identified self-regulatory behaviors as components of metacognition during comprehension tasks. These self-regulatory behaviors include comprehension monitoring, or self-checking during reading in order to detect errors and monitor understanding and comprehension regulation, or the active use of strategies to help regulate the reader's comprehension.

Given the importance of reading comprehension, it is no wonder that much effort has been invested in providing text enhancements as well as developing instructional programs for teaching effective strategies to students. Several features of text appear to be helpful in improving comprehension and retention of material, including representational illustrations, imagery, spatial organization, and mnemonic illustrations (Mastropieri & Scruggs, 1997). Representational illustrations and imagery may provide an additional mode of information to be encoded; however, to date, representational illustrations have produced small effect sizes while other interventions have demonstrated more utility (Mastropieri & Scruggs, 1997). Teaching students to use a spatial organizer or providing such illustrations organizes information in a concise, visual manner for students to refer to. Advance organizers, which are used prior to reading to organize the material to be learned, can be helpful if the student already has the prerequisite knowledge to understand them (Mayer, 1987). Mnemonic illustrations can be an aid when committing material to memory (Scruggs & Mastropieri, 1992). Aside from illustrations, Mastropieri and Scruggs (1997) identified several adjunct aids that appear to improve comprehension. The thought is that these aids, including study guides, audiotapes, underlining, and semantic feature relationship charts, help students to discern more important facts, providing an additional chance for encoding.

Questioning techniques have also yielded promising results for both students with learning disabilities and normally achieving students (Mastropieri and Scruggs, 1997; Rosenshine, Meister, and Chapman, 1996). While these strategies can be quite different, they each involve teaching students to improve their comprehension by questioning themselves before, during, or after reading. Mastropieri and Scruggs (1997) concluded that

> The following all facilitate the recall and comprehension of reading: (a) preteaching vocabulary and completing relevant group and independent work on the content, (b) presenting graphic or advance organizers containing the main ideas prior to reading the content and generating relevant questions, and (c) finding answers to questions about the story prior to reading. (p. 204)

Providing questions prior to or embedded within the text can also cue students as to what information is most important and assist in later retention (Duchastel & Nungester, 1984; Pressley, Tanenbaum, McDaniel, & Wood, 1990). Summarization and main idea strategies have included techniques such as a student asking questions such as "Who?" and "What's happening?" while reading, then summarizing the text in their own words (Gajria & Salvia, 1992; Jenkins, Heliotis, Stein, & Haynes, 1987). Use of these techniques has generally been effective. Summarization has also been combined with self-monitoring and attribution training, yielding positive results (Mastropieri & Scruggs, 1997).

One instructional approach that has increased academic performance was termed the Question Answer Relationship (QAR; Ezell, Hunsicker, & Quinque, 1997). Developed by Pearson and Johnson (1978) and Raphael and Pearson (1985), QAR teaches students the need to use both their previously acquired knowledge and the information from the text. Students learn (a) how to locate information, (b) how to recognize text structures and how they present important information, and (c) how to decide whether an inference is required or invited (Raphael, 1986). QAR appears to have good external validity, even as a single strategy intervention (Gersten et al., 2001).

To help students recognize expository text, Bakken and Whedon (2002) recommended that teachers instruct students how to recognize the structure text by looking for signal words or phrases, developing goals for understanding based on the purpose of the text, and selecting study strategies best suited for the structure. Recognizing structures and using them to understand text has been more effective than paragraph restatement and retelling the main idea and incidental information (Bakken, 1995 as cited in Bakken & Whedon, 2002).

Rosenshine, Meister, and Chapman (1996) conducted a review of studies teaching one type of procedural prompt—question generation strategies. Of the 26 studies included, 17 were interventions in which question generation was the sole strategy taught; the remaining 9 studies were reciprocal teaching studies that taught several cognitive strategies, one being question generation. They were interested not only in the effectiveness of different types of prompts, but also in establishing the instructional methods most likely to be effective in teaching such strategies.

Five kinds of prompts were examined: signal words, generic question stems/generic questions, main idea, question types, and story grammar categories. Effect sizes obtained indicated that signal words and generic stems/generic questions were the most effective prompts used. Story grammar prompts were the third highest. The authors suggested the effectiveness of these three types

of prompts may be because they were easy to use, and they provided students with a guide and a way to focus their attention without requiring strong cognitive skills. While the other types of prompts were not as successful, Rosenshine and his colleagues (1996) felt that more intensive instruction might help to improve results. Use of generic questions were given more value than signal words "because they promote deeper processing, initiate recall of background knowledge, require integration of prior knowledge, and provide more direction for processing than might be obtained through the use of the more simplified signal words" (Rosenshine et al., 1996, p. 200).

While reading comprehension strategies have much variation, Billingsley and Wildman (1990) identified instructional methods that appear to be most effective, regardless of the strategy being taught. These steps include the teacher (1) modeling the strategy to be learned, (2) providing guided practice and feedback regarding performance, and (3) gradually increasing the student's responsibility as he becomes more proficient at using the strategy. These steps are considered to be crucial in developing metacognition, particularly the student's understanding and control over learned skills. Strategies taught should include the following elements: "(1) What the strategy is, (2) Why the strategy should be learned, (3) How to use the strategy, (4) When and where the strategy is to be used, and (5) How to evaluate the use of the strategy" (Winograd & Hare, 1988, pp. 123–124).

Writing/Research Skills

Like reading comprehension, effective writing has become a benchmark for success in school. From a scholarly perspective, it is perhaps the best means of communicating understanding of concepts as well as one's ideas or feelings. As such, it has become a target for measuring academic achievement and is used as part of most state tests required for grade advancement or graduation. A key element in learning complex material in particular (and in nearly every professional form of employment), writing and research skills become more and more crucial as students progress through school. Having students conduct research and then organize and present what they learn is one form of discovery learning, a process that tends to lead to improved comprehension and recall (e.g., see Alexander & Murphy, 1999). Writing involves the "coordination and integration of multiple processes, including planning, production, editing, and revision. Composing requires prior knowledge of topic, genre, conventions, and rules as well as the ability to access, use and organize that knowledge when writing" (Montague and Leavell, 1994, p. 21).

Research skills are the skills necessary to complete increasingly complex research tasks using various resources. As children are encouraged early in life to use libraries to increase general reading skills and interest in reading, they should be learning basic skills to use other aspects of the library (Krapp, 1988). Resources available in libraries can include Internet resources, reference books and materials, audio/video materials, archival documents, and others. In college, students will need to be able to effectively use scholarly databases to obtain the sources they need. Given the amount of resources at their disposal, it is more important than ever to teach students how to discern which sources are credible as well as how to effectively organize and narrow the information available (Quarton, 2003). These research skills are essential beginning skills in the process of writing. The process of writing begins long before the first words are written on paper.

Numerous descriptions of the writing process exist. Gall et al. (1990) pointed to several models (e.g., Neubert & McNelis, 1986; Romano, 1987; Schumm & Radencich, 1984) as well as delineating what they consider to be the 12 skills necessary to write a paper:

> 1. Defining the writing task, 2. Specifying the paper topic, 3. Developing a writing plan, 4. Generating ideas, 5. Collecting information, 6. Organizing ideas into a plan for the paper, 7. Drafting the paper, 8. Getting feedback on the draft, 9. Revising the paper, 10. Editing the paper and producing a neat final copy, 11. Publishing the paper, and 12. Using the computer to write the paper. (p. 150)

More recent models are similar to these, ranging in degrees of specificity (Tompkins, 1994). All involve some degree of planning and organizing information prior to writing, writing at least one draft, and revising drafts both for content and grammar before producing a final copy. While these models are presented in linear format, many steps may be revisited during the process.

Writing strategies are needed throughout the writing process. During prewriting, students might plan their task by reading or interviewing others (Scott & Vitale, 2003). They might then collect information by brainstorming, answering appropriate questions, using software, or reading more information (Roberts, 2002; Scott & Vitale, 2003). Information gathered would then be organized into a coherent plan or outline for writing (Scott & Vitale, 2003). In later steps, strategies would include narrowing the topic, recognizing the need for new information, or adapting a paper for a specific audience.

Hillocks (1986) conducted an extensive metanalysis of writing strategies. His examination of the literature included more than 500 studies published between 1963 and 1982. Of these, 60 studies with 75 experimental treatments met the criteria for inclusion (i.e., the study must involve a treatment, employ a scale of writing quality rather than standardized tests, and control for differences between groups). When evaluating teaching modes, Hillocks described the most effective mode of teaching the writing process as *environmental*. This method was much more effective than the far more common method of *presentational* teaching and the *natural process* mode, which involves primarily student feedback and fails to have the teacher develop specific writing strategies. The environmental presentation method incorporates both of the other modes while also emphasizing student involvement and structured problem-solving activities (Hillocks, 1986).

Results examining the focus of instruction again produced results in contrast to common practice (Hillocks, 1986). Traditional school grammar, which might arguably consume the most time in language arts classes, was determined to have no effect in improving quality of writing. Activities more effective than traditional or free writing included those of building more complex sentences as well as using and internalizing scales, criteria, or specific questions to generate material. The most effective activities were inquiry treatments, which include those of analyzing data, problem-solving, and generating arguments.

Much of the research on writing strategies has been conducted with students identified as having learning disabilities. Students with learning disabilities frequently do not use writing strategies to the extent that nondisabled students do. They are not as purposeful in prewriting or revision and tend to focus on grammar, spelling, and handwriting (Faigley, Cherry, Jolliffee, & Skinner, 1985; Graham, Schwartz, & MacArthur, 1993). When given instructions to plan their papers and then write, students with learning disabilities spent less than one minute on average prior to beginning their drafts (MacArthur & Graham, 1987). They tended to write without pausing to rethink or read what had been written (Faigley et al., 1985). Graham et al. (1993) found that such students were less likely than normally achieving peers to emphasize the process of writing or writing strategies as being important. When asked how they would modify their writing for a different audience, they were much more likely to stress surface level aspects of writing, whereas normally achieving students typically suggested changes to the substance of the material. Problems with written expression are in no way limited to children with learning disabilities, however; only 23% of fourth graders are considered to be proficient at completing grade-level work, while 60% have just some of the skills necessary to work on grade-level (Greenwald, Persky, Ambell, & Mazzeo, 1999).

Graham and Harris (1989) taught a small group of sixth grade students with learning disabilities how to use a strategy including a series of self-directed prompts. Elements included considering their audience, developing a plan, evaluating the impact of content, and continuing to generate new content during the writing process. Participants included all the basic elements of an essay on 10% of papers written prior to the intervention, but they improved to 80% following the intervention. Most importantly, measures of maintenance and generalization yielded promising results. A larger sample of students with learning disabilities was taught self-regulated learning strategies including how to brainstorm, semantic webbing, setting writing goals, and revision (Chalk, Hagan-Burke, & Burke, 2005). The training yielded significant improvements in word production and quality of writing.

Test-Taking Strategies

Assessment of academic skills plays an ever-increasing role in accountability for schools. Several states have developed assessments as standards for progressing to the next grade and measuring minimum standards for graduation. Further, minimum performance on standardized tests remains a part of the requirements for acceptance at most colleges and universities. As such, educators, parents, and students have placed a premium on improving performance on tests.

While evaluating content knowledge is most often the objective of a test, several factors may affect a person's score. These include the student's level of confidence, his motivation for success, and test-taking skills. Test-taking strategies are a set of skills that allow a student to recognize differences in test format and the entire testing situation in order to improve his or her score (Millman, Bishop, & Ebell, 1965). Six major types of test-taking skills have been identified, four of which can be applied to most testing situations. These include: time-using strategies, error avoidance strategies, guessing strategies, and deductive reasoning strategies (Millman et al., 1965). Intent consideration strategies and cue using strategies are more specific to a particular testing situation or test author.

Time-using strategies are those designed to make effective and efficient use of time during a test. Examples of such strategies might include monitoring time, answering questions you know, and not spending too much time on one item or one section. Error avoidance strategies are designed to minimize the points lost due to mistakes. They include accurately reading and understanding directions, accurately selecting answers, and checking for mistakes. Guessing strategies are intended to increase a student's chance of answering a question correctly. Deductive reasoning strategies help a student arrive at an answer by using the item content, eliminating unlikely answers, and recognizing similar responses. Intent consideration indicates a student's awareness of the intent behind the test or individual item. Finally, cue using strategies involve the test taker's understanding of the idiosyncrasies of the specific author (Mastropieri & Scruggs, 1992).

Mastropieri and Scruggs (1992) made a distinction between teaching test-taking skills and "teaching to the test". While test-taking skills can help to improve a person's test score by reducing the extraneous effect of test taking, "teaching to the test" can inflate a student's score by teaching students the exact items to be included on the test. Some researchers have argued that there is a distinction between test-taking skills and test wiseness (Millman et al., 1965; Scruggs, White, & Bennion, 1986; Towns & Robinson, 1993). Test wiseness involves skills that would inflate the score obtained by a student based on his savvy in recognizing such things as grammatical cues and choosing the longer length option. The difficulty is that many researchers continue to use these two terms synonymously, and various test-taking skills training programs can contain both. Furthermore, many researchers do not include specifics about the components of their programs, complicating comparisons of the effectiveness of skills taught (Scruggs et al., 1986).

It has been demonstrated that instruction in test-taking strategies can be helpful for all students, particularly special populations such as students with learning disabilities and those with emotional and behavioral disorders as well as minority students (Hughes, 1993; Scruggs & Mastropieri, 1986; Scruggs & Tolfa, 1985). In a meta-analysis, Scruggs and Mastropieri (1986) determined small overall effect sizes for test-taking skills instruction. However, several differences appear to increase the effectiveness of an intervention. For example, studies with interventions lasting longer than four hours produced significantly higher effect sizes than those lasting less than four hours. Also, when combining age and length of instruction, older children's performance is much less dependent on length of instruction than younger children. Older elementary children appear to benefit from even short instruction periods. Interestingly, they estimate that children of low socioeconomic status appear to benefit more than two times as much as their peers of higher socioeconomic status.

Scruggs and Mastropieri (1986) demonstrated the effectiveness of teaching test-taking strategies to students with learning disabilities or behavioral disabilities. Elementary students were taught strategies that included "attending to directions, marking answers carefully, choosing the best answer carefully, using error avoidance strategies, and deciding appropriate situations for soliciting teacher attention" (Scruggs & Mastropieri, 1986, p. 65). Significant increases were obtained on the Stanford Achievement Test Word Study subtest. This subtest appeared to be more amenable to changes due to the skills taught than the Reading Comprehension test. Researchers hypothesized that the skills required for these two subtests were different and that the skills needed for the reading comprehension subtest were more difficult to remediate.

In a much smaller study, Hughes (1993) taught eight middle school students identified as having an emotional behavioral disability test-taking strategies using a mnemonic device to help students remember the steps during a test situation in a mainstream class. Maintenance was observed up to 11 weeks following instruction, and general improvements were demonstrated on probe and classroom tests.

One of few studies looking at cultural factors examined cultural differences in students' test preparation, test-strategy use, and self-efficacy and their effects on a cognitive ability test (Ellis & Ryan, 2003). Caucasians and African Americans both reported use of effective test-taking skills, but African Americans reported much more frequent use of ineffective strategies. Such findings are interesting and highlight the need for additional study in this area.

Note-Taking/Listening Strategies

Note taking begins in later elementary years and becomes a very important skill in secondary school and college as class sizes increase and the preferred method of instruction becomes teacher lecture. Note-taking skills as well as text marking strategies are specific learning strategies associated with good listening skills and the ability to discern important versus nonimportant information. Rather than verbatim recording of information presented, effective note taking often requires manipulating information or reconstructing it in a way that is most meaningful for efficient learning (Porte, 2001). Important strategies include teaching students how to become aware of their listening ability, understand common barriers to listening, and listen to directions and discriminate information.

Earlier research examining the utility of note taking has taken two traditional approaches. From an information processing perspective, research focuses on the process or actual recording of information (Kiewra, 1985). Many studies have been conducted to determine whether it is the encoding process that is constructive in increasing achievement. This would be assessed by comparing students who do take notes with students who do not take notes on a given measure (Kiewra, 1985). The second approach, the "product" or "external storage" perspective, views the utility of note taking in terms of whether it improves achievement by aiding in review of the information recorded (Kiewra, 1985). This would be assessed by comparing students who review their notes prior to assessment with those who are not given the opportunity to review their notes.

Meta-analyses conducted by Kiewra (1985) and Hartley (1983) indicated limited support for the efficacy of both the encoding and product functions of note taking. Kiewra, Mayer, Christensen, Kim and Risch (1991) reported that 61 encoding studies were reviewed by at least one of these analyses. Of these, 35 supported encoding effects, 23 revealed no significant differences from control groups, and 3 actually appeared to produce detrimental effects. Somewhat more heartening, of 32 product studies, 24 indicated positive effects of reviewing, while the remaining 8 studies failed to yield significant differences between groups. Use of note-taking strategies has generally been supported, although some differences are seen between students with low ability and students with high ability (Shrager & Mayer, 1989; Kiewra & Benton, 1985; Wade & Trathen, 1989).

Note takers can differ in their ability to take effective notes, relate new information to that already learned, make note taking an active process, and determine priorities of relevant information (Faber et al., 2000). Students are able to shift their focus and the learning strategies they employ with repetition of lecture material, suggesting that "students are active learners who have some metacognitive control over their learning strategies" (Kiewra et al., 1991, p. 123). Students with learning disabilities have reported significant difficulties with note taking, including recording notes with sufficient speed, focusing their attention on lectures, and using appropriate strategies such as a shorthand method (Suritsky, 1992).

More recent research on note taking has suggested that students may not be very proficient in their self-regulation of learning (Peverly, Brobst, Graham, & Shaw, 2003). Students who took notes and reviewed them scored higher on academic measures; however, they generally had a difficult time predicting their performance beforehand as well as estimating how well they performed after completing the tests. Students' relative background knowledge and macropropositions contained in their notes accounted for a significant amount of variance on test measures. Peverly et al. (2003) suggested that students who processed the information likely had a better sense of what they knew as well as what they did not know.

Faber et al. (2000) pointed out that note taking is a developmental process, particularly with respect to the role that students encode information as they hear and write it. They highlighted the importance of both encoding and external storage in learning. In the encoding process, the learner must process the new information and assimilate it with previous related knowledge. Self-questioning is also important to monitor comprehension and to make associations with other information (Faber et al., 2000). Given research suggesting that students gradually transition from using notes in a primarily external storage function to a more efficient use of encoding, Faber and his colleagues investigated whether younger students could be taught this more active encoding process by teaching ninth graders (a) how to apply prior knowledge to the current subject matter, (b) how to detect and write main ideas, and (c) how to monitor themselves for understanding. Particularly on low-interest passages, students who were taught note-taking strategies performed significantly better as compared to peers who had not received this instruction. Of note, students with both high and low ability benefited from instruction in note taking. Other methods used to help students develop complete and effective notes include learning shorthand, writing faster, previewing the subject before class, using guided notes provided by the teacher, and strategic note taking that cues the student what questions to ask himself about the lecture (Boyle, 2001).

Attention/Concentration

Attention is a fundamental component of learning (e. g., see Riccio, Reynolds, Lowe, & Moore, 2002), so it is fundamental to success on any academic task. Most theories of learning include as their first step, the ability to attend adequately to the material to be learned. Attention is a precursor to memory and learning—a student must attend before learning can occur (e. g., see Reynolds & Voress, 2007). Students must attend to lectures and other academic tasks, adjust levels of attention as tasks may require them, self-monitor attention to academic tasks, and be able to avoid distractions.

Inattention in school children is often attributed only to children with ADHD. Indeed, prevalence rates ranging from 3% (American Psychiatric Association, 1994) to 10–20% of school-age children (Shaywitz & Shaywitz, 1992) certainly suggest this is a common problem in most classrooms. However, attention problems plague many children, including those suffering from other psychological disorders. The relationships between both internalizing and externalizing disorders and academic underachievement appear to be mediated by attention (Barriga, et al., 2002; Hinshaw, 1992). Given these effects, it is imperative to include assessment of attention with children who are struggling academically (Barriga et al., 2002). Many times, attention problems are eclipsed by more overt and disruptive behavioral symptoms, such as hyperactivity or defiance or by the severity of internalizing symptoms. Given the significant effects of attention on achievement, however, it should clearly be targeted for intervention.

The ability to self-monitor and adjust in a learning environment is also seen by cognitive psychologists as an important skill in the development of effective learning strategies (e.g., Alexander & Murphy, 1999). Strategies are dependent upon the processes of identifying important information, allocating attention, and monitoring comprehension (Reynolds & Shirey, 1988). In turn, increasing a student's skills in study, note-taking, and test-taking strategies is likely to increase a student's perception that attention and performance can be controlled. Increasing a student's interest in subject matter also may be helpful. Without intervention, the effects can be significant, both on the use of learning strategies and emotional adjustment as well (Borden, Brown, Jenkins, & Clingerman, 1987).

Numerous classroom strategies appear to be helpful in engaging children with attention problems. These techniques target areas such as getting attention, focusing attention, sustaining attention, reducing distractions, teaching organizational skills, increasing time management skills, and increasing specific skills in content areas (Teeter, 1998).

Organizational Techniques

Organizational difficulties have been most notably discussed with regard to children with ADHD. Certainly, some children without ADHD have problems with organization without the concomitant difficulties associated with the disorder. Zentall, Harper, and Stormont-Spurgin (1993) defined organizational behaviors as being able "to (a) plan and manage activities within a time framework, (b) systematically arrange objects and assignments within space for rapid retrieval, and (c) structure an approach to a task" (p. 112). This definition of organizational behavior delineates three separate types of organization: idea, time, and object. Object organization is a student's ability to maintain his possessions, including supplies needed for schoolwork. It is most synonymous with what is commonly thought of as organizational techniques. Time organization is typically referred to as time management. Idea organization refers to the management and structure of academic information to be learned. In terms of intervention, each of these constructs is distinct.

Organizational strategies refer to specific techniques used to organize materials to be learned. They range from being prepared for class to keeping daily assignments in a designated place. Teaching students basic techniques better

prepares them for more complex organization tasks (Slade, 1986). Students with a strategy for organizing their work in various school and home environments are likely to be more effective and to have more time to devote to academic tasks. They are more likely to complete homework assignments and to turn in their work (Hughes, Ruhl, Schumaker, & Deshler, 2002). Object organizational strategies are essential to learning the effective use of other skills including time management, in academic settings and later in work activities (Richards, 1987).

Zentall et al. (1993) developed two scales for assessing student organization, specifically for children with ADHD. The Child Organization Scale (COS) is a self-report measure for children to determine a student's perception of his (a) organization of inanimate objects and (b) organization of time. Designed for concurrent use with the COS, the Child Organization Parent Perception Scale (COPPS) was developed to assess a student's organization of time and objects. Both scales indicated spatial and temporal organizational difficulties for students with ADHD (Zentall et al., 1993). Psychopathology also has been correlated with regulating the study environment (Brackney & Karabenick, 1995).

Gall et al. (1990) included organizational skills as part of teaching overall self-management skills to students, highlighting goals such as "filing and transporting classroom materials" (p. 62) and "organizing a home study space" (p. 62). Methods teachers might employ for teaching students these skills include requiring the use of a three-ring binder, providing lessons and games regarding organization of their desk at school, teaching students ways to define and organize a place to study at home, providing incentives for using appropriate skills, and eliciting parent support. Stormont-Spurgin (1997) also recommended the use of routines in the classroom and cooperation with parents. In addition, lists of daily materials could be provided to students. Teachers could use cooperative homework teams that might compare students who have good organizational skills with students who may lack effective use of such skills. Such teams would be reinforced for completing work in a timely manner. Positive reinforcement, even the use of contracts with specific goals for using good organizational skills in the classroom, could be a helpful reminder for students to practice good habits. Finally, the use of assignment folders and daily planners would help students to keep papers organized and to see at a glance what materials are necessary to complete a task (i.e., geometry homework might require a pencil, protractor, calculator).

Time Management

Weissberg, Berentsen, Cote, Cravey, and Heath (1982) found that 62% of undergraduates at a university identified their greatest need to be managing their time more effectively. Therefore, it is not surprising that numerous books and learning strategies classes for college students have included efficient time management skills as a focus. Most sources have offered very similar suggestions for improving these skills (Macan, Shahani, Dipboye, & Phillips, 1990). Effective time management, often included as a self-regulatory strategy, has been associated with higher course grades (Brackney & Karabenick, 1995; Zimmerman, Greenberg, & Weinstein, 1994).

Britton and Tesser (1991) presented time management from an information processing perspective. Given a limited amount of time and a set of tasks to be completed, it makes sense that a student who is able to efficiently allocate time to prioritized tasks would be able to accomplish more academically. Many different factors of tasks must be taken into account when prioritizing tasks, including task length, complexity, deadlines, and resources needed.

Measures of time management as a behavior have been used primarily for research rather than intervention. Macan and colleagues (1990) developed a measure of time management called the Time Management Behavior Scale (TMB). Items on the scale were based on behaviors recommended by various sources on time management. Factor analyses indicated four separate factors. Macan et al. (1990) examined the correlation of time management behaviors measured by the TMB with numerous factors including role ambiguity, role overload, job tension, somatic tension, job and life satisfaction, and grade point average. Results indicated that students' report of effective general time management behaviors were significantly correlated with role ambiguity, somatic tension, job and life satisfaction, self-rated performance, and GPA. Greater perceived control over time was associated with less role ambiguity, job-induced tension and somatic tension; it was also associated with higher scores on life and job satisfaction measures as well as self-reports of achievement and grade point average (Macan et al. 1990). Correlations

with the remaining three factors ranged from two (Factor 1—Setting Goals & Priorities) to four (Factor 2—Mechanics, Planning & Scheduling). With regard to intervention, students who have attended a time management seminar obtained higher TMB scores. No differences were found for those who had only read a book on time management.

Britton and Tesser (1991) also demonstrated promising effects of time management skills and attitudes for college students. Regression analyses of their time management questionnaire yielded three factors: short-range planning, time attitudes, and long-range planning. The first two factors were more predictive of subsequent academic grade point average than SAT scores.

Gall et al. (1990) discussed time management skills as part of overall self-management goals to be included when teaching study skills. Such skills include learning to organize a schedule, setting attainable goals and accurate timelines, deciding on priorities, arriving on time for class or other obligations, completing work on time, providing rewards or incentives for work completion, and breaking an assignment into manageable parts. They offer several suggestions for incorporating time management skills in the classroom. For example, teachers might have students use an assignment sheet to keep track of tasks to be completed in their various classes. Students should be taught specifically how to schedule their time and encouraged to monitor how well they stay on schedule. It would be helpful to show students ways to break larger tasks into smaller more manageable ones. Whenever possible, it is important to draw the connection between students' goals and their academic effort. Incentives are helpful in reinforcing the use of good skills. Finally, Gall et al. (1990) suggested involving parents by having them provide for and monitor study time, model good time management behavior, provide tools such as "to do" lists and assignment planners, and reinforce good time management practices at home.

Academic Motivation

As asserted earlier, Weinstein et al.'s (2000) model of strategic learning includes three components: skill, will, and self-regulation. "Will" encompasses the motivation to learn. To overlook this factor when looking at success or failure in the classroom would be short-sighted. Yet, some researchers and teachers of learning strategies ignore the crucial role that motivation plays in terms of students' learning in general and the selection and use of learning strategies specifically. Among other things, motivation determines investment in the process of learning, which strategies are used, and the amount of effort put into carrying them out. In addition, understanding motivation helps to explain the differential use of learning strategies, both between students and in one student across learning situations.

Motivation can be seen as the "process by which the individuals' needs and desires are activated and, thus, directs their thoughts and their behaviors" (Alexander & Murphy, 1998, p. 33). Dembo & Eaton (1996) define motivation as "an internal state that arouses, directs, and maintains behavior" (p. 68) and view internal factors of motivation in terms of three components: (a) expectancy, or the student's attributions and self-efficacy for success/failure, (b) value, or the importance placed on the task, and (c) affective, or the emotional processes associated with the learning situation. Self-motivational beliefs are also included as part of a cyclical model of self-regulation (Zimmerman, 2002). Such beliefs are important in the forethought phase of learning and include self-efficacy, outcome expectations, intrinsic interest or value, and goal orientation. Academic achievement motivation is a construct of motivation that relates specifically to academic learning. Theories of achievement motivation abound, including self-efficacy, attribution, and goal theories as well as self-determination and intrinsic motivation. Many have argued that much can be learned from integrating the practical points of these theories when the aim is for successful interventions in the classroom (Brophy, 2004; Roeser & Galloway, 2002). Others feel that there is merit in viewing academic motivation as a multidimensional construct (Bong, 2001). Brophy (2004) asserted that self-efficacy, attribution, and goal theories can all be conceptualized in the expectancy part of expectancy-value theory.

Expectancy-value theory suggests that "individuals' expectancies for success and the value they have for succeeding are important determinants of their motivation to perform different achievement tasks, and their choices which tasks to pursue" (Wigfield & Tonks, 2002, p. 54). A student's expectancy for success may depend largely on his or her self-efficacy for the task. Self-efficacy is defined as "People's judgments of their capabilities to organize and execute courses of action required to attain designated types of performances" (Bandura, 1986, p. 391). It is the product of perceived performance in previous tasks and perceived control that a person feels he has had. Self-efficacy is independent of ability, and it affects a child's choice of tasks, persistence, future performance, and his or her emotional reaction to the task or situation (Collins, 1982). Increased self-efficacy has been associated with improved coping with stress and academic performance (Chemers, Hu, & Garcia, 2001).

Learning strategies interventions can have a direct effect on self-efficacy (Corno & Mandinach, 1983). Being able to use a strategy to accomplish a task provides a sense of control over performance outcomes. If the strategy is successful, then the student's self-efficacy is improved and the learner is more likely to use the strategy again. In several studies, efficacy has been positively correlated with the use of learning strategies (Pintrich & De Groot, 1990; Zimmerman & Martinez-Pons, 1990). Even vicarious experience through modeled use of strategies improved efficacy and motivation (Schunk & Gunn, 1985).

Attribution theory refers to a person's natural desire to understand why things happen and their beliefs about the causes of success or failure (Dembo & Eaton, 1996). Therefore, with regard to learning, attribution theory refers to a student's perceptions of the causes of academic success or failure. Weiner's (1979, 1986) achievement motivation theory is the most commonly accepted theory of attribution. Her model provides for classification of attributions in three dimensions: internal/external, stable/unstable, controllable/uncontrollable. Subsequent beliefs and future actions depend on the student's judgment of events in these dimensions. The attributions students make will affect their expectancy of future performance, persistence in similar tasks, emotional responses, which tasks they choose, and students' self-efficacy (Dembo & Eaton, 1996; Weiner, 1976).

Attribution retraining as an intervention has met with mixed results when combined with learning strategies instruction. Retraining improved use of reading strategies in a group of children with learning disabilities (Borkowski, Weyhing, & Carr, 1988). Similarly, attribution-based intervention with a group of college freshmen produced an 18% higher rate of passing final exams (Van Overwalle & De Metsenaere, 1990). However, attribution retraining was only partially supported (Craske, 1985) or not supported by similar studies (Miranda, Villaescusa, & Vidal-Abarca, 1997; Short & Ryan, 1984). Miranda et al.

(1997) suggested that the self-regulation procedures included in their training may have fostered sufficient self-confidence, circumventing the need for additional training with a group of children with learning disabilities.

It has been argued that perhaps goal theory can provide the best conceptualization of student motivation (Brophy, 2004). Traditionally, goal theory suggested that students adopt one of two distinct goals—performance or mastery. Performance goals, also known as task or ability goals, include a view of learning as a means to an end. These goals focus on "one's ability and sense of self-worth" pairing evaluation of one's ability with the process of learning (Ames, 1992, p. 262). Mastery goals, also known as learning or task goals, are those in which "individuals are oriented toward developing new skills, trying to understand their work, improving their level of competence, or achieving a sense of mastery based on self-referenced standards" (Ames, 1992, p. 262). Church, Elliot, & Gable (2001) found that adoption of mastery goals was associated with perceived lecture engagement and lack of a harsh or evaluative environment. The latter were associated with adoption of performance goals. The classroom environment helped to determine which goal orientation was adopted, which in turn affected students' grades.

Ames (1992) has conceptualized performance and mastery goals as contrasting goals that do not coexist. Some subsequent studies have suggested that this is a simplistic view. More recently a 2×2 model has been suggested that takes into account approach/avoidance goals as well as mastery/performance (Kaplan & Maehr, 2002). Brophy (2004) pointed out that learning or mastery approach goals appear to facilitate achievement while performance avoidance goals hinder achievement. The role of performance approach goals is less clear. Some argue that they may be helpful, while others suggest that they are a hindrance. Still others suggest that their usefulness or detrimental nature may be related to situational factors including the age of the students (Pintrich, 2000). Research on mastery avoidance goals is lacking (Kaplan & Maehr, 2002). What little research exists suggests that mastery avoidance goals may be associated with disorganized learning and test anxiety (Elliot & McGregor, 2001). Many studies suggest that these goals are not adopted in isolation (Kaplan & Maehr, 2002). Students may adopt multiple goals depending on the situation. While the 2×2

conceptualization of goal theory is compelling, it should be noted that it fails to take into account other goals that students have endorsed, such as work completion and social goals. Recently, Kaplan and Maehr (2002) have presented a model that takes into account personal and situational characteristics when determining goal orientation. Three major components comprise what they term a "personal achievement goal": perceived purpose in the situation, self-processes (i.e., self-efficacy, social identity), and the available possibilities for action in the situation.

Somewhat similar to a mastery orientation is academic intrinsic motivation. Gottfried, Fleming, and Gottfried (2001) describe academic intrinsic motivation as concerning "enjoyment of school learning characterized by a mastery orientation; curiosity; persistence; task endogeny; and the learning of challenging, difficult, and novel tasks" (p. 4). Findings of their longitudinal study suggest that academic intrinsic motivation increases in stability over time; however, intrinsic academic motivation decreases with age in general, and its effects are dependent on the academic subject. Factors in this decline may be increased extrinsic consequences for failure, increasing anxiety in school, and changing parental demands (Gottfried et al., 2001).

While an ultimate goal for teachers might be intrinsic motivation, a more realistic conceptualization of fostering academic motivation would "include encouraging (students) to use thoughtful information-processing and skill-building strategies when they are learning. This is quite different from merely offering them incentives for good performance later." (Brophy, 2004, p. 15).

Self-determination theory (SDT) has been used extensively in academic motivation research. Developed by Deci and Ryan (1985), this theory proposes that humans have an innate desire to learn. This desire may be encouraged or discouraged by a person's environment. Fulfillment of three basic psychological needs—competency, relatedness, and autonomy—is necessary in order for intrinsic motivation to develop (Deci & Ryan, 1985). In addition to intrinsic and extrinsic motivation, SDT also proposes the existence of amotivation or the absence of any desire to pursue an activity. Rather than a simple dichotomy, these three states exist on a continuum, with varying degrees of extrinsic motivation: external regulation, introjected regulation, identified regulation, and integrated regulation. Vallerand, Pelletier, Blais, and Brière (1992) have further divided intrinsic motivation into three categories: intrinsic motivation to know, intrinsic motivation to accomplish, and intrinsic motivation to experience stimulation. The Academic Motivation Scale (AMS, Vallerand et al., 1992) was developed as a measure of academic motivation based on SDT. Somewhat like mastery versus performance goals, some researchers have argued that validity studies of the AMS suggest that the constructs of SDT may not fit well along a continuum. Rather, they might be better conceptualized in a hierarchical manner (Fairchild, Horst, Finney, & Barron, 2005).

Strategies for improving academic motivation are numerous and often vary according to the theoretical orientation adopted. Individual strategies used to facilitate academic motivation include self-talk, goal setting, and time management (Dembo & Eaton, 1996). Classroom management strategies can also have a profound effect on students' academic achievement motivation (Brophy, 2004; Church et al., 2001). The reader is referred to Brophy (2004) for an integrated review of theories of academic achievement motivation with a strong emphasis on how teachers can use aspects of each of these theories to adapt their teaching style and classroom environments to maximize student effort.

Test Anxiety

The increasing reliance on mandated testing in schools (especially those near-end-of-year programs known as high-stakes testing programs) further highlights the need for an accurate understanding of test anxiety. Test anxiety can be debilitating for students of all ages. In addition to lower test scores, test anxiety has been associated with lower self-esteem (Marsh, 1990; Newbegin & Owens, 1996). In addition, students scoring high on test anxiety measures are more likely to report more pervasive psychological difficulties, including anxiety disorders and depressive symptoms (Beidel, Turner, & Trager, 1994; King, Mietz, Tinney, & Ollendick, 1995).

Four main theories have evolved in the study of test anxiety: the cognitive-attentional model, the learning deficit model, the dual deficit model, and the social learning model (Jones & Petruzzi, 1995). More recently integrative models have been proposed that incorporate previous theories (Jones & Petruzzi, 1995, Spielberger & Vagg, 1995). The cognitive-attentional model encompasses the worry-emotionality constructs, asserting that excessive worries, self-coping statements,

concern regarding physiological reactions, and other task-irrelevant thoughts interfere with optimal task performance (Naveh-Benjamin, 1991; Wine, 1971). Second, the learning deficit model proposed that test anxiety arises from a lack of adequate study and test-taking skills (Hodapp & Henneberger, 1983). While the relationship between poor study habits and test anxiety has been supported, Tobias (1985) has pointed out that the model does not explain how high-achieving students who have good study skills can also experience test anxiety. The dual deficit or information processing model seeks to bridge the gap between the cognitive-attentional model and the learning deficit model, indicating that both task-irrelevant thoughts and skills deficits can contribute to feelings of anxiety (Jones & Petruzzi, 1995). As the term information processing suggests, test anxiety appears to be caused by difficulties encoding and organizing material as well as retrieval during an evaluation (Naveh-Benjamin, 1991). Finally, the social learning model suggests that the etiology of test anxiety lies with a student's self-efficacy regarding a task and motivation to perform well.

Integrative models include Spielberger and Vagg's (1995) Transactional Process Model, which describes the relationships among antecedents, student dispositions, cognitive processes, and the consequences associated with test anxiety. Antecedents considered are the subject matter of the test, study skills, and test-taking skills. During the evaluation, a student retrieves and processes information, continually appraises his situation, and may respond with an increase in worry and/or emotionality. The result of these processes will either be behavior that is relevant to the task or not relevant to the task.

Anxiety may be experienced differently for high-achieving students than for low-achieving students (Wigfield and Eccles, 1989). High-achieving students may be anxious due to unrealistic expectations placed on them by parents, peers, or self. Less able students may be anxious due to previous experiences of and future expectations of failure. Further, some anxious students may have good study habits but suffer from the pressure of being evaluated, whereas other students have poor study strategies which inhibit their learning (Naveh-Benjamin, McKeachie, & Lin, 1987). The significance of these differences is that changing test conditions may help students with fears of evaluation; however, those whose learning process has been impaired would not benefit from such changes.

Research has suggested that a student with high anxiety divides his or her attention between task-relevant and task-irrelevant thoughts (Wine 1971). Irrelevant thoughts reported by adults in Galassi, Frierson, & Sharer (1981) might include comparing oneself to others, poor concentration, and a desire to escape the testing situation. It is interesting to note, however, that in that study, highly anxious adults reported more on-task thoughts than their less anxious peers.

Highly anxious children are similar to anxious adults in their increased reporting of negative self-evaluations (Galassi et al., 1981; Zatz & Chassin, 1983; Zatz & Chassin, 1985). Contrary to what one might think, coping statements made by test-anxious children do not appear to improve their performance (Zatz & Chassin, 1985). Students with high test anxiety report more self-coping statements than low test-anxious students, likely because they perceived the situation as stressful (Prins, Groot, & Hanewald, 1994). It appears, in fact, that it is the absence of negative thoughts rather than the presence of positive thoughts that improves performance. This finding has significant implications for programs designed to decrease test anxiety, suggesting the need to focus on decreasing negative and off-task cognitions in intervention programs.

Hembree (1988) conducted a meta-analysis of 562 reports of research examining the causes, correlates, and effects of test anxiety. His main conclusions regarding relationships of test anxiety to other variables included the following: (a) an inverse relationship between test anxiety and achievement exists from third grade onward, (b) worry tends to be more associated with achievement than emotionality, (c) no gender differences exist regarding the relationship between anxiety and achievement, (d) females report higher levels of anxiety, but with no corresponding achievement differences, (e) test anxiety increases significantly in later elementary years, (f) some racial differences exist relative to age, and (g) lower test anxiety is associated with higher ability in general.

A complicating factor to consider in the measurement of test anxiety is that anxiety as it relates to performance is likely not linear. Ball (1995) summarized the following suggestions regarding the relationship between test performance and test anxiety: (a) "that test anxiety may be facilitating" (for some students), (b) that moderator variables including test difficulty and "the proficiency of the test taker" may be present, and

(c) "the relation between test anxiety and performance may be curvilinear" (p. 109). In addition, students who are test anxious demonstrate poor study habits and organizational difficulties which inhibit information processing (Culler & Holahan, 1980; Naveh-Benjamin et al., 1987).

Self-report methods are most commonly used to assess test anxiety, likely due, in part, to their efficiency and ease of administration. Such measures appear to be used primarily for research purposes rather than for diagnostic or intervention purposes. The most commonly used measures are the Test Anxiety Scale for Children (TASC; Sarason, Davidson, Lighthall, & Waite, 1958) and the Test Anxiety Inventory (TAI; Spielberger, 1980).

Given the detrimental effects that test anxiety has on task performance, what is considered to be the most effective method of achieving this goal? A cursory glance at the literature might leave one with the impression that W. J. McKeachie was left with early in his studies of test anxiety: "anxious students are made anxious by almost anything one does to try to help them" (McKeachie, 1984, p. 193). As with studies regarding the antecedents and correlates of test anxiety, there is a lack of good research investigating the effectiveness of intervention with children and adolescents who experience test anxiety (Ergene, 2003). Wilson and Rotter (1986) cited several studies that have suggested the superiority of combining study skills training and treatment for test anxiety in improving academic performance and decreasing anxiety. In their own study, they used sixth and seventh graders with high scores on the TASC to compare several different treatment methods. The modified anxiety management training group, which received anxiety management training combined with "suggestions for strengthening the ego and developing memory and concentration, with a focus on study habits" (Wilson & Rotter, 1986, p.22), most effectively reduced test anxiety and increased self-esteem and academic performance.

Multicomponent approaches of test anxiety have included training in cognitive restructuring, relaxation, time management, attention control, test taking, and study skills (Decker, 1987; Dendato and Diener, 1986; Glanz, 1994). These approaches, particularly used in combination, appear to decrease test anxiety while improving academic performance. Cavallaro and Meyers (1986) identified three main approaches for alleviating test anxiety and thereby improving academic performance: (a) rational-emotive therapy and cognitive restructuring, (b) desensitization, relaxation, and self-control techniques, and (c) training in study or test-taking skills. In their study of adolescent females, the cognitive restructuring and relaxation intervention was the more effective intervention overall. However, for students with poor study strategies, the relaxation and study skills intervention was somewhat effective. It should be noted, however, that several possible reasons for the differential effects of the treatment groups, including the overly didactic nature of the study skills training, possible differences in length of time needed to learn, and discrepancies in group sizes, were suggested.

Hembree's (1988) meta-analysis asserted that a variety of cognitive and behavioral interventions have had lasting effects in reducing anxiety and increasing academic performance. The discovery that interventions overall improve test anxiety was inconsistent with previous reviews. Hembree attributed the failure to find such effects to generally low sample sizes which would not detect modest effects. Test-taking strategies training was also helpful for students who have poor skills.

ASSESSMENT MEASURES

While several measures currently exist that purport to measure learning strategies and/or self-regulated learning, most have significant limitations in their utility. The three most commonly used assessment measures are the Learning and Study Strategies Inventory (LASSI, Weinstein, 1987), the Motivated Strategies for Learning Questionnaire (MSLQ; Pintrich, Smith, Garcia, & McKeachie, 1991), and more recently, the School Motivation and Learning Strategies Inventory (SMALSI; Stroud & Reynolds, 2006). Unfortunately, the MSLQ was created solely for college students. The LASSI also was originally designed for use with college students (Weinstein, 1987). The LASSI for high school students is a downward extension of a college-level version of the same instrument. While the LASSI has proven to be an excellent measure of learning strategies, it leaves much unanswered about children and the development of learning strategies.

An inventory to assess learning strategies and study habits has several purposes. Weinstein, Zimmerman, and Palmer (1988) identified three historic purposes for such an inventory: "(1) prediction of academic performance, (2) counseling students concerning their study practices, and (3) screening or criterion measures for study skills courses" (p. 26). They proposed additional purposes for the development of the LASSI which included: assessment of a wide variety of topics related to and including learning strategies with sound reliability and validity, assessment of behaviors that could be changed, representing current research in cognitive psychology, and use as a diagnostic instrument (Weinstein et al., 1988).

The SMALSI (Stroud & Reynolds, 2006) was developed for the purposes identified by Weinstein et al. (1988) in addition to several others. First, little is known about special populations and their individual needs. Those mentioned previously include children with ADHD, cancer, learning disabilities, or children with traumatic brain injuries. Second, and probably the greatest potential for contribution that the SMALSI will make is that it covers a wider range of child development. The ability to measure these constructs across ages will provide a greater understanding of the development of certain cognitive skills as well as an understanding of motivational factors and how they change from childhood to adolescence. It allows educators to assess and monitor learning strategies as they develop, rather than only targeting them for remediation after a problem already exists.

The SMALSI was intended to help to identify which behaviors are consistent with academic success and how or if these behaviors vary according to age, gender, intelligence, motivation, attributions, and other relevant variables. Existing inventories have provided a reasonable understanding of learning strategies from a remedial perspective. Weinstein et al. (2000) has called for research to help understand the development of learning strategies in younger children. An established means of measuring such strategies and their associated features such as the SMALSI was necessary in order to accomplish this goal.

Finally, it has been argued that learning strategies naturally increase as a student matures, regardless of instruction. While true for many strategies, this is not the case for all learning strategies. Reading comprehension strategies such as making up questions while reviewing texts or making visual representations of information do not improve over time (Thomas & Rowher, 1986). Self-regulated learning strategies appear to change as students progress through school, some increasing while others increase then decrease over time (Zimmerman & Martinez-Pons, 1990). Furthermore, the changing frequency of use of some strategies appears to be dependent on how often other strategies are used. For example, Zimmerman and Martinez-Pons (1990) found that students reported a decline in the practice of reviewing textbooks from junior high to high school and an increase in reviewing notes. These two trends suggest a shift in use of strategies based on the nature of their changing learning activities. A better understanding of these changes in learning strategies and related constructs was the final reason for the development of the SMALSI.

The Student Motivation and Learning Strategies Inventory

The SMALSI has two forms: one for children ages 8–12 (SMALSI-Child) and one for adolescents ages 13–18 (SMALSI-Teen). The SMALSI may be group or individually administered in an academic or clinical setting. Typical administration time is 20–30 minutes. The SMALSI is comprised of seven strengths scales and three liabilities scales. Student Strengths scales include: Study Strategies, Reading/Comprehension Strategies, Note-taking/Listening Strategies, Writing/

Research Strategies, Test-Taking Strategies, Organizational Techniques, and Time Management. Student Liabilities scales include Low Academic Motivation, Attention/Concentration, and Test Anxiety. On the Child Form, the Time Management and Organizational Techniques scales are combined to reflect developing but not yet distinct organizational behaviors. Scales are reported as T-scores, which allows for comparison of performance among constructs as well as for monitoring development or the effectiveness of an intervention. The SMALSI also includes an Inconsistent Responding Index (INC) to aid in detecting responses that are inconsistent due to noncompliance, poor understanding, or carelessness. Definitions of these scales as used in the SMALSI are given in Table 34.2.

Validity studies have yielded promising psychometric properties for the SMALSI Form C and Form T (Stroud & Reynolds, 2006). More specifically, internal consistencies for the final scales produced estimates consistently above .7, indicating support for the structure of the SMALSI Form C and Form T scales. These findings were consistent with regard to age and grade with the exception of the SMALSI Form C Writing/Research Strategies scale. Younger children in the sample obtained had the most

TABLE 34.2   **Definitions of the SMALSI Scales**

Scale	Definition
Study Strategies	Selecting important information, relating new to previously learned information, and memory strategies for encoding
Note-Taking/Listening Skills	Discriminating important material when taking notes, organizing notes, efficiency in note taking
Reading and Comprehension Strategies	Previewing, monitoring, and reviewing texts, including self-testing to ensure understanding
Writing-Research Skills	Researching topics in a variety of ways, organizing writing projects as well as monitoring and self-checking for errors
Test-Taking Strategies	Increasing efficiency in test taking, including eliminating unlikely answers and strategic guessing
Organizational Techniques	Organizing class and study materials, structuring assignments including homework and other projects
Time Management	Effectively using time to complete assignments, understanding of time needed for academic tasks
Academic Motivation	Level of intrinsic motivation to engage and succeed in academic tasks
Test Anxiety	Student's experience of debilitating symptoms of test anxiety, lower performance on tests due to excessive worry
Attention/Concentration	Attending to lectures and other academic tasks, monitoring and adjusting attention to performance, concentrating, and avoiding distractions

difficulty responding reliably regarding their use of writing strategies. While this was the lowest scale in general, reliability on this scale tended to increase with age as would be expected from a developmental perspective. With this exception, younger children tended to respond in the same manner as older children to SMALSI constructs. These findings are particularly important in that they support the argument that younger children are capable of reliably reporting their own attitudes and behaviors (Reynolds & Kamphaus, 1992, 2004; Reynolds & Richmond, 1985).

The reliability of the SMALSI scales was also robust across gender and across ethnicity with one exception (Stroud & Reynolds, 2006). When ethnicity was taken into account, results were generally commensurate with the exception of the American Indian sample which produced higher reliability coefficients on several scales to a small but consistent degree. This difference was present across SMALSI Form C and Form T, with the difference being somewhat larger on Form T. While this small difference did not indicate significant implications for interpretation, it does invite further study with regard to differences in response patterns for different ethnic groups. Overall, results of initial standardization and validity studies suggest sufficient reliability for the SMALSI, indicating good confidence that the items comprising the SMALSI scales are accurate in estimating a student's standing on each construct.

Of equal importance is evidence that the SMALSI measures the constructs it purports to measure. SMALSI constructs were determined by thorough review of literature in education, psychology, and related fields. As discussed earlier, each construct has empirical support spanning several decades to support its role in fostering academic success. The content validity of the scales and items was also supported by expert review from multiple sources (Stroud & Reynolds, 2006).

The structure of the SMALSI as measuring individual constructs falling within the two areas of student strengths and student liabilities was supported by correlations between the SMALSI scales (Stroud & Reynolds, 2006). Results were similar across Form C and Form T, indicating the presence of both common and distinctive constructs. More specifically, scales within the student strengths scales were correlated with each other, and scales within the student liabilities were correlated.

The validity of the SMALSI scales was also supported by divergence of the SMALSI scales from clinical dimensions (i.e., depression, general anxiety, etc.) and convergence with academic measures (i.e., math and reading). Correlations between the SMALSI scales and measures of emotional, academic, and social adjustment indicated that School Liability scales were positively correlated with measures of clinical, personal, and school maladjustment. In like form, the School Strength scales had negative associations with these scales. This pattern was evident in both Form C and Form T. Of note, academic motivation was highly correlated with both attitude to school and teachers, highlighting the importance between school motivation and the classroom environment. This is consistent with previous literature asserting the critical roles that academic environment and characteristics of the teacher play in the level of students' academic motivation (e.g., Brophy, 2004; Pajares & Urdan, 2002). Also of importance was the application that children who report increased depression evidenced poorer study strategies such as test-taking strategies and note-taking strategies but also decreased concentration, attention skills, and academic motivation. The trend between depression and motivation in the adolescent sample was somewhat decreased but still evident. This finding lends support to Brackney & Karabenick (1995), who asserted the need to teach learning strategies to students with psychiatric disorders. Children and adolescents who reported decreased sense of control over events in their surroundings (external locus of control) also reported increased levels of test-related anxiety, further highlighting the relations of the SMALSI with social-emotional functioning. As such, the relations between the SMALSI scores and Behavior Assessment System for Children Self-report of Personality scores (Reynolds & Kamphaus, 1992) indicated a pattern of divergence and convergence that was supportive of the content of the scales.

Results examining the relationships between the SMALSI constructs and academic achievement as measured by a state-developed assessment also provided some promising information regarding the utility of the SMALSI in the academic arena. The curriculum-based assessment used designed to assess students' attainment of minimum levels of competence for each grade level demonstrated significant correlations with several of the SMALSI scales. More specifically, in child samples, children's use of study strategies, writing skills, and time management/organizational techniques were linked with reading abilities. Writing skills also were associated positively with math abilities, while test anxiety impaired math performance. In the adolescent group, though, a shift was noted with test anxiety playing a more prominent role, negatively impacting reading, social studies, and science academic abilities. Academic motivation also played a more significant role in the adolescent sample, particularly in the areas of reading and social studies.

Examining the validity of the measure in relation to the performance of different demographic groups on the SMALSI also produced interesting results. With regard to gender, girls consistently scored higher on both the Child and Teen forms on scales suggesting better use of note-taking and listening skills, writing and research strategies, and test-taking strategies. Differences for gender comparison of adolescents were more prevalent, with girls scoring higher on all student strengths scales. Adolescent girls also tended to report higher test anxiety. While these differences are consistent, effect sizes were all small but consistent with previous research (Reynolds & Kamphaus, 1992, 2002, and 2004).

In relation to age, the SMALSI scores demonstrated reliability and validity across age and grades. In the child sample, scores on the SMALSI were stable, with little deviation aside from minor score fluctuations around the mean T-score of 50. In the teen group, there was evidenced a general trend by which adolescent's study strategies increased with age and grade. This is as would be expected, as individual's study strategies and abilities tend to improve with increased practice and refinement of skills gained through exposure to the academic setting. Of note, though, was an evidenced trend of eighth grade students demonstrating decreased study and learning strategies than other teen groups. This trend invites future research and exploration in adolescent samples.

Implications and Uses of the SMALSI

While the SMALSI will inevitably lead to new possibilities in research, the most exciting aspect of the instrument is certainly the wealth of information it provides for professionals working directly with children. The SMALSI was intentionally designed for use by a wide variety of individuals in a number of different settings.

For example, teachers may use this measure in a group format with his class to identify trends in academic motivation or to identify specific problem areas such as ineffective note taking or poorly developed writing skills for the class as a whole that might be incorporated into the teacher's curriculum. In this way, the SMALSI can be applied as a preventive measure at the classroom level. School-level teams designed to help implement interventions prior to referral for special education services may use the SMALSI with a struggling child to identify specific areas that may be impeding academic performance. They may then be able to provide the necessary intervention without the need for additional levels of academic support. The SMALSI will have applications in response-to-intervention as well since the teaching and improvement of learning strategies may improve academic performance, in conjunction with models such as direct instruction, to the point that special education services are not required.

School psychologists and other assessment staff, in some cases including teachers with sufficient training in assessment, can use the SMALSI in a more diagnostic manner depending upon their level of training. It is important to maximize the effectiveness of the interventions chosen in order to minimize the level of assistance needed. Information from the SMALSI can be used by clinicians to make meaningful academic recommendations regarding interventions to use and classroom accommodations to make in the Individualized Education Plan (IEP). Without such information, much of this process can often be the product of trial and error rather than the result of objective assessment. Students who are struggling academically but do not meet eligibility criteria under the Individuals with Disabilities Education Act or Section 504 equal access services are particularly vulnerable to academic failure. Teachers will need specific recommendations about what areas to target given the constraints general education modifications (i.e., tutoring, reading programs, skill-building programs) pose.

Psychologists can use the SMALSI as part of a comprehensive assessment battery. The valuable relationships among constructs measured by the SMALSI and more global behavioral and emotional difficulties have been demonstrated in this study. Results of the SMALSI can add valuable insight into possible academic causes, consequences, or correlates for emotional and behavioral disorders.

Given the increased use of high-stakes testing emerging across the United States used in determining grade promotion and school funding, the SMALSI also holds value more directly in the classroom setting. As states transition to requiring passing scores on state tests such as the TAKS (Texas Assessment of Knowledge and Skills) in Texas and the FCAT (Florida Comprehensive Assessment Test) to determine school funding and pupil progress, teachers and school personnel are faced with the increasing demands of promoting children and adolescents' academic knowledge as well as their test-taking abilities. The use of the SMALSI can be a valuable tool for teachers to help identify children's individual strengths and weaknesses in these areas to help tailor interventions to their needed area. This measure provides a user-friendly method for teachers and administrators to assess multiple children's skills at one time, without the need for comprehensive one-on-one testing.

It should be noted that, too often in an attempt to find out "what is wrong" with a child, clinicians find only that—a child's weaknesses. While this information is a necessary component to assessment, the value and importance of identifying a child's strengths cannot be understated. The SMALSI has been designed with the intent to do both by providing both positive and negative indicators and by offering objective assessment in areas that previously have been difficult to assess. Given the research reviewed in the opening sections of this chapter, more emphasis on teaching children how to be strategic learners seems appropriate, and the SMALSI can monitor success in this endeavor. Knowing how to learn and having effective strategies becomes more and more imperative to vocational success with each passing generation. Jobs and the skills needed to perform them are more likely to change over a student's lifetime. Becoming a strategic learner will give students the necessary flexibility and problem-solving ability to adapt successfully to these changes.

REFERENCES

Alexander, P. A., & Murphy, P. K. (1998). The research base for APA's learner-centered psychological principles. In N. M. Lamberst & B. L. McCombs (Eds.), *How students learn: Reforming schools through learner-centered education* (pp. 25–60). Washington, DC: American Psychological Association.

Alexander, P. A., & Murphy, P. K. (1999). What cognitive psychology has to say to school psychology: Shifting perspectives and shared purposes. In C. R. Reynolds & T. B. Gutkin (Eds.), *The handbook of school psychology* (3rd ed., pp. 167–193). New York: Wiley.

American Psychiatric Association. (1994). *Diagnostic and statistical manual of mental disorders* (4th ed.). Washington, DC: Author.

Ames, C. (1992). Classrooms: Goals, structures, and student motivation. *Journal of Educational Psychology, 84*(3), 261–271.

Baker, L., and Brown, A. (1984). Metacognitive skills in reading. In P. D. Pearson, R. Barr, M. L. Kamil, & P. Morenthal, P. (Eds.), *Handbook of reading research*. New York: Longman.

Bakken, J. P., Mastropieri, M. A., & Scruggs, T. E. (1997). Reading comprehension of expository science material and students with learning disabilities: A comparison of strategies. *Journal of Special Education, 31*(3), 300–324.

Bakken, J. P., & Whedon, C. K. (2002). Teaching text structure to improve reading comprehension. *Intervention in School and Clinic, 37*(4), 229–233.

Ball, S. (Ed.). (1995). *Anxiety and test performance.* Philadelphia, PA: Taylor & Francis.

Bandura, (1986). *Social foundations of thought and action: A social cognitive theory.* Englewood Cliffs, NJ: Prentice-Hall.

Barriga, A. Q., Doran, J. W., Newell, S. R., Morrison, E. M., Barbetti, V., & Robbins, B. D. (2002). Relationships between problem behaviors and academic achievement in adolescents: The unique role of attention problems. *Journal of Emotional and Behavioral Disorders, 10*(4), 233–240.

Beidel, D. C., Turner, M. W., & Trager, K. N. (1994). Test anxiety and childhood anxiety in African American and white school children. *Journal of Anxiety Disorders, 8*(2), 169–179.

Billingsley, B. S., & Wildman, T. M. (1990). Facilitating reading comprehension in learning disabled students: Metacognitive goals and instructional strategies. *RASE: Remedial & Special Education, 11*(2), 18–31.

Bong, M. (2001). Between- and within-domain relations of academic motivation among middle and high school students' self-efficacy, task-value, and achievement goals. *Journal of Educational Psychology, 93*(1), 23–34.

Borden, K. B., Brown, R. T., Jenkins, P., & Clingerman, S. R. (1987). Achievement attributions and depressive symptoms in attention deficit-disordered and normal children. *Journal of School Psychology, 25*(4), 399–404.

Borkowski, J. G., Weyhing, R. S., & Carr, M. (1988). Effects of attributional retraining on strategy-based reading comprehension in learning-disabled students. *Journal of Educational Psychology, 80*(1), 46–53.

Boyle, J. R. (2001). Enhancing the note-taking skills of students with mild disabilities. *Intervention of School and Clinic, 36*(4), 221–224.

Brackney, B. E., & Karabenick, S. A. (1995). Psychopathology and academic performance: The role of motivation and learning strategies. *Journal of Counseling Psychology*, *42*(4), 456–465.

Britton, B. K., & Tesser, A. (1991). Effects of time-management practices on college grades. *Journal of Educational Psychology*, *83*(3), 405–410.

Brophy, J. (2004). *Motivating students to learn*, 2nd ed. Mahwah, NJ: Lawrence Erlbaum Associates.

Bygrave, P. L. (1994). Development of listening skills in students in special education settings. *International Journal of Disability, Development and Education*, *41*(1), 51–60.

Cassady, J. C., & Johnson, R. E. (2002). Cognitive test anxiety and academic performance. *Contemporary Educational Psychology*, *27*(2), 270–295.

Cavallaro, D. M., & Meyers, J. (1986). Effects of study habits on cognitive restructuring and study skills training in the treatment of test anxiety with adolescent females. *Techniques: A Journal for Remedial Education and Counseling*.

Chalk, J. C., Hagan-Burke, S., & Burke, M. D. (2005). The effects of self-regulated strategy development on the writing process for high school students with learning disabilities. *Learning Disability Quarterly*, *28*(1), 75–87.

Chemers, M. M., Hu, L., & Garcia, B. F. (2001). Academic self-efficacy and first-year college student performance and adjustment. *Journal of Educational Psychology*, *93*(1), 55–64.

Church, M. A., Elliot, A. J., & Gable, S. L. (2001). Perceptions of classroom environment, achievement goals, and achievement outcomes. *Journal of Educational Psychology*, *93*(1), 43–54.

Collins, W. (1982). Some correlates of achievement among students in a supplemental instruction program. *Journal of Learning Skills*, *2*(1), 19–28.

Corno, L., & Mandinach, E. B. (1983). Using existing classroom data to explore relationships in a theoretical model of academic motivation. *Journal of Educational Research*, *77*(1), 33–42.

Craske, M. L. (1985). Improving persistence through observational learning and attribution retraining. *British Journal of Educational Psychology*, *55*, 138–147.

Culler, R. E., & Holahan, C. J. (1980). Test anxiety and academic performance: The effects of study-related behaviors. *Journal of Educational Psychology*, *72*(1), 16–20.

De Beni, R., & Palladino, P. (2000). Intrusion errors in working memory tasks: Are they related to reading comprehension ability? *Learning and Individual Differences*, *12*(2), 131–143.

Deci, E. L., & Ryan, R. M. (1985). The general causality orientations scale: Self-determination in personality. *Journal of Research in Personality*, *19*(2), 109–134.

Decker, T. W. (1987). Multi-component treatment for academic underachievers. *Journal of College Student Psychotherapy*, *1*(3), 29–37.

Dembo, M. H., & Eaton, M. J. (1996). School learning and motivation. In G. D. Phye (Ed.), *Handbook of academic learning: Construction of knowledge*, (pp. 66–105). San Diego: Academic Press.

Dendato, K. M., & Diener, D. (1986). Effectiveness of cognitive/relaxation therapy and study-skills training in reducing self-reported anxiety and improving the academic performance of test-anxious students. *Journal of Counseling Psychology*, *33*(2), 131–135.

Duchastel, P. C., & Nungester, R. J. (1984). Adjunct question effects with review. *Contemporary Educational Psychology*, *9*(2), 97–103.

DuPaul, G. J., & Stoner, G. D. (1994). *ADHD in the schools: Assessment and intervention strategies*. New York: Guilford Press.

Durkin, D. (1979). What classroom observations reveal about reading comprehension instruction. *Reading Research Quarterly*, *14*(4), 481–533.

Elliot, A. J., & McGregor, H. A. (2001). A 2 × 2 achievement goal framework. *Journal of Personality and Social Psychology*, *80*(3), 501–519.

Ellis, A. P., & Ryan, A. M. (2003). Race and cognitive-ability test performance: The mediating effects of test preparation, test-taking strategy use and self-efficacy. *Journal of Applied Social Psychology*, *33*(12), 2607–2629.

Ergene, G. (2003). Effective interventions on test anxiety reduction: A meta-analysis. *School Psychology International*, *24*(3), 313–328.

Ezell, H. K., Hunsicker, S. A., & Quinque, M. M. (1997). Comparison of two strategies for teaching reading comprehension skills. *Education and Treatment of Children*, *20*(4), 365–82.

Faber, J. E., Morris, J. D., & Lieberman, M. G. (2000). The effect of note taking on ninth grade students' comprehension. *Reading Psychology*, *21*, 257–270.

Faigley, L., Cherry, R. D., Jolliffee, D. A., & Skinner, A. M. (1985). *Assessing writers' knowledge and processes of composing*. Norwood, NJ: Ablex.

Fairchild, A. J., Horst, S. J., Finney, S. J., & Barron, K. E. (2005). Evaluating existing and new validity evidence for the academic motivation scale. *Contemporary Educational Psychology*, *30*(3), 331–358.

Gajria, M., & Salvia, J. (1992). The effects of summarization instruction on text comprehension of students with learning disabilities. *Exceptional Children*, *58*(6), 508–516.

Galassi, J. P., Frierson, H. T., & Sharer, R. (1981). Behavior of high, moderate, and low test anxious students during an actual test situation. *Journal of Consulting and Clinical Psychology*, *49*, 51–62.

Gall, M. D., Gall, J. P., Jacobsen, D. R., & Bullock, T. L. (1990). *Tools for learning: A guide to teaching study skills*. Alexandria, VA: Association for Supervision and Curriculum Development.

Garner, R. (1988). Verbal-report data on cognitive and metacognitive strategies. In C. E. Weinstein, E. T. Goetz, & P. A. Alexander (Eds.), *Learning and study strategies: Issues in assessment, instruction, and evaluation* (pp. 63–76). San Diego: Academic Press.

Gersten, R., Fuchs, L. S., Williams, J. P., & Baker, S. (2001). Teaching reading comprehension strategies to students with learning disabilities: A review of research. *Review of Educational Research*, *71*(2), 279–320.

Gettinger, M., & Seibert, J. K. (2002). Contributions of study skills to academic competence. *School Psychology Review*, *31*(3), 350–365.

Glanz, J. (1994). Effects of stress reduction strategies on reducing test-anxiety among learning-disabled students. *Journal of Instructional Psychology*, *21*(4), 313–317.

Goll, P. S. (2004). Mnemonic strategies: Creating schemata for learning enhancement. *Education*, *125*(2), 306.

Gottfried, A. E., Fleming, J. S., & Gottfried, A. W. (2001). Continuity of academic intrinsic motivation from childhood through late adolescence: A longitudinal study. *Journal of Educational Psychology*, *93*(1), 3–13.

Graham, S., & Harris, K. R. (1989). Improving learning disabled students' skills at composing essays: Self-instructional strategy training. *Exceptional Children*, *56*(3), 201–214.

Graham, S., Schwartz, S. S., & MacArthur, C. A. (1993). Knowledge of writing and the composing process, attitude toward writing, and self-efficacy for students with and without learning disabilities. *Journal of Learning Disabilities*, *26*(4), 237–249.

Greenwald, E., Persky, H., Ambell, J., & Mazzeo, J. (1999). *National assessment of educational progress: 1998 report card for the nation and the states*. Washington, DC: U.S. Department of Education.

Hartley, J. (1983). Note-taking research: Resetting the scoreboard. *Bulletin of the British Psychological Society*, *36*, 13–14.

Hembree, R. (1988). Correlates, causes, effects, and treatment of test anxiety. *Review of Educational Research*, *58*(1), 47–77.

Hinshaw, S. P. (1992). Externalizing behavior problems and academic underachievement in childhood and adolescence: Causal relationships and underlying mechanisms. *Psychological Bulletin*, *111*(1), 127–155.

Hillocks, G. (1986). *Research on written composition: New directions for teaching*. Urbana, IL: ERIC Clearinghouse on Reading and Communication Skills and the National Conference on Research in English.

Ho, R., & McMurtrie, J. (1991). Attributional feedback and underachieving children: Differential effects on causal attributions, success expectancies, and learning processes. *Australian Journal of Psychology*, *43*(2), 93–100.

Hodapp, V., & Henneberger, A. (1983). Test anxiety, study habits, and academic performance. In H. M. van der Ploeg, R. Schwarzer, & E. D. Spielberger (Eds.), *Advances in test anxiety research*, *Vol. 2* (pp. 119–127). Hillsdale, NJ: Erlbaum.

Hughes, C. A. (1993). Test-taking strategy instruction for adolescents with emotional and behavioral disorders. *Journal of Emotional & Behavioral Disorders*, *1*(3), 189–198.

Hughes, C. A., Ruhl, K. L., Schumaker, J. B., & Deshler, D. D. (2002). Effects of instruction in an assignment completion strategy on the homework performance of students with learning disabilities in general education classes. *Learning Disabilities Research & Practice*, *17*(1), 1–18.

Hughes, C. A., & Suritsky, S. K. (1994). Note-taking skills of university students with and without learning disabilities. *Journal of Learning Disabilities*, *27*(1), 20–24.

Jannoun, L., & Chessells, J. M. (1987). Long-term psychological effects of childhood leukemia and its treatment. *Pediatric Hematology and Oncology*, *4*, 293–308.

Jenkins, J. R., Heliotis, J. D., Stein, M. L., & Haynes, M. C. (1987). Improving reading comprehension by using paragraph restatements. *Exceptional Children*, *54*, 54–59.

Jones, L., & Petruzzi, D. C. (1995). Test anxiety: A review of theory and current treatment. *Journal of College Student Psychotherapy*, *10*(1), 3–15.

Kaplan, A., & Maehr, M. L. (2002). *Adolescents' achievement goals: Situating motivation in sociocultural contexts*. Greenwich, CT: Information Age Publishing.

Keefe, J. W. (1979). Learning style: An overview. In J. W. Keefe (Ed.), *Student learning styles: Diagnosing and prescribing programs*. Reston, VA: National Association of Secondary School Principals.

Kiewra, K. A. (1985). Learning from a lecture: An investigation of note-taking, review and attendance at a lecture. *Human Learning: Journal of Practical Research & Applications*, *4*(1), 73–77.

Kiewra, K. A., & Benton, S. L. (1985). The effects of higher-order review questions with feedback on achievement among learners who take notes or receive the instructor's notes. *Human Learning: Journal of Practical Research & Applications*, *4*(3), 225–231.

Kiewra, K. A., Mayer, R. E., Christensen, M., Kim, S. and Risch (1991). Effects of repetition on recall and note-taking: Strategies for learning from lectures. *Journal of Educational Psychology*, *83*(1), 20–123.

King, N. J., Mietz, A., Tinney, L., & Ollendick, T. H. (1995). Psychopathology and cognition in adolescents experiencing severe test anxiety. *Journal of Clinical Child Psychology, 24*(1), 49–54.

Kleinheksel, K. A., & Summy, S. E. (2003). Enhancing student learning and social behavior through mnemonic strategies. *Teaching Exceptional Children, 36*(2), 30–35.

Krapp, J. V. (1988). Teaching research skills: A critical-thinking approach. *School Library Journal, 34*(5), 32–35.

Macan, T. H., Shahani, C., Dipboye, R. L., & Phillips, A. P. (1990). College students' time management correlations with academic performance and stress. *Journal of Educational Psychology, 82*(4), 760–768.

MacArthur, C., & Graham, S. (1987). Learning disabled students' composing with three methods: Handwriting, dictation, and word processing. *Journal of Special Education, 21,* 22–42.

Marsh, H. W. (1990). Causal ordering of academic self-concept and academic achievement: A multiwave, longitudinal panel analysis. *Journal of Educational Psychology, 82*(4), 646–656.

Mastropieri, M. A., & Scruggs, T. E. (1992). Science for students with disabilities. *Review of Educational Research, 62*(4), 377–411.

Mastropieri, M. A., & Scruggs, T. E. (1997). Best practices in promoting reading comprehension in students with learning disabilities: 1976 to 1996. *RASE: Remedial and Special Education, 18*(4), 197–214.

Mastropieri, M. A., & Scruggs, T. E. (1998). Enhancing school success with mnemonic strategies. *Intervention in School and Clinic, 33*(4), 201–208.

Mayer, R. E. (1987). Instructional variables that influence cognitive processes during reading. In B. K. Britton & S. M. Glynn (Eds.), *Executive control processes in reading* (pp. 201–216). Hillsdale, NJ: Erlbaum.

McKeachie, W. J. (1984). Does anxiety disrupt information processing or does poor information processing lead to anxiety? *International Review of Applied Psychology, 33,* 187–203.

Millman, J., Bishop, C. H., & Ebel, R. (1965). An analysis of test-wiseness. *Educational and Psychological Measurement, 25*(3), 707–726.

Miranda, A., Villaescusa, M. I., & Vidal-Abarca, E. (1997). Is attribution retraining necessary? Use of self-regulation procedures for enhancing the reading comprehension strategies of children with learning disabilities. *Journal of Learning Disabilities, 30*(5), 503–512.

Montague, M., & Leavell, A. G. (1994). Improving the narrative writing of students with learning disabilities. *RASE: Remedial & Special Education, 15*(1), 21–33.

Naveh-Benjamin, M. (1991). A comparison of training programs intended for different types of test-anxious students: Further support for an information-processing model. *Journal of Educational Psychology, 83*(1), 134–139.

Naveh-Benjamin, M., McKeachie, W. J., & Lin, Y. (1987). Two types of test-anxious students: Support for an information processing model. *Journal of Educational Psychology, 79*(2), 131–136.

Neubert, G. A., & McNelis, S. J. (1986). Improving writing in the disciplines. *Educational Leadership, 43*(7), 54–58.

Newbegin, I., & Owens, A. (1996). Self-esteem and anxiety in secondary school achievement. *Journal of Social Behavior and Personality, 11*(3), 521–530.

Pajares, F., & Urdan, T., Eds. (2002). *Academic motivation of adolescents.* Greenwich, CT: Information Age Publishing.

Paris, S. G., Lipson, M. Y., & Wixson, K. K. (1983). Becoming a strategic reader. *Contemporary Educational Psychology, 8*(3), 293–316.

Paris, S. G., & Winegrad, P. (1990). Dimensions of thinking and cognitive intervention. In B. F. Jones & L. Idol (Eds.), *How metacognition can promote academic learning and instruction* (pp. 15–51). Hillsdale, NJ: Erlbaum.

Pearson, P. D., Johnson, D. D. (1978). *Teaching Reading Comprehension.* New York: Holt, Rinehart Winston.

Peverly, S. T., Brobst, K. E., Graham, M., & Shaw, R. (2003). College adults are not good at self-regulation: A study on the relationship of self-regulation, note taking, and test taking. *Journal of Educational Psychology, 95*(2), 335–346.

Pintrich, P. R. (2000). The role of goal orientation in self-regulated learning. In M. Boekaerts, P. R. Pintrich, & M. Zeidner (Eds.), *Handbook of self-regulation* (pp. 451–502), San Diego: Academic Press.

Pintrich, P. R., & De Groot, E. V. (1990). Motivational and self-regulated learning components of classroom academic performance. *Journal of Educational Psychology, 82,* 33–40.

Pintrich, P., Smith, D. E., Garcia, T., & McKeachie, W. (1991). *A manual for the use of the Motivated Strategies for Learning Questionnaire (MSLQ).* Ann Arbor, MI: The Regents of the University of Michigan.

Porte, L. K. (2001). Cut and paste 101: New strategies for note-taking and review. *Teaching Exceptional Children, 34*(2), 14–20.

Powers, S. W., Vanetta, K., Noll, R. B., Cool, V. A., & Stehbens, J. A. (1995). Leukemia and other childhood cancers. In M. C. Roberts (Ed.), *Handbook of pediatric psychology* (2nd ed., pp. 310–326). New York: The Guilford Press.

Pressley, M., Tanenbaum, R., McDaniel, M. A., & Wood, E. (1990). What happens when university students try to answer prequestions that accompany textbook material? *Contemporary Educational Psychology*, *15*(1), 27–35.

Prins, P. J., Groot, M. J., & Hanewald, G. J. (1994). Cognition in test-anxious children: The role of on-task and coping cognition reconsidered. *Journal of Consulting and Clinical Psychology*, *62*(2), 404–409.

Purdie, N., Hattie, J., & Douglas, G. (1996). Student conceptions of learning and their use of self-regulated learning strategies: A cross-cultural comparison. *Journal of Educational Psychology*, *88*(1), 87–100.

Quarton, B. (2003). Research skills and the new undergraduate. *Journal of Instructional Psychology*, *30*(2), 120–124.

Rabiner, D., & Coie, J. D. (2000). Early attention problems and children's reading achievement: A longitudinal investigation. *Journal of the American Academy of Child & Adolescent Psychiatry*, *39*(7), 859–867.

Raphael, T. E., (1986). Teaching question answer relationships, revisited. *The Reading Teacher*, *39*, 516–522.

Raphael, T. E., & Pearson, P. D. (1985). Increasing students' awareness of sources of information for answering questions. *American Educational Research Journal*, *22*, 217–233.

Reynolds, C. R., & Kamphaus, R. W. (1992). *Behavior assessment system for children: BASC*. Circle Pines, MN: American Guidance Service.

Reynolds, C. R., & Kamphaus, R. W. (2002). *Reynolds intellectual assessment scales*. Lutz, FL: Par, Inc.

Reynolds, C. R., & Kamphaus, R. W. (2004). *Behavior Assessment System for Children–Second edition: BASC-2*. Circle Pines, MN: American Guidance Service.

Reynolds, C. R., & Richmond, B. O. (1985). *Revised Children's Manifest Anxiety Scale*. Los Angeles: Western Psychological Services.

Reynolds, C. R. & Voress, J. (2007). *Test of Memory and Learning—2*. Austin, TX: Pro-Ed.

Reynolds, R. E. & Shirey, L. L. (1988). The role of attention in studying and learning. In C. E. Weinstein, E. T. Goetz, & P. A. Alexander (Eds.), *Learning and study strategies: Issues in assessment, instruction, and evaluation* (pp. 77–100). San Diego: Academic Press.

Riccio, C. A., Reynolds, C. R., Lowe, P., & Moore, J. J. (2002). The continuous performance test: A window on the neural substrates for attention? *Archives of Clinical Neuropsychology*, *17*(3), 235–272.

Richards, J. H. (1987). Time management: A review. *Work & Stress*, *1*(1), 73–78.

Roberts, S. K. (2002). Taking a technological path to poetry prewriting. *Reading Teacher*, *55*(7), 678–688.

Roeser, R. W., & Galloway, M. K. (2002). *Studying motivation to learn during early adolescence: A holistic perspective*. Greenwich, CT: Information Age Publishing.

Romano, T. (1987). *Clearing the way: Working with teenage writers*. Portsmouth, NH: Heinemann Educational Books, Inc.

Rosenshine, B., Meister, C., & Chapman, S. (1996). Teaching students to generate questions: A review of the intervention studies. *Journal of Educational Research*, *66*(2), 181–221.

Samuels, S. J. (1989). Training students how to understand what they read. *Reading Psychology*, *10*(1), 1–17.

Sarason, S. B., Davidson, K., Lighthall, F., & Waite, R. (1958). A test anxiety scale for children. *Child Development*, *29*, 105–113.

Schmeck, R. R. (1988). Individual differences and learning strategies. In C. E. Weinstein, E. T. Goetz, & P. A. Alexander (Eds.), *Learning and study strategies: Issues in assessment, instruction, and evaluation* (pp. 171–192). San Diego: Academic Press.

Schumm, J. S., & Radencich, M. C. (1984). Readers'/Writers' workshops: An antidote to term paper terror. *Journal of Reading*, *28*(1), 13–19.

Schunk, D. H. (1991). Self-efficacy and academic motivation. *Educational Psychologist*, *26*(3–4), 207–231.

Schunk, D. H., & Gunn, T. P. (1985). Modeled importance of task strategies and achievement beliefs: Effects on self-efficacy and skill development. *Journal of Early Adolescence*, *5*, 247–258.

Scott, B. J., & Vitale, M. R., (2003). Teaching the writing process to students with LD. *Intervention in School & Clinic*, *38*(4), 31–42.

Scruggs, T. E., & Mastropieri, M. A. (1986). Improving the test-taking skills of behaviorally disordered and learning disabled children. *Exceptional Children*, *53*(1), 63–68.

Scruggs, T. E., & Mastropieri, M. A. (1992). *Teaching test-taking skills: Helping children show what they know*. Brookline, MA: Brookline Books.

Scruggs, T. E., & Mastropieri, M. A. (2000). The effectiveness of mnemonic instruction for students with learning and behavior problems: An update and research synthesis. *Journal of Behavioral Education*, *10*(2–3), 163–173.

Scruggs, T. E., & Tolfa, D. (1985). Improving the test-taking skills of learning-disabled students. *Perceptual & Motor Skills*, *60*(3), 847–850.

Scruggs, T. E., White, K. R., & Bennion, K. (1986). Teaching test-taking skills to elementary-grade students: A meta-analysis. *Elementary School Journal*, *87*(1), 69–82.

Shapiro, E. S., DuPaul, G. J., & Bradley-Klug, K. L. (1998). Self-management as a strategy to improve the classroom behavior of adolescents with ADHD. *Journal of Learning Disabilities*, *31*(6), 545–555.

Shaywitz, S.E., & Shaywitz, B.A. (1992). *Attention-deficit disorder comes of age*. Austin, TX: Pro-Ed.

Short, E. J., & Ryan, E. B. (1984). Metacognitive differences between skilled and less skilled readers: Remediating deficits through story grammar and attribution training. *Journal of Educational Psychology, 76*(2), 225–235.

Shrager, L., & Mayer, R. E. (1989). Note-taking fosters generative learning strategies in novices. *Journal of Educational Psychology, 81*(2), 263–264.

Slade, D. L. (1986). Developing foundations for organizational skills. *Academic Therapy, 21*(3), 261–66.

Spielberger, C. D. (1980). *Preliminary professional manual for the Test Anxiety Inventory*. Palo Alto, CA: Consulting Psychologists Press.

Spielberger, C. D., & Vagg, P. R., Eds. (1995). *Test anxiety: A transactional process model*. Philadelphia, PA: Taylor & Francis.

Stormont-Spurgin, M. (1997). I lost my homework: Strategies for improving organization in students with ADHD. *Intervention in School and Clinic, 32*(5), 270–74.

Stroud, K. C., & Reynolds, C. R. (2006). *School motivation and learning strategies inventory*. Los Angeles: Western Psychological Services.

Suritsky, S. K. (1992). Notetaking approaches and specific areas of difficulty reported by university students with learning disabilities. *Journal of Postsecondary Education and Disability, 10*, 3–10.

Sweidel, G. B. (1996). Study strategy portfolio: A project to enhance study skills and time management. *Teaching of Psychology, 23*(4), 246–248.

Teeter, P. A. (1998). *Interventions for ADHD: Treatment in developmental context*. New York: The Guilford Press.

Thomas, J. W., & Rowher, W. D. (1986). Academic studying: The role of learning strategies. *Educational Psychologist, 21*, 19–41.

Tobias, S. (1985). Test anxiety: Interference, defective skills, and cognitive capacity. *Educational Psychologist, 20*(3), 135–142.

Tompkins, G. E. (1994). *Teaching writing: Balancing process and product* (2nd ed.). New York: Macmillan.

Towns, M. H., & Robinson, W. R. (1993). Student use of test-wiseness strategies in solving multiple-choice chemistry examinations. *Journal of Research in Science Teaching, 30*(7), 709–722.

U.S. Department of Education. (1999). *Twenty-first annual report to Congress on the implementation of the Individuals with Disabilities Education Act*. Washington DC: U.S. Government Printing Office.

Vallerand, R. J., Pelletier, L. G., Blais, M. R., & Brière, N. M. (1992). The academic motivation scale: A measure of intrinsic, extrinsic, and amotivation in education. *Educational and Psychological Measurement, 52*(4), 1003–1017.

Van Overwalle, F. & De Metsenaere, M. (1990). The effects of attribution-based intervention and study strategy training on academic achievement in college freshmen. *British Journal of Educational Psychology, 60*, 299–311.

Wade, S. E. & Trathen, W. (1989). Effect of self-selected study methods on learning. *Journal of Educational Psychology, 81*(1), 40–47.

Weiner, B. (1976). Attribution theory, achievement motivation, and the educational process. *Review of Educational Research, 42*, 201–215.

Weiner, B. (1979). A theory of motivation for some classroom experiences. *Journal of Educational Psychology, 71*, 3–25.

Weiner, B. (1986). *Attribution, emotion, and action*. New York: The Guilford Press.

Weinstein, C. E. (1987). *Learning and Study Strategies Inventory (LASSI)*. Clearwater, FL: H & H Publishing.

Weinstein, C. E. (1994). Strategic learning/strategic teaching: Flip sides of a coin. In P. R. Pintrich, D. R. Brown, & C. E. Weinstein (Eds.), *Student motivation, cognition, and learning: Essays in honor of Wilbert J. McKeachie* (pp. 257–273). Hillsdale, NJ: Erlbaum.

Weinstein, C. E., & Hume, L. M. (1998). *Study strategies for lifelong learning*. Washington, DC: American Psychological Association.

Weinstein, C. E., Husman, J., & Dierking, D. R. (Eds.). (2000). Self-regulation interventions with a focus on learning strategies. In M. Boekaerts, P. R. Pintrich, & M. Zeidner (Eds.), *Handbook of self-regulation*. (pp. 727–747). San Diego: Academic Press.

Weinstein, C. E., & Mayer, R. F. (1986). The teaching of learning strategies. In M. C. Wittrock (Ed.), *Handbook of research on teaching*. New York: MacMillan.

Weinstein, C. E., Schulte, A. C., & Palmer, D. R. (1987). *LASSI: Learning and Study Strategies Inventory*. Clearwater, FL: H & H Publishing.

Weinstein, C. E. Zimmerman, S. A., and Palmer, D. R. (1988). Assessing learning strategies: The design and development of the LASSI. In C. E. Weinstein, E. T. Goetz, & P. A. Alexander (Eds.), *Learning and study strategies: issues in assessment, instruction, and evaluation* (pp. 25–40). San Diego: Academic Press.

Weissberg, M., Berentsen, M., Cote, A., Cravey, B. & Heath, K. (1982). An assessment of the personal, career, and academic needs of undergraduate students. *Journal of College Student Personnel, 23*, 115–122.

Wigfield, A., & Eccles, J. S. (1989). Test anxiety in elementary and secondary school students. *Educational Psychologist, 24*(2), 159–183.

Wigfield, A., & Tonks, S. (2002). *Adolescents' expectancies for success and achievement task values during the middle and high school years*. Greenwich, CT: Information Age Publishing.

Wilson, N. H., & Rotter, J. C. (1986). Anxiety management training and study skills counseling for students on self-esteem and test anxiety and performance. *The School Counselor*, (Sept.), 18–31.

Wine, J. (1971). Test anxiety and direction of attention. *Psychological Bulletin*, 76(2), 92–104.

Winne, P. H., & Hadwin, A. F. (Eds.). (1998). *Studying as self-regulated learning*. Mahwah, NJ: Lawrence Erlbaum Associates.

Winne, P. H., & Perry, N. E. (Eds.). (2000). *Measuring self-regulated learning*. San Diego: Academic Press.

Winograd, P., & Hare, V. C. (1988). Direct instruction of reading comprehension strategies: The nature of teacher explanation. In C. E. Weinstein, E. T. Goetz, & P. A. Alexander (Eds.), *Learning and study strategies: Issues in assessment, instruction, and evaluation*. (pp. 121–139). San Diego: Academic Press.

Zatz, S., & Chassin, S. (1983) Cognitions of test-anxious children. *Journal of Consulting and Clinical Psychology*, 51, 526–534.

Zatz, S., & Chassin, L. (1985). Cognitions of test-anxious children under naturalistic test-taking conditions. *Journal of Consulting and Clinical Psychology*, 53(3), 393–401.

Zentall, S. S., Harper, G. W., and Stormont-Spurgin, M. (1993). Children with hyperactivity and their organizational abilities. *Journal of Educational Research*, 87(2), 112–117.

Zimmerman, B. J. (1998). Academic studying and the development of personal skill: A self-regulatory perspective. *Educational Psychologist*, 33(2–3), 73–86.

Zimmerman, B. J. (2002). Achieving self-regulation: The trial and triumph of adolescence. In F. Pajares & T. Urdan (Eds.), *Academic motivation of adolescents*. Greenwich, CT: Information Age Publishing.

Zimmerman, B. J., Greenberg, D., & Weinstein, C. E. (Eds.). (1994). *Self-regulating academic study time: A strategy approach*. Hillsdale, NJ; England: Lawrence Erlbaum Associates, Inc.

Zimmerman, B. J. & Martinez-Pons, M. (1990). Student Differences in Self- Regulated Learning: Relating Grade, Sex, and Giftedness to Self-Efficacy and Strategy Use. *Journal of Educational Psychology*, 82(1), 51–59.

INTERVENTION: FOCUS ON SYSTEMS

CHAPTER 35

EFFECTIVE TEACHING AND EFFECTIVE SCHOOLS

MARIBETH GETTINGER
University of Wisconsin–Madison

KAREN STOIBER
University of Wisconsin–Milwaukee

INTRODUCTION

Education directly or indirectly affects the lives of almost everyone in contemporary society. Furthermore, schools account for a substantial proportion of both public and private expenditure. Thus, it is not surprising that there is intense interest among both researchers and policy makers in knowing the degree to which schooling is effective and how it can be improved. For decades, educational researchers have engaged in studies to identify instructional and environmental variables that contribute to effective teaching and effective schools. Specifically, researchers have sought to identify and quantify teacher and school variables that influence student achievement.

The purpose of this chapter is to summarize important findings from research on schooling conducted during the past 40 years. First, we provide a historical review of research on teaching to trace the evolution of diverse paradigms and conceptualizations of effective teaching. Second, we summarize key findings related to effective teaching and schools in six major areas of scientifically based practice. Next, we provide an overview of current reform movements in education resulting from research on effective teaching. Finally, we conclude with cautions and considerations for future directions in research and practice.

HISTORY OF RESEARCH ON EFFECTIVE TEACHING AND EFFECTIVE SCHOOLS

Empirical studies on effective teaching and effective schools have a relatively short history in educational research. In their 1974 review, Dunkin and Biddle identified four types of variables that influence the teaching-learning process; these have been the focus of the majority of research on effective teaching over the last 40 years. In Dunkin and Biddle's categorization, *presage* variables are those associated with the teacher. These include teacher characteristics such as age, sex, social class, training experiences, attitudes, beliefs, expectations, and abilities teachers bring to the teaching-learning situation. *Context* variables are attributed primarily to the students, school, or community, and, as such, are not totally under the control of the teacher. These include grade level, subject matter, class size, student diversity, and other features of the context within which teaching and learning take place. *Process* variables refer to what takes place in the classroom. They include behaviors or events that transpire during the teaching-learning process, including ways in which teachers and students behave and interact with one another. Finally, *product* variables describe the desired outcomes of education. These are the measurable indices of the outcomes of instruction, such as students' achievement, attitudes, or classroom behavior. This categorization of variables is useful for tracing the evolution of diverse paradigms for research on teaching.

Trait Theories

The earliest studies of factors associated with quality of teaching occurred during the 1950s and 1960s, and focused primarily on presage variables such as teachers' verbal ability, warmth, enthusiasm, intelligence, and appearance (Shulman, 1986). Collectively, this work contributed to "trait theories" of effective teaching. Research on teachers' personality traits and intelligence produced few consistent findings, with the exception of studies finding a recurring positive relationship between student learning and teachers' creativity and, to a lesser extent, verbal ability (Darling-Hammond, 1999). Most trait theories are no longer of interest in research on teaching; however, investigators have demonstrated a renewed interest in other types of presage variables. In particular, researchers increasingly argue that teaching is a form of expert work which requires extensive professional preparation, strong subject-matter knowledge, and a variety of pedagogical skills, all of which are necessary to be effective in the complex and dynamic environment of classrooms (Borko, 2004; Darling-Hammond, Wise, & Klein, 1995). This contemporary view that teaching requires expert pedagogical knowledge has encouraged researchers, once again, to investigate the effects of presage variables (i.e., teacher expert knowledge) on student achievement.

Process-Product Research

A process-product, or process-outcome, approach to the study of teaching was initiated during the late 1960s, partly in response to a perceived overemphasis on presage variables in early research on teaching. Process-product research increased significantly throughout the 1970s and 1980s (Hoffman, 1986). During this time, researchers concentrated on identifying teacher actions or school characteristics (processes) linked directly to student learning and behavior (products or outcomes).

Two forms of process-outcome research were prominent during the 1970s (Brophy, 1997). The first was school-effects research, initiated primarily in reaction to the national Coleman report (Coleman et al., 1966), which concluded that family background factors, such as poverty level, were the major determinants of student achievement. Claiming that schools *do* make a difference in predicting student achievement, school-effects researchers sought to identify system-level characteristics of schools that were successful in promoting high achievement and positive classroom behavior among students (Rutter & Maughan, 2002). Correlates of effective schools include schoolwide variables that relate to positive student outcomes, such as strong administrative leadership; positive teacher attitudes; safe, orderly school environments; and communication among

school, home, and community (Bickel, 1999). The results from this research contributed significantly to school improvement and reform efforts during the 1990s (Lezotte, 1997; Mortimore, 1998).

The second type of process-outcome research initiated during the 1970s was teacher-effects research. Similar to school-effects research, this work sought to describe teacher behaviors and patterns of teacher-student interactions associated with student performance. Using primarily teacher observation instruments and measures of student achievement, researchers identified specific skills or behaviors exhibited among teachers who were effective in promoting high student performance (Good, 1996). The results of this process-product tradition yielded findings that continue to influence teaching and teacher education today.

The primary goal of process-outcome research is to determine relationships between classroom processes and student performance, with the intent of identifying teaching practices or school variables associated with students' learning and appropriate classroom behavior. Early process-outcome research focused primarily on overt, low-inference teacher behaviors, and the relation between the frequency of these behaviors and measurable student outcomes. Although more recent research has included additional process measures such as high-inference ratings, teacher interviews, and narrative recordings, variables quantified through low-inference coding procedures are more prominent in published reports because they typically demonstrate the strongest association with student outcomes (Floden, 2001).

Process-product research can be characterized on the basis of several methodological features (Hoffman, 1986; Shulman, 1986). In a prototypical study, teachers are observed at work in their classrooms. Teaching and classroom interactions are described in a series of low-inference behavioral categories, often mutually exclusive and exhaustive, such that any classroom event may be coded in one and only one way. Which teaching processes to observe are often predetermined on the basis of extant research or hypothesized relationships. For example, if growth in reading comprehension is an expected outcome, the researcher may select levels of teacher questioning as one process to observe. In this instance, the researcher attempts to discover the degree to which certain kinds of teacher questions relate to growth in reading comprehension. Coded frequencies of behaviors are aggregated across teachers, and then correlated with student achievement measures. Relationships between patterns of teaching behaviors and student outcomes are determined statistically by correlating process variables that depict what occurs during teaching (teacher behaviors, teaching methods, teacher-student interactions) with specific products or learner outcomes, such as performance on achievement tests. In this regard, effective teaching means engaging in behaviors that match as closely as possible a list of prescriptive approaches (Richardson, 1994).

Despite important contributions to an understanding of effective teaching, process-outcome research has been criticized on multiple grounds (Gage & Needels, 1989). Many critics believe that a process-outcome perspective perpetuates a mechanistic conceptualization of the teaching-learning process, i.e., that teaching is "acting out" a set of predetermined behaviors. They contend that process-outcome research views teaching as a linear activity, such that if a teacher performs certain actions, then students will achieve high outcomes. Similarly, process-outcome research has been criticized because it fails to take into account important context variables relating to both teaching and student outcomes, such as students' social class and ability level, as well as instructional features such as the degree of teacher- versus student-initiated learning, nature of tasks (new information versus recitation and drill), and context within which feedback occurs (e.g., following correct, incorrect, versus no response). A search for universal process-product relationships may disregard important presage and context variables. Indeed, the generality of any process-outcome relationship is variable. Some findings may have wide generality, whereas others may be specific to particular grade levels or types of students. Furthermore, the stability of classroom process measures from one observation to another may depend as much on the context as on observer accuracy. Thus, process-product research, by necessity, is confined to specific classroom contexts.

The most critical concerns with process-outcome research relate to how findings have been interpreted and utilized, *not* the manner in which the research has been conducted. Some school districts, for example, provide professional development based on limited results of process-outcome research and have attempted to translate research findings directly into instruments for evaluating teachers. Such efforts represent a misapplication of process-outcome research and tend to enforce a prescriptive set of uniform teaching behaviors with limited regard to diverse content, curriculum or student ability (Good, 1996; Richardson, 1994). Even process-outcome researchers agree that the application of findings should avoid an oversimplification of results and naïve misuse by policymakers, particularly because different teaching behaviors may lead to similar student outcomes. Data linking specific teaching behaviors to student performance ought not to be the sole basis for teacher evaluation. For example, in some classrooms, students demonstrate above-average math achievement even when high levels of off-task talking and behavior are coded during independent math work periods. In this case, teachers should not be penalized for failing to follow behavioral prescriptions derived from process-outcome research to increase observed rates of on-task behavior.

Interpretive Paradigm

Due to concerns surrounding a narrow application of process-product findings, combined with an expanding focus on context variables and growing emphasis on teaching for understanding, the 1980s and 1990s witnessed the emergence of an alternate research paradigm. Referred to as the interpretive paradigm, this line of inquiry focused on understanding the complexity of teachers' actions, their interactions with students, and diverse teaching-learning contexts (Shulman, 1986). The shift away from a strict process-product paradigm was catalyzed, in part, by concerns that process-product relationships failed to reflect the dynamic nature of classroom contexts. Within an interpretive perspective, the key to effective teaching is to encourage students to develop knowledge by allowing them to see how new ideas help them make better sense of their world (Edelson, 2001). Merely contradicting students' ideas or giving them correct answers is not sufficient for learning to occur. Interpretive researchers focus on indicators of effectiveness that are context-specific (e.g., teachers' decision making within content-specific domains) and utilize measures of higher-order outcomes that go beyond what can be observed or measured on a standardized test (e.g., students' problem solving). For example, within an interpretive approach, teachers may be interviewed about their thinking while engaged in lesson planning, and students are asked to describe their approaches to solving problems or learning concepts.

Embedded in the interpretive paradigm are descriptive approaches to understanding classroom life. Researchers have relied predominantly on qualitative or case-study methodology to build a rich knowledge of teaching that considers learning in different contexts and subject domains, and examines the role of teachers' planning, beliefs, and decision making. Researchers focus on teachers' thinking and how they accommodate diverse learners or domain-specific content. Effective teaching typically involves adaptive teaching (rather than adherence to a prescribed teaching method) that facilitates students' understanding of academic content and application of knowledge. According to Shulman (1986), the changes introduced by interpretive researchers were more than methodological; rather, a conceptual shift in the focus of inquiry and the conceptualization of effective teaching was evident. What interpretive researchers have uncovered is that teaching for understanding does not follow a step-by-step prescriptive package. Rather, teaching requires sophisticated knowledge and expertise (Brophy, 1997). These findings highlight the importance of being able to understand diverse characteristics of learners and educational contexts. Interpretive researchers examine how teachers make sense of their students and their classrooms and, in so doing, advocate student-centered pedagogy (Driver, Aasoko, Leach, Mortimer & Scott, 1999). Within an interpretive framework, effective teachers are those who engage students in meaningful tasks that allow them to make choices. They use students' strengths as a point of entry for enhancing motivation and interest in learning, while challenging students with projects and concepts about which to think. This conception of teaching as a complex task and nonlinear process of many overlapping demands, constraints, and opportunities, represents the most important contribution of interpretive research during the 1980s and 1990s.

Contemporary Constructs

Efforts to ensure learner-responsive teaching in schools have shaped research on effective teaching and effective schools since the 1990s. Although contemporary research builds on established results which indicate that teachers and schools play a vital role in promoting learning, it places greater emphasis on the role of students, the social context of teaching and learning, and the importance of accommodating diverse learning needs. Within contemporary views of effective

teaching, teachers are required to possess a deep understanding of student learning, to be flexible and responsive to individual differences, and to have knowledge of scientifically based practices. In addition, they must possess a capacity for critical analysis of classrooms to prioritize goals for each teaching situation. In many ways, the concept of effective teaching has been replaced with the notion of expert teaching (Darling-Hammond, 1999). Expert teachers are able to implement teaching methods that build on students' background knowledge and promote understanding, while also strengthening skills and competence. Several new variables have emerged in recent research that reflect the notion of expert teaching, including responsiveness to cultural and ability differences, monitoring of students' progress, and evidence-based practice (Ellis, Farmer, & Newman, 2005). Each variable, in turn, has contributed to the development of school reform initiatives, to be described later.

FINDINGS FROM RESEARCH ON EFFECTIVE TEACHING AND EFFECTIVE SCHOOLS

Our knowledge about effective teaching and effective schools has expanded significantly since the 1960s; however, the complexities of the teaching-learning process are such that there is variability across classrooms and schools in the implementation of practices that contribute to student achievement. Nonetheless, researchers have been successful in identifying critical teaching and school variables that contribute to positive student outcomes, academic as well as social. In the following sections we examine six areas of effective teaching, including teacher behaviors, teacher beliefs, grouping strategies, motivation, self-regulated learning, and schoolwide characteristics.

Teaching Behaviors and Classroom Practices

Research on effective teaching underscores the importance of teaching behaviors, as well as environmental and instructional variables, in promoting students' success in school. Regardless of the context in which it occurs, teaching that has a positive influence on student achievement incorporates four key components: (a) high student engagement; (b) teacher-directed instruction; (c) guided practice and feedback; and (d) effective classroom management.

Student Engagement

One of the most highly researched aspects of effective teaching and effective schools is student engagement, or time on task. The amount of time students spend actively engaged in learning is a strong determinant of achievement. In 1963, John Carroll expressed the relationship of time and learning in an equation wherein the degree of learning is a function of the ratio of time spent relative to time needed. According to Carroll's model, the closer students come to achieving equilibrium between time spent and time needed, the higher their degree of learning. Few, if any, learners spend exactly the amount of time they need to learn a particular concept or unit of information. Teachers and schools must strive to create classroom environments in which learners can maximize their learning time.

The relevant causal agent maximizing student learning is *not* the amount of time allocated to learning but rather how teachers use instructional time. Researchers have identified specific teaching behaviors and classroom practices that have the potential to increase engaged learning time (Clark & Linn, 2003). Using learning time efficiently and keeping students engaged in learning are critical, yet challenging, goals for effective classrooms. Noninstructional activities can consume up to 50% of available instructional time (Jones & Jones, 2001). Inevitably, teachers "lose" some portion of each school day to noninstructional tasks, such as procedural activities (e.g., sharpening pencils, distributing papers) and noninstructional waiting or transition time. It is possible, however, for teachers to minimize the loss of available instructional time by engaging in interactive teaching behaviors, which allow them to maintain continuous interaction with students and support engagement in learning. Examples of interactive teaching behaviors include (a) moving about the room to monitor performance and communicate awareness of students' behavior and progress; (b) using written rules and fast-paced, routinized classroom procedures to facilitate smooth transitions; and, (c) implementing proactive management methods to prevent the occurrence of disruptive behaviors that interfere with classroom learning and contribute to lost instructional time (Gettinger & Seibert, 2002).

In addition to specific teaching behaviors, the nature of teaching activities and types of instructional methods are related to high engagement among students. For example, high-participation formats that encourage active responding, such as discussion, group problem-solving activities, cooperative learning, and peer-assisted learning, are more strongly associated with student engagement than low-participation activities, such as reading silently, listening or watching other students, or working alone (Gettinger & Seibert, 2002). Frequent teacher-directed questioning and student responding are also associated with high levels of engagement, especially in the acquisition of basic arithmetic and reading skills (Phillips, Fuchs, Fuchs, & Hamlett, 1996). Effective teachers ask many questions to sustain active student involvement and time on task. In a study of junior high school mathematics and English instruction, for example, the most effective teachers (i.e., high levels of student engagement and achievement) asked an average of 24 questions during a 50-minute period, whereas the least effective teachers asked an average of only 8.6 questions (Evertson, Anderson, Anderson, & Brophy, 1980).

Teacher-Directed Instruction

Research has consistently documented a strong connection between teacher-directed instruction and student achievement and learning behaviors (Leinhardt, 1992; Good & Brophy, 2000). Teacher-directed instruction occurs when teachers spend significant time in any format that directly teaches students (e.g., lecturing, demonstrating, leading discussions) in contrast to teaching routines in which students work independently or are engaged in nonacademic work. The concept of teacher-directed instruction is generic in that such teaching looks similar across academic subjects and positively affects student achievement across a range of grade levels and subject areas. At the same time, however, the concept of teacher-directed instruction does not imply that one particular instructional format, such as lecture and demonstration, is generally more effective than another. In fact, the particular method a teacher uses to provide instruction is not as critical as the teacher simply being an active agent of instruction. Three instructional features are most characteristic of teacher-directed instruction: (a) instructional clarity; (b) academic focus; and (c) opportunity to learn.

Instructional clarity relates to how teachers organize academic content and the degree to which achievement expectations are communicated and understood by learners. High clarity is achieved when explanations of content proceed in a step-by-step fashion; illustrations and applications of content are provided; and, questions are posed to assess, develop, and extend students' understanding (Good & Brophy, 2000). Clear instruction also contributes to higher-order learning and helps students make connections among ideas, both within and across lessons. Whether in textbooks or through teacher presentations, information is easier to learn when it is coherent, i.e., the sequence of ideas makes sense and the relationships among ideas are explicit. Lessons in which students perceive linkages among concepts (through using advance organizers, highlighting connections, or summarizing key concepts) contribute to better understanding, retention, and application of knowledge compared to lessons in which these interconnections are not explicit (Suppovitz, 2001).

Academic focus, the second characteristic of teacher-directed instruction, refers to the degree to which teaching is oriented toward maximizing students' opportunities to learn and the extent to which lessons and activities are related to learning goals (Schuell, 1996). In general, students learn more when the majority of available instructional time is allocated to curriculum-related activities and when the classroom management system is effective in maintaining engagement in those activities. Students of effective teachers spend more hours each year on curriculum-related activities than do students of teachers who are less focused on academic goals (Waxman, Huang, Anderson, & Weinstein, 1997). Teachers with a strong academic focus also convey a sense of purposefulness and importance for maximizing the effectiveness of available time. For example, they begin and end lessons on time, teach students how to get started on activities quickly, and maintain students' focus when working on assignments through cuing, questioning, or redirecting (Fuchs, Fuchs, & Phillips, 1994).

Finally, effective teachers and schools are clearly oriented toward maximizing students' opportunity to learn (OTL). Teachers who maximize OTL incorporate systematic, goal-oriented activities; provide lessons and content related to attaining specific learning goals; and make a variety of learning materials easily accessible to all learners. They also emphasize in-depth content coverage, or a focus on "big ideas" (Kameenui & Carnine, 1998). The degree of overlap between content covered in a classroom and content tested is a consistent predictor of student achievement scores (Stedman, 1997). Recently, Gamoran, Porter, Smithson, and White (1997) assessed curriculum coverage on two dimensions—what topics are covered and, for each topic, the level of cognitive demand (i.e., rating of the complexity of work students are required to undertake in studying the topic). These researchers found that the addition of a cognitive-demand dimension to the topic-covered dimension increased the power of measures of content coverage to predict student achievement.

Guided Practice and Feedback

Effective teaching incorporates guided student practice and performance feedback. The primary purpose of guided practice is to scaffold students' learning and sustain task engagement. In using guided practice, teachers incorporate multiple and varied opportunities for students to apply new knowledge, and they provide error-correction and reteaching as needed (Rosenshine & Meister, 1992). Skills that are practiced to the point of automaticity are more easily retained and applied more successfully than skills that are mastered only partially. Thus, effective teachers incorporate periodic practice and review, and provide opportunities for students to use knowledge and skills in a variety of application contexts.

How teachers guide student practice is also linked to student performance. The effectiveness of practice is enhanced when teachers first explain the work and demonstrate practice examples before releasing students to work independently. Effective teachers then circulate to monitor progress and provide help when needed. Guided practice involves providing assistance that students need to engage in learning activities productively and independently, including explanations, modeling, coaching, and other forms of scaffolding. It also involves a systematic and gradual diminishing of teacher guidance as students' competence develops (Rosenshine & Meister, 1992).

Finally, to be useful, guided practice must involve opportunities not only to apply skills, but also receive timely feedback. The mere repetition of tasks by students is unlikely to lead to sustained learning or deep understanding of content. Effective use of guided practice relies on frequent assessments of students' understanding and their ability to apply skills or strategies, combined with feedback that is informative, rather than evaluative. Such feedback helps students evaluate their progress relative to goals and to correct errors or misunderstanding. Although students perform better and are more engaged in classrooms in which they receive frequent feedback about their performance, observational research reveals that teachers may not always use feedback appropriately (Kluger & DeNisi, 1996). The key to effectiveness lies in the quality rather than frequency of corrective feedback. Simply knowing whether an answer is correct or incorrect has a limited effect on learning and performance. To be effective, feedback (including praise) should incorporate (a) a high degree of specificity, with explicit reference to the standard or objective to be achieved; (b) information about accuracy, or the results achieved in meeting the standard; and (c) recommendations about alternate methods for meeting the objective. In addition, there must be time for students to reflect on the feedback they receive, to make adjustments, and to try again (Kluger & DeNisi, 1996).

Classroom Management

The fourth component of effective teaching behaviors relates to classroom management. Effective teachers have good control of their classrooms and achieve this control through several structural and organizational classroom processes that contribute to positive student outcomes, such as consistent classrooms rules and smooth transitions between activities (Rosenshine, 1997).

Classroom rules are an integral part of effective classroom management. Rules refer to general expectations or standards for classroom conduct for all students. The manner in which teachers are successful in establishing, teaching, and enforcing rules has been well documented (Evertson, 1987). First, effective teachers approach the teaching of classroom rules as systematically and methodically as teaching academic content. They explain, practice, and review classroom rules until students master them. Second, effective teachers communicate clearly to students their expectations for behavior; they provide explicit information about what "good behavior" is and how students can achieve it. Rules that are stated positively are taught and enforced more effectively than long lists of prohibited behaviors. For example, "raise your hand to speak" is preferable to "no talking" because this rule clearly explains the desired behavior and what action students should take. Furthermore, effective teachers are likely to have rules in a written form, either posted or provided to students to include in a notebook (Rhode, Jenson, & Reavis, 1993). Finally, several researchers have demonstrated that simply stating rules is ineffective in preventing problem behavior; teachers must also demonstrate a willingness

and ability to act when rules are violated (Evertson, 1987; Rhode et al., 1993). Thus, effective teachers inform students about the consequences of breaking rules, carefully monitor compliance, and enforce rule-violation consequences consistently.

More than 30 transitions occur every day in elementary classrooms, accounting for approximately 15% of classroom time (Burns, 1984). Thus, increasing compliance during transition from one task to another is particularly important for effective schools. Transitions disrupt time flow in classrooms, and disruptive behaviors increase significantly during unstructured transitions. To facilitate smooth transitions, skilled teachers foreshadow and clearly signal the onset of transitions, actively structure and orchestrate transitions, and minimize the loss of momentum during these changes in activities. Less effective managers, conversely, tend to blend activities together; they fail to monitor events during transitions and take excessive time to complete the movement between activities (Waxman et al., 1997).

Effective teachers also employ strategies to move through transitions rapidly, in ways that minimize student frustration and disruption. These include providing students with beginning-of-year instruction and practice in how to execute transition routines efficiently; training students to respond to a standard signal for initiating transitions; and, providing students with overlapping assignments in a sequence. Results from one study documented the benefits of a high-probability instructional sequence for increasing group compliance during transition periods (Ardoin, Martens, & Wolfe, 1999). This procedure involves the rapid presentation of three high-probability instructions (directives with which students are likely to comply), immediately preceding a directive with a low probability of compliance. For example, in directing students to transition to a new activity, a teacher might instruct students to "touch their head," "shake their fingers," "clap their hands," and, finally, "take out their morning calendars." According to Ardoin et al. (1999), this type of high-probability sequence increases the likelihood of compliance with low-probability directives to make transitions to academic activities.

Teacher Knowledge and Beliefs

Dissatisfaction with characterizations of effective teaching based primarily on observable behavior and classroom practices led to a surge of interest in how teachers' knowledge and beliefs also affect the teaching-learning process (Kagan, 1992; Nietfeld & Enders, 2003). Within the last decade, researchers have expanded the key components of effective teaching and effective schools to include teachers' pedagogical knowledge or expertise, as well as their beliefs about teaching and learning. Three categories of teacher knowledge and beliefs play an essential role in contributing to effective teaching: (a) confidence in one's ability to bring about positive change in students' performance; (b) scientifically based knowledge about instruction in content domains; and, (c) sophisticated awareness of students' strengths and ability to accommodate individual needs (Calderhead, 1996).

Self-Efficacy

Perhaps the most widely studied belief construct related to teaching is self-efficacy. Self-efficacy is defined as a judgment of one's ability to perform a task within a specific domain (Bandura, 1997). The study of self-efficacy in teaching has brought to light the importance of not only considering teacher behaviors, but also teachers' beliefs that they will be effective in the classroom. Teacher self-efficacy, in particular, has been shown to contribute directly to classroom teaching (Pajares, 1996). Teachers with high self-efficacy are focused on students' needs and able to accommodate students who have difficulty learning. High self-efficacy heightens teachers' commitment to instructional activities and sustains their efforts when faced with failure or disappointment. In contrast, teachers with low self-efficacy spend less time teaching subject areas in which they feel less competent, devote less time to academic content, and are less likely to persevere when students do not grasp concepts readily (Chester & Beaudin, 1996; Pajares, 1996).

Related to teacher self-efficacy is the notion of accountability. Effective schools are accountable for student learning. According to effective-schools research, schools that elicit high achievement among students have staff who accept responsibility for doing so (Lezotte, 1997). In effective schools, there is a climate of uniformly high academic expectations. Staff members believe that all students can succeed and that schools have the capability to help students achieve. Research has shown a positive association between teacher accountability and individual student performance (Rutter & Maughan, 2002). Specifically, if students do not learn something the first time,

accountable teachers teach it again; and, if the regular curriculum materials do not do the job, accountable teachers find or develop other materials that will.

Pedagogical Knowledge and Expertise

Teachers' pedagogical knowledge and expertise are central to teaching effectiveness (Ellis et al., 2005). In large-scale research, teaching expertise is often measured by reference to teachers' educational background, credentials, and years or type of experience, which are viewed as proxies for the actual knowledge and expertise teachers bring to bear in their classrooms (Rowan, Correnti, & Miller, 2002). Researchers have typically been interested in assessing whether teachers with varied levels of expertise perform differently in the classroom. Although research on the impact of teachers' qualifications and their students' academic achievement has yielded somewhat mixed results, it appears that certification status and content-domain knowledge are more powerful predictors of student achievement than overall education level (Darling-Hammond, 1999). Studies have assessed the effects of teachers' subject-matter knowledge on student achievement by examining differences in student outcomes for teachers with different academic majors. Most studies have been conducted in high schools and have shown that in classes where teachers have an academic major in the subject area being tested, students have higher achievement (Rowan et al., 2002). Similarly, the number of classes in subject-matter pedagogy taken by teachers has positive effects on high school students' achievement (Darling-Hammond et al., 1995; Monk, 1994). Finally, some research has found positive effects of direct measures of teachers' knowledge on student achievement. For example, teachers' scores on content knowledge tests are significantly correlated to students' achievement scores (Ferguson & Brown, 2000).

Classroom-based research on teachers' expertise goes beyond a concern with proxy variables to index teachers' expertise, and focuses instead on the use of observational measures to assess the extent to which teachers implement research-based instructional practice in a content domain (Baker, Gersten, Dimino, & Griffiths, 2004; Wray, Medwell, Fox, & Poulson, 2000). Teachers' ability to create classrooms that promote learning depends, in large part, on their knowledge and use of scientifically based teaching practices. Instructional interventions often go beyond their research base, such that programs may be implemented without sufficient support (Stoiber & Kratochwill, 2000). To address this concern, principles of evidence-based intervention have evolved over the last decade and provide a set of criteria for evaluating interventions. One subject domain in which scientifically based practices have been clearly delineated is reading instruction, especially early literacy development. Several comprehensive reports have synthesized the converging evidence about how literacy develops among young children and should be taught (e.g., National Reading Panel, 2000; Snow, Burns & Griffin, 1998). Collectively, these sources provide evidence that learning to read is based on the foundation skills of phonological processing, print awareness, alphabet knowledge, and oral language. Effective teachers of early literacy draw upon this expert knowledge base in providing instruction (Pressley, 2002). In sum, knowledge of scientifically based instructional approaches for a content domain is essential to effective teaching.

Accommodating Individual Learners

Finally, effective teaching is founded on an understanding of the learner. Effective teaching requires knowledge of how to represent content to different kinds of learners in ways that produce learning and extend understanding. Current research highlights the importance of teachers being able to vary their practices according to their knowledge of individual students' strengths and instructional needs. As such, effective teaching requires diverse types of knowledge on which to draw when making individual decisions about students. Successful teachers are those who are able to use a range of teaching strategies and who use a range of interactions styles, rather than a single set of teaching behaviors or classroom practices (Floden, 2001). Good teachers are good decision makers. They adjust their teaching to fit the needs of different students and the demands of different instructional goals and topics. For example, effective teachers do not rely exclusively on scripted teaching interactions, but instead individualize their curriculum materials and lesson sequences to match learner's needs (Wang, Haertel, & Walberg, 1994). Effective teachers follow a systematic, yet flexible, approach to classroom teaching. They use lecture and demonstration formats to present new information and concepts; they engage students in recitation and discussion by asking questions and providing feedback; they

adequately prepare students for independent seatwork by giving explicit instructions and modeling with practice examples; they carefully monitor students' progress during independent work periods; and, they provide appropriate feedback and reteaching when necessary.

For any type of instruction to be effective, it must be appropriate to the students' ability levels. Differentiating instruction for groups or individual students is particularly necessary when the classroom composition is heterogeneous. In general, as the heterogeneity of a classroom increases, the amount of whole-class instruction is reduced, and teachers rely more on individual assignments, peer-assisted learning, and small-group work. Daly, Martens, Kilmer, and Massie (1996) found, for example, that the greatest gains in oral reading accuracy occurred when instructional reading materials were matched to the students' skill level.

Finally, accommodating individual students involves complementary changes in teacher and student roles that occur as learning progresses. Early in the learning process, teachers assume primary responsibility for structuring learning and providing explanation, practice and scaffolding for students. As students develop greater knowledge and skills, teachers gradually release responsibility for learning to students themselves. That is, as the teaching-learning process progresses, students begin to regulate their own learning and work on tasks with increasing degrees of autonomy. The teacher continues to provide scaffolding and support as needed until students assume primary responsibility for learning (Hogan & Pressley, 1997).

Classroom Grouping Strategies

Cooperative learning is one of the best researched of all classroom practices and has gained popularity in schools in the last decade. Approximately 80% of elementary teachers and more than 60% of middle school teachers report making some sustained use of cooperative learning (Antil, Jenkins, Wayne, & Vadasy, 1997). Studies demonstrate that learners of all ages who have opportunities to work collaboratively with their peers in small groups learn faster and more efficiently, have greater retention, and feel more positive about the learning experience than if they do not participate in small-group learning (Antil et al., 1997). In contrast to competitive learning situations, cooperative learning groups are characterized by joint goals, shared resources, complementary roles among group members, and mutual rewards. Small-group learning has positive effects on both task engagement and student achievement, especially when instruction is carefully structured, individual students are accountable for performance, and a well-defined group reward system is used (Slavin, 1994). In addition, cooperative learning strategies promote student responsibility for learning.

Learning in classrooms is fundamentally a social and interactive process. The collaborative nature of inquiry—especially in math and science—is reinforced by frequent group activity in the classroom. Individuals naturally seek out others to help them solve problems and perform tasks. Students in all grade levels learn naturally from their peers, exploiting each others' skills while providing social support and assistance for students who need it. One approach that has gained considerable support in recent years that builds on the social nature of teaching and learning is classwide peer tutoring. Results from a 12-year longitudinal study demonstrate that classwide peer tutoring significantly increases students' engagement during instruction, contributes to student achievement gains, reduces the number of students needing special education services, and reduces the number of dropouts by twelfth grade (Greenwood & Delquadri, 1995). Small-group, student-centered learning also has the advantage of permitting greater opportunities for teachers to interact with individual students to maintain a strong academic focus and enable teachers to be more responsive to diversity in learners (Fuchs, Fuchs, Mathes & Simmons, 1997).

Research examining the effects of the nature of students' interaction during group learning has contributed significantly to our understanding of effective cooperative learning structures. Work by Webb and her colleagues, in particular, demonstrates that the type and quality of interaction during group learning affects student achievement (e.g., Webb, Troper, & Fall, 1995). Students who know what questions to ask and how to succeed in getting their questions answered are more likely to learn material than students who do not have skills for giving and receiving explanations. Although students benefit from both giving and receiving explanations, there is stronger evidence of achievement gains for students who give explanations. Webb et al. (1995) also found that the more students engage in finding solutions to a problem, the better their achievement. Students are motivated to provide high-quality explanations and less prone to simply

supply answers to peers when they understand that each group member is accountable for learning the content (Slavin, 1994). This suggests that both group goals and individual responsibility are important features of cooperative group work and account for the observed gains in student achievement.

Student Motivation, Self-Efficacy, and Goal Orientation

The role of motivation in education, particularly as it relates to student outcomes, has been the focus of considerable research in recent years (Otis, Grouzet, & Pelletier, 2005; Pintrich, 2003). Motivation is an important disposition that affects students' learning and thinking (Brophy, 2004). Furthermore, the construct of student motivation is essential to a discussion of effective teaching in that teachers, their instructional style, and the learning environment can either enhance or deter a student's motivation.

Research has examined two motivational components, intrinsic motivation and extrinsic motivation (Lepper, Corpus, & Iyengar, 2005). Intrinsic motivation represents engaging in behavior for no other reason than for enjoyment, interest, curiosity, or challenge. In contrast, extrinsic motivation refers to a reliance on extrinsic incentives, rewards, and contingencies. There is disagreement among scholars regarding whether and how educational approaches that emphasize extrinsic motivation, such as the use of rewards, may undermine intrinsic motivation. In recent years, a multidimensional perspective of educational motivation has emerged focusing on three forms of extrinsic motivation: (a) external regulation, (b) introjected regulation, and (c) identified regulation (Deci & Ryan, 2002). Students who are controlled by external sources, such as those who study to get a good grade, attain teacher recognition, or avoid being punished by their parents, are externally regulated. This is typically described in the literature as extrinsic motivation. With introjected regulation, students behave in a certain way because they believe this is what they must do, although it may not be what they truly want to do. An example is when a student works due to self-imposed pressure to achieve and to avoid feelings of guilt or inadequacy. Identified regulation occurs in students when they recognize that learning has advantages for them, such as making them feel important, successful, or intelligent; they choose to engage in an activity or task due to its perceived value and personal importance. Identified regulation is most closely aligned with intrinsic motivation.

An additional construct proposed by Deci and colleagues (Deci & Ryan, 2002) that has relevance for classroom learning is amotivation, which occurs when students believe that no matter what they do, it will amount to nothing. Amotivated students, similar to those described as having learned helplessness, believe they are incompetent, lack control over desired outcomes, and that outside forces are working against them (Deci & Ryan, 2002; Otis et al., 2005). Students who experience low levels of achievement and/or drop out of school are more prone to be amotivated toward education and oriented toward external regulation than are persistent, self-determined students (Vallerand, Fortier, & Guay, 1997). In contrast, students with more self-determination or intrinsic motivation demonstrate greater educational adjustment and interest in school, and they report more positive emotions in the classroom and at school (Otis et al., 2005).

More than 150 studies over the past three decades have focused on the role of rewards (praise, gold stars) as they relate to classroom learning. Recent meta-analytic reviews have identified the conditions under which rewards enhance or maintain intrinsic motivation (Cameron, Pierce, Banko, & Gear, 2005). Specifically, if a task initially is of low interest, then rewards can lead students to become interested in the task, which in turn increases intrinsic motivation and performance (Hidi, 2000). A possible interpretation of this finding is that as interest increases, individuals see themselves as being intrinsically motivated, or having self-determination. On high-interest tasks, rewards produce positive effects when provided as verbal praise for work, indicative of competence, and linked to achieving performance standards or goals.

In educational settings, rewards are typically given for task performance or for outperforming others, rather than for progress toward a learning goal or for effort. Although such use of rewards may increase one's perceived competence and self-efficacy, students may also experience these conditions as controlling. Teachers' use of rewards in the following ways increases task involvement, enhances positive evaluations of performance, and heightens perceived competence: (a) rewarding progress toward a valued goal and not merely task completion; (b) clearly defining the desired behavior to be rewarded; and, (c) focusing on quality of performance and on purposeful learning.

Researchers have consistently demonstrated a positive relation between intrinsic motivation and student performance, both in class and on standardized outcome measures (Lepper et al., 2005). Being interested and actively engaged in learning, which typically occurs when students are intrinsically motivated, contributes to higher achievement. Unfortunately, research has documented a steady decline in intrinsic motivation as students progress through elementary and secondary school (Gottfried, Fleming, & Gottfried, 2001), suggesting a progressive erosion of their positive academic beliefs and interest in school. Gottfried et al. found that students from 9 to 17 years old showed gradual decreases in intrinsic motivation for reading, math and science. Pajares and Graham (1999) found a similar developmental trend for students' perceptions of the importance they attach to subject areas, with decreases for math across first through twelfth grade. Interestingly, researchers have also observed that starting in third grade there is a linear increase in students reporting a desire for easy work, which may suggest that students gradually adopt a work-avoidance orientation. Children who report a desire for easy work and to please their teachers perform more poorly on standardized achievement and classroom assessment measures (Ginsburg & Bronstein, 1993).

Another key construct for understanding student motivation is students' self-efficacy beliefs or perceptions of competence (Bandura, 1997). Similar to findings from research on teachers' self-efficacy beliefs, there is a positive association between self-efficacy and school success among students (Wilkins, 2004). Indeed, students' self-efficacy can be as powerful as cognitive ability in predicting achievement (Pajares & Kranzler, 1995). As students engage in tasks and self-reflect, they evaluate their competence by comparing their progress to their goals. Self-evaluations of positive progress enhance motivation and lead to sustained engagement. Based on their self-evaluations, students decide whether to continue with the same goals, modify their goals, or establish new ones. Although self-efficacy predicts students' motivation, effective learning does not necessarily require one's efficacy to be extremely high. According to Schunk (2003), having some level of doubt about one's capacity to achieve can mobilize effort and lead to better use of strategies than when overly confident. Low self-efficacy, however, is clearly detrimental to learning.

Even when students perceive themselves to be competent in school tasks, they may not be motivated to engage in schoolwork in a manner that promotes their deep understanding and learning. Students adopt one of two goal orientations as they approach tasks, mastery or performance goal orientation. Whereas a mastery orientation reflects a focus on learning and improving, a performance orientation reflects a focus on besting others or demonstrating one's competence. In general, mastery goals tend to be associated with positive learner dispositions, such as cognitive engagement and achievement; in contrast, students with personal performance goals show more maladaptive motivational and learning behavior patterns.

Students' decisions to pursue particular types of achievement goals depend, at least in part, on the perceived goal structures in the learning environment (Bong, 2005). Students perceive mastery goal structures in classrooms where student investment in effort is valued and understanding of material is emphasized over test scores. When teachers emphasize performance evaluation and when students are evaluated against their peers, students tend to pursue performance-oriented goals. Students with performance-approach goals strive to demonstrate their competencies, whereas those with performance-avoidance goals seek to conceal their relative incompetence and avoid help-seeking as it suggests failure. Students with a performance-approach orientation may switch to performance-avoidance goals if learning becomes too challenging and achievement is unsatisfactory. In the long run, therefore, adopting performance-approach goals can have a negative impact on student motivation and efficacy.

Most agree that a goal of education is for children to come to school eager to enjoy learning, feeling capable of mastering challenges, and able to sustain active engagement in tasks. Together the research on motivation, self-efficacy, and goal orientation provides support for several key instructional characteristics. First, teachers should help students feel autonomous and develop a sense of self-determination by providing opportunities for students to make choices and to guide their own learning. Teachers can facilitate students' personal control when they (a) recognize students for learning and improving; (b) emphasize intrinsic reasons for learning rather than stress performance outcomes such

as grades; (c) select and assign activities that are varied and include novel, interesting, fantasy, and game-like characteristics; (d) ask students to perform authentic tasks with an intermediate level of difficulty or challenge; (e) assign project-based and hands-on activities of personal relevance that result in completion of a meaningful product; and (f) provide feedback that is informational as opposed to evaluative (Brophy, 2004). The goal of such strategies is to promote motivation and to foster the belief among students that they have control of their learning.

Finally, as schools become more accountable for positive student outcomes, there is increasing emphasis on enhancing students' motivation by addressing their affective needs. The underlying assumption is that students are more likely to thrive in schools in which they feel they belong and have a sense of connection. Teachers can enhance student learning by balancing children's fundamental needs for autonomy and competence with their need to feel connected. Effective teachers and schools emphasize personalization, or the goal of "knowing students well." Several leaders in effective schooling practices propose that knowing students well is second only to autonomy in fostering student success (Cotton, 2001). The strategy of placing children in classrooms with small class size or in smaller high schools is not enough. Rather, teachers need to implement strategies that enable them to know their students well, including (a) making personal, positive contact on a daily basis (e.g., warmly greeting students with their name as they arrive); (b) fostering an inviting and caring classroom environment; (c) incorporating opportunities for peer connections through peer coaching, peer tutoring and cooperative groups; (d) closely monitoring students' progress toward curriculum goals as well as their affective status; and (e) providing social supports and interventions as needed. In addition to promoting individualized knowledge of students and higher student retention, a focus on personalization has been linked to increases in school safety and decreases in misbehavior (Cotton, 2001).

Self-Regulation and Strategic Learning

Most educational scholars and practitioners agree that students who self-regulate and engage in effective problem solving usually attain educational success (Schunk, 2005). Self-regulation refers to an individual's active involvement in generating goals; monitoring and evaluating their own progress toward acquiring knowledge, skill, or information; and adjusting purposeful actions for meeting goals (Schunk, 2005; Zimmerman, 2001).

Self-regulated learners are metacognitively aware of what they are doing and whether the strategies they have deployed will lead to goal attainment. Consider the middle school student who wants an "A" in social studies, but realizes after the first few exams that his approach to studying is likely to result in a lower grade. If the student is confident in his ability to do better, he might self-regulate by monitoring whether information is being understood during teacher instruction, seeking assistance from the teacher or a peer tutor, or reviewing notes taken during class. These self-regulation strategies may boost the student's odds of reaching the goal. If the student's initial efforts at making improved progress fail, he may readjust the original goal to a grade of "B." Self-regulation may also involve raising one's standards after experiencing early success if the student initially established modest goals. In this case, the student constructs a new challenge that is aligned with performance feedback. In these sequences of regulation, the student may begin by regulating effort, and then regulate the goal standard itself or vice versa. Thus, self-regulated students approach tasks with confidence, diligence, and resourcefulness, as well as flexibility in altering their effort, learning strategies, and goals as they receive feedback about goal attainment.

Effective teaching involves promoting students' strategic use of self-regulation. Three instructional components help students self-regulate: (a) modeling, (b) goal setting, and (3) self-monitoring (Schunk, 2003). Modeling informs how and why students should be cognitively engaged. Models provide useful, and often step-by-step, information about what actions will likely lead to success and, conversely, which ones will produce undesirable consequences. For modeling to be effective, students must attend to the model, code the presented information (retain it), be capable of performing it, and be motivated. Cognitive modeling, which involves modeled explanations for actions along with verbalizations of one's thoughts or reasons for performing the action, is considered especially effective when teaching new skills, concepts, or for demonstrating problem-solving skills (Schunk, 2003). When modeling, it is helpful to highlight the functional

value of an action, such as leading to a positive outcome. In addition, when models are perceived as relevant or similar to the student, they help the student form appropriate expectancies. Thus, under certain instructional conditions, peer models may be more potent in producing desirable effects than teacher models.

Goal setting is the second component of self-regulation. Stated simply, goals establish direction for learning. As noted previously, there are multiple types of achievement goals, that is, mastery, performance-approach, and performance-avoidance goals. Students sometimes pursue more than one goal at a time, for example, to learn new information, satisfy curiosity, and obtain a good grade; therefore, they may need to regulate multiple goals. In addition, goals can be short-term (e.g., attend to the teacher for 5 minutes) or distal (e.g., outperform all other students on a test). As short-term proximal goals can be achieved more quickly, they may enhance efficacy and motivation toward related, future-oriented goals. There is support for students developing subgoals (e.g., understanding information presented in a daily reading assignment) within the framework of a larger goal (e.g., read an entire book). Short-term goals are typically necessary for young children who cannot yet represent distal outcomes in thought.

Although it is important for teachers to set goals for students, goals should not be at a level of specificity that fails to accommodate the learner's constructivist nature. The difficulty level of a goal is an important consideration in that students expend greater effort to attain challenging goals than easier ones. The most appropriate goals are those students perceive as moderately difficult; reaching such goals conveys a clear sense of accomplishment and raises one's efficacy. For learners to evaluate their progress, they need to receive feedback about progress toward goals. Such feedback is especially important for reading and writing, areas in which students often struggle to "see" their own improvement or determine appropriate benchmarks (Schunk, 2003). The most useful feedback is informative and timely (i.e., the greater the delay in feedback the less improvement in achievement), and should involve opportunities for the student to achieve mastery to a specific criterion.

Self-monitoring or self-evaluation, the third component of self-regulation, increases active engagement and academic productivity. Self-monitoring typically involves periodically assessing one's skill level or progress toward a goal or knowledge acquisition. For this to occur, performance benchmarks need to be clear to the student. Effective teachers provide prompts or cues for students to self-assess as well as standards to gauge their goal progress. Students should be encouraged to record their own progress since the perception of progress in learning is crucial for sustaining active engagement and positive motivation. Students typically need to be taught self-evaluation strategies, for example, how to complete a scale on which they rate a behavior or check off the problem-solving steps followed. It is typically beneficial for students to discuss their self-ratings with teachers or peers, who provide productive feedback. Teaching students strategies for self-evaluation is an important skill for continued learning because it contributes to both effective problem solving and content-specific learning.

School-Level Characteristics

The passage of the No Child Left Behind Act (NCLB) requires states to have in place a system of accountability that includes large-scale assessment, graduation rates, and other indicators of student success. With the current movement for greater accountability and student success, hundreds of schools are being identified as not making adequate yearly progress (AYP) and needing improvement. Even generally high-performing American schools have gaps in their capacity to meet the needs of all students, and for various reasons, have not effectively prepared students with the social, academic, and long-term readiness skills needed for making productive contributions. As the focus on school improvement has gained more visibility through NCLB, so has the press to design and implement school-level educational improvement plans.

Recent estimates indicate that some 4 million American children attend over 8,000 public schools that are not educating students at expected levels (Brady, 2003). Some states estimate that 40% or more of their schools are low performing (Brady; U.S. Department of Education, 2003). The need for school improvement efforts are indicated at all levels. For example, a recent study of Head Start indicated that most staff could not define research-based markers of early literacy (e.g., phonemic awareness) and typically spend less than 10 minutes each day engaged in storytelling activities, which is viewed as the single most effective practice to promote early literacy. Of approximately 16,000 high schools nationwide, recent data indicated that approximately 2,100 high schools promoted fewer than 60% of their students to twelfth grade on time (U.S. Department of Education, 2003). Poverty does not constitute the cause of low performance; more than 4,500 high-poverty and high-minority schools across the U.S. also are high performing (U.S. Department of Education, 2003). In that causes for low-performing schools are complex, solutions must take a comprehensive and research-based approach.

A starting place for determining school improvement strategies is to examine the characteristics of highly effective schools. In *No Excuses: Lessons from 21 High-Performing, High-Poverty Schools*, Carter (2000) outlined seven common traits of effective schools: (a) principals who have the freedom to allocate their resources; (b) principals who establish a culture of achievement through the use of measurable goals; (c) presence of master teachers who model and bring out the best in other staff; (d) rigorous and regular assessment focused on continuous student achievement; (e) principals who promote parent involvement so as to make homes centers of learning; (f) a clear focus on achievement; and (g) commitment and hard work by all school staff and students. Whereas such characteristics can be identified and described, it is much more difficult to transform low-performing schools into high-performing schools. Furthermore, although some turnaround efforts have improved schools, success is not the norm. Rather, most school-level improvement efforts yield a success rate of less than 50% (Brady, 2003). Brady reviewed more than 100 sources of data (e.g., books, journal articles, research reports) to compile school improvement approaches that are effective. Among some 17 intervention approaches that emerged, no strategy was found to be markedly better than another in terms of overall effectiveness. Rather, what appears to be most important is to create an improvement focus that can be supported and sustained by a critical group of stakeholders. Examples of effective school improvement efforts include reorganizing the school, providing tutoring, extending school time, providing professional development, and developing school improvement plans. Different types and levels of intensity for such improvement efforts are indicated based on the degree to which a school is considered to be low performing.

Although no particular school improvement effort alone leads to a high success rate, Brady

(2003) found that strong *school leadership* was a common component across schools that have undertaken successful turnaround efforts. Thus, strong school leadership emerges as a key characteristic of positive change. In addition, the literature indicates that committed, high-quality, energized staff, who collaboratively support high learner expectations, is another key component of excellence in schools (Borman, Hewes, Overman, & Brown, 2002).

School climate also emerges as a critical indicator of school effectiveness (Freiberg, 1999). School climate generally refers to the degree to which the school environment feels "welcoming" or "inviting." More specifically, school climate is conceptualized as (a) the quality of interpersonal relations between students and teachers, (b) the extent to which the school is perceived as safe and caring, and (c) the collaborative nature of school decisions. Schools that create more positive learning environments through implementing universal intervention approaches, such as positive behavior support programs, have been shown to promote better student performance outcomes (e.g., fewer disciplinary problems, increased instructional time) (Bohanon et al., 2006; Leedy, Bates, & Safran, 2004; Nelson, Martella, Marchand-Martella, 2002). School size and class size have also been linked to school climate and achievement outcomes (Blatchford, Bassett, & Brown, 2005). Schools that are organized into smaller learning communities and/or have smaller class size often demonstrate higher rates of engaged students, in part, by providing greater opportunities for relevant curriculum, teacher-student relationships, and individual attention. In addition, small schools typically have lower incidences of negative social behaviors than do large schools, regardless of whether it is measured by truancy, aggressive behavior, vandalism, or classroom disruption (Oxley, 2004).

Professional learning teams (PTLs) and participatory action research (Suppovitz, 2002) have emerged as viable strategies for promoting positive school-level professional development. PLTs typically (a) include a self-selected group of staff who establish yearly goals for improving student achievement, (b) meet weekly or biweekly for 60–90 minutes, (c) discuss their instruction and examine student work with the purpose of better understanding how students learn, (d) read and discuss research-based practices, and (e) attempt new instructional strategies and collect student data to inform their inquiry. As with any form of professional development, school-improvement initiatives must be a schoolwide priority (e.g., 80% or more of staff know and acknowledge that the focus for change is needed), with administrative support and leadership provided for integration across the school (Northwest Regional Educational Laboratory, 2001; Sugai & Horner, 1999). Although schools that implement PLTs show promise in promoting higher levels of interaction and collaboration among staff and greater involvement in school-related decisions, the practice of organizing teachers into teams does not necessarily lead to improved instructional practices or improved student achievement. Rather, for PLTs to lead to productive student outcomes, there must be a clearly articulated focus on instructional practices (Suppovitz, 2002).

SCHOOL REFORM INITIATIVES

As policymakers become increasingly involved in school reform, issues of effective teaching and effective schools take on greater significance. Many reform initiatives rely on presumed relationships between education-related factors and learning outcomes. As new standards for student learning are introduced across the states, greater attention is being given to the role that teachers and schools play in promoting student achievement (Slavin & Madden, 2001). Two recent initiatives, response to intervention (RTI) and evidence-based intervention (EBI), have contributed significantly to current teaching practices for students with and without disabilities.

Response to Intervention

A response-to-intervention (RTI) model for special education identification and intervention planning builds on concepts put forth in the Individuals with Disabilities Education Improvement Act (IDEIA) as well as the No Child Left Behind Act (NCLB). The NCLB specifies that students must receive effective instruction (i.e., scientific- or evidence-based programs and interventions) for the purpose of educational accountability prior to entering special education. Perhaps the most compelling rationale for RTI is the failure of traditional methods to guide the selection of effective and ongoing teaching interventions which contribute to positive outcomes among students (Barnett, Daly, Jones, & Lentz, 2004). Decision-making models based on RTI use the quality and degree of student response to effective teaching as key criteria for determining student need and/or disability.

Successful application of an RTI model incorporates a high-quality design that includes: (a) a standard process for making sequential decisions regarding student need; (b) goals for teaching that represent socially or academically significant progress toward classroom expectations; (c) ongoing monitoring of student progress; (d) analysis of desired change in student performance; and (5) data-based decision making regarding student need and eligibility for special services (Barnett et al., 2004; Stoiber & Kratochwill, 2002). Inherent in the concept of RTI is a focus on the child within the instructional context. An RTI model recognizes that a child's difficulty in school may be due, in part, to the learning environment and instruction he or she receives. Data collected through the progress-monitoring component of RTI should ultimately expand the research base concerning how children learn and how teaching can be effective in meeting children's needs (Denton, Vaughn, & Fletcher, 2003).

RTI methods represent several critical changes in the functioning of schools and teachers. First, educators must be able to reliably document that the child has received high-quality instruction and scientifically based intervention. Identifying such strategies and ensuring they have been implemented as intended is no small challenge. It is reasonable for schools to, first, initiate less intrusive interventions at the school and classroom level, and then move to more comprehensive and intensified interventions as needed (O'Shaughnessy, Lane, Gresham, & Beebe-Frankenberger, 2003). Constructing such hierarchies of intensity requires an understanding of effective instructional procedures (Barnett et al., 2004). Second, schools must establish socially and empirically valid outcomes that can be measured repeatedly and reliably across the duration of the intervention. This step requires educators to know and understand educational benchmarks that are validated in relation to long-term outcomes. Third, the level of intervention intensity must be defined to determine whether special services are indicated for the child to perform at expected levels.

Within an RTI model, a child is identified as having a disability when (a) pre- and post-intervention performance does not change significantly despite implementation of validated effective teaching practices, or (b) intensive teaching intervention is required for the child

to demonstrate an expected level of performance (Barnett et al., 2004). Intensive instruction differs significantly from regular education in terms of the resources or support needed, time required, amount of professional involvement beyond the classroom teacher, and other factors necessary for facilitating progress. Implementation of RTI should contribute to positive educational outcomes for all students. To improve outcomes for students, however, increased knowledge and use of evidence-based interventions and practices must occur.

Evidence-Based Interventions

The recent emphasis on evidence-based interventions (EBI) and empirically or scientifically based practices is connected closely to the current focus in NCLB and general emphasis on accountability in intervention selection and implementation. The NCLB legislation was partly a reaction to the observation that education as a field has produced limited research reflecting well-designed and scientifically credible methodologies (Shavelson & Towne, 2002). A research base on effective instruction is critical for understanding and determining student response to intervention. At a broader level, evidence-based interventions are necessary for effective practice to be integrated into the everyday instruction of all children attending our nation's schools.

In education, interventions are developed typically to alter, and often improve, student performance. Educational interventions target a broad range of student outcomes, including those in cognitive, behavioral, and affective areas. Although intervention research has been evident since the early 1900s, the interest in translating research findings into effective instructional and intervention practices has intensified with the evidence-based intervention movement (Kratochwill & Stoiber, 2002; Shavelson & Towne, 2002; Stoiber & Kratochwill, 2000).

Despite the need for evidence-based practices to improve educational outcomes, there are fewer educational intervention studies being conducted in schools today than during the 1970s and 1980s (Hsieh et al., 2005). Educational researchers have recently called for an improvement in the overall quality of teaching intervention studies (Kratochwill & Stoiber, 2002; Phye, Robinson, & Levin, 2005). Researchers have criticized the quantity and quality of research in important areas affecting student educational outcomes, such as reading (Troia, 1999), early childhood

(Snyder, Thompson, McLean, & Smith, 2002), emotional disturbance (Mooney, Epstein, Reid, & Nelson, 2003), learning disabilities (Tunmer, Chapman, Greaney, & Prochnow, 2002), and special education (Seethaler & Fuchs, 2005). For example, Seethaler and Fuchs (2005) examined five prominent special education journals and recorded the proportion of articles that involved mathematics and reading interventions; only 5% of all articles included a focus on mathematics or reading interventions. Such a finding is remarkable given that interventions in the area of early literacy development and reading comprehension are among those considered most needed for improving long-term student outcomes (Denton et al., 2003).

The primary basis for the EBI movement is to translate research into effective practices and thus address the research-practice gap. Therefore, it is important to consider specific qualities of intervention research. The following criteria have been considered pertinent in determining effectiveness of instructional interventions: (a) used an experimental and/or quasi-experimental design; (b) occurred for a reasonable length of time; (c) incorporated multiple outcome measures; (d) collected postintervention as well as follow-up data after a specified period of time subsequent to program implementation; (e) assessed treatment integrity (intervention implemented as intended); (f) employed appropriate statistical methods; (g) had a sufficient sample size to measure effects; and (h) showed significant positive effects on appropriate outcomes (e.g., improved reading comprehension, school attendance, attitude to school, compliance to teacher directions).

Thus, for an instructional or intervention strategy to be considered "evidence based" or "effective" it should be supported by research meeting specified criteria. For this to occur, considerable changes in the characteristics of intervention research are indicated. Recent examinations of education intervention studies (in learning disabilities, early childhood, and autism) indicated that less than 15% measured treatment integrity (Snyder et al., 2002; Wolery & Garfinkle, 2002). Whereas typical school- and classroom-based interventions need to occur over a substantial period of time to produce meaningful and long-term effects, Hsieh et al. (2005) reported that the typical intervention study reported in educational psychology journals was brief, with less than 16% of studies reported in 2004 lasting more than one day. Other trends

were noted by Hsieh et al., specifically that the typical intervention study (a) assessed intervention effects immediately following the intervention rather than after a period of time, (b) did not evaluate intervention integrity, and (c) typically included adults (i.e., college students) rather than children.

The dearth of intervention studies involving students as participants, and in particular students performing within classroom contexts, is likely due to several obstacles that present important limitations to the documentation and use of evidence-based interventions. For example, teachers and administrators typically resist random assignment of students to classrooms for experimental purposes, especially for an extended period of time. Attrition presents another problem in that children may change classrooms and even schools during the intervention period. Perhaps the greatest obstacle to the EBI movement pertains to issues of acceptance, feasibility, and sustainability (Stoiber & Kratochwill, 2002). Regardless of how effective an intervention may be, school administrators will likely assess the cost-benefit ratio to ensure the intervention is practical to implement. Questions regarding a range of costs, such as those for materials, time, and training, must be addressed. For schools and staff to "buy in," such costs must be balanced against the expected "pay-offs" of the intervention.

Support is emerging for a "practitioner-as-researcher" or evidence-based practice (EBP) approach to determining effective schooling practices (Stoiber, Lewis-Snyder & Miller, 2005). This approach recognizes that different schools reflect diverse ecological and complex qualities, which cannot be captured through the use of traditional laboratory procedures and methodologies. EBPs have broader application in actual classrooms as they include strategies based on scientific principles and empirical data, as well as those with a strong theoretical base. As such, practitioners function as researchers by applying data-based approaches for systematic planning, monitoring, and evaluating outcomes of their own teaching and classrooms practices. Kratochwill and Stoiber (2002) argued that such an approach is indicated due to a general lack of evidence for using particular interventions with particular children in particular contexts (i.e., situated knowledge).

Practitioner-as-researcher and other EBP approaches hold considerable promise as they target several important barriers to the dissemination of educational interventions, including issues of (a) acceptability, the degree to which consumers find the intervention procedures and outcomes acceptable in their daily lives; (b) feasibility, the degree to which intervention components can be implemented in naturalistic contexts; and (c) sustainability, the extent to which the intervention can be maintained without support from external agents. EBP initiatives have the potential to result in widespread improvement in instructional practices and educational success for all children.

SUMMARY AND FUTURE DIRECTIONS

Research from both the process-outcome and interpretive perspectives has identified multiple instructional and environmental variables that relate to effective schooling. Research within a process-outcome view has identified behaviors and practices associated with high student achievement. Specifically, effective teachers sustain high levels of student engagement, implement teacher-directed instruction, provide sufficient practice and feedback, and practice good classroom management techniques. The interpretive paradigm has added other principles of effective teaching and learning which include ways to promote understanding and application of knowledge. Finally, research suggests that effective schools also establish supportive, yet challenging learning environments, and encourage students to be responsible and independent learners. In sum, effective teaching involves more than the simple transmission of information. It includes being responsive to individual students and creating a productive environment for all learners. Furthermore, recent reform initiatives underscore the importance of teachers' knowledge of scientifically based strategies and student-monitoring procedures.

It is clear that no single variable accounts for classroom-to-classroom differences in teaching and school effectiveness. Instead, multiple variables combine to produce effectiveness in terms of student achievement. The key for improving teaching effectiveness lies in finding situations in which as many instructionally desirable conditions as possible coexist in classrooms and in schools. Recent work has pointed to the need for evaluating the efficacy of comprehensive, schoolwide models of teaching (Floden, 2001). The aggregation of findings into a composite model of effective schooling rests on some key assumptions.

First, different types of learning call for different types of classroom processes; therefore, no single approach can be the method of choice for all classroom learning. The most effective classroom teaching features a balanced mix of research-based instructional methods. Second, within any content domain, students' instructional needs change as their expertise and abilities develop. What constitutes an optimal mix of instructional methods will change as students advance through school. Third, few, if any, universal models of effective teaching are uniformly effective in all teaching circumstances. Even a potentially useful process of praising students may lead to variable outcomes, depending on the age and attitude of learners. A "one-size-fits-all" approach is rarely effective. Instead, effective teaching requires incorporating multiple research findings to creating productive schools.

In sum, teachers and schools can be effective in promoting student achievement when they follow pedagogical principles derived from a variety of perspectives and research paradigms. The current challenge is to continue to seek ways to facilitate the application and sustained use of research-based practices. The knowledge base on teaching will have positive effects only to the extent that it is understood and implemented accurately. On one hand, researchers need to present findings accurately and qualify them appropriately. On the other hand, educators need to appreciate the complexity of teaching and not seek simplistic approaches to teaching practice. Research on teaching should empower schools by enabling them to act more confidently on the basis of well-established principles and practices. Thus, future efforts should be directed toward identifying the type of supports necessary to help schools implement practices and approaches that have been validated by research.

CONCLUSION

Teachers and schools can succeed with diverse students when they follow sound pedagogical principles that contribute to effectiveness. The best teaching and the most effective schools are flexible—able to adapt to the context and needs of individual learners. Researchers are continuing to make progress in learning about the complexities of school and learning contexts and the implications for teaching. Research-based knowledge can inform teachers and schools about these complexities. It is teachers and schools that must decide what goals to pursue and what combinations of methods and activities will be most effective in helping their students accomplish these goals.

REFERENCES

Antil, L., Jenkins, J., Wayne, S., & Vadasy, P. (1997). Cooperative learning: Prevalence, conceptualizations, and the relationship between research and practice. *American Educational Research Journal, 35,* 419–454.

Ardoin, S. P., Martens, B. K., & Wolfe, L. A. (1999). Using high-probability instruction sequences with fading to increase student compliance during transitions. *Journal of Applied Behavior Analysis, 32,* 339–351.

Baker, S., Gersten, R., Dimino, J., & Griffiths, R. (2004). The sustained use of research-based instructional practice. *Remedial and Special Education, 35,* 5–24.

Bandura, A. (1997). *Self-efficacy: The exercise of control.* New York: W.H. Freeman and Company.

Barnett, D. W., Daly, E. J., Jones, K. M., & Lentz, F. E. (2004). Response to intervention: Empirically-based special service decisions from single-case designs of increasing and decreasing intensity. *The Journal of Special Education, 38,* 66–79.

Bickel, W. E. (1999). The implications of the effective schools literature for school restructuring. In C. R. Reynolds & T. B. Gutkin (Eds.), *The handbook of school psychology* (3rd ed., pp. 959–983). New York: John Wiley.

Blatchford, P., Bassett, P., & Brown, P. (2005). Teachers' and pupils' behavior in large and small classes: A systematic observation study of pupils aged 10 and 11 years. *Journal of Educational Psychology, 97,* 454–467.

Bohanon, H., Fenning, P., Carney, K., Minnis-Kim, M. J., Anderson-Harriss, S. A., Moroz, K. B., et al. (2006). Schoolwide application of positive behavior support in an urban high school: A case study. *Journal of Positive Behavior Interventions, 8,* 131–145.

Bong, M. (2005). Within-grade changes in Korean girls' motivation and perceptions of the learning environment across domains and achievement levels. *Journal of Educational Psychology, 97,* 656–673.

Borko, H. (2004). Professional development and teacher learning. *Educational Researcher, 33,* 3–15.

Borman, G. D., Hewes, G. M., Overman, L. T., & Brown, S. (2002). *Comprehensive school reform and student achievement: A meta-analysis.* Baltimore, MD: Center for Research on Education of Students Placed At Risk.

Brady, R. C. (2003). Can facility schools be fixed? Retrieved from www.edexcellence.net.

Brophy, J. (2004). *Motivating students to learn* (2nd ed.). Mahwah, NJ: Erlbaum.

Brophy, J. E. (1997). Effective instruction. In H. J. Walberg & G. D. Haertel (Eds.), *Psychology and educational practice* (pp. 212–232). Berkeley, CA: McCutchan.

Burns, R. B. (1984). How time is used in elementary schools: The activity structure of classrooms. In L. W. Anderson (Ed.), *Time and school learning: Theory, research, and practice* (pp. 52–71). London: Croom Helm.

Calderhead, J. (1996). Teachers: Beliefs and knowledge. In D. C. Berliner & R. C. Calfee (Eds.), *Handbook of educational psychology* (pp. 167–199). New York: Macmillan.

Cameron, J., Pierce, W. D., Banko, K. M., & Gear, A. (2005). Achievement-based rewards and intrinsic motivation: A test of cognitive mediators. *Journal of Educational Psychology, 97,* 641–655.

Carroll, J. C. (1963). A model of school learning. *Teachers College Record, 64,* 723–733.

Carter, S. C. (2000). *No excuses: Lessons from 21 high-performing, high-poverty schools.* Washington, DC: The Heritage Foundation.

Chester, M. D., & Beaudin, B. Q. (1996). Efficacy beliefs of newly hired teachers in urban schools. *American Educational Research Journal, 33,* 233–257.

Clark, D., & Linn, M. C. (2003). Design for knowledge integration: The impact of instructional time. *Journal of the Learning Sciences, 6,* 271–315.

Coleman, J. S., Campbell, E. Q., Hobson, C. J., McPartland, J., Mood, A. M., Weinfeld, F. D., & York, R. L. (1966). *Equality of educational opportunity.* Washington, DC: U.S. Government Printing Office.

Cotton, K. (2001). *New small learning communities: Findings from recent literature.* Portland, OR: Northwest Regional Educational Laboratory. Retrieved from www.nwrel.org.

Daly, E. J., Martens, B. K., Kilmer, A., & Massie, D. R. (1996). The effects of instructional match and content overlap on generalized reading performance. *Journal of Applied Behavior Analysis, 29,* 507–518.

Darling-Hammond, L. (1999). *Teacher quality and student achievement: A review of state policy evidence.* Seattle: University of Washington, Center for the Study of Teaching and Policy.

Darling-Hammond, L., Wise, A. E., & Klein, S. P. (1995). *A license to teach: Building a profession for 21st-century schools.* San Francisco: Westview Press.

Deci, E. L., & Ryan, R. M. (2002). *Handbook of self-determination research.* Rochester, NY: University of Rochester Press.

Denton, C. A., Vaughn, S., & Fletcher, J. M. (2003). Bringing research-based practice in reading intervention to scale. *Learning Disabilities Research & Practice, 18*, 201–211.

Driver, R., Aasoko, H., Leach, J., Mortimer, E., & Scott, P. (1999). Constructing scientific knowledge in the classroom. *Educational Researcher, 23*(7), 5–12.

Dunkin, M. J., & Biddle, B. J. (1974). *The study of teaching.* New York: Holt, Rinehart, and Winston.

Edelson, D. C. (2001). Learning-for-use: A framework for integrating content and process learning in the design of inquiry activities. *Journal of Research in Science Teaching, 38*, 355–385.

Ellis, E., Farmer, T., & Newman, J. (2005). Big ideas about teaching big ideas. *Teaching Exceptional Children, 38*(1), 34–39.

Evertson, C. M. (1987). Creating conditions for learning: From research to practice. *Theory into Practice, 26*(1), 44–50.

Evertson, C., Anderson, C., Anderson, L., & Brophy, J. (1980). Relationships between classroom behaviors and student outcomes in junior high mathematics and English classes. *American Educational Research Journal, 17*, 43–60.

Ferguson, R. F., & Brown, J. (2000). Certification test scores, teacher quality, and student achievement. In D. W. Grissmer & J. M. Ross (Eds.), *Analytic issues in the assessment of student achievement* (pp. 45–61). Washington, DC: U.S. Department of Education.

Floden, R. E. (2001). Research on effects of teaching: A continuing model for research on teaching. In V. Richardson (Ed.), *Handbook of research on teaching* (4th ed., pp. 3–16). Washington, DC: American Educational Research Association.

Freiberg, H. J. (1999). *School climate: Measuring, improving, and sustaining healthy learning environments.* London: Falmer.

Fuchs, D., Fuchs, L., Mathes, P., & Simmons, D. (1997). Peer-assisted learning strategies: Making classrooms more responsive to diversity. *American Educational Research Journal, 34*, 174–206.

Fuchs, L. S., Fuchs, D., & Phillips, N. B. (1994). The relation between teachers' beliefs about the importance of good student work habits, teacher planning, and student achievement. *The Elementary School Journal, 94*, 331–345.

Gage, N. L., & Needels, M. C. (1989). Process-product research on teaching: A review of criticisms. *The Elementary School Journal, 89*, 253–297.

Gamoron, A., Porter, A. C., Smithson, J., & White, P. (1997). Upgrading high school mathematics instruction: Improving learning opportunities for low-achieving, low-income youth. *Educational Evaluation and Policy Analysis, 19*(4), 325–338.

Gettinger, M., & Seibert, J. (2002). Best practices in increasing academic learning time. In A. Thomas & J. Grimes (Eds.), *Best practices in school psychology IV* (pp. 773–787). Bethesda, MD: National Association of School Psychologists.

Ginsburg, G. S., & Bronstein, P. (1993). Family factors related to children's intrinsic/extrinsic motivational orientation and academic performance. *Child Development, 64*, 1461–1474.

Good, T. (1996). Teacher effectiveness and teacher evaluation. In J. Sikula, T. Buttery, & E. Guyton (Eds.), *Handbook of research on teacher education* (2nd ed., pp. 617–665). New York: Macmillan.

Good, T., & Brophy, J. (2000). *Looking in classrooms* (9th ed.). New York: Longman.

Gottfried, A. E., Fleming, J. S., & Gottfried, A. W. (2001). Continuity of academic intrinsic motivation from childhood though late adolescence: A longitudinal study. *Journal of Educational Psychology, 93*, 3–13.

Greenwood, C. R., & Delquadri, J. (1995). Peer tutoring and the prevention of school failure. *Preventing School Failure, 39*(4), 21–25.

Hidi, S. (2000). An interest research's perspective: The effects of extrinsic and intrinsic factors on motivation. In C. Sansone & J. M. Harackiewicz (Eds.), *Intrinsic and extrinsic motivation: The search for optimal motivation and performance* (pp. 311–342). San Diego, CA: Academic Press.

Hoffman, J. V. (1986). Process-product research on effective teaching: A primer for a paradigm. In J. V. Hoffman (Ed.), *Effective teaching of reading: Research and practice* (pp. 39–51). Newark, DE: International Reading Association.

Hogan, K., & Pressley, M. (Eds.). (1997). *Scaffolding student learning: Instructional approaches and issues.* Boston, MA: Brookline.

Hsieh, P., Acee, T., Chung, W., Hsieh, Y., Kim, H., Thomas, G. D., et al. (2005). Is educational intervention research on the decline? *Journal of Educational Psychology, 97*, 523–529.

Jones, V. F., & Jones, L. S. (2001). *Comprehensive classroom management* (6th ed.). Boston: Allyn & Bacon.

Kagan, D. M. (1992). Implications of research on teacher belief. *Educational Psychologist, 27*, 65–90.

Kameenui, E. J., & Carnine, D. W. (1998). *Effective teaching strategies that accommodate diverse learners.* Upper Saddle River, NJ: Prentice Hall.

Kluger, A. N., & DeNisi, A. (1996). The effects of feedback interventions on performance: A historical review, a meta-analysis, and a preliminary feedback intervention theory. *Psychological Bulletin, 119*, 254–284.

Kratochwill, T. R., & Stoiber, K. C. (2002). Evidence-based intervention in school psychology: Conceptual foundations of the procedural and coding manual of Division 16 and the Society of the Study of School Psychology Task Force. *School Psychology Quarterly, 17*, 314–389.

Lepper, M. R., Corpus, J. H., & Iyengar, S. S. (2005). Intrinsic and extrinsic motivational orientations in the classroom: Age differences and academic correlates. *Journal of Educational Psychology, 97,* 184–196.

Lezotte, L. W. (1997). *Learning for all.* Okemos, MI: Effective Schools Products.

Leinhardt, G. (1992). What research on learning tells us about teaching. *Educational Leadership, 49*(7), 20–25.

Leedy, A., Bates, P., & Safran, S. P. (2004). Bridging the research-to-practice gap: Improving hallway behavior using positive behavior support. *Behavior Disorders, 29,* 131–139.

Monk, D. H. (1994). Subject area preparation of secondary mathematics and science teachers and student achievement. *Economics of Education Review, 13*(2), 125–145.

Mooney, P., Epstein, M. H., Reid, R., & Nelson, R. J. (2003). Status and trends in academic intervention research for students with emotional disturbance. *Remedial and Special Education, 24,* 273–287.

Mortimore, P. (1998). *The road to improvement: Reflections on school effectiveness.* Lisse, Netherlands: Swets & Zeitlinger.

National Reading Panel. (2000). *Teaching children to read: An evidence-based assessment of the scientific research literature on reading and its implications for reading instruction.* Washington, DC: Author.

Nelson, J. R., Martella, R. M., & Marchand-Martella, N. (2002). Maximizing student learning: The effects of a comprehensive school-based programs for preventing problem behaviors. *Journal of Emotional and Behavioral Disorders, 10,* 136–148.

Nietfeld, J. L., & Enders, C. K. (2003). An examination of student teacher beliefs: Interrelationships between hope, self-efficacy, goal-orientations, and beliefs about learning. *Current Issues in Education, 6*(5). Retrieved from cie.ed.asu.edu/volume6/number5.

Northwest Regional Educational Laboratory. (2001). Professional learning teams. Retrieved from nwrel.org/qualityteaching/PLT/index.asp.

O'Shaughnessy, T. E., Lane, K. L., Gresham, F. M., & Beebe-Frankenberger, M. E. (2003). Children placed at risk for learning and behavior difficulties. *Remedial and Special Education, 24,* 27–35.

Otis, N., Grouzet, F. M. E., & Pelletier, L. G. (2005). Latent motivational change in an academic setting: A 3-year longitudinal study. *Journal of Educational Psychology, 97,* 170–183.

Oxley, D. (2004). *Smaller learning communities: Implementing and deepening practice.* Retrieved from www.nwrel.org.

Pajares, F. (1996). Self-efficacy beliefs in academic settings. *Review of Educational Research, 66,* 543–578.

Pajares, F., & Graham, L. (1999). Self-efficacy, motivation constructs, and mathematics performance of entering middle school students. *Contemporary Educational Psychology, 24,* 124–139.

Pajares, F., & Kranzler, J. (1995). Self-efficacy beliefs and general mental ability in mathematical problem-solving. *Contemporary Educational Psychology, 26,* 426–443.

Phillips, N. B., Fuchs, L. S., Fuchs, D., & Hamlett, C. L. (1996). Instructional variables affecting student achievement: Case studies of two contrasting teachings. *Learning Disabilities Research and Practice, 11,* 24–33.

Phye, G. D., Robinson, D. H., & Levin, J. R. (Eds.). (2005). *Empirical methods for evaluating educational interventions.* San Diego: Academic Press.

Pintrich, P. R. (2003). A motivational science perspective on the role of student motivation in learning and teaching contexts. *Journal of Educational Psychology, 95,* 667–686.

Pressley, M. (2002) *Reading instruction that works: The case for balanced teaching* (2nd ed.) New York: Guilford Press.

Rhode, G., Jenson, R. J., & Reavis, H. K. (1993). *The tough kid book: Practical classroom management strategies.* Longmont, CA: Sopris West.

Richardson, V. (1994). Conducting research on practice. *Educational Researcher, 23*(5), 5–10.

Rosenshine, B. (1997). Advances in research on instruction. In J. W. Lloyd, E. J. Kameenuui, & D. Chard (Eds.), *Issues in educating students with disabilities* (pp. 197–221). Mahwah, NJ: Lawrence Erlbaum Associates.

Rosenhine, B., & Meister, C. (1992). The use of scaffolds for teaching higher-level cognitive strategies. *Educational Leadership, 29*(7), 26–33.

Rowan, B., Correnti, R., & Miller, R. J. (2002). *What large-scale, survey research tells us about teacher effects on student achievement.* Philadelphia: University of Pennsylvania, Consortium for Policy Research in Education.

Rutter, M., & Maughan, B. (2002). School effectiveness findings, 1979–2002. *Journal of School Psychology, 40,* 451–475.

Schuell, T. (1996). Teaching and learning in a classroom context. In D. Berliner & R. Calfee (Eds.), *Handbook of educational psychology* (pp. 726–764). New York: Macmillan.

Schunk, D. H. (2003). Self-efficacy for reading and writing: Influence of modeling, goal setting, and self-evaluation. *Reading and Writing Quarterly, 19,* 159–172.

Schunk, D. H. (2005). Commentary on self-regulation in school contexts. *Learning and Instruction, 15,* 173–177.

Seethaler, P. M., & Fuchs, L. S. (2005). A drop in the bucket: Randomized controlled trials testing reading and math interventions. *Learning Disabilities Research & Practice, 20,* 98–102.

Shavelson, R. J., & Towne, L. (2002). *Scientific research in education*. Washington, DC: National Academic Press.

Shulman, L. S. (1986). Paradigms and research programs in the study of teaching: Contemporary perspective. In M. Wittrock (Ed.), *Handbook of research on teaching* (3rd ed., pp. 3–36). New York: Macmillan.

Slavin, R. E. (1994). *Cooperative learning: Theory, research, and practice* (2nd ed.), Boston: Allyn & Bacon.

Slavin, R. E., & Madden, N. A. (Eds.). (2001). *Success for all: Research and reform in elementary education*. Hillsdale, NJ: Lawrence Erlbaum.

Snow, C. E., Burns, M. S., & Griffin, P. (Eds.). (1998). *Preventing reading difficulties in young children*. Washington, DC: National Academy Press.

Snyder, P., Thompson, B., McLean, M. E., & Smith, B. J. (2002). Examination of quantitative methods used in early intervention research: Linkages with recommended practices. *Journal of Early Intervention, 25*, 137–150.

Stedman, L. C. (1997). International achievement differences: An assessment of a new perspective. *Educational Researcher, 26*(3), 4–15.

Stoiber, K. C., & Kratochwill, T. R. (2000). Empirically supported interventions and school psychology: Rationale and methodological issues. *School Psychology Quarterly, 15*, 75–105.

Stoiber, K. C., & Kratochwill, T. R. (2002). *Outcomes: Planning, Monitoring, Evaluating*. San Antonio, TX: PsychCorp.

Stoiber, K. C., Lewis-Snyder, G., & Miller, M. A. (2005). Evidence-based interventions. In S. W. Lee (Ed.), *Encyclopedia of school psychology* (pp. 196–199). Thousand Oaks, CA: Sage.

Sugai, G., & Horner, R. H. (1999). Discipline and behavioral support: Preferred processes and practices. *Effective School Practices, 17*(4), 10–22.

Suppovitz, J. A. (2001). Translating teaching practice into improved student performance. In S.H. Fuhrman (Ed.), *100th yearbook of the National Society for the Study of Education, Part II* (pp. 81–98). Chicago: University of Chicago Press.

Suppovitz, J. A. (2002). Developing communities of instructional practice. *Teachers College Record, 104*, 1591–1626.

Troia, G. A. (1999). Phonological awareness intervention research: A critical review of the experimental methodology. *Reading Research Quarterly, 34*, 28–51.

Tunmer, W. E., Chapman, J. W., Greaney, K. T., & Prochnow, J. E. (2002). The contribution of educational psychology to intervention research and practice. *International Journal of Disability, Development and Education, 49*, 11–29.

U.S. Department of Education. (2003). *The high school leadership summit*. Retrieved from www.ed.gov/about/offices/list/ovae/pi/hsinit/index.html.

Vallerand, R. J., Fortier, M. S., & Guay, F. (1997). Self-determination and persistence in real-life setting: Toward a motivational model of high school dropout. *Journal of Personality and Social Psychology, 72*, 1161–1176.

Wang, M. C., Haertel, G. D., & Walberg, H. J. (1994). What helps students learn? *Educational Leadership, 51*(4), 74–79.

Waxman, H., Huang, S., Anderson, L., & Weinstein, T. (1997). Classroom process differences in inner-city elementary schools. *Journal of Educational Research, 91*, 49–59.

Webb, N. M., Troper, J. D., & Fall, R. (1995). Constructive activity and learning in collaborative small groups. *Journal of Educational Psychology, 87*, 406–423.

Wilkins, J. L. M. (2004). Mathematics and science self-concept: An international investigation. *Journal of Experimental Education, 72*, 331–346.

Wolery, M., & Garfinkle, A. N. (2002). Measures in intervention research with young children. *Journal of Autism and Developmental Disorders, 32*, 463–478.

Wray, D., Medwell, J., Fox, R., & Poulson, L. (2000). The teaching practices of effective teachers of literacy. *Educational Review, 52*(1), 75–84.

Zimmerman, B. J. (2001). Theories of self-regulated learning and academic achievement: An overview and analysis. In B. J. Zimmerman & D. H. Schunk (Eds.), *Self-regulated learning and academic achievement: Theoretical perspectives* (pp. 1–37). Mahwah, NJ: Erlbaum.

CHAPTER 36

EFFECTIVE CLASSROOMS: CLASSROOM LEARNING ENVIRONMENTS THAT FOSTER SCHOOL SUCCESS

BETH DOLL, COURTNEY LECLAIR, AND SARAH KURIEN
University of Nebraska–Lincoln

EFFECTIVE CLASSROOMS

In 2000, 11.6% of the 18-year-olds who left school were dropouts instead of high school graduates (National Center for Educational Statistics, 2002). Their trajectories to dropping out of school began in early elementary grades with excessive absences, poor attention, uncompleted work, discipline problems, unsatisfactory peer relationships, and low achievement. Their gradual disengagement from learning is important to understand, not only because it precedes dropping out of school, but also because it describes a set of passive behaviors that restrict students' learning even while they are sitting in classrooms. Examples of passive disengagement behaviors include making no effort to learn, not asking for help when it is needed, and avoiding new and unfamiliar tasks (Turner et al., 2002). These passive strategies for avoiding learning have also been called "artful dodges" (Covington, 1992) to acknowledge their apparent function of protecting students from publicly acknowledging ignorance or learning failures. High-quality curriculum and instruction has minimal impact for such disengaged students.

The phenomenon of academic disengagement is important to the practice of school psychology since it defines, in stark terms, the critical interface between psychological wellness and learning. Children having social, emotional, and personal competence are more available for learning, while those who are less competent may not take full advantage of classroom instruction and struggle against "barriers to learning" (Adelman & Taylor, 2006). Adelman and Taylor identify a principal purpose of school mental health services to be breaking down these barriers, especially with children who are at high social risk and particularly for very young children.

Mounting evidence shows that very early school experiences are especially important in establishing children's patterns of learning. Current paradigms assume that children travel along a "path of learning" that extends from infancy into adulthood, and very early shifts in the slope or direction of this trajectory can ultimately result in dramatic differences in adolescent and adult competence. Intriguing evidence suggests that high-quality learning environments can shift these trajectories and may even have the potential to "close the gap" in learning between advantaged students and students growing up under conditions of social disadvantage (Hamre & Pianta, 2005). Examinations of students' learning will be incomplete unless these carefully consider the processes that influence students' learning trajectories, and efforts to strengthen student learning will be underpowered unless they also include strategies to strengthen classroom learning environments.

There is nothing radical about the idea that children's success in school emerges, in part, out of the learning environments that exist in their classrooms. Prominent educational leaders have often demanded that schools pay closer attention to the adequacy of learning contexts that promote active participation in the curriculum (Kavale & Forness, 1999; President's Commission on Excellence in Special Education, 2002). Still, traditional research on school success sought to identify the *instructional* characteristics of successful classrooms as these interact with the *intellectual* and *cognitive* competencies of child learners. For example, Carroll's (1963) classic model of school learning emphasized students' learning ability and instructional adequacy. Adaptive instruction models emphasized instructional delivery and implementation (Wang & Walberg, 1985), while Glaser (1982) emphasized the efficient allocation of teacher and student time.

An important criticism of these early models was that they overlooked the social and psychological influences on school learning (Haertel, Walberg, & Weinstein, 1983; Masten et al., 2005). Thus, recent researchers have worked to identify the *social, psychological*, and *behavioral* characteristics of classrooms and students that interact to prompt school success. These new-generation studies recognize that academic achievement is a critical developmental task of children that is integral to, rather than independent of, other facets of developmental competence. They use elaborated models of classroom learning that include social, emotional, behavioral, and attitudinal measures as possible predictors of academic success. They acknowledge the importance of contextual as well as individual variables as possible predictors of school achievement, and use innovative empirical measures of context in their models. Finally, they redefine school success as a complex composite variable that is comprised of academic engagement or participation as well as academic achievement. Examples of these studies include Wang, Haertel, and Walberg's (1990) meta-review of the factors that influence learning; Kellam, Ling, Merisca, Brown, and Ialongo's (1998) classic study of the effects of classroom aggression in first grade on students' aggressive behavior in middle school; Ladd, Birch, and Buhs' (1999) examination of the social and scholastic lives of kindergarteners; Barth, Dunlap, Dane, Lochman, and Wells' (2004) study of classroom environments; and Wentzel and Caldwell's (1997) examination of the relations between social competence and achievement.

The particular sociopsychological contexts that contribute to children's developmental competence have also been well documented by several longitudinal studies of developmental risk (Coie et al., 1993; Doll & Lyon, 1998). Risk is defined both demographically (e.g., growing up in communities of poverty, violence, and limited education) and functionally (e.g., showing early evidence of learning, behavior, or adjustment problems; Hamre & Pianta, 2005). These studies show that children develop competence despite adversity when given nurturing relationships with adults; coaching in self-efficacy, self-regulation,

and achievement orientation; caring and effective peer relationships; and "connectedness" within and among families and communities. In the *Fifteen Thousand Hours* study, Rutter and his colleagues (Rutter, Maughan, Mortimore, Ouston, & Smith, 1979; Rutter & Maughan, 2002) linked these contextual variables to academic achievement, and demonstrated that most of the alterable predictors of academic success were school characteristics. Because school contexts are far more alterable than those of families, schools remain a natural focus of academic intervention. Wang et al.'s (1990) careful analysis of the school learning research showed that social and affective variables, as well as classroom climate variables, rivaled traditional instructional and cognitive measures in their influence on learning. The relationship is one of interdependence: success in school is both caused by and causes success in behavioral and social domains (Masten et al., 2005). Promotion of mental health and psychological wellness depends, at least in part, on the enhancement of school success.

This chapter will examine features of the classroom learning environment that promote psychological wellness and developmental competence and, concurrently, promote students' active participation in classroom learning and ultimately their school success (Ladd et al., 1999). Our analysis will build upon both developmental risk and school context studies to construct an operational definition of effective classroom learning environments that emphasizes relationship-enhancing and autonomy-promoting characteristics of classrooms. Three important relational features of classrooms will be discussed including the relationships that teachers have with their students, students have with each other, and parents have with the teachers and students. Similarly, three important autonomy characteristics of classrooms will be described, including the students' shared expectations for success, goals for learning, and behavioral self-control. In each case, we will first describe the characteristics more fully. Then, we will describe the relation between these features and children's school success, including the mechanism underlying the relation. Finally, we will describe the implications that these hold for the practice of school psychology. Ultimately, we will argue that the academic engagement and subsequent academic achievement of children is stronger when their classroom environments support socially competent and autonomous learning.

RELATIONAL CHARACTERISTICS OF EFFECTIVE CLASSROOMS

Interpersonal relationships have long been recognized as essential building blocks of psychological wellness, and so it is not surprising that relationships are essential to effective classrooms. Learning is, at its core, a social activity that emerges out of interpersonal interactions between and among adults and children. However, the relationships in classrooms have a peculiar quality because they are necessarily constructed among a very few adult teachers and many students. Relationships among students are also peculiar, in that school settings almost always represent the earliest opportunity for children to interact with each other outside of the close monitoring of their families. Both adult-child and child-child relationships can be characterized by either positive (prosocial) or negative (conflictual) features, and it is increasingly apparent that these are isomorphic features. Conflict does not always signify the absence of caring, and prosocial interactions are not necessarily conflict-free.

Teachers' Relationships with Students

Of all the different people that students interact with at school, it is their relationships with teachers that contribute most to their school success. The teacher-student relationship is frequently described as an attachment bond that is similar to but less intense than the parent-child bond (Kesner, 2000). In fact, the 30 to 35 hours per week that students spend with their teachers can amount to more adult interaction than they have with their own parents. Fortunately, the relationship that most teachers form with their students is an exceptionally strong feature of classroom learning environments (Doll, 2005). In a three-state study that used anonymous written surveys, almost all students answered with an unequivocal "yes" when asked whether their teacher respected them (86%), listened carefully to them (82%), thought they were an important member of their class (81%), and helped them (79%). Similar to relationships with their parents, students can find social and emotional security with their teachers and may also internalize teachers' values as their own.

Teacher-student relationships are necessarily asymmetrical, in that students are the less mature participants (Pianta, 1999). By virtue of their authority, teachers are responsible for the initiation, maintenance and promotion of the positive relationship. Still, the relationships are also dyadic, in that they are affected by the behavior of both students and teachers (Greene, Abidin, & Kmetz, 1997). For example, students who are cooperative, cautious, and engaged in responsible behavior are viewed more positively by their teachers (Birch & Ladd, 1998), as are young children who seek help and comfort from their teacher in appropriate ways (Pianta & Nimetz, 1991). Conversely, students who are aggressive, defiant, or disorderly generally have negative relationships with their teachers (Hughes & Cavell, 1999). Likewise, young children who consistently engaged in intense, "needy," attention-seeking behaviors are described by their teachers as especially challenging (Pianta & Nimetz, 1991).

A special attribute of teacher-student relationships is that there are so many students relative to a single teacher, such that teachers' relationships with any one student are interdependent with their relationships with all other students in the class. A single negative teacher-relationship has the potential to color a teacher's relationships with all other students in a classroom. Imagine students witnessing a classmate, possibly a friend, being criticized and embarrassed by a new teacher. Such an experience would likely impact their future perceptions of that teacher. Continued negativity could "ripple" throughout the classroom, and subsequent students may arrive in class with stereotypically negative expectations of the teacher.

Teachers can influence the course of their relationships with students in many different ways. First and foremost, teachers who are warm and caring towards their students foster strong personal bonds with them. Teachers demonstrate their caring through helpfulness, friendliness (Breckelmans, Wubbels, & Levy, 1993), and by going out of their way for students (Bosworth, 1995). Second, like authoritative parents (Baumrind, 1989, 1991), effective teachers are fair and even-tempered leaders who hold students accountable at the same time that they model responsible decision making (Damon, 1992; Wentzel, 2002). Third, relationships with students are enhanced when teachers are frank and truthful, sharing their ideas, opinions, experiences, and feelings with students (Damon, 1992). Finally, democratic teacher behaviors are important to their relationships with students, as when teachers encourage student freedoms or empower students to participate in problem solving and conflict resolution (Breckelmans et al., 1993).

Recent research suggests that the presence of conflict or discord in teachers' relationships with their students is more destructive to learning than the absence of positive interactions. For example, the correlation between antisocial student behaviors and a negative teacher-student relationship is stronger than the relation between prosocial youth behaviors and a positive teacher-student bond (Ladd et al., 1999; Murray & Murray, 2004). Similarly, kindergarten teachers' reports of negativity in their relationships with students uniquely predicted students' grades, test scores, and work habits in the lower elementary grades, and behavioral success in the upper grades (Hamre & Pianta, 2001). Likewise, the *absence* of teacher conflict and negative interactions with teachers is predictive of students' academic success (Ang, 2005). These findings establish that the presence of negativity in teacher-student relationships is not equivalent to the absence of positive interactions, and that reducing negative interactions might be more important than increasing positive interactions between teachers and their students. Moreover, negative classroom relationships have the potential to cascade over time, when the mutually negative beliefs held by teachers and students are reinforced during behavioral interactions, such that each sees the other as increasingly problematic (Pianta, 1999).

Both academic achievement and behavioral competence improve when relationships between teachers and students are strong and effective, but at least one study has shown that the relationships of early elementary students with their teachers are stronger predictors of *behavioral* than *academic* outcomes (Hamre & Pianta, 2001; Pianta & Stuhlman, 2004). In particular, while a negative teacher-student relationship made it more likely that students would show inadequate academic progress, negative behavioral outcomes for such students were even more likely (Hamre & Pianta, 2001). In another study, closeness, dependence, and lack of conflict within the teacher-student relationship significantly predicted children's successful academic performance, feelings about school, and active involvement in school activities (Birch & Ladd, 1997). Evidence also links positive teacher-student relationships with ease of transition from one grade or school to the next, and to future successful interactions with other teachers (Birch & Ladd, 1998; Stuhlman & Pianta, 2001). For students identified as having behavior

disorders, strong teacher-student relationships have led to moderate increases in grade point average (Murray & Malmgren, 2005).

When they are strong and effective, the bond between teachers and their students also influences students' social success. Students' positive relationships with their teacher are associated with better peer relationships and, conversely, poor teacher-student relationships have been linked to negative peer interactions (Birch, 2002). In early elementary students, teacher-student relationships predict a small to moderate portion of the variance in social skills in young students (Pianta & Stuhlman, 2004) and conflict with teachers predicts later increases in peer aggression (Birch & Ladd, 1998).

Relationships between teachers and their students are frequently mentioned as sources of resilience for children who live in high-risk communities (Hamre & Pianta, 2005). The single most common factor associated with childhood resilience is a supportive relationship with a caring adult, and teachers are the most frequently cited sources of this support (Doll & Lyon, 1998; Resnick et al., 1997). Thus, it is not surprising that the impact of high-quality teacher-student relationships is more pronounced for students who are socially disadvantaged or show early signs of behavior or adjustment problems. In one particularly well-designed study, students with and without high demographic risk were assigned to classrooms with high and low teacher support (Hamre & Pianta, 2005). At-risk students who were placed in the highly supportive classrooms fared significantly better than those placed in classrooms with low teacher support, and within one year their developmental competence and achievement was similar to that of low-risk students. In a different study, children who were experiencing harsh discipline and high parental conflict at home benefited more from a supportive teacher-student relationship than students with supportive homes (Meehan, Hughes, & Cavell, 2003).

While the links between teacher-student relationships and school success have been repeatedly studied, there is relatively little research examining the mechanism that underlies this correlation. One hypothesis is that the "approachability" of the teacher increases as the teacher-student bond strengthens, such that students are more comfortable asking questions and participating actively in class, and consequently experience greater academic success. An alternative hypothesis, based upon social motivational theory, argues that students adopt the goals of prominent individuals in their lives (Wentzel, 2002). For example, students become more academically motivated if they have strong bonds with teachers who value school success highly. Yet another hypothesis posits that strong teacher-student relationships reduce student anxiety and consequently increase student participation in learning. Still other researchers have suggested that students who have a strong bond with their classroom teachers are better able to access the instructional and social supports that a dynamic classroom environment offers, and so experience increased rates of school success (Hamre & Pianta, 2001).

The enhancement of teacher-student relationships is best conceptualized as a transactional enterprise. First, the *students* can be taught to behave in ways that develop and sustain supportive relationships with their teachers (Consortium on the School-based Promotion of Social Competence, 1994; Greenburg, Kusche, Cook, & Quamma, 1995; Murray & Murray, 2004). Second, *teachers* can be helped to understand the significance of their relationships with students and to act in ways that encourage formation of the bond (Pianta, 1999). The most powerful strategies are multilevel and multicomponent interventions that simultaneously shift *both* student and teacher behaviors to strengthen their relationship (Murray & Murray, 2004).

Students' Relationships with Each Other

Classmates represent a second important source of social support for students in schools, by providing each other with caring, assistance, company, and simple enjoyment (Johnson, Johnson, Buckman, & Richards, 1998). The adequacy of their peer interactions is simultaneously shaped by the social competence of each student and by the social ecological context that defines their classroom and school (Ladd et al., 1999). Effective peer relationships will be evidenced in two ways within classrooms: through high rates of peer friendships and competent management of social conflicts that occur between classmates (Birch & Ladd, 1998; Doll, Murphy, & Song, 2003). Both friendship and conflict management abilities are constructed out of individual student attributes including strong preferences for social affiliation, skilled social judgment and problem solving, strong social empathy, and effective social behaviors (Doll, 1996). However, these attributes are more likely to support flourishing friendships when the classroom has a strong climate of mutual acceptance, frequent and enjoyable opportunities to have fun together, and routines and practices that facilitate conflict management.

In a three-state study, the availability of friendships was the second strongest feature of most classrooms' learning environments (Doll, 2005). Using anonymous written surveys, most students reported that they had friends in class to play with (80%) or eat lunch with (75%). Having a friend in class makes it easier for students to enjoy daily activities in the classroom, easier to ask for assistance in times of stress, and much more likely that students will receive help when they ask (Doll, 1996). In a typical classroom, only 4% of children are not identified as a friend by any classmate, and approximately 8% are actively disliked by their classmates (Asher, 1995; Doll et al., 2003). Most children in most classrooms enjoy frequent and satisfying interactions with their classmates.

At the same time, disturbing levels of interpersonal conflict characterized many elementary classrooms (Doll, 2005). The majority of students reported that they sometimes or always struggled with other kids teasing them (60%) or arguing with them (67%), although rates of physical conflict were much lower. Studies of peer coercion and victimization suggest that between 10% and 20% of students encounter bullying regularly (Nansel, Overpeck, & Pilla, 2001). Conflict in classrooms' peer relationships can contribute to overall student stress, and subsequently to diminished participation in schooling (Ladd et al., 1999). At first glance, it might be difficult to reconcile classrooms' high rates of friendship with high levels of conflict. However, conflicts among friends are common, and most of the time friends will successfully resolve their conflicts, forgive each other, compromise, and continue their friendships (Grotpeter & Crick, 1996). Conflicts occurring between nonfriends are more difficult for children to resolve, either because peers are less ready to forgive nonfriends for social mistakes or because they attribute malevolent intentions to the social actions of classmates outside their own circle of friends. It is the failure to resolve conflicts, and not the prevalence of conflicts, that diminishes a classroom's social climate.

Repeated studies have established that children's peer relationships are significantly related to their academic achievement in classrooms (Coie, Dodge & Kupersmidt, 1990; DeRosier, Kupersmidt & Patterson, 1994; Wentzel &

Caldwell, 1997). Having friends in class prompts students to actively participate in learning and stay interested in academic tasks (Malecki & Elliott, 2002; Wentzel & Watkins, 2002). Inner-city schools showing the largest improvements in student achievement were the same schools where students reported the strongest affiliations with classmates (Waxman, Anderson, Huang & Weinstein, 2001). Tenth grade students' grades and achievement test scores were significantly related to judgements of social competence by their fourth grade teachers (Fleming et al., 2005). Perhaps most importantly, peer relationships are critical determinants of the attachment bonds that students form with their schools: students who are unliked in elementary school drop out of middle school at five times the rate of liked students (Barclay, 1966; Kupersmidt, Coie & Dodge, 1990).

Still, the mechanism underlying this association of academic success with peer relationships is not altogether clear. Friends may directly help each other in school through informal tutoring or mentoring (Wentzel, 1991). They might become each others' peer models for academic responsibility or reinforce each others' commitment to being in school and doing well there (Berndt, 1999; Clark, 1991). Alternatively, students who are friends may shape each other's enjoyment of school and learning (Wentzel, 1991). Prosocial behaviors such as sharing, helping and cooperating provide the foundation for such crucial academic activities as problem solving and cooperative learning (Wentzel & Watkins, 2002), while conflict in the classroom can contribute to student stress, and subsequently to diminished participation in schooling (Ladd et al., 1999). It is also possible that students' social competence and academic competence could both relate to a third factor of cooperation or behaving in social responsible ways (Ladd et al., 1999; Wentzel & Caldwell, 1997).

The difficulty in intervening to enhance classroom peer relationships is that authentic interpersonal interactions cannot be engineered. Instead, facilitating peer friendships requires a shift in classroom opportunities for friendships by providing frequent opportunities for classmates to have fun together. Students can have fun working together, learning together, or performing classroom chores, such that friendships do not necessarily require more class play or leisure time. Friendships also increase when cooperative learning instructional strategies are used in the classroom (Johnson et al., 1998). On the recess playground, friendships are enhanced when there are more games and more interesting games, when these games are most enjoyable when played in groups, and when the recess games are noncompetitive (Siemers, 2006). Classroom management of peer conflict is more straightforward, since students can benefit from explicit instruction in recognizing conflicts, finding mutually satisfactory resolutions, and mediating conflicts among classmates (Smith, Daunic, & Miller, 2002). Alternatively, classroom meetings can be used to identify classroom routines that eliminate frequent sources of classroom conflict (Murphy, 2002).

Parents' Relationships with Teachers and Students

Both families and schools believe that the home-school relationship is critical to children's classroom success. Ideally, parents want to be informed about their children's schooling, and expect the school to recognize them as key players in their children's education. Schools concur, acknowledging that relationships with students' parents provide additional support for the school's goals (Fan, 2001). Consequently, a significant emphasis of national and local school policies is the promotion of strong communication and collaboration between children's families and their schools (Hill & Taylor, 2004). Indeed, strong home-school partnerships are required in the No Child Left Behind Act (Epstein, 2005), for Title I funding (Kessler-Sklar & Baker, 2000), and for participation in Head Start (Hill & Taylor, 2004). Further, home-school relationships are emphasized by the National Education Goals Panel, United States Department of Education and the National Parent Teacher Association (Esler, Godber, & Christenson, 2002). Despite this emphasis, parental involvement in children's schooling is historically quite low, especially with economically disadvantaged families and for families of secondary students (Izzo, Weissberg, Kasprow, & Fendrich, 1999; Mapp, 2003).

Discussions about parental involvement in their children's schooling have been complicated by the lack of any consistent definition of a high-quality home-school relationship. Instead, the activities comprising parental involvement differ from one researcher to the next. Epstein and Sheldon (2002) have proposed one of the broadest definitions by describing six kinds of parental involvement: providing effective parenting to their children, volunteering in the school and classroom, actively communicating with the teacher and school, engaging children in learning activities at home, participating in decision making related to school policies and practices, and using community resources to strengthen their family. These six types include the obvious examples of parental involvement that occur within the school, including attending parent-teacher conferences, going to school assemblies, helping with instruction in the classroom, and participating in a parent-teacher organization (Hill & Taylor, 2004). Epstein's definition also includes less obvious ways that parents support their children's educational success outside of school, such as assisting with homework, limiting television watching time, or enforcing bedtime (Carter & Wojtkiewicz, 2000; Shumow & Miller, 2001).

Diverse studies have shown that students are more successful when their parents are involved in their schooling. High rates of parental involvement are linked to higher educational and career aspirations of their children (Hill et al., 2004). Students' homework completion increases when parents are involved (Epstein & Van Voorhis, 2001) and students with involved parents have higher grades and test scores (Fan, 2001; Hill et al., 2004). When parents are involved, students have better attendance, lower suspension rates, and higher rates of school completion (Anguiano, 2004, Epstein & Sheldon, 2002; Fan, 2001; Hill et al., 2004).

Still, conclusions about the strength of associations between home-school relationships and academic success vary widely. Conflicting results may be due to a variety of methodological differences in the research (Fan, 2001). First, researchers include different activities within their definitions of parental involvement, making it difficult to compare results across studies. Moreover, very similar activities can have dramatically different meanings when the context changes. For example, teachers may telephone students' parents to report discipline problems and, in this case, increased communication would not necessarily correlate with positive student outcomes. Second, different studies used different methods (rating scales, interviews, diaries) and different sources (parents, teachers, or students) to gather information about the home-school relationship, and reports from these sources are not necessarily comparable. Third, studies have not used consistent methods for measuring achievement. Those studies that measured school success using

grades did not yield the same correlation as test scores, and studies that assessed subject-specific achievement had different results than those measuring general achievement Fourth, the strength of correlations between home-school relationships and school success differs depending upon family factors such as income level (Anguiano, 2004) or parents' education (Anguiano, 2004; Hill et al, 2004; Shumow & Miller, 2001); and student factors such as age, grade, gender (Sartor & Youniss, 2002), or ethnicity (Anguiano, 2004). As one example, the quality of home-school relationships is much stronger in elementary than secondary classrooms, and studies comparing rates of parent involvement over several years could erroneously detect a group difference that would disappear once this age-related change was considered (Fan, 2001). Indeed, some studies have failed to detect any association between school success and home-school relationships. The ultimate evidence that home-school relationships contribute meaningfully to school success would come from experimental studies, but there are few or no controlled studies that manipulated rates of parental involvement and observed changes in achievement (Hoover-Dempsey & Sandler, 1995; Mattingly, Prislin, McKenzie, Rodriguez, & Kayzar, 2002; McWayne, Hampton, Fantuzzo, Cohen, & Sekino, 2004). Thus, despite the extensive literature on parent involvement in schooling, there is no clear consensus as to the nature or strength of this relationship.

Three alternative explanations have been offered as rationales for the possible link between parental involvement and children's school success: modeling, reinforcement and direct instruction (Hoover-Dempsey & Sandler, 1995). The first hypothesis is that when home-school communication is effective, the school's emphasis on school success is echoed at home and children are more likely to understand that success in school will be valued (McWayne et al., 2004). The second hypothesis is that parents who are involved with their children's schooling provide reinforcement through attention, praise and rewards for achievement-enhancing behaviors like attending school and finishing homework. The third hypothesis is that collaboration with children's schools provides parents with valuable information and opportunities to engage in direct academic instruction with children. This additional instruction on top of their classroom instruction encourages school success (Hill & Taylor, 2004).

Effective strategies to strengthen parents' involvement in classrooms take advantage of the control that schools, and particularly classrooms, have over the home-school relationships. With the assistance and cooperation of students in the class, teachers can initiate interactions with parents, invite parents to reciprocate, and be meticulously responsive to any parental overture. Parent-centered practices accommodate classroom expectations and tasks to parental realities, and promote more involvement than when classrooms expect parents to work around the school (Hoover-Dempsey & Sandler, 1997; Kessler-Sklar & Baker, 2000). Parent-centered practices are especially important for minority families, those with limited English proficiency, or other families that are less familiar with school practices and procedures (Kessler-Sklar & Baker, 2000). For example, homework assignments can be planned so that they do not require parents to teach their child specific skills that parents may not have uniformly mastered (Epstein & Van Voorhis, 2001). High expectations of involvement can convey to parents that they play a significant role in their children's schooling (Hoover-Dempsey & Sandler, 1997).

AUTONOMY CHARACTERISTICS OF EFFECTIVE CLASSROOMS

Students' growing capacity for autonomous, self-regulated learning is one of the most important developmental tasks that they master in schools. Ladd and his colleagues (1999) describe autonomy as the second component of academic success, and compare it to intrinsic motivation (Gottfried, Fleming, & Gottfried, 1994), autonomous orientation (Solomon & Kendall, 1977), or learning goal orientation (Dweck, 1989). Bandura (1989) refers, instead, to human agency when describing a very similar phenomenon. This confusion of terms may be one reason why schools frequently overlook autonomy and focus principally on the social characteristics of classroom learning environments, even though educational and psychological research thoroughly documents the critical role that self-regulatory skills play in psychological wellness and academic success. Still, classrooms are important contexts for the emergence of autonomy, not only because of the number of hours that children spend in school classrooms, but also because the work that students accomplish in classrooms is less closely monitored by adults. Regardless of the terminology that is used to describe it, autonomy emerges out of cognitive, attitudinal, and behavioral processes (Rudolph, Lambert, Clark, & Kurlakowsky, 2001).

Shared Expectations of Success

Academic efficacy describes the beliefs that students hold about their ability to learn and be successful in the classroom (Bandura, 1997). Efficacy works as a self-fulfilling prophecy; when students believe that they can succeed, they will, and when they believe that they cannot succeed, they will not. Families are the first to offer children mastery experiences and feedback, and parents serve as models for how to persevere when facing a challenge (Pastorelli et al., 2001). Once they enter school, students regularly perform tasks that their teachers will evaluate; the feedback that they receive and their experiences of success and failure fosters their own beliefs in their ability to succeed in school. Ultimately, students' beliefs about their ability can be as important as their actual ability in predicting their achievement (Pajares & Schunk, 2001; Schunk & Pajares, 2005).

Students who possess high levels of academic efficacy behave differently than those with low self-efficacy. Efficacious students pursue more challenging tasks because they believe they can excel (Pajares & Schunk, 2002). They persist longer and are willing to devote more effort to learning. If they encounter problems and need assistance, efficacious students are more likely to ask for help (Ryan, Patrick, & Shim, 2005). Students with high self-efficacy also develop self-regulated learning skills that help them succeed: goal setting, using appropriate academic strategies, self-monitoring, and self-evaluation (Linnenbrink & Pintrich, 2002; Zimmerman, 2000).

Efficacy also contributes to academic success by shaping student's thoughts and feelings about learning (Pajares & Schunk, 2002). Students with lower efficacy believe that tasks are too difficult and identify fewer possible solutions to a problem. They are more likely to become anxious and stressed and may have difficulty recovering from failures that they often attribute to their own lack of ability. In contrast, highly efficacious students are more optimistic, feel less anxious, and are calm when approaching a challenging task. Students with high efficacy for a specific subject are more interested in learning that subject and possess a strategic flexibility when solving problems (Pajares, 2003). They attribute failures to a lack of effort or a lack of information, and since they can put forth more effort or seek out more information, they understand failure to be a temporary event rather than a permanent state (Pajares & Schunk, 2002). Overall, highly efficacious students are better equipped to succeed.

Self-efficacy develops from four kinds of classroom experiences: students' personal experience with learning success, vicarious experience of classmates' success, verbal persuasion by classmates and teachers, and emotional arousal. Past experiences with success or failure are the most influential of these (Pajares, 1996). Self-efficacy increases after successful classroom learning experiences, particularly when students attribute their success to their own effort, since they can choose to engage in similar effort in the future. Though less salient than personal experience, watching classmates succeed or fail at tasks also influences efficacy, especially when students believe that they are similar to the classmate and that the classmate's performance is indicative of how they would perform. Vicarious experiences are particularly useful when new and unfamiliar tasks are introduced, and students feel unsure about their skills (Bandura, 1997; Schunk & Pajares, 2005). Verbal persuasion from teachers or classmates can enhance students' self-efficacy if the appraisal is believable and accurate (Bandura, 1997; Linnenbrink & Pintrich, 2002; Schunk & Pajares, 2005). Positive encouragement can convince students to try new and harder tasks or to increase their effort, all ideally leading to more success. Finally, students' emotional arousal impacts their efficacy. Stress and other aversive emotions are detrimental to personal efficacy (Bandura, 1997; Schunk & Pajares, 2005).

Within the classroom, efficacy is contagious. Students with high academic efficacy prompt high efficacy in their classmates through vicarious learning and mutual appraisal. The accuracy and believability of teachers' and classmates' appraisals are critically important. If students overestimate their ability, they are likely to attempt and fail at tasks above their true ability level, but if they underestimate their ability they will not approach tasks that could provide opportunities for success (Multon, Brown, & Lent, 1991). Moreover, strong teacher-student relationships increase self-efficacy because if teachers believe that a student can succeed, students are also more likely to believe that they can (Bandura, Caprara,

Barbaranelli, Gerbino, & Pastorelli, 2003). Like classrooms, schools can develop collective efficacy beliefs about the ability of their teachers to be successful and their students' ability to learn (Schunk & Pajares, 2005), and efficacious schools are more capable of producing successful students (Bandura, 1997).

The underlying mechanism of efficacy is a cycle of beliefs, feelings and behaviors. Believing that they can succeed encourages students' skill development and enhances learning behaviors that promote success and lead, in turn, to the development of stronger efficacy. Similar to a domino effect, efficacy in one subject or task contributes to students' general sense of efficacy and so can generalize to other, less familiar tasks (Lorsbach & Jinks, 1999).

Efficacious classrooms provide an environment in which students frequently engage in evaluative tasks and practice self-regulatory skills under conditions of strong support and encouragement (Pajares & Schunk, 2001). Feedback is immediate and frequent, especially when students work on challenging tasks (Pajares & Schunk, 2001), and focuses on skill development and effort rather than outcomes (Pintrich, 2003). Skillful management of classrooms' academic tasks and assessment methods provides strong student models for efficacy, and frequent persuasive comments from classmates and teachers regarding students' likely success. Classrooms with a range of learning tasks make it possible to challenge students, while still ensuring that they have frequent success experiences (Pintrich, 2003).

Shared Goals for Learning

Learning is self-determined when students have personal goals for their learning and take purposeful actions to meet these goals (Wehmeyer & Metzler, 1995). Self-determined learners identify with the importance of academic learning and regulate the time and the effort that they give to learning (Masten, 2001; Masten et al., 1999). They consider learning to be their own responsibility, take credit for their successes, and react to temporary failures with revised goals, new action plans, or strengthened strategies for improvement.

Ideally, students choose to participate in classroom learning activities because they are interested in them and believe that the activities matter for their current lives or their personal goals for their future (Deci, Koestner, & Ryan, 2001; Ladd et al., 1999). When this occurs, learning is an intrinsically motivating activity for the students and the teacher's role shifts to that of a guide and mentor rather than an enforcer of extrinsic goals. This is a crucial shift for students because it presages their development into self-regulated learners for whom the acquisition of knowledge and skills is self-selected. When learning is volitional, it is prompted by interest and sustained by spontaneous thoughts (Black & Deci, 2000).

Some classroom learning activities are immediately rewarding for students. In particular, students are more likely to become actively engaged in achieving classroom goals when these are goals to master the task (Mastery Goals) rather than goals to do better than classmates (Performance or Competitive Goals; Pajares & Schunk, 2002). One well-designed study examined students' academic disengagement under conditions of mastery goals, competitive goals, neither, or both (Turner et al., 2002). Results suggested that when there were no classroom mastery goals, many at-risk students actively avoided learning by withdrawing their effort from the task, refusing to participate in unfamiliar tasks, and not asking for help. Surprisingly, these learning avoidance strategies did not occur in classrooms with competitive goals as long as the classrooms also had mastery goals for learning. These results suggest that it is the absence of mastery goals, more than the presence of performance goals, that undermines students' active engagement in learning.

Learning is also more purposeful when classroom goals are specific (e.g., describing the number of problems to be completed), proximal (e.g., having deadlines of tomorrow or next week), and attainable (Pajares & Schunk, 2001). Classroom process goals describe strategies and procedures to use in challenging tasks, and are useful in bridging the gap between immediate short-term goals and more distal, outcome goals (Zimmerman & Kitsantas, 1999).

Learning that is initially extrinsic can become intrinsic if students come to understand the purpose of the learning, and recognize its importance (Assor, Kaplan, & Roth, 2002). In particular, describing the relevance of classroom learning to children's lives outside the classroom is the most important thing that prompts self-directed learning. Teachers encourage students' independent thinking with searching questions, enthusiastic rejoinders to innovative ideas, and explicit permission for divergent comments. Conversely,

they discourage intrinsic learning by forcing instruction through meaningless and uninteresting activities, criticizing independent thinking, or intruding and disrupting students once they've found a rhythm of learning. Of course, some learning requires rote memory and practice (such as memorizing the multiplication tables), but even these tasks can become more intrinsic if students are allowed to choose the most acceptable option from a slate of tasks.

Research on goal setting and self-determination has established that the best learning is voluntary. Still, students may not immediately aspire to master the classroom tasks of academic learning. When this occurs, coercion strategies will be the least powerful ways to secure active participation in learning. In contrast, classroom strategies that engage students as partners in their learning will be more effective; these include strategies that offer choices in how to learn or how to demonstrate mastery, if and when choices in what to learn are not possible. Rationales that explain the connections between academic tasks and student-set goals are also persuasive. Finally, classroom practices that challenge students to master a task are more convincing than those that pit one student against another in competitive learning "contests."

Behavioral Self-Control

Behavioral self-control is the environmental feature of classrooms that is most widely acknowledged to affect academic achievement. At the most basic level, it is the degree to which students' classroom conduct is appropriate and self-regulated (Doll, Zucker, & Brehm, 2004). Within a classroom setting, students' ability to control their behavior emerges out of characteristics internal to the students, such as their desire to succeed and please, and factors external to the students, such as classroom routines and procedures. Any instance of self-control is comprised of three phases: forethought or thinking about the action to be carried out, control or behaving as planned, and self-reflection or thinking back on what was achieved (Zimmerman, 2000). Thus, behavioral self-control depends on students making behavioral choices, setting standards for results, and judging whether their behavior met these self-imposed standards (Bandura, 1989; Bear, Telzrow, & deOliveira, 1997).

The past thirty years of research on developmental risk has shown that success in school is both caused by and causes success in behavioral competence (Masten et al., 2005). The interactions are complex and transactional. For example, antisocial behavior clearly undermines academic achievement in the early school years while academic failures in secondary schools contribute to increases in rule-breaking behaviors (Hawkins et al., 2003; Masten et al., 1995). The reverse is also true; prevention programs that increase school success have the potential to reduce future behavior problems (Hawkins et al., 1999). Classroom behavioral control is closely linked to other features of effective classrooms. For example, a consistent finding is that students who lack self-control often have impaired relationships with their teachers and peers (Lane, Pierson, & Givner 2003).

Behavioral self-control is ultimately an individual student decision, although it occurs within complex ecological social environments that predispose students to be well controlled or disruptive. Indeed, students frequently report that their classmates' work behaviors are not well controlled (Doll, 2005). Fewer than half of students said "yes" when asked whether: "most kids do their work when they're supposed to in this class" (49%), "most kids follow the rules in this class" (42%), "most kids in this class pay attention when they are supposed to" (41%), and "most kids work quietly and calmly in this class" (41%). Any single student's lack of control can disrupt learning for the rest of a class. Students who consistently make loud comments, are out of seat, and poke or prod classmates make learning difficult for everyone in class. Additionally, the behavior of one or two disruptive students can seriously limit teacher time for and attention to instruction. Further, disruptive students can become negative role models for their classmates since misbehavior of one student, if rewarded with attention, can inadvertently influence the behavior of other students in the class.

Students who are attentive, regulated, and persistent in their work receive higher grades, while lack of behavioral self-control contributes to academic underachievement (Doll et al., 2004; Lane et al., 2003). Disciplined classroom behavior is a better predictor of students' grades than intellectual ability, suggesting that self-control can lead to academic success (McDermott, Mordell, & Stoltzfus, 2001). Both secondary and elementary teachers viewed student self-control as critical to student success within the classroom (Lane et al., 2003). Teachers' judgments about the self-control of kindergarten students predicted their promotion into and academic success in first grade (Agostin & Bain, 1997).

The mechanism underlying the relationship between self-control and academic success is not clear. One hypothesis posits that students who are better able to control their behavior are also more likely to actively participate in class instruction. Conversely, students who lack self-control may miss out on much classroom instruction that occurs while they are inattentive, engaged in competing behaviors, or out of the classroom for disciplinary actions. A few researchers have suggested that self-regulation might be a manifestation of intelligence, and so more intelligent students would also be more self-regulated and show greater school success (Sanz de Acedo Lizarraga, Ugarte, Iriarte, & Sanz de Acedo Baquedano, 2003). A third, cyclical hypothesis speculates that disruptive behavior leads to frequent negative feedback from teachers and peers, which leads in turn to increased feelings of frustration. Frustrated or upset students often are unable to control their behavior, leading to additional negative relational feedback. This cycle of negativity leads to increased dysfunction within relationships, and less controlled behavior. In contrast, strong teacher-student relationships are likely to lead to increased student behavioral self-control, as students are more apt to try to "please" and get positive feedback from teachers with whom they have a relationship.

The prominence of behavioral control in the educational literature is evident in the large number of empirically supported programs that have a common purpose of improving students' compliance with classroom behavior rules. Positive behavior support strategies developed and reinforced classwide rules (Sugai, Horner & Gresham, 2002), while classwide instructional programs have taught students increased behavioral self-control (Camp & Bash, 1981) and social problem solving (Shure, 2001; Shure & Spivac, 1980, 1982). Collaborative teams of parents and teachers have created and implemented behavioral interventions to reduce aggressive student behaviors (McConaughy, Kay, & Fitzgerald, 1999). Peers have been grouped to monitor each other on appropriate academic and behavioral goals, provide feedback to each other about their behavioral disruptions, and deliver reinforcement and feedback as consequences (Fantuzzo & Rohrbeck, 1992; Greenwood, Maheady, & Delquadri, 2002; Mitchem, Young, West, & Benyo, 2001).

SUMMARY

Children's school success emerges, in part, out of the social and psychological characteristics of the classrooms where they learn. The relationships and autonomy-promoting features that were reviewed here strengthen students' active participation in learning and, ultimately, contribute to academic success. Notably, the impact of these learning environments may be especially important for vulnerable students who come into the classroom under conditions of demographic or functional risk. There is some evidence that high-risk students are more sensitive to classroom learning goals, more dependent on strong relationships with their teachers, and more reactive to the peer social environment.

Regardless, once academic disengagement begins, it contributes further to the cycle of risk because poor academic competence disadvantages students. Conversely, active participation in classroom learning activities contributes to a cycle of success by feeding students' sense of academic efficacy, strengthening their relationships with teachers, raising their esteem in the eyes of their classmates, and enhancing their classroom behavioral competence.

It is not surprising that interpersonal relationships in the classroom are important to learning. Relationships have long been recognized as the foundation of personal strength and wellness, and schools have traditionally emphasized relationships when evaluating the school and classroom climate. However, a recent but important finding is that the absence of negative features in classroom relationships may have weightier impact on school success than the presence of positive features. The importance of autonomy to school success is less widely recognized than that of relationships, but is no less significant. Personal autonomy is the hallmark of one's development into a competent adult. Still, while it has been useful to divide this chapter into six sections for purposes of explanation, the reality is that these characteristics of classrooms are interconnected. Academic efficacy grows or ebbs depending, in part, on the social interactions that color a students' learning experiences. Teachers' relationships with students emerge, in part, out of students' behavioral competence. While we have presented convincing research that documents the relation of each of these classroom features with success, very little of this research has examined multiple classroom features simultaneously. Consequently, the relative and independent importance of each feature is difficult to judge at the present time.

It is important to recognize that these features of classrooms are not necessarily features of teacher competence. As the guiding authority of a classroom, teachers often have more influence over the classrooms' social and psychological environment than does any single student. However, the learning environment is also heavily affected by the collective influence of all students in the class and by the impact of the classrooms' school and community contexts. The goal of intervention is not necessarily to improve teacher behaviors, but to support teachers in their efforts to strengthen the classroom environment for learning. Fortunately, there is evidence that each of these classroom features can be strengthened and that strengthening them can improve school success.

All of which brings us back to the opening premise of this chapter. Examinations of student learning must include information about the relationships and the autonomy-enhancing features of the classrooms where students are learning. Without this information, an understanding of student ability and instructional quality will never be sufficient to explain learning problems when these arise. Finally, efforts to strengthen student learning must include efforts to foster stronger relationships and promote more autonomous learning within the classroom. When this happens, classrooms will become resilient places where all children can learn.

REFERENCES

Adelman, H. S. & Taylor, L. (2006). *The school leader's guide to student learning supports: New directions for addressing barriers to learning*. Thousand Oaks, CA: Corwin Press.

Agostin, T. & Bain, S. (1997). Predicting early school success with developmental and social skills screeners. *Psychology in the Schools, 34,* 219–228.

Ang, R. (2005). Development and validation of the Teacher-Student Relationship Inventory using exploratory and confirmatory factor analysis. *Journal of Experimental Education, 74,* 55–73.

Anguiano, R. P. V. (2004). Families and schools: The effect of parental involvement on high school completion. *Journal of Family Issues, 25,* 61–85.

Asher, S. R. (1995, June). Children and adolescents with peer relationship problems. A workshop presented at the Annual Summer Institute in School Psychology: Internalizing Disorders in Children and Adolescents. Denver, Colorado.

Assor, A., Kaplan, H., & Roth, G. (2002). Choice is good, but relevance is excellent: Autonomy-enhancing and suppressing teacher behaviours predicting students' engagement in schoolwork. *British Journal of Educational Psychology 72*, 261–278.

Bandura, A. (1989). Human agency in cognitive theory. *American Psychologist, 44*, 1175–1184.

Bandura, A. (1997). *Self-efficacy: The exercise of control.* New York: W. H. Freeman.

Bandura, A., Caprara, G. V., Barbaranelli, C., Gerbino, M., & Pastorelli, C. (2003). Role of affective self-regulatory efficacy in diverse spheres of psychosocial functioning. *Child Development, 74*, 769–782.

Barclay, J. R. (1966). Sociometric choices and teacher ratings as predictors of school dropouts. *Journal of School Psychology, 4*, 40–44.

Barth, J. M., Dunlap, S. T., Dane, H., Lochman, J. E., & Wells, K. C. (2004). Classroom environment influences on aggression, peer relations, and academic focus. *Journal of School Psychology, 42*, 115–133.

Baumrind, D. (1989). Rearing competent children. In W. Damon (Ed.), *Child development today and tomorrow* (pp. 349–378). San Francisco: Jossey-Bass.

Baumrind, D. (1991). Effective parenting during the early adolescent transition. In P. A. Cowan and E. M. Hetherington (Eds.), *Family transitions* (pp. 111–163). Hillsdale, NJ: Lawrence Erlbaum Associates, Inc.

Bear, G. G., Telzrow, C. F., & deOliveira, E. A. (1997). Socially responsible behavior. In G. G. Bear, K. M. Minke, & A. Thomas (Eds.), *Children's needs II: Development, problems and alternatives* (pp. 51–63). Bethesda, MD: National Association of School Psychologists.

Berndt, T. J. (1999). Friends' influence on students' adjustment to school. *Educational Psychologist, 34*, 15–29.

Birch, S. H. (2002). Children's relationships with peers and teachers: Assessment, linkages between relationship systems, and associations with school adjustment. *Dissertation Abstracts International Section A: Humanities and Social Sciences, 62*, 8A.

Birch, S. H., & Ladd, G. W. (1997). The teacher-child relationship and children's early school adjustment. *Journal of School Psychology, 35*, 61–79.

Birch, S. H., & Ladd, G. W. (1998). Children's interpersonal behaviors and the teacher-child relationship. *Developmental Psychology, 34*, 934–946.

Black, A. E., & Deci, E. L. (2000). The effects of instructors' autonomy support and students' autonomous motivation on learning organic chemistry: A self-determination theory perspective. *Science Educator, 84*, 740–756.

Bosworth, K. (1995). Caring for others and being cared for: Students talk caring in school. *Phi Delta Kappan, 76*, 686–693.

Breckelmans, M., Wubbels, T., & Levy, J. (1993). Student performance, attitudes, instructional strategies and teacher-communication style. In T. Wubbels & J. Levy (Eds.), *Do you know what you look like? Interpersonal relationships in education* (pp. 56–63). Washington, DC: The Falmer Press.

Camp, B. W., & Bash, M. A. (1981). *Think Aloud: Increasing social and cognitive skills—A problem-solving program for children.* Champaign, IL: Research Press.

Carroll, J. (1963). A model of school learning. *Teachers College Record, 64*, 723–733.

Carter, R. S., & Wojtkiewicz, R. A. (2000). Parental involvement with adolescents' education: Do daughters or sons get more help? *Adolescence, 35*, 29–44.

Clark, M. L. (1991). Social identity, peer relations and academic competence of African-American adolescents. *Education and Urban Society, 24*, 41–52.

Coie, J. D., Dodge, K. A., & Kupersmidt, J. B. (1990). Peer group behavior and social status. In S. R. Asher & J. D. Coie (Eds.), *Peer rejection in childhood* (pp. 17–59). New York: Cambridge University Press.

Coie, J. D., Watt, N. F., West, S. G., Hawkins, J. D., Asarnow, J. R., Markan, H. J., et al. (1993). The science of prevention: A conceptual framework and some directions for a national research program. *American Psychologist, 48*, 1013–1022.

Consortium on the School-based Promotion of Social Competence. (1994). The school-based promotion of social competence: Theory, research, practice, and policy. In R. J. Haggerty, L. R. Sherrod, N. Germezy, & M. Rutter (Eds.), *Stress, risk, and resilience in children and adolescents* (pp. 268–316). New York: Cambridge University Press.

Covington, M. V. (1992). *Making the grade: A self-worth perspective on motivation and school reform.* New York: Cambridge University Press.

Damon, W. (1992). Teaching as a moral craft and developmental expedition. In F. K. Oser, A. Dick, & J. Patry (Eds.), *Effective and responsible teaching: The new synthesis* (pp. 139–153). San Fransisco: Jossey-Bass Publishers.

Deci, E. L., Koestner, R., & Ryan, R. M. (2001). Extrinsic rewards and intrinsic motivation in education: Reconsidered once again. *Review of Educational Research, 71*, 1–27.

DeRosier, M. E., Kupersmidt, J. B., & Patterson, C. J. (1994). Children's academic and behavioral adjustment as a function of the chronicity and proximity of peer rejection. *Child Development, 65*, 1799–1813.

Doll, B. (1996). Children without friends: Implications for practice and policy. *School Psychology Review, 25,* 165–183.

Doll, B. (2005, July). Resilient classrooms: Places where all kids succeed. A keynote address presented at the Second Annual Summer Conference of the National Association of School Psychologists, Philadelphia, PA.

Doll, B., & Lyon, M. (1998). Risk and resilience: Implications for the practice of school psychology. *School Psychology Review, 27,* 348–363.

Doll, B., Murphy, P., & Song, S. (2003). The relation between children's self-reported recess problems, and peer acceptance and friendships. *Journal of School Psychology, 41,* 113–130.

Doll, B., Zucker, S., & Brehm, K. (2004). *Resilient classrooms: Creating healthy environments for learning.* New York: Guilford Press.

Dweck, C. S. (1989). Motivation. In A. Lesgold & R. Glaser (Eds.), *Foundations for a psychology of education* (pp. 87–136). Hillsdale, NJ: Erlbaum.

Epstein, J. L. (2005). Attainable goals? The spirit and letter of the No Child Left Behind Act on parental involvement. *Sociology of Education, 78,* 179–182.

Epstein, J. L., & Sheldon, S. B. (2002). Present and accounted for: improving student attendance through family and community involvement. *Journal of Educational Research, 95,* 308–318.

Epstein, J. L., & Van Voorhis, F. L. (2001). More than minutes: Teachers' roles in designing homework. *Educational Psychologist, 36,* 181–193.

Esler, A. N., Godber, Y., & Christenson, S. L. (2002). Best practices in supporting home-school collaboration. In A. Thomas & J. Grimes (Eds.), *Best Practices in School Psychology IV* (pp. 389–411). Bethesda, MD: National Association of School Psychologists.

Fan, X. (2001). Parental involvement and students' academic achievement: A growth modeling analysis. *Journal of Experimental Education, 70,* 27–61.

Fantuzzo, J. W., & Rohrbeck, C. A. (1992). Self-managed groups: Fitting self-management approaches into classroom systems. *School Psychology Review, 21,* 255–263.

Fleming, C. B., Haggerty, K. P., Catalano, R. F., Harachi, T. W., Mazza, J. J., & Gruman, D. H. (2005). Do social and behavioral characteristics targeted by preventive interventions predict standardized test scores and grades? *Journal of School Health, 75,* 342–349.

Glaser, R. (1982). Instructional psychology: Past, present, and future. *American Psychologist, 37,* 292–305.

Gottfried, A. E., Fleming, J. S., & Gottfried, A. W. (1994). Role of parental motivational practices in children's academic intrinsic motivation and achievement. *Journal of Educational Psychology, 86,* 104–113.

Greenburg, M. T., Kusche, C. A., Cook, E. T., & Quamma, J. P. (1995). Promoting emotional competence in school-aged children: The effects of the PATHS curriculum. *Development and Psychopathology, 7,* 117–136.

Greene, R. W., Abidin, R. R., & Kmetz, C. (1997). The Index of Teaching Stress: A measure of student-teacher compatibility. *Journal of School Psychology, 35,* 239–259.

Greenwood, C. R., Maheady, L., & Delquadri, J. C. (2002). Classwide peer tutoring programs. In M. R. Shinn, H. M. Walker, & G. Stoner (Eds.), *Interventions for academic and behavior problems II: Preventative and remedial approaches* (pp. 611–649). Bethesda, MD: National Association of School Psychologists.

Grotpeter, J. K. & Crick N. R. (1996). Relational aggression, overt aggression, and friendship. *Child Development, 67,* 2328–2338.

Haertel, G. D., Walberg, H. J., & Weinstein, T. (1983). Psychological models of educational performance: A theoretical synthesis of constructs. *Review of Educational Research, 53,* 75–92.

Hamre, B. & Pianta, R. (2001). Early teacher-child relationships and the trajectory of children's school outcomes through eighth grade. *Child Development, 72,* 625–638.

Hamre, B. & Pianta, R. (2005). Can instructional and emotional support in the first-grade classroom make a difference for children at-risk for school failure? *Child Development, 76,* 949–967.

Hawkins, J. D., Catalano, R. F., Kosterman, R., Abott, R. D., & Hill, K. G. (1999). Preventing adolescent health-risk behavior by strengthening protection during childhood. *Archives of Pediatrics and Adolescent Medicine, 153,* 226–234.

Hawkins, J. D., Smith, B. H., Hill, K. G., Kosterman, R. F. C., Catalano, F. C., & Abbott, R. D. (2003). Understanding and preventing crime and violence: Findings from the Seatle Social Development Project. In T. P. Thornberry & M. D. Krohn (Eds.), *Taking stock of delinquency: An overview of findings from contemporary longitudinal studies* (pp. 255–312). New York: Kluwer Academic/Plenum Press.

Hill, N. E., Castellino, D. R., Lansford, J. E., Nowlin, P., Dodge, K. A., Bates, J. E., & Pettit, G. S. (2004). Parent academic involvement as related to school behavior, achievement, and aspirations: Demographic variations across adolescence. *Child Development, 75,* 1491–1509.

Hill, N. E., & Taylor, L. C. (2004). Parental school involvement and children's academic achievement. *Current Directions in Psychological Science, 13,* 161–164.

Hoover-Dempsey, K. V., & Sandler, H. M. (1995). Parental involvement in children's education: Why does it make a difference? *Review of Educational Research, 97,* 310–333.

Hoover-Dempsey, K. V., & Sandler, H. M. (1997). Why do parents become involved in their children's education? *Review of Educational Research, 67*, 3–42.

Hughes, J. N., & Cavell, T. A. (1999). Influence of the teacher-student relationship in childhood conduct problems: A prospective study. *Journal of Clinical Child Psychology, 28*, 173–185.

Izzo, C. V., Weissberg, R. P., Kasprow, W. J., & Fendrich, M. (1999). A longitudinal assessment of teacher perceptions of parental involvement in children's education and school performance. *American Journal of Community Psychology, 27*, 817–839.

Johnson, D. W., Johnson, R. T., Buckman, L. A., & Richards, P. S. (1998). The effect of prolonged implementation of cooperative learning on social support within the classroom. *The Journal of Psychology, 119*, 405–411.

Kavale, K. A., & Forness, S. R. (1999). *Efficacy of Special Education and Related Services*. Washington, DC: American Association on Mental Retardation.

Kellam, S. G., Ling, X., Merisca, R., Brown, C. H., & Ialongo, N. (1998). The effect of the level of aggression in the first grade classroom on the course and malleability of aggressive behavior into middle school. *Development and Psychopathology, 10*, 165–185.

Kesner, J. E. (2000). Teacher characteristics and the quality of child-teacher relationships. *Journal of School Psychology, 28*, 133–149.

Kessler-Sklar, S. L., & Baker, A. J. L. (2000). School district parent involvement policies and programs. *The Elementary School Journal, 101*, 101–120.

Kupersmidt, J., Coie, J., & Dodge, K. (1990). The role of poor peer relationships in the development of disorder. In S. R. Asher & J. D. Coie (Eds.), *Peer rejection in childhood* (pp. 274–308). New York: Cambridge University Press.

Ladd, G. W., Birch, S. H., & Buhs, E. S. (1999). Children's social and scholastic lives in kindergarten: Related spheres of influence? *Child Development, 70*, 1373–1400.

Lane, K., Pierson, M., & Givner, C. (2003). Teacher expectations of student behavior: Which skills do elementary and secondary teachers deem necessary for success in the classroom? *Education and Treatment of Children, 26*, 413–430.

Linnenbrink, E. A., & Pintrich, P. R. (2002). Motivation as an enabler for academic success. *School Psychology Review, 31*, 313–327.

Lorsbach, A. W., & Jinks, J. L. (1999). Self-efficacy theory and learning environment research. *Learning Environments Research, 2*, 157–167.

Malecki, C. K., & Elliott, S. N. (2002). Children's social behaviors as predictors of academia achievement: a longitudinal analysis. *School Psychology Quarterly, 17*, 1–23.

Mapp, K. L. (2003). Having their say: Parents describe why and how they are engaged in their children's learning. *The School Community Journal, 13*, 35–64.

Masten, A. S. (2001). Ordinary Magic: Resilience processes in development. *American Psychologist, 56*, 227–238.

Masten, A. S., Coatsworth, J. D., Neemann, J., Gest, S. D., Tellegen, A., & Garmezy, N. (1995). The structure of competence in favorable and unfavorable environments. In D. Cicchetti & D. J. Cohen (Eds.), *Developmental Psychopathology* (pp. 715–752). New York: Wiley.

Masten, A. S., Hubbard, J. J., Gest, S. D., Tellegen A., Garmezy, N., & Ramirez, M. (1999). Competence in the context of adversity: Pathways to resilience and maladaptation from childhood to late adolescence. *Development and Psychopathology, 11*, 143–169.

Masten, A., S., Roisman, G. I., Long, J. D., Burt, K. B., Obradovic, J., Riley, J. R., et al. (2005). Developmental cascades: Linking academic achievement and externalizing and internalizing symptoms over 20 years. *Developmental Psychology, 41*, 733–746.

Mattingly, D. J., Prislin, R., McKenzie, T. L., Rodriguez, J. L., & Kayzar, B. (2002). Evaluating evaluations: The case of parent involvement programs. *Review of Educational Research, 72*, 549–576.

McConaughy, S., Kay, P., & Fitzgerald, M. (1999). The achieving, behaving, caring project for preventing ED: Two-year outcomes. *Journal of Emotional and Behavioral Disorders, 7*, 224–240.

McDermott, P. A., Mordell, M., & Stoltzfus, J. (2001). The organization of student performance in American schools: Discipline, motivation, verbal learning, and nonverbal learning. *Journal of Educational Psychology, 93*, 65–76.

McWayne, C., Hampton, V., Fantuzzo, J., Cohen, H. L., & Sekino, Y. (2004). A multivariate examination of parent involvement and the social and academic competencies of urban kindergarten children. *Psychology in the Schools, 41*, 363–377.

Meehan, B., Hughes, J., & Cavell, T. (2003). Teacher-student relationships as compensatory resources for aggressive children. *Child Development, 74*, 1145–1157.

Mitchem, K. J., Young, K. R., West, R. P., & Benyo, J. (2001). CWPASM: A Classwide Peer-Assisted Self-Management Program for general education classrooms. *Education and Treatment of Children, 24*, 111–141.

Multon, K. D., Brown, S. D., & Lent, R. W. (1991). Relation of self-efficacy beliefs to academic outcomes: A meta-analytic investigation. *Journal of Counseling Psychology, 38*, 30–38.

Murphy, P. (2002). The effect of classroom meetings on the reduction of recess problems: A single case design. Unpublished doctoral dissertation, University of Denver, Denver, CO.

Murray, C. & Malmgren, K. (2005). Implementing a teacher-student relationship program in a high-poverty urban school: Effects on social, emotional, and academic adjustment and lessons learned. *Journal of School Psychology, 43*, 137–152.

Murray, C. & Murray, K. (2004). Child level correlates of teacher-student relationships: An examination of demographic characteristics, academic orientations, and behavioral orientations. *Psychology in the Schools, 41*, 751–762.

Nansel, T. R., Overpeck, M., & Pilla, R. S. (2001). Bullying behaviors among U.S. youth: Prevalence and association with psychosocial adjustment. *Journal of the American Medical Association, 285*, 2094–2100.

National Center for Educational Statistics. (2002). *Dropout Rates in the United States: 2000.* Washington DC: U.S. Department of Education.

Pajares, F. (1996). Self-efficacy beliefs in academic settings. *Review of Educational Research, 66*, 543–578.

Pajares, F. (2003). Self-efficacy beliefs, motivation, and achievement in writing: A review of the literature. *Reading & Writing Quarterly: Overcoming Learning Difficulties, 19*, 139–158.

Pajares, F., & Schunk, D. H. (2001). Self-beliefs and school success: Self-efficacy, self-concept, and school achievement. In R. J. Riding & S. G. Rayner (Eds.), *Self perception* (pp. 239–265). Westport, CT: Ablex Publishing.

Pajares, F., & Schunk, D. H. (2002). Self and self-belief in psychology and education: A historical perspective. In J. Aronson (Ed.), *Improving academic achievement: Impact of psychological factors on education* (pp. 3–21). San Diego: Academic Press.

Pastorelli, C., Caprara, G. V., Barbaranelli, C., Rola, J., Rozsa, S., & Bandura, A. (2001). The structure of children's perceived self-efficacy: A cross-national study. *European Journal of Psychological Assessment, 17*, 87–97.

Pianta, R. C. (1999). *Enhancing relationships between children and teachers.* Washington, DC: American Psychological Association.

Pianta, R. C., & Nimetz, S. L. (1991). Relationships between children and teachers: Associations with classroom and home behavior. *Journal of Applied Developmental Psychology, 12*, 379–393.

Pianta, R. C. & Stuhlman, M. W. (2004). Teacher-child relationships and children's success in the first years of school. *School Psychology Review, 33*, 444–458.

Pintrich, P. R. (2003). A motivational science perspective on the role of student motivation in learning and teaching contexts. *Journal of Educational Psychology, 95*, 667–686.

President's Commission on Excellence in Special Education. (2002). *A new era: Revitalizing special education for children and their families.* Washington, DC: U.S. Department of Education.

Resnick, M. D., Bearman, P. S., Blum, R. W., Bauman, K. E., Harris, K. M., Jones, J., et al. (1997). Protecting adolescents from harm: Findings from the National Longitudinal Study on Adolescent Health. *Journal of the American Medical Association, 278*, 823–832.

Rudolph, K., Lambert, S., Clark, A., & Kurlakowsky, K. (2001). Negotiating the transition to middle school: The role of self-regulatory processes. *Child Development, 72*, 929–946.

Rutter, M., & Maughan, B. (2002). School effectiveness findings, 1979–2002. *Journal of School Psychology, 40*, 451–475.

Rutter, M., Maughan, B., Mortimore, P., Ouston, J., & Smith, A. (1979). *Fifteen thousand hours: Secondary schools and their effects on children.* Cambridge, MA: Harvard University Press.

Ryan, A. M., Patrick, H., & Shim, S. O. (2005). Differential profiles of students identified by their teacher as having avoidant, appropriate, or dependent help-seeking tendencies in the classroom. *Journal of Educational Psychology, 97*, 275–285.

Sanz de Acedo Lizarraga, M. L., Ugarte, M. D., Iriarte, M. D., & Sanz de Acedo Baquedano, M. T. (2003). Immediate and long-term effects of a cognitive intervention on intelligence, self-regulation, and academic achievement. *European Journal of Psychology of Education, 18*, 59–74.

Sartor, C. E., & Youniss, J. (2002). The relationship between positive parental involvement and identity achievement during adolescence. *Adolescence, 37*, 221–234.

Schunk, D. H., & Pajares, F. (2005). Competence perceptions and academic functioning. In A. J. Elliot & C. S. Dweck (Eds.), *Handbook of competence and motivation* (pp. 85–104). New York: Guilford Publications, Inc.

Shumow, L., & Miller, J. D. (2001). Parents' at-home and at-school academic involvement with young adolescents. *Journal of Early Adolescence, 21*(1), 68–91.

Shure, M. B. (2001). What's right with prevention? Commentary on "Prevention of mental disorders in school-aged children." *Prevention and Treatment, 4*, np.

Shure, M. B., & Spivac, G. (1980). Interpersonal problem solving as a mediator of behavioral adjustment in preschool and kindergarten children. *Journal of Applied Developmental Psychology, 1*, 29–44.

Shure, M. B. & Spivac, G. (1982). Interpersonal problem solving in young children: A cognitive approach to prevention. *American Journal of Community Psychology, 10*, 341–355.

Siemers, E. (2006). Children's aggression at recess: Examining the relation between the playground environment and aggressive behavior. Unpublished doctoral dissertation, University of Nebraska, Lincoln, NE.

Smith, S. W., Daunic, A. P., & Miller, M. D. (2002). Conflict resolution and peer mediation in middle schools: Extending the process and outcome knowledge base. *Journal of Social Psychology, 142*, 567–586.

Soloman, D., & Kendall, A. J. (1977). Dimensions of children's classroom behavior as perceived by teachers. *American Educational Research Journal, 14*, 411–421.

Stuhlman, M., & Pianta, R. (2001). Teachers' narratives about their relationships with children: Associations with behavior in classrooms. *School Psychology Review, 31*, 148–163.

Sugai, G., Horner, R. H., & Gresham, F. M. (2002). Behaviorally effective school environments. In M. R. Shinn, H. M. Walker, & G. Stoner (Eds.), *Interventions for academic and behavior problems II: Preventive and remedial approaches* (pp. 315–350). Bethesda, MD: National Association of School Psychologists.

Turner, J. C., Midgley, C., Meyer, D. K., Gheen, M., Anderman, E. M., Kang, Y., & Patrick, H. (2002). The classroom environment and students' reports of avoidance strategies in mathematics: A multimethod study. *Journal of Educational Psychology, 94*, 88–106.

Wang, M. C., Haertel, G. D., & Walberg, H. J. (1990). What influences learning? A content analysis of review literature. *Journal of Educational Research, 84*, 30–43.

Wang, M. C., & Walberg, H. J. (1985). *Adapting instruction to individual differences.* Berkeley, CA: McCutchan.

Waxman, H. C., Anderson, L., Huang, S. L., & Weinstein, T. (2001). Classroom process differences in inner-city elementary schools. *Journal of Educational Research, 91*, 49–59.

Wehmeyer, M. L., & Metzler, C. A. (1995). How self-determined are people with mental retardation? The National Consumer Survey. *Mental Retardation, 33*, 111–119.

Wentzel, K. R. (1991). Relations between social competence and academic achievement in early adolescence. *Child Development, 62*, 1066–1078.

Wentzel, K. R. (2002). Are effective teachers like good parents? Teaching styles and student adjustment in early adolescence. *Child Development, 73*, 287–301.

Wentzel, K. R., & Caldwell, K. (1997). Friendships, peer acceptance, and group membership: Relations to academic achievement in middle school. *Child Development, 68*, 1198–1209.

Wentzel, K. R., & Watkins, D. E. (2002). Peer relationships and collaborative learning as contexts for academic enablers. *School Psychology Review, 31*, 366–377.

Zimmerman, B. J. (2000). Self-efficacy: An essential motive to learn. *Contemporary Educational Psychology, 25*, 82–91.

Zimmerman, B. J., & Kitsantas, A. (1999). Acquiring writing revision skill: Shifting from process to outcome self-regulatory goals. *Journal of Educational Psychology, 91*, 241–250.

CHAPTER 37

TEAMS AS VALUE-ADDED CONSULTATION SERVICES

TODD A. GRAVOIS, SARAH GROFF, AND SYLVIA ROSENFIELD
University of Maryland, College Park

Finding a team in today's schools is not a difficult prospect. Teams that promote student assistance, teacher support and schoolwide services have proliferated since the passage of the Education for All Handicapped Children Act (Public Law 94-142). Beginning with the mandated multidisciplinary team (MDT), which was designated as the primary decision-making body for referrals, eligibility, and placements to special education, the use of teams has expanded into supporting students and teachers prior to referral. Teams are now problem solving units for the inclusion of students already identified for special education (e.g., Fuchs & Fuchs, 1989, Thousand & Villa, 1992) and providing general support for students struggling within the general education classroom (e.g., Chalfant & Pysh, 1989; Graden, Casey, & Christenson, 1985; Kovaleski, Tucker, & Duffy, 1995; Rosenfield & Gravois, 1996).

With the recent reauthorization of the Individuals with Disabilities Education Improvement Act of 2004 (IDEIA), the number and use of teams in schools for a variety of purposes will, without doubt, increase. The reauthorized IDEIA has granted increased flexibility to local districts in determining decision-making procedures for special education eligibility (i.e., Response to Intervention; Gresham et al., 2005). A central feature of the law endorses a group of professionals making those decisions. These mandates cement the use of teams for prereferral activities and for eligibility for at least another decade.

While teams have been a mainstay in education for well over thirty years, the empirical research relating to teams in schools remains limited (Burns & Symington, 2002). And, even as the research on teams and their impact in schools begins to grow, it remains difficult to effectively interpret or attribute the observed effects found in the research to any particular aspect of the team structure itself. For example, in the literature there is often an assumption that anytime multiple professionals work together, it is considered a team. This lack of conceptual clarity about the essential components of team-based services casts a shadow on the ability of both practitioners and researchers to interpret existing research effectively and also hinders future research efforts.

Further, an additional question is rarely addressed: "Is there an added value of delivering support services through teams versus individual consultation?" Such a question challenges team developers and researchers to create causal theories that specify team model components, indicate the links between the defined components and expected outcomes, and conduct research that establishes how the model of teaming presented leads to the observed outcomes.

Considering the potential for a new wave of teaming structures facing education as a result of changes in the special education law, the primary focus of this chapter is to provide a context for team use in schools and offer a framework for program developers and researchers interested in promoting the successful adoption of teams by schools, districts and states. A summary of the current state of teams in schools will be conducted by reviewing models of teams and the associated research literature; following the summary, a framework that conceptualizes teams as a form of consultation service delivery will be introduced. Specifically, it is proposed that teams can be identified as a third dimension of general consultation services. This conceptualization allows for establishing a theoretical model that justifies the use and importance of delivering services through teams. It also assists in organizing the variation of team models presented in the literature. Finally, and most important, this conceptual framework can frame a research agenda that will support the future investigation of the impact of team services within the larger educational arena.

CURRENT STATE OF THE FIELD

Burns and Symington's (2002) recent meta-analysis of research on prereferral intervention teams epitomizes the state of the field of school-based teams. Their review confirmed two aspects of team research. First, they concluded that much of the research is descriptive of program components with few rigorous studies. Second, the few studies with attempts at empirical analyses did find positive outcomes.

For example, Burns and Symington's search of the literature resulted in a pool of 72 articles to be considered for the meta-analysis. However, only about one-third of the articles reviewed presented data related to outcomes of team implementation. Further, there was a noted lack of rigor in the research on teams with only nine articles meeting the methodological criteria required to conduct the analysis (i.e., availability of means, standard deviations and statistical analysis).

However, the analysis of these nine articles did find relatively strong effect sizes after categorizing the results based upon methodological design used, source of implementation (i.e., university initiated versus field initiated) and dependent variable. The dependent variables in these studies included both student variables (e.g., time on task, teacher ratings of student behavior) and systemic variables (e.g., referrals to and placement in special education, number of students retained in grade, an increase in consultative activity by school psychologists). Burns and Symington's (2002) analysis found a mean effect size of 1.43 for research studies on teams that utilized a design incorporating randomized control and a mean effect size of 1.15 for research focusing upon student outcomes (Burns and Symington, 2002).

Research on Teams

Additional review of the literature provides a representation of the types of studies that generally investigate the impact of teams upon several common outcomes. While such studies do not always conform to the rigor sought by Burns and Symington (2002), they do provide insight into the potential impact that teams have on special education referral patterns, student behavior, teacher satisfaction, and teacher skills and knowledge.

Special Education Patterns (General)

A major impetus for the development of school-based teams was to support teachers' and students' prior referral for special education services. Hence it is not surprising that the most commonly reported impact of school teams appears to center on the impact that such teams have upon systemic patterns of referral and placement into special education. Reduction in special education referrals has been demonstrated in a number of studies that have examined a variety of team models including Teacher Assistance Teams (Bay, Bryan, & O'Connor, 1994; Chalfant & Pysh, 1989; Short & Talley, 1996), Prereferral Intervention Teams (Graden, Casey, and Bonstrom, 1985; Ingalls & Hammond, 1996), Building Educational Support Teams (Henning-Stout, Lucas, & McCary, 1993), Peer Intervention Teams (Saver & Downes, 1991), Instructional Support Teams (Kovaleski et al., 1995), Project ACHIEVE (Knoff & Batsche, 1995), Instructional Consultation Teams (Gravois & Rosenfield, 2002), Mainstream Assistance Teams (Fuchs, Fuchs, & Bahr, 1990), and School Based-Intervention Teams (McDougal, Moody, Clonan, & Martens, 2000).

Special Education Patterns (Minority Populations)

Related to reduction of overall special education referrals, a second goal of many problem-solving teams is to reduce the disproportional representation of minority students in special education. To date, few studies have examined the referral patterns of minority versus nonminority students. However, Gravois and Rosenfield (2002) found that fewer African American students referred to the Instructional Consultation Team (IC Teams) were subsequently referred to special education, compared to African American students initially referred to the existing school-based team. A subsequent study by Gravois and Rosenfield (2006) found significant reductions in the referral and placement of minority students in special education when comparing schools implementing IC Teams with comparison schools that continued to implement their existing support team models. Thus, there is preliminary evidence that a team-based consultation approach to problem solving is effective in reducing the overrepresentation of minority students in special education.

Student Behavior

In addition to reducing the number of referrals to special education, there is evidence that problem-solving teams have a positive influence on student behavior. In a highly controlled school-based study, Fuchs and Fuchs (1989) reported mixed findings regarding the influence of Mainstream Assistance Teams (MATs). They found that teachers participating in the MAT indicated significantly more improvement in their students' problem behaviors than did nonparticipating teachers. However, direct behavioral observations did not corroborate the teacher reports. In a study published a year later (Fuchs, Fuchs, & Bahr 1990), two types of teacher rating scales as well as direct observations of student behavior revealed significant gains for students involved in MAT but not students in the control group. These findings were replicated in two additional studies (Fuchs, Fuchs, Bahr, Fernstrom, & Stecker, 1990; Fuchs, Fuchs, Harris, & Roberts, 1996).

Student Achievement

Whereas the MAT focuses on problem behaviors, other models put a stronger emphasis on improving academic behaviors. For example, the Instructional Support Team (IST) was developed as an early intervention program for students struggling in school (Kovaleski, Gickling, Morrow, & Swank, 1999). In a study investigating the effectiveness of the IST related to program integrity, Kovaleski and colleagues (1999) found that over time students in IST schools demonstrated significant improvement in their academic learning time, as measured by time on task, task completion, and task comprehension. However, it was found that such gains were significant only in the schools that had high implementation of the IST program. High implementation schools were defined as those schools that scored in the top 30% on a measure of implementation of various elements of the IST process. Low-implementation IST schools (those schools scoring in the bottom 30% on the measure of implementation), on the other hand, showed virtually the same patterns as schools with no IST.

Teacher Satisfaction, Skills, and Knowledge

Teachers participating in Teacher Assistance Teams (TATs) have reported satisfaction with the team and cited appreciation of moral support and reinforcement provided by the team, usefulness of the group problem solving to generate intervention strategies, and improvement in student performance and behavior (Chalfant & Pysh, 1989). Teachers participating in TATs have also been shown to use new and different strategies in their classrooms more so than nonparticipating teachers (Bay, Bryan, & O'Connor, 1994). Research on Peer Intervention Teams indicated that teachers reported alleviation of feelings of frustration and isolation, being treated as an equal collaborator in the problem-solving process, and promotion of a collaborative school atmosphere (Saver & Downes, 1991). Fuchs et al. (1990) found that teachers who participated in the MAT were satisfied with the process, particularly with the consultants.

Essential Team Elements

While research findings provide evidence that teams do impact relevant outcomes (e.g., student behavior, teaching practices), there is less understanding as to what elements were critical in the development and implementation of these teams to produce the stated outcomes. Indeed, a major challenge in reviewing the research on teams is that there is not always sufficient detail in the descriptions of the particular team models to decipher which essential elements are critical to the effective functioning of the team.

Clarity about what constitutes an effective team will help in the development, training, implementation and replication of these efforts. For example, components that are often cited in the general literature as essential in effective team functioning include: (a) observable definition of the target behavior, (b) baseline data, (c) measurable goals, (d) specified intervention plans, (e) data collection after intervention implementation, and (f) comparison of the student's postintervention performance with baseline (Donovan & Cross, 2002; Kovaleski, 2002; Telzrow, McNamara, & Hollinger, 2000).

Some research has been conducted to support these components. Telzrow, McNamara, and Hollinger (2000) examined implementation fidelity of eight problem-solving components in 227 problem-solving teams. The six components listed previously and two additional components (generating a hypothesized reason for the problem and intervention integrity) were examined. Using ratings of work products submitted by the problem-solving teams, they found that six of the eight components (all but "hypothesized reason for the problem" and "treatment integrity") were significantly, positively correlated with student outcomes (as measured by student goal attainment). It was also found that two of the components ("clearly identified goal" and "data indicating student response to intervention") were the most significant predictors of student outcomes.

CREATING A CONCEPTUAL MODEL FOR TEAM-BASED SERVICES

The review of the literature presents a unique dilemma that is emerging in the research on team-based services. The initial research findings suggest teams do have a positive impact on select student, teacher and school variables. However, the essential elements that are most frequently cited for effective team-based services are largely characteristic of individually delivered consultation (i.e., use of systematic problem-solving stages) and cannot be considered exclusive to team functioning. This overlap presents both a challenge and opportunity. It reveals a gap in a theoretical or causal model that questions the need to deliver support services via a team rather than simply provide individual consultation. If the elements that are cited for effective teams are the same elements that are essential for effective consultation, what is the added value of using team-based services?

As an example of this interplay between team and individual consultation services, Fuchs et al. (1996), in their own work with MAT's, initially used a full team combined with team members working with teachers in consultant-consultee dyads. However, as their research evolved, the role of the full team was diminished since it appeared more efficient and effective to have only the consultant-consultee structure.

This theoretical gap is also evident in practice. For example, Truscott, Cohen, Sams, Sanborn, and Frank (2005) found wide variation in the stated focus and function of school-based teams. They found that members of the same teams rarely agreed as to the purpose or function of the team. Indeed less than 30% of team members surveyed indicated a common goal or purpose for the team functioning.

These research findings challenge the added value of using team-based services rather than individual consultation. However, there is also an opportunity to strengthen the value of teams as a vehicle for service if a conceptual framework can be established that promotes consistency

and theoretical validity across the large number of team-based models presented within the literature. We propose that a majority of teams that operate in schools can be conceptualized as an extension of individual consultation service that have the potential of adding value to the effectiveness of support services in schools. There is a strong relationship between teams and consultation services in the literature. For example, consultation, defined as a "nonsupervisory relationship between professionals from different fields established to aid one in his or her professional functioning" (Conoley & Conoley, 1982, p. 1), relates closely to the definition often used to describe prereferral teams: "a schoolwide method of systematically providing and documenting interventions developed through consultation and implemented in the regular classroom prior to consideration of a referral for traditional psychoeducational assessment and decision making" (Ponti, Zins, & Graden, 1988, p. 89). Further, teams and individual consultation are often considered indirect forms of service whereby support is provided to the teacher who in turn supports the student.

Teams as a Third Dimension of Consultation Service Delivery

The similarities between consultation and team services provide an opportunity to create an explicit conceptual connection. Whereas consultation services have traditionally been described as operating along the two major dimensions: focus and function (see for example, Meyers, 2002; Meyers & Nastasi, 1999), Figure 37.1 extends this to include a third dimension, that of *form*. Form incorporates the structure by which consultation services are delivered within schools (i.e., individual, group or team).

Focus

The first dimension, focus, refers to level of impact that the consultation service hopes to achieve. Within school settings for example, client-centered consultation services are provided to the teacher for the primary purpose of impacting change in student behavior and achievement (Gutkin & Curtis, 1999) while at other times, the focus of consultation is consultee-centered, to primarily impact the teacher's current and future knowledge and skills (Knotek & Sandoval, 2003). In many client-centered models, the outcome of the consultation process can be recommendations for direct service to the student

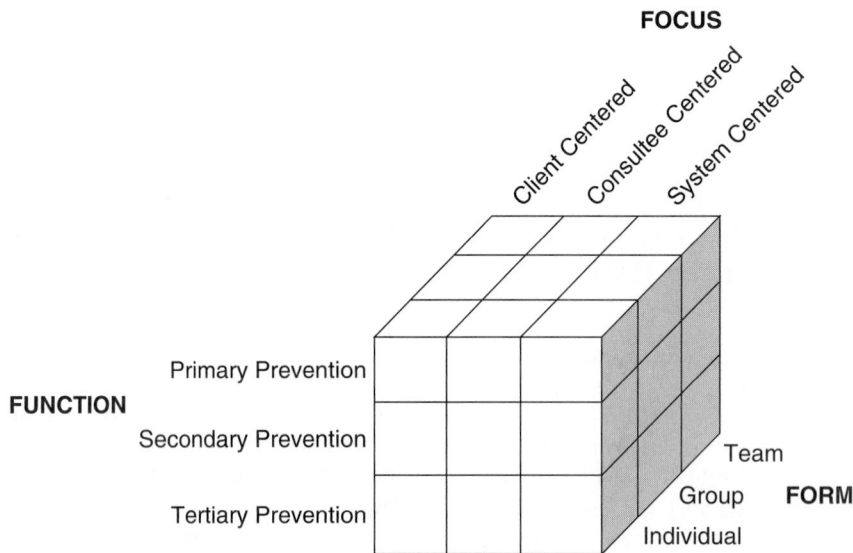

FIGURE 37.1   Dimensions of Consultation Services.

that is delivered by a specialist outside of the classroom, rather than supporting the classroom teacher to address the concerns differently. In consultee-centered consultation, however, the consultation relationship serves as an arena not only in which interventions are developed, but where the teacher can gain new skills, receive feedback on whether he or she is implementing the intervention correctly, and help design an intervention that is acceptable to the teacher and that fits with the ecology of the classroom. Still at other times, the consultant works with a variety of individuals within the school setting to impact the process and procedures of the larger school functioning (e.g., system centered, see for example Illback, Zins, & Maher, 1999; Curtis & Stollar, 2002).

Regardless of the level focused upon, Meyers (2002) argues that all three levels of impact remain models of indirect service delivery since the ultimate outcome of the service is for someone other than the consultant to implement an intervention or program. The defined focus of particular consultation services represents a major decision since the skills and knowledge used by the consultant are influenced in part by target individual(s) the consultant intends to impact. For example, consultee-centered consultation presumes that the service delivered will impact the teacher as a primary outcome rather than the student directly. The defined focus of consultation service is also important in designing research, since it ultimately provides guidance as to the unit of analysis when evaluating the effectiveness of the service.

Function

The second dimension of consultation depicted in Figure 37.1 stresses the function or desired outcome. Specifically, consultation services can function as (a) primary prevention, or the prevention of problems before they occur; (b) secondary prevention, or intervention with groups or individuals who are at risk for a particular problem or in cases where the presenting concern is in the early stages; and/or (c) tertiary prevention, or intervention to remediate or support performance for those having an identified problem (Meyers & Nastasi, 1999; Strein, Hoagwood & Cohn, 2003). The defined function of a consultation service not only provides critical direction as to the skills and knowledge required of the consultant but, again, also provides direction for research.

Form

In order to conceptually connect the use of teams to consultation, we introduce a third dimension of consultation services, that of form. *Form* refers to the structure and cohesiveness of consultation services that exist in schools. Borrowing from the field of design, the form should have some stated connection to the function proposed by the developer (i.e., form follows function). The concept of form is intended to offer greater clarity when program developers describe the structure by which consultation services are being delivered. Such clarity will allow program developers to articulate how the form conceptually supports and advances both the focus and function intended. While some variation may exist, at least three general forms of consultation can be identified.

Individual

The first form, individual delivery, fits neatly within the current literature for consultation services (e.g., Behavioral Consultation, Bergan & Kratochwill, 1990; Conjoint Consultation, Sheridan & Kratochwill, 2007; Instructional Consultation, Rosenfield, 2002; Mental Health Consultation, Caplan & Caplan, 1993). This represents one individual, or several individuals working independently of one another, to deliver consultation services along the other two dimensions (i.e., focus and function). Individual delivery does not simply mean only one individual is providing consultation services within a school or that there is no interaction among the various individual consultants. Indeed, many individuals may be acting as consultants within the same school and may in fact meet together at times. However, there is no coordination as to the focus or function of these consultation services across the various individuals.

As an example, a school psychologist conducting consultee-centered consultation with a teacher in an effort to promote the teachers' use of risk reduction strategies (secondary prevention) with a group of students experiencing reading difficulties may be working in the same school with a school social worker conducting client-centered consultation in an effort to provide treatment for a student who has been abused by a family member. While these two consultants may or may not professionally interact, the focus and/or function of their consultation services are not coordinated.

Groups

Group problem solving represents a second form of consultation. While the terms group and team are often used interchangeably, there is growing agreement in the literature that there are differences (e.g., Iverson, 2002; Katzenbach & Smith, 1993). One distinction of groups is that the group exists as a collective unit and adheres to broad participation structures (Iverson, 2002). The group only exists when members are working together on a common focus and function. When members are functioning outside of the group

structure they do not represent the group, do not speak for the group nor hold responsibility for the group's functioning. Instead when outside of the group, members are defined by their professional role within the school, not by their membership on the group. While members may have other professional roles outside of the group (e.g., principal, special educator), decision making related to the group's mission is only made within the context of the group setting.

A second distinguishing feature is rather than each member developing a common set of knowledge and skills, each individual contributes unique knowledge and skills toward the operation of the group. Individual members combine their unique knowledge and skills to operate as a *single unit* with a common purpose to impact a particular focus (i.e., client, consultee, or system) with a particular function (e.g., prevention, early intervention). In essence, the parts constitute the whole when thinking of groups.

Teams

Team structures can be conceptualized as a third form of service delivery. There are notable distinctions between broad participation group models and teams. As Katzenbach and Smith (1993) suggest, teams share "a common purpose, set of performance goals, and approach for which they hold themselves mutually accountable" (p. 112). An important characteristic of teams then, is that members agree to develop a common set of knowledge and skills to effectively achieve the explicit shared purpose of the team (Katzenbach and Smith, 1993).

Each member adheres to the purpose and outcomes of the larger team, even if they are operating on behalf of the team *outside* of the physical presence of other members. In addition, there are clearly established performance goals that allow team members to continually evaluate their effectiveness as individual members and as a team collectively. In this way, being a member of a team means that the effectiveness of any individual members' performance is a reflection upon oneself *and* the team.

A common purpose, a clearly defined function *and* an agreed upon approach allows individual members to smoothly transition between operating as a collective unit and working as a representative of the team in dyadic interactions. A compelling rationale, or added value, for providing consultation in the form of team services as opposed to individual consultation is that the team concept provides organizational support, which has been documented as a key factor in effective service delivery (Kruger & Struzierro, 1995; McDougal et al., 2000).

As Gravois and Rosenfield (2002) describe in their work with Instructional Consultation Teams, the team delivery system both ensures the continued development of individual members' skills as effective consultants, but also creates a culture of acceptance for consultation services within the larger school setting. The concept of a critical mass of individuals all skilled in and practicing a common form of consultation services creates the "norm" for problem solving and professional collaboration and serves as a model for professionals within the larger school setting (Fullan, 1991; Gravois & Rosenfield, 2002).

Rosenfield and Gravois (1996) outlined six major roles that link the interdependent relationship between team-based and consultation services when describing Instructional Consultation Teams. First, the team meets regularly for business and team maintenance. Second, the team assesses individual member needs and plans for ongoing training. Third, the team represents the central point in the organization for teachers to request assistance. Fourth, the team facilitates organizational interventions based on patterns noted in requests from teachers. For example, if multiple teachers ask for assistance related to students struggling in the area of writing, this may reflect system-wide problems that can be identified and addressed through professional and staff development. Fifth, the team documents proceedings and outcomes. Finally, and most important, although team members provide one-to-one consultation services to teachers, the entire team remains responsible to monitor and evaluate the effectiveness of individual case consultation.

Distinguishing Individual Consultation, Groups and Teams

The distinction between the three forms of consultation offered here cannot always be determined by the title of a particular model. Indeed, many models described as teams (e.g., multidisciplinary teams) are in reality groups; they are broad participation models only existing when all members are present within the context of the group's purpose. This distinction between group and team frameworks has recently been elevated within the recent reauthorization of special education (IDEIA, 2004). The 1997 IDEA wording "a *team* may determine that a child has a specific

learning disability..." has been updated in 2004 IDEIA with the notable change in wording to "the *group* may determine that a child has a specific learning disability..." The decision to change the wording may simply represent semantics or may be a recognition that the functioning of a MDT more closely aligns with broad participation models we have described here as "groups."

The distinction being offered between groups (broad participation) and teams (coordinated case consultation) may seem minor, yet there is a growing recognition that such differences do matter. For example, in a review of outcome research on prereferral intervention models, Sindelar, Griffin, Smith, and Watanabe (1992) distinguished between teams (individually organized) and collaborative (group-based) models. This review revealed that these two forms of service have demonstrated success in different areas. Specifically, research on models formed as teams that use coordinated case management have documented direct student gains and reductions in special education referrals. The strengths of groups (i.e., broad participation models), on the other hand, include high consumer satisfaction, and widespread adoption and acceptance (Sindelar et al., 1992). While such research does not suggest that one form of consultation service is better than the other, these results create a compelling rationale to explicitly distinguish models that are formed as groups or teams.

Examples of Consultation Services Categorized by Form, Focus and Function

Consumers (e.g., schools and districts) will be better informed and better able to select a particular model of service delivery that matches their unique needs when developers specify the form, function and focus of the particular model. While by no means exhaustive, the following section attempts to provide examples of various permutations of the three-dimensional framework presented in Figure 37.1 in order to facilitate specification by future developers of school-based services.

Group/Client Centered/Tertiary

The most salient example of a group that is student centered for the purpose of remediation of an existing disorder is that of multidisciplinary teams (MDTs). The stated purpose of the MDT is to ensure appropriate placement in special education via a group composed of various school professionals who would work collaboratively to make eligibility and placement decisions based on multiple criteria. Conceptually then, MDT's are designed to provide services for students already failing within the classroom (focus), by deciding which intervention or remedial services to provide (function) and are delivered as a broad participation model with the group only existing within the confines of the decision-making function (form).

Group/Client Centered/Secondary

Many schools have mandated prereferral processes generically termed Student Support Teams (SST), Pupil Services Teams (PST) or Child Study Teams (CST). Such groups operate in the form of group problem solving using broad participation in which all members work as a collective unit. The function of such groups is to implement, document and evaluate interventions or strategies for referred students who have been identified as struggling or at risk, but prior to consideration for special education services. In such models, teachers refer students to the group and schedule discussions in which ideas for strategies can be shared. Once shared, the teacher remains largely responsible for implementing and evaluating such strategies and possibly reporting back to the group.

While it is noted that the teacher may also benefit from such interactions, the primary focus of this type of broad participation team is to positively impact the individual targeted student. One key indicator of its client versus consultee focus is that information about the student and the students' performance is the focus of the discussion, with less discussion about the performance of the teacher.

Team/Consultee Centered/Primary and Secondary

Rosenfield and Gravois (1996) proposed the Instructional Consultation Team (IC Team) model that specifically employs a team *form* by using a case management structure. The IC Team is comprised of key school-based resources including the principal, classroom teachers, special educators, and school psychologists. Teachers can request assistance for instructional and student concerns. Instead of group problem solving, an IC Team member volunteers and offers one-to-one collaboration and consultation to the teacher. Case managers develop a set of skills and

knowledge in problem solving, instructional assessment and collaboration in order to provide uniform support services to teachers. Each case manager represents the team in these one-on-one interactions with the teacher and yet always has the option to access the full team if assistance is required for the case.

Unlike individual consultation, the case manager is accountable to the team for the service to the teacher and likewise the team holds individual members accountable for providing effective support services. The team monitors the progress of each case through case updates at weekly meetings and intervenes if a case requires support. Progress on individual cases provides the foundation for team goals and further team member skill development.

The primary *focus* of the IC Team is to support the professional development of classroom teacher skills (i.e, consultee centered) in meeting the needs of students within their classroom. By engaging in collaborative consultation, the IC Team *functions* to increase and enhance the teacher's skills and knowledge in dealing with the presenting concern (secondary prevention) but more important, in developing the necessary skill and knowledge to prevent future concerns (primary prevention).

IMPLICATIONS FOR PRACTICE AND RESEARCH

Implications for Practice

Unless explicitly stated by program developers, educators are often left to draw their own assumptions as to form, function and/or focus of the service model being adopted. The lack of specificity on the part of developers has several implications for those who adopt, work with or receive services from teams or groups.

Meeting Organizational Needs

The lack of specificity by developers may result in a mismatch between what a school or district requires in terms of impact or outcome and what a given model can actually produce. Such mismatches due to lack of clarity about form, function and focus can result in decreased use of the model by teachers within a school, resistance in adopting additional team- or group-based services, or just plain frustration when the expected results aren't achieved.

Professional Development of Service Providers

Possibly the most pressing implication of clarifying the form, function, and focus of services is the ability to better match the type of professional development that service providers will require. For example, services that focus on teacher skill development (consultee centered) will require service providers who are skilled at establishing collaborative relationships with teachers. However, service providers that are primarily client centered (i.e., focused upon students) will likely seek and receive professional development that is content focused and follows an expert model. Further, services that are formed as groups may provide little professional development to members since the underlying assumption of the group form is that each member contributes his or her existing, unique professional expertise. However, team-based services require a commonality of service delivery across team members and therefore demand professional development activities to assure each member has the agreed-upon skills and knowledge.

Implications for Research

Organizing the Extant Literature

Conceptualizing the form of service as individual, group- or team-based within the domain of consultation can bring needed order to the current literature. A framework will be helpful in categorizing the current literature according to the form, function, and focus of the service being described. Explicit description of the form, function, and focus of services will also aid consumers (i.e, schools and districts) to more accurately interpret the research results before investing time and resources in adoption.

There is no attempt here to organize the extant team and group literatures according to the conceptual framework presented for two primary reasons. First, the existing literature often lacks sufficient description of the focus, function, and form to effectively categorize the services. This lack of specificity most certainly assures errors between developers' intentions and the authors' categorization. Second, it is our position that developers of services hold the responsibility to explicitly consider and describe the function, focus, and form of their services in order to promote clarity for consumers and the field at large.

Framing Future Research

While existing research is difficult to categorize due to lack of specificity, the conceptual framework presented in Figure 37.1 could help to ensure that future research of school consultation services progress in a meaningful and coherent manner. Developers will need to describe their model, and also provide a rationale for the particular form, function, and focus chosen. Finally, developers will then be challenged to research how their chosen design components connect to and produce the intended outcomes rather than just reporting generic outcomes (e.g., use logic and causal modeling).

Logic Models

In recent years, social and educational service delivery systems have been faced with demands from government and funding agencies to not only demonstrate the effectiveness of their programs, but also to justify their strategies for achieving the desired results (Hernandez, 2000; Millar, Simeone, & Carnevale, 2001). This increased emphasis on accountability necessitates clear methods for demonstrating the theory behind a program, and critically examining whether program services lead to the intended outcomes.

The increased calls for accountability in education demand that team developers explain their rationale of form chosen and make a concerted effort to substantiate their decision within their research. At a basic level, developers have a responsibility to research the impact of their service on students or teachers (dependent variable). However, developers also have an equal responsibility to specify how the form, function and focus of the service represent relevant independent variables.

One potentially useful tool for facilitating the development and evaluation of school-based groups and teams is the logic model, a technique frequently utilized by program developers and evaluators. A logic model is a visual representation of program theory that specifies the components of a given program (e.g., resources, activities, outcomes) and depicts how the resources and activities are linked to the desired outcomes (Rossi, Freeman, & Lipsey, 2004). There are several advantages to using a logic model to represent program theory. In many social and educational programs, such as those based on school groups and teams, the underlying structures are often implicit.

In a logic model, these implicit structures are made explicit (Millar et al., 2001). When program personnel, researchers, and evaluators come together to develop the logic of the program, they are also encouraged to articulate the theory and assumptions underlying the program (Scheirer, 2000).

Not only does this create a shared and accurate understanding of the program theory, but it also offers an opportunity to recognize flaws in the program logic. Further, logic models illustrate the connections among the various components of the program, thus revealing how resources are linked to activities and how activities, in turn, are linked to short- and long-term outcomes. Finally, by laying out the logic of the program in this way, it becomes easier to identify questions that the evaluation might appropriately address. For example, one can ask questions related to the resources, activities, implementation, outputs, and outcomes. It is often helpful to develop measurable standards for each of these components.

Program logic models have been used by evaluators in developing and assessing a variety of social programs, from large urban social service organizations such as the United Way (Julian, 1997) to a middle school curriculum service delivery system (Cooksy, Gill, & Kelly, 2001).

However, there are few examples in education, and fewer still related specifically to team-based services.

Example of Logic Model for Team-Based Services

Gravois and Rosenfield (2002) have provided an initial example of using a logic model to research team-based services (see Figure 37.2). In their research and development of Instructional Consultation Teams over a period of 20 years, the developers have presented a causal model that explicitly states the underlying theory of IC Teams linked directly to the extant consultation, instruction, and professional development literatures. While Figure 37.2 depicts hypothesized expected long-term outcomes at the client and system level (e.g., increased student achievement, collaborative school climates), these are considered second-order impacts. The primary *focus* of the IC Team service is the classroom teacher (i.e., consultee centered).

IC Teams are clearly defined as a team *form* of consultation utilizing equally skilled case managers (see also Rosenfield & Gravois, 1996). Rather than simply offering services by a single instructional consultant, Rosenfield and Gravois

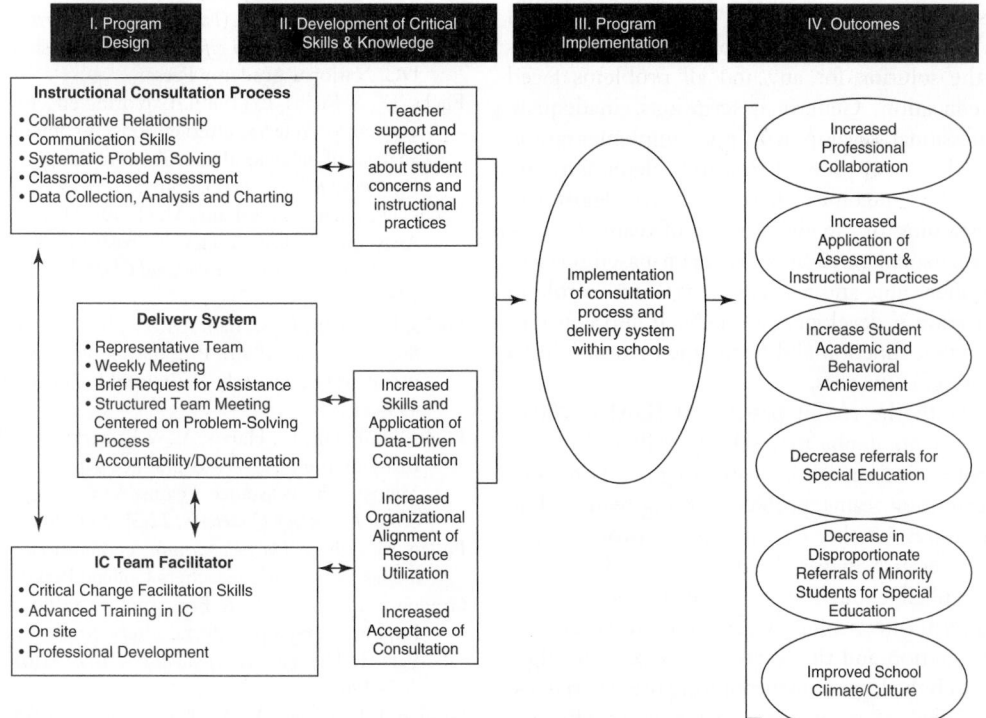

FIGURE 37.2 Instructional Consultation Team Logic Model.

(1996) explicitly describe added value of a team form of service delivery. For example, Rosenfield and Gravois hypothesize that the commonality of skill, knowledge and approach used by team members both strengthens individual team members' skills and creates a climate in the school that expects and accepts consultation as a service, thereby increasing teachers' request and use of these services.

The *function* of the IC Team service is both primary and secondary prevention. The IC Team's primary prevention function is directly grounded in theory and structure of Instructional Consultation (Rosenfield, 1987) and explicitly acknowledges the role that reflective and collaborative consultation plays in changing the teachers' frame of reference and practice (see also Knotek, Rosenfield, Gravois, & Babinski, 2003). While secondary prevention is the function of the immediate consultation, it is hypothesized that primary prevention is a long-term outcome. Through multiple experiences of instructional consultation with a variety of team members offering the same approach, teachers gain knowledge and skills that influence present and future instructional delivery.

THE FUTURE

Historically, the promoters of teams have tried to be all things to all people, advancing teams as the solution for any and all problems faced in education. Generic descriptions, inadequate professional development, poor implementation, and the slow pace of research demonstrating effective outcomes have led to legitimate questioning of the added value of team services. Our personal position is that team-based services *can* offer value and *will* have a productive role in education if developers are explicit and consider the focus, function and form when researching a team's effectiveness.

With the recent passage of IDEIA (2004), there is no doubt that schools will create and adopt an assortment of teams (e.g., response-to-intervention teams, problem-solving teams). The question is whether we will repeat history or take a new course in service delivery. If developers are explicit about the rationale for using teams as a form of consultation service delivery, specify the function and the focus of services, and then research the logic of incorporating these variables, the added value of using teams as an effective model of service delivery will be demonstrated.

REFERENCES

Bay, M., Bryan, T., & O'Connor, R. (1994). Teachers assisting teachers: A prereferral model for urban educators. *Teacher Education and Special Education*, *17*(1), 10–21.

Bergan, J. R., & Kratochwill, T. R. (1990). *Behavioral consultation in applied settings*. New York: Plenum.

Burns, M., & Symington, T. (2002). A meta-analysis of prereferral intervention teams: Student and systemic outcomes. *Journal of School Psychology*, *40*(5), 437–447.

Caplan, G., & Caplan, R. B. (1993). *Mental health consultation and collaboration*. San Francisco: Jossey-Bass.

Chalfant, J. C., & Pysh, M. V. (1989). Teacher Assistance Teams: Five descriptive studies on 96 teams. *Remedial and Special Education*, *10*(6), 49–58.

Conoley, J. C., & Conoley, C. W. (1982). *School consultation: A guide to practice and training*. New York: Pergamon.

Cooksy, L. J., Gill, P., & Kelly, P. A. (2001). The program logic model as an integrative framework for a multimethod evaluation. *Evaluation and Program Planning*, *24*, 119–128.

Curtis, M., & Stollar, S. (2002). Best practices in system-level change. In A. Thomas & J. Grimes (Eds.), *Best Practices in School Psychology IV*: Vol. 1. (pp. 223–254). Bethesda, MD: National Association of School Psychologists.

Donovan, S. & Cross, C. (Eds.) (2002). *Minority students in special and gifted education*. Washington, DC: National Academy Press.

Fuchs, D., & Fuchs, L. (1989). Exploring effective and efficient prereferral interventions: A component analysis of behavioral consultation. *School Psychology Review*, *18*(2), 260–279.

Fuchs, D., Fuchs, L., & Bahr, M. (1990). Mainstream Assistance Teams: A scientific basis for the art of consultation. *Exceptional Children*, *57*(2), 128–139.

Fuchs, D., Fuchs, L. S., Bahr, M. W., Fernstrom, P., & Stecker, P. M. (1990). Prereferral intervention: A prescriptive approach. *Exceptional Children*, *56*(6), 493–513.

Fuchs, D., Fuchs, L., Harris, A., & Roberts, H. (1996). Bridging the research-to-practice gap with Mainstream Assistance Teams: A cautionary tale. *School Psychology Quarterly*, *11*(3), 244–266.

Fullan, M. (1991). *The new meaning of educational change*. New York: Teachers College Press.

Graden, J. L., Casey, A., & Bonstrom, O. (1985). Implementing a prereferral intervention system: Part II. The data. *Exceptional Children*, *51*(6), 487–496.

Graden, J. L., Casey, A., & Christenson, S. (1985). Implementing a prereferral intervention system:

Part I. The model. *Exceptional Children, 51*(5), 377–384.

Gravois, T. A., & Rosenfield, S. A. (2002). A multi-dimensional framework for evaluation of Instructional Consultation Teams. *Journal of Applied School Psychology, 19*(1).

Gravois, T. A., & Rosenfield, S. (2006). Impact of instructional consultation teams on the disproportionate referral and placement of minority students in special education. *Journal of Remedial and Special Education, 27*, 42–52.

Gresham, F. M., Reschly, D. J., Tilly, W. D., Fletcher, J., Burns, M., Christ, T., et al. (2005). Comprehensive evaluation of learning disabilities: A response to intervention perspective. *The School Psychologist, 59*(1), 26–29.

Gutkin, T., & Curtis, M. (1999). School-based consultation theory and practice: The art and science of indirect service delivery. In C. Reynolds & T. Gutkin (Eds.), *Handbook of school psychology* (3rd ed., pp. 598–637). New York: John Wiley & Sons.

Henning-Stout, M., Lucas, D. A., & McCary, V. L. (1993). Alternative instruction in the regular classroom: A case illustration and evaluation. *School Psychology Review, 22*(1), 81–98.

Hernandez, M. (2000). Using logic models and program theory to build outcome accountability. *Education and Treatment of Children, 23*, 24–40.

Illback, R., Zins, J., & Maher, C. (1999). Program planning and evaluation: Principles, procedures and planned change. In C. Reynolds & T. Gutkin (Eds.), *Handbook of school psychology* (3rd ed., pp. 907–932). New York: John Wiley & Sons.

Individuals with Disabilities Education Improvement Act of 2004, H.R. 1350, 108 Cong., 2nd Sess.

Ingalls, L., & Hammond, H. (1996). Prereferral school-based teams: How effective are they? *Rural Special Education Quarterly, 15*(2), 9–18.

Iverson, A. M. (2002). Best practices in problem-solving team structure and process. In A. Thomas & J. Grimes (Eds.), *Best Practices in School Psychology IV*: Vol. 1. (pp. 657–669). Bethesda, MD: National Association of School Psychologists.

Julian, D. A. (1997). The utilization of the logic model as a system level planning and evaluation device. *Evaluation and Program Planning, 20*, 251–257.

Katzenbach, J. R., & Smith, D. K. (1993). The discipline of teams. *Harvard Business Review, 7*, 162–171.

Kovaleski, J. F. (2002). Best practices in operating pre-referral intervention teams. In A. Thomas & J. Grimes (Eds.) *Best Practices in School Psychology* (4th ed., pp. 645–655). Bethesda, MD: National Association of School Psychology.

Kovaleski, J. F., Gickling, E. E., Morrow, H., & Swank, P. R. (1999). High versus low implementation of Instructional Support Teams: A case for maintaining program fidelity. *Remedial and Special Education, 20*(3), 170–183.

Kovaleski, J. F., Tucker, J. A., & Duffy, D. J. (1995). School reform through instructional support: The Pennsylvania Initiative: Part I: The Instructional Support Team (IST). *Communique, 23*(8), 1, 11, 14–18.

Knoff, H. M., & Batsche, G. M. (1995). Project ACHIEVE: Analyzing a school reform process for at-risk and underachieving students. *School Psychology Review, 244*, 579–603.

Knotek, S. E., Rosenfield, S. A., Gravois, T. A., & Babinski, L. M. (2003). The process of fostering consultee development during Instructional Consultation. *Journal of Educational and Psychological Consultation, 14*(3&4), 303–328.

Knotek, S., & Sandoval, J. (2003). Current research in consultee-centered consultation. *Journal of Educational and Psychological Consultation, 14*, 243–250.

Kruger, L. J., & Struzziero, J. (1995). The relationship between organizational support and satisfaction with teacher assistance teams. *Remedial and Special Education, 16*(4), 203–212.

McDougal, J. L., Moody Clonan, S., & Martens, B. K. (2000). Using organizational change procedures to promote the acceptability of prereferral intervention services: The school-based intervention team project. *School Psychology Quarterly, 15*, 149–171.

Meyers, J. (2002). A 30 year perspective on best practices for consultation training. *Journal of Educational and Psychological Consultation, 13*, 35–54.

Meyers, J. & Nastasi, B. (1999). Primary prevention in school settings. In C. Reynolds & T. Gutkin (Eds.), *Handbook of school psychology* (3rd ed., pp. 764–799). New York: John Wiley & Sons.

Millar, A. M., Simeone, R. S., & Carnevale, J. T. (2001). Logic models: A systems tool for performance management. *Evaluation and Program Planning, 24*, 73–81.

Ponti, C. R., Zins, J. E., & Graden, J. L. (1988). Implementing a consultation-based service delivery system to decrease referrals for special education: A case study of organizational considerations. *School Psychology Review, 17*, 89–100.

Rosenfield, S. (2002). Best practices in instructional consultation. In A. Thomas & J. Grimes (Eds.), *Best Practices in School Psychology* (4th ed., pp. 609–623). Bethesda, MD: National Association of School Psychologists.

Rosenfield, S. A. (1987). *Instructional Consultation*. Hillsdale, NJ: Erlbaum

Rosenfield, S. A., & Gravois, T. A. (1996). *Instructional Consultation Teams: Collaborating for Change*. New York: Guilford.

Rossi, P. H., Freeman, H. E., & Lipsey, M. W. (2004). *Evaluation: A systematic approach* (7th ed.). Thousand Oaks, CA: Sage.

Saver, K., & Downes, B. (1991). PIT Crew: A model for teacher collaboration in an elementary school. *Intervention in School and Clinic, 27*(2), 116–122.

Scheirer, M. A. (2000). Getting more 'bang' for your performance measures 'buck.' *American Journal of Evaluation, 21,* 139–150.

Sheridan, S. M., & Kratochwill, T. R. (2007). *Conjoint behavioral consultation: Promoting family-school connections and interventions.* New York: Springer.

Short, R. J., & Talley, R. C. (1996). Effects of teacher assistance teams on special education referrals in elementary schools. *Psychological Reports, 79,* 1431–1438.

Sindelar, P. T., Griffin, C. C., Smith, S. W., & Watanabe, A. K. (1992). Preferral intervention: Encouraging notes on preliminary findings. *The Elementary School Journal, 92*(3), 245–259.

Strein, W., Hoagwood, K., & Cohn, A. (2003). School psychology: A public health perspective I. Prevention, populations, and systems change. *Journal of School Psychology, 41,* 23–38.

Telzrow, C. F., McNamara, K., & Hollinger, C. L. (2000). Fidelity of problem-solving implementation and relationship to student performance. *School Psychology Review, 29,* 443–462.

Thousand, J. S., & Villa, R. A. (1992). Collaborative teams: A powerful tool in school restructuring. In R. A. Villa, J. S. Thousand, W. Stainback, & S. Stainback (Eds.), *Restructuring for caring and effective education: An administrative guide to creating heterogeneous schools* (pp. 73–108). Baltimore, MD: Paul H. Brookes.

Truscott, S. D., Cohen, C. E., Sams, D. P., Sanborn, K. J., & Frank, A. J. (2005). The current state(s) of prereferral intervention teams. *Remedial and Special Education, 26,* 130–140.

Chapter 38

Promoting Inclusive Practice in Schools:
A Challenging Role for School Psychologists

Peter T. Farrell and Andy J. Howes
University of Manchester

Shane R. Jimerson
University of California, Santa Barbara

Sue M. Davies
Trinity College

This chapter reviews theory and research relevant to promoting inclusive practice in schools. Each of the following topics are addressed sequentially: (a) a brief review of previous and current definitions of the term "inclusion," as consensus regarding the term has been elusive; (b) historical foundations related to the inclusion of children with disabilities in regular education classrooms, including legislation and research from the United States and the United Kingdom; (c) challenges faced by school psychologists[1] as they strive to make education more inclusive for all learners; (d) recent evidence on the current role of school psychologists and the extent to which it is inclusive in orientation; (e) the origins of the traditional practices of school psychologists, much of which is based on a reliance on the use of norm referenced psychometric tests, and the extent to which working in this way might promote policies and practices which are anti-inclusive; and (f) the findings of a two-year research project in seven secondary schools in England and Wales to illustrate how school psychologists, who draw on their skills and expertise as facilitators of collaborative action research projects, can work at the schoolwide level to promote effective inclusive practice in schools. The chapter concludes with a discussion of how the profession can draw on these findings so as to broaden the range of school psychologists' work and help schools to become more inclusive.

Defining Inclusion

Definitions of inclusion within the educational context have varied, representing diverse perspectives and ideologies (e.g., Clair, Church, & Batshaw, 2002; Falvey & Givner, 2005; Gee, 2004; Giangreco, 2006; Lewis & Doorlag, 2006; Turnbull, Turnbull, Erwin, & Soodak, 2006). Indeed, up until the early 1990s, the term "inclusion" was hardly used. Instead the terms "integration" or "mainstreaming" were employed and these referred exclusively to the placement of pupils with special needs in regular education classes in mainstream schools. There were of course different degrees of integration, from full-time placement of a child with disabilities in a mainstream class in his/her local school (functional integration) to the placement of a pupil in a special class or unit attached to a mainstream school (locational integration) (Hegarty, 1991).

---

[1] Throughout this chapter the term "school psychologist" is used to refer to the work of both school psychologists in the United States and educational psychologists in the United Kingdom, recognizing the fact that the job roles undertaken by both groups are similar.

An obvious problem with defining integration solely in terms of the location of service provision (i.e., the setting in which a pupil is placed), is that it doesn't say anything about the quality of the education that is received. Are pupils placed in units attached to a mainstream school, an example of locational integration, more "integrated" than if they were taught in a special school? Jupp (1992) argued that such units can be just as segregating. Indeed, even pupils placed in a regular mainstream class may be isolated from the rest of the class and not truly "integrated" within the group, particularly if they work with a support worker in one-to-one sessions for the majority of each day. Integrated placements, therefore, may still leave the pupil "segregated" (Harrower, 1999).

Partly for these reasons, the term "inclusion" has become a more usual way of describing the extent to which a pupil, categorized as needing to receive special education services, is truly "integrated." Used in this way the term refers to the extent to which a school or community welcomes such pupils as full members of the group and values them for the contribution which they make. This implies that for inclusion to be seen to be "effective," all pupils with disabilities must actively belong to, be welcomed by, and participate in a mainstream school and community. Their diversity of interests, abilities and attainment should be welcomed and be seen to enrich the school community.

Giangreco (2006) reflects this broader view of inclusion and offers a definition that addresses all students, describes special education as a process, highlights the rights of students, emphasizes the responsibilities of all schools and education professionals, and recognizes that the school is a community context.

All students are welcomed in general education. The general education class in the school the student would attend if not disabled is the first placement option considered. Appropriate supports, regardless of disability type or severity, are available.

Students are educated in classes where the number of those with and without disabilities is proportional to the local population (e.g., 10% to 12% have identified disabilities).

Students are educated with peers in the same age groupings available to those without disability labels.

Students with varying characteristics and abilities (e.g., those with and without disability labels) participate in shared

educational experiences while pursuing individually appropriate learning outcomes with necessary supports and accommodations.

Shared educational experiences take place in settings predominantly frequented by people without disabilities (e.g., general education classes, community work sites, community recreational facilities).

Educational experiences are designed to enhance individually determined valued life outcomes for students and therefore seek an individualized balance between the academic-functional and social-personal aspects of schooling.

Inclusive education exists when each of the previously listed characteristics occurs on an ongoing, daily basis. (p. 4)

In the United Kingdom, definitions of inclusion have widened still further. Booth and Ainscow (1998), for example, take the view that policies on inclusion should not be restricted to the education of pupils thought to have special needs. Inclusion, they argue, is a process in which schools, communities, local authorities and governments strive to reduce barriers to the participation and learning for all citizens. Looked at in this way, inclusive policies and practices should consider ways in which marginalized groups in society, for example people from ethnic minorities and those who are socially and economically disadvantaged, can participate fully in the educational process within mainstream contexts.

This view of inclusion is also reflected in guidance from the UK government on the inspection of schools in England and Wales (Ofsted, 2000). In addressing what they refer to as "educational inclusion," this document focuses attention on a wide range of vulnerable groups. It states:

An educationally inclusive school is one in which the teaching and learning, achievements, attitudes and well-being of every young person matters. Effective schools are educationally inclusive schools. This shows, not only in their performance, but also in their ethos and their willingness to offer new opportunities to pupils who may have experienced previous difficulties . . . The most effective schools do not take educational inclusion for granted. They constantly monitor and evaluate the progress each pupil makes. They identify any pupils who may be missing out, difficult to engage, or feeling in some way apart from what the school seeks to provide. (p. 65)

Here the sentence "the most effective schools are inclusive schools" is particularly significant. In essence it redefines the way school effectiveness will be determined, drawing attention to the need for inspectors to go beyond an analysis of aggregate performance scores in order to determine the extent to which a school is supporting the learning of all individuals within a school.

The UK government guidance is therefore important for two reasons. First of all, it reinforces a much broader view of inclusion in that the concept is widened to include pupils other than those thought to have Special Educational Needs (SEN). Second, it forces schools to focus on the achievements of all of their pupils and, indeed, to pay attention to a wider range of outcomes than those reflected in test or examination results.

One way to bring some coherence to this developing and sometimes confusing picture, is to conceptualize inclusion around its impact on pupil outcomes in relation to the following key concepts: presence, acceptance, participation and achievement. *Presence* refers to extent to which pupils attend lessons in mainstream settings in local schools and committees. (This is similar to the previous notion of "integration.") *Acceptance* refers to the extent to which other staff and pupils welcome all pupils as full and active members of their community. *Participation* refers to the extent to which all pupils contribute actively in all the school's activities. *Achievement* refers to the extent to which pupils learn and develop positive views of themselves.

It is argued that for a school to be truly inclusive, all four conditions should apply to all children in the schools regardless of their abilities and disabilities, ethnic origin, social class or gender. It is not, for example, sufficient for children to simply be *present* in a school. They need to: (a) be *accepted* by their peers and by staff, (b) *participate* in all the school's activities, and (c) attain satisfactory levels of *achievement* in their work and behavior. This formulation is proactive in the sense that it sets goals for schools, local authorities, communities and governments and can act as a benchmark against which to judge the extent to which inclusive policies and practices are working.

CONTEXT OF INCLUSION IN THE UNITED STATES AND THE UNITED KINGDOM

The following provides a brief synopsis of salient historical foundations that resulted in an emphasis on inclusion in the United States and the United Kingdom, respectively. In addition, information is presented from research on the extent to which schools have been able to include more students with disabilities in regular classrooms, as well as research regarding potential benefits of inclusion for these students. Hence the emphasis in this section is on research and developments as they relate to the inclusion of children with disabilities, and this reflects the fact that a key aspect of the role of schools psychologists is in carrying out special educational evaluations and in making recommendations for extra service provision (Jimerson et al., 2004; Jimerson et al., 2006; Jimerson, Graydon, Curtis, & Staskal, 2007).

Inclusion in the United States

Prior to the 1970s many children with disabilities in the United States were educated in segregated special schools or special-needs programs on regular school campuses. In 1972, courts in the United States ruled that public schools must extend an equal education opportunity to children with disabilities (*PARC v. Pennsylvania*; *Mills v. Board of Education*, 1972). Thus, separating children solely on the basis of disability became a practice that was both unacceptable and illegal. Soon thereafter, both state and federal legislation was established that required an equal educational opportunity for children with disabilities, and also required that the education be provided in the least restrictive environment. The Education for All Handicapped Children Act (Public Law 94–142) in 1975 (reauthorized most recently in 2004 as the Individuals with Disabilities Education Improvement Act [IDEA]) clearly set the stage for inclusive schooling, delineating that every child is eligible to receive a free and appropriate public education and to learn in the least restrictive environment possible. Specifically, the law ensures "that to the maximum extent appropriate, children with disabilities, including children in public or private institutions and other care facilities, are educated with children who are not disabled" (Individuals with Disabilities Education Act, 20 U.S.C. § 1412 [a][5]). Establishing guidelines to determine the least restrictive environments has been very challenging for educational professionals. The 1997 version of the Individuals with Disabilities Education Act defines the least restrictive environment as: "To the maximum extent appropriate, children with disabilities, including children in pubic or private institutions or other care facilities, are [1] educated with children who are not disabled and [2] special classes, separate schooling, or other removal of children with disabilities from the regular educational environment occurs only when the nature of the severity of the disability of the child is such that education in the regular classes with the use of supplementary aids and services cannot be achieved satisfactorily" (Sec 612 (a)(5)(A)).

The courts have continued to further refine the criteria related to the least restrictive environment mandate of IDEA (see for instance, *A. W. v. Northwest R-1 School District* [1987], *Daniel R. R. v. State Board of Education* [1989], *Devries v. Fairfax Conty School Board* [1989], *Greer v. Rome City School District* [1992], *Doe v. Board of Education of Tullahoma City School* [1993]). The Fifth Circuit Court of Appeals ruling in the *Daniel R. R. v. State Board of Education* (1989) case established a two-part test to determine compliance with the least restrictive environment mandate: "First, we ask whether education in the regular classroom, with use of supplemental aids and services, can be achieved satisfactorily for a given child. If it cannot and the school intends to provide special education or to remove the child from regular education, we ask, second, whether the school has mainstreamed the child to the maximum extent appropriate" (p. 1048). Subsequent cases also emphasized the importance of individualized needs and considerations. For instance, in *Board of Education v. Holland* (1992) the court stated, "Thus the decision as to whether any particular child should be educated in a regular classroom setting, all of the time, part of the time, or none of the time, is necessarily an inquiry into the needs and abilities of one child, and does not extend to a group or category of handicapped children" (p. 878). The court rulings have varied with respect to the optimal education setting, with some supporting the regular classroom (see for instance, *Mavis v. Sobol*, [1994], *Corey H. v. Chicago Public Schools and the Illinois State Board of Education* [1998]) and others recommending self-contained programs or special schools (see for instance, *Poolaw v. Bishop* [1994], *M. R. v. Lincolnwood Board of Education, District 74* [1994], *School District of Wisconsin Dells v. Z. S.* [2002]).

Thus, the courts examine the facts in individual cases to determine whether school districts have offered an appropriate placement for each child with disabilities.

Despite the federal legislation and both state and federal court decisions in the United States during the 12 years between 1977 and 1990, the number of students with intellectual disabilities in regular education or resource classrooms increased by only 1.2 percent (Karagiannis, Stainback, & Stainback, 1996). In 1992, a Report Card on Inclusion in Education of Children with Mental Retardation (Davis, 1992) revealed that most states received grades of D's and F's and called for full inclusion of 50% of students with intellectual disabilities by 1995, and the full inclusion of all students with intellectual disabilities by 2000. A national study in the United States examined the extent to which students with intellectual disabilities were included in regular education classrooms during 2002–2003 (Smith, 2007). Using data from the U.S. Department of Education's Office of Special Education and Rehabilitative Services (OSERS), full inclusion was defined as students who were outside of the regular classroom less than 21% of the school day. Findings from this study revealed fewer than 11% of students with intellectual disabilities were fully included in regular education classrooms. This represented only a 3.44% increase from 1992 to 1993 (Smith, 2007).

While it is important to understand the justification and prevalence of inclusion, it is essential to understand the extent to which children with disabilities benefit from inclusion, including both academic achievement and social outcomes. In the United States, there is a paucity of empirical evidence to support inclusive practices. To our knowledge, there are no experimental studies examining student outcomes based on their placement in inclusive versus noninclusive settings. However, numerous comparative studies have been published in the United States and proponents of inclusion often highlight studies revealing positive academic and social outcomes (see for instance, Agran, Blanchard, Wehmeyer, & Hughes, 2002; Burstein, Sears, Wilcoxen, Cabello, & Spagna, 2004; Cole, 2006; Cole, Waldron, & Majd, 2004; Deno, Maruyama, Espin, & Cohen, 1990; Doré, Dion, Wagner, & Brunet, 2002; Downing & Eichinger, 2003; Downing, Spencer, & Cavallaro, 2004; Dymond & Orelove, 2001; Fisher & Meyer, 2002; Freeman & Alkin, 2000; Giangreco, Dennis, Cloninger,

Edelman, & Schattman, 1993; Giangreco, Edelman, Cloninger, & Dennis, 1993; Helmstetter, Peck, & Giangreco, 1994; Hunt & Goetz, 1997; Hunt, Staub, Alwell, & Goetz, 1994; Janney & Snell, 1996; Kozleski & Jackson, 1993; Peck, Donaldson, & Pezzoli, 1990; Peck, Staub, Gallucci, & Schwartz, 2004; Rea, Mclaughlin, & Walther-Thomas, 2002; Salisbury, Palombaro, & Hollowood, 1993; Sharpe, York, & Knight, 1994; York, Vandercook, Macdonald, Heise-Neff, & Caughey, 1992; Zigmond & Baker, 1990). Giangreco (1997) offers numerous examples of positive impacts that inclusive education has been reported to have on students with disabilities (e.g., access to peer models, new relationships and friendships, raised expectations), their classmates without disabilities (e.g., increased appreciation of human diversity, increased comfort interacting with people with disabilities), their teachers (e.g., increased ownership and accountability for students with disabilities, learned skills to teach all children better), and their families (e.g., increased family involvement in planning the educational program, created new social opportunities for families through the social networks of their child). Meta-analyses reveal a small beneficial effect of inclusion education on the academic and social outcome of students with special needs (Baker, Wang, & Walberg, 1995; Carlberg & Kavale, 1980).

There have also been numerous critical reviews of inclusive educational practices (see for instance, Baines, Baines, & Masterson, 1994; Gerber, 1995; Kauffmann & Hallahan, 1995; Kozleski & Jackson, 1993; McDonnell, McDonnell, Hardman, & McCune, 1991; Smelter, Rasch, & Yudewitz, 1994; Villa & Thousand, 1992; Winzer, 2000). Critical reviews raise concerns regarding the impact of inclusion. For instance, Gerber (1995) wrote, "Despite differences in approach, the effect of implementing 'inclusion' in each of these schools was to diminish and subordinate the role of the special education teacher, reduce the potential effectiveness of special education as a program of specialized instructional effort, and remove the academic press for achievement by students with learning disabilities" (p. 181). In the United States, inclusion remains a controversial topic, whereas most education professionals embrace the moral imperative of inclusion, implementation of inclusive practices and policies remains varied throughout schools in the country.

Inclusion in the United Kingdom

The development of more inclusive provision for children with special needs in the United Kingdom has many parallels with developments in the United States. A key milestone was the publication of a government Report on SEN known as the Warnock Report (Department of Education and Science [DES], 1978). This report covered a whole range of issues to do with definitions and conceptualizations of SEN, assessment arrangements, the role and development of support services and the need to develop more integrated assistance. Prior to the Warnock Report the common view in the United Kingdom was that 2% of the child population had SEN, with about 1.5% placed in special schools and units and 0.5% in mainstream schools. Warnock widened the definition of SEN to include children who experienced difficulties in learning and behavior, but whose problems were never seen as being so severe as to warrant placement in a special school. She argued that the traditional view of SEN tended to exclude these children and that this could have a deleterious effect on services. In Warnock's view about 20% of all children could have SEN with only 1.5% being in special schools.

In relation to "integrating" children with SEN, the Warnock Report (DES, 1978) suggested that many children in special schools could, and should, be educated in mainstream schools with appropriate levels of support. This drive to develop more integrated services was reflected in the 1981 Education Act which among other things stipulated that, where possible, all children with SEN should be educated in mainstream schools. This was the first legislative signal from the government supporting integration/inclusion movement. Since the 1981 Act there has been a plethora of government guidance, further amendments to the Act and two Codes of Practice giving detailed guidance to parents, schools, local authorities and other agencies on the interpretation and implementation of the 1981 Act and subsequent legislation. (Readers who would like to learn more should consult the following documents: DES, 1980; DES, 1983; Department for Education [DfE], 1994; Department for Education and Employment [DfEE], 1997; DfEE, 1998; Department for Education and Skills [DfES], 2001a; DfES, 2001b; DfES, 2001c; DfES, 2004.)

Government regulations regarding provision for children with SEN in mainstream schools have remained more or less consistent since the 1981 legislation. For example, the most recent revision, incorporated within the 2001 SEN and Disability Act, states that all children with SEN "should be educated in a mainstream school, unless this is against the wishes of the child's parents or is incompatible with the efficient education of other children" (DfES, 2001c). Hence, like the United States, decisions about whether or not a child should be placed in a mainstream school are not related to a child's diagnosed condition but to his or her assessed needs, whether these can be met in a mainstream setting without affecting the education of other children and the parents' wishes. The emphasis on parents' wishes and the "efficient education of other children" inevitably results in children with very similar needs being placed in completely different types of settings. In the United Kingdom, parents, in particular, often express strong views about where they would like their child with SEN to be educated. However, for some parents these views are very pro-special schools while for others it is the opposite.

In the 10 years following the implementation of the 1981 Education Act there was a fall in the numbers of pupils attending special schools and segregated units from around 1.5% in 1981 to 0.95% in 1991. Since then there has only been a gradual decline in the numbers attending segregated settings to 0.82% in 2004 (House of Commons Education and Skills Committee, 2006; Rustemier & Vaughn, 2005). The House of Commons report states that the vast majority of these children are described as having severe or moderate learning difficulties or severe behavior, emotional and social difficulties.

As in the United States, research on the effectiveness of inclusion for pupils with SEN in the United Kingdom is beset with methodological problems as it is extremely difficult, and sometime ethically inappropriate, to set up carefully controlled studies. In an earlier review of research, Farrell (2000) concluded that there was some evidence indicating that pupils with SEN benefited socially from being included in mainstream schools but that academic benefits were much less clear cut. Teachers in mainstream schools appeared to be generally positive about the idea of inclusion, but their views can become more negative once they experience having a child with SEN in their class, particularly if he or she has severe emotional and behavioral

difficulties (Ainscow, Farrell, Tweddle & Malki, 2000; Farrell & Tskalidou, 1999). A key factor that seems to relate to the success of inclusion is the availability and expertise of support staff, in particular teaching assistants, and the quality of the working relations between these staff and mainstream teachers (Balshaw & Farrell, 2002; Farrell, Balshaw, & Polat, 2000; Fox, Farrell, & Davis, 2004).

In a more recent study Farrell, Dyson, Polat, Hutcheson, and Gallannaugh (2007a, 2007b) used multilevel modeling combined with in-depth case studies to investigate the relationship between the inclusion of pupils with SEN in mainstream schools and the achievements of their peers. The findings indicated that despite concerns expressed by teachers in mainstream schools about the negative consequences of placing pupils with special needs in their class, there was little or no impact, positive or negative, on the achievements of all pupils. This study was also supported by the findings of a systematic review of the literature in this area (Kalambouka, Farrell, Dyson, & Kaplan, 2007).

The most up-to-date systematic review on the impact of inclusion has been carried out by Lindsay (2007). Like other researchers quoted above, Lindsay concludes that there is an absence of powerful evidence on the positive impact of inclusion. He also considers that the inclusion policy has been strongly influenced by concerns about children's rights. In his view, future research should focus on the "mediators and moderators" that enable inclusion to be effective in practice and that this would help to develop an approach to the education of children with SEN that was evidence based.

SCHOOL PSYCHOLOGISTS AND INCLUSIVE PRACTICES

In recent years there have been a number of publications and reports suggesting that school psychologists are striving to become more inclusive in their work (Farrell, Woods, Lewis, Rooney, Squires, & O'Connor, 2006; Hayes, 2002; Hick, 2005). For example, in the United Kingdom there is a nationwide interest group known as Educational Psychologists for Inclusion that meets regularly to share ideas and recent developments. In addition a number of chapters in a forthcoming book (Hick, Kerhsner, & Farrell, in press) focus on specific approaches that school psychologists have adopted to support inclusion in schools in the United Kingdom and overseas. Furthermore the proceedings of the annual colloquium of the International School Psychology Association in 2002 indicate the rich and varied ways in which school psychologists can support the development of more inclusive practices in schools and local authorities (ISPA, 2002).

Some professional associations representing school psychologists, in the United Kingdom, United States, and elsewhere, have also been active in promoting inclusion. In England, for example, the Association of Educational Psychologists (AEP), one of the professional associations that advises the government, local authorities, and educational psychologists about the development of the profession, has provided written guidance for its members on ways to foster inclusion (AEP, 1999). Similar policy guidance has been issued in the United States by the National Association of School Psychologists (NASP, 1999). This emphasizes NASP's continuing support for the development of inclusive programs for all children and young people. It also provides guidance for how school psychologists can develop inclusive education for students with disabilities.

This guidance from the professional associations is reflected in the growing number of published accounts of school psychologists actively promoting one or more aspects of inclusive practice in their work. Among these are papers on helping mainstream schools to support children with behavior problems (e.g., Barrett & Randall, 2004; Burton, 2004; Frydenburg, et al., 2004; Hutchings, Lane, Owen, & Gwyn, 2004; Maddern, Franey, McLaughlin, & Cox, 2004; Young & Holdorf, 2003). There are also accounts of how school psychologists can help to support pupils with learning difficulties in mainstream schools (e.g., Brooks, Weeks, & Everatt, 2002; Dole, 2003; Hodson, Baddeley, Laycock, & Williams, 2005; Medcalf, Glynn, & Moore, 2004). Other examples include work that school psychologists have done to help schools develop general policies on inclusion (e.g., Dunsmuir, Frederickson, & Lang, 2004; Hayes, 2002; Hick, 2005; Roffey, 2004) and there are also examples of school psychologists working with government agencies to develop country-wide inclusive strategies (e.g., Mnkandla & Matruse, 2002; Muthukrishna & Baez, 2002; van Kraayenoord, 2002).

These developments suggest that school psychologists are embracing the inclusion agenda and that this is embedded in, and underpinned by, all of their work. However evidence from recent research presents a more complex picture. For example, a survey of school psychology practice in different countries (Jimerson et al. 2004; Jimerson et al. 2006; Jimerson, Graydon, Curtis, & Staskal, 2007) indicates that school psychologists continue to have a key role in the assessment of children with special educational needs with this being the most commonly performed task in eight of the countries that took part in the survey. Furthermore, over the past 20 years or so, a number of surveys of teachers' perceptions of the school psychologist's role in the United Kingdom and United States indicate that, generally, they expect them to carry out special education assessments (DfEE, 2000; Dowling & Leibowitz, 1994; Evans & Wright, 1987; Ford & Migles, 1979). Moreover, this finding is replicated in a survey of teachers' views of school psychologists in Estonia (Kikas, 1999), in a major survey of the views of 1,100 teachers in eight different countries (Farrell, Jimerson, Kalambouka, & Benoit, 2005) and in the chapters of the *International Handbook on School Psychology* (Jimerson, Oakland, & Farrell, 2006). In addition Gilman and Gabriel (2004) found that education administrators in the United States were even more committed than teachers to the view that the school psychologist's main role was to carry out assessments of children with special needs and to make recommendations for them to be placed in some form of special education.

Thus the evidence suggests that many school psychologists continue to work in a traditional paradigm where the key focus is on responding to the referrals of individual children who may have special educational needs. This paradigm encourages school psychologists to emphasize a summative rather than formative role, where problems are seen to be centered "within the child," where they can be explored through the psychologist working in a separate room, testing the child and using the results to predict educational performance. This approach to assessment tends to ignore the contribution that the school or family, with the ongoing involvement of the school psychologist, can make towards prevention and intervention for individuals, groups, families and communities.

Challenges for School Psychologists in Promoting Inclusive Practices

Farrell (2006) makes the case that the origins of the traditional school psychology paradigm are profoundly *anti-inclusive* in orientation. It reflects an historical view of the work of school psychologists as being one where their key task was the identification and placement of children with special needs in segregated special schools and classrooms. This key and unique task, which is inexorably associated with the use of IQ tests to categorize such children, has had a major impact on the development of segregated education. As Guillemard (2006) reminds us, the earliest example of this comes from the pioneering work in France of Alfred Binet. In 1899, along with Pierre Vaney, Alfred Binet opened a pedagogical and psychological laboratory in a Parisian primary school and, in 1905, he was asked by the Ministry of Public Instruction in France to study problems exhibited by children who could not follow the regular school curriculum. He developed the Binet-Simon test which was assumed to be an entirely valid measure of intelligence and hence a legitimate tool to detect children with mental retardation and to direct them toward special classes. This test formed the basis of the well known Stanford-Binet test. In the United Kingdom, during the 1920s, the London County Council employed Cyril Burt as a psychologist to help solve the problem of classifying children's suitability for schooling. He was the United Kingdom's first educational psychologist and he saw the role as primarily being one of giving children an IQ test to see if they needed to be educated in a special school.

Furthermore, if IQ tests serve this purpose, then there is a need to employ professionals to use them and this helps to explain the origins of the development of school psychology as a profession. As Oakland (2000) emphasizes, the rise in the numbers of school psychologists in different countries around the world closely mirrors the extent to which these countries have embraced the concept of intelligence and IQ testing as being indispensable tools for the identification of children with special needs and in the legitimization of placing children, so identified, in special schools. As an emerging profession it was crucial to identify a task that could only be performed by someone from that profession, and IQ testing provided the perfect example. Here was a task that had respectable roots in academic psychology and was seen to be of value to schools, parents and other professionals, and which therefore should rightly be something that must be administered by trained psychologists. In the United Kingdom, this position was greatly strengthened by an agreement that individually administered IQ tests should be "closed" (i.e., only for use in clinical settings by appropriately trained applied psychologists). Hence, IQ testing was something that no other professional could do, a truly distinctive task and one which therefore contributed significantly to the development and identity of the profession of school and other applied psychologists.

In addition, categories of special schools for pupils with learning difficulties have developed where the IQ score provides the main criteria for admission. Twenty years ago in the United Kingdom it was common for special schools for children with severe learning difficulties to select children whose IQ scores were less than 50 and for schools for pupils with moderate learning difficulties to use cut-off points in the 50–70 IQ range. Hence, if children were placed in special schools on the basis of their IQ score, and if school psychologists were the only professional who could administer IQ tests, then it was logical for local authorities to employ them so as to ensure that only "eligible" pupils were admitted to such schools. Indeed, Reschly (2000) points out that the rapid development of the profession of school psychology can, to a great extent, be explained by school psychologists being assigned a unique role in IQ testing and by the requirement in many countries for them to be involved in special education assessments.

As mentioned previously in this chapter, evidence indicates that in general school psychologists still maintain this way of working and spend the bulk of their time undertaking formal special education evaluations using IQ tests (see, for example, Burns, 2004; Farrell, Harraghy, & Petrie, 1996; Rees, Rees, & Farrell, 2003; Shapiro, Angello, & Eckert, 2004; Woods & Farrell, 2006). This is in spite of the wealth of literature that is critical of the role and negative impact of IQ testing that goes back over many years (see for example Brown & Ferrara, 1985; Gillham, 1978; Howe, 1998; Leadbetter; 2005; Lokke, Gersch, M'Gadzah, & Frederickson, 1997; Mercer, 1973, 1974; Ysseldyke, 1987); and of the inappropriateness of the medical model (e.g., Poplin, 1988; Sheridan & Gutkin, 2000).

It could be argued, of course, that, despite its anti-inclusive origins, the traditional paradigm underpinning school psychology practice, which relies predominately on individual assessments using IQ tests, is quite compatible with the more recent moves to make education more inclusive for all learners. For instance, instead of recommending segregated education, school psychologists could use their psychometric and other findings to plan and support inclusive arrangements. However, this presents a continuing challenge for school psychologists, because the within-child nature of traditional assessment practices can direct attention away from questions about how a mainstream school can accommodate a child with special needs and toward a discussion about the availability of alternative segregated placements. This is because most traditional psychometric assessments focus on the child's difficulties and not on the school setting. Furthermore, it is sometimes easier for school psychologists to attribute a child's failure to learn to within-child problems or perhaps to poor parenting. It is much harder to focus on failings in the instructional strategies in the classroom or contextual influences of the school.

Despite the fact that survey findings suggest that school psychologists still rely on traditional within-child models that run the risk of promoting anti-inclusive practice, there are other approaches that draw on alternative theories in psychology which are entirely compatible with the inclusion movement. In particular there are instructional, social, and organizational theories that encourage school psychologists, and others, to take a holistic view of learning and behavior, which take account of context and where problems are not placed with one individual (e.g., the child). These include, for example, Vygotskian (1986) theories, such as cultural-historical activity theory, Bruner's (1966) theory of instruction and Bandura's (1977) social learning theory. Through informing their practice by drawing on these and similar theories, school psychologists can actively pursue the inclusion agenda and through this they will adopt other approaches which take them away from within-child medical models.

USING COLLABORATIVE ACTION RESEARCH TO PROMOTE INCLUSION

In this section we discuss the findings of a UK-based study, involving three of the authors (Farrell, Howes, Davies), which provides an illustration of how school psychologists can work with schools to promote inclusion. The aim is to offer a detailed illustration of how, by adopting alternative paradigms, school psychologists can use their knowledge and skills to bring about

system change in secondary schools and help teachers to engage in inclusive practices.

The methodology for this project was drawn from that used in an earlier 3-year study involving Manchester, Newcastle and Canterbury Universities. This was a 3-year program of action research and collaborative enquiry with 24 schools in three local districts (Ainscow et al., 2006). A team of researchers from each university worked with individual schools to help them to reflect on and develop inclusive policies and practices. Working as consultants, the role of the researchers was to help staff in the schools to engage in a process of action research, reflecting on the work that they were doing, questioning some of their assumptions and evaluating progress. As Ainscow et al. indicate, the findings from this complex longitudinal study were extremely varied but, taken together, they offered a range of insights into how schools could engage more actively in inclusive practice. There were, however, two key overarching themes that were evident throughout the study. The first of these was the clear finding that staff in mainstream secondary schools found it far more difficult to change their practice to embrace the inclusion agenda than those from primary schools. Secondly, none of the schools involved had regular access to a consultant who could work with them to develop their inclusive practice. The researchers thought this had an adverse affect on their success in bringing about sustainable change. In order to develop and refine the methodology for the secondary school context, this project was extended to involve seven schools, five from Wales and two from England, where the action research projects were facilitated by a school psychologist, with support from research staff in Trinity College Carmarthen, Wales and the University of Manchester, England.

This extension study "Prosiect Dysgu Cydradd[2]: Facilitating Teacher Engagement in More Inclusive Practice" lasted two years and the final report will be published in 2008 (Davies, Howes, & Farrell, in press). The project's research questions focused upon what helps and hinders teachers in secondary schools to engage in action

---

[2] The portion of the project title in Welsh "Prosiect Dysgu Cydradd" embodies an inclusive aspiration to learn and teach on equal terms, with and from each other. The Welsh word "Dysgu" means both "teaching" and "learning," whilst "cydradd" means "equal"—the stem "cyd" means "together." ("Prosiect" is "Project.")

research to develop inclusion, and the impact of this on their pupils. As the study developed it became evident that the facilitation of school psychologists was a crucial part of this process and, as a result, additional questions were asked about the facilitators and barriers facing school psychologists working systemically in secondary schools using this approach.

At the start of the study, groups of teachers (often from a subject department) within the seven schools set up collaborative action research projects facilitated by their school psychologist, the aim of which was to focus on bringing about improvements in one aspect of inclusive practice in the school. In accordance with the fundamental principles of action research, the teachers and school psychologists were encouraged to work on projects that were chosen by the teachers and not by the researchers based in the universities. Hence the choice reflected the views of the school staff and school psychologist about the aspect of inclusive practice in their school that they should address and the methods they should use to address it. The only constraints imposed by the researchers were that the projects had to be completed in one year, with a second group of teachers working on a different project during year 2 of the research. This design was implemented in this way in order to provide opportunities in year 2 to explore solutions to issues and problems identified during the first round of school projects.

The school psychologists received some guidance and support in how to facilitate collaborative action research at the start of the study, and they met every 6 months during the course of the research. Between these meetings, the four school psychologists working in the Welsh schools met together as did the two school psychologists working in the English schools.

Given that the choice of collaborative action research projects was left to the school and the psychologist, it was not surprising, as the following examples indicate, that the areas chosen were extremely varied and reflected the broad definition of inclusion and inclusive practice which is prevalent across the United Kingdom at the present time. There were projects which focused on:

- Enhancing pupil participation using interactive whiteboards
- Addressing girls' underachievement in history

- Obtaining pupil perspective about science lessons so as to enhance motivation and their involvement in the subject
- Making humanities lessons more inclusive for second-language speakers using visual teaching approaches
- Developing peer mentoring to support pupils in danger of exclusion
- Including all pupils in literacy learning through using color coding and color overlays

This list of projects reflects the fact that, in the United Kingdom, the concept of inclusion has moved away from an explicit focus on educational services for pupils with special educational needs and now encompasses a much wider agenda. The emphasis is on how to reduce barriers to participation and learning for all pupils so that the needs of *all* children can be met, including those with special needs but also other pupils who are at risk of being marginalized. Hence the inclusion agenda should be embedded within the fabric of all schools where all staff have a role to play. For these reasons collaborative action research projects that address systemic issues within a school are particularly appropriate if the school is to improve its inclusive practice.

However, consistent with change literature, there are a number of prerequisites that need to be in place for systemic change to be successful. These include the following:

- The presence of a consultant who can lead and support the process
- Focusing on a specific aspect of the system
- Working with a committed staff team
- Having the support of senior management
- Setting clear goals
- Being prepared to take risks
- Being self critical
- Having a clear time line with built in evaluation

In carrying out these one-year action research projects the school staff and psychologists collected a range of data that reflected the aims and scope of their particular projects. This included testing the impact of the projects on pupil attitudes (e.g., pupil opinion questionnaires), behavior (e.g., classroom observation schedules), or achievement (e.g., monitoring class work or tests). It also included interview data (e.g., from teachers, pupils, parents, support staff) and evidence of changes in policies and procedures across the school.

In addition to collating analyses and findings from the seven school projects, the university researchers collected additional contextual data, mainly using questionnaires, interviews and focus groups that was consistent across all sites. Among other things, this included data on changes in a school's approach to inclusion and to teacher development in this area. In addition, the views of those directly involved in the specific projects were sought through questionnaires, interviews and focus groups, and included data from teachers and students. Finally, the school psychologists' perspective on the process was also obtained through questionnaires, discussions and a reflective journal.

This wide ranging project has gathered a wealth of data that has formed the basis of several conference papers and publications. These focus not only on the experience of the action research process for teachers (Howes, Fox, & Davies, 2006), but also on other important aspects of the project methodology and outcomes: for example a critique of the use of a design study (Howes & Davies, 2006) and theory of change (Howes, Fox & Davies, 2006). Activity theory has been used as a model to explore the barriers facing school psychologists and teachers when working systemically in schools (Howes & Davies 2006; Davies, Howes & Farrell, in press). The challenges for teachers and school psychologists of using action research to develop inclusion is fully discussed in a forthcoming book (Davies et al., in preparation), and a practical toolkit for facilitators is to follow (Howes, Davies, Fox, Davies, & Swann, in preparation).

Key Themes Emerging From the Study

The following provides a summary of the key themes that emerged from the study that relate to the role of the school psychologists in using collaborative action research to bring about system change and more inclusive practices in the six secondary schools (see Table 38.1).

Uncertainty and Conflicting Expectations

Almost none of the teachers were familiar with, or had knowledge about, action research. They had little experience of trying to improve or change their practice in a collaborative and open-ended way, while at the same time following a systematic process. As a result there was a certain amount of teacher uncertainty and conflicting expectations of the process. Unfamiliarity with action research and perceptions that it might be too vague and open-ended meant that teachers valued direction from their school psychologist to guide them through the process.

For most of the school psychologists, using action research and working with a systemic process with teachers was also a novel experience. It was different from the usual casework orientation of their everyday contact with teachers. This meant that some school psychologists found it difficult to respond effectively to the challenge of facilitation and provide the direction that the teachers wanted.

Values and Assumptions

A key element of the change process involved teachers and school psychologists being willing to discuss issues and problems in a free and relatively uninhibited manner. The interview and focus group findings suggest that teachers, in particular, tended to talk extensively about external causes of problems and about possible actions that others might take to resolve them and that there was a reluctance to talk about their own values and assumptions and how these might be part of the problem. Part of this process involved teachers being "unsettled" by questions arising from

---

TABLE 38.1 Key Themes that Relate to the Role of the School Psychologists in Using Collaborative Action Research to Bring About System Change and More Inclusive Practices

1. Uncertainty and conflicting expectations
2. Values and assumptions
3. Evaluating change introduced by the school-based projects
4. The value of having time for discussion
5. School leadership structure
6. Collaborating, owning, noticing and reflecting
7. The value of the school psychologist as a consultant

their project. For example, we found that some teachers felt a little threatened when encouraged to question their own practice and to try working in a different way. The support of the schools psychologist and others was important in helping them reflect on their values and assumptions.

Evaluating Change Introduced by the School-Based Projects

Most school groups found it difficult (strange, awkward, untypical) to evaluate systematically the success of the changes they had introduced. School psychologists' knowledge of assessment and methods for evaluating pupil change were a valuable resource for teachers developing empirical attention to what was happening in their classrooms.

The Value of Having Time for Discussion

The groups of teachers who fully engaged in an action research project valued the opportunity to decide on the focus for change themselves, rather than having the focus or the solution imposed upon them. For some of those teachers, such engagement appears to be a refreshing change from their usual diet of professional development activities. Having the "space" to stand back and reflect on practice was a beneficial outcome that was evident to teachers and school managers alike. However it was important that this space was used productively, and the direction and structure created by good facilitation played a crucial role in making this happen.

School Leadership Structure

There were a number of factors that influenced the ability of a group to identify an issue, get started, and persist with a project. These included the quality of leadership within the group and departmental hierarchies and senior management. Indeed, lessons from successful projects were sometimes ignored by senior staff and teachers in other departments, unless there were powerful brokers, frequently the school psychologist, seeing and taking opportunities to involve other staff in the school.

Collaborating, Owning, Noticing and Reflecting

In the more successful projects it was clear that the process of collaborative action research had worked well when attention was given to the following three components: *collaboration*, *ownership*, and *noticing and reflecting*. (These three elements and the challenges they present to consultants are summarized in Table 38.2).

Collaboration

When school psychologists and teachers worked well together, they could draw on the insights and ideas of others and make changes in the way they worked that would be impossible for one person to sustain on their own. They could also share the risks and encourage each other to be systematic. School psychologists contributed to this collaboration as a coprofessional but also as one who could offer nondirectional questioning, psychological knowledge, guidance about the process and other aspects of facilitation when needed.

Owning

When teachers and school psychologists assumed shared ownership of an issue, they put energy into thinking through the consequences for them and their practice and they were prepared to take some risks in trying to resolve problems. When a group owned an issue, they could create space together to follow it through—and part of that involved persuading others in school that it was valuable and worth prioritizing. The challenge to the school psychologist was to help to maintain direction and momentum without taking ownership.

Noticing and Reflecting

When teachers and school psychologists agreed on the specific focus of a project, it made them more alert. They talked more with others about what they noticed and checked it out with each other. They searched out reasons for what was happening, and all this helped them to develop their understanding and to refine what they were doing. The school psychologist could offer expertise that would inform systematic evaluation. They could also help create the right balance between teacher action and reflection which could make the space for reflection productive and valuable.

The Value of the School Psychologist as a Consultant

All teachers welcomed the involvement of the school psychologist in working on projects to promote the agenda for inclusion in their school. Furthermore the school psychologists themselves reported that they had improved their skills as consultants in order to meet the particular demands and challenges of the school context. In further informal discussion among school psychologists,

TABLE 38.2   Three Essential Elements and Their Challenge to Consultants

Key Element	Challenge for Consultants
Collaboration between teachers is necessary if they are to tackle action research in the context of their working life in school, making use of the resources they have available, and become more fully engaged in working on pupil learning and participation.	• Identify and work with a group with the explicit intention of addressing something of shared importance to the group • Facilitate the group while maintaining a collaborative relationship of different professionals working together
Ownership — Teacher identification and ownership of an issue is necessary if teachers are to engage in an open-ended way, and to do so in the face of obvious and rational professional risks. Ownership by the school (and school leadership) makes it more likely that as an initiative it will be able to compete for priority against external agendas.	• Help the group to identify a focus meaningful to them which they can connect to pupils' engagement in and attitude to learning • Contribute to the maintenance of momentum without taking ownership
Attention and reflection — Systematic evaluation of the consequences of actions is necessary if teachers are to refine and develop their current interpretations and solutions.	• Offer nondirective support for this process • Enable a balance between action and reflection that nurtures teacher engagement

a number of specific themes relating to their role as consultants emerged. These included: (a) their multiple and flexible role as chair, counselor, support, sounding board and information provider; (b) their skills in "carrying the baggage of theory . . . with a backpack of ideas;" (c) safeguarding teacher ownership; (d) seeking clarity of purpose; (e) maintaining attention on the project; and (f) guiding the evaluation.

Overall Findings From the Study

Findings from eleven school projects indicated both the challenges and resources involved for teachers engaging in a process of action research, and how facilitation and support in school can make that engagement easier and more effective for pupils. The processes elaborated in this project can help teachers to engage effectively with issues of inclusion in secondary schools, in a way which is accessible to all teachers, requires minimal additional training, and utilizes existing resources (in school, and from psychological services). In summary, therefore, the project has developed an understanding of how to improve the context for inclusion in secondary schools, both at the teacher and whole-school level.

At the teacher level the study has shown that by creating and structuring a space for teachers to engage in discussions about how to develop inclusive practice in their schools, they can apply the key principals of collaborative action research and, as a result, bring about sustainable change. This process was not always easy to manage in view of the fact that collaboratively owned action research can only partly be a rational, planned and systematic activity. It is also an emergent process, in which possibilities are created and socially constructed over time. Clear structure and expectations are helpful but surprises occur, and the facilitator needs to tap into modes of change as they emerge by remaining flexible and alert to opportunities. Groups require different elements of facilitation at various times, including consolidating the group itself, asking critical questions, maintaining momentum, and sustaining the process through the inevitable difficulties. Facilitators need to be responsive, without assuming ownership. Their tangential relationship to management appeared helpful here.

In many schools, inclusion is not a sustained theme; it is in focus at particular moments (e.g. in policy making) and unconsidered at other times, rather than being addressed as a systematic and creative process. Collaboratively owned empirical action research proved to be a means of extending the range of time scales over which teachers developed and maintained their inclusive practices.

At the whole-school level the findings indicated that structuring a space for teachers to engage in discussions about how to develop inclusive practice was necessary, but insufficient, to guarantee impact. In several projects the space was well structured, but poorly connected, and had less impact on the wider institution than was merited. Teachers' work on some projects was undervalued whereas in others teachers' engagement was celebrated, with outcomes understood by other teachers and senior staff. In the more successful school-based projects the study identified a stepwise process of facilitation to anchor the group process in the management and practice of the whole school. This involved managers and teachers working together to *prepare the ground*, to *shape the project*, to *keep it going*, and to plan for *closure and sustainability* so that the projects could be embedded within the school's policies and practices.

Taken as a whole, the findings have helped to advance theory and practice in relation to the factors that can help schools to become reflective learning organizations that have the capacity to develop and maintain sustainable change towards inclusion. In particular, this project has demonstrated that, through working as school-based consultants, school psychologists can help staff to feel confident in developing, implementing and evaluating projects which help them and their school become more inclusive. Although the collaborative action research projects in which the schools engaged were varied and reflected a broad view of inclusion, there is no reason why school psychologists could not use this approach to focus on the more traditional special needs area. Indeed there were projects for the original study (Ainscow et al., 2006) which indicated that through using collaborative action research teachers were able to facilitate the inclusion of children with behavior, emotional, and social difficulties, as well as those with hearing impairments (see also Farrell, 2006).

CONCLUSION

This chapter has reviewed current definitions of the term inclusion and the sociopolitical zeitgeist in which inclusion emerged in the United States and the United Kingdom, and has considered some research evidence on the impact of inclusion in relation to the education of children with special needs. Following was a discussion of some of the problems school psychologists face as they strive to develop a more inclusive orientation within their work. Perhaps one of the key barriers to progress in this direction lies in the history of the profession, being strongly linked to a "within-child" model of school psychology practice, where individual IQ testing still plays a major role and where recommendations for segregated provision are made on the basis of IQ scores. In addition, despite a growing body of literature providing examples of school psychologists working in more inclusive ways, evidence from surveys (e.g., Jimerson et al., 2004, 2006, 2007) seems to suggest that many school psychologists continue to engage in traditional practices.

A key concluding question that emerges from the discussion concerns the extent to which school psychologists can be persuaded to abandon some of their traditional ways of working and adopt alternative practices drawing on social constructivist paradigms. These paradigms, which require school psychologists to abandon the medical model, provide a basis for making a more positive contribution towards driving the inclusive agenda forward.

The key themes and overall findings described above from the collaborative action research project in which school psychologists worked with seven secondary schools present a more optimistic picture about the potential role for the profession. Results indicate that school psychologists can work successfully as consultants on collaborative action research projects that encourage secondary schools to develop their inclusive practices and hence improve the life chances of vulnerable learners.

This positive finding is mirrored by some other hopeful signs that the profession is moving forward and is now in a better position to embrace the inclusion agenda. First, there is some recent evidence suggesting that teachers in different countries would like school psychologists to spend less time on individual assessments and more on consultative and preventative work (Farrell et al., 2005), and this in itself could act as a lever to change. Second, the advent of approaches to assessment based on Response to Intervention (RTI) will, according to Jimerson and Oakland (2006), have the potential to reduce school psychologists' reliance on using IQ tests. Third, developments in school psychology training in the United Kingdom and overseas (ISPA, 2003) indicate how training programs are drawing on a much broader range of areas in academic psychology, in particular social and organizational psychology, and there is much less reliance on the study of individual differences and psychometrics.

Hence, in relation to the role of school psychologists in developing inclusive practices, optimism appears warranted. Countries around the world are striving to develop more inclusive practices (Mitchell, 2005; Vitello & Mithaug, 1998); there is a growing literature on the role of school psychologists that is critical of traditional ways of working and which strongly supports such a move. There is an increasing body of evidence that school psychologists can make a difference in supporting inclusion. All of this indicates that the time is ripe for school psychologists to throw off the shackles that the medical model of working has imposed upon them and to join the inclusion movement with confidence and enthusiasm.

REFERENCES

Agran, M., Blanchard, C., Wehmeyer, M., & Hughes, C. (2002). Increasing the problem solving skills of students with developmental disabilities participating in general education. *Remedial and Special Education, 23,* 279–288.

Ainscow, M., Booth, T, Dyson, A., Howes, A., Gallannaugh, F, Smith, R., et al. (2006). *Improving Schools; Developing Inclusion.* London: Routledge.

Ainscow, M., Farrell, P., Tweddle, D., & Malki, G. (2000). Developing policies for inclusive education: a study of the role of local education authorities. *The International Journal of Inclusive Education, 4,* 232–242.

Association of Educational Psychologists (1999). *Increasing inclusion: ASP position paper.* Durham: The Association of Educational Psychologists.

Baines, L., Baines, C., & Masterson, C. (1994). Mainstreaming: One school's reality. *Phi Delta Kappan, 76*(1), 39–40, 57–64.

Baker, E. T., Wang, M. C., & Walberg, H. J. (1995). The effects of inclusion on learning. *Educational Leadership, 52*(4), 33–35.

Balshaw, M., & Farrell, P. (2002). *Teaching Assistants: Practical Strategies for Effective Classroom Support.* London: Fulton.

Bandura, A. (1977). *Social learning theory.* Englewood Cliffs, N.J.: Prentice Hall.

Barrett, W., & Randall, L. (2004). Investigating the circle of friends approach: adaptations and implications for practice. *Educational Psychology in Practice, 20,* 353–368.

Booth, T., & Ainscow, M. (Eds). (1998). *From Them to Us: An International Study of Inclusion in Education.* London: Routlege.

Brooks, P., Weeks, S., & Everatt, J. (2002). Individual of learning in mainstream schoolchildren. *Educational and Child Psychology, 19*(4), 63–74.

Brown, A. L., & Ferrara, R. A. (1985). Diagnosing zones of proximal development. In J. Wertsch (Ed.), *Culture, communication and cognition: Vygotskian perspectives* (pp. 272–305). New York: Cambridge University Press.

Bruner, J. S. (1966). *Towards a theory of instruction.* New York: Norton.

Burns, M. K. (2004). Using curriculum-based assessment in consultation: A review of three levels of research. *Journal of Educational and Psychological Consultation, 15,* 63–78.

Burstein, N., Sears, S., Wilcoxen, A., Cabello, B., & Spagna, M. (2004). Moving toward inclusive practices. *Remedial and Special Education, 25,* 104–116.

Burton, S. (2004). Self-esteem groups for secondary pupils with dyslexia. *Educational Psychology in Practice, 20,* 55–73.

Carlberg, C., & Kavale, K. (1980). The efficacy of special versus regular class placement for exceptional students: A meta-analysis. *Journal of Special Education, 14,* 295–309.

Clair, E., Church, R., & Batshaw, M. (2002). Special education services. In M. Batshaw (Ed.), *Children with disabilities* (5th ed., pp. 589–606). Baltimore: Brookes.

Cole, C. (2006). Closing the achievement gap series, Part III: What is the impact of NCLB on the inclusion of students with disabilities? *Center for Evaluation and Education Policy Brief, 4*(11), 1–12.

Cole, C., Waldron, N., & Majd, M. (2004). Academic progress of students across inclusive and traditional settings. *Mental Retardation, 42,* 136–144.

Davies, S., Howes, A., Christopher, A., Davies, B., Davies, H., Farrell, P., et al. forthcoming. *Collaborative action research for inclusion: A guide for practitioners.* Routledge, London.

Davies, S. M. B., Howes, A. & Farrell, P. forthcoming. "I haven't got time to think!" Contradictions as drivers for change in an analysis of joint working between teachers and school psychologists. *School Psychology International.*

Davis, S. (1992). *Report card to the nation on inclusion in education of students with mental retardation.* Arlington, TX: The Arc.

Deno, S., Maruyama, G., Espin, C., & Cohen, C. (1990). Educating students with mild disabilities in general education classrooms: Minnesota alternatives. *Exceptional Children, 57,* 150–161.

Department of Education and Science (1978). *Special Educational Needs: Report of the Committee of Inquiry into the Education of Handicapped Children and Young People.* London: HMSO.

Department of Education and Science (1980). *Special Needs in Education. Cmnd 7996.* London: HMSO.

Department of Education and Science (1983). *Assessments and Statements of Special Educational Needs, Circular 1/83*. London: DES/DHSS.

Department for Education (1994). *Code of Practice on the Identification and Assessment of Special Educational Needs*. London: Department for Education.

Department for Education and Employment (1997). *Excellence for All Children: Meeting special educational needs*. London: The Stationery Office.

Department for Education and Employment (1998). *Meeting Special Educational Needs: A Programme for Action*. London: Department for Education and Employment.

Department for Education and Employment (2000). *Educational psychology services (England): Current role, good practice, and future directions—The research report (DfEE 0133/2000)*. Nottingham: Department for Education and Employment.

Department for Education and Skills (2001a). *Inclusive Schooling: Children with special educational needs*. London: DfES.

Department for Education and Skills (2001b). *Special Educational Needs Code of Practice*. London: DfES.

Department for Education and Skills (2001c). *SEN and Disability Act (SENDA)*. London: DfES.

Department for Education and Skills (2004). *Removing Barriers to Achievement*. London: DfES.

Dole, S. (2003). Applying psychological theory to helping students overcome learned difficulties in mathematics: An alternative approach to intervention. *School Psychology International, 24*, 95–114.

Doré, R., Dion, E., Wagner, S., & Brunet, J.-P. (2002). High school inclusion of adolescents with mental retardation: A multiple case study. *Education and Training in Mental Retardation and Developmental Disabilities, 37*, 253–261.

Dowling, J., & Leibowitz, D. (1994). Evaluation of educational psychology services: Past and present. *Educational Psychology in Practice, 9*, 241–250.

Downing, J., & Eichinger, J. (2003). Creating learning opportunities for students with severe disabilities in inclusive classrooms. *Teaching Exceptional Children, 36*(1), 26–31.

Downing, J., Spencer, S., & Cavallaro, C. (2004). The development of an inclusive charter elementary school: Lessons learned. *Research & Practice for Persons with Severe Disabilities, 29*, 11–24.

Dunsmuir, S. Frederickson, N., & Lang, J. (2004). Building home-school trust. *Educational and Child Psychology, 21*, 109–128.

Dymond, S., & Orelove, F. (2001). What constitutes effective curricula for students with severe disabilities? *Exceptionality, 9*, 109–122.

Evans, M. E., & Wright, A. K. (1987). The Surrey school psychological service: An evaluation through teacher perceptions. *Educational Psychology in Practice, 3*, 12–20.

Falvey, M. A., & Givner, C. C. (2005). What is an inclusive school? In R. Villa & J. S. Thousand (Eds.), *Creating an inclusive school* (3rd ed.). Alexandria, VA: Association for Supervision and Curriculum.

Farrell, P. (2000). The impact of research on developments in inclusive education. *The International Journal of Inclusive Education, 4*, 153–162.

Farrell, P. (2006). Developing inclusive practices among educational psychologists: Problems and possibilities. *European Journal of the Psychology of Education, 21*, 293–305.

Farrell, P., Balshaw, M., & Polat, F. (2000). Effective practice in the work of learning support assistants: Implications for educational psychologists. *Educational and Child Psychology. 17*, 66–77.

Farrell, P., Dyson, A., Polat, F., Hutcheson, G. & Gallannaugh, F. (2007a). Inclusion and achievement in mainstream schools. *European Journal of Special Needs Education, 22*, 131–147.

Farrell, P., Dyson, A., Polat, F., Hutcheson, G. & Gallannaugh, F. (2007b). The relationship between inclusion and academic achievement in English mainstream schools. *School Effectiveness and School Improvement, 18*(3), 335–352.

Farrell, P., Harraghy, J., & Petrie, B. (1996). The statutory assessment of children with emotional and behavioural difficulties. *Educational Psychology in Practice, 12*, 80–85.

Farrell P., Jimerson, S., Kalambouka, A., & Benoit, J. (2005). Teachers' perceptions of school psychologists in different countries. *School Psychology International, 26*(5), 525–544.

Farrell, P. & Tskalidou, K. (1999). Recent trends in the re-integration of pupils with emotional and behavioural difficulties. *School Psychology International, 20*, 323–338.

Farrell, P., Woods, K., Lewis, S., Rooney, S., Squires, G., & O'Connor, M. (2006). *A Review of the Functions and Contribution of Educational Psychologists in England and Wales in Light of "Every Child Matters: Change for Children."* London: HMSO.

Fisher, M., & Meyer, L. (2002). Development and social competence after two years for students enrolled in inclusive and self-contained educational programs. *Research and Practice for Persons With Severe Disabilities, 27*, 165–174.

Ford, J. D., & Migles, M. (1979). The role of the school psychologist: Teachers' preferences as a function of personal professional characteristics. *Journal of School Psychology, 17*, 372–378.

Fox, S., Farrell, P., & Davis, P. (2004). Factors affecting the successful inclusion of pupils with Down's syndrome. *British Journal of Special Education, 4*, 184–190.

Freeman, S., & Alkin, M. (2000). Academic and social attainments of children with mental retardation in general education and special education settings. *Remedial and Special Education*, *21*, 3–18.

Frydenburg, E., Lewis, R., Bugalski, K., Cotta, A., McCarthy, C., Luscombe-Smith, N., & Poole, C. (2004). Prevention is better than cure: coping skills training for adolescents at school. *Educational Psychology in Practice*, *20*, 117–134.

Gee, K. (2004). Developing curriculum and instruction. In F. Orelove, D. Sobsey, & R. Silberman (Eds.), *Educating children with multiple disabilities: A collaborative approach* (4th ed., pp. 67–114). Baltimore: Brookes.

Gerber, M. M. (1995). Inclusion at the high-water mark? Some thoughts on Zigmond and Baker's case studies of inclusive educational programs. *Journal of Special Education*, *29*, 181–191.

Giangreco, M. F. (2006). Foundational concepts and practices for educating students with severe disabilities. In M. E. Snell & F. Brown (Eds.), *Instruction of students with severe disabilities* (6th ed., pp. 1–27). Upper Saddle River, NJ: Pearson Education/Prentice-Hall.

Giangreco, M. F. (1997). Key lessons learned about inclusive education: Summary of the 1996 Schonell Memorial Lecture. *International Journal of Disability, Development & Education*, *44*, 193–206.

Giangreco, M. F., Dennis, R., Cloninger, C., Edelman, S. & Schattman, R. (1993). "I've counted Jon": Transformational experiences of teachers educating students with disabilities. *Exceptional Children*, *59*, 359–372.

Giangreco, M. F., Edelman, S., Cloninger, C., & Dennis, R. (1993). My child has a classmate with severe disabilities: What parents of nondisabled children think about full inclusion. *Developmental Disabilities Bulletin*, *21*, 77–91.

Gillham, W. (Ed.). (1978). *Reconstructing educational psychology*. London: Virago.

Gilman, R., & Gabriel, S. (2004). Perceptions of school psychological services by education professionals: results from a multi-state survey pilot study. *School Psychology Review*, *33*, 271–287.

Guillemard, J. C. (2006). School psychology in France. In S. Jimerson, T. Oakland, & P. Farrell (Eds.), *The Handbook of international school psychology*. London: Sage.

Harrower, J. K. (1999). Educational inclusion of children with severe disabilities. *Journal of Positive Behavioural Interventions*, *1*, 215–230.

Hayes, B. (2002). Community, cohesion, inclusive education. *Educational and Child Psychology*, *19*(4), 75–90.

Hegarty, S. (1991). Towards an agenda for research in special education. *European Journal of Special Needs Education*, *6*, 87–99.

Helmstetter, E., Peck, C., & Giangreco, M. F. (1994). Outcomes of interactions with peers with moderate or severe disabilities: A statewide survey of high school students. *The Journal of the Association for Persons with Severe Handicaps*, *19*, 263–276.

Hick, P. (2005). Supporting the development of more inclusive practices using the index for inclusion. *Educational Psychology in Practice*, *21*, 117–122.

Hick, P., Kerhsner, R., & Farrell, P. (Eds.). Forthcoming. *A psychology for inclusion*. London: Routledge-Falmer.

Hodson, P., Baddeley, A., Laycock, S., & Williams, S. (2005). Helping secondary schools to be more inclusive of year 7 pupils with SEN. *Educational Psychology in Practice*, *21*(1), 53–67.

House of Commons Education and Skills Committee (2006). *Special Educational Needs: Vol. 1*. London: HMSO.

Howe, M. (1998). *IQ in question: The truth about intelligence*. London: Sage.

Howes, A., & Davies, S. M. B. (2006, September). *Designing for complex change? Critically evaluating an application of design study in relation to teachers developing more inclusive practices*. British Educational Research Association Conference, Warwick.

Howes, A., Davies, S., Fox, S., Davies, H., & Swann, S. forthcoming. *Improving the context for inclusion: How teachers and educational psychologists can use action research to work together to develop inclusion*, Routledge, London.

Howes, A., Fox, S. & Davies, S. M. B. (2006, September). *Understanding action research with professionals in schools: accounting for legitimate and persistent discourses as part of the real-world experience of changing practice*. British Educational Research Association Conference, Warwick.

Hunt, P., & Goetz, L. (1997). Research on inclusive educational programs, practices and outcomes for students with severe disabilities. *Journal of Special Education*, *31*, 3–29.

Hunt, P., Staub, D., Alwell, M., & Goetz, L. (1994). Achievement of all students within the context of cooperative learning groups. *The Journal of the Association for Persons with Severe Handicaps*, *19*, 290–301.

Hutchings, J., Lane, E., Owen, R., & Gwyn, R. (2004). The introduction of the Webster-Stratton incredible years classroom dinosaur school programme in Gwynedd, North Wales: a pilot study. *Educational and Child Psychology*, *21*, 4–15.

International School Psychology Association (2002). Proceedings of the 2002 International School Psychology Colloquium, Denmark. Available online at www.ispaweb.org

International School Psychology Association (2003). Guidelines for the Accreditation of School Psychology Training Programmes. Available online at www.ispaweb.org

Janney, R., & Snell, M. (1996). How teachers use peer interactions to include students with moderate and severe disabilities in elementary general education classes. *The Journal of the Association for Persons with Severe Handicaps, 21*, 72–80.

Jimerson, S. R., Graydon, K., Curtis, M., & Staskal, R. (2007). The international school psychology survey: Insights from school psychologists around the world. In S. Jimerson, T. Oakland, & P. Farrell, (Eds.), *Handbook of international school psychology* (pp. 481–500). London: Sage.

Jimerson, S. R., Graydon, K., Farrell, P., Kikas, E., Hatzichristou, S., Boce, E., & Bashi, G., (2004). The international school psychology survey: Development and data. *School Psychology International, 25*, 259–286.

Jimerson, S. R., Graydon, K., Yuen, M., Lam, S. F., Thurm, J., Klueva, N., et al. (2006). The international school psychology survey: Data from Australia, China, Germany, Italy and Russia. *School Psychology International, 27*, 5–32.

Jimerson, S. R. & Oakland, T. D. (2006). School psychology in the United States. In S. Jimerson, T. Oakland, & P. Farrell (Eds.), *The handbook of international school psychology* (pp. 415–426). London: Sage.

Jimerson, S. R., Oakland, T. D., & Farrell, P., (Eds). (2006). *The handbook of international school psychology*. London: Sage.

Jupp, K. (1992). *Everyone Belongs*. London: Souvenir Press.

Kalambouka, A., Farrell, P., Dyson, A., & Kaplan, I. (2007). The impact of placing pupils with special educational needs in mainstream schools on the achievements of their peers. *Educational Research, 39*, 365–382.

Karagiannis, A., Stainback, S., & Stainback, W. (1996). Historical overview of inclusion. In S. Stainback & W. Stainback (Eds.), *Inclusion: A guide for educators* (pp. 17–28). Baltimore: Brookes.

Kauffmann, J. M., & Hallahan, D. P. (Eds.) (1995). *The illusion of full inclusion: A comprehensive critique of a current special education bandwagon*. Austin, TX: Pro-Ed.

Kikas, E. (1999). School psychology in Estonia: expectations of teachers and school psychologists. *School Psychology International, 20*, 352–365.

Kozleski, E. B., & Jackson, L. (1993). Taylor's story: Full inclusion in her neighborhood elementary school. *Exceptionality, 4*, 153–175.

Leadbetter, J. (2005). Activity theory as a conceptual framework and analytical tool within the practice of educational psychology. *Educational and Child Psychology, 22*, 18–28.

Lewis, R., & Doorlag, D. (2006). *Teaching special students in general education classrooms* (7th ed.). Upper Saddle River, NJ: Pearson Prentice Hall.

Lindsay, G. (2007). Educational psychology and the effectiveness of inclusive education/ mainstreaming, *British Journal of Educational Psychology, 77*, 1–24

Lokke, C., Gersch, I., M'Gadzah, H., & Frederickson, N. (1997). The resurrection of psychometrics: fact or fiction ? *Educational Psychology in Practice, 12*, 222–233.

Maddern, L., Franey, J., McLaughlin, V., & Cox, S. (2004). An evaluation of the impact of an inter-agency intervention programme to promote social skills in primary school children. *Educational Psychology in Practice, 20*(2), 135–155.

McDonnell, A., McDonnell, J., Hardman, M., & McCune, G. (1991). Educating students with severe disabilities in their neighborhood school: The Utah Elementary Integration Model. *Remedial and Special Education, 12*(6), 34–45.

Medcalf, J., Glynn, T., & Moore, D. (2004). Peer tutoring in writing: a school systems approach. *Educational Psychology in Practice, 20*, 157–178.

Mercer, J. R. (1973). *Labeling the mentally retarded*. Berkeley: University of California Press.

Mercer, J. R. (1974). A policy statement on assessment procedures and the rights of children. *Harvard Education Review, 44*, 125–141.

Mitchell, D. (Ed). (2005). *Contextualizing inclusive education: Evaluating old and new international paradigms*. London: Routledge.

Mnkandla, M., & Matruse, K. (2002). The impact of inclusion policy on school psychology practices in Zimbabwe. *Educational and Child Psychology, 19*, 12–24.

Muthukrishna, N., & Baez, M. (2002). Building an inclusive education and training system. What is next for educational psychologists in South Africa? *Educational and Child Psychology, 19*, 24–33.

National Association of School Psychologists (1999). *The role of the school psychologist in inclusive education*. Retrieved from www.naSPweb.org/ information/misc/inclusion.htm

Oakland, T. (2000). International school psychology. In T. Fagan & T. Wise (Eds.), *School psychology: past, present & future*. National Association of School Psychologists.

Ofsted (2000). *Educational Inclusion: Guidance for Inspectors and Schools*. London: Ofsted.

Peck, C., Donaldson, J. & Pezzoli, M. (1990). Some benefits non-handicapped adolescents perceive for themselves from their social relationships with peers who have severe handicaps. *The Journal of the Association for Persons with Severe Handicaps, 15*, 241–249.

Peck, C., Staub, D., Gallucci, C., & Schwartz, I. (2004). Parent perception of the impacts of inclusion on their nondisabled child. *Research & Practice for Persons with Severe Disabilities, 29*, 135–143.

Poplin, M. S. (1988). The reductionistic fallacy in learning disabilities: Replicating the past by reducing the present. *Journal of Learning Disabilities, 21*, 401–416.

Rea, P., Mclaughlin, V., & Walther-Thomas, C. (2002). Outcomes for students with learning disabilities in inclusive and pullout programs. *Exceptional Children, 68*, 203–222.

Rees, C., Rees, P., & Farrell, P. (2003). Methods used by psychologists to assess pupils with emotional and behavioural difficulties. *Educational Psychology in Practice, 19*, 203–214.

Reschly, D. J. (2000). The present and future status of school psychology in the United States. *School Psychology Review, 29*, 507–522.

Roffey, S. (2004). The home-school interface for behaviour: a conceptual framework for co-constructing reality. *Educational and Child Psychology, 21*, 95–108.

Rustemier, S., & Vaughn, M. (2005). *Segregation trends—LEAs in England 2002–2004*. Bristol: Centre for Studies on Inclusive Education.

Salisbury, C., Palombaro, M., & Hollowood, T. (1993). On the nature and change of an inclusive elementary school. *Journal of the Association for Persons with Severe Handicaps, 18*, 75–84.

Shapiro, E. S., Angello, L. M., & Eckert, T. L. (2004). Has curriculum based assessment become the staple of school psychology practice? An update and extension of knowledge, use and attitudes from 1990–2000. *School Psychology Review, 33*, 249–258.

Sharpe, M., York, J., & Knight, J. (1994). Effects of inclusion on the academic performance of classmates without disabilities: A preliminary study. *Remedial and Special Education, 15*, 281–287.

Sheridan, S. M., & Gutkin, T. B. (2000). The ecology of school psychology: examining and changing our paradigm for the 21st century. *School Psychology Review, 29*, 485–502.

Smelter, R. W., Rasch, B. W., & Yudewitz, G. J. (1994). Thinking of inclusion for all special needs students? Better think again. *Phi Delta Kappan, 76*(1), 35–38.

Smith, P. (2007). Have we made any progress? Including students with intellectual disabilities in regular education classrooms. *Intellectual and Developmental Disabilities, 45*, 297–309.

Turnbull, A., Turnbull, R., Erwin, E., & Soodak, L. (2006). *Families, professionals, and exceptionality: Positive outcomes through partnerships and trust*. Upper Saddle River, NJ: Pearson Prentice Hall.

van Kraayenoord, C. E. (2002). The roles of the educational psychologist in inclusion in Australia. *Educational and Child Psychology, 19*, 46–59.

Villa, R. A., & Thousand, J. S. (1992). How one district integrated special and general education. *Educational Leadership, 50*(2), 39–41.

Vitello, S. J., & Mithaug, D. E. (1998). *Inclusive schooling: National and international perspective*. Mahawah, NJ: Lawrence Erlbaum Associates.

Vygotsky, L. S. (1986). *Thought and language*. Cambridge, MA: Massachusetts Institute of Technology Press.

Winzer, M. (2000). The inclusion movement: Review and reflections on reform in special education. In Winzer M, Mazurek K (Eds.), *Special education in the 21st century: Issues of inclusion and reform* (pp. 5–26). Washington, DC: Gallaudet University Press.

Woods, K., & Farrell, P. (2006). Current approaches used by educational psychologists in the assessment of children with learning and behaviour problems. *School Psychology International, 27*, 387–404.

Ysseldyke, J. E. (1987). Do tests help in teaching? *Journal of the Association of Child Psychology and Psychiatry, 28*, 21–25.

York, J., Vandercook, T., Macdonald, C., Heise-Neff, C., & Caughey, E. (1992). Feedback about integrating middle school students with severe disabilities in general education classes. *Exceptional Children, 58*, 260–269.

Young, S., & Holdorf, G. (2003). Using solution focused brief therapy in individual referrals for bullying. *Educational Psychology in Practice, 19*, 271–282.

Zigmond, N., & Baker, J. (1990). Mainstream experiences for learning disabled students (Project MELD): Preliminary report. *Exceptional Children, 57*, 176–185.

THINKING DIVERSITY: A HABIT OF MIND FOR SCHOOL PSYCHOLOGY

MARY M. CLARE
Lewis & Clark College

Today we are faced with the preeminent fact that if civilization is to survive, we must cultivate the science of human relationships—the ability of all peoples, of all kinds, to live together and work together in the same world, at peace.

Franklin D. Roosevelt
Undelivered Speech, 1945

We share a common knowledge base with others in our discipline, but our codification and application of that knowledge is mediated by who we are and how we know.

Michael-Anthony Brown-Cheatham

Janette is 22. She has a 2-year-old son who, soon after his birth, was diagnosed with an extremely rare digestive disorder that will require him to follow a precise medical regimen his entire life. Janette lives in an urban area where services for her son are available through public assistance. She is a young woman of the Tlingit, Apache and Klamath tribes married to a white man, her son's father. These young parents have agreed to raise their son in the ways of his mother's traditions.

Janette and her older brother George were raised by a lesbian couple who served as their foster parents. The couple, a Mayan woman and a white woman of Irish ancestry, were supported by the tribes as good parents committed to fully involving the children in tribal traditions. Because they were lesbian, however, the tribes would not approve adoption. Janette and George had been removed from their mother by the state when they were 4 and 6 because of repeated incidents of neglect linked in large part with poverty. Both children received services for specific learning disabilities during their schooling.

Janette was nonetheless successful in elementary and middle school with ambition and capacity for becoming a psychologist. By 16, Janette's beauty, budding sexuality, and experimentation with substances combined with her internalization of a profound sense of hopelessness and limitation to show up in a series of reckless and self-destructive behaviors. Three years later, she was in a work-release program for juvenile felons after causing an automobile accident in which an elderly man was killed. It was in this program she met her future husband. Together they solve the myriad problems of a young family with the additional and weighty realities of living with felonies and raising a medically fragile son. Janette was recently accepted to nursing school.

These three paragraphs give only a preliminary sense of the richness and complexity of this young woman's life—the profound challenges she faces and the resiliency she musters again and again. She is a real woman. She has been a student in public and private schools and is the parent of a child who already qualifies for public school services. Janette's life, its texture, pain, and promise is one of 6 billion. This is the reality of human circumstance and its vast diversity. This is the reality school psychology serves.

For school psychologists, for schools, and for communities in the United States and across the globe, Janette's story is one in the chorus of whispers, the cacophony of cries that arise from the presence and insistence of human diversity. Individual and group differences and variations in sociopolitical circumstances are real and present. They demand that our profession employ dynamic ways of knowing and being to identify, refine and revise practice so that learning may be enjoyed across all differences. Diversity thus stands as an essential variable affecting all of our work in schools and communities. It both transcends and includes constructs of dignity, equity, and sensitivity to serve as a core source for the integrated knowledge and responsible expression of our work.

School psychology must respond to diversity with particular interventions and other technologies. At the same time we are wise to recognize diversity as a powerful guide and, perhaps most accurately, as a wise and enduring habit of mind for our profession. In service to such a broad view, this chapter forgoes an extensive inventory or assessment of current practices. Very useful surveys of school psychology practices related to diversity are readily available (e.g., Esquivel, Lopez, & Nahari, 2006; Frisby & Reynolds, 2005). Instead, these pages hold an attempt at investigating the context that is set with the fact of diversity by acknowledging and exploring the bearing of that fact on school psychology research, training and practice. I begin with reconsideration of our necessary but dynamic limitation for ever fully addressing diversity's demands given the ways in which our own enculturation and diverse experiences mediate our work. Though not explicitly discussed here, this perspective draws from understandings of the complicated location of any knowing within sociopolitical (Harding, 1991; Sloan, 2001), sociocultural (Salzman, 2001), social-psychological (e.g., Solomon, Greenberg, & Pyszcynski, 1991), and phenomenological (e.g., Hein & Austin, 2001) variables.

To initiate this inquiry, I start with ideas Michael-Anthony Brown-Cheatham and I (Henning-Stout & Brown-Cheatham, 1998) proposed in the third edition of *The Handbook of School Psychology*. Those ideas highlight the influence that individual experience, cultural values, and social circumstances have on the development and practice of our profession.

WHY DIVERSITY?

We hear the term daily in our work. We speak it. To differing degrees, by various qualities, and across the range of awareness, we all live within the realities of diversity. Ten years ago, Michael-Anthony Brown-Cheatham and I initiated a conceptual investigation of diversity's implications for the profession of school psychology (Henning-Stout & Brown-Cheatham, 1998). At the point of the chapter's composition, I found myself writing alone from my best memory of our conversations and of Michael-Anthony's brilliant ideas. He had died with AIDS. Life and death intervene.

This fact may provide the most poignant articulation of diversity's presence, power and invitation. Each of us lives, each of us dies and each of us moves into and through these experiences somewhat differently. As psychologists we are especially attentive to variation in human experience. Our profession follows from our wish to identify ways of responding well in support of the diverse lives we encounter. As scholars and practitioners interested in education, learning, and schools our individual and collective stores of knowledge guide our practice: the strategies, technologies, and art of our work. Our practice is unavoidably influenced by and reflective of who we are as citizens; as parents, children, relatives, and partners; as professionals, scholars and community leaders. Life and death intervene.

In our conversations ten years ago, Michael-Anthony and I were compelled by this intervention. We were most curious about the evolving construct of *diversity* as a collection of variables at the core of the discipline and practice of school psychology. We considered how the lives and cultures of school psychologists signify and mediate that construct as fundamentally as do the circumstances and behaviors of the people we serve. *Diversity* is the term we use to hold our observation of the variety in ways of knowing and being. *Diversity* is a container for our rapidly expanding awareness in formal scholarship and professional practice of the influence, persistence and significance of these variations. Understandings and experiences of diversity vary according to life circumstances (of culture, geography, economics, gender, sexuality, age, physical ability, political environment, etc.). In turn, these understandings and experiences influence both idiosyncratic and systemically normative definitions of what diversity itself connotes (Clare, 2002).

This discussion of definition alongside the suggestion that our work and our disciplinary knowledge base are mediated by our culture echoes arguments associated with postmodernism from the past half century (Ellis, 1986; Harding, 1991, Hyussen, 1990). For example, the notion of *constructivism* recognizes individual and collective knowledge as reflective of idiosyncrasy, culture, education, socioeconomic status, and related distributions of social power; that is, constructivism recognizes diversity itself. Observations of situated knowledge, constructed meaning, and individually mediated renditions of what is real link back to questions of whether objectivity is subjective (Hyussen, 1990) and even to the illusive unknown (perhaps unknowable and certainly controversial) variable in intelligence, "*g*" (Jensen, 1998; Jorion, 1999; Kush, 1999). Uncontained by postmodern considerations of knowledge, however, is the subtle yet enduring implication of human diversity as a constant to which our profession must respond. Considering diversity in this way requires moving beyond postmodern perspectives to understand human diversity as an essential reality having, among myriad effects, dynamic and perpetual impact as both a mediator of experience and an essential stimulus for the continued extension and improvement of ways of knowing and being.

Following from our thinking ten years ago (Henning-Stout & Brown-Cheatham, 1998) and drawing from the substantial and growing work of our colleagues in the meantime, it seems both possible and useful to consider diversity as a dynamic constant influencing all areas of school psychology. To do this, I will offer a brief survey of contemporary responses to diversity in the research and practice of school psychology. In this context, I will review ideas linked with postmodernism as evident in our profession's engagement with diversity's challenges. I will explore ways in which diversity may be understood as a dynamic constant in school psychology by considering possibilities for thought, research and action beyond postmodernism. To illustrate these ideas I will specifically reference and describe two emerging areas of theory and practice: the growing conceptualization and advancement of decolonization (e.g., Smith, 1999) and practical applications of multicontextuality (Ibarra, 2001). Both of these areas contain substantive scholarly advancements originating in the perspectives and experiences of scholars from historically marginalized cultural and sociopolitical backgrounds. As such, they serve to stimulate and extend our individual and collective receptivity to diversity's influence in the research and practice of school psychology.

CONTEMPORARY RESPONSES TO DIVERSITY

The past decade's literature on diversity in school psychology seems to take five general tacks: (a) articulation and development of theory, (b) systematic anecdotal reflections on historically marginalized groups in relation to current practices, (c) demographic cataloguing of social and cultural differences vis-a-vis measures of learning or mental health, (d) description of technical interventions to address diversity (curricula and instructional practices, behavioral and clinical methodologies, organizational and consultation strategies), and (e) emerging efforts to establish cross-cultural research strategies in our discipline. Each of these forms of scholarship has been crucial for extending the responsiveness and relevance of school psychology research and practice to the range of human experience.

Several exceptional publications have provided useful and compelling documentation of the interventions and strategies that have emerged over the past years reflecting the ways our profession has developed to better address the interests and concerns of diverse learners (e.g., Esquivel et al., 2006; Frisby & Reynolds, 2005). Both emergent and established, these practices support interventions for behavior (e.g., Harris & Goldstein, 2006; Sheridan, 2000) and academic success (e.g., Reyes-Carrasquillo, 2006), strategies for consultation with diverse teachers and parents and administrators (e.g., Ingraham, 2000; Lopez, 2000; Nahari, Martines, & Marquez, 2006), and a strong and growing collection of empirical studies guiding culturally fair assessment (e.g., Flanagan & Ortiz, 2000; Gottlieb & Hamayan, 2006; Ochoa, Rivera, & Ford, 1997). Additional work on the validation of cross-cultural research approaches in school psychology has included emphasis on and elaboration of mixing the methods of quantitative and qualitative research methodologies for greatest sensitivity to culture-specific phenomena (e.g., Hitchcock et al., 2005).

Each of these areas of scholarship has direct and immediate bearing on the content of graduate preparation programs in school psychology. In a careful analysis of the current practices in graduate instruction, Rogers (2005) reminds us that school psychology's practice is linked significantly with the training programs through which practitioners enter the field. Based on her analysis, Rogers urges our intelligent and self-conscious attention in three specific areas: (1) fairly researching, representing and supporting the development of responsive practices across diverse populations; (2) actively recruiting graduate students from underrepresented cultural groups; and (3) adjusting all educational systems to be accessible, navigable and dignifying of people across the range of human experience. Rogers' (2005) observations are particularly salient in a profession that has seen no increase in the diversity of its membership over the past ten years while the population of our country becomes increasingly varied. Each of her suggestions warrants serious consideration and committed response by our profession. In particular, scholars of historically marginalized groups are needed to extend the perspectives from which research data are generated, interpreted, and linked with practice.

Apropos of the enhancement to knowledge available with the entry into school psychology of scholars from historically marginalized groups, this chapter invites a temporary shift of attention to regard diversity as a dynamic constant for our profession—as a growing habit of mind. The fact of our work being situated in our lives and in the epistemologies emerging from there may make such a shift in attention crucial to our continued growth individually and as a profession.

One danger of this kind of inquiry is relegating the discussion to the ethers of philosophical pondering. Diversity, however, refuses to be abstract. Our successes and failures, our insights and blindness as individuals and as a profession touch real lives in real ways on a daily basis. In schools people of the dominant and marginalized groups are affected by overt and covert messages carried in curricula, instructional practices, general communication norms, and values expressed in applied notions of intelligence, social skill, and talent. All of these message systems and their content affect and are purveyed by school psychology. As Jackson (2005) has observed, "For decades school psychology has been shaped by a form of monoculturalism.... The functional perspective of psychological services delivery has been (and continues to be) based on the assumption that middle-class Euro-American cultural standards are superior and preferred.... Youth of groups outside this standard were then variously described as deprived, different, culturally neutral—negatively despite positive intentions (e.g., of school psychologists)" (p. 15).

The impact and subtlety of what Jackson refers to as our profession's "functional perspective" has begun to be addressed through theoretical unpacking of the bias inherent in our discipline, and through empirical investigations of the impact of and responses to inequity in educational and psychological practices. In their important text, *Comprehensive Handbook of Multicultural School Psychology*, Frisby and Reynolds (2005) engage the voices of scholars and practitioners from across the field to consider the empirical literature addressing these issues. This text illustrates the energy and action school psychology has generated in response to diversity's mandate. In their introductory essay, Frisby and Reynolds (2005) argue that human diversity and multicultural realities are best understood as elemental to our work. "We are uncomfortable with characterizing multicultural school psychology as a subspecialty area, because this implies that the subject matter is relevant to only a subset of training programs or applied settings in the field." Many of the contributors to their volume carry forward the editors' position but the tension between values considered generalizably "American" and historically overlooked values of marginalized groups gains illustration in warnings against overapplication of multicultural consideration. For example, in an opening essay, Oakland (2005) cautions against the reification of multiculturalism suggesting that "our nation's struggle [has been] to find ways to uphold important values yet not show disrespect for cultures and subgroups that hold different values" (p. 12). Later, Frisby (2005) refers to the observations of Naylor (1998) reminding readers that "at the level of individuals, cultural differences between persons are not mutually exclusive, as persons can share the same culture according to one set of characteristics while simultaneously being culturally different according to another set of characteristics" (p. 87).

EVIDENCE OF POSTMODERNISM IN DISCUSSIONS OF DIVERSITY

The care and caution communicated with each of the warnings mentioned above stand as examples, intended or not, of the effect of postmodern philosophies on the sensibilities of theoreticians and empiricists in school psychology. These sensibilities, in turn, necessarily guide our profession particularly with relation to multicultural and more broadly construed diversity considerations.

Before discussing the evidence of postmodernism in school psychology, a brief digression into definitions may be helpful. *Postmodernism* is a post facto designation given a set of philosophies that have developed in reaction to philosophies related to positivism (these, sometimes referred to as *modernism*). The dominant Western tradition of empirical positivism (modernism) originated with Copernicus and was modified and further reified with Newton. Modernist views of absolutely discernable cause and effect persist in many contemporary scientific, political and social practices and are based on celebration of reason as an independent, neutral, unbiased, and objective instrument by which absolute truths can and will be found. In reaction, postmodernism turns the objective gaze back toward the observer to ask where any thought, idea, or scientific hypothesis originates thus suggesting that "reality" is a construct always and necessarily mediated through human cognition and thereby rendering objectivity subjective.

So, what does this have to do with school psychology and the effect of the constant presence of human diversity in the context of our discipline? Needless to say, entire books could be devoted to this question. Given the limitations of a chapter, I've selected initial considerations of three concepts emerging from postmodernism and its critical extensions: situated knowledge, constructed meaning, and individually mediated understandings. I will illustrate each as it affects school psychology practice. The essential redundancy of these three terms is important to note. Each serves the function, in a slightly different way, of shifting the gaze from its usual direction toward the techniques, circumstances and people we study or serve to investigating the influence of diversity on the way we as individuals and as a profession construct and enact what we know.

The term *situated knowledge* refers to the location or situation of knowledge bases (e.g., psychology, history, philosophy, mathematics, science) in the sensibilities and circumstances from which they are authored (Harding, 1991). It asks the question, "Where does knowledge originate?" The content of knowledge bases has historically been produced by scholars and leaders representing a narrow band of human experience (i.e., educated European and European American men of financial means). To situate knowledge differently would, in the case of human diversity, require broad inclusion of thought originating in and developing from groups excluded from the dominant perspective. Response to this challenge has often involved attempts to "give voice" to the disenfranchised. Speaking specifically to the knowledge of women, Harding (1991) warns, "Starting from women's lives is something that both men and women must *learn* to do [emphasis in original]. Women's telling their experiences

is not the same as thinking from the perspective of women's lives" (p. 150). This is so for any historically marginalized group. Discerning knowledge as it arises from the epistemologies, and thus from the lives of people who have experienced oppression, vastly extends the collective knowledge available for guiding social, political, and educational practices.

Illustrating the spirit of situated knowledge, Frisby and Reynolds' (2005) suggestion that multicultural perspectives are relevant across and throughout the research and practice of school psychology calls attention to the fact of our work being situated in multicultural realities. The fact of cultural variation, the fact of diversity may not yet (and likely cannot) be fully captured in the knowledge base of school psychology or any profession. Rather, as these authors imply, diversity serves much as human development, communication, or social organization. It is an overarching and dynamic variable to which our work must respond. In the history of social science in general and school psychology in particular, we have tended toward referring to these realities as intervening variables and quite often have avoided dealing with them by theorizing their random and therefore irrelevant effects. To suggest as Frisby and Reynolds do, that multicultural school psychology is not a subspecialty of the profession but rather a pervasive and constantly relevant consideration, situates the knowledge of school psychology in the social and political practices and circumstances that reflect contemporary responses to diversity.

A more conventional illustration of situated knowledge is evident in Oakland's (2005) caution against discarding dominant culture values. While his warning to balance all perspectives is of essential wisdom, his notion of the "important values" (p. 12) our nation struggles to uphold is necessarily situated in the perspective and culture of the few who define both *value* and *importance*. To assign absolute value without collective discussion across cultural groups fails to fulfill the tenants of democracy. Frisby and Reynold's (2005) suggestion that multicultural considerations pervade school psychology represents a broader situation of knowledge within an ongoing dialogue across cultural experiences, values and related perspectives.

Like *situated knowledge, constructed meaning* points to individual and collective ways of knowing as essential building blocks for any public knowledge. While the terms are in many ways synonymous, *constructed meaning* carries a more active focus. This term asks the question, "How is thought built and what determines its content?" The way any school psychologist constructs knowledge is mediated through training, exposure to the research and literature of the profession, and experience in the schools and in one's life generally. The overriding strength of organizational and professional consensus as reflected in the literature and articulated practice of school psychology (all constructed) has profound and often unseen influence on the meaning individual professionals construct—on how and what we know. As Jackson (2005) observes in the quote above, school psychology must be understood for the source of its functional perspectives. The strategies of our profession, the techniques of assessment, consultation and counseling alongside the content and process of graduate preparation programs reflect the values and perspectives of their authors. Given the persistent overrepresentation of white people of European ancestry in school psychology, more women in practice and more men in academe, it is impossible to avoid considering the way white cultural values serve as the fundamental and sometimes exclusive building blocks of our empirical and practical functions.

Popular notions of *readiness to learn* in politics and educational policy stand as examples of meaning that is culturally constructed. The vast majority of 5-year-old children (all those free of severe cognitive impairment) step across the thresholds of their schools not only ready but astonishingly accomplished as learners. They bring with them functional and expertly acquired linguistic, numeric, and spatial forms along with the social behaviors with which they have successfully navigated their preschool years. Once across the threshold, however, only those whose culture matches that of the curriculum and staff find easy recognition for their readiness as learners. In general, educators fail to recognize the construction of meaning behind *readiness* as rooted primarily in the reification of curricula. Because curricula are made and delivered by people, they may only be cultural expressions, even as portions of their content or purpose may arguably be constants (e.g., both phonics and comprehension are vital to reading). Nonetheless, and in general, the strategies and narrative used for conveying both curricula and instructional practices cannot stand the test of cross-cultural validity. In the curricular contexts of most contemporary schools, children of unrepresented cultures appear less

ready for learning when actually the curriculum is not prepared to support and sustain the learning they, like their peers, have already accomplished.

The third concept, the idea of *individually mediated knowledge*, is arguably a defining notion of our profession—one that creates space for addressing situations like the incomplete conceptualization of school readiness described above. School psychology exists to aid educators' capacities to support learning of the students that one master practitioner, Sue Klapstein, refers to as "the most puzzling learners in schools and communities" (personal communication, January 31, 2006). We understand well that individual learners may make sense of that which is to be learned in very different ways. Our focus tends to be on cognition and affect, but lately we are attending, too, to culture and language. With awareness of these considerations school psychologists and school psychology are coming increasingly to sense as relevant the vast complexity and array of human diversity.

The fact of *individually mediated knowledge*, from a postmodern perspective, must also be understood as a continuous influence on those of us who are researching and responding to the diversity among learners. This term, though again largely redundant with the first two ideas, brings consideration of the influence of worldview even closer to the individual scholar or practitioner. To consider this influence fully, we can bring forward the suggestion that the knowledge base of school psychology is *situated* in the understandings and sociocultural worldviews of its authors. We can bring forward the suggestion that recognized diagnostic and intervention strategies or the applied functions of this knowledge are *constructed*—they are developed and advocated by scholars, trainers and practitioners who share general understandings of their content, meaning, and purpose. School psychology is culturally constructed at the level of our profession, its knowledge base, standards, and shared practices. At the level of the individual researcher or practitioner, *individual mediation* further filters constructed meanings and practical function.

In the school psychology literature, development in the practices of consultation provides illustration of individual mediation of meaning. In her extensive identification and description of cross-cultural interactions in consultation, Ingraham (2000) focuses on the in-the-moment sensitivities and adjustments required of consultants in cross-cultural consultation situations. Ingraham unveils nuances in various cross-cultural constellations (e.g., dominant culture consultant with consultee and client of historically marginalized groups) in order to identify when, how and what efforts may be made to extend the epistemology and social parameters of a consultation interaction as it is happening. Whatever the activity of a school psychologist (e.g., consultation, counseling, assessment, leading team meetings, conducting research of any kind), the decisions made in real time must be mediated by individual judgment.

Whereas positivism, realism, reductionism, and classical applications of the scientific method have downplayed variables of diversity as they operate in the thoughts and actions of scholars and professionals, the sensibilities associated with postmodernism point out the subjectivity inherent in any generation or application of knowledge. School psychology has flexed to contain and improve with these sensibilities. The effect seems to be a profession simultaneously more inclusive and more humble. There are certainly exceptions with some research and practice still tied closely to strict rationalist orientations (e.g., Jensen, 1998). But even in the most reductionistic traditions within our profession (e.g., Gresham, 2002), the influence of postmodernism and a related recognition of the real and present demands of diversity can be seen. Well-established behaviorist scholars in our discipline, for example, have elaborated the notion of *treatment validity* (Gresham, 2002; Reschly & Ysseldyke, 2002). Though not intentionally grounded in the postmodern ideas described above, this notion represents shifts in the perspective of behaviorist researchers and theorists in that the values, interests, concerns and by extension the generally overlooked perspective of a teacher, parent, or learner are taken into account when developing, implementing and refining intervention strategies. Treatment validity is present when the treatment works, and these more positivist scholars have noted that treatment acceptability is essential to validity (Boothe, Borrego, Hill & Anhalt, 2005; Gresham, 2002; Reschly & Ysseldyke, 2002).

More recently, Boothe et al. (2005) have extended the investigation of treatment acceptability explicitly to consider the impact of ethnicity on the acceptability of interventions offered by school psychologists and other educators. They note the lack of representation of people of color in the studies of this construct and note further, "More important than the lack of examining ethnic differences is the lack of examining cultural factors that might lead to differences with regard to treatment acceptability and treatment compliance" (p. 967). The concept of treatment validity already reflects the incorporation of postmodern calls to consider the situation, construction, and mediation of knowing (or, in this case, acceptability of and compliance with professional instruction). Boothe and her colleagues (2005) take this concept explicitly into the considerations necessitated with the fact of diversity.

Finally, Frisby (2005) offers a specific call for a more anthropological sensibility in school psychology research. He extends the observation that "all culture is local" (p. 121) to identify the practical and ethical necessity for locating research closer to the learners, schools, and communities it effects. This call and school psychology's response signify a profound step in the direction of honoring, representing and responding to the fact of diversity by recognizing variation in the way learners, families and communities live, learn and know. Jackson (2005) offers a similar observation: "This is another way of saying that multicultural school psychology proposes to treat the individual client from the reality base of where he or she actually lives. This in contrast to the client being treated against a cultural background that is not his or her own, as is the rule under monocultural school psychology" (p. 19).

DIVERSITY BEYOND POSTMODERNISM: THEORETICAL BASES FOR SCHOOL PSYCHOLOGY'S NEXT STEPS

When the best of empirical positivism combines with the best of constructivism the result is the epistemological capacity of a mature profession for using reason and improvisation to support human well-being. In the case of school psychology, drawing on the strength of both ways of knowing helps us dignify and learn from the broad range of children, youth, families, communities and social organizations. The fact of diversity only enhances our work. School psychology, alongside other professions linked with psychology and education, has benefited greatly from the presence and insistence of human diversity. Diversity may be what has brought us to this humble, artistic, and rigorous point in the development of our discipline.

In a primarily white profession, we are coming increasingly to recognize the privilege that makes access to education and professional status more open to white people, especially of the middle and upper social classes. We are coming gradually to see that our privilege as professionals of any ethnicity and economic background must be used to undo systems of privilege that waste the minds and talents of people for whom access is limited (Henning-Stout, 1994). In the United States, our years of struggle toward living the democracy we prize has led slowly to increased awareness of the costs of social marginalization.

To respond well to this urgent challenge, school psychology must integrate our empirical and constructivist skills. We must expand and apply our science and practice to reveal and remove the disproportionate obstruction faced by children, youth and adults not raised in the dominant culture. The integration of our thinking with diversity's realities is urgent because reductionistic strategies of measurement and diagnosis have never been reliable indicators of treatment (e.g., Boothe, Borrego, Hill & Anhalt, 2005; Reschly & Ysseldyke, 2002)—they are valuable tools, but they are not the truth. This integration is also urgent because the deconstruction of measurement, diagnosis and intervention, while helpful for revealing epistemological and practical limitations, does not of itself address the crushing realities in the everyday lives of so many learners, educators, families and communities.

As our profession works to remain on track by expanding awareness of and responsiveness to diversity's demands, two developing theoretical perspectives seem worth noting. The ideas and initiatives of *decolonization* (e.g., Smith, 1999) and *multicontextuality* (e.g., Ibarra, 2001) arise from the research agendas of scholars who were raised in historically marginalized groups and choose consciously to apply their scholarly prowess to the articulation and representation of rigorous ways of knowing that fall outside the recognized knowledge traditions of the dominant culture.

Decolonization

Colonialism is an historical term associated with the international assertion of political and economic power and control by the recognized government of a nation. Historically colonialism has been particularly associated with many countries of Western Europe and later by the United States. Those stories of national imperialism and related colonization span more than 500 years and vary greatly according to the storyteller (e.g., Cooper, 2005; Mamdani, 2002; Said,

1978; Smith, 1999). Over the past century, resistance to colonization, its historical impact and contemporary persistence, has gained strength among indigenous people across the world (e.g., Chief Seattle, Mohandas Ghandi, Nelson Mandela). Recently, scholars like Linda Tuhiwai Smith (1999) have brought this resistance to bear in the articulation of approaches to research that may serve to repair and preserve cultures and epistemologies damaged by colonization while at the same time extending those epistemologies into the active conceptualization, enactment and interpretation of research agendas and data. Consideration of decolonization by school psychology calls us to look carefully at the ways the practices of our discipline dignify the ways of knowing brought by each learner and family or serve to further the negation, erasure, disrespect and harm of colonization by failing at seeing cultural difference.

Smith (1999) locates herself in the Maori tradition, culture and history, a "vantage point of the colonized, a position from which I write and choose to privilege" (p. 1). From this worldview, her articulation of methodologies for research that support the decolonization of indigenous peoples represents the step beyond postmodernism. The research sensibility she describes acknowledges the vital necessity for postmodern deconstruction. At the same time, decolonizing methodologies require explicit and concrete links between research and the real lives and pressing concerns of the people and communities who self-identify as indigenous. This kind of responsiveness requires practical effort often based in recognition of measurable and reducible (positivist) concerns. "In a decolonizing framework, deconstruction is part of a much larger intent. Taking apart the story, revealing underlying texts, and giving voice to things that are often known intuitively does not help people to improve their current conditions. It provides words, perhaps, and insight that explain current experiences—but it does not prevent someone from dying" (p. 3).

In school psychology, we are interested in supporting learning—in nurturing the development of each learner's unique capacities. Two questions arise for our profession when the questions of decolonization are considered: (1) To what extent do barriers to learning reside in the collective history of groups harmed by colonialism? (2) What are the actions that can be taken in policy and practice to remove these barriers? Both are research questions and, according to

Smith (1999), both will be researched differently by scholars and practitioners who are themselves indigenous. "When indigenous peoples become researchers and not merely the researched, the activity of research is transformed. Questions are framed differently, priorities are ranked differently, problems are defined differently, people participate on different terms" (p. 193).

The perspective and methodologies Smith (1999) advocates underscore the vital necessity of consciously and systematically bringing into our research community the scholarly eyes and cultural sensibilities of indigenous academics. This is an immense challenge to both our profession and to indigenous scholars, practitioners and graduate students. Bridging the gap between indigenous ways of knowing and the requirements and content of our graduate curricula is an enormous undertaking. As Smith and others (e.g., Huffman, 2003; Little & McCarty, 2006; Tafarondi & Walters, 1999) demonstrate, it is costly to indigenous people who must continue to learn and demonstrate the values and practices of the dominant culture at the risk of losing ready contact with their culture of origin and its practices. The energy required for navigating the dominant system as an indigenous person is also substantial. For most indigenous people, this mobilization of attention and energy represents a persistent, weighty and additional requirement in graduate school, practice in the dominant culture, or junior academic posts. These circumstances are rarely considered by university and employment systems or by nonindigenous people who, in any of these roles, experience their own stresses and are not inclined to understand the qualitative difference in the barriers and detours consistently encountered by people outside the dominant group.

One of these barriers is maintained by a reluctance on the part of established (dominant culture) scholars to recognize as valuable the investigations and findings emerging from indigenous perspectives. As Smith (1999) observes, "A dilemma posed by such a thorough critical approach to history, writing and theory [as with indigenous standpoints] is that whilst we may reject or dismiss them, this does not make them go away, nor does the critique necessarily offer [immediately applicable] alternatives. We live simultaneously within such views while needing to pose, contest and struggle for legitimacy of oppositional or alternative histories, theories and ways of writing" (pp. 38–39).

The dilemma is also a vital opportunity for supporting the social-emotional well-being of entire communities. In the press toward better science in assessment and intervention, for example, dominant culture school psychologists may overlook the relationship between the act of research investigation and the health of a culture. When one's culture is taken as the standard, as with white culture, the link between research and cultural preservation becomes invisible because it is not urgent. Yet the knowledge base of a profession is a storehouse of cultural values and practices and pursuing research questions of social, emotional and cognitive well-being is always evidence of interest in and commitment to knowing and enhancing one's community and culture. For indigenous people the stakes are higher and more overt than for the dominant culture. One profound and immediate illustration of this urgency is the connection between the articulation and preservation of culture and reduction in the incidence of suicide, addiction, drop out and disease in indigenous communities (Little & McCarty, 2006; Smith, 1999). This sort of evidence and its cultural implications are most apparent with the conscious application of decolonizing methodologies.

Alongside research supporting cultural recovery, Smith (1999) identifies the equally vital necessity for dialogue across indigenous and dominant boundaries. She identifies clearly the multiple responsibilities and perspectives required of indigenous researchers themselves who must hold central their curiosity about and devotion to their own culture while developing ways of opening dialogue in the dominant culture of scholarship and professional practice. "This has to be because we constantly collide with dominant views while we are attempting to transform our lives on a larger scale than our own localized circumstances. This means struggling to make sense of our own world while also attempting to transform what counts as important in the world of the powerful" (p. 39). Consistent across Smith's observations regarding the decolonization of research methodology and Ibarra's (2001) work on *multicontextuality* discussed below, is a clear recognition of the importance of drawing from the strongest and best expressions and practices of all cultural traditions. As Smith writes, "Decolonization, however, does not mean and has not meant a total rejection of all theory or research or Western knowledge. Rather, it is about centering our concerns and world views and then coming to know and understand theory and research from our own perspectives and for our own purposes" (p. 39).

Multicontextuality

The simultaneous development of research methodologies within and across the wisdom of diverse human experience is obstructed by strict adherence to any one way of knowing. Jackson (2005) calls us to see the threat of monoculturalism in the knowledge base and practices of school psychology. This threat results directly from the maintenance of a dominant culture practiced by insiders as the unseen and default standard for all. Helms (1992) addresses this problem when she observes the tendency among white people not to see ourselves as having a race. This occurs because of the invisibility of politically and socially dominant cultural values to those who benefit from and set those values as the standard for what defines, for example, *common sense* (Hall, 1977). Because ours is the culture represented in the political and social organization of contemporary life (from the U.S. Congress to suburban malls to K–12 classrooms), those of us who were raised white often do not, without significant shifts in perspective, see many of the overt and covert expressions of our own way of being. By contrast, people historically and currently marginal to the dominant culture see its characteristics, rules and demands, and the features of their own cultures that do not fit with dominant values, practices and ways of being and knowing. For some of these people, the mismatch may be managed or overcome in ways that make fitting with the dominant system possible. Many marginalized groups have language for this kind of assimilation, perhaps most descriptively called *passing*. For some groups passing is not possible, and for most people of historically marginalized backgrounds, passing is not desirable.

Investigations of the impact of this pervasive social dynamic on the lives of learners have revealed its substantial cost (Bowen & Bok, 1998; Little & McCarty, 2006; Ramirez & Casteneda, 1974, Tafarondi & Walters, 1999). Reflective of the resilience, creativity and dauntless vigor of historically marginalized groups and cultures, newer research and practice offers indications of practical ways dominant educational practices in general and school psychology practices in particular may be revised and extended to benefit all learners (e.g., Boothe, Borrego, Hill & Anhalt,

2005; Bowen & Bok, 1998; Ibarra, 2001; Little & McCarthy, 2006; Ochoa, 2005; Sandoval, 2006).

Robert Ibarra's (2001) development of the idea of *multicontextuality* stands as a promising example of these visionary, optimistic and immediately practical ways of thinking. Ibarra speaks to the ways in which capacity for functioning in multiple cultural contexts serves individuals even as recognition and substantive reflection of multiple world views enhances educational systems. His empirical focus on the experiences of Latino academics and graduate students has direct bearing on the questions raised by Rogers (2005) in her reflection on multicultural considerations for training in school psychology.

Ibarra (2001) first reviews the literature on the experiences of Latinos in academe. He emphasizes two exemplary studies, one measuring the challenges and successes of "the first affirmative action generation... between 1967 and 1979" (Cuadraz, 1993, p. 21) and one focused on resiliency factors in high-achieving Chicano(a)s with advanced degrees and backgrounds in low-income Mexican American families (Gandara, 1995). In both of these studies success in graduate school was linked with consistent exposure to and growing confidence within Latino and dominant culture experiences. To extend the literature on Latinos in higher education, Ibarra (2001) employs qualitative research methods (semistructured personal interviews, $n = 77$, *Latino* = 41, *Latina* = 36) to imbed questions of the individual experiences of Latino graduate students and faculty in the larger context of academic and institutional culture. The extensive data from this study reveal cultural mismatches that interfere with full contribution and participation, and impede the success of Latino scholars in contemporary academic environments.

Both the theoretical foundation and the data of Ibarra's inquiry underscore the persistence of the world views of both Latino and white graduate students and faculty in dominant culture academic settings. Ibarra draws on Edward T. Hall's research to differentiate the overt and covert meaning conveyed by behaviors or held in the cultural reasoning that underlies them. The subtler rules of any cultural group are described by Hall (1977) as "the most important paradigms or rules governing behavior, the ones that control our lives, function below the level of conscious awareness and [are] not generally available for analysis" (p. 43). While overt meaning resides in behaviors that are more visible and include habits of dress and speech, common and celebrated pastimes, and ways of organizing time and space, covert meaning exists in what would be called *common sense* to any given cultural group—conventions of communication, proximity, sense of privacy, and signs of morality or immorality.

Perhaps best known of Hall's findings are his descriptions of the contrast between low- and high-context language. The English and German languages provide the strongest examples of low-context language—language that relies heavily on the value and function of words with less attention to nuances of nonverbal and other contextual information (e.g., legal briefs, research journals, nutritional labeling on foods). Most other languages, and indigenous languages in particular, are more high context—relying as significantly on what is not said with particular attention to the communications of behavior (i.e., action or inaction). Academic and scholarly settings are typified by low-context language.

In early work on the phenomena involved in building capacity for thinking in both language contexts, Ramirez and Casteneda (1974) identified the skill some students from high-context language groups developed for cognitive switching or flex. From this came the theoretical construct of *bicognition*, or the capacity to function well within two distinct cognitive styles. The reflections and stories offered by Ibarra's (2001) interviewees point to this capacity as a highly functional individual skill. Ibarra clarifies the somewhat elaborated nature of his interviewees' reports by identifying their skill as *multicontextual* and evident in the behaviors of "bicognitive individuals [who are] able to demonstrate flex by interacting selectively across cultural contexts and cognitive styles. They are equipped with a versatility that enables them to adjust or adapt at any time to a variety of activities, tasks, or social environments" (p. 65). In keeping with Smith's (1999) suggestions regarding decolonized thinking, multicontextuality *is not* acculturation. Rather, by virtue of the capacity for interacting successfully in multiple cultural contexts, multicontextuality simultaneously preserves one's culture and ethnicity of origin while facilitating productive interaction with another (e.g., dominant) culture or ethnic group. The flexibility afforded for communication, understanding, diplomacy or scholarly dialogue at any level is enhanced with multicontextuality. The presence of this skill in an individual or group automatically places requirements for echoed flexibility in those who tend to function from a more unitary context. "It is not like a one-way street that directs the flow of cultural adjustment and demands that less-dominant culture or ethnic group adopt the ways of a dominant culture. In fact, a multicontextual individual is likely to have a pluralistic ethnic identity and be sensitive to [all] gender perspectives" (Ibarra, p. 65). In this way and regardless of any person's culture of origin, multicontextuality affords deep cultural and ethnic knowledge and pride alongside a self-confident capacity for interacting respectfully across cultural variations. The motive is communication and maintenance of relationships rather than any assertion of control or manipulation.

Ibarra's (2001) study has as its explicit objective the illustration of human social systems and organizations as reflective of the cultural patterns of the individuals who established and sustained them. He invites our considered attention to ways in which organizations, specifically schools (kindergarten through the professoriate) might develop their own multicontextual capacity. The implications of Ibarra's work for extending investigations in school psychology are a matter of our own creativity. Ibarra's investigation and discussion provide a compelling example of our opportunity to engage in long-term efforts for building practical understandings and practices of multicontextuality into school psychology, its practices and technologies, and into the educational and community systems we serve.

Summary: Listening

When Linda Tuhiwai Smith (1999) worked as a community health researcher, she heard countless expressions of the experiences of Maori people giving profound impetus to her desire to reflect their ways of knowing in the research bearing directly on their health. "'We know we are dying,' someone said, 'but tell me why we are living?' 'Our health will not improve unless we address the fact that we have no sovereignty,' 'We're sick of hearing what's wrong with us, tell us something good for a change,' or 'why do they always think by looking at us they will find the answers to our problems, why don't they look at themselves?'" (p. 198).

Ibarra's (2001) research and theory development invite dominant culture educators, administrators and policy makers to listen differently—to be open to the legitimacy of multiple ways of constructing meaning and recognizing truth. The stories of his interviewees indicated consistently that in higher education, "We are caught at a cultural crossroads with a one-dimensional vision of the future. We have yet to comprehend the multicontextual world that looms out there and exists in the shadows all around us. That concept could unlock enormous untapped potential in human diversity and new critical knowledge" (p. 259). He concludes that it is only a matter of time and attention for academe to realize the innovation and wealth of knowledge available to science with the inclusion of multiple worldviews, in part as a result of the application of what Smith (1999) names *decolonizing methodologies*.

Time is moving and the local, national and global demands of a diverse citizenry require schools and community services to respond. As for the matter of attention, both Ibarra and Smith urge listening to the experiences of people from historically and contemporarily marginalized social groups as the most robust and responsive practice for guiding professional practice. Speaking specifically to the interests and concerns of low-income families in schools, Lott (2003) calls for our listening to the stories of these people *from the standpoint of their lives*. "One major theme that emerged from [low income] parents' stories was how often they had to cope with environmental damage to their children's health, as with lead poisoning, that had serious implications for school progress. Another major theme was how eager the schools seemed to be to suggest diagnostic labels for their children's problems in school" (Lott, 2003, p. 101).

In addition to listening to groups and communities, Smith (1999) and Ibarra (2001) ask that we listen also to colleagues who were raised in historically marginalized social groups. Echoing the experiences noted by Ibarra's interviewees regarding the pressure they feel as faculty to act as if they are no longer of their culture, Smith notes, "In traveling around other places I have met indigenous people who have experienced similar histories as researchers. Their tertiary education was alienating and disconnected from the needs of their own communities. The more educated they became the more it was assumed that they would not want to return to their own communities. Assimilation policies in education were intended to provide one-way roads out for those indigenous people who 'qualified'" (p. 199). Quite in contrast to the assimilation agendas they experienced in higher education, the scholars encountered by both Ibarra and Smith engaged with academe to preserve and enhance their cultures of origin, not to overcome them.

The professional organizations of school psychology have built operational structures that increasingly address the kind of listening that acknowledges and enhances culture. Division 16 (School Psychology) of the American Psychological Association (APA) has long maintained a vice presidency for Social and Ethical Responsibility and Ethnic Minority Affairs within which committees focused on the interests and concerns of ethnic minorities, women, and sexual minorities. The investigations and activities of these committees have influenced APA policy while at the same time affecting the research and practice of school psychology. The National Association of School Psychologists (NASP) has also developed committee and task force structures to support multicultural dialogue and related practice (e.g., the Native American Task Force; Committee on Gay, Lesbian and Bisexual Issues; the Multicultural Committee; the Task Force on Social Justice). The inclusion demonstrated by APA and NASP with the maintenance of these formal structures has the potential for going beyond offering simple invitation to historically marginalized people to participate in the dominant group. That is, these structures may be, and at times have been, employed to designate formal space and time for convening discussion among members of particular social groups. The opportunity for more homogenous conversation and professional support makes more likely the entry and continuance of people from these backgrounds in the profession of school psychology.

Diversity never goes away. For people of historically marginalized groups ethnicity, linguistic background, social class, sexual orientation, age, religious and/or physical difference are active variables in their everyday experience. Less apparently, the dominant culture privileges of white people of all genders, ages and sexual orientations provides daily comforts and access of which we are largely unaware. LaTina Lewis, a recent university graduate, offered a story illustrating this contrast between the experiences of dominant and nondominant groups. "For three years," she said, "I was an officer for the Black Student Union on campus. We were always an active and productive organization, but only in February—only in Black History Month did the staff of the university's student paper come around for a story. The third year this happened, I mentioned the pattern to the reporter. They never really understood that we celebrate black history every day" (LaTina Lewis, personal communication, February 2, 2006).

CONCLUSION

School psychology research, training (learning) and practice are all mediated by social, economic and spiritual values. They are mediated by the capacity and limitations of the language with which they are originated and by which they are conveyed. They are mediated by the individual, regional and global social conditions of school psychologists and of the people and systems where research data are collected and where practices are applied. We are all in the relationship and our profession serves best when it is intentionally and consistently grounded in the twin realities of our interdependence and diversity.

Past advances in empirical and postmodern constructivist philosophies and research methods provide us with great tools. The situation of school psychology at this point in the stream of historical moments gives us the immediate opportunity to draw on the best of all ways of knowing. With this synthesis, we can move beyond exclusive reliance on either mindset and into creative and responsive research and practice drawing on the best of both. Diversity demands this maturity of us. The wisdom and humility of listening to multiple ways of knowing can provide the stability our profession needs for engaging productively the misunderstandings guaranteed with the actual and persistent variation in human experience, circumstance, and allegiance.

Our willingness to listen for the higher expression of all ways of knowing has bearing at every level of school psychology research and practice. This willingness is also urgently needed in the troubling circumstances of our times. Michael Salzman refers to the three major Western religious traditions (Judaism, Islam and Christianity) to emphasize this point. He describes each tradition as having its highest expression. For Judaism that expression is social justice, for Islam it is mercy, for Christianity it is love and kindness. The lowest expressions of each are alarmingly similar with absolute identification of "in" and "out" groups associated aggressively with identifying those who deserve to live and those who deserve to die (or at least to be defeated and subdued). Based on these observations Salzman suggests, "So then all traditions must 'prime' the higher values so that... when the blood flows and mortality is salient, we will become

more loving, just, compassionate and merciful" (personal communication, October 23, 2002).

War, terrorism and economic exploitation belie the urgency of our bringing collective intelligence, wisdom, creativity and unwavering commitment into engagement with the local circumstances of our everyday work as school psychologists. Given our positions in the academy, school and community systems, we have the influence and capacity to lead the way by recognizing and acting on the urgent necessity for listening and learning across cultures. Beyond studying and responding to human differences from exclusively empirical or postmodern worldviews, we will best serve the pressing needs of learners and communities by bringing our clearest and most creative thinking to our work. Across school psychology and the people and communities we serve, clear thinking will best be guided with the recognition and tending of diversity as a state of mind for our profession and for its practice.

REFERENCES

Boothe, J., Borrego, J. Jr., Hill, C., & Anhalt, K. (2005). Treatment acceptability and treatment compliance in ethnic minority populations. In C. L. Frisby & C. R. Reynolds (Eds.), *Comprehensive handbook of multicultural school psychology* (pp. 945–972). Hoboken, NJ: Wiley.

Bowen, W. G., & Bok, D. (1998). *The shape of the river: Long-term consequences of considering race in college and university admissions*. Princeton, NJ: Princeton University Press.

Clare, M. M. (2002). Diversity at a dependent variable: Considerations for research and practice in consultation. *Journal of Educational and Psychological Consultation, 13*, 251–263.

Cooper, F. (2005). *Colonialism in question: Theory, knowledge, history*. Berkeley, CA: University of California Press.

Cuadraz, G. H. (1993). *Meritocracy (un)challenged: The making of a Chicano and Chicana professoriate and professional class*. Unpublished doctoral dissertation, University of California, Berkeley.

Ellis, R. D. (1986). *An ontology of consciousness*. Dordrecht: Kluwer/Martinus Nijhoff.

Esquivel, G. B., Lopez, E. C., & Nahari, S. G., Eds. (2006). *Handbook of Multicultural School Psychology: An Interdisciplinary Perspective*. Mahwah, NJ: Erlbaum.

Flanagan, D. P., & Ortiz, S. O. (2000). *Essentials of cross-battery assessment*. New York: Wiley & Sons.

Frisby, C. L. (2005). The politics of multiculturalism in school psychology: Part 2. In C. L. Frisby & C. R. Reynolds (Eds.), *Comprehensive handbook of multicultural school psychology* (pp. 81–134). Hoboken, NJ: Wiley.

Frisby, C. L. & Reynolds, C. R. (Eds.) (2005). *Comprehensive handbook of multicultural school psychology* (pp. 945–972). Hoboken, NJ: Wiley.

Gandara, P. (1995). *Over the ivy walls: The educational mobility of low-income Chicanos*. Albany: SUNY Press.

Gottlieb, M. & Hamayan, E. (2006). Assessing oral and written language proficiency: A guide for psychologists and teachers. In G. B. Esquivel, E. C. Lopez, & S. G. Nahari (Eds.), *The Handbook of multicultural school psychology: An interdisciplinary perspective*. Mahwah, NJ: Erlbaum.

Gresham, F. M. (2002). Responsiveness to intervention: An alternative approach to the identification of learning disabilities. In R. Bradley, L. Danielson, & D. P. Hallahan (Eds.) *Identification of learning disabilities: Research to practice* (pp. 467–519). Mahwah, NJ: Lawrence Erlbaum.

Hall, E. T. (1977). *Beyond culture* (2nd ed.). New York: Anchor.

Harding, S. (1991). *Whose science? Whose knowledge? Thinking from women's lives*. Ithaca, NY: Cornell University Press.

Harris, K. C., & Goldstein, B. C. (2006). Implementing culturally sensitive interventions in classroom settings. In G. B. Esquivel, E. C. Lopez, & S. G. Nahari (Eds.), *The handbook of multicultural school psychology: An interdisciplinary perspective*. Mahwah, NJ: Erlbaum.

Hein, S., & Austin, W. (2001). Empirical and hermeneutic approaches to phenomenological research in psychology—a comparison. *Psychological Methods, 6*(1), 3–17.

Helms, J. E. (1992). *A race is a nice thing to have: A guide to being a white person or understanding the white persons in your life*. Topeka, KA: Content Communications.

Henning-Stout, M., (1994). Thoughts on being a white consultant. *Journal of Educational and Psychological Consultation, 5,* 269–273.

Henning-Stout, M., & Brown-Cheatham, M. (1998). School psychology in a diverse world: Considerations for practice, research and training. In C. R. Reynolds and T. B. Gutkin (Eds.), *The handbook of school psychology*, 3rd ed. (pp. 1041–1055). New York: Wiley.

Hitchcock, J. H., Nastasi, B. K., Dai, D. Y., Newman, J., Jayasena, A., Bernstein-Moore, R., et al., (2005). Illustrating a mixed-method approach for validating culturally specific constructs. *Journal of School Psychology, 43,* 259–278.

Huffman, T. (2003). A comparison of personal assessments of college experience among reservation and non-reservation American Indian students. *Journal of American Indian Education, 42,* 1–16.

Hyussen, A. (1990). Mapping the postmodern. In L. Nicholson (Ed.), *Feminism/Postmodernism* (pp. 234–280). New York: Routledge.

Ibarra, R. A. (2001). *Beyond affirmative action: Reframing the context of higher education*. Madison, WI: University of Wisconsin Press.

Ingraham, C. L. (2000). Consultation through a multicultural lens: Multicultural and cross-cultural consultation in schools. *School Psychology Review, 29,* 320–343.

Jackson, J. H. (2005). Commentary #2: What is multicultural school psychology? In C. L. Frisby & C. R. Reynolds (Eds.), *Comprehensive handbook of multicultural school psychology* (pp. 14–29). Hoboken, NJ: Wiley.

Jensen, A. (1998). *The g factor: The science of mental ability*. Westport, CT: Praeger.

Jorion, P. J. M. (1999) Intelligence and race: The house of cards. *Psycoloquy, 10,* p. 64.

Kush, J. C. (1999) The g factor: Implications for school psychologists. *Psycoloquy, 10,* p. 67.

Little, M. E. R., & McCarty, T. L. (2006). *Language planning challenges and prospects in Native American communities and schools*. Tempe, AZ: Education Policy Studies Laboratory.

Lopez, E. C. (2000). Conducting instructional consultation through interpreters. *School Psychology Review, 29,* 378–388.

Lott, B. (2003). Recognizing and welcoming the standpoint of low-income parents in the public schools. *Journal of educational and psychological consultation, 14,* 91–104.

Mamdani, M. (2002). *When victims become killers: Colonialism, nativism, and the genocide in Rwanda*. Princeton, NJ: Princeton University Press.

Nahari, S., Martines, D., & Marquez, G. (2006). Consulting with culturally and linguistically diverse parents. In G. B. Esquivel, E. C. Lopez, & S. G. Nahari (Eds.), *The handbook of multicultural school psychology: An interdisciplinary perspective*. Mahwah, NJ: Erlbaum.

Naylor, L. (1998). *American culture: Myth and reality of a culture of diversity*. Westport, CT: Bergin & Garvey.

Oakland, T. (2005). Commentary #1: What is multicultural psychology? In C. L. Frisby & C. R. Reynolds (Eds.), *Comprehensive handbook of multicultural school psychology* (pp. 3–13). Hoboken, NJ: Wiley.

Ochoa, S. H. (2005). The effectiveness of bilingual education programs in the United States: A review of empirical literature. In C. L. Frisby & C. R. Reynolds (Eds.), *Comprehensive handbook of multicultural school psychology* (pp. 329–356). Hoboken, NJ: Wiley.

Ochoa, S. H., Rivera, B. D., & Ford, L. (1997). An investigation of school psychology training pertaining to bilingual psycho-educational assessment of primarily Hispanic students:

Twenty-five years after Diana v. California. *Journal of School Psychology, 35,* 329–349.

Ramirez, M. III & Casteneda, A. (1974). *Cultural democracy, bicognitive development, and education.* New York: Academic Press.

Reschly, D. J., & Ysseldyke, J. E. (2002). Paradigm shift: The past is not the future. In A. Thomas & J. Grimes (Eds.) *Best practices in school psychology IV* (pp. 3–20). Bethesda, MD: National Association of School Psychologists.

Reyes-Carrasquillo, A. (2006). Multicultural educational practices. In G. B. Esquivel, E. C. Lopez, & S. G. Nahari (Eds.), *The handbook of multicultural school psychology: An interdisciplinary perspective.* Mahwah, NJ: Erlbaum.

Rogers, M. (2005). Multicultural training in school psychology. In C. L. Frisby & C. R. Reynolds (Eds.), *Comprehensive handbook of multicultural school psychology* (pp. 993–1022). Hoboken, NJ: Wiley.

Said, E. (1978). *Orientalism.* London: Vintage Books.

Salzman, M. B. (2001). Globalization, culture and anxiety: Perspectives and predictions from Terror Management Theory. *The Journal of Social Distress and the Homeless, 10,* 337–352.

Sandoval, J. H. (2006). Professional standards, guidelines and ethical issues within a multicultural context. In G. B. Esquivel, E. C. Lopez, & S. G. Nahari (Eds.), *The handbook of multicultural school psychology: An interdisciplinary perspective.* Mahwah, NJ: Erlbaum.

Sheridan, S. M. (2000). Considerations of multiculturalism and diversity in behavioral consultation with parents and teachers. *School Psychology Review, 29,* 344–353.

Sloan, T. S. (2001). Ideology criticism in theory and practice. *International Journal of Critical Psychology, 1*(2), 163–168.

Smith, L. T. (1999). *Decolonizing methodologies: Research and indigenous peoples.* New York: Zed Books.

Solomon, S., Greenberg, J., & Pyszcynski, T. (1991). A terror management theory of social behavior: The psychological foundations of self-esteem and cultural worldview. *Advances in Experimental Social Psychology, 24,* 93–159.

Tafarondi, R. W., & Walters, P. (1999). Individualism, collectivism, life events and self-esteem: A test of two trade-offs. *European Journal of Social Psychology, 29,* 797–814.

CHAPTER 40

CULTURAL COMPETENCE IN SCHOOL PSYCHOLOGY:
ESTABLISHED OR ELUSIVE CONSTRUCT?

CRAIG L. FRISBY
University of Missouri

Contemporary school psychologists are saturated with messages extolling the importance of "cultural competence." According to Sue, Bingham, Porche-Burke, and Vasquez (1999), the increasing racial and ethnic diversity in American society calls for "revolutionary changes in [psychology's] science, education and training, and practice," which, when applied to psychology training programs, involves "faculty and student preparation in the development of cultural competence" (p. 1067). The American Psychological Association's (APA) *Guidelines and Principles for Accreditation of Programs in Professional Psychology* (APA, 2005) stipulate that training programs "[implement] a clear and coherent curriculum plan that provides the means whereby all students can acquire and demonstrate substantial understanding of and competence in . . . issues of cultural and individual diversity" (p. 10).

According to one National Association of School Psychologists (NASP) webpage, appropriately designed consultation, intervention, and assessment services that "meet student, staff, and parental needs" is ensured by culturally competent school psychologists (NASP, 2000a). As a corollary, Ortiz and Flanagan (2002) argue that school psychologists' lack of adequate comfort and competence in dealing with culturally different children and families "can often lead to conflict, miscommunication, and misunderstanding, having tremendous impact on the nature and effectiveness of service delivery" (p. 339). Adopting a more dire prediction, D'Andrea, Daniels, and Noonan (2003) argue that the lack

of cultural competence by educators, counselors and psychologists "prevents many children and adolescents from realizing their educational and intellectual potential during their formative years" and "impedes their ability to secure the resources necessary to achieve a heightened sense of mental health and personal well-being" (p. 156). In short, the message to school psychologists is blunt and to the point: "To meet the needs of an increasingly diverse clientele, school psychologists must develop cross-cultural competencies" (Rogers & Lopez, 2002, p. 115).

Given these strong statements, it comes as little surprise that an overwhelming majority of cultural competence articles (across a variety of disciplines) reflect little more than print advertisements for why cultural competence is important (Ehrhardt-Padgett, Hatzichristou, Kitson, & Meyers, 2004), how it is defined (Burchum, 2002), how it should be measured (Ruelas, 2003), what professional organizations are doing to make sure you get it (Sue, Arredondo, & McDavis, 1992), how to address barriers to getting it (Taylor, 2005), how to know if you have it (Mason, 1995), and problems that are likely to occur if you don't have it (Tarver-Behring & Ingraham, 1998).

Readers expecting this chapter to reflect more of the same will surely be disappointed. With rare exceptions (e.g., Braden & Shah, 2005; Bruni, 1988; Dreher & MacNaughton, 2002), there is a virtual absence in the literature of critical analyses that evaluates evidence for the construct validity of the cultural competence concept. The general purpose of this chapter is to critically evaluate the contribution of cultural competence, both as a concept and as a movement in school psychology. The chapter begins with a brief overview of the history of the cultural competence movement in school psychology. Strengths and weaknesses of this movement are then discussed, followed by a closing summary.

Cultural competence (hereafter abbreviated as CC) is the generic term used in this chapter that also refers to such similar terms as "intercultural competence" (Lustig & Koester, 2006), "cross-cultural competence" (Lynch & Hanson, 2004), and "multicultural competence" (Huang & Gibbs, 1992). CC is used as a noun, but sometimes it is used as an adjective (e.g., "culturally competent services"). No attempt will be made to explicitly untangle CC from its cousin terms "cultural sensitivity," "culturally responsive services," "cultural awareness," "culturally congruent practices," and the like (which are sometimes used as synonyms for CC). A brief sampling of CC definitions from various sources, relevant to school psychology training, are given in Table 40.1.

BRIEF HISTORY OF THE CULTURAL COMPETENCE MOVEMENT IN SCHOOL PSYCHOLOGY

Identifying the first appearance of the phrase "cultural competence" (CC) in school psychology literature is difficult, as this phrase (or a derivative) may have appeared in school psychology articles or chapters in which a different topic is the explicit main focus (e.g., Huang & Gibbs, 1992, p. 83). Readers are encouraged to consult Rogers (2005) for a broad overview of the multicultural demographic trends in school psychology, multicultural advocacy and initiatives affecting school psychology, and multicultural training research in school psychology. This section has a narrower focus, tracing the historical evolution of cultural competency content areas that are most familiar to a school psychology audience. For the sake of brevity, only the most salient milestones in the field, sorted by decade, are highlighted.

TABLE 40.1 Sample Cultural Competence Definitions

- "[P]ractitioners' ability to respond respectfully, reciprocally, and responsively to children and families in ways that acknowledge the richness and limitations of families' and practitioners' sociocultural contexts" (Barrera & Corso, 2003, p. 34)

- "The development of skills that enable the professional to be competent, sensitive, and knowledgeable of the critical factors related to issues of cultural diversity to best serve minority students" (Miranda, 2002, p. 356; quoting Gopaul-McNicol, 1997, p. 17)

- "(T)he ability to think, feel, and act in ways that acknowledge, respect, and build upon ethnic, sociocultural, and linguistic diversity" (Lynch & Hanson, 2004, p. 43)

- "Cultural competence is defined as a set of congruent behaviors, attitudes, and policies that come together in a system, agency, or among professionals and enables that system, agency, or those professionals to work effectively in cross-cultural situations" (NASP, 2003b).

- "Cultural competence is the integration and transformation of knowledge about individuals and groups of people into specific standards, policies, practices, and attitudes used in appropriate cultural settings to increase the quality of services; thereby producing better outcomes" (NASP, 2003b).

- "[Cultural competence helps service providers to] (1) feel comfortable and effective in their interactions and relationships with families whose cultures and life experiences differ from their own, (2) interact in ways that enable families from different cultures and life experiences to feel positive about the interactions with service providers, and (3) accomplish the goals that each family and service provider establish" (Lynch & Hanson, 2004, p. 44)

- "[Cultural Competence] refer(s) to the ability to function effectively with members of ethnic minorities and immigrant groups by dint of insights into the local community's idiosyncratic prejudices, fears and assumptions, insofar as these differed from the norms of middle-class white society" (Levitt, 2005)

1960–1969

Discussions of ethnic or racial diversity issues were nonexistent in many of the early school psychology textbooks from this decade (e.g., Eisere, 1963; White & Harris, 1961). In some early school psychology texts, however, fleeting references to "culturally deprived" children can be identified (e.g., Reger, 1965). Here, racial differences were referred to indirectly, but rarely stated explicitly. The earliest discussion in a school psychology text that conforms to the spirit of the modern CC movement occurs in Gray (1963). In a discussion that compares different responses to classroom teaching from middle-class versus lower-class "slum" students, school psychologists are given suggestions for how they can assist teachers to incorporate these differences in how they respond to students (see discussion on p. 219).

1970–1979

At the opening of this decade, the dawning of a growing social awareness on behalf of inner cities was beginning to be evident. Zach (1970) reported experiences learned from a National Institute of Mental Health funded training grant awarded to Yeshiva University for preparing school psychologists to work with disadvantaged (primarily black) children in urban "slum" schools. The article describes the annual sequence of training experiences for school psychology students, as well as the unique benefits and frustrations that occurred as a result of exposure to urban settings.

In *Contemporary School Psychology* (Herron, Green, Guild, Smith, & Kantor, 1970), signs of a more militant advocacy on behalf of "disadvantaged" children is reflected in the following passage:

> School psychologists need an intense awareness that cultural deprivation, race riots, unemployment, the antiseptic environment of the suburbs, and the volatile nature of the cities directly affect the quality of available education, and the mental health of our children. School psychologists must be intimately concerned with and actively involved in these issues. . . .There is little evidence as yet that school psychologists are activists in these critical social issues. . . .The school psychologist can help teachers who work with disadvantaged children simply by challenging many of the accepted stereotypes of the lower-class child. . . . In

order to work effectively with people that are different in some respects, there must be a willingness to accept the difference as a state of being, rather than as an omission of some cherished middle-class trait. Implicit in much of the literature on the deprived child is the suggestion that society turn them into middle-class carbon copies. Before blithely following this path, schools should stop and consider the implications of such an approach. (p. 185)

In addition, this decade inaugurated the era of intense interest in "nondiscriminatory assessment" for cultural minority children, so named in recognition of school psychology's response to highly publicized court cases such as *Diana v. California State Board of Education* (see Oakland & Laosa, 1977), *Larry P. v. Riles* (see *School Psychology Review*, Vol. 9, No. 2 miniseries), and *Lau v. Nichols* (see Garcia, 1990) that were litigated or decided in this decade. Oakland and Gallegos (2005) provide more recent updates of these and other relevant court decisions affecting minority students.

The Psychological and Educational Assessment of Minority Children (Oakland, 1977) is the first major text, oriented to a school psychology audience, to capitalize on the nondiscriminatory assessment theme in school psychology. The edited text negotiates a difficult balance between the recognition that over- and under-representation of black and Hispanic children and youth in special education and gifted classes may be attributed to the inappropriate use of tests, versus the recognition that informal and formal assessment techniques serve a useful function in educational decision making. To successfully navigate this delicate balancing act, the text covers historical issues, legal and professional issues and standards, and diagnostic intervention models related to serving minority children.

In Winter 1979, *School Psychology Digest* (now School Psychology Review) published a series of papers supporting and critiquing the System of Multicultural Pluralistic Assessment, or SOMPA (Mercer & Lewis, 1978). The SOMPA was developed by its authors to address the "nondiscriminatory testing" language of the Education of the Handicapped Act (P.L. 94–142), and consists of a collection of tests that obtain information directly from the examinee (i.e., WISC-R, Bender Gestalt Test, Physical Dexterity Battery, Snellen Test of visual acuity, weight, height measurements) and data collected from parents (i.e., Adaptive Behavior Inventory for Children, Health History Inventories, and Sociocultural Scales). By using regression formulas from Sociocultural Scales data, a minority child's WISC-R score can be "adjusted" by transforming them into "estimated learning potential" scores (derived in comparison to children from a similar sociocultural background).

1980–1989

A major shift in the testing and assessment literature occurred in 1980, with the groundbreaking publication of *Bias in Mental Testing* (Jensen, 1980). Many innovative studies on test bias can be identified prior to the 1970s (see review by Reynolds & Kaiser, 2003). As a whole, however, early research on test bias was often unsystematic, frequently suffered from faulty assumptions and imprecise definitions, and lacked conceptual coherence (Jensen, 1984). Beginning in the 1970s, a large body of research studies using objective methods and more sophisticated methodology began to appear (Berk, 1982). *Bias in Mental Testing* exhaustively reviewed bias research up to its 1980 publication date, and concluded that well-constructed tests of intelligence and aptitude were not biased (i.e., do not show systematic group effects due to construct-irrelevant variance) toward American-born, English-speaking groups.

The impact of *Bias in Mental Testing* (Jensen, 1980) created noticeable tensions in school psychology oriented publications that insisted on clinging to the "IQ tests are discriminatory" theme. On the one hand, publications were obligated to acknowledge Jensen's findings, yet on the other hand they could not abandon the philosophical conviction that alternative testing is diagnostically preferable to traditional IQ testing for minority children. The alternative testing movement of this decade culminated in the edited text *Psychoeducational Assessment of Minority Group Children: A Casebook* (Jones, 1988). This text showcased applications of Learning Potential ("Dynamic") Assessment, the System of Multicultural Pluralistic Assessment (SOMPA), adaptive behavior assessment, behavioral observation, bilingual assessment, Piagetian assessment, and curriculum-based assessment in evaluating minority group children.

In the first *Handbook of School Psychology* (Reynolds & Gutkin, 1982), Torrance (1982) contributed a chapter entitled *Identifying and Capitalizing on the Strengths of Culturally Different Children*. He begins with the assertion that "There is also growing agreement that existing school programs are biased against culturally different groups" (p. 481). Building on this assumption, Torrance posits 18 behavioral characteristics of culturally different children (Torrance, 1977) that, in his view, are overlooked by traditional tests and school curricula. In Torrance's view, school psychologists display CC when they reject "traditional" assessment and curriculum practices for use with culturally different and disadvantaged children, use their consultation skills to encourage "creative problem solving" among educators, redefine giftedness to align with the mores of multicultural communities, and use alternative assessment measures such as the SOMPA, Torrance Tests of Creative Thinking (Torrance, 1974), and various learning style measures.

Henderson and Valencia's (1985) chapter on nondiscriminatory school psychological services in *School Psychology in Contemporary Society*, and Argulewicz's (1986) chapter on school psychology service delivery in bicultural (i.e., Hispanic and American Indian) settings in *The Delivery of Psychological Services in Schools*, are notable as the first publications of their kind to introduce more elaborate discussions of culture theory and knowledge as important components of the school psychologist's effectiveness with culturally diverse children. Saigh and Oakland (1989) published *International Perspectives on Psychology in the Schools*, which represents the first textbook of its kind that describes the state of school psychology in 25 countries throughout the world.

This decade also marks the beginning of school psychology publications that articulate taxonomies of specific competencies needed to work with Hispanic and/or bilingual children (Esquivel, 1985; Figueroa, Sandoval, & Merino, 1984; Rosenfield & Esquivel, 1985).

1990–1999

The beginning of this decade witnessed the publication of *Children at Risk: Poverty, Minority Status, and Other Issues in Educational Equity* (Barona & Garcia, 1990). This 20-chapter edited text, published under the auspices of NASP, represented a major scholarly contribution at that time to the CC movement in school psychology. The text introduced the theme of "educational equity," which is conceptualized as education's efforts to ensure that students who are "vulnerable" due to poverty and language/cultural minority status receive special and regular education assessment and intervention services that are appropriate and nondiscriminatory. Particularly noteworthy is the text's clear emphasis on bilingual and language issues (particularly as this relates to Hispanics), which is the main focus of approximately half of the chapters.

Three chapters applicable to cultural competence issues in school psychology (Dornbusch & Ritter, 1992; Frisby, 1992; Huang & Gibbs, 1992) appeared in NASP's edited text *Home School Collaboration: Enhancing Children's Academic and Social Competence* (Christenson & Conoley, 1992). In 1992, *School Psychology Review* published a miniseries (Vol. 21, No. 4) on *Understanding and Meeting the Psychological and Educational Needs of African-American and Spanish-Speaking Students.* The miniseries showcased literature reviews on the meaning of culture in analyzing educational needs and problems of African American students, the role of alternative intelligence testing with culturally diverse children, the psycho-educational adjustment of English-speaking Caribbean and Central American immigrant children, and the role of cooperative learning and culturally prescriptive pedagogy in education for African Americans.

The literature on the testing of bilingual and limited English-speaking (LEP) students continues to mature during this decade, providing the field with key guidelines related to the importance of language proficiency measurement, the use of test translations, and the use of nonverbal tests (Lopez, 1997). During this decade, the SOMPA (Mercer & Lewis, 1978) had largely disappeared from the school psychology literature. The Learning Potential Assessment Device (LPAD; Feuerstein, Rand, & Hoffman, 1979) was featured in the 1997 first edition of *Contemporary Intellectual Assessment: Theories, Tests, & Issues* (Feuerstein, Feuerstein, & Gross, 1997), but its absence from the second edition (Flanagan & Harrison, 2005) most likely signals its slow demise in the school psychology literature as well.

The finding that individually administered tests of academic and cognitive ability measure intended constructs and predict equally well with English-speaking, American-born groups continues to be supported in literature reviews published after Jensen's (1980) *Bias in Mental Testing* (Brown, Reynolds, & Whitaker, 1999; Reynolds & Kaiser, 2003; Reynolds, Lowe, & Saenz, 1999). Despite these consistent findings, there is still a subculture of writers affiliated with school psychology who accept these findings only reluctantly (if

at all). These "purveyors of doubt" (a phrase coined by Gottfredson, 2005a, p. 518) continued to criticize aptitude tests as being suspect for use with English-speaking minority groups on any number of idiosyncratic grounds (e.g., see Armour-Thomas, 1992; Armour-Thomas & GoPaul-McNicol, 1998; Helms, 1992, 1997). One effort to evaluate such claims was reflected in a *School Psychology Quarterly* (Vol. 14, No. 3) miniseries entitled *Straight Talk About Cognitive Assessment and Diversity.* The miniseries reviewed empirical literature on alternative assessment techniques used with culturally diverse children (e.g., performance assessment, curriculum-based assessment), in addition to literature on related issues (e.g., culture and test session behavior).

Although minority issues have received limited coverage in survey studies during the 1980s (e.g., Barona & Flores, 1984; Yoshida, Cancelli, Sowinski, & Bernhardt, 1989; Zins & Halsell, 1986), Rogers, Ponterotto, Conoley, and Wiese (1992) published the first comprehensive survey of multicultural training in school psychology during this decade, based on a national sample of directors of school psychology training programs. Ochoa, Rivera, and Ford (1997) surveyed over 1,500 school psychologists from eight states having large concentrations of Hispanics and Spanish speakers. The survey asked respondents to provide information related to perceptions of the adequacy of their bilingual assessment training, their ability to interpret results from a bilingual assessment, number of courses in bilingual assessment taken in graduate school, and the frequency with which they conducted bilingual assessments in their current jobs.

Barnett et al. (1995) introduced the concept of "ethnic validity," which they defined as "the degree to which problem identification and problem solving are acceptable to the client in respect to the client's belief and value systems, as these are associated with the client's ethnic/cultural group" (p. 221). GoPaul-McNicol (1997) advanced a theory-based framework within which school psychologists can be trained to work with multilingual/multicultural children. This framework included 15 domains (ethics, awareness of cultural values and biases, cross-cultural awareness, understanding interracial issues, language competencies, ability to work with interpreters, assessment, counseling, conflict resolution, special education prevention, knowledge of bilingual education curriculum, consultation, research, empowering families, and pediatric/health psychology). Rogers and Ponterotto (1997) developed the Multicultural

School Psychology Counseling Competencies Scale (MSPCCS), which is an 11-item self-report scale designed to be used by trainers to assess the multicultural counseling competencies of school psychology program graduates.

The American Psychological Association (APA) Division 16 Task Force on Cross-Cultural School Psychology was convened to create recommendations for adapting the APA (1993) *Guidelines for Providers of Psychological Services to Ethnic, Cultural, and Linguistically Diverse Populations* to better meet the needs of school psychologists working in schools (Rogers et al., 1999). The adaptation covers primary categories of expertise and specific issues within six major domains of multicultural service delivery (Legal and Ethical Issues; School Culture, Educational Policy and Institutional Advocacy; Psycho-educational Assessment and Related Issues; Academic, Therapeutic and Consultative Interventions; Working with Interpreters; Research). According to Rogers et al. (1999), the task force recommendations for practice were accepted by the APA Division 16 Executive Council in January 1997.

2000–2007

Comprehensive discussions of legal/ethical issues related to the assessment of language minorities (Oakland & Gallegos, 2005), the nature of second language acquisition (Ochoa, 2003; Rhoades, Ochoa, & Ortiz, 2005), the assessment of language proficiency (Ochoa, 2003), working with interpreters (Ochoa, 2003), and factors related to dual-language instruction and bilingual education (Ochoa, 2003, 2005) are abundant in textbooks oriented to school psychology audiences during this decade. Some publications during this decade continue to promote skepticism about the appropriateness of intelligence test use and interpretation with culturally diverse groups (e.g., GoPaul-McNicol & Armour-Thomas, 2002; Ortiz & Dynda, 2003; Valencia & Suzuki, 2001).

In 2000, *School Psychology Review* published a nine-article miniseries on the topic of *Multicultural and Cross-cultural Consultation in the Schools* (Ingraham & Meyers, 2000). The miniseries articles are representative of conceptual/theoretical analyses of consultation models, reports of empirical research in multicultural settings, and discussions of professional and training issues. In 2005, the *Comprehensive Handbook of Multicultural School Psychology* (Frisby & Reynolds, 2005)

was published. Modeled after the *Handbook of School Psychology* series (Gutkin & Reynolds, 1990; Reynolds & Gutkin, 1982, 1999), the multicultural handbook contains empirical literature reviews on sociopolitical issues in multicultural school psychology; cultural variation within broad ethnic/racial groups; educational and psychological foundations of practice with multicultural populations; testing, assessment, and training issues; and international school psychology. An additional *Handbook of Multicultural School Psychology: An Interdisciplinary Perspective* (Esquivel, Lopez, & Nahari, 2007) was published in 2007. This handbook emphasizes both interdisciplinary literature reviews and discussions of specific competencies closely related to practice with multicultural populations.

In a departure from survey studies that identify what training programs *are doing* in the area of multicultural training, Rogers and Lopez (2002) used empirical methods to identify what programs *should be doing* in multicultural training. They expanded upon earlier work by broadening the scope of investigation to include a wider literature base and a more complete spectrum of school psychological services. Rogers and Lopez had a national sample of "cross-cultural experts" (school psychology faculty, practitioners, and school administrators) rate the importance of literature-based competencies, as well as generate their own competencies gleaned from professional experience. This resulted in 260 distinct CC items whose importance was rated during a second round of surveys. This resulted in a reduced pool of 102 competencies, covered across 14 major domains, that were rated as critical for school psychology practice. A sampling of critical competencies identified in this research is shown in Table 40.2.

Many of the themes of the CC movement in school psychology converge in a package of multimedia training materials entitled *Portraits of the Children: Culturally Competent Assessment*, offered through NASP (NASP, 2003a). The development of the *Portraits of the Children* materials was funded by the U.S. Department of Education Office of Special Education Programs through the ASPIIRE (Associations of Service Providers Implementing IDEA Reforms in Education Partnership) Project at the Council for Exceptional Children. The actual training package includes a videotape and a CD-ROM that contains the

TABLE 40.2 **School Psychology Cultural Competencies Rated as Most Critical by Experts**

Competency Category, Ranking of Category Importance,* and Sample Critical Items**

Assessment (Ranked 1st)
Cross-culturally skilled school psychologists should have knowledge or skills about:

- Nonbiased assessment and the process of adapting available instruments to assess linguistically and culturally diverse (hereafter referred to as LCD) students
- Alternative assessment methods (e.g., dynamic, ecological)
- Using instruments sensitive to cultural and linguistic differences
- Using assessment results to formulate recommendations that facilitate language acquisition

Report Writing (Ranked 2nd)
Cross-culturally skilled school psychologists should have knowledge or skills about:

- The importance of integrating cultural and language background of the family and child, language proficiency, and learning style information into the report
- Incorporating information about family origins, family composition, parental attitudes about education and handicapping conditions, and level of acculturation into report (if relevant)
- Reporting the use of translations during assessment
- Reporting the use of an interpreter during the assessment process and describing the scope of the interpreters involvement in the assessment

Laws and Regulations (Ranked 3rd)
Cross-culturally skilled school psychologists should have skills about:

- Applying laws and regulations to protect LCD children from sources of bias and discrimination
- Interpreting legal and regulatory decisions that are relevant to LCD children and their families

Working With Interpreters (Ranked 4th)
Cross-culturally skilled school psychologists should have knowledge or skills about:

- The dynamics of the translation procedure
- The competencies needed by interpreters (e.g., language skills, knowledge of intercultural communication, translation techniques, professional conduct, school-relevant knowledge)
- Assessing students through interpreters
- Interpreting information obtained through interpreters
- Speaking directly to the parents, not the interpreter

Working With Parents (Ranked 5th)
Cross-culturally skilled school psychologists should have knowledge or skills about:

- Differences in family structures across cultures (e.g., extended families)
- Differences in authority, hierarchies, communication patterns, belief systems, values, and gender roles
- The attitudes of culturally diverse parents towards different forms of interventions and types of interventions
- The attitudes that culturally diverse parents have toward educational institutions and teachers
- Implementing home-school collaboration programs and interventions

Theoretical Paradigms (Ranked 6th)
Cross-culturally skilled school psychologists should have knowledge about:

- The strengths and limitations of the major theoretical paradigms that operate in school psychology and the appropriateness of their applications to LCD individuals/groups

(Continued)

TABLE 40.2 *(Continued)*

Counseling (Ranked 7th)
Cross-culturally skilled school psychologists should have knowledge or skills about:

- Differences that exist between counselor and client that can impact the counseling relationship
- Recognizing that helping styles and methods may be culture-bound
- Assessing acculturation of the client and responding to the client's self-presentation rather than the counselor's inferred identity of the client

Professional Characteristics (Ranked 8th)
Cross-culturally skilled school psychologists should have knowledge or skills about:

- The client's culture, cultural context, values, worldview and social norms
- Viewing clinical information within a contextual perspective (i.e., depression among gay populations)
- Engaging in ongoing efforts to reduce and eliminate biased beliefs and behaviors

Consultation (Ranked 9th)
Cross-culturally skilled school psychologists should have knowledge or skills about:

- Cultural and linguistic factors that can influence the input, process, and outcome of consultation
- Working with LCD parents, children, and school staff
- Using a variety of data collection techniques for problem identification and clarification, and planning and implementing interventions that are culturally and linguistically sensitive
- Recognizing prejudice and prevalent obstacles that may effect consultation (e.g., racism, sexism)

Culture (Ranked 10th)
Cross-culturally skilled school psychologists should have knowledge or skills about:

- The cultural context of the client
- The interaction of culture and assessment
- Assessing the norms of the cultural group that they work with and modifying behavior to become culturally congruent when appropriate
- Working with all the cultural groups served

Academic Interventions (Ranked 11th)
Cross-culturally skilled school psychologists should have knowledge or skills about:

- The most successful instructional strategies used with LCD students
- The factors linked to high dropout rates among diverse students and techniques aimed at retention
- Second language acquisition and its impact on acquisition of academic skills
- Making curriculum and classroom management recommendations that are culturally relevant

Research Methods (Ranked 12th)
Cross-culturally skilled school psychologists should have knowledge or skills about:

- The need to consider sociocultural variables and perspectives that impact data analysis and interpretation
- Translating traditional theoretical paradigms into relevant and sensitive research that benefits LCD populations

Working with Organizations (Ranked 13th)
Cross-culturally skilled school psychologists should have knowledge or skills about:

- Applying institutional intervention skills and working to elimi- nate biases, prejudices, and discriminatory practices

---

(Continued)

TABLE 40.2 *(Continued)*

Language (Ranked 14th)
Cross-culturally skilled school psychologists should have knowledge or skills about:

- Second language acquisition process
- Using culturally sensitive verbal and nonverbal communication styles when communicating with LCD children and their families
- The use of translators

*Determined by calculating, for each of 102 critical competencies, its mean ranking of importance, then averaging means for all critical competencies within categories. Categories are ranked from most (ranked 1st) to least (ranked 14th) important
**Only 45 of 102 critical competencies identified by Rogers and Lopez (2002) are shown
Source: Adapted with permission from Rogers & Lopez, 2002.

entire videotape presentation, a printable user's guide and assorted reference lists and hand-outs. The core of the videotape presentation consists of four case studies involving "culturally diverse" (i.e., nonwhite) students, representing preschool to high school age levels, who experience learning problems requiring intervention from school psychologists and multidisciplinary school-based teams. Throughout each case study, a narrator describes the referral problem and problem-solving steps taken by the multidisciplinary team in working through the case. The narration highlights the ways in which multicultural issues may apply to problem conceptualization and intervention. Brief commentaries from school psychologists, administrators, teachers, parents, assessment experts, and multicultural educators are interspersed throughout each of the four case studies.

STRENGTHS ASSOCIATED WITH THE CULTURAL COMPETENCE MOVEMENT IN SCHOOL PSYCHOLOGY

The CC Movement Helps Focus Attention on Cultural Diversity Issues

The CC movement is one of many initiatives in school psychology that promote and reinforce implicit messages that (1) minorities are welcome in the profession, (2) multicultural issues are to be taken seriously, (3) cultural differences should be accommodated, and (4) the profession desires minority groups to succeed and experience positive outcomes. From a purely public relations perspective, the steady increase in scholarly writing on cultural competence in the school psychology literature since 1970 testifies to the importance of these messages.

Testing and Assessment Problems and Solutions Can Be Empirically Evaluated

Individual testing and assessment is generally considered to be the "bread and butter" of school psychology practice. Therefore, it comes as no surprise that calls for CC occur most frequently in the context of testing and assessment issues. There is a logical role for school psychologists to share their measurement knowledge with educators in schools (Kamphaus, 1995)—particularly as this knowledge relates to the testing of cultural minority groups. Efforts to correct real or imagined abuses in testing and assessment has a growing knowledge base developed through the application of objective empirical methods. Test companies have begun to routinely develop instruments that are normed and empirically validated on non-English-speaking populations (Wechsler, 2004). Test translation techniques can be used to determine the extent to which items from tests developed in one language can be adapted to another language while maintaining the integrity of the construct measured (Hambleton & Li, 2005). Tests can be evaluated for statistical bias using a variety of methods, in order to ensure that the test measures the same construct and predicts equally well across all relevant groups, both before and after a test is published (Reynolds & Carson, 2005). Other test developers will create instruments involving items that do not require behaviors (e.g., verbal responses, paper-and-pencil format, or speeded responses) that would unfairly penalize culturally different groups (McCallum & Bracken, 2005). Data from measures of test session behavior can be analyzed by modern statistical techniques to determine if examiners rate examinees differently as a function of examinees' group membership (Frisby, 1999; Glutting, Oakland, & Konold, 1994). Testing conditions can be experimentally manipulated to determine if the manipulation effects test performance differentially as a function of group membership (Evans-Hampton, Skinner, Henington, Sims, & McDaniel, 2002). In short, school psychology excels in showcasing scholarship that employs rigorous, empirical methods to ensure multicultural sensitivity and fairness at the test development, test usage, and test interpretation stages.

The Cultural Competence Movement Highlights the Need for Bilingual Service Providers

Cross-cultural communication is arguably the most important subskill in the development of CC (Figueroa et al., 1984). In the year 2000, approximately 18% of the United States population between the ages of 5 and 17 spoke a language other than English at home (U.S. Census Bureau, 2003). Of this group, approximately 35% reported speaking English less than "very well." In the state of California alone, nearly 30% of the entire state's English Language Learner (ELL) students reside in just five school districts (Gershberg, Danenberg, & Sanchez, 2004). Although Spanish is spoken by the overwhelming majority of ELL students in these five California districts, Filipino, Southeast and East Asian, Eastern and Western European, African, Middle Eastern, and Pacific Island languages are also spoken.

According to responses returned from a random sampling of 20% of the membership of NASP, about 1 in 10 school psychologists (from a total $N = 1922$) reported being able to fluently speak a language other than English (Curtis, Hunley, Walker, & Baker, 1999). However, the extent to which these psychologists' language skills are proficient enough to use in school psychology practice with non-English speakers remains unknown. According to the NASP 2000 Bilingual Directory (as reported from Lopez & Paez, 2005), only 612 school psychologists reported being able to speak at least 1 foreign language, and 97 school psychologists reported being able to speak at least 2 or more foreign languages.

Due to the high cost of retaining on-site translators for students belonging to low-incidence language groups, districts must rely instead on the interpreter/translation services of nonspecialists living in the local community or working at nearby universities (Gershberg et al., 2004). Although these individuals are helpful to some degree, they are not trained to deliver psychological services. Numerous authors have documented the unique challenges that arise from the use of nonspecialist interpreters (e.g., Paez, 2004; Rhoades, 2000). The CC movement underscores the obvious need for well-trained bilingual school psychologists to fill these urgent gaps.

Cultural Competence Needs Are Most Salient in the Context of International Cross-Cultural Interactions

Unique cultural challenges arise whenever American school psychologists come into sustained contact with clients from foreign countries. This occurs whenever American school psychologists travel to school systems in foreign countries to deliver psychological services (e.g., Mishra & Dejud, 2006), or when clients from foreign countries enroll in American schools (e.g., Pilon, 1992).

School psychologists who have worked overseas often describe fundamental differences, compared to the United States, in the government's role in public education, the procedures used to assign students to schools, the administrative structure of special education, the financial resources available to purchase current assessment and curriculum materials, and cultural conditions that shape educators' expectations concerning the best methods for educating pupils (e.g., see Lam, 2005; Mpofu, Peltzer, Shumba, Serpell, & Mogaji, 2005; Ricord-Griesemer, Warnick, Hawk, & Jarzab, 2006; Saigh & Oakland, 1989). Thus, assumptions about the role of school psychology in education require some degree of reexamination and adjustment in international settings, depending on the degree of similarity to American cultural norms (e.g., see Ricord-Griesemer et al., 2006).

On the other hand, the CC movement correctly anticipates the important role that school psychologists can play in helping schools assist new immigrants' adjustment to the American education system. For example, Gershberg, Danenberg, and Sanchez (2004) interviewed school teachers, administrators, and psychologists in five large urban California school districts with large immigrant student populations. In many cases, the extent to which the influx of new immigrants creates problems for schools is a function of the extent to which schools prepare in advance for these potential stressors. Gershberg et al. found wide differences in the extent to which schools developed formal or informal programs, practices, and policies to effectively address the educational needs of recent immigrant students (facilitated through use of federal Emergency Immigrant Education Program funds). These include, but are not limited to, establishing educational facilities and assessment centers which offer physical exams, vaccinations, academic evaluations and counseling specifically for immigrants; transportation services for children of migrant workers; parent/neighborhood resource centers that can broker access to welfare, child protection, health, and other family services; district computerized data base of translators from school, university, and other advocacy groups; sheltered English immersion classes in regular schools; language support personnel who assist mainstreamed immigrants; and peer tutors who can serve as language/cultural brokers.

In addition to the obvious language barriers, immigrant families are overwhelmed by the effort and skill required to navigate a large bureaucratic school system. Some districts do not provide a general orientation to American public schools for newly arrived immigrant families. Basic school information documents and important school notices are often not translated into a language that immigrant parents can understand. American educators find that long-established expectations for high parental involvement in the schooling process clashes with some immigrants' cultural expectations of minimal involvement with schools—which requires cultural mediation. Recent immigrant families bring older children who have had little or no previous schooling in their native countries, which requires knowledgeable intervention by school psychologists, among others. Olsen (1997) and Lee (2005) provide interesting and colorful (although somewhat politicized) narrative observations of adjustment and identity problems faced by older immigrant adolescents in high schools.

At the turn of the twentieth century, the French Minister of Public Instruction called on a psychologist (Alfred Binet) to assist with massive numbers of school children in need of a reliable evaluation for mental retardation (Wasserman & Tulsky, 2005). The current immigrant situation in America presents a somewhat similar opportunity for school psychologists working in areas highly impacted by immigration. This role is tailor-made for the "School and Systems Organization" requirement in the NASP training standards (National Association of School Psychologists, 2000c), which states in part: "School psychologists work with individuals and groups to facilitate policies and practices that create and maintain safe,

supportive, and effective learning environments for children and others" (p. 16).

PROBLEM AREAS ASSOCIATED WITH THE CULTURAL COMPETENCE MOVEMENT IN SCHOOL PSYCHOLOGY

Despite these strengths of the CC movement, there are significant conceptual, empirical, and philosophical problems that are evident in this movement - particularly as applied to the field of school psychology. Three broad categories of problem areas are described next.

Weak Empirical Support for the Construct Validity of Cultural Competence
Conceptual Problems Related to the CC Construct

When conducting construct validity studies, researchers must show how the new construct correlates positively to some established constructs, correlates negatively with other established constructs, or is unrelated to still other established constructs (DeVellis, 1991). One construct that appears to most closely approximate CC is *social competence*. The origins for the serious study of social competence as an individual difference variable can be traced to E. L. Thorndike's (1920) notion of social intelligence—defined as "the ability to ... act wisely in human relations" (Jensen, 1998, p. 576). Subsequent research since Thorndike has concluded that social competence overlaps somewhat with general intelligence, but it is a distinct and differentiable construct (Schneider, Ackerman, & Kanfer, 1996). In their review of multifaceted dimensions of the social competence construct, Schneider et al. (1996) defined social competence as "socially effective behavior and its cognitive, affective and conative antecedents" (p. 471). Using comprehensive correlational analyses of adjective rating and personality questionnaires and academic performance indicators, their empirical research suggests that social competence is a "compound trait ... [composed of] a linear combination of dimensions not all of which covary" (p. 478). In addition, they state that social competence overlaps substantially with personality constructs, more so than cognitive ability constructs. Seven dimensions of social competence were identified: (a) Extraversion, (b) Warmth, (c) Social

Influence, (d) Social Insight, (e) Social Openness, (f) Social Appropriateness, and (g) Social Maladjustment (Schneider et al., 1996). Of particular interest is Schneider et al.'s (1996) description of implications of high scores on the "Social Openness" factor: "*social openness will become increasingly important in this age of multiculturalism. For example, it may facilitate success in organizational environments where individuals of various ethnicities must work together effectively*" (p. 478).

Given these comments, it is important to distinguish the CC construct from the social competence construct. Three broad models that may clarify this distinction are possible:

Model 1: Social Competence Subsumes Cultural Competence

This model hypothesizes that social competence is the primary variable responsible for success or failure in professional situations involving cross-cultural interactions. Here, CC can be thought of as a narrower construct that represents one of many manifestations of social competence. That is, the successful school psychologist is one who has a natural or developed propensity to pick up social cues accurately and demonstrate care and concern for others; knows how to help persons feel at ease in social interactions; is not prone to make socially embarrassing mistakes; and is genuinely interested in learning how to best adapt their services to clients in a manner that incorporates sensitivity to clients' experiential backgrounds. In this model, the fact that particular clients may belong to a different cultural group is a largely irrelevant factor that does not warrant a fundamentally different approach to dealing with people. Stated succinctly, this model assumes that a person who is socially competent will automatically be culturally competent. Dreher and MacNaughton (2002) favor this model as applied to the nursing profession. They argue that "culturally competent care" is little more than a repackaged version of "individualized patient care" (p. 185).

Model 2: Social Competence is a Necessary but Not Sufficient Condition for Cultural Competence

This model hypothesizes that social and cultural competence may overlap somewhat, but they are distinct constructs. The personal traits that characterize social competence are a necessary foundation for effectively interacting with people, but there is an additional set of specific cultural knowledge and skills that must be mastered in order to function effectively in cross-cultural situations. Without these culturally specific skills, the school psychologist is not as likely to be effective with culturally diverse clients, even if s/he is socially competent. Tarver-Behring and Ingraham (1998) appear to favor this model, and give an example of how this model can apply to a cross cultural consultation scenario.

Model 3: Social Competence and Cultural Competence Are Independent Constructs

This model hypothesizes that individual differences in social competence are uncorrelated with a school psychologist's competence in cross cultural situations, because the two constructs are assumed to be largely independent. Here, the cultural competence construct includes knowledge and skills that will enable the school psychologist to be effective in cross-cultural situations regardless of his/her level of social competence. This model is implied whenever publications portray cultural competence as an original construct without acknowledging prior research in social competence.

CC advocates bear a responsibility to elaborate, compare and contrast these models given the rich empirical history of established research in the social competence construct. From this discussion, research agendas must be designed that test competing hypotheses that derive from these models. Unfortunately, current writing on cultural competence in school psychology rarely, if ever, acknowledeges previous scholarship in related constructs. This impairs the field's ability to evaluate whether CC is indeed an original construct that adds incremental knowledge to previous research (e.g., see Lonner & Hayes, 2004), or if it is merely an old construct given a new name.

Problems Establishing Consensus Definitions of the CC Construct

There are two well-executed studies designed to evaluate empirically the degree of professional consensus surrounding the nature of CC and its components. In one study (Cunningham, Foster, & Henggeler, 2002), two groups of experts (professionals nominated by peer scholars as having expertise in CC, and therapists with extensive experience and training working with African Americans) were asked to judge the extent to which items from three psychotherapy process measures (number of items = 120) were relevant to the construct of CC. When the first group was asked to judge the extent to which each item was relevant to culturally competent practice, the level of agreement between all expert pairs was no better than chance (mean kappa statistic of .07). Only 32 out of 120 items were rated as having relevance to culturally competent practice. When the first expert group was asked to rate these 32 items as to their degree of "representativeness" to CC using a 7-point Likert scale, the intraclass correlation was .27 (indicating low relationship among the items). The second group of experts was asked to classify each of the 120 items into 9 cultural competence skill categories. Kappa statistics calculated for all possible expert pairs revealed a mean value of .13, with the majority of the statistics being nonsignificant (Cunningham, Foster, & Henggeler, 2002).

In a second study, Davis (2004) used concept mapping methodology to identify models of cultural competence in four children's mental health systems of care communities in one state. Family caregivers, family advocates, service providers, administrators, and community stakeholders ($N = 188$) were brought together within each of the four communities and asked to respond (in English or Spanish) to the following sentence stems:

I know services to families are culturally competent when _____.
I know services to families are respectful when _____.
I know services are culturally responsive when _____.

This process resulted in a total of 117 statements (combined across all four systems). Participants within each of the four systems then sorted the responses into conceptually similar groupings, then rated their importance on Likert scales. The researchers then compared the concept maps generated across each of the four community groups. Although there were some similarities in map elements across communities, the researchers found that no one community practice model accounted for all concepts that were generated. By association, measures developed using any one community model would not be completely generalizable to any other system of care community. The author concluded:

(A)ssessing cultural competence is a difficult task when the concept under study remains elusive to the researcher. The lack of clarity around the conceptual meaning of cultural competence raises questions about the constructs underlying the practice models

advanced and the measurement instruments developed based on these models. Furthermore, the dearth of empirical support for culturally related concepts and practice models raises troubling questions about the foundations upon which social work students are being educated about culturally responsive practice. (p. 220)

Disconnect Between the CC Construct and Its Measurement

According to Schultheiss and Brunstein (2005), *competence* is a multifaceted concept that refers to "skills and abilities a person has developed," the "degree to which a person is effective in her or his transactions with the environment," and "how successfully a person performs" (p. 42). Concepts such as *skill, ability,* and *performance* require certain conditions for objective measurement (adapted from Jensen, 1992). First, the construct to be measured must involve observable units of behavior (i.e., something spoken, written, or acted out). Second, the behavior must be intentional, as opposed to an involuntary reflex. Third, there must be a high degree of agreement among different observers that the behavior occurred. Fourth, the units of behavior must be classifiable (e.g., judged as poor, fair, or excellent) or quantifiable in terms of a standard (e.g., running a race of a given length within a given time limit). Fifth, there must be a high degree of agreement among different observers in judging the quality of the behavior. Sixth, the behaviors must be demonstrated across fairly fixed conditions for all respondents, so that individual differences in performance can be attributed to differences in skill level, rather than to differences in the conditions. Seventh, the units of behavior must demonstrate some degree of consistency and temporal stability (as opposed to displaying random patterns) in order to infer mastery. Eighth, this consistency must be displayed across similar classes of observable behaviors, in order to infer a generalized ability.

At the time of this writing, *there exist no published measures that enable examiners to observe and score an examinee's "competence" in cross-cultural situations (in school psychology or a related field) according to all eight criteria previously described.* The *Racial Ethical Sensitivity Test* (REST; Brabeck et al., 2000, reported in Ponterotto, Mendelsohn, & Belizaire, 2003), however, is one example of a CC scale that comes closest to satisfying a few of the eight criteria for objective measurement previously discussed. Here, respondents view videotaped vignettes depicting "acts of racial/ethnic and gender intolerance" (Ponterotto et al., 2003, p. 197). For each vignette, examiners use a structured interview protocol to score examinee's verbally reported awareness of the ethical problems embedded in the vignettes. According to Ponterotto et al. (2003), however, "the REST is in need of additional testing, particularly in regard to test-retest stability, interrater agreement, and criterion-related validity" (p. 198).

Scholars in counseling psychology have developed self-report scales that assess respondent's *opinions or perceptions* about their own cultural competence (e.g., D'Andrea et al., 2003; Ponterotto et al., 2003; Ponterotto & Potere, 2003), however self-report instruments have been criticized for their failure to address social desirability effects (Constantine & Ladany, 2000). Social desirability is the tendency for respondents on self-report measures to give responses that are more in line with current social mores, rather than reporting their true opinions. Constantine and Ladany (2000) controlled for social desirability effects before correlating several self-report multicultural counseling competence measures and a behavioral measure of multicultural case conceptualization ability. They found that none of the self-report CC measures were significantly related to multicultural case conceptualization ability. Thus, these and other researchers (Pope-Davis & Coleman, 1997; Sodowsky, Kuo-Jackson, Richardson, & Corey, 1998) speculate that high scores on self-report cultural competence measures may actually reflect the desire to be perceived as competent, or high self-efficacy (strong confidence in one's competence), rather than *actual competence*. Unfortunately, using a self-report paradigm to measure CC is analogous to a school psychologist who assumes that a child's intellectual functioning has been assessed merely from asking children their *perceptions of, or how they feel about*, their ability to solve intelligence test tasks.

For school psychology, comprehensive checklists have been developed that rate the extent to which school psychology training programs adhere to CC standards (e.g., Kearns, Ford, & Brown, 2002). Others have designed scales for supervisors to provide their perceptions of the quality of trainees' accumulation of multicultural counseling competencies after they have graduated from training (e.g., Multicultural School Psychology Counseling Competency Scale, or MSPCCS; Rogers & Ponterotto, 1997).

Unfortunately, the MSPCCS requires trainers to rate the extent to which graduates demonstrate "respect," "sensitivity," "awareness," and "understanding," which reflect constructs that are difficult to operationalize, let alone objectively measure according to the criteria discussed previously.

Evaluating the Ethnic Matching Doctrine

According to *School Psychology: A Blueprint for Training and Practice II* (Ysseldyke et al., 1997): "As the composition of the student population changes, so too should the cultural and ethnic makeup of educators who instruct, provide models for, and counsel these youngsters" (p. 4). There is a presumption that "minority status automatically instills school psychologists with special sensitivities and skills that will make them more effective in their work with minority clients compared to European American school psychologists" (Braden & Shah, 2005, p. 1027). Since practitioner/client ethnic parity in school psychology is not likely to be realized in the near future (Rogers, 2005), this is viewed by some as a strong justification for the urgency of CC training for Caucasian, English-speaking school psychologists. Thus, an empirical evaluation of the ethnic matching hypothesis provides an indirect evaluation of one of the central justifications for CC advocacy.

Maramba and Hall (2002) identified seven ethnic-matching psychotherapy studies (six with adults; one with children and adolescents) with nonoverlapping samples between 1977 and 1999. All studies involved three dependent variables: (1) dropping out, defined as failure of the client to return for a second session after the initial session; (2) utilization, defined as the number of sessions attended, and (3) Global Assessment Score, which measures the degree of overall functioning on a continuum from psychiatric disturbance to health. The authors found very small effect sizes in favor of ethnic matching (ES = .01–.04), but concluded that these effect sizes were too small to provide support for ethnic matching as a promising variable for improving client outcomes.

Braden and Shah (2005) reviewed counseling psychology literature addressing the multiplicity of factors associated with clients' preferences for service providers of the same ethnicity. At the end of their review, they conclude that "the assumption that individuals of minority status will necessarily provide better services to clients of similar status is not supported by the current research" (p. 1028).

Meta-Analysis of the Effects of Multicultural Education

Smith, Constantine, Dunn, Dinehart, and Montoya (2006) conducted two meta-analyses of multicultural education research studies published between 1973 and 2002 in the counseling (including school counseling) and counseling psychology disciplines. The first meta-analysis examined 45 survey studies of persons (average age = 37) who reported taking or not taking multicultural education courses in the past, and how this status affects performance on self-report multicultural competence, racial identity, racial prejudice, and client/counselor relationship measures. The second meta-analysis examined 37 pre- and posttest studies that examined the effects of multicultural education (or general coursework) on counselors' self-report measures of multicultural competence or observer ratings (average age of respondents = 30). The estimated average effect sizes for both meta-analyses, adjusted for attenuation due to measurement error, was .53 and .98 standard deviations, respectively. Smith et al. (2006) concluded that these results show support for "positive outcomes" (p. 139) related to multicultural education for counselors. However, a closer evaluation of these results reveals a more sobering truth. The authors translate the findings for the first meta-analysis as equivalent to a mere 1-point increase (on a Likert scale) on 8 out of 60 questions on the self-report Multicultural Awareness/Knowledge/Skills Survey (D'Andrea, Daniels, & Heck, 1991). In addition, the authors state:

> [A] conspicuous deficiency in the multicultural education literature is that none of the studies included in this meta-analysis evaluated client retention or clinical outcome data. Does multicultural education translate into tangible benefits (e.g., increased well-being) for mental health consumers, particularly those from historically oppressed backgrounds? (p. 141)

The obvious answer to this rhetorical question, at the time of this writing, is that such information remains unknown. The 82 studies reviewed by Smith et al. (2006) were selected from a parent pool of over 2,000 citations on multicultural issues in counseling, due to their amenability to a quantitative meta-analysis (i.e., by including appropriate statistical information). *This means that 96% of the citations reviewed by Smith et al. were not in a format amenable to identifying its effects in any systematic way.*

A Construct in Search of Empirical Integrity

Atkinson and Israel (2003) argue that multicultural counseling competencies (MCC) have strong intuitive appeal, but lack a strong empirical base. They state that the policy initiatives on behalf of the MCC movement have jumped ahead of its research base, and "the reality is that very little research actually supports either the policy changes that have been implemented by the APA and other professional organizations or the MCC training models that have been an important feature of the movement" (pp. 593–594). They state "there is currently no research evidence to support the validity of the 31 MCC described in Sue et al. (1992)." These observations suggest that the MCC movement is analogous to a huge and elaborately built castle, but with its foundation firmly planted in mid-air.

Given these conceptual and empirical problems, the exact nature and structure of the CC construct (as applied to school psychology) remains ambiguous. Is CC a nominal dichotomous variable, which clearly categorizes practitioners into those that are culturally competent versus those who are not? Or, are there degrees of cultural competence? If there are degrees of CC, how does the field characterize persons who have "more" CC from those who have less? Is cultural competence a generalized continuous variable analogous to having a "cultural competence IQ"? Or, is cultural competence simply the accumulation of discrete uncorrelated skills? Can a person be culturally competent only in certain settings with certain groups, but also be culturally incompetent in other settings with different groups? Finally, who or what decides the criteria for evaluating cultural competence, and is the basis of this authority earned, conferred, or capricious?

Justifications for Cultural Competence Are Often Built on Ill-Defined Concepts, Vague Generalizations and Unexamined Assumptions

The CC movement in school psychology portrays increasing American diversity (premise) and the need for CC (conclusion) as a short move from Step A to Step B. This merely juxtaposes a premise and a conclusion, without any analysis of the mediating steps that should logically tie the conclusion to the premises. In reality, however, this reflects a *giant leap* from Step A to Step Z, with mediating assumptions B through Y left largely unexamined. What follows is a brief discussion of some mediating assumptions (and their inherent problems) that are often left unexamined in the CC movement.

Mediating Assumption: Cultural Differences Between Groups Are Inherently Problematic for Schools

"The United States is a nation composed largely of immigrants and their ancestors" (Oakland, 2005, p. 3) is an oft-repeated phrase that nevertheless carries an important truth - namely, that racial and ethnic diversity in American schools is nothing new or unusual in American history (Sowell, 1981). The CC movement in school psychology does not specify exactly what kinds of cultural differences are inherently problematic; how such differences are problematic; for which kinds of schools; for which grade levels; which "cultural" groups; or under what conditions. The meshing of ethnic, racial, or cultural groups together in schools occurs in a variety of different contexts: the occasional transfer of a foreign student to a culturally homogeneous school; natural diversity determined by school-attendance zoning patterns; court-ordered school desegregation (e.g., Bankston & Caldas, 2002); the slow changing of neighborhood demographics, or the more aggressive influx of illegal immigration in select vulnerable communities (e.g., Camarota, 2001). Although all of these situations can be lumped together as instances of "diversity in schools," there are large qualitative differences in the kinds of social and pedagogical tensions that can put a strain (if at all) on school systems.

Some schools have been "culturally diverse" for decades and do not experience any significantly higher levels of racial/ethnic tensions arising from cultural differences. Greene (2005) demonstrates how the level of racial conflict and positive integration in schools varies as a function of school type (public versus private; with the advantage going to private schools). Miller (1998) describes a case study where a school district changed policies from offering elaborate bilingual Spanish language classes to English immersion classes for its Spanish-speaking students. The change

initially split the community along racial and ethnic lines. As early as one year after the policy change, however, the district reported significant increases in parent satisfaction levels, children's proficiency in English, and levels of academic achievement. In contrast, school districts that are overwhelmed by immigration report struggling with vexing problems that include, but are not limited to, high levels of school overcrowding, communication/language issues, health issues, parents' difficulties with navigating the school system and understanding school policies, children needing to work outside of school or not living with parents, gang activity, low levels of parental involvement, family evasions due to fear of illegal status exposure, and transportation problems (Gershberg et al., 2004).

To summarize, the factors that influence whether or not cultural differences pose problems for educators are extremely complex, yet an appreciation of this complexity is virtually absent in simplistic justifications for CC training.

Mediating Assumption: The Nation's Increasing Diversity Impacts All American Schools, Generally, and All School Psychologists, Specifically, in a Uniform Manner

A typical prediction states that by the year 2050, half of the U.S. population will be nonwhite (Miranda, 2002). According to one writer, by the year 2091 the proportion of ethnic groups in America will mirror the world (Ibrahim, 1991). It is beyond the scope of this chapter to evaluate the accuracy and validity of these statistical claims (for a brief discussion, see Frisby, 2005b). However, a reasonable question can be raised as to whether this incoming diversity affects all areas of the country, schools, and school psychologists in the same fashion.

William Frey (2001), a leading research demographer, chronicled migration and settling patterns of major racial/ethnic groups within America's counties from 1990 to 2000. According to his data, ethnic settling patterns are *overwhelmingly regional in character and pattern*. When county data are organized according to a group's overrepresentation compared to their national proportions, black representation dominates in Southern counties and select Northeast and Midwest urban centers; Hispanic representation dominates in Western states stretching from California to Texas; Asian representation, though small, dominates in isolated pockets of California and the Pacific Northwest; and Native American representation dominates in selected pockets in Oklahoma, the Southeast, Northern Midwest, and the West. According to Frey, there is a broad swath of counties stretching from the upper West and Rocky Mountains to the Midwest and Northeast that remain mostly white. In these counties, none of the nonwhite minority groups comes close to approximating their national percentage of the population. "Rainbow" cities, defined as metropolitan areas in which white percentages are less than the national figure (69.1%) and at least two of its minority groups exceed national figures (12.5% for Hispanics, 12.6% for blacks, 5% for Asians and Native Americans), appear to be concentrated in only ten key states: Arizona, California, Florida, Illinois, Nevada, New Mexico, New Jersey, New York, Oklahoma, and District of Columbia.

Some school psychology training programs that are known for their multicultural emphasis tend to be located in states near metropolitan areas where nonwhite diversity is strong (e.g., Palmer, Hughes, & Juarez, 1991). Other training programs are located in states and metropolitan communities that have minimal levels of multicultural diversity, or are characterized by black/white diversity but minimal non-English language diversity. This raises a question of why a school psychology training program, situated in regions with minimal multicultural diversity, should require extensive training in second language competencies. Even if a potential school psychologist selects a training program in more linguistically diverse regions, this is no guarantee that second language competencies will be emphasized in the training program (see Ochoa et al., 1997). Furthermore, there is no guarantee that the mere presence of culturally diverse language minority groups in a school system compels development of CC in English-speaking school psychologists, when the tendency is to funnel the majority of second language cases to school psychologists who have been hired specifically for their bilingual skills (Bainter & Tollefson, 2003).

Mediating Assumption: Disproportionalities in Social and Educational Problems Among "Culturally Diverse" Groups Must Have "Cultural" Explanations and "Cultural" Remedies

"Cultural" explanations for why some racial/ethnic groups perform better or worse than other groups

on school achievement variables is a popular theme in the education literature. According to the "cultural discontinuity" or "cultural incompatibility" hypothesis, ethnic/racial groups succeed or fail in proportion to the extent to which the minority group's culture is congruent with the host culture (Delgado-Gaitan, 1991; Trueba, 1988), culture of the school (Allen & Boykin, 1992; Cortese, 1992), or their voluntary versus involuntary immigrant status (Ogbu, 1987). These explanations can adequately explain disproportionate failure in some, but not all situations. There are countless examples, both in the United States and abroad, where immigrant or other minority groups with cultural and linguistic traits that are aberrant from the mainstream nevertheless flourish and exceed the host culture in achievement levels (Bankston, Caldas, & Zhou, 1997; Kao & Thompson, 2003; Sowell, 1994, 1996, 1998). A normal distribution of academic achievement can be found within all groups, and subgroup differences in academic achievement within broad racial groups are salient. For example, black students attending Catholic schools tend to academically outperform black students attending public schools (e.g., Johnson, 1999). Although roughly 57% of Latino youth complete high school, dropout rates and levels of high school/college degree attainment tend to be highest for Puerto Ricans and Cubans and lowest for Mexican Americans (Lopez, Lopez, Suarez-Morales, & Castro, 2005). "Confucian values" of hard work, respect for elders, self-restraint, and educational achievement are often cited as responsible for higher success levels (relative to other groups) of Asian immigrants in the United States (e.g., Winnick, 1990). Nevertheless, there exist wide variations within Asian immigrant groups in school dropout rates and other indicators of academic achievement (Thao, 2005; Yoon & Cheng, 2005).

Some of the so-called "cultural difference" problems identified by educators in schools are little more than "IQ difference" problems. IQ variation is certainly not the only variable that is responsible for achievement outcomes, as many other important variables contribute in major ways to worldly success (see discussion in Jensen, 1998, pp. 572–578). However, a voluminous body of evidence exists showing how IQ variation is superior to almost all other alternative explanations for explaining a significant portion of the variance in individual and group differences in academic achievement both within and outside of school; rates of under- and over-identification in special education and gifted classes; occupational and job performance outcomes; and health outcomes (Gottfredson, 2000, 2004, 2005b; Herrnstein & Murray, 1994; Kuncel, Hezlett, & Ones, 2004; Rushton & Jensen, 2005).

Culture can be useful to the extent that it *describes* behavior and its variations within certain groups (e.g., see Fong, 2004; Frisby & Reynolds, 2005; Lynch & Hanson, 2004). However, culture falters as a reliable explanation for predicting individual differences in variables of interest to school psychologists. Dreher and MacNaughton (2002) articulate this problem as follows:

> [A]lthough humans are indeed "culture carriers, most are born, live, and die having assumed only some features of their reference culture. Some members of a culture may embrace its traditional norms, others may reject them, and still others may deploy cultural values situationally. (p. 182)

According to Dreher and MacNaughton (2002), the assumption that individuals who belong to the same ethnic/racial group are influenced in the same way by their reference culture is to commit the "ecologic fallacy." The ecologic fallacy is committed when inappropriate generalizations are made about individuals based on data about groups (Bernard, 2002). The ecologic fallacy can be seen in scholars' attempts to explain, and suggest remedies for, disproportionate representation of certain minority groups in classes for the emotionally and behaviorally disordered (e.g., see Osher et al., 2004). Here, disproportionate representation is partially blamed on "teacher bias and ignorance," "limited understanding of cultural differences," and "lack of respect for and responsiveness to students' experiential backgrounds" (Osher et al., 2004). Here, culture is viewed as a factor that partially explains overidentification rates. However, such theories cannot explain why the *majority* of children within these "cultural" groups are *not referred to, or subsequently placed in, classes for the emotionally and behaviorally disordered* (since nonreferred students should possess the same cultural traits as referred and identified students). The ecologic fallacy will continue to be committed as long as scholars continue the habit of attributing disproportionalities to exclusively cultural explanations.

Mediating Assumption: *Whatever School Psychologists are Doing Currently in Response to Cultural Diversity, It Is Inadequate for Meeting the Needs of Culturally Diverse Groups Absent Specialized Training in CC*

According to Rogers et al. (1999), the neglect of culturally competent practice recommendations for culturally diverse groups: *"can lead to inappropriate referrals for services, misassessments of needs and issues, ineffective interventions and therapeutic approaches, and erroneous research results"* (p. 243). Rogers and Lopez (2002) cite two examples that illustrate how the lack of CC can lead to impaired outcomes. One example involved a simulated cross-cultural consultation (Tarver-Behring & Ingraham, 1998), and the other example involved a blatant error involving the administration of an English test to Spanish-speaking students (Gersten & Woodward, 1994). However, it remains unknown how widespread such examples are to date. Studies that may be relevant to this issue are rare but appear to be limited to the psychology of refer/test/placement decisions. For example, Huebner (1989) found that a sample of NASP members were *not* biased in their referral decisions by a child's race or socioeconomic status. Literature reviews do not support the hypothesis that the race of the test examiner differentially influences cognitive test scores of black examinees (Jensen, 1984; Graziano, Varca, & Levy, 1982). Examiners' mean ratings of the test session behavior for test takers from different English-speaking ethnic groups are either statistically nonsignificant, or significant differences fall well within normal behavior ranges (Frisby, 1999; Glutting et al., 1994). A simulation study that investigated the effects of a student's race and assessment data on psycho-educational expectations and diagnostic/placement decisions found that psychologists were *not* influenced by a student's racial status (Huebner & Cummings, 1986).

It remains unclear as to where, how often, and under what conditions abuses are occurring for immigrant (particularly non-English-speaking) children. If multidisciplinary teams ultimately recommend special education placement for linguistically diverse children, then it remains unknown the extent to which the individual school psychologist can be held as directly responsible for the kinds of malpractice feared by Rogers et al. (1999).

Given the fact that the numbers of immigrant children in impacted districts have been increasing steadily in the last two decades, the occurrence of malpractice would assume gross incompetence throughout all levels of the school system. As discussed previously, the first line of defense for handling immigrant issues falls squarely on district policies (e.g., by funding "newcomer" programs, providing bilingual instruction, hiring translators/interpreters), followed by individual school policies (e.g., organizing English learner advisory committees, hosting orientation meetings prior to school enrollment, hiring school/community liasons), followed by teachers' classroom practices (e.g., modifying instruction for English language learners, reaching out to immigrant families). Assuming that these mechanisms are functioning adequately, those few students who come to the attention of school psychologists would have experienced significant academic problems *over and above what would be reasonably predicted from their immigrant status.*

As shown in Tables 40.1 and 40.2, definitions for the cultural competence construct include "feelings-oriented" competencies (e.g., "sensitivity," "awareness," "respect," "comfort"). In order to accept the notion of widespread abuse in feelings-oriented competencies, one must imagine scenarios in which school psychologists (a) grow up in communities with no natural contacts with cultural minorities; (b) have had no meaningful friendships with persons from groups different from their own; (c) have had no exposure to television, books, radio, Internet, or newspapers that discuss cultural issues; (d) are so inept socially that they are incapable of regulating behavior for interacting successfully with culturally different persons; and (e) possess no spontaneous professional or personal curiosity for learning about different cultures. This author is unaware of any survey studies that have documented such conditions in the background characteristics of school psychologists.

Mediating Assumption: There Is a Direct Relationship Between CC and Improved Outcomes for Culturally Different Clients in the Workplace

According to Kanfer and Ackerman (2005), competence in the workplace refers to "the potential for, or demonstration of, coordinated actions that accomplish *organizationally valued tasks*" (p. 336). Thus, the evaluation of competency in the workplace varies as a function of job and professional role demands. For example, a school psychologist may be able to administer and interpret the Universal Nonverbal Intelligence Test (McCallum & Bracken, 2005) to a Thai-speaking student, but know virtually nothing about Thai culture. Although CC advocates would most likely view this as a lack of cultural competence, the school psychologist's employer may view this as exemplary cultural competence, because proficiency with the UNIT is valued by the school district (while familiarity with Thai culture is not).

Kanfer and Ackerman (2005) argue that successful or unsuccessful performance or outcomes in the workplace are influenced by a complex combination of a person's abilities and skills (e.g., the ability to speak Spanish or conduct a functional behavior assessment), the quality of resources in the workplace (e.g., district funds to purchase updated tests, time allowed in service contract to meet with parents, availability of appropriate translators), and unanticipated random events (e.g., parents who fail to show up for IEP meetings, a child that is arrested in the middle of an intervention). An intervention may be successful for reasons that have nothing to do with the CC of the school psychologist, and an intervention may fail despite exemplary CC of the school psychologist. Thus, the relationship between CC (as conceptualized by academia) and workplace outcomes is deceptively complex.

The Cultural Competence Movement Is Dominated by Ideologically Driven Advocacy Rather Than Research-Based Evidence

Weak empirical support for the CC construct, and the lack of research-based answers for troubling gaps in the justification for CC advocacy, should temper the urgency with which the CC movement is promoted in school psychology. Yet, the urgency with which professional organizations in school psychology promote CC training far exceeds its current level of conceptual clarity and empirical support (Braden & Shah, 2005). This paradox can be attributed to a much deeper problem, from which the previous two problems are merely symptoms. This deeper problem is symptomatic of ideologically driven advocacy movements that influence psychology generally, and school psychology particularly.

Various scholars have provided different, yet somewhat correlated interpretations of the ideological factors that drive CC advocacy despite its lack of a solid research foundation. Frisby (2005a, 2005b) argues that an accurate picture of cultural diversity issues is distorted by *multiculturalism*, defined as a sociopolitical ideology that reflects "a coherent system of clearly identifiable assumptions, beliefs, attitudes, and practices associated with intergroup relations within a society" (Frisby, 2005a, p. 45). Just as a fish does not consciously realize that it is wet, Frisby opines that school psychologists may not be consciously aware that the content of scholarly articles, training texts, and organizational position/policy statements are unavoidably shaped by six unspoken but ideologically driven doctrines (for a complete discussion of these doctrines, see Frisby, 2005a). These doctrines are implicit "authoritative beliefs that give (multiculturalism) ideology its force" (p. 47). Only by making these doctrines explicit, and challenging their validity in light of available research, can school psychology begin to appreciate how its assumptions, interpretations, and practices may be based on a distorted picture of reality (Frisby, 2005b).

Redding (2001) identifies the root of CC advocacy bias as originating ultimately in a clash of worldviews between a liberal versus conservative political orientation among professional psychologists, and within its largest organization, the American Psychological Association. A liberal political ideology sees racism, prejudice and discrimination from society as the primary problem responsible for minority group difficulties (Kerlinger, 1984). It then logically follows that government largesse, affirmative action policies, political and judicial activism, antidiscrimination laws, and the acquisition of political power are believed to be the best means through which minority groups can achieve protection and advancement in society. In contrast, a conservative political orientation favors limited government. Conservatism sees minority group advancement is achieved primarily through hard work, entrepreneurship, law abidingness, good citizenship, and personal responsibility. Whereas a liberal political orientation sees the maintenance of racial/ethnic group cultural distinctions from mainstream culture as preferable (e.g., bilingual education), a conservative political orientation tends to view acculturation

and assimilation into the mainstream as preferable (e.g., English immersion). According to Redding (2001), a significant majority of both academic and practicing psychologists are more politically liberal compared to the general population, and a majority of social policy articles in psychology journals espouse liberal sociopolitical views. The consequences of a liberal sociopolitical imbalance, according to Redding, is that policy and "best practice" positions on social issues advocated by a professional psychology groups inevitably reflect politically liberal values. According to Redding, this linkage ultimately undermines the ecological validity of psychological research (Redding, 1998), undermines the accuracy of scientific theories (Lillis et al., 2005; Redding & Reppucci, 1999), and weakens psychology's credibility as an intellectually honest science in public policy and scientific arenas (Gottfredson, 2005a; Redding, 1998; Suedfeld & Tetlock, 1992).

Cummings and O'Donohue (2005) attribute advocacy bias to the pervasive influence of *political correctness* in contemporary psychology. Political correctness can be defined as a social phenomenon that prescribes how language and terminology should be modified in order to provide a minimum of offense to racial, cultural, or other identity groups, which ultimately sets parameters around which discussion topics are or are not considered acceptable for public discourse. Political correctness is a term that is almost always used in a pejorative sense. Conservatives accuse liberals of using political correctness to avoid discussions of painful realities (Cummings & O'Donohue, 2005), while liberals accuse conservatives of using political correctness as a straw man to oppose progressive social change (Owusu-Bempah, 2003). Both liberal and conservative ideologues have been accused of using political correctness to stifle important research (Hunt, 1999). The political correctness phenomenon is seen as a worthy topic of psychological study in its own right, which has resulted in a special series of scholarly papers in such journals as the *Journal of Social Distress and the Homeless* (1996, Vol. 5(2)) and *Canadian Psychology* (1997, Vol. 38(4)).

The need to adhere to political correctness shapes both implicit and explicit assumptions about which among the many conditions in multicultural education are judged as urgent problems (for which CC is seen as the solution); which among many perspectives is the preferred interpretation of problems; and how the content of CC training is decided. This point can be illustrated by the following thought experiment. Shown in Table 40.3 are two columns, each of which represent two very different sets of beliefs related to the knowledge, skills, and attitude components of CC training in school psychology. In the first step of this thought experiment, readers can cover the entries on the right hand column, then slowly read down the list of entries in the left hand column ("Politically Correct" beliefs). Although readers may disagree to some extent with specific entries in the left column, chances are high that nothing in the left column will be perceived as unusually provocative or controversial when viewed against the backdrop of mainstream thought on CC in school psychology. In contrast, when this procedure is repeated for the right hand column ("Politically Incorrect" beliefs), chances are high that one or more entries in the right column will engender a more visceral reaction. Some readers may be offended at some of the entries, believing that these beliefs should be vigorously excluded from the realm of acceptable discourse in school psychology. Others may recognize that some right column entries are more empirically supported than their counterparts on the left column, but know all too well that offences will be taken if these beliefs were aired and defended publicly. Still others will

TABLE 40.3 **Politically "Correct" vs. "Incorrect" Beliefs Associated with the Cultural Competence Movement in School Psychology**

Knowledge	
"Politically Correct" Beliefs	**"Politically Incorrect" Beliefs**
1. Cultural diversity inherently presents serious challenges to effective schooling	1. The *politicization* of cultural diversity presents serious challenges to effective schooling
2. Discrimination can result in group inequalities; and group inequalities are evidence of discrimination	2. Discrimination can result in group inequalities; but group inequalities are not necessarily evidence of discrimination
3. Understanding how groups are different is more useful for school psychologists than understanding how groups are similar	3. Understanding how groups are similar is more useful for school psychologists than understanding how groups are different
4. Ethnic and racial group mean differences in intelligence test scores are caused by inherent bias in culturally insensitive tests	4. Ethnic and racial group mean differences in intelligence test scores are caused by real group differences in the underlying trait measured by unbiased tests
5. Cultural and language differences between ethnic and racial groups is the root of most school problems involving culturally diverse learners	5. Differences in the prevalence of social problems among ethnic and racial groups is the root of most school problems involving culturally diverse learners
6. Knowledge of ethnic/racial group norms is indispensable for understanding behavioral, academic, and emotional problems of culturally diverse individuals	6. Knowledge of ethnic/racial group norms creates blind spots where potentially effective interventions for culturally diverse individuals are overlooked or ignored
7. Immersion in a different culture helps to combat stereotypes	7. Immersion in a different culture can sometimes reinforce stereotypes
Skills	
"Politically Correct" Beliefs	**"Politically Incorrect" Beliefs**
1. Multicultural experts and professional organizations know best how to develop cultural competence in school psychologists	1. Job and life experience, common sense, and good interpersonal skills are best for developing cultural competence in school psychologists

(Continued)

TABLE **40.3** (*Continued*)

Skills	
"Politically Correct" Beliefs	**"Politically Incorrect" Beliefs**
2. An increase in educators' and psychologists' cultural competence skills will significantly reduce statistical disparities among ethnic/racial groups in school outcomes	2. Variability in educators' and psychologists' cultural competence skills bears little to no relationship to statistical disparities among ethnic/racial groups in school outcomes
3. The best way for teachers to educate culturally diverse children equally is to treat them differently as a function of their culture	3. The best way for teachers to educate culturally diverse children equally is to treat them equally without regard to their culture
4. Interventional empirically validated on predominantly white, English-speaking samples are *ipso facto* not appropriate for application to non-white, English-speaking samples—until proven otherwise	4. Interventions empirically validated on predominantly white, English-speaking samples can be reasonably assumed to be appropriate for application to non-white, English-speaking samples—until proven otherwise.
5. Information from the assessment of perceived racism, acculturation, cultural worldview, and ethnic identity provides significant incremental utility necessary for facilitating school success and adjustment of cultural minority children	5. Information collected from well constructed behavioral assessments and ability, achievement, language, and personality tests are sufficient for serving the psycho-educational needs of *all* children

Attitudes/Dispositions	
"Politically Correct" Beliefs	**"Politically Incorrect" Beliefs**
1. Educators and school psychologists have a moral obligation to eradicate disproportionate representation of racial and ethnic groups in special education and gifted programs	1. Educators and school psychologists do not have a moral obligation to eradicate disproportionate representation of racial and ethnic groups in special education and gifted programs
2. "Tolerance" is a universal value, applied unconditionally, for which all persons should be held accountable	2. "Tolerance" has its limits, and these limits are determined by personal, family, school, religious, and/or community standards
3. The values, beliefs and behaviors of all cultures should be respected	3. Some cultural values, beliefs, and behaviors do not deserve respect. To require unilateral respect that is not earned is to rob respect of its meaning
4. Resistance to sensitivity training can be attributed to trainees' racism, the need to maintain "white privilege," cultural blindness or cultural insensitivity	4. Resistance to sensitivity training can be attributed to its lack of demonstrated utility, low quality of instruction, or trainees' aversion to the politicized nature of such training
5. Training in cultural sensitivity empowers professionals to work effectively with clients from different backgrounds in order to facilitate positive outcomes	5. Training in cultural sensitivity enables professionals to feel morally virtuous, without the concrete skills and knowledge to do anything tangible that leads to real solutions for problems
6. Good intentions, a concern for "social justice," and compassion for the needy is a self-evident justification for CC training	6. The ability to demonstrate empirically validated outcomes should determine the need for CC training

sense an immediate philosophical kinship with the right column entries, and will experience these viscerally as a welcome "breath of fresh air."

The point here is not to recommend replacing presuppositions on the left column with those on the right. A presuppositional "worldview" should not be the foundation on which CC (if it exists at all) is built. The advancement of CC as an intellectually respectable movement requires that the full range of presuppositions be available for review, discussion, debate, and rigorous evaluation. If evidence appears to overwhelmingly support a presupposition in one column, then scholars and practitioners in school psychology should have the strength of conviction to reject the corresponding presupposition in the opposing column, regardless of its emotional popularity in professional school psychology. It may be that truth does not lie exclusively in one column or the other. It is possible that with careful research, scholars may discover that select entries in one column are supported only under certain conditions and for certain outcomes, but that corresponding entries in the opposing column are more strongly supported under a different set of conditions or outcomes. At the time of this writing, this level of sophistication in evaluating CC knowledge claims has not been realized in school psychology.

SUMMARY

Interest in cultural competence (CC) is currently ubiquitous in the applied social and behavioral sciences. CC is a concept that appears to have been invented in response to recognition of America's increasing ethnic and racial diversity, made particularly salient by legal and illegal immigration of limited or non-English speakers. Although the application of CC to practice is naturally discipline specific, most (if not all) conceptualizations appear to define CC as a combination of knowledge, skills, and attitudes. Even before CC entered the school psychology lexicon, the field had a rich history of discussing cultural diversity issues, which appeared to hit its stride in the 1990s and has not shown signs of abating. The question of whether professional consensus exists as to the definition of CC ironically depends upon the definition of "consensus." As shown in this chapter, the solicitation of expert or consumer opinion often results in a lack of consensus as to the most important components of CC. If the researcher retains and showcases only those competencies that appear to have the highest degree of agreement across respondents, however, then it can be argued that the retained competencies can represent consensus. Unfortunately, a different outcome often emerges when this procedure is reversed. When researchers present experts with a predetermined list of competencies, their ratings of the competencies (on any number of criteria) often result in unacceptably low levels of agreement.

The truth be told, CC policy initiatives on behalf of both APA and NASP are vigorously promoted at a speed and intensity that far exceeds its validation from empirical research. There exists too many intervening factors that have not received adequate research attention, which is necessary in order to inspire confidence in CC as (1) a validated construct, and (2) as an undisputed training need for all school psychologists. The widening chasm between its vigorous promotion by professional organizations versus its weak research support can be attributable partly to the influence of multiculturalism ideology, a one-sided (i.e., liberal) political orientation, or political correctness. School psychologists must first learn to recognize the existence of these influences, and use this awareness as a springboard for understanding the extent to which these influences may or may not distort reality.

At the time of this writing, it is not known whether CC, as a hypothesized attribute of practitioners, is a dichotomous variable, a generalized continuous variable, a collection of discrete skills, or a variable that simply reflects a new name given to an old concept. Even if the phrase "cultural competence" had never been invented, there still remains an important role for school psychologists in applying their measurement expertise in testing and assessment issues to problems involving culturally different groups. As always, the need for well-trained bilingual school psychologists will continue to be a perennial problem. The very urgent pressures that some districts experience as a result of both legal and illegal immigration can create opportunities for school psychologists to consult with school/district administrators to help ease immigrants' difficult transition to an alien school culture. Whether or not school psychologists who meet these needs should be called "culturally competent" is a largely irrelevant issue. Until serious research can be conducted, CC will remain an impressionistic rather than precise concept that exists in the eye of the beholder.

REFERENCES

Allen, B. A., & Boykin, A. W. (1992). African-American children and the educational process: Alleviating cultural discontinuity through prescriptive pedagogy. *School Psychology Review, 21*(4), 586–596.

American Psychological Association (1993). Guidelines for providers of psychological services to ethnic, linguistic, and culturally diverse populations. *American Psychologist, 48*, 45–48.

American Psychological Association (2005). *Guidelines and principles for accreditation of programs in professional psychology.* Washington, DC: Author. Retrieved June 20, 2006 from www.apa.org/ed/G&P2.pdf.

Argulewicz, E. N. (1986). School psychology in bicultural settings: Implications for service delivery. In S. N. Elliott & J. C. Witt (Eds.), *The delivery of psychological services in schools: Concepts, processes, and issues* (pp. 227–247). Hillsdale, NJ: Lawrence Erlbaum.

Armour-Thomas, E. (1992). Intellectual assessment of children from culturally diverse backgrounds. *School Psychology Review, 21*(4), 552–565.

Armour-Thomas, E., & GoPaul-McNicol, S. (1998). *Assessing intelligence: Applying a biocultural model.* Thousand Oaks, CA: Sage.

Atkinson, D. R., & Israel, T. (2003). The future of multicultural counseling competence. In D. B. Pope-Davis, H. L.K. Coleman, W. M. Liu, & R. L. Toporek (Eds.), *Handbook of multicultural competencies in counseling and psychology* (pp. 591–606). Thousand Oaks, CA: Sage Publications.

Azar, B. (1997, August). When research is swept under the rug. *APA Monitor, 18.*

Bainter, T. R., & Tollefson, N. (2003). Intellectual assessment of language minority students: What do school psychologists believe are acceptable practices? *Psychology in the Schools, 40*(6), 599–603.

Bankston, C. L., Caldas, S. J., & Zhou, M. (1997). The academic achievement of Vietnamese American students: Ethnicity as social capital. *Sociological Focus, 30*(1), 1–16.

Bankston, C. L., & Caldas, S. J. (2002). *A troubled dream: The promise and failure of school desegregation in Louisiana.* Nashville, TN: Vanderbilt University Press.

Barnett, D. W., Collins, R., Coulter, C., Curtis, M. J., Ehrhardt, K, Glaser, A., et al. (1995). Ethnic validity and school psychology: Concepts and practices associated with cross-cultural professional competence. *Journal of School Psychology, 33*(3), pp. 219–234.

Barona, A., & Flores, A. A. (1984). Critical variables in the recruitment of ethnic minorities to APA school psychology doctoral programs. Unpublished manuscript, Texas A & M University.

Barona, A., & Garcia, E. E. (Eds.). (1990). *Children at risk: Poverty, minority status, and other issues in educational equity.* Washington, DC: National Association of School Psychologists.

Barrera, I., & Corso, R. M. (2003). Skilled dialogue: Strategies for responding to cultural diversity in early childhood. Baltimore: Paul H. Brookes.

Berk, R. A. (Ed.). (1982). *Handbook of methods for detecting test bias.* Baltimore, MD: Johns Hopkins.

Bernard, H. R. (2002). *Research methods in anthropology* (3rd ed.). Walnut Creek, CA.: Alta Mira Press.

Braden, J. P., & Shah, K. G. (2005). A critique of multicultural training in school psychology: Rationale, strategies, and tactics. In C. L. Frisby & C. R. Reynolds (Eds.), *Comprehensive handbook of multicultural school psychology* (pp. 1023–1047). New York: Wiley.

Brown, R. T., Reynolds, C. R., & Whitaker, J. S. (1999). Bias in mental testing since Bias In Mental Testing. *School Psychology Quarterly, 14*(3), 208–238.

Bruni, N. (1988). A critical analysis of transcultural theory. *Australian Journal of Advanced Nursing, 5*(3), 26–32.

Burchum, J. (2002). Cultural competence: An evolutionary perspective. *Nursing Forum, 37*(4), 5–15.

Camarota, S. A. (2001). *Immigration from Mexico: Assessing the impact on the United States.* Washington, DC: Center for Immigration Studies.

Christenson, S. L., & Conoley, J. C. (Eds), (1992) *Home-school collaboration: Enhancing children's academic and social competence.* Silver Spring, MD: National Association of School Psychologists.

Constantine, M. G., & Ladany, N. (2000). Self report multicultural counseling competence scales: Their relation to social desirability attitudes and multicultural case conceptualization ability. *Journal of Counseling Psychology, 47,* 155–164.

Cortese, A. (1992). Academic achievement in Mexican Americans: Sociolegal and cultural factors. *Latino Studies Journal, 3*(1), 31–47.

Cummings, N. A., & O'Donohue, W. T. (2005). Psychology's surrender to political correctness. In R. H. Wright & N. A. Cummings (Eds.), *Destructive trends in mental health: The well-intentioned path to harm* (pp. 3–27). New York, NY: Routledge.

Cunningham, P. B., Foster, S. L., & Henggeler, S.W. (2002). The elusive concept of cultural competence. *Children's Services: Social Policy, Research, and Practice, 5*(3), 231–243.

Curtis, M. J., Hunley, S. A., Walker, K. J., & Baker, A. C. (1999). Demographic characteristics and professional practices in school psychology. *School Psychology Review, 28*, 104–116.

D'Andrea, M., Daniels, J., & Heck, R. (1991). Evaluating the impact of multicultural training. *Journal of Counseling & Development, 70*, 143–150.

D'Andrea, M., Daniels, J., & Noonan, M. J. (2003). New developments in the assessment of multicultural competence: The Multicultural Awareness-Knowledge-Skills Survey-Teachers Form. In D. B. Pope-Davis, H. L. K. Coleman, W. M. Liu, & R. L. Toporek (Eds.), *Handbook of multicultural competencies in counseling and psychology* (pp. 154–167). Thousand Oaks, CA: Sage Publications.

Davis, T. S. (2004). Viability of concept mapping for assessing cultural competence in children's mental health systems of care: A comparison of theoretical and community conceptualizations. *Dissertation Abstracts International, 65*(1), 287-A (UMI No. DA3119665).

Delgado-Gaitan, C. (1991). *Crossing cultural borders.* London: Falmer Press.

DeVellis, R. F. (1991). *Scale development: Theory and applications.* Newbury Park, CA: Sage.

Dornbusch, S. M., & Ritter, P. L. (1992). Home-school processes in diverse ethnic groups, social classes, and family structures. In S. L. Christenson & J. C. Conoley (Eds.), *Home-school collaboration: Enhancing children's academic and social competence* (pp. 111–126). Silver Spring, MD: National Association of School Psychologists.

Dreher, M., & MacNaughton, N. (2002). Cultural competence in nursing: Foundation or fallacy? *Nursing Outlook, 50*, pp. 181–186.

Ehrhardt-Padgett, G. N., Hatzichristou, C., Kitson, J., & Meyers, J. (2004). Awakening to a new dawn: Perspectives of the future of school psychology. *School Psychology Review, 33*(1), 105–114.

Eisere, P. E. (1963). *The school psychologist.* Washington, DC: Center for Applied Research in Education.

Esquivel, G. B. (1985). Best practices in the assessment of limited English proficient and bilingual children. In A. Thomas & J. Grimes (Eds.), *Best practices in school psychology* (pp. 113–123). Washington, DC: National Association of School Psychologists.

Esquivel, G. B., Lopez, E. C., & Nahari, S. (2007). *Handbook of multicultural school psychology: An interdisciplinary perspective.* Mahwah, NJ: Lawrence Erlbaum.

Evans-Hampton, T. N., Skinner, C. H., Henington, C., Sims, S., & McDaniel, C. E. (2002). An investigation of situational bias: Conspicuous and covert timing during curriculum-based measurement of mathematics across African American and Caucasian students. *School Psychology Review, 31*(4), 529–539.

Feuerstein, R., Feuerstein, & Gross, S. (1997). The Learning Potential Assessment Device. In D. P. Flanagan, J. L. Genshaft, & P. L. Harrison (Eds.), *Contemporary intellectual assessment: Theories, tests, and issues* (pp. 297–313). New York: Guilford.

Feuerstein, R., Rand, Y., & Hoffman, M. (1979). *The Dynamic Assessment of Retarded Performers: The Learning Potential Assessment Device (LPAD).* Baltimore, MD: University Park Press.

Figueroa, R. A., Sandoval, J., & Merino, B. (1984). School psychology and limited-English proficient (LEP) children: New competencies. *Journal of School Psychology, 22*, 131–143.

Flanagan, D. P., & Harrison, P. L. (Eds.). (2005). *Contemporary intellectual assessment: Theories, tests, and issues* (2nd ed). New York: Guilford.

Fong, R. (Ed.). (2004). *Culturally competent practice with immigrant and refugee children and families.* New York: Guilford Press.

Frey, W. (2001). *Metro magnets for minorities and whites: Melting pots, the new sunbelt, and the heartland (Research Report).* Ann Arbor, MI: University of Michigan Population Studies Center. Retrieved May 30, 2006 from www.prcdc.org/summaries/frey.html.

Frisby, C. L. (1992). Parent education as a means for improving the school achievement of low-income African American children. In S. L. Christenson & J. C. Conoley (Ed.), *Home-school collaboration: Enhancing children's academic and social competence* (pp. 127–155). Silver Spring, MD: National Association of School Psychologists.

Frisby, C. (1999). Culture and test session behavior: Part I. *School Psychology Quarterly, 14*(3), 263–280.

Frisby, C. L. (2005a). The politics of multiculturalism in school psychology: Part I. In C. L. Frisby & C. R. Reynolds (Eds.), *Comprehensive handbook of multicultural school psychology* (pp. 45–80). New York: John Wiley.

Frisby, C. L. (2005b). The politics of multiculturalism in school psychology: Part II. In C. L. Frisby & C. R. Reynolds (Eds.), *Comprehensive handbook of multicultural school psychology* (pp. 81–136). New York: John Wiley.

Frisby, C. L., & Reynolds, C. R. (Eds.), (2005). *Comprehensive handbook of multicultural school psychology.* New York: John Wiley.

Garcia, E. E. (1990). Language-minority education litigation policy: "The law of the land". In A. Barona & E. E. Garcia (Ed.), *Children at risk: Poverty, minority status, and other issues in educational equity* (pp. 53–63). Washington, DC.: National Association of School Psychologists.

Gershberg, A. I., Danenberg, A., & Sanchez, P. (2004). *Beyond "bilingual" education: New immigrants and public school policies in California.* Washington, DC: Urban Institute Press.

Gersten, R., & Woodward, J. (1994). The language-minority student and special education: Issues, trends, and paradoxes. *Exceptional Children, 60,* 310–322.

Glutting, J., Oakland, T., & Konold, T. R. (1994). Criterion-related bias with the Guide to the Assessment of Test-Session Behavior for the WISC-III and WIAT: Possible race/ethnicity, gender, and SES effects. *Journal of School Psychology. 32*(4), 355–369.

GoPaul–McNicol, S. (1997). A theoretical framework for training monolingual school psychologists to work with multilingual/multicultural children: An exploration of the major competencies. *Psychology in the Schools, 34*(1), pp. 17–29.

GoPaul-McNicol, S., & Armour-Thomas, E. (2002). *Assessment and culture: Psychological tests with minority populations.* San Diego, CA: Academic Press.

Gottfredson, L. S. (2000). Skills gaps, not tests, make racial proportionality impossible. *Psychology, Public Policy, and Law, 6*(1), 129–143.

Gottfredson, L. S. (2004). Intelligence: Is it the epidemiologists' elusive "fundamental cause" of social class inequalities in health? *Journal of Personality and Social Psychology, 86*(1), 174–199.

Gottfredson, L. S. (2005a). Suppressing intelligence research: Hurting those we intend to help. In R. H. Wright & N. A. Cummings (Eds.), *Destructive trends in mental health: The well-intentioned path to harm* (pp. 155–186). New York, NY: Routledge.

Gottfredson, L. S. (2005b). Implications of cognitive difference for schooling within diverse societies. In C. L. Frisby & C. R. Reynolds (Eds.), *Comprehensive handbook of multicultural school psychology* (pp. 517–554). New York: Wiley.

Gray, S. W. (1963). *The psychologist in the schools.* New York: Holt, Rinehart & Winston.

Graziano, W. G., Varca, P. E., & Levy, J. (1982). Race of examiner and the validity of intelligence tests. *Review of Educational Research, 52*(4), 469–497.

Greene, J. P. (2005). *Education myths: What special interest groups want you to believe about our schools—and why it isn't so.* Lanham, MD: Rowman & Littlefield.

Gutkin, T. B., & Reynolds, C. R. (Eds.). (1990). *The handbook of school psychology* (2nd ed.). New York: Wiley.

Halstead, J. M. (2005). Religion, culture, and schooling. In C. L. Frisby & C. R. Reynolds (Eds.), *Comprehensive handbook of multicultural school psychology* (pp. 394–424). New York: John Wiley.

Hambleton, R. K., & Li, S. (2005). Translation and adaptation issues and methods for educational and psychological tests. In C. L. Frisby & C. R. Reynolds (Eds.), *Comprehensive handbook of multicultural school psychology* (pp. 881–903). New York: John Wiley.

Hanley, J. H. (1999). Beyond the tip of the iceberg: Five stages toward cultural competence. *Reaching Today's Youth, 3*(2), 9–12.

Helms, J. E. (1992). Why is there no study of cultural equivalence in standardized cognitive ability testing? *American Psychologist, 47,* 1083–1101.

Helms, J. E. (1997). The triple quandary of race, culture, and social class in standardized cognitive ability testing. In D. P. Flanagan, J. L. Genshaft, & P. L. Harrison (Eds.), *Contemporary intellectual assessment: Theories, tests, and issues* (pp. 517–532). New York: Guilford.

Helms, J. E. (1995). An update of Helm's White and people of color racial identity models. In J. G. Ponterotto, J. M. Casas, L. A. Suzuki, & C. M. Alexander (Eds.), *Handbook of multicultural counseling* (pp. 181–198). Thousand Oaks, CA: Sage.

Henderson, R. W., & Valencia, R. R. (1985). Nondiscriminatory school psychological services: Beyond nonbiased assessment. In J. R. Bergan (Ed.), *School psychology in contemporary society: An introduction.* Columbus, OH: Charles E. Merrill.

Herron, W. G., Green, M., Guild, M., Smith, A. & Kantor, R. E. (1970). *Contemporary school psychology.* Seranton, PA: Intext Educational Publishers.

Herrnstein, R. J., & Murray, C. (1994). *The bell curve.* New York: Free Press.

Huang, L. N., & Gibbs, J. T. (1992). Partners or adversaries? Home-school collaboration across culture, race, and ethnicity. In S. L. Christenson & J. C. Conoley (Eds.), *Home-school collaboration: Enhancing children's academic and social competence* (pp. 81–109). Silver Spring, MD: National Association of School Psychologists.

Huebner, E. S. (1989). Factors influencing the decision to administer psychoeducational tests. *Psychology in the Schools, 26*(4), 365–369.

Huebner, E. S., & Cummings, J. A. (1986). Influence of race and test data ambiguity upon school psychologists' decisions. *School Psychology Review, 15*(3), 410–417.

Hunt, M. (1999). *The new know-nothings: The political foes of the scientific study of human nature.* New Brunswick, NJ: Transaction.

Ibrahim, F. (1991). Contribution of cultural world view to generic counseling and development. *Journal of Counseling and Development, 70,* 13–19.

Ingraham, C. L., & Meyers, J. (2000). Introduction to multicultural and cross-cultural consultation in schools: Cultural diversity issues in school consultation. *School Psychology Review, 29*(3), 315–319.

Jensen, A. R. (1980). *Bias in mental testing.* New York: Free Press.

Jensen, A. R. (1984). Test bias: Concepts and criticisms. In C. R. Reynolds & R. T. Brown

(Eds.), *Perspectives on Bias in Mental Testing* (pp. 507–586). New York: Plenum.

Jensen, A. R. (1992). Psychometric G and achievement. In B. R. Gifford & M. C. O'Conner (Eds.), *Changing assessments: Alternative views of aptitude, achievement, and instruction* (pp. 117–227). Boston, MA: Kluwer Academic Publishers.

Jensen, A. R. (1998). *The g factor: The science of mental ability*. Westport, CT: Praeger.

Johnson, K. A. (1999). *Comparing math scores of black students in D.C.'s public and Catholic schools*. Washington, DC: Heritage Foundation.

Jones, R. (1988). *Psychoeducational assessment of minority group children: A casebook*. Berkeley, CA: Cobb & Henry.

Kamphaus, R. (1995). Measurement consultation. In R. C. Talley, T. Kubiszyn, M. Brassard, & R. J. Short (Eds.), *Making psychologists in schools indispensable: Critical questions and emerging perspectives* (pp. 153–158). Washington, DC: American Psychological Association.

Kanfer, R., & Ackerman, P. L. (2005). Work competence: A person-oriented perspective. In A. J. Elliot & C. S. Dweck (Eds.), *Handbook of competence and motivation* (pp. 336–353). New York: Guilford Press.

Kao, G., & Thompson, J. S. (2003). Racial and ethnic stratification in educational achievement and attainment. *Annual Review of Sociology, 29*, 417–442.

Kearns, T., Ford, L., & Brown, K. (2002). *Multicultural training in doctoral school psychology programs: In search of the model program?* ERIC Document Reproduction Service No. ED 465 930.

Kerlinger, F. N. (1984). *Liberalism and conservatism: The nature and structure of social attitudes*. Hillsdale, NJ: Erlbaum.

Kuncel, N. R., Hezlett, S. A., & Ones, D. S. (2004). Academic performance, career potential, creativity, and job performance: Can one construct predict them all? *Journal of Personality and Social Psychology, 86*(1), 148–161.

Lam, S. (2005). The growth and development of school psychology in Hong Kong. In C. L. Frisby & C. R. Reynolds (Eds.), *Comprehensive handbook of multicultural school psychology* (pp. 1107–1127). New York: John Wiley.

Lee, S. J. (2005). *Up against whiteness: Race, school, and immigrant youth*. New York: Teachers College Press.

Levitt, N. (2005, October 12). Academic strife: The American university in the slough of despond. *Spiked Essays*. Retrieved April 4, 2006 from www.spiked-online.com/Articles/0000000CADAC.htm.

Lillis, J., O'Donohue, W., Cucciare, M., & Lillis, E. (2005). Social justice in community psychology. In R. H. Wright & N. A. Cummings (Eds.), *Destructive trends in mental health: The well*

intentioned path to harm (pp. 283–302). New York: Routledge.

Lonner, W. J., & Hayes, S. A. (2004). Understanding the cognitive and social aspects of intercultural competence. In R. J. Sternberg & E. L. Grigorenko (Eds.), *Culture and competence: Contexts of life success* (pp. 89–110). Washington, DC: American Psychological Association.

Lopez, E. C. (1997). The cognitive assessment of limited English proficient and bilingual children. In D. P. Flanagan, J. L. Genshaft, & P. L. Harrison (Eds.), *Contemporary intellectual assessment: Theories, tests, and issues* (pp. 517–532). New York: Guilford.

Lopez, E., & Paez, D. (2005). Excerpts from practicing the three C's: Cross-cultural competence in school psychological services. [Powerpoint presentation]. Retrieved June 7, 2006 from www.nasponline.org/culturalcompetence/threeCs.ppt.

Lopez, C., Lopez, V., Suarez-Morales, L., & Castro, F. (2005). Cultural variation within Hispanic American families. In C. L. Frisby & C. R. Reynolds (Eds.), *Comprehensive handbook of multicultural school psychology* (pp. 234–264). New York: John Wiley.

Lustig, M. W., & Koester, J. (2006). *Intercultural competence: Interpersonal communication across cultures*. Boston, MA: Pearson.

Lynch, F.R. (1997). *The diversity machine: The drive to change the "White male workplace."* New York: Free Press.

Lynch, E. W., & Hanson, M. J. (2004). *Developing cross cultural competence* (3rd ed.). Baltimore, MD: Brookes.

Maramba, G. G., & Hall, G. N. (2002). Meta-analyses of ethnic match as a predictor of dropout, utilization, and level of functioning. *Cultural Diversity and Ethnic Minority Psychology, 8*(3), 290–297.

Mason, J. L. (1995). *Cultural Competence Self Assessment Questionnaire: A manual for users*. Portland, OR: Oregon State University, Research and Training Center on Family Support and Children's Mental Health.

McCallum, R. S., & Bracken, B. A. (2005). The Universal Nonverbal Intelligence Test: A multidimensional measure of intelligence. In D. P. Flanagan & P. L. Harrison (Eds.), *Contemporary intellectual assessment: Theories, tests, and issues* (pp. 425–440). New York: Guilford Press.

Mercer, J. R., & Lewis, J. F. (1978). *System of multicultural pluralistic assessment*. New York: The Psychological Corporation.

Miller, J. (1998). *The unmaking of Americans: How multiculturalism has undermined the assimilation ethic*. New York: Free Press.

Milofsky, C. (1989). *Testers and testing: The sociology of school psychology*. New Brunswick, NJ: Rutgers University Press.

Miranda, A. H. (2002). Best practices in increasing cross-cultural competence. In A. Thomas & J. Grimes (Eds.), *Best practices in school psychology IV: Volume 1* (pp. 353–362). Bethesda, MD: National Association of School Psychologists.

Mishra, S. P., & Dejud, C. (2006). The University of Arizona's summer program for bilingual school psychologists. *NASP Communique, 34*(8), 5–6.

Mpofu, E., Peltzer, K., Shumba, A., Serpell, R., & Mogaji, A. (2005). School psychology in sub-saharan Africa: Results and implications of a six-county survey. In C. L. Frisby & C. R. Reynolds (Eds.), *Comprehensive handbook of multicultural school psychology* (pp. 1128–1150). New York: John Wiley.

National Association of School Psychologists (2000a). *Mission statement.* Retrieved March 28, 2006 from www.nasponline.org/culturalcompetence/mission.html.

National Association of School Psychologists (2000b). *Minority demographics in school psychology.* Retrieved March 28, 2006 from www.nasponline.org/culturalcompetence/minority_demog.html.

National Association of School Psychologists (2000c). *Standards for training and field placement programs in school psychology.* Bethesda, MD: Author. Retrieved June 20, 2006 from www.nasponline.org/certification/FinalStandards.pdf.

National Association of School Psychologists (2003a). *Portraits of the children: Culturally competent assessment.* Bethesda, MD: Author.

National Association of School Psychologists (2003b). Defining cultural competence. Handout from *Portraits of the children: Culturally competent assessment.* Bethesda, MD: Author.

National Association of School Psychologists (2003c). Defining culture. Handout from *Portraits of the children: Culturally competent assessment.* Bethesda, MD: Author.

National Association of School Psychologists (2003d). *Position statement on minority recruitment.* Bethesda, MD: Author. Retrieved June 22, 2006 from www.nasponline.org/information/pospaper_mr.html.

Nieto, S. (1992). *Affirming diversity: The sociopolitical context of multicultural education.* New York: Longman.

Nunez, A., & Robertson, C. (2006). Cultural competency. In D. Satcher & R. J. Pamies (Eds.), *Multicultural medicine and health disparities* (pp. 371–388). New York: McGraw Hill.

Oakland, T. (Ed.). (1977). *Psychological and educational assessment of minority children.* New York: Brunner/Mazel.

Oakland, T. (2005). Commentary #1: What is multicultural school psychology? In C. L. Frisby & C. R. Reynolds (Eds.), *Comprehensive handbook of multicultural school psychology* (pp. 3–13). New York: Wiley.

Oakland, T., & Gallegos, E. M. (2005). Selected legal issues affecting students from multicultural backgrounds. In C. L. Frisby & C. R. Reynolds (Eds.), *Comprehensive handbook of multicultural school psychology* (pp. 1048–1078). New York: Wiley.

Oakland, T., & Laosa, L. M. (1977). Professional, legislative, and judicial influences on psychoeducational assessment practices in schools. In T. Oakland (Ed.), *Psychological and educational assessment of minority children* (pp. 21–51). New York: Brunner/Mazel.

Ochoa, S. H. (2003). Assessment of culturally and linguistically diverse children. In C. R. Reynolds & R. W. Kamphaus (Eds.), *Handbook of psychological and educational assessment of children: Intelligence, aptitude, and achievement* (pp. 563–583). New York: Guilford.

Ochoa, S. H. (2005). The effectiveness of bilingual education programs in the United States: A review of the empirical literature. In C. L. Frisby & C. R. Reynolds (Eds.), *Comprehensive handbook of multicultural school psychology* (pp. 329–356). New York: Wiley.

Ochoa, S. H., Rivera, B., & Ford, L. (1997). An investigation of school psychology training pertaining to bilingual psycho-educational assessment of primarily Hispanic students: Twenty-five years after Diana v. California. *Journal of School Psychology, 35,* 329–349.

Ogbu, J. (1987). Variability in minority school performance: A problem in search of an explanation. *Anthropology and Education Quarterly, 18*(4), 312–334.

Olsen, L. (1997). *Made in America: Immigrant students in our public schools.* New York: New Press.

Ortiz, S. O., & Dynda, A. M. (2003). Use of intelligence tests with culturally and linguistically diverse populations. In D. P. Flanagan & P. L. Harrison (Eds.), *Contemporary intellectual assessment: Theories, tests, and issues* (2nd ed., pp. 545–556). New York: Guilford Press.

Ortiz, S. O., & Flanagan, D. P. (2002). Best practices in working with culturally diverse children and families. In A. Thomas & J. Grimes (Eds.), *Best practices in school psychology IV: Volume 1* (pp. 337–351). Bethesda, MD.: National Association of School Psychologists.

Osher, D., Cartledge, G., Oswald, D., Sutherland, K. S., Artiles, A. J., & Coutinho, M. (2004). Cultural and linguistic competency and disproportionate representation. In R. B. Rutherford, M. M. Quinn, & S. R. Mathur (Eds.), *Handbook of research in emotional and behavioral disorders* (pp. 54–77). New York: Guildford Press.

Owusu-Bempah, K. (2003). Political correctness: In the interest of the child? *Educational and Child Psychology, 20*(1), 53–63.

Pachter, L. M. (2005). Cultural competence. In S. Parker, B. Zuckerman, & M. Augustyn (2005), *Developmental and behavioral pediatrics: A handbook for primary care (Second Edition)* (pp. 389–391). Philadelphia, PA: Lippincott Williams & Wilkins.

Paez, D. (2004). *Culturally competent assessment of English language learners: Strategies for school personnel.* Bethesda, MD: National Association of School Psychologists. Retrieved June 7, 2006 from www.nasponline.org/culturalcompetence/cca_personnel.pdf.

Palmer, D. J., Hughes, J. N., & Juarez, L. (1991). School psychology training and the education of minority at-risk youth: The Texas A&M University program emphasis on handicapped Hispanic children and youth. *School Psychology Review, 20,* 472–484.

Piatek, T. K. (2006). Cultural competence for teachers. Retrieved April 5, 2006 from http://www.opb.org/education/minisites/culturalcompetence/teachers.html.

Pilon, B. (1992). Serving the whole immigrant student in L.A.'s Newcomer Center. *NASP Communique, 21*(2), 13–14.

Ponterotto, J. G., Mendelsohn, J., & Belizaire, L. (2003). Assessing teacher multicultural competence: Self-report instruments, observer report evaluations, and a portfolio assessment. In D. B. Pope-Davis, H. Coleman, W. M. Liu, & R. L. Toporek (Eds.), *Handbook of multicultural competencies in counseling and psychology* (pp. 191–210). Thousand Oaks, CA: Sage.

Ponterotto, J. G., & Potere, J. C. (2003). The multicultural counseling knowledge and awareness scale (MCKAS): Validity, reliability, and user guidelines. In D. B. Pope-Davis, H. Coleman, W. M. Liu, & R. L. Toporek (Eds.), *Handbook of multicultural competencies in counseling and psychology* (pp. 137–153). Thousand Oaks, CA: Sage.

Pope-Davis, D. B., & Coleman, H. (1997). *Multicultural counseling competencies: Assessment, education and training, and supervision.* Thousand Oaks, CA: Sage.

Proctor, E. K., & Davis, L. E. (1989). *Race, gender, and class: Guidelines for practice with individuals, families, and groups.* Englewood Cliffs, NJ: Prentice Hall.

Ramirez, A. G. (1990). Perspectives on language proficiency assessment. In A. Barona & E. E. Garcia (Ed.), *Children at risk: Poverty, minority status, and other issues in educational equity* (pp. 305–323). Washington, DC.: National Association of School Psychologists.

Redding, R. E. (1998). How common-sense psychology can inform law and psycholegal research. *University of Chicago Law School Roundtable, 5,* 107–142.

Redding, R. E. (2001). Sociopolitical diversity in psychology: A case for pluralism. *American Psychologist, 56*(3), 205–215.

Redding, R. E., & Reppucci, N. D. (1999). Relationships between lawyers' sociopolitical attitudes and their judgments of social science in legal decision making. *Law and Human Behavior, 23,* 317–54.

Reger, R. (1965). *School psychology.* Springfield, Ill: Thomas.

Reynolds, C. R., & Carson, A. D. (2005). Methods for assessing cultural bias in tests. In C. L. Frisby & C. R. Reynolds (Eds.), *Comprehensive handbook of multicultural school psychology* (pp. 795–823). New York: Wiley.

Reynolds, C. R., & Gutkin, T. B. (Eds.) (1982). *The handbook of school psychology.* New York: John Wiley.

Reynolds, C. R. & Gutkin, T. B. (Eds.). (1999). *The handbook of school psychology* (3rd ed.). New York: Wiley.

Reynolds, C. R., & Kaiser, S. M. (2003). Bias in the assessment of aptitude. In C. R. Reynolds & R. W. Kamphaus (Eds.), *Handbook of psychological and educational assessment of children: Intelligence, aptitude, and achievement* (pp. 519–562). New York: Guilford Press.

Reynolds, C. R., Lowe, P. A., & Saenz, A. L. (1999). The problem of bias in psychological assessment. In C. R. Reynolds & T. B. Gutkin (Eds.), *Handbook of school psychology* (3rd ed., pp. 549–595). New York: Wiley.

Rhodes, R. (2000). Legal and professional issues in the use of interpreters: Guidelines for school psychologists. *NASP Communique, 29*(1), 28.

Rhodes, R., Ochoa, S. H., & Ortiz, S. O. (2005). *Assessment of culturally and linguistically diverse students: A practical guide.* New York: The Guilford Press.

Ricord-Griesemer, S., Warnick, K., Hawk, M. H., & Jarzab, M. J. (2006). Lessons in culturally competent practice: Summer in Costa Rica. *NASP Communique, 34*(6), 7–8.

Rogers, M. R. (2005). Multicultural training in school psychology. In C. L. Frisby & C. R. Reynolds (Eds.), *Comprehensive handbook of multicultural school psychology* (pp. 993–1022). New York: John Wiley.

Rogers, M. R., Ingraham, C. L., Bursztyn, A., Cajigas-Segredo, N., Esquivel, G., Hess, R., et al. (1999). Providing psychological services to racially, ethnically, culturally, and linguistically diverse individuals in the schools. *School Psychology International, 20*(3), 243–264.

Rogers, M. R., & Lopez, E. C. (2002). Identifying critical cross-cultural school psychology competencies. *Journal of School Psychology, 40*(2), 115–141.

Rogers, M. R., & Ponterotto, J. G. (1997). Development of the multicultural school psychology counseling competencies scale. *Psychology in the Schools, 34*(3), 211–217.

Rogers, M. R., Ponterotto, J. G., Conoley, J. C., & Wiese, M. J. (1992). Multicultural training in school psychology: A national survey. *School Psychology Review, 21*(4), 603–616.

Rosenfield, S., & Esquivel, G. B. (1985). Educating school psychologists to work with bilingual bicultural populations. *Professional Psychology: Research and Practice, 16*, 199–208.

Ruelas, S. (2003). Objectively measured multicultural counseling competencies: A preliminary study. In D. B. Pope-Davis, H. Coleman, W. M. Liu, & R. L. Toporek (Eds.), *Handbook of multicultural competencies in counseling and psychology* (pp. 283–300). Thousand Oaks, CA: Sage.

Rushton, J. P. & Jensen, A. (2005). Thirty years of research on race differences in cognitive ability. *Psychology, Public Policy, and Law, 11*(2), 235–294.

Saigh, P. A., & Oakland, T. (Eds.). (1989). *International perspectives on psychology in the schools*. Hillsdale, NJ: Lawrence Erlbaum.

Satel, S. (1996, May 8). Psychiatric apartheid. *The Wall Street Journal*, p. A14.

Satcher, D., & Pamies, R.J. (Eds.) (2006). *Multicultural medicine and health disparities*. New York: McGraw-Hill.

Schultheiss, O. C., & Brunstein, J. C. (2005). An implicit motive perspective on competence. In A. J. Elliot & C. S. Dweck (Eds.), *Handbook of competence and motivation* (pp. 31–51). New York: Guilford Press.

Seymer, L. (1954). *Selected writings of Florence Nightingale*. New York: McMillan.

Schneider, R. J., Ackerman, P. L. & Kanfer, R. (1996). To "act wisely in human relations:" Exploring the dimensions of social competence. *Personality and individual differences, 21*(4), 469–481.

Smith, T. B., Constantine, M. G., Dunn, T. W., Dinehart, J. M., & Montoya, J. A. (2006). Multicultural education in the mental health professions: A meta-analytic review. *Journal of Counseling Psychology, 53*(1), 132–145.

Sodowsky, G. R., Kuo-Jackson, P. Y., Richardson, M. F., & Corey, A. T. (1998). Correlates of self-reported multicultural competencies: Counselor multicultural social desirability, race, social inadequacy, locus of control racial ideology, and multicultural training. *Journal of Counseling Psychology, 45*, 256–264.

Sowell, T. (1981). *Ethnic America: A history*. New York: Basic Books.

Sowell, T. (1994). *Race and culture: A world view*. New York: Basic Books.

Sowell, T. (1996). *Migrations and culture: A world view*. New York: Basic Books.

Sowell, T. (1998). *Conquests and cultures: An international history*. New York: Basic Books.

Sue, D. W., Arredondo, P., & McDavis, R. J. (1992). Multicultural counseling competencies and standards: A call to the profession. *Journal of Counseling and Development, 70*, 477–486.

Sue, D. W., Bingham, R. P., Porche-Burke, L., & Vasquez, M. (1999). The diversification of psychology: A multicultural revolution. *American Psychologist, 54*, 1061–1069.

Suedfeld, P., & Tetlock, P. E. (1992). *Psychology and social policy*. New York: Hemisphere.

Tarver-Behring, S., & Ingraham, C. L. (1998). Culture as a central component of consultation: A call to the field. *Journal of Educational and Psychological Consultation, 9*, 57–72.

Taylor, R. (2005). Addressing barriers to cultural competence. *Journal For Nurses in Staff Development, 21*(4), 135–142.

Thao, P. (2005). Cultural variation within southeast Asian American families. In C. L. Frisby & C. R. Reynolds (Ed.), *Comprehensive handbook of multicultural school psychology* (pp. 173–204). New York: John Wiley.

Thorndike, E. L. (1920). Intelligence and its uses. *Harper's Magazine, 140*, 217–235.

Torrance, E. P. (1974). *The Torrance Tests of Creative Thinkin–Norms–Technical Manual Research Edition–Verbal Tests, Forms A and B–Figural Tests, Forms A and B*. Princeton NJ: Personnel Press.

Torrance, E. P. (1977). *Discovery and nurturance of giftedness in the culturally different*. Reston, VA: Council for Exceptional Children.

Torrance, E. P. (1982). Identifying and capitalizing on the strengths of culturally different children. In Reynolds, C. R., & Gutkin, T. B., *The handbook of school psychology* (pp. 481–500). New York: John Wiley.

Tripp-Reimer, T., & Dougherty, M. C. (1985). Cross-cultural nursing research. In H. H. Werley & J. J. Fitzpatrick (Eds.), *Annual review of nursing research, 3*, 77–104.

Trueba, H. (1988). Culturally-based explanations of minority students' academic achievement. *Anthropology and Education Quarterly, 19*(3), 270–287.

U. S. Census Bureau (2003). *Language use, English ability, and linguistic isolation for the population 5 to 17 years by state: 2000*. Washington, DC: Author. Retrieved June 7, 2006 from www.census.gov/population/cen2000/phc-t20/tab02.pdf.

UO Office of Institutional Equity and Diversity (2005). *Five year diversity plan draft*. Retrieved June 16, 2005 from http://darkwing.uoregon.edu/~ncp/DiversityPlan/DiversityPlan_Small.pdf

Valencia, R. R., & Suzuki, L. A. (2001). *Intelligence testing and minority students: Foundations, performance factors, and assessment issues*. Thousand Oaks, CA: Sage.

Wasserman, J. D., & Tulsky, D. S. (2005). A history of intelligence assessment. In D. P. Flanagan & P. L. Harrison (Eds.), *Contemporary intellectual assessment: Theories, tests, and issues* (pp. 3–22). New York: Guilford Press.

Wechsler, D. (2004). *WISC-IV Spanish*. San Antonio, TX: Harcourt.

White, M. A., & Harris, M. W. (1961). *The school psychologist*. New York: Harper.

Winnick, L. (1990). America's model minority. *Commentary, 90*(2), 22–29.

Yoon, J. S., & Cheng, L. L. (2005). Cultural variation within East Asian American families. In C. L. Frisby & C. R. Reynolds (Ed.), *Comprehensive handbook of multicultural school psychology* (pp. 265–302). New York: John Wiley.

Yoshida, R. K., Cancelli, A. A., Sowinski, J., & Bernhardt, R. (1989). Differences in information sent to minority and non-minority prospective applicants to clinical, counseling, and school psychology programs. *Professional Psychology: Research and Practice, 20,* 179–184.

Ysseldyke, J., Dawson, P., Lehr, C., Rechsly, D., Reynolds, M., & Telzrow, C. (1997). *School Psychology: A blueprint for training and practice II.* Bethesda, MD: National Association of School Psychologists. Retrieved May 26, 2006 from www.naspcenter.org/pdf/blue2.pdf.

Zach, L. (1970). Training psychologists for the urban slum school. *Psychology in the Schools, 7,* 345–350.

Zigler, E., & Kanzer, P. (1962). The effectiveness of two classes of verbal reinforcers on the performance of middle and lower class children. *Journal of Personality, 30*(2), 157–163.

Zins, J. E., & Halsell, A. (1986). Status of ethnic minority group members in school psychology training programs. *School Psychology Review, 15,* 76–83.

CHAPTER **41**

MANAGING CRISIS: PREVENTION, INTERVENTION, AND TREATMENT

JONATHAN SANDOVAL
University of the Pacific
STEPHEN E. BROCK
California State University, Sacramento

In spite of our best efforts to keep the world safe for children and to provide a secure place for them to be educated, crisis events happen. A fire or an earthquake occurs damaging a community or school, terrorism or other forms of violence victimize children, or accidents cripple, maim or kill. Unfortunately, negative events are an unavoidable part of life.

Most children and adults are resilient and have ways of coping with stressful events. In fact, according to the National Institute of Mental Health (NIMH, 2001) recovery from crisis exposure is the norm. Children need minimal assistance from family members, teachers, clergy or other caring adults. Others, particularly those with few social supports, enter into a crisis state (Barenbaum, Ruchkin, & Schwab-Stone, 2004; Caffo & Belaise, 2003; Litz, Gray, Bryant, & Alder, 2002; Ozer, Best, Lipsey, & Weiss, 2003).

This chapter addresses ways to prepare for emergencies and potentially traumatic events, discusses the dynamics and definitions of crisis, and outlines how children may be helped to manage hazardous events, once they are affected.

What happens when a child has been exposed to a crisis event? Children in crisis suddenly function with a greatly diminished capacity for meeting everyday demands. They suddenly become disorganized, depressed, hyperactive, confused, and/or hysterical (Litz et al., 2002; Pynoos, 1994), whereas previously others have seen them behaving competently and efficiently. Children's customary problem-solving activities and resources seem to evaporate, and performance in school may suffer accordingly.

People in crisis are in what Caplan (1964) terms a state of psychological disequilibrium. They often behave irrationally and withdraw from normal social contacts. They cannot be helped using usual counseling or teaching techniques. Nevertheless, children in crisis are usually also in school. School psychologists and other guidance personnel must be able to support teachers, parents, and the children themselves during periods of crisis. In addition, school personnel must be forward thinking and anticipate that crises will occur. Thus, they must be prepared to act and find ways to help children master the challenges of traumatic events when they do occur.

DEFINITIONS AND DISTINCTIONS

The term crisis is used generically to stand for both the event and the reaction. It is useful, however, to make a distinction between the event and the reaction. Donald C. Klein and Erich Lindemann (1961) offered the following definition:

> An emotionally hazardous situation (or emotional hazard) refers to any sudden alteration in the field of social forces within which the individual exists, such that the individual's expectations of himself and his relationships with others undergo change. Major categories of hazards include: (1) a loss or threatened loss of significant relationship; (2) the introduction of one or more new individuals into social orbit; (3) transitions in social status and role relationships as a consequence of such factors as (a) maturation (e.g., entry into adolescence),

(b) achievement of a new social role (e.g., marriage), or (c) horizontal or vertical social mobility (e.g., job promotion). (p. 284)

Klein and Lindemann (1961) use the term *hazard* to capture the notion that many individuals are able to pass through such alterations with little difficulty or with a minimum amount of stress. Others, however, find themselves immobilized or damaged by the hazard. Natural disasters and acts of terrorism would be included in their definition of hazard. These kinds of hazards typically involve the loss of relationships through death or injury or loss of security and a sense of safety.

When used to define an individual's reaction to an event, Klein and Lindemann (1961) reserve the term crisis "for the acute and often prolonged disturbance that may occur in an individual or social orbit as a result of an emotional hazard" (p. 284). Emotional hazards faced by school children include losses in significant relationships associated with the death of a parent; parental divorce and remarriage; death of a sibling or the loss of a parent to illness; maturational challenges such as the beginning of puberty; and transitions such as those accompanying movement into new schools, or new educational programs. Failing a grade is a hazard, but so is promotion to a new grade with its separation from a known, possibly favored teacher and the adjustment to change and an unknown, new teacher or school.

Disasters typically bring about these same disruptions since they often result in loss of life or of status, such as becoming homeless. Most children will navigate these hazards with little or no ill effect. Others will develop crisis reactions and come to the attention of school psychologists and other school personnel.

Caplan (1964) offers a general view of an emotional crisis as a "psychological disequilibrium in a person who confronts a hazardous circumstance that for him constitutes an important problem which he can, for the time being, neither escape nor solve with his customary problem solving resources" (p. 53). Caplan views a crisis as being a period when the individual is temporarily out of balance. This state of disequilibrium provides an opportunity for psychological growth as well as a danger of psychological deterioration. Although there are great risks to the future mental well-being of an individual who passes through a crisis, there is also an opportunity for an individual to change. It is an old but traditional cliché to point out that the Chinese character for

crisis includes ideographs related to the concept of danger as well as the concept of opportunity.

The primary goal in helping an individual who is undergoing a crisis is to intervene in such a way as to restore the individual to a previous level of functioning, although it may be possible to use the situation to enhance personal growth. The immediate goal is not to reorganize completely the individual's major dimensions of personality, but to restore the individual to creative problem solving. Of course by successfully resolving a crisis an individual will most likely acquire new coping skills that will lead to improved functioning in new situations, but that is only a desired, possible outcome, not the sole objective of the process.

Because failure to cope is at the heart of a crisis, and the promotion of coping is an overall objective of crisis intervention, it is useful to consider what normal coping entails. Moos and Billings (1984) have identified a taxonomy of coping skills organized into three domains, each with three skills. The first is appraisal-focused coping. The three skills in this domain enable the individual to find meaning and to understand the crisis, that is, to apprehend it in a productive manner. They are (a) logical analysis and mental preparation, (b) cognitive redefinition, and (c) cognitive avoidance or denial. Thus, in first becoming aware of a hazardous event, a child may think it through rationally, step by step, and prepare for what will probably happen next; may reframe the hazard in a variety of ways; or may keep all or part of it at a distance, mentally, until he or she is ready to deal with it. This last skill has important intervention implications. Use of it suggests that crisis intervention should be sensitive to the importance of not asking an individual to confront crisis facts before they are ready to do so.

The second domain is problem-focused coping. The three skills in this domain enable the individual to confront the reality brought about by the crisis. These are (a) seeking information and support, (b) taking problem-solving action, and (c) identifying alternative rewards. This last skill involves changing activities and relationships so there may be substitutions for the sources of satisfaction lost by the hazardous event.

The third domain is emotion-focused coping. Here, the three skills enable the child to manage the feelings generated by the crisis and to maintain affective equilibrium. The three skills are (a) affective regulation, (b) emotional discharge, and (c) resigned acceptance. These skills allow one to maintain control of emotions, or to vent them in a way that brings relief. Many situations cannot be controlled, however, and resigned acceptance may lead to avoidance and withdrawal as a way to protect oneself. As we will argue later, much of crisis intervention is directed at stimulating one or more of these coping skills in all domains, or even teaching them depending on the individual and the type of hazard he or she is attempting to negotiate.

There has been a great deal of interest in the concept of *resilience*, or the internal and external resources that enable some children to overcome difficult situations or events (Werner, 1989). Children who are able to adaptively cope with hazardous situations may be characterized as having active (or approach) oriented coping styles, mental health, good self-regulation of emotion and problem solving skills, self-confidence and esteem, an internal locus of control, and/or resilient belief systems. They also come from supportive family and school environments with high expectations and encouragement of participation in meaningful activities. Thus, some children will be vulnerable to hazardous events and transitions, and others, who are resilient, will not (Brock, 2002b).

Types of Crises

Although there are a number of ways that crises may be defined and categorized, most authorities distinguish between developmental and situational crises (Slaikeu, 1990). Developmental crises occur when an individual moves from one developmental stage to another (e.g., from middle childhood to adolescence). Situational crises, however, are incidents that are unexpected and accidental. Because of their potential to impact many students simultaneously, situational crises are the events that have generated the need for school crisis response team formation (Brock, Sandoval, & Lewis, 2001).

Examples of situational crises include severe illness and/or injury, violent and/or unexpected death, threatened death and/or injury, acts of war and/or terrorism, and natural and man-made/industrial disasters (Brock et al., 2001). It is important to acknowledge that not all of these events have equivalent potential to generate crisis reactions. Simply put, some types of crises are more traumatic then are others. Specifically, events that have a predictable/gradual onset, involve nonassaultive injury and/or threatened

injury, are considered natural disasters, and/or do not involve any fatalities are less traumatic. Conversely, those types of crises that have an unpredictable/sudden onset, involve assaultive injury and/or threatened injury, are considered man-made disasters, and/or result in fatalities are likely to me more traumatic (Brock, 2002a).

Knowledge of the traumatic potential of different types of crises is critical given the problems that are associated with both over- and underreacting to a crisis event. If a school underreacts then it is likely that some student crisis intervention needs will go unmet. At the same time, overreacting may actually generate anxiety among students. Younger children, in particular, are very sensitive to the anxiety of adults in their environment (Nader & Pynoos, 1993). Thus, if school personnel behave as if a crisis event is highly traumatic, when in fact it is not, students may be unnecessarily stressed (Brock, 2002a).

GENERAL CRISIS INTERVENTION

Goals

According to the National Child Traumatic Stress Network (2006) there are eight goals for the immediate crisis intervention response. These goals are offered in Table 41.1.

The goals offered in Table 41.1 are the essence of the immediate crisis intervention response to traumatized youth. Further, flexibility is key and specific strategies for obtaining these goals should be tailored to the particular needs of crisis victims. Finally, it is suggested that the time spent addressing each goal will vary according to the needs of the person in crisis.

Principles and Procedures

General principles and procedures of crisis intervention include the following:

1. *Facilitate the reestablishment of a social support network.* This is an especially important crisis intervention for children. If possible, get the child to accept some help from others. It is usually possible to find either a group of peers or family members who can provide emotional support and temporary physical assistance during the crisis. In this way the pupil's energies may be devoted to coping with the crisis. Being with and sharing crisis experiences with positive social support systems facilitates recovery. Conversely, lower levels of social support often

TABLE 41.1   Goals of the Immediate Crisis Intervention Response

1. *Contact and Engagement.* Respond to contacts initiated by affected persons, or initiate contacts in a nonintrusive, compassionate, and helpful manner.

2. *Safety and Comfort.* Enhance immediate and ongoing safety, and provide physical and emotional comfort.

3. *Stabilization (if needed).* Calm and orient emotionally overwhelmed/distraught survivors.

4. *Information Gathering: Current Needs and Concerns.* Identify immediate needs and concerns, gather additional information, and tailor psychological first aid interventions.

5. *Practical Assistance.* Offer practical help to the survivor in addressing immediate needs and concerns.

6. *Connection with Social Supports.* Help establish brief or ongoing contacts with primary support persons or other sources of support, including family members, friends, and community helping resources.

7. *Information on Coping.* Provide information (about stress reactions and coping) to reduce distress and promote adaptive functioning

8. *Linkage with Collaborative Services.* Link survivors with needed services, and inform them about available services that may be needed in the future.

Source: Adapted from The National Child Traumatic Stress Network (2006, p. 10).

predict traumatic stress reactions (Barenbaum et al., 2004; Caffo & Belaise, 2003; Litz et al., 2002; Ozer et al., 2003). If family is not available, there are often community resources that may substitute and the crisis intervenor should be knowledgeable about them.

2. *Engage in focused problem solving.* Once the crisis intervenor has been able to formulate an accurate, comprehensive statement about the student's perception of the situation, identifying all of the sources of concern, it will be possible to begin the process of exploring potential strategies to improve or resolve the emotionally hazardous situation. Jointly, the crisis intervenor and pupil review the strategies explored and select one for trial. The outcome should be an action plan. This is much like the problem solving that occurs in counseling, but must be preceded by the steps previously mentioned. Moving too quickly to problem solving is a common mistake of novices. However effective the problem solution is, the very process of turning attention to the future, away from the past, is beneficial in and of itself. Some solutions may involve actions by others such as teachers or school administrators. To the extent necessary, the crisis intervenor may act as an intermediary communicating with authorities on the child's behalf.

3. *Focus on self-concept.* Any action strategies must be implemented in the context of

what the student thinks is possible to accomplish. The crisis situation often leads to a diminution in self-esteem and the acceptance of blame for the crisis. With an emphasis on how well the child coped given the situation so far and how the person has arrived at a strategy for moving forward, there can be a restoration of the damaged view of the self. Crisis intervenors can emphasize what positive there is in the situation, even if it seems relatively minor. Even the victim of a sexual assault can be acknowledged for at least surviving physically.

4. *Encourage self-reliance.* During the process of crisis intervention, the student will have temporarily become dependent on the crisis intervenor for direct advice, for stimulating action, and for supplying hope. This is a temporary situation and before the crisis intervention is over, the crisis intervenor must spend some time planning ways to restore the student to self-reliance and self-confidence. As indicated in crisis intervention this is done by consciously moving into a position of equality with the student, sharing the responsibility and authority. Although earlier the crisis intervenor may have been very directive, eventually he or she strives to return to a more democratic stance. Techniques such as one-downsmanship, where the counselor acknowledges the pupil's contribution to problem solving, while minimizing the

counselor's own contribution (Caplan, 1970), permit the counselee to leave the crisis intervention with a sense of accomplishment. Helping individuals to find alternative rewards and sources of satisfaction (i.e., using problem-focused coping), is most helpful.

Developmental Issues in Crisis Counseling

A child of 5 and an adolescent of 16 have radically different faculties for dealing with information and reacting to events. Differences in cognitive, social, and emotional development mean that they will respond differently to hazards and will need to be counseled differently should they develop a crisis reaction. The same event, the death of a parent for example, may be a crisis for a preschooler as well as a high school senior, but each will react and cope with the event differently.

Counseling with younger children often involves the use of nonverbal materials, many more directive leads in order to elicit and reflect feelings, and a focus on concrete concerns as well as fantasy. The use of drawing for example has proved very effective in getting children to express what has happened to them (Morgan & White, 2003).

Traditional talk therapies such as nondirective counseling capitalize on a client's capacity for rational thought and high level of moral development and are more likely to be effective with adolescents. With adolescents, the school psychologist can also acknowledge and use the age-appropriate crisis of establishing an identity.

In reviewing the crisis intervention principles and procedures just outlined, it seems reasonable to expect that younger children would have a greater difficulty acknowledging a crisis, and would be more prone to use immature defenses such as denial and projection to avoid coping with a crisis (Allen, Dlugokinski, Cohen, & Walker, 1999). In contrast, an adolescent might use more advanced defenses such as rationalization and intellectualization. In counseling children, more time might be spent on exploring reactions and feelings to the crisis situation and establishing support systems that engage in lengthy problem solving. With older adolescents, then, it may be possible to focus much more on establishing reasonable expectations and avoiding false reassurance, as well as spending more time on focused problem-solving activities.

SPECIFIC RESPONDING TO VIOLENCE AND DISASTER

Crisis intervention and counseling for children and youth subject to the traumatic stress of acts of violence is not greatly different from the generic principles of counseling and intervention outlined above. The impact of disasters and acts of violence is typically a loss for the affected individual. The loss may be of human life or of a sense of safety and security or of shelter. Grieving and mourning these losses will be among the objectives of the counseling intervention. It is important, however, to acknowledge that the combination of traumatic stress and grief generated by a sudden traumatic loss create unique problems for crisis counselors. Associated with traumatic stress are emotional numbing and avoidance of trauma reminders. These symptoms can greatly interfere with the process of grieving. Given this reality it is typically a good idea that trauma work takes precedence over grief work.

The common goal of responding to children experiencing situational crises is to prevent the formation of posttraumatic stress disorder (PTSD). This syndrome, first identified among military combat veterans, also manifests itself in children. Their reaction is similar to that in adults, although their reactions may be somewhat different and the symptoms will vary with age (American Psychiatric Association, 2000).

Three clusters of symptoms are typically associated with PTSD: (a) reexperiencing through dreams and nightmares or flashbacks, (b) numbing/avoidance with a resulting loss of positive affect, and (c) hyperarousal and nervousness. In the United States, survivors of Hurricane Hugo were characterized by (a) intrusive phenomena coupled with active avoidance of negative experiences (bad dreams, repetitive images, upset thoughts, fear reactions); (b) emotional numbing along with passive avoidance of emotionally unrewarding activities (anhedonia, isolation, avoidance); and (c) arousal problems (somatic complaints, easy startling, sleep disturbance, and attention deficits). It should be noted that anhedonia (the absence of pleasurable feelings in situations where they are normally present), learning/memory problems and attention problems, although common following a traumatic event, are associated problems and do not predict later PTSD status. Children are more likely than adults to have symptomotology related to aggression, anxiety, depression and regression (Mazza

& Overstreet, 2000). It is important to note that traumatic stress reactions are to a significant extent dependent upon the child's level of development (Joshi & Lewin, 2004). Especially among younger children, traumatic stress reactions are less connected to the stressor and more likely to take the form of generalized fear and anxiety.

It is certainly not true that all children, if untreated, will develop PTSD. In fact, as was mentioned at the beginning of this chapter recovery is the norm (NIMH, 2001). Estimates vary by extent and type of trauma, but a conservative estimate is that 12–15% of children may develop PTSD six or more months following a disaster (La Greca, Silverman, Vernberg, & Prinstein, 1996; McDermott & Palmer, 1999). In a review of the literature Saigh, Yasik, Sack & Koplewicz (1999) report that rates of psychological trauma among children and adolescents (as indicated by the presence of PTSD) vary considerably both within and between crisis event types (with rates of PTSD ranging from 0–95%). Some may even develop long-term characterological patterns of behavior following a disaster, such as fearfulness (Honig, Grace, Lindy, Newman, & Titchener, 1999). These character traits, exhibited later in life, may originate as negative coping responses to the trauma.

Severity of symptoms is related to the magnitude of exposure to the event itself. However, symptoms in children may be more severe if there is parental discord or distress and if there are subsequent stressors, such as lack of housing following a disaster (La Greca et al., 1996). The traumatic death of a family member also increases the risk of stress reactions (Applied Research and Consulting et al., 2002; Bradach & Jordan, 1995). Symptoms may also be heightened among ethnic minorities (La Greca et al., 1996).

La Greca and her colleagues (1996) discuss five factors which are related to the development of severe symptomatology: (a) exposure to disaster-related experiences, including perceived life threats; (b) preexisting child characteristics such as poverty and illness; (c) the recovery environment including social support; (d) the child's coping skills; and (e) intervening stressful life events during recovery.

With this model in mind, intervention must proceed to supply an appropriate recovery environment that is suited to a child's characteristics and facilitates coping. Determination of what intervention is appropriate for a given student should be based on assessment of risk for psychological traumatization ("psychological triage"). When it comes to the immediate crisis intervention response it is clear that one size does not fit all (McNally, Bryant, & Ehlers, 2003).

Psychological Triage

Following acts of violence or a disaster, the medical workers who first arrive and find widespread injury will perform medical triage to establish who is most in need of help. The process of psychological triage (which is obviously secondary in importance to medical triage) is similar and involves deciding who is at risk for psychological trauma following a traumatic event. The following are factors that need to be taken into account in deciding which students need what specific crisis interventions.

Physical Proximity

All individuals directly experiencing or witnessing an act of violence or an injury or loss during a disaster should be considered to be at high-risk to be significantly affected by the event. The physically closer the individual is, the greater the likelihood of the person becoming a psychological trauma victim (Galea et al., 2002; Pynoos et al., 1987).

Emotional Proximity

In addition to physical proximity, emotional proximity is also a consideration when attempting to identify the psychological victims of violence. Individuals who have an emotional attachment to someone who was injured or killed are at risk for psychological trauma. The stronger the attachment, the more likely it is that the individual will be traumatized (Galea et al., 2002; Kolaitis et al., 2004; NIMH, 2001; Pfefferbaum et al., 2000).

Perception of danger or threat may also increase emotional proximity. Following a disaster or violence, children who have developed a concern for the well-being and safety of themselves, a family member, or other emotionally significant person may also be at risk for psychological trauma (Shaw, 2003). The trauma is likely to heighten the fears for others, since there is concrete evidence now available that bad things can happen to people

Previous Trauma

Individuals known to be vulnerable because of previous trauma, loss or preexisting psychopathology should be considered at high risk (Galea et al., 2000). Special attention needs to be given to students who have experienced other traumas within the past year and/or those who have experienced prior crises similar in nature to the current crisis event. How an individual perceives a crisis event will have a lot to do with his or her frame of reference at the time of the event. If the individual has experienced numerous recent significant traumas and losses, a relatively minor or remote crisis event might be sufficient to cause psychological trauma. For example, Nader, Pynoos, Fairbanks, & Frederick (1990) reported that children who have experienced previous traumas had renewed posttraumatic stress disorder symptoms related to the previous experience, following a sniper attack at their school.

Acute Stress Reactions

Any individual whose response to the event is out of proportion to the degree of exposure to the crisis event should be evaluated next. These individuals may not have the intellectual or emotional problem solving skills necessary to cope with the experience (Brock, 2006). Those conducting psychological triage must determine whether the psychological victims are either *over-* or *underreacting* to the event based upon their degree of exposure. Denial, blocking, and/or emotional numbing of the unpleasant reality of an act of violence is often part of the early reactions to a crisis event. For example, individuals directly exposed to a shooting and not reacting to it, should be monitored closely. We should also be aware that delayed stress reactions are possible following a trauma.

Psychopathology

Although the acute stress associated with psychological trauma is not necessarily a sign of mental illness (it is typically a common reaction to abnormal circumstances), a history of emotional disturbance can lower one's capacity to cope with an unforeseen crisis (American Psychiatric Association, 2000; Brock, 2002b).

The family's mental health should also be considered. For example, following a school bus kidnapping, Terr (1983) found "relationships between the clinical severity of the children's posttraumatic conditions and their preexisting family pathology" (p. 1550). If family members are not functioning well to support the child's coping, it will obviously be more difficult for the child to surmount a traumatic event.

Lack of Resources

A lack of resources can make it much more difficult for children and adults to cope with traumatic events. For example, a lack of material resources such as money, food, housing, and transportation can turn a moderately stressful event into a crisis. According to the American Psychiatric Association (2000), "There is some evidence that social supports . . . may influence the development of Acute Stress Disorder" (p. 470). Internal resources include intelligence, skill in problem solving, personality, and temperament. Individuals with disabilities may use up these resources in coping with their disability and not have extra resources available to deal with violence, disasters, and terrorism. These internal personal resources must also be evaluated in the attempt to identify children and adults at risk for psychological trauma (Brock, 2002b).

Secondary Screening

All individuals classified as being at risk should be closely monitored to assess their need for mental health referrals (Brock, 2006). Crisis intervention will be provided by school and community mental health professionals, unless the disaster is so widespread that state or national assistance is forthcoming. It may or may not be provided at school site. The goals of triage include identification of students and staff members most significantly affected by crisis and then providing these individuals with immediate psychological first-aid assistance.

Screening

After the initial psychological triage has identified all individuals judged to be at risk due to either involvement and exposure or other risk factors, the next step is to survey the entire school population for signs of posttraumatic stress (Brock, 2006). Mass screening is especially important following crises that affect large numbers of students. During these situations it is unlikely that the crisis workers will be able to identify all students significantly affected by the event. Thus, teachers and parents should be enlisted in the process. Parents and teachers are the most likely to see and be affected by a student's crisis reactions. In his discussion of mass screening, Klingman (1988) suggests using "observation of signs of behavior maladaptation, child paper-and-pencil products (e.g., free writing, drawing), anxiety scales administered to children, and the identification of absentees" (pp. 210–211).

An effective referral system needs to educate teachers and other adults about reactions to look for among youth following a crisis. Staff in-service, both during and before a crisis event, would be important for teachers. School newsletter articles both before and during a crisis event would serve a similar purpose for parents. Finally, it is important to note that the media can be very helpful. Newspapers and broadcast media can quickly and efficiently alert parents and the community in general to signs, symptoms, and reactions suggesting the need for crisis intervention and where assistance can be obtained (Brock, 2006).

Self-Referral

All students need to be informed about the availability of assistance in coping with acts of violence or disasters. Especially following crises affecting large numbers of students, it is possible that crisis workers, teachers, and parents may overlook or fail to recognize signs suggesting the need for a crisis intervention. Other students may not display behavioral signs of distress. Thus, students need to know where to go for assistance on their own. This information can be disseminated in a variety of ways, such as public address announcements, school assemblies, and teacher-led discussions (Brock et al., 2001).

Parent Involvement

Because of the sudden and unexpected nature of situational crises, it is not always possible to contact a student's family right away. Some students will need to be seen immediately and in a crisis situation this is an appropriate action. However, we recommend as soon as possible, crisis workers obtain parent permission for referral or continuing crisis intervention. Parents also need to know about the distress their children are experiencing so that they may participate in lending their child emotional and physical support. Natural disasters often strike parents as well as children. Since parent adjustment is related to a child's recovery (Qouta, Punamäki, & El Sarraj, 2003), seeing that parents get assistance and counseling also is important.

Disaster Response Counseling

Young and his colleagues (Young, Ford, Ruzek, Friedman, & Gusman, 1999) emphasize three concepts in intervention: Protect, Direct, and Connect. It is important to *protect* children from further harm by moving them to a secure location, and attending to their basic needs for food,

drink, sleep, and shelter. To relieve tension, it is also helpful to provide a place for play and relaxation. Children need to be protected from the gaze of onlookers and the curious, and they need to be spared watching scenes of the traumatic event replayed on television. Helpers need to be *direct* with children and take an active role in managing their environment. Since parents may be disabled by the disaster, it is comforting to see some adult taking control and making decisions. *Connecting* means to establish a relationship through verbal and nonverbal means with the child. This relationship will be important to help the child manage fear, anxiety, panic and grief. Simply being physically present with the child can lessen anxiety. Connecting also refers to the need to reunite children with parents and loved ones, and connecting children to knowledge and resources through anticipatory guidance.

An important intervention goal following a disaster is to restore social resources. Providing social supports is particularly difficult during times of crisis. With a disaster, whole communities are affected. There is a disruption of both schools and social services. There is often an absence of adults with whom children can process feelings of loss, dread, and vulnerability. Support groups can provide one vehicle for feeling connected to others and working through these feelings. Ceballo (2000) describes a short-term supportive intervention group based in the school for children exposed to urban violence. Her groups are designed to (a) validate and normalize children's emotional reactions to violence, (b) help children restore a sense of control over certain aspects of their environment, (c) develop safety skills for dealing with the environment in the future, (d) understand the process of grief and mourning, and (e) minimize the influence of PTSD symptoms on educational tasks and other daily life events. Such structured support groups can promote resiliency and promote constructive coping with problems.

Bibliotherapy may also be useful following a disaster. A particularly useful resource for children is a book entitled *I'll Know What To Do: A Kid's Guide to Natural Disasters* by Mark, Layton and Chesworth (1997). The authors focus on four concepts they view as fundamental to recovery: information, communication, reassurance, and the reestablishment of routine. They explore children's feelings that often emerge in the aftermath of a disaster, and offer useful techniques to help young people cope with them.

Galante and Foa (1986) worked in groups with children in one school throughout the school year following a major Italian earthquake. The children were encouraged to explore fears, mistaken understandings, and feelings connected to death and injury from the disaster using discussion, drawing, and role playing. Most participants, except those who experienced a death in the family, showed a reduction in symptoms.

Another feature of disasters and terrorist acts is a lowered sense of control over one's destiny and heightened fear of the unknown. Thus, a focus on returning a sense of empowerment to children will be important. If children can be directed to participate in restorative activities and take some actions to mitigate the results of the disaster, no matter how small, they can begin to rebuild an important sense of efficacy.

Finally, there may be issues of survivor guilt, if there is widespread loss of life or property. Survivor guilt is a strong feeling of culpability often induced among individuals who survive a situation that results in the death of valued others. Those spared, but witnessing the devastation of others, may have extreme feelings of guilt that will need to be addressed. Children, particularly ascribe fantastical causes to the effects they see. Consequently, some may need to explore their magical thinking in counseling or play therapy about why they escaped injury or loss.

The Crisis Intervenor in Crisis

It is most important to consider a crisis intervenor's feelings and adaptive behavior at a time of crisis. Crisis intervenors are human and often forced to witness horrible things happening to children. School psychologists, just as other emergency workers, will exhibit symptoms of stress (Bolnik & Brock, 2005). For example, it is clear that disaster workers such as fire fighters are adversely affected by responding to a crisis (Everly, Lating, & Mitchell, 2000). Those responding to airline disasters seem to have a particularly difficult time, but all emergency workers are subject to the same reactions as the victims of the crisis. Responses of crisis intervenors are individual and may not be apparent to an observer or supervisor. Often working in the aftermath of traumatic event can stimulate the recall of a crisis intervenor's own past experience of trauma and loss. Training and supervision permits the avoidance or reduction of countertransference while serving as a helper during a crisis.

In a sense, then, a crisis in a child is also a time of crisis for the crisis intervenor. Because the event may have come up suddenly and unexpectedly and because the child's problem may be quite serious, the crisis intervenor is likely to experience heightened anxiety and momentary disorganization. A number of principles for the crisis intervenor's behavior may also be identified.

1. *Remove distracters and other stressors acting on you.* Set aside your other duties and roles. Order your priorities and realize your limits. Give as much time as you can to the crisis and put off what is not urgent.

2. *Avoid impulsive action.* You must act quickly but you should also take time to plan in a time of crisis. Gather your thoughts and think through the possibilities prior to seeing the affective parties in a crisis situation.

3. *Delegate authority.* The medical response to a crisis is the triage process. Not only are the most important risks to the patient assessed and identified, but also roles are assigned to various medical personnel. In the schools there is the ideal of the multidisciplinary team, and with effort it can be a reality. In times of crisis, by delegating authority among school psychologists, counselors, social workers, school nurses, administrators, and teachers, there will be a minimum of duplication of effort and a greater likelihood that professionals will be tackling those tasks they can do best.

4. *Model calmness in a way consonant with your personality.* Although Carl Rogers (1957), for example, argues that the counselor should always be genuine and honest with the client, there are times when such openness may not be in the best interest of the client. If you are overly upset and angry about the child's predicament and act it out in front of the client, it may have the effect of getting in the way of emotion-focused coping.

5. *Be prepared.* The more you are informed about the particular crisis the child is experiencing, the easier will be the process of working with him or her. School psychologists should anticipate that various crises will occur and to expend some energy into planning and executing prevention programs that will keep hazardous situations from developing into crises for large numbers of children.

6. ***Seek supervision and debriefing.*** You may help yourself and others cope in the aftermath of a crisis by knowing yourself and respecting your limitations; by asking for special support from your family; by taking care of yourself physically, by supporting other members of the team; by using humor; by recognizing that you, yourself, will be impacted by the crisis; and by talking to others. In doing these things you are serving as an important model to children and other adults.

The goal of a debriefing is to detect burnout among crisis workers and move toward an individualized stress management intervention when it is detected. The debriefing itself can provide emotion-focused coping, in that it permits the expression of ideas and emotions in a psychologically safe environment.

Other Adults in Crisis

An important feature of a traumatic event is the fact that the adults in the school as well as the children are effected. For example, the teachers, administrators and guidance staff would be equally traumatized by an earthquake or an airplane crashing into the school. The school caregivers can be as traumatized as the children. They will need assistance in coping with the aftermath of the crisis as much as the children will. It is likely that outside crisis response assistance will be needed to help an entire community deal with disaster and mayhem associated with violence.

PREVENTION ACTIVITIES

Most traumatic events and other emotional hazards are not very common. The rarity of the events also leads to problems in prevention. Prevention usually is based on understanding the dynamics and causes of the precipitating event. Because these events are unusual, and many disasters are considered "Acts of God," it may not be very cost effective to address preventing the specific event. This is not to say that there are not things to be done with respect to primary prevention (e.g., upgrading building codes to reduce the impact of earthquakes and wind storms); rather the focus of prevention is secondary, and more focused on generic preparation to respond to all kinds of crisis rather than on preventing specific events from occurring.

Drawing heavily from an earlier account of crisis response planning (Brock et al., 2001; Brock,

Nickerson, Reeves, & Jimerson, 2008) and the (U.S. Department of Homeland Security, 2004), this next section reviews how to prepare for the crisis response following situational crises.

Creating a Crisis Response Team

A critical prevention activity for a crisis is to be prepared in advance to respond. A single person can be prepared, but an effective response demands that a team of professionals be developed and trained to fill specific roles. The teams can be made up locally, regionally or even nationally, depending on resources available. It is recommended that more than one individual be designated to fill each of the roles described below. This is designed to account for the possible physical or psychological unavailability of crisis response team members (e.g., due to illness, injury, or psychological traumatization stemming from the crisis event).

Defining Crisis Response Roles and Responsibilities

The first step in building a team of individuals to manage a crisis when it occurs is to define specific crisis response roles. As indicated by the Incident Command Structure (ICS; U.S. Department of Homeland Security, 2004), individuals should be identified to be responsible for each of the crisis team components indicated in Figure 41.1.

Incident Command

This component includes the School Incident Commander. Typically a school administrator, the incident commander is the person who coordinates the response to crises. When a crisis response involves multiple agencies (e.g., school, police, fire), the ICS will employ a unified command. Within the command section, a Public Information Officer works with the media and/or other agencies that require information about the crisis. This individual is responsible for establishing procedures for working with broadcast and print journalists. In districts that have a media spokesperson, this individual will naturally fill this role. Immediately following a crisis, the public information officer would be responsible for the dissemination of crisis facts (Nye, 1997) and for ensuring that the media is able to assist and not hinder the response.

Operations

Individuals working in this section are responsible for immediate response needs, establishing

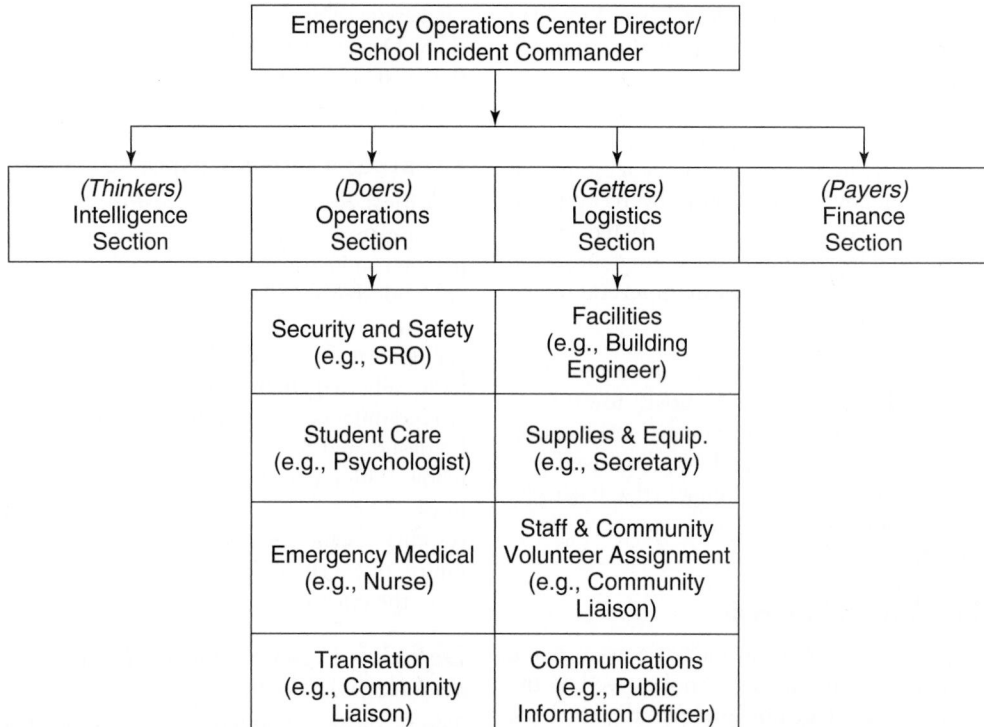

FIGURE 41.1 The Incident Command Structure (ICS) and examples of school staff members who may fill these roles.

situational control, and restoring a normal school routine. The school psychologist is a particularly important member of this section as activities typically viewed as "crisis intervention" would be placed within the Operations section.

Working within the Operations section within Student Care, the Crisis Intervention Coordinator should have a clear understanding of the objectives, methods, and limitations of school crisis intervention. Typically, an individual with a background in school social work, psychology or counseling would be assigned to this position. The crisis intervention coordinator would have several planning responsibilities. These would include the development of psychological triage and crisis intervention referral procedures, the development of psychological first aid resources, and the identification of community mental health referral sources. Immediately following a crisis event the crisis intervention coordinator's responsibilities would include identifying psychological trauma victims, ensuring the provision of psychological first aid and identifying those who may need professional mental health interventions.

Also working within the Operations Section, the Emergency Medical Coordinator is typically a school nurse. Specific preparedness responsibilities would include providing first aid training (e.g., CPR), ensuring that medical first aid materials and equipment are available, and establishing communication links with local doctors, hospitals, and emergency medical personnel. In some cases the medical liaison's secondary prevention responsibilities may include participation in, or management of, the medical triage of crisis victims. However, in most cases emergency medical personnel (e.g., paramedics) will take up this role. In these instances the medical liaison would facilitate communication between paramedics and the crisis response team. Once immediate medical needs are taken care of, the medical liaison would facilitate communication between hospitals, doctors, and other medical personnel and the crisis response team. Additionally, the medical liaison would assist in communicating to parents and staff the medical conditions of those who were injured.

Another key member of the Operations Section is the Security and Safety Coordinator. Although often a school administrator, in some cases a school and/or a district may have its own security personnel who will fill this role. Ideally this person will have ongoing contacts with local police and/or sheriff's departments. Planning activities would include general safety planning, the development of plans designed to ensure student safety following a crisis (e.g., staff identification, bomb threat procedures, student evacuation procedures, etc.), and working with law enforcement to ensure that they are familiar with school crisis response team procedures. During a crisis response this individual would implement safety and security procedures, and facilitate communication between local law enforcement and the school.

Intelligence

Individuals working in this section are charged with the tasks of (a) collecting, evaluating, and disseminating incident information (crisis facts) and intelligence to the incident commander(s); (b) preparing status reports; (c) knowing the status of resources assigned to an incident; and (d) developing/documenting the plan, including incident objectives and strategies. Members of this section are constantly asking questions; evaluating information; planning; and making use of recorders, logs, radios, campus maps, and buses.

Logistics

Individuals working in this section are responsible for obtaining the resources needed to manage the crisis. These resources include personnel, equipment/supplies, and services. When members of the Operations section needs something, they get it from Logistics. Members of this section also work with the Intelligence section to develop resources for future needs.

Finance/Administration

Individuals working in this section are responsible for keeping a record of all expenses, and establishing when the agency requires finance and other administrative support services (e.g., payroll, claims and reimbursements). The records of expense become particularly important if federal or state funds are later allocated to the response.

After having begun to acquire the knowledge necessary to prepare for the school crisis response, response planners will be in a position to begin team-building efforts. Although each of the team-building activities discussed in this section are essential to the comprehensive school crisis response, obtaining administrative support is prerequisite to system-wide crisis preparedness. Thus, while all of the activities described in this section may occur simultaneously, this action comes first.

Obtaining Administrative Support

If the crisis response planning effort is a "top-down" effort (i.e., it is initiated by school administration), then this step will be relatively straightforward. It will require administration to be aware of factors important to initiation and implementation of any school change effort. On the other hand, if the crisis response planning effort is a "bottom-up" effort, then obtaining administrative support will be more involved.

When crisis response planning is initiated by nonadministrative personnel, the authors recommend as a first step the formation of a Crisis Response Planning Committee (CRPC). This committee should be representative of the district or the school(s) within which the planning takes place. CRPC efforts should focus on obtaining and disseminating the knowledge needed to undertake crisis response planning, and then begin to develop an outline of a crisis preparedness procedure. At this point the committee will find itself in a position to approach school and/or district administration regarding the desire to institutionalize crisis response planning.

It may not be surprising to find some administrations cool to this type of planning. There are many competing demands placed on today's schools. This fact combined with the unpleasant feelings generated by considering traumatic circumstances, may understandably result in resistance to crisis planning. As with any school change effort, timing is critical to the initiation of school crisis response preparedness. It is important to keep in mind that there will come a time in the life of every school and school district when it is more receptive to crisis preparedness. Unfortunately, this is often immediately after a significant crisis event.

Making the School Safe in a Crisis
Danger Procedures

Each school should have a way of announcing that danger is imminent. It may be a siren or a particular bell sequence. Usually one is already in place to warn of fires. To be prepared, school staff members need to be trained to recognize and know exactly what to do when a signal indicates that an act of violence or disaster is occurring. During a terrorist attack, for example, staff must know that students are to be directed to a secure room, doors locked, cover taken underneath tables or desks, windows closed, and curtains drawn. Drills will be helpful in reinforcing these instructions.

Emergency Evacuations

Some acts of school violence and many disasters (e.g., fire, plane crash, toxic waste or chemical spills, bomb threats, etc.) may necessitate the evacuation of students from one location to another. The first step in developing an evacuation plan is to identify potential safe areas that students could be moved to in the event that their school and/or their classrooms are no longer safe. Ideally, the area chosen would be large enough to accommodate the entire student body. Examples of such locations include shopping centers, community recreation facilities, business offices, and churches. In most cases, existing fire drill evacuation routes can be adapted to other potential emergencies requiring evacuation. However, the evacuation procedure should contain alternative evacuation routes in the event that the primary evacuation routes or safe areas are affected by the crisis event. In addition, be aware that terrorists have been known to study these evacuation routes and cause an evacuation in order to concentrate potential victims in a particular location.

Accounting for Students and Staff

It is also important to develop plans and procedures that will allow the school to quickly and efficiently account for students and staff members following acts of violence or other crises. Reporting methods may include the use of alphabetical listings of all students and staff or class lists.

Reuniting Students with Parents

Facilitating the development of procedures for reuniting students with their families following crisis events is yet another task. The authors have seen literally hundreds of parents arriving simultaneously to locate their children following a school shooting, which resulted in incredible confusion and great emotional distress when reunification did not occur efficiently.

Crowd Control

Crowd control procedures complement student and parent reunion procedures. In advance of a crisis areas need to be designated where parents can wait until they can be reunited with their children. Possible locations may include school cafeterias, multipurpose rooms, playground areas, and libraries. The school will need to be able to communicate with large groups of people at one time. This will mean making sure that bullhorns or public address systems are available.

Traffic Management

Traffic management issues include plans for keeping driveways clear to allow emergency response vehicle access to school grounds. As a rule, traffic management procedures should encourage school visitors to park on side streets during times of crisis. The need to clear a location for an emergency medical helicopter landing site may also play a role in traffic management.

Involving Community Resources

It is useful to obtain a prior written agreement regarding coordination of the law enforcement or medical personnel in response to school crisis events. This document should detail the point at which responsibility for a situation would be assumed by law enforcement or other civil agencies. When preparing for the involvement of law enforcement in school crisis events (such as school shootings), it is important to provide them with a detailed floor plan of the school showing entrances, windows, roof latches, ventilation systems, and so on, and current estimates of the number and identities of staff and students in each class area. Often school yearbooks or class pictures become handy tools for helping law enforcement to identify students. Police should also have a master key to the school and know if there are parking permits used to identify student and staff cars.

Referral Planning Procedures

Preparing for the crisis intervention response is yet another critical crisis preparedness procedures. Clearly, it will be difficult to meet the needs of those who have been psychologically traumatized by acts of violence or disaster without carefully developed crisis intervention referral options.

Referral planning procedures will typically involve staff in-service and training. Given that an effective crisis intervention provides such support immediately, it is clearly desirable to have as many staff members as possible receive in-service instruction. At a minimum, every member of the school's guidance staff should have a clear understanding of the principles, goals, and limitations of psychological first aid.

In addition, professional mental health counseling resources need to be identified. The identification of community resources will involve the survey of both community mental health agencies and private practitioners. Community agencies are typically well known to most school psychologists, social workers, and counselors. School district personnel should have little difficulty developing a comprehensive list of local community mental health agencies, but it will be important to verify expertise in crisis intervention. The identification of private mental health practitioner referrals is more difficult, especially in urban communities where there are large numbers of licensed professionals.

Referral planning must acknowledge that not all individuals exposed to crises will require immediate individual assistance or eventually require a professional mental health referral. Depending on circumstances and resources, many students and staff members may be able to independently integrate the trauma into their lives. Although individuals not obviously in crisis or at high risk will not be made intervention priorities when it comes to making treatment decisions, there are clearly ways in which schools can and should facilitate the process of crisis resolution. Referred to by Brock et al. (2006) as psychological education, large numbers of students can effectively receive intervention through group and classroom discussions of the crisis event. With preparation, and if comfortable in the role, the classroom teacher can be an effective provider of this type of crisis intervention.

Making the School Safe in Advance of a Traumatic Event

Individuals who are not part of the school community may commit acts of terrorism and violence. They come from the outside and commit their crimes on the school site. Aside from making it difficult to enter the school grounds, it is difficult to do more in terms of prevention for these types of events. More can be done, however, in reducing the violence that takes place in schools instigated by students. But school violence does not only come from children who are bullies; alienated, isolated and rejected children are also capable of explosive violence. To create safer schools, there must be a close examination of student discipline, the openness of the school to outsiders, the school climate, and the physical arrangement of the campus.

Student Discipline

The School Safety Check Book (National School Safety Center, 1990) advocates the establishment of written discipline rules that clearly differentiate between an infraction (unacceptable behavior such as lying and inappropriate language) and a crime (behavior that violates the law such as assault and vandalism). Rules need to identify specific unacceptable behaviors and their consequences. Rules must be reasonable, and should allow for due process and appeal. In particular, school disciplinary codes must cover school fights. There is a fine line between a schoolyard altercation involving pushing and shoving and criminal assault or battery. Increasingly schools are moving the line by identifying battery when it occurs. One school district experienced a dramatic decrease in the number of fights after implementing a policy requiring students involved in fights to make a court appearance and pay a $200 fine.

Campus Visitors

Schools as public institutions are open to visitors, but the school can require that visitors identify themselves and can set guidelines for access. Signs should be posted at all school entry points directing visitors to check in at the school office. It is important to establish policies that ask all staff members to approach and identify unfamiliar campus visitors and ask them to sign in, if they have not already done so. After having signed in, all campus visitors should be issued identification badges. Staff should be trained to, and be comfortable with, challenging visitors without badges.

Employee and Student Identification

To further assist in the identification of campus visitors, it is also helpful if students and employees are issued their own personal identification cards. If funds are available, a system of photo-identification badges increases security.

School Climate

Positive school climates are both the result of, and contribute to, secure and safe schools. Stephens (1994) advocates creating a positive school climate by building pride and ownership in the school, making the campus welcoming (e.g., by having staff greet students as they arrive and being present during class changes), and having high administrator visibility (including class visitations and attendance at special events).

On the other hand, Hyman and Snook (1999) argue that educator policies and practices, such as corporal punishment, and discipline that is administered inconsistently, can contribute to student misbehavior. These practices lead to student alienation, which in turn leads to acts of violence.

Resiliency and school climate research provide important data regarding factors influencing the climate of the school. Resiliency and school climate improves as children are able to form a positive relationship with a caring adult. Many vehicles are available for making this kind of adult-child interaction possible, including schools within schools, use of community mentors and providing sufficient numbers of school counselors. Dwyer, Osher, and Warger (1998) and Strepling (1997) have reviewed the school climate literature. Their findings on the characteristics of effective schools, and safe and secure classrooms are summarized in Table 41.2. Students feel secure when there is a sense of community and there is sufficient routine for students to know what to expect.

School Environment

Often a relationship exists between student and staff behavior, and their surroundings. Crowe (1990) describes the *Crime Prevention Through Environmental Design* theory, which asserts that the appropriate physical "design" and effective use of the "built environment" decreases the incidence of crime and prevalence of fear. Crowe identifies significant problem areas on school campuses, including parking lots and lockers, and suggests potential remedies.

Brooks (1993) suggests evaluating patterns of student congregation, paying particular attention to shifts in clusters of students, rival groups binding together, students attending events they normally do not attend, sudden appearance of underground publications, and parents withdrawing their children from school due to fear that something might happen. These are warning signs from the physical environment that should be monitored.

School Security

Many schools have their own security personnel or have become "beats" for local police. Models of campus security, described by Grant (1993), include "officer friendly" and "campus cop." In the former the police officer has a public relations role; educates children on safety, gangs, and

TABLE 41.2 Characteristics of Effective Schools and Safe/Secure Classrooms

1. Focus on academic achievement and foster enthusiasm for learning
2. Involve families in meaningful ways
3. Develop links to the community
4. Emphasize positive relationships among students and staff. Teachers and students learn and use each other's names
5. Treat students with equal respect
6. Discuss safety issues openly
7. Create ways for students to share their concerns and help students feel safe expressing their feelings
8. Have in place a system for referring children who are suspected of being abused or neglected
9. Offer extended day programs for children
10. Promote good citizenship and character, and build a community of learners (using collaboration between students and teacher, school, and home)
11. Identify problems and assess progress toward solutions. Classroom meetings are held to discuss issues and solve problems
12. Support students in making the transition to adult life and the workplace
13. Develop and consistently enforce school wide rules that are clear, broad-based, and fair
14. Classroom management includes firm, fair, and consistent rules and procedures
15. Use of learning centers and the opportunity for cooperative group work
16. Leisure areas exist for discussions, down time, and reading
17. Books and magazines readily available
18. Displays of students' in-progress and completed work
19. Plants and objects that assist students in developing an identity of the classroom space as "ours"

substance abuse; and is viewed as a positive role model. In the later model, the officer's role is to enforce laws. Combining both models, Grant also describes the development of the *School Liaison Officer Program* in Richmond, British Columbia. In this program police officers attend sporting events, dances, field trips; have casual conversations with students; investigate school crimes; follow up on disclosures; and provide enforcement. Schools have also invoked technology for surveillance as part of their security approach. The ultimate, perhaps, is the use of metal detectors to screen for weapons. A balance must be struck between adequate monitoring for safety and the establishment of a friendly, caring school climate. There is a trade-off between control and sensitivity to educational needs and traditions.

RESOURCES FOR MANAGING CRISES

Internet Resources

A resource for obtaining background knowledge that has become increasingly valuable is the Internet. Recently there has been significant growth in the number of web sites of interest to school crisis response planners. A specific site the authors have found to be helpful is the National Center for PTSD (www.dartmouth.edu/dms/ptsd). This Center and its web site are supported by the U.S. Department of Veteran Affairs. It provides information on a broad range of research and training programs. A helpful document found within this site is "Information About PTSD." Also found on its "Fact Sheets" page are the following: "PTSD in Children," "Survivors of Natural Disasters," and "PTSD and the Family." Viewers can download a PDF file titled "Disaster Mental Health Services: A Guidebook for Clinicians and Administrators." This document, which is in the public domain, addresses the reactions of survivors; how to help survivors, helpers and organizations; and mental health team and program development. PDF files for the *PTSD Research Quarterly* can also be viewed.

Another helpful resource is the U.S. Department of Education's website (www.ed.gov). From the Department's home page, viewers can connect to the "School Safety Resources and Statistics" page. Here the document "Early Warning, Timely Response: A Guide to Safe Schools" can be accessed. A similar resource, the School Violence Virtual Library (www.uncg.edu/edu/

ericcass/violence/index.htm), is produced by the ERIC Counseling and Student Services Clearing house. This web site includes pages for students, parents and practitioners. Topics include "Punishment and Intervention," "School Environment," "Security Measures," "Avoiding Violence," "Dealing with Violent Children," "Crisis Intervention," and "Media Impact."

Finally, in the authors' opinion, one of the best web sites for crisis response planners is operated by the Federal Emergency Management Agency (www.fema.gov). Available in both English and Spanish, it contains a variety of resources which parents and students will also find helpful. By accessing this site's Virtual Library and Electronic Reading Room viewers can browse *FEMA for Kids*, which contains disaster preparedness activities, curriculums and games for children. It also includes resources for adults such as a mental health checklist and a discussion of how to help child victims. Viewers can download a PDF file titled "How to Help Children After a Disaster: A Guidebook for Teachers." The *Preparedness, Training and Exercise* room includes an emergency preparedness checklist and a disaster supply kit list. It also includes suggestions for how to prepare for and respond to a variety of specific crisis events (e.g., nuclear disaster, hazardous materials, wildfires, hurricanes, landslides, mudflows, flood and flash floods, fire, extreme heat, earthquakes, thunderstorms and lightening, tornadoes, tsunamis, volcanoes, and terrorism). Another download is a PDF file titled "Disaster Preparedness Coloring Book." This document includes coloring activities for children and "Action Steps for Adults" on helping children respond to and prepare for a variety of disasters. For additional review of Internet web sites of interest to the school crisis response planner the reader may consult Brock et al. (2001).

Professional Organizations

Both the National Association of School Psychologists (National Emergency Assistance Team, NEAT) and the American Psychological Association (Disaster Response Network) have set up groups of psychologists with special training in crisis intervention. They offer consultation and training prior to disaster and services to victims following a disaster. Many state school psychological associations also have interest groups or committees. Of course, the American Red Cross has been a leader in preparing volunteers of mental health workers to respond during times of crisis and conduct a two-day training course for mental health professionals to help them adapt their existing skills to address the needs of disaster workers and victims. The course leads to becoming a Red Cross Disaster Mental Health Services Volunteer. There are many opportunities for school psychologist with an interest and skill in crisis intervention to helpful beyond the borders of their school districts and to join with others for training, supervision and support. Crisis intervention is an integral role for school psychologists who are first responders during emergencies that occur in children's lives.

REFERENCES

Allen, S. F., Dlugokinski, E L., Cohen, L. A., & Walker, J. L. (1999). Assessing the impact of a traumatic community event on children and assisting with their healing. *Psychiatric Annals*, *29*, 93–98.

American Psychiatric Association. (2000). *Diagnostic and statistical manual of mental disorders* (4th ed., Text Rev.). Washington, DC: Author.

Applied Research and Consulting, Columbia University Mailman School of Public Health, & New York Psychiatric Institute. (2002, May 6). *Effects of the World Trade Center attack on NYC public school students: Initial report to the New York City Board of Education*. New York: New York City Board of Education.

Barenbaum, J., Ruchkin, V., & Schwab-Stone, M. (2004). The psychosocial aspects of children exposed to war: Practice and policy initiatives. *Journal of Child Psychology and Psychiatry*, *45*, 41–62.

Bolnik, L., & Brock, S. E. (2005). The self-reported effects of crisis intervention work on school psychologists. *The California School Psychologist*, *10*, 117–124.

Bradach, K. M., & Jordan, J. R. (1995). Long-term effects of a family history of traumatic death on adolescent individuation. *Death Studies*, *19*, 315–336.

Brock, S. E. (2002a). Estimating the appropriate crisis response. In S. E. Brock, P. J. Lazarus, & S. R. Jimerson (Eds.), *Best practices in school crisis prevention and intervention* (pp. 355–366). Bethesda, MD: National Association of School Psychologists.

Brock, S. E. (2002b). Identifying individuals at risk for psychological trauma. In S. E. Brock, P. J. Lazarus, & S. R. Jimerson (Eds.), *Best practices in school crisis prevention and intervention* (pp. 367–384). Bethesda, MD: National Association of School Psychologists.

Brock, S. E. (2006). *Crisis intervention and recovery: The roles of school-based mental health professionals*. Besthesda, MD: National Association of School Psychologists.

Brock, S. E., Nickerson, A. B., Reeves, M. A., & Jimerson, S. R. (2008). Best practices for school psychologists as members of crisis teams: The PREPaRE Model. In A. Thomas & J. Grimes (Eds.), *Best practices in school psychology* (Vol. 4; pp. 1487–1504). Bethesda, MD: National Association of School Psychologists.

Brock, S. E., Sandoval, J., & Lewis, S. (2001). *Preparing for crises in the schools: A manual for building school crisis response teams* (2nd ed.). New York: Wiley.

Brooks, R. D. (1993, Winter). Signs of the times. *School Safety*, 4–7.

Caffo, E., & Belaise, C. (2003). Psychological aspects of traumatic injury in children and adolescents. *Child & Adolescent Psychiatric Clinics of North America*, *12*, 493–535.

Caplan, G. (1964). *Principles of preventative psychiatry*. New York: Basic Books.

Caplan, G. (1970). *Theory and practice of mental health consultation*. New York: Basic Books.

Ceballo, R. (2000). The neighborhood club: A supportive intervention group for children exposed to urban violence. *American Journal of Orthopsychiatry*, *70*, 401–407.

Crowe, T. D. (1990, Fall). Designing safer schools. *School Safety*, 9–13.

Dwyer, K., Osher, D., & Wagner, C. (1998). *Early warning, timely response: A guide to safe schools*. Washington, DC: U.S. Department of Education.

Everly, G. S., Lating, J. M. & Mitchell, J. T. (2000). Innovations in group crisis intervention. In A. R. Roberts (Ed.), *Crisis intervention handbook: Assessment, treatment and research*. (pp. 77–94). New York: Oxford University Press.

Galante, R., & Foa, D. (1986). An epidemiological study of psychic trauma and treatment effectiveness for children after a natural disaster. *Journal of the American Academy of Child Psychiatry*, *25*, 357–363.

Galea, S., Ahern J., Resnick, H., Kilpatrick, D., Bucuvalas, M., Gold, J., & Vlahov, D. (2002). Psychological sequelae of the September 11 terrorist attacks in New York City. *New England Journal of Medicine*, *346*, 982–987.

Grant, S. A. (1993, Winter). Students respond to "campus cops." *School Safety*, 15–17.

Honig, R. G., Grace, M. C., Lindy, J. D., Newman, C. J., & Titchener, J. L. (1999). Assessing the long-term effects of disasters occurring during childhood and adolescence: Questions of perspective and methodology. In M. Sugar (Ed.), *Trauma and adolescence* (pp. 203–224). Madison, CT: International Universities Press.

Hyman, I., & Snook, P. (1999). *Dangerous schools: What we can do about the physical and emotional abuse of our children*. San Francisco: Jossey-Bass.

Joshi, P. T., & Lewin, S. M. (2004). Disaster, terrorism and children. *Psychiatric Annals, 34,* 710–716.

Klein, D. C., & Lindemann, E. (1961). Preventive intervention in individual and family crisis situations. In G. Caplan (Ed.), *Prevention of mental disorders in children.* (pp. 283–306). New York: Basic Books.

Klingman, A. (1988). School community in disaster: Planning for intervention. *Journal of Community Psychology, 16,* 205–216.

Kolaitis, G., Kotsopoulos, J., Tsiantis, J., Haritaki, S., Rigizou, R., Zacharaki, L., et al. (2003). Posttraumatic stress reactions among children following the Athens earthquake of September 1999. *European Child & Adolescent Psychiatry, 12,* 273–280.

La Greca, A. M., Silverman, W. K., Vernberg, E. M., & Prinstein, M. J. (1996). Symptoms of posttraumatic stress in children after Hurricane Andrew: A prospective study. *Journal of Consulting & Clinical Psychology, 64,* 712–723.

Litz, B. T., Gray, M. J., Bryant, R. A., & Adler, A. (2002). Early intervention for trauma: Current status and future directions. *Clinical Psychology: Science and Practice, 9,* 112–134.

Mark, B. S., Layton, A., & Chesworth, M. (1997). *I'll know what to do: A kid's guide to natural disaster.* Washington DC: Magination Press/American Psychological Association.

Mazza, J. J., & Overstreet, S. (2000). Children and adolescents exposed to community violence: A mental health perspective for school psychologists. *School Psychology Review, 29,* 86–101.

McDermott, B. M. C., & Palmer, L. J. (1999). Post-disaster service provision following proactive identification of children with emotional distress and depression. *Australian & New Zealand Journal of Psychiatry, 33,* 855–863.

McNally, R. J., Bryant, R. A., & Ehlers, A. (2003). Does early psychological intervention promote recovery from posttraumatic stress? *Psychological Sciences in the Public Interest, 4,* 45–80.

Moos, R., & Billings, A. (1984). Conceptualizing and measuring coping resources and processes. In L. Goldberger & S. Breznitz (Eds.), *Handbook of stress: Theoretical and clinical aspects* (pp. 109–145). New York: Macmillan.

Morgan, K. E., & White, P. R. (2003). The functions of art-making in CISD with children and youth. *International Journal of Emergency Mental Health, 5,* 61–76.

Nader, K., Pynoos, R., Fairbanks, L., & Frederick, C. (1990). Children's post-traumatic stress disorder reactions one year after a sniper attack at their school. *American Journal of Psychiatry, 147,* 1526–1530.

Nader, K., & Pynoos, R. (1993). School disaster: Planning and initial interventions. Handbook of

post-disaster interventions. *Journal of Social Behavior and Personality, 8,* 299–320.

National Child Traumatic Stress Network. (2006). *Psychological First Aid: Field Operation Guide,* 2nd Ed. Author: Retrieved August 16, 2008, from www.nctsnet.org/nccts/nav.do?pid=ctr_rsch_prod.

National School Safety Center. (1990). *School safety check book.* Westlake Village, CA: Author.

Nye, K. P. (1997). He's got a gun! *American School Board Journal, 18,* 43–45.

Ozer, E. J., Best, S. R., Lipsey, T. L., & Weiss, D. S. (2003). Predictors of posttraumatic stress disorder and symptoms in adults: A meta-analysis. *Psychological Bulletin, 129,* 52–73.

Pfefferbaum, B., Seale, T. W., McDonald, N. B., Brandt, E. N., Rainwater, S. M., Maynard, B. T., et al. (2000). Posttraumatic stress two years after the Oklahoma City bombing in youths geographically distant from the explosion. *Psychiatry: Interpersonal & Biological Processes, 63,* 358–370.

Pynoos, R. S. (1994). *Traumatic stress and developmental psychopathology in children and adolescents.* Lutherville, MD: Sidran Press.

Pynoos, R. S., Frederick, C., Nader, K., Arroyo, W., Steinberg, A., Eth, S., et al. (1987). Life threat and post traumatic stress in school-age children. *Archives of General Psychiatry, 44,* 1057–1063.

Qouta, S., Punamäki, R. L., & El Sarraj, E. (2003). Prevalence and determinants of PTSD among Palestinian children exposed to military violence. *European Child & Adolescent Psychiatry, 12,* 265–272.

Rogers, C. R. (1957). The necessary and sufficient conditions of therapeutic personality change. *Journal of Consulting Psychology, 21,* 95–103.

Saigh, P. A., Yasik, A. E., Sack, W. H., & Koplewicz, H. S. (1999). Child-adolescent posttraumatic stress disorder: Prevalence, risk factors, and comorbidity. In P. A. Saigh & J. D. Bremner (Eds.), *Posttraumatic stress disorder: A comprehensive text* (pp. 18–43). Boston: Allyn & Bacon.

Shaw, J. A. (2003). Children exposed to war/terrorism. *Clinical Child and Family Psychology Review, 6,* 237–246.

Slaikeu, K. A. (1990). *Crisis intervention: A handbook for practice and research* (2nd ed.). Newton, MA: Allyn & Bacon.

Stephens, R. D. (1994). Planning for safer and better schools: School violence prevention and intervention strategies. *School Psychology Review, 23,* 204–215.

Strepling, S. H. (1997). The low-aggression classroom: A teacher's view. In A. P. Goldstein & J. C. Conoly (Eds.), *School violence intervention: A practical handbook* (pp. 23–45). New York: Guilford Press.

Terr, L. C. (1983). Chowchilla revisited: The effects of psychic trauma four years after a school-bus kidnapping. *American Journal of Psychiatry, 140*, 1543–1555.

U.S. Department of Homeland Security. (2004, March). *National incident management system*. Retrieved August 16, 2008, from www.fema .gov/pdf/emergency/nims/nims_doc_full.pdf.

Werner, E. (1989). High-risk children in young adulthood: A longitudinal study from birth to 32 years. *American Journal of Orthopsychiatry, 59*, 72–81.

Young, B. H., Ford, J. D., Ruzek, J. I., Friedman, M. L., & Gusman, F. D. (1999). *Disaster mental health services: A guidebook for clinicians and administrators*. Retrieved August 16, 2008, from www.ncptsd.va.gov/ncmain/ncdocs/nc_prod/ Cover.pdf.

CHAPTER 42

PREVENTION PROGRAMS

JOSEPH A. DURLAK
Loyola University

CURRENT STATUS

Prevention programs have reached a high water mark in American schools. Virtually every school district in the country hosts at least one prevention program, and many schools offer multiple programs targeting such areas as drug use, bullying, AIDS/HIV, diet and nutrition, human sexuality, personal safety and injury prevention, conflict resolution or violence prevention, and suicide prevention (Durlak, 1997). Several developments have fueled this interest. For example, research evidence continues to mount indicating that many school-based prevention efforts have been successful in reducing the future rate of negative outcomes that are pertinent to students' academic, personal or social development. As educators have learned more about the possible benefits of prevention, they have become more interested in offering programs in their schools. Some funding has been made available through both private and governmental agencies for school-based prevention (e.g., Safe and Drug-Free Schools, Title I programs for high-risk students) prompting many schools to take advantage of these resources. As a result, it is reasonable to assume that prevention programs will be a part of the American primary and secondary educational landscape for the foreseeable future. This is the good news.

At the same time, there are two important limitations in the way school-based prevention is currently practiced. First, there is a large gap between research and practice. For a variety of reasons, many schools do not chose to use evidence-based programs, that is, programs whose effectiveness has been supported by scientific research. Instead, many schools chose either other programs that have not been carefully evaluated, or they develop their own initiatives. In neither of these latter cases, however, do schools usually

evaluate the impact of their alternative choices. As a result, each year millions of school children participate in prevention programs whose impact is unknown, and may be of little or no merit. For example, one survey found that only 14% of schools were offering drug prevention programs whose content and method of delivery were consistent with empirical research (Ennett et al., 2003). Another survey of private and public American schools that inquired about several different types of prevention programs found that, at best, less than 50% of school-based prevention programs followed recommended practices (Gottfredson & Gottfredson, 2002). Furthermore, the quality of programming was often hampered by poor implementation, leading to the conclusion that "the quality of school-based prevention practices as they are implemented in the typical school is low" (p. 3).

A second major limitation in current school-based prevention is its uncoordinated nature. Often, new prevention programs are added in piecemeal fashion without integrating them with existing curricula. As noted above, schools may offer more than one prevention program, but do not usually consider how different programs can be integrated for maximum effectiveness. This lack of strategic planning means that schools are not using their limited resources most efficiently to enhance students' academic, personal and social development.

This chapter summarizes current findings on school-based prevention programs and is divided into four major sections. First, prevention is defined and three conceptual frameworks for understanding many prevention efforts are identified. Second, the results for school-based prevention programs are summarized, and representative programs are described. This section also discusses general principles associated with successful programs and some important future research directions. Third, the importance of effective implementation of prevention programs is emphasized by discussing research on the influence of implementation on outcomes and the factors that promote the effective use of evidence-based programs in schools. This section describes the capacity that most schools need to do prevention successfully. Finally, issues related to the coordination of school-based services and new roles for school psychologists are discussed.

WHAT IS PREVENTION?

The three major categories of prevention are universal (also called primary), selective, and indicated (formerly called secondary prevention). All three types of prevention seek to reduce the future occurrence of negative outcomes in a target population, but they vary in how the target population is chosen for intervention. Universal prevention is applied to all in a target population (e.g., all first graders, all high school students). Selective prevention focuses on a subgroup of the total population who is at higher risk for later problems due to life circumstances, but is not yet showing problems. For example, children from low-income families, children undergoing school transitions, children of divorce, or children from immigrant families are selected for intervention based on longitudinal research indicating that children in these selected groups are more likely to have later problems than other children. Finally, indicated prevention is prompt intervention for early-detected problems. A population of school children would be evaluated in some way (sometimes using screening instruments, sometimes through principal or teacher referrals), and only those identified as having mild to moderate adjustment problems would receive intervention. The distinctions among the three forms of prevention are not always clear. However, it is helpful to consider these forms of intervention in terms of whether the children who receive attention are showing some early difficulties (indicated prevention), are not demonstrating difficulties, but as a group are at higher risk to do so later (selective prevention), or do not fit either of these circumstances (universal prevention).

Three Frameworks for Understanding Current Prevention Efforts

Most current approaches in prevention can be understood by considering the perspectives of three major theoretical and conceptual frameworks. These perspectives are ecological theory, the risk and protective factor paradigm, and more recently, competency promotion (sometimes identified as health promotion, social and emotional learning, positive youth development, or most broadly, as positive psychology).

In brief, ecological theory stresses that behavior must be viewed within the context in which it occurs, and that there are multiple levels of interacting influences (or systems) that affect behavior (Bronfenbrenner, 1979). For example, child and adolescent development is affected by multiple interacting social environments or systems. The microsystem includes the family, school, and peer group; the mesosystem is represented by the interaction of different environments (e.g., family-school partnerships); the exosystem includes community-level processes such as available resources and services at the neighborhood or local level. Finally, broader societal-level factors such as policies, cultural values and norms are part of the macrosystem. These social systems and their interactions can either promote or hinder child development. For instance, effective family-school partnerships can enhance children's academic development, whereas association with a deviant peer group can disrupt school performance. At the exosystemic and macrosystemic levels, educational mandates strongly influence what curricula and services schools offer, while local and federal funding and policies affect a school's ability to offer enriching and diversified educational programs and resources, to attract and retain competent staff, and to improve its physical facilities.

The risk and protective factor paradigm guides prevention through its identification of variables that increase the probabilities of negative outcomes (i.e., risk factors) or that reduce such probabilities (i.e., protective factors).

Research indicates that one single risk or protective factor rarely has a large effect on adjustment. Rather, it is the accumulation and interaction of risk and protective factors that are critical. A risk or protective factor can be associated with an individual (e.g., behavioral self-control, risky sexual behavior) or with an environmental setting (e.g., supportive teachers, harsh parenting practices).

Table 42.1 lists several major risk and protective factors that are associated with schools.

Most recently, competency promotion strategies have been emphasized in many interventions. Instead of a focus on pathology, competency

TABLE 42.1   Examples of Risk and Protective Factors Associated with School[1]

	Risk Factors
In Term of Individual Behavior:	Early behavior problems
	Early academic failure
Factors Associated with Peers:	Peer rejection
	Association with deviant peers
Neighborhood/Family Factors:	Neighborhood disorganization
	Economic deprivation

	Protective Factors
Individual Characteristics and Behaviors:	Bonding to school
	Personal and social competencies
	(Examples include behavioral and emotional self-control, conflict resolution skills, drug refusal skills, and problem-solving skills.)
School/Family Factors:	Safe and orderly school campus
	Caring, supportive school staff
	High academic expectations
	Challenging educational curriculum
	Parental involvement in child's school life
	Strong school-family partnerships

[1] Further information on these factors is available in Durlak (1997).

promotion stresses the importance of developing the multiple competencies (e.g., assets, skills) that youth need to become productive, contributing members of society. These competencies relate to four major areas in young people's lives: namely, their physical, cognitive, social, and personal (or psychological) development.

The personal and social skills frequently targeted in programs include self-awareness, self-management, social awareness, relationship skills, and responsible decision making (Collaborative for Academic, Social, and Emotional Learning, 2005). More specifically, those programs which promote social and emotional learning focus on self-control of behaviors and emotions, self-efficacy, effective coping strategies, perspective taking, empathy, interpersonal problem solving, conflict resolution, decision making, and positive connections to school, family, and to other adult role models. Competency promotion efforts stress that promoting competencies is a worthy objective in its own right, and research has found that competency enhancement can also lead to a reduction in later negative outcomes (Catalano, Berglund, Ryan, Lonczak & Hawkins, 2002; Durlak, 2000; Durlak & Weissberg, 2005; Weissberg & Greenberg, 1998).

There is overlap and sometimes confusion over the difference between a protective factor and a competency. In some cases, for example at the individual level, they are often the same thing. Teaching children effective methods of behavioral or emotional self-control is a protective factor *and* a competency. Those interested in protective factors tend to emphasize how self-control reduces the likelihood of later negative outcomes. Competency-oriented researchers appreciate the negative relationship that exists between enhanced competencies and later problems, but also value the contribution of better self-control to children's overall well-being and to their later positive functioning.

The three perspectives of ecological theory, the risk and protective factor paradigm, and competency promotion are not mutually exclusive and can be combined in various ways in interventions. For example, some programs work directly with school children to promote competencies in one or more areas; others attempt ecological change by modifying classroom structure and organization or through schoolwide changes in curricula and policies, and some combine these strategies in a more comprehensive effort. In each case, the intervention may also focus specifically on reducing certain risk factors, increasing specific protective factors, or targeting both risk and protective factors.

In sum, many current approaches to school-based prevention or competency promotion emphasize one or more of three key concepts: (1) It is helpful to build competencies in school children (i.e., to focus on the positive); (2) The school, family, peer, and neighborhood environments influence development and are appropriate targets for intervention; (3) Interventions should strive to create conditions that lessen risk and increase protection for children in order to increase the later odds of more positive outcomes and fewer negative outcomes.

IMPACT OF SCHOOL-BASED PREVENTION

The research literature on prevention has become so extensive and diversified that it is impossible to do justice to all this work in one chapter. Based on this author's own surveys and the number of research reviews that have appeared, a conservative estimate is that over 1500 outcome studies have been conducted by the end of 2005 evaluating one form or another of school-based prevention (Durlak, 1995, 1997). Collectively, there is strong empirical support for the value of school-based prevention in reducing the rate of many different types of problems that include both internalizing and externalizing difficulties (e.g., anxiety, depression, conduct problems, aggression, school suspensions), poor academic achievement, and drug use. Moreover, many positive outcomes have been produced by prevention and competency promotion programs such as enhanced bonding to school, better teacher and peer relationships, improved academic performance (as opposed to fewer academic problems), and higher levels of self-esteem and self-efficacy. Several notable programs have been able to simultaneously prevent the later incidence of one or more problems and increase positive outcomes in participating students (multiple reviews of the prevention literature are identified at www.oslc.org/spr/apa/summaries.html). In sum, research offers extensive empirical support for school-based prevention and promotion.

There are some caveats to the above conclusion. Not every prevention program has been successful, so it is important to understand the parameters that increase the chances of success, which are identified below. Prevention has

been more successful in some areas than others. School-based suicide prevention programs have not demonstrated their impact on suicide-related behaviors (Mazza, 1997; Miller & duPaul, 1996), although it is extremely difficult to detect significant changes in such low-rate behaviors unless very large sample sizes are evaluated. Although some investigations have found that program effects endure and may even increase over time, more follow-up studies are needed. There are some important unknowns about prevention programs. Do programs benefit some participants more than others based on such characteristics as ethnicity, age, or gender? What are the crucial ingredients of interventions that should be emphasized in replications in different school districts? There have been very few cost-benefit analyses, and the results of such analyses would be extremely helpful to school districts in their choice of programming.

Finally, although many individual studies report statistically significant outcomes and meta-analytic reviews have quantified the magnitude of impact from prevention by calculating effect sizes, it is difficult to translate research findings into practical terms. How much of a difference does prevention make for school children?

One way to begin to understand the practical benefits of intervention is to explore its value added benefits. Table 42.2 summarizes the findings from several meta-analytic reviews of universal, selective, or indicated school-based prevention or competency promotion efforts. Collectively, these reviews evaluate more than 1600 studies involving over 150,000 school children. Each review has concluded that prevention or competency promotion has been effective. The mean effect sizes obtained on different categories of outcomes in these reviews are presented along with percentages in the last column indicating the value-added benefits of intervention. The value added benefits of intervention are portrayed by estimating the additional percentage of students who could improve on various outcomes if an effective prevention or competency-promotion program was introduced, compared to what is currently happening or occurring in schools.

The value-added data are relevant to the decision facing each school: "Should we offer a new prevention or competency promotion program or should we simply continue doing what we are doing? In other words, on average, how *many more* students might benefit if schools were to offer a new program directed at sexual abuse,

TABLE 42.2 Summary of Meta-Analytic Reviews of the Outcomes for School-Based Prevention or Competency Promotion Programs[1]

Review	Type of Prevention	Focus of Review	Number of Interventions/ participants	Mean Effect Size	Value Added Benefit (%)
Davis & Gidycz (2000)	Universal	sexual abuse	16/8115	0.71—knowledge & self-protective skills	35.5%
Derzon (2006)	Universal & Indicated	antisocial behavior	74/?	0.11—disruptive behavior	5.5%
				0.44—crimes	22.0%
				0.14—fighting	7.0%
				0.24—suspensions	12.0%
Durlak & Weissberg (2005)	Competency Promotion	school adjustment	379/33352	0.27—bonding to school	13.5%
				0.39—acad performance	19.5%
				0.22—aggression	11.0%
				0.41—personal & social competencies	20.5%
Durlak, Weissberg, Kawashima, Dupre, & Pachan (2005)	Universal & Indicated	aggression	163/12388	0.29—aggression	14.5%
				0.33—academic performance	17.0%
				0.29—suspensions	14.5%
Durlak & Wells (1997)	Universal	mental health	177/22,125	0.30—internalizing symptoms	15.0%
				0.32—behavior problems	16.0%
				0.30—academic performance	15.0%
Durlak & Wells (1998)	Indicated	mental health	130/9862	0.44—behavior problems	22.0%
				0.34—personal & social competencies	17.0%
Mytton, DiGuiseppi, Gough, Taylor, & Logan (2002)	Indicated	aggression	28/2096	0.36—aggression	18.0%
				0.59—suspensions	29.5%
Tobler et al. (2000)	Universal	drug use	207/?	0.13—drug use	6.5%
Wilson, Gottfredson, & Najaka (2001)	Universal & Selective	problem behaviors	216/?	0.07—universal programs	2.5%
				0.20—selective programs	10.0%
Wilson, Lipsey, & Derzon (2003)	Universal & Indicated	conduct problems	522/56,000	0.09—universal programs	4.5%
				0.41—indicated	20.5%

[1]Value-added benefit refers to the percentage of additional school children who could improve on each outcome compared to the benefits they receive from current school programming. A "?" indicates that total sample sizes were not reported.

drugs, aggression, general school adjustment, and so on, compared to what is currently occurring.[1] These value added data are in the last column of Table 42.2.

The differential percentages are compelling in many respects. For example, 22% fewer children would engage in criminal behavior (Derzon, 2006) and between10% and 22% would demonstrate fewer problem behaviors such as acting out, disruptiveness, or noncompliance depending on the review (Durlak & Wells, 1997; Durlak & Wells, 1998; Wilson, Gottfredson & Najaka, 2001; Wilson, Lipsey & Derzon (2003). More specifically, between 7% and 18% would show less aggression (Durlak & Weissberg, 2005; Durlak, Weissberg, Kawashima, Dupre & Pachan, 2005; Mytton, DiGuiseppi, Gough, Taylor & Logan, 2002). In other cases, 6.5% fewer children would use drugs, and there would be between 12% to 29.5% fewer school suspensions and disciplinary actions (Derzon, 2006; Durlak et al., 2005; Mytton et al., 2002).

In terms of positive outcomes, up to 35.5% more children would have more knowledge and self-protective skills relative to sexual abuse (Davis & Gidycz, 2000). Between 17% (Durlak & Wells, 1998) to 20.5% (Durlak & Weissberg, 2005) more children would demonstrate personal and social competencies in such areas as interpersonal problem solving, communication, assertiveness and conflict resolution skills, and 13.5% would show stronger bonds and attachments to school (Durlak & Weissberg, 2005). Finally, the academic performance of up to 19.5% more children would improve (Durlak & Weissberg, 2005; Durlak et al., 2005; Durlak & Wells, 1997). The above changes have occurred in universal, selective and indicated prevention programs.

Unfortunately, it is not possible to predict which students will benefit, or exactly how much change would occur for each student. Nevertheless, the percentages in the last column of Table 42.2 are a convincing demonstration of the practical benefits that can be derived from prevention or competency promotion. Most schools would welcome an intervention that can produce

the percentage changes listed in Table 42.2 in areas such as aggression, school suspensions, problem behaviors, and academic performance.

Although current research indicates the value of school-based prevention in general, programs have varied in their overall effects and on which outcomes they are most likely to achieve their best results, so schools must select which program to offer. The issue of which program is most appropriate for which school is complicated, and some relevant issues are discussed in the later section on program diffusion. However, it is possible to describe the principles that are most consistently associated with effective programs.

Principles of Effective Prevention and Competency Promotion Programs

There is substantial agreement on the principles of effective prevention and competency promotion. Table 42.3 lists nine principles that have been distilled from various sources (Bond & Hauf, 2004; Durlak, 2003; Nation et al., 2003). These principles overlap and are interdependent, but several merit attention.

The first principle, that interventions should be guided by an established theory and be based on previous empirical support, is probably the most important because of its influence on several principles related to the conceptualization, execution and evaluation of programs. Theory offers a framework for deciding what should be done to whom, by whom, when, for how long, and with what expected benefits. A good theory leads to a logic model for intervention that contains clear program goals, a specification of what activities should be used to accomplish program goals, and a plan for measuring how well desired goals have been achieved. As a result, programs can be evaluated systematically, and effective programs can be continued and ineffective ones improved or eliminated.

It is important to use effective change strategies in the intervention, which relates to principles 3, 4 and 5 in Table 42.3. Effective prevention focuses on behavior change and often attends as much or more to promoting personal and social competencies as reducing problems. As Allensworth (1993) has indicated, "Acquisition of basic skills at appropriate ages appears to be a primary component of all prevention" (p. 17). Social learning and cognitive behavioral techniques have consistently emerged as successful ways to improve competencies or skills. These techniques emphasize active forms of learning

---

[1] Of course, if a school has done a good evaluation of their local programming then they would have to balance the effectiveness of their current efforts with introducing a new intervention. However, most prevention or competency promotion programs operating in schools have not been empirically evaluated.

TABLE 42.3 Principles Guiding Effective Prevention and Competency Promotion Programs[1]

Effective Prevention and Competency Promotion Programs are:

1. Theory-driven and empirically based
2. Well-timed and developmentally appropriate
3. Emphasize behavior change and the promotion of personal and social competencies
4. Use effective methods to change behavior and competencies
5. Recognize the importance of multiple environmental influences
6. Foster connections to adults and prosocial peers
7. Permit adaptations to fit the needs, preferences and values of the target population and setting
8. Carefully evaluated
9. Planned carefully for effective program implementation

[1] Further details are available in Bond & Hauf (2004), Durlak (2003), and Nation et al. (2003).

whereby students practice skills that have been modeled or explained to them and then they receive feedback and positive support until behavioral mastery is attained.

At the same time, it is also clear what strategies are ineffective. Programs that rely on information or on changing attitudes to the exclusion of behavioral change have not been effective in any area of prevention in which they have been tried (Durlak, 1997). School children need knowledge to understand what is expected of them, but they require active practice and social support in changing their behavior if prevention is to be effective.

Although some programs that have worked directly and exclusively with students (i.e., have taken an individual focus) have been successful, there is growing evidence that ecologically oriented interventions that modify the classroom, school environment or the family environment may have more enduring effects (Weissberg & Greenberg, 1998). This is probably because newly learned behaviors are less likely to be sustained unless the environment supports and reinforces behavioral change. Principles 7 and 9 from Table 42.3 relate to program implementation and are discussed in that section of this chapter.

EXAMPLES OF SUCCESSFUL PREVENTION PROGRAMS

In order to provide readers with some details about specific programs, this section describes several different types of successful universal and indicated school-based interventions. Some of the following programs have very specific goals such as preventing future drug use or aggression,

whereas others seek to prevent behavioral or academic problems more generally. The programs also vary in terms of the number of components they contain, their attempts at ecological change, and the inclusion of parents in the intervention. The following programs illustrate the success that can be achieved in preventing different types of negative outcomes when interventions are carefully conceptualized, executed, and evaluated. Many of the following programs feature a well-articulated theory of intervention, random assignment to conditions, large sample sizes, use of multiple and psychometrically sound outcome measures, and the collection of follow-up data, although each study does not contain all these characteristics. Universal programs are discussed first followed by indicated prevention programs.

Universal Interventions

The Life Skills Training (LST) program has been the most extensively evaluated drug abuse prevention program (Botvin, 2000). LST uses an individual-level approach and trains students in a set of personal and social skills that are potentially applicable to many situations, including drug use. These skills include communication and assertiveness, decision making and goal setting, self-directed behavioral change strategies, and coping techniques to deal with anxiety and social pressure. The prototypical LST program is begun in sixth grade and contains booster sessions for seventh and eighth graders. LST has been effective in reducing future drug use, sometimes to a considerable degree (between 40 to 80% depending on the study). LST has also been shown to reduce more serious drug-related problems such as risky driving, binge drinking and polydrug use, and has obtained good results regardless of the school's geographical setting (e.g., urban, suburban or rural) and general population (Caucasian, African American, or Hispanic). Follow-up effects have been obtained for periods ranging from 3 months to 6 years (Botvin, 2000; Botvin & Griffin, 2005).

The Social Development Program (SDP) has been successful in preventing multiple academic and behavioral problems by combining school- and home-based components. SDP is an intensive program that operates during the first six years of elementary school. The classroom setting is targeted for change as teachers learn proactive classroom management techniques, and use mastery learning teaching practices and cooperative learning strategies during much of their academic instruction. Teachers also conduct social skills training in their classrooms. SDP also involves a parent component in which parents learn more effective parenting practices. At the end of sixth grade, positive results have occurred on such outcomes as students' bonding to school, rates of positive class participation, and school achievement (O'Donnell, Hawkins, Catalano, Abbott & Day, 1995). Most impressively, data collected 7 and 10 years following intervention have shown positive effects on sexual behavior (e.g., pregnancies, safe sexual practices), school achievement, and various adult outcomes such as crime, drug use, and mental health problems (Hawkins, Kosterman, Catalano, Hill & Abbott, 2005; Lonczak, Abbott, Hawkins, Kosterman & Catalano, 2002)

Gottfredson, Gottfredson and Hybl (1993) described the success of a schoolwide effort to improve middle and high school students' prosocial behaviors in order to prevent later delinquency and improve academic achievement. The 2-year intervention attempted schoolwide changes through an organizational development approach that sought to clarify school rules, improve classroom management, involve parents more actively in their child's school life, and make the school environment more engaging and positive for students. Teachers, school administrators, students, and parents met in teams to design and carry out school improvement programs. Teachers were also trained in effective management procedures in order to improve order and enhance classroom climate.

Findings suggested significant improvement in school administration and functioning and perceptions of school climate by both teachers and students. For example, teachers' morale and feelings about classroom order and efficiency increased; students felt less alienated, reported a greater sense of belonging to school, felt safer at school, and believed there were improvements in the fairness and clarity of school rules. Students also reported receiving more positive reinforcement at school. Most important, students' rebellious behavior decreased, and their attention to academic work increased.

The Child Development Project (CDP) is a notable, successful effort at school reform that seeks to create a supportive and inclusive school-wide environment that maximizes personal, social and academic growth (Solomon, Battistich, Watson, Schaps, & Lewis, 2000). The interventions emphasizes several principles such as warm and supportive interpersonal relationships; student autonomy, influence and self-direction; collaborative learning and shared decision making; a consistently engaging, relevant, and challenging curriculum; and attention to such values as justice, responsibility and caring. CDP involves a classroom component emphasizing curriculum and social climate, a schoolwide component focused on school policies, practices and events, and a family involvement program to foster a stronger family-school partnership.

A series of evaluations have documented significant changes in the school system and corresponding positive changes in children following successful implementation of CDP. For example, observational data indicate that the behaviors of program teachers change significantly in accordance with project principles, and students perceive improvements in the classroom and school environment. Other indications that the school environment was effectively modified have been reflected in students' reports of improved relations with teachers, a more positive sense of school community, and fewer instances of being victimized or bullied at school. In turn, teachers' reports have indicated students are more engaged in learning and school activities, and more considerate and respectful of others. Benefits to children have been seen in peer relations, prosocial behaviors, academic achievement, and reductions in school misconduct and drug use (Battistich, Schaps, Watson, Solomon, & Lewis, 2000; Battistich, Schaps & Wilson, 2004; Solomon et al., 2000).

Positive Action is an integrated attempt at changing aspects of school, family and community systems to promote students' personal, academic, and social competencies (Flay & Allred, 2003;

Flay, Allred & Ordway, 2001). Positive Action targets such skills as effective self-management, social skills, goal setting, and decision making through developmentally appropriate classroom curricula for kindergarten to sixth graders. These classroom lessons are coordinated with attempted changes in school organization, teacher-student relations, and parent and community involvement. The classroom component emphasizes active learning and effective classroom management procedures. The schoolwide component focuses on social climate, and how school policies and actions can foster and reinforce children's skills. In addition, activities for parents and local community members and organizations are designed to support and generalize students' new learning. Several evaluations of Positive Action has been conducted indicating effective implementation of the program model and multiple gains for students after intervention that include improved conduct at school and better academic achievement (Flay et al., 2001).

Examples of Indicated Prevention

The Montreal Experiment (Tremblay, Pagani-Kurtz, Masse, Vitaro & Pihl, 1995; Tremblay et al., 1992) is a good illustration of how indicated prevention can achieve positive short and long-term results for children displaying early signs of disruptive behavior. Researchers used teacher ratings to identify disruptive kindergarten children and offered intervention to these children and their parents during first and second grade. Teachers conducted social skills training in the classroom emphasizing issues related to appropriate emotional and behavioral control, and parents received child management training in their homes.

In one program evaluation, outcome data from multiple sources were pooled to evaluate the adjustment status of intervention and control children. Compared to controls, the intervention was able to increase the percentage of children judged to be well-adjusted by 53%, and to reduce the percentage of children with serious overall difficulties by 50% (Tremblay et al., 1992). Six-year follow-up data indicated that by age 15, the intervention continued to have positive effects in terms of modifying school performance and delinquent behavior (Tremblay et al., 1995).

The use of an indicated prevention approach to target internalizing problems is reflected in the work of Clarke and colleagues (Clarke et al., 1995). Adolescents who had subclinical symptoms of depression and who were identified through a series of teacher and student ratings and personal interviews participated in a 15-session program. The cognitive-behavioral intervention taught students how to develop more adaptive cognitive styles to deal with stressful situations. Over a 17-month follow-up period, the intervention was successful in reducing the rate of diagnosed mood disorders by 56%.

PROGRAM IMPLEMENTATION

The value-added data that were presented in Table 42.2 indicate that students would benefit if their schools decided to offer an effective prevention or competency promotion program compared to doing nothing about a particular problem or issue. This information, however, does not help schools decide what specific program to offer, or how to conduct or evaluate the program they have chosen.

It is now clear that developing an effective intervention is only the first step in bringing better services to our nation's school children. As noted earlier, effective programs are not used routinely in many U.S. schools, and even when they are, program quality can be compromised by poor implementation (Ennett et al., 2003; Gottfredson & Gottfredson, 2002). This section is devoted to the topic of program diffusion, which, in general, refers to transporting new ideas, technologies, or evidence-based interventions into real world settings, such as schools, where they can be used and then maintained by local providers (Rogers, 2003).

Program diffusion is a complicated long-term process that involves at least five interrelated steps: dissemination, adoption, implementation, evaluation and, for programs that are successful during their demonstration period, maintenance. In other words, if effective prevention programs are to gain widespread use in our nation's schools, then several things must happen. First, schools need clear, accurate information about the existence of various programs, their relative value, and their possible benefits (dissemination). Second, schools must make a good choice about which program to try (adoption). Third, the program must be conducted carefully so its value can be adequately assessed (implementation). Fourth, schools must collect accurate data on the impact of the programs they conduct (evaluation). Fifth, based on the results of the local evaluation, schools must then decide to continue the program as is, make modifications to improve its functioning, or abandon the program and make another choice.

Unfortunately, problems can occur at each step of the diffusion process. For example, schools may not receive helpful information about existing programs; they might not make good choices when they adopt a particular program; problems can develop during implementation that compromise a program's impact; the resources to conduct local program evaluations might not be available; and some successful programs are not maintained because of political, administrative or financial issues. The multiple difficulties encountered during the diffusion process are one of the reasons that a wide gap remains between the existence of many potentially successful prevention programs that could be used in schools and the interventions that are offered in many school districts.

Over 5000 studies have appeared on program diffusion (Rogers, 2003), so it is impossible to discuss the entire diffusion process from adoption to maintenance. In addition to the Rogers (2003) text, which covers all phases of diffusion, several useful references related to the adoption, implementation, and maintenance of school-based interventions are available (Durlak & Dupre, 2008; Han & Weiss, 2005; Ringwalt, Ennett, Vincus, Rohrbach, & Simons-Rudolph, 2004; Rohrbach, Ringwalt, Ennett & Vincus, 2005). The next section focuses specifically on implementation, and is based on Durlak and Dupre's (2008) findings.

What Is Implementation?

In general, implementation refers to what a program consists of when it is put into practice. Although implementation can be viewed in different ways, the most frequently studied dimensions are fidelity, which is the extent to which the program that is eventually delivered corresponds to the originally intended program (sometimes also called integrity, adherence, or faithful replication), and dosage, which refers to how much (and sometimes which components) of a proposed program were actually conducted. A third important dimension that has more recently received more attention is program adaptation, which as the term implies refers to changes that are made to the original program when it is delivered in another setting.

Research Findings on Implementation

There is consistent evidence supporting five main conclusions about implementation that tend to hold across a broad array of programs and settings.

1. The level of implementation obtained influences the outcomes of prevention and competency promotion programs for children and adolescents. This is reflected in two patterns of findings: (1) higher levels of implementation lead to much stronger benefits for participants than lower levels; or (2) unless a certain level of implementation is successfully attained (a level that can differ from program to program), significant positive benefits for participants do not occur.

   For example, evaluations of the CDC project (see above) have found that when all intervention conditions are combined the outcomes are very modest, and sometimes nonsignificant on several measures. However, when schools with better and poorer implementation are evaluated separately, students in the former schools do significantly better than controls and show very positive outcomes (Battitisch et al., 2000; Solomon et al., 2000).

2. It is unrealistic to expect perfect or near-perfect implementation. Positive results have often been achieved with implementation levels of 60% or more; achieving implementation between 80% and 90% is very good; and no study has reported 100% implementation for all providers. For example, Botvin and colleagues have found that implementation levels of 60% are usually sufficient to produce positive results for LST programs (Botvin & Griffin, 2005).

3. There is marked variability in the level of implementation achieved across providers within the same study. For example, in school-based studies figures have ranged from 17% to 100%, indicating that some teachers are much better at implementation than others.

4. Levels of implementation tend to deteriorate over time. One can expect that some teachers will drift farther and farther away from the originally intended program in the absence of steps taken to maintain implementation through monitoring, and then retraining, support, and consultation as needed.

5. Adaptation is the norm for school-based programs. Most teachers will change some part of the original program to suit local preferences, needs, and interests. Based on their national survey of schools, Ringwalt et al., (2004) offered this conclusion: "We can thus say now with confidence that some measure of adaptation is inevitable and that for curriculum developers to oppose it categorically, even for the best of conceptual or empirical reasons, would appear to be futile" (p. 387).

As the Ringwalt et al., (2004) conclusion suggests, there are some who believe that fidelity must be emphasized in program implementation. A higher degree of fidelity is more likely to be achieved for interventions that are carefully structured and have accompanying lesson plans or program manuals, but many interventions do not have these features. Yet, fidelity and adaptation are not mutually exclusive. In fact, in most cases, fidelity and adaptation co-occur during implementation. That is, teachers often replicate some parts of a program faithfully while modifying other parts.

Data and extensive field experiences suggest that striking the proper balance between fidelity and adaptation may be the most effective strategy. For example, some data indicate that program adaptations made by teachers can improve program outcomes (e.g., Kerr, Kent & Lam, 1988; McGraw et al., 1996). Because fidelity is not 100%, there is room for adaptation to have a positive effect. Much depends on careful measurement of the implementation process to determine which program features are conducted faithfully, and what changes are made to other program features so that the effect of both fidelity and adaptation can be assessed in each case.

What Factors Affect Implementation?

Because of the consistent influence that implementation has on the outcomes of prevention programs, it is important to understand the factors that affect implementation. There is a growing consensus that it is helpful to focus on factors that affect the capacity of host organizations to conduct interventions. Capacity is often viewed in reference to the entire process of program diffusion and is defined as the motivation and ability to plan, select, implement, evaluate, and continue effective interventions. In this section, the focus is on capacity specific to the implementation process and generally refers to the willingness

and available resources (e.g., facilities, funds, time, personnel) to achieve an acceptable level of implementation. What affects the capacity of schools to implement prevention programs successfully?

Research has identified at least 23 factors that affect implementation and these factors can be placed into five categories (see Durlak & Dupre, 2008). The five categories consist of variables related to communities, providers, innovations, organizational features of the host organization, and the resources that are provided with respect to initial training and continual technical assistance.

One way of viewing the confluence of these factors is to consider factors in these five categories as contributing to effective implementation either directly or through their interaction with other factors. Ideally, the factors ultimately contribute to an efficient and effective system for implementation. In other words, strategic planning is necessary for effective implementation, and if all goes well then relevant factors will coalesce and lead to sufficient capacity to conduct the intervention.

A few examples will help clarify this complex constellation of issues that affect implementation. Other sources contain more detailed discussions of relevant issues (Bellig et al., 2004; Fixsen, Naoom, Blasé, Friedman, & Wallace, 2005; Greenhalgh et al., 2005).

Two characteristics of the innovation that frequently affect implementation are its compatibility with the setting and its flexibility. Compatibility generally refers to the fit that exists between the intervention and local norms, needs, preferences and resources. Flexibility refers to the extent to which an innovation can be modified when it is implemented. These two factors frequently interact, as schools are likely to implement a program because it can be flexibly changed to fit local circumstances. Both these factors may also interact with organizational factors such as integration of new programming. Schools are more likely to implement programs successfully when the program can be easily integrated into existing practices as opposed to requiring substantial modifications in policy and procedures.

At the individual level, program implementation is generally enhanced if teachers feel the program serves a local need, will produce some desired benefits, and if they feel they have the necessary skills and will be able to implement the more challenging aspects of the program. The latter two issues are usually addressed during training and through technical assistance but these issues are best broached when new programs are being offered to schools. Teachers might balk at adopting programs if they perceive the intervention requires skills they do not possess.

Schools are complex organizations and some organizational features that have been most consistently related to implementation include a positive work climate, openness to change, good leadership, the presence of a program champion, effective managerial support, and collaborative decision making. A program champion is someone at the school who is generally well respected by other staff and who can advocate successfully for the program, help in problem solving when difficulties arise, and can rally and maintain support for the program if motivational levels drop.

Several studies have emphasized the importance of collaborative decision making. Interventions that are characterized by collaborative decision making are more likely to be implemented more successfully. Collaboration refers to a process characterized by mutual trust, respect and open lines of communication among all involved parties (e.g., administrators, teachers, researchers, consultants, and in some cases, parents and students). The group collectively shares responsibility for what is to be implemented and how. For example, teachers who have meaningful input into the programs they will eventually have to conduct tend to implement the programs more effectively than those who have no or little say, or who may be pressured or asked to conduct elements of a program they find objectionable or impractical in whole or in part.

Some researchers who bring programs into schools do not solicit input from school staff for fear that fidelity will be compromised. Yet, as noted earlier, teachers can offer ideas that can increase program impact if their views are solicited and considered. After all, staff have valuable "inside" information about the school setting and what is realistic given local circumstances.

Collaborative decision making has the additional benefit of increasing local ownership of a program. That is, under collaborative circumstances, school staff are more likely to feel they are conducting "their" program rather than someone else's, and thus, under most circumstances, would be more disposed to continuing an effective program after its demonstration period. As a result, effective programs can be sustained in schools (Weissberg & Greenberg, 1998).

Two very most important aspects of implementation are the quality of training and ongoing technical assistance that is provided. Good training procedures create clear lines of communication, explain what aspects of an intervention are most important and why, clarify expectations and responsibilities, and provide teachers with necessary hands-on practice, especially in learning the more difficult aspects of program delivery. Ongoing technical assistance (ideally provided promptly and in person) is essential to help those who struggle with implementation (and there always will be some who do), shore up morale and motivation, and encourage those who are doing well.

Before concluding the discussion of program implementation, the practical realities of school life cannot be ignored. Some school staff are so overwhelmed by competing demands on their time, limited resources, or lack of administrative support that such barriers can severely impede program implementation. If program demands exceed local capacity, the program will not be implemented very well or continued regardless of its initial impact. The issue of program scale is also important. It might be wise to begin on a small scale with only a few participating teachers in one or more schools to test the feasibility of the intervention in a new setting. If the smaller scale effort is successful then "word of mouth" from those in the pilot program can be the best advertising to encourage more widespread adoptions and implementations. Finally, time is important. Program implementation cannot be rushed and it is far better to wait and work to have several relevant factors positively disposed toward program success than to move too quickly. For example, taking time to secure necessary administrative support and establishing trust during collaborative meetings are often well worth the effort. Unfortunately, funding agencies do not always provide sufficient time or financial support to lay the groundwork for effective implementation.

Need for Coordinated Programming

Several authors have stressed the need for coordination of school-based competency promotion and prevention programs to create a more effective school system that truly speaks to educating the whole person (e.g., Adelman & Taylor, 2002; Elias et al., 1997; Greenberg et al., 2003; Osher, Dywer & Jackson, 2004). Findings from prevention and competency promotion programs have supported the idea that students' academic, social and personal development are interrelated. Some educational policies have been drafted in recognition of this fact. For example, New Jersey and Illinois have developed statewide educational standards directing schools to incorporate the teaching of personal and social skills throughout their curriculum (New Jersey Department of Education, 1996; isbe.net/ils/social_emotional/standards/htm).

The need for coordinated programming actually extends to the entire continuum of services offered by schools including competency promotion, prevention and the treatment of more severe and chronic problems. In effect, the issue becomes one of whole school reform that requires careful strategic planning, systemic policy and organizational changes, involvement of multiple stakeholders from schools and the local community, supports for professional staff development, and consideration of the many issues involved in the implementation and sustainability of innovations. As daunting as the task appears, there are several noteworthy success stories that indicate the positive results that can be achieved when interested parties possess the motivation and can generate the necessary capacity for enduring change (e.g., Collaborative for Academic, Social, and Emotional Learning, 2005; Elias et al., 1997; Osher et al., 2004; www.smhp.psych.ucla.edu).

SOME IMPLICATIONS FOR SCHOOL PSYCHOLOGISTS

In concluding this chapter, it is important to emphasize how current developments in school-based competency promotion and prevention suggest new roles for school psychologists. For example, Sheridan and Gutkin (2000) have argued forcefully that "school psychologists should be substantially *less* concerned with identifying what is wrong with a child, measuring problems, and delivering remedial services and substantially *more* concerned with *prevention and promoting wellness*" (p. 490, author italics). School psychologists can advance competency promotion and prevention in their schools by applying their skills related to assessment, particularly needs assessment, program evaluation, consultation and training of others.

For example, school psychologists can help develop a common vision among school staff and create realistic expectations regarding new programs, assist in the choice and implementation of interventions by acting as trainers and consultants, and contribute to local evaluation efforts. This, of course, assumes that psychologists have kept abreast of the latest research developments

so they can also help their schools make the best initial choices regarding evidence-based programs and the allocation of resources.

School psychologists can also play a vital role by becoming the local program champion of new programming. As noted earlier, a program champion who can advocate successfully for new programs and can motivate and support staff during training and implementation can be extremely influential. Sheridan and Gutkin (2000) have also stressed that psychologists should adopt an ecological perspective in their new roles, and this perspective includes attention to educational policies that affect staff roles, school curricula and school services.

Others have spoken of the need for school psychologists and all educators to understand the value of competency promotion and the inseparable connection that exists in the development of students' academic, personal and social skills (Collaborative for Academic, Social, and Emotional Learning, 2005; Elias et al., 1997; Ross, Powell & Elias, 2003; Zins, Weissberg, Wang & Wahlberg, 2004). In sum, those who work in and with schools and are willing to embrace new roles related to prevention and competency promotion, advocacy, ecological change, and strategic planning can play an influential role in improving the lives of our nation's school children.

REFERENCES

Adelman, H. S., & Taylor, L. (2002). Building comprehensive, multifaceted, and integrated approaches to reducing barriers to learning. *Childhood Education, 78,* 261–268.

Allensworth, D. D. (1993). Health education: State of the art. *Journal of School Health, 63,* 14–20.

Battisch, V., Schaps, E., Watson, M., Solomon, D., & Lewis, C. (2000). Effect of the Child Development Project on students' drug use and other problem behaviors. *The Journal of Primary Prevention, 21,* 75–99.

Battistich, V., Schaps, E., & Wilson, N. (2004). Effects of an elementary school intervention on students' "connectedness" to school and social adjustment during middle school. *The Journal of Primary Prevention, 24,* 243–262.

Bellig, A., Borrelli, B., Resnick, B., Hecht, J., Minicucci, D. S., & Ory, M. et al. (2004). Enhancing treatment fidelity in health behavior change studies: Best practices and recommendations from the NIH behavior change consortium. *Health Psychology, 23,* 443–451.

Bond, J. A., & Hauf, A. M. C. (2004). Taking stock and putting stock in primary prevention:

Characteristics of effective programs. *Journal of Primary Prevention, 24,* 199–221.

Botvin, G. J. (2000). Preventing drug abuse in schools: Social and competence enhancement approaches targeting individual-level etiologic factors. *Addictive Behaviors, 25,* 887–897.

Botvin, G. J., & Griffin, K. W. (2005). Prevention science, drug abuse prevention, and Life Skills Training: Comments on the state of the science. *Journal of Experimental Criminology, 1,* 63–78.

Bronfenbrenner, U. (1979). *The ecology of human development: Experiments by nature and design.* Cambridge, MA: Harvard University Press.

Catalano, R. F., Berglund, M. L., Ryan, J. A., Lonczak, H. S., & Hawkins, D. (2002). Positive youth development in the United States: Research findings on evaluations of positive youth development programs. *Prevention & Treatment, 5,* Article 15. Retrieved July 14, 2004, from www.journals.apa.org/prevention/volume5/pre0050015a.html.

Clarke, G. N., Hawkins, W., Murphy, M., Sheeber, L. B., Lewinsohn, P. M., & Seeley, J. R. (1995). Targeted prevention of unipolar depressive disorder in an at-risk sample of high school adolescents: A randomized trial of a group cognitive intervention. *Journal of the American Academy of Child and Adolescent Psychiatry, 34,* 312–321.

Collaborative for Academic, Social, and Emotional Learning. (2005). *Safe and sound: An educational leader's guide to evidence-based social and emotional learning programs: The Illinois Edition.* Chicago, IL: Author.

Davis, M. K., & Gidycz, C. A. (2000). Child sexual abuse prevention programs: A meta-analysis. *Journal of Clinical Child Psychology, 29,* 257–265.

Derzon, J. (2006). How effective are school-based violence prevention programs in preventing and reducing violence and other antisocial behaviors? A meta-analysis. In S. R. Jimerson & J. J. Furlong (Eds.), *The handbook of school violence and school safety: From research to practice* (pp. 429–441). Mahwah, NJ: Lawrence Earlbaum.

Durlak, J. A. (1995). *School-based prevention programs for children and adolescents.* Thousand Oaks, CA: Sage.

Durlak, J. A. (1997). *Successful prevention programs for children and adolescents.* New York: Plenum.

Durlak, J. A. (2000). Health promotion as a preventive strategy. In D. Cicchetti, J. Rappaport, I. Sandler, & R. P. Weissberg (Eds.), *The promotion of wellness in children and adolescents* (pp. 221–241). Washington, DC: Child Welfare League of America Press.

Durlak, J. A. (2003). Generalizations regarding effective prevention and health promotion programs. In T. P. Gullotta & M. Bloom (Eds.), *The encyclopedia of primary prevention and health promotion* (pp. 61–69). New York: Kluver Academic/Plenum.

Durlak, J. A., & Dupre, E. P. (2008). Implementation matters: A review of research on the influence of implementation on program outcomes and the factors affecting implementation. *American Journal of Community Psychology, 41,* 327–330.

Durlak, J. A., & Weissberg, R. P. (2005, August). *A major meta-analysis of positive youth development programs.* Paper presented at the meeting of the American Psychological Association, Washington, DC.

Durlak, J. A., Weissberg, R. P., Kawashima, K., Preheim Dupre, E., & Pachan, M. (June 2005). Violence prevention for children. In M. A. Fuentes (Chair), *Violence prevention across the life span.* Symposium presented at the 10th Biennial Conference of the Society for Social Research and Action, Champaign-Urbana, Il.

Durlak, J. A., & Wells, A. M. (1997). Primary prevention mental health programs for children and adolescents: A meta-analytic review. *American Journal of Community Psychology, 25,* 115–152.

Durlak, J. A., & Wells, A. M. (1998). Evaluation of indicated preventive intervention (secondary prevention) mental health programs for children and adolescents. *American Journal of Community Psychology, 26,* 775–802.

Elias, M. J., Zins, J. E., Weissberg, R. P., Frey, K. S., Greenberg, M. T., Kessler, R., et al. (1997). *Promoting social and emotional learning: Guidelines for educators.* Alexandria, VA: Association for Supervision and Curriculum Development.

Ennett, S. T., Ringwalt, C. L., Thorne, J., Rohrbach, L. A., Vincus, A., Simons-Rudolph, A., et al. (2003). A comparison of current practice in school-based substance use prevention programs with meta-analysis findings. *Prevention Science, 4,* 1–14.

Fixsen, D. L., Naoom, S. F., Blasé, K. A., Friedman, R. M., & Wallace, F. (2005). *Implementation research: A synthesis of the literature.* Tampa, FL: University of South Florida, Louis de la Parte Florida Mental Health Institute, The National Implementation Research Network (FMHI Publication #231). Retrieved November 1, 2006, from nirn.fmhi.usf.edu/resources/publications/Monograph/pdf/monograph_full.pdf.

Flay, B. R., & Allred, C. G. (2003). Long-term effects of the Positive Action Program—A Comprehensive, Positive Youth Development Program. *American Journal of Health Behavior, 27(Supp 1),* S6–S21.

Flay, B. R., Allred, C. G., & Ordway, N. (2001). Effects of the Positive Action Program on achievement and discipline: Two matched-control comparisons. *Prevention Science, 2,* 71–89.

Gottfredson, D. C., & Gottfredson, G. D. (2002). Quality of school-based prevention programs:

Results from a national survey. *Journal of Research in Crime and Delinquency, 39,* 3–35.

Gottfredson, D. C., Gottfredson, G. D., & Hybl, L. G. (1993). Managing adolescent behavior: A multiyear, multischool study. *American Educational Research Journal, 30,* 179–215.

Greenberg, M. T., Weissberg, R. P., O'Brien, M. U., Zins, J. E., Fredericks, L., Resnik, H., & Elias, M. J. (2003). Enhancing school-based prevention and youth development through coordinated social, emotional, and academic learning. *American Psychologist, 58,* 466–474.

Greenhalgh, T., Robert, G., Macfarlane, F., Bate, P., Kyriakidou, O., & Peacock, R. (2005). *Diffusion of innovations in health service organizations: A systematic literature review.* Oxford: Blackwell.

Han, S. S., & Weiss, B. (2005). Sustainability of teachers' implementation of school-based mental health programs. *Journal of Abnormal Child Psychology, 33,* 665–679.

Hawkins, J. D., Kosterman, R., Catalano, R. F., Hill, K. G., & Abbott, R. D. (2005). Promoting positive adult functioning through social development intervention in childhood: Long term effects from the Seattle Social Development Project. *Archives of Pediatric and Adolescent Medicine, 159,* 25–31.

Kerr, D. M., Kent, L., & Lam, T. C. M. (1985). Measuring program implementation with a classroom observation instrument: The interactive teaching map. *Evaluation Review, 9,* 461–482.

Lonczak, H. S., Abbott, R. D., Hawkins, J. D., Kosterman, R., & Catalano, R. (2002). Effects of the Seattle Social Development Project on sexual behavior, pregnancy, birth, and sexually transmitted disease outcomes by age 21 years. *Archives of Pediatric and Adolescent Medicine, 156,* 438–447.

Mazza, J. J. (1997). School-based suicide prevention programs: Are they effective? *School Psychology Review, 26,* 382–296.

McGraw, S., Sellers, D., Stone, E., Bebchuk, J., Edmundson, E., Johnson, C., et al. (1996). Using process data to explain outcomes: An illustration from the child and adolescent trial for cardiovascular health (CATCH). *Evaluation Review, 20,* 291–312.

Miller, D. N., & DuPaul, G. J. (1996). School-based prevention of adolescent suicide: Issues, obstacles, and recommendations for practice. *Journal of Emotional and Behavioral Disorders, 4,* 221–230.

Mytton, J. A., DiGuiseppi, C., Gough, D. A., Taylor, R. S., & Logan, S. (2002). School-based violence prevention programs: Systematic review of secondary prevention trials. *Archives of Pediatric and Adolescent Medicine, 156,* 752–762.

Nation, M., Crusto, C., Wandersman, A., Kumpfer, K. L., Seybolt, D., Morrissey-Kane, E., et al. (2003). What works in prevention: Principles of effective prevention programs. *American Psychologist, 58,* 449–456.

New Jersey Department of Education (1996). *New Jersey Core Curriculum Content Standards.* Trenton, NJ: Author.

O'Donnell, J., Hawkins, J. D., Catalano, R. F., Abbott, R., & Day, L. E. (1995). Preventing school failure, drug use, and delinquency among low-income children: Long-term intervention in elementary schools. *American Journal of Orthopsychiatry, 65,* 87–100.

Osher, D., Dwyer, K., & Jackson, S. (2004). *Safe, supportive and successful school: Step by step.* Boston: MA: Sopris West Educational Services.

Ringwalt, C., Ennett, S. T., Vincus, A. A., Rohrbach, L. A., & Simons-Rudolph, A. (2004). Who's calling the shots? Decision-makers and the adoption of effective school-based substance use prevention curricula. *Journal of Drug Education, 34,* 19–31.

Rohrbach, L., A., Ringwalt, C. L., Ennett, S. T., & Vincus, A. A. (2005). Factors associated with adoption of evidence-based substance use prevention curricula in US school districts. *Health Education Research, 20,* 514–526.

Rogers, E. M. (2003). *Diffusions of innovations* (5th ed.). New York: Free Press.

Ross, M. R., & Powell, S. R., & Elias, M. J. (2002). New roles for school psychologists: Addressing the social and emotional learning needs of students. *School Psychology Review, 31,* 43–52.

Sheridan, S. M., & Gutkin, T. B. (2000). The ecology of school psychology: Examining and changing our paradigm for the 21st century. *School Psychology Review, 29,* 485–502.

Solomon, D., Battistich, V., Watson, M., Schaps, E., & Lewis, C. (2000). A six-district study of educational change: Direct and mediated effects of the Child Development Project. *Social Psychology of Education, 4,* 3–51.

Tobler, N. S., Roona, M. R., Ochshorn, P., Marshall, D. G., Streke, A. V., & Stackpole, K. M. (2000). School-based adolescent drug prevention programs: 1998 meta-analysis. *Journal of Primary Prevention, 20,* 275–336.

Tremblay, R. E., Pagani-Kurtz, L. Masse, L. C., Vitaro, F., & Pihl, R. O. (1995). A bimodal preventive intervention for disruptive kindergarten boys: Its impact through mid-adolescence. *Journal of Consulting and Clinical Psychology, 63,* 560–568.

Tremblay, R. E., Vitaro, F. Betrand, L. Leblanc, M., Beauchesne, H., Boileau, H., & David, L. (1992). Parent and child training to prevent early onset of delinquency: The Montreal longitudinal-experimental study. In. J. McCord & R. E. Tremblay (Eds.), *Preventing antisocial behavior: Interventions from birth through adolescence* (pp. 117–131). New York: Guilford.

Weissberg, R. P., & Greenberg, M. T. (1998). School and community competence-enhancement and prevention programs. In W. Damon (Series Editor) and I. E. Siegel & L. A. Renninger (Vol. Eds.), *Handbook of child psychology: Vol. 4. Child psychology in practice* (5th ed., pp. 877–954). New York: Wiley.

Wilson, D., B., Gottfredson, D. C., & Najaka, S. S. (2001). School-based prevention of problem behaviors: A meta-analysis. *Journal of Quantitative Criminology, 17,* 247–272.

Wilson, D. B., Lipsey, M. W., & Derzon, J. H. (2003). The effects of school-based intervention programs on aggressive behavior: A meta-analysis. *Journal of Consulting and Clinical Psychology, 71,* 136–149.

Zins, J. E., Weissberg, R. P., Wang, M. C., & Walberg. H. J. (Eds.). (2004). *Building academic success on social and emotional learning: What does the research say?* New York: Teachers College Press.

CHAPTER 43

ORGANIZATIONAL CONSULTATION

AND SYSTEMS INTERVENTION

JOEL MEYERS, SHERRIE LYNN PROCTOR, AND EMILY COOK GRAYBILL
Georgia State University

ADENA B. MEYERS
Illinois State University

As noted elsewhere in this volume, consultation represents an important role for psychologists in schools (Gutkin & Curtis, Chapter 28). Consultation can focus on the child, the classroom, or the system (Meyers, 1995; Meyers, Meyers & Grogg, 2004). Organizational development and systemic intervention can be viewed as consultation methods that address issues relevant to the system. Throughout the chapter these approaches will be referred to as "organizational consultation" and that will serve as the focus of this chapter.

It has been argued that the potential preventive contributions of consultation have not received sufficient attention in the scholarly literature (Meyers et al., 2004). Organizational consultation offers an opportunity for psychologists in schools to maximize their preventive efforts, while attaining widespread effects by using organizational strategies to support preventive goals that affect a maximum number of children and staff. The purpose of this chapter is to facilitate understanding of organizational consultation, to delineate the important issues that influence effective implementation of organizational consultation, to review the relevant research literature, and to create a research agenda that might enhance future work with organizational consultation.

Organizational consultation can be applied to a range of community settings, and in this chapter, it is discussed in the context of school-based consultation. School-based organizational consultation involves a relationship in which a consultant (or team of consultants) works with a system (school or school district) in an effort to promote growth and solve problems affecting the students, staff (i.e., teachers, administrators, other educators, nonprofessional staff), and other people (i.e., parents, community members) affected by the system. The goal is to strengthen the overall functioning of the system with positive effects for its members, particularly students. School-based organizational consultants seek to help schools and/or school districts to implement systems interventions related to school leadership, team problem solving, interpersonal relationships, school climate, curriculum, instruction, student academic performance, social-emotional development of children, home-school relationships, school-community relationships and so forth.

HISTORICAL OVERVIEW OF ORGANIZATIONAL CONSULTATION AND SYSTEMS INTERVENTION

There are at least four historical influences that have led to the development of school-based organizational consultation. These include "field theory" (Lewin, 1951), organization development consultation (Schmuck, 1995), mental health consultation (Caplan, 1970), and models of school reform (Fullan, 1991; Sarason, 1971; 1990).

Field Theory

Kurt Lewin (1951) developed "field theory" as a basis for conducting "action research" that uses a problem-solving process in which the researcher seeks to define the research focus, collects data to plan an intervention, evaluates the intervention, and revises the intervention based on evaluation data. "Field theory" forms one important foundation for organizational consultation because it helps to conceptualize systems and develop effective interventions.

According to this theory, the environment serves as a field that includes forces resulting in various outcomes. When working toward a given goal, the consultant examines the environment (i.e., field) to determine which of the existing forces support the goal (moving forces) and which forces inhibit goal attainment (restraining forces). Action plans are then developed to change the system by enhancing moving forces and reducing restraining forces. Lewin's approaches to force field analysis and action research have initiated many of the methods currently used for organizational consultation.

Organization Development Consultation

Organization development was one of the first approaches to organizational consultation to appear in the professional literature, with much of the initial work focusing on applications to business settings. Various authors have provided definitions for organization development (e.g., see Bennis, 1969; Dougherty, 1990; French & Bell, 1973; Fullan, Miles, & Taylor, 1980; Lippitt & Lippitt, 1986; Schein, 1988; Schmuck, 1995). Within the school consultation literature, organizational development has been defined as "the application of behavioral science knowledge, particularly social psychological principles of group dynamics, to the problems of organizations.... The application of this knowledge by the (organizational consultation) has as its goal a more adaptive, flexible and self-renewing organization" (Meyers, Parsons, & Martin, 1979). A hallmark of this approach is the substantial time investment necessary to accomplish the systemic changes believed to be required to create meaningful and sustained organizational change (e.g., see Kelly, 2004; Walters & Henkleman, 1990).

While organization development can be useful in schools, there are times when briefer and more targeted systems interventions are needed

and can be effective to create organizational change in schools. As a result, this chapter is designed to consider a range of approaches to school-based organizational consultation that can include but are not limited to the long-term and comprehensive interventions involved in organization development. We use the term organizational consultation to refer to all of these approaches.

Caplan's Consultation Model

Gerald Caplan (1970) also influenced school-based organizational consultation (Erchul, 1993; Lambert, Hylander, & Sandoval, 2004). Caplan's model of mental health consultation was targeted to a wide range of community settings, and some have worked to apply this model specifically to school settings (Alpert, 1976; Erchul, 1993; Lambert et al., 2004; Meyers, 1995; Meyers et al., 2004; Meyers et al., 1979). His initial framework included four types of consultation, two of which were directly relevant to organizational consultation (i.e., "program-centered administrative consultation" and "consultee-centered administrative consultation"). These are discussed in more detail later in this chapter in the section that introduces our model of organizational consultation.

School Reform

There is a long history of system-wide, statewide, and federal efforts to reform various aspects of the education offered to children in American public schools. Inevitably these efforts include some form of systemic intervention as well as the goals of sustaining the reforms over time. While this literature is generally separate from the literature on organizational consultation, there are numerous common features as noted in the works of Michael Fullan (1991) and Seymour Sarason (1971; 1990).

ISSUES AFFECTING ORGANIZATIONAL CONSULTATION AND SYSTEMS INTERVENTION

Prevention

Caplan's (1964) prevention framework, which distinguishes between primary, secondary and tertiary prevention, has important implications for organizational consultation. While there have been modifications of this framework (e.g., see Meyers & Nastasi, 1999), the essential components of Caplan's approach have had a continuing impact on school-based mental health services (see Chapter 42). Although organizational consultation has the potential to achieve goals associated with each type of prevention, there is a particular opportunity to accomplish goals associated with primary prevention because of the focus on the system as a whole (or some clearly defined subcomponent of the system).

Ecological Theory, Prevention, and Systems Intervention

Albee (1988) presented a formula that provides a conceptual guide for developing systems interventions to prevent mental health problems. Modifications of Albee's formula have been proposed for application to the practice of psychology in schools (Meyers & Meyers, 2003; Meyers & Nastasi, 1999). The implications are that comprehensive efforts to prevent educational and health disorders should be designed to enhance variables such as self-esteem, subjective well-being, and competence as well as educational, social and/or medical supports, while attempting to reduce the impact of individual predispositions, stress, and systemic exploitation. In this context, ecological theory is important because effective school-based preventive interventions are likely to target interactions between the person and the setting (Bronfenbrenner, 1989; Meyers & Nastasi, 1999).

Assumptions of Process Consultation

The model of organizational consultation presented in this chapter overlaps in several ways with Schein's (1988) model of *process consultation*. A number of the assumptions underlying that model are also applicable to our model of school-based organizational consultation. These assumptions are presented below with particular attention to their application to school-based practice.

Beliefs about Human Nature

Much of the organizational consultation literature assumes that approaches to organizational leadership are based on the organization's beliefs about human nature. Schein (1988) discusses two models of human nature that may influence the behaviors of school leaders, as well as teachers and students in turn. The first is McGregor's Theory X, hypothesizing that people work for money and must be controlled and motivated to do a good job. Control would be exerted though administrative directive and economic incentives. In contrast, applied to teachers, McGregor's Theory Y suggests that teachers work to do the best they can

for children and to meet their own professional goals in the context of good supportive relationships with colleagues. Schein (1988) adds that people in organizations have a range of motives, knowledge and skills and can change and grow on these dimensions. Further, he argues that organizations will be most effective if there are structures designed to meet these needs on an individual basis.

Organizational Structures and Processes

Organizational structures include formally defined positions and roles such as administrator, teacher, student, psychologist, and so forth. While structures provide insight to organizational consultants, they tend to be static. To create systems change, it is assumed that organizational consultants must also attend to those processes in the organization that are dynamic and change over time (e.g., curriculum, instructional methods, discipline procedures, leadership styles, group problem-solving approaches, and so forth).

Knowledge That Organization Members May Lack

It is assumed that administrators and teachers often do not know what the organizational problem is, how to diagnose the problem, or what assistance can be offered by organizational consultants. While administrators and other educators often intend to improve their instructional environment and climate, they may not know how to identify what needs improvement or how to improve it. This is particularly true for such issues as leadership, school climate, interpersonal relationships, group problem-solving methods and so forth.

Empowerment

Process consultation includes the assumption that schools function best if they learn to diagnose and manage their own strengths and weaknesses. Generally, organizational consultants do not know enough about the organization, its procedures, and its cultures to make optimal suggestions without input. Therefore, interventions must be developed jointly with members of the organization. If interventions are to be implemented successfully and on a sustained basis, educators must learn to see the problem for themselves and think through intervention options. A goal of our model of organizational consultation is to develop the organization's capacity related to diagnosis and intervention so that the organization has greater potential to solve its own problems in the future. Consultants who adopt this perspective view the consultees in the organization as professional colleagues who are equal in the problem-solving process (i.e., a nonhierarchical and coordinate relationship; Caplan, 1970; Meyers, 1995). This approach is consistent with Rappaport's (1981) ideas about empowerment, and is radically different from a directive approach in which the consultant is viewed as the expert who controls the consultation process.

Constructivism

Social constructivism suggests that knowledge is constructed by the individual in the context of social or cultural circumstances (Sexton & Griffin, 1997; Vygotsky, 1978). There are several constructivist principles that are important for organizational consultation (see Sandoval, 1996; 2003 for discussions of constructivism and consultation). For example, prior knowledge is important in understanding change during organizational consultation. According to constructivist theory, prior knowledge is organized in unique cognitive structures referred to as *schemas* (Vygotsky, 1978) and the social context adds to meaning as members of the social or cultural group share knowledge (in the form of schemas). This shared cultural knowledge can be exchanged between cultures (or may be difficult to exchange) based on the extent to which these groups are similar. This is important for organizational consultation because the consultant seeks to promote knowledge exchange between multiple cultural groups (such as consultants, consultees, clients, ethnic groups, different socioeconomic status (SES) levels, gender, and so forth) that vary in the extent to which they are similar (Ingraham, 2000).

New knowledge developed from the collaboration of consultants and members of the organization must be within the realm of the conceivable (zone of proximal development) or it will be dismissed by some participants (Vygotsky, 1978). The zone of proximal development is where new knowledge is developed through social mediation that occurs in formal and informal interactions among the participants in organizational consultation. This framework suggests that members of the organization can learn and change based on support they receive in areas just beyond their existing knowledge or schemas (i.e., the *zone of proximal development*). The organizational consultant seeks to find ways to provide such

support for members of the organization to enhance their learning. This is referred to as *scaffolding* because new knowledge is built on prior knowledge. Further, to *accommodate* new knowledge that is obtained in consultation through scaffolding, it is necessary for the learner to act on this knowledge. In other words, new knowledge developed through organizational consultation must be acted upon by participants in the organization if this knowledge is to be incorporated into the members' schemas. This implies that participants in organizational consultation must be actively engaged during consultation (Sexton & Griffin, 1997).

Multicultural Influences on Organizational Consultation

Cultural factors can have a significant impact on the process and outcome of school consultation (Ingraham, 2000). This is particularly important for organizational consultation because of its focus on groups. Culture includes a range of factors in addition to ethnicity or race (e.g., SES, acculturation status, gender, professional role, sexual orientation, disability status). Culture has been discussed as an "organized framework of thoughts, beliefs, and norms for interaction and communication patterns" (Ingraham, 2000, p. 325). Organizational consultants need to display attitudes, skills, and knowledge relevant to multicultural practice, including awareness of their own and other cultures, and skills in cross-cultural communication and collaboration. This is an area that needs further investigation.

Strong Objectivity: A Link Between Organizational Consultation, Culture and Prevention

"Strong objectivity" has the potential to strengthen multicultural consultation (Henning-Stout & Meyers, 2000). According to this perspective, the most objective and accurate perspectives on any mainstream theory come from the most marginalized people in the system or culture that generated the theory (Harding, 1991). As applied to organizational consultation, the least powerful and most disenfranchised participants would help to provide an accurate and objective perspective, leading to methods that are most responsive and relevant with high potential for success (Henning-Stout & Meyers, 2000). As a result, in organizational consultation the application of "strong objectivity" would encourage the active involvement of consultees, clients, and others who traditionally lacked power in the organization that is the target of consultation. Such marginalized groups have been referred to elsewhere as "missing voices" (Meyers, Dowdy, & Paterson, 2000) and might include teachers, parents, nonprofessional staff, or students.

A Model of Organizational Consultation and Systems Intervention

As noted throughout this chapter our model of organizational consultation is derived from others' approaches to implementing organizational consultation or systems intervention. It is also based on our experiences providing various forms of organizational consultation. We have distilled information from all of these sources to create the model that is presented in this chapter. Based on Caplan (1970), and in contrast to the literature on organization development, we believe that there are two essential types of organizational consultation. One is analogous to Caplan's "program-centered administrative consultation" and the other is analogous to Caplan's "consultee-centered administrative consultation." However, we prefer to use the term "organizational consultation" rather than "administrative consultation," because of the principle that organizational consultation must be offered to all relevant levels of the system, rather than being directed only to the administrative levels of the organization. As a result, we conceptualize two distinct sets of goals in organizational consultation by considering *program-centered organizational consultation* and *consultee-centered organizational consultation*.

The focus of *program-centered organizational consultation* is to assist the organization with a specifically defined component of its work. Examples include helping a school system examine and strengthen its existing reading curriculum, discipline system, or program for home-school collaboration. Other examples might be to help a school system develop and implement new programs designed to promote social skills, prevent alcohol and drug abuse, prevent bullying and so forth. For this type of consultation, it can be important that the consultant (or a member of the consultation team) have expertise related to the content of the consultation (e.g., reading curriculum, discipline systems, home-school collaboration, prevention of bullying and so forth).

School-based *consultee-centered organizational consultation* is an approach where the consultant helps the school address issues that are fundamental to the effective functioning of organizations. These might include interpersonal relationships among staff, leadership strategies, approaches to group problem-solving methods, and so forth. The goals of consultee-centered organizational consultation overlap substantially with the goals of process consultation and organization development consultation (Lippitt & Lippitt, 1986; Schein, 1988).

We believe that the distinction between program-centered and consultee-centered organizational consultation is important because it draws attention to the wide range of goals that can be the focus of organizational consultation, and because it helps to distinguish between specific program-related goals and broader goals that can influence the functioning of the school as a system. This distinction may also be important because of the implications for internal and external consultants discussed below. When implementing this model there may be instances where both program-centered and consultee-centered organizational consultation occur simultaneously. That is, after beginning to work toward one type of organizational consultation goal (i.e., program-centered or consultee-centered), it may become apparent that there are also needs for the other type of goal. For example, if systemic decision making and communication problems were uncovered as interfering with effectiveness of program-centered organizational consultation, it might be necessary to conduct consultee-centered consultation to address these decision making and communication problems, while continuing to work toward program-centered goals.

Implications of the Model for Organizational Consultants Who Are Internal or External to the System

The literature on school-based consultation has devoted some attention to the consultant's status as being either internal or external to the system (Dubrow, Wocher, & Austin, 2001). An internal consultant would be an employee of the school system with a clearly defined role, while an external consultant would not be a regular employee of the school system and would be brought in for the express purpose of providing some form of organizational consultation.

Much of the literature on organizational consultation refers to the organizational consultant as being external to the system (i.e., Schein, 1988) and in our experience an external consultant can have certain advantages as an organizational consultant. These advantages include expertise readily attributed to those who come from outside of the system; lack of competing job responsibilities within the system that can enhance the person's perception as an organizational consultant and can allow the consultant to engage 100% in organizational consultation; and organizational commitment to the consultation based on money spent on consultation. In addition, external consultants may have the advantage of being able to offer a different or more objective perspective on circumstances that those internal to the system have trouble seeing clearly. They may also be less likely to encounter problems related to dual roles or conflicts of interest. However, as in all approaches to consultation, internal organizational consultants would have the advantage of an insider's knowledge and understanding of the system and how it works, and they may have previously developed trusting relationships with key personnel within the system that would provide open and ready access to these personnel. Internal consultants may also have more of a vested interest in the outcome of consultation that could enhance their motivation. Also, internal consultants may be in a better position than external consultants to facilitate long-term systems change and provide follow-up services as needed.

Our experience suggests that while external consultants might have equal opportunities to engage in program-centered and consultee-centered organizational consultation, internal consultants would have an easier time engaging in program-centered organizational consultation when compared to consultee-centered approaches. Often the kinds of problems that come up in consultee-centered organizational consultation have the potential to be highly sensitive, particularly when addressing issues such as the system's approaches to leadership, problem solving, collaboration, interpersonal communication, and conflict. When these types of issues require consultation, it is difficult for members of the organization to be sanctioned and trusted to carry out organizational consultation. In contrast, in program-centered organizational consultation, when the focus of attention is on developing and implementing new programs or modifying existing programs, the consultant's expertise in the content of the consultation may become more important than whether they are external to the system.

IMPLEMENTING ORGANIZATIONAL CONSULTATION

There is not adequate space to present all aspects of implementing organizational consultation in sufficient detail within the context of this chapter. As a result, readers are referred to other sources for more detailed information (i.e., Dougherty, 1990; Lippitt & Lippitt, 1986; Schein, 1988; Schmuck, 1995). The following sections present some of the key methods and strategies that are applicable for effective implementation of both program-centered and consultee-centered organizational consultation in the schools.

Collaborative Strategies

Active Engagement of Participants

A key principle that underlies most models of organizational consultation is that the members of the organization must be actively engaged in the consultation process (Caplan, 1970; Dougherty, 1990; Lambert et al., 2004; Meyers et al., 2004; Meyers et al., 1979; Schein, 1988). This may enhance the probability that participants will be committed to the goals of consultation and the intervention plans. As a result, organizational consultants seek to promote the active involvement of participants in establishing problem definition and goal statements, collecting and analyzing data, and developing as well as implementing intervention plans resulting from consultation. These forms of active involvement are expected to maximize the effectiveness of both program-centered and consultee-centered organizational consultation.

Effective Interpersonal Communication

To effectively engage participants in the consultation process, organizational consultants must be skilled in the area of interpersonal communication (Schein, 1988). In addition to standard interpersonal skills such as empathy, open invitation to talk, and facilitative confrontation, it is important that organizational consultants understand how political and systemic factors can complicate interpersonal communication. Further, these skills are needed to underscore with consultees the collaborative, coordinate and nonhierarchial nature of their relationship with the consultant.

Recursive Process

Our model is based on the understanding that organizational consultation is a recursive process that can result in changing problem definitions and intervention plans based on ongoing data collection and reinterpretation of conclusions.

One required component of this recursive process is that organizational consultants must collect and analyze data continuously throughout the consultation process. After data are collected and initial efforts are made to analyze the data, findings are presented to participants for feedback (referred to as "member checking" by qualitative researchers; Meyers, Truscott, Meyers, Varjas & Collins, 2008), that is used to modify interpretations of the findings. In turn, additional data are collected and presented to participants in a cyclical process until consensus is reached about the meaning of findings. This recursive process is ongoing throughout the problem definition and intervention phases, and continues until clarity is reached about the problems, goals, and interventions in organizational consultation. An advantage of this recursive approach is that various political, cultural, or personal factors that could cause problems or interfere with organizational consultation may be identified and addressed as they arise.

Entry Issues

Entry issues are relevant to all types of consultation and a number of these issues are particularly important for both program-centered and consultee-centered organizational consultation. It is important for organizational consultants to understand and use cultural, ecological and political circumstances to enhance consultation. While these issues are always important in consultation, it is particularly important for organizational consultants to assess carefully the cultural factors that are relevant to the system they are approaching. This may include awareness of cultural issues pertinent to ethnic groups represented among the school staff, students, or community that may have an impact on the organizational consultation. Similarly, the consultant must collect sufficient information to develop a thorough understanding of how the school's ecology may influence organizational consultation. This might include aspects of the physical structure of the school layout, the economic support for education in the system, the impact of the local community on education, and so forth. Given that organizational consultants must work at the highest levels of the system, it is also important that the consultant develop an in-depth understanding of the politics that influence decisions in the school or school system; and it is important to understand the impact of local community politics as well.

Given the emphasis on culture, ecology, and politics it is important for organizational consultants to consider how they may be perceived to be aligned with key members of the school/system culture. Organizational consultants should strive to avoid playing favorites with certain participants, and to use perceptions of their relationships with members of the organization in ways that facilitate their entry.

A critically important aspect of the entry phase of organizational consultation is to negotiate a clear agreement about the consultation services to be offered. This can be referred to as contract negotiation, which can be written and formal or can be accomplished verbally with less formality depending on the circumstances. Regardless of whether it is formal or informal, agreement about the services to be provided must be reached with all parties involved. In schools, it is often important to include administrators, pupil services personnel, teachers, and even parents and students in some cases. Including the highest relevant levels of administration is critical since organizational consultation will inevitably involve administrators as well as various administrative or organizational changes. However, it is advisable to include all relevant groups during entry and contract negotiation as this sets a tone that may increase participants' active engagement throughout the consultation stages.

Problem Definition

One of the first steps in organizational consultation is to develop an initial definition of the problem. Sometimes this is done within the context of contract negotiation and at other times it requires more extended work immediately following contract negotiation. Early efforts to define the problem seek input from multiple members of the organization to create an operational definition that has clear implications for goals to be achieved. We view problem definition as an ongoing process during organizational consultation and expect that the goals and definitions may be modified periodically in response to data that are collected.

Needs Assessment

Often, an early component of organizational consultation is a needs assessment that is used to obtain information regarding the problems and goals of consultation. In an effort to gain an accurate understanding of the system, the problem being addressed, and related goals, the needs assessment seeks input from all relevant constituent groups. Needs assessment(s) often use mixed-methods approaches to data collection, which may include individual and group interviews, surveys, observations, and review of extant records. Data collection methods are developed based on initial efforts to define the problem and establish consultation goals. Once data have been collected and analyzed, organizational consultants systematically feed back the findings to the participants and solicit their assistance in interpreting the findings.

Develop and Implement Interventions

As implied throughout this discussion, interventions are developed jointly by the organizational consultant and members of the organization based on their analysis of data collected as a component of consultation.

Challenges Related to Use of Empirically Supported Interventions

The literature on school intervention has included substantial attention to the importance of using empirically supported methods (Kratochwill & Shernoff, 2004). We agree that, other things being equal, there are advantages to using interventions with established or probable efficacy, based on research findings. However, there are important limitations to this approach when applied in the context of our model. These are considered here by discussing program-centered and consultee-centered consultation separately.

The empirical literature on consultee-centered organizational consultation is extremely limited. While many procedures used to implement this approach to consultation have a good deal of support in the literature, this is generally based on theory and the experience of consultants rather than a systematic body of empirical research. As a result, at the present time it may not be possible to apply reasonable standards from the literature on empirically supported interventions to consultee-centered organizational consultation methods.

While there is a much more substantial empirical literature evaluating the efficacy of a wide range of school-based interventions that might be recommended and implemented as a result of program-centered organizational consultation, our model does not support the blind implementation of such approaches without careful consideration of the ecological and cultural circumstances of the school settings where these interventions may be implemented. In fact, we assume that interventions will have to be modified

to be implemented effectively in any specific context, and this view has some support in recent literature on school-based intervention (Meyers et al., 2008; Nastasi, Moore, & Varjas et al., 2006). Ultimately, although empirical support is desirable, it is not the only important criterion in selection of interventions. If a program's methods are not acceptable to relevant constituent groups, such as parents, students, administrators, teachers, or community leaders, its effectiveness will be greatly compromised. Thus it is essential that organizational consultants work collaboratively with members of the organization to select or develop interventions that make sense locally.

Changing School Structures and School Culture

Organizational consultants using our model are encouraged to work collaboratively to develop interventions that are designed to create change in school structures and school culture. We believe that structural and cultural changes increase the potential that interventions will be implemented effectively and sustained over time. For example, changing school structures to create a new role that supports an intervention might create important changes in school culture while helping to promote desired short-term and long-term outcomes. This might be done by including a new teacher with responsibility for social skills training in the school, a new staff position providing an educator responsible for staff development concerning key preventive interventions in the school, and so forth. For example, hiring substitute teachers or rearranging the schedule to free up teachers to participate in problem-solving teams may enhance a school's culture of collaboration, as general education teachers take ownership for solving learning and behavioral problems.

Person-Centered Interventions

A number of preventive interventions are person-centered (e.g., see Meyers & Nastasi, 1999) in the sense that they seek to increase participants' knowledge and skills. Examples might include efforts to increase social skills in order to prevent violence (Edwards, Hunt, Meyers, Grogg, & Jarrett, 2005) or efforts to increase life skills in order to prevent drug and alcohol abuse (Botvin & Dusenbury, 1989; Meyers & Nastasi, 1999). A key strategy that can increase the effectiveness of such person-centered approaches to preventive intervention is to provide environmental supports designed to increase the likelihood that participants practice using their new knowledge and skills in a range of interpersonal situations. The use of environmental supports is based on the assumption that personal factors interact with environmental factors to create meaningful change through preventive programs (Meyers & Nastasi, 1999). A good example of this principle is Shure and Spivack's discussion of "dialoguing" as a way in which adults can talk with children who have been taught social skills in an effort to support their acquisition and use of these skills (Meyers & Nastasi, 1999; Shure, 1988).

Staff Training

Another key element for effective implementation of interventions is to provide systematic staff training to support school change on a continuing basis over a number of years. In this way, all staff members can be informed about the preventive interventions that are being implemented, and those responsible for service delivery can be taught how to implement the program with integrity and how to support children's use of newly acquired skills. Such training is usually needed on a periodic basis (e.g., annually) to orient any new staff to the program and to provide booster sessions for those with prior experience.

Evaluation of Intervention

Effective implementation of program-centered and consultee-centered organizational consultation requires systematic evaluation of the interventions' *acceptability, integrity, and efficacy* (Meyers & Nastasi, 1999; Meyers et al., 2008). Evaluation of *efficacy* can be accomplished through content tests that measure the knowledge taught to participants, questionnaires that measure the attitudes and feelings of participants that are relevant to the interventions used, behavior rating scales filled out by adults knowledgeable about the participating children's behaviors, interviews of students and adults to assess gains in knowledge, as well as changes in attitudes and behaviors, and school records relevant to program outcomes.

Evaluation of the *acceptability* of organizational consultation can be accomplished through interviews and surveys that seek to obtain information about participants' perceptions of various aspects of the organizational consultation process and the resulting interventions. Acceptability surveys and interviews would be directed to students, staff, and parents. This information provides an indication of the system's support for the key components of organizational consultation.

Evaluation of the *integrity* of organizational consultation is also conducted with surveys or interviews. The purpose is to obtain detailed information about how organizational consultation and any resulting interventions are implemented. We assume that any school-based intervention such as organizational consultation will need to be modified in order to be implemented successfully in a given local setting. The purpose of evaluating treatment integrity is to learn about the implementation process. This information can be used to facilitate the interpretation of positive or negative outcome data and the design of changes to implementation when needed (e.g., see Meyers et al., 2008).

RESEARCH RELATED TO ORGANIZATIONAL CONSULTATION

There has been limited research on school-based organizational consultation, particularly in the past twenty years. As a result, we have expanded the time frame for the literature review in this chapter to include some work from the 1980s. In addition, rather than limiting the review to research on school-based organizational consultation, we have included a few investigations of organizational consultation in public settings outside of the public schools such as universities, mental health agencies, and so forth. We also present results from some case studies that do not report clear research deigns. Throughout this review, we emphasize investigations that shed light on the processes needed to conduct organizational consultation successfully. The review is organized into two primary sections, the first focusing on program-centered organizational consultation, and the second focusing on consultee-centered organizational consultation. The chapter concludes by presenting an agenda for future research and overall conclusions about future directions for organizational consultation.

Review of Research about Program-Centered Organizational Consultation

While there has been little research about organizational consultation, most of the literature that does exist focuses on program-centered (as opposed to consultee-centered) consultation. This is due, in part, to the fact that some of the school reform literature has implications for program-centered organizational consultation. Also, program-centered organizational consultation may occur more frequently because of the focus on specific programs or innovations, rather than on underlying problems of the organization such as communication, leadership, or interpersonal conflict. We review a sample of this research to illustrate findings and point to future directions for research and practice. In general, several recurrent themes are evident in the recent literature on program-centered organizational consultation. These include the use of qualitative research methods, efforts to address or understand cultural issues, efforts to address or understand resistance, and description of consultation stages. Although most of this literature is primarily descriptive, a few studies address questions about the contributions of specific strategies (e.g., contract negotiation and treatment acceptability) to consultation outcomes. Also, although program-centered consultation tends to emphasize changes in program content as opposed to influencing interpersonal, emotional and systemic processes in the organization, the literature reveals the important role that individual change and systemic process variables can play in program-centered organizational consultation.

B. Meyers (2002) reports a case study using qualitative methods to investigate the contract negotiation stage of school-based, cross-cultural organizational consultation. This empirical study examines how particular aspects of contract negotiation may have contributed to a majority white faculty at a predominantly white elementary school withdrawing from a school reform project that sought to provide excellent education to low-income, African American students.

Qualitative methods were used to code data from multiple sources (e.g., needs assessment, focus group and exit interviews, documents, logs and commentaries). Emergent themes illustrated two factors that contributed to the school's withdrawal from the project. First, participants believed that the project's exclusive focus on the education of African American students was not a good fit given that African American students represented a minority of their student population, and that pedagogical beliefs of the faculty were often in conflict with methods espoused by the school reform project.

The second contributing factor was a series of failures during the contracting phase of organizational consultation (B. Meyers, 2002).

Themes specific to contract negotiation problems included: different expectations and beliefs of consultants and the school's faculty, faculty dissatisfaction with project procedures and policies, misunderstandings concerning money, failure to solicit meaningful teacher input during contract negotiation, and expeditious contracting with this school in order to initiate the project rather than seeking the best match. These findings concerning the importance of contract negotiation provide support for Remley's (1993) suggestions about factors that should be included when developing a consultation contract (e.g., clearly specify work to be completed by consultant, establish a time line for completion, delineate the lines of authority, describe compensation and method of payment). The data collected by B. Meyers (2002) illustrate how focusing on the content of the project (exemplary education of for African American students) to the exclusion of the processes needed for effective organizational consultation (e.g., application of effective interpersonal skills and communication, clear and thoroughly understood contract negotiation, accurate problem definition) can impede desired outcomes.

In addition, this investigation raises important issues concerning cultural variables in consultation. In this instance, the cultural dynamics involved a team of predominantly African American school reformers attempting to conduct program-centered organizational consultation with a school including a predominantly white faculty, administration, and student body. Similar to many other examples of cross-cultural consultation, this situation required the use of culturally sensitive approaches to consultation, but in this case it would have been necessary for the minority group consultants to be sensitive to the culture of this predominantly majority-group school setting. However, the reformers were so committed to the content of the reform (exemplary education for African American students) that they were unwilling to adhere to best practices in organizational consultation by modifying the contract to fit the school's needs.

As noted earlier in this section, the Participatory Culture-Specific Intervention Model (Nastasi et al., 2004) also has implications for cultural issues in organizational consultation because of its use of qualitative and ethnographic methodology, collaborative consultation, and action research methods. Importantly, culture is not defined simply by this model as ethnic, racial, or geographical factors. Instead, culture is defined in terms of such factors (e.g., ethnicity, SES, religion) as they interact with specific local circumstances of the organization or community. Further, there is an emphasis on within group differences as well as differences between various cultural groups.

This model of organizational consultation is a component of the Sri Lanka Mental Health Project (i.e., Nastasi et al., 2004; Nastasi, Varjas, Bernstein, & Jayasena, 2000), a mental health intervention program implementing culturally specific mental health services in schools using a number of stages (i.e., Understand Existing Theory, Research, Practice; Learn the Culture; Form Partnerships; Identify Problems/Goals; Collect Data & Define Problems/Goals; Generate Culture-Specific Hypotheses; Design & Implement Culture-Specific Interventions; Evaluate Intervention & Consultation; and Institutionalization). In-depth interviews with key participants facilitated a collaborative approach to problem identification. This process generated hypotheses specific to the local cultural setting that led to the collaborative development of interventions targeted specifically to the local culture. Evaluation addressed the acceptability, integrity, and effectiveness of intervention using data from student work, teacher session logs, group process evaluations from students, informal interviews on site, and formal periodic consultation sessions with teachers. Institutionalization efforts sought to enhance the participants' skills and empower them to continue the intervention. This research would have been strengthened by greater attention to efficacy, particularly how specific components of the consultation model were related empirically to outcome.

O'Neil and Conyne (1992) describe an example of program-centered organizational consultation addressing cultural issues within a university setting. In this case, a campus diversity committee developed recommendations to reduce racist and sexist stereotypes. The consultant, an internal consultant who served as an original member of that committee, then worked with the university to make the committee's recommendations public and facilitate their implementation. Procedures from Lippitt and Lippitt's (1986) model of organizational consultation were used, although timing required that the phases of this model were implemented in a nonsequential manner. For example, problem identification and action plans were developed by the committee before the consultation contract was established with the internal consultant. The consultation

occurred over 18 months and the consultant followed up with the university after consultation was concluded. Evaluation included the percentage of recommendations that were implemented and accepted by the university. Additionally, administrators completed a follow-up questionnaire assessing their knowledge of the committee's action and the impact of the recommendations on their jobs. While 73% of the recommendations to reduce stereotypes were implemented, many of the administrators reported they had little knowledge of the committee's actions and recommendations. Half of the participants noted that the recommendations affected their jobs and provided specific examples of the differences observed.

An additional example of program-centered consultation offered to a university occurred in the aftermath of the attacks on the World Trade Center buildings on September 11, 2001. In this case, there was little time for contract negotiation when a university faculty member served as an internal consultant to facilitate an action plan for crisis intervention designed to meet the mental health needs of the university community (Knotek, 2006). Instead, all consultation steps were implemented in an expedited manner (i.e., Entry, Data Gathering, Problem Definition, Intervention and Short-Term Action Plans, and Feedback to the System).

The author describes how the consultant used organizational consultation methods to coordinate crisis intervention services for the student population in the days following 9/11. Specific issues discussed include how the consultant and organization gathered data regarding the college's existing crisis plans, as well as how consultees (i.e., college staff) responded to the crisis. Furthermore, the author detailed how crisis team members from various facets of the college community came together to develop a short-term action plan. Finally, resistance to the action plan is described (i.e., lack of knowledge and skills among members of the system, consultees' lack of objectivity, and existing conflicts between faculty and administration).

There are few studies that document large-scale program-centered organizational consultation in the schools. One example presented by Zins (1992) reports a retrospective analysis of organizational consultation conducted over a five-year period to develop psychological consultative services based on a model of prereferral intervention (i.e., Truscott, Cosgrove, Meyers, & Eidle-Barkman, 2000). While focusing on the content of consultation (improving the system's psychological consultation services by changing approaches and enhancing skills of consultants and consultees), it was necessary to engage in consultation processes that empowered consultees, facilitated their active engagement in the consultation process, and enhanced the commitment of teachers and staff to the new consultation services. To do this the organizational consultant engaged in collaborative, problem-solving activities with the teachers to build trust and create commitment to the new model of psychological consultation. The author discussed how the following steps of organizational consultation were implemented: Entry and Relationship Establishment; Contractual Arrangements, Goal Setting and Action Planning; Taking Action and Establishing Feedback; and Program Evaluation.

One important contribution of this report is the discussion of barriers and resistance faced throughout consultation. For example, the school system's past negative experiences with consultants, the time demands on consultants, and external factors (i.e., a teacher in the school system being sued) all served as barriers to consultation. It is noteworthy that the author underscored the importance of long-term consultation (five years in this case). The author argues that the extended period of time with the system contributed to the consultant's rapport and facilitated efforts to teach problem-solving processes to the staff.

Zins (1992) concludes that organizational consultants must engage flexibly in a variety of consultative roles (e.g., joint problem solver, expert, program or process evaluator). Data-based evaluation and marketing efforts proved to be important. Significantly, the effective consultation process led to solutions developed by the consultees.

As noted earlier, conceptual change in the consultee(s) may be a goal of either consultee-centered or program-centered organizational consultation. Some "consultee-centered" approaches include conceptual change in the consultee as a key component of the definition of organizational consultation (Lambert et al., 2004). We argue that conceptual change can also be a significant outcome of program-centered organizational consultation. This is demonstrated in research on school-based Instructional Consultation Teams (e.g., see Knotek, Rosenfield, Gravois, & Babinski, 2003).

Rosenfield (1992) describes instructional consultation teams as an approach to maximize

students' academic performance. These teams can be implemented systemically using a series of stages that are similar to those discussed in the literature on organizational consultation: initiation, implementation, institutionalization, and evaluation. This innovation has been implemented in schools for more than 20 years, and there is evidence supporting the model's effectiveness (Gravois & Rosenfield, 2002; Gravois & Rosenfield, 2006; Rosenfield, 1992).

Knotek et al. (2003) sought to determine whether conceptual change resulted from this educational reform. Qualitative research methods were used including interviews, direct observations, consultation documents, and training documents. Thematic analysis revealed four primary themes that described the conceptual changes in the participants.

1. **Problem solving as initially paradoxical.** Teachers felt initially that they were being guided to consider narrow, data-based, instructionally focused concerns during problem identification; in contrast, they had more global and multifaceted views of their students' problems. The paradox is that these specific questions about students often led teachers to think about students in a more global, complex manner.

2. **Collaborative nature of instructional consultation.** Teachers viewed the instructional consultation process as a collaborative interchange between the consultant and educator. This was particularly true for the communication between consultant and teacher and for the problem-solving components.

3. **The problem and appropriate interventions.** Teachers modified their views of the problem and effective interventions.

4. **Letting go of the consultant's expert role.** Teachers endorsed a collaborative view of consultation in which they no longer relied on the consultant as the expert who would hand them the simple solution to the problem.

Conceptual change was observed on two levels: the teacher-consultees and the case managers who served as instructional consultants. Consultees changed in the way they conceptualized student issues and thought about problem identification. For some case managers, change occurred in how they viewed their professional roles as they shifted from viewing themselves as the content experts to consultants who collaborated with teacher-consultees in a nonhierarchical relationship. The organizational consultation process, staff development, and instructional consultation were all viewed as contributing to the conceptual change.

Despite the strengths of this research on the effectiveness of Instructional Consultation Teams, limitations include the reliance on self-report data from participants regarding consultation. While the authors include helpful discussion about the processes that were used in the problem-identification stage of instructional consultation, one limitation is the lack of systematic data-based evidence about the impact of particular components (e.g., stages) of organizational consultation on the outcomes of this reform. This is a weakness throughout much of the research on organizational consultation, including both program-centered and consultee-centered approaches.

There have been a few beginning efforts to document empirically the linkages between specific organizational consultation methods and consultation outcomes. For example, as noted earlier, B. Meyers (2002) infers a relationship between the contract negotiation stage and consultation outcome by studying a consultation failure. A direct effort to examine the relationships between consultation methods and outcomes is presented by Truscott et al. (2000) using systematic qualitative methodology.

These researchers examine acceptability of the organizational consultation methods used to help a school system develop and implement school-based prereferral intervention teams (Truscott et al., 2000). Poor treatment acceptability is thought to be one reason why well-designed programs may not work well. This investigation was designed to evaluate the acceptability of consultation methods used. Participants reported high levels of acceptability for the consultation methods. The relationships between consultation method, acceptability and outcome were examined and the researchers report temporal sequences of consultation methods followed by related organizational changes that provide evidence that highly acceptable consultation methods resulted in important organizational changes as teams adopted a preventive model. These findings were used by the authors to suggest that there may be a relationship between acceptability and changes made by these prereferral intervention teams.

At the one-year follow up, most changes were still in place (e.g., teachers as team members, preventive focus, team composition, mission statements, goals). While some changes were more difficult to institute (e.g., team use of an effective problem-solving process) the participants continued to express support for these ideas. These findings suggest the need for ongoing consultative and administrative support along with staff development to sustain the results from organizational consultation and support the continued acceptability of newly adopted concepts.

Taken together, these investigations illustrate the complexity of program-centered organizational consultation. It is evident that numerous interacting cultural, contextual, and interpersonal factors that are difficult to measure and poorly understood can influence the processes and outcomes of organizational consultation. In the context of these challenging circumstances, it seems reasonable to assume that the strategies described by many of these authors (e.g., systematic stage-based approaches, iterative use of data, collaboration with members of the organization) may all help increase the success of consultation. However, very little is known about the causal impact of these strategies.

Review of Research on Consultee-Centered Organizational Consultation

While there was some research on approaches consistent with consultee-centered organizational consultation in the 1970s (Fullan et al., 1980) and into the early 1990s (Schmuck, 1995), overall there is a dearth of research on consultee-centered organizational consultation, and importantly, there has been very little research to advance the field in the past 20 years. Much of the more recent published work in this area tends to consist of case studies that vary in quality (e.g., Dubrow et al., 2001; Conway, 1990; Walters & Henkelman, 1990), while some have used systematic qualitative methodology (Kelly, 2004).

One factor limiting both the research and application of consultee-centered approaches to organizational consultation is that schools do not often specifically request these services. As a result, consultants must be creative and flexible in their use of strategies to help schools recognize the need for consultee-centered organizational consultation. One common method is to begin with other more readily accepted approaches, such as program-centered consultation, before negotiating to use consultee-centered organizational consultation. Conway (1990) describes a case study that exemplifies this process. In this case, district-wide staff development was initially focused on program-centered goals (i.e., school-based planning and applying research on effective schools). Later, consultation was modified to focus on consultee-centered goals after it became clear that there was a need to address conflicts involving principals and members of the district's central office.

This case illustrates methods that are used in consultee-centered organizational consultation such as observation, diagnosis, treatment, evaluation, and follow-up. For example, the consultant used data from document reviews, observations, and interviews for problem analysis and diagnosis. An organizational health framework facilitated the consultant's analysis of the problem. Intervention involved feeding back observation and interview data, and using these data to help the administrators develop a collaborative mission statement, clarify roles, and confront group members' behaviors that did not facilitate successful role functioning. Observational data collected by the consultant at five months follow-up indicated that positive group changes occurred (e.g., diminished differences across roles, increased openness in interaction, greater mutual influence among participants).

Rosenbach, Robert, and Taylor (1983) report the results of an investigation that occurred when a school superintendent requested consultation to facilitate better understanding of interpersonal dynamics and school climate as they affected supervision and educational change in the school district. An organizational climate survey was administered to district-level administrators, principals, faculty, secretarial and custodial staff, librarians, cooks and bus drivers. The survey explored such things as employees' satisfaction with supervision, perceptions of feedback from supervisors, and overall job satisfaction. Feedback based on the results was provided to the system in an effort to strengthen communication, enhance effective school leadership, and maximize relations between work groups. This project makes an important contribution by illustrating how performance feedback can be used with administrators and schools to facilitate strategic decision-making in educational settings.

Walters and Henkleman (1990) report on a large-scale organizational development effort where the state department of education supported school districts by using organizational development procedures to (a) improve

instruction and classroom management, and (b) develop a process to facilitate change. State-level staff, knowledgeable about organizational development, provided consultation to participating schools. Initially, consultants encouraged each school's staff to take ownership of their change process and define, for themselves, what needed to be changed. Then consultants assisted schools in collecting, analyzing, and feeding back data that were used as the basis for decision making. Improvements in group functioning were sought by developing team members' problem-solving skills using team-building activities. Consultants served as models by demonstrating positive interpersonal skills such as listening, and giving and receiving feedback and emphasizing that organizational development consultation was a long-term process, lasting three years for each school. Evaluation data revealed positive outcomes (e.g., increased confidence by school teams regarding their problem-solving ability, improved staff morale, development of change agent skills by school team members). The researchers conclude that organizational development strategies can help to ensure the effective and sustained implementation of school reform efforts.

Another example of school-based consultee-centered organizational consultation is reported by Ruch, Oehler, and Bost (1982), who provided organizational consultation to three urban parochial schools. The goal of consultation was to develop a planning process that would facilitate and sustain effective planning and problem solving in the schools. The authors briefly described the components of organizational consultation that were utilized (training, site consultation, survey feedback, force field analysis, and action planning). The evaluation components included the Schein Group Process Inventory (see Schein, 1988) and a concerns-based questionnaire developed using the Concerns Based Adoption Model (Newlove & Hall, 1976). According to this model, after exposure to an innovation (e.g., the new planning process), educators initially experience personal concerns about their ability to incorporate the new innovation into their repertoire. Based on exposure to, knowledge about, and experience with the innovations, their concerns are expected to become more "task related" over time (i.e., concerns about the effectiveness of the implementation). Consistent with this prediction, the participants developed more task-related concerns as the project continued. Based on results of the Schein Group Process Inventory, it was concluded that the participants viewed the training as effective. Also, each school developed and sustained its own plan.

Dubrow et al. (2001) present a case study describing the steps taken to introduce organizational development in a human services agency. This case study focused primarily on the entry stage of consultation. The organization created a new permanent, full-time position for an organizational consultant who served as an internal consultant. This position was designed to facilitate organizational efforts to implement reforms to the state welfare system. The organizational consultant sought to improve communication within the organization, enhance team decision making, and help team leaders design effective team meeting methods. A key method was to feed back data to members of the organization.

Before the consultant could work effectively with the organization, entry issues had to be addressed (e.g., gaining acceptance, and responding to resistance from members of the organization). Entry was accomplished by gradually introducing the consultant to participants, acknowledging reasons for resistance, and framing problems as systems issues to clarify that the consultants did not seek to address the personal aspects of each individual's job performance. A conclusion is presented about the entry process, suggesting that consultants should take time and energy to establish close working relationships with members of the organization. Further, the authors consider some of the challenges involved in implementing organizational development in the public sector (i.e., regulatory constraints, the range of people involved in decision making, and lack of clear outcomes).

Another reason consultee-centered organizational consultation can be difficult to implement is that the organization or particular consultees may not see the need for consultation or may be opposed to working with a consultant. This is described in a study of consultation that was provided to a state-owned South African organization soon after apartheid was ended (Kaminstein, Smith, & Miller, 2000). Because of prior negative experiences with consultation, the organization initially requested an educational program rather than organizational consultation. Predictably, the educational program was unsuccessful, and subsequently, the consultants were able to convince the organization to engage in consultation. Consultation was designed to overcome leadership weaknesses while reducing racial tensions in the organization. The consultation procedures included creating an inventory of leadership skills required for change, facilitating staff introspection, and developing a transformational leadership group. Evaluation was incomplete, as the consultation was still in process at the time of the article's publication. Anecdotal evidence indicated that racial tensions within the organization's leadership had begun to subside.

The authors reach several conclusions from this study. They suggest that interventions, while being grounded in theory and data, need to be redesigned several times to ensure a good fit with the organization. This is consistent with the participatory culture-specific intervention model (Nastasi et al., 2004) as well as our model of organizational consultation. Additionally, the authors concluded that when working with international settings, a consultant should avoid acting like the expert who knows what is wrong and how the organization should be "fixed." They refer to this as "enacting an aspect of colonialism and imperialism" (Kaminstein et al., 2000, p. 59).

A particularly important component of this investigation is its focus on how organizational consultation can be used in the context of racial/ ethnic tensions and how it can help organizations cope with such tensions. By setting ground rules for moderating the group's behaviors during consultation, providing self-reflective opportunities, and providing a safe environment for the organization's leaders to form and establish cross-racial relationships, the organization was able to make small steps toward functioning effectively as a multiracial system (Kaminstein et al., 2000).

One potentially productive way to conduct research on consultee-centered organizational consultation is to use collaborative action research methods. One example is provided by Kelly (2004) who reported using consultee-centered consultation to build the leadership of African Americans in an inner-city community. Kelly and his colleagues describe their work in this community from 1989 to 1999 and discuss their use of action research methods to conduct consultee-centered consultation while helping to strengthen leadership of African Americans in this community (Kelly, 2004; Kelly et al., 2004; Kelly, Mock, & Tandon, 2001). They describe their methodology as collaborative action research because community members were treated as active and equal participants in the research and they attempted to create change while studying the change process. Qualitative interviews were used to collect data. One conclusion from their research is that sustained, effective consultation requires access and support from those with key leadership positions (administrators). It was also found that effective entry into this community required that organizational consultants work to eliminate stereotyped thinking by the organization (i.e., negative views that members and groups in the system had toward consultants or other subgroups in the system). Finally, Kelly and his colleagues conclude that effective consultee-centered consultation requires that consultants understand the culture of the consultee system and translate findings in ways that help consultees meet their role requirements.

Research Agenda

The most compelling finding from this review is that there has been very little research about program-centered or consultee-centered approaches to organizational consultation. As a result, any increase in this research would be a welcome addition to the literature. While data on the outcomes of organizational consultation may help to advance the field, a priority must be to conduct research that investigates the specific processes that are needed for effective organizational consultation. In this section, we present a research agenda that we believe has the greatest potential to advance the field of school-based organizational consultation.

Most of the previous research on program-centered organizational consultation has relied primarily on studies that examine the outcomes of various school interventions, with few studies examining empirically the processes relevant to implementing organizational consultation. Some retrospective case studies consider the impact of variables that may be relevant to the process of program-centered organizational consultation. However, there is a substantial need for prospective research designs that investigate the uses of consultation methods associated with each of the stages of consultation (e.g., entry, problem definition, data collection and analysis, intervention development, intervention implementation, evaluation of intervention, disengagement from the system), as well as the acceptability, integrity, and efficacy of these methods. Additional research questions to be addressed include: What are the contexts in which program-centered organizational consultation methods are used effectively? Which of these

methods are most acceptable and effective for consultation directed to particular goals (e.g., goals related to academic instruction, prevention, and remediation of violent behavior and drug abuse; prevention of social-emotional deficits like depression and anxiety; and poor social skills)?

Even though there have been initial attempts to investigate conceptual changes that may occur during organizational consultation (Knotek et al., 2003), there is a need for more research on this topic. For example, more data are needed to determine whether and what kinds of conceptual changes occur as a result of different approaches to organizational consultation (i.e., consultee-centered as compared to program-centered approaches). Also, future researchers should seek innovative, practical and effective ways to measure conceptual changes occurring in consultees as well as the organization as a whole.

Another clear area of need for research concerns diversity issues in organizational consultation. Only a few published studies in this area have addressed multicultural issues (e.g., Kaminstein et al., 2000; B. Meyers, 2002; Nastasi et al., 2000; O'Neil & Conyne, 1992) and research is needed to sensitize organizational consultants to best practices regarding multicultural factors. Steward (1996) found that many organizational consultants are not prepared during their graduate training to handle multicultural and cross-cultural issues in organizational consultation. As diversity increases in the schools, workforce and the general population, special attention must be given to this topic in future research and in training school-based organizational consultants (Jeltova & Fish, 2005; Steward, 1996).

Some prior investigations have led to hypotheses about factors that may interfere with organizational consultation and these include: lack of clear outcome measures, the range of people involved in decision making, lack of knowledge and skills among members of the system, cosultees' lack of objectivity, inflexible systems, the system's past negative experiences with consultants, a greater demand for the consultant's services than the available time, a range of external factors (e.g., legal and economic factors), as well as conflicts between faculty and administration. Systematic research is needed to identify these sources of resistance and to evaluate strategies designed to overcome such resistance.

In addition to program-centered organizational consultation, all of the issues presented earlier in this research agenda can be applied to consultee-centered organizational consultation. This needs to be done by addressing these same basic research issues in the context of the challenging goals associated with consultee-centered organizational consultation (e.g., organizational leadership, communication and problem solving, interpersonal dynamics that affect systems).

One potential way to study organizational consultation is to use qualitative methodology (Hylander, 2003; Meyers et al., 2008) and/or action research methods (Meyers et al., 2008). Qualitative methods are well suited to research about school-based organizational consultation because of the complex nature of the relationships among teachers, administrators, students, communities and consultants in the context of schools as dynamic systems. Further, collaborative action research models have the potential to increase research about organizational consultation while facilitating more effective practice (e.g., Kelly, 2004; Kelly et al., 2004; Kelly et al., 2001; Meyers et al., 2008; Reason & Bradbury, 2001; Varjas et al., 2004).

Researchers who use qualitative and action research methods to investigate organizational consultation must be careful to employ rigorous methods. Several of the case studies reviewed for this chapter provide some description of consultation but do not report strong, well designed research with high degrees of scientific trustworthiness. Of course, some investigations do include evidence about scientific trustworthiness (e.g., B. Meyers, 2002; Knotek et al., 2003; Truscott et al., 2000). Information about strong research designs to investigate school-based organizational consultation using qualitative methodology and other innovative designs can be found in the literature (e.g., Gravois & Rosenfield, 2002; Meyers et al., 2008).

It could be argued that research on organizational consultation has not made much progress since Fullan et al.'s (1980) review, though there have been some promising efforts to investigate causal connections between particular methods, their acceptability, and outcomes (i.e., Truscott et al., 2000). Some of the research reviewed by Fullan et al. examined the entry stages of consultation, reported data related to entry and considered how those factors were related to sustained implementation. Some of those studies used quantitative or quasi-experimental designs. Future research on school-based organizational consultation should build on these efforts and use quantitative designs as well as qualitative and mixed methods designs, while including experimental controls to document the efficacy of various methods.

CONCLUSIONS AND FUTURE DIRECTIONS IN ORGANIZATIONAL CONSULTATION

Caplan's (1970) distinction between consultee-centered and program-centered approaches to organizational consultation is important because it brings attention to those goals that are applicable to the organization as a whole (e.g., organizational communication, problem solving, leadership, decision making, interpersonal relationships), as compared to those goals that are tied to particular programmatic efforts (enhance social skills, strengthen the reading curriculum, and so forth). These are both important sets of goals, and it is likely that effective strategies may vary depending on which goals are primary (of course, this is an empirical question).

While this distinction may be productive to enhance practice and research, it is important to recognize that both program-centered and consultee-centered organizational consultation seek to promote conceptual and/or attitudinal changes in individual members of the organization (e.g., teachers, administrators, parents, students) who are sometimes referred to as consultees (e.g., teachers, educators) or clients (e.g., students) (see Knotek et al., 2003; Lambert et al., 2004). Future work on organizational consultation should include research, training, and practice in both program-centered and consultee-centered approaches, while considering the kinds of changes sought in individual members of the organization.

Multicultural approaches to any kind of educational or psychological practice are challenging and are a growing priority for school settings in the United States. This is particularly true for organizational consultants who simultaneously encounter multiple cultures when they work with schools. We have already suggested that this is an important goal for future research. In addition organizational consultants need training in effective multicultural strategies, and professional consultants must make systematic efforts to work with cultural sensitivity. In this context, professionals in organizational consultation must avoid the error of oversimplifying constructs like "culture" by viewing it simply as a static variable such as ethnicity, social class, geographic background, and so forth. Multicultural perspectives that recognize the complexity of culture are more likely to lead to effective research and practice in organizational consultation. For example, Nastasi et al. (2004) uses a "culture specific" approach to mold interventions and consultation practices to fit the unique and complex cultural circumstances of each school and community setting that is the focus of consultation.

Effective organizational consultants need to use systematic problem-solving approaches and the strategies for implementing organizational consultation presented in this chapter provide a useful framework. The problem solving stages included in this model can enhance the systematic implementation of organizational consultation (i.e., entry issues, problem definition, development and implementation of interventions, and evaluation). Other components of our implementation model are equally important (i.e., recursive process, active engagement of participants, effective interpersonal communication, and seek out problems during organizational consultation). The emphasis on active engagement of participants who are treated in a collaborative and collegial manner, and who are viewed as professional colleagues with equal status as the consultant, is congruent with prior literature in his area (i.e., see Caplan, 1970; Lambert et al., 2004). The recursive process that uses data to continuously learn about consultation impediments while modifying and strengthening interventions may be a unique addition to the organizational consultation literature and it is congruent with Nastasi et al.'s (2004) approach to participatory culture specific interventions. Taken together, these strategies have the potential to enhance effective implementation of organizational consultation.

REFERENCES

Albee, G. W. (1988). A model for classifying prevention programs. In G. W. Albee, J. M. Joffe, & L. A. Dusenbury (Eds.), *Prevention, powerlessness, and politics: Readings on social change* (pp. 13–22). Newbury Park, CA: Sage.

Alpert, J. L. (1976). Conceptual bases of mental health consultation in the schools. *Professional Psychology, 7*, 619–626.

Bennis, W. G. (1969). *Organizational development: Its nature, origins and prospects*. Reading, MA: Addison-Wesley.

Botvin, G. J., & Dusenbury, L. (1989). Substance abuse prevention and promotion of competence. In

L. A. Bond & B. E. Compas (Eds.), *Primary prevention and promotion in the schools* (pp. 147–178). Newbury Park, CA: Sage.

Bronfenbrenner, U. (1989). Ecological systems theory. In R. Vasta (Ed.), *Annals of child development* (Vol. 6, pp. 187–249). Greenwich, CT: JAI Press.

Caplan, G. (1964). *Principles of preventive psychiatry*. New York: Basic Books.

Caplan, G. (1970). *The theory and practice of mental health consultation*. New York: Basic Books.

Conway, J. A. (1990). Lessons for staff developers from an organization development consultation. *Journal of Staff Development, 11* (1), 8–13.

Dougherty, A. M. (1990). *Consultation: Practice and perspectives*. Pacific Grove, CA: Brooks-Cole.

Dubrow, A., Wocher, D. M., & Austin, M. J. (2001). Introducing organizational development (OD) practices into a country human services agency. *Administration in Social Work, 25*(4), 63–83.

Edwards, D., Hunt, M. H., Meyers, J., Grogg, K. R., & Jarrett, O. (2005). Acceptability and student outcomes of a violence prevention curriculum. *Journal of Primary Prevention, 26*(5), 401–418.

Erchul, W. P. (Ed.). (1993). *Consultation in community, school and organizational practice: Gerald Caplan's contributions to professional psychology*. Washington, DC: Taylor and Francis.

French, W. L., & Bell, C. H., Jr. (1973). *Organization development: Behavioral science interventions for organizational improvement*. Englewood Cliffs, N.J.: Prentice Hall.

Fullan, M.G. (with Stiegelbauer, S.) (1991). *The new meaning of educational change*. New York: Teachers College Press.

Fullan, M., Miles, M., & Taylor, G. (1980). Organization development in schools: The state of the art. *Review of Educational Research, 50*(1), 121–183.

Gravois, T., & Rosenfield, S. (2002). A multidimensional framework for evaluation of instructional support teams. *Journal of Applied School Psychology, 19*(1), 5–30.

Gravois, T., & Rosenfield, S. (2006). Impact of Instructional Support Teams on the Disproportionate Referral and Placement of Minority Children in Special Education. *Remedial & Special Education, 27*(1), 42–52.

Harding, S. (1991). *Whose science? Whose knowledge? Thinking from women's lives*. NY: Cornell University Press.

Henning-Stout, M., & Meyers, J. (2000). Consultation and human diversity: First things first. *School Psychology Review, 29*, 419–425.

Hylander, I. (2003). Toward a grounded theory of the conceptual change process in consultee-centered consultation. *Journal of Educational & Psychological Consultation, 14*, 263–280.

Ingraham, C. L. (2000). Consultation through a multicultural lens: Multicultural and cross-cultural consultation in schools. *School Psychology Review, 29*, 320–343.

Jeltova, I., & Fish, M. C. (2005). Creating school environments responsive to gay, lesbian, bisexual, and transgender families: Traditional and systemic approaches for consultation. *Journal of Educational and Psychological Consultation, 16*(1 & 2), 17–23.

Kaminstein, D., Smith, K. K., & Miller, R. (2000). Quiet chaos: An organizational consultation in Mandela's South Africa. *Consulting Psychology Journal: Practice and Research, 52*, 49–62.

Kelly, J. G. (2004). The legacy of consultee-centered consultation for the process of collaborative research. In N. M. Lambert, I. Hylander, & J. H. Sandoval (Eds.), *Consultee-centered consultation: Improving the quality of professional services in schools and community organizations* (pp. 213–244). Mahwah, New Jersey: Erlbaum.

Kelly, J. G., Azelton, S. L., Lardon, C., Mock, L. O., Tandon, S. D., & Thomas, M. (2004). On community leadership: Stories about collaboration in action research. *American Journal of Community Psychology, 33*, 205–216.

Kelly, J. G., Mock, L. O., & Tandon, S. D. (2001). Collaborative inquiry with African American community leaders: Comments on a participatory action research process. In P. Reason & H. Bradbury (Eds.), *Handbook of action research* (pp. 348–355). London: Sage.

Knotek, S. (2006). Administrative crisis consultation after 9/11: A university's systems response. *Consulting Psychology Journal: Practice and Research, 58*(3), 162–173.

Knotek, S., Rosenfield, S. A., Gravois, T., & Babinski, L. M. (2003). The process of fostering consultee development during instructional consultation. *Journal of Educational and Psychological Consultation, 14*(3/4), 303–328.

Kratochwill, T. R., & Shernoff, E. S. (2004). Evidence-based practice: Promoting evidence-based interventions in school psychology. *School Psychology Review, 33*, 34–48.

Lambert, N. M., Hylander, I., & Sandoval, J., (2004). *Consultee-centered consultation: Improving the quality of professional services in schools and community organizations*. Mahwah, NJ: Erlbaum.

Lewin, K. (1951). *Field theory in social sciences*. New York: Harper and Row.

Lippitt, G. L., & Lippitt, R. (1986). *The consulting process in action* (2nd ed.). San Diego, CA: University Associates.

Meyers, B. (2002). The contract negotiation stage of a school-based, cross-cultural organizational consultation: A case study. *Journal of Educational and Psychological Consultation, 13*, 151–183.

Meyers, B., Dowdy, J., Paterson, T. (2000). Missing voices: Perspectives of the least visible families and their willingness and capacity for school involvement. *Current Issues in Middle Level Education, 7*(2), 59–79.

Meyers, J. (1995). A consultation model for school psychological services: Twenty years later. *Journal of Educational and Psychological Consultation, 6*, 73–81.

Meyers, J., & Meyers, B. (2003). Bi-directional influences between positive psychology and primary prevention. *School Psychology Quarterly, 18*, 222–229.

Meyers, J., Meyers, A. B., & Grogg, K. (2004). Prevention through consultation: A model to guide future developments in the field of school psychology. *Journal of Educational and Psychological Consultation, 15*, 257–276.

Meyers, J., & Nastasi, B. K. (1999). Primary prevention in school settings. In T. B. Gutkin & C. R. Reynolds (Eds.), *The Handbook of School Psychology* (3rd ed., pp. 764–799). NY: Wiley.

Meyers, J., Parsons, R. D., and Martin, R. P. (1979). *Mental health consultation in the schools*. San Francisco, CA: Jossey-Bass.

Meyers, J., Truscott, S. D., Meyers, A. B., Varjas, K., & Collins, A. S. (2008). Qualitative and mixed methods designs in consultation research. In W. P. Erchul & S. M. Sheridan (Eds.). *Handbook of research in school consultation: Empirical foundations for the field (Chapter 5)*. New York, NY: Routledge.

Nastasi, B. K., Moore, R. B., & Varjas, K. M. (2004). *School-based mental health services: Creating comprehensive and culturally specific programs*. Washington, DC: American Psychological Association.

Nastasi, B. K., Varjas, K., Bernstein, R., & Jayasena, A. (2000). Conducting participatory culture-specific consultation: A global perspective on multicultural consultation. *School Psychology Review 29*, 401–413.

Newlove, B., & Hall, G. (1976). *A manual for assessing open-ended statements of concern about an innovation*. Austin, TX: University of Texas.

O'Neil, J. M., & Conyne, R. K. (1992). Reducing racism and sexism in a university setting through organizational consultation. In R. K. Conyne & J. M. O'Neil (Eds.), *Organizational consultation: A casebook* (pp. 146–183).

Rappaport, J. (1981). In praise of paradox: A social policy of empowerment over prevention. *American Journal of Community Psychology, 9*, 1–25.

Reason, P., & Bradbury, H. (Eds.). (2001). *Handbook of action research*. London: Sage.

Remley, T. (1993). Consultation contracts. *Journal of Counseling and Development, 72*(2), 157–158.

Rosenbach, W. E., Robert, A., & Taylor, R. L. (1983). Survey feedback as an organization development strategy in a public school district. *Education, 103*, 316–325.

Rosenfield, S. (1992). Developing school based consultation teams: A design for organizational change. *School Psychology Quarterly, 7*(1), 27–46.

Ruch, C. P., Oehler, J. S., & Bost, W. A. (1982). Training for planning: Organizational consultation to design and install constituency-based planning. *Planning and Changing, 13,* 234–244.

Sandoval, J. (1996). Construcivism, consultee-centered consultation, and conceptual change. *Journal of Educational and Psychological Consultation, 7,* 89–97.

Sandoval, J. (2003). Constructing conceptual change in consultee-centered consultation. *Journal of Educational and Psychological Consultation, 14,* 231–242.

Sarason, S. B. (1971). *The culture of the school and the problem of change.* Boston: Allyn & Bacon.

Sarason, S. B. (1990). *The predictable failure of educational reform: Can we change course before it's too late?* San Francisco: Jossey-Bass.

Schein, E. H. (1988). *Process consultation: Its role in organization development* (Vol. 1, 2nd ed.). Reading, MA: Addison-Wesley.

Schmuck, R. A. (1995). Process consultation and organization development. *Journal of Educational & Psychological Consultation, 6,* 199–205.

Sexton, T. L., & Griffin, B. L. (Eds.). (1997). *Constructivist thinking in counseling practice, research and training.* NY: Teachers College Press.

Shure, M. B. (1988). How to think, not what to think: A cognitive approach to prevention. In L. A. Bond & B. M. Wagner (Eds.), *Families in transition: Primary prevention programs that work.* Newbury Park, CA: Sage.

Steward, R. J. (1996). Training consulting psychologists to be sensitive to multicultural issues in organizational consultation. *Consulting Psychology Journal: Practice and Research, 48*(3), 180–189.

Truscott, S. D., Cosgrove, G., Meyers, J., & Eidle-Barkman, K. A. (2000). The acceptability of organizational consultation with prereferral intervention teams. *School Psychology Quarterly, 15,* 172–206.

Varjas, K., Meyers, J., Henrich, C. C., Graybill, E. C., Dew, B. J., Marshall, M. L., et al. (2006). Using a participatory culture-specific intervention model to develop a peer victimization intervention. *Journal of Applied School Psychology, 22*(2), 35–58. Copublished in B. K. Nastasi (Ed.), *Multicultural Issues in School Psychology.* New York: The Haworth Press, Inc.

Vygotsky, L. (1978). *Mind in society.* Cambridge, MA: Harvard University Press.

Walters, P., & Henkleman, J. (1990). Organization development and the process of school improvement in Maryland. *Journal of Staff Development, 11,* 14–19.

Zins, J. E. (1992). Implementing school-based consultation services: An analysis of five years of practice. In R. K. Conyne & J. M. O'Neil (Eds.), *Organizational consultation: A casebook* (pp. 50–79). Newbury Park, CA: Sage.

NAME INDEX

Page references followed by *n* indicate material in footnotes. Page references have been conflated to conserve space. A range of page numbers may not necessarily indicate a continuous discussion over the whole range, just that the name was mentioned at least once on each page of the range.

A
Aaron, P. G., 526–527
Abebimpe, V. R., 340
Aber, J. L., 108
Abidin, R. R., 793
Abikoff, H., 683
Aboud, F. E., 147
Abramowitz, J. S., 514
Abramson, L. Y., 145, 728
Abu-Saad, H. H., 478
Achenbach, T. M., 66, 173, 179, 191, 201–202, 289–292, 296, 376, 413, 474
Ackerman, P. L., 68, 865, 873
Acklin, M., 216
Adams, G. R., 95, 113, 421
Adams, K., 423
Adams, M. J., 539
Adams, R. B., 164
Adams, W., 162
Addis, M. E., 640
Adelman, H. S., 791
Adler, A., 886
Adler, T. F., 112
Adolphs, R., 164
Agostin, T. M., 264, 801
Agran, M., 824
Aiken, L. S., 5
AIMSweb, 437
Ainscow, M., 822, 826
Ainsworth, M. D. S., 146
Ajzen, I., 141–143
Albee, G. W., 488–489
Alberto, P. A., 96, 569, 571, 577–580, 582–583
Alden, J., 326
Alderman, M. K., 135, 137
Alessi, G., 94, 218
Alexander, K. L., 108, 112, 659
Alexander, P. A., 66, 130, 134, 742, 744, 749, 751

Alexander, S. P., 639
Alfonso, V. C., 257–258, 264, 271
Algozzine, B., 211, 218, 415, 420–421, 426, 552, 593
Alkin, M., 824
Allard, G., 210
Allen, B. A., 871
Allen, J. C., 297
Allen, J. G., 211
Allen, J. P., 117–118
Allen, S. F., 890
Allen, S. J., 606
Allensworth, D. D., 710, 910
Alley, G., 340–341
Allison, J., 391
Alloy, L. B., 145
Allport, G. W., 139–141
Aloia, G. F., 342
Alper, S., 425
Alpert, J. L., 922
Al-Shabbout, M., 694
Altham, P. E., 177
Altman, D. G., 214
Alvarez, B., 658
Alvarez, J. M., 147
Alvord, G. W., 485
Alwin, J., 110
Amador-Campos, J. A., 474
Ambady, N., 164
Ambell, J., 746
Ambrosini, P. J., 641, 694
Amedi, A., 163
American Academy of Pediatrics, 322, 683, 686
American Association on Mental Retardation, 195–197
American Educational Research Association, 340
American Psychiatric Association, 178, 192, 197, 291–292, 295, 298–299, 301,

464, 466, 468, 472–475, 508, 682, 748, 890, 892
American School Counselor Association, 592
Ames, C., 752
Amir, Y., 147
Anastasi, A., 335, 341, 351
Anastopoulos, A. D., 657
Anderman, E. M., 131
Anderman, L. H., 116
Andersch, S., 691
Anderson, C. A., 141, 149, 385, 773
Anderson, J. R., 125–126
Anderson, L. M., 419, 774, 796
Anderson, R. C., 528, 533
Anderson, R. E., 211
Anderson, S. W., 165
Anderson, T. K., 599
Anderson, V. A., 326
Andorfer, R., 377
Andrade, A. R., 640
Andrews, H. B., 391
Andrews, L. W., 142, 593, 606
Andrews, T. J., 166
Ang, R., 794
Anglin, T. M., 637
Angoff, W. H., 344
Angold, A., 300
Anguiano, R. P. V., 797
Annan, J., 592, 611
Annett, J., 538
Antil, L., 777
Apter, A., 692
Apter, S. J., 479, 483, 692
Arbuckle, J. L., 13
Archer, A. L., 485
Ardoin, S. P., 95, 398, 579, 775
Arend, R., 202
Arkes, H. R., 212, 218, 224
Armbrister, R. C., 144
Armenteros, J. L., 698

SUBJECT INDEX

Page references followed by a *t* indicate material in tables, those followed
by an *f* indicate figures, and those followed by an *n* indicate material in footnotes.